UNIVERSITY CASEBOOK SERIES®

HART AND WECHSLER'S

THE FEDERAL COURTS AND THE FEDERAL SYSTEM

SEVENTH EDITION

by

RICHARD H. FALLON, JR.
Ralph S. Tyler, Jr. Professor of Constitutional Law
Harvard Law School

JOHN F. MANNING
Bruce Bromley Professor of Law
Harvard Law School

DANIEL J. MELTZER
Story Professor of Law
Harvard Law School

DAVID L. SHAPIRO
William Nelson Cromwell Professor of Law, Emeritus
Harvard Law School

FOUNDATION
PRESS

K

University Casebook Series is a trademark registered in the U.S. Patent and Trademark Office.

© 1953, 1973, 1988, 1996, 2003 FOUNDATION PRESS
© 2009 By THOMSON REUTERS/FOUNDATION PRESS
© 2015 LEG, Inc. d/b/a West Academic
    444 Cedar Street, Suite 700
    St. Paul, MN 55101
    1-877-888-1330

Printed in the United States of America

ISBN: 978-1-60930-427-0

Richard Fallon, John Manning, and David Shapiro dedicate this Edition to the memory of Daniel J. Meltzer, whose luminous scholarship so enriched our field, and whose contributions and wise counsel so enriched this book.*

---

*   Dan Meltzer died on May 24, 2015, after completing work on this Edition.

PREFACE TO THE SEVENTH EDITION

I

In this Seventh Edition we have tried above all to carry on the great intellectual and scholarly tradition bequeathed to us by the authors of the First Edition, Henry Hart and Herbert Wechsler, and sustained by successive editors. As in previous editions, we have not only kept up with developments in the Supreme Court, but also provided relevant background and called attention to important scholarship.

Of nearly equal importance, we have worked hard to make this edition as user-friendly and teachable as possible. In a number of places, we have prefaced leading cases with brief introductory notes, to explain to students how cases and materials that they are about to read fit into an emerging historical or doctrinal picture. We have trimmed and in many instances eliminated discussions of old cases. In addition, users of prior editions will notice that although our Notes continue to probe the most challenging problems that lawyers, judges, and lawmakers confront, we have reduced the number of sentences that end in question marks. Where we think we have guidance to offer, we have more frequently stated our views explicitly. Many questions remain, but few are rhetorical or repetitive.

We have also continued the policy of recent editions of relegating to footnotes material that we have included in the book primarily for those interested in pursuing further research. We tell students in our classes that they need not read footnotes—apart, of course, from those that are parts of Supreme Court opinions that we have retained in principal cases—unless we specifically ask them to do so. We would encourage other instructors to adopt a similar policy.

As part of our commitment to continuity, we have retained the core structure of the previous edition, including the organization of most chapters, and have retained most (but not all) of the principal cases. With regret, we have omitted what in prior editions were Chapters XIV and XV. The former largely addressed matters of process and venue, including removal procedures, and the latter dealt with obligatory and discretionary review in the Supreme Court. Consultation with a number of friends and colleagues persuaded us that few intructors have actually taught the material in those chapters, the subject matters of which are more than adequately addressed in other sources. When material from the former Chapters XIV and XV was relevant to topics covered in other chapters of this book, we moved it accordingly.

As a result of our efforts to make the book as concise as possible without sacrificing depth of analysis, this edition is slightly shorter than its precedecessor, despite a minor increase in font size. Our selective trimming in producing this edition marks the continuation of a self-conscously adopted policy. Each of the two prior editions was more than 100 pages shorter than the one that came before.

II

Beyond our elimination of two chapters, developments since the publication of the Sixth Edition have occasioned several significant changes in our selection and organization of materials. Stern v. Marshall (2011), which raises important questions about the constitutional permissibility of adjudication by non-Article III tribunals both in the bankruptcy area and more generally, appears as a principal case in Chapter IV. We have also undertaken major revisions in Chapter XI's habeas corpus materials on executive detention. In addition to clarifying changes and reorganizations, we have added Hamdi v. United States (2004) as a principal case. Ongoing ferment concerning the availability of "facial challenges" to statutes has triggered significant revisions in Chapter II—though, in this case, with a small overall reduction in the number of pages devoted to the topic. These revisions should make it easier for instructors to address the leading issues surrounding the distinction between facial and as-applied challeges in a single class discussion based on a single reading assignment. Other, smaller changes occur throughout the book, including in the materials on plaintiffs' standing and qualified immunity.

In making these and other revisions, we have benefited immeasurably from comments and suggestions by a number of colleagues and friends. Our thanks go to Brad Clark, Allan Erbsen, Willy Fletcher, Barry Friedman, Amanda Frost, Jack Goldsmith, Abner Greene, Tara Grove, Vicki Jackson, Gillian Metzger, Henry Monaghan, Caleb Nelson, John Parry, Judith Resnik, Neil Siegel, Gil Seinfeld, Amanda Tyler, Carlos Vázquez, Steve Vladeck, Brian Wolfman, and Larry Yackle.

III

No two instructors using this book are likely to select the same materials for study, but all must make choices in compiling their syllabi. We therefore offer some brief comments about the possible contents of a three-or four-(or more) credit course. Chapter I provides important background reading, but none of us devotes class time to discussion of its contents. In three-or four-credit courses, each of us teaches some of Chapter II, primarily in the section on standing, but we also rely on exposure to issues of justiciability in courses on Civil Procedure, Constitutional Law, and Administrative Law. None of us teaches Chapter III (on the Supreme Court's original jurisdiction), but we all teach at least Sections 1 and 3 of Chapter IV, involving congressional control of judicial jurisdiction. (Section 2, relating to non-judicial federal tribunals, is challenging and important, but almost impossible to teach in its entirety in a three-credit course.) We also cover Sections 1 and 2 of Chapter V (Supreme Court review of state court judgments), dip into Chapter VI (discussing at least the Erie decision), and assign much of Chapters VII (federal common law), VIII (federal question jurisdiction), IX (suits against federal and state governments and their officials), and X (dealing with limitations on federal jurisdiction or its exercise), especially Sections 1 and 2(A–C). Chapter XI on habeas corpus, may either be taught as a unit or divided by focusing on collateral federal review of state court decisions in conjunction with Chapter V, on direct review.

In four-credit courses (or for those with the even greater luxury of five credits), we recommend consideration of the materials in Chapter XII (problems of res judicata and other aspects of successive or concurrent jurisdiction), and in Chapter XIII (especially the sections relating to class actions and supplemental jurisdiction). We also suggest expanding coverage of Chapters II, IV, and IX.

IV

Although every chapter is the product of extensive review and comment among the four authors, primary responsibility is divided among us as follows:

Fallon   Chapters I, II(3)(B), IX, X

Manning   Chapters II (except Section (3)(B)), V, VII

Meltzer   Chapters III, IV, VI, VIII, XI, XII, XIII

David Shapiro read and commented on drafts of every chapter.

V

A few notes on form and related matters: In many instances, we adhere not to the Bluebook but to the style of previous editions.[1] With respect to principal cases and quotations in our Notes, no indication of omitted footnotes or citations is normally given; those footnotes that have been retained carry their original numbers. All other omissions, whether of a few words, a paragraph, or several pages, are indicated by spaced asterisks.

Several of the authors of this and prior editions took part in various ways as counsel or amici curiae in some of the cases in this book. As in prior editions, we concluded that it would constitute an excess of caution to advert, in each case, to such participation. We believe that our editorial process has fairly guarded us against resulting bias (or undue leaning over backwards). Each of us who is an active member of the Harvard Law School faculty has a webpage on the Harvard Law School website that discloses any of our involvements with cases related to the materials covered in this book within the previous three years.

VI

We are grateful to a number of our present and former students for their research and for invaluable assistance in checking the manuscript for this edition: Evelyn Blacklock, Niko Bowie, William Burgess, Erin Cady, Gabe Daly, Michael Decker, Caitlin Halpern, Lucas Issacharoff, Mark Jia, Rachel Kenigsberg, Janet Kim, Jeremy Kreisberg, Jordan Moran, Jason Neal, Kevin Neylan, Allison Ray, Owen Roberts, Max Rosen, Matthew Rowen, Rachel Siegel, Josh Tannen, and Jason Yen. Our thanks go also to Carol Bateson, Peggy Flynn, Maura Kelley, Kimberly O'Hagan, and Matthew Rose for their splendid secretarial assistance, and to the Library Reference Staff at Harvard Law School for their help on a number of difficult problems.

VII

Readers may be interested in the dedications of earlier editions of this book. The first was dedicated to Felix Frankfurter, "who first opened our minds to these problems"; the second to the memory of Henry M. Hart, Jr., "profound and passionate student and teacher"; the third to the

---

[1] For example, we do not use first names of authors, unless necessary to avoid confusion; we do not italicize case names (or case "nicknames") in either text or footnotes, and we do not indicate that certiorari was denied except in the few instances where it has special relevance. And despite some criticism from watchful colleagues and students, we adhere in our own text to the British practice of putting inside a quote only that punctuation that is part of the quote, since we believe that practice is more informative to the reader.

memory of Henry J. Friendly, "man for all seasons in the law; master of this subject"; the fourth to Herbert Wechsler, "source of inspiration and wisdom, epitome of a grand tradition"; the fifth "by a 2–1 vote," to David L. Shapiro, "lawyer's lawyer, exemplary teacher and scholar, who continues to show us the way"; and the sixth to "our families."

R.H.F.

J.F.M.

D.J.M.

D.L.S.

April 2015

SUMMARY OF CONTENTS

TABLE OF CONTENTS

TABLE OF CASES

The principal cases are in bold type.

TABLE OF AUTHORITIES

THE CONSTITUTION OF THE UNITED STATES OF AMERICA

We the people of the United States, in order to form a more perfect union, establish justice, insure domestic tranquility, provide for the common defense, promote the general welfare, and secure the blessings of liberty to ourselves and our posterity, do ordain and establish this Constitution for the United States of America.

Article I

Section 1. All legislative powers herein granted shall be vested in a Congress of the United States, which shall consist of a Senate and House of Representatives.

Section 2. [1] The House of Representatives shall be composed of members chosen every second year by the people of the several states, and the electors in each state shall have the qualifications requisite for electors of the most numerous branch of the state legislature.

[2] No person shall be a Representative who shall not have attained to the age of twenty five years, and been seven years a citizen of the United States, and who shall not, when elected, be an inhabitant of that state in which he shall be chosen.

[3] Representatives and direct taxes shall be apportioned among the several states which may be included within this union, according to their respective numbers, which shall be determined by adding to the whole number of free persons, including those bound to service for a term of years, and excluding Indians not taxed, three fifths of all other Persons. The actual Enumeration shall be made within three years after the first meeting of the Congress of the United States, and within every subsequent term of ten years, in such manner as they shall by law direct. The number of Representatives shall not exceed one for every thirty thousand, but each state shall have at least one Representative; and until such enumeration shall be made, the state of New Hampshire shall be entitled to chuse three, Massachusetts eight, Rhode Island and Providence Plantations one, Connecticut five, New York six, New Jersey four, Pennsylvania eight, Delaware one, Maryland six, Virginia ten, North Carolina five, South Carolina five, and Georgia three.

[4] When vacancies happen in the Representation from any state, the executive authority thereof shall issue writs of election to fill such vacancies.

[5] The House of Representatives shall choose their speaker and other officers; and shall have the sole power of impeachment.

Section 3. [1] The Senate of the United States shall be composed of two Senators from each state, chosen by the legislature thereof, for six years; and each Senator shall have one vote.

[2] Immediately after they shall be assembled in consequence of the first election, they shall be divided as equally as may be into three classes. The seats of the Senators of the first class shall be vacated at

the expiration of the second year, of the second class at the expiration of the fourth year, and the third class at the expiration of the sixth year, so that one third may be chosen every second year; and if vacancies happen by resignation, or otherwise, during the recess of the legislature of any state, the executive thereof may make temporary appointments until the next meeting of the legislature, which shall then fill such vacancies.

[3] No person shall be a Senator who shall not have attained to the age of thirty years, and been nine years a citizen of the United States and who shall not, when elected, be an inhabitant of that state for which he shall be chosen.

[4] The Vice President of the United States shall be President of the Senate, but shall have no vote, unless they be equally divided.

[5] The Senate shall choose their other officers, and also a President pro tempore, in the absence of the Vice President, or when he shall exercise the office of President of the United States.

[6] The Senate shall have the sole power to try all impeachments. When sitting for that purpose, they shall be on oath or affirmation. When the President of the United States is tried, the Chief Justice shall preside: And no person shall be convicted without the concurrence of two thirds of the members present.

[7] Judgment in cases of impeachment shall not extend further than to removal from office, and disqualification to hold and enjoy any office of honor, trust or profit under the United States: but the party convicted shall nevertheless be liable and subject to indictment, trial, judgment and punishment, according to law.

Section 4. [1] The times, places and manner of holding elections for Senators and Representatives, shall be prescribed in each state by the legislature thereof; but the Congress may at any time by law make or alter such regulations, except as to the places of choosing Senators.

[2] The Congress shall assemble at least once in every year, and such meeting shall be on the first Monday in December, unless they shall by law appoint a different day.

Section 5. [1] Each House shall be the judge of the elections, returns and qualifications of its own members, and a majority of each shall constitute a quorum to do business; but a smaller number may adjourn from day to day, and may be authorized to compel the attendance of absent members, in such manner, and under such penalties as each House may provide.

[2] Each House may determine the rules of its proceedings, punish its members for disorderly behavior, and, with the concurrence of two thirds, expel a member.

[3] Each House shall keep a journal of its proceedings, and from time to time publish the same, excepting such parts as may in their judgment require secrecy; and the yeas and nays of the members of either House on any question shall, at the desire of one fifth of those present, be entered on the journal.

[4] Neither House, during the session of Congress, shall, without the consent of the other, adjourn for more than three days, nor to any other place than that in which the two Houses shall be sitting.

Section 6. [1] The Senators and Representatives shall receive a compensation for their services, to be ascertained by law, and paid out of the treasury of the United States. They shall in all cases, except treason, felony and breach of the peace, be privileged from arrest during their attendance at the session of their respective Houses, and in going to and returning from the same; and for any speech or debate in either House, they shall not be questioned in any other place.

[2] No Senator or Representative shall, during the time for which he was elected, be appointed to any civil office under the authority of the United States, which shall have been created, or the emoluments whereof shall have been increased during such time: and no person holding any office under the United States, shall be a member of either House during his continuance in office.

Section 7. [1] All bills for raising revenue shall originate in the House of Representatives; but the Senate may propose or concur with amendments as on other Bills.

[2] Every bill which shall have passed the House of Representatives and the Senate, shall, before it become a law, be presented to the President of the United States; if he approve he shall sign it, but if not he shall return it, with his objections to that House in which it shall have originated, who shall enter the objections at large on their journal, and proceed to reconsider it. If after such reconsideration two thirds of that House shall agree to pass the bill, it shall be sent, together with the objections, to the other House, by which it shall likewise be reconsidered, and if approved by two thirds of that House, it shall become a law. But in all such cases the votes of both Houses shall be determined by yeas and nays, and the names of the persons voting for and against the bill shall be entered on the journal of each House respectively. If any bill shall not be returned by the President within ten days (Sundays excepted) after it shall have been presented to him, the same shall be a law, in like manner as if he had signed it, unless the Congress by their adjournment prevent its return, in which case it shall not be a law.

[3] Every order, resolution, or vote to which the concurrence of the Senate and House of Representatives may be necessary (except on a question of adjournment) shall be presented to the President of the United States; and before the same shall take effect, shall be approved by him, or being disapproved by him, shall be repassed by two thirds of the Senate and House of Representatives, according to the rules and limitations prescribed in the case of a bill.

Section 8. [1] The Congress shall have power to lay and collect taxes, duties, imposts and excises, to pay the debts and provide for the common defense and general welfare of the United States; but all duties, imposts and excises shall be uniform throughout the United States;

[2] To borrow money on the credit of the United States;

[3] To regulate commerce with foreign nations, and among the several states, and with the Indian tribes;

[4] To establish a uniform rule of naturalization, and uniform laws on the subject of bankruptcies throughout the United States;

[5] To coin money, regulate the value thereof, and of foreign coin, and fix the standard of weights and measures;

[6] To provide for the punishment of counterfeiting the securities and current coin of the United States;

[7] To establish post offices and post roads;

[8] To promote the progress of science and useful arts, by securing for limited times to authors and inventors the exclusive right to their respective writings and discoveries;

[9] To constitute tribunals inferior to the Supreme Court;

[10] To define and punish piracies and felonies committed on the high seas, and offenses against the law of nations;

[11] To declare war, grant letters of marque and reprisal, and make rules concerning captures on land and water;

[12] To raise and support armies, but no appropriation of money to that use shall be for a longer term than two years;

[13] To provide and maintain a navy;

[14] To make rules for the government and regulation of the land and naval forces;

[15] To provide for calling forth the militia to execute the laws of the union, suppress insurrections and repel invasions;

[16] To provide for organizing, arming, and disciplining, the militia, and for governing such part of them as may be employed in the service of the United States, reserving to the states respectively, the appointment of the officers, and the authority of training the militia according to the discipline prescribed by Congress;

[17] To exercise exclusive legislation in all cases whatsoever, over such District (not exceeding ten miles square) as may, by cession of particular states, and the acceptance of Congress, become the seat of the government of the United States, and to exercise like authority over all places purchased by the consent of the legislature of the state in which the same shall be, for the erection of forts, magazines, arsenals, dockyards, and other needful buildings;—And

[18] To make all laws which shall be necessary and proper for carrying into execution the foregoing powers, and all other powers vested by this Constitution in the government of the United States, or in any department or officer thereof.

Section 9. [1] The migration or importation of such persons as any of the states now existing shall think proper to admit, shall not be prohibited by the Congress prior to the year one thousand eight hundred and eight, but a tax or duty may be imposed on such importation, not exceeding ten dollars for each person.

[2] The privilege of the writ of habeas corpus shall not be suspended, unless when in cases of rebellion or invasion the public safety may require it.

[3] No bill of attainder or ex post facto Law shall be passed.

[4] No capitation, or other direct, tax shall be laid, unless in proportion to the census or enumeration herein before directed to be taken.

[5] No tax or duty shall be laid on articles exported from any state.

[6] No preference shall be given by any regulation of commerce or revenue to the ports of one state over those of another: nor shall vessels bound to, or from, one state, be obliged to enter, clear or pay duties in another.

[7] No money shall be drawn from the treasury, but in consequence of appropriations made by law; and a regular statement and account of receipts and expenditures of all public money shall be published from time to time.

[8] No title of nobility shall be granted by the United States: and no person holding any office of profit or trust under them, shall, without the consent of the Congress, accept of any present, emolument, office, or title, of any kind whatever, from any king, prince, or foreign state.

Section 10. [1] No state shall enter into any treaty, alliance, or confederation; grant letters of marque and reprisal; coin money; emit bills of credit; make anything but gold and silver coin a tender in payment of debts; pass any bill of attainder, ex post facto law, or law impairing the obligation of contracts, or grant any title of nobility.

[2] No state shall, without the consent of the Congress, lay any imposts or duties on imports or exports, except what may be absolutely necessary for executing it's inspection laws: and the net produce of all duties and imposts, laid by any state on imports or exports, shall be for the use of the treasury of the United States; and all such laws shall be subject to the revision and control of the Congress.

[3] No state shall, without the consent of Congress, lay any duty of tonnage, keep troops, or ships of war in time of peace, enter into any agreement or compact with another state, or with a foreign power, or engage in war, unless actually invaded, or in such imminent danger as will not admit of delay.

Article II

Section 1. [1] The executive power shall be vested in a President of the United States of America. He shall hold his office during the term of four years, and, together with the Vice President, chosen for the same term, be elected, as follows:

[2] Each state shall appoint, in such manner as the Legislature thereof may direct, a number of electors, equal to the whole number of Senators and Representatives to which the State may be entitled in the Congress: but no Senator or Representative, or person holding an office of trust or profit under the United States, shall be appointed an elector.

[3] The electors shall meet in their respective states, and vote by ballot for two persons, of whom one at least shall not be an inhabitant of the same state with themselves. And they shall make a list of all the persons voted for, and of the number of votes for each; which list they shall sign and certify, and transmit sealed to the seat of the government of the United States, directed to the President of the Senate.

The President of the Senate shall, in the presence of the Senate and House of Representatives, open all the certificates, and the votes shall then be counted. The person having the greatest number of votes shall be the President, if such number be a majority of the whole number of electors appointed; and if there be more than one who have such majority, and have an equal number of votes, then the House of Representatives shall immediately choose by ballot one of them for President; and if no person have a majority, then from the five highest on the list the said House shall in like manner choose the President. But in choosing the President, the votes shall be taken by States, the representation from each state having one vote; A quorum for this purpose shall consist of a member or members from two thirds of the states, and a majority of all the states shall be necessary to a choice. In every case, after the choice of the President, the person having the greatest number of votes of the electors shall be the Vice President. But if there should remain two or more who have equal votes, the Senate shall choose from them by ballot the Vice President.

[4] The Congress may determine the time of choosing the electors, and the day on which they shall give their votes; which day shall be the same throughout the United States.

[5] No person except a natural born citizen, or a citizen of the United States, at the time of the adoption of this Constitution, shall be eligible to the office of President; neither shall any person be eligible to that office who shall not have attained to the age of thirty five years, and been fourteen Years a resident within the United States.

[6] In case of the removal of the President from office, or of his death, resignation, or inability to discharge the powers and duties of the said office, the same shall devolve on the Vice President, and the Congress may by law provide for the case of removal, death, resignation or inability, both of the President and Vice President, declaring what officer shall then act as President, and such officer shall act accordingly, until the disability be removed, or a President shall be elected.

[7] The President shall, at stated times, receive for his services, a compensation, which shall neither be increased nor diminished during the period for which he shall have been elected, and he shall not receive within that period any other emolument from the United States, or any of them.

[8] Before he enter on the execution of his office, he shall take the following oath or affirmation:—'I do solemnly swear (or affirm) that I will faithfully execute the office of President of the United States, and will to the best of my ability, preserve, protect and defend the Constitution of the United States.'

Section 2. [1] The President shall be commander in chief of the Army and Navy of the United States, and of the militia of the several states, when called into the actual service of the United States; he may require the opinion, in writing, of the principal officer in each of the executive departments, upon any subject relating to the duties of their respective offices, and he shall have power to grant reprieves and pardons for offenses against the United States, except in cases of impeachment.

[2] He shall have power, by and with the advice and consent of the Senate, to make treaties, provided two thirds of the Senators present concur; and he shall nominate, and by and with the advice and consent of the Senate, shall appoint ambassadors, other public ministers and consuls, judges of the Supreme Court, and all other officers of the United States, whose appointments are not herein otherwise provided for, and which shall be established by law: but the Congress may by law vest the appointment of such inferior officers, as they think proper, in the President alone, in the courts of law, or in the heads of departments.

[3] The President shall have power to fill up all vacancies that may happen during the recess of the Senate, by granting commissions which shall expire at the end of their next session.

Section 3. He shall from time to time give to the Congress information of the state of the union, and recommend to their consideration such measures as he shall judge necessary and expedient; he may, on extraordinary occasions, convene both Houses, or either of them, and in case of disagreement between them, with respect to the time of adjournment, he may adjourn them to such time as he shall think proper; he shall receive ambassadors and other public ministers; he shall take care that the laws be faithfully executed, and shall commission all the officers of the United States.

Section 4. The President, Vice President and all civil officers of the United States, shall be removed from office on impeachment for, and conviction of, treason, bribery, or other high crimes and misdemeanors.

Article III

Section 1. The judicial power of the United States, shall be vested in one Supreme Court, and in such inferior courts as the Congress may from time to time ordain and establish. The judges, both of the supreme and inferior courts, shall hold their offices during good behaviour, and shall, at stated times, receive for their services, a compensation, which shall not be diminished during their continuance in office.

Section 2. [1] The judicial power shall extend to all cases, in law and equity, arising under this Constitution, the laws of the United States, and treaties made, or which shall be made, under their authority;—to all cases affecting ambassadors, other public ministers and consuls;—to all cases of admiralty and maritime jurisdiction;—to controversies to which the United States shall be a party;—to controversies between two or more states;— between a state and citizens of another state;—between citizens of different states;—between citizens of the same state claiming lands under grants of different states, and between a state, or the citizens thereof, and foreign states, citizens or subjects.

note - no "all"

[2] In all cases affecting ambassadors, other public ministers and consuls, and those in which a state shall be party, the Supreme Court shall have original jurisdiction. In all the other cases before mentioned, the Supreme Court shall have appellate jurisdiction, both as to law and

fact, with such exceptions, and under such regulations as the Congress shall make.

[3] The trial of all crimes, except in cases of impeachment, shall be by jury; and such trial shall be held in the state where the said crimes shall have been committed; but when not committed within any state, the trial shall be at such place or places as the Congress may by law have directed.

Section 3. [1] Treason against the United States, shall consist only in levying war against them, or in adhering to their enemies, giving them aid and comfort. No person shall be convicted of treason unless on the testimony of two witnesses to the same overt act, or on confession in open court.

[2] The Congress shall have power to declare the punishment of treason, but no attainder of treason shall work corruption of blood, or forfeiture except during the life of the person attainted.

Article IV

Section 1. Full faith and credit shall be given in each state to the public acts, records, and judicial proceedings of every other state. And the Congress may by general laws prescribe the manner in which such acts, records, and proceedings shall be proved, and the effect thereof.

Section 2. [1] The citizens of each state shall be entitled to all privileges and immunities of citizens in the several states.

[2] A person charged in any state with treason, felony, or other crime, who shall flee from justice, and be found in another state, shall on demand of the executive authority of the state from which he fled, be delivered up, to be removed to the state having jurisdiction of the crime.

[3] No person held to service or labor in one state, under the laws thereof, escaping into another, shall, in consequence of any law or regulation therein, be discharged from such service or labor, but shall be delivered up on claim of the party to whom such service or labor may be due.

Section 3. [1] New states may be admitted by the Congress into this union; but no new states shall be formed or erected within the jurisdiction of any other state; nor any state be formed by the junction of two or more states, or parts of states, without the consent of the legislatures of the states concerned as well as of the Congress.

[2] The Congress shall have power to dispose of and make all needful rules and regulations respecting the territory or other property belonging to the United States; and nothing in this Constitution shall be so construed as to prejudice any claims of the United States, or of any particular state.

Section 4. The United States shall guarantee to every state in this union a republican form of government, and shall protect each of them against invasion; and on application of the legislature, or of the executive (when the legislature cannot be convened) against domestic violence.

Article V

The Congress, whenever two thirds of both houses shall deem it necessary, shall propose amendments to this Constitution, or, on the application of the legislatures of two thirds of the several states, shall call a convention for proposing amendments, which, in either case, shall be valid to all intents and purposes, as part of this Constitution, when ratified by the legislatures of three fourths of the several states, or by conventions in three fourths thereof, as the one or the other mode of ratification may be proposed by the Congress; provided that no amendment which may be made prior to the year one thousand eight hundred and eight shall in any manner affect the first and fourth clauses in the ninth section of the first article; and that no state, without its consent, shall be deprived of its equal suffrage in the Senate.

Article VI

[1] All debts contracted and engagements entered into, before the adoption of this Constitution, shall be as valid against the United States under this Constitution, as under the Confederation.

[2] This Constitution, and the laws of the United States which shall be made in pursuance thereof; and all treaties made, or which shall be made, under the authority of the United States, shall be the supreme law of the land; and the judges in every state shall be bound thereby, anything in the Constitution or laws of any State to the contrary notwithstanding.

[3] The Senators and Representatives before mentioned, and the members of the several state legislatures, and all executive and judicial officers, both of the United States and of the several states, shall be bound by oath or affirmation, to support this Constitution; but no religious test shall ever be required as a qualification to any office or public trust under the United States.

Article VII

The ratification of the conventions of nine states, shall be sufficient for the establishment of this Constitution between the states so ratifying the same.

ARTICLES IN ADDITION TO, AND AMENDMENT OF, THE CONSTITUTION OF THE UNITED STATES OF AMERICA, PROPOSED BY CONGRESS, AND RATIFIED BY THE LEGISLATURES OF THE SEVERAL STATES PURSUANT TO THE FIFTH ARTICLE OF THE ORIGINAL CONSTITUTION.

Amendment I [1791]

Congress shall make no law respecting an establishment of religion, or prohibiting the free exercise thereof; or abridging the freedom of speech, or of the press; or the right of the people peaceably to assemble, and to petition the government for a redress of grievances.

Amendment II [1791]

A well regulated militia, being necessary to the security of a free state, the right of the people to keep and bear arms, shall not be infringed.

Amendment III [1791]

No soldier shall, in time of peace be quartered in any house, without the consent of the owner, nor in time of war, but in a manner to be prescribed by law.

Amendment IV [1791]

The right of the people to be secure in their persons, houses, papers, and effects, against unreasonable searches and seizures, shall not be violated, and no warrants shall issue, but upon probable cause, supported by oath or affirmation, and particularly describing the place to be searched, and the persons or things to be seized.

Amendment V [1791]

No person shall be held to answer for a capital, or otherwise infamous crime, unless on a presentment or indictment of a grand jury, except in cases arising in the land or naval forces, or in the militia, when in actual service in time of war or public danger; nor shall any person be subject for the same offense to be twice put in jeopardy of life or limb; nor shall be compelled in any criminal case to be a witness against himself, nor be deprived of life, liberty, or property, without due process of law; nor shall private property be taken for public use, without just compensation.

Amendment VI [1791]

In all criminal prosecutions, the accused shall enjoy the right to a speedy and public trial, by an impartial jury of the state and district wherein the crime shall have been committed, which district shall have been previously ascertained by law, and to be informed of the nature and cause of the accusation; to be confronted with the witnesses against him; to have compulsory process for obtaining witnesses in his favor, and to have the assistance of counsel for his defense.

Amendment VII [1791]

In suits at common law, where the value in controversy shall exceed twenty dollars, the right of trial by jury shall be preserved, and no fact tried by a jury, shall be otherwise reexamined in any court of the United States, than according to the rules of the common law.

Amendment VIII [1791]

Excessive bail shall not be required, nor excessive fines imposed, nor cruel and unusual punishments inflicted.

Amendment IX [1791]

The enumeration in the Constitution, of certain rights, shall not be construed to deny or disparage others retained by the people.

Amendment X [1791]

The powers not delegated to the United States by the Constitution, nor prohibited by it to the states, are reserved to the states respectively, or to the people.

Amendment XI [1798]

The judicial power of the United States shall not be construed to extend to any suit in law or equity, commenced or prosecuted against one of the United States by citizens of another state, or by citizens or subjects of any foreign state.

Amendment XII [1804]

The electors shall meet in their respective states and vote by ballot for President and Vice-President, one of whom, at least, shall not be an inhabitant of the same state with themselves; they shall name in their ballots the person voted for as President, and in distinct ballots the person voted for as Vice-President, and they shall make distinct lists of all persons voted for as President, and of all persons voted for as Vice-President, and of the number of votes for each, which lists they shall sign and certify, and transmit sealed to the seat of the government of the United States, directed to the President of the Senate;—The President of the Senate shall, in the presence of the Senate and House of Representatives, open all the certificates and the votes shall then be counted;—the person having the greatest number of votes for President, shall be the President, if such number be a majority of the whole number of electors appointed; and if no person have such majority, then from the persons having the highest numbers not exceeding three on the list of those voted for as President, the House of Representatives shall choose immediately, by ballot, the President. But in choosing the President, the votes shall be taken by states, the representation from each state having one vote; a quorum for this purpose shall consist of a member or members from two-thirds of the states, and a majority of all the states shall be necessary to a choice. And if the House of Representatives shall not choose a President whenever the right of choice shall devolve upon them, before the fourth day of March next following, then the Vice-President shall act as President, as in the case of the death or other constitutional disability of the President. The person having the greatest number of votes as Vice-President, shall be the Vice-President, if such number be a majority of the whole number of electors appointed, and if no person have a majority, then from the two highest numbers on the list, the Senate shall choose the Vice-President; a quorum for the purpose shall consist of two-thirds of the whole number of Senators, and a majority of the whole number shall be necessary to a choice. But no person constitutionally ineligible to the office of President shall be eligible to that of Vice-President of the United States.

Amendment XIII [1865]

Section 1. Neither slavery nor involuntary servitude, except as a punishment for crime whereof the party shall have been duly convicted, shall exist within the United States, or any place subject to their jurisdiction.

Section 2. Congress shall have power to enforce this article by appropriate legislation.

Amendment XIV [1868]

Section 1. All persons born or naturalized in the United States, and subject to the jurisdiction thereof, are citizens of the United States and of the state wherein they reside. No state shall make or enforce any law which shall abridge the privileges or immunities of citizens of the United States; nor shall any state deprive any person of life, liberty, or property, without due process of law; nor deny to any person within its jurisdiction the equal protection of the laws.

Section 2. Representatives shall be apportioned among the several states according to their respective numbers, counting the whole number of persons in each state, excluding Indians not taxed. But when the right to vote at any election for the choice of electors for President and Vice President of the United States, Representatives in Congress, the executive and judicial officers of a state, or the members of the legislature thereof, is denied to any of the male inhabitants of such state, being twenty-one years of age, and citizens of the United States, or in any way abridged, except for participation in rebellion, or other crime, the basis of representation therein shall be reduced in the proportion which the number of such male citizens shall bear to the whole number of male citizens twenty-one years of age in such state.

Section 3. No person shall be a Senator or Representative in Congress, or elector of President and Vice President, or hold any office, civil or military, under the United States, or under any state, who, having previously taken an oath, as a member of Congress, or as an officer of the United States, or as a member of any state legislature, or as an executive or judicial officer of any state, to support the Constitution of the United States, shall have engaged in insurrection or rebellion against the same, or given aid or comfort to the enemies thereof. But Congress may by a vote of two-thirds of each House, remove such disability.

Section 4. The validity of the public debt of the United States, authorized by law, including debts incurred for payment of pensions and bounties for services in suppressing insurrection or rebellion, shall not be questioned. But neither the United States nor any state shall assume or pay any debt or obligation incurred in aid of insurrection or rebellion against the United States, or any claim for the loss or emancipation of any slave; but all such debts, obligations and claims shall be held illegal and void.

Section 5. The Congress shall have power to enforce, by appropriate legislation, the provisions of this article.

Amendment XV [1870]

Section 1. The right of citizens of the United States to vote shall not be denied or abridged by the United States or by any state on account of race, color, or previous condition of servitude.

Section 2. The Congress shall have power to enforce this article by appropriate legislation.

Amendment XVI [1913]

The Congress shall have power to lay and collect taxes on incomes, from whatever source derived, without apportionment among the several states, and without regard to any census of enumeration.

Amendment XVII [1913]

[1] The Senate of the United States shall be composed of two Senators from each state, elected by the people thereof, for six years; and each Senator shall have one vote. The electors in each state shall

have the qualifications requisite for electors of the most numerous branch of the state legislatures.

[2] When vacancies happen in the representation of any state in the Senate, the executive authority of such state shall issue writs of election to fill such vacancies: Provided, that the legislature of any state may empower the executive thereof to make temporary appointments until the people fill the vacancies by election as the legislature may direct.

[3] This amendment shall not be so construed as to affect the election or term of any Senator chosen before it becomes valid as part of the Constitution.

Amendment XVIII [1919]

Section 1. After one year from the ratification of this article the manufacture, sale, or transportation of intoxicating liquors within, the importation thereof into, or the exportation thereof from the United States and all territory subject to the jurisdiction thereof for beverage purposes is hereby prohibited.

Section 2. The Congress and the several states shall have concurrent power to enforce this article by appropriate legislation.

Section 3. This article shall be inoperative unless it shall have been ratified as an amendment to the Constitution by the legislatures of the several states, as provided in the Constitution, within seven years from the date of the submission hereof to the states by the Congress.

Amendment XIX [1920]

[1] The right of citizens of the United States to vote shall not be denied or abridged by the United States or by any state on account of sex.

[2] Congress shall have power to enforce this article by appropriate legislation.

Amendment XX [1933]

Section 1. The terms of the President and Vice President shall end at noon on the 20th day of January, and the terms of Senators and Representatives at noon on the 3d day of January, of the years in which such terms would have ended if this article had not been ratified; and the terms of their successors shall then begin.

Section 2. The Congress shall assemble at least once in every year, and such meeting shall begin at noon on the 3d day of January, unless they shall by law appoint a different day.

Section 3. If, at the time fixed for the beginning of the term of the President, the President elect shall have died, the Vice President elect shall become President. If a President shall not have been chosen before the time fixed for the beginning of his term, or if the President elect shall have failed to qualify, then the Vice President elect shall act as President until a President shall have qualified; and the Congress may by law provide for the case wherein neither a President elect nor a Vice President elect shall have qualified, declaring who shall then act as President, or the manner in which one who is to act shall be selected, and such person shall act accordingly until a President or Vice President shall have qualified.

Section 4. The Congress may by law provide for the case of the death of any of the persons from whom the House of Representatives may choose a President whenever the right of choice shall have devolved upon them, and for the case of the death of any of the persons from whom the Senate may choose a Vice President whenever the right of choice shall have devolved upon them.

Section 5. Sections 1 and 2 shall take effect on the 15th day of October following the ratification of this article.

Section 6. This article shall be inoperative unless it shall have been ratified as an amendment to the Constitution by the legislatures of three-fourths of the several states within seven years from the date of its submission.

Amendment XXI [1933]

Section 1. The eighteenth article of amendment to the Constitution of the United States is hereby repealed.

Section 2. The transportation or importation into any state, territory, or possession of the United States for delivery or use therein of intoxicating liquors, in violation of the laws thereof, is hereby prohibited.

Section 3. This article shall be inoperative unless it shall have been ratified as an amendment to the Constitution by conventions in the several states, as provided in the Constitution, within seven years from the date of the submission hereof to the states by the Congress.

Amendment XXII [1951]

Section 1. No person shall be elected to the office of the President more than twice, and no person who has held the office of President, or acted as President, for more than two years of a term to which some other person was elected President shall be elected to the office of the President more than once. But this article shall not apply to any person holding the office of President when this article was proposed by the Congress, and shall not prevent any person who may be holding the office of President, or acting as President, during the term within which this article becomes operative from holding the office of President or acting as President during the remainder of such term.

Section 2. This article shall be inoperative unless it shall have been ratified as an amendment to the Constitution by the legislatures of three- fourths of the several states within seven years from the date of its submission to the states by the Congress.

Amendment XXIII [1961]

Section 1. The District constituting the seat of government of the United States shall appoint in such manner as the Congress may direct:

A number of electors of President and Vice President equal to the whole number of Senators and Representatives in Congress to which the District would be entitled if it were a state, but in no event more than the least populous state; they shall be in addition to those appointed by the states, but they shall be considered, for the purposes of the election of President and Vice President, to be electors appointed by a state; and they shall meet in the District and perform such duties as provided by the twelfth article of amendment.

Section 2. The Congress shall have power to enforce this article by appropriate legislation.

Amendment XXIV [1964]

Section 1. The right of citizens of the United States to vote in any primary or other election for President or Vice President, for electors for President or Vice President, or for Senator or Representative in Congress, shall not be denied or abridged by the United States or any state by reason of failure to pay any poll tax or other tax.

Section 2. The Congress shall have power to enforce this article by appropriate legislation.

Amendment XXV [1967]

Section 1. In case of the removal of the President from office or of his death or resignation, the Vice President shall become President.

Section 2. Whenever there is a vacancy in the office of the Vice President, the President shall nominate a Vice President who shall take office upon confirmation by a majority vote of both Houses of Congress.

Section 3. Whenever the President transmits to the President pro tempore of the Senate and the Speaker of the House of Representatives his written declaration that he is unable to discharge the powers and duties of his office, and until he transmits to them a written declaration to the contrary, such powers and duties shall be discharged by the Vice President as Acting President.

Section 4. Whenever the Vice President and a majority of either the principal officers of the executive departments or of such other body as Congress may by law provide, transmit to the President pro tempore of the Senate and the Speaker of the House of Representatives their written declaration that the President is unable to discharge the powers and duties of his office, the Vice President shall immediately assume the powers and duties of the office as Acting President.

Thereafter, when the President transmits to the President pro tempore of the Senate and the Speaker of the House of Representatives his written declaration that no inability exists, he shall resume the powers and duties of his office unless the Vice President and a majority of either the principal officers of the executive department or of such other body as Congress may by law provide, transmit within four days to the President pro tempore of the Senate and the Speaker of the House of Representatives their written declaration that the President is unable to discharge the powers and duties of his office. Thereupon Congress shall decide the issue, assembling within forty-eight hours for that purpose if not in session. If the Congress, within twenty-one days after receipt of the latter written declaration, or, if Congress is not in session, within twenty-one days after Congress is required to assemble, determines by two-thirds vote of both Houses that the President is unable to discharge the powers and duties of his office, the Vice President shall continue to discharge the same as Acting President; otherwise, the President shall resume the powers and duties of his office.

Amendment XXVI [1971]

Section 1. The right of citizens of the United States, who are 18 years of age or older, to vote, shall not be denied or abridged by the United States or any state on account of age.

Section 2. The Congress shall have the power to enforce this article by appropriate legislation.

Amendment XXVII [1992]

No law varying the compensation for the services of the Senators and Representatives shall take effect until an election of Representatives shall have intervened.

UNIVERSITY CASEBOOK SERIES®

THE FEDERAL COURTS AND THE FEDERAL SYSTEM

SEVENTH EDITION

CHAPTER I

THE DEVELOPMENT AND STRUCTURE OF THE FEDERAL JUDICIAL SYSTEM

INTRODUCTORY NOTE: THE JUDICIARY ARTICLE IN THE CONSTITUTIONAL CONVENTION AND THE RATIFICATION DEBATES

Article III, the judiciary article of the Constitution, emerged from the Convention that met in Philadelphia during the summer of 1787.[1] In the words of a leading scholar, however, to "one who is especially interested in the judiciary, there is surprisingly little on the subject to be found in the records of the convention".[2] For most of the delegates, the judiciary was a secondary or even a tertiary concern. To understand the Convention's deliberations about Article III, attention to context is therefore vital.

A. Background of the Convention

On the whole, the period from the end of the Revolution to the ratification of the Constitution was one of economic growth.[3] Nonetheless, a downturn in the middle of the 1780s caused significant dislocations, especially for debtors. For this among other reasons, "the Critical Period", as it has been called,[4] was a time of frustration, tension, and anxiety.[5]

By all accounts, the prevailing structure of "national" government, the Articles of Confederation, had proved inadequate to the challenges confronting the new nation. The Articles provided no executive branch and

---

[1] Farrand, The Records of the Federal Convention 20–23 (1911) (hereinafter cited as Farrand), is the basic document for the study of the Convention. Three volumes were published in 1911; a fourth, published in 1937, has been revised and expanded. Hutson, Supplement to Max Farrand's Records of the Federal Convention of 1787 (1987).

Secondary sources include Amar, America's Constitution: A Biography (2006); Farrand, The Framing of the Constitution of the United States (1913) (hereinafter cited as Farrand, Framing); Goebel, History of the Supreme Court of the United States: Antecedents and Beginnings to 1801, at 196–250 (1971); McDonald, Novus Ordo Seclorum: The Intellectual Origins of the Constitution (1985); Rakove, Original Meanings: Politics and Ideas in the Making of the Constitution (1996); Stewart, The Summer of 1787: The Men Who Invented the Constitution (2007); and Warren, The Making of the Constitution 3–54 (1937 ed.).

Professors Kurland and Lerner have assembled a five-volume anthology, The Founders' Constitution (1987), which presents views expressed on constitutional problems before, during, and after the Convention, through 1835. The volumes are keyed to the provisions of the Constitution and the first twelve amendments.

[2] Farrand, Framing, note 1, *supra*, at 154.

[3] See generally Wood, The Creation of the American Republic, 1776–1787, at 393–96 (1969); Jensen, The New Nation: A History of the United States During the Articles of Confederation, 1781–1789, at 256, 339–40, 423–24 (1950).

[4] The label apparently originated with Fiske, The Critical Period of American History, 1783–89 (1883).

[5] See generally Wood, note 3, *supra*, at 393–467.

no system of courts. Each state had equal representation in Congress, and the concurrence of nine was needed for most important matters, including the appropriation of money. To levy a tariff required unanimous consent, which was never forthcoming. Perhaps the most basic problem, however, was that Congress lacked mechanisms to enforce its mandates. It could pass resolutions and make recommendations, but had to rely on the states to implement them. The states proved increasingly unwilling to do so.

Efforts to enforce the Treaty of Paris with Great Britain illustrated the difficulty. The treaty guaranteed the integrity of some of the private debts owed to British subjects, provided for post-war return of certain British property interests acquired before the war, and limited private causes of action against British subjects arising out of legitimate war activities. Yet nearly all the states enacted statutes that violated these and other provisions of the treaty. Even when states formally allowed suits by aliens, the cherished right to trial by jury often functioned as an instrument of nullification, as it sometimes did in other debtor-creditor actions.[6]

Under the circumstances, the nation suffered a series of humiliations in foreign affairs. In addition, the need for a national power to tax and to regulate commerce was increasingly obvious. By 1787 "[a]lmost every political leader in the country, including most of the later opponents of the Constitution, wanted something done to strengthen the Articles of Confederation".[7]

Related to the problems issuing from national weakness, but possessing a dynamic of their own, were anxieties about emerging political currents in the state legislatures and elsewhere.[8] By the 1780s, a burgeoning commercialism had broadly expanded networks of credit and debt, and resentments accumulated around debtor-creditor relations, including those between the states—most of which had borrowed heavily during the Revolution—and their debt holders. At least six states responded by authorizing paper money, which was widely expected to yield inflation.[9] Some feared that it would spawn a broad-based financial instability. In the state legislatures, movements were afoot to pass debtor relief laws. In Massachusetts, Shays' Rebellion—a revolt of western debtors—broke out.

To many of those who came to be called Federalists, "the rage for paper money, for an abolition of debts",[10] and similar proposals reflected not only bad policy, but also a form of political immorality—a breach of honor, if not of natural right, and one that threatened to spawn both financial and political turmoil.[11] From this perspective, a new, national constitution was necessary to restore a regime of virtuous government—or, failing that, a scheme that would protect individual rights and the public good by ensuring

---

[6] See Holt, *"To Establish Justice": Politics, The Judiciary Act of 1789, and the Invention of the Federal Courts*, 1989 Duke L.J. 1421, 1427–58.

[7] Wood, Empire of Liberty: A History of the Early Republic, 1789–1815, at 15 (2009).

[8] See *id.* at 15–20; Holton, Unruly Americans and the Origins of the Constitution 21–123 (2007).

[9] See, *e.g.*, Reisman, *Money, Credit, and Federalist Political Economy*, in Beeman, Botein, & Carter, Beyond Confederation: Origins of the Constitution and American National Identity 128, 150–51 (1987); Jensen, note 3, *supra*, at 313–26.

[10] The Federalist, No. 10 (Madison).

[11] See Wood, note 7, *supra*, at 15–20.

that faction would be checked by faction[12] and ambition set against ambition.[13]

When the Constitutional Convention met in Philadelphia with a charge to amend the Articles of Confederation, it agreed immediately to ignore the limits on its mandate and instead to draft an entirely new Constitution.[14] With the agenda thus framed, the central questions involved the extent to which a new Constitution should create and empower a truly national government to replace the existing confederation. At one pole stood the nationalists.[15] At the other were those who preferred more minor departures from the existing confederated structure, with authority concentrated in the sovereign states and delegated to a federal government by the states for limited purposes only.[16]

As historical studies of "republican" ideology[17] have emphasized, this division tended to correlate with, and at least partly reflected, a more profound disagreement about the foundations of legitimate government. The nationalists—or "Federalists", as they came to be called—generally favored centralized institutions in which enlightened representatives would be at least partly insulated from, and reasonably asked to rise above, the play of passions and factional interests that often characterized local politics. By contrast, those wishing to retain the central significance of more local institutions tended to be suspicious of political and economic elites and supportive of democratic egalitarianism.[18]

Against this backdrop, perhaps the most crucial decision of the Constitutional Convention was that a federal government should be established with powers to act directly on individuals, not just on the member states. The most important implementing decisions were those defining the powers of the national government, allocating representation

---

[12] See The Federalist, No. 10 (Madison).

[13] See The Federalist, No. 51 (Madison).

[14] On the relationships among formal legality and illegality, popular sovereignty, and the theory of political legitimacy reflected in the framing and ratification of the Constitution, and on the implications of the implicit constitutional theory of the founding for subsequent American constitutional history, see Ackerman, 1 We the People: Foundations (1991); Ackerman & Katyal, *Our Unconventional Founding*, 62 U.Chi.L.Rev. 475 (1995); Amar, *Philadelphia Revisited: Amending the Constitution Outside Article V*, 55 U.Chi.L.Rev. 1043 (1988); Amar, *The Consent of the Governed: Constitutional Amendment Outside Article V*, 94 Colum.L.Rev. 457 (1994); Rakove, *The Super-Legality of the Constitution, or, A Federalist Critique of Bruce Ackerman's Neo-Federalism*, 108 Yale L.J. 1931 (1999). Professor Ackerman generally sees the founders as breaking sharply with existing legal forms, in the name of higher law or "We the People", whereas Professors Amar and Rakove assert the availability of legal justifications for the course of action followed at the Convention and after.

[15] Crosskey, Politics and the Constitution in the History of the United States (1953), makes especially strong claims about the nationalism of the Constitution that emerged from the Convention. On the general dismissal of Crosskey's work by a later generation of historians, see Beeman, *Introduction*, in Beeman, Botein, & Carter, note 9, *supra*, at 6–8.

[16] Middlekauff, The Glorious Cause: The American Revolution, 1763–1789 (2005).

[17] The pathbreaking works are Bailyn, The Ideological Origins of the American Revolution (1967); Wood, note 3, *supra*; and Pocock, The Machiavellian Moment: Florentine Political Thought and the Atlantic Republican Tradition (1975). For valuable overviews, see Appleby, Liberalism and Republicanism in the Historical Imagination (1992); Kloppenberg, The Virtues of Liberalism (1998); and Rodgers, *Republicanism: The Career of a Concept*, 79 J.Am.Hist. 11 (1992).

[18] See generally Wood, note 3, *supra*, at 393–615; Wood, note 7, *supra*; Ellis, Founding Brothers: The Revolutionary Generation (2001). For a more skeptical survey, see Holton, note 8, *supra*, at 162–98.

among the states, and distributing responsibilities between the national legislature and the national executive. Almost without exception, decisions regarding the judiciary were ancillary, and reflected settlements and divisions concerning more deeply controversial issues.

B. The Convention

The Convention's main decisions concerning the federal courts may be grouped under six headings:

First, that there should be a federal judicial power operating, like the legislative and executive powers, upon both states and individuals;

Second, that the power should be vested in a Supreme Court and in such inferior federal courts as Congress might establish;

Third, that the federal judiciary should be as "independent as the lot of humanity will admit"[19];

Fourth, that its power should be judicial only but should include the power to pass upon the constitutionality of both state and federal legislation;

Fifth, that the power should extend to nine specified classes of cases; and

Sixth, that in certain cases the Supreme Court should have original jurisdiction and in the remainder "appellate Jurisdiction, both as to Law and Fact, with such Exceptions, and under such Regulations as the Congress shall make."

To understand the judicial structure chosen at the Convention, however, one must have a general picture of the way the Convention worked. Its deliberations divided into three main phases.

The settlement of general principles (May 30 to July 26). Although the Convention was scheduled to convene on May 14, a quorum did not arrive until May 25, and the Convention did not begin its substantive business until four days later. On May 29, Governor Edmund Randolph of Virginia presented fifteen resolutions, variously referred to as the "Virginia Plan" or the "Randolph Plan", that as amended and expanded ultimately became the Constitution of the United States.[20]

Jointly drafted by the Virginia delegation, but with Madison exerting a heavy influence,[21] the Randolph Plan called for a national government consisting of legislative, executive, and judicial branches. It provided national legislative authority "in all cases to which the separate States are incompetent, or in which the harmony of the United States may be interrupted by individual legislation"; and it conferred a legislative veto over state legislation. The national legislature was to consist of two houses, each apportioned according to the states' free population or their contributions to the national treasury. The Randolph Plan contemplated a national executive and a judiciary "to consist of one or more supreme tribunals, and of inferior tribunals to be chosen by the National Legislature".[22]

Randolph's resolutions became the order of business when, on May 30, the Convention resolved itself into a Committee of the Whole to begin serious

---

[19]   Article XXIX of the Declaration of Rights of the Massachusetts Constitution of 1780.

[20]   1 Farrand, note 1, *supra*, at 20–23.

[21]   See Banning, The Sacred Fire of Liberty: James Madison and the Founding of the Federal Republic 111–37 (1995).

[22]   1 Farrand, note 1, *supra*, at 21–22.

deliberation. On the same day, Charles Pinckney of South Carolina proposed a draft constitution that was also referred to the committee.[23] As discussed and amended through two weeks of debate, the Randolph Plan provided the substance of the first report of the Committee of the Whole to the Convention on June 13.

Randolph's plan had a distinctly nationalist thrust, and, unsurprisingly, it precipitated a counter-proposal (by William Paterson of New Jersey),[24] which would have retained the existing unicameral Congress, with each state continuing to possess an equal vote. Even the Paterson Plan, however, would have created a national executive and a national judiciary. During this period, Alexander Hamilton of New York presented the fourth and last of the complete plans before the Convention.[25] As a final contribution to the mix, the Convention probably had before it a draft, of a judiciary article only, in the handwriting of John Blair of Virginia.[26]

But it was the Randolph Plan, and to a lesser extent the Paterson alternative, on which the delegates principally focused. Upon the introduction of the Paterson Plan, both it and the Randolph Plan were returned to the Committee of the Whole. Following four days of debate, the Committee voted on June 19, seven states to three with Maryland divided,[27] to adhere to its original report of the Randolph resolutions.

There followed the second major round of debate, in the Convention proper, on the report of the Committee of the Whole. At the outset, progress stalled for nearly a month, as—amid threats that delegates from the small states would pull out—the Convention wrestled with the divisive issue of proportional versus equal representation of the states. Finally, on July 16, the delegates reached a compromise under which representation would be proportional in the House but equal in the Senate. Remaining disagreements were resolved, frequently by compromise, over the next ten days.

The elaboration of detail (July 27 to September 10).[28] The Convention adjourned from July 27 to August 6 while a Committee of Detail, chaired by John Rutledge, prepared the first definite draft of the Constitution.[29] The Committee built upon the votes of the Convention adopting or modifying Randolph's Virginia Plan, but it drew also on the other plans that had been submitted, on the provisions of various state constitutions, and on a report drafted in 1781 by a committee of the Continental Congress that had sought to revise the Articles of Confederation. The report of the Committee of Detail introduced the third major round of debate, during which the Convention finally came to agreement on all remaining problems of general principle.

Final settlement and polishing (September 10 to 17).[30] A Committee on Style, which made more than stylistic changes, reported to the Convention

---

[23] 3 *id.* 595–609 (Appendix D).

[24] 1 *id.* 242–45, 3 *id.* 611–16 (Appendix E).

[25] 1 *id.* 291–93, 3 *id.* 617–30 (Appendix F).

[26] Blair's draft was later found in the papers of George Mason. 2 *id.* 432–33.

[27] 1 *id.* 313, 322.

[28] This phase is described in Farrand, Framing, note 1, *supra*, at 124–75, and Warren, note 1, *supra*, at 368–685.

[29] 2 Farrand, note 1, *supra*, at 177–89.

[30] For this final phase, see Farrand, Framing, note 1, *supra*, at 176–95, and Warren, note 1, *supra*, at 686–721.

on September 12.[31] There ensued a final review, which produced minor amendments and culminated in the signing of the engrossed Constitution on Monday, September 17.

C.   The Judiciary Article

1.   A Federal Judicial Power

On the first day of substantive debate (May 30), the Committee of the Whole accepted Randolph's resolution "that a national government ought to be established consisting of a supreme Legislative, Judiciary, and Executive".[32] Again on June 4, Madison records in his notes, the first clause of Randolph's ninth resolution—"Resolved that a national Judiciary be established"—passed unanimously.[33] Without discussion or further question, the delegates thereby agreed to a substantial innovation in American experience. The new states had tried to settle border disputes by the device of *ad hoc* tribunals.[34] In addition, Congress had possessed the power to "appoint" state courts for the trial of "piracies and felonies on the high seas",[35] and it had even established a distinctively national court to handle appeals in cases of capture.[36] But what was now proposed was much

---

[31] 2 Farrand, note 1, *supra*, at 590–603.

[32] Connecticut alone opposed, with New York divided. 1 *id*. 30–32.

[33] Madison's Journal 108 (Scott ed. 1895). See also 1 Farrand, note 1, *supra*, at 104.

[34] The Articles of Confederation provided a cumbersome machinery for resolving disputes between states, under which the disputing states selected seven judges by joint consent, any five of whom constituted a quorum. If judges could not be agreed upon, Congress was to select three candidates from each state, and the court would be arrived at by alternate striking of names. The judgment of the court was to be final. Articles of Confederation, Art. IX.

The only case ever decided under this provision involved a dispute between Connecticut and Pennsylvania over territory on the banks of the Susquehanna River. In 1775, prior to the enactment of the Articles, a special committee of Congress was appointed, which recommended the terms of an armistice that should govern until the dispute could be settled. When a court was appointed in 1782, by joint consent, it sat for forty-two days in Trenton, New Jersey, then rendered a unanimous judgment against Connecticut. Although Connecticut acquiesced, individual Connecticut settlers were unwilling to cede their lands, and uncertainty persisted. Carson, The Supreme Court of the United States 67–74 (1891).

[35] Articles of Confederation, Art. IX. Congress exercised the power by providing for trial of such offenses by designated state judges in 1781. See Carson, note 34, *supra*, at 42–43. In all such cases an appeal was to lie to Congress, or such person or persons as Congress should appoint. All the states but New York complied, and even New York ultimately appears to have come into partial compliance. See *id*. at 45.

[36] The first appeal from a state tribunal came up in August of 1776, and Congress appointed a special committee to hear it. The practice of appointing special committees continued until January, 1777, when a five-member Standing Committee was established. At length, however, in January, 1780, Congress resolved "that a Court be established for trial of all appeals from the Courts of Admiralty in these United States, in cases of capture, to consist of 3 Judges appointed and commissioned by Congress * * *." See *id*. at 41–64.

Although this was the first national court, several needed powers were stricken from its authorizing provisions, including those of fining and imprisoning for contempt and disobedience and directing that the state admiralty courts should execute its decrees. *Id*. at 56. Indeed, the court was never really independent of its creator. In the case of the brig "Lusanna", involving a delicate question of national power arising out of conflict between a New Hampshire statute and the act of Congress creating the Court of Appeals, Congress ordered that all proceedings upon the sentence of the court be stayed, and attempted to determine the dispute itself. Congress never took any final action in the case, but it defeated a motion stating that it was improper for Congress in any manner to reverse or control the court's decisions. In December, 1784, business had dwindled; the court had cleared its docket; and after a few more occasional sessions, the court ceased to function on May 16, 1787. *Id*. at 58–60.

more than a specialized tribunal. It was a national judicial power joined with executive and legislative powers as part of a national government.

The Convention's unhesitating initial agreement about the need for a national judiciary was only a prelude to serious disagreements about the kinds of tribunals that should exercise the judicial power and about the scope of the jurisdiction that these tribunals should possess. Nonetheless, the unanimity bespoke a general understanding that an efficacious government requires courts.

2. The Tribunals Exercising the Power

Having agreed to the establishment of a national judiciary, the Convention proceeded swiftly to vote that the judicial branch should "consist of one supreme tribunal, and of one or more inferior tribunals."[37] The vote of June 4, reiterated on June 5, reflected an uncontroversial agreement, never to be reconsidered, that there should be one Supreme Court.[38] The decision concerning inferior federal courts proved less stable.[39]

On June 5, after an inconclusive discussion about where the power to appoint inferior tribunals should lie, Rutledge moved to reconsider the provision for their establishment at all. He urged that "the State Tribunals might and ought to be left in all cases to decide in the first instance the right of appeal to the supreme national tribunal being sufficient to secure the national rights & uniformity of Judgments: that it was making an unnecessary encroachment on the jurisdiction of the States, and creating unnecessary obstacles to their adoption of the new system".[40] Sherman, supporting him, dwelled on the expense of an additional set of courts.[41]

Madison strongly opposed the motion. He argued that "unless inferior federal tribunals were dispersed throughout the Republic with *final* jurisdiction in *many* cases, appeals would be multiplied to a most oppressive degree".[42] Besides, he maintained, "an appeal would not in many cases be a remedy." "What was to be done after improper Verdicts in State tribunals obtained under the biassed directions of a dependent Judge, or the local prejudices of an undirected jury? To remand the cause for a new trial would answer no purpose. To order a new trial at the supreme bar would oblige the parties to bring up their witnesses, tho' ever so distant from the seat of the Court. An effective Judiciary establishment commensurate to the legislative

---

Nonetheless, "some 118 cases were disposed of by the congressional committees and the Court of Appeals, and the idea became well fixed that admiralty and maritime cases pertained to federal jurisdiction". Hockett, The Constitutional History of the United States 157 (1939).

[37] 1 Farrand, note 1, *supra*, at 104–05 (June 4), 119 (June 5).

[38] All the plans submitted to the Convention provided for a Supreme Court. See *id.* 21, 244, 292; 2 *id.* 432; 3 *id.* 600.

[39] Although the Randolph and Pinckney plans called for mandatory establishment of inferior federal courts, the Paterson plan did not provide for any such courts at all. Hamilton's plan empowered Congress to create them if it so chose. John Blair's plan provided only for lower courts of admiralty. See 3 *id.* 593–94 (Randolph); *id.* 600 (Pinckney); *id.* 612 (Paterson); *id.* 618 (Hamilton); 2 *id.* 432 (Blair).

[40] 1 Farrand, note 1, *supra*, at 124.

[41] *Id.* 125.

[42] *Id.* 124.

authority, was essential."[43] Wilson and Dickinson spoke in the same vein, with the former emphasizing the special need for an admiralty jurisdiction.[44]

Despite these appeals, Rutledge's motion to strike out "inferior tribunals" carried, five states to four with two divided.[45] This, however, was not the end of the matter. Picking up on a suggestion by Dickinson, Wilson and Madison moved a compromise resolution, which provided that "the National Legislature [should] be empowered" to "institute"—the verb recorded in Madison's notes[46]—or "appoint"—the word in the Convention Journal[47] and another set of contemporary notes[48]—"inferior tribunals". According to Madison, he and Wilson "observed that there was a distinction between establishing such tribunals absolutely, and giving a discretion to the Legislature to establish or not establish them".[49]

Pierce Butler objected even to this compromise proposal: "The people will not bear such innovations. The States will revolt at such encroachments." Despite this protest, "the Madisonian Compromise", as it has come to be called, was agreed to, eight states to two with one divided.[50]

Opposition to a system of inferior federal courts was renewed when the report of the Committee of the Whole came before the Convention on July 18. But it was milder, with Sherman saying that he "was willing to give the power to the Legislature but wished them to make use of the State Tribunals whenever it could be done with safety to the general interest". This time the vote accepting the compromise was unanimous,[51] and the decision stood without further question.[52] The Committee of Detail reported a draft prescribing that the judicial power "shall be vested in one Supreme Court and in such inferior Courts as shall, when necessary, from time to time, be

---

43 *Id.*

44 *Id.* 124 (Wilson), 125 (Dickinson).

45 *Id.* 125.

46 *Id.*

47 *Id.* 118.

48 *Id.* 127 (Yates).

49 *Id.* 125.

50 *Id.* 124–25 (June 5). Professor Collins sees a puzzle in the sequence of the Convention's actions on June 4–5: Why, within so short a span, did the Convention swing from unanimous approval of constitutionally mandated lower federal courts, to preclusion of lower federal courts altogether, to approval of a compromise apparently authorizing Congress to "appoint" or "establish" lower federal courts? See Collins, *Article III Cases, State Court Duties, and the Madisonian Compromise*, 1995 Wisc.L.Rev. 35, 116–19. During the interval between the vote to approve mandatory federal courts and adoption of Rutledge's motion to reconsider, the Convention voted to delete the provision of the Randolph Plan that the national judiciary should be elected by the national legislature and to leave open for the time being the question of judicial selection. Emphasizing this background, Collins speculates that Rutledge's motion to reconsider may have been motivated by the intervening debate on the selection of the federal judiciary; if the power did not lie with the legislature, the Convention might have considered it too dangerous to be vested elsewhere.

A related suggestion ascribes significance to the contested wording of Madison's and Wilson's compromise resolution: if the congressional power was one to "appoint" inferior tribunals, this formulation may hark back to the practice under the Articles of Confederation by which Congress "appointed" existing state courts, rather than creating independent federal courts, to conduct certain forms of judicial business. See Goebel, note 1, *supra*, at 211–12. On the subsequent alteration of the language to its final form, see *infra*.

51 2 Farrand, note 1, *supra*, at 45–46 (July 18).

52 In the debate on the report of the Committee of Detail, a motion, recorded only in the Journal, was made and seconded to give the inferior federal courts only an appellate jurisdiction over decisions of state courts, but the motion was withdrawn. *Id.* 424 (August 27).

constituted by the Legislature of the United States."[53] The Committee of Style further altered the language to its current form.

3.   Separation and Independence of the Judicial Power

a.   Appointment of Judges

The method of appointing federal judges occasioned significant controversy. The Randolph Plan called for appointment by the legislature, but Madison objected that many legislators would be incompetent to assess judicial qualifications and proposed appointment by the "less numerous & more select" Senate.[54] The Committee of the Whole agreed to Madison's suggested amendment on June 13. The Convention adhered to this decision on July 21, when it rejected another proposal by Madison, who now feared that senatorial appointment would confer too much power on the states, and instead urged appointment by the national executive, with or without the approval of the Senate.[55] In the closing days the issue was reopened yet again and finally resolved, as part of a general settlement on appointments, in favor of appointment by the executive with the advice and consent of the Senate.[56]

b.   Tenure and Salary

The provisions protecting the tenure and salary of judges received almost complete assent.[57] There was minor controversy over whether to prevent the temptation of pay increases. The Committee of the Whole first accepted language barring increase as well as diminution in salary during tenure in office,[58] but the prohibition against increases was rejected in the subsequent debate in the Convention and again in the debate on the report of the Committee of Detail.[59] Rejection rested largely on the practical ground that the cost of living might rise.

---

[53] *Id.* 186. According to Pfander, Federal Supremacy, State Court Inferiority, and the Constitutionality of Jurisdiction-Stripping Legislation, 101 Nw.U.L.Rev. 191 (2007), a full understanding of the significance of the report of the Committee of Detail requires attention not only to the judiciary article, but also to the provision of Article I, § 8, cl. 9 authorizing Congress "[t]o constitute Tribunals inferior to the supreme Court." Pfander maintains that when Articles I and III are read in conjunction, the import of the report of the Committee of Detail was that "Congress could proceed either by appointing state courts to serve as tribunals under Article I (as Sherman hoped), or by creating new federal courts under Article III (as Madison hoped)". Insofar as Congress fails to vest federal courts with jurisdiction to rule on federal claims, Pfander maintains, state courts should be regarded as having been constituted as "Tribunals inferior to the supreme Court". For critical discussion of this thesis, see pp. 321 n.27, 389–390 n.8, *infra*.

[54] 1 Farrand, note 1, *supra*, at 233 (June 13).

[55] The first proposal for appointment by the President with the concurrence of the Senate was made by Hamilton on June 5. Motions for executive appointment alone, or executive appointment subject to Senate approval, were defeated on several occasions thereafter. See *id.* 128, 224, 232–33; 2 *id.* 80–83; Warren, note 1, *supra*, at 327–29.

[56] Appointment by the Senate was retained in the draft reported by the Committee of Detail. 2 Farrand, note 1, *supra*, at 132, 155, 169, 183. The final compromise was worked out between August 25 and September 7. See *id.* 498, 538–40; Warren, note 1, *supra*, at 639–42. For Hamilton's comments on the matter, see The Federalist, Nos. 76, 77.

[57] All four of the principal plans provided that the judges should hold office during good behavior, and the Randolph, Pinckney, and Paterson plans forbade either a decrease or an increase in salary during continuance in office.

[58] 1 Farrand, note 1, *supra,* at 121.

[59] 2 *id.* 44–45, 429–30; Warren, note 1, *supra,* at 532–34. See also Rosenn, The Constitutional Guaranty Against Diminution of Judicial Compensation, 24 UCLA L.Rev. 308, 311–18 (1976).

The lone assault on the principle of tenure during good behavior occurred in the debate on the report of the Committee of Detail, when Dickinson of Delaware, seconded by Gerry and Sherman, moved that the judges "may be removed by the Executive on the application by the Senate and House of Representatives". The motion drew strong opposition, however, and only Connecticut ultimately supported it.[60]

c. Extra-Judicial Functions

Randolph's eighth resolution proposed to create a council of revision composed of "the Executive and a convenient number of the National Judiciary" with authority, first, "to examine every act of the National Legislature before it shall operate", and, second, to review every negative exercised by the National Legislature upon an act of a state legislature, pursuant to a power proposed in the sixth resolution, before it "shall be final". The dissent of the council was to "amount to a rejection, unless the Act of the National Legislature be again passed, or that of a particular Legislature be again negatived by [blank] of the members of each branch".[61]

In an early vote of 8–2, the Committee of the Whole rejected this plan to mingle executive and judicial functions, and substituted a purely executive veto of national legislation.[62] Madison and Wilson renewed the proposal for a council of revision on three subsequent occasions, but the Convention defeated it each time.[63]

In the view of Madison and Wilson, judicial participation in a council of revision would have furnished a necessary check upon legislative aggrandizement and provided an assurance of wiser laws. The arguments that prevailed against it were concisely stated by Gerry and King:

"Mr. Gerry doubts whether the Judiciary ought to form a part of [the council of revision], as they will have a sufficient check agst. encroachments on their own department by their exposition of the laws, which involved a power of deciding on their Constitutionality. In some States the Judges had actually set aside laws as being agst. the Constitution. This was done too

---

[60] 2 Farrand, note 1, *supra*, at 428–29; Warren, note 1, *supra*, at 532. For an extensive analysis of the problems of tenure and removal in the Constitution, see Berger, Impeachment: The Constitutional Problems (1973). Prakash & Smith, *How to Remove a Federal Judge*, 116 Yale L.J. 72 (2006), challenges the traditional assumption that Article III permits the removal of a judge only by impeachment. The authors argue that Article III should be read, in light of established English and colonial practice, to embody standards of "good Behaviour" under which various public and private officers could be removed from office pursuant to the judgment of an ordinary court. According to them, the "good Behaviour" standard is "more general and less severe" than that of "high Crimes and Misdemeanors". *But see* Redish, *Response: Good Behavior, Judicial Independence, and the Foundations of American Constitutionalism*, 116 Yale L.J. 139 (2006) (defending the traditional position by arguing that the interpretation urged by Prakash & Smith is not linguistically necessary, is incompatible with the commitment to strong judicial independence reflected in the overall constitutional structure, and finds little support in post-ratification evidence); Pfander, *Removing Federal Judges*, 74 U.Chi.L.Rev. 1227 (2007) (arguing that the Constitution's provision for a judicial tenure in office rules out any removal mechanism not specified by the Constitution).

[61] 1 Farrand, note 1, *supra*, at 21.

[62] *Id.* 97–104, 108–110 (June 4).

[63] The Committee of the Whole adhered to the rejection, eight votes to three, on June 6. *Id.* 138–140 (June 6). The Convention did likewise in the later debate on the report of the Committee of the Whole, this time by four votes to three with two states divided. 2 *id.* 73–80 (July 21). Madison and Wilson made their final attempt in the debate on the report of the Committee of Detail, but their proposal, which this time took a somewhat different form, again failed. *Id.* 298 (August 15).

with general approbation. It was quite foreign from the nature of ye. office to make them judges of the policy of public measures."

King added "that the Judges ought to be able to expound the law as it should come before them, free from the bias of having participated in its formation".[64]

The last important reference to extra-judicial functions occurred near the close of the Convention, when Dr. Johnson moved to extend the judicial power to cases arising under the Constitution of the United States, as well as under its laws and treaties.[65] Madison, responding, "doubted whether it was not going too far to extend the jurisdiction of the Court generally to cases arising under the Constitution, & whether it ought not to be limited to cases of a Judiciary Nature. The right of expounding the Constitution in cases not of this nature ought not to be given to that Department." Madison's concern notwithstanding, "The motion of Docr. Johnson was agreed to [without opposition]: it being generally supposed that the jurisdiction given was constructively limited to cases of a Judiciary nature."[66]

4.   The Power to Declare Statutes Unconstitutional

At no time did the Constitutional Convention systematically discuss the availability or scope of judicial review, but the subject drew recurrent mention in debates over related issues. As in Madison's comment on Dr. Johnson's motion, the existence of a power of judicial review appears to have been taken for granted by most if not all delegates.[67] The point became perhaps most explicit in a debate over the proposed congressional negative of state laws, during which the existence of a power in the federal courts to invalidate unconstitutional state laws was common ground. The crux of the controversy was whether this was a sufficient safeguard.[68] Resolution came through acceptance of Luther Martin's proposal of the Supremacy Clause,

---

[64]   1 *id.* 97–98, 109 (June 4).

[65]   The Convention permitted two other plans for using judges non-judicially to die without coming to votes. The first was a suggestion advanced by Ellsworth and elaborated by Gouverneur Morris to make the Chief Justice a member of the projected Privy Council of the President. See Warren, note 1, *supra*, at 643–50. The second was a proposal by Charles Pinckney that "Each branch of the Legislature, as well as the Supreme Executive shall have authority to require the opinions of the supreme Judicial Court upon important questions of law, and upon solemn occasions". 2 Farrand, note 1, *supra*, at 340–41 (August 20). Pinckney's proposal went to the Committee of Detail, but was never reported out.

[66]   2 Farrand, note 1, *supra*, at 430 (August 27). On whether the limitation of judicial authority to cases of a judiciary nature clearly precluded advisory opinions, see Chap. II, Sec. 1, *infra*.

[67]   Berger, Congress v. The Supreme Court (1969), marshals the supporting evidence. Snowiss, Judicial Review and the Law of the Constitution 40 (1990), which deals much more broadly with shifting historical understandings concerning the Constitution's nature and judicial enforceability, concludes that "[t]here was more support than opposition for judicial authority over legislation in the convention, and this was probably an accurate reflection of the strength of the contending sides outside the convention." For historical discussions on the origins of judicial review prior to the Convention, see Bilder, The Transatlantic Constitution: Colonial Legal Culture and the Empire (2005); Smith, Appeals to the Privy Council from the American Plantations (1950); and Wood, note 3, *supra*, at 453–63.

[68]   Wilson summarized the proponents' case: "The power of self-defence had been urged as necessary for the State Governments—It was equally necessary for the General Government. The firmness of Judges is not of itself sufficient. Something further is requisite—It will be better to prevent the passage of an improper law, than to declare it void when passed." 2 Farrand, note 1, *supra*, at 391 (August 23).

which strengthened the judicial check by express statement of the parallel power and responsibility of state judges.[69]

The existence of a judicial safeguard against unconstitutional federal laws was similarly recognized on both sides in the debates over the proposal for a council of revision of acts of the national legislature. Gerry's statement presupposing a power of judicial review, already quoted, was substantially echoed at least eight times.[70]

The only note of challenge came in the fourth and last debate on the proposal when Mercer, a recently arrived delegate, speaking in support of the alternative plan of judicial participation in the veto, said that he "disapproved of the Doctrine that the Judges as expositors of the Constitution should have authority to declare a law void". Dickinson then observed that he was impressed with Mr. Mercer's remark and "thought no such power ought to exist" but "he was at the same time at a loss what expedient to substitute". Gouverneur Morris at once said that he could not agree that the judiciary "should be bound to say that a direct violation of the Constitution was law", and there the discussion ended.[71]

Meanwhile, the final version of the Supremacy Clause had been approved. The Convention's matter-of-course approval of the express grant of jurisdiction in cases arising under the Constitution gives further indication that some form of judicial review was contemplated.[72]

There was no exchange of views, even indirectly, concerning appropriate judicial methodology in constitutional interpretation.[73]

---

[69] The proposal of a legislative negative, first advanced and vigorously supported throughout by Madison, was embodied in Randolph's sixth resolution, which authorized a negative only of state laws "contravening in the opinion of the National Legislature the articles of Union". 1 *id.* 21. In this form it was initially approved by the Committee of the Whole on May 31 without debate or dissent. *Id.* 54. The plan was first discussed on June 8, when the Committee rejected Charles Pinckney's motion to extend the negative to "all laws which they shd. judge to be improper". *Id.* 171. Rumblings of opposition then appeared and culminated in a debate in the Convention of July 17, when the plan was rejected. 2 *id.* 21–22.

Madison, in support, urged that states "can pass laws which will accomplish their injurious objects before they can be repealed by the Genl Legislre, or be set aside by the National Tribunals". Sherman and Gouverneur Morris, in opposition, relied upon the courts to set aside unconstitutional laws, with Sherman saying that the proposal "involves a wrong principle, to wit, that a law of a State contrary to the articles of the Union, would if not negatived, be valid and operative". None doubted the judicial power. When the negative was defeated, Luther Martin at once proposed the first version of the Supremacy Clause, "which was agreed to" without opposition. *Id.* 27–29. See also *id.* 390–91. For a discussion of the relationship between the Supremacy Clause, Madison's "federal negative," and the controversial pre-Revolution practice of Parliamentary nullification of legislation by the colonies, see LaCroix, The Ideological Origins of American Federalism (2010).

[70] See Rufus King, 1 Farrand, note 1, *supra,* at 109 (June 4); Wilson, 2 *id.* 73 (July 21); Madison, *id.* 74 (July 21), 92–93 (July 23); Martin, *id.* 76 (July 21); Mason, *id.* 78 (July 21); Pinckney, *id.* 298 (August 15); G. Morris, *id.* 299 (August 15). See also Williamson, *id.* 376 (August 22). *Cf.* Snowiss, note 67, *supra,* at 39–40: "It was not always clear, however, whether speakers endorsing judicial review were supporting a general power over legislation or one limited to defense of the courts' constitutional sphere. Gerry's observation was immediately preceded by the remark that the judiciary 'will have a sufficient check against encroachments on their own department * * *' ".

[71] 2 Farrand, note 1, *supra,* at 298–99 (August 15).

[72] See text at note 66, *supra.*

[73] Several prominent scholars have argued that it was widely understood during the 1780s and 1790s that judicial nullification should occur only in cases of plain unconstitutionality. See, *e.g.,* Snowiss, note 67, *supra,* at 13–44; Kramer, *Putting the Politics Back into the Political Safeguards of Federalism,* 100 Colum.L.Rev. 215, 240 (2000); Wood, *The Origin of Judicial*

5. The Scope of Jurisdiction

As initially formulated, the Randolph Plan contemplated apparently mandatory federal jurisdiction of "all piracies & felonies on the high seas, captures from an enemy; cases in which foreigners or citizens of other States applying to such jurisdictions may be interested, or which respect the collection of the National revenue; impeachments of any National officers, and questions which may involve the national peace and harmony".[74] When the Committee of the Whole first discussed this subject on June 12 and 13, however, Randolph concluded that it was "the business of a subcommittee to detail" the jurisdiction. He "therefore moved to obliterate such parts of the resolve so as only to establish the principle, to wit, that the jurisdiction of the national judiciary shall extend to all cases of national revenue, impeachment of national officers, and questions which involve the national peace or harmony". The Committee agreed to this proposal by unanimous vote.[75]

In considering the report of the Committee of the Whole on July 18, the Convention again confined itself to general principle. But "several criticisms having been made on the definition [of jurisdiction]; it was proposed by Mr. Madison so to alter as to read thus—'that the jurisdiction shall extend to all cases arising under the Natl. laws: And to such other questions as may involve the Natl. peace & harmony.' which was agreed to [without opposition]."[76]

With only this general direction, the Committee of Detail took the lead in defining the categories to which the federal judicial power would extend. The nine heads of federal jurisdiction that eventually emerged in Article III, § 2 can be grouped in various ways. Thematically, for example, the jurisdictional categories appear to contemplate federal judicial power to promote four central purposes: (i) to protect and enforce federal authority (jurisdiction of federal question cases and cases to which the United States is a party); (ii) to resolve disputes relating to foreign affairs (jurisdiction of suits affecting foreign envoys, admiralty cases, cases arising under treaties, and suits involving foreign nations); (iii) to provide an interstate umpire (suits between states or involving their conflicting land grants); and (iv) to furnish an impartial tribunal where state court bias was feared (party-based cases involving citizens of different states, a state and a non-citizen, or an alien).

On the face of the text, however, a linguistically striking divide exists between the first three and the last six jurisdictional categories. For the first three categories, which are defined mostly if not exclusively by subject

---

Review Revisited, or How the Marshall Court Made More out of Less, 56 Wash. & Lee L.Rev. 787, 798–99 (1999). Larry Kramer has also argued, separately, that many in the founding generation subscribed to a "departmental" theory of constitutional interpretation, under which each branch of government would decide for itself how to construe the Constitution in discharging its responsibilities. See Kramer, The People Themselves: Popular Constitutionalism and Judicial Review (2004). According to the departmental theory, disputes among the branches would need to be resolved politically, with ultimate responsibility residing in "the people themselves".

[74] 1 Farrand, note 1, *supra*, at 22. All of the plans respecting the judiciary that were put before the Convention specified various definite heads of federal jurisdiction.

[75] *Id.* 238 (June 13, Yates' notes). See also *id.* 220 (June 12), 223–24, 232 (June 13).

[76] 2 *id.* 46 (July 18).

matter,[77] Article III, § 2 provides that the judicial power shall extend to "all Cases". By contrast, in the last six categories, which are defined primarily by reference to the status of the parties, the "all" disappears, and the judicial power is extended to "Controversies", not "Cases".

The shift in language seems sufficiently sharp to require explanation. Yet no recorded discussion occurred in the Committee of the Whole or on the floor of the Convention.[78] Partly as a result, whether the change of language marks a distinction of constitutional intent—especially with reference to Congress' power over the jurisdiction of the federal courts—is much controverted and will be explored more fully in later Chapters.[79]

Regardless of its intended significance, the linguistic division provides a useful framework for examining the scope of federal jurisdiction authorized, if not required, by Article III.

a.   Jurisdiction Based Primarily on Subject Matter: The First Three Headings

(i) Cases Arising Under the Constitution, Laws, and Treaties of the United States. Faithful to the vote of July 18, the Committee of Detail placed at the head of its list of subjects of jurisdiction "all cases arising under laws passed by the Legislature of the United States".[80] Except for the change in wording by the Committee of Style, this provision was accepted and incorporated into the Constitution without further question or discussion.[81]

But the provision for jurisdiction of cases "arising under [federal] laws" was not left standing alone. As already noted, in a general discussion of the judiciary article as crafted by the Committee of Style, Dr. Johnson moved to insert an express provision for jurisdiction of cases under "this Constitution", and the motion carried without opposition.[82] Immediately thereafter, according to Madison's notes, Rutledge moved to extend the jurisdictional category to encompass cases involving "treaties made or which shall be

---

[77] The jurisdiction for the first and third of these categories, involving "all Cases * * * arising under" the Constitution, laws, and treaties of the United States and "all Cases of admiralty and maritime Jurisdiction", is based unequivocally on subject matter. By contrast, the second category of "all Cases affecting Ambassadors, other public Ministers and Consuls" arguably straddles the distinction between subject-matter-based and party-based jurisdiction.

[78] *But cf.* Amar, *A Neo-Federalist View of Article III: Separating the Two Tiers of Federal Jurisdiction*, 65 B.U.L.Rev. 205, 242–45 (1985) (arguing that documents used in drafting by the Committee of Detail, coupled with the Convention's specific reinsertion of the word "all" in the clause setting out the Supreme Court's appellate jurisdiction, after it had been omitted by the Committee of Style, reflect deliberate advertence to this point and an intention to make federal jurisdiction mandatory in the first three jurisdictional categories).

[79] For discussion of the possible significance of the distinction for Congress' power to define and limit federal jurisdiction in the various categories of cases, see Chap. IV, Sec. 1, *infra*.

[80] 2 Farrand, note 1, *supra*, at 186 (August 6). The clause had antecedents, partial or complete, in all of the judiciary plans: Randolph: cases "which respect the collection of the National revenue", 1 *id.* 22; Pinckney: "all cases arising under the laws of the United States", 3 *id.* 600; Paterson: all cases "which may arise on any of the Acts for regulation of trade, or the collection of the federal Revenue", 1 *id.* 244; Hamilton: "all causes in which the revenues of the general Government * * * are concerned", with power in the legislature "to institute Courts in each State for the determination of all matters of general concern", *id.* 292; Blair: "all cases in law and equity arising under * * * the laws of the United States", 2 *id.* 432.

[81] 2 *id.* 600 (committee report), 628 (September 15, entire Article approved).

[82] See note 66, *supra*, and accompanying text. Among the plans presented to the Convention, only the Blair plan had included such a provision. 2 Farrand, note 1, *supra*, at 432.

made" under the authority of the United States. The vote to adopt the motion was again unanimous.[83]

(ii) Cases Affecting Ambassadors, Other Public Ministers, or Consuls. Under the Articles of Confederation, the United States could give no assurance of legal protection to the representatives of foreign countries living in the United States. "The Convention was convinced that if foreign officials were either to seek justice at law or be subjected to its penalties, it should be at the hand of the national government."[84] The present clause was reported out of the Committee of Detail and passed without dispute, and, again without dispute, was included in the Supreme Court's original jurisdiction.[85]

(iii) Admiralty and Maritime Cases. The inclusion of admiralty and maritime jurisdiction in the report of the Committee of Detail went unchallenged.[86] The principal commerce of the period was, of course, maritime; and as Wilson pointed out on the floor, it was in the admiralty jurisdiction that disputes with foreigners were most likely to arise.[87] In addition, maritime law had been administered by British vice-admiralty rather than colonial courts before the war,[88] and state courts had therefore not been accustomed to exercising general maritime jurisdiction. Following the break with England, some states established courts with general admiralty jurisdiction, but others did not.[89] Moreover, experience during the Revolution with state court adjudication of prize cases had shown the need for a federal tribunal.[90]

---

[83] 2 Farrand, note 1, *supra*, at 431 (August 27). This amendment could easily be viewed as implementing the Convention's earlier determination that federal judicial power should extend to "questions which involve the national peace and harmony". In his early proposal to settle the scope of jurisdiction in terms of general principle, Randolph made clear that this language was intended to include questions of "the security of foreigners where treaties are in their favor". 1 *id.* 238 (June 13). Nevertheless, the Committee of Detail omitted any express reference to treaties, perhaps because of the provisions giving jurisdiction when foreigners were parties.

By all indications, the Convention regarded federal judicial power to enforce treaties as possessing vital importance. All the other plans except Pinckney's contemplated a similar jurisdiction. Paterson: appellate jurisdiction where construction of a treaty was involved, 1 *id.* 244; Hamilton: where "citizens of foreign nations are concerned", *id.* 292; Blair: cases arising under a treaty, 2 *id.* 432. In addition, the Convention at one time had extended the proposed negative on state laws, upon motion by Benjamin Franklin, to include laws contravening "any treaties subsisting under the authority of the Union". 1 *id.* 54 (May 31).

[84] Frank, *Historical Bases of the Federal Judicial System*, 13 Law & Contemp.Prob. 3, 14 (1948). All the plans contemplated such a jurisdiction. The Paterson plan gave the Supreme Court appellate jurisdiction in cases "touching the rights of ambassadors", as well as in cases "in which foreigners may be interested". 1 Farrand, note 1, *supra*, at 244. The Pinckney plan gave the Court original jurisdiction in cases "affecting Ambassadors & other public Ministers". 3 *id.* 600. The Blair plan added consuls, in substantially the language of the present grant. 2 *id.* 432. The Randolph and Hamilton plans provided generally for jurisdiction where foreigners were concerned. 1 *id.* 22, 292.

[85] 2 Farrand, note 1, *supra*, at 186, 431.

[86] *Id.* 186. See The Federalist No. 80 (Hamilton): "The most bigoted idolizers of state authority, have not thus far shown a disposition to deny the National Judiciary the cognizance of maritime causes".

[87] 1 Farrand, note 1, *supra*, at 124 (June 5).

[88] See Benedict on Admiralty § 61 (7th ed.rev.2007).

[89] See *id.* at §§ 83–89.

[90] See note 36, *supra*.

b. Jurisdiction Based on Party Status: The Remaining Categories

(i) United States a Party. Under the Articles of Confederation, the United States had to go into state courts for enforcement of its laws and collection of its claims.[91] Of the five plans before the Convention, however, only Blair's included a general grant of jurisdiction in cases to which the United States was a party.[92] Possibly the clause was omitted in the others, and in the initial report of the Committee of Detail, because the problem was thought to be addressed through jurisdiction in cases arising under various federal laws. But responding to a motion by Charles Pinckney, the committee later specially recommended, on August 22, that jurisdiction be given in controversies "between the United States and an individual State or the United States and an individual person".[93] The provision as it stands was inserted on the floor on August 27, on a motion by Madison and G. Morris apparently intended to reflect this recommendation. Soon after, on the same day, it was moved that "in cases in which the United States shall be a party the jurisdiction shall be original or appellate as the Legislature may direct", but the motion failed,[94] with the result that the jurisdiction of the Supreme Court was made appellate only.

(ii) Two or More States. Border disputes had plagued the new states.[95] In a speech introducing his resolutions, Governor Randolph said: "Are we not on the eve of war, which is only prevented by the hopes from the convention?"[96] Though not specifically mentioned, a jurisdiction in controversies between states could be viewed as implicit in Randolph's "national peace and harmony" provision.

The Committee of Detail's report qualified its proposed grant of jurisdiction to the Supreme Court in "controversies between two or more States" with an exception for "such as shall regard Territory or Jurisdiction". For these disputes, the Committee retained an analogue to the cumbersome machinery of the Articles of Confederation, which the Senate was charged with implementing.[97] On the floor, in the debate on the legislative articles,

---

[91] Thus, even treason against the United States had to be tried in state courts under state law. In 1781, Congress recommended that the state legislatures pass laws punishing infractions of the law of nations, and erect courts or clothe existing courts with authority to decide what constituted such an offense. Where an official of the United States Post Office was guilty of misdemeanor in office, Congress could only prescribe penalties and let the Postmaster General bring an action in debt in a state court to recover them. In settling accounts of the military and in recovering debts from individuals, Congress recommended that the state legislatures pass laws empowering Congress' agents to bring such actions in state courts. Carson, note 34, *supra*, at 83–86.

[92] 2 Farrand, note 1, *supra*, at 432. One version of the Paterson plan included a resolution that "provision ought to be made for hearing and deciding upon all disputes arising between the United States and an individual State respecting territory". 3 *id.* 611.

[93] 2 *id.* 367 (August 22). This report was distributed to the members, *id.* 376, but seems not to have been acted upon. For Pinckney's earlier motion, see *id.* 342 (August 20).

[94] *Id.* 424–25, 430.

[95] See note 34, *supra*.

[96] 1 Farrand, note 1, *supra*, at 26 (May 29). This view was by no means singular. When the Convention was close to complete impasse, Gerry appealed to the members to keep trying. Without a Union, "We should be without an Umpire to decide controversies and must be at the mercy of events". *Id.* 515 (July 2). Sherman listed a national power to prevent internal disputes and resorts to force as one of the four basic objects of a Union. *Id.* 133 (June 6).

[97] See the proposed Art. IX, Sec. 3, 2 Farrand, note 1, *supra*, at 183–84. The provision seems to have originated in Randolph's draft in the Committee of Detail. *Id.* 144.

Rutledge moved to strike these provisions, saying that they were "necessary under the Confederation, but will be rendered unnecessary by the National Judiciary now to be established". Some expressed doubts whether the judiciary was appropriate, since "the Judges might be connected with the States being parties". But the motion to strike carried eight states to two, with only North Carolina and Georgia dissenting.[98]

(iii) A State and Citizens of Another State. The grant of jurisdiction in controversies between a state and citizens of another state had no specific forerunner in any of the five plans before the Convention.[99] The clause first appears in a marginal note in Rutledge's handwriting on Randolph's draft for the Committee of Detail,[100] and it was reported out by that committee in its present form.[101] No discussion occurred, though concern about prejudice seems the only possible explanation.

(iv) Citizens of Different States. The grant of diversity jurisdiction aroused bitter opposition in the ratification debates, and the controversy has continued intermittently ever since.[102] Strangely, the clause passed without question in the Convention, and thus without clarification of its purposes.

Randolph's initial plan provided for jurisdiction in "cases in which foreigners or citizens of other States applying to such jurisdictions may be interested",[103] in contrast with Paterson's, Hamilton's, and Blair's, which protected only foreigners, and Pinckney's, which had no provision against bias. When the Committee of the Whole first considered Randolph's proposal on June 12, it voted to give jurisdiction in "cases in which foreigners or citizens of two distinct States of the Union" may be interested.[104] This specification was submerged in the more general votes of principle on June 13 and July 18. But it reappeared in its present form in the report of the Committee of Detail, and the Convention accepted it without challenge on August 27.[105]

(v) Citizens of the Same State, Claiming Lands Under Grants of Different States. The Committee of Detail proposed the same mode of settling these controversies as for controversies over territory or jurisdiction between the states themselves, and both proposals were stricken by the same vote.[106] Sherman's motion to insert the present provision during the later debate passed unanimously.[107]

(vi) States, or Citizens Thereof, and Foreign States, Citizens or Subjects. All the plans except Pinckney's provided for jurisdiction where

---

[98] *Id.* 400–01 (August 24).

[99] Randolph's original resolution would have given jurisdiction to inferior federal courts in "cases in which foreigners or citizens of other States applying to such jurisdictions may be interested". 1 *id.* 22. But this provision would not have guarded against the possibility of antagonism when a state was suing in the courts of another state. Moreover, if Hamilton was right in The Federalist, No. 81, that the Convention did not contemplate that a state could be sued by a citizen of another state without its consent (at least on causes of action not based on federal law), it would have been of no assistance to an out-of-state citizen as plaintiff.

[100] 2 Farrand, note 1, *supra,* at 147.

[101] *Id.* 186.

[102] The problem is more fully treated in Chap. XIII, *infra.*

[103] See note 99, *supra.*

[104] 2 Farrand, note 1, *supra,* at 431–32.

[105] 1 *id.* 22.

[106] See note 98, *supra,* and accompanying text.

[107] 2 Farrand, note 1, *supra,* at 431–32 (August 27).

foreigners were interested,[108] and the need for a grant going beyond cases involving treaties and foreign representatives seems to have aroused no dispute. The clause came out of the Committee of Detail in its present form.[109]

6.   Jurisdiction of the Supreme Court

a.   Original Jurisdiction

The Randolph plan, which required the establishment of lower federal courts, made no provision for an original jurisdiction of the Supreme Court, but all the other plans did.[110] In the Committee of Detail, one draft of the Constitution in Randolph's handwriting gave the Supreme Court original jurisdiction in cases of impeachment and such other cases as the legislature might prescribe.[111] A later draft in Wilson's handwriting, and the draft submitted to the Convention, provided for original jurisdiction in cases of impeachment, in cases affecting ambassadors and other public ministers and consuls, and in cases in which a state was a party. This grant, however, was subject to a general power in the legislature to assign this jurisdiction, except for a trial of the President, to inferior federal courts.[112] The provision for impeachments and the legislative power of assignment were stricken on the floor.[113]

b.   Appellate Jurisdiction

The decisions as to the scope of the Supreme Court's original jurisdiction settled that the balance of its jurisdiction should be appellate.[114]

The important provision that the appellate jurisdiction should be subject to exceptions and regulations by Congress appeared in none of the plans.[115] It emerged for the first time in the report of the Committee of Detail and, remarkably, provoked no discussion on the floor of the Convention at the time of its acceptance. There are few clues even to the thinking of the Committee of Detail.[116]

Discussions on the floor of the Convention do speak, however, to another question that would later occasion bitter political controversy. In debates about whether lower federal courts should be constitutionally mandatory or

---

[108] See note 83, *supra.*

[109] 2 Farrand, note 1, *supra*, at 186.

[110] Paterson's plan, contemplating primarily an appellate jurisdiction from state courts, provided for original jurisdiction in cases of impeachment. *Id.* 244. Pinckney's gave original jurisdiction in impeachment and in cases affecting ambassadors and other public ministers, see 3 *id.* 600; Hamilton's, in cases of captures, see 1 *id.* 292; and Blair's, "in all cases affecting ambassadors, other public ministers and consuls, and those in which a State shall be a party, and suits between persons claiming lands under grants of different states", see 2 *id.* 432.

[111] 2 *id.* 147.

[112] *Id.* 173, 186–87.

[113] See *id.* 423–24, 430–31 (August 27).

[114] 1 *id.* 243–44; 2 *id.* 433.

[115] All the plans appear to have made the appellate jurisdiction a constitutional requirement, and Blair's even went to the point of prescribing a constitutional jurisdictional amount.

[116] The Exceptions Clause is foreshadowed in Randolph's draft for the committee and then appears in a later draft in Wilson's handwriting in substantially the form in which the committee reported it. 2 Farrand, note 1, *supra*, at 147, 173, 186. For an argument that the clause has its origins in the legal system of Scotland—where Wilson was born and educated— see Pfander & Birk, *Article III and the Scottish Judiciary*, 124 Harv.L.Rev. 1613, 1671–84 (2011).

prohibited, it was universally assumed that the Supreme Court would have jurisdiction to review the decisions of state courts on matters of federal concern.[117] Indeed, it was the staunchest partisans of state authority who most insistently urged the appropriateness of this method of protecting federal interests.

The provision that the jurisdiction should extend to both law and fact was added on the floor of the Convention.[118] G. Morris asked if the appellate jurisdiction extended to matters of fact as well as law, and Wilson said he thought that was the intention of the Committee of Detail. Dickinson then moved to add the words "both as to law and fact", and his motion passed unanimously.[119]

The phrase "and fact" opened the Constitution to the charge that the Supreme Court was authorized to re-examine jury verdicts.[120] The charge was made even as to criminal cases, where the right of trial by jury was guaranteed, but more especially as to civil cases, where it was not.[121] The protests bore fruit in the Seventh Amendment, which not only established the right of trial by jury in civil cases, but also provided that "no fact tried by a jury, shall be otherwise re-examined in any Court of the United States, than according to the rules of the common law".

D. The Ratification Debates and Proposals for Amendment

The judiciary article, which had aroused only relatively minor disagreement in the Convention, became a center of controversy in the ratification debates. The conventions of six of the initially ratifying states suggested amendments, and all of these but South Carolina wanted changes in Article III.[122] Indeed, no fewer than 19 of the 103 amendments proposed

---

[117] See text accompanying notes 39–53, *supra*.

[118] Paterson's plan included a similar provision. 1 Farrand, note 1, *supra*, at 243. Blair's plan gave jurisdiction as to law only, except in cases of equity and admiralty. 2 *id*. 433. But the point was not touched on in the report of the Committee of Detail.

[119] 2 *id*. 431 (August 27).

[120] According to Ritz, Rewriting the History of the Judiciary Act of 1789, at 6 (Holt & LaRue eds. 1990), for the framing generation "there was no clear distinction between the *functions* of an 'appellate' court and a 'trial' court", since appellate courts routinely retried entire cases. "Distinctness and hierarchy did not characterize the [then familiar] court structures, and 'superior' usually meant only that a reviewing court had more judges sitting on it." *Id*.

[121] Of the five plans, only Blair's referred to trial by jury. While contemplating the trial of crimes in state courts, it required the use of juries. Blair's plan said nothing of civil cases. 2 Farrand, note 1, *supra*, at 433.

The provision in Article III for trial of crimes by jury first appears in a draft for the Committee of Detail in Wilson's handwriting, *id*. 173, and was included in the Committee's report. *Id*. 187. It was amended in the Convention to provide for the venue of trial for crimes not committed in any state and approved unanimously on August 28. *Id*. 438.

On September 12, while the report of the Committee of Style was being printed, Mr. Williamson "observed to the House that no provision was yet made for juries in Civil cases and suggested the necessity of it". Gorham said it was impossible "to discriminate equity cases from those in which juries are proper", and added that the "Representatives of the people may be safely trusted in this matter". Gerry supported Williamson. Mason said he saw the difficulty of specifying jury cases, but, broadening the discussion, said that a bill of rights "would give great quiet to the people"; and Gerry and Mason moved that a committee be appointed to prepare such a bill. Sherman thought the state bills of rights sufficient, and repeated Gorham's points about juries. The Convention voted down the motion unanimously. *Id*. 587–88.

[122] Rhode Island's belated convention in 1790 also proposed amendments to Article III. Ames, Proposed Amendments to the Constitution, 1789–1889, at 310 (1897).

by these six states related to the judiciary or judicial proceedings.[123] According to Charles Warren, "The principal Amendments which were regarded as necessary, relative to the Judiciary, were (a) an express provision guaranteeing jury trials in civil as well as criminal cases; (b) the confinement of appellate power to questions of law, and not of fact; (c) the elimination of any Federal Courts of first instance, or, at all events, the restriction of such original Federal jurisdiction to a Supreme Court with very limited original jurisdiction; (d) the elimination of all jurisdiction based on diverse citizenship and status as a foreigner."[124]

Ames lists 173 amendments proposed in the first session of the first Congress, although this figure includes many repetitions. Of the total, 48 were primarily concerned with courts and court proceedings; most had to do with trial by jury and various rights of defendants in criminal proceedings.[125] The Fourth, Fifth, Sixth, Seventh, and Eighth Amendments respond to the central concerns. The House approved a proposal to exclude appeals to the Supreme Court "where the value in controversy shall not amount to one thousand dollars", but it failed in the Senate.[126]

NOTE ON THE ORGANIZATION AND DEVELOPMENT OF THE FEDERAL JUDICIAL SYSTEM

A.   The First Judiciary Act

The judiciary article of the Constitution was not self-executing, and the first Congress therefore faced the task of structuring a court system and, within limits established by the Constitution, of defining its jurisdiction. The job was daunting. Among other things, the controversies that had flared during the ratification debates made it clear that the definition of federal jurisdiction was freighted with political ramifications.

The Judiciary Act of 1789,[1] the twentieth statute enacted by the first Congress, responded to multiple pressures.[2] The Act is of interest today

---

For a comprehensive and illuminating examination of the ratification debates, see Maier, Ratification: The People Debate The Constitution, 1787–1788 (2010). Older but still useful works on the ratification process, and especially on the character of anti-federalist opinion, include Main, The Anti-Federalists: Critics of the Constitution, 1781–1788 (1961); Mason, The States Rights Debate: Antifederalism and the Constitution (1964); Kenyon, The Anti-Federalists (1966); Rutland, The Ordeal of the Constitution: The Anti-Federalists and the Ratification Struggle of 1787–1788 (1966); Goebel, note 1, *supra*, at 251–91; Storing, The Complete Anti-Federalist (1981); and Wood, note 3, *supra*. On the debate over the judiciary during the ratification process, see Clinton, *A Mandatory View of Federal Court Jurisdiction: A Guided Quest for the Original Understanding of Article III*, 132 U.Pa.L.Rev. 741, 797–829 (1984).

[123] Ames, note 122, *supra*, at 307–10.

[124] Warren, New Light on the History of the Federal Judiciary Act of 1789, 37 Harv.L.Rev. 49, 56 (1923).

[125] Ames, note 122, *supra*, at 310–21 (Nos. 135–38, 140, 142–43, 169–76, 183–86, 188–89, 213–14, 221–24, 226–27, 254–55, 258, 292–94, 297).

[126] Ames, note 122, *supra*, at 316 (No. 225, drawn from Nos. 141, 181, 182); Senate Journal, p. 130.

[1]   Act of Sept. 24, 1789, 1 Stat. 73.

[2]   On the 1789 Act, see, *e.g.*, Goebel, History of the Supreme Court of the United States: Antecedents and Beginnings to 1801, at 457–508 (1971); Ritz, Rewriting the History of the Judiciary Act of 1789 (Holt & LaRue eds. 1990); Amar, *The Two-Tiered Structure of the Judiciary Act of 1789*, 138 U.Pa.L.Rev. 1499 (1990); Holt, *"To Establish Justice": Politics, the*

along at least two dimensions. First, the 1789 Act reflects the beginning of an organic development. It is impossible to understand the current judicial structure without a basic awareness of the foundations from which it evolved.[3] Second, the first Judiciary Act is widely viewed as an indicator of the original understanding of Article III and, in particular, of Congress' constitutional obligations concerning the vesting of federal jurisdiction.

1. Court Organization

a. The Supreme Court

The first section of the 1789 Act provided that "the supreme court of the United States shall consist of a chief justice and five associate justices". It called for two sessions annually at the seat of government, with one commencing the first Monday of February and the other the first Monday of August.

b. The Circuit and District Courts

The "transcendent achievement"[4] of the First Judiciary Act lay in its exercise of the constitutional option to establish a system of federal trial courts.[5] Nonetheless, the original statutory scheme seems a curious one today. The Act provided for two tiers of trial courts: district courts, each with its own district judge, and circuit courts, without judges of their own. The circuit courts, which were to hold two sessions a year in each district within the circuit, were to be staffed by one district judge and two Supreme Court justices sitting on circuit.

The Act divided the eleven states then in the Union into thirteen districts with boundaries corresponding to state lines, except that the parts of Massachusetts and Virginia that later became Maine and Kentucky were made into separate districts. The Act thus established a precedent, still almost invariably observed, against the crossing of state lines in setting the boundaries of federal judicial districts. Eleven of the thirteen districts were in turn grouped into three circuits, with special provision made for the remote Maine and Kentucky districts.[6]

Judiciary Act of 1789, and the Invention of the Federal Courts, 1989 Duke L.J. 1421; Clinton, *A Mandatory View of Federal Court Jurisdiction: Early Implementation of and Departures from the Constitutional Plan*, 86 Colum.L.Rev. 1515 (1986); Casto, *The First Congress's Understanding of Its Authority over the Federal Courts' Jurisdiction*, 26 B.C.L.Rev. 1101 (1985); Warren, *New Light on the History of the Federal Judiciary Act of 1789*, 37 Harv.L.Rev. 49 (1923); and Collins, *The Federal Courts, the First Congress, and the Non-Settlement of 1789*, 91 Va.L.Rev. 1515 (2005).

[3] Still perhaps the most valuable source on the sequence of federal judiciary acts is Frankfurter & Landis, The Business of the Supreme Court (1928). For a useful summary, see Bator, *Judicial System, Federal*, 3 Encyclopedia of The American Constitution 1068–75 (1986). For a brief but valuable description of the historical development of the jurisdiction of the lower federal courts, see Frankfurter, *Distribution of Judicial Power Between United States and State Courts*, 13 Corn.L.Q. 499, 507–15 (1928).

[4] Frankfurter & Landis, note 3, *supra*, at 4.

[5] See Frank, *Historical Bases of the Federal Judicial System*, 13 Law & Contemp.Prob. 3, 9–11 (1948).

[6] The district courts in those two districts were authorized to sit also as circuit courts, a device afterward used repeatedly in outlying areas.

2. Jurisdiction of the District and Circuit Courts

The jurisdiction of the district courts was entirely original. Part of the jurisdiction was exclusive of the state courts, and part was concurrent.[7]

The circuit courts also had an important original jurisdiction, as well as authority to review on writ of error final decisions of the district courts in civil cases in which the matter in controversy exceeded $50, and, on appeal, final decrees in admiralty and maritime cases in which the matter in controversy exceeded $300.

The original jurisdiction of both sets of courts can usefully be considered together, as the jurisdiction of the Supreme Court will be below, under the nine jurisdictional headings of Article III.

a. Jurisdiction Based Primarily on Subject Matter

(i) Cases Arising Under the Constitution, Laws, and Treaties of the United States. In the sphere of private civil litigation, the 1789 Act, curiously, made no use of the grant of judicial power over cases arising under the Constitution or laws of the United States.[8] The district courts were, however, given "exclusive original cognizance of all seizures on land, or other waters than as aforesaid, made, and of all suits for penalties and forfeitures incurred, under the laws of the United States."[9]

The Act vested the circuit courts with "exclusive cognizance of all crimes and offences cognizable under the authority of the United States", subject to a concurrent jurisdiction of the district courts to try certain minor criminal offenses.[10]

The only reference to suits arising under treaties came in a provision conferring district court jurisdiction, concurrent with the state courts or the circuit courts, of "all Causes where an Alien sues for a tort only in violation of * * * a Treaty of the United States".[11]

(ii) Cases Affecting Ambassadors, Other Public Ministers, and Consuls. Suits affecting ambassadors came within the original jurisdiction of the Supreme Court.[12] But the Act conferred district court jurisdiction, exclusive of the state courts, of all suits against consuls and vice-consuls (except criminal cases triable in the circuit courts).[13]

(iii) Admiralty Jurisdiction. In terms that in substance survive today, the 1789 Act gave the district courts "exclusive original cognizance of

---

[7]   For a discussion of exclusive federal jurisdiction, see Chap. IV, Sec. 3, *infra.*

[8]   Engdahl, *Federal Question Jurisdiction Under the 1789 Judiciary Act*, 14 Okla.City U.L.Rev. 521, 522 (1989), argues that "all cases which could then have been contemplated as within" the "federal question" category of Article III were in fact provided for under the Act, although the jurisdiction had to be established under various grants of party-based and subject matter jurisdiction. But this position depends on a number of doubtful claims. Compare Casto, *An Orthodox View of the Two-Tier Analysis of Congressional Control over Federal Jurisdiction,* 7 Const. Commentary 89, 97 (1990) (stating that the 1789 Act "completely excluded a number of federal question cases from original and appellate federal jurisdiction"). For further discussion, see pp. 25–26, *infra.*

The development of later statutory grants of "arising under" jurisdiction is traced in Chap. VIII, pp. 779–784, *infra.*

[9]   § 9, 1 Stat. 73, 77.

[10]   § 10, 1 Stat. 73, 78–79.

[11]   § 9, 1 Stat. 73, 77. For discussion, see Chap. VII, pp. 717–722, *infra.*

[12]   See p. 24, *infra.*

[13]   § 9, 1 Stat. 73, 77.

all civil causes of admiralty and maritime jurisdiction, * * * saving to suitors, in all cases, the right of a common law remedy, where the common law is competent to give it".[14] This grant included jurisdiction of "all seizures under laws of impost, navigation or trade of the United States, where the seizures are made, on waters which are navigable from the sea by vessels of ten or more tons burthen, within their respective districts as well as upon the high seas."

b. Jurisdiction Based on Party Status

(i) United States a Party. The Act did not in terms contemplate the possibility of suits against the United States.

In addition to the jurisdiction for civil and criminal enforcement actions by the United States arising under federal law, discussed above, the 1789 Act gave the circuit courts concurrent jurisdiction with the state courts of all civil suits at common law or in equity in which "the United States are plaintiffs, or petitioners" and the matter in dispute exceeded five hundred dollars.[15] The district courts were given jurisdiction, similarly concurrent, "of all suits at common law where the United States sue, and the matter in dispute amounts * * * to the sum or value of one hundred dollars."[16]

(ii) Diversity Jurisdiction. Although the Act made use of the constitutional grant of judicial power in cases of diverse citizenship, the initial grant was limited to controversies "between a citizen of the State where the suit is brought, and a citizen of another State".[17] Strawbridge v. Curtiss, 7 U.S. (3 Cranch) 267 (1806), p. 1422, *infra*, soon construed this language to require "complete diversity" when there are multiple parties on one or more sides of a case. In addition, to prevent defendants from being summoned long distances to defend small claims, the jurisdiction was restricted to cases in which the matter in dispute exceeded five hundred dollars. The jurisdiction was concurrent with state courts.[18]

The circuit courts received a further jurisdiction dependent upon the character of the parties, also concurrent with the state courts, in all suits of a civil nature at common law or equity where an alien was a party, again when more than five hundred dollars was in dispute.[19] As noted above, the 1789 Act also gave the district courts jurisdiction, concurrent with the circuit courts, "of all causes where an alien sues for a tort only in violation of the law of nations or a treaty of the United States."[20]

These party-based grants of jurisdiction were qualified by the "assignee clause", framed to avoid collusive assignments to create jurisdiction, which with various changes survived until 1948. Under its terms, no district or circuit court had "cognizance of any suit to recover the contents of any promissory note or other chose in action in favor of any assignee, unless a

---

[14] *Id.* For the current provision, see 28 U.S.C. § 1333; see also pp. 872–876, *infra*.

[15] § 11, 1 Stat. 73, 78.

[16] § 9, 1 Stat. 73, 77.

[17] § 11, 1 Stat. 73, 78.

[18] For the development of the diversity jurisdiction, see Chap. XIII, *infra*.

[19] § 11, 1 Stat. 73, 78.

[20] § 9, 1 Stat. 73, 77. The successor provision is 28 U.S.C. § 1350. See Chap. VII, Sec. 1, pp. 717–722, *infra*.

suit might have been prosecuted in such court * * * if no assignment had been made, except in cases of foreign bills of exchange."[21]

The First Judiciary Act also originated the policy, which has endured ever since, of authorizing the removal to a federal court, before trial, of certain proceedings begun in the state courts.[22] The statute provided for removal to a circuit court, subject to the jurisdictional amount requirement of five hundred dollars. The privilege of removing was given to three classes of parties: (i) a defendant who was an alien; (ii) a defendant who was a citizen of another state, when sued by a plaintiff who was a citizen of the state where suit was brought; and (iii) either party, where title to land was in dispute, if one party claimed under a grant from another state and the other party claimed under a grant of the state in which the suit was brought.

3.   Jurisdiction of the Supreme Court

a.   Original Jurisdiction[23]

Possibly not foreseeing the later-established doctrine that the original jurisdiction of the Supreme Court derives directly from the Constitution, the framers of the First Judiciary Act provided for the Court's original jurisdiction in terms that are nearly but not exactly coextensive with the constitutional grant. Under the 1789 Act, the original jurisdiction included:[24]

(1) "all controversies of a civil nature, where a state is a party, except between a state and its citizens;" and

(2)(a) "all such jurisdiction * * * as a court of law can have or exercise consistently with the law of nations" of suits "against ambassadors, or other public ministers, or their domestics, or domestic servants"; and

(b) "all suits brought by ambassadors, or other public ministers, or in which a consul, or vice consul, shall be a party."[25]

The Act distinguished, as have all later acts, between instances in which this original jurisdiction was exclusive of other courts and those in which it was not. The jurisdiction was exclusive in the cases in clause (1), above, except suits "between a state and citizens of other states, or aliens", and in all the cases in clause 2(a).

b.   Appellate Jurisdiction[26]

The 1789 Act did not provide for Supreme Court review of all decisions of the lower federal courts. Final judgments or decrees of the circuit courts in civil cases were reviewable on writ of error only if "the matter in dispute exceeds the sum or value of two thousand dollars, exclusive of costs".[27] There was no provision for review of federal criminal cases. The Act did, however, confer on the Supreme Court a habeas corpus jurisdiction, which the Court

---

[21] § 11, 1 Stat. 73, 79. The successor provision is 28 U.S.C. § 1359. See Chap. XIII, Sec. 5, *infra.*

[22] § 12, 1 Stat. 73, 79. For the later history of the removal provisions, see Chap. VIII, Sec. 4, *infra.*

[23] See generally Chap. III, *infra.*

[24] § 13, 1 Stat. 73, 80–81.

[25] The jurisdiction conferred by clause 2 was thus framed in terms of party status, rather than echoing the broader constitutional language authorizing jurisdiction in all cases "*affecting* Ambassadors, other public Ministers and Consuls" (emphasis added).

[26] See Chap. V, *infra.*

[27] § 22, 1 Stat. 73, 84.

later classified as appellate, through which it could review federal decisions resulting in detentions.[28]

With respect to state court decisions, Section 25 provided for Supreme Court review of final judgments or decrees "in the highest court of law or equity of a State in which a decision in the suit could be had," in three classes of cases:

(1) " * * * where is drawn in question the validity of a treaty or statute of, or an authority exercised under the United States, and the decision is against their validity;" or

(2) " * * * where is drawn in question the validity of a statute of, or an authority exercised under any State, on the ground of their being repugnant to the constitution, treaties or laws of the United States, and the decision is in favor of such their validity;" or

(3) " * * * where is drawn in question the construction of any clause of the constitution, or of a treaty, or statute of, or commission held under the United States, and the decision is against the title, right, privilege or exemption specially set up or claimed" thereunder.[29]

In all cases within the Court's appellate jurisdiction, review occurred by "writ of error". This limitation "eliminate[d] all possibility of a second trial of the facts, by jury or otherwise", in the Supreme Court.[30]

4. The Overall Scope of Federal Jurisdiction Under the First Judiciary Act

When the respective jurisdictions of district and circuit courts and the Supreme Court are viewed together, the 1789 Act fell short of vesting federal jurisdiction in "all Cases" in which Article III would have permitted jurisdiction based primarily on subject matter.

(i) In the category of cases arising under federal law, Congress provided no general federal question jurisdiction in the lower federal courts. Nor, under section 25, did the Supreme Court's appellate jurisdiction extend to cases originating in the state courts in which the federal claim was *upheld*. Further, habeas corpus aside, the Supreme Court lacked appellate jurisdiction over federal criminal cases.

(ii) In the category of cases affecting foreign envoys, section 13 conferred original Supreme Court jurisdiction over a broad category of suits to which denominated officials, and in some cases their servants, were *parties*. It did not, however, extend to all suits by which ambassadors, other public ministers, and consuls might be "affect[ed]".

(iii) In the category of admiralty and maritime jurisdiction, section 9 gave the federal courts exclusive jurisdiction in admiralty, but saved "to suitors, in all cases, the right of a common law remedy". In practice, this provision has meant that claims that can be enforced in a federal court in admiralty can typically also be enforced in a state court in personam action.

With respect to Article III's authorizations of jurisdiction based on party status, the 1789 Act did not provide in terms for suits against the United States. By contrast, the Act did authorize jurisdiction of a variety of civil

---

[28] See Chap. III, Sec. 3, *infra.*

[29] For the later development, see Chap. V, Sec. 1, *infra.*

[30] Ritz, note 2, *supra,* at 88.

suits to which states were parties, "except between a state and its citizens", without expressly limiting the grant to cases in which the states were plaintiffs or petitioners. The diversity jurisdiction included a significant amount-in-controversy limitation, and was construed by the Supreme Court as limited to cases of "complete diversity" in cases involving multiple parties.

The scope of these jurisdictional provisions and limitations continues to be much controverted, as does the question of the first Congress' understanding of the scope of its constitutional obligation, if any, to vest federal jurisdiction in various classes of cases. For further discussion, see Chap. IV, Sec. 1, *infra*.

B.   The Antebellum Years

The antebellum years witnessed the emergence of two enduring patterns in the judicial history of the United States. The first involved the relative stability of the structure of courts established by the First Judiciary Act—at least at its base in the district courts and its apex in the Supreme Court.[31] The circuit courts quickly emerged as a weak spot, due to their lack of any judges of their own and the inordinate burden that circuit riding cast upon Supreme Court Justices. The burden was reduced in 1793 by requiring only one Justice per circuit court;[32] but the reduction came at the cost of establishing a two-judge court, which created a problem of split decisions.

A second emerging pattern concerned the incremental adjustment of federal jurisdiction to reflect shifting political currents and, in particular, preferences for greater or lesser national authority vis-a-vis the states. The famous Law of the Midnight Judges,[33] enacted by a lame duck Federalist Congress after the Federalist party had lost control of both Congress and the Presidency in the elections of 1800,[34] furnishes an egregious example. The new Act, which aimed in part to protect the nationalist values of the outgoing administration, gave the district and circuit courts, taken together, a jurisdiction almost coextensive with the constitutional authorization. The Act also abolished circuit riding by Supreme Court Justices and provided instead that five of the circuit courts would each have a bench of three circuit judges and that the sixth (the western circuit) would have a single circuit judge. The new judges, appointed by President Adams and confirmed by the outgoing Senate, were all Federalists.

The incoming Jeffersonians, their anger heightened by the behavior of some of the new judges, repealed the act and abolished the judgeships.[35] For the most part, the new Act of April 29, 1802,[36] prescribed a return to the *status quo ante*. Although the repeal raised serious constitutional questions,

---

[31] For a detailed account of the administration and business of the district and circuit courts under the First Judiciary Act from 1789 to 1801, see Henderson, Courts for a New Nation (1971); see also Goebel, note 2, *supra*, at 552–661.

[32] Act of March 2, 1793, 1 Stat. 333. See Frankfurter & Landis, note 3, *supra*, at 14–30, and 1 Warren, The Supreme Court in United States History 85–90 (1926), for discussions of contemporary criticisms of the circuit riding obligation.

[33] Act of February 13, 1801, 2 Stat. 89. See generally Surrency, The Judiciary Act of 1801, 2 Am.J.Legal Hist. 53 (1958); Turner, *The Midnight Judges*, 109 U.Pa.L.Rev. 494 (1961); Turner, *Federalist Policy and the Judiciary Act of 1801*, 22 Wm. & Mary Q. 3 (1965).

[34] For further discussion, see Wood, Empire of Liberty: A History of the Early Republic, 1789–1815, at 400–32 (2009), and pp. 68–69, *infra*.

[35] Act of March 8, 1802, 2 Stat. 132. See Frankfurter & Landis, note 3, *supra*, at 24–30; 1 Warren, note 32, *supra*, at 184–230.

[36] 2 Stat. 156, as amended by the Act of March 3, 1803, 2 Stat. 244.

none of the ousted judges appears to have pressed a challenge in the courts, and the Supreme Court, in Stuart v. Laird, rejected a constitutional objection to the requirement that Supreme Court Justices resume acting as circuit judges.[37]

Among its innovations, the 1802 Act authorized the circuit courts, in cases where the judges were divided, to certify questions to the Supreme Court.[38] In addition to its old jurisdiction to entertain a writ of error, the Supreme Court was empowered to hear appeals from the circuit courts in equity, admiralty, and prize cases where the amount in dispute exceeded $2,000.

In the wake of the 1802 Act, however, the circuit courts grew more and more rickety. Though Congress remained attached to circuit riding as a means of keeping Supreme Court Justices in touch with the people, the burgeoning number of judicial districts put increasing strains on the system. To allow for circuit court sessions in each district, the Act had reduced the number of Supreme Court sessions to one a year and authorized the holding of the circuit court by a single district judge. As the country grew, however, the Justices increasingly invoked the privilege of non-attendance in remote districts. Correspondingly, circuit court review of district court decisions became increasingly futile.

In 1807 Congress created a seventh circuit to meet the needs of Kentucky, Tennessee, and Ohio.[39] This action automatically triggered the appointment of a sixth associate Justice for the new circuit. With the size of the Supreme Court tied to the circuit system, Congress proved unable to agree upon similar action for later-entering states for more than twenty years. As a result, these states remained outside the circuit system. In 1837, Congress re-divided the country into nine circuits and increased the membership of the Supreme Court to nine.[40] California (joined soon after by Oregon) became a tenth circuit in 1855;[41] and in 1863 Congress briefly added a tenth Justice to the Supreme Court,[42] before shortly reorganizing the districts into nine circuits[43] and reducing the number of Justices.[44]

Meanwhile, a series of collisions between federal and state authority had provoked Congress to extend federal jurisdiction to meet threats to federal interests. New England's resistance to the War of 1812 led Congress to provide for removal of suits against federal officers and others enforcing

---

[37] 5 U.S. (1 Cranch) 299 (1803). For a provocative study of the location of Stuart v. Laird in the constitutional politics surrounding the 1800 presidential election and its aftermath, see Ackerman, The Failure of the Founding Fathers: Jefferson, Marshall, and the Rise of Presidential Democracy (2005).

[38] Certification was optional in civil and mandatory in criminal cases. Professor White reports that in the early nineteenth century, the Justices sometimes deliberately created divisions when riding circuit, in order to permit Supreme Court review on certificate of decisions that otherwise were not reviewable. See White, III–IV History of the Supreme Court of the United States: The Marshall Court and Cultural Change, 1815–35, at 173–74 (1988).

[39] Act of Feb. 24, 1807, 2 Stat. 420, amended by the Act of March 22, 1808, 2 Stat. 477, and the Act of Feb. 4, 1809, 2 Stat. 516.

[40] Act of March 3, 1837, 5 Stat. 176.

[41] Act of March 2, 1855, 10 Stat. 631.

[42] Act of March 3, 1863, 12 Stat. 794, amended by the Act of Feb. 19, 1864, 13 Stat. 4.

[43] Act of July 23, 1866, § 2, 14 Stat. 209.

[44] In 1866, the number of Justices was reduced to seven, *id.*, § 1, to keep President Johnson from filling vacancies; but three years later the number was restored to nine, Act of April 10, 1869, 16 Stat. 44, where it has remained ever since.

customs duties from state to federal court.[45] Similarly, the "Force Bill" of 1833[46] responded to South Carolina's threats of nullification by authorizing removal of suits and prosecutions based on acts done under federal customs laws[47] and conferring federal habeas corpus jurisdiction in cases of confinement "for any act done, or omitted to be done, in pursuance of a law of the United States".[48] The advent of the Civil War occasioned further removal acts.[49]

C. Reconstruction

Reconstruction Congresses complemented the profound changes in constitutional structure wrought by the Civil War amendments with a compendious series of statutes extending the jurisdiction of the federal courts.[50] Notably, Congress authorized federal courts to issue writs of habeas corpus on behalf of prisoners held by state authorities in violation of the Constitution, laws, and treaties of the United States.[51] In addition, the various civil rights acts included jurisdictional grants. At least twelve pieces of removal legislation were enacted during the Reconstruction era.[52] Most sweepingly, the Judiciary Act of 1875 conferred on the federal judiciary a general jurisdiction over all civil cases "arising under" federal law, subject only to an amount-in-controversy requirement.[53] With the enactment of this statute, the Supreme Court later observed, "the lower federal courts * * * 'became the primary and powerful reliances for vindicating every right given by the Constitution, the laws, and treaties of the United States' ".[54]

D. Structural Reforms

The surge in federal judicial business in the years following the Civil War and Reconstruction created untenable strains on the federal judicial structure. Congress enacted a minor reform in 1869, when it finally provided for the permanent appointment of circuit judges and authorized one judge for each of the nine circuits.[55] At the same time, it reduced the circuit-riding duty of the Supreme Court Justices to attendance at one term every two years in each district of the circuit to which the Justice was assigned.

Nonetheless, docket pressures continued to mount. Growth in the Supreme Court's caseload resulted both from an increased population and from congressional additions to the Court's jurisdiction, including civil

---

[45] See Act of Feb. 4, 1815, § 8, 3 Stat. 195, 198. For further discussion, see pp. 853–854 n.6, *infra.*

[46] Act of March 2, 1833, 4 Stat. 632.

[47] For discussion of the removal provisions, see pp. 853–854 n.6, *infra.*

[48] For discussion of the habeas corpus provisions, see pp. 1197 *infra.*

[49] See pp. 853–854 n.6, *infra.*

[50] For useful overviews, see Kutler, Judicial Power and Reconstruction Politics (1968); Wiecek, *The Reconstruction of Federal Judicial Power, 1863–1875*, 13 Am.J.Legal Hist. 333 (1969).

[51] See Act of Feb. 5, 1867, ch. 28, § 1, 14 Stat. 385. See generally Chap. XI, *infra.*

[52] See Kutler, note 50, *supra*, at 147.

[53] See pp. 781–782, *infra.*

[54] Steffel v. Thompson, 415 U.S. 452, 464 (1974) (quoting Frankfurter & Landis, note 3, *supra*, at 65).

[55] Act of April 10, 1869, 16 Stat. 44.

rights,[56] habeas corpus,[57] and patent and copyright[58] cases. In 1875 Congress restricted the Court's appellate jurisdiction by increasing the jurisdictional amount to $5,000.[59] Yet even this restriction was partially offset by further enlargements in the years immediately following.[60] By 1890, the number of cases on the Court's docket was nearly three times as large as in 1870.[61]

In the lower federal courts, which were the principal feeders of the stream, similar conditions prevailed. In 1873, there were 29,013 cases pending in the circuit and district courts, including 5,180 bankruptcy cases. By 1880, the total had increased to 38,045, even though the repeal of the Bankruptcy Act had eliminated the inward flow of bankruptcy cases. The year 1890 saw a further upward surge to 54,194 filings.[62]

Congress finally responded with the Judiciary Acts of 1887–88, which put a series of curbs on access to the lower federal courts.[63] Two years later, it fundamentally reshaped the federal judicial system, and substantially established the framework of the contemporary system, when it enacted the Evarts Act (the Circuit Court of Appeals Act of 1891).[64] The Act, which finally absolved the Justices of the Supreme Court of their obligation to "ride circuit", established circuit courts of appeals, consisting of three judges each, for each of the nine existing circuits. The legislation also created an additional circuit judgeship in each circuit, thus providing two circuit judges

---

[56] Act of April 9, 1866, § 10, 14 Stat. 27, 29; Act of April 20, 1871, 17 Stat. 13.

[57] Act of Feb. 5, 1867, § 1, 14 Stat. 385, 386. Congress abolished appeals to the Supreme Court under this law by the Act of March 27, 1868, § 2, 15 Stat. 44, see Ex parte McCardle, p. 304, *infra*, but restored them by the Act of March 3, 1885, 23 Stat. 437.

[58] Act of Feb. 18, 1861, 12 Stat. 130.

[59] Act of Feb. 16, 1875, § 3, 18 Stat. 315.

[60] To the matters reviewable without regard to the amount in controversy, Congress added more civil rights cases by the Act of March 1, 1875, § 5, 18 Stat. 335, 337, and jurisdictional questions by the Act of Feb. 25, 1889, 25 Stat. 693. In 1889, writs of error were for the first time permitted in cases of capital crime. Act of Feb. 6, 1889, § 6, 25 Stat. 655, 656.

[61] The figures in this paragraph are all taken from Frankfurter & Landis, note 3, *supra*, at 60.

[62] *Id.*

[63] See Act of March 3, 1887, 24 Stat. 552, corrected by Act of Aug. 13, 1888, 25 Stat. 433. The specific restrictions of jurisdiction that the Act introduced were each relatively minor, but they had considerable aggregate effect:

(1) The Act raised the jurisdictional amount to $2,000.

(2) The privilege of removal was withdrawn from plaintiffs and confined to defendants; in diversity cases it was confined to nonresident defendants.

(3) Specific language made clear that the general removal jurisdiction did not extend to any cases except those that might have been brought originally in a federal court.

(4) No longer was venue proper in any district in which the defendant "shall be found", but only in the district of which the defendant was an "inhabitant", with an option in diversity cases of the district of either the plaintiff's or the defendant's residence.

(5) Banking associations were no longer allowed to sue in federal courts merely on the ground that they were incorporated under the laws of the United States.

(6) The Act broadened the assignee clause limiting diversity jurisdiction.

These restrictions of the 1887 act, however, were partly offset by the Tucker Act, 24 Stat. 505, which was signed into law on the same day. See Chap. IX, Sec. 1(C), *infra*.

[64] Act of March 3, 1891, 26 Stat. 826. For the view that the Evarts Act was one of a package of post-Reconstruction measures by which the Republican Party attempted to expand federal power as a means of promoting national economic development—and thereby helped to lay the foundation for the Lochner era—see Gilman, *How Political Parties Can Use the Courts to Advance Their Agendas: Federal Courts in the United States, 1875–1891*, 96 Am.Pol.Sci.Rev. 511 (2002).

in all the circuits except the second, which, having received an additional judge in 1887,[65] now had three. The Evarts Act provided for the third place on court of appeals' panels ordinarily to be filled by a district judge, but Supreme Court Justices also remained eligible to sit.[66]

With respect to the Supreme Court's appellate jurisdiction, the Evarts Act introduced the then revolutionary, but now familiar, principle of discretionary review of federal judgments on writ of certiorari.[67] The Act also made circuit court of appeals' decisions "final" in diversity litigation, in suits under the revenue and patent laws, in criminal prosecutions, and in admiralty suits. In such cases, however, the Supreme Court, "by certiorari or otherwise," was authorized, regardless of the amount in controversy, to order the judgment brought before it for review. Despite this innovation, the Act continued to permit Supreme Court review as of right in important classes of cases, subject in general to a jurisdictional amount requirement of $1,000. In addition, as remains true today, a circuit court of appeals was authorized to "certify to the Supreme Court * * * any questions or propositions of law concerning which it desires the instruction of that court for its proper decision."

The principle of discretionary review also served as an important feature of the structurally significant Act of December 23, 1914.[68] Animated at least partly by hostility to state court decisions invalidating legislation under the Due Process Clause,[69] Congress expanded the Supreme Court's appellate jurisdiction to encompass for the first time cases in which a state court rendered a decision favorable to a claim of federal right. To protect the Court from further docket overload, the statute provided for review of such cases by writ of certiorari. Congress further expanded the scope of discretionary Supreme Court review in the so-called Judges' Bill, enacted in 1925,[70] which was drafted by a committee of Supreme Court Justices (led by Justice Van Devanter). Since then, the principle of review at the Court's discretion has become ever more dominant until, today, mandatory appellate jurisdiction has entirely disappeared in cases originating in state courts and has virtually disappeared in federal cases.[71]

E.   Political Responses to Federal Jurisdiction and Judicial Administration: The Lochner Era and Beyond

In the late nineteenth and early twentieth centuries, during the so-called Lochner era, the federal courts began to engage in broader and potentially more intrusive scrutiny of state and federal legislation than ever before. The substantive constitutional theory underlying judicial review of

---

[65] Act of March 3, 1887, 24 Stat. 492.

[66] In deference to the traditionalists, the Act did not abolish the old circuit courts, although it took away their appellate jurisdiction over the district courts. For another twenty years there remained two sets of federal trial courts. The Circuit Courts were finally abolished by the Judicial Code of 1911. See Act of March 3, 1911, 36 Stat. 1087.

[67] The Evarts Act did not alter the prevailing scheme of review of state court judgments by writ of error.

[68] Act of Dec. 23, 1914, 38 Stat. 790.

[69] See Frankfurter & Landis, note 3, *supra*, at 187–98.

[70] Act of Feb. 13, 1925, 43 Stat. 936. See generally Frankfurter & Landis, note 3, *supra*, at 255–94; Mason, William Howard Taft: Chief Justice 88–120 (1964). For a critical history of the Judges' Act's genesis and enactment, see Hartnett, *Questioning Certiorari: Some Reflections Seventy-Five Years After the Judges' Bill*, 100 Colum.L.Rev. 1643, 1660–1704 (2000).

[71] On review of state court decisions, see Chap. V, Sec. 1, *infra*.

economic legislation occasioned controversy from the outset, and critics viewed federal injunctions against the enforcement of state law as a special irritant in the structure of American federalism.

Congress responded with a number of jurisdictional enactments. In 1910, Congress provided that federal interlocutory injunctions against the enforcement of state statutes on constitutional grounds could be issued only by special, three-judge district courts, with direct appeal as of right to the Supreme Court.[72]

The Johnson Act, passed in 1934, sharply circumscribed the district courts' jurisdiction to issue injunctions interfering with state regulation of public utilities whenever "[a] plain, speedy, and efficient remedy may be had at law or in equity in the courts of" the state.[73] The Tax Injunction Act of 1937 similarly forbade federal injunctions against "the assessment, levy or collection of any tax imposed by or pursuant to the laws of any State" as long as "a plain, speedy, and efficient remedy may be had at law or in equity in the courts of such state."[74]

Another congressional enactment of the same era, the Norris-LaGuardia Act of 1932,[75] sought to protect unions and their right to strike by narrowly restricting the authority of the federal courts to issue injunctions in "a case involving or growing out of a labor dispute". The Act further provided that "yellow-dog" contracts under which employees promised not to join a labor union "shall not be enforceable in any court of the United States", despite Supreme Court precedent holding that state legislation similarly limiting employers' remedies violated the Due Process Clause.[76]

In 1937, after decisions of the Supreme Court in 1934–36 had invalidated important portions of the New Deal program[77] and raised apprehensions concerning the remainder, President Franklin Roosevelt sought to salvage the situation by "packing" the federal courts and especially the Supreme Court with New Deal sympathizers.[78] The plan that he submitted to Congress[79] would have authorized the President to appoint one additional judge to the federal courts, including the Supreme Court, for any federal judge who had served 10 years and who, after reaching the age of 70, did not retire or resign.[80]

---

[72]   36 Stat. 557. For a discussion of this statute and its subsequent history, see Chap. X.

[73]   48 Stat. 775, now codified at 28 U.S.C. § 1342. See Chap. X, § 1, *infra*.

[74]   50 Stat. 738, now codified at 28 U.S.C. § 1341. See Chap. X, § 1, *infra*.

[75]   47 Stat. 70, now codified at 29 U.S.C. §§ 101–115.

[76]   For discussion, see Chap. IV, Sec. 1, pp. 312–314, *infra*.

[77]   See, *e.g.*, Panama Refining Co. v. Ryan, 293 U.S. 388 (1935); Railroad Retirement Board v. Alton R. Co., 295 U.S. 330 (1935); A.L.A. Schechter Poultry Corp. v. United States, 295 U.S. 495 (1935); United States v. Butler, 297 U.S. 1 (1936); Carter v. Carter Coal Co., 298 U.S. 238 (1936).

[78]   Before settling on this plan, the Administration canvassed other possible measures, including restrictions on the courts' jurisdiction and substantive constitutional amendments. See Leuchtenburg, *The Origins of Franklin D. Roosevelt's "Court-Packing" Plan*, 1966 Sup.Ct.Rev. 347. See also Burns, Roosevelt: The Lion and the Fox ch. 15 (1956).

[79]   S. 1392, 75th Cong., 1st Sess. (1937), printed in Sen.Rep. No. 711, 75th Cong., 1st Sess. (1937) (Reorganization of the Federal Judiciary).

[80]   Not more than 50 additional judges were to be so appointed, and the membership of the Supreme Court was to be limited to 15. The proposal would have allowed President Roosevelt to add six Justices to the Supreme Court if none of the sitting members over 70 had stepped down.

But the Court-packing proposal, which the President initially defended on the dubious ground that it was needed to keep the Supreme Court abreast of its work,[81] aroused wide-spread opposition as an attack on the independence of the federal judiciary and on the principle of judicial review.[82] The Senate Judiciary Committee reported the plan adversely in June, 1937,[83] and in late July the Senate allowed it to die.[84] In the meantime, the Supreme Court had upheld the constitutionality of a number of regulatory statutes,[85] Justice Van Devanter had retired, and the Lochner era had come to an end. Scholars continue to debate whether the Court-packing scheme, Roosevelt's overwhelming victory in the 1936 election, or related political pressures influenced Justice Roberts' "switch in time", which provided the critical fifth vote to uphold New Deal legislation.[86]

After only a brief respite from the vortex of controversy, the substance of federal judicial action again began to occasion proposals to curb federal jurisdiction during the years of the Warren Court.[87] None of the proposals was enacted, however.

F.   Further Reforms

The defeat of the Court-packing plan left the basic organization of the federal court system in the form established by the Evarts Act and the

---

[81] See the President's Message to Congress of February 5, 1937, printed in Sen.Rep. No. 711, note 79, *supra*, at 25–27. Subsequently the President became much more forthright in justifying his plan on the ground that the Court's decisions were an intolerable obstacle to his program. See generally Burns, note 78, *supra*. See also 6 The Public Papers and Addresses of Franklin D. Roosevelt lxv (1941): "I made one major mistake when I first presented the plan. I did not place enough emphasis upon the real mischief—the kind of decisions which, as a studied and continued policy, had been coming down from the Supreme Court. I soon corrected that mistake—in the speeches which I later made about the plan."

[82] The suggestion that the plan was justified by the needs of judicial administration was strongly rebutted by Chief Justice Hughes, speaking also for Justices Brandeis and Van Devanter, in a celebrated letter to Senator Wheeler, which stated that the Court was abreast of its work and that the appointment of additional Justices would impair the Court's effectiveness. See Sen.Rep. No. 711, note 79, *supra*, at 38–40 (quoting the letter).

[83] Sen.Rep. No. 711, note 79, *supra*.

[84] See Burns, note 78, *supra*, at 306–09.

[85] See, in particular, West Coast Hotel Co. v. Parrish, 300 U.S. 379 (1937); NLRB v. Jones & Laughlin Steel Corp., 301 U.S. 1 (1937).

[86] Contemporaneous discussions almost invariably attributed the Court's apparent turnaround to political pressures, including the Court-packing plan. Later, however, Justice Frankfurter reported having received a memo from Justice Roberts that detailed the sequence of events and established that Roberts had cast his crucial votes in the West Coast Hotel and Jones & Laughlin cases, note 85, *supra*, before the President's announcement of his court-packing proposal. See Frankfurter, *Mr. Justice Roberts*, 104 U.Pa.L.Rev. 311 (1955). *Cf.* Ariens, *A Thrice-Told Tale, or Felix the Cat*, 107 Harv.L.Rev. 620 (1994) (doubting Frankfurter's claims). Notwithstanding the Roberts memo, some historians have continued to maintain that political factors including the 1936 election—even if not the Court-packing plan in particular—provide the best explanation for Justice Roberts' 1937 votes to uphold key New Deal legislation. See, e.g., Leuchtenburg, The Supreme Court Reborn: The Constitutional Revolution in the Age of Roosevelt (1995). Revisionist works that attribute the "switch in time" less to immediate political pressure than to gradually unfolding changes in constitutional doctrine and prevailing jurisprudential assumptions include Cushman, Rethinking the New Deal: The Structure of a Constitutional Revolution (1998), and White, The Constitution and the New Deal (2000). For a masterly review of the scholarly debate between those who attribute the turn-around to "external" political or "internal" legal forces, and a search for common ground, see Kalman, *The Constitution, the Supreme Court, and the New Deal*, 110 Am.Hist.Rev. 1052 (2005).

[87] For discussion, see Chap. IV, Sec. 1, p. 297, *infra*. For a broader discussion of the relation of Warren Court decisionmaking to surrounding political currents, see Powe, The Warren Court and American Politics (2000).

Judges' Bill of 1925.[88] The Judicial Code of 1948 (the present codification of the organization and business of the federal courts) retained that structure while making a number of important but interstitial changes.

Since the 1948 recodification, the major legislative changes in the federal judicial system have included:

1. Elimination in 1980 of the amount-in-controversy requirement in federal question cases brought under 28 U.S.C. § 1331.[89]

2. Increases in the amount-in-controversy requirement in diversity cases under 28 U.S.C. § 1332 from $3,000 to $10,000 in 1958,[90] from $10,000 to $50,000 in 1988, see 102 Stat. 4642, 4646, and then to $75,000 in 1996.[91]

3. Legislation adopted in 1958 redefining corporate citizenship[92] and permitting certain interlocutory appeals to the courts of appeals from the district courts.[93]

4. The virtual elimination of the requirement that certain cases be heard before a district court of three judges, with a right of direct appeal to the Supreme Court.[94] The story of the rise and fall of this requirement is told in Chap. X, Sec. 1(B), *infra*.

5. Elimination of several other provisions for direct appeal to the Supreme Court of federal district court decisions.[95]

6. Division of the Fifth Circuit into a new Fifth Circuit (Louisiana, Mississippi, and Texas) and a new Eleventh Circuit (Alabama, Florida, and Georgia).[96]

7. Numerous changes in the character and scope of the specialized federal courts, including the creation of a new Court of Appeals for the Federal Circuit. These changes are described in Parts G and H of this Note.

8. Elimination of the Supreme Court's mandatory appellate jurisdiction in the general jurisdictional statutes governing review of state and lower federal court judgments and substitution of discretionary review by writ of certiorari. The major amendments are described at p. 463, *infra*.

---

[88] The present Tenth Circuit had been created in 1929. Act of Feb. 28, 1929, 45 Stat. 1346.

[89] Act of Dec. 1, 1980, 94 Stat. 2369.

[90] Act of July 25, 1958, 72 Stat. 415.

[91] See the Federal Courts Improvement Act of 1996, 110 Stat. 3847. The Judicial Improvements Act of 1990, 104 Stat. 5089, besides creating 85 new judgeships (11 at the appellate level and 74 at the district court level) (§§ 201–06, 104 Stat. 5098–5104), required that each district court formulate a plan to reduce the cost and delay of civil litigation (§ 103, 104 Stat. 5090, adding §§ 471–482 to Title 28).

[92] Act of July 25, 1958, 72 Stat. 415. (amending 28 U.S.C. § 1332 to provide that a corporation shall be considered a citizen of both its state of incorporation and the state in which it maintains its principal place of business).

[93] Act of Sept. 2, 1958, 72 Stat. 1770 (amending 28 U.S.C. § 1292 to permit district courts to certify questions for interlocutory appeal).

[94] Act of Aug. 12, 1976, 90 Stat. 1119.

[95] See, *e.g.*, Omnibus Crime Control Act of 1970, 18 U.S.C. § 3731, as amended by Act of Jan. 2, 1971, § 14(a), 84 Stat. 1890; Act of Dec. 21, 1974, 88 Stat. 1708–09 (amending the Expediting Act).

[96] Act of Oct. 14, 1980, 94 Stat. 1994.

G.   Specialized Courts Under Article III

For the most part, the Article III courts have been courts of broad-based, although not "general", jurisdiction,[97] and many have viewed the diversity of the federal docket as a large asset in attracting able lawyers to the bench and achieving cross-pollination among different areas of the law.[98] There are important exceptions to the norm of relatively general jurisdiction, however, as well as continuing debate about whether the benefits of specialization (with respect to at least some subject matters) outweigh the drawbacks.[99]

1.   The Court of International Trade

In 1926 the old Board of General Appraisers, which had been established to hear appeals from decisions of customs collectors, received formal status as a specialized court with the name of the United States Customs Court.[100] Congress vested the court with Article III status in 1956[101] and in 1980 redesignated it the United States Court of International Trade.[102]

2.   The Court of Appeals for the Federal Circuit

In 1982, Congress created the United States Court of Appeals for the Federal Circuit.[103] This court has exclusive jurisdiction to hear appeals from (1) the Court of Federal Claims,[104] (2) the Federal Merit System Protection Board, (3) agency boards of contract appeals under the Contract Disputes Act of 1978, (4) the Court of International Trade, (5) the Patent Office in patent and trademark cases,[105] (6) the district courts in certain actions in which district court jurisdiction was based in whole or in part on the "Little Tucker Act" (28 U.S.C. § 1346(a)(2)), involving claims against the United States that, *inter alia*, neither exceed $10,000 nor sound in tort, and (7) the

---

[97] By contrast, there are a number of specialized Article I courts—a concept discussed in Part H of this Note—that are created by Congress exercising Article I power and that are staffed by judges who lack the tenure and salary protection provided by Article III.

[98] See, *e.g.*, Posner, The Federal Courts: Challenge and Reform 249–50 (1996).

[99] With *id.*, compare Bator, *The Judicial Universe of Judge Richard Posner* (Book Review), 52 U.Chi.L.Rev. 1146, 1154–56 (1985) (advocating "increase[d] specialization at the court of appeals level" and arguing that specialization would "attract more real lawyers and fewer pseudo-politicians" to the bench and would subject them to the "kind of intellectual discipline that comes from having to demonstrate detailed substantive mastery over a field").

[100] Act of May 28, 1926, 44 Stat. 669. See also Act of June 17, 1930, § 518, 46 Stat. 590, 737; Act of Oct. 10, 1940, 54 Stat. 1101; Act of June 2, 1970, § 110, 84 Stat. 274, 278.

[101] Act of July 14, 1956, 70 Stat. 532.

[102] Act of Oct. 10, 1980, 94 Stat. 1727. The provisions governing its organization are collected in Chapter 11 of the Judicial Code and the jurisdictional provisions in Chapter 95.

[103] The Federal Courts Improvement Act of 1982, § 127, 96 Stat. 25, 37–38. The jurisdictional provision appears in the Judicial Code at 28 U.S.C. § 1295.

[104] For further discussion of the Court of Federal Claims and its history, see Chap. II, Sec. 2, pp. 89–90, and Chap. IX, Sec. 1, pp. 897–899, *infra*.

[105] Items (4) and (5) embrace the jurisdiction of the former Court of Customs and Patent Appeals. The Court of Customs Appeals was established in 1909 as the second of the specialized federal courts with nationwide jurisdiction to hear appeals from the Board of General Appraisers—appeals that were then swamping some of the regular courts. Act of Aug. 5, 1909, § 29, 36 Stat. 11, 105. The court continued to hear these appeals after the board became the Customs Court in 1926, and in 1929 Congress gave the court the jurisdiction over appeals from the Patent Office that had been vested in the Court of Appeals of the District of Columbia. Act of March 2, 1929, 45 Stat. 1475. See also Act of June 17, 1930, § 646, 46 Stat. 590, 762; Act of Dec. 24, 1970, § 143, 84 Stat. 1542, 1558. Congress designated the Court of Customs and Patent Appeals an Article III court in 1958, see 72 Stat. 848, and the Supreme Court recognized the validity of that designation in Glidden Co. v. Zdanok, 370 U.S. 530 (1962).

district courts in all patent cases in which district court jurisdiction was based in whole or in part on 28 U.S.C. § 1338.[106]

3.   Special Courts with Non-Specialist Judges

In addition to creating specialized courts whose judges are nominated by the President and confirmed by the Senate to do those courts' specialized business, Congress has from time to time constituted tribunals with specialized jurisdiction but staffed with Article III judges drawn from the regular district courts and courts of appeals. Past examples include an Emergency Court of Appeals with exclusive jurisdiction to entertain challenges to orders and regulations issued under the Emergency Price Control Act of 1942[107] and a Temporary Emergency Court of Appeals, created by the 1971 amendments to the Economic Stabilization Act of 1970,[108] to hear all appeals from district court decisions arising under the Act or its implementing regulations.

Today, the Foreign Intelligence Surveillance Court (FISC), which consists of Article III judges assigned by the Chief Justice, has the responsibility of ruling on applications for electronic surveillance and certain physical searches relating to suspected foreign intelligence agents and international terrorists within the United States.[109] Denials of such applications are reviewable by the Foreign Intelligence Surveillance Court of Review, made up of three Article III judges also selected by the Chief Justice.

After leaked reports of U.S. intelligence-gathering practices spawned a public controversy, President Obama appointed a Review Group on Intelligence and Communications Technologies to examine current policies and recommend changes. With respect to the Foreign Intelligence Surveillance Court, the Review Group recommended: (1) the creation of a Public Interest Advocate with the authority to intervene to represent privacy and civil liberties interests; (2) provision to the FISC of greater access to technological experts to assist it in decision-making; (3) alteration of declassification procedures to increase FISC transparency by making more FISC opinions public in a timely manner; and (4) division of the power to

---

[106] See Christianson v. Colt Industries Operating Corp., 486 U.S. 800 (1988) (deciding whether a federal action arises under the patent or antitrust laws, which in turn determines whether the Federal Circuit or the regional court of appeals has appellate jurisdiction); United States v. Hohri, 482 U.S. 64 (1987) (ambiguity in 1982 Act is resolved by holding that Federal Circuit has exclusive jurisdiction over "mixed cases" involving claims under both the Little Tucker Act and the Federal Tort Claims Act).

Assessments of the performance of the Federal Circuit have tended to be mixed, with friendly commentary emphasizing its contribution to doctrinal consistency and critics questioning the substantive quality of its decisions, especially with respect to patent law. See, e.g., Dreyfuss, *In Search of Institutional Identity: The Federal Circuit Comes of Age*, 23 Berkeley Technology L.J. 787, 788–92 (2008). Gugliazza, *Rethinking Federal Circuit Jurisdiction,* 100 Geo.L.J. 1437 (2012), maintains that the narrowness of the Federal Circuit's non-patent jurisdiction adversely affects both its development of patent law and its performance in non-patent-law cases and calls for a major reshaping of the court's non-patent jurisdiction. For discussion of a variety of issues involving the nature of the Federal Circuit and its performance, see Symposium: The Federal Circuit as an Institution, 43 Loy.L.A.L.Rev. 749 (2010).

[107] Act of Jan. 29, 1942, 56 Stat. 23. See pp. 341–345, *infra.*

[108] Act of Dec. 22, 1971, 85 Stat. 743.

[109] See 50 U.S.C. § 1803

appoint FISC members among the Justices of the Supreme Court, acting in their capacity as Circuit Justices.[110]

The Alien Terrorist Removal Court, which Congress established in 1996 and which consists of five Article III judges chosen by the Chief Justice, determines whether to grant applications by the Attorney General for removal of suspected alien terrorists, first in a private, *ex parte* review by one judge, and then, upon a finding of probable cause, in an open, public hearing before the Removal Court.[111]

H.   Non-Article III Courts and Adjudicators

Although this Note has so far focused on the Article III federal courts, Congress, from the very first, has asserted a power to organize tribunals under Article I.[112] Judges of these Article I tribunals lack the Article III guarantees of tenure during good behavior and non-reduction in salary, but the tribunals' functions are frequently indistinguishable from those of the Article III courts.

Almost no one disputes the highly general principle that Article III imposes some limits on Congress' authority to vest judicial power in non-Article III federal tribunals, but there is much less consensus or certainty concerning precisely what those limits are. The relevant doctrine and its perplexities are explored in Chap. IV, Sec. 2, *infra*.

For present purposes, it will be useful to distinguish three broad categories: (i) legislative courts, (ii) administrative agencies, and (iii) non-Article III adjudicators appointed by and subject to the supervision of Article III judges .

1.   Legislative Courts

Legislative courts—so-called because they are established not under Article III, but pursuant to Congress' legislative powers under Article I— typically are charged with adjudicating disputes involving specialized subject matters or with exercising jurisdiction in discrete geographical enclaves, such as the federal territories. They are characteristically constituted as "courts" and are seldom assigned significant executive or legislative functions.[113]

a.   Courts of the District of Columbia

The organization of the District of Columbia compelled the establishment of tribunals to perform the functions of local courts as well as of ordinary federal courts. From the beginning the District has had inferior courts with distinctively local jurisdiction.[114] From 1863 to 1893, this judicial system was headed by a Supreme Court of the District of Columbia, which was comparable both to a federal circuit court and to a state supreme court. In 1893, Congress established the Court of Appeals of the District of Columbia as a superior tribunal corresponding to the new circuit courts of

---

[110] See Report and Recommendations of the President's Review Group on Intelligence and Communications Technologies, Recommendation 28 (Dec. 12, 2013), *available at* http://www. whitehouse.gov/sites/default/files/docs/2013-12-12_rg_final_report.pdf.

[111] See 8 U.S.C. §§ 1532–37.

[112] See Chap. IV, Sec. 2, *infra*.

[113] For further generalizations about the characteristic nature of legislative courts, as well as some qualifications, see Chap. IV, Sec. 2, p. 379–380, *infra*.

[114] For an overview of the history, see Bloch & Ginsburg, *Celebrating the 200th Anniversary of the Federal Courts of the District of Columbia*, 90 Geo.L.J. 549 (2002).

appeals.[115] Both of these appellate tribunals had a local as well as a federal jurisdiction. But by successive steps the former District supreme court was given the title and status of a district court of the United States, and the former court of appeals became a United States Court of Appeals.[116]

In 1970 the District of Columbia Court Reorganization Act[117] ended the system of combining federal and local jurisdictions in the courts of the District. Under this Act, the United States District Court for the District of Columbia and the United States Court of Appeals for the District of Columbia Circuit exercise only the jurisdiction exercised by other federal district courts and circuit courts of appeals. The Act transferred the remaining local jurisdiction to two non-Article III courts. The highest local court continues to be the District of Columbia Court of Appeals,[118] an appellate tribunal whose judgments are reviewable by the Supreme Court under 28 U.S.C. § 1257(b) as if they were rendered by the highest court of a state. The Superior Court of the District of Columbia is now the trial court of general jurisdiction,[119] analogous to a state's trial courts. The judges of both these local courts serve for 15-year terms.[120]

b. The Territorial and Related Courts

The statutes organizing each of the territories have likewise had to make provision for courts of local as well as federal jurisdiction. Today the Commonwealth of Puerto Rico has a system of local courts, headed by the Supreme Court of Puerto Rico;[121] decisions of the latter are reviewed by the United States Supreme Court much as state court judgments are.[122] In addition, a United States District Court for the District of Puerto Rico, exercising federal jurisdiction, sits in the Commonwealth. Its decisions are reviewable in the United States Court of Appeals for the First Circuit.[123]

Guam, the Virgin Islands, and the Northern Mariana Islands all have courts, designated as "district courts" but organized under Article I, that exercise both local and federal jurisdiction.[124] The judgments of the district courts of the Virgin Islands and those of Guam and the Northern Mariana

---

[115] Act of Feb. 9, 1893, 27 Stat. 434. For the history of this court and of the old District supreme court, see O'Donoghue v. United States, 289 U.S. 516, 548–49 (1933).

[116] For the present provisions, see 28 U.S.C. §§ 41, 43 (court of appeals), and §§ 88, 132 (district court).

[117] Act of July 29, 1970, 84 Stat. 473.

[118] D.C.Code §§ 11–701 *et seq.*

[119] D.C.Code §§ 11–901 *et seq.*

[120] D.C.Code § 11–1502. For discussion of the constitutional status of the courts of the District of Columbia, see Palmore v. United States, 411 U.S. 389 (1973).

[121] See Puerto Rico Constitution Art. V, superseding 48 U.S.C. § 861.

[122] 28 U.S.C. § 1258.

[123] 28 U.S.C. § 41. This district court is constituted among the regular district courts by Chapter 5 of the Judicial Code, 28 U.S.C. §§ 119, 132. Its judges have life tenure by virtue of the Act of September 12, 1966, 80 Stat. 764, amending 28 U.S.C. § 134(a).

[124] See 48 U.S.C. §§ 1611–14 (Virgin Islands), 1424 (Guam), 1821–24 (Northern Mariana Islands).

The Court held in Nguyen v. United States, 539 U.S. 69 (2003), that judges of the non-Article III district courts are ineligible to sit on federal courts of appeals under 28 U.S.C. § 292(a), which provides that "[t]he chief judge of a circuit may designate and assign one or more district judges within the circuit to sit upon the court of appeals * * * whenever the business of that court so requires".

Islands are reviewable by the Third and Ninth Circuits respectively.[125] These territories also have local inferior courts.

c. The Tax Court

Until 1969 the United States Tax Court, which hears taxpayer petitions contesting deficiency determinations, was an independent agency in the Executive Branch. Congress then declared it to be a "court".[126] Decisions of the Tax Court are reviewed by the courts of appeals "in the same manner and to the same extent as decisions of the district courts in civil action tried without a jury".[127]

d. The Court of Federal Claims

The story of the establishment of the Court of Claims by statutes of 1855, 1863, and 1866, and its replacement in 1982 by the United States Claims Court, which was itself retitled the United States Court of Federal Claims a decade later, is summarized in Chap. II, Sec. 2.[128] The court's decisions are reviewed by the Article III Court of Appeals for the Federal Circuit.[129]

e. Court of Veterans Appeals

In 1988 Congress created the Court of Appeals for Veterans Claims, with exclusive jurisdiction to review decisions of the Board of Veterans' Appeals. Decisions of the Court of Appeals for Veterans Claims are reviewable by the Article III Court of Appeals for the Federal Circuit.[130]

f. Military Courts

Throughout American history, Congress has provided a separate set of military courts with jurisdiction over offenses arising from military service.[131] In addition, Congress and the President have from time to time established special military courts or "commissions" to dispense justice in areas subject to martial law or military occupation and to try alleged illegal combatants under the laws of war. The use of such special military courts or commissions is discussed in Chap. IV, Sec. 2, *infra*.

The more regularized and enduring system of military courts exercising jurisdiction over the service-related offenses of American service members comprises three tiers. At the trial level, the least serious form of court-martial may be presided over by a commissioned officer, but trials of more serious offenses usually require a military judge—a position that has formally existed only since 1968—as presiding officer.[132] The trial-level judges do not serve for fixed terms and perform judicial duties only when

---

[125] See 28 U.S.C. §§ 1291, 1294(3), 1294(4), and 48 U.S.C. § 1821(a).

[126] Act of Dec. 30, 1969, § 951, 83 Stat. 487, 730, amending 26 U.S.C. § 7441. Tax Court judges are appointed for 15-year terms. 26 U.S.C. § 7443(e).

[127] 26 U.S.C. § 7482(a)(1). For discussion and defense of this non-deferential standard of review despite the Tax Court's expertise, see Lederman, *(Un)appealing Deference to the Tax Court,* 63 Duke L.J. 1835 (2014).

[128] See also Glidden Co. v. Zdanok, 370 U.S. 530 (1962).

[129] See 28 U.S.C. § 1295(a)(3). Under the 1982 statute, Court of Federal Claims judges are appointed for 15-year terms. 28 U.S.C. § 172(a).

[130] See 38 U.S.C. §§ 7104, 7251–56, 7292.

[131] For a discussion of military justice and its relation to Article III, see Note, 103 Harv.L.Rev. 1909 (1990).

[132] See Art. 26, Uniform Code of Military Justice ("UCMJ"), 10 U.S.C. § 826.

assigned to do so by the Judge Advocate General of the service of which they are members.[133]

At the first appellate tier are Courts of Criminal Appeals for each of the services. The appellate judges may be either military officers or civilians. They do not serve for fixed terms and are assigned by the appropriate Judge Advocate General.[134]

At the top of the system sits a five-member, all-civilian Court of Appeals for the Armed Forces, the judges of which are appointed by the President, with the advice and consent of the Senate, to 15-year terms.[135] The Court of Appeals' decisions are subject to review on certiorari by the Supreme Court of the United States.[136]

2.   Administrative Agencies

Administrative agencies frequently adjudicate rights and obligations under their organic statutes. In classic regimes of agency adjudication, ultimate adjudicative authority resides in "the agency" or its head. Agencies characteristically differ from legislative courts along several dimensions,[137] perhaps the most important of which is that agencies frequently perform a mix of functions, including rulemaking and enforcement as well as adjudication. In the modern agency, initial adjudication is typically performed by an "administrative law judge" or "administrative judge", who enjoys relative insulation from pressure by officials performing other functions, but nonetheless is an employee of the agency.

Though administrative adjudication is often overlooked in portrayals of the "judicial" system, by 2012 the federal government employed almost 1,600 officials denominated as "administrative law judges",[138] as well as a further group of so-called "administrative judges" or "presiding officers" that numbered roughly 3370 in 2002.[139] Although a current figure is hard to come by, in 1989 this latter group rendered decisions in roughly 350,000 on-the-record adjudications per year.[140] All by itself, the Social Security Administration conducted nearly 800,000 hearings in fiscal 2013[141]—a caseload larger than the civil docket of all Article III courts combined.

---

[133] As of 2013, there were roughly 130 judges, all attorneys and all commissioned officers, certified to preside at various types of courts-martial. See Joint Annual Report of the Code Committee (2013), *available at* http://www.armfor.uscourts.gov/newcaaf/annual/FY12Annual Report.pdf; U.S. Army Trial Judiciary e-Docket, https://www.jagcnet.army.mil/Apps/TJeDocket/usatjedocket.nsf/xpPub_Judges.xsp.

[134] See Art. 66, UCMJ, 10 U.S.C. § 866.

[135] Arts. 67, 142, UCMJ, 10 U.S.C. §§ 867, 942.

[136] See 28 U.S.C. § 1259. There is also a limited opportunity to test the judgments of military courts in federal habeas corpus actions.

[137] The differences are explored in Chap. IV, Sec. 2, *infra*.

[138] Administrative Law Judges: Protecting Justice and Due Process for the American People: Hearing Before the Subcomm. on Social Security of the H. Comm. on Ways and Means, 112th Cong. 1 (2012) (statement of D. Randall Frye, President, Association of Administrative Law Judges).

[139] See Limon, The Federal Administrative Judiciary: Then and Now: A Decade of Change, 1992–2002, at 4–5 (2002) (published by the Office of Administrative Law Judges in the Office of Personnel Management).

[140] See Verkuil, *Reflections upon the Federal Administrative Judiciary*, 39 UCLA L.Rev. 1341, 1345–46 (1992).

[141] Information About Social Security's Hearings and Appeals Process, SSA, http://ssa.gov/appeals/#a0=2.

The adjudicative decisions of federal administrative agencies are generally reviewable in the Article III courts—often directly by the courts of appeals, but in some instances by the district courts. According to at least one commentator, this relationship between agencies and the Article III courts demonstrates that traditional thought about the federal judicial system has lagged behind the reality: Reconceptualization is needed to account for a fourth tier of federal adjudication (beneath the federal district courts, the courts of appeals, and the Supreme Court). See Resnik, *Rereading "The Federal Courts": Revising the Domain of Federal Courts Jurisprudence at the End of the Twentieth Century*, 47 Vand.L.Rev. 1021 (1994). For further consideration of administrative adjudication and constitutional limits on its permissibility, see Chap. IV, Sec. 2, *infra*.

3.   Non-Article III Adjudicators Appointed by and Subject to the Supervision of Article III Judges

a.   Magistrate Judges

The Federal Magistrates Act of 1968, 82 Stat. 1107, as amended, 28 U.S.C. §§ 631 *et seq.*, created the position of "magistrate", which was subsequently retitled as "magistrate judge".[142] Magistrate judges are appointed by the federal district judges, in such numbers as the Judicial Conference of the United States may determine. They may be appointed on a full-time basis for an eight-year term, or on a part-time basis for a four-year term. Magistrate judges were initially given (a) the powers previously exercised by United States commissioners (*e.g.*, issuing warrants, conducting probable cause and other preliminary hearings in criminal cases), (b) jurisdiction to try "minor offenses", and (c) "such additional duties as are not inconsistent with the Constitution and laws" and as might be established at the district court level, including service as special masters in civil cases, assistance in discovery or other pretrial proceedings, and preliminary review of applications for post-conviction relief.[143]

Congress further expanded the role of magistrates in the Federal Magistrate Act of 1979,[144] which authorized magistrates to hear, determine, and enter final judgment in both jury and nonjury civil cases if all parties consent. Magistrate judges may also try criminal misdemeanor cases if the defendant consents. Aggrieved parties may appeal to the court of appeals. 28 U.S.C. § 636(c)(3).

In 2013, there were 531 full-time and 40 part-time magistrate judges, supplemented by 58 retired magistrate judges who had been temporarily recalled to service and three clerks of court who doubled as magistrate judges.[145] Altogether these officials disposed of more than one million judicial matters in 2013 alone.[146] For more discussion of the kinds of matters handled by magistrate judges, see p. 42, *infra*. For discussion of the statutory and especially constitutional issues that the role of magistrate judges presents, see *Note on Magistrate Judges*, p. 390, *infra*.

---

[142] See the Judicial Improvements Act of 1990, § 321, 104 Stat. 5089, 5117.

[143] § 636, 82 Stat. 1107, 1113.

[144] 93 Stat. 643, amending 28 U.S.C. §§ 604, 631, 633–36, 1915(b), and 18 U.S.C. § 3401.

[145] Administrative Office of the U.S. Courts, 2013 Judicial Business, Table 13.

[146] *Id.*, Table S–17.

b.   Bankruptcy Courts

Until enactment of the Bankruptcy Reform Act of 1978, the district courts acted as bankruptcy courts. Proceedings were generally conducted before court-appointed referees; the district court could at any time withdraw the case from the referee; and the referee's final order was appealable to the district court. In the 1978 Act, however, Congress created, as "an adjunct to the district court" for each district, a "court of record known as the United States Bankruptcy Court." The judges of the new courts were appointed by the President and confirmed by the Senate to serve 14-year terms; they were removable by the judicial councils of the circuits; and their salaries were not protected against diminution.

The Supreme Court invalidated the system of bankruptcy courts created by this statute in Northern Pipeline Construction Co. v. Marathon Pipe Line Co., 458 U.S. 50 (1982). After considerable delay and controversy, Congress in 1984 changed the system once again. Under the law as revised, bankruptcy judges are appointed as officers of the district courts for a term of fourteen years; appointments are made by the courts of appeals for the districts within their respective circuits, and the judges in each district "constitute a unit of the district court to be known as the bankruptcy court for that district." 28 U.S.C. §§ 151, 152. As of September 30, 2013, there were 350 authorized and funded bankruptcy judgeships, 20 of which were vacant. In addition, 47 retired judges had been called to temporary service.[147]

Issues involving the constitutionally permissible functions of bankruptcy judges have arisen recurrently in the decades since the Northern Pipeline case. For discussion of the relevant decisions and surrounding uncertainties, see Chap. IV, Sec. 2, *infra*.

I.   The Article III Courts Today

1.   The District Courts

Chapter 5 of the Judicial Code of 1948 (Title 28, U.S. Code) codified the statutes establishing the district courts. It now provides for 94 district courts: 92 for the fifty states, and one each for the District of Columbia and Puerto Rico.

Each state has at least one district court. The more populous states are divided into two, three, or four districts. Many districts are in turn divided into divisions. On September 30, 2013, there were 677 authorized district judgeships. In addition, 346 senior district judges continued to hear cases following their retirement from full-time status.[148]

The current business of the district courts (as well as of other federal courts) is described in detail by the Director of the Administrative Office of the United States Courts in the Annual Reports of the Director: Judicial Business of the United States Courts.[149] Although nothing ages more quickly than statistics, this and the following subsections of this Part attempt to give a summary picture of the work of the Article III courts.

---

[147] *Id.*, Table 12.

[148] *Id.*, Table 11.

[149] These reports are available on-line at http://www.uscourts.gov/statistics-reports/judicial-business-2014.

In the 2013 fiscal year, 284,604 civil and 91,266 criminal cases were commenced in the district courts, for a total of 375,870.[150] (By contrast, 313,615 civil and criminal cases were filed in 2001, 287,864 in 1994, 296,318 in 1986, 127,280 in 1970, and 89,091 in 1960.) In addition, the district courts received 1,107,699 bankruptcy petitions.[151]

On the civil side, 236,362 cases involved private disputes. Of these, 89,305 came within the diversity jurisdiction and 147,057 within the federal question jurisdiction (including admiralty).[152] The United States appeared as a plaintiff in 7,694 civil cases and as a defendant in 40,545 actions.[153]

Two factors are crucial in permitting the federal district courts to handle the current volume of business. First, most cases never come to trial. Of the 255,260 civil cases terminated in the district courts in 2013, trials occurred in only 5,027 (of which 2,025 were before a jury).[154] On the criminal side, federal cases terminated in 2013 involved 91,234 defendants.[155] Cases involving 7,181 defendants were dismissed, and 81,567 other defendants pleaded guilty.[156] (Of those whose cases actually went to trial, 344 were acquitted, and 2,142 were convicted.)[157]

Second, a growing volume of business is handled by magistrate judges. In 2013, magistrate judges disposed of 374,229 civil matters and received 202,252 references (mostly involving motions, hearings, and conferences) in criminal felony cases.[158] These figures include final dispositions of 15,804 civil cases with the consent of the parties (in comparison with 4,931 in 1986, 7,835 in 1994, and 12,024 in 2001), 455 of which involved a trial.[159]

By most if not all accounts, the federal district courts are seriously overtaxed by their current caseloads, and thoughtful and much discussed reform proposals have emerged, *inter alia*, from the American Law Institute in 1969;[160] from the Federal Courts Study Committee, appointed by the Chief Justice at the direction of Congress, in 1990;[161] and from the Committee on Long Range Planning of the Judicial Conference of the United States in

---

[150] Administrative Office of the U.S. Courts, 2013 Judicial Business, Tables 3, 5.

[151] *Id.*, Table 6.

[152] *Id.*, Table 4.

[153] *Id.*

[154] *Id.*, Tables 3, T–1.

[155] *Id.*, Table D–4.

[156] *Id.*

[157] *Id.*

[158] *Id.*, Table S–17.

[159] *Id.*

[160] See American Law Institute, Study of the Division of Jurisdiction Between State and Federal Courts (1969). For appraisals, see Wright, *Restructuring Federal Jurisdiction: The American Law Institute Proposals*, 26 Wash. & Lee L.Rev. 185 (1969); Currie, *The Federal Courts and the American Law Institute*, 36 U.Chi.L.Rev. 1, 268 (1969).

[161] Report of the Federal Courts Study Committee (1990). Among its recommendations were (1) substantial reduction of the diversity jurisdiction, (2) vesting of nearly exclusive tax jurisdiction in the Article I Tax Court (coupled with the creation of an Article III appellate division of that court), (3) creation of a new Article I Court of Disability Claims, and (4) reliance on non-judicial, or at least non-Article III, fora for resolving some disputes. For comment, see, *e.g.*, Symposium, *The Federal Court Docket: Issues and Solutions*, 22 Conn.L.Rev. 615 (1990).

1995.[162] The leading studies have all recommended substantial curtailments in the diversity jurisdiction, but Congress has not agreed.[163]

One obvious response to the problem of growing federal caseloads would be to increase substantially the number of federal judges. Although this mode of reform has not wanted for champions, it was viewed with distaste by the Committee on Long Range Planning of the Judicial Conference and was rejected in strong terms by the Federal Courts Study Committee, which regarded the preservation of elite status as crucial to maintaining the quality of the federal bench.[164] The Committee also argued that an expanded federal bench would increase the difficulties of coordination: more district judges would generate more appeals, and more appeals would heighten the obstacles to maintaining uniformity both within and among the circuits.[165]

2.   The Courts of Appeals

Chapter 3 of the Judicial Code of 1948 changed the name of the former circuit courts of appeals to the United States Courts of Appeals and codified the provisions establishing them. There are currently thirteen judicial circuits: eleven in the various states; one for the District of Columbia; and one for the Federal Circuit, which has a nationwide but specialized jurisdiction and is located in the District of Columbia and other places as the court may direct by rule. The number of judges per circuit ranges from six (First) to 29 (Ninth). 28 U.S.C. § 44(a). As of September 30, 2013, 179 judgeships were authorized, and there were an additional 89 senior judges.[166]

The principal business of the courts of appeals consists of review of the district courts, including the district courts in the territories.[167] The most important provision governing appeals from the district courts is 28 U.S.C. § 1291, which provides for jurisdiction of appeals from those courts' "final decisions". This limitation aims to avoid excessive appeals, especially of issues that may be mooted by settlement or by the ultimate outcome after trial.

---

[162] See Long Range Plan for the Federal Courts, as approved by the Judicial Conference of the United States (1995) (reprinted in 166 F.R.D. 49 (1995)).

[163] For an iconoclastic examination of the federal judicial docket and of the role of the federal courts in the American legal system, see Resnik, *Building the Federal Judiciary (Literally and Legally): The Monuments of Chief Justices Taft, Warren, and Rehnquist,* 87 Ind.L.J. 823 (2012). Professor Resnik emphasizes that although the size of the federal docket has continued to grow, the rate of increase has flattened in recent decades, as a result, among other factors, of jurisdictional doctrines developed by the Supreme Court and congressional legislation.

[164] The Committee wrote: "The independence secured to federal judges by Article III is compatible with responsible and efficient performance of judicial duties only if federal judges are carefully selected from a pool of competent and eager applicants and only if they are sufficiently few in number to feel a personal stake in the consequences of their actions." Were the judiciary greatly enlarged, "[t]he process of presidential nomination and senatorial confirmation would become pro forma * * *, [and] a sufficient number of highly qualified applicants could not be found unless the salaries of federal judges were greatly increased * * *."

[165] The Report posited that the total number of judgeships (then at 750) should not exceed 1000—a view shared by Judge Newman, among others. See Newman, *1,000 Judges—The Limit for an Effective Federal Judiciary,* 76 Judicature 187 (1993).

[166] Administrative Office of the U.S. Courts, Judicial Business 2013, Table 11.

[167] For a comprehensive survey and analysis of this topic see 15, 15A & 16, Wright, Miller & Cooper, Federal Practice and Procedure.

The Supreme Court has given the statutory limitation a pragmatic construction, however. Under "the collateral order doctrine", a decision may be considered final for purposes of appeal if it disposes of a matter that is "separable from, and collateral to" the merits of the main proceeding, is "too important to be denied review", and is "too independent of the case itself to require that appellate consideration be deferred until the whole case is adjudicated." Cohen v. Beneficial Industrial Loan Corp., 337 U.S. 541, 546 (1949).[168] In addition, Congress, in 28 U.S.C. § 1292(a)(1), has authorized appeals of interlocutory decisions in a number of situations, including those involving orders "granting, continuing, modifying, refusing or dissolving injunctions, or refusing to modify or dissolve injunctions". Section 1292(b) allows additional interlocutory appeals, but only when the district judge in a civil action is of the opinion that an appeal from an otherwise unappealable order "involves a controlling question of law as to which there is substantial ground for difference of opinion" and immediate appeal "may materially advance the ultimate termination of the litigation". Even then, the court of appeals has discretion to accept or reject the appeal. Although the circuits vary somewhat in the standards applied, permission for such appeals is difficult to obtain.

A last resort for a litigant seeking appellate review is the All Writs Act (28 U.S.C. § 1651), which authorizes extraordinary writs including those of prohibition and mandamus. Although the courts of appeals vary somewhat in their willingness to use these writs for purposes of review, the standard imposed by the Supreme Court is a restrictive one: in referring to the availability of mandamus, the Court has said that the writ is traditionally used "only 'to confine an inferior court to a lawful exercise of its prescribed jurisdiction or to compel it to exercise its authority when it is its duty to do so.' * * * Only exceptional circumstances amounting to a judicial 'usurpation of power' will justify the invocation of an extraordinary remedy." Will v. United States, 389 U.S. 90 (1967).

Finally, some statutes limit or prohibit the appeal even of final judgments. See, e.g., 28 U.S.C. § 2253(c) (habeas corpus), p. 1269, infra; 28 U.S.C. § 1447(d) (remand orders).

Cases in the courts of appeals are normally heard and determined by panels of three judges, but each court may, by vote of a majority of the judges in regular active service, order a hearing or rehearing by the court en banc. 28 U.S.C. § 46(c).[169] Rehearings en banc are rare; original hearings en banc

---

[168] In rare circumstances appeals from orders that do not "end the litigation" are specifically allowed by rule. Thus, Fed.R.Civ.P. 23(f) authorizes a court of appeals to permit an appeal from an order granting or denying class action certification, and Fed.R.Civ.P.54(b) permits a district court to "direct entry of a final judgment as to one or more, but fewer than all, claims or parties" if "the court expressly determines that there is no just reason for delay".

[169] A court en banc consists of all circuit judges in regular active service, except that (a) a senior circuit judge who sat on the decision being reviewed is also eligible to participate, and (b) circuits with more than fifteen active judges—currently the fifth, sixth and ninth—may prescribe by rule the number of members required to perform en banc functions.

are even rarer.[170] A number of circuits, however, have specified that panel decisions may be overruled only by the full bench sitting en banc.[171]

The number of appeals filed in the courts of appeals rose from 3,899 in 1960, to 11,662 in 1970, to 34,292 in 1986, to 48,322 in 1994, to 66,618 in 2006, before falling to 56,475 in 2013.[172] In another measure of the volume of cases, "[w]hereas in 1950 circuit judges had to review an average of only 73 appeals, their modern counterparts must decide four times that many, with an average of 329 appeals per annum today."[173] The increased volume has triggered large changes in the courts of appeals' traditional procedures.[174] Most circuits have sharply restricted opportunities for oral argument,[175] and the proportion of cases decided without any opinion, or by per curiam opinion, has increased.[176] Indeed, of the 37,820 cases (including those consolidated with other cases) decided on the merits during the year ending September 30, 2013 (by courts of appeals other than the Court of Appeals for the Federal Circuit), only 3,850—roughly 10%—resulted in signed, published opinions.[177] Although most circuits once had rules, adopted at the urging of the Judicial Conference of the United States, that restricted the citation of their "unpublished" opinions and orders as precedents, this practice attracted significant criticism,[178] and gradually the circuits began to

---

[170] En banc courts were responsible for only a little more than 0.1% of decisions rendered on the merits by the courts of appeals in the year ending September 30, 2013. See Administrative Office of the U.S. Courts, 2013 Judicial Business, Table S–1. Stein, *Uniformity in the Federal Courts: A Proposal for Increasing the Use of En Banc Appellate Review*, 54 U.Pitt.L.Rev. 805, 808–819 (1993), provides interesting historical background.

[171] See, *e.g.*, Bonner v. City of Prichard, 661 F.2d 1206, 1209–11 (11th Cir.1981); United States v. Fatico, 603 F.2d 1053, 1058 (2d Cir.1979). For examples of some of the difficulties that have arisen in the en banc process, see 16A Wright, Miller, Cooper & Gressman, Federal Practice and Procedure § 3981.

[172] Administrative Office of the U.S. Courts, 2013 Judicial Business, Table 1.

[173] Levy, *Judging Justice on Appeal*, 123 Yale L.J. 2386 (2014). There is a large literature on the increased caseload and its consequences. For an informative collection of statistics, discussion of changes in procedures that the increased caseload has provoked, and suggestions for reform, see Richman & Reynolds, Injustice on Appeal: The United States Court of Appeals Crisis (2013).

[174] See generally Richman & Reynolds, note 173, *supra,* at 83–127. Apart from more formal changes, one commentator, who examined the flood of immigration appeals following reforms passed in the wake of the September 11, 2001, terrorist attacks, has argued that increased caseload pressure leads to lower rates of reversal of district courts. See Huang, *Lightened Scrutiny*, 124 Harv.L.Rev. 1109 (2011).

[175] In the year ending September 30, 2013, the percentage of decisions on the merits rendered without oral argument ranged from 62% in the Seventh Circuit to 89% in the Fourth Circuit. The nationwide percentage stood at 80%. See *id.*, Table S–1.

[176] See Administrative Office of the U.S. Courts, 2013 Judicial Business, Table S–3. For a study of the case management systems through which different circuits determine which cases will receive oral argument, which dispositions will initially be drafted by staff attorneys rather than judges, and which opinions will be unpublished, see Levy, *The Mechanics of Federal Appeals: Uniformity and Case Management in the Circuit Courts*, 61 Duke L.J. 315 (2011). Finding a nearly pervasive lack of formal transparency, Professor Levy bases her conclusions on extensive interviews that reveal considerable variation among the circuits.

[177] Administrative Office of the U.S. Courts, 2013 Judicial Business, Table S-3. Of the unpublished opinions and orders, 6,737 were "written, signed"; 19,684 were "written, reasoned, unsigned"; and 4,716 were "written, unsigned, without comment". *Id.* As one mark of change over time, Judge Posner has reported that of all "contested terminations"—terminations after hearing or submission—74% were disposed of by written, signed opinions in 1960. Posner, The Federal Courts: Crisis and Reform 69–70 (1985).

[178] Critics raised serious questions about the desirability and even the constitutionality of such rules. See, *e.g.*, Carrington, Meador & Rosenberg, Justice on Appeal 36–41 (1976); Reynolds & Richman, *An Evaluation of Limited Publication in the United States Courts of Appeals: The*

reverse themselves. The heated debate generated by the practice has been mooted, at least for now, by the Supreme Court's adoption in 2006 of a new Federal Rule of Appellate Procedure 32.1, under which "[a] court may not prohibit or restrict the citation of federal judicial opinions" designated as "unpublished" or "the like" that are "issued on or after January 1, 2007". The problem of congestion in the courts of appeals has also led to increased reliance on "central" legal staffs.[179]

As with the district courts, crowded appellate dockets have prompted a number of calls for reform, including proposals to replace appeal as of right with a system of discretionary review.[180] Also generating reform pressures in recent years have been the size of the Ninth Circuit and a worry by some that it has grown bureaucratically unwieldy and non-collegial.[181]

Price of Reform, 48 U.Chi.L.Rev. 573 (1981). See also Pether, *Inequitable Injunctions: The Scandal of Private Judging in the U.S. Courts*, 56 Stan.L.Rev. 1435 (2004). *But see* Martineau, *Restrictions on Publication and Citation of Judicial Opinions: A Reassessment*, 28 U.Mich.J.L.Ref. 119 (1994) (summarizing and answering objections to rules restricting publication of judicial opinions and citation of unpublished opinions).

In a decision subsequently vacated on mootness grounds, a panel of the Eighth Circuit held that a rule denying precedential effect to "unpublished" opinions violates Article III. See Anastasoff v. United States, 223 F.3d 898, vacated, 235 F.3d 1054 (2000) (en banc). The panel opinion had concluded that the doctrine of precedent was implicit in the original understanding of "the judicial power" and that it embraced unpublished as well as published opinions. The panel emphasized that the issue was not whether all opinions should be published, "but whether they ought to have precedential effect, whether published or not". For a rejection of the view of the Anastasoff panel on the merits and a determination that a prohibition against the citation of unpublished opinions does not violate Article III, see Hart v. Massanari, 266 F.3d 1155 (9th Cir.2001).

[179] For a comprehensive account of this and related developments in one circuit, see Hellman, Restructuring Justice: The Innovations of the Ninth Circuit and the Future of the Federal Courts (1990); Oakley, *The Screening of Appeals: The Ninth Circuit's Experience in the Eighties and Innovations for the Nineties*, 1991 B.Y.U.L.Rev. 859.

[180] See, *e.g.*, Federal Judicial Center, Structural and Other Alternatives for the Federal Courts of Appeals: Report to the United States Congress and the Judicial Conference of the United States (1993), which included as alternative proposals creation of a writ system that would have introduced discretionary review at the appeals court level and what it described as a "two-track" appellate review structure, under which parties would submit 15-page briefs at the Track One stage, and many cases would be summarily disposed of at this point. For a critical survey of other reform proposals, see Baker, *Imagining the Alternative Futures of the U.S. Courts of Appeals*, 28 Ga.L.Rev. 913 (1994).

[181] In response to concerns such as these and to congressional proposals to split the Ninth Circuit, in 1997 Congress established a Commission on Structural Alternatives for the Federal Courts of Appeals. 111 Stat. 2440, 2491. The Commission, composed of five members appointed by the Chief Justice of the United States and chaired by retired Justice Byron White, proposed retention of the Ninth Circuit's current boundaries, but called for it to be restructured into three regional divisions, each including seven to eleven active circuit judges and each capable of performing en banc functions. Commission on Structural Alternatives for the Federal Courts of Appeals: Final Report 40–45 (1998). More generally, the Commission recommended that any Circuit with more than 15 judges should be authorized to restructure itself into adjudicative divisions. Congress took no action on the proposals advanced by the White Commission, however, and debate about dividing or restructuring the Ninth Circuit continues. See, *e.g.*, Roll, *The 115 Year-Old Ninth Circuit—Why a Split Is Necessary and Inevitable*, 7 Wyo.L.Rev. 109 (2007) (asserting, *inter alia*, that the Ninth Circuit has the highest reversal rate among the circuits in the Supreme Court and attributing this phenomenon partly to the circuit's unique en banc procedures, necessitated by its size, which call for the participation of fewer than all active circuit judges).

3.   The Supreme Court

The Supreme Court maintains an original[182] and an appellate docket.[183] Original cases are few, but characteristically laborious and prolonged. Cases that are fully heard are invariably referred to a master, whose findings the Court then determines whether to accept.[184] The staple of the Court's docket is appellate cases, virtually all of which come within the discretionary certiorari jurisdiction.

The number of cases filed annually in the Court has risen over time. During the 2013 Term, which ended in June 2014, 8,580 cases were docketed[185] (in comparison with 1,957 in the 1960, 3,419 in the 1970, 4,174 in the 1980, 5,502 in the 1990, and 7,924 in the 2001 Terms). Of the total for the 2013 Term, five came within the Court's original jurisdiction.[186]

While the number of docketed cases has climbed quite steadily, the number disposed of by written opinion, including per curiam opinions containing substantial discussion, has varied considerably. The Court rendered opinions in 72 cases in the 2013 Term,[187] in comparison with 132 in the 1960, 141 in the 1970, 159 in the 1980, 129 in the 1990, 95 in the 1994, and 88 in the 2001 Terms. Some of the decline in the more recent figures reflects Congress' virtual abolition of the Court's mandatory appellate jurisdiction in 1988. But other factors appear to have played a role. For a provocative, though dated, analysis, see Hellman, *The Shrunken Docket of the Rehnquist Court*, 1996 Sup.Ct.Rev. 403. For a more recent analysis, see Owens & Simon, *Explaining the Supreme Court's Shrinking Docket*, 53 Wm. & Mary L.Rev. 1219 (2012).

Especially during the years when the Court was producing well in excess of 100 written dispositions per year, a variety of proposals emerged to lighten the Justices' workload. Perhaps the most recurring suggestion called for the development of a national court of appeals, subordinate to the Supreme Court, but with jurisdiction to review decisions of the existing circuit courts of appeals.[188] None of the proposals to create a national court of appeals has come to a vote in Congress.

---

[182] The Court's original jurisdiction is discussed in Chap. III, *infra*.

[183] The development of the provisions for review of state court decisions is described in Chap. V, Sec. 1, *infra*.

[184] See generally *Note on Procedure in Original Actions*, Chap. III, p. 271, *infra*.

[185] *The Supreme Court, 2013 Term—The Statistics*, 128 Harv.L.Rev. 401, 409 (2014).

[186] *Id.* at 401, 409.

[187] This figure includes 67 signed opinions and five per curiam decisions. See *id.*

[188] See, *e.g.*, Federal Judicial Center, Report of the Study Group on the Caseload of the Supreme Court (1972) (proposing elimination of the Court's obligatory review jurisdiction and creation of a new national court of appeals with the authority, *inter alia*, to screen cases for the Supreme Court's docket). This proposal by the so-called Freund Committee met a predominantly critical response. See, *e.g.*, Warren, *Let's Not Weaken The Supreme Court*, 60 A.B.A.J. 677 (1974); Black, *The National Court of Appeals: An Unwise Proposal*, 83 Yale L.J. 883 (1974). For a defense, see Freund, *Why We Need the National Court of Appeals*, 59 A.B.A.J. 247 (1973). Nevertheless, variations have subsequently appeared in a report by the Commission on Revision of the Federal Court Appellate System, Structure and Internal Procedures: Recommendations for Change (1975) (reprinted in 67 F.R.D. 195 (1975)), and as part of a comprehensive package of reform proposals by the Federal Courts Study Committee, which proposed a five-year pilot project authorizing the Supreme Court to refer intercircuit conflicts to a court of appeals for an en banc, nationally binding decision. Report of the Federal Courts Study Committee 125–29 (1990). *Cf.* George & Guthrie, *"The Threes": Re-Imagining Supreme Court Decisionmaking*, 61 Vand.L.Rev. 1825 (2008) (advocating statutory reform to allow the Supreme Court to sit in panels of three (with or without en banc review) and thereby expand the number of cases that the Court can hear).

CHAPTER II

THE NATURE OF THE FEDERAL JUDICIAL FUNCTION: CASES AND CONTROVERSIES

1. INTRODUCTION AND HISTORICAL CONTEXT

This chapter examines questions of justiciability—a cluster of related issues that define the scope of federal judicial power through categories such as standing, ripeness, mootness, and the political question doctrine. These categories deal respectively with questions such as who constitutes a proper plaintiff to invoke federal judicial power (standing); when is a matter sufficiently immediate and concrete to justify judicial consideration (ripeness); what should a court do when a crucial element of a live dispute goes away during the adjudication process (mootness); and what sorts of legal disputes, if any, does the Constitution mark off for exclusive resolution by branches other than the judiciary (political question doctrine). Viewed together, these doctrines help define the role of the federal courts in our constitutional structure—a goal that entails not only identifying the judicial function but also understanding how it relates to the powers of the coordinate branches.

Needless to say, there is no intrinsically correct or universally accepted idea of appropriate judicial power. The Constitution, moreover, says little about the matter. The document has no Standing, Ripeness, Mootness, or Political Question Clause. Although Article III vests in the federal courts "the judicial Power" and grants jurisdiction to exercise it in various "cases" or "controversies", it nowhere defines those terms. The Philadelphia Convention and the thirteen state ratifying conventions do not offer much guidance either. Nevertheless, these open-ended terms both reflect and embody legal traditions, practices, and understandings that help define the role of Article III courts.

Because the operative terms of Article III are so open-ended, this chapter begins with the historical context in which "the judicial Power" first came to be understood. In reading the materials that follow, consider the following questions. First, to what extent should one assume that those who adopted the Constitution—all of whom were raised in the English legal tradition—understood technical legal terms (such as "judicial Power" or "case") in their common-law English sense?[1] Second,

---

[1] The Court has frequently stated that legal concepts informed the understanding of technical legal terms used in drafting the Constitution. See, *e.g.*, Ex parte Grossman, 267 U.S. 87, 110 (1925); Myers v. United States, 272 U.S. 52, 118 (1926); United States v. Wilson, 32 U.S. (7 Pet.) 150, 160 (1833) (Marshall, C.J.). The Court has also recognized, however, that in many respects the American constitutional structure deviates from and is incompatible with English premises about government, making certain English common law traditions inapposite to aspects of the U.S. Constitution. See, *e.g.*, Grosjean v. American Press Co., 297 U.S. 233, 248–

to what extent is constitutional meaning revealed by practical constructions given to the document by those officials who were charged with implementing it? Third to what extent, if any, should original understanding and early practice guide the interpretation of Article III's language more than two centuries later?[3]

Starting from the premise that the early historical context supplies at least a relevant data point for understanding, refining, and critiquing some of the constitutional traditions that have taken shape around "the judicial Power", this Section begins by exploring practical controversies that gave rise to certain established conceptions of federal judicial power.

INTRODUCTORY NOTE

This discussion of judicial power begins with President Washington's efforts to ascertain the legal rights and duties of the United States in relation to those involved in the late-eighteenth-century European hostilities that had spilled into North America. Secretary of State Jefferson propounded the following questions to the Court. Today, the prohibition against the Court's issuing "advisory opinions" is taken for granted. It is an uncontroversial and central element of our understanding of federal judicial power. As you read the materials below, ask yourself to what extent the conventional tools of legal interpretation dictated the result that we take as a given today. In other words, how much is the embedded understanding a matter of historical contingency?

CORRESPONDENCE OF THE JUSTICES (1793)[1]

Letter from Thomas Jefferson, Secretary of State, to Chief Justice Jay and Associate Justices:

Philadelphia, July 18, 1793.

---

49 (1936); Belknap v. Schild, 161 U.S. 10, 15 (1896); Fleming v. Page, 50 U.S. (9 How.) 603, 618 (1850).

[2]   See Knowlton v. Moore, 178 U.S. 41, 56 (1900) (crediting early practical constructions of the Constitution by public officials because "all questions which related to the Constitution and its adoption must have been, at that early date, vividly impressed in their minds"). See also, *e.g.*, Wisconsin v. Pelican Ins. Co., 127 U.S. 265, 297 (1888); The Laura, 114 U.S. 411, 416 (1885); Cohens v. Virginia, 19 U.S. (6 Wheat.) 264, 420 (1821). Some early Supreme Court cases treated the political branches' practical constructions as conclusively settling the Constitution's meaning. See Stuart v. Laird, 5 U.S. (1 Cranch) 299, 309 (1803) (upholding statutorily required circuit riding by Supreme Court Justices); United States v. Hudson & Goodwin, 11 U.S. (7 Cranch) 32 (1812), p. 636, *infra* (rejection of federal common law crimes).

[3]   See, *e.g.*, Brest, *The Misconceived Quest for the Original Understanding*, 60 B.U.L.Rev. 204, 225 (1980) (arguing that the reliance on original meaning violates Lockean premises because our present society "did not adopt the Constitution, and those who did are dead and gone"); Strauss, *Common Law Constitutional Interpretation*, 63 U. Chi.L.Rev. 877, 880 (1996) ("Following a written constitution means accepting the judgments of people who lived centuries ago in a society that was very different from ours.").

[1]   The letters are respectively taken from 3 Correspondence and Public Papers of John Jay 486–89 (Johnston ed. 1891) and 15 The Papers of Alexander Hamilton 111 n. 1 (H. Syrett ed. 1969), and the questions from 10 Sparks, Writings of Washington 542–45 (1836).

Gentlemen:

The war which has taken place among the powers of Europe produces frequent transactions within our ports and limits, on which questions arise of considerable difficulty, and of greater importance to the peace of the United States. These questions depend for their solution on the construction of our treaties, on the laws of nature and nations, and on the laws of the land, and are often presented under circumstances *which do not give a cognizance of them to the tribunals of the country.* Yet their decision is so little analogous to the ordinary functions of the executive, as to occasion much embarrassment and difficulty to them. The President therefore would be much relieved if he found himself free to refer questions of this description to the opinions of the judges of the Supreme Court of the United States, whose knowledge of the subject would secure us against errors dangerous to the peace of the United States, and their authority insure the respect of all parties. He has therefore asked the attendance of such of the judges as could be collected in time for the occasion, to know, in the first place, their opinion, whether the public may, with propriety, be availed of their *advice on these questions?* And if they may, to present, for their advice, the abstract questions which have already occurred, or may soon occur, from which they will themselves strike out such as any circumstances might, in their opinion, forbid them to pronounce on. I have the honour to be with sentiments of the most perfect respect, gentlemen,

> Your most obedient and
> humble servant,
>
> Thos. Jefferson.

Anticipating that the Justices would proffer the requested "advice", the President's Cabinet agreed to address no fewer than twenty-nine specific questions to the Court. It is unclear whether those questions were appended to Jefferson's letter, but the Justices were surely aware of the questions' "general content". Jay, Most Humble Servants: The Advisory Role of Early Judges 136–37 (1997). The following are some of the questions prepared by the President and his Cabinet for submission to the Justices:

"1. Do the treaties between the United States and France give to France or her citizens a *right*, when at war with a power with whom the United States are at peace, to fit out originally in and from the ports of the United States vessels armed for war, with or without commission?

"2. If they give such a *right*, does it extend to all manner of armed vessels, or to particular kinds only? If the latter, to what kinds does it extend?

"3. Do they give to France or her citizens, in the case supposed, a right to refit or arm anew vessels, which, before their coming within any port of the United States, were armed for war, with or without commission?

"4. If they give such a right, does it extend to all manner of armed vessels, or to particular kinds only? If the latter, to what kinds does it extend? Does it include an *augmentation* of force, or does it only extend to replacing the vessel *in statu quo*? * * *

"17. Do the laws of neutrality, considered as aforesaid, authorize the United States to permit France, her subjects, or citizens, the sale within their ports of prizes made of the subjects or property of a power at war with

France, before they have been carried into some port of France and there condemned, refusing the like privilege to her enemy?

"18. Do those laws authorize the United States to permit to France the erection of courts within their territory and jurisdiction for the trial and condemnation of prizes, refusing that privilege to a power at war with France? * * *

"20. To what distance, by the laws and usages of nations, may the United States exercise the right of prohibiting the hostilities of foreign powers at war with each other within rivers, bays, and arms of the sea, and upon the sea along the coasts of the United States?

"22. What are the articles, by name, to be prohibited to both or either party? * * *

"25. May we, within our own ports, sell ships to both parties, prepared merely for merchandise? May they be pierced for guns? * * *

"29. May an armed vessel belonging to any of the belligerent powers follow *immediately* merchant vessels, enemies, departing from our ports, for the purpose of making prizes of them? If not, how long ought the former to remain, after the latter have sailed? And what shall be considered as the place of departure from which the time is to be counted? And how are the facts to be ascertained?"

On July 20, 1793, Chief Justice Jay and the Associate Justices wrote to President Washington expressing their wish to postpone the answer to Jefferson's letter until the sitting of the Court. On August 8, 1793, they wrote to the President as follows:

"Sir:

"We have considered the previous question stated in a letter written to us by your direction by the Secretary of State on the 18th of last month. The lines of separation drawn by the Constitution between the three departments of the government—their being in certain respects checks upon each other—and our being judges of a court in the last resort—are considerations which afford strong arguments against the propriety of our extrajudicially deciding the questions alluded to; especially as the power given by the Constitution to the President of calling on the heads of departments for opinions, seems to have been *purposely* as well as expressly limited to the *executive* departments."

NOTE ON ADVISORY OPINIONS

(1) Foundations. The prohibition against advisory opinions has been termed "the oldest and most consistent thread in the federal law of justiciability." Wright & Kane, Law of Federal Courts 65–66 (7th ed.2011). But how clear was the Justices' decision from the Constitution's language and history?[1] The English judicial practice with which early Americans were familiar had long permitted the Crown to solicit advisory opinions from judges. See Jay, p. 51, *supra*, at 12. As Professor Jay further notes, neither the constitutional text nor the discussions at the Constitutional Convention

---

[1] For an illuminating discussion of the Correspondence of the Justices, see Wheeler, *Extrajudicial Activities of the Early Supreme Court*, 1973 Sup.Ct.Rev. 123, 144–58.

reflected any clear prohibition against advisory opinions. Consider, also, whether the position taken in the Correspondence accords with early American practice.

In 1790, Chief Justice Jay and a minority of the Justices were said to have sent a letter to President Washington advising him of their view that circuit riding was unconstitutional. See 4 Am.Jur. & L.Mag. 293 (1830). But see Wheeler, note 1, *supra*, at 148 (suggesting that the letter was never sent). Chief Justice Jay himself regularly gave informal legal advice to the Washington Administration. Jay, p. 51, *supra*. Some of the advice pertained to sensitive questions of foreign affairs, including the international law ramifications of a potential British request to cross over American soil to attack Spain during the Nootka Sound crisis of 1790. At Alexander Hamilton's initiation, moreover, Chief Justice Jay prepared a draft of the Neutrality Proclamation declaring the Nation to be impartial toward the belligerent powers, and he advised the national government to commence criminal prosecutions of those who violated the proclamation. Well after the Correspondence of the Justices, Chief Justice Ellsworth gave an opinion to Senator Trumbull on an aspect of the Jay Treaty and another to Secretary of State Pickering on the legality of the Sedition Act. See Casto, The Supreme Court in the Early Republic: The Chief Justiceships of John Jay and Oliver Ellsworth 71–72, 74–75. 97–98, 148–49 (1995). The conflicting early practices suggest the absence of constitutional consensus on the question addressed by the Correspondence.[2]

Does the separation of powers justify the now well-settled rejection of judicial power to give advisory opinions? In the Correspondence, the Justices generally invoked the "lines of separation" among the branches and the background understanding that each branch would serve as a check on the others. After invoking separation-of-powers considerations more generally, the Justices added that "the power given by the Constitution to the President of calling on the heads of departments for opinions, seems to have been *purposely* as well as expressly limited to the *executive* departments." See p. 52, *supra*. In other words, the Justices apparently believed that the Opinion Clause of Article II—which provides that the President "may require the Opinion, in writing, of the principal Officer in each of the executive Departments, upon any Subject relating to the Duties of their respective Offices" (U.S. Const. Art. II, § 2, cl. 1)—carried a negative implication that the President could not ask *judges* for such opinions. Is that general inference from the constitutional structure sufficient to justify deviation from the specific expectations that early Americans likely held about judicial power, given the longstanding tradition of English judges' issuing advisory opinions? Compare Amar, *Some Opinions on the Opinion Clause*, 82

---

[2] Based on the historical precedents, Professor Casto would minimize the significance of the Correspondence. He thus argues that "the early Justices clearly believed that they had a discretionary power" to furnish advisory opinions for the executive branch and that "[t]he only absolute rule that can be teased out of their 1793 letter to President Washington, is that the President is not empowered to require the federal judiciary to provide an advisory opinion." Casto, *The Early Supreme Court Justices' Most Significant Opinion*, 29 Ohio Northern U.L.Rev. 173, 201 (2002). Professor Jay argues that the Correspondence reflected idiosyncratic considerations, such as the desire of the Justices, who wished to be relieved of circuit riding responsibilities, to avoid entanglement in a potentially divisive political controversy. Jay, p. 51, *supra*, at 149–70. But see Pushaw, *Why the Supreme Court Never Gets Any "Dear John" Letters: Advisory Opinions in Historical Perspective*, 87 Geo.L.J. 473 (1998) (book review) (arguing that the Correspondence of the Justices is best explained by constitutional considerations unrelated to the immediate political context).

Va.L.Rev. 847 (1996) (arguing that the Opinion Clause meant to distinguish the President from the Crown, *inter alia*, by precluding the former from treating the other branches as his or her subordinates).

Perhaps due to these historical complexities, Felix Frankfurter defended the prohibition against advisory opinions based on the policies implicit in Article III, rather than on historical pedigree. Frankfurter, *Advisory Opinions*, 1 Encyc. of the Social Sciences 475, 476 (1937). What are these policies? Perhaps the prohibition serves the interest, discussed below, in making federal judicial power available only to resolve concrete disputes based on private rights. See pp. 73–74, *infra*. Or it might serve the interest, also discussed below, in ensuring that cases and controversies satisfy the "functional requisites" of effective adjudication. See p. 75, *infra*. To what extent could the Court address objections to advisory opinions by restricting itself to giving advisory rulings on definite states of fact, real or assumed? If the Justices had answered questions like those presented to them by Jefferson, would the Court's prestige, and the acceptability of its decisions, have been enhanced or diminished?

(2) Identifying Advisory Opinions. How does one distinguish a forbidden advisory opinion from, on the one hand, the adjudication of a proper "case" or "controversy", and, on the other hand, permissible nonjudicial pronouncements by the Justices in books, articles, lectures, and the like? Consider how the idea of "advisory opinions" bears on the following questions:

(a) Would a purely prospective decision, which did not apply a newly propounded rule of decision to the parties in the case, constitute an advisory opinion forbidden by Article III?[3] The question of prospectivity typically has arisen when a ruling of the Court overrules a past decision or departs significantly from settled understandings and establishes rights and obligations not previously recognized in our history. Until fairly recently, the Court's tradition had been to give even novel rulings full retroactivity— applying them not only to the case before it but also to other cases pending on direct review. Perhaps because of the pathbreaking character of many of its criminal procedure rulings, the Warren Court broke with that tradition in criminal cases. In Linkletter v. Walker, 381 U.S. 618 (1965), the Court held that the rule in Mapp v. Ohio, 367 U.S. 643 (1961), though applied to the case in which it was announced, would not be applied in collateral review of a final state court conviction. In so doing, moreover, Linkletter suggested in dictum that nothing in Article III precluded even a "purely prospective" decision. The next year, in Johnson v. New Jersey, 384 U.S. 719 (1966), the Court asserted power to make rules of criminal procedure nonretroactive, by which it meant that the new rule would be applied in the case before it but otherwise would not apply in cases pending on direct review. In civil cases, too, the Court also gestured toward very expansive judicial discretion to announce new rules prospectively. See Chevron Oil Co. v. Huson, 404 U.S.

---

[3] For general discussion of questions concerning the retroactivity or prospectivity of judicial decisions, see Beytagh, *Ten Years of Non-retroactivity: A Critique and a Proposal*, 61 Va.L.Rev. 1557 (1975); Fallon & Meltzer, *New Law, Non-Retroactivity, and Constitutional Remedies*, 104 Harv.L.Rev. 1731 (1991); Mishkin, *Foreword: The High Court, The Great Writ, and the Due Process of Time and Law*, 79 Harv.L.Rev. 56 (1965); Schwartz, *Retroactivity, Reliability, and Due Process: A Response to Professor Mishkin*, 33 U.Chi.L.Rev. 719 (1966); Note, 71 Yale L.J. 907 (1962).

97, 107 (1971); England v. Louisiana St. Bd. of Med. Examiners, 375 U.S. 411, 422 (1964).

In that same period, the Court also began to voice some concerns about pure prospectivity, stating in Stovall v. Denno, 388 U.S. 293, 301 (1967), that "[s]ound policies of decision-making, rooted in the command of Article III of the Constitution that we resolve issues solely in cases or controversies, * * * militate against" pure prospectivity. More recently, the Court expressly reconsidered its authority to make rules of criminal procedure nonretroactive to cases pending on direct review. In Griffith v. Kentucky, 479 U.S. 314, 322–23 (1987), the Court wrote: "[F]ailure to apply a newly declared constitutional rule to criminal cases pending on direct review violates basic norms of constitutional adjudication. * * * [A]fter we have decided a new rule in the case selected, the integrity of judicial review requires that we apply that rule to all similar cases pending on direct review." (While the Court continues to insist upon the presumptive nonretractivity of new rules on collateral review of final state court convictions, its decision to do so rests squarely upon the special characteristics of the habeas remedy. See Chap. XI, Sec. 3, *infra*.) The Court has also drawn back from any suggestion in civil cases that pure prospectivity is appropriate. See, *e.g.*, American Trucking Ass'ns, Inc. v. Smith, 496 U.S. 167 (1990); James B. Beam Distilling Co. v. Georgia, 501 U.S. 529 (1991); Harper v. Virginia Dep't of Taxation, 509 U.S. 86 (1993); Reynoldsville Casket Co. v. Hyde, 514 U.S. 749 (1995); Ryder v. United States, 515 U.S. 177 (1995). In Harper, the Court explained that even in civil cases, non-retroactive decisionmaking is a legislative function, and that such decisionmaking denies equal treatment to similarly situated litigants.

Despite all of these developments, the Court has never squarely held that purely prospective judicial decisionmaking would violate Article III. Would a purely prospective ruling violate the prohibition against advisory opinions? When a court first identifies a constitutional violation, then denies relief under the harmless error or analogous doctrines, has it rendered a constitutionally impermissible advisory opinion? See Teague v. Lane, *supra*, at 318 (1989) (Stevens, J., concurring in part and concurring in the judgment); Fallon & Meltzer, note 3, *supra*, at 1798–1800.[4]

(b) When a Court renders alternative holdings, has it violated constitutional norms? Settled practice surely suggests not, but why not? Consider the relevance of the following factors: (i) a concretely framed dispute, (ii) adverse parties, (iii) adversarial presentation of competing arguments, (iv) res judicata and stare decisis effects in subsequent judicial actions; and (v) conclusiveness of the determination for other branches of government.

(c) In Steel Co. v. Citizens for a Better Environment, 523 U.S. 83 (1998), Justice Scalia's opinion for the Court invoked the specter of an "advisory opinion" in holding that federal courts must resolve questions of subject matter jurisdiction—in this case standing—at the threshold. Under the rubric of "hypothetical jurisdiction", several courts of appeals had found "it

---

[4] For an argument that many non-retroactivity issues should be analyzed as involving the necessity or appropriateness of particular judicial remedies for constitutional violations, see Fallon & Meltzer, *supra*. For criticism of that position, see Roosevelt, *A Little Theory is a Dangerous Thing: The Myth of Adjudicative Retroactivity*, 31 Conn.L.Rev. 1075 (1999); Liebman & Ryan, *"Some Effectual Power": The Quantity and Quality of Decisionmaking Required of Article III Courts*, 98 Colum.L.Rev. 696 (1998).

proper to proceed immediately to the merits question, despite jurisdictional objections, at least where (1) the merits question is more readily resolved, and (2) the prevailing party on the merits would be the same as the prevailing party were jurisdiction denied." Justice Scalia reasoned, however, that "[h]ypothetical jurisdiction produces nothing more than a hypothetical judgment—which comes to the same thing as an advisory opinion". When the decision of a question conclusively resolves a lawsuit, in what sense could a judicial opinion deciding that question count as "advisory"?[5]

(d) Despite the general acceptance of the view that advisory opinions fall without "the judicial Power of the United States", see Wright & Kane, p. 52, *supra*, individual Justices have engaged in extrajudicial expression of their legal views on innumerable occasions. For later examples, see: Opinion given by Justice Johnson, with the approval of other members of the Court, to President Monroe, in 1 Warren, The Supreme Court in United States History 596–97 (1937 ed.); Letter of Chief Justice Hughes to Senator Wheeler, Chairman of the Senate Judiciary Committee, concerning President Roosevelt's proposals for reorganizing the Supreme Court, Sen.Rep. No. 711, 75th Cong., 1st Sess. (1937), at 38–40; Letter of Chief Justice Taney to Secretary of the Treasury Chase concerning the 1862 tax levied upon the salaries of federal judges, in Tyler, Memoir of Roger B. Taney 432–34 (1872). In recent years, sitting Justices have published numerous books, articles, and lectures commenting on legal issues.[6] Does this practice contradict the view that advisory opinions are constitutionally prohibited?

(e) Is it possible to specify necessary or sufficient conditions for identifying advisory opinions that lie outside Article III judicial power? According to Lee, *Deconstitutionalizing Justiciability: The Example of Mootness*, 105 Harv.L.Rev. 603, 644–45 (1992), the Supreme Court has used the term "advisory opinion" to embrace "[a]ny judgment subject to review by a co-equal branch of government", "[a]dvice to a coequal branch of government prior to the other branch's contemplated action", "Supreme Court review of any state judgment for which there is or may be an adequate and independent state ground", "[a]ny opinion, or portion thereof, not truly necessary to the disposition of the case at bar (that is, dicta)", and "[a]ny decision on the merits of a case that is moot or unripe or in which one of the parties lacks standing". Lee concludes that "only the first two of these usages denote a constitutional bar. The other three usages are a function of judicial discretion".

(3) Declaratory Judgments. The Federal Declaratory Judgment Act of 1934, 48 Stat. 955, provides that federal courts "may declare the rights and legal relations of any interested party seeking such declaration" in "a case of actual controversy." For the present provisions, see 28 U.S.C. §§ 2201–02. Prior to the Act's adoption, there had been some division of authority on the question whether declaratory judgments constitute advisory opinions. Compare Willing v. Chicago Auditorium Ass'n, 277 U.S. 274, 289 (1928) (holding that federal courts lacked jurisdiction to resolve a lessee's doubts

---

[5] For a case that seems to qualify Steel Co., see Sinochem Int. Co. Ltd. v. Malaysia Int. Shipping Corp., 549 U.S. 422 (2007) (holding that a district court may dismiss a case on forum non conveniens grounds without first determining whether it has subject matter jurisdiction and noting that a forum non conveniens determination is not "on the merits").

[6] For a comprehensive review and compilation of informal comments through 1962, see Westin, *Out-of-Court Commentary by United States Supreme Court Justices, 1790–1962: Of Free Speech and Judicial Lockjaw*, 62 Colum.L.Rev. 633 (1962).

about its rights under a lease and that a request for "simply a declaratory judgment" lies "beyond the power conferred upon the federal judiciary"), with Nashville, C. & St. L. Ry. v. Wallace, 288 U.S. 249 (1933) (finding jurisdiction to review a state court declaratory judgment action on the ground that it had all of the elements of a bill of injunction except a request for a coercive decree and a claim of irreparable injury, neither of which was essential to the existence of a "case" or "controversy" in an Article III sense).

The Court put the question to rest when it unanimously upheld the Declaratory Judgment Act's constitutionality in Aetna Life Ins. Co. v. Haworth, 300 U.S. 227 (1937). Aetna had brought the action to secure a declaration that four policies held by the defendant had lapsed for nonpayment of premiums, and that the company's only obligation was to pay $45 on the insured's death as extended insurance on one policy. The complaint asserted that the defendant claimed to be totally and permanently disabled, in which event all of the policies would be in full force, and two of them would oblige the company presently to pay disability benefits. The complaint added that the defendant, while making this claim repeatedly against the insurer, had failed to institute any action in which the company could prove its falsity. The complaint pointed to the danger posed by the possible disappearance, illness, or death of witnesses, and to the necessity meanwhile of maintaining reserves against the policies in excess of $20,000.[7]

Chief Justice Hughes, for the Court, said:

" * * * The Declaratory Judgment Act of 1934, in its limitation to 'cases of actual controversy,' manifestly has regard to the constitutional provision and is operative only in respect to controversies which are such in the constitutional sense. The word 'actual' is one of emphasis rather than of definition. Thus the operation of the Declaratory Judgment Act is procedural only. In providing remedies and defining procedure in relation to cases and controversies in the constitutional sense the Congress is acting within its delegated power over the jurisdiction of the federal courts which the Congress is authorized to establish. * * * Exercising this control of practice and procedure the Congress is not confined to traditional forms or traditional remedies. * * *

"There is here a dispute between parties who face each other in an adversary proceeding. The dispute relates to legal rights and obligations arising from the contracts of insurance. The dispute is definite and concrete, not hypothetical or abstract. * * * It calls, not for an advisory opinion upon a hypothetical basis, but for an adjudication of present right upon established facts. * * *

"If the insured had brought suit to recover the disability benefits currently payable under two of the policies there would have been no question that the controversy was of a justiciable nature, whether or not the amount involved would have permitted its determination in a federal court. * * * [T]he character of the controversy and of the issue to be determined is essentially the same whether it is presented by the insured or by the insurer."

---

[7]   Bray, *Preventive Adjudication*, 77 U.Chi.L.Rev. 1275 (2010), contends that such actions are appropriate when the administrative and error costs of anticipatory litigation are outweighed by the benefits of legal clarification, as he concludes is true in cases involving legal status (such as citizenship) and clouds on title. Is this use of cost-benefit analysis judicially manageable? Consistent with the text of the statute?

Would it be safe to say that an actual controversy always exists if either party could maintain an action for coercive relief?[8]

(4) Advisory Opinions by State Courts. Article III's prohibition against advisory opinions by federal courts does not extend to state courts, a number of which are authorized to render such opinions.[9] For example, part 2, ch. 3, art. 2 of the constitution of Massachusetts (1780) provides: "Each branch of the legislature, as well as the governor or the council, shall have authority to require the opinions of the justices of the supreme judicial court, upon important questions of law, and upon solemn occasions."[10] There are variants of this provision in the constitutions of Colorado, Florida, Maine, Michigan, New Hampshire, Rhode Island, and South Dakota. In three states— Alabama, Delaware, and Oklahoma—advisory opinions are authorized, in certain circumstances, by statute. "Ten other states have rejected or abandoned the practice." Hershkoff, *State Courts and the "Passive Virtues": Rethinking the Judicial Function*, 114 Harv.L.Rev. 1833, 1840 n.68 (2001). According to Professor Hershkoff, advisory opinions perform a useful dialogic function within state constitutional regimes by "allow[ing] state courts to articulate constitutional principles, while effectively 'remanding' disputes back to the other branches" for a considered response. Her judgment rests partly on an assumption about the nature of state constitutional practice: "[A]dvisory opinions suit the conditional nature of all state constitutional decisions, which are easily amended and frequently experimental in approach."

If a state court renders an advisory opinion on a question of federal law, that opinion may significantly affect the operations of state government. How may federal interests be protected in such a case? See pp. 158–160, *infra.*

———

[8] A recent case suggests that the capacity to request coercive relief may not be necessary, as long as the Court's opinion resolves the plaintiff's *potential* liability. In MedImmune, Inc. v. Genentech, Inc., 549 U.S. 118 (2007), a patent licensee (Medimmune) received a demand letter from the patent holder (Genentech) stating that its patent covered Synagis, a drug manufactured by Medimmune. Medimmune paid royalties under protest and brought a declaratory judgment action seeking to establish that the patent was invalid and did not apply. Although Medimmune's payment of royalties meant that it had no "reasonable apprehension" of liability, the Court held that the suit constituted a proper declaratory judgment action. If Medimmune had declined to pay, and Genentech had successfully sued for patent infringement, Medimmune could have been liable for treble damages and attorneys' fees and could have been enjoined from selling Synagis, which accounted for eighty percent of its sales. Invoking the principle that plaintiffs who wish to challenge the validity of state criminal statutes need not first violate those statutes in order to have actionable controversies under the Declaratory Judgment Act or Article III, the Court rejected the idea that a plaintiff must "risk treble damages and the loss of 80 percent of its business, before seeking a declaration of its actively contested legal rights". Justice Thomas dissented, arguing that for so long as a patent licensee continued to pay royalties, neither the licensor nor the licensee had a justiciable controversy with the other concerning the patent's scope or validity.

[9] For discussion of the evolving use of advisory opinions versus other forms of adjudication in European constitutional practice, see Gardbaum, *The Myth and the Reality of American Constitutional Exceptionalism*, 107 Mich.L.Rev. 391, 411–16 (2008). See also Jackson & Tushnet, Comparative Constitutional Law, Chap. 6 (3d ed.2009).

[10] See Farina, *Supreme Judicial Court Advisory Opinions: Two Centuries of Interbranch Dialogue*, in The History of the Law in Massachusetts: The Supreme Judicial Court 1692–1992, at 353 (Osgood ed. 1992) (giving a generally favorable assessment of advisory opinion practice in Massachusetts).

INTRODUCTORY NOTE ON MARBURY V. MADISON

Typically, one thinks of the case that follows—Marbury v. Madison—as establishing conclusively the federal courts' authority to invalidate Acts of Congress as unconstitutional. It did that, to be sure. But Chief Justice Marshall's opinion for the Court also grappled with another question that we take as a given today: judicial authority to judge the legality of actions by the officer of a coordinate branch and to direct that officer to comply with federal law. In wrestling with both issues—judicial review and mandamus— the Court in Marbury necessarily articulated a vision of the role of the federal judiciary in our system of separation of powers. Perhaps because of Marbury's canonical status, scholars today offer competing views of what vision the Court, in fact, articulated. As you read the case, try to identify theory of judicial power on which the Court justifies its role in assessing the legality of both statutes and executive action.

Marbury v. Madison

5 U.S. (1 Cranch) 137, 2 L.Ed. 60 (1803).
On Petition for Mandamus.

■ * * * [T]he following opinion of the Court was delivered by the CHIEF JUSTICE:

Opinion of the Court. At the last term on the affidavits then read and filed with the clerk, a rule was granted in this case, requiring the secretary of state to show cause why a *mandamus* should not issue, directing him to deliver to William Marbury his commission as a justice of the peace for the county of Washington, in the district of Columbia.

No cause has been shown, and the present motion is for a *mandamus*. The peculiar delicacy of this case, the novelty of some of its circumstances, and the real difficulty attending the points which occur in it, require a complete exposition of the principles on which the opinion to be given by the court is founded. * * *

In the order in which the court has viewed this subject, the following questions have been considered and decided.

1st. Has the applicant a right to the commission he demands?

2d. If he has a right, and that right has been violated, do the laws of his country afford him a remedy?

3d. If they do afford him a remedy, is it a *mandamus* issuing from this court?

The first object of inquiry is,

1st. Has the applicant a right to the commission he demands?

His right originates in an act of congress passed in February 1801, concerning the district of Columbia. [The statute authorizes the appointment of justices of the peace, "to continue in office for five years."] * * * In order to determine whether [Marbury] is entitled to this commission, it becomes necessary to enquire whether he has been appointed to the office. For if he has been appointed, the law continues him in office for five years, and he is entitled to the possession of those evidences of office, which, being completed, became his property.

[The Court then discussed the constitutional and statutory provisions governing the appointment of Officers of the United States. As relevant here, the Appointments Clause, U.S. Const. Art. II, § 2, cl. 2, provides that the President "shall nominate, and by and with the Advice and Consent of the Senate, shall appoint * * * Officers of the United States." Under Article 2, § 3, the President "shall commission all the officers of the United States." Finally, the statute establishing the Department of State provided that the Secretary of State must affix the seal of the United States to "all civil commissions" after the President signed them.]

Some point of time must be taken when the power of the executive over an officer, not removable at his will, must cease. That point of time must be when the constitutional power of appointment has been exercised. And this power has been exercised when the last act, required from the person possessing the power, has been performed. This last act is the signature of the commission. * * * The signature is a warrant for [the Secretary of State's] affixing the great seal to the commission; and the great seal is only to be affixed to an instrument which is complete. It attests, by an act supposed to be of public notoriety, the verity of the Presidential signature. * * *

[The Court then rejected the argument] that the transmission of the commission, and the acceptance thereof, might be deemed necessary to complete the right of the plaintiff. * * * The appointment is the sole act of the President * * *. A commission is transmitted to a person already appointed; not to a person to be appointed or not, as the letter enclosing the commission should happen to get into the post-office and reach him in safety, or to miscarry. * * * If the transmission of a commission be not considered as necessary to give validity to an appointment; still less is its acceptance. * * *

Mr. Marbury, then, since his commission was signed by the President, and sealed by the secretary of state, was appointed; and as the law creating the office, gave the officer a right to hold for five years, independent of the executive, the appointment was not revocable; but vested in the officer legal rights, which are protected by the laws of this country. * * * To withhold his commission, therefore, is an act deemed by the court not warranted by law, but violative of a vested legal right.

This brings us to the second enquiry; which is,

2dly. If he has a right, and the right has been violated, do the laws of the country afford him a remedy?

The very essence of civil liberty consists in the right of every individual to claim the protection of the laws, whenever he receives an injury. One of the first duties of government is to afford that protection. In Great Britain the king himself is sued in the respectful form of a petition, and he never fails to comply with the judgment of his court. * * *

The government of the United States has been emphatically termed a government of laws and not of men. It will certainly cease to deserve this high appellation, if the laws furnish no remedy for the violation of a vested legal right. * * * If this obloquy is to be cast on the jurisprudence of our country, it must arise from the peculiar character of the case.

[In concluding that our jurisprudence did not merit that "obloquy," the Court first found that Marbury's case was not "one of *damnum absque injuria*; a loss without an injury."] This description of cases never has been considered, and it is believed never can be considered, as comprehending offices of trust, of honor or of profit. The office of justice of peace in the district of Columbia * * * has been created by special act of congress, and has been secured, so far as the laws can give security to the person appointed to fill it, for five years. It is not then on account of the worthlessness of the thing pursued, that the injured party can be alleged to be without remedy.

Is it in the nature of the transaction? Is the act of delivering or withholding a commission to be considered a mere political act, belonging to the executive department alone, for the performance of which, entire confidence is placed by our constitution in the supreme executive; and for any misconduct concerning which the injured individual has no remedy.

That there be such cases is not to be questioned; but that every act of duty, to be performed in any of the great departments of government, constitutes such a case, is not to be admitted.

* * * [T]he question, whether the legality of an act of the head of a department be examinable in a court of justice or not, must always depend on the nature of that act * * *. If some acts be examinable, and others not, there must be some rule of law to guide the court in the exercise of its jurisdiction. * * *

By the Constitution of the United States, the President is invested with certain important political powers, in the exercise of which he is to use his own discretion, and is accountable only to his country in his political character, and to his conscience. To aid him in the performance of these duties, he is authorized to appoint certain officers, who act by his authority and in conformity with his orders.

In such cases, their acts are his acts; and whatever opinion may be entertained of the manner in which executive discretion may be used, still there exists, and can exist, no power to control that discretion. The subjects are political: they respect the nation, not individual rights, and being entrusted to the executive, the decision of the executive is conclusive. * * *

But when the legislature proceeds to impose on that officer other duties; when he is directed peremptorily to perform certain acts; when the rights of individuals are dependent on the performance of those acts; he is so far the officer of the law; is amenable to the laws for his conduct; and cannot at his discretion sport away the vested rights of others.

The conclusion from this reasoning is that, where the heads of departments are the political or confidential agents of the executive, merely to execute the will of the President, or rather to act in cases in which the executive possesses a constitutional or legal discretion, nothing can be more perfectly clear than that their acts are only politically examinable. But where a specific duty is assigned by law, and individual rights depend upon the performance of that duty, it seems equally clear that the individual who considers himself injured, has the right to resort to the laws of his country for a remedy. * * *

[Mr. Marbury's right having been established,] it remains to be inquired whether,

3d. He is entitled to the remedy for which he applies. This depends on,

1st. The nature of the writ applied for; and,

2d. The power of this court.

1st. The nature of the writ.

* * * [T]o render the *mandamus* a proper remedy, the officer to whom it is to be directed, must be one to whom, on legal principles, such writ may be directed; and the person applying for it must be without any other specific and legal remedy.

1st. With respect to the officer to whom it would be directed. The intimate political relation subsisting between the president of the United States and the heads of departments, necessarily renders any legal investigation of the acts of one of those high officers peculiarly irksome, as well as delicate; and excites some hesitation with respect to the propriety of entering into such investigation. Impressions are often received without much reflection or examination and it is not wonderful that in such a case as this the assertion, by an individual, of his legal claims in a court of justice, to which claims it is the duty of that court to attend, should at first view be considered by some, as an attempt to intrude into the cabinet, and to intermeddle with the prerogatives of the executive.

It is scarcely necessary for the court to disclaim all pretensions to such a jurisdiction. An extravagance, so absurd and excessive, could not have been entertained for a moment. The province of the court is, solely, to decide on the rights of individuals, not to inquire how the executive, or executive officers, perform duties in which they have a discretion. Questions in their nature political, or which are, by the constitution and laws, submitted to the executive, can never be made in this court.

But, if this be not such a question; if, so far from being an intrusion into the secrets of the cabinet, it respects a paper which, according to law, is upon record, and to a copy of which the law gives a right, on the payment of ten cents; if it be no intermeddling with a subject over which the executive can be considered as having exercised any control; what is there in the exalted station of the officer, which shall bar a citizen from asserting, in a court of justice, his legal rights, or shall forbid a court to listen to the claim, or to issue a *mandamus*, directing the performance of a duty, not depending on executive discretion, but on particular acts of congress, and the general principles of law?

If one of the heads of departments commits any illegal act, under colour of his office, by which an individual sustains an injury, it cannot be pretended that his office alone exempts him from being sued in the ordinary mode of proceeding, and being compelled to obey the judgment of the law. How, then, can his office exempt him from this particular mode of deciding on the legality of his conduct, if the case be such a case as would, were any other individual the party complained of, authorize the process?

It is not by the office of the person to whom the writ is directed, but the nature of the thing to be done, that the propriety or impropriety of issuing a *mandamus* is to be determined. Where the head of a department acts in a case, in which executive discretion is to be exercised; in which he is the mere organ of executive will; it is again repeated, that any application to a court to control, in any respect, his conduct would be rejected without hesitation.

But where he is directed by law to do a certain act affecting the absolute rights of individuals, in the performance of which he is not placed under the particular direction of the president, and the performance of which the president cannot lawfully forbid, and therefore is never presumed to have forbidden; as for example, to record a commission, or a patent for land, which has received all the legal solemnities; or to give a copy of such record; in such cases, it is not perceived on what ground the courts of the country are further excused from the duty of giving judgment that right be done to an injured individual, than if the same services were to be performed by a person not the head of a department. * * *

This, then, is a plain case for a *mandamus*, either to deliver the commission, or a copy of it from the record; and it only remains to be inquired,

Whether it can issue from this court.

The act to establish the judicial courts of the United States authorizes the supreme court, "to issue writs of *mandamus*, in cases warranted by the principles and usages of law, to any courts appointed or persons holding office, under the authority of the United States."

The secretary of state being a person holding an office under the authority of the United States, is precisely within the letter of the description; and if this court is not authorized to issue a writ of *mandamus* to such an officer, it must be because the law is unconstitutional, and therefore, absolutely incapable of conferring the authority, and assigning the duties which its words purport to confer and assign.

The constitution vests the whole judicial power of the United States in one supreme court, and such inferior courts as congress shall, from time to time, ordain and establish. This power is expressly extended to all cases arising under the laws of the United States; and, consequently, in some form, may be exercised over the present case; because the right claimed is given by a law of the United States.

In the distribution of this power it is declared, that "the supreme court shall have original jurisdiction in all cases affecting ambassadors, other public ministers and consuls, and those in which a state shall be a party. In all other cases, the supreme court shall have appellate jurisdiction."

It has been insisted, at the bar, that as the original grant of jurisdiction, to the supreme and inferior courts, is general, and the clause, assigning original jurisdiction to the supreme court, contains no negative or restrictive words, the power remains to the legislature, to assign original jurisdiction to that court in other cases than those specified in the article which has been recited; provided those cases belong to the judicial power of the United States.

If it had been intended to leave it in the discretion of the legislature to apportion the judicial power between the supreme and inferior courts according to the will of that body, it would certainly have been useless to have proceeded further than to have defined the judicial power, and the tribunals in which it should be vested. The subsequent part of the section is mere surplusage, is entirely without meaning, if such is to be the construction. If congress remains at liberty to give this court appellate jurisdiction where the constitution has declared their jurisdiction shall be original; and original jurisdiction where the constitution has declared it shall be appellate; the distribution of jurisdiction, made in the constitution, is form without substance.

Affirmative words are often, in their operation, negative of other objects than those affirmed; and in this case, a negative or exclusive sense must be given to them, or they have no operation at all.

It cannot be presumed that any clause in the constitution is intended to be without effect; and therefore, such a construction is inadmissible, unless the words require it.

If the solicitude of the convention, respecting our peace with foreign powers, induced a provision that the supreme court should take original jurisdiction in cases which might be supposed to affect them; yet the clause would have proceeded no further than to provide for such cases, if no further restriction on the powers of congress had been intended. That they should have appellate jurisdiction in all other cases, with such exceptions as congress might make, is no restriction; unless the words be deemed exclusive of original jurisdiction.

When an instrument organizing fundamentally a judicial system, divides it into one supreme, and so many inferior courts as the legislature may ordain and establish; then enumerates its powers, and proceeds so far to distribute them, as to define the jurisdiction of the supreme court, by declaring the cases in which it shall take original jurisdiction, and that in others it shall take appellate jurisdiction; the plain import of the words seems to be, that in one class of cases its jurisdiction is original, and not appellate; in the other it is appellate, and not original. If any other construction would render the clause inoperative, that is an additional reason for rejecting such other construction, and for adhering to their obvious meaning.

To enable this court, then, to issue a *mandamus*, it must be shown to be an exercise of appellate jurisdiction, or to be necessary to enable them to exercise appellate jurisdiction. * * *

It is the essential criterion of appellate jurisdiction, that it revises and corrects the proceedings in a cause already instituted, and does not create that cause. Although, therefore, a *mandamus* may be directed to courts, yet to issue such a writ to an officer for the delivery of a paper, is in effect the same as to sustain an original action for that paper, and, therefore, seems not to belong to appellate, but to original jurisdiction. Neither is it necessary in such a case as this, to enable the court to exercise its appellate jurisdiction.

The authority, therefore, given to the supreme court by the act establishing the judicial courts of the United States, to issue writs of *mandamus* to public officers, appears not to be warranted by the constitution; and it becomes necessary to inquire whether a jurisdiction so conferred can be exercised.

The question, whether an act, repugnant to the constitution, can become the law of the land, is a question deeply interesting to the United States; but, happily, not of an intricacy proportioned to its interest. It seems only necessary to recognize certain principles, supposed to have been long and well established, to decide it.

That the people have an original right to establish, for their future government, such principles, as in their opinion, shall most conduce to their own happiness is the basis on which the whole American fabric has been erected. The exercise of this original right is a very great exertion; nor can it, nor ought it, to be frequently repeated. The principles, therefore, so established, are deemed fundamental. And as the authority from which they proceed is supreme, and can seldom act, they are designed to be permanent.

This original and supreme will organizes the government, and assigns to different departments their respective powers. It may either stop here, or establish certain limits not to be transcended by those departments.

The government of the United States is of the latter description. The powers of the legislature are defined and limited; and that those limits may not be mistaken, or forgotten, the constitution is written. To what purpose are powers limited, and to what purpose is that limitation committed to writing, if these limits may, at any time, be passed by those intended to be restrained? The distinction between a government with limited and unlimited powers is abolished, if those limits do not confine the persons on whom they are imposed, and if acts prohibited and acts allowed, are of equal obligation. It is a proposition too plain to be contested, that the constitution controls any legislative act repugnant to it; or, that the legislature may alter the constitution by an ordinary act.

Between these alternatives, there is no middle ground. The constitution is either a superior paramount law, unchangeable by ordinary means, or it is on a level with ordinary legislative acts, and, like other acts, is alterable when the legislature shall please to alter it.

If the former part of the alternative be true, then a legislative act, contrary to the constitution, is not law: if the latter part be true, then written constitutions are absurd attempts, on the part of the people, to limit a power in its own nature, illimitable.

Certainly all those who have framed written constitutions contemplate them as forming the fundamental and paramount law of the nation, and, consequently, the theory of every such government must be, that an act of the legislature, repugnant to the constitution, is void.

This theory is essentially attached to a written constitution, and is consequently, to be considered, by this court, as one of the fundamental principles of our society. It is not therefore to be lost sight of, in the further consideration of this subject.

If an act of the legislature, repugnant to the constitution, is void, does it, notwithstanding its invalidity, bind the courts, and oblige them to give it effect? Or, in other words, though it be not law, does it constitute a rule as operative as if it was a law? This would be to overthrow in fact what was established in theory; and would seem, at first view, an absurdity too gross to be insisted on. It shall, however, receive a more attentive consideration.

It is emphatically the province and duty of the judicial department to say what the law is. Those who apply the rule to particular cases, must of necessity expound and interpret that rule. If two laws conflict with each other, the courts must decide on the operation of each.

So, if a law be in opposition to the constitution; if both the law and the constitution apply to a particular case, so that the court must either decide that case conformably to the law, disregarding the constitution; or conformably to the constitution, disregarding the law; the court must determine which of these conflicting rules governs the case. This is of the very essence of judicial duty.

If then, the courts are to regard the constitution, and the constitution is superior to any ordinary act of the legislature, the constitution, and not such ordinary act, must govern the case to which they both apply.

Those, then, who controvert the principle that the constitution is to be considered, in court, as a paramount law, are reduced to the necessity of maintaining that courts must close their eyes on the constitution, and see only the law. This doctrine would subvert the very foundation of all written constitutions. It would declare that an act which, according to the principles and theory of our government, is entirely void, is yet, in practice, completely obligatory. It would declare that if the legislature shall do what is expressly forbidden, such act, notwithstanding the express prohibition, is in reality effectual. It would be giving to the legislature a practical and real omnipotence, with the same breath which professes to restrict their powers within narrow limits. It is prescribing limits, and declaring that those limits may be passed at pleasure.

That it thus reduces to nothing, what we have deemed the greatest improvement on political institutions, a written constitution, would of itself be sufficient, in America, where written constitutions have been viewed with so much reverence, for rejecting the construction. But the peculiar expressions of the constitution of the United States furnish additional arguments in favour of its rejection.

The judicial power of the United States is extended to all cases arising under the constitution.

Could it be the intention of those who gave this power, to say that in using it the constitution should not be looked into? That a case arising under the constitution should be decided, without examining the instrument under which it arises?

This is too extravagant to be maintained.

In some cases, then, the constitution must be looked into by the judges. And if they can open it at all, what part of it are they forbidden to read or to obey?

There are many other parts of the constitution which serve to illustrate this subject.

It is declared, that "no tax or duty shall be laid on articles exported from any state." Suppose, a duty on the export of cotton, of tobacco, or of flour; and a suit instituted to recover it. Ought judgment to be rendered in such a case? ought the judges to close their eyes on the constitution, and only see the law?

The constitution declares "that no bill of attainder or *ex post facto* law shall be passed."

If, however, such a bill should be passed, and a person should be prosecuted under it; must the court condemn to death those victims whom the constitution endeavors to preserve?

"No person," says the constitution, "shall be convicted of treason unless on the testimony of two witnesses to the same overt act, or on confession in open court."

Here the language of the constitution is addressed especially to the courts. It prescribes, directly for them, a rule of evidence not to be departed from. If the legislature should change that rule, and declare *one* witness, or a confession *out* of court, sufficient for conviction, must the constitutional principle yield to the legislative act?

From these, and many other selections which might be made, it is apparent, that the framers of the constitution contemplated that instrument as a rule for the government of courts, as well as of the legislature.

Why otherwise does it direct the judges to take an oath to support it? This oath certainly applies in an especial manner, to their conduct in their official character. How immoral to impose it on them, if they were to be used as the instruments, and the knowing instruments, for violating what they swear to support!

The oath of office, too, imposed by the legislature, is completely demonstrative of the legislative opinion on this subject. It is in these words: "I do solemnly swear that I will administer justice without respect to persons, and do equal right to the poor and to the rich; and that I will faithfully and impartially discharge all the duties incumbent on me as ___, according to the best of my abilities and understanding, agreeably to the *constitution* and laws of the United States."

Why does a judge swear to discharge his duties agreeably to the constitution of the United States, if that constitution forms no rule for his government? if it is closed upon him, and cannot be inspected by him?

If such be the real state of things, this is worse than solemn mockery. To prescribe, or to take this oath, becomes equally a crime.

It is also not entirely unworthy of observation, that in declaring what shall be the *supreme* law of the land, the *constitution* itself is first mentioned; and not the laws of the United States, generally, but those only which shall be made in *pursuance* of the constitution, have that rank.

Thus, the particular phraseology of the constitution of the United States confirms and strengthens the principle, supposed to be essential to all written constitutions, that a law repugnant to the constitution is void; and that *courts*, as well as other departments, are bound by that instrument.

The rule must be discharged.

NOTE ON MARBURY V. MADISON

(1) Historical Background.[1] Control of the national government passed from Federalist to Republican hands for the first time in the national elections of 1800. The lines of political division were sharp. The Federalists generally favored a strong national government, a sound currency, and domestic and foreign policies promoting mercantile interests. The Republicans, by contrast, were the party of states' rights and political and economic democracy.

Before the Republican Thomas Jefferson assumed office as President, the outgoing Federalists took a variety of measures to preserve their party's influence through the life-tenured federal judiciary. First, President John Adams appointed his Secretary of State, John Marshall, as Chief Justice of the United States, and the Senate quickly confirmed him. Marshall, while continuing to serve as Secretary of State, took office as Chief Justice on February 4, 1801. Second, a new Circuit Court Act of February 13, 1801, relieved Supreme Court Justices of their circuit-riding duties and created sixteen new circuit court judgeships. With only two weeks remaining in his term, Adams hurried to nominate Federalists to the newly created positions, and the Senate confirmed the "midnight judges" with equal alacrity. Finally, on February 27, Congress enacted legislation authorizing the President to appoint justices of the peace for the District of Columbia. Adams nominated forty-two justices on March 2, and the Senate confirmed them on March 3, the day before the conclusion of Adams' term. Adams signed the commissions, and John Marshall, as Secretary of State, affixed the great seal of the United States. Nonetheless, some of the commissions, including that of William Marbury, were not delivered before Adams' term expired, and the new President refused to honor those appointments.

While Marbury's suit was pending in the Supreme Court, the newly installed Republicans worked on a number of fronts to frustrate the outgoing Federalists' designs for the federal judiciary. Congress repealed the Circuit Court Act of 1801 and abolished the sixteen judgeships that it had created. By statute, Congress also abolished the Supreme Court's previously scheduled June and December Terms and provided that there be only one Term, in February. As a result, the Supreme Court did not meet at all in 1802. Having received Marbury's petition in December 1801, it could not hear his case until February 1803. Even more menacingly, the Jeffersonians embarked on a program of judicial impeachments. Early in 1802, the House voted articles of impeachment against the Federalist district judge John Pickering of New Hampshire, who apparently was burdened by mental infirmity and an alcohol problem. On the day after Pickering's conviction by the Senate in March 1804, the House impeached Supreme Court Justice Samuel Chase. The case against Chase failed in the Senate. Had it succeeded, the impeachment of John Marshall was widely expected to follow.

---

[1] For contrasting views of Marshall's opinion, compare Van Alstyne, *A Critical Guide to Marbury v. Madison*, 1969 Duke L.J. 1 (1969), with Haggard, *Marbury v. Madison: A Concurring/Dissenting Opinion*, 10 J. Law & Pol. 543 (1994). For additional historical background, see Ackerman, The Failure of the Founding Fathers: Jefferson, Marshall, and the Rise of Presidential Democracy (2005); Simon, What Kind of Nation: Thomas Jefferson, John Marshall, and the Epic Struggle to Create a United States (2002); Haskins & Johnson, Foundations of Power: John Marshall, 1801–15 (1981); Ellis, The Jeffersonian Crisis: Courts and Politics in the Young Republic (1971); McCloskey, The American Supreme Court 36–44 (1960).

In this charged political climate, it seems doubtful, at least, that James Madison, Thomas Jefferson's Secretary of State, would have obeyed a judicial order to deliver Marbury's commission as a justice of the peace. Might this consideration have influenced Marshall's decision of the case?[2] In light of his involvement in the events leading up to the case, should Marshall have recused himself?

(2) A Political Masterstroke? The Marbury opinion is widely regarded as a political masterstroke. Marshall seized the occasion to uphold the institution of judicial review,[3] but he did so in the course of reaching a judgment that his political opponents could neither defy nor protest.[4]

Is it ironic if Marbury, which authorizes the courts to hold some issues outside the bounds of permissible political decisionmaking, was itself a political decision? See generally Fallon, *Marbury and the Constitutional Mind: A Bicentennial Essay on the Wages of Doctrinal Tension*, 91 Calif.L.Rev. 1 (2003). Does the answer depend on sorting out various possible senses of "political" and determining in which sense, if any, Marbury should be so characterized?

(3) Marbury's Jurisdictional Holdings. Marbury ultimately holds that the Supreme Court lacked jurisdiction to decide the case before it.

The jurisdictional analysis proceeds in two steps. First, Marshall concludes that section 13 of the 1789 Judiciary Act—which authorized the

---

[2] Commentators have overwhelmingly thought that Marshall's decision was motivated by political considerations. See Pfander, *Marbury, Original Jurisdiction, and the Supreme Court's Revisory Powers*, 101 Colum.L.Rev. 1515, 1515–18 (2001) (summarizing views and collecting citations). Among the corroborating evidence is the Court's decision the week after Marbury in Stuart v. Laird, 5 U.S. (1 Cranch) 299 (1803), declining to consider the constitutionality of the Repeal Act of 1802, which abolished the sixteen circuit court judgeships created by the Circuit Court Act of 1801. See, *e.g.*, Alfange, *Marbury v. Madison and Original Understandings of Judicial Review: In Defense of Traditional Wisdom*, 1993 Sup.Ct.Rev. 329, 362–68, 409–10 (treating Stuart v. Laird as strongly probative of the Court's awareness of the political sensitivity of its situation and its willingness to shape its decisions accordingly). See also Ackerman, note 1, *supra*, at 163–98 (discussing the relationship between the Marbury and Stuart decisions). For the contrary view that Marshall's Marbury opinion was essentially innocent of political motivation, see Clinton, Marbury v. Madison and Judicial Review 79–138 (1989).

[3] The issue, however, was "by no means new", according to Currie, *The Constitution in the Supreme Court: The Powers of the Federal Courts, 1801–1835*, 49 U.Chi.L.Rev. 646, 655–56 (1982): "The Supreme Court itself had measured a state law against a state constitution in Cooper v. Telfair, 4 U.S. (4 Dall.) 14 (1800), and had struck down another under the Supremacy Clause in Ware v. Hylton, 3 U.S. (3 Dall.) 199 (1796); in both cases the power of judicial review was expressly affirmed. Even acts of Congress had been struck down by federal circuit courts [as in Hayburn's Case, p. 82, *infra*], and the Supreme Court, while purporting to reserve the question of its power to do so, had reviewed the constitutionality of a federal statute in Hylton v. United States, 3 U.S. (3 Dall.) 171 (1796). Justice James Iredell had explicitly asserted this power both in Chisholm v. Georgia, 2 U.S. (2 Dall.) 419 (1793), and in Calder v. Bull, 3 U.S. (3 Dall.) 386 (1798), and Chase had acknowledged it in Cooper. * * * Yet though Marshall's principal arguments echoed those of Hamilton [in Federalist No. 78,] he made no mention of any of this material, writing as if the question had never arisen before." In a detailed study of early case law, Treanor, *Judicial Review Before Marbury*, 58 Stan.L.Rev. 455 (2005), concludes that judicial review was exercised by state and federal courts in more than thirty cases before Marbury. On the understanding of the Convention, see Chap. I, pp. 11–12, *supra*. See also Klarman, *How Great Were the "Great" Marshall Court Decisions?*, 87 Va.L.Rev. 1111, 1114–15 (2001) (observing that judicial review "became far less controversial" during the period between the Convention and the decision in Marbury).

[4] For a detailed critical review of Marshall's opinion, culminating in the conclusion that "[j]ust about everything in Marbury is wrong", see Paulsen, *Marbury's Wrongness*, 20 Const.Comm. 343, 343 (2003).

Court "to issue * * * writs of mandamus, in cases warranted by the principles and usages of law, to any courts appointed, or persons holding office, under the authority of the United States", 1 Stat. 73, 81—confers original Supreme Court jurisdiction in actions for mandamus. Some believe that Marshall misread Section 13. Professor Amar, for example, argues that "the mandamus clause is best read as simply giving the Court remedial authority—for both original and appellate cases after jurisdiction * * * has been independently established". Amar, *Marbury, Section 13, and the Original Jurisdiction of the Supreme Court*, 56 U.Chi.L.Rev. 443, 456 (1989). See also Van Alstyne, note 1, *supra*, at 15. In contrast, Professor Pfander contends that "supreme" courts traditionally possessed a supervisory authority over lower courts and governmental officers, exercised through writs of mandamus and prohibition, and that against this background "section 13 appears to confer precisely the sort of freestanding power on the Court that Marshall attributed to it in Marbury". Pfander, note 2, *supra*, at 1535. Should the Court have adopted Amar's construction under the principle favoring interpretations that render statutes constitutional?[5]

Second, Marshall finds that the second paragraph of Article III, § 2 restricts the permissible scope of the Supreme Court's original jurisdiction to cases "affecting Ambassadors, other public Ministers and Consuls, and those in which a State shall be a Party." According to Van Alstyne, *supra* note 1, at 31, this clause "readily supports the interpretation that the Court's original jurisdiction may not be *reduced* by Congress, but that it may be supplemented". *Cf.* Amar, *supra*, at 469–76 (arguing that the Court's original jurisdiction was limited partly to spare parties from the burden of traveling to the seat of government to litigate their disputes). For further discussion of the Supreme Court's original jurisdiction, see Chap. III, *infra*.[6]

(4) Marbury's Arguments for Judicial Review. Consider the arguments Marshall offers to support the power of judicial review and whether those arguments are persuasive.

A common criticism is developed in Bickel, The Least Dangerous Branch 2–14 (1962). Everyone accepted the proposition that the Constitution was binding on the national government. Dispute centered on the quite separate proposition that the courts were authorized to enforce their interpretations of the Constitution against the conflicting interpretations of Congress and the President. Marshall's arguments prove the first, undisputed proposition,

---

[5] For discussion of that principle, see pp. 79–81, *infra*.

[6] With the Supreme Court lacking jurisdiction in Marbury v. Madison, would any other court have had jurisdiction to entertain Marbury's claim? A state court could not have issued mandamus relief against a federal official, see McClung v. Silliman, 19 U.S. (6 Wheat.) 598 (1821), and the 1789 Judiciary Act failed to vest the lower federal courts with mandamus jurisdiction, see McIntire v. Wood, 11 U.S. (7 Cranch) 504 (1813). In Kendall v. United States ex. rel. Stokes, 37 U.S. (12 Pet.) 524 (1838), the Supreme Court held that the Circuit Court for the District of Columbia, which had been established by a special act, was uniquely authorized to issue writs of mandamus in original actions against federal officials. Based on Kendall, Bloch, *The Marbury Mystery: Why Did William Marbury Sue in the Supreme Court?*, 18 Const.Comment. 607 (2002), concludes unequivocally that the Circuit Court would have had jurisdiction had Marbury chosen to file there. Professor Bloch further speculates that Marbury may have deliberately bypassed the Circuit Court in order to permit John Marshall to issue the precise rulings about Supreme Court jurisdiction and judicial review for which Marbury v. Madison is famous. Compare Fallon, Paragraph (2), *supra*, at 52 n. 271 (2003) (finding it "highly doubtful that the [Supreme] Court, in the politically charged atmosphere of 1803, would have upheld the authority of the D.C. courts to order mandamus relief for William Marbury against James Madison").

but furnish no support for the second. In sum, Marshall's arguments beg the only question really in issue.

In support of this criticism, note that there are issues on which, without further inquiry, courts accept a formally correct determination of the legislative or executive branches—*e.g.*, a statement that a certain statute has in fact been enacted in accordance with the prescribed procedure or an executive determination that a certain government is the established government of a country. See Sec. 6, *infra* (discussing "political questions"). Would it not be possible for courts, in all cases, similarly to accept the determination of Congress and the President (or in the case of a veto, of a super majority of Congress) that a statute is duly authorized by the Constitution?

On the other hand, does Congress in voting to enact a bill, or the President in approving it, typically make or purport to make such a determination? With respect to the validity of the statute as applied in particular situations, how could they?[7]

(5) Judicial Supremacy in Historical Perspective. Conventional wisdom now treats the federal judiciary as "supreme in the exposition of the law of the Constitution" and traces that premise back to Marbury itself. Cooper v. Aaron, 358 U.S. 1, 18 (1958). See also, *e.g.*, United States v. Morrison, 529 U.S. 598, 616 n.7 (2000); United States v. Nixon, 418 U.S. 683, 703 (1974). Recent historical studies, however, have suggested that the present conventional wisdom may reflect an ahistorical understanding of Marbury and of the intellectual and legal context that preceded it. Some historians contend, in particular, that the founding generation initially distinguished between fundamental or constitutional law (embodying the basic terms of the social compact) and ordinary law (interpreted and enforced by courts through ordinary means). See, *e.g.*, Snowiss, Judicial Review and the Law of the Constitution 13–89 (1990); Wood, *The Origins of Judicial Review Revisited, or How the Marshall Court Made More Out of Less*, 56 Wash. & Lee L.Rev. 787, 796–99 (1999). Under this conception of judicial review, moreover, courts and commentators of the time apparently thought it proper for courts to invalidate legislation on constitutional grounds only in cases of such relatively clear legislative or executive overreaching that little or no "interpretation" was required.[8] According to Snowiss, "Marshall's key innovations [to that set of understandings] did not come in Marbury," in which he said little about *how* the Constitution should be interpreted, but in opinions of the 1810s and 1820s in which he subjected the Constitution to "rules of statutory interpretation" and "transformed explicit fundamental

originally
j.r. was
more restrained

---

[7]   For an attempt to "provide a clear and persuasive derivation of Marbury's conclusion from the constitutional text", see Harrison, *The Constitutional Origins and Implications of Judicial Review*, 84 Va.L.Rev. 333 (1998). See also Prakash & Yoo, *The Origins of Judicial Review*, 70 U.Chi.L.Rev. 887 (2003) (arguing that the Constitution's text, structure, and history all support the practice of judicial review).

[8]   With respect to the circumstances under which courts would hold statutes unconstitutional, see also Alfange, note 2, *supra*, at 342–49 (noting the expectation of the founding generation that judicial invalidation of statutes would occur only in cases of clear mistake); Casto, *James Iredell and the American Origins of Judicial Review*, 27 Conn.L.Rev. 329, 341–48 (1995) (same); Klarman, note 3, *supra*, at 1120–21.

law, different in kind from ordinary law, into supreme written law, different only in degree" and enforceable by the courts in all cases.[9]

In a similar vein, former Dean Larry Kramer argues that when viewed in proper historical context, Marbury represented the application of an earlier, modest understanding of judicial review rather than a bold articulation of the idea of judicial supremacy. See Kramer, The People Themselves: Popular Constitutionalism and Judicial Review 93–127 (2004). Kramer notes that judicial review arose against a backdrop of popular constitutionalism—the notion, inherited from British constitutional theory, that ultimate responsibility for the enforcement of constitutional law lay with the community through political action, protest, and even revolution. From this starting point, Kramer maintains that many early Americans embraced a "departmental" theory of judicial review under which Congress and the President, no less than the judiciary, had an obligation to decide for themselves how the duties imposed by the Constitution constrained their authority. On that view, the interpretations by one branch—such as the judiciary—did not necessarily bind the others; ultimately, "the people themselves" would have to resolve conflicts among the branches about the Constitution's meaning through popular action.[10] Kramer contends that Marbury, properly understood, is consistent with departmentalism rather than the judicial supremacy with which many now associate it.

These historical accounts, of course, have not gone unchallenged.[11] But even if historians such as Snowiss, Wood, and Kramer are correct in their understanding of Marbury and its historical context, is the modern conception of Marbury too well entrenched to reconsider?[12]

---

[9] For a more traditional account of the development of judicial review, in which the distinction between fundamental and ordinary law is not emphasized, see Corwin, *The Establishment of Judicial Review*, 9 Mich.L.Rev. 102–25, 283–316 (1910–11).

[10] For a sweeping historical account of both the Court's role as a catalyst of political debate and the influence of public opinion on the development of constitutional doctrine, see Friedman, The Will of the People: How Public Opinion Has Influenced the Supreme Court and Shaped the Meaning of the Constitution (2009).

[11] For recent interventions, see, *e.g.*, Hamburger, Law and Judicial Duty (2008) (arguing that what we now think of as judicial review was merely an aspect of a more general common law judicial duty to decide in accordance with the law of the land and to respect the hierarchical character of law by treating inferior law as void when it conflicted with superior law); Bilder, *The Corporate Origins of Judicial Review*, 116 Yale.L.J. 502 (2006) (arguing that judicial review originated in the common law practice of invalidating corporate charters that were "repugnant" to the law of nations and that the seamless adaptation of that practice to the context of judicial review leaves us little useful founding-era evidence about questions such as "departmentalism" or the standard of review in constitutional cases); Treanor, note 3, *supra*, at 458 (arguing that in pre-Marbury cases, "the standard of review varied with subject matter" and that courts were especially aggressive in rebuffing threats to judicial power and in invalidating state statutes).

[12] See, *e.g.*, White, *The Constitutional Journey of Marbury v. Madison*, 89 Va.L.Rev. 1463 (2003) (tracing historically evolving interpretations of Marbury); Whittington & Rinderle, *Making a Mountain out of a Molehill? Marbury and the Construction of the Constitutional Canon*, 39 Hastings Const.L.Q. 823 (2012) (arguing that while courts and commentators cited Marbury for various purposes in the nineteenth century, the case attained its status as the cornerstone of judicial review nearer the turn of the twentieth century).

NOTE ON MARBURY V. MADISON AND THE FUNCTION OF ADJUDICATION

(1) Marbury and Judicial Power: Marbury is often quoted for the observation that "[i]t is emphatically the province and duty of the judicial department to say what the law is." But how far does the law declaration power extend? Imagine that Marbury, although wishing to take office as justice of the peace, had no interest in litigating Madison's refusal to deliver his commission. Given the tenor of Chief Justice Marshall's opinion, could a concerned citizen of the District of Columbia have brought suit to establish that Madison acted unlawfully and to compel him to deliver Marbury's commission (assuming that Congress had vested appropriate jurisdiction in a federal court)? What if it were instead a concerned citizen living in Boston who—like many others—felt aggrieved that Madison, as an officer of the United States, had failed to comply with the law? Should it matter whether Congress explicitly authorized such suits?

(2) Dispute Resolution Model. Chief Justice Marshall's opinion in Marbury treats the law declaration power as incidental to the resolution of a concrete dispute occasioned by Marbury's claim to a "private right" to take possession of the office. Marshall emphasizes this recurrent theme, moreover, in ways that seem obviously calculated to make two aspects of his decision more palatable: first, the assertion of judicial authority to grant affirmative relief against a senior political officer of the executive branch; and, second, the claimed authority to invalidate an Act of Congress. The Court, in Marshall's view, had the authority to impose in those ways on the coordinate branches because doing so was an unavoidable consequence of its obligations to adjudicate Marbury's claim of right.

In response to the charge that the relief requested against Secretary of State Madison would "intrude into the cabinet, and * * * intermeddle with the prerogatives of the executive," Marshall parried that "[t]he province of the court is, solely, to decide on the rights of individuals." While the Court could "never" resolve "political" questions that the Constitution or laws assigned to the executive's "discretion," the fact that Madison occupied public office did not "exempt[ ] him from being sued in the ordinary mode of proceeding". On this view, the suit did not rest upon the notion that the Court's special function was to bring public officials into conformity with the rule of law. On the contrary, the Court granted the requested relief to vindicate Marbury's private right, just as it could if the defendant had been a private citizen.

Marshall's discussion of the authority to engage in judicial review similarly assumed that the Court had no choice but to interpret and apply the Constitution when presented with a proper case requiring decision. Hence, in deeming it "emphatically the province and duty of the judicial department to say what the law is", Marshall took pains to elaborate in the very next sentence that "[t]hose who apply the rule to particular cases, must of necessity expound and interpret that rule."

This "dispute resolution" model—under which the Court treats its law declaration power as incidental to its responsibility to resolve concrete disputes—recurs in several related aspects of the Court's justiciability case law. First, to avoid intrusion upon the prerogatives of the other branches, leading cases affirm that courts should eschew any role as a general overseer of government conduct; that is, the federal judiciary's function is not to

vindicate abstract interests in the government's compliance with the rule of
law. See, *e.g.*, FEC v. Akins, 524 U.S. 11, 23–24 (1998); Lujan v. Defenders
of Wildlife, 504 U.S. 555, 573–574 (1992). Second, justiciable "cases" should
be restricted to disputes in which a defendant's violation of a legal duty has
caused a distinct and palpable injury to a concrete, legally protected interest
of the plaintiff. See, *e.g.*, Allen v. Wright, 468 U.S. 737 (1984); Warth v.
Seldin, 422 U.S. 490 (1975). These themes are taken up in detail in Sections
3, 4, and 5 of this Chapter.

(3) Law Declaration Model. In the past half century, a competing account
of the courts has found considerable support in the commentary and also,
albeit less than completely, in several aspects of the law of justiciability.
Rather than treating law declaration as an incidental function of resolving
concrete claims of individual right, the "law declaration" account of the
judicial function presupposes that federal courts (and especially the Supreme
Court) have a special function of enforcing the rule of law, independent of
the task of resolving concrete disputes over individual rights.[1] This approach
questions the importance of requiring that the plaintiff have a personal stake
in the outcome of a lawsuit; in its purest form, it would permit any citizen to
bring a "public action" to challenge allegedly unlawful government conduct.
Under this view, the judiciary should be recognized not as a mere settler of
disputes, but rather as an institution with a distinctive capacity to declare
and explicate norms that transcend individual controversies.[2]

At least three historical phenomena have contributed to the emergence
of the law declaration model. First, the vast increase in the modern
administrative state has created diffuse rights shared by large groups and
new legal relationships that are hard to capture in traditional, private law
terms. At the same time, a need has arisen for judicial control of
administrative power.[3] Encouraged by statutes authorizing judicial review
of administrative action, leading administrative law decisions gradually
departed from the dispute resolution model and accorded "standing" to
persons asserting interests not protected at common law in order to
represent the "public interest" in statutory enforcement. See, *e.g.*, FCC v.
Sanders Bros. Radio Station, 309 U.S. 470 (1940); Scripps-Howard Radio,
Inc. v. FCC, 316 U.S. 4 (1942). For further discussion, see pp. 145–146, *infra*.

Second, the substantive expansion of constitutional rights, especially
under the Warren Court in the 1960s, has broadened the conception of

---

[1] Support for the law declaration approach, particularly in constitutional adjudication, is
found by some commentators in Marbury itself. See, *e.g.*, Monaghan, *Constitutional
Adjudication: The Who and When*, 82 Yale L.J. 1363 (1973); Fallon, *Marbury and the
Constitutional Mind: A Bicentennial Essay on the Wages of Doctrinal Tension*, 91 Calif.L.Rev. 1
(2003).

[2] For a range of commentary elaborating aspects of this approach, see, *e.g.*, Vining, Legal
Identity: The Coming of Age of Public Law (1978); Bandes, *The Idea of a Case*, 42 Stan.L.Rev.
227 (1990); Chayes, *The Role of the Judge in Public Law Litigation*, 89 Harv.L.Rev. 1281 (1976);
Chayes, *Foreword: Public Law Litigation and the Burger Court*, 96 Harv.L.Rev. 4 (1982);
Dworkin, Taking Rights Seriously 131–49 (1977); Fiss, *Foreword: The Forms of Justice*, 93
Harv.L.Rev. 1 (1979); Jaffe, *The Citizen as Litigant in Public Actions: The Non-Hohfeldian or
Ideological Plaintiff*, 116 U.Pa.L.Rev. 1033 (1968); Pushaw, *Article III's Case/Controversy
Distinction and the Dual Functions of Federal Courts*, 69 Notre Dame L.Rev. 447 (1994);
Sunstein, *Standing and the Privatization of Public Law*, 88 Colum.L.Rev. 1432 (1988); Tushnet,
The New Law of Standing: A Plea for Abandonment, 62 Cornell L.Rev. 633 (1977).

[3] See generally Jaffe, *Standing to Secure Judicial Review: Public Actions*, 74 Harv.L.Rev.
1265, 1282–84 (1961); Stewart, *The Reformation of American Administrative Law*, 88
Harv.L.Rev. 1667, 1674–81 (1975).

legally cognizable interests. For example, the widely shared interests of voters in challenging a malapportioned legislative district, see Baker v. Carr, 369 U.S. 186 (1962), p. 250, *infra*, or of public school pupils in challenging school prayer, see School Dist. v. Schempp, 374 U.S. 203 (1963), differ markedly from the liberty and economic interests recognized at common law.

Third, one contemporary notion of constitutional rights treats them not merely as shields against governmental coercion, but as swords authorizing the award of affirmative relief to redress injury to constitutionally protected interests. That understanding, the origins of which can be traced in part to the landmark decision in Ex parte Young, 209 U.S. 123 (1908), p. 922, *infra*, also finds expression in the institutional reform litigation following Brown v. Board of Education, 347 U.S. 483 (1954). After the recognition of such rights as those to school desegregation, courts inevitably found themselves awarding remedies of a kind difficult to square with at least some of the premises of the private rights or dispute resolution model.

(4) Overlap of the Approaches. No two stylized and oversimplified models can capture the full historical or functional complexity of the role of the federal judiciary. School desegregation cases, for example, have their origin in individual grievances that seemingly require the reshaping of institutions. But such cases resolve questions about the structure of legal and social institutions that far transcend the context of any individual's claimed deprivation of private right. The devices of the class action, like other techniques for broadening the scope of litigation, frequently also meld the two functional models, and many of the tensions about the proper role of the courts have been felt in the resulting cases and doctrines.[4]

The distinction between the dispute resolution and law declaration models blurs, moreover, because the law declaration model, sensibly construed, cannot be understood to license judicial review at the behest of any would-be litigant on the basis of any hypothesized set of facts or indeed no facts whatsoever. For there to be a constitutionally justiciable case under the public rights approach, at least "the functional requisites of effective adjudication" must be satisfied. See Fallon, *Of Justiciability, Remedies, and Public Law Litigation: Notes on the Jurisprudence of Lyons*, 59 N.Y.U.L.Rev. 1, 51 (1984). These requisites cannot be reduced to a determinate list, but involve such considerations as: (a) the importance of a concrete set of facts to permit the accurate formulation of the legal issue to be decided and the limits of the ruling ultimately issued and (b) adversary presentation as an aid to the accurate determination of factual and legal issues. In the end, disputes about the comparative merits of the competing models are not so much about the appropriate formula for deciding cases as about the basic attitude toward the proper role of the federal judiciary.

(5) The Supreme Court and the Models. The Supreme Court has never explicitly rejected the dispute resolution model. Indeed, its formal pronouncements have been consistently to the contrary. There are, however,

---

[4] For further discussion of such complex litigation, compare, *e.g.*, Fuller, *The Forms and Limits of Adjudication*, 92 Harv.L.Rev. 353 (1978) (arguing that adjudication is not well adapted to resolve "polycentric" disputes, which he claims have too many interdependent aspects to yield to rational, properly judicial solution), with Sabel & Simon, *Destabilization Rights: How Public Law Litigation Succeeds*, 117 Harv.L.Rev. 1015, 1019 (2004) (arguing that institutional reform remedies have become more successful as they have moved from "from command-and-control injunctive regulation toward experimentalist intervention" that combines "more flexible and provisional norms with procedures for ongoing stakeholder participation and measured accountability").

some holdings that may be seen as reflecting, though not in explicit terms, a shift in conception of the judicial role. See, *e.g.*, the developments discussed in the *Note on Mootness in Class Actions*, p. 208, *infra*, and in the *Note on the Scope of the Issue in First Amendment Cases and Related Problems Involving "Facial Challenges"*, p. 177, *infra*. See also Fallon & Meltzer, *New Law, Non-Retroactivity, and Constitutional Remedies*, 104 Harv.L.Rev. 1731, 1779–1800 (1991) (citing, *inter alia*, harmless error practice, the practice of providing alternative grounds for decision, and the exception to mootness doctrine for cases "capable of repetition, yet evading review" in support of the conclusion that "there exists a substantial body of case law, rising almost to the level of a general tradition, in which adjudication * * * functions more as a vehicle for the pronouncement of norms than for the resolution of particular disputes").

In a bolder argument, Professor Monaghan maintains that the Supreme Court now substantially embraces the law declaration model as the dominant approach to its own jurisdiction. First, in addition to noting some of the examples cited in the previous paragraph, Professor Monaghan argues that the Court's special rules governing review of official immunity decisions (see pp. 1051–1054, *infra*) and its qualification of the statutory "final judgment" rule of 28 U.S.C. § 1257 (see pp. 546–558, *infra*) show that the Court will often find a way around jurisdictional constraints that would otherwise limit its ability to review important propositions of law. Second, he catalogues a broad array of "agenda control" devices—making limited grants of certiorari, reformulating questions presented, injecting new questions into cases, appointing amici to defend positions abandoned by the litigants, and strategically accepting or rejecting party stipulations, waivers, or concessions. Based on these phenomena, he concludes that the Court has defined "its current place in our constitutional order" in a way that establishes "a 'final say' default position." Monaghan, *On Avoiding Avoidance, Agenda Control, and Related Matters*, 112 Colum. L. Rev. 665 (2012). To the extent that these innovations deviate from the assumptions about justiciability that govern the lower courts, does the Court have an obligation to specify some basis in the text or history of Article III for treating its own jurisdiction differently? Do the practices identified by Professor Monaghan raise concerns about judicial self-aggrandizement? Cf. Vermeule, *The Judicial Power in the State (and Federal) Courts*, 2000 Sup. Ct. Rev. 357, 361 (discussing "cognitive pressures that cause judges to press judicial prerogatives to implausible extremes").[5]

(6) Discretion, Prudence, and the Judicial Function. Does the power of judicial review upheld in Marbury carry with it a correlative duty to decide any claims of unconstitutionality in a properly presented case, or is there some measure of discretion to abstain from rendering such decisions? In Cohens v. Virginia, 19 U.S. (6 Wheat.) 264, 404 (1821), Chief Justice Marshall said: "It is most true that this Court will not take jurisdiction if it should not: but it is equally true, that it must take jurisdiction, if it should. * * * We have no more right to decline the exercise of jurisdiction which is

---

[5] For contrasting views on whether the federal courts should have discretion to reframe the issues by the parties, compare Frost, *The Limits of Advocacy*, 59 Duke L.J. 447 (2009) (arguing that such judicial discretion avoids potential distortions of law by the parties), with Lawson, *Stipulating the Law*, 109 Mich.L.Rev. 1191 (2011) (arguing that allowing the parties to structure the case promotes judicial restraint and minimalism).

given, than to usurp that which is not given. The one or the other would be treason to the constitution".

Shapiro, *Jurisdiction and Discretion*, 60 N.Y.U.L.Rev. 543 (1985), argues (in discussing a wide range of traditional and contemporary doctrines, including equitable discretion, abstention doctrines, prudential components of justiciability doctrines, forum non conveniens, and others) that Marshall's dictum cannot be taken at face value: On many issues, courts have exercised a "principled discretion" in refusing to exercise jurisdiction seemingly granted by Congress. The discretion of which Shapiro approves is not ad hoc, but rather constitutes a fine-tuning of legislative enactments in accordance with criteria that are openly applied and that are "drawn from the relevant statutory * * * grant of jurisdiction or from the tradition within which the grant arose". Compare Redish, The Federal Courts in the Political Order: Judicial Jurisdiction and American Political Theory 47–74 (1991) (arguing that federal judicial jurisdiction is mandatory and that failure to exercise jurisdiction conferred is an illegitimate usurpation of Congress' lawmaking power).

Beyond the "principled discretion" defended by Professor Shapiro, is there a further judicial power to decline to exercise jurisdiction on a more ad hoc basis, for what might loosely be termed "prudential" reasons?[6]

According to Fallon, note 1, *supra*, at 16–20, a prudential tradition in constitutional adjudication can be traced back to Marbury itself: "In Marbury, the Court reached the only prudent conclusion: It could not, indeed must not, issue a quixotic order to Madison to deliver Marbury's commission." Moreover, Fallon writes, "[e]ven if the face of prudence is typically one of judicial self-abnegation, there may be occasions when prudence counsels an otherwise constitutionally dubious assertion of judicial power. In Marbury itself, for example, the Court arguably invented a non-existent statutory jurisdiction in order to be able to hold * * * that Congress had overstepped constitutional bounds" and thereby to establish what the Justices believed to be a functionally desirable tradition of judicial review. For a classic defense of judicial "prudence" in deciding jurisdictional questions, see Bickel, The Least Dangerous Branch (1962).

(7) Marbury and Constitutional Avoidance. Is the power of judicial review so fraught that federal courts should exercise it only when truly necessary to resolve the case before it? The so-called doctrine of constitutional avoidance holds that it is. See, *e.g.*, Department of Commerce v. United States House of Representatives, 525 U.S. 316, 343 (1999) (" 'If there is one doctrine more deeply rooted than any other in the process of constitutional adjudication, it is that we ought not to pass on questions of constitutionality * * * unless such adjudication is unavoidable.' ") (quoting Spector Motor Service v. McLaughlin, 323 U.S. 101, 105 (1944)).

The nearly canonical citation for the avoidance doctrine is Justice Brandeis' concurring opinion in Ashwander v. Tennessee Valley Authority, 297 U.S. 288, 345–48 (1936).[7] Although his famous opinion included among the avoidance devices a number of the justiciability doctrines discussed

---

[6]   For further discussion, see Paragraph (7), p. 78 n. 8, *infra*.

[7]   The majority opinion in Ashwander considered on the merits and rejected a constitutional challenge to the existence and authority of the Tennessee Valley Authority. Concurring, Justice Brandeis argued that the Court should have avoided the constitutional issues, principally on equitable grounds.

below (doctrines we now think of as the prohibition of feigned cases and the requirements of ripeness and standing),[8] Justice Brandeis also identified several avoidance devices that the Court had applied "to cases confessedly within its own jurisdiction". First, Brandeis noted that the Court will not " 'formulate a rule of constitutional law broader than is required by the precise facts to which it is to be applied' " (quoting Liverpool, N.Y. & Phila. Steamship Co. v. Emigration Commissioners, 113 U.S. 33, 39 (1885)). Second, he emphasized that federal courts "will not pass upon a constitutional question although properly presented by the record, if there is also present some other ground upon which the case may be disposed of." Third, and perhaps most important in modern terms, he invoked avoidance in matters of statutory interpretation: " 'When the validity of an act of the Congress is drawn in question, and even if a serious doubt of constitutionality is raised, it is a cardinal principle that this Court will first ascertain whether a construction of the statute is fairly possible by which the question may be avoided' " (quoting Crowell v. Benson, 285 U.S. 22, 62 (1932)). How closely do these principles follow from the approach to constitutional adjudication articulated by Chief Justice Marshall in Marbury?

(a) Breadth of Decision. The principle that the Court should not "formulate a rule of constitutional law broader than is required by the precise facts" necessarily includes a judgmental element, involving the appropriate specification of the applicable rule of decision. What rationale supports this principle? Would it *always* be sound practice for the Court to decide cases on the narrowest possible grounds?[9]

(b) Last Resort Rule. The principle that the Court should avoid ruling on constitutional issues "if there is also present some other ground on which the case may be disposed of" has been termed the "last resort" rule. Kloppenberg, *Avoiding Constitutional Questions*, 35 B.C.L.Rev. 1003, 1004 (1994). This rule continues to be much invoked when a party claiming relief on federal constitutional grounds also asserts a right to relief under a federal statute or regulations or on state law grounds. See, *e.g.*, Department of

---

[8] Although such doctrines of justiciability might sometimes result in the avoidance of constitutional questions, those doctrines are not framed to serve that purpose directly. Could they legitimately be adapted to such ends? In his famous "passive virtues" argument, Professor Bickel suggests that the Court might properly rely, at times, on a result-oriented approach to justiciability as a way to achieve avoidance. Bickel, Paragraph (6), *supra*, at 127 (1969). According to Bickel, this technique of constitutional avoidance is necessary to reconcile the Court's role as the ultimate enforcer of constitutional "principle" with competing demands of "prudence" and expediency that counsel the Court sometimes to avoid constitutional decisions that aroused political constituencies would be unwilling to accept. In contrast, Gunther, *The Subtle Vices of the "Passive Virtues"—A Comment on Principle and Expediency in Judicial Review*, 64 Colum.L.Rev. 1 (1964), argues that Bickel's proposed approach tends "to blur the fact that jurisdiction under our system is rooted in Article III, that it is not a domain solely within the Court's keeping." He adds that in cases within the Court's jurisdiction, proper avoidance techniques "are devices which go to the choice of the ground of decision of a case, not devices which avoid decision on the merits, not devices which 'decline to exercise' the jurisdiction to decide."

[9] Sunstein, One Case at a Time: Judicial Minimalism on the Supreme Court (1999), argues that a minimalist approach to judicial decision making tends "to make judicial errors less frequent and (above all) less damaging" and to maximize the space for the operation of political democracy. Sunstein acknowledges, however, that sometimes broad clear rules are necessary or at least desirable to avoid chilling the exercise of constitutional freedoms and to facilitate advance planning.

Commerce v. U.S. House of Representatives, 525 U.S. 316 (1999); United States v. Locke, 471 U.S. 84, 93 (1985).

In some contexts, however, the Court has taken a different approach, one that is more consistent with the law declaration model. See, *e.g.*, United States v. Leon, 468 U.S. 897, 925–26 (1984) (determining first whether a search violated the Fourth Amendment and then asking whether reasonable reliance on a warrant would negate the remedy of the exclusionary rule despite the unconstitutional search). Consider, in particular, the Court's approach to the "qualified immunity" doctrine, which provides that governmental officials who are sued in their personal capacities typically are immune from suits for money damages under federal law unless they violated "clearly established" federal rights. See generally Chap. IX, Sec. 3, *infra*. In ruling on qualified immunity defenses, the Court has stated that lower courts have discretion to decide initially whether the plaintiff has stated a valid constitutional claim and then to determine whether the plaintiff's rights were clearly established for purposes of qualified immunity. See Pearson v. Callahan, 555 U.S. 223 (2009) pp. 1052–1053, *infra*. Although acknowledging circumstances that would warrant addressing those issues in the opposite order (for example, "cases in which it is plain that the constitutional right is not clearly established but far from obvious whether there is in fact such a right"), the Court noted that deciding the underlying constitutional question first may "promote[ ] the development of constitutional precedent", which "is especially valuable with respect to questions that do not frequently arise in cases in which a qualified immunity defense is unavailable." Is there a general constitutional interest in achieving judicial articulation of legal norms that may outweigh the interest in avoiding "unnecessary" decisions of constitutional law? In light of the exceptions to the "last resort" rule, would it be fair to say that whether to apply the rule is simply a policy question, to be decided on a case-by-case basis? See Kloppenberg, *supra*.[10]

(c) The Canon of Avoidance. Among the avoidance rules offered by Justice Brandeis, the most important and controversial is the last: "When the validity of an act of the Congress is drawn in question, and even if a serious doubt of constitutionality is raised, it is a cardinal principle that this Court will first ascertain whether a construction of the statute is fairly possible by which the question may be avoided." In tracing the history of this principle, commentators have noted a slide from what might be termed an "unconstitutionality" to a "doubts" canon of statutory interpretation. Nagle, *Delaware & Hudson Revisited*, 72 Notre Dame L.Rev. 1495, 1495–97 (1997). See also Kelley, *Avoiding Constitutional Questions as a Three-Branch Problem*, 86 Cornell L.Rev. 831 (2001); Vermeule, *Saving Constructions*, 85 Geo.L.J. 1945 (1997). Under the unconstitutionality approach, which was commonly practiced during the nineteenth century, the courts adopted an alternative interpretation only after first deciding that the preferred interpretation would render the statute unconstitutional. See Nagle, *supra*. Modern avoidance, which can be traced back to United States v. Delaware & Hudson Co., 213 U.S. 366, 407–08 (1909), rejects the unconstitutionality approach on the ground that the former practice still required an

---

[10] See also Katyal, *Judges as Advicegivers*, 50 Stan.L.Rev. 1709 (1998); Mikva, *Why Judges Should Not Be Advicegivers: A Response to Professor Neal Katyal*, 50 Stan.L.Rev. 1825 (1998); Healy, *The Rise of Unneccessary Constitutional Rulings*, 83 N.C.L.Rev. 847 (2005); Kamin, *An Article III Defense of Merits-First Decisionmaking in Civil Rights Litigation: The Continued Viability of Saucier v. Katz*, 16 Geo. Mason L.Rev. 53 (2008).

unnecessary constitutional ruling. Instead, the Court now holds that "where an otherwise acceptable construction of a statute would raise constitutional problems, the Court will construe the statute to avoid such problems unless such construction is plainly contrary to the intent of Congress." Edward J. DeBartolo Corp. v. Florida Gulf Coast Bldg. and Constr. Trades Council, 485 U.S. 568, 575 (1988).

How closely is the modern canon tied to Marbury's premises that judicial review is justified because (and, thus, presumably only when) necessary to resolve a case? The Court has suggested that, in the interest of judicial restraint, the modern canon seeks "to minimize disagreement between the branches by preserving congressional enactments that might otherwise founder on constitutional objections." Almendarez-Torres v. United States, 523 U.S. 224, 238 (1998). A second prominent rationale rests on an empirical assumption that the canon respects Congress' presumed intent not "to press ahead into dangerous constitutional thickets in the absence of firm evidence that it courted those perils." Public Citizen v. United States Dep't of Justice, 491 U.S. 440, 466 (1989). A third rationale argues that the modern avoidance canon represents a "resistance norm" disfavoring interpretations of statutes that press close to the border of actual unconstitutionality. See Young, *Constitutional Avoidance, Resistance Norms, and the Preservation of Judicial Review*, 78 Tex.L.Rev. 1549, 1585 (2000). See also Eskridge & Frickey, *Quasi-Constitutional Law: Clear Statement Rules as Constitutional Lawmaking*, 45 Vand.L.Rev. 593 (1992) (presenting a related justification); Stephenson, *The Price of Public Action: Constitutional Doctrine and the Judicial Manipulation of Enactment Costs*, 118 Yale L.J. 2 (2008) (same); Sunstein, *Interpreting Statutes in the Regulatory State*, 103 Harv.L.Rev. 405, 468–69 (1989) (same).[11]

Although the Court has stated that the modern avoidance canon "has so long been applied by this Court that it is beyond debate," Edward J. DeBartolo Corp., *supra*, the canon has in fact become the subject of growing debate and criticism. Some have argued that the doctrine contradicts, rather than implements, principles of judicial restraint. First, Professor Schauer has maintained that "it is by no means clear that a strained interpretation of a federal statute that avoids a constitutional question is any less a judicial intrusion than the judicial invalidation on constitutional grounds of a less strained interpretation of the same statute." Schauer, *Ashwander Revisited*, 1995 Sup.Ct.Rev. 71, 74. Accordingly, Schauer concludes that the canon permits judges to use disingenuous interpretations of statutes "to substitute their judgment for that of Congress" without assuming responsibility for rendering a constitutional holding.[12] Second, because the modern avoidance

---

[11] The avoidance canon sometimes overlaps with other precepts of statutory interpretation, including "clear statement" rules under which the Court will not read federal statutes to preclude all judicial review of administrative action, see Chap. IV, pp. 329–330, *infra*, or to impose duties or liabilities on the states, see Chap. IX, p. 959, *infra*, in the absence of clear statutory statements mandating that effect. For contrasting views on the legitimacy of clear statement rules generally, compare, *e.g.*, Manning, *Clear Statement Rules and the Constitution*, 110 Colum.L.Rev. 339 (2010) (arguing that clear statement rules impermissibly abstract constitutional values from the limits placed upon them by the constitutional text), with Sunstein, *Nondelegation Canons*, 67 U.Chi.L.Rev.315 (2000) (suggesting that such canons merely require Congress to take responsibility for decisions that push against accepted constitutional values).

[12] Jerry Mashaw suggests that the strategic misconstruction of a statute may intrude upon legislative supremacy more severely than would the decision to strike down an unconstitutional statute. See Mashaw, Greed, Chaos, and Governance: Using Public Choice To Improve Public

canon is triggered by mere constitutional doubt rather than a finding of actual unconstitutionality, its effect is "to enlarge the already vast reach of constitutional prohibition beyond even the most extravagant modern interpretation of the Constitution—to create a judge-made 'penumbra' that has much the same prohibitory effect as * * * [the already extravagantly interpreted] Constitution itself." Posner, *Statutory Interpretation—In the Classroom and in the Courtroom*, 50 U.Chi.L.Rev. 800, 816 (1983). Third, when the Court practices avoidance in reviewing an agency's interpretation of its own organic act, see, *e.g.*, Edward J. DeBartolo Corp., *supra*, the Court's reliance on the canon may devalue the executive's own responsibility to determine the constitutionality of action that it undertakes pursuant to authority delegated by Congress. See Kelley, *supra*.

The Court has frequently emphasized that the canon is "not a license for the judiciary to rewrite language enacted by the legislature," United States v. Monsanto, 491 U.S. 600, 611 (1989) (internal quotations omitted), and that in no case should a court "press statutory construction to the point of disingenuous evasion even to avoid a constitutional question." United States v. Locke, 471 U.S. 84, 96 (1985) (internal quotations omitted). But does that premise correspond to the reality of the cases? Compare Ullman v. United States, 350 US 422, 433 (1956) (emphasizing that "the Court has stated that words may be strained 'in the candid service of avoiding a serious constitutional doubt' ").

---

2. ISSUES OF PARTIES, THE REQUIREMENT OF FINALITY, AND THE PROHIBITION AGAINST FEIGNED AND COLLUSIVE SUITS

INTRODUCTORY NOTE

Helping to define the appropriate scope of an Article II "case" or "controversy" are a set of technical requirements that include the Court's insistence that federal courts have the capacity to enter final judgments and its prohibition against the parties' colluding to invoke federal jurisdiction, not to resolve a genuine dispute but to secure a judicial ruling on a subject of interest to one or more of the litigants. As you read the following materials, ask yourself how readily one can derive these doctrines from the standard constitutional materials and how readily one can subject the doctrines to principled limits.

Law 105 (1997). According to Mashaw, if the Court invalidates a statute, that course of action returns matters to the pre-statutory status quo. To fill the policy vacuum created by such a judicial ruling, the legislature must go back to the drawing board in a process that requires the House, the Senate, and the President to bargain afresh. If, however, the Court relies on avoidance to misread a statute, the resultant misinterpretation will remain in place if any one of those three actors prefers it to the likely outcome of corrective legislation.

Hayburn's Case

2 U.S. (2 Dall.) 408, 1 L.Ed. 436 (1792).
On Petition for Mandamus.

Mandamus

This was a motion for a *mandamus* to be directed to the *Circuit Court* for the district of *Pennsylvania*, commanding the said court to proceed in a certain petition of *Wm. Hayburn*, who had applied to be put on the pension list of the *United States*, as an invalid pensioner.

Pensions Act

Sec. not bound

[The Invalid Pensions Act of 1792,[1] which provided financial assistance to injured veterans of the Revolutionary War, charged the federal circuit courts with entertaining petitions from would-be pensioners. The courts were to receive evidence of the petitioners' military service, their war injuries, their resulting disabilities, and the proportion of their monthly pay corresponding to those disabilities. If the court found that a petitioner qualified for a pension, it was directed to submit the petitioner's name, as well as a recommended sum, to the Secretary of War. The statute directed the Secretary to place any applicant certified by a circuit court on the pension list, except that, in cases of suspected "imposition or mistake", the Secretary was to withhold the suspected petitioner's name and so report to Congress.]

not from specific person (ex officio)

The Attorney General (Randolph) who made the motion for the *mandamus*, having premised that it was done *ex officio*, without an application from any particular person, but with a view to procure the execution of an act of Congress, particularly interesting to a meritorious and unfortunate class of citizens, THE COURT declared that they entertained great doubt upon his right, under such circumstances, and in a case of this kind, to proceed *ex officio*; and directed him to state the principles on which he attempted to support the right. The Attorney General, accordingly, entered into an elaborate description of the powers and duties of his office:—

But the COURT being divided in opinion on that question, the motion, made *ex officio*, was not allowed.

Hayburn

The Attorney General then changed the ground of his interposition, declaring it to be at the instance, and on behalf of Hayburn, a party interested; and he entered into the merits of the case, upon the act of Congress, and the refusal of the Judges to carry it into effect.

Legislative fix

The COURT observed, that they would hold the motion under advisement, until the next term; but no decision was ever pronounced, as the Legislature, at an intermediate session, provided, in another way, for the relief of the pensioners.

[The following was added by the reporter as a footnote to the above report:]

As the reasons assigned by the Judges, for declining to execute the first act of Congress, involve a great Constitutional question, it will not be thought improper to subjoin them, in illustration of Hayburn's case.

---

[1] [Ed.] Act of March 23, 1792, ch. 11, 1 Stat. 243 (1792) (repealed in part and amended by Act of Feb. 28, 1793, ch. 17, 1 Stat. 324 (1793)).

■ The Circuit Court for the district of New York (consisting of JAY, CHIEF JUSTICE, CUSHING, JUSTICE, and DUANE, DISTRICT JUDGE) * * * were * * * unanimously, of opinion and agreed.

"That by the Constitution of the United States, the government thereof is divided into *three* distinct and independent branches, and that it is the duty of each to abstain from, and to oppose, encroachments on either.

"That neither the *Legislative* nor the *Executive* branches, can constitutionally assign to the *Judicial* any duties, but such as are properly judicial, and to be performed in a judicial manner.

"That the duties assigned to the Circuit courts, by this act, are not of that description, and that the act itself does not appear to contemplate them as such; in as much as it subjects the decisions of these courts, made pursuant to those duties, first to the consideration and suspension of the Secretary [of] War, and then to the revision of the Legislature; whereas by the Constitution, neither the Secretary [of] War, nor any other Executive officer, nor even the Legislature, are authorized to sit as a court of errors on the judicial acts or opinions of this court.

"As, therefore, the business assigned to this court, by the act, is not judicial, nor directed to be performed judicially, the act can only be considered as appointing commissioners for the purposes mentioned in it, by *official* instead of *personal* descriptions.

"That the Judges of this court regard themselves as being the commissioners designated by the act, and therefore as being at liberty to accept or decline that office.

"That as the objects of this act are exceedingly benevolent, and do real honor to the humanity and justice of Congress; and as the Judges desire to manifest, on all proper occasions, and in every proper manner, their high respect for the National Legislature, they will execute this act in the capacity of commissioners. * * *"

■ The Circuit court for the district of Pennsylvania, (consisting of WILSON, and BLAIR, JUSTICES, and PETERS, DISTRICT JUDGE) made the following representation, in a joint letter to the President of the United States, on the 18th of April, 1792.

" * * * It is a principle important to freedom, that in government, the *judicial* should be distinct from, and independent of, the legislative department. To this important principle the people of the United States, in forming their Constitution, have manifested the highest regard. * * *

"Upon due consideration, we have been unanimously of opinion, that, under this act, the Circuit court held for the Pennsylvania district could not proceed;

"1st. Because the business directed by this act is not of a judicial nature. It forms no part of the power vested by the Constitution in the courts of the United States; the Circuit court must, consequently, have proceeded *without* constitutional authority.

"2d. Because, if, upon that business, the court had proceeded, its *judgments* (for its *opinions* are its judgments) might, under the same act, have been revised and controuled by the legislature, and by an officer in the executive department. Such revision and controul we deemed radically inconsistent with the independence of that judicial power which is vested in the courts; and, consequently, with that important principle which is so strictly observed by the Constitution of the United States. * * * "

■ The Circuit court for the district of North Carolina, (consisting of IREDELL, JUSTICE, and SITGREAVES, DISTRICT JUDGE) made the following representation in a joint letter to the President of the United States, on the 8th of June, 1792. * * *

"1. That the Legislative, Executive, and Judicial departments, are each formed in a separate and independent manner; and that the ultimate basis of each is the Constitution only, within the limits of which each department can alone justify any act of authority.

"2. That the Legislature, among other important powers, unquestionably possess that of establishing courts in such a manner as to their wisdom shall appear best, limited by the terms of the constitution only; and to whatever extent that power may be exercised, or however severe the duty they may think proper to require, the Judges, when appointed in virtue of any such establishment, owe implicit and unreserved obedience to it.

"3. That at the same time such courts cannot be warranted, as we conceive, by virtue of that part of the Constitution delegating *Judicial power*, for the exercise of which any act of the legislature is provided, in exercising (even under the authority of another act) any power not in its nature *judicial*, or, if *judicial*, not provided for upon the terms the Constitution requires.

"4. That whatever doubt may be suggested, whether the power in question is properly of a judicial nature, yet inasmuch as the decision of the court is not made final, but may be at least suspended in its operation by the Secretary [of] War, if he shall have cause to suspect imposition or mistake; this subjects the decision of the court to a mode of revision which we consider to be unwarranted by the Constitution; for, though Congress may certainly establish, in instances not yet provided for, courts of appellate jurisdiction, yet such courts must consist of judges appointed in the manner the Constitution requires, and holding their offices by no other tenure than that of their good behaviour, by which tenure the office of Secretary [of] War is not held. And we beg leave to add, with all due deference, that no decision of any court of the United States can, under any circumstances, in our opinion, agreeable to the Constitution, be liable to a reversion [sic], or even suspension, by the Legislature itself, in whom no judicial power of any kind appears to be vested, but the important one relative to impeachments. * * * "

[The judges then indicated that they were of the opinion that they could not regard the Act as appointing them commissioners for the purpose of its execution, since the Act appeared to confer power on the circuit courts and not on the judges personally. Acknowledging their doubts as to the propriety of giving an advisory opinion (no application under the Act had as yet been made to them), they concluded that the present situation called for an exception, "upon every principle of humanity and justice", but stated that they would "most attentively hear" argument on the points on which an opinion had been expressed in the event that an actual application were made.]

NOTE ON HAYBURN'S CASE

(1) Jurisdictional Basis. Jurisdiction in the mandamus proceeding in the Supreme Court was no doubt premised on the statute later held unconstitutional in Marbury v. Madison. Is this case distinguishable? See Ex parte Peru and materials in Chap. III, pp. 289–290, *infra*.

(2) The Ex Officio Action by the Attorney General. Why did three Justices conclude that the Attorney General could not proceed *ex officio*? Was the problem that the Attorney General lacked a personal stake or interest in the outcome? Surely the Attorney General can enforce both the criminal law and federal regulatory statutes. See Hartnett, *The Standing of the United States: How Criminal Prosecutions Show That Standing Doctrine is Looking for Answers in All the Wrong Places*, 97 Mich.L.Rev. 2239 (1999).

In Pasadena City Bd. of Educ. v. Spangler, 427 U.S. 424 (1976), high school students and their parents brought an action seeking injunctive relief from allegedly unconstitutional segregation in the Pasadena schools. The United States intervened as a party plaintiff pursuant to 42 U.S.C. § 2000h–2, which provides that upon such intervention, "the United States shall be entitled to the same relief as if it had instituted the action." By the time the case reached the Supreme Court, all the student plaintiffs had graduated. The Court held that the continued presence of the United States was authorized by the statute, and that the case was therefore not moot. Was the Attorney General's problem in Hayburn's Case merely a lack of statutory authorization to sue? For suggestions to that effect, see Bloch, *The Early Role of the Attorney General in Our Constitutional Scheme: In the Beginning There Was Pragmatism*, 1989 Duke L.J. 561, 608–18; Marcus & Teir, *Hayburn's Case: A Misinterpretation of Precedent*, 1988 Wis.L.Rev. 527, 540–41.

[handwritten margin note: statutory auth.]

(3) Advisory Opinion? The Supreme Court never pronounced a judgment on the motion for mandamus in Hayburn's Case, and the opinions of the Justices on the merits emerge only through the reporter's footnote, which includes an opinion of the Circuit Court for the District of New York and letters from the Circuit Courts for the Districts of Pennsylvania and North Carolina to President Washington. Were the latter two communications, at least, advisory opinions? How can the issuance of these letters be reconciled with the formal position taken in the Correspondence of the Justices, p. 52, *supra*? At least one theme links the Correspondence of the Justices and the opinions expressed in the reporter's footnote in Hayburn's Case: Judicial independence requires that the Article III courts not be subject to requisition by Congress or the executive to act as subordinates to those two branches in the performance of their characteristic functions.[1]

(4) Adverse Parties. Apart from concerns about executive and legislative revision, discussed in the immediately following Note, why did the Justices and district judges consider the functions assigned to the circuit courts by the Invalid Pensions Act of 1792 to be nonjudicial? Was it because a "case" or "controversy" requires at least two parties who are adverse to each other? Is there any intrinsic difficulty in making a "case" out of an application by a

---

[1] See also Pfander, *Judicial Compensation and the Definition of Judicial Power in the Early Republic*, 107 Mich.L.Rev. 1 (2007), which argues that in the Correspondence of the Justices, p. 52, *supra*, and in Hayburn's Case, the Justices may have reacted in part against efforts by the political branches to add significant, but uncompensated, duties to what the Justices regarded as an already heavy workload and burdensome circuit riding responsibilities.

private person for a grant by the government of money or other tangible
property or an intangible permission?

contra case

Tutun v. United States, 270 U.S. 568 (1926), held that rulings on
petitions for naturalization satisfy the case or controversy requirement. The
Court recognized that many petitions are uncontested, but observed that
"the proceeding is instituted and is conducted throughout according to the
regular course of judicial procedure", with the United States "always a
possible adverse party." After Tutun, would Hayburn's Case remain a bar to
Congress' charging an Article III court with routine determinations of
eligibility for disability benefits under the Social Security Act? Certainly, the
United States is always a possible adverse party in such proceedings.
Hayburn's Case, however, seems to reject rather decisively Congress' effort
to enlist federal courts to act as administrative agencies by applying law to
fact outside the context of a concrete dispute between adverse parties. Is
there way to understand Tutun that does not contradict that premise? The
Court in Tutun noted that "[t]he function of admitting to citizenship has been
conferred exclusively on courts since the foundation of our government. See
Act of March 26, 1790, c. 3. * * * The constitutionality of this exercise of
jurisdiction has never been questioned." What role should such a
consideration play in constitutional adjudication? Compare Ex parte Quirin,
317 U.S. 1, 41–42 (1942) (a legislative construction of the Constitution
"which has been followed since the founding of our government * * * is
entitled to the greatest respect"); The Laura, 114 U.S. 411, 416 (1885) ("[T]he
practice [under federal legislation] and acquiescence under it, 'commencing
with the organization of the judicial system, affords an irresistible answer,
and has, indeed, fixed the construction.' ") (quoting Stuart v. Laird, 5 U.S. (1
Cranch) 299, 308 (1803)). When, if ever, should a deep historical pedigree
sustain a practice if the Court would otherwise find it unconstitutional?

(5) Intragovernmental Litigation. In Hayburn's Case, the original
parties in the Supreme Court were the Attorney General and the Circuit
Court for the District of Pennsylvania. Does the idea of a "case" entirely
between the government and its own officials smack too much of the
government's litigating with itself?

In United States v. Nixon, 418 U.S. 683 (1974), enforcement of a
subpoena against the President was sought by the Watergate Special
Prosecutor, who was appointed—and also (under specified conditions)
removable—by the Attorney General, an official directly answerable to the
President within the executive branch. In finding the action justiciable, the
Court relied heavily on the fact that the Attorney General had promulgated
a regulation providing that the Special Prosecutor would not be removed
except for "extraordinary improprieties". Although the Attorney General
could revoke the regulation, it had the force of law as long as it remained in
effect. Because the President could not, therefore, control the litigation
decisions of the Special Prosecutor, the Court found that the action to enforce
the subpoena possessed the requisite adverseness. How important was what
the Court described as "the uniqueness of the setting in which the conflict
arises"—the need to devise some efficacious way for the executive branch to
conduct a criminal investigation of alleged wrongdoing that potentially
involved the President himself?[2] For discussion of potential pathologies of

---

[2] The Court has also deemed justiciable certain actions between an independent agency,
whose principal officers are insulated by statute from presidential removal, and executive
agencies, whose officers the President may remove at will. See United States v. ICC, 337 U.S.

intragovernmental litigation, see Kelley, *The Constitutional Dilemma of Litigation Under the Independent Counsel System*, 83 Minn.L.Rev. 1197 (1999).

NOTE ON HAYBURN'S CASE AND THE PROBLEM OF REVISION OF JUDICIAL JUDGMENTS

Among the concerns in the opinions of the Justices and the district judges in Hayburn's Case was the possibility of "revision" of a judicial judgment by the executive or legislative branch. Similar concerns have been said to raise issues about the existence of a justiciable case or controversy under Article III in other cases.

A.   Executive Revision

(1) Doctrinal Foundations. Why did the judges in the circuit courts in Hayburn's Case think that the existence of an executive power of revision was fatal to the exercise of "judicial power"? Note that the statutory scheme made short-run practical sense. The judges were in a better position than the Secretary of War to appraise the personal good faith of claimants and the extent of their disability, which was the job they were given to do, but the Secretary was in a better position to check the official military records. Did the objection to executive revision rest simply on judicial dignity and a desire to keep face, or on more fundamental concerns about the integrity of the judicial process?[1]

(a) Pursuant to the treaty of 1819 between the United States and Spain, Congress directed the judge of the territorial court, and later of the district court, in Florida to "receive, examine and adjudge" claims for losses suffered by certain Spanish citizens through operations of the American army in Florida. The judge was to report decisions in favor of the claimants, together with the supporting evidence, to the Secretary of the Treasury, who, if satisfied that the awards were just and within the provisions of the treaty, was to authorize payment. 3 Stat. 768, 6 *id.* 569, 9 *id.* 788. In United States v. Ferreira, 54 U.S. (13 How.) 40 (1851), the Supreme Court dismissed an appeal by the United States from an award by the district judge "for want of jurisdiction". The Court said that the judge was not acting judicially, but as a commissioner—a non-Article III administrative official charged with adjusting claims against the United States. See Chap. IV, Sec. 2, *infra.* It noted but did not decide the question whether the judge could be appointed in that capacity by statute rather than by the President with the advice and consent of the Senate.

(b) In Chicago & Southern Air Lines v. Waterman S.S. Corp., 333 U.S. 103 (1948), the question was whether an order of the Civil Aeronautics Board denying to one American air carrier and granting to another a certificate of

---

426 (1949) (action by the United States, as shipper, to set aside reparations order of ICC, an independent agency); United States ex rel. Chapman v. FPC, 345 U.S. 153 (1953) (action by Secretary of Interior challenging authority of the FPC, an independent agency, to grant license). See generally Herz, *United States v. United States: When Can the Federal Government Sue Itself?*, 32 Wm. & Mary L.Rev. 893 (1991).

[1]   For historical discussion, see Tushnet, *Dual Office Holding and the Constitution: A View from Hayburn's Case*, in Origins of the Federal Judiciary: Essays on the Judiciary Act of 1789, at 196 (Marcus ed. 1992).

convenience and necessity for an overseas air route was subject to judicial review. Section 801 of the Act provided that such an order must be submitted to the President before publication and was unconditionally subject to presidential approval. The judicial review section of the Act provided that "any order, affirmative or negative, issued by the Board under this Act, except any order in respect of any *foreign* air carrier subject to the approval of the President as provided in section 801 of this Act, shall be subject to review by the circuit courts of appeals * * *."

In a 5–4 decision, the Court held that final orders approved by the President could not be reviewed because such orders "embody Presidential discretion as to political matters beyond the competence of the courts to adjudicate". The court of appeals had avoided this difficulty by holding that after it had reviewed the final order, the case should be resubmitted to the President so "that his power to disapprove would apply after as well as before the court acts". In rejecting this approach, the Court said:

"But if the President may completely disregard the judgment of the court, it would be only because it is one the courts were not authorized to render. Judgments, within the powers vested in courts by the Judiciary Article of the Constitution, may not lawfully be revised, overturned or refused faith and credit by another Department of Government.

"To revise or review an administrative decision which has only the force of a recommendation to the President would be to render an advisory opinion in its most obnoxious form—advice that the President has not asked, tendered at the demand of a private litigant, on a subject concededly within the President's exclusive, ultimate control. This Court early and wisely determined that it would not give advisory opinions even when asked by the Chief Executive. It has also been the firm and unvarying practice of Constitutional Courts to render no judgments not binding and conclusive on the parties and none that are subject to later review or alteration by administrative action."

(2) A Contemporary Application: Extradition Proceedings. To effect an extradition under 18 U.S.C. § 3184, the government must file a complaint with "any justice or judge of the United States, or any magistrate," or with any judge of a state court of general jurisdiction, who then conducts a hearing. Upon a finding of probable cause that the accused has committed an extraditable crime, the presiding judge certifies this finding to the Secretary of State, who then determines whether to deliver the accused to the country seeking extradition. Although the Supreme Court has not addressed the question, the courts of appeals thus far have rejected Hayburn's Case objections to this procedure, reasoning that judges in extradition proceedings act as extradition officers in their individual rather than judicial capacities. See, *e.g.*, Lopez-Smith v. Hood, 121 F.3d 1322, 1327 (9th Cir.1997); Lo Duca v. United States, 93 F.3d 1100 (2d Cir.1996).[2] Is it relevant that § 3184, although permitting the Secretary of State to exercise a power analogous to clemency in cases found to satisfy the statutory requirements, does not allow the Secretary to "revise" a finding that the statutory requirements of extradition have not been satisfied?

---

[2]   For criticism of this position, see generally Parry, *The Lost History of International Extradition Litigation*, 43 Va.J.Int'l L. 93 (2002) (attacking the purported historical foundations for the view that the judicial role in extradition proceedings falls outside Article III).

B.   Legislative Revision

(1) The Problem Defined. Recall that in Hayburn's Case, the Pension Act provided that, if the Secretary of War found that the circuit court's determination was mistaken, the Secretary would withhold the pensioner from the pension rolls and report the case to Congress. Was Congress' power to revise the decision of the judges open to the same objections as the Secretary's power to do so? What if the Secretary had been directed to put all names certified by the courts on the pension roll, and Congress had simply retained power to refuse to pay any particular pension by virtue of its power over appropriations? Unsurprisingly, the issue of congressional revision of final judicial judgments has arisen many times in our history, most commonly when Congress determines whether to appropriate money to pay judgments against the United States. Consider the examples follow.

(2) Claims Against the United States. Article I, § 9, clause 7 of the Constitution provides that "[n]o Money shall be drawn from the Treasury, but in Consequence of Appropriations made by Law". Because the payment of any judgment against the United States thus requires a specific or general appropriation by Congress, suits against the United States present especially complex issues involving legislative revision of judicial judgments. Many of the Supreme Court's encounters with those issues have been further complicated by Congress' recurrent use of non-Article III tribunals—whose judges lack life tenure and whose powers are not subject to Article III justiciability doctrines—either to adjudicate or to recommend to Congress whether to pay claims against the United States. The Court has assumed these arrangements are valid. (Issues involving non-Article III courts are discussed in Chap. IV, Sec. 2, *infra*.) But when Congress provides for review of the decisions of non-Article III tribunals by Article III courts, Article III justiciability rules apply to the appeal, and the Court has had to determine whether its own judgment might be subject to impermissible legislative revision. What follows is a brief history of Congress' approach to funding judgments against the United States and the Court's reaction to any resultant prospect of legislative revisions of federal judicial judgments.

(a) Before 1855, no general statute waived the sovereign immunity of the United States on claims for money, and a claimant's only recourse was to petition Congress for a private act. In order to relieve the burden posed by the need to consider numerous private acts, Congress in 1855 established a non-Article III Court of Claims with authority to "hear and determine" most types of money claims not sounding in tort. Initially, this court embodied its decisions not in judgments but in reports to Congress and drafts of private bills requiring congressional action. In 1863, Congress enacted new legislation to permit the Court of Claims to render judgments, but the statutory scheme continued to provide that "no money shall be paid out of the Treasury for any claim passed on by the Court of Claims till after an appropriation therefor shall have been estimated for by the Secretary of the Treasury." In Gordon v. United States, 69 U.S. 561 (1865), the Court construed this provision as authorizing executive revision of judgments against the United States and, accordingly, held that Supreme Court review of Court of Claims judgments was barred by Article III.[3] Congress responded by amending the statute once again, omitting the "objectionable section", and

---

[3] The Court did not question the authority of Congress to vest non-judicial functions in the non-Article III Court of Claims. As a result, the only issue in Gordon was whether the Supreme Court could review Court of Claims decisions.

the Court upheld its own jurisdiction to entertain appeals from decisions of the Court of Claims in United States v. Jones, 119 U.S. 477 (1886). (Note the assumption that Supreme Court review of a "judicial" decision by a "legislative court" was an exercise of "appellate jurisdiction" within the meaning of Article III.)[4]

(b) From 1956 to 1977, Congress provided that judgments of $100,000 or less were to be paid by the General Accounting Office; judgments in excess of that amount were to be certified by the Secretary of the Treasury to Congress for consideration. The effect of that provision on the justiciability of money claims against the United States in Article III courts was considered by the Supreme Court on two occasions:

(i) Glidden Co. v. Zdanok, 370 U.S. 530 (1962), the Court's opinion dealt with two consolidated cases, one addressing the Article III status of the former Court of Claims. In determining that the Court of Claims could constitutionally exercise Article III power, Justice Harlan's plurality opinion found claims against the United States were justiciable even when they exceeded $100,000.[5] In so doing, he referred to a study (46 Harv.L.Rev. 677, 685–86 n. 63 (1933)) that discovered only 15 instances in 70 years when Congress had refused to pay a judgment. "This historical record", he said, "surely more favorable to prevailing parties than that obtaining in private litigation, may well make us doubt whether the capacity to enforce a judgment is always indispensable for the exercise of judicial power." Justice Harlan noted that a similar insecurity marked the Court's ability to execute monetary judgments awarded by it in suits between states, given "the Court's recognition of judicial impotence to compel a levy of taxes or otherwise by process to enforce [such an] award." He thus concluded that "[i]f this Court may rely on the good faith of state governments or other public bodies to respond to its judgments, there seems to be no sound reason why the Court of Claims may not rely on the good faith of the United States."

Does Justice Harlan's reasoning effectively sanction the issuance of advisory opinions? If Congress has no binding legal obligation to comply with money judgments in excess of $100,000, in what way does a Court of Claims judgment for such a sum change the legal status quo? Certainly, Congress could appropriate the money to satisfy a claim with or without a Court of Claims' judgment finding liability.[6]

(ii) The Regional Rail Reorganization cases (Blanchette v. Connecticut General Ins. Corp., 419 U.S. 102 (1974)) involved a challenge to the constitutionality of amendments to the Bankruptcy Act enacted after eight northeastern railroads had filed for reorganization. The amendments

---

[4]   On the history of the Court of Claims, see generally Richardson, History, Jurisdiction and Practice of the Court of Claims (2d ed. 1885); Cowen, Section I: 1855–1887, in Cowen et al., The United States Court of Claims: A History 1–34 (1978). The United States Court of Federal Claims (an Article I court), along with the Court of Appeals for the Federal Circuit (an Article III court), has succeeded to the jurisdiction of the Court of Claims. For further discussion, see Symposium, *Proceedings of the 15th Judicial Conference Celebrating the 20th Anniversary of the United States Court of Federal Claims*, 71 Geo.Wash.L.Rev. 529 (2003).

[5]   In 1953, the Court of Claims was congressionally "declared to be a court established under article III", 28 U.S.C. § 171, and the departmental reference responsibility (28 U.S.C. § 1493) repealed. 67 Stat. 226. Glidden upheld the general Article III characterization.

[6]   For discussion of the relationship early in United States history between federal jurisdiction and Congress' appropriations power, see Pfander & Hunt, *Public Wrongs and Private Bills: Indemnification and Government Accountability in the Early Republic*, 85 N.Y.U.L.Rev. 1862, 1920–22 (2010).

required creditors and shareholders of the railroads to exchange their interests for stock and debt in Conrail (a government-created but private, for-profit corporation) and also required the railroads to continue operating until the exchange occurred. The Court held that the previously discussed remedy in the Court of Claims remained available to compensate for any deficiency in the value of the Conrail securities and for losses incurred by reason of the mandatory continued operation. Justice Brennan, for the Court, relied on the above-quoted language in Glidden to answer the contention that this remedy was inadequate. Justice Douglas' dissent, joined on this issue by Justice Stewart, argued that while Congress ordinarily pays judgments over $100,000 as a matter of routine, "this is an exceptional case, involving the possibility of judgments in the billions of dollars."

(c) In 1977, Congress eliminated the dollar amount limitation in the statute. The current version, 31 U.S.C. § 1304, provides generally for payment by the Secretary of the Treasury of final judgments, awards, and compromise settlements against the United States.

(d) As long as Congress makes lump sum appropriations, whether for judgments already entered or to be entered, particular judgments can be questioned only by means of an additional, separate legislative act. In the instances mentioned in the Harvard Note cited by Justice Harlan in Glidden, such a special act was the means actually used. Given its constitutional responsibility for appropriations, could Congress always defeat a particular judgment against the United States by the adoption of later legislation forbidding its payment, or might such legislation itself be unconstitutional?

(e) Many cases have upheld statutes limiting the binding effect of judgments in favor of the United States. *E.g.*, Cherokee Nation v. United States, 270 U.S. 476 (1926) (waiving effect of res judicata with respect to a former judgment concerning interest on a judgment in favor of the Cherokee Nation); Pope v. United States, 323 U.S. 1 (1944) (upholding a statute directing the Court of Claims to rehear a claim after adverse judgment for the claimant and to give judgment according to a different principle of proof); United States v. Sioux Nation of Indians, 448 U.S. 371 (1980) (upholding a statute providing for de novo review, by the Court of Claims, of Native Americans' claims against the United States without regard to defenses of res judicata or collateral estoppel based on a prior Court of Claims proceeding). Similarly, if the United States, acting through Congress, has permissibly defined a public right on which an injunctive decree rests, the Court has held that Congress has the authority to modify that public right going forward. See Pennsylvania v. Wheeling & Belmont Bridge Co., 59 U.S. (18 How.) 421 (1855) (sustaining a statute that declared a bridge not to be an obstruction to navigation, even though the Supreme Court had previously enjoined the bridge's maintenance on grounds of such obstruction).[7]

(3) Other Legislative Revision of Final Judgments. In Plaut v. Spendthrift Farm, Inc., 514 U.S. 211 (1995), the Supreme Court ruled that a federal statute directing federal courts to reopen final judgments in private lawsuits violated Article III and the separation of powers. The original action

---

[7]   In an article tracing the history and constitutional implications of the idea of "public rights," Professor Nelson notes the traditional understanding that such rights—like the right to unobstructed use of navigable waterways—were "held in common by the public at large" and "belong[ed] to the body politic". Nelson, *Adjudication in the Political Branches*, 107 Colum.L.Rev. 559, 562 (2007). Should that understanding affect Congress's ability to waive judgments based on public rights claims?

between the parties, involving allegations of securities fraud, was dismissed with prejudice after the Supreme Court held in Lampf, Pleva, Lipkind, Prupis & Petigrow v. Gilbertson, 501 U.S. 350, 364 (1991), that the suit was time-barred. The decision in the Lampf case surprised many litigants by establishing a shorter limitations period than most courts had previously applied, and Congress responded by enacting legislation that authorized reinstatement of certain actions dismissed as time-barred under Lampf. Relying on the congressional enactment, the plaintiffs moved to reopen their lawsuit. But the Supreme Court held that Congress had trenched on the judicial power. In an opinion for six Justices, Justice Scalia found that the Framers, having "lived among the ruins of a system of intermingled legislative and judicial powers," wished to insulate *final* judicial judgments—those by the highest courts possessing jurisdiction or lower court decisions from which the time for appeal has expired—from legislative revision. The Court distinguished from the case before it those in which Congress (a) had changed the applicable law while a case was pending but prior to entry of a final judgment, (b) had waived the res judicata effect of a prior judgment in favor of the government, or (c) had annulled judgments rendered by legislative (rather than Article III) courts. Justice Breyer filed a concurring opinion. Justice Stevens, joined by Justice Ginsburg, dissented.

In the absence of a final judgment dismissing a lawsuit, the Court in Plaut did not question Congress' power to enact laws establishing the retroactive liability of one private party to another or to authorize suits that otherwise would be time-barred. What purposes are served by attaching so much significance to the form of a final judgment of an Article III court?

(4) Changes of Law and Orders Mandating Ongoing Relief. The Court distinguished both Plaut and Hayburn's Case in Miller v. French, 530 U.S. 327 (2000), which sharply differentiated judgments in suits for damages from judgments providing ongoing injunctive relief. The Prison Litigation Reform Act of 1995, 110 Stat. 1321 (1996), provides in part that "in any civil action with respect to prison conditions, a defendant * * * shall be entitled to the immediate termination of any prospective relief if the relief was approved or granted in the absence of a finding by the court that the relief * * * extends no further than necessary to correct the violation of the Federal right, and is the least intrusive means necessary to correct the violation of the Federal right." 18 U.S.C. § 3626(b)(2). A further provision of the PLRA, § 3626(e)(2), establishes that a motion to terminate injunctive relief in prison cases "shall operate as a stay" of any previously entered remedial order beginning 30 days after the filing of the motion (extendable up to 90 days for "good cause"). Assuming without holding that § 3626(b)(2) establishes a substantively valid standard for the termination of injunctive remedies, Miller held that the "automatic stay" provision of § 3626(e)(2) does not infringe the judicial role under the separation of powers.

Speaking on this point for seven Justices, Justice O'Connor's opinion began by holding that the "automatic stay" provision was mandatory. Then, for a majority of five, she concluded that nothing in Plaut or Hayburn's Case restricted Congress' authority "to alter the prospective effect of previously entered injunctions." Rather, past cases established that where Congress validly alters the substantive law on which an injunction was predicated, entitlement to the injunction lapses without Congress' having impermissibly revised a "final" judgment: "The provision of prospective relief is subject to the continuing supervisory jurisdiction of the court, and therefore may be altered according to subsequent changes in the law."

Justice Souter, joined by Justice Ginsburg, concurred in the part of the Court's opinion construing the statute, but dissented from the disposition. He would have remanded the case to the district court to determine whether the "automatic stay" provision gave the court too little time to determine whether the extant injunction remained valid under the changed substantive standard. If so, he saw "a serious question"—which he thought should be decided by the district court in the first instance—"whether Congress has in practical terms assumed the judicial function." The majority, too, left open whether the time limit would be constitutionally valid, "particularly in a complex case", but treated the question as one of due process, not separation of powers, and thus as "not before [the Court]." (Justice Breyer, joined by Justice Stevens, dissented on statutory grounds.)

Does the Court's reasoning leave any doubt about the constitutional validity of § 3626(b)(2), the underlying PLRA provision that provides for termination of injunctive orders not found to be narrowly tailored to correct proven constitutional violations?

C. Judicial Revision

(1) Res Judicata Effect and the Judicial Function. Judicial judgments are obviously subject to judicial revision until they become "final" following the completion of appellate review or the expiration of the period for appeal. After the judgments of Article III courts have become final, mustn't they have at least some res judicata effect in order to avoid being forbidden advisory opinions? See Shapiro, Preclusion in Civil Actions 14 (2001). The Supreme Court has seldom had to consider how much res judicata effect is necessary.

(2) Patent and Trademark Rulings. For many years the U.S. Court of Appeals of the District of Columbia had jurisdiction of appeals from certain decisions of the Patent Office denying patent applications and disposing of claims of interference, and also from similar decisions of the Commissioner of Patents in trademark proceedings. The statute provided that the decision on appeal "shall govern the further proceedings in the case. But no opinion or decision of the court in any such case shall preclude any person interested from the right to contest the validity of such patent in any court wherein the same may be called in question." Rev.Stat. § 4914, 35 U.S.C. § 62 (1946).

In Postum Cereal Co. v. California Fig Nut Co., 272 U.S. 693 (1927), the Court held that it lacked jurisdiction under the Constitution to review a decision of the Court of Appeals of the District of Columbia in a trademark proceeding to which § 62 applied. (Since that lower court was not then viewed as limited in its jurisdiction by Article III, no question was raised as to its power under the Constitution to hear such appeals.) Chief Justice Taft wrote for the Court:

"The decision of the Court of Appeals * * * is not a judicial judgment. It is a mere administrative decision. It is merely an instruction to the Commissioner of Patents by a court which is made part of the machinery of the Patent Office for administrative purposes. In the exercise of such function, it does not enter a judgment binding parties in a case as the term case is used in the third article of the Constitution * * *. Neither the opinion nor decision of the Court of Appeals * * * precludes any person interested from having the right to contest the validity of such patent or trade-mark in any court where it may be called in question. This result prevents an appeal to this Court, which can only review judicial judgments."

Postum's holding has since eroded. In one of the consolidated cases reviewed in Glidden Co. v. Zdanok, discussed at p. 90, *supra*, Justice Harlan revisited the question decided in Postum. At issue was whether judges of the Court of Customs and Patent Appeals were Article III judges. That tribunal, established in 1929, had inherited from the Court of Appeals for the District of Columbia jurisdiction over patent appeals exercised pursuant to § 62.[8] Although the revision of the statute at least raised a question about whether appeals to the Court of Customs and Patent Appeals had the same limited preclusive effect as the ones at issue in Postum, the plurality in Glidden proceeded on the assumption that they did and then noted that limited preclusive effect "alone is insufficient to make [that court's] decisions nonjudicial."

In so concluding, the plurality relied tellingly on precedents from the naturalization context. Treating Tutun v. United States, 270 U.S. 568 (1926), p. 86, *supra*, as "controlling authority," the plurality noted:

"Mr. Justice Brandeis, the author of the Tutun opinion, had also prepared the Court's opinion in United States v. Ness, 245 U.S. 319, which upheld the Government's right to seek denaturalization even upon grounds known to and asserted unsuccessfully by it in the naturalization court. Proceedings in that court, the opinion explained, were relatively summary, with no right of appeal, whereas the denaturalization suit was plenary enough to permit full presentation of all objections and was accompanied with appeal as of right. These differences made it reasonable for Congress to allow the Government another chance to contest the applicant's eligibility.

"The decision in Tutun, coming after Ness, draws the patent and trademark jurisdiction now exercised by the Court of Customs and Patent Appeals fully within the category of cases or controversies. * * * Like naturalization proceedings in a District Court, appeals from Patent Office decisions [to the Court of Customs and Patent Appeals] are relatively summary—since the record is limited to the evidence allowed by that office— and are not themselves subject to direct review by appeal as of right. It was as reasonable for Congress, therefore, to bind only the Patent Office on appeals and to give private parties whether or not participants in such appeals a further opportunity to contest the matter on plenary records developed in litigation elsewhere. * * * We conclude that the Postum decision must be taken to be limited to the statutory scheme in existence before the transfer of patent and trademark litigation to that court."

INTRODUCTORY NOTE ON ADVERSARINESS

A proper Article III "case" or "controversy" requires genuine adversity. Even if parties to a lawsuit have nominally adverse interests, they cannot obtain a judgment from an Article III court if one party controls or dominates the other party's conduct of the litigation. As you read the case below and the

---

[8]   From 1929 to 1982 this jurisdiction was vested in the Court of Customs and Patent Appeals. Act of March 2, 1929, 45 Stat. 1476. In 1982, that court was abolished and its jurisdiction transferred to the new United States Court of Appeals for the Federal Circuit. See p. 34–35, *supra*.

material that follows, ask how consistent the Court has been in enforcing the resulting principle against "feigned" or "collusive" lawsuits. Does the pattern of enforcement and nonenforcement reveal anything about the interests that principle is meant to serve?

———

United States v. Johnson
319 U.S. 302, 63 S.Ct. 1075, 87 L.Ed. 1413 (1943).
Appeal from the District Court of the United States for the
Northern District of Indiana.

■ PER CURIAM. One Roach, a tenant of residential property belonging to appellee, brought this suit in the district court alleging that the property was within a "defense rental area" established by the Price Administrator pursuant to §§ 2(b) and 302(d) of the Emergency Price Control Act of 1942; that the Administrator had promulgated Maximum Rent Regulation No. 8 for the area; and that the rent paid by Roach and collected by appellee was in excess of the maximum fixed by the regulation. The complaint demanded judgment for treble damages and reasonable attorney's fees, as prescribed by § 205(e) of the Act. The United States, intervening pursuant to 28 U.S.C. § 401, filed a brief in support of the constitutionality of the Act, which appellee had challenged by motion to dismiss. The district court dismissed the complaint on the ground—as appears from its opinion and judgment—that the Act and the promulgation of the regulation under it were unconstitutional because Congress by the Act had unconstitutionally delegated legislative power to the Administrator.

Before entry of the order dismissing the complaint, the Government moved to reopen the case on the ground that it was collusive and did not involve a real case or controversy. This motion was denied. The Government brings the case here on appeal, and assigns as error both the ruling of the district court on the constitutionality of the Act, and its refusal to reopen and dismiss the case as collusive. * * *

The affidavit of the plaintiff, submitted by the Government on its motion to dismiss the suit as collusive, shows without contradiction that he brought the present proceeding in a fictitious name; that it was instituted as a "friendly suit" at appellee's request; that the plaintiff did not employ, pay, or even meet, the attorney who appeared of record in his behalf; that he had no knowledge who paid the $15 filing fee in the district court, but was assured by appellee that as plaintiff he would incur no expense in bringing the suit; that he did not read the complaint which was filed in his name as plaintiff; that in his conferences with the appellee and appellee's attorney of record, nothing was said concerning treble damages and he had no knowledge of the amount of the judgment prayed until he read of it in a local newspaper.

Appellee's counter-affidavit did not deny these allegations. It admitted that appellee's attorney had undertaken to procure an attorney to represent the plaintiff and had assured the plaintiff that his presence in court during the trial of the cause would not be necessary. It appears from the district court's opinion that no brief was filed on the plaintiff's behalf in that court.

The Government does not contend that, as a result of this cooperation of the two original parties to the litigation, any false or fictitious state of facts was submitted to the court. But it does insist that the affidavits disclose the absence of a genuine adversary issue between the parties, without which a court may not safely proceed to judgment, especially when it assumes the grave responsibility of passing upon the constitutional validity of legislative action. Even in a litigation where only private rights are involved, the judgment will not be allowed to stand where one of the parties has dominated the conduct of the suit by payment of the fees of both.

Here an important public interest is at stake—the validity of an Act of Congress having far-reaching effects on the public welfare in one of the most critical periods in the history of the country. That interest has been adjudicated in a proceeding in which the plaintiff has had no active participation, over which he has exercised no control, and the expense of which he has not borne. He has been only nominally represented by counsel who was selected by appellee's counsel and whom he has never seen. Such a suit is collusive because it is not in any real sense adversary. It does not assume the "honest and actual antagonistic assertion of rights" to be adjudicated—a safeguard essential to the integrity of the judicial process, and one which we have held to be indispensable to adjudication of constitutional questions by this Court. Chicago & G.T. Ry. Co. v. Wellman, 143 U.S. 339, 345. Whenever in the course of litigation such a defect in the proceedings is brought to the court's attention, it may set aside any adjudication thus procured and dismiss the cause without entering judgment on the merits. It is the court's duty to do so where, as here, the public interest has been placed at hazard by the amenities of parties to a suit conducted under the domination of only one of them. The district court should have granted the Government's motion to dismiss the suit as collusive. We accordingly vacate the judgment below with instructions to the district court to dismiss the cause on that ground alone. * * *

Judgment vacated with directions.

———

NOTE ON FEIGNED AND COLLUSIVE CASES

(1) Collusive Litigation. In principle it is easy to see why an important constitutional issue should not be determined in a proceeding in which one nominal party has dominated the conduct of the other. But why didn't the government's intervention in the Johnson case, pursuant to what is now 28 U.S.C. § 2403, cure the difficulty?

(2) Background to the Johnson Case. The Supreme Court's current approach to feigned and collusive litigation reflects an apparent departure from some of its early precedents.

(a) In at least two early cases, the Court reached the merits despite evidence that the controversy was feigned or collusive. See Hylton v. United States, 3 U.S. (3 Dall.) 171 (1796);[1] Fletcher v. Peck, 10 U.S. (6 Cranch) 87

---

[1]   Hylton was an apparently contrived suit to settle the constitutionality of a federal tax, in which the Supreme Court overlooked a number of potential obstacles to justiciability, among

(1810).[2] Indeed, according to Bloch, *The Early Role of the Attorney General in Our Constitutional Scheme: In the Beginning There Was Pragmatism*, 1989 Duke L.J. 561, 612, "[f]eigned and contrived suits were reasonably common in * * * [the 1790s], and appear to have raised no red flags". Does this history suggest any parallels to the conventional wisdom about advisory opinions? See pp. 50–54, *supra*. Isn't it predictable that it would sometimes— perhaps often—take the institutions responsible for implementing the Constitution a long period of time to come to rest on how to understand certain elements of a highly complex constitutional structure?[3]

(b) Compare Lord v. Veazie, 49 U.S. (8 How.) 251 (1850), in which Veazie had executed a deed to Lord warranting that he had certain rights claimed by third persons, and an action on the covenant by Lord against Veazie "was docketed by consent". The circuit court "gave judgment for the defendant *pro forma*, at the request of the parties, in order that the judgment and question might be brought before" the Supreme Court. On a third person's motion, the Court dismissed the case, saying that the judgment below was a nullity upon which no writ of error would lie, and that "the whole proceeding was in contempt of the court, and highly reprehensible". What accounts for the change in the Court's attitude?

(3) Test Cases. Does the rule against feigned cases defeat the planning of a test case by the parties to a real controversy? See Evers v. Dwyer, 358 U.S. 202 (1958), in which the plaintiff (who was black) boarded a bus once, refused to obey an order to sit in the rear, got off, and brought a class action for a declaratory judgment against the enforced segregation. The Court held the action justiciable despite findings by the district court that the plaintiff had ridden a city bus on only that one occasion, for the purpose of instituting the litigation.[4]

(4) Test Cases Framed by Congress. Is it constitutionally objectionable for Congress to frame a case for judicial resolution or to provide specifically for decision of a case by an Article III court?

In the puzzling case of Muskrat v. United States, 219 U.S. 346 (1911), the Court refused to entertain a suit that Congress had specifically authorized. In 1902, Congress had provided for the transfer of Cherokee property from tribal to private ownership. Every citizen of the Cherokee Nation as of September 1, 1902, was entitled to be enrolled and, upon

---

them that the government had evidently paid Hylton's lawyers. See Currie, *The Constitution in the Supreme Court: 1789–1801*, 48 U.Chi.L.Rev. 819, 854 (1981).

[2] See 1 Warren, The Supreme Court in United States History 392–99 (rev.ed.1926). But *cf.* the dissenting opinion filed in the Fletcher case by Justice Johnson, 10 U.S. (6 Cranch) at 147–48 (noting that although the case "bear[s] strong evidence" of being "feigned", "[m]y confidence * * * in the respectable gentlemen who have been engaged by the parties, has induced me to abandon my scruples, in the belief that they would never consent to impose a mere feigned case upon this court").

[3] At least some of the Constitution's architects expected as much. See, *e.g.*, The Federalist No. 37, at 229 (Madison) (Rossiter ed. 1961) ("All new laws, though penned with the greatest technical skill and passed on the fullest and most mature deliberation, are considered as more or less obscure and equivocal, until their meaning be liquidated and ascertained by a series of particular discussions and adjudications.").

[4] See also Bankamerica Corp. v. United States, 462 U.S. 122, 124 (1983), in which the Court decided an issue of federal antitrust law after noting that the proceedings before it were "companion test cases" brought by the United States against ten corporations and five individuals. *Cf.* Buchanan v. Warley, 245 U.S. 60 (1917), a challenge to a segregated housing law that had every appearance of a test case and in which the Court reached the merits without discussion of justiciability.

enrollment, to receive an allotment equal in value to 110 acres of the average allottable lands of the tribe (plus a proportionate share of any tribal funds on deposit in the U.S. Treasury and, presumably, of any land remaining after the allotments). In 1906, Congress extended the time for completion of the roll by permitting enrollment of minor children living on March 4, 1906. At the same time, it imposed new restraints on alienation by the original allottees. The Secretaries of the Interior and of the Treasury were charged with implementation of various aspects of these statutes.

In 1907, Congress authorized certain named original allottees—David Muskrat, Levi Gritts, and two others—to bring suit against the United States in the Court of Claims, with a right of appeal by either party to the Supreme Court, "to determine the validity of any acts of Congress" passed after the 1902 act that purported to diminish their rights as allottees. Attorneys' fees for plaintiffs, if they prevailed, were to be paid by the Treasury out of tribal funds. Pursuant to this statute, Muskrat and other allottees brought suit in the Court of Claims, challenging the 1906 act on the ground that it deprived them of property without due process of law. The Court of Claims rejected this contention, and the case came to the Supreme Court on appeal. The Court ordered the suit dismissed for want of jurisdiction:

"The right to declare a law unconstitutional arises because an act of Congress relied upon by one or the other of such parties in determining their rights is in conflict with the fundamental law. The exercise of this, the most important and delicate duty of this court, is not given to it as a body with revisory power over the action of Congress, but because the rights of the litigants in justiciable controversies require the court to choose between the fundamental law and a law purporting to be enacted within constitutional authority, but in fact beyond the power delegated to the legislative branch of the government. This attempt to obtain a judicial declaration of the validity of the act of Congress is not presented in a 'case' or 'controversy,' to which, under the Constitution of the United States, the judicial power alone extends. It is true the United States is made a defendant to this action, but it has no interest adverse to the claimants. The object is not to assert a property right as against the government, or to demand compensation for alleged wrongs because of action upon its part. The whole purpose of the law is to determine the constitutional validity of this class of legislation, in a suit not arising between parties concerning a property right necessarily involved in the decision in question, but in a proceeding against the government in its sovereign capacity, and concerning which the only judgment required is to settle the doubtful character of the legislation in question. Such judgment will not conclude private parties, when actual litigation brings to the court the question of the constitutionality of such legislation. In a legal sense the judgment could not be executed, and amounts in fact to no more than an expression of opinion upon the validity of the acts in question."

Why didn't Muskrat present a justiciable controversy? Assuming the plaintiffs had a plausible due process claim, whom should they have sued? Was the Court's decision influenced by doubts that a request for a declaratory judgment, without more, was a sufficient basis for the invocation of judicial power? See pp. 56–58, *supra*. If so, Muskrat would lack contemporary significance. Yet the Supreme Court continues occasionally to cite the decision, with apparent acceptance of its authority, if not actual approval. See, *e.g.*, Raines v. Byrd, 521 U.S. 811, 819 (1997); Steel Co. v.

Citizens for a Better Environment, 523 U.S. 83, 101 (1998). Was it a problem in Muskrat that Congress specifically designated both the plaintiffs and the defendant *and* provided for the payment of both of their attorneys?

(5) Parties in Agreement. If one party agrees with the position of the other, does that necessarily preclude the presence of a case or controversy?

(a) In Moore v. Charlotte-Mecklenburg Bd. of Educ., 402 U.S. 47 (1971), "confronted with the anomaly that both litigants desire precisely the same result, namely, a holding that the anti-busing statute is constitutional," the Court held that "[t]here is, therefore, no case or controversy within the meaning of Art. III of the Constitution."[5]

How does Moore square with the accepted judicial practice of entering consent decrees, resulting from a negotiated settlement among the parties, that are invested with the force of law? See, *e.g.*, New Hampshire v. Maine, 426 U.S. 363 (1976). See generally Schwarzschild, *Public Law by Private Bargain: Title VII Decrees and the Fairness of Negotiated Institutional Reform*, 1984 Duke L.J. 887, 902–03.[6] Of granting uncontested naturalization decrees? See Tutun v. United States, p. 86, *supra*. Of expunging convictions? For an illuminating discussion of issues raised by practices such as these, see Resnik, *Whose Judgment? Vacating Judgments, Preferences for Settlement, and the Role of Adjudication at the Close of the Twentieth Century*, 41 UCLA L.Rev. 1471 (1994).

(b) Issues arising from agreement among the parties have frequently drawn notice in cases involving the government. Government counsel who becomes convinced that the other side deserves to prevail can settle a case before judgment or, if the government is seeking review, withdraw the appeal or other petition. When the government has prevailed below, the problem becomes stickier; in a number of such instances the Solicitor General has confessed error in the judgment and asked the Supreme Court to vacate or reverse. These confessions are generally accepted, but the Court not infrequently recites that it does so "upon an independent examination of the record." See, *e.g.*, Pope v. United States, 392 U.S. 651 (1968); Rosengart

---

[5]   As authority, the Court cited Muskrat v. United States, Paragraph (4), *supra*. Did the Court cite Muskrat fairly?

[6]   The threat of "collusion" in framing consent decrees may be particularly acute in mass tort litigation. See, *e.g.*, Coffee, *Class Wars: The Dilemma of the Mass Tort Class Action*, 95 Colum.L.Rev. 1343 (1995), arguing that as a result of recent legal developments, corporate defendants often prefer to be sued in class actions (in order to establish an upper limit on liability, for example), and sometimes collude with accommodating plaintiffs' attorneys to arrange for such suits to be filed—and then settled on favorable terms—by nominal plaintiffs.

The Supreme Court addressed related issues concerning Fed.R.Civ.P. 23 in Amchem Products, Inc. v. Windsor, 521 U.S. 591 (1997). After holding that the existence of a settlement agreement was "relevant to class certification", the Court ruled that requirements of Rule 23 "designed to protect absentees by blocking unwarranted or overbroad class definition * * * demand undiluted, even heightened, attention in the settlement context", since there is no opportunity for the court "to adjust the class, informed by proceedings as they unfold." See also Ortiz v. Fibreboard Corp., 527 U.S. 815 (1999) (applying the heightened scrutiny of settlement classes and refusing to certify a settlement class under Rule 23(b)(3)).

The Class Action Fairness Act of 2005 sought to address some of the concerns about collusion. See Class Action Fairness Act of 2005, Pub.L.No. 109–2, 109th Cong., 1st Sess., 119 Stat. 4 (2005). For example, the Act requires that appropriate state and federal officials receive notice and an opportunity to comment on proposed class settlements. See 28 U.S.C. § 1715. See also S.Rep.No. 14, 109th Cong., 1st Sess. 35 (2005), as reprinted in 2005 U.S.C.C.A.N. 3, 34 (arguing that the notice required by § 1715 "will * * * deter collusion between class counsel and defendants to craft settlements that do not benefit the injured parties."). For further discussion of the Act, see Chap. XIII, Sec. 2, *infra*.

v. Laird, 405 U.S. 908 (1972). In Casey v. United States, 343 U.S. 808 (1952), the Court, without an independent examination, accepted a confession of error that there had been an unreasonable search and seizure, saying that to do so "in this case * * * would not involve the establishment of any precedent." Three justices dissented vigorously, arguing that "[w]hatever action we take is a precedent" and that "[o]nce we accept a confession of error at face value and make it the controlling and decisive factor in our decision, we no longer administer a system of justice under a government of laws." See also Mariscal v. United States, 449 U.S. 405 (1981); Watts v. United States, 422 U.S. 1032 (1975); Note, 82 Geo.L.J. 2079 (1994) (surveying government confessions of error).

(c) What are the justiciability implications of the executive's decision to enforce a statute whose constitutionality it will not defend? In United States v. Windsor, 133 S.Ct. 2675 (2013), the plaintiff, who had entered a lawful same-sex marriage, challenged the constitutionality of § 3 of the Defense of Marriage Act (DOMA), 110 Stat. 2419, which excluded partners in a same-sex marriage from the definition of "spouse" for federal law purposes. This provision rendered Windsor ineligible for the "surviving spouse" exclusion from the federal estate tax. Windsor paid $363,053 in federal estate taxes under protest and filed suit in federal district court challenging DOMA and seeking a refund.

While the case was pending, the President instructed the Department of Justice not to defend the constitutionality of § 3 of DOMA. He simultaneously directed the executive branch to continue to enforce § 3 and thus to refuse to provide the refund. The President's directive made clear that this approach was designed to "recogniz[e] the judiciary as the final arbiter" of constitutionality. The House committee that advises the Speaker of the House on legal matters—the Bipartisan Legal Advisory Group (BLAG)—intervened in the district court to defend the statute's constitutionality.

The district court found § 3 unconstitutional and ordered the Treasury to refund the plaintiff's estate tax payments. Although the United States agreed with the merits of the district court's decision, it refused to comply with the judgment and appealed to the Second Circuit. After the Second Circuit affirmed, the United States sought review in the Supreme Court.

In an opinion by Justice Kennedy (joined by Justices Ginsburg, Breyer, Sotomayor, and Kagan), the Court found that a justiciable controversy existed between Windsor and the United States. The Court reasoned that whatever commonality the parties had concerning the law, the government's continued enforcement of § 3 meant that Windsor's "injury (failure to obtain a refund allegedly required by law) was concrete, persisting, and unredressed." The United States continued to have a justiciable interest in the suit as well; however much the government might welcome a ruling that § 3 is unconstitutional, such a ruling would inflict injury upon it by requiring a refund of several hundred thousand dollars in taxes.

In the Court's view, the parties' agreement that DOMA was unconstitutional implicated only the "prudential limits" that the judiciary has traditionally placed on the exercise of its own power. See pp. 76–77, *supra*, & pp. 156–158, *infra*. Thus, the Court needed only to assure itself that the case presented the concrete adverseness necessary to ensure sharp presentation of the issues. Here, the fact that the attorneys for BLAG presented "a substantial argument" for DOMA's constitutionality fully addressed the "prudential concerns" that might otherwise counsel against hearing a case in this unusual posture.[7] The Court added that a failure to address the question presented would leave the district courts in "94 districts throughout the Nation * * * without precedential guidance not only in tax refund suits but also in cases involving the whole of DOMA's sweep involving over 1,000 federal statutes and a myriad of federal regulations." Finally, Justice Kennedy's opinion emphasized that "if the Executive's agreement with a plaintiff that a law is unconstitutional is enough to preclude judicial review, then the Supreme Court's primary role in determining the constitutionality of a law that has inflicted real injury on a plaintiff * * * would become only secondary to the President's."

In a dissent joined by Chief Justice Roberts and Justice Thomas, Justice Scalia wrote that "[i]n the more than two centuries that this Court has existed * * *, we have never suggested that we have the power to decide a question when every party agrees with both its nominal opponent *and the court below* on that question's answer." In Justice Scalia's view, the matter should not have come before the judiciary in this posture, and the proper course for the government was to decline to enforce a statute that it regarded as unconstitutional. He concluded by stressing that Justice Kennedy's concern about preserving the Court's law declaration function conflicted with the founders' vision of the Court as a dispute resolver and reflected an ahistorical "desire to place this Court at the center of the Nation's life."

---

3. SOME PROBLEMS OF STANDING TO SUE

A. PLAINTIFFS' STANDING

INTRODUCTORY NOTE

Standing is one of the key components of the modern definition of the judicial power to decide "cases" or "controversies." Standing doctrine rations the exercise of judicial power by determining *who* is entitled to invoke the power of the federal courts to decide cases. In particular, a plaintiff wishing to sue in federal court must be able to identify a concrete injury (a) that he or she has sustained, (b) that the defendant has caused, and (c) that a properly framed judicial decree can redress. Despite the clarity with which the Court articulates the elements of standing, the Constitution contains no Standing Clause. Nor, as it turns out, does the standing doctrine, at least as presently conceived, run deep in our history. Among the many questions raised by the following materials are these: What structural, functional, and

---

[7] Having determined that the suit between Windsor and the United States satisfied constitutional and prudential requirements for standings, the Court found it unnecessary to determine whether BLAG would have standing in its own right. Because Justice Scalia and Alito found that there was no justiciable controversy between Windsor and the United States, both found it necessary to address the question whether BLAG had standing to oppose Windsor on appeal. For discussion, see pp. 131–132, *infra*.

other arguments might justify the Court's current doctrine? How much do conventional rationales for standing doctrine help us evaluate how to apply the doctrine in particular cases?

Fairchild v. Hughes

258 U.S. 126, 42 S.Ct. 274, 66 L.Ed. 499 (1922).
Appeal from the Court of Appeals of the District of Columbia.

■ MR. JUSTICE BRANDEIS delivered the opinion of the Court.

On July 7, 1920, Charles S. Fairchild, of New York, brought this suit in the Supreme Court of the District of Columbia against the Secretary of State and the Attorney General. The prayers of the bill are that "the so-called Suffrage Amendment [the Nineteenth to the federal Constitution] be declared unconstitutional and void"; that the Secretary of State be restrained from issuing any proclamation declaring that it has been ratified; and that the Attorney General be restrained from enforcing it. There is also a prayer for general relief and for an interlocutory injunction. The plaintiff, and others on whose behalf he sues, are citizens of the United States, taxpayers and members of the American Constitutional League, a voluntary association which describes itself as engaged in diffusing "knowledge as to the fundamental principles of the American Constitution, and especially that which gives to each state the right to determine for itself the question as to who should exercise the elective franchise therein."

The claim to relief was rested upon the following allegations: The Legislatures of 34 of the states have passed resolutions purporting to ratify the Suffrage Amendment; and from one other state the Secretary of State of the United States has received a certificate to that effect purporting to come from the proper officer. The proposed amendment cannot, for reasons stated, be made a part of the Constitution through ratification by the Legislatures, and there are also specific reasons why the resolutions already adopted in several of the states are inoperative. But the Secretary has declared that he is without power to examine into the validity of alleged acts of ratification, and that, upon receiving from one additional state the customary certificate, he will issue a proclamation declaring that the Suffrage Amendment has been adopted. Furthermore, "a force bill" has been introduced in the Senate, which provides fine and imprisonment for any person who refuses to allow women to vote, and, if the bill is enacted, the Attorney General will be required to enforce its provisions. The threatened proclamation of the adoption of the amendment would not be conclusive of its validity, but it would lead election officers to permit women to vote in states whose Constitutions limit suffrage to men. This would prevent ascertainment of the wishes of the legally qualified voters, and elections, state and federal, would be void. Free citizens would be deprived of their right to have such elections duly held, the effectiveness of their votes would be diminished, and election expenses would be nearly doubled. Thus irremediable mischief would result. * * *

Plaintiff's alleged interest in the question submitted is not such as to afford a basis for this proceeding. It is frankly a proceeding to have the

Nineteenth Amendment declared void. In form it is a bill in equity; but it is not a case, within the meaning of section 2 of article 3 of the Constitution, which confers judicial power on the federal courts, for no claim of plaintiff is "brought before the court[s] for determination by such regular proceedings as are established by law or custom for the protection or enforcement of rights, or the prevention, redress, or punishment of wrongs." See In re Pacific Railway Commission (C. C.) 32 Fed. 241, 255 (1887), quoted in Muskrat v. United States, 219 U.S. 346, 357 (1911). The alleged wrongful act of the Secretary of State, said to be threatening, is the issuing of a proclamation which plaintiff asserts will be vain, but will mislead election officers. The alleged wrongful act of the Attorney General, said to be threatening, is the enforcement, as against election officers, of the penalties to be imposed by a contemplated act of Congress which plaintiff asserts would be unconstitutional. * * * Plaintiff has only the right, possessed by every citizen, to require that the government be administered according to law and that the public moneys be not wasted. Obviously this general right does not entitle a private citizen to institute in the federal courts a suit to secure by indirection a determination whether a statute, if passed, or a constitutional amendment, about to be adopted, will be valid.

———

Allen v. Wright

468 U.S. 737, 104 S.Ct. 3315, 82 L.Ed.2d 556 (1984).
Certiorari to the United States Court of Appeals for the District of Columbia Circuit.

■ JUSTICE O'CONNOR delivered the opinion of the Court.

Parents of black public school children allege in this nation-wide class action that the Internal Revenue Service (IRS) has not adopted sufficient standards and procedures to fulfill its obligation to deny tax-exempt status to racially discriminatory private schools. They assert that the IRS thereby harms them directly and interferes with the ability of their children to receive an education in desegregated public schools. The issue before us is whether plaintiffs have standing to bring this suit. We hold that they do not.

I

The IRS denies tax-exempt status under §§ 501(a) and (c)(3) of the Internal Revenue Code, 26 U.S.C. §§ 501(a) and (c)(3)—and hence eligibility to receive charitable contributions deductible from income taxes under §§ 170(a)(1) and (c)(2) of the Code, 26 U.S.C. §§ 170(a)(1) and (c)(2)—to racially discriminatory private schools.[1] The IRS policy requires that a school applying for tax-exempt status show that it [does not engage in discrimination. Moreover,] the IRS has established guidelines and procedures for determining whether a particular school is

---

[1] As the Court explained last Term in Bob Jones University v. United States, 461 U.S. 574, 579 (1983), the IRS announced this policy in 1970 and formally adopted it in 1971. This change in prior policy was prompted by litigation over tax exemptions for racially discriminatory private schools in the State of Mississippi, litigation that resulted in the entry of an injunction against the IRS largely if not entirely coextensive with the position the IRS had voluntarily adopted. * * *

in fact racially nondiscriminatory. Failure to comply with the guidelines "will ordinarily result in the proposed revocation of" tax-exempt status.

* * * [T]he school must annually certify, under penalty of perjury, compliance with [the applicable] requirements. * * *

In 1976 respondents challenged these guidelines and procedures in a suit filed in Federal District Court against the Secretary of the Treasury and the Commissioner of Internal Revenue. The plaintiffs named in the complaint are parents of black children who, at the time the complaint was filed, were attending public schools in seven States in school districts undergoing desegregation. They brought this nation-wide class action "on behalf of themselves and their children, and * * * on behalf of all other parents of black children attending public school systems undergoing, or which may in the future undergo, desegregation pursuant to court order [or] HEW regulations and guidelines, under state law, or voluntarily." They estimated that the class they seek to represent includes several million persons.

Respondents allege in their complaint that many racially segregated private schools were created or expanded in their communities at the time the public schools were undergoing desegregation. According to the complaint, many such private schools, including 17 schools or school systems identified by name in the complaint (perhaps some 30 schools in all), receive tax exemptions either directly or through the tax-exempt status of "umbrella" organizations that operate or support the schools. Respondents allege that, despite the IRS policy of denying tax-exempt status to racially discriminatory private schools and despite the IRS guidelines and procedures for implementing that policy, some of the tax-exempt racially segregated private schools created or expanded in desegregating districts in fact have racially discriminatory policies. [App.] 17–18 (IRS permits "schools to receive tax exemptions merely on the basis of adopting and certifying—but not implementing—a policy of nondiscrimination"); id., at 25 (same).[11] Respondents allege that the IRS grant of tax exemptions to such racially discriminatory schools is unlawful.[12]

Respondents allege that the challenged Government conduct harms them in two ways. The challenged conduct

"(a) constitutes tangible federal financial aid and other support for racially segregated educational institutions, and

"(b) fosters and encourages the organization, operation and expansion of institutions providing racially segregated educational opportunities for white children avoiding attendance in desegregating public school districts and thereby interferes with the efforts of federal courts, HEW and local

---

[11] * * * Contrary to Justice Brennan's statement, the complaint does not allege that each desegregating district in which they reside contains one or more racially discriminatory private schools unlawfully receiving a tax exemption.

[12] The complaint alleges that the challenged IRS conduct violates several laws: § 501(c)(3) of the Internal Revenue Code, 26 U.S.C. § 501(c)(3); Title VI of the Civil Rights Act of 1964, 42 U.S.C. § 2000d et seq.; 42 U.S.C. § 1981; and the Fifth and Fourteenth Amendments to the United States Constitution.

Last Term, in Bob Jones University v. United States, 461 U.S. 574 (1983), the Court concluded that racially discriminatory private schools do not qualify for a tax exemption under § 501(c)(3) of the Internal Revenue Code.

school authorities to desegregate public school districts which
have been operating racially dual school systems."

Thus, respondents do not allege that their children have been the victims
of discriminatory exclusion from the schools whose tax exemptions they
challenge as unlawful. Indeed, they have not alleged * * * that their
children have ever applied or would ever apply to any private school.
Rather, respondents claim a direct injury from the mere fact of the
challenged Government conduct and, as indicated by the restriction of
the plaintiff class to parents of children in desegregating school districts,
injury to their children's opportunity to receive a desegregated education.
The latter injury is traceable to the IRS grant of tax exemptions to
racially discriminatory schools, respondents allege, chiefly because
contributions to such schools are deductible from income taxes * * * and
the "deductions facilitate the raising of funds to organize new schools and
expand existing schools in order to accommodate white students avoiding
attendance in desegregating public school districts."

Respondents * * * ask for a declaratory judgment that the challenged
IRS tax-exemption practices are unlawful. They also ask for an
injunction requiring the IRS to deny tax exemptions to a considerably
broader class of private schools than the class of racially discriminatory
private schools, [including those with "insubstantial" minority
populations that were "established or expanded at or about the same
time" as local public schools were desegregating]. * * * Finally,
respondents ask for an order directing the IRS to replace its 1975
guidelines with standards consistent with the requested injunction.

* * * [P]rogress in the lawsuit was stalled for several years. During
this period, the IRS reviewed its challenged policies and proposed new
Revenue Procedures to tighten requirements for eligibility for tax-
exempt status for private schools. In 1979, however, Congress blocked
any strengthening of the IRS guidelines at least until October 1980.[16]
The District Court thereupon considered and granted the defendants'
motion to dismiss the complaint, concluding that respondents lack
standing, that the judicial task proposed by respondents is
inappropriately intrusive for a federal court, and that awarding the
requested relief would be contrary to the will of Congress expressed in
the 1979 ban on strengthening IRS guidelines.

The United States Court of Appeals for the District of Columbia
Circuit reversed, concluding that respondents have standing to maintain
this lawsuit. * * *

We granted certiorari, and now reverse.

---

[16] [Provisions in appropriations acts] specifically forbade the use of funds to carry out the
IRS's proposed Revenue Procedures * * * [and] more generally forbade the use of funds to make
the requirements for tax-exempt status of private schools more stringent than those in effect
prior to the IRS's proposal of its new Revenue Procedures.

These provisions expired on October 1, 1980, but * * * were reinstated for the period
December 16, 1980, through September 30, 1981. For fiscal year 1982, Congress specifically
denied funding for carrying out not only administrative actions but also court orders entered
after the date of the IRS's proposal of its first revised Revenue Procedure. No such spending
restrictions are currently in force.

II

A

Article III of the Constitution confines the federal courts to adjudicating actual "cases" and "controversies." As the Court explained in Valley Forge Christian College v. Americans United for Separation of Church and State, Inc., 454 U.S. 464, 471–476 (1982), the "case or controversy" requirement defines with respect to the Judicial Branch the idea of separation of powers on which the Federal Government is founded. The several doctrines that have grown up to elaborate that requirement are "founded in concern about the proper—and properly limited—role of the courts in a democratic society." Warth v. Seldin, 422 U.S. 490, 498 (1975).

> "All of the doctrines that cluster about Article III—not only standing but mootness, ripeness, political question, and the like—relate in part, and in different though overlapping ways, to an idea, which is more than an intuition but less than a rigorous and explicit theory, about the constitutional and prudential limits to the powers of an unelected, unrepresentative judiciary in our kind of government." Vander Jagt v. O'Neill, 699 F.2d 1166, 1178–1179 ([D.C.Cir.] 1983) (Bork, J., concurring).

The case-or-controversy doctrines state fundamental limits on federal judicial power in our system of government.

The Art. III doctrine that requires a litigant to have "standing" to invoke the power of a federal court is perhaps the most important of these doctrines. "In essence the question of standing is whether the litigant is entitled to have the court decide the merits of the dispute or of particular issues." Warth v. Seldin, *supra*, at 498. Standing doctrine embraces several judicially self-imposed limits on the exercise of federal jurisdiction, such as the general prohibition on a litigant's raising another person's legal rights, the rule barring adjudication of generalized grievances more appropriately addressed in the representative branches, and the requirement that a plaintiff's complaint fall within the zone of interests protected by the law invoked. The requirement of standing, however, has a core component derived directly from the Constitution. A plaintiff must allege personal injury fairly traceable to the defendant's allegedly unlawful conduct and likely to be redressed by the requested relief.

Like the prudential component, the constitutional component of standing doctrine incorporates concepts concededly not susceptible of precise definition. The injury alleged must be, for example, "distinct and palpable," Gladstone, Realtors v. Village of Bellwood, 441 U.S. 91, 100 (1979) (quoting Warth v. Seldin, *supra*, at 501), and not "abstract" or "conjectural" or "hypothetical," Los Angeles v. Lyons, 461 U.S. 95, 101–102 (1983). The injury must be "fairly" traceable to the challenged action, and relief from the injury must be "likely" to follow from a favorable decision. See Simon v. Eastern Kentucky Welfare Rights Org., 426 U.S. [26,] 38, 41 [(1976)]. These terms cannot be defined so as to make application of the constitutional standing requirement a mechanical exercise.

The absence of precise definitions, however, * * * hardly leaves courts at sea in applying the law of standing. Like most legal notions, the standing concepts have gained considerable definition from developing case law. * * * More important, the law of Art. III standing is built on a single basic idea—the idea of separation of powers. It is this fact which makes possible the gradual clarification of the law through judicial application. * * *

Determining standing in a particular case may be facilitated by clarifying principles or even clear rules developed in prior cases. Typically, however, the standing inquiry requires careful judicial examination of a complaint's allegations to ascertain whether the particular plaintiff is entitled to an adjudication of the particular claims asserted. Is the injury too abstract, or otherwise not appropriate, to be considered judicially cognizable? Is the line of causation between the illegal conduct and injury too attenuated? Is the prospect of obtaining relief from the injury as a result of a favorable ruling too speculative? These questions and any others relevant to the standing inquiry must be answered by reference to the Art. III notion that federal courts may exercise power only "in the last resort, and as a necessity," Chicago & Grand Trunk R. Co. v. Wellman, 143 U.S. 339, 345 (1892), and only when adjudication is "consistent with a system of separated powers and [the dispute is one] traditionally thought to be capable of resolution through the judicial process," Flast v. Cohen, 392 U.S. 83, 97 (1968).

B

Respondents allege two injuries in their complaint to support their standing to bring this lawsuit. First, they say that they are harmed directly by the mere fact of Government financial aid to discriminatory private schools. Second, they say that the federal tax exemptions to racially discriminatory private schools in their communities impair their ability to have their public schools desegregated. * * *

Alleged Injury

We conclude that neither suffices to support respondents' standing. The first fails under clear precedents of this Court because it does not constitute a judicially cognizable injury. The second fails because the alleged injury is not fairly traceable to the assertedly unlawful conduct of the IRS.[19]

1

Respondents' first claim of injury * * * might be a claim simply to have the Government avoid the violation of law alleged in respondents' complaint. Alternatively, it might be a claim of stigmatic injury, or denigration, suffered by all members of a racial group when the

Claim 1

---

[19] The "fairly traceable" and "redressability" components of the constitutional standing inquiry were initially articulated by this Court as "two facets of a single causation requirement." C. Wright, Law of Federal Courts § 13, p. 68, n. 43 (4th ed. 1983). To the extent there is a difference, it is that the former examines the causal connection between the assertedly unlawful conduct and the alleged injury, whereas the latter examines the causal connection between the alleged injury and the judicial relief requested. Cases such as this, in which the relief requested goes well beyond the violation of law alleged, illustrate why it is important to keep the inquiries separate if the "redressability" component is to focus on the requested relief. Even if the relief respondents request might have a substantial effect on the desegregation of public schools, whatever deficiencies exist in the opportunities for desegregated education for respondents' children might not be traceable to IRS violations of law—grants of tax exemptions to racially discriminatory schools in respondents' communities.

Government discriminates on the basis of race. Under neither interpretation is this claim of injury judicially cognizable.

This Court has repeatedly held that an asserted right to have the Government act in accordance with law is not sufficient, standing alone, to confer jurisdiction on a federal court. In Schlesinger v. Reservists Committee to Stop the War, 418 U.S. 208 (1974), for example, the Court rejected a claim of citizen standing to challenge Armed Forces Reserve commissions held by Members of Congress as violating the Incompatibility Clause of Art. I, § 6, of the Constitution. As citizens, the Court held, plaintiffs alleged nothing but "the abstract injury in nonobservance of the Constitution. . . . " More recently, in Valley Forge, *supra*, we rejected a claim of standing to challenge a Government conveyance of property to a religious institution. Insofar as the plaintiffs relied simply on "their shared individuated right" to a Government that made no law respecting an establishment of religion, we held that plaintiffs had not alleged a judicially cognizable injury. * * *

Neither do they have standing to litigate their claims based on the stigmatizing injury often caused by racial discrimination. There can be no doubt that this sort of noneconomic injury is one of the most serious consequences of discriminatory government action and is sufficient in some circumstances to support standing. Our cases make clear, however, that such injury accords a basis for standing only to "those persons who are personally denied equal treatment" by the challenged discriminatory conduct. * * *

If [an] abstract stigmatic injury were cognizable, standing would extend nationwide to all members of the particular racial groups against which the Government was alleged to be discriminating by its grant of a tax exemption to a racially discriminatory school, regardless of the location of that school. * * * A black person in Hawaii could challenge the grant of a tax exemption to a racially discriminatory school in Maine. Recognition of standing in such circumstances would transform the federal courts into "no more than a vehicle for the vindication of the value interests of concerned bystanders." United States v. SCRAP, 412 U.S. 669, 687 (1973). Constitutional limits on the role of the federal courts preclude such a transformation.

2

It is in their complaint's second claim of injury that respondents allege harm to a concrete, personal interest that can support standing in some circumstances. The injury they identify—their children's diminished ability to receive an education in a racially integrated school—is, beyond any doubt, not only judicially cognizable but, as shown by cases from Brown v. Board of Education, 347 U.S. 483 (1954), to Bob Jones University v. United States, 461 U.S. 574 (1983), one of the most serious injuries recognized in our legal system. Despite the constitutional importance of curing the injury alleged by respondents, however, the federal judiciary may not redress it unless standing requirements are met. In this case, respondents' second claim of injury cannot support standing because the injury alleged is not fairly traceable to the Government conduct respondents challenge as unlawful.[22]

---

[22] Respondents' stigmatic injury, though not sufficient for standing in the abstract form in which their complaint asserts it, is judicially cognizable to the extent that respondents are

The illegal conduct challenged by respondents is the IRS's grant of tax exemptions to some racially discriminatory schools. The line of causation between that conduct and desegregation of respondents' schools is attenuated at best. From the perspective of the IRS, the injury to respondents is highly indirect and "results from the independent action of some third party not before the court." Simon v. Eastern Kentucky Welfare Rights Org., 426 U.S., at 42. * * *

The diminished ability of respondents' children to receive a desegregated education would be fairly traceable to unlawful IRS grants of tax exemptions only if there were enough racially discriminatory private schools receiving tax exemptions in respondents' communities for withdrawal of those exemptions to make an appreciable difference in public school integration. Respondents have made no such allegation. It is, first, uncertain how many racially discriminatory private schools are in fact receiving tax exemptions. Moreover, it is entirely speculative, as respondents themselves conceded in the Court of Appeals, whether withdrawal of a tax exemption from any particular school would lead the school to change its policies. It is just as speculative whether any given parent of a child attending such a private school would decide to transfer the child to public school as a result of any changes in educational or financial policy made by the private school once it was threatened with loss of tax-exempt status. It is also pure speculation whether, in a particular community, a large enough number of the numerous relevant school officials and parents would reach decisions that collectively would have a significant impact on the racial composition of the public schools.

The links in the chain of causation between the challenged Government conduct and the asserted injury are far too weak for the chain as a whole to sustain respondents' standing. * * *

The idea of separation of powers that underlies standing doctrine explains why our cases preclude the conclusion that respondents' alleged injury "fairly can be traced to the challenged action" of the IRS. That conclusion would pave the way generally for suits challenging, not specifically identifiable Government violations of law, but the particular programs agencies establish to carry out their legal obligations. Such suits, even when premised on allegations of several instances of violations of law, are rarely if ever appropriate for federal-court adjudication. * * *

The same concern for the proper role of the federal courts is reflected in cases like O'Shea v. Littleton, 414 U.S. 488 (1974), Rizzo v. Goode, 423 U.S. 362 (1976), and Los Angeles v. Lyons, 461 U.S. 95 (1983). In all three cases plaintiffs sought injunctive relief directed at certain systemwide law enforcement practices. The Court held in each case that, absent an allegation of a specific threat of being subject to the challenged practices,

---

personally subject to discriminatory treatment. See Heckler v. Mathews, 465 U.S. 728, 739–740 (1984) [involving the denial of monetary benefits on an allegedly discriminatory basis]. The stigmatic injury thus requires identification of some concrete interest with respect to which respondents are personally subject to discriminatory treatment. That interest must independently satisfy the causation requirement of standing doctrine.

* * * In this litigation, respondents identify only one interest that they allege is being discriminatorily impaired—their interest in desegregated public school education. Respondents' asserted stigmatic injury, therefore, is sufficient to support their standing in this litigation only if their school-desegregation injury independently meets the causation requirement of standing doctrine.

plaintiffs had no standing to ask for an injunction. Animating this Court's holdings was the principle that "[a] federal court * * * is not the proper forum to press" general complaints about the way in which government goes about its business.

Case-or-controversy considerations, the Court observed in O'Shea v. Littleton, *supra*, at 499, "obviously shade into those determining whether the complaint states a sound basis for equitable relief." The latter set of considerations should therefore inform our judgment about whether respondents have standing. Most relevant to this case is the principle articulated in Rizzo v. Goode, *supra*, at 378–379:

> "When a plaintiff seeks to enjoin the activity of a government agency, even within a unitary court system, his case must contend with 'the well-established rule that the Government has traditionally been granted the widest latitude in the' dispatch of its own internal affairs."

When transported into the Art. III context, that principle, grounded as it is in the idea of separation of powers, counsels against recognizing standing in a case brought, not to enforce specific legal obligations whose violation works a direct harm, but to seek a restructuring of the apparatus established by the Executive Branch to fulfill its legal duties. The Constitution, after all, assigns to the Executive Branch, and not to the Judicial Branch, the duty to "take Care that the Laws be faithfully executed." U.S. Const., Art. II, § 3. We could not recognize respondents' standing in this case without running afoul of that structural principle.[26]

C

The Court of Appeals relied for its contrary conclusion on Gilmore v. City of Montgomery, 417 U.S. 556 (1974), [and] Norwood v. Harrison, 413 U.S. 455 (1973) * * *. * * * [No case], however, requires that we find standing in this lawsuit.

In Gilmore v. City of Montgomery, *supra*, the plaintiffs * * * alleged that the city was violating [their] equal protection right by permitting racially discriminatory private schools and other groups to use the public parks. The Court recognized plaintiffs' standing to challenge this city policy insofar as the policy permitted the exclusive use of the parks by racially discriminatory private schools * * *.

Standing in Gilmore thus rested on an allegation of direct deprivation of a right to equal use of the parks. * * *

In Norwood v. Harrison, *supra*, parents of public school children in Tunica County, Miss., filed a statewide class action challenging the State's provision of textbooks to students attending racially discriminatory private schools in the State. The Court held the State's practice unconstitutional because it breached "the State's acknowledged duty to establish a unitary school system." The Court did not expressly address the basis for the plaintiffs' standing.

---

[26] We disagree with Justice Stevens' suggestions that separation of powers principles merely underlie standing requirements, have no role to play in giving meaning to those requirements, and should be considered only under a distinct justiciability analysis. Moreover, our analysis of this case does not rest on the more general proposition that no consequence of the allocation of administrative enforcement resources is judicially cognizable. Rather, we rely on separation of powers principles to interpret the "fairly traceable" component of the standing requirement.

In Gilmore, however, the Court identified the basis for standing in Norwood: "The plaintiffs in Norwood were parties to a school desegregation order and the relief they sought was directly related to the concrete injury they suffered." 417 U.S., at 571, n.10. Through the school-desegregation decree, the plaintiffs had acquired a right to have the State "steer clear" of any perpetuation of the racially dual school system that it had once sponsored. 413 U.S., at 467. The interest acquired was judicially cognizable because it was a personal interest, created by law, in having the State refrain from taking specific actions. * * *

III

"The necessity that the plaintiff who seeks to invoke judicial power stand to profit in some personal interest remains an Art. III requirement." Simon v. Eastern Kentucky Welfare Rights Org., 426 U.S., at 39. Respondents have not met this fundamental requirement. The judgment of the Court of Appeals is accordingly reversed, and the injunction issued by that court is vacated.

It is so ordered.

■ JUSTICE MARSHALL took no part in the decision of these cases.

■ JUSTICE BRENNAN, dissenting.

* * *

II

A

In these cases, the respondents have alleged at least one type of injury that satisfies the constitutional requirement of "distinct and palpable injury."[3] In particular, they claim that the IRS's grant of tax-exempt status to racially discriminatory private schools directly injures their children's opportunity and ability to receive a desegregated education. * * *

The Court acknowledges that this alleged injury is sufficient to satisfy constitutional standards. * * *

B

* * * Viewed in light of the injuries they claim, the respondents have alleged a direct causal relationship between the Government action they challenge and the injury they suffer: their inability to receive an education in a racially integrated school is directly and adversely affected by the tax-exempt status granted by the IRS to racially discriminatory schools in their respective school districts. Common sense alone would recognize that the elimination of tax-exempt status for racially

---

[3] Because I conclude that the second injury alleged by the respondents is sufficient to satisfy constitutional requirements, I do not need to reach what the Court labels the "stigmatic injury." I note, however, that the Court has mischaracterized this claim of injury * * *. In particular, the respondents have not simply alleged that, as blacks, they have suffered the denigration injury "suffered by all members of a racial group when the Government discriminates on the basis of race." Rather, the complaint, fairly read, limits the claim of stigmatic injury from illegal governmental action to black children attending public schools in districts that are currently desegregating yet contain discriminatory private schools benefiting from illegal tax exemptions. Thus, the Court's "parade of horribles" concerning black plaintiffs from Hawaii challenging tax exemptions granted to schools in Maine is completely irrelevant for purposes of Art. III standing in this action. Indeed, even if relevant, that criticism would go to the scope of the class certified or the relief granted in the lawsuit, issues that were not reached by the District Court or the Court of Appeals and are not now before this Court.

discriminatory private schools would serve to lessen the impact that those institutions have in defeating efforts to desegregate the public schools.

The Court admits that "[t]he diminished ability of respondents' children to receive a desegregated education would be fairly traceable to unlawful IRS grants of tax exemptions . . . if there were enough racially discriminatory private schools receiving tax exemptions in respondents' communities for withdrawal of those exemptions to make an appreciable difference in public school integration," but concludes that "[r]espondents have made no such allegation." With all due respect, the Court has either misread the complaint or is improperly requiring the respondents to prove their case on the merits in order to defeat a motion to dismiss. For example, the respondents specifically refer by name to at least 32 private schools that discriminate on the basis of race and yet continue to benefit illegally from tax-exempt status. Eighteen of those schools * * * are located in the city of Memphis, Tenn., which has been the subject of several court orders to desegregate. * * * [T]here can be little doubt that the respondents have identified communities containing "enough racially discriminatory private schools receiving tax exemptions * * * to make an appreciable difference in public school integration."[6]

Moreover, the Court has previously recognized the existence, and constitutional significance, of such direct relationships between unlawfully segregated school districts and government support for racially discriminatory private schools in those districts. In Norwood v. Harrison, 413 U.S. 455 (1973), for example, we considered a Mississippi program that provided textbooks to students attending both public and private schools, without regard to whether any participating school had racially discriminatory policies. In declaring that program constitutionally invalid, we * * * [observed]:

"The District Court laid great stress on the absence of a showing by appellants that 'any child enrolled in private school, if deprived of free textbooks, would withdraw from private school and subsequently enroll in the public schools.' * * * *We do not agree with the District Court in its analysis of the legal consequences of this uncertainty, for the Constitution does not permit the State to aid discrimination even when there is no precise causal relationship between state financial aid to a private school and the continued well-being of that school. A State may not grant the type of tangible financial aid here involved if that aid has a significant tendency to facilitate, reinforce, and support private discrimination.*" Id., at 465–466 (citations omitted) (emphasis added).

The Court purports to distinguish Norwood from the present litigation because "[t]he plaintiffs in Norwood were parties to a school desegregation order" and therefore "had acquired a right to have the State 'steer clear' of any perpetuation of the racially dual school system that it had once sponsored," whereas the "[r]espondents in this lawsuit * * * have no injunctive rights against the IRS that are allegedly being harmed." * * * Given that many of the school districts identified in the

---

[6] Even if the Court were correct in its conclusion that there is an insufficient factual basis alleged in the complaint, the proper disposition would be to remand in order to afford the respondents an opportunity to amend their complaint.

respondents' complaint have also been the subject of court-ordered integration, the standing inquiry in these cases should not differ. And, although the respondents do not specifically allege that they are named parties to any outstanding desegregation orders, that is undoubtedly due to the passage of time since the orders were issued, and not to any difference in the harm they suffer.

Even accepting the relevance of the Court's distinction, moreover, that distinction goes to the injury suffered by the respective plaintiffs, and not to the causal connection between the harm alleged and the governmental action challenged. The causal relationship existing in Norwood between the alleged harm (*i.e.*, interference with the plaintiffs' injunctive rights to a desegregated school system) and the challenged governmental action (*i.e.*, free textbooks provided to racially discriminatory schools) is indistinguishable from the causal relationship existing in the present cases, unless the Court intends to distinguish the lending of textbooks from the granting of tax-exempt status. * * *

III

More than one commentator has noted that the causation component of the Court's standing inquiry is no more than a poor disguise for the Court's view of the merits of the underlying claims. The Court today does nothing to avoid that criticism. * * *

■ JUSTICE STEVENS, with whom JUSTICE BLACKMUN joins, dissenting.

Three propositions are clear to me: (1) respondents have adequately alleged "injury in fact"; (2) their injury is fairly traceable to the conduct that they claim to be unlawful; and (3) the "separation of powers" principle does not create a jurisdictional obstacle to the consideration of the merits of their claim.

I

Respondents, the parents of black schoolchildren, have alleged that their children are unable to attend fully desegregated schools because large numbers of white children in the areas in which respondents reside attend private schools which do not admit minority children. The Court, JUSTICE BRENNAN and I all agree that this is an adequate allegation of "injury in fact." * * *

II

In final analysis, the wrong respondents allege that the Government has committed is to subsidize the exodus of white children from schools that would otherwise be racially integrated. The critical question in these cases, therefore, is whether respondents have alleged that the Government has created that kind of subsidy.

* * * Only last Term we explained the effect of * * * preferential [tax] treatment:

> "Both tax exemptions and tax deductibility are a form of subsidy that is administered through the tax system. A tax exemption has much the same effect as a cash grant to the organization of the amount of tax it would have to pay on its income. Deductible contributions are similar to cash grants of the amount of a portion of the individual's contributions." Regan v. Taxation With Representation of Washington, 461 U.S. 540, 544 (1983).

* * * If the granting of preferential tax treatment would "encourage" private segregated schools to conduct their "charitable" activities, it must follow that the withdrawal of the treatment would "discourage" them, and hence promote the process of desegregation. * * *

This causation analysis is nothing more than a restatement of elementary economics: when something becomes more expensive, less of it will be purchased. * * * [W]ithout tax-exempt status, private schools will either not be competitive in terms of cost, or have to change their admissions policies, hence reducing their competitiveness for parents seeking "a racially segregated alternative" to public schools, which is what respondents have alleged many white parents in desegregating school districts seek. In either event the process of desegregation will be advanced in the same way that it was advanced in Gilmore and Norwood—the withdrawal of the subsidy for segregated schools means the incentive structure facing white parents who seek such schools for their children will be altered. * * *

III

Considerations of tax policy, economics, and pure logic all confirm the conclusion that respondents' injury in fact is fairly traceable to the Government's allegedly wrongful conduct. The Court therefore is forced to introduce the concept of "separation of powers" into its analysis. The Court writes that the separation of powers "explains why our cases preclude the conclusion" that respondents' injury is fairly traceable to the conduct they challenge.

The Court could mean one of three things by its invocation of the separation of powers. First, it could simply be expressing the idea that if the plaintiff lacks Art. III standing to bring a lawsuit, then there is no "case or controversy" within the meaning of Art. III and hence the matter is not within the area of responsibility assigned to the Judiciary by the Constitution. * * * While there can be no quarrel with this proposition, in itself it provides no guidance for determining if the injury respondents have alleged is fairly traceable to the conduct they have challenged.

Second, the Court could be saying that it will require a more direct causal connection when it is troubled by the separation of powers implications of the case before it. That approach confuses the standing doctrine with the justiciability of the issues that respondents seek to raise. The purpose of the standing inquiry is to measure the plaintiff's stake in the outcome, not whether a court has the authority to provide it with the outcome it seeks * * *.

Thus, the " 'fundamental aspect of standing' is that it focuses primarily on the *party* seeking to get his complaint before the federal court rather than 'on the issues he wishes to have adjudicated,' " United States v. Richardson, 418 U.S. 166, 174 (1974) (emphasis in original) (quoting Flast, 392 U.S., at 99). * * * If a plaintiff presents a nonjusticiable issue, or seeks relief that a court may not award, then its complaint should be dismissed for those reasons, and not because the plaintiff lacks a stake in obtaining that relief and hence has no standing. Imposing an undefined but clearly more rigorous standard for redressability for reasons unrelated to the causal nexus between the injury and the challenged conduct can only encourage undisciplined, ad hoc litigation * * *.

Third, the Court could be saying that it will not treat as legally cognizable injuries that stem from an administrative decision concerning how enforcement resources will be allocated. This surely is an important point. Respondents do seek to restructure the IRS's mechanisms for enforcing the legal requirement that discriminatory institutions not receive tax-exempt status. Such restructuring would dramatically affect the way in which the IRS exercises its prosecutorial discretion. The Executive requires latitude to decide how best to enforce the law, and in general the Court may well be correct that the exercise of that discretion, especially in the tax context, is unchallengeable.

However, as the Court also recognizes, this principle does not apply when suit is brought "to enforce specific legal obligations whose violation works a direct harm." For example, despite the fact that they were challenging the methods used by the Executive to enforce the law, citizens were accorded standing to challenge a pattern of police misconduct that violated the constitutional constraints on law enforcement activities in Allee v. Medrano, 416 U.S. 802 (1974). Here, respondents contend that the IRS is violating a specific constitutional limitation on its enforcement discretion. There is a solid basis for that contention. In Norwood, we wrote:

"A State's constitutional obligation requires it to steer clear, not only of operating the old dual system of racially segregated schools, but also of giving significant aid to institutions that practice racial or other invidious discrimination." * * *

Respondents contend that these cases limit the enforcement discretion enjoyed by the IRS. They establish, respondents argue, that the IRS cannot provide "cash grants" to discriminatory schools through preferential tax treatment without running afoul of a constitutional duty to refrain from "giving significant aid" to these institutions. Similarly, respondents claim that the Internal Revenue Code itself, as construed in Bob Jones, constrains enforcement discretion. It has been clear since Marbury v. Madison that "[i]t is emphatically the province and duty of the judicial department to say what the law is." Deciding whether the Treasury has violated a specific legal limitation on its enforcement discretion does not intrude upon the prerogatives of the Executive, for in so deciding we are merely saying "what the law is." * * *

In short, I would deal with the question of the legal limitations on the IRS's enforcement discretion on its merits, rather than by making the untenable assumption that the granting of preferential tax treatment to segregated schools does not make those schools more attractive to white students and hence does not inhibit the process of desegregation. I respectfully dissent.

———

NOTE ON STANDING TO SUE

(1) What Is Standing? The Supreme Court has frequently stated that standing questions relate to parties—to the nature and sufficiency of the litigant's concern with the subject matter of the litigation—rather than to the fitness for adjudication of the legal issues tendered for decision. See, *e.g.*, Flast v. Cohen, 392 U.S. 83, 95 (1968), p. 128, *infra*. Consider whether Allen

v. Wright and the decisions discussed in this Note are consistent with that statement.

(2) The Modern Origins of Standing Doctrine. Although one can identify at least some apparent precursors to modern standing doctrine in cases such as Fairchild, "[t]he word *'standing'* * * * does not appear to have been commonly used until the middle of * * * [the twentieth] century." Vining, Legal Identity: The Coming of Age of Public Law 55 (1978).[1] The absence of such discussion should perhaps come as little surprise. Traditionally, most litigants had challenged official action on the ground that it unlawfully invaded legal interests plainly recognized at common law, such as contract and property rights. See Stewart, *The Reformation of American Administrative Law*, 88 Harv.L.Rev. 1667, 1717–18, 1723–24 (1975).[2] For instance, if a food packing company wished to allege that public health officials seized (allegedly adulterated) food without due process, the alleged unlawful invasion of the company's property interests provided the basis for maintaining suit. See North American Cold Storage v. Chicago, 211 U.S. 306 (1908).

During the twentieth century, courts became self-conscious about the concept of standing only after developments in the legal culture subjected the traditional model to unfamiliar strains.[3] Two sources of strain had special importance. One involved the advent of the administrative state and the enactment of statutes to protect interests, unprotected at common law, that were shared by large numbers of people.[4] The other was the increasing

---

[1]   On the history of standing as a concept, see Winter, *The Metaphor of Standing and the Problem of Self-Governance*, 40 Stan.L.Rev. 1371, 1418–25 (1988).

[2]   At times, the prerogative writs or other forms of action seem to have permitted suit by litigants not asserting traditional common law interests. See pp. 151–153, *infra*. For the intriguing suggestion that the legal system's earlier focus on common law causes of action and prerogative writs would provide a more workable framework than contemporary standing law's emphasis on injury in fact, see Mashaw, *Rethinking Judicial Review of Administrative Action: A Nineteenth Century Perspective*, 32 Cardozo L.Rev. 2241 (2011). Professor Mashaw adds that Congress should have the authority to supplement these nineteenth century sources with fresh statutory causes of action. For further discussion of this possibility, see pp. 132–156, *infra*.

[3]   Professor Sunstein argues that "the principal early architects of * * * standing limits were Justices Brandeis and Frankfurter," whose aim in so doing "was to insulate progressive New Deal legislation from frequent judicial attack." Sunstein, *What's Standing After Lujan? Of Citizen Suits, "Injuries," and Article III*, 91 Mich.L.Rev. 163, 179 (1992). See also Pushaw, *Justiciability and Separation of Powers: A Neo-Federalist Approach*, 81 Cornell L.Rev. 394, 458–63 (1996). Based on an empirical study of more than 1,500 standing cases decided between 1921 and 2006, Ho and Ross conclude that attributing the rise of standing doctrine to the progressive goals of Justices Brandeis and Frankfurter misstates the history. See Ho & Ross, *Did Liberal Justices Invent the Standing Doctrine? An Empirical Study of the Evolution of Standing*, 1921–2006, 62 Stan.L.Rev. 591 (2010). In particular, they argue that the early standing cases (1921–1930) had no political valence; many were unanimous or at least included some of the conservative Justices associated with the Lochner era and, later, with the Court's resistance to the New Deal. During the New Deal, however, Ho and Ross's study finds that the doctrine shifted, and that voting blocs substantiate the liberal reliance on standing to insulate administrative agencies from judicial review. After 1950, the valence of standing doctrine shifted again, as it became more associated with conservative efforts to insulate government action from public interest challenges. For discussion of the current political valence of standing doctrine, see Elliott, *Standing Lessons: What We Can Learn When Conservative Plaintiffs Lose Under Article III Standing Doctrine*, 87 Ind.L.J. 551 (2012), which argues that standing limitations increasingly filter out not merely progressive interest group litigation, but also litigation by conservative interest groups seeking to challenge laws dealing with same-sex marriage, health care reform, and stem cell research.

[4]   See generally Sunstein, *Standing and the Privatization of Public Law*, 88 Colum.L.Rev. 1432 (1988).

recognition of substantive constitutional rights, such as voting rights and rights to educational equality, that were broadly shared and that were not associated with the kind of liberty or property interests protected by the common law. Once the Court recognized more widely held constitutional rights, the question arose who, if anyone, should be able to sue to ensure governmental compliance with statutory and constitutional provisions intended to protect broadly shared interests of large numbers of citizens. See *Note on Marbury v. Madison and the Function of Adjudication*, p. 73, *supra*.

(3) Injury in Fact: General Principles. As Allen v. Wright makes plain, the Court has for many years relied on concrete and personalized injury as a test of Article III standing. The Court's cases have articulated a range of purposes served by the injury-in-fact requirement: (a) ensuring the stakes and the limits of any resulting ruling are well understood;[5] (b) limiting the judicial process to litigants who will be energetic adversaries;[6] (c) assigning the right to sue to those most immediately affected by a government policy in order to ensure that their interests will be adequately represented;[7] (d) protecting democratic prerogatives by ensuring both that the judicial process is invoked only when necessary and that generalized grievances widely shared by the public are vindicated through the political process;[8] and (e) preserving the constitutional powers of the executive—including the law enforcement authority prescribed by Article II—from unnecessary interference by federal court adjudication.[9] Consider whether the lines drawn by the cases that follow correspond well to these asserted purposes.

(a) In Sierra Club v. Morton, 405 U.S. 727 (1972), the Sierra Club sued the United States Forest Service, claiming that its approval of the development of a ski resort in the Sequoia National Forest violated federal statutes and regulations. Alleging that it had "a special interest in the conservation and sound maintenance of the national parks, game refuges, and forests of the country" and that the project would adversely affect the aesthetics and ecology of the area, the Club claimed to be "adversely affected or aggrieved" under § 10 of the Administrative Procedure Act (APA), 5 U.S.C. § 702.[10]

The Court ruled that the plaintiff lacked standing because it had not alleged that it would suffer "injury in fact" from the challenged action. Although acknowledging that the Court allows organizations to litigate as representatives of their members (if some members themselves would have standing to sue),[11] the Court emphasized that "[n]owhere * * * did the Club

---

[5]   See, *e.g.*, Valley Forge Christian College v. Americans United for Separation of Church and State, Inc., 454 U.S. 464, 475–479 (1982); Schlesinger v. Reservists Committee to Stop the War, 418 U.S. 208, 222 (1974).

[6]   See, *e.g.*, Flast v. Cohen, 392 U.S. 83, 101 (1968); Baker v. Carr, 369 U.S. 186, 204 (1962).

[7]   See, *e.g.*, Diamond v. Charles, 476 U.S. 54, 62 (1986); Sierra Club v. Morton, 405 U.S. 727, 740 (1972). See also Brilmayer, *The Jurisprudence of Article III: Perspectives on the "Case or Controversy" Requirement*, 93 Harv.L.Rev. 297, 302 (1979).

[8]   See, *e.g.*, Lujan v. Defenders of Wildlife, 504 U.S. 555, 576 (1992); Lewis v. Casey, 518 U.S. 343, 357 (1996).

[9]   See, *e.g.*, Laird v. Tatum, 408 U.S. 1, 15 (1972).

[10]   That section provides: "A person suffering legal wrong because of agency action, or adversely affected or aggrieved by agency action within the meaning of a relevant statute, is entitled to judicial review thereof." For further discussion of standing under the APA, see p. 157, *infra*.

[11]   See Hunt v. Washington State Apple Advertising Comm'n, 432 U.S. 333, 343 (1977) (holding "that an association has standing to bring suit on behalf of its members when: (a) its members would otherwise have standing to sue in their own right; (b) the interests it seeks to

state that its members use [the area in question] for any purpose, much less that they use it in any way that would be significantly affected by the proposed actions of the [defendants]." The Court termed the requirement of injury a "rough attempt to put the decision as to whether review will be sought in the hands of those who have a direct stake in the outcome". Justice Stewart added for the Court that the goals of the injury-in-fact requirement would be "undermined" if organizations were permitted to sue under the APA merely to "vindicate their own value preferences through the judicial process."

Justice Blackmun (joined by Justice Brennan) dissented, calling for "an imaginative expansion of our traditional concepts of standing in order to enable an organization such as the Sierra Club, possessed, as it is, of pertinent, bona fide and well-recognized attributes and purposes in the area of the environment, to litigate environmental issues."[12] Would it be proper for the Court to make ad hoc judgments about the litigating capacity of particular parties?[13] Do the courts do so, in effect, when deciding whether to certify class actions under Fed.R.Civ.P. 23? Did the Sierra Club's incentives or capacity to litigate depend on whether some members used the relevant part of the national forest?

(b) United States v. Richardson, 418 U.S. 166 (1974), held (5–4) that the plaintiff lacked standing to litigate whether the CIA was violating Article I, § 9, cl. 7 (requiring "a regular Statement and Account of the Receipts and Expenditures of all public Money") by accounting for its expenditures, in accordance with a federal statute, "solely on the certificate of the Director." Chief Justice Burger wrote: "The respondent's claim is that without detailed information on CIA expenditures—and hence its activities—he cannot intelligently follow the actions of Congress or the Executive, nor can he properly fulfill his obligations as a member of the electorate in voting for candidates seeking national office."

"This is surely [a] * * * generalized grievance * * * since the impact on him is plainly undifferentiated and 'common to all members of the public.' While we can hardly dispute that this respondent has a genuine interest in the use of funds and that his interest may be prompted by his status as a taxpayer, he has not alleged that, as a taxpayer, he is in danger of suffering any concrete injury as a result of the operation of the statute."

The Chief Justice continued: "It can be argued that if respondent is not permitted to litigate this issue, no one can do so. In a very real sense, the

---

protect are germane to the organization's purpose; and (c) neither the claim asserted nor the relief requested requires the participation of individual members in the lawsuit"). For decisions refusing to authorize organizational standing, see Harris v. McRae, 448 U.S. 297, 320–21 (1980); Warth v. Seldin, 422 U.S. 490, 515–16 (1975). Does Hunt's broad endorsement of organization standing make an end run around the procedural protections that Fed.R.Civ.P. 23 imposes on plaintiffs seeking to represent those whose claims present common questions of law and fact against the same defendant? For a decision reaffirming Hunt in the face of such an objection, see International Union, UAW v. Brock, 477 U.S. 274 (1986).

[12] Justice Douglas also dissented; he would have upheld standing "in the name of the inanimate object about to be despoiled, defaced, or invaded by roads and bulldozers and where injury is the subject of public outrage."

[13] Compare Stearns, *Standing Back from the Forest: Justiciability and Social Choice*, 83 Cal.L.Rev. 1309 (1995) (arguing that because ideological litigants have an incentive to seek to determine the "path" of the law by bringing cases at early or otherwise opportune moments, standing doctrine is needed to "render[ ] the inevitable path dependency of legal doctrine * * * more fair by preventing ideological litigants from manipulating the path in which cases are presented for consideration").

absence of any particular individual or class to litigate these claims gives support to the argument that the subject matter is committed to the surveillance of Congress, and ultimately to the political process. * * * Slow, cumbersome, and unresponsive though the traditional electoral process may be thought at times, our system provides for changing members of the political branches when dissatisfied citizens convince a sufficient number of their fellow electors that elected representatives are delinquent in performing duties committed to them.''

Justice Powell elaborated on this theme in his concurring opinion:

''[R]epeated and essentially head-on confrontations between the life-tenured branch and the representative branches of government will not, in the long run, be beneficial to either. The public confidence essential to the former and the vitality critical to the latter may well erode if we do not exercise self-restraint in the utilization of our power to negative the actions of the other branches. * * * The irreplaceable value of the power [of judicial review] * * * lies in the protection it has afforded the constitutional rights and liberties of individual citizens and minority groups against oppressive or discriminatory government action. It is this role, not some amorphous general supervision of the operations of government, that has maintained public esteem for the federal courts and has permitted the peaceful coexistence of the countermajoritarian implications of judicial review and the democratic principles upon which our Federal Government in the final analysis rests.''

Does the fact that a grievance is widely shared ensure that the political branches will respond to it—or that, if they do not, the grievance must not be very serious? Should the lack of any other or better plaintiff count in favor of upholding a litigant's standing?[14]

(c) In Heckler v. Mathews, 465 U.S. 728 (1984), Congress had provided larger benefit awards under the Social Security Act to certain women than to similarly situated men. A severability clause provided that if the provision in question were found to deny equal protection, men and women alike should receive the smaller amount. Despite the unavailability of any material compensation for the male plaintiff, the Court upheld his standing to challenge the unequal treatment. Because he asserted ''the right to receive 'benefits * * * distributed according to classifications which do not without sufficient justification differentiate * * * solely on the basis of sex,' and not a substantive right to any particular amount of benefits, [plaintiff's] standing does not depend on his ability to obtain increased Social Security payments. * * * [D]iscrimination itself, by perpetuating 'archaic and stereotypic notions' or by stigmatizing members of the disfavored group as 'innately inferior,' * * * can cause serious noneconomic injuries.'' Can Mathews be squared with the refusal in Allen v. Wright to find that the stigma alleged by the plaintiffs was a cognizable injury?[15]

(4) Injury in Fact: Probabilistic Harms. The Court has said that injury in fact must be concrete, imminent, and not speculative. Yet, in many instances, the injury that litigation seeks to prevent may reflect merely a

---

[14] See Meltzer, *Deterring Constitutional Violations by Law Enforcement Officials: Plaintiffs and Defendants as Private Attorneys General*, 88 Colum.L.Rev. 247, 297–306 (1988).

[15] For the argument that the Supreme Court has implicitly recognized stigmatic harm as a basis for standing in cases other than Allen v. Wright, and that it ought to do so more broadly, see Healy, *Stigmatic Harm and Standing*, 92 Iowa L.Rev. 417 (2007).

statistical probability of harm. Social scientists routinely calculate the expected value of alternative courses of action by reference to the harm or benefit of an event multiplied by its probability. The Court, however, has taken varying positions on whether and when a plaintiff can predicate Article III standing on the objective probability of sustaining harm and the reasonable concerns flowing from such a probability.

(a) In Summers v. Earth Island Institute, Inc., 555 U.S. 488 (2009), the Court (5–4) rejected efforts by environmental organizations to base standing on the statistical probability that some of their members would suffer harms by virtue of the U.S. Forest Service's pervasive application of challenged regulations to sites throughout a park system frequented by the organizations' members. The Forest Service Decision Making and Appeals Reform Act, 16 U.S.C. § 1612, afforded interested parties the right to notice and comment and to an appellate process concerning certain land and resource management plans implemented by the Forest Service. The plaintiffs sought to enjoin the enforcement of Forest Service regulations that excluded fire-rehabilitation activities and salvage-timber sales of a certain size from those procedures. Consistent with the requirements of Sierra Club v. Morton, pp. 117–118, *supra*, a member of one of the plaintiff groups had filed an affidavit stating that he had visited and intended again to visit the site of a particular salvage-timber sale that the challenged regulations exempted from the Act's procedures. Because the litigation concerning that site had been settled, however, the plaintiff groups could not rely on that injury to sustain injunctive relief. Compare City of Los Angeles v. Lyons, p. 232, *infra*. Nor, said the Court, could the plaintiff organizations establish the requisite concrete, particularized injury by relying on the affidavit of another member who simply averred that he has visited many National Forests and plans to visit several unnamed National Forests in the future.

In a dissent joined by Justices Stevens, Souter, and Ginsburg, Justice Breyer argued that given the sweep of the Forest Service's policy and the vast membership of the plaintiff organizations, establishing the requisite injury in this case should not necessarily depend on whether any identifiable individual member of the plaintiff organizations had alleged a sufficiently concrete injury. In particular, he contended that the government's application of the challenged regulations to thousands of projects in the future sufficed to establish a realistic threat of injury to the plaintiffs' many thousands of members who, according to uncontested allegations in the complaint, have used and intend to use the National Forests to which the regulations apply. The majority responded that "[t]his novel approach to the law of organizational standing would make a mockery of our prior cases, which have required plaintiff-organizations to make specific allegations establishing that at least one identified member had suffered or would suffer harm."[16]

---

[16] In contrast to Summers, in Monsanto Co. v. Geertson Seed Farms, 561 U.S. 139 (2010), the Court held that conventional alfalfa growers had standing to challenge the Secretary of Agriculture's deregulation of genetically-engineered alfalfa, given the "reasonable probability" that such action would result in cross-contamination of conventional and organic alfalfa with the altered gene. This risk of cross-contamination concretely injured the conventional growers in at least two ways. First, in order to continue marketing their product to consumers "who wish to buy non-genetically-engineered alfalfa, [the growers] would have to conduct testing to find out whether and to what extent their crops have been contaminated." Second, "the risk of gene flow [from genetically altered to conventional alfalfa] will cause them to take certain measures to minimize the likelihood of potential contamination and to ensure an adequate supply of non-

(b) In Clapper v. Amnesty International USA, 133 S.Ct. 1138 (2013), the Court signaled a renewed caution about finding injury in fact based on probabilistic injury and the reasonable concerns that flow from it. Pursuant to the Foreign Intelligence Surveillance Act of 1978, as amended, 50 U.S.C. § 1881a, the Attorney General and the Director of National Intelligence may seek an order from the Foreign Intelligence Surveillance Court (FISC) that enables them to "authorize jointly, for a period of up to 1 year * * *, the targeting [for surveillance] of persons reasonably believed to be located outside the United States to acquire foreign intelligence information." The statute prescribes safeguards to prevent surveillance of persons in the United States or U.S. persons abroad but permits retention of communications between a proper foreign target and a U.S. person. It also specifies that acquisitions of data must comply with Fourth Amendment requirements.

The plaintiffs—who alleged that § 1881a violates the First and Fourth Amendments and the constitutional separation of powers—were attorneys and human rights, labor, legal and media organizations who work with clients and sources abroad. The plaintiffs' declarations averred that their work requires them to communicate by telephone or email with individuals abroad whom the government believes to be affiliated with terrorist groups, who live in areas that are the "special focus" of U.S. counterterrorism efforts, or who actively oppose U.S.-supported governments. These circumstances, the plaintiffs claimed, created an objectively reasonable likelihood that their communications would be intercepted pursuant to § 1881a. The plaintiffs' declarations also stated that their apprehension of being monitoring compelled them to take costly and burdensome measures to maintain confidentiality, in some cases traveling abroad to communicate with individuals rather than using email or telephone communication.

Justice Alito's opinion for a closely divided Court (5–4) concluded that the plaintiffs lacked standing. The Court found it "speculative" (a) that the government would target parties with whom the plaintiffs communicated, (b) that it would rely on § 1881a rather than some other source of authority, (c) that FISC would authorize the surveillance, (d) that the surveillance would successfully intercept the intended communications, and (e) that the interceptions would include the plaintiffs' communications. This "speculative chain of possibilities," in the Court's view, did not establish that injury based on potential future surveillance is "certainly impending." Rebuffing the plaintiffs' assertions that they felt compelled to take costly measures in order to preserve confidentiality, the Court admonished that plaintiffs cannot "manufacture" standing through their responses to "fears of hypothetical future harm."[17] Finally, the Court added that "we have often found a lack of

---

genetically-engineered alfalfa" for customers who insist on such crops. The Court found these harms sufficed to confer standing, even if the growers' crops were not actually infected.

Why does the reasonable probability of an injury suffice to confer standing here if it did not in the Summers case? Does the difference flow from the costly precautions that the plaintiffs in Monsanto had to take to avoid those concerns—a harm that was certain and not merely probabilistic?

[17] In so holding, the Court in Clapper distinguished Friends of the Earth Inc. v. Laidlaw Environmental Services (TOC) Inc., 528 U.S. 167 (2000), in which the Court—over a dissent by Justice Scalia (joined by Justice Thomas)—held that plaintiffs had standing to challenge the defendant's alleged violation of the Clean Water Act, even though the district court had found that the defendant's actions had not "result[ed] in any health risk or environmental harm". The plaintiffs alleged that the defendants' actions concretely harmed their recreational and aesthetic interests, and Justice Ginsburg explained for the Court that "[t]he relevant showing for Article

standing in cases in which the Judiciary has been requested to review actions of the political branches in the fields of intelligence gathering and foreign affairs."

Justice Breyer's dissent, joined by Justices Ginsburg, Sotomayor, and Kagan, argued that the probability that the plaintiffs' communications would be intercepted was hardly speculative. At least two plaintiffs were attorneys who represented high profile detainees at Guantanamo Bay and whose work required communications with the detainees' family, friends, acquaintances, and other associates abroad. Justice Breyer argued that the government would have a strong motive to intercept such communications, which might lead to information about crimes or terrorist plots, and that past governmental behavior showed the government's propensity and capacity to intercept such communications. Justice Breyer also disputed the majority's suggestion that a future harm must be "certainly impending" before it could sustain standing. "Would federal courts," he asked, "deny standing to a plaintiff who seeks to enjoin as a nuisance the building of a nearby pond which, the plaintiff believes, will very likely, but not inevitably, overflow his land?"

Responding in a footnote, the majority conceded that the Court's cases have sometimes permitted standing based on a "substantial risk" of harm rather than a "literally certain" injury. The Court explained, however, that the plaintiffs' asserted injuries were too speculative to reach even the "substantial risk" threshold. What probability should the Court insist upon before finding standing based on the threat of a future harm? What is the significance of the fact that the classified nature of the program in Clapper limited the plaintiffs' ability and the government's willingness to present evidence bearing on likelihood? For perspectives on the challenges posed by such litigation, see, *e.g.*, Michelman, *Who Can Sue over Government Surveillance?*, 57 UCLA L.Rev. 71 (2009); Rubenfeld, *The End of Privacy*, 61 Stan.L.Rev. 101, 138 (2008).

(c) In Susan B. Anthony List v. Driehaus, 134 S.Ct. 2334 (2014), the Court held that the "substantial risk" of administrative proceedings against an advocacy group, if backed by the "additional threat of criminal prosecution," sufficed to establish standing. The Susan B. Anthony List (the SBA List) is an advocacy group that opposes abortion. In the 2010 election cycle, the SBA List ran advertisements against Rep. Steven Driehaus stating that his vote for the Affordable Care Act (ACA) constituted a vote for "taxpayer-funded abortion." Under Ohio election law, knowingly or recklessly making a false statement about a candidate is a criminal offense. A candidate may file a complaint with the Ohio Election Commission. If the Commission finds probable cause, it conducts a hearing into the alleged violation. If the Commission then finds "clear and convincing evidence" of a prohibited false statement, it "shall" refer the matter to the District Attorney.

III standing is not injury to the environment but injury to the plaintiff", which existed because of the plaintiffs' "reasonable concern" that pollution damaged land that they otherwise would have used. The Court in Clapper distinguished Laidlaw on the ground that, in that case, the defendant's environmental discharges into the waterway were ongoing, and the only question was whether the plaintiffs, who were nearby residents, "acted reasonably in refraining from using the polluted area." Is that distinction convincing, or does Clapper evince a new skepticism toward standing based on a plaintiff's "reasonable concerns"?

Driehaus filed a complaint with the Commission, which found probable cause to hold a hearing. The SBA List filed suit seeking declaratory and injunctive relief, under the First Amendment, against the enforcement of the false statement statute. After Driehaus lost his bid for reelection, he withdrew his complaint. The SBA List, however, continued to press its constitutional challenge, seeking injunctive relief against future enforcement of the false statement law.

A unanimous Court found that the "substantial" threat of future enforcement of the false statement act sufficed to permit the SBA List to bring a pre-enforcement challenge to the statute's enforcement. The SBA List had alleged that it would make substantially similar claims about the ACA against candidates in future elections. The Court concluded that the SBA List's future conduct was arguably prohibited by the statute. And since "any person" could file a complaint, the Court deemed the "threat" of a future enforcement action against the SBA List to be substantial, especially since the Commission had found probable cause to conduct a hearing on Rep. Driehaus' complaint. Although a Commission enforcement action could in and of itself disrupt the target's political speech and divert its resources during an election, the Court found it unnecessary to determine if standing could rest on the threat of administrative proceedings alone. Instead, because "burdensome Commission proceedings . . . are backed by the additional threat of criminal prosecution," the Court found that "the combination of those two threats suffices to create an Article III injury under the circumstances of this case."

Driehaus confirms that, despite the "certainly impending" language in Clapper, a "substantial" risk of injury suffices to establish standing. Do the differing results in the two cases reflect the Court's intuition that the risk of harm was more substantial in the latter than in the former? Or is the Court more prone to permit pre-enforcement challenges when the plaintiff avers that it will violate a criminal statute?

(d) The Court's recent cases seem to vary in their willingness to treat probabilistic harms as a basis for granting standing. Is there anything at play other than the Court's own rough judgment about how realistic the threat of a contingent harm might be for the plaintiff in question? Despite the Court's stated reluctance to allow standing for "speculative" events, should it recognize standing for low probability events if their realization would produce catastrophic consequences? Compare the discussion of Massachusetts v. EPA, pp. 149–151, *infra*. See also Nash, *Standing's Expected Value*, 111 Mich.L.Rev. 1283 (2013).

(5) Causation and Redressability Requirements. Allen v. Wright holds that Article III requires more than merely a cognizable injury. Rather, the injury must be (i) "fairly traceable" in a causal sense to the challenged action and (ii) redressable by a favorable decision.[18]

(a) Linda R.S. v. Richard D., 410 U.S. 614 (1973), was a class action, brought by the mother of a child born out of wedlock, against state officials whose policy was to bring non-support prosecutions against only the fathers of children born in wedlock. Asserting that the policy violated the Equal

---

[18] For critical commentary on the Court's early development of the "causation" and "redressability" requirements, see Chayes, *Foreword: Public Law Litigation and the Burger Court*, 96 Harv.L.Rev. 4, 17–19 (1982); Nichol, *Causation as a Standing Requirement: The Unprincipled Use of Judicial Restraint*, 69 Ky.L.Rev. 185 (1981); Tushnet, *The New Law of Standing: A Plea for Abandonment*, 62 Cornell L.Rev. 663, 680–88 (1977).

Protection Clause, the complaint sought an injunction requiring prosecution of the fathers of out-of-wedlock children. Justice Marshall's opinion for the Court found no standing: "[I]n the unique context of a challenge to a criminal statute, appellant has failed to allege a sufficient nexus between her injury and the government action which she attacks to justify judicial intervention. * * * [T]he requested relief * * * would result only in the jailing of the child's father. The prospect that prosecution will, at least in the future, result in payment of support can, at best, be termed only speculative." The opinion also rested on the proposition that "in American jurisprudence at least, a private citizen lacks a judicially cognizable interest in the prosecution or nonprosecution of another."

Since the suit was brought as a class action, is the result of prosecuting non-supporting fathers any more speculative than the general theory that the criminal law deters? Compare the Court's reasoning in Linda R.S. with its conclusion in Allen v. Wright that it was "speculative" whether the withdrawal of a challenged tax exemption would produce less of the behavior subsidized by the exemption. See also Simon v. Eastern Ky. Welfare Rights Organization, 426 U.S. 26 (1976) (deeming it "purely speculative" whether the IRS' abandonment of a requirement that nonprofit hospitals provide services to indigents in order to receive favorable tax treatment caused "the denial of access to hospital services" complained of by the plaintiffs).

(b) In contrast, Regents of the University of California v. Bakke, 438 U.S. 265 (1978), granted standing to a white plaintiff to challenge the defendant's operation of a special admissions program for minority applicants to medical school. Some amici argued that Bakke lacked standing because he had not shown that his asserted injury—exclusion from medical school—would be redressed by a favorable decision, since he might not have been admitted even absent any preference for minority applicants. In a portion of his opinion endorsed by four other Justices, Justice Powell affirmed Bakke's standing, arguing that relief would redress the injury Bakke had suffered by having been deprived, simply because of his race, of the chance to *compete* for every place in the entering class. The four Justices dissenting on the merits did not address the standing question. See also Northeastern Florida Chapter of the Associated General Contractors of America v. City of Jacksonville, 508 U.S. 656 (1993) (taking a similar approach in an action by a non-minority bidder on municipal contracts who wished to challenge a municipal ordinance that set aside 10% of city contracts for "minority business enterprises").[19]

In light of Bakke and Associated General Contractors, consider Sunstein, note 4, *supra*, at 1464–69: "The central problem [is] how to characterize the relevant injury. [In Simon,] for example, the plaintiffs might have characterized their injury as an impairment of the opportunity to obtain medical services under a regime undistorted by unlawful tax incentives. In Allen, the plaintiffs themselves argued that their injury should

---

[19] In Texas v. Lesage, 528 U.S. 18 (1999) (per curiam), the Court held that a rejected applicant challenging an affirmative action program could not recover damages where the defendant proved that it would have made the same decision to exclude the applicant even in the absence of an affirmative action program. Under these circumstances, the Court said, "there is no cognizable injury warranting relief". If the injury grounding standing in Bakke and Associated General Contractors is "the denial of equal treatment" rather than "the ultimate inability to obtain the benefit", why will that injury support injunctive but not damages relief? See Bhagwat, *Injury Without Harm: Texas v. Lesage and the Strange World of Article III Injuries*, 28 Hastings Const.L.Q. 445 (2001).

be characterized as the deprivation of an opportunity to undergo desegregation in school systems unaffected by unlawful tax deductions. Thus recharacterized, the injuries are not speculative at all." To what extent could the standing difficulties in cases like Simon and Allen be solved by more artful pleading?

(c) Although inquiries into causation and redressability often overlap, they do not inevitably do so. Because of distinctive concerns about redressability, a plaintiff may have standing to seek some forms of relief but not others. See, *e.g.*, Friends of the Earth Inc. v. Laidlaw Environmental Services (TOC), Inc., 528 U.S. 167, 185 (2000) (holding that "a plaintiff must demonstrate standing separately for each form of relief sought"); Lewis v. Casey, 518 U.S. 343, 358, n.6 (1996) ("[S]tanding is not dispensed in gross."). For example, in Los Angeles v. Lyons, 461 U.S. 95 (1983) (discussed in greater detail at p. 232–234, *infra*), the plaintiff alleged that officers in the Los Angeles Police Department had used an illegal chokehold on him, without any provocation, when they stopped him for a traffic offense. Lyons sought damages, as well as declaratory and injunctive relief against the future use of chokeholds absent the immediate threat of deadly force by a detainee. The district court had held, and the parties agreed, that the damages claim could be severed from the claim for equitable relief, and the Court proceeded on the assumption that Lyons would have standing to pursue his damages remedy on remand. The Court concluded, however, that he was required to establish standing for each element of relief he sought, and that the equitable relief he requested would not redress the harms he alleged. The fact that he had been choked once, the Court explained, "does nothing to establish a real and immediate threat that he would again be stopped for a traffic violation, or for any other offense, by an officer or officers who would illegally choke him into unconsciousness without any provocation or resistance on his part." Because the requested relief would therefore not redress Lyons' alleged injury, the Court found that he was "no more entitled to an injunction than any other citizen of Los Angeles".[20]

(6) Are Standing Requirements Judicially Manageable? In light of the cases discussed thus far in this Note, consider the following contentions about the objectivity, determinacy, and efficacy of standing requirements:[21]

i. "In classifying some harms as injuries in fact and other harms as purely ideological, courts must inevitably rely on some standard that is normatively laden and independent of facts. * * * When blacks challenge a grant or tax deductions to segregated schools, they believe that the grant is an injury in fact, not that it is purely ideological. When an environmentalist complains about the destruction of a pristine area, he believes that the loss of that area is indeed an injury to him. When we deny these claims, we are

---

[20] For decisions resting on similar reasoning, see, *e.g.*, Rizzo v. Goode, 423 U.S. 362 (1976); O'Shea v. Littleton, 414 U.S. 488 (1974); Golden v. Zwickler, 394 U.S. 103 (1969). Fallon, *The Linkage Between Justiciability and Remedies—And Their Connections to Substantive Rights*, 92 Va.L.Rev. 633 (2006), argues that the Court treats a particular set of remedies—injunctions directing executive officials to enforce the law against third parties (as in Allen v. Wright, p. 103, *supra*, and Linda R.S. v. Richard D., p. 123, *supra*)—as especially problematic, though not as categorically forbidden, and that this consideration has influenced the Court's development and application of the causation and redressability requirements.

[21] Some commentators suggest that the Court uses standing to pursue unarticulated strategic aims unrelated to the doctrine's stated goals. *See, e.g.*, Pierce, Is Standing Law or Politics?, 77 N.C.L.Rev. 1741, 1742–43 (1999); Staudt, *Modeling Standing*, 79 N.Y.U.L.Rev. 612 (2004); Varat, *Variable Justiciability and the Duke Power Case*, 58 Tex.L.Rev. 273 (1980).

making a judgment based not on any fact, but instead on an inquiry into what should count as a judicially cognizable injury." Sunstein, note 3, *supra*, at 188–190.

ii. "The factors relevant to the case determination exist on a continuum, and the Court must unavoidably make choices about where on the continuum a line should be drawn. * * * The Court must make distinctions of degree, not of kind." Bandes, *The Idea of a Case*, 43 Stan.L.Rev. 227, 264 (1990).

iii. "One way of describing the Court's mistake in standing cases is to say that it has tried to formulate standing principles at too high a level of generality. Lawyers and judges usually try to formulate principles at as high a level of generality as the nature of the material will permit, but there is a limit on the generality of any given principle. That limit is passed when too many bad results are obtained by following the principle, or when the principle is too often evaded by subterfuge." Fletcher, *The Structure of Standing*, 98 Yale L.J. 221, 290 (1988).

Do those criticisms seem well grounded? Even strong proponents of the Court's modern injury-in-fact requirement acknowledge its variability. See Valley Forge Christian College v. Americans United for the Separation of Church and State, 454 U.S. 464, 475 (1982) (Rehnquist, J): "We need not mince words when we say that the concept of 'Art. IIII standing' has not been defined with complete consistency in all of the various cases decided by this Court which have discussed it, nor when we say that this very fact is probably proof that the concept cannot be reduced to a one-sentence or one-paragraph definition." But similar complaints are often leveled at the Supreme Court's jurisprudence in other areas.

Assuming a lack of a tight connection between the lines drawn in particular standing cases and the background goals articulated in those cases, might the Court's approach still plausibly promote a sound conception of the limits on Article III power? The Court has consistently made clear that an abstract interest in the government's "proper application of the Constitution and laws" cannot alone justify Article III standing. Lujan v. Defenders of Wildlife, 504 U.S. 555, 573–74 (1992). See also, *e.g.*, Schlesinger v. Reservists Committee to Stop the War, 418 U.S. 208, 217 (1974); Valley Forge Christian College v. Americans United for Separation of Church and State, Inc., 454 U.S. 464, 475–479 (1982). As one of the first modern standing cases, Fairchild v. Hughes, p. 102, *supra*, put it, the judicial power cannot be invoked to vindicate "the [general] right, possessed by every citizen, to require that the government be administered according to law". Might the Court's modern cases be understood as a crude, imperfect way of trying to fulfill that broad purpose, namely, to filter out plaintiffs who really wish only to vindicate the rule of law?

Finally, consider the following alternative framework: Judge (formerly Professor) Fletcher has argued that the standing inquiry should focus on the *meaning* of the particular constitutional or statutory provision relied upon and on the question whether such provision should be construed to grant the plaintiff a right to sue. See Fletcher, *supra*. See also Warth v. Seldin, 422 U.S. 490, 500 (1975) (suggesting that the standing question "is whether the constitutional or statutory provision on which the claim rests properly can be understood as granting persons in the plaintiff's position a right to judicial relief"). Does this approach solve some of the apparent anomalies in the case law? Consider, for example, the contrast between the Court's treatment of psychic harm in Allen v. Wright and in Heckler v. Matthews. Would a shift to an approach inquiring whether particular constitutional or statutory provisions create rights in plaintiffs prove more reliable or administrable than the present framework? Wouldn't many of the same disputes about plaintiffs' standing recur, recast as arguments about which specific constitutional rights plaintiffs do and do not have? In Allen v. Wright, for example, mightn't the question whether the plaintiffs had an enforceable right under the Equal Protection Clause to have Treasury officials enforce the law against third parties depend on whether the officials' actions and inactions had caused them harm and on whether relief would redress that harm?

NOTE ON SPECIALIZED STANDING DOCTRINES: TAXPAYER AND LEGISLATOR STANDING

(1) Introductory Note. The Court has had to deal repeatedly with the concreteness and cognizability of injuries suffered by plaintiffs purporting to sue as taxpayers or legislators. Though these areas present different considerations from each other, each provides a valuable case study in the Court's development of theories of injury, causation, and redressability for a particular type of plaintiff. Consider whether these areas, in fact, present special considerations or whether they present the exact same concerns about fact-bound judgment as the other cases described above.

(2) Taxpayer Standing. In a series of cases going back to the early twentieth century, the Court has considered whether a taxpayer has standing to challenge expenditures from the public fisc.

(a) In Frothingham v. Mellon, 262 U.S. 447 (1923), a federal taxpayer challenged the Maternity Act of 1921, which provided federal financial support for state programs to reduce maternal and infant mortality, as beyond Congress' Article I powers and an invasion of state prerogatives under the Tenth Amendment. The plaintiff alleged that the Maternity Act would increase her tax liability and "thereby take her property without due process of law." Distinguishing cases that had allowed suits by municipal taxpayers, the Court found that the plaintiff's "interest in the moneys of the [federal] treasury" was "comparatively minute and indeterminable" and that "the effect upon future taxation of any payment out of" federal funds was "remote, fluctuating and uncertain".[1] To accept jurisdiction of Frothingham's

---

[1] For cases endorsing municipal taxpayer standing, see, *e.g.*, Everson v. Board of Education, 330 U.S. 1 (1947); Crampton v. Zabriskie, 101 U.S. 601, 609 (1879). Although municipal taxpayer standing doctrine is well settled, the Court has not applied it without reservation. In Doremus v. Board of Education, 342 U.S. 429 (1952), the Court refused to recognize a (state and) municipal taxpayer's standing to challenge a state statute requiring teachers to read five verses of the Old Testament, without comment, at the beginning of each school day. The plaintiffs had nowhere alleged that reading the verses would add to school costs. On review from the state supreme court, the Court's 6–3 decision reasoned: "The taxpayer's action can meet [the case-or-controversy] test * * * only when it is a good-faith pocketbook action. It is apparent that the grievance which it is sought to litigate here is not a direct dollars-and-cents injury but is a religious difference. If appellants established the requisite special injury necessary to a taxpayer's case or controversy, it would not matter that their dominant inducement to action was more religious than mercenary. It is not a question of motivation but of possession of the requisite financial interest that is, or is threatened to be, injured by the unconstitutional conduct."

Doremus also rejected state taxpayer standing, noting that absent "direct pecuniary injury, * * * what the [Frothingham] Court said of a federal statute is equally true when a state Act is assailed." The Court has repeatedly upheld that line of demarcation. See, *e.g.*, DaimlerChrysler

case "would be not to decide a judicial controversy, but to assume a position of authority over the governmental acts of another and co-equal department, an authority which plainly we do not possess." See also Fairchild v. Hughes, p. 102, *supra*.

(b) In Flast v. Cohen, 392 U.S. 83 (1968), a suit by federal taxpayers alleging that a federal statute violated the Establishment Clause by providing financial support for educational programs in religious schools, the Court distinguished Frothingham and upheld standing. Emphasizing that standing turns on whether "the dispute sought to be adjudicated will be presented in an adversary context and in a form historically viewed as capable of judicial resolution", Chief Justice Warren concluded that Frothingham did not erect "an absolute bar" to federal taxpayer standing. Rather, the problem at hand entailed "determining the circumstances under which a federal taxpayer will be deemed to have [the requisite] personal stake and interest" to satisfy those criteria. In a case in which standing rested upon the plaintiff's status (*e.g.*, as taxpayer), the Court reasoned that part of its task was "to determine whether there was a logical nexus between the status asserted and the claim sought to be adjudicated." The Court continued: "The nexus demanded of federal taxpayers has two aspects to it. First, the taxpayer must establish a logical link between that status and the type of legislative enactment attacked. * * * Secondly, the taxpayer must establish a nexus between that status and the precise nature of the constitutional infringement alleged."

On the facts, the Court found both nexus requirements to be satisfied. It perceived a link between taxpayer status and the alleged "unconstitutionality only of exercises of congressional power under the taxing and spending clause of Art. I, § 8 of the Constitution." With respect to the second nexus, the Court found that the Establishment Clause at least partly resulted from concern that "the taxing and spending power would be used to favor one religion over another or to support religion in general." The Court thus distinguished Frothingham as involving no allegation that Congress "had breached a specific limitation upon its taxing and spending power."

Dissenting, Justice Harlan argued that "the Court's standard for the determination of standing", which focused on whether the plaintiff had the requisite personal stake in the outcome, was "entirely unrelated" to its double nexus test for whether this standard was satisfied. "I am quite unable to understand how, if a taxpayer believes that a given public expenditure is unconstitutional, and if he seeks to vindicate that belief in a federal court, his interest in the suit can be said necessarily to vary according to [the nature of the spending program that he attacks or] the constitutional provision under which he states his claim."

Justice Harlan was correct, wasn't he, about the transparent artificiality of Flast's double-nexus test for taxpayer standing? How is that artificiality to be explained? Surely, Flast fits uneasily, at best, with the traditional, dispute resolution model of standing that underlay Frothingham. Or, thinking back to Professor Fletcher's rights-based approach to standing (see pp. 126–127, *supra*), can Flast and Frothingham

---

Corp. v. Cuno, 547 U.S. 332, 345 (2006); ASARCO Inc. v. Kadish, 490 U.S. 605, 613–14 (1989) (plurality opinion). Is it obvious that a municipal taxpayer's stake in the constitutionality of a local expenditure or tax subsidy is more particularized or less conjectural than a state taxpayer's stake in a comparable state policy?

be distinguished on the ground that Flast claimed a violation of her personal constitutional rights under the Establishment Clause, whereas Frothingham sought standing to enforce an essentially structural constitutional provision? For elaboration of this distinction, see Flast v. Cohen, *supra*, at 114 (Stewart, J., concurring).

(c) In the years following Flast v. Cohen, the Supreme Court has grown increasingly wary of federal citizen and taxpayer standing. In Valley Forge Christian College v. Americans United for Separation of Church and State, Inc., 454 U.S. 464 (1982), plaintiffs challenged an *executive* decision to transfer surplus property worth $577, 500 to a religious institution.[2] The Court ruled that the taxpayer plaintiffs failed the first prong of Flast's test— permitting challenges only to "exercises of congressional power under the taxing and spending clause"—for two reasons: first, "the source of their complaint is not a congressional action, but a decision by HEW to transfer a parcel of federal property"; second, the authorizing statute was "an * * * exercise of Congress' power under the Property Clause, Art. IV, § 3, cl. 2", rather than under the Taxing and Spending Clause. In dissent, Justice Brennan rejected the Court's distinction of Flast as unconvincing.

(d) The Roberts Court has divided over the continuing reach of Flast v. Cohen and over whether it remains—or should remain—good law. In Hein v. Freedom from Religion Foundation, Inc., 551 U.S. 587 (2007), a plurality read Flast narrowly. The President, by executive order, had created a White House office and several centers within federal agencies to ensure that faith-based community groups would be eligible to apply for federal funding for activities that were not inherently religious. Suing as taxpayers, the respondents challenged a number of executive actions that, they said, violated the Establishment Clause by expending public funds to promote religious community groups over secular ones. The plurality opinion by Justice Alito, joined by Chief Justice Roberts and Justice Kennedy, held Flast distinguishable on the ground that the expenditures at issue were not made pursuant to any specific Act of Congress, as in Flast, but rather occurred under general appropriations to the Executive Branch.

Concurring in the judgment, Justice Scalia (joined by Justice Thomas) argued that Flast ultimately rested on the principle, indefensible in his view, that "Psychic Injury", rather than "Wallet Injury", sufficed to establish standing. Arguing that efforts to distinguish Flast had been arbitrary and unconvincing, he maintained that the precedent's lack of a logical theoretical underpinning has rendered our taxpayer standing doctrine such a jurisprudential disaster that it ought to be overruled. Justice Souter's dissent (joined by Justices Stevens, Ginsburg, and Breyer) agreed that efforts to distinguish Flast were unconvincing and contended that the respondents sought "not to 'extend' Flast, but merely to apply it. When executive agencies spend identifiable sums of tax money for religious purposes, no less than when Congress authorizes the same thing, taxpayers suffer injury."

(e) In Arizona Christian School Tuition Org. v. Winn, 131 S.Ct. 1436 (2011), the Court again divided over Flast's meaning. Under Arizona law,

---

[2] On Valley Forge, see Nichol, *Standing on the Constitution: The Supreme Court and Valley Forge*, 61 N.C.L.Rev. 798 (1983). For earlier commentary on taxpayer standing, see Bittker, *The Case of the Fictitious Taxpayer: The Federal Taxpayer's Suit Twenty Years After Flast v. Cohen*, 36 U.Chi.L.Rev. 364 (1969); Davis, *The Case of the Real Taxpayer: A Reply to Professor Bittker*, 36 U.Chi.L.Rev. 375 (1969).

taxpayers earn tax credits for money they contribute to "school tuition organizations" (STOs) that fund scholarships for children attending private schools, including sectarian ones. Arizona taxpayers challenged the state statute, arguing that it violates the Establishment Clause. In an opinion by Justice Kennedy, a closely divided Court held that the plaintiffs could not "take advantage of Flast's narrow exception to the general rule against taxpayer standing." In particular, the Court noted that Flast had relied on James Madison's influential Memorial and Remonstrance Against Religious Assessments (1785), which had objected to public funding for religion on the ground that it "would coerce [taxpayers into] a form of religious devotion in violation of conscience." Since the STO program consisted entirely of voluntary contributions by taxpayers, the Court reasoned that, in contrast with the expenditures challenged in Flast, the program did not forcibly extract money from religious dissenters.

In dissent, Justice Kagan, joined by Justices Ginsburg, Breyer, and Sotomayor, argued that the Court's position was unsupported by precedent or fiscal reality. In particular, she emphasized that the Court had resolved five cases involving state tax expenditures (the use of tax relief rather than direct expenditures to achieve public purposes) but had not once questioned Flast's applicability. In addition, she maintained that "targeted tax breaks" are economically no different from a direct appropriation because each requires the diversion of tax revenues to support religion. As Justice Kagan elaborated, "Suppose a State desires to reward Jews—by, say, $500 per year—for their religious devotion. Should the nature of the taxpayers' concern vary if the State allows Jews to claim the aid on their tax returns in lieu of receiving an annual stipend?" Justice Kagan would have reaffirmed Flast and upheld standing in Winn. In an opinion concurring in the Court's opinion, Justices Scalia and Thomas again urged that Flast be overruled.

(f) Has the Court engaged in a "stealth" overruling of Flast by drawing thin, and sometimes arbitrary, distinctions that essentially limit Flast to its facts? See, *e.g.*, Friedman, *The Wages of Stealth Overruling (With Particular Attention to Miranda v. Arizona)*, 99 Geo.L.J. 1, 9–11, 34–36, 47–49 (2010); Sherry, *The Four Pillars of Constitutional Doctrine*, 32 Cardozo L.Rev. 969, 977–81 (2011).

(3) Actions by Legislators. Another specialized area of standing doctrine involves actions by legislators challenging intrusions upon their prerogatives. These cases present two related considerations. First, the Court must articulate what type of injury to a legislator's vote is legally actionable. Second, the Court must determine precisely what types of actions inflict such injuries. Consider whether the Court's handling of those questions in the following cases reflect a discernible theory of separation of powers.

(a) In Coleman v. Miller, 307 U.S. 433 (1939), a bare majority of the Court held that Kansas state legislators who had voted against ratification of the Child Labor Amendment had standing to seek review of a state court's refusal to enjoin state officials from certifying that Kansas had ratified the amendment. One of the grounds of suit was that the amendment had been approved in the state senate only by virtue of the vote of the lieutenant-governor, as presiding officer, to break a tie, and that under the federal Constitution such a vote was ineffectual. The Court recognized not only the standing of state senators to raise this issue, in protection of their official vote, but also the standing of both state senators and representatives to urge that the ratification was invalid because a previous rejection by Kansas was final, and because the proposed amendment, having been outstanding for what was claimed to be more than a reasonable time, was no longer susceptible of ratification. In so holding, the Court reasoned: "[T]he plaintiffs include twenty senators, whose votes against ratification have been overridden and virtually held for naught although if they are right in their contentions their votes would have been sufficient to defeat ratification. We think that these senators have a plain, direct and adequate interest in maintaining the effectiveness of their votes."

(b) In Raines v. Byrd, 521 U.S. 811 (1997), the Court rejected the standing of six present and former members of the House and Senate to challenge the constitutionality of the Line Item Veto Act, which authorized the President to "cancel" certain spending and tax benefit measures after signing them into law. The Act specifically authorized suit for declaratory and injunctive relief by "[a]ny Member of Congress or any individual adversely affected". Plaintiffs brought suit the day after the Act took effect, claiming that the statute " 'dilute[d] their Article I voting power' ". The Court noted that "our standing inquiry has been especially rigorous when reaching the merits of the dispute would force us to decide whether an action taken by one of the other two branches of the Federal Government was unconstitutional." The Court then concluded that plaintiffs based their claim of standing on a "type of institutional injury"—"a loss of political power"—and did "not claim that they have been deprived of something to which they *personally* are entitled—such as their seats as members of Congress after their constituents had elected *them*" (emphasis in original). The Court distinguished Coleman as standing "at most * * * for the proposition that legislators whose votes would have been sufficient to defeat (or enact) a specific legislative act have standing to sue if that legislative action goes into effect (or does not go into effect), on the ground that their votes have been completely nullified." Although plaintiffs alleged that the Line Item Veto Act diluted the significance of their votes for bills subject to presidential cancellation, there was a "vast difference" between the "level of vote nullification" in this case and that in Coleman.[3]

Is the majority's attempted distinction of "personal" and "institutional" injuries convincing? If not, is the degree of difference in the "institutional" injuries in the two cases sufficient to support the divergent results, or has Coleman effectively been limited to its facts?

(c) The issue of congressional standing arose again in Windsor v. United States, 133 S.Ct. 2675 (2013), which considered the constitutionality of the Defense of Marriage Act's exclusion of same-sex married couples from the definition of "spouses" for purposes of federal law. As discussed at pp. 100–101, *supra*, the President directed the Attorney General not to defend the Act's constitutionality but also directed the executive branch to continue to enforce the Act in order to give Congress an opportunity to defend its validity. Pursuant to the rules of the House, the Speaker consulted with the Bipartisan Legal Advisory Group (BLAG) to discuss the proper course of action. By a 3–2 party line vote, BLAG in 2011 recommended that the Speaker direct the House General Counsel to intervene in Windsor to defend

---

[3]   Justice Souter, joined by Justice Ginsburg, concurred in the judgment that the plaintiffs lacked standing. Justice Stevens, dissenting, would have sustained standing and invalidated the Act on the merits. Justice Breyer, who also dissented, argued that the case was not distinguishable from Coleman.

DOMA's constitutionality. After the Supreme Court had granted certiorari, the House itself passed a resolution "authoriz[ing] [BLAG] * * * to defend [DOMA's] constitutionality * * * including in the case of Windsor v. United States."

Because the Court found that there remained a justiciable controversy between Windsor and the United States, it declined to reach the question whether BLAG had standing. The dissenting Justices, however, not only reached the question but also disagreed about its resolution. Justice Alito concluded that BLAG had standing because the House, which authorized BLAG to represent it, suffered a concrete, justiciable injury. Justice Alito noted that when the executive declined to defend the legislative veto in INS v. Chadha, 462 U.S. 919 (1983), the Court held that the House and Senate had standing to defend the statute authorizing such a veto. Justice Alito reasoned that just as invalidation of the legislative veto injured Congress' institutional power, so too did the refusal to defend DOMA. "[B]ecause legislating is Congress' central function," he wrote, "any impairment of that function is a more grievous injury than the impairment of a procedural add-on." Justice Alito distinguished Raines v. Byrd, *supra*, in part, on the ground that the six individual Members of Congress who sought to challenge the Item Veto Act neither had the institutional backing of the House nor the status of pivotal actors whose votes would have altered legislative outcomes absent the challenged procedure.

In an opinion joined by Chief Justice Roberts and Justice Thomas, Justice Scalia rejected Justice Alito's analysis of congressional standing. Because DOMA, unlike the legislative veto, did not regulate Congress' institutional authority as such, he argued that Justice Alito's position would permit Congress to "hale the Executive before the courts not only to vindicate its own institutional powers to act, but to correct a perceived inadequacy in the execution of its laws." This approach, he added, would permit Congress to "pop immediately into Court" not only when "the President refuses to implement a statute he believes to be unconstitutional," but also when he or she "implements a law in a manner that is not to Congress' liking." Such matters, in Justice Scalia's view, have long been properly "left for political resolution" between Congress and the President.[4]

(4) Standing and the Merits. To what extent does the reasoning in the foregoing cases collapse with the merits, as Judge Fletcher's work suggests it should? See pp. 126–127, *supra*. To the extent that taxpayers or legislators may sue when the particular constitutional provision at issue gives them an implied "cause of action," perhaps it would clarify standing doctrine for the Court to analyze the question explicitly in those terms. Compare Chapter VII, Sec. (2)(A), *infra*.

INTRODUCTORY NOTE ON CONGRESSIONAL POWER TO REGULATE STANDING

If standing reflects an irreducible constitutional minimum that authorizes judges to measure the existence of injury in fact, causation, and

-----

[4] For an argument that a single House should have standing to go to court to enforce its own subpoenas but not to defend legislation against constitutional attack, see Grove & Devins, *Congress's (Limited) Power to Defend Itself in Court*, 99 Cornell L.Rev. 571 (2014).

redressability against a constitutional ideal of what constitutes a "case" or "controversy", then the availability of standing may not depend upon the way Congress defines new rights of action. If, however, standing turns on the articulation of a *legal* injury, then Congress has greater leeway to define injuries and chains of causation that will create standing where none would otherwise exist. In the materials that follow, consider (i) where Congress derives its authority to create novel forms of standing and (ii) where the judiciary derives its authority to displace Acts of Congress that give particular classes of plaintiffs the right to sue.

———

Lujan v. Defenders of Wildlife

504 U.S. 555, 112 S.Ct. 2130, 119 L.Ed.2d 351 (1992).
Certiorari to the United States Court of Appeals for the Eighth Circuit.

■ JUSTICE SCALIA delivered the opinion of the Court with respect to Parts I, II, III–A, and IV, and an opinion with respect to Part III–B, in which THE CHIEF JUSTICE, JUSTICE WHITE, and JUSTICE THOMAS join.

I

The ESA, 87 Stat. 884, as amended, 16 U.S.C. § 1531 *et seq.*, seeks to protect species of animals against threats to their continuing existence caused by man. * * * Section 7(a)(2) of the Act * * * provides, in pertinent part:

> "Each Federal agency shall, in consultation with and with the assistance of the Secretary [of the Interior], insure that any action authorized, funded, or carried out by such agency . . . is not likely to jeopardize the continued existence of any endangered species or threatened species or result in the destruction or adverse modification of habitat of such species which is determined by the Secretary, after consultation as appropriate with affected States, to be critical." 16 U.S.C. § 1536(a)(2).

In 1978, the Fish and Wildlife Service (FWS) and the National Marine Fisheries Service (NMFS), on behalf of the Secretary of the Interior and the Secretary of Commerce respectively, promulgated a joint regulation stating that the obligations imposed by § 7(a)(2) extend to actions taken in foreign nations. * * * [In 1986, the Interior Department promulgated a "revised joint regulation, reinterpreting § 7(a)(2) to require consultation only for actions taken in the United States or on the high seas."]

Shortly thereafter, respondents, organizations dedicated to wildlife conservation and other environmental causes, filed this action against the Secretary of the Interior, seeking a declaratory judgment that the new regulation is in error as to the geographic scope of § 7(a)(2) and an injunction requiring the Secretary to promulgate a new regulation restoring the initial interpretation. The District Court granted the Secretary's motion to dismiss for lack of standing. The Court of Appeals for the Eighth Circuit reversed by a divided vote. On remand, the Secretary moved for summary judgment on the standing issue, and respondents moved for summary judgment on the merits. The District

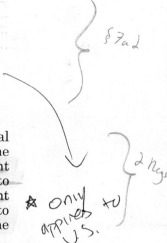

Court denied the Secretary's motion, on the ground that the Eighth Circuit had already determined the standing question in this case; it granted respondents' merits motion, and ordered the Secretary to publish a revised regulation. The Eighth Circuit affirmed. We granted certiorari.

II

* * * Over the years, our cases have established that the irreducible constitutional minimum of standing contains three elements. First, the plaintiff must have suffered an "injury in fact"—an invasion of a legally protected interest which is (a) concrete and particularized, [see Allen v. Wright, 468 U.S. 737, 756 (1984)]; and (b) "actual or imminent, not 'conjectural' or 'hypothetical.' " Whitmore [v. Arkansas, 495 U.S. 149, (1990)] (quoting Los Angeles v. Lyons, 461 U.S. 95, 102 (1983)). Second, there must be a causal connection between the injury and the conduct complained of—the injury has to be "fairly . . . trace[able] to the challenged action of the defendant, and not . . . th[e] result [of] the independent action of some third party not before the court." Simon v. Eastern Ky. Welfare Rights Organization, 426 U.S. 26, 41–42 (1976). Third, it must be "likely," as opposed to merely "speculative," that the injury will be "redressed by a favorable decision." *Id.*, at 38, 43.

The party invoking federal jurisdiction bears the burden of establishing these elements. * * * [O]n a motion to dismiss we "presum[e] that general allegations embrace those specific facts that are necessary to support the claim." [Lujan v. National Wildlife Federation, 497 U.S. 871, 889 (1990)]. In response to a summary judgment motion, however, the plaintiff can no longer rest on such "mere allegations," but must "set forth" by affidavit or other evidence "specific facts," Fed.Rule Civ.Proc. 56(e), which for purposes of the summary judgment motion will be taken to be true. And at the final stage, those facts (if controverted) must be "supported adequately by the evidence adduced at trial."

When the suit is one challenging the legality of government action or inaction, the nature and extent of facts that must be averred (at the summary judgment stage) or proved (at the trial stage) in order to establish standing depends considerably upon whether the plaintiff is himself an object of the action (or forgone action) at issue. If he is, there is ordinarily little question that the action or inaction has caused him injury, and that a judgment preventing or requiring the action will redress it. When, however, as in this case, a plaintiff's asserted injury arises from the government's allegedly unlawful regulation (or lack of regulation) of *someone else*, much more is needed. In that circumstance, causation and redressability ordinarily hinge on the response of the regulated (or regulable) third party to the government action or inaction—and perhaps on the response of others as well. The existence of one or more of the essential elements of standing "depends on the unfettered choices made by independent actors not before the courts and whose exercise of broad and legitimate discretion the courts cannot presume either to control or to predict," ASARCO Inc. v. Kadish, 490 U.S. 605, 615 (1989) (opinion of KENNEDY, J.); and it becomes the burden of the plaintiff to adduce facts showing that those choices have been or will be made in such manner as to produce causation and permit redressability of injury. Thus, when the plaintiff is not himself the object of the government action or inaction he challenges, standing is not precluded, but it is ordinarily "substantially more difficult" to establish. Allen, *supra*, 468 U.S., at 758.

III

We think the Court of Appeals failed to apply the foregoing principles in denying the Secretary's motion for summary judgment. Respondents had not made the requisite demonstration of (at least) injury and redressability.

A

Respondents' claim to injury is that the lack of consultation with respect to certain funded activities abroad "increas[es] the rate of extinction of endangered and threatened species." Of course, the desire to use or observe an animal species, even for purely esthetic purposes, is undeniably a cognizable interest for purpose of standing. See, *e.g.*, Sierra Club v. Morton, 405 U.S. [727, 734 (1972)]. "But the 'injury in fact' test requires more than an injury to a cognizable interest. It requires that the party seeking review be himself among the injured." *Id.*, at 734–735. To survive the Secretary's summary judgment motion, respondents had to submit affidavits or other evidence showing, through specific facts, not only that listed species were in fact being threatened by funded activities abroad, but also that one or more of respondents' members would thereby be "directly" affected apart from their " 'special interest' in th[e] subject." *Id.*, at 735, 739. * * *

With respect to this aspect of the case, the Court of Appeals focused on the affidavits of two Defenders' members—Joyce Kelly and Amy Skilbred. Ms. Kelly stated that she traveled to Egypt in 1986 and "observed the traditional habitat of the endangered nile crocodile there and intend[s] to do so again, and hope[s] to observe the crocodile directly," and that she "will suffer harm in fact as the result of [the] American . . . role . . . in overseeing the rehabilitation of the Aswan High Dam on the Nile . . . and [in] develop[ing] . . . Egypt's . . . Master Water Plan." Ms. Skilbred averred that she traveled to Sri Lanka in 1981 and "observed th[e] habitat" of "endangered species such as the Asian elephant and the leopard" at what is now the site of the Mahaweli project funded by the Agency for International Development (AID), although she "was unable to see any of the endangered species"; "this development project," she continued, "will seriously reduce endangered, threatened, and endemic species habitat including areas that I visited . . . [, which] may severely shorten the future of these species"; that threat, she concluded, harmed her because she "intend[s] to return to Sri Lanka in the future and hope[s] to be more fortunate in spotting at least the endangered elephant and leopard." When Ms. Skilbred was asked at a subsequent deposition if and when she had any plans to return to Sri Lanka, she * * * confessed that she had no current plans * * *.

We shall assume for the sake of argument that these affidavits contain facts showing that certain agency-funded projects threaten listed species—though that is questionable. They plainly contain no facts, however, showing how damage to the species will produce "imminent" injury to Mses. Kelly and Skilbred. That the women "had visited" the areas of the projects before the projects commenced proves nothing. * * * And the affiants' profession of an "inten[t]" to return to the places they had visited before—* * * without any description of concrete plans, or indeed even any specification of *when* the some day will be—do not support a finding of the "actual or imminent" injury that our cases require.

Besides relying upon the Kelly and Skilbred affidavits, respondents propose a series of novel standing theories. The first, inelegantly styled "ecosystem nexus," proposes that any person who uses *any part* of a "contiguous ecosystem" adversely affected by a funded activity has standing even if the activity is located a great distance away. This approach, as the Court of Appeals correctly observed, is inconsistent with our opinion in National Wildlife Federation, which held that a plaintiff claiming injury from environmental damage must use the area affected by the challenged activity and not an area roughly "in the vicinity" of it. 497 U.S., at 887–889. It makes no difference that the general-purpose section of the ESA states that the Act was intended in part "to provide a means whereby the ecosystems upon which endangered species and threatened species depend may be conserved," 16 U.S.C. § 1531(b). To say that the Act protects ecosystems is not to say that the Act creates (if it were possible) rights of action in persons who have not been injured in fact, that is, persons who use portions of an ecosystem not perceptibly affected by the unlawful action in question.

Respondents' other theories are called, alas, the "animal nexus" approach, whereby anyone who has an interest in studying or seeing the endangered animals anywhere on the globe has standing; and the "vocational nexus" approach, under which anyone with a professional interest in such animals can sue. Under these theories, anyone who goes to see Asian elephants in the Bronx Zoo, and anyone who is a keeper of Asian elephants in the Bronx Zoo, has standing to sue because the Director of the Agency for International Development (AID) did not consult with the Secretary regarding the AID-funded project in Sri Lanka. This is beyond all reason. * * * It is clear that the person who observes or works with a particular animal threatened by a federal decision is facing perceptible harm, since the very subject of his interest will no longer exist. It is even plausible—though it goes to the outermost limit of plausibility—to think that a person who observes or works with animals of a particular species in the very area of the world where that species is threatened by a federal decision is facing such harm, since some animals that might have been the subject of his interest will no longer exist, see Japan Whaling Assn. v. American Cetacean Society, 478 U.S. 221, 231, n.4 (1986). It goes beyond the limit, however, and into pure speculation and fantasy, to say that anyone who observes or works with an endangered species, anywhere in the world, is appreciably harmed by a single project affecting some portion of that species with which he has no more specific connection.

B.

Besides failing to show injury, respondents failed to demonstrate redressability. Instead of attacking the separate decisions to fund particular projects allegedly causing them harm, respondents chose to challenge a more generalized level of Government action (rules regarding consultation) * * *. * * * Since the agencies funding the projects were not parties to the case, the District Court could accord relief only against the Secretary: He could be ordered to revise his regulation to require consultation for foreign projects. But this would not remedy respondents' alleged injury unless the funding agencies were bound by the Secretary's regulation, which is very much an open question. * * * When the Secretary promulgated the regulation at issue here, he thought it was binding on the agencies. The Solicitor General, however, has repudiated that position here, and the agencies themselves apparently deny the Secretary's authority. * * * The short of the matter is that redress of the only injury in fact respondents complain of requires action (termination of funding until consultation) by the individual funding agencies; and any relief the District Court could have provided in this suit against the Secretary was not likely to produce that action.

A further impediment to redressability is the fact that the agencies generally supply only a fraction of the funding for a foreign project. AID, for example, has provided less than 10% of the funding for the Mahaweli project. Respondents have produced nothing to indicate that the projects they have named will either be suspended, or do less harm to listed species, if that fraction is eliminated. As in Simon, 426 U.S., at 43–44, it is entirely conjectural whether the nonagency activity that affects respondents will be altered or affected by the agency activity they seek to achieve. There is no standing.

IV

The Court of Appeals found that respondents had standing for an additional reason: because they had suffered a "procedural injury." The so-called "citizen-suit" provision of the ESA provides, in pertinent part, that "any person may commence a civil suit on his own behalf (A) to enjoin any person, including the United States and any other governmental instrumentality or agency . . . who is alleged to be in violation of any provision of this chapter." 16 U.S.C. § 1540(g). The court held that, because § 7(a)(2) requires interagency consultation, the citizen-suit provision creates a "procedural righ[t]" to consultation in all "persons"—so that *anyone* can file suit in federal court to challenge the Secretary's (or presumably any other official's) failure to follow the assertedly correct consultative procedure, notwithstanding his or her inability to allege any discrete injury flowing from that failure. To understand the remarkable nature of this holding one must be clear about what it does *not* rest upon: This is not a case where plaintiffs are seeking to enforce a procedural requirement the disregard of which could impair a separate concrete interest of theirs (*e.g.*, the procedural requirement for a hearing prior to denial of their license application, or the procedural requirement for an environmental impact statement before a federal facility is constructed next door to them).[7] Nor is it simply a case where concrete injury has been suffered by many persons, as in mass fraud or mass tort situations. Nor, finally, is it the unusual case in

---

[7]   There is this much truth to the assertion that "procedural rights" are special: The person who has been accorded a procedural right to protect his concrete interests can assert that right without meeting all the normal standards for redressability and immediacy. Thus, under our case law, one living adjacent to the site for proposed construction of a federally licensed dam has standing to challenge the licensing agency's failure to prepare an environmental impact statement, even though he cannot establish with any certainty that the statement will cause the license to be withheld or altered, and even though the dam will not be completed for many years. (That is why we do not rely, in the present case, upon the Government's argument that, *even if* the other agencies were obliged to consult with the Secretary, they might not have followed his advice.) What respondents' "procedural rights" argument seeks, however, is quite different from this: standing for persons who have no concrete interests affected—persons who live (and propose to live) at the other end of the country from the dam.

which Congress has created a concrete private interest in the outcome of a suit against a private party for the government's benefit, by providing a cash bounty for the victorious plaintiff. Rather, the court held that the injury-in-fact requirement had been satisfied by congressional conferral upon *all* persons of an abstract, self-contained, noninstrumental "right" to have the Executive observe the procedures required by law. We reject this view.

We have consistently held that a plaintiff raising only a generally available grievance about government—claiming only harm to his and every citizen's interest in proper application of the Constitution and laws, and seeking relief that no more directly and tangibly benefits him than it does the public at large—does not state an Article III case or controversy. * * *

To be sure, our generalized-grievance cases have typically involved Government violation of procedures assertedly ordained by the Constitution rather than the Congress. But there is absolutely no basis for making the Article III inquiry turn on the source of the asserted right. Whether the courts were to act on their own, or at the invitation of Congress, in ignoring the concrete injury requirement described in our cases, they would be discarding a principle fundamental to the separate and distinct constitutional role of the Third Branch—one of the essential elements that identifies those "Cases" and "Controversies" that are the business of the courts rather than of the political branches. "The province of the court," as Chief Justice Marshall said in Marbury v. Madison, 5 U.S. (1 Cranch) 137, 170 (1803), "is, solely, to decide on the rights of individuals." Vindicating the *public* interest (including the public interest in Government observance of the Constitution and laws) is the function of Congress and the Chief Executive. The question presented here is whether the public interest in proper administration of the laws (specifically, in agencies' observance of a particular, statutorily prescribed procedure) can be converted into an individual right by a statute that denominates it as such, and that permits all citizens (or, for that matter, a subclass of citizens who suffer no distinctive concrete harm) to sue. If the concrete injury requirement has the separation-of-powers significance we have always said, the answer must be obvious. To permit Congress to convert the undifferentiated public interest in executive officers' compliance with the law into an "individual right" vindicable in the courts is to permit Congress to transfer from the President to the courts the Chief Executive's most important constitutional duty, to "take Care that the Laws be faithfully executed," Art. II, § 3. It would enable the courts, with the permission of Congress, "to assume a position of authority over the governmental acts of another and co-equal department," Frothingham v. Mellon, 262 U.S. [447, 489 (1923)], and to become " 'virtually continuing monitors of the wisdom and soundness of Executive action.' " Allen, 468 U.S., at 760 (quoting Laird v. Tatum, 408 U.S. 1, 15 (1972)). We have always rejected that vision of our role * * *

Nothing in this contradicts the principle that "[t]he . . . injury required by Art. III may exist solely by virtue of 'statutes creating legal rights, the invasion of which creates standing.' " Warth [v. Seldin, 422 U.S. [490,] 500 [(1975)]] (quoting Linda R. S. v. Richard D., 410 U.S. 614, 617, n.3 (1973)). Both of the cases used by Linda R. S. as an illustration of that principle involved Congress' elevating to the status of legally cognizable injuries concrete, *de facto* injuries that were previously inadequate in law (namely, injury to an individual's personal interest in living in a racially integrated community, see Trafficante v. Metropolitan Life Ins. Co., 409 U.S. 205, 208–212 (1972), and injury to a company's interest in marketing its product free from competition, see Hardin v. Kentucky Utilities Co., 390 U.S. 1, 6 (1968)). As we said in Sierra Club, "[Statutory] broadening [of] the categories of injury that may be alleged in support of standing is a different matter from abandoning the requirement that the party seeking review must himself have suffered an injury." 405 U.S., at 738. Whether or not the principle set forth in Warth can be extended beyond that distinction, it is clear that in suits against the Government, at least, the concrete injury requirement must remain. * * *

It is so ordered.

■ JUSTICE KENNEDY, with whom JUSTICE SOUTER joins, concurring in part and concurring in the judgment.

Although I agree with the essential parts of the Court's analysis, I write separately to make several observations.

I agree with the Court's conclusion in Part III–A that, on the record before us, respondents have failed to demonstrate that they themselves are "among the injured." Sierra Club v. Morton, 405 U.S. 727, 735 (1972). * * *

While it may seem trivial to require that Mses. Kelly and Skilbred acquire airline tickets to the project sites or announce a date certain upon which they will return, this is not a case where it is reasonable to assume that the affiants will be using the sites on a regular basis, nor do the affiants claim to have visited the sites since the projects commenced. With respect to the Court's discussion of respondents' "ecosystem nexus," "animal nexus," and "vocational nexus" theories, I agree that on this record respondents' showing is insufficient to establish standing on any of these bases. I am not willing to foreclose the possibility, however, that in different circumstances a nexus theory similar to those proffered here might support a claim to standing.

In light of the conclusion that respondents have not demonstrated a concrete injury here sufficient to support standing under our precedents, I would not reach the issue of redressability that is discussed by the plurality in Part III–B.

I also join Part IV of the Court's opinion with the following observations. As Government programs and policies become more complex and farreaching, we must be sensitive to the articulation of new rights of action that do not have clear analogs in our common-law tradition. Modern litigation has progressed far from the paradigm of Marbury suing Madison to get his commission, Marbury v. Madison, 5 U.S. (1 Cranch) 137 (1803), or Ogden seeking an injunction to halt Gibbons' steamboat operations, Gibbons v. Ogden, 22 U.S. (9 Wheat.) 1 (1824). In my view, Congress has the power to define injuries and articulate chains of causation that will give rise to a case or controversy where none existed before, and I do not read the Court's opinion to suggest a contrary view. In exercising this power, however, Congress must at the very least identify the injury it seeks to vindicate and relate the injury to the class of persons entitled to bring suit. The citizen-suit provision of the Endangered Species Act does not meet these minimal requirements, because while the statute purports to confer a right on "any person . . . to enjoin . . . the United States and any other governmental instrumentality or agency . . . who is alleged to be in violation of any provision of this chapter," it does not of its own force establish that there is an injury in "any person" by virtue of any "violation." 16 U.S.C. § 1540(g)(1)(A).

The Court's holding that there is an outer limit to the power of Congress to confer rights of action is a direct and necessary consequence of the case and controversy limitations found in Article III. I agree that it would exceed those limitations if, at the behest of Congress and in the absence of any showing of concrete injury, we were to entertain citizen suits to vindicate the public's nonconcrete interest in the proper administration of the laws. While it does not matter how many persons have been injured by the challenged action, the party bringing suit must show that the action injures him in a concrete and personal way. This requirement is not just an empty formality. It preserves the vitality of the adversarial process by assuring both that the parties before the court have an actual, as opposed to professed, stake in the outcome, and that "the legal questions presented . . . will be resolved, not in the rarified atmosphere of a debating society, but in a concrete factual context conducive to a realistic appreciation of the consequences of judicial action." Valley Forge Christian College v. Americans United for Separation of Church and State, Inc., 454 U.S. 464, 472 (1982). In addition, the requirement of concrete injury confines the Judicial Branch to its proper, limited role in the constitutional framework of Government.

An independent judiciary is held to account through its open proceedings and its reasoned judgments. In this process it is essential for the public to know what persons or groups are invoking the judicial power, the reasons that they have brought suit, and whether their claims are vindicated or denied. The concrete injury requirement helps assure that there can be an answer to these questions; and, as the Court's opinion is careful to show, that is part of the constitutional design.

■ JUSTICE STEVENS, concurring in the judgment.

[Justice Stevens concurred in the judgment on the ground that he did not believe that § 7(a)(2) of the Endangered Species Act of 1973 (ESA), 16 U.S.C. § 1536(a)(2), required consultation about projects in foreign countries. He believed, however, that respondents had established their standing to sue. First, he contended that "injury to an individual's interest in studying or enjoying a species and its natural habitat occurs when someone (whether it be the Government or a private party) takes action that harms that species and habitat." Accordingly, the affidavits sufficed to survive summary judgment even though they did not specify a date for the plaintiffs' return to the habitats. Justice Stevens also rejected the plurality's conclusions about redressability on two grounds. First, he argued that the Court "must presume that if [we] hold[ ] that § 7(a)(2) requires consultation, all affected agencies would abide by that interpretation and engage in the requisite consultations." Second, he argued that the Court should credit Congress' judgment that consultation would affect the allocation of funds. And despite the varying levels of federal aid to different foreign projects, he argued that "it is not mere speculation to think that foreign governments, when faced with the threatened withdrawal of United States assistance, will modify their projects to mitigate the harm to endangered species."]

■ JUSTICE BLACKMUN, with whom JUSTICE O'CONNOR joins, dissenting.

I part company with the Court in this case in two respects. First, I believe that respondents have raised genuine issues of fact—sufficient to survive summary judgment—both as to injury and as to redressability. Second, I question the Court's breadth of language in rejecting standing for "procedural" injuries. I fear the Court seeks to impose fresh limitations on the constitutional authority of Congress to allow citizen suits in the federal courts for injuries deemed "procedural" in nature. I dissent.

I

To survive petitioner's motion for summary judgment on standing, respondents * * * need show only a "genuine issue" of material fact as to standing. Fed.Rule Civ.Proc. 56(c). This is not a heavy burden. A "genuine issue" exists so long as "the evidence is such that a reasonable jury could return a verdict for the nonmoving party [respondents]." Anderson v. Liberty Lobby, Inc., 477 U.S. 242, 248 (1986). * * *

1

I think a reasonable finder of fact could conclude from the information in the affidavits and deposition testimony that either Kelly or Skilbred will soon return to the project sites, thereby satisfying the "actual or imminent" injury standard. * * * By requiring a "description of concrete plans" or "specification of *when* the some day [for a return visit] will be," the Court, in my view, demands what is likely an empty formality. No substantial barriers prevent Kelly or Skilbred from simply purchasing plane tickets to return to the Aswan and Mahaweli projects. This case differs from other cases in which the imminence of harm turned largely on the affirmative actions of third parties beyond a plaintiff's control. * * * I fear the Court's demand for detailed descriptions of future conduct will do little to weed out those who are genuinely harmed from those who are not. More likely, it will resurrect a code-pleading formalism in federal court summary judgment practice, as federal courts, newly doubting their jurisdiction, will demand more and more particularized showings of future harm. * * *

2

The Court also concludes that injury is lacking, because respondents' allegations of "ecosystem nexus" failed to demonstrate sufficient proximity to the site of the environmental harm. To support that conclusion, the Court mischaracterizes our decision in Lujan v. National Wildlife Federation as establishing a general rule that "a plaintiff claiming injury from environmental damage must use the area affected by the challenged activity." In National Wildlife Federation, the Court required specific geographical proximity because of the particular type of harm alleged in that case: harm to the plaintiff's visual enjoyment of nature from mining activities. One cannot suffer from the sight of a ruined landscape without being close enough to see the sites actually being mined. Many environmental injuries, however, cause harm distant from the area immediately affected by the challenged action. * * *

The Court also rejects respondents' claim of vocational or professional injury. The Court says that it is "beyond all reason" that a zoo "keeper" of Asian elephants would have standing to contest his Government's participation in the eradication of all the Asian elephants in another part of the world. I am unable to see how the distant location of the destruction *necessarily* (for purposes of ruling at summary judgment) mitigates the harm to the elephant keeper. If there is no more access to a future supply of the animal that sustains a keeper's livelihood, surely there is harm.

B

A plurality of the Court suggests that respondents have not demonstrated redressability * * *: The plurality identifies two obstacles. The first is that the "action agencies" * * * cannot be required to undertake consultation with petitioner Secretary, because they are not directly bound as parties to the suit and are otherwise not indirectly bound by being subject to petitioner Secretary's regulation. Petitioner, however, officially and publicly has taken the position that his regulations regarding consultation under § 7 of the Act are binding on action agencies. 50 CFR § 402.14(a) (1991). And he has previously taken the same position in this very litigation * * *. I cannot agree with the plurality that the Secretary (or the Solicitor General) is now free, for the convenience of this appeal, to disavow his prior public and litigation positions. * * *

The second redressability obstacle relied on by the plurality is that "the [action] agencies generally supply only a fraction of the funding for a foreign project." What this Court might "generally" take to be true does not eliminate the existence of a genuine issue of fact to withstand summary judgment. Even if the action agencies supply only a fraction of the funding for a particular foreign project, it remains at least a question for the finder of fact whether threatened withdrawal of that fraction would affect foreign government conduct sufficiently to avoid harm to listed species.

[T]he relevant inquiry is not, as the plurality suggests, what will happen if AID or other agencies stop funding projects, but what will happen if AID or other agencies comply with the consultation requirement for projects abroad. Respondents filed suit to require consultation, not a termination of funding. Respondents have raised at least a genuine issue of fact that the projects harm endangered species and that the actions of AID and other United States agencies can mitigate that harm.

II

The Court concludes that any "procedural injury" suffered by respondents is insufficient to confer standing. It rejects the view that the "injury-in-fact requirement . . . [is] satisfied by congressional conferral upon *all* persons of an abstract, self-contained, noninstrumental 'right' to have the Executive observe the procedures required by law." Whatever the Court might mean with that very broad language, it cannot be saying that "procedural injuries" *as a class* are necessarily insufficient for purposes of Article III standing.

Most governmental conduct can be classified as "procedural." * * * When the Government, for example, "procedurally" issues a pollution permit, those affected by the permittee's pollutants are not without standing to sue. Only later cases will tell just what the Court means by its intimation that "procedural" injuries are not constitutionally cognizable injuries. In the meantime, I have the greatest of sympathy for the courts across the country that will struggle to understand the Court's standardless exposition of this concept today.

The Court expresses concern that allowing judicial enforcement of "agencies' observance of a particular, statutorily prescribed procedure" would "transfer from the President to the courts the Chief Executive's most important constitutional duty, to 'take Care that the Laws be faithfully executed,' Art. II, § 3." In fact, the principal effect of foreclosing judicial enforcement of such procedures is to transfer power into the hands of the Executive at the expense—not of the courts—but of Congress, from which that power originates and emanates.

Under the Court's anachronistically formal view of the separation of powers, Congress legislates pure, substantive mandates and has no business structuring the procedural manner in which the Executive implements these mandates. To be sure, in the ordinary course, Congress does legislate in black-and-white terms of affirmative commands or negative prohibitions on the conduct of officers of the Executive Branch. In complex regulatory areas, however, Congress often legislates, as it were, in procedural shades of gray. That is, it sets forth substantive policy goals and provides for their attainment by requiring Executive Branch officials to follow certain procedures, for example, in the form of reporting, consultation, and certification requirements. * * *

The consultation requirement of § 7 of the Endangered Species Act is [an] * * * action-forcing statute. Consultation is designed as an integral check on federal agency action, ensuring that such action does not go forward without full consideration of its effects on listed species. Once consultation is initiated, the Secretary is under a duty to provide to the action agency "a written statement setting forth the Secretary's opinion, and a summary of the information on which the opinion is based, detailing how the agency action affects the species or its critical habitat." 16 U.S.C. § 1536(b)(3)(A). The Secretary is also obligated to suggest "reasonable and prudent alternatives" to prevent jeopardy to listed species. *Ibid.* The action agency must undertake as well its own "biological assessment for the purpose of identifying any endangered species or threatened species" likely to be affected by agency action. § 1536(c)(1). After the initiation of consultation, the action agency "shall not make any irreversible or irretrievable commitment of resources" which would foreclose the "formulation or implementation of any reasonable and prudent alternative measures" to avoid jeopardizing listed species. § 1536(d). These action-forcing procedures are "designed to protect some threatened concrete interest," of persons who observe and work with endangered or threatened species. That is why I am mystified by the Court's unsupported conclusion that "[t]his is not a case where plaintiffs are seeking to enforce a procedural requirement the disregard of which could impair a separate concrete interest of theirs." * * *

To prevent Congress from conferring standing for "procedural injuries" is [for Justice Scalia] another way of saying that Congress may not delegate to the courts authority deemed "executive" in nature. * * *

Here Congress seeks not to delegate "executive" power but only to strengthen the procedures it has legislatively mandated. * * *

It is to be hoped that over time the Court will acknowledge that some classes of procedural duties are so enmeshed with the prevention of a substantive, concrete harm that an individual plaintiff may be able to demonstrate a sufficient likelihood of injury just through the breach of that procedural duty. For example, in the context of the NEPA requirement of environmental-impact statements, this Court has acknowledged "it is now well settled that NEPA itself does not mandate particular results [and] simply prescribes the necessary process," but *"these procedures are almost certain to affect the agency's substantive decision."* Robertson v. Methow Valley Citizens Council, 490 U.S. [332, 350 (1989)] (emphasis added). * * *

In short, determining "injury" for Article III standing purposes is a fact-specific inquiry. * * * There may be factual circumstances in which a congressionally imposed procedural requirement is so insubstantially connected to the prevention of a substantive harm that it cannot be said to work any conceivable injury to an individual litigant. But, as a general matter, the courts owe substantial deference to Congress' substantive purpose in imposing a certain procedural requirement. In all events, * * * [t]here is no room for a *per se* rule or presumption excluding injuries labeled "procedural" in nature.

III

In conclusion, I cannot join the Court on what amounts to a slash-and-burn expedition through the law of environmental standing. In my view, "[t]he very essence of civil liberty certainly consists in the right of every individual to claim the protection of the laws, whenever he receives an injury." Marbury v. Madison, 1 Cranch 137, 163 (1803).

I dissent.

NOTE ON CONGRESSIONAL POWER TO CONFER STANDING TO SUE

(1) Prior Congressional Grants of Standing. With the possible exceptions of the Court's cryptic opinion in Muskrat v. United States, 219 U.S. 346 (1911), p. 97, *supra*, and its unexplained summary affirmance in McClure v. Reagan, 454 U.S. 1025 (1981),[1] Lujan represents the first time that the Court clearly invalidated an Act of Congress on the ground that it unconstitutionally conferred standing upon someone who did not meet the requisite injury requirements.[2] Indeed, prior Court opinions suggested that

---

[1] Despite a relevant congressional authorization to sue, McClure v. Carter, 513 F.Supp. 265 (D.Idaho 1981), summarily affirmed *sub nom.* McClure v. Reagan, 454 U.S. 1025 (1981), the Court denied Senator McClure standing to challenge the appointment of former Congressman Mikva to the United States Court of Appeals for the D.C. Circuit as a violation of the Emoluments Clause. See U.S. Const. Art. I, § 6, cl. 2 (prohibiting the appointment of any Senator or Representative to any federal office whose emoluments were increased during the time for which the Senator or Representative was elected). For further discussion of congressional standing, see pp. 131–132, *supra*.

[2] Following Lujan, the Court again found an absence of standing, despite a congressional authorization to sue, in Raines v. Byrd, 521 U.S. 811 (1997), discussed p. 131, *supra*. For critical discussion of Lujan, see Sunstein, *What's Standing After Lujan? Of Citizen Suits, "Injuries," and Article III*, 91 Mich.L.Rev. 163 (1992); Pierce, *Lujan v. Defenders of Wildlife: Standing as a*

the determination about who possessed a judicially cognizable right to sue ultimately lay within congressional control. See Warth v. Seldin, 422 U.S. 490, 500–01 (1975) (dictum) (stating that "[t]he actual or threatened injury required by Art. III may exist solely by virtue of 'statutes creating legal rights, the invasion of which creates standing' "); Sierra Club v. Morton, 405 U.S. 727, 732 n.3 (1972) ("[W]here a dispute is otherwise justiciable, the question whether the litigant is a 'proper party to request an adjudication of a particular issue,' is one within the power of Congress to determine.").

As Justice Harlan noted in his influential separate opinion in Flast v. Cohen, 392 U.S. 83, 120 (1968), administrative law decisions of the 1940s had recognized significant congressional power to confer standing where none otherwise would have existed. In the absence of an authorizing statute, standing to challenge administrative action had generally depended on the coercive infringement of a liberty or property interest recognized at common law. See Sunstein, *Standing and the Privatization of Public Law*, 88 Colum.L.Rev. 1432 (1988). In effect, this common law approach to standing meant that the targets of regulatory action, but not the intended beneficiaries of regulatory statutes, possessed standing to sue. In a series of pathbreaking decisions, however, the Supreme Court held that Congress could authorize standing to protect the "public interest" in statutory enforcement. Consider the following pre-Lujan examples.

(a) Competitors' Standing. The evolution of competitors' standing provides the paradigmatic example of Congress' recognized power to create standing where none previously existed. The traditional rule was that the proprietor of a business lacks standing to object to the government's support of competing activities, because the common law does not recognize an interest in freedom from competition. See Tennessee Elec. Power Co. v. Tennessee Valley Auth., 306 U.S. 118, 137–38 (1939) (power companies that sell electricity lack standing to enjoin the TVA's competing operations, which are alleged to be unconstitutional); see also Alabama Power Co. v. Ickes, 302 U.S. 464 (1938). A major shift occurred in FCC v. Sanders Bros. Radio Station, 309 U.S. 470 (1940), where a radio station sought judicial review of the FCC's award of a broadcast license to a competitor. Section 402(b) of the Communications Act allowed an appeal "by any * * * person aggrieved or whose interests are adversely affected by a decision of the Commission granting or refusing any such application." The complainant argued that the Act created a legal interest in freedom from competition, which required consideration by the FCC of the economic impact of the award on existing licensees. The Court rejected this argument on the merits, but upheld the complainant's standing to protect the public interest: "Congress * * * may have been of opinion that one likely to be financially injured by the issue of a license would be the only person having a sufficient interest to bring to the attention of the appellate court errors of law in the action of the Commission in granting the license. It is within the power of Congress to confer such standing to prosecute an appeal." See also Scripps-Howard Radio, Inc. v. FCC, 316 U.S. 4, 14 (1942) (under Sanders, "these private litigants have standing only as representatives of the public interest"). Even if injury to the plaintiff's competitive position did not count as an injury to a legally

---

Judicially Imposed Limit on Legislative Power, 42 Duke L.J. 1170 (1993); and Nichol, *Justice Scalia, Standing, and Public Law Litigation*, 42 Duke L.J. 1141 (1993). For more favorable commentary, see Breger, *Defending Defenders: Remarks on Nichol and Pierce*, 42 Duke L.J. 1202 (1993); Roberts, *Article III Limits on Statutory Standing*, 42 Duke L.J. 1219 (1993).

protected interest, does the economic impact on the aggrieved party seem like concrete and personalized injury in fact, as that concept has come to be understood? For a thoughtful historical analysis suggesting that the competitor standing cases reflected—and, at the time, were generally understood by the legal community to reflect—the Court's view that Congress could authorize those without *any* private legal interest to sue on the public's behalf, see Magill, *Standing for the Public: A Lost History*, 95 Va.L.Rev. 1131 (2009).

(b) Civil Rights Enforcement. In Trafficante v. Metropolitan Life Ins. Co., 409 U.S. 205 (1972), a white and an African-American tenant were held to have standing under § 810 of the Civil Rights Act of 1968, 42 U.S.C. § 3610, to seek injunctive relief and damages from their landlord for discriminating against non-white rental applicants. Section 810(d) of the Act provides that a "person aggrieved" may bring suit in federal court "to enforce rights granted or protected" by the Act. Section 810(a) defines "person aggrieved" to mean one "who claims to have been injured by a discriminatory housing practice". The plaintiffs here claimed damages for (1) lost social benefits of living in an integrated community, (2) lost business and professional advantages, and (3) embarrassment and economic injury from being "stigmatized" as residents of a "white ghetto."

Justice Douglas, for a unanimous Court, held that the statute "showed 'a congressional intention to define standing as broadly as is permitted by Article III * * *' insofar as tenants of the same housing unit * * * are concerned." The opinion further inferred from the Civil Rights Act's structure that, in achieving compliance, "the main generating force must be private suits in which * * * the complainants act not only on their own behalf but also 'as private attorneys general in vindicating a policy that Congress considered to be of the highest priority.' "

Justice White, joined by Justices Blackmun and Powell, concurred in the opinion of the Court but wrote specially to note: "Absent the Civil Rights Act of 1968, I would have great difficulty in concluding that petitioners' complaint in this case presented a case or controversy within the jurisdiction of the District Court under Article III of the Constitution. But with that statute purporting to give all those who are authorized to complain to the agency the right also to sue in court, I would sustain the statute insofar as it extends standing to those in the position of the petitioners in this case."

In Havens Realty Corp. v. Coleman, 455 U.S. 363, 372–74 (1982), the Court held that an African-American "tester"—who posed as a renter or purchaser of housing to collect evidence of racial steering practices—had standing to seek equitable and monetary relief against private parties under § 804 of the Fair Housing Act of 1968, 42 U.S.C. § 3604. The Court reasoned that the Act conferred on the tester an enforceable legal right not to be denied, because of racial steering, truthful information about the availability of housing. (A white tester, to whom the defendant had given truthful information, was held to lack standing under this theory.)

Even if the plaintiffs in Trafficante can be said to have sustained concrete and personalized injury within the meaning of today's cases, can the testers in Havens be understood as having an interest beyond gathering evidence of illegal conduct to help ensure enforcement of the law?

(2) Congressional Power to Define "Injury" After Lujan. After Lujan, uncertainty surrounds the question of how much authority Congress possesses to define judicially cognizable injuries that will provide Article III standing. Justices Kennedy and Souter joined the Lujan Court's opinion, but then concurred separately to note that "Congress has the power to define injuries and articulate chains of causation that will give rise to a case or controversy where none existed before, and I do not read the Court's opinion to suggest a contrary view." What kind of authority does this language imagine? Consider the following hypothetical amendment to the Endangered Species Act: "Every citizen has a right to preservation of all species throughout the world against threats to which actions of the United States government contribute in any way. Any citizen may bring suit in federal court for all appropriate relief for violations of that right." If the Kennedy-Souter position represents the Court's center of gravity, could such a statute support a citizen plaintiff's standing to sue to enjoin an overseas project funded in part by the United States, when the plaintiff never has been and never will be in the project's vicinity? Two subsequent cases cast some (albeit imperfect) light on the question.

(a) In Federal Election Commission v. Akins, 524 U.S. 11 (1998), the Court held that a group of voters had standing to challenge a determination by the Federal Election Commission (FEC) that the American Israel Public Affairs Committee (AIPAC) is not a "political committee" within the meaning of the Federal Election Campaign Act of 1971, 2 U.S.C. § 431(4) (FECA). Based on that determination, the FEC "ha[d] refused to require AIPAC to make disclosures regarding its membership, contributions, and expenditures that FECA would otherwise require." As a group of voters whose views often contradicted those of AIPAC, respondents had filed a complaint with the FEC arguing that AIPAC was a "political committee" within the meaning of the Act and asking the FEC to order AIPAC to make the disclosures required of such a committee under the Act. When the FEC dismissed the complaint on the ground that AIPAC was an advocacy organization rather than a political committee, respondents filed an action in federal court seeking review.

In an opinion by Justice Breyer, the Court held that the respondent-voters had standing to challenge the FEC's decision: "Congress has specifically provided in FECA that 'any person who believes a violation of this Act . . . has occurred, may file a complaint with the Commission.' § 437g(a)(1). It has added that 'any party aggrieved by an order of the Commission dismissing a complaint filed by such party . . . may file a petition' in district court seeking review of that dismissal. § 437g(8)(A)." The Court reasoned that the statute was intended "to cast the standing net broadly—beyond the common-law interests and substantive statutory rights upon which 'prudential' standing traditionally rested." Finding, in particular, that Congress had sought "to protect voters such as respondents from suffering the kind of injury here at issue", the Court rejected contentions that Congress lacked power to authorize such an action:

"The 'injury in fact' that respondents have suffered consists of their inability to obtain information—lists of AIPAC donors (who are, according to AIPAC, its members), and campaign-related contributions and expenditures—that, on respondents' view of the law, the statute requires that AIPAC make public. There is no reason to doubt their claim that the information would help them (and others to whom they would communicate it) to evaluate candidates for public office, especially candidates who received assistance from AIPAC, and to evaluate the role that AIPAC's financial assistance might play in a specific election. Respondents' injury consequently seems concrete and particular."

Rejecting an analogy to the Court's prior decision in United States v. Richardson, p. 118, *supra*, the Court concluded that the present pursuit of information differed importantly from Richardson's efforts to ascertain the CIA's budget by virtue of the Accounts Clause, U.S. Const. Art. I, § 9, cl. 7 ("[A] regular Statement and Account of the Receipts and Expenditures of all public Money shall be published from time to time."). First, the plaintiff in Richardson had sued in his capacity as a taxpayer, and the Court found no "logical nexus" (as required by Flast, p. 128, *supra*) between his status as a taxpayer and the government's failure to provide a detailed statement of account. Second, even if Richardson had asserted a particular interest in such information as a voter, Justice Breyer noted, "the Court would * * * have had to consider whether 'the Framers . . . ever imagined that the *general directives* [of the Constitution] . . . would be subject to enforcement by an individual citizen.'" That determination, Justice Breyer added, "would have rested in significant part upon the Court's view of the Accounts Clause".

The Court then considered but rejected the FEC's contention that Akins presented "a generalized grievance." Justice Breyer first observed: "Whether styled as a constitutional or prudential limit on standing, the Court has sometimes determined that where large numbers of Americans suffer alike, the political process, rather than the judicial process, may provide the more appropriate remedy for a widely shared grievance." But the generalized grievance concern "invariably appears in cases where the harm at issue is not only widely shared, but is also of an abstract and indefinite nature—for example, harm to the 'common concern for obedience to law' " (quoting L. Singer & Sons v. Union Pacific R. Co., 311 U.S. 295, 303 (1940)). Acknowledging that abstractness often corresponds with an injury's being widely shared, Justice Breyer explained that "their association is not invariable, and where a harm is concrete, though widely shared, the Court has found 'injury in fact.' "

Justice Breyer added: "This conclusion seems particularly obvious where (to use a hypothetical example) large numbers of individuals suffer the same common-law injury (say, a widespread mass tort), or where large numbers of voters suffer interference with voting rights conferred by law. We conclude that similarly, the informational injury at issue here, directly related to voting, the most basic of political rights, is sufficiently concrete and specific such that the fact that it is widely shared does not deprive Congress of constitutional power to authorize its vindication in the federal courts."

In dissent, Justice Scalia argued that the analogy to Richardson was closer than the Court recognized, and, indeed, that "the aggrievement there was more direct, since the Government already had the information in its possession, whereas here the respondents seek enforcement action that will bring information within the Government's possession and then require the information to be made public." He also contested the Court's analysis of the generalized grievance prohibition, noting that "if concrete generalized grievances (like concrete particularized grievances) are OK, and abstract generalized grievances (like abstract particularized grievances) are bad[,] * * * one must wonder why we ever developed the superfluous distinction

between generalized and particularized grievances at all."[3] He argued that
even if many people suffer the same type of harm—*e.g.*, interference with the
right to vote or a personal injury—each has still suffered "a particularized
and differentiated harm." In contrast, he reasoned, a generalized grievance
is "undifferentiated": "the * * * harm caused to Mr. Akins by the allegedly
unlawful failure of FECA is precisely the same as the harm caused to
everyone else: unavailability of a description of AIPAC's activities." Invoking
concerns about intrusion upon the President's prerogative to "take Care that
the Laws be faithfully executed," Justice Scalia concluded by observing that
"[i]f today's decision is correct, it is within the power of Congress to authorize
any interested person to manage (through the courts) the Executive's
enforcement of any law that includes a requirement for the filing and public
availability of a piece of paper."

How much does Akins undermine Lujan conceptually? Consider the
following possible ways to understand the conjunction of Akins with Lujan:
(a) an injury sufficient for purposes of Article III may exist simply by virtue
of the invasion of a legal right created by Congress; (b) Congress has the
power, by statute, to transform into cognizable injuries concrete harms that
had been "previously inadequate in law," Lujan, p. 133, *supra*; or (c)
whatever else one might say about Congress's authority to create judicially
cognizable injuries, the inability to procure information to which Congress
has created a right itself constitutes a concrete injury that gives rise to
Article III standing.

By itself, congressional power to confer "informational standing" is of
large importance. See Sunstein, *Informational Regulation and
Informational Standing: Akins and Beyond*, 147 U.Pa.L.Rev. 613 (1999).
(Under Justice Scalia's view, who could bring suit under the Freedom of
Information Act?) Beyond statutes conferring rights to information, does
Akins suggest that the barriers to congressionally authorized citizen
standing established by Lujan can nearly always be surmounted by a
properly drafted statute—for example, in the way suggested by Justice
Kennedy's concurring opinion in Lujan?[4]

(b) In Massachusetts v. EPA, 549 U.S. 497 (2007), the Court upheld the
standing of a state to challenge a refusal by the EPA to issue regulations
governing greenhouse gas emissions by new motor vehicles. In an opinion
joined by four other Justices, Justice Stevens reasoned that Congress had
authorized "this type of challenge to EPA action". In so holding, he
emphasized that the Clean Air Act not only required the EPA to prescribe
emissions standards in specified circumstances (42 U.S.C. § 7521(a)(1)), but
also conferred upon parties the "procedural right" to challenge the EPA's
denial of their petition to promulgate such standards (*id.* § 7607(b)(1)).
Quoting Lujan v. Defenders of Wildlife, 504 U.S. 555, 572 n. 7 (1992), Justice
Stevens added that "a litigant to whom Congress has 'accorded a procedural

---

[3]   The Court has gone back and forth on the question of whether a "generalized grievance"
constitutes an element of the Article III requirements for a "case" or "controversy" or a
prudential doctrine of judicial self-restraint. For further discussion, see pp. 156–158, *infra*.

[4]   Citing the Court's invalidation of congressional efforts to redefine the (judicially settled)
scope of individual rights under § 5 of the Fourteenth Amendment (see City of Boerne v. Flores,
p. 959, *infra*), one commentator deems it "almost inconceivable * * * that the Court would accept
congressional efforts to redefine the constitutional limits of standing." Elliott, *Congress's
Inability to Solve Standing Problems*, 91 B.U.L.Rev. 159, 192 (2011). Does Congress'
identification of a novel injury "redefine" standing law or merely establish a right of action
where none existed before?

right to protect his interests' * * * 'can assert that right without meeting all the normal standards for redressability and immediacy.' When a litigant is vested with a procedural right, that litigant has standing if there is some possibility that the requested relief will prompt the injury-causing party to reconsider the decision that allegedly harmed the litigant." The Court further noted that "[g]iven [the existence of a statutorily conferred] procedural right and Massachusetts' stake in protecting its quasi-sovereign interests", which set it apart from ordinary litigants, "the Commonwealth is entitled to special solicitude in our standing analysis." (For discussion of this aspect of the Court's analysis and of the standing of states to sue to protect their citizens' interests as well as their own, see pp. 279–286, *infra*.) With the framework for standing analysis thus apparently loosened, Justice Stevens' opinion for the Court concluded that Massachusetts had alleged "a particularized injury in its capacity as a landowner," involving the threatened loss of state-owned coastal property as a result of global warming traceable to greenhouse gas emissions and a consequent rise in sea levels; that domestic greenhouse gas traceable to automobile emissions contributed causally to the threat of loss by making "a meaningful contribution to greenhouse gas concentrations," even if "predicted increases in greenhouse gas emissions from developing nations, particularly China and India, are likely to offset any marginal domestic decrease"; and that the redressability requirement was met because the risk of catastrophic environmental damage "would be reduced to some extent if the petitioners received the relief they seek."

Dissenting, Chief Justice Roberts, joined by Justices Scalia, Thomas, and Alito, argued that the state had alleged no threat of imminent or particularized injury: "Global warming is a phenomenon 'harmful to humanity at large,' and the redress petitioners seek is focused no more on them than on the public generally—it is literally to change the atmosphere of the world." The Chief Justice also maintained that "[p]etitioners are never able to trace their alleged injuries * * * to the fractional amount of global emissions that might have been limited with EPA standards" and that "given events elsewhere in the world * * * the Court never explains" why the injury resulting from its alleged, impending loss of land would be redressed by such standards. The Chief Justice concluded: "The good news is that the Court's 'special solicitude' for Massachusetts limits the future applicability of the diluted standing requirements applied in this case. The bad news is that the Court's self-professed relaxation of * * * Article III requirements has caused us to transgress 'the proper—and properly limited—role of the courts in a democratic society' " (quoting Allen v. Wright, 468 U.S. 737, 750 (1984)).

Given the importance that the Court's opinion attached to the statutory right to sue, one might read Massachusetts v. EPA to signal further erosion of Lujan.[5] It might also be viewed as distinguishable on the ground that the

---

[5] Recall that in Summers v. Earth Island Institute, Inc., 555 U.S. 488 (2009), discussed at p. 120, *supra*, a 5–4 Court rebuffed efforts by environmental organizations to base standing on the statistical probability that at least some of their members would suffer harms from the U.S. Forest Service's application of challenged regulations to parklands frequented by the organizations' members. Five Justices, however, hinted that the case might come out differently if Congress created a right of action for such probabilistic harms to the enjoyment of the national parks. In a concurring opinion, Justice Kennedy wrote that "[t]his case would present different considerations if Congress had sought to provide redress for a concrete injury 'giv[ing] rise to a case or controversy where none existed before' " (quoting Lujan v. Defenders of Wildlife, p. 139, *supra* (Kennedy, J., concurring in part and concurring in the judgment)). Similarly, in dissent, Justice Breyer (joined by Justices Stevens, Souter, and Ginsburg) posited a hypothetical statute

case involved "special solicitude" for a state plaintiff protecting its quasi-sovereign interests, but the Court's subsequent analysis of the harm to Massachusetts focused on its ownership of coastal land—in which respect it differs little from any private landowner. The decision might also reflect the idea, discussed above, that a lack of imminence and uncertainty about the realization of harm must be counterbalanced against the extent of the consequences of the alleged harm, if realized. See pp. 119–123, *supra*. See also Nash, *Standing and the Precautionary Principle*, 108 Colum.L.Rev. 494 (2008) (arguing for such an approach under the rubric of "precautionary-principle standing"). Which understanding of Massachusetts v. EPA should the Court emphasize in future cases?

(3) The (Contested) Historical Understanding of the Judicial Power.

With the doctrine surrounding congressional power to establish standing in flux, how much significance should be attached to the conclusions of recent legal scholarship suggesting that the treatment of injury in fact as a constitutional requirement contradicts the historical understanding of judicial power, both at the founding era and as that idea later unfolded?[6]

Most commentators, while not agreeing in all respects, have found that English judicial practice at the time of the founding permitted so-called "strangers" (i.e., private litigants with no personalized injury) to file various prerogative writs to test the legality of the exercise of public authority. See, *e.g.*, Berger, *Standing to Sue in Public Actions: Is It a Constitutional Requirement?*, 78 Yale L.J. 816 (1969); Sunstein, note 2, *supra*, at 171–73; Winter, *The Metaphor of Standing and the Problem of Self-Governance*, 40 Stan.L.Rev. 1371, 1396–99 (1988). For example, such litigants could seek writs of prohibition or certiorari in the courts at Westminster to challenge action in excess of jurisdiction by other courts (such as ecclesiastical tribunals) or by local administrative tribunals. English law prior to the founding also authorized informers' actions, which gave strangers financial inducements to prosecute unlawful conduct, and relators' actions, which allowed private parties to bring actions against public authorities in the name of the Attorney General. See Berger, *supra*, at 816–26.[7] Although this

---

that "expressly permitted environmental groups * * * to bring cases just like the present one, provided (1) that the group has members who have used salvage-timber parcels in the past and are likely to do so in the future, and (2) that the group's members have opposed Forest Service timber sales in the past (using notice, comment, and appeal procedures to do so) and will likely use those procedures to oppose salvage-timber sales in the future." Citing both Massachusetts v. EPA and Sierra Club v. Morton, the dissent then observed that "[t]he majority cannot, and does not, claim that such a statute would be unconstitutional."

[6] In his influential separate opinion in Coleman v. Miller, 307 U.S. 433, 460 (1939), Justice Frankfurter wrote: "Judicial power could come into play only in matters that were the traditional concern of the courts at Westminster and only if they arose in ways that to the expert feel of lawyers constituted 'Cases' or 'Controversies.' " That idea has framed subsequent analysis, even in cases widely regarded to take a generous view of Article III power. See, *e.g.*, Federal Election Commission v. Akins, 524 U.S. 11, 24 (1998); Flast v. Cohen, 392 U.S. 83, 101 (1968).

[7] Berger further noted that strangers could bring writs of quo warranto to prosecute those who usurped the franchise, and that, while the evidence is less clear, they apparently could also file writs of mandamus "to compel action by one who was under a duty to act". Berger, *supra*, at 823–25.

Professor Jaffe believed that the English history was somewhat less conclusive. See Jaffe, *Standing to Secure Judicial Review: Public Actions*, 74 Harv.L.Rev. 1265, 1269–75, 1308 (1961). But he found, at minimum, that "in prerogative proceedings in the King's Bench the character of the relator was often obscure or unstated" and that "[a] number of notable statements [in the eighteenth century English case law] expressed the King's general concern for legality, and in

view of the history has come under some challenge,[8] it is fair to say, at the very least, that the English common law background in the founding era does not reliably supply a basis for the Court's modern position that concrete and personalized injury is a prerequisite to invoking "the judicial Power".

In a highly influential book published in 1965, moreover, Professor Jaffe wrote that despite some initial "doubts and misgivings," "the public action has become broadly established in this country in a large and continually increasing majority of jurisdictions." Jaffe, *Judicial Control of Administrative Action* 467 (1965). In particular, the "very considerable weight of [state court] authority" came over time to support "the citizen-mandamus suit", and taxpayer's injunction actions "have become even more acclimated in this country than the citizen's mandamus." *Id.* at 468–70. Winter, *supra*, similarly maintains that, until the twentieth century, courts did not view injury in fact either as part of the case or controversy requirement or as a prerequisite for seeking review of official action, but instead granted relief whenever a plaintiff asserted a right for which one of the forms of action afforded a remedy.[9]

Professors Woolhandler and Nelson, however, suggest that although early American courts did not speak in the terms employed by modern standing doctrine, they nonetheless determined proper parties by distinguishing "public rights" (those belonging to the public as a whole, such as free passage on waterways and public highways or the interests protected by penal laws) from "private rights" (those held by particular individuals, such as the common law rights to property or bodily integrity). Woolhandler & Nelson, *Does History Defeat Standing Doctrine?*, 102 Mich.L.Rev. 689, 691, 693–705 (2004). On that view of early American common law practice, a private individual could not vindicate public rights unless suffering special damage not shared by the public at large. Moreover, although relevant federal case law from the early days of the Republic is sparse and mixed, at least some of it suggests that the Supreme Court subscribed to that distinction.[10]

---

the writ of prohibition, at least, there is overt authority for allowing anyone to initiate the proceeding."

[8] One commentator has argued that the actual practice of the courts at Westminster offers only scant evidence to support the proposition that parties without any personal interest could bring prerogative writs. See Clanton, *Standing and the English Prerogative Writs: The Original Understanding*, 63 Brook.L.Rev. 1001 (1997).

[9] But see Bellia, *Article III and the Cause of Action*, 89 Iowa L.Rev. 777, 855 (2004) (arguing that modern standing doctrine "attempt[s] to generalize * * * in constitutional terms" certain limits on the reach of judicial power that were embedded in historic forms of action but then were eliminated by the merger of law and equity).

[10] For example, Professors Woolhandler and Nelson argue that while jurisdictional statutes sharply limited the availability of federal mandamus jurisdiction until well into the twentieth century, the small number of federal court opinions that did address mandamus in the nineteenth century (including Marbury) assumed that private relators must allege private injury. They also note that various nineteenth century cases involving the Supreme Court's original jurisdiction seemed to adopt the private injury requirement. While acknowledging that the First Congress passed statutes authorizing qui tam actions, which permitted litigants (informers) with no personal interest to sue for penalties that were to be shared between the sovereign and the informer, Woolhandler and Nelson maintain that such actions constitute, at most, a limited exception to the nation's dominant judicial tradition. See Woolhandler & Nelson, *supra*, at 707, 713–17, 724–31.

When the evidence of relevant practice is sparse, how does one determine which practices should count as the exception and which as the rule?

Insofar as historical understandings—whether from the founding era or subsequent periods—inform modern standing doctrine, how can one make sense of the foregoing history? If Lujan rests on a claim of constitutional authority to invalidate Acts of Congress granting standing in the absence of concrete and particularized injury, should any significant indeterminacy in the evidence of original meaning and early constitutional practice tip the balance in favor of Congress? See generally Manning, *Foreword: The Means of Constitutional Power*, 128 Harv.L.Rev. 1 (2014) (arguing that, by virtue of the Necessary and Proper Clause, Congress should have the final say on the means of implementing federal powers—including the judicial power—where evidence of constitutional meaning is unclear). Or, given the now-long line of precedents treating injury in fact as a constitutional requirement of an Article III case or controversy, does stare decisis counsel against abandoning that requirement unless the historical record convincingly shows that the precedents misread Article III?

In general, consider the potential difficulties inherent in translating historical evidence from English and state contexts into the distinctive context of federal judicial power under the United States Constitution. For example, the prerogative writs "were conceived of as public proceedings brought in the King's name" and, "in their origin and until the middle of the nineteenth century, were used primarily to control authorities below the level of the central government." Jaffe, *Judicial Control*, *supra*, at 462. Does this context cast doubt on the relevance of English practice, without more, to understanding an American constitutional structure predicated on quite different assumptions about sovereignty and the allocation of powers? How much weight should one give to the state court practice when the design of the federal government so frequently deviates from state structural premises, including state structural premises about the judiciary?

(4) Standing, Injury, and the Separation of Powers. Congress has often given the Attorney General or other federal officials power to bring suit for the purpose of enforcing laws that do not benefit the agency or officials empowered to sue. See, *e.g.*, § 301 of the Voting Rights Act Amendments of 1975, 42 U.S.C. § 1973bb; Title VII of the Civil Rights Act of 1964, §§ 706–07, as amended, 42 U.S.C. §§ 2000e–5 to 2000e–6. Hartnett, *The Standing of the United States: How Criminal Prosecutions Show That Standing Doctrine is Looking for Answers in All the Wrong Places*, 97 Mich.L.Rev. 2239, 2255–58 (1999), argues that the recognized standing of the United States to bring criminal suits demonstrates that personal injury to the party initiating a case is not a requirement for Article III standing. If that is correct, should Congress have equal power to use the device of suits by *private* attorneys general?[11] Or do separation of powers considerations distinguish private from public enforcement actions?

In Allen v. Wright, p. 103, *supra*, Justice O'Connor introduced the idea that a standing regime that makes it too easy for private attorneys general to sue to enforce the legality of executive action could interfere with the President's constitutionally assigned responsibility to "take Care that the Laws be faithfully executed". In cases such as Lujan and Akins, Justice Scalia has repeatedly emphasized that point in questioning statutory

---

[11] Compare Fallon, *Of Justiciability, Remedies, and Public Law Litigation: Notes on the Jurisprudence of Lyons*, 59 N.Y.U.L.Rev. 1, 30–35, 54–56 (1984), with Krent & Shenkman, *Of Citizens Suits and Citizen Sunstein*, 91 Mich.L.Rev. 1793 (1993).

authorizations of private standing either to compel enforcement actions by the executive or to enforce what he regards as public rights.[12]

How persuasive is this view? Some scholars have argued that the Take Care Clause imposes a duty but does not create a power. See, *e.g.*, May, *Presidential Defiance of "Unconstitutional" Laws: Reviving the Royal Prerogative*, 21 Hastings Const.LQ. 865, 873–74 (1994); Tiefer, *The Constitutionality of Independent Officers as Checks on Abuses of Executive Power*, 63 BU.L.Rev. 59, 90 (1983). Others believe that it provides the President with significant authority to oversee the Executive Branch's interpretations of law. See, *e.g.*, Paulsen, *The Most Dangerous Branch: Executive Power To Say What the Law Is*, 83 Geo.L.J. 217, 261–62 (1994). Professor Sunstein finds it "clear" from both "its text and history" that "the Take Care Clause confers both a duty and a power". Sunstein, note 2, *supra*, at 212–13. While he believes that the power element of the Clause gives the President some oversight authority over the bureaucracy's implementation of the law, Sunstein emphasizes that the duty element "imposes on the President both a responsibility to be faithful to the law and an obligation to enforce the law as it has been enacted". Accordingly, he believes that when a plaintiff "establishes that an agency has enforced the law in an unlawful way," the President has violated the Take Care Clause, and judicial enforcement does no violence to presidential authority.

If the Take Care Clause establishes some presidential superintendence over the bureaucracy's legal decisionmaking, is Sunstein correct to assume that the Take Care Clause is violated every time a court concludes that an agency acts unlawfully? A great deal of modern law hinges on the proposition that reasonable people can differ about the best answer to a legal interpretive question.[13] The idea is captured by Justice Jackson's famous aphorism about the Supreme Court: "We are not final because we are infallible, but we are infallible only because we are final." Brown v. Allen, 344 U.S. 443, 540 (1953) (Jackson, J., concurring in the result). If so, the mere fact that a reviewing court disagrees with the executive's legal interpretation does not mean that that interpretation violates the President's duty under the Take Care Clause. Does Sunstein's point have greater force if the pertinent standard of judicial review precludes reversal of the agency as long as its position is reasonable? Compare Chevron U.S.A., Inc. v. Natural Resources Defense Council, Inc., 467 U.S. 837, 844 (1984) (court must accept agency's "reasonable" interpretation of organic act even if the court would have reached a different result on its own).

Finally, even if the Take Care Clause does provide a reason to ration judicial power, how well does the injury-in-fact requirement serve that purpose? Consider Professor Sunstein's further question: "If a court [faced with the claims in Lujan] could set aside executive action at the behest of plaintiffs with a plane ticket, why does the Take Care Clause forbid it from doing so at the behest of plaintiffs without a plane ticket?" Sunstein, note 2, *supra*, at 213; accord, Siegel, *A Theory of Justiciability*, 86 Tex.L.Rev. 73,

---

[12] See also Scalia, *The Doctrine of Standing as an Element of the Separation of Powers*, 17 Suffolk U.L.Rev. 881 (1983).

[13] See, *e.g.*, Sawyer v. Smith, 497 U.S. 227, 234 (1990) (application of the bar against applying "new law" on federal habeas review of state court convictions depends on whether "reasonable" people could differ about the law when a state court conviction became final); Anderson v. Creighton, 483 U.S. 635, 640 (1987) (qualified immunity is available unless right is "sufficiently clear that a reasonable official would understand that what he [or she] is doing violates that right").

100–01 (2007). Is that a problem endemic to tests that depend on line drawing? Consider the observation that all of the overlapping justiciability criteria try to implement "an idea, which is more than an intuition but less than a rigorous and explicit theory, about the constitutional and prudential limits to the powers of an unelected, unrepresentative judiciary in our kind of government." Allen v. Wright, 468 U.S. 737, 751 (1984) (quoting Vander Jagt v. O'Neill, 699 F.2d 1166, 1178–1179 (D.C.Cir. 1982) (Bork, J., concurring)).

Can a restrictive approach to congressional authorizations of standing be justified on the view that "overenforcement" of regulatory statutes is a greater problem than "underenforcement"? On what basis could such a judgment be made?[14]

(5) Qui Tam Actions. The False Claims Act (FCA), a federal statute with antecedents nearly as old as the republic itself, authorizes private citizens—called "relators"—to bring "qui tam" actions on behalf of the United States seeking civil penalties and damages payable to the Treasury against "any person" who procured payment on a false claim against the United States. When a qui tam action succeeds, the relator receives a percentage of the money payable to the government. Although divided on other issues, the Court held without dissent in Vermont Agency of Natural Resources v. United States ex rel. Stevens, 529 U.S. 765 (2000), that a relator has Article III standing. Justice Scalia's majority opinion first rejected the suggestion that a relator's interest in recovering a bounty for successful prosecution could support standing. Where no previous injury existed, "an interest that is merely a 'byproduct' of the suit itself" did not satisfy the injury requirement. But the opinion then concluded that the relator, as the assignee of the Government's claim, "has standing to assert the injury in fact suffered by the assignor." The Court pronounced itself "confirmed in this conclusion by the long tradition of qui tam actions in England and the American Colonies." Justice Scalia termed the historical practice "particularly relevant * * * since * * * Article III's restriction of the judicial power to 'Cases' and 'Controversies' is properly understood to mean 'cases and controversies of the sort traditionally amenable to * * * the judicial process.' "[15]

---

[14] Friends of the Earth, Inc. v. Laidlaw Environmental Services (TOC), Inc., 528 U.S. 167 (2000), may undercut the premise that standing doctrine rests significantly upon concerns about judicial intrusion upon prosecutorial discretion assigned to the executive by Article II. Laidlaw upheld the plaintiffs' standing under the citizen suit provision of the Clean Water Act to bring an action seeking civil money penalties payable to the government. In an opinion by Justice Ginsburg, the Court ruled, 7–2, that "the civil penalties sought by [the plaintiffs] carried with them a deterrent effect that made it likely, as opposed to merely speculative, that the penalties would redress [plaintiffs'] injuries by abating current violations and preventing future ones." Dissenting, Justice Scalia (joined by Justice Thomas) argued that this reasoning was inconsistent with Linda R.S. v. Richard D., p. 123, *supra*: "The principle that 'in American jurisprudence . . . a private citizen lacks a judicially cognizable interest in the prosecution or nonprosecution of another' applies no less to prosecution for civil penalties payable to the State than to prosecution for criminal penalties owing to the State." In response, the majority distinguished Linda R.S. on the ground that criminal prosecutions enjoy a "special status" and that the relief sought there—prosecution and ultimately incarceration of a delinquent father—"would scarcely remedy the plaintiff's lack of child support payments." For further discussion of the use of standing doctrine to channel prosecutorial discretion, see Grove, *Standing as an Article II Nondelegation Doctrine*, 11 U.Pa.J.Const.L. 781 (2009).

[15] In Sprint Communications Co. v. APCC Services, Inc., 554 U.S. 269 (2008), the Court appears to extend Vermont Agency. In Sprint, pay telephone operators assigned to a litigation service numerous small claims against long-distance carriers for nonpayment of fees owed to the operators for certain types of pay telephone calls. The litigation service received a periodic fee for its services rather than a percentage of the recovery it collected as assignee of the claims.

With the standing question thus resolved, Justice Scalia dropped a footnote: "In so concluding, we express no view on the question whether qui tam suits violate Article II, in particular the Appointments Clause of § 2 and the 'Take Care' Clause of § 3." In support of this reservation he quoted Steel Co. v. Citizens for a Better Environment, 523 U.S. 83, 102 (1998), for the proposition that " '[O]ur standing jurisprudence, * * * though it may sometimes have an impact on Presidential powers, derives from Article III and not Article II.' "[16]

If, in light of the historical practice, a plaintiff has a sufficient personal stake in the outcome to satisfy Article III's injury and redressability requirements, are Article II objections based on the Appointments and Take Care Clauses necessarily obviated?[17]

The assignment in Vermont Agency involved a "proprietary" or financial interest of the United States. Could Congress also confer standing by providing for the assignment of a more paradigmatically "sovereign" interest, such as that in enforcing the criminal law? See Gilles, *Representational Standing: U.S. ex rel. Stevens and the Future of Public Law Litigation*, 89 Cal.L.Rev. 315, 341–45 (2001) (arguing not).

(6) Congressional Authority and Prudential Standing. How does the Court's recent emphasis on Congress' power to determine who has standing affect, if at all, judge-made doctrines *limiting* standing? Recall the Court has long exercised judicial authority to apply prudential limitations on its power to hear cases that otherwise satisfy Article III case or controversy requirements. See pp. 76–77, *supra*. For example, two frequently invoked aspects of standing doctrine—the bars against raising generalized grievances and asserting the legal rights of third parties—have often been described as prudential, rather than constitutional elements of standing doctrine. See, *e.g.*, Warth v. Seldin, 422 U.S. 490, 499–500 (1975); see also p. 106, *supra*, & p. 162, *infra*. On that basis, such limitations might be understood to fit within a wide array of traditional doctrines of judicial self-governance, such as equitable discretion, abstention, and forum non conveniens—and, thus, to be appropriate qualifications upon a general judicial obligation to hear cases within a federal court's jurisdiction. See Shapiro, *Jurisdiction and Discretion*, 60 N.Y.U.L.Rev. 543 (1985). In Lexmark Int'l, Inc. v. Static Control Components, Inc., 134 S.Ct. 1377 (2014),

---

Any actual sums recovered went straight to the operators themselves. Relying in significant part on its understanding of "history and tradition", the Court determined, 5–4, that such a suit fit among "the types of cases that Article III empowers federal courts to consider", even though the assignee lacked a "personal stake" in the outcome of the litigation. The Court added that the assignee's economic interest as a litigation service provider assured that it would litigate with the concrete adverseness required by Article III. Notably, all nine Justices agreed that standing would exist if a small portion of the assigned claim itself, perhaps even "a dollar or two," had been reserved to the assignee. Given the majority's and dissent's apparent agreement on the sufficiency of even a small personal stake in a lawsuit, could Congress create standing by authorizing a "dollar or two" in damages against a party for past noncompliance with a disclosure requirement, or even a regulatory requirement?

[16] Justice Ginsburg concurred in the judgment only. Justice Stevens, joined by Justice Souter, dissented on other grounds.

[17] See, e.g., Shane, *Returning Separation-of-Powers Analysis to Its Normative Roots: The Constitutionality of Qui Tam Actions and Other Private Suits to Enforce Civil Fines*, 30 Envtl.L.Rep. 11081 (2000) (arguing that qui tam actions do not violate Article II); Craig, *Will Separation of Powers Challenges "Take Care" of Environmental Citizen Suits? Article II, Injury-in-Fact, Private "Enforcers," and Lessons from Qui Tam Litigation*, 72 U.Colo.L.Rev. 93 (2001) (same); Johnson, *Private Plaintiffs, Public Rights: Article II and Environmental Citizen Suits*, 49 Kan.L.Rev. 383 (2001) (same).

however, the Court called into question the continuing validity of prudential standing doctrine.

At issue in Lexmark was whether the plaintiff fell within the "zone of interests" protected by the Lanham Act. The zone of interests test had first developed in cases arising under the Administrative Procedure Act (APA). In a pivotal decision in Association of Data Processing Service Organizations, Inc. v. Camp, 397 U.S. 150 (1970), the Court sought to reorient the standing inquiry in administrative law away from the question of whether the plaintiff had suffered the invasion of a "legal interest"—an inquiry that, in the Court's view, went to the merits. Instead, the Court insisted first that the plaintiff demonstrate the "injury in fact" necessary to sustain Article III standing. The Court added that after satisfying that Article III minimum, the plaintiff also had to assert a claim "arguably within the zone of interests to be protected or regulated by the statute or constitutional guarantee in question." The Court, however, left the source of that test unclear. At times, the Court described the zone-of-interests requirement as a gloss on the judicial review provisions of the APA. See, *e.g.*, Clarke v. Sec. Indus. Ass'n, 479 U.S. 388, 400 n.16 (1987). But the Court also applied the test outside the APA context, see, *e.g.*, Dennis v. Higgins, 498 U.S. 439, 449 (1991); Boston Stock Exchange v. State Tax Comm'n, 429 U.S. 318, 320–321 n.3 (1977), and often described it as a prudential doctrine of judicial self-restraint. See, *e.g.*, Allen v. Wright, p. 103, *supra*, at 751. The Court's approach left a number of questions unanswered, including the relationship of the zone-of-interests test to the Court's evolving criteria for identifying implied rights of action in non-APA cases.[18] See pp. 723–747, *infra*.

The Court in Lexmark purported to resolve the confusion by recharacterizing the zone-of-interests question as one of statutory interpretation—an inquiry that turns on whether the claim filed by the plaintiff falls within the scope of the right of action established by the Act. This understanding, the Court reasoned, fit better with what it described as the federal judiciary's "virtually unflagging" obligation to hear cases within its jurisdiction.[19] In so holding, the Court in Lexmark noted that it had sometimes also characterized generalized grievance standing doctrine as prudential but had in other decisions held that suits raising generalized grievances "do not present constitutional 'cases' or 'controversies.' " Turning to third-party standing, the Court noted that its cases sometimes framed the issue as being whether someone in the plaintiff's position had a right of action but that other cases treated that question as one of prudence. Because Lexmark presented no third-party standing issue, the Court did not attempt resolve the status of that doctrine.

One might read Lexmark as the Court's attempt to safeguard Congress' effective control over the means of implementing federal power—including

---

[18] Perhaps because of the Court's ambiguity about the nature of the zone-of-interests test, the doctrine has provoked an extensive body of scholarly writing. See, *e.g.*, Albert, *Standing to Challenge Administrative Action: An Inadequate Surrogate for Claim for Relief*, 83 Yale L.J. 425 (1974); Anthony, *Zone-Free Standing for Private Attorneys General*, 7 Geo.Mason L.Rev. 237 (1999); Davis, *The Liberalized Law of Standing*, 37 U.Chi.L.Rev. 450, 455–56 (1970) Jaffe, *Standing Again*, 84 Harv.L.Rev. 633 (1971); Scott, *Standing in the Supreme Court—A Functional Analysis*, 86 Harv.L.Rev. 645 (1973); Siegel, *Zone of Interests*, 92 Geo.L.J. 317, 368 (2004); Stewart, *The Reformation of American Administrative Law*, 88 Harv.L.Rev. 1667, 1723–47 (1975); Vining, Legal Identity: The Coming of Age of Public Law 34–35 (1978).

[19] In Susan B. Anthony List v. Driehaus, 134 S.Ct. 2334 (2014), the Court raised similar concerns about prudential limitations in the context of ripeness. See p. 227, *infra*.

the power to determine when, and by what means, a party can invoke federal jurisdiction. See Manning, Paragraph (3), *supra*, at 73 n.415. But an unyielding rejection of prudential standing doctrine would have further-reaching implications. Consider Elk Grove Unified School Dist. v. Newdow, 542 U.S. 1 (2004), in which the Court cited a desire not to interfere with family relations structured by state law as its "prudential" ground for denying a divorced father's standing to challenge a school district's policy of commencing each school day with a recitation of the Pledge of Allegiance, including the words "under God". Newdow, the father of a girl in the school system, sued to enjoin the practice, which he claimed interfered with his right to communicate his atheistic beliefs to his daughter. But the girl's mother opposed the action, and as a matter of California law Newdow could therefore not bring his action as his daughter's next friend, but only on his own behalf. In an opinion joined by four other Justices, Justice Stevens found on prudential grounds that Newdow lacked standing. Without denying that Newdow suffered injury in fact, the Court emphasized that the outer reaches of Newdow's rights and interests as a parent were governed by uncertain state law and that his interests were potentially adverse to those of his daughter. In finding that federal adjudication would be imprudent, Justice Stevens drew an analogy to the so-called "domestic relations exception" to federal diversity jurisdiction, under which federal courts generally lack jurisdiction to issue divorce, alimony, or child custody decrees even within cases otherwise subject to federal jurisdiction. See Chap. X, Sec. 2(E), *infra*. Applying that federalism concern to standing doctrine, the Court deemed it "improper * * * to entertain a claim by a plaintiff whose standing to sue is founded on family law rights that are in dispute when prosecution of the lawsuit may have an adverse effect on the person who is the source of the plaintiff's claimed standing."[20]

(7) The Bearing of State Law on Standing. To what extent can state law create Article III standing where none would otherwise exist? Compare the two cases that follow.

In ASARCO Inc. v. Kadish, 490 U.S. 605 (1989), the Supreme Court held that "[w]hen a state court has issued a judgment in a case where plaintiffs in the original action had no standing to sue under the principles governing the federal courts, we may exercise our jurisdiction on certiorari if the judgment of the state court causes direct, specific, and concrete injury to the parties who petition for our review, where the requisites of a case or controversy are also met." In ASARCO, state taxpayers and an association of public school teachers challenged a state statute governing mineral leases on state school lands as void under federal law. Some of the private leaseholders intervened as defendants. The state supreme court found the statute invalid and remanded for entry of a declaratory judgment and consideration of injunctive relief. On certiorari, the Supreme Court held that it had power to review the judgment. Justice Kennedy's opinion (for four Justices) first concluded that in a federal court action, the plaintiffs would lack standing. Even accepting the plaintiffs' premise that the state's issuance of mineral leases in violation of federal law had cost state school trust funds millions of dollars, the Court deemed it "pure speculation" whether the relief

---

[20] Chief Justice Rehnquist, whose opinion on this issue was joined by Justices O'Connor and Thomas, would have upheld standing based on the injury to Newdow's right to expose his daughter to his religious views. He thought the abstention doctrine for domestic relations cases flatly inapplicable: "This case does not involve diversity jurisdiction, and it does not ask this Court to issue a divorce, alimony, or child custody decree." (Justice Scalia did not participate.)

sought would result in tax reductions for the plaintiff-taxpayers or pay increases for the plaintiff-teachers. Accordingly, the plaintiff-respondents would not have had standing to bring their action in federal district court in the first instance. Nevertheless, Justice Kennedy (here speaking for a majority of six) ruled that given the way the proceedings had unfolded, the Supreme Court could review the state court decision, which had proceeded to final judgment under the state's more liberal standing rules. Because the state court judgment invalidated mineral leases held by the private leaseholders who had petitioned for certiorari, it had produced "the kind of injury [to them] cognizable in this Court on review from the state courts." Chief Justice Rehnquist, joined by Justice Scalia, dissented in relevant part.

In Hollingsworth v. Perry, 133 S.Ct. 2652 (2013), by contrast, the Court held that state law cannot transform a "generalized grievance" into a justiciable controversy by designating the official proponents of a state ballot initiative to defend its constitutionality when state officials decline to do so. Pursuant to the initiative process set forth in the California Constitution, voters enacted Proposition 8, which limited marriage to opposite-sex couples. Respondents, same-sex couples who wished to marry, filed suit in district court challenging Proposition 8's constitutionality and seeking to enjoin the governor and other state officials from enforcing it. After the district court held the initiative unconstitutional, state officials refused to defend the law further, and the initiative's proponents—those who got it on the ballot and shepherded it through the election process—successfully moved to intervene. When the intervenors sought to appeal, the Ninth Circuit certified to the California Supreme Court a question about the state law status of the proponents of a ballot initiative; the state court replied that as a matter of California statutory and constitutional law, proponents of a ballot initiative have authority to defend the initiative's constitutionality when state officials do not do so. The Ninth Circuit accordingly held that the proponents had standing to appeal.

In an opinion by Chief Justice Roberts, joined by Justices Scalia, Breyer, Ginsburg, and Kagan, the Supreme Court reversed. The Court noted that because the proponents' involvement with the initiative ended with its adoption, "[t]heir only interest in having the District Court order reversed was to vindicate the constitutional validity of a generally applicable California law." Such a "generalized grievance" could not support standing. Nor could the premise that the proponents were authorized by state law to sue on the state's behalf. The Court acknowledged that the state has a "cognizable interest" in defending Proposition 8 and that it may vindicate that interest by "designat[ing] agents to represent it in federal court." The Court found, however, that despite the California Supreme Court's ruling, the proponents were not acting as agents of the state. The Court stressed that under the Restatement of Agency, an agent owes a fiduciary duty to a principal, and the principal must be able to control the agent—elements wholly lacking in the proponents' relationship to the California government. Nor did the proponents take an oath of office or receive attorney's fees from the state. The Court stressed that whatever state law might say, "standing in federal court is a question of federal law," and "the fact that a State thinks a private party should have standing to seek relief for a generalized grievance cannot override this Court's settled law to the contrary."

Justice Kennedy, joined by Justices Thomas, Alito, and Sotomayor dissented. The dissent stressed that California law gave the proponent of an initiative "authority to appear in court and assert the State's interest in defending an enacted initiative," at least when public officials would not do so. Justice Kennedy added that nothing in Article III requires a state "to comply with the Restatement of Agency or with this Court's view of how a state should * * * structure its government." He further reasoned that because the purpose of a ballot initiative was to establish a lawmaking process that "does not depend upon state officials," the Court's insistence upon the presence of state officials or others answerable to them would undermine the initiative process. "A prime purpose of justiciability is to ensure vigorous advocacy," the dissent concluded, "yet the Court insists upon litigation conducted by state officials whose preference is to lose the case."

Does ASARCO differ from Hollingsworth simply because Arizona's idiosyncratic standing rules ended up inflicting a "wallet injury" on ASARCO? Does the distinction between the two cases suggest the continuing importance of the plaintiff's showing a concrete and individualized "injury in fact" rather than merely a legally defined harm?

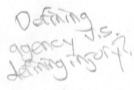

————————

B. STANDING TO ASSERT THE RIGHTS OF OTHERS AND RELATED ISSUES INVOLVING "FACIAL CHALLENGES" TO STATUTES

————————

INTRODUCTORY NOTE

The standing issues considered thus far have involved whether a party may invoke the jurisdiction of an Article III court at all. In some cases, however, a further question may arise concerning whether parties with Article III standing—including, in some cases, criminal defendants—may rely on the rights of third parties as a basis for their claims to relief. The next principal case and the materials that immediately follow it address the issues presented when one party tries to assert the rights of others or seeks to establish what is often referred to as "third-party" or "*jus tertii*" standing.

Subsequent principal cases then take up the questions whether, and if so under what circumstances, a party may challenge a statute on the ground that it is unconstitutional "on its face." Although parties can always argue that statutes are unconstitutional as applied to them, the standards governing facial challenges are complex and often controverted. Among the central questions to be considered are why this is so and what the pertinent standards for the availability of facial challenges ought to be.

————————

Craig v. Boren

429 U.S. 190, 97 S.Ct. 451, 50 L.Ed.2d 397 (1976).
Appeal from the District Court for the Western District of Oklahoma.

■ JUSTICE BRENNAN delivered the opinion of the Court.

[Oklahoma law prohibited the sale of a low-alcohol, 3.2% beer to males under the age of 21 and to females under the age of 18. On the merits, the question was whether this gender-based disparity violated the Equal Protection Clause. Suit was initially brought by two named plaintiffs—Craig, a male between the ages of 18 and 21, and a licensed vendor of 3.2% beer. After the Supreme Court noted probable jurisdiction to review a decision upholding the statutory scheme, Craig turned 21, and his challenge became nonjusticiable under the mootness doctrine, discussed in Sec. 4, *infra*. The question thus arose] whether appellant Whitener, the beer vendor, who has a live controversy against enforcement of the statute, may rely upon the equal protection objections of males 18–20 years of age to establish her claim of unconstitutionality of the age-sex differential. We conclude that she may.

Initially, it should be noted that, despite having had the opportunity to do so, appellees never raised before the District Court any objection to Whitener's reliance upon the claimed unequal treatment of 18–20-year-old males as the premise of her equal protection challenge to Oklahoma's 3.2% beer law.

Indeed, at oral argument Oklahoma acknowledged that appellees always "presumed" that the vendor, subject to sanctions and loss of license for violation of the statute, was a proper party in interest to object to the enforcement of the sex-based regulatory provision. While such a concession certainly would not be controlling upon the reach of this Court's constitutional authority to exercise jurisdiction under Art. III, our decisions have settled that limitations on a litigant's assertion of jus tertii are not constitutionally mandated, but rather stem from a salutary "rule of self-restraint" designed to minimize unwarranted intervention into controversies where the applicable constitutional questions are ill-defined and speculative. See, *e.g.*, Barrows v. Jackson, 346 U.S. 249, 255, 257 (1953). These prudential objectives, thought to be enhanced by restrictions on third-party standing, cannot be furthered here, where the lower court already has entertained the relevant constitutional challenge and the parties have sought—or at least have never resisted—an authoritative constitutional determination. In such circumstances, a decision by us to forgo consideration of the constitutional merits in order to await the initiation of a new challenge to the statute by injured third parties would be impermissibly to foster repetitive and time-consuming litigation under the guise of caution and prudence. Moreover, insofar as the applicable constitutional questions have been and continue to be presented vigorously and "cogently," Holden v. Hardy, 169 U.S. 366, 397 (1898), the denial of jus tertii standing in deference to a direct class suit can serve no functional purpose. * * *

In any event, we conclude that appellant Whitener has established independently her claim to assert jus tertii standing. The operation of [the challenged statutory provisions] plainly has inflicted "injury in fact" upon appellant sufficient to guarantee her "concrete adverseness," Baker v. Carr, 369 U.S. 186, 204 (1962), and to satisfy the constitutionally based

standing requirements imposed by Art. III. The legal duties created by
the statutory sections under challenge are addressed directly to vendors
such as appellant. She is obliged either to heed the statutory
discrimination, thereby incurring a direct economic injury through the
constriction of her buyers' market, or to disobey the statutory command
and suffer, in the words of Oklahoma's Assistant Attorney General,
"sanctions and perhaps loss of license." This Court repeatedly has
recognized that such injuries establish the threshold requirements of a
"case or controversy" mandated by Art. III. See, *e.g.*, Singleton v. Wulff,
428 U.S. 106, 113 (1976) (doctors who receive payments for their abortion
services are "classically adverse" to government as payer); Barrows v.
Jackson, *supra*, at 255–256.

As a vendor with standing to challenge the lawfulness of [applicable
Oklahoma statutes], appellant Whitener is entitled to assert those
concomitant rights of third parties that would be "diluted or adversely
affected" should her constitutional challenge fail and the statutes remain
in force. Griswold v. Connecticut, 381 U.S. 479, 481 (1965); see Note,
Standing to Assert Constitutional Jus Tertii, 88 Harv.L.Rev. 423, 432
(1974). Otherwise, the threatened imposition of governmental sanctions
might deter appellant Whitener and other similarly situated vendors
from selling 3.2% beer to young males, thereby ensuring that
"enforcement of the challenged restriction against the [vendor] would
result indirectly in the violation of third parties' rights." Warth v. Seldin,
422 U.S. 490, 510 (1975). Accordingly, vendors and those in like positions
have been uniformly permitted to resist efforts at restricting their
operations by acting as advocates of the rights of third parties who seek
access to their market or function. See, *e.g.*, Eisenstadt v. Baird, 405 U.S.
438 (1972).[4]

Indeed, the jus tertii question raised here is answered by our
disposition of a like argument in Eisenstadt v. Baird, *supra*. There, as
here, a state statute imposed legal duties and disabilities upon the
claimant, who was convicted of distributing a package of contraceptive
foam to a third party.[5] Since the statute was directed at Baird and
penalized his conduct, the Court did not hesitate—again as here—to
conclude that the "case or controversy" requirement of Art. III was
satisfied. In considering Baird's constitutional objections, the Court fully
recognized his standing to defend the privacy interests of third parties.

---

[4]   The standing question presented here is not answered by the principle stated in United
States v. Raines, 362 U.S. 17, 21 (1960), that "one to whom application of a statute is
constitutional will not be heard to attack the statute on the ground that impliedly it might also
be taken as applying to other persons or other situations in which its application might be
unconstitutional." In Raines, the Court refused to permit certain public officials of Georgia to
defend against application of the Civil Rights Act to their official conduct on the ground that the
statute also might be construed to encompass the "purely private actions" of others. The Raines
rule remains germane in such a setting, where the interests of the litigant and the rights of the
proposed third parties are in no way mutually interdependent. Thus, a successful suit against
Raines did not threaten to impair or diminish the independent private rights of others, and
consequently, consideration of those third-party rights properly was deferred until another day.

[5]   The fact that Baird chose to disobey the legal duty imposed upon him by the
Massachusetts anticontraception statute, resulting in his criminal conviction, does not
distinguish the standing inquiry from that pertaining to the anticipatory attack in this case. In
both Eisenstadt and here, the challenged statutes compel jus tertii claimants either to cease
their proscribed activities or to suffer appropriate sanctions. The existence of Art. III "injury in
fact" and the structure of the claimant's relationship to the third parties are not altered by the
litigative posture of the suit. * * *

Deemed crucial to the decision to permit jus tertii standing was the recognition of "the impact of the litigation on the third-party interests." *Id.*, at 445. Just as the defeat of Baird's suit and the "[e]nforcement of the Massachusetts statute will materially impair the ability of single persons to obtain contraceptives," *id.*, at 446, so too the failure of Whitener to prevail in this suit and the continued enforcement of [the challenged statutes] will "materially impair the ability of" males 18–20 years of age to purchase 3.2% beer despite their classification by an overt gender-based criterion. Similarly, just as the Massachusetts law in Eisenstadt "prohibit[ed], not use, but distribution," and consequently the least awkward challenger was one in Baird's position who was subject to that proscription, the law challenged here explicitly regulates the sale rather than use of 3.2% beer, thus leaving a vendor as the obvious claimant.

We therefore hold that Whitener has standing to raise relevant equal protection challenges to Oklahoma's gender-based law. * * *

[The Court went on to hold the statute unconstitutional.]

■ CHIEF JUSTICE BURGER, dissenting.

* * * I cannot agree that appellant Whitener has standing arising from her status as a saloon-keeper to assert the constitutional rights of her customers. In this Court "a litigant may only assert his own constitutional rights or immunities." United States v. Raines, 362 U.S. 17, 22 (1960). There are a few, but strictly limited exceptions to that rule; despite the most creative efforts, this case fits within none of them.

This is not * * * Barrows v. Jackson, 346 U.S. 249 (1953) [which permitted the seller of property to challenge the validity of a covenant barring the sale of that property to non-whites by asserting the equal protection rights of racial minorities], for there is here no barrier whatever to Oklahoma males 18–20 years of age asserting, in an appropriate forum, any constitutional rights they may claim to purchase 3.2% beer. Craig's successful litigation of this very issue was prevented only by the advent of his 21st birthday. There is thus no danger of interminable dilution of those rights if appellant Whitener is not permitted to litigate them here.

Nor is this controlled by Griswold v. Connecticut, 381 U.S. 479 (1965), [in which a doctor was allowed to assert the constitutional rights of his patients]. It borders on the ludicrous to draw a parallel between a vendor of beer and the intimate professional physician-patient relationship which undergirded relaxation of standing rules in that case.

Even in Eisenstadt, the Court carefully limited its recognition of third-party standing to cases in which the relationship between the claimant and the relevant third party "was not simply the fortuitous connection between a vendor and potential vendees, but the relationship between one who acted to protect the rights of a minority and the minority itself." 405 U.S., at 445. This is plainly not the case here.

In sum, permitting a vendor to assert the constitutional rights of vendees whenever those rights are arguably infringed introduces a new concept of constitutional standing to which I cannot subscribe. * * **

---

* [Ed.] The concurring opinions of Justices Powell, Stevens, Blackmun, and Stewart and the dissenting opinion of Justice Rehnquist—none of which addressed standing issues—are omitted.

NOTE ON ASSERTING THE RIGHTS OF OTHERS

(1) Jus Tertii Doctrine. (a) In Craig v. Boren the appellant Whitener was threatened with criminal prosecution if she sold low alcohol beer in violation of an Oklahoma statute and, thus, concededly satisfied the Article III requirement of injury in fact. The only standing question was whether Whitener could argue that the statute under which she was threatened with prosecution violated the equal protection rights of 18-to-20-year-old males—a question often described as one of third-party standing.

(b) For purposes of analytical clarity, it may help to restrict the label of third-party standing or *jus tertii* to cases in which litigants claim that the application of a law against them will also harm the very third parties whose rights the litigants seek to raise. If observed, this conceptual limitation permits a distinction between the doctrine governing *jus tertii* standing and that applicable to overbreadth challenges, discussed at pp. 177–195, *infra*: "The most common example of * * * an [overbreadth] attack arises under the first amendment, when a litigant whose speech may not itself be constitutionally protected claims that the relevant statute must be struck down because it could be applied to restrict speech that cannot constitutionally be burdened. Thus, overbreadth attacks involve both the application of the challenged law to the claimant and a different, hypothetical application of the law to third parties. Quite different from this sort of third party claim is an assertion of jus tertii—a litigant's claim that a single application of a law both injures him and impinges upon the constitutional rights of third persons." Note, *Standing to Assert Constitutional Jus Tertii*, 88 Harv.L.Rev. 423, 423–24 (1974).

(2) The Traditional View. The traditional rule, from which Craig and the precedents that it relied on deviated, was that parties to a lawsuit could only assert their own rights or immunities.

(a) In Tileston v. Ullman, 318 U.S. 44 (1943) (per curiam), the Connecticut Supreme Court had rejected, on the merits, a physician's constitutional challenge to the application to him of a state statute prohibiting the use or distribution of contraceptives. The Supreme Court dismissed his appeal on the ground that the only constitutional attack on the statute—that it worked a deprivation of liberty without due process—was based on the rights not of the physician but of his patients, which he had no standing to assert.[1]

(b) McGowan v. Maryland, 366 U.S. 420 (1961), involved a prosecution of department store employees for Sunday sales in violation of the state's "Blue Laws". The Court denied the defendants' standing to assert their customers' First Amendment right to free exercise of religion: "[A]ppellants * * * allege only economic injury to themselves; they do not allege any

---

[1]   Although Tileston is often cited as holding that a litigant may not assert the rights of third persons, some have read the case more narrowly, as resting on the absence of any injury to the doctor himself: he failed to allege that the statute injured him economically, and the risk of a criminal prosecution was insufficiently ripe to constitute redressable injury. See Bickel, The Least Dangerous Branch 143–45 (1962); Scott, *Standing in the Supreme Court—A Functional Analysis*, 86 Harv.L.Rev. 645, 649 n.14 (1973). On this view, the case stands merely for the proposition that a party not personally injured may not start a lawsuit solely to alleviate harm to others.

infringement of their own religious freedoms due to Sunday closing. * * * Those persons whose religious rights are allegedly impaired by the statutes are not without effective ways to assert these rights. Cf. NAACP v. Alabama, 357 U.S. 449, 459–460 (1958); Barrows v. Jackson, 346 U.S. 249, 257 (1953). Appellants present no weighty countervailing policies here to cause an exception to our general principles."[2]

(3) Doctrinal Evolution. Although subsequent cases have continued to describe jus tertii standing as a departure from the norm, the post-Craig pattern has been for the Court almost routinely to permit assertions of third-party rights upon finding (i) some sort of "relationship" between the litigants seeking third-party standing and those whose rights they want to assert and (ii) some sort of impediment to third parties' effective assertion of their own rights through litigation. See, *e.g.*, Powers v. Ohio, 499 U.S. 400 (1991) (upholding a criminal defendant's standing to assert prospective jurors' rights not to be peremptorily challenged on grounds of race, in light of the "relation" between the defendant and jurors that "continues throughout the entire trial" and the significant practical barriers to the assertion by prospective jurors of their own rights)[3]; United States Dept. of Labor v. Triplett, 494 U.S. 715, 720 (1990) (holding that an attorney who was resisting state court disciplinary proceedings for receiving prohibited contingent fees from claimants under the Federal Black Lung Benefits Act had standing to assert the constitutional rights of his clients and stating that when "enforcement of a restriction against the litigant prevents a third party from entering into a relationship with the litigant (typically a contractual relationship), to which relationship the third party has a legal entitlement (typically a constitutional entitlement), third-party standing has been held to exist").

But the Court has not enforced either of these requirements with consistent stringency. In Powers, for example, the "relation" between a criminal defendant and a prospective juror is attenuated at best, and perhaps the most characteristic "impediment" to third parties' enforcement of their own rights is the cost of bringing a lawsuit. According to Fallon, *As-Applied and Facial Challenges and Third-Party Standing*, 113 Harv.L.Rev. 1321, 1361 n.202 (2000), the Court has almost invariably upheld third-party standing to assert plausibly meritorious claims. But there are exceptions, including Kowalski v. Tesmer, 543 U.S. 125 (2004). The Kowalski plaintiffs were lawyers who sought to challenge provisions of Michigan law that made the appointment of appellate counsel discretionary, rather than a matter of right (as before), for indigent state defendants who pleaded guilty or nolo contendere. In an opinion by Chief Justice Rehnquist, the Court assumed that the plaintiffs had Article III standing, based on the likelihood of lost revenues, but refused to accord them third-party standing to assert the rights of indigent defendants—rights that it recognized and enforced when an indigent defendant appeared as the petitioner in Halbert v. Michigan, 545 U.S. 605 (2005), a case decided during the same Term. Writing for a 6–3 majority in Kowalski, Chief Justice Rehnquist reasoned that "[t]he attorneys before us do not have a 'close relationship' with their alleged clients; indeed,

---

[2] In a companion case to McGowan involving Orthodox Jewish merchants, the Court rejected the free exercise challenge on the merits. See Braunfeld v. Brown, 366 U.S. 599 (1961).

[3] The Court found that the criminal defendant had suffered injury in fact because forbidden discrimination "places the fairness of a criminal proceeding in doubt". Powers was followed in Georgia v. McCollum, 505 U.S. 42 (1992), which held that prosecutors may challenge a criminal defendant's exercise of peremptory challenges on the basis of race.

they have no relationship at all". Nor had the attorneys "demonstrated that there is a 'hindrance' to the indigents' advancing their own constitutional rights". That "hypothesis" was disproved, the Court said, by the success of pro se defendants in asserting their rights in Michigan's appellate courts: "While we agree that an attorney would be valuable to a criminal defendant challenging the constitutionality of the scheme, we do not think that the lack of an attorney here is the type of hindrance necessary to allow another to assert the indigent defendants' rights".

Justice Ginsburg, joined by Justices Stevens and Souter, dissented. She noted that "the Court has found an adequate 'relation' between litigants alleging third-party standing and those whose rights they seek to assert when nothing more than a buyer-seller connection was at stake", and she emphasized the difficulties confronting "indigent and poorly educated defendants" attempting to present constitutional claims in a pro se appeal.

In light of earlier cases authorizing third-party standing, is the result in Kowalski defensible on any principled ground?

(4) Attempted Re-conceptualizations. It was established well before Craig—by authorities that Craig cited—that the rule against third-party standing is a discretionary and waivable "rule of self-restraint", not a mandate of Article III. By what authority does the Court craft jurisdictional rules that are not mandated by Article III, by any other provision of the Constitution, or by federal statute?

(a) Professors Monaghan and Sedler have argued forcefully that many of the cases viewed by the Court as involving assertions of third-party rights would be better conceptualized as presenting first-party claims. See Sedler, *The Assertion of Constitutional Jus Tertii: A Substantive Approach*, 70 Calif.L.Rev. 1308, 1329 (1982); Monaghan, *Third Party Standing*, 84 Colum.L.Rev. 277, 299 (1984). See also Warth v. Seldin, 422 U.S. 490, 501 (1975), citing Pierce v. Society of Sisters, 268 U.S. 510 (1925), as an example of the Court's having "found, in effect, that the constitutional or statutory provision in question implies a right of action in the plaintiff." According to Monaghan, a litigant "asserts his own rights (not those of a third person) when he seeks to void restrictions that directly impair his freedom to interact with a third person who himself could not be legally prevented from engaging in the interaction."

In support of his view, Professor Monaghan suggests that the "first party" approach is preferable because it eliminates "unanalyzed and ungrounded notions of judicial 'discretion.' " 84 Colum.L.Rev. at 278. A further asserted benefit of Monaghan's approach is that it supplies a straightforward answer to some troubling questions of judicial power, such as the source of a federal court's authority to provide relief to which a party has no personal "right".

Consider, however, whether judicial power to provide remedies to parties with no personal right to relief, as a means of ensuring that the rights of others are not harmed, has not been implicitly recognized by such well-established doctrines as the First Amendment overbreadth doctrine, see pp. 177–184, *infra*, and the exclusionary rule. The Supreme Court has concluded that the Fourth Amendment's exclusionary rule does not prevent or redress any harm to the criminal defendant who invokes it, but instead simply helps to protect the citizenry at large by generally deterring constitutional violations. See, *e.g.*, United States v. Calandra, 414 U.S. 338, 353–54 (1974).

On this view, isn't the criminal defendant, in moving to suppress evidence, given standing to claim a remedy whose purpose is to safeguard the rights of others?[4]

(b) Building on a suggestion by Professor Monaghan,[5] Professor Fallon goes even farther in recharacterizing some purportedly third-party rights as first-party rights. See Fallon, Paragraph (3), *supra*, at 1331–32. He argues that under the presuppositions of Marbury v. Madison, everyone has a *personal* constitutional right not to be sanctioned except pursuant to a constitutionally valid rule of law. In Craig v. Boren, for example, the beer vendor had a personal right not to be punished criminally for violating the constitutionally invalid Oklahoma statute that she challenged in the Supreme Court. See also Bond v. United States, 131 S.Ct. 2355 (2011) (Ginsburg, J., concurring) (joining a Court opinion that permitted a criminal defendant to attack a statute on the ground that it exceeded congressional authority under Article I and the Tenth Amendment and explaining that "Bond, like any other defendant, has a personal right not to be convicted under a constitutionally invalid law").

If the premise is granted that everyone has a personal right not to be sanctioned under a constitutionally invalid rule of law, Fallon maintains, then all actual and potential *defendants* in legal enforcement proceedings are entitled (once the Article III requirement of injury-in-fact is satisfied) to challenge the constitutional validity of the rules of law invoked against them; in other words, distinctions between first- and third-party standing do not arise in cases involving actual or possible defendants, for all are asserting personal rights not to be sanctioned under invalid statutes.

Although Professor Fallon attempts to fit many third-party standing claims into a first-party mold, his view does not wholly eliminate the category of third-party standing (as Professor Monaghan's appears to do). According to Fallon, it is only actual and potential defendants who enjoy a Marbury-based entitlement to challenge the validity of rules invoked against them; questions remain about whether and to what extent *plaintiffs* who face no threat of legal coercion—such as the lawyer plaintiffs in Kowalski v. Tesmer, Paragraph (3), *supra*—should be able to assert third-party rights. In addition, some defendants may plausibly claim entitlements to assert rights best conceptualized as those of third-parties—for example, in cases in which a white criminal defendant challenges the use of peremptory challenges to exclude potential black jurors on the basis of race.[6]

Acceptance of Fallon's view would call for a re-conceptualization of many decided cases, but he asserts that virtually all of the Supreme Court's results can be explained as consistent with his theory.[7] While nearly all of

---

[4] See generally Meltzer, *Deterring Constitutional Violations by Law Enforcement Officials: Plaintiffs and Defendants as Private Attorneys General*, 88 Colum.L.Rev. 247 (1988); Monaghan, *supra*, at 279–82, 310–15.

[5] See Monaghan, *Overbreadth*, 1981 Sup.Ct.Rev. 1, 3; see also Monaghan, *Harmless Error and the Valid Rule Requirement*, 1989 Sup.Ct.Rev. 195.

[6] For criticism of Fallon's argument, see Adler, *Rights, Rules, and the Structure of Constitutional Adjudication: A Response to Professor Fallon*, 113 Harv.L.Rev. 1371 (2000). Adler argues that all constitutional rights are rights against rules; that it is a mistake to think of litigants as having "personal" rights in the sense assumed by Fallon's argument; and that Fallon particularly errs in assuming that there is a well-grounded personal right not to be sanctioned except pursuant to a constitutionally valid rule of law.

[7] Note that private litigants are often permitted to raise questions of federalism or separation of powers in challenging as invalid a law or a government action that harms their

the cases denying standing (including Kowalski v. Tesmer) really are ones in which one party sought to assert another party's rights, many if not most of the cases upholding third-party standing, including Craig v. Boren, can be explained alternatively as involving the personal right of an actual or potential defendant not to be sanctioned pursuant to a constitutionally invalid statute. Questions of prudence and judicial administration aside, would it have been a constitutionally tolerable situation in Craig for the plaintiff beer vendor to have been jailed for violating a statute that was constitutionally invalid under the Equal Protection Clause and would have been held to be such in a case involving a different challenger?

(c) In Lexmark Int'l, Inc. v. Static Control Components, Inc., 134 S.Ct. 1377, 1386 (2014), also discussed pp. 156–157, *supra,* a unanimous Court noted "some tension" between prudential standing doctrine and the "principle that a federal court's obligation to hear and decide cases within its jurisdiction is virtually unflagging," as affirmed, for example, in Sprint Communications, Inc. v. Jacobs, 134 S.Ct. 584, 591 (2013) (internal quotations omitted), pp. 1167, 1169, *infra.* In a footnote to its Lexmark decision, the Court then quoted an earlier case as having recognized that "third-party standing is closely related to the question whether a person in the litigant's position will have a right of action on the claim," but also acknowledged that "most of our cases have not framed the inquiry in that way." 134 S.Ct. at 1387 n.3 (internal quotations and citations omitted). The footnote concluded: "This case does not present any issue of third-party standing, and consideration of that doctrine's proper place in the standing firmament can await another day."

Yazoo & Mississippi Valley R. R. v. Jackson Vinegar Co.

226 U.S. 217, 33 S.Ct. 40, 57 L.Ed. 193 (1912).
Appeal from the Circuit Court of Hinds County, Mississippi.

■ MR. JUSTICE VAN DEVANTER delivered the opinion of the Court.

This was an action to recover damages from a railway company for the partial loss of a shipment of vinegar carried over the company's line from one point to another in the state of Mississippi. * * * The position of the railway company, unsuccessfully taken in the state court and now renewed, is that the Mississippi statute providing for the penalty is repugnant to the due process of law and equal protection clauses of the 14th Amendment to the Constitution of the United States. The statute reads:

---

interests. See, *e.g.,* San Diego Bldg. Trades Council v. Garmon, 359 U.S. 236 (1959) (private litigant permitted to assert that state law under which he was sued is preempted by the National Labor Relations Act); INS v. Chadha, 462 U.S. 919 (1983) (permitting an alien to challenge a legislative veto of a decision suspending a deportation order against him, on the ground that the veto violated the separation of powers); Bond v. United States, 131 S.Ct. 2355, 2364 (2011) (holding the prohibition against third-party standing inapplicable to a criminal defendant challenging the law being enforced against her as exceeding congressional power under Article I and the Tenth Amendment because "[s]tates are not the sole intended beneficiaries of federalism").

"Railroads, corporations, and individuals engaged as common carriers in this state are required to settle all claims for lost or damaged freight which has been lost or damaged between two given points on the same line or system, within sixty days from the filing of written notice of the loss or damage with the agent at the point of destination * * *. A common carrier failing to settle such claims as herein required shall be liable to the consignee for $25 damages in each case, in addition to actual damages, all of which may be recovered in the same suit: Provided that this section shall only apply when the amount claimed is $200 or less."

The facts showing the application made of the statute are these: The plaintiff gave notice of its claim in the manner prescribed, placing its damages at $4.76, and, upon the railway company's failure to settle within sixty days, sued to recover that sum and the statutory penalty. Upon the trial the damages were assessed at the sum stated in the notice, and judgment was given therefor, with the penalty. Thus, the claim presented in advance of the suit, and which the railway company failed to settle within the time allotted, was fully sustained.

As applied to such a case, we think the statute is not repugnant to either the due process of law or the equal protection clause of the Constitution, but, on the contrary, merely provides a reasonable incentive for the prompt settlement, without suit, of just demands of a class admitting of special legislative treatment.

Although seemingly conceding this much, counsel for the railway company urge that the statute is not confined to cases like the present, but equally penalizes the failure to accede to an excessive or extravagant claim; in other words, that it contemplates the assessment of the penalty in every case where the claim presented is not settled within the time allotted, regardless of whether, or how much, the recovery falls short of the amount claimed. But it is not open to the railway company to complain on that score. It has not been penalized for failing to accede to an excessive or extravagant claim, but for failing to make reasonably prompt settlement of a claim which, upon due inquiry, has been pronounced just in every respect. Of course, the argument to sustain the contention is that, if the statute embraces cases such as are supposed, it is void as to them, and, if so void, is void *in toto*. But this court must deal with the case in hand, and not with imaginary ones. It suffices, therefore, to hold that, as applied to cases like the present, the statute is valid. How the state court may apply it to other cases, whether its general words may be treated as more or less restrained, and how far parts of it may be sustained if others fail, are matters upon which we need not speculate now.

The judgment is accordingly affirmed.

————

PRELIMINARY NOTE ON AS-APPLIED AND FACIAL CHALLENGES AND THE PROBLEM OF SEPARABILITY

(1) As-Applied Versus Facial Challenges. Judges and scholars have traditionally distinguished between two types of challenges to statutes—as-applied challenges and facial challenges. As a first approximation, a party presenting an as-applied challenge argues that a statute cannot be applied to her because its application would violate her personal constitutional rights. By contrast, a party making a facial challenge seeks to have a statute declared unconstitutional in all possible applications. Although these concepts may seem straightforward, they have generated substantial controversy and debate, and the line between them is not always clear.

(2) Underlying Policies. Is the Yazoo approach, which generally precludes consideration of a statute's constitutionality as applied to the facts of other cases, a sound one? Consider Fallon, *Making Sense of Overbreadth*, 100 Yale L.J. 853, 860–61 (1991): "The Yazoo rule is harsh and in some ways counterintuitive. The challenged statute imposed pressure on railroads to settle even frivolous cases. The Court, in prescribing the approach that it did, bypassed a clear opportunity to consider the permissibility of the statutory policy and, if it found injustice, to end it."

According to Fallon, at least three policy reasons support the Yazoo approach. First, if the defendant's conduct may constitutionally be forbidden, the defendant has no personal right to escape punishment, at least as long as a statute's valid applications are severable from its invalid application. Second, to permit adjudication to turn on hypothetical disputes would give too abstract a flavor to constitutional litigation. Third, it is a fundamental premise of constitutional federalism that state courts may provide narrowing constructions of state statutes, and state courts should therefore be given the opportunity to do so.

(3) Separability. The Yazoo approach depends on the premise that statutes are typically "separable" or "severable", and that invalid applications can somehow be severed from valid applications without invalidating the statute as a whole—a premise that is deeply rooted in American constitutional law.[1] Sometimes the separability question is whether a linguistically identifiable part of a statute can survive after another part has been found invalid— whether, for example, a statute prohibiting the sale of "lewd or obscene" materials can be enforced against sellers of "obscene" materials if a prohibition against materials that are merely "lewd" violates the First Amendment. In other instances, as in Yazoo, the question will be whether a statutory provision that does not on its face reflect divisible linguistic units— such as a requirement that railroads must settle "all claims"—can nonetheless be severed into valid and invalid elements, or whether valid applications can be separated from invalid ones.[2] According to conventional

---

[1] The classic study of separability is Stern, *Separability and Separability Clauses in the Supreme Court*, 51 Harv.L.Rev. 76 (1937); a useful more recent discussion is Nagle, *Severability*, 72 N.C.L.Rev. 203 (1993).

[2] Fallon, *As-Applied and Facial Challenges and Third-Party Standing*, 113 Harv.L.Rev. 1321, 1331–33 (2000), maintains that the Court's frequent refusals to adjudicate facial challenges involves an implicit assumption that statutory rules are reducible to what might be characterized as statutory "sub-rules". In a case such as Yazoo, he suggests, the Court assumes that the statutory requirement that the railroad settle "all claims" should be viewed as potentially encompassing multiple sub-rules, including the sub-rule "(i) settle all valid and non-exorbitant claims", as well as possible further sub-rules such as "(ii) settle all frivolous and excessive claims". If the statute is viewed as comprising a number of sub-rules, it becomes comprehensible that sub-rule (i) could survive even if sub-rule (ii) were constitutionally invalid and had to be severed.

Fallon emphasizes, however, that a statute's full meaning is not always obvious. For example, one of the open questions in Yazoo was whether the statute should be "specified", in Fallon's terms, as applying to frivolous and excessive claims at all. According to Fallon, recognition that a statute can be separated into separately specified sub-rules, some of which are valid even if others are not, is necessary to explain why courts, in cases such as Yazoo, can

understandings, a "presumption" of statutory severability applies. See Dorf, *Facial Challenges to State and Federal Statutes*, 46 Stan.L.Rev. 235, 250 (1994); Monaghan, *Overbreadth*, 1981 Sup.Ct.Rev. 1, 6–7.

Challenging the conventional view, Fallon, *Fact and Fiction About Facial Challenges,* 99 Cal.L.Rev. 915 (2011), argues that the ascription to Yazoo of a nearly categorical presumption of severability "leaves open the question of how Yazoo related to such cases as the nearly contemporaneous Lochner v. New York, [198 U.S. 45 (1905),] which upheld a facial challenge to a law regulating the hours of employment of bakery workers under the same Due Process Clause that was involved in Yazoo. In Lochner, the Court made no suggestion that the possibility of statutory severing limited the challenger to asserting as-applied claims." According to Fallon, a general presumption of severability would make it impossible for courts ever to hold a statute irrational or otherwise invalid because it is too broadly written, but "Yazoo is easily distinguishable from cases that have held statutes irrationally overinclusive * * * because in Yazoo, unlike those cases, there was an obvious surgical cure [that would remove the problem of irrational overbreadth] if severing turned out to be necessary in a future case. Even if the challenged statute was invalid as applied to cases involving frivolous, excessive, or disputable claims for damages, it could have been so severed as to remain enforceable in cases involving admittedly valid claims, such as the one before the Court." If a truly general presumption of severability applied, what would be the point of asking whether a *statute*—as opposed to an *application* of a statute—was rationally related to a legitimate state interest, or narrowly tailored to a compelling state interest, or satisfied a similar test of constitutional validity?

(4) Deference to State Interpretations. (a) Although federal courts apply a presumption of severability, questions about the meaning and thus the separability of state statutes are primarily questions of state law. In Dorchy v. Kansas, 264 U.S. 286 (1924), a criminal defendant sought review of his conviction under § 19 of the Court of Industrial Relations Act of Kansas, which he claimed was an unconstitutional restriction of the right to strike. Pending the decision of this case, the Supreme Court held in another case that other provisions of the statute (providing for compulsory arbitration of labor disputes) violated the federal Constitution as there applied. After pointing out that it would be unnecessary to consider Dorchy's objections to § 19 if that section were inseparable from the arbitration provisions, it vacated the state court's judgment and remanded the case for a determination of that question:

"Whether § 19 is so interwoven with the system held invalid that the section cannot stand alone, is a question of interpretation and of legislative intent. * * * The task of determining the intention of the state legislature in this respect, like the usual function of interpreting a state statute, rests primarily upon the state court. Its decision as to the severability of a provision is conclusive upon this Court. * * * In cases coming from the state courts, this Court, in the absence of a controlling state decision, may, in passing upon the claim under the federal law, decide, also, the question of severability. But it is not obliged to do so. The situation may be such as to

---

postpone questions about whether a statute might apply to cases not currently before the Court and about whether it would be constitutional as so applied.

make it appropriate to leave the determination of the question to the state court. We think that course should be followed in this case."

(b) In Ayotte v. Planned Parenthood of Northern New England, 546 U.S. 320 (2006), also discussed p. 186, *infra*, the Court reviewed a lower federal court judgment facially invalidating a state statute that barred minors from having abortions in the absence of parental notification or judicial authorization unless "necessary to prevent the minor's death". Agreeing with the lower court that the Constitution required further exceptions for non-life-threatening health emergencies, the majority opinion said that "[a]fter finding an application or portion of a statute unconstitutional, we must next ask: Would the legislature have preferred what is left of its statute to no statute at all?" Without reference to the applicable state law of severability, it then remanded the case for a determination whether an injunction merely prohibiting invalid applications of the statute would accord with the preferences of the New Hampshire legislature. Scoville, *The New General Common Law of Severability*, 91 Tex.L.Rev. 543 (2013), reads Ayotte as rejecting the rule that the severability of state statutes is a matter of state law and replacing it with a new general common law rule—which the author thinks difficult to square with Erie R. Co. v. Tompkins, p. 584, *infra*—that federal courts should prefer partial to facial invalidations of state statutes. Even if Ayotte is read more cautiously, Professor Scoville seems correct that there may be a tension in some cases among the Supreme Court's asserted preference for as-applied over facial challenges, its insistence that federal courts must not re-write statutes in order to save them, and its long-held stance that state law governs the separability of state statutes.

(5) Separability of Federal Statutes. The separability of a federal statute is, of course, a purely federal issue. Although many federal statutes contain separability clauses directing that the judicial invalidation of one provision should not preclude enforcement of others, even in the absence of such clauses the Supreme Court generally presumes that invalid statutory applications should be severed and the remainder of a statute enforced whenever possible.

(a) In United States v. Jackson, 390 U.S. 570 (1968), the district court had dismissed a federal kidnapping indictment after holding unconstitutional the statute's death penalty provision. The Supreme Court agreed that the death penalty could not be imposed, but ruled that the kidnapping charge was nonetheless valid: "Unless it is evident that the legislature would not have enacted those provisions which are within its power, independently of that which is not, the invalid part may be dropped if what is left is fully operative as a law." Though the statute at issue had no separability clause, the Court remarked that "the ultimate determination of severability will rarely turn on the presence or absence of such a clause".[3]

Exactly what is the question of legislative intent that the Court asks in severability cases? Can it be resolved on the basis of a statute's text, or does it inevitably require an assessment of legislative purposes and legislative history—one that adherents of textualist theories of statutory interpretation would ordinarily resist? See generally pp. 652–656, *infra*.

---

[3] Accord, Buckley v. Valeo, 424 U.S. 1, 108 (1976); Regan v. Time, Inc., 468 U.S. 641, 653 (1984) (plurality opinion) (severability "is largely a question of legislative intent, but the presumption is in favor of severability").

(b) After holding that a federal statute violates equal protection principles by conferring benefits on one class but not another, the Supreme Court has occasionally recognized that "the choice between 'extension' [to the disfavored class] and 'nullification' is within the 'constitutional competence of a federal district court.'" Heckler v. Mathews, 465 U.S. 728, 739 n.5 (1984), quoting Califano v. Westcott, 443 U.S. 76, 91 (1979). But it has also said that "ordinarily 'extension, rather than nullification, is the proper course'", although "the court should not, of course, 'use its remedial powers to circumvent the intent of the legislature,'" Heckler, 465 U.S. at 739 n.5, quoting Califano, 443 U.S. at 94 (opinion of Powell, J.). In Heckler, which involved a constitutional challenge to a statutory formula that provided more generous Social Security benefits to certain women than to men with similar employment histories, the Court thus declined to invalidate the statute and instead extended the more generous benefits to men. When a court opts for "extension" of a statute that would otherwise be invalid, is it "severing" a constitutionally invalid limitation or doing something else?

(c) In National Federation of Independent Business v. Sebelius, 132 S.Ct. 2566 (2012), the Court held that a provision of the Patient Protection and Affordable Care Act violated principles of constitutional federalism by coercively requiring states to dramatically expand their Medicaid coverage or potentially forfeit all Medicaid funds. But that problem could be adequately remedied, Chief Justice Roberts held (writing for a plurality only on this point), by barring any cut-offs of pre-existing funds that were unconnected with the challenged expansion mandate. This limitation was supported, he argued, by a separability clause in the chapter of the U.S. Code in which the provision authorizing funds cutoffs was codified.

In a joint dissenting opinion, Justices Scalia, Kennedy, Thomas, and Alito concluded that two major provisions of the Act—the Medicaid extension and a mandate to otherwise uninsured individuals to purchase health insurance—were both unconstitutional. (The majority had found the latter to be valid under the Taxing and Spending Clause.) Having so determined, the joint opinion would have held the Act inseverable and therefore invalid in toto. According to the dissent, severability is improper unless "Congress would have enacted" the otherwise valid provisions of a partially invalidated law "standing alone". A number of the Act's otherwise unchallenged "major provisions" were inseparable because they could not "operate as Congress intended without the Individual Mandate and Medicaid Expansion." With respect to a number of "minor provisions"—including such matters as break times at work for nursing mothers and taxes on tanning booths and some medical devices—the dissenting Justices quoted a statement by the Senate majority leader in support of the conclusion that "[o]ften, a minor provision will be the price paid for support of a major provision. So, if the major provision were unconstitutional, Congress would not have passed the minor one."

According to the four dissenting Justices, "[a]n automatic or too cursory severance of statutory provisions risks 'rewrit[ing] a statute'" and "impos[ing] on the Nation, by the Court's decree, its own new statutory regime" in contravention of the separation of powers. Do cases in which the Court holds statutes unconstitutional as applied but declines to entertain facial challenges pose comparable risks? Is the inquiry into which provisions Congress would have passed "standing alone" a judicially manageable one?

(d) In thinking about the large separability issues framed by the dissent in National Federation of Independent Business v. Sebelius, one might begin by considering the respective attractions of two polar alternatives: (i) never sever and (ii) always sever. For a close approximation of (i), see Campbell, *Severability of Statutes*, 62 Hastings L.J. 1495 (2011), arguing that severability doctrine should be abolished, with the effect that any statute with even a single invalid application would be deemed invalid in toto. If Dean Campbell's proposal were adopted, would there be any way of avoiding constitutional litigation based on bizarre hypotheticals involving potentially invalid statutory applications?

In an approximation of (ii), Walsh, *Partial Unconstitutionality*, 85 N.Y.U.L.Rev. 738 (2010), argues that early courts declined to enforce statutory provisions insofar as they were "repugnant" to the Constitution, but did not frame the further "severability" question of whether a partially unconstitutional statute could survive. Professor Walsh argues for a return to the earlier approach, under which courts would enforce all partially (un)constitutional federal statutes to the extent of their constitutional validity unless Congress had enacted a non-severability clause. In comparison with the older model, he argues, the function of modern severability doctrine is not to "save" statutes from invalidity, but instead to authorize judicial invalidation of statutes in toto based on judicial ascriptions of counterfactual congressional intent.

Between these polar alternatives, is there any coherent and otherwise satisfactory middle position that would not require some kind of inquiry into what Congress intended or whether it would have enacted particular provisions if it had known that others would be invalidated? Speaking descriptively rather than prescriptively, Fallon, *Fact and Fiction About Facial Challenges,* Paragraph (2), *supra,* argues that the Supreme Court is often inattentive to severability issues and that although it is possible to offer rationalizing generalizations about the Court's approach, determinate rules cannot be extracted from the Court's cases.[4]

---

[4] The Supreme Court divided sharply over tangled questions involving the separability of a federal statute in United States v. Booker, 543 U.S. 220 (2005). In the "merits" part of Booker, the Court held (by 5–4) in an opinion by Justice Stevens that statutorily mandated impositions of enhanced sentences under the federal Sentencing Guidelines, based on the sentencing judge's determination of a fact not found by the jury, violate the Sixth Amendment. In a separate (5–4) opinion addressing the appropriate remedy, with only Justice Ginsburg joining both majorities, Justice Breyer held invalid the statutory provision that made the Sentencing Guidelines mandatory and determined that this provision should be "severed", with the result that the guidelines became "effectively advisory". (All agreed that, in the light of history, the Sixth Amendment did not bar the exercise of sentencing discretion by judges.) Dissenting from the remedial holding, Justice Stevens (joined by Justice Souter and in pertinent parts by Justice Scalia) protested that the statutory provision making the guidelines mandatory was not facially unconstitutional; although it was invalid as applied to cases in which judges based *enhanced* sentences on facts not found by the jury, it was not invalid as applied to other cases. According to Justice Stevens, the appropriate remedy was therefore to invalidate only those sentence enhancements forbidden by the Constitution and, thus, effectively to force the government to prove to a jury all facts on which it wished to rely at the sentencing stage. (Justice Thomas also dissented from the Court's severability analysis.)

In rejecting the dissenters' approach, the majority appealed to congressional intent: "In our view, it is more consistent with Congress' likely intent in enacting the Sentencing Reform Act (1) to preserve important elements of that system while severing and excising [the provision making the guidelines mandatory] * * * than (2) to maintain all provisions of the Act and engraft today's constitutional requirement [that juries must find all facts pertinent to sentence enhancement] onto that statutory scheme". How persuasive is the argument that a Congress that imposed mandatory sentencing guidelines would have preferred judicial discretion in

---

Board of Airport Commissioners v. Jews for Jesus, Inc.

482 U.S. 569, 107 S.Ct. 2568, 96 L.Ed.2d 500 (1987).
Certiorari to the United States Court of Appeals for the Ninth Circuit.

■ JUSTICE O'CONNOR delivered the opinion of the Court.

The issue presented in this case is whether a resolution banning all "First Amendment activities" at Los Angeles International Airport (LAX) violates the First Amendment.

I.

On July 13, 1983, the Board of Airport Commissioners (Board) adopted Resolution No. 13787, which provides in pertinent part:

"NOW, THEREFORE, BE IT RESOLVED by the Board of Airport Commissioners that the Central Terminal Area at Los Angeles International Airport is not open for First Amendment activities by any individual and/or entity; * * * and

"BE IT FURTHER RESOLVED that if any individual or entity engages in First Amendment activities within the Central Terminal Area at Los Angeles International Airport, the City Attorney of the City of Los Angeles is directed to institute appropriate litigation against such individual and/or entity to ensure compliance with this Policy statement of the Board of Airport Commissioners. . . ."

* * * On July 6, 1984, Alan Howard Snyder, a minister of the Gospel for Jews for Jesus, [a nonprofit religious corporation,] was stopped by a Department of Airports peace officer while distributing free religious literature on a pedestrian walkway in the Central Terminal Area at LAX. The officer showed Snyder a copy of the resolution, explained that Snyder's activities violated the resolution, and requested that Snyder leave LAX. The officer warned Snyder that the city would take legal action against him if he refused to leave as requested. Snyder stopped distributing the leaflets and left the airport terminal.

Jews for Jesus and Snyder then filed this action in the District Court for the Central District of California, challenging the constitutionality of the resolution under * * * the First Amendment to the United States Constitution because it bans all speech in a public forum * * * [and is] unconstitutionally vague and overbroad. * * *

II.

[Although the challengers argue that the resolution is unconstitutional under the stringent standards governing restrictions on free speech in a public forum, there is no need to determine whether LAX is a public forum in order to resolve this case because] the resolution is facially unconstitutional under the First Amendment overbreadth doctrine. * * * Under the First Amendment overbreadth doctrine, an

---

sentencing to a requirement that juries find all pertinent facts? Even if the Court is right about Congress' "likely intent", what is the source of judicial authority to invalidate and sever a statutory provision that is not facially unconstitutional?

individual whose own speech or conduct may be prohibited is permitted to challenge a statute on its face "because it also threatens others not before the court—those who desire to engage in legally protected expression but who may refrain from doing so rather than risk prosecution or undertake to have the law declared partially invalid." Brockett v. Spokane Arcades, Inc., 472 U.S. 491, 503 (1985). A statute may be invalidated on its face, however, only if the overbreadth is "substantial." New York v. Ferber, 458 U.S. 747, 769 (1982); Broadrick v. Oklahoma, 413 U.S. 601, 615 (1973). The requirement that the overbreadth be substantial arose from our recognition that application of the overbreadth doctrine is, "manifestly, strong medicine," Broadrick v. Oklahoma, *supra*, at 613, and that "there must be a realistic danger that the statute itself will significantly compromise recognized First Amendment protections of parties not before the Court for it to be facially challenged on overbreadth grounds." City Council of Los Angeles v. Taxpayers for Vincent 466 U.S. 789, 801 (1984).

On its face, the resolution at issue in this case reaches the universe of expressive activity, and, by prohibiting *all* protected expression, purports to create a virtual "First Amendment Free Zone" at LAX. * * * The resolution therefore does not merely reach the activity of respondents at LAX; it prohibits even talking and reading, or the wearing of campaign buttons or symbolic clothing. Under such a sweeping ban, virtually every individual who enters LAX may be found to violate the resolution by engaging in some "First Amendment activit[y]." We think it obvious that such a ban cannot be justified even if LAX were a nonpublic forum because no conceivable governmental interest would justify such an absolute prohibition of speech.

Additionally, we find no apparent saving construction of the resolution. The resolution expressly applies to all "First Amendment activities," and the words of the resolution simply leave no room for a narrowing construction. * * * The difficulties in adopting a limiting construction of the resolution are not unlike those found in Baggett v. Bullitt, 377 U.S. 360 (1964). At issue in Baggett was the constitutionality of several statutes requiring loyalty oaths. The Baggett Court * * * held the statutes unconstitutional on their face under the First Amendment overbreadth doctrine. We observed that the challenged loyalty oath was not "open to one or a few interpretations, but to an indefinite number," and concluded that "[i]t is fictional to believe that anything less than extensive adjudications, under the impact of a variety of factual situations, would bring the oath within the bounds of permissible constitutional certainty." *Id.*, at 378. Here too, it is difficult to imagine that the resolution could be limited by anything less than a series of adjudications, and the chilling effect of the resolution on protected speech in the meantime would make such a case-by-case adjudication intolerable.

The petitioners suggest that the resolution is not substantially overbroad because it is intended to reach only expressive activity unrelated to airport-related purposes. Such a limiting construction, however, is of little assistance in substantially reducing the overbreadth of the resolution. Much nondisruptive speech—such as the wearing of a T-shirt or button that contains a political message—may not be "airport related," but is still protected speech even in a nonpublic forum. See

Cohen v. California, 403 U.S. 15 (1971). Moreover, the vagueness of this suggested construction itself presents serious constitutional difficulty. The line between airport-related speech and nonairport-related speech is, at best, murky. The petitioners, for example, suggest that an individual who reads a newspaper or converses with a neighbor at LAX is engaged in permitted "airport-related" activity because reading or conversing permits the traveling public to "pass the time." We presume, however, that petitioners would not so categorize the activities of a member of a religious or political organization who decides to "pass the time" by distributing leaflets to fellow travelers. In essence, the result of this vague limiting construction would be to give LAX officials alone the power to decide in the first instance whether a given activity is airport related. Such a law that "confers on police a virtually unrestrained power to arrest and charge persons with a violation" of the resolution is unconstitutional because "[t]he opportunity for abuse, especially where a statute has received a virtually open-ended interpretation, is self-evident." Lewis v. City of New Orleans, 415 U.S. 130, 135–136 (1974) (Powell, J., concurring).

We conclude that the resolution is substantially overbroad, and is not fairly subject to a limiting construction. Accordingly, we hold that the resolution violates the First Amendment. The judgment of the Court of Appeals is

Affirmed.[*]

NOTE ON THE SCOPE OF THE ISSUE IN FIRST AMENDMENT CASES AND RELATED PROBLEMS INVOLVING "FACIAL CHALLENGES"

(1) Distinguishing Overbreadth and Vagueness. The Jews for Jesus case exemplifies the First Amendment overbreadth doctrine that governs the permissibility of facial challenges to statutes brought on the ground that they reach constitutionally protected speech or expressive conduct by parties not before the court. There was also a First Amendment vagueness issue in the case, which arose only upon consideration of a possible limiting judicial construction of the otherwise overbroad regulation. As the Court's separate consideration of overbreadth and vagueness suggests, the doctrines are distinct. A statute may be overbroad without being vague. For example, a statute making it a crime to use the words "kill" and "President" in the same sentence is not vague, but is clearly overbroad. By contrast, a vague statute may or may not be overbroad; the vices of vague statutes are their failure to give notice of what conduct is forbidden and their conferral of excessive discretion on enforcement officials. For example, a statute prohibiting "all speech not protected by the First Amendment" is not overbroad—it prohibits all of the speech the Constitution permits legislatures to ban, no more—but it is vague. On the question whether and when statutes can be subjected to facial challenges on grounds of vagueness, see Paragraph (8), *infra*, and pp. 191–192, *infra*.

(2) Overbroad Federal Statutes. If a litigant challenges a federal statute as overbroad, a federal court can of course give a narrowing construction,

---

[*]   [Ed.] The concurring opinion of Justice White, in which Chief Justice Burger joined, is omitted.

and indeed should presumably apply the canon of statutory construction that "where an otherwise acceptable construction of a statute will raise serious constitutional problems, * * * [the court should] construe the statute to avoid such problems unless such construction is plainly contrary to the intent of Congress." Edward J. DeBartolo Corp. v. Florida Gulf Coast Bldg. & Constr. Trades Council, 485 U.S. 568, 575 (1988).[1] But the Court will not rewrite a statute in the guise of interpreting it. See, *e.g.*, Reno v. ACLU, 521 U.S. 844, 884 (1997) (declining to provide a narrowing construction of parts of a federal statute where the "open-ended character" of the challenged provision, which prohibited transmission of certain "indecent" messages over the Internet, gave "no guidance whatever for limiting its coverage").

If a statute cannot be saved by construction, the question arises whether the invalid portions or applications can be severed. For discussions of separability, see pp. 169–174, *supra*.

(3) The Rationale of the Doctrine. As developed and enforced in cases such as Jews for Jesus, the First Amendment overbreadth doctrine appears to reflect at least three assumptions.[2] First, as stated in Gooding v. Wilson, 405 U.S. 518, 521 (1972), constitutionally protected speech possesses "transcendent value to all society" and therefore merits special protection. (But should that protection be provided by licensing overbreadth attacks, rather than through broad substantive rules privileging expression?) Second, if overbroad restrictions on speech could not be challenged on their face, persons whose expression is constitutionally protected might be chilled from exercising their rights for fear of criminal sanctions. Third, regulations of speech that fail to establish clear standards are likely to be enforced in invidiously discriminatory ways. See, *e.g.*, City of Lakewood v. Plain Dealer Pub. Co., 486 U.S. 750, 757–69 (1988). Are these assumptions well-founded?[3]

Consider how the likelihood of "chill" is affected by the prevailing doctrine concerning "narrowing constructions". Just as federal courts can give narrowing constructions to federal statutes, state courts can give authoritative constructions of state statutes. Accordingly, the overbreadth doctrine applies to statutes as construed, not as written. See, *e.g.*, Osborne v. Ohio, 495 U.S. 103, 119–20 (1990). Indeed, the Supreme Court has held that a state court may provide a narrowing construction in the course of applying and enforcing a statute that, if read literally, would be unconstitutionally overbroad. See *id.*; Cox v. New Hampshire, 312 U.S. 569 (1941).[4]

Isn't either a federal or a state statute that is overbroad on its face (prior to a narrowing judicial construction) likely to chill protected speech and conduct? If so, why should a narrowing construction defeat an overbreadth challenge? One possible answer would be that by the time an overbreadth

---

[1]   For further discussion of this canon, see pp. 77–81, *supra*. For decisions upholding federal statutes after narrowing constructions, see, *e.g.*, Hamling v. United States, 418 U.S. 87, 114–15 (1974); Buckley v. Valeo, 424 U.S. 1, 44, 76–80 (1976).

[2]   The origins of the doctrine are usually traced to Thornhill v. Alabama, 310 U.S. 88 (1940).

[3]   For a discussion of the importance of speech relative to other fundamental rights or preferred liberties, see *Note on Facial Challenges and Overbreadth Beyond the First Amendment*, p. 184, *infra*.

[4]   *But cf.* Shuttlesworth v. Birmingham, 394 U.S. 147, 155–58 (1969) (invalidating a conviction for parading without a permit as part of a civil rights protest where "[i]t would have taken extraordinary clairvoyance for anyone to perceive that [the ordinance] meant what the Supreme Court of Alabama was destined to find that it meant").

challenge is presented, any such chill necessarily occurred in the past; a narrowing construction should help to avert chill in the future; and a forward-looking remedy is sufficient.[5] But how realistic is it to think that parties who might otherwise be chilled will be aware of a narrowing construction?

Is it an aim of the overbreadth doctrine to create incentives for legislatures to write narrow statutes and for state courts to develop narrowing constructions at the earliest opportunity? See Fallon, note 5, *supra.*

The possibility that a state statute might be subject to a narrowing construction can raise formidable difficulties for lower federal courts in suits to enjoin enforcement of state statutes on grounds of overbreadth. An overbreadth attack should not succeed if the statute is "readily subject to a narrowing construction by the state courts." Erznoznik v. City of Jacksonville, 422 U.S. 205, 216 (1975). But how can a federal court know what construction a state court would adopt? Sometimes a federal court that is asked to provide declaratory or injunctive relief may wish to abstain, or certify the question of state law to a state court, in order to obtain that court's authoritative construction of the statute—a possibility to which the Court alluded briefly in Jews for Jesus. See generally Chap. X, Sec. 2(B). Because either course of action is likely to occasion delay, however, courts—as in Jews for Jesus—must sometimes make delicate judgments about when there is sufficient likelihood of a state court narrowing construction (that a federal court cannot readily anticipate) to make abstention or certification appropriate.

(4) The Substantiality Requirement. In Broadrick v. Oklahoma, 413 U.S. 601, 615 (1973), the Supreme Court laid down the rule, echoed in Jews for Jesus, that "where conduct and not merely speech is involved, * * * the overbreadth of a statute must not only be real, but substantial as well, judged in relation to the statute's plainly legitimate sweep", for a facial challenge to prevail.[6] New York v. Ferber, 458 U.S. 747 (1982), then extended the demand for "substantial" overbreadth to a case in which "merely speech" was involved. In rejecting a facial challenge to a New York statute that prohibited the distribution of materials depicting sexual performances by children under 16, Ferber held that even if the statute possibly reached some constitutionally protected materials, any overbreadth was not substantial.

Conceived in the abstract, the substantiality requirement is surely sound. As Justice Brennan conceded in a dissenting opinion in Broadrick, statutes should not be invalidated based on a few aberrant, hypothetical applications. But does it make sense to measure substantial overbreadth, as the Court has sometimes suggested, as a kind of algebraic proportion

---

[5] Compare Note, *The First Amendment Overbreadth Doctrine*, 83 Harv.L.Rev. 844 (1970), and Note, *The Chilling Effect in Constitutional Law*, 69 Colum.L.Rev. 808 (1969), both supporting the premise that narrowing constructions help to alleviate chill, with Redish, The *Warren Court, The Burger Court, and the First Amendment Overbreadth Doctrine*, 78 Nw.U.L.Rev. 1031 (1983), questioning it. See also Fallon, *Making Sense of Overbreadth*, 100 Yale L.J. 853, 885–87 (1991), arguing that the degree of chill is likely to vary with the nature of the statute in question. For example, behavior targeted by a prohibition against "opprobrious language" is likely to be too spontaneous and emotional to be chilled, whereas a statute barring picketing affects conduct that is more likely to be planned in advance by groups with access to legal advice concerning potentially applicable statutes.

[6] Broadrick rejected a facial attack on Oklahoma's "Little Hatch Act," which restricted political activity by state employees.

between constitutional and unconstitutional applications? Is this a manageable inquiry? Would it be preferable for courts frankly to weigh on a relatively ad hoc basis (i) the state's substantive interest in being able to employ a particular legal standard as opposed to some other, less restrictive substitute, against (ii) the First Amendment interest in encouraging narrow statutes and avoiding chill?[7]

(5) Challenges by Protected Speakers. In Brockett v. Spokane Arcades, Inc., 472 U.S. 491 (1985), only four days after the effective date of a Washington statute regulating obscenity, purveyors of sexually oriented books and movies brought a federal court challenge. The court of appeals ruled that the statute extended to protected as well as unprotected speech, and, finding that it "did not lend itself to a saving construction", declared it to be unconstitutional *in toto*. (In the court of appeals' view, the statute's vice was that it defined "prurient" to include "that which incites * * * lust" and thereby reached material that merely stimulated normal sexual responses.) The Supreme Court reversed. Though Justice O'Connor, joined by Chief Justice Burger and Justice Rehnquist, argued for abstention to permit the state courts to construe the new statute, the Court, per Justice White, rejected that course. Instead, the Court ruled that the court of appeals should have invalidated the statute, but only insofar as it reached protected expression. In a departure from earlier cases,[8] Justice White said the Court would not entertain an overbreadth claim "where the parties challenging the statute are those who desire to engage in protected speech that the overbroad statute purports to punish, or who seek to publish both protected and unprotected material. There is then no want of a proper party to challenge the statute, no concern that an attack on the statute will be unduly delayed or protected speech discouraged. The statute may forthwith be declared invalid to the extent it reaches too far, but otherwise left intact".

Total invalidation would be proper, the Court said, only if the state legislature had passed an inseverable statute or would not have passed the statute had its partial invalidity been recognized. Under Washington law, however, there was a presumption of severability, and the statute included a severability clause.

Note that the Court failed to follow the Brockett prescription in Jews for Jesus, in which it upheld a facial challenge without first considering whether the LAX regulation was constitutional as applied to the plaintiffs. See also United States v. Stevens, 559 U.S. 460 (2010), in which the Court held a statute criminalizing the commercially motivated creation, sale, or possession of depictions of animal cruelty to be invalid on its face without first conducting an as-applied assessment.[9]

---

[7] See Alexander, *Is There an Overbreadth Doctrine*, 22 San Diego L.Rev. 541, 553–54 (1985). See also Redish, note 5, *supra* (advocating a balancing analysis). Compare Gunther, *Reflections on Robel*, 20 Stan.L.Rev. 1140, 1147–48 (1968), criticizing overbreadth decisions for suggesting, when striking down overbroad laws, that less sweeping enactments would be valid without providing any guidance concerning how to draft them.

[8] In Secretary of State of Maryland v. Joseph H. Munson Co., Inc., 467 U.S. 947 (1984), the majority cited 10 cases that it described as permitting facial rather than partial invalidation at the behest of litigants claiming that their own conduct was protected.

[9] In Citizens United v. Federal Election Commission, 558 U.S. 310 (2010), the Court sustained a facial challenge to a statutory provision that barred corporations and unions from expending funds on "electioneering communications" relating to candidates for federal office within 30 days of a primary or 60 days of a general election. The challenger, a not-for-profit corporation that wished to fund cable on-demand viewings of a 90-minute film about a

(6) The Strength of Overbreadth Medicine. In Jews for Jesus, the Supreme Court referred to First Amendment overbreadth doctrine as "strong medicine" that ought to be applied sparingly. See also Osborne v. Ohio, 495 U.S. 103, 122 (1990) ((same) quoting Broadrick, *supra*, 413 U.S. at 613). Redish, note 5, *supra*, at 1040. Note, however, that a federal court has no authority to excise a law from a state's statute book. The authority of its ruling in a subsequent action depends on the doctrines of claim and issue preclusion and of precedent. In future cases involving those who were not parties to the action in which a federal court pronounced a state statute facially invalid, the doctrine of claim preclusion will not apply, and the doctrine of issue preclusion may be inapplicable as well, depending on who the parties to the first and the subsequent action are. Moreover, because state courts and lower federal courts stand in a coordinate rather than a hierarchical relationship, the doctrine of precedent would not normally oblige a state court to follow a lower federal court's determinations. Even after the Supreme Court has held a statute unconstitutionally overbroad, state authorities remain free to seek narrowing constructions in state court actions for declaratory judgments. See, *e.g.*, Younger v. Harris, 401 U.S. 37, 50–51 (1971); Dombrowski v. Pfister, 380 U.S. 479, 491–92 (1965). If an adequately narrow construction is obtained, the state can proceed with criminal prosecutions based on conduct occurring *after*, and possibly even based on conduct occurring *before*, the time that the narrowing construction was obtained. See Dombrowski, 380 U.S. at 491 n.7, quoted in Osborne, 495 U.S. at 115: "Our cases indicate that once an acceptable limiting construction is obtained, it may be applied to conduct occurring prior to the construction * * * provided such application affords fair warning to the defendants."

When all of these factors are taken into account, is it possible that the Supreme Court has overestimated the strength of the overbreadth medicine? See generally Fallon, note 5, *supra* (so arguing).

(7) Characterizations of Overbreadth Doctrine. Overbreadth doctrine is frequently characterized as an exception to the rule against third-party standing. See Virginia v. Hicks, 539 U.S. 113, 118 (2003); Members of the City Council v. Taxpayers for Vincent, 466 U.S. 789, 798–99 (1984); Broadrick v. Oklahoma, 413 U.S. 601, 610–12 (1973). When the doctrine is so described, questions arise concerning the source of a court's authority to provide relief to a party whose own speech or expressive conduct is not constitutionally protected.

Fallon, *As-Applied and Facial Challenges and Third-Party Standing*, 113 Harv.L.Rev. 1321, 1359–64 (2001), argues that overbreadth doctrine is closely analogous to a variety of "substantive" doctrines that do not perfectly

---

presidential candidate (Hillary Clinton), had challenged the statute only "as applied" to its case. But the Court, in an opinion by Justice Kennedy, held the applicable provision invalid on its face. Justice Kennedy's reasoning included three strands. First, the Court could not "resolve this case on a narrower ground without chilling political speech". Second, a party's pleadings could not "prevent[ ] the Court from considering certain remedies if those remedies are necessary to resolve a claim [of unconstitutionality] that has been preserved". Third, "we cannot easily address [the issue of whether the statute would be unconstitutional as applied] without assuming a premise—the permissibility of restricting corporate political speech—that is itself in doubt." In a dissenting opinion, Justice Stevens—who would have upheld the statute both on its face and as applied—also objected to the majority's sustaining a facial challenge when it could have found the state unconstitutional as applied to a feature-length video-on-demand film or to a not-for-profit corporation.

Neither the majority nor the dissenting opinion characterized Citizens United as an overbreadth case. Is there any way in which such a characterization would have been inapt?

reflect underlying constitutional norms but are properly crafted by courts to implement those norms meaningfully. Consider the analogy of overbreadth doctrine to the rule of New York Times v. Sullivan, 376 U.S. 254, 279–80 (1964), which protects false allegations against public officials as long as they are not uttered with knowledge of their falsity or reckless disregard for the truth—even though "there is no constitutional value in false statements of fact." Gertz v. Robert Welch, Inc., 418 U.S. 323, 340 (1974).

Compare the argument in Monaghan, *Overbreadth*, 1981 Sup.Ct.Rev. 1, that there is neither justification nor need for a special "standing" doctrine in First Amendment overbreadth cases. Professor Monaghan argues that litigants are always permitted to attack as constitutionally invalid the rule of law under which they are being sanctioned, whether or not the First Amendment is implicated, and whether or not their conduct is itself constitutionally protected. In his view, First Amendment overbreadth doctrine merely applies the requirement of a constitutionally valid rule in light of the substantive demands of the First Amendment. Although statutes are ordinarily assumed to be separable, and whatever remains of statutes after their invalid applications are severed will qualify as a constitutionally valid rule, Monaghan maintains that the First Amendment mandates a substantive exception to ordinarily applicable separability principles. When parties claim First Amendment rights, a court must specifically articulate the constitutionally valid rule of law under which a defendant may be subject to sanctions; if an enforcement court fails to do so, it must be presumed that no constitutionally valid rule exists.[10]

(8) Vagueness. The threat of a chill on protected speech and expression can arise as readily from statutes that are vague as from those that are overbroad. The Due Process Clause establishes requirements of fair notice; criminal prohibitions, in particular, may not be enforced against defendants who would need to guess at whether their conduct was prohibited. *E.g.*, Connally v. General Constr. Co., 269 U.S. 385, 391 (1926) (holding that state minimum wage requirements tied to the "current rate" in a "locality" were "fatally vague"). As with statutes that are overbroad, the doctrinally harder question is when, if ever, litigants can mount a facial attack on statutes that—whether or not vague as applied to their conduct—would be vague as to some substantial range of conduct that might be engaged in by others. For example, a statute barring all speech "not protected by the First Amendment" would clearly apply to someone who falsely cried fire in a crowded theater and thereby caused a panic, but could a false crier of fire seek to have the statute declared facially invalid on the ground that it would be vague as applied to others?

---

[10] In Massachusetts v. Oakes, 491 U.S. 576 (1989), the Massachusetts Supreme Court reversed a conviction under a statute making it a crime to photograph a minor "in a state of nudity" on the ground that the statute was unconstitutionally overbroad. Following this decision, the Massachusetts legislature amended the statute to include a "lascivious intent" requirement, but the state's attorney general continued to seek U.S. Supreme Court reversal of the Massachusetts court's overbreadth ruling. Writing for a plurality of four, Justice O'Connor found that the overbreadth doctrine did not apply to statutes that have been amended or repealed. The purpose of the doctrine, according to the plurality, was to avert chill. Because chill was no longer a concern, the defendant was not entitled to an overbreadth defense. Did the Oakes plurality overlook (or implicitly reject) the defendant's right, as framed by Professor Monaghan, not to be punished except pursuant to a constitutionally valid rule of law? What if the Massachusetts court had deemed the original statute constitutionally overbroad because it was not, as a matter of state law, susceptible of a narrowing construction?

(a) Although the Warren Court, in particular, held a large number of statutes regulating speech and expression to be void for vagueness,[11] later cases convey mixed messages with respect to whether parties may challenge a statute that clearly applies to their conduct on the ground that the statute would be vague as applied to others. Compare Gooding v. Wilson, 405 U.S. 518, 521 (1972) (suggesting an affirmative answer), with Broadrick v. Oklahoma, 413 U.S. 601, 608 (1973) (suggesting a negative answer).

(b) United States v. Williams, 553 U.S. 285 (2008), rejected a vagueness challenge to a federal statute that makes it a crime to offer any material for sale "in a manner that reflects the belief, or that is intended to cause another to believe" that the material is child pornography, regardless of whether it is in fact child pornography. "Whether someone held a belief or had an intent is a true-or-false determination, not a subjective judgment," and a statute clearly defining a factual question cannot be vague, Justice Scalia wrote for the majority. "What renders a statute vague is not the possibility that it will sometimes be difficult to determine whether the incriminating fact it establishes has been proved; but rather the indeterminacy of precisely what that fact is."

As a prelude to this conclusion, Justice Scalia described the applicable vagueness doctrine as follows: "Vagueness doctrine is an outgrowth not of the First Amendment, but of the Due Process Clause of the Fifth Amendment. A conviction fails to comport with due process if the statute under which it is obtained fails to provide a person of ordinary intelligence fair notice of what is prohibited, or is so standardless that it authorizes or encourages seriously discriminatory enforcement. * * * Although ordinarily '[a] plaintiff who engages in some conduct that is clearly proscribed cannot complain of the vagueness of the law as applied to the conduct of others,' we have relaxed that requirement in the First Amendment context, permitting plaintiffs to argue that a statute is overbroad because it is unclear whether it regulates a substantial amount of protected speech. Hoffman Estates v. Flipside, Hoffman Estates, Inc., 455 U.S. 489, 494–95 (1982)."

Does this formulation imply that vagueness challenges in the First Amendment context are subject to a "substantial vagueness" test analogous to that for "substantial overbreadth"? If so, is there any significance to Justice Scalia's insistence that vagueness doctrine is rooted in the Due Process Clause, not the First Amendment?

More generally, if—as stated in Kolender v. Lawson, 461 U.S. 352, 359 n.8 (1983), which is further discussed on p. 191, *infra*—vagueness is "logically related and similar" to overbreadth, shouldn't all of the rules governing First Amendment overbreadth challenges apply equally to First Amendment vagueness cases? See Fallon, note 5, *supra*, at 903–07 (so arguing).

(c) With United States v. Williams, in which the Court said that it had "relaxed the requirement" that a plaintiff whose own conduct is clearly proscribed "cannot complain of the vagueness of the law as applied to the conduct of others", compare Holder v. Humanitarian Law Project, 561 U.S. 1 (2010). There, as a prelude to rejecting an as-applied First Amendment challenge to a statute that makes it a federal crime to "knowingly provid[e] material support or resources to a foreign terrorist organization", Chief

---

[11] See BeVier, *Intersection and Divergence: Some Reflections on the Warren Court, Civil Rights, and the First Amendment*, 59 Wash. & Lee L.Rev. 1075, 1090–91 (2002).

Justice Roberts' majority opinion flatly asserted that "even to the extent a heightened vagueness standard applies" to expressive conduct, "a plaintiff whose speech is clearly proscribed cannot raise a successful vagueness claim under the Due Process Clause of the Fifth Amendment * * * [a]nd he certainly cannot do so based on the speech of others." Although dissenting on the merits, Justice Breyer, joined by Justices Ginsburg and Sotomayor, agreed with regard to vagueness, saying that, "[l]ike the Court, and substantially for the reasons it gives, I do not think this statute is unconstitutionally vague."

If the Court will allow facial challenges to overbroad statutes that threaten to chill third-party speech, does it make sense not to allow vagueness challenges predicated on the possible chilling of third-party speech? In Holder v. Humanitarian Law Project, Chief Justice Roberts suggested that if the Court were to adopt a special vagueness rule for First Amendment cases, the First Amendment overbreadth and Fifth Amendment vagueness doctrines "would be substantially redundant." Do you agree? If an interest in avoiding the chilling of speech provides a sound basis for First Amendment overbreadth doctrine, why would some redundancy with regard to vagueness doctrine be improper?

NOTE ON FACIAL CHALLENGES AND OVERBREADTH BEYOND THE FIRST AMENDMENT

(1) The Salerno Decision. Are the considerations supporting First Amendment overbreadth doctrine any less forceful when applied to statutes whose overbreadth violates other fundamental rights? In United States v. Salerno, 481 U.S. 739, 746 (1987), the Supreme Court confronted arguments that the Bail Reform Act of 1984, which establishes a mandatory scheme of pretrial detention for certain arrestees, violated the guarantees of substantive due process and the Excessive Bail Clause of the Eighth Amendment. In rejecting both challenges, Chief Justice Rehnquist wrote: "A facial challenge to a legislative Act is, of course, the most difficult challenge to mount successfully, since the challenger must establish that no set of circumstances exists under which the Act would be valid. The fact that the Bail Reform Act might operate unconstitutionally under some conceivable set of circumstances is insufficient to render it wholly invalid, since we have not recognized an 'overbreadth' doctrine outside the limited context of the First Amendment." See also Schall v. Martin, 467 U.S. 253, 269 n.18 (1984).

Although Justices Brennan, Marshall, and Stevens dissented on the merits in Salerno, none of the dissenting Justices challenged the Court's framing of the rules governing the availability of facial challenges outside the First Amendment.

(2) Uncertainty and Controversy. The Salerno standard is not impossible to satisfy in all cases. For example, a statute that has an unconstitutional motivation is presumably invalid under all "conceivable * * * circumstances". In other cases, however, the Salerno formulation's meaning may be less than pellucid. Consider, for example, how the Salerno formulation would apply to a statutory classification such as that in Craig v. Boren, p. 161, *supra*, under which young men who wished to buy low alcohol beer were disadvantaged relative to young women. If there are any circumstances under which a particular young man might be more prone to drive dangerously as a result of drinking low alcohol beer than would most young women, should a facial challenge fail under the Salerno standard? If not, why not?

In a challenge to the conventional wisdom that successful facial challenges are rare outside of First Amendment cases, and to Salerno's description of the normally applicable standard, Fallon, *Fact and Fiction About Facial Challenges,* 99 Cal.L.Rev. 915 (2011), maintains that "facial challenges to statutes are common, not anomalous". Based on an examination of "every case decided by the Supreme Court in the 2009, 2004, 1999, 1994, 1989, and 1984 Terms", he concludes: "In all of those Terms, the Court adjudicated more facial challenges on the merits than it did as-applied challenges". In the sample as a whole, moreover, facial challenges had a 44% success rate compared with 38% for as-applied challenges. According to Fallon, another "convincing measure of the frequency of facial challenges emerges from an informal survey of leading Supreme Court cases establishing and applying doctrinal tests, many if not most of which direct attention to a statute on its face, not as applied." These include the familiar strict scrutiny, intermediate scrutiny, and rational basis tests, tests of validity under the First Amendment's Free Speech and Religion Clauses, and tests of congressional authority under Article I and the separation of powers. The real puzzle, Fallon argues, is to explain how the rhetoric in a few leading cases has either generated or supported the conventional but mistaken understanding that facial challenges are disfavored. As you read the remainder of this Note, consider whether any clear and general principles have emerged to govern the availability of facial challenges outside the First Amendment.

(3) Right to Travel. In Aptheker v. Secretary of State, 378 U.S. 500 (1964), two leaders of the Communist Party brought suit to enjoin the State Department's efforts to revoke their passports under § 6 of the Subversive Activities Control Act of 1950, which prohibited the use of a passport by any person who belonged to an organization that the person knew to be required to register under the Act. The Supreme Court held the statute "unconstitutional on its face" because it "too broadly and indiscriminately restricts the right to travel and thereby abridges the liberty guaranteed by the Fifth Amendment". Though it did not deny that a statutory ban on passport use by leaders of the Party might be valid, the Court refused to uphold the statute as applied to the plaintiffs: "[S]ince freedom of travel is a constitutional liberty closely related to rights of free speech and association, we believe that appellants in this case should not be required to assume the burden of demonstrating that Congress could not have written a statute constitutionally prohibiting their travel". Should Aptheker be regarded as a First Amendment case?[1]

(4) Abortion. (a) In a long string of abortion cases beginning with Roe v. Wade, the Supreme Court treated the issues before it as involving the facial validity of challenged statutes. See, *e.g.*, Ohio v. Akron Ctr. for Reprod. Health, 497 U.S. 502 (1990); Hodgson v. Minnesota, 497 U.S. 417 (1990); Webster v. Reprod. Health Services, 492 U.S. 490 (1989). But see H.L. v.

---

[1]   Without attempting to clarify the standard governing the availability of facial challenges asserting freedom of association claims, Washington State Grange v. Washington State Republican Party, 552 U.S. 442 (2008), rejected (7–2) a facial challenge to a scheme under which candidates running and nominated in nonpartisan primaries may express a party "preference" on the ballot. The majority reasoned that any burden on the party's freedom of association rights that might arise from voter confusion about a candidate's actual association with the party should be gauged on an as-applied basis.

Matheson, 450 U.S. 398 (1981) (holding that the plaintiff, an unmarried 15-year-old girl living with and dependent on her parents, could not present a facial challenge to a statute requiring parental notification).

Dissenting from a denial of certiorari in Janklow v. Planned Parenthood, 517 U.S. 1174 (1996), in which the lower court had sustained a facial challenge to a statute regulating the availability of abortions, Justice Scalia, joined by Chief Justice Rehnquist and Justice Thomas, contended that the circuits were split over the permissibility of facial challenges to abortion legislation. He maintained that Salerno, Paragraph (1), *supra,* had correctly stated the applicable principle, under which abortion regulations should not be vulnerable to facial challenges unless invalid in all conceivable circumstances. Justice Scalia would have granted the writ in order to resolve the issue.[2]

(b) By unanimous vote, the Court held in Ayotte v. Planned Parenthood of Northern New England, 546 U.S. 320, 331 (2006), that a state statute requiring parental notification before the performance of an abortion on a minor was unconstitutional insofar as it made no exception for cases of non-life-threatening medical emergency. Nonetheless, the Court held that the lower federal courts had erred in enjoining all enforcement of the statute: "Only a few applications of New Hampshire's parental notification statute would present a constitutional problem. So long as they are faithful to legislative intent, * * * the lower courts can issue a declaratory judgment and an injunction prohibiting the statute's unconstitutional application".

On the Ayotte remand, if the lower court found that severing the statute would accord with the intent of the New Hampshire legislature, how should an injunction be written? The lower court could presumably enjoin the application of the statute to any abortion necessary to avert a threat to a minor's health. But does the Constitution give minors a right to abortion without parental consent (or judicial bypass) no matter how small or speculative the threat to health might be? In order to write an injunction, do the lower courts now need to determine precisely where the line lies between constitutionally permissible and impermissible infringements on abortion rights—rather than, as before, assessing the constitutional validity of the line that a state had drawn?

(c) The Court, by 5–4, again rejected a facial challenge to a statute regulating abortions in Gonzales v. Carhart, 550 U.S. 124 (2007). The case involved a federal statute that bans a particular late-term abortion procedure, often dubbed "partial-birth abortion", but leaves other abortion options intact. Plaintiffs argued, *inter alia*, that the statute should be struck down on its face because it included no exception for cases in which the banned procedure would be necessary to protect the health of the mother.

---

[2] In a memorandum supporting the denial of certiorari in Janklow, Justice Stevens characterized Salerno's assertion that "a facial challenge must fail unless there is 'no set of circumstances' in which the statute could be validly applied" as an unfortunate "dictum" and a "rigid and unwise" departure from the Court's precedents. Before the "rhetorical flourish" to which he objected, Salerno had stated what Justice Stevens believed to be the "long established" and appropriate principle: " 'The fact that [a legislative] Act might operate unconstitutionally under some conceivable set of circumstances is insufficient [by itself] to render it wholly invalid.' " Explaining his vote to deny certiorari, Justice Stevens saw "no need for this Court affirmatively to disavow [Salerno's] unfortunate language, in the abortion context or otherwise, until it is clear that a federal court has ignored the appropriate principle and applied the draconian 'no circumstance' dictum to deny relief in a case in which a facial challenge would otherwise be successful", apparently on the ground that a statute swept excessively broadly.

(The statute did include an exception for cases involving threats to the mother's life.) Justice Kennedy's majority opinion "assume[d]" that the statute would be unconstitutional if it subjected women to "significant health risks". But the majority found medical "uncertainty" about whether the congressionally forbidden procedure "is ever necessary to preserve a woman's health" and ruled that, under the circumstances, a facial challenge must fail: "In these circumstances [involving medical uncertainty] the proper means to consider exceptions is by as-applied challenge * * * if it can be shown that in discrete and well-defined instances a particular condition has or is likely to occur in which the procedure prohibited by the Act must be used. In an as-applied challenge the nature of the medical risk can be better quantified and balanced than in a facial attack.

"The latitude given facial challenges in the First Amendment context is inapplicable here. Broad challenges of this type impose 'a heavy burden' upon the parties maintaining the suit. Rust v. Sullivan, 500 U.S. 173, 183 (1991). What that burden consists of in the specific context of abortion statutes has been a subject of some question. Compare Ohio v. Akron Center for Reproductive Health, 497 U.S. 502, 514 (1990) ('[B]ecause appellees are making a facial challenge to a statute, they must show that no set of circumstances exists under which the Act would be valid * * * '), with [Planned Parenthood of Southeastern Pa. v.] Casey, 505 U.S. [833,] 905 [(1992)] (opinion of the Court) (indicating a spousal-notification statute would impose an undue burden 'in a large fraction of the cases in which [it] is relevant' and holding the statutory provision facially invalid). * * * We need not resolve that debate.

"As the previous sections of this opinion explain, respondents have not demonstrated that the Act would be unconstitutional in a large fraction of relevant cases. * * * The Act is open to a proper as-applied challenge in a discrete case".

Justice Ginsburg, joined by Justices Stevens, Souter, and Breyer, dissented: "The Court * * * confuses our jurisprudence when it declares that 'facial attacks' are not permissible * * * where medical uncertainty exists. * * * Casey makes clear that, in determining whether any restriction poses an undue burden on a 'large fraction' of women, the relevant class is *not* 'all women,' nor 'all pregnant women,' nor even all women 'seeking abortions.' Rather, a provision restricting access to abortion, 'must be judged by reference to those [women] for whom it is an actual rather than an irrelevant restriction.' * * * The very purpose of a health *exception* is to protect women in *exceptional* cases".

Moreover, Justice Ginsburg continued, as-applied challenges were an inadequate substitute for facial challenges: "Surely the Court cannot mean that no suit may be brought until a woman's health is immediately jeopardized * * *. A woman 'suffer[ing] from medical complications' needs access to the medical procedure at once and cannot wait for the judicial process to unfold. * * * The Court appears, then, to contemplate another lawsuit by the initiators of the instant actions * * * demonstrating that 'in discrete and well-defined instances a particular condition has or is likely to occur in which the procedure prohibited by the Act must be used.' * * * [But e]ven if courts were able to carve-out exceptions through piecemeal litigation * * * women whose circumstances have not been anticipated by prior litigation could well be left unprotected. * * * The Court is thus gravely mistaken to conclude that narrow as-applied challenges are 'the proper manner to protect the health of the woman' ".

By assuming that the challenged statute would be unconstitutional if it subjected women to "significant health risks" and that any woman actually subjected to a significant health risk ought to prevail on an "as applied" challenge, did the Court in effect hold the law unenforceable in any case posing a significant risk to maternal health? If the Constitution mandates an exception to pre-viability abortion prohibitions for cases of significant risk to health, and if doctors and pregnant women have been so advised, then why should anyone care whether the statute expressly recognizes a maternal-health exception? The dissent protests that unless a facial challenge can be brought successfully, doctors and pregnant women may be unable to predict with confidence whether a particular abortion would be adjudged necessary to preserve maternal health, but wouldn't the same uncertainty exist if the statute said specifically, but without further elaboration, that the prohibition was subject to a health exception?

(5) The Commerce Clause. In United States v. Lopez, 514 U.S. 549, 551 (1995), the Court held that a federal statute making it a crime knowingly to possess a gun in a school zone exceeded Congress' authority under the Commerce Clause and was therefore invalid. If Congress could validly have forbidden the possession within a school zone of any gun that had traveled in interstate commerce, as seems likely under the Court's precedents,[3] why was Lopez permitted to raise a facial challenge, rather than being required to argue that the statute was unconstitutional as applied to him?

Compare Gonzales v. Raich, 545 U.S. 1, 23 (2005), in which the Court rejected an argument that the Controlled Substances Act, which prohibits cultivation and use of marijuana, exceeds Congress' power under the Commerce Clause as applied to the non-commercial cultivation and use of home-grown marijuana for wholly medical purposes: " 'Where the class of activities is regulated and that class is within the reach of federal power, the courts have no power 'to excise, as trivial, individual instances' of the class' " (quoting Perez v. Unites States, 402 U.S. 146, 154 (1971)). Does Raich hold, in effect, that plaintiffs challenging statutes as beyond congressional authority under the Commerce Clause can *only* mount facial attacks? See Franklin, *Facial Challenges, Legislative Purpose, and the Commerce Clause*, 92 Iowa L.Rev. 41 (2006).

(6) Section Five of the Fourteenth Amendment. Questions involving the conditions for the success of facial attacks have arisen recurrently in recent cases challenging legislation enacted by Congress pursuant to § 5 of the Fourteenth Amendment. As is discussed in detail in Chapter 9, *infra*, states ordinarily enjoy sovereign immunity from suits naming them (rather than their officers) as defendants, but Congress can strip the states of their immunity when exercising its power to "enforce" the Fourteenth Amendment. In City of Boerne v. Flores, 521 U.S. 507 (1997), the Court established the test for the validity of § 5 legislation, including legislation stripping the states of their sovereign immunity and thus making them vulnerable to suit, especially for money damages: In order to qualify as

---

[3]   See Scarborough v. United States, 431 U.S. 563, 575–77 (1977) (finding that a nexus with interstate commerce existed under a federal statute criminalizing possession of a firearm by a convicted felon so long as the firearm had at any point in time traveled in interstate commerce). Following the Supreme Court's decision in Lopez, Congress re-enacted the statute that the Court had invalidated with the addition of such a jurisdictional element.

validly "enforc[ing]" the Fourteenth Amendment, a statute must exhibit "congruence and proportionality between the [constitutional violations] to be prevented or remedied and the means"—including abrogation of the states' immunity—"adopted to that end." Does the congruence and proportionality test inherently require facial challenges by prescribing an inquiry into whether a *statute* is congruent and proportional to the pattern of constitutional violations that it seeks to remedy or prevent? Or can the question sensibly be asked with respect to discrete statutory provisions or even with respect to particular applications?

(a) Florida Prepaid Postsecondary Education Expense Board v. College Savings Bank, 527 U.S. 627 (1999), also discussed p. 959, *infra*, appeared to hold a federal statute purporting to abrogate the states' sovereign immunity in suits for patent infringement to be facially invalid. The majority opinion, by Chief Justice Rehnquist, acknowledged that patent rights are a species of property. It concluded, however, that the statute exceeded the scope of congressional power under § 5 of the Fourteenth Amendment in part because the statute purported to abrogate the states' immunity even in cases of "negligent" patent infringements, and merely negligent deprivations of property do not violate the Due Process Clause (see Daniels v. Williams, p. 1026, *infra*). The Court made no mention of the Salerno test. Justice Stevens dissented, partly on the ground that because the plaintiff had alleged a *willful* patent infringement, the only question properly before the Court was whether the challenged statute could constitutionally be applied to such a case, and he thought that it could.

(b) Justice Stevens, who had dissented in Florida Prepaid, wrote for the majority in rebuffing a facial challenge to a statute argued to exceed Congress' power under § 5 in Tennessee v. Lane, 541 U.S. 509 (2004), also discussed at p. 961, *infra*, with only Justice O'Connor having shifted in the alignment of Justices. Lane arose under Title II of the Americans With Disabilities Act (ADA), which generally bars state and local governments from discriminating on the basis of disability in providing access to their "services, programs or activities" and purports to abrogate the sovereign immunity of offending states. The defendants argued that under Boerne's congruence and proportionality test, Title II swept far too broadly by requiring governments to accommodate those with handicaps in contexts in which failure to do so would not violate the Constitution and that it was therefore unconstitutional on its face. The Court disagreed: The case before it involved a state's failure to provide any mode of access, other than stairs, to a courtroom, and "[b]ecause we find that Title II unquestionably is valid § 5 legislation as it applies to the class of cases implicating the accessibility of judicial services, we need go no further". According to Justice Stevens, prior cases upholding facial challenges under § 5 had involved legislation crafted to enforce a single constitutional right, and a judicial finding that the legislation failed the congruence and proportionality test therefore marked it as invalid in all its applications. By contrast, Justice Stevens reasoned, Title II was designed to protect due process rights of access to courts as well as equal protection rights to freedom from irrational discrimination, and the question whether it validly enforced constitutional rights without redefining them must be determined on a right-by-right basis.

In a dissenting opinion joined by Justices Kennedy and Thomas, Chief Justice Rehnquist argued that Title II exhibited "massive overbreadth" in its extension of rights of access to the disabled in all governmental services and programs, and he would have declared it facially invalid on that basis. Justice Scalia dissented separately.

The Court's approach in Tennessee v. Lane appears to ask not whether a statute is valid as applied to particular facts, but whether it is valid insofar as it attempts to enforce one "constitutional guarantee" (such as the right of access to courts) rather than another (such as the right to be free from irrational discrimination). Under this approach, won't outcomes often depend on how the pertinent "constitutional guarantees" are described?[4]

(c) The Court again took an as-applied approach in another case involving Title II of the ADA, United States v. Georgia, 546 U.S. 151 (2006), in which the plaintiff, a paraplegic prison inmate, sought money damages from the state based, *inter alia*, on conduct that allegedly also violated his constitutional right not to be subjected to cruel and unusual punishment. According to Justice Scalia's opinion for a unanimous Court, the plaintiff's pleading of a constitutional violation differentiated his case from "our other cases addressing Congress' ability to abrogate sovereign immunity pursuant to its § 5 powers" because "no one doubts" Congress' power under § 5 to create "private remedies against the States for *actual* violations" of the Constitution. The Court thus remanded for the lower courts to "determine in the first instance, on a claim-by-claim basis, (1) which aspects of the State's alleged conduct violated Title II; (2) to what extent such misconduct also violated the Fourteenth Amendment; and (3) insofar as such misconduct violated Title II but did not violate the Fourteenth Amendment, whether Congress's purported abrogation of sovereign immunity as to that class of conduct is nevertheless valid".

Although the Justices were unanimous in distinguishing prior § 5 cases on the ground that none alleged an actual constitutional violation, Justice Stevens's dissenting opinion in Florida Prepaid had argued—without contradiction on this point at the time—that the Court's opinion "has nothing to do with the facts of this case", which he said involved an alleged willful violation of the plaintiff's constitutionally protected property interests and thus a violation of the Due Process Clause.

Does United States v. Georgia, especially when viewed in conjunction with Ayotte v. Planned Parenthood of Northern New England, *supra*, signal a renewed wariness about facial challenges? About some kinds of facial challenges (which kinds?) but not others?

(d) In Shelby County v. Holder, 133 S.Ct. 2612 (2013), the Court, by 5 to 4, sustained a facial challenge to the coverage provision of the Voting Rights Act of 1965 (VRA), which identified jurisdictions, mostly in the south, that could not change their voting procedures without seeking prior clearance from the Department of Justice. Chief Justice Roberts' majority opinion reasoned that the coverage formula, which remained unchanged from the 1960s and 1970s through 2006, when Congress most recently re-enacted the VRA, did not bear sufficient relation to current conditions to pass muster under Section 2 of the Fifteenth Amendment. (Like Section 5 of the Fourteenth Amendment, Section 2 of the Fifteenth Amendment authorizes Congress to enforce the provisions in the amendment through "appropriate legislation".) In one of just two paragraphs explaining why facial invalidation

---

[4] For approving commentary on Tennessee v. Lane, maintaining that no justification exists for abandoning the "ordinary" presumption of statutory severability in § 5 cases, see Metzger, *Facial Challenges and Federalism*, 105 Colum.L.Rev. 873 (2005).

was appropriate, the Chief Justice concluded that "[w]e cannot * * * try our hand at updating the statute ourselves, based on the new record compiled by Congress." Although the dissenting Justices would have upheld the coverage formula in toto, they also argued that facial invalidation would be inappropriate even if the coverage formula had invalid applications. According to Justice Ginsburg, a number of relatively recent episodes of discrimination by Alabama and its subdivisions demonstrated that "as applied to Shelby County, the VRA's preclearance requirement is hardly contestable." Justice Ginsburg also emphasized that the VRA includes a severability provision, which directs that "[i]f any provision of [this Act] or the application thereof * * * is held invalid, the remainder of [the Act] and the application of the provision to other persons not similarly situated or to other circumstances shall not be affected thereby." Did the Court impliedly hold the VRA's severability clause unconstitutional, at least as applied to the case before it?[5]

(7) Facial Challenges Based on Vagueness. In Kolender v. Lawson p. 183, *supra*, the plaintiff brought a facial attack against a California statute prohibiting loitering. The lower federal courts enjoined the law on the grounds that it was vague and that it violated the Fourth Amendment, and the Supreme Court affirmed on vagueness grounds. In dissent, Justice White, joined by Justice Rehnquist, argued that the statute did not implicate First Amendment concerns, and that because the statute was not vague in all of its possible applications, the Court's facial invalidation was inconsistent with the Court's precedents governing facial attacks. Writing for the majority, Justice O'Connor responded that Justice White's description of the precedents was inaccurate because (i) the Court permits facial challenges to laws that reach "a substantial amount of constitutionally protected conduct," and (ii) the standard of certainty is higher for criminal statutes.[6]

In City of Chicago v. Morales, 527 U.S. 41 (1999), the Court, by a 6–3 vote, sustained a facial challenge to a municipal ordinance that made it a crime to "loiter" in a public place following a dispersal order by a police officer who reasonably believes one of the persons present to be a gang member. In a majority opinion joined by four other Justices, Justice Stevens held the ordinance invalid on vagueness grounds, because it failed adequately to cabin police discretion. Justice Stevens also concluded (here joined only by Justices Souter and Ginsburg) that the ordinance was facially invalid because it did not provide clear enough notice of the conduct that it

---

[5] For a range of perspectives on doctrines governing facial and as-applied challenges and emerging trends in their application, see Symposium, *The Roberts Court: Distinguishing As-Applied Versus Facial Challenges*, 36 Hastings Const.L.Q. 563 (2009) (including articles by Professors Borgmann, Faigman, Franklin, Manian, and Walsh). See also O'Grady, *The Role of Speculation in Facial Challenges*, 53 Ariz.L.Rev. 867 (2011) (concluding that the Roberts Court is especially reluctant to uphold facial challenges predicated on speculative claims about the behavior that untested statutes are likely to trigger). Metzger, *Facial and As-Applied Challenges Under the Roberts Court*, 36 Fordham Urb.L.J. 773, 798 (2009), asserts that Chief Justice Roberts and Justices Kennedy and Alito have a "greater affinity for as-applied challenges" than the other Justices but that, even for them, "substantive constitutional law drives the Court's approach to facial and as-applied challenges" and determines which statutes are constitutional or unconstitutional in whole and which in part.

[6] For discussions of vagueness doctrine, see generally *Symposium: Void for Vagueness*, 82 Cal.L.Rev. 487 (1994); Jeffries, *Legality, Vagueness, and the Construction of Penal Statutes*, 71 Va.L.Rev. 189 (1985); Note, *The Void-for-Vagueness Doctrine in the Supreme Court*, 109 U.Pa.L.Rev. 67 (1960).

prohibited. In dissent, Justice Scalia contended (without contradiction) that the challengers had not demonstrated that the statute was vague as applied to their conduct or that they had suffered any personal abuse of police discretion. He added that neither precedent nor respect for the judicial role permitted a facial challenge under these circumstances to a statute that, as the majority conceded, did not trench on First Amendment rights. Justice Stevens (again speaking only for a plurality) appeared to offer alternative responses to this objection: (i) the challenge was to "a criminal law" that was "permeate[d]" by vagueness, "that contains no mens rea requirement * * * and infringes on constitutionally protected rights"; and (ii) the case arose on review from a state court, which had entertained and upheld a facial challenge. Two of the concurring Justices (O'Connor and Kennedy) did not specifically explain their grounds for permitting a facial challenge. In his concurring opinion, Justice Breyer reasoned that the challengers were invoking their own rights, not those of third parties, because the ordinance's pervasive vagueness rendered it incapable of constitutional application to anyone.

It certainly makes sense that the standards of fair individual notice should be higher in criminal than in other cases, but how does the interest in fair notice justify the authorization of facial attacks? And doesn't the concern about uneven application exist equally when laws are clear on their faces? Consider the threat of arbitrary and unequal enforcement with respect to speed limits.

(8) Facial Challenges and Narrowing Constructions. The Court propounded a saving construction of a federal statute that had been subjected to a facial challenge on vagueness grounds in Skilling v. United States, 561 U.S. 358 (2010). That statute, 18 U.S.C. § 1346, makes it a crime to fraudulently "deprive another of the intangible right of honest services." In an opinion by Justice Ginsburg, the Court acknowledged that Skilling's argument that the statute was unconstitutionally vague "has force" in light of the "disarray" among prior judicial opinions. "To preserve the statute" under the doctrine that calls for courts to consider "limiting constructions" that might avert holdings of constitutional invalidity under the avoidance doctrine, pp. 77–81, *supra,* the Court held that "§ 1346 criminalizes *only*" the bribery and kickbacks that constituted the "core of the * * * caselaw" that Congress had meant to codify. "Apprised that a broader reading of § 1346 could render the statute impermissibly vague, Congress, we believe, would have drawn the honest-services line, as we do now, at bribery and kickback schemes", Justice Ginsburg wrote.

In an opinion concurring in part and concurring in the judgment, Justice Scalia, joined by Justice Thomas and in part by Justice Kennedy, argued that the majority's "paring down" of the statute was "clearly beyond judicial power." In his view, the Court had not chosen between "fair alternative[ ]" interpretations of § 1346—as would have been proper under the doctrine of constitutional avoidance—but simply rewritten it.

The majority appears to have advanced its saving construction in response to Skilling's argument that § 1346 was so vague as to be facially invalid. Was that argument well founded? Suppose that neither Skilling nor any other defendant could challenge § 1346 on its face, but only as applied. Would the statutory prohibition against fraudulently "depriv[ing] another of the intangible right of honest services" be unconstitutionally vague as applied to an employee who accepted bribes and kickbacks? If not, is the net effect of Skilling possibly to achieve in one step, via a "saving construction," the same result that might have emerged from a series of cases adjudicating claims that § 1346 was unconstitutional as applied—namely, a situation in which § 1346 can be applied to cases involving bribes and kickbacks but not those predicated on other conduct?

(9) Conceptualizing Efforts. Commentators have attempted to clarify issues involving non-First Amendment overbreadth and vagueness by conceptualizing the grounds on which "facial challenges" may be brought.

(a) Fallon, *As-Applied and Facial Challenges and Third-Party Standing*, 113 Harv.L.Rev. 1321 (2000), maintains that there is no single distinctive category of facial, as opposed to as-applied, litigation. According to Fallon, all challenges arise when litigants claim that a statute cannot be constitutionally enforced against them. In ruling on such challenges, courts then typically apply doctrinal tests—such as the strict scrutiny formula or the congruence and proportionality test—and it is these tests, rather than trans-substantive rules governing facial challenges, that determine when facial challenges can and cannot succeed.[7]

In a subsequent article, *Fact and Fiction About Facial Challenges,* Paragraph (2), *supra,* Fallon emphasizes that the tests operate in conjunction with severability principles. In particular, the Court sometimes rebuffs facial challenges to statutes under tests such as the strict scrutiny formula, without determining whether the statutes on their faces might fail those tests, when the Justices can anticipate in advance the relatively "surgical" lines along which a statute might be severed if necessary and thus saved from invalidity. For example, in United States v. Georgia, Paragraph (6)(c), the Court could foresee that even if Title II of the ADA swept too broadly to be upheld in its entirety under § 5 of the Fourteenth Amendment, the statute could be severed in a subsequent case in a way that would leave it valid as applied to cases—such as the one before it—in which plaintiffs' alleged statutory violations also constituted constitutional violations.

(b) Gans, *Strategic Facial Challenges*, 85 B.U.L.Rev. 1333 (2005), argues that the Supreme Court permits facial challenges on a "strategic" basis when, in its view, the costs of remitting challengers to as-applied adjudication would be too great: "Like prophylactic rules, strategic facial challenges aim to better enforce constitutional rights by preempting case-by-case review because of the fear that such review will not adequately protect constitutional norms". According to Gans, "there are three strategic bases for facial invalidation that recur throughout constitutional adjudication": "(i) a chilling effect theory, featured not only in First Amendment overbreadth doctrine, but also in privacy * * * cases [such as those involving abortion]; (ii) an excessive discretion theory that condemns statutes that confer too much discretion on actors to violate constitutional rights * * *; and (iii) a stigma theory, which calls for facial invalidation of laws that send a message of

---

[7] Fallon's argument builds in part on Isserles, *Overcoming Overbreadth: Facial Challenges and the Valid Rule Requirement*, 48 Am.U.L.Rev. 359 (1998), which argues that statutes may be subjected to facial challenges on either of two bases. (i) An "overbreadth" challenge asserts that a statute is facially invalid because "an otherwise valid rule of law" would have too many unconstitutional applications. (ii) A "valid rule facial challenge" asserts that a statute, as measured against a doctrinally applicable constitutional test, possesses some defect *other than overbreadth* that renders it invalid in all its applications—for example, that it has a constitutionally forbidden purpose.

inequality because case-by-case review does not promise to eliminate expeditiously the law's stigmatic message".

As a descriptive matter, how would one test the proposition that the Court determines whether to permit facial challenges pursuant to a case-by-case balancing of costs and benefits? As a normative matter, would it be attractive to recognize a judicial power to make "strategic" judgments about whether to uphold facial challenges?[8]

(c) Rosenkranz, *The Subjects of the Constitution*, 62 Stan.L.Rev. 1209 (2010), argues that some of the Constitution's language inherently calls for facial challenges by designating Congress as the relevant actor and thus making any constitutional violation one that can be committed only by Congress at the time when it enacts a challenged a law. This is true, Professor Rosenkranz maintains, of all provisions of the First Amendment, of the Commerce Clause, and of Section 5 of the Fourteenth Amendment. When Congress violates one of these provisions, he concludes, its attempted lawmaking is void, and a court should invalidate the failed effort by deeming it no law it all. See also Meier, *Facial Challenges and the Separation of Powers,* 83 Ind.L.J. 1557 (2010) (similarly maintaining that challenges to Congress' power to enact a law under the Constitution's power-conferring provisions, such as the Commerce Clause or Section 5 of the Fourteenth Amendment, are inherently facial).

If a court were to adopt Professor Rosenkranz's framework, what should count as a "law" that was inherently and necessarily open to facial attack? Suppose a multi-page revenue bill provides in one section for a special tax on the press. Should a court invalidate the entire bill (on the assumption that it is all one "law"), or should it treat the offending provision as the "law" that violates the First Amendment? Might it be said that Congress violated the First Amendment insofar, but only insofar, as the law that it enacted abridges constitutionally protected expression?[9] *Cf.* Hartnett, *Modest Hope for a Modest Roberts Court: Deference, Facial Challenges, and the Comparative Competence of Courts*, 59 S.M.U.L.Rev. 1735 (2006) (arguing that because courts do a better job than legislatures primarily in applying

---

[8] Gans does not discuss the appropriateness of facial challenges to statutes on the ground that they overreach congressional power under the Commerce Clause or Section Five of the Fourteenth Amendment.

[9] Meier, *supra,* would permit the severance of linguistically distinct bits of statutory text—so that each provision of a multi-part enactment could stand or fall separately from the rest—but not of statutory "applications".

In *The Objects of the Constitution,* 63 Stan.L.Rev. 1005 (2011), Professor Rosenkranz extends the analysis of his earlier article by arguing that the Constitution's grammar and structure sometimes mark either the President or the judicial branch as the object of a prohibition and that in such cases a constitutional challenge is necessarily as-applied (because rights against those branches are not rights against the enactment of "laws"). For a skeptical assessment, see Fallon, *Appraising the Significance of the Subjects and Objects of the Constitution: A Case Study in Textual and Historical Revisionism,* 16 U.Pa.J.Const.L. 453 (2013); see also Harrison, *Power, Duty, and Facial Invalidity,* 16 U.Pa.J.Const.L. 501 (2013) (maintaining that when Congress has implicitly or explicitly provided a "fallback" rule to replace a primary rule that is invalid on its face, as contemplated by severability doctrine, total facial invalidity need not result).

Keller & Tseytlin, *Applying Constitutional Decision Rules Versus Invalidating in Toto,* 98 Va.L.Rev. 301 (2012), argue that Professor Rosenkranz—along with other commentators—errs by failing to distinguish "constitutional decision rules", which determine whether statutes are constitutionally valid or invalid, from "invalidation rules", which determine whether the appropriate remedy for an invalid statute is severance or total nullification.

specific provisions to specific facts, courts should prefer as-applied to facial challenges).

_____

4. MOOTNESS

_____

INTRODUCTORY NOTE

If the requisite injury exists at the outset of a lawsuit, must it persist throughout the life of the litigation? Settled Supreme Court case law suggests that a live controversy must exist throughout. In reading the materials that follow, ask yourself where the mootness doctrine originates, whether its essential elements mirror or deviate from those of standing, and how your answers to those questions affect your view of the choice between the dispute resolution and law declaration models of judicial authority discussed above. See pp. 73–76, *supra*.

_____

DeFunis v. Odegaard

416 U.S. 312, 94 S.Ct. 1704, 40 L.Ed.2d 164 (1974).
Certiorari to the Supreme Court of Washington.

■ PER CURIAM.

In 1971 the petitioner Marco DeFunis, Jr., applied for admission as a first-year student at the University of Washington Law School, a state-operated institution. The size of the incoming first-year class was to be limited to 150 persons, and the Law School received some 1,600 applications for these 150 places. DeFunis was eventually notified that he had been denied admission. He thereupon commenced this suit in a Washington trial court, contending that the procedures and criteria employed by the Law School Admissions Committee invidiously discriminated against him on account of his race in violation of the Equal Protection Clause of the Fourteenth Amendment to the United States Constitution.

DeFunis brought the suit on behalf of himself alone, and not as the representative of any class, against the various respondents, who are officers, faculty members, and members of the Board of Regents of the University of Washington. He asked the trial court to issue a mandatory injunction commanding the respondents to admit him as a member of the first-year class entering in September 1971, on the ground that the Law School admissions policy had resulted in the unconstitutional denial of his application for admission. The trial court agreed with his claim and granted the requested relief. DeFunis was, accordingly, admitted to the Law School and began his legal studies there in the fall of 1971. On appeal, the Washington Supreme Court reversed the judgment of the trial court and held that the Law School admissions policy did not violate the Constitution. By this time DeFunis was in his second year at the Law School.

He then petitioned this Court for a writ of certiorari, and Mr. Justice Douglas, as Circuit Justice, stayed the judgment of the Washington Supreme Court pending the "final disposition of the case by this Court." By virtue of this stay, DeFunis has remained in law school, and was in the first term of his third and final year when this Court first considered his certiorari petition in the fall of 1973. Because of our concern that DeFunis' third-year standing in the Law School might have rendered this case moot, we requested the parties to brief the question of mootness before we acted on the petition. In response, both sides contended that the case was not moot. The respondents indicated that, if the decision of the Washington Supreme Court were permitted to stand, the petitioner could complete the term for which he was then enrolled but would have to apply to the faculty for permission to continue in the school before he could register for another term.[2]

We granted the petition for certiorari on November 19, 1973. The case was in due course orally argued on February 26, 1974.

In response to questions raised from the bench during the oral argument, counsel for the petitioner has informed the Court that DeFunis has now registered "for his final quarter in law school." Counsel for the respondents have made clear that the Law School will not in any way seek to abrogate this registration. In light of DeFunis' recent registration for the last quarter of his final law school year, and the Law School's assurance that his registration is fully effective, the insistent question again arises whether this case is not moot, and to that question we now turn.

The starting point for analysis is the familiar proposition that "federal courts are without power to decide questions that cannot affect the rights of litigants in the case before them." North Carolina v. Rice, 404 U.S. 244, 246 (1971). The inability of the federal judiciary "to review moot cases derives from the requirement of Art. III of the Constitution under which the exercise of judicial power depends upon the existence of a case or controversy." Liner v. Jafco, Inc., 375 U.S. 301, 306 n. 3 (1964). Although as a matter of Washington state law it appears that this case would be saved from mootness by "the great public interest in the continuing issues raised by this appeal," the fact remains that under Art. III "[e]ven in cases arising in the state courts, the question of mootness is a federal one which a federal court must resolve before it assumes jurisdiction." North Carolina v. Rice, supra, at 246.

The respondents have represented that, without regard to the ultimate resolution of the issues in this case, DeFunis will remain a student in the Law School for the duration of any term in which he has already enrolled. Since he has now registered for his final term, it is evident that he will be given an opportunity to complete all academic and other requirements for graduation, and, if he does so, will receive his diploma regardless of any decision this Court might reach on the merits of this case. In short, all parties agree that DeFunis is now entitled to complete his legal studies at the University of Washington and to receive his degree from that institution. A determination by this Court of the legal issues tendered by the parties is no longer necessary to compel that

---

2   By contrast, in their response to the petition for certiorari, the respondents had stated that DeFunis "will complete his third year [of law school] and be awarded his J.D. degree at the end of the 1973–74 academic year regardless of the outcome of this appeal."

result, and could not serve to prevent it. DeFunis did not cast his suit as a class action, and the only remedy he requested was an injunction commanding his admission to the Law School. He was not only accorded that remedy, but he now has also been irrevocably admitted to the final term of the final year of the Law School course. The controversy between the parties has thus clearly ceased to be "definite and concrete" and no longer "touch[es] the legal relations of parties having adverse legal interests." Aetna Life Ins. Co. v. Haworth, 300 U.S. 227, 240–241 (1937).

It matters not that these circumstances partially stem from a policy decision on the part of the respondent Law School authorities. The respondents, through their counsel, the Attorney General of the State, have professionally represented that in no event will the status of DeFunis now be affected by any view this Court might express on the merits of this controversy. And it has been the settled practice of the Court, in contexts no less significant, fully to accept representations such as these as parameters for decision. See Gerende v. Election Board, 341 U.S. 56 (1951) * * *.

There is a line of decisions in this Court standing for the proposition that the "voluntary cessation of allegedly illegal conduct does not deprive the tribunal of power to hear and determine the case, *i.e.*, does not make the case moot." United States v. W.T. Grant Co., 345 U.S. 629, 632 (1953); United States v. Trans-Missouri Freight Assn., 166 U.S. 290, 308–310 (1897) * * *. These decisions and the doctrine they reflect would be quite relevant if the question of mootness here had arisen by reason of a unilateral change in the *admissions procedures* of the Law School. For it was the admissions procedures that were the target of this litigation, and a voluntary cessation of the admissions practices complained of could make this case moot only if it could be said with assurance "that 'there is no reasonable expectation that the wrong will be repeated.'" United States v. W.T. Grant Co., *supra*, at 633. Otherwise, "[t]he defendant is free to return to his old ways," *id.*, at 632, and this fact would be enough to prevent mootness because of the "public interest in having the legality of the practices settled." *Ibid.* But mootness in the present case depends not at all upon a "voluntary cessation" of the admissions practices that were the subject of this litigation. It depends, instead, upon the simple fact that DeFunis is now in the final quarter of the final year of his course of study, and the settled and unchallenged policy of the Law School to permit him to complete the term for which he is now enrolled.

It might also be suggested that this case presents a question that is "capable of repetition, yet evading review," Southern Pacific Terminal Co. v. ICC, 219 U.S. 498, 515 (1911); Roe v. Wade, 410 U.S. 113, 125 (1973), and is thus amenable to federal adjudication even though it might otherwise be considered moot. But DeFunis will never again be required to run the gantlet of the Law School's admission process, and so the question is certainly not "capable of repetition" so far as he is concerned. Moreover, just because this particular case did not reach the Court until the eve of the petitioner's graduation from law school, it hardly follows that the issue he raises will in the future evade review. If the admissions procedures of the Law School remain unchanged, there is no reason to suppose that a subsequent case attacking those procedures will not come with relative speed to this Court, now that the Supreme Court of Washington has spoken. This case, therefore, in no way presents the exceptional situation in which the Southern Pacific Terminal doctrine might permit a departure from "[t]he usual rule in federal cases * * * that an actual controversy must exist at stages of appellate or certiorari review, and not simply at the date the action is initiated." Roe v. Wade, *supra*, at 125; United States v. Munsingwear, Inc., 340 U.S. 36 (1950).

Because the petitioner will complete his law school studies at the end of the term for which he has now registered regardless of any decision this Court might reach on the merits of this litigation, we conclude that the Court cannot, consistently with the limitations of Art. III of the Constitution, consider the substantive constitutional issues tendered by the parties.[5] Accordingly, the judgment of the Supreme Court of Washington is vacated, and the cause is remanded for such proceedings as by that court may be deemed appropriate.

It is so ordered.

■ MR. JUSTICE DOUGLAS, dissenting.

I agree with MR. JUSTICE BRENNAN that this case is not moot, and because of the significance of the issues raised I think it is important to reach the merits. * * *

■ MR. JUSTICE BRENNAN, with whom MR. JUSTICE DOUGLAS, MR. JUSTICE WHITE, and MR. JUSTICE MARSHALL concur, dissenting.

I respectfully dissent. Many weeks of the school term remain, and petitioner may not receive his degree despite respondents' assurances that petitioner will be allowed to complete this term's schooling regardless of our decision. Any number of unexpected events—illness, economic necessity, even academic failure—might prevent his graduation at the end of the term. Were that misfortune to befall, and were petitioner required to register for yet another term, the prospect that he would again face the hurdle of the admissions policy is real, not fanciful; for respondents warn that "Mr. DeFunis would have to take some appropriate action to request continued admission for the remainder of his law school education, and *some discretionary action by the University on such request would have to be taken.*" (Emphasis supplied). Thus, respondents' assurances have not dissipated the possibility that petitioner might once again have to run the gantlet of the University's allegedly unlawful admissions policy. The Court therefore proceeds on an erroneous premise in resting its mootness holding on a supposed inability to render any judgment that may affect one way or the other petitioner's completion of his law studies. For surely if we were to reverse the Washington Supreme Court, we could insure that, if for some reason petitioner did not graduate this spring, he would be entitled to re-enrollment at a later time on the same basis as others who have not faced the hurdle of the University's allegedly unlawful admissions policy.

In these circumstances, and because the University's position implies no concession that its admissions policy is unlawful, this controversy falls squarely within the Court's long line of decisions

---

[5] It is suggested in dissent that "[a]ny number of unexpected events—illness, economic necessity, even academic failure—might prevent his graduation at the end of the term." "But such speculative contingencies afford no basis for our passing on the substantive issues [the petitioner] would have us decide," Hall v. Beals, 396 U.S. 45, 49 (1969), in the absence of "evidence that this is a prospect of 'immediacy and reality.' " Golden v. Zwickler, 394 U.S. 103, 109 (1969) * * *.

holding that the "[m]ere voluntary cessation of allegedly illegal conduct does not moot a case." United States v. Phosphate Export Assn., 393 U.S. 199, 203 (1968) * * *. Since respondents' voluntary representation to this Court is only that they will permit petitioner to complete this term's studies, respondents have not borne the "heavy burden," [*id.*], at 203, of demonstrating that there was not even a "mere possibility" that petitioner would once again be subject to the challenged admissions policy. United States v. W.T. Grant Co., *supra*, at 633. On the contrary, respondents have positioned themselves so as to be "free to return to [their] old ways." *Id.*, at 632.

I can thus find no justification for the Court's straining to rid itself of this dispute. While we must be vigilant to require that litigants maintain a personal stake in the outcome of a controversy to assure that "the questions will be framed with the necessary specificity, that the issues will be contested with the necessary adverseness and that the litigation will be pursued with the necessary vigor to assure that the constitutional challenge will be made in a form traditionally thought to be capable of judicial resolution," Flast v. Cohen, 392 U.S. 83, 106 (1968), there is no want of an adversary contest in this case. Indeed, the Court *[adverseness]* concedes that, if petitioner has lost his stake in this controversy, he did so only when he registered for the spring term. But petitioner took that action only after the case had been fully litigated in the state courts, briefs had been filed in this Court, and oral argument had been heard. The case is thus ripe for decision on a fully developed factual record with *[ripe]* sharply defined and fully canvassed legal issues. *Cf.* Sibron v. New York, 392 U.S. 40, 57 (1968).

Moreover, in endeavoring to dispose of this case as moot, the Court clearly disserves the public interest. The constitutional issues which are avoided today concern vast numbers of people, organizations, and colleges and universities, as evidenced by the filing of twenty-six *amicus curiae* briefs. Few constitutional questions in recent history have stirred as much debate, and they will not disappear. * * * Because avoidance of repetitious litigation serves the public interest, that inevitability counsels against mootness determinations, as here, not compelled by the record. Although the Court should, of course, avoid unnecessary decisions of constitutional questions, we should not transform principles of avoidance of constitutional decisions into devices for sidestepping resolution of difficult cases. *Cf.* Cohens v. Virginia, 6 Wheat. 264, 404–405 (1821) (Marshall, C.J.).

NOTE ON MOOTNESS: ITS RATIONALE AND APPLICATIONS

(1) The Relation of Mootness and Standing. In an influential article, Professor Henry Monaghan characterized mootness as "the doctrine of standing set in a time frame. The requisite personal interest that must exist at the commencement of the litigation (standing) must continue through its existence (mootness)." Monaghan, *Constitutional Adjudication: The Who and When*, 82 Yale L.J. 1363, 1384 (1973). After quoting that formulation on two

previous occasions,[1] the Court later rejected it in *Friends of the Earth v.
Laidlaw Environmental Services (TOC), Inc.*, 528 U.S. 167, 190 (2000).

The case arose when Friends of the Earth sued under the citizen suit
provision of the Clean Water Act to enjoin a violation of the environmental
laws and to secure a civil penalty payable to the government. After the
defendant's violations ceased subsequent to the filing of suit, the Court of
Appeals held the case moot; it reasoned that all elements of Article III
standing must persist throughout litigation and that the only remedy
available once the defendant's violations had stopped—civil penalties
payable to the government—would not redress any injury to the plaintiff. In
an opinion by Justice Ginsburg, the Court reversed, holding that "the Court
of Appeals confused mootness with standing." Justice Ginsburg described
this confusion as "understandable, given this Court's repeated statements
that the doctrine of mootness can be described as 'the doctrine of standing
set in a time frame' " (citing cases that had quoted Professor Monaghan's
formulation). But "[c]areful reflection on the long-recognized exceptions to
mootness," such as that allowing adjudication of issues capable of repetition
yet evading review, revealed that "there are circumstances in which the
prospect that a defendant will engage in (or resume) harmful conduct may
be too speculative to support standing, but not too speculative to overcome
mootness. * * * Standing doctrine functions to ensure, among other things,
that the scarce resources of the federal courts are devoted to those disputes
in which the parties have a concrete stake. In contrast, by the time mootness
is an issue, the case has been brought and litigated, often (as here) for years.
To abandon the case at an advanced stage may prove more wasteful than
frugal. This argument from sunk costs does not license courts to retain
jurisdiction over cases in which one or both of the parties plainly lacks a
continuing interest * * * [but it] surely highlights an important difference
between the two doctrines."

Justice Scalia, joined by Justice Thomas, dissented on the ground that
the plaintiffs never had standing. Assuming arguendo that standing existed,
he did "not disagree" with the Court's conclusion as to mootness on the facts
of the case, but was "troubled by the Court's too-hasty retreat from our
characterization of mootness as 'the doctrine of standing set in a time
frame.' " In his view, that conception correctly emphasized that "[b]ecause
the requirement of a continuing case or controversy derives from the
Constitution * * * it may not be avoided when inconvenient * * * or, as the
Court suggests, to save 'sunk costs' ".[2]

In addition to the "sunk costs" cited by Justice Ginsburg, consider the
following reasons for treating mootness doctrine differently from standing:
(i) an actual course of conduct, even if past, continues to frame litigation in
a factual context and thereby focus judicial decisionmaking; (ii) the unlawful
causation of a past injury deprives a defendant of any moral entitlement to
freedom from judicial intervention; (iii) since a defendant who has caused
wrongful conduct would otherwise remain free to repeat it, a judicial decision
forbidding such conduct is not an advisory opinion in any objectionable sense;

---

[1] Arizonans for Official English v. Arizona, 520 U.S. 43, 68 n. 22 (1997); U.S. Parole
Comm'n v. Geraghty, 445 U.S. 388, 397 (1980).

[2] For earlier discussions of the relation of standing and mootness doctrines, see
Chemerinsky, *A Unified Approach to Justiciability*, 22 Conn.L.Rev. 677 (1990); Fallon, *Of
Justiciability, Remedies, and Public Law Litigation: Notes on the Jurisprudence of Lyons*, 59
N.Y.U.L.Rev. 1, 24–30 (1984).

and (iv) there is an important public interest in protecting the legal system against manipulation by parties, especially those prone to involvement in repeat litigation, who might contrive to moot cases that otherwise would be likely to produce unfavorable precedents.

(iv B brg) [handwritten margin note]

In light of considerations such as these, should the mootness doctrine bar adjudication only when the functional requisites of effective adjudication, such as effective adversarial presentation of sharply framed issues, are absent?

(2) Foundations of Mootness Doctrine. The Court in DeFunis viewed the mootness doctrine as a function of the Article III case or controversy requirement. The Court apparently made this link explicit for the first time in 1964, in Liner v. Jafco, Inc., 375 U.S. 301 (1964), discussed in Paragraph (8), *infra*. Concurring in Honig v. Doe, 484 U.S. 305, 330 (1988), Chief Justice Rehnquist conceded that "our recent cases have taken that position" but argued that the Court had erred; mootness doctrine, he contended, is rooted in policy judgments, not "forced upon us by the case or controversy requirement of Art. III itself." The Chief Justice rested his position partly on history; he thought it "very doubtful that the earliest case I have found discussing mootness, Mills v. Green, 159 U.S. 651 (1895), was premised on constitutional constraints; Justice Gray's opinion in that case nowhere mentions Art. III." Chief Justice Rehnquist also maintained that the recognized exceptions to mootness doctrine for cases involving voluntary cessation of challenged conduct and for acts "capable of repetition, yet evading review", see Paragraphs (3) and (4), *infra*, could not be justified if Article III barred the adjudication of moot cases.[3]

Art. III [handwritten margin note]

Rhenquist Arg. [handwritten margin note]

By contrast, Justice Scalia had "little doubt that the Court [in Mills v. Green] believed the [mootness] doctrine called into question the Court's power and not merely its prudence, for (in an opinion by the same Justice who wrote Mills) it had said two years earlier: '[T]he Court is not *empowered* to decide moot questions. * * * No stipulation of the parties or counsel * * * can enlarge the *power*, or affect the duty, of the court in this regard.'

Scalia Arg. [handwritten margin note]

---

[3]   For further discussion of Chief Justice Rehnquist's position, see Nichol, *Moot Cases, Chief Justice Rehnquist, and the Supreme Court*, 22 U.Conn.L.Rev. 703, 706 (1990). In Pacific Bell Telephone Co. v. Linkline Communications, Inc., 555 U.S. 438 (2009), the plaintiffs in an antitrust action conceded in the Supreme Court that they now agreed with the defendants on the question presented. At the same time, they asked the Court to vacate the court of appeals decision in their favor and to remand the case to the district court in order to seek relief on a different antitrust theory from the one on which they had prevailed in the court of appeals. Even though the parties were no longer adverse on the question presented, the Court concluded that the case was not moot because the parties still sought different outcomes and because there remained some ambiguity in the plaintiffs' position. Because amici continued to defend the plaintiffs' now-abandoned position, the Court had no difficulty concluding that it should proceed to the merits. Consider the Court's unabashedly pragmatic arguments for proceeding to the question on which the Court had originally granted certiorari:

> Plaintiffs defended the Court of Appeals' decision at the certiorari stage, and the parties have invested a substantial amount of time, effort, and resources in briefing and arguing the merits of this case. In the absence of a decision from this Court on the merits, the Court of Appeals' decision would presumably remain binding precedent in the Ninth Circuit, and the Circuit conflict we granted certiorari to resolve would persist. Two amici have submitted briefs defending the Court of Appeals' decision on the merits, and we granted the motion of one of those amici to participate in oral argument. We think it appropriate to proceed to address the question presented.

Given the parties' agreement on the *only* question before the Court, does the Court's decision in Linkline Communications—relying on amici to present the plaintiffs' case on the merits—suggest that the Court regards mootness, at least in the Supreme Court, as grounded in prudential rather than constitutional concerns?

California v. San Pablo & Tulare R. Co., 149 U.S. 308, 314 (1893) (Gray, J.)"
(emphasis added by Justice Scalia).

Whoever had the better of the argument, should historical practice be
dispositive of the constitutional authority of Article III courts to decide moot
cases?[4]

(3) Voluntary Cessation. As noted in DeFunis, a long line of cases holds
that an action for an injunction, or other judgment with continuing force,
does not become moot merely because the conduct immediately complained
of has terminated, if there is a sufficient possibility of a recurrence that
would be barred by a proper decree.[5] But the Court has given mixed signals
concerning how likely recurrence needs to be for this exception to mootness
doctrine to apply. See, *e.g.*, the various formulations quoted in the majority
and dissenting opinions in DeFunis and in the cases that follow.

(a) According to Iron Arrow Honor Society v. Heckler, 464 U.S. 67, 72
(1983) (per curiam), a case mooted by the voluntary act of a non-party,
"[d]efendants face a heavy burden to establish mootness" in voluntary
cessation cases "because otherwise they would be 'free to return to [their] old
ways' after the threat of a lawsuit had passed" (quoting United States v. W.T.
Grant Co., 345 U.S. 629, 632 (1953)).

(b) In Vitek v. Jones, 445 U.S. 480 (1980), a convicted felon brought a
federal court action challenging (on procedural grounds) his transfer from a
prison to a mental hospital. While the case was pending, he was
retransferred to prison, placed in the psychiatric ward, paroled on condition
that he accept psychiatric treatment at a V.A. hospital, and subsequently
returned to prison for violation of parole. The Court, by 5–4, agreed with both
parties that the case was not moot, stating that against the background of
Jones' mental illness, it was not "absolutely clear" that the challenged wrong
would not recur. Justice Stewart, for three dissenters, argued that the case
was moot because there was "no demonstrated probability" of recurrence.

(c) In City of Erie v. Pap's A.M., 529 U.S. 277 (2000), the state court
enjoined the enforcement of the city's anti-nudity ordinance. However, the
nude dancing establishment that brought the challenge had closed by the
time the case reached the Supreme Court, and the proprietor submitted an
affidavit attesting that he did not intend to resume business. By a vote of 7–
2, the Court held the case not moot. Writing for the majority, Justice
O'Connor reasoned that "this is not a run of the mill voluntary cessation
case." The majority noted, *inter alia*, that the city suffered "an ongoing injury
because it [was] barred from enforcing" its public nudity prohibitions; Pap's
was "still incorporated" and "could again decide to operate a nude dancing
establishment in Erie"; Pap's failed to raise the mootness issue in its brief in
opposition to the petition for certiorari, even though the nude dancing
establishment was already closed; and the "interest in preventing litigants

---

[4] See, *e.g.*, Hall, *The Partially Prudential Doctrine of Mootness*, 77 Geo.Wash.L.Rev. 562
(2009) (arguing that the Court has long treated post-filing events that moot the issue underlying
the claim as a jurisdictional bar negating a case or controversy, while treating events that
merely moot the plaintiff's personal stake in the matter as a prudential limitation on the
exercise of judicial power); Lee, *Deconstitutionalizing Justiciability: The Example of Mootness*,
105 Harv.L.Rev. 603 (1992) (suggesting that though there might be statutory, doctrinal, or
prudential impediments to the adjudication of moot cases, they remain "cases" within the
meaning of Article III).

[5] See, *e.g.*, United States v. Concentrated Phosphate Export Ass'n, 393 U.S. 199, 202–04
(1968); United States v. W.T. Grant Co., 345 U.S. 629 (1953); United States v. Trans-Missouri
Freight Ass'n, 166 U.S. 290, 307–09 (1897).

from attempting to manipulate the Court's jurisdiction to insulate a favorable decision from review further counsels against a finding of mootness."

(4) Capable of Repetition, Yet Evading Review. Closely related to the "voluntary cessation" decisions are cases, also discussed in DeFunis, in which the alleged wrong has ceased but the wrong is capable of repetition, yet evading review.[6] Consider, for example, Federal Election Commission v. Wisconsin Right to Life, Inc. ("WRTL"), 551 U.S. 449 (2007). During the 2004 election cycle, respondents filed suit challenging the constitutionality, as applied to them, of a provision of a federal prohibition on running advertisements that referred by name to a candidate for federal office within 30 days of a primary election. Despite the passing of the 2004 election, the Court held (in an opinion by Chief Justice Roberts) that the case was not moot because (1) it would have been unreasonable to expect the respondents' challenge to make its way through the courts within a single election cycle and (2) similar issues were likely to arise between the parties in the future.

Does the Court's willingness to decide such cases suggest a kind of justiciability by necessity where there may otherwise be no way to obtain review of an important issue? But *cf.* United States v. Richardson, discussed at p. 118, *supra*, denying standing to challenge the constitutionality of official conduct under the Accounts Clause, despite recognizing the probability that "if respondent is not permitted to litigate this issue, no one can do so." Do you agree with Chief Justice Rehnquist that acceptance of jurisdiction in such cases is incompatible with viewing mootness as an Article III requirement? See Honig v. Doe, 484 U.S. at 331 (Rehnquist, C.J., concurring).

The Court has stressed for some time that, in the absence of a class action, the relevant question turns on the possibility of recurrence with respect to the complaining party. See Weinstein v. Bradford, 423 U.S. 147, 149 (1975); Murphy v. Hunt, 455 U.S. 478, 482 (1982). Earlier cases seemed satisfied by the likelihood of recurrence between the defendant and another member of the public. See, *e.g.*, Southern Pac. Term. Co. v. ICC, 219 U.S. 498, 515 (1911); Rosario v. Rockefeller, 410 U.S. 752, 756 n. 5 (1973); Dunn v. Blumstein, 405 U.S. 330, 333 n. 2 (1972).

The requisite degree of likelihood is unclear. The Court has spoken of a "reasonable expectation" or "demonstrated probability" that the controversy would recur and insisted that a "mere physical or theoretical possibility" was insufficient. See, *e.g.*, Murphy v. Hunt, *supra*, at 482. Yet in Southern Pac. Term. Co. v. ICC, *supra*, where the Commission had issued a short-term cease-and-desist order that had expired, there was no showing that the Commission proposed to issue similar short-term orders in the future. And in Roe v. Wade, 410 U.S. 113, 124–25 (1973), a challenge to an abortion statute was held not moot even though the woman who had initiated the action was no longer pregnant. "Pregnancy", the Court said, "often comes

---

[6]   See, *e.g.*, Globe Newspaper Co. v. Superior Court, 457 U.S. 596 (1982) (order excluding press and public from certain portions of rape trial had expired with the completion of the trial); Nebraska Press Ass'n v. Stuart, 427 U.S. 539 (1976) (short-term judicial orders restricting press coverage of criminal proceedings had expired prior to Supreme Court review); Moore v. Ogilvie, 394 U.S. 814 (1969) (challenge to signature requirement on nominating petitions; election had occurred before Supreme Court review); Carroll v. President and Com'rs of Princess Anne, 393 U.S. 175 (1968) (ten-day injunction restraining white supremacist organization from holding public rallies had expired two years before).

more than once to the same woman * * * [and] truly could be 'capable of repetition, yet evading review.' "[7] *Cf.* Honig v. Doe, 484 U.S. at 318–19 n. 6 (finding, over two dissenting votes, that a "reasonable expectation" of recurrence may suffice to avoid mootness, even if there is no "demonstrated probability" of recurring, challengeable action).

(5) Mootness in Criminal Cases. Although the doctrines discussed in this Note apply generally to criminal as well as civil cases, two issues unique to criminal proceedings merit separate discussion: the ability of convicted defendants to attack their convictions after serving their sentences and the effect of a defendant's death on the justiciability of such an attack.

(a) For many years, the general rule in the federal courts was that after criminal defendants had served their sentences, their cases were moot because "there was no longer a subject matter on which the judgment * * * could operate." St. Pierre v. United States, 319 U.S. 41, 42 (1943). But that rule gradually eroded because of recognition, first, that issues characteristically involving only short sentences might forever escape review and, second, that criminal convictions have collateral consequences (recidivism statutes, testimonial impeachment, civil disabilities, etc.) that continue after a sentence is served. See, *e.g.*, Sibron v. New York, 392 U.S. 40, 50–58 (1968).[8] Quite apart from any post-sentence collateral consequences, should the stigma of a criminal conviction itself be regarded as an answer to the argument that an attack on the conviction is moot, at least while the defendant is alive? *Cf.* Hart, *The Aims of the Criminal Law*, 23 Law & Contemp.Probs. 401, 404 (1958).

(b) The death of a criminal defendant ordinarily moots the defendant's case on direct or collateral review. See, *e.g.*, Singer v. United States, 323 U.S. 338, 346 (1945).[9] In Robinson v. California, 370 U.S. 660 (1962), a divided Court held in a novel decision that a law making drug addiction a crime constituted "cruel and unusual punishment" in violation of the Eighth and Fourteenth Amendments. Subsequently, the state informed the Court that the defendant in the case had died ten days before the appeal to the Supreme Court was taken, and it petitioned for rehearing and abatement of the judgment. The petition was denied without opinion. 371 U.S. 905 (1962). Three justices dissented, arguing that the judgment should be vacated as moot.

(6) Disposition of Mooted Cases in the Federal System. When a case in the federal system becomes moot on appeal, the disposition depends on the nature of the events that mooted the dispute.

(a) United States v. Munsingwear, Inc., 340 U.S. 36, 39 (1950), pronounced that "[t]he established practice of the Court in dealing with a civil case from a court in the federal system which has become moot * * * is to reverse or vacate the judgment below and remand with a direction to

*vacate/
forbe*

---

[7] Since Roe was brought as a class action, the mootness question would presumably not be difficult today. See *Note on Mootness in Class Actions*, p. 194, *infra*.

[8] Although the defendant's interest in attacking a *conviction* surely guarantees the requisite adverseness in most instances, the Court has sustained claims of mootness in attacks on *sentences* already served. See Lane v. Williams, 455 U.S. 624 (1982); North Carolina v. Rice, 404 U.S. 244 (1971).

[9] But *cf.* Wetzel v. Ohio, 371 U.S. 62 (1962) (per curiam decision granting motion on appeal in criminal case to substitute deceased appellant's wife as appellant; as administratrix and probable heir of appellant's estate, she had a substantial interest in protecting the estate from costs to be levied against it if conviction stood).

dismiss [citing many cases, together with four 'exceptions']." The Munsingwear case had been mooted by a change in the applicable law, not any conduct of the parties intended to terminate the dispute, and the Court reasoned that vacatur was appropriate in such cases on the motion of a party to "clear[ ] the path for future relitigation of the issues between the parties and eliminate[ ] a judgment, review of which was prevented through happenstance."

Munsingwear remains the controlling authority for *civil* cases that—through happenstance, conduct not attributable to the parties, or the unilateral action of the prevailing party in the lower court—become moot either (i) on appeal, (ii) during the pendency of a petition for certiorari, or (iii) after the grant of such a petition but prior to decision by the Supreme Court.

(b) In federal criminal cases, the Supreme Court held for a time that death abated "not only the appeal but also all proceedings had in the prosecution from its inception", thus requiring dismissal of the indictment. Durham v. United States, 401 U.S. 481, 483 (1971). But in Dove v. United States, 423 U.S. 325 (1976), the Court overruled this holding without discussion and dismissed a petition for a writ of certiorari on learning of petitioner's death.[10] Does any good reason support the disparity in the Court's practices concerning civil and criminal cases?

(c) In United States Bancorp Mortgage Co. v. Bonner Mall Partnership, 513 U.S. 18 (1994), the Supreme Court granted certiorari to resolve a question under the Bankruptcy Code, and the parties thereafter reached a settlement that mooted the case. Relying on Munsingwear, *supra*, Bancorp, the losing party in the court of appeals, asked the Supreme Court to vacate the judgment below as well as dismissing the writ. Bonner opposed the motion. Following briefing and argument, the Court, in an opinion by Justice Scalia, unanimously found Munsingwear distinguishable and ruled that "mootness by reason of settlement does not [ordinarily] justify vacatur of a judgment under review."

Justice Scalia began by rejecting an argument that, when a case becomes moot, a federal court loses jurisdiction to take any action, including entry of a vacatur order. Although mootness nullifies jurisdiction to pronounce on the merits, the court retains authority to take such ancillary action, including vacatur and the award of costs, as justice may require. The decision whether to vacate a judgment or simply to dismiss the case is thus governed by equitable principles. And while such principles generally support vacatur when one party has lost the opportunity to seek review of an adverse judgment as the result of happenstance, the "voluntary forfeiture of review" through settlement ordinarily shifts the balance of equities. "Judicial precedents are presumptively correct and valuable to the legal community as a whole. They are not merely the property of private litigants and should stand unless a court concludes that the public interest would be served by vacatur."

The Bancorp decision is mostly of concern to litigants likely to be involved in a number of similar disputes, who have a keen interest not only in the outcome of any particular case, but also in the preclusive or precedential effects of any judicial resolution. Isn't there something

---

[10] Dove was a case before the Supreme Court on direct review; the procedure was later followed on collateral review as well. Warden v. Palermo, 431 U.S. 911 (1977).

unseemly about letting repeat players "buy up" judgments that they dislike by settling cases pending on appeal and seeking vacatur?[11]

(d) In Alvarez v. Smith, 558 U.S. 87 (2009), the Court made clear that the Bancorp exception to vacatur would not apply if the circumstances demonstrated that the parties had not arranged their affairs to render the case moot. In Alvarez, the plaintiffs (six individuals) had brought a due process challenge to the procedures used under Illinois law to seize property used to facilitate a drug crime and had prevailed on their claims in the Seventh Circuit. The Supreme Court, however, found that the case was moot. The plaintiffs had sought only injunctive and declaratory relief. By the time the case reached the Supreme Court, the plaintiffs had agreed on the disposition of the forfeited property. The agreements were reached not in the federal court lawsuit then before the Court, but rather in the state court actions whose procedures the federal case challenged. In an opinion by Justice Breyer, the Court held that the federal case was moot because the dispute over the validity of the Illinois law was no longer embedded in any actual controversy about the plaintiffs' particular legal rights.

Although the case had been mooted by the settlement of the state proceedings that underlay the federal challenge, the Court concluded that Bancorp did not govern. First, the Court found it significant that the parties did not settle the federal case itself; rather, "[t]he six individual cases proceeded through a different court system without any procedural link to the federal case before us." Second, the plaintiffs had not raised their federal claims in the state forfeiture cases themselves. Third, "[t]he disparate dates at which plaintiffs' forfeiture proceedings terminated—11, 14, 27, and 40 months after the seizures—indicate that the [state] did not coordinate the resolution of plaintiffs' state court cases, either with each other or with plaintiffs' federal civil rights case." Accordingly, the Court concluded that the presence of this federal case played no role at all in producing the state court terminations and followed its ordinary practice of vacating the judgment of the court of appeals. Justice Stevens dissented.

Given the difficulty of identifying the motives underlying the settlement of a case, does a bright-line rule precluding vacatur in cases of settlement make more sense than Alvarez's fact-bound inquiry into whether the settlement was driven by a desire to vacate the lower court judgment?[12]

---

[11] For illuminating discussions, see, e.g., Fisch, *The Vanishing Precedent: Eduardo Meets Vacatur*, 70 Notre Dame L.Rev. 325 (1994); Resnik, *Whose Judgment? Vacating Judgments, Preferences for Settlement, and the Role of Adjudication at the Close of the Twentieth Century*, 41 UCLA L.Rev. 1471 (1994).

[12] In Camreta v. Greene, 131 S.Ct. 2020 (2011), which is further discussed at pp. 1053–1054, *infra*, the Court addressed the appropriateness of a Munsingwear order in a qualified immunity case in which the lower court had ruled both on the merits and on grounds of qualified immunity. As discussed, Pearson v. Callahan, pp. 1052–1053, *infra*, had held that in order to "promote[ ] the development of constitutional precedent", federal courts in constitutional tort actions have discretion to reach the merits of a constitutional claim before deciding whether the defendants are entitled to qualified immunity on the ground that the asserted rights were not "clearly established". In Camreta, the Court held that when a lower court applying Pearson ruled against a state official on the merits but for him or her on qualified immunity grounds, the official could, at least in some circumstances, seek certiorari despite having prevailed in the court below. Of interest here, because Camreta became moot while the defendants' case was pending before the Supreme Court, the Court issued a Munsingwear order vacating the court of appeals' adverse merits decision. In so doing, the Court rejected the argument that vacatur was inappropriate in this context because it would undermine Pearson's goal of giving the court of appeals discretion to resolve constitutional questions for future cases. The Court reasoned that because "a constitutional ruling in a qualified immunity case is a legally consequential decision"

not moot

(7) Mootness and the Merits. In Chafin v. Chafin, 133 S.Ct. 1017 (2013), Chief Justice Roberts' opinion for the Court admonished lower courts not to hold a case moot because the claim at issue reflected a low probability of success on the merits, or because the judgment was unlikely to be executed if the plaintiff prevailed. The case involved an international child custody battle. Lynn Chafin, a citizen of the United Kingdom, filed an action against Jeffrey Chafin seeking the return of her daughter to Scotland under the Hague Convention on the Civil Aspects of International Child Abduction and U.S. legislation implementing the Convention. Pursuant to an order of the district court, Lynn Chafin returned to Scotland with the child. Jeffrey Chafin appealed to the Eleventh Circuit, which held that an appeal under the Convention is moot once the child has been returned to a foreign country.

The Supreme Court reversed. Lynn Chafin argued that the case was moot because the district court lacked authority under the Convention, and had no inherent equitable powers, to order the return of the child if the court of appeals reversed. The Court held that this argument's dependence on the proper interpretation of the Convention confused the question of mootness with that of the merits, adding that Jeffrey Chafin's claim "cannot be dismissed as so implausible that it is insufficient to preserve jurisdiction." The Court also rejected the contention that the case was moot because Scottish courts would "ignore" any district court order to return the child to the United States. "A re-return order," said the Court, "may not result in the return of [the child] to the United States, just as an order that an insolvent defendant pay $100 million may not make the plaintiff rich." Whatever the "potential difficulties in enforcement," the Court found that Jeffrey Chafin retained a sufficiently "concrete" interest in the case to defeat mootness.

(8) Mootness and State Court Litigation. In DeFunis, after concluding that the action was moot, the Supreme Court vacated the judgment and remanded "for such proceedings [in the state supreme court] as * * * may be deemed appropriate." In ASARCO Inc. v. Kadish, 490 U.S. 605, 621 n. 1 (1989), discussed p. 158, *supra*, the Court noted its decision in DeFunis to vacate and remand for further proceedings in state court, but said that its more recent practice has been to dismiss cases that become moot on review from the state courts, leaving undisturbed the state court judgment (citing Kansas Gas & Elec. Co. v. State Corp. Comm'n of Kansas, 481 U.S. 1044 (1987); Times-Picayune Pub. Corp. v. Schulingkamp, 420 U.S. 985 (1975)).

If a state court holds moot a case involving a federal question, is Supreme Court review precluded? In Liner v. Jafco, Inc., 375 U.S. 301 (1964), a state court enjoined picketing in a labor dispute, despite a contention that its jurisdiction was federally preempted. Pending decision on appeal, construction at the site was completed, and the state appellate court held that the case had become moot (though it also expressed an opinion on the merits). The Supreme Court unanimously held, per Justice Brennan, that "in this case the question of mootness is itself a question of federal law upon which we must pronounce final judgment." In holding the case not moot, the Court cited an indemnity bond requiring payment if the injunction was "wrongfully" sued out, but also relied on the frustration of federal policy that might result if the state court's ruling on the preemption claim were

---

that entitles even a prevailing defendant to Supreme Court review, the normal rule of vacatur should apply when "happenstance prevents that review from occurring".

immunized from review. See also, *e.g.*, Gannett Co., Inc. v. DePasquale, 443 U.S. 368 (1979).

Is mootness always a "federal" question, or only when the state court's view of mootness is broader than that under federal law?

NOTE ON MOOTNESS IN CLASS ACTIONS

(1) The Geraghty Case. The leading case on mootness in class actions is United States Parole Commission v. Geraghty, 445 U.S. 388 (1980), in which a federal prisoner who was refused parole filed a class action challenging the applicable parole guidelines. The district court declined to certify a class action and granted summary judgment for the defendants on all the claims. Geraghty then appealed the denial of class certification, but before any briefs were filed in the court of appeals, he was released from prison for reasons unrelated to the lawsuit. Despite Geraghty's release, the U.S. Court of Appeals for the Third Circuit found the dispute not moot, reversed the judgment of the district court, and remanded for further proceedings. The Supreme Court, 5–4, agreed that Geraghty's appeal of the denial of class certification was not moot. Writing for the majority, Justice Blackmun concluded that a review of prior decisions demonstrated the "flexible character of the Art. III mootness doctrine. As has been noted in the past, Art. III justiciability is 'not a legal concept with a fixed content or susceptible of scientific verification.' Poe v. Ullman, 367 U.S. 497, 508 (1961) (plurality opinion)."

Justice Blackmun continued: "A plaintiff who brings a class action presents two separate issues for judicial resolution. One is the claim on the merits; the other is the claim that he is entitled to represent a class. * * *

"In order to achieve the primary benefits of class suits, the Federal Rules of Civil Procedure give the proposed class representative the right to have a class certified if the requirements of the rules are met. This 'right' is more analogous to the private attorney general concept than to the type of interest traditionally thought to satisfy the 'personal stake' requirement.

" * * * [T]he purpose of the 'personal stake' requirement is to assure that the case is in a form capable of judicial resolution. The imperatives of a dispute capable of judicial resolution are sharply presented issues in a concrete factual setting and self-interested parties vigorously advocating opposing positions. * * * We conclude that these elements can exist with respect to the class certification issue notwithstanding the fact that the named plaintiff's claim on the merits has expired. * * * In Sosna v. Iowa, [419 U.S. 393 (1975),] it was recognized that a named plaintiff whose claim on the merits expires *after* class certification may still adequately represent the class. Implicit in that decision was the determination that vigorous advocacy can be assured through means other than the traditional requirement of a 'personal stake in the outcome.' * * *

"We therefore hold that an action brought on behalf of a class does not become moot upon expiration of the named plaintiff's substantive claim, even though class certification has been denied. The proposed representative retains a 'personal stake' in obtaining class certification sufficient to assure that Art. III values are not undermined. If the appeal results in reversal of the class certification denial, and a class subsequently is properly certified, the merits of the class claim then may be adjudicated pursuant to the holding in Sosna.

"Our holding is limited to the appeal of the denial of the class certification motion. A named plaintiff whose claim expires may not continue to press the appeal on the merits until a class has been properly certified. * * * If, on appeal, it is determined that class certification properly was denied, the claim on the merits must be dismissed as moot. * * * "

Justice Powell wrote a sharp dissent, joined by Chief Justice Burger and Justices Stewart and Rehnquist, protesting both the Court's pronouncement "that mootness is a 'flexible' doctrine which may be adapted as we see fit to 'nontraditional' forms of litigation" and its holding "that the named plaintiff has a right 'analogous to the private attorney general concept' to appeal the denial of class certification even when his personal claim for relief is moot."

Justice Powell wrote: "Art. III contains no exception for class actions. Thus, we have held that a putative class representative who alleges no individual injury 'may not seek relief on behalf of himself or any other member of the class.' O'Shea v. Littleton, 414 U.S. 488, 494 (1974). Only after a class has been certified in accordance with Rule 23 can it 'acquir[e] a legal status separate from the interest asserted by [the named plaintiff].' Sosna v. Iowa, *supra*, 419 U.S. at 399 (1975)."

He continued: "The Court splits the class aspects of this action into two separate 'claims': (i) that the action may be maintained by respondent on behalf of a class, and (ii) that the class is entitled to relief on the merits. Since no class has been certified, the Court concedes that the claim on the merits is moot. But respondent is said to have a personal stake in his 'procedural claim' despite his lack of a stake in the merits.

"The Court makes no effort to identify any injury to respondent that may be redressed by, or any benefit to respondent that may accrue from, a favorable ruling on the certification question. Instead, respondent's 'personal stake' is said to derive from two factors having nothing to do with concrete injury or stake in the outcome. First, the Court finds that the Federal Rules of Civil Procedure create a 'right,' 'analogous to the private attorney general concept,' to have a class certified. Second, the Court thinks that the case retains the 'imperatives of a dispute capable of judicial resolution' * * *.

"The Court's reliance on some new 'right' inherent in Rule 23 is misplaced. We have held that even Congress may not confer federal court jurisdiction when Art. III does not. * * * Far less so may a rule of procedure which 'shall not be construed to extend * * * the jurisdiction of the United States district courts.' Fed.Rule Civ.Proc. 82. Moreover, the 'private attorney general concept' cannot supply the personal stake necessary to satisfy Art. III. It serves only to permit litigation by a party who has a stake of his own but otherwise might be barred by prudential standing rules. * * *

"Although we have refused steadfastly to countenance the 'public action,' the Court's redefinition of the personal stake requirement leaves no principled basis for that practice."[1]

---

[1] For forceful criticism of the Geraghty majority's reliance on a Rule 23 right to seek class certification (but a defense of the decision on other grounds), see Greenstein, *Bridging the Mootness Gap in Federal Court Class Actions*, 35 Stan.L.Rev. 897, 907–08 (1983). Does the Court's reliance on the rule raise a question under the Rules Enabling Act? See Chap. VI, Sec. 1, *infra*.

(2) Evolution of Mootness Doctrine in Class Actions. Though Geraghty is the most important decision governing mootness in the class action context, its approach fits comfortably with that of cases decided both before and after it.

(a) In Sosna v. Iowa, 419 U.S. 393 (1975), the Court announced that certification as a class action could save litigation from mootness when thereafter the named plaintiff no longer had an individual claim. The Court, however, appeared to require that the controversy (over a state durational residency requirement for obtaining a divorce) be within the "capable of repetition, yet evading review" category (not for the named plaintiff but for the remaining members of the class).

(b) Franks v. Bowman Transp. Co., 424 U.S. 747 (1976), was a class action in which the sole issue before the Supreme Court was a demand for retroactive seniority in employment and in which the plaintiff, the only named representative of the class, had been lawfully discharged by the employer after certification. In holding the case not moot, the Court, which was unanimous on this point, said: "[N]othing in our Sosna * * * [or other] opinions holds or even intimates that the fact the named plaintiff no longer has a personal stake in the outcome of a certified class action renders the class action moot unless there remains an issue 'capable of repetition, yet evading review.' * * * Given a properly certified class action, Sosna contemplates that mootness turns on whether, in the specific circumstances of the given case at the time it is before this Court, an adversary relationship sufficient to [ensure that the 'concrete adverseness which sharpens the presentation of issues'] exists. In this case, that adversary relationship obviously obtained as to unnamed class members * * *."

How significant was it that other members of the class in the Franks case were "individually named in the record" and actively sought relief?

(c) In Gerstein v. Pugh, 420 U.S. 103 (1975), a putative class action challenging pretrial detention procedures was held by a unanimous Court not to be moot even though the named plaintiffs had evidently been tried before the district court certified the class. The Court said: "Such a showing [that the case was not moot as to all named plaintiffs at the time of certification] ordinarily would be required to avoid mootness under Sosna. But this case is a suitable exception to that requirement. * * * It is by no means certain that any given individual, named as plaintiff, would be in pretrial custody long enough for a district judge to certify the class. Moreover, in this case the constant existence of a class of persons suffering deprivation is certain. The attorney representing the named respondents [plaintiffs] is a public defender, and we can safely assume that he has other clients with a continuing live interest in the case."

(d) Genesis Healthcare Corp. v. Symczyk, 133 S.Ct. 1523 (2013), emphasizes the filing of a motion for certification as the pivotal moment in determining whether a collective action becomes moot when the named plaintiff's claim is mooted. There, the plaintiff sued under the Fair Labor Standards Act (FLSA), 29 U.S.C. § 201 et seq., on the ground that the employer illegally deducted thirty minutes for an unpaid lunch break each day, even when the employee performed compensable work during that time. Under the FLSA, a plaintiff may file an action on behalf of him- or herself and "other employees similarly situated." 29 U.S.C. § 216(b). Before Symczyk moved for "conditional certification," Genesis Healthcare tendered a settlement offer that purported to satisfy the full amount of the plaintiff's individual claim. Because the lower courts had held that this tender mooted the plaintiff's individual claim (even though she did not accept the offer), and a majority of the Justices thought the plaintiff had failed to preserve a challenge to that finding, the Court, in an opinion by Justice Thomas, accepted the premise that her claim was moot.[2] Given that premise, the Court held that the plaintiff could not maintain the collective action on behalf of other similarly situated employees under the FLSA. The Court emphasized that Geraghty had "explicitly limited its holding to cases in which the named plaintiff's claim remains live at the time the district court denies class certification." The plaintiff in Genesis Healthcare, however, had not even moved for conditional certification under § 216(b) when her claim became moot.[3]

(e) Geraghty and Genesis Healthcare make clear that filing a motion for certification defines the moment after which a plaintiff may maintain a putative class action even though his or her individual claim has become moot. Did the Court draw the proper line? What constitutional or prudential interests would have been served by holding, as Justice Powell would have in Geraghty, that the named plaintiff may continue to represent the class only if formal certification has taken place before the individual claim has become moot? After all, a class may be certified without any real contest between the parties, since certification sometimes works to the advantage of both sides. Even after certification, moreover, other members of the class may be able to opt out (see Fed.R.Civ.P. 23(c)(2)), or to challenge the adequacy of representation and thus the binding effect of the judgment in a collateral proceeding (see Hansberry v. Lee, 311 U.S. 32 (1940)). Conversely, what interests, if any, are served by insisting, as Genesis Healthcare seems to, that the motion for certification be filed before the individual claim becomes moot? Will the Court's position prevent strategic litigation behavior or merely ensure that plaintiffs move for class certification when they file their complaints?

(3) Possible Significance of a Plaintiff with a Personal Stake. The constitutional argument for nonjusticiability in a case such as Geraghty centers on the lack of an ongoing dispute involving the class member before the court. Whether or not that argument is accepted, does the absence of a named plaintiff with a stake in the outcome invoke prudential considerations favoring a refusal to adjudicate? Consider whether the central goal of the class action—more vigorous and effective enforcement of group rights— requires that the litigation be prosecuted by a representative of the group who continues to share its concerns or whether it suffices that members of the group not themselves before the court have an ongoing dispute. See Deposit Guar. Nat'l Bank v. Roper, 445 U.S. 326, 342–44 (1980) (Stevens, J., concurring). See also Shapiro, *Class Actions: The Class as Party and Client*, 73 Notre Dame L.Rev. 913 (1998). Indeed, in some instances, insistence that class counsel have an identifiable client with an ongoing interest may lead only to the naming of a class representative with little or no knowledge of

---

[2]   In dissent, Justice Kagan (joined by Justices Ginsburg, Breyer, and Sotomayor) argued that the mootness of the individual claim was properly before the Court, and that the employer's tender of a settlement offer could not moot the individual claim if the plaintiff did not accept it.

[3]   The Court also emphasized that the premise of cases such as Geraghty and Sosna was that "a putative class acquires an independent legal status once it is certified under [Fed.R.Civ.P.] 23." In contrast, certification under the FLSA procedure merely resulted in sending notice to employees, who could then become parties by filing written consent with the court.

the case who will play no role in the course of the litigation. Does it follow that such insistence is always and necessarily a sterile formalism? For discussion of the role of lawyers in class litigation, see, for example, Hay & Rosenberg, *"Sweetheart" and "Blackmail" Settlements in Class Actions: Reality and Remedy*, 75 Notre Dame L.Rev. 1377 (2000); Rhode, *Class Conflicts in Class Actions*, 34 Stan.L.Rev. 1183 (1982).

(4) State Class Action Doctrine and Mootness on Appeal. Richardson v. Ramirez, 418 U.S. 24 (1974), was a state court action against state election officials challenging a law disenfranchising convicted felons. The Supreme Court concluded that the state courts had treated the case as a class action and that, as such, it presented a justiciable controversy; even though the named plaintiffs had received all the relief that they sought, there was a continuing dispute involving "the unnamed members of the classes represented below by petitioner and respondents". The Court observed that if the suit had been brought in federal court, there "would be serious doubt as to whether it could have proceeded as a class action * * *. But California is at liberty to prescribe its own rules for class actions". (Quite apart from any remaining differences between state court versus federal court class actions, would there still be "serious doubt" after Franks v. Bowman Transp. Co., p. 210, *supra*, if the suit had commenced in federal court?) The Court saw strong practical arguments militating against a holding of mootness, especially the fact that were the state judgment for the plaintiffs allowed to stand, the defendant officials would be "permanently bound by [the state court's] conclusion on a matter of federal constitutional law"—a conclusion that the U.S. Supreme Court went on to reverse. *Cf.* ASARCO Inc. v. Kadish, 490 U.S. 605 (1989), p. 158, *supra*.

(5) Implications for Standing Doctrine? Should Geraghty's recognition that mootness is a "flexible" doctrine and its characterization of justiciability doctrine more generally as "not a legal concept with a fixed content" have any implications for standing and ripeness, either generally or in class action cases? For example, would and should the Court uphold standing in a class action—perhaps alleging raced-based targeting of motorists for traffic stops—in which no individual plaintiff could establish the requisite likelihood of individual injury but in which the practice, if proved to exist, would be certain to affect at least some members of the plaintiff class? To date, the indications from the Court are negative. See *Note on "Ripeness" and Related Issues in Public Actions Challenging Patterns or Practices in the Administration of the Law*, p. 232, *infra*. If Geraghty is accepted, is this an intellectually tenable position? Compare Meltzer, *Deterring Constitutional Violations by Law Enforcement Officials: Plaintiffs and Defendants as Private Attorneys General*, 88 Colum.L.Rev. 247, 301–03 (1988) (discussing implications of modern mootness doctrine for justiciability doctrine generally).

5. RIPENESS

INTRODUCTORY NOTE

Understood as a temporal aspect of justiciability, the ripeness doctrine seeks to prevent the adjudication in federal court of disputes that remain too ill-defined for proper judicial resolution. The classic example of a ripeness concern involves the plaintiff who wishes to challenge the validity of a governmental policy that has not yet been enforced against him or her and may never be. In the pages that follow, consider in what ways ripeness differs from the law of standing.

United Public Workers v. Mitchell

330 U.S. 75, 67 S.Ct. 556, 91 L.Ed. 754 (1947).

Appeal from the District Court for the District of Columbia.

■ MR. JUSTICE REED delivered the opinion of the Court.

[The appellant federal employees and their union sought declaratory and injunctive relief from a provision of the Hatch Act and an implementing civil service rule that forbade executive officers and employees to "take any active part in political management or in political campaigns." This prohibition was claimed to violate the First, Fifth, Ninth, and Tenth Amendments to the Constitution.]

* * * It is alleged that the individuals desire to engage in acts of political management and in political campaigns. Their purposes are as stated in the excerpt from the complaint set out in the margin.[11] From the affidavits it is plain, and we so assume, that these activities will be carried on completely outside of the hours of employment. * * *

None of the appellants, except George P. Poole, has violated the provisions of the Hatch Act. They wish to act contrary to its provisions and those of * * * the Civil Service Rules and desire a declaration of the legally permissible limits of regulation. Defendants moved to dismiss the complaint for lack of a justiciable case or controversy. The [three-judge] District Court determined that each of these individual appellants had an interest in their claimed privilege of engaging in political activities, sufficient to give them a right to maintain this suit. The District Court further determined that the questioned provision of the Hatch Act was valid and * * * accordingly dismissed the complaint and granted summary judgment to defendants. * * *

Second. At the threshold of consideration, we are called upon to decide whether the complaint states a controversy cognizable in this Court. We defer consideration of the cause of action of Mr. Poole until section *Three* of this opinion. The other individual employees have elaborated the grounds of their objection in individual affidavits for use in the hearing on the summary judgment. We select as an example one

---

[11] "In discharge of their duties of citizenship, of their right to vote, and in exercise of their constitutional rights of freedom of speech, of the press, of assembly, and the right to engage in political activity, the individual plaintiffs desire to engage in the following acts: write for publication letters and articles in support of candidates for office; be connected editorially with publications which are identified with the legislative program of UFWA [former name of the present union appellant] and candidates who support it; solicit votes, aid in getting out voters, act as accredited checker, watcher, or challenger; transport voters to and from the polls without compensation therefor; participate in and help in organizing political parades; initiate petitions, and canvass for the signatures of others on such petitions; serve as party ward committeeman or other party official; and perform any and all acts not prohibited by any provision of law other than the second sentence of Section 9(a) and Section 15 of the Hatch Act, which constitute taking an active part in political management and political campaigns."

that contains the essential averments of all the others and print below the portions with significance in this suit.[18] Nothing similar to the fourth paragraph of the printed affidavit is contained in the other affidavits. The assumed controversy between affiant and the Civil Service Commission as to affiant's right to act as watcher at the polls on November 2, 1943, had long been moot when this complaint was filed. We do not therefore treat this allegation separately. The affidavits, it will be noticed, follow the generality of purpose expressed by the complaint. They declare a desire to act contrary to the rule against political activity but not that the rule has been violated. In this respect, we think they differ from the type of threat adjudicated in Railway Mail Association v. Corsi, 326 U.S. 88. In that case, the refusal to admit an applicant to membership in a labor union on account of race was involved. Admission had been refused. Definite action had also been taken in Hill v. Florida, 325 U.S. 538. In the Hill case an injunction had been sought and allowed against Hill and the union forbidding Hill from acting as the business agent of the union and the union from further functioning as a union until it complied with the state law. The threats which menaced the affiants of these affidavits in the case now being considered are closer to a general threat by officials to enforce those laws which they are charged to administer than they are to the direct threat of punishment against a named organization for a completed act that made the Mail Association and the Hill cases justiciable.

As is well known, the federal courts established pursuant to Article III of the Constitution do not render advisory opinions. For adjudication

---

[18] "At this time, when the fate of the entire world is in the balance, I believe it is not only proper but an obligation for all citizens to participate actively in the making of the vital political decisions on which the success of the war and the permanence of the peace to follow so largely depend. For the purpose of participating in the making of these decisions it is my earnest desire to engage actively in political management and political campaigns. I wish to engage in such activity upon my own time, as a private citizen.

"I wish to engage in such activities on behalf of those candidates for public office who I believe will best serve the needs of this country and with the object of persuading others of the correctness of my judgments and of electing the candidates of my choice. This objective I wish to pursue by all proper means such as engaging in discussion, by speeches to conventions, rallies and other assemblages, by publicizing my views in letters and articles for publication in newspapers and other periodicals, by aiding in the campaign of candidates for political office by posting banners and posters in public places, by distributing leaflets, by 'ringing doorbells', by addressing campaign literature, and by doing any and all acts of like character reasonably designed to assist in the election of candidates I favor.

"I desire to engage in these activities freely, openly, and without concealment. However, I understand that the second sentence of Section 9(a) of the Hatch Act and the Rules of the C.S.C. provide that if I engage in this activity, the Civil Service Commission will order that I be dismissed from federal employment. Such deprivation of my job in the federal government would be a source of immediate and serious financial loss and other injury to me.

"At the last Congressional election I was very much interested in the outcome of the campaign and offered to help the party of my choice by being a watcher at the polls. I obtained a watcher's certificate but I was advised that there might be some question of my right to use the certificate and retain my federal employment. Therefore, on November 1, 1943, the day before the election, I called the regional office of the Civil Service Commission in Philadelphia and spoke to a person who gave his name as * * *. Mr. * * * stated that if I used my watcher's certificate, the Civil Service Commission would see that I was dismissed from my job at the * * * for violation of the Hatch Act. I, therefore, did not use the certificate as I had intended.

"I believe that Congress may not constitutionally abridge my right to engage in the political activities mentioned above. However, unless the courts prevent the Civil Service Commission from enforcing this unconstitutional law, I will be unable freely to exercise my rights as a citizen." [Identifying words omitted.]

of constitutional issues, "concrete legal issues, presented in actual cases, not abstractions" are requisite. This is as true of declaratory judgments as any other field. These appellants seem clearly to seek advisory opinions upon broad claims of rights protected by the First, Fifth, Ninth and Tenth Amendments to the Constitution. As these appellants are classified employees, they have a right superior to the generality of citizens, compare Fairchild v. Hughes, 258 U.S. 126, but the facts of their personal interest in their civil rights, of the general threat of possible interference with those rights by the Civil Service Commission under its rules, if specified things are done by appellants, does not make a justiciable case or controversy. Appellants want to engage in "political management and political campaigns", to persuade others to follow appellants' views by discussion, speeches, articles and other acts reasonably designed to secure the selection of appellants' political choices. Such generality of objection is really an attack on the political expediency of the Hatch Act, not the presentation of legal issues. It is beyond the competence of courts to render such a decision.

The power of courts, and ultimately of this Court to pass upon the constitutionality of acts of Congress arises only when the interests of litigants require the use of this judicial authority for their protection against actual interference. A hypothetical threat is not enough. We can only speculate as to the kinds of political activity the appellants desire to engage in or as to the contents of their proposed public statements or the circumstances of their publication. It would not accord with judicial responsibility to adjudge, in a matter involving constitutionality, between the freedom of the individual and the requirements of public order except when definite rights appear upon the one side and definite prejudicial interferences upon the other.

The Constitution allots the nation's judicial power to the federal courts. Unless these courts respect the limits of that unique authority, they intrude upon powers vested in the legislative or executive branches. * * * Should the courts seek to expand their power so as to bring under their jurisdiction ill-defined controversies over constitutional issues, they would become the organ of political theories. Such abuse of judicial power would properly meet rebuke and restriction from other branches. * * * No threat of interference by the Commission with rights of these appellants appears beyond that implied by the existence of the law and the regulations. * * * These reasons lead us to conclude that the determination of the trial court, that the individual appellants, other than Poole, could maintain this action, was erroneous.

Third. The appellant Poole does present by the complaint and affidavit matters appropriate for judicial determination. The affidavits filed by appellees confirm that Poole has been charged by the Commission with political activity and a proposed order for his removal from his position adopted subject to his right under Commission procedure to reply to the charges and to present further evidence in refutation. We proceed to consider the controversy over constitutional power at issue between Poole and the Commission as defined by the charge and preliminary finding upon one side and the admissions of Poole's affidavit upon the other. Our determination is limited to those facts. This proceeding so limited meets the requirements of defined rights and a definite threat to interfere with a possessor of the menaced rights by a penalty for an act done in violation of the claimed restraint.

Because we conclude hereinafter that the prohibition of § 9 of the Hatch Act and Civil Service Rule 1, * * * are valid, it is unnecessary to consider, as this is a declaratory judgment action, whether or not this appellant sufficiently alleges that an irreparable injury to him would result from his removal from his position. Nor need we inquire whether or not a court of equity would enforce by injunction any judgment declaring rights. Since Poole admits that he violated the rule against political activity and that removal from office is therefore mandatory under the act, there is no question as to the exhaustion of administrative remedies. * * * Under such circumstances, we see no reason why a declaratory judgment action, even though constitutional issues are involved, does not lie. * * *

[The Court held that Poole had violated the Act, and that the Act as applied to him was valid.

[MR. JUSTICE FRANKFURTER delivered a concurring opinion dealing with a point of appellate procedure.

[MR. JUSTICE BLACK delivered a dissenting opinion, expressing the view that all the complaints stated a case or controversy, and that the Act as applied in all the cases was invalid.]

■ MR. JUSTICE DOUGLAS, dissenting in part.

I disagree with the Court on two of the four matters decided.

First. There are twelve individual appellants here asking for an adjudication of their rights. The Court passes on the claim of only one of them, Poole. It declines to pass on the claims of the other eleven on the ground that they do not present justiciable cases or controversies. With this conclusion I cannot agree. * * *

The declaratory judgment procedure is designed "to declare rights and other legal relations of any interested party * * * whether or not further relief is or could be prayed." Judicial Code, § 274d, 28 U.S.C. § 400. The fact that equity would not restrain a wrongful removal of an office holder but would leave the complainant to his legal remedies is, therefore, immaterial. A judgment which, without more, adjudicates the status of a person is permissible under the Declaratory Judgment Act. Perkins v. Elg, 307 U.S. 325, 349, 350. * * * The right to hold an office or public position against such threats is a common example of its use. Borchard, Declaratory Judgments (2d ed.), pp. 858 *et seq.* Declaratory relief is the singular remedy available here to preserve the status quo while the constitutional rights of these appellants to make these utterances and to engage in these activities are determined. The threat against them is real not fanciful, immediate not remote. The case is therefore an actual not a hypothetical one. And the present case seems to me to be a good example of a situation where uncertainty, peril, and insecurity result from imminent and immediate threats to asserted rights.

Since the Court does not reach the constitutionality of the claims of these eleven individual appellants, a discussion of them would seem to be premature. * * *

Abbott Laboratories v. Gardner

387 U.S. 136, 87 S.Ct. 1507, 18 L.Ed.2d 681 (1967).
Certiorari to the United States Court of Appeals for the Third Circuit.

■ MR. JUSTICE HARLAN delivered the opinion of the Court.

In 1962 Congress amended the Federal Food, Drug, and Cosmetic Act * * * to require manufacturers of prescription drugs to print the "established name" of the drug "prominently and in type at least half as large as that used thereon for any proprietary [or brand] name * * * " on labels and other printed material * * *. The underlying purpose of the 1962 amendment was to bring to the attention of doctors and patients the fact that many of the drugs sold under familiar trade names are actually identical to drugs sold under their "established" or less familiar trade names at significantly lower prices. The Commissioner of Food and Drugs, exercising authority delegated to him by the Secretary, * * * promulgated [a regulation providing] * * *:

> "If the label or labeling of a prescription drug bears a proprietary name or designation for the drug or any ingredient thereof, the established name, if such there be, corresponding to such proprietary name or designation, shall accompany each appearance of such proprietary name or designation."

A similar rule was made applicable to advertisements for prescription drugs * * *.

The present action was brought by a group of 37 individual drug manufacturers and by the Pharmaceutical Manufacturers Association, of which all the petitioner companies are members, and which includes manufacturers of more than 90% of the Nation's supply of prescription drugs. They challenged the regulations on the ground that the Commissioner exceeded his authority under the statute by promulgating an order requiring labels, advertisements, and other printed matter relating to prescription drugs to designate the established name of the particular drug involved every time its trade name is used anywhere in such material.

The District Court, on cross motions for summary judgment, granted the declaratory and injunctive relief sought, finding that the statute did not sweep so broadly as to permit the Commissioner's "every time" interpretation. * * * The Court of Appeals for the Third Circuit reversed without reaching the merits of the case. * * * [T]he Court of Appeals held [*inter alia*] that no "actual case or controversy" existed * * *.

I.

[Congress did not] * * * intend to forbid pre-enforcement review of this sort of regulation promulgated by the Commissioner. * * * [Based on applicable precedents], only upon a showing of "clear and convincing evidence" of a contrary legislative intent should the courts restrict access to judicial review [quoting Rusk v. Cort, 369 U.S. 367, 379–80 (1962)]. * * *

Given this standard, we are wholly unpersuaded that the statutory scheme in the food and drug area excludes this type of action. * * *

II.

A further inquiry must, however, be made. The injunctive and declaratory judgment remedies are discretionary, and courts traditionally have been reluctant to apply them to administrative determinations unless these arise in the context of a controversy "ripe" for judicial resolution. Without undertaking to survey the intricacies of the ripeness doctrine it is fair to say that its basic rationale is to prevent the courts, through avoidance of premature adjudication, from entangling themselves in abstract disagreements over administrative policies, and also to protect the agencies from judicial interference until an administrative decision has been formalized and its effects felt in a concrete way by the challenging parties. The problem is best seen in a twofold aspect, requiring us to evaluate both the fitness of the issues for judicial decision and the hardship to the parties of withholding court consideration.

As to the former factor, we believe the issues presented are appropriate for judicial resolution at this time. First, all parties agree that the issue tendered is a purely legal one: whether the statute was properly construed by the Commissioner to require the established name of the drug to be used *every time* the proprietary name is employed. Both sides moved for summary judgment in the District Court, and no claim is made here that further administrative proceedings are contemplated. It is suggested that the justification for this rule might vary with different circumstances, and that the expertise of the Commissioner is relevant to passing upon the validity of the regulation. This of course is true, but the suggestion overlooks the fact that both sides have approached this case as one purely of congressional intent, and that the Government made no effort to justify the regulation in factual terms.

Second, the regulations in issue we find to be "final agency action" within the meaning of § 10 of the Administrative Procedure Act, 5 U.S.C. § 704, as construed in judicial decisions. * * *

This is also a case in which the impact of the regulations upon the petitioners is sufficiently direct and immediate as to render the issue appropriate for judicial review at this stage. These regulations purport to give an authoritative interpretation of a statutory provision that has a direct effect on the day-to-day business of all prescription drug companies; its promulgation puts petitioners in a dilemma that it was the very purpose of the Declaratory Judgment Act to ameliorate. As the District Court found on the basis of uncontested allegations, "Either they must comply with the every time requirement and incur the costs of changing over their promotional material and labeling or they must follow their present course and risk prosecution." 228 F.Supp. 855, 861. The regulations are clear-cut, and were made effective immediately upon publication; as noted earlier the agency's counsel represented to the District Court that immediate compliance with their terms was expected. If petitioners wish to comply they must change all their labels, advertisements, and promotional materials; they must destroy stocks of printed matter; and they must invest heavily in new printing type and new supplies. The alternative to compliance—continued use of material which they believe in good faith meets the statutory requirements, but which clearly does not meet the regulation of the Commissioner—may be even more costly. That course would risk serious criminal and civil penalties for the unlawful distribution of "misbranded" drugs.

It is relevant at this juncture to recognize that petitioners deal in a sensitive industry, in which public confidence in their drug products is especially important. To require them to challenge these regulations only as a defense to an action brought by the Government might harm them severely and unnecessarily. Where the legal issue presented is fit for judicial resolution, and where a regulation requires an immediate and significant change in the plaintiffs' conduct of their affairs with serious penalties attached to noncompliance, access to the courts under the Administrative Procedure Act and the Declaratory Judgment Act must be permitted, absent a statutory bar or some other unusual circumstance, neither of which appears here. * * *

[The Court also upheld pre-enforcement review of an administrative regulation in the companion cases of Gardner v. Toilet Goods Ass'n, 387 U.S. 167 (1967), but reached a different conclusion as to ripeness in Toilet Goods Ass'n, Inc. v. Gardner, 387 U.S. 158 (1967), discussed p. 220, *infra*.*

[■ MR. JUSTICE FORTAS, joined by CHIEF JUSTICE WARREN and JUSTICE CLARK, concurred in the judgment in Toilet Goods Ass'n v. Gardner, but dissented from the decisions finding the controversies in Abbott Laboratories and Gardner v. Toilet Goods Ass'n ripe for review.]

* * * Those challenging the regulations have a remedy and there are no special reasons to relieve them of the necessity of deferring their challenge to the regulations until enforcement is undertaken. In this way, and only in this way, will the administrative process have an opportunity to function—to iron out differences, to accommodate special problems, to grant exemptions, etc. The courts do not and should not pass on these complex problems in the abstract and the general—because these regulations peculiarly depend for their quality and substance upon the facts of particular situations. We should confine ourselves—as our jurisprudence dictates—to actual, specific, particularized cases and controversies, in substance as well as in technical analysis.

NOTE ON "RIPENESS" IN PUBLIC LITIGATION CHALLENGING THE VALIDITY OR APPLICATION OF STATUTES AND REGULATIONS

(1) The Nature of Ripeness. Why did the Court hold that the plaintiffs in UPW v. Mitchell (except for Poole) had failed to present a justiciable controversy? The Court refers to the impermissibility of advisory opinions, but would a decision on the merits have been "advisory"? The rights of the parties would have been determined, and the judgment would have had res judicata effect in any subsequent litigation between them.

Was the problem, then, that there was no threat of "actual interference" by the defendants with any constitutional rights of the plaintiffs? Inquiries into the presence or absence of actual threats are by no means unfamiliar in

---

*   Justice Brennan did not take part in any of the three cases. Justice Douglas dissented in Toilet Goods Association v. Gardner.

ripeness cases, but doesn't this focus substantially replicate the standing inquiry?

By contrast, there is a real issue in UPW v. Mitchell about whether the dispute was too "ill-defined" to be appropriate for judicial resolution until further developments had more sharply framed the issues for decision. If ripeness doctrine has a distinctive role or focus, mustn't this be it?

(2) The Abbott Labs Test. Abbott Laboratories is invariably cited as the leading case on the ripeness of challenges to federal administrative regulations, and its two-part test is often applied in cases involving constitutional attacks on state and federal statutes. How do the two parts of its test relate to each other? If a court first determines that "the issues tendered are appropriate for judicial resolution", may it still deem the case unripe because there would be no substantial "hardship to the parties if judicial relief is denied at that stage"?

(a) A companion case to Abbott Laboratories, Toilet Goods Ass'n, Inc. v. Gardner, 387 U.S. 158 (1967), involved a pre-enforcement challenge to a regulation that required manufacturers of color additives to give "free access" to FDA inspectors; if access were denied, the regulation authorized the Commissioner to suspend the certification needed for manufacturers to market their products. With Justice Harlan again writing for the majority, the Court concluded that "the legal issue as presently framed" was "not appropriate for judicial resolution." The Court reasoned that "[t]he regulation serves notice only that the Commissioner *may* under certain circumstances order inspection of certain facilities and data, and that further certification of additives *may* be refused to those who decline to permit a duly authorized inspection until they have complied in that regard." In the face of such uncertainty about the circumstances in which the Commissioner would order inspections, the Court concluded that awaiting application of the regulation would place judicial review "on a much surer footing". The Court also found that the regulation would not "be felt immediately by [manufacturers] in conducting their day-to-day affairs" because they were already under a "statutory duty to permit reasonable inspections" and because the only consequence of refusing to admit an inspector was "a suspension of certification services", which the manufacturers could promptly challenge before the agency.

(b) In Lujan v. National Wildlife Federation, 497 U.S. 871 (1990), the Court held that the Interior Department's "land withdrawal review program" was not "agency action" or "final agency action" within the meaning of the APA and thus was not "ripe" for review. A "wholesale" attack on an administrative program, wrote Justice Scalia for the majority, was inappropriate: "Under the terms of the APA, [plaintiff] must direct its attack against some particular 'agency action' that causes it harm. * * * [Absent a statutory provision permitting judicial review of broad regulations or policies], a regulation is not ordinarily considered the type of agency action 'ripe' for judicial review under the APA until the scope of the controversy has been reduced to more manageable proportions, and its factual components fleshed out, by some concrete action applying the regulation to the claimant's situation in a fashion that harms or threatens to harm him. (The major exception, of course [citing Abbott Laboratories, *supra*, and Toilet Goods, *supra*], is a substantive rule which as a practical matter requires the plaintiff to adjust his conduct immediately. Such agency action is 'ripe' for review at once, whether or not explicit statutory review apart from the APA is provided.)"

How would Lujan's standard for determining ripeness deal with a regulation that does not require anything of the party seeking review, or of anyone else, but that causes others to change their conduct toward that party? What of a case in which nothing more will be learned by waiting for the regulation to be applied in a particular case?

(c) A stringent conception of ripeness was also at work in Reno v. Catholic Social Services, Inc., 509 U.S. 43 (1993), which involved disputes under the Immigration Reform and Control Act of 1986—legislation that permitted certain undocumented aliens to apply for and obtain authorization to reside permanently in the United States. In two class actions, undocumented aliens challenged as unduly restrictive certain INS regulations interpreting the Act. In an opinion by Justice Souter, the Court ruled, *sua sponte*, that the challenges were not ripe, stressing that the regulations imposed no penalty upon class members, but merely limited the availability of a benefit. Emphasizing that class members might have their applications for adjustment of status denied because they failed to meet eligibility criteria unrelated to the challenged regulations, the Court ruled that plaintiffs would have a ripe claim only if their application were denied *because* of the challenged regulations. If and when that occurred, plaintiffs could obtain adequate judicial review on appeal of a deportation order, as provided by the Act.

The Court recognized that in some instances applications from aliens had been excluded from the formal review process altogether on grounds of facial ineligibility: In such cases no further judicial review was available under the Act, and some exclusions may have been based on the challenged regulations. The Court ruled that in such circumstances challenges to the regulations would be ripe, but it remanded the case because the record did not reveal whether any class members had been rejected on that basis.

The majority did not suggest that the legal issues relating to the regulations' validity were not appropriate for judicial resolution. Justice Stevens' dissenting opinion, joined by Justices White and Blackmun, argued forcefully that legal uncertainty alone caused considerable hardship to the plaintiffs—a continued need to live in a "shadow" status.[1] Is the Court's differential treatment of regulated parties (who, under Abbott Laboratories, will often and perhaps typically be able to obtain immediate review of regulations) and regulatory beneficiaries (who, under this decision, will frequently be able to obtain review of regulations only after the benefit is denied) justifiable?

(d) Mashaw, *Improving the Environment of Agency Rulemaking: An Essay on Management, Games, and Accountability*, 57 Law & Contemp.Probs. 185, 235–36 (1994), argues that Abbott Labs has made pre-enforcement review of administrative regulations "the norm" in suits by regulated parties. Professor Mashaw believes that such pre-enforcement review (i) creates incentives for the targets of regulation to litigate immediately rather than attempt to develop technologies needed to comply with regulations while maintaining economic viability; (ii) invites "the invocation of a laundry list of potential frailties in a rule's substantive

---

[1]   Justice O'Connor concurred in the judgment, though disagreeing with much of the ripeness analysis.

content or procedural regularity", rather than a focused challenge to particular applications; (iii) deprives agencies of an enforcement record on which to defend a rule as applied, confronts courts with increased uncertainties, and thereby increases the likelihood of judicial invalidation; and (iv) as a result, promotes "defensive" rulemaking or avoidance of rulemaking altogether. Mashaw traces these difficulties not only to Abbott Labs, but also to a variety of statutes making specific agencies' rules immediately appealable. He sees the need for a context-sensitive legislative solution, rather than a blanket prohibition of—or even a presumption against—pre-enforcement review.[2]

(e) Is the Abbott Labs approach to ripeness more or less appropriate in constitutional challenges to statutes than in challenges to administrative regulations? In his opinion in the Food, Drug, and Cosmetic Act cases, Justice Fortas suggested that at least some constitutional attacks might be entertained under a less restrictive standard than otherwise applied. He also said: "Where personal status or liberties are involved, the courts may well insist upon a considerable ease of challenging administrative orders or regulations."[3]

(3) Ripeness and the Merits. What is the relationship between ripeness determinations and the merits of the underlying substantive claims?

(a) First Amendment Overbreadth Challenges. Adler v. Board of Education, 342 U.S. 485 (1952), was a state court action challenging New York statutes that required the dismissal of public school teachers who advocated the "doctrine that any government in the United States should be overthrown or overturned by force or violence" or who belonged to any organization so advocating. After the issuance of implementing rules, but before any enforcement actions or even the publication of a list of organizations deemed subversive, the plaintiffs (including four teachers) sued to enjoin enforcement. They contended, *inter alia*, that the statute imposed invalid limitations on freedom of speech, press, and assembly and that the presumptive significance attached to membership in listed organizations denied due process of law. The New York Court of Appeals rejected these attacks, and the Supreme Court affirmed.

Justice Minton, for the Court, held that the statute and the rules did not deprive teachers of "any right to free speech or assembly"; that the presumption of disqualification based on knowing membership in a listed organization did not offend due process; and that the term "subversive" as used in the statute was not unconstitutionally vague. Justice Douglas, joined by Justice Black, dissented on the merits.

Justice Frankfurter alone perceived a ripeness problem: "The allegations in the present action fall short of those found insufficient in the Mitchell case. These teachers do not allege that they have engaged in

---

[2] The costs and benefits of anticipatory adjudication are interestingly modeled in Landes & Posner, *The Economics of Anticipatory Adjudication*, 23 J.Leg.Stud. 683 (1994). For general discussions of the issue of ripeness in administrative law, see Jaffe, Judicial Control of Administrative Action 395–417 (1965); 2 Pierce, Administrative Law Treatise, Chap. 15 (5th ed. 2010); Vining, *Direct Judicial Review and the Doctrine of Ripeness in Administrative Law*, 69 Mich.L.Rev. 1443 (1971). Note too the related concepts of exhaustion of administrative remedies and finality of administrative decision, both discussed in 2 Pierce, *supra*, as prerequisites to the availability of judicial review.

[3] Compare *Note on the Scope of the Issue in First Amendment Cases and Related Problems Involving "Facial Challenges"*, p. 177, *supra*. See also Paragraph (3), *infra*.

proscribed conduct or that they have any intention to do so. * * * They do not assert that they are threatened with action under the law, or that steps are imminent whereby they would incur the hazard of punishment for conduct innocent at the time, or under standards too vague to satisfy due process of law. * * * Since we rightly refused in the Mitchell case to hear government employees whose conduct was much more intimately affected by the law there attacked than are the claims of plaintiffs here, this suit is wanting in the necessary basis for our review."

In the Adler case, could the decision on the available record mean any more than that the challenged statutes were susceptible of valid applications or, insofar as the challenge rested on the First Amendment, that the statutes were not constitutionally overbroad?[4] Insofar as Adler is viewed as an overbreadth case, however, does it become obvious that the issue presented required little if any factual framing in order to be ripe?[5]

If overbreadth cases require little factual illumination, does it follow that UPW v. Mitchell, which also presented an overbreadth challenge, implicitly held that the Hatch Act was *not* unconstitutionally overbroad?[6]

Consider the discussion of Adler in Scharpf, *Judicial Review and the Political Question: A Functional Analysis*, 75 Yale L.J. 517, 532 (1966): "For [Justice Minton, writing for the majority], the statute was clearly constitutional because it in no way deprived teachers of their freedoms of speech and association—it merely put before them the choice of either exercising these freedoms or continuing their employment in the public school system which, after all, was not a right but merely a privilege. * * *

---

[4] In Keyishian v. Board of Regents, 385 U.S. 589 (1967), the Court overturned Adler on the merits. Adler was characterized as "a declaratory judgment suit in which the Court held, in effect, that there was no constitutional infirmity in [the challenged New York statutes] on their faces and that they were capable of constitutional application."

[5] See also Times Film Corp. v. Chicago, 365 U.S. 43 (1961). The plaintiff motion picture distributor refused to submit a film to the censorship board. After being denied a permit to show the movie, it sought injunctive relief from a federal court on the ground that the ordinance was void on its face as a prior restraint. Both lower courts dismissed the suit as unripe, but the Supreme Court found "that a justiciable controversy exists. * * * The claim is that this concrete and specific statutory requirement, the production of the film at the office of the Commissioner for examination, is invalid as a previous restraint on freedom of speech. * * * [T]he broad justiciable issue is therefore present as to whether the ambit of constitutional protection includes complete and absolute freedom to exhibit, at least once, any and every kind of motion picture. It is that question alone which we decide." The ordinance was upheld, over sharp dissent on the merits.

[6] In United States Civil Service Comm'n v. National Ass'n of Letter Carriers, 413 U.S. 548 (1973), the Court, without discussing ripeness, entertained and rejected on the merits anticipatory attacks on § 9(a) of the Hatch Act as facially vague and overbroad. The pleadings in Letter Carriers were somewhat more specific than in UPW v. Mitchell. In addition, there had been substantial experience under the statute, as well as continual interpretation by the Civil Service Commission, in the interim between the two cases. The Court relied on these facts in deciding the merits. Are they also relevant to ripeness?

In Clements v. Fashing, 457 U.S. 957 (1982), the Court unanimously upheld the justiciability of a challenge by state judicial officers to state constitutional provisions (a) making them ineligible to run for the state legislature during their term of office and (b) providing that an announcement of candidacy for any other office would result in automatic loss of their judicial post. The plaintiffs alleged that but for (b), they would announce their candidacy for higher judicial office and one said that but for (a), he would run for the legislature during his term. In a brief section of the opinion, the Court said that the challenge to (a) was not abstract or hypothetical and that as to (b): "Unlike the situation in Mitchell, [plaintiff] appellees have alleged in a precise manner that, but for the sanctions of the constitutional provision they seek to challenge, they would engage in the very acts that would trigger the enforcement of the provision."

For [Justices Black and Douglas, dissenting,] the statute was clearly unconstitutional because it penalized teachers for the exercise of their 'absolute' freedoms of speech and association. The conclusion seems inevitable that Justice Frankfurter alone advocated avoidance because he alone defined the substantive issues in terms of a close balance between the equally legitimate interests of society in its self-preservation and of the teachers in their freedom of thought, inquiry and expression. Thus, in order to strike this balance in the particular case, Frankfurter would have had to know much more about the actual practices of enforcement and the degree of surveillance to which the teachers would be subjected than the bare text of an unenforced statute permitted him to know."

(b) Takings Claims. In Williamson County Regional Planning Comm'n v. Hamilton Bank, 473 U.S. 172 (1985), the Supreme Court held that a Fifth Amendment takings claim, challenging various zoning regulations, was not ripe because the plaintiff had failed to institute an inverse condemnation action under state law and had not applied for potentially available variances. Could the Court's decision be viewed as a holding, on the merits, that no taking should be imputed to the defendant until these steps had been taken?[7] See Nichol, *Ripeness and the Constitution*, 54 U.Chi.L.Rev. 153, 167 (1987) (stating that "the takings clause demands a showing by the challenger that the regulating authority has foreclosed all economically viable options").[8]

The bite of Williamson's holding that a just compensation claim is not ripe until a claimant has sought compensation through available state procedures was felt in San Remo Hotel, L.P. v. City and County of San Francisco, 545 U.S. 323 (2005). In an opinion by Justice Stevens, the Court held that after a state court had rejected an as-applied takings claim, its

---

[7] Does Williamson require exhaustion of state procedures when doing so would be "futile" or "pointless"? The Court unanimously distinguished Williamson, and held a takings claim ripe on that ground, in Suitum v. Tahoe Regional Planning Agency, 520 U.S. 725 (1997). Because agency regulations conclusively forbade building on Suitum's undeveloped lot, the Court concluded that she did not need to take the futile step of applying for a variance. And although Suitum was entitled to valuable "Transferable Development Rights" (TDRs) that she could sell to other landowners, Justice Souter's majority opinion found that she did not need to find a buyer and seek agency approval of the transfer in order for her suit to be ripe; the valuation of her TDRs was "simply an issue of fact about possible market prices" that the district court was competent to resolve. Justice Scalia, joined by Justices O'Connor and Thomas, concurred in part and concurred in the judgment.

In Lucas v. South Carolina Coastal Council, 505 U.S. 1003 (1992), a property owner sought, *inter alia*, just compensation for a "temporary" taking under a (later amended) state statute that had barred all habitable development of his beachfront property. In a 5–4 decision, the Court held that Williamson did not bar the action, even though the plaintiff had not filed a development plan or challenged the relevant state agency's decision to include his property in a no-building zone under the former statute. Justice Scalia reasoned that "such a submission would have been pointless, as the [defendant] stipulated below that no building permit would have been issued under the 1988 Act, application or no application."

The Court again distinguished Williamson in Palazzolo v. Rhode Island, 533 U.S. 606 (2001), ruling that a plaintiff who was denied a land-use permit for a "substantial project" need not file further applications or seek a variance for a smaller project when applicable regulations left "no doubt" that "no structures and no development" would be allowed. Justice Ginsburg's dissenting opinion, joined by Justices Souter and Breyer, did not dispute the majority's formulation of the applicable ripeness standard, but argued that a further permit application was needed to establish the allowable uses and thus the value of a fractional portion of the plaintiff's property on which development was unquestionably permitted.

[8] See also Yee v. City of Escondido, 503 U.S. 519 (1992); Pennell v. City of San Jose, 485 U.S. 1 (1988).

decision was entitled to preclusive effect in federal court. Noting other contexts in which a plaintiff who would have preferred to proceed in federal court may be required to litigate in state court instead, the Court termed it "hardly a radical notion to recognize that, as a practical matter, a significant number of plaintiffs will necessarily litigate their federal takings claims in state courts." Concurring in the judgment, Chief Justice Rehnquist, joined by Justices O'Connor, Kennedy, and Thomas, opined that the Court, in an appropriate case, "should reconsider whether plaintiffs asserting a Fifth Amendment takings claim based on the final decision of a state or local government entity must first seek compensation in state courts."

(4) Constitutional or Discretionary? The Supreme Court has frequently associated the ripeness doctrine with Article III's case or controversy requirement. See, *e.g.*, Babbitt v. United Farm Workers Nat. Union, 442 U.S. 289, 297 (1979); Duke Power Co. v. Carolina Environmental Study Group, Inc., 438 U.S. 59, 82 (1978). Should considerations of the adequacy of factual framing, fitness of issues for review, and hardship to parties be elevated to constitutional stature?[9] Consider, in this regard, the justiciability questions in Buckley v. Valeo, 424 U.S. 1 (1976). Buckley was an action for declaratory and injunctive relief attacking the constitutionality of all the major elements of the Federal Election Campaign Act of 1971, as amended in 1974, including limitation of political contributions and expenditures, requirements of disclosure and recordkeeping of many such contributions and expenditures, public financing of national party conventions and presidential campaigns, and the establishment of a Federal Election Commission with responsibility for administering the Act. The plaintiffs included a presidential candidate and a committee organized on his behalf, a United States Senator running for re-election, a potential contributor, and a number of political organizations. The action, instituted shortly after enactment of the amending statute, was based in part on § 315(a) of the Act, 2 U.S.C. § 437h, which provided: "The Commission, the national committee of any political party, or any individual eligible to vote in any election for the office of President of the United States may institute such actions in the appropriate district court of the United States, including actions for declaratory judgment, as may be appropriate to construe the constitutionality of any provision of this Act [or related sections of the Criminal Code]." Because of the special expediting provisions of that section, the case was argued before the Supreme Court on November 10, 1975, and decided on January 30, 1976, near the beginning of the first national election campaign to be governed by the amended Act.

The Court passed on the merits of all the contentions with only the briefest treatment of the justiciability of the case as a whole, concluding: "In our view, the complaint in this case demonstrates that at least some of the appellants have a sufficient 'personal stake' in a determination of the constitutional validity of each of the challenged provisions to present 'a real and substantial controversy admitting of specific relief through a decree of conclusive character, as distinguished from an opinion advising what the law would be upon a hypothetical state of facts.' "

Should Congress' direction for speedy adjudication be relevant to the ripeness inquiry? See Buckley, *supra*, at 117 (noting, in one of its ripeness determinations, that Congress was "most concerned with obtaining a final adjudication of as many issues as possible litigated pursuant to the

---

[9]   For a negative answer, see Nichol, Paragraph (3)(b), *supra*.

provisions of § 437h"). Should it matter if the consequences of deferring adjudication—possibly until after the 1976 campaign—would have been unusually troublesome?

(5) Criminal Statutes. Anticipatory challenges to state criminal laws must confront the traditional doctrine—often honored in the breach—that equity will not enjoin a criminal prosecution. Should there be any special reluctance to entertain preventive attacks on criminal laws? On *state* criminal laws? See generally Chap. X, Sec. 2(C), *infra*. Prior to these questions, however, suits seeking declaratory or injunctive relief from criminal statutes often present ripeness issues, which substantially overlap those already discussed. Consider the leading cases that follow:

(a) In Pierce v. Society of Sisters, 268 U.S. 510 (1925), two private schools were allowed to sue to enjoin enforcement of a criminal statute requiring parents to send their children to public school, even though the measure was not to be effective for several years. The complaints alleged that the defendant officials had announced their intention to proceed under the law, and that as a result parents were withdrawing children or refusing to enter them in complainants' schools, to their immediate and irreparable injury.

(b) In Poe v. Ullman, 367 U.S. 497 (1961), married persons and their doctor brought a state court action for a declaratory judgment of the unconstitutionality of the state's law prohibiting the use of contraceptive devices or the giving of medical advice about them. An appeal from the state supreme court's decision upholding the statute was dismissed for nonjusticiability, with the plurality emphasizing the absence of any specific threat of enforcement, as well as the long history of non-enforcement.[10]

(c) In Doe v. Bolton, 410 U.S. 179, 188 (1973), the Court allowed physicians consulted by pregnant women to challenge a state anti-abortion statute without any showing that they had been prosecuted or threatened with prosecution. But in the companion case of Roe v. Wade, 410 U.S. 113, 127–29 (1973), the Court refused to allow a similar challenge by a childless couple who alleged that they feared pregnancy for medical and personal reasons and that the inability to obtain a legal abortion in the state was forcing them to " 'the choice of refraining from normal sexual relations or of endangering [the plaintiff wife's] health through a possible pregnancy.' " The Court said that the alleged injury was too speculative, resting as it did on possible contraceptive failure, possible pregnancy, and possible future impairment of health.

(d) In Holder v. Humanitarian Law Project, 561 U.S. 1 (2010), plaintiffs challenged on due process vagueness and First Amendment grounds a statute making it a crime "knowingly [to] provid[e] material support or resources to a foreign terrorist organization". 18 U.S.C. § 2339B(a)(1). The plaintiffs alleged that they were seeking to provide support for the nonviolent and lawful activities of two groups that had been designated as foreign terrorist organizations by the Secretary of State, and that the material-support statute prevented them from doing so. The Court found the case to be ripe because the plaintiffs faced "a credible threat of prosecution" (quoting Babbitt v. United Farm Workers National Union, 442 U.S. 289

---

[10] Justice Brennan, concurring in the result, said that the "true controversy", not presented by the parties in the case, was "over the opening of birth-control clinics on a large scale". There were four dissents.

(1979)). In so holding, the Court relied on two central considerations: (a) the plaintiffs alleged "that they provided support to [the relevant groups] before the enactment of § 2339B and that they would provide similar support again if the statute's allegedly unconstitutional bar were lifted", and (b) the government advised the Court "that it has charged about 150 persons with violating § 2339B, and that several of those prosecutions involved the enforcement of the statutory terms at issue here."

(e) In Susan B. Anthony List v. Driehaus, 134 S.Ct. 2334 (2014), the Court held that the Susan B. Anthony List—a political advocacy group— could bring a pre-enforcement challenge under the First Amendment to the application of a criminal false statement statute to the group's election advocacy activities. The Court's opinion dealt primarily with the question of whether the plaintiff faced a substantial threat of enforcement giving rise to Article III standing. See *supra* pp. 122–123. The Court, however, also addressed the contention that the plaintiff's suit did not meet "prudential" ripeness requirements—namely, those relating to (a) the fitness of the case for adjudication and (b) the hardship to the parties if the Court denied relief at this stage. Noting that its decision in Lexmark Int'l, Inc. v. Static Control Components, Inc., 134 S.Ct. 1377 (2014) (see *supra* pp. 156–158), had called into question the legitimacy of "prudential" limitations in standing cases, the Court in *Driehaus* suggested that enforcing prudential ripeness requirements was in tension with its earlier observation that federal courts have a "virtually unflagging" obligation to exercise the jurisdiction Congress confers. But because the suit before it clearly satisfied both the fitness and hardship requirements, the Court in *Driehaus* found it unnecessary to resolve whether it would continue to enforce prudential requirements in ripeness cases generally.

* * *

Do the foregoing cases suggest that the question of ripeness is inherently fact-bound or is it possible to articulate meaningfully constraining principles to guide the application of ripeness doctrine to anticipatory challenges to criminal statutes?

O'Shea v. Littleton

414 U.S. 488, 94 S.Ct. 669, 38 L.Ed.2d 674 (1974).
Certiorari to the United States Court of Appeals for the Seventh Circuit.

■ MR. JUSTICE WHITE delivered the opinion of the Court.

[Nineteen citizens of Cairo, Illinois, brought a civil rights action (alleging violations of various provisions of the Constitution and of 42 U.S.C. §§ 1981–83) against various government officials, including the city's police commissioner, the state's attorney for Alexander County, and a magistrate and judge of the county court. The complaint alleged a longstanding and continuing pattern of discriminatory law enforcement against African-Americans and, in particular, an effort to deter participation in an economic boycott of city merchants believed to engage in race discrimination. The magistrate and judge were alleged, *inter alia*, to set bond in criminal cases and to impose sentences on a discriminatory basis. The complaint cited examples of unlawful conduct committed against named plaintiffs by the state's attorney and his investigator, but contained only general allegations against the magistrate and judge. The plaintiffs sought to bring the case as a class action and requested injunctive (but no damages) relief.

[The district trial court dismissed the case, partly on grounds of lack of jurisdiction to award the relief requested. The court of appeals reversed, ruling that] in the event respondents proved their allegations, the District Court should proceed to fashion appropriate injunctive relief to prevent petitioners from depriving others of their constitutional rights in the course of carrying out their judicial duties in the future.[1] We granted certiorari.

I

We reverse the judgment of the Court of Appeals. The complaint failed to satisfy the threshold requirement imposed by Art. III of the Constitution that those who seek to invoke the power of federal courts must allege an actual case or controversy. * * * Plaintiffs * * * "must allege some threatened or actual injury resulting from the putatively illegal action before a federal court may assume jurisdiction." Linda R.S. v. Richard D., 410 U.S. 614, 617 (1973). The injury or threat of injury must be both "real and immediate," not "conjectural" or "hypothetical." Golden v. Zwickler, 394 U.S. 103 (1969); United Public Workers v. Mitchell, 330 U.S. 75, 89–91 (1947). Moreover, if none of the named plaintiffs purporting to represent a class establishes the requisite of a case or controversy with the defendants, none may seek relief on behalf of himself or any other member of the class. * * *

In the complaint that began this action, the sole allegations of injury are that petitioners "have engaged in and continue to engage in, a pattern and practice of conduct * * * all of which has deprived and continues to deprive plaintiffs and members of their class of their" constitutional rights and, again, that petitioners "have denied and continue to deny to plaintiffs and members of their class their constitutional rights" by illegal bond-setting, sentencing, and jury-fee practices. None of the named plaintiffs is identified as himself having suffered any injury in the manner specified. In sharp contrast to the claim for relief against the State's Attorney where specific instances of misconduct with respect to particular individuals are alleged, the claim against petitioners alleges injury in only the most general terms. At oral argument, respondents' counsel stated that some of the named plaintiffs-respondents, who could be identified by name if necessary, had actually been defendants in proceedings before petitioners and had suffered from the alleged unconstitutional practices. Past exposure to illegal conduct does not in itself show a present case or controversy regarding injunctive relief, however, if unaccompanied by any continuing, present adverse effects. Neither the complaint nor respondents' counsel suggested that any of the named plaintiffs at the time the complaint was filed were themselves serving an allegedly illegal sentence or were on trial or awaiting trial before petitioners. Indeed, if any of the respondents were then serving an assertedly unlawful sentence, the complaint would inappropriately be seeking relief from or modification of current, existing custody. See

---

[1] While the Court of Appeals did not attempt to specify exactly what type of injunctive relief might be justified, it at least suggested that it might include a requirement of "periodic reports of various types of aggregate data on actions on bail and sentencing." * * *

Preiser v. Rodriguez, 411 U.S. 475 (1973). Furthermore, if any were then on trial or awaiting trial in state proceedings, the complaint would be seeking injunctive relief that a federal court should not provide. We thus do not strain to read inappropriate meaning into the conclusory allegations of this complaint.

Of course, past wrongs are evidence bearing on whether there is a real and immediate threat of repeated injury. But here the prospect of future injury rests on the likelihood that respondents will again be arrested for and charged with violations of the criminal law and will again be subjected to bond proceedings, trial, or sentencing before petitioners. Important to this assessment is the absence of allegations that any relevant criminal statute of the State of Illinois is unconstitutional on its face or as applied or that respondents have been or will be improperly charged with violating criminal law. If the statutes that might possibly be enforced against respondents are valid laws, and if charges under these statutes are not improvidently made or pressed, the question becomes whether any perceived threat to respondents is sufficiently real and immediate to show an existing controversy simply because they anticipate violating lawful criminal statutes and being tried for their offenses, in which event they may appear before petitioners and, if they do, will be affected by the allegedly illegal conduct charged. Apparently, the proposition is that *if* respondents proceed to violate an unchallenged law and *if* they are charged, held to answer, and tried in any proceedings before petitioners, they will be subjected to the discriminatory practices that petitioners are alleged to have followed. But it seems to us that attempting to anticipate whether and when these respondents will be charged with crime and will be made to appear before either petitioner takes us into the area of speculation and conjecture. See Younger v. Harris, [401 U.S. 37, 41–42 (1971)]. The nature of respondents' activities is not described in detail and no specific threats are alleged to have been made against them. Accepting that they are deeply involved in a program to eliminate racial discrimination in Cairo and that tensions are high, we are nonetheless unable to conclude that the case-or-controversy requirement is satisfied by general assertions or inferences that in the course of their activities respondents will be prosecuted for violating valid criminal laws. We assume that respondents will conduct their activities within the law and so avoid prosecution and conviction as well as exposure to the challenged course of conduct said to be followed by petitioners.

* * * We can only speculate whether respondents will be arrested, either again or for the first time, for violating a municipal ordinance or a state statute, particularly in the absence of any allegations that unconstitutional criminal statutes are being employed to deter constitutionally protected conduct. * * * Under these circumstances, where respondents do not claim any constitutional right to engage in conduct proscribed by therefore presumably permissible state laws, or indicate that it is otherwise their intention to so conduct themselves, the threat of injury from the alleged course of conduct they attack is simply too remote to satisfy the case-or-controversy requirement and permit adjudication by a federal court. * * *

II

The foregoing considerations obviously shade into those determining whether the complaint states a sound basis for equitable relief; and even if we were inclined to consider the complaint as presenting an existing case or controversy, we would firmly disagree with the Court of Appeals that an adequate basis for equitable relief against petitioners had been stated. The Court has recently reaffirmed the "basic doctrine of equity jurisprudence that courts of equity should not act, and particularly should not act to restrain a criminal prosecution, when the moving party has an adequate remedy at law and will not suffer irreparable injury if denied equitable relief." Younger v. Harris, [*supra*, at] 43–44. Additionally, recognition of the need for a proper balance in the concurrent operation of federal and state courts counsels restraint against the issuance of injunctions against state officers engaged in the administration of the State's criminal laws in the absence of a showing of irreparable injury which is "both great and immediate." *Id.*, at 46. * * *

Respondents do not seek to strike down a single state statute, either on its face or as applied; nor do they seek to enjoin any criminal prosecutions that might be brought under a challenged criminal law. In fact, respondents apparently contemplate that prosecutions will be brought under seemingly valid state laws. What they seek is an injunction aimed at controlling or preventing the occurrence of specific events that might take place in the course of future state criminal trials. The order the Court of Appeals thought should be available if respondents proved their allegations would be operative only where permissible state prosecutions are pending against one or more of the beneficiaries of the injunction. Apparently the order would contemplate interruption of state proceedings to adjudicate assertions of noncompliance by petitioners. This seems to us nothing less than an ongoing federal audit of state criminal proceedings which would indirectly accomplish the kind of interference that Younger v. Harris, *supra*, and related cases sought to prevent.

A federal court should not intervene to establish the basis for future intervention that would be so intrusive and unworkable. * * * [B]ecause an injunction against acts which might occur in the course of future criminal proceedings would necessarily impose continuing obligations of compliance, the question arises of how compliance might be enforced if the beneficiaries of the injunction were to charge that it had been disobeyed. Presumably, any member of respondents' class who appeared as an accused before petitioners could allege and have adjudicated a claim that petitioners were in contempt of the federal court's injunction order, with review of adverse decisions in the Court of Appeals and, perhaps, in this Court. Apart from the inherent difficulties in defining the proper standards against which such claims might be measured, and the significant problems of proving noncompliance in individual cases, such a major continuing intrusion of the equitable power of the federal courts into the daily conduct of state criminal proceedings is in sharp conflict with the principles of equitable restraint which this Court has recognized in the decisions previously noted.

Respondents have failed, moreover, to establish the basic requisites of the issuance of equitable relief in these circumstances—the likelihood of substantial and immediate irreparable injury, and the inadequacy of remedies at law. We have already canvassed the necessarily conjectural nature of the threatened injury to which respondents are allegedly subjected. And if any of the respondents are ever prosecuted and face trial, or if they are illegally sentenced, there are available state and federal procedures which could provide relief from the wrongful conduct alleged. * * *

Considering the availability of other avenues of relief open to respondents for the serious conduct they assert, and the abrasive and unmanageable intercession which the injunctive relief they seek would represent, we conclude that, apart from the absence of an existing case or controversy presented by respondents for adjudication, the Court of Appeals erred in deciding that the District Court should entertain respondents' claim.

Reversed.

■ MR. JUSTICE BLACKMUN, concurring in part.

I join the judgment of the Court and Part I of the Court's opinion which holds that the complaint "failed to satisfy the threshold requirement imposed by Art. III of the Constitution that those who seek to invoke the power of federal courts must allege an actual case or controversy."

When we arrive at that conclusion, it follows, it seems to me, that we are precluded from considering any other issue presented for review. Thus, the Court's additional discussion of the question whether a case for equitable relief was stated amounts to an advisory opinion that we are powerless to render. * * *

■ MR. JUSTICE DOUGLAS, with whom MR. JUSTICE BRENNAN and MR. JUSTICE MARSHALL concur, dissenting.

* * * The allegations [in the complaint] support the likelihood that the named plaintiffs as well as members of their class will be arrested in the future and * * * subjected to the alleged discriminatory practices in the administration of justice.

These allegations of past and continuing wrongdoings clearly state a case or controversy in the Art. III sense. They are as specific as those alleged in Jenkins v. McKeithen, 395 U.S. 411, and in Doe v. Bolton, 410 U.S. 179, where we held that cases or controversies were presented.

Specificity of proof may not be forthcoming: but specificity of charges is clear.

What has been alleged here is not only wrongs done to named plaintiffs, but a recurring pattern of wrongs which establishes, if proved, that the legal regime under control of the whites in Cairo, Illinois, is used over and over again to keep the blacks from exercising First Amendment rights, to discriminate against them, to keep from the blacks the protection of the law in their lawful activities, to weight the scales of justice repeatedly on the side of white prejudices and against black protests, fears, and suffering. This is a more pervasive scheme for suppression of blacks and their civil rights than I have ever seen. It may not survive a trial. But if this case does not present a "case or controversy" involving the named plaintiffs, then that concept has been so watered down as to be no longer recognizable. This will please the white superstructure, but it does violence to the conception of evenhanded justice envisioned by the Constitution.

* * * It will be much more appropriate to pass on the nature of any equitable relief to be granted after the case has been tried. * * *

NOTE ON "RIPENESS" AND RELATED ISSUES IN PUBLIC ACTIONS CHALLENGING PATTERNS OR PRACTICES IN THE ADMINISTRATION OF THE LAW

(1) Scope of the Issue. The distinction between the matters discussed in the preceding Note and those considered in this one is more a matter of degree than one of kind. But a case such as O'Shea differs from a case such as United Public Workers v. Mitchell or Roe v. Wade in several respects. First, in O'Shea there is no challenged statute or regulation but rather a pattern of past events (and their implication for the future) that form the basis of the complaint and the prayer for equitable relief. Second, in a case such as O'Shea, in which the matters complained of consist of official practices in law enforcement, it is especially difficult to identify the individuals who are likely to be harmed by those practices in the future. Third, such cases may also involve requests for "structural relief"—for the shaping of a decree designed to modify significantly the way in which an arm of government (or, in some instances, a private institution) conducts its affairs. The Court's evident reluctance to become enmeshed in disputes of this kind, especially when state institutions are at the bar, has been expressed, in part, in terms of justiciability doctrines—notably ripeness and standing.[1] Which if any of the problems in these cases is properly viewed as ones of justiciability under Article III?

Consider O'Shea itself. Did the Court take adequate account of plaintiffs' allegation that the effect of defendants' continuing practices was "to deter them [plaintiffs] from engaging in their boycott and similar activities"? If this allegation was true, and the boycott and related activities had ceased as a result of the challenged practices, should the controversy have been deemed premature?

(2) The Lyons Case. In City of Los Angeles v. Lyons, 461 U.S. 95 (1983), Lyons, an African-American male, brought a civil rights action against the city and certain of its police officers in federal district court, claiming that he

---

[1] See also Rizzo v. Goode, 423 U.S. 362 (1976), in which the Supreme Court, partly on grounds of nonjusticiability, set aside a lower court order requiring Philadelphia police authorities to institute comprehensive civilian complaint procedures in accordance with specified guidelines. The order was based on some 19 instances in one year in which the police were found to have violated citizens' constitutional rights. The majority, per Justice Rehnquist, said that the considerations expressed in O'Shea "apply here with even more force, for the individual [plaintiffs'] claim to 'real and immediate' injury rests not upon what the named [defendants] might do to them in the future—such as set a bond on the basis of race—but upon what one of a small, unnamed minority of policemen might do to them in the future because of that unknown policeman's perception of departmental disciplinary procedures."

In Laird v. Tatum, 408 U.S. 1 (1972), plaintiffs sought to enjoin Army surveillance of civilian political activity, claiming they had been subjected to such surveillance and that the practice exerted a "chilling effect" on the exercise of First Amendment rights. The Court, 5–4, held the action not justiciable, stating that "[a]llegations of a subjective 'chill' are not an adequate substitute for a claim of specific present objective harm or a threat of specific future harm."

had been unconstitutionally subjected to a "chokehold" after being stopped for a traffic violation. He alleged that pursuant to official authorization, chokeholds were routinely applied in situations where they were not warranted and that many people had suffered injury as a consequence. (Since 1975, sixteen people, twelve of whom were African-American, had died as a result of police chokeholds.) Lyons sought both damages and declaratory and injunctive relief. The district court granted a preliminary injunction against the use of chokeholds "under circumstances which do not threaten death or serious bodily injury"—an injunction that was to continue in effect until an improved training and reporting program had been approved by the court—and the court of appeals affirmed.

The Supreme Court reversed on the ground that Lyons had "failed to demonstrate a case or controversy" that "would justify the equitable relief sought". Noting that only the question of an injunctive remedy was before it, and that the damages claim could be severed on remand, the Court relied on O'Shea and on Rizzo v. Goode, note 1, *supra*, in concluding that there was no jurisdiction to entertain the claim for equitable relief.

First, the Court concluded that Lyons was not immediately threatened, finding it to be "no more than speculation to assert either that Lyons himself will again be involved in one of those unfortunate instances, or that he will be arrested in the future and provoke the use of a chokehold by resisting arrest, attempting to escape, or threatening deadly force or serious bodily injury."

Second, the Court decided that precedents including O'Shea could not be distinguished on the basis that in those proceedings, unlike the present one, "massive structural relief" had been sought.

Still relying on O'Shea, the Court went on to conclude that even if Lyons' standing based on his pending damage suit permitted him also "to seek an injunction as a remedy", the showing of irreparable injury prerequisite to that remedy had not been made: "We decline the invitation to slight the preconditions for equitable relief; for as we have held, recognition of the need for a proper balance between state and federal authority counsels restraint in the issuance of injunctions against state officers engaged in the administration of the States' criminal laws in the absence of irreparable injury which is both great and immediate [citing O'Shea and Younger v. Harris, p. 1127, *infra*]".

Justice Marshall, for four dissenters, focused on the majority's claim of lack of "standing" and argued that cases such as O'Shea were not controlling because the plaintiffs in those cases had not sought damages for past injury: "In addition to the risk that he will be subjected to a chokehold in the future, Lyons has suffered past injury. Because he has a live claim for damages, he need not rely solely on the threat of future injury to establish his personal stake in the outcome of the controversy.

" * * * The Court provides no justification for departing from the traditional treatment of remedial issues and demanding a separate threshold inquiry into each form of relief a plaintiff seeks. It is anomalous to require a plaintiff to demonstrate 'standing' to seek each particular form of relief requested in the complaint when under Rule 54(c) the remedy to which a party may be entitled need not even be demanded in the complaint."

As to the majority's alternative ground—involving the failure to satisfy the traditional prerequisites for equitable relief—Justice Marshall objected, *inter alia*, that the majority's approach "immunizes from prospective equitable relief any policy that authorizes persistent deprivations of constitutional rights as long as no individual can establish with substantial certainty that he will be injured, or injured again, in the future."

(3) Standing, Ripeness, Mootness. The Court treated Lyons as a standing case. The request for a forward-looking injunction failed the redressability requirement because no injunction could redress the past harm. Is this a sound analysis? No one disputed Lyons' standing to seek damages. Why shouldn't his past injury have established the existence of a case or controversy focused largely on the appropriateness of equitable relief?

Alternatively, why wasn't Lyons a mootness case?[2] At the time he was being choked, Lyons surely would have had a live controversy concerning the constitutionality of the city's alleged chokehold policy. Why, then, was he unable to benefit from the "flexible character of the Art. III mootness doctrine" (United States Parole Commission v. Geraghty, p. 208, *supra*)? Do all mootness cases also raise standing questions about whether declaratory or injunctive relief would redress past injuries that may or may not be repeated? *Cf.* Friends of the Earth v. Laidlaw Environmental Services (TOC), Inc., 528 U.S. 167 (2000), p. 121 n.17, *supra*, which held that "there are circumstances in which the prospect that a defendant will engage in (or resume) harmful conduct may be too speculative to support standing, but not too speculative to overcome mootness".

Or does it make more sense to view Lyons as a ripeness case, concerned with whether the threat of future injury to the plaintiff was sufficiently real and imminent to warrant immediate adjudication? See Little, *It's About Time: Unraveling Standing and Equitable Ripeness*, 41 Buff.L.Rev. 933, 988–90 (1993). The Court cited Lyons as authority for denying standing in McConnell v. Federal Election Commission, 540 U.S. 93 (2003), in which it held that a Senator could not challenge a statutory provision that would allegedly impede his re-election effort in a campaign nearly five years off. In finding that standing required an injury that was not temporally "remote", Chief Justice Rehnquist's opinion for the Court made no reference to ripeness. Neither did Justice Stevens, joined by Justices Ginsburg and Breyer, who dissented on the standing question.

Do the various justiciability doctrines fit together in a way that makes sense in light of underlying values and concerns?[3]

(4) Justiciability and Institutional Remedies. Although the injunction sought in Lyons was, as the Court conceded, less intrusive in scope than the injunction sought in O'Shea, it was nonetheless designed to effectuate a significant change in the practices of a local governmental agency. Judicial efforts to reform or restructure governmental institutions seem imperative in at least some instances, but undoubtedly place great if not excessive demands on the practical competence of courts, and sometimes may even prove dysfunctional.[4]

---

[2] See Fallon, *Of Justiciability, Remedies, and Public Law Litigation: Notes on the Jurisprudence of Lyons*, 59 N.Y.U.L.Rev. 1 (1984), arguing that in cases where past injury has occurred, the justiciability question in an action for equitable relief should be viewed, under the rubric of mootness, as a question of the likelihood of recurrence.

[3] See generally Chemerinsky, *A Unified Approach to Justiciability*, 22 Conn.L.Rev. 677 (1990).

[4] For analysis of the issues raised by institutional or structural reform litigation, see, *e.g.*, Feeley & Rubin, Judicial Policy Making and the Modern State: How the Courts Reformed

Is it appropriate for the Supreme Court to employ justiciability doctrines as a means of shielding the federal courts from the hazards of institutional reform litigation? See generally Fallon, *The Linkage Between Justiciability and Remedies—And Their Connections to Substantive Rights*, 92 Va.L.Rev. 633 (2006) (arguing that concerns about "unacceptable" and occasionally "necessary" remedies pervasively influence the formulation and application of justiciability doctrines). Justiciability questions are generally resolved at the outset of litigation. By contrast, framing the central question as involving the law of remedies would allow a balancing of affected public and private interests upon a full record. Why has the Supreme Court rejected this approach? Is it significant that the doctrine of "remedial discretion" makes it difficult for appellate courts to set aside lower courts' remedial decrees and that a Supreme Court that is skeptical of institutional reform litigation—and possibly of the good judgment of lower federal courts—can exercise more effective appellate control through the blunter instrument of justiciability doctrine? See Fallon, note 2, *supra*, at 39–43.

As a way of highlighting the remedial question, consider whether the Court in Lyons or in O'Shea might have taken a different view of the justiciability issue if the plaintiffs had sought only a declaration of the unlawfulness of the conduct engaged in.[5]

(5) Justiciability and Class Actions. What significance, if any, should attach to the fact that Lyons did not file a class action? Even if Lyons could not establish a sufficient likelihood that he personally, or any individual class member, would be subjected to another chokehold, would there nevertheless have been a justiciable controversy if he had established his membership in an identifiable class at least some of whose members were virtually certain to be subjected to chokeholds in the near future?

In considering this question, note that there is language in O'Shea—in which the plaintiffs had *sought* class certification—that can be taken to suggest that a named plaintiff must individually satisfy the case or controversy requirement before being able to seek either individual or class relief: "None of the named plaintiffs is identified as himself having suffered any injury in the manner specified". See also Simon v. Eastern Kentucky Welfare Rights Org., 426 U.S. 26, 40 n. 20 (1976) ("That a suit may be a class action * * * adds nothing to the question of standing, for even plaintiffs who represent a class 'must allege and show that they personally have been injured, not that injury has been suffered by other, unidentified members of the class to which they belong and which they purport to represent.' "). Is the conclusion toward which such statements point a sound one?

America's Prisons (1998); Rosenberg, The Hollow Hope: Can Courts Bring About Social Change? (1991); Sandler & Schoenbrod, Democracy by Decree: What Happens When Courts Run Government (2003); Chayes, *Foreword: Public Law Litigation and the Burger Court*, 96 Harv.L.Rev. 4 (1982); Eisenberg & Yeazell, *The Ordinary and the Extraordinary in Institutional Litigation*, 93 Harv.L.Rev. 465 (1980); Fletcher, *The Discretionary Constitution: Institutional Remedies and Judicial Legitimacy*, 91 Yale L.J. 635 (1982); Friedman, *When Rights Encounter Reality: Enforcing Federal Remedies*, 65 S.Cal.L.Rev. 735 (1992); Jeffries & Rutherglen, *Structural Reform Revisited*, 95 S.Cal.L.Rev. 1387 (2007); Mishkin, *Federal Courts as State Reformers*, 35 Wash. & Lee L.Rev. 949 (1978); Nagel, *Separation of Powers and the Scope of Federal Equitable Remedies*, 30 Stan.L.Rev. 661 (1978); Sabel & Simon, *Destabilization Rights: How Public Law Litigation Succeeds*, 117 Harv.L.Rev. 1015, 1019 (2004); Schlanger, *Civil Rights Injunctions Over Time: A Case Study of Jail and Prison Court Orders*, 81 N.Y.U.L.Rev. 550 (2006).

[5]   *Cf.* Steffel v. Thompson, 415 U.S. 452 (1974), p. 1144, *infra*.

Would the constitutional requirements of standing doctrine be satisfied by a class action on behalf of all persons who have been exposed to toxic chemicals, some of whom are sick and others of whom are at risk of contracting serious illness, brought in a bankruptcy proceeding to protect the class's interests vis-a-vis other claimants to a debtor's assets? See Coffee, *Class Wars: The Dilemma of the Mass Tort Class Action*, 95 Colum.L.Rev. 1343, 1422–33 (1995). Is the problem posed by the hypothetical properly considered one of justiciability or proper class certification? Compare Amchem Products, Inc. v. Windsor, 521 U.S. 591 (1997) (avoiding justiciability issues posed by a class suit on behalf of plaintiffs who had not yet become sick, as well as others who had manifested more concrete injuries, by finding that there was no certifiable class under Fed.R.Civ.Pro. 23). Or is it more appropriately handled by tailoring the scope of judicial relief at the back end of the litigation? Compare Lewis v. Casey, 518 U.S. 343, 357 (1996) (holding that the remedy in a class action lawsuit alleging violations of prisoners' rights to legal assistance must "be limited to the inadequacy that produced the injury in fact that the plaintiff has established").

Consider the relevance of class certification in Gratz v. Bollinger, 539 U.S. 244 (2003), a case in which the Court upheld the justiciability of a class action challenging the affirmative action policies of the University of Michigan with respect to freshman admissions, even though the class representative claimed continuing harm only from the school's policy concerning transfer admissions. After having been turned down for admission as a freshman, the petitioner Hamacher filed suit challenging the University's undergraduate affirmative action policies. Although he matriculated at another institution, he represented that he would apply to transfer to the University of Michigan if it ceased to consider race as a factor in admissions. The district court certified Hamacher as the representative of a class consisting of all non-beneficiaries of the University's undergraduate affirmative action policies, including both freshman and transfer admissions, who had either been rejected in the past or intended to apply in the future. Thereafter, the Gratz litigation centered almost exclusively on the freshman admission policy, which included the assignment of 20 points on a 150-point scale on the basis of race.

In an opinion by Chief Justice Rehnquist, the Supreme Court held that Hamacher had standing to seek injunctive relief against the use of race in both freshman and transfer admissions, even though he suffered no imminent threat of injury from the freshman policy. The Court reasoned that Hamacher contested the constitutionality of any reliance on race as a component of undergraduate admissions decisions and that reliance on race was a common element of the freshman and transfer admissions policies. Although the transfer policy did not include the point system that crucially distinguished freshman admissions, the Court held that the difference went to the merits of whether the policy was narrowly tailored to a compelling state interest, not to Hamacher's standing.

Following this ruling with respect to standing, the Court held, by 6–3, that the freshman admissions policy was unconstitutional because it was not "narrowly tailored" to the University's compelling interest in promoting diversity. The Court did not address the constitutionality of the transfer admissions policy.

In his dissenting opinion, Justice Stevens, joined by Justice Souter, cited the Lyons case, p. 232, *supra*, in arguing that although Hamacher would have standing to seek damages resulting from his denial of admission as a freshman, he lacked standing to seek an injunction against the freshman admissions policy, because he would never again file an application under it. As the majority noted, however, an obvious difference between the cases is that Gratz was certified as a class action, whereas Lyons was not. Is the real issue whether Hamacher was appropriately certified to represent a class consisting of challengers to *both* the freshman admissions and the transfer admissions policies? The Gratz majority appeared to acknowledge this question, but gave no clear answer, pronouncing it unnecessary to resolve whether Hamacher's entitlement to challenge the freshman admissions policy should be treated as "a matter of Article III standing" or as an issue involving "the propriety of class certification pursuant to Federal Rule of Civil Procedure 23(a)".

_____

6. POLITICAL QUESTIONS

_____

Among the most controversial elements of justiciability, the political question doctrine comes into play only in a case that otherwise has a proper plaintiff with a live claim. Despite the presence of all of the other elements of an Article III case or controversy, the Court forbears on the ground that something about the subject matter of the case makes it inappropriate for judicial resolution. Sometimes, this conclusion entails a determination that the constitutional text, read in context, assigns resolution of the controversy to a branch of government other than the federal judiciary. Other times, the determination of a political question touches on pragmatic or prudential questions about the appropriateness of judicial intervention. Which factors predominate in the case that follows?

_____

Nixon v. United States
506 U.S. 224, 113 S.Ct. 732, 122 L.Ed.2d 1 (1993).
Certiorari to the United States Court of Appeals for the District of Columbia Circuit.

■ CHIEF JUSTICE REHNQUIST delivered the opinion of the Court.

Petitioner Walter L. Nixon, Jr., asks this court to decide whether Senate Rule XI, which allows a committee of Senators to hear evidence against an individual who has been impeached and to report that evidence to the full Senate, violates the Impeachment Trial Clause, Art. I, § 3, cl. 6. That Clause provides that the "Senate shall have the sole Power to try all Impeachments." But before we reach the merits of such a claim, we must decide whether it is "justiciable," that is, whether it is a claim that may be resolved by the courts. We conclude that it is not.

Nixon, a former Chief Judge of the United States District Court for the Southern District of Mississippi, was convicted by a jury of two counts of making false statements before a federal grand jury and sentenced to prison. * * * The grand jury investigation stemmed from reports that Nixon had accepted a gratuity from a Mississippi businessman in exchange for asking a local district attorney to halt the prosecution of the businessman's son. Because Nixon refused to resign from his office as a United States District Judge, he continued to collect his judicial salary while serving out his prison sentence. * * *

On May 10, 1989, the House of Representatives adopted three articles of impeachment for high crimes and misdemeanors. The first two articles charged Nixon with giving false testimony before the grand jury and the third article charged him with bringing disrepute on the Federal Judiciary. * * *

After the House presented the articles to the Senate, the Senate voted to invoke its own Impeachment Rule XI, under which the presiding officer appoints a committee of Senators to "receive evidence and take testimony." The Senate committee held four days of hearings, during which 10 witnesses, including Nixon, testified. * * * Pursuant to Rule XI, the committee presented the full Senate with a complete transcript of the proceeding and a report stating the uncontested facts and summarizing the evidence on the contested facts. * * * Nixon and the House impeachment managers submitted extensive final briefs to the full Senate and delivered arguments from the Senate floor during the three hours set aside for oral argument in front of that body. Nixon himself gave a personal appeal, and several Senators posed questions directly to both parties. * * * The Senate voted by more than the constitutionally required two-thirds majority to convict Nixon on the first two articles. * * * The presiding officer then entered judgment removing Nixon from his office as United States District Judge.

Nixon thereafter commenced the present suit, arguing that Senate Rule XI violates the constitutional grant of authority to the Senate to "try" all impeachments because it prohibits the whole Senate from taking part in the evidentiary hearings. See Art. I, § 3, cl. 6. Nixon sought a declaratory judgment that his impeachment conviction was void and that his judicial salary and privileges should be reinstated. The District Court held that his claim was nonjusticiable, and the Court of Appeals for the District of Columbia Circuit agreed.

A controversy is nonjusticiable—*i.e.*, involves a political question— where there is "a textually demonstrable constitutional commitment of the issue to a coordinate political department; or a lack of judicially discoverable and manageable standards for resolving it. . . . " Baker v. Carr, 369 U.S. 186, 217 (1962). But the Courts must, in the first instance, interpret the text in question and determine whether and to what extent the issue is textually committed. See *ibid*; Powell v. McCormack, 395 U.S. 486 (1969). As the discussion that follows makes clear, the concept of a textual commitment to a coordinate political department is not completely separate from the concept of a lack of judicially discoverable and manageable standards for resolving it; the lack of judicially manageable standards may strengthen the conclusion that there is a textually demonstrable commitment to a coordinate branch.

In this case, we must examine Art. I, § 3, cl. 6, to determine the scope of authority conferred upon the Senate by the Framers regarding impeachment. It provides:

"The Senate shall have the sole Power to try all Impeachments. When sitting for the Purpose, they shall be on

Oath or Affirmation. When the President of the United States is tried, the Chief Justice shall preside: And no Person shall be convicted without the Concurrence of two thirds of the Members present."

The language and structure of this Clause are revealing. The first sentence is a grant of authority to the Senate, and the word "sole" indicates that this authority is reposed in the Senate and nowhere else. The next two sentences specify requirements to which the Senate proceedings shall conform: the Senate shall be on oath or affirmation, a two-thirds vote is required to convict, and when the President is tried the Chief Justice shall preside.

Petitioner argues that the word "try" in the first sentence imposes by implication an additional requirement on the Senate in that the proceedings must be in the nature of a judicial trial. From there petitioner goes on to argue that this limitation precludes the Senate from delegating to a select committee the task of hearing the testimony of witnesses, as was done pursuant to Senate Rule XI. " '[T]ry' means more than simply 'vote on' or 'review' or 'judge.' In 1787 and today, trying a case means hearing the evidence, not scanning a cold record." * * * Petitioner concludes from this that courts may review whether or not the Senate "tried" him before convicting him.

There are several difficulties with this position which lead us ultimately to reject it. The word "try," both in 1787 and later, has considerably broader meanings than those to which petitioner would limit it. Older dictionaries define try as "[t]o examine" or "[t]o examine as a judge." See 2 S. Johnson, A Dictionary of the English Language (1785). In more modern usages the term has various meanings. For example, try can mean "to examine or investigate judicially," "to conduct the trial of," or "to put to the test by experiment, investigation, or trial." Webster's Third New International Dictionary 2457 (1971). Petitioner submits that "try," as contained in T. Sheridan, Dictionary of the English Language (1796), means "to examine as a judge; to bring before a judicial tribunal." Based on the variety of definitions, however, we cannot say that the Framers used the word "try" as an implied limitation on the method by which the Senate might proceed in trying impeachments. "As a rule the Constitution speaks in general terms, leaving Congress to deal with subsidiary matters of detail as the public interests and changing conditions may require * * *." Dillon v. Gloss, 256 U.S. 368, 376 (1921).

The conclusion that the use of the word "try" in the first sentence of the Impeachment Trial Clause lacks sufficient precision to afford any judicially manageable standard of review of the Senate's actions is fortified by the existence of the three very specific requirements that the Constitution does impose on the Senate when trying impeachments: the members must be under oath, a two-thirds vote is required to convict, and the Chief Justice presides when the President is tried. These limitations are quite precise, and their nature suggests that the Framers did not intend to impose additional limitations on the form of the Senate proceedings by the use of the word "try" in the first sentence.

Petitioner devotes only two pages in his brief to negating the significance of the word "sole" in the first sentence of Clause 6. As noted above, that sentence provides that "[t]he Senate shall have the sole Power to try all Impeachments." We think that the word "sole" is of

"sole"

considerable significance. Indeed, the word "sole" appears only one other time in the Constitution—with respect to the House of Representatives' "*sole* Power of Impeachment." Art. I, § 2, cl. 5 (emphasis added). The common sense meaning of the word "sole" is that the Senate alone shall have authority to determine whether an individual should be acquitted or convicted. The dictionary definition bears this out. "Sole" is defined as "having no companion," "solitary," "being the only one," and "functioning * * * independently and without assistance or interference." Webster's Third New International Dictionary 2168 (1971). If the courts may review the actions of the Senate in order to determine whether that body "tried" an impeached official, it is difficult to see how the Senate would be "functioning * * * independently and without assistance or interference." * * *

The history and contemporary understanding of the impeachment provisions support our reading of the constitutional language. The parties do not offer evidence of a single word in the history of the Constitutional Convention or in contemporary commentary that even alludes to the possibility of judicial review in the context of the impeachment powers. * * * This silence is quite meaningful in light of the several explicit references to the availability of judicial review as a check on the Legislature's power with respect to bills of attainder, *ex post facto* laws, and statutes. See The Federalist No. 78, p. 524 (J. Cooke ed. 1961) ("Limitations . . . can be preserved in practice no other way than through the medium of the courts of justice.").

The Framers labored over the question of where the impeachment power should lie. Significantly, in at least two considered scenarios the power was placed with the Federal Judiciary. Indeed, Madison and the Committee of Detail proposed that the Supreme Court should have the power to determine impeachments. Despite these proposals, the Convention ultimately decided that the Senate would have "the sole Power to Try all Impeachments." Art. I § 3, cl. 6. According to Alexander Hamilton, the Senate was the "most fit depository of this important trust" because its members are representatives of the people. See The Federalist No. 65, p. 440 (J. Cooke ed. 1961). The Supreme Court was not the proper body because the Framers "doubted whether the members of that tribunal would, at all times, be endowed with so eminent a portion of fortitude as would be called for in the execution of so difficult a task" or whether the Court "would possess the degree of credit and authority" to carry out its judgment if it conflicted with the accusation brought by the Legislature—the people's representative. See *id.*, at 441. In addition, the Framers believed the Court was too small in number: "The awful discretion, which a court of impeachments must necessarily have, to doom to honor or to infamy the most confidential and the most distinguished characters of the community, forbids the commitment of the trust to a small number of persons." *Id.*, at 441–442.

There are two additional reasons why the Judiciary, and the Supreme Court in particular, were not chosen to have any role in impeachments. First, the Framers recognized that most likely there would be two sets of proceedings for individuals who commit impeachable offenses—the impeachment trial and a separate criminal trial. In fact, the Constitution explicitly provides for two separate proceedings. See

Art. I, § 3, cl. 7. The Framers deliberately separated the two forums to avoid raising the specter of bias and to ensure independent judgments:

> "Would it be proper that the persons, who had disposed of his fame and his most valuable rights as a citizen in one trial, should in another trial, for the same offence, be also the disposers of his life and his fortune? Would there not be the greatest reason to apprehend, that error in the first sentence would be the parent of error in the second sentence? That the strong bias of one decision would be apt to overrule the influence of any new lights, which might be brought to vary the complexion of another decision?" The Federalist No. 65, p. 442 (J. Cooke ed. 1961).

Certainly judicial review of the Senate's "trial" would introduce the same risk of bias as would participation in the trial itself.

Second, judicial review would be inconsistent with the Framers' insistence that our system be one of checks and balances. In our constitutional system, impeachment was designed to be the *only* check on the Judicial Branch by the Legislature. * * *

Judicial involvement in impeachment proceedings, even if only for purposes of judicial review, is counterintuitive because it would eviscerate the "important constitutional check" placed on the Judiciary by the Framers. See *id.*, No. 81, p. 545. Nixon's argument would place final reviewing authority with respect to impeachments in the hands of the same body that the impeachment process is meant to regulate.

Nevertheless, Nixon argues that judicial review is necessary in order to place a check on the Legislature. Nixon fears that if the Senate is given unreviewable authority to interpret the Impeachment Trial Clause, there is a grave risk that the Senate will usurp judicial power. The Framers anticipated this objection and created two constitutional safeguards to keep the Senate in check. The first safeguard is that the whole of the impeachment power is divided between the two legislative bodies, with the House given the right to accuse and the Senate given the right to judge. *Id.*, No. 66, p. 446. This split of authority "avoids the inconvenience of making the same persons both accusers and judges; and guards against the danger of persecution from the prevalency of a factious spirit in either of those branches." The second safeguard is the two-thirds supermajority vote requirement. Hamilton explained that "[a]s the concurrence of two-thirds of the senate will be requisite to a condemnation, the security to innocence, from this additional circumstance, will be as complete as itself can desire." *Ibid.*

In addition to the textual commitment argument, we are persuaded that the lack of finality and the difficulty of fashioning relief counsel against justiciability. See Baker v. Carr, 369 U.S., at 210. We agree with the Court of Appeals that opening the door of judicial review to the procedures used by the Senate in trying impeachments would "expose the political life of the country to months, or perhaps years, of chaos." * * * This lack of finality would manifest itself most dramatically if the President were impeached. The legitimacy of any successor, and hence his effectiveness, would be impaired severely, not merely while the judicial process was running its course, but during any retrial that a differently constituted Senate might conduct if its first judgment of conviction were invalidated. Equally uncertain is the question of what relief a court may give other than simply setting aside the judgment of conviction. Could it order the reinstatement of a convicted federal judge, or order Congress to create an additional judgeship if the seat had been filled in the interim?

Petitioner finally contends that a holding of nonjusticiability cannot be reconciled with our opinion in Powell v. McCormack, [*supra*]. The relevant issue in Powell was whether courts could review the House of Representatives' conclusion that Powell was "unqualified" to sit as a Member because he had been accused of misappropriating public funds and abusing the process of the New York courts. We stated that the question of justiciability turned on whether the Constitution committed authority to the House to judge its members' qualifications, and if so, the extent of that commitment. 395 U.S. at 519, 521. Article I, § 5 provides that "Each House shall be the Judge of the Elections, Returns and Qualifications of its own Members." In turn, Art. I, § 2 specifies three requirements for membership in the House: The candidate must be at least 25 years of age, a citizen of the United States for no less than seven years, and an inhabitant of the State he is chosen to represent. We held that, in light of the three requirements specified in the Constitution, the word "qualifications"—of which the House was to be the Judge—was of a precise, limited nature. *Id.*, at 522.

Our conclusion in Powell was based on the fixed meaning of "[q]ualifications" set forth in Art. I, § 2. The claim by the House that its power to "be the Judge of the Elections, Returns and Qualifications of its own Members" was a textual commitment of unreviewable authority was defeated by the existence of this separate provision specifying the only qualifications which might be imposed for House membership. The decision as to whether a member satisfied these qualifications *was* placed with the House, but the decision as to what these qualifications consisted of was not.

In the case before us, there is no separate provision of the Constitution which could be defeated by allowing the Senate final authority to determine the meaning of the word "try" in the Impeachment Trial Clause. We agree with Nixon that courts possess power to review either legislative or executive action that transgresses identifiable textual limits. As we have made clear, "whether the action of [either the Legislative or Executive Branch] exceeds whatever authority has been committed, is itself a delicate exercise in constitutional interpretation, and is a responsibility of this Court as ultimate interpreter of the Constitution." Baker v. Carr, *supra*, 369 U.S., at 211; accord, Powell, *supra*, 395 U.S., at 521. But we conclude, after exercising that delicate responsibility, that the word "try" in the Impeachment Clause does not provide an identifiable textual limit on the authority which is committed to the Senate.

For the foregoing reasons, the judgment of the Court of Appeals is

Affirmed.

■ JUSTICE STEVENS, concurring.

* * *

■ JUSTICE WHITE, with whom JUSTICE BLACKMUN joins, concurring in the judgment.

Petitioner contends that the method by which the Senate convicted him on two articles of impeachment violates Art. I, § 3, cl. 6 of the Constitution, which mandates that the Senate "try" impeachments. The Court is of the view that the Constitution forbids us even to consider his contention. I find no such prohibition and would therefore reach the merits of the claim. I concur in the judgment because the Senate fulfilled its constitutional obligation to "try" petitioner.

I

It should be said at the outset that, as a practical matter, it will likely make little difference whether the Court's or my view controls this case. This is so because the Senate has very wide discretion in specifying impeachment trial procedures and because it is extremely unlikely that the Senate would abuse its discretion and insist on a procedure that could not be deemed a trial by reasonable judges. Even taking a wholly practical approach, I would prefer not to announce unreviewable discretion in the Senate to ignore completely the constitutional direction to "try" impeachment cases. When asked at oral argument whether that direction would be satisfied if, after a House vote to impeach, the Senate, without any procedure whatsoever, unanimously found the accused guilty of being "a bad guy," counsel for the United States answered that the Government's theory "leads me to answer that question yes." Especially in light of this advice from the Solicitor General, I would not issue an invitation to the Senate to find an excuse, in the name of other pressing business, to be dismissive of its critical role in the impeachment process.

Practicalities aside, however, since the meaning of a constitutional provision is at issue, my disagreement with the Court should be stated.

II

The majority states that the question raised in this case meets two of the criteria for political questions set out in Baker, [supra]. It concludes first that there is "a textually demonstrable constitutional commitment of the issue to a coordinate political department." It also finds that the question cannot be resolved for "a lack of judicially discoverable and manageable standards." * * *

Of course the issue in the political question doctrine is not whether the Constitutional text commits exclusive responsibility for a particular governmental function to one of the political branches. There are numerous instances of this sort of textual commitment, e.g., Art. I, § 8, and it is not thought that disputes implicating these provisions are nonjusticiable. Rather, the issue is whether the Constitution has given one of the political branches final responsibility for interpreting the scope and nature of such a power. * * *

A

The majority finds a clear textual commitment in the Constitution's use of the word "sole" in the phrase "the Senate shall have the sole Power to try all impeachments." Art. I, § 3, cl. 6. It attributes "considerable significance" to the fact that this term appears in only one other passage in the Constitution. * * *

In disagreeing with the Court, I note that the Solicitor General stated at oral argument that "[w]e don't rest our submission on sole power to try." The Government was well advised in this respect. The significance of the Constitution's use of the term "sole" lies not in the infrequency with which the term appears, but in the fact that it appears exactly twice, in parallel provisions concerning impeachment. That the word "sole" is found only in the House and Senate Impeachment Clauses demonstrates that its purpose is to emphasize the distinct role of each in the impeachment process. As the majority notes, the Framers, following English practice, were very much concerned to separate the prosecutorial from the adjudicative aspects of impeachment. * * * Giving each House "sole" power with respect to its role in impeachments effected this division of labor. While the majority is thus right to interpret the term "sole" to indicate that the Senate ought to "functio[n] independently and without assistance or interference," it wrongly identifies the judiciary, rather than the House, as the source of potential interference with which the Framers were concerned when they employed the term "sole."

Even if the Impeachment Trial Clause is read without regard to its companion clause, the Court's willingness to abandon its obligation to review the constitutionality of legislative acts merely on the strength of the word "sole" is perplexing. Consider, by comparison, the treatment of Art. I, § 1, which grants "All legislative powers" to the House and Senate. As used in that context "all" is nearly synonymous with "sole"—both connote entire and exclusive authority. Yet the Court has never thought it would unduly interfere with the operation of the Legislative Branch to entertain difficult and important questions as to the extent of the legislative power. * * *

The historical evidence reveals above all else that the Framers were deeply concerned about placing in any branch the "awful discretion, which a court of impeachments must necessarily have." The Federalist No. 65, p. 441 (J. Cooke ed. 1961). Viewed against this history, the discord between the majority's position and the basic principles of checks and balances underlying the Constitution's separation of powers is clear. In essence, the majority suggests that the Framers conferred upon Congress a potential tool of legislative dominance yet at the same time rendered Congress' exercise of that power one of the very few areas of legislative authority immune from any judicial review. While the majority rejects petitioner's justiciability argument as espousing a view "inconsistent with the Framers' insistence that our system be one of checks and balances," it is the Court's finding of nonjusticiability that truly upsets the Framers' careful design. In a truly balanced system, impeachments tried by the Senate would serve as a means of controlling the largely unaccountable judiciary, even as judicial review would ensure that the Senate adhered to a minimal set of procedural standards in conducting impeachment trials.

B

The majority also contends that the term "try" does not present a judicially manageable standard. It notes that in 1787, as today, the word "try" may refer to an inquiry in the nature of a judicial proceeding, or, more generally, to experimentation or investigation. * * *

Th[e] argument * * * that one simply cannot ascertain the sense of "try" which the Framers employed and hence cannot undertake judicial review, is clearly untenable. To begin with, one would intuitively expect that, in defining the power of a political body to conduct an inquiry into official wrongdoing, the Framers used "try" in its legal sense. That intuition is borne out by reflection on the alternatives. The third clause of Art. I, § 3 cannot seriously be read to mean that the Senate shall "attempt" or "experiment with" impeachments. It is equally implausible to say that the Senate is charged with "investigating" impeachments given that this description would substantially overlap with the House of Representatives' "sole" power to draw up articles of impeachment. Art. I, § 2, cl. 5. That these alternatives are not realistic possibilities is finally evidenced by the use of "tried" in the third sentence of the Impeachment Trial Clause ("[w]hen the President of the United States is tried * * *"), and by Art. III, § 2, cl. 3 ("[t]he Trial of all Crimes, except in Cases of Impeachment * * *").

The other variant of the majority position focuses not on which sense of "try" is employed in the Impeachment Trial Clause, but on whether the legal sense of that term creates a judicially manageable standard. The majority concludes that the term provides no "identifiable textual limit." Yet, as the Government itself conceded at oral argument, the term "try" is hardly so elusive as the majority would have it. Were the Senate, for example, to adopt the practice of automatically entering a judgment of conviction whenever articles of impeachment were delivered from the House, it is quite clear that the Senate will have failed to "try" impeachments. Indeed in this respect, "try" presents no greater, and perhaps fewer, interpretive difficulties than some other constitutional standards that have been found amenable to familiar techniques of judicial construction, including, for example, "Commerce * * * among the several States," Art. I, § 8, cl. 3, and "due process of law." Amdt. 5.[3]

III

The majority's conclusion that "try" is incapable of meaningful judicial construction is not without irony. One might think that if any class of concepts would fall within the definitional abilities of the judiciary, it would be that class having to do with procedural justice. Examination of the remaining question—whether proceedings in accordance with Senate Rule XI are compatible with the Impeachment Trial Clause—confirms this intuition.

Petitioner bears the rather substantial burden of demonstrating that, simply by employing the word "try," the Constitution prohibits the Senate from relying on a factfinding committee. It is clear that the Framers were familiar with English impeachment practice and with that

---

[3] The majority's *in terrorem* argument against justiciability—that judicial review of impeachments might cause national disruption and that the courts would be unable to fashion effective relief—merits only brief attention. In the typical instance, court review of impeachments would no more render the political system dysfunctional than has this litigation. Moreover, the same capacity for disruption was noted and rejected as a basis for not hearing Powell, [*supra*], at 549. The relief granted for unconstitutional impeachment trials would presumably be similar to the relief granted to other unfairly tried public employee-litigants. Finally, as applied to the special case of the President, the majority's argument merely points out that, were the Senate to convict the President without any kind of a trial, a constitutional crisis might well result. It hardly follows that the Court ought to refrain from upholding the Constitution in all impeachment cases. Nor does it follow that, in cases of Presidential impeachment, the Justices ought to abandon their Constitutional responsibilities because the Senate has precipitated a crisis.

of the States employing a variant of the English model at the time of the Constitutional Convention. Hence there is little doubt that the term "try" as used in Art. I, § 3, cl. 6 meant that the Senate should conduct its proceedings in a manner somewhat resembling a judicial proceeding. Indeed, it is safe to assume that Senate trials were to follow the practice in England and the States, which contemplated a formal hearing on the charges, at which the accused would be represented by counsel, evidence would be presented, and the accused would have the opportunity to be heard.

Petitioner argues, however, that because committees were not used in state impeachment trials prior to the Convention, the word "try" cannot be interpreted to permit their use. It is, however, a substantial leap to infer from the absence of a particular device of parliamentary procedure that its use has been forever barred by the Constitution. And there is textual and historical evidence that undermines the inference sought to be drawn in this case. * * *

[That] evidence reveals that the Impeachment Trial Clause was not meant to bind the hands of the Senate beyond establishing a set of minimal procedures. Without identifying the exact contours of these procedures, it is sufficient to say that the Senate's use of a factfinding committee under Rule XI is entirely compatible with the Constitution's command that the Senate "try all impeachments." Petitioner's challenge to his conviction must therefore fail.

IV

Petitioner has not asked the Court to conduct his impeachment trial; he has asked instead that it determine whether his impeachment was tried by the Senate. The majority refuses to reach this determination out of a laudable respect for the authority of the legislature. Regrettably, this concern is manifested in a manner that does needless violence to the Constitution.[4] The deference that is owed can be found in the Constitution itself, which provides the Senate ample discretion to determine how best to try impeachments.

---

[4] Although our views might well produce identical results in most cases, the same objection may be raised against the prudential version of the political question doctrine presented by Justice Souter. According to the prudential view, judicial determination of whether the Senate has conducted an impeachment trial would interfere unacceptably with the Senate's work and should be avoided except where necessitated by the threat of grave harm to the constitutional order. As articulated, this position is missing its premise: no explanation is offered as to why it would show disrespect or cause disruption or embarrassment to review the action of the Senate in this case as opposed to, say, the enactment of legislation under the Commerce Clause. * * *

In any event, the prudential view cannot achieve its stated purpose. The judgment it wishes to avoid—and the attendant disrespect and embarrassment—will inevitably be cast because the courts still will be required to distinguish cases on their merits. Justice Souter states that the Court ought not to entertain petitioner's constitutional claim because "[i]t seems fair to conclude," that the Senate tried him. In other words, on the basis of a preliminary determination that the Senate has acted within the "broad boundaries" of the Impeachment Trial Clause, it is concluded that we must refrain from making that determination. At best, this approach offers only the illusion of deference and respect by substituting impressionistic assessment for constitutional analysis.

■ JUSTICE SOUTER, concurring in the judgment. ("Soft" pol. q. doctrine.)

I agree with the Court that this case presents a nonjusticiable political question. Because my analysis differs somewhat from the Court's, however, I concur in its judgment by this separate opinion.

As we cautioned in Baker v. Carr, [*supra*, at] 210–211, "the 'political question' label" tends "to obscure the need for case-by-case inquiry." The need for such close examination is nevertheless clear from our precedents, which demonstrate that the functional nature of the political question doctrine requires analysis of "the precise facts and posture of the particular case," and precludes "resolution by any semantic cataloguing," *id.*, at 217. * * *

Whatever considerations feature most prominently in a particular case, the political question doctrine is "essentially a function of the separation of powers," *ibid.*, existing to restrain courts "from inappropriate interference in the business of the other branches of Government," United States v. Munoz-Flores, 495 U.S. 385, 394 (1990), and deriving in large part from prudential concerns about the respect we owe the political departments. See Goldwater v. Carter, 444 U.S. 996, 1000 (1979) (Powell, J., concurring in the judgment); A. Bickel, The Least Dangerous Branch 125–126 (2d ed.1986); Finkelstein, Judicial Self-Limitation, 37 Harv.L.Rev. 338, 344–345 (1924). Not all interference is inappropriate or disrespectful, however, and application of the doctrine ultimately turns, as Learned Hand put it, on "how importunately the occasion demands an answer." L. Hand, The Bill of Rights 15 (1958).

This occasion does not demand an answer. The Impeachment Trial Clause commits to the Senate "the sole Power to try all Impeachments," subject to three procedural requirements: the Senate shall be on oath or affirmation; the Chief Justice shall preside when the President is tried; and conviction shall be upon the concurrence of two-thirds of the Members present. U.S. Const., Art. I, § 3, cl. 6. It seems fair to conclude that the Clause contemplates that the Senate may determine, within broad boundaries, such subsidiary issues as the procedures for receipt and consideration of evidence necessary to satisfy its duty to "try" impeachments. Other significant considerations confirm a conclusion that this case presents a nonjusticiable political question: the "unusual need for unquestioning adherence to a political decision already made," as well as "the potentiality of embarrassment from multifarious pronouncements by various departments on one question." Baker, *supra*, 369 U.S., at 217. As the Court observes, * * * judicial review of an impeachment trial would under the best of circumstances entail significant disruption of government.

One can, nevertheless, envision different and unusual circumstances that might justify a more searching review of impeachment proceedings. If the Senate were to act in a manner seriously threatening the integrity of its results, convicting, say, upon a coin-toss, or upon a summary determination that an officer of the United States was simply "a bad guy," (White, J., concurring in the judgment), judicial interference might well be appropriate. In such circumstances, the Senate's action might be so far beyond the scope of its constitutional authority, and the consequent impact on the Republic so great, as to merit a judicial response despite the prudential concerns that would ordinarily counsel silence. "The political question doctrine, a tool for maintenance of governmental order, will not be so applied as to promote only disorder." Baker, *supra*, at 215.

NOTE ON POLITICAL QUESTIONS

(1) Political Questions and the Judicial Function. What, exactly, did the Supreme Court mean in dismissing Nixon's lawsuit as raising a "political question"? Nixon's standing was not in question. He presented a live controversy, which was neither moot nor unripe, and there was no lack of adverse parties. How does the political question relate to Marbury v. Madison, p. 59, *supra*, and its assertions that it is "the province and duty of the judicial department to say what the law is" and that for every violation of a vested right there should be a legal remedy?[1]

Note that in Marbury, Chief Justice Marshall suggested that questions should be deemed "political", and therefore not subject to judicial review, if non-judicial officials possessed "discretion". Does the political question doctrine refer only to questions that are "political" in this sense? If so, a judicial holding that a suit was governed by the political question doctrine would amount to a decision that no "legal" rights of the plaintiff had been violated—that the challenged action lay within the legal discretion of the officials who took it.

To some extent, competing views of the political question doctrine mirror debates about whether doctrines such as standing or ripeness, in fact, represent implicit judgments about the merits of the underlying legal disputes or, instead, more purely reflect inferences about the reach of Article III power. Hence, one prominent conception—the "classical" position—maintains that political question decisions, properly understood, consist of a series of interpretations of the substantive meaning of particular clauses of the Constitution. The leading exponent of that position, Herbert Wechsler, thus wrote: "[A]ll the [political question] doctrine can defensibly imply is that the courts are called upon to judge whether the Constitution has committed to another agency of government the autonomous determination of the issue raised, a finding that itself requires an interpretation. * * * [T]he only proper judgment that may lead to an abstention from decision is that the Constitution has committed the determination of the issue to another agency of government than the courts. Difficult as it may be to make that judgment wisely, whatever factors may be rightly weighed in situations where the answer is not clear, what is involved is in itself an act of constitutional interpretation, to be made and judged by standards that should govern the interpretive process generally. That, I submit, is *toto caelo* different from a broad [judicial] discretion to abstain or intervene." See Wechsler, Principles, Politics and Fundamental Law 11–14 (1961).

A competing theory—the "prudential" position—is associated with Alexander Bickel, who argued that the political question doctrine, in fact, appropriately reflects prudential concerns about the exercise of judicial power. Bickel wrote: "[O]nly by means of a play on words can the broad discretion that the courts have in fact exercised be turned into an act of

---

[1] For an argument that the political question doctrine cannot be reconciled with the judicial function as it has descended from Marbury and should therefore be abandoned, see Redish, *Judicial Review and the "Political Question"*, 79 Nw.U.L.Rev. 1031 (1985).

constitutional interpretation governed by the general standards of the interpretive process. The political-question doctrine simply resists being domesticated in this fashion. There is * * * something different about it, in kind not in degree; something greatly more flexible, something of prudence, not construction and not principle. And it is something that cannot exist within the four corners of Marbury v. Madison. * * *

"Such is the foundation, in both intellect and instinct, of the political-question doctrine: the Court's sense of lack of capacity, compounded in unequal parts of (a) the strangeness of the issue and its intractability to principled resolution; (b) the sheer momentousness of it, which tends to unbalance judicial judgment; (c) the anxiety, not so much that the judicial judgment will be ignored, as that perhaps it should but will not be; (d) finally ('in a mature democracy'), the inner vulnerability, the self-doubt of an institution which is electorally irresponsible and has no earth to draw strength from." Bickel, The Least Dangerous Branch 125–26, 184 (1962).

In Bickel's view, a fundamental problem of American constitutionalism lies in the necessity to reconcile adherence to principle, on which the legitimacy of judicial review depends, with the demands of sensible, prudent governance. He thought he found the key in a distinction between judicial judgments on the merits, which he argued must be unyieldingly principled, and determinations of justiciability, which he thought could and should turn largely on prudential concerns. Are both the Wechsler and Bickel positions reflected in the various opinions in Nixon? Properly so?[2]

Although they are perhaps the two most prominent theories of the political question doctrine, the classical and prudential theories do not, of course, exhaust the field. Professor Scharpf, for example, offered a functional theory that explains the doctrine in terms of "the Court's acknowledgment of the limitations of the American judicial process." Scharpf, *Judicial Review and the Political Question: A Functional Analysis*, 75 Yale L.J. 517, 566 (1966). The factors relevant under that theory include, but are not limited to, the difficulty of securing the information needed "to assure the correct determination of particular issues" or the need for inter-branch uniformity "when the Court would have to question the position taken by the government in an international dispute." *Id.* Another significant position, advanced by Professor Henkin, is that the political question doctrine is "an unnecessary, deceptive packaging of several established doctrines" whose "proper content" relates to such matters as the obligation of the courts to "accept decisions by the political branches within their constitutional authority" and the ability of the courts to "refuse some (or all) remedies for want of equity". Henkin, *Is There a Political Question Doctrine?*, 85 Yale L.J. 597, 622–23 (1976).[3]

---

[2] Compare Brown, *When Political Questions Affect Individual Rights: The Other Nixon v. United States*, 1993 Sup.Ct.Rev. 125, 126 which argues that the the Court should not invoke the political question doctrine to foreclose judicial review of a separation-of-powers question implicating individual rights.

[3] For other accounts of the political question doctrine, see, *e.g.*, Choper, *The Political Question Doctrine: Suggested Criteria*, 54 Duke L.J. 1457 (2005); Field, *The Doctrine of Political Questions in the Federal Courts*, 8 Minn.L.Rev 485 (1924); Finkelstein, *Further Notes on Judicial Self-Limitation*, 39 Harv.L.Rev. 338 (1924); Seidman, *The Secret Life of the Political Question Doctrine*, 37 J. Marshall L.Rev. 441 (2004); Tushnet, *Law and Prudence in the Law of Justiciability: The Transformation of the Political Question Doctrine*, 80 N.C.L.Rev. 1203 (2002); Weston, *Political Questions*, 38 Harv.L.Rev. 296 (1925).

(2) Baker v. Carr. A leading modern political question case is Baker v. Carr, 369 U.S. 186 (1962), which the Court applied in Nixon. Baker presented the question whether an equal protection challenge to the apportionment of the Tennessee legislature raised a nonjusticiable political question. At the time the suit was brought, representation in both houses of the legislature was based on an apportionment scheme adopted in 1901. Since then, population shifts had resulted in gross imbalances in the number of voters in various districts, with the result that even a substantial majority of the state's voters might fail to elect a majority in the legislature. At least partly as a consequence, every political effort to procure reapportionment had failed. As Justice Clark wrote in a concurring opinion: "The majority of voters have been caught up in a legislative strait jacket. * * * [The existing apportionment scheme] has riveted the present seats in the assembly to their respective constituencies, and by the votes of their incumbents a reapportionment of any kind is prevented."

In Colegrove v. Green, 328 U.S. 549 (1946), a narrowly divided Supreme Court had found that a challenge to congressional districting in Illinois, based on the Guarantee Clause, presented a nonjusticiable political question. Districting questions, the Court reasoned, were questions of political power and thus "not fit for judicial determination".[4]

In Baker, the Court distinguished Colegrove on the ground that it was a Guarantee Clause case, which had no relevance to a suit under the Equal Protection Clause. "Judicial standards under the Equal Protection Clause", Justice Brennan wrote, "are well developed and familiar".

In a dissenting opinion joined by Justice Harlan, Justice Frankfurter charged that Baker presented "a Guarantee Clause claim masquerading under a different label". In his view, the Equal Protection Clause provided no clearer standards for apportioning electoral power than did the Guarantee Clause. For a court to enter the dispute without such standards would embroil the judicial process in politics and threaten judicial legitimacy. Justice Harlan, in a separate dissenting opinion also joined by Justice Frankfurter, argued that Tennessee's apportionment scheme offended no applicable constitutional standard and that the plaintiffs had therefore failed to state a valid claim on the merits. Were the dissenting opinions of Justices Frankfurter and Harlan, each joined by the other, mutually consistent?

At the time Baker was decided, numerous commentators echoed Justice Frankfurter's concerns that the Supreme Court had plunged into a political thicket and put its legitimacy at risk. Although these criticisms did not immediately abate with the pronouncement of the Warren Court's "one person, one vote" formula, see Reynolds v. Sims, 377 U.S. 533 (1964), that formula proved reasonably manageable in practice. Was this formula itself a result of the inability of the majority to discern or agree on any judicially manageable standard short of substantial arithmetical equality?

Baker v. Carr is notable, among other things, for its canvas of prior political question decisions. The Court began by identifying entire subject areas in which challenges to congressional or executive authority had

---

[4] In several cases, however, the Supreme Court had upheld judicial challenges to alleged racial discrimination in the drawing of election districts and in the organization of state political parties. See, e.g., Gomillion v. Lightfoot, 364 U.S. 339 (1960) (drawing of political boundaries to disenfranchise African-Americans); Terry v. Adams, 345 U.S. 461 (1953) (discrimination by political party); Smith v. Allwright, 321 U.S. 649 (1944) (same).

sometimes been thought to raise non-justiciable political questions: foreign relations, questions involving dates of duration of hostilities, the formal validity of legislative enactments, the status of the Native American tribes, and questions about whether a republican form of government exists in the states. But the categorical divides were misleading, the Court concluded. "Much of the confusion results from the capacity of the 'political question' label to obscure the need for case-by-case inquiry." From its survey, the Court distilled a list of governing criteria:

> "Prominent on the surface of any case held to involve a political question is found a textually demonstrable constitutional commitment of the issue to a coordinate political department; or a lack of judicially discoverable and manageable standards for resolving it; or the impossibility of deciding without an initial policy determination of a kind clearly for nonjudicial discretion; or the impossibility of a court's undertaking independent resolution without expressing lack of the respect due coordinate branches of government; or an unusual need for unquestioning adherence to a political decision already made; or the potentiality of embarrassment from multifarious pronouncements by various departments on one question."

These criteria are frequently cited, as they were in Nixon v. United States, but the division over their applicability in that case was by no means unusual. No single criterion seems to control, and some appear to reflect the classical position ("textually demonstrable commitment", "lack of judicially discoverable or manageable standards") while others have a more prudential or functional feel to them (*e.g.*, "an unusual need for unquestioning adherence to a political decision already made" and "the potentiality of embarrassment from multifarious pronouncements by various departments on one question").

But the Baker factors may not lend themselves to such sharp categorical differentiation.[5] At the time the Court decided Baker, the prevailing approach to statutory interpretation—the Legal Process school—instructed interpreters to "assume, unless the contrary unmistakably appears, that the legislature was made up of reasonable persons pursuing reasonable purposes reasonably." Hart & Sacks, The Legal Process: Basic Problems in the Making and Application of Law 1378 (1958) (Eskridge & Frickey eds., 1994). The various Baker factors might be understood to represent a similar philosophical approach to interpreting the Constitution—an effort to identify the set of factors a reasonable founder would take into account in determining whether a particular clause, such as the Impeachment Clause, should be regarded as assigning exclusive interpretive authority, or at least broad discretion, over a particular question to one of the political branches.

(3) Textually Demonstrable Commitment to Another Branch. The Nixon majority found a "textually demonstrable constitutional commitment of the issue" presented "to a coordinate political department"—but only after conducting an inquiry into the "history and contemporary understanding of the impeachment provisions." Are those contextual considerations always necessary to make sense of the textual commitment factor?[6]

---

[5] For a broad-ranging critique of the political question doctrine, see Paulsen, *The Constitutional Power to Interpret International Law*, 118 Yale L.J. 1762, 1817–1823 (2009).

[6] Bradley & Morrison, *Historical Gloss and the Separation of Powers*, 126 Harv.L.Rev. 411, 429–430 (2012), argues that finding "a textually demonstrable constitutional commitment of [an] issue to a coordinate political department" often depends on an assessment of historical practice. For example, they explain, historical practice largely accounts for the constitutional

The notion of textual commitment may connote two distinct ideas. First, textual commitment, within the formulation of Marbury v. Madison, may serve as shorthand for describing the textual assignment of some significant element of "discretion" to another branch. On that view, even if the Impeachment Clause commits to the Senate "discretion" to decide how to "try" an impeachment, could the Senate's textually committed discretion plausibly be treated as constitutionally unbounded? (Recall Justice Souter's coin-toss example.) Second, textual commitment could suggest a constitutional assignment of exclusive interpretive authority to a branch other than the judiciary. On that view, the Nixon Court would have to accept the Senate's understanding of "try" as conclusive, even if the Court thinks it means something else.[7] Under both versions of textual commitment—the "discretion theory" and the "interpretive authority theory"—the Court's application of the political question doctrine still requires an interpretation of the underlying constitutional provision to determine where the relevant discretion or interpretive authority is vested. Does that process itself satisfy Marbury's requirement that the judiciary "say what the law is" in resolving cases or controversies? Compare Baker, Paragraph (2), *supra*, at 64: "Deciding whether a matter has in any measure been committed by the Constitution to another branch of government, or whether the action of that branch exceeds whatever authority has been committed, is itself a delicate exercise in constitutional interpretation, and is a responsibility of this Court as ultimate interpreter of the Constitution."

Compare Powell v. McCormack, 395 U.S. 486 (1969), which presented the question whether an unbounded discretion was conferred on the House of Representatives by Art. I, § 5, which provides that "Each House shall be the Judge of the * * * Qualifications of its own Members." At issue was whether Adam Clayton Powell, Jr. was constitutionally entitled to take the seat in the House of Representatives to which he had been elected. It was conceded that he met the age, citizenship, and residence requirements of Art. I, § 2, but he had been denied his seat by a House resolution on the basis of findings by a Select Committee that he "had asserted an unwarranted privilege and immunity from the processes of the courts of New York; that he had wrongfully diverted House funds for the use of others and himself; and that he had made false reports on expenditures of foreign currency to the Committee on House Administration." Together with some voters in his district, Powell sued for a declaration that his exclusion was unconstitutional (and for back salary).

Chief Justice Warren, for the Court, held that the claim did not present a political question. After a lengthy historical examination, he concluded that the provision of Art. I, § 5, is "at most a 'textually demonstrable commitment' to Congress to judge only the qualifications expressly set forth in the Constitution".[8]

---

principle that the Article II power to "receive Ambassadors" (U.S. Const. Art. II, § 3) also confers upon the President exclusive power to recognize foreign governments.

[7] For discussion of the two different approaches to textual commitment, see, *e.g.*, Redish, note 1, *supra*, at 1039–43; Seidman, note 3, *supra*, at 444–59.

[8] The Court also rejected several other arguments for concluding that the case presented a political question. Justice Stewart alone dissented on the ground that the case was moot.

For other cases involving claims of a textually demonstrable commitment to another branch, see, *e.g.*, INS v. Chadha, 462 U.S. 919, 940–43 (1983) (rejecting a claim that the constitutionality of a one-House veto of a suspension of deportation was a political question; the grant of power to Congress to "establish an uniform Rule of Naturalization" did not preclude the

In light of Powell, was Justice White correct that the Court in Nixon should have examined more carefully the constitutional bounds on the Senate's power? If courts always had to inquire into whether other branches had acted within the bounds of their constitutionally permissible discretion, wouldn't every political question argument collapse (as Professor Wechsler contends it should) into an argument on the merits about how the Constitution should be applied to a particular, challenged action by a non-judicial official?

(4) Judicially Manageable Standards. The Nixon Court observed that "the lack of judicially manageable standards may strengthen the conclusion that there is a textually demonstrable commitment to a coordinate branch." If the Court dismisses a case because it is unable to identify standards for evaluating the claimed invalidity of another branch's action, does that suggest that there is simply no law to apply and, thus, no basis for displacing a coordinate branch's judgment? Compare Citizens to Preserve Overton Park v. Volpe, 401 U.S. 402, 410 (1971) (holding that agency action is "committed to agency discretion" within the meaning of a statutory exception to the Administrative Procedure Act's reviewability provisions when the reviewing court finds "no law to apply").[9]

What if, to use Justice Souter's example, the Senate had "tried" Nixon by accepting the outcome of a coin-toss? Even under the majority's approach, wouldn't there be judicially manageable standards for determining that such a procedure lay beyond the outer boundaries of any plausible constitutional understanding of what it means to "try" someone?

The jurisprudence on partisan gerrymanders has produced an extended debate among the Justices over judicially manageable standards. In Davis v. Bandemer, 478 U.S. 109 (1986), the Court concluded that while no arithmetic formula was available to resolve such cases, the equal protection principles articulated in the Baker line of decisions, as well as in several racial gerrymandering cases, suggested that judicially manageable standards might be developed to address the question whether a gerrymander violates equal protection norms. After so holding, however, the six-member majority in Bandemer could not agree among themselves on what those standards should be. Justice O'Connor, joined by two other Justices, dissented on the ground that the question was a political one, due largely to the lack of manageable standards, since "the legislative business of apportionment is inherently a political affair". How much does Justice O'Connor's view depend on the conclusion that the Equal Protection Clause does not address the particular problem? Certainly, challenges to other forms of gerrymandering are justiciable. Compare Rogers v. Lodge, 458 U.S. 613 (1982) (racial gerrymandering claim is justiciable).

In Vieth v. Jubelirer, 541 U.S. 267 (2004), Justice Scalia's plurality opinion cited an absence of judicially manageable standards as its ground for

---

Court from considering whether Congress had chosen a permissible means of implementing that power); United States v. Nixon, 418 U.S. 683, 692–97 (1974) (rejecting the argument, in an action to enforce a subpoena against the President, that his claim of executive privilege raised a political question; the question was one arising in the regular course of a federal criminal prosecution and thus was "within the traditional scope of Art. III power"); Gilligan v. Morgan, 413 U.S. 1 (1973).

[9] Might the Court lack judicially manageable standards if there is law to apply but it is articulated at too high a level of abstraction? See Huq, *Removal as a Political Question*, 65 Stan.L.Rev. 1 (2013).

holding that a challenge to the political gerrymander of Pennsylvania voting districts presented a nonjusticiable political question. Writing for himself, Chief Justice Rehnquist, and Justices O'Connor and Thomas, Justice Scalia concluded that Bandemer had not led to the articulation of judicially manageable standards and should be overruled. He did not dispute that "severe partisan gerrymanders violate the Constitution", but he concluded that there were no constitutionally appropriate and judicially manageable standards for determining when state legislatures, which are entitled to give some weight to partisan considerations in designing voting districts, have gone "too far". The plurality opinion examined a number of possible tests and found each of them wanting.

Justice Kennedy concurred in the judgment ordering dismissal of the plaintiffs' challenge. He agreed with the plurality that no judicially manageable standard for identifying forbidden partisan gerrymanders "has emerged in this case", but he declined to pronounce partisan gerrymandering claims categorically non-justiciable: "[There] are * * * weighty arguments for holding cases like these to be nonjusticiable; and those arguments may prevail in the long run. In my view, however, the arguments are not so compelling that they require us now to bar all future claims of injury from a partisan gerrymander. * * * That no [adequate] standard has emerged in this case should not be taken to prove that none will emerge in the future."

Writing in dissent, Justice Stevens maintained that partisan gerrymanders should be scrutinized under the same framework that the Court found manageable in evaluating allegations of racial gerrymandering—including consideration of the irregularity of district lines, "the purpose behind the line drawing", "the process by which the districting schemes were enacted", and "other evidence demonstrating that purely improper considerations motivated the [line-drawing] decision". Justices Souter (joined by Justice Ginsburg) and Breyer also disagreed with the plurality about the absence of judicially manageable standards and indeed identified the (different) standards that they would apply.[10]

In the eyes of the plurality, the difficulty with Justice Stevens' proposed standard was not that it was judicially unmanageable, but that it was not "discernible in the Constitution". Are familiar judicial standards such as strict scrutiny and rational basis review, and the multi-part tests used to apply various constitutional provisions, "discernible in the Constitution", or are they better viewed as formulas devised by courts to implement the Constitution? Compare Reynolds v. Sims, p. 250, *supra*. If so, when the Court cites an absence of judicially manageable standards, is it simply acknowledging its own inability to craft standards that it regards as both sound and judicially manageable?[11]

(5) Respect for Coordinate Branches. A further consideration cited by Baker is "the impossibility of a court's undertaking independent resolution without expressing lack of the respect due coordinate branches of government." Is this criterion too conclusory to do independent work in identifying a political question?

---

[10] In League of United Latin American Citizens v. Perry, 548 U.S. 399 (2006), the Court divided once again about whether there are judicially manageable standards to gauge the constitutionality of partisan gerrymanders.

[11] For discussion of these and related questions, see Fallon, *Judicially Manageable Standards and Constitutional Meaning*, 119 Harv.L.Rev. 1274 (2006).

In United States v. Munoz-Flores, 495 U.S. 385 (1990), the Court considered on the merits a challenge to the validity of a provision of the Victims of Crime Act requiring those convicted of federal crimes to pay a special assessment to a Crime Victims Fund established by that Act. Munoz-Flores contended that the provision had originated in the Senate and therefore violated the requirement of the Origination Clause of the Constitution (Art. I, § 7, cl. 1) that "all Bills for raising Revenue shall originate in the House of Representatives." The Court rejected the position of the United States that the case presented a nonjusticiable political question. With respect to the suggestion that invalidation of a law on Origination Clause grounds would evidence a "lack of respect" for the House that passed the bill, the Court said: "[D]isrespect, in the sense the Government uses the term, cannot be sufficient to create a political question. If it were, *every* judicial resolution of a constitutional challenge to a congressional enactment would be impermissible. * * * Nor do the House's incentives to safeguard its origination prerogative obviate the need for judicial review. * * * [T]he fact that one institution of government has mechanisms available to guard against incursions into its power by other governmental institutions does not require that the judiciary remove itself from the controversy by labeling the issue a political question."

The Court then rejected the government's argument that judicial intervention was inappropriate since the case did not involve a question of individual rights. The argument, the Court said, is "simply irrelevant to the political question doctrine. * * * Furthermore, * * * [p]rovisions for separation of powers within the Legislative Branch are * * * *not* different in kind from provisions concerning relations between the branches: both sets of provisions safeguard liberty."[12]

On the merits, the Court held that, even if the bill did not originate in the House, it did not violate the Origination Clause because a statute that does not raise revenue to support government generally, but rather creates and raises revenue to support a particular program, is not a "Bill for raising Revenue."

Justice Stevens, joined by Justice O'Connor, concurred on the ground that a bill that passes both Houses and is signed by the President becomes law even if it originated unconstitutionally. Justice Scalia, also concurring, argued that any enacted law that bears an attestation that it originated in the House (as this law did) should "establish[ ] that fact as officially and authoritatively as it establishes the fact that its recited text was adopted by both Houses." Although neither concurring opinion rested in terms on the political question doctrine, both interpreted and applied the constitutional text in a manner that immunizes from judicial review certain actions of the legislature even when those actions violate the Constitution.

(6) Speaking with One Voice. In his concurring opinion in Nixon, Justice Souter noted that "significant considerations" suggested "the 'unusual need

---

[12] Compare Choper, Judicial Review and the National Political Process (1980), which contends that questions involving the proper relationship of Congress to the President (as well as questions involving the proper relationship between the states and the federal government) should be nonjusticiable. Professor Choper maintains that the political process is capable of protecting the relevant interests and that the courts should preserve their institutional capital for the protection of individual rights. See also Choper, note 3, *supra* (proposing functional criteria to guide application of the political question doctrine based on notions of comparative judicial competence).

Uniformity of pronouncements

for unquestioning adherence to a political decision already made,' as well as 'the potentiality of embarrassment from multifarious pronouncements by various departments on one question' " (quoting Baker v. Carr). He added, however, that such considerations might not carry the day "[i]f the Senate were to act in a manner seriously threatening the integrity of its results, convicting, say, upon a coin toss".

Consider Black, Impeachment: A Handbook 61–62 (1974): "If the Supreme Court [were] to order reinstatement of an impeached and convicted president, there would be, to say the least, a very grave and quite legitimate doubt whether that decree had any title to being obeyed, or whether it was [as] widely outside judicial jurisdiction as would be a judicial order to Congress to increase the penalty for counterfeiting. To cite the most frightening consequence, our military commanders would have to decide for themselves which president they were bound to obey, the reinstated one or his successor. * * * It would be most unfortunate if the notion got about that the Senate's verdict was somewhat tentative. * * * No senator should be encouraged to think he can shift to any court responsibility for an unpalatable or unpopular decision."[13]

Do functional concerns about the role of the judiciary in our constitutional scheme explain these grounds for forbearance? If so, from what source does this understanding of the judicial role derive?

def. to Congress

(7) Constitutional Challenges to Statutes. Zivotofsky v. Clinton, 132 S.Ct. 1421 (2012), suggests that the Court may be especially reluctant to find a political question where the question at issue is whether an Act of Congress is unconstitutional. Zivotofsky presented a question involving the constitutionality of Section 214(d) of the Foreign Relations Authorization Act, Fiscal Year 2003, 116 Stat. 1350, which provides that an American citizen born in Jerusalem may list Israel as his or her place of birth on a U.S. Passport. Given the contested status of that city, State Department policy had long provided that American citizens born in Jerusalem could list Jerusalem, but not Israel or Jordan, as their place of birth. Born in Jerusalem to American parents, Zivotofsky (through his parents) sued the Secretary of State under the statute, seeking to enjoin her to designate Israel as the place of birth on his passport. The court of appeals held that Zivotofsky's complaint presented a political question because the Constitution assigns the executive unreviewable discretion to recognize foreign sovereigns and because the State Department's determination fell within that power.

After describing the political question doctrine as a "narrow exception" to its presumptive duty to hear cases within its jurisdiction, the Supreme Court reversed. The Court focused only on the first two Baker factors—textual commitment of the question to a coordinate branch and the absence of judicially manageable standards. The Court reasoned that Zivotofsky's invocation of an Act of Congress made both of those criteria harder to establish. First, the Court argued that whether or not the President has exclusive authority to recognize foreign governments and thus to make appropriate designations on U.S. Passports, "there is, of course, no exclusive commitment to the Executive of the power to determine the constitutionality

---

[13] Compare Berger, Impeachment: The Constitutional Problems 103–21 (1973) (arguing, primarily in the context of non-presidential impeachment proceedings, that the scope and content of the terms "other high Crimes and Misdemeanors" in Art. II, § 4, is a question of law subject to judicial review).

of a statute." The judiciary, the Court made clear, must properly resolve any conflicts between Congress and the President over the contested allocation of power over passports.

Second, the Court suggested that if it had been asked to determine the political status of Jerusalem in the absence of a statute, it would have lacked judicially manageable standards to do so. But the problem "dissipate[d] * * * when the issue is recognized to be the more focused one of the [statute's] constitutionality." In arguing that the contested power lay exclusively with the President, the executive branch relied on the constitutional text, longstanding executive practice, congressional acquiescence in that practice, and judicial precedent. Zivotofsky, by contrast, contended that the power to designate a citizen's place of birth fell squarely within Congress' authority over immigration and foreign commerce, and that Congress had traditionally exercised extensive control over the form and content of passports. Relying on passages from the Federalist Papers, moreover, Zivotofsky argued that the recognition power is not exclusively executive and that, even if it were, designating a citizen's place of birth does not intrude on that power. After cataloguing (but not resolving) these competing arguments, the Court concluded that Zivotofsky's claims "sound in familiar principles of constitutional interpretation" and, while difficult, did not leave the Court without manageable standards.

Justice Sotomayor, joined in part by Justice Breyer, concurred in the judgment. She criticized the Court for failing to consider whether its assertion of jurisdiction would impinge on Baker's prudential factors, such as the need for the government to speak with one voice. She added that, in her view, the political question doctrine could, under proper circumstances, apply to a constitutional challenge to a statute. Finally, she noted that the Court should not have held that the case presented judicially manageable standards simply because the parties made textual, structural, and historical arguments—something that the parties in Nixon v. United States, p. 237, *supra*, had also done. She argued that when "parties' textual, structural, and historical evidence is inapposite or wholly unilluminating, rendering judicial decision no more than guesswork, a case relying on the ordinary kinds of arguments offered to courts might well still present justiciability concerns." Justice Breyer also dissented. Invoking the prudential Baker factors, he concluded that "this case is unusual both in its minimal need for judicial intervention and in its more serious risk that intervention will bring about 'embarrassment,' show lack of 'respect' for the other branches, and potentially disrupt sound foreign policy decisionmaking."

By framing the political question inquiry wholly in terms of the first two Baker factors—textual commitment and absence of judicially manageable standards—did Zivotofsky signal the Roberts Court's endorsement of Professor Wechsler's "classical" position over Professor Bickel's "prudential" one? Justice Sotomayor also accurately notes that the Court's test for a judicially manageable standard seems more forgiving in Zivotofsky than in Nixon, where the Court found a political question despite the availability of conventional textual, structural, and historical evidence about the nature of the Impeachment Power.

NOTE ON SPECIFIC SUBJECT MATTER AREAS IMPLICATING THE POLITICAL QUESTION DOCTRINE

(1) The Political Question Doctrine as Applied. The political question doctrine plays a recurring role in several subject matter areas. Even within these areas, relatively fine distinctions often seem to separate cases treated as nonjusticiable from cases adjudicated on the merits. When engaging in judicial review in an area potentially governed by the political question doctrine, the Court frequently does not even address the doctrine's applicability. See generally Barkow, *More Supreme Than Court? The Fall of the Political Question Doctrine and the Rise of Judicial Supremacy*, 102 Colum.L.Rev. 237 (2002). Do the diverse results in the subject matter areas discussed below suggest that the political question doctrine cannot be applied in a principled manner? Or does the variance merely suggest that the inquiry is fine-grained enough to produce different results in cases that have superficial similarities but that ultimately involve important differences in terms of textual commitment, judicially manageable standards, or relevant practical considerations?

(2) The Guarantee Clause. The leading early case on the political question doctrine, Luther v. Borden, 48 U.S. (7 How.) 1 (1849), involved Article IV, § 4, which provides that "[t]he United States shall guarantee to every State in the Union a Republican Form of Government". The case grew "out of the unfortunate political differences which agitated the people of Rhode Island in 1841 and 1842". Despite popular unrest with a "charter" government elected under a state constitution that predated the American Revolution, incumbent officials thwarted reform, and the "Dorr Rebellion" broke out. As an aspect of that rebellion, Dorr was elected governor under the purported authority of a new constitution adopted outside established legal forms. But his effort to take power by force was repulsed, and the charter government implemented martial law. The charter government did, finally, call a constitutional convention, and a new constitution was peaceably introduced in May of 1843.

Meantime, however, Borden and other state officers broke into the house of Luther, a Dorr supporter. When Luther sued for trespass, the forced entry was admitted. The claim turned on whether the defendants were lawfully authorized to enter. This, the plaintiff maintained, depended on whether the charter government was indeed, as the defendants asserted and the plaintiff denied, the lawfully constituted, "republican" government of Rhode Island at the time of the entry. Rejecting the plaintiff's demand that it inquire into the charter government's lawful authority under the Guarantee Clause, the lower court entered judgment for the defendants, and the Supreme Court affirmed.

In an opinion by Chief Justice Taney, the Supreme Court offered several reasons for holding the issue nonjusticiable, including the practical difficulties that would ensue if judicial challenges to the lawful authority of state governments were invited. The Court's holding was that the question presented was one for congressional, not judicial, resolution: "Congress must necessarily decide what government is established in the state before it can determine whether it is republican or not. And when the senators and representatives of a state are admitted into the councils of the Union, the authority of the government under which they are appointed, as well as its republican character, is recognized by the proper constitutional authority."

And its decision is binding on every other department of government, and could not be questioned in a judicial tribunal."

Since the Luther decision, the Supreme Court has never expressly found a Guarantee Clause claim to present a justiciable question, and indeed on several occasions has held such claims to be nonjusticiable. *E.g.*, Pacific States Tel. & Tel. Co. v. Oregon, 223 U.S. 118 (1912) (holding the question whether state laws enacted by initiative and referendum procedures were consistent with "republican" government to be nonjusticiable). Other decisions, however, are more ambiguous in their import. *E.g.*, Texas v. White, 74 U.S. (7 Wall.) 700 (1868) (a state engaged in rebellion against the Union in violation of the Constitution was depriving its citizens of a republican form of government);[1] Coyle v. Smith, 221 U.S. 559 (1911) (holding that Congress could not rely on the Guarantee Clause—or any other provision—as a basis for conditioning the entry of a state into the Union on the state's agreement to locate its capital in a particular city for at least a decade). Is there a good reason why all Guarantee Clause claims should be deemed political questions? Is the Guarantee Clause any less definite than the Equal Protection Clause to which the Baker Court shifted its analysis of reapportionment? See generally Symposium, *Guaranteeing a Republican Form of Government*, 65 Colo.L.Rev. 709 (1994).

(3) Constitutional Amendments. In Coleman v. Miller, 307 U.S. 433 (1939), the Court "affirmed" a judgment of the Supreme Court of Kansas refusing to restrain the Kansas Secretary of State from certifying that Kansas had ratified the Child Labor Amendment. Chief Justice Hughes, in an opinion for three Justices, said (a) that the question whether Kansas, once having rejected the amendment, could later ratify it was a question that Congress had the ultimate authority to decide, and (b) that while ratification of a proposed amendment must occur within a "reasonable time" after promulgation of the proposal, decision of that question was "essentially political and not justiciable. * * * In determining whether a question falls within that category [of political questions], the appropriateness under our system of government of attributing finality to the action of the political departments and also the lack of satisfactory criteria for a judicial determination are dominant considerations."

Justice Black, in an opinion for four Justices, said that "Congress has sole and complete control over the amending process, subject to no judicial review", and thus no opinion should be expressed even on the question whether ratification must take place within a reasonable time.[3]

---

[1]   The Court in White went on to say that it did not need to determine whether every step taken by Congress to restore the state government after the rebellion complied with the Guarantee Clause, because the power to effectuate that clause was "primarily" a legislative power. 74 U.S. at 730.

[2]   See generally Shapiro, Federalism: A Dialogue 21–22, 60–61, 110–13 (1995); Merritt, *The Guarantee Clause and State Autonomy: Federalism for a Third Century*, 88 Colum.L.Rev. 1 (1988); Bonfield, *The Guarantee Clause of Article IV, Section 4: A Study in Constitutional Desuetude*, 46 Minn.L.Rev. 513 (1962). Professor Shapiro contends that in New York v. United States, 505 U.S. 144 (1992), which held that Congress may not require states to adopt legislation providing nuclear waste disposal, the Court implied that the Guarantee Clause was relevant to its decision. See Shapiro, *supra*, at 68 n.46 (citing lower court cases relying on the Guarantee Clause as well).

[3]   Compare Professor Dellinger's argument for a substantially expanded judicial role in reviewing amending process issues, *The Legitimacy of Constitutional Change: Rethinking the Amendment Process*, 97 Harv.L.Rev. 386 (1983); Professor Tribe's reply, *A Constitution We Are*

Can Coleman be reconciled with the Court's earlier decision in Hawke v. Smith, 253 U.S. 221 (1920), which reviewed the constitutionality of a provision of the Ohio Constitution requiring that the state legislature's ratification of a federal constitutional amendment be subject to a popular referendum in the state. The Court held that Ohio's referendum provision contradicts the procedures for adopting constitutional amendments prescribed by Article V of the United States Constitution. Article V provides that when two thirds of each House of Congress propose a federal constitutional amendment, that amendment shall be considered part of the Constitution "when ratified by the Legislatures of three-fourths of the several states". Finding the language of Article V to be "plain", the Court held that "the method of ratification is the exercise of a national power specifically granted by the Constitution" and that it "is not the function of courts or legislative bodies, national or state, to alter the method which the Constitution has fixed." This conclusion left only the question of what constitutes the "Legislatures * * * of the several States". The Court then concluded that this term excluded any role for state referenda in the Article V process.

Does the difference between Coleman and Hawke come down to the fact that the Court in Hawke read Article V to speak unambiguously to the question of state ratification procedure, whereas the questions in Coleman lacked "satisfactory criteria for a judicial determination"? If correct, does that conclusion suggest that the political question doctrine tracks the merits, at least in some important instances?

(4) External Relations. In its survey of political question cases in Baker v. Carr, the Court observed that "[t]here are sweeping statements to the effect that all questions touching foreign relations are political questions", but then rejected this conclusion. "Our cases in this field seem invariably to show a discriminating analysis of the particular question posed, in terms of the history of its management by the political branches, of its susceptibility to judicial handling in light of its nature and posture in the specific case, and of the possible consequences of judicial action".[4]

(a) In Goldwater v. Carter, 444 U.S. 996 (1979), the Court, summarily and without opinion, vacated a lower court judgment holding, on the merits, that the President had authority to terminate a mutual defense treaty with Taiwan without the approval of either two-thirds of the Senate or a majority of both Houses of Congress. Justice Rehnquist, in an opinion for four Justices, concurred in the judgment. He argued that since the Constitution speaks only of the ratification of treaties, and not of their termination, the question of the President's power unilaterally to terminate a treaty is a political one. "[In] light of [the] fact that different termination procedures may be appropriate for different treaties, the [case] 'must surely be

---

Amending: In Defense of a Restrained Judicial Role, 97 Harv.L.Rev. 433 (1983); and Professor Dellinger's response, Constitutional Politics: A Rejoinder, 97 Harv.L.Rev. 446 (1983).

    [4] On the justiciability of foreign affairs issues, see generally Ely, War and Responsibility: Constitutional Lessons of Vietnam and Its Aftermath 55–58 (1993); Franck, Political Questions/Judicial Answers: Does the Rule of Law Apply to Foreign Affairs? (1992); Tigar, Judicial Power, the "Political Question Doctrine," and Foreign Relations, 17 UCLA L.Rev. 1135 (1970); Champlin & Schwarz, Political Question Doctrine and the Allocation of Foreign Affairs Power, 13 Hofstra L.Rev. 215 (1985). For a thoughtful critique of lower court cases invoking the political question doctrine to justify judicial deference to the executive in the foreign relations context, see Note, Developments in the Law—Access to Courts, 122 Harv.L.Rev. 1151, 1193–1204 (2009).

controlled by political standards' " (quoting Dyer v. Blair, 390 F.Supp. 1291, 1302 (N.D.Ill.1975)). Justice Rehnquist also emphasized that the question involved the politically sensitive area of foreign affairs and that, especially in this field, judicial intervention in "a dispute between coequal branches of our Government, each of which has resources available to protect and assert its interests", was inappropriate.

Justice Powell, in a concurring opinion, disagreed with the view that the question was a political one; he argued that the case was not ripe—that prudential considerations militated against judicial involvement in a quarrel between the other two branches until and unless those branches were more at loggerheads than was indicated by the record before the Court.

Justice Brennan, who dissented, would have affirmed on the merits. Although the political question doctrine bars judicial review of some executive decisions in the field of foreign policy, he argued that "the doctrine does not pertain when a court is faced with the *antecedent* question whether a particular branch has been constitutionally designated as the repository of political decisionmaking power". After addressing that antecedent question, he concluded that the Court should decide the question of presidential authority to terminate a treaty.[5]

(b) In Japan Whaling Ass'n v. American Cetacean Society, 478 U.S. 221 (1986), the Court (unanimously on this point) rejected the government's argument that it should not review a decision of the Secretary of Commerce refusing to certify that Japan's whaling practices diminished the effectiveness of an international conservation program. "[U]nder the Constitution," the Court said, "one of the judiciary's characteristic roles is to interpret statutes, and we cannot shirk this responsibility merely because our decision may have significant political overtones" bearing on American relations with Japan.

When, if ever, could the political question doctrine be properly invoked in a statutory interpretation case? *Cf.* Chicago & S. Air Lines v. Waterman S.S. Corp., 333 U.S. 103, 111 (1948).

(c) The Court has long shown reluctance to entertain challenges to the President's military judgment. In Martin v. Mott, 25 U.S. (12 Wheat.) 19 (1827), the Court refused to review the legality of the President Madison's decision to call the New York militia into the active service of the United States during the War of 1812. Article I, § 8, clause 15 of the Constitution authorizes Congress "[t]o provide for calling forth the Militia to execute the Laws of the Union, suppress Insurrections and repel Invasions". Pursuant to that authority, Congress enacted the Militia Act of 1792, 1 Stat. 264, 264, stating "that whenever the United States shall be invaded, or be in imminent danger of invasion from any foreign nation or Indian tribe, it shall be lawful for the President of the United States to call forth such number of the militia of the State or States most convenient to the place of danger, or scene of action, as he may judge necessary to repel such invasion, and to issue his order for that purpose to such officer or officers of the militia as he shall think proper."

A court martial had convicted Jacob Mott for refusing to enter into the service of the United States pursuant to an order calling up the New York

---

[5]   Justice Marshall concurred in the result. Justices White and Blackmun, dissenting from the summary disposition, would have "set the case for oral argument and give[n] it the plenary consideration it so obviously deserves".

militia in 1812. After refusing to pay the fine imposed by court martial, Mott was sentenced to a year in prison. Mott then challenged the order calling him into service, in relevant part, on the ground that President Madison had not made findings of the statutory conditions for calling the militia into service. In rejecting Mott's objection, the Court concluded that the Constitution and the statute confided the determination of such exigencies to the President's judgment alone. In his opinion for the Court, Justice Story wrote:

"The power thus confided by Congress to the President, is, doubtless, of a very high and delicate nature. * * * It is, in its terms, a limited power, confined to cases of actual invasion, or of imminent danger of invasion. If it be a limited power, the question arises, by whom is the exigency to be judged of and decided? * * * We are all of opinion, that the authority to decide whether the exigency has arisen, belongs exclusively to the President, and that his decision is conclusive upon all other persons. We think that this construction necessarily results from the nature of the power itself, and from the manifest object contemplated by the act of Congress. The power itself is to be exercised upon sudden emergencies, upon great occasions of state, and under circumstances which may be vital to the existence of the Union. A prompt and unhesitating obedience to orders is indispensable to the complete attainment of the object. * * * Besides, in many instances, the evidence upon which the President might decide that there is imminent danger of invasion, might be of a nature not constituting strict technical proof, or the disclosure of the evidence might reveal important secrets of state, which the public interest, and even safety, might imperiously demand to be kept in concealment.

"* * * [The President] is necessarily constituted the judge of the existence of the exigency in the first instance, and is bound to act according to his belief of the facts. * * * The law does not provide for any appeal from the judgment of the President * * *. Whenever a statute gives a discretionary power to any person, to be exercised by him upon his own opinion of certain facts, it is a sound rule of construction, that the statute constitutes him the sole and exclusive judge of the existence of those facts. * * *

"* * * When the President exercises an authority confided to him by law, the presumption is, that it is exercised in pursuance of law. * * * It is not necessary to aver, that the act which he may rightfully do, was so done. If the fact of the existence of the exigency were averred, it would be traversable, and of course might be passed upon by a jury; and thus the legality of the orders of the President would depend, not on his own judgment of the facts, but upon the finding of those facts upon the proofs submitted to a jury."

Does Martin v. Mott merely represent a judgment that the Militia Act gave the President unreviewable power to determine the appropriateness of calling the militia into service, or does Justice Story's opinion reflect a broader functional assessment of the permissibility of judicial review of the President's military judgment? See Baker v. Carr, p. 250, *supra* (describing Martin v. Mott as a political question case).

During the late 1960s and early 1970s, a number of suits were brought attacking the legality of the Vietnam War and related executive actions in the absence of a formal declaration of war. The Supreme Court never gave plenary consideration to the justiciability of any of these challenges, though in one case it summarily affirmed a three-judge court's holding of nonjusticiability,[6] and in another it summarily denied leave to file an original complaint.[7] But several lower courts did pass on this question and invariably held all or a substantial part of the issues raised to be nonjusticiable.[8] Factors cited included the lack of manageable standards, commitment of final authority to other branches of the federal government, and the difficulty of gaining access to and determining the relevant facts. Several commentators urged, however, that at least some of the challenges presented justiciable issues concerning the scope of executive power. See, *e.g.,* Henkin, p. 249, *supra,* at 623–24.[9]

If American actions in Vietnam and Cambodia had been held to violate the Constitution, what consequences would have flowed from the decision? Do problems of judicial enforcement and confrontation with other branches loom larger in a case challenging executive actions in Vietnam than in a case such as Powell?[10] Have challenges to more recent military actions confirmed the lesson of the Vietnam-era cases or left the door open for reconsideration?[11]

---

[6] Atlee v. Richardson, 411 U.S. 911 (1973). Justices Douglas, Brennan, and Stewart would have noted probable jurisdiction.

[7] Massachusetts v. Laird, 400 U.S. 886 (1970). Justices Harlan, Stewart, and Douglas dissented; Justice Douglas, in a separate opinion, considered the justiciability issue at some length. In several other cases involving similar challenges, there were dissents from decisions denying certiorari. *E.g.,* Mora v. McNamara, 389 U.S. 934 (1967); Da Costa v. Laird, 405 U.S. 979 (1972).

[8] *E.g.,* Mitchell v. Laird, 488 F.2d 611 (D.C.Cir.1973); Orlando v. Laird, 443 F.2d 1039 (2d Cir.1971); Massachusetts v. Laird, 451 F.2d 26 (1st Cir.1971). In Orlando, the court held that there was a manageable standard "imposing on the Congress a duty of mutual participation in the prosecution of war", but that the question of "[t]he form which congressional authorization should take is one of policy, committed to the discretion of Congress and outside the power and competency of the judiciary".

[9] For echoes of the Vietnam decisions, see Crockett v. Reagan, 720 F.2d 1355 (D.C.Cir.1983), and Sanchez-Espinoza v. Reagan, 770 F.2d 202 (D.C.Cir.1985), holding nonjusticiable challenges to the Reagan Administration's activities in El Salvador and Nicaragua.

[10] Some earlier cases suggest that, at least in some contexts, the presence of a political question cannot rest on the asserted absence of judicially manageable standards for determining the existence of a "war". See, *e.g.,* Fleming v. Mohawk Wrecking Co., 331 U.S. 111, 115 (1947) (determining whether after the cessation of hostilities in World War II, the President retained authority to redistribute functions within the executive branch under the First War Powers Act, whose authorization expired six months after "the termination of the war"); Prize Cases, 67 U.S. 635, 669 (1863) (holding that despite the absence of a congressional declaration of war, the Civil War constituted a "war" for purposes of determining the question whether a right to prize exists); Bas v. Tingy, 4 U.S. (4 Dall.) 37 (1800) (determining whether hostilities between the United States and France constituted "war" for purposes of the law of capture).

[11] In challenges to post-Vietnam era conflicts, lower court decisions have relied on various justiciability doctrines to avoid passing on the legality of military actions undertaken by the executive. See, *e.g.,* Dellums v. Bush, 752 F.Supp. 1141 (D.D.C.1990) (holding that a suit challenging the constitutional authority of the Bush administration to launch the Gulf War without congressional authorization was unripe because Congress had not acted with respect to the issue); Campbell v. Clinton, 203 F.3d 19, 25 (D.C. Cir.2000) (holding that members of Congress lacked standing to challenge whether the Clinton administration's intervention in Kosovo violated the War Powers Resolution); Doe v. Bush, 323 F.3d 133, 140–41 (1st Cir.2003) (holding unripe a suit seeking to enjoin second Bush administration from launching war against Iraq without a declaration of war by Congress). These actions have expressed a variety of views on the political question doctrine. In Dellums, the district court declined to hold that the political question doctrine precluded review of a challenge to the President's launching a war without a congressional declaration of war, reasoning that the Supreme Court had in many contexts determined whether the country was at war and that it would be inappropriate for the judiciary to disregard "the clause granting to the Congress, and to it alone, the authority 'to declare war' ". Compare also, *e.g.,* Campbell v. Clinton, *supra,* at 25 (Silberman, J., concurring) (arguing in

Despite concerns about confronting the President on questions of military judgment in a time of armed conflict, the Court has also, at times, shown a willingness to do just that. The Court, of course, famously ordered the federal government to relinquish control over steel mills seized during the Korean Conflict, notwithstanding President Truman's executive order specifically finding that seizure of the mills in the face of an impending labor strike was essential to the Nation's military efforts. See Youngstown Sheet & Tube Co. v. Sawyer, 343 U.S. 579 (1952). Justice Black's opinion for the Court held that the power to seize the mills did not lie within the President's Article II commander-in-chief power (§ 2, cl. 1) or within the more general grant of "the executive Power" (§ 1, cl. 1), but rather fell squarely within Congress' Article I authority to enact laws "necessary and proper" to carry into execution its other powers (§ 8, cl. 18), presumably including the power (as Justice Jackson noted in his concurrence) to "raise and support Armies" and to "provide and maintain a Navy" (§ 8, cls. 12–13). Justice Black noted that whatever the scope of the President's authority as commander-in-chief in theaters of war, "we cannot with faithfulness to our constitutional system hold that the Commander in Chief of the Armed Forces has the ultimate power as such to take possession of private property in order to keep labor disputes from stopping production." Given Justice Jackson's observation, in concurrence, that "what our forefathers * * * envision[ed] [about executive war powers], or would have envisioned had they foreseen modern conditions, must be divined from materials almost as enigmatic as the dreams Joseph was called upon to interpret for Pharaoh", how did the Justices derive judicially manageable standards for drawing the necessary lines?[12] Even though the government argued that the power to seize the mills was committed to the President by virtue of the commander-in-chief power, none of the Justices found it controversial to determine the scope of that commitment. Although the government did not raise the political question doctrine in Youngstown, how different are the factors that the Court handled easily in that case from the factors that come into play in classic political question doctrine cases?

(d) In reviewing military judgments that implicate individual rights, the Court has frequently (and, sometimes, infamously) given significant deference to the political branches' decisions. See, e.g., Hirabayashi v. United States, 320 U.S. 81 (1943) (holding that an executive order imposing a curfew on Japanese Americans during World War II did not result from an unconstitutional delegation of legislative power or violate the equal protection component of the Due Process Clause and noting that "[w]here, as they did here, the conditions call for the exercise of judgment and discretion and for the choice of means by those branches of the Government on which the Constitution has placed the responsibility of warmaking, it is not for any

---

connection with challenge to Kosovo intervention that no judicially manageable standards are available to determine applicability of War Powers Resolution and what counts as "war" under the Constitution), with id. at 37 (Tatel, J., concurring) (concluding that historical practice and precedent provides judicially manageable standard to determine what counts as a "war" in a constitutional sense and to apply the less exacting statutory trigger for the War Powers Resolution).

[12] For an in-depth historical study of the President's war powers, see Barron & Lederman, *The Commander in Chief at the Lowest Ebb—A Constitutional History*, 121 Harv.L.Rev. 941 (2008); Barron & Lederman, *The Commander in Chief at the Lowest Ebb—Framing the Problem, Doctrine, and Original Understanding*, 121 Harv.L.Rev. 689 (2008). For a contrasting view, see Yoo, *The Continuation of Politics by Other Means: The Original Understanding of War Powers*, 84 Cal.L.Rev. 167 (1999).

court to sit in review of the wisdom of their action or substitute its judgment for theirs"); Korematsu v. United States, 323 U.S. 214 (1944) (reviewing legality of the internment of Japanese Americans during World War II and relying on Hirabayashi for the conclusion that " 'we cannot reject as unfounded the judgment of the military authorities and of Congress' " that resulted in the challenged relocation order); Rostker v. Goldberg, 453 U.S 57 (1981) (rejecting a challenge under the equal protection component of the Due Process Clause to the application of the Military Selective Service Act to males only and noting that "perhaps in no other area has the Court accorded Congress greater deference" than in cases involving "Congress' authority over national defense and military affairs"). Is the political question doctrine just the ultimate exhibition of deference—of complete deference—by the courts to the political branches?

Should a textually demonstrable commitment of power to Congress or the President under a power-conferring provision of the Constitution ever preclude judicial review of an alleged violation of individual rights under another provision of the Constitution? What would have been the result in the Nixon case if Nixon had alleged a due process or equal protection violation involving race-based discrimination? Choper, *The Political Question Doctrine: Suggested Criteria*, 54 Duke L.J. 1457 (2005), contends that allegations of individual rights violations should never be deemed to present political questions.[13]

(5) Political Questions and Political Cases. The mere fact that a case has political stakes or has generated political controversy clearly does not render it nonjusticiable under the political question doctrine. "The doctrine of which we treat is one of 'political questions,' not one of 'political cases.' " Baker v. Carr, 369 U.S. 186, 217 (1962).

The Court's willingness to decide cases charged with political consequences was dramatically manifest in two decisions arising from the 2000 presidential election in the state of Florida, Bush v. Palm Beach County Canvassing Board, 531 U.S. 70 (2000) (per curiam), and Bush v. Gore, 531 U.S. 98 (2000) (per curiam), the latter of which reversed a decision of the Florida Supreme Court ordering a manual recount of ballots that had failed to register any presidential choice in a machine count. The Court ruled that a hand recount in which election officials were directed only to attempt to discern "the will of the voter" would lead to counting disparities and violate the Due Process and Equal Protection Clauses. Apart from the obvious political ramifications, there were colorable arguments, raised in amicus curiae briefs, that the cases involved political questions in the technical sense.[14] In particular, amici argued that the Twelfth Amendment commits to Congress the question whether a state's electors have been chosen in accord with the constitutionally specified requirements of Article II. Nonetheless, the Court opinions did not refer to the political question

---

[13] In Hamdi v. Rumsfeld, 542 U.S. 507, 578 (2004), Justice Scalia, joined by Justice Stevens and with the endorsement of Justice Thomas, asserted in dissent that if Congress were to suspend the writ of habeas corpus, any challenge to its action would present a political question under the Suspension Clause, Article I, § 9, cl. 2. For further discussion, see Chap. XI, Sec. 2, *infra*.

[14] See also Barkow, *More Supreme Than Court? The Fall of the Political Question Doctrine and the Rise of Judicial Supremacy*, 102 Colum.L.Rev. 237, 273–300 (2002); Chemerinsky, *Bush v. Gore Was Not Justiciable*, 76 Notre Dame L.Rev. 1093, 1105–09 (2001); Tribe, *Hsub v. Erog and Its Disguises: Freeing Bush v. Gore From Its Hall of Mirrors*, 115 Harv.L.Rev. 170, 276–87 (2001).

doctrine in either decision, and the concurring and dissenting opinions in Bush v. Gore dealt with the doctrine only glancingly.

(a) Commentators on Bush v. Gore have argued that the current Court—much more than its predecessors—holds a Court-centered view of constitutionalism and regards itself as central and indispensable in ensuring the correctness and legitimacy of constitutional decisions. *See, e.g.*, Barkow, note 14, *supra* (characterizing Bush v. Gore and the relative decline of the political question doctrine as reflecting the modern Court's assumption that it alone has the competency to identify constitutional meaning); Tribe, note 14, *supra*, at 288 (citing, *inter alia*, Bush v. Gore and the Court's rulings that Congress has no interpretive latitude to define constitutional rights in enacting legislation under Section 5 of the Fourteenth Amendment, see pp. 959–962, *infra*, as evidence that "[t]he Court's self-confidence in matters constitutional is matched only by its disdain for the meaningful participation of other actors in constitutional debate"); Kramer, *Foreword: We The Court*, 115 Harv.L.Rev. 4, 153, 158 (2001) (terming Bush v. Gore an "emblematic" decision of the Rehnquist Court and "the capstone of [its] campaign to control all things constitutional").

(b) In a partial inversion of Professor Bickel's famous argument that courts should avoid decision of certain momentous issues for prudential reasons (see Note on Political Questions, Paragraph (1), *supra*), Posner, Breaking the Deadlock: The 2000 Election, the Constitution, and the Courts 143 (2001), suggests that there were compelling "pragmatic" reasons for the Court to accept jurisdiction and to resolve Bush v. Gore as it did: If Gore emerged victorious in the Florida recount, Florida's legislature was prepared to appoint an alternate slate of electors pledged to Bush. Because of a predictable split between the Republican-controlled House and the Democrat-controlled Senate, "there was a real and disturbing *potential* for disorder and temporary paralysis", and "[w]hatever Congress did would have been regarded as the product of raw politics, with no tincture of justice". The circumstances, Judge Posner argues, called for a "a reverse political questions doctrine. Political considerations in a broad, nonpartisan sense will sometimes counsel the Court to abstain, but sometimes to intervene".[15]

(c) It is surely a colorable argument that the justiciability of the equal protection claims upheld in Bush v. Gore was established by Baker v. Carr and subsequent voting rights cases under the Equal Protection Clause. But those cases could also have been distinguished—for example, on the basis of the special role assigned to Congress in counting electoral votes under the Twelfth Amendment. In the face of these competing arguments, what considerations ought the Court to have weighed in determining whether Bush v. Gore presented non-justiciable political questions?

---

[15] For a critique of this argument based within the same "pragmatic" framework that Posner advocates, see Farnsworth, *"To Do a Great Right, Do a Little Wrong": A User's Guide to Judicial Lawlessness*, 86 Minn.L.Rev. 227 (2001).

CHAPTER III

THE ORIGINAL JURISDICTION OF THE SUPREME COURT

Marbury v. Madison

5 U.S. (1 Cranch) 137, 2 L.Ed. 60 (1803).
On Petition for Mandamus.

[See p. 59, *supra*.]

INTRODUCTORY NOTE ON THE POWER OF CONGRESS TO REGULATE THE ORIGINAL JURISDICTION OF THE SUPREME COURT

(1) The Constitutional and Statutory Grants. Article III, Sec. 2, cl. 2 declares: "In all Cases affecting Ambassadors, other public Ministers and Consuls, and those in which a State shall be Party, the supreme Court shall have original Jurisdiction." The Supreme Court has repeatedly said that exercise of this jurisdiction does not require enabling action by Congress. See, *e.g.*, Arizona v. California, 373 U.S. 546, 564 (1963). Nevertheless, beginning with the provision at issue in Marbury, § 13 of the Judiciary Act of 1789, Congress has specified the Court's original jurisdiction. The current provision, 28 U.S.C. § 1251, reads:

(a) The Supreme Court shall have original and exclusive jurisdiction of all controversies between two or more States.

(b) The Supreme Court shall have original but not exclusive jurisdiction of:

(1) All actions or proceedings to which ambassadors, other public ministers, consuls, or vice consuls of foreign states are parties;

(2) All controversies between the United States and a State;

(3) All actions or proceedings by a State against the citizens of another State or against aliens.

The congressional grants of jurisdiction, taken collectively from 1789 to the present, have given rise to three central questions. First, may Congress *expand* the original jurisdiction by assigning to it cases beyond those described in Article III, Sec. 2, cl. 2? Second, may Congress *contract* the original jurisdiction by excluding from it cases that are described in Article III, Sec. 2, cl. 2? Third, may Congress prescribe that the Supreme Court's original jurisdiction is concurrent with the jurisdiction of state and/or lower federal courts, thereby contracting its mandatory scope? The three succeeding Paragraphs of this Note discuss each of those three questions in order.

(2) Congressional Expansion of the Original Jurisdiction. Marbury's statutory ruling, that § 13 purported to vest the Supreme Court with a general, original jurisdiction in mandamus actions, was controversial.[1] No less controversial was its constitutional ruling that § 13 was invalid because it purported to confer original jurisdiction over a case other than one of those described by Article III, Sec. 2, cl. 2.

To understand the controversy over the constitutional holding, consider that the prevailing understanding of the reason for the original jurisdiction is that the exercise of jurisdiction over another sovereign (here, over one of the states, or, in the case of the foreign-envoy jurisdiction, over cases so intimately affecting a sovereign) is so sensitive that only the court of greatest dignity—the Supreme Court—should exercise it. That rationale can explain why Article III might bar Congress from depriving states or foreign envoys of an original hearing before the Supreme Court. See, *e.g.*, Ames v. Kansas ex rel. Johnston, 111 U.S. 449, 464 (1884). But why should Article III preclude Congress from giving other litigants direct access to the Court? To protect the Court from a crushing burden imposed by an irresponsible Congress? To protect litigants from a possibly inconvenient forum?[2]

---

[1] For a defense of Chief Justice Marshall's interpretation of § 13 as consistent with English practice, in which superior courts used mandamus to exercise supervisory authority over ministerial officers as well as lower courts, see Pfander, *Marbury, Original Jurisdiction, and the Supreme Court's Supervisory Powers*, 101 Colum.L.Rev. 1515, 1523–49 (2001). For arguments that § 13 could have been read merely to authorize mandamus in cases in which the Court otherwise possessed appellate or original jurisdiction, see, *e.g.*, Currie, The Constitution in the Supreme Court: The First Hundred Years, 1789–1888, at 67–68 (1985); Van Alstyne, *A Critical Guide to Marbury v. Madison*, 1969 Duke L.J. 1, 14–16.

[2] Professor Amar has defended Marbury's holding that Congress may not add to the original jurisdiction, while offering the unorthodox view that Congress has some power to limit the exercise of original jurisdiction. The latter contention flows from his general view, described at pp. 319–322, *infra*, that the nine heads of jurisdiction defined in Article III, Sec. 2, cl. 1 fall into two tiers: a first tier (comprising admiralty and federal question cases and cases affecting foreign envoys) based on subject matter and over which federal jurisdiction is mandatory; and a second tier (comprising the remaining six heads of jurisdiction) based on party status and over which federal jurisdiction is optional. Because controversies to which a state is a party fall within the optional second tier, Congress need not confer federal court jurisdiction over them, notwithstanding their inclusion in the Original Jurisdiction Clause.

In Amar's view, the Original Jurisdiction Clause operates as a kind of constitutional venue provision. It requires that cases against foreign envoys, and cases to which a state is a party (if Congress has chosen to confer federal court jurisdiction over such cases) must be heard by the Supreme Court. Amar contends that in both classes of cases, original Supreme Court jurisdiction would be convenient: foreign envoys are likely to reside in the nation's capital, and states are likely to have representatives there. In other cases, however, "venue" before the Supreme Court would be inconvenient, which supports Marbury's holding that Congress may not expand the original jurisdiction. See Amar, *Marbury, Section 13, and the Original Jurisdiction of the Supreme Court*, 56 U.Chi.L.Rev. 443, 467–88 (1989).

Amar's theory raises many questions. Beyond the fact that the Constitution does not require the Supreme Court to sit in the capital, if geographic convenience were the key concern, then the Original Jurisdiction Clause could have explicitly referred to venue; after all, a lower federal court in the capital (which could have heard Marbury's suit) is no less convenient than the Supreme Court. Furthermore, for many cases within the original jurisdiction—those involving consuls (many of whom resided outside the capital) or those between two distant states—the Supreme Court would be less convenient than a lower federal court nearer the place of controversy. Moreover, Amar's approach would yield the surprising result that Congress could leave the resolution of controversies involving a state—even actions between two states—to the state courts. See Meltzer, *The History and Structure of Article III*, 138 U.Pa.L.Rev. 1569, 1608

Despite dicta in Marbury that the original and the appellate jurisdictions are mutually exclusive, Chief Justice Marshall's opinion for the Court in Cohens v. Virginia, 19 U.S. (6 Wheat.) 264, 392–405 (1821), held in the alternative that Congress may grant appellate jurisdiction over cases falling within the original jurisdiction. Given that, why can it not do the reverse, even though the effect would be to expand the original jurisdiction?

(3) Congressional Restriction of the Original Jurisdiction. Consider now the opposite situation, in which Congress purports to contract the scope of original jurisdiction set forth in Article III, Sec. II, cl. 2. The question is not merely hypothetical. Indeed, today 28 U.S.C. § 1251, like its predecessor in the First Judiciary Act, falls short of the constitutional grant. For example, § 1251 does not include cases *affecting* foreign envoys but to which they are not parties,[3] nor does it include disputes between a state and a foreign nation.

(a) Elimination of Jurisdiction Altogether. Doubts that Congress may limit the constitutional grant were expressed in California v. Arizona, 440 U.S. 59 (1979), an original action by California against Arizona and the United States to quiet title to land. One question presented was whether the Supreme Court's exercise of original jurisdiction was barred by 28 U.S.C. §§ 1346(f), 2409a(a), which together had the effect of (i) waiving the United States' sovereign immunity, rendering it liable to a quiet title action, but (ii) conferring on the federal district courts *exclusive* jurisdiction over actions falling within the scope of the waiver. The Court refused to read the exclusivity provision as purporting to divest the Supreme Court of original jurisdiction, interpreting it instead merely to bar state court jurisdiction. Any other construction, the Court said, would raise constitutional difficulties: although Congress need not waive the United States' immunity from suit, once it had done so, it was far from clear that Congress could "withdraw the constitutional jurisdiction of this Court over such suits." The Framers, the Court said, seemed to wish to match the dignity of the parties— States and the envoys of foreign nations—to the status of the Court, and "[e]limination of this Court's original jurisdiction would require those sovereign parties to go to another court, in derogation of this constitutional purpose."[4]

(1990) (Hamilton's view in The Federalist No. 80—that Article III's grant of jurisdiction where a state is a party is grounded on the premise that "[n]o man ought certainly to be a judge in his own cause"—is "hard to square with Amar's view that the state courts, but not the lower federal courts, are free to entertain such actions."). For critical discussion, see Harrison, *The Power of Congress to Limit the Jurisdiction of Federal Courts and the Text of Article III*, 64 U.Chi.L.Rev. 203, 247–50 (1997); Pfander, *Rethinking the Supreme Court's Original Jurisdiction in State-Party Cases*, 82 Cal.L.Rev. 555, 568–72 (1994); Meltzer, *supra*, at 1604–06 & nn. 126, 128, 130. For a defense, see Pushaw, *Congressional Power over Federal Court Jurisdiction: A Defense of the Neo-Federalist Interpretation of Article III*, 1997 B.Y.U.L.Rev. 847, 890–91.

[3] But *cf.* United States v. Ortega, 24 U.S. (11 Wheat.) 467 (1826), holding that an indictment for "offering violence" to a public minister was not a case "affecting" the minister.

[4] The draft of Article III reported by the Committee of Detail included a provision, eliminated on the floor, permitting the legislature to assign to the lower federal courts cases within the Supreme Court's original jurisdiction (excepting trial of the President in an impeachment, which that draft allocated to the Supreme Court rather than to the Senate). See p. 18, *supra*.

See also South Carolina v. Katzenbach, 383 U.S. 301 (1966), in which the state filed suit in the Supreme Court against Attorney General Katzenbach (a New Jersey citizen), seeking to enjoin enforcement of various provisions of the Voting Rights Act of 1965. In deciding the case, the Court did not mention § 14(b) of the Act, which provided that only the District Court for the

(b) Remedial or Procedural Limitations on the Exercise of Jurisdiction. The Supreme Court has not decided whether, or to what extent, the constitutional concern expressed in California v. Arizona extends to congressional efforts to regulate, for example, the procedures followed or the remedies available in original action. But individual Justices have suggested that congressional power is sharply restricted.

In Kansas v. Colorado, 556 U.S. 98 (2009), a suit between two states heard in the Supreme Court's original jurisdiction, Kansas, the prevailing party, sought to have the costs of its expert witness fees awarded against Colorado. A federal statute, 28 U.S.C. § 1821(b), authorizes the award of $40/day as witness fees for proceedings in "any court of the United States". Kansas, in seeking more than $40/day for its expert witnesses, argued first that the statute does not apply to an original action in the Supreme Court, and second that Congress lacked the constitutional power to limit the Court's ultimate authority to set its own procedures for original actions.

In an opinion by Justice Alito, the Court found it unnecessary to address either the statutory or the constitutional issue. "[A]ssuming for the sake of argument that the matter is left entirely to [its] discretion," the Court decided to apply the limitations found in § 1821(b) on the ground that "the best approach is to have a uniform rule that applies in all federal cases." Chief Justice Roberts, joined by Justice Souter, wrote a concurrence to address the constitutional question. Noting that Article III, Sec. 2, authorizes Congress to make "Exceptions" and "Regulations" concerning the Court's appellate jurisdiction but says no such thing about its original jurisdiction, the Chief Justice wrote that "[i]t is accordingly our responsibility to determine matters related to our original jurisdiction, including the availability and amount of witness fees." He agreed that the statutory rate was reasonable, but stressed that "the choice is ours."[5]

District of Columbia "shall have jurisdiction to issue * * * any restraining order or temporary or permanent injunction" against enforcement of the Act. Justice Black, in dissent, stated that he thought § 14(b) was unconstitutional insofar as it purported to restrict the Supreme Court's original jurisdiction.

    [5]   A similar question was raised in South Carolina v. Regan, 465 U.S. 367 (1984), where the state sought to enjoin, as a violation of its Tenth Amendment rights, federal income taxation of the interest on certain state-issued bonds. A federal statute, 26 U.S.C. § 7421(a), bars injunctions in suits in any court challenging the assessment or collection of any federal tax. The Court did not address § 7421(a)'s applicability to original actions in the Supreme Court, finding instead that the statute did not apply when an aggrieved party, like South Carolina, lacks an alternative forum for litigating a tax's validity. Justice O'Connor, concurring in the judgment, disagreed with that reading of § 7421(a), but agreed that the statute did not bar South Carolina's action; to rule otherwise would raise the "grave" question "whether Congress constitutionally can impose remedial limitations so jurisdictional in nature that they effectively withdraw the original jurisdiction of this Court."

    Can it be that no congressional regulation of procedure or remedies can have effect of its own force in original actions in the Supreme Court, and that the statutory rule will be followed only if, as the Chief Justice suggested in Kansas v. Colorado, the Court chooses in its discretion to do so? Consider statutes providing that "all process issuing from a court of the United States shall be under the seal of the court and signed by the clerk thereof" (28 U.S.C. § 1691), that certified copies of the Journals of the Senate and the House of Representatives "shall be received in evidence with the same effect as the originals would have" (28 U.S.C. § 1736), or that the interest rate allowed on a money judgment shall be calculated in a particular way (28 U.S.C. § 1961). One might question whether it is sensible to require the Supreme Court to decide each of these matters on its own, reaching an independent resolution.

    For discussion of whether statutory restrictions on the exercise of federal habeas corpus jurisdiction apply to the Supreme Court when entertaining "original" writs of habeas corpus, see pp. 287–288, *infra*.

(4) Concurrent Jurisdiction. Since 1789, Congress has assumed that the Supreme Court's original jurisdiction could be made concurrent with the jurisdiction of the lower federal courts or of state courts. Today, § 1251(a) makes the Supreme Court's original jurisdiction exclusive only for controversies between states. Section 1251(b) makes the remainder of the Court's original jurisdiction concurrent. But § 1251(b) does not itself confer concurrent jurisdiction on any other court; instead, it simply permits the operation of any jurisdiction otherwise granted. In Ames v. Kansas ex rel. Johnston, 111 U.S. 449 (1884), the Court put to rest any doubts about the constitutionality of concurrent jurisdiction, leaning heavily on the understanding of the First Congress and on an unbroken line of judicial authority. The opinion also stressed the inconvenience to the parties that would arise if the Supreme Court had to hear every small claim involving a state or a foreign envoy; an obvious additional concern, though not stated explicitly, was the potential burden on the Court itself.

A case falling within the Court's concurrent jurisdiction but filed in lower federal court, or filed in state court but turning on a federal question, is subject to Supreme Court review. But the Supreme Court has not doubted the validity of concurrent jurisdiction even when there is no prospect of such review—for example, when a state brings an action raising only state law issues against a citizen of another state. See Plaquemines Tropical Fruit Co. v. Henderson, 170 U.S. 511, 520–21 (1898). When the plaintiff is a state or a foreign envoy, might that result be rationalized on the basis that the "right" to file suit in the Supreme Court is a waivable privilege of the sovereign, and that the privilege was waived by filing the suit within a state court's concurrent jurisdiction?

But suppose a foreign envoy or a state is sued as a defendant in state court. Ordinarily, diplomatic or sovereign immunity will bar such actions. But those immunity doctrines have limits. Thus, in Nevada v. Hall, 440 U.S. 410 (1979), the Supreme Court held that Nevada was not immune from suit in a California state court with regard to an automobile accident, in California, involving a Nevada state employee driving a state-owned car. Because the question whether the federal Constitution barred the state court from acting was unresolved, the Supreme Court could decide the matter. But with that issue resolved, a subsequent case like Nevada v. Hall could be litigated in state court without the prospect of Supreme Court review.

NOTE ON PROCEDURE IN ORIGINAL ACTIONS

Supreme Court Rule 17.3 states that "[t]he initial pleading in an original action shall be preceded by a motion for leave to file." The Court often disposes of major jurisdictional issues when ruling on the motion for leave to file. Although four votes suffice to grant a writ of certiorari, a majority seems to be needed to grant a motion for leave to file. Oklahoma ex rel. Williamson v. Woodring, 309 U.S. 623 (1940) (motion denied by evenly divided Court). From 1961–93, 50 of the 102 motions for leave to file were denied, generally without opinion. See McKusick, *Discretionary Gatekeeping: The Supreme Court's Management of Its Original Jurisdiction Docket Since 1961*, 45 Me.L.Rev. 185, 188–90 (1993).

Although the Seventh Amendment applies to trials at common law in the Supreme Court (as 28 U.S.C. § 1872 recognizes), no jury trial seems to have been held since the eighteenth century,[1] as original cases have usually been equitable in character. Invariably, the Court appoints a special master to take evidence and prepare findings of fact, which, though in theory only advisory, the Court regularly accepts. See United States v. Raddatz, 447 U.S. 667, 683 n.11 (1980). But *cf.* Maryland v. Louisiana, 451 U.S. 725, 765 (1981) (Rehnquist, J., dissenting) (referring to the "appellate-type review which this Court necessarily gives to a [special master's] findings and recommendations"). See generally Shapiro et al., Supreme Court Practice ch. 10 (10th ed.2013).

INTRODUCTORY NOTE ON THE SUPREME COURT'S POWER TO DECLINE TO EXERCISE ORIGINAL JURISDICTION

In cases that do fall within the Supreme Court's original jurisdiction, what is the scope of the Court's power to decline to hear the case, thereby relegating the litigants to an alternative forum? The next case presents that issue in a particularly sharp relief.

Louisiana v. Mississippi
488 U.S. 990, 109 S.Ct. 551, 102 L.Ed.2d 579 (1988).
On Motion for Leave to File a Bill of Complaint.

The motion for leave to file a bill of complaint is denied.

■ JUSTICE WHITE, with whom JUSTICE STEVENS and JUSTICE SCALIA join, dissenting.

Louisiana's complaint against Mississippi is plainly within our original jurisdiction and alleges a boundary dispute with Mississippi, the very kind of a dispute that countless times the Court has * * * adjudicated under its original jurisdiction. Furthermore, as 28 U.S.C. § 1251(a) prescribes, the Court has exclusive jurisdiction over controversies between States. No other court may entertain Louisiana's complaint against Mississippi.

It is true that Louisiana intervened in a dispute between private parties over the ownership of land on an island in the Mississippi River, claiming that the land was in that State. That suit might settle the dispute among the parties and the State, but a judgment that the island is in Louisiana would not bind Mississippi. For that reason, I suppose, Louisiana filed a third-party complaint against Mississippi and also sought leave to file an original action in this Court. We prefer to have disputes within our original jurisdiction settled in other fora where possible. But this boundary dispute between two States is exclusively our business and, as such, may not be adjudicated in the District Court. Had Louisiana not intervened in the private action, denying leave to file

---

[1]   See Georgia v. Brailsford, 3 U.S. (3 Dall.) 1 (1794). A recent study of Brailsford found that the jury in that case was a "special jury" of merchants, who could provide expertise and insight about mercantile custom. See Note, 123 Yale L.J. 208 (2013). See also 1 Carson, History of the Supreme Court of the United States 169 n.1 (1902) (describing two unreported jury trials in 1795 and 1797).

would surely be indefensible. Perhaps denial of leave to file rests on the possibility that the private action will go forward with Louisiana as a party and that a judgment unfavorable to, but binding on, Louisiana will be entered. For me, however, this is no way to treat a sovereign State that wants its dispute with another State settled in this Court. I would grant leave to file.

JUSTICE BRENNAN took no part in the consideration or decision of this motion.

––––––––––

NOTE ON THE ORIGINAL JURISDICTION AS AN INAPPROPRIATE FORUM

(1) The Wyandotte Chemicals Corporation Decision. The leading discussion of the Court's power to decline to exercise jurisdiction, Ohio v. Wyandotte Chemicals Corp., 401 U.S. 493 (1971), involved a case within the Court's concurrent jurisdiction under § 1251(b).[1] There, Ohio sued chemical companies alleged to be responsible for pollution of Lake Erie, seeking compensatory and injunctive relief. Justice Harlan's opinion for the Court expressed no doubt that the case, between a state and citizens of other states or of a foreign nation, fell within the original jurisdiction. The Court acknowledged the "time-honored maxim of the Anglo-American common-law tradition that a court possessed of jurisdiction generally must exercise it. Cohens v. Virginia, 6 Wheat. 264, 404 (1821). Nevertheless, although it may initially have been contemplated that this Court would always exercise its original jurisdiction when properly called upon to do so, * * * changes in the American legal system and the development of American society have rendered untenable, as a practical matter, the view that this Court must stand willing to adjudicate all or most legal disputes that may arise between one State and a citizen or citizens of another * * *." States have increasingly been drawn into legal disputes with noncitizens, often bottomed on local law as to which the Supreme Court has no special competence; "[t]his Court's paramount responsibilities to the national system lie almost without exception in the domain of federal law," but nothing in the complaint suggested that it raised important questions of federal law. He added that the Court is "structured to perform as an appellate tribunal, ill-equipped for the task of factfinding and so forced, in original cases, awkwardly to play the role of factfinder without actually presiding over the introduction of evidence." Thus, he concluded that the Court may properly exercise discretion to decline to hear a case not merely or primarily to protect the Court from vexatious or unfamiliar tasks, but also, and primarily, to preserve the Court's capacity as an appellate tribunal resolving matters of federal law. He noted that exercising this power of declination would not require a state to bring suit in the courts of another state, given the prevalence of long-arm statutes under which a state like Ohio could sue the defendants in its own courts.

Justice Douglas alone dissented, finding this to be "a classic type of case congenial to our original jurisdiction. It is to abate a public nuisance." He cited a number of other cases involving interstate environmental problems

––––––––––

[1]   For an earlier declination of concurrent jurisdiction, see Massachusetts v. Missouri, 308 U.S. 1 (1939).

that the Court had entertained. He also pointed to several complex cases that the Court had decided, in his view successfully, on the basis of a Special Master's report.

(2) Declining to Exercise Concurrent Jurisdiction. The Court followed Wyandotte the next year in declining to exercise original jurisdiction, and remitting to federal district courts, both another interstate pollution case, Illinois v. City of Milwaukee, 406 U.S. 91 (1972), and a different case in which 18 states sought to bring antitrust claims against automobile manufacturers and their trade association, Washington v. General Motors Corp., 406 U.S. 109 (1972). The following year, in United States v. Nevada, 412 U.S. 534 (1973), the Court applied the Wyandotte doctrine to a suit by the United States that involved a dispute over the waters of the Truckee River, noting, *inter alia*, that its jurisdiction over the case was not exclusive and that private users of the disputed waters could participate in a district court litigation but could not intervene in an original action in the Supreme Court.[2] Recognizing that the United States could not sue California in an action against Nevada in the Nevada district court, the Court characterized the controversy between the United States and California as "remote" and capable of resolution in separate actions in lower federal courts in California.

(3) Questions About the Wyandotte Doctrine.

(a) The Court in California v. Arizona, p. 269, *supra*, explained that it would be in "derogation" of the purpose of the Framers—"matching the dignity of the parties to the status of the court"—for *Congress* to narrow the Court's original jurisdiction. Is it less in derogation of that purpose for the *Court* to remit "sovereign parties" to another tribunal? For both a general discussion and criticism of the Court's approach when its jurisdiction is exclusive, see Shapiro, *Jurisdiction and Discretion*, 60 N.Y.U.L.Rev. 543, 560–61, 576 (1985).[3]

(b) If the Court may legitimately decline to exercise jurisdiction, what factors should inform its discretion? The few original cases that the Court handles each year tend to be disproportionately lengthy and difficult, often involving elaborate factual issues, as in Wyandotte itself. But that may simply indicate that any court would find these cases extremely difficult rather than showing that the Supreme Court is a particularly inappropriate forum. And it is unusual to rely on the doctrine of forum non conveniens to serve the convenience of the Court rather than of the litigants.

(4) Actions Within the Supreme Court's Exclusive Jurisdiction. The application of the Wyandotte doctrine in Louisiana v. Mississippi, p. 272, *supra*, is surely a dramatic expansion of the Wyandotte doctrine, given that the case falls within § 1251(a)'s grant of *exclusive* original jurisdiction.[4] The dissenters suggest it is not merely dramatic but unjustifiable.

---

[2] Apparently the only previous denial of leave to the United States to file, United States v. Alabama, 382 U.S. 897 (1965), occurred on the same day that the Court granted leave in another original action, South Carolina v. Katzenbach, 382 U.S. 898 (1965), p. 284, *infra*, that raised identical questions.

[3] In dissenting for himself, Chief Justice Rehnquist, and Justice Scalia in Wyoming v. Oklahoma, 502 U.S. 437, 474 n.* (1992), Justice Thomas cited both the Third Edition of this book and Shapiro, *supra*, in support of the view that the Court lacked discretion to refuse to exercise its exclusive, though not its concurrent, original jurisdiction.

[4] An earlier refusal to exercise exclusive original jurisdiction, Arizona v. New Mexico, 425 U.S. 794 (1976), was based on the pendency in New Mexico state court of a lawsuit, brought by Arizona companies, challenging the same New Mexico statute that Arizona's original action

The exclusivity provision of § 1251(a) appears to preclude state courts and federal district courts alike from exercising jurisdiction. Does that mean there is no alternative forum in which the state may bring suit? (A plaintiff state might try to circumvent the Supreme Court's exclusive jurisdiction over suits between states by instead suing state officials.)

In considering whether a more appropriate forum exists, is it enough that, as in Louisiana v. Mississippi, the *issues* that a state seeks to litigate before the Supreme Court are under consideration in proceedings to which the state is not a party? If so, the apparent result is that the state loses the opportunity to litigate those issues itself—an opportunity that Congress apparently afforded in § 1251(a).

The denouement in Louisiana v. Mississippi highlights these concerns. After the Court denied leave to file, the federal district court in Mississippi upheld its jurisdiction over Louisiana's third-party complaint against Mississippi (and reached the merits). Ultimately, however, the Supreme Court disagreed that the district court had jurisdiction, ordering the claim dismissed because § 1251(a)'s "uncompromising language" of exclusivity "necessarily denies jurisdiction * * * to any other federal court." Mississippi v. Louisiana, 506 U.S. 73 (1992). In so ruling, the Court rejected the argument that its earlier declination of original jurisdiction over that claim necessarily established that the district court was a proper forum to hear it. One might doubt that § 1251(a)'s language is any less "uncompromising" in requiring the Supreme Court to hear such disputes than in forbidding lower federal courts from doing so.

Perhaps the Court ultimately realized the problem that its pair of rulings created, for when Louisiana thereafter sought to file a new original action in the Supreme Court, it granted leave to file the bill of complaint. See Louisiana v. Mississippi, 510 U.S. 941 (1993), *decided on the merits*, 516 U.S. 22 (1995).

NOTE ON THE SCOPE OF JURISDICTION OVER CASES IN WHICH A STATE IS A PARTY: JURISDICTION ONLY WHEN INDEPENDENTLY CONFERRED BY STATE PARTY STATUS

(1) The Broadest Position and Its Rejection: Jurisdiction Whenever a State is a Party. How broadly does Article III confer original jurisdiction on the Supreme Court in cases in which a State is a party? Recall that the first sentence of Article III, Sec. 2, extends the federal judicial power to nine specified heads of jurisdiction. Section 2's subsequent provision for original jurisdiction in "those [cases] in which a State shall be Party" might have been construed as an independent grant of jurisdiction to hear *any* such case, whether or not it fell within one of the previously specified nine heads of jurisdiction. However, this broadest of possible constructions has been uniformly rejected. See, *e.g.*, Pennsylvania v. Quicksilver Co., 77 U.S. (10 Wall.) 553, 554–56 (1870).

(2) The Narrow Position and Its Rejection: Jurisdiction Only When Conferred by the State's Party Status. At the other extreme, a very narrow interpretation of the jurisdiction in cases in which a state is a party

---

sought to invalidate. See also Maryland v. Louisiana, 451 U.S. 725 (1981) (asserting but not exercising the power to decline to hear a case within the exclusive original jurisdiction).

might have begun by noting that, of the nine heads of jurisdiction, three are based on subject matter (admiralty, federal question, and cases affecting foreign envoys); the remaining six rest on party status, and three of those six require that a state be a party. It could be argued that the original jurisdiction should be limited to those cases in which the state's presence as a party is necessary to bring the case within the federal judicial power at all—cases between two states, between a state and a citizen of another state, or between a state and an alien.

The Supreme Court rejected that narrow construction in United States v. Texas, 143 U.S. 621 (1892) (7–2), a boundary dispute filed by the United States (as sovereign over the territory of Oklahoma) against Texas. Because the federal judicial power embraces any case in which the United States is a party, and because the case raised federal questions, the existence of federal court jurisdiction did not depend on the fact that Texas was also a party. In upholding the constitutionality of its exercise of original jurisdiction, the Court first stressed the importance of the United States-as-party jurisdiction, adding that it would be odd if the Court could resolve a dispute between one state and another, or between a state and a foreign nation, but not one between a state and the United States. The Court emphasized that it best comported with the dignity of a state and the momentous trust involved in adjudicating a dispute between state and union to vest jurisdiction in the Supreme Court.

(3) Rejection of an Intermediate Position: Whenever a State Is Party to a Case Falling Within the Federal Judicial Power. The decision in United States v. Texas, *supra*, is consistent with an intermediate position on the reach of the Original Jurisdiction Clause, under which the Supreme Court could exercise original jurisdiction in any case that falls within one of the nine heads of subject matter jurisdiction and in which a state is a party. However, that position was rejected in Texas v. ICC, 258 U.S. 158 (1922), involving a federal question claim by the state, which sued two agencies of the United States. There, the Court held that the case could not go forward without the presence, as defendants, of citizens of Texas whose interests were directly at issue, but that adding Texas citizens as parties opposed to Texas would destroy the diversity of citizenship (as Article III confers jurisdiction in suits by a state against *non-citizens* of the state).[1] Left unexplained was why, even if party-based jurisdiction could not be established between Texas and these in-state indispensable parties, it did not suffice that party-based jurisdiction could rest separately on the presence of the United States as a party.

It is not easy to reconcile Texas v. ICC with United States v. Texas, but the lessons seem to be these: (a) a case that raises a federal question and in which a state is party is not, without more, within the original jurisdiction; (b) for original jurisdiction to exist, the case must be one to which a state is a party and in which the basis for federal subject matter jurisdiction is the status of the parties (*e.g.*, state vs. state or state vs. non-citizen of the state) rather than subject matter (*e.g.*, federal question or admiralty); (c) the party-based jurisdiction that can support original jurisdiction includes those in which the United States is a party (establishing federal judicial power) and in which a state is also a party (establishing original jurisdiction); but (d) as in Texas v. ICC, the presence of the United States as a party does not suffice

---

[1]   An earlier decision pointing this way is California v. Southern Pac. Co., 157 U.S. 229 (1895), Paragraph (4), *infra.*

if not only the United States but also non-diverse parties are opposed to the state; and (e) while federal question jurisdiction alone does not suffice, its presence does not disqualify a case that otherwise falls within categories (b) or (c) above.[2]

The rationale for this set of rules, however, is anything but clear. And the limitation of the original jurisdiction in cases to which a state is a party to those in which federal judicial power exists because of party status rather than subject matter is hard to reconcile with the Original Jurisdiction Clause's extension of jurisdiction, by subject matter, to cases *affecting* foreign envoys.

(4) "Supplemental" Original Jurisdiction. In interpreting its original jurisdiction, the Supreme Court has adopted something akin to the "complete diversity rule" embodied by 28 U.S.C. § 1332, which governs the scope of diversity jurisdiction between private parties. (That, indeed, was the basis for dismissal in Texas v. ICC, Paragraph (3), *supra*.) The leading case establishing this proposition is California v. Southern Pac. Co., 157 U.S. 229 (1895). There, after California sued a citizen of another state, the Court determined that the rights of other parties, who were citizens of California, were so bound up in the action that the litigation should not proceed in their absence. In turn, the Court denied jurisdiction: although there would have been original jurisdiction in an action by California against the non-citizen defendant alone, the addition as defendants of California citizens, who could not have been sued independently in the Supreme Court, was fatal to the jurisdiction.[3]

Was the Court wise to reject the argument that joinder should be allowed to permit resolution of the entire matter in controversy? Could Congress override decisions like Southern Pacific and authorize exercise of "supplemental" original jurisdiction?

Notwithstanding Southern Pacific, in actions by the United States against a state, the Court has repeatedly (and without discussion) permitted the joinder of individual defendants whom the United States could not have sued separately in the original jurisdiction. See, *e.g.*, United States v. Wyoming, 331 U.S. 440 (1947); United States v. West Virginia, 295 U.S. 463 (1935). Here, too, the basis for the Court's position is anything but clear.

(5) Jurisdiction over Intervening Nonstate Parties. The Supreme Court has ruled that once it has original jurisdiction, it has authority to permit intervention by (and thereby to exercise jurisdiction over) non-state parties. In South Carolina v. North Carolina, 558 U.S. 256 (2010), South Carolina sued North Carolina, seeking an equitable apportionment of a river's waters. Three nonstate entities, all citizens of North Carolina—the Catawba River Water Supply Project, Duke Energy Carolinas, and the city of Charlotte, North Carolina—moved to intervene.

---

[2]   For criticism of the course of the decisions, and particularly of the conclusion that the original jurisdiction does not reach federal question or admiralty cases that do not also fall within the party-based heads of jurisdiction, see Pfander, p. 268, note 1, *supra*. Pfander contends more broadly that the state-as-party original jurisdiction was "at the center of the framers' plan to secure the effective enforcement of federal law against the states."

[3]   In Louisiana v. Cummins, 314 U.S. 577 (1941) (per curiam), the Court denied leave to file a complaint, rejecting the state's argument that dismissal in cases like Southern Pacific was required only when the ineligible party was "indispensable" (a term whose meaning is essentially the same as that of a party whose joinder is required under Fed.R.Civ.P. 19) and that here the Court had jurisdiction to proceed without the in-state defendant.

Had South Carolina's original complaint named any of the three intervenors as defendants, there would have been no original jurisdiction under the "complete diversity" approach of the Southern Pacific decision. Nonetheless, the Supreme Court ruled that nothing in Article III posed an absolute impediment to intervention. But stressing the burdens imposed on the Court's limited resources by original proceedings that require the Court to serve as factfinder, the opinion noted the high bar that the Court had traditionally applied when considering motions to intervene. " 'An intervenor whose state is already a party should have the burden of showing some compelling interest in his own right, apart from his interest in a class with all other citizens and creatures of the state, which interest is not properly represented by the state' " (quoting New Jersey v. New York, 345 U.S. 369, 373 (1953) (per curiam)). The Court concluded that two of the three intervenors satisfied this strict standard. Chief Justice Roberts, joined by Justices Thomas, Ginsburg, and Sotomayor, dissented on the intervention issue, reasoning that original jurisdiction was meant to resolve "sovereign" disputes and noting that "this Court has never before granted intervention in such a case to an entity other than a State, the United States, or an Indian tribe."

Since 28 U.S.C. § 1251(a) confers "original and exclusive jurisdiction of all controversies between two or more States," what is the source of the Court's authority to permit (and, if it has such authority, to limit) intervention by nonstate entities? *Cf.* UMW v. Gibbs, p. 861, *infra*, and the Note following the Gibbs decision.[4]

(6) "Penal" Actions. A state's criminal prosecution of a noncitizen falls within the literal wording of the constitutional grant of original jurisdiction and of § 1251.[5] But in Wisconsin v. Pelican Ins. Co., 127 U.S. 265, 297–98 (1888), the Court concluded that Article III's grant of jurisdiction in state-as-party cases "is limited to controversies of a civil nature" and does not extend to "a suit or prosecution by the one state, of such a nature that it could not, on the settled principles of public and international law, be entertained by the judiciary of the other state at all".[6]

---

[4]   On a related note, the Court in Alabama v. North Carolina, 560 U.S. 330 (2010), held that sovereign immunity does not bar suit by a nonstate plaintiff (in this case, an interstate compact commission), provided that the nonstate plaintiff "assert[s] the same claims and request[s] the same relief" as a plaintiff state whose claims are not barred by sovereign immunity under existing case law. See p. 921, *infra*. Chief Justice Roberts, joined by Justice Thomas, dissented, reasoning that the commission's ability as a party to "object to settlement, seek taxation of costs, advance arguments we are obliged to consider, and plead the judgment as res judicata in future litigation" violated the defendant state's immunity.

In view of the Court's strict posture toward intervention in South Carolina v. North Carolina, does its forgiving view of sovereign immunity in this case make sense? Quite apart from sovereign immunity, if the Court is reluctant to permit nonstate parties to intervene under 28 U.S.C. § 1251, why should a compact commission be able to join the action as a plaintiff simply because its claims and interests are aligned with those of a plaintiff state?

[5]   But *cf.* Fletcher, *Exchange on the Eleventh Amendment*, 57 U.Chi.L.Rev. 131, 133 (1990), and Meltzer, *The History and Structure of Article III*, 138 U.Pa.L.Rev. 1569, 1575–76 & nn.18, 22 (1990) (noting evidence that the word "controversy", used in Article III to define the state-as-party jurisdiction, was understood in the 18th century to encompass only civil cases); pp. 320–322, *infra*.

[6]   The Pelican case was disapproved in part in Milwaukee County v. M.E. White Co., 296 U.S. 268 (1935), which held that a federal district court in Illinois should take jurisdiction of an action by a Wisconsin county against an Illinois citizen on a judgment for taxes. The Court reserved opinion as to actions, outside the obligation-creating state, to enforce revenue laws or to enforce judgments "for an obligation created by a penal law, in the international sense".

The Pelican Court stressed the traditional reluctance of one jurisdiction to enforce the penal laws of another. Is that an adequate justification? (Note that (i) Cohens v. Virginia, p. 269, *supra*; pp. 920–921, *infra*, rejected the argument that Article III does not permit the exercise of the Supreme Court's *appellate* jurisdiction to review state criminal cases, and (ii) federal courts have removal jurisdiction over some state law criminal prosecutions.) Is the Pelican decision justified by docket concerns? By the desire to provide convenient venues and local juries for criminal trials? By the limitation to "civil" cases in the jurisdiction over state-as-party cases granted by § 13 of the Judiciary Act of 1789? See generally Woolhandler & Collins, *State Standing*, 81 Va.L.Rev. 387, 422–46 (1995); Meltzer, note 5, *supra*, at 1576.

NOTE ON A STATE'S STANDING TO SUE AND ON PARENS PATRIAE STANDING

A. Overview

States can bring suit in a number of different capacities—and sometimes in more than one capacity in a single litigation. States sometimes sue in their own proprietary capacity, much like private parties—for example, to enforce an interstate contract. In boundary disputes, the state's interest—preserving its sovereignty over property owned by others—is more intangible and less analogous to private interests. See Section B, *infra*.

The most difficult standing cases, discussed in Section C, *infra*, are those in which a state sues as *parens patriae* (literally translated as parent of the country), seeking to assert what is sometimes called a quasi-sovereign interest—an interest in the well-being of its citizens generally, as, for example, when a state sues to prevent pollution of water or air that is enjoyed by large numbers of state citizens. A distinct aspect of *parens patriae* standing is presented in suits *against the United States* and is discussed in Section D, *infra*.

B. Standing of a State to Sue as Proprietor or Sovereign

(1) The Real Party in Interest Rule. Although a state may sue to vindicate its own property rights, it has no standing to sue either another state or a private party when it is merely sponsoring the claims of a small number of individual citizens. Thus, in New Hampshire v. Louisiana, 108 U.S. 76 (1883), the plaintiff states sued on defaulted bonds, as assignees for collection only, on behalf of certain of their citizens. Although in general a state is not immune from suit by another state, the Court held the real parties in interest were the private citizens, whose claims against Louisiana were barred by state sovereign immunity. But in South Dakota v. North Carolina, 192 U.S. 286 (1904), South Dakota, having learned a lesson from the decision in New Hampshire v. Louisiana, acquired absolute title (by gift from an individual) to defaulted North Carolina bonds and was able to obtain judgment on them.[1]

(2) States as Tax Collectors. Without suggesting that in general a state can establish standing merely by asserting that its economy, and hence its

---

[1] See generally Siegel, *Congress's Power to Authorize Suits Against States*, 68 Geo.Wash.L.Rev. 44, 100 (1999) (reading the two decisions as indicating that "what matters is whether the plaintiff has a proper interest that entitles it to bring the suit, not whether plaintiff has an appropriate motive").

tax collections, have been harmed by another state, a divided Court upheld standing to complain of a reduction in tax revenues in the circumstances presented in Wyoming v. Oklahoma, 502 U.S. 437 (1992). There, Wyoming successfully challenged, as a violation of the dormant Commerce Clause, an Oklahoma law requiring that at least 10% of the coal burned by certain private utility plants within the state be Oklahoma-mined. The Court stressed that the law deprived Wyoming of "specific tax revenues" from its severance tax on coal mined in Wyoming. And the Court rejected the view (endorsed by Justice Scalia in dissent) that Wyoming, because it was not engaged in commerce in coal, had not suffered the *kind* of injury cognizable under the dormant Commerce Clause.[2]

(3) States as Sovereigns: Boundary and Water Cases. When suing a neighboring state about water rights or boundaries, a state asserts a distinctive interest in sovereignty. Although Chief Justice Taney's dissent in Rhode Island v. Massachusetts, 37 U.S. (12 Pet.) 657, 752 (1838), argued that such cases were therefore not justiciable, the prevailing view is that these interstate disputes, though not justiciable at common law, were made justiciable by the Constitution, see, *e.g.*, Hans v. Louisiana, 134 U.S. 1, 15 (1890).

In Kansas v. Colorado, 533 U.S. 1 (2001), the Court held that when Colorado violated an interstate compact regulating use of the waters of the Arkansas River, sovereign immunity did not preclude awarding Kansas damages that were measured in part by the losses suffered by Kansas' citizens (who would themselves be barred, by sovereign immunity, from suing Colorado). The Court reaffirmed the rule of New Hampshire v. Louisiana—that a state may not sue to advance the claims of citizens who are the real parties in interest. But the Court noted that Kansas fully controlled the litigation, that the injury to Kansas farmers was only one component of the damages calculation, and that the ultimate measure of damages cannot "retrospectively negate our jurisdiction". Nor, the Court added, would jurisdiction be affected if, after judgment, Kansas distributed the damages awarded to injured citizens.

C.   Standing of a State to Sue as *Parens Patriae*

(1) Introduction. Once the boundary and water cases recognized that states could sue to protect sovereign interests, the question arose whether or when a state may also litigate as *parens patriae* to protect quasi-sovereign interests, a kind of interest which the Supreme Court has acknowledged is "a judicial construct that does not lend itself to a simple or exact definition." Alfred L. Snapp & Son, Inc. v. Puerto Rico ex rel. Barez, 458 U.S. 592, 601

---

[2]   The Court took a more restrictive approach in Pennsylvania v. New Jersey, 426 U.S. 660 (1976) (per curiam), which involved two different lawsuits by neighboring states alleging that commuter income taxes were unconstitutional under the Privileges and Immunities and Equal Protection Clauses. In one case, Maine, Massachusetts, and Vermont alleged that, because of the credit they afforded their residents for income taxes paid to other states, the New Hampshire commuter tax had diverted $13.5 million of revenue from their respective treasuries to New Hampshire. In the second case, Pennsylvania (which provided a similar tax credit) alleged that New Jersey's commuter income tax was invalid. The Court denied leave to file in both cases. It held, first, that "[t]he injuries to the plaintiffs' fiscs" were not caused by the defendant states but were "self-inflicted," resulting from their own tax credits. Second, it held that no state has standing to complain of violations of the Privileges and Immunities Clause or the Equal Protection Clause, both of which "protect people, not States." Finally, the Court held that Pennsylvania could not sue as *parens patriae*, as the action was "nothing more than a collectivity of private suits against New Jersey for taxes withheld from private parties."

(1982). The basic notion, however, seems to be that the state is suing to protect public interests that concern the state's citizens at large.

(2) The Early *Parens Patriae* Cases. The early *parens patriae* decisions appeared to rest on two premises. First, a state not complaining of injury to its own property could not sue merely because its citizens were injured by (a) actions of another state, see Louisiana v. Texas, 176 U.S. 1 (1900) (rejecting a complaint by Louisiana alleging that a Texas embargo on commerce from New Orleans, although predicated on health concerns, was a pretext and harmed Louisiana citizens), or (b) by actions of private persons, see Oklahoma v. Atchison, Topeka and Santa Fe Ry. Co., 220 U.S. 277 (1911) (Oklahoma could not sue to enjoin railroad rates alleged to hinder growth in the state and to injure the property rights of its inhabitants).

Second, suits were permitted to challenge physical intrusions into the plaintiff state that harmed state citizens. Thus, in Missouri v. Illinois, 180 U.S. 208, 241 (1901), the Court refused to dismiss Missouri's action to enjoin the dumping of Chicago's sewage into a canal whose waters flowed to Missouri and harmed its water supply and land: "[I]f the health and comfort of the inhabitants of a state are threatened, the state is the proper party to represent and defend them." Notably, the Court reasoned that because Missouri, in joining the nation, had surrendered to the national government the power that a foreign nation would possess to seek redress by negotiation and, failing that, by force, the national government was obliged to provide a remedy. This approach was extended, in Georgia v. Tennessee Copper Co., 206 U.S. 230 (1907), to the state of Georgia's lawsuit for redress for injury to its lands and those of its citizens caused by a private company whose discharge of noxious gas in Tennessee passed into Georgia.

(3) The Extension of *Parens Patriae* Standing. Beginning in the 1920s, a series of decisions extended *parens patriae* standing to situations in which the harm to the plaintiff state's citizens did not arise from physical intrusion but rather from regulations adopted within the defendant state. In Pennsylvania v. West Virginia, 262 U.S. 553 (1923), a divided Court enjoined enforcement of a West Virginia statute designed to limit the export of natural gas. The Court said that Pennsylvania and Ohio, the complaining states, each "sues to protect a twofold interest—one as the proprietor of various public institutions and schools whose supply of gas * * * [could be curtailed], and the other as the representative of the consuming public whose supply will be similarly affected. * * * [T]he state, as the representative of the public, has an interest apart from that of the individuals affected. It is not merely a remote or ethical interest, but one which is immediate and recognized by law." The extension of standing that this decision represents is apparent when it is compared to the decision in Louisiana v. Texas, Paragraph C(2), *supra*, where the Court, in denying standing, had stated that "the vindication of the freedom of interstate commerce is not committed to the [complaining state]". See also Maryland v. Louisiana, 451 U.S. 725 (1981) (permitting eight states to challenge the constitutionality of a Louisiana tax on the "first use" of previously untaxed natural gas coming into the state, a tax whose incidence fell on many customers in the plaintiff states).

Georgia v. Pennsylvania R.R., 324 U.S. 439 (1945) (5–4), extended the more liberal attitude to standing to a state's action against private defendants. There, Georgia was permitted, on behalf of its citizens, to sue twenty railroads to enjoin an alleged rate-fixing conspiracy, because the high rates impaired the state economy's development and because of "the measures taken by the State to promote * * * the general progress and welfare of its people". Noting that Oklahoma v. Atchison, Topeka, and Santa Fe Ry. Co., Paragraph C(2), *supra*, had refused thirty-four years earlier to permit a state to challenge railroad rates, the Court said: "This is not a suit in which a State is a mere nominal plaintiff, individual shippers being the real complainants. This is a suit in which Georgia asserts claims arising out of federal laws and the gravamen of which runs far beyond the claim of damage to individual shippers."[3]

Compare the broad language in Alfred L. Snapp & Son, Inc. v. Puerto Rico ex rel. Barez, 458 U.S. 592 (1982), upholding a *district* court action by Puerto Rico, as *parens patriae*, against apple growers in eastern states who allegedly had illegally preferred Jamaican over Puerto Rican temporary workers. The Court discussed its original jurisdiction precedents but noted that the special considerations limiting *parens patriae* suits in the original jurisdiction may not apply to district court actions—a point four concurring Justices emphasized. The Court also stated that in determining whether a state may sue as *parens patriae* to redress injury to its citizens' health and welfare, "[o]ne helpful indication * * * is whether the injury is one that the State, if it could, would likely attempt to address through its sovereign lawmaking powers." The concurrence suggested that the state, "no ordinary litigant", should be able to determine which injuries to its citizens warrant protection. Does either notion place any serious limit on *parens patriae* standing?

(4) The Adequacy of State Representation. In Maryland v. Louisiana, 451 U.S. 725 (1981), Paragraph (3), *supra*, the Court suggested that it is desirable to empower states to bring original actions when many citizens have suffered small claims for which individual redress is impractical. But note that there are no safeguards, similar to those set forth in Fed.R.Civ.Proc. 23 for class actions, that require courts to determine whether a state will be an adequate representative in any particular lawsuit—even though judgment in a *parens patriae* action ordinarily will preclude separate claims by the citizens whose interests were represented.[4] Professor Lemos finds the absence of such safeguards troubling given the numerous reasons to believe that state attorneys general will often not be good representatives of private claimants. See Lemos, *Aggregate Litigation Goes Public: Representative Suits by State Attorneys General*, 126 Harv.L.Rev. 486 (2012). Those reasons include conflicts of interest arising

---

[3]   The Court also distinguished Massachusetts v. Mellon, Paragraph D(1), *infra*, which refused to permit a state to sue to protect her citizens from the operation of federal statutes; here, by contrast, the state sought not to invalidate federal laws but to assert rights based on them.

[4]   See, *e.g.*, Washington v. Washington State Commercial Passenger Fishing Vessel Ass'n, 443 U.S. 658, 692 n.32 (1979), and City of Tacoma v. Taxpayers of Tacoma, 357 U.S. 320, 340–41 (1958), both involving former lower court judgments in suits by states as *parens patriae*. In Badgley v. City of New York, 606 F.2d 358, 364–66 (2d Cir.1979), involving a prior judgment in an original action in the Supreme Court, the court precluded private parties from raising claims not only for injunctive relief but also for damages. But *cf.* Satsky v. Paramount Communications, Inc., 7 F.3d 1464, 1470 (10th Cir.1993) (prior judgment in *parens patriae* action does not preclude citizens from suing for private damages not recoverable in the earlier action).

Compare Hawaii v. Standard Oil Co. of Cal., 405 U.S. 251 (1972), a *district* court treble damages action under the federal antitrust laws for injuries to the state's "economy and prosperity". The Supreme Court ruled that Hawaii could sue in its "proprietary capacity", but that permitting it to obtain damages as *parens patriae* for injury to the state's "general economy" would open the door to duplicate recoveries. The Court did not discuss the possibility of preclusion.

from the attorneys general's (i) responsibility to represent the distinct interests of state agencies, (ii) concern about the effect of litigation on the public interest, (iii) electoral ambitions, and (iv) inclination to accept inadequate but quick settlements given their lack of personal financial incentive to seek larger recoveries and the limited resources most offices possess. But however imperfect such litigation may be, is there a better alternative?

(5) Questions About the *Parens Patriae* Decisions. The question of a state's standing has not generally been answered by reference to the doctrines governing the standing of private parties in the district courts. See generally Woolhandler & Collins, *State Standing*, 81 Va.L.Rev. 387, 450–55, 464–78 (1995), who suggest that some of the foregoing decisions upholding standing embraced a "public law" model (see pp. 74–75, *supra*) long before it became available in actions by private individuals. See also Massachusetts v. EPA, 549 U.S. 497 (2007), discussed at pp. 149–151, *infra*. Numerous recent Supreme Court decisions reject a "public law" model—for example, those holding that private plaintiffs who present a generalized grievance lack standing to sue. See pp. 118–119, 164–168, *supra*. But many of the *parens patriae* decisions can be viewed as assertions by the state of generalized grievances of its citizens. Should standards of justiciability be more liberal in actions by states than in actions by individuals? Does it matter whether the defendant is another state (in which case the original jurisdiction substitutes for war or diplomacy) or a private party? Or should state standing be narrowly defined because many suits will fall within the original jurisdiction, burdening the Court and depriving it of the chance to have issues first percolate in the lower courts? (And if so, should *parens patriae* standing be broader if a state sues in a district court that has concurrent jurisdiction, as in Alfred L. Snapp & Son, Inc. v. Puerto Rico ex rel. Barez, Paragraph C(3), *supra*?) How do the considerations noted in Paragraph C(4), *supra*—that private suits may be impractical, but also that attorneys general may not be good representatives—bear on these questions?

D.   Standing of a State as *Parens Patriae* to Sue the Federal Government

A distinct set of cases involves states as *parens patriae* suing not other states or private parties but rather the federal government or its officials. The decisions seem to depend in part upon the kind of claim that the state advances, but they are hard to reconcile.

(1) Massachusetts v. Mellon. In Massachusetts v. Mellon, 262 U.S. 447 (1923), the Court unanimously found that Massachusetts lacked standing to sue the Secretary of the Treasury on a claim that a federal grant program exceeded Congress' Article I powers and thus violated the Tenth Amendment. The Court reasoned that the state's claim, if brought on its own behalf, involved "not rights of person or property, not rights of dominion over physical domain, not quasi-sovereign rights actually invaded or threatened, but abstract questions of political power, of sovereignty, of government." As for a suit representing the state's citizens, the Court said that "[w]e need not go so far as to say that a State may never intervene by suit to protect its citizens against any form of enforcement of unconstitutional acts of Congress; but we are clear that the right to do so does not arise here. * * * While the State, under some circumstances, may sue [as *parens patriae*] for the protection of its citizens, it is no part of its duty or power to enforce their rights in respect of their relations with the Federal Government. In that field it is the United States, and not the State, which represents them as *parens patriae*."

(2) South Carolina v. Katzenbach. Some forty years later, the Court relied on Massachusetts v. Mellon in denying South Carolina the right to sue on two claims to enjoin the Attorney General from enforcing the Voting Rights Act of 1965. South Carolina v. Katzenbach, 383 U.S. 301 (1966). But while holding that the state, as *parens patriae*, could not invoke the Due Process and Bill of Attainder Clauses, the Court, without discussing standing, reached the merits of (and rejected) a third claim, based on the Fifteenth Amendment, that the Act invaded the reserved power of the states to determine voter qualifications and regulate elections. It is anything but clear that the handling of the standing questions was internally consistent or consistent with the Mellon decision. See Bickel, *The Voting Rights Cases*, 1966 Sup.Ct.Rev. 79, 80–93.

(3) Nebraska v. Wyoming. In Nebraska v. Wyoming, 515 U.S. 1 (1995), the state of Wyoming advanced a different kind of interest from those advanced in the cases just described, and the Supreme Court permitted the state to file a cross-claim against the United States. The Court in 1945 had entered a decree, apportioning water among several states, that was predicated on compliance by the United States (which had intervened in the action) with certain obligations regarding its handling of storage water. When Wyoming later moved to enjoin the United States from violating those obligations, the Court rejected the United States' argument that Wyoming was merely seeking to benefit individuals who were parties to storage contracts. Relying on Georgia v. Tennessee Copper Co., Paragraph C(2), *supra*, the Court said that Wyoming could sue to vindicate the state's "quasi-sovereign" interests, which are independent of those of its citizens, in the physical environment within its domain.

(4) Massachusetts v. EPA. Most recently in Massachusetts v. EPA, 549 U.S. 497 (2007), a closely divided Court recognized a state's standing to sue to require the federal government to comply with a federal statute. The state's standing was based both on a claim of injury to the state's own real property and on its quasi-sovereign interests. In rejecting the contention that these allegations of injury failed to satisfy Article III's standing requirement, the Court suggested that a state's standing is broader than that of a private citizen.

Along with private organizations and other governments, Massachusetts challenged the EPA's determinations that (i) it lacked statutory authority to regulate greenhouse gas emissions from new motor vehicles and (ii) it would not exercise regulatory authority in any event. Justice Stevens' majority opinion reasoned that Massachusetts had adequately alleged that global warming could cause rising sea levels that would threaten the considerable coastal land owned by the state and that the relief sought would reduce the risk of harm to Massachusetts.

As a prelude to that analysis, the Court quoted language from Georgia v. Tennessee Copper Co., Paragraph C(2), *supra*, at 237, stressing that that case was not one merely between private parties and that Georgia was suing for an injury to its quasi-sovereign interest "in all the earth and air within its domain." Similarly, the Court reasoned, Massachusetts has a "well-founded desire to preserve its sovereign territory today. * * * That Massachusetts does in fact own a great deal of the 'territory alleged to be affected' only reinforces the conclusion that its stake in the outcome of this case is sufficiently concrete to warrant the exercise of federal judicial power."

Having discussed both the state's quasi-sovereign and proprietary interests, the Court then turned to political theory. Massachusetts, by joining the union, had surrendered to the national government such sovereign prerogatives as invading a neighboring state, or negotiating with foreign nations, in an effort to reduce emissions of greenhouse gases; moreover, in some cases a state's regulatory power is preempted by federal law. In this connection, the Court quoted the statement in Alfred L. Snapp & Son, Inc. v. Puerto Rico ex rel. Barez, Paragraph C(3), *supra*, that one " 'helpful indication' " of a state's capacity to sue *parens patriae* is whether the state would likely try to address the injury in question through its lawmaking powers if it could. Suggesting that recognition of state standing was therefore all the more important, the Court concluded this portion of its analysis by stating that Massachusetts "is entitled to special solicitude in our standing analysis."

In dissent, Chief Justice Roberts, joined by Justices Scalia, Thomas, and Alito, objected that Georgia v. Tennessee Copper distinguished states from private litigants only with respect to the availability of equitable relief, not with respect to standing. In that case, he said, the inquiry was not whether the state could sue where private standing was doubtful but whether the state had articulated a quasi-sovereign interest beyond the interests of private citizens who clearly had standing. He also complained that the Court, while purporting to extend special solicitude for the state's quasi-sovereign injury, proceeded to analyze Massachusetts' standing based on its status as landowner, a nonsovereign interest. And he accused the Court of overlooking the doubts expressed in prior decisions that a state may assert a quasi-sovereign right as *parens patriae* when, as here, the defendant is the federal government.

It is difficult to ascertain how much the majority's decision turned on the proposition that a state is not bound by the standing rules that apply to private plaintiffs, especially since the Court, after referring to the state's quasi-sovereign interests, devoted considerable attention to its proprietary interest as the owner of coastal land. But insofar as the decision heralds a relaxation of standing for states (at least when suing in a quasi-sovereign capacity), does it make sense? Professor Massey thinks so, *inter alia*, because such an approach creates a further level of accountability for the federal executive, at the behest of discrete polities of the union. Massey, *Of Sovereignty, States, and Standing*, 61 Fla.L.Rev. 249 (2009). Professors Freeman and Vermeule disagree, contending that the states have greater ability to mobilize congressional power vis-a-vis agencies than do private litigants. They suggest that the majority may have included that statement in order to secure Justice Kennedy's vote, but that it is hard to square with the faith, expressed by the other members of the majority in other decisions, in the political safeguards of federalism. See Freeman & Vermeule, *Massachusetts v. EPA: From Politics to Expertise*, 2007 Sup.Ct.Rev. 51, 67–71.[5]

---

[5]   See also Merrill, *Global Warming as a Public Nuisance*, 30 Colum.J.Envtl.L. 293, 299–306 (2005), noting that states, when enforcing their criminal laws, have never been required to satisfy the same standing rules that govern private plaintiffs and that public nuisance actions might be viewed as the civil analogue of criminal prosecution. He proposes that traditional private party standing doctrines should apply to *parens patriae* suits only when not filed in a

An additional uncertainty relates to the statutory provision, 42 U.S.C. § 7606(b)(1), that authorized the filing of "[a] petition for review of * * * final action taken" by EPA. The majority said that provision "is of critical importance to the standing inquiry", because Congress may " 'define injuries and articulate chains of causation that will give rise to a case or controversy where none existed before' " (quoting Lujan v. Defenders of Wildlife, 504 U.S. 555, 580 (1992) (Kennedy, J., concurring in part and concurring in the judgment)). Insofar as Massachusetts' standing rested on § 7606(b)(1), was it convincing for the Court to suggest that standing is broader for states than for private litigants, when all of the challengers sued under the same review provision?

The statute may be relevant along a different dimension. In Maryland People's Counsel v. FERC, 760 F.2d 318, 320–22 (D.C.Cir.1985), then Judge Scalia characterized the Mellon decision's barrier to *parens patriae* suits against the federal government as prudential, not constitutional, and hence subject to override by Congress, at least when the citizen interests represented by the state are concrete and the state challenges executive compliance with statutory requirement in an area in which the states have long shared responsibility with the federal government.[6]

———

NOTE ON THE SUPREME COURT'S ISSUANCE OF ORIGINAL WRITS

(1) Original Writs: Original Versus Appellate Jurisdiction. Although, as noted at the outset of this Chapter, Article III directly grants original jurisdiction to the Supreme Court, ever since 1789 Congress has nonetheless enacted legislation conferring original jurisdiction on the Supreme Court. That legislation has not only prescribed jurisdiction in the provision now codified in 28 U.S.C. § 1251 but also authorized the Court to issue "extraordinary" writs—mandamus, prohibition, common-law certiorari, quo warranto, and habeas corpus. Issuance of such writs in a case that otherwise falls within the original jurisdiction—one affecting a foreign envoy or in which a state is a party—raises little difficulty. But as Marbury v. Madison famously held, Congress may not authorize the Supreme Court to issue a writ, as an exercise of original jurisdiction, in a case beyond the scope of Article III's grant of original jurisdiction.

When, unlike in Marbury, mandamus or some other writ is sought in connection with a pending proceeding in a state or a lower federal *court*, the Supreme Court's issuance of the writ can be viewed as an exercise (in advance) of the Court's appellate jurisdiction. Article III confers that jurisdiction, "with such Exceptions, and under such Regulations as the

---

sovereign's own courts. He recognizes, however, that his approach does not fit the decided cases—notably the long history of adjudication by federal courts of interstate nuisance disputes.

Professor Mank, in *Should States Have Greater Standing Rights Than Ordinary Citizens?: Massachusetts v. EPA's New Standing Test for States*, 49 Wm. & Mary L.Rev. 1701 (2008), argues that Massachusetts v. EPA is soundly grounded in *parens patriae* precedents, even though they do not address standing issues as such. He contends that when states sue to protect quasi-sovereign interests, which typically implicate generalized grievances, courts should not require a showing of particularized injury and should apply more lenient immediacy and redressability requirements.

  [6] In Lexmark Intern., Inc. v. Static Control Components, Inc., 134 S.Ct. 1377 (2014), pp. 156–158, 168, *supra*, Justice Scalia, writing for a unanimous Supreme Court, cast doubt on the continued validity of prudential limits on standing generally.

Congress shall make." In Durousseau v. United States, 10 U.S. (6 Cranch) 307 (1810), the Court construed the Judiciary Act of 1789 as impliedly withdrawing the Supreme Court's appellate jurisdiction in every situation in which jurisdiction was not expressly conferred. As a result, the power to issue an extraordinary writ as an exercise of appellate jurisdiction, if outside the affirmative grant of authority by statute, may be deemed to have impliedly been precluded by Congress.[1]

(2) Early Developments: Habeas Corpus Practice and Ex parte Bollman. The ancient writ of habeas corpus *ad subjiciendum* requires the respondent, ordinarily a government official, to appear in court to justify the legality of the detention of the individual who petitions for the writ. It has a long history as an important protection of liberty in England. The Constitution appears at least to presuppose that American courts would have jurisdiction to entertain habeas corpus petitions, and the Supreme Court has held that the Suspension Clause of the Constitution guarantees the availability of habeas corpus in some circumstances. See pp. 335–341, 1200–1203, *infra*. The Judiciary Act of 1789, consistently with those understandings, conferred habeas jurisdiction on the federal courts. Section 14 of that Act, 1 Stat. 81–82, provided in relevant part: "That all the before-mentioned courts of the United States, shall have power to issue writs of *scire facias*, *habeas corpus*, and all other writs not specially provided for by statute, which may be necessary for the exercise of their respective jurisdictions, and agreeable to the principles and usages of law. And that either of the justices of the supreme court, as well as judges of the district courts, shall have power to grant writs of *habeas corpus* for the purpose of an inquiry into the cause of commitment."

In Ex parte Bollman, 8 U.S. (4 Cranch) 75 (1807), the federal circuit court had found probable cause to order the petitioners committed to stand trial for treason. The petitioners then challenged the legality of their detention by seeking an original writ of habeas corpus from the Supreme Court. Chief Justice Marshall's opinion upheld the Court's jurisdiction to entertain the application for the writ of habeas corpus. He first rejected the view that § 14 authorized the courts to issue the writ only as an auxiliary to jurisdiction otherwise conferred upon them.[2] Rather, he read that provision as authorizing an independent action in habeas corpus. The power that § 14 expressly conferred on the *Justices* and *judges* was held to be vested by implication in the courts.

---

[1] In *Not the King's Bench*, 20 Const.Comment. 283 (2003), Professor Hartnett contends that the Supreme Court did not inherit the power of the King's Bench in England to issue prerogative writs, absent legislative authorization. Among the decisions on which Hartnett relies are those holding that, absent congressional authorization, prerogative writs may not be issued either (a) by the inferior federal courts or (b) by the Supreme Court when acting within its appellate jurisdiction. But since the lower federal courts have only such jurisdiction as Congress affirmatively provides, their need for statutory authorization in order to issue prerogative writs is hardly surprising. And as to the Supreme Court, given the approach of Durousseau, affirmative grants of *appellate* jurisdiction impliedly create an exception for that which is not granted. Neither example, then, establishes the need for congressional authorization of extraordinary writs issued under the Supreme Court's original jurisdiction, which is given directly by the Constitution but is not subject to a congressional power to make exceptions.

[2] For the contrary view—that § 14 merely ratified a court's power to employ habeas corpus in aid of jurisdiction otherwise conferred—see Paschal, *The Constitution and Habeas Corpus*, 1970 Duke L.J. 605.

Marshall next declared that when (as in Bollman) an application filed directly in the Supreme Court challenges the legality of a detention that is based on a lower court's order, the matter falls within the appellate jurisdiction of the Supreme Court: "The decision that the individual shall be imprisoned must always precede the application for a writ of *habeas corpus*, and this writ must always be for the purpose of revising that decision, and therefore appellate in its nature." Section 14 was recognized as conferring appellate jurisdiction via the writ of habeas corpus, even though no statute conferred on the Supreme Court a direct right to review the lower court decision through a more conventional mechanism (an appeal or a writ of error or a writ of certiorari). See also Ex parte Watkins, 32 U.S. (7 Pet.) 568 (1833).

Subsequently, in Ex parte Yerger, 75 U.S. (8 Wall.) 85 (1868), where a circuit court had granted and thereafter dismissed the writ sought by a military prisoner, the Supreme Court again found that its consideration of a petition for a writ of habeas corpus was an exercise of appellate jurisdiction—despite congressional repeal of the statute that had authorized an ordinary appeal from the denial of the writ by lower courts.[3] Felker v. Turpin, 518 U.S. 651 (1996), similarly upheld the Court's power to issue a writ to review a lower federal court decision, notwithstanding a statutory provision that the decision below "shall not be appealable and shall not be the subject of a petition for * * * writ of certiorari." 28 U.S.C. § 2244(b)(3)(E). In finding that a congressional limitation on the Supreme Court's jurisdiction to review (via appeal or certiorari) a lower federal court decision did not prelude the Court from entertaining an original writ of habeas corpus, both decisions avoided difficult constitutional questions under Article III and, at least in Yerger, under the Suspension Clause.

(3) The Development of Mandamus Jurisdiction. Section 13 of the Judiciary Act of 1789 gave the Supreme Court "power to issue writs of prohibition to the district courts, when proceeding as courts of admiralty and maritime jurisdiction, and writs of mandamus, in cases warranted by the principles and usages of law, to any courts appointed, or persons holding office, under the authority of the United States." Marbury, of course, held the last clause—authorizing mandamus to be issued to persons holding office under the authority of the United States—to be unconstitutional. But the Marbury decision did not resolve the scope of the Court's authority to issue such writs to lower federal courts.

More than a century ago, the Court seemed to have thought that it could issue mandamus or prohibition, in the exercise of appellate jurisdiction, only when the writ was in aid of the proper disposition of a case then pending in the Supreme Court. See Ex parte Warmouth, 84 U.S. (17 Wall.) 64 (1872). But in In re Massachusetts, 197 U.S. 482 (1905), the Court recognized the propriety of issuing a writ in aid of the disposition of a case that was pending in a lower federal court and over which the Supreme Court had a power of direct review.

(4) Ex parte Peru. After Congress in 1891 created the circuit courts of appeals as an intermediate level between federal trial courts and the Supreme Court, the question arose whether it was a proper exercise of the Supreme Court's appellate jurisdiction to issue an original writ with respect

---

[3]   See also Ex parte Siebold, 100 U.S. 371 (1880). But see Ex parte Barry, 43 U.S. (2 How.) 65 (1844) (no appellate jurisdiction to issue writ to test confinement by a private party in a child custody case).

to a proceeding pending in a federal district court—and thus one step away from being directly reviewable by the Supreme Court. In the leading decision of Ex parte Republic of Peru, 318 U.S. 578 (1943), the Court upheld its jurisdiction, under the successor provisions to the First Judiciary Act's §§ 13 (quoted in Paragraph (3), *supra*) and 14 (quoted in Paragraph (2), *supra*), to issue mandamus and/or prohibition in connection with a federal district court admiralty proceeding. In that case, the nation of Peru had filed a motion in the Supreme Court, seeking leave to file a petition for an original writ of prohibition or a writ of mandamus against a federal district judge, requiring him to recognize Peru's claim of sovereign immunity in pending litigation.

In an opinion by Chief Justice Stone, the Court cited numerous cases in which it had issued such writs in aid of its appellate jurisdiction. The Chief Justice acknowledged that issuance of the writ is within the Court's sound discretion, and further acknowledged since the creation of the circuit courts of appeals, the Court had often refused to issue a writ to a district court, without prejudice to the petitioner's application in the court of appeals, which also has power to issue a writ. But those exercises of discretion did not deprive the Supreme Court of jurisdiction to issue the writ in an exceptional case of public importance like the present one, involving the "dignity and rights of a friendly sovereign state."

Only Justice Frankfurter disagreed with the Court's jurisdictional ruling, stressing the Court's unwillingness, since the circuit courts of appeals were created, to issue writs of mandamus to district courts when the case had not (yet) been taken to the court of appeals. The decisions on which the majority relied were distinguishable; none involved a case in which a ruling had not yet been, but could be, reviewed in the court of appeals.[4]

(5) Writs Issued in Connection with State Court Decisions. Does the Court have the same authority to issue an extraordinary writ with regard to a case pending in a state court, if the case presents a federal issue that is potentially reviewable by the Supreme Court? (Section 13 of the Judiciary Act of 1789 permitted writs to be issued only to "courts appointed * * * under the authority of the United States", but the surviving authority in 28 U.S.C. § 1651(a) lacks that restriction.) The only decisions are two cases where the Court had already exercised appellate jurisdiction over the merits, and, without discussion of jurisdiction, subsequently granted leave to file a petition for a writ of mandamus ordering the state court to conform its decision to the Supreme Court's mandate. Deen v. Hickman, 358 U.S. 57 (1958); General Atomic Co. v. Felter, 436 U.S. 493 (1978); see p. 476–477, *infra*.[5]

---

[4] See Wolfson, *Extraordinary Writs in the Supreme Court Since Ex parte Peru*, 51 Colum.L.Rev. 977, 991 (1951) (in Ex parte Peru, "the Court found that, with respect to cases coming from the federal courts, its power was practically limitless. Thus, * * * the conflict moved into the area of discretion").

For discussion of the authority of non-Article III federal appellate tribunals—particularly tribunals authorized by Congress to review military prosecutions—to issue writs in cases that will ultimately come before them on appeal, see Vladeck, *Military Courts and the All Writs Act*, 17 Green Bag 2d 191 (2014).

[5] What of cases pending in a federal administrative agency, directly reviewable in a lower federal court? *Cf.* CAB v. American Air Transport, 344 U.S. 4 (1952), refusing to decide questions of law certified by the court of appeals under the predecessor provision to 28 U.S.C. § 1254(2), in a case coming from an administrative agency. See also FTC v. Dean Foods Co., 384 U.S. 597 (1966).

(6) Statutory Authority for the Issuance of Extraordinary Writs. Five years after the Ex parte Peru decision, the 1948 revision of the Judicial Code repealed the successor provision to § 13 of the Judiciary Act of 1789; the revisers explained that it was "omitted as unnecessary". Thus, at present the only statutory authority for the issuance of extraordinary writs other than habeas corpus (which is specifically authorized in 28 U.S.C. § 2241(a)) is the famous all-writs section, 28 U.S.C. § 1651(a), which today covers the ground initially covered by §§ 13 and 14 of the 1789 Act.

In LaBuy v. Howes Leather Co., 352 U.S. 249, 265–66 (1957), Justice Brennan's dissent, in discussing the powers of the courts of appeals (which were never covered by § 13), argued that the mandamus power granted by § 1651(a) is significantly narrower than that formerly granted by § 13. But he did not have to face the question whether the elimination of § 13 narrowed the *Supreme Court*'s power to issue mandamus.[6] See also Chandler v. Judicial Council of the Tenth Circuit, 398 U.S. 74, 89, 117 n. 15 (1970) (Harlan, J., concurring).[7]

(7) Supreme Court Practice. The Supreme Court Rules address the circumstances in which an original writ will issue. The 1980 revision of those Rules dispensed with the requirement that a petition for an extraordinary writ be preceded by a motion for leave to file. However, the Rules provide that issuance of extraordinary writs under § 1651(a) "is not a matter of right,

---

[6] Professor Pfander, in *Jurisdiction-Stripping and the Supreme Court's Power to Supervise Inferior Tribunals*, 78 Tex.L.Rev. 1433 (2000), does not view § 1651 as having narrowed the Supreme Court's authority to supervise lower federal court decisions, an authority he believes inheres in the *Supreme* Court and is not subject to congressional limitation. He reads § 1651's authorization to federal courts to issue writs "in aid of their respective jurisdictions" to mean, in the case of the Supreme Court, in aid of its appellate jurisdiction *as defined by Article III.* Under this view, he acknowledges, § 1651 would mean something different when applied to the Supreme Court (freestanding authority to issue a writ to review an inferior court, so long as the case is "appellate" within the meaning of the *Constitution*) than when applied to the inferior courts (authority to issue a writ only when the inferior court otherwise has jurisdiction conferred by *statute*). He justifies this difference by noting that Article III confers appellate jurisdiction directly on the Supreme Court but leaves it to Congress to create and confer jurisdiction upon the inferior courts. (Does this suggest, notwithstanding Pfander's emphasis on supervision of inferior *federal* courts, that the Supreme Court is authorized, whether by § 1651 or Article III itself, to issue writs to supervise *state* court decisions—review of which is equally within the appellate jurisdiction directly conferred by Article III?)

[7] The Chandler case raised but did not answer important questions about the Court's power to issue extraordinary writs in connection with the discipline of lower court judges. The Tenth Circuit Judicial Council found District Judge Chandler "unable or unwilling" to discharge his duties, and ordered that cases pending before him be reassigned and that no new cases be assigned to him. Judge Chandler filed a motion in the Supreme Court for leave to file a petition for writs of mandamus or prohibition, arguing that the Council's orders were illegal.

The Court said that it would be "no mean feat" to find that the Judicial Council's action was reviewable as a "judicial act or decision by a judicial tribunal", "without doing violence to the constitutional requirement that [the Court's] review be appellate." However, it ruled that the question need not be resolved, since other, though unspecified, avenues of relief on the merits "may yet be open to Judge Chandler."

Justice Harlan would have granted leave to file, finding that the Judicial Council's orders were an exercise of judicial power, that Chandler lacked other remedies, and that the Supreme Court had appellate jurisdiction. He acknowledged that prior Supreme Court invocations of § 1651(a) to issue a writ "in aid of [its jurisdiction]" involved cases over which the Court would later have statutory jurisdiction to review. By contrast, here the Judicial Council's action "affects hundreds of cases over which the Court has appellate . . . jurisdiction", and the orders reassigning cases "constitute a usurpation of power that cannot adequately be remedied on final review of those cases by certiorari or appeal." Application of § 1651(a) in such circumstances, while lacking direct precedent, "seems to me wholly in line with the history of that statute and consistent with the manner in which it has been interpreted both here and in the lower courts."

but of discretion sparingly exercised. To justify the granting of any such writ, the petition must show that the writ will be in aid of the Court's appellate jurisdiction, that exceptional circumstances warrant the exercise of the Court's discretionary powers, and that adequate relief cannot be obtained in any other form or from any other court" (Rule 20.1). The rule governing issuance of the writ of habeas corpus repeats that limitation and adds: "This writ is rarely granted" (Rule 20.4(a)). "[N]ot since 1925 has any petitioner been successful in obtaining release on a habeas petition filed directly with the Court." Shapiro et al., Supreme Court Practice 672 (10th ed.2013). See generally Oaks, *The "Original" Writ of Habeas Corpus in the Supreme Court*, 1962 Sup.Ct.Rev. 153; pp. 1195–1196 n.1, *infra*.

On the rarest of occasions, the Supreme Court will transfer a petition for an original writ of habeas corpus to a federal district court for hearing and determination, as 28 U.S.C. § 2241(b) authorizes. It did so most recently in In re Davis, 557 U.S. 952 (2009) (per curiam), directing the district court to receive testimony and determine whether evidence not obtainable at trial clearly established the innocence of the petitioner, a death row inmate. Objecting to the Court's decision on the ground that the petition lacked merit and did not satisfy the standards of Supreme Court Rule 20, Justice Scalia's dissent (joined by Justice Thomas) stated that the Court had not taken this extraordinary step since 1962.[8]

Had Davis filed his petition in the district court, various statutory rules would have limited that court's exercise of habeas jurisdiction, including (1) a ban, in 28 U.S.C. § 2254(d)(1), on the award of relief unless the state court decision was contrary to, or an unreasonable application of, clearly established federal law as determined by the Supreme Court; and (2) sharp limits on consideration of successive petitions. See pp. 1301–1319, 1346–1349, *infra*. Justice Scalia's dissent focused on the former of these limits in characterizing the petition as a "sure loser". In response, a concurring opinion of Justice Stevens (joined by Justices Ginsburg and Breyer) suggested, *inter alia*, that § 2254(d)(1) might not apply, or might not apply "with the same rigidity", to an original habeas petition.

Recall that the so-called "original writ" of habeas corpus in the Supreme Court is an exercise of appellate jurisdiction.[9] See Paragraph (2), *supra*. (The Court in Davis did not specify, but the petition could have been viewed as an appeal from the federal court of appeals' decision denying Davis permission to file a successive habeas petition.) Accordingly, whatever constitutional limits restrict congressional power to regulate the Supreme Court's exercise of its *original* jurisdiction, see p. 267–271, *supra*, how strong is the claim that Congress' restrictions on habeas petitions did not apply to Davis' petition? (And if statutory limits apply to the district courts but not to original writs sought from the Supreme Court, do they apply when, as in Davis, a district court entertains a case transferred to it by the Supreme Court?)

Insofar as Davis claimed a constitutional right to access to a court (or a federal court) to present a colorable claim of innocence, see pp. 1288–1290,

---

[8]   See Byrnes v. Walker, 371 U.S. 937 (1962); Chaapel v. Cochran, 369 U.S. 869 (1962).

[9]   Does that suggest that the district court would also be exercising appellate jurisdiction when adjudicating the petition transferred by the Supreme Court?

infra, would it be sensible to provide that any such right as might exist may be vindicated only in the Supreme Court and not in the district court?[10]

_____

NOTE ON THE WAR CRIMES CASES

(1) Introduction. After World War II, the Supreme Court received more than a hundred petitions for original writs of habeas corpus, by or on behalf of persons convicted by or held for trial before various American or international military tribunals abroad.[1] Such cases, not involving foreign envoys or a state, did not fall within the original jurisdiction. And in almost none of these cases was relief first sought in a lower federal court.[2] Could they be entertained on the theory that the Court could exercise its appellate jurisdiction to entertain what was, in substance, an appeal not from a federal or state court but from an American or multinational military tribunal?

(2) The Initial Denials. Between 1946 and early 1948, dozens of cases were dismissed by order. In some cases want of jurisdiction was cited by the Court or by some Justices as the basis for dismissal. See Ex parte Betz, 329 U.S. 672 (1946); Everett v. Truman, 334 U.S. 824 (1948); see generally Fairman, note 1, *supra*, at 591–604. But others simply stated that the petition was denied, see Brandt v. United States, 333 U.S. 836 (1948); In re Eichel, 333 U.S. 865 (1948), or that the Court was evenly divided (with Justice Jackson taking no part in view of his role at the Nuremberg trials), see Milch v. United States, 332 U.S. 789 (1947).

(3) Hirota v. MacArthur.

(a) In December of 1948, motions for leave to file original petitions of habeas corpus were filed on behalf of a group of Japanese, including former Premier Hirota, who had been convicted by the International Military Tribunal of the Far East. The short per curiam order denying leave to file first stated that the tribunal sentencing the petitioners was not a tribunal of the United States, but rather was established by General Douglas MacArthur as Supreme Commander of the Allied Powers that were occupying Japan. Hirota v. MacArthur, 338 U.S. 197 (1948). The Court then said that "[u]nder the foregoing circumstances the courts of the United States have no power or authority to review, to affirm, set aside or annul the

_____

[10]   For discussion of some of these issues and a more general review of the original writ of habeas corpus, see Kovarsky, *Original Habeas Redux*, 97 Va.L.Rev. 61 (2011).

[1]   See generally Fairman, *Some New Problems of the Constitution Following the Flag*, 1 Stan.L.Rev. 587 (1949). See also Oaks, *supra*, at 169–73.

[2]   An exception was Ex parte Quirin, 317 U.S. 1 (1942), p. 405–406, *infra*, involving the trial of German saboteurs by a military commission appointed by President Roosevelt. During argument in the Supreme Court on a motion for leave to file petitions for habeas corpus, counsel perfected appeals in the court of appeals from the district court's denial of the writ and petitioned for certiorari before judgment. The Supreme Court denied permission to file the habeas petitions but granted the petitions for certiorari.

In re Yamashita, 327 U.S. 1 (1946), like Quirin, did not involve direct Supreme Court review of military tribunals. There, a Japanese general on trial for war crimes before an American military tribunal in the Philippines sought leave to file petitions for writs of habeas corpus and prohibition in the Supreme Court. The Court stayed the case, 326 U.S. 693 (1945), pending receipt of a petition for certiorari from a decision of the Supreme Court of the Philippines that had denied similar relief. Subsequently the Court denied certiorari and leave to file, opining that Yamashita was not entitled to relief on the merits. In dictum, Chief Justice Stone, citing Ex parte Vallandigham, 68 U.S. (1 Wall.) 243 (1863), stated that the decisions of military tribunals authorized by Congress are not subject to Supreme Court review.

judgments and sentences imposed on these petitioners * * *." Justice Murphy noted his dissent. Justice Rutledge stated that he reserved decision and the announcement of his vote until a later time. (He died nine months later without having announced his vote.) Justice Jackson "took no part in the final decision on these motions".

  (b) Concurring in the result, Justice Douglas said that "the capture and control of those who were responsible for the Pearl Harbor incident was a political question on which the President * * * had the final say." But he thought that the District Court for the District of Columbia had jurisdiction to hear the motions, and that "[t]he appropriate course would be to remit the parties to it, reserving any further questions until the cases come here by certiorari." He objected to the sweep of the Court's decision that jurisdiction was barred merely because the committing tribunal was international. In his view, the appropriate course was to "ascertain whether, so far as American participation is concerned, there was authority to try the defendants for the precise crimes with which they are charged."[3]

(4) The Implications of Hirota. On one reading, Hirota was a narrow holding that the petition fell outside both the original and appellate jurisdiction of the Supreme Court.[4] That would have left Hirota free to petition in a district court, *if* there was a district court with jurisdiction. Justice Douglas' premise that the District Court for the District of Columbia had jurisdiction over cases involving aliens held abroad was anything but clear under the statutory grant of habeas jurisdiction then in effect.[5]

  Note, however, that in Hirota, even on Justice Douglas' assumption that a district court did have jurisdiction, there was no pending lower court case. Was Justice Douglas on firm ground in contending that the Supreme Court

---

[3] In 1949 and 1950, the Court denied leave to file petitions in a further set of war crimes cases. In one group of cases, four Justices again relied on the lack of original jurisdiction, In re Dammann and companion cases, 336 U.S. 922 (1949); In re Muhlbauer and companion cases, 336 U.S. 964 (1949); In re Steimle, 337 U.S. 913 (1949); In re Felsch, 337 U.S. 953 (1949), while in other cases the Court unanimously denied the application "without prejudice to the right to apply to any appropriate court that may have jurisdiction," In re Bush, 336 U.S. 971 (1949), or without explanation, In re Hans, 339 U.S. 976 (1950).

[4] The D.C. Circuit has read Hirota more broadly, as suggesting a barrier to the exercise of judicial power not by the Supreme Court in particular but by American courts generally, and relied on that reading in dismissing a habeas petition filed by a German businessman convicted by a military tribunal and detained in Germany. Flick v. Johnson, 174 F.2d 983 (D.C. Cir.1949). Distinguishing its own decision in Eisentrager v. Forrestal, 174 F.2d 961 (D.C. Cir.1949), upholding jurisdiction over petitions from aliens detained abroad, the court of appeals said that Flick was held by an "international court" and, relying on Hirota, ruled that no American court has power to review the conviction. For discussion, see Huq, *The Hirota Gambit*, 63 NYU Ann.Surv.Am.L. 63 (2007); Vladeck, *Deconstructing Hirota: Habeas Corpus, Citizenship, and Article III*, 95 Geo.LJ. 1497 (2007); pp. 1263–1264, *infra*.

[5] He relied on the D.C. Circuit's decision upholding such jurisdiction in Eisentrager v. Forrestal, 174 F.2d 961 (D.C. Cir.1949), but the following year the Supreme Court reversed, with Justice Douglas, as well as Justices Black and Burton, dissenting. Johnson v. Eisentrager, 339 U.S. 763 (1950), p. 1246, *infra*.

In Munaf v. Geren, 553 U.S. 674 (2008), the Supreme Court did uphold the jurisdiction of that District Court to entertain a petition on behalf of an American citizen held by the multinational forces in Iraq. Chief Justice Roberts' opinion for a unanimous Court described Hirota as a "slip of a case" that could not bear the weight the government placed on it. The Court distinguished Hirota on two grounds: first, the government had argued that General MacArthur did not serve under U.S. Authority, whereas here the government conceded that the petitioner was in the direct physical custody of American forces that were subject to control by the President and the Defense Department; and second, unlike the petitioners in Hirota, Munaf was an American citizen.

has "appellate jurisdiction", in the constitutional sense, in any case within the *potential* jurisdiction of a lower federal court? On that assumption, if a lower court would have had jurisdiction over the dispute that gave rise to Marbury v. Madison, couldn't the Supreme Court in Marbury have issued a writ of mandamus as an exercise of appellate jurisdiction?

(5) Concluding Questions: Review of Military Tribunals and of Other Non-Article III Federal Tribunals. A similar question about the Supreme Court's jurisdiction to review a criminal conviction before a military tribunal is raised by 28 U.S.C. § 1259. That provision authorizes direct Supreme Court review (on writ of certiorari) of decisions of the United States Court of Appeals for the Armed Services. That tribunal, like its predecessor, the Court of Military Appeals, is not an Article III court, and the cases it decides do not fall within Article III's definition of the original jurisdiction. Yet the Supreme Court has reviewed decisions of the Court of Military Appeals without addressing this jurisdictional issue. See, *e.g.*, Solorio v. United States, 483 U.S. 435 (1987).

State courts, of course, are not Article III courts either, and yet Supreme Court review of state court decisions is not thought to be an exercise of original jurisdiction. But does it follow that Supreme Court review of *any* adjudicatory decision—even by a non-Article III federal tribunal—is an exercise of appellate jurisdiction?

With respect to military tribunals, the Yamashita decision, note 2, *supra*, relied in part on the decision in Ex parte Vallandigham, 68 U.S. 243 (1863), which held that neither section 14 of the First Judiciary Act nor Article III permitted the Supreme Court to entertain a petition for a writ of certiorari directly from a military commission that had convicted the prisoner of disloyalty during the Civil War.[6]

Could Congress provide for direct Supreme Court review of an NLRB decision in an unfair labor practice proceeding? If not, what distinguishes the NLRB from the Court of Appeals for the Armed Services? The label "court"? The fact that the court, unlike the NLRB, engages exclusively in adjudication?[7]

Finally, consider the trend toward greater use of multinational tribunals, in which American officials participate, to adjudicate disputes arising under international agreements to which the United States is a party. Could the Supreme Court review a decision rendered by such a tribunal?

In connection with the questions in this Paragraph, see Chap. IV, Section 2, *infra*.

---

[6]   Today there is in place a statutory mechanism for review by the D.C. Circuit of military commission convictions, see pp. 1199–1200, *infra*, and the Supreme Court can review judgments of the D.C. Circuit.

[7]   And if the Supreme Court could review directly a decision of the NLRB, could it also review directly a determination made not by a five-member federal agency but by a single federal official—and if so, why couldn't the Supreme Court review Secretary of State Madison's "adjudication" that Marbury was not entitled to his commission?

CHAPTER IV

CONGRESSIONAL CONTROL OF THE DISTRIBUTION OF JUDICIAL POWER AMONG FEDERAL AND STATE COURTS

1. CONGRESSIONAL REGULATION OF FEDERAL JURISDICTION

INTRODUCTORY NOTE ON CONGRESSIONAL POWER OVER THE JURISDICTION OF THE ARTICLE III COURTS

(1) The Question Facing Congress and Possible Options. Imagine that Congress enacted a statute that requires federal contractors to pay all employees a "living wage" (as prescribed by a federal administrative agency) and that authorizes employees to bring actions against the contractors who violate that requirement. Congress might seek to assign authority to adjudicate such actions to a variety of different tribunals.

(a) Congress could prescribe that such suits may be filed in federal court—and could further prescribe that federal court jurisdiction either is concurrent with state court jurisdiction (thus leaving the ultimate choice of forum to the parties) or is exclusive (thus prohibiting state courts from exercising jurisdiction).

(b) Congress could prescribe that such suits be filed only in state court. In doing so, it would have to consider the extent to which state courts would be free to refuse to hear such cases.

(c) A distinct possibility would be to channel initial adjudication before a federal adjudicative body other than a regular Article III court—for example, a federal administrative agency—with judicial review provided in Article III courts.

(d) In any of the foregoing cases, Congress might or might not purport to limit the capacity of the Supreme Court ultimately to review the matter.

This chapter considers the scope of congressional power in making decisions like these—a scope that might vary with the kind of case at issue.

(2) Sources of Congressional Power. That Congress possesses significant powers to define and limit the jurisdiction of federal and state courts is not in question, but the precise limits of Congress' authority are controverted. Four sources of congressional authority are particularly important.

(a) The Madisonian Compromise. Article III, § 1 vests the federal judicial power in "one supreme Court, and in such inferior Courts as the Congress may from time to time ordain and establish". At the Constitutional Convention, establishment of the Supreme Court generated little controversy. But delegates sharply disagreed about lower federal courts: some urged that the Constitution mandate their existence, while others opposed any power to create such courts. See pp. 7–9, *supra*. Under the resolution reached by the "Madisonian Compromise", Congress is authorized but not obliged to "ordain and establish" federal tribunals "inferior" to the Supreme Court—a power that has generally been understood to permit establishing lower federal courts whose jurisdiction is more limited than the Constitution would allow.

(b) The Exceptions Clause. Article III, § 2, cl. 2 specifies that the appellate jurisdiction of the Supreme Court shall be subject to "such Exceptions, and under such Regulations as the Congress shall make".

(c) Limitation of State Court Jurisdiction. Under the Necessary and Proper Clause, Congress may limit state court jurisdiction, by providing for exclusive federal jurisdiction in some cases and for removal in others.

(d) Legislative Courts. Under its legislative authority in Article I (and in Article IV, Sec. 3, relating to the governance of territories), Congress has been understood to have power to assign at least the initial adjudication of some claims to "legislative courts"—federal tribunals whose judges lack the tenure and salary protections afforded to the Article III judiciary.

(3) Some Historical Limits on Federal Court Jurisdiction. Beginning with the Judiciary Act of 1789, Congress has never vested the federal courts with the entire "judicial Power" that Article III would permit. A *partial* list of historical exclusions includes the following:

(a) Jurisdiction of the Lower Federal Courts.

(i) Federal Question Cases.[1] The First Judiciary Act did not provide for any general federal question jurisdiction in civil cases "arising under" the Constitution, laws, or treaties of the United States. Federal question cases that did not fall within one of the small number of specialized grants of jurisdiction had to be litigated in state court, subject to Supreme Court review. Only in 1875 did Congress provide an enduring grant of general federal question jurisdiction, now found in 28 U.S.C. § 1331.

Even today, § 1331 confers jurisdiction only when the federal question appears on the face of the plaintiff's well-pleaded complaint. Thus, for example, cases raising federal defenses, although they arise under federal law within the meaning of Article III, generally may not be litigated in the lower federal courts. See generally pp. 806–816, *infra*.

From 1875 to 1980, the general federal question statute included an amount-in-controversy requirement. During that period, many "small" federal question claims could be adjudicated only in state court.

(ii) Diversity Jurisdiction.[2] Beginning in 1789, lower federal courts have had jurisdiction to hear many diversity cases. But the general statutory grant has always required "complete diversity" when there are multiple

---

[1] The statutory history is discussed more fully in Chapter VIII, Sec. 1, *infra*.

[2] The statutory history is discussed more fully in Chapter XIII, Sec. 1, *infra*.

parties on one or more sides of a case, see Strawbridge v. Curtiss, 7 U.S. (3 Cranch) 267 (1806), p. 1422, *infra*—a requirement not imposed by Article III.

The diversity statute has always had an amount-in-controversy requirement, set at $500 in 1789 (a significant sum) and increasing over time to $75,000.

Finally, in-state defendants are prohibited from removing cases filed in state court, even when the other requisites of diversity jurisdiction are met.

(b) Supreme Court Jurisdiction. From 1789–1914, the Supreme Court could review only those state court decisions that denied a claim of federal right; state court decisions upholding federal claims were thus excluded from the Court's appellate jurisdiction. See Chap. V, Sec. 1, *infra*. Nor, until 1891, did the Supreme Court possess statutory authority to review most decisions of lower federal courts in criminal cases.

(4) Congressional Authority and Constitutional Controversy. The most controversial proposals to limit federal court jurisdiction have been those reflecting a substantive disagreement with the way those courts (especially the Supreme Court) have resolved particular substantive issues. The subject matters of the proposed curbs have varied widely. "In the Marshall Court years, especially during the 1820's, those who perceived a tendency toward centralization in the Court's decisions proposed repealing section 25 of the 1789 Judiciary Act, which authorized Supreme Court review of certain state court judgments." Gunther, *Congressional Power to Curtail Federal Court Jurisdiction: An Opinionated Guide to the Ongoing Debate*, 36 Stan.L.Rev. 895, 896–97 (1984).

In the late 1950s and 1960s, bills were introduced to curb federal jurisdiction to review the admissibility of confessions in state criminal cases,[3] state legislative apportionments,[4] and legislation regulating or restricting subversive activities.[5] Beginning in the early 1970s, a number of bills sought to limit federal court jurisdiction to order busing to remedy school segregation.[6] In the 1980s, two efforts to limit jurisdiction concerned abortion and school prayer. [7] In 2004, the House of Representatives passed bills that would have eliminated federal jurisdiction over challenges to the Defense of Marriage Act and to recitations of the Pledge of Allegiance.[8] But

---

[3]   See, *e.g.*, S. 917, 90th Cong., 2d Sess. (1968).

[4]   See, *e.g.*, H.R. 11926, 88th Cong., 2d Sess. (1964) (eliminating federal district court jurisdiction; one of more than fifty bills introduced in 1964 to restrict jurisdiction in reapportionment cases). See generally McKay, *Court, Congress, and Reapportionment*, 63 Mich.L.Rev. 255 (1964).

[5]   See, *e.g.*, the Jenner bill, S. 2646, 85th Cong., 1st Sess. (1957) (eliminating Supreme Court jurisdiction in cases relating to functions or practices of a congressional committee or state laws relating to subversive activities or to admission to the practice of law). The Jenner bill was defeated 49–41. See 104 Cong.Rec. 18687 (1958). For discussion of court-curbing proposals during the Warren era, see Ross, *Attacks on the Warren Court by State Officials: A Case Study of Why Court-Curbing Movements Fail*, 50 Buff.L.Rev. 483 (2002).

[6]   See, *e.g.*, Student Transportation Moratorium Act of 1972, S.3388, 92d Cong., 2d Sess.; H.R.13916, 92d Cong., 2d Sess.; Equal Educational Opportunities Act of 1972, S.3395, 92d Cong., 2d Sess.; H.R.13915, 92d Cong., 2d Sess.

[7]   See, *e.g.*, H.R. 326, 97th Cong., 1st Sess. (1981) (school prayer); H.R. 865, 97th Cong., 1st Sess. (1981) (school prayer); H.R. 867, 97th Cong., 1st Sess. (1981) (abortion).

[8]   For discussion of these and other proposals, see Norton, *Reshaping Federal Jurisdiction: Congress's Latest Challenge to Judicial Review*, 41 Wake Forest L.Rev. 1003 (2006).

jurisdiction-stripping bills, though not infrequently introduced, have almost invariably failed of passage.[9]

Over the centuries, in only one area has proposed legislation stripping the federal courts of jurisdiction with respect to a particular substantive area actually been enacted. The Detainee Treatment Act of 2005,[10] as amended by the Military Commissions Act of 2006,[11] prohibited federal (and state) courts from entertaining habeas corpus and all other actions filed by aliens being detained as enemy combatants or awaiting a determination of enemy combatant status. (Habeas corpus is a traditional form of relief whose purpose is to permit the courts to determine if the petitioner's detention is lawful, and if not, to order that the petitioner be released from custody.) Congress substituted for habeas corpus a limited judicial review procedure in the D.C. Circuit. In Boumediene v. Bush, 553 U.S. 723 (2008), the Supreme Court held that withdrawal to be an unconstitutional restriction of the guarantee of the privilege of habeas corpus contained in the "Suspension Clause" of Article I, Sec. 9. See pp. 338, 1224, infra.

Only one other decision has held a statute framed as depriving a federal court of jurisdiction to be unconstitutional. See United States v. Klein, 80 U.S. (13 Wall.) 128 (1871). That decision, however, may be best read as resting on a different substantive ground—that the measure required courts to render decisions that conflicted with the President's power to pardon. See p. 323, infra.

It is unclear, then, how generalizable either decision is to other congressional enactments depriving the federal courts of jurisdiction. The question of the limits of congressional power to regulate federal court jurisdiction has generated few precedents but a body of literature that Professor Van Alstyne described as "choking on redundancy."[12]

(5) Residual Jurisdiction in the State Courts. Although jurisdiction-stripping proposals vary in form, a common approach is reflected in several bills providing that, notwithstanding any other provision of Title 28 of the United States Code, neither (a) the Supreme Court nor (b) any federal district court shall have jurisdiction of any case arising out of any state or local law or rule "which relates to voluntary prayer in public schools and buildings".[13] If enacted, such legislation would not impair state court jurisdiction.

If federal jurisdiction over challenges to school prayer were eliminated, would state courts be obliged to entertain such cases? To accept Supreme Court precedents as authoritative interpretations of constitutional meaning? Compare Wechsler, *The Courts and the Constitution*, 65 Colum.L.Rev. 1001, 1006–07 (1965) (so arguing), with Caminker, *Why Must Inferior Courts Obey*

---

[9]   Professor Grove explains this pattern of failure by contending that political actors in a competitive political system have long-term incentives to maintain an independent judiciary that can check the opposition party when it becomes dominant, and that the hurdles erected by Article I's bicameralism and presentment requirements generally allow the minority faction to block attempts by the majority to strip jurisdiction. Grove, *The Structural Safeguards of Federal Jurisdiction*, 124 Harv.L.Rev. 869 (2011). In a subsequent article, she argues that the President and the Department of Justice also have strong incentives to oppose jurisdiction stripping bills. See Grove, *The Article II Safeguards of Federal Jurisdiction*, 112 Colum.L.Rev. 250 (2012).

[10]   119 Stat. 2739, codified at 10 U.S.C. § 801 note.

[11]   120 Stat. 2600.

[12]   Quoted in Gunther, *supra*, at 897 n.9.

[13]   See, *e.g.*, S.481, 97th Cong., 1st Sess. (1981); S.1742, 97th Cong., 1st Sess. (1981).

Superior Court Precedents?, 46 Stan.L.Rev. 817, 868–69 (1994) (contending that state and lower courts could disregard a Supreme Court precedent from which they believe the Court itself would have departed). Is it realistic to expect that all courts would follow Supreme Court authority under such circumstances?

(6) The "Parity" Debate. A decision by Congress whether to assign a set of cases to the federal courts or instead to the state courts implicates important questions about the "parity" or disparity of state and federal courts. Various forms of the question of parity can be distinguished.

(a) Constitutional Requirements Versus Legislative Policy. One question about "parity" is constitutional: it asks whether the Constitution (particularly Article III) is indifferent about whether adjudication of a particular case occurs before a federal court or a state court. But a distinct question is one of legislative policy: it asks, insofar as the Constitution permits Congress to choose between federal and state courts, how Congress should assess the capacities of federal courts and state courts in deciding how to allocate jurisdiction. The answers to the two questions might differ: one might conclude, for example, that state courts are good enough to satisfy the Constitution but need not be viewed by legislators or lawyers as on a par with federal courts.[14]

(b) What Do We Mean by Parity? Whether as a matter of constitutional requirement or legislative policy, one must specify more clearly what one means by parity. One framing of the question would ask whether state courts are as likely as federal courts to resolve a case (like one challenging the constitutionality of school prayer) correctly. The answer to that question is bound up with normative issues—how broadly should the Constitution, or the Establishment Clause, be interpreted?—that are not subject to empirical measurement. Nonetheless, some have suggested as a general matter that, in the words of Judge Posner, it is widely believed "by the practicing bar that federal judges are, on average (an important qualification), of higher quality than their state counterparts". Posner, The Federal Courts: Challenge and Reform 216 (2d ed.1996); see also Neuborne, *Parity Revisited: The Uses of a Judicial Forum of Excellence*, 44 DePaul L.Rev. 797 (1995). It is difficult, however, to assess judicial competence independently from normative commitments.

A second way to frame the parity question, to which an empirical answer seems more appropriate, focuses on comparative receptiveness to federal claims: are state courts as likely as federal courts to uphold either a particular federal right or federal rights in general? Some commentators have suggested that state courts fall short of their federal counterparts, see, *e.g.*, Neuborne, *The Myth of Parity*, 90 Harv.L.Rev. 1105, 1105 (1977), although sometimes they smuggle in the further normative (and contestable) premise that a broader scope for federal rights is necessarily better, see, *e.g.*, Bator, *The State Courts and Federal Constitutional Litigation*, 22 Wm. & Mary L.Rev. 605 (1981).

---

[14]   See, *e.g.*, Wells, *Behind the Parity Debate: The Decline of the Legal Process Tradition in the Law of Federal Courts*, 71 B.U.L.Rev. 609 (1991); Wells, *Who's Afraid of Henry Hart?*, 14 Const.Commt. 175 (1997). Professor Wells offers a "weak parity" thesis—that state courts afford litigants a constitutionally adequate hearing on federal claims but "are not interchangeable with federal courts" and sometimes provide a "home court advantage" to state defendants. See also Solimine & Walker, Respecting State Courts 58–59 (1999) (also endorsing a "weak parity" thesis).

Several studies have tried to address this empirical question. Some have purported to find parity or a degree of disparity that was unimportant.[15] Others have looked at particular issues. One study of takings litigation found similar results in federal and state courts. (Are takings claims likely to be representative of constitutional claims generally?)[16] Another studied gay rights claims and concluded that they generally fared better in state courts; although the state court victories almost invariably rested on state law grounds, the author argued that the experience raises doubts about the thesis that federal courts are generally more protective of civil rights.[17]

In a 1988 review of the reported empirical studies, Professor Chemerinsky concluded that the methodological difficulties confronting inquiries of this kind—including those of controlling for differences in the types and difficulty of federal questions characteristically raised in state and federal court and of studying outcomes in state trial courts, which frequently fail to write opinions—are so daunting that "[a]lthough parity is an empirical question, no empirical answer seems possible". Chemerinsky, note 15, *supra*, at 261–69.

Putting aside empirical studies, one's more intuitive assessment of parity may depend upon the period in question. The conventional wisdom in the Warren Court era was that federal courts were more rights-protective than state courts. But by the early 1990s, Republicans, who had occupied the Presidency since 1981, had appointed a large percentage of federal judges. At about the same time, state supreme courts were increasingly reported to be upholding claims of rights, as a matter of state constitutional law, that had been rejected by the United States Supreme Court under the federal Constitution. See, *e.g.*, Schuman, *The Right to "Equal Privileges and Immunities": A State's Version of "Equal Protection,"* 13 Vt.L.Rev. 221, 221 (1988); Wachtler, *Our Constitutions—Alive and Well*, 61 St. John's L.Rev. 381, 397 (1987). *But cf.* Neuborne, p. 299, *supra*, at 799 (noting mounting difficulties in winning novel individual rights case anywhere, but maintaining that federal courts remain advantageous for plaintiffs). Following those developments, the press reported a large decline in the number of civil rights claims filed in federal courts and a corresponding increase in the number of such claims filed in state courts. See, *e.g.*, Cullen, *Scales Tip to State Courts*, The Boston Globe, p. 1, Dec. 28, 1991.

Any general claim about the relative receptivity of federal and state courts to federal rights may be hard to sustain if over time there are major

---

[15] Solimine & Walker, *Constitutional Litigation in Federal and State Courts: An Empirical Analysis of Judicial Parity*, 10 Hastings Const.L.Q. 213 (1983), compared the decisions of federal district courts and state appellate courts concerning selected constitutional issues, finding that federal courts upheld the constitutional claim in 41% of the cases within their sample, while state courts did so in only 32% of the cases. Although this difference was "statistically significant", the authors viewed it as "unimportant", interpreting the data as showing that state courts exhibit no clear reluctance to uphold federal claims that a federal district court would uphold. Among its weaknesses, however, this study compared state appellate courts with federal trial courts and did not attempt to correct for possible differences in the content of the cases in state and federal court. For further criticisms, see Chemerinsky, *Parity Reconsidered: Defining a Role for the Federal Judiciary*, 36 UCLA L.Rev. 233, 261–69 (1988).

[16] Gerry, *Parity Revisited: An Empirical Comparison of State and Lower Federal Court Interpretations of Nollan v. California Coastal Commission,* 23 Harv.J.L. & Pub.Pol'y 233 (1999*)*, examined all reported cases applying a single Supreme Court decision involving a claim of an unconstitutional taking—Nollan v. California Coastal Comm'n, 483 U.S. 825 (1987)—from 1987–97 and concluded that "[t]he aggregate findings are startling in their similarity".

[17] Rubenstein, *The Myth of Superiority*, 16 Const.Commt. 599 (1999).

shifts, arising from the politics of judicial appointments, in the outlook of federal judges.

(c) Institutional Understandings Bearing on the Parity Debate. One argument for parity as a constitutional concept rests on the Madisonian Compromise and the structure of Article III: since Congress need not create any lower federal courts, state courts must be regarded as enjoying constitutional parity with the lower federal courts.[18] But not everyone accepts that analytical starting point.

(i) Distinctive Characteristics of Federal Judges. A number of commentators have advanced linguistic and structural arguments that Article III rejects parity and compels that the judicial power "shall be vested" in federal courts. Some of these arguments draw on an influential article by Professor Neuborne, *The Myth of Parity, supra,* which argued that three characteristics of federal judges tend to make them more sympathetic to federal claims than their state court counterparts: (a) federal judgeships are generally more prestigious and better paid than state judgeships and thus tend to be filled by more technically competent lawyers, who are better able to grasp complex and novel arguments; (b) federal judges, unlike the judges in all but a handful of states, enjoy life tenure and are therefore more insulated from majoritarian pressures to decide cases adversely to unpopular claims; and (c) federal judges are participants in a proud tradition of protecting constitutional rights that may create a "psychological tilt" in favor of upholding constitutional claims.

(ii) The Selection of State Judges. In the Founding era, "in a vast majority of states—covering a full 85% of the population by 1790—state judges enjoyed the same tenure as federal judges: life with good behavior." Fitzpatrick, *The Constitutionality of Federal Jurisdiction-Stripping Legislation and the History of State Judicial Selection and Tenure,* 98 Va.L.Rev. 839, 857 (2012). The Jacksonian era launched a movement favoring judicial elections and limited terms, which became common in the 1850s. Professor Shugerman has argued that the movement sought to end a system in which appointments had become a tool of political cronyism; elections were designed not to subject judges to popular control but rather to strengthen the exercise of the power of judicial review, and they proved to have that effect. See Shugerman, *Economic Crisis and the Rise of Judicial Elections and Judicial Review,* 123 Harv.L.Rev. 1063 (2010).

[handwritten margin note: intended to improve quality, probably didn't]

In the 20th century, progressive-era reformers urged non-partisan elections to reduce the control of party bosses.[19] In 1940, Missouri adopted a merit selection plan, under which the governor chooses one of several names on a list developed by a nominating commission, and sitting judges face retention elections in which they run not against an opponent but on their record. Both approaches were adopted elsewhere. A recent tally of selection methods for state supreme court justices finds that two states use gubernatorial appointment, two legislative appointment, eight partisan elections, 14 non-partisan elections, and 24 merit selection.[20] (Although

---

[18] See, e.g., Bator, *supra*; Hart, *The Power of Congress to Limit the Jurisdiction of Federal Courts: An Exercise in Dialectic,* 66 Harv.L.Rev. 1362 (1953).

[19] See Shugerman, *The Twist of Long Terms: Judicial Elections, Role Fidelity, and American Tort Law,* 98 Geo.L.J. 1349 (2010).

[20] On state selection methods, see Am. Judicature Soc'y, Judicial Selection in the States: Appellate and General Jurisdiction Courts (2013), *available at* www.judicialselection.com/uploads/documents/Judicial_Selection_Charts_1196376173077.pdf. Methods for lower state

there are many variations, a common approach to merit selection involves creation of a non-partisan commission of citizens that evaluates applicants and submits a list of well-qualified individuals to the Governor, who chooses one of the listed individuals; when the term of the initial appointment expires, a judge is evaluated for retention either by a commission or in a non-partisan election.)

Many observers believe that in recent years, state elections have become more "politicized".[21] Campaign expenditures by candidates, and hence fundraising from individuals and groups, have mushroomed, as have direct expenditures (including TV attack ads) by groups seeking to influence elections. Successful candidates sometimes later sit on cases involving campaign contributors. In Republican Party of Minnesota v. White, 536 U.S. 765 (2002) (5–4), the Court held that a canon of judicial conduct prohibiting "a candidate for judicial office", not currently a judge, from "announc[ing] his or her views on disputed legal or political issues" violated the First Amendment. Following that decision, many interest groups, which had already been increasingly active in judicial election campaigns, began to submit questionnaires to judicial candidates on a range of issues, and candidates' advertisements increasingly stressed not only qualifications but also positions.[22]

Justice O'Connor, concurring in White, expressed concern that "the very practice of electing judges undermines" the important governmental interest in actual and perceived judicial impartiality.[23] Indeed, a number of studies (most of which have focused on criminal sentencing in capital and other cases) have found evidence that an impending election has an effect on the

---

courts differ, with merit selection used less often than for state supreme courts. See generally Schotland, *New Challenges to States' Judicial Selection*, 95 Geo.L.J. 1077, 1084–86 (2007).

[21] See Pozen, *The Irony of Judicial Elections*, 108 Colum.L.Rev. 265 (2008).

[22] See generally Sample et al., The New Politics of Judicial Elections 2000–2009 (Brennan Center for Justice; Charles Hall ed. 2010), *available at* http://www.brennancenter.org/sites/default/files/legacy/JAS-NPJE-Decade-ONLINE.pdf; Running for Judge: The Rising Political, Financial, and Legal Stakes of Judicial Elections (Streb ed. 2007); Brown, *Political Judges and Popular Justice: A Conservative Victory of a Conservative Dilemma?*, 49 Wm. & Mary L.Rev. 1543, 1552–53 (2008). Some courts have read White as invalidating ethics rules that bar candidates from making promises (other than faithful performance of judicial duties) about their conduct in office if elected. See, *e.g.*, North Dakota Alliance, Inc. v. Bader, 361 F.Supp.2d 1021 (D.N.D.2005).

Defenders of partisan elections contend that non-partisan elections provide insufficient information to promote accountability; that retention elections, lacking opponents and partisan affiliation, generate little voter knowledge or interest and little turnover; and that because politics inevitably plays a key role in judicial selection, even under merit-based systems, those systems have little to recommend themselves over elections. More broadly, defenders of elections contend that making judges accountable through partisan elections is appropriate given the broad policymaking discretion that they possess.

[23] For a forceful expression of similar concerns, see Croley, *The Majoritarian Difficulty: Elective Judiciaries and the Rule of Law*, 62 U.Chi.L.Rev. 689 (1995). See also Bright, *Can Judicial Independence be Attained in the South? Overcoming History, Elections, and Misperceptions About the Role of the Judiciary*, 14 Ga.St.U.L.Rev. 817 (1998) (stressing that many "vestiges of discrimination * * * still infect [southern state] courts and affect their decisions"); Carrington, *Judicial Independence and Democratic Accountability in Highest State Courts*, 61 Law & Contemp.Probs. 79 (Summer 1998, No. 3) (arguing that selection processes for states' highest courts have become increasingly politicized and canvassing possible correctives); Frost & Lindquist, *Countering the Majoritarian Difficulty*, 96 Va.L.Rev. 719 (2010) (urging heightened review of elected (rather than appointed) state court judges by the Supreme Court, as well as by lower federal courts exercising habeas corpus jurisdiction).

behavior of sitting judges,[24] although other studies suggest that the quality of judges varies little under electoral or merit-based systems. Do the changes since 1789 in state judicial selection methods and the character of state judicial elections call into question arguments, based on the original understanding and the Madisonian Compromise, that state courts must be viewed as on a par with federal courts for purposes of Article III? See *Fitzpatrick*, p. 301, *supra*.

For general discussion, see Symposium, *Fair and Independent Courts: A Conference on the State of the Judiciary*, 95 Geo.L.J. 895 (2007), and 137 Daedalus No. 4 (2008) (articles concerning judicial independence).

Sheldon v. Sill

49 U.S. (8 How.) 441, 12 L.Ed. 1147 (1850).
Appeal from the Circuit Court for the District of Michigan.

■ MR. JUSTICE GRIER delivered the opinion of the Court.

The only question which it will be necessary to notice in this case is, whether the Circuit Court had jurisdiction.

[Sill, a New York citizen, sued Sheldon, a Michigan citizen, to recover on a bond and mortgage that had been assigned to Sill by Hastings, also a Michigan citizen. Sheldon's answer contended that the statutory grant of diversity jurisdiction did not reach a case like this one in which diverse citizenship exists only because of the assignment of rights to the plaintiff.]

The eleventh section of the Judiciary Act, which defines the jurisdiction of the Circuit Courts, restrains them from taking "cognizance of any suit to recover the contents of any promissory note or other chose in action, in favor of an assignee, unless a suit might have been prosecuted in such court to recover the contents, if no assignment had been made, except in cases of foreign bills of exchange."

The third article of the Constitution declares that "the judicial power of the United States shall be vested in one Supreme Court, and such inferior courts as the Congress may, from time to time, ordain and establish." The second section of the same article enumerates the cases and controversies of which the judicial power shall have cognizance, and, among others, it specifies "controversies between citizens of different States."

It has been alleged, that this restriction of the Judiciary Act, with regard to assignees of choses in action, is in conflict with this provision of the Constitution, and therefore void.

---

[24] For studies relating to decisions in capital cases, see Gordon & Huber, *Accountability and Coercion: Is Justice Blind When It Runs for Office?*, 48 Am.J.Pol.Sci. 247 (2004); Hall, *Electoral Politics and Strategic Voting in State Supreme Courts*, 54 J.Pol. 427 (1992); Brace & Boyea, *State Public Opinion, the Death Penalty, and the Practice of Electing Judges*, 52 Am.J.Pol.Sci. 360 (2008). See also, e.g., Gordon & Huber, *The Effect of Electoral Competitiveness on Incumbent Behavior*, 2 Q.J.Pol.Sci. 107 (2007); Pinello, The Impact of Judicial Selection Method on State-Supreme-Court Policy (1995). But see Blume & Eisenberg, *Judicial Politics, Death Penalty Appeals, and Case Selection*, 72 S.C.L.Rev. 465 (1999) (showing no significant effect of selection methods).

It must be admitted, that if the Constitution had ordained and established the inferior courts, and distributed to them their respective powers, they could not be restricted or divested by Congress. But as it has made no such distribution, one of two consequences must result,— either that each inferior court created by Congress must exercise all the judicial powers not given to the Supreme Court, or that Congress, having the power to establish the courts, must define their respective jurisdictions. The first of these inferences has never been asserted, and could not be defended with any show of reason, and if not, the latter would seem to follow as a necessary consequence. And it would seem to follow, also, that, having a right to prescribe, Congress may withhold from any court of its creation jurisdiction of any of the enumerated controversies. Courts created by statute can have no jurisdiction but such as the statute confers. * * *

The Constitution has defined the limits of the judicial power of the United States, but has not prescribed how much of it shall be exercised by the Circuit Court; consequently, the statute which does prescribe the limits of their jurisdiction, cannot be in conflict with the Constitution, unless it confers powers not enumerated therein.

Such has been the doctrine held by this court since its first establishment. To enumerate all the cases in which it has been either directly advanced or tacitly assumed would be tedious and unnecessary.

In the case of Turner v. Bank of North America, 4 Dall. 10, [another case involving diversity created only by assignment,] * * * the court said,—"The political truth is, that the disposal of the judicial power (except in a few specified instances) belongs to Congress: and Congress is not bound to enlarge the jurisdiction of the Federal courts to every subject, in every form which the Constitution might warrant." This decision was made in 1799; since that time, the same doctrine has been frequently asserted by this court * * *.

[Finding that Sill was an assignee of a "chose in action" within the meaning of the statute, the Court held that jurisdiction was lacking.] * * *

The judgment of the Circuit Court must therefore be reversed, for want of jurisdiction.

Ex Parte McCardle

74 U.S. (7 Wall.) 506, 19 L.Ed. 264 (1869).
Appeal from the Circuit Court for the Southern District of Mississippi.

[On February 5, 1867, Congress enacted legislation authorizing federal judges "to grant writs of habeas corpus in all cases where any person may be restrained of his or her liberty in violation of the constitution, or of any treaty or law of the United States". The Act's principal purpose was to establish federal habeas corpus jurisdiction to review detentions of persons held under *state and local authority*— especially newly freed African-Americans, their supporters, and federal officials, all of whom were subjected to harassment and baseless arrests in southern states. (Habeas jurisdiction to review detention under *federal* authority had existed since 1789.) Among its provisions, the 1867 Act authorized a right of appeal from decisions of the circuit courts to the Supreme Court of the United States.

[McCardle, the editor of the *Vicksburg Times* in Mississippi, was arrested by federal military authorities acting pursuant to the Military Reconstruction Act, enacted in March of 1867. The charges against him, based solely on editorials published in his newspaper, included disturbing the peace, libel, incitement to insurrection, and impeding reconstruction. While he was awaiting trial before a military commission, McCardle filed a habeas corpus petition in the federal Circuit Court for the Southern District of Mississippi. He contended that it was unconstitutional to try him before a military tribunal rather than an Article III court—a contention to which the Court's decision in Ex parte Milligan, 71 U.S. (4 Wall.) 2 (1867), though not conclusive, gave some support. McCardle also contended more broadly that the provisions of the Military Reconstruction Act, placing ten states under military jurisdiction, were unconstitutional. The Supreme Court ruled that two prior challenges to the Act were not fit for judicial resolution,[1] but McCardle's case did not pose the same barriers to adjudication on the merits.

[After the circuit court denied the petition, McCardle appealed to the Supreme Court. Following oral argument there but before the case was decided, Congress, over the President's veto, passed the Act of March 27, 1868, ch. 34, § 2, 15 Stat. 44, which provided: " * * * That so much of the act approved [February 5, 1867], entitled 'An act to amend "An act to establish the judicial courts of the United States," approved [September 24, 1789],' as authorizes an appeal from the judgment of the circuit court to the Supreme Court of the United States, or the exercise of any such jurisdiction by said Supreme Court on appeals which have been or may hereafter be taken, be, and the same is, hereby repealed."]

The attention of the court was directed to this statute at the last term, but counsel having expressed a desire to be heard in argument upon its effect, and the Chief Justice being detained from his place here, by his duties in the Court of Impeachment, the cause was continued under advisement. Argument was now heard upon the effect of the repealing act. * * *

■ THE CHIEF JUSTICE [CHASE] delivered the opinion of the Court.

The first question necessarily is that of jurisdiction; for, if the act of March, 1868, takes away the jurisdiction defined by the act of February, 1867, it is useless, if not improper, to enter into any discussion of other questions.

It is quite true, as was argued by the counsel for the petitioner, that the appellate jurisdiction of this court is not derived from acts of Congress. It is, strictly speaking, conferred by the Constitution. But it is conferred "with such exceptions and under such regulations as Congress shall make."

It is unnecessary to consider whether, if Congress had made no exceptions and no regulations, this court might not have exercised general appellate jurisdiction under rules prescribed by itself. For among

---

[1]   [Ed.] See Mississippi v. Johnson, 71 U.S. (4 Wall.) 475, 501 (1867), and Georgia v. Stanton, 73 U.S. (6 Wall.) 50, 76–77 (1867).

the earliest acts of the first Congress, at its first session, was the act of September 24th, 1789, to establish the judicial courts of the United States. That act provided for the organization of this court, and prescribed regulations for the exercise of its jurisdiction.

The source of that jurisdiction, and the limitations of it by the Constitution and by statute, have been on several occasions subjects of consideration here. In the case of Durousseau v. The United States,[12] particularly, the whole matter was carefully examined, and the court held, that while "the appellate powers of this court are not given by the judicial act, but are given by the Constitution," they are, nevertheless, "limited and regulated by that act, and by such other acts as have been passed on the subject." The court said, further, that the judicial act was an exercise of the power given by the Constitution to Congress "of making exceptions to the appellate jurisdiction of the Supreme Court." "They have described affirmatively," said the court, "its jurisdiction, and this affirmative description has been understood to imply a negation of the exercise of such appellate power as is not comprehended within it."

The principle that the affirmation of appellate jurisdiction implies the negation of all such jurisdiction not affirmed having been thus established, it was an almost necessary consequence that acts of Congress, providing for the exercise of jurisdiction, should come to be spoken of as acts granting jurisdiction, and not as acts making exceptions to the constitutional grant of it.

The exception to appellate jurisdiction in the case before us, however, is not an inference from the affirmation of other appellate jurisdiction. It is made in terms. The provision of the act of 1867, affirming the appellate jurisdiction of this court in cases of *habeas corpus* is expressly repealed. It is hardly possible to imagine a plainer instance of positive exception.

We are not at liberty to inquire into the motives of the legislature. We can only examine into its power under the Constitution; and the power to make exceptions to the appellate jurisdiction of this court is given by express words.

What, then, is the effect of the repealing act upon the case before us? We cannot doubt as to this. Without jurisdiction the court cannot proceed at all in any cause. Jurisdiction is power to declare the law, and when it ceases to exist, the only function remaining to the court is that of announcing the fact and dismissing the cause. And this is not less clear upon authority than upon principle. * * *

It is quite clear, therefore, that this court cannot proceed to pronounce judgment in this case, for it has no longer jurisdiction of the appeal; and judicial duty is not less fitly performed by declining ungranted jurisdiction than in exercising firmly that which the Constitution and the laws confer.

Counsel seem to have supposed, if effect be given to the repealing act in question, that the whole appellate power of the court, in cases of *habeas corpus*, is denied. But this is an error. The act of 1868 does not except from that jurisdiction any cases but appeals from Circuit Courts

dodge

---

[12] 6 Cranch, 312 [(1810)].

under the act of 1867. It does not affect the jurisdiction which was previously exercised.[17]

The appeal of the petitioner in this case must be dismissed for want of jurisdiction.*

NOTE ON THE POWER OF CONGRESS TO LIMIT THE JURISDICTION OF FEDERAL COURTS

The question of Congress' power to limit federal court jurisdiction is not a unitary one. This Note considers three different issues: (i) the power of Congress to limit the jurisdiction of the lower federal courts, leaving cases to be decided initially by the state courts and then subject to Supreme Court review; (ii) the power of Congress to limit the appellate jurisdiction of the Supreme Court over cases that continue to be within the jurisdiction of the lower federal courts; and (iii) the power of Congress to withdraw certain matters from the jurisdiction of all *federal* courts (with state courts continuing to exercise jurisdiction over those matters).

A. Congressional Power to Exclude Cases from the Lower Federal Courts

(1) Background Premise: The Madisonian Compromise. As *Sheldon v. Sill* suggests, congressional power to prescribe limits on the lower federal courts' jurisdiction—for example, by excluding cases involving school prayer—seems plainly contemplated by Article III and the Madisonian Compromise. Would it "make nonsense of" the compromise to hold that "the only power to be exercised is the all-or-nothing power to decide whether *none* or *all* of the cases to which the federal judicial power extends need the haven of a lower federal court"? Bator, *Congressional Power Over the Jurisdiction of the Federal Courts*, 27 Vill.L.Rev. 1030, 1031 (1982).[1]

If that is so, any ground for objection under Article III would seemingly have to involve the *basis* for Congress' exercise of its acknowledged power. Do you agree with Professor Bator that Article III and the Madisonian Compromise contemplate a general congressional power to make "political" judgments about the desirability of federal jurisdiction in particular classes

---

[17] Ex parte McCardle, 6 Wallace 324.

[Ed.] Later that year, another Mississippi journalist detained by the military sought a writ of habeas corpus. After the circuit court denied the writ, the detainee followed the suggestion in the penultimate paragraph of the McCardle opinion and filed in the Supreme Court an application for an original writ of habeas corpus, as authorized by Section 14 of the Judiciary Act of 1789, 1 Stat. 81–82. In Ex parte Yerger, 75 U.S. (8 Wall.) 85 (1869), the Court upheld its jurisdiction to entertain the application, reasoning that the 1868 repealer act affected only the Court's appellate jurisdiction under the Habeas Corpus Act of 1867 and left intact its jurisdiction, dating from 1789, to entertain *original* applications, directly to the Supreme Court, for a writ of habeas corpus. Technicalities aside, § 14 of the 1789 Act permitted the Court to review the Circuit Court's decision, through a procedural form different from an appeal.

Following the Supreme Court's decision, the government transferred Yerger from military custody to the local civil authority, thereby again avoiding adjudication of the merits of challenges to military Reconstruction. See Fairman, History of the Supreme Court of the United States: Reconstruction and Reunion, 1864–88, Part One, at 589 (1971).

[1] But see Goebel, History of the Supreme Court of the United States: Antecedents and Beginnings to 1801, at 246–47 (1971) (arguing that Congress must create lower federal courts and vest them with the full possible jurisdiction).

of cases?[2] Does that view give too much weight to the Convention history leading to the Madisonian compromise, which was not known to those who ratified the Constitution, or can it be supported simply by the constitutional text and structure?

(2) Mandatory Theories of Article III: Justice Story's Views. Notwithstanding the Madisonian Compromise and the historical practice reflected in decisions like Sheldon v. Sill, various theories supported a constitutional requirement of lower federal court jurisdiction in at least some cases. Nearly all of these theories build on dictum in Justice Story's opinion for the Court in Martin v. Hunter's Lessee, 14 U.S. (1 Wheat.) 304 (1816). Justice Story's exposition was complex and arguably internally contradictory. Although it did not focus exclusively on Congress' power to limit lower federal court jurisdiction in cases that, after state court litigation, remain subject to Supreme Court review, the principal focus of this Paragraph is on that issue.

In Martin v. Hunter's Lessee, Justice Story wrote:

" * * * The language of [Article III] throughout is manifestly designed to be mandatory upon the legislature. * * * The judicial power of the United States *shall be vested* (not may be vested) in one supreme court, and in such inferior courts as congress may, from time to time, ordain and establish. Could congress have lawfully refused to create a supreme court, or to vest in it the constitutional jurisdiction? * * *

"If, then, it is a duty of congress to vest the judicial power of the United States, it is a duty to vest the *whole judicial power*. The language, if imperative as to one part, is imperative as to all. If it were otherwise, this anomaly would exist, that congress might successively refuse to vest the jurisdiction in any one class of cases enumerated in the constitution, and thereby defeat the jurisdiction as to all; for the constitution has not singled out any class on which congress are bound to act in preference to others.

" * * * It is manifest, that a supreme court must be established; but whether it is equally obligatory to establish inferior courts, is a question of some difficulty. If congress may lawfully omit to establish inferior courts, it might follow, that in some of the enumerated cases, the judicial power could nowhere exist. * * * [I]f in any of the cases enumerated in the constitution, the state courts did not then possess jurisdiction, the appellate jurisdiction of the supreme court * * * could not reach those cases, and, consequently, the injunction of the constitution, that the judicial power *'shall be vested'*, would be disobeyed. It would seem, therefore, to follow, that congress are bound to create some inferior courts, in which to vest all that jurisdiction which, under the constitution, is *exclusively* vested in the United States, and of which the supreme court cannot take original cognizance. * * * [T]he power of the United States should be, at all times, vested either in an original or appellate form, in some courts created under its authority.

"This construction will be fortified by an attentive examination of the second section of the third article. The words are 'the judicial power *shall extend*,' & c. Much minute and elaborate criticism has been employed upon these words. It has been argued that they are equivalent to the words 'may

---

[2] Compare Engdahl, *Intrinsic Limits of Congress' Power Regarding the Judicial Branch*, 1999 B.Y.U.L.Rev. 75 (arguing, based on debates at the Constitutional Convention, that Congress' power to limit the jurisdiction of the federal courts rests on the Necessary and Proper Clause, not Article III, and that total exclusions of categories of cases cannot be justified).

extend,' and that 'extend' means to widen to new cases not before within the scope of the power. For the reasons which have been already stated, we are of opinion that the words are used in an imperative sense. * * * "

A few pages later, Justice Story analyzed the text of Article III, Section 2:

"[T]here are two classes of cases enumerated in the constitution, between which a distinction seems to be drawn. The first class includes cases arising under the constitution, laws, and treaties of the United States; cases affecting ambassadors, other public ministers and consuls, and cases of admiralty and maritime jurisdiction. In this class the expression is, and that the judicial power shall extend to *all cases*; but in the subsequent part of the clause which embraces all the other cases of national cognizance, and forms the second class, the word '*all*' is dropped seemingly *ex industria*. Here the judicial authority is to extend to controversies (not to *all* controversies) to which the United States shall be a party, & c. From this difference of phraseology, perhaps, a difference of constitutional intention may, with propriety, be inferred. * * * [I]t is not very difficult to find a reason sufficient to support the apparent change of intention. In respect to the first class, it may well have been the intention of the framers of the constitution imperatively to extend the judicial power either in an original form or appellate form to *all cases;* and in the latter class to leave it to congress to qualify the jurisdiction, original or appellate, in such manner as public policy might dictate.

"The vital importance of all the cases enumerated in the first class to the national sovereignty, might warrant such a distinction. * * * All these cases, then, enter into the national policy, affect the national rights, and may compromit the national sovereignty. * * *

"A different policy might well be adopted in reference to the second class of cases; for although it might be fit that the judicial power should extend to all controversies to which the United States should be a party, yet this power might not have been imperatively given, least it should imply a right to take cognizance of original suits brought against the United States as defendants in their own courts. It might not have been deemed proper to submit the sovereignty of the United States, against their own will, to judicial cognizance, either to enforce rights or to prevent wrongs; and as to the other cases of the second class, they might well be left to be exercised under the exceptions and regulations which congress might, in their wisdom, choose to apply. It is also worthy of remark, that congress seem, in a good degree, in * * * [the Judiciary Act of 1789] to have adopted this distinction. In the first class of cases, the jurisdiction is not limited except by the subject matter; in the second, it is made materially to depend upon the value in controversy".

Note the three different positions suggested in these excerpts. First, Justice Story argues that Congress must vest all of the judicial power "either in an original or appellate form" in some federal court. Second, he argues that if any cases described in Article III are beyond the jurisdiction of the state courts, and thus cannot be reviewed by the Supreme Court on appeal from a state court, Congress must vest jurisdiction over them in the inferior federal courts, so that they can be heard in some federal court.[3] (His

---

[3] In this connection, see Collins, *The Federal Courts, the First Congress, and the Non-Settlement of 1789*, 91 Va.L.Rev. 1515, 1560 (2005) (maintaining that debates over the Judiciary Act of 1789 reflected widely shared assumptions of state court incapacity to entertain certain

argument rests on the premise that such cases fall outside the Supreme Court's own original jurisdiction, which is limited to cases in which a state is a party and those affecting foreign envoys.) Third, he appears to limit any congressional obligation to the first three categories of cases described in Article III, as to which the Constitution uses the adjective "all".

(3) Contemporary Relevance of Justice Story's Arguments. Each of the three positions just described assumes that Article III is satisfied so long as a case falls within *either* the lower federal courts' jurisdiction or the Supreme Court's appellate jurisdiction over state court decisions.

(a) In connection with Justice Story's assumption, consider first a diversity case like Sheldon v. Sill. Suppose, following the Supreme Court's decision in that case, the dispute is litigated in state court. The Supreme Court has never exercised jurisdiction to review a state court decision, governed entirely by non-federal law, solely on the basis that the parties are diverse. Notwithstanding the decision in Erie R.R. Co. v. Tompkins, p. 584, *infra,* could the Court second-guess a state supreme court on an issue of state law? In Sheldon, if the Supreme Court lacks appellate jurisdiction over any state court decision, then the situation would run afoul of the first position attributed to Justice Story: that some federal court must have jurisdiction to review every case within the federal judicial power.

Professor Clinton has embraced a variant of this first position, contending that "Congress [must] allocate to the federal judiciary as a whole each and every type of case or controversy" within the scope of Article III, "excluding, possibly, only those cases that Congress deemed to be so trivial that they would pose an unnecessary burden." Clinton, *A Mandatory View of Federal Court Jurisdiction: A Guided Quest for the Original Understanding of Article III*, 132 U.Pa.L.Rev. 741, 749–50 (1984).[4] But he is hard-pressed to explain the gaps left in federal jurisdiction by the Judiciary Act of 1789, see pp. 25–26, *supra*, notably with respect to diversity cases. Indeed, if the Supreme Court cannot review state court decisions based on diversity, would Clinton's view oblige Congress to vest essentially the full scope of diversity jurisdiction in the lower federal courts, eliminating, for example, the statutory requirement of complete diversity?[5] Apart from requiring a striking expansion of diversity jurisdiction, could such an obligation be squared with the Madisonian Compromise?

(b) Consider next limiting lower federal court jurisdiction over a set of federal question cases (for example, cases challenging school prayer under the Establishment Clause). So long as suit can be filed in state court and the Supreme Court has the power to review, the allocation of jurisdiction squares with the thrust of Justice Story's views, subject to two qualifications.

---

federal claims, but not necessarily the further conclusion that Congress was obliged to create federal courts in which such cases could be heard).

[4] See also Clinton, *A Mandatory View of Federal Court Jurisdiction: Early Implementation of and Departures from the Constitutional Plan*, 86 Colum.L.Rev. 1515 (1986). Clinton's view is challenged, based on a study of the first Judiciary Act, in Casto, *The First Congress's Understanding of Its Authority over the Federal Courts' Jurisdiction*, 26 B.C.L.Rev. 1101 (1985).

[5] Sitting as a circuit judge in White v. Fenner, 1 Mason 520, 29 F.Cas. 1015 (C.C.D.R.I.1818) (No. 17,547), Justice Story dismissed a diversity suit excluded from the statutory grant. Although pronouncing it "somewhat singular, that the jurisdiction actually conferred on the courts of the United States should have stopped so far short of the constitutional extent," he held the "court has no jurisdiction, which is not given by some statute".

The first qualification builds on Justice Story's assumption, which is hotly contested, that the Constitution may preclude state courts from exercising jurisdiction in at least some cases that fall within Article III. (Possible examples are federal criminal cases and suits seeking specific relief against federal officials. See pp. 427–437, *infra*.) A case outside state court jurisdiction can make its way into the federal judiciary (aside from the few cases within the Supreme Court's original jurisdiction) only by way of original jurisdiction in the lower federal courts. Accordingly, Justice Story argued that in such cases Congress must vest jurisdiction in the lower federal courts.[6] But that position is in tension with the Madisonian Compromise and the language of Article III, both of which reflected the understanding that the decision whether to create lower federal courts should be a matter for discretionary decision by Congress.

The second qualification arises from changes in the Supreme Court's jurisdiction. When Justice Story wrote, the Court's jurisdiction to review state court decisions was mandatory. Since 1914, that jurisdiction has been discretionary, and in recent years the Court has rarely decided more than a dozen of the several thousand cases from the state courts in which review is sought. Is certiorari jurisdiction, especially when exercised so rarely, a sufficient "vesting" of the federal judicial power in the federal judiciary?[7]

(4) Internal and External Restraints. Consider the statement in Sheldon v. Sill that a statute defining the jurisdiction of the lower federal courts "cannot be in conflict with the Constitution, unless it confers powers not enumerated therein." That statement presumably refers only to a conflict with Article III—what commentators sometimes call "internal restraints" on Congress' power to define federal court jurisdiction.

But consider a statute that removed federal jurisdiction over claims brought by plaintiffs who were black, or female, or Jewish. Even if such a statute does not violate Article III, it would surely run afoul of "external" restrictions imposed by other constitutional provisions, such as the equal protection component of the Fifth Amendment's Due Process Clause.

The statute at issue in Sheldon v. Sill did not violate any "external" limit on congressional power over jurisdiction. Would any provision of the Constitution besides Article III bar Congress from withdrawing federal district court jurisdiction over challenges to prayer in public schools? Professor Tribe has argued that to single out a particular category of constitutional claims, like challenges to school prayer, for exclusion from the federal courts imposes an impermissible burden on the underlying constitutional right being asserted.[8] But how convincing is Tribe's premise—that it is an unconstitutional "burden" to send a case to a state court—in light of the Madisonian Compromise? Is there a substantial argument that

---

[6]   For one version of this argument, see Redish & Woods, *Congressional Power to Control the Jurisdiction of Lower Federal Courts: A Critical Review and a New Synthesis*, 124 U.Pa.L.Rev. 45 (1975).

[7]   See Eisenberg, *Congressional Authority to Restrict Lower Federal Court Jurisdiction*, 83 Yale L.J. 498 (1974), who asserts that the federal judiciary was intended to be able to hear all cases within its jurisdiction under Article III. According to Eisenberg, since the Supreme Court no longer has the capacity to review all cases originating in the state courts, he contends that it is "no longer reasonable to assert that Congress may simply abolish the lower federal courts". Eisenberg concludes that "[t]he power to curtail [federal court jurisdiction] is limited to prudent steps which help avoid case overloads."

[8]   See Tribe, *Jurisdictional Gerrymandering: Zoning Disfavored Rights Out of the Federal Courts*, 16 Harv.C.R.–C.L.L.Rev. 129, 142–43 (1981).

the Reconstruction Amendments, although directed at the states rather than at Congress, have relevantly altered the constitutional framework?[9]

(5) The Norris-LaGuardia Act. There is little precedent that considers the constitutionality of congressional exclusion of a class of constitutional cases from lower federal court jurisdiction. But one decision possibly implicating such a situation involved the Norris-LaGuardia Act of 1932, 29 U.S.C. §§ 101–115, which sharply restricts the jurisdiction of "courts of the United States" to issue temporary or permanent injunctions in "a case involving or growing out of a labor dispute". The term "court of the United States" is defined to mean "any court of the United States whose jurisdiction has been or may be conferred or defined or limited by Act of Congress".

Before the Act's adoption, Truax v. Corrigan, 257 U.S. 312 (1921), had found *state* legislation similarly limiting employers' remedies to be unconstitutional. More specifically, Truax found that (a) the denial of *all* effective remedies for violation of common law rights would offend due process, and (b) state legislation depriving employers in labor disputes of injunctive remedies against the invasion of common law property rights, when injunctions were available to others who suffered similar invasions, denied equal protection.

Relying on those precedents, in Lauf v. E.G. Shinner & Co., 303 U.S. 323 (1938), an employer challenged the constitutionality of the Norris-LaGuardia Act insofar as it sharply restricted, but did not completely abolish, the authority of a federal court to enjoin allegedly unlawful picketing and related activities. As the Supreme Court noted, the substantive rights of the parties were governed by state law and federal jurisdiction rested on diversity. The district court (affirmed by the court of appeals) had issued an injunction, finding that there was no labor dispute regulated by the Act. The Supreme Court reversed, ruling that the Act did apply and that the district court, because it had not made the findings required by the Act in order to issue an injunction in a labor dispute, had exceeded its jurisdiction. "There can be no question," the Court said, "of the power of Congress thus to define and limit the jurisdiction of the inferior courts of the United States". But the Court did not discuss the Truax decision, even though both the employer's brief and the two dissenting Justices relied upon it, nor did the Court directly address the constitutionality of statutory limits on the provision of injunctive relief to employers.

With respect to internal restraints, given that the employer could have sued in state court, where the Norris-LaGuardia Act does not apply, does Lauf v. Shinner establish that the Constitution does not "give people any right to proceed or be proceeded against, in the first instance, in a federal rather than a state court"? Hart, *The Power of Congress to Limit the Jurisdiction of Federal Courts: An Exercise in Dialectic*, 66 Harv.L.Rev. 1362, 1363 (1953) (hereinafter cited as "Hart, *Dialogue*").[10] Or should Lauf be read

---

[9]   See generally Fallon, *Reflections on the Hart and Wechsler Paradigm*, 47 Vand.L.Rev. 953, 980–83 (1994), arguing that the Civil War Amendments reflected a conception of federalism different from that embodied in the original Constitution generally, and possibly Article III specifically, and claiming that Federal Courts scholars should attend more self-consciously to resulting problems of "intertemporal synthesis".

[10]   The Senate and House Judiciary Committees that drafted the Norris-LaGuardia Act believed that the availability of state remedies satisfied the Constitution. S.Rep. No. 163, 72d Cong., 1st Sess. 10 (1932); H.R.Rep. No. 669, 72d Cong., 1st Sess. 3 (1932). See also Frankfurter & Greene, The Labor Injunction 210–14 (1930). Is it fair to say that the theory of the legislation

more narrowly—for example, as resting on the ground that the limits imposed by the Act on issuance of a federal injunctive remedy were constitutionally unexceptionable? The latter view is supported by Young, *A Critical Reassessment of the Case Law Bearing on Congress's Power to Restrict the Jurisdiction of the Lower Federal Courts*, 54 Md.L.Rev. 132 (1995). He argues, *inter alia*, that by 1938, when Lauf was decided, the Supreme Court no longer would have thought that the Due Process Clause required labor injunctions in any more than (at most) a narrow class of cases, to which Lauf did not belong. And he adds that the relevant holding of Truax v. Corrigan was that a *state* had denied the employer equal protection, a significant point given that the Court did not subject *federal* action to equal protection scrutiny until 1954, see Bolling v. Sharpe, 347 U.S. 497 (1954). On this view, the Norris-LaGuardia Act did not prevent the federal courts from awarding any relief that was constitutionally required by either the Due Process or Equal Protection Clauses.

What does Lauf v. Shinner imply about external restraints? The Norris-LaGuardia Act was clearly motivated by objections to the substance of federal judicial decisions (including constitutional decisions like Truax) in labor disputes. See Cox, Law and National Labor Policy 4–8 (1960). Does the Act therefore unconstitutionally "burden" federal constitutional rights? Does it unconstitutionally discriminate against employers, or the particular rights asserted by employers, by denying them an injunctive remedy in federal court that was available to others who seek redress for constitutional violations?

Note that within a few years of the Norris-LaGuardia Act, Congress passed two other measures that also sharply limit federal court power in particular subject matter areas. The Tax Injunction Act, 28 U.S.C. § 1341, limits authority to issue injunctions in disputes about state taxes, and the Johnson Act, 28 U.S.C. § 1342, limits authority to enjoin state public utility rate orders. See generally Chap. X, Sec. 1(B), *infra*.

Do these statutes, and the Supreme Court's acceptance of their constitutionality, establish that "the basic structure of article III affords" Congress the power to "redraw[ ] jurisdictional lines in part because it dislikes certain federal court decisions"? Gunther, *Congressional Power to Curtail Federal Court Jurisdiction: An Opinionated Guide to the Ongoing Debate*, 36 Stan.L.Rev. 895, 919–20 (1984). Would the analysis change if Congress' motive in withdrawing federal jurisdiction were to send cases to state courts that were viewed as less receptive to constitutional challenges?[11] If Congress sought to invite state court defiance of Supreme Court precedents interpreting the Constitution?[12] Consider in this regard a bill introduced in 2005 (but not enacted) that not only stripped the lower federal courts and the Supreme Court of jurisdiction to entertain challenges to governmental "acknowledgment of God as the sovereign source of law, liberty, or government", but also provided that any federal court or Supreme

---

was that the Constitution may impose more stringent limitations on state power to restrict state court jurisdiction than on federal power to restrict federal jurisdiction? Does this make sense?

[11] There is limited evidence in the legislative record that some opponents of the Johnson Act feared that the state courts were less likely to vindicate the federal constitutional claims over which the Act eliminated federal jurisdiction. See 78 Cong.Rec. 2,029 (1934).

[12] See Ely, *Legislative and Administrative Motivation in Constitutional Law*, 79 Yale L.J. 1205, 1306–08 (1970). See also Gressman & Gressman, *Necessary and Proper Roots of Exceptions to Federal Jurisdiction*, 51 Geo.Wash.L.Rev. 495 (1983).

Court decision on such an issue (whether rendered before or after the effective date of the Act) "is not binding precedent on any State court".[13]

B. Congressional Power over the Supreme Court's Appellate Jurisdiction

(1) History. Article III's provision that Congress may create "exceptions" to the Supreme Court's appellate jurisdiction was added to the Constitutional Convention's working draft by the Committee of Detail. Its purposes and possible limits were not discussed on the floor of the Convention. See p. 18, *supra*.[14]

(2) Can "Exceptions" Swallow the Rule? Congress' power to limit the Supreme Court's appellate jurisdiction is presumably subject to the same "external" limits as is the power to define the lower courts' jurisdiction. (Recall in this regard McCardle's broad statement: "We are not at liberty to inquire into the motives of the legislature.") But does Article III impose any "internal" limits on Congress' authority to create "exceptions"?[15]

In his provocative and influential *Dialogue*, Professor Hart offered the following exchange:

"Q. * * * The *McCardle* case says that the appellate jurisdiction of the Supreme Court is entirely within Congressional control.

"A. You read the *McCardle* case for all it might be worth rather than the least it has to be worth, don't you?

"Q. No, I read it in terms of the language of the Constitution and the antecedent theory that the Court articulated in explaining its decision. This seems to me to lead inevitably to the same result, whatever jurisdiction is denied to the Court.

"A. You would treat the Constitution, then, as authorizing exceptions which engulf the rule, even to the point of eliminating the appellate jurisdiction altogether? How preposterous!

"Q. If you think an 'exception' implies some residuum of jurisdiction, Congress could meet that test by excluding everything but patent cases. This is so absurd, and it is so impossible to lay down any measure of a necessary

---

[13] Constitutional Restoration Act of 2005, S. 520, 109th Cong., 1st Sess.

[14] Glashausser, *A Return to Form for the Exceptions Clause*, 51 B.C.L.Rev. 1383 (2010), argues that the first draft of what became the Exceptions Clause sought only to permit Congress to transfer cases from the Court's appellate to its original jurisdiction, an objective that was obscured by revisions that culminated in the current language.

[15] Pfander, *Jurisdiction-Stripping and the Supreme Court's Power to Supervise Inferior Tribunals*, 78 Tex.L.Rev. 1433 (2000), argues that Congress may not restrict Supreme Court oversight of the lower *federal* courts so as to undermine the constitutional premise that they must be "inferior" to the Supreme Court. He argues that historically, supervisory authority was available through "discretionary writs, such as mandamus, habeas corpus, and prohibition" and hence need not be provided by a formal appeal. Does this view give too little significance to the Exceptions Clause? In a subsequent article, Pfander & Burk, *Article III and the Scottish Judiciary*, 124 Harv.L.Rev. 1613 (2011), contend that the example of the Scottish judiciary supports the view that the Constitution requires a single Supreme Court with supervisory authority over inferior courts.

See also Claus, *The One Court that Congress Cannot Take Away: Singularity, Supremacy, and Article III*, 96 Geo.L.J. 59 (2007) (arguing that the Exceptions Clause permits Congress to transfer cases from the Supreme Court's appellate to its original jurisdiction, but does not authorize the removal of the Court's ability to have the ultimate judgment on matters within the federal judicial power).

reservation, that it seems to me the language of the Constitution must be taken as vesting plenary control in Congress.

"A. It's not impossible for me to lay down a measure. The measure is simply that the exceptions must not be such as will destroy the essential role of the Supreme Court in the constitutional plan. * * *

"Q. The measure seems pretty indeterminate to me.

"A. Ask yourself whether it is any more so than the tests which the Court has evolved to meet other hard situations. But whatever the difficulties of the test, they are less, are they not, than the difficulties of reading the Constitution as authorizing its own destruction?"

This last statement is assumed to reflect Hart's own view. In an elaboration of Hart's theory that Congress may not destroy the Supreme Court's "essential role", Professor Ratner argues that, to be constitutionally valid, "exceptions" to the Court's appellate jurisdiction must not "negate" the Court's "essential constitutional functions of maintaining the uniformity and supremacy of federal law." Ratner, *Congressional Power over the Appellate Jurisdiction of the Supreme Court*, 109 U.Pa.L.Rev. 157, 201–02 (1960). "[L]egislation that precludes Supreme Court review in every case involving a particular subject is an unconstitutional encroachment", he concludes. See also Ratner, *Majoritarian Constraints on Judicial Review: Congressional Control of Supreme Court Jurisdiction*, 27 Vill.L.Rev. 929 (1982).

Consider the extent to which historic practice squares with Professor Ratner's "essential functions" thesis. With respect to maintaining the uniform application of federal law, recall the significant gaps in Supreme Court jurisdiction left by the Judiciary Act of 1789—both the lack of jurisdiction to review state court decisions *upholding* claims of federal right and the lack of a general jurisdiction to review federal criminal cases.[16] With respect to maintaining the supremacy of federal law, is any scope left for the exceptions power when state conduct is asserted to violate federal law? In light of difficulties such as these, Professor Gunther suggests that essential functions arguments confuse "the familiar with the necessary, the desirable with the constitutionally mandated". Gunther, *supra*, at 905.[17]

---

[16] See pp. 24–25 *supra. Cf.* Felker v. Turpin, 518 U.S. 651, 667 (1996) (Souter, J., joined by Stevens and Breyer, JJ., concurring) (terming it an "open" question whether a statute limiting the Supreme Court's appellate jurisdiction would be unconstitutional if, in practice, it stopped the Court from reviewing "divergent interpretations" of a federal statute).

Frost, *Overvaluing Uniformity*, 94 Va.L.Rev. 1567 (2008), finds little evidence that the Framers were concerned with promoting uniformity, contends that the Supreme Court may never have had, and today surely lacks, the capacity to maintain uniformity, and argues that the benefits of uniformity have been greatly exaggerated.

[17] According to Calabresi & Lawson, *The Unitary Executive, Jurisdiction Stripping, and the Hamdan Opinions: A Textualist Response to Justice Scalia*, 107 Colum.L.Rev. 1002 (2007), the Exceptions Clause is not a *grant* of power to limit the Supreme Court's appellate jurisdiction but rather an *acknowledgment* of limited congressional authority to do so under the Necessary and Proper Clause. The authors maintain, based on an originalist analysis, that Congress' Article I power may not undermine the Supreme Court's status as superior to any "inferior" courts within the federal system, which requires the Supreme Court to "have the final judicial word in *all* cases * * * that raise federal issues" (emphasis in original). Under the Exceptions and Necessary and Proper Clauses, Congress may move cases back and forth between the Supreme Court's original and appellate jurisdiction but may not remove them from Supreme Court jurisdiction altogether. The authors thus conclude that Marbury v. Madison erred in holding that Congress may not expand the constitutionally specified original jurisdiction of the Supreme Court and that the First Judiciary Act was unconstitutional insofar as it failed to

Hart's view failed to persuade his collaborator, Professor Wechsler, who thought it "antithetical to the plan of the Constitution for the courts—which was quite simply that the Congress would decide from time to time how far the federal judicial institution should be used within the limits of the federal judicial power; or, stated differently, how far judicial jurisdiction should be left to the state courts, bound as they are by the [Supremacy Clause]. Federal courts, including the Supreme Court, do not pass on constitutional questions because there is a special function vested in them to enforce the Constitution or police the other agencies of the government. They do so rather for the reason that they must decide a litigated issue that is otherwise within their jurisdiction and in doing so must give effect to the supreme law of the land. That is, at least, what Marbury v. Madison was all about." Wechsler, *The Courts and the Constitution*, 65 Colum.L.Rev. 1001, 1005–06 (1965).[18]

(3) The Political Context of McCardle. The McCardle decision arose in a period of deep constitutional and political controversy. (Indeed, isn't that likely to be true when legislation limiting federal jurisdiction is not merely proposed but actually enacted?) The case appeared to require the Supreme Court to resolve the vital question of the constitutionality of the Military Reconstruction Act of 1867's authorization of criminal trials before military commissions. A decision might also reach broader issues concerning the legality of that Act, which had displaced Southern governments with military rule. Rumors swirled that the Court would uphold McCardle's appeal.

Some of the language in McCardle suggests few if any limits on Congress' power to make exceptions to the appellate jurisdiction, and many have viewed the Court as having caved in to the political dominance of the congressional Republicans, who had not only passed the Repealer Act over a presidential veto but also impeached and nearly convicted President Johnson, and who proceeded to capture the Presidency with Grant's election in 1868.[19] On the other hand, the Court's penultimate paragraph, reaching out in dictum to deny that all aspects of its jurisdiction had been withdrawn, could be viewed as a significant qualification to any broad reading of the Exceptions Clause as well as a notable assertion of power vis-a-vis Congress. The Republicans who passed the Repealer Act undoubtedly expected to block the Court from ruling on McCardle's case and would have been surprised that the Act left someone like McCardle free to reach the Supreme Court by filing an original writ of habeas corpus under § 14 of the First Judiciary Act.

---

confer either original or appellate jurisdiction on the Supreme Court in all cases presenting federal issues.

[18] The McCardle decision gave effect to a statute withdrawing jurisdiction over a case after the Supreme Court had obtained jurisdiction. Compare Hamdan v. Rumsfeld, 548 U.S. 557 (2006), p. 408, *infra*, where a statute limiting lower federal court jurisdiction over a habeas corpus action by an alien detained at Guantánamo Bay was enacted after certiorari was granted. The majority held that the statute did not withdraw jurisdiction over the pending case; in dissent, Justice Scalia contested the majority's statutory construction and, in rejecting the argument that removing jurisdiction over a pending case posed a constitutional problem, contended that the Exceptions Clause "explicitly permits" Congress to do just that.

[19] For discussion of McCardle's political context, see Fairman, History of the Supreme Court of the United States: Reconstruction and Reunion, 1864–88, Part One, ch. X (1971); Friedman, *The History of the Countermajoritarian Difficulty, Part II: Reconstruction's Political Court*, 91 Geo.L.J. 1, 25–38 (2002); Meltzer, *The Story of Ex parte McCardle: The Power of Congress to Limit the Supreme Court's Appellate Jurisdiction*, in Federal Courts Stories (Jackson & Resnik eds. 2010); Van Alstyne, *A Critical Guide to Ex Parte McCardle*, 15 Ariz.L.Rev. 229 (1973).

(4) Constitutional Avoidance. In Felker v. Turpin, 518 U.S. 651 (1996), the Court avoided potential constitutional questions about congressional restriction of the Supreme Court's appellate jurisdiction by holding that a statute withdrawing the Court's certiorari jurisdiction in certain habeas corpus cases did not restrict the Court's authority to review the case before it by entertaining a petition for an original writ of habeas corpus. In this respect, Felker echoed the penultimate paragraph of the McCardle decision. But rather than merely mentioning in passing, as in McCardle, that alternative means of review existed, the Felker Court, and in particular the concurring Justices, placed far greater reliance on it.

Under the provision at issue in Felker, 28 U.S.C. § 2244(b), a state prisoner may file a second or successive habeas petition in federal district court only after having obtained, from the court of appeals, a "gatekeeping" determination that the petition satisfies stringent statutory criteria. Section 2244(b) also declares that decisions by the courts of appeals in this gatekeeping capacity "shall not be appealable and shall not be the subject of a petition for rehearing or for a writ of certiorari".

The court of appeals denied Felker, a state prisoner, authorization to file a successive petition. He then filed in the Supreme Court a document styled "Petition for Writ of Habeas Corpus, for Appellate or Certiorari Review * * *, and for Stay of Execution". The Court, per Rehnquist, C.J., held unanimously that the Act's preclusion of certiorari review of the court of appeals' gatekeeping decisions did not offend Article III, § 2. But the Court reached that conclusion only after having interpreted § 2244(b) as not withdrawing the Court's authority to entertain original habeas petitions under 28 U.S.C. § 2241 (the successor provision in this respect to § 14 of the First Judiciary Act). That interpretation of § 2244(b) rested on the principle, which the Court drew from Ex parte Yerger, p. 307 n. *, *supra*, that implied repeals of the Supreme Court's appellate jurisdiction are disfavored.

The Court next held that § 2244(b)'s stringent requirements for the authorization of successive petitions in the district courts, whether or not they formally limited the Court's power to issue writs of habeas corpus under § 2241, should "inform our authority to grant such relief as well" and were well within the permissible range of congressional judgments. Finding that the petitioner failed to satisfy those requirements, "let alone" the requirements of the Supreme Court's Rule 20.4(a) that there must be "exceptional circumstances" justifying issuance of original writs, the Court dismissed Felker's petition.

Concurring, Justice Stevens (joined by Justices Souter and Breyer) described the Court's response "to the argument that [§ 2244(b)] has deprived this Court of appellate jurisdiction in violation of Article III, § 2" as "incomplete", and noted additional statutes that might authorize Supreme Court review of a gatekeeping decision, including the All Writs Act, 28 U.S.C. § 1651, and 28 U.S.C. § 1254(2), which authorizes a court of appeals to certify a question for the Court's review. Justice Souter's separate concurring opinion (joined by Justices Stevens and Breyer) reserved the question that would be presented if the courts of appeals "adopted divergent interpretations of the gatekeeper standard" and in practice "statutory avenues other than certiorari for reviewing a gatekeeping determination were closed".

The Court's opinion in Felker does not expressly invoke the maxim that statutes should be construed to avoid difficult constitutional questions, but can the result be explained on any other basis?[20] Consider Tushnet, *"The King of France with Forty Thousand Men": Felker v. Turpin and the Supreme Court's Deliberative Processes*, 1996 Sup.Ct.Rev. 163, 182: "Congress's attempt to speed up executions was rendered almost entirely toothless: Every prospective applicant denied leave to file a second petition by a court of appeals now can file an application for leave to file an original writ in the Supreme Court, instead of filing a petition for certiorari." Is it harder to satisfy the "exceptional circumstances" standard of Sup.Ct.R. 20.4(a) than the Court's normal standard for granting review, see Sup.Ct.R. 10 ("A petition for a writ of certiorari will be granted only for compelling reasons")? If not, why would Congress enact a provision whose only practical effect was (a) to preclude a petition for rehearing in the court of appeals, and (b) to require that a petition in the Supreme Court be labeled one for an original writ of habeas corpus rather than for a writ of certiorari?

(5) Uncertainty and Its Consequences. Professor Bator contends that for Congress to withdraw the Supreme Court's appellate jurisdiction would "violate the spirit of the Constitution, even if it would not violate its letter * * * because the structure contemplated by the instrument makes sense * * * only on the premise that there would be a federal Supreme Court with the power to pronounce uniform and authoritative rules of federal law." Bator, *Congressional Power over the Jurisdiction of the Federal Courts*, 27 Vill.L.Rev. 1030, 1039 (1982). Others, including some strong supporters of broad judicial protection of individual rights, view the power to withdraw jurisdiction as an important political counterweight whose existence gives legitimacy to judicial review. See, *e.g.*, Black, *The Presidency and Congress*, 32 Wash. & Lee L.Rev. 841, 846 (1975). Of course, the political branches can exercise some control over the Court in other ways—by selecting new Justices or by changing the size of the Court (which has happened seven times over the years, see Orth, *How Many Judges Does It Take to Make a Supreme Court?*, 19 Const.Comment. 681 (2002)). Is jurisdiction stripping, or at least the threat of jurisdiction stripping, an appropriate means for the people's representatives to seek accountability from Justices with life tenure? Does the answer to this question depend upon one's view of the appropriate role of the courts in exercising the power of judicial review?[21] Is

---

[20] Tyler, *Continuity, Coherence, and the Canons*, 99 Nw.U.L.Rev. 1389, 1443–47 (2005), argues that Felker is best explained not by constitutional avoidance but by "stare decisis and the canon against implied repeals." Professor Tyler suggests that these "broader principles of statutory continuity and harmonization" have animated the Court's approach to integrating the framework established in § 2241 with new statutes such as the AEDPA.

[21] Consider, in this regard, the argument of proponents of "popular constitutionalism" that constitutional understanding should be less concentrated in the courts and informed more broadly by the views of officials in other branches of government and of the people. See, *e.g.*, Kramer, The People Themselves: Popular Constitutionalism and Judicial Review 246–48 (2004); Tushnet, Taking the Constitution Away from the Courts (1999). Dean Kramer views Reconstruction as a high point in popular constitutionalism: the Supreme Court, after it had issued rulings that were deeply unpopular with the Republicans who dominated Congress, was "threatened with 'annihilation' in Congress, and on important matters it was forced to back down in various ways—including both jurisdiction stripping and court packing, to which it meekly submitted." Kramer, *The Supreme Court 2000 Term—Foreword: We the Court*, 115 Harv.L.Rev. 5, 117–18 (2001). Is Kramer right to view the Court in McCardle as caving to congressional pressure? Or could one view it as "slightly bloodied but emphatically unbowed", Wiecek, *The Great Writ and Reconstruction: The Habeas Corpus Act of 1867*, 36 J.S.Hist. 530, 543 (1970), and, indeed, as somewhat assertive in refusing to read the Repealer Act as precluding the exercise of habeas corpus jurisdiction under the Judiciary Act of 1789?

it perhaps politically healthy that the limits of congressional power over Supreme Court appellate jurisdiction have never been completely clarified?

C.   Congressional Power to Withdraw All Federal Jurisdiction

(1) Framing the Issue. Would *simultaneous* restrictions on Supreme Court and lower federal court jurisdiction over matters that remain subject to adjudication in state court raise distinctive issues under Article III? Such limits have been accepted historically with respect to diversity cases, for example, but debate has swirled around the cases arising under federal law, and the Supreme Court appears never to have addressed directly the issues thus presented.

(2) Constitutional Arguments. As noted in Paragraphs (A)(2–3), *supra,* Justice Story argued that denial of all federal jurisdiction to hear cases within Article III would offend the Constitution. If understood to apply to every case falling within the federal judicial power, Justice Story's argument is hard to square with the Judiciary Act of 1789—which is frequently viewed as a repository of insight into the original understanding of Article III—and with historical practice surrounding the diversity jurisdiction. See pp. 20–26, 296–297, *supra.*

In modern times, some more limited versions of Story's argument—that Article III requires the vesting of federal jurisdiction in either original or federal appellate form in *some,* but not all, categories of cases—have been put forward.

(a) Professor Sager has argued that the Constitution requires either original or appellate federal jurisdiction over *constitutional* claims. See Sager, *The Supreme Court, 1980 Term—Foreword: Constitutional Limitations on Congress' Authority to Regulate the Jurisdiction of the Federal Courts,* 95 Harv.L.Rev. 17 (1981). He rests largely on the premise that these cases present the largest constitutional interest in adjudication by a judge with the safeguards from political influence established by Article III. How firmly is this appeal to "history and logic" anchored in the constitutional text?[22]

(b) Professor Amar has argued that Article III requires vesting either original or appellate federal jurisdiction in three of the nine categories of cases listed in Article III, § 2. See, *e.g.,* Amar, *A Neo-Federalist View of Article III: Separating the Two Tiers of Federal Jurisdiction,* 65 B.U.L.Rev. 205 (1985); Amar, *The Two-Tiered Structure of the Judiciary Act of 1789,* 138 U.Pa.L.Rev. 1499 (1990); Amar, *Reports of My Death Are Greatly Exaggerated: A Reply,* 138 U.Pa.L.Rev. 1651 (1990). Following Justice Story, Amar stresses the language of Article III, § 1 directing that the "judicial Power *shall* be vested" (emphasis added), but relies even more heavily on the selective use of the word "all" in Article III, § 2. With respect to the first three of the nine listed categories—federal question cases, cases affecting foreign envoys, and admiralty cases—Article III, § 2 says that the judicial power shall extend to "*all* Cases". With respect to the remaining six categories, Article III omits "all" and says simply that the judicial power shall extend to the denominated categories of "Controversies". According to Amar, Article III thus establishes two "tiers" of federal jurisdiction: a first tier, comprising the first three categories, in which federal jurisdiction (in either original or

---

[22]   For criticism, see Redish, *Constitutional Limitations on Congressional Power to Control Federal Jurisdiction: A Reaction to Professor Sager,* 77 Nw.U.L.Rev. 143 (1982).

appellate form) is mandatory in "all Cases"; and a second tier, consisting of the remaining six categories, in which the decision whether to vest federal jurisdiction is a matter for Congress to decide.

This interpretation leaves a role for congressional discretion, as contemplated by the Madisonian Compromise, about whether to create lower federal courts, for even in their absence, the Supreme Court's exercise of appellate jurisdiction would satisfy Article III's mandate. The two-tier thesis also recognizes Congress' power to create "exceptions" to the Supreme Court's appellate jurisdiction even within Amar's first tier; exceptions are permissible wherever there is original jurisdiction in the lower federal courts. But what Congress may not do, Amar contends, is exercise its power to deny *both* Supreme Court and lower federal court jurisdiction with respect to the same class of cases within the mandatory first tier.[23]

Amar buttresses his reading of Article III with a wide range of supporting arguments.

(i) At the Convention, all of the central drafts of the judiciary article, in describing the cases to which the federal judicial power would extend, referred to "all" actions arising under federal law but omitted "all" in listing other cases.

(ii) Despite some gaps, the Judiciary Act of 1789 was reasonably consistent with the two-tier thesis.

(iii) Language said to support the two-tier thesis appears not only in Martin v. Hunter's Lessee but also in other early Supreme Court opinions.[24]

(iv) The theory ensures adjudication by federal judges, whose tenure and salary are protected, in the cases of most profound national consequence.

Each of these arguments by Amar is skeptically probed in Meltzer, *The History and Structure of Article III*, 138 U.Pa.L.Rev. 1569 (1990), who contends:

(i) As to use of the word "all", some evidence suggests that the founding generation understood the word "cases"—in contrast to the word "controversies"—to include criminal as well as civil actions, and the word "all" might have been used to emphasize that both were encompassed.[25]

---

[23] Consider whether the following regime comports with Amar's thesis. In Santa Clara Pueblo v. Martinez, 436 U.S. 49 (1978), the Court held that federal courts possess no jurisdiction over suits to enforce the federal Indian Civil Rights Act, 28 U.S.C. §§ 1301–03, the express purpose of which is to "protect individual Indians from arbitrary and unjust actions of tribal governments" by imposing "limitations on an Indian tribe in the exercise of its powers of self-government". S. Rep. No. 841, 90th Cong., 1st Sess. 6 (1967). In general enforcement actions, although they arise under federal law, can be filed only in tribal courts, see Worthen, *Shedding New Light on an Old Debate: A Federal Indian Law Perspective on Congressional Authority to Limit Federal Question Jurisdiction*, 75 Minn.L.Rev. 65, 90–91 (1990), and there is no possibility of Supreme Court review. Are tribal matters simply sui generis?

[24] Amar cites American Ins. Co. v. 356 Bales of Cotton, 26 U.S. (1 Pet.) 511, 515 (1828); Osborn v. Bank of the United States, 22 U.S. (9 Wheat.) 738, 821–22 (1824); Cohens v. Virginia, 19 U.S. (6 Wheat.) 264, 378 (1821). See 138 U.Pa.L.Rev. at 1513 n.37. See also The Moses Taylor, 71 U.S. (4 Wall.) 411, 428–29 (1866); Stevenson v. Fain, 195 U.S. 165, 167 (1904).

[25] Harrison, *The Power of Congress to Limit the Jurisdiction of Federal Courts and the Text of Article III*, 64 U.Chi.L.Rev. 203 (1997), offers a sustained textual critique of Amar's thesis; see also Velasco, *Congressional Control Over Federal Court Jurisdiction: A Defense of the Traditional View*, 46 Cath.U.L.Rev. 671, 763 (1997) (advancing a textual and historical defense of "the orthodox position that Congress possesses nearly plenary authority to regulate" federal jurisdiction). For a point-by-point response to Professor Harrison, see Pushaw, *Congressional*

What is more, Meltzer argues, there is virtually no support in either the Convention's records or the ratification debates for Amar's understanding.

(ii) The fit between Amar's thesis and the Judiciary Act of 1789 is not as close as Amar suggests, especially insofar as section 25 of that Act allowed review of federal questions decided by the state courts only when the decision was adverse to a claim of federal right.[26] (See p. 25, *supra*.)

(iii) Meltzer views early Supreme Court dicta as much less probative than Amar suggests.

(iv) Amar's first mandatory tier, which does not reach cases in which the United States is a party and those between states, does not include the cases most important to the union. Meltzer also notes that "Charles Black, the dean of structural constitutional interpretation, has argued that congressional power to control federal court jurisdiction 'is the rock on which rests the legitimacy of the judicial work in a democracy.' " (quoting Black, p. 318, *supra*, at 846).[27]

Judge Fletcher offers a distinct challenge to Amar's interpretation of the significance of the use of the word "all". Noting that "all" also appears in the

---

Power Over Federal Court Jurisdiction: A Defense of the Neo-Federalist Interpretation of Article III, 1997 BYU L.Rev. 847.

[26] Amar contends that in fact Section 25 covered all federal questions, because whenever one party claimed a federal right, the other party could claim a federal immunity (*e.g.*, that the other party lacked a federal right). In response, Meltzer acknowledges that some twentieth century cases seemed to take that view, but pointed to Marshall and Taney Court decisions dismissing appeals for want of jurisdiction when the state court had upheld federal rights. More recently, Professor Woolhandler advanced a middle ground, finding that the Court was more likely to accept the expansive view in cases involving the scope of federal statutes. She acknowledges that "no one seems to have thought review was available when [in 1911] the New York Court of Appeals struck down the state workers' compensation statute on federal constitutional grounds"—the decision that motivated Congress in 1914 to eliminate the restriction on Supreme Court review of state court decisions against the claimed federal right. Woolhandler, *Power, Rights, and Section 25*, 86 Notre Dame L.Rev.1241, 1286 (2011).

[27] For other critical commentary, see Redish, *Text, Structure, and Common Sense in the Interpretation of Article III*, 138 U.Pa.L.Rev. 1633 (1990).

See also Liebman & Ryan, *"Some Effectual Power": The Quantity and Quality of Decisionmaking Required of Article III Courts*, 98 Colum.L.Rev. 696 (1998) (arguing that the Framers intended to allow assignment of federal question cases to the state courts without Supreme Court review, but to preclude Congress from imposing "qualitative" restrictions that would limit independent judicial decisionmaking in cases assigned to Article III courts).

Pfander, *Federal Supremacy, State Court Inferiority, and the Constitutionality of Jurisdiction-Stripping Legislation*, 101 Nw.U.L.Rev. 191 (2007), argues on historical and structural grounds that the scope of Congress' power to control federal jurisdiction comes into view only when Article III is read in conjunction with the provision of Article I, § 8, cl. 9, authorizing Congress "[t]o constitute Tribunals inferior to the supreme Court." Pfander says the provision for inferior tribunals "appears to implement the Madisonian Compromise by giving Congress a choice either to create Article III courts or to rely on appointed state courts instead (as the old Congress had done under the Articles of Confederation)". In his view, legislation purporting to strip federal courts of all power to decide federal issues "should be seen as 'constitut[ing]' the state courts as [inferior] tribunals within the meaning of Article I" and therefore trigger a requirement of enough Supreme Court oversight of state court decisionmaking to implement "the inferiority requirement of Article I". Even if Pfander is correct that Article III authorizes Congress to "constitute" state courts as federal tribunals for limited purposes, does it follow that legislation limiting federal jurisdiction should be read as doing so?

Compare Calabresi & Lawson, *The Unitary Executive, Jurisdiction Stripping, and the Hamdan Opinions: A Textualist Response to Justice Scalia*, 107 Colum.L.Rev. 1002, 1034 (2007), who contend that in the eighteenth century, the term "court" had a broader meaning than the term "tribunal".

clause defining the Supreme Court's original jurisdiction as embracing cases involving foreign envoys and those in which a state is a party, Fletcher contends that Article III's use of "all authorizes, but does not require, Congress to confer exclusive jurisdiction on the federal courts" over the cases in Amar's first tier (and to confer exclusive jurisdiction on the Supreme Court in cases affecting foreign envoys or those in which a state is a party). See Fletcher, *Congressional Power Over the Jurisdiction of Federal Courts: The Meaning of the Word "All" in Article III*, 59 Duke L.J. 929, 934 (2010). He asserts that his interpretation is consistent with Article III's text and with the Judiciary Acts of 1789 and 1801, and is somewhat, though not perfectly, consistent with Hamilton's views in Federalist No. 82 and with Justice Story's opinion in Martin v. Hunter's Lessee.

(3) The Limits of Originalism, and the Significance of Unconstitutional Motivation, in Assessing Jurisdiction-Stripping Legislation. Despite widespread acknowledgement that the materials from the founding period are quite limited and cryptic with regard to disputed issues about the meaning of Article III, much of the debate about Article III's interpretation has been heavily originalist in approach. Professor Fallon, in *Jurisdiction-Stripping Reconsidered,* 96 Va.L.Rev. 1043 (2010), criticizes an interpretive approach based on "exclusive originalism." He finds support for his criticism in the Supreme Court's 2008 decision in Boumediene v. Bush, pp. 298, 1224, 1249. There, the Court, in ruling that Congress had violated the Suspension Clause of the Constitution when it sought to preclude both federal and state courts from exercising habeas corpus jurisdiction in specified cases, found the eighteenth century history indeterminate and resolved the case based on principles derived from recent decisions and functional considerations.

Fallon proceeds to contend that an unconstitutional purpose can render a jurisdiction-stripping statute invalid, noting more broadly the prevalence of motive-based inquiries in constitutional adjudication. He argues that it would be unconstitutional for Congress to withdraw previously conferred jurisdiction over a constitutional issue from both the lower federal courts and the Supreme Court, based on anticipated disagreement with federal court decisions; such a statute would have "the purpose of encouraging state courts to ignore, reject, or defy pertinent precedents." Fallon discounts the Court's declaration in McCardle that it may not inquire into Congress' motive, noting that the McCardle decision can be read narrowly in view of the existence of another route to Supreme Court review.

Fallon does not assume that it would necessarily be unconstitutional for Congress, with respect to a particular set of cases, either to withdraw the Supreme Court's appellate jurisdiction without disturbing lower court jurisdiction, or to eliminate the original jurisdiction of the lower federal courts, which is consistent with settled practice.

Is a congressional decision to assign cases to state courts, motivated by concern about the substance of federal court constitutional decisions, necessarily an invitation to defy precedent, rather than an effort to choose a forum that legislators think is more likely to reach sound constitutional results? And if legislation precluding *all* federal court jurisdiction is constitutionally infirm on the basis that Fallon suggests, isn't legislation that strips lower federal courts alone of jurisdiction likely to rest on the same suspect motivation—especially given the infrequency of Supreme Court review of state court decisions?

D.   The Klein Decision

The first Supreme Court case to invalidate a statutory limitation on federal court power framed in jurisdictional terms is United States v. Klein, 80 U.S. (13 Wall.) 128 (1871). Unfortunately, the Court's opinion raises more questions than it answers, and it can be read to support a wide range of holdings.[28] The decision may have more to do with efforts by Congress to tell a court *how* to decide—and in particular, to tell a court to decide in a way that conflicts with the Constitution—than *whether* it may exercise jurisdiction to decide.

During the Civil War, agents of the government, acting pursuant to wartime legislation, seized and sold a large quantity of cotton that belonged to a Southerner named Wilson. The legislation provided, however, that those whose property had been seized could recover the proceeds from its sale in the Court of Claims, if they could prove that they had "never given any aid or comfort to the present rebellion." After Wilson's death, Klein, the administrator of his estate, prevailed in an action in the Court of Claims, which awarded the considerable sum of $125,300. The Supreme Court had previously held that one who, like Wilson, had received a presidential pardon must be treated as loyal, and the Court of Claims' ultimate judgment reaffirming the award seemed consistent with the Supreme Court's decision, although it was not cited.

While an appeal by the United States from that judgment was pending, Congress passed an act providing that no pardon should be admissible as proof of loyalty and, further, that acceptance of a pardon without a protest that the claimant took no part in the rebellion was conclusive evidence of the claimant's *disloyalty*. The statute directed the Court of Claims and the Supreme Court to dismiss "for want of jurisdiction" any claim based on a pardon.[29] The United States quickly asked the Supreme Court to remand Klein's case to the Court of Claims with instructions to dismiss for want of jurisdiction. Instead, the Court held the supervening statute to be unconstitutional and proceeded to exercise jurisdiction, affirming the judgment below. The brief and delphic opinion includes at least four strands.

(1) The opinion stresses that Congress' attempt to regulate jurisdiction is not a talisman that renders any such legislative effort constitutional. The Court says that the "denial of jurisdiction to this court, as well as to the Court of Claims, is founded solely on the application of a rule of decision, in causes pending, prescribed by Congress. The court has jurisdiction of the cause to a given point; but when it ascertains that a certain state of things exists, its jurisdiction is to cease and it is required to dismiss the cause for want of jurisdiction. * * * It seems to us that this is not an exercise of the acknowledged power of Congress to make exceptions and prescribe regulations to the appellate power".

---

[28] For a useful overview, see Tyler, *The Story of Klein: The Scope of Congress's Authority to Shape the Jurisdiction of the Federal Courts*, in Federal Courts Stories 87 (Jackson & Resnik eds.2010).

[29] The statute provided that, with respect to any pending appeal in which a claimant had prevailed on proof of loyalty other "than such as is above required and provided, * * * the Supreme Court shall, on appeal, have no further jurisdiction of the cause, and shall dismiss the same for want of jurisdiction." Act of July 12, 1870, 16 Stat. 230, 235. Senator Edmunds, in response to a question whether this provision would simply require dismissal of the appeal (leaving the lower court judgment intact), said: "No; * * * we say they shall dismiss the case out of court for want of jurisdiction; not dismiss the appeal, but dismiss the case—everything." Cong.Globe, 41st Cong., 2d Sess. 3824 (1870).

Whatever else the Court may have had in mind, it is surely right, isn't it, that not every congressional attempt to influence the outcome of cases, even if phrased in jurisdictional language, can be justified as a valid exercise of a power over jurisdiction?

(2) The opinion continues by broadly questioning the power of Congress to "prescribe rules of decision to the Judicial Department of the government in cases pending before it". It is doubtful, however, that this language can be taken at face value, for congressional power to make valid statutes retroactively applicable to pending cases has often been recognized. See p. 89, *supra*.

Consider the situation presented in Robertson v. Seattle Audubon Soc'y, 503 U.S. 429 (1992). Two lawsuits alleged that that the U.S. Forest Service's plan to permit some timber harvesting in areas that were home to the Northern Spotted Owl violated the Endangered Species Act. While those cases were pending, Congress, as part of an appropriations bill, enacted a provision, known as Section 318, that contained a management plan for timber harvesting only in the areas that were home to the Northern Spotted Owl. Section 318, which expired at the end of the fiscal year, declared that management of the forests in accordance with the plan set forth in that section constituted "adequate consideration" for the purposes of the legal requirements governing the two pending lawsuits, which Section 318 identified by docket number.

The Ninth Circuit, citing Klein, held Section 318 unconstitutional, concluding that Congress had not repealed or amended the environmental laws underlying the pending lawsuits, but instead attempted to direct a result contrary to the law as judicially interpreted and thereby violated Article III. The Supreme Court, however, unanimously disagreed, contending that Section 318 did not instruct a court in how to apply pre-existing legal standards to a pending case, but rather amended the pre-existing standards. The Court thus found it unnecessary to consider whether Klein precludes Congress from directing a decision in a pending case without amending the governing law.

Professor Redish argues that Congress should not be able to dictate an outcome without changing the applicable law, because to do so would go beyond the legislative function of laying down general rules for which the legislature must accept political responsibility and intrude on the judicial function of deciding individual cases. See Redish, *Federal Judicial Independence: Constitutional and Political Perspectives*, 46 Mercer L.Rev. 697, 718–21 (1995). If Professor Redish's argument seeks to bound the legislative function, how clear are the boundary lines? Would Congress violate the principles he endorses by passing an amendment that swept no more broadly than the range of applications of an existing statute to a single pending case, which the amendment identified by docket number?

(3) The Court found that the rule of decision in question impaired the effect of a presidential pardon and thus "infring[ed] the constitutional power of the Executive". More broadly, one could read Klein as supporting a conception of judicial integrity: Congress may not, in the guise of enacting jurisdictional legislation, direct a federal court to decide a case in a fashion that conflicts with the Constitution.[30]

---

[30] Professor Young reads Klein as suggesting that Congress may not regulate a federal court's deliberative processes in a variety of ways. Young, *United States v. Klein, Then and Now*,

(4) The Court suggested that jurisdiction-stripping legislation enacted "as a means to an end" that is itself constitutionally impermissible "is not an exercise of the acknowledged power of Congress to make exceptions and prescriptive regulations to the appellate power". (No mention was made of the Court's statement in McCardle, two years earlier, that it could not inquire into the motives of the legislature.)[31]

Does this language support arguments that legislation precluding Supreme Court jurisdiction, or jurisdiction of all federal courts, in cases challenging school prayer, for example, would be in service of a forbidden purpose and therefore beyond Congress' power to make exceptions to the Court's appellate jurisdiction?[32] If so, how strong is that support given that the Klein judgment is adequately supported by narrower reasoning, including the entirely plausible understanding that the rule of decision whose application Congress directed would have required the courts to abridge the President's pardon power?

---

44 Loy.U.Chi.L.J. 265 (2012). Among the prohibited regulations would be some restrictions on fact-finding in constitutional cases (*e.g.*, conclusive presumptions or rebuttable presumptions that are probabilistically unreasonable) and some prescription of the interpretive methods followed when interpreting the Constitution and statutes.

A still broader version of this understanding of Klein is offered by Professor Sager: "The judiciary will not allow itself to be made to speak and act against its own best judgment on matters within its competence which have great consequence for our political community." Sager, *Klein's First Principle: A Proposed Solution*, 86 Geo.L.J. 2525, 2529 (1998). As an example, he mentions the Religious Freedom Restoration Act, which enacted by statute a rule of decision for religious freedom that the Court had rejected as a constitutional standard under the Free Exercise Clause. But isn't there a difference between statutes (arguably like that in Klein) that direct courts how to apply the Constitution, and statutes, like RFRA, that create statutory rules of decision whose content differs from that of the Constitution? See Meltzer, *Congress, Courts and Constitutional Remedies*, 86 Geo. L.J. 2537, 2540–41 (1998) (suggesting that Sager's reading of Klein is overly broad and would endanger other statutes—such as the Voting Rights Act of 1982 and the Pregnancy Discrimination Act of 1978—that created statutory bans on conduct that the Supreme Court had ruled was not unconstitutional).

[31] Another reading of Klein sees it as establishing that Congress may not deceive the electorate about the way in which legislation operates—a principle that Congress was said to have violated by enacting evidentiary rules whose effect was to transform the meaning of the law that provided compensation to loyal owners of property. See Redish & Pudelski, *Legislative Deception, Separation of Powers, and the Democratic Process: Harnessing the Political Theory of United States v. Klein*, 100 Nw.U.L.Rev. 437 (2006); accord, Vladeck, *Why Klein (Still) Matters: Congressional Deception and the War on Terrorism*, 5 J.Nat'l Security L. & Pol'y 251 (2011). Professor Young, note 30, *supra*, casts doubt on this view of Klein and questions the appropriateness of judicial evaluation of purported legislative deceptiveness. (Moreover, how deceptive, really, was the statute at issue in Klein?)

[32] Roughly contemporaneous cases decided on the authority of Klein include Armstrong v. United States, 80 U.S. (13 Wall.) 154 (1872), and Witkowski v. United States, 7 Ct.Cl. 393 (1872), in both of which the courts refused to be bound by the provision of the statute involved in Klein ordering courts to dismiss suits for want of jurisdiction upon the introduction of a pardon. According to Professor Young, these decisions take an important step beyond Klein, which in his terms involved a "puppeteering" provision of the statute ordering the Supreme Court to reverse a decision rendered by a lower court. See Young, *A Critical Reassessment of the Case Law Bearing on Congress's Power to Restrict the Jurisdiction of the Lower Federal Courts*, 54 Md.L.Rev. 132, 158–59 (1995). By contrast, Young argues, Armstrong and Witkowski involved a "court-stripping" portion of the statute purporting to deprive *trial* courts of jurisdiction over a defined class of cases. He concludes that "[i]t seems impossible to distinguish * * * the plaintiff in Armstrong from plaintiffs today who might seek federal court enforcement of modern constitutional rights, such as busing or abortion rights, despite a statute which purports to close off the federal courts".

Under a statute that authorizes lower courts to entertain claims, but orders them to dismiss those claims for want of jurisdiction upon proof of a presidential pardon, is the line between "puppeteering" and "court stripping" as clear as Young suggests?

INTRODUCTORY NOTE ON CONGRESSIONAL PRECLUSION OF BOTH STATE AND FEDERAL COURT JURISDICTION

The preceding discussion of congressional regulation of federal court jurisdiction has assumed in each case that, whatever the limits on federal court jurisdiction, the state courts remained open to litigate the merits of any claim. The next case raises the question of the constitutionality of congressional efforts to preclude the jurisdiction of both the federal courts and the state courts, leaving a litigant with no court in which to bring suit.[1]

Battaglia v. General Motors Corp.

169 F.2d 254 (2d Cir. 1948).
Appeals from the District Court of the United States for the
Western District of New York.

Before SWAN, AUGUSTUS N. HAND and CHASE, CIRCUIT JUDGES.

■ CHASE, CIRCUIT JUDGE:

[The Fair Labor Standards Act of 1938 (FLSA), 29 U.S.C. §§ 201–219, requires that covered employees be paid at least one and one-half times their regular wage rate for hours worked in excess of a 40-hour work week. The Act makes employers liable for unpaid overtime and for an additional, equal amount as liquidated damages.

[In three decisions in 1946, the Supreme Court unexpectedly interpreted the statutory term "work week" as including underground travel, and similar preliminary activities, of employees in iron ore mines. Under these decisions, many employees' work week now exceeded forty hours, resulting in monetary liability under the FLSA.

[Between July 1, 1946, and January 31, 1947, nearly two thousand lawsuits based on the Supreme Court's decisions were filed in federal district courts. Collectively, these actions sought more than $5 billion; the potential liability of the United States, on War Department cost-plus contracts, was estimated at $1.4 billion.

[Moved by these facts, on May 14, 1947, Congress enacted the Portal-to-Portal Act of 1947, 29 U.S.C. §§ 251–62. Finding that the recent decisions created immense and unexpected liabilities that would ruin many employers, bestow windfalls on employees, and seriously affect the United States Treasury, sections 2(a) and (b) of the Act eliminated the substantive liability that the Supreme Court had recognized. These subsections provided (with limited exceptions) that "[n]o employer shall be subject to any liability" under the FLSA for the failure to compensate employees for the preliminary work at issue.

---

[1] The constitutional issues arising from the substitution of non-Article III federal tribunals for Article III courts are discussed in Section 2 of this Chapter. This Note addresses issues arising when Congress tries to withdraw jurisdiction from all "courts", with that term here understood to encompass so-called "Article I" or "legislative" courts—which are discussed extensively in Section 2—as well as Article III courts and state courts.

[In addition, section 2(d) of the Act provided: "No court of the United States, of any State, Territory, or possession of the United States, or of the District of Columbia, shall have jurisdiction of any action or proceeding, whether instituted prior to or on or after May 14, 1947, to enforce liability or impose punishment for or on account of the failure of the employer to pay minimum wages or overtime compensation under the Fair Labor Standards Act of 1938 * * * to the extent that such action or proceeding seeks to enforce any liability or impose any punishment with respect to an activity which was not compensable under subsections (a) and (b) of this section."]

[The Battaglia decision involved four lawsuits filed against General Motors by employees alleging that the company had violated their right, under the Supreme Court's 1946 trio of decisions, to time and a half for hours over forty per week. While the actions were pending in the district court, the Portal-to-Portal Act was adopted. General Motors then moved to dismiss the complaints,] on the grounds that no cause of action was alleged and that the court was without jurisdiction by virtue of section 2 of the Portal-to-Portal Act. * * * [T]he appellants then questioned this statute upon constitutional grounds * * *. [Ultimately, the district court granted the motions to dismiss.]

* * * [T]he issue of the constitutionality of this section of the Portal-to-Portal Act has been presented by these appeals. * * * It was the duty of the court to ascertain whether it had jurisdiction before proceeding to hear and decide the case on the merits. * * * If subdivision (d) of section 2 of the Act is valid the lack of jurisdiction is clear and if subdivisions (a) and (b) of section 2 are valid it is equally apparent that no cause of action on the merits was alleged. We think the dismissal of each cause of action right, for the following reasons.

A few of the district court decisions sustaining section 2 of the Portal-to-Portal Act have done so on the ground that since jurisdiction of federal courts other than the Supreme Court is conferred by Congress, it may at the will of Congress be taken away in whole or in part. * * * [T]hese district court decisions would, in effect, sustain subdivision (d) of section 2 of the Act regardless of whether subdivisions (a) and (b) were valid. We think, however, that the exercise of Congress of its control over jurisdiction is subject to compliance with at least the requirements of the Fifth Amendment. That is to say, while Congress has the undoubted power to give, withhold, and restrict the jurisdiction of courts other than the Supreme Court,[4] it must not so exercise that power as to deprive any person of life, liberty, or property without due process of law or to take private property without just compensation. Thus, regardless of whether subdivision (d) of section 2 had an independent end in itself, if one of its effects would be to deprive the appellants of property without due process or just compensation, it would be invalid. Under this view, subdivision (d) on the one hand and subdivisions (a) and (b) on the other will stand or fall together. We turn then to a consideration of the question whether the appellants have been unconstitutionally deprived of any substantive rights.

---

[4] It also has the power, of course, to make "exceptions" to and "regulations" regarding the Supreme Court's appellate jurisdiction. Const. Art. III, § 2.

[After examining the statute and the employees' contracts, the court noted] three ways in which the employees' rights to compensation for these activities may be viewed: first, as wholly statutory up to the time the Portal-to-Portal Act was enacted; second, as purely statutory up to the time of the Supreme Court decisions and contractual thereafter; and finally, as wholly contractual from the beginning. * * * [W]e think that however appellants' rights are considered, the Portal-to-Portal Act is constitutional.

This seems plain enough, if we take the view that the claims rested purely on statute up to the time the Portal-to-Portal Act was enacted. Clearly, the general rule is that "powers derived wholly from a statute are extinguished by its repeal." Flanigan v. County of Sierra, 196 U.S. 553, 560. * * * This being true, so long as the claims, if they were purely statutory, had not ripened into final judgment, regardless of whether the activities on which they were based had been performed, they were subject to whatever action Congress might take with respect to them.

If however, the rights were statutory up to the time of the Supreme Court decisions and contractual thereafter, or if they were founded upon contract from the time of the enactment of the Fair Labor Standards Act, the problem is not so simple, for there are a number of cases holding that it is a violation of due process to deprive an individual of previously vested contractual rights.

But the solution to the problem seems quite as clear. * * * [If the FLSA previously made the employees' contracts include the right to compensation for portal-to-portal activities, the Portal-to-Portal Act did away with that aspect of the contracts.] Very closely in point is Louisville & Nashville R. Co. v. Mottley, 219 U.S. 467, where a contract to furnish transportation free of charge—valid when made * * *—was held unenforceable when Congress later * * * made it unlawful for railroads to provide such transportation. * * * The Supreme Court there said: "The agreement between the railroad company and the Mottleys must necessarily be regarded as having been made subject to the possibility that, as some future time, Congress might so exert its * * * power in regulating interstate commerce as to render that agreement unenforceable * * *. * * * If that principle be not sound, the result would be individuals and corporations could, by contracts between themselves, in anticipation of legislation, render of no avail the exercise of Congress, to the full extent authorized by the Constitution, of its power to regulate commerce. No power of Congress can be thus restricted." 219 U.S. at pages 482, 485, 486. * * *

Nor is the Portal-to-Portal Act a violation of Article III of the Constitution or an encroachment upon the separate power of the judiciary. True enough, decisions of the Supreme Court played their part in creating the conditions Congress undertook to remedy * * *. But those decisions were construing a previously enacted statute. The regulatory legislation did not attempt to change these decisions in any way, or to impose upon the courts any rule of decision not in conformity with basic legal concepts, as in United States v. Klein, 13 Wall. 128. On the contrary, it left express private contracts and those implied in fact, except to the extent that they may be said to have had reference to prior statutory law, untouched and enforceable in the courts as before under the applicable legal principles. It did not require repayment of any money paid in reliance upon the decisions of the Supreme Court. It left valid final judgments for portal-to-portal pay. Since Congress, for the reasons heretofore stated, otherwise had the power to enact the Portal-to-Portal Act, the fact that one of the Act's incidental effects is to prevent the courts from following the [Supreme Court's decisions interpreting the FLSA] is of no importance. * * *

Judgments affirmed.

NOTE ON PRECLUSION OF ALL JUDICIAL REVIEW AND ON THE RIGHT TO SEEK JUDICIAL REDRESS

(1) The Reach of the Battaglia Principle. Although the court of appeals found plaintiff's constitutional claim wanting on the merits, it did not treat Congress' preclusion of federal and state court jurisdiction as barring it from examining the merits. Does Battaglia illustrate Professor Hart's contention that it is "a necessary postulate of constitutional government" that "a court must always be available to pass on claims of constitutional right to judicial process, and to provide such process if the claim is sustained"? Hart, *The Power of Congress to Limit the Jurisdiction of Federal Courts: An Exercise in Dialectic*, 66 Harv.L.Rev. 1362, 1372 (1953) (hereinafter cited as "Hart, *Dialogue*").

(2) Constitutional Avoidance by the Supreme Court. The Supreme Court has ordinarily found ways to avoid squarely facing the question whether Congress may strip all courts of jurisdiction to entertain constitutional claims. Thus, in Webster v. Doe, 486 U.S. 592 (1988), an action by a former CIA employee against the CIA Director alleging an unlawful discharge, the Court interpreted a statutory review provision as barring consideration of non-constitutional challenges but not constitutional challenges. In finding that the provision did not satisfy the "heightened showing" of intent required to construe it as barring judicial review of constitutional challenges, the Court noted the " 'serious constitutional question' that would arise if a federal statute were construed to deny any judicial forum for a colorable constitutional claim".

Other cases have similarly strained to construe statutes to permit judicial review of constitutional questions. See, *e.g.*, Bowen v. Michigan Academy of Family Physicians, 476 U.S. 667, 681 n.12 (1986) (finding that a statutory bar of judicial review of certain Medicare awards did not encompass constitutional challenges—a ruling that avoided the "serious constitutional question" that would otherwise be presented); Johnson v. Robison, 415 U.S. 361, 366–67 (1974) (holding that a statute making benefits decisions of the Veterans Administration "final" and nonreviewable did not apply to constitutional challenges to the validity of legislative classifications, since preclusion of such challenges would raise serious questions about the provision's constitutionality).

(3) Preclusion of Review and Rights to Remedies. A litigant's claim to possess a right to judicial redress for a constitutional violation necessarily has two components. First, was there a constitutional violation: for example, does a challenged government action abridge free speech or deny equal protection? Second, even where there is a constitutional violation, to what remedy, if any, is the litigant constitutionally entitled?

Any claim that the Constitution guarantees any particular remedy, or indeed even that it guarantees some remedy, for a constitutional violation can be in some tension with well-established doctrines. In Webster v. Doe, Paragraph (2), *supra*, Justice Scalia's dissent noted that the Court has "found some constitutional claims to be beyond judicial review because they involve 'political questions' ". A second pertinent doctrine is that of sovereign immunity, which loosely holds that neither the states nor the United States can be sued in their own names without their consent—even for constitutional violations.[1] In Bartlett v. Bowen, 816 F.2d 695, 719–20 (D.C.Cir.1987), Judge Bork's dissent asserted that "the Supreme Court had never suggested * * * that there might be a constitutional difficulty in a statute that merely invoked sovereign immunity with respect to suits challenging the constitutionality of a statutory denial of government benefits."

The constitutional text refers to only two remedies: (1) a right to just compensation for takings and (2) the privilege of the writ of habeas corpus, a means of contesting the legality of executive detention. In Marbury v. Madison, 5 U.S. (1 Cranch) 137, 163 (1803), Chief Justice Marshall, quoting Blackstone, famously said that " 'it is a general and indisputable rule, that where there is a legal right, there is also a legal remedy by suit or action at law, whenever that right is invaded.' " But Marbury, of course, claimed a violation of a *non-constitutional* right to a judicial commission. And as a statement about remedies for constitutional violations, Marshall's dictum is more of an aspiration than a hard and fast rule. In numerous situations, there is no remedy for an acknowledged violation of constitutional rights—notably in cases in which damages seem to be the only appropriate remedy, but all defendants are immune from damages liability, the government because of sovereign immunity, and individual officials because of official immunity. See generally Fallon, *Some Confusions About Due Process, Judicial Review, and Constitutional Remedies*, 93 Colum.L.Rev. 309, 329–39, 366–72 (1993); Fallon & Meltzer, *New Law, Non-Retroactivity, and Constitutional Remedies*, 104 Harv.L.Rev. 1731 (1991). By contrast, the right to seek a petition of habeas corpus, at least in circumstances falling within the core of the historical understanding of the writ, is more firmly grounded.[2] Thus, the question whether one has a constitutional right to a remedy is neither a single nor a simple question.[3]

(4) Professor Hart's Views. Consider the following, suggestive remarks from Professor Hart's *Dialogue*, 66 Harv.L.Rev. at 1366–71:

"Q. The power of Congress to regulate jurisdiction gives it a pretty complete power over remedies, doesn't it? To deny a remedy all Congress needs to do is to deny jurisdiction to any court to give the remedy.

---

[1]   Sovereign immunity is extensively discussed in Chap. IX, Secs. 1 and 2A, *infra*.

[2]   Questions involving rights to damages and injunctive relief are explored more fully in Chap. VII, pp. 752–777, *infra*. The distinctive questions relating to claims of a constitutional right to habeas corpus are explored in the immediately following *Further Note on Preclusion of All Judicial Review and on the Right to Seek Judicial Redress: Habeas Corpus and the Suspension Clause.*

[3]   For an analysis of congressional power to control jurisdiction, stressing its interconnection with the scope of Congress' power to preclude the award of a particular remedy, or in some cases to preclude any and all remedies, and suggesting that Congress may sometimes lack a valid source of legislative authority to strip all courts of jurisdiction, see Fallon, *Jurisdiction-Stripping Reconsidered*, 96 Va.L.Rev. 1043 (2010).

"A. That question is highly multifarious. If what you are asking is whether the power to regulate jurisdiction isn't, in effect, a power to deny rights which otherwise couldn't be denied, why don't you come right out and ask it?

"Before you do, however, I'll * * * make a point that may help in the later discussion. The denial of *any* remedy is one thing—that raises the question we're postponing. But the denial of one remedy while another is left open, or the substitution of one for another, is very different. It must be plain that Congress necessarily has a wide choice in the selection of remedies, and that a complaint about action of this kind can rarely be of constitutional dimension.

"Q. Why is that plain?

"A. History has a lot to do with it. Take, for example, the tradition of our law that preventive relief is the exception rather than the rule. That naturally makes it hard to hold that anybody has a constitutional right to an injunction or a declaratory judgment.

"But the basic reason * * * is the great variety of possible remedies and the even greater variety of reasons why in different situations a legislature can fairly prefer one to another. That usually makes it hard to say, when one procedure has been provided, that it was unreasonable to make it exclusive. * * *

"Q. Please spell that out a little bit.

"A. Tax remedies furnish one of the best illustrations.

"More than a hundred years ago * * * the Supreme Court distressed Justice Story and many other people by holding that Congress had withdrawn the traditional right of action against a collector of customs for duties claimed to have been exacted illegally. [Cary v. Curtis, 44 U.S. (3 How.) 236 (1845).] Congress soon showed that it had never intended to do this, by restoring the right of action. But meanwhile the misunderstanding of the statute had produced a notable constitutional decision.

"* * * The majority opinion by Justice Daniel poses very nicely the apparent dilemma which is the main problem of this discussion. It states the contention that the construction adopted would attribute to Congress purposes which 'would be repugnant to the Constitution, inasmuch as they would debar the citizen of his right to resort to the courts of justice'. In a bow to this position, it said: 'The supremacy of the Constitution over all officers and authorities, both of the federal and state governments, and the sanctity of the rights guarantied by it, none will question. These are *concessa* on all sides.'

"But then Justice Daniel stated the other horn of the dilemma as if it were an answer:

" 'The objection above referred to admits of the most satisfactory refutation. This may be found in the following positions, * * * viz: that the government, as a general rule, claims an exemption from being sued in its own courts. * * * Secondly, in the doctrine * * * that the judicial power of the United States, although it has its origin in the Constitution, is (except in enumerated instances, applicable exclusively to this court) dependent for its distribution and organization, and for the modes of its exercise, entirely upon the action of Congress, who possess the sole power of creating tribunals (inferior to the Supreme Court) * * * and of investing them with jurisdiction either limited, concurrent, or exclusive, and of withholding jurisdiction from them in the exact degrees and character which to Congress may seem proper for the public good. To deny this position would be to elevate the judicial over the legislative branch of the government, and to give to the former powers limited by its own discretion merely.'

"Q. I can't see how to reconcile those two horns. How did Justice Daniel do it?

"A. He escaped by way of the power to select remedies. He said:

" 'The claimant had his option to refuse payment; the detention of the goods for the adjustment of duties, being an incident of probable occurrence, to avoid this it could not be permitted to effect the abrogation of a public law, or a system of public policy essentially connected with the general action of the government. The claimant, moreover, was not without other modes of redress, had he chosen to adopt them. He might have asserted his right to the possession of the goods, or his exemption from the duties demanded, either by replevin, or in an action of detinue, or perhaps by an action of trover, upon his tendering the amount of duties admitted by him to be legally due. The legitimate inquiry before this court is not whether all right of action has been taken away from the party, and the court responds to no such inquiry.'

"Q. Why bother with an old case that ducked the issue that way? What is today's law? Has a taxpayer got a constitutional right to litigate the legality of a tax or hasn't he?

"A. Personally, I think he has. But I can't cite any really square decision for the very reason I'm trying to tell you. The multiplicity of remedies, and the fact that Congress has seldom if ever tried to take them all away, has prevented the issue from ever being squarely presented.

"For example, history and the necessities of revenue alike make it clear that the Government must have constitutional power to make people pay their taxes first and litigate afterward. Summary distraint to compel payment is proper. And injunctions against collection can be forbidden. But these decisions all proceeded on the express assumption that the taxpayer had other remedies.

"Correspondingly, a remedy after payment may be denied if the taxpayer had a remedy before, as Cary v. Curtis shows. Or the remedy may be conditioned upon following exactly a prescribed procedure. Rock Island, Ark. & La. Ry. v. United States, 254 U.S. 141 (1920).

"Q. The taxpayer has to watch out, then, or he'll lose his rights.

"A. He certainly does. As Justice Holmes said in the Rock Island case, 'Men must turn square corners when dealing with the government.' That's true of constitutional rights generally. * * * There isn't often a constitutional right to a second bite at the apple. * * *

"Q. * * * Granting [that there might be a constitutional right to litigate the constitutionality of taxes], you still have to reckon separately with the power of Congress to prevent its vindication by controlling jurisdiction. May I remind you of Sheldon and McCardle?

"A. There you go oversimplifying again.

" * * * The Bearing of Sovereign Immunity

"Q. Well, if it's too simple for you, let me complicate it a little bit. Justice Daniel mentioned sovereign immunity in Cary v. Curtis. That gives a double reason, doesn't it, why Congress has an absolute power over legal relations between the government and private persons? If it doesn't want to defeat private rights by regulating the jurisdiction of the federal courts, it can do it by withholding the Government's consent to suit.

"A. I can't deny that that does complicate things. But the power of withholding consent isn't as nearly absolute as it seems.

"Q. What mitigates it?

"A. You have to remember * * * that the immunity is only to suits against the Government. * * * [T]he possibility remains, as Cary v. Curtis indicates, of a personal action against an official who commits a wrong in the name of the Government.[4] Wherever the applicable substantive law allows such a remedy, the Government may be forced to protect its officers by providing a remedy against itself. The validity of any protection it tries to give may depend on its providing such a remedy and, indeed, the validity of other parts of its program. Consider, for example, the possibility that summary collection of taxes might be invalid if the Government did not waive its immunity to a suit for refund.

"Too, the Government may be under other kinds of practical pressure not to insist on its immunity. Take Government contracts, for example. * * * The business of the Government requires that people be willing to contract with it. * * * [T]his pressure made itself felt even before the Civil War and resulted in a blanket consent to suit [that has stood ever since] * * *.[5]

"Finally, no democratic government can be immune to the claims of justice and legal right. The force of those claims of course varies in different situations. If private property is taken, for example, the claim for just compensation has the moral sanction of an express constitutional guarantee; and it is not surprising that there is a standing consent to that kind of suit. 28 U.S.C. §§ 1346(a)(2), 1491(1). And where constitutional rights are at stake the courts are properly astute, in construing statutes, to avoid the conclusion that Congress intended to use the privilege of immunity, or of withdrawing jurisdiction, in order to defeat them."

(5) Developments Since the Dialogue.

(a) Refund Remedies for Unconstitutionally Exacted Taxes. Four decades after Professor Hart wrote the *Dialogue*, the Supreme Court took a major step in the direction of holding that "a taxpayer [has] a constitutional right to litigate the legality of a tax", but then took at least half a step back. In Reich v. Collins, 513 U.S. 106, 109–10 (1994), the Court stated that " 'a denial by a state court of a recovery of [state] taxes exacted in violation of the laws or Constitution of the United States by compulsion is itself in contravention of the Fourteenth Amendment,' *the sovereign immunity States traditionally enjoy in their own courts notwithstanding*" (emphasis added; quoting Carpenter v. Shaw, 280 U.S. 363, 369 (1930)). More recently, however, in Alden v. Maine, 527 U.S. 706, 740 (1999), the Court

---

[4] [Ed.] On the personal responsibility of government officials in damages, see Chap. IX, Sec. 3, *infra*.

[5] [Ed.] See Chap. II, Sec. 2, pp. 89–90, *supra*. Some of the bracketed material in the text appeared in a footnote in the *Dialogue* as originally published.

characterized Reich as having held that state sovereign immunity had to
yield only because the state, in requiring taxpayers to pay first and litigate
later, had effectively promised to provide a post-deprivation remedy and was
bound by the Due Process Clause to satisfy its promise. These decisions are
discussed more fully at pp. 757, 967–976, *infra*. The Court's shifting
rationale highlights Professor Hart's observation that the doctrine of
sovereign immunity is difficult to integrate with constitutional
understandings that one has a right to a remedy for a constitutional
violation.

    (b) Just Compensation Claims. A similar equivocation about
whether the Constitution mandates judicial remedies has occurred in
Takings Clause cases. In First English Evangelical Lutheran Church of
Glendale v. Los Angeles County, 482 U.S. 304, 316 (1987), the Court stated
that "in the event of a taking, the compensation remedy is required by the
Constitution". Because the First English case involved a county government
that, unlike the United States or a state government, does not enjoy
sovereign immunity, the question whether sovereign immunity could
preclude the "required" compensation remedy was not squarely presented.
But in dictum, the Court rejected the United States' argument, as amicus,
that (especially in view of sovereign immunity) the Takings Clause does not
itself furnish the basis for a court to award damages. But in City of Monterey
v. Del Monte Dunes at Monterey, Ltd., 526 U.S. 687, 714 (1999), Justice
Kennedy's plurality opinion (joined by Chief Justice Rehnquist and Justices
Stevens and Thomas) treated it as an open question whether "the sovereign
immunity rationale retains its vitality" with respect to just compensation
claims and offered a "cf." citation to First English.[6]

(6) A Theory of Constitutional Remedies. Consider the argument of
Fallon & Meltzer, Paragraph (3), *supra*, at 1778–79, that the constitutional
tradition (which includes recognition of immunities for governments and
their officials) reflects two remedial principles. The first prescribes that there
should be individually effective redress for all violations of constitutional
rights; it is strong but not unyielding, and is sometimes outweighed by
practical imperatives, such as those that underlie immunity doctrines. The
second, more structural principle "demands a system of constitutional
remedies adequate to keep government generally within the bounds of law";
it is "more unyielding in its own terms, but can tolerate the denial of
particular remedies, and sometimes of [any] individual redress to the victim
of a constitutional violation".

    Note that the position of Fallon and Meltzer is entirely consistent with
Professor Hart's contention that it is "a necessary postulate of constitutional
government" that "a court must always be available to pass on claims of
constitutional right to judicial process, and to provide such process if the
claim is sustained" (*Dialogue*, at 1372).[7] Their formulation simply leaves
open whether due process requires access to a court and an individually

---

    [6]   Two circuit courts have dismissed reverse condemnation actions against a state or state
officials in *federal* court, concluding, in the words of one, that a "State may be sued in its own
courts (but not in federal court) for damages arising from violation of a self-executing
constitutional clause." Seven Up Pete Venture v. Schweitzer, 523 F.3d 948, 956 (9th Cir.2008);
see also DLX, Inc. v. Kentucky, 381 F.3d 511, 528 (6th Cir.2004) (finding that "where the
Constitution requires a particular remedy, such as through the Due Process Clause for the tax
monies at issue in Reich, or through the Takings Clause as indicated in First English, the state
is required to provide that remedy in its own courts, notwithstanding sovereign immunity").

    [7]   See also Fallon, Paragraph (3), *supra*, at 367–68.

effective constitutional remedy in some cases involving alleged constitutional violations.

(7) Statutory Violations. So far we have considered claims of right to a remedy for a violation of a *constitutional* right. Would a serious constitutional question be presented by preclusion of all jurisdiction, in both federal and state courts, over suits alleging only that the defendant violated a *federal statute*?

In the Portal-to-Portal Act, Congress both extinguished a substantive statutory right and eliminated jurisdiction to enforce it. Suppose Congress had enacted a provision barring state and federal courts from exercising jurisdiction over FLSA claims grounded on the failure to compensate for incidental and preliminary work, but had not amended the substance of the FLSA, thereby leaving in place the Supreme Court's decisions that such work is compensable. Could employees overcome the denial of federal court jurisdiction by arguing that Congress may not direct an Article III court to decide a case other than in accordance with the law? *Cf.* United States v. Klein, p. 323, *supra*. Or would such congressional action be unproblematic because the practical effect of precluding all state and federal court jurisdiction is the same as amending the statute?

———————

FURTHER NOTE ON PRECLUSION OF ALL JUDICIAL REVIEW AND ON THE RIGHT TO SEEK JUDICIAL REDRESS: HABEAS CORPUS AND THE SUSPENSION CLAUSE

(1) The Writ and the Suspension Clause. A distinctive question about congressional power to preclude judicial review in both state and federal court concerns limitations on judicial authority to award the writ of habeas corpus. First developed in English common law courts, the writ is a means of testing the lawfulness of detention. Historically its central role was to permit a court to oversee the legality of detention imposed extra-judicially by executive officials. If detention is deemed to be unlawful, a court exercising habeas corpus jurisdiction orders that the prisoner be discharged from confinement.

Any effort by Congress to preclude courts from providing the remedy of habeas corpus implicates not only Article III and the Due Process Clause but also the Suspension Clause of the Constitution, Article I, § 9, cl. 2, which states: "The Privilege of the Writ of Habeas Corpus shall not be suspended, unless when in Cases of Rebellion or Invasion the public Safety may require it." The provision testifies to the founding generation's understanding that the writ was an established and fundamental guarantee of liberty. Yet while the Clause plainly was designed to confine power to suspend the writ, the meaning of the "Privilege of the Writ" is obscure. See pp. 1200–1206, *infra*. One uncertainty is whether the Suspension Clause, though not worded as an affirmative guarantee that habeas corpus will be available, should be so understood. Because Congress, beginning with the Judiciary Act of 1789, has vested habeas corpus jurisdiction in the federal courts, the question whether the Constitution requires the availability of such jurisdiction has rarely arisen. But more than two centuries after the Founding, the Supreme Court addressed that question when confronted by two different legislative schemes curtailing the availability of habeas corpus for particular classes of detainees.

(2) Immigration Detainees and the St. Cyr Case. In Immigration and Naturalization Serv. v. St. Cyr, 533 U.S. 289 (2001), the Court for the first time stated that the Suspension Clause restricts Congress' power to preclude review of the legality of federal executive detentions. St. Cyr, a Haitian citizen lawfully resident in the United States, pled guilty to a criminal charge, triggering a provision of the immigration laws that in early 1996 presumptively required his deportation. At that time, however, the Attorney General had broad discretion to waive deportation. But the INS commenced deportation proceedings against St. Cyr after the effective dates of two 1996 statutes: the Antiterrorism and Effective Death Penalty Act of 1996 (AEDPA) and the Illegal Immigration Reform and Immigrant Responsibility Act of 1996 (IIRIRA). The Attorney General took the position that those statutes withdrew her discretion to waive deportation.

St. Cyr brought a federal habeas corpus proceeding challenging this interpretation of the statutes. His claim was that he had a statutory right to have the Attorney General consider (in her discretion) whether to waive deportation; that the Attorney General's contrary view was legally mistaken; and hence St. Cyr's deportation, a form of custody, was contrary to law. In response, the government argued that the court lacked jurisdiction to consider St. Cyr's legal arguments, because all judicial review was expressly precluded by a provision of the AEDPA titled "Elimination of Custody Review by Habeas Corpus" and by three separate provisions of the IIRIRA, including 8 U.S.C. § 1252(a)(2)(c): "Notwithstanding any other provision of law, no court shall have jurisdiction to review any final order of removal against an alien who is removable by reason of having committed [one or more enumerated] criminal offense[s]", which included the offense of which St. Cyr had been convicted.

The statutes appeared to preclude judicial review of the deportation order in the federal court of appeals (as the Court held in a companion case, Calcano-Martinez v. INS, 533 U.S. 348 (2001)) and in the state courts. The question in the St. Cyr case was whether the statutes also precluded federal district courts from exercising habeas corpus jurisdiction and thus left St. Cyr with no court in which he could make his legal argument. The Supreme Court held that the 1996 amendments had not foreclosed jurisdiction under the pre-existing general grant of habeas corpus jurisdiction in 28 U.S.C. § 2241. In reaching that conclusion, the Court relied heavily on a series of interpretive presumptions: "the strong presumption in favor of judicial review of administrative action" (citing, *e.g.*, Bowen v. Michigan Academy of Family Physicians, p. 329, *supra*);[1] "the longstanding rule requiring a clear statement of congressional intent to repeal habeas jurisdiction" (citing Ex parte Yerger, p. 307 n.*, *supra*, and Felker v. Turpin, p. 317, *supra*); and most important of all, the presumption that statutes should be construed, where possible, to avoid serious constitutional problems.

For present purposes, the key statement in Justice Stevens' majority opinion was that a finding of preclusion of review "of a pure question of law by any court would give rise to substantial constitutional questions" under the Suspension Clause: "[A]t the absolute minimum, the Suspension Clause

---

[1] For a sustained critique of the presumption of reviewability, see Bagley, *The Puzzling Presumption of Reviewability*, 127 Harv.L.Rev. 1385 (2014).

protects the writ 'as it existed in 1789.' * * * At its historical core, the writ of habeas corpus has served as a means of reviewing the legality of executive detention * * *. [Historically,] the issuance of the writ was not limited to challenges to the jurisdiction of the custodian, but encompassed detentions based on errors of law, including the erroneous application or interpretation of statutes."

On the more specific question whether habeas corpus was available "to redress the improper exercise of official discretion", Justice Stevens viewed the historical evidence as equivocal, but noted the "substantial evidence to support the proposition that pure questions of law like the one raised by [St. Cyr] could have been answered in 1789 by a common law judge with power to issue the writ of habeas corpus. It necessarily follows that a serious Suspension Clause issue would be presented if we were to accept the INS's submission that the 1996 statutes have withdrawn that power from federal judges and provided no adequate substitute for its exercise."

Turning at last to the statutory provisions at issue, Justice Stevens held that the language of the IIRIRA precluding "judicial review" of and "jurisdiction to review" removal orders did not withdraw federal habeas corpus jurisdiction: "In the immigration context, 'judicial review' and 'habeas corpus' have historically distinct meanings." Justice Stevens similarly found that the key provision of the AEDPA merely repealed a specialized grant of habeas corpus jurisdiction for immigration cases and, because it did not refer expressly to the general grant of habeas corpus jurisdiction under § 2241, it should not be construed to have eliminated it. The Court proceeded to rule, on the merits, that the elimination of the Attorney General's authority to grant discretionary relief did not apply retroactively to persons like St. Cyr who might have pled guilty in reliance on their eligibility at that time to seek waivers of deportation.

In a vigorous dissent, Justice Scalia (joined by Chief Justice Rehnquist and Justice Thomas and in part by Justice O'Connor) protested that the majority found "ambiguity in the utterly clear" language of the IIRIRA only by "fabricat[ing] a superclear statement, 'magic words' requirement * * * unjustified in law and unparalleled in any other area of our jurisprudence". He argued that constitutional avoidance was not implicated, as the Suspension Clause does not "guarantee[ ] any particular habeas right that enjoys immunity from suspension" but ensures only that whatever privileges of habeas corpus may exist at any particular time may not be suspended except in cases of rebellion or invasion. "In the present case, of course, Congress has not temporarily withheld operation of the writ, but has permanently altered its content. That is, to be sure, an act subject to majoritarian abuse * * *. But that is not the majoritarian abuse against which the Suspension Clause was directed." Justice Scalia also brusquely rejected arguments that preclusion of any review of St. Cyr's claim would violate the Due Process Clause or Article III.[2]

Many commentators sympathetic to the majority's decision would not dispute Justice Scalia's claim that the Court's statutory interpretation bordered on a demand for "magic words".[3] Thus, although St. Cyr is formally

---

[2] Justice O'Connor, who did not join Justice Scalia's discussion of the Suspension Clause, wrote her own dissent, arguing that even if the Suspension Clause guarantees some minimum habeas review, St. Cyr's claim falls outside the scope of that review.

[3] See also Demore v. Kim, 538 U.S. 510 (2003) (6–3) (quoting Justice Scalia's claim in St. Cyr as *supporting* the need for a "particularly clear statement" of congressional intent to bar

a statutory ruling on the meaning of the jurisdictional provisions in the immigration laws, that ruling was driven by the Court's constitutional reasoning.[4]

Consider how that constitutional reasoning relates to the understanding that Congress need not create lower federal courts. Does St. Cyr presuppose that if Congress creates lower federal courts, it must vest them with the full scope of habeas corpus jurisdiction protected by the Suspension Clause? Or does the Suspension Clause apply only when Congress purports to restrict the jurisdiction of *both* federal and state courts? In pondering the last question, consider the significance of Tarble's Case, p. 427, *infra*, whose much-criticized reasoning appears to suggest that the Constitution precludes state courts from issuing writs of habeas corpus to federal officials.[5]

(3) Habeas Corpus, the Suspension Clause, and Detention Under the Laws of War. St. Cyr's constitutional reasoning became a constitutional holding seven years later in Boumediene v. Bush, 553 U.S. 723 (2008). Boumediene is the only Supreme Court decision clearly holding that a congressional enactment restricting jurisdiction—in that case, of both federal and state courts—is unconstitutional.[6]

The background to Boumediene began in Rasul v. Bush, 542 U.S. 466 (2004), p. 1247, *infra*, where the Court held, as a matter of statutory interpretation, that the general grant of habeas corpus jurisdiction, 28

---

habeas review and finding no such statement in a different provision of the immigration laws barring judicial review of decisions regarding the detention of aliens pending removal proceedings).

[4] For an expansive view of St. Cyr's implications, see Neuman, *The Habeas Corpus Suspension Clause After INS v. St. Cyr*, 33 Colum.Hum.Rts.L.Rev. 555 (2002). For earlier articles, both cited by Justice Stevens, supporting his suggestion that the writ's protected historical core encompassed not just constitutional errors but also errors of law, including the erroneous application or interpretation of statutes, see Neuman, *Habeas Corpus, Executive Detention, and the Removal of Aliens*, 98 Colum.L.Rev. 961 (1998), and Neuman, *Jurisdiction and the Rule of Law After the 1996 Immigration Act*, 113 Harv.L.Rev. 1963 (2000).

[5] In assessing St. Cyr's arguments under the Due Process Clause and Article III, consider the case, suggested by Meltzer, *Congress, Courts, and Constitutional Remedies*, 86 Geo.L.J. 2537, 2573 (1998), of a resident alien with legal claims identical to those involved in St. Cyr, but who is physically removed from the country before filing a challenge to a removal order. Because the alien is no longer in federal detention, the Suspension Clause presumably no longer applies. Would preclusion of judicial review raise no serious constitutional issue? Compare the Court's dictum in Zadvydas v. Davis, 533 U.S. 678 (2001), which held as a matter of statutory construction, in light of the "avoidance" canon, that Congress had not authorized the indefinite detention of a removable alien whom no other country would accept: "This Court has suggested * * * that the Constitution may well preclude granting 'an administrative body the unreviewable authority to make determinations implicating fundamental rights' ".

The St. Cyr majority did not discuss Supreme Court decisions suggesting that aliens "excluded" from the United States (including those detained at a port of entry or "paroled" into the country after being denied formal admission at a port of entry)—in contrast with those, like St. Cyr, who have entered the country and wish to resist removal—have no *constitutional* rights to habeas corpus or any other judicial proceeding. See, *e.g.*, Moon Sing v. United States, 158 U.S. 538, 546, 548 (1895); United States ex rel. Knauff v. Shaughnessy, 338 U.S. 537, 544 (1950). The rights of aliens may of course differ from those of citizens, but it is a different question whether *excluded* aliens may be denied any judicial forum whatsoever in which they may assert a claim of right. If those cases remain good law, do they suggest that excluded aliens simply fall outside the protection of the Suspension Clause? See also pp. 1259–1261, *infra*.

[6] The decision in United States v. Klein, p. 323, *supra*, also invalidated a congressional statute framed in jurisdictional terms. But as discussed at p. 324, *supra*, the constitutional basis for Klein is murky, and the decision may be best understood as holding that Congress sought to enact *substantive* rules of decision that violated the Constitution.

U.S.C. § 2241, embraced petitions filed on behalf of aliens detained by the United States as enemy combatants at Guantánamo Bay, Cuba. Congress reacted by enacting the Detainee Treatment Act of 2005 (DTA)[7] and the Military Commissions Act of 2006 (MCA).[8] The MCA purported to eliminate habeas corpus jurisdiction for any alien, wherever held, who has "been determined by the United States to have been properly detained as an enemy combatant or is awaiting such a determination." *Id.*, § 7(a) (codified at 28 U.S.C. § 2241(e)(1)). In place of habeas jurisdiction, these statutes authorized the D.C. Circuit to review, *inter alia*, decisions of military Combatant Status Review Tribunals (CSRTs) finding that a particular detainee is in fact an enemy combatant, subject to non-punitive detention under the laws of war. Judicial review was limited to whether the CSRT's determination conforms to the applicable military standards and procedures "including the requirement that the conclusion of the Tribunal be supported by a preponderance of the evidence" and, "to the extent the Constitution and laws of the United States are applicable, whether the use of such standards and procedures to make the determination is consistent with the Constitution and laws of the United States."

In Boumediene, petitions for habeas corpus were filed on behalf of detainees at Guantánamo Bay who had been determined by CSRTs to be enemy combatants. The government argued that their petitions were barred by the MCA's jurisdiction-stripping provision; in turn, the detainees contended that the jurisdiction-stripping provision violated the Suspension Clause. The Supreme Court (5–4), per Justice Kennedy, found the MCA's provision to be unconstitutional, on the ground that the Suspension Clause affirmatively guarantees, for those detainees who fall within its scope, the right of habeas corpus (or an adequate substitute). Unlike in St. Cyr, in Boumediene that premise was not merely part of reasoning informing interpretation of a statute; instead, it formed the basis for a constitutional holding invalidating § 7 of the MCA.

The Court said that the Suspension Clause "ensures that, except during periods of formal suspension, the Judiciary will have a time-tested device, the writ, to maintain the 'delicate balance of governance' that is itself the surest safeguard of liberty. See Hamdi [v. Rumsfeld, 542 U.S. 507, 536 (2004)] (plurality opinion). The Clause protects the rights of the detained by affirming the duty and authority of the Judiciary to call the jailer to account."

Chief Justice Roberts and Justice Scalia both wrote dissents, joined by each other and by Justices Thomas and Alito. Unlike Justice Scalia's dissent in St. Cyr, neither dissent questioned that the Suspension Clause affirmatively guarantees habeas review. Instead, each advanced a reason why the Suspension Clause guarantee was not violated in the circumstances before the Court.

Justice Scalia's dissent contended that the Suspension Clause guarantee does not extend to aliens alleged to be enemy combatants and detained in a location like Guantánamo Bay that falls outside the formal territorial sovereignty of the United States. On that issue, the majority and Justice Scalia both extensively reviewed historical materials. In doing so, Justice Kennedy said that "[t]he Court has been careful not to foreclose the possibility that the protections of the Suspension Clause have expanded"

---

[7] Pub.L.No. 109–148, 119 Stat. 2739.

[8] Pub.L.No. 109–366, 120 Stat. 2600.

since the Founding but that "the analysis may begin with precedents as of 1789, for the Court has said that 'at the absolute minimum' the Clause protects the writ as it existed when the Constitution was drafted and ratified" (quoting St. Cyr). Finding the historical evidence inconclusive, he concluded that the petitioners were within the protection of the Suspension Clause on the basis of a functional understanding of the writ as part of the scheme of separation of powers.

Chief Justice Roberts' dissent started from the uncontroversial proposition that Congress may eliminate habeas corpus jurisdiction as long as it provides an adequate substitute. He contended that the judicial review in the D.C. Circuit authorized by the DTA sufficed. The majority disagreed, pointing specifically to the inability of a detainee seeking review under the DTA to introduce exculpatory evidence that became available only after conclusion of the military's CSRT proceeding. More generally, Justice Kennedy said: "We do not endeavor to offer a comprehensive summary of the requisites for an adequate substitute for habeas corpus. We do consider it uncontroversial, however, that the privilege of habeas corpus entitles the prisoner to a meaningful opportunity to demonstrate that he is being held pursuant to 'the erroneous application or interpretation' of relevant law. St. Cyr, 533 U.S., at 302. And the habeas court must have the power to order the conditional release of an individual unlawfully detained * * *. These are the easily identified attributes of any constitutionally adequate habeas corpus proceeding. But, depending on the circumstances, more may be required."

The foregoing aspects of the Boumediene decision, and many of the questions that it leaves open, are explored at greater length in Chap. XI, Sec. 2. For present purposes, Boumediene's central importance relates to the scope of congressional power to regulate the jurisdiction of the federal courts. Although it rests on the distinctive protections of the Suspension Clause, does the decision support Professor Hart's general contention, in his celebrated *Dialogue* (see p. 334, *supra*) that, notwithstanding congressional enactments purporting to withdraw jurisdiction, it is "a necessary postulate of constitutional government" that "a court must always be available to pass on claims of constitutional right to judicial process, and to provide such process if the claim is sustained"?

On the other hand, Professor Hart also argued that the *state* courts are the ultimate guardian of constitutional rights, a position with which the Boumediene opinion (like the St. Cyr opinion) does not even engage. See Fallon, *Jurisdiction-Stripping Reconsidered,* 96 Va.L.Rev. 1043, 1061 (2010). Does the Court's assumption in both cases that any review should occur in federal court rather than state court undercut Professor Hart's position and even suggest a right that any constitutionally-required review be provided by federal court? Or can the Court's assumption be explained on a narrower basis resting on statutory construction and severability analysis? In both cases, had Congress realized that it could bar judicial review of executive action in either federal court or state court but not both, surely it would have preferred that the ban on federal court review rather than on state court review be the one that was invalidated. The point is only reinforced in light of the suggestion (much criticized, but never repudiated) in Tarble's Case, p. 427, *supra*, that state courts lack authority to entertain habeas actions against federal custodians. And once the specific provisions purporting to eliminate habeas corpus and other judicial review in federal courts were viewed as unconstitutional (or in St. Cyr interpreted narrowly in light of constitutional concerns), there remained in place the pre-existing general grant of habeas corpus jurisdiction in § 2241, under which the petitions could be entertained.

NOTE ON CONGRESSIONAL APPORTIONMENT OF JURISDICTION AMONG FEDERAL COURTS AND RESULTING LIMITATIONS ON THE AUTHORITY OF ENFORCEMENT COURTS[1]

(1) Introduction. The preceding material has focused on the scope of congressional power to restrict federal court jurisdiction, either to adjudicate at all or to provide particular remedies. This Note considers a distinct question: the scope of congressional power to confer jurisdiction on a court while limiting its authority to consider particular issues that are relevant to the controversy.

That question has sometimes arisen in connection with legislation to establish specialized courts. Under its broad authority to apportion jurisdiction among federal courts, Congress can create specialized courts and vest them with exclusive jurisdiction over particular categories of cases. See Chap. I, p. 34, *supra*, and Paragraph (2), *infra*. But hard issues can arise when Congress gives a federal court jurisdiction over a case while simultaneously providing that one or more issues in that case may be decided only by a different federal court.

[handwritten margin note: special courts]

(2) Specialized Courts.

(a) The Emergency Price Control Act. To combat wartime inflation, the Emergency Price Control Act of 1942, 56 Stat. 23, created the office of Price Administrator with the authority to issue regulations and orders fixing maximum prices and rents. The Act created an Article III court called the Emergency Court of Appeals (ECA), consisting of three or more federal district or circuit judges. The ECA was given "the powers of a district court with respect to the jurisdiction conferred on it", except that it had no power to issue any temporary restraining order or interlocutory decree staying the effectiveness of any order, regulation, or price schedule issued under the Act. The Act permitted a challenge to any order, regulation, or price schedule by filing a protest with the Administrator (§ 204(c));[2] if the protest was denied, the aggrieved party had thirty days to file a complaint with the ECA. Section 204(d) made the jurisdiction of the ECA in reviewing the denial of a protest exclusive of all other federal and of state courts. ECA decisions were subject to Supreme Court review.

But the ECA lacked jurisdiction over other actions under the Act. In particular, federal district courts had jurisdiction over (i) actions by the Administrator to enjoin violations of the Act or secure an order directing compliance; (ii) treble damage actions by the Administrator or a buyer for

---

[1]   For a thoughtful discussion of Congress' power to divide aspects of the judicial function among Article III courts, see Caminker, *Allocating the Judicial Power in a "Unified Judiciary"*, 78 Tex.L.Rev. 1513 (2000).

[2]   As originally enacted, the statute required such a protest to be filed within 60 days after the issuance of the regulation or after the grounds of protest had arisen, but this time limit was removed in the Stabilization Extension Act of June 30, 1944, 58 Stat. 632.

over-ceiling sales; and (iii) criminal prosecutions for willful violations. The state courts had concurrent jurisdiction except in criminal prosecutions.[3]

(b) The Lockerty Decision. The Act's conferral of exclusive jurisdiction to the ECA over actions to enjoin regulations, orders, or price schedules was challenged in Lockerty v. Phillips, 319 U.S. 182 (1943), a suit by wholesale meat dealers in a federal district court to restrain the United States Attorney from prosecuting them for violations of certain price regulations. The district court dismissed the suit on the ground that the ECA had exclusive jurisdiction over such an action. The Supreme Court affirmed, with Chief Justice Stone writing:

"The Congressional power to ordain and establish inferior courts includes the power 'of investing them with jurisdiction either limited, concurrent, or exclusive, and of withholding jurisdiction from them in the exact degrees and character which to Congress may seem proper for the public good.' Cary v. Curtis, 3 How. 236, 245; Lauf v. E.G. Shinner & Co., 303 U.S. 323, 330. * * * [I]t is plain that Congress has power to provide that the equity jurisdiction to restrain enforcement of the Act, or of regulations promulgated under it, be restricted to the Emergency Court, and, upon review of its decisions, to this Court. * * *

"Appellants also contend that the review in the Emergency Court is inadequate to protect their constitutional rights, and that § 204 is therefore unconstitutional, because § 204(c) prohibits all interlocutory relief by that court. We need not pass upon the constitutionality of this restriction. For, in any event, the separability clause of § 303 of the Act would require us to give effect to the other provisions of § 204, including that withholding from the district courts authority to enjoin enforcement of the Act—a provision which as we have seen is subject to no unconstitutional infirmity.

"Since appellants seek only an injunction which the district court is without authority to give, their bill of complaint was rightly dismissed."

Given that the jurisdiction of the ECA was explicitly defined to exclude the power to grant such relief, would the plaintiffs' position have been stronger there than in the district court? If not, does the foundation for the Court's separability ruling collapse?

(c) The Voting Rights Act of 1965. In South Carolina v. Katzenbach, 383 U.S. 301 (1966), the Court upheld a provision of the Voting Rights Act of 1965, 42 U.S.C. § 1973, requiring that actions to exempt states from the coverage of the Act and actions to permit certain "suspended" state voting regulations to go into effect be brought in the District Court for the District of Columbia. In declaring that "Congress might appropriately limit litigation under this provision to a single court in the District of Columbia, pursuant to its constitutional power under Art. III, § 1, to 'ordain and establish' inferior federal tribunals", the Court relied on the Lockerty decision and several others.

Assume that Congress' motivation for requiring litigation in the District of Columbia, rather than, for example, in federal court in South Carolina,

---

[3] As originally enacted, the statute made no provision for a stay of enforcement proceedings by the government either to permit a regulatee to file a protest or to await the disposition of a protest previously filed. The Stabilization Extension Act of June 30, 1944, 58 Stat. 632, however, added a new § 204(e), which directed a stay of enforcement suits pending action on a protest already filed or review of its denial; it also gave a narrow scope for stays in some cases to permit suits to be filed in the ECA where no protest had been filed.

was a belief that the former was less likely to uphold a state's constitutional objection to the Voting Rights Act. Does that motivation call the constitutionality of the jurisdictional provision into question? Does the answer to that question bear on the constitutionality of congressional limits on federal court jurisdiction over particular constitutional claims, leaving them to be adjudicated in state courts that Congress may believe are less likely to uphold those claims?

(3) Jurisdictional Limits on Enforcement Courts. When a federal court has jurisdiction to determine whether a defendant has violated federal law and, if so, to impose a sanction, may Congress limit the issues that may be raised by way of defense?

    (a) The Yakus Decision. Yakus v. United States, 321 U.S. 414 (1944), presented the question whether a defendant prosecuted for a violation of the Price Control Act may defend the criminal case by challenging the validity of the Act or of a regulation. Section 204(d) was interpreted to bar attack upon a regulation (at least one not invalid on its face) but not upon the Act itself. Thus construed, the provision was sustained against contentions that it denied due process, violated the Sixth Amendment right to trial by a jury of the state and district where a crime was committed, and worked an unconstitutional legislative interference with judicial power.

    On the due process issue, Chief Justice Stone's opinion for the Court treated as the central question whether the procedure for review in the ECA "affords to those affected a reasonable opportunity to be heard and present evidence". Concluding that it did, the opinion further held that in "the circumstances of this case" there was "no denial of due process in the statutory prohibition of a temporary stay or injunction. * * * If the alternatives, as Congress could have concluded, were wartime inflation or the imposition on individuals of the burden of complying with a price regulation while its validity is being determined, Congress could constitutionally make the choice in favor of the protection of the public interest from the dangers of inflation".

    On the other issues, the opinion stated, *inter alia*: "[W]e are pointed to no principle of law or provision of the Constitution which precludes Congress from making criminal the violation of an administrative regulation, by one who has failed to avail himself of an adequate separate procedure for the adjudication of its validity, or which precludes the practice, in many ways desirable, of splitting the trial for violations of an administrative regulation by committing the determination of the issue of its validity to the agency which created it, and the issue of violation to a court which is given jurisdiction to punish violations. Such a requirement presents no novel constitutional issue * * *

    " * * * Nor has there been any denial * * * of the right, guaranteed by the Sixth Amendment, to a trial by a jury of the state and district where the crime was committed. * * * The indictment charged a violation of the regulation in the district of trial, and the question whether petitioners had committed the crime thus charged in the indictment and defined by Congress, namely, whether they had violated the statute by willful disobedience of a price regulation promulgated by the Administrator, was properly submitted to the jury".

    Justice Rutledge's dissent, joined by Justice Murphy, found "the crux" of the case to lie in "the question whether Congress can confer jurisdiction upon federal and state courts in the enforcement proceedings, more particularly the criminal suit, and at the same time deny them 'jurisdiction or power to consider the validity' of the regulations for which enforcement is thus sought".

dissent

"It is one thing for Congress to withhold jurisdiction. It is entirely another to confer it and direct that it be exercised in a manner inconsistent with constitutional requirements or, what in some instances may be the same thing, without regard to them. * * * There are limits to the judicial power. Congress may impose others. And in some matters Congress or the President has final say under the Constitution. But whenever the judicial power is called into play, it is responsible directly to the fundamental law and no other authority can intervene to force or authorize the judicial body to disregard it. The problem therefore is not solely one of individual right or due process of law. It is equally one of the separation and independence of the powers of government and of the constitutional integrity of the judicial process, more especially in criminal trials".

After questioning the constitutional adequacy of the statutory procedure in the ECA, even in cases where it is pursued and the regulation under protest is declared invalid, Justice Rutledge found a "deeper fault" in a conviction "on a trial in two parts, one so summary and civil and the other criminal or, in the alternative, on a trial which shuts out what may be the most important of the issues material to * * * guilt". Quoting the guarantee of jury trial in the Sixth Amendment and Article III, as well as the definition of the judicial power in Article III, he stated: "By these provisions the purpose hardly is to be supposed to authorize splitting up a criminal trial into separate segments, with some of the issues essential to guilt triable before one court in the state and district where the crime was committed and others, equally essential, triable in another court in a highly summary civil proceeding held elsewhere, or to dispense with trial on them because that proceeding has not been followed. * * * If Congress can remove these questions, it can remove also all questions of validity of the statute, or, it would seem, of law".

(b) Subsequent Developments. Absent the exigency presented by the threat of wartime inflation, would a scheme like that involved in Yakus survive constitutional scrutiny? See United States v. Mendoza-Lopez, 481 U.S. 828, 839 n.15 (1987), p. 359, *infra*, which distinguished Yakus in part on the basis that it rested on the exigencies of wartime, and proceeded to hold that an enforcement court could not predicate a finding of criminal violation on a previous administrative determination where there had been no meaningful opportunity to seek judicial review of the administrative ruling.

distinguished

Is there a division of responsibilities among courts whenever a claim of issue preclusion is upheld? Is it especially troubling to allow issue preclusion against a criminal defendant?[4] Especially troubling when the precluded

---

[4] Bowles v. Willingham, 321 U.S. 503 (1944), decided the same day as Yakus, sustained preclusion of a challenge by the defendant to the validity of an Office of Price Administration regulation in a civil action brought by the Administrator to enjoin a landlord's state court suit to restrain the Administrator's issuance of an order reducing certain rentals. Concurring in the result, Justice Rutledge distinguished between such a civil enforcement proceeding and enforcement by criminal prosecution. He insisted, however, upon the following limitations, which he found to be satisfied: "(1) The order or regulation must not be invalid on its face; (2) the previous opportunity must be adequate for the purpose prescribed, in the constitutional sense; and (3) * * * the circumstances and nature of the substantive problem dealt with by the

issue was not fully and fairly litigated, even though there was an opportunity for full and fair litigation?[5]

2. CONGRESSIONAL AUTHORITY TO ALLOCATE JUDICIAL POWER TO NON-ARTICLE III FEDERAL TRIBUNALS

INTRODUCTORY NOTE

The Yakus decision involved the division of a case between two Article III courts. Even though Congress precluded the district court from deciding some issues, those issues could be resolved by the Emergency Court of Appeals. Thus all issues in the case could be decided within the Article III judiciary.

A different question is raised when Congress divides a case between an Article III court and a federal tribunal other than an Article III court—that is, a tribunal whose judges lack tenure and salary protection. To the extent that the Article III court, when reviewing the other tribunal's determination, is limited to reviewing only certain issues, or to reviewing issues under a deferential standard, Congress has limited the authority of the Article III judiciary to fully adjudicate the matter.

This section considers the scope of congressional power to assign to non-Article III tribunals some role in adjudicating cases or controversies that fall within the scope of federal judicial power as defined by Article III, and, conversely, the extent to which the Constitution requires that an Article III court have authority to review the non-Article III tribunal's determinations.

---

legislature must be such that they justify both the creation of the special remedy and the requirement that it be followed to the exclusion of others normally available".

[5] Compare Custis v. United States, 511 U.S. 485 (1994), holding that a federal criminal defendant generally has no constitutional right to challenge previous *state* convictions that are used for sentence enhancement. Writing for the Court, Chief Justice Rehnquist distinguished precedents allowing defendants in sentence enhancement proceedings to attack prior convictions allegedly obtained without the assistance of counsel on the basis that the complete failure to appoint counsel was a "unique" constitutional violation rising to the level of "a jurisdictional defect." By contrast, the petitioner's claim that his state court conviction was invalid because his attorney had not provided effective assistance of counsel "would require sentencing courts to rummage through frequently nonexistent or difficult to obtain state court transcripts or records". Justice Souter, joined by Justices Blackmun and Stevens, dissented on statutory grounds.

Crowell v. Benson

285 U.S. 22, 52 S.Ct. 285, 76 L.Ed. 598 (1932).
Certiorari to the Circuit Court of Appeals for the Fifth Circuit.

■ MR. CHIEF JUSTICE HUGHES delivered the opinion of the Court.

This suit was brought in the District Court to enjoin the enforcement of an award made by petitioner Crowell, as Deputy Commissioner of the United States Employees' Compensation Commission, in favor of the petitioner Knudsen and against the respondent Benson. The award was made under the Longshoremen's and Harbor Workers' Compensation Act [33 U.S.C. §§ 901–950], and rested upon the finding of the deputy commissioner that Knudsen was injured while in the employ of Benson and performing service upon the navigable waters of the United States. The complainant alleged that the award was contrary to law for the reason that Knudsen was not at the time of his injury an employee of the complainant and his claim was not "within the jurisdiction" of the Deputy Commissioner. An amended complaint charged that the act was unconstitutional upon the grounds that it violated the due process clause of the Fifth Amendment, the provision of the Seventh Amendment as to trial by jury, * * * and the provisions of Article III with respect to the judicial power of the United States. The District Judge denied motions to dismiss and granted a hearing de novo upon the facts and the law, expressing the opinion that the act would be invalid if not construed to permit such a hearing. [After the case was transferred to the admiralty docket,] the District Court decided that Knudsen was not in the employ of the petitioner and restrained the enforcement of the award. The decree was affirmed by the Circuit Court of Appeals and this Court granted writs of certiorari.

The question of the validity of the act may be considered in relation to (1) its provisions defining substantive rights and (2) its procedural requirements. * * *

[The first part of the opinion sustained the substantive provisions of the Act as a proper exercise of "the general authority of the Congress to alter or revise the maritime law which shall prevail throughout the country".

[The second part of the opinion began by describing the procedural provisions of the Act and the provisions for judicial review. Awards may be made by a deputy commissioner only after investigation, notice, and hearing. They may be enforced by a federal district court, on application of beneficiaries or of the deputy commissioner, if found to have been "made and served in accordance with law". Or they may be suspended or set aside, in whole or in part, on application of a respondent if "not in accordance with law".]

Second. The objections to the procedural requirements of the act relate to the extent of the administrative authority which it confers. * * *

1. The contention under the due process clause of the Fifth Amendment relates to the determination of questions of fact. Rulings of the deputy commissioner upon questions of law are without finality. * * *

Apart from cases involving constitutional rights to be appropriately enforced by proceedings in court, there can be no doubt that the act contemplates that as to questions of fact, arising with respect to injuries to employees within the purview of the act, the findings of the deputy commissioner, supported by evidence and within the scope of his authority, shall be final. To hold otherwise would be to defeat the obvious purpose of the legislation to furnish a prompt, continuous, expert, and inexpensive method for dealing with a class of questions of fact which are peculiarly suited to examination and determination by an administrative agency specially assigned to that task. The object is to secure within the prescribed limits of the employer's liability an immediate investigation and a sound practical judgment, and the efficacy of the plan depends upon the finality of the determinations of fact with respect to the circumstances, nature, extent, and consequences of the employee's injuries and the amount of compensation that should be awarded. And this finality may also be regarded as extending to the determination of the question of fact whether the injury "was occasioned solely by the intoxication of the employee or by the willful intention of the employee to injure or kill himself or another." While the exclusion of compensation in such cases is found in what are called "coverage" provisions of the act (section 3 [33 U.S.C. § 903]), the question of fact still belongs to the contemplated routine of administration, for the case is one of employment within the scope of the act, and the cause of the injury sustained by the employee as well as its character and effect must be ascertained in applying the provisions for compensation. The use of the administrative method for these purposes, assuming due notice, proper opportunity to be heard, and that findings are based upon evidence, falls easily within the principle of the decisions sustaining similar procedure against objections under the due process clauses of the Fifth and Fourteenth Amendments. * * *

2. The contention based upon the judicial power of the United States, as extended "to all cases of admiralty and maritime jurisdiction" (Const. Art. III), presents a distinct question. * * *

The question in the instant case, in this aspect, can be deemed to relate only to determinations of fact. The reservation of legal questions is to the same court that has jurisdiction in admiralty, and the mere fact that the court is not described as such is unimportant. * * * The Congress did not attempt to define questions of law, and the generality of the description leaves no doubt of the intention to reserve to the Federal court full authority to pass upon all matters which this Court had held to fall within that category. There is thus no attempt to interfere with, but rather provision is made to facilitate, the exercise by the court of its jurisdiction to deny effect to any administrative finding which is without evidence, or "contrary to the indisputable character of the evidence," or where the hearing is "inadequate," or "unfair," or arbitrary in any respect. * * *

As to determinations of fact, the distinction is at once apparent between cases of private right and those which arise between the government and persons subject to its authority in connection with the performance of the constitutional functions of the executive or legislative departments. The Court referred to this distinction in Murray's Lessee v. Hoboken Land & Improvement Company, 59 U.S. (18 How.) 272, 284 (1856), pointing out that "there are matters, involving public rights, which may be presented in such form that the judicial power is capable of acting on them, and which are susceptible of judicial determination, but which Congress may or may not bring within the cognizance of the courts of the United States, as it may deem proper." Thus the Congress, in exercising the powers confided to it, may establish "legislative" courts (as distinguished from "constitutional courts in which the judicial power conferred by the Constitution can be deposited") which are to form part of the government of territories or of the District of Columbia, or to serve as special tribunals "to examine and determine various matters, arising between the government and others, which from their nature do not require judicial determination and yet are susceptible of it." But "the mode of determining matters of this class is completely within congressional control. Congress may reserve to itself the power to decide, may delegate that power to executive officers, or may commit it to judicial tribunals." Ex parte Bakelite Corporation, 279 U.S. 438, 451. Familiar illustrations of administrative agencies created for the determination of such matters are found in connection with the exercise of the congressional power as to interstate and foreign commerce, taxation, immigration, the public lands, public health, the facilities of the post office, pensions, and payments to veterans.

The present case does not fall within the categories just described, but is one of private right, that is, of the liability of one individual to another under the law as defined. But, in cases of that sort, there is no requirement that, in order to maintain the essential attributes of the judicial power, all determinations of fact in constitutional courts shall be made by judges. On the common-law side of the federal courts, the aid of juries is not only deemed appropriate but is required by the Constitution itself. In cases of equity and admiralty, it is historic practice to call to the assistance of the courts, without the consent of the parties, masters, and commissioners or assessors, to pass upon certain classes of questions, as, for example, to take and state an account or to find the amount of damages. * * *

The statute has a limited application, being confined to the relation of master and servant, and the method of determining the questions of fact, which arise in the routine of making compensation awards to employees under the act, is necessary to its effective enforcement. The act itself, where it applies, establishes the measure of the employer's liability, thus leaving open for determination the questions of fact as to the circumstances, nature, extent and consequences of the injuries sustained by the employee for which compensation is to be made in accordance with the prescribed standards. Findings of fact by the deputy commissioner upon such questions are closely analogous to the findings of the amount of damages that are made according to familiar practice by commissioners or assessors, and the reservation of full authority to the court to deal with matters of law provides for the appropriate exercise of the judicial function in this class of cases. For the purposes stated, we are unable to find any constitutional obstacle to the action of the Congress in availing itself of a method shown by experience to be essential in order to apply its standards to the thousands of cases involved, thus relieving the courts of a most serious burden while preserving their complete authority to insure the proper application of the law.

3. What has been said thus far relates to the determination of claims of employees within the purview of the act. A different question is

presented where the determinations of fact are fundamental or "jurisdictional,"[17] in the sense that their existence is a condition precedent to the operation of the statutory scheme. These fundamental requirements are that the injury occur upon the navigable waters of the United States and that the relation of master and servant exist. These conditions are indispensable to the application of the statute, not only because the Congress has so provided explicitly (section 3), but also because the power of the Congress to enact the legislation turns upon the existence of these conditions. * * *

In relation to these basic facts, the question is not the ordinary one as to the propriety of provision for administrative determinations. Nor have we simply the question of due process in relation to notice and hearing. It is rather a question of the appropriate maintenance of the federal judicial power in requiring the observance of constitutional restrictions. It is the question whether the Congress may substitute for constitutional courts, in which the judicial power of the United States is vested, an administrative agency—in this instance a single deputy commissioner—for the final determination of the existence of the facts upon which the enforcement of the constitutional rights of the citizen depend. The recognition of the utility and convenience of administrative agencies for the investigation and finding of facts within their proper province, and the support of their authorized action, does not require the conclusion that there is no limitation of their use, and that the Congress could completely oust the courts of all determinations of fact by vesting the authority to make them with finality in its own instrumentalities or in the Executive Department. That would be to sap the judicial power as it exists under the Federal Constitution, and to establish a government of a bureaucratic character alien to our system, wherever fundamental rights depend, as not infrequently they do depend, upon the facts, and finality as to facts becomes in effect finality in law. * * *

In cases brought to enforce constitutional rights, the judicial power of the United States necessarily extends to the independent determination of all questions, both of fact and law, necessary to the performance of that supreme function. The case of confiscation is illustrative, the ultimate conclusion almost invariably depending upon the decisions of questions of fact. This court has held the owner to be entitled to "a fair opportunity for submitting that issue to a judicial tribunal for determination upon its own independent judgment as to both law and facts." Ohio Valley Water Company v. Ben Avon Borough, 253 U.S. 287 (1920). * * * Jurisdiction in the executive to order deportation exists only if the person arrested is an alien, and, while, if there were jurisdiction, the findings of fact of the executive department would be conclusive, the claim of citizenship "is a denial of an essential jurisdictional fact" both in the statutory and the constitutional sense, and a writ of habeas corpus will issue "to determine the status." Persons claiming to be citizens of the United States "are entitled to a judicial determination of their claims," said this Court in Ng Fung Ho v. White, 259 U.S. 276, 285 (1922), and in that case the cause was remanded to the

---

[17] The term "jurisdictional," although frequently used, suggests analogies which are not complete when the reference is to administrative officials or bodies. In relation to administrative agencies, the question in a given case is whether it falls within the scope of the authority validly conferred.

federal District Court "for trial in that court of the question of citizenship." * * *

[The Court then determined that, in order to avoid the serious constitutional question that would otherwise arise, the statute should be construed to permit the court "in determining whether a compensation order is in accordance with law" to "determine the fact of employment which underlies the operation of the statute".]

Assuming that the federal court may determine for itself the existence of these fundamental or jurisdictional facts, we come to the question, Upon what record is the determination to be made? * * * We think that the essential independence of the exercise of the judicial power of the United States in the enforcement of constitutional rights requires that the federal court should determine such an issue upon its own record and the facts elicited before it. * * *

Decree affirmed.

■ MR. JUSTICE BRANDEIS, dissenting.

[The following excerpt from the long dissenting opinion indicates only one of the grounds of dissent.]

Sixth. Even if the constitutional power of Congress to provide compensation is limited to cases in which the employer-employee relation exists, I see no basis for a contention that the denial of the right to a trial de novo upon the issue of employment is in any manner subversive of the independence of the federal judicial power. Nothing in the Constitution, or in any prior decision of this Court to which attention has been called, lends support to the doctrine that a judicial finding of any fact involved in any civil proceeding to enforce a pecuniary liability may not be made upon evidence introduced before a properly constituted administrative tribunal, or that a determination so made may not be deemed an independent judicial determination. Congress has repeatedly exercised authority to confer upon the tribunals which it creates, be they administrative bodies or courts of limited jurisdiction, the power to receive evidence concerning the facts upon which the exercise of federal power must be predicated, and to determine whether those facts exist. The power of Congress to provide by legislation for liability under certain circumstances subsumes the power to provide for the determination of the existence of those circumstances. It does not depend upon the absolute existence in reality of any fact.

It is true that, so far as Knudsen is concerned, proof of the existence of the employer-employee relation is essential to recovery under the act. But under the definition laid down in Noble v. Union River Logging R. Co., 147 U.S. 165, 173, 174, that fact is not jurisdictional. It is quasi-jurisdictional. The existence of a relation of employment is a question going to the applicability of the substantive law, not to the jurisdiction of the tribunal. Jurisdiction is the power to adjudicate between the parties concerning the subject-matter. Obviously, the deputy commissioner had not only the power but the duty to determine whether the employer-employee relation existed. * * *

The "judicial power" of Article III of the Constitution is the power of the federal government, and not of any inferior tribunal. There is in that article nothing which requires any controversy to be determined as of first instance in the federal district courts. The jurisdiction of those courts is subject to the control of Congress. Matters which may be placed within their jurisdiction may instead be committed to the state courts. If there be any controversy to which the judicial power extends that may not be subjected to the conclusive determination of administrative bodies or federal legislative courts, it is not because of any prohibition against the diminution of the jurisdiction of the federal district courts as such, but because, under certain circumstances, the constitutional requirement of due process is a requirement of judicial process. An accumulation of precedents, already referred to, has established that in civil proceedings involving property rights determination of facts may constitutionally be made otherwise than judicially; and necessarily that evidence as to such facts may be taken outside of a court. I do not conceive that Article III has properly any bearing upon the question presented in this case. * * *

■ MR. JUSTICE STONE and MR. JUSTICE ROBERTS join in this opinion.

NOTE ON CROWELL V. BENSON AND ADMINISTRATIVE ADJUDICATION

(1) Historical Significance. Henry Hart claimed that "[m]ost people * * * reading Crowell concentrate on what it said Congress could *not* do", but criticized this emphasis as a "simple mistake". Hart, *The Power of Congress to Limit the Jurisdiction of Federal Courts: An Exercise in Dialectic*, 66 Harv.L.Rev. 1362, 1374–75 (1953) (hereinafter cited as "Hart, *Dialogue*"). What did the Court say in Crowell that Congress *could* do by way of investing federal administrative agencies with adjudicative authority?

In considering Professor Hart's statement, note that as of 2010, the federal government employed at least 1584 "administrative law judges" (ALJs)—executive branch officials assigned to various federal agencies. See Free Enter. Fund. v. Pub. Co. Accounting Oversight Bd., 561 U.S. 477, 542–43 (2010) (Breyer, J., dissenting). ALJs perform exclusively adjudicative functions and enjoy some statutory safeguards of decisional independence, but they lack life tenure and the Article III guarantee against reduction in salary. Indeed, a federal agency is frequently a party to proceedings before ALJs in whose selection the agency has participated and against whom the agency can initiate removal proceedings (although in practice removal is extraordinarily rare).[1] In addition, as of 2002, there were another 3370 federal administrative judges (AJs), who, although not designated as "administrative law judges" under the Administrative Procedure Act, nonetheless conducted either oral or written adjudications. See Limon, The Federal Administrative Judiciary: Then and Now: A Decade of Change, 1992–2002 4–5 (2002) (published by the Office of Administrative Law Judges in the Office of Personnel Management). The study reports that approximately 1370 of the 3370 AJs were lawyers.

Because administrative adjudication is studied extensively in courses on Administrative Law, the discussion in this Note is brief and occasionally oversimplified. Nonetheless, any account of the contemporary role of the federal courts would be incomplete if it did not reckon with (i) the vast scope

---

[1] See generally Barnett, *Resolving the ALJ Quandary*, 66 Vand.L.Rev. 797 (2013) (describing the selection and removal of ALJs and the debate about their independence).

of administrative adjudication, (ii) the relationship between administrative adjudicators and the Article III courts, and (iii) the strains that acceptance of administrative adjudication puts on efforts to develop a coherent theory of the necessary role of courts under Article III, the separation of powers, and the Due Process Clause.

(2) **Historical Foundations of Agency Adjudication.** In assessing whether Congress' vesting of any form of adjudicative power in federal administrative agencies is justified under Article III, note that the first Congress assigned responsibilities to executive officials—including resolution of disputes involving veterans' benefits and customs duties—that might instead have been vested in constitutional courts. See Fallon, *Of Legislative Courts, Administrative Agencies, and Article III*, 101 Harv.L.Rev. 915, 919 (1988). Beyond the history lies a conceptual point, well-expressed in Bator, *The Constitution as Architecture: Legislative and Administrative Courts Under Article III*, 65 Ind.L.J. 233, 264–65 (1990): "Every time an official of the executive branch, in determining how faithfully to execute the laws, goes through the process of finding facts and determining the meaning and application of the relevant law, he is doing something which functionally is akin to the exercise of judicial power. Every time the Commissioner of Internal Revenue makes a determination that, on X facts, the Tax Code requires the collection of Y tax, and issues a tax assessment on that basis, or the Immigration Service determines that Z is a deportable alien and issues an order to deport, an implicit adjudicatory process is going on. Of course, many such executive determinations are informal. But it is only a step—and one quite consistent with the ideal of 'faithful' execution of the laws—from informal, implicit adjudication to the notion that in making these determinations the official should hear the parties, make a record of the evidence, and give explicit formulations to his interpretation of the law. Determinations by the executive to apply law and judicial adjudication have a symbiotic relationship and flow naturally from and into each other. There is no *a priori* wall between them. * * * It is history and custom and expediency, rather than logic—or the text of the Constitution—that determine what needs to be the participation of the judges in the adjudicatory enterprise. * * * The judicial power is neither a platonic essence nor a pre-existing empirical classification. It is a purposive institutional concept, whose content is a product of history and custom distilled in the light of experience and expediency."

Since not every application of law to fact to determine legal rights can be deemed inherently judicial, isn't the question whether administrative adjudication is permissible under Article III a bit phony? Consider whether the real questions are not: (i) the extent to which the Constitution requires judicial *remedies* for injuries resulting from erroneous or unlawful actions by executive and administrative officials, and (ii) the extent to which administrative findings of fact and law can be made *conclusive* on a court in subsequent litigation, including litigation to enforce an administrative judgment.

(3) Constitutional Values at Stake. Justice Brandeis, dissenting in Crowell, apparently viewed the Due Process Clause as the only constitutional limitation on Congress' power to vest in administrative agencies authority to adjudicate matters that could instead have been vested in Article III courts. And for the most part, he thought, the Constitution is satisfied if the administrative process is sufficiently fair to satisfy due process, though occasionally "the constitutional requirement of due process is a requirement of judicial process".

In contending that "Article III has properly [no] bearing upon the question presented", he noted that Congress could leave adjudication of cases like Crowell exclusively to the state courts, whose judges typically lack life tenure and salary protection (and none of whom enjoys such protection under the Constitution). If state court adjudication satisfies Article III, he reasoned, so too should adjudication before a federal administrative agency.

By contrast, the Court's opinion in Crowell reasoned that Article III was implicated when Congress assigned adjudication to an administrative agency but not when it relied on state courts. One possible distinction is that federal agencies may be more susceptible than state courts to influence by Congress or the President.[2] A second possible distinction relates back to the thesis, discussed at pp. 319–322, *supra*, that Congress must vest jurisdiction in "*all*" cases arising under federal law in some Article III court; if that premise were accepted, Supreme Court review of state court decisions might suffice, but federal agency decisions would require some federal *appellate* jurisdiction.

Consider the argument of Fallon, *supra*, that there are at least three Article III values at stake in cases such as Crowell: (i) ensuring fair adjudication to individual litigants, (ii) maintaining a system of judicial review and judicial remedies that suffices to keep government generally within the bounds of law, and (iii) preserving judicial integrity by not requiring a court to accept an agency's erroneous decision as conclusive of a legal issue and to make that decision a predicate for the judicial imposition of civil or criminal penalties.[3]

(4) Public Rights and Private Rights. Crowell suggests broadly that public rights cases could be committed exclusively to administrative adjudication. Although as we shall see, that suggestion may be somewhat overbroad, there is little doubt that the categorical distinction drawn in Crowell between public rights and private rights remains important in fixing the bounds of constitutionally permissible adjudication by federal administrative agencies.[4] The Court's discussion in Crowell relied on the foundational decision in Murray's Lessee v. Hoboken Land & Improvement Co., 59 U.S. (18 How.) 272 (1855), which upheld the power of an executive official to audit the accounts of a federal employee and, upon finding a deficit, to impose a summary attachment. In response to the argument that these

---

[2] Meltzer, *Legislative Courts, Legislative Power, and the Constitution*, 65 Ind.L.J. 291 (1990), argues that review of federal administrative decisions is sometimes required by the Constitution, and, moreover, that if the constitutionally required review is by a federal tribunal, the judges must be Article III judges. Since due process does not generally require judges with life tenure (as, for example, in state court), Meltzer concludes that Article III must, at least in such cases, impose a requirement that the Due Process Clause does not impose.

[3] Ordinarily, these values are promoted by review of agency decisions in Article III courts. But if Congress need not create lower federal courts, could it provide that state courts have exclusive jurisdiction, for example, to review federal administrative adjudications denying claims for disability benefits under the Social Security Act? To review Federal Trade Commission cease-and-desist orders (which impose enforceable duties whose violation can lead to contempt citations)? Though stressing how unusual such arrangements would be, Meltzer, note 2, *supra*, argues that they would satisfy Article III because the reviewing courts would be free from control by Congress or the federal executive.

[4] For a valuable history of the public rights doctrine, see Young, *Public Rights and the Federal Judicial Power: From Murray's Lessee Through Crowell to Schor*, 35 Buff.L.Rev. 765 (1986).

were judicial acts that could be performed only by a court, the Court in Murray's Lessee said:

"[W]e do not consider congress can either withdraw from judicial cognizance any matter which, from its nature, is the subject of a suit at the common law, or in equity, or admiralty; nor, on the other hand, can it bring under the judicial power a matter which, from its nature, is not a subject for judicial determination. At the same time there are matters, involving public rights, which may be presented in such form that the judicial power is capable of acting on them, and which are susceptible of judicial determination, but which congress may or may not bring within the cognizance of the courts of the United States, as it may deem proper."

(a) Defining Public Rights. Despite its historical lineage, the public rights category has never received a canonical formulation. Historically, however, three main classes of cases have formed the doctrine's core.

(i) The first category is "claims against the United States" for "money, land or other things." Ex parte Bakelite Corp., 279 U.S. 438, 452 (1929). Perhaps because the doctrine of sovereign immunity broadly bars suit against the United States (absent its consent), adjudication of such matters could be undertaken outside of Article III courts.

(ii) The second category is disputes arising from coercive governmental conduct outside of the criminal law. Customs disputes are illustrative: the government may coerce payment of duties at the border or seize disputed property and force the disputant to litigate later. See Bakelite, *supra*, 279 U.S. at 458. Here, too, settled Supreme Court decisions hold that Congress can provide for subsequent litigation in federal tribunals other than Article III courts. *Id.*

(iii) The third category is immigration cases, "[a]pparently because of the longstanding assumption that the executive and legislative branches possess plenary power over immigration issues". Fallon, *supra*, at 967.[5]

(b) Public Rights and Judicial Review. Although the Supreme Court has sometimes suggested that public rights disputes can be removed from the purview of the courts altogether, that broad pronouncement fits uneasily with recent cases suggesting that there may be a right to judicial review of claims that administrative officials have violated constitutional rights. See pp. 329–330, *supra*. Moreover, quite apart from suits against the United States itself, the legal background has always included a range of common law and equitable remedies against government officers. See pp. 877–895, *infra*. A striking example is the writ of habeas corpus, through

---

[5] Nelson, *Adjudication in the Political Branches*, 107 Colum.L.Rev. 559 (2007), offers a different account, arguing that the public rights category historically consisted mostly if not entirely of interests belonging to the community in its "aggregate capacity" (quoting 4 Blackstone, Commentaries *5). In his view, most citizen claims against the government lay outside the necessary reach of judicial power not because they involved "public rights" but because they asserted mere "privileges"—as did immigration disputes. He contends that the government's capacity to collect taxes coercively without resort to the judicial process also lay outside the public rights category, but fell within an exception to "the traditional framework" that otherwise required judicial determination of all "core" private rights disputes.

Professor Nelson does not make it wholly clear to what extent he seeks to describe the vocabulary used by 18th and 19th century jurists and to what extent he means to reconstruct and rationalize the foundations for 18th and 19th century doctrines. He thus leaves unexplained the Supreme Court's invocation of the term "public rights" to justify its rulings in a number of cases, such as Murray's Lessee v. Hoboken Land & Improvement Co., that he regards as lying outside the public rights category.

which individuals whose liberty has been restrained may sue the government official who is responsible for the custody. Historically, this tradition of "officer suits" has diminished, but by no means eradicated, the tension between the public rights category on the one hand and, on the other, the ideal of the rule of law and the dictum of Marbury v. Madison promising a legal remedy for every deprivation of a legal right. And recall that in INS v. St. Cyr, 533 U.S. 289, 300 (2001), p. 336, *supra*, the majority reasoned that because of the Suspension Clause, Article I, § 9, cl. 2, "some 'judicial intervention in deportation cases' is unquestionably 'required by the Constitution' " (quoting Heikkila v. Barber, 345 U.S. 229, 235 (1953)).

A decision like St. Cyr surely qualifies the broadest statements that public rights matters may always be decided with no judicial involvement. Nonetheless, there is little doubt that Congress generally has greater latitude to limit judicial involvement in the resolution of matters that involve public as compared to private rights. (As we shall see, the distinction, though still important, is often quite difficult to draw. See pp. 384–387, *infra*.)

(5) The Judicial Power in Private Rights Cases. Crowell was a private rights case, involving the liability of one private party to another. The dictum in Murray's Lessee suggests that Congress could not in such a case wholly preclude judicial consideration of the correctness of the administrative decision—at least in an action by a prospective defendant (here, the employer, Benson) seeking to forestall an enforcement proceeding. The relevant question was thus what effect courts, in the judicial review proceedings, should give to the administrative decision.

(a) Questions of Fact. As summarized by Professor Hart, "the apparently solid thing about Crowell is the holding that administrative findings of non-constitutional and jurisdictional facts may be made conclusive upon the courts, if not infected with any error of law, as a basis for judicial enforcement of a money liability of one private person to another". Hart, *Dialogue*, 66 Harv.L.Rev. at 1375. Indeed, without this degree of agency conclusiveness, administrative adjudication would seem to be little more than a dry run for a later determination in court.

Congress' reasons for vesting at least initial adjudicatory responsibility in administrative agencies have varied over time and across statutory regimes. Recurrent themes include a desire to take advantage of specialized expertise, to adapt law and administration swiftly to changing priorities, to unite in a single body the power to adjudicate and to promulgate regulations, and to avoid having to increase the number of Article III judges, thereby diminishing their prestige. An additional impetus has been the belief that regulatory statutes (like the one at issue in Crowell) should be applied purposively, that adjudication furnishes a fitting occasion for the elaboration of agency policy, and that fact-finding should promote statutory purposes. (Recall that the Article III courts of the "Lochner era" were widely thought to have frustrated remedial schemes that departed from common law allocations of rights and responsibilities.) Is this last cluster of rationales in tension with constitutional values? See Strauss, *Article III Courts and the Constitutional Structure*, 65 Ind.L.J. 307, 308–09 (1990).

In light of all of these underpinnings of agency adjudication, the Court's suggestion in Crowell that that the agency functioned as little more than a fact-finding "adjunct" seems naïve or disingenuous. How persuasive are the Court's analogies to the traditional judicial reliance on factfinding by juries, masters, and commissioners—all of whom operate more directly under judicial supervision and with far greater insulation from influence of the political branches?

(b) Questions of "Jurisdictional Fact." The Court in Crowell insisted that constitutional values required de novo judicial review of questions of "jurisdictional fact"—that is, of those facts on which the jurisdiction of the agency depends. Earlier decisions had required de novo judicial review of agency determinations of "jurisdictional" facts, see Ng Fung Ho v. White, 259 U.S. 276 (1922) (involving the fact of citizenship in an immigration case), and also of "constitutional" facts—those facts on which the adjudication of constitutional rights depends, see Ohio Valley Water Co. v. Ben Avon Borough, 253 U.S. 287 (1920). In Crowell, the Court viewed the questions whether the injury occurred on navigable waters, and whether a master-servant relationship existed, as going to the jurisdiction of the agency. Justice Brandeis, by contrast, first called them quasi-jurisdictional, and then said, as to the master-servant issue, that it "go[es] to the applicability of the substantive law, not to the jurisdiction of the tribunal." Whenever an agency's action violates its governing statute, it seems possible to characterize the agency either as having exceeded its jurisdiction or as having erred substantively. As a result, any effort to distinguish those categories will be elusive. *Cf.* City of Arlington v. FCC, 133 S.Ct. 1863 (2013) ("Because the question—whether framed as an incorrect application of agency authority or an assertion of authority not conferred—is always whether the agency has gone beyond what Congress has permitted it to do, there is no principled basis for carving out some arbitrary subset of [legal] claims as 'jurisdictional.' ").

In Northern Pipeline Constr. Co. v. Marathon Pipe Line Co., 458 U.S. 50, 82 n.34 (1982), the plurality opinion summarized post-Crowell developments by stating: "Crowell's precise holding, with respect to the review of 'jurisdictional' and 'constitutional' facts that arise within ordinary administrative proceedings, has been undermined by later cases." Soon after Crowell, the decision in St. Joseph Stock Yards Co. v. United States, 298 U.S. 38, 54 (1936), did not jettison the category of jurisdictional fact, but it did reject any requirement that the court must conduct its own evidentiary hearing; instead, the opinion suggested that all relevant evidence should ordinarily be submitted to the agency and that review on the agency's record would suffice in all but extraordinary cases. More recent cases have refused to require courts to engage in de novo review of agency determinations of issues that are no less "jurisdictional" than the master-servant relationship in Crowell. See, *e.g.*, Myers v. Bethlehem Shipbuilding Corp., 303 U.S. 41, 49–50 (1938) (although the NLRB's jurisdiction over a labor dispute depends upon whether it affects interstate commerce, that question is for the Board to determine, with judicial review limited to whether the Board's finding lacks adequate evidence or is contrary to law). Thus, today any requirement of independent judicial judgment on questions of jurisdictional fact is at best infrequently applied, and independent judicial fact-finding—rather than redetermination of facts on the administrative record, ordinarily with considerable deference to the agency's determination—virtually never occurs. See generally Monaghan, *Constitutional Fact Review*, 85 Colum.L.Rev. 229 (1985).

(c) Questions of Law. The Court in Crowell appeared to assume that the Constitution required independent judicial decision of questions of law in private rights cases. But beginning as early as the 1940s, cases such as

Gray v. Powell, 314 U.S. 402 (1941), and NLRB v. Hearst Publications., Inc., 322 U.S. 111 (1944), suggested that courts should defer to agency interpretations of their governing statutes. More recently, the important decision in Chevron v. Natural Resources Defense Council, 467 U.S. 837, 842–43 (1984), elaborates a two-step process to be followed by courts reviewing agency interpretations:

"When a court reviews an agency's construction of the statute which it administers, it is confronted with two questions. First, always, is the question whether Congress has directly spoken to the precise question at issue. If the intent of Congress is clear, that is the end of the matter * * *. If, however, the court determines Congress has not directly addressed the precise question at issue, the court does not simply impose its own construction on the statute, as would be necessary in the absence of an administrative interpretation. Rather, if the statute is silent or ambiguous with respect to the specific issue, the question for the court is whether the agency's answer is based on a permissible construction of the statute."

Numerous questions have arisen about the meaning and reach of the Chevron decision.[6] But there is no doubt that it often requires a reviewing court to accept any reasonable agency construction, even if the court does not regard that construction as the best one. Are Chevron and other decisions calling for some kind of deference to agency interpretations of law consistent with Crowell—or does deference result in vesting at least part of the judicial power of the United States in administrative agencies? Consider the following colloquy from Hart, *Dialogue*, 66 Harv.L.Rev. at 1377–78:

"Q. The Crowell case * * * has a dictum that questions of law * * * must be open to judicial consideration. And * * * Brandeis * * * [said] *that* was necessary to the supremacy of law. Have those statements stood up? * * *

"A. [Whether agencies are permitted 'to make final decisions of questions of law'] depends on how you define 'law'. * * *

"In recent years we've recognized increasingly a permissible range of administrative discretion in the shaping of judicially enforceable duties. How wide that discretion should be, and what are the appropriate ways to control it, are crucial questions in administrative law. But so long as the courts sit to answer the questions, the spirit of Brandeis' statement is maintained. And, since discretion by hypothesis is not law, the letter of it is not in question."

Compare Monaghan, *Marbury and the Administrative State*, 83 Colum.L.Rev. 1, 29, 33 (1983), arguing that "[t]he opposition of 'discretion' to 'law' cannot dissolve Hart's problem," since "the result of the exercise of discretion is * * * an administrative formulation of a rule of law". Professor Monaghan concludes, however, that "there has never been a pervasive notion that limited government mandated an all-encompassing judicial duty to supply all of the relevant meaning of statutes. Rather, the judicial duty is to ensure that the administrative agency stays within the zone of discretion committed to it by its organic act". And the Chevron decision, which postdated Monaghan's article, can surely be viewed through the lens of legislative delegation: when an Act of Congress has not addressed the precise question, the statute will be viewed as implicitly delegating authority to the

---

[6] For a fuller catalogue of questions, more than a few answers, and a valuable bibliography, see Manning & Stephenson, Legislation and Regulation 768–72 (2d ed.2013).

agency, and agency lawmaking under that delegation is subject to review only for whether it falls within the scope of the statutory delegation.

(6) Agency Adjudication in Criminal Cases. Criminal cases have always been treated as "private rights" cases,[7] despite the involvement of the government as a party, and there seems to be no doubt that an administrative agency may not directly impose criminal punishments.[8] But may an Article III court, in imposing criminal punishment, rely in whole or in part on an agency's determination of fact or law? That question differs from the circumstances (a) in Yakus v. United States, p. 343, *supra*, where the Court held that Congress could require a criminal enforcement court to give conclusive effect to the decisions of a prior *judicial* proceeding, and (b) in Crowell, where the Court held that in a *civil* action, a federal court could defer to agency determinations of the facts.

(a) Falbo, Estep, and the Views of Professor Hart. Consider the following excerpts from Professor Hart's *Dialogue*, 66 Harv.L.Rev. at 1380–83. Hart, who accepted Crowell without much difficulty but was troubled by Yakus, was even more troubled by the idea that federal criminal courts might accept the findings of federal agencies without searching independent inquiry:

"Q. Does Yakus mark the maximum inroad on the rights of a criminal defendant to judicial process?

"A. No, unfortunately it doesn't. We have to take account of two World War II selective service cases, Falbo v. United States, 320 U.S. 549 (1944), and Estep v. United States, 327 U.S. 114 (1946). 'By the terms of' the selective service legislation, as Justice Douglas put it in Estep, 'Congress enlisted the aid of the federal courts only for enforcement purposes.' And so the question was sharply presented on what terms that could be done.

"The Court held in Falbo, with only Justice Murphy dissenting, that a registrant who was being prosecuted for failure to report for induction (or for work of national importance) could not defend on the ground that he had been wrongly classified and was entitled to a statutory exemption.

"Q. Doesn't that pretty well destroy your notion that there has to be some kind of reasonable means for getting a judicial determination of questions of law affecting liability for criminal punishment? All Congress has to do is to authorize an administrative agency to issue an individualized order, make the violation of the order a crime in itself, and at the same time immunize the order from judicial review. On the question of the violation of the order, all the defendant's rights are preserved in the criminal trial, except that they don't mean anything.

"A. Whoa! Falbo doesn't go that far. In Estep, after the fighting was over, the case was explained—and perhaps it had actually been decided—on the basis that the petitioner in failing to report for induction had failed to exhaust his administrative remedies. Considering the emergency, the

---

[7] See, *e.g.*, Northern Pipeline Construction Co. v. Marathon Pipe Line Co., 458 U.S. 50, 70 n.23 (1982), p. 356, *supra*.

[8] Under at least some circumstances, however, it has been held that *other* non-Article III federal tribunals—characteristically denominated as "legislative courts"—may do so. For discussion of the permissible use of "legislative courts" and the necessity, if any, of review of their judgments by Article III courts, see pp. 361–390, *infra*.

requirement that claims be first presented at the induction center was pretty clearly a reasonable procedure.[9]

"Q. How about Estep?

"A. The petitioner there went to the end of the administrative road, and was indicted for refusing to submit to induction. The Court held that he was entitled to make the defense that the local board had 'acted beyond its jurisdiction'. Justice Douglas, speaking for himself and Justices Reed and Black, said:

" 'The provision making the decisions of the local boards "final" means to us that Congress chose not to give administrative action under this Act the customary scope of judicial review which obtains under other statutes. It means that the courts are not to weigh the evidence to determine whether the classification made by the local boards was justified. The decisions of the local boards made in conformity with the regulations are final even though they may be erroneous. The question of jurisdiction of the local board is reached only if there is no basis in fact for the classification which it gave the registrant.'

"Justices Murphy and Rutledge concurred specially on the ground that the Court's construction was required by the Constitution. Justice Frankfurter thought the construction wrong but concurred on the ground that there were other errors in the trial. Justice Burton and Chief Justice Stone dissented.

"Q. Well, the holding in the end wasn't such a departure after all, was it?

"A. Stop and think before you say that.

"Except for two Justices who are now dead, the whole Court dealt with the question as if it were merely one of statutory construction. Three Justices of the Supreme Court of the United States were willing to assume that Congress has power under Article I of the Constitution to direct courts created under Article III to employ the judicial power conferred by Article III to convict a man of a crime and send him to jail without his ever having had a chance to make his defenses. No decision in 164 years of constitutional history, so far as I know, had ever before sanctioned such a thing. Certainly no such decision was cited. For these three didn't even see it as a problem. There is ground to doubt whether the first three in the majority did either.

"Bear in mind that the three dissenters from the Court's construction expressly recognized that the order of induction might have been erroneous in law. They said that the remedy for that was habeas corpus after induction. They seemed to say that the existence of the remedy of habeas corpus saved the constitutionality of the prior procedure. That turns an ultimate safeguard of law into an excuse for its violation. And it strikes close to the heart of one of the main theses of this discussion—that so long at least as Congress feels impelled to invoke the assistance of courts, the supremacy of law in their decisions is assured."

(b) The Mendoza-Lopez Case. In United States v. Mendoza-Lopez, 481 U.S. 828 (1987), the Court held that a statutory provision that purported to prevent a federal court in a criminal case from reconsidering an

---

[9] [Ed.] More recent cases indicate that even this "exhaustion" aspect of Falbo will be only selectively enforced, at least when the nation is not fully engaged in war. Compare McKart v. United States, 395 U.S. 185 (1969), with McGee v. United States, 402 U.S. 479 (1971).

administrative determination denied due process on the facts of the case. There, an alien was prosecuted for the crime of re-entering the United States after having previously been deported. The question was whether he was entitled, in the criminal proceeding, to challenge the validity of the administrative agency's prior deportation order, on the ground that the hearing conducted by the immigration judge failed to afford due process. Although he failed to seek judicial review of that order at the time of its issuance, he contended that he had not understood his rights, that the administrative judge did not adequately apprise him of his right to appeal, and that any waiver of that right was not knowing and intelligent.

The Court first ruled that the statute criminalizing re-entry purported to preclude this form of collateral attack on the earlier deportation orders. But resolution of that statutory question "does not end our inquiry". Turning to constitutional issues, the Court first cited Yakus (and other cases) for the proposition that "where a determination made in an administrative proceeding is to play a critical role in the subsequent imposition of a criminal sanction, there must be *some* meaningful review of the administrative proceeding". In a footnote, the Court added: "Even with this safeguard, the use of the result of an administrative proceeding to establish an element of a criminal offense is troubling. While the Court has permitted criminal conviction for violation of an administrative regulation where the validity of the regulation could not be challenged in the criminal proceeding, Yakus v. United States, the decision in that case was motivated by the exigencies of wartime, dealt with the propriety of regulations rather than the legitimacy of an adjudicative procedure, and, most significantly, turned on the fact that adequate judicial review of the validity of the regulation was available in another forum. Under different circumstances, the propriety of using an administrative ruling in such a way remains open to question. We do not reach this issue here, however, holding that, at a minimum, the result of an administrative proceeding may not be used as a conclusive element of a criminal offense where the judicial review that legitimated such a practice in the first instance has effectively been denied."

The Court proceeded to hold, 5–4, that when defects in a prior deportation proceeding "effectively eliminate[d] the right of [an] alien to obtain judicial review"—apparently because the immigration judge had failed to make clear the consequences of a deportation order and the availability of appeal—due process required that the alien be allowed to make a collateral challenge to the use of that proceeding as an element of a subsequent criminal offense.

In dissent, Chief Justice Rehnquist, joined by Justices White and O'Connor, agreed that "there may be exceptional circumstances where the Due Process Clause prohibits the Government from using an alien's prior deportation as a basis for imposing criminal liability", but argued that in this case the initial deportation proceedings did not violate due process and that there was no bar to relying on the prior deportation order.

In a separate dissent, Justice Scalia contended that no prior decision of the Court "squarely holds that the Due Process Clause invariably forbids reliance upon the outcome of unreviewable administrative determinations in subsequent criminal proceedings". He continued: "The Court's apparent adoption of that conclusion today seems to me wrong. To illustrate that point * * *, imagine that a State establishes an administrative agency that (after investigation and full judicial-type administrative hearings) periodically publishes a list of unethical businesses. Further imagine that the State, having discovered that a number of previously listed businesses are bribing the agency's investigators to avoid future listing, passes a law making it a felony for a business that has been listed to bribe agency investigators. It cannot be that the Due Process Clause forbids the State to punish violations of that law unless it either makes the agency's listing decisions judicially reviewable or permits those charged with violating the law to defend themselves on the ground that the original listing decisions were in some way unlawful."

(c) Questions about Mendoza-Lopez.

(i) Does the Court's decision effectively vindicate Professor Hart's position, including his criticisms of the opinions in Falbo and Estep?

(ii) How broad is the Court's holding? In a prosecution for re-entry, could an alien collaterally attack a deportation order if the immigration judge did explain the right to seek judicial review of the deportation order, but because the alien could not afford a lawyer, no appeal was filed? If an alien, represented by counsel, had moved unsuccessfully to remove the immigration judge on the basis of alleged bias, but the lawyer failed to seek judicial review of the denied motion?

(iii) If agency findings can play a lesser role in criminal than in civil enforcement courts, why exactly is that? Because of Article III? The Due Process Clause? Presuppositions about the role of courts as guarantors of constitutional liberty that are reflected in Article III, the Due Process Clause, and the Suspension Clause? *Cf.* INS v. St. Cyr, p. 336, *supra.*

(7) Transitional Questions. In Mendoza-Lopez, as in Crowell, the statutory scheme gave ultimate responsibility for enforcing federal law to an Article III court, and the question therefore arose to what extent an "enforcement court" could rely on an agency's determination of fact or law. But may Congress bypass both Article III federal courts and state courts altogether, by authorizing a non-Article III federal tribunal to issue directly binding and enforceable rulings in private rights cases? (A non-Article III federal tribunal simply means a body in which a federal official vested with authority to adjudicate lacks the constitutional guarantees of life tenure and salary protection enjoyed by judges in the "regular" Article III courts.) In criminal prosecutions? Does the permissibility of using non-Article III tribunals depend upon the existence and extent of judicial review in an Article III court?

Although Congress has seldom purported to vest administrative "agencies" with powers that present this constitutional question, it has much more frequently done so through its use of so-called "legislative courts"—the subject of the materials that directly follow this Note.

INTRODUCTORY NOTE ON LEGISLATIVE COURTS

(1) The Concept of a "Legislative Court". Congress has vested adjudicative authority not only in administrative agencies, but also in "legislative courts"—federal tribunals denominated as "courts" but not as Article III courts, and staffed by judges lacking life tenure and salary protection. (They are sometimes called Article I courts, as most often Congress creates them under its Article I legislative authority, but territorial courts, for example, are legislative courts created under Congress' Article IV powers.)

(2) Historical Practice. Longstanding examples of legislative courts fall into three main but not necessarily exclusive categories.

(a) Territorial Courts. In American Ins. Co. v. Canter, 26 U.S. (1 Pet.) 511 (1828), Chief Justice Marshall upheld employment of non-Article III courts to adjudicate an admiralty dispute in the then-territory of Florida. Territorial courts, the Chief Justice said, were created in virtue of every government's general right of sovereignty, or in virtue of Article IV, Sec. 3's conferral on Congress of authority to "make all needful Rules and Regulations respecting the Territory * * * belonging to the United States." While noting that the "admiralty jurisdiction can be exercised in the states [only in Article III courts], the same limitation does not extend to the territories. In legislating for them, Congress exercises the combined powers of the general, and of a state government."

As courts of general jurisdiction, territorial courts resemble state courts, which need not satisfy Article III's strictures. Moreover, had Congress established only Article III courts in the territory of Florida, hard questions might have arisen about whether all cases filed in those courts came within one of Article III's nine heads of jurisdiction. Do these considerations justify assigning a case like Canter, which clearly falls within one of those nine heads, to a non-Article III federal tribunal?

The Court relied on Canter, among other authorities, in Palmore v. United States, 411 U.S. 389 (1973), which upheld the constitutionality of a criminal prosecution before the local, non-Article III courts that Congress created in the District of Columbia, pursuant to Article I's conferral of legislative authority over the District.[1]

(b) Military Courts. From 1789 to the present, Congress has authorized military tribunals, whose judges are commissioned officers not protected by life tenure, to conduct courts martial to enforce military discipline and punish service members.[2] Their constitutionality was upheld in Dynes v. Hoover, 61 U.S. (20 How.) 65 (1858), and as a practical matter seems to be beyond question today,[3] although some issues have arisen at the margin about the reach of court-martial jurisdiction.[4] The justifications for establishing such a system outside of Article III have included (i) the physical separation of civilian society from the military, the latter of which requires a tribunal staffed with military officers to permit a quick determination of guilt; (ii) a concern that the military system differs from civilian society and that civilian officials unfamiliar with or even antagonistic to military life might misapply the legal standards of the military justice system; and (iii)

---

[1] For descriptions of other territorial and related courts, see p. 37, *supra*.

[2] See Schlueter, *The Court-Martial: An Historical Survey*, 87 Mil.L.Rev. 129, 150 (1980).

[3] For a discussion of the relation of military justice to Article III, see Note, 103 Harv.L.Rev. 1909 (1990).

[4] The holding of O'Callahan v. Parker, 395 U.S. 258 (1969), that a soldier may be tried by a court martial only for "service-connected" offenses, was overruled by Solorio v. United States, 483 U.S. 435 (1987). The Supreme Court has barred the use of military courts to try civilians, including the civilian dependents of service members, at least for non-military offenses in peacetime. See, *e.g.*, Kinsella v. United States ex rel. Singleton, 361 U.S. 234 (1960). In 2006, Congress extended court-martial jurisdiction to reach civilian contractors "serving with or accompanying an armed force in the field" during a "contingency operation". 10 U.S.C. § 802(a)(10); see United States v. Ali, 71 M.J. 256 (C.A.A.F. 2012).

the view that the goals of civilian and military justice differ, as the latter serves to preserve good order and discipline in the military as much as to punish, deter, incapacitate and rehabilitate offenders. See generally Vladeck, *Military Courts and Article III*, 103 Geo.L.J. ___ (forthcoming 2015).

Other military tribunals have also been used from time to time to try enemy spies and other alleged unlawful combatants under the laws of war, to conduct trials under conditions of martial law, and to administer justice in foreign territories subject to military occupation. For discussion, see *Note on Military Tribunals or Commissions*, p. 402, *infra*.

(c) **Courts to Adjudicate Public Rights Disputes.** Numerous bodies fall within the elusive category of federal tribunals that adjudicate public rights. Current examples include the Court of Federal Claims,[5] the Tax Court,[6] and the United States Court of Appeals for Veterans Claims.[7] The contours of the public rights doctrine have never been clearly defined, although most if not all public rights disputes involve civil claims by or against the government.

(3) Legislative Courts and Article III Subject Matter. Plainly, legislative courts hear cases that could have been heard by Article III courts. Territorial courts (and the D.C. local courts) decide diversity and federal question cases; Canter was an admiralty case. In both criminal prosecutions before courts martial and public rights cases, typically the United States is a party and the case arises under federal law. Although past Supreme Court decisions have occasionally, if unconvincingly, suggested otherwise,[8] for some time the Court has acknowledged that legislative courts hear Article III judicial business and instead has sought to rationalize that fact.[9]

The broad range of matters that have been, or might be, assigned to legislative courts raises the question of what limits the Constitution places on Congress' power to deploy such tribunals. The natural import of Article III is that that judges hearing Article III judicial business must enjoy the guarantee of independence supplied by life tenure and protection against reduction in salary. To what extent can a series of historical exceptions, such as those just discussed, or a set of functional needs, overcome the natural import of Article III?

---

[5] For discussions of the status and history of this court, see pp. 38, 89–90, *supra*.

[6] See p. 38, *supra*.

[7] See p. 38, *supra*. Earlier statutes also assigned adjudicative responsibilities to a Court of Private Land Claims and a Court of Customs Appeals. See Ex parte Bakelite Corp., 279 U.S. 438 (1929).

[8] See, *e.g.*, Williams v. United States, 289 U.S. 553, 571–77 (1933) (appearing to assume that legislative courts are incapable of resolving cases within the jurisdictional headings of Article III).

[9] See Glidden Co. v. Zdanok, 370 U.S. 530, 549–51 (1962) (opinion of Harlan, J.).

Stern v. Marshall

___ U.S. ___, 131 S.Ct. 2594, 180 L.Ed.2d 475 (2011).
Certiorari to the U.S. Court of Appeals for the Ninth Circuit.

■ CHIEF JUSTICE ROBERTS delivered the opinion of the Court.

* * *

* * * This is the second time we have had occasion to weigh in on this long-running dispute between Vickie Lynn Marshall and E. Pierce Marshall over the fortune of J. Howard Marshall II * * *. [A] Texas state probate court and the Bankruptcy Court for the Central District of California * * * have reached contrary decisions on [the Marshalls' litigation.] * * *

* * * The Bankruptcy Court in this case exercised the judicial power of the United States by entering final judgment on a common law tort claim, even though the judges of such courts enjoy neither tenure during good behavior nor salary protection. We conclude that, although the Bankruptcy Court had the statutory authority to enter judgment on Vickie's counterclaim, it lacked the constitutional authority to do so.

I

* * * Known to the public as Anna Nicole Smith, Vickie was J. Howard's third wife and married him about a year before his death. Although J. Howard bestowed on Vickie many * * * gifts during their courtship and marriage, he did not include her in his will. Before J. Howard passed away, Vickie filed suit in Texas state probate court, asserting that Pierce—J. Howard's younger son—fraudulently induced J. Howard to sign a living trust that did not include her, even though J. Howard meant to give her half his property. * * *

After J. Howard's death, Vickie filed a petition for bankruptcy in the Central District of California. Pierce filed a complaint in that bankruptcy proceeding, contending that Vickie had defamed him by inducing her lawyers to tell members of the press that he had engaged in fraud to gain control of his father's assets. The complaint sought a declaration that Pierce's defamation claim was not dischargeable in the bankruptcy proceedings. Pierce subsequently filed a proof of claim for the defamation action, meaning that he sought to recover damages for it from Vickie's bankruptcy estate. Vickie responded to Pierce's initial complaint by * * * filing a counterclaim for tortious interference with the gift she expected from J. Howard. * * *

* * * [The Bankruptcy Court awarded Vickie $400 million in compensatory damages and $25 million in punitive damages.]

In post-trial proceedings, Pierce argued that [Vickie's counterclaim was not a "core proceeding" under 28 U.S.C. § 157(b)(2)(C) and hence was outside the Bankruptcy Court's statutory jurisdiction. Ultimately, the Court of Appeals for the Ninth Circuit agreed with Pierce's jurisdictional objection, in part because of doubts the Bankruptcy Court could constitutionally adjudicate Vickie's counterclaim.]

II

[In this part of the opinion, the Court ruled that Vickie's counterclaim was a "core proceeding" within the Bankruptcy Court's statutory jurisdiction, and that the statutory text was so clear on this point as to leave no room to construe the statute otherwise in order to avoid a constitutional question.]

III

Although we conclude that § 157(b)(2)(C) permits the Bankruptcy Court to enter final judgment on Vickie's counterclaim, Article III of the Constitution does not.

A

* * *

* * * Article III is "an inseparable element of the constitutional system of checks and balances" that "both defines the power and protects the independence of the Judicial Branch." Northern Pipeline [Constr. Co. v. Marathon Pipe Line Co,] 458 U.S. [50,] 58 [(1982)] (plurality opinion). * * *

In establishing the system of divided power in the Constitution, the Framers considered it essential that "the judiciary remain[ ] truly distinct from both the legislature and the executive." The Federalist No. 78, p. 466 (C. Rossiter ed. 1961) (A. Hamilton). * * *

We have recognized that the three branches are not hermetically sealed from one another, but it remains true that Article III imposes some basic limitations that the other branches may not transgress. Those limitations serve two related purposes. "Separation-of-powers principles are intended, in part, to protect each branch of government from incursion by the others. Yet the dynamic between and among the branches is not the only object of the Constitution's concern. The structural principles secured by the separation of powers protect the individual as well. Bond v. United States, 564 U.S. ___, ___ (2011).

* * *

B

This is not the first time we have faced an Article III challenge to a bankruptcy court's resolution of a debtor's suit. In Northern Pipeline, we considered whether bankruptcy judges serving under the Bankruptcy Act of 1978—appointed by the President and confirmed by the Senate, but lacking the tenure and salary guarantees of Article III—could "constitutionally be vested with jurisdiction to decide [a] state-law contract claim" against an entity that was not otherwise part of the bankruptcy proceedings. 458 U.S., at 53, 87, n. 40 (plurality opinion); see id., at 89–92 (Rehnquist, J., concurring in judgment). The Court concluded that assignment of such state law claims for resolution by those judges "violates Art. III of the Constitution." Id., at 52, 87 (plurality opinion); id., at 91 (Rehnquist, J., concurring in judgment).

The plurality in Northern Pipeline recognized that there was a category of cases involving "public rights" that Congress could constitutionally assign to "legislative" courts for resolution. That opinion concluded that this "public rights" exception extended "only to matters arising between" individuals and the Government "in connection with the performance of the constitutional functions of the executive or legislative departments . . . that historically could have been determined exclusively by those" branches. Id. at 67–68 (internal quotation marks omitted). A full majority of the Court, while not agreeing on the scope of the exception, concluded that the doctrine did not encompass adjudication of the state law claim at issue in that case. *Id.,* at 69–72; see *id.,* at 90–91 (Rehnquist, J., concurring in judgment) * * *.[5]

A full majority of Justices in Northern Pipeline also rejected the debtor's argument that the bankruptcy court's exercise of jurisdiction was constitutional because the bankruptcy judge was acting merely as an adjunct of the district court or court of appeals.

After our decision in Northern Pipeline, Congress revised the statutes governing bankruptcy jurisdiction and bankruptcy judges. In the 1984 Act, Congress provided that the judges of the new bankruptcy courts would be appointed by the courts of appeals for the circuits in which their districts are located. And * * * Congress permitted the newly constituted bankruptcy courts to enter final judgments only in "core" proceedings.

With respect to such "core" matters, however, the bankruptcy courts under the 1984 Act exercise the same powers they wielded under the Bankruptcy Act of 1978 (1978 Act). As in Northern Pipeline, for example, the newly constituted bankruptcy courts are charged * * * with resolving "[a]ll matters of fact and law in whatever domains of the law to which" a counterclaim may lead. 458 U.S., at 91 (Rehnquist, J., concurring in judgment). * * * And, as in Northern Pipeline, the district courts review the judgments of the bankruptcy courts in core proceedings only under the usual limited appellate standards. That requires marked deference to, among other things, the bankruptcy judges' findings of fact. See § 158(a); Fed. Rule Bkrtcy. Proc. 8013 (findings of fact "shall not be set aside unless clearly erroneous").

C

* * * Vickie argues that this case is different [from Northern Pipeline] because the defendant is a creditor in the bankruptcy. But the debtors' claims in the cases on which she relies were themselves federal claims under bankruptcy law, which would be completely resolved in the bankruptcy process of allowing or disallowing claims. Here Vickie's claim is a state law action independent of the federal bankruptcy law and not necessarily resolvable by a ruling on the creditor's proof of claim in bankruptcy. * * *

Nor can the bankruptcy courts under the 1984 Act be dismissed as mere adjuncts of Article III courts, any more than could the bankruptcy courts under the 1978 Act. The judicial powers the courts exercise in cases such as this remain the same, and a court exercising such broad powers is no mere adjunct of anyone.

1

Vickie's counterclaim cannot be deemed a matter of "public right" that can be decided outside the Judicial Branch. * * * [I]n Northern Pipeline we rejected the argument that the public rights doctrine permitted a bankruptcy court to adjudicate a state law suit brought by a debtor against a company that had not filed a claim against the estate. Although our discussion of the public rights exception since that time has not been entirely consistent, and the exception has been the subject of

---

[5]   The dissent is thus wrong in suggesting that less than a full Court agreed on the points pertinent to this case.

some debate, this case does not fall within any of the various formulations of the concept that appear in this Court's opinions.

We first recognized the category of public rights in Murray's Lessee v. Hoboken Land & Improvement Co., 59 U.S. 272 (1856). That case involved the Treasury Department's sale of property belonging to a customs collector who had failed to transfer payments to the Federal Government that he had collected on its behalf. The plaintiff * * * objected that the Treasury Department's calculation of the deficiency and sale of the property was void, because it was a judicial act that could not be assigned to the Executive under Article III.

* * * [T]he Court * * * confirmed that Congress cannot "withdraw from judicial cognizance any matter which, from its nature, is the subject of a suit at the common law, or in equity, or admiralty." [*Id.* at 284.] The Court also recognized that "[a]t the same time there are matters, involving public rights, which may be presented in such form that the judicial power is capable of acting on them, and which are susceptible of judicial determination, but which congress may or may not bring within the cognizance of the courts of the United States, as it may deem proper." *Ibid.*

As an example of such matters, the Court referred to "[e]quitable claims to land by the inhabitants of ceded territories" and cited cases in which land issues were conclusively resolved by Executive Branch officials. *Ibid.* In those cases "it depends upon the will of congress whether a remedy in the courts shall be allowed at all," so Congress could limit the extent to which a judicial forum was available. Murray's Lessee, 18 How., at 284. The challenge in Murray's Lessee to the Treasury Department's sale of the collector's land likewise fell within the "public rights" category of cases, because it could only be brought if the Federal Government chose to allow it by waiving sovereign immunity.

Subsequent decisions from this Court contrasted cases within the reach of the public rights exception—those arising "between the Government and persons subject to its authority in connection with the performance of the constitutional functions of the executive or legislative departments"—and those that were instead matters "of private right, that is, of the liability of one individual to another under the law as defined." Crowell v. Benson, 285 U.S. 22, 50, 51 (1932).[6] * * *

Shortly after Northern Pipeline, the Court rejected the limitation of the public rights exception to actions involving the Government as a party. The Court has continued, however, to limit the exception to cases in which the claim at issue derives from a federal regulatory scheme, or in which resolution of the claim by an expert government agency is

---

[6] Although the Court in Crowell went on to decide that the facts of the private dispute before it could be determined by a non-Article III tribunal in the first instance, subject to judicial review, the Court did so only after observing that the administrative adjudicator had only limited authority to make specialized, narrowly confined factual determinations regarding a particularized area of law and to issue orders that could be enforced only by action of the District Court. In other words, the agency in Crowell functioned as a true "adjunct" of the District Court. That is not the case here.

Although the dissent suggests that we understate the import of Crowell in this regard, the dissent itself recognizes—repeatedly—that Crowell by its terms addresses the determination of facts outside Article III. Crowell may well have additional significance in the context of expert administrative agencies that oversee particular substantive federal regimes, but we have no occasion to and do not address those issues today. * * *

deemed essential to a limited regulatory objective within the agency's authority. In other words, it is still the case that what makes a right "public" rather than private is that the right is integrally related to particular federal government action.

Our decision in Thomas v. Union Carbide Agricultural Products Co., for example, involved a data-sharing arrangement between companies under a federal statute providing that disputes about compensation between the companies would be decided by binding arbitration. 473 U.S. 568, 571–575 (1985). This Court held that the scheme did not violate Article III, explaining that "[a]ny right to compensation . . . results from [the statute] and does not depend on or replace a right to such compensation under state law." *Id.*, at 584.

Commodity Futures Trading Commission v. Schor concerned a statutory scheme that created a procedure for customers injured by a broker's violation of the federal commodities law to seek reparations from the broker before the Commodity Futures Trading Commission (CFTC). 478 U.S. 833, 836 (1986). A customer filed such a claim to recover a debit balance in his account, while the broker filed a lawsuit in Federal District Court to recover the same amount as lawfully due from the customer. The broker later submitted its claim to the CFTC, but after that agency ruled against the customer, the customer argued that agency jurisdiction over the broker's counterclaim violated Article III. This Court disagreed, but only after observing that (1) the claim and the counterclaim concerned a "single dispute"—the same account balance; (2) the CFTC's assertion of authority involved only "a narrow class of common law claims" in a "'particularized area of law'"; (3) the area of law in question was governed by "a specific and limited federal regulatory scheme" as to which the agency had "obvious expertise"; (4) the parties had freely elected to resolve their differences before the CFTC; and (5) CFTC orders were "enforceable only by order of the district court." *Id.*, at 844, 852–855 (quoting Northern Pipeline, 458 U.S., at 85). Most significantly, given that the customer's reparations claim before the agency and the broker's counterclaim were competing claims to the same amount, the Court repeatedly emphasized that it was "necessary" to allow the agency to exercise jurisdiction over the broker's claim, or else "the reparations procedure would have been confounded." *Id.*, at 856.

The most recent case in which we considered application of the public rights exception * * * is Granfinanciera, S.A. v. Nordberg, 492 U.S. 33 (1989). In Granfinanciera we rejected a bankruptcy trustee's argument that a fraudulent conveyance action filed on behalf of a bankruptcy estate against a noncreditor in a bankruptcy proceeding fell within the "public rights" exception. We explained that, "[i]f a statutory right is not closely intertwined with a federal regulatory program Congress has power to enact, and if that right neither belongs to nor exists against the Federal Government, then it must be adjudicated by an Article III court." *Id.*, at 54–55. We reasoned that fraudulent conveyance suits were "quintessentially suits at common law that more nearly resemble state law contract claims brought by a bankrupt corporation to augment the bankruptcy estate than they do creditors' hierarchically ordered claims to a pro rata share of the bankruptcy res." *Id.*, at 56. As a consequence, we concluded that fraudulent conveyance actions were "more accurately characterized as a private rather than a public right as we have used those terms in our Article III decisions." *Id.,* at 55.[7]

Vickie's counterclaim—like the fraudulent conveyance claim at issue in Granfinanciera—does not fall within any of the varied formulations of the public rights exception in this Court's cases. It is not a matter that can be pursued only by grace of the other branches, as in Murray's Lessee, or one that "historically could have been determined exclusively by" those branches, Northern Pipeline, *supra,* at 68 (citing Ex parte Bakelite Corp., 279 U.S. [438,] 458 [(1929)]. The claim is instead one under state common law between two private parties. * * *

In addition, Vickie's claimed right to relief does not flow from a federal statutory scheme, as in Thomas * * *. It is not "completely dependent upon" adjudication of a claim created by federal law, as in Schor. And in contrast to the objecting party in Schor, Pierce did not truly consent to resolution of Vickie's claim in the bankruptcy court proceedings. He had nowhere else to go if he wished to recover from Vickie's estate.[8]

Furthermore, the asserted authority to decide Vickie's claim is not limited to a "particularized area of the law," as in Crowell, Thomas, and Schor. Northern Pipeline, 458 U.S., at 85 (plurality opinion). We deal here not with an agency but with a court, with substantive jurisdiction reaching any area of the *corpus juris.* This is not a situation in which Congress devised an "expert and inexpensive method for dealing with a class of questions of fact which are particularly suited to examination and determination by an administrative agency specially assigned to that task." Crowell, 285 U.S., at 46. The "experts" in the federal system at resolving common law counterclaims such as Vickie's are the Article III courts * * *.

The dissent reads our cases differently, and in particular contends that more recent cases view Northern Pipeline as " 'establish[ing] only that Congress may not vest in a non-Article III court the power to adjudicate, render final judgment, and issue binding orders in a traditional contract action arising under state law, without consent of the litigants, and subject only to ordinary appellate review.' " *Post,* at 2624 (quoting Thomas, *supra,* at 584). Just so: Substitute "tort" for "contract," and that statement directly covers this case.

We recognize that there may be instances in which the distinction between public and private rights—at least as framed by some of our recent cases—fails to provide concrete guidance as to whether, for example, a particular agency can adjudicate legal issues under a substantive regulatory scheme. Given the extent to which this case is so

---

[7] We noted that we did not mean to "suggest that the restructuring of debtor-creditor relations is in fact a public right." 492 U.S., at 56, n. 11. Our conclusion was that, "even if one accepts this thesis," Congress could not constitutionally assign resolution of the fraudulent conveyance action to a non-Article III court. *Ibid.* Because neither party asks us to reconsider the public rights framework for bankruptcy, we follow the same approach here.

[8] Contrary to the claims of the dissent, Pierce did not have another forum in which to pursue his claim to recover from Vickie's prebankruptcy assets, rather than take his chances with whatever funds might remain after the Title 11 proceedings. Creditors who possess claims that do not satisfy the requirements for nondischargeability under 11 U.S.C. § 523 have no choice but to file their claims in bankruptcy proceedings if they want to pursue the claims at all. That is why * * * the notion of "consent" does not apply in bankruptcy proceedings as it might in other contexts.

markedly distinct from the agency cases discussing the public rights exception in the context of such a regime, however, we do not in this opinion express any view on how the doctrine might apply in that different context.

What is plain here is that this case involves the most prototypical exercise of judicial power: the entry of a final, binding judgment *by a court* with broad substantive jurisdiction, on a common law cause of action, when the action neither derives from nor depends upon any agency regulatory regime. * * *

2

Vickie and the dissent next attempt to distinguish Northern Pipeline and Granfinanciera on the ground that Pierce, unlike the defendants in those cases, had filed a proof of claim in the bankruptcy proceedings. * * * Vickie argues [that] the Bankruptcy Court had the authority to adjudicate her counterclaim under our decisions in Katchen v. Landy, 382 U.S. 323 (1966), and Langenkamp v. Culp, 498 U.S. 42 (1990) (*per curiam*).

We do not agree. * * *

* * * Katchen permitted a bankruptcy referee acting under the Bankruptcy Acts of 1898 and 1938 (akin to a bankruptcy court today) to exercise what was known as "summary jurisdiction" over a voidable preference claim brought by the bankruptcy trustee against a creditor who had filed a proof of claim in the bankruptcy proceeding. A voidable preference claim asserts that a debtor made a payment to a particular creditor in anticipation of bankruptcy, to in effect increase that creditor's proportionate share of the estate. The preferred creditor's claim in bankruptcy can be disallowed as a result of the preference, and the amounts paid to that creditor can be recovered by the trustee.

* * * [T]his Court concluded that summary adjudication in bankruptcy was appropriate, because it was not possible for the referee to rule on the creditor's proof of claim without first resolving the voidable preference issue. * * * Once the referee did that, "nothing remains for adjudication in a plenary suit"; such a suit "would be a meaningless gesture." *Id.*, at 334. * * *

It was in that sense that the Court stated that "he who invokes the aid of the bankruptcy court by offering a proof of claim and demanding its allowance must abide the consequences of that procedure." *Id.*, at 333, n. 9. * * *

Our *per curiam* opinion in Langenkamp is to the same effect. * * *

* * * There was some overlap between Vickie's counterclaim and Pierce's defamation claim that led the courts below to conclude that the counterclaim was compulsory, or at least in an "attenuated" sense related to Pierce's claim. But there was never any reason to believe that the process of adjudicating Pierce's proof of claim would necessarily resolve Vickie's counterclaim. [The Court here noted the questions relating to Vickie's tortuous interference claim that would remain to be decided even after Vickie succeeded in defeating Pierce's defamation claim.]

In both Katchen and Langenkamp, moreover, the trustee bringing the preference action was asserting a right of recovery created by federal bankruptcy law. * * * Vickie's claim, in contrast, is in no way derived from or dependent upon bankruptcy law; it is a state tort action * * *.

3

Vickie additionally argues that the Bankruptcy Court's final judgment was constitutional because bankruptcy courts under the 1984 Act are properly deemed "adjuncts" of the district courts. We rejected a similar argument in Northern Pipeline, and our reasoning there holds true today.

* * * The new bankruptcy courts, like the old, do not "ma[k]e only specialized, narrowly confined factual determinations regarding a particularized area of law" or engage in "statutorily channeled factfinding functions." Northern Pipeline, 458 U.S., at 85 (plurality opinion). Instead, bankruptcy courts under the 1984 Act resolve "[a]ll matters of fact and law in whatever domains of the law to which" the parties' counterclaims might lead. Id., at 91 (Rehnquist, J., concurring in judgment).

In addition, whereas the adjunct agency in Crowell v. Benson "possessed only a limited power to issue compensation orders . . . [that] could be enforced only by order of the district court," Northern Pipeline, supra, at 85, a bankruptcy court resolving a counterclaim under 28 U.S.C. § 157(b)(2)(C) has the power to enter "appropriate orders and judgments"—including final judgments—subject to review only if a party chooses to appeal. * * * Given that authority, a bankruptcy court can no more be deemed a mere "adjunct" of the district court than a district court can be deemed such an "adjunct" of the court of appeals. * * *

It does not affect our analysis that * * * bankruptcy judges under the current Act are appointed by the Article III courts, rather than the President. If—as we have concluded—the bankruptcy court itself exercises "the essential attributes of judicial power [that] are reserved to Article III courts," Schor, 478 U.S., at 851 (internal quotation marks omitted), it does not matter who appointed the bankruptcy judge * * *.

D

Finally, Vickie and her amici predict as a practical matter that restrictions on a bankruptcy court's ability to hear and finally resolve compulsory counterclaims will create significant delays and impose additional costs on the bankruptcy process. It goes without saying that "the fact that a given law or procedure is efficient, convenient, and useful in facilitating functions of government, standing alone, will not save it if it is contrary to the Constitution." INS v. Chadha, 462 U.S. 919, 944 (1983).

* * * The dissent asserts that it is important that counterclaims such as Vickie's be resolved "in a bankruptcy court," and that, "to be effective, a single tribunal must have broad authority to restructure [debtor-creditor] relations." Post, at 2628, 2629 (emphasis deleted). But the framework Congress adopted in the 1984 Act already contemplates that certain state law matters in bankruptcy cases will be resolved by judges other than those of the bankruptcy courts. Section 1334(c)(2), for example, requires that bankruptcy courts abstain from hearing specified non-core, state law claims that "can be timely adjudicated[ ] in a State forum of appropriate jurisdiction." Section 1334(c)(1) similarly provides that bankruptcy courts may abstain from hearing any proceeding,

including core matters, "in the interest of comity with State courts or respect for State law."

* * *

If our decision today does not change all that much, then why the fuss? Is there really a threat to the separation of powers where Congress has conferred the judicial power outside Article III only over certain counterclaims in bankruptcy? The short but emphatic answer is yes. A statute may no more lawfully chip away at the authority of the Judicial Branch than it may eliminate it entirely. * * * We cannot compromise the integrity of the system of separated powers and the role of the Judiciary in that system, even with respect to challenges that may seem innocuous at first blush.

* * *

* * * The Bankruptcy Court below lacked the constitutional authority to enter a final judgment on a state law counterclaim that is not resolved in the process of ruling on a creditor's proof of claim. Accordingly, the judgment of the Court of Appeals is affirmed.

It is so ordered.

■ JUSTICE SCALIA, concurring.

I agree with the Court's interpretation of our Article III precedents, and I accordingly join its opinion. I adhere to my view, however, that—our contrary precedents notwithstanding—"a matter of public rights . . . must at a minimum arise between the government and others," Granfinanciera, S.A. v. Nordberg, 492 U.S. 33, 65 (1989) (SCALIA, J., concurring in part and concurring in judgment) (internal quotation marks omitted).

The sheer surfeit of factors that the Court was required to consider in this case should arouse the suspicion that something is seriously amiss with our jurisprudence * * *. I count at least seven different reasons * * * for concluding that an Article III judge was required to adjudicate this lawsuit: that it was one "under state common law" which was "not a matter that can be pursued only by grace of the other branches," *ante,* at 2614; that it was "not 'completely dependent upon' adjudication of a claim created by federal law," *ibid.*; that "Pierce did not truly consent to resolution of Vickie's claim in the bankruptcy court proceedings," *ibid.*; that "the asserted authority to decide Vickie's claim is not limited to a 'particularized area of the law,'" *ante,* at 2615; that "there was never any reason to believe that the process of adjudicating Pierce's proof of claim would necessarily resolve Vickie's counterclaim," *ante,* at 2617; that the trustee was not "asserting a right of recovery created by federal bankruptcy law," *ante,* at 2618; and that the Bankruptcy Judge "ha[d] the power to enter 'appropriate orders and judgments'—including final judgments—subject to review only if a party chooses to appeal," *ante,* at 2619.

Apart from their sheer numerosity, the more fundamental flaw in the many tests suggested by our jurisprudence is that they have nothing to do with the text or tradition of Article III. For example, Article III gives no indication that state-law claims have preferential entitlement to an Article III judge; nor does it make pertinent the extent to which the area of the law is "particularized." * * *

Leaving aside certain adjudications by federal administrative agencies, which are governed (for better or worse) by our landmark decision in Crowell v. Benson, 285 U.S. 22 (1932), in my view an Article III judge is required in all federal adjudications, unless there is a firmly established historical practice to the contrary. For that reason—and not because of some intuitive balancing of benefits and harms—I agree that Article III judges are not required in the context of territorial courts, courts-martial, or true "public rights" cases. Perhaps historical practice permits non-Article III judges to process claims against the bankruptcy estate; the subject has not been briefed, and so I state no position on the matter. But Vickie points to no historical practice that authorizes a non-Article III judge to adjudicate a counterclaim of the sort at issue here.

■ JUSTICE BREYER, with whom JUSTICE GINSBURG, JUSTICE SOTOMAYOR, and JUSTICE KAGAN join, dissenting.

* * *

I

My disagreement with the majority's conclusion stems in part from my disagreement about the way in which it interprets, or at least emphasizes, certain precedents. In my view, the majority overstates the current relevance of statements this Court made in * * * Murray's Lessee v. Hoboken Land & Improvement Co., 59 U.S. 272 (1856), and it overstates the importance of an analysis that did not command a Court majority in Northern Pipeline Constr. Co. v. Marathon Pipe Line Co., 458 U.S. 50 (1982), and that was subsequently disavowed. At the same time, I fear the Court understates the importance of a watershed opinion widely thought to demonstrate the constitutional basis for the current authority of administrative agencies to adjudicate private disputes, namely, Crowell v. Benson, 285 U.S. 22 (1932). And it fails to follow the analysis that this Court more recently has held applicable to the evaluation of claims of a kind before us here * * *. See Thomas v. Union Carbide Agricultural Products Co., 473 U.S. 568 (1985); Commodity Futures Trading Comm'n v. Schor, 478 U.S. 833 (1986).

* * *

A

In Murray's Lessee, the Court held that the Constitution permitted an executive official, through summary, nonjudicial proceedings, to attach the assets of a customs collector whose account was deficient. * * * In the course of its opinion, the Court wrote:

> "[W]e do not consider congress can either withdraw from judicial cognizance any matter which, from its nature, is the subject of a suit at the common law, or in equity, or admiralty; nor, on the other hand, can it bring under the judicial power a matter which, from its nature, is not a subject for judicial determination. At the same time there are matters, involving public rights, which may be presented in such form that the judicial power is capable of acting on them, and which are susceptible of judicial determination, but which congress may or may not bring within the cognizance of the courts of the United States, as it may deem proper." *Id.*, at 284.

The majority reads the first part of the statement's first sentence as authoritatively defining the boundaries of Article III. I would read the statement in a less absolute way. For one thing, the statement is in effect dictum. For another, it is the remainder of the statement, announcing a distinction between "public rights" and "private rights," that has had the more lasting impact. Later Courts have seized on that distinction when upholding non-Article III adjudication, not when striking it down. [Citing cases.] The one exception is Northern Pipeline * * *. But in that case [it was] a plurality, not a majority, [that] read the statement roughly in the way the Court does today.

B

At the same time, I believe the majority places insufficient weight on Crowell * * *. The Court assumed that an Article III court would review the agency's decision de novo in respect to questions of law but it would conduct a less searching review (looking to see only if the agency's award was "supported by evidence in the record") in respect to questions of fact. The Court pointed out that the case involved a dispute between private persons (a matter of "private rights") and (with one exception not relevant here) it upheld Congress' delegation of primary factfinding authority to the agency.

* * *

Crowell has been hailed as "the greatest of the cases validating administrative adjudication." Bator, *The Constitution as Architecture: Legislative and Administrative Courts Under Article III*, 65 .Ind. L.J. 233, 251 (1990) Yet, in a footnote, the majority distinguishes Crowell as a case in which the Court upheld the delegation of adjudicatory authority to an administrative agency simply because the agency's power to make the "specialized, narrowly confined factual determinations" at issue arising in a "particularized area of law," made the agency a "true 'adjunct' of the District Court." *Ante,* at 2612, n. 6. Were Crowell's holding as narrow as the majority suggests, one could question the validity of Congress' delegation of authority to adjudicate disputes among private parties to other agencies such as the National Labor Relations Board, the Commodity Futures Trading Commission, the Surface Transportation Board, and the Department of Housing and Urban Development * * *.

C

The majority, in my view, overemphasizes the precedential effect of the plurality opinion in Northern Pipeline. There, * * * [f]our Members of the Court wrote that Congress could grant adjudicatory authority to a non-Article III judge only where (1) the judge sits on a "territorial cour[t]" (2) the judge conducts a "court-martial," or (3) the case involves a "public right," namely, a "matter" that "at a minimum arise[s] 'between the government and others.'" 458 U.S., at 64–70 (plurality opinion) (quoting Ex parte Bakelite Corp., *supra,* at 451). Two other Members of the Court, without accepting these limitations, agreed with the result because the case involved a breach-of-contract claim brought by the bankruptcy trustee on behalf of the bankruptcy estate against a third party who was not part of the bankruptcy proceeding, and none of the Court's preceding cases (which, the two Members wrote, "do not admit of easy synthesis") had "gone so far as to sanction th[is] type of adjudication." 458 U.S., at 90–91 (Rehnquist, J. concurring in judgment).

Three years later, the Court held that Northern Pipeline

"establishes only that Congress may not vest in a non-Article III
court the power to adjudicate, render final judgment, and issue
binding orders in a traditional contract action arising under
state law, without consent of the litigants, and subject only to
ordinary appellate review." Thomas, 473 U.S., at 584.

D

* * * I would look to this Court's more recent Article III cases Thomas
and Schor—cases that commanded a clear majority. In both cases the
Court took a more pragmatic approach to the constitutional question. It
sought to determine whether, in the particular instance, the challenged
delegation of adjudicatory authority posed a genuine and serious threat
that one branch of Government sought to aggrandize its own
constitutionally delegated authority by encroaching upon a field of
authority that the Constitution assigns exclusively to another branch.

1

In Thomas, * * * [t]he statute in question required pesticide
manufacturers to submit to binding arbitration claims for compensation
owed for the use by one manufacturer of the data of another to support
its federal pesticide registration. * * * [T]he Court stated that "practical
attention to substance rather than doctrinaire reliance on formal
categories should inform application of Article III." Thomas, 473 U.S., at
587 (emphasis added). It indicated that Article III's requirements could
not be "determined" by "the identity of the parties alone," ibid., or by the
"private rights"/"public rights" distinction, id., at 585–586. And it upheld
the arbitration provision of the statute.

The Court pointed out that the right in question was created by a
federal statute, it "represent[s] a pragmatic solution to the difficult
problem of spreading [certain] costs," and the statute "does not preclude
review of the arbitration proceeding by an Article III court." Id., at 589–
592. The Court concluded:

"Given the nature of the right at issue and the concerns
motivating the Legislature, we do not think this system
threatens the independent role of the Judiciary in our
constitutional scheme." Id., at 590.

2

* * * The question at issue in Schor involved a delegation of authority
to an agency to adjudicate a counterclaim. A customer brought before the
Commodity Futures Trading Commission (CFTC) a claim for reparations
against his commodity futures broker. The customer noted that his
brokerage account showed that he owed the broker money, but he said
that the broker's unlawful actions had produced that debit balance, and
he sought damages. The broker brought a counterclaim seeking the
money that * * * the customer owed. This Court had to decide whether
agency adjudication of such a counterclaim is consistent with Article III.

In doing so, the Court expressly "declined to adopt formalistic and
unbending rules." Schor, 478 U.S., at 851. Rather, it "weighed a number
of factors, none of which has been deemed determinative, with an eye to
the practical effect that the congressional action will have on the
constitutionally assigned role of the federal judiciary." Ibid. Those

relevant factors include (1) "the origins and importance of the right to be adjudicated"; (2) "the extent to which the non-Article III forum exercises the range of jurisdiction and powers normally vested only in Article III courts"; (3) the extent to which the delegation nonetheless reserves judicial power for exercise by Article III courts; (4) the presence or "absence of consent to an initial adjudication before a non-Article III tribunal"; and (5) "the concerns that drove Congress to depart from" adjudication in an Article III court. *Id.*, at 849, 851.

The Court added that where "private rights," rather than "public rights" are involved, the "danger of encroaching on the judicial powers" is greater. *Id.*, at 853–854 (internal quotation marks omitted). Thus, while non-Article III adjudication of "private rights" is not necessarily unconstitutional, the Court's constitutional "examination" of such a scheme must be more "searching." *Ibid.*

Applying this analysis, the Court upheld the agency's authority to adjudicate the counterclaim. The Court conceded that the adjudication might be of a kind traditionally decided by a court and that the rights at issue were "private," not "public." *Id.*, at 853. But, the Court said, the CFTC deals only with a " 'particularized area of law' "; the decision to invoke the CFTC forum is "left entirely to the parties"; Article III courts can review the agency's findings of fact under "the same 'weight of the evidence' standard sustained in *Crowell*" and review its "legal determinations . . . de novo"; and the agency's "counterclaim jurisdiction" was necessary to make "workable" a "reparations procedure," which constitutes an important part of a congressionally enacted "regulatory scheme." *Id.*, at 852–856. The Court concluded that for these and other reasons "the magnitude of any intrusion on the Judicial Branch can only be termed de minimis." *Id.*, at 856.

II

A

This case law, as applied in *Thomas* and *Schor*, requires us to determine pragmatically whether a congressional delegation of adjudicatory authority to a non-Article III judge violates the separation-of-powers principles inherent in Article III. * * * [The relevant] factors include (1) the nature of the claim to be adjudicated; (2) the nature of the non-Article III tribunal; (3) the extent to which Article III courts exercise control over the proceeding; (4) the presence or absence of the parties' consent; and (5) the nature and importance of the legislative purpose served by the grant of adjudicatory authority to a tribunal with judges who lack Article III's tenure and compensation protections. The presence of "private rights" does not automatically determine the outcome of the question but requires a more "searching" examination of the relevant factors. *Schor*, *supra*, at 854.

Insofar as the majority would apply more formal standards, it simply disregards recent, controlling precedent.

B

Applying *Schor*'s approach here, I conclude that * * * [a] grant of authority to a bankruptcy court to adjudicate compulsory counterclaims does not violate any constitutional separation-of-powers principle related to Article III.

First, I concede that *the nature of the claim to be adjudicated* argues against my conclusion. Vickie Marshall's counterclaim—a kind of tort suit—resembles "a suit at the common law." Murray's Lessee, 18 How., at 284. * * *

At the same time the significance of this factor is mitigated here by the fact that bankruptcy courts often decide claims that similarly resemble various common-law actions. * * *

[Here, although the state law question arises in a counterclaim, that counterclaim is "compulsory" and thus its resolution will turn on facts at least related to those] at issue in a creditor's claim that is undisputedly proper for the bankruptcy court to decide.

Second, *the nature of the non-Article III tribunal* argues in favor of constitutionality. * * * [T]he tribunal is made up of judges who enjoy considerable protection from improper political influence. Unlike the 1978 Act which provided for the appointment of bankruptcy judges by the President with the advice and consent of the Senate, current law provides that the federal courts of appeals appoint federal bankruptcy judges. Bankruptcy judges are removable by the circuit judicial counsel (made up of federal court of appeals and district court judges) and only for cause. Their salaries are pegged to those of federal district court judges, and the cost of their courthouses and other work-related expenses are paid by the Judiciary. * * * [F]unctionally, bankruptcy judges can be compared to magistrate judges, law clerks, and the Judiciary's administrative officials, whose lack of Article III tenure and compensation protections do not endanger the independence of the Judicial Branch.

Third, *the control exercised by Article III judges over bankruptcy proceedings* argues in favor of constitutionality. * * * Any party may appeal * * * to the federal district court, where the federal judge will review all determinations of fact for clear error and will review all determinations of law de novo. But for the here-irrelevant matter of what Crowell considered to be special "constitutional" facts, the standard of review for factual findings here ("clearly erroneous") is more stringent than the standard at issue in Crowell (whether the agency's factfinding was "supported by evidence in the record"). 285 U.S., at 48; see Dickinson v. Zurko, 527 U.S. 150, 152, 153 (1999) ("unsupported by substantial evidence" more deferential than "clearly erroneous" (internal quotation marks omitted)). * * *

Moreover, in one important respect Article III judges maintain greater control over the bankruptcy court proceedings at issue here than they did over the relevant proceedings in any of the previous cases in which this Court has upheld a delegation of adjudicatory power. The District Court here may "withdraw, in whole or in part, any case or proceeding referred [to the Bankruptcy Court] . . . on its own motion or on timely motion of any party, for cause shown." 28 U.S.C. § 157(d).

Fourth, the fact that *the parties have consented* to Bankruptcy Court jurisdiction argues in favor of constitutionality, and strongly so. Pierce Marshall * * * appeared voluntarily in Bankruptcy Court as one of Vickie Marshall's creditors * * *. He need not have filed a claim, * * * for he says his claim is "nondischargeable," in which case he could have litigated it in a state or federal court after distribution. * * *

* * * In Granfinanciera, the Court held that when a bankruptcy trustee seeks to void a transfer of assets from the debtor to an individual [as] an unlawful "preference," the question of whether the individual has a right to a jury trial "depends upon whether the creditor has submitted a claim against the estate." The following year in Langenkamp v. Culp, 498 U.S. 42 (1990) (per curiam), the Court emphasized that when the individual files a claim against the estate, that individual has

> "trigger[ed] the process of 'allowance and disallowance of claims,' thereby subjecting himself to the bankruptcy court's equitable power. If the creditor is met, in turn, with a preference action from the trustee, that action becomes part of the claims-allowance process which is triable only in equity. In other words, the creditor's claim and the ensuing preference action by the trustee become integral to the restructuring of the debtor-creditor relationship through the bankruptcy court's equity jurisdiction." *Id.*, at 44 (quoting Granfinanciera, 492 U.S., at 58 (citations omitted).

As we have recognized, the jury trial question and the Article III question are highly analogous. And to that extent, Granfinanciera's and Langenkamp's basic reasoning and conclusion apply here: Even when private rights are at issue, non-Article III adjudication may be appropriate when both parties consent. The majority argues that Pierce Marshall "did not truly consent" to bankruptcy jurisdiction, but filing a proof of claim was sufficient in Langenkamp and Granfinanciera [and should be so here.]

Fifth, the nature and importance of the legislative purpose served by the grant of adjudicatory authority to bankruptcy tribunals argues strongly in favor of constitutionality.

* * * [T]o be effective, a single tribunal must have broad authority to restructure those relations, "having jurisdiction of the parties to controversies brought before them," "decid[ing] all matters in dispute," and "decree[ing] complete relief." Katchen v. Landy, 382 U.S. 323, 335 (1966) (internal quotation marks omitted).

The restructuring process requires a creditor to file a proof of claim in the bankruptcy court. In doing so, the creditor "triggers the process of 'allowance and disallowance of claims,' thereby subjecting himself to the bankruptcy court's equitable power." Langenkamp, *supra*, at 44 (quoting Granfinanciera, *supra,* at 58). By filing a proof of claim, the creditor agrees to the bankruptcy court's resolution of that claim, and if the creditor wins, the creditor will receive a share of the distribution of the bankruptcy estate. When the bankruptcy estate has a related claim against that creditor, that counterclaim may offset the creditor's claim, or even yield additional damages that augment the estate and may be distributed to the other creditors.

* * *

Consequently a bankruptcy court's determination of [counterclaims] * * * plays a critical role in Congress' constitutionally based effort to create an efficient, effective federal bankruptcy system. At the least, that is what Congress concluded. We owe deference to that determination, which shows the absence of any legislative or executive motive * * * to encroach upon areas that Article III reserves to judges to whom it grants tenure and compensation protections.

Considering these factors together, I conclude that, as in Schor, "the magnitude of any intrusion on the Judicial Branch can only be termed *de minimis.*" 478 U.S., at 856. * * *

III

The majority predicts that as a "practical matter" today's decision "does not change all that much." *Ante,* at 2619–2620. But I doubt that is so. Consider a typical case: A tenant files for bankruptcy. The landlord files a claim for unpaid rent. The tenant asserts a counterclaim for damages suffered by the landlord's (1) failing to fulfill his obligations as lessor, and (2) improperly recovering possession of the premises by misrepresenting the facts in housing court. (These are close to the facts presented in In re Beugen, 81 B.R. 994 (Bkrtcy.Ct.N.D.Cal.1988).) This state-law counterclaim does not "ste[m] from the bankruptcy itself," *ante,* at 2618, it would not "necessarily be resolved in the claims allowance process," *ibid.*, and it would require the debtor to prove damages suffered by the lessor's failures, the extent to which the landlord's representations to the housing court were untrue, and damages suffered by improper recovery of possession of the premises, cf. *ante,* at 2617–2618. Thus, under the majority's holding, the federal district judge, not the bankruptcy judge, would have to hear and resolve the counterclaim.

Why is that a problem? * * * Because the volume of bankruptcy cases is staggering, involving almost 1.6 million filings last year, compared to a federal district court docket of around 280,000 civil cases and 78,000 criminal cases. Because unlike the "related" non-core state law claims that bankruptcy courts must abstain from hearing, see *ante,* at 2619, compulsory counterclaims involve the same factual disputes as the claims that may be finally adjudicated by the bankruptcy courts. Because under these circumstances, a constitutionally required game of jurisdictional ping-pong between courts would lead to inefficiency, increased cost, delay, and needless additional suffering among those faced with bankruptcy.

For these reasons, with respect, I dissent.

FURTHER NOTE ON LEGISLATIVE COURTS

(1) Distinguishing Legislative Courts from Administrative Agencies. Chief Justice Roberts emphasized that the non-Article III tribunal in Stern was a *court*, not an agency, and calls its adjudication a "prototypical exercise of judicial power". What is the difference between a legislative court and an administrative agency, and how does it bear on the appropriateness of adjudication outside of Article III? Indeed, aren't bankruptcy judges far freer from control by the political branches than adjudicators in administrative agencies, which are subject to congressional oversight and some measure of presidential influence and are typically led by political appointees?

Consider the relevance of the following generalizations (which are subject to significant exceptions):

(a) Policymaking Functions. Administrative agencies typically engage in rulemaking as well as adjudication, and are permitted to choose between and coordinate those processes to serve policy goals. See Shapiro, *The Choice of Rulemaking or Adjudication in the Development of Administrative Policy*, 78 Harv.L.Rev. 921 (1965). (Administrative law judges (ALJs), who characteristically make initial or recommended decisions, generally are not policymakers, but policymaking officials often review, and/or have some authority to establish standards and procedures governing, ALJs' decisions.) By contrast, legislative courts are less likely to have policymaking responsibilities.

(b) Enforceability of Judgments. The decisions of administrative agencies often are not self-executing, but (as in Crowell v. Benson) instead require an enforcement action in a federal court. By contrast, the decisions of legislative courts (including the bankruptcy courts) are typically final and enforceable unless appealed. See Redish, *Legislative Courts, Administrative Agencies, and the Northern Pipeline Decision*, 1983 Duke L.J. 197, 216–17.

(c) Traditions of Justification. According to Fallon, *Of Legislative Courts, Administrative Agencies, and Article III*, 101 Harv.L.Rev. 915, 920–26, 946–47 (1988), agency adjudication, at least since Crowell v. Benson, has frequently been justified *under* Article III on the theory that agencies are "adjuncts" or that judicial review of the agency's decisionmaking retains "the essential elements" of the judicial power in an Article III court. By contrast, legislative courts have usually been justified as permissible "exceptions" to Article III's requirement of tenure and salary protection (although they are sometimes subject to Article III review as well).

(2) Why Not Article III Status?

(a) Bankruptcy Judges. Congress could have constituted the bankruptcy courts as Article III courts. But in connection with the Bankruptcy Reform Act of 1978 (the statute that was invalidated in Northern Pipeline), the organized federal judiciary lobbied against doing so, arguing that the Article III judiciary must remain relatively small to retain the elite status that has traditionally attracted first-rate lawyers to the federal bench. See Countryman, *Scrambling to Define Bankruptcy Jurisdiction: The Chief Justice, the Judicial Conference, and the Legislative Process*, 22 Harv.J. On Legis. 1, 7–12 (1985). (For a brief discussion and citations to some of the relevant literature addressing this argument, see pp. 42–43, *supra*.) Could Congress have addressed that concern by making bankruptcy judgeships less remunerative or prestigious in various respects than other Article III judgeships? In the end, how strong is the argument for making bankruptcy courts non-Article III courts?

(b) Administrative Adjudicators. Note the difficulties with trying to reconstitute other non-Article III tribunals—including the literally thousands of officials exercising adjudicative authority in administrative agencies—as Article III courts whose decisionmakers have life tenure: (i) a large, new cost to phasing programs in and out would be introduced; (ii) it would obstruct agencies from using adjudication as a policymaking vehicle and from coordinating rulemaking and adjudication, for policymakers could not control Article III administrative judges, while any appeal of decisions by an ALJ to "the agency" would raise a problem of impermissible executive revision of the judgment of an Article III tribunal; and (iii) the number of adjudicators who would have to be approved by the (sometimes dysfunctional) Senatorial confirmation process would mushroom. See generally Chap. II, Sec. 2, pp. 87–88, *supra*. Do these considerations provide stronger arguments for non-Article III adjudication than were present in Stern? On the other hand, to what extent is the point of Article III to deny politically responsive policymakers the authority to control adjudication?

(3) The (In)Significance of Crowell v. Benson. Northern Pipeline and Stern v. Marshall treat legislative courts and adjuncts as distinct categories, and view Crowell as involving the latter. That approach limits the generative force of Crowell as a precedent that can validate non-Article III tribunals that do not fit the agency model. By contrast, cases like Thomas and Schor tended to run the categories together and look at a wide range of factors in determining the constitutionality of a particular tribunal, and Justice Breyer's dissent takes that approach. But did his argument concerning Congress' power to substitute legislative courts for constitutional courts contain any limiting principle?

Was this also a problem with the government's "adjuncts" argument? Was the degree of oversight by Article III courts really that much less in Stern v. Marshall than in Crowell v. Benson? With respect to adjudicatory independence, how significant is it that judgments of the bankruptcy court were self-executing unless appealed, whereas the orders of the agency in Crowell required judicial enforcement? That bankruptcy courts' jurisdiction is not specialized but ranges broadly over diverse areas of law? That the tribunal in Stern, unlike the one in Crowell, resolved state rather than federal law claims?

On the last point, note that federal territorial courts (including the local courts of the District of Columbia) exercise jurisdiction over state law claims, and that the political branches might be more tempted to compromise adjudicatory independence with respect to federal law issues arising in congressionally created programs.

(4) Developments Between Northern Pipeline and Stern v. Marshall. As both the Chief Justice and Justice Breyer note, between Northern Pipeline and Stern the Supreme Court addressed the validity of an Article I tribunal in several cases.

(a) Thomas v. Union Carbide Agricultural Products Co. This 1985 decision arose under the Federal Insecticide, Fungicide, and Rodenticide Act (FIFRA), 7 U.S.C. § 136 *et seq.*, which requires manufacturers of pesticides, in order to obtain the registration necessary to market a new product, to submit extensive data to the EPA concerning the product's health and environmental effects. The statute permits the EPA to use data previously submitted by another registrant in considering the application of a later ("me-too" or "follow-on") registrant—but only if the later registrant agrees to compensate the original data submitter. If the original and follow-up registrants cannot agree on appropriate compensation, the issue must be submitted to binding arbitration before a private arbitrator, whose decision is subject to judicial review only for "fraud, misrepresentation, or other misconduct". 7 U.S.C. § 136a(c)(1)(D)(ii).

In upholding the statute's arbitration provision, Justice O'Connor's opinion for the Court stated that "an absolute construction of Article III is not possible" and "the Court has long recognized that Congress is not barred from acting pursuant to its powers under Article I to vest decisionmaking authority in tribunals that lack the attributes of Article III courts". The lead opinion in Northern Pipeline had spoken only for a plurality, Justice

O'Connor emphasized. In addition, it adopted too categorical an approach in suggesting that the public rights/private rights dichotomy provides a bright-line test for determining the requirements of Article III and that the public rights category includes only cases in which the government is a party. Instead, "[t]he enduring lesson of Crowell is that practical attention to substance rather than doctrinaire reliance on formal categories should inform application of Article III."

Turning to the dispute before it, the Court distinguished Northern Pipeline because here the claim rested on federal law, and distinguished Crowell because the federal claim did not replace a pre-existing state law right to compensation. Although the liability of one private party to another was at stake, the right to compensation under FIFRA "is not a purely 'private' right but bears many of the characteristics" of a public rights dispute, apparently because it arose under a complex regulatory scheme. The crucial point did not involve categorization, however. The administrative scheme represented "a pragmatic solution to the difficult problem of spreading the costs of generating adequate information regarding the safety, health, and environmental impact of a potentially dangerous product". The arbitration mechanism "incorporates its own system of internal sanctions and relies only tangentially, if at all, on the Judicial Branch for enforcement. The danger of Congress or the Executive encroaching on the Article III judicial powers is at a minimum when no unwilling defendant is subjected to judicial enforcement". Finally, "FIFRA limits but does not preclude review of the arbitration proceeding by an Article III court", since awards can be set aside for "fraud, misconduct or misrepresentation" and "review of constitutional error is preserved".[1]

Justice Brennan, joined by Justices Blackmun and Marshall, concurred in the judgment. After noting that the Northern Pipeline plurality (which he wrote) had "concluded that at a minimum public rights disputes must arise 'between the Government and others' ", he seemed to shift gears, stating that (though the matter was not free from doubt) the FIFRA compensation scheme "should be viewed as involving a matter of public rights * * *. [T]he dispute arises in the context of a federal regulatory scheme that virtually occupies the field. * * * This case * * * involves not only the congressional prescription of a federal rule of decision to govern a private dispute but also the active participation of a federal regulatory agency in resolving the dispute. Although a compensation dispute under FIFRA ultimately involves a determination of the duty owed one private party by another, at its heart the dispute involves the exercise of authority by a Federal Government arbitrator in the course of administration of FIFRA's comprehensive regulatory scheme."

Note that in Thomas, the majority treated the restricted scope of judicial review as a virtue rather than a possible defect, stressing that the arbitration mechanism "relies only tangentially, if at all, on the Judicial Branch for enforcement." Does that have matters backwards? But consider the restricted scope of review party by party. The follow-on registrant consented to arbitration, thereby perhaps waiving at least aspects of its rights to Article III review. And the original registrant, who did not consent, is not a defendant in an enforcement proceeding, where rights to Article III review

---

[1]   Because the parties had abandoned any due process claim, the Court did not consider that question, but said that because "review of constitutional error is preserved", FIFRA "does not obstruct whatever judicial review might be required by due process".

are at their apex, but instead a claimant seeking affirmative relief. Justice O'Connor did note that "[t]he danger of Congress or the Executive encroaching on the Article III judicial powers is at a minimum when no unwilling defendant is subjected to judicial enforcement". Can a distinction between the Article III rights of plaintiffs and defendants bear the weight the Court places on it?

(b) CFTC v. Schor. This decision, handed down one year after Thomas, is described by both the majority and dissenting opinions in Stern v. Marshall. The majority opinion in Schor stressed that the CFTC regime differed from the traditional agency model of Crowell in just one respect: the authorization of a permissive state law counterclaim by the broker against its customer. Acknowledging that the Court's scrutiny has been searching when private rights under state law are involved, the majority found no substantial threat to the separation of powers and refused to endorse a prohibition on an agency's exercising a form of supplemental jurisdiction out of fear of a slippery slope. The Schor Court both noted how limited the departure from Crowell was (as Chief Justice Roberts' opinion in Stern stresses) and endorsed the Thomas decision's "practical attention to substance rather than doctrinaire reliance on formal categories" in assessing whether a particular scheme is constitutional (as Justice Breyer's dissent in Stern stresses).

(c) Granfinanciera, S.A. v. Nordberg. This 1989 decision was actually about whether there is a right to jury trial, in a bankruptcy proceeding, with respect to a fraudulent conveyance action, based on federal statutory law, filed on behalf of a bankruptcy estate against a noncreditor. The Court suggested that the jury trial question tracked the question of the constitutionality of using a non-Article III tribunal: in an action at law, "if Congress may assign the adjudication of a statutory cause of action to a non-Article III tribunal, then the Seventh Amendment poses no independent bar to the adjudication of that action by a nonjury factfinder". The decision is particularly confusing, but for present purposes its significance lies (a) in its assigning greater importance to the public/private distinction than had Thomas or Schor, and also (b) in its reliance, in Justice Brennan's opinion for the Court, on the reformulation of the public rights doctrine offered in his concurring opinion in Thomas, which "rejected the view that 'a matter of public right must at a minimum arise between the government and others'. * * * The crucial question, in cases not involving the Federal Government, is whether 'Congress * * * [has] create[d] a seemingly 'private' right that is so closely integrated into a public regulatory scheme as to be a matter appropriate for agency resolution with limited involvement by the Article III judiciary' ". The Court found that the fraudulent conveyance action was a private right.)[2]

[handwritten margin note: 7 am. only applies to art. III]

[handwritten margin note: public reg. scheme involvement]

---

[2] In Granfinanciera, the lower courts had rejected the defendants' claimed right to a jury trial on the ground that an action to recover a fraudulent conveyance is equitable, not legal. The Supreme Court reversed that determination. Justice Brennan's opinion for the Court then declared that under both Article III and the Seventh Amendment, the crucial inquiry was whether the right to recover a fraudulent conveyance should be viewed as "public" or "private". Finally, having determined that the right was private and hence that defendants were entitled to a jury trial, Justice Brennan noted two questions to be decided upon remand: (i) whether the bankruptcy courts possessed statutory authority to conduct jury trials in fraudulent conveyance actions, and (ii) whether it is consistent with the Seventh Amendment, and Article III, for non-Article III bankruptcy judges to conduct jury trials, subject to the oversight of federal district courts.

(5) What Is a Public Right? If you don't feel that you know a public right when you see it, or that you don't understand how significant the public/private distinction is, that may be because of the dizzying array of formulations that the Court has offered in recent decisions. Some decisions, like Crowell and Justice Scalia's opinion in Stern v. Marshall, suggest that it is a necessary condition that the United States be a party to the case. Thomas rejected that idea, stating that even though the case involved the liability of one private party to another, it was not a "purely" private right, and bore many characteristics of a public right, apparently because it arose under a complex federal regulatory scheme; Thomas also downplayed the significance of the distinction, a viewpoint that was echoed in Schor. In Stern, the Court notes the varied formulations of past cases and does not offer its own, simply arguing that the circumstances there are distinguishable from prior cases finding that a claim was a public right or that it bore many characteristics of one.

Although Stern uses the public/private line as a basis for invalidation, that line has frequently been drawn for the express purpose of excluding from the courts altogether civil disputes between citizens and the government.[3] Isn't the public rights tradition, if deployed in order to protect the role of Article III courts in enforcing citizens' rights, a two-edged sword at best?

If one were to return to first principles, is the public/private distinction intelligible, and useful, in considering the appropriateness of adjudication outside of Article III?[4] Consider whether the presence of the United States

---

Justice Scalia concurred in part and concurred in the judgment, advancing themes similar to those expressed in his concurring opinion in Stern v. Marshall. Justice White's dissent (with which Justices Blackmun and O'Connor expressed general agreement) took a far broader view of public rights, and criticized the Court for "call[ing] into question the longstanding assumption * * * that the equitable proceedings of [bankruptcy] courts, adjudicating creditor-debtor disputes," involve public rights. Justice White also argued that "[h]istory and our cases support the proposition that the right to a jury trial depends not solely on the nature of the issue to be resolved, but also on the forum in which it is to be resolved". He concluded that in a court of equity, where a jury trial would be anomalous, the Seventh Amendment does not apply.

If the jury trial and Article III questions are coextensive, as the Court says in an early part of the Granfinanciera opinion, then how can the Court (a) go on to determine that there is a jury trial right under the Seventh Amendment because the matter is one of private right, and at the same time (b) leave open the question whether the jury trial may be conducted in a bankruptcy court before a non-Article III bankruptcy judge?

Would trial by jury, even in a non-Article III federal court, alleviate many of the concerns about political pressure that underlie Article III? (Pub.L.No. 103–394, 108 Stat. 4106, § 112 amends 28 U.S.C. § 157 to provide: "(e) If the right to a jury trial applies in a proceeding that may be heard * * * by a bankruptcy judge, the bankruptcy judge may conduct the jury trial if specially designated to exercise such jurisdiction by the district court and with the express consent of all the parties.")

[3] See, *e.g.*, Strauss, *The Place of the Agencies in Government: Separation of Powers and the Fourth Branch*, 84 Colum.L.Rev. 573, 632 (1984). See also Nelson, *Adjudication in the Political Branches*, 107 Colum.L.Rev. 559, 627 (2007) (arguing that "[a]s a matter of both historical practice and current doctrine, the line between political and judicial power in our democracy depends crucially on" whether "core private rights of individuals" are at stake).

[4] For an argument that confusion will persist as long as the law is organized around this distinction, see Chemerinsky, *Ending the Marathon: It Is Time to Overrule Northern Pipeline*, 65 Am.Bankr.L.J. 311, 314–16 (1991). See also Redish & LaFave, *Seventh Amendment Right to Jury Trial in Non-Article III Proceedings: A Study in Dysfunctional Constitutional Theory*, 4 Wm. & Mary Bill Rts.J. 407 (1995), and Klein, *The Validity of the Public Rights Doctrine in Light of the Historical Rationale of the Seventh Amendment*, 21 Hast.Const.L.Q. 1013 (1994), both arguing, *inter alia*, that the public rights exception to the Seventh Amendment lacks sound foundations in history and doctrine.

as a party, if not a sufficient condition, should at least be a necessary one in order for a case to fall into the public rights category. If so, then the law might sharply distinguish between (a) an agency like the NLRB, in which the United States commences agency proceedings (but does so after having received a complaint by a private party), and (b) an agency like those in Crowell, Thomas, and Schor, in which one private party commences agency proceedings against another.

If the United States must be a party, does that call into question the longstanding jurisdiction of bankruptcy courts to adjudicate claims against the estate and to work out priorities and confer discharges? Note that Chief Justice Roberts states that no party asked the Court to consider that question. If a party in a future case does ask, what weight should the Court give to the tradition, which has deep roots in English and American practice, that bankruptcy adjudication extends to the administration of the estate and to the disposition of claims against it, but not to actions seeking to obtain property to augment the estate? See Brubaker, *Article III's Bleak House (Part I): The Statutory Limits of Bankruptcy Judges' Core Jurisdiction*, 31 No.8 Bankr.L.Letter 1 (2011).

Should the idea of public rights be limited to situations in which the matter can be resolved with no judicial involvement—in which case, there can be little complaint about providing (gratuitously) some judicial review? This might be true, for example, of an individual's claim for monetary relief to be paid by the government; direct judicial review of the Executive Branch's resolution of such claims is ordinarily barred by sovereign immunity (assuming Congress has not waived it).[5] On that view, much agency adjudication, in which the government is imposing a sanction against an individual, would have to be rationalized on a different basis—perhaps on an adjunct theory or some variant of it. Indeed, note that Justice Breyer's dissent in Stern fears that the Court calls into question the validity of a range of longstanding administrative agencies like the NLRB, CFTC, and HUD, while the majority simply says that those tribunals are distinguishable without necessarily blessing them; and Justice Scalia injects a note of skepticism when he mentions "certain adjudications by federal administrative agencies, which are governed (for better or worse) by our landmark decision in *Crowell v. Benson*".

(6) Formal Versus Functional Approaches and the Search for Constitutional Limits.

(a) The functional approach of Justice Breyer's dissent and the cases on which it relies (Thomas and Schor) is hard to square with the rigid view of the separation of powers adopted in INS v. Chadha, 462 U.S. 919 (1983) (holding legislative veto provisions constitutionally invalid), and Bowsher v. Synar, 478 U.S. 714 (1986) (invalidating a statute designed to trigger federal budgets cuts on the ground that it vested executive functions in an employee potentially subject to congressional influence). At the same time, the "formalist" approach of Chadha and Bowsher may be difficult to reconcile with Crowell v. Benson, more generally with the assignment of a mix of executive, rulemaking, and adjudicative functions to administrative agencies, see generally Strauss, *Formal and Functional Approaches to*

---

[5] Sovereign immunity would not necessarily bar a claim against a federal official involving the same matter in dispute, but that claim differs from one against the government itself.

Separation of Powers Questions—A Foolish Inconsistency?, 72 Cornell L.Rev. 488 (1987), and most generally with a capacity for institutional innovation.

Chief Justice Roberts touted his more formal approach as a protection against a series of pragmatic decisions, each seemingly innocuous, that collectively deprive the courts of their fundamental role in the constitutional scheme. He worried that Vickie Marshall, and the dissent, had failed to furnish an adequate "limiting principle".

On the other hand, the Court's opinion, while distinguishing prior cases, does not set forth a generalized understanding about how to assess the constitutionality of a diverse array of existing (not to mention possible future) institutions. And as Justice Scalia noted, it adverts to a large number of considerations whose relative importance is unclear. Those considerations include:

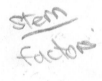

(i) the claim did not fall under any of the varying formulations of a public right (*e.g.*, its pursuit did not depend upon the grace of the political branches, it did not derive from a federal regulatory scheme, or its resolution by an expert government agency was not essential to a limited regulatory objective within the agency's authority);

(ii) the claim rested on state common law rather than federal law;

(iii) the claim was independent of bankruptcy law and would not necessarily be resolved by other aspects of the bankruptcy court's adjudication;[6]

(iv) the tribunal at issue was a court, not an agency;

(v) the jurisdiction of the bankruptcy courts is not particularized but reaches any area of the law;

(vi) the bankruptcy court can enter orders and judgments—including final judgments—subject to review only if a party chooses to appeal; and

(vii) at least one party (Pierce) did not voluntarily consent.

(b) While defending its more formal approach, the Court also contends that its decision will not have dire consequence. Chief Justice Roberts

---

[6] For an effort to define the appropriate scope of jurisdiction exercised by bankruptcy judges, see Casey & Huq, *The Article III Problem in Bankruptcy*, 82 U.Chi.L.Rev. ___ (forthcoming 2015). After highlighting the Stern Court's statement that a bankruptcy judge may resolve only those matters whose resolution "is integral to the restructuring of the debtor-creditor relationship", the authors rely on the "creditors' bargain" theory of bankruptcy to identify those matters. That theory, widely but not universally endorsed by scholars, views bankruptcy law as responding to a collective action problem faced by creditors when a debtor is under financial distress. Substantive bankruptcy rules, this theory posits, should mirror a hypothetical bargain that creditors would have made with each other *ex ante* absent transaction costs. On this view, however, bankruptcy law should not otherwise alter the parties' rights and obligations. Casey and Huq contend that the creditors' bargain theory has implications not only for substantive rules but also for the procedures followed in bankruptcy cases. In their view, if an issue does not affect the creditors' collective relationship, the creditors' hypothetical bargain would not have provided for bankruptcy jurisdiction over that issue and hence such jurisdiction should not be exercised.

Casey and Huq contend that their approach would not only respect the separation of powers, but would also be sensitive to a federalism concern at which the Stern Court gestured— the problem of having bankruptcy courts deciding state law questions. Bankruptcy jurisdiction, they say, has the potential to cast a shadow on state-court adjudication of state-created rights. They assert that Article III judges will be more sensitive than bankruptcy judges to the risk that bankruptcy jurisdiction could distort parallel state processes, because Article III judges are not only nominated by the President and confirmed by the Senate, but also are tasked with enforcing constitutional federalism values.

suggests that claims like the counterclaim in Stern, which the jurisdictional statute unconstitutionally assigns to bankruptcy courts for final adjudication, may instead be initially assigned to the bankruptcy courts to make proposed findings of fact and conclusions of law, to be reviewed de novo by the district court. In Executive Benefits Ins. Agency v. Arkison, 134 S.Ct. 2165 (2014), a unanimous Court held that the jurisdictional statute authorizes that approach. But given the volume of cases noted by Justice Breyer, is it realistic to expect that district judges will truly engage in de novo decisionmaking?

7. The Significance of Consent. To what extent can litigant consent validate an adjudication that might otherwise be constitutionally questionable?

(a) Individual Versus Structural Interests. The Stern decision contends that Article III protects both the personal rights of litigants and the structural interest in the separation of powers. The Schor decision, after drawing the same distinction, argued that litigants can waive their personal rights, but when the structural concern is implicated, consent cannot cure any constitutional difficulty. In his dissent in Schor, Justice Brennan contended that the distinction between personal and structural interests was artificial: individual interests are at risk only when federal adjudicators are subject to congressional or executive pressure. He then contended that consent should have no weight in assessing the validity of non-Article III adjudication.

Could one accept Justice Brennan's view that the two interests are inseparable without accepting his conclusion that consent is not relevant? Justice Brennan viewed the matter as similar to the inability of litigants to consent to Article III adjudication when the courts lack subject matter jurisdiction. But consider other analogies: (a) litigants who consent to private arbitration of a matter that otherwise would have fallen within the jurisdiction of the Article III courts; or (b) a litigant who might have a valid constitutional argument resting on the separation of powers but chooses not to assert that argument. (For example, even if the scheme in Crowell v. Benson was constitutional only if appellate review in an Article III tribunal is required, no litigant is obliged to seek such review.) Which analogy is more convincing? See also p. 393, *infra*.

The Stern decision, because it finds that Pierce did not really consent to bankruptcy court adjudication, does not clearly indicate what role consent should play when it does in fact exist. That question is discussed further in the Note on Magistrate Judges that follows this Note.

(b) The Voluntariness of Consent. What constitutes *valid* consent? On the facts of Schor, the claim of consent was very strong, given Schor's motion to dismiss the parallel Article III court proceeding because of the pendency of the CFTC proceeding. But the Court said more broadly that merely proceeding before the CFTC constituted consent to a counterclaim. When federal programs provide for compulsory arbitration of disputes, has every participant consented to arbitration simply by participating in the program? See generally Bruff, *Public Programs, Private Deciders: The Constitutionality of Arbitration in Federal Programs*, 67 Tex.L.Rev. 441 (1989).

But in Stern, the Court is far more skeptical about notions of constructive consent. On the facts there presented, doesn't the Chief Justice have the better of the argument? Pierce's initial request for a declaration of non-dischargeability very likely stemmed from uncertainty on that score. If his choice was either to file in bankruptcy court or to accept a non-trivial risk of forfeiting his claim if it was later deemed to have been discharged, how "voluntary" was his consent to counterclaim jurisdiction?

(8) The Right to Jury Trial Before Non-Article III Tribunals. To what extent does the right to jury trial constrain Congress' ability to establish non-Article III tribunals? Until the Granfinanciera decision, the precedents suggested that the Seventh Amendment has little if any applicability to adjudication before administrative agencies.

(a) In NLRB v. Jones & Laughlin Steel Corp., 301 U.S. 1 (1937), in rejecting a Seventh Amendment challenge to an NLRB decision awarding back pay and reinstatement to union members whom the company had unlawfully dismissed, the Court said: "[The Seventh Amendment] has no application to cases where recovery of money damages is an incident to equitable relief even though damages might have been recovered in an action at law. It does not apply where the proceeding is not in the nature of a suit at common law.

"The instant case is not a suit at common law or in the nature of such a suit. The proceeding is one unknown to the common law. Reinstatement of the employee and payment for time lost are requirements imposed for violation of the statute and are remedies appropriate to its enforcement."

(b) Several decades later, the Court said that Jones & Laughlin "merely stands for the proposition that the Seventh Amendment is generally inapplicable in administrative proceedings, where jury trials would be incompatible with the whole concept of administrative adjudication and would substantially interfere with the NLRB's role in the statutory scheme". Curtis v. Loether, 415 U.S. 189, 194 (1974). But in Curtis, the Court held that Jones & Laughlin did not govern, as the action—one between private parties, under a federal civil rights law—was brought in a regular Article III court. The Supreme Court ruled that the Seventh Amendment conferred a right to jury trial.

(c) Finally, in Atlas Roofing Co. v. Occupational Safety & Health Review Comm'n, 430 U.S. 442 (1977), the Court upheld an agency's assessment of a civil money penalty for violation of workplace safety regulations. Relying on the distinction between public and private rights, the Court said: "At least in cases in which public rights are being litigated—*e.g.*, cases in which the Government sues in its sovereign capacity to enforce public rights created by statutes within the power of Congress to enact—the Seventh Amendment does not prohibit Congress from assigning the factfinding function and initial adjudication to an administrative forum with which the jury would be incompatible".[7]

(9) Surveying the Landscape. Few observers would view the Supreme Court's shifting decisions in this area as having provided a coherent

---

[7]   Sward, *Legislative Courts, Article III, and the Seventh Amendment*, 77 N.C.L.Rev. 1037 (1999), argues that the Seventh Amendment serves values distinct from those reflected in Article III—including citizen participation and securing deliberative, unanimous decisions. More generally, she finds "good reasons" for upholding a far broader right to jury trial than is currently recognized, "regardless of the nature of the [tribunal] in which the matter is pending". But acknowledging that a broader right would seriously disrupt administrative agencies and legislative courts, she concludes that "maintaining the status quo, however weak its constitutional base, may be more pragmatic and therefore more attractive."

approach to the general question of the constitutionality of non-Article III
adjudication. Consider the plausibility of the following alternatives:

(a) **Article III Exclusivity.** A polar position would read Article III as
mandating that all federal adjudicative tribunals must be Article III courts.
As the early development of "exceptions" indicates, however, it is highly
doubtful that this approach represented the original understanding of
Congress' power, and as Professor Bator noted, there is a deep conceptual
problem in seeking to distinguish adjudication from routine execution of the
laws. (You may wish to review his discussion quoted on p. 352, *supra*.) In any
event, by the time of the Northern Pipeline decision, wasn't it clearly too late
to upset the myriad schemes of federal non-Article III adjudication—by both
legislative courts and administrative agencies—already in existence?

(b) **Historical Exceptions.** The cases appear, for the moment, to
accept a short list of exceptions to Article III (territorial courts, courts
martial, and some combination of public rights cases and agency
adjudication) as having been legitimated by a mixture of textual analysis
and tradition. But the approach in Stern, like that in Northern Pipeline,
strongly suggests that further exceptions will be hard if not impossible to
justify. Isn't this categorical approach hard to apply and to justify without
the identification of some guiding principles?

(c) **Necessary and Proper Test.** At the opposite pole from Article III
exclusivity would be an approach that views Article III as indifferent as to
whether jurisdiction is vested in an Article III court, a legislative court, or
an administrative agency. The only relevant questions would be whether use
of a non-Article III federal tribunal was "necessary and proper" under Article
I and whether it offended some other constitutional provision, such as the
Due Process Clause or the Seventh Amendment.

(d) **Balancing.** Justice White, who dissented in Northern Pipeline,
appeared there to endorse a case-by-case balancing approach, in which
Article III values are weighed against the interests supporting adjudication
by a non-Article III federal tribunal. All balancing tests raise a question
whether courts can adequately specify which interests ought to count in the
balance and how they ought to be weighed. Is that problem especially
difficult in this context?

(e) **Appellate Review.** A final position, resting on the approach in
Crowell v. Benson, would treat sufficiently searching appellate review by an
Article III court as both necessary and sufficient to legitimate initial
adjudication by a federal legislative court or administrative agency. See
Fallon, p. 380, *supra*.[8] This approach claims the virtue of drawing only clear

---

8 Professor Merrill, in *Article III, Agency Adjudication, and the Origins of the Appellate
Review Model of Administrative Law*, 111 Colum.L.Rev. 939 (2011), provides a careful historical
study of the origins of the appellate review model of agency adjudication, which he views as hardly
inevitable. The nineteenth century, he suggests, featured a "bipolar", all-or-nothing model in which
courts either reviewed administrative action under one of the prerogative writs (like mandamus
or habeas corpus), on a record produced in court, or afforded no review at all. He locates the origins
of the modern appellate review model in the Supreme Court's retreat from its aggressive, and
politically controversial, review of decisions of the Interstate Commerce Commission in the 1890s
and 1900s, and contends that the approach then spread to other areas. Merrill suggests that while
today scholars worry about whether the appellate review model permits the dilution of judicial
power, the earlier concern was that Article III courts would be contaminated by being drawn into
matters of administration, a concern that the appellate review model largely eliminated. Moving
to the present, he doubts that the current allocation of authority—in which judges decide legal
issues, while deferring to agencies on factual matters—is optimal, given the close ties of law to
policy and the greater expertise and accountability of agencies as policymakers. (The Chevron

and enforceable lines.[9] As the price for doing so, it eschews efforts to inquire closely into the necessity or desirability of initial adjudication by a legislative court or administrative agency in a particular case. Compare Saphire & Solimine, *Shoring Up Article III: Legislative Court Doctrine in the Post CFTC v. Schor Era*, 68 B.U.L.Rev. 85, 135–51 (1988) (suggesting that review by an Article III court should be viewed as necessary, but not sufficient, to validate adjudication by a legislative court or administrative agency); Meltzer, *Legislative Courts, Legislative Power, and the Constitution*, 65 Ind.L.J. 291 (1990) (same). Moreover, as one of its advocates, Professor Fallon, acknowledges, the requirement of Article III review, if it is at all robust, could call into question the validity of a number of extant and seemingly accepted regimes. See Fallon, *Jurisdiction-Stripping Reconsidered,* 96 Va.L.Rev. 1043 (2010).

NOTE ON MAGISTRATE JUDGES

(1) The Institution of Magistrates. Ever since 1789, the federal courts have employed officials other than Article III judges—sometimes called magistrates, sometimes commissioners—to handle certain adjudicative functions.[1] The current regime was established by the Federal Magistrates Act of 1968, codified at 28 U.S.C. § 631 *et seq.* That Act, which replaced a system of "commissioners" that was widely regarded as ineffective, contemplated a major expansion in the functions that could be delegated by federal district judges. See Spaniol, *The Federal Magistrates Act: History and*

---

doctrine, Merrill suggests, is a partial but incomplete recognition of agency primacy in policymaking.) But he acknowledges that the appellate review model is so deeply entrenched as to make unlikely any significant departure from it.

Pfander, *Article I Tribunals, Article III Courts, and the Judicial Power of the United States,* 118 Harv.L.Rev. 643 (2004), notes that Article I empowers Congress "[t]o constitute *Tribunals* inferior to the supreme Court", while Article III provides that the judicial power "shall be vested in one supreme Court, and in such inferior *Courts*" as Congress establishes (emphasis added). The "Tribunals" contemplated by Article I, he contends, are non-Article III tribunals. (Others dispute his linguistic claim that "tribunals" reaches farther than "courts". See Calabresi & Lawson, *The Unitary Executive, Jurisdiction Stripping, and the Hamdan Opinions: A Textualist Response to Justice Scalia,* 107 Colum.L.Rev. 1002, 1034 (2007).) Pfander contends that the "inferior" status of non-Article III tribunals requires oversight by Article III courts, either through appeals or in some cases by writs such as habeas corpus or mandamus. But he contends that non-Article III tribunals may not adjudicate any disputes that would have lain "at the traditional core of the judicial power of the United States", even were appellate review provided. By contrast, he approves of adjudication by administrative agencies on the separate theory that they are "adjuncts" to Article III courts. Pfander's approach is thus less demanding than appellate review theory in some respects but more demanding in others.

This brief summary does not capture all of Pfander's complex argument. But doesn't his approach, like that of the Northern Pipeline plurality, raise this question: If administrative adjudication can be justified by the fiction that agencies are "adjuncts" to Article III courts, why cannot adjudication by other non-Article III tribunals be justified on the same basis?

[9]   Note, however, that hard questions would remain about the necessary scope of review. See Fallon, *supra,* at 974–92.

[1]   The Judiciary Act of 1789 authorized magistrates to fix bail for those accused of federal crimes. In 1817, Congress redesignated magistrates as commissioners and modestly expanded their functions. Periodic revisions and expansions of commissioners' functions were enacted before passage of the 1968 Act. For historical background and analysis of the permissible role of federal magistrate judges, see Silberman, *Masters and Magistrates,* 50 N.Y.U.L.Rev. 1070 (*Part I: The English Model*), 1297 (*Part II: The American Analogue*) (1975).

Development, 1974 Ariz.L.Rev. 566. A 1990 amendment renamed magistrates as magistrate judges.[2]

Today, magistrate judges are appointed for a term of eight years by the judges of the federal judicial district in which they are employed. 28 U.S.C. § 631(a), (e). During this term, a magistrate judge may be removed, by the judges of the judicial district, "only for incompetency, misconduct, neglect of duty, or physical or mental disability". *Id.* § 631(i).

(2) Statutory History and the Scope of Authority.

(a) The Federal Magistrates Act of 1968 authorized magistrates to serve as special masters, to provide "assistance to district judges in the conduct of pretrial or discovery proceedings in civil or criminal actions", and to conduct "preliminary review of motions for posttrial relief". See Pub.L.No. 90–578, 82 Stat. 1107, 1287 (1968). The 1968 Act also contained an open-ended grant of authority to district judges to charge magistrates with additional duties.

(b) Amendments enacted in 1976 significantly expanded the range of functions that magistrate judges are expressly authorized to perform. Overruling the decision in Wingo v. Wedding, 418 U.S. 461 (1974), the 1976 amendments permit magistrate judges to conduct evidentiary hearings in habeas corpus cases and to "hear and determine" non-dispositive pre-trial motions, subject to review only to ensure that the decision is not "clearly erroneous or otherwise contrary to law", 28 U.S.C. § 636(b)(1)(A). The amendments further specify that "dispositive" motions may be referred to a magistrate judge, but only for "proposed findings of fact and recommendations for the disposition"; the presiding judge must make a "de novo" determination of those findings to which objection is raised. *Id.* § 636(b)(1)(B). A catch-all provision, still in effect, provides that magistrate judges "may be assigned such additional duties as are not inconsistent with the Constitution and laws of the United States". *Id.* § 636(b)(3).

(c) The Federal Magistrates Act of 1979 took yet a further step by establishing that magistrate judges, with the consent of the parties, "may conduct any or all proceedings in a jury or nonjury civil matter and order the entry of judgment in the case, when specifically designated to exercise such jurisdiction by the district court". *Id.* § 636(c)(1).[3] Aggrieved parties then may appeal to the court of appeals. *Id.* § 636(c)(3).

(3) The Significance of Magistrate Judges.
As of 2012, there were 531 full-time and 39 part-time magistrate judges.[4] (By comparison, there were 678 authorized federal district judgeships.) The magistrate judges disposed of 1,068,153 judicial matters that year, including social security "appeals" and habeas petitions, and handled 199,686 references in criminal felony cases (involving motions, conferences, and other pretrial matters).[5] Magistrate judges conducted 499 civil trials with the consent of the parties.[6]

---

[2]   Judicial Improvements Act of 1990, Pub.L.No. 101–650, § 321, 104 Stat. 5089 (1990).

[3]   "The court may, for good cause shown on its own motion, or under extraordinary circumstances shown by any party, vacate a reference of a civil matter to a magistrate". 28 U.S.C. § 636(c)(6).

[4]   U.S. Federal Courts, Judicial Facts and Figures (Sept. 30, 2012), at Table 1.1, http:// www.uscourts.gov/statistics/table/11/judicial-facts-and-figures/2012/09/30.

[5]   See Judicial Business of the United States Courts: 2012 Annual Report of the Director of the Administrative Office of the United States Courts, at Table S-17, http://www.uscourts. gov/statistics/table/s-17/judicial-business/2012/09/30.

[6]   See *id.* For further discussion, see p. 40, *supra*.

(4) The Raddatz Case. United States v. Raddatz, 447 U.S. 667 (1980), presented questions about the statutory and constitutional authority of magistrates (as they were then called). There, after the defendant in a felony prosecution moved to suppress incriminating statements, the district judge referred the motion to a magistrate, who conducted an evidentiary hearing. The defendant's account of the encounters at which the statements were made differed sharply from that of federal agents. Crediting the latter, the magistrate proposed findings of fact and recommended that the motion be denied. Following a review of the magistrate's findings and recommendation, but not an independent review of the evidence, the district judge denied the motion.

In considering the defendant's challenge to this procedure, the Supreme Court first ruled that the Act does not require an Article III judge to hear the evidence of witnesses on a suppression motion, even when "determination" of the motion turned on issues of demeanor and credibility. The Act required a de novo decision by an Article III judge, but not a de novo hearing of the evidence. The Court then held that the Act, as so interpreted, did not deny due process. Writing for the majority, Chief Justice Burger noted that administrative agencies frequently follow an analogous procedure, with the agencies themselves making the ultimate findings based upon evidence presented to a hearing officer. Finally, the Court rejected the suggestion that Crowell v. Benson, p. 346, *supra*, requires an Article III trial de novo on the "constitutional facts" at stake in a suppression motion. The district court had "plenary discretion" whether to use a magistrate, to accept or reject the magistrate's recommendation, and to hear evidence de novo. It sufficed that "the entire process takes place under the district court's total control and jurisdiction".

In an elaborate dissent, Justice Marshall, joined by Justice Brennan, argued that the due process principle that the "one who decides must hear" is violated when a judge resolves a matter without hearing the witnesses in a case where "the factual issues turned on issues of credibility that cannot be fairly resolved on the basis of the record". He argued further that under Crowell and Ng Fung Ho v. White, p. 356, *supra*, an Article III court must make an independent determination of "case-dispositive facts", including credibility issues, in cases where individual liberty is at stake.[7]

---

[7] In a separate dissent, Justice Stewart, joined by Justices Brennan and Marshall, concluded that the statute required a de novo hearing where credibility issues are critical. In another opinion, Justice Powell dissented on the basis of the Due Process Clause.

The Raddatz Court assumed that it was unlikely that a district court, without conducting its own evidentiary hearing, would reject a magistrate's proposed finding of fact that is dispositive and that depends on a determination of credibility. But it turns out that district courts do just that with some regularity. In turn, six courts of appeals have held that such rejections of a magistrate's finding deny due process when they likely will lead to a defendant's criminal conviction. The cases are discussed in Pierce, *District Court Review of Findings of Fact Proposed by Magistrates: Reality Versus Fiction*, 81 Geo.Wash.L.Rev. 1236 (2013). Professor Pierce criticizes these appellate decisions as (i) inconsistent with the settled practice in administrative agencies of rejecting ALJs' credibility-based determinations, (ii) burdensome and at odds with the rationale for assigning factfinding to magistrates in the first instance, (iii) resting on a premise—that an observer can reliably determine from demeanor whether a person is telling the truth—that the empirical evidence belies, and (iv) inconsistent with Raddatz's argument that factfinding by magistrates comports with Article III because the entire process falls under the complete supervisory control of the district courts.

(5) Jurisdiction with Consent.

(a) The courts of appeals have been unanimous in upholding the validity of 28 U.S.C. § 636(c), which permits magistrate judges to adjudicate any civil case brought in a federal district court if both parties consent, see, *e.g.*, Gairola v. Commonwealth of Virginia Department of General Services, 753 F.3d 1281 (4th Cir. 1985) & cases cited, and the Supreme Court must have implicitly agreed when it decided that consent could be inferred from a party's conduct in litigation. Roell v. Withrow, 538 U.S. 580 (2003).[8]

(b) In Peretz v. United States, 501 U.S. 923 (1991), the Court considered whether a magistrate judge may preside over jury selection in a felony trial when the parties consent.[9] Just two years earlier, in Gomez v. United States, 490 U.S. 858 (1989), a unanimous Court had ruled that presiding over jury selection in such a case, without the defendant's consent, is not among those "additional duties" that under 28 U.S.C. § 636 district courts may assign to magistrate judges. In so ruling the Court had adverted to the doctrine of constitutional avoidance as well as to its "serious doubts" about the feasibility of conducting meaningful review of determinations made by a magistrate judge in the course of jury selection.

But in the Peretz case, the Court held, 5–4, that consent rendered the assignment of jury selection constitutional. Any personal right of a defendant to an Article III judge may be waived, the Court found, and "[e]ven assuming that a litigant may not waive structural protections provided by Article III, we are convinced that such structural protections are not implicated by the procedure followed in this case. Magistrates are appointed and subject to removal by Article III judges. * * * Because 'the entire process takes place under the district court's total control and jurisdiction,' [quoting Raddatz, Paragraph (4), *supra*,] there is no danger that use of the magistrate involves" an attempt to transfer jurisdiction for purposes of crippling the Article III courts. As to review before an Article III judge, "nothing in the statute precludes a district judge from providing the review that the Constitution requires". (The Court did not explain what the content of such a requirement might be in this setting.)

Justice Marshall, joined by Justices White and Blackmun, dissented. His opinion protested that the Court had not explained how the "serious doubts" about meaningful review expressed in Gomez were now resolved and concluded that, in the absence of such review, the district court could not be said to have "total control and jurisdiction".[10]

---

[8] At least three federal circuits have upheld § 636(c) consent jurisdiction in class actions, based on the consent of the class representative(s) and the defendant(s), rejecting the view that unnamed class members are "parties" whose consent is required. See Williams v. Gen. Elec. Capital Auto Lease, Inc., 159 F.3d 266, 268–70 (7th Cir.1998); Dewey v. Volkswagen Aktiengesellschaft, 681 F.3d 170, 180–81 (3d Cir.2012); Day v. Persels & Associates, LLC, 729 F.3d 1309, 1324–25 (11th Cir.2013).

[9] Although the government had relied on a *waiver* theory, the Court rested on the conceptually distinct basis of *consent*. Should the distinction make a difference under Article III?

[10] For an argument that Peretz gives insufficient attention to the structural concerns embodied in Article III—concerns that might be analogized to the non-waivability of subject matter jurisdiction defects—see, *e.g.*, Note, 33 Wm. & Mary L.Rev. 253 (1991), and Note, 70 N.C.L.Rev. 1334 (1992). But see Meltzer, *Legislative Courts, Legislative Power, and the Constitution*, 65 Ind.L.J. 291, 304 (1990), concluding that "there is no inconsistency between an emphasis on Article III as the source of a right to judicial review * * * and a willingness to validate non-Article III adjudication to which litigants have consented".

(6) The Underlying Issues. As courts and commentators have recognized, questions pertaining to the use of magistrate judges and other judicial auxiliaries within the Article III system are analytically distinct from the issue of the validity of legislative and administrative tribunals.

On the one hand, the congressional need to substitute magistrate judges for Article III judges might be thought to be weak. Because magistrate judges function just like Article III judges, the assignment of work to non-Article III officials cannot be justified on grounds that it requires specialized expertise, or the combination of adjudicatory and rulemaking functions, or different procedures (for example, arbitration) from those followed in Article III courts. Indeed, could one say Congress has *no* reason for providing for the assignment of adjudicative functions to magistrate judges, except that it prefers not to create more Article III judgeships? Is this a constitutionally adequate justification?

There have been strong dissents from the decisions of the courts of appeals upholding the consent jurisdiction under § 636(c). One theme of the dissents is that although there have always been judicial adjuncts like magistrates or special masters, their role should be to advise and assist, not to displace, the real judge. See, *e.g.*, Geras v. Lafayette Display Fixtures, Inc., 742 F.2d 1037 (7th Cir. 1984) (Posner, J., dissenting); Pacemaker Diagnostic Clinic of America, Inc. v. Instromedix, Inc., 725 F.2d 537 (9th Cir. 1984) (en banc) (Schroeder, J., dissenting).

On the other hand, the threat to judicial independence might be thought to be relatively minor. Magistrate judges are selected by Article III judges rather than by the political branches; they operate within the Article III judicial structure; and Article III judges not only review the decisions of magistrate judges but also have an unusually broad array of levers for supervising them.

But if those factors reduce any threat to independence from the political branches, do they create risks to independence from within the judicial branch? A provocative student Note, 88 Yale L.J. 1023, 1052–58 (1979), argues that caseload pressures will lead to appointment of more magistrate judges, with the matters referred to them disproportionately involving "simple cases and needy litigants". The upshot, the author fears, will be a form of discrimination both among classes of litigants and areas of the law. "In addition to the familiar 'control' of appellate review that all higher federal tribunals exercise over the judges of lower courts, the magistrate is also subject to a qualitatively different form of bureaucratic control that may attend district court authority to determine his reappointment prospects and, more importantly, the day-to-day contents of his docket. Moreover, district judges must evaluate the magistrate's decisional record in the course of exercising their administrative functions, if only in order to maintain the standards of the court. The ongoing, informal oversight creates the risk of impermissible intrusion on the magistrate's substantive decisions. The danger is not that magistrates will come to function as judicial alter egos, but rather that they may be encouraged to adopt a risk-averse strategy of adjudication by the pressure of judicial scrutiny, a strategy eschewing unconventional decisions that might otherwise be prompted by novel legal claims or pressing factual idiosyncracies [sic]. Such 'judicious' decisionmaking would be inconsistent with the * * * policy of autonomous adjudication within the federal courts that underlies the Article III judicial office".

NOTE ON ADJUDICATION BEFORE MULTINATIONAL TRIBUNALS

(1) Multilateral and International Tribunals. The United States is a party to numerous treaties and conventions that contemplate the use of non-Article III tribunals to resolve disputes. In several instances, the United States has participated in establishing multilateral tribunals to adjudicate disputes, including disputes arising under the laws of the United States, and has either foreclosed or limited review of those tribunals' decisions by the Article III courts. Arrangements such as these present a broad range of questions about both appropriate policy and constitutional validity.

(2) The North American Free Trade Agreement (NAFTA). A notable example involves the North American Free Trade Agreement (NAFTA), which establishes a free trade zone among the United States, Canada, and Mexico.[1]

(a) NAFTA retains authority in administrative agencies of the signatory nations to enforce domestic "antidumping" rules (forbidding the sale of under-priced goods) and to impose "countervailing" duties on subsidized imports. In the United States, the relevant determinations, which can occur in proceedings initiated by aggrieved private parties, are made in the first instance by the International Trade Administration and the International Trade Commission. Following an agency's decision whether federal law was violated and whether countervailing duties should be imposed, review can take either of two tracks. One track involves judicial review by the Article III Court of International Trade and the Court of Appeals for the Federal Circuit. The other, which can be triggered by either the United States or one of the other signatory nations (but not by private parties), leads to review by a panel of five non-Article III judges from the two affected nations, with the American judges appointed by the United States Trade Representative. There is an extremely limited provision for further multilateral review of the panel's decision, but no opportunity for an Article III court to review whether the panel correctly applied federal law. (A private party may, however, obtain review by the Article III Court of International Trade "with respect to a determination solely concerning a constitutional issue". 19 U.S.C. § 1516a(g)(4)(B) (2006).)

(b) Articles 1102 and 1105(1) require each signatory nation, *inter alia*, to treat the others' investors (i) consistently with international law, including the provision of fair and equitable treatment and full protection and security, and (ii) no less favorably than it treats its own investors. The Treaty also generally prohibits expropriation of investments. Foreign investors who believe those guarantees have been violated are given a private right of action to file a claim against a signatory state before a NAFTA arbitral panel, ordinarily consisting of one arbitrator appointed by each party and a third by agreement of the disputing parties. A disputing

---

[1] The parties entered the agreement in December 1992, and Congress enacted implementing legislation a year later. See North American Free Trade Implementation Act, Pub.L.No. 103–182, 107 Stat. 2057 (1993).

An earlier example is the Canada-United States Free Trade Agreement, from which NAFTA's provisions for the adjudication of disputes were adapted. See Metropoulos, *Constitutional Dimensions of the North American Free Trade Agreement*, 27 Cornell Int'l L.J. 141, 145–46 (1994).

party may bring an action to set aside or annul an arbitral award under the law of the jurisdiction that was the official place of arbitration. See Alvarez & Park, *The New Face of Investment Arbitration: NAFTA Chapter 11*, 28 Yale J.Int'l L. 365, 374–75 (2003).

A prominent case under this provision, Loewen Group, Inc. v. United States, 42 I.L.M. 811 (2003), began as a lawsuit in Mississippi state court by an American funeral home company against Loewen, a Canadian rival with operations in Mississippi. The American plaintiff made overt anti-foreign statements in the litigation and although its complaint sought $5 million in compensatory damages, the jury awarded a total of $500 million (including $400 million in punitive damages). In order to stay execution of that judgment pending appeal, Mississippi law required posting a bond of 125% of the judgment. After the Mississippi courts failed to relieve Loewen of that requirement, Loewen settled the matter for $175 million.

Loewen then filed an arbitration claim under NAFTA against the United States, seeking $725 million on the basis that the state court proceeding and the bond requirement violated the treaty. The arbitration panel agreed that "the conduct of the trial by the trial judge was so flawed that it constituted a miscarriage of justice" amounting to a manifest injustice as that expression is understood in international law, but in the end ruled against Loewen on narrow procedural grounds.[2]

(3) Questions of Constitutional and Legal Policy. Does NAFTA raise constitutional concerns by assigning cases within the federal judicial power to non-Article III tribunals?

(a) Boyer, *Article III, The Foreign Relations Power, and the Binational Panel System of NAFTA*, 13 Int'l Tax & Bus.Lawyer 101, 131–34 (1996), argues that the NAFTA provisions on countervailing tariffs are permissible under Article III, largely because the questions whether the United States should take retaliatory action against another nation and seek the payment of countervailing duties involve "public" rather than "private" rights. By contrast, Chen, *Appointments with Disaster: The Unconstitutionality of Binational Arbitral Review Under the United States-Canada Free Trade Agreement*, 49 Wash. & Lee L.Rev. 1455 (1992), contends that a similar adjudicatory scheme under an earlier bilateral agreement between the United States and Canada (see note 1, *supra*) violates both Article III and the Appointments Clause.

(b) In a case like Loewen, although the NAFTA arbitral process is not formally an appeal that reviews the decision of a national court, it has some of that flavor, and the arbitral panel, in determining whether the Treaty provided for compensation, to some extent second-guessed the Mississippi courts' application of Mississippi law. Professor Young fears that NAFTA proceedings are more threatening than Supreme Court review of state court judgments, in part because of what he views as a lack of appropriate deference to a state court's decision of state law (which he attributes in part to the fact that NAFTA panels are one-time rather than permanent tribunals) and in part because the review is as of right rather than discretionary (as with Supreme Court review via certiorari). He

---

[2] Loewen had failed to exhaust an available domestic American remedy: a petition for certiorari to the United States Supreme Court. Moreover, Loewen had gone bankrupt (in part due to the Mississippi litigation), and because the entity that emerged from bankruptcy was a U.S. corporation, there was not the requisite continuity of national identity from the time of the actions complained of through the resolution of the claim.

acknowledges, however, that in the Loewen case, the Mississippi courts engaged in what he terms "home cooking".

(c) Justice O'Connor, in *Federalism of Free Nations*, 28 N.Y.U.J.Int'l L. & Pol. 35, 42 (1995–96), states that "the vesting of certain adjudicatory authority in international tribunals presents a very significant constitutional question * * *. Article III * * * reserves to federal courts the power to decide cases and controversies, and the U.S. Congress may not delegate to another tribunal 'the essential attributes of judicial power.' " Is it clear that the concerns about multinational arrangements are properly analogized to concerns about non-Article III adjudication in a purely domestic context?

The range of political controls over multinational tribunals is far more limited than the range of controls—including the appointment power, budgetary authority, congressional and presidential oversight, and judicial review—over American administrative agencies. (Does that argue for heightened concern about multinational tribunals, because of fear of their lack of accountability, or lessened concern, because of their greater independence?) At the same time, the regulatory impulse for many multinational arrangements may rest less on the attractions of delegation and more on the need for nations to transfer some sovereignty to a polity that transcends existing national boundaries. And some have argued that these arrangements can be upheld based upon "separation of powers 'flexibility' unique to the foreign affairs area". Note, 88 Va.L.Rev. 1529, 1532 (2002). As a generalization, constitutional anxieties about delegating power to multinational bodies are more intense in the United States than in most of our treaty partners.[3]

(d) Multinational tribunals, although increasingly important in an era of globalization, are not a new phenomenon. Monaghan, *Article III and Supranational Judicial Review*, 107 Colum.L.Rev. 833 (2007), rests largely on historical practice in arguing that "NAFTA-like trade tribunals raise no serious problems under Article III * * *. * * * Since the Jay Treaty of 1794, it has been clear that claims of American nationals espoused by the United States against foreign sovereigns could be adjudicated by state-state mixed arbitration commissions". Professor Monaghan notes that the 1871 Treaty of Washington between the United States and Britain gave a binational commission jurisdiction over a wide range of claims by U.S. and British nationals against the two governments; the commissioners even "purported to 'review' prize decisions of the United States Supreme Court (and the House of Lords)". Equivocating slightly about the extent to which historical practice alone should be dispositive of Article III issues, Professor Monaghan apparently accords weight to the practical desirability of multinational tribunals as part of the emerging world economic order. And he emphasizes that the public rights doctrine provides at least a partial rationale for upholding adjudication by an international adjudicator, without which "any suit by an American citizen against a foreign state would be barred by sovereign immunity". Accordingly, he suggests, the waiver of such immunity can be conditioned upon adjudication in a non-Article III tribunal.

Monaghan adds: "[O]ne important systemic role for the Article III courts remains: the power to confine other organs of government within the bounds

---

[3]   For an informative canvass of some of the constitutional issues presented by agreements establishing international and multilateral tribunals, see Symposium, *The Interaction Between National Courts and International Tribunals*, 28 N.Y.U.J.Int'l L. & Pol. 1 (1995–96).

of their authority. If NAFTA-like arbitration processes compromise that function, they do so only at the margin. Far more important issues for our constitutional order are raised by the delegation of lawmaking authority to international bodies. Issues of national sovereignty and democratic accountability are surely raised by this increasingly widespread practice. But that bell having been rung, it cannot be unrung".

Has the bell rung as clearly as Professor Monaghan suggests? Does his assessment reflect an artful synthesis of doctrine and good judgment, a confession of the bankruptcy of current doctrine and judicial methodology in this area, or elements of both?

Is it a necessary element of a multinational regime like NAFTA that a multinational tribunal be empowered to sit in judgment of domestic institutions, including, sometimes, domestic courts? Is the key question not whether to permit such claims but rather how to define the bases for them, the composition of the multinational tribunal, and the appropriate degree of deference to domestic tribunals? See Young, *Institutional Settlement in a Globalizing Judicial System*, 54 Duke L.J. 1143, 1174, 1193–97 (2005).

(e) Do international *criminal* tribunals raise distinctive questions? Kontorovich, *The Constitutionality of International Courts: The Forgotten Precedent of Slave-Trade Tribunals*, 158 U.Pa.L.Rev. 39, 75–81, 102, 104–05, 114 (2009), identifies two relevant historical precedents. First, from the end of the War of 1812 through at least 1825, the United States repeatedly rebuffed British entreaties to join a system of international courts to punish participants in the slave trade; both executive and congressional officials cited objections founded on Article III and the Bill of Rights. Second, in 1862, the Senate ratified the Lyons-Seward Treaty, which authorized international courts that included American judges to exercise a civil jurisdiction over vessels seized in the slave trade, but withheld criminal jurisdiction to try the crew. According to Professor Kontorovich, the central thread of consistency is that "[a]t all times there was consensus that [participation in international] *criminal* tribunals would be unconstitutional", except possibly in cases involving "universally cognizable offenses by service members".

However, Martinez, *International Courts and the U.S. Constitution: Reexamining the History*, 159 U.Pa.L.Rev. 1069 (2011), disputes Kontorovich's argument that these episodes suggest that contemporary participation in the International Criminal Court would be constitutionally suspect. In her view, the initial U.S. rejection of international slave-trade tribunals rested on objections not to criminal jurisdiction over Americans but rather to the tribunals' trying Americans for conduct that at that time violated *American* but not *international* law. By 1862, when the United States ratified the Lyons-Seward Treaty, the slave trade *was* understood to violate international law, alleviating the initial concern. As a result, Professor Martinez argues, neither the initial resistance to nor later acceptance of the slave-trade tribunals by the United States casts constitutional doubt on participation in the International Criminal Court.[4]

---

[4]   Kontorovich continues the debate in *Three International Courts and Their Constitutional Problems*, 99 Cornell L.Rev. 1353 (2014), where he also examines the Senate's rejection, at the beginning of the 20th century, of a treaty that would have established an International Prize Court that would have applied the international law of maritime warfare. He contends that the Senate concluded that the treaty would violate Article III because the Prize Court would have power to review U.S. Supreme Court decisions.

Whoever has the better of the historical argument, how much weight should extra-judicial constitutional analysis more than century ago carry in current legal debates?[5]

(4) The Interpretation of International Agreements. Whatever the reach of constitutional power to assign final adjudicative authority to non-United States tribunals, a related and important question is whether an international agreement to which the United States is a party does in fact assign final adjudicative authority to a multinational tribunal. Recent decisions involving the Vienna Convention suggest that at present the Supreme Court will not readily interpret treaties as having done so.

The Vienna Convention requires signatory nations promptly to inform aliens who are being detained that they have a right to ask the detaining authorities to inform the consulate of their home country. The United States was a party not only to the Convention but also to an Optional Protocol, under which disputes concerning the Convention were submitted to the "compulsory jurisdiction" of the International Court of Justice (ICJ).

For many years, American states' record of compliance with the Convention has been poor. Foreign nations have been particularly concerned about non-compliance in criminal cases imposing the death penalty (which many foreign nations have abolished). Accordingly, foreign countries have sought redress on behalf of their citizens from both American courts and the ICJ.

(a) In 1998, the Supreme Court, in a brief per curiam opinion, rebuffed a last minute challenge by Paraguay to the scheduled execution of one its citizens, whose rights under the Convention had been violated and who had thereafter been sentenced to death in Virginia. Breard v. Greene, 523 U.S. 371 (1998). (Paraguay had instituted proceedings before the ICJ only eleven days before the Supreme Court's decision, and the ICJ had not yet taken any action.)

(b) Thereafter, Germany and Mexico filed proceedings against the United States before the ICJ, on behalf of several of their citizens who had not been informed of their right to consular notification and then were sentenced to death in American state court proceedings. The ICJ proceedings challenged state court decisions holding that aliens who had not raised a timely objection to the denial of consular notification had, under state law, procedurally defaulted and thereby had forfeited the rights provided by the Vienna Convention. Ruling for Germany and Mexico, the ICJ held that the application of state court procedural default rules violated the requirement of Article 36 of the Convention that signatories give "full effect . . . to the purposes for which the rights accorded under this Article are intended," 21 U.S.T. 77, 100–01, as the practice of American states "prevented [courts] from attaching any legal significance" to the fact that the violation of Article 36 kept the foreign governments from assisting in their nationals' defense. LaGrand Case, 2001 I.C.J. 466, 497, ¶ 91 (Judgment of June 27) (LaGrand); see also Case Concerning Avena and other Mexican Nationals, 2004 I.C.J. 12 (Judgment of Mar. 31) (Avena).

(c) Following those ICJ decisions, the Supreme Court considered a case in which the Oregon courts had held that an alien convicted of a crime had waived his rights under the Vienna Convention by failing to assert them

---

[5] For a thoughtful general discussion, see Bradley & Morrison, *Historical Gloss and the Separation of Powers*, 126 Harv.L.Rev. 411 (2012).

until filing a state court petition for habeas relief. (The petitioner was not one whose claim had been espoused by Germany and Mexico before the ICJ.). In Sanchez-Llamas v. Oregon, 548 U.S. 331 (2006), the Court, diverging from the view of the ICJ, ruled that Oregon's application of its normal procedural default rules did not violate the Vienna Convention. Chief Justice Roberts cited Marbury v. Madison for the proposition that the "judicial power includes the duty 'to say what the law is' ", a power that extends to treaties. Nothing in the Vienna Convention, he declared, suggests that ICJ decisions were intended to be conclusive on American courts. Those decisions bind only the parties and thus are not even precedents before the ICJ itself. While under the U.N. Charter, members agree to comply with ICJ judgments, "the Charter's procedure for noncompliance—referral to the Security Council by the aggrieved state—contemplates quintessentially *international* remedies." Moreover, the Chief Justice noted that American courts typically give weight to the interpretations of treaties by the political branches, and the Executive Branch had not taken the view that the ICJ's interpretation of Article 36 binds American courts. Indeed, "shortly after Avena, the United States withdrew from the Optional Protocol concerning Vienna Convention disputes. Whatever the effect of Avena and LaGrand before this withdrawal, it is doubtful that our courts should give decisive weight to the interpretation of a tribunal whose jurisdiction in this area is no longer recognized by the United States.

"LaGrand and Avena are therefore entitled only to the 'respectful consideration' due an interpretation of an international agreement by an international court." The Court proceeded to find that Article 36, properly interpreted, did not displace state court procedural default rules, for reasons summarized at pp. 401–402, *infra*.

The general question raised in the Sanchez-Llamas case—the appropriate allocation of interpretive authority between U.S. courts and multinational tribunals whose jurisdiction the United States has recognized—can arise under any number of international regimes. There is a range of alternatives, from that followed in Sanchez-Llamas—which essentially gives the international tribunal's views weight only insofar as its reasoning is persuasive—to treating such views as authoritative. See generally Alford, *Federal Courts, International Tribunals, and the Continuum of Deference*, 43 Va.J.Int'l L. 675 (2003). Is the latter position more attractive in view of the power of the United States to withdraw from a treaty? Or is the "exit" option less attractive given the political and diplomatic friction involved?

An intermediate suggestion, put forward in the context of adjudication under NAFTA, would treat the decision of a supranational tribunal as deserving deference but not as being conclusive—much like the deference that courts pay to legal determinations by administrative agencies. See Young, *Toward a Framework Statute for Supranational Adjudication*, 57 Emory L.J. 93 (2007).[6]

---

[6]   Paulsen, *The Constitutional Power to Interpret International Law*, 118 Yale L.J. 1762 (2009), draws on earlier work of other scholars and a detailed structural analysis of the Constitution to conclude that foreign and international tribunals cannot issue interpretations of international law (including treaties to which the United States is party) or judgments that bind American courts, and that the United States government cannot delegate that power to such tribunals.

(d) In the next case to reach the Supreme Court under the Vienna Convention, *Medellín v. Texas*, 552 U.S. 491 (2008), the petitioner *was* one of the individuals whose claims had been espoused by Mexico before the ICJ in the Avena litigation. The case thus raised the question whether American courts were bound to respect the *judgment* of the ICJ, even if it rested on an interpretation of Article 36 with which the Supreme Court disagreed. Dividing 6–3, the Court said no. Chief Justice Roberts' majority opinion stated that the Optional Protocol was most naturally read as a bare grant of jurisdiction to the ICJ, not as a commitment of signatories to comply with ICJ judgments. Article 94 of the U.N. Charter does provide that each member nation "undertakes to comply with the decision of the [ICJ] in any case to which it is a party." But taking an approach that the dissent criticized as overly textual, the Chief Justice stated that in general, a treaty is self-executing—in the sense that it has automatic effect as federal law without implementing legislation—only when "the treaty itself conveys an intention that it be 'self-executing' " and is ratified on that basis. Article 94, he said, was not a directive to domestic courts, but a compact among nations, enforceable through diplomacy and a referral to the U.N. Security Council.

A lengthy dissent by Justice Breyer (joined by Justices Souter and Ginsburg) began by stating: "The Constitution's Supremacy Clause provides that 'all Treaties . . . which shall be made . . . under the Authority of the United States, shall be the supreme Law of the Land; and the Judges in every State shall be bound thereby.' The Clause means that the 'courts' must regard 'a treaty . . . as equivalent to an act of the legislature, whenever it operates of itself without the aid of any legislative provision.' *Foster v. Neilson*, 2 Pet. 253, 314 (1829) (majority opinion of Marshall, C.J.)." Justice Breyer accused the Court of placing too much emphasis on language and too little on precedents that treated other treaty commitments as self-executing. (An appendix to the dissent cited 29 treaty provisions held or assumed to be self-executing, many of which, he said, lack the textual clarity demanded by the Court.) Clear language in treaties regarding the issue of "self-execution" is rare, he argued, because different nations approach the issue so differently: some, unlike the United States, routinely incorporate treaties signed by the executive directly into domestic law; others require legislative approval of treaties and legislative implementation of them. Justice Breyer argued for a practical, context-specific approach in which the question whether a treaty is self-executing would depend upon such factors as the treaty's subject matter (treaties pertaining to war and peace are less likely to be self-executing than treaties conferring private rights), whether it creates specific rights that courts are capable of enforcing, and whether judicial enforcement would provoke conflict with the political branches. In response, the Chief Justice characterized the dissent's approach as "arrestingly indeterminate" and as vesting an ad hoc power in the courts to pick and choose which treaty obligations are, in the absence of clear language approved by the political branches, binding law enforceable in American courts.

(e) Should American courts give more respect to a *judgment* of a multinational tribunal than to the tribunal's interpretation of a treaty? If a French court properly exercising jurisdiction had to interpret a federal statute and entered a judgment, no American court would think it should accept the French court's interpretation of the statute as authoritative, but a court might view it as appropriate to enforce the judgment, even if it rested on a doubtful construction of federal law. However, one commentator reports that international authority on the domestic effect of a judgment of an international tribunal is sparse: one Belgian decision refused to give such a judgment binding effect; a Japanese and an Italian court each viewed such a judgment as persuasive but not binding; and the only national court to treat an ICJ judgment as binding domestically was one in Morocco (and even there a second court disagreed two years later as to the same judgment). See Note, 29 Fordham Int'l L.J. 865, 898–900 (2006).

(f) Given Sanchez-Llamas and Medellín, it appears that interpretations or judgments rendered by international tribunals will have binding effect in American courts only when Congress, or the text of the treaty, clearly so specifies. Should one welcome that assignment of responsibility, particularly given the distinctive importance of political involvement in matters concerning foreign affairs? Does it disregard the language of the Supremacy Clause, which makes treaties (like the Constitution and statutes) the supreme law of the land?[7] Or if Justice Breyer is right that not all treaties (and not all provisions in a particular treaty) are automatically self-executing (or automatically not), does the Court's approach impose a burden of legislative specification, and require a degree of legislative foresight, that is impractical? Compare the question of the appropriate role of courts in formulating federal common law, discussed at length in Chap. VII, and, more specifically, in recognizing implied rights of action for violations of federal law, see pp. 723–752, *infra*.

Note on Military Tribunals or Commissions

(1) Introduction. Distinct from the courts-martial employed to try members of the U.S. military are military tribunals or "commissions" that have been constituted from time to time by the Executive Branch to deal with exigencies associated with war and whose jurisdiction embraces persons outside of the U.S. military. When authorized by Congress, they may be viewed as another form of legislative court. But the Executive Branch has established some commissions without clear legislative authorization.

The judges of such tribunals are typically military officers, and by their nature, military commissions involve adjudication outside the bounds of Article III. Moreover, the full safeguards of the Bill of Rights (for example, the jury trial right) do not apply. Although the Supreme Court has ruled that military commissions must afford due process, see Paragraph (2), *infra*, the Court has not resolved just how due process, and possibly other constitutional rights, apply before military tribunals.

Military commissions have most often been used abroad, in connection with military occupations of foreign territory, but they have sometimes been used domestically as well. They were employed during the Mexican-American War and more commonly during the Civil War "to enforce military discipline among civilian populations and to punish spies, saboteurs, provocateurs, and those that seriously disturbed public order." Bederman, *Article II Courts*, 44 Mercer L.Rev. 825, 835 (1993). During and after World

---

[7] Professor Vázquez so argues, asserting that treaties should be "presumptively enforceable in court in the same circumstances as constitutional and statutory provisions of like content." Vázquez, *Treaties as Law of the Land: The Supremacy Clause and the Judicial Enforcement of Treaties*, 122 Harv.L.Rev. 599, 601–02 (2008).

War II, the Supreme Court sustained the use of military tribunals to try both alleged war criminals[1] and civilians charged with ordinary criminal offenses in zones occupied by American forces.[2]

Following the 9/11 attack, military tribunals have been used to ascertain whether an individual is an enemy combatant who, under the laws of war, may be detained (without being subjected to criminal punishment) until the cessation of hostilities. After some delays, military commissions are now being used to prosecute alleged terrorists for violations of the laws of war.

(2) The Constitutionality of Military Tribunals. The most fundamental question raised by military commissions is whether adjudication before them, rather than before an Article III court, is ever constitutionally permissible. As is elaborated below, both history and Supreme Court precedent suggest that the answer to that question is yes. But that answer does not mean that every use of such commissions is constitutional. A range of variables may affect the constitutionality of their use, including:

(a) Whether the individual under its jurisdiction is a citizen or an alien;

(b) Whether the tribunal is located abroad or in the United States;

(c) What procedural protections a particular commission affords;

(d) The existence and scope of review in an Article III court;

(e) Whether Congress has authorized the Executive Branch to use a particular kind of tribunal, or, conversely, has prohibited its use.

The present discussion is somewhat summary, seeking simply to provide an overview of the use of these non-Article III tribunals and to explore some of the questions they raise in connection with the themes of this Chapter—notably, the scope of congressional power to assign adjudication to particular tribunals. More detail on these matters is presented in Chapter XI, Sec. 2.

(3) 9/11, the War on Terror, and the Hamdi Decision. In Hamdi v. Rumsfeld, 542 U.S. 507 (2004), the Court addressed the constitutionality of the contemporary use of military tribunals—in that case, to detain an American citizen as an enemy combatant under the laws of war. Hamdi was captured in a field of combat in Afghanistan but then moved to the United States. Military officials determined that he was an "enemy combatant" and claimed the authority to detain him on that basis. When his challenge to his detention reached the Supreme Court, five Justices agreed that an enemy combatant, even if a citizen, could be lawfully detained. Justice O'Connor's plurality opinion (joined by Chief Justice Rehnquist and Justices Kennedy and Breyer) concluded that Congress, in enacting, one week after 9/11, an authorization for the use of military force, had validly authorized the seizure of enemy combatants (including citizens) in Afghanistan, in accordance with the laws and usages of war. But she also concluded that the Due Process Clause gave Hamdi the right to challenge, before an impartial adjudicator, his designation as an enemy combatant. Justice O'Connor referred without elaboration to "the possibility" that the process to which Hamdi was constitutionally entitled could be provided "by an appropriately authorized

---

[1] See, *e.g.*, Application of Yamashita, 327 U.S. 1 (1946).

[2] See, *e.g.*, Madsen v. Kinsella, 343 U.S. 341 (1952) (upholding a murder trial of an American civilian before a military tribunal in occupied Germany following World War II).

and properly constituted military tribunal". But because the hearing that Hamdi had previously been afforded was not adequate, she concluded that the decision below denying him any relief must be reversed and the case remanded for further proceedings. (Justices Souter and Ginsburg concluded that Hamdi's detention was not legislatively authorized, but in order to create a majority they joined the plurality's disposition.[3])

Justice Thomas agreed that Hamdi was not immune from detention at the hands of the Executive. He would have affirmed the denial of relief, however, because on his broad view of the scope of executive power, he found no constitutional shortcoming in the hearing that Hamdi had previously been afforded.

In dissent, Justice Scalia (joined by Justice Stevens) maintained that the traditions underlying the Constitution's guarantees of due process and of the privilege of the writ of habeas corpus barred Hamdi's non-punitive detention by the military. In his view, the government must either try Hamdi for an ordinary crime in an Article III court or release him. He explicitly stated, however, that his views applied only to citizens who are detained within the territorial jurisdiction of a federal court and that in wartime, aliens may lawfully be detained by the military outside of the ordinary criminal process.[4]

The Hamdi decision left open many questions, a number of which are addressed in Chapter XI, Sec. 2. But a majority of the Justices affirmed that there is a constitutionally valid role for military commissions to play, even with respect to American citizens.

(4) The Precedents at Issue in Hamdi. The various opinions in Hamdi discussed, and disagreed about the significance of, two important precedents on the use of military tribunals within the United States: Ex parte Milligan and Ex parte Quirin. Those two decisions are difficult to reconcile with each other.

---

[3]   Justice Souter contended that because the government had not shown that its policy of incommunicado detention was consistent with the Geneva Conventions, it could not claim to be acting in accordance with the laws of war that Congress had authorized to be applied against citizens.

[4]   Powerful support for Justice Scalia's position is provided by Tyler, *The Forgotten Core Meaning of the Suspension Clause*, 125 Harv.L.Rev. 901 (2012). Tyler reviews the history of the writ of habeas corpus, and its suspension, from the Stuart period in Britain through the American Founding and up to the Civil War and Reconstruction. She concludes that persons owing allegiance to the government and thereby enjoying the protection of its law—most especially citizens—could not, absent suspension of the writ, be detained domestically except by the normal criminal process. That understanding extended, she argues, to persons suspected of aiding the enemy. Although most of her evidence involves persons seized within a nation's sovereign territory, she contends that the extraterritorial seizure of Hamdi did not deprive him of protection and hence that he could not be detained outside of the criminal process absent suspension of the writ.

A quite different conclusion is offered by Professor Harrison, in *The Habeas Corpus Suspension Clause and the Right to Natural Liberty*, *available at* http://papers.ssrn.com/sol3/papers.cfm?abstract_id=1852745. Harrison argues that neither the text of the Suspension Clause nor historical practice places citizens outside the scope of permissible detention, noting in particular that during the Revolutionary War, both the British and the Americans held captured citizens as prisoners of war. His review of English and early American history concludes that the Suspension Clause, despite its language, is not primarily about habeas corpus but rather about a substantive right to natural liberty. At the Founding, he argues, the paradigmatic case of a suspension was a law that conferred on the executive extremely broad discretion to detain—whether or not the judicial remedy of habeas corpus remained intact, and whether or not the detainee was a citizen.

(a) The Milligan Decision. In Ex parte Milligan, 71 U.S. (4 Wall.) 2 (1866), the Court held that a military tribunal lacked jurisdiction to try a U.S. citizen, living in Indiana, of conspiring to aid the Confederacy. Justice Davis' majority opinion began with the historical context: "During the late wicked Rebellion [when military tribunals were broadly employed], the temper of the times did not allow that calmness in deliberation and discussion so necessary to a correct conclusion of a purely legal question". The Court emphasized the status of the rights to jury trial and of the Fourth, Fifth, and Sixth Amendments as "the birthright of every American citizen". Then, coming finally to the government's principal argument that the military tribunal could exercise jurisdiction whenever prosecutions were brought "under the 'laws and usages of war' ", the Court replied that those "laws and usages * * * can never be applied to citizens in states which have upheld the authority of the government, and where the courts are open and their process unobstructed. This court has judicial knowledge that, in Indiana, the Federal authority was always unopposed, and its courts always open to hear criminal accusations and redress grievances, and no usage of war could sanction a military trial there for any offence whatever of a citizen in civil life, in nowise connected with the military service."

Chief Justice Chase, joined by Justices Wayne, Swayne, and Miller, concurred in the judgment solely on the ground that Congress had not authorized trial by military commission on the facts of the case: "We think that Congress had power, though not exercised, to authorize the military commission which was held in Indiana".

(b) The Quirin Decision. The Court next addressed the use of military commissions in the midst of World War II. In Ex parte Quirin, 317 U.S. 1 (1942), it unanimously upheld the jurisdiction of a military tribunal to try eight German service members who, after landing on Long Island from a German submarine, buried their German military uniforms and set off on their sabotage mission in civilian garb. The Court determined that Congress, by statute, as well as the President, by proclamation, had "authorized trial of offenses against the law of war before [military] commissions", and then added: "the law of war draws a distinction between * * * lawful and unlawful combatants. Lawful combatants are subject to capture and detention as prisoners of war by opposing military forces. Unlawful combatants are likewise subject to capture and detention, but in addition they are subject to trial and punishment by military tribunals for acts which render their belligerency unlawful. The spy who secretly and without uniform passes the military lines of a belligerent in time of war * * * or an enemy combatant who without uniform comes secretly through the lines for purpose of waging war by destruction of life or property, are familiar examples of belligerents who are generally deemed not to be entitled to the status of prisoners of war, but to be offenders against the law of war subject to trial and punishment by military tribunals."

The Court then held that the historical practice of trying such charges before military tribunals was conclusive of the question of constitutional validity: "§ 2 of Article III and the Fifth and Sixth Amendments cannot be taken to have extended the right to demand a jury to trials by military commission, or to have required that offenses against the law of war not triable by jury at common law be tried only in the civil courts." That conclusion applied equally, the Court said, to one of the saboteurs who claimed American citizenship.

The Court distinguished Ex parte Milligan in the following opaque passage: "Petitioners, and especially [the one claiming American citizenship], stress the pronouncement in the Milligan case that the law of war 'can never be applied to citizens in states which have upheld the authority of the government, and where the courts are open and their process unobstructed.' Elsewhere in its opinion the Court was at pains to point out that Milligan * * * was not an enemy belligerent either entitled to the status of a prisoner of war or subject to the penalties imposed upon unlawful belligerents. We construe the Court's statement as to the inapplicability of the law of war to Milligan's case as having particular reference to the facts before it. From them the Court concluded that Milligan, not being a part of or associated with the armed forces of the enemy, was a non-belligerent, not subject to the law of war save as—in circumstances found not there to be present, and not involved here—martial law might be constitutionally established."

(c) Hamdi's Discussion of Precedent. Unlike Quirin and Milligan, which involved *prosecutions for war crimes* before military tribunals, the Hamdi case involved the *non-criminal* detention of an enemy combatant during an armed conflict. Nonetheless, the Justices in Hamdi viewed Milligan and Quirin as the key precedents, although the various opinions differed sharply in their assessments of those decisions.

(i) Justice O'Connor's plurality opinion in Hamdi rested heavily on Quirin as establishing the constitutionality of military tribunals being used in accordance with the laws of war, even as to an American citizen. She emphasized that Quirin was a unanimous decision that "postdates and clarifies" Milligan. Justice Thomas' opinion went slightly further, asserting that "Quirin overruled Milligan to the extent that those cases are inconsistent."

(ii) By contrast, Justice Scalia's dissent contended that Quirin sought "to revise Milligan rather than describe it." He viewed Milligan as the more foundational precedent, one that resonated with the history of habeas corpus. Justice Scalia stressed Milligan's declaration that the "laws and usages [of war] * * * can never be applied to citizens in states which have upheld the authority of the government, and where the courts are open and their process unobstructed." Quirin, he said, was not the Court's "finest hour", noting that the denial of relief was announced the day after oral argument but the decision justifying it was not issued for several months.[5] Justice Scalia added that Quirin was distinguishable in any event because there it was uncontested that the defendants were members of enemy forces; but when, as in Hamdi, that question is in dispute, a citizen is entitled to a trial before an Article III court.

(d) Reconciling Milligan and Quirin. It is not certain that Milligan and Quirin can be reconciled. But consider these possible distinctions:

(i) One concerns the individual's relationship to the enemy. In the Milligan case, the "substance" of the charges included "holding communications with the enemy" and "conspiring to seize munitions of war stored in the arsenals" during the Civil War. But does a charge of providing

---

[5] See also Katyal & Tribe, *Waging War, Deciding Guilt: Trying the Military Tribunals*, 111 Yale L.J. 1259, 1291 (2002) (suggesting that "some highly questionable ex parte arm-twisting by the executive may have spurred the Supreme Court's unanimous decision", and arguing that "Quirin plainly fits the criteria typically offered for judicial confinement or reconsideration").

support to or conspiring with the enemy fall short of a charge that an individual was a "part of or associated with" enemy forces? On some views, only a person charged with the latter may be detained under the laws of war. If that is a basis for distinction, the facts of Hamdi would seem to fall on the Quirin side of the line.

(ii) Justice Scalia suggests a distinction between cases of conceded and contested enemy status. (Quirin, of course, did not distinguish Milligan on this basis.) As he notes, on that view Hamdi falls on the Milligan side of the line.

(iii) Quirin found that Congress had authorized the use of military tribunals, whereas Milligan found the contrary. (But five of the nine Justices in Milligan expressed the view that any congressional authorization would have been invalid in any event.)

(5) Military Tribunals to Try Defendants Abroad. The use of military tribunals abroad to detain or punish individuals has provoked less controversy. During the occupations of Germany and Japan following World War II, the United States used military tribunals extensively, trying over 1600 persons in Germany and 1000 persons in the Far East.[6] The use of such tribunals seems to have rested on one of two bases: An occupying power may use military tribunals to try ordinary criminal offenses (including those committed by U.S. citizens) until domestic civil government is restored, see Madsen v. Kinsella, note 2, *supra*, or to try alleged violations of the laws of war (usually by aliens), even after hostilities have ended, see, *e.g.*, Application of Yamashita, note 1, *supra*.

In Johnson v. Eisentrager, 339 U.S. 763, 788–89 (1950), however, Justice Jackson's opinion for the Court can be read as going further; he suggested that challenges to the use of military tribunals to try aliens in foreign territories are challenges to the "conduct of diplomatic and foreign affairs, for which the President [at least insofar as authorized by Congress] is exclusively responsible". He coupled this suggestion of constitutional authority with a further suggestion that enemy aliens detained on foreign soil have no constitutional right to be free from detention and trial by military commissions.

(6) The Relationship of Congress and the President in Determining the Appropriate Use of Military Tribunals. Insofar as the Constitution does not prohibit the use of military commissions, to what extent may the President constitute them without congressional authorization or in a fashion that conflicts with statutorily prescribed provisions?

(a) Quirin and Hamdi. That question did not arise in Quirin, where the Court unanimously found congressional authorization. And five of the Justices in Hamdi concluded, in the plurality's words, that at least in the circumstances there presented, Congress' authorization to the President to use "all necessary and appropriate force" against those responsible for the 9/11 attacks implicitly authorized the detention of enemy combatants, given that wartime detention was "so fundamental and accepted an incident to war". They declined to decide whether such authorization was necessary. But the other four Justices, who found no statutory authorization on varying

---

[6] American Bar Association Task Force on Terrorism and the Law, Report and Recommendations on Military Commissions (Jan. 4, 2002).

bases,[7] appeared to assume that absent congressional authorization, the tribunals were not valid.

(b) Conflict Between President and Congress: Hamdan v. Rumsfeld. When President Bush established military commissions after 9/11 to try enemy combatants for alleged violations of the laws of war, the Supreme Court found both that those tribunals violated statutorily rooted requirements that had taken effect after Quirin, and that as a result those tribunals lacked the power to proceed. In Hamdan v. Rumsfeld, 548 U.S. 557 (2006), a Yemeni national alleged to have been the bodyguard and driver for Osama bin Laden was captured during hostilities in Afghanistan, transported by the U.S. military to Guantánamo Bay, Cuba, and charged with conspiracy to commit war crimes. While those charges were pending, he filed suit in federal court challenging the jurisdiction of the military commission. On review, the Supreme Court upheld Hamdan's claim that the military commission lacked lawful authority to try him. Justice Stevens' opinion for the Court found that "[t]he [Uniform Code of Military Justice (UCMJ)] conditions the President's use of military commissions on compliance not only with the American common law of war, but also with * * * the 'rules and precepts of the law of nations,' Quirin, 317 U.S., at 28— including, *inter alia*, the four Geneva Conventions signed in 1949," seven years after the Quirin decision. The Court proceeded to find that the commission established to try Hamdan violated the UCMJ in two respects, both relating to the failure of the commission to conform to procedures that the UCMJ expressly prescribed for courts martial and that, the Court ruled, also applied to the proceedings in Hamdan's case.[8]

Dissents by Justices Scalia, Thomas, and Alito (each joined in full or in part by the others) disagreed with many aspects of the majority's reasoning. Justice Thomas contended that history and precedent supported the President's powers under the common laws of war to prescribe the procedures for military commissions and questioned the majority's premise that Congress, in enacting the UCMJ, "intended to deprive [the President] of particular powers not specifically enumerated".

Some months after the Hamdan decision, Congress enacted the Military Commissions Act of 2006 (MCA), Pub.L.No. 109–366, 120 Stat. 2600, which expressly authorizes trials before military commissions of aliens alleged to be unlawful enemy combatants and which includes provisions that cured the legal defects identified in the Hamdan decision. For discussion, see pp. 1244–1245, *infra*.

(c) The Framework of the Steel Seizure Case. In Hamdan, all of the Justices appeared to agree that the validity of military commissions

---

[7] Justice Souter's dissent (joined by Justice Ginsburg) argued that at most Congress authorized detention consistent with the laws of war, which, in hiw view, Hamdi's incommunicado detention violated. Justice Scalia's dissent focused on constitutional issues, but he also said that in view of the constitutional concerns, the congressional authorization of force was not sufficiently clear to warrant interpreting it to authorize the detention of a citizen.

[8] First, the Court interpreted the UCMJ as requiring that the procedures used before military commissions be uniform with the procedures used before courts martial except to the extent that the President found them to be impracticable, a finding the Court concluded that the President had not made. Second, the Court interpreted the UCMJ as requiring compliance with Common Article 3 of the Geneva Conventions, which requires trial before a "regularly constituted court affording all the judicial guarantees which are recognized as indispensable by civilized peoples." The Court then determined that military commissions were not regularly constituted because they deviated from court martial practice without an adequate justification.

should be resolved within the framework of Justice Jackson's celebrated concurring opinion in Youngstown Sheet & Tube Co. v. Sawyer, 343 U.S. 579 (1952), which viewed presidential authority as (i) broadest when taken with the explicit or implicit authorization of Congress, (ii) uncertain when taken in the absence of either a congressional grant or denial of authority, and (iii) at its lowest ebb when taken contrary to the express or implied will of Congress. The Justices in Hamdan disagreed, however, about which of Justice Jackson's three categories the case occupied. The dissenters read the UCMJ and AUMF as broad authorizations of executive reliance on military tribunals, whereas the majority interpreted the UCMJ, in particular, as limiting presidential power.

When Congress and the Executive are in agreement, what limits are there on the scope of authority that can be vested in military tribunals rather than in Article III courts? Article I, § 8, cl. 10 gives Congress the power to "define and punish * * * Offences against the Law of Nations." Some have argued that Congress' power is limited to defining and specifying the punishment for offenses that are recognized as such by the international laws of war,[9] at least when there are no exigent circumstances arising, for example, from martial law or from the occupation of enemy territory. But the government has at times taken the view that the political branches may assign for trial before military tribunals a broader set of offenses, as recognized either by past U.S. practice or by legislation under Article I, § 8, cl. 10.[10]

(d) The Question of Executive Authority. When Congress has neither authorized nor prohibited the use of military commissions, what is the scope of the President's power unilaterally to establish them?

(7) Judicial Review and Habeas Corpus. Article III courts have not typically had statutory jurisdiction to engage in appellate review of the decisions of military tribunals. But in some instances, the federal courts, in the exercise of their general habeas corpus jurisdiction, have reviewed whether "the Constitution or laws of the United States withhold [from the military] authority to proceed with the trial." Application of Yamashita, note 1, *supra*, 327 U.S. at 9. The decisions in Milligan, Quirin, Hamdi and Hamdan all arose under the habeas corpus jurisdiction.

Recall that in Boumediene v. Bush, p. 338, *supra*, the Court, after first determining that an alien detained at Guantánamo Bay had a constitutional right to habeas corpus review, and that a procedure for appellate review in an Article III court of appeals was not an adequate substitute for habeas review, held that a congressional enactment purporting to bar all federal and state courts from exercising habeas corpus jurisdiction over detainees like the petitioner violated the Suspension Clause. The Boumediene decision left

---

[9] See, e.g., Vladeck, *The Laws of War as a Constitutional Limit on Military Jurisdiction*, 4 J.Nat'l Security L. & Pol'y 295 (2010); Hafetz, *Policing the Line: International Law, Article III, and the Constitutional Limits of Military Jurisdiction*, 2014 Wis.L.Rev. 681.

[10] See, *e.g.*, Al Bahlul v. United States, 767 F.3d 1 (D.C.Cir. 2014) (en banc). The decision in that case left a great deal unresolved. The seven judges participating issued five separate opinions. Moreover, some of petitioner's contentions that particular offenses of which he was convicted by a military commission were beyond that tribunal's proper jurisdiction were not directly addressed, either because the petitioner had failed properly to raise the issue below (and hence appellate review was limited to plain error) or because the conviction was held to violate the Ex Post Facto Clause (thus leaving unresolved whether a similar conviction raising no ex post facto problem would be valid).

open, however, a broad range of questions about the appropriate timing and scope of judicial inquiry. See generally pp. 1237–1239, *infra*.

NOTE ON THE TIDEWATER PROBLEM

It has usually been taken for granted that Congress may not confer jurisdiction on the federal courts to hear a case that does not fall within one of the nine heads of subject matter jurisdiction listed in Article III. But that understanding was put to a test in National Mutual Insurance Co. v. Tidewater Transfer Co., 337 U.S. 582 (1949). There, a District of Columbia citizen brought suit in federal district court in Maryland against a Virginia corporation on an insurance contract; the dispute involved only issues of Maryland law. A 1940 statute gave the district courts jurisdiction in actions between citizens of the states and citizens of the District, even though, in the venerable case of Hepburn & Dundas v. Ellzey, 6 U.S. (2 Cranch) 445 (1805), Chief Justice Marshall had ruled that a citizen of the District was not a citizen of a "State" within the meaning of the Diversity Clause.

The Supreme Court upheld the constitutionality of the statutory grant of jurisdiction. But the Justices whose votes were necessary to the judgment reached their conclusions by radically different paths.

(1) Justices Rutledge and Murphy thought that Hepburn should be overruled and hence that there was diversity within the meaning of Article III. The other seven Justices would have followed Hepburn and found no diversity.

(2) Justice Jackson's plurality opinion, joined by Justices Black and Burton, supplied the other three votes to uphold the statute. He contended that Congress, pursuant to its Article I powers, may authorize Article III courts to adjudicate cases beyond Article III's nine heads of jurisdiction. He relied partly on the view that Congress had previously done so when it gave the district courts jurisdiction over cases that could also be heard by legislative courts (for example, consented suits against the United States, also cognizable in the non-Article III Court of Claims). Resting on the dubious proposition that legislative courts are "incapable of receiving" Article III judicial power, see Williams v. United States, 289 U.S. 553 (1933), p. 363 n. 8, *supra*, he concluded that in such cases, both the legislative courts and the district courts must exercise an Article I judicial power entirely outside the scope of Article III.

Justice Jackson also cited Schumacher v. Beeler, 293 U.S. 367 (1934), and Williams v. Austrian, 331 U.S. 642 (1947), in which the Court had upheld provisions authorizing a district court to entertain non-diversity suits by bankruptcy trustees against debtors of the bankrupt based on state-law causes of action. Rejecting the view that these actions could be viewed as cases "arising under" federal law,[1] Justice Jackson reasoned that the power over bankruptcy in Article I "can supply a source of judicial power for their adjudication".

Although he concluded that Congress is free to give the federal courts judicial business that lies outside the enumeration of Article III, Justice

---

[1] Here Justice Jackson cited cases such as Gully v. First National Bank, discussed in Chap. VIII, Sec. 3, *infra*, construing the statutory grant of "arising under" jurisdiction to the district courts. On the bankruptcy jurisdiction, see pp. 794–795, *infra*.

Jackson contended that it must be *judicial* business. He asserted that Congress lacks any similar power to authorize federal courts to decide matters that are not cases or controversies within the meaning of Article III.[2]

(3) The other six Justices objected strongly to Justice Jackson's opinion. Justice Rutledge's dissent called it a "dangerous doctrine". Chief Justice Vinson, joined by Justice Douglas, also disagreed and dissented.

Justice Frankfurter, joined by Justice Reed, wrote a passionate dissent reaffirming the classical proposition that the federal courts are courts of limited jurisdiction with no authority to adjudicate except in the instances specifically enumerated in Article III. He asked: "what justification is there for interpreting Article III as imposing one restriction in the exercise of those other powers of the Congress—the restriction to the exercise of 'judicial power'—yet not interpreting it as imposing the restrictions that are most explicit, namely, the particularization of the 'cases' to which 'the judicial Power shall extend' "? He continued:

"Power to adjudicate between citizens of different states, merely because they are citizens of different states, has no relation to any substantive rights created by Congress. * * * The diversity jurisdiction of the federal courts was probably the most tenuously founded and most unwillingly granted of all the heads of federal jurisdiction which Congress was empowered by Article III to confer. * * * The process of reasoning by which this result is reached invites a use of the federal courts which breaks with the whole history of the federal judiciary and disregards the wise policy behind that history. It was because Article III defines and confines the limits of jurisdiction of the courts which are established under Article III that the first Court of Claims Act fell, Gordon v. United States, 69 U.S. (2 Wall.) 561.

"To find a source for 'the judicial Power,' therefore, which may be exercised by courts established under Article III of the Constitution outside that Article would be to disregard the distribution of powers made by the Constitution. * * *

"A substantial majority of the Court agrees that each of the two grounds urged in support of the attempt by Congress to extend diversity jurisdiction to cases involving citizens of the District of Columbia must be rejected—but not the same majority. And so, conflicting minorities in combination bring to pass a result—paradoxical as it may appear—which differing majorities of the Court find insupportable."

Justice Frankfurter is clearly correct about the last point. Would it be fair to say that Tidewater stands for the proposition that Congress may *not* give an Article III court jurisdiction over a non-Article III case or function— with the case itself being a counterexample to the proposition for which it stands?

What outcome would Tidewater call for if a citizen of Puerto Rico sued a citizen of a state in a case raising no federal question?

------

[2] Professor Seinfeld has recently elaborated upon Justice Jackson's argument. For discussion, see p. 803, *infra*.

3. FEDERAL AUTHORITY AND STATE COURT JURISDICTION

INTRODUCTORY NOTE

So far, the material in this Chapter has focused on the power of Congress to vest, or deny, jurisdiction in federal tribunals. But there are closely related issues about congressional control of the jurisdiction of the state courts.

Four principal questions are addressed in this section. The first, addressed in the next two principal cases, Tafflin v. Levitt and Tennessee v. Davis, concerns the scope of congressional power to preclude states from exercising jurisdiction, either by making federal court jurisdiction exclusive or by authorizing removal of cases from state to federal court. The second, which is provoked by Tarble's Case, asks whether the Constitution itself precludes the exercise of state court jurisdiction in any way. The third concerns the extent to which state courts are obliged, by virtue of congressional action or the Supremacy Clause, to exercise jurisdiction over federal cases, even when state law does not authorize state court adjudication; the principal case here is Testa v. Katt. And the last question, raised by Dice v. Akron, Canton & Youngstown R.R., concerns the extent to which federal law governs the procedures and remedies followed by the state courts when litigating federal rights.

Tafflin v. Levitt

493 U.S. 455, 110 S.Ct. 792, 107 L.Ed.2d 887 (1990).
Certiorari to the United States Court of Appeals for the Fourth Circuit.

■ JUSTICE O'CONNOR delivered the opinion of the Court.

* * *

I

[Suit was brought in federal court against the officers and directors of a failed state-chartered savings and loan, and other defendants, by holders of unpaid certificates of deposit. The complaint included claims under the Racketeer Influenced and Corrupt Organizations Act (RICO), which prohibits various forms of participation in a criminal enterprise that is connected to a "pattern of racketeering activity." RICO is an unusual federal statute, as liability for a pattern of racketeering is based on the existence of at least two predicate acts, which are not defined by RICO itself. Instead, a predicate act can be any of a long list of federal or state crimes listed in the RICO statute. A person who violates RICO is subject not only to criminal prosecution, but also to private civil actions in which injured parties may collect treble damages and attorney's fees.

[The question before the Supreme Court in Tafflin was whether a state court may exercise jurisdiction over civil RICO actions. That question arose when, upon the defendants' motion, the lower federal courts held that they should "abstain" from resolving the RICO claims, effectively requiring them to be litigated in the state court.] The lower courts reasoned that since (i) the underlying causes of action had been raised in pending litigation in Maryland state court, and (ii) Maryland had a "comprehensive scheme for the rehabilitation and liquidation of insolvent state-chartered savings and loan associations", abstention was appropriate under the doctrine of Burford v. Sun Oil Co., pp. 1120–1123, *infra.* The Supreme Court granted certiorari to determine whether the lower courts were correct in concluding, as a predicate for their abstention decision, that the state courts have concurrent jurisdiction over civil RICO actions.] We hold that they do * * *.

II

We begin with the axiom that, under our federal system, the States possess sovereignty concurrent with that of the Federal Government, subject only to limitations imposed by the Supremacy Clause. Under this system of dual sovereignty, we have consistently held that state courts have inherent authority, and are thus presumptively competent, to adjudicate claims arising under the laws of the United States. See, *e.g.,* Claflin v. Houseman, 93 U.S. 130, 136–137 (1876); Charles Dowd Box Co. v. Courtney, 368 U.S. 502, 507–508, 522–523 (1962); Gulf Offshore Co. v. Mobil Oil Corp., 453 U.S. 473, 477–478 (1981). As we noted in Claflin, "if exclusive jurisdiction be neither express nor implied, the State courts have concurrent jurisdiction whenever, by their own constitution, they are competent to take it." 93 U.S., at 136; see also Dowd Box, *supra,* 368 U.S. at 507–508 ("We start with the premise that nothing in the concept of our federal system prevents state courts from enforcing rights created by federal law. Concurrent jurisdiction has been a common phenomenon in our judicial history, and exclusive federal court jurisdiction over cases arising under federal law has been the exception rather than the rule."). See generally * * * The Federalist No. 82 (A. Hamilton) * * *.

This deeply rooted presumption in favor of concurrent state court jurisdiction is, of course, rebutted if Congress affirmatively ousts the state courts of jurisdiction over a particular federal claim. As we stated in Gulf Offshore:

> "In considering the propriety of state-court jurisdiction over any particular federal claim, the Court begins with the presumption that state courts enjoy concurrent jurisdiction. Congress, however, may confine jurisdiction to the federal courts either explicitly or implicitly. Thus, the presumption of concurrent jurisdiction can be rebutted by an explicit statutory directive, by unmistakable implication from legislative history, or by a clear incompatibility between state-court jurisdiction and federal interests." 453 U.S., at 478 (citations omitted).

* * * These principles, which have "remained unmodified through the years," Dowd Box, *supra,* 368 U.S. at 508, provide the analytical framework for resolving this case.

III

The precise question presented, therefore, is whether state courts have been divested of jurisdiction to hear civil RICO claims "by an explicit statutory directive, by unmistakable implication from legislative history, or by a clear incompatibility between state-court jurisdiction and federal interests." Gulf Offshore, *supra,* 453 U.S. at 478. * * *

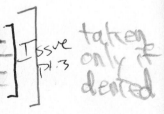

At the outset, petitioners concede that there is nothing in the language of RICO—much less an "explicit statutory directive"—to suggest that Congress has, by affirmative enactment, divested the state courts of jurisdiction to hear civil RICO claims. The statutory provision authorizing civil RICO claims provides in full:

> "Any person injured in his business or property by reason of a violation of section 1962 of this chapter *may* sue therefor in any appropriate United States district court and shall recover threefold the damages he sustains and the cost of the suit, including a reasonable attorney's fee." 18 U.S.C. § 1964(c) (emphasis added).

This grant of federal jurisdiction is plainly permissive, not mandatory, for "[t]he statute does not state nor even suggest that such jurisdiction shall be exclusive. * * *" Dowd Box, *supra*, 368 U.S., at 506. Indeed, "[i]t is black letter law . . . that the mere grant of jurisdiction to a federal court does not operate to oust a state court from concurrent jurisdiction over the cause of action." Gulf Offshore, *supra*, 453 U.S., at 479 * * *.

Petitioners thus rely solely on the second and third factors suggested in Gulf Offshore, arguing that exclusive federal jurisdiction over civil RICO actions is established "by unmistakable implication from legislative history, or by a clear incompatibility between state-court jurisdiction and federal interests," 453 U.S., at 478.

Our review of the legislative history, however, reveals no evidence that Congress even considered the question of concurrent state court jurisdiction over RICO claims, much less any suggestion that Congress affirmatively intended to confer exclusive jurisdiction over such claims on the federal courts. * * * Petitioners nonetheless insist that if Congress had considered the issue, it would have granted federal courts exclusive jurisdiction over civil RICO claims. This argument, however, is misplaced, for even if we could reliably discern what Congress' intent might have been had it considered the question, we are not at liberty to so speculate; the fact that Congress did not even *consider* the issue readily disposes of any argument that Congress unmistakably intended to divest state courts of concurrent jurisdiction.

Sensing this void in the legislative history, petitioners rely, in the alternative, on our decisions in Sedima, S.P.R.L. v. Imrex Co., 473 U.S. 479 (1985), and Agency Holding Corp. v. Malley-Duff & Assocs., 483 U.S. 143 (1987), in which we noted that Congress modeled § 1964(c) after § 4 of the Clayton Act, 15 U.S.C. § 15(a). * * * Petitioners assert that, because we have interpreted § 4 of the Clayton Act to confer exclusive jurisdiction on the federal courts, see, *e.g.*, General Investment Co. v. Lake Shore & M.S.R. Co., 260 U.S. 261, 286–288 (1922), and because Congress may be presumed to have been aware of and incorporated those interpretations when it used similar language in RICO, Congress intended, by implication, to grant exclusive federal jurisdiction over claims arising under § 1964(c).

This argument is also flawed. To rebut the presumption of concurrent jurisdiction, the question is not whether any intent at all may be divined from legislative silence on the issue, but whether Congress in its deliberations may be said to have affirmatively or unmistakably intended jurisdiction to be exclusively federal. In the instant case, the lack of any indication in RICO's legislative history that Congress either considered or assumed that the importing of remedial language from the Clayton Act into RICO had any jurisdictional implications is dispositive. The "mere borrowing of statutory language does not imply that Congress also intended to incorporate all of the baggage that may be attached to the borrowed language." Lou [v. Belzberg, 834 F.2d 730, 737 (9th Cir.1987)]. Indeed, to the extent we impute to Congress knowledge of our Clayton Act precedents, it makes no less sense to impute to Congress knowledge of Claflin and Dowd Box, under which Congress, had it sought to confer exclusive jurisdiction over civil RICO claims, would have had every incentive to do so expressly. * * *

Petitioners finally urge that state court jurisdiction over civil RICO claims would be clearly incompatible with federal interests. We noted in Gulf Offshore that factors indicating clear incompatibility "include the desirability of <u>uniform interpretation</u>, the expertise of federal judges in federal law, and the assumed <u>greater hospitality</u> of federal courts to peculiarly federal claims." 453 U.S., at 483–484 (citation and footnote omitted). Petitioners' primary contention is that concurrent jurisdiction is clearly incompatible with the federal interest in uniform interpretation of federal criminal laws, see 18 U.S.C. § 3231, because state courts would be required to construe the federal crimes that constitute predicate acts defined as "racketeering activity," see 18 U.S.C. §§ 1961(1)(B), (C), and (D) * * * [and the federal courts would] consequently lose control over the orderly and uniform development of federal criminal law.

We perceive no "clear incompatibility" between state court jurisdiction over civil RICO actions and federal interests. * * * [C]oncurrent jurisdiction over § 1964(c) suits is clearly not incompatible with § 3231 itself, for civil RICO claims are not "offenses against the laws of the United States," § 3231, and do not result in the imposition of criminal sanctions—uniform or otherwise. * * *

* * * Although petitioners' concern with the need for uniformity and consistency of federal criminal law is well-taken, see Ableman v. Booth, 62 U.S. 506, 517–518 (1859), federal courts, pursuant to § 3231, would retain full authority and responsibility for the interpretation and application of federal criminal laws, for they would not be bound by state court interpretations of the federal offenses constituting RICO's predicate acts. State courts adjudicating civil RICO claims will, in addition, be guided by federal court interpretations of the relevant federal criminal statutes, just as federal courts sitting in diversity are guided by state court interpretations of state law * * *. State court judgments misinterpreting federal criminal law would, of course, also be subject to direct review by this Court. * * *

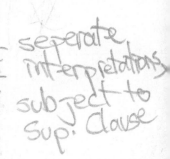

Moreover, contrary to petitioners' fears, we have full faith in the ability of state courts to handle the complexities of civil RICO actions, particularly since many RICO cases involve asserted violations of state law, such as state fraud claims, over which state courts presumably have greater expertise. See * * * BNA, Civil RICO Report, Vol. 2, No. 44, p. 7 (Apr. 14, 1987) (54.9% of all RICO cases after Sedima involved "common law fraud" and another 18.0% involved either "nonsecurities fraud" or "theft or conversion"). * * *

Finally, we note that, far from disabling or frustrating federal interests, "[p]ermitting state courts to entertain federal causes of action facilitates the enforcement of federal rights." Gulf Offshore, 453 U.S., at 478, n. 4 * * *. Thus, to the extent that Congress intended RICO to serve broad remedial purposes, * * * concurrent state court jurisdiction over civil RICO claims will advance rather than jeopardize federal policies underlying the statute.

For all of the above reasons, we hold that state courts have concurrent jurisdiction to consider civil claims arising under RICO. * * * The judgment of the Court of Appeals is accordingly

Affirmed.

■ JUSTICE WHITE, concurring.

* * *

■ JUSTICE SCALIA, with whom JUSTICE KENNEDY joins, concurring.

I join the opinion of the Court, addressing the issues before us on the basis argued by the parties, which has included acceptance of the dictum in Gulf Offshore Co. v. Mobil Oil Corp., 453 U.S. 473, 478 (1981), that "the presumption of concurrent jurisdiction can be rebutted by an explicit statutory directive, by unmistakable implication from legislative history, or by a clear incompatibility between state-court jurisdiction and federal interests." * * * I write separately, before this * * * [dictum] has become too entrenched, to note my view that in one respect it is not a correct statement of the law, and in another respect it may not be.

State courts have jurisdiction over federal causes of action not because it is "conferred" upon them by the Congress; nor even because their inherent powers permit them to entertain transitory causes of action arising under the laws of foreign sovereigns, see, *e.g.*, McKenna v. Fisk, 1 How. 241, 247–249 (1843); but because "[t]he laws of the United States are laws in the several States, and just as much binding on the citizens and courts thereof as the State laws are. . . . The two together form one system of jurisprudence, which constitutes the law of the land for the State; and the courts of the two jurisdictions are not foreign to each other. . . ." Claflin v. Houseman, 93 U.S. 130, 136–137 (1876).

It therefore takes an affirmative act of power under the Supremacy Clause to oust the States of jurisdiction—an exercise of what one of our earliest cases referred to as "the power of congress to *withdraw*" federal claims from state-court jurisdiction. Houston v. Moore, 5 Wheat. 1, 26 (1820) (emphasis added).

As an original unqualified proposition, it would be eminently arguable that depriving state courts of their sovereign authority to adjudicate the law of the land must be done, if not with the utmost clarity, *cf.* Atascadero State Hospital v. Scanlon, 473 U.S. 234, 243 (1985) (state sovereign immunity can be eliminated only by "clear statement"), at least *expressly.* That was the view of Alexander Hamilton:

> "When . . . we consider the State governments and the national governments, as they truly are, in the light of kindred systems, and as parts of ONE WHOLE, the inference seems to be conclusive that the State courts would have a concurrent jurisdiction in all cases arising under the laws or the Union, where it was not expressly prohibited." The Federalist No. 82, p. 132 (E. Bourne ed. 1947).

* * * Although as early as Claflin, and as late as Gulf Offshore, we had *said* that the exclusion of concurrent state jurisdiction could be achieved by implication, the only cases in which to my knowledge we have acted upon such a principle are those relating to the Sherman Act and the Clayton Act—where the full extent of our analysis was the less than compelling statement that provisions giving the right to sue in United States District Court "show that [the right] is to be exercised *only* in a 'court of the United States.' " General Investment Co. v. Lake Shore & Michigan Southern R. Co., 260 U.S. 261, 287 (1922) (emphasis added). * * * In the standard fields of exclusive federal jurisdiction, the governing statutes specifically recite that suit may be brought "only" in federal court, Investment Company Act of 1940, as amended, 15 U.S.C. § 80a–35(b)(5); that the jurisdiction of the federal courts shall be "exclusive," Securities Exchange Act of 1934, as amended, 15 U.S.C. § 78aa; Natural Gas Act of 1938, 15 U.S.C. § 717u; Employee Retirement Income Security Act of 1974, 29 U.S.C. § 1132(e)(1); or indeed even that the jurisdiction of the federal courts shall be "exclusive of the courts of the States," 18 U.S.C. § 3231 (criminal cases); 28 U.S.C. §§ 1333 (admiralty, maritime, and prize cases), 1334 (bankruptcy cases), 1338 (patent, plant variety protection, and copyright cases), 1351 (actions against consuls or vice consuls of foreign states), 1355 (actions for recovery or enforcement of fine, penalty, or forfeiture incurred under Act of Congress), 1356 (seizures on land or water not within admiralty and maritime jurisdiction).

Assuming, however, that exclusion by implication is possible, surely what is required is implication in the text of the statute, and not merely, as the second part of the Gulf Offshore dictum would permit, through "unmistakable implication from legislative history." 453 U.S., at 478. Although Charles Dowd Box Co. v. Courtney, 368 U.S. 502 (1962), after concluding that the statute "does not state nor even suggest that [federal] jurisdiction shall be exclusive," *id.*, at 506, proceeded quite unnecessarily to examine the legislative history, it did so to reinforce rather than contradict the conclusion it had already reached. We have never found state jurisdiction excluded by "unmistakable implication" from legislative history. * * * What is needed to oust the States of jurisdiction is congressional *action* (*i.e.*, a provision of law), not merely congressional discussion.

It is perhaps also true that implied preclusion can be established by the fact that a statute expressly mentions only federal courts, plus the fact that state-court jurisdiction would plainly disrupt the statutory scheme. That is conceivably what was meant by the third part of the Gulf Offshore dictum, "clear incompatibility between state-court jurisdiction and federal interests." 453 U.S., at 478. If the phrase is interpreted more broadly than that, however—if it is taken to assert some power on the part of this Court to exclude state-court jurisdiction when systemic federal interests make it undesirable—it has absolutely no foundation in our precedent. * * *

In sum: As the Court holds, the RICO cause of action meets none of the three tests for exclusion of state-court jurisdiction recited in Gulf Offshore. Since that is so, the proposition that meeting any one of the tests would have sufficed is dictum here, as it was there. In my view meeting the second test is assuredly not enough, and meeting the third may not be.

NOTE ON TAFFLIN V. LEVITT AND CONGRESSIONAL EXCLUSION OF STATE COURT JURISDICTION

(1) Federalist No. 82. Both the majority and the concurrence in Tafflin cite Federalist No. 82. In that paper, Alexander Hamilton started from the principles in Federalist No. 32, regarding legislative authority, writing that the states "will retain all *pre-existing* authorities" that are not exclusively delegated to the national government, either by (i) an express grant of exclusivity to the national government, (ii) a grant of authority to the union where "the exercise of a like authority is prohibited to the States," or (iii) an authority granted to the Union, with which the exercise of state authority would be utterly incompatible. Being inclined to think these principles apply to the judiciary with similar force as to the legislature, he concluded that the "State courts will *retain* the jurisdiction they now have, unless it appears to be taken away in one of the enumerated modes."

He then said that Article III's language—in particular, that "[t]he JUDICIAL POWER of the United States *shall be vested* in one Supreme Court, and in *such* inferior courts as the Congress shall from time to time ordain and establish"—should not suggest that the federal judicial power is exclusive, as that would "amount to an alienation of State power by implication." Instead, he preferred interpreting the quoted language as merely identifying the courts that will exercise the judicial power.

Hamilton next seemed at first to state that "this doctrine of concurrent jurisdiction is only clearly applicable" to those causes of action "of which the State courts have previous cognizance" and that to deny state court jurisdiction over "cases which may grow out of, and be *peculiar* to, the Constitution * * * can hardly be considered as the abridgement of a pre-existing authority." But while proceeding to declare that the United States could, if it thought it expedient, make federal jurisdiction exclusive over "causes arising upon a particular regulation" (of which the RICO action in Tafflin would be an example), he then said that state courts would have concurrent jurisdiction not only of pre-existing causes but also of causes of action to which federal acts of Congress "may give birth." He noted that the judicial power of every government, in civil cases, "looks beyond its own * * * laws" and may apply the laws of foreign nations; when one considers that the state and federal governments are parts of "One Whole, the inference seems to be conclusive, that the State courts would have a concurrent jurisdiction in all cases arising under the laws of the Union, where it was not expressly prohibited."

(2) Constitutionally Mandated Exclusivity? The unqualified proposition that, absent congressional exclusion, state courts may adjudicate federal causes of action has not always appeared self-evident. Justice Story, for example, believed that Article III makes federal jurisdiction "unavoidably * * * exclusive" in at least some classes of cases. He clearly placed federal criminal cases and admiralty and maritime cases within with that category, and suggested somewhat less clearly that the same might be true more generally of cases over which the state courts would not have had jurisdiction prior to adoption of the Constitution. See Martin v. Hunter's Lessee, 14 U.S.

(1 Wheat.) 304, 337 (1816).[1] Tafflin v. Levitt and the cases on which it relies decisively reject the notion of constitutionally-based exclusivity. For additional discussion of whether the Constitution requires exclusive federal jurisdiction in particular classes of cases, see pp. 431–432, *infra*.

(3) Foundations of Congressional Authority. The Judiciary Act of 1789 provided for exclusive federal jurisdiction of cases involving "crimes and offenses cognizable under the authority of the United States," "seizures" on land or water, "suits for penalties and forfeitures, incurred under the laws of the United States," "suits against consuls or vice-consuls", and "civil causes of admiralty and maritime jurisdiction * * * saving to suitors, in all cases, the right of a common law remedy, where the common law is competent to give it". Act of Sept. 24, 1789, §§ 9, 11, 1 Stat. 76, 78. The Act also conferred exclusive *original* Supreme Court jurisdiction in many civil actions to which states were parties. *Id.* § 13. Pockets of exclusive jurisdiction have existed ever since.[2] Justice Scalia's opinion in Tafflin lists most of the important statutes that make federal jurisdiction exclusive. (One important grant of exclusive jurisdiction that he does not list governs common law tort actions against the United States, brought under the Federal Tort Claims Act. See 28 U.S.C. § 1346(b).)

Because Congress' power to create exclusive federal jurisdiction has seldom been challenged, the Supreme Court did not discuss the question until The Moses Taylor, 71 U.S. (4 Wall.) 411 (1867). In reversing a state court judgment sustaining an *in rem* proceeding against a vessel, the Court held that such relief fell within the exclusive grant of federal admiralty jurisdiction. With respect to the constitutional question, Justice Field said:

"The Judiciary Act of 1789 * * * is framed upon the theory that in all cases to which the judicial power of the United States extends, Congress may rightfully vest exclusive jurisdiction in the Federal courts. It declares that in some cases, from their commencement, such jurisdiction shall be exclusive; in other cases it determines at what stage of procedure such jurisdiction shall attach, and how long and how far concurrent jurisdiction of the State courts shall be permitted. * * *

"The constitutionality of these provisions cannot be seriously questioned, and is of frequent recognition by both State and Federal courts."[3]

Under which grant(s) of authority might Congress exclude state court jurisdiction of federal claims? Could Congress make diversity jurisdiction exclusive?

---

[1]   Justice Story's view appears to have rested in part on a distinction between jurisdiction that existed in state courts "previous to the adoption of the constitution", which they retained, and jurisdiction over cases that could not previously have arisen, which "could not afterwards be directly conferred on them". 14 U.S. (1 Wheat.) at 335. Whether intentionally or not, Justice Story's formulation echoes some of the language (though not the conclusion reached) in The Federalist No. 82. *Cf.* 3 Story, Commentaries on the Constitution § 1666, at 533 (1833) (noting the "peculiar wisdom in giving to the national government" admiralty jurisdiction, but stating that in many admiralty cases "the same reasons do not exist, as in cases of prize, for an exclusive jurisdiction; and, therefore, whenever the common law is competent to give a remedy in the state courts, they may retain their accustomed concurrent jurisdiction in the administration of it").

[2]   Section 256 of the former Judicial Code (28 U.S.C. § 371, 1940 ed.) purported to enumerate the areas from which state courts had been excluded, but the enumeration was incomplete and the section was repealed in the 1948 revision.

[3]   For similar affirmations, see Houston v. Moore, 18 U.S. (5 Wheat.) 1, 25–26 (1820); Lockerty v. Phillips, p. 342, *supra*; Bowles v. Willingham, 321 U.S. 503, 511–12 (1944).

(4) The Scope of Implied Exclusion.

(a) The Claflin Presumption of Concurrency and Departures from It. The 1876 decision in Claflin v. Housman established the presumption, generally followed ever since, that a grant of federal jurisdiction, unless explicitly exclusive, does not preclude the exercise of concurrent state court jurisdiction.[4] As noted in the Tafflin opinion, however, the Supreme Court has occasionally held that grants of federal jurisdiction *impliedly* exclude state jurisdiction. In the antitrust decision discussed by Justice Scalia, General Inv. Co. v. Lake Shore & M.S. Ry., 260 U.S. 261 (1922), and the subsequent decision in Freeman v. Bee Machine Co., 319 U.S. 448 (1943), the Court did not refer to the Claflin presumption. Indeed, the Court's discussion of implied exclusivity was cursory.

Other statutes construed as impliedly excluding state court jurisdiction include 28 U.S.C. §§ 1346(a) (U.S. as defendant in suits for recovery in tax and certain non-tax cases), 1491(a)(1) (Court of Federal Claims jurisdiction over express or implied contract actions where U.S. is the defendant), and 2321–22 (enforcement of Surface Transportation Board orders).

(b) The Current Law on Implied Exclusion. In Yellow Freight System, Inc. v. Donnelly, 494 U.S. 820 (1990), decided only a few months after Tafflin, a unanimous Court expressed stronger disfavor of implied exclusion. Holding that state courts have concurrent jurisdiction over private civil actions brought under Title VII of the 1964 Civil Rights Act, Justice Stevens' opinion said that the omission of any express provision making federal jurisdiction exclusive "is strong, and arguably sufficient, evidence that Congress had no such intent". The Court discussed only briefly the other two factors set forth in the Gulf Offshore decision—an "unmistakable implication from legislative history" or a "clear incompatibility between state-court jurisdiction and federal interests"—and attached little weight to statements in the legislative history indicating an expectation that all Title VII cases would be tried in federal courts or to the frequent statutory references to procedures applicable in federal courts.

Professor Solimine suggests that this decision implicitly abandons the three-part test employed in the Gulf Offshore and Tafflin cases and instead adopts Justice Scalia's view that only a clear statement by Congress suffices to oust state court jurisdiction. See Solimine, *Rethinking Exclusive Federal Jurisdiction*, 52 U.Pitt.L.Rev. 383, 385 (1991).[5]

---

[4] The Court has also held that an express statutory recognition of state court jurisdiction does not bar the exercise of federal court jurisdiction. See Mims v. Arrow Financial Services, LLC, 132 S.Ct. 740 (2012), p. 815, *infra*. Congress, when prohibiting certain telemarketing practices, specified that a person "may, if otherwise permitted by the laws or rules of court of a State, bring in an appropriate court of that State" an action for damages and/or an injunction. In the Mims case, the Court held that the textual recognition of state court jurisdiction did not bar the federal courts from exercising federal question jurisdiction.

[5] The later decision in Nevada v. Hicks, 533 U.S. 353 (2001), can be viewed as raising the question whether the presumption of concurrent jurisdiction applies to tribal courts. There, the Court held that the tribal court lacked jurisdiction to adjudicate a federal civil rights claim under 42 U.S.C. § 1983 that was premised on the allegedly tortious conduct of a state warden executing, on tribal land, a search warrant for an off-reservation crime. Justice Scalia's majority opinion reasoned that the "historical and constitutional assumption of concurrent state-court jurisdiction is completely missing with respect to tribal courts", which, unlike state courts, are not courts of general jurisdiction. Rather, "a tribe's inherent adjudicative jurisdiction over nonmembers is at most only as broad as its legislative jurisdiction". Finding that "tribal court jurisdiction would create serious anomalies * * * because the general federal-question removal

(5) Implied Exclusion and the Judicial Function. What *should* be the courts' role in determining whether a grant of federal jurisdiction should be construed to exclude state jurisdiction? One approach insists that only Congress may oust state court jurisdiction. (Some might add that Congress must make its intention evident in the statutory text.) A second approach would have courts eschew any such interpretive presumption and simply use ordinary methods of statutory interpretation. A final approach urges courts to exercise a "creative lawmaking function" and determine whether federal jurisdiction is impliedly exclusive in light of "the potential impingement on important federal interests and programs that might result from [adjudication] by state judges who lack sufficient background, expertise or— on occasion—competence to deal with * * * uniquely federal concerns". Redish & Muench, *Adjudication of Federal Causes of Action in State Courts*, 75 Mich.L.Rev. 311, 329 (1976).

(6) Congressional Policy. The conjunction of congressional powers to define the scope of federal jurisdiction (discussed in Section 1 of this Chapter) and to make federal jurisdiction exclusive leaves Congress with an array of policy options. These include: (a) exclusive state original jurisdiction; (b) concurrent federal and state jurisdiction; (c) concurrent state and federal jurisdiction, but with a right of state court defendants to remove to federal court; and (d) exclusive federal jurisdiction.

Each of these options is employed for some kinds of federal claims. The considerations that Congress might weigh in choosing among them are complex. But one must bear in mind that cases frequently involve a mix of state and federal issues. For example, a plaintiff may assert both state and federal causes of action, or a federal issue may come into a case only by way of defense or reply to a defense. In considering the appropriate forum for cases involving a mixture of state and federal issues, questions arise about how to weigh the competing state and federal interests in adjudicating the entire case, see generally Chapter VIII, *infra*, and about the benefits and drawbacks of carving a case into parts so that the state elements can be adjudicated in state court and federal issues resolved in federal court, see generally Chapter X, *infra*.[6]

(a) Exclusive State Original Jurisdiction. State jurisdiction is necessarily exclusive in cases not within the jurisdictional headings of Article III (for example, state law claims between non-diverse parties), as it is in cases in which Congress has not seen fit to confer federal jurisdiction (for example, claims not satisfying a federal amount-in-controversy requirement).

---

statute refers only to removal from state court", the Court concluded that unlike state courts, "tribal courts cannot entertain § 1983 claims".

[6] Thus, Friedman, *Under the Law of Federal Jurisdiction: Allocating Cases Between State and Federal Courts*, 104 Colum.L.Rev. 1211, 1228–35 (2004), argues that "multijurisdictional models", which involve some division of authority between state and federal courts for a single case, should be used more extensively. Among the possibilities are "reference" models, under which a federal court exercising jurisdiction can refer certain state law issues to a state court for authoritative resolution (see pp. 1113–1116, *infra*); "collateral review" models, under which a federal court effectively reviews state court decisions of federal law (as, for example, in the case of federal habeas corpus review of state court decisions, see pp. 1265–1355, *infra*); and "sequencing" models, under which a party to state court litigation reserves federal issues for subsequent litigation in federal court (as occasionally happens under federal "abstention" doctrine, see pp. 1113–1116, *infra*).

(b) Concurrent Jurisdiction. Concurrent federal and state jurisdiction may promote convenience when it is easier for litigants to appear in a state court than in a federal court. Concurrent jurisdiction also "permits plaintiffs a relatively free choice of forum in the expectation that enlightened self-interest" will lead plaintiffs "into the forum most likely to enunciate an expansive vision of the rights of the individual". Neuborne, *Toward Procedural Parity in Constitutional Litigation*, 22 Wm. & Mary L.Rev. 725, 730 (1981).

(c) Concurrent Jurisdiction with Right of Removal. In civil cases arising under federal law, the most common jurisdictional arrangement is concurrent state and federal jurisdiction, subject to a right of the defendant to remove from state to federal court.[7] (When there are multiple defendants, the general removal statute, § 1441, requires the agreement of all of them to effect removal.) Ordinarily, the right to remove depends on the contents of the plaintiff's well-pleaded complaint; with a few exceptions, removal is not allowed based on a federal counterclaim, a federal defense, or a federal reply to a defense. For extensive consideration of the intricacies of this scheme and of policy arguments for and against it, see Chap. VIII, Sec. 3, *infra*.

The general diversity statute likewise couples original jurisdiction with a right of defendant(s) to remove, although in diversity actions the removal right is denied to in-state defendants.

(d) Exclusive Federal Jurisdiction. Arguments in favor of exclusive federal jurisdiction frequently invoke the desirability of uniform interpretation of federal law, the presumptive expertise of federal judges in dealing with federal issues, and the likelihood that federal courts will be more sympathetic to federal purposes than will state courts. To a considerable extent, these arguments assume lack of parity between state and federal courts. See Fallon, *The Ideologies of Federal Courts Law*, 74 Va.L.Rev. 1141, 1202–07 (1988); see generally pp. 299–303, *supra* (discussing the concept of "parity"). Insofar as that assumption is warranted, can the concern about the relative sympathy of state and federal tribunals to federal claims be adequately met by providing for concurrent state and federal jurisdiction and a right of removal? Putting the question differently, if all litigants prefer state court, what justifies overriding those preferences and insisting on exclusive federal jurisdiction?[8]

---

[7] See 28 U.S.C. § 1441. In some situations, statutes prelude removal of a federal question case that was initially filed in state court. See p. 850, note 2, *infra*.

[8] See Redish, *Reassessing the Allocation of Federal Judicial Business Between State and Federal Courts: Federal Jurisdiction and "The Martian Chronicles"*, 78 Va.L.Rev. 1769, 1812 (1992) (urging the virtual abandonment of exclusive jurisdiction).

The existing pattern of exclusive jurisdiction is limited in its capacity to achieve uniformity by the combination of the well-pleaded complaint rule, which applies to original jurisdiction, and the general removal statute, which ties removal to original jurisdiction. Thus, for example, in Lear, Inc. v. Adkins, 395 U.S. 653 (1969), a patent holder sued for breach of a patent license agreement; the licensee raised as a defense that the patent was invalid and hence that federal law precluded the award of damages. The rule barring removal based on a federal defense meant that the case remained in the state court, which had to resolve the issue of patent validity—an issue central to the regime of federal patent regulation. Of course, Congress could authorize removal at the point at which an issue of federal patent law arises.

Tennessee v. Davis

100 U.S. (10 Otto) 257, 25 L. Ed. 648 (1880).
Certificate of division in opinion between the judges of the Circuit Court of the
United States for the Middle District of Tennessee.

[Davis, a federal revenue official, was indicted for murder in Tennessee state court. Before trial, he filed in the Circuit Court of the United States a petition to remove the case from the state court. The judges of the Circuit Court were divided in opinion, and certified to the Supreme Court, *inter alia*, the question, "Whether an indictment of a revenue officer (of the United States) for murder, found in a State court, under the facts alleged in the petition for removal in this case, is removable to the Circuit Court of the United States, under § 643 of the Revised Statutes."*]

■ MR. JUSTICE STRONG delivered the opinion of the court.

The first of the questions certified is one of great importance, bringing as it does into consideration the relation of the general government to the government of the States, and bringing also into view not merely the construction of an act of Congress, but its constitutionality. That * * * the defendant's petition for removal * * * was in the form prescribed by the act of Congress admits of no doubt. It represented that * * * he was acting by and under the authority of the internal-revenue laws of the United States; that what he did was done under and by right of his office, to wit, as deputy collector of internal revenue; that it was his duty to seize illicit distilleries and the apparatus that is used for the illicit and unlawful distillation of spirits; and that while so attempting to enforce the revenue laws of the United States, * * * he was assaulted and fired upon by a number of armed men, and that in defence of his life he returned the fire. * * * The language of the statute * * * is as follows: "When any civil suit or criminal prosecution is commenced in any court of a State against any officer appointed under, or acting by authority of, any revenue law of the United States, * * *, or against any person acting by or under authority of any such officer, on account of any act done under color of his office or of any such law, or on account of any right, title, or authority claimed by such officer or other person under any such law," the case may be removed into the Federal court. * * *

We come, then, to the inquiry * * * whether sect. 643 is a constitutional exercise of the power vested in Congress. * * *

By the last clause of the eighth section of the first article of the Constitution, Congress is invested with power to make all laws necessary and proper for carrying into execution not only all the powers previously specified, but also all other powers vested by the Constitution in the government of the United States, or in any department or officer thereof. Among these is the judicial power of the government. That is declared by the second section of the third article to "extend to all cases in law and equity arising under the Constitution, the laws of the United States, and treaties made or which shall be made under their authority," & c. This

---

*   [Ed.] At the time of this decision, no statute gave the Supreme Court appellate jurisdiction over decisions of federal circuit courts in criminal cases. However, the judges of a circuit court—which was a trial court composed of two judges—could certify to the Supreme Court for decision a question on which the circuit judges disagreed.

provision embraces alike civil and criminal cases arising under the Constitution and laws. Cohens v. Virginia, 6 Wheat. 264. Both are equally within the domain of the judicial powers of the United States, and there is nothing in the grant to justify an assertion that whatever power may be exerted over a civil case may not be exerted as fully over a criminal one. And a case arising under the Constitution and laws of the United States may as well arise in a criminal prosecution as in a civil suit. What constitutes a case thus arising was early defined in the case cited from 6 Wheaton. It is not merely one where a party comes into court to demand something conferred upon him by the Constitution or by a law or treaty. A case consists of the right of one party as well as the other, and may truly be said to arise under the Constitution or a law or a treaty of the United States whenever its correct decision depends upon the construction of either. Cases arising under the laws of the United States are such as grow out of the legislation of Congress, whether they constitute the right or privilege, or claim or protection, or defense of the party, in whole or in part, by whom they are asserted. * * *

The constitutional right of Congress to authorize the removal before trial of civil cases arising under the laws of the United States has long since passed beyond doubt. It was exercised almost contemporaneously with the adoption of the Constitution, and the power has been in constant use ever since. The Judiciary Act of Sept. 24, 1789, was passed by the first Congress, many members of which had assisted in framing the Constitution; and though some doubts were soon after suggested whether cases could be removed from State courts before trial, those doubts soon disappeared. Whether removal from a State to a Federal court is an exercise of appellate jurisdiction, as laid down in Story's Commentaries on the Constitution, sect. 1745, or an indirect mode of exercising original jurisdiction, as intimated in Railway Company v. Whitton (13 Wall. 270), we need not now inquire. Be it one or the other, it was ruled in the case last cited to be constitutional. But if there is power in Congress to direct a removal before trial of a civil case arising under the Constitution or laws of the United States, and direct its removal because such a case has arisen, it is impossible to see why the same power may not order the removal of a criminal prosecution, when a similar case has arisen in it. * * *

The argument so much pressed upon us, that it is an invasion of the sovereignty of a State to withdraw from its courts into the courts of the general government the trial of prosecutions for alleged offences against the criminal laws of a State, even though the defense presents a case arising out of an act of Congress, ignores entirely the dual character of our government. It assumes that the States are completely and in all respects sovereign. But when the national government was formed, some of the attributes of State sovereignty were partially, and others wholly, surrendered and vested in the United States. Over the subjects thus surrendered the sovereignty of the States ceased to extend. Before the adoption of the Constitution, each State had complete and exclusive authority to administer by its courts all the law, civil and criminal, which existed within its borders. Its judicial power extended over every legal question that could arise. But when the Constitution was adopted, a portion of that judicial power became vested in the new government created, and so far as thus vested it was withdrawn from the sovereignty of the State. Now the execution and enforcement of the laws of the United

States, and the judicial determination of questions arising under them, are confided to another sovereign, and to that extent the sovereignty of the State is restricted. The removal of cases arising under those laws, from State into Federal courts, is, therefore, no invasion of State domain. On the contrary, a denial of the right of the general government to remove them, to take charge of and try any case arising under the Constitution or laws of the United States, is a denial of the conceded sovereignty of that government over a subject expressly committed to it. * * *

It follows that the first question certified to us from the Circuit Court of Tennessee must be answered in the affirmative. * * *

■ MR. JUSTICE CLIFFORD, with whom concurred MR. JUSTICE FIELD, dissenting. * * *

NOTE ON THE POWER OF CONGRESS TO PROVIDE FOR REMOVAL FROM STATE TO FEDERAL COURTS

(1) Constitutional Background and Statutory Foundations. The constitutionality of removal before judgment has long been accepted,[1] as has broad congressional power in specifying how removal operates. See City of Greenwood v. Peacock, 384 U.S. 808, 833 (1966) ("We may assume that Congress has constitutional power to provide that all federal issues be tried in the federal courts, that all be tried in the courts of the States, or that jurisdiction of such issues be shared. And in the exercise of that power, we may assume that Congress is constitutionally fully free to establish the conditions under which civil or criminal proceedings involving federal issues may be removed from one court to another.").

(2) Current Statutes and Issues.[2]

(a) Civil Cases. The general removal statute applicable to civil cases, 28 U.S.C. § 1441, permits the defendant(s) to remove only when the action is one that could originally be filed in federal court.[3]

(b) Criminal Cases. No *general* provision, similar to § 1441, authorizes removal of state criminal cases. But where a more specialized provision authorizes removal of a criminal case, the notice of removal must be filed

---

[1]   Though declared to be beyond doubt in The Moses Taylor, 71 U.S. (4 Wall.) 411, 429–30 (1867), the power was not directly determined in a civil action until The Mayor v. Cooper, 73 U.S. (6 Wall.) 247 (1868), a tort action challenging a seizure under claim of federal authority during the Civil War. Railway Co. v. Whitton, 80 U.S. (13 Wall.) 270 (1872), reaffirmed this decision in a case in which removal rested on diversity of citizenship.

In Martin v. Hunter's Lessee, 14 U.S. (1 Wheat.) 304 (1816), in challenging the power of the Supreme Court to review state court judgments, counsel conceded the authority of Congress to provide for removal before final judgment of a case within the federal judicial power. In response, Justice Story's opinion treated removal as an exercise of "appellate jurisdiction" and thus used counsel's concession to refute the attack. See Chap. V, Sec. 1, *infra*.

[2]   For additional materials on removal, see pp. 849–860, *infra*.

[3]   Unlike most removal statutes, the Act of March 3, 1863, 12 Stat. 755, applied after as well as before judgment in the state court. In The Justices v. Murray, 76 U.S. (9 Wall.) 274 (1870), an action for assault and battery and false imprisonment, that was removed after a jury trial and verdict for the plaintiff, the Court held that the Seventh Amendment governed and that "so much of the * * * Act of Congress * * * as provides for the removal of a judgment in a State court, and in which the cause was tried by a jury, to the Circuit Court of the United States for a retrial on the facts and law, is not in pursuance of the Constitution, and is void".

within thirty days of arraignment "or at any time before trial, whichever is earlier, except that for good cause shown the * * * [federal court] may enter an order granting the defendant or defendants leave to file the notice at a later time." 28 U.S.C. § 1455.

(c) Federal Officer Removal. The statute at issue in Davis authorized particular federal officials—those enforcing the revenue laws—to remove state court actions to federal court. Since 1948, 28 U.S.C. § 1442 has permitted removal of any civil or criminal action against any federal "officer" or "person acting under the officer" for "any act under color of such office". A later amendment extended the removal right to the United States or any agency thereof.

The scope of removal authorized by § 1442 is broader than that under § 1441, both because § 1442 applies to criminal as well as civil cases and because it permits removal not merely when the action could have been filed in federal court but also when the defendant asserts a federal defense. Tennessee v. Davis exemplifies both features of the broader coverage of the federal officer removal provision. And § 1442 has in general been broadly construed. See, *e.g.*, Willingham v. Morgan, 395 U.S. 402 (1969) (allowing the warden and chief medical officer of a federal penitentiary to remove to federal court on a showing that their only contact with a prisoner who alleged a range of abuses had occurred inside the penitentiary).

But in Mesa v. California, 489 U.S. 121 (1989), p. 803, *infra*, the Court recognized an important limit on § 1442's reach, holding that it authorized removal only when the defendant federal officer raises a federal defense, rather than, as in Mesa, when the officer simply contests a state law criminal charge. In arguing for a broader interpretation, the United States contended that the defendant in Davis had not asserted a federal defense to the killing but only a state law self-defense claim. The Government argued, accordingly, that despite language in Davis about the importance of federal adjudication of federal defenses, in fact the decision upheld removal in the absence of a federal defense. In Mesa, the Court rejected that interpretation of Davis, reasoning that whether Davis was acting in self-defense depended on whether he was lawfully trying to seize the still or was merely a thief; proof that he was not a simple thief depended on the federal revenue laws; and hence, adjudication of the self-defense claim required the application of federal law.

Clearly in the background in Mesa was a concern that, if § 1442 were construed to permit removal in the absence of a federal defense, the case might not "aris[e] under" federal law in the constitutional sense, and thus would not come within any of the authorized categories of federal jurisdiction under Article III. But at least as long as there is some issue of federal law in a case, are there any "external" limits (arising from the Tenth Amendment or the Constitution's structure) on Congress' authority to provide for federal jurisdiction of civil and criminal actions rooted in state law? In this regard, consider whether any of the Supreme Court decisions of the Burger, Rehnquist, and Roberts Courts that have stressed state sovereignty and the limits of national power suggest any limits upon the strong view of national supremacy articulated in the Davis decision.

INTRODUCTORY NOTE ON TARBLE'S CASE

The preceding cases concerned the scope of *congressional* power, in authorizing exclusive federal jurisdiction or removal jurisdiction, to divest the state courts of jurisdiction over federal cases. The next principal case raises the question whether the *Constitution* (rather than congressional legislation) sometimes precludes state courts from exercising jurisdiction.

———

Tarble's Case

80 U.S. (13 Wall.) 397, 20 L.Ed. 597 (1872).
Error to the Supreme Court of Wisconsin.

This was a proceeding on habeas corpus for the discharge of one Edward Tarble, held in the custody of a recruiting officer of the United States as an enlisted soldier, on the alleged ground that he was a minor, under the age of eighteen years at the time of his enlistment, and that he enlisted without the consent of his father.

[The writ was issued by a Wisconsin state court commissioner whom state law authorized to issue a writ of habeas corpus.] It was issued in this case upon the petition of the father of Tarble, in which he alleged that his son, who had enlisted under the name of Frank Brown, was confined and restrained of his liberty by Lieutenant Stone, of the United States army, in the city of Madison, in that State and county * * *.

[The Supreme Court of Wisconsin affirmed] * * * the order of the commissioner discharging the prisoner. This judgment was now before this court for examination on writ of error prosecuted by the United States. * * *

■ MR. JUSTICE FIELD, after stating the case, delivered the opinion of the court, as follows:

The important question is presented by this case, whether a State court commissioner has jurisdiction, upon habeas corpus, to inquire into the validity of the enlistment of soldiers into the military service of the United States, and to discharge them from such service when, in his judgment, their enlistment has not been made in conformity with the laws of the United States. The question presented may be more generally stated thus: Whether any judicial officer of a State has jurisdiction to issue a writ of habeas corpus, or to continue proceedings under the writ when issued, for the discharge of a person held under the authority, or claim and color of the authority, of the United States, by an officer of that government. * * *

The decision of this court in the two cases which grew out of the arrest of Booth, that of Ableman v. Booth, and that of United States v. Booth,[3] disposes alike of the claim of jurisdiction by a State court, or by a State judge, to interfere with the authority of the United States, whether that authority be exercised by a Federal officer or be exercised by a Federal tribunal. * * * [The Supreme Court's 1859 decision in these consolidated cases involved one Booth, a federal prisoner charged with aiding in the escape of a fugitive slave. Booth filed a habeas corpus

———
[3]   21 Howard 506.

petition in Wisconsin state court, challenging his arrest and detention by federal officials on the ground, *inter alia*, that the federal Fugitive Slave Act was unconstitutional. While federal criminal charges under that Act were pending against Booth, the Wisconsin courts held in his favor and ordered his release. Booth was thereafter tried and convicted in a federal court for violating the Fugitive Slave Act. He then filed a second habeas corpus petition in state court, attacking the Act on the same grounds, and the state court again ordered his discharge. Federal officials then filed writs of error in the U.S. Supreme Court, seeking review of both judgments of the Wisconsin Supreme Court.] * * * The cases were afterwards heard and considered together, and the decision of both was announced in the same opinion. In that opinion the Chief Justice [Taney] details the facts of the two cases at length, and comments upon the character of the jurisdiction asserted by the State judge and the State court * * *.

And in answer to this assumption of judicial power by the judges and by the Supreme Court of Wisconsin thus made, the Chief Justice said as follows: If they "possess the jurisdiction they claim, they must derive it either from the United States or the State. It certainly has not been conferred on them by the United States; and it is equally clear it was not in the power of the State to confer it, even if it had attempted to do so; for no State can authorize one of its judges or courts to exercise judicial power, by habeas corpus or otherwise, within the jurisdiction of another and independent government. And although the State of Wisconsin is sovereign within its territorial limits to a certain extent, yet that sovereignty is limited and restricted by the Constitution of the United States. And the powers of the General government and of the State, although both exist and are exercised within the same territorial limits, are yet separate and distinct sovereignties, acting separately and independently of each other, within their respective spheres. And the sphere of action appropriated to the United States, is as far beyond the reach of the judicial process issued by a State judge or a State court, as if the line of division was traced by landmarks and monuments visible to the eye. And the State of Wisconsin had no more power to authorize these proceedings of its judges and courts, than it would have had if the prisoner had been confined in Michigan, or in any other State of the Union, for an offence against the laws of the State in which he was imprisoned."

It is in the consideration of this distinct and independent character of the government of the United States, from that of the government of the several States, that the solution of the question presented in this case, and in similar cases, must be found. There are within the territorial limits of each State two governments, restricted in their spheres of action, but independent of each other, and supreme within their respective spheres. * * *

Such being the distinct and independent character of the two governments, within their respective spheres of action, it follows that neither can intrude with its judicial process into the domain of the other, except so far as such intrusion may be necessary on the part of the National government to preserve its rightful supremacy in cases of conflict of authority. In their laws, and mode of enforcement, neither is responsible to the other. How their respective laws shall be enacted; how they shall be carried into execution; and in what tribunals, or by what officers; and how much discretion, or whether any at all shall be vested in their officers, are matters subject to their own control, and in the regulation of which neither can interfere with the other.

Now, among the powers assigned to the National government, is the power "to raise and support armies," and the power "to provide for the government and regulation of the land and naval forces." The execution of these powers falls within the line of its duties; and its control over the subject is plenary and exclusive. * * * Probably in every county and city in the several States there are one or more officers authorized by law to issue writs of habeas corpus on behalf of persons alleged to be illegally restrained of their liberty; and if soldiers could be taken from the army of the United States, and the validity of their enlistment inquired into by any one of these officers, such proceeding could be taken by all of them, and no movement could be made by the National troops without their commanders being subjected to constant annoyance and embarrassment from this source. The experience of the late rebellion has shown us that, in times of great popular excitement, there may be found in every State large numbers ready and anxious to embarrass the operations of the government, and easily persuaded to believe every step taken for the enforcement of its authority illegal and void. Power to issue writs of habeas corpus for the discharge of soldiers in the military service, in the hands of parties thus disposed, might be used, and often would be used, to the great detriment of the public service. In many exigencies the measures of the National government might in this way be entirely bereft of their efficacy and value. An appeal in such cases to this court, to correct the erroneous action of these officers, would afford no adequate remedy. Proceedings on habeas corpus are summary, and the delay incident to bringing the decision of a State officer, through the highest tribunal of the State, to this court for review, would necessarily occupy years, and in the meantime, where the soldier was discharged, the mischief would be accomplished. It is manifest that the powers of the National government could not be exercised with energy and efficiency at all times, if its acts could be interfered with and controlled for any period by officers or tribunals of another sovereignty.

It is true similar embarrassment might sometimes be occasioned, though in a less degree, by the exercise of the authority to issue the writ possessed by judicial officers of the United States, but the ability to provide a speedy remedy for any inconvenience following from this source would always exist with the National legislature. * * *

This limitation upon the power of State tribunals and State officers furnishes no just ground to apprehend that the liberty of the citizen will thereby be endangered. The United States are as much interested in protecting the citizen from illegal restraint under their authority, as the several States are to protect him from the like restraint under their authority * * *. Their courts and judicial officers are clothed with the power to issue the writ of habeas corpus in all cases, where a party is illegally restrained of his liberty by an officer of the United States, whether such illegality consists in the character of the process, the authority of the officer, or the invalidity of the law under which he is held. And there is no just reason to believe that they will exhibit any hesitation to exert their power, when it is properly invoked. Certainly there can be

Isn't there though?

no ground for supposing that their action will be less prompt and efficient in such cases than would be that of State tribunals and State officers.

It follows, from the views we have expressed, that the court commissioner of Dane County was without jurisdiction to issue the writ of habeas corpus for the discharge of the prisoner in this case * * *. * * *

Judgment reversed.

■ THE CHIEF JUSTICE [CHASE], dissenting.

I cannot concur in the opinion just read. I have no doubt of the right of a State court to inquire into the jurisdiction of a Federal court upon habeas corpus, and to discharge when satisfied that the petitioner for the writ is restrained of liberty by the sentence of a court without jurisdiction. If it errs in deciding the question of jurisdiction, the error must be corrected in the mode prescribed by the 25th section of the Judiciary Act; not by denial of the right to make inquiry.

I have still less doubt, if possible, that a writ of habeas corpus may issue from a State court to inquire into the validity of imprisonment or detention, without the sentence of any court whatever, by an officer of the United States. The State court may err; and if it does, the error may be corrected here. The mode has been prescribed and should be followed.

 To deny the right of State courts to issue the writ, or, what amounts to the same thing, to concede the right to issue and to deny the right to adjudicate, is to deny the right to protect the citizen by habeas corpus against arbitrary imprisonment in a large class of cases; and, I am thoroughly persuaded, was never within the contemplation of the Convention which framed, or the people who adopted, the Constitution. That instrument expressly declares that "the privilege of the writ of habeas corpus shall not be suspended, unless when, in case of rebellion or invasion, the public safety may require it."

NOTE ON TARBLE'S CASE AND STATE COURT PROCEEDINGS AGAINST FEDERAL OFFICIALS

(1) Historical Practice. The decisions in Ableman v. Booth and Tarble's Case departed from historic practice. Beginning in 1789, state courts, "for a period of eighty years, continued to assert a right, through the issue of writs of *habeas corpus*, to take persons out of the custody of federal officials". Warren, *Federal and State Court Interference*, 43 Harv.L.Rev. 345, 353 (1930). Many of these cases, like Tarble's Case, involved petitions seeking to free individuals from service in the military. See Oaks, *Habeas Corpus in the States—1776–1865*, 32 U.Chi.L.Rev. 243 (1965); Pettys, *State Habeas Relief for Federal Extrajudicial Detainees*, 92 Minn.L.Rev. 265 (2007).[1]

(2) Ableman v. Booth and Tarble's Case Distinguished. The Wisconsin courts in Booth, in holding the Fugitive Slave Act unconstitutional, were acting in the teeth of Supreme Court and lower court decisions that that Act

---

[1] There were also prominent instances of refusal to interfere with federal enforcement activities, notably with respect to the Fugitive Slave Law, even in areas where its validity was most contested. See, *e.g.*, Passmore Williamson's Case, 26 Pa. 9 (1855); Warren, *supra*, at 355–56.

was valid. By contrast, Tarble's Case involved no such frontal state court defiance, however nobly motivated, of governing precedent.

Perhaps a more significant distinction between the cases rests on the fact that in Booth, the state court's second writ of habeas corpus, issued after the federal court conviction, threatened the finality of federal judgments;[2] Tarble's Case posed no such threat, as there the state court challenged only the legality of extra-judicial detention—the historic core of the writ of habeas corpus. And in the thirteen years that separated the two decisions, although some state courts read the Booth decision broadly as denying them any power to issue habeas relief to individuals in federal custody, most read it more narrowly, as confined to cases in which detention was under the authority of a federal court judgment. See Pettys, *supra*, at 284–88. Thus, Professor Warren observes that "during the Civil War, New York, Ohio, Iowa and Maine judges granted *habeas corpus* for persons serving in the United States Army. And as late as 1871, one Massachusetts court said that this power was so well settled by judicial opinion and long practice that it was not 'to be now disavowed, unless in obedience to an express act of congress, or to a direct adjudication of the supreme court of the United States.' " Warren, *supra*, at 357, quoting Gray, J., in McConologue's Case, 107 Mass. 154, 160 (1871).[3]

(3) Constitutionally Mandated Exclusion? Much of the reasoning in Tarble's Case appears to rest on the proposition that the Constitution, of its own force, precludes the exercise of state habeas corpus jurisdiction against federal officials. Can such a proposition be squared with the Madisonian Compromise and the language of Article III making the establishment of "inferior" federal courts a matter of congressional discretion?

Imagine a case in which a petitioner seeking habeas corpus alleges that federal officials are detaining him unconstitutionally. Article I, § 9, which provides that "[t]he Privilege of the Writ of Habeas Corpus shall not be suspended, unless when in Cases of Rebellion or Invasion the public Safety may require it", has been interpreted as conferring a constitutional right to habeas review of detention by federal officials (or to an adequate substitute therefor) that would apply in many situations. See pp. 335–341, *supra*; 1201–1203, *infra*. Tarble, of course, had the option of seeking a writ of habeas corpus from a federal court. But suppose Congress had not vested jurisdiction over his case, or some other case implicating the Suspension Clause, in the federal courts. If the state courts are not competent to entertain a petition, the detainee would lack any court in which to seek to vindicate his constitutional right.[4] That situation would conflict with

---

[2] Following the Supreme Court's decision, the Wisconsin courts refused to issue a third writ of habeas corpus, after which an armed crowd freed Booth from federal custody. See generally Note, 93 Va.L.Rev. 1315 (2007).

[3] The departure from historic practice in Ableman v. Booth might be ascribed to the political division that two years later ignited the Civil War. Professor Cover, in an illuminating study of some Northern judges who opposed slavery yet hesitated to press judicial challenges to the Fugitive Slave Act, raises "the issue of whether the modern lawyer and scholar must forsake all the slavery cases as too infused with a substantive issue to be of any use in understanding our federal system" today. Cover, Justice Accused: Antislavery and the Judicial Process 166 n.* (1975). Tarble's Case was decided after the war's end and the Thirteenth Amendment's abolition of slavery. But might the Justices have had the recent rebellion in mind when considering the issues of state and national power in 1872?

[4] According to Duker, A Constitutional History of Habeas Corpus 126–80 (1980), a principal purpose of the Suspension Clause was to protect state habeas corpus jurisdiction from federal abrogation. That view would obviously create more serious tensions with Tarble's Case

Professor Hart's premise, p. 329, *supra*, that "a court must always be available to pass on claims of constitutional right to judicial process, and to provide such process if the claim is sustained." See pp. 330–333, *supra*.

Professor Hart further thought that in cases of jurisdictional foreclosure the state courts were the ultimate guardians of constitutional rights—a position hard to square with Tarble's Case. Consider in this regard the Boumediene decision, p. 338, *supra*, which involved a statutory provision purporting to bar all judicial review, in federal or state courts, of the detention of aliens as enemy combatants. The Court found the provision invalid, but proceeded to rule that the detainees had a right to habeas corpus review in *federal* court; there was no discussion of Tarble's Case or of whether any constitutionally required review could be provided in state court. Thus, the Boumediene opinion is not clear whether the detainees had (a) a constitutional right to federal court review (perhaps because Tarble's Case would preclude state court review), or, instead, (b) a constitutional right to judicial review that either federal or state courts could provide. If the latter, there were reasonably powerful statutory and historical arguments that any constitutionally required review should be undertaken by federal courts, even if Tarble's Case was wrongly decided and state courts were not disempowered from providing such review. See p. 434, *infra*. None of this, however, is discussed in the Boumediene opinion, and thus its implications for Tarble's Case, and for theories critical of Tarble's Case, remain uncertain.

(a) Historical Evidence. Professor Collins offers a *historical* argument that members of the generation that framed and ratified the Constitution, and of its immediate successors, widely understood that some categories of federal jurisdiction—including federal criminal cases and suits against federal officers for specific relief—were inherently exclusive of state court jurisdiction. See Collins, *Article III Cases, State Court Duties, and the Madisonian Compromise*, 1995 Wisc.L.Rev. 39, 46–135. Justice Story, Collins contends, was the most prominent but hardly the only example. According to Collins, as to cases in which the state courts lacked a "pre-existing" jurisdiction before the Constitution's ratification, the Constitution neither directly conferred jurisdiction nor empowered Congress to vest jurisdiction in state courts. He adds it appeared plausible to many eighteenth and nineteenth century lawyers that if Congress wished to see federal law enforced in cases in which the Constitution precluded state court jurisdiction, the solution could be to create lower federal courts—though such lawyers would not necessarily have endorsed the further conclusion that Congress was obliged to create lower federal courts. See Collins, *The Federal Courts, the First Congress, and the Non-Settlement of 1789*, 91 Va.L.Rev. 1515, 1560 (2005).

The actual historical practice is contested but poses some challenges for Collins' thesis. Professor Warren has mustered evidence that early Congresses authorized state courts to entertain actions seeking fines and other penalties, including criminal penalties, under a variety of federal laws. See Warren, *Federal Criminal Laws and the State Courts*, 38 Harv.L.Rev. 545, 550–55, 570–73 (1925). Collins quarrels with Warren's characterization of the scope of state *criminal* jurisdiction contemplated by these federal statutes, see Collins, *supra*, 1995 Wisc.L.Rev. at 86–89, and in a subsequent

---

than alternative views that suggest, notwithstanding the Madisonian Compromise, that in some circumstances federal courts are constitutionally obliged to exercise habeas corpus jurisdiction. See generally *Note on the Suspension Clause of the Constitution*, pp. 1200–1206, *infra*.

article, Collins and co-author Nash argue that the evidence from the Founding era—particularly the debate about the First Judiciary Act—is hard to square with state court authority to entertain federal criminal prosecutions. Collins & Nash, *Prosecuting Federal Crimes in State Courts*, 97 Va.L.Rev. 243 (2011).[5]

Another historical practice that poses a challenge for Collins is the state courts' exercise, during the antebellum period, of habeas jurisdiction against federal officials, as already described in Paragraph (1), *supra*.

(b) Constitutional Conundrums. Suppose, however, that it could be determined that Article III's public meaning at the time of the Founding precluded state court jurisdiction of certain classes of claims. Would that *specific* determination necessarily dispose of the constitutional question? Would it be consistent with the structural logic of the constitutional plan for there to be no remedy available in any court for unconstitutional detentions or other unconstitutional actions by federal officials?

Redish & Woods, *Congressional Power to Control the Jurisdiction of Lower Federal Courts: A Critical Review and a New Synthesis*, 124 U.Pa.L.Rev. 45 (1975), give a negative answer to the latter question. They argue that Congress would violate the Constitution if it failed to create lower courts invested with jurisdiction to entertain suits that state courts may not entertain, unless Congress also expressly authorized the state courts to exercise jurisdiction in cases, like Tarble's Case, in which state court jurisdiction would otherwise be constitutionally forbidden. On this view, Tarble's Case does not establish an absolute constitutional bar to state court jurisdiction in the circumstances there presented, but only a constitutional default rule, subject to displacement by a clear congressional statement.

In assessing this argument, suppose that Congress neither created lower federal courts nor expressly authorized state courts to entertain suits seeking to compel action by federal officials. In that case, if the Suspension Clause gives individuals a right to habeas review in some court, as the Supreme Court has held, see pp. 338–341, *supra*, then wouldn't it follow either that the state courts must be able to hear such an action (in which case, even the "default rule" reading of Tarble's Case cannot be right) or that Congress must create lower federal courts and vest them with jurisdiction (a result at odds with the Madisonian Compromise)?[6]

Recall that the decision in the Boumediene case assumed that the habeas review constitutionally guaranteed by the Suspension Clause would be in federal court. But when that case was decided in 2008, not only had the lower federal courts long been established, but after the Court invalidated the jurisdiction-stripping provision there was also arguably a backstop

---

[5]   The authors contend that only one federal statute plainly authorized federal criminal prosecutions in state courts, and they point to two state court decisions suggesting a lack of jurisdiction under it.

[6]   Hartnett, *The Constitutional Puzzle of Habeas Corpus*, 46 B.C.L.Rev. 251 (2005), argues that any demand for federal habeas jurisdiction under the Suspension Clause could be, and historically has been, reconciled with the Madisonian Compromise by a statute authorizing individual Justices of the Supreme Court to issue writs of habeas corpus. But that is not an exercise of the Supreme Court's original jurisdiction (and under Marbury v. Madison, it could not be), nor is it an exercise of appellate jurisdiction, and so it must be viewed as the exercise of jurisdiction of an inferior court. (Recall that the Justices initially sat on the Circuit Courts as well as on the Supreme Court.) As such, that grant could be repealed as easily as the grant of habeas jurisdiction to the lower courts themselves. Thus, doesn't this suggestion fail to resolve the conundrum posed by Tarble's Case?

statutory grant of federal court habeas corpus jurisdiction on which to rely. See pp. 338–340, *supra*.

(4) Alternative Views of Tarble's Case. The foregoing discussion highlights the difficulties of any reading of Tarble's Case that suggests that the *Constitution* barred the exercise of state court jurisdiction in that case.

    (a) Implied Exclusivity of Federal Jurisdiction? Could the narrow holding of Tarble's Case that the state court lacked jurisdiction be justified on the ground that federal *statutes* impliedly establish habeas corpus for persons in federal custody as a domain of exclusive federal jurisdiction? Might this attribution of congressional intent be warranted by the acts of Congress granting the federal courts habeas corpus jurisdiction? The acts of Congress governing the army? The conjunction of the two?

[handwritten margin note: implication theory]

    In the period after the Civil War, the authority of state courts (particularly in the states that had joined the Confederacy) to issue writs of habeas corpus or other orders to federal officials would seem to have posed a distinctive threat to national authority. And at that time, unlike today, the federal officials sued in Tarble's Case were unable to remove the matter to federal court. Perhaps the decision can be understood, and defended, as presuming that state courts are not sufficiently trustworthy to issue mandatory orders to federal officials, but as leaving open the prospect that the presumption could be overridden when Congress has either provided a sufficiently clear statement or has failed to confer federal jurisdiction.[7]

    Such a rationale for the result in Tarble's Case would, however, find federal jurisdiction to be exclusive without any clear statement to that effect in a statutory text. As such, that rationale would be in tension with the approach to exclusivity taken in recent decisions like Tafflin v. Levitt and Yellow Freight System, Inc. v. Donnelly, pp. 412, 420, *supra*. If those two approaches are in tension, which one is to be preferred?

    (b) Was Tarble's Case Wrongly Decided? Alternatively, perhaps there is no justification, constitutional or sub-constitutional, for the result in Tarble's Case. Professor Pettys, Paragraph (1), *supra*, considers this question with particular attention to habeas corpus claims by those detained by the federal government in connection with the war on terror. He contends that state courts today should reject a constitutional basis for the result in Tarble's Case and should follow the modern approach (as set forth in a decision like Tafflin) in determining whether the grant of federal habeas jurisdiction excludes state court jurisdiction. Pettys notes that (1) Congress, in enacting the Judiciary Act of 1789, knew how to make federal court jurisdiction exclusive, as it did in jurisdictional grants other than the grant of habeas corpus jurisdiction; (2) the legislative history of the Judiciary Act reflected a general concern to limit federal displacement of state court authority; and (3) state court habeas jurisdiction is not incompatible with federal purposes given that the state courts are presumptively competent to adjudicate federal rights and that, today at least, federal officials sued in state court may remove the action to federal court under § 1442.

    On the last point, had a provision like today's § 1442 permitted the federal military officials to remove Tarble's habeas corpus action from state court to federal court, no decision on state court power would have been needed. Conversely, precisely because Congress had not provided for removal at that time, the legitimate concerns about potential state court interference

---

    [7]   But *cf.* McClung v. Silliman, Paragraph (5)(a), *infra*.

with national policy may have made Tarble's a hard case that in turn made bad law.

(5) State Jurisdiction in Other Proceedings Against Federal Officials. How far does or should the rationale of Tarble's Case extend in barring state courts from issuing remedies other than a writ of habeas corpus in actions challenging the legality of federal official action? Any such action could have the potential, in the words of the Court in Tarble's Case, to place "the sphere of action appropriated to the United States" improperly within "the reach of the judicial process issued by a State judge or a State court". Yet one commentator, summarizing the decisions described in more detail below, suggested some years ago that various remedies line up along a spectrum, with mandamus joining habeas corpus jurisdiction as forbidden at one end, with jurisdiction to award damages and common law writs like replevin and ejectment that seek specific relief being just as clearly permitted at the other, and with injunctions from a court of equity in an uncertain middle. See Arnold, *The Power of State Courts to Enjoin Federal Officers*, 73 Yale L.J. 1385, 1397 (1964). Consider, as you read the materials below, whether any coherent policy supports such a pattern, or whether the pattern itself may be the product of historical accident.[8]

(a) Mandamus. In McClung v. Silliman, 19 U.S. (6 Wheat.) 598 (1821), the Court held that a state court lacked jurisdiction over a suit for mandamus to compel the register of a federal land office to make a conveyance. The Court's opinion seemed to rest on several intersecting lines of reason. The first was that because the federal courts lacked authority to issue mandamus to a federal executive official,[9] the states did also: "no one will seriously contend, it is presumed, that it is among the reserved powers of the states, because not communicated by law to the courts of the United States". The second, which resonates with the opinion in Tarble's Case, was that the conduct of a federal official implementing a federal statute "can only be controlled by the power that created him." The third, building on the first, stressed that mandamus was an extraordinary remedy, and the absence of federal court power to issue it implied that those complaining that federal officials had violated their rights "should be referred to the ordinary mode of obtaining justice", such as damages or actions to recover specific property. McClung has been interpreted to exclude state court mandamus against federal officials under any circumstances.[10]

---

[8]   For an illuminating discussion and a powerful argument in favor of jurisdiction, see Arnold, *supra*. See also Warren, *Federal and State Court Interference*, 43 Harv.L.Rev. 345 (1930); Note, 53 Cornell L.Rev. 916, 926–29 (1968).

[9]   See McIntire v. Wood, 11 U.S. (7 Cranch) 504 (1813).

[10]   See, *e.g.*, Armand Schmoll, Inc. v. Federal Reserve Bank, 286 N.Y. 503, 37 N.E.2d 225 (1941); Ex parte Shockley, 17 F.2d 133 (N.D.Ohio 1926). In at least one case, however, the Supreme Court has decided on the merits a state-court mandamus action against a federal officer. Northern Pac. Ry. Co. v. North Dakota ex rel. Langer, 250 U.S. 135 (1919). See generally Arnold, *supra*, at 1391–92. And the Court held in Kendall v. United States ex rel. Stokes, 37 U.S. (12 Pet.) 524 (1838), that the territorial courts for the District of Columbia, apparently uniquely among the courts in the nation, possessed authority to issue writs of mandamus against federal officials.

The Court's premise in McClung v. Silliman that the power to issue mandamus to enforce the laws of the United States was not "among the reserved powers of the states" might seem to be consistent with the statement of Hamilton, in The Federalist No. 82, that the "doctrine of concurrent jurisdiction is only clearly applicable to those descriptions of cases of which the state courts have previous cognizance"—for mandamus suits against federal officials fall outside this category. Yet The Federalist No. 82 went on to suggest that "in every case in which * * * [state

Note the tension between one interpretation of Tarble's Case noted above—that state court jurisdiction was excluded because the federal courts _possessed_ habeas jurisdiction—and the holding in McClung that state court jurisdiction is excluded because the federal courts _lacked_ mandamus jurisdiction.

In 1962, Congress authorized federal district courts to issue mandamus against federal officers. See 28 U.S.C. § 1361. Can McClung's rationale survive after that enactment and the broad removal authority conferred by § 1442?

(b) Injunctions. The Supreme Court has not yet decided whether state courts have jurisdiction to entertain injunction actions against federal officers.[11] State and lower federal court decisions are divided, but "[t]he weight of reasoned opinion * * * supports the general denial of state court power" to enjoin federal officers. Redish & Woods, Paragraph (3)(b), _supra_, at 89.[12] See also General Atomic Co. v. Felter, 434 U.S. 12 (1977) (per curiam).

(c) Actions at Law for Specific Relief. Slocum v. Mayberry, 15 U.S. (2 Wheat.) 1 (1817), sustained a state court action for replevin of cargo illegally detained by federal customs officers. Chief Justice Marshall said that "the act of congress neither expressly, nor by implication, forbids the state courts to take cognizance of suits instituted for property in possession of an officer of the United States, not detained under some law of the United States; consequently their jurisdiction remains". The Court has also assumed that state courts may try ejectment actions against federal officers. See, _e.g._, Scranton v. Wheeler, 179 U.S. 141 (1900). See generally Arnold, _supra_, at 1397. But _cf._ Malone v. Bowdoin, p. 894, _infra_ (finding such actions barred by the distinct doctrine of sovereign immunity).

How should modern courts consider the widely varying approaches to varying forms of specific relief? Insofar as, following the merger of law and equity, common law writs like replevin and ejectment have been displaced by injunctive relief, what sense is there to the distinctions in the cases just noted?

(d) Damages Actions. The Supreme Court has routinely sustained state court jurisdiction in damages actions averring tortious conduct by

---

courts are] not expressly excluded by future acts of the national legislature, they will, of course, take cognizance of the causes to which those acts may give birth". If that is right, should the _failure_ of Congress to confer mandamus jurisdiction on the federal courts be taken to have divested the state courts of power?

[11] A dictum in Keely v. Sanders, 99 U.S. 441, 443 (1878), stated that "no State court could, by injunction or otherwise, prevent federal officers from collecting Federal taxes." The government could have raised the question, but did not, in Tennessee Elec. Power Co. v. TVA, 306 U.S. 118 (1939). The issue was raised in Brooks v. Dewar, 313 U.S. 354, 360 (1941), but the Court was unwilling to resolve an "asserted conflict touching issues of so grave consequence" where there was no case for injunction on the merits.

[12] _Cf._ Donovan v. City of Dallas, 377 U.S. 408 (1964), holding that a state court lacked authority to enjoin a person from prosecuting an in personam action in a federal district court. Justice Black's majority opinion reasoned: "While Congress has seen fit to authorize courts of the United States to restrain state-court proceedings in some special circumstances, it has in no way relaxed the old and well-established judicially declared rule that state courts are completely without power to restrain federal-court proceedings in in personam actions like the one here. And it does not matter that the prohibition here was addressed to the parties rather than to the federal court itself * * * ". Justice Harlan's dissent, joined by Justices Stewart and Clark, argued that the Court's precedents recognized state court power to enjoin a resident state court suitor from "conducting vexatious and harassing litigation in another forum".

federal officials that was not authorized by federal law. See, *e.g.*, Teal v. Felton, 53 U.S. (12 How.) 284 (1852); Buck v. Colbath, 70 U.S. (3 Wall.) 334 (1866). But *cf.* Davis v. Passman, 442 U.S. 228, 245 n.23 (1979).[13]

INTRODUCTORY NOTE ON THE OBLIGATION OF STATE COURTS TO ENFORCE FEDERAL LAW

The preceding material discusses issues arising when federal law limits the *power* of *willing* state courts to exercise jurisdiction over federal rights of action. The material that follows concerns the opposite problem: issues that arise when federal law imposes an *obligation* on *unwilling* state courts to exercise jurisdiction over federal rights of action.

Testa v. Katt

330 U.S. 386, 67 S.Ct. 810, 91 L.Ed. 967 (1947).
Certiorari to the Superior Court for Providence and Bristol Counties, Rhode Island.

■ MR. JUSTICE BLACK delivered the opinion of the Court.

Section 205(e) of the Emergency Price Control Act provides that a buyer of goods above the prescribed ceiling price may sue the seller "in any court of competent jurisdiction" for not more than three times the amount of the overcharge plus costs and a reasonable attorney's fee. Section 205(c) provides that federal district courts shall have jurisdiction of such suits "concurrently with State and Territorial courts." Such a suit under § 205(e) must be brought "in the district or county in which the defendant resides or has a place of business * * *."

The respondent was in the automobile business in Providence, * * * Rhode Island. In 1944 he sold an automobile to petitioner Testa * * * for $1100, $210 above the ceiling price. The petitioner later filed this suit against respondent in the State District Court in Providence. Recovery was sought under § 205(e). The court awarded a judgment of treble damages and costs to petitioner. On appeal to the State Superior Court, where the trial was de novo, the petitioner was again awarded judgment, but only for the amount of the overcharge plus attorney's fees. * * * On appeal, the State Supreme Court reversed. It interpreted § 205(e) to be "a penal statute in the international sense." It held that an action for violation of § 205(e) could not be maintained in the courts of that State. The State Supreme Court rested its holding on its earlier decision in Robinson v. Norato, 1945, 71 R.I. 256, 43 A.2d 467, 468, in which it had reasoned that: A state need not enforce the penal laws of a government

---

[13] Whether sued in state or federal court, federal officials can ordinarily invoke qualified or absolute immunity as a shield from damages liability. See Chap. IX, Sec. 3.

In Clinton v. Jones, 520 U.S. 681, 691 (1997), a unanimous Court held that the President was not immune from a damages suit in federal court based on acts committed before he took office, but explicitly avoided the question whether a comparable claim of immunity might succeed in state court. Such a state court case would raise issues of federalism and comity, "as well as the interest in protecting federal officers from possible local prejudice that underlies the authority to remove certain cases brought against federal officials * * *. Whether those concerns would present a more compelling case for immunity is a question that is not before us".

which is "foreign in the international sense"; § 205(e) is treated by Rhode Island as penal in that sense; the United States is "foreign" to the State in the "private international" as distinguished from the "public international" sense; hence Rhode Island courts, though their jurisdiction is adequate to enforce similar Rhode Island "penal" statutes, need not enforce § 205(e). Whether state courts may decline to enforce federal laws on these grounds is a question of great importance. For this reason, and because the Rhode Island Supreme Court's holding was alleged to conflict with this Court's previous holding in Mondou v. New York, N.H. & H.R. Co., 223 U.S. 1, we granted certiorari.

For the purposes of this case, we assume, without deciding, that § 205(e) is a penal statute in the "public international," "private international," or any other sense. * * * For we cannot accept the basic premise on which the Rhode Island Supreme Court held that it has no more obligation to enforce a valid penal law of the United States than it has to enforce a penal law of another state or a foreign country. Such a broad assumption flies in the face of the fact that the States of the Union constitute a nation. It disregards the purpose and effect of Article VI, § 2 of the Constitution which provides: "This Constitution, and the Laws of the United States which shall be made in Pursuance thereof; and all Treaties made, or which shall be made, under the Authority of the United States, shall be the supreme Law of the Land; and the Judges in every State shall be bound thereby, any Thing in the Constitution or Laws of any State to the Contrary notwithstanding."

It cannot be assumed, the supremacy clause considered, that the responsibilities of a state to enforce the laws of a sister state are identical with its responsibilities to enforce federal laws. Such an assumption represents an erroneous evaluation of the statutes of Congress and the prior decisions of this Court in their historic setting. Those decisions establish that state courts do not bear the same relation to the United States that they do to foreign countries. The first Congress that convened after the Constitution was adopted conferred jurisdiction upon the state courts to enforce important federal civil laws,[4] and succeeding Congresses conferred on the states jurisdiction over federal crimes and actions for penalties and forfeitures.[5]

Enforcement of federal laws by state courts did not go unchallenged. Violent public controversies existed throughout the first part of the Nineteenth Century until the 1860's concerning the extent of the constitutional supremacy of the Federal Government. During that period there were instances in which this Court and state courts broadly questioned the power and duty of state courts to exercise their jurisdiction to enforce United States civil and penal statutes or the power of the Federal Government to require them to do so. But after the fundamental issues over the extent of federal supremacy had been resolved by war, this Court took occasion in 1876 to review the phase of the controversy concerning the relationship of state courts to the Federal

---

[4]   Judiciary Act of 1789, 1 Stat. 73, 77 (suits by aliens for torts committed in violation of federal laws and treaties; suits by the United States).

[5]   1 Stat. 376, 378 (1794) (fines, forfeitures and penalties for violation of the License Tax on Wines and Spirits); 1 Stat. 373, 375 (1794) (the Carriage Tax Act); 1 Stat. 452 (penalty for purchasing guns from Indians); 1 Stat. 733, 740 (1799) (criminal and civil actions for violation of the postal laws).

Government. Claflin v. Houseman, 93 U.S. 130. The opinion of a unanimous court in that case was strongly buttressed by historic references and persuasive reasoning. It repudiated the assumption that federal laws can be considered by the states as though they were laws emanating from a foreign sovereign. Its teaching is that the Constitution and the laws passed pursuant to it are the supreme laws of the land, binding alike upon states, courts, and the people, "anything in the Constitution or Laws of any State to the contrary notwithstanding." It asserted that the obligation of states to enforce these federal laws is not lessened by reason of the form in which they are cast or the remedy which they provide. And the Court stated that "If an act of Congress gives a penalty to a party aggrieved, without specifying a remedy for its enforcement, there is no reason why it should not be enforced, if not provided otherwise by some act of Congress, by a proper action in a state court." Id. 93 U.S. at page 137.

The Claflin opinion thus answered most of the arguments theretofore advanced against the power and duty of state courts to enforce federal penal laws. And since that decision, the remaining areas of doubt have been steadily narrowed. There have been statements in cases concerned with the obligation of states to give full faith and credit to the proceedings of sister states which suggested a theory contrary to that pronounced in the Claflin opinion. But when in Mondou v. New York, N.H. & H.R. Co., supra, this Court was presented with a case testing the power and duty of states to enforce federal laws, it found the solution in the broad principles announced in the Claflin opinion.

The precise question in the Mondou case was whether rights arising under the Federal Employers' Liability Act, 36 Stat. 291, could "be enforced, as of right, in the courts of the states when their jurisdiction, as prescribed by local laws, is adequate to the occasion. * * * " Id. 223 U.S. at page 46. The Supreme Court of Connecticut had decided that they could not. Except for the penalty feature, the factors it considered and its reasoning were strikingly similar to that on which the Rhode Island Supreme Court declined to enforce the federal law here involved. But this Court held that the Connecticut court could not decline to entertain the action. The contention that enforcement of the congressionally created right was contrary to Connecticut policy was answered as follows:

"The suggestion that the act of Congress is not in harmony with the policy of the State, and therefore that the courts of the state are free to decline jurisdiction, is quite inadmissible, because it presupposes what in legal contemplation does not exist. When Congress, in the exertion of the power confided to it by the Constitution, adopted that act, it spoke for all the people and all the states, and thereby established a policy for all. That policy is as much the policy of Connecticut as if the act had emanated from its own legislature, and should be respected accordingly in the courts of the state." Mondou v. New York, N.H. & H.R. Co., supra, 223 U.S. at page 57.

So here, the fact that Rhode Island has an established policy against enforcement by its courts of statutes of other states and the United States which it deems penal, cannot be accepted as a "valid excuse." Cf. Douglas v. New York, N.H. & H.R. Co., 279 U.S. 377, 388. For the policy of the federal Act is the prevailing policy in every state. Thus, in a case which chiefly relied upon the Claflin and Mondou precedents, this Court stated that a state court cannot "refuse to enforce the right arising from the law of the United States because of conceptions of impolicy or want of wisdom on the part of Congress in having called into play its lawful powers." Minneapolis & St. L.R. Co. v. Bombolis, 241 U.S. 211, 222.

The Rhode Island court in its Robinson decision on which it relies cites cases of this Court which have held that states are not required by the full faith and credit clause of the Constitution to enforce judgments of the courts of other states based on claims arising out of penal statutes. But those holdings have no relevance here, for this case raises no full faith and credit question. Nor need we consider in this case prior decisions to the effect that federal courts are not required to enforce state penal laws.

* * * [T]hose decisions did not bring before us our instant problem of the effect of the supremacy clause on the relation of federal laws to state courts. Our question concerns only the right of a state to deny enforcement to claims growing out of a valid federal law.

It is conceded that this same type of claim arising under Rhode Island law would be enforced by that State's courts. Its courts have enforced claims for double damages growing out of the Fair Labor Standards Act, 29 U.S.C.A. § 201 et seq. Thus the Rhode Island courts have jurisdiction adequate and appropriate under established local law to adjudicate this action. Under these circumstances the State courts are not free to refuse enforcement of petitioners' claim. See McKnett v. St. Louis & S.F.R. Co., 292 U.S. 230; and compare Herb v. Pitcairn, 324 U.S. 117; 325 U.S. 77. * * *

Reversed.

———

NOTE ON THE OBLIGATION OF STATE COURTS TO ENFORCE FEDERAL LAW

(1) From Power to Obligation. How long is the leap from Claflin v. Houseman, discussed in Testa, which upheld the *power* of a *willing* state court to exercise concurrent jurisdiction over a federal claim, to the holding of Testa itself that an *unwilling* state court was under an *obligation* to do so?[1]

---

[1]   The question of congressional power to obligate the states to exercise jurisdiction was apparently first discussed by the Supreme Court in Prigg v. Pennsylvania, 41 U.S. (16 Pet.) 539 (1842), where the precise issue involved Congress' authority to impose a mandatory, concurrent jurisdiction to enforce the Fugitive Slave Act. Writing for himself and Justices Catron and McKinley, Justice Story—echoing a position he had taken in Martin v. Hunter's Lessee, 14 U.S. (1 Wheat.) 304, 337 (1816)—suggested that Congress lacked power to force the states to exercise jurisdiction over federal criminal matters. Although Justice Story's opinion was styled as that of "the Court", "no five judges concurred in all of its reasoning." Cover, Justice Accused: Antislavery and the Judicial Process 166–68 (1975). The Court did not need to resolve this issue to reverse Prigg's conviction on the ground that the state kidnapping statute violated Article IV's Fugitive Slave Clause insofar as it forbade the forcible removal of an African-American from the state.

For a collection of nineteenth century cases expressing doubts about Congress' power to impose jurisdiction on the state courts, see Collins, *Article III, State Court Duties, and the Madisonian Compromise*, 1995 Wisc.L.Rev. 39, 145–94.

For general discussion of state court obligations, see Jordan & Bader, *State Power to Define Jurisdiction*, 47 Ga.L.Rev. 1161 (2013); Katz, *State Judges, State Officers, and Federal*

(2) State Obligations of Non-Discrimination.

(a) The Decisions. For more than a century, the Supreme Court has ruled that state courts may not discriminate against federal causes of action. Thus, Mondou v. New York, N.H. & H.R.R., 223 U.S. 1 (1912) (sometimes known as the Second Employers' Liability Cases), held unanimously that the state could not discriminate against a claim under the Federal Employers' Liability Act (FELA) by refusing to entertain it because of disagreement with the underlying federal policy.[2] (You may wish to review the lengthy quotation from Mondou in the Testa opinion.)

In line with Mondou is McKnett v. St. Louis & S.F. Ry., 292 U.S. 230 (1934), another FELA case, where an Alabama statute for the first time opened the state courts to suits against foreign corporations based on an out-of-state accident, but only for suits under the laws of sister states, not for those under federal law. The Court held that the state statute unlawfully discriminated against federal rights: "While Congress has not attempted to compel states to provide courts for the enforcement of the [FELA], the Federal Constitution prohibits state courts of general jurisdiction from refusing to do so solely because the suit is brought under a federal law. * * * A state may not discriminate against rights arising under federal laws."[3]

(b) The Source of the Non-Discrimination Principle. What federal law is the source of the non-discrimination obligation? One possibility is the Supremacy Clause. But that provision is often viewed merely as a rule of priority: when federal and state law conflict, federal law prevails. On that understanding, with what rule of federal law does a discriminatory state law conflict?

Commands After Seminole Tribe and Printz, 1998 Wisc.L.Rev. 1465; Neuborne, *Toward Procedural Parity in Constitutional Litigation,* 22 Wm. & Mary L.Rev. 725, 753–66 (1981); Redish & Muench, *Adjudication of Federal Causes of Action in State Court,* 75 Mich.L.Rev. 311, 340–61 (1976); Sandalow, *Henry v. Mississippi and the Adequate State Ground: Proposals for a Revised Doctrine,* 1965 Sup.Ct.Rev. 187, 203–09. See also Warren, *New Light on the History of the Federal Judiciary Act of 1789,* 37 Harv.L.Rev. 49 (1923); Warren, *Federal Criminal Laws and the State Courts,* 38 Harv.L.Rev. 545 (1925); Note, 73 Harv.L.Rev. 1551 (1960).

[2] The FELA, enacted in 1908, provides a federal right of action for railroad workers in interstate commerce who are injured on the job due to their employer's negligence. At the time it was enacted, the FELA was designed to facilitate recovery by employees, by eliminating certain defenses that the employer might otherwise have had in a tort action. The most important of these defenses was the "fellow servant" rule, which barred recovery in tort when the damage was caused by a fellow employee. Some courts have understood the FELA to embody a decidedly pro-plaintiff policy.

In the years since the FELA was enacted, virtually every American jurisdiction has moved to compensating victims of workplace injuries through workers' compensation schemes. The FELA stands as an exception to this general movement; thus, employees of railroads in interstate commerce have their tort claims decided according to federal law standards under a negligence standard in an ordinary jury trial, rather than by a state administrative agency administering a workers' compensation system. Recoveries in FELA actions tend to far exceed workers' compensation awards.

Federal and state courts have concurrent jurisdiction over FELA actions. A special provision (28 U.S.C. § 1445(a)) denies to defendants in a state court FELA action the usual right to remove a federal cause of action to federal court.

[3] Could Congress, if it relaxed the exclusivity of federal court jurisdiction over federal criminal cases, require state courts to entertain federal criminal cases? The Long Range Plan for the Federal Courts of the Judicial Conference of the United States, 166 F.R.D. 49, 86–87 (1996), proposed that some categories of federal criminal cases be heard nearly exclusively in state court. See also Bellia, Jr., *Congressional Power and State Court Jurisdiction,* 94 Geo.L.J. 949 (2006); Carrington, *Federal Use of State Institutions in the Administration of Criminal Justice,* 49 S.M.U.L.Rev. 557, 560 (1996); Collins & Nash, p. 433, *supra.*

A second possibility is an implicit rule that every federal statutory right of action implicitly bars states from discriminating. Is that a plausible interpretive canon to apply across the board to all federal rights of action?

(c) Challenges to the Non-Discrimination Principle. Although some Justices have occasionally questioned application of the non-discrimination rule, few have doubted its validity. (Note that Testa was a unanimous decision.)[4] But in a dissent in Haywood v. Drown, 556 U.S. 729 (2009), discussed in more detail in Paragraph (4), *infra*, Justice Thomas, speaking in this respect only for himself, broadly challenged the idea that federal law can *ever* oblige state courts to entertain an action over which they lack jurisdiction under state law. Distinguishing state court refusals to adjudicate based on disagreements with federal policy from those based on a lack of jurisdiction, he viewed Mondou and Testa as correctly decided: in both cases the state courts refused because of a policy disagreement to exercise jurisdiction they possessed. By contrast, he thought McKnett was wrongly decided because the Alabama statutes did not give the state courts jurisdiction over the FELA action there at issue.

Justice Thomas' approach drew on the drafting history at the Constitutional Convention. (You may wish to review pp. 1–20, *supra*.) After adopting the Madisonian Compromise (embodied in the Virginia Plan), which left to Congress the decision whether to create lower federal courts, the Convention considered and rejected the New Jersey Plan, whose judiciary article would have expressly required state courts to entertain federal actions for punishments, fines, forfeitures and penalties. Justice Thomas argued that in view of the defeat of the New Jersey approach and the absence of any language in Article III expressly imposing obligations on state courts, the widespread assumption at the Convention that state courts would ordinarily entertain federal causes of action cannot be viewed as indicating that state courts had a federal obligation to do so. He buttressed his conclusion with discussion of cases from the early Republic suggesting that the states had plenary authority to decide whether to entertain federal causes of action.

How probative is the Convention history? Many motivations other than a rejection of state court obligation (including doubts that the Constitution itself should mandate state court jurisdiction over federal *crimes*, see note 3, *supra*) might have underlain the rejection of the New Jersey Plan. In other contexts, Justice Thomas has joined his colleagues in expressing skepticism about seeking to draw meaning from legislative inaction, see, *e.g.*, Brecht v. Abrahamson, 507 U.S. 619, 623–33 (1993), and that concern is especially

---

[4]   Consider, however, Justice Frankfurter's view, concurring, in Brown v. Gerdes, 321 U.S. 178, 188 (1944): "Since 1789, rights derived from federal law could be enforced in state courts unless Congress confined their enforcement to the federal courts. This has been so precisely for the same reason that rights created by the British Parliament or by the Legislature of Vermont could be enforced in New York courts. Neither Congress nor the British Parliament nor the Vermont Legislature has power to confer jurisdiction upon the New York courts. But the jurisdiction conferred upon them by * * * the State of New York * * * enables them to enforce rights no matter what the legislative source of the right may be." Is that view consistent with Testa (which Justice Frankfurter joined)?

Pfander, *Federal Supremacy, State Court Inferiority, and the Constitutionality of Jurisdiction-Stripping Legislation*, 101 Nw.U.L.Rev. 191, 228 (2007), contends that Article I, § 8, cl. 9's authorization "[t]o constitute Tribunals inferior to the supreme Court" does indeed permit Congress to "appoint" state courts to act as inferior federal tribunals and in that role to entertain federal claims. For critical discussion, see p. 321, note 27, *supra*.

potent with respect to inaction by the Convention, whose secret decisions were unknown to those in the state ratification conventions.

Suppose, however, that Justice Thomas is correct that neither the Supremacy Clause nor any other constitutional provision requires state courts to exercise jurisdiction over federal causes of action. How does that specific conclusion fit with foundational understandings of the constitutional structure? Consider, for example, the situation in which an individual has a constitutional right to judicial redress in some court, but Congress has not conferred jurisdiction on any federal court. Justice Thomas' approach would leave the state courts free to refuse jurisdiction, thereby foreclosing all relief for the individual. Is that a sensible understanding of the constitutional plan? Would his approach be more convincing if it were joined with the view that lower federal courts are constitutionally required in some cases?

(d) The Limits of the Non-Discrimination Rule: Cases Involving State Sovereign Immunity. One modern Supreme Court decision refused to invalidate what appeared to be state court discrimination against federal causes of action. Alden v. Maine, 527 U.S. 706 (1999) (5–4), p. 967, *infra*, upheld the authority of a state, which is generally immune from suit, to waive its immunity in state court from state law actions but not from analogous federal law actions.[5] Rather than suggesting a general qualification of the rule against discrimination, however, Alden may be best understood as limited to cases involving state sovereign immunity, a doctrine to which the Court is strongly committed, and as reflecting the Court's desire to address what it viewed as an effort to make an end run around that doctrine.

(3) Valid Excuses. Several Supreme Court decisions have upheld, as a "valid excuse," non-discriminatory refusals by a state court to entertain a federal cause of action. The leading cases have involved rules relating in some way to the convenience of the state as a forum for resolving the case in question, and the refusal to adjudicate has typically left the courts of another, putatively more convenient state, as well as the federal courts, open to hear the dispute.

The leading example is Douglas v. New York, N.H. & H.R.R., 279 U.S. 377 (1929), where the New York courts had dismissed an FELA action by a Connecticut resident against a Connecticut corporation based on an accident in Connecticut. A New York statute permitted actions by a nonresident against a foreign corporation only in certain cases, of which this was not one. On appeal, Justice Holmes said that the FELA "does not purport to require State Courts to entertain suits arising under it, but only to empower them to do so, so far as the authority of the United States is concerned. It may very well be that if the Supreme Court of New York were given no discretion, being otherwise competent, it would be subject to a duty. But there is nothing in the Act of Congress that purports to force a duty upon such Courts as against an otherwise valid excuse [citing Mondou]."

---

[5]   In this action, state employees contended that Maine had failed to pay overtime wages as required by the Fair Labor Standards Act. The Supreme Court ruled that under the Constitution, the state enjoys sovereign immunity from suit in its own courts under federal causes of action. Seeking to avoid that conclusion, the plaintiffs had argued that Maine was discriminating against the federal cause of action because Maine had waived its immunity to permit its state courts to entertain wage claims based on state law. In response, the Court offered only the cryptic observation that "there is no evidence that the State has manipulated its immunity in systematic fashion to discriminate against federal causes of action".

Consider also Herb v. Pitcairn, 324 U.S. 117 (1945), an FELA action in an Illinois city court that, under state law, lacked jurisdiction of causes of action, such as this one, arising outside the city. Before action on plaintiff's motion for a change of venue, the FELA's two-year statute of limitations had run. The state court dismissed on the ground that there was no timely filed action to transfer, and the Supreme Court affirmed. Acknowledging the state's authority to allocate jurisdiction among its courts, the Court found no violation of the "qualification that the cause of action must not be discriminated against because it is a federal one". (Other decisions generally in accord with Douglas and Herb are noted in the footnote below.)[6]

(4) Nondiscriminatory Rules that Are Not a Valid Excuse: Haywood v. Drown. In its most recent decision on state court obligation, a closely divided Court held that a state court's dismissal of a federal cause of action, based on a state jurisdictional rule that did not discriminate against federal rights, was not a valid excuse for refusing to adjudicate the matter. Haywood v. Drown, 556 U.S. 729 (2009), involved a provision of New York's Correction Law that, responding to concerns about vexatious and frivolous prisoner lawsuits, stripped New York's trial courts of jurisdiction over suits by prisoners seeking damages from state corrections officials. (The statute did not bar actions for declaratory or injunctive relief against corrections officials, nor did it bar damages actions against police officers.) For damages actions against corrections officials, the statute substituted an action directly against the state in the state's court of claims, although this remedy was hedged with substantive and procedural limitations. The state's jurisdiction stripping law applied equally to federal and state law claims, and so when Haywood, an inmate, brought a federal civil rights action against prison officials, seeking damages under 42 U.S.C. § 1983, the state trial court dismissed his action. The state appellate courts affirmed.

The Supreme Court reversed, holding (5–4) that the state rule at issue was not a valid excuse. Justice Stevens' majority opinion stressed that states may in no case withhold jurisdiction over federal claims based on substantive disagreement with federal law, and stated: "It is principally on this basis that [the New York law] violates the Supremacy Clause." The state's policy on prisoner suits, "whatever its merits, is contrary to Congress' judgment that *all* persons who violate federal rights while acting under color of state law shall be held liable for damages." Acknowledging that the rule was evenhanded, he declared that "[e]nsuring equality of treatment" of state and federal causes of action is "the beginning, not the end, of the Supremacy Clause analysis", for "[a] jurisdictional rule cannot be used as a device to undermine federal law,

---

[6] In Missouri ex rel. Southern Ry. v. Mayfield, 340 U.S. 1 (1950), the state supreme court had quashed writs of mandamus to compel a state trial judge to exercise his discretion, on a plea of forum non conveniens, to dismiss FELA actions. The U.S. Supreme Court relied on its statement in the Douglas case that the FELA does not purport to force state courts to entertain FELA actions "against an otherwise valid excuse". Because the nondiscriminatory application of the doctrine of forum non conveniens constitutes a valid excuse, and because the state supreme court might have acted under a misapprehension of a federal duty, the state court judgment was vacated and the cause remanded for further proceedings.

Mayfield permits state courts to apply forum non conveniens doctrine to federal causes of action, but American Dredging Co. v. Miller, 510 U.S. 443 (1994), held, 7–2, that federal law does not require states to do so. There, a state procedural rule rendered forum non conveniens doctrine inapplicable in Jones Act and maritime cases filed in state court under the "saving to suitors" clause. Although a federal district court would apply a different forum non conveniens rule, the Court ruled that forum non conveniens doctrine is procedural, not substantive, and that the policies of federal maritime law do not require complete procedural uniformity.

no matter how evenhanded it may appear." Thus, " '[t]he fact that a rule is denominated jurisdictional does not provide a court an excuse to avoid the obligation to enforce federal law if the rule does not reflect the concerns of power over the person and competence over the subject matter that jurisdictional rules are designed to protect' " (quoting Howlett v. Rose, 496 U.S. 356, 381 (1990)). The Court noted that the state courts were open to § 1983 damages actions against other officials and to injunctive actions against corrections officials; "[i]t is only a particular species of suits—those seeking damages relief against corrections officers—that the State deems inappropriate for its trial courts." He concluded that "having made the decision to create courts of general jurisdiction that regularly sit to entertain analogous suits, New York is not at liberty to shut the courthouse door to federal claims that it considers at odds with its local policy" of disfavoring prisoner litigation.

Justice Thomas, joined in part by the Chief Justice and Justices Scalia and Alito, dissented. (The portion of his dissent in which he spoke only for himself is discussed in Paragraph (2)(c), *supra*.) In the portion of his opinion that the other dissenters joined, Justice Thomas maintained that the majority mistakenly pressed beyond the Court's precedents by invalidating a "neutral" statute that deprived state "courts of subject-matter jurisdiction over a particular class of claims on terms that treat federal and state actions equally." Acknowledging that the Court's precedents forbade the states to enforce substantive rules that nullify a federal right, even if the rules are labeled jurisdictional, he said the critical question is whether the rule operates jurisdictionally. A true jurisdictional statute such as New York's is "incapable of undermining federal law" because it requires dismissal of the plaintiff's case without prejudice, leaving him free to re-file in another forum (likely a federal court). The rule's jurisdictional character did not depend on its breadth, and so the majority's observation that New York's rule excluded only a particular species of suit from the courts' jurisdiction was beside the point.

(5) Questions About Haywood v. Drown. Haywood is the only decision in which the Court acknowledged that it was invalidating a nondiscriminatory jurisdictional rule. (One other decision, Felder v. Casey, 487 U.S. 131 (1988), also appears to have invalidated a nondiscriminatory rule, although the Court's opinion included an unconvincing contention that the state rule was discriminatory.[7])

Consider these questions raised by the Haywood decision:

(a) What Counts as Jurisdictional? Justice Stevens' opinion described the New York rule as jurisdictional, but he also said that in many respects it operates more as an immunity from damages than a jurisdictional rule; at another point he called it "an immunity statute cloaked in

---

[7]   Felder involved a state law requiring that before a state court action can be filed against a governmental body or its officials, the plaintiff must first have given the defendant notice of the claim within 120 days of the alleged injury. The plaintiff brought a federal civil rights action under 42 U.S.C. § 1983, naming a city and a police official as defendants. The state supreme court upheld dismissal of the action for failure to comply with the notice-of-claim statute. The Supreme Court reversed. Part of the Court's opinion argued that the statute, although it treated state law and federal law claims against governmental defendants identically, discriminated against the precise type of civil rights action that Congress had created in § 1983; that claim is not very persuasive. But the Court also argued that the statute would burden civil rights plaintiffs in order to serve a purpose—minimizing governmental liability—that was impermissible under federal law. In particular, the Court reasoned that enforcement of the statute was inconsistent with the decision in Patsy v. Board of Regents, p. 1097, *infra*, that exhaustion of state administrative remedies is not required in § 1983 actions. For further discussion of Felder, see pp. 455–457, *infra*.

jurisdictional garb." In response, Justice Thomas essentially suggested that whatever substantive concerns might have motivated the rule, the key point was that a genuinely jurisdictional rule results in a dismissal without prejudice (thus permitting suit to go forward in another court), whereas a substantive immunity would result in dismissal with prejudice, which would preclude further pursuit of the claims.[8]

One possible reply to Justice Thomas is that in view of the § 1983 suits that New York courts do entertain, the rule doesn't seem, in Justice Stevens' terms, to regulate judicial power over persons or competence over subject matter. But why can't a narrow rule depriving courts of a particular remedy be jurisdictional? A different reply to Justice Thomas might be that the policy underlying New York's law differs from the federal policy underlying § 1983. Compare the statement in the Mondou decision, quoted in Testa v. Katt: "When Congress, in the exertion of the power confided to it by the Constitution, adopted that act, it spoke for all the people and all the states, and thereby established a policy for all. That policy is as much the policy of Connecticut as if the act had emanated from its own legislature, and should be respected accordingly in the courts of the state."

(b) Why Displace Nondiscriminatory Rules? If application of the New York rule would merely have led to dismissal without prejudice of Haywood's action, what federal interest requires New York's courts to entertain it? Is it that a state court might be more convenient, speedier, or less costly than a federal court and that Congress wanted to give plaintiffs a forum choice? (The majority does not rely on that argument.) That state court resolution of the action helps reduce the federal courts' caseload, permitting their limited capacity to be directed elsewhere and avoiding burdens that might require an unwanted expansion of the federal judiciary? Does the latter rationale suggest that Congress is imposing an unfunded mandate upon the state courts? If so, is that problematic?

On the other hand, on Justice Thomas' view, are the state courts free to enforce any jurisdictional limitation that does not discriminate against federal rights so long as it requires a dismissal without prejudice? Consider a rule depriving state courts of jurisdiction over any employment discrimination case seeking more than $50,000 in damages, or over any actions challenging marriage rules under the state or federal constitution, or over any action challenging voting rules that relies on statistical evidence?[9]

---

[8]   Both opinions in Haywood endorsed the decision in Howlett v. Rose, 496 U.S. 356 (1990), where the Court unanimously ruled that the Florida state courts were obliged to entertain a federal civil rights action under 42 U.S.C. § 1983 against a local school board. Since a state statute had waived sovereign immunity in comparable actions under state law, the Court found the state's excuse—that the waiver of immunity did not extend to § 1983 actions— discriminatory and therefore invalid. Justice Stevens read Howlett as standing for the proposition that a state "cannot employ a jurisdictional rule 'to dissociate [itself] from federal law because of disagreement with its content or a refusal to recognize the superior authority of its source' " (quoting Howlett). Justice Thomas viewed the state rule there as being an effort to redefine the substantive rights and liabilities in § 1983 actions; though phrased in jurisdictional terms, the fact that the state courts had dismissed the claim *with prejudice* confirmed the rule's substantive nature.

[9]   Seinfeld, *The Jurisprudence of Union*, 89 Notre Dame L.Rev. 1085 (2014), echoes Justice Thomas' arguments that the New York rule did not undermine the § 1983 cause of action, given that a dismissal without prejudice left the plaintiff free to sue in federal court. He distinguishes the Court's claim that the New York rule undermined federal law from a second, and more persuasive, argument offered by the Court: that New York could not craft jurisdictional rules based on disagreement with federal policy. The latter argument, Professor Seinfeld suggests,

(6) Statutory Interpretation Versus Constitutional Power. When the Supreme Court decides that a state rule is a valid excuse (as in Douglas) or is not (as in Haywood), exactly what federal law is the Court applying? Is the Court determining whether a federal statute (like § 1983 in Haywood) and its associated policy are incompatible with the state's refusal to exercise jurisdiction? Recall Justice Holmes' statement in Douglas that the FELA does not purport to oblige states to open their courts to an FELA suit involving litigants and an accident that were all out-of-state. And in a case like Douglas, Congress would have lacked any apparent reason to oblige the New York state courts to entertain the action, especially when another (likely more convenient) state court was open.

But suppose that New York eliminated all state court jurisdiction over civil rights actions, federal and state, and in turn Congress purported to compel the states to entertain § 1983 actions. Both Justice Stevens and Justice Thomas agreed that the Haywood case, in Justice Stevens' words, "does not require us to decide whether Congress may compel a State to offer a forum, otherwise unavailable under state law, to hear suits brought pursuant to § 1983."

A series of Supreme Court decisions on constitutional federalism bear on the question of the ultimate scope of congressional power.

(a) Usery and Garcia. In National League of Cities v. Usery, 426 U.S. 833 (1976), the Court had ruled that substantive federal regulation of traditional state governmental functions involving matters "essential to [the] separate and independent existence" of the states lay beyond Congress' power under the Commerce Clause and the Tenth Amendment. Nine years later, the Usery decision was overruled in Garcia v. San Antonio Metropolitan Transit Auth., 469 U.S. 528 (1985). Both cases involved application of the Fair Labor Standards Act, and both resulted in 5–4 decisions.

(b) New York v. United States. In New York v. United States, 505 U.S. 144 (1992) (6–3), the Court made clear that, despite Garcia, it had not abandoned judicial enforcement of constitutional limits on Congress' power to regulate the states.[10] The Court invalidated, as outside the commerce

---

correctly treats a rule like New York's as invalid "not because it is tantamount to the nullification of federal law, but because it is corrosive to the sense of union that our Constitution seeks to foster." He finds that value of union recognized in the opinions in Testa, Mondou, Paragraph (2)(a), *supra*, and Howlett v. Rose (p. 446, n. 8, *supra*), as well as in other constitutional doctrines.

[10] Even before Usery was overruled, in Federal Energy Regulatory Comm'n [FERC] v. Mississippi, 456 U.S. 742 (1982), the Court rebuffed a Tenth Amendment challenge to the Public Utilities Regulatory Policies Act of 1978, 16 U.S.C. §§ 2601 *et seq.* That Act, *inter alia*, directed state utility regulatory authorities to implement certain federal rules, to "consider" the adoption of certain rate design and regulatory standards, and to follow specified procedures when considering these proposed standards. The Court distinguished Usery, and relied heavily on Testa v. Katt, in upholding the federal requirements. The Court stressed that Congress could choose to preempt state public utility regulation altogether and that the states could avoid the federal obligation by opting not to regulate.

In a partial dissent whose themes were later echoed by the majority in the New York decision and in Printz v. United States, Paragraph (6)(c), *infra*, Justice O'Connor, joined by Chief Justice Burger and Justice Rehnquist, argued that "[a]pplication of Testa to legislative power [such as that exercised by state utility regulatory commissions] * * * vastly expands the scope of that decision. Because trial courts of general jurisdiction do not choose the cases that they hear, the requirement that they evenhandedly adjudicate state and federal claims falling within their jurisdiction does not infringe any sovereign authority to set an agenda. * * * [But]

power, a federal statute requiring states that failed to provide for disposal of internally generated radioactive waste by a certain date to take title to the waste and thereby to assume associated liabilities. In the Court's view, Congress lacked power either to "commandeer" the states into regulating waste disposal or to require states to take title to waste; accordingly, Congress lacked power to offer the states a choice between those two options. Garcia was distinguished because it involved a statute that, unlike the "take title" provision, "subjected a State to the same legislation applicable to private parties".

The Court distinguished Testa on the following basis: "Federal statutes enforceable in state courts do, in a sense, direct state judges to enforce them, but this sort of federal 'direction' of state judges is mandated by the text of the Supremacy Clause. No comparable constitutional provision authorizes Congress to command state legislatures to legislate".

(c) The Printz Decision. The Court extended the "anti-commandeering" principle of New York v. United States in Printz v. United States, 521 U.S. 898 (1997) (5–4). Justice Scalia's opinion for the Court held that Congress overstepped constitutional bounds by directing local law enforcement officials to conduct background checks on would-be purchasers of handguns. The Court said that just as the federal government may not order the states to legislate, it may not "command the States' officers, or those of their political subdivisions, to administer or enforce a federal regulatory program". The Court in Printz distinguished Testa on the same basis that it had in New York v. United States.

(d) The Import of the Decisions. Do the New York and Printz decisions, notwithstanding their distinction of Testa, suggest that the Justices are concerned about preserving state autonomy in a way that might limit congressional power to require state courts to hear federal claims?

(7) The Interpretation of Federal Statutes. Insofar as the question presented in cases like Testa, Douglas, and Haywood is one of statutory construction, consider the relevance of the decision in Gregory v. Ashcroft, 501 U.S. 452 (1991). There, the Court relied on some of the themes of the Usery decision and the anti-commandeering decisions in holding that the federal Age Discrimination in Employment Act, which forbids age-based mandatory retirement, does not apply to Missouri state judges, who are required by the state constitution to retire at age 70. Justice O'Connor's majority opinion reasoned that "[c]ongressional interference with this decision of the people of Missouri, defining their constitutional officers, would upset the usual constitutional balance of federal and state powers". Without questioning Congress' power to do so, Justice O'Connor held that "[i]f Congress intends to alter 'the usual constitutional balance between the States and the Federal Government' it must make its intention to do so 'unmistakably clear in the language of the statute' " (quoting Will v. Michigan Dep't of State Police, 491 U.S. 58, 65 (1989)).

Given Gregory, does it upset the usual constitutional balance to override a discriminatory state jurisdictional rule? A non-discriminatory state rule? Should courts require that the statutory text include some language suggesting that state courts are *obliged* to hear a federal action? Recall that

---

the power to choose subjects for legislation is a fundamental attribute of legislative power, and interference with this power unavoidably undermines state sovereignty".

For further consideration of FERC, see p. 457, *infra*.

in deciding whether state courts are *precluded* from exercising jurisdiction, the Supreme Court has come close to holding that only statutory text can render a grant of federal jurisdiction exclusive.[11]

Is Justice Stevens' approach in Haywood, which assesses whether the state jurisdictional rule conflicts with federal policy, more appropriate, given the limited capacity of Congress both to anticipate how state jurisdictional rules might limit adjudication of federal actions and to decide up front whether those limitations should be overridden?[12]

Dice v. Akron, Canton & Youngstown R.R.

342 U.S. 359, 72 S.Ct. 312, 96 L.Ed. 398 (1952).
Certiorari to the Supreme Court of Ohio.

■ MR. JUSTICE BLACK delivered the opinion of the Court.

Petitioner, a railroad fireman, was seriously injured when an engine in which he was riding jumped the track. Alleging that his injuries were due to respondent's negligence, he brought this action for damages under the Federal Employers' Liability Act, in an Ohio court of common pleas. Respondent's defenses were (1) a denial of negligence and (2) a written document signed by petitioner purporting to release respondent in full for $924.63. Petitioner admitted that he had signed several receipts for payments made him in connection with his injuries but denied that he had made a full and complete settlement of all his claims. He alleged that the purported release was void because he had signed it relying on respondent's deliberately false statement that the document was nothing more than a mere receipt for back wages.

* * * [T]he jury found in favor of petitioner and awarded him a $25,000 verdict. The trial judge later entered judgment notwithstanding the verdict. In doing so he reappraised the evidence as to fraud, found that petitioner had been "guilty of supine negligence" in failing to read the release, and accordingly held that the facts did not "sustain either in law or in equity the allegations of fraud by clear, unequivocal and convincing evidence." This judgment notwithstanding the verdict was reversed by the Court of Appeals of Summit County, Ohio, on the ground that under federal law, which controlled, the jury's verdict must stand because there was ample evidence to support its finding of fraud. The Ohio Supreme Court, one judge dissenting, reversed the Court of Appeals' judgment and sustained the trial court's action, holding that: (1) Ohio, not federal, law governed; (2) under that law petitioner, a man of ordinary intelligence who could read, was bound by the release even

---

[11] In Mims v. Arrow Financial Services, LLC, 132 S.Ct. 740 (2012), p. 420, n. 4, *supra,* the Court held that a statutory provision specifying that a person "may, if otherwise permitted by the laws or rules of court of a State, bring in an appropriate court of that State" an action for violation of a federal statute, did not bar the federal courts from exercising federal question jurisdiction. In response to the argument that the language authorizing state court suit would be superfluous, given the presumption of concurrent jurisdiction, unless it excluded federal jurisdiction, the Court said that Congress "arguably gave States leeway they would otherwise lack" to decide whether to exercise jurisdiction over such actions. Should that language be read to authorize states to invoke any non-discriminatory basis for declining to hear federal actions brought under this statute? To refuse to hear such actions even if their courts entertain analogous state law actions?

[12] See generally Meltzer, *Textualism and Preemption*, 112 Mich.L.Rev. 1 (2013).

though he had been induced to sign it by the deliberately false statement that it was only a receipt for back wages; and (3) under controlling Ohio law factual issues as to fraud in the execution of this release were properly decided by the judge rather than by the jury. We granted certiorari because the decision of the Supreme Court of Ohio appeared to deviate from previous decisions of this Court that federal law governs cases arising under the Federal Employers' Liability Act.

First. We agree with the Court of Appeals of Summit County, Ohio, and the dissenting judge in the Ohio Supreme Court and hold that validity of releases under the Federal Employers' Liability Act raises a federal question to be determined by federal rather than state law. Congress * * * granted petitioner a right to recover against his employer for damages negligently inflicted. State laws are not controlling in determining what the incidents of this federal right shall be. * * * Manifestly the federal rights affording relief to injured railroad employees under a federally declared standard could be defeated if states were permitted to have the final say as to what defenses could and could not be properly interposed to suits under the Act. Moreover, only if federal law controls can the federal Act be given that uniform application throughout the country essential to effectuate its purposes. Releases and other devices designed to liquidate or defeat injured employees' claims play an important part in the federal Act's administration. Their validity is but one of the many interrelated questions that must constantly be determined in these cases according to a uniform federal law.

Second. In effect the Supreme Court of Ohio held that an employee trusts his employer at his peril, and that the negligence of an innocent worker is sufficient to enable his employer to benefit by its deliberate fraud. Application of so harsh a rule to defeat a railroad employee's claim is wholly incongruous with the general policy of the Act to give railroad employees a right to recover just compensation for injuries negligently inflicted by their employers. And this Ohio rule is out of harmony with modern judicial and legislative practice to relieve injured persons from the effect of releases fraudulently obtained. * * * We hold that the correct federal rule is that announced by the Court of Appeals of Summit County, Ohio, and the dissenting judge in the Ohio Supreme Court—a release of rights under the Act is void when the employee is induced to sign it by the deliberately false and material statements of the railroad's authorized representatives made to deceive the employee as to the contents of the release. The Trial Court's charge to the jury correctly stated this rule of law.

Third. Ohio provides and has here accorded petitioner the usual jury trial of factual issues relating to negligence. But Ohio treats factual questions of fraudulent releases differently. It permits the judge trying a negligence case to resolve all factual questions of fraud "other than fraud in the factum." The factual issue of fraud is thus split into fragments, some to be determined by the judge, others by the jury.

It is contended that since a state may consistently with the Federal Constitution provide for trial of cases under the Act by a nonunanimous verdict, Minneapolis & St. Louis R. Co. v. Bombolis, 241 U.S. 211, Ohio may lawfully eliminate trial by jury as to one phase of fraud while allowing jury trial as to all other issues raised. The Bombolis case might be more in point had Ohio abolished trial by jury in all negligence cases including those arising under the federal Act. But Ohio has not done this. It has provided jury trials for cases arising under the federal Act but seeks to single out one phase of the question of fraudulent releases for determination by a judge rather than by a jury. Compare Testa v. Katt, 330 U.S. 386.

We have previously held that "The right to trial by jury is 'a basic and fundamental feature of our system of federal jurisprudence' " and that it is "part and parcel of the remedy afforded railroad workers under the Employers' Liability Act." Bailey v. Central Vermont R. Co., 319 U.S. 350, 354. We also recognized in that case that to deprive railroad workers of the benefit of a jury trial where there is evidence to support negligence "is to take away a goodly portion of the relief which Congress has afforded them." It follows that the right to trial by jury is too substantial a part of the rights accorded by the Act to permit it to be classified as a mere "local rule of procedure" for denial in the manner that Ohio has here used. Brown v. Western R. Co., 338 U.S. 294.

The trial judge and the Ohio Supreme Court erred in holding that petitioner's rights were to be determined by Ohio law and in taking away petitioner's verdict when the issues of fraud had been submitted to the jury on conflicting evidence and determined in petitioner's favor. * * * The cause is reversed and remanded to the Supreme Court of Ohio for further action not inconsistent with this opinion. * * *

■ MR. JUSTICE FRANKFURTER, whom MR. JUSTICE REED, MR. JUSTICE JACKSON and MR. JUSTICE BURTON join, concurring for reversal but dissenting from the Court's opinion.

Ohio, as do many other States, maintains the old division between law and equity even though the same judge administers both. The Ohio Supreme Court has told us what, on one issue, is the division of functions in all negligence actions brought in the Ohio courts: "Where it is claimed that a release was induced by fraud (other than fraud in the factum) or by mistake, it is * * * necessary, before seeking to enforce a cause of action which such release purports to bar, that equitable relief from the release be secured." 155 Ohio St. 185, 186, 98 N.E.2d 301, 304. Thus, in all cases in Ohio the judge is the trier of fact on this issue of fraud, rather than the jury. * * * To require Ohio to try a particular issue before a different fact-finder in negligence actions brought under the Employers' Liability Act from the fact-finder on the identical issue in every other negligence case disregards the settled distribution of judicial power between Federal and State courts where Congress authorizes concurrent enforcement of federally-created rights.

It has been settled ever since the Second Employers' Liability Cases (Mondou v. New York, N.H. & H.R. Co.) 223 U.S. 1, that no State which gives its courts jurisdiction over common law actions for negligence may deny access to its courts for a negligence action founded on the Federal Employers' Liability Act. Nor may a State discriminate disadvantageously against actions for negligence under the Federal Act as compared with local causes of actions in negligence. Conversely, however, simply because there is concurrent jurisdiction in Federal and State courts over actions under the Employers' Liability Act, a State is under no duty to treat actions arising under that Act differently from the way it adjudicates local actions for negligence, so far as the mechanics of litigation, the forms in which law is administered, are concerned. This surely covers the distribution of functions as between judge and jury * * *.

In 1916 the Court decided without dissent that States in entertaining actions under the Federal Employers' Liability Act need not provide a jury system other than that established for local negligence actions. States are not compelled to provide the jury required of Federal courts by the Seventh Amendment. Minneapolis & St. L. R. Co. v. Bombolis, 241 U.S. 211. * * * [T]he Bombolis case has often been cited by this Court but never questioned. Until today its significance has been to leave to States the choice of the fact-finding tribunal in all negligence actions, including those arising under the Federal Act. * * *

Although a State must entertain negligence suits brought under the Federal Employers' Liability Act if it entertains ordinary actions for negligence, it need conduct them only in the way in which it conducts the run of negligence litigation. The Bombolis case directly establishes that the Employers' Liability Act does not impose the jury requirements of the Seventh Amendment on the States *pro tanto* for Employers' Liability litigation. If its reasoning means anything the Bombolis decision means that if a State chooses not to have a jury at all, but to leave questions of fact in all negligence actions to a court, certainly the Employers' Liability Act does not require a State to have juries for negligence actions brought under the Federal Act in its courts. Or, if a State chooses to retain the old double system of courts, common law and equity—as did a good many States until the other day, and as four States still do—surely there is nothing in the Employers' Liability Act that requires traditional distribution of authority for disposing of legal issues as between common law and chancery courts to go by the board. And if States are free to make a distribution of functions between equity and common law courts, it surely makes no rational difference whether a State chooses to provide that the same judge preside on both the common law and the chancery sides in a single litigation, instead of in separate rooms in the same building. So long as all negligence suits in a State are treated in the same way, by the same mode of disposing equitable, non-jury, and common law, jury issues, the State does not discriminate against Employers' Liability suits nor does it make any inroad upon substance.

Ohio and her sister States with a similar division of functions between law and equity are not trying to evade their duty under the Federal Employers' Liability Act; nor are they trying to make it more difficult for railroad workers to recover, than for those suing under local law. The States merely exercise a preference in adhering to historic ways of dealing with a claim of fraud; they prefer the traditional way of making unavailable through equity an otherwise valid defense. The State judges and local lawyers who must administer the Federal Employers' Liability Act in State courts are trained in the ways of local practice; it multiplies the difficulties and confuses the administration of justice to require, on purely theoretical grounds, a hybrid of State and Federal practice in the State courts as to a single class of cases. * * * The fact that Congress authorized actions under the Federal Employers' Liability Act to be brought in State as well as in Federal courts seems a strange basis for the inference that Congress overrode State procedural arrangements controlling all other negligence suits in a State, by imposing upon State courts to which plaintiffs choose to go the rules prevailing in the Federal courts regarding juries. Such an inference is admissible, so it seems to me, only on the theory that Congress included as part of the right created by the Employers' Liability Act an assumed likelihood that trying all issues to juries is more favorable to plaintiffs. At least, if a plaintiff's right to have all issues decided by a jury rather than the court is "part and parcel of the remedy afforded railroad workers under the Employers Liability Act," the Bombolis case should be overruled explicitly instead of left as a derelict bound to occasion collisions on the waters of the law. We have put the questions squarely because they seem to be precisely what will be roused in the minds of lawyers properly pressing their clients' interests and in the minds of trial and appellate judges called upon to apply this Court's opinion. It is one thing not to borrow trouble from the morrow. It is another thing to create trouble for the morrow.

Even though the method of trying the equitable issue of fraud which the State applies in all other negligence cases governs Employers' Liability cases, two questions remain for decision: Should the validity of the release be tested by a Federal or a State standard? And if by a Federal one, did the Ohio courts in the present case correctly administer the standard? If the States afford courts for enforcing the Federal Act, they must enforce the substance of the right given by Congress. They cannot depreciate the legislative currency issued by Congress—either expressly or by local methods of enforcement that accomplish the same result. Davis v. Wechsler, 263 U.S. 22, 24. In order to prevent diminution of railroad workers' nationally-uniform right to recover, the standard for the validity of a release of contested liability must be federal. * * *

NOTE ON "SUBSTANCE" AND "PROCEDURE" IN THE ENFORCEMENT OF FEDERAL RIGHTS OF ACTION IN STATE COURTS

(1) State Court Procedures: Rule and Exceptions. Justice Frankfurter's general claim that state courts apply state procedures when adjudicating federal rights, although stated in dissent in Dice, is plainly correct. The Dice decision, then, is an exceptional departure from that general rule. This Note will discuss a handful of other cases recognizing such exceptions, but one should keep in mind that these relatively few decisions depart from an otherwise consistent practice in which state courts, when adjudicating federal rights, apply the same procedures that apply when state law rights are adjudicated.

(2) The Relationship of Dice to Testa v. Katt. The issue in Dice—whether states may follow their procedural rules in entertaining federal rights—echoes the issue in cases like Testa—whether states may follow their own jurisdictional or related rules in deciding whether to entertain federal causes of action. In both instances, there are questions of statutory interpretation or judicial policymaking, as well as questions of the ultimate scope of the constitutional authority of Congress.

Justice Frankfurter stressed that Ohio's rule on the division of factfinding authority did not discriminate against federal rights. But the Court has displaced nondiscriminatory procedural rules somewhat more freely than nondiscriminatory jurisdictional rules. As you read the material that follows, consider whether good reason exists for the difference in treatment. (Recall in this respect Justice Thomas' argument in his dissent in

Haywood that applying state jurisdictional rules so as to dismiss a claim without prejudice does not harm federal rightholders. That argument plainly does not apply equally to the enforcement of state procedures.)

(3) The FELA and Jury Trial. In what sense is jury trial "part and parcel of the remedy afforded railroad workers under the Employers' Liability Act"? The FELA's only textual reference to jury trial is in a provision stating that contributory negligence shall not bar a recovery "but the damages shall be diminished by the jury in proportion to the amount of negligence" attributable to the employee. 45 U.S.C. § 53. Why then does the opinion say: "[T]o deprive railroad workers of the benefit of a jury trial where there is evidence to support negligence 'is to take away a goodly portion of the relief which Congress has afforded them'" (quoting Bailey v. Central Vermont Ry., 319 U.S. 350, 354 (1943))? Because juries tend strongly to favor injured railroad workers? See Hill, *Substance and Procedure in State FELA Actions—The Converse of the Erie Problem?*, 17 Ohio St.L.J. 384, 397 (1956).[1]

If the federal rule with respect to the jury's role in FELA cases is correctly seen as implementing congressional policy regarding risk-distribution, doesn't it follow that the Court was correct in imposing that rule on the state courts?

(4) Federal Rights and Federal "Procedures" Under the FELA. A number of the Supreme Court's cases concerning the displacement of state court procedures when hearing federal causes of action have, like Dice, arisen under the FELA. Because for some years the Court evinced special solicitude for FELA plaintiffs, its FELA decisions on displacement of state procedures may not be generalizable to cases brought under the full range of federal statutes. Moreover, the FELA decisions do not seem to set forth a consistent standard that explains when state procedures are, and are not, found wanting.

(a) Burden of Proof. Central Vermont Ry. Co. v. White, 238 U.S. 507 (1915), held that a state rule requiring the plaintiff to prove freedom from contributory negligence did not apply in FELA actions: the burden of proof on contributory negligence is not a "mere matter of state procedure", and Congress intended that the FELA be interpreted in light of the federal court decisions that uniformly required the defendant to prove contributory negligence.

(b) Non-Unanimous Juries. In Minneapolis & St. Louis R.R. v. Bombolis, 241 U.S. 211 (1916), another FELA action, the Court upheld a provision for a civil verdict by five-sixths of the jury, after failure for twelve hours to achieve unanimity.[2] Why is that state rule valid but not a state rule on burden of proof? Can the difference be explained by whether each state rule was consistent with the (pro-plaintiff) policies of the FELA?[3]

---

[1]   There is some evidence that congressional policy favored jury trials in FELA cases, and possibly for plaintiff-favoring reasons, but it is far from conclusive. See Tiller v. Atlantic Coast Line R.R., 318 U.S. 54, 58–67 (1943); Rogers v. Missouri Pac. R.R., 352 U.S. 500, 508–09 (1957), and sources cited.

[2]   Companion cases upheld verdicts by three-fourths, St. Louis & San Francisco R.R. v. Brown, 241 U.S. 223 (1916); Louisville & Nashville R.R. v. Stewart, 241 U.S. 261 (1916), and trial to a jury of seven, Chesapeake & Ohio Ry. v. Carnahan, 241 U.S. 241 (1916).

[3]   Despite the Bombolis decision, the Court has reversed state court judgments directing a verdict for the railroad, where the Court deemed the evidence sufficient to create an issue for the jury, although it would not overturn a jury verdict in defendant's favor. See, *e.g.*, Bailey v. Central Vermont Ry., 319 U.S. 350 (1943); Wilkerson v. McCarthy, 336 U.S. 53 (1949).

Suppose a state provided no jury in negligence actions. If the denial of a jury trial as to "one phase of fraud" diminishes a federal right in Dice, wouldn't the failure to provide any jury at all do so *a fortiori*? On the other hand, requiring state courts to convene juries when they otherwise would not have one is a greater burden than requiring submission of one additional issue to a jury that has already been convened. Does (should) the question whether a state procedure is displaced depend on a balancing of federal and state interests?

(c) State Pleading Rules. In still another FELA case, Brown v. Western Ry., 338 U.S. 294 (1949), the plaintiff alleged injuries caused by "the negligence of the defendant" when he stepped on "a large clinker [the incombustible residue from burning coal] lying beside the tracks"; the railroad, he averred, had allowed clinkers and other debris to collect, "well knowing that * * * yards in such condition were dangerous". The Georgia courts dismissed the complaint for failure to state a claim, apparently interpreting a rule that complaints must be construed "most strongly against the pleader" as requiring a specific pleading that the particular clinker inflicting the harm was not in plain view and therefore easily avoidable or that the railroad was negligent in allowing the particular clinker to be there. The Supreme Court reversed. Justice Black's opinion acknowledged the "impossibility of laying down a precise rule to distinguish 'substance' from 'procedure'," but found that the Court did not need to try to do so, as it was obliged to interpret the averments itself "to determine whether petitioner has been denied a right of trial granted him by Congress. This federal right cannot be defeated by the forms of local practice. * * * And we cannot accept as final a state court's interpretation of allegations in a complaint asserting it." He added: "Strict local rules of pleading cannot be used to impose unnecessary burdens upon rights of recovery authorized by federal laws."

Justice Frankfurter, joined by Justice Jackson, dissented, arguing that a litigant who chooses to enforce a federal right in state court cannot object to being treated no differently, with respect to the form in which the claim must be stated, from a litigant raising a state law claim, so long as the state requirement "does not add to, or diminish, the right as defined by Federal law, nor burden the realization of this right in the actualities of litigation." He stressed that "Congress has authorized State courts to enforce Federal rights, and Federal courts State-created rights. Neither system of courts can impair these respective rights, but both may have their own requirements for stating claims (pleading) and conducting litigation (practice)."[4]

(5) Notice of Claim Requirements in § 1983 Actions. Not all of the handful of Supreme Court decisions displacing state procedures arose under the FELA. In Felder v. Casey, 487 U.S. 131 (1988), state law required that a plaintiff suing a governmental body or its officials must have first given the defendant notice of the claim within 120 days of the alleged injury. The state supreme court upheld dismissal of Felder's federal civil rights action under 42 U.S.C. § 1983 for failure to comply with the notice-of-claim statute. The

---

[4] Given that Brown could have amended his complaint to provide greater particularity, Professor Hill suggests that the real problem was not burdensome state pleading rules but rather "a misconception concerning the minimum quantum of evidence needed in an FELA case." Hill, Paragraph (3), *supra*, at 407 & n.143. Compare Meltzer, *State Court Forfeitures of Federal Rights*, 99 Harv.L.Rev. 1128, 1142–43 n.65 (1986), arguing that on Hill's view, the proper disposition would have been a remand to permit the state courts to decide whether, on a proper understanding of federal law, the plaintiff had complied with state pleading rules, rather than a direction to the state courts to treat the plaintiff as having complied.

Supreme Court reversed, concluding, *inter alia*, that the state statute burdened civil rights plaintiffs in order to serve a purpose—minimizing governmental liability—that was impermissible under federal law, and that enforcement of the statute was inconsistent with the decision in Patsy v. Board of Regents, p. 1097, *infra*, that exhaustion of state administrative remedies is not required in § 1983 actions. Justice Brennan's majority opinion, quoting Brown v. Western Ry., reasoned that "[f]ederal law takes state courts as it finds them only insofar as those courts employ rules that do not 'impose unnecessary burdens upon rights of recovery authorized by federal laws.' * * * [T]he notice-of-claim statute in § 1983 actions brought in state court so interferes with and frustrates the substantive right Congress created that, under the Supremacy Clause, it must yield to the federal interest". The Court assumed that the notice-of-claim statute would not have applied in a federal court action. Comparing the question before it to the application of the Erie doctrine, the Court said that the state could not "demand[ ] compliance with outcome-determinative rules that are inapplicable when such claims are brought in federal court".

Justice O'Connor, joined by Chief Justice Rehnquist, dissented, finding that the state statute, unlike the rule in Brown, did not "diminish or alter any substantive right cognizable under § 1983".[5]

(6) Reverse-Erie? Cases like Dice are often seen as raising "reverse-Erie" issues about the permissibility of state courts applying state procedural rules when enforcing federal rights. Recall Justice Brennan's reference to reverse-Erie in his Felder opinion.[6] Professor Clermont argues that cases such as Dice and Felder are properly viewed as exemplifying a broad reverse-Erie doctrine central to understanding the relation of state and federal law in the federal system. Clermont, *Reverse-Erie*, 82 Notre Dame L.Rev. 1 (2006). Criticizing Federal Courts casebooks (including earlier editions of this book) for treating the issue as solely one of preemption, he argues that there exists a zone of discretion in which judges must resolve "choice-of-law" issues, determining whether state or federal interests predominate, pursuant to a

---

[5]   Insofar as Felder could be read to suggest that state courts hearing § 1983 actions must follow (at least important) federal procedural rules, the Court unanimously rejected any such implication in Johnson v. Fankell, 520 U.S. 911 (1997). There, the Court ruled that in a suit against a state official under § 1983, an Idaho court need not provide an interlocutory appeal from a trial judge's denial of a motion for summary judgment based on qualified immunity. Had the plaintiff filed her § 1983 action in federal court, such an appeal would have been permitted, on the theory that qualified immunity is " 'an entitlement not to stand trial or face the other burdens of litigation' ". Behrens v. Pelletier, 516 U.S. 299, 306 (1996). Nonetheless, the Court ruled in Johnson that Idaho rules precluding interlocutory appeals were not preempted in § 1983 actions. A key point was that the interlocutory appeal in federal court actions was provided to protect the state and its officials from overenforcement of federal rights. The state courts' failure to provide a similar protection "is thus less an interference with federal interests than a judgment about how best to balance the competing state interests of limiting interlocutory appeals and providing state officials with immediate review of the merits of their defense". The Court also found that Idaho's rules were "not 'outcome determinative' in the sense" used in Felder, since "postponement of the appeal until after final judgment will not affect the ultimate outcome of the case". Is that argument persuasive in view of the characterization of the purpose of immunity doctrine in the Behrens decision?

Would the Court's reasoning in Johnson apply to a federal civil rights action in state court filed against a *federal* officer (in an action under Bivens v. Six Unknown Named Agents, p. 762, *infra*) who had failed to remove the case to a federal court?

[6]   The term apparently originated in Baxter, *Choice of Law and the Federal System*, 16 Stan.L.Rev. 1, 34 (1963).

"balancing" test prescribed by the Supreme Court, apparently as a matter of federal common law.

Might the "reverse-Erie" label distract attention from a pertinent asymmetry, one that Clermont does acknowledge: Federal law can and frequently does preempt otherwise valid and applicable state law, whereas state law cannot preempt otherwise valid and applicable federal law? See generally Meltzer, note 4, *supra*, at 1176–85; Weinberg, *The Federal State Conflict of Laws: "Actual" Conflicts*, 70 Tex.L.Rev. 1743, 1773–96 (1992). However one answers that question, is Professor Clermont correct that the decisions such as Dice and Felder are better characterized as reflecting a judicial balancing of competing state and federal interests, conducted as a matter of federal common law, than as determining whether federal law preempts otherwise applicable state law?

(7) Power, Policy, and Statutory Construction. In considering the decisions summarized in this Note, consider the perspective of Hart, *The Relations Between State and Federal Law*, 54 Colum.L.Rev. 489, 508 (1954):

"The general rule, bottomed deeply in belief in the importance of state control of state judicial procedure, is that federal law takes the state courts as it finds them. * * * The Supreme Court in recent years has been disturbed by the recognition that differences between state and federal procedure may sometimes lead to different results in actions to enforce federally-created rights of which state and federal courts have concurrent jurisdiction. [Citing Dice and other FELA cases.] * * * Some differences in remedy and procedure are inescapable if the different governments are to retain a measure of independence in deciding how justice should be administered. If the differences become so conspicuous as to affect advance calculations of outcome, and so to induce an undesirable shopping between forums, the remedy does not lie in the sacrifice of the independence of either government. It lies rather in provision by the federal government, confident of the justice of its own procedure, of a federal forum equally accessible to both litigants."

[handwritten margin note: SCOTUS' concern (forum shopping)]

Professor Hart's view has been clearly rejected by the Supreme Court in cases like Dice, Brown, and Felder. But whose position is sounder?

(a) Congressional Power to Prescribe Procedures in State Court. What is the scope of Congress' authority under Article I to require state courts to follow federally mandated procedures in adjudicating federal causes of action? In FELA cases, could Congress require state courts (a) to convene juries of 12, even though the state usually uses six-person juries; (b) to follow federal discovery rules, or (c) to use judges appointed by the governor (even though the state has long elected its judges)?

Consider in this regard the decision in Federal Energy Regulatory Comm'n [FERC] v. Mississippi, 456 U.S. 742 (1982), also noted at p. 447, n. 10, *supra*, where the Court upheld provisions of the Public Utility Regulatory Policies Act of 1978 that imposed important federal procedural requirements on state commissions regulating energy (as well as requiring the commissions to "consider" the adoption of federal substantive standards). The Court acknowledged that the Act's procedural provisions were "more intrusive" than its "hortatory" substantive provisions, but said: "If Congress can require a state administrative body to consider proposed regulations as a condition to its continued involvement in a pre-emptible field—and we hold today that it can—there is nothing unconstitutional about Congress' requiring certain procedural minima as that body goes about undertaking its tasks". Justice Powell's dissent stated that "I know of no other attempt by the Federal Government to supplant state-prescribed procedures that in part define the nature of their administrative agencies". Justice O'Connor's dissent objected that "[s]tate legislative and administrative bodies are not field offices of the national bureaucracy".

Neither the Court nor the dissenters alluded to Dice or the other FELA cases. Does the nature or scope of Congress' power to specify procedures that state adjudicators must follow differ for state agencies and state courts?

(b) Subconstitutional Questions: Statutory Interpretation and Judicial Policymaking. Would Professor Hart's argument be more tenable or attractive if understood to address not the *power* of Congress to impose obligations on state courts, but (i) the policies that Congress ought to follow in enacting substantive and jurisdictional legislation, (ii) the principles of statutory construction that courts should adopt in identifying the obligations that Congress has imposed, and/or (iii) the principles that should govern a judge-made federal common law of state-federal relations?

In this regard, recall that the Court in Dice was unanimous in holding that the standard governing the validity of the release is federal. If state law governing the validity of a release can be displaced as conflicting with federal purposes—even absent express statutory language so providing—why should the same not be true of state procedures? Perhaps Hart would have responded that state court procedures applied to the run of state and federal claims are unlikely to conflict with federal purposes. But even if that is true in general, what of cases where it is not? If one accepts Professor Clermont's view that these matters require interest balancing, does the state have a weightier interest in following its procedural rules than its rules on the validity of fraudulently obtained releases?[7]

(c) The Relevance of Plaintiff's Forum Choice. Professor Hart suggests that Dice, having chosen to file his FELA action in state rather than federal court, should be stuck with Ohio's allocation of responsibility between judge and jury. If the exercise of choice is the key, then should a state court *defendant* in an FELA action (who is barred from removing the case to

---

[7] The decisions discussed in text involved state law rules thought to impair enforcement of federal rights in state courts. Does federal law ever preclude state courts from following procedural rules that make enforcement of those rights easier?

In Norfolk & Western Ry. Co. v. Liepelt, 444 U.S. 490 (1980), a state court wrongful death action under the FELA, the Illinois appellate court had followed Illinois law, under which evidence of the effect of income taxes on the decedent's projected future earnings could be excluded and no instruction on the effect of income taxes was required. In reversing this plaintiff-friendly approach, the Supreme Court said that federal law governs the measure of damages in FELA actions, and proceeded to rule that the Illinois courts must (i) allow the defendant to introduce evidence about the effect of income taxes on the decedent's projected future earnings, and (ii) on request, instruct the jury that its award will not be taxable. In dissent, Justice Blackmun, joined by Justice Marshall, said that Illinois law should apply.

In Monessen Southwestern Ry. Co. v. Morgan, 486 U.S. 330 (1988), another FELA action, the Court ruled that federal law barred prejudgment interest and required that damages for loss of future earnings be discounted to present value; conflicting state law was accordingly displaced. Justices Blackmun and Marshall, dissenting in part, urged a federal rule providing prejudgment interest. Justice O'Connor and Chief Justice Rehnquist also dissented in part; while generally agreeing with the Court, they would have given the states greater latitude in selecting a method for determining present value.

Even if questions about the measure of damages are "federal in character", must there be a uniform federal rule? An alternative would be for federal law to "adopt" state law insofar as it is not incompatible with federal policy. See generally Chap. VII, Sec. 1(B), *infra*. Is the argument for a federal ceiling on FELA damages as strong as the argument for a federal floor?

federal court, see 28 U.S.C. § 1445(a)) be able to insist on a jury trial on the question of fraud in obtaining a release?

In assessing Hart's position, note that Congress may wish to give litigants the convenience of using state courts to enforce federal rights (a particularly salient point in FELA cases given the unusual statutory bar on removal) but may not be able to anticipate all of the procedural issues that might arise in the litigation of federal causes of action in state court. (After all, some state procedural rules may have been adopted after enactment of the FELA.) Moreover, isn't it doubtful to treat decisions about forum choice, which are motivated by many factors (for example, length of dockets; location of the court; geographical size of jury pool; identity and quality of judge) as if the parties and their lawyers had comprehensively analyzed every possible difference in state and federal procedure at the outset? Indeed, in Dice itself, when suit was filed in state court neither the plaintiff nor his lawyer may have known that the plaintiff had signed a paper that purported to be a release.

(8) The Regulation of State Procedures When Adjudicating State Law Claims. What is the scope and appropriate use of congressional power to regulate state court procedures used in adjudicating *state law* claims? Only a few Supreme Court decisions bear directly on this question.[8]

(a) The Pierce County Decision. In Pierce County v. Guillen, 537 U.S. 129 (2003), the Court ruled unanimously that Congress possesses power under the Commerce Clause to enact a federal statute barring, in state as well as federal trials, the discovery or introduction into evidence of information "compiled or collected" in connection with certain federal highway safety programs. But the Court declined to decide (because the question had not been addressed by the lower court) whether the challenged statute "violates the principles of dual sovereignty embodied in the Tenth Amendment because it prohibits a State from exercising its sovereign powers to establish discovery and admissibility rules to be used in state court for a state cause of action".

(b) The Jinks Decision. In Jinks v. Richland County, 538 U.S. 456 (2003), the Court upheld a provision of the supplemental jurisdiction statute, 28 U.S.C. § 1367(d), that (under some circumstances) tolls the statute of limitations on state law claims while they are pending in federal court. The tolling provision requires state courts to hear claims, over which a federal court has declined to exercise supplemental jurisdiction, after the otherwise applicable state limitations period has expired. Justice Scalia's unanimous opinion first found the tolling provision "necessary and proper for carrying into execution Congress's power '[t]o constitute Tribunals inferior to the supreme Court' ", because, he said, it promotes the fair and efficient administration of justice by the federal courts. He then rejected a claim that, in light of principles of state sovereignty, it was not "proper" for Congress to prescribe procedural rules for the adjudication of state law claims in state courts: assuming arguendo that federal laws regulating state-court "procedure" could be distinguished from laws changing the "substance" of state-law rights of action, "we do not think that state-law limitations periods

---

[8] For expressions of doubt about congressional power in this context, see Parmet, *Stealth Preemption: The Proposed Federalization of State Court Procedures*, 44 Vill.L.Rev. 1 (1999); Bellia, Jr., *Federal Regulation of State Court Procedures*, 110 Yale L.J. 947 (2001). For discussion of related issues, see Weinberg, *The Power of Congress Over Courts in Nonfederal Cases*, 1995 BYU L.Rev. 731; Steinman, *Reverse Removal*, 78 Iowa L.Rev. 1029 (1993).

fall into the category of 'procedure' immune from congressional regulation". The Court cautioned, however, that "[t]o sustain § 1367(d) in this case, we need not (and do not) hold that Congress has unlimited power to regulate practice and procedure in state courts".

(c) Unresolved Questions. How should Congress understand the Court's reservation in both cases of the question of the ultimate scope of legislative power? As a suggestion that it is prepared to enforce as yet unstated limits on congressional action? An effort to forestall intrusive congressional action that might, however, ultimately be upheld? Or simply as a form of judicial minimalism, leaving undecided a broad question whose resolution was unnecessary to the cases at hand?

Suppose that Congress agreed with business interests that the procedures followed by certain state courts in adjudicating state law class actions are overly pro-plaintiff, have a harmful effect on interstate commerce, and are a much greater problem than the substantive law of tort or contract applied in such actions. Could Congress require state courts entertaining state law class actions to follow the procedures established in Fed. R. Civ. Proc. 23? (Note that rather than trying to regulate the state courts directly, Congress instead broadened the availability of removal of state court class actions to federal court, where federal procedures govern. See the Class Action Fairness Act of 2005 (CAFA), Pub.L. 109–2, 119 Stat. 4, discussed at p. 1066, *infra*.)

CHAPTER V

REVIEW OF STATE COURT DECISIONS BY THE SUPREME COURT

1. THE ESTABLISHMENT OF THE JURISDICTION

DEVELOPMENT OF THE STATUTORY PROVISIONS

(1) The Judiciary Act of 1789 and the Amendments of 1867. Section 25 of the Judiciary Act of 1789[1] gave the Supreme Court mandatory jurisdiction to review specified state court judgments via a writ of error. (A writ of error was limited to matters in the record and, unlike a modern appeal, permitted review only of legal issues.[2]) The following text and accompanying footnotes show the original form of § 25 and the 1867 amendments to that provision:[3]

"Sec. 25. And be it further enacted, That a final judgment or decree in any suit, in the highest court [of law or equity][4] of a State in which a decision in the suit could be had, where is drawn in question the validity of a treaty or statute of, or an authority exercised under the United States, and the decision is against their validity; or where is drawn in question the validity of a statute of, or an authority exercised under any State, on the ground of their being repugnant to the constitution, treaties or laws of the United States, and the decision is in favour of such their validity, [or where is drawn in question the construction of any clause of the constitution, or of a treaty, or statute of, or commission held under the United States,][5] and the decision is against the title, right, privilege or [exemption][6] specially set up or claimed by either party, under such [clause of the said][4] Constitution, treaty, statute [or] commission,[7] may be re-examined and reversed or affirmed in the

---

[1] 1 Stat. 73, 85.

[2] See Cohens v. Virginia, 19 U.S. (6 Wheat.) 264, 409–10 (1821); Wiscart v. D'Auchy, 3 U.S. (3 Dall.) 321, 327–29 (1796) (Elsworth, C.J.).

[3] Act of February 5, 1867 (14 Stat. 385, 386). The text is reproduced from Frankfurter & Shulman, Cases on Federal Jurisdiction and Procedure 627–28 (rev.ed.1937).

The 1867 version was re-enacted in substantially the same form as § 709 of the Revised Statutes (1874) and § 237 of the Judicial Code (1911); for the relevant texts, see Robertson & Kirkham, Jurisdiction of the Supreme Court of the United States, Appendix A, 931–41 (Wolfson & Kurland eds.1951).

[4] The 1867 Act deleted these words.

[5] The 1867 Act substituted: "or where any title, right, privilege, or immunity is claimed under the constitution, or any treaty or statute of or commission held, or authority exercised under the United States".

[6] The 1867 Act substituted "immunity".

[7] The 1867 Act added "or authority".

Supreme Court of the United States upon a writ of error, the citation being signed by the chief justice, or judge or chancellor of the court rendering or passing the judgment or decree complained of, or by a justice of the Supreme Court of the United States, in the same manner and under the same regulations, and the writ shall have the same effect, as if the judgment or decree complained of had been rendered or passed in a [Circuit Court][8] and the proceeding upon the reversal shall also be the same, except that the Supreme Court, [instead of remanding the cause for a final decision as before provided,][4] may at their discretion, [if the cause shall have been once remanded before,][4] proceed to a final decision of the same, and award execution.[9] [But no other error shall be assigned or regarded as a ground of reversal in any such case as aforesaid, than such as appears on the face of the record, and immediately respects the before mentioned questions of validity or construction of the said constitution, treaties, statutes, commissions, or authorities in dispute.][4]"

(2) The Judiciary Act of 1914. The Judiciary Act of 1914 introduced two important features to the Supreme Court's jurisdiction. First, Congress for the first time authorized review of state court decisions *upholding* a claim of federal right;[10] previously, review extended only to judgments denying federal rights. This amendment was prompted largely by the decision in Ives v. South Buffalo Ry., 201 N.Y. 271, 94 N.E. 431 (1911), which held that the first American workers' compensation act violated both federal and state constitutional guarantees of due process. The state court's decision invalidating social legislation provoked widespread criticism and drew attention to the consequences of withholding Supreme Court review of state court decisions invalidating legislation on federal grounds. This limitation threatened disuniformity in the content of federal constitutional law among the states.[11]

Second, the 1914 Act introduced the discretionary writ of certiorari as a means of review of state court judgments.[12] While mandatory review via a writ of error was preserved for cases within the pre-1914 jurisdiction, the newly-conferred jurisdiction was discretionary.

(3) Expansion of Certiorari Jurisdiction. Congress further extended the scope of discretionary review via certiorari in succeeding Acts in 1916[13] and

---

8   The 1867 Act substituted "court of the United States".

9   The 1867 Act added "or remand the same to an inferior court".

10   Act of December 23, 1914, c. 2, 38 Stat. 790. See Meltzer, *The History and Structure of Article III*, 138 U.Pa.L.Rev. 1569, 1585–92 (1990) (discussing decisions interpreting and often denying review under the pre-1914 jurisdictional statute); Hartnett, *Why Is the Supreme Court of the United States Protecting State Judges from Popular Democracy?*, 75 Tex.L.Rev. 907 (1997) (viewing the 1914 Act as a means of counteracting political pressure faced by state court judges rendering unpopular decisions, and taking the surprising view that under the Act, state officials should not have the same right as private litigants to seek Supreme Court review of unfavorable state court judgments).

11   See Frankfurter & Landis, The Business of the Supreme Court 193–98 (1928).

12   Thus, the Act made review discretionary where the state court decision was "in favor of the validity of the treaty or statute or authority exercised under the United States" or "against the validity of the State statute or authority claimed to be repugnant to the Constitution, treaties, or laws of the United States" or "in favor of the title, right, privilege, or immunity claimed under the Constitution, treaty, statute, commission, or authority of the United States."

The Evarts Act of 1891 had earlier provided for review via writ of certiorari of decisions of the federal circuit courts of appeals. See p. 30, *supra*.

13   The Act of September 6, 1916, c. 448, § 2, 39 Stat. 726, substituted review on certiorari for the writ of error in cases where "any title, right, privilege or immunity is claimed under the

1925;[14] the latter preserved mandatory review only for state judgments invalidating a treaty or Act of Congress or upholding a state statute attacked on federal grounds. That distribution of mandatory and discretionary jurisdiction remained for more than a half century, with some minor changes in other provisions—most notably, the substitution, in 1928, of an appeal for a writ of error in all cases reviewable as of right.[15]

In 1988, Congress completed the gradual transition from mandatory to discretionary review of state court decisions by amending 28 U.S.C. § 1257 to eliminate appeals as of right and to make all state court judgments reviewable only by writ of certiorari.[16]

In the years since that change, the Supreme Court has reduced the number of cases that it hears annually, and a recent study found that the decline was particularly sharp in cases from the state courts. While the Court reviewed and decided with full opinions 41 cases from the state courts in 1989, 28 in 1990, and 25 in 1991, in 1997–99 the number ranged from 10 to 12, see Solimine, *Supreme Court Monitoring of State Courts in the Twenty-First Century*, 35 Ind.L.Rev. 335 (2002). During the 2013 Term, the Court decided with full opinions only 8 cases from state courts. See *The Supreme Court, 2013 Term—The Statistics*, 122 Harv.L.Rev. 401, 411 (2014).

Current SCOTUS figures

Constitution, or any treaty or statute of, or commission held or authority exercised under the United States, and the decision is either in favor of or against the title, right, privilege, or immunity especially set up or claimed." The Act retained review on writ of error for decisions against the validity of "an authority exercised under the United States" and for decisions refusing to invalidate "an authority exercised under any State" as "repugnant to the Constitution, treaties, or laws of the United States". Review of the validity of claims asserted *under* an "authority", as distinguished from the validity of the authority itself, was only on certiorari. See, *e.g.*, Yazoo & Mississippi Valley R.R. v. Clarksdale, 257 U.S. 10, 15–16 & cases cited (1921). For discussion of the sometimes elusive distinction between review of the validity of legislation and review of the application of legislation, see Frankfurter & Landis, note 11, *supra*, at 211–16.

[14] See Judges' Bill (Act of February 13, 1925, 43 Stat. 936). The Act abandoned the 1916 Act's subtle, and difficult, distinction between cases under an authority and those challenging the validity of an authority. See note 13, *supra*. A new § 237(c) authorized the Supreme Court to treat as a petition for a writ of certiorari papers improperly seeking a writ of error.

For an elaborate discussion of the Judges' Bill and its aftermath, see Hartnett, *Questioning Certiorari: Some Reflections Seventy-Five Years After the Judges' Bill*, 100 Colum.L.Rev. 1643 (2000). Hartnett is critical of the certiorari jurisdiction, and notes that while a denial of certiorari in a federal case merely allocates judicial power among federal courts, a denial in a state court case determines whether "the judicial power of the United States shall be called into play at all."

[15] Act of January 31, 1928, c. 14, 45 Stat. 54, as amended, 45 Stat. 466. The 1948 revision of the Judicial Code reformulated, in 28 U.S.C. § 1257, the basic provisions conferring jurisdiction, without significant change in substance. Three clauses of former § 237 were made separate sections among Title 28's miscellaneous procedural provisions relating to Supreme Court review: § 2103 (treatment under certiorari jurisdiction of improper effort to obtain review of right), § 2104 (appeal from state court to be taken in same manner and with same effect as if judgment rendered by court of the United States), and § 2106 (power to affirm, modify, vacate, reverse, remand, direct entry of judgment, or require further proceedings).

Under § 2101(c), the time in which to seek Supreme Court review in civil cases is 90 days, and within this period, a Justice may extend the time to apply for not more than 60 days. Section 2101(d) defines the time in criminal cases as that "prescribed by rules of the Supreme Court", which state that a petition for a writ of certiorari is timely if filed within 90 days after the entry of the judgment of which review is sought (Rule 13.1) and that "[f]or good cause," an application to extend the time to file may be made but "is not favored" (Rule 13.5).

[16] Act of June 27, 1988, 102 Stat. 662. As part of this change, § 2103, permitting the Court to treat an improvidently taken appeal as a petition for certiorari, was repealed as superfluous.

(4) Rules of the Supreme Court. Supreme Court Rules 10–16 set out the procedure on petitions for certiorari.[17] Among the considerations that the Court weighs in deciding whether to grant a petition are whether "a state court of last resort has decided an important federal question in a way that conflicts with the decision of another state court of last resort or of a United States court of appeals", and whether "a state court * * * has decided an important question of federal law that has not been, but should be, settled by this Court, or has decided an important federal question in a way that conflicts with relevant decisions of this Court." Rule 10.

INTRODUCTORY NOTE

The two principal cases that follow, Martin v. Hunter's Lessee and Murdock v. City of Memphis, are the twin pillars on which Supreme Court review of state court judgments rests. Martin is generally taken to affirm the Court's power to review *federal* issues decided in state court, while Murdock is taken to establish limits on the Court's power to review *non-federal* issues decided in state court. Both points are correct but require qualification: in the first round of Supreme Court review in Martin, the Court appears to have reviewed a non-federal issue, while in Murdock the Court discusses, at the end of its opinion, limitations on its power to review federal issues. Those complexities will be explored in more detail in Sec. 2(A), *infra*.

Martin v. Hunter's Lessee
14 U.S. (1 Wheat.) 304, 4 L.Ed. 97 (1816).
Error to the Court of Appeals of Virginia.

[At issue in this complex litigation was a portion of a partially unappropriated tract of Virginia land known as the Northern Neck. The land originally belonged to Lord Fairfax, a British subject but also a loyal citizen of Virginia. In 1781, Lord Fairfax bequeathed the Northern Neck to his nephew, Denny Martin Fairfax, who was a British subject. By virtue of a 1779 state statute providing for escheat of land held by a British subject, the vacant unappropriated lands of the Northern Neck became liable for escheat. Complicating Virginia's subsequent disposition of the land, however, was the fact that the commonwealth had never invoked the "inquest of office" procedure for escheat that the 1779 statute required, nor had it effected escheat by any equivalent legislative act. In 1785, the Virginia General Assembly passed legislation stating that the commonwealth had the right to grant the unappropriated lands of the Northern Neck.* In 1789, Virginia granted a portion of the Northern Neck to David Hunter.

[In 1791, Hunter initiated on behalf of his lessee an action for ejectment, which he pursued against Denny Martin Fairfax and later

---

[17] An authoritative work on Supreme Court practice is Shapiro et al., Supreme Court Practice (10th ed.2013).

*   [Ed.] See Hobson, *John Marshall and the Fairfax Litigation: The Background of Martin v. Hunter's Lessee*, 1996 J.Sup.Ct.Hist. 36, 38 (vol. 2), from which some of the description is taken.

Philip Martin, who inherited Fairfax's interests. In the course of what turned out to be very drawn out litigation, Hunter's claim would rest at various points upon (a) the 1789 grant; (b) the assertion that Denny Martin Fairfax, as an alien, could not validly take ownership of the land and that his land had, in any case, escheated to the state pursuant to the 1779 state statute; and (c) that any claims had been resolved by a 1796 state statute styled as an "Act of Compromise," which purported to settle the controversy, in part, by confirming Hunter's interest in the disputed lands. A potential conflict between state and federal law arose from Martin's counterarguments that the Commonwealth had not taken the steps necessary for escheat under the 1779 state statute and that the Treaty of Paris, adopted in 1783, and later the Jay Treaty of 1794 invalidated all subsequent attempts by the commonwealth to transfer the Fairfax-Martin interests to Hunter.

[Writing for the Virginia Court of Appeals in 1810, Judge Spencer Roane—Marshall's political enemy—concluded that the Commonwealth had validly obtained title prior to ratification of the Treaty of Paris. He also ruled that the Act of Compromise was binding. Hunter v. Fairfax's Devisee, 15 Va. (1 Munf.) 218, 231–32. Judge Fleming concurred solely on the basis of the Act of Compromise.

[On writ of error, the Supreme Court reversed. Fairfax's Devisee v. Hunter's Lessee, 11 U.S. (7 Cranch) 603 (1813). Justice Story's opinion held that none of the Virginia acts altered the common law requirement of "inquest of office" to vest title in the Commonwealth; hence, the Fairfax-Martin title was undivested at the time of the 1794 Jay Treaty, which protected the property interests of British subjects who owned American land. Justice Johnson dissented on the ground that the Virginia legislature was competent to dispense with an inquest of office; he agreed, however, that under § 25 of the Judiciary Act an inquiry into title was necessary and "must, in the nature of things, precede the consideration how far the law, treaty and so forth, is applicable to it; otherwise an appeal to this court would be worse than nugatory". Neither Story nor Johnson mentioned the Act of Compromise. (Chief Justice Marshall, who had been a member of a syndicate that purchased part of the Fairfax estate, did not participate.)

[The Supreme Court mandate, which was directed to "the Honorable the Judges of the Court of Appeals in and for the Commonwealth of Virginia," "adjudged and ordered, that the judgment of the Court of Appeals * * * in this case be, and the same is hereby reversed and annulled, and that the judgment of the [Superior Court] be affirmed, with costs; and it is further ordered, that the said cause be remanded to the said Court of Appeals * * * with instructions to enter judgment for the appellant." It ended with the formal provision: "You therefore are hereby commanded that such proceedings be had in said cause, as according to right and justice, and the laws of the United States, and agreeably to said judgment and instructions of said Supreme Court ought to be had, the said writ of error notwithstanding". Hunter v. Martin, Devisee of Fairfax, 18 Va. (4 Munf.) 2–3.

["The question, whether this mandate should be obeyed, excited all that attention from the bench and bar, which its great importance truly merited"; and after oral argument, on December 16, 1815, the judges

(Cabell, Brooke, Roane and Fleming) expressed their separate opinions *seriatim* but unanimously joined in the following conclusion:

["[T]he appellate power of the Supreme Court of the United States, does not extend to this court, under a sound construction of the constitution of the United States;—that so much of the 25th section of the act of Congress * * * as extends the appellate jurisdiction of the Supreme Court to this court, is not in pursuance of the constitution of the United States; that the writ of error in this case was improvidently allowed under the authority of that act; that proceedings thereon in the Supreme Court were *coram non judice* in relation to this court; and that obedience to its mandate be declined by this court."

[The common grounds for this conclusion of the Virginia judges are indicated by the following excerpts from Judge Cabell's opinion:

["The present government of the United States, grew out of the weakness and inefficacy of the confederation, and was intended to remedy its evils. Instead of a government of requisition, we have a government of power. But how does the power operate? On individuals in their individual capacity. No one presumes to contend, that the state governments can operate compulsively on the general government or any of its departments, even in cases of unquestionable encroachment on state authority. * * * I can perceive nothing in the constitution which gives to the Federal Courts any stronger claim to prevent or redress, by any procedure acting on the state courts, an equally obvious encroachment on the Federal jurisdiction. The constitution of the United States contemplates the independence of both governments and regards the residuary sovereignty of the states, as not less inviolable, than the delegated sovereignty of the United States. It must have been foreseen that controversies would sometimes arise as to the boundaries of the two jurisdictions. Yet the constitution has provided no umpire, has erected no tribunal by which they shall be settled. The omission proceeded, probably, from the belief, that such a tribunal would produce evils greater than those of the occasional collisions which it would be designed to remedy. * * *

["If this Court should now proceed to enter a judgment in this case, according to instructions of the Supreme Court, the Judges of this Court, in doing so, must act either as Federal or as State Judges. But we cannot be made Federal Judges without our consent, and without commissions. * * * We must, then, in obeying this mandate, be considered still as State Judges. We are required, as State Judges to enter up a judgment, not our own, but dictated and prescribed to us by another Court. * * * But, before one Court can dictate to another, the judgment it shall pronounce, it must bear, to that other, the relation of an appellate Court. The term appellate, however, necessarily includes the idea of superiority. But one Court cannot be correctly said to be superior to another, unless both of them belong to the same sovereignty. It would be a misapplication of terms to say that a Court of Virginia is superior to a Court of Maryland, or vice versa. The Courts of the United States, therefore, belonging to one sovereignty, cannot be appellate Courts in relation to the State Courts, which belong to a different sovereignty * * *. * * *

["If, therefore, I am correct in this position, the appellate jurisdiction of the Supreme Court of the United States [under the constitution], must have reference to the inferior Courts of the United States, and not to the

State Courts. * * * It has been contended that the constitution contemplated only the objects of appeal, and not the tribunals from which the appeal is to be taken * * * But this argument proves too much * * *. It would give appellate jurisdiction, as well over the courts of England or France, as over the State courts; for, although I do not think the State Courts are foreign Courts in relation to the Federal Courts, yet I consider them not less independent than foreign Courts."

[To the argument that Supreme Court review of state decisions was necessary to ensure uniformity, Judge Cabell replied: "All the purposes of the constitution of the United States will be answered by the erection of Federal Courts, into which any party, plaintiff or defendant, concerned in a case of federal cognizance, may carry it for adjudication". Judges Brooke and Fleming apparently shared this opinion, on which Judge Roane expressed no view.

[Judges Roane and Fleming offered an additional ground for decision—that the case fell outside § 25 since the record did not show that the decision turned upon the federal treaty (see the last sentence of the text of section 25 on p. 462, *supra*) and that if the Supreme Court "had held itself at liberty, to go outside of the record", the report of the decision of the Virginia Court would have shown that it was based on the Act of Compromise.

[The case returned to the Supreme Court on a second writ of error brought by Philip Martin.**]

■ STORY, J., delivered the opinion of the court. * * *

The constitution of the United States was ordained and established, not by the states in their sovereign capacities, but emphatically, as the preamble of the constitution declares, by "the People of the United States." There can be no doubt, that it was competent to the people to invest the general government with all the powers which they might deem proper and necessary * * * and to give them a paramount and supreme authority. As little doubt can there be, that the people had a right to prohibit to the states the exercise of any powers which were, in their judgment, incompatible with the objects of the general compact; to make the powers of the state governments, in given cases, subordinate to those of the nation, or to reserve to themselves those sovereign authorities which they might not choose to delegate to either. The constitution was not, therefore, necessarily carved out of existing state sovereignties, nor a surrender of powers already existing in state institutions * * *. On the other hand, it is perfectly clear, that the sovereign powers vested in the state governments, by their respective constitutions, remained unaltered and unimpaired, except so far as they were granted to the government of the United States.

These deductions do not rest upon general reasoning, plain and obvious as they seem to be. They have been positively recognized by one of the articles in amendment of the constitution, which declares, that "the powers not delegated to the United States by the constitution, nor prohibited by it to the *states*, are reserved to the states respectively, or *to the people*." * * *

** [Ed.] For the claim that John Marshall drafted the second petition for a writ of error, see White, The Marshall Court and Cultural Change, 1815–35, at 167–68 (1988); Hobson, note *, *supra*, at 48 (also contending that Marshall helped prepare arguments for the use of counsel).

The third article of the constitution is that which must principally attract our attention. * * *

[Here, Justice Story developed the view that Article III's language is "designed to be mandatory" upon Congress. See pp. 308–310, *supra*.]

* * * [A]ppellate jurisdiction is given by the constitution to the supreme court in all cases where it has not original jurisdiction; subject, however, to such exceptions and regulations as congress may prescribe. It is, therefore, capable of embracing every case enumerated in the constitution, which is not exclusively to be decided by way of original jurisdiction. But the exercise of appellate jurisdiction is far from being limited by the terms of the constitution to the supreme court. There can be no doubt that congress may create a succession of inferior tribunals, in each of which it may vest appellate as well as original jurisdiction. * * *

As, then, by the terms of the constitution, the appellate jurisdiction is not limited as to the supreme court, and as to this court it may be exercised in all other cases than those of which it has original cognizance, what is there to restrain its exercise over state tribunals in the enumerated cases? The appellate power is not limited by the terms of the third article to any particular courts. The words are, "the judicial power (which includes appellate power) shall extend *to all cases*," & c., and "in all other cases before mentioned the supreme court shall have appellate jurisdiction." It is the *case*, then, and not *the court*, that gives the jurisdiction. * * *

If the constitution meant to limit the appellate jurisdiction to cases pending in the courts of the United States, it would necessarily follow that the jurisdiction of these courts would, in all the cases enumerated in the constitution, be exclusive of state tribunals. How otherwise could the jurisdiction extend to *all* cases arising under the constitution, laws, and treaties of the United States, or *to all cases* of admiralty and maritime jurisdiction? If some of these cases might be entertained by state tribunals, and no appellate jurisdiction as to them should exist, then the appellate power would not extend to *all*, but to *some*, cases. If state tribunals might exercise concurrent jurisdiction over all or some of the other classes of cases in the constitution without control, then the appellate jurisdiction of the United States might, as to such cases, have no real existence, contrary to the manifest intent of the constitution. Under such circumstances, to give effect to the judicial power, it must be construed to be exclusive; and this not only when the *casus foederis* should arise directly, but when it should arise, incidentally, in cases pending in state courts. This construction would abridge the jurisdiction of such court far more than has been ever contemplated in any act of congress.

On the other hand, if, as has been contended, a discretion be vested in congress to establish, or not to establish, inferior courts at their own pleasure, and congress should not establish such courts, the appellate jurisdiction of the supreme court would have nothing to act upon, unless it could act upon cases pending in the state courts. Under such circumstances it must be held that the appellate power would extend to state courts; for the constitution is peremptory that it shall extend to certain enumerated cases, which cases could exist in no other courts. Any other construction, upon this supposition, would involve this strange contradiction, that a discretionary power vested in congress, and which they might rightfully omit to exercise, would defeat the absolute injunctions of the constitution in relation to the whole appellate power. * * *

A moment's consideration will show us the necessity and propriety of this provision in cases where the jurisdiction of the state courts is unquestionable. * * * Suppose an indictment for a crime in a state court, and the defendant should allege in his defence that the crime was created by an *ex post facto* act of the state, must not the state court, in the exercise of a jurisdiction which has already rightfully attached, have a right to pronounce on the validity and sufficiency of the defence? It would be extremely difficult, upon any legal principles, to give a negative answer * * *. Innumerable instances of the same sort might be stated, in illustration of the position; and unless the state courts could sustain jurisdiction in such cases, this clause of the sixth article would be without meaning or effect, and public mischiefs, of a most enormous magnitude, would inevitably ensue.

It must, therefore, be conceded that the constitution not only contemplated, but meant to provide for cases within the scope of the judicial power of the United States, which might yet depend before state tribunals. It was foreseen that in the exercise of their ordinary jurisdiction, state courts would incidentally take cognizance of cases arising under the constitution, the laws, and treaties of the United States. Yet to all these cases the judicial power, by the very terms of the constitution, is to extend. It cannot extend by original jurisdiction if that was already rightfully and exclusively attached in the state courts * * *. It would seem to follow that the appellate power of the United States must, in such cases, extend to state tribunals * * *.

It is further argued, that no great public mischief can result from a construction which shall limit the appellate power of the United States to cases in their own courts: first, because state judges are bound by an oath to support the constitution of the United States, and must be presumed to be men of learning and integrity; and, secondly, because congress must have an unquestionable right to remove all cases within the scope of the judicial power from the state courts to the courts of the United States, at any time before final judgment, though not after final judgment. As to the first reason—admitting that the judges of the state courts are, and always will be, of as much learning, integrity, and wisdom, as those of the courts of the United States, (which we very cheerfully admit,) it does not aid the argument. It is manifest that the constitution has proceeded upon a theory of its own, and given or withheld powers according to the judgment of the American people, by whom it was adopted. We can only construe its powers, and cannot inquire into the policy or principles which induced the grant of them. The constitution has presumed (whether rightly or wrongly we do not inquire) that state attachments, state prejudices, state jealousies, and state interests, might sometimes obstruct, or control, or be supposed to obstruct or control, the regular administration of justice. Hence, in controversies between states; between citizens of different states; between citizens claiming grants under different states; between a state and its citizens, or foreigners, and between citizens and foreigners, it enables the parties, under the authority of congress, to have the controversies heard, tried, and determined before the national tribunals.

No other reason than that which has been stated can be assigned, why some, at least, of those cases should not have been left to the cognizance of the state courts. In respect to the other enumerated cases—the cases arising under the constitution, laws, and treaties of the United States, cases affecting ambassadors and other public ministers, and cases of admiralty and maritime jurisdiction—reasons of a higher and more extensive nature, touching the safety, peace, and sovereignty of the nation, might well justify a grant of exclusive jurisdiction.

uniformity

This is not all. A motive of another kind, perfectly compatible with the most sincere respect for state tribunals, might induce the grant of appellate power over their decisions. That motive is the importance, and even necessity of *uniformity* of decisions throughout the whole United States * * *. Judges of equal learning and integrity, in different states, might differently interpret a statute, or a treaty of the United States, or even the constitution itself. If there were no revising authority to control these jarring and discordant judgments, and harmonize them into uniformity, the laws, the treaties, and the constitution of the United States would be different in different states * * *. The public mischiefs that would attend such a state of things would be truly deplorable; * * * and the appellate jurisdiction must continue to be the only adequate remedy for such evils.

Concern for Ds

There is an additional consideration, which is entitled to great weight. * * * The judicial power was * * * not to be exercised exclusively for the benefit of parties who might be plaintiffs, and would elect the national forum, but also for the protection of defendants who might be entitled to try their rights, or assert their privileges, before the same forum. Yet, if the construction contended for be correct, it will follow, that as the plaintiff may always elect the state court, the defendant may be deprived of all the security which the constitution intended in aid of his rights. Such a state of things can, in no respect, be considered as giving equal rights. To obviate this difficulty, we are referred to the power which it is admitted congress possess to remove suits from state courts to the national courts; and this forms the second ground upon which the argument we are considering has been attempted to be sustained.

This power of removal is not to be found in express terms in any part of the constitution; if it be given, it is only given by implication * * *. [I]t presupposes an exercise of original jurisdiction to have attached elsewhere. * * * If, then, the right of removal be included in the appellate jurisdiction, it is only because it is one mode of exercising that power, and as congress is not limited by the constitution to any particular mode, or time of exercising it, it may authorize a removal either before or after judgment. * * * A writ of error is, indeed, but a process which removes the record of one court to the possession of another court, and enables the latter to inspect the proceedings, and give such judgment as its own opinion of the law and justice of the case may warrant. * * *

The remedy, too, of removal of suits would be utterly inadequate to the purposes of the constitution, if it could act only on the parties, and not upon the state courts. * * * If state courts should deny the constitutionality of the authority to remove suits from their cognizance, in what manner could they be compelled to relinquish the jurisdiction? In respect to criminal cases, there would at once be an end of all control, and the state decisions would be paramount to the constitution; and though in civil suits the courts of the United States might act upon the parties, yet the state courts might act in the same way; and this conflict of jurisdictions would not only jeopardise private rights, but bring into imminent peril the public interests.

On the whole, the court are of opinion, that the appellate power of the United States does extend to cases pending in the state courts; and that the 25th section of the judiciary act, which authorizes the exercise of this jurisdiction in the specified cases, by a writ of error, is supported by the letter and spirit of the constitution. * * * *Holding*

Strong as this conclusion stands upon the general language of the constitution, it may still derive support from other sources. It is an historical fact, that this exposition of the constitution, extending its appellate power to state courts, was, previous to its adoption, uniformly and publicly avowed by its friends, and admitted by its enemies, as the basis of their respective reasonings, both in and out of the state conventions. It is an historical fact, that at the time when the judiciary act was submitted to the deliberations of the first congress, composed, as it was, not only of men of great learning and ability, but of men who had acted a principal part in framing, supporting, or opposing that constitution, the same exposition was explicitly declared and admitted by the friends and by the opponents of that system. It is an historical fact, that the supreme court of the United States have, from time to time, sustained this appellate jurisdiction in a great variety of cases, brought from the tribunals of many of the most important states in the union, and that no state tribunal has ever breathed a judicial doubt on the subject, or declined to obey the mandate of the supreme court, until the present occasion. * * *

The next question which has been argued, is, whether the case at bar be within the purview of the 25th section of the judiciary act, so that this court may rightfully sustain the present writ of error. * * * *Writ of Error ?*

That the present writ of error is founded upon a judgment of the court below, which drew in question and denied the validity of a statute of the United States, is incontrovertible, for it is apparent upon the face of the record. * * *

But it is contended, that the former judgment of this court was rendered upon a case not within the purview of this section of the judicial act, and that as it was pronounced by an incompetent jurisdiction, it was utterly void, and cannot be a sufficient foundation to sustain any subsequent proceedings. * * * [I]n ordinary cases a second writ of error has never been supposed to draw in question the propriety of the first judgment * * *. * * *

In this case, however, from motives of a public nature, we are entirely willing to wa[i]ve all objections, and to go back and re-examine the question of jurisdiction as it stood upon the record formerly in judgment. * * *

The objection urged at the bar is, that this court cannot inquire into the title, but simply into the correctness of the construction put upon the treaty by the court of appeals; and that their judgment is not re-examinable here, unless it appear on the face of the record that some construction was put upon the treaty. If, therefore, that court might have decided the case upon the invalidity of the title, (and, *non constat*, that they did not,) independent of the treaty, there is an end of the appellate jurisdiction of this court. In support of this objection much stress is laid upon the last clause of [§ 25, see p. 462, *supra*], which declares, that no other cause shall be regarded as a ground of reversal than such as appears *on the face* of the record and *immediately* respects the construction of the treaty, & c., in dispute.

If this be the true construction of the section, it will be wholly inadequate for the purposes which it professes to have in view, and may be evaded at pleasure. But we see no reason for adopting this narrow construction; and there are the strongest reasons against it, founded upon the words as well as the intent of the legislature. What is the case for which the body of the section provides a remedy by writ of error? The answer must be in the words of the section, a suit where is drawn in question the construction of a treaty, and the decision is against *the title set up by the party*. It is, therefore, the decision against the title set up with reference to the treaty, and not the mere abstract construction of the treaty itself, upon which the statute intends to found the appellate jurisdiction. * * *

The restraining clause was manifestly intended for a very different purpose. It was foreseen that the parties might claim under various titles, and might assert various defences, altogether independent of each other. The court might admit or reject evidence applicable to one particular title, and not to all, and in such cases it was the intention of congress to limit what would otherwise have unquestionably attached to the court, the right of revising all the points involved in the cause. It therefore restrains this right to such errors as respect the questions specified in the section; and in this view, it has an appropriate sense, consistent with the preceding clauses. We are, therefore, satisfied, that, upon principle, the case was rightfully before us, and if the point were perfectly new, we should not hesitate to assert the jurisdiction. * * *

It has been asserted at the bar that, in point of fact, the court of appeals did not decide either upon the treaty or the title apparent upon the record, but upon a compromise made under an act of the legislature of Virginia. If it be true (as we are informed) that this was a private act, to take effect only upon a certain condition, viz. the execution of a deed of release of certain lands, which was matter *in pais*, it is somewhat difficult to understand how the court could take judicial cognizance of the act, or of the performance of the condition, unless spread upon the record. At all events, we are bound to consider that the court did decide upon the facts actually before them. The treaty of peace was not necessary to have been stated, for it was the supreme law of the land, of which all courts must take notice. And at the time of the decision in the court of appeals and in this court, another treaty had intervened, which attached itself to the title in controversy, and, of course, must have been the supreme law to govern the decision, if it should be found applicable to the case. It was in this view that this court did not deem it necessary to rest its former decision upon the treaty of peace, believing that the title of the defendant was, at all events, perfect under the treaty of 1794. * * *

We have not thought it incumbent on us to give any opinion upon the question, whether this court have authority to issue a writ of mandamus to the court of appeals to enforce the former judgments, as we do not think it necessarily involved in the decision of this cause.

It is the opinion of the whole court, that the judgment of the court of appeals of Virginia, rendered on the mandate in this cause, be reversed, and the judgment of the district court, held at Winchester, be, and the same is hereby affirmed.

■ JOHNSON, J., * * * In this act I can see nothing which amounts to an assertion of the inferiority or dependence of the state tribunals. The presiding judge of the state court is himself authorized to issue the writ of error, if he will, and thus give jurisdiction to the supreme court: and if he thinks proper to decline it, no compulsory process is provided by law to oblige him. The party who imagines himself aggrieved is then at liberty to apply to a judge of the United States, who issues the writ of error, which (whatever the form) is, in substance, no more than a mode of compelling the opposite party to appear before this court, and maintain the legality of his judgment obtained before the state tribunal. An exemplification of a record is the common property of every one who chooses to apply and pay for it, and thus the case and the parties are brought before us; and so far is the court itself from being brought under the revising power of this court, that nothing but the case, as presented by the record and pleadings of the parties, is considered, and the opinions of the court are never resorted to unless for the purpose of assisting this court in forming their own opinions.

The absolute necessity that there was for congress to exercise something of a revising power over cases and parties in the state courts, will appear from this consideration.

Suppose the whole extent of the judicial power of the United States vested in their own courts, yet such a provision would not answer all the ends of the constitution, for two reasons:

1st. Although the plaintiff may, in such case, have the full benefit of the constitution extended to him, yet the defendant would not; as the plaintiff might force him into the court of the state at his election.

2dly. Supposing it possible so to legislate as to give the courts of the United States original jurisdiction in all cases arising under the constitution, laws, & c., in the words of the 2d section of the 3d article, (a point on which I have some doubt, and which in time might, perhaps, under some *quo minus* fiction, or a willing construction, greatly accumulate the jurisdiction of those courts,) yet a very large class of cases would remain unprovided for. Incidental questions would often arise, and as a court of competent jurisdiction in the principal case must decide all such questions, whatever laws they arise under, endless might be the diversity of decisions throughout the union upon the constitution, treaties, and laws, of the United States * * *.

I should feel the more hesitation in adopting the opinions which I express in this case, were I not firmly convinced that they are practical, and may be acted upon without compromising the harmony of the union, or bringing humility upon the state tribunals. God forbid that the judicial power in these states should ever, for a moment, even in its humblest departments, feel a doubt of its own independence. Whilst adjudicating on a subject which the laws of the country assign finally to the revising power of another tribunal, it can feel no such doubt. An anxiety to do justice is ever relieved by the knowledge that what we do is not final between the parties. And no sense of dependence can be felt from the knowledge that the parties, not the court, may be summoned before another tribunal. With this view, by means of laws, avoiding judgments obtained in the state courts in cases over which congress has constitutionally assumed jurisdiction, and inflicting penalties on parties who shall contumaciously persist in infringing the constitutional rights of others—under a liberal extension of the writ of injunction and the *habeas corpus ad subjiciendum*, I flatter myself that the full extent of the constitutional revising power may be secured to the United States, and the benefits of it to the individual, without ever resorting to compulsory or restrictive process upon the state tribunals; a right which, I repeat again, congress has not asserted, nor has this court asserted, nor does there appear any necessity for asserting. * * *

NOTE ON THE ATTACKS UPON THE JURISDICTION

(1) State Resistance to § 25. Between 1789 and 1860 the courts of Virginia, Ohio, Georgia, Kentucky, South Carolina, California, and Wisconsin denied that the Supreme Court had the power to review state court judgments on writs of error. The legislatures of all these states (except California), and of Pennsylvania and Maryland, adopted measures denying this power to the Supreme Court. Bills were introduced in Congress on at least ten occasions between 1821 and 1882 to deprive the Court of such jurisdiction.[1] The arguments advanced in these attacks ranged from the relatively narrow grounds adduced in the Martin case to the extreme position that each state had an equal right to stand on its interpretation of the Constitution.[2] The Court's position, as defined by Justice Story, did not change throughout the period of controversy.[3]

---

[1]   Warren, *Legislative and Judicial Attacks on the Supreme Court of the United States—A History of the Twenty-Fifth Section of the Judiciary Act, Part I*, 47 Am.L.Rev. 1, 3–4 (1913); see also Part II of Warren's article, 47 *id.* 161 (1913). For an argument that the jurisdiction conferred upon the Supreme Court by § 25 may be constitutionally required by the political compromise that made the Supremacy Clause (rather than a congressional veto) the mechanism for enforcing federal supremacy, see LaCroix, *On Being "Bound Thereby"*, 27 Const.Comm. 507 (2011). Does that structural inference represent a plausible implied limitation on congressional power given Article III's Exceptions Clause? See pp. 314–319, *supra.*

[2]   See generally Haines, The Role of the Supreme Court in American Government and Politics 499–577 (1944); Reference Note, *Interposition vs. Judicial Power—A Study of Ultimate Authority in Constitutional Questions*, 1 Race Rel.L.Rep. 465 (1956); Goldstein, Constituting Federal Sovereignty: The European Union in Comparative Context 20, 22–33, 161–71 (2001).

Goldstein contends that the "American states, intermittently but in a steady, and not regionally concentrated stream, resisted federal authority when feelings in particular states on particular issues ran high. * * * Tax laws, debtor laws, controversies over land ownership, embargo laws, laws concerning Native Americans, laws concerning the banking system, laws concerning judicial procedures, laws regulating speech and press, fugitive slave laws—all at one time or another provoked state denial of federal judicial authority." She details more than fifty instances of resistance (defined to include formal public pronouncements by governors, majority decisions of state appellate courts, or majority votes or resolutions of legislative bodies) by 20 of the 33 states admitted to the Union prior to the Civil War.

[3]   In Cohens v. Virginia, 19 U.S. (6 Wheat.) 264 (1821), a writ of error to review a state court judgment affirming a criminal conviction, Chief Justice Marshall reiterated, for the Court, the position taken in Martin. He also rejected two additional contentions urged against the jurisdiction. The first was that the Eleventh Amendment (or general notions of state sovereign immunity) barred the writ of error as a prohibited suit against the state. (For a recent reaffirmation of this aspect of Cohens, see McKesson Corp. v. Division of ABT, 496 U.S. 18, 26–28 (1990).) The second was that Article III's grant of original jurisdiction to the Supreme Court in

The remedies proposed by dissidents included repeal of § 25, *e.g.*, H.R.Rep. No. 43, 21st Cong., 2d Sess. (1831), and constitutional amendments depriving the courts of authority to annul legislation, vesting jurisdiction in the Senate, or establishing a new tribunal to mediate between the nation and the states.[4]

(2) Supreme Court Review Today. The constitutional validity of the Court's jurisdiction to review state court decisions has not been seriously challenged in recent years. For example, while the Court's decision in Bush v. Gore, 531 U.S. 98 (2000), sparked great controversy, it did not generate attacks on the Court's jurisdiction.[5]

A half century earlier, however, Brown v. Board of Education, 347 U.S. 483 (1954), did provoke challenges to the authoritativeness of Court decisions, including "interposition" resolutions by state legislatures reminiscent of the pre-Civil War pattern.[6] There have also been relatively recent attempts—none successful—to restrict the Court's jurisdiction over specific controversial subjects (*e.g.*, reapportionment, school prayer, abortion). See p. 465, *supra*.

(3) Review by Lower Federal Courts. Justice Story's opinion describes removal as an exercise of appellate jurisdiction. Does that suggest that Congress may authorize lower federal courts to review state court judgments? Hamilton, in Federalist No. 82, perceived "no impediment" in Article III to such an arrangement. See The Federalist No. 82, at 495 (Rossiter ed.1961). Under current law, a state court is not obliged to follow

---

cases in which a state is a party precludes the Court's exercise of *appellate* jurisdiction in such a case. The Court did not respond to Virginia's third objection—that Article III's grant of federal question jurisdiction does not extend to criminal cases.

See generally Graber, *The Passive-Aggressive Virtues: Cohens v. Virginia and the Problematic Establishment of Judicial Power*, 12 Const.Comm. 67 (1995) (suggesting that the ruling on the merits in Cohens—that the state court conviction did not violate federal law—was implausible, but may have reflected the same strategy deployed in Marbury v. Madison: to make an assertion of judicial power politically palatable by refusing in the end to award relief); Newmyer, *John Marshall, McCulloch v. Maryland, and the Southern States' Rights Tradition*, 33 John Marshall L.Rev. 875 (2000) (discussing Cohens in the context of Marshall's response to anti-Court sentiment). For further discussion of Cohens, see LaCroix, *Federalists, Federalism, and Federal Jurisdiction*, 30 Law & Hist.Rev. 205, 237–40 (2012).

[4] See Ames, The Proposed Amendments to the Constitution of the United States During the First Century of its History 158–63 (1896).

[5] In fact, some commentators believe that the Court's exercise of "vertical" authority to review state-court judgments helped it to establish and maintain "horizontal" authority to review the actions by the coordinate federal branches. For example, to the extent that national political leaders found it necessary to bolster the Court's final authority to enforce the supremacy of federal law against the states, those leaders often incidentally bolstered the Court's position as the final arbiter of legality more generally. In addition, particularly after the Court incorporated the Bill of Rights against the states, the exercise of federal judicial power to invalidate state statutes under provisions such as the First Amendment made it harder for Congress and the President to resist judicial enforcement of similar limitations against the federal government. See Friedman & Delaney, *Becoming Supreme: The Federal Foundation of Judicial Supremacy*, 111 Colum.L.Rev. 1137 (2011). Is this claim one of historical contingency or is there a tight conceptual link between judicial review of state and federal action?

[6] See, *e.g.*, Driver, *Supremacies and the Southern Manifesto*, 92 Tex.L.Rev. 1053, 1089–93 (2014) (discussing the range of post-Brown positions taken toward the Court's authority by various southern states and by the congressional signatories of the so-called "Southern Manifesto"). For the Supreme Court's response to post-Brown challenges to its authority, see, for example, Cooper v. Aaron, 358 U.S. 1 (1958); Bush v. Orleans Parish Sch. Bd., 364 U.S. 803 (1960) (summarily rejecting the assertion that certain state statutes should be sustained on the ground that Louisiana "has interposed itself in the field of public education over which it has exclusive control").

the decisions of any federal court of appeals on issues of federal law. Would it be constitutional for Congress to require a state court to treat as controlling precedent the decisions of the federal circuit court of appeals within whose boundaries the state sits?

NOTE ON ENFORCEMENT OF THE MANDATE

(1) The Supreme Court's Mandate. Normally the Supreme Court, when reversing a state court judgment, remands the case for proceedings "not inconsistent" with the Court's opinion. The state court is thus free to resolve any undecided questions or even to alter its determination of underlying state law. The reversal may not, therefore, be decisive of the final judgment.

Compare this form of decree with the firmness of the mandate issued in Fairfax's Devisee v. Hunter's Lessee (the Supreme Court's first decision in the Martin/Fairfax litigation), p. 465, *supra*. In what circumstances is each form preferable?

(2) Mandamus to Enforce Compliance. If a state court deviates from the Supreme Court's mandate, the proper remedy is to seek a new review of the judgment, as in Martin v. Hunter's Lessee. So long as such review is possible, issuance of a writ of mandamus as a means of obtaining compliance has been considered inappropriate. In re Blake, 175 U.S. 114 (1899).

When immediate review is precluded by the absence of a final judgment in the state court, the aggrieved party may seek leave from the Supreme Court to file a petition for mandamus. Even in such instances, the Court has generally denied leave without explanation. *E.g.*, Lavender v. Clark, 329 U.S. 674 (1946); Ex parte Kedroff, 346 U.S. 893 (1953); International Ass'n of Machinists v. Duckworth, 368 U.S. 982 (1962). On at least two occasions, however, the Court has taken a further step.

In Deen v. Hickman, 358 U.S. 57 (1958), the Supreme Court granted leave to file after determining that the Texas courts were treating as open an issue it considered foreclosed by its prior decision. The writ itself was not issued, however, since the Court assumed that the Texas court "will of course conform to the disposition we now make". The opinion did not discuss the Court's power to issue mandamus to a state court.

The Court again granted leave to file a petition for mandamus in General Atomic Co. v. Felter, 436 U.S. 493 (1978). There, the Court determined that a state trial court "has again done precisely what we held [in a prior decision] that it lacked the power to do". The opinion invoked the principle that "a lower court" that fails to "give full effect" to the Court's mandate may be controlled by writ of mandamus (without discussing the assumption that state courts fall within this principle). As in Deen v. Hickman, the Court did not issue the formal writ, assuming that the state court "will now conform to our previous judgment".

(3) Entry of Judgment. Another means by which the Supreme Court can deal with state recalcitrance is to enter judgment, as in Martin v. Hunter's Lessee, McCulloch v. Maryland, 17 U.S. (4 Wheat.) 316, 437 (1819), and Gibbons v. Ogden, 22 U.S. (9 Wheat.) 1, 239 (1824); to award execution, as in Tyler v. Magwire, 84 U.S. (17 Wall.) 253 (1873); or to remand with directions to enter a specific judgment, as in Stanley v. Schwalby, 162 U.S. 255 (1896), and Poindexter v. Greenhow, 114 U.S. 270 (1885).[1]

In NAACP v. Alabama ex rel. Flowers, 377 U.S. 288 (1964), after eight years of litigation (including four considerations by the Supreme Court) and obvious state court recalcitrance, the Court still refused the request to formulate its own decree for entry in the state courts. Accepting that it "undoubtedly" has the power to enter judgment, the Court "prefer[red] to follow our usual practice and remand the case to the Supreme Court of Alabama for further proceedings not inconsistent with this opinion." The opinion concluded: "Should we unhappily be mistaken in our belief that the Supreme Court of Alabama will promptly implement this disposition, leave is given the Association to apply to this Court for further appropriate relief"—which proved to be unnecessary, see 167 So.2d 171 (Ala.1964).

(4) Remedies for Violation of Mandates. If a state court were to defy a mandate to enter a specific judgment, which of the following procedures, if any, might be pursued: (a) recall of mandate and entry of judgment with award of execution or other process (28 U.S.C. §§ 561–66, 672, 1651, 2241); (b) mandamus to the state court to enter the proper judgment; or (c) punishment for contempt under 18 U.S.C. § 401 for disobedience to a "lawful * * * order * * * or command"?

In one instance, state *executive* officials have been punished for contempt of a Supreme Court order. In United States v. Shipp, 203 U.S. 563 (1906), 214 U.S. 386 (1909), 215 U.S. 580 (1909), the Court had ordered a stay of execution of an African-American man who had been convicted of rape in Tennessee, pending an appeal, which the Court had allowed, from a federal circuit court's denial of the prisoner's habeas corpus petition. A group of men (including a state sheriff with custody of the prisoner), with knowledge of the Supreme Court's order, lynched the prisoner. After the Attorney General of the United States filed an information charging contempt of the Supreme Court, the Court appointed a commissioner to take testimony, rendered judgments of conviction, and sentenced the defendants to prison.

Should state judges, in a case of clear defiance, be any less subject to contempt sanctions than state executive officials?

Murdock v. City of Memphis   U.S.

87 U.S. (20 Wall.) 590, 22 L.Ed. 429 (1875).
Error to the Supreme Court of Tennessee.

[Murdock filed a bill in Tennessee chancery court against the city of Memphis. He alleged that in July of 1844, after Congress had authorized establishment of a naval depot in Memphis and appropriated money for that purpose, Murdock's ancestors—"by ordinary deed of bargain and sale, without any covenants or declaration of trust on which the land was to be held by the city, but referring to the fact of 'the location of the naval

---

[1]   The First Judiciary Act authorized the Supreme Court to enter judgment and award execution if the case had previously been remanded once; the requirement of one remand was eliminated in 1867, see pp. 461–462, *supra. Cf.* Judicial Code § 237(a), 28 U.S.C. § 344(a) (1940). In combination, 28 U.S.C. §§ 1651(a), 2104, and 2106 presumably confer no less authority than the Court had before the 1948 revision.

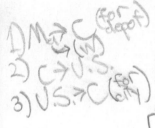

depot lately established by the United States at said town'—conveyed to the city certain land 'for the location of the naval depot aforesaid.' By the same instrument (a quadrupartite one) both the grantors and the city conveyed the same land to one Wheatley, in fee, in trust for the grantors and their heirs 'in case the same shall not be appropriated by the United States for that purpose.' "

[On September 14, 1844, the city sold the land to the United States. The conveyance included a covenant of general warranty; nothing in the deed to the United States designated any purpose to which the land was to be applied or any conditions precedent or subsequent. The United States took possession of the land for the purpose of establishing a naval depot and made various improvements for that purpose. Ten years later, by an Act of Congress dated August 5, 1854, the United States transferred the land back to the city. The act stated: "All the grounds and appurtenances thereunto belonging, known as the Memphis Navy Yard, in Shelby County, Tennessee, be, and the same is hereby, ceded to the mayor and aldermen of the city of Memphis, *for the use and benefit of said city.*"

[Murdock's bill alleged that when the United States abandoned any intention to establish a naval depot, the land came within the clause of the deed of July 1844 conveying it to Wheatley in trust—or, if not, that the land was held by the city in trust for the original grantors. The bill prayed to subject the land to those trusts.

[The city's answer disputed Murdock's construction of the 1844 deed, asserted that the land had been appropriated by the United States as a naval depot within the meaning of that deed, and contended that the perpetual occupation of it was not a condition subsequent; thus, the United States' abandonment of the land as a naval depot was not a breach of a condition that divested the title that had been conveyed by the deed. The city also demurred to the bill as seeking to enforce a forfeiture for breach of a condition subsequent. In addition, the city pleaded the statute of limitations.

[The trial court sustained the demurrer, and also ruled that the city had a perfect title to the land against the complainant under both the act of Congress and the statute of limitations, and dismissed the bill. The Supreme Court of Tennessee affirmed that decree, stating that the act of Congress "cedes the property in controversy in this cause to the mayor and aldermen of the city of Memphis, for the use of the city only, and not in trust for the complainant; and that the complainant takes no benefit under the said act."

[Murdock sued out a writ of error to the Supreme Court.]

■ MR. JUSTICE MILLER * * * delivered the opinion of the court.

In the year 1867 Congress passed an act * * * entitled an act to amend "An act to establish the judicial courts of the United States, approved September the 24th, 1789." This act consisted of two sections, the first of which conferred upon the Federal courts * * * additional power in regard to writs of habeas corpus, and regulated appeals and other proceedings in that class of cases. The second section was a reproduction, with some changes, of the twenty-fifth section of the act of 1789, to which, by its title, the act of 1867 was an amendment, and it related to the appellate jurisdiction of this court over judgments and decrees of State courts. * * *

The proposition is that by a fair construction of the act of 1867 this court must, when it obtains jurisdiction of a case decided in a State court, by reason of one of the questions stated in the act, proceed to decide every other question which the case presents which may be found necessary to a final judgment on the whole merits. To this has been added the further suggestion that in determining whether the question on which the jurisdiction of this court depends has been raised in any given case, we are not limited to the record which comes to us from the State court * * * but we may resort to any such method of ascertaining what was really done in the State court as this court may think proper, even to *ex parte* affidavits. * * *

[After an initial argument, the Court propounded the following questions to counsel on reargument]:

1.   Does the second section of the act of February 5th, 1867, repeal all or any part of the twenty-fifth section of the act of 1789, commonly called the Judiciary Act?

2.   Is it the true intent and meaning of the act of 1867, above referred to, that when this court has jurisdiction of a case, by reason of any of the questions therein mentioned, it shall proceed to decide all the questions presented by the record which are necessary to a final judgment or decree?

3.   If this question be answered affirmatively, does the Constitution of the United States authorize Congress to confer such a jurisdiction on this court? * * *

1.   [The Court answered the first question in the affirmative.]

2.   The affirmative of the second question propounded above is founded upon the effect of the omission or repeal of the last sentence of the twenty-fifth section of the act of 1789. That clause in express terms limited the power of the Supreme Court in reversing the judgment of a State court, to errors apparent on the face of the record and which respected questions, that for the sake of brevity, though not with strict verbal accuracy, we shall call Federal questions, namely, those in regard to the validity or construction of the Constitution, treaties, statutes, commissions, or authority of the Federal government.*

The argument may be thus stated: 1. That the Constitution declares that the judicial power of the United States shall extend to *cases* of a character which includes the questions described in the section, and that by the word *case* is to be understood all of the cases in which such a question arises. 2. That by the fair construction of the act of 1789 in regard to removing those cases to this court, the power and the duty of re-examining the whole case would have been devolved on the court, but for the restriction of the clause omitted in the act of 1867; and that the same language is used in the latter act regulating the removal, but omitting the restrictive clause. And, 3. That by re-enacting the statute in the same terms as to the removal of cases from the State courts, without the restrictive clause, Congress is to be understood as conferring the power which that clause prohibited.

---

*   [Ed.] For the text of this change, see pp. 461–462, *supra*.

We will consider the last proposition first.

What were the precise motives which induced the omission of this clause it is impossible to ascertain with any degree of satisfaction. In a legislative body like Congress, it is reasonable to suppose that among those who considered this matter at all, there were varying reasons for consenting to the change. No doubt there were those who, believing that the Constitution gave no right to the Federal judiciary to go beyond the line marked by the omitted clause, thought its presence or absence immaterial; and in a revision of the statute it was wise to leave it out, because its presence implied that such a power was within the competency of Congress to bestow. There were also, no doubt, those who believed that the section standing without that clause did not confer the power which it prohibited, and that it was, therefore, better omitted. It may also have been within the thought of a few that all that is now claimed would follow the repeal of the clause. But if Congress, or the Framers of the bill, had a clear purpose to enact affirmatively that the court *should consider* the class of errors which that clause forbids, nothing hindered that they should say so in positive terms; and in reversing the policy of the government from its foundation in one of the most important subjects on which that body could act, it is reasonably to be expected that Congress would use plain, unmistakable language in giving expression to such intention.

There is, therefore, no sufficient reason for holding that Congress, by repealing or omitting this restrictive clause, intended to enact affirmatively the thing which that clause had prohibited. * * *

There is * * * nothing in the language of the act, as far as we have criticized it, which in express terms defines the extent of the re-examination which this court shall give to such cases.

But we have not yet considered the most important part of the statute, namely, that which declares that it is only upon the existence of certain questions in the case that this court can entertain jurisdiction at all. Nor is the mere existence of such a question in the case sufficient to give jurisdiction—the question must have been *decided* in the State court. Nor is it sufficient that such a question was raised and was decided. It must have been decided in a certain way, that is, against the right set up under the Constitution, laws, treaties, or authority of the United States. The Federal question may have been erroneously decided. It may be quite apparent to this court that a wrong construction has been given to the Federal law, but if the right claimed under it by plaintiff in error has been conceded to him, this court cannot entertain jurisdiction of the case, so very careful is the statute, both of 1789 and of 1867, to narrow, to limit, and define the jurisdiction which this court exercises over the judgments of the State courts. Is it consistent with this extreme caution to suppose that Congress intended, when those cases came here, that this court should not only examine those questions, but all others found in the record?—questions of common law, of State statutes, of controverted facts, and conflicting evidence. Or is it the more reasonable inference that Congress intended that the case should be brought here that *those questions* might be decided and *finally* decided by the court established by the Constitution of the Union, and the court which has always been supposed to be not only the most appropriate but the only proper tribunal for their final decision? No such reason nor any necessity exists for the decision by this court of other questions in those cases. The jurisdiction has been exercised for nearly a century without serious inconvenience to the due administration of justice. The State courts are the appropriate tribunals, as this court has repeatedly held, for the decision of questions arising under their local law, whether statutory or otherwise. And it is not lightly to be presumed that Congress acted upon a principle which implies a distrust of their integrity or of their ability to construe those laws correctly.

Let us look for a moment into the effect of the proposition contended for upon the cases as they come up for consideration in the conference-room. If it is found that no such question is raised or decided in the court below, then all will concede that it must be dismissed for want of jurisdiction. But if it is found that the Federal question was raised and was decided against the plaintiff in error, then the first duty of the court obviously is to determine whether it was correctly decided by the State court. Let us suppose that we find that the court below was right in its decision on that question. What, then, are we to do? Was it the intention of Congress to say that while you can only bring the case here on account of this question, yet when it is here, though it may turn out that the plaintiff in error was wrong on that question, and the judgment of the court below was right, though he has wrongfully dragged the defendant into this court by the allegation of an error which did not exist, and without which the case could not rightfully be here, he can still insist on an inquiry into all the other matters which were litigated in the case? This is neither reasonable nor just.

In such case both the nature of the jurisdiction conferred and the nature and fitness of things demand that, no error being found in the matter which authorized the re-examination, the judgment of the State court should be affirmed, and the case remitted to that court for its further enforcement.

* * * We are of opinion that upon a fair construction of the whole language of the section the jurisdiction conferred is limited to the decision of the questions mentioned in the statute, and, as a necessary consequence of this, to the exercise of such powers as may be necessary to cause the judgment in that decision to be respected.

We will now advert to one or two considerations apart from the mere language of the statute, which seem to us to give additional force to this conclusion.

It has been many times decided by this court, on motions to dismiss this class of cases for want of jurisdiction, that if it appears from the record that the plaintiff in error raised and presented to the court * * * one of the questions specified in the statute, and the court ruled against him, the jurisdiction of this court attached, and we must hear the case on its merits. * * * But if when we once get jurisdiction, everything in the case is open to re-examination, it follows that every case tried in any State court, from that of a justice of the peace to the highest court of the State, may be brought to this court for final decision on all the points involved in it. * * *

It is impossible to believe that Congress intended this result, and equally impossible that they did not see that it would follow if they intended to open the cases that are brought here under this section to reexamination on all the points involved in them and necessary to a final judgment on the merits.

The twenty-fifth section of the act of 1789 has been the subject of innumerable decisions * * *. These form a system of appellate jurisprudence relating to the exercise of the appellate power of this court over the courts of the States. That system has been based upon the fundamental principle that this jurisdiction was limited to the correction of errors relating solely to Federal law. And though it may be argued with some plausibility that the reason of this is to be found in the restrictive clause of the act of 1789, which is omitted in the act of 1867, yet an examination of the cases will show that it rested quite as much on the conviction of this court that without that clause and on general principles the jurisdiction extended no further. It requires a very bold reach of thought, and a readiness to impute to Congress a radical and hazardous change of a policy vital in its essential nature to the independence of the State courts, to believe that that body contemplated, or intended, what is claimed, by the mere omission of a clause in the substituted statute, which may well be held to have been superfluous, or nearly so, in the old one.

Another consideration, not without weight in seeking after the intention of Congress, is found in the fact that where that body has clearly shown an intention to bring the whole of a case which arises under the constitutional provision as to its subject-matter under the jurisdiction of a Federal court, it has conferred its cognizance on Federal courts of original jurisdiction and not on the Supreme Court. * * *

There may be some plausibility in the argument that [rights under federal law] cannot be protected in all cases unless the Supreme Court has final control of the whole case. But the experience of eighty-five years of the administration of the law under the opposite theory would seem to be a satisfactory answer to the argument. It is not to be presumed that the State courts, where the rule is clearly laid down to them on the Federal question, and its influence on the case fully seen, will disregard or overlook it, and this is all that the rights of the party claiming under it require. Besides, by the very terms of this statute, when the Supreme Court is of opinion that the question of Federal law is of such relative importance to the whole case that it should control the final judgment, that court is authorized to render such judgment and enforce it by its own process. It cannot, therefore, be maintained that it is in any case necessary for the security of the rights claimed under the Constitution, laws, or treaties of the United States that the Supreme Court should examine and decide other questions not of a Federal character.

And we are of opinion that the act of 1867 does not confer such a jurisdiction.

This renders unnecessary a decision of the question whether, if Congress had conferred such authority, the act would have been constitutional. It will be time enough for this court to inquire into the existence of such a power when that body has attempted to exercise it in language which makes such an intention so clear as to require it. * * *

It is proper, in this first attempt to construe this important statute as amended, to say a few words on another point. What shall be done by this court when the question has been found to exist in the record, and to have been decided against the plaintiff in error, and *rightfully* decided, we have already seen, and it presents no difficulties.

But when it appears that the Federal question was decided erroneously against the plaintiff in error, we must then reverse the case undoubtedly, if there are no other issues decided in it than that. It often has occurred, however, and will occur again, that there are other points in the case than those of Federal cognizance, on which the judgment of the court below may stand; those points being of themselves sufficient to control the case.

Or it may be, that there are other issues in the case, but they are not of such controlling influence on the whole case that they are alone sufficient to support the judgment.

It may also be found that notwithstanding there are many other questions in the record of the case, the issue raised by the Federal question is such that its decision must dispose of the whole case.

In the two latter instances there can be no doubt that the judgment of the State court must be reversed, and under the new act this court can either render the final judgment or decree here, or remand the case to the State court for that purpose.

But in the other cases supposed, why should a judgment be reversed for an error in deciding the Federal question, if the same judgment must be rendered on the other points in the case? And why should this court reverse a judgment which is right on the whole record presented to us; or where the same judgment will be rendered by the court below, after they have corrected the error in the Federal question?

We have already laid down the rule that we are not authorized to examine these other questions for the purpose of deciding whether the State court ruled correctly on them or not. We are of opinion that on these subjects not embraced in the class of questions stated in the statute, we must receive the decision of the State courts as conclusive.

But when we find that the State court has decided the Federal question erroneously, then to prevent a useless and profitless reversal, which can do the plaintiff in error no good, and can only embarrass and delay the defendant, we must so far look into the remainder of the record as to see whether the decision of the Federal question alone is sufficient to dispose of the case, or to require its reversal; or on the other hand, whether there exist other matters in the record actually decided by the State court which are sufficient to maintain the judgment of that court, notwithstanding the error in deciding the Federal question. In the latter case the court would not be justified in reversing the judgment of the State court.

But this examination into the points in the record other than the Federal question is not for the purpose of determining whether they were correctly or erroneously decided, but to ascertain if any such have been decided, and their sufficiency to maintain the final judgment, as decided by the State court. * * *

Finally, we hold the following propositions on this subject as flowing from the statute as it now stands:

1. That it is essential to the jurisdiction of this court over the judgment of a State court, that it shall appear that one of the questions

mentioned in the act must have been raised, and presented to the State court.

2.   That it must have been decided by the State court, or that its decision was necessary to the judgment or decree, rendered in the case.

3.   That the decision must have been against the right claimed or asserted by plaintiff in error under the Constitution, treaties, laws, or authority of the United States.

4.   These things appearing, this court has jurisdiction and must examine the judgment so far as to enable it to decide whether this claim of right was correctly adjudicated by the State court.

5.   If it finds that it was rightly decided, the judgment must be affirmed.

6.   If it was erroneously decided against plaintiff in error, then this court must further inquire, whether there is any other matter or issue adjudged by the State court, which is sufficiently broad to maintain the judgment of that court, notwithstanding the error in deciding the issue raised by the Federal question. If this is found to be the case, the judgment must be affirmed without inquiring into the soundness of the decision on such other matter or issue.

7.   But if it be found that the issue raised by the question of Federal law is of such controlling character that its correct decision is necessary to any final judgment in the case, or that there has been no decision by the State court of any other matter or issue which is sufficient to maintain the judgment of that court without regard to the Federal question, then this court will reverse the judgment of the State court, and will either render such judgment here as the State court should have rendered, or remand the case to that court, as the circumstances of the case may require.

Applying the principles here laid down to the case now before the court, we are of opinion that this court has jurisdiction, and that the judgment of the Supreme Court of Tennessee must be affirmed. * * *

The complainants, in their bill, and throughout the case, insisted that the effect of the act of 1854 was to vest the title in the mayor or aldermen of the city in trust for them.

It may be very true that it is not easy to see anything in the deed by which the United States received the title from the city, or the act by which they ceded it back, which raises such a trust, but the complainants claimed a right under this act of the United States, which was decided against them by the Supreme Court of Tennessee, and this claim gives jurisdiction of that question to this court.

But we need not consume many words to prove that neither by the deed of the city to the United States, which is an ordinary deed of bargain and sale for a valuable consideration, nor from anything found in the Act of 1854, is there any such trust to be inferred. The act, so far from recognizing or implying any such trust, cedes the property to the mayor and aldermen *for the use of the city*. We are, therefore, of opinion that this, the only Federal question in the case, was rightly decided by the Supreme Court of Tennessee.

[As for any claim based on the 1844 deed, it is] to be determined by the general principles of equity jurisprudence, and is unaffected by anything found in the Constitution, laws, or treaties of the United States. Whether decided well or otherwise by the State court, we have no authority to inquire. According to the principles we have laid down as applicable to this class of cases, the judgment of the Supreme Court of Tennessee must be

Affirmed.

■ MR. JUSTICE CLIFFORD, with whom concurred MR. JUSTICE SWAYNE, dissenting:

I dissent from so much of the opinion of the court as denies the jurisdiction of this court to determine the whole case, where it appears that the record presents a Federal question and that the Federal question was erroneously decided to the prejudice of the plaintiff in error; as in that state of the record it is, in my judgment, the duty of this court, under the recent act of Congress, to decide the whole merits of the controversy, and to affirm or reverse the judgment of the State court. * * *

■ MR. JUSTICE BRADLEY, dissenting:

* * * Proving that the government did not appropriate the land for a navy yard is a very different thing from setting up a claim to the land under an act of Congress.

I think, therefore, that in this case there was no title or right claimed by the appellants under any statute of, or authority exercised under, the United States; and consequently that there was no decision against any such title; and, therefore, that this court has no jurisdiction.

But supposing, as the majority of the court holds, that it has jurisdiction, I cannot concur in the conclusion that we can only decide the Federal question raised by the record. * * *

The clause by its presence in the original act meant something, and effected something. * * * The omission of the clause, according to a well-settled rule of construction, must necessarily have the effect of removing the restriction which it effected in the old law.

In my judgment, therefore, if the court had jurisdiction of the case, it was bound to consider not only the Federal question raised by the record, but the whole case. As the court, however, has decided otherwise, it is not proper that I should express any opinion on the merits.

[The Chief Justice, who was appointed only after reargument, took no part in the judgment.]

NOTE ON MURDOCK V. MEMPHIS

(1) Murdock and Reconstruction. Is it possible that the Reconstruction Congress was so highly mistrustful of state courts that it did mean to authorize Supreme Court review of state law issues?[1] Although Murdock concerned only the second section of the Act of 1867, the first section of the Act gave the federal courts, for the first time, a general power to issue writs

---

[1] See generally Matasar & Bruch, *Procedural Common Law, Federal Jurisdictional Policy, and Abandonment of the Adequate and Independent State Grounds Doctrine*, 86 Colum.L.Rev. 1291, 1319 (1986) (so arguing). For a different perspective, see Collins, *Reconstructing Murdock v. Memphis*, 98 Va.L.Rev 1439 (2012).

of habeas corpus to state prisoners. See Chap. XI, Sec. 3, *infra*.[2] Was the Court justified in requiring a clearer statement than the Act's deletion of the restrictive language of section 25? Would a statute mandating the contrary result in Murdock have been constitutional?

(2) Appellate Versus Original Federal Jurisdiction. Former Justice Benjamin R. Curtis, in an amicus curiae brief, argued in support of the extended jurisdiction that the Court ultimately rejected. On the question of the constitutionality of Supreme Court review of non-federal issues, Curtis asserted: "Unless, therefore, some distinction can be made between the power of Congress to confer original and appellate jurisdiction, and neither the Constitution nor the decisions of this court permit this distinction, it is clear that Congress may confer appellate power over all cases to which the judicial power of the United States extends, and is not restricted by the Constitution to particular questions, by reason of which the cases are brought within the judicial power * * *."[3]

Doesn't the Curtis syllogism ignore a fundamental structural difference between original and appellate adjudication? A federal trial court exercising original jurisdiction must decide the entire case, including state-law questions, in order to come to judgment. By contrast, when the Supreme Court exercises appellate jurisdiction, it need not decide state law issues to ensure complete adjudication; those issues have been decided (or will be decided on remand) by the state courts.

Consider, for example, whether the undoubted power of a federal district court to entertain a diversity action based entirely on state law necessarily implies that the Supreme Court could exercise appellate jurisdiction over such an action that had been litigated in a state court.[4]

(3) The Dissent's Position. Suppose Murdock had been decided the other way, permitting the Supreme Court, in a case otherwise within its appellate jurisdiction, to review a state's highest court on an issue of state law. What

---

[2]   Professor Wiecek argues that Congress, in deleting the proviso to § 25, may have approved a bill with far-reaching effects on American federalism without knowing what it was doing. He observes that many commentators believe that Congress did intend the expansion of jurisdiction implicit in deletion of § 25's proviso. Wiecek views Murdock as one of a group of decisions in the 1870s that narrowed federal jurisdiction and retreated from federal protection of the newly freed slaves. He asserts that the Court, already feeling overworked, was leery of taking on the added caseload that a contrary decision in Murdock would have generated. He concludes, however, that Murdock "was * * * a godsend for the American federal system". Wiecek, *Murdock v. Memphis: Section 25 of the 1789 Judiciary Act and Judicial Federalism*, in Marcus (ed.), Origins of the Federal Judiciary 223, 243 (1992).

[3]   The brief is summarized at 87 U.S. (20 Wall.) at 602–06 and printed in Curtis, Jurisdiction, Practice and Peculiar Jurisprudence of the Courts of the United States 54–58 (1880). *Cf.* 2 Crosskey, Politics and the Constitution in the History of the United States 711–817 (1953) (arguing on a much broader basis for the Court's power to decide state law). But see Hart, *The Relations Between State and Federal Law*, 54 Colum.L.Rev. 489, 499–506 (1954).

[4]   Mitchell, *Reconsidering Murdock: State-Law Reversals as Constitutional Avoidance*, 77 U.Chi.L.Rev.1335 (2010), argues that nothing in the language of Article III or 28 U.S.C. § 1257(a) forecloses Supreme Court review of state law issues, and that the Court already reviews questions of state law in many contexts. Starting from those premises, Professor Mitchell argues that the Supreme Court should review state law rulings of state courts when necessary to avoid a "novel and contentious" federal constitutional question. Such an approach, he contends, would serve the interests of the avoidance doctrine and allow the Court to forestall error costs sometimes incurred in difficult constitutional cases. Can Professor Mitchell's reading of Article III be squared with the premises about our federal system that underlie Erie R. Co. v. Tompkins, p. 584, *infra*?

would be the future precedential authority of such a Supreme Court determination, if the identical issue of state law arose:

(a) in the state's courts, in a case that did not involve any issue of federal law and was not otherwise within the federal judicial power?

(b) in the state's courts, in a case that, because there was a federal question presented, would potentially be subject to the Supreme Court's appellate jurisdiction?

(c) in the state's courts, in a case in which there was no federal question but there was diversity of citizenship?

(d) in a federal district court of that state, in a diversity action in which there was not (or, alternatively, there was) also a federal question?

(e) in a state court of a second state that, under applicable choice of law principles, would apply the law of the first state, and in which there was not (or, alternatively, there was) also a federal question?

Do these questions shed light on the correctness of Murdock as a matter of statutory interpretation? On whether the dissent's interpretation of the jurisdictional statute was constitutionally permissible?[5]

(4) Murdock and Erie. The Court's recognition in Murdock that it lacks authority to review a state court on issues of state law was echoed when the Court ruled, in Erie R. Co. v. Tompkins, 304 U.S. 64 (1938), that the grant of diversity jurisdiction does not give federal courts a general lawmaking power to fashion common law. Why did it take so long after Murdock for Erie to be decided?

(5) "Antecedent" Versus "Distinct" State Law Grounds. In Murdock, the non-federal issue of trust law was logically (and functionally) quite distinct from any issue of federal law; answering the state law question was not a necessary antecedent to any question of federal law. Put differently, had the Supreme Court resolved the federal issue in favor of Murdock (the purported federal rightholder) and held that the 1854 Act of Congress conferred good title on him, he would have obtained all the relief he sought, regardless of the state court's resolution of the non-federal issues.

In Martin v. Hunter's Lessee, by contrast, the state law question (did the Commonwealth of Virginia obtain title by escheat before any federal treaty took effect) was an essential antecedent to the application of the federal treaty provisions giving protection to then-existing land titles. Put differently, to obtain the relief he sought, Martin had to prevail on both the non-federal issue (that his chain of title had not been divested at the time of the Treaty of Peace) and the federal law issue (that the Treaty protected that title against the Act of Compromise and other efforts to divest it).

The distinction between these two types of cases is critical to understanding this area of the law. Where the state issue is wholly distinct, as in Murdock, is there any plausible argument that the Supreme Court, as a corollary to its authority over federal issues, needs power to review the

---

[5] Compare Field, *The Differing Federalisms of Canada and the United States*, 55 L. & Contemp.Probs. 107 (1992) (noting that in Canada's federal system, the highest national court— the Canadian Supreme Court—has authority to review decisions of the provincial courts even on issues of provincial law). For an argument (stimulated by Bush v. Gore) that Article III permits the Supreme Court to review issues of state law in a case like Murdock, or in a state court case that involves diversity of citizenship, see Harrison, *Federal Appellate Jurisdiction Over Questions of State Law in State Courts*, 7 Green Bag 2d 353 (2004).

correctness of the state ruling? On the other hand, where a state law ruling serves as an antecedent for determining whether a federal right has been violated, some review of the basis for the state court's determination of the state-law question is essential if the federal right is to be protected against evasion and discrimination—as Martin itself exemplifies. See Wechsler, *The Appellate Jurisdiction of the Supreme Court: Reflections on the Law and Logistics of Direct Review*, 34 Wash. & Lee L.Rev. 1043, 1050–56 (1977).

(6) The Disposition in Murdock. Justice Miller's seven propositions do not represent the Court's contemporary practice. Proposition (3) was the law prior to 1914, but that year Congress extended Supreme Court review to embrace state decisions that uphold as well as those that deny claims of federal right. Propositions (4)–(6) suggest an order of decision (first decide the federal issue, and if there was error, then determine whether the state judgment can nonetheless stand on the basis of a state law ground) that is the opposite of current practice. See the next principal case, Fox Film Corp. v. Muller.

Moreover, given the statute of limitations issue in Murdock, which appears to have been viewed as one of non-federal law, there is an argument (at least under current practice) that the Court should not have reached the merits of even the federal issue. Return to this question after reading Sec. 2(A) of this Chapter.

2. The Relation Between State and Federal Law

A. Substantive Law

Introductory Note

(1) The Relationship of State and Federal Law. The material in this Section concerns the scope of Supreme Court review of state court decisions, but it also demands analysis of the diverse ways in which state and federal law interact. Only such analysis can illuminate why the Court sometimes lacks power to review issues of federal law decided by a state court,[1] and on other occasions may review (at least on a limited basis) determinations of state law.[2]

(2) The Interstitial Nature of Federal Law. A central aspect of the relationship of state and federal law was highlighted in the following discussion in the First Edition of this book, published in 1953:

"Federal law is generally interstitial in its nature. It rarely occupies a legal field completely, totally excluding all participation by the legal systems of the states. This was plainly true in the beginning when the federal legislative product (including the Constitution) was extremely small. It is significantly true today, despite the volume of Congressional enactments,

---

[1] See, *e.g.*, Fox Film Corp. v. Muller, p. 490, *infra.*

[2] See, *e.g.*, Indiana ex rel. Anderson v. Brand, p. 509, *infra.*

and even within areas where Congress has been very active. Federal legislation, on the whole, has been conceived and drafted on an *ad hoc* basis to accomplish limited objectives. It builds upon legal relationships established by the states, altering or supplanting them only so far as necessary for the special purpose. Congress acts, in short, against the background of the total *corpus juris* of the states in much the way that a state legislature acts against the background of the common law, assumed to govern unless changed by legislation.

"That this is so was partially affirmed in § 34 of the First Judiciary Act, now 28 U.S.C. § 1652, but an attentive canvass of the total product of the Congress would establish its surprising generality and force. Indeed, the strength of the conception of the central government as one of delegated, limited authority is most significantly manifested on this mundane plane of working, legislative practice.

"The point involved is vital to appreciation of the legal issues posed by the materials in this and later chapters (especially [Chapters VI and VII]), concerned with the relationship between the law of the United States and of the states. It explains why frequently in litigation federal law bears only partially upon the case: the basis of a right asserted by the plaintiff which is open to defenses grounded in state law, the basis of a defense when a state-created right has been advanced, the foundation of a replication to a state defense or only of the rejoinder to a replication that would otherwise be good. It explains why federal law often embodies concepts that derive their content, or some portion of their content, from the states. It makes it less anomalous, at least, that substantive rights may be defined by Congress but the remedies for their enforcement left undefined or relegated wholly to the states; or that *per contra* national law may do no more than formulate remedies for vindicating rights that have their source and definition in state law.

"The diversity of these relationships is shown most plainly in cases that reach the Supreme Court from the authorized expositors of state law, the state courts."

In the more than sixty years since the First Edition was published, the expansion of federal legislation and administrative regulation noted in this discussion has accelerated; today one finds many more instances in which federal enactments supply both right and remedy in, or wholly occupy, a particular field. This same period has witnessed a broad extension of federal laws (constitutional and statutory) that protect individual rights and provide remedies for violations thereof. Thus, at present federal law appears to be more primary than interstitial in numerous areas. Nonetheless, consider, in reading the material in this Section, whether the First Edition's thesis does not remain accurate over an extremely broad range of applications.[3]

---

[3]   See generally Hart *The Relations Between State and Federal Law*, 54 Colum.L.Rev. 489 (1954). For analysis of relevant institutional factors that help to preserve the primacy of state law in many areas, see, *e.g.*, Wechsler, *The Political Safeguards of Federalism: The Role of the States in the Composition and Selection of the National Government*, 54 Colum.L.Rev. 543 (1954); Choper, Judicial Review and the National Political Process (1980); Shapiro, Federalism: A Dialogue (1995); Baker, *Putting the Safeguards Back Into the Political Safeguards of Federalism*, 46 Vill.L.Rev. 951 (2001); Kaden, *Politics, Money, and State Sovereignty: The Judicial Role*, 79 Colum.L.Rev. 847 (1979); Kramer, *Understanding Federalism*, 47 Vand.L.Rev. 1485 (1994); Kramer, *Putting the Politics Back into the Political Safeguards of Federalism*, 100 Colum.L.Rev. 215 (2000).

Fox Film Corp. v. Muller

296 U.S. 207, 56 S.Ct. 183, 80 L.Ed. 158 (1935).
Certiorari to the Supreme Court of Minnesota.

■ MR. JUSTICE SUTHERLAND delivered the opinion of the Court.

This is an action * * * by the Film Corporation against Muller, to recover damages for an alleged breach of two contracts by which Muller was licensed to exhibit certain moving-picture films belonging to the corporation. Muller answered, setting up the invalidity of the contracts under the Sherman Anti-trust Act. It was and is agreed that these contracts are substantially the same as the one involved in United States v. Paramount Famous Lasky Corp., 34 F.(2d) 984, *aff'd* 282 U.S. 30; that petitioner was one of the defendants in that action; and that the "arbitration clause" * * * of each of the contracts sued upon, is the same as that held in that case to be invalid. * * *

The court of first instance held that each contract sued upon violated the Sherman Anti-trust Act, and dismissed the action. In a supplemental opinion, that court put its decision upon the grounds, first, that the arbitration plan is so connected with the remainder of the contract that the entire contract is tainted; and, second, that the contract violates the Sherman Anti-trust law. The state supreme court affirmed. * * *

In its opinion, the state supreme court * * * said: "The question presented on this appeal is whether the arbitration clause is severable from the contract, leaving the remainder of the contract enforceable, or not severable, permeating and tainting the whole contract with illegality and making it void." That court then proceeded to * * * discuss a number of decisions of state and federal courts, some of which took the view that the arbitration clause was severable, and others that it was not * * *. After reviewing the opinion and decree of the federal district court in the Paramount case, the lower court reached the conclusion that the holding of the federal court was that the entire contract was illegal; and upon that view and upon what it conceived to be the weight of authority, held the arbitration plan was inseparable from the other provisions of the contract. Whether this conclusion was right or wrong we need not determine. It is enough that it is, at least, not without fair support.

Respondent contends that the question of severability was alone decided and that no federal question was determined by the lower court. This contention petitioner challenges, and asserts that a federal question was involved and decided. We do not attempt to settle the dispute; but, assuming * * * that petitioner's view is the correct one, the case is controlled by the settled rule that where the judgment of a state court rests upon two grounds, one of which is federal and the other nonfederal in character, our jurisdiction fails if the nonfederal ground is independent of the federal ground and adequate to support the judgment. This rule had become firmly fixed at least as early as Klinger v. State of Missouri, 13 Wall. 257, 263, and has been reiterated in a long line of cases since that time. [Citing numerous decisions.]

Whether the provisions of a contract are non-severable, so that if one be held invalid the others must fall with it, is clearly a question of general and not of federal law. The invalidity of the arbitration clause which the present contracts embody is conceded. It was held invalid * * * in the Paramount case, and its judgment was affirmed here. * * * [T]he primary question to be determined by the court below was whether the concededly invalid clause was separable from the other provisions of the contract. The ruling of the state supreme court that it was not, is sufficient to conclude the case without regard to the determination, if, in fact, any was made, in respect of the federal question. It follows that the non-federal ground is adequate to sustain the judgment.

The rule * * * to the effect that our jurisdiction attaches where the nonfederal ground is so interwoven with the other as not to be an independent matter, does not apply. The construction put upon the contracts did not constitute a preliminary step which simply had the effect of bringing forward for determination the federal question, but was a decision which automatically took the federal question out of the case if otherwise it would be there. The nonfederal question in respect of the construction of the contracts, and the federal question in respect of their validity under the Anti-trust Act, were clearly independent of one another. The case, in effect, was disposed of before the federal question said to be involved was reached. A decision of that question then became unnecessary; and whether it was decided or not, our want of jurisdiction is clear.

Writ dismissed for want of jurisdiction.

■ THE CHIEF JUSTICE took no part in the consideration or decision of this case.

PRELIMINARY NOTE ON THE INDEPENDENT AND ADEQUATE STATE GROUND

(1) Early Development and Present Administration of the Rule. In the early decisions after Murdock, the rule that the Court would not review a judgment resting on an adequate and independent state ground was apparently regarded merely as prudential (why decide an issue that could not affect the judgment?). Later cases placed the rule squarely on lack of jurisdiction, *e.g.*, Enterprise Irrigation Dist. v. Farmers' Mut. Canal Co., 243 U.S. 157, 164 (1917), and in Herb v. Pitcairn, 324 U.S. 117, 126 (1945), the Court suggested that the jurisdictional barrier might be not merely statutory but constitutional: "[O]ur power is to correct wrong judgments, not to revise opinions. * * * [I]f the same judgment would be rendered by the state court after we corrected its view of federal laws, our review could amount to nothing more than an advisory opinion."[1]

Because, as Fox Film indicates, the Court regards the presence of an adequate and independent state ground as depriving it of jurisdiction to review the state court judgment, the proper disposition is to dismiss for lack of jurisdiction, rather than (as Murdock suggested) to affirm; and this has

---

[1] For endorsements of this suggestion, see, *e.g.*, Coleman v. Thompson, 501 U.S. 722, 729 (1991); Ake v. Oklahoma, 470 U.S. 68, 75 (1985); Fountaine, *Article III and the Adequate and Independent State Grounds Doctrine*, 48 Am.U.L.Rev. 1053 (1999) (arguing that the doctrine is demanded by the Article III standing requirement that the harm complained of be redressable).

been the Court's practice since Eustis v. Bolles, 150 U.S. 361 (1893). Today, the Court will simply deny a petition for certiorari that it lacks jurisdiction to entertain, without noting a reason, jurisdictional or otherwise.

(2) Application of the Rule. It is now an accepted principle that the Supreme Court will not review a federal question when the state court's decision of a state law issue precludes the Court from altering the outcome below, no matter how the Court might resolve the federal question.[2] But administration of that principle engenders impressive difficulties and requires careful analysis of the relationship between state and federal law in the case at hand.[3] (In Fox Film, was the premise for finding no jurisdiction—that the question of separability was governed exclusively by state law—as obvious as the Court seemed to think?)

In analyzing the relation of state and federal law, it is critical to keep in mind the key distinction (discussed at pp. 487–488, Paragraph (5), *supra*, and also noted in the last substantive paragraph of the Fox Film opinion) between (i) state law as antecedent to federal law and (ii) state law as a distinct basis for relief.

(3) State Law as Antecedent to Federal Law. In cases like Martin v. Hunter's Lessee, the federal rightholder must prevail on both state and federal grounds in order to obtain relief. This is what is meant by stating that state law is antecedent to the federal question. In such a case, if (i) the state court denies relief to the federal rightholder by deciding the issue of state law adversely, (ii) that ground is broad enough to support the judgment, and (iii) there is no basis for questioning or setting aside the state court's decision of the state law issue, then the Supreme Court lacks jurisdiction to review the federal question, because federal review could not change the judgment.[4] The hard question here, explored at pp. 509–524, 529–546, *infra*, relates to the third of these conditions—is the state ground "adequate" to support the judgment, or is there reason (as Justice Story thought there was in Martin) to set aside the state court's determination of

---

[2]   Camreta v. Greene, 131 S.Ct. 2020 (2011), may be in tension with the Court's position on the adequate-and-independent-state-grounds doctrine. As discussed below, see pp. 1053–1054, *infra*, Camreta was a § 1983 action alleging that the defendants—a child protective services worker and a deputy sheriff—violated a schoolchild's Fourth Amendment rights by interviewing her without a warrant or parental consent. The court of appeals held that the defendants (a) violated the Fourth Amendment but (b) were entitled to qualified immunity. Even though the defendant state officials thus prevailed below, Justice Kagan's opinion for the Court held that the Court had jurisdiction to grant their petition for certiorari. Noting that the lower court's merits decision would constrain the petitioners in the future conduct of their public duties, the Court concluded that the petitioners had an injury sufficient to give rise to Article III standing. Relying on Herb v. Pitcairn, Paragraph (1), *supra*, Justice Kennedy dissented.

Does Camreta suggest that the Court should now exercise jurisdiction over state court cases that contain an adequate and independent state ground but, like Camreta, impose federal constitutional limitations on state officials who prevailed below? Or do federalism concerns distinguish the adequate-and-independent-state-ground doctrine from the Camreta doctrine?

[3]   See generally Hill, *The Inadequate State Ground*, 65 Colum.L.Rev. 943 (1965); Wechsler, *The Appellate Jurisdiction of the Supreme Court: Reflections on the Law and Logistics of Direct Review*, 4 Wash. & Lee L.Rev. 1043 (1977); Note, 74 Harv.L.Rev. 1375 (1961).

[4]   This principle has been recognized in a variety of decisions refusing to review state court judgments resting on lack of remedial authority or similar quasi-procedural grounds. See, *e.g.*, Utley v. City of St. Petersburg, 292 U.S. 106 (1934) (laches is an adequate state ground); Enterprise Irrigation Dist. v. Farmers' Mutual Canal Co., 243 U.S. 157 (1917) (estoppel is an adequate state ground). The same principle operates when there is an antecedent state law *procedural* ground—ordinarily, that the party seeking Supreme Court review failed to raise the federal question in state court in accordance with state procedural rules. See Sec. 2(B), *infra*.

the antecedent state law issue? Resolution of that question may require the Supreme Court to engage in some review of the correctness of the state court's decision of state law issues (again, as in Martin) to ensure that federal rights are not undercut by serious misapplications of state law.

However, if the state court resolves the state law issue *in favor* of the federal rightholder, it must then determine the federal issue—and the Supreme Court has jurisdiction to review that determination, however the issue is resolved. Thus, federal reviewability depends on who prevailed on the state law issue in state court.

(4) State Law as a Distinct Basis for Relief. More complex possibilities are posed by cases like Fox Film and Murdock, in which state law provides a basis for relief that is entirely distinct from federal law—so that the federal rightholder can obtain the relief sought by prevailing on *either* state or federal grounds. Suppose, for example, that a taxpayer contends, in a state-court refund action, that a state tax violates both the federal and state constitutions.

(a) If the state supreme court invalidates the tax under the state constitution, without reaching the federal question, the Supreme Court lacks jurisdiction to review. (This situation parallels the defendant's interpretation of the state court's decision in Fox Film.)

(b) If the state supreme court holds the tax invalid under the U.S. Constitution and independently invalid under the state constitution, there is no jurisdiction to review. (This situation parallels the plaintiff's interpretation of the state court's decision in Fox Film.) Is it a problem that the state court's interpretation of federal law may be erroneous but unreviewable, thereby misleading other litigants or other courts? Is correcting such errors reason enough to justify Supreme Court review, even though the state court's judgment ordering a refund would not change, however the Supreme Court decided the federal issue? Compare Camreta v. Greene, note #, *supra*.

(c) If the state court holds the tax *valid* under both constitutions, the state ground cannot independently support the judgment, and the federal-law ruling is plainly subject to review.

(d) If the state court invalidates the tax under the federal Constitution without reaching the state-law issue, the settled rule is that the judgment is reviewable: Supreme Court jurisdiction depends on the state court's actual grounds of decision rather than on possible grounds. See, *e.g.*, Grayson v. Harris, 267 U.S. 352, 358 (1925); Regents of the Univ. of California v. Bakke, 438 U.S. 265, 279–80 (1978); Orr v. Orr, 440 U.S. 268, 274–77 (1979). If it reverses the state court with respect to the federal question, the Supreme Court will remand to permit the state court to resolve the undetermined state law issue. See, *e.g.*, California v. Ramos, 463 U.S. 992, 997–98 n. 7 (1983). The state court remains free to reinstate its prior judgment on that state-law ground. See, *e.g.*, Washington v. Chrisman, 455 U.S. 1 (1982), *reinstated on remand*, 676 P.2d 419 (Wash.1984); South Dakota v. Neville, 459 U.S. 553 (1983), *reinstated on remand*, 346 N.W.2d 425 (S.D.1984).

The Supreme Court's practice in cases like these has not been uniform, however. On occasion the Court, rather than deciding the federal constitutional question, has instead vacated the state court judgment and remanded for consideration of state grounds whose decision might obviate the need to reach the federal constitutional question. See Kirkpatrick v.

Christian Homes of Abilene, Inc., 460 U.S. 1074 (1983); Musser v. Utah, 333 U.S. 95 (1948). What would justify use of this technique in some cases but not in others?[5]

(5) The Responsibility of State Courts. In a case like the hypothetical challenge to a state tax, if a state court views the tax as invalid under both the federal and state constitutions, the state court may choose to rest its decision on state grounds alone, on federal grounds alone, or on both. In such cases, do state courts have an obligation to avoid decision of the federal constitutional issue if possible?[6] May the Supreme Court mandate such a canon of avoidance? May Congress?[7]

(6) Further Problems in Application. Three further difficulties in the administration of the adequate and independent state ground rule are explored in the remaining materials in this Section:

(a) With the Court's jurisdiction turning on whether a given issue is one of federal or state law, surprisingly difficult questions of categorization sometimes arise.

(b) Once state and federal issues have been sorted out, the question may arise whether a state law ground is genuinely "independent" of the federal issue. Suppose, for example, that a state court rules that the state constitutional guarantee of free speech protects exactly what the federal First Amendment protects—no more and no less—and then strikes down a state statute as invalid under the state's constitutional guarantee. Is the state ground truly independent of federal law so as to bar Supreme Court review?

(c) Finally, a state court's opinion may be unclear about whether the judgment rested on an independent state-law ground, on federal law, or on both—a problem posed in the case that follows.

———

Michigan v. Long

463 U.S. 1032, 103 S.Ct. 3469, 77 L.Ed.2d 1201 (1983).
Certiorari to the Supreme Court of Michigan.

■ JUSTICE O'CONNOR delivered the opinion of the Court.

* * * In the present case, respondent David Long was convicted for possession of marihuana found by police in the passenger compartment

———

[5] Consider Paschall v. Christie-Stewart Inc., 414 U.S. 100, 101–02 (1973), in which the Court declined to review a state court decision resting squarely on the Due Process Clause, deciding instead to remand because the suit might have been time-barred under state law, and asserting that if so, "any decision by this Court would be advisory and beyond our jurisdiction." Though Paschall was a case in which state law (the statute of limitations) was antecedent to the federal right, rather than a case like the tax refund illustration, in which state law provides a distinct basis for relief, the Court's reason for remanding has more general applicability.

[6] For a variety of views, see Kahn, *Interpretation and Authority in State Constitutionalism*, 106 Harv.L.Rev. 1147 (1993); Linde, *First Things First: Rediscovering the States' Bills of Rights*, 9 U.Balt.L.Rev. 379 (1980); Pollock, *State Constitutions as Separate Sources of Fundamental Rights*, 35 Rutgers L.Rev. 707 (1983); Utter, *Swimming in the Jaws of the Crocodile: State Court Comment on Federal Constitutional Issues When Disposing of Cases on State Constitutional Grounds*, 63 Tex.L.Rev. 1025 (1985). See also Kloppenberg, *Avoiding Constitutional Questions*, 35 B.C.L.Rev. 1003, 1061–65 (1994).

[7] See Wechsler, note 3, *supra*, at 1056.

and trunk of the automobile that he was driving. The police searched the passenger compartment because they had reason to believe that the vehicle contained weapons potentially dangerous to the officers. We hold that the protective search of the passenger compartment was reasonable under the principles articulated in Terry [v. Ohio, 392 U.S. 1 (1968),] and other decisions of this Court. We also examine Long's argument that the decision below rests upon an adequate and independent state ground, and we decide in favor of our jurisdiction.

I

* * * [The trial court denied Long's motion to suppress the marihuana. Long's conviction for possession of marihuana was affirmed by the Michigan Court of Appeals. The Michigan Supreme Court reversed, however, holding that "the sole justification of the Terry search, protection of the police officers and others nearby, cannot justify the search in this case."]

We granted certiorari * * *.

II

Before reaching the merits, we must consider Long's argument that we are without jurisdiction to decide this case because the decision below rests on an adequate and independent state ground. The court below referred twice to the State Constitution in its opinion, but otherwise relied exclusively on federal law.[3] Long argues that the Michigan courts have provided greater protection from searches and seizures under the State Constitution than is afforded under the Fourth Amendment, and the references to the State Constitution therefore establish an adequate and independent ground for the decision below.

* * * Although we have announced a number of principles in order to help us determine whether various forms of references to state law constitute adequate and independent state grounds,[4] we openly admit that we have thus far not developed a satisfying and consistent approach for resolving this vexing issue. In some instances, we have taken the strict view that if the ground of decision was at all unclear, we would dismiss the case. See, *e.g.*, Lynch v. New York ex rel. Pierson, 293 U.S. 52 (1934). In other instances, we have vacated, see, *e.g.*, Minnesota v. National Tea Co., 309 U.S. 551 (1940), or continued a case, see, *e.g.*, Herb

---

[3] On the first occasion, the court merely cited in a footnote both the State and Federal Constitutions. On the second occasion, at the conclusion of the opinion, the court stated: "We hold, therefore, that the deputies' search of the vehicle was proscribed by the Fourth Amendment to the United States Constitution and art. 1, § 11 of the Michigan Constitution."

[4] For example, we have long recognized that "where the judgment of a state court rests upon two grounds, one of which is federal and the other non-federal in character, our jurisdiction fails if the non-federal ground is independent of the federal ground and adequate to support the judgment." Fox Film Corp. v. Muller, 296 U.S. 207, 210 (1935). We may review a state case decided on a federal ground even if it is clear that there was an available state ground for decision on which the state court could properly have relied. Beecher v. Alabama, 389 U.S. 35, 37, n. 3 (1967). Also, if, in our view, the state court " 'felt compelled by what it understood to be federal constitutional considerations to construe * * * its own law in the manner it did,' " then we will not treat a normally adequate state ground as independent, and there will be no question about our jurisdiction. Delaware v. Prouse, 440 U.S. 648, 653 (1979) (quoting Zacchini v. Scripps-Howard Broadcasting Co., 433 U.S. 562, 568 (1977)). Finally, "where the non-federal ground is so interwoven with the [federal ground] as not to be an independent matter, or is not of sufficient breadth to sustain the judgment without any decision of the other, our jurisdiction is plain." Enterprise Irrigation District v. Farmers Mutual Canal Co., 243 U.S. 157, 164 (1917).

v. Pitcairn, 324 U.S. 117 (1945), in order to obtain clarification about the nature of a state court decision. See also California v. Krivda, 409 U.S. 33 (1972). In more recent cases, we have ourselves examined state law to determine whether state courts have used federal law to guide their application of state law or to provide the actual basis for the decision that was reached. See Texas v. Brown, 460 U.S. 730, 732–733, n. 1 (1983) (plurality opinion). *Cf.* South Dakota v. Neville, 459 U.S. 553, 569 (1983) (Stevens, J., dissenting). In Oregon v. Kennedy, 456 U.S. 667, 670–671 (1982), we rejected an invitation to remand to the state court for clarification even when the decision rested in part on a case from the state court, because we determined that the state case itself rested upon federal grounds. We added that "[e]ven if the case admitted of more doubt as to whether federal and state grounds for decision were intermixed, the fact that the state court relied to the extent it did on federal grounds requires us to reach the merits." *Id.*, at 671.

This ad hoc method of dealing with cases that involve possible adequate and independent state grounds is antithetical to the doctrinal consistency that is required when sensitive issues of federal-state relations are involved. Moreover, none of the various methods of disposition that we have employed thus far recommends itself as the preferred method that we should apply to the exclusion of others, and we therefore determine that it is appropriate to reexamine our treatment of this jurisdictional issue in order to achieve the consistency that is necessary.

The process of examining state law is unsatisfactory because it requires us to interpret state laws with which we are generally unfamiliar, and which often, as in this case, have not been discussed at length by the parties. Vacation and continuance for clarification have also been unsatisfactory both because of the delay and decrease in efficiency of judicial administration, see Dixon v. Duffy, 344 U.S. 143 (1952), and, more important, because these methods of disposition place significant burdens on state courts to demonstrate the presence or absence of our jurisdiction. See Philadelphia Newspapers, Inc. v. Jerome, 434 U.S. 241, 244 (1978) (Rehnquist, J., dissenting); Department of Motor Vehicles v. Rios, 410 U.S. 425, 427 (1973) (Douglas, J., dissenting). Finally, outright dismissal of cases is clearly not a panacea because it cannot be doubted that there is an important need for uniformity in federal law, and that this need goes unsatisfied when we fail to review an opinion that rests primarily upon federal grounds and where the *independence* of an alleged state ground is not apparent from the four corners of the opinion. * * *

Respect for the independence of state courts, as well as avoidance of rendering advisory opinions, have been the cornerstones of this Court's refusal to decide cases where there is an adequate and independent state ground. It is precisely because of this respect for state courts, and this desire to avoid advisory opinions, that we do not wish to continue to decide issues of state law that go beyond the opinion that we review, or to require state courts to reconsider cases to clarify the grounds of their decisions. Accordingly, when, as in this case, a state court decision fairly appears to rest primarily on federal law, or to be interwoven with the federal law, and when the adequacy and independence of any possible state law ground is not clear from the face of the opinion, we will accept

interwoven or primarily Fed ⇨ Fed determinative

as the most reasonable explanation that the state court decided the case the way it did because it believed that federal law required it to do so. If a state court chooses merely to rely on federal precedents as it would on the precedents of all other jurisdictions, then it need only make clear by a plain statement in its judgment or opinion that the federal cases are being used only for the purpose of guidance, and do not themselves compel the result that the court has reached. * * * If the state court decision indicates clearly and expressly that it is alternatively based on bona fide separate, adequate, and independent grounds, we, of course, will not undertake to review the decision.

This approach obviates in most instances the need to examine state law in order to decide the nature of the state court decision, and will at the same time avoid the danger of our rendering advisory opinions.[6] It also avoids the unsatisfactory and intrusive practice of requiring state courts to clarify their decisions to the satisfaction of this Court. We believe that such an approach will provide state judges with a clearer opportunity to develop state jurisprudence unimpeded by federal interference, and yet will preserve the integrity of federal law. "It is fundamental that state courts be left free and unfettered by us in interpreting their state constitutions. But it is equally important that ambiguous or obscure adjudications by state courts do not stand as barriers to a determination by this Court of the validity under the federal constitution of state action." National Tea Co., *supra*, at 557.

The principle that we will not review judgments of state courts that rest on adequate and independent state grounds is based, in part, on "the limitations of our own jurisdiction." Herb v. Pitcairn, 324 U.S. 117, 125 (1945). The jurisdictional concern is that we not "render an advisory opinion, and if the same judgment would be rendered by the state court after we corrected its views of federal laws, our review could amount to nothing more than an advisory opinion." *Id.*, at 126. Our requirement of a "plain statement" that a decision rests upon adequate and independent state grounds does not in any way authorize the rendering of advisory opinions. Rather, in determining, as we must, whether we have jurisdiction to review a case that is alleged to rest on adequate and independent state grounds, we merely assume that there are no such grounds when it is not clear from the opinion itself that the state court relied upon an adequate and independent state ground and when it fairly appears that the state court rested its decision primarily on federal law.[8]

Our review of the decision below under this framework leaves us unconvinced that it rests upon an independent state ground. Apart from

---

6   There may be certain circumstances in which clarification is necessary or desirable, and we will not be foreclosed from taking the appropriate action.

8   * * * In dissent, Justice Stevens proposes the novel view that this Court should never review a state court decision unless the Court wishes to vindicate a federal right that has been endangered. The rationale of the dissent is not restricted to cases where the decision is arguably supported by adequate and independent state grounds. Rather, Justice Stevens appears to believe that even if the decision below rests exclusively on federal grounds, this Court should not review the decision as long as there is no federal right that is endangered.

The state courts handle the vast bulk of all criminal litigation in this country. * * * The state courts are required to apply federal constitutional standards, and they necessarily create a considerable body of "federal law" in the process. It is not surprising that this Court has become more interested in the application and development of federal law by state courts in the light of the recent significant expansion of federally created standards that we have imposed on the States. * * *

its two citations to the State Constitution, the court below relied *exclusively* on its understanding of Terry and other federal cases. Not a single state case was cited to support the state court's holding that the search of the passenger compartment was unconstitutional. Indeed, the court declared that the search in this case was unconstitutional because "[t]he Court of Appeals erroneously applied the principles of Terry v. Ohio * * * to the search of the interior of the vehicle in this case." The references to the state constitution in no way indicate that the decision below rested on grounds in any way *independent* from the state court's interpretation of federal law. Even if we accept that the Michigan Constitution has been interpreted to provide independent protection for certain rights also secured under the Fourth Amendment, it fairly appears in this case that the Michigan Supreme Court rested its decision primarily on federal law.

Rather than dismissing the case, or requiring that the state court reconsider its decision on our behalf solely because of a mere possibility that an adequate and independent ground supports the judgment, we find that we have jurisdiction in the absence of a plain statement that the decision below rested on an adequate and independent state ground. It appears to us that the state court "felt compelled by what it understood to be federal constitutional considerations to construe * * * its own law in the manner it did." Zacchini v. Scripps-Howard Broadcasting Co., 433 U.S. 562, 568 (1977).[10]

III

[The Court held that the search was valid under Terry v. Ohio.]

IV

[The Court concluded that a remand was necessary to permit the Michigan Supreme Court to address a different federal constitutional question that that court had not resolved in its earlier decision.]

V

The judgment of the Michigan Supreme Court is reversed, and the case is remanded for further proceedings not inconsistent with this opinion.

It is so ordered.

■ JUSTICE BLACKMUN, concurring in part and concurring in the judgment.

I join Parts I, III, IV, and V of the Court's opinion. While I am satisfied that the Court has jurisdiction in this particular case, I do not join the Court, in Part II of its opinion, in fashioning a new presumption of jurisdiction over cases coming here from state courts. Although I agree with the Court that uniformity in federal criminal law is desirable, I see

---

[10] There is nothing unfair about requiring a plain statement of an independent state ground in this case. Even if we were to rest our decision on an evaluation of the state law relevant to Long's claim, as we have sometimes done in the past, our understanding of Michigan law would also result in our finding that we have jurisdiction to decide this case. Under state search and seizure law, a "higher standard" is imposed under art. 1, § 11 of the 1963 Michigan Constitution. See People v. Secrest, 413 Mich. 521, 525, 321 N.W.2d 368, 369 (1982). If, however, the item seized is, *inter alia*, a "narcotic drug * * * seized by a peace officer outside the curtilage of any dwelling house in this state," art. 1, § 11 of the 1963 Michigan Constitution, then the seizure is governed by a standard identical to that imposed by the Fourth Amendment. See People v. Moore, 391 Mich. 426, 435, 216 N.W.2d 770, 775 (1974). * * *

little efficiency and an increased danger of advisory opinions in the Court's new approach.

■ [JUSTICE BRENNAN, with whom JUSTICE MARSHALL joined, dissented on the merits of the Fourth Amendment issue. On the jurisdictional question, he said only: "I agree that the Court has jurisdiction to decide this case. See [footnote 10 of the Court's opinion]."]

■ JUSTICE STEVENS, dissenting.

The jurisprudential questions presented in this case are far more important than the question whether the Michigan police officer's search of respondent's car violated the Fourth Amendment. The case raises profoundly significant questions concerning the relationship between two sovereigns—the State of Michigan and the United States of America.

The Supreme Court of the State of Michigan expressly held "that the deputies' search of the vehicle was proscribed by the Fourth Amendment to the United States Constitution and *art 1, § 11 of the Michigan Constitution*." (Emphasis added). The state law ground is clearly adequate to support the judgment, but the question whether it is independent of the Michigan Supreme Court's understanding of federal law is more difficult. Four possible ways of resolving that question present themselves: (1) asking the Michigan Supreme Court directly, (2) attempting to infer from all possible sources of state law what the Michigan Supreme Court meant, (3) presuming that adequate state grounds are independent unless it clearly appears otherwise, or (4) presuming that adequate state grounds are *not* independent unless it clearly appears otherwise. This Court has, on different occasions, employed each of the first three approaches; never until today has it even hinted at the fourth. In order to "achieve the consistency that is necessary," the Court today undertakes a reexamination of all the possibilities. It rejects the first approach as inefficient and unduly burdensome for state courts, and rejects the second approach as an inappropriate expenditure of our resources. Although I find both of those decisions defensible in themselves, I cannot accept the Court's decision to choose the fourth approach over the third * * *.

If we reject the intermediate approaches, we are left with a choice between two presumptions: one in favor of our taking jurisdiction, and one against it. Historically, the latter presumption has always prevailed. See, *e.g.*, Durley v. Mayo, 351 U.S. 277, 285 (1956); Lynch v. New York ex rel. Pierson, 293 U.S. 52 (1934). The rule, as succinctly stated in Lynch, was as follows:

> "Where the judgment of the state court rests on two grounds, one involving a federal question and the other not, or if it does not appear upon which of two grounds the judgment was based, and the ground independent of a federal question is sufficient in itself to sustain it, this Court will not take jurisdiction." *Id.*, at 54–55.

The Court today points out that in several cases we have weakened the traditional presumption by using the other two intermediate approaches identified above. Since those two approaches are now to be rejected, however, I would think that *stare decisis* would call for a return to historical principle. Instead, the Court seems to conclude that because some precedents are to be rejected, we must overrule them all. * * *

The nature of the case before us hardly compels a departure from tradition. These are not cases in which an American citizen has been deprived of a right secured by the United States Constitution or a federal statute. Rather, they are cases in which a state court has upheld a citizen's assertion of a right, finding the citizen to be protected under both federal and state law. The attorney for the complaining party is an officer of the State itself, who asks us to rule that the state court interpreted federal rights too broadly and "overprotected" the citizen.

Such cases should not be of inherent concern to this Court. The reason may be illuminated by assuming that the events underlying this case had arisen in another country, perhaps the Republic of Finland. If the Finnish police had arrested a Finnish citizen for possession of marihuana, and the Finnish courts had turned him loose, no American would have standing to object. If instead they had arrested an American citizen and acquitted him, we might have been concerned about the arrest but we surely could not have complained about the acquittal, even if the Finnish court had based its decision on its understanding of the United States Constitution. That would be true even if we had a treaty with Finland requiring it to respect the rights of American citizens under the United States Constitution. We would only be motivated to intervene if an American citizen were unfairly arrested, tried, and convicted by the foreign tribunal.

In this case the State of Michigan * * * simply provided greater protection to one of its citizens than some other State might provide or, indeed, than this Court might require throughout the country.

I believe that in reviewing the decisions of state courts, the primary role of this Court is to make sure that persons who seek to *vindicate* federal rights have been fairly heard. That belief resonates with statements in many of our prior cases. * * *

Until recently we had virtually no interest in cases [like the present one]. Thirty years ago, this Court reviewed only one. Nevada v. Stacher, 346 U.S. 906 (1953). Indeed, that appears to have been the only case during the entire 1953 Term in which a State even sought review of a decision by its own judiciary. Fifteen years ago, we did not review any such cases, although the total number of requests had mounted to three. Some time during the past decade, * * * our priorities shifted. The result is a docket swollen with requests by States to reverse judgments that their courts have rendered in favor of their citizens.[3] I am confident that a future Court will recognize the error of this allocation of resources. When that day comes, I think it likely that the Court will also reconsider the propriety of today's expansion of our jurisdiction.

The Court offers only one reason for asserting authority over cases such as the one presented today: "an important need for uniformity in federal law [that] goes unsatisfied when we fail to review an opinion that rests primarily upon federal grounds and where the independence of an alleged state ground is not apparent from the four corners of the opinion" (emphasis omitted). Of course, the supposed need to "review an opinion" clashes directly with our oft-repeated reminder that "our power is to

_____

[3]   This Term, we devoted argument time to [twelve such cases], as well as this case. And a cursory survey of the United States Law Week index reveals that so far this Term at least 80 petitions for certiorari to state courts were filed by the States themselves.

correct wrong judgments, not to revise opinions." Herb v. Pitcairn, 324 U.S. 117, 126 (1945). The clash is not merely one of form; the "need for uniformity in federal law" is truly an ungovernable engine. That same need is no less present when it is perfectly clear that a state ground is both independent and adequate. In fact, it is equally present if a state prosecutor announces that he believes a certain policy of nonenforcement is commanded by federal law. Yet we have never claimed jurisdiction to correct such errors, no matter how egregious they may be, and no matter how much they may thwart the desires of the state electorate. We do not sit to expound our understanding of the Constitution to interested listeners in the legal community; we sit to resolve disputes. If it is not apparent that our views would affect the outcome of a particular case, we cannot presume to interfere.

Finally, I am thoroughly baffled by the Court's suggestion that it must stretch its jurisdiction and reverse the judgment of the Michigan Supreme Court in order to show "[r]espect for the independence of state courts." Would we show respect for the Republic of Finland by convening a special sitting for the sole purpose of declaring that its decision to release an American citizen was based upon a misunderstanding of American law?

I respectfully dissent.

NOTE ON REVIEW OF STATE DECISIONS UPHOLDING CLAIMS OF FEDERAL RIGHT

(1) Justice Stevens' Argument. Justice Stevens' dissent argues, quite apart from the problem of ambiguity (which is explored in the following Note), that the Court should not review state-court judgments that *uphold* claims of federal right.[1] He returned to this theme in his dissent in Delaware v. Van Arsdall, 475 U.S. 673 (1986), where the Court reviewed a Delaware decision that had found a violation of the Confrontation Clause of the Sixth Amendment. Agreeing that the federal Constitution had been violated, the Supreme Court nonetheless vacated the state court's judgment reversing the conviction. The Court concluded that (a) as a matter of federal law, the violation was not grounds for automatic reversal if the error was "harmless"; (b) the state court's reversal did not clearly rest on a state-law "automatic reversal" rule; and (c) the case should therefore be remanded to allow the state court to determine whether the error was "harmless" under federal standards.

Justice Stevens objected that this disposition "operates to expand this Court's review of state remedies that over-compensate for violations of federal constitutional rights", adding that "the claim of these cases on our docket is secondary to the need to scrutinize judgments disparaging those rights." He also complained that reviewing such cases puts pressure on the state courts to confine *state* constitutional protections to the level required by the federal Constitution, and noted that on remand the Delaware courts were free to apply an automatic reversal rule on the basis of state law. Despite these arguments, the Court has adhered to the position that it has

---

[1] In Minnesota v. Clover Leaf Creamery, 449 U.S. 456 (1981), and City of Revere v. Massachusetts Gen. Hosp., 463 U.S. 239 (1983), Justice Stevens voiced the same objection.

both the power and responsibility to review state court decisions that uphold individual claims of federal right. See, *e.g.*, Arkansas v. Sullivan, 532 U.S. 769, 772 (2001) (per curiam). For an extended defense of Justice Stevens' position, see Mazzone, *When the Supreme Court is Not Supreme*, 104 Nw.U.L.Rev. 979 (2010).

(2) The 1914 Expansion of Supreme Court Jurisdiction. As Justice Stevens acknowledged in Van Arsdall (but not in Long), the Judiciary Act of 1914 gave the Supreme Court power for the first time to review state court determinations upholding claims of federal right. See p. 462, *supra*. Justice Stevens described that Act as designed to permit the Supreme Court to review "Lochner-style" overenforcement of supposed federal limits on the states' power to enact social legislation. Is there a principled distinction between review in "Lochner-style" cases and in Long or Van Arsdall?

Or does the absence of review in cases of "overenforcement" before 1914 support the view (advanced by Justice Stevens in Van Arsdall) that the Court should adopt a systematic policy (as against the normal case-by-case operation of the certiorari practice) disfavoring review in such cases? If Justice Stevens' "low priority" approach is justified, should the Court, in its Rules, state that approach to be its policy—much as the Rules identify, for example, the priority assigned to reviewing cases involving conflicts among the lower courts?

(3) Uniformity Versus Federalism. The conventional wisdom is that a significant purpose of Article III (now implemented by § 1257) is to permit the Supreme Court to unify federal law by reviewing state court decisions of federal questions—a point stressed, for example, by Hamilton in Federalist No. 82 and by Justice Story in Martin v. Hunter's Lessee, see p. 464, *supra*. Assuming that to be the case,[2] how effectively can the Court play that role given that it rarely reviews state court decisions at all, much less those upholding claims of federal right? See p. 463, *supra*.

Beyond the uniformity problem lie other, deeper issues. Justice Stevens evidently assumes that the Constitution's guarantees of individual rights represent the only significant constitutional norms. Even were this true of the Bill of Rights and the other amendments when viewed in isolation, consider whether the Constitution as a whole "contains other sorts of values as well. It gives the federal government powers, but also enacts limitations on those powers. *The limitations, too, count as setting forth constitutional values.* * * * When a court upholds a state criminal statute against the claim that it violates the first amendment, it is rejecting one sort of constitutional claim, but it is also upholding principles of separation of powers and federalism which themselves have constitutional status." Bator, *The State Courts and Federal Constitutional Litigation*, 22 Wm. & Mary L.Rev. 605, 631–633 (1981). Does Justice Stevens' reference to Lochner illustrate these points?

Consider, also, the distinct point that states, when they complain of "overenforcement" of federal constitutional norms, often represent important individual or collective interests—as, for example, in Regents of the University of California v. Bakke, 438 U.S. 265, 279–80 (1978), where a state

---

[2]   Compare Frost, *Overvaluing Uniformity*, 94 Va.L.Rev. 1567, 1619–20 (2008), which argues that, "[a]t best, Article III appears to be neutral with regard to uniformity, and [that] several of its provisions can be read as antithetical to the idea that the federal judiciary was to devote significant resources to that project."

agency challenged a state court's invalidation under the federal Constitution of an affirmative action plan. See Shapiro, Federalism: A Dialogue 99–104 (1995). But see Sager, *Fair Measure: The Legal Status of Underenforced Constitutional Norms*, 91 Harv.L.Rev. 1212, 1242–63 (1978) (*inter alia*, urging the Stevens position while discussing a number of the objections to it).

(4) Supreme Court Review to "Unfreeze" State Political Processes. If a state's highest court provides broader protection of individual rights, under state statutory or constitutional provisions, than the federal Constitution demands, political actors in the state may express their disagreement by amending the state statute or constitution to be narrower. But some have objected that a state court judgment that the federal Constitution bars the state government from action, if unreviewable by the Supreme Court, would effectively freeze the law in that state (subject only to an amendment of the United States Constitution): no change in state law could overcome the decision. (The possibility that the state court would, in a subsequent case, reconsider and reverse its own judgment on the federal issue may be remote, as may be the possibility that the United States Supreme Court would review the same issue in a case from another state court that *denied* the same federal claim.) Would this be a tolerable situation?

Consider the concerns expressed by then-California Attorney General Deukmejian, who criticized his state's highest court for improperly insulating its decisions from any review by relying on state and federal grounds: the presence of a state ground bars Supreme Court review of the federal ground, while the presence of a federal ground makes futile, or at least discourages, popular review of the state law ground. See Deukmejian & Thompson, *All Sail and No Anchor—Judicial Review Under the California Constitution*, 6 Hast.Const.L.Q. 975, 996–97 (1979). Should the Court review such cases, even though reversal of the federal ground could not change the judgment below, in order to avoid "freezing" the state's political processes? Compare Bice, *Anderson and the Adequate State Ground*, 45 S.Cal.L.Rev. 750 (1972) (so arguing), with Falk, *The State Constitution: A More than "Adequate" Nonfederal Ground*, 61 Cal.L.Rev. 273 (1973) (criticizing the argument).

NOTE ON AMBIGUOUS STATE DECISIONS AND TECHNIQUES FOR CLARIFYING THEM

(1) Possible Approaches to Ambiguous State Court Judgments. When, as in Michigan v. Long, it is uncertain whether a state decision rested on a federal ground, a state ground, or both, the Court can (a) seek clarification from the state court (by vacating and remanding with a request for clarification);[1] (b) try to resolve the ambiguity itself by examining the

---

[1] See, *e.g.*, Philadelphia Newspapers, Inc. v. Jerome, 434 U.S. 241, 242 (1978); Minnesota v. National Tea Co., 309 U.S. 551, 556–57 (1940). Although rarely done, the Court might also hold the case or defer consideration of the petition for a writ of certiorari so that counsel can apply to the state court for a certificate as to whether its judgment was intended to rest on an adequate and independent state ground. See, *e.g.*, Lynum v. Illinois, 368 U.S. 908 (1961), 372 U.S. 528, 535–36 (1963) (consideration of certiorari petition deferred for counsel to seek certificate from state court; certificate treated as conclusive to establish jurisdiction); Herb v. Pitcairn, 324 U.S. 117, 128 (1945).

relevant state-law materials;[2] (c) dismiss on the ground that, in view of the ambiguity, the obligation affirmatively to establish jurisdiction has not been satisfied;[3] or (d) presume that the decision rested on a federal ground (the opposite stance from alternative "(c)"). Over the years, the Court oscillated among the first three alternatives; Long was the first time it embraced the fourth.

(2) The Alternative of Vacation. In Long, none of the Justices favored vacation and remand. Yet might that approach best serve the two concerns that Justice O'Connor identified as underlying the adequate and independent state ground doctrine—the avoidance of unnecessary decisions of federal law (especially federal constitutional law) and respect for the independence of state courts? See Minnesota v. National Tea Co., 309 U.S. 551, 557 (1940) (so arguing). As Justice Jackson famously contended, where the state court opinion is unclear, "it seems consistent with the respect due the highest courts of states of the Union that they be asked rather than told what they have intended. If this imposes an unwelcome burden it should be mitigated by the knowledge that it is to protect their jurisdiction from unwitting interference as well as to protect our own from unwitting renunciation." Herb v. Pitcairn, 324 U.S. 117, 128 (1945). Indeed, even though the Court in Long declined to vacate and remand for clarification, its decision nevertheless required the Michigan Supreme Court, on remand, to clarify the basis for its original decision in order to dispose of the case. Hence, if the Court wishes to avoid "advisory opinions" or, at least, unnecessary decisions of federal law, isn't vacation and remand superior to the Court's current position?

The principal problem with vacation and remand is that it causes delay. Given that the Supreme Court is not a court of errors, and given the purposes for which it exercises its certiorari jurisdiction, how serious is that problem?

(3) Other Justifications for Long. If one looks beyond respect for state courts and the avoidance of possibly unnecessary decisions, do any of the following arguments offer convincing justifications for the approach adopted in Long?

(a) The certiorari jurisdiction assumes that Supreme Court review should be provided not because it is "necessary" to resolve a particular dispute but rather to decide important issues of federal law. By increasing the number of cases eligible for review, Long maximizes the Court's flexibility in managing its docket and in finding the right vehicle for resolving important federal issues.

(b) Unlike most federal laws, the federal Constitution has not had a merely interstitial role; the federal Constitution is the primary protection of individual rights, and it remains so despite the recent invigoration of state constitutional guarantees. Thus, as a matter of probability, an ambiguous state court opinion is more likely to have rested on federal than on state

---

[2]   See, e.g., South Dakota v. Neville, 459 U.S. 553 (1983); Jankovich v. Indiana Toll Road Com'n, 379 U.S. 487 (1965); compare footnote 10 of the Court's opinion in Long. As early as Johnson v. Risk, 137 U.S. 300 (1890), the Court examined prior state decisions before concluding that a state court judgment (rendered without opinion) could have rested on the state statute of limitations; it added that the party seeking review, if claiming that a federal question was in fact dispositive, should have obtained a certificate to that effect from the state supreme court.

[3]   This was the approach of the earliest cases. See, e.g., Klinger v. Missouri, 80 U.S. (13 Wall.) 257 (1871); Eustis v. Bolles, 150 U.S. 361 (1893). See also, e.g., Lynch v. New York ex rel. Pierson, 293 U.S. 52, 54 (1934); Durley v. Mayo, 351 U.S. 277 (1956).

constitutional law. (Note, however, that Long appears to apply to all ambiguous state court decisions, not merely to those involving federal constitutional questions.)

(c) Long makes it more likely that, in order to avoid the possibility of reversal, state judges will clearly elaborate a state law ground when it exists. Since it is uniquely within the power of state courts to supply such clarity, does Long in effect operate as a penalty default rule—subjecting state court decisions to Supreme Court review unless they clearly articulate that the decision rests on an adequate and independent state ground? Compare Elhauge, Statutory Default Rules 151–53 (2008) (discussing such rules in the context of statutes).

(d) If the Court reversed the Long presumption and instead held that ambiguity about the basis for a state court decision precludes Supreme Court review, then state courts might be better able to evade accountability for their decisions. As Professors Vikram Amar and Alan Brownstein have written, in that hypothetical regime, "state courts * * * might fuzz up their opinions to foreclose U.S. Supreme Court reversal of results they favor, but at the same time invoke enough federal law to suggest—even when such federal law isn't really constraining—federal responsibility for the outcome of controversial disputes." Amar & Brownstein, *When Avoiding Federal Questions Shouldn't Evade Federal* Review, 12 Green Bag 2d 381, 384 (2009). Because an ambiguous state court decision *might* rest on federal grounds, "attempts by state electorates to amend their constitutions or to impose electoral sanctions on state court judges could be discouraged by the not-unrealistic possibility that the state law options were constrained by federal requirements." Does that concern seem substantial enough to sustain the Long presumption?

(4) The Meaning of Long. How significant a change in practice did Long introduce? Note that the application of Long's presumption depends on two "soft" requirements: the state decision must (a) "fairly appear" to rest "primarily" on federal law or be "interwoven" with federal law, *and* (b) the independence of the state ground must be "not clear" from the face of the state court opinion. These are not self-applying concepts. Subsequent decisions, however, have articulated the Long presumption more broadly than did the Long opinion.

(a) In Ohio v. Johnson, 467 U.S. 493, 497 n. 7 (1984), the Court stated Long's holding in the disjunctive: "we have jurisdiction * * * when the decision 'appears to rest primarily on federal law or to be interwoven with the federal law,' or if the 'adequacy and independence of any possible state law ground is not clear from the face of the opinion' " (emphasis added). Long said *and* rather than *or*. When might that difference in phrasing matter?

(b) In Pennsylvania v. Labron, 518 U.S. 938 (1996) (per curiam), the Court ruled that a state court opinion that rested on the state constitution but cited federal constitutional precedents did not contain "a 'plain statement' sufficient to tell us 'the federal cases [were] being used only for the purpose of guidance, and d[id] not themselves compel the result that the court had reached' " (quoting Long). Justice Stevens' dissent (joined by Justice Ginsburg) objected that the state court had not rested "primarily" on federal law, nor was its holding "interwoven" with federal law; thus the Court's ruling "extends Michigan v. Long beyond its original scope".

(5) Long and Judicial Discretion. Since Long, the Court has often accepted jurisdiction in the face of ambiguities in the state court opinion. However, does the Court's reservation of the right to seek clarification from the state court where "necessary or desirable" (see footnote 6 of the Long opinion) suggest that the underlying policy tensions responsible for prior oscillations could still overcome the effort to work out a uniform approach?

In Capital Cities Media, Inc. v. Toole, 466 U.S. 378 (1984) (per curiam), the Court reverted to the practice of vacating and remanding. There, a state trial judge had restricted media access to a criminal trial. The Supreme Court of Pennsylvania, without opinion, denied a media petition (based on the First Amendment) for a writ of prohibition—a decision that might have rested on the ground that Pennsylvania law did not permit appellate review via writ of prohibition. The United States Supreme Court, after noting that "the record does not disclose whether the Supreme Court of Pennsylvania passed on petitioners' federal claims or whether it denied their petition * * * on an adequate and independent state ground," vacated and remanded to the state court for clarification.

Can this shift in technique be explained by the different relationship between state and federal law in Long and in Capital Cities? In Long, state and federal constitutional provisions provided distinct grounds of relief. See p. 494, *supra*. In such cases, ambiguity about the presence of an adequate and independent state ground arises when the state court has upheld the position of the federal rightholder.

In Capital Cities, by contrast, the possible state ground (lack of jurisdiction to issue a writ of prohibition) was antecedent to the federal right. In such cases, ambiguity about the presence of an adequate and independent state ground arises when the state court has denied the relief sought by the federal rightholder.

The different approach followed in Capital Cities might seem to substantiate the many critics of Long who complained that the Burger Court, not generally known for its expansive view of federal jurisdiction, was extending Supreme Court jurisdiction in Long in order to permit review of a state court decision challenged as overprotecting federal rights.[4] By contrast, the Court refused to apply Long's broad view of jurisdiction in Capital Cities at the behest of a petitioner complaining that the state court failed to protect federal rights.

The Court has also shown unevenness in three post-Long decisions concerning federal habeas applications by state prisoners. The district courts' habeas jurisdiction, for present purposes, should be thought of as, in substance, a form of federal review of a state court conviction. But habeas jurisdiction, unlike Supreme Court review, is (a) as of right rather than discretionary, and (b) one way—*i.e.*, a prisoner in custody may challenge a conviction as in violation of the federal Constitution, but the state may not use habeas to complain that a state court decision overprotected federal rights. See generally Chap. XI, Sec. 3, *infra*.

---

[4]   Consider the statistics noted in Sager, p. 503, *supra*, at 1244: from 1960–69, the Supreme Court reviewed only eight cases in which state courts had upheld federal rights, affirming the state court in four of them; from 1970–78, the Court granted review in 25 such cases, affirming the state court in only one. See also Hellman, *Case Selection in the Burger Court: A Preliminary Inquiry*, 60 Notre Dame L.Rev. 947, 1044–46 (1985); Hellman, *The Shrunken Docket of the Rehnquist Court*, 1996 Sup.Ct.Rev. 403.

Initially, the Court in Harris v. Reed, 489 U.S. 255 (1989), indicated that Long would apply in federal habeas proceedings to determine whether an ambiguous state court ruling had rested on a state prisoner's procedural default or on a rejection of the federal constitutional merits in denying postconviction relief. (If so, under established habeas rules, the prisoners would ultimately be barred from asserting their defaulted claims, subject only to extremely narrow exceptions.) In so holding, Justice Blackmun's opinion for the Court in Harris rejected the contention that heightened interests in "finality, federalism, and comity" counseled against extending Long to this context. The Court noted that the Long presumption would impose only a minimal burden on state courts (articulating a clear basis for their decision), but that a different rule would impose significant costs on federal habeas courts (sifting through state-court records to determine if a procedural default was asserted and/or researching state law to determine the potential existence of a procedural default). Justice Kennedy dissented, contending that it was not realistic to expect judges in lower state courts to internalize Long's plain statement rule and that the Court's approach would encourage prisoners "to burden state courts with a never-ending stream of petitions for postconviction relief."

Although Harris has never been overruled, the Court's subsequent habeas decisions appear to have significantly diluted its force by making it easier for the state to establish that an ambiguous state court decision rested on a finding of procedural default. See, *e.g.*, Coleman v. Thompson, 501 U.S. 722 (1991) (refusing to apply the Harris presumption in a capital case where the state court order dismissing a petition for postconviction relief "fairly appear[ed]" to rest primarily on state law because it did not mention federal law and because the motion to dismiss had relied solely on the tardiness of a notice of appeal to the state trial court); Ylst v. Nunnemaker, 501 U.S. 797 (1991) (announcing, in an another capital case, the presumption that where the last reasoned state court opinion on a federal question rested on a finding of procedural default, subsequent state court summary orders denying relief also relied on the default rather than the merits, even if the orders and their surrounding circumstances gave no indication of such reliance).

Does the pattern described in this Paragraph suggest that jurisdictional rules tend to move in the direction of allowing more intensive supervision of areas where the Supreme Court is in the process of changing the relevant substantive rules and wants to assure itself that the state courts are in compliance?

(6) The Importance of Long? Many commentators reacted to the Long decision with hostility.[5] But in the end, how important is Long, given that a state court that in fact relies on state law can, by simply so stating, avoid Supreme Court review? While many post-Long state court decisions fail to

---

[5] See, *e.g.*, Matasar & Bruch, *Procedural Common Law, Federal Jurisdictional Policy, and Abandonment of the Adequate and Independent State Grounds Doctrine*, 86 Colum.L.Rev. 1291, 1367–82 (1986); Seid, *Schizoid Federalism, Supreme Court Power and Inadequate Adequate State Ground Theory: Michigan v. Long*, 18 Creighton L.Rev. 1 (1984); Welsh, *Reconsidering the Constitutional Relationship Between State and Federal Courts: A Critique of Michigan v. Long*, 59 Notre Dame L.Rev. 1118 (1984). For more favorable treatments, see Althouse, *How to Build a Separate Sphere: Federal Courts and State Power*, 100 Harv.L.Rev. 1485 (1987); Baker, *The Ambiguous Independent and Adequate State Ground in Criminal Cases: Federalism Along a Möbius Strip*, 19 Ga.L.Rev. 799 (1985); Redish, *Supreme Court Review of State Court "Federal" Decisions: A Study in Interactive Federalism*, 19 Ga.L.Rev. 861 (1985); Solimine, *Supreme Court Monitoring of State Courts in the Twenty-First Century*, 35 Ind.L.Rev. 335 (2002).

indicate clearly whether they rest on state or federal grounds (why do you think such ambiguity persists?), the New Hampshire Supreme Court routinely adds a declaration like the following: "when this court cites federal or other State court opinions in construing provisions of the New Hampshire Constitution or statutes, we rely on those precedents merely for guidance and do not consider our results bound by those decisions. See Michigan v. Long * * *." See, *e.g.*, State v. Ball, 471 A.2d 347, 352 (N.H.1983); see generally Gardner, *The Failed Discourse of State Constitutionalism*, 90 Mich.L.Rev. 761, 785–88, 801, 803–04 (1992).

Even when the Supreme Court does review an ambiguous decision and reverses on the federal issue, the state courts retain the power on remand to consider independent state-law grounds and, indeed, to rely on such grounds in reinstating their initial judgment. Of course, there is always the possibility that a Supreme Court decision on the merits of the federal issue might influence the state court's resolution, on remand, of an uncertain question of state constitutional law. For example, in See v. Commonwealth, 746 S.W.2d 401, 402 (Ky.1988), a criminal defendant claimed a violation of a constitutional right to confrontation that the Kentucky Supreme Court had recognized as a matter of federal law in a prior decision that in turn had been reversed by the Supreme Court. On remand, the state court recognized that it remained free under the Kentucky Constitution to uphold the claimed right, but, in refusing to do so, stated that it was "not convinced that the [alleged error] is so violative of a basic right guaranteed by the Kentucky Constitution that we should place ourselves in direct opposition to an opinion of the United States Supreme Court".

(7) State Incorporation of Federal Law. The discussion so far has assumed that, however ambiguous a state court opinion may be, the content of state law does not depend on the content of federal law. But when a state court believes that its interpretation of a state constitutional or statutory provision is compelled by federal law, it would be difficult to regard that determination as an "independent" state ground. In Delaware v. Prouse, 440 U.S. 648 (1979), for example, the state supreme court affirmed the trial court's suppression of evidence after finding a violation of both the Fourth Amendment and the Delaware Constitution. On certiorari, the Supreme Court upheld its jurisdiction: "As we understand the opinion below, Art I, § 6, of the Delaware Constitution will automatically be interpreted at least as broadly as the Fourth Amendment; that is, every police practice authoritatively determined to be contrary to the Fourth and Fourteenth Amendments will, without further analysis, be held to be contrary to Art. I, § 6." In Prouse the state supreme court had done no more than give effect to what it perceived to be the compulsion of federal law.

In Prouse, the Fourth Amendment applied to the case of its own force, without regard to the content of state law. But sometimes federal law applies only because the state has gratuitously adopted federal criteria as the touchstone for the meaning of a state law. In such a case of gratuitous incorporation, what is the federal interest in reviewing the state court's (mis)interpretation? Consider some examples. If a state income tax statute piggybacked, as many do, on the federal definition of taxable income, does every question of taxable income in state tax returns present a reviewable federal question? Or if a state adopted as its rules of civil procedure the Federal Rules of Civil Procedure and indicated that they should be interpreted in the same fashion, would every interpretation of a state rule present a reviewable federal question? For the suggestion that in all such cases, the Court has an "implicit power to choose" whether the case is reviewable in light of "the strength of the federal interest", see Shapiro, *Jurisdiction and Discretion*, 60 N.Y.U.L.Rev. 543, 565 (1985). For a narrower conception of the authority of the Court to review state incorporation of federal law, see Greene, *Hybrid State Law in the Federal Courts*, 83 Harv.L.Rev. 289, 321 (1969) (suggesting that Supreme Court review of state law incorporating federal law is warranted "where harmonization of state and federal law serves federal objectives" or "where the state has determined to act to the full extent of its constitutional powers, thus transmuting every question of state law into a constitutional issue").[6]

To the extent that the Supreme Court can review the state court's determination of federal law when a question of state law turns on that interpretation, it does not necessarily follow that such claims fall within the arising-under jurisdiction of the district courts. See Chap. VIII, Sec. 3, considering issues of federal law embedded in state law claims.

INTRODUCTORY NOTE ON STATE LAW ANTECEDENTS TO FEDERAL RIGHTS

Indiana ex. rel. Anderson v. Brand, which arises under the Contract Clause, exemplifies the distinctive issues that can be presented when federal law protects interests created *primarily* by state law. Prominent examples include liberty and property interests, which the Fourteenth Amendment protects against deprivation without due process, and property interests, which the Takings Clause protects against taking without just compensation.

Indiana ex rel. Anderson v. Brand

303 U.S. 95, 58 S.Ct. 443, 82 L.Ed. 685 (1938).
Certiorari to the Supreme Court of Indiana.

■ MR. JUSTICE ROBERTS delivered the opinion of the Court.

The petitioner sought a writ of mandate to compel the respondent to continue her in employment as a public school teacher. Her complaint alleged that as a duly licensed teacher she entered into a contract in September, 1924, to teach in the township schools and, pursuant to successive contracts, taught continuously to and including the school year 1932–1933; that her contracts for the school years 1931–1932 and 1932–1933 contained this clause: "It is further agreed by the contracting parties that all of the provisions of the Teachers' Tenure Law, approved March 8, 1927, shall be in full force and effect in this contract"; and that

---

[6] Sometimes a state court's interpretation of state law is influenced by a misconception about federal law, even if state law has not formally incorporated the federal provision—and in such cases, a correct Supreme Court resolution of the federal issue will permit the state court on remand to provide a sound interpretation of state law, free from any misconception. Consider, *e.g.*, Ohio v. Reiner, 532 U.S. 17 (2001) (per curiam); Three Affiliated Tribes v. Wold Engineering, P.C., 467 U.S. 138 (1984); St. Martin Evangelical Lutheran Church v. South Dakota, 451 U.S. 772 (1981).

by force of that Act she had a contract, indefinite in duration, which could be canceled by the respondent only in the manner and for the causes specified in the Act. She charged that in July, 1933, the respondent notified her he proposed to cancel her contract for cause; that, after a hearing, he adhered to his decision and the County Superintendent affirmed his action; that, despite what occurred in July, 1933, the petitioner was permitted to teach during the school year 1933–1934 and the respondent was presently threatening to terminate her employment at the end of that year. The complaint alleged the termination of her employment would be a breach of her contract with the school corporation. The respondent demurred on the grounds that (1) the complaint disclosed the matters pleaded had been submitted to the respondent and the County Superintendent who were authorized to try the issues and had lawfully determined them in favor of the respondent; and (2) the Teachers' Tenure Law had been repealed in respect of teachers in township schools. The demurrer was sustained and the petitioner appealed to the State Supreme Court which affirmed the judgment. The court did not discuss the first ground of demurrer * * *, but rested its decision upon the second, that, by an act of 1933, the Teachers' Tenure Law had been repealed as respects teachers in township schools; and held that the repeal did not deprive the petitioner of a vested property right and did not impair her contract within the meaning of the Constitution. * * *

The court below holds that in Indiana teachers' contracts are made for but one year; that there is no contractual right to be continued as a teacher from year to year; that the law grants a privilege to one who has taught five years and signed a new contract to continue in employment under given conditions; that the statute is directed merely to the exercise of their powers by the school authorities and the policy therein expressed may be altered at the will of the legislature; that in enacting laws for the government of public schools, the legislature exercises a function of sovereignty and the power to control public policy in respect of their management and operation cannot be contracted away by one legislature so as to create a permanent public policy unchangeable by succeeding legislatures. In the alternative the court declares that if the relationship be considered as controlled by the rules of private contract the provision for re-employment from year to year is unenforceable for want of mutuality.

As in most cases brought to this court under the contract clause of the Constitution, the question is as to the existence and nature of the contract and not as to the construction of the law which is supposed to impair it. The principal function of a legislative body is not to make contracts but to make laws which declare the policy of the state and are subject to repeal when a subsequent legislature shall determine to alter that policy. Nevertheless, it is established that a legislative enactment may contain provisions which, when accepted as the basis of action by individuals, become contracts between them and the State or its subdivisions within the protection of Art. 1, § 10. If the people's representatives deem it in the public interest they may adopt a policy of contracting in respect of public business for a term longer than the life of the current session of the Legislature. This the petitioner claims has been done with respect to permanent teachers. The Supreme Court [of

Indiana] has decided, however, that it is the state's policy not to bind school corporations by contract for more than one year.

On such a question, one primarily of state law, we accord respectful consideration and great weight to the views of the state's highest court but, in order that the constitutional mandate may not become a dead letter, we are bound to decide for ourselves whether a contract was made, what are its terms and conditions, and whether the State has, by later legislation, impaired its obligation. This involves an appraisal of the statutes of the State and the decisions of its courts.

Deference, yet reviewable

The courts of Indiana have long recognized that the employment of school teachers was contractual and have afforded relief in actions upon teachers' contracts. * * *

In 1927, the State adopted the Teachers' Tenure Act under which the present controversy arises. * * * By this Act it was provided that a teacher who has served under contract for five or more successive years, and thereafter enters into a contract for further service with the school corporation, shall become a permanent teacher and the contract, upon the expiration of its stated term, shall be deemed to continue in effect for an indefinite period * * * and shall remain in force unless succeeded by a new contract or canceled as provided in the Act. The corporation may cancel the contract, after notice and hearing, for incompetency, insubordination, neglect of duty, immorality, justifiable decrease in the number of teaching positions, or other good or just cause, but not for political or personal reasons. The teacher may not cancel the contract during the school term nor for a period of thirty days previous to the beginning of any term (unless by mutual agreement) and may cancel only upon five days' notice.

By an amendatory Act of 1933 township school corporations were omitted from the provisions of the Act of 1927. The court below construed this Act as repealing the Act of 1927 so far as township schools and teachers are concerned and as leaving the respondent free to terminate the petitioner's employment. But we are of opinion that the petitioner had a valid contract with the respondent, the obligation of which would be impaired by the termination of her employment.

Where the claim is that the State's policy embodied in a statute is to bind its instrumentalities by contract, the cardinal inquiry is as to the terms of the statute supposed to create such a contract. The State long prior to the adoption of the Act of 1927 required the execution of written contracts between teachers and school corporations * * *. These were annual contracts, covering a single school term. The Act of 1927 announced a new policy that a teacher who had served for five years under successive contracts, upon the execution of another was to become a permanent teacher and the last contract was to be indefinite as to duration and terminable by either party only upon compliance with the conditions set out in the statute. The policy which induced the legislation evidently was that the teacher should have protection against the exercise of the right, which would otherwise inhere in the employer, of terminating the employment at the end of any school term without assigned reasons and solely at the employer's pleasure. The state courts in earlier cases so declared.

History of Tenure

The title of the Act is couched in terms of contract. It speaks of the making and cancelling of indefinite contracts. In the body the word "contract" appears ten times in § 1, defining the relationship; eleven times in § 2, relating to the termination of the employment by the employer, and four times in § 4, stating the conditions of termination by the teacher.

The tenor of the act indicates that the word "contract" was not used inadvertently or in other than its usual legal meaning. By § 6 it is expressly provided that the act is a supplement to that of March 7, 1921, requiring teachers' employment contracts to be in writing. By § 1 it is provided that the written contract of a permanent teacher "shall be deemed to continue in effect for an indefinite period and shall be known as an indefinite contract." Such an indefinite contract is to remain in force unless succeeded by a new contract signed by both parties or cancelled as provided in § 2. No more apt language could be employed to define a contractual relationship. By § 2 it is enacted that such indefinite contracts may be cancelled by the school corporation only in the manner specified. The admissible grounds of cancellation, and the method by which the existence of such grounds shall be ascertained and made a matter of record, are carefully set out. Section 4 permits cancellation by the teacher only at certain times consistent with the convenient administration of the school system and imposes a sanction for violation of its requirements. Examination of the entire act convinces us that the teacher was by it assured of the possession of a binding and enforceable contract against school districts.

Until its decision in the present case the Supreme Court of the State had uniformly held that the teacher's right to continued employment by virtue of the indefinite contract created pursuant to the act was contractual. [The opinion here reviews four decisions of the Indiana Supreme Court explicitly referring to teachers' contractual rights and indicating that mandamus to compel reinstatement was available.]

We think the decision in this case runs counter to the policy evinced by the Act of 1927, to its explicit mandate and to earlier decisions construing its provisions. * * *

The respondent urges that every contract is subject to the police power and that in repealing the Teachers' Tenure Act the legislature validly exercised that reserved power of the state. The sufficient answer is found in the statute. By § 2 of the Act of 1927 power is given to the school corporation to cancel a teacher's indefinite contract for incompetency, insubordination (which is to be deemed to mean wilful refusal to obey the school laws of the State or reasonable rules prescribed by the employer), neglect of duty, immorality, justifiable decrease in the number of teaching positions or other good and just cause. The permissible reasons for cancellation cover every conceivable basis for such action growing out of a deficient performance of the obligations undertaken by the teacher, and diminution of the school requirements. Although the causes specified constitute in themselves just and reasonable grounds for the termination of any ordinary contract of employment, to preclude the assumption that any other valid ground was excluded by the enumeration, the legislature added that the relation might be terminated for any other good and just cause. Thus in the declaration of the state's policy, ample reservations in aid of the efficient administration of the school system were made. * * * It is significant that the Act of 1933 left the system of permanent teachers and indefinite contracts untouched as respects school corporations in cities and towns of the state.* * *

Our decisions recognize that every contract is made subject to the implied condition that its fulfillment may be frustrated by a proper exercise of the police power but we have repeatedly said that, in order to have this effect, the exercise of the power must be for an end which is in fact public and the means adopted must be reasonably adapted to that end, and the Supreme Court of Indiana has taken the same view in respect of legislation impairing the obligation of the contract of a state instrumentality. The causes of cancellation provided in the Act of 1927 and the retention of the system of indefinite contracts in all municipalities except townships by the Act of 1933 are persuasive that the repeal of the earlier Act by the latter was not an exercise of the police power for the attainment of ends to which its exercise may properly be directed.

As the court below has not passed upon one of the grounds of demurrer which appears to involve no federal question, and may present a defense still open to the respondent, we reverse the judgment and remand the cause for further proceedings not inconsistent with this opinion.

Reversed.

■ MR. JUSTICE CARDOZO took no part in the consideration or decision of this case.

■ MR. JUSTICE BLACK, dissenting. * * *

The Indiana Supreme Court has consistently held, even before its decision in this case, that the right of teachers, under the 1927 Act, to serve until removed for cause, was *not given by contract, but by statute.* Such was the express holding in the two cases cited in the majority opinion * * *.

* * * In order to hold in this case that a contract was impaired, it is necessary to create a contract unauthorized by the Indiana Legislature and declared to be non-existent by the Indiana Supreme Court. * * *

The clear purport of Indiana law is that its legislature cannot surrender any part of its plenary constitutional right to repeal, alter or amend existing legislation relating to the school system whenever the conditions demand change for the public good. Under Indiana law the legislature can neither barter nor give away its constitutional investiture of power. * * * The construction of the constitution of Indiana by the Supreme Court of Indiana *must be accepted as correct.* That court * * * has here held that the legislature did not attempt or intend to surrender its constitutional power by authorizing *definite* contracts which would prevent the future exercise of this continuing, constitutional power. If the constitution and statutes of Indiana, as construed by its Supreme Court, prohibit the legislature from making a contract which is inconsistent with a continuing power to legislate, there could have been no *definite* contracts to be impaired. * * *

NOTE ON FEDERAL PROTECTION OF STATE-CREATED RIGHTS

How should the Supreme Court treat decisions involving federal interests established primarily or even exclusively by state law? At one extreme, one can imagine an approach under which the existence of a protected interest, for purposes of a particular federal provision, is defined by *federal* law; under that approach, the existence of a contract for purposes of the Contract Clause would be a matter of federal law. At the other extreme, the existence of a protected interest like a contractual right would depend only upon whether state law recognizes it. An intermediate approach, which Professor Merrill has called a "patterning definition" strategy, first establishes federal criteria that a protected interest must satisfy to merit federal protection, and then examines state law to determine if such an interest has been created. See generally Merrill, *The Landscape of Constitutional Property*, 86 Va.L.Rev. 885 (2000).

Which of these approaches (or which combination of them) is followed in a particular setting is a matter of interpretation of the federal provision that is the source of protection (in Brand, for example, the Contract Clause). But the choice of approach, once made, plainly affects the scope of review. For example, insofar as the federally protected interests are defined entirely by federal law, the Supreme Court would presumably engage in de novo review of a state court's determination whether a protected interest exists. Insofar as the existence of a protected interest depends only upon state law, a state court determination would presumably be reviewed more deferentially. The intermediate, patterning definition approach might involve de novo review of the content of the federal criteria and deferential review of a state court's determination whether those criteria have been satisfied.

Note that federal constitutional provisions may also protect liberty or property interests created by *federal* statutory law. For example, the Takings Clause or the Due Process Clause might provide protection against a statute or other government action that threatens a patent or other intellectual property rights that are created by federal statutes. Cases involving rights created by federal statute are considered here only insofar as they shed light on the primary focus of this material, which is Supreme Court review of state court judgments involving state-created entitlements.

With that background, consider the following materials.

A.   The Contract Clause

(1) Choice of Law and Scope of Review. The question whether an acknowledged contractual obligation has been impaired, within the meaning of the Contract Clause, involves only interpretation of the Constitution. See, *e.g.*, El Paso v. Simmons, 379 U.S. 497, 506–08 (1965); Wright, The Contract Clause of the Constitution (1938); Hale, *The Supreme Court and the Contract Clause*, 57 Harv.L.Rev. 512, 621, 852 (1944).

But whose law governs the antecedent question whether there was a contract in the first place? The Brand opinion says that "the existence and nature of the contract" claimed to be impaired is a question "primarily of state law".[1]

Note that the key question under the Contract Clause is not what state law currently *is* but rather what it *was* in the past. And because the Clause

---

[1] Accord, Ogden v. Saunders, 25 U.S. 213, 256–59, 326 (1827); Appleby v. City of New York, 271 U.S. 364, 380 (1926).

prohibits impairment only by legislation, not by judicial decision, see Frankfurter & Landis, The Business of the Supreme Court 199–202 (1928), the critical time for judging whether an obligation existed would seem to be when the allegedly impairing legislation was enacted. The Court, however, appears to have emphasized the date of the agreement. See, *e.g.*, El Paso v. Simmons, *supra*. Does that explain why in Brand the Supreme Court did not accept the Indiana court's determination? Is a state court less authoritative an expositor of what state law was than of what it now is?

Brand affirms an "independent judgment" rule, but as the Court noted, it usually accords respectful weight to the state court's determination. Does independent review that accords great weight to the state court's views differ from limited review of the state court's decision for obvious error? Compare Hale v. Iowa State Bd., 302 U.S. 95, 101 (1937), where the Court said that it would accept the state court's judgment as to "the effect and meaning of the contract as well as its existence * * * unless manifestly wrong." Can a state court be "manifestly wrong" on a matter primarily involving state law absent earlier decisions setting forth a different view?

In General Motors Corp. v. Romein, 503 U.S. 181 (1992), the Court, in reviewing a state court determination that no contract existed, seemed to take a further step away from reliance on state law: "The question whether a contract was made is a federal question for purposes of Contract Clause analysis, * * * and 'whether it turns on issues of general or purely local law, we cannot surrender the duty to exercise our own judgment' " (quoting Appleby v. City of New York, 271 U.S. 364, 380 (1926)). At the same time, the Court in Romein acknowledged the "great weight" that it accords to— and in the end "saw no reason to disagree with"—the state court's views. Isn't it difficult to justify the view that the existence of a contract is governed only by federal law? Are the federal courts in a position to formulate a complete body of federal contract law for purposes of the Contract Clause? And should the question whether a particular contract creates an obligation be governed by one set of rules (state law) in a suit for breach and by another (federal law) in litigation under the Contract Clause? *Cf.* the discussion of Murdock v. Memphis, p. 477, *supra*.

(2) Brand and Murdock. How can the Supreme Court's willingness in the Brand case to review a state court's determination of an issue of state law be squared with Murdock v. Memphis? Note that in Brand, as in Martin v. Hunter's Lessee, state law is antecedent to the claim for relief under federal law, whereas in Murdock, state and federal law provided distinct avenues for the relief sought. See pp. 487–488, *supra*.

(3) Review of Decisions Upholding Contractual Obligations. In United States Mortgage Co. v. Matthews, 293 U.S. 232 (1934), the state court affirmed that a contractual obligation existed as a matter of state law and proceeded to invalidate the alleged impairment. The Supreme Court reversed, finding no contractual obligation. When the state court's determination poses no threat to the enforcement of federal rights, what justifies Supreme Court review of that determination? See Monaghan, *Of Liberty and Property*, 62 Cornell L.Rev. 405, 436 n. 201 (1977).

B. The Due Process and Takings Clauses

More complex is the question of whose law governs the existence of property or liberty interests that are protected by the Fifth or Fourteenth

Amendments against deprivation without due process or (in the case of property) against a taking without just compensation.

(1) "Old Property." The early cases involved traditional ("old") property interests. In Demorest v. City Bank Farmers Trust Co., 321 U.S. 36 (1944), the claimants argued that a New York statute retroactively deprived them of a property right, in violation of the Due Process Clause, by allocating to the income beneficiaries of a trust certain proceeds of mortgage salvage operations that, under prior case law, would have been apportioned to the remaindermen. A divided New York Court of Appeals sustained the statute, denying that those holding remainder interests in fact enjoyed, prior to enactment of the statute, the property interest they alleged. In affirming, the Supreme Court (per Jackson, J.) concluded that even when the claim of constitutional deprivation turned on a determination of state law, the Court's role was merely "to inquire whether the decision of the state court rests upon a fair or substantial basis." The Court added that "if there is no evasion of the constitutional issue, . . . and the nonfederal ground of decision has fair support, . . . this Court will not inquire whether the rule applied by the state court is right or wrong".[2] Is that approach consistent with the approach in Brand to determining whether a contractual right existed?

A plurality opinion by Justice Scalia (joined by Chief Justice Roberts and Justices Thomas and Alito) in Stop the Beach Renourishment, Inc. v. Florida Department of Environmental Protection, 560 U.S. 702 (2010), struck what seems to be a middle position between Brand and Demorest. At issue was whether Florida's filling in of state-owned submerged lands to restore previous erosion deprived riparian property owners of their common law right to any natural accretions that might have accrued to their property in the absence of the state-owned landfill. The Florida Supreme Court held that the statute that mandated the filling did not take the beach owners' property because a competing common law doctrine of avulsion allowed the state to reclaim restored beach land on behalf of the public.

In reviewing the state court's decision, the plurality addressed the state's contention that the U.S. Supreme Court should not find a taking unless the state court decision lacked a "fair and substantial basis." The plurality noted that "we make our own determination, without deference to state judges, whether the challenged decision deprives the claimant of an established property right" and that this was part and parcel of the Court's more general obligation to determine "state-court compliance with *all* constitutional imperatives." Still, the plurality added, one could expect "a considerable degree of deference to state courts", in practice, under a test asking whether the state court decision resulted in the "deprivation of an *established* property right". As the plurality elaborated, no property right can be "established if there is doubt about its existence; and when there is doubt we do not make our own assessment but accept the determination of the state court."

Justice Kennedy (joined by Justice Sotomayor) and Justice Breyer (joined by Justice Ginsburg) wrote separately to express disagreement with the plurality on a different point. But all eight participating Justices (Justice Stevens did not participate) joined the part of Justice Scalia's opinion holding that the Florida Supreme Court had not effected a taking of property because

---

[2]   See also Muhlker v. New York & Harlem R.R., 197 U.S. 544 (1905); Sauer v. New York, 206 U.S. 536 (1907); Fox River Paper Co. v. R.R. Comm'n of Wisconsin, 274 U.S. 651 (1927).

"[t]he Takings Clause only protects property rights as they are established under state law," and "[w]e cannot say that the Florida Supreme Court's decision eliminated a right of accretion established under Florida law." Does Stop the Beach's insistence upon identifying an "established" property interest under state law provide a way of reconciling Brand and Demorest? How does the Court's approach in Stop the Beach compare with its treatment of the Contract Clause question in General Motors Corp. v. Romein, Paragraph (1), *supra*?

(2) "New" Property and Liberty. Most of the recent decisions involve alleged deprivations of so-called "new property" interests or of analogous liberty interests—when, for example, the government fires an employee, denies an individual social welfare benefits, or disadvantages a prisoner (for example, by denial of parole or transfer to less desirable conditions of confinement).[3] Where a protected "property" or "liberty" interest exists, federal law governs the questions (i) whether there has been a deprivation, and (ii) if so, whether due process was afforded. The more complicated issue is whose law governs the determination whether, in the first instance, a protected interest exists.

    (a) Property Interests. The Supreme Court has held that state law generally governs the question whether a "property" interest exists. In Board of Regents v. Roth, 408 U.S. 564 (1972), a state university teacher alleged that the failure to re-appoint him at the end of his one-year term, without a statement of reasons or a hearing, deprived him of property without due process of law. In rejecting that claim, the Court stated: "Property interests, of course, are not created by the Constitution. Rather they are created and their dimensions are defined by existing rules or understandings that stem from an independent source such as state law". Because nothing in the plaintiff's appointment, any state statute, or any university policy or rule created any legitimate claim to reemployment, the Court found that "he did not have a *property* interest sufficient to require the University authorities to give him a hearing". Compare, *e.g.*, Memphis Light, Gas & Water Div. v. Craft, 436 U.S. 1, 9–12 (1978) (holding that a state law prohibiting the termination of utility service except "for cause" created a property interest in the non-termination of such service).[4]

---

    [3]   See generally Merrill, p. 514, *supra*; Farina, *Conceiving Due Process*, 3 Yale J.L. & Feminism 189 (1991); Monaghan, Paragraph A(3), *supra*; Van Alstyne, *Cracks in "The New Property": Adjudicative Due Process in the Administrative State*, 62 Cornell L.Rev. 445 (1977); Herman, *The New Liberty*, 59 N.Y.U.L.Rev. 482 (1984).

    [4]   Even where state law itself creates a "new property" interest, the Court has made clear that the state cannot qualify the resultant interest by specifying in advance that it may impaired as long as certain procedures are followed. Compare Arnett v. Kennedy, 416 U.S. 134 (1974) (plurality opinion) (arguing that a new property holder must "take the bitter with the sweet"), with Cleveland Bd. of Educ. v. Loudermill, 470 U.S. 532 (1985) (8–1) (repudiating the bitter-with-the-sweet test and noting that state law defines the property interest but the Due Process Clause determines the procedural requirements for the deprivation). By the same token, because the procedures prescribed by state law do not define the *scope* of a liberty or property interest, a claimant cannot establish a due process violation merely by showing that the state has not complied with such procedures. In Swarthout v. Cooke, 562 U.S. 216 (2011) (per curiam), a prisoner filed a federal habeas petition alleging that the California state parole board had improperly denied his application for parole and that the state court had misapplied the state law standard of review requiring "some evidence" for the board's determinations. Treating the "some evidence" standard as a "component" of the state-created liberty interest in parole, the Ninth Circuit held that the state courts' failure to apply that standard denied the petitioner due process. The Supreme Court reversed, explaining that while the liberty interest at stake was the product of state law, the process due depended upon federal constitutional law, and not upon

In Webb's Fabulous Pharmacies, Inc. v. Beckwith, 449 U.S. 155 (1980), however, the Court held that state law is not the sole determinant of property interests under the Due Process Clause. Webb's involved the issue of whether there was a property interest supporting a claim under the Takings Clause. The lawsuit alleged that a Florida statute, which authorized a county to take the interest accruing on an interpleader fund deposited in state court, constituted a taking of property from the claimants to the fund. The state court held that under the statute the interest was the property of the county, not of the claimants. The Supreme Court reversed. It acknowledged (citing Roth) that property rights are created not by the Constitution but by an independent source like state law. The Court, however, proceeded to cite numerous cases from jurisdictions other than Florida as supporting the proposition that, in the circumstances presented, the interest belonged to the claimants. Without examining Florida law further, the Court ruled that "a State, by *ipse dixit*, may not transform private property into public property without compensation".

Does Webb's Fabulous Pharmacies suggest that, despite Roth, there is a core conception of "property" in the Due Process or Takings Clause that state law must respect? For an affirmative answer, see Monaghan, Paragraph A(3), *supra*, at 440; Fallon, *Some Confusions About Due Process, Judicial Review, and Constitutional Remedies*, 93 Colum.L.Rev. 309, 328–29 (1993). Does the same idea of constitutional constraint apply in the other direction—that is, are there federally derived constraints on what a state can recognize as a property right?[5] Professor Fallon argues that "no constitutional value typically precludes a state from choosing as expansive a conception [of property] as it may wish; a state court that found a 'property' interest in a public employee's job, under circumstances in which the federal Constitution would not compel that characterization, should be deemed to commit no constitutional error." If property is merely whatever "bundle of sticks" finds recognition in state law, doesn't Fallon's point have considerable force? On the other hand, could affording constitutional protection to whatever entitlement a state creates, no matter how unimportant, give rise to a flood of due process claims asserting the deprivation of quite trivial interests?

(b) Liberty Interests. The respective roles of state and federal law in defining entitlements are at least as complicated in cases involving "liberty" as in those involving "property". Significant authority recognizes a federal constitutional dimension to liberty, quite apart from entitlements based on positive law. Thus, without referring to state law, the Court has recognized a liberty interest of a student in freedom from corporal punishment, see Ingraham v. Wright, 430 U.S. 651 (1977), of a parent in not having parental rights terminated, see Santosky v. Kramer, 455 U.S. 745, 754 (1982), and of

---

state-law criteria. To treat state procedure as a judicially enforceable component of the resultant liberty interest, the Court explained, "would subject to federal-court merits review the application of all state-prescribed procedures in cases involving liberty or property interests, including (of course) those in criminal prosecutions." This, the Court added, would contradict the settled principle that violations of state law do not necessarily violate the federal requirements of due process.

[5]   *Cf.* Town of Castle Rock v. Gonzales, 545 U.S. 748 (2005) (7–2) (holding that given the public and traditionally discretionary character of law enforcement, a state court restraining order did not give the complainant a state-created property interest in its enforcement, even though a state statute provided that a peace offer "*shall* use every reasonable means to enforce [such an] order").

a mentally disabled individual in the conditions of involuntary confinement, see Youngberg v. Romeo, 457 U.S. 307 (1982).

At the same time, state law can create "liberty" interests, just as it can create property interests. See, *e.g.*, Board of Pardons v. Allen, 482 U.S. 369, 370–81 (1987) (state-law entitlement to parole). But the Court's cases have tended to be fairly parsimonious in recognizing a liberty interest on that basis.[6] In particular, in Sandin v. Conner, 515 U.S. 472 (1995), a prisoner filed suit in *federal* court, objecting to his placement in disciplinary segregation for 30 days after having been found to have violated prison rules. Mandatory language in a state regulation (i) gave the prisoner a right to present evidence and (ii) permitted discipline only if the charge was supported by substantial evidence or admitted by the prisoner. But with Chief Justice Rehnquist writing for a bare majority, the Court held that the prisoner lacked a liberty interest in freedom from disciplinary segregation and thus could not challenge the discipline as a denial of due process. Acknowledging that it was departing from its precedents, the Court refused to treat mandatory language alone as sufficient to generate a state-created liberty interest. Doing so, the Court contended, "creates disincentives for States to codify prison management procedures" and leads "to the involvement of federal courts in the day-to-day management of prisons". Instead, the Court held that a state-created liberty interest "will be generally limited to freedom from restraint which, while not exceeding the sentence in such an unexpected manner as to give rise to protection by the Due Process Clause of its own force, nonetheless imposes atypical and significant hardship on the inmate in relation to the ordinary incidents of prison life." No such finding could be made here: the conditions of disciplinary segregation, when compared to ordinary prison life, did not "work a major disruption in [the prisoner's] environment."

Four Justices dissented. Justice Breyer (joined by Justice Souter) would have followed prior law, which he viewed as establishing three categories: deprivations so severe in kind or degree that as a matter of federal law they infringe liberty interests protected by the Due Process Clause directly; deprivations about minor matters (for example, the kind of lunch to be served) that are unprotected by the Due Process Clause, even if official conduct violated a clear-cut regulation; and an intermediate category of deprivations—like the one in this case—in which the existence of a liberty interest depends upon state law. He argued forcefully that the disciplinary segregation here was not a mere "minor matter" that should be deemed unprotected despite the state regulation. Justice Ginsburg, joined by Justice Stevens, agreed with Justice Breyer that the deprivation was serious, but took the view that the prisoner had a liberty interest rooted in the Due Process Clause itself—a result that avoided the concern (voiced by the majority) that states that formulate more rules subject themselves to stricter constitutional constraints.[7]

---

[6]   See, *e.g.*, Paul v. Davis, 424 U.S. 693 (1976) (state government official's defamation of private individual does not invade liberty interest); Connecticut Bd. of Pardons v. Dumschat, 452 U.S. 458, 465 (1981) (liberty interest in clemency does not arise out of institutional practice); Kentucky Dep't of Corrections v. Thompson, 490 U.S. 454, 462–63 (1989) (liberty interest is created only where official decisions are governed by "explicitly mandatory language" establishing "substantive predicates" whose satisfaction requires a particular outcome).

[7]   A claim of deprivation of *life* without due process was at issue in Ohio Adult Parole Authority v. Woodard, 523 U.S. 272 (1998). In that case, a death row inmate challenged the adequacy of the hearing procedures followed by the parole authority, which makes clemency

Sandin is a prime example of what Professor Merrill terms a patterning approach—in which the Court first establishes constitutional criteria that a protected interest must satisfy (put differently, sets a constitutional floor of importance that interests created by the state must rise above to merit federal protection) and then examines state law to determine if such an interest has been created. Merrill defends that approach as preferable to the alternatives; in particular, he says that leaving the definition of entitlements entirely to state law risks generating increasing numbers of claims based on insubstantial or trivial state-created interests.

Under Sandin, what is the scope of review of a state court's decision that the state has not created "atypical and significant hardship"? Compare Wilkinson v. Austin, 545 U.S. 209 (2005), in which a unanimous Court recognized a state-created liberty interest in avoiding assignment to Ohio's "supermax" facility.[8]

C. Presidential Elections: The Role of State Legislatures and the Interpretation of State Statutes

(1) The Concurring Opinion in Bush v. Gore. Article II, § 1, cl. 2 provides: "Each State shall appoint, in such Manner as the Legislature thereof may direct," electors for the President and Vice President. In the litigation over the 2000 presidential election in Florida, arguments were made that this constitutional provision (a) protects a state-created "right" of a different sort—the right to a have a presidential election conducted under the system established by the state legislature, unmodified by the state courts, and (b) demands Supreme Court review without the customary deference to state court determinations of state law.

The argument was made most clearly in a concurring opinion in Bush v. Gore, 531 U.S. 98 (2000) (per curiam). There, after Florida officials had certified Governor George Bush as having won that state's electoral votes, Vice President Al Gore sued under Florida statutes authorizing a "contest"

---

recommendations to the Governor. In ruling against the prisoner, Chief Justice Rehnquist (for a plurality of four) declared that Connecticut Bd. of Pardons v. Dumschat, note 6, *supra*, which held that non-capital prisoners have no protected entitlement to clemency, was fully applicable to capital cases. He noted that the Governor had unfettered discretion and that denial of clemency does not impose " 'atypical and significant hardship on the inmate' ", but merely requires a prisoner to serve the sentence originally imposed (quoting Sandin). Finally, the plurality rejected the claim that clemency was an integral part of the state's criminal justice system and hence that due process protections necessarily attached.

The other five Justices disputed the Woodward plurality's suggestion that no procedural protections are ever required in clemency proceedings. Four Justices, in an opinion by Justice O'Connor, concluded that the state's clemency procedures comported with whatever limits the Due Process Clause may impose. Justice Stevens would have remanded the case to permit the district court to determine the constitutional adequacy of the procedures.

[8] Acknowledging the general difficulty of determining the appropriate baseline against which to measure whether a hardship is "atypical and significant", the Court in Wilkinson determined that "under any plausible baseline", assignment to the supermax prison qualified: "[A]lmost all human contact is prohibited, even to the point that conversation is not permitted from cell to cell; the light, though it may be dimmed, is on for 24 hours; exercise is for 1 hour per day, but only in a small indoor room. Save perhaps for the especially severe limitations on all human contact, these conditions likely would apply to most solitary confinement facilities, but here there are two added components. First is the duration. Unlike the 30-day placement in Sandin, placement * * * is indefinite and, after an initial 30-day review, is reviewed just annually. Second is that placement disqualifies an otherwise eligible inmate for parole consideration. While any of these conditions standing alone might not be sufficient to create a liberty interest, taken together they impose an atypical and significant hardship within the correctional context." The Court proceeded to hold that the state's procedures for assigning inmates to the supermax prison satisfied due process requirements.

of the certification of an election. The Florida Supreme Court ordered manual recounts in Florida counties in which ballots that voting machines had read as not casting a vote had not been manually tabulated. The state supreme court also ordered a change in vote totals previously certified by state officials, to take account of votes that had been tallied in manual recounts in two counties as part of pre-certification "protests" but that had been excluded from the certified total because they had been submitted only after the deadline for the counties to file their election returns with Florida's Secretary of State.

Although the Supreme Court reversed on equal protection grounds and ordered an end to the recounts, Chief Justice Rehnquist, joined by Justices Scalia and Thomas, filed a concurring opinion contending that the Florida Supreme Court's interpretation of Florida election law modified the scheme established by the Florida legislature and thereby violated Article II. The constitutional premise for that argument—that Article II provides a basis for federal review of the correctness of a state court's interpretation of state statutes regulating the selection of presidential electors—is hardly free from question.[9] But operating on that premise, the Chief Justice argued that the state court's decision "empties certification of virtually all legal consequence during the contest," "virtually eliminat[es] both the [certification] deadline and the Secretary [of State]'s discretion to disregard recounts that violate it", and fails to defer to the Secretary's reasonable interpretation of what counts as a "legal vote," instead embracing the "peculiar reading of the statutes" that includes as a legal vote an improperly punched ballot.

As Chief Justice Rehnquist explained, "[t]hough we generally defer to state courts on the interpretation of state law, there are of course areas in which the Constitution requires this Court to undertake an independent, if still deferential, analysis of state law." Emphasizing that Article II, § 1, cl. 2 provides for the appointment of each state's presidential electors " 'in such Manner as the *Legislature* thereof may direct,' " the Chief Justice stressed that "the text of the election law itself, and not just its interpretation by the courts of the States, takes on independent significance." From that starting point, his concurring opinion concluded "that the Florida Supreme Court's interpretation of the Florida election laws impermissibly distorted them beyond what a fair reading required, in violation of Article II."

(2) The Response of the Dissenters. In separate dissents, Justices Stevens, Souter, and Breyer disputed that the Florida Supreme Court had changed, rather than merely interpreted, state law. All three of the dissents viewed differences between the Florida Supreme Court and the Secretary of State as routine disagreements about the interpretive merits. In still another dissent, Justice Ginsburg (joined in this respect by the other dissenters) argued less about the specifics of Florida law and more about the need to defer to state court interpretations of state law. Mere disagreement with a state court's interpretation of state law, she stressed, "does not warrant the conclusion that the justices of that court have legislated." She continued:

"Unavoidably, this Court must sometimes examine state law in order to protect federal rights. But we have dealt with such cases ever mindful of the

---

[9] Moreover, this premise necessarily raises the question whether a state's compliance with Article II presents a political question to be determined by Congress. See pp. 265–266, *supra.*

full measure of respect we owe to interpretations of state law by a State's highest court. * * *

"The Chief Justice says that Article II * * * authorizes federal superintendence over the relationship between state courts and state legislatures, and licenses a departure from the usual deference we give to state-court interpretations of state law. * * * The Framers of our Constitution, however, understood that in a republican government, the judiciary would construe the legislature's enactments. * * * Yet * * * [b]y holding that Article II requires our revision of a state court's construction of state laws in order to protect one organ of the State from another, the Chief Justice contradicts the basic principle that a State may organize itself as it sees fit."

(3) Questions. Bush v. Gore was obviously an extraordinary case. Moreover, the complexities of Florida election law make it difficult to judge whether the Florida Supreme Court's interpretations were correct, were debatable but reasonable, or were, as the Chief Justice argued, "absurd" and "peculiar".[10] But was the basic problem facing the Supreme Court different from other cases involving federal protection of state-created rights? Do you agree with the Chief Justice that the Court should accord less deference to the Florida Supreme Court's interpretation of state election law than the Court would accord, for example, to a state court's interpretation of contract law underlying a Contract Clause claim?

It is true, of course, that Article II can be read as a directive to state *legislatures* to enact statutes establishing a method of appointing presidential electors; by contrast, the Contract Clause, although it presupposes that states will have a law of contracts, does not by its terms direct a particular branch of state government to create one. But does that difference bear on the appropriate degree of deference?[11]

---

[10] For differing perspectives on that issue, compare, *e.g.*, Tribe, *Erog v. Hsub and its Disguises: Freeing Bush v. Gore from Its Hall of Mirrors*, 115 Harv.L.Rev. 170, 184–217 (2001), and Klarman, *Bush v. Gore Through the Lens of Constitutional History*, 89 Cal.L.Rev. 1721, 1741–46 (2001) (both defending the Florida Supreme Court's interpretations of state law as correct or at least reasonable), with Posner, Breaking the Deadlock: The 2000 Election, the Constitution, and the Courts 92–128, 150–88 (2001), and Epstein, *Bush v. Gore: "In Such Manner as the Legislature Thereof May Direct": The Outcome in Bush v. Gore Defended*, 68 U.Chi.L.Rev. 613 (2001) (both sharply critical of those interpretations).

[11] For articles arguing that the Florida Supreme Court's rulings on issues of state law were not entitled to deference, see, *e.g.*, Wells, *Were There Adequate State Grounds in Bush v. Gore?*, 18 Const.Comm. 403 (2001); Wells & Netter, *Article II and the Florida Election Case: A Public Choice Perspective*, 61 Md.L.Rev. 711 (2002). For those critical of the Supreme Court's scope of review of Florida law, see, *e.g.*, Krent, *Judging Judging: The Problem of Second-Guessing State Judges' Interpretation of State Law in Bush v. Gore*, 29 Fla.St.U.L.Rev. 493 (2001); Schapiro, *Conceptions and Misconceptions of State Constitutional Law in Bush v. Gore*, 29 Fla.St.U.L.Rev. 661, 662 (2001); Smith, *History of the Article II Independent State Legislature Doctrine*, 29 Fla.St.U.L.Rev. 731 (2001); Solimine, *Supreme Court Monitoring of State Courts in the Twenty-First Century*, 35 Ind.L.Rev. 335 (2002).

Compare Schapiro, *Article II as Interpretive Theory: Bush v. Gore and the Retreat from Erie*, 34 Loy.U.Chi.L.J. 89, 109 (2002) (contending that the concurring opinion's implicit reliance on a textualist method of statutory interpretation, which was not based specifically on Florida law, harkens back to the era of Swift v. Tyson, "when federal courts invoked general common law, rather than the law of a particular state, to decide certain nonfederal disputes"), with Harrison, *Federal Appellate Jurisdiction Over Questions of State Law in State Courts*, 7 Green Bag 2d 353 (2004) (contending that all cases involving federal office arise under federal law within the meaning of Article III, and that the Supreme Court has plenary power to review questions of state law).

D. Other Federal Protections of State-Created Entitlements

The foregoing discussion of cases under the Contract, Due Process, and Takings Clauses, and under Article II, merely exemplifies a broad set of situations in which federal constitutional or statutory law operates to protect an entitlement created primarily, if not exclusively, by state law. Another such situation was that involved in Martin v. Hunter's Lessee—where a federal treaty protected state-created rights in land against confiscation.

Other examples abound. The Full Faith and Credit Clause and implementing legislation (28 U.S.C. § 1738) protect entitlements under state-created judgments against non-recognition;[12] the Federal Arbitration Act protects state-created contractual rights to arbitrate against non-enforcement;[13] various federal constitutional provisions protect against criminal punishment except in accordance with previously enacted state laws.[14]

As the cases in this Note demonstrate, the Court has not embraced a consistent approach to reviewing state law issues embedded in questions of federal entitlement. Sometimes the Court has engaged in de novo review, sometimes settled for limited review, and sometimes deferred altogether to the state court determination. Is there any reason why the scope of review, on the question of the existence of an antecedent state-created entitlement, should not be the same in all cases?[15]

For a wide-ranging discussion of the problems raised in this Note, see Monaghan, *Supreme Court Review of State-Court Determinations of State*

---

[12] See, *e.g.*, Clark v. Williard, 292 U.S. 112 (1934); Ford v. Ford, 371 U.S. 187 (1962). In Adam v. Saenger, 303 U.S. 59 (1938), the Texas courts denied enforcement to a California judgment on the ground that the California court that had rendered it lacked jurisdiction under California law. On review, Justice Stone said: "While this Court reexamines such an issue with deference after its determination by a state court, it cannot, if the laws and Constitution of the United States are to be observed, accept as final the decision of the state tribunal as to matters alleged to give rise to the asserted federal right. This is especially the case where the decision is rested * * * upon the law of another state, as readily determined here as in a state court."

[13] Compare, *e.g.*, Volt Info. Sciences, Inc. v. Board of Trustees of Leland Stanford Jr. Univ., 489 U.S. 468 (1989) (deferring to a state court's decision, notwithstanding the Federal Arbitration Act, not to enforce a contractual arbitration clause and to enforce instead a distinct contractual clause incorporating state statutory choice-of-law rules under which arbitration was not compelled), with Green Tree Financial Corp. v. Bazzle, 539 U.S. 444 (2003) (plurality opinion) (declining to defer to a state court's determination that state law permits class arbitration when a contractual arbitration clause was silent on the question and concluding, instead, that ambiguities in such a clause were subject, in the first instance, to decision by the arbitrator).

[14] See, *e.g.*, Splawn v. California, 431 U.S. 595, 600 (1977) (holding that in the Supreme Court's own assessment of an alleged retroactive expansion of a state law criminal prohibition, the state court's ruling on state law issues "is entitled to great weight in evaluating petitioner's constitutional contentions" under the Ex Post Facto and Due Process Clauses); Ricketts v. Adamson, 483 U.S. 1 (1987) (holding that the Court would not "second-guess" the state courts' determination that new charges against the defendant were permissible because he had breached a plea agreement, and asserting that "[w]hile we assess independently the plea agreement's effect on [the defendant's] double jeopardy rights, the construction of the plea agreement and the concomitant obligations flowing therefrom are, within broad bounds of reasonableness, matters of state law").

[15] For an argument that the Court has too readily set aside state court rulings on issues of antecedent state law and should reverse state-law determinations only where it can substantiate a concrete reason to suspect that the state court deliberately manipulated state law, see Fitzgerald, *Suspecting the States: Supreme Court Review of State-Court State-Law Judgments*, 101 Mich.L.Rev. 80 (2002).

Law in Constitutional Cases, 103 Colum.L.Rev. 1919 (2003). Monaghan stresses the prevalence of what he calls "characterization" issues—*e.g.*, the question, in Sandin v. Conner, p. 519, *supra*, whether disciplinary segregation implicates "liberty", or the question, in Webb's Fabulous Pharmacies, Inc. v. Beckwith, p. 518, *supra*, whether the interest on an interpleader fund is property. He contends that such questions do not involve redetermination of state law but simply questions of federal constitutional interpretation.

The heart of Professor Monaghan's article, however, addresses cases that do involve redetermination of state law—cases in which the Constitution assigns significance to a state's fidelity to state law as it stood at some point in the past. For example, referring to the state law questions raised by the Article II issue in Bush v. Gore, Monaghan argues that the Supreme Court had power to engage in de novo review to determine what state law was at the critical time. He finds support for that view in numerous cases, including Fairfax's Devisee (the prelude to Martin v. Hunter's Lessee) and Brand. Though he believes that ordinarily deferential review is the appropriate stance, more intrusive review may be necessary, he suggests, "particularly in times of change, or in certain controversial areas of the law." Uncertain whether criteria can be articulated to specify when de novo review should be exercised, he would leave it to the Court's sense of the situation, though he adds that de novo review would rarely be appropriate in cases involving federal statutory rather than constitutional provisions. Absent evidence that a state court's decision was unreasonable, motivated by hostility to federal rights, or lacking in fair support, is a "sense of the situation" an adequate basis for the Supreme Court to disregard a state court's view of state law?

B. PROCEDURAL REQUIREMENTS

Cardinale v. Louisiana

394 U.S. 437, 89 S.Ct. 1161, 22 L.Ed. 398 (1969).
Certiorari to the Supreme Court of Louisiana.

■ MR. JUSTICE WHITE delivered the opinion of the Court.

Petitioner brutally murdered a woman near New Orleans. * * * His confession [to the police] was introduced in its entirety in the subsequent trial for murder in which petitioner was convicted and sentenced to death. Petitioner does not now contend that his confession was involuntary or that his admission of guilt * * * was inadmissible in evidence. He objects solely to the admission of those parts of his confession which he argues were both irrelevant and prejudicial in his trial for murder. A Louisiana statute requires that confessions must be admitted in their entirety, and petitioner contends that this is unconstitutional.

Although certiorari was granted to consider this question, the fact emerged in oral argument that the sole federal question argued here had never been raised, preserved, or passed upon in the state courts below. It was very early established that the Court will not decide federal *rule* constitutional issues raised here for the first time on review of state court decisions. In Crowell v. Randell, 10 Pet. 368 (1836), Justice Story reviewed the earlier cases commencing with Owings v. Norwood's Lessee, 5 Cranch 344 (1809), and came to the conclusion that the Judiciary Act of 1789, § 25, vested this Court with no jurisdiction unless a federal question was raised and decided in the state court below. * * * The Court has consistently refused to decide federal constitutional issues raised here for the first time on review of state court decisions both before the Crowell opinion, Miller v. Nicholls, 4 Wheat. 311, 315 (1819), and since, e.g., Safeway Stores, Inc. v. Oklahoma Retail Grocers Assn., Inc., 360 U.S. 334, 342, n. 7 (1959); [citing additional cases].

In addition to the question of jurisdiction arising under the statute controlling our power to review final judgments of state courts, 28 U.S.C. § 1257, there are sound reasons for this. Questions not raised below are those on which the record is very likely to be inadequate, since it certainly was not compiled with those questions in mind. And in a federal system it is important that state courts be given the first opportunity to consider the applicability of state statutes in light of constitutional challenge, since the statutes may be construed in a way which saves their constitutionality. Or the issue may be blocked by an adequate state ground. Even though States are not free to avoid constitutional issues on inadequate state grounds, they should be given the first opportunity to consider them.

In view of the petitioner's admitted failure to raise the issue he presents here in any way below, the failure of the state court to pass on this issue, the desirability of giving the State the first opportunity to apply its statute on an adequate record, and the fact that a federal habeas remedy may remain if no state procedure for raising the issue is available to petitioner, the writ is dismissed for want of jurisdiction.

It is so ordered.

■ MR. JUSTICE BLACK, MR. JUSTICE DOUGLAS, and MR. JUSTICE FORTAS concur in the dismissal of the writ, believing it to have been improvidently granted.

NOTE ON THE PRESENTATION AND PRESERVATION OF FEDERAL QUESTIONS

(1) The Sources of the Rule. As sources for the rule it follows, Cardinale invokes both 28 U.S.C. § 1257 (which requires that the federal question have been "drawn in question" or "specially set up or claimed") and a variety of policy concerns.[1] Despite such references to § 1257, the Court in recent years

---

[1] See also Webb v. Webb, 451 U.S. 493, 499–501 (1981), elaborating on these sources. Supreme Court Rule 14.1(g)(i) provides that a petition for certiorari to a state court shall contain "specification of the stage in the proceedings, both in the court of first instance and in the appellate courts, when the federal questions sought to be reviewed were raised; the method or manner of raising them and the way in which they were passed on by those courts; and pertinent quotations of specific portions of the record or summary thereof, with specific reference to the places in the record where the matter appears (e.g., court opinion, ruling on exception, portion of court's charge and exception thereto, assignment of errors), so as to show that the federal

has repeatedly acknowledged that it is unsettled whether the rule is a jurisdictional requirement or is merely prudential. The Court has also stressed, however, that whatever its precise nature, the rule is strictly enforced and exceptions to it are extraordinarily rare.[2] (For discussion of two decisions hard to square with the rule, see Paragraph (4), *infra*.)

(2) The Governing Standard. The requirement that a federal question have been presented to the state courts is often framed as one governed by federal-law standards: "There are various ways in which the validity of a state statute may be drawn in question on the ground that it is repugnant to the Constitution of the United States. No particular form of words or phrases is essential, but only that the claim of invalidity and the ground therefor be brought to the attention of the state court with fair precision and in due time." New York ex rel. Bryant v. Zimmerman, 278 U.S. 63, 67 (1928).[3]

(3) Problems in Application. The requirement of presentation to the state courts has been applied with varying strictness. A central difficulty in application is determining whether an issue raised before the Supreme Court is the same as one that was raised before and decided by the state courts.

(a) New Claims Versus New Arguments. One set of cases has addressed the question whether a particular federal issue raised for the first time before the Supreme Court was subsumed in a slightly different federal issue that was raised in state court. For example, in Yee v. City of Escondido, 503 U.S. 519, 532 (1992), the Court reiterated the proposition that if a federal *claim* was properly raised in state court, a party can raise before the Supreme Court any *argument* in support of that claim, even if the *argument* was not raised in state court. The Court proceeded to hold that the argument that a rent control ordinance constituted a "regulatory taking" could be raised for the first time in the Supreme Court, since the litigant had raised, in state court, the claim that the ordinance was a "physical taking".[4] However, a substantive due process challenge to the ordinance was deemed to be a different claim not raised below and hence not reviewable.

The distinction between a new claim and a new argument is hardly clear-cut. For decisions in which the Justices divided on the question, see, *e.g.*, Eddings v. Oklahoma, 455 U.S. 104, 113–14 n. 9 (1982) (defendant's claim that imposition of the death penalty in his particular circumstances violated the Eighth Amendment sufficed to put in issue the legality of the trial judge's refusal to consider mitigating evidence as required by Lockett v. Ohio, 438 U.S. 586 (1978)—despite the failure to mention Lockett in state

---

question was timely and properly raised and that this Court has jurisdiction to review the judgment on a writ of certiorari."

    [2] See, *e.g.*, Adams v. Robertson, 520 U.S. 83, 86–88 (1997); Bankers Life & Cas. Co. v. Crenshaw, 486 U.S. 71, 79 (1988); Illinois v. Gates, 462 U.S. 213, 217–24 & cases cited (1983).

    [3] In Street v. New York, 394 U.S. 576, 582 (1969), the Court said that it is not bound by the state court's determination as to whether the federal question was sufficiently raised, but added: "[I]t is not entirely clear whether in such cases the scope of our review is limited to determining whether the state court has 'by-passed the federal right under forms of local procedure' or whether we should decide the matter '*de novo* for ourselves.' Ellis v. Dixon, 349 U.S. 458, 463 (1955)." See also Herndon v. Georgia, 295 U.S. 441, 443 (1935), p. 535, *infra*, which appears to recite a federal standard in articulating "[t]he long-established general rule * * * that the attempt to raise a federal question after judgment [of the state's highest court], upon a petition for rehearing, comes too late".

    [4] The Court nonetheless refused to decide the regulatory taking claim, on the distinct ground that it was not included within the question presented in the petition for certiorari (which was limited to the physical taking issue). See Paragraph (4)(a), *infra*.

court); Terminiello v. Chicago, 337 U.S. 1, 6 (1949) (defendant's objection that "his speech was protected by the first amendment" sufficed to put in issue before the Supreme Court the question of the constitutionality of the ordinance under which he was prosecuted as it had been construed in the jury instructions).

(b) Federal Versus State Law Claims. A second set of cases has focused on whether a litigant adequately indicated in state court that a claim was based on federal rather than on state law. The Court has long required a litigant to show "that some provision of the Federal, as distinguished from the state, Constitution was relied upon," New York Central & H.R.Co. v. New York, 186 U.S. 269, 273 (1902), and claims that a state statute violates the Constitution or denies due process, without more, have been treated as referring to state and not federal provisions. See, *e.g.*, New York ex rel. Bryant v. Zimmerman, 278 U.S. at 67–68; Bowe v. Scott, 233 U.S. 658, 664–65 (1914). (Is that treatment consistent with Michigan v. Long, p. 494, *supra*?)

The requirement that a litigant make clear that a claim rests on federal law is not limited to cases involving parallel federal and state constitutional provisions, and is sometimes applied with exorbitant rigor. For example, in Webb v. Webb, note 1, *supra*, the Court, over Justice Marshall's lone dissent, held that a litigant who had complained in a state court custody suit about a failure to give "full faith and credit" to a prior judgment, but who had not mentioned the Full Faith and Credit Clause, had presented only a state law issue under the Uniform Child Custody Jurisdiction Act, and thus could not raise the federal constitutional issue in the Supreme Court.

In Howell v. Mississippi, 543 U.S. 440 (2005), the petitioner argued that he had presented his federal claim in state court by implication, because the state-law rule on which he had relied was identical to the federal rule. The Court assumed without deciding that identical standards might overcome a failure to have identified as federal a claim pressed in state court, but ruled that state and federal law in fact differed and hence dismissed the petition.

(4) Exceptions to the Rule. While exceptions to the rule that Cardinale reaffirms are extraordinarily rare, two relatively modern decisions may be examples.

(a) Vachon v. New Hampshire. In Vachon v. New Hampshire, 414 U.S. 478 (1974), the defendant had been convicted of willfully contributing to the delinquency of a minor, for having sold a 14-year-old girl a button containing a sexual slogan. On appeal to the state supreme court, he had unsuccessfully challenged the sufficiency of the evidence of willfulness. The Supreme Court, in a brief per curiam opinion, reversed, relying on the federal constitutional principle that due process is denied when there is "no evidence" to support one element of a crime (here, willfulness).

In dissent, Justice Rehnquist protested: "A litigant seeking to preserve a constitutional claim for review in this Court must not only make clear to the lower courts the nature of his claim, but he must also make it clear that the claim is constitutionally grounded. The closest that appellant came in his brief on appeal to the Supreme Court of New Hampshire to discussing the issue on which this Court's opinion turns is in the sixth section, which is headed: 'The State's failure to introduce any evidence of scienter should have resulted in dismissal of the charge following the presentation of the State's case.' Appellant in that section makes the customary appellate arguments of insufficiency of the evidence and does not so much as mention either the United States Constitution or a single case decided by this Court. The Supreme Court of New Hampshire treated these arguments as raising a classic state law claim of insufficient evidence of scienter; nothing in that court's opinion remotely suggests that it was treating the claim as having a basis other than in state law."

In response, the Court relied on provisions in the Supreme Court's Rules stating that questions raised in the brief that were not presented in the jurisdictional papers "will be disregarded, save as the court, at its option, may notice a plain error not presented."[5] However, as Justice Rehnquist objected, that provision appeared only to authorize the Court, once it has previously noted probable jurisdiction or granted certiorari, to hear an issue properly raised in state court but not presented in the application for Supreme Court review, rather than an issue not raised at all in state court.

The Vachon decision takes an unusually flexible view of the requirement that the federal issue be raised in state court. Compare, *e.g.*, Bailey v. Anderson, 326 U.S. 203 (1945), ruling that a state court challenge to the denial of interest in a condemnation action could not be converted, in the Supreme Court, into a federal constitutional question under the Takings Clause. Note, however, that Vachon fell within the Court's then-existing mandatory appellate jurisdiction. By permitting itself to dispose of the case on the fact-specific basis that there was "no evidence" of one element of the crime, the Court avoided the obligation it would otherwise have had to decide more difficult constitutional claims (under the void-for-vagueness doctrine and the First Amendment) that the appellant had properly raised. Today, the Court would have the option, in a case like Vachon, of simply denying certiorari. But do the circumstances in Vachon suggest that the Court's jurisdictional determinations are likely to be influenced by whether the Court is eager (or reluctant) to reach a particular issue? Is that appropriate? Inevitable?

(b) Wood v. Georgia. In Wood v. Georgia, 450 U.S. 261 (1981), the Court decided an issue that all the Justices acknowledged had not been raised in state court. There, three employees of "adult" establishments had been convicted of distributing obscene materials. Their sentence of probation was conditioned on their making installment payments of substantial fines. When those payments were not made, probation was revoked. The Supreme Court granted review to decide whether imprisonment of a probationer who is unable to make such payments denies equal protection.

But the Court (per Powell, J.) vacated the convictions on a different ground. Noting that the employees had been represented by a lawyer paid by their employer, and that the employer had promised to pay any fines imposed, the Court found that there was a potential conflict of interest that might have denied the employees due process. The Court accordingly remanded the case so that the state courts could determine the nature and implications of any such conflict.

In dissent, Justice White objected that the Court lacked jurisdiction to resolve the due process issue. The Court responded that the lack of any

---

[5]   For the current provisions, see Rule 14.1(a) (the Court will consider on the merits only those questions presented for its review in the petition) and Rule 24.1(a) (reserving to the Court the power to "consider a plain error not among the questions presented but evident from the record *and otherwise within its jurisdiction to decide*") (emphasis added).

presentation of the issue "merely emphasize[s] * * * why it *is* appropriate for us to consider the issue. The party who argued the appeal and prepared the petition for certiorari was the lawyer on whom the conflict-of-interest charge focused. It is unlikely that he would contend that he had continued improperly to act as counsel." And, the Court continued, the state could not claim lack of notice, as it had pointed out the conflict at the probation revocation hearing. He concluded: "In this context, it is appropriate to treat the due process issue as one 'raised' below, and proceed to consider it here. Even if one considers that the conflict-of-interest question was not technically raised below, there is ample support for a remand required in the interests of justice. See 28 U.S.C. § 2106 (authorizing the Court to 'require such further proceedings to be had as may be just under the circumstances')".

What is the holding of Wood? In Webb v. Webb, note 1, *supra*, at 502, Justice Powell, in a concurring opinion joined by Justice Brennan, characterized Wood as having "reaffirmed * * * that the Court has jurisdiction to review plain error unchallenged in the state court when necessary to prevent fundamental unfairness." Should Wood be limited to circumstances in which some defect in the state process prevented the litigant from raising the issue in the first instance?[6]

Staub v. City of Baxley

355 U.S. 313, 78 S.Ct. 277, 2 L.Ed.2d 302 (1958).
Appeal from the Court of Appeals of Georgia.

■ MR. JUSTICE WHITTAKER delivered the opinion of the Court.

Appellant, Rose Staub, was convicted in the Mayor's Court of the City of Baxley, Georgia, of violation of a city ordinance and was sentenced to imprisonment for 30 days or to pay a fine of $300. The Superior Court of the county affirmed the judgment of conviction; the Court of Appeals of the State affirmed the judgment of the Superior Court; and the Supreme Court of the State denied an application for certiorari. The case comes here on appeal.

The ordinance in question is set forth in the margin.[1] Its violation, which is not denied, arose from the following undisputed facts * * *:

---

    6   Compare the cases discussed at p. 535–537, Paragraph (4), *infra*.

    1   [Section I of the ordinance required written application to the Mayor and City Council for a permit before acting to "solicit membership for any organization, union or society of any sort which requires from its members the payments of membership fees" from citizens of Baxley.

    [Section II required specific information about the organization and its representative (including places of residence for the past ten years and the names of three character references).

    [Section III described the procedure for a hearing before the Mayor and Council of City of Baxley on the application.

    [Section IV stated: "In passing upon such application the Mayor and Council shall consider the character of the applicant, the nature of the business of the organization for which members are desired to be solicited, and its effects upon the general welfare of citizens of the City of Baxley."

    [Section V provided that the decision on granting a permit shall be determined "in the same manner as other matters are so granted or denied by the vote of the Mayor and Council."

Appellant was a salaried employee of the International Ladies' Garment Workers Union which was attempting to organize the employees of a manufacturing company located in the nearby town of Hazelhurst. A number of those employees lived in Baxley. On February 19, 1954, appellant * * * went to Baxley and, without applying for permits required under the ordinance, talked with several of the employees at their homes about joining the union. * * * Later that day a meeting was held at the home of one of the employees, attended by three other employees, at which, in the words of the hostess, appellant "just told us they wanted us to join the union, and said it would be a good thing for us to do . . . and went on to tell us how this union would help us." * * * No money was asked or received from the persons at the meeting, but they were invited "to get other girls . . . there to join the union" and blank membership cards were offered for that use. Appellant further explained that the immediate objective was to "have enough cards signed to petition for an election . . . with the [National Labor Relations Board]."

On the same day a summons was issued and served by the Chief of Police commanding appellant to appear before the Mayor's Court three days later to answer "to the offense of Soliciting Members for an Organization without a Permit & License."

Before the trial, appellant moved to abate the action upon a number of grounds, among which were the contentions that the ordinance "shows on its face that it is repugnant to and violative of the 1st and 14th Amendments to the Constitution of the United States in that it places a condition precedent upon, and otherwise unlawfully restricts, the defendant's freedom of speech as well as freedom of the press and freedom of lawful assembly" by requiring, as conditions precedent to the exercise of those rights, the issuance of a "license" which the Mayor and city council are authorized by the ordinance to grant or refuse in their discretion, and the payment of a "license fee" which is discriminatory and unreasonable in amount * * *. [After conviction in the Mayor's Court, the appellant made the same contentions in the Superior Court, which affirmed the conviction.]

Those contentions were renewed in the Court of Appeals but that court declined to consider them. It stated that "[t]he attack should have been made against specific sections of the ordinance and not against the ordinance as a whole; * * * and that since it 'appears that * * * the defendant has made no effort to comply with any section of the ordinance . . . it is not necessary to pass upon the sufficiency of the evidence, the constitutionality of the ordinance, or any other phase of the case. . . .' " The court * * * affirmed the judgment of conviction.

* * * At the threshold, appellee urges that this appeal be dismissed because, it argues, * * * we are * * * without jurisdiction to entertain it. * * *

[Section VI provided that an applicant who is salaried by the organization for which the applicant solicits members, or receives a fee from obtaining members, must pay $2,000 a year, and also $500.00 for each member obtained, in order to obtain a permit.

[Section VII stated that anyone who, without having obtained a permit, solicits, as members of an organization, citizens of Baxley or persons employed therein is subject to punishment.

[Section VIII repealed all city ordinances in conflict with this ordinance, while Section IX contained a separability provision.]

Appellee * * * contends that the holding of the Court of Appeals, that appellant's failure to attack "specific sections" of the ordinance rendered it unnecessary, under Georgia procedure, "to pass upon . . . the constitutionality of the ordinance, or any other phase of the case . . . ," constitutes an adequate "non-federal ground" to preclude review in this Court. We think this contention is "without any fair or substantial support" (Ward v. Love County, [253 U.S. 17, 22 (1920)]) and therefore does not present an *adequate* nonfederal ground of decision in the circumstances of this case. The several sections of the ordinance are interdependent in their application to one in appellant's position and constitute but one complete act for the licensing and taxing of her described activities. For that reason, no doubt, she challenged the constitutionality of the whole ordinance, and in her objections used language challenging the constitutional effect of all its sections. She did, thus, challenge all sections of the ordinance, though not by number. To require her, in these circumstances, to count off, one by one, the several sections of the ordinance would be to force resort to an arid ritual of meaningless form. Indeed, the Supreme Court of Georgia seems to have recognized the arbitrariness of such exaltation of form. Only four years ago that court recognized that an attack on such a statute was sufficient if "the [statute] so challenged was invalid in every part for some reason alleged." Flynn v. State, 209 Ga. 519, 522 (1953). In enunciating that rule the court was following a long line of its own decisions. [Citing four decisions of the Georgia Supreme Court.]

We conclude that the decision of the Court of Appeals does not rest on an adequate nonfederal ground and that we have jurisdiction of this appeal. * * *

[The Court reversed the conviction on the ground that the ordinance violated the First Amendment.]

■ MR. JUSTICE FRANKFURTER, whom MR. JUSTICE CLARK joins, dissenting.

This is one of those small cases that carry large issues, for it concerns the essence of our federalism—due regard for the constitutional distribution of power as between the Nation and the States, and more particularly the distribution of judicial power as between this Court and the judiciaries of the States. * * *

While the power to review the denial by a state court of a nonfrivolous claim under the United States Constitution has been centered in this Court, carrying with it the responsibility to see that the opportunity to assert such a claim be not thwarted by any local procedural device, equally important is observance by this Court of the wide discretion in the States to formulate their own procedures for bringing issues appropriately to the attention of their local courts * * *. Such methods and procedures may, when judged by the best standards of judicial administration, appear crude, awkward and even finicky or unnecessarily formal when judged in the light of modern emphasis on informality. But so long as the local procedure does not discriminate against the raising of federal claims and, in the particular case, has not been used to stifle a federal claim to prevent its eventual consideration here, this Court is powerless to deny to a State the right to have the kind of judicial system it chooses and to administer that system in its own way. It is of course for this Court to pass on the substantive sufficiency of a claim of federal right, but if resort is had in the first instance to the state judiciary for the enforcement of a federal constitutional right, the State is not barred from subjecting the suit to the same procedures, *nisi prius* and appellate, that govern adjudication of all constitutional issues in that State. * * *

* * * The [United States Supreme] Court has long insisted, certainly in precept, on rigorous requirements that must be fulfilled before it will pass on the constitutionality of legislation, on avoidance of such determinations even by strained statutory construction, and on keeping constitutional adjudication, when unavoidable, as narrow as circumstances will permit. * * * [T]his Court will consider only those very limited aspects of a statute that alone may affect the rights of a particular litigant before the Court. * * * Surely a state court is not to be denied the like right to protect itself from the necessity—sometimes even the temptation—of adjudicating overly broad claims of unconstitutionality. Surely it can insist that such claims be formulated under precise (even if, in our view, needlessly particularized) requirements and restricted to the limited issues that concrete and immediately pressing circumstances may raise.

* * * The cases relied upon by the Georgia court in this case are part of a long line of decisions holding a comprehensive, all-inclusive challenge to the constitutionality of a statute inadequate and requiring explicit particularity in pleadings in order to raise constitutional questions. * * * Thus, allegations of unconstitutionality directed at a group of 16 sections of the Criminal Code, Rooks v. Tindall, 138 Ga. 863; a single named "lengthy section" of a statute, Crapp v. State, 148 Ga. 150; a single section of a city charter amendment, Glover v. City of Rome, 173 Ga. 239; a named Act of the General Assembly, Wright v. Cannon, 185 Ga. 363; and a 5-section chapter of the Code, Richmond Concrete Products Co. v. Ward, 212 Ga. 773, were held "too general" or "too indefinite" to raise constitutional questions * * *. * * *

There is nothing frivolous or futile (though it may appear "formal") about a rule insisting that parties specify with arithmetic particularity those provisions in a legislative enactment they would ask a court to strike down. This is so, because such exactitude helps to make concrete the plaintiffs' relation to challenged provisions. First, it calls for closer reflection and greater responsibility on the part of one who challenges legislation, for, in formulating specific attacks against each provision for which an infirmity is claimed, the pleader is more likely to test his claims critically and to reconsider them carefully than he would be if he adopted a "scatter-shot" approach. Secondly, the opposing party, in responding to a particularized attack, is more likely to plead in such a way as to narrow or even eliminate constitutional issues, as where he admits that a specific challenged provision is invalid.[6] Finally, where the parties identify particular language in a statute as allegedly violating a constitutional provision, the court will often be able to construe the words in such a way as to render them inoffensive. * * *

---

[6]   One of the most vulnerable provisions of this ordinance, the drastically high license fee, was taken out of controversy in this suit by the respondent's admission of its invalidity. It is not out of question that more specific pleading might have drawn similar admissions as to other allegedly objectionable portions of the ordinance.

It may be—but it certainly is not clearly so—that with little expenditure of time and effort, and with little risk of misreading appellant's charges, a court could determine exactly what it is about the Baxley ordinance that allegedly infringes upon appellant's constitutional rights. But rules are not made solely for the easiest cases they govern. The fact that the reason for a rule does not clearly apply in a given situation does not eliminate the necessity for compliance with the rule. So long as a reasonable rule of state procedure is consistently applied, so long as it is not used as a means for evading vindication of federal rights, see Davis v. Wechsler, 263 U.S. 22, 24–25, it should not be refused applicability. * * *

The local procedural rule which controlled this case should not be disregarded by reason of a group of Georgia cases which, while recognizing and reaffirming the rule of pleading relied on by the Court of Appeals below, suggest a limited qualification. It appears that under special circumstances, where a generalized attack is made against a statute without reference to specific provisions, the court will inquire into the validity of the entire body of legislation challenged. The cases on which the Court relies as establishing this as the prevailing rule in Georgia strongly indicate that this approach will be used only where an allegation of unconstitutionality can be disposed of (one way or the other) relatively summarily and not where, as here, difficult issues are raised. In the only case cited by the Court in which the Georgia Supreme Court overturned a statute on the basis of generalized allegations, Atlantic Loan Co. v. Peterson, 181 Ga. 266, the result was "plainly apparent." 181 Ga., at 274. In the other cases cited, the court gave varying degrees of recognition to this approach, refusing altogether to apply it in [Flynn v. State, 209 Ga. 519, 522], where the court declined to accept "the burden of examining the act section by section and sentence by sentence." Certainly it cannot be said that the Court of Appeals was out of constitutional bounds in failing to bring the instant case within the purview of whatever exception can be said to have been spelled out by these cases or that it is for this Court to formulate exceptions to the valid Georgia rule of procedure.

The record before us presents not the remotest basis for attributing to the Georgia court any desire to limit the appellant in the fullest opportunity to raise claims of federal right or to prevent an adverse decision on such claims in the Georgia court from review by this Court. Consequently, this Court is left with no proper choice but to give effect to the rule of procedure on the basis of which this case was disposed of below. "Without any doubt it rests with each State to prescribe the jurisdiction of its appellate courts, the mode and time of invoking that jurisdiction, and the rules of practice to be applied in its exercise; and the state law and practice in this regard are no less applicable when Federal rights are in controversy than when the case turns entirely upon questions of local or general law." John v. Paullin, 231 U.S. 583, 585.

The appeal should be dismissed.

———

NOTE ON THE ADEQUACY OF STATE PROCEDURAL GROUNDS

(1) Cardinale and Staub Compared. There is a subtle difference, not always appreciated in the decisions, between the jurisdictional questions in Cardinale and in Staub. In Cardinale, the federal issue was never raised or considered in any fashion in state court. The Supreme Court's refusal to hear the issue was based on the litigant's failure to have complied with a *federal* rule requiring that some presentation be made in the state court.

In Staub (and the other cases discussed in this Note), the federal issue was raised, but in a fashion that, the state court found, did not comply with state procedural law. With the state court having ruled that it could not reach the merits of the federal claim because of the procedural default, the question for the Supreme Court was whether that *state law ruling* constituted an adequate state procedural ground barring Supreme Court review.

(2) The Adequate State Procedural Ground and the Primacy of State Practice. Justice Frankfurter is surely correct that, in general, state rules of practice presumptively determine the time when, and the mode by which, federal claims must be asserted in the state courts. Thus, ordinarily when a state court litigant has committed a procedural default—that is, has failed to raise a federal question in accordance with state procedural rules—the state court will refuse to decide the federal question, and any effort to obtain Supreme Court review will be rejected on the basis that there is an adequate and independent state procedural ground precluding the exercise of jurisdiction. Decisions so holding are legion. See generally Shapiro et al., Supreme Court Practice 141–231 (10th ed.2013). And in many other such instances, the Court simply denies certiorari, without noting specifically that jurisdiction was wanting.

(3) The Inadequate State Ground. The decision in Staub is thus one of a small set of cases forming a limited exception to the general rule—cases in which the Supreme Court upholds its jurisdiction to review the federal issue in the case on the basis that the state procedural ground is "inadequate" to support the judgment below. The remainder of this Note examines this set of cases.[1]

Many of the cases discussed in this Note involved a refusal by courts in southern states to adjudicate the federal rights of African-American criminal defendants, or, as in Staub, of members of unpopular social or political movements. Consider these questions: Did the Court bend its usual jurisdictional rules in order to give itself the capacity to deal with a pressing set of social, legal and political problems—and if so, was that appropriate?[2]

---

[1] See generally Hill, *The Inadequate State Ground*, 65 Colum.L.Rev. 943 (1965); Meltzer, *State Court Forfeitures of Federal Rights*, 99 Harv.L.Rev. 1128 (1986); Sandalow, *Henry v. Mississippi and the Adequate State Ground: Proposals for a Revised Doctrine*, 1965 Sup.Ct.Rev. 187.

[2] *Cf.* the story related by Professors Eskridge & Frickey in their *Historical and Critical Introduction* to Hart & Sacks, The Legal Process: Basic Problems in the Making and Application of Law cxiii (Eskridge & Frickey eds.1994): "When Henry Hart taught 'Federal Courts' for the last time, during the Spring Term of 1965, he brought into class the Supreme Court's opinion in Hamm v. City of Rock Hill[, 379 U.S. 306 (1964)]. The Court applied the just-enacted Civil Rights Act of 1964 to abate Southern prosecutions of sit-in demonstrators. Hart stated the facts and relevant authorities, including a federal statute creating a presumption against finding abatement of prosecutions by new statutes. It was apparent from the professor's statement of the case and the authorities that the decision was about to be analytically dissected. But, rather than launching into the sort of devastating critique of which he was capable, Hart paused and

Or did the Court fail to go far enough in protecting federal rights from being undermined in state court litigation? (Recall that, in criminal cases, an additional difficulty is the poor quality of representation afforded to many defendants, resulting in manifold failures by counsel properly to raise federal issues.[3]) In theory, Congress might have addressed defects in state court proceedings by strengthening the collateral relief available in federal habeas actions. See Chap. XI, Sec. 3, *infra*. In the absence of such congressional action, how much discretion did the Supreme Court have to respond to the underlying problems? Compare Hart, *The Relations Between State and Federal Law*, 54 Colum.L.Rev. 489, 508 (1954), with Meltzer, note 1, *supra*, at 1176–78.

(4) Due Process Violations. Supreme Court review plainly cannot be foreclosed by a litigant's noncompliance with a state procedural rule that, on its face or as applied, violates the Due Process Clause. Rather, the validity of a state procedural rule under the Due Process Clause raises an independent federal question that the Court has jurisdiction to review, apart from any other federal issue in the case.

    (a) Unforeseeable Appellate Court Rulings. In Brinkerhoff-Faris Trust & Savings Co. v. Hill, 281 U.S. 673 (1930), an equal protection challenge to a state tax was denied by the state appellate court because the taxpayer had failed first to seek administrative relief (which was no longer available)—even though earlier state decisions had held that the state administrative body lacked power to award relief. The taxpayer's petition to the state appellate court, objecting to this shift of course, was denied. The Supreme Court viewed the state court's action as a denial of due process, and thus, brushing aside claims of procedural default, reversed and remanded for the state court to consider the equal protection issue on the merits.[4]

    But the Court rejected a similar attack on a state court's change of position in Herndon v. Georgia, 295 U.S. 441 (1935). Herndon, an organizer for the Communist Party, was convicted of attempting to incite insurrection, after the trial court instructed the jury that the defendant must have expected or advocated immediate serious violence against the state. The Supreme Court of Georgia, in rejecting Herndon's contention that the evidence was insufficient to convict him under the statute as interpreted by

---

reflected to himself, his eyes focused on his reprint of the Court's opinion. The class stopped for thirty breathless seconds. Finally, Hart looked up at the class and said: 'Sometimes, sometimes, you just have to do the right thing.' " For a slightly different report on that same class, see Harper, *Public and Private Clients in the 1990s*, 46 Yale L.Rpt. #1, at 56 (Winter 1999) (describing a far more elaborate discussion of the Hamm decision, which Hart defended as correct, stating that at times constitutional heroes are needed and that this was such a time). See also Glennon, *The Jurisdictional Legacy of the Civil Rights Movement*, 61 Tenn.L.Rev. 869 (1994) (arguing that in the mid-1950s and the 1960s, the Supreme Court modified doctrines, including that of the adequate state ground, that would otherwise have presented jurisdictional obstacles to the Court's support of the civil rights movement, and that subsequent changes in the southern states' legal and political systems have substantially diminished the need for expansive federal jurisdiction).

    [3] Givelber, *Litigating State Capital Cases While Preserving Federal Questions: Can It Be Done Successfully?*, 29 St. Mary's L.J. 1009 (1998), explains the frequency with which federal issues are not successfully preserved in state criminal, and especially capital, cases on the bases, *inter alia*, that (i) trial counsel, who often do not serve as counsel on appeal or in federal postconviction review, may overlook the need to raise and properly identify federal objections, and (ii) defense counsel may be wary of resting on federal law when the claim might also be based on state law that appears to be more favorable or clear-cut.

    [4] See also, *e.g.*, Saunders v. Shaw, 244 U.S. 317 (1917); *cf.* Missouri v. Gehner, 281 U.S. 313 (1930); Cole v. Arkansas, 333 U.S. 196 (1948).

the trial court, construed the statute as not in fact requiring proof of the immediacy of violence. Herndon then challenged that construction of the statute as a violation of his First Amendment rights—first on a motion for rehearing in the state supreme court (which was denied), and then on appeal to the United States Supreme Court.

The Supreme Court refused to hear the First Amendment issue, ruling that Herndon had defaulted by not having challenged the statute until filing his motion for rehearing. The Court reasoned that while Herndon's motion for a new trial was pending in the trial court, the Supreme Court of Georgia had decided another case that, in the Court's view, had construed the statute as not requiring proof of the immediacy of violence; thus, the Georgia Supreme Court was justified in holding that Herndon should have anticipated the construction of which he complained and should have challenged it in his initial appeal in state court. In a powerful dissent, Justice Cardozo objected that "[i]t is novel doctrine that a defendant who has had the benefit of all he asks, and indeed of a good deal more, must place a statement on the record that if some other court at some other time shall read the statute differently, there will be a denial of liberties that at the moment of the protest are unchallenged and intact." He also argued persuasively that no decision of the Georgia courts had in fact put Herndon on notice of the construction of the statute later adopted on appeal in his case. Thus, he concluded (citing, *inter alia*, Brinkerhoff-Faris) that Herndon had given "seasonable notice" of his First Amendment claim.

(b) Strict Time Limits for Pre-Trial Motions. Reece v. Georgia, 350 U.S. 85 (1955), and Michel v. Louisiana, 350 U.S. 91 (1955), decided on the same day, both involved due process challenges by criminal defendants who failed to comply with state rules requiring prompt challenges to grand juries.

(i) Reece, an African-American man, "was convicted [in state court] of the rape of a white woman in Cobb County, Georgia." In the Supreme Court of the United States, he sought to challenge his conviction on the ground that African-Americans had been "systematically excluded" from grand jury service, in violation of the Equal Protection Clause. The state argued that this claim was procedurally barred because it was not timely raised in state court. The trial court had not appointed Reece's lawyers until the day after his indictment. Six days later, they moved to quash the indictment based on discrimination in the grand jury's selection. The Georgia courts nonetheless treated the motion as untimely under a longstanding state rule requiring such challenges to be made prior to indictment. Without holding the rule facially invalid, the Supreme Court unanimously ruled that its application here denied due process: "Reece is * * * semi-illiterate [and] of low mentality. We need not decide whether, with the assistance of counsel, he would have had an opportunity to raise his objection during the two days he was in jail before indictment. But it is utterly unrealistic to say that he had such opportunity when counsel was not provided for him until the day after he was indicted. * * * The effective assistance of counsel in [a capital] case is a constitutional requirement of due process * * *. Georgia should have considered Reece's motion to quash on its merits."

Nothing in the Reece opinion suggests that the defendant argued in the state courts that a refusal to hear his grand jury discrimination claim would deny due process. Should he have been required to "present" the due process claim in state court?

(ii) The Michel case involved three defendants who, the Louisiana courts found, had failed to comply with a state rule requiring that objections to the composition of the grand jury be raised before the expiration of the third judicial day following the end of the grand jury's term, or before trial, whichever was earlier.

One defendant had a lawyer who, when the judge purported to appoint him (on the day the grand jury expired), told the judge of his reluctance and asked for a week to look the case over; the lawyer did not receive more definite notice of his appointment until three days after the grand jury had expired. Five days later, the lawyer filed a motion alleging racial discrimination in selecting the grand jury.

A second defendant had fled shortly after the crime with which he was charged, and was not returned to the state until 22 months after his indictment. His motion respecting the grand jury was filed more than a month after his return, and 11 days after his arraignment (where he was represented by counsel).

The third defendant was represented by an elderly lawyer whose first and only action in the case, coming 12 months after his appointment, was to move to withdraw.

In reviewing the state court's findings of procedural default, the Supreme Court declared that the state rule in question did not "raise[ ] an insuperable barrier to one making claim to federal rights. The test is whether the defendant has had 'a reasonable opportunity to have the issue as to the claimed right heard and determined by the state court.' Parker v. Illinois, 333 U.S. 571, 574"—a test that the Court appeared to equate with the meaning of due process. Over three dissents, the Court ruled that the application of the Louisiana rule was not "unreasonable" as to any of the defendants.

(5) Nonconstitutional Bases for Finding State Grounds Inadequate.
The opinion in the Michel case, Paragraph (4)(b), *supra*, appears to assume that a state procedural ground is inadequate only if it denies due process. In general, however, the Court's decisions do not equate the two doctrines.[5] For example, no language in Staub suggests that Georgia's application of its rule requiring the defendant to specify the sections of the ordinance she was challenging denied due process. And if a state procedural rule denies due process, presumably it could not be enforced to prevent hearing a state law claim any more than it could prevent hearing a federal claim; but the Staub opinion does not suggest that Georgia was barred from applying its procedural rule to a challenge based on state constitutional grounds. Other decisions are more explicit that an inadequate procedural ground may not block litigation of federal rights even when it might block litigation of state law claims. See Davis v. Wechsler, Paragraph (5)(b), *infra*.

The "nonconstitutional" bases for inadequacy can be broadly placed in two categories:

(a) The State Procedural Ground Is Not Fairly Supported by State Law Because the Requirement Is Novel or Has Been Inconsistently Applied.
Part of the reasoning in Staub was that the procedural ruling was inadequate because the Georgia precedents did not

---

[5]   See generally Fay v. Noia, 372 U.S. 391, 448, 465–66 (1963) (Harlan, J., dissenting); Meltzer, note 1, *supra*, at 1159–60; Note, 74 Harv.L.Rev. 1375 (1961). But *cf.* Hill, note 1, *supra*, at 971–80.

support it—a point vigorously disputed by Justice Frankfurter. Note the detailed examination of state law necessary to make such a determination.

Just five months after deciding Staub, the Court handed down NAACP v. Alabama ex rel. Patterson, 357 U.S. 449 (1958). There, the NAACP was held in contempt for failing to produce its membership lists, as required by a trial court order that the NAACP assailed as unconstitutional. The NAACP petitioned the Alabama Supreme Court for certiorari to review the contempt judgment. That court refused to consider the constitutional issues, holding that the Association should have sought appellate review prior to the contempt adjudication, by filing a petition for mandamus to quash the discovery order.

The Supreme Court unanimously held that the state court's procedural ground was inadequate to bar consideration of the federal constitutional claims. That ground, the Court said, could not be reconciled with the Alabama court's "past unambiguous holdings as to the scope of review available upon a writ of certiorari addressed to a contempt judgment." Although the Alabama authorities indicated that an order requiring production of evidence could be reviewed on a petition for mandamus, the Court found "nothing in the prior state cases which suggests that mandamus is the *exclusive* remedy for reviewing court orders after disobedience of them has led to contempt judgments. Nor, so far as we can find, do any of these prior decisions indicate that the validity of such orders can be drawn in question by way of certiorari only in instances where a defendant had no opportunity to apply for mandamus. * * * Even if that is indeed the rationale of the Alabama Supreme Court's present decision, such a local procedural rule, although it may now appear in retrospect to form a part of a consistent pattern of procedures to obtain appellate review, cannot avail the State here, because petitioner could not fairly be deemed to have been apprised of its existence. Novelty in procedural requirements cannot be permitted to thwart review in this Court applied for by those who, in justified reliance upon prior decisions, seek vindication in state courts of their federal constitutional rights. *Cf.* Brinkerhoff-Faris Co. v. Hill, 281 U.S. 673."[6]

Inadequacy is similarly established by a demonstration that the state courts had not previously applied their stated rule "with the pointless severity" shown in the present case. See, *e.g.*, Rogers v. Alabama, 192 U.S. 226 (1904) (two-page motion to quash indictment stricken as prolix); NAACP v. Alabama ex rel. Flowers, 377 U.S. 288, 294–302 (1964) (formal arrangement of points in brief); Barr v. City of Columbia, 378 U.S. 146, 149–50 (1964) (generality of stated exceptions; same form accepted in other cases).

Note that a state ruling that is novel or inconsistent could be characterized either as a misapplication of state law or as an implicit revision of state law. Under either view, the state procedural ground will be inadequate and thus will not block Supreme Court review in the present case; but the latter characterization would presumably permit the new ruling to be applied to future cases "once notice of the new interpretation is provided." Meltzer, note 1, *supra*, at 1139 n. 44.

(b) The State Procedural Requirement Is Unacceptably Burdensome. On rare occasions, the Court finds state grounds inadequate

---

[6] For more recent decisions along similar lines, see, *e.g.*, Ford v. Georgia, 498 U.S. 411 (1991); James v. Kentucky, 466 U.S. 341, 345–48 (1984); Hathorn v. Lovorn, 457 U.S. 255 (1982).

not because state rules are applied in an inconsistent or novel fashion but rather because they are burdensome. In Davis v. Wechsler, 263 U.S. 22 (1923), a federal official defending a state court action entered a general denial and also pleaded a special federal jurisdictional objection. The official's successor, substituting as defendant, entered an appearance and adopted the previous pleadings. The state court ruled that the appearance, coming just before the adoption of the pleadings, was a general one and waived the jurisdictional objection. The Supreme Court found the state ground unduly burdensome and therefore inadequate. In a much-quoted passage, Justice Holmes said: "Whatever springes the State may set for those who are endeavoring to assert rights that the State confers, the assertion of federal rights, when plainly and reasonably made, is not to be defeated under the name of local practice."

For examples of other decisions resting on undue burden, see Lee v. Kemna, 534 U.S. 362 (2002) (failing to comply with requirements that a motion for a continuance be in writing and make certain showings is not adequate in the particular circumstances of the case); Osborne v. Ohio, 495 U.S. 103, 123–25 (1990) (requiring a specific objection to jury instructions when the defendant had in substance previously raised the same objection in a motion to dismiss would " 'force resort to an arid ritual of meaningless form' " and would serve no perceivable state interest) (quoting Staub); Douglas v. Alabama, 380 U.S. 415, 422–23 (1965) (rejecting as inadequate a requirement that the defendant repeat, after every question to a witness, a constitutional objection that had been thrice made and whose repetition would have been futile and strategically harmful); Shuttlesworth v. City of Birmingham, 376 U.S. 339 (1964) (failing to use proper paper for petition to review criminal conviction; state forfeiture ruling held inadequate).[7]

(c) Relationship of the Varying Rubrics of Inadequacy. Individual cases may fit within more than one rubric of inadequacy. In Staub, some of the majority's language—"To require her, in these circumstances, to count off, one by one, the several sections of the ordinance would be to force resort to an arid ritual of meaningless form"—suggests that the state court's ruling would have been deemed inadequate (because unduly burdensome) even had the Court thought it was fairly supported by precedent.

(6) State Court "Discretionary" Refusals to Excuse a Procedural Default. A handful of Supreme Court decisions raise the question whether a state court's failure to exercise "discretion" to excuse a litigant's failure to comply with state procedural rules calls into question the adequacy of a state procedural ground.

---

[7] In International Longshoremen's Ass'n v. Davis, 476 U.S. 380 (1986), a labor union, after it had been found liable in tort in state court, objected for the first time that the action was preempted under the federal labor laws. The state courts refused to entertain the preemption defense, holding that it was untimely. The Supreme Court disagreed, ruling 5–4 that a claim of "Garmon preemption" under the federal labor laws goes to the state court's jurisdiction and could not, as a matter of federal law, be waived, notwithstanding the state's procedural rules.

Does the fact that the federal courts treat the lack of federal subject matter jurisdiction as a non-waivable defect necessarily require state courts to do likewise with respect to the question whether their jurisdiction is preempted by federal law? Doesn't the Davis decision risk giving a defendant with a good preemption defense a free roll of the dice: it can take its chances at trial, knowing that it will be able, should the verdict go against it, to raise a preemption defense on appeal? For criticism of Davis, see Holzhauer, *Longshoremen v. Davis and the Nature of Labor Law Pre-Emption*, 1986 Sup.Ct.Rev. 135.

(a) In Williams v. Georgia, 349 U.S. 375 (1955) (6–3), after Williams, an African-American man, had been convicted of an inter-racial murder, the U.S. Supreme Court held in a different case from the same county that the system used there to select juries was unconstitutional. Williams' counsel first raised a jury discrimination claim six months later, in an extraordinary new trial motion filed after affirmance of the conviction. The state courts held the motion untimely on the ground that state practice required a challenge to the array before trial and that there had not been the due diligence necessary to justify an exception to that rule.

The Supreme Court, per Frankfurter, J., vacated and remanded. Although acknowledging the validity of the state rule, the Court said that "where a State allows questions of this sort to be raised at a later stage and be determined by its courts as a matter of discretion, we are not concluded from assuming jurisdiction and deciding whether the state court action in the particular circumstances is, in effect, an avoidance of the federal right." Noting numerous cases in which Georgia courts had exercised discretion to entertain extraordinary motions challenging individual jurors, and finding no basis for distinguishing challenges to the array, the Court stated that "the discretionary decision to deny the motion does not deprive this Court of jurisdiction to find that the substantive issue is properly before us."

"But the fact that we have jurisdiction does not compel us to exercise it." Stressing that life was at stake and that the state had conceded the constitutional violation, the Court concluded that "orderly procedure requires a remand * * *. Fair regard for the principles which the Georgia courts have enforced in numerous cases and for the constitutional commands binding on all courts compels us to reject the assumption that the courts of Georgia would allow this man to go to his death as the result of a conviction secured from a jury which the State admits was unconstitutionally impaneled."[8]

Was the Williams majority seeking "to cajole the Georgia court into reversing itself where the United States Supreme Court lacked grounds to do so"? Note, 69 Harv.L.Rev. 158, 160 (1955). On remand, the Georgia Supreme Court, without briefing or argument, "[a]dhered to" its earlier

---

[8]   To similar effect is Patterson v. Alabama, 294 U.S. 600 (1935), an appeal arising out of the infamous Scottsboro trials. In Patterson, African-American defendants (including Patterson) had been convicted of raping a white girl and sentenced to death for a third time after earlier convictions had been overturned. The Supreme Court of Alabama held that Patterson's challenge to the exclusion of African-Americans from the jury had not been made in timely fashion; in a companion case, that court rejected the same claim of jury discrimination on the merits. Granting review in both cases, the Supreme Court held in the companion case that discrimination was established. Norris v. Alabama, 294 U.S. 587 (1935). In Patterson's case, the Court found the state procedural ruling supported by earlier Alabama decisions, but nonetheless vacated the judgment: "We are not convinced that the [state] court, * * * confronting the anomalous and grave situation which would be created by a reversal of the judgment against Norris, and an affirmance of the judgment of death in the companion case of Patterson, * * * would have considered itself powerless to * * * provide appropriate relief. * * * At least the state court should have an opportunity to examine its powers in the light of the situation which has now developed."

Do you agree that in Patterson, "the technical requirements of law were subordinated to the ends of justice"? Hendel, Charles Evans Hughes and the Supreme Court 161 (1951). A new trial was thereafter granted and a conviction sustained in Patterson v. State, 175 So. 371 (Ala.), cert. denied, 302 U.S. 733 (1937).

judgment, while protesting that the Supreme Court had lacked jurisdiction. 88 S.E.2d 376 (Ga. 1954). Certiorari was denied. 350 U.S. 950 (1956).[9]

(b) In Sullivan v. Little Hunting Park, Inc., 396 U.S. 229 (1969), the trial court dismissed plaintiffs' suit alleging violations of federal civil rights laws. The Supreme Court of Appeals of Virginia denied plaintiffs' appeals, finding a failure to comply with a Virginia rule requiring that opposing counsel be given reasonable notice of the tendering of the transcript and reasonable opportunity to examine it. The Supreme Court (per Douglas, J.) reversed, stating that although the procedural ruling was not novel, the Virginia decisions "do not enable us to say that the Virginia court has so consistently applied its notice requirement as to amount to a self-denial of the power to entertain the federal claim here presented if the Supreme Court of Appeals desires to do so. * * * Such a rule, more properly deemed discretionary than jurisdictional, does not bar review here by certiorari." The Court proceeded to reach the merits and reverse.

In a separate opinion, Justice Harlan, joined by Chief Justice Burger and Justice White, agreed with the conclusion that the state ground was inadequate, but for the different reason that the state court had applied its rule here much more strictly than in prior cases, in violation of the principle of NAACP v. Alabama, Paragraph (5)(a), *supra*. However, he disagreed with the majority's reasoning:

"I am not certain what the majority means in its apparent distinction between rules that it deems 'discretionary' and those that it deems 'jurisdictional.' Perhaps the majority wishes to suggest that the dismissals of petitioners' writs of error by the Supreme Court of Appeals were simply *ad hoc* discretionary refusals to accept plenary review of the lower court's decisions, analogous to this Court's denial of certiorari. If this were all the Virginia Supreme Court of Appeals had done, review of a federal question properly raised below would of course not be barred here. * * *

"But this case clearly does not present this kind of discretionary refusal of a state appellate court to accept review. * * *

"The majority * * * may be suggesting that 'reasonable written notice,' and 'reasonable opportunity to examine' are such flexible standards that the Virginia Supreme Court of Appeals has the 'discretion' to decide a close case either of two ways * * *. * * * This kind of 'discretion' is nothing more than 'the judicial formulation of law,' for a court has an obligation to be reasonably consistent and 'to explain the decision, including the reason for according different treatment to the instant case.' Surely a state ground is no less adequate simply because it involves a standard that requires a judgment of what is reasonable, and because the result may turn on a close analysis of the facts of a particular case in light of competing policy considerations."

(c) In recent years, the Court's habeas case law seems to have moved toward Justice Harlan's position on the relationship between state court discretion and the adequate-and-independent-state-ground doctrine. In Beard v. Kindler, 558 U.S. 53 (2009), Kindler had been convicted of murder

[9]   Dickson, *State Court Defiance and the Limits of Supreme Court Authority: Williams v. Georgia Revisited*, 103 Yale L.J. 1423, 1478 (1994), argues that the Justices failed to respond to the challenge offered on remand by the Georgia Supreme Court because they "feared that a showdown with the Southern states over this case would cost the Court too dearly in terms of image and authority, undermining the Court's efforts to secure Southern compliance with Brown [v. Board of Education]."

in Pennsylvania state court in 1985. While his post-verdict motions were pending, he escaped to Canada, where he was captured, again escaped, and was recaptured. After fighting extradition for several years, Kindler was extradited to the United States in 1991. The Pennsylvania trial court had dismissed Kindler's original postverdict motions because of his escape. In 1991, the trial court rejected his motion to reinstate those earlier motions, reasoning that the original trial judge had not abused his discretion in dismissing them. The Pennsylvania Supreme Court affirmed, concluding that the trial court's dismissal of Kindler's postverdict motions constituted a "reasonable response" to his escape under Pennsylvania's fugitive forfeiture law. On state collateral review, the state courts again rejected Kindler's claims. Kindler then filed a petition for a writ of habeas corpus in federal court. The U.S. Court of Appeals for the Third Circuit held that because Pennsylvania's fugitive forfeiture law gave state courts "discretion" to hear an appeal by a fugitive who had been returned to custody, the fugitive forfeiture rule was not sufficiently "firmly established" to provide an adequate and independent state ground.

In reversing the court of appeals, Chief Justice Roberts, speaking for a unanimous Court, explained: "[A] discretionary state procedural rule can serve as an adequate ground to bar federal habeas review. Nothing inherent in such a rule renders it inadequate for purposes of the adequate state ground doctrine. To the contrary, a discretionary rule can be 'firmly established'—and 'regularly followed' even if the appropriate exercise of discretion may permit consideration of a federal claim in some cases but not others" (citing Meltzer, n.1, *supra*). The Court emphasized that a contrary principle would put states to a terrible choice. They "could preserve flexibility by granting courts discretion to excuse procedural errors, but only at the cost of undermining the finality of state court judgments." Alternatively, they could protect finality "by withholding such discretion, but only at the cost of precluding any flexibility in applying the rules." Noting that federal procedural norms frequently give the trial judge "broad discretion," the Court suggested that "the federalism and comity concerns that motivate the adequate state ground doctrine" would make it "particularly strange to disregard state procedural rules that are substantially similar to those to which we give full force in our own courts." For a similar approach to discretion and procedural default in habeas, see Walker v. Martin, 562 U.S. 307 (2011).

Is there any reason to think that the Court's reasoning in Kindler should have less force in the context of applying the adequate-state-ground doctrine on direct review? If not, what criteria should the Court apply in determining whether the exercise of such discretion negates an adequate and independent state ground?

(7) Henry v. Mississippi. The Court's decision in Henry v. Mississippi, 379 U.S. 443 (1965), may represent the high point of its assertion of power to hear federal claims despite their apparent forfeiture in state court. Two years earlier, in Fay v. Noia, 372 U.S. 391 (1963), the Court had held that when a federal district court heard a petition for a writ of habeas corpus—a device for collaterally attacking custody pursuant to a state court conviction—it was free to reach the merits, despite a procedural default, unless the defendant had personally "waived" a federal constitutional claim in state court. See pp. 1324–1326, *infra*. Henry then seemingly imported Noia's forgiving standards for judging procedural default into the context of direct review of state court convictions. In Henry, the defendant, a prominent NAACP leader in Mississippi, was prosecuted for what many viewed as a baseless charge, in proceedings in which segregation lingered. (Henry's lawyer, unlike the prosecutor, was not given a water pitcher in the hot courtroom but was told he could use the fountain "for colored only" outside the courtroom.) Henry had moved at the close of the state's case for a directed verdict; his motion objected in passing to the admission of evidence derived from an allegedly unconstitutional search. The Mississippi Supreme Court ultimately refused to reach the Fourth Amendment issue because of the defendant's failure to have made a contemporaneous objection when the evidence was admitted.

In a confusing opinion by Justice Brennan, the Supreme Court declared that a state court may not forfeit a litigant's federal rights unless the procedural requirement that the litigant failed to satisfy serves a "legitimate state interest." Although conceding that Mississippi's contemporaneous objection rule itself satisfied this test (which was more stringent than prior conditions for adequate state grounds), Justice Brennan went on to find that the purpose underlying this rule might have been substantially served by Henry's objection in his motion for a directed verdict. Ultimately, however, rather than deciding whether the state court's application of the contemporaneous objection rule in these circumstances constituted an adequate state ground, the Court noted that Henry's lawyer might have deliberately waived his federal claim, in which case federal review would be barred. The Court vacated the judgment to permit a hearing on the waiver issue.

Justice Harlan's dissent (joined by Justices Clark and Stewart) argued, *inter alia*, (i) that Henry's lengthy motion for a directed verdict, only one sentence of which referred to the search and seizure issue, did not realistically alert the trial judge to the claim, and (ii) that a contemporaneous objection rule, by focusing attention on the disputed evidence when introduced, minimizes the risk of error and the potential for a mistrial.

Despite its radical potential, Henry had little effect on the standards applied on direct review in judging the adequacy of state procedural grounds; for the most part Henry has been ignored in subsequent cases. Some decisions cited Henry while resting on more traditional formulations of inadequacy, see, *e.g.*, James v. Kentucky, 466 U.S. 341, 345–48 (1984). Others decisions finding state grounds inadequate failed to cite Henry, even though it seemed pertinent. See Douglas v. Alabama, 380 U.S. 415 (1965); Parrot v. Tallahassee, 381 U.S. 129 (1965). In Monger v. Florida, 405 U.S. 958 (1972), the state supreme court dismissed an appeal because the defendant filed his notice of appeal too *soon*: the notice was filed on the day the trial judge pronounced an oral judgment and imposed sentence (January 12), but the written judgment was entered on January 18, "*nunc pro tunc* January 12.*" The Supreme Court entered the following per curiam order: "The petition for writ of certiorari is denied, it appearing that judgment [sic] of the Supreme Court of Florida rests upon an adequate state ground." Justice Douglas, joined by Justices Brennan and Stewart, dissented, citing Henry and arguing that "no state interest * * * would be served by rejecting a notice of appeal filed after an oral pronouncement of judgment but before a written order." Isn't Justice Douglas correct that the disposition of Monger cannot be squared with Henry? What might explain Henry's lack of generative capacity?

(8) The Source of Power to Find State Grounds Inadequate. What is the basis for the Supreme Court's assertion of the power to review a case where the state judgment rests on a procedural ruling that the Court finds "inadequate"? Could Supreme Court review of federal questions be adequately effectuated if state procedural rulings, once found constitutional, wholly insulated federal issues from review? See Wechsler, *The Appellate Jurisdiction of the Supreme Court: Reflections on the Law and Logistics of Direct Review*, 34 Wash. & Lee L.Rev. 1043, 1053–56 (1977). Consider whether the following justifications are persuasive.

(a) Traditional Explanations. First, one might ascribe to the Due Process Clause judicial power to find state grounds inadequate if (a) a state procedural bar denies a litigant a reasonable opportunity to raise the federal claim, or (b) if the novelty or inconsistency of a state procedural bar's application results in arbitrary decisionmaking. But the Due Process Clause, although occasionally invoked in the Court's decisions, see Paragraph (4), *supra*, provides at best a partial explanation for the doctrine. As Professor Meltzer writes, the Court has never held that mere inconsistency or lack of uniformity, standing alone, violates due process. In addition, he notes, if due process were the source of the inadequate state ground doctrine, it would provide a federal constitutional basis for challenging the application of state court procedural bars against *state* claims—something that the Court has not yet endeavored to do. See Meltzer, note 1, *supra*, at 1159–61.

Second, to the extent that the inadequate state ground doctrine suggests a purpose to prevent the use of state procedural rules to evade or deny federal claims of right, the source of judicial power to apply that doctrine might originate in the Supremacy Clause, U.S. Const. Art. VI. As Professor Hill puts it, that theory would rest on the proposition "that there is jurisdiction to determine whether the state court has given federal law its due". Hill, note 1, *supra*, at 959. The anti-discrimination theory, however, does not necessarily account for cases that find inadequacy on the basis of an undue burden on the presentation of federal claims. See Paragraph 5(b), *supra*. Moreover, Professor Meltzer writes: "The supremacy clause is usually viewed * * * as creating not a substantive rule of federal law, but a rule of priority: if state and federal law conflict, federal law prevails. But this priority tells us little about what the federal law should be. For these reasons, it is hard to view the inadequate state ground doctrine simply as an interpretation of a constitutional provision barring discrimination." Meltzer, note 1, *supra*, at 1162.

Third, the source of the doctrine may be traced to the jurisdictional statute authorizing Supreme Court review—28 U.S.C. § 1257—which requires that "any title, right, privilege, or immunity [be] specially set up or claimed under the Constitution or the treaties or statutes of * * * the United States." Professor Roosevelt thus suggests that when the Supreme Court decides the adequacy of the ground for a state court procedural default, it is determining, as a matter of federal law, whether the federal right was "specially set up or claimed" in state court within the meaning of § 1257. Federal law, he adds, in general incorporates applicable state law, so as not to interfere with a state's ability to establish its own procedural rules. When, however, the federal statutory standard does not incorporate state rules (because the state ground is inadequate), that decision governs only the Supreme Court's jurisdiction; it does not preclude the state court from continuing to follow the rule in similar cases. See Roosevelt, *Light from Dead*

Stars: The Procedural Adequate and Independent State Ground Reconsidered, 103 Colum.L.Rev. 1888 (2003).

One might plausibly attribute to § 1257 a purpose to maintain federal supremacy through the development of the inadequate state ground doctrine. But such an interpretation of § 1257 is "not closely tied to the text or other indicia of legislative intent." Meltzer, note 1, *supra*, at 1163. And treating § 1257 as the source of the doctrine would give rise to the odd situation in which a state court might correctly apply a state procedural bar to a federal claim, only to have the Supreme Court, on review, correctly reverse the state court's decision on the merits on the basis that the state court's application of state procedural law cannot bar Supreme Court consideration of the federal claim. Is it consistent with the broader implications of Murdock and Erie to have the applicable law in a single litigation change as the case moves up the appellate ladder to the Supreme Court?

(b) The Inadequate State Ground Doctrine as Federal Common Law. Could one explain the inadequate state ground doctrine as a form of "federal common law" that places limits, beyond those demanded by the Due Process Clause, on the freedom of states to refuse to entertain federal claims because not presented in compliance with state procedural rules? See Meltzer, note 1, *supra*, which adopts such a theory and then uses the reformulation to advocate somewhat more forgiveness in excusing state procedural defaults.[10]

According to Professor Meltzer, "special institutional factors" mitigate "inherent concerns about the legitimacy of federal common law"—concerns that center on the separation-of-powers and federalism implications of federal judicial lawmaking. See Chap. VII, Sec. 1(B), *infra*. First, because judges are experts in procedure, they have a comparative advantage in crafting a doctrine of inadequate state grounds. Second, separation of powers concerns are minimized because "doctrines excusing procedural default" necessarily depend heavily on "factual nuance", which makes such doctrines "notoriously difficult to encapsulate in clear and specific codes". Hence, even if Congress wished to address the question legislatively, federal judges would necessarily retain a great deal of policymaking discretion in filling in the interstices of any such statute. Third, federalism concerns about federal common lawmaking could be significantly mitigated if state courts participated in the formulation of a federal common law of state court forfeitures of federal rights.

Assuming that Professor Meltzer's take on the institutional factors is correct, what is the source of authority for the formulation of such federal common law rules? Article III? § 1257? Some other source?

Consider the implications of the federal common law approach if, just after the decision in Staub v. Baxley, a case raising an indistinguishable procedural issue were to arise in Georgia with respect to the forfeiture of a federal claim. Professor Meltzer argues that the Supreme Court's decision in Staub—finding inadequate the Georgia rule that a litigant must object to each separate section of the statute—should not be regarded simply as

---

[10] Noting, however, that federal common law should be guided by federal legislative policy, Meltzer argues that the standards for excusing procedural defaults in the state courts should not be more forgiving than the standards applied in the federal courts, which themselves have numerous procedural rules whose violation results in the forfeiture of federal rights. Meltzer, note 1, *supra*, at 1202–08.

regulating Supreme Court jurisdiction to review, but rather as establishing a federal common law rule that must be honored in the state courts. Compare Dice v. Akron, Canton & Youngstown R.R., 342 U.S. 359 (1952), p. 449, *supra* (holding that in FELA actions, state courts must follow a federal procedural rule requiring jury trial on the issue whether a purported release of the claim was fraudulently obtained—even though the federal rule was not set forth in any federal constitutional or statutory enactment).[11]

(9) State Court Excuse of Procedural Default. In the cases already discussed, the state courts enforced their procedural rules by refusing to reach federal claims that were not properly presented. But when a state court chooses instead to excuse a procedural violation and proceeds to reach the merits of the federal claim, the Supreme Court's jurisdiction to review the decision is secure.[12] This rule creates an obvious risk that the record may not be adequately developed, but the elimination of mandatory appeals in 1988 permits the Court to deny certiorari whenever that problem might exist.

(10) State Court Ambiguity. Sometimes it is unclear whether a state court's denial of relief rests on a state procedural ground (which would ordinarily foreclose Supreme Court review) or on the merits of the federal issue (which would permit such review). In such cases, the earlier decisions declined jurisdiction, presuming that the state judgment rested on the procedural default. See, *e.g.*, Mutual Life Ins. Co. v. McGrew, 188 U.S. 291, 309–10 (1903); Bailey v. Anderson, 326 U.S. 203, 206–07 (1945). The Court's decision in Harris v. Reed, p. 507, *supra*, suggests that the ordinary presumption may now be just the reverse, so as to permit Supreme Court review. But compare the subsequent decisions in Coleman v. Thompson and Ylst v. Nunnemaker, p. 507, *supra*, which qualify Harris' approach. *Cf.* Capital Cities Media, Inc. v. Toole, p. 506, *supra* (instead of presuming one way or the other, vacating and remanding to the state court for clarification).

―――――

3.   FINAL JUDGMENTS AND THE HIGHEST STATE COURT

―――――

Cox Broadcasting Corp. v. Cohn
420 U.S. 469, 95 S.Ct. 1029, 43 L.Ed.2d 328 (1975).
Appeal from the Supreme Court of Georgia.

■ MR. JUSTICE WHITE delivered the opinion of the Court.

[During a criminal prosecution for rape and murder, a television reporter broadcasted a news story reporting the victim's name, which he had learned from records publicly available at the court. The victim's father sued the reporter and the television station for invasion of privacy, relying on Ga. Code Ann. § 26–9901, which made publication or broadcast of the identity of a rape victim a misdemeanor. Despite the defendants'

―――――

[11] The question whether a finding of "inadequacy" should bind the state courts in future cases has divided the commentators. See Meltzer, note 1, *supra*, at 1150–52, 1202 n. 70.

[12] See, *e.g.*, Whitney v. California, 274 U.S. 357, 360–63 (1927); Orr v. Orr, 440 U.S. 268, 274–75 (1979); Payton v. New York, 445 U.S. 573, 582 n. 19 (1980).

claim that the imposition of civil liability would violate the First Amendment, the state trial court held that § 26–9901 implicitly created a civil remedy and granted summary judgment for the plaintiff on liability, with damages to be determined at a jury trial.

[On appeal, the Georgia Supreme Court initially ruled that the trial court's recognition of an implied right of action under § 26–9901 was in error (and therefore it did not further discuss the statute's constitutionality). The court added, though, that the complaint did state a cause of action for invasion of privacy or for the common law tort of public disclosure. The award of summary judgment, however, was improper, because whether public disclosure of the name actually invaded plaintiff's "zone of privacy," and if so, to what extent, were issues to be determined by the trier of fact. The court went on to say that "in formulating such an issue for determination by the fact-finder, it is reasonable to require the appellee to prove that the appellants invaded his privacy with willful or negligent disregard for the fact that reasonable men would find the invasion highly offensive." The Georgia Supreme Court agreed with the trial court, however, that the First and Fourteenth Amendments did not, as a matter of law, require judgment for defendants.]

Upon motion for rehearing the Georgia court countered the argument that the victim's name was a matter of public interest and could be published with impunity by relying on § 26–9901 as an authoritative declaration of state policy that the name of a rape victim was not a matter of public concern. This time the court felt compelled to determine the constitutionality of the statute and sustained it as a "legitimate limitation on the right of freedom of expression contained in the First Amendment." * * *

We postponed decision as to our jurisdiction over this appeal to the hearing on the merits. We conclude that the Court has jurisdiction, and reverse the judgment of the Georgia Supreme Court.

II

* * * Since 1789, Congress has granted this Court appellate jurisdiction with respect to state litigation only after the highest state court in which judgment could be had has rendered a "[f]inal judgment or decree." Title 28 U.S.C. § 1257 retains this limitation on our power to review cases coming from state courts. The Court has noted that "[c]onsiderations of English usage as well as those of judicial policy" would justify an interpretation of the final-judgment rule to preclude review "where anything further remains to be determined by a State court, no matter how dissociated from the only federal issue that has finally been adjudicated by the highest court of the State." Radio Station WOW, Inc. v. Johnson, 326 U.S. 120, 124 (1945). But the Court there observed that the rule had not been administered in such a mechanical fashion and that there were circumstances in which there has been "a departure from this requirement of finality for federal appellate jurisdiction." *Ibid.*

These circumstances were said to be "very few," *ibid.*; but as the cases have unfolded * * * [t]here are now at least four categories of * * * cases in which the Court has treated the decision on the federal issue as a final judgment for the purposes of 28 U.S.C. § 1257 and has taken jurisdiction without awaiting the completion of the additional proceedings anticipated in the lower state courts. * * *

In the first category are those cases in which there are further proceedings—even entire trials—yet to occur in the state courts but where for one reason or another the federal issue is conclusive or the outcome of further proceedings preordained. In these circumstances, because the case is for all practical purposes concluded, the judgment of the state court on the federal issue is deemed final. In Mills v. Alabama, 384 U.S. 214 (1966), for example, a demurrer to a criminal complaint was sustained on federal constitutional grounds by a state trial court. The State Supreme Court reversed, remanding for jury trial. This Court took jurisdiction on the reasoning that the appellant had no defense other than his federal claim and could not prevail at trial on the facts or any nonfederal ground. To dismiss the appeal "would not only be an inexcusable delay of the benefits Congress intended to grant by providing for appeal to this Court, but it would also result in a completely unnecessary waste of time and energy in judicial systems already troubled by delays due to congested dockets." (footnote omitted).

Second, there are cases such as Radio Station WOW, *supra*, and Brady v. Maryland, 373 U.S. 83 (1963), in which the federal issue, finally decided by the highest court in the State, will survive and require decision regardless of the outcome of future state-court proceedings. In Radio Station WOW, the Nebraska Supreme Court directed the transfer of the properties of a federally licensed radio station and ordered an accounting, rejecting the claim that the transfer order would interfere with the federal license. The federal issue was held reviewable here despite the pending accounting on the "presupposition * * * that the federal questions that could come here have been adjudicated by the State court, and that the accounting which remains to be taken could not remotely give rise to a federal question * * * that may later come here * * *." * * * Nothing that could happen in the course of the accounting, short of settlement of the case, would foreclose or make unnecessary decision on the federal question. Older cases in the Court had reached the same result on similar facts. * * *9

In the third category are those situations where the federal claim has been finally decided, with further proceedings on the merits in the state courts to come, but in which later review of the federal issue cannot be had, whatever the ultimate outcome of the case. Thus, in these cases, if the party seeking interim review ultimately prevails on the merits, the federal issue will be mooted; if he were to lose on the merits, however, the governing state law would not permit him again to present his federal claims for review. * * * California v. Stewart, 384 U.S. 436 (1966) (decided with Miranda v. Arizona), epitomizes this category. There the state court reversed a conviction on federal constitutional grounds and remanded for a new trial. Although the State might have prevailed at trial, we granted its petition for certiorari and affirmed, explaining that the state judgment was "final" since an acquittal of the defendant at trial would preclude, under state law, an appeal by the State.

---

9   In Brady v. Maryland, 373 U.S. 83 (1963), the Maryland courts had ordered a new trial in a criminal case but on punishment only, and the petitioner asserted here that he was entitled to a new trial on guilt as well. We entertained the case, saying that the federal issue was separable and would not be mooted by the new trial on punishment ordered in the state courts.

A recent decision in this category is North Dakota State Board of Pharmacy v. Snyder's Drug Stores, Inc., 414 U.S. 156 (1973), in which the Pharmacy Board rejected an application for a pharmacy operating permit relying on a state statute specifying ownership requirements which the applicant did not meet. The State Supreme Court held the statute unconstitutional and remanded the matter to the Board for further consideration of the application, freed from the constraints of the ownership statute. * * * [When the Board sought review, we exercised jurisdiction.] The federal issue would not survive the remand, whatever the result of the state administrative proceedings. The Board might deny the license on state-law grounds, thus foreclosing the federal issue, and the Court also ascertained that under state law the Board could not bring the federal issue here in the event the applicant satisfied the requirements of state law except for the invalidated ownership statute. Under these circumstances, the issue was ripe for review.[10]

Lastly, there are those situations where the federal issue has been finally decided in the state courts with further proceedings pending in which the party seeking review here might prevail on the merits on nonfederal grounds, thus rendering unnecessary review of the federal issue by this Court, and where reversal of the state court on the federal issue would be preclusive of any further litigation on the relevant cause of action rather than merely controlling the nature and character of, or determining the admissibility of evidence in, the state proceedings still to come. In these circumstances, if a refusal immediately to review the state-court decision might seriously erode federal policy, the Court has entertained and decided the federal issue, which itself has been finally determined by the state courts for purposes of the state litigation.

In Local No. 438 Construction and General Laborers' Union v. Curry, 371 U.S. 542 (1963), the state courts temporarily enjoined labor union picketing over claims that the National Labor Relations Board had exclusive jurisdiction of the controversy. The Court took jurisdiction for two independent reasons. First, the power of the state court to proceed in the face of the preemption claim was deemed an issue separable from the merits and ripe for review in this Court, particularly "when postponing review would seriously erode the national labor policy requiring the subject matter of respondents' cause to be heard by the * * * Board, not by the state courts." Second, the Court was convinced that in any event the union had no defense to the entry of a permanent injunction other than the preemption claim that had already been ruled on in the state courts. Hence the case was for all practical purposes concluded in the state tribunals.

In Mercantile National Bank v. Langdeau, 371 U.S. 555 (1963), two national banks [that had been sued in a particular county asserted that, under a federal venue statute,] they could properly be sued only in another county. Although trial was still to be had and the banks might

---

[10]   Cohen v. Beneficial Industrial Loan Corp., 337 U.S. 541 (1949), was a diversity action in the federal courts in the course of which there arose the question of the validity of a state statute requiring plaintiffs in stockholder suits to post security for costs as a prerequisite to bringing the action. The District Court held the state law inapplicable, the Court of Appeals reversed, and this Court, after granting certiorari, held that the issue of security for costs was separable from and independent of the merits and that if review were to be postponed until the termination of the litigation, "it will be too late effectively to review the present order, and the rights conferred by the statute, if it is applicable, will have been lost, probably irreparably."

well prevail on the merits, the Court, relying on Curry, entertained the issue as a "separate and independent matter, anterior to the merits and not enmeshed in the factual and legal issues comprising the plaintiff's cause of action." Moreover, it would serve the policy of the federal statute "to determine now in which state court appellants may be tried rather than to subject them * * * to long and complex litigation which may all be for naught if consideration of the preliminary question of venue is postponed until the conclusion of the proceedings."

Miami Herald Publishing Co. v. Tornillo, 418 U.S. 241 (1974), is the latest case in this category. There a candidate for public office sued a newspaper for refusing, allegedly contrary to a state statute, to carry his reply to the paper's editorial critical of his qualifications. The trial court held the act unconstitutional, denying both injunctive relief and damages. The State Supreme Court reversed, sustaining the statute against the challenge based upon the First and Fourteenth Amendments and remanding the case for a trial and appropriate relief, including damages. The newspaper brought the case here. We sustained our jurisdiction, relying on the principles elaborated in the North Dakota case and observing:

> "Whichever way we were to decide on the merits, it would be intolerable to leave unanswered, under these circumstances, an important question of freedom of the press under the First Amendment; an uneasy and unsettled constitutional posture of § 104.38 could only further harm the operation of a free press."

In light of the prior cases, we conclude that we have jurisdiction to review the judgment of the Georgia Supreme Court * * *, [which] is plainly final on the federal issue and is not subject to further review in the state courts. Appellants will be liable for damages if the elements of the state cause of action are proved. They may prevail at trial on nonfederal grounds, it is true, but if the Georgia court erroneously upheld the statute, there should be no trial at all. Moreover, even if appellants prevailed at trial and made unnecessary further consideration of the constitutional question, there would remain in effect the unreviewed decision of the State Supreme Court that a civil action for publishing the name of a rape victim disclosed in a public judicial proceeding may go forward despite the First and Fourteenth Amendments. Delaying final decision of the First Amendment claim until after trial will "leave unanswered * * * an important question of freedom of the press under the First Amendment," "an uneasy and unsettled constitutional posture [that] could only further harm the operation of a free press." Tornillo, *supra*, at 247 n. 6. On the other hand, if we now hold that the First and Fourteenth Amendments bar civil liability for broadcasting the victim's name, this litigation ends. Given these factors—that the litigation could be terminated by our decision on the merits[13] and that a failure to decide

---

13 Mr. Justice Rehnquist is correct in saying that this factor involves consideration of the merits in determining jurisdiction. But it does so only to the extent of determining that the issue is substantial and only in the context that if the state court's final decision on the federal issue is incorrect, federal law forecloses further proceedings in the state court. That the petitioner who protests against the state court's decision on the federal question might prevail on the merits on nonfederal grounds in the course of further proceedings anticipated in the state court and hence obviate later review of the federal issue here is not preclusive of our jurisdiction. Curry, Langdeau, North Dakota State Board of Pharmacy, California v. Stewart, 384 U.S. 436 (1966) (decided with Miranda v. Arizona), and Miami Herald Publishing Co. v. Tornillo, 418

the question now will leave the press in Georgia operating in the shadow of the civil and criminal sanctions of a rule of law and a statute the constitutionality of which is in serious doubt—we find that reaching the merits is consistent with the pragmatic approach that we have followed in the past in determining finality. * * *

[The Court proceeded to invalidate § 26–9901 and the common-law privacy action on the merits, holding that the First and Fourteenth Amendments preclude states from basing liability on the publication of truthful information contained in official court records open to public inspection.]

Reversed.

■ [JUSTICE POWELL wrote a concurring opinion. CHIEF JUSTICE BURGER concurred in the judgment without opinion. JUSTICE DOUGLAS wrote an opinion concurring in the judgment.]

■ MR. JUSTICE REHNQUIST, dissenting.

* * * Over the years, * * * this Court has steadily discovered new exceptions to the finality requirement, such that they can hardly any longer be described as "very few." * * * Although the Court's opinion today does accord detailed consideration to this problem, I do not believe that the reasons it expresses can support its result.

I

The Court has taken what it terms a "pragmatic" approach to the finality problem presented in this case. In so doing, it has relied heavily on Gillespie v. United States Steel Corp., 379 U.S. 148 (1964). As the Court acknowledges, Gillespie involved 28 U.S.C. § 1291, which restricts the appellate jurisdiction of the federal courts of appeals to "final decisions of the district courts." Although acknowledging this distinction, the Court accords it no importance and adopts Gillespie's approach without any consideration of whether the finality requirement for this Court's jurisdiction over a "judgment or decree" of a state court is grounded on more serious concerns than is the limitation of court of appeals jurisdiction to final "decisions" of the district courts. * * *

Were judicial efficiency the only interest at stake there would be less inclination to challenge the Court's resolution in this case, although, as discussed below, I have serious reservations that the standards the Court has formulated are effective for achieving even this single goal. The case before us, however, is an appeal from a state court, and this fact introduces additional interests which must be accommodated in fashioning any exception to the literal application of the finality requirement. I consider § 1257 finality to be but one of a number of congressional provisions reflecting concern that uncontrolled federal judicial interference with state administrative and judicial functions would have untoward consequences for our federal system. This is by no means a novel view of the § 1257 finality requirement. In Radio Station WOW, Inc. v. Johnson, 326 U.S. [120, 124 (1945),] Mr. Justice Frankfurter's opinion for the Court explained the finality requirement as follows:

U.S. 241 (1974), make this clear. In those cases, the federal issue having been decided, arguably wrongly, and being determinative of the litigation if decided the other way, the finality rule was satisfied. * * *

*" * * * This prerequisite to review derives added force when the jurisdiction of this Court is invoked to upset the decision of a State court.* Here we are in the realm of potential conflict between the courts of two different governments. And so, ever since 1789, Congress has granted this Court the power to intervene in State litigation only after 'the highest court of a State in which a decision in the suit could be had' has rendered a 'final judgment or decree.' § 237 of the Judicial Code, 28 U.S.C. § 344(a). *This requirement is not one of those technicalities to be easily scorned. It is an important factor in the smooth working of our federal system."* (Emphasis added.) * * *

[W]e have in recent years emphasized and re-emphasized the importance of comity and federalism in dealing with a related problem, that of district court interference with ongoing state judicial proceedings. See Younger v. Harris, 401 U.S. 37 (1971). Because these concerns are important, and because they provide "added force" to § 1257's finality requirement, I believe that the Court has erred by simply importing the approach of cases in which the only concern is efficient judicial administration.

II

But quite apart from the considerations of federalism which counsel against an expansive reading of our jurisdiction under § 1257, the Court's holding today enunciates a virtually formless exception to the finality requirement, one which differs in kind from those previously carved out. * * *

While the totality of [the exceptions previously recognized by the Court] certainly indicates that the Court has been willing to impart to the language "final judgment or decree" a great deal of flexibility, each of them is arguably consistent with the intent of Congress in enacting § 1257, if not with the language it used, and each of them is relatively workable in practice.

To those established exceptions is now added one so formless that it cannot be paraphrased, but instead must be quoted:

"Given these factors—that the litigation could be terminated by our decision on the merits and that a failure to decide the question now will leave the press in Georgia operating in the shadow of the civil and criminal sanctions of a rule of law and a statute the constitutionality of which is in serious doubt—we find that reaching the merits is consistent with the pragmatic approach that we have followed in the past in determining finality."

There are a number of difficulties with this test. One of them is the Court's willingness to look to the merits. It is not clear from the Court's opinion, however, exactly how great a look at the merits we are to take. On the one hand, the Court emphasizes that if we reverse the Supreme Court of Georgia the litigation will end, and it refers to cases in which the federal issue has been decided "arguably wrongly." On the other hand, it claims to look to the merits "only to the extent of determining that the issue is substantial." If the latter is all the Court means, then the inquiry is no more extensive than is involved when we determine whether a case is appropriate for plenary consideration; but if no more is meant, our decision is just as likely to be a costly intermediate step in the litigation as it is to be the concluding event. If, on the other hand, the Court really intends its doctrine to reach only so far as cases in which our decision in all probability will terminate the litigation, then * * * henceforth in determining our own jurisdiction we may be obliged to determine whether or not we agree with the merits of the decision of the highest court of a State.

Yet another difficulty with the Court's formulation is the problem of transposing to any other case the requirement that "failure to decide the question now will leave the press in Georgia operating in the shadow of the civil and criminal sanctions of a rule of law and a statute the constitutionality of which is in serious doubt." Assuming that we are to make this determination of "serious doubt" at the time we note probable jurisdiction of such an appeal, is it enough that the highest court of the State has ruled against any federal constitutional claim? If that is the case, then because § 1257 by other language imposes that requirement, we will have completely read out of the statute the limitation of our jurisdiction to a "final judgment or decree." Perhaps the Court's new standard for finality is limited to cases in which a First Amendment freedom is at issue. The language used by Congress, however, certainly provides no basis for preferring the First Amendment, as incorporated by the Fourteenth Amendment, to the various other Amendments which are likewise "incorporated," or indeed for preferring any of the "incorporated" Amendments over the due process and equal protection provisions which are embodied literally in the Fourteenth Amendment.

Another problem is that in applying the second prong of its test, the Court has not engaged in any independent inquiry as to the consequences of permitting the decision of the Supreme Court of Georgia to remain undisturbed pending final state-court resolution of the case. * * * In this case nothing more is at issue than the right to report the name of the victim of a rape. No hindrance of any sort has been imposed on reporting the fact of a rape or the circumstances surrounding it. Yet the Court unquestioningly places this issue on a par with the core First Amendment interest involved in Miami Herald Publishing Co. v. Tornillo, 418 U.S. 241 (1974), and Mills v. Alabama, [384 U.S. 214 (1966),] that of protecting the press in its role of providing uninhibited political discourse.

But the greatest difficulty with the test enunciated today is that it totally abandons the principle that constitutional issues are too important to be decided save when absolutely necessary, and are to be avoided if there are grounds for decision of lesser dimension * * *. [That principle is] primarily designed, not to benefit the lower courts, or state-federal relations, but rather to safeguard this Court's own process of constitutional adjudication. * * *

In this case there has yet to be an adjudication of liability against appellants, and unlike the appellant in Mills v. Alabama, they do not concede that they have no nonfederal defenses. Nonetheless, the Court rules on their constitutional defense. * * *

III

This Court is obliged to make preliminary determinations of its jurisdiction at the time it votes to note probable jurisdiction. * * * [S]uch determinations must of necessity be based on relatively cursory acquaintance with the record of the proceedings below. * * * It is thus especially disturbing that the rule of this case, unlike the more workable and straightforward exceptions which the Court has previously formulated, will seriously compound the already difficult task of accurately determining, at a preliminary stage, whether an appeal from a state-court judgment is a "final judgment or decree." * * *

I would dismiss for want of jurisdiction.

————

NOTE ON THE FINAL JUDGMENT RULE AND THE HIGHEST STATE COURT REQUIREMENT

(1) Evolution of the Finality Doctrine. As Cox indicates, out of the deceptively simple language "final judgment or decree," enacted in 1789 in Section 25 of the first Judiciary Act and found today in 28 U.S.C. § 1257 ("final judgments or decrees"), the Court has developed a complicated body of doctrine.

For many years, the Court permitted review only when nothing was left to be done except entry or execution of judgment. See, *e.g.*, Houston v. Moore, 16 U.S. (3 Wheat.) 433 (1818). The first major inroad came with Carondelet Canal & Navigation Co. v. Louisiana, 233 U.S. 362 (1914), in which the state supreme court's judgment ordered the transfer of the company's property, despite its claim of federal protection, and remanded for an accounting. In reviewing that judgment, the Supreme Court noted that the remaining issue on remand was narrow and that the state supreme court's judgment disposed of the federal right asserted. Over time, a "penumbral area" developed within which state court judgments that left something to be adjudicated were nevertheless deemed final—often when they resolved a federal question in a manner threatening immediate and irreparable harm to a party. *E.g.*, Radio Station WOW, Inc. v. Johnson, 326 U.S. 120, 124 (1945).

The 1963 decisions in Curry and Langdeau (both discussed in Cox) substantially expanded the penumbra of finality. Curry's loose formulation, which treated as final cases where "postponing review would seriously erode" national policy, established the foundation for the fourth Cox category.

(2) The First Cox Category. The first Cox category—cases in which, despite a state court's remand to a lower state court, the federal question finally decided by the state court is likely to be decisive—has not been very controversial.[1] For example, in Duquesne Light Co. v. Barasch, 488 U.S. 299 (1989), the state PUC authorized a rate increase to permit a utility to recoup costs incurred from canceled nuclear plants. The state supreme court reversed, remanding for the PUC to set lower rates excluding those costs, and rejecting the utility's argument that the lower rates constituted an unconstitutional "taking". In hearing the utility's appeal, the Supreme Court (with only Justice Blackmun dissenting) ruled that the state court had finally adjudicated the constitutional challenge, leaving for remand only "straight-forward application of [the state supreme court's] clear directive to otherwise complete rate orders."

————

[1]   See, *e.g.*, the Mills case discussed in Cox; Richfield Oil Corp. v. State Bd. of Equalization, 329 U.S. 69 (1946); Abood v. Detroit Bd. of Educ., 431 U.S. 209, 216 n. 8 (1977).

(3) The Second Cox Category. The second Cox category allows review of federal claims that will eventually require decision no matter what happens during further state court proceedings. Consider the suggestions (a) that each of the cases cited in Cox in support of this second category "arguably involved elements of hardship in addition to the simple burden of proceedings that might prove unnecessary" and that this category should be restricted to such situations, 16B Wright, Miller, & Cooper, Federal Practice and Procedure § 4010, at 174, and (b) that in practice the prediction necessitated under this category is too difficult to make reliably, see Note, 91 Harv.L.Rev. 1004, 1017–20 (1978).

(4) The Third Cox Category. The third Cox exception allows immediate review where further proceedings may render the federal question effectively unreviewable. Typical, and routinely reviewed, are criminal cases where the state court has decided a federal question in favor of the defendant—either in an interlocutory appeal or in reversing a conviction and remanding for retrial. See, *e.g.*, New York v. Quarles, 467 U.S. 649 (1984), California v. Trombetta, 467 U.S. 479 (1984), and Florida v. Meyers, 466 U.S. 380 (1984) (all reviewing decisions suppressing evidence on federal constitutional grounds).

(5) The Fourth Cox Category. The fourth Cox category requires that (i) reversal of the state court on the federal issue would end the litigation, and (ii) a refusal to review the federal issue would immediately threaten serious erosion of a significant federal policy. The range of federal policies encompassed has been broad. See, *e.g.*, Bullington v. Missouri, 451 U.S. 430 (1981), and Harris v. Washington, 404 U.S. 55 (1971) (constitutional policy against double jeopardy threatened if defendant tried a second time); Goodyear Atomic Corp. v. Miller, 486 U.S. 174 (1988) (federal preemption of state safety rules for nuclear facilities threatened by workers' compensation award based on violation of those rules); Southland Corp. v. Keating, 465 U.S. 1 (1984) (Federal Arbitration Act's policy of requiring arbitration eroded by decision refusing to compel arbitration and ordering state judicial proceedings); Belknap, Inc. v. Hale, 463 U.S. 491 (1983) (to permit state proceedings would erode federal policy giving the NLRB exclusive jurisdiction); Shaffer v. Heitner, 433 U.S. 186, 195–96 n. 12 (1977), and Calder v. Jones, 465 U.S. 783 (1984) (due process limits on state court personal jurisdiction threatened if, after decision upholding jurisdiction, trial were to follow).

(6) First Amendment Cases. The Court has been especially willing to relax finality requirements in order to protect speech interests against the erosion that can attend delay. Such cases typically are accommodated by the fourth Cox category.

(a) A notable example, which built on earlier decisions,[2] is National Socialist Party v. Skokie, 432 U.S. 43 (1977). There, Illinois appellate courts refused to stay a trial court order prohibiting petitioners from marching or parading. The U.S. Supreme Court, treating an application for a stay as a petition for certiorari from the order of the Illinois Supreme Court denying a stay, granted certiorari and reversed: "The order is a final judgment for purposes of our jurisdiction * * *. It finally determined the merits of petitioners' claim that the outstanding injunction will deprive them of rights

---

[2] See Organization for a Better Austin v. Keefe, 402 U.S. 415 (1971); Nebraska Press Ass'n v. Stuart, 423 U.S. 1319 (1975) (Blackmun, J., in chambers).

protected by the First Amendment during the period of appellate review, which in the normal course may take a year or more to complete. If a State seeks to impose a restraint of this kind, it must provide strict procedural safeguards * * * including immediate appellate review * * *." Three Justices dissented, distinguishing Cox on the ground that there the state supreme court had finally decided the federal claim.[3]

(b) In Fort Wayne Books, Inc. v. Indiana, 489 U.S. 46 (1989), the Court came close to holding reviewable any interlocutory order affecting the exercise of First Amendment rights. In a state RICO prosecution predicated on obscenity offenses, the trial court had dismissed the charges on the ground that the statute was unconstitutionally vague as applied to obscenity offenses. The Indiana Court of Appeals reversed, reinstating the charges. The Supreme Court (per White, J.) upheld its jurisdiction to review. Although acknowledging the general rule that in criminal cases finality is defined by judgment of conviction and imposition of sentence, the Court concluded that the case fell within Cox's fourth category. A decision for the defendants at trial would preclude review of their First Amendment challenges to the RICO statute, and, the Court argued, would intolerably erode federal policy by leaving unresolved the question of First Amendment limits on government efforts to apply RICO laws in obscenity cases.

In dissent, Justice O'Connor (with whose views Justice Blackmun expressed agreement) relied heavily on Flynt v. Ohio, 451 U.S. 619 (1981) (per curiam) (5–4). There, after the state courts had denied defendants' motion to dismiss an obscenity prosecution on the ground that it constituted selective prosecution in violation of the First Amendment, the Supreme Court held the judgment not final. Although it arguably fell within the fourth Cox category, "there is no identifiable federal policy that will suffer if the state criminal proceeding goes forward. * * * The resolution of this [equal protection] question can await final judgment without any adverse effect upon important federal interests. A contrary conclusion would permit the fourth exception [of Cox] to swallow the rule."[4]

In the Fort Wayne case, the majority distinguished Flynt as involving a selective prosecution rather than a First Amendment claim—albeit in the context of a trial raising First Amendment issues. The majority added: "[N]o member of the Court concluded in Flynt—as Justice O'Connor does today— that where an important First Amendment claim *is* before us, the Court should refuse to invoke Cox's fourth exception".[5]

---

[3] For similar rulings, see, *e.g.*, M.I.C. Ltd. v. Bedford Township, 463 U.S. 1341 (1983) (Brennan, J., in chambers); Seattle Times Co. v. Rhinehart, 467 U.S. 20 (1984); Oklahoma Pub. Co. v. District Ct., 429 U.S. 967 (1976).

The cases in this line assume that the power of the Court (or of a Justice) to grant a stay is limited to cases where the state decision is "final". That assumption is plainly correct where the stay is sought pursuant to 28 U.S.C. § 2101(f), which authorizes a stay of a final judgment subject to Supreme Court review on writ of certiorari. But Sup.Ct.R. 23.1 says more generally that "[a] stay may be granted by a Justice as permitted by law." Does the All Writs Act, 28 U.S.C. § 1651, permit the Court to stay a concededly non-final state court judgment? See Shapiro et al., Supreme Court Practice 878–81 (10th ed.2013).

[4] The four dissenters in Flynt found in the First Amendment an identifiable federal policy of preventing this sort of prosecution.

[5] In Fort Wayne, a second proceeding was before the Court—a civil RICO action brought by the state, which had obtained an ex parte pretrial seizure order under which the defendants' stores were padlocked and their contents hauled away. On interlocutory appeal, the state supreme court upheld the constitutionality of the obscenity statute (the same constitutional issue presented in the criminal case) and of the pretrial seizure. Without dissent, the Supreme

(c) Neither the criminal prosecution in the Fort Wayne case nor the tort action in Cox involved an injunction against speech. Was Supreme Court review urgently needed in either case? Does the Court's approach in these cases echo First Amendment overbreadth doctrine in trying to prevent the "chilling effect" from statutes that purport to prohibit protected activity? In this regard, recall Justice Rehnquist's invocation, in his dissent in Cox, of the policy of constitutional avoidance. Does the Court's approach in First Amendment cases reflect a quite different conception of its role, in which articulation of constitutional values is to be encouraged rather than avoided? See generally pp. 177–184, *supra*.

(7) Finality and Statutory Interpretation. Does the Court's assertion of a power to create desirable exceptions to a strict conception of finality (a) unjustifiably disregard a statutory limitation on its own jurisdiction, or (b) properly try to accommodate a necessarily general legislative directive to situations that Congress could not have anticipated?[6]

The Court in Cox does not make clear whether the four categories it identifies exhaust the exceptions to the final judgment rule. Indeed, Justice White speaks of "at least" four categories of exceptions. In Florida v. Thomas, 532 U.S. 774 (2001), however, the Court said that Cox "divided cases [in which further state court proceedings were to occur] into four categories. None fits the judgment of the Florida Supreme Court, however, and we therefore conclude that its judgment is not final."[7] Does the elimination in 1988 of mandatory appellate jurisdiction over state court judgments argue for a less strict interpretation of finality—because the Court can simply deny certiorari in any case?

(8) Finality and Federalism. In Cox, Justice Rehnquist's dissent argued that the finality rule of § 1257 should be more strictly construed than the analogous finality requirement in § 1291, governing review of district court decisions in the federal courts of appeals. The tradition has been to draw no distinction between the two statutes, and cases arising under them are apparently cited interchangeably.[8] Are there good reasons to distinguish between the finality rules of § 1257 and § 1291? If so, which way do they cut?

(9) Reviewability of Issues Not Previously Reviewable. If a state court judgment is not final for purposes of Supreme Court review, the federal questions it determines will (if not mooted) be open in the Supreme Court on review of a later, final judgment—whether or not under state law the initial adjudication is the law of the case on the second state review. See, *e.g.*, Great

---

Court upheld its jurisdiction to review that judgment. Justice O'Connor's separate opinion expressed her agreement, noting that pretrial sanctions had already been imposed, and adding: "Where First Amendment interests are actually affected, we have held that such interlocutory orders are immediately reviewable by this Court." She asserted, however, that the availability of review in the civil case was another argument against the Court's decision that the criminal proceeding was reviewable.

[6] For defense of the Court's departures from a strict view of finality, see Matasar & Bruch, *Procedural Common Law, Federal Jurisdictional Policy, and Abandonment of the Adequate and Independent State Grounds Doctrine*, 86 Colum.L.Rev. 1291, 1355 (1986); Shapiro, *Jurisdiction and Discretion*, 60 N.Y.U.L.Rev. 543, 565–66 (1985).

[7] For a particularly mysterious finding of finality that is hard to fit into any of the Cox categories, see American Export Lines, Inc. v. Alvez, 446 U.S. 274 (1980).

[8] In Cox, Justice White cited Forgay v. Conrad, 47 U.S. (6 How.) 201 (1848), for the proposition that the final judgment rule is to be given a liberal, non-technical construction, and relied significantly on Gillespie v. United States Steel Corp., 379 U.S. 148 (1964). Both cases dealt with the question of finality of federal trial court decisions under what is now 28 U.S.C. § 1291.

Western Tel. Co. v. Burnham, 162 U.S. 339 (1896); Jefferson v. City of Tarrant, 522 U.S. 75 (1997). "[A] contrary rule would insulate interlocutory state court rulings on important federal questions from our consideration." Hathorn v. Lovorn, 457 U.S. 255, 262 (1982).

(10) The Highest State Court Requirement. The "highest court of a State in which a decision could be had" (28 U.S.C. § 1257) may be the lowest court in the state system, *e.g.*, the city's Police Court in Thompson v. City of Louisville, 362 U.S. 199 (1960), or the order of a judge in chambers, as in Betts v. Brady, 316 U.S. 455 (1942). The sole criterion is whether further appellate review is possible within the state; if it is, even if such review is discretionary, it must have been sought to confer jurisdiction on the Supreme Court.[9]

In Pacific Gas & Elec. Co. v. PUC, 475 U.S. 1, 7 (1986), an order of the state utility commission was reviewable only in the discretion of the state supreme court, which had refused to accept the appeal. The Supreme Court noted probable jurisdiction and decided the appellant's First Amendment challenge. Was this an exercise of the Supreme Court's original jurisdiction? (If so, it would appear to lack authorization under 28 U.S.C. § 1251 and to violate the Eleventh Amendment.) Before answering "yes", consider whether any federal criterion distinguishes state "courts" (review of whose decisions clearly falls within the Supreme Court's *appellate* jurisdiction) from other state tribunals that engage in adjudication. See Meltzer, *Legislative Courts, Legislative Power, and the Constitution*, 65 Ind.L.J. 291, 297–301 (1990).

---

[9]   See, *e.g.*, Costarelli v. Massachusetts, 421 U.S. 193 (1975); Gotthilf v. Sills, 375 U.S. 79 (1963) (leave to appeal on certified questions must be sought); Gorman v. Washington Univ., 316 U.S. 98 (1942) (review of judgment of division of state highest court by the court *en banc* is available and must be applied for).

CHAPTER VI

THE LAW APPLIED IN CIVIL ACTIONS IN THE DISTRICT COURTS

SECTION 34, JUDICIARY ACT OF 1789
1 Stat. 92, Rev.Stat. § 721

That the laws of the several states, except where the constitution, treaties, or statutes of the United States shall otherwise require or provide, shall be regarded as rules of decision in trials at common law in the courts of the United States in cases where they apply.

28 U.S.C. § 1652

The laws of the several states, except where the Constitution or treaties of the United States or Acts of Congress otherwise require or provide, shall be regarded as rules of decision in civil actions in the courts of the United States, in cases where they apply.

1. PROCEDURE

NOTE ON THE HISTORICAL DEVELOPMENT OF THE STATUTES AND RULES OF COURT

In each of the major fields of federal court jurisdiction—bankruptcy, admiralty, and civil actions in equity or at law—while some matters of procedure are controlled directly by statute or constitutional provision, for the most part general rules, promulgated by the Supreme Court pursuant to delegation of authority by Congress, govern. Such rules also govern the procedure in all cases in the courts of appeals. But the proliferation of local rules issued by each district court and by the individual circuits has to some extent undermined the goal of uniformity across the entire federal court system.

Section 2071 of the Judicial Code confers on the Supreme Court and on all courts established by act of Congress general authority to prescribe rules for the conduct of their own business. The Supreme Court is given specific authority to prescribe rules of procedure for the lower federal courts in bankruptcy by 28 U.S.C. § 2075, and in other civil actions by 28 U.S.C.

§ 2072. Section 2072 also delegates to the Supreme Court authority to prescribe rules of evidence.[1]

In equity, admiralty, and bankruptcy, there was an early consensus that federal procedure should be uniform, rather than conforming to the varied practices among the states. In civil actions at law, the move toward uniformity was considerably slower.[2]

A. Equity Before Merger

For nearly a century and a half, before law and equity were merged in 1938, equity had its own history as a distinctive branch of federal practice. From the outset, federal equity had to administer the substantive law of the states as well as of the United States. Particularly where rights under state law were at issue, state procedure, in principle, had a claim for acceptance. But in 1789 equity was either non-existent or undeveloped in the courts of many of the states. Federal procedure was thus able to establish itself without serious challenge.

Even the Rules of Decision Act—the famous § 34 of the Judiciary Act of 1789—did not apply in terms to equity. Not until the 1948 revision was the language broadened to cover all "civil actions". 28 U.S.C. § 1652.

In the Process Act of September 29, 1789, 1 Stat. 93, 94, the first Congress provided that "the forms and modes of proceedings in causes of equity * * * shall be according to the course of the civil law". The second Congress replaced this stopgap measure with a formulation that lasted until 1938. The forms of process in equity, except their style, and the forms and modes of proceedings were to be "according to the principles, rules and usages which belong to courts of equity * * *, as contradistinguished from

---

[1] Congress has also conferred certain rulemaking powers on the judicial councils of the circuits in connection with complaints of judicial misconduct and disability. See 28 U.S.C. § 372(c)(11); Burbank, *Procedural Reform Under the Judicial Conduct and Disability Act of 1980*, 131 U.Pa.L.Rev. 283 (1982). In 2002, Public Law No. 107–273, Div. C, Title I, § 11043(a)(1)(B), 116 Stat. 1855, repealed former § 372(c)(11), replacing it with a provision codified at 28 U.S.C. § 358.

[2] This Chapter focuses on civil cases. In criminal cases, before adoption of the Rules of Criminal Procedure, federal practice was a hodgepodge of judicial elaboration, common law rules, constitutional provisions, and *ad hoc* legislation. The general uniformity was limited by specific statutory provisions or judicial interpretations calling for application of state law.

In 1933, Congress authorized the Supreme Court to prescribe rules as to proceedings after verdict. Act of February 24, 1933, 47 Stat. 904, as amended by the Act of March 8, 1934, 48 Stat. 399. See 18 U.S.C. § 3772. The Court issued the first rules in 1934. 292 U.S. 661. The Act of June 29, 1940, 54 Stat. 688, enlarged the Court's authority to include the promulgation of rules of procedure for criminal proceedings prior to and including verdict. See 18 U.S.C. § 3771. The Court exercised this authority in 1944. 323 U.S. 821.

The Rules of Criminal Procedure, which became effective on March 21, 1946, merged the 1934 post-verdict rules with the new rules. 327 U.S. 821 (1946). Since then, the rules have often been amended. (The current rulemaking authority for criminal cases is found in 28 U.S.C. § 2072.) As the pace of rulemaking increased and the subjects of rulemaking became more controversial, Congress became more deeply enmeshed in the process, especially in the 1970s, when it not infrequently modified, postponed, or disapproved particular rules.

The Supreme Court has also promulgated rules governing habeas corpus and other collateral proceedings under 28 U.S.C. §§ 2254 and 2255—which became effective, with changes by Congress, in 1977—as well as rules for the trial of misdemeanors before United States magistrates. (The latter are authorized by 18 U.S.C. § 3402. See 445 U.S. 975 (1980)).

For an exploration of the limitations imposed on the Court as rulemaker by the Rules Enabling Act and related principles of the separation of powers, and a discussion of a number of examples involving the Federal Rules of Criminal Procedure, see Minzner, *The Criminal Rules Enabling Act*, 46 U. Richmond L.Rev. 1047 (2012).

courts of common law". Act of May 8, 1792, § 2, 1 Stat. 275, 276. But an important qualification provided needed flexibility: " * * * subject however to such alterations and additions as the said courts respectively shall in their discretion deem expedient, or to such regulations as the supreme court of the United States shall think proper from time to time by rule to prescribe to any circuit or district court concerning the same".[3] The Court first prescribed rules for lower federal courts in 1822, when it promulgated thirty-three Equity Rules. 20 U.S. (7 Wheat.) xvii. Twenty years later these were replaced with ninety-two rules. 42 U.S. (1 How.) xli. These rules assumed the existence of traditional chancery practice, and undertook only *ad hoc* modification or clarification of points of detail. The 1842 rules lasted for seventy years, long after they had become archaic.

The Equity Rules of 1912 (226 U.S. 627) worked a major reform. Three years later, Congress enacted the Law and Equity Act of 1915, 38 Stat. 956, making equitable defenses available in actions at law and providing for the transfer of cases brought on the wrong side of the court.

B.   Admiralty

In many respects, the story in admiralty parallels that in equity. Admiralty was thought of in 1789 as a distinct body of law, quasi-international in character. This traditional law of admiralty comprised not only distinctive principles of liability and distinctive remedies but also a distinctive set of procedures.

Nonetheless, state law played a significant role in admiralty by virtue of the provision in § 9 of the Judiciary Act of 1789 (1 Stat. 73, 76), conferring on the district courts "exclusive original cognizance of all civil causes of admiralty and maritime jurisdiction", while "saving to suitors, in all cases, the right of a common law remedy, where the common law is competent to give it". The saving clause preserved remedies in the state courts and on the law side of the federal courts. But it did not affect the federal character of proceedings on the admiralty side of the federal courts.

The first Congress provided that in admiralty, as in equity, the forms and modes of proceedings "shall be according to the course of the civil law", and the second Congress provided in 1792 that they should be "according to the principles, rules and usages which belong * * * to courts of admiralty * * *, as contradistinguished from courts of common law". 1 Stat. 93, 94. Given content by exercise of the same rulemaking powers that applied in equity, this formulation survived until 1948, when it was swallowed entirely by the general rulemaking authorizations in 28 U.S.C. §§ 2071 and 2073. In 1966, the general Enabling Act provision, § 2072, was extended to admiralty, and § 2073 was repealed. (The present version of § 2073 deals with other matters.)

For more than half a century after the 1792 Act, the Supreme Court left rulemaking in admiralty to the district courts, and divergent practices developed. Spurred apparently by the reaffirmation of its rulemaking authority in § 6 of the Act of August 23, 1842, see note 3, *supra*, the Court in 1844 promulgated forty-seven "Rules of Practice of the Courts of the United States in Causes of Admiralty and Maritime Jurisdiction on the Instance

---

[3]   The Supreme Court's rulemaking power was affirmed, in language that swept beyond the confines of equity (and admiralty) and extended to "suits at common law", in § 6 of the Act of August 23, 1842, 5 Stat. 516, 518.

Side of the Court". 44 U.S. (3 How.) ix. Like the first Equity Rules, the Admiralty Rules presupposed a traditional framework of procedure.

The 1844 rules remained in effect, with rather frequent amendments, until they were superseded in 1921. 254 U.S. 671. The 1921 rules, in turn, were frequently amended until in 1966 admiralty procedure was merged with civil procedure. 383 U.S. 1029. The Federal Rules of Civil Procedure now apply in admiralty, but there are a number of special provisions and "supplemental rules for certain admiralty and maritime claims".

C. Bankruptcy

As in equity and admiralty, Congress has authorized the Supreme Court to promulgate general rules. (The authority is codified today at 28 U.S.C. § 2075.) Within five months of the enactment of the Bankruptcy Act of July 1, 1898 (30 Stat. 544), the Court adopted the first "General Orders and Forms in Bankruptcy" (172 U.S. 653). The Court completely revised these rules in 1939 (305 U.S. 677), following enactment of the Chandler Act of 1938 (52 Stat. 840), and once again promulgated new rules in the 1970s as a result of the work of the Advisory Committee on Bankruptcy Rules.

When Congress in 1978 enacted a comprehensive revision of the bankruptcy laws, 92 Stat. 2549, it provided that existing bankruptcy rules, to the extent not inconsistent with the new law, were to remain effective until "repealed or superseded" by new rules. 11 U.S.C. § 405(d). In Northern Pipeline Const. Co. v. Marathon Pipe Line Co., 458 U.S. 50 (1982), p. 356, *supra*, the Supreme Court held that the 1978 Act's broad grant of jurisdiction to bankruptcy judges who lacked tenure and salary protection violated Article III. After a period of uncertainty, Congress made a number of changes in the bankruptcy laws as part of the Bankruptcy Amendments and Federal Judgeship Act of 1984. In 1985, an Advisory Committee proposed extensive amendments to the bankruptcy rules to conform to those statutory changes and for other purposes (107 F.R.D. 403 (1985)), and in March 1987, the Supreme Court approved amendments based on those proposals (114 F.R.D. 193 (1987)). Since then, a number of further changes in the rules have taken effect.

D. Actions at Law Before Merger

(1) Origins. The Rules of Decision Act, § 34 of the Judiciary Act of 1789, specified that state law would apply in a wide area in actions at law in federal courts but left uncertain whether this area included procedure. The Process Act immediately following it (Act of Sept. 29, 1789), however, clearly called for application of state law: "That * * * except where by this act or other statutes of the United States is otherwise provided, the forms of writs and executions, except their style, and modes of process and rates of fees, except fees to judges, in the circuit and district courts, in suits at common law, shall be the same in each state respectively as are now used or allowed in the supreme courts of the same." The Act of May 8, 1792, reaffirmed this provision but made it subject to the same rulemaking power, both in the Supreme Court and the lower courts, that applied in equity and admiralty.

(2) Static Conformity. The enactments just discussed created a static conformity, calling for application of state law as it stood on the date of the federal enactment. And, except for the rulemaking power, the provisions had no application to federal courts sitting in states that entered the union after 1789.

As time passed, state procedure changed (notably, in many states, in favor of debtors). Nonetheless, Congress, in the Process Act of May 19, 1827, 4 Stat. 278, continued to provide for static conformity. But both the Supreme Court and the lower courts retained their rulemaking authority throughout this period—an authority they were reluctant to use. The adoption of the Field Code by New York in 1848 and the spread of the code system to other states complicated the problem, and the situation became increasingly unsatisfactory.

(3) Wayman v. Southard. In Wayman v. Southard, 23 U.S. (10 Wheat.) 1 (1825), the Court issued two important holdings about procedures followed in federal courts. The question presented was whether a federal court sitting in Kentucky should apply a Kentucky statute requiring a judgment plaintiff either to accept Kentucky bank notes in payment of the judgment or else to take a replevin bond from the defendant for the debt.

(a) In an opinion by Chief Justice Marshall, the Court ruled that the procedure on executions in the federal courts, as well as the procedure before judgment, was governed by the Process Act of 1792, which continued the Process Act of 1789. These acts adopted the state law "as it existed in September, 1789, * * * not as it might afterwards be made". The Court acknowledged that the Rules of Decision Act, by contrast, called for a dynamic rather than a static conformity. But it rejected the claim that that Act applied to executions.

(b) The Court recognized that its holding that the process acts governed entailed the conclusion that the matters in issue could be regulated by rule of court. Then, in a pioneering discussion of delegation of legislative power, it went out of its way to consider and sustain the validity of this rulemaking authority. The discussion is highly relevant both to the inherent power of courts to make rules governing their own procedures for the resolution of controversies within their jurisdiction and to the broad congressional delegations of rulemaking authority that were to follow in the next century[4]:

"That the power claimed for the state is not given by the 34th section of the judiciary act, has been fully stated in the preceding part of this opinion. That it has not an independent existence in the state legislatures, is, we think, one of those political axioms, an attempt to demonstrate which, would be a waste of argument * * *. Its utter inadmissibility will at once present itself to the mind, if we imagine an act of a state legislature for the direct and sole purpose of regulating proceedings in the courts of the Union, or of their officers in executing their judgments. No gentleman, we believe, will be so extravagant as to maintain the efficacy of such an act. It seems not much less extravagant, to maintain, that the practice of the federal courts, and the conduct of their officers, can be indirectly regulated by the state legislatures, by an act professing to regulate the proceedings of the state courts, and the conduct of the officers who execute the process of those courts. It is a general rule, that what cannot be done directly, from defect of power, cannot be done indirectly. The right of congress to delegate to the courts the power of altering the modes (established by the process act) of proceedings in suits,

---

[4] In a comprehensive analysis, Professor Barrett concludes that while "[u]niform procedural regulation is ultimately in the control of Congress", judicial authority to develop "[f]ederal procedural common law is supported by the twin justifications that federal courts can develop uniform common law rules in enclaves of constitutional preemption and that Article III impliedly grants each federal court power to regulate procedure in the course of adjudicating cases." Barrett, *Procedural Common Law*, 94 Va.L.Rev. 813, 888 (2008).

has been already stated; but, were it otherwise, we are well satisfied that the state legislatures do not possess that power."

(4) The Shift to Dynamic Conformity. The Conformity Act of June 1, 1872, 17 Stat. 196, withdrew the unused rulemaking authority, and adopted, with qualifications, the principle of dynamic conformity. Section 5 of the Act provided: "That the practice, pleadings, and forms and modes of proceeding, in other than equity and admiralty causes in the circuit and district courts of the United States shall conform, as near as may be, to the practice, pleadings, and forms and modes of proceeding existing at the time in like causes in the courts of record of the State within which such circuit or district courts are held, any rule of court to the contrary notwithstanding: *Provided, however,* That nothing herein contained shall alter the rules of evidence under the laws of the United States, and as practiced in the courts thereof."

The Conformity Act eliminated the anachronism of federal adherence to no-longer-existent state practice. On more matters than not, a lawyer in a federal court in a particular state could now follow the procedure currently prevailing in the courts of that state—an advantage particularly appreciated in the code states. But this conformity was confined to actions at law, and even as to such actions, exceptions and qualifications soon appeared.

The earlier process acts did not affect "jurisdiction", and the Conformity Act was similarly construed. See, *e.g.*, Davenport v. County of Dodge, 105 U.S. 237 (1881). When the Act did plainly apply, it required the federal courts to conform to state procedure only "as near as may be", a phrase that opened a wide door for adherence to distinctive federal practices. See generally Clark & Moore, *A New Federal Civil Procedure*, 44 Yale L.J. 387, 401–11 (1935).

Partly in reliance on this latter phrase and partly by a restrictive interpretation of the three categories of "practice, pleadings, and forms and modes of proceedings", the Court held that the Act did not reach a wide area of particularly important matters affecting the administration of federal justice. See, *e.g.*, McDonald v. Pless, 238 U.S. 264 (1915) (approving a district court's refusal, when ruling on a motion to set aside a verdict as having been reached by compromise, to permit a juror to testify about proceedings in the jury room, and concluding that state practice on the question did not control).

E.　The Enabling Act, Merger, and Beyond

(1) The Aspiration for Uniformity. A desire to dispel the confusion created by the uneasy co-existence of several systems of procedure in the federal courts helped spur the next movement to reform federal procedure. Those who sought change believed that effective reform could be achieved only through the promulgation of nationwide court rules, drafted with the assistance of bench and bar. Federal-state conformity, they hoped, would not have to be sacrificed, if the federal rules served as a model for the states to follow. See generally Sunderland, *The Grant of Rule-Making Power to the Supreme Court of the United States*, 32 Mich.L.Rev. 1116 (1934).[5]

The bill that became the Act of June 19, 1934 (now principally contained in 28 U.S.C. § 2072) followed several decades of debate and proposals for reform.[6] In both the House and Senate, the favorable committee reports were brief, see S.Rep. No. 1048, H.R.Rep. No. 1829, 73d Cong., 2d Sess. (1934),

---

[5]　Virtually every state has been influenced by the federal model, and many have followed that model quite closely. See Wright & Kane, Federal Courts § 62, at 431 (7th ed. 2011).

[6]　For an exhaustive and informative study of the pre-1934 efforts at reform, see Burbank, *The Rules Enabling Act of 1934*, 130 U.Pa.L.Rev. 1015, 1035–98 (1982).

and the discussion on the floor consumed only a few minutes. In each House, the floor manager claimed the unanimous support of bar associations. In each, the objection that lawyers would have to learn two systems of practice was made by one member but was quickly withdrawn, and the bill was passed by unanimous consent. 78 Cong.Rec. 9362–63 (Senate); *id.* at 10866 (House).[7]

(2) The Exercise of Rulemaking Authority. On June 3, 1935, the Court appointed a distinguished Advisory Committee to draw up proposed rules. 295 U.S. 774. The Committee's proposals were subjected to considerable scrutiny and criticism, through the medium, among others, of special committees of the bench and bar established in the various circuits and districts. With minor changes, the Court approved the final proposals, and the rules became effective September 16, 1938. See 308 U.S. 645–766.

In 1958, in an amendment to 28 U.S.C. § 331, Congress instructed the Judicial Conference of the United States to "carry on a continuous study of the operation and effect of the general rules of practice and procedure now or hereafter in use as prescribed by the Supreme Court for the other courts of the United States pursuant to law. Such changes in and additions to those rules as the Conference may deem desirable * * * shall be recommended by the Conference from time to time to the Supreme Court for its consideration and adoption, modification or rejection, in accordance with law."

Pursuant to this provision, the Judicial Conference in 1960 established a Standing Committee on Rules of Practice and Procedure, together with five Advisory Committees (Civil, Criminal, Appellate, Bankruptcy, and Admiralty). The task of an Advisory Committee is to draft proposals, solicit public comment, and submit a report to the Standing Committee. The Standing Committee in turn reports to the Conference, which makes its recommendations to the Supreme Court.

(3) The Rules of Evidence. In 1965, the Conference appointed a sixth Advisory Committee, on Rules of Evidence, and after several drafts were submitted for public comment, see 46 F.R.D. 161 (1969); 51 F.R.D. 315 (1971), the Supreme Court transmitted the Federal Rules of Evidence to Congress in November 1972. 56 F.R.D. 183 (1972). Almost immediately, congressional opposition surfaced, centering both on the content of certain rules and on the question whether the Court was empowered by the Rules Enabling Act to promulgate rules of evidence at all. This opposition culminated in an enactment staying the effectiveness of the proposed rules until they should be affirmatively approved by Congress. 87 Stat. 9 (1973). Following this resolution, Congress redrafted the rules, leaving much of the

---

[7]   The Act provided:

"That the Supreme Court of the United States shall have the power to prescribe, by general rules, for the district courts of the United States and for the courts of the District of Columbia, the forms of process, writs, pleadings, and motions, and the practice and procedure in civil actions at law. Said rules shall neither abridge, enlarge, nor modify the substantive rights of any litigant. They shall take effect six months after their promulgation, and thereafter all laws in conflict therewith shall be of no further force or effect.

"SEC. 2. The court may at any time unite the general rules prescribed by it for cases in equity with those in actions at law so as to secure one form of civil action and procedure for both: *Provided, however,* That in such union of rules the right of trial by jury as at common law and declared by the seventh amendment to the Constitution shall be preserved to the parties inviolate. Such united rules shall not take effect until they shall have been reported to Congress by the Attorney General at the beginning of a regular session thereof and until after the close of such session." 48 Stat. 1064.

original Court text substantially unchanged, but making significant modifications, *inter alia*, in the rules relating to privileges and presumptions. Finally, the Federal Rules of Evidence were enacted in statutory form. 88 Stat. 1926 (1975).[8]

The same statute contained a new "Enabling Act" (designated 28 U.S.C. § 2076) to govern amendments to the Rules of Evidence. This new Act extended the time allowed for congressional review of Supreme Court amendments to those rules from the ninety days of § 2072 (the general Enabling Act) to one hundred eighty days, and authorized *either* House of Congress to disapprove or defer a Supreme Court amendment. (The "one-House veto" was successfully challenged, in another context, in INS v. Chadha, 462 U.S. 919 (1983), and eventually was eliminated in this context in 1988.)

(4) The 1988 Revision of the Enabling Acts. Congress amended the Enabling Acts in 1988, repealing § 2076 and consolidating the rulemaking power with respect to civil procedure and evidence. Section 2074(a) now provides that no changes in the rules shall take effect until they have been reported to Congress and until the expiration of a specified period. In § 2074(b), however, Congress preserved the provision (formerly in § 2076) that any revision of the rules governing evidentiary privilege shall have no force unless approved by an Act of Congress.

(5) Growing Controversy About Rulemaking. The pace of rulemaking in all areas has increased dramatically in recent years. But at the same time, criticism of the process and the product has also increased, and Congress' responses to these criticisms have in turn generated their own critiques.

From the beginning, a number of Supreme Court Justices have been skeptical or disapproving of their role in the process. In 1938, Justice Brandeis stated without explanation that he did not approve of the adoption of the original civil rules. See 308 U.S. at 649. And Justices Black and Douglas together on several occasions voiced objections, on grounds ranging from the undesirability of specific rules or amendments, to the inappropriateness of the Court's role in the rulemaking process, to the possible unconstitutionality of that role.[9]

The Court itself, in promulgating changes in the civil, criminal, appellate, and evidence rules in April 1993, expressed reservations about its role. (Some of these rules, especially as they related to lawyer discipline for filing or pursuing matters thought to be frivolous and to radical changes in the rules governing discovery, were significant and controversial.) Each of the transmittal letters to Congress, signed by the Chief Justice "[b]y direction of the Supreme Court", stated: "While the Court is satisfied that the required procedures [pursuant to 28 U.S.C. § 2072] have been observed, this transmittal does not necessarily indicate that the Court itself would have proposed these amendments in the form submitted." See, *e.g.*, 146 F.R.D. 401, 403 (1993). A separate statement of Justice White noted that "[s]ome of us * * * have silently shared Justice Black's and Justice Douglas' suggestion that the enabling statutes be amended" to eliminate the Court's

---

[8]   Several of the rules of evidence refer to state law in cases in which state law supplies the rule of decision. See Rule 302 (presumptions); Rule 501 (privileges); Rule 601 (competency of witnesses).

[9]   See, *e.g.*, 368 U.S. 1012 (1961); 374 U.S. 865 (1963); 383 U.S. 1032 (1966); 383 U.S. 1089 (1966); 398 U.S. 979 (1970); 401 U.S. 1019 (1971).

participation in rulemaking. Justice White added that if the rulemaking process were not changed, he believed the Court's role was "to transmit the Judicial Conference's recommendations without change and without careful study, as long as there is no suggestion that the committee system has not operated with integrity"—even though on several occasions he had "serious questions about the wisdom of particular proposals to amend certain rules." 146 F.R.D. 401, 503, 505 (1993). In an order issued on April 28, 2010, approving certain proposed changes in the Rules of Criminal Procedure, the Court took the rare action of recommitting to the Advisory Committee for further consideration a proposed amendment to Rule 15 (dealing with depositions). 130 S.Ct. Ct.R. 179 (2010). There was no explanation.

Other critics contend that public notice and participation were inadequate and urged that the process be made more open.[10] In addition, some have faulted the predominance of judges in the rulemaking process, or have noted that those practitioners who are given a role tend to constitute a section of the bar more likely to represent the "haves" than the "have-nots."[11] Still others have decried the lack of adequate empirical investigation, or of cost-benefit analysis, as a basis for proposed rule changes, especially for those changes of more than technical significance.[12] Other criticisms of the federal rules include (1) skepticism about "trans-substantive" rules that prescribe a uniform procedure for the entire range of cases,[13] (2) the failure

---

[10] See, *e.g.*, Weinstein, Reform of Court Rule-Making Procedures (1977); Lesnick, *The Federal Rule-Making Process: A Time for Reexamination*, 61 A.B.A.J. 579 (1975); Hazard, *Undemocratic Legislation*, 87 Yale L.J. 1284 (1978) (reviewing Judge Weinstein's book).

[11] See, *e.g.*, Macey, *Judicial Preferences, Public Choice, and the Rules of Procedure*, 23 J.Leg.Stud. 627 (1994) (arguing that judges engaged in rulemaking will try to serve their self-interest in a variety of ways); Yeazell, *Judging Rules, Ruling Judges*, 61 Law & Contemp.Probs. 229 (Summer 1998) (criticizing the increased involvement of judges in rulemaking and advocating adoption of a two-step rulemaking process in which lawyers draft and propose, while judges approve or disapprove). Stancil, *Close Enough for Government Work: The Committee Rulemaking Game*, 96 Va.L.Rev. 69 (2010), applies game theory in concluding that the existing rulemaking system may lead Congress to accept rules that have substantive consequences "some distance away from its 'real' preferences" in order "to avoid incurring the costs associated with informing itself and then acting." The present structure, he contends, "may reduce certain other risks of strategic behavior, most notably interest-group hijacking of the rulemaking process".

A recent study of the Advisory Committee for Civil Rules between 1960 and 2013 included these findings: (1) judges moved from being a relatively small minority of members in 1960 to a majority in 1971 and most every year thereafter, with a corresponding decline in the proportion of practitioner and academic members; (2) the practitioner members in 1960 predominantly represented plaintiffs and individuals, though many had heterogeneous practices defying categorization; over time, there was a steady shift toward practitioners who predominantly represent defendants and organizations; (3) between 1971 and 2013, after adjusting for the number of judges appointed by Republican or Democratic Presidents, those appointed by Republican Presidents had served on the Committee at a 161% higher rate than their colleagues appointed by Democratic Presidents; and (4) the prospect that Committee proposals relating to private enforcement of federal rights would favor plaintiffs went from highly likely at the outset of the study period to zero at the end. Burbank & Farhang, *Federal Court Rulemaking and Litigation Reform: An Institutional Approach*, 15 Nev.L.J. (forthcoming 2014–15).

[12] One of the leaders of this group has been Laurens Walker who, in a series of articles, proposed various techniques for avoiding changes that result in undue surprise or unintended consequences. See, *e.g.*, *Perfecting Federal Civil Rules: A Proposal for Restricted Field Experiments*, 51 Law & Contemp.Probs. 67 (Summer 1988); *A Compromise Reform for Federal Civil Rulemaking*, 61 Geo.Wash.L.Rev. 455 (1993); *Avoiding Surprise From Civil Rule Making: The Role of Economic Analysis*, 23 J.Legal Stud. 569 (1994).

[13] But see Marcus, *The Past, Present, and Future of Trans-Substantivity in Federal Civil Procedure*, 59 DePaul L.Rev. 371 (2010) (arguing that despite mounting legislation that has

openly to acknowledge that the rulemaking process is necessarily political in its implications; (3) the failure of the rulemakers to develop a "coherent normative theory of civil adjudication,"[14] (4) a concern that the goal in 1938 of rapidly advancing to resolution on the merits has been displaced by a desire to dispose of cases as quickly as possible, often by private resolution short of trial,[15] and (5) a concern that many rules have transgressed the limits imposed by the Enabling Act and even that the Enabling Act itself raises constitutional difficulties because it insulates policy choices from politically accountable branches of government.[16] From a different direction, the Supreme Court has been criticized for some of its decisions that re-interpreted the rules in a fashion that circumvents the rulemaking process.[17]

(6) Changes in the Rulemaking Process. Some of these criticisms led to proposals for legislative change, and Congress has responded to these proposals on several occasions.

(a) The 1988 amendments to the Enabling Acts (see 28 U.S.C. §§ 2071–2077) specified procedures to be followed by the Judicial Conference and its committees (including the holding of open meetings by committees); provided mechanisms for the modification and abrogation of district and appellate court rules; and required notice and opportunity for comment as part of the rulemaking processes of the district and appellate courts. The new openness, while generally praised, led some to question whether the broadening of participation might increase the politicization of the process.[18]

(b) In 1990, Congress enacted the Civil Justice Reform Act (CJRA), codified as amended at 28 U.S.C. §§ 471–82. This Act required every federal district to create an advisory group (which was to include attorneys and representatives of major categories of litigants) to assess the causes of "cost and delay" in civil litigation and to formulate recommendations based at least in part on an assessment of certain specified factors. Each district was

---

joined substantive change with substance-specific procedural change, trans-substantivity can and should continue to operate "as an institutional restraint on court-supervised rulemakers").

[14] Bone, *Making Effective Rules: The Need for Procedure Theory*, 61 Okla.L.Rev. 319 (2008).

[15] Perschbacher & Bassett, *The Revolution of 1938 and Its Discontents*, 61 Okla.L.Rev. 275 (2008).

[16] See the Symposium on Rulemaking in 59 Brook.L.Rev. No. 3 (1993), especially (on the first two of the criticisms) the articles by Richard Marcus, *Of Babies and Bathwater* (p. 761), and Burbank, *Ignorance and Procedural Law Reform: A Call for a Moratorium* (p. 841); see also, on the third criticism, Redish & Amarulu, *The Supreme Court, the Rules Enabling Act, and the Politicization of the Federal Rules: Constitutional and Statutory Interpretation*, 90 Minn.L.Rev. 1303 (2006).

Richard Marcus, *Not Dead Yet*, 61 Okla.L.Rev. 299 (2008), contends that despite these criticisms, the rulemaking process is alive and well and it continues to lead and to innovate.

[17] Carrington, *Politics and Civil Procedure Rulemaking: Reflections and Experience*, 60 Duke L.J. 597 (2010). See also Burbank & Farhang, *Litigation Reform: An Institutional Approach*, 162 U.Pa.L.Rev. 1543 (2014) (arguing that conservative efforts to limit private enforcement actions have had more success in adjudication (by obtaining restrictive readings of the Federal Rules) that in efforts to change the Federal Rules).

[18] See, *e.g.*, Mullenix, *Hope Over Experience: Mandatory Informal Discovery and the Politics of Rulemaking*, 69 N.C.L.Rev. 796 (1991); Bone, *The Process of Making Process: Court Rulemaking, Democratic Legitimacy, and Procedural Efficacy*, 87 Geo.L.J. 887 (1999) (rejecting as exaggerated the concerns about the substantive effects of the rules and arguing that political accountability and public participation are unnecessary to what he views as a deliberative process akin to common law adjudication).

then required to adopt a plan, addressed to these problems, which would be reviewed by the Judicial Conference and evaluated annually.

The CJRA resulted in the adoption and implementation of a variety of plans to reduce cost and delay, many of which focused on such matters as early control and scheduling by judges and/or magistrate judges, mandatory or optional use of alternative dispute resolution techniques (such as mediation or non-binding arbitration), and other devices for encouraging settlement or expedition. See *Reformers Tout ADR Programs*, A.B.A.J. 28 (Aug. 1994). When the CJRA expired, Congress made certain of its provisions permanent, including 28 U.S.C. § 476(a), which requires that the Director of the Administrative Office of the United States Courts prepare a semiannual report listing certain delayed matters on each judicial officer's docket. See 111 Stat. 1173 (1997).[19]

(7) The Scope of Rulemaking Authority. Sibbach v. Wilson, the principal case immediately following this Note, was decided shortly after promulgation of the Federal Rules under the Enabling Act, and remains one of the leading decisions interpreting the scope of the authority conferred by that Act.

Sibbach v. Wilson & Co., Inc.
312 U.S. 1, 61 S.Ct. 422, 85 L.Ed. 479 (1940).
Certiorari to the Circuit Court of Appeals for the Seventh Circuit.

■ MR. JUSTICE ROBERTS delivered the opinion of the Court.

This case calls for decision as to the validity of Rules 35 and 37 of the Rules of Civil Procedure for District Courts of the United States.

In an action brought by the petitioner in the District Court for Northern Illinois to recover damages for bodily injuries, inflicted in Indiana, respondent * * * moved for an order requiring the petitioner to submit to a physical examination by one or more physicians appointed by the court to determine the nature and extent of her injuries. The court ordered that the petitioner submit to such an examination by a physician so appointed.

Compliance having been refused, the respondent obtained an order to show cause why the petitioner should not be punished for contempt. In response the petitioner challenged the authority of the court to order her to submit to the examination, asserting that the order was void. It appeared that the courts of Indiana, the state where the cause of action arose, hold such an order proper, whereas the courts of Illinois, the state in which the trial court sat, hold that such an order cannot be made. Neither state has any statute governing the matter.

The court adjudged the petitioner guilty of contempt, and directed that she be committed until she should obey the order for examination or

---

[19] For retrospectives on the CJRA, see Symposium, *Evaluation of the Civil Justice Reform Act*, 49 Ala.L.Rev. No. 1 (1997); Cavanagh, *The Civil Justice Reform Act of 1990: Requiescat in Pace*, 173 F.R.D. 565 (1997). In addition, the RAND Institute conducted detailed studies of the effectiveness of various CJRA reforms. See RAND Institute, Just, Speedy, and Inexpensive? An Evaluation of Judicial Case Management Under the CJRA (1996).

otherwise should be legally discharged from custody. The petitioner appealed.

The Circuit Court of Appeals decided that Rule 35, which authorizes an order for a physical examination in such a case, is valid, and affirmed the judgment. The writ of certiorari was granted * * *

The contention of the petitioner, in final analysis, is that Rules 35 and 37 are not within the mandate of Congress to this court. This is the limit of permissible debate, since argument touching the broader questions of Congressional power and of the obligation of federal courts to apply the substantive law of a state is foreclosed.

Congress has undoubted power to regulate the practice and procedure of federal courts,[6] and may exercise that power by delegating to this or other federal courts authority to make rules not inconsistent with the statutes or Constitution of the United States; but it has never essayed to declare the substantive state law, or to abolish or nullify a right recognized by the substantive law of the state where the cause of action arose, save where a right or duty is imposed in a field committed to Congress by the Constitution. On the contrary it has enacted that the state law shall be the rule of decision in the federal courts.

Hence we conclude that the Act of June 19, 1934, was purposely restricted in its operation to matters of pleading and court practice and procedure. Its two provisos or caveats emphasize this restriction. The first is that the court shall not "abridge, enlarge, nor modify the substantive rights", in the guise of regulating procedure. The second is that if the rules are to prescribe a single form of action for cases at law and suits in equity, the constitutional right to jury trial inherent in the former must be preserved. There are other limitations upon the authority to prescribe rules which might have been, but were not mentioned in the Act; for instance, the inability of a court, by rule, to extend or restrict the jurisdiction conferred by a statute.

Whatever may be said as to the effect of the Conformity Act while it remained in force, the rules, if they are within the authority granted by Congress, repeal that statute, and the District Court was not bound to follow the Illinois practice respecting an order for physical examination. On the other hand if the right to be exempt from such an order is one of substantive law, the Rules of Decision Act required the District Court, though sitting in Illinois, to apply the law of Indiana, the state where the cause of action arose, and to order the examination. To avoid this dilemma the petitioner admits, and, we think, correctly, that Rules 35 and 37 are rules of procedure. She insists, nevertheless, that by the prohibition against abridging substantive rights, Congress has banned the rules here challenged. In order to reach this result she translates "substantive" into "important" or "substantial" rights. And she urges that if a rule affects such a right, albeit the rule is one of procedure merely, its prescription is not within the statutory grant of power embodied in the Act of June 19, 1934. * * *

[The Court here discussed and distinguished several cases, including Union Pac. Ry. v. Botsford, 141 U.S. 250 (1891), in which, the Court said,

---

6   Wayman v. Southard, 10 Wheat. 1, 21; Bank of United States v. Halstead, 10 Wheat. 51, 53; Beers v. Haughton, 9 Pet. 329, 359, 361.

the refusal to order plaintiff to submit to a physical examination was based on a lack of authority for the issuance of such an order.]

We are thrown back, then, to the arguments drawn from the language of the Act of June 19, 1934. Is the phrase "substantive rights" confined to rights conferred by law to be protected and enforced in accordance with the adjective law of judicial procedure? It certainly embraces such rights. One of them is the right not to be injured in one's person by another's negligence, to redress infraction of which the present action was brought. The petitioner says the phrase connotes more; that by its use Congress intended that in regulating procedure this court should not deal with important and substantial rights theretofore recognized. Recognized where and by whom? The state courts are divided as to the power in the absence of statute to order a physical examination. In a number such an order is authorized by statute or rule. * * *

The asserted right, moreover, is no more important than many others enjoyed by litigants in District Courts sitting in the several states, before the Federal Rules of Civil Procedure altered and abolished old rights or privileges and created new ones in connection with the conduct of litigation. The suggestion that the rule offends the important right to freedom from invasion of the person ignores the fact that as we hold, no invasion of freedom from personal restraint attaches to refusal so to comply with its provisions. If we were to adopt the suggested criterion of the importance of the alleged right we should invite endless litigation and confusion worse confounded. The test must be whether a rule really regulates procedure,—the judicial process for enforcing rights and duties recognized by substantive law and for justly administering remedy and redress for disregard or infraction of them. That the rules in question are such is admitted.

Finally, it is urged that Rules 35 and 37 work a major change of policy and that this was not intended by Congress. Apart from the fact already stated, that the policy of the states in this respect has not been uniform, it is to be noted that the authorization of a comprehensive system of court rules was a departure in policy, and that the new policy envisaged in the enabling act of 1934 was that the whole field of court procedure be regulated in the interest of speedy, fair and exact determination of the truth. The challenged rules comport with this policy. Moreover, in accordance with the Act, the rules were submitted to the Congress so that that body might examine them and veto their going into effect if contrary to the policy of the legislature.

The value of the reservation of the power to examine proposed rules, laws and regulations before they become effective is well understood by Congress. It is frequently, as here, employed to make sure that the action under the delegation squares with the Congressional purpose. * * * [T]his specific rule was attacked and defended before the committees of the two Houses. The Preliminary Draft of the rules called attention to the contrary practice indicated by the Botsford case, as did the Report of the Advisory Committee and the Notes prepared by the Committee to accompany the final version of the rules. That no adverse action was taken by Congress indicates, at least, that no transgression of legislative policy was found. We conclude that the rules under attack are within the authority granted.

The District Court treated the refusal to comply with its order as a contempt and committed the petitioner therefor. Neither in the Circuit Court of Appeals nor here was this action assigned as error. We think, however, that in the light of the provisions of Rule 37 it was plain error of such a fundamental nature that we should notice it. * * * Rule 37 exempts from punishment as for contempt the refusal to obey an order that a party submit to a physical or mental examination. The District Court was in error in going counter to this express exemption. The remedies available under the rule in such a case are those enumerated in [the rule itself]. For this error we reverse the judgment and remand the cause to the District Court for further proceedings in conformity to this opinion.

Reversed and remanded.

■ MR. JUSTICE FRANKFURTER, dissenting.

* * * [I]t does not seem to me that the answer to our question is to be found by an analytic determination whether the power of examination here claimed is a matter of procedure or a matter of substance, even assuming that the two are mutually exclusive categories with easily ascertainable contents. The problem seems to me to be controlled by the policy underlying the Botsford decision. Its doctrine was not a survival of an outworn technicality. It rested on considerations akin to what is familiarly known in the English law as the liberties of the subject. To be sure, the immunity that was recognized in the Botsford case has no constitutional sanction. It is amenable to statutory change. But the "inviolability of a person" was deemed to have such historic roots in Anglo-American law that it was not to be curtailed "unless by clear and unquestionable authority of law". * * *

So far as national law is concerned, a drastic change in public policy in a matter deeply touching the sensibilities of people or even their prejudices as to privacy, ought not to be inferred from a general authorization to formulate rules for the more uniform and effective dispatch of business on the civil side of the federal courts. I deem a requirement as to the invasion of the person to stand on a very different footing from questions pertaining to the discovery of documents, pre-trial procedure and other devices for the expeditious, economic and fair conduct of litigation. That disobedience of an order under Rule 35 cannot be visited with punishment as for contempt does not mitigate its intrusion into an historic immunity of the privacy of the person. Of course the Rule is compulsive in that the doors of the federal courts otherwise open may be shut to litigants who do not submit to such a physical examination.

In this view little significance attaches to the fact that the Rules, in accordance with the statute, remained on the table of two Houses of Congress without evoking any objection to Rule 35 and thereby automatically came into force. * * * Having due regard to the mechanics of legislation and the practical conditions surrounding the business of Congress when the Rules were submitted, to draw any inference of tacit approval from non-action by Congress is to appeal to unreality. And so I conclude that to make the drastic change that Rule 35 sought to introduce would require explicit legislation.

Ordinarily, disagreement with the majority on so-called procedural matters is best held in silence. Even in the present situation I should be loath to register dissent did the issue pertain merely to diversity litigation. But Rule 35 applies to all civil litigation in the federal courts, and thus concerns the enforcement of federal rights and not merely of state law in the federal courts.

■ MR. JUSTICE BLACK, MR. JUSTICE DOUGLAS, and MR. JUSTICE MURPHY agree with these views.

―――――

NOTE ON CHALLENGES TO THE VALIDITY OF THE FEDERAL RULES

(1) Decisions Rejecting Challenges Under the Enabling Act. In Mississippi Pub. Corp. v. Murphree, 326 U.S. 438 (1946), a federal district court had held that a provision of Rule 4, permitting service of process anywhere within the state in which the district court sits, rather than only within the district, was invalid because it was beyond the authority granted by the Enabling Act. The Supreme Court, while upholding the rule, was at pains to point out that "[t]he fact that this Court promulgated the rules as formulated and recommended by the Advisory Committee does not foreclose consideration of their validity, meaning or consistency".[1]

In several cases, the Court has given a rule a strained interpretation, apparently to avoid questions about its validity under the Enabling Act. See, *e.g.*, Palmer v. Hoffman, 318 U.S. 109 (1943) (Fed.Rule 8(c)); Anderson v. Yungkau, 329 U.S. 482 (1947) (Fed.Rules 6(b) and 25(a)); Walker v. Armco Steel Corp., 446 U.S. 740 (1980) (Fed.Rule 3); Semtek Int'l, Inc. v. Lockheed Martin Corp., 531 U.S. 497 (2001) (Fed.Rule 41(b)); see generally pp. 619–621, *infra*. But to date, the Court has never squarely invalidated a provision of the civil rules.[2]

(2) Allocation of Authority Between the Legislative and Judicial Branches. The Enabling Act in § 2072(b) specifies that "[a]ll laws in conflict [with rules promulgated under the Act] shall be of no further force or effect." Does this provision raise a constitutional issue? Does the Supreme Court's rulemaking power allow it to supersede acts of Congress passed *after* the rules became effective? If Congress overrides a particular rule, may the Court thereafter reinstate the rule? (Note that the opinion in Sibbach, surprisingly, characterized the Enabling Act as giving the courts only the

―――――――――――――

[1] For criticism of the rationale in Murphree, and arguments that aspects of Rule 4 relating to amenability to jurisdiction exceed the Court's rulemaking authority, see Whitten, *Separation of Powers Restrictions on Rule Making: A Case Study of Federal Rule 4*, 40 Me.L.Rev. 41 (1988); Kelleher, *Amenability to Jurisdiction as a "Substantive Right": The Invalidity of Rule 4(k) Under the Rules Enabling Act*, 75 Ind.L.J. 1191 (2000).

[2] In Business Guides, Inc. v. Chromatic Communications Enterprises, Inc., 498 U.S. 533 (1991), the Court took seriously, but ultimately rejected, an Enabling Act challenge to its interpretation of revised Rule 11 of the Federal Rules of Civil Procedure. See also Marek v. Chesny (and especially Justice Brennan's dissent), discussed in Paragraph (4), *infra*.

In Ortiz v. Fibreboard Corp., 527 U.S. 815, 862 (1999), the Court cautioned against—but did not explicitly reject—an application of Rule 23 that would permit certification of a "mandatory" (non-opt out) class action solely on the basis that the defendant might lack sufficient assets to satisfy all potential claims against it. The Court emphasized that the combination of the Enabling Act's limiting provisions and the effect on absent class members of certifying such a mandatory proceeding militated against so expansive an interpretation of the rule.

authority "to make rules not inconsistent with the statutes or Constitution of the United States".)

The relationship between the Enabling Act and an Act of Congress arose in an unusual context in Henderson v. United States, 517 U.S. 654 (1996). In a provision unchanged since its enactment in 1920, the Suits in Admiralty Act (SAA), 46 U.S.C. App. § 742, permits certain actions in admiralty to be brought against the United States and further states that the plaintiff shall "forthwith" serve a copy of the complaint on the U.S. Attorney and shall mail a copy to the Attorney General. Rule 4 of the Federal Rules of Civil Procedure, however, as enacted by Congress in 1982, 96 Stat. 2527, authorizes an extendable 120-day period for service of process in all cases. In an action under the SAA, service of process was effected in accordance with Rule 4 but (the Court assumed) too late to meet the SAA requirement that service be made "forthwith".

The Court held that the "procedural" provision of Rule 4 governing the time available for service superseded the shorter period specified in the SAA. Observing that the question did not arise squarely under the Enabling Act because Rule 4, as amended, had been enacted by Congress, the Court said: "As the United States acknowledges, * * * a Rule made law by Congress supersedes conflicting laws no less than a Rule this Court prescribes."[3]

Note that, despite arguments that the Enabling Act's delegation of authority to override statutes is unconstitutional,[4] all the Justices assumed that such authority could be exercised, at least in areas not involving subject matter jurisdiction or statutory limitations on the waiver of sovereign immunity.

(3) Sibbach and the Substance-Procedure Distinction. The substantive right asserted in the Sibbach case was state-created. What, if any, are the constitutional limits upon the power of Congress to regulate practice and procedure in actions for the enforcement of such rights? Does the Sibbach opinion yield a satisfactory test of what constitutes practice and procedure? Of when regulation of the former may transgress limits on the validity or appropriateness of federal regulation of the latter? Does the opinion cast any light on the difference, if any, between the constitutional power of Congress in this area and the power delegated by Congress to the Supreme Court? Do you agree with the Sibbach Court's statement that if the right asserted were one of "substantive law", the Rules of Decision Act would require the application of Indiana law?

Some light is shed on all these questions in the materials in Sections 2 and 3, *infra* (including materials on the significance of the Enabling Act and rules promulgated pursuant to it).[5]

---

[3] Justice Thomas, joined by Chief Justice Rehnquist and Justice O'Connor in dissent, argued that the SAA's requirement of service "forthwith" was a jurisdictional limitation on the waiver of sovereign immunity (1) that could not be changed by a rule promulgated under the Enabling Act and (2) that had not been impliedly repealed by Congress in 1982.

[4] See, *e.g.*, Clinton, *Rule 9 of the Federal Habeas Corpus Rules: A Case Study on the Need for Reform of the Rules Enabling Acts*, 63 Iowa L.Rev. 15, 64–77 (1977).

[5] Redish & Murashko, *The Rules Enabling Act and the Procedural-Substantive Tension: A Lesson in Statutory Interpretation*, 93 Minn.L.Rev. 26 (2008), advocate an interpretation that "permits rules to impact substantive rights if and only if they do so incidentally." As an example of a case effectively implementing their approach, the authors cite Burlington N.R.R. v. Woods, 480 U.S. 1 (1987), p. 619 n.7, *infra* (holding that a federal appellate rule giving discretion to impose a penalty on a losing party preempts a state rule mandating such a penalty). Can this position be squared with the 2010 decision in the Shady Grove case, p. 621, *infra*? Compare

(4) Marek v. Chesny and the Limits of Rulemaking Authority. The tension between the rulemaking authority and the legislative powers of Congress was highlighted by the controversy in Marek v. Chesny, 473 U.S. 1 (1985). In that case the plaintiff, after prevailing in a civil rights action under 42 U.S.C. § 1983, moved for an award of attorney's fees as authorized by 42 U.S.C. § 1988. The district court denied the motion with respect to attorney's fees incurred after an offer of settlement by the defendant, since Rule 68 provided that when, as here, the amount recovered after trial was less than the amount of the offer, "the offeree must pay the costs incurred after the making of the offer." The Supreme Court agreed with the district court, holding that (a) the term "costs" in Rule 68 includes attorney's fees whenever the underlying statute (here § 1988) defines costs to include those fees, and (b) as so construed Rule 68's policy of encouraging settlements is wholly consistent with § 1988's policy of encouraging meritorious civil rights suits.

Justice Brennan (joined by Justices Marshall and Blackmun) dissented on both grounds. He argued that the automatic provisions of Rule 68, if applied to attorney's fees, would put severe pressure on civil rights plaintiffs to settle even meritorious suits without adequate information and were thus wholly inconsistent with the broad discretion conferred by § 1988. He concluded that "[as] construed by the Court * * * Rule 68 surely will operate to 'abridge' and to 'modify' [the] statutory right to reasonable attorney's fees. * * * [Thus] the Rules Enabling Act requires that the Court's interpretation give way".[6]

---

2. THE POWERS OF THE FEDERAL COURTS IN DEFINING PRIMARY LEGAL OBLIGATIONS THAT FALL WITHIN THE LEGISLATIVE COMPETENCE OF THE STATES

Swift v. Tyson

41 U.S. (16 Pet.) 1, 10 L.Ed. 865 (1842).
Certificate of Division from the Circuit Court for the Southern District of New York.

■ STORY, JUSTICE, delivered the opinion of the court.—This cause comes before us from the circuit court of the southern district of New York, upon a certificate of division of the judges of that court. The action was brought by the plaintiff, Swift, as indorsee, against the defendant, Tyson, as

---

Hendricks, *In Defense of the Substance-Procedure Dichotomy*, 89 Wash.U.L.Rev. 103 (2011) (acknowledging that many legal rules have both substantive and procedural aspects, but arguing that the REA and transparency require federal courts to classify each legal rule as either one or the other).

[6] Justice Brennan's position finds support in Professor Burbank's study of the history of the Rules Enabling Act. See Burbank, *The Rules Enabling Act of 1934*, 130 U.Pa.L.Rev. 1015 (1982). In a later article, Burbank concludes that while the rules may *authorize* the award of fees and other costs in such circumstances, they may not *require* their imposition without running afoul of the Enabling Act. Burbank, *Sanctions in the Proposed Amendments to the Federal Rules of Civil Procedure: Some Questions About Power*, 11 Hofstra L.Rev. 997 (1983).

acceptor, upon a bill of exchange dated at Portland, Maine, on [May 1,] 1836, for the sum of $1540.30, payable six months after date, and grace, drawn by one Nathaniel Norton and one Jairus S. Keith upon and accepted by Tyson, at the city of New York, in favor of the order of Nathaniel Norton, and by Norton indorsed to the plaintiff. The bill was dishonored at maturity.

At the trial, the acceptance and indorsement of the bill were admitted, and the plaintiff there rested his case. The defendant then introduced in evidence the answer of Swift to a bill of discovery, by which it appeared, that Swift took the bill, before it became due, in payment of a promissory note due to him by Norton & Keith; that he understood, that the bill was accepted in part payment of some lands sold by Norton to a company in New York; that Swift was a *bona fide* holder of the bill, not having any notice of anything in the sale or title to the lands, or otherwise impeaching the transaction, and with the full belief that the bill was justly due. * * *. The defendant then offered to prove, that the bill was accepted by the defendant, as part consideration for the purchase of certain lands in the state of Maine, which Norton & Keith represented themselves to be the owners of, and also represented to be of great value, and contracted to convey a good title thereto; and that the representations were in every respect fraudulent and false, and Norton & Keith had no title to the lands, and that the same were of little or no value. The plaintiff objected to the admission of such testimony, or of any testimony, as against him, impeaching or showing a failure of the consideration, on which the bill was accepted, under the facts admitted by the defendant, and those proved by him, by reading the answer of plaintiff to the bill of discovery. The judges of the circuit court thereupon divided in opinion upon the following point or question of law—Whether, under the facts last mentioned, the defendant was entitled to the same defence to the action, as if the suit was between the original parties to the bill, that is to say, Norton, or Norton & Keith, and the defendant; and whether the evidence so offered was admissible as against the plaintiff in the action. And this is the question certified to us for our decision. * * *

In the present case, the plaintiff is a *bona fide* holder, without notice, for what the law deems a good and valid consideration, that is, for a pre-existing debt; and the only real question in the cause is, whether, under the circumstances of the present case, such a pre-existing debt constitutes a valuable consideration, in the sense of the general rule applicable to negotiable instruments. * * * [T]he argument on behalf of the defendant is, that the contract is to be treated as a New York contract, and therefore, to be governed by the laws of New York, as expounded by its courts, as well upon general principles, as by the express provisions of the 34th section of the judiciary act of 1789, ch. 20. And then it is further contended, that by the law of New York, as thus expounded by its courts, a pre-existing debt does not constitute, in the sense of the general rule, a valuable consideration applicable to negotiable instruments.

[The Supreme Court first expressed doubt that the doctrine asserted can "be treated as finally established" by the New York cases.]

But, admitting the doctrine to be fully settled in New York, it remains to be considered, whether it is obligatory upon this court, if it differs from the principles established in the general commercial law. It is observable, that the courts of New York do not found their decisions upon this point, upon any local statute, or positive, fixed or ancient local usage; but they deduce the doctrine from the general principles of commercial law. It is, however, contended, that the 34th section of the judiciary act of 1789, ch. 20, furnishes a rule obligatory upon this court to follow the decisions of the state tribunals in all cases to which they apply. That section provides "that the laws of the several states, except where the constitution, treaties or statutes of the United States shall otherwise require or provide, shall be regarded as rules of decision, in trials at common law, in the courts of the United States, in cases where they apply." In order to maintain the argument, it is essential, therefore, to hold, that the word "laws," in this section, includes within the scope of its meaning, the decisions of the local tribunals. In the ordinary use of language, it will hardly be contended, that the decisions of courts constitute laws. They are, at most, only evidence of what the laws are, and are not, of themselves, laws. They are often re-examined, reversed and qualified by the courts themselves, whenever they are found to be either defective, or ill-founded, or otherwise incorrect. The laws of a state are more usually understood to mean the rules and enactments promulgated by the legislative authority thereof, or long-established local customs having the force of laws. In all the various cases, which have hitherto come before us for decision, this court have uniformly supposed, that the true interpretation of the 34th section limited its application to state laws, strictly local, that is to say, to the positive statutes of the state, and the construction thereof adopted by the local tribunals, and to rights and titles to things having a permanent locality, such as the rights and titles to real estate, and other matters immovable and intraterritorial in their nature and character. It never has been supposed by us, that the section did apply, or was designed to apply, to questions of a more general nature, not at all dependent upon local statutes or local usages of a fixed and permanent operation, as, for example, to the construction of ordinary contracts or other written instruments, and especially to questions of general commercial law, where the state tribunals are called upon to perform the like functions as ourselves, that is, to ascertain, upon general reasoning and legal analogies, what is the true exposition of the contract or instrument, or what is the just rule furnished by the principles of commercial law to govern the case. And we have not now the slightest difficulty in holding, that this section, upon its true intendment and construction, is strictly limited to local statutes and local usages of the character before stated, and does not extend to contracts and other instruments of a commercial nature, the true interpretation and effect whereof are to be sought, not in the decisions of the local tribunals, but in the general principles and doctrines of commercial jurisprudence. Undoubtedly, the decisions of the local tribunals upon such subjects are entitled to, and will receive, the most deliberate attention and respect of this court; but they cannot furnish positive rules, or conclusive authority, by which our own judgments are to be bound up and governed. The law respecting negotiable instruments may be truly declared in the language of Cicero, adopted by Lord Mansfield in Luke v. Lyde, 2 Burr. 883, 887, to be in a great measure, not the law of a single country only, but of the commercial world. * * *

It becomes necessary for us, therefore, upon the present occasion, to express our own opinion of the true result of the commercial law upon the question now before us. And we have no hesitation in saying, that a pre-existing debt does constitute a valuable consideration, in the sense of the general rule already stated, as applicable to negotiable instruments. * * * And why, upon principle, should not a pre-existing debt be deemed such a valuable consideration? It is for the benefit and convenience of the commercial world, to give as wide an extent as practicable to the credit and circulation of negotiable paper, that it may pass not only as security for new purchases and advances, made upon the transfer thereof, but also in payment of, and as security for, pre-existing debts. The creditor is thereby enabled to realize or to secure his debt, and thus may safely give a prolonged credit, or forbear from taking any legal steps to enforce his rights. The debtor also has the advantage of making his negotiable securities of equivalent value to cash. But establish the opposite conclusion, that negotiable paper cannot be applied in payment of, or as security for, pre-existing debts, without letting in all the equities between the original and antecedent parties, and the value and circulation of such securities must be essentially diminished, and the debtor driven to the embarrassment of making a sale thereof, often at a ruinous discount, to some third person, and then, by circuity, to apply the proceeds to the payment of his debts. What, indeed, upon such a doctrine, would become of that large class of cases, where new notes are given by the same or by other parties, by way of renewal or security to banks, in lieu of old securities discounted by them, which have arrived at maturity? Probably, more than one-half of all bank transactions in our country, as well as those of other countries, are of this nature. The doctrine would strike a fatal blow at all discounts of negotiable securities for pre-existing debts.

This question has been several times before this court, and it has been uniformly held, that it makes no difference whatsoever, as to the rights of the holder, whether the debt, for which the negotiable instrument is transferred to him, is a pre-existing debt, or is contracted at the time of the transfer. * * * In England, the same doctrine has been uniformly acted upon. * * *

In the American courts, so far as we have been able to trace the decisions, the same doctrine seems generally, but not universally, to prevail. * * * We are all, therefore, of opinion, that the question on this point, propounded by the circuit court for our consideration, ought to be answered in the negative; and we shall, accordingly, direct it so to be certified to the circuit court.

■ [JUSTICE CATRON concurred in a separate statement limiting his agreement to "the case made by the record".]

———

NOTE ON SWIFT V. TYSON, ITS ANTECEDENTS AND RISE, AND THE INTIMATIONS OF ITS FALL

(1) Decisions Prior to Swift. The first volume of American law reports was Kirby's Connecticut reports, published in 1789. Given the paucity of reported decisions and the difficulties of establishing the grounds of unreported ones, the problem of the authority of state decisions arose infrequently in the early years. See the account of the antecedents of Swift v. Tyson in 2 Crosskey,

Politics and the Constitution in the History of the United States 822–62 (1953).[1]

In Jackson v. Chew, 25 U.S. (12 Wheat.) 153 (1827), a dispute over a testamentary disposition, the Court for the first time squarely recognized an obligation to conform to post-1789 decisions of state courts on matters of unwritten law. Justice Thompson said:

"After such a settled course of decisions, and two of them in the highest court of law in the state, * * * a contrary decision by this court would present a conflict between the state courts and those of the United States, productive of incalculable mischief. * * * And * * * to establish a contrary doctrine here, would be repugnant to the principles which have always governed this court in like cases.

"It has been urged, however, at the bar, that this court applies this principle only to state constructions of their own statutes.[2] * * * But the same rule has been extended to other cases; and there can be no good reason assigned, why it should not be, when it is applying settled rules of real property. This court adopts the state decisions, because they settle the law applicable to the case; and the reasons assigned for this course, apply as well to rules of construction growing out of the common law, as the statute law of the state, when applied to the title of lands."

A few years before Swift, the Court decided Wheaton v. Peters, 33 U.S. (8 Pet.) 591 (1834), a federal court copyright action in which the plaintiff's claim for relief rested in part on the common law. The majority said: "It is clear, there can be no common law of the United States. The federal government is composed of twenty-four sovereign and independent states; each of which may have its local usages, customs and common law. There is no principle which pervades the Union and has the authority of law, that is not embodied in the constitution or laws of the Union. The common law could be made a part of our federal system, only by legislative adoption. When,

---

[1] In Brown v. Van Bramm, 3 U.S. (3 Dall.) 344 (1797), the plaintiff, in an action on bills of exchange in the United States Circuit Court for Rhode Island, obtained a default judgment for the principal, together with interest, protest charges, and (pursuant to a Rhode Island statute) damages of 10 per cent of the principal. The Supreme Court affirmed the judgment with a brief statement that the result was warranted "under the laws, and the practical construction of the courts, of Rhode Island", and with the following footnote: "Chase, Justice, observed, that he concurred in the opinion of the court; but that it was on common law principles, and not in compliance with the laws and practice of the state."

Professor Conant argues that this case was correctly decided under Rhode Island law not because of § 34, which the Court did not cite, but "because of a rule of the international conflicts of law, an integral part of the international law merchant", and that Justice Chase was "surely referring" not to domestic common law but to "the entire Common-Law legal system that incorporates maritime and merchant law." See letter from Prof. Michael Conant to David Shapiro (3/3/97). See generally Conant, The Constitution and the Economy, Ch. 7 (1991).

[2] [Ed.] Both before and after Jackson v. Chew, the Supreme Court acknowledged the authority of state court decisions construing state statutes. See, particularly, Elmendorf v. Taylor, 23 U.S. (10 Wheat.) 152, 159–60 (1825); Green v. Neal's Lessee, 31 U.S. (6 Pet.) 291 (1832).

In Huidekoper's Lessee v. Douglass, 7 U.S. (3 Cranch) 1 (1805), Chief Justice Marshall, speaking for a unanimous Court, decided an important question of title to lands turning upon the construction of a 1792 Pennsylvania statute, without reference to two contrary decisions of the Supreme Court of Pennsylvania. But the Supreme Court of Pennsylvania was not the highest court of the state in 1805, and state law at the time was apparently unsettled. See Bridwell & Whitten, The Constitution and the Common Law 101–05 (1977).

therefore, a common law right is asserted, we must look to the state in which the controversy originated".[3]

(2) The Rationale of Swift. The decisions just noted are in tension with the meaning that Justice Story attributed to the term "laws" in the Rules of Decision Act. In Swift, he distinguished "local" law (both statutes and some aspects of unwritten laws, sometimes called usages), on the one hand, from "general commercial law", on the other. A conception of the common law as a single system, and especially of the law merchant as "a branch of the law of nations" that did not emanate from the sovereign command of any particular state, had a substantial foundation in the thinking of his time and an even stronger foundation in eighteenth century thought.[4]

Under the approach of Swift, federal decisions concerning the general common law were not viewed as federal law. Thus, one year after Swift, a New York state judge refused to follow Swift's commercial law ruling,[5] distinguishing that ruling from Supreme Court decisions about the meaning of the federal Constitution, law, or treaties.[6] Nor was a state court's decision concerning the general common law considered "federal" law for purpose of the Supreme Court's appellate jurisdiction to review state court judgments.[7] Still, even if not binding, federal decisions were often influential and thus, in some domains (such as commercial law), may have led to greater uniformity among the state courts in practice than would have otherwise existed.[8]

In 1842, however, the problems of conflicting applications of common law principles, even on matters of commerce, were already fully apparent. Consider the basic character of those rules of law that guide people in everyday affairs, advising them, in advance of any dispute, of their primary duties and powers and of their corresponding rights and vulnerabilities. Swift appears to have had the effect of leaving people uncertain about such

---

[3] United States v. Mundell, 27 F.Cas. 23 (C.C.D.Va.1795) (No. 15,834), is a little known Circuit Court decision by Supreme Court Justice James Iredell that is discussed in Collins, *Justice Iredell, Choice of Law, and the Constitution—A Neglected Encounter*, 23 Const. Comment. 163 (2006). Collins finds in the decision "strong early constitutional and statutory [*i.e.*, Judiciary Act, Section 34] authority for the application of a particular state's statutory *and common law* in civil litigation in the federal courts" (emphasis added).

[4] See, *e.g.*, Hoffman, Course of Legal Study (2 vols., 2d ed. 1836), particularly Vol. I, pp. 415–16; and the materials in Crosskey, Paragraph (1), *supra*, particularly Chap. XVIII. See also Clark, *Erie's Constitutional Source*, 95 Calif.L.Rev. 1289 (2007); Fletcher, *The General Common Law and Section 34 of the Judiciary Act of 1789: The Example of Marine Insurance*, 97 Harv.L.Rev. 1513 (1984). See also Sosa v. Alvarez-Machain, 542 U.S. 692, 725–26 (2004) (stating that in 1789, the common law was "outside of any particular State"); *id.* at 739–40 (Scalia, J., concurring in part and concurring in the judgment) (viewing the general common law of Swift as neither federal nor state law).

An alternative conception of the general common law applied in cases like Swift did view it as the law of the state, but did not view state court decisions about the common law as authoritative; instead, they were evidence of what the common law was, but a federal court could exercise its independent judgment about the meaning of the common law. See, *e.g.*, Harrison, *The Power of Congress over the Rules of Precedent*, 50 Duke L.J. 503, 526 (2000); Nelson, *A Critical Guide to Erie Railroad Co. v. Tompkins*, 54 Wm. & Mary L.Rev. 921, 927–28 (2013).

[5] See Stalker v. McDonald, 6 Hill 93 (N.Y. 1843).

[6] *Id.* at 95. Some state courts chose to follow federal decisions as a matter of policy. See Nelson, note 4, *supra*, at 949.

[7] See, *e.g.*, San Francisco v. Itsell, 133 U.S. 65, 67 (1890); N.Y. Life Ins. v. Hendren, 92 U.S. 286 (1876).

[8] See Fletcher, note 4, *supra*, at 1562–63.

matters—of telling them that the rules by which they are to be judged, with respect even to basic obligations and powers, will depend upon the unpredictable circumstance of what court they can get into, or may be haled into. Does the problem created by such uncertainty vary significantly as between questions of local property law, on the one hand, and commercial law or other types of obligations, on the other?

Would Congress have had power to enact the holding of Swift v. Tyson as a rule of decision in the federal courts? As a rule of decision in diverse citizenship cases in the state courts? As a rule of conduct between diverse citizens? As a general rule of conduct? Would a federal court in New York have been free to disregard a New York statute enacting a rule contrary to Swift v. Tyson?[9]

(3) Contemporary Controversy. There is a continuing debate among legal historians about the rationale and significance of the Swift decision. And these issues are in turn part of a larger debate about the nature of law and the role played by judges in nineteenth century American society.

Professor Horwitz, in The Transformation of American Law, 1780–1860, at 245–52 (1977), argues that the Swift decision is a leading example of the instances in which Justice Story and other judges of the period employed judicial powers as an instrument to aid in the redistribution of wealth and to promote commercial and industrial growth. Justice Story, he suggests, was well aware that the common law was not a brooding omnipresence—an awareness demonstrated by the approach taken in his treatise on Conflict of Laws in 1834—but was eager to provide the shelter of the federal courts against the application of state policies hostile to commercial interests.

In response, Professors Bridwell and Whitten, in The Constitution and the Common Law (1977), argue that Professor Horwitz's thesis misconstrues both the Swift decision and the perceptions of its author. They suggest that in the first half of the nineteenth century, Story and his contemporaries viewed the law of commercial transactions and contracts not as the command of the sovereign, but rather as the embodiment of prevailing customs and practices and as a process for applying them to the case at hand. To allow local customs to prevail over general practice, in the absence of some strong reason for doing so, would frustrate the understandings on which the transaction was based. Swift v. Tyson, they conclude, is "a prime example of how the diversity jurisdiction operated to preserve the intentions and

---

[9] Professor Crosskey, an important but much-criticized historian and student of the Constitution, appeared to answer all the questions in the last two paragraphs in the affirmative. See 1 Crosskey, Paragraph (1), *supra*, Part III, entitled "A Unitary View of the National Governing Powers". He read the Constitution as providing for a national legislature with plenary powers to pass laws for the general welfare and a national judiciary with plenary powers to establish justice. (In support of this reading he argued that the "laws of the United States" referred to in the jurisdictional provisions of Article III included the common law, and that Congress should have provided for the exercise of jurisdiction in all common law cases.)

Sherry, *Wrong, Out of Step, and Pernicious: Erie as the Worst Decision of All Time*, 39 Pepp.L.Rev. 129 (2011), contends that when Congress enacted the Rules of Decision Act, it "probably did not intend for federal courts sitting in diversity to apply *either* state statutory law or state common law, but rather to apply federal common law" (emphasis added). She goes on to contend that (1) Erie's rejection of Swift cannot be grounded in constitutional principles of federalism or separation of powers, and (2) Erie's pernicious effect is that by placing a "murky constitutional imprimatur" on judicial restraint, it "threatens to deprive us of one of our oldest and most effective tools for avoiding majority tyranny."

expectations of the parties intact when their dealings had taken place against the assumed background of general commercial practice".[10]

(4) Developments Following Swift. After Swift, the Court generally continued to follow state law on matters of construction of state statutes. See Note, 37 Harv.L.Rev. 1129 (1924). But there were some notable exceptions. See, *e.g.*, Watson v. Tarpley, 59 U.S. (18 How.) 517, 521 (1855) ("[A]ny state law or regulation, the effect of which would be to impair the rights [under and defined by the general commercial law] * * * or to devest the federal courts of cognizance thereof, * * * must be nugatory and unavailing.").

    (a) The Bond Cases. Controversy over the Swift decision did not become intense until the period during and after the Civil War. Among the most controversial of the Court's decisions were those governing federal court actions on defaulted municipal bonds.[11] In Gelpcke v. City of Dubuque, 68 U.S. (1 Wall.) 175 (1863), the Court declined to follow a state-court construction of the state constitution that would have invalidated the state bonds. The Court rested its decision on the fact that the state's construction overruled decisions outstanding at the time the bonds were issued. Justice Swayne said for the Court: "We are not unmindful of the importance of uniformity in the decisions of this court, and those of the highest local courts, giving constructions to the laws and constitutions of their own States. It is the settled rule of this court in such cases, to follow the decisions of the State courts. But there have been heretofore, in the judicial history of this court, as doubtless there will be hereafter, many exceptional cases. We shall never immolate truth, justice, and the law, because a State tribunal has erected the altar and decreed the sacrifice."

    Did the state court's overruling decision violate any federal constitutional provision? If not, can the Gelpcke decision be defended?[12]

    (b) Further Extensions of Swift Before 1938. The principle of Swift v. Tyson held sway for nearly a century in a wide area of commercial law, marked off only with difficulty from property and other matters of "local" law.

    (i) Extension to Contract and Tort Cases. Consistently with Swift's language, the Court also relied on general principles rather than state precedents in "the construction of ordinary contracts or other written instruments" like deeds and wills. *E.g.*, Lane v. Vick, 44 U.S. (3 How.) 464 (1845). And in an extension of the doctrine much criticized even by Swift's

---

[10] See also Freyer, Harmony and Dissonance: The Swift and Erie Cases in American Federalism xiii (1981) ("Swift was thoroughly consistent with antebellum notions of American constitutionalism and federalism"); Conant, The Constitution and the Economy, Ch. 7 (1991) (arguing that Swift was a case arising under the interstate-international law merchant—"general commercial law"—and not what was then viewed as "the common law"); Fletcher, note 4, *supra* (drawing on early nineteenth century diversity cases involving marine insurance to show that well before Swift, state and federal courts succeeded in developing a uniform system of common law in the adjudication of these commercial disputes under the law merchant, and arguing that § 34, and the lex loci principle it was thought to embody, were never seen as precluding the application of general common law in such cases).

[11] See Freyer, note 10, *supra*, at 58–61. According to one report, "the total of defaulted bonds across the nation amounted to between $100,000,000 and $150,000,000." Some 300 bond cases came to the Supreme Court in the last third of the nineteenth century.

[12] A study of diversity cases construing state constitutions during the Swift era concludes that the federal courts developed a body of uniform (but "nonfederal") constitutional law that sharply limited legislative power. Collins, *Before Lochner—Diversity Jurisdiction and the Development of General Constitutional Law*, 74 Tul.L.Rev. 1263 (2000). See also Woolhandler, *The Common Law Origins of Constitutionally Compelled Remedies*, 107 Yale L.J. 77 (1997).

present-day defenders,[13] the Court applied Swift's approach to a tort case as early as 1862. Chicago v. Robbins, 67 U.S. (2 Black) 418 (1862). Reliance on Swift in Baltimore & O.R.R. v. Baugh, 149 U.S. 368 (1893), to uphold the fellow-servant defense in a federal court action evoked a strenuous dissent by Justice Field.[14]

(ii) Displacement of "Uncertain" State Law. In Burgess v. Seligman, 107 U.S. 20 (1883), an action to recover on a debt owed by a corporation that later had been dissolved, the Court refused to follow a state court's decisions that had interpreted a state *statute* as applied to the very transactions in dispute. The Court noted that those decisions post-dated the transactions but claimed more generally the same power to exercise its own judgment that it exercises in cases involving the commercial and general law.

In Kuhn v. Fairmont Coal Co., 215 U.S. 349 (1910), the Court applied in a common law case a doctrine akin to that applied in Gelpcke and Burgess in statutory fields. With Justices Holmes, White, and McKenna dissenting, it held itself free to take its own view of the legal effect of a deed of land when the state decisions had been unsettled at the time of the conveyance.

(c) Corporations and the Diversity Jurisdiction. Corporations were especially successful in taking advantage of the existence of different rules in state and federal courts. A striking and notorious example was Black & White Taxicab & Transfer Co. v. Brown & Yellow Taxicab & Transfer Co., 276 U.S. 518 (1928), where a company had reincorporated itself in another state in order to establish diversity of citizenship with its rival. The Court declined to follow state decisions holding that a railroad's agreement to give exclusive taxicab privileges was contrary to public policy, declaring the question to be one of general law, under which the reincorporated company prevailed.[15]

In an important study embracing the post-Swift era, the Erie decision, and the work and thought of Justice Brandeis, Professor Purcell views the expansion of the Swift doctrine as part of the Supreme Court's effort to use the diversity jurisdiction both to protect the interests of (corporate) capital and to assert federal judicial authority even in areas falling outside the legislative authority of Congress. Purcell, Brandeis and the Progressive Constitution: Erie, the Judicial Power, and the Politics of the Federal Courts in Twentieth-Century America (2000). (See also Post, note 15, *supra.*) Purcell emphasizes the aggressive application of the Swift doctrine in the field of insurance, which at that time had been held to fall outside the authority of Congress to regulate commerce, and the similarly aggressive use of the injunctive power to protect business from the efforts of labor unions to organize and to strike.

---

[13] *E.g.*, Bridwell & Whitten, Paragraph (3), *supra*, at 119–27.

[14] For a suggestion that this dissent (excerpted in the Erie opinion, p. 587, *infra*) was motivated more by dislike of the fellow-servant rule than by considerations of jurisprudential theory, see Freyer, note 10, *supra*, at 173 n. 41.

[15] In the course of an extensive examination of the Taft Court, Professor Post uses the Taxicab case as an illustration of "the manner in which the Court interpreted federal common law to reflect the same preoccupations as the Court's substantive due process jurisprudence." Post, *Federalism in the Taft Court Era: Can It Be "Revived"?*, 51 Duke L.J. 1513, 1599–1600 (2002). "Federal common law and federal constitutional rights", he concludes, "were equally policies of 'judicial centralization' ".

(5) Increasing Criticism. In the decade following the Black & White case there was a perceptible erosion of Swift v. Tyson.[16]

In Burns Mortgage Co. v. Fried, 292 U.S. 487 (1934), for example, the circuit court of appeals had held that the construction by a state court of last resort of a state statute that was merely declaratory of the common law or law merchant did not bind the federal courts, and hence refused to follow a decision interpreting the Uniform Negotiable Instruments Law. The Supreme Court reversed, asserting "that there is no valid distinction * * * between an act which alters the common law and one which codifies or declares it. Both are within the letter of § 34 of the Judiciary Act * * *. And a declaratory act is no less an expression of the legislative will because the rule it prescribes is the same as that announced in prior decisions of the courts of the state. Nor is there a difference in this respect between a statute prescribing rules of commercial law and one concerned with some other subject of narrower scope."

And in Mutual Life Ins. Co. v. Johnson, 293 U.S. 335 (1934), Justice Cardozo built some prior expressions of the Court into a principle of large if indeterminate potential. The question was whether an insured's physical and mental condition excused his failure to give notice of his disability before his default in the payment of premiums. The opinion said: "[W]e yield to the judges of Virginia expounding a Virginia policy and adjudging its effect. * * * All that is here for our decision is the meaning, the tacit implications, of a particular set of words, which, as experience has shown, may yield a different answer to this reader and to that one. With choice so 'balanced with doubt', we accept as our guide the law declared by the state where the contract had its being."

(6) Prelude to Erie. On April 24, 1938, the day before the Erie decision, it is doubtful that anyone could have provided an intelligible formulation, consistent with the decided cases, concerning the power and duty of federal judges to disregard decisions of a state's highest court on questions of state law.

Erie Railroad Co. v. Tompkins

304 U.S. 64, 58 S.Ct. 817, 82 L.Ed. 1188 (1938).
Certiorari to the Circuit Court of Appeals for the Second Circuit.

■ MR. JUSTICE BRANDEIS delivered the opinion of the Court.

The question for decision is whether the oft-challenged doctrine of Swift v. Tyson shall now be disapproved.

Tompkins, a citizen of Pennsylvania, was injured on a dark night by a passing freight train of the Erie Railroad Company while walking along its right of way at Hughestown in that state. He claimed that the accident occurred through negligence in the operation, or maintenance, of the train; that he was rightfully on the premises as licensee because on a commonly used beaten footpath which ran for a short distance alongside

---

[16] For a discussion of legislative efforts in 1928 and 1929 to overrule Swift, see Burbank, *The Rules Enabling Act of 1934*, 130 U.Pa.L.Rev. 1015, 1109–10 n. 433 (1982). Burbank notes that one of the bills introduced was "drafted by * * * [then Professor Frankfurter] and sent to Senator Walsh at the suggestion of Justice Brandeis."

the tracks; and that he was struck by something which looked like a door projecting from one of the moving cars. To enforce that claim he brought an action in the federal court for Southern New York, which had jurisdiction because the company is a corporation of that state. * * *

The Erie insisted that its duty to Tompkins was no greater than that owed to a trespasser. It contended, among other things, that its duty to Tompkins, and hence its liability, should be determined in accordance with the Pennsylvania law; that under the law of Pennsylvania, as declared by its highest court, persons who use pathways along the railroad right of way—that is, a longitudinal pathway as distinguished from a crossing—are to be deemed trespassers; and that the railroad is not liable for injuries to undiscovered trespassers resulting from its negligence, unless it be wanton or willful. Tompkins denied that any such rule had been established by the decisions of the Pennsylvania courts; and contended that, since there was no statute of the state on the subject, the railroad's duty and liability is to be determined in federal courts as a matter of general law.

The trial judge refused to rule that the applicable law precluded recovery. The jury brought in a verdict of $30,000; and the judgment entered thereon was affirmed by the Circuit Court of Appeals, which held that it was unnecessary to consider whether the law of Pennsylvania was as contended, because the question was one not of local, but of general, law, and that "upon questions of general law the federal courts are free, in absence of a local statute, to exercise their independent judgment as to what the law is; and it is well settled that the question of the responsibility of a railroad for injuries caused by its servants is one of general law. * * * Where the public has made open and notorious use of a railroad right of way for a long period of time and without objection, the company owes to persons on such permissive pathway a duty of care in the operation of its trains. * * * It is likewise generally recognized law that a jury may find that negligence exists toward a pedestrian using a permissive path on the railroad right of way if he is hit by some object projecting from the side of the train."

The Erie had contended that application of the Pennsylvania rule was required, among other things, by section 34 of the Federal Judiciary Act of September 24, 1789 * * *.

Because of the importance of the question whether the federal court was free to disregard the alleged rule of the Pennsylvania common law, we granted certiorari.

First. Swift v. Tyson held that federal courts exercising jurisdiction on the ground of diversity of citizenship need not, in matters of general jurisprudence, apply the unwritten law of the state as declared by its highest court; that they are free to exercise an independent judgment as to what the common law of the state is—or should be * * *.

The Court in applying the rule of section 34 to equity cases, in Mason v. United States, 260 U.S. 545, 559, said: "The statute, however, is merely declarative of the rule which would exist in the absence of the statute." The federal courts assumed, in the broad field of "general law," the power to declare rules of decision which Congress was confessedly without power to enact as statutes. Doubt was repeatedly expressed as to the correctness of the construction given section 34, and as to the soundness of the rule which it introduced. But it was the more recent research of a competent scholar, who examined the original document, which established that the construction given to it by the Court was erroneous; and that the purpose of the section was merely to make certain that, in all matters except those in which some federal law is controlling, the federal courts exercising jurisdiction in diversity of citizenship cases would apply as their rules of decision the law of the state unwritten as well as written.[5]

Criticism of the doctrine became widespread after the decision of Black & White Taxicab & Transfer Co. v. Brown & Yellow Taxicab & Transfer Co., 276 U.S. 518 [see p. 583, *supra*] * * *.

Second. Experience in applying the doctrine of Swift v. Tyson, had revealed its defects, political and social; and the benefits expected to flow from the rule did not accrue. Persistence of state courts in their own opinions on questions of common law prevented uniformity; and the impossibility of discovering a satisfactory line of demarcation between the province of general law and that of local law developed a new well of uncertainties.[8]

On the other hand, the mischievous results of the doctrine had become apparent. Diversity of citizenship jurisdiction was conferred in order to prevent apprehended discrimination in state courts against those not citizens of the state. Swift v. Tyson introduced grave discrimination by noncitizens against citizens. It made rights enjoyed under the unwritten "general law" vary according to whether enforcement was sought in the state or in the federal court; and the privilege of selecting the court in which the right should be determined was conferred upon the noncitizen. Thus, the doctrine rendered impossible equal protection of the law. In attempting to promote uniformity of law throughout the United States, the doctrine had prevented uniformity in the administration of the law of the state.

The discrimination resulting became in practice far-reaching. This resulted in part from the broad province accorded to the so-called "general law" as to which federal courts exercised an independent judgment. In addition to questions of purely commercial law, "general law" was held to include the obligations under contracts entered into and to be performed within the state, the extent to which a carrier operating within a state may stipulate for exemption from liability for his own negligence or that of his employee; the liability for torts committed within the state upon persons resident or property located there, even where the question of liability depended upon the scope of a property right conferred by the state; and the right to exemplary or punitive damages. Furthermore, state decisions, construing local deeds, mineral conveyances, and even devises of real estate, were disregarded.

In part the discrimination resulted from the wide range of persons held entitled to avail themselves of the federal rule by resort to the

---

[5]   Charles Warren, New Light on the History of the Federal Judiciary Act of 1789 (1923) 37 Harv. L. Rev. 49, 51–52, 81–88, 108.

[8]   Compare 2 Warren, The Supreme Court in United States History (rev. ed. 1935) 89: "Probably no decision of the Court has ever given rise to more uncertainty as to legal rights; and though doubtless intended to promote uniformity in the operation of business transactions, its chief effect has been to render it difficult for business men to know in advance to what particular topic the Court would apply the doctrine. * * *."

diversity of citizenship jurisdiction. Through this jurisdiction individual citizens willing to remove from their own state and become citizens of another might avail themselves of the federal rule. And, without even change of residence, a corporate citizen of the state could avail itself of the federal rule by reincorporating under the laws of another state, as was done in the Taxicab Case.

The injustice and confusion incident to the doctrine of Swift v. Tyson have been repeatedly urged as reasons for abolishing or limiting diversity of citizenship jurisdiction. Other legislative relief has been proposed. If only a question of statutory construction were involved, we should not be prepared to abandon a doctrine so widely applied throughout nearly a century. But the unconstitutionality of the course pursued has now been made clear, and compels us to do so.

Third. Except in matters governed by the Federal Constitution or by acts of Congress, the law to be applied in any case is the law of the state. And whether the law of the state shall be declared by its Legislature in a statute or by its highest court in a decision is not a matter of federal concern. There is no federal general common law. Congress has no power to declare substantive rules of common law applicable in a state whether they be local in their nature or "general," be they commercial law or a part of the law of torts. And no clause in the Constitution purports to confer such a power upon the federal courts. As stated by Mr. Justice Field when protesting in Baltimore & Ohio R.R. Co. v. Baugh, 149 U.S. 368, 401, against ignoring the Ohio common law of fellow-servant liability: "I am aware that what has been termed the general law of the country—which is often little less than what the judge advancing the doctrine thinks at the time should be the general law on a particular subject—has been often advanced in judicial opinions of this court to control a conflicting law of a state. I admit that learned judges have fallen into the habit of repeating this doctrine as a convenient mode of brushing aside the law of a state in conflict with their views. And I confess that, moved and governed by the authority of the great names of those judges, I have, myself, in many instances, unhesitatingly and confidently, but I think now erroneously, repeated the same doctrine. But, notwithstanding the great names which may be cited in favor of the doctrine, and notwithstanding the frequency with which the doctrine has been reiterated, there stands, as a perpetual protest against its repetition, the constitution of the United States, which recognizes and preserves the autonomy and independence of the States—independence in their legislative and independence in their judicial departments. Supervision over either the legislative or the judicial action of the states is in no case permissible except as to matters by the constitution specifically authorized or delegated to the United States. Any interference with either, except as thus permitted, is an invasion of the authority of the state, and, to that extent, a denial of its independence."

The fallacy underlying the rule declared in Swift v. Tyson is made clear by Mr. Justice Holmes. The doctrine rests upon the assumption that there is "a transcendental body of law outside of any particular State but obligatory within it unless and until changed by statute," that federal courts have the power to use their judgment as to what the rules of common law are; and that in the federal courts "the parties are entitled to an independent judgment on matters of general law":

"But law in the sense in which courts speak of it today does not exist without some definite authority behind it. The common law so far as it is enforced in a State, whether called common law or not, is not the common law generally but the law of that State existing by the authority of that State without regard to what it may have been in England or anywhere else. * * *

"The authority and only authority is the State, and if that be so, the voice adopted by the State as its own [whether it be of its Legislature or of its Supreme Court] should utter the last word."

Thus the doctrine of Swift v. Tyson is, as Mr. Justice Holmes said, "an unconstitutional assumption of powers by the Courts of the United States which no lapse of time or respectable array of opinion should make us hesitate to correct." In disapproving that doctrine we do not hold unconstitutional section 34 of the Federal Judiciary Act of 1789 or any other act of Congress. We merely declare that in applying the doctrine this Court and the lower courts have invaded rights which in our opinion are reserved by the Constitution to the several states.

Fourth. The defendant contended that by the common law of Pennsylvania * * *, the only duty owed to the plaintiff was to refrain from willful or wanton injury. The plaintiff denied that such is the Pennsylvania law. * * * The Circuit Court of Appeals ruled that the question of liability is one of general law; and on that ground declined to decide the issue of state law. As we hold this was error, the judgment is reversed and the case remanded to it for further proceedings in conformity with our opinion.

Reversed.

■ [JUSTICE REED delivered a concurring opinion joining "in the conclusions reached in this case, in the disapproval of the doctrine of Swift v. Tyson, and in the reasoning of the majority opinion except in so far as it relies upon the unconstitutionality of the 'course pursued' by the federal courts." JUSTICE BUTLER dissented in an opinion in which JUSTICE MCREYNOLDS joined. JUSTICE CARDOZO did not participate.]

NOTE ON THE RATIONALE OF THE ERIE DECISION

(1) The "First" Ground of Decision. Under its *"First"* heading, the Court relies heavily on Warren, *New Light on the History of the Federal Judiciary Act of 1789*, 37 Harv.L.Rev. 49, 51–52, 81–88, 108 (1923). In that article Warren notes that Section 34 was "not contained in the Draft Bill, as introduced in the Senate, but was proposed, probably by [Senator, later Chief Justice] Ellsworth, as an amendment * * *." Warren's examination of the records of the Senate revealed a slip of paper, believed to be in Ellsworth's handwriting, on which an earlier version of the amendment (including the italicized material in the following quotation) was written:

"And be it further enacted, That the *Statute law of the several states in force for the time being and their unwritten or common law now in use, whether by adoption from the common law of England, the ancient statutes of the same or otherwise*, except where the Constitution, Treaties or Statutes of the United States shall otherwise require or provide, shall be regarded as rules of decision in the trials at common law in the courts of the United States in cases where they apply."

Warren's conclusion, endorsed by the Court in Erie, was that in light of the earlier draft, the phrase "laws of the several states" (which Ellsworth had written in as a substitute for the italicized phrase) was plainly designed to cover unwritten law. That conclusion has been widely criticized. See, *e.g.,* Nelson, p. 580, note 4, *supra,* at 956 & n. 104 and sources cited. But even if you accept Warren's conclusion, could you still defend the result of Swift v. Tyson? See Friendly, *In Praise of Erie—And of the New Federal Common Law,* 39 N.Y.U.L.Rev. 383, 389–91 (1964).[1]

(2) The "Second" Ground. In discussing the "political and social" defects of Swift v. Tyson, under his "*Second*" heading, Justice Brandeis emphasized the "grave discrimination by noncitizens against citizens" introduced by the decision. The point is oddly phrased, since every citizen of a state is a noncitizen of other states. Moreover, the Court seems to suggest that only noncitizens of a state may invoke the diversity jurisdiction. This is true of removal but not of original jurisdiction, and the statutory ban on removal by in-state defendants, see 28 U.S.C. § 1441(b)(2), could be eliminated by Congress. Moreover, the Court's claim that the Swift approach "rendered impossible equal protection of the law" must be taken with a grain of salt, if for no other reason than that the Equal Protection Clause is directed at the states and it was not until 1954 that the Court held that the Fifth Amendment's Due Process Clause, which does regulate the federal government, embodies principles of equal protection. See Bolling v. Sharpe, 347 U.S. 497 (1954).

Note, moreover, that the Erie holding and rationale are not limited to issues arising in litigation between citizens of different states. Consider, for example, a state law claim, joined to a federal law claim, that a federal court hears under its supplemental jurisdiction. In such a case, the Second Circuit said: "[I]t is the *source* of the right sued upon, and not the ground on which federal jurisdiction over the case is founded, which determines the governing law. * * * Thus, the Erie doctrine applies, whatever the ground for federal jurisdiction, to any issue or claim which has its source in state law." Maternally Yours v. Your Maternity Shop, 234 F.2d 538, 540–41 n. 1 (2d Cir.1956). That understanding has gained general acceptance.

Another "defect" of the Swift doctrine that Justice Brandeis discusses is the murkiness of the distinction between general and local unwritten law. But the Erie decision requires federal courts to apply a murky distinction between substance and procedure,[2] as is discussed at length below, and in many cases, to apply murky choice of law principles to determine which state's law applies. See pp. 591–596, *infra.*

In his study of Erie and of Justice Brandeis, discussed at p. 583, *supra,* Professor Purcell contends that Justice Brandeis was aware of the difficulties

---

[1] For a broader challenge to the conventional readings of § 34, see Ritz, Rewriting the History of the Judiciary Act of 1789, at 8–12, 126–48 (Holt & LaRue eds., 1990) (contending that the statutory phrase "laws of the several states", as distinguished from a reference to the laws of the "respective" states, referred to the law of the states in general, not to the law of any specific state). For a powerful response to Ritz, see Young, p. 590, *infra,* at 38–45.

[2] The Conformity Act, see p. 564, *supra,* had required federal courts generally to follow state practice and procedure in actions at law, and thus to distinguish practice and procedure from substance (on which it might follow the general common law). The Act was repealed in 1948.

of this part of the argument but, for a variety of reasons (including the need to secure a majority), refrained from clearly stating his real objections to the Swift doctrine: that it had been used by the federal courts to assert judicial power to regulate matters that fell outside the legislative authority of Congress and to protect corporate interests against reform movements in the states.

(3) The "Third" Ground. In a letter to Justice Reed written before the Erie decision was handed down, Justice Brandeis insisted that his opinion did not "pass upon or discuss the constitutionality of section 34 as construed in Swift v. Tyson"; rather the *"Third"* section of the opinion was "addressed to showing that the action of the Court in disregarding state law is unconstitutional" (quoted in Freyer, Harmony and Dissonance: The Swift and Erie Cases in American Federalism 136 (1981)). What is the distinction?

From the time of its rendition to the present day, controversy has surrounded the scope and meaning of Erie as a constitutional holding.[3] Is the Court saying that Congress itself could not have enacted a rule of decision to govern a case like Erie? It certainly is true that under the Swift regime, federal courts determined the substantive law to govern some matters that Congress, under the prevailing constitutional wisdom of the time, would have lacked the power to regulate. But even if in 1938 (and perhaps today as well), Congress would not have possessed authority to enact legislation purporting to govern the rights of *any* trespasser solely on the basis that the case was brought in a federal court (especially under the diversity jurisdiction), there was little doubt that Congress had power to prescribe a narrower rule of decision to govern the rights of trespassers on railroads whose activities affect interstate commerce.

Against this background, does any constitutional ruling in Erie rest on the notion that no branch of the federal government (including Congress) may declare the rights and duties of a litigant solely on the basis that a federal court has jurisdiction over a case involving that litigant? See p. 592, *infra.* Or does it depend on the proposition that the federal courts do not possess the same lawmaking power as Congress? See Mishkin, *Some Further Last Words on Erie: The Thread*, 87 Harv.L.Rev. 1682 (1974); Young, *A General Defense of Erie Railroad Co. v. Tompkins*, 10 J.L.Econ. & Pol'y 17, 68–76 (2013).[4]

---

[3]   See generally Wright & Kane, Federal Courts § 56 and authorities cited nn. 15, 16 (7th ed.2011); Chemerinsky, Federal Jurisdiction § 5.3 and authorities cited n. 161 (6th ed.2012).

[4]   In recent years, the controversy has not only been rekindled but has extended to a debate over the impact of Erie on the proper limits of modern federal common law in areas of predominantly federal concern—a subject dealt with in Chapter VII, *infra.* For arguments that Erie's constitutional basis significantly affects those limits, see Clark, p. 580 n.4, *supra* (finding the basis of Erie in the structure of the Constitution, including the Supremacy Clause); Goldsmith & Walt, *Erie and the Irrelevance of Legal Positivism*, 84 Va.L.Rev. 673 (1998) (contending that Erie is best understood as grounded not in changes in the perception of the common law since Swift but as an exercise in constitutional interpretation). In 2008, two articles by Professor Craig Green challenge what the author describes as Erie's "old myth" (that Erie rests on constitutional grounds), and Erie's "new myth" (that Erie imposes constitutional limits on "federal common-law authority regardless of state law"). Green, *Repressing Erie's Myth*, 96 Calif.L.Rev. 595 (2008); Green, *Erie and Problems of Constitutional Structure*, 96 Calif.L.Rev. 661 (2008). For Clark's response, reviewing and expanding on his view that there is a close relationship between Erie and the Supremacy Clause and that "[p]roperly understood, Erie implicates both separation of powers and federalism", see Clark, *Federal Lawmaking and the Role of Structure in Constitutional Interpretation*, 96 Calif.L.Rev. 699 (2008). The implications

Other explanations of Erie's constitutional holding have been put forward.[5] Is it possible that both Swift and Erie were correctly decided, but that changes occurring over the roughly 100 years between them—expansion of the reach of Swift, growing disuniformity, and decisionmaking by the federal judges that reflected their own views of policy rather than an effort to capture "the general law" as commonly understood, as well as the nature and sources of law[6]—called for different outcomes?

NOTE ON THE KLAXON DECISION AND PROBLEMS OF HORIZONTAL CHOICE OF LAW IN CASES INVOLVING STATE-CREATED RIGHTS

(1) The Klaxon Decision. The Erie decision assumed that, on remand, a New York federal court should apply Pennsylvania law in the case before it. But was this assumption grounded in another assumption: that a New York state court would apply Pennsylvania law on the facts of Erie, or was it premised on the assumption that the question of *which* state's law applied was one for the federal court to decide for itself, even in a diversity case? This issue was squarely addressed by the Court in Klaxon Co. v. Stentor Elec. Mfg. Co., 313 U.S. 487 (1941), where the Court began its opinion by stating: "The principal question in this case is whether in diversity cases the federal courts must follow conflict of laws rules prevailing in the states in which they sit".

The precise issue in Klaxon was whether—in a diversity action brought in a Delaware federal court for breach of an agreement executed in New York and partially performed there—the federal court could look to New York law in determining whether interest should be added to the judgment, whether or not a Delaware state court would look to New York law on that question.

---

of this debate for federal common law generally are also explored in *Symposium, Separation of Powers as a Safeguard of Federalism*, 83 Notre Dame L.Rev. No. 4 (2008).

[5] Professor Roosevelt suggests that the constitutional defect that Erie remedied was the application of law without a lawgiver. His premise is that the court of appeals in Erie, operating as it was under the Swift regime, was not applying either state law or a federal statute; nor, he says, did it purport to be making federal law. Hence, the imposition of liability on the railroad, based on a legal rule that was invalid because not given by any sovereign, denied due process. Roosevelt, *Valid Rule Due Process Challenges: Bond v. United States and Erie's Constitutional Source*, 54 Wm. & Mary L.Rev. 987, 999–1000 (2013). Does his premise, however, presuppose an answer to the central question: must judge-made rules applied by federal courts be like modern federal common law (that is, applicable in state as well as federal courts and consciously "made") to be valid, rather than representing the federal courts' view of what the general common law requires?

Roosevelt's premise does accord with Justice Brandeis' claim in Erie that it is a fallacy to believe "that there is a 'transcendental body of law outside of any particular State but obligatory within it unless and until changed by statute,'" because "'law in the sense in which courts speak of it today does not exist without some definite authority behind it'" (quoting Justice Holmes' dissent in the Black & White Taxicab case). Brandeis' view, which associates Erie's holding with a commitment to a version of legal positivism, has been broadly accepted. For a challenge to this conventional wisdom, see Goldsmith & Walt, note 4, *supra*.

For still another understanding of the constitutional basis for the Erie decision—that Congress cannot constitutionally authorize federal courts to formulate substantive law governing the Nation's commerce without providing an intelligible principle to limit the courts' exercise of that authority—see Nielson, *Erie as Nondelegation*, 72 Ohio St.L.J. 239 (2011).

[6] See Casto, *The Erie Doctrine and the Structure of Constitutional Revolutions*, 62 Tul.L.Rev. 907 (1998) (relating the overruling of Swift to changes in the prevailing intellectual climate).

A unanimous Court, in an opinion by Justice Reed, held that the federal court was required to apply the rule that a Delaware state court would apply, and that Delaware was not constitutionally required (under the Full Faith and Credit Clause) to look to New York law on the issue of interest. On the first of these questions, the Court said:

"Any other ruling would do violence to the principle of uniformity within a state upon which the Tompkins decision is based. Whatever lack of uniformity this may produce between federal courts in different states is attributable to our federal system, which leaves to a state, within the limits permitted by the Constitution, the right to pursue local policies diverging from those of its neighbors. It is not for the federal courts to thwart such local policies by enforcing an independent 'general law' of conflict of laws. Subject only to review by this Court on any federal question that may arise, Delaware is free to determine whether a given matter is to be governed by the law of the forum or some other law. * * * And the proper function of the Delaware federal court is to ascertain what the state law is, not what it ought to be."

(2) Klaxon and the Constitution. Assuming that the right to prejudgment interest at issue in Klaxon is substantive and thus is governed by state law under Erie, the choice of *which* state's law applies in a federal court is surely a matter of federal concern. Indeed, even if it could not have legislated the substantive decisional rule for all diversity cases encompassed by Erie, Congress, acting under its power to make laws "necessary and proper" to the exercise of jurisdiction under Article III, could certainly enact, or authorize the formulation of, federal choice-of-law rules for the federal courts.

The point is buttressed by the fact that at least in civil cases, the Constitution does not prohibit the territorial jurisdiction of the federal district courts from cutting across state boundaries. If Congress were to eliminate the district courts of New York and Delaware, and to create a single "Federal District Court for the Middle Atlantic States", the Klaxon rule could not operate on the facts of the case itself. See Hill, *The Erie Doctrine and the Constitution*, 53 Nw.U.L.Rev. 541, 558 (1958).

Moreover, Congress is generally believed to have authority under the Full Faith and Credit Clause to federalize choice of law by enacting conflicts rules binding on state as well as federal courts. See, *e.g.*, Friendly, *In Praise of Erie—And of the New Federal Common Law*, 39 N.Y.U.L.Rev. 383, 401–02 (1964).[1]

Note that these points go no further than to criticize the rather simplistic extension of Erie in the Klaxon opinion. They do not make an affirmative case for a contrary result, since it may be desirable, even if not constitutionally compelled, to apply the choice-of-law rules of the forum state.

(3) The First Edition's Criticism of Klaxon. In the First Edition of this book (pp. 634–35), the authors marshaled the arguments against Klaxon:

"Consider the application of Erie and of Klaxon to problems of the choice of plainly substantive rules of decision, such as those involved in Erie itself and in Swift v. Tyson.

---

[1]   The American Law Institute has proposed a federal choice of law code for complex cases involving state-created causes of action. See ALI, Complex Litigation: Statutory Recommendations and Analysis §§ 6.01–6.07 (1994).

" * * * [T]hese rules do much more than provide the underlying premises of a decision on the merits when litigation occurs. They help to organize and guide people's everyday lives. * * * [C]onfusion and uncertainty about the rules of law which are relevant at this stage of primary private activity is far more serious than uncertainty about rules which become material only if litigation eventuates. This is so, if for no other reason, because the number of instances of the application of law at the primary stage bears to the number of instances of its application in litigation the ratio of thousands or hundreds of thousands to one.

"As applied in non-conflicts situations, Erie might have been regarded, might it not, as based at least in significant part on the proposition that it is intolerable to have two different systems of courts deciding questions of 'plainly substantive' law differently, where it is unpredictable which system will acquire jurisdiction, since that not only introduces an element of retroactivity into every judicial disposition of such disputes as develop but confuses basic legal relations throughout the area of primary activity affected by the overlap? Notice that it was in the context of questions of this kind that Justice Brandeis spoke of the 'unconstitutionality' of the course which the federal courts had pursued.

"If this view of Erie had been taken, the problem of marking out the scope of its application in non-conflicts situations would have reduced itself, would it not, to one of distinguishing between (a) those rules of law which characteristically and reasonably affect people's conduct at the stage of primary private activity and should therefore be classified as substantive or quasi-substantive, and (b) those rules which are not of significant importance at the primary stage and should therefore be regarded as quasi-procedural or procedural?

"Consider the bearing which such an analysis of Erie would have had in situations involving state-versus-state conflicts of plainly substantive law.

"Notice that Swift v. Tyson had solved the problem of uncertainty about the applicable substantive law for people who could anticipate access to a federal court. Erie destroyed this assurance, but mitigated the damage with an alternative assurance of the uniform enforcement in any federal court of whatever state law was applicable. Klaxon destroyed the mitigation, did it not?

"Erie must largely have proceeded upon the assumption, must it not, that the prime need was for an assurance of state-federal conformity in the interest of people who could not be sure of a federal forum? Klaxon cut down the value of this new assurance, did it not, largely to those situations in which it is possible to foresee the state in which litigation will take place? In what proportion of situations *is* this possible, when the people involved are of diverse citizenship?

"Would it be accurate to conclude that Klaxon, in effect, treats Erie as if it had been unconcerned with the problem of uncertainty about the applicable substantive law at the stage of primary private activity? Why should forum-shopping between different courts in the same state have been regarded as the *summum malum* of diversity litigation while forum-shopping among courts in different geographical areas was dismissed as an inescapable weakness of a federal system? Did the Rules of Decision Act have to be read as authorizing the plaintiff, and the courts of the state he selects, to decide which state's laws are the laws which 'apply', rather than the federal court?"

The authors' assumption—thinly concealed behind veils of rhetorical questions—was that horizontal uniformity among federal courts on choice of law issues, which Klaxon impedes, is at least as important as vertical uniformity between state and federal courts in a given state, which Klaxon promotes. Is it more likely that forum shopping for a favorable choice-of-law rule would occur within a given state or among states? To what extent is horizontal disuniformity among state courts, and under Klaxon, among federal courts sitting in different states, not only inevitable but the very "*essence* of a federal system"? Young, p. 590, *supra*, at 45.

But note the scope of a plaintiff's opportunity to benefit from horizontal disuniformity. The increase in multistate transactions and actors, together with the growth of long-arm statutes, permits many plaintiffs to choose among a number of states in deciding where to file; accordingly, plaintiffs enjoy a broad opportunity to select a state whose choice of law rules are favorable. To be sure, had Klaxon been decided differently, removal to federal court would have permitted defendants to negate that advantage. But removal is often unavailable—because the plaintiff has chosen to sue one defendant who is non-diverse, the requisite amount in controversy is lacking, or for other reasons—and in such cases the plaintiff can maintain its forum-selection advantage.

(4) Further Arguments Bearing on the Klaxon Rule. Consider the argument that the federal courts in diversity cases are in a special and strategic position, as a disinterested forum, to work out solutions to problems of interstate conflict of laws that are consistent with the presuppositions of a federal judicial system. See Hart, *The Relations Between State and Federal Law*, 54 Colum.L.Rev. 489, 513–15 (1954). This argument rests on the premise that a state's choice-of-law rules are likely to discriminate (unfairly, even if not unconstitutionally) against out-of-staters and that this is precisely the kind of prejudice that the diversity jurisdiction was designed to prevent. To paraphrase one commentator, allowing the state in which the action happens to be brought to resolve a conflict with another state is like allowing the pitcher to call balls and strikes whenever he manages to beat the batter to the call.[2]

Such an argument suggests that all choice-of-law questions in actions between diverse citizens should be federal questions, whether they arise in state or federal court. But even if the argument need not carry that far, it raises some problems about the supremacy of state policy in matters of essentially state concern. Consider a case in which a product made in State X is sold in State Y, where a consumer is injured in the course of using it.[3] State X holds manufacturers liable only on a showing of negligence, or privity of warranty, while State Y holds them strictly liable for personal injuries caused by a defective product. If litigation occurs in State Y, should Y's rule of liability apply? What is the relevance of state court decisions in Y holding that the rule should have "extra-territorial" application in such a case? Can a federal court in State Y disregard the state's choice of its own law without seriously undermining a substantive state policy? See Hill, Paragraph (2), *supra*, at 546–68. Bear in mind that an out-of-state defendant would

---

[2]   See Baxter, *Choice of Law and the Federal System*, 16 Stan.L.Rev. 1, 23 (1963).

[3]   See *id.* at 7–11.

undoubtedly remove a state court action if there were any advantage in doing so. Suppose the legislature of Y had enacted a statute explicitly imposing strict liability on all manufacturers, wherever located, whose products cause personal injury within the state. If a federal court in Y were to choose X's law in such a case, would that not, in effect, be a holding that, as a matter of federal law, Y could not furnish this substantive protection to those injured within its borders?[4]

Is it an answer to these arguments that if the Y federal court disregards X's law limiting the manufacturer's liability in such a case, it is also frustrating a significant state policy? Note that the suit in this hypothetical case is almost certain to take place in Y if the state has a long-arm statute permitting out-of-state service of process, and that the decisions upholding the constitutionality of the reach of state process in such a case are themselves a recognition of the substantiality of Y's interest. Do they also suggest the appropriateness, or at least the permissibility, of applying Y's laws?[5]

(5) Existing Constitutional Limits on Horizontal Choice of Law. The Due Process and Full Faith and Credit Clauses place some limitations, but not strict ones, on the choice of law by state courts. Compare, *e.g.*, Phillips Petroleum Co. v. Shutts, 472 U.S. 797, 821–22 (1985) (since state lacks "significant contact or significant aggregation of contacts" with respect to claims of many members of plaintiff class, application of that state's law to those claims is "sufficiently arbitrary and unfair as to exceed constitutional limits"), with, *e.g.*, Allstate Ins. Co. v. Hague, 449 U.S. 302 (1981), and cases cited therein; Sun Oil Co. v. Wortman, 486 U.S. 717 (1988) (holding that the forum state could constitutionally apply its own, relatively long statute of limitations to claims as to which, under Shutts, it could not apply its own substantive law). Federal courts are controlled by the same limitations in administering the Klaxon doctrine—at least to the extent those limitations derive from the Due Process Clauses.

(6) Klaxon and Transfer of Venue. Consider actions that are transferred to another federal court under 28 U.S.C. § 1404 (providing for transfer from a federal court in which the action was properly brought), § 1406 (providing discretion to transfer (in lieu of dismissal) from a federal court in which venue was improper), or § 1407 (providing for transfer of multidistrict

---

[4] Professor Roosevelt, in *Choice of Law in the Federal Courts: From Erie and Klaxon to CAFA and Shady Grove*, 106 Nw.U.L.Rev. 1 (2012), lends some support to the argument in text. He contends that Erie itself "is best understood as a choice-of-law case." Thus, in resolving an Erie problem, as in choice of law cases generally, a court should first determine "which sovereigns might attach legal consequences to the events and which have in fact done so"—a question of the scope of the relevant sovereigns' laws. Then, if more than one sovereign has such an interest, the court "must decide which of the competing rights will get priority." Applying this analysis to Klaxon, he argues that, as to step one, a federal court "must respect the [forum] state definition of rights and obligations, and choice-of-law rules about the scope of state law are part of that definition." As to step two, federal courts should "usually incorporate the rules of priority of the states in which they sit, but they reserve a 'federal veto'—the power to diverge from a state rule of priority that unreasonably disfavors foreign law."

[5] Klaxon has its defenders, see, *e.g.*, Cavers, *The Changing Choice-of-Law Process and the Federal Courts*, 28 Law & Contemp.Probs. 732 (1963); Ely, p. 604, *infra*, at 714–15 n. 125, but also has continued to have its critics, see, *e.g*, Bridwell & Whitten, The Constitution and the Common Law 135 (1977); Trautman, *The Relation Between American Choice of Law and Federal Common Law*, 41 Law & Contemp.Probs. No. 2, at 105, 120 n. 58 (Spring 1977); Borchers, *The Origins of Diversity Jurisdiction, the Rise of Legal Positivism, and a Brave New World for Erie and Klaxon*, 72 Tex.L.Rev. 79 (1993).

litigation for coordinated or consolidated pretrial proceedings). Under Klaxon, what choice-of-law rules should the transferee court apply?

In Van Dusen v. Barrack, 376 U.S. 612 (1964), the Court held (in a case involving transfer under § 1404) that the choice-of-law rules followed by the courts in the transferor state would apply. The defendants in that case were seeking the transfer, and the law of the transferee state would have been more favorable to them. "The legislative history of § 1404(a)", the Court said, "certainly does not justify the rather startling conclusion that one might 'get a change of law as a bonus for a change of venue' ". See also Ferens v. John Deere Co., 494 U.S. 516 (1990) (holding that the transferor state's law governs in *all* cases transferred under § 1404, whether the transfer is initiated by the plaintiff, the defendant, or the court).[6]

Does the very existence of the issue raised in Van Dusen cast doubt on the soundness of the Klaxon result? Given Klaxon, was the Van Dusen holding the best of the available alternatives?

(7) The Applicability of Klaxon in Special Circumstances.

(a) In most diversity actions, the reach of federal process does not exceed that of the forum state.[7] Thus, application of the forum state's choice-of-law rules does not alter the resolution of conflicting interests among states that would be reached if there were no federal diversity jurisdiction. But sometimes a federal court in a diversity case exercises jurisdiction over a defendant who is beyond the reach of process issuing from the forum state's own courts. (Examples of such cases include interpleader actions under 28 U.S.C. § 2361, and actions in which additional parties across state lines but within 100 miles of the federal courthouse are brought in under Fed.R.Civ.Proc. 4(k)(1)(B)).

In Griffin v. McCoach, 313 U.S. 498 (1941), decided the same day as Klaxon, the Court held that the forum state's choice of law rules must be applied in a statutory interpleader case. The Court did not mention the fact that at least one of the claimants to the fund was almost certainly beyond the reach of the forum state's process.

(b) Another context in which the Klaxon rule has been questioned is that of class actions, especially those arising under the Class Action Fairness Act of 2005 (CAFA), which dramatically increased the availability of federal jurisdiction in diversity class actions. For discussion of the Act, see pp. 1426–1429, *infra*.

(c) For contrasting views on the need for, and extent of, federal preemption of state choice of law rules when the choice of law question is international in scope, see Childress, *When Erie Goes International*, 105 Nw.U.L.Rev. 1531 (2011) (contending that, contrary to Day & Zimmerman, Inc. v. Challoner, 423 U.S. 3 (1975), federal courts should develop "specialized federal common law in international conflict-of-laws cases"), with Green, *Erie's International Effect*, 107 Nw.U.L.Rev. 1485 (2013) (arguing that the need for federal preemption in international choice of law

---

[6]   But *cf.* Atlantic Marine Constr. Co. v. United States Dist. Court, 134 S.Ct. 568 (2013) (holding that whenever a transfer of venue is made on the basis of a forum selection clause, the transferee court should apply the choice-of-law-rules of the state in which it sits; a party that files in a forum other than the one specified in a forum selection clause should not be able to gain possible advantage from application of the transferor court's choice of law rules).

[7]   See Fed.R.Civ.Proc. 4(k)(1)(A).

cases should be based solely on the existence of a federal interest and that the existence of such an interest is likely to be rare).

———

NOTE ON THE WAYS OF ASCERTAINING STATE LAW

(1) Unresolved Questions of State Law. If a federal court confronts a question of state law not plainly resolved by the state's highest court, a range of issues can arise, including what weight should be given to state lower court decisions or to dicta in state decisions, even from the highest state court. There are also questions about whether the federal court should assume the same sense of responsibility for the creative development of law that a state court would have, and whether a federal court may disregard an applicable decision of the highest state court on the basis that the state court would not follow it today.

(2) Lower State Court Decisions. Two years after Erie, the Supreme Court held, in Fidelity Union Trust Co. v. Field, 311 U.S. 169 (1940), that a federal court in New Jersey was bound to follow a decision of the New Jersey Court of Chancery, a trial court of state-wide jurisdiction, "in the absence of more convincing evidence of what the state law is". But eight years after the Fidelity Union decision, in King v. Order of United Commercial Travelers, 333 U.S. 153 (1948), the Court unanimously upheld the refusal of a federal court of appeals to follow an unreported decision of a South Carolina court of common pleas (a trial court of limited territorial jurisdiction).

Eight years later, in Bernhardt v. Polygraphic Co., 350 U.S. 198 (1956), one issue was whether a 1910 Vermont Supreme Court decision represented the state law on the question in 1956. The United States Supreme Court held that it did, stating: "Were the question in doubt * * *, we would of course remand the case to the Court of Appeals to pass on this question of Vermont law. But * * * there appears to be no confusion in the Vermont decisions, no developing line of authorities that casts a shadow over the established ones, no dicta, doubts or ambiguities in the opinions of Vermont judges on the question, no legislative development that promises to undermine the judicial rule."

Wright and Kane, summarizing the state of the law since King and Bernhardt, say that a federal judge "need no longer be a ventriloquist's dummy. Instead he or she is free, just as state judges are, to consider all the data the highest court of the state would use in an effort to determine how the highest court of the state would decide." Wright & Kane, Federal Courts § 58, at 394 (7th ed.2011).

But a welter of issues lies behind this general statement. Should a federal court (as some do) follow federal circuit precedent on the meaning of state law, even when one or more intervening state appellate court decisions have taken a different view? Should a federal trial court seek to predict how the state's highest court would rule in a state whose trial courts would not do so but instead would follow precedent of a state intermediate court? Insofar as different states articulate different approaches for their courts at various levels to take in addressing unsettled questions, should a federal court in a diversity case seek to mirror the practice and allocation of responsibility of the particular state in which it sits? See Erbsen, *Erie's Four*

Functions: Reframing Choice of Law in Federal Courts, 89 Notre Dame L.Rev. 579, 646–59 (2013).[1]

(3) Abstention and Other Refusals to Decide State Law Questions. In some cases, a federal court will abstain from determining a state law question because of the question's uncertainty and difficulty. Relatedly, nearly every state authorizes its highest court to answer questions that federal appellate courts, and often federal district courts, refer to it. For discussion of the use of abstention and certification by federal courts, see Chap. X, Sec. 2, *infra*.

(4) Appellate Review of District Court Decisions. In Salve Regina College v. Russell, 499 U.S. 225 (1991), the Court held that a federal court of appeals should provide de novo review of the district court's determination of state law. The opinion relied not only on the traditional scope of review on questions of law and the "reflective dialogue and collective judgment" that attend appellate consideration, but also on the purposes of the Erie doctrine—to discourage forum shopping and to avoid inequitable administration of the laws. "[D]eferential appellate review," the Court said, "invites divergent development of state law among the federal trial courts even within a single State".

Is the rule of Salve Regina required by Erie? If not, is it preferable to a rule that in the absence of a conflict among district court decisions in a district, the circuit court will ordinarily defer to the district court's understanding of the content of local law—an interpretation usually rendered by a judge who hails from the state in question? See Nash, *Resuscitating Deference to Lower Federal Court Judges' Interpretations of State Law*, 77 S.Cal.L.Rev. 975 (2004).

---

3. ENFORCING STATE-CREATED OBLIGATIONS— EQUITABLE REMEDIES AND PROCEDURE

Guaranty Trust Co. v. York

326 U.S. 99, 65 S.Ct. 1464, 89 L.Ed. 2079 (1945).
Certiorari to the Circuit Court of Appeals for the Second Circuit.

■ MR. JUSTICE FRANKFURTER delivered the opinion of the Court.

[Petitioner Guaranty Trust Co. was trustee for the holders of notes issued by a corporation. When it became apparent that the corporation could not meet its obligations on the notes, Guaranty negotiated an offer of exchange for less than the face value of the notes. After the offer had

---

[1] There are also important questions, which are related to the questions raised in text, concerning whether federal courts, in applying state statutory law, should follow the rules of statutory interpretation adopted by the courts of the relevant state. Gluck, *Intersystemic Statutory Interpretation: Methodology as "Law" and the Erie Doctrine*, 120 Yale L.J. 1898 (2011), criticizes the failure of most federal courts to recognize that the interpretive rules adopted by a state are integral to its substantive law. For her further exploration of the question of interpretive methodology, see Gluck, *The Federal Common Law of Statutory Interpretation: Erie for the Age of Statutes*, 54 Wm. & Mary L.Rev. 753 (2013).

expired, respondent York, a noteholder, brought a diversity action against Guaranty in a New York federal court.]

The suit, instituted as a class action on behalf of non-accepting noteholders * * *, is based on an alleged breach of trust by Guaranty in that it failed to protect the interests of the noteholders in assenting to the exchange offer and failed to disclose its self-interest when sponsoring the offer. Petitioner moved for summary judgment, which was granted * * *. On appeal, the Circuit Court of Appeals, one Judge dissenting, * * * held that in a suit brought on the equity side of a federal district court that court is not required to apply the State statute of limitations that would govern like suits in the courts of a State where the federal court is sitting even though the exclusive basis of federal jurisdiction is diversity of citizenship. The importance of the question for the disposition of litigation in the federal courts led us to bring the case here.

* * *

In exercising their jurisdiction on the ground of diversity of citizenship, the federal courts, in the long course of their history, have not differentiated in their regard for State law between actions at law and suits in equity. Although § 34 of the Judiciary Act of 1789 directed that the "laws of the several States * * * shall be regarded as rules of decision in trials of common law * * *", this was deemed, consistently for over a hundred years, to be merely declaratory of what would in any event have governed the federal courts and therefore was equally applicable to equity suits. Indeed, it may fairly be said that the federal courts gave greater respect to State-created "substantive rights", Pusey & Jones Co. v. Hanssen, 261 U.S. 491, 498, in equity than they gave them on the law side, because rights at law were usually declared by State courts and as such increasingly flouted by extension of the doctrine of Swift v. Tyson, while rights in equity were frequently defined by legislative enactment and as such known and respected by the federal courts.

Partly because the States in the early days varied greatly in the manner in which equitable relief was afforded and in the extent to which it was available, * * * Congress provided that "the forms and modes of proceeding in suits * * * of equity" would conform to the settled uses of courts of equity. Section 2, 1 Stat. 275, 276. But this enactment gave the federal courts no power that they would not have had in any event when courts were given "cognizance", by the first Judiciary Act, of suits "in equity". From the beginning there has been a good deal of talk in the cases that federal equity is a separate legal system. And so it is, properly understood. The suits in equity of which the federal courts have had "cognizance" ever since 1789 constituted the body of law which had been transplanted to this country from the English Court of Chancery. But this system of equity "derived its doctrines, as well as its powers, from its mode of giving relief". Langdell, Summary of Equity Pleading (1877) xxvii. * * * Congress never gave, nor did the federal courts ever claim, the power to deny substantive rights created by State law or to create substantive rights denied by State law.

This does not mean that whatever equitable remedy is available in a State court must be available in a diversity suit in a federal court, or conversely, that a federal court may not afford an equitable remedy not available in a State court. Equitable relief in a federal court is of course subject to restrictions: the suit must be within the traditional scope of equity as historically evolved in the English Court of Chancery, Payne v. Hook, 7 Wall. 425, 430; a plain, adequate and complete remedy at law must be wanting, § 16, 1 Stat. 73, 82, 28 U.S.C. § 384; explicit Congressional curtailment of equity powers must be respected; the constitutional right to trial by jury cannot be evaded, Whitehead v. Shattuck, 138 U.S. 146. That a State may authorize its courts to give equitable relief unhampered by any or all such restrictions cannot remove these fetters from the federal courts. State law cannot define the remedies which a federal court must give simply because a federal court in diversity jurisdiction is available as an alternative tribunal to the State's courts.[3] Contrariwise, a federal court may afford an equitable remedy for a substantive right recognized by a State even though a State court cannot give it. Whatever contradiction or confusion may be produced by a medley of judicial phrases severed from their environment, the body of adjudications concerning equitable relief in diversity cases leaves no doubt that the federal courts enforced State-created substantive rights if the mode of proceeding and remedy were consonant with the traditional body of equitable remedies, practice and procedure, and in so doing they were enforcing rights created by the States and not arising under any inherent or statutory federal law.

Inevitably, therefore, the principle of Erie R. Co. v. Tompkins, an action at law, was promptly applied to a suit in equity. Ruhlin v. New York Life Ins. Co., 304 U.S. 202.

And so this case reduces itself to the narrow question whether, when no recovery could be had in a State court because the action is barred by the statute of limitations, a federal court in equity can take cognizance of the suit because there is diversity of citizenship between the parties. Is the outlawry, according to State law, of a claim created by the States a matter of "substantive rights" to be respected by a federal court of equity when that court's jurisdiction is dependent on the fact that there is a State-created right, or is such statute of "a mere remedial character", Henrietta Mills v. Rutherford Co., supra, 281 U.S. at page 128, which a federal court may disregard?

Matters of "substance" and matters of "procedure" are much talked about in the books as though they defined a great divide cutting across the whole domain of law. But, of course, "substance" and "procedure" are the same key-words to very different problems. Neither "substance" nor "procedure" represents the same invariants. Each implies different variables depending upon the particular problem for which it is used. And the different problems are only distantly related at best, for the terms are in common use in connection with situations turning on such different considerations as those that are relevant to questions pertaining to ex post facto legislation, the impairment of the obligations

---

[3] In Pusey & Jones Co. v. Hanssen, 261 U.S. 491 (1923), the Court had to decide whether a Delaware statute had created a new right appropriate for enforcement in accordance with traditional equity practice or whether the statute had merely given the Delaware Chancery Court a new kind of remedy. * * * [T]he Court construed the Delaware statute merely to extend the power to an equity court to appoint a receiver on the application of an ordinary contract creditor. By conferring new discretionary authority upon its equity court, Delaware could not modify the traditional equity rule in the federal courts that only someone with a defined interest in the estate of an insolvent person, e.g., a judgment creditor, can protect that interest through receivership. * * *

of contract, the enforcement of federal rights in the State courts and the multitudinous phases of the conflict of laws. * * *

Here we are dealing with a right to recover derived not from the United States but from one of the States. When * * * such a right is enforceable in a federal as well as in a State court, the forms and mode of enforcing the right may at times, naturally enough, vary because the two judicial systems are not identic. But since a federal court adjudicating a state-created right solely because of the diversity of citizenship of the parties is for that purpose, in effect, only another court of the State, it cannot afford recovery if the right to recover is made unavailable by the State nor can it substantially affect the enforcement of the right as given by the State.

And so the question is not whether a statute of limitations is deemed a matter of "procedure" in some sense. The question is whether such a statute concerns merely the manner and the means by which a right to recover, as recognized by the State, is enforced, or whether such statutory limitation is a matter of substance in the aspect that alone is relevant to our problem, namely does it significantly affect the result of a litigation for a federal court to disregard a law of a State that would be controlling in an action upon the same claim by the same parties in a State court?

It is therefore immaterial whether statutes of limitation are characterized either as "substantive" or "procedural" in State court opinions in any use of those terms unrelated to the specific issue before us. Erie R. Co. v. Tompkins was not an endeavor to formulate scientific legal terminology. It expressed a policy that touches vitally the proper distribution of judicial power between State and federal courts. In essence, the intent of that decision was to insure that, in all cases where a federal court is exercising jurisdiction solely because of the diversity of citizenship of the parties, the outcome of the litigation in the federal court should be substantially the same, so far as legal rules determine the outcome of a litigation, as it would be if tried in a State court. The nub of the policy that underlies Erie R. Co. v. Tompkins is that for the same transaction the accident of a suit by a non-resident litigant in a federal court instead of in a State court a block away, should not lead to a substantially different result. And so, putting to one side abstractions regarding "substance" and "procedure", we have held that in diversity cases the federal courts must follow the law of the State as to burden of proof, Cities Service Oil Co. v. Dunlap, 308 U.S. 208, as to conflict of laws, Klaxon Co. v. Stentor Co., 313 U.S. 487, as to contributory negligence, Palmer v. Hoffman, 318 U.S. 109, 117. Erie R. Co. v. Tompkins has been applied with an eye alert to essentials in avoiding disregard of State law in diversity cases in the federal courts. A policy so important to our federalism must be kept free from entanglements with analytical or terminological niceties.

Plainly enough, a statute that would completely bar recovery in a suit if brought in a State court bears on a State-created right vitally and not merely formally or negligibly. As to consequences that so intimately affect recovery or nonrecovery a federal court in a diversity case should follow State law. * * *

To make an exception to Erie R. Co. v. Tompkins on the equity side of a federal court is to reject the considerations of policy which, after long travail, led to that decision. * * *

Diversity jurisdiction is founded on assurance to non-resident litigants of courts free from susceptibility to potential local bias. * * * The source of substantive rights enforced by a federal court under diversity jurisdiction, it cannot be said too often, is the law of the States. Whenever that law is authoritatively declared by a State, whether its voice be the legislature or its highest court, such law ought to govern in litigation founded on that law, whether the forum of application is a State or a federal court and whether the remedies be sought at law or may be had in equity.

Dicta may be cited characterizing equity as an independent body of law. To the extent that we have indicated, it is. But insofar as these general observations go beyond that, they merely reflect notions that have been replaced by a sharper analysis of what federal courts do when they enforce rights that have no federal origin. * * *

Reversed.

■ MR. JUSTICE ROBERTS and MR. JUSTICE DOUGLAS took no part in the consideration or decision of this case.

■ MR. JUSTICE RUTLEDGE.

I dissent.

* * *

If any characteristic of equity jurisprudence has descended unbrokenly from and within "the traditional scope of equity as historically evolved in the English Court of Chancery," it is that statutes of limitations, often in terms applying only to actions at law, have never been deemed to be rigidly applicable as absolute barriers to suits in equity as they are to actions at law. That tradition, it would seem, should be regarded as having been incorporated in the various Acts of Congress which have conferred equity jurisdiction upon the federal courts. So incorporated it has been reaffirmed repeatedly by the decisions of this and other courts. It is now excised from those Acts. If there is to be excision, Congress, not this Court, should make it. * * *

■ MR. JUSTICE MURPHY joins in this opinion.

─────────

NOTE ON STATE LAW AND FEDERAL EQUITY

(1) Equity as a Separate Legal System. Traditional equity was not a system merely of distinctive remedies without distinctive substantive consequences. As Dean Langdell noted in his *Summary of Equity Pleading,* "there are many extensive doctrines in equity, and some whole branches of law, which are unknown to the common-law courts". And he went on to give familiar examples, such as trusts (the subject of suit in Guaranty Trust), the mortgagee's equity of redemption, and the doctrine of equitable election, in which equity was able to recognize and enforce an interest that the law entirely denied. Compare also the many equitable defenses, enforced by a separate bill in equity, by which the chancellor, having as always the last word, destroyed interests recognized at law, so as to reach a wholly different substantive result.

(2) Origins of Federal Equity. The first Congress not only gave the circuit courts diversity jurisdiction in suits "in equity" (Act of Sept. 24, 1789, § 11, 1

Stat. 73, 78), but refrained from making the Rules of Decision Act (§ 34) applicable in such proceedings. Congress provided instead, in § 16 (repealed in 1948), only that "suits in equity shall not be sustained in either of the courts of the United States, in any case where plain, adequate and complete remedy may be had at law." And as Justice Frankfurter notes, in 1787 many states had no separate systems of equity and only rudimentary equitable doctrines. In this context, it seems likely that federal courts sitting in states lacking courts of equity jurisdiction claimed, and were intended to claim, "the power to deny substantive rights created by State law or to create substantive rights denied by State law".

(3) The Case Law Prior to Guaranty Trust. Some of the early cases are inconclusive about whether federal equity was its own system, free to disregard state law. Compare, *e.g.*, Neves v. Scott, 54 U.S. (13 How.) 268, 272 (1851) (dictum), with, *e.g.*, Meade v. Beale, 16 F.Cas. 1283, No. 9,371, at 1291 (C.C.Md.1850) (Taney, C.J., on circuit). But Guffey v. Smith, 237 U.S. 101 (1915), was clear in this regard. There, lessees under an oil and gas lease brought a federal diversity action to enjoin operations under a later lease and to obtain discovery and an accounting. The complainants' lease gave them an option to surrender it at any time, and though this provision did not, under state law, render the lease "void as wanting in mutuality", the state courts would have regarded the lease as "so lacking in mutuality" that the lessee's only remedy would have been one at law for damages.

The Supreme Court held that federal equitable relief was available. State decisions denying equitable relief in such a case, the Court said, did not govern. "By the legislation of Congress and repeated decisions of this court it has long been settled that the remedies afforded and modes of proceeding pursued in the Federal courts, sitting as courts of equity, are not determined by local laws or rules of decision, but by general principles, rules and usages of equity having uniform operation in those courts wherever sitting".[1]

A thorough study of federal equity prior to merger in 1938 concludes that Guffey's approach was not unusual: "federal courts [sitting in equity] generally applied a uniform body of nonstate, judge-made equity principles with respect to procedure, remedial laws, and—in certain instances—the primary rights and liabilities of litigants." Collins, *"A Considerable Surgical Operation": Article III, Equity, and Judge-Made Law in the Federal Courts*, 60 Duke L.J. 249 (2010). Professor Collins concludes that Justice Frankfurter's opinion in Guaranty Trust "[sought] to diminish federal equity's robust past" in order to further Erie's aim of allowing the states more leeway to pursue their (progressive) agendas. Whatever the motivation, Guaranty Trust and subsequent cases have discarded the concept of a uniform federal equity practice that disregards state created rights in diversity actions.

(4) The Bernhardt Case and Federal Equity. The Court moved far away from the Guffey approach in Bernhardt v. Polygraphic Co., 350 U.S. 198 (1956). There, the defendant, after removing a breach of contract action to a Vermont federal court on diversity grounds, moved to stay the proceedings

---

[1]   See also Payne v. Hook, 74 U.S. (7 Wall.) 425, 430 (1868) (in federal diversity actions, "[i]f legal remedies are sometimes modified to suit the changes in the laws of the States, and the practice of their courts, it is not so with equitable. The equity jurisdiction conferred on the Federal courts * * * is subject to neither limitation or restraint by State legislation, and is uniform throughout the different States of the Union.").

pending arbitration, pursuant to an arbitration clause in the contract. The district court denied the motion on the ground that under Vermont law an agreement to arbitrate was revocable at any time prior to an award and was therefore not enforceable. The Second Circuit reversed, but the Supreme Court agreed with the district court, saying: "If the federal court allows arbitration where the state court would disallow it, the outcome of litigation might depend on the courthouse where suit is brought. * * * The nature of the tribunal where suits are tried is an important part of the parcel of rights behind a cause of action."

The Court held, as a matter of statutory interpretation, that the provisions in the Federal Arbitration Act (FAA), 9 U.S.C. §§ 1–14, that authorize judicial enforcement of certain agreements to arbitrate did not apply to the case at hand. The Court noted that "[i]f respondent's contention [that the Act applied] is correct, a constitutional question might be presented. Erie R. Co. v. Tompkins indicated that Congress does not have the constitutional authority to make the law that is applicable to controversies in diversity of citizenship cases."[2]

Professor Ely, while agreeing with Bernhardt's conclusion that state law applies, was highly critical of the Court's suggestion that a contrary interpretation of the FAA would probably be unconstitutional. Ely contended that Erie did not fence off local law as immune from displacement by otherwise valid federal statutes, and that application of the FAA to diversity cases would be unconstitutional "only if it were so plainly nonprocedural as to fall outside Congress' undoubted power to formulate procedure for federal courts, which it quite clearly is not." See Ely, *The Irrepressible Myth of Erie,* 87 Harv.L.Rev. 693, 705–06 (1974).

(5) The Effect of the FAA. The constitutional concern raised in Bernhardt was dispelled, in part, in Prima Paint Corp. v. Flood & Conklin Mfg. Co., 388 U.S. 395 (1967). In this diversity action, Prima sought rescission of an agreement on the basis of fraudulent inducement. Flood & Conklin, relying on the FAA, moved to stay the action pending arbitration of the issue of fraud under an arbitration clause in the contract. The Supreme Court held, 6–3, that a stay was properly granted, even though it might not have been available in a state court action. The FAA applied because the contract here, unlike the one in Bernhardt, "evidenc[ed] a transaction involving commerce" within the meaning of § 2 of the Act. Application of the Act was constitutionally permissible because the question was "not whether Congress may fashion federal substantive rules to govern questions arising in simple diversity cases", but "whether Congress may prescribe how federal courts are to conduct themselves with respect to subject matter [interstate commerce] over which Congress plainly has power to legislate". The answer, the Court concluded, "can only be in the affirmative". But the Court carefully

---

[2] Scholars have disagreed on the appropriateness of recognizing a special role for federal equity in fashioning remedies in cases falling within the scope of the Erie doctrine. See, *e.g.,* Hill, *The Erie Doctrine in Bankruptcy,* 66 Harv.L.Rev. 1013, 1024–35 (1953) (concluding that insofar as the federal courts overrode state substantive law in equity they did so on the basis of assumptions concerning the nature of law and the nature of federal judicial power common both to law and equity; for these reasons the implications of Erie are essentially the same in law and equity); Cross, *The Erie Doctrine in Equity,* 60 La.L.Rev. 173, 175 (1999) (arguing that "the Article III judicial power includes the authority to exercise the type of discretion practiced by courts of equity in the late eighteenth century. As long as that exercise of discretion does not result in the creation of new substantive rights or the abolition of existing rights, it falls within a federal court's inherent constitutional authority.").

avoided any explicit endorsement of the view that the FAA embodied substantive policies that were to be applied to all contracts within its scope, whether sued on in state or federal courts.

The result in Prima Paint, which evidently contemplated different remedies in federal and state courts for breach of the same contract, was unstable and did not endure. In Southland Corp. v. Keating, 465 U.S. 1 (1984), the Court held that a state law rendering certain claims in franchise agreements not arbitrable directly conflicted with § 2 of the Act and therefore could not be applied by a state court to a contract within the scope of that Act. This reversal of the state court's judgment effectively required that court to compel arbitration.[3]

(6) The Significance of State Law Favoring Equitable Relief. Do Erie, Klaxon, and Guaranty Trust require federal courts to mirror state courts when the availability of an equitable remedy in state court is urged not as a reason for denying federal equitable relief but for granting it? In Pusey & Jones Co. v. Hanssen, 261 U.S. 491 (1923) (discussed in footnote 3 of the Guaranty Trust opinion), the court refused to enforce a Delaware statute authorizing the appointment of a receiver upon the application of a simple contract creditor. In a much-cited opinion for the Court, Justice Brandeis said:

"That this suit could not be maintained in the absence of the statute is clear. * * * That a remedial right to proceed in a federal court sitting in equity cannot be enlarged by a state statute is likewise clear. * * * The federal court may therefore be obliged to deny an equitable remedy which the plaintiff might have secured in a state court. * * * [I]t is not true that this statute confers upon the creditor a substantive right. * * * Insolvency is made a condition of the Chancellor's jurisdiction; but it does not give rise to any substantive right in the creditor. It makes possible a new remedy because it confers upon the Chancellor a new power. * * * Whatever its exact nature, the power enables the Chancellor to afford a remedy which therefore would not have been open to an unsecured simple contract creditor. But because that which the statute confers is merely a remedy, the statute cannot affect proceedings in the federal courts sitting in equity."

---

[3] Southland has been reaffirmed, and extended, in several subsequent decisions. See, *e.g.*, Allied-Bruce Terminix Companies, Inc. v. Dobson, 513 U.S. 265 (1995); Preston v. Ferrer, 552 U.S. 346 (2008). Justice Thomas, joined in dissent by Justice Scalia in Dobson, argued vigorously that Southland should be overruled and that the FAA should be held inapplicable in state courts. Justice Thomas has continued to dissent in subsequent cases.

Scholars disagree on the soundness of these decisions. Compare Carrington & Haagen, *Contract and Jurisdiction*, 1996 Sup.Ct.Rev. 331, and Moses, *How the Supreme Court Created a Federal Arbitration Act Law Never Enacted by Congress*, 34 Fla.St.U.L.Rev. 1 (2006) (sharply criticizing the decisions), with Drahozal, *In Defense of Southland: Reexamining the Legislative History of the Federal Arbitration Act*, 78 Notre Dame L.Rev. 101, 169 (2002) (concluding, on the basis of a detailed examination of the legislative history of the Act, that "while the 'primary purpose' of the FAA was to make arbitration agreements enforceable in federal court, a secondary purpose was to make arbitration agreements enforceable in state court").

Some courts skeptical of arbitration have turned to state unconscionability doctrine as a means of restricting the spread of arbitration. See Bruhl, *The Unconscionability Game: Strategic Judging and the Evolution of Federal Arbitration Law*, 83 N.Y.U.L.Rev. 1420 (2008). But such use of state unconscionability doctrine suffered a severe setback in AT&T Mobility LLC v. Concepcion, 131 S.Ct. 1740 (2011). In a 5–4 decision, the Court held, in the context of a contracting party's effort to compel arbitration, that the FAA preempts a state's rule treating contractual class action waivers as unconscionable in certain consumer contracts of adhesion.

Pusey & Jones was cited and relied on, over 70 years later, in Grupo Mexicano de Desarrollo, S.A. v. Alliance Bond Fund, Inc., 527 U.S. 308 (1999). In this case, the Court held, 5–4, that under Fed.R.Civ.Proc. 65 and federal equity principles, a federal district court lacked authority to issue a preliminary injunction preventing a defendant from disposing of its assets pending adjudication of a breach of contract claim against it. The Court reasoned that (a) such a remedy was unavailable in a court of equity at the time the Judiciary Act of 1789 was enacted, and (b) neither the merger of law and equity in 1938 nor any specific authority granted in the federal rules affected this historical limitation on the equity powers of a federal court.

Grupo Mexicano was a diversity case, but the Court declined petitioner's request to consider the effect of the Erie doctrine because the issue had not been raised below. If the relevant state law did allow the preliminary relief sought, and the Erie question had been properly raised, how should it have been decided? In considering this question, do you think it relevant that the majority in Grupo Mexicano, in concluding that the result was unaffected by the adoption of the federal rules in 1938, reasoned that the limitation on federal equitable power "was a product, not just of the procedural requirement [of exhaustion of legal remedies] * * * but also of the *substantive* rule that a general creditor (one without a judgment) had no cognizable interest, either at law or in equity, in the property of his debtor" (emphasis added)?[4]

(7) Door-Closing Provisions. May an objection be raised under Erie if the federal courts, without passing on the merits, simply close their doors to a complainant seeking equitable relief? Does it matter whether the federal door-closing policy is based on decisional law, a Federal Rule of Civil Procedure, or an act of Congress (like the anti-injunction provisions of the Norris-LaGuardia Act)? Or whether the policy is stated in terms of a limitation on subject-matter jurisdiction, as in the case of the jurisdictional amount requirement?[5]

A door-closing rule creates special problems if the defendant is able to remove a state court action and then have the case dismissed. Compare Cates v. Allen, 149 U.S. 451 (1893) (holding in such a case that the proper disposition was not to dismiss but rather to remand, since the case had been improperly removed), with Venner v. Great Northern Ry., 209 U.S. 24 (1908) (upholding the existence of federal jurisdiction but affirming dismissal of the bill for "want of equity"). *Cf.* Sec. 4, *infra*.

---

[4]　For an insightful analysis of the issues in Grupo Mexicano, see Burbank, *The Bitter with the Sweet: Tradition, History, and Limitations on Federal Judicial Power—A Case Study*, 75 Notre Dame L.Rev. 1291 (2000).

For a later 5–4 decision in which the majority again relied on what Justice Ginsburg, in dissent, criticized as a static conception of equity jurisdiction, see Great-West Life Ins. Co. v. Knudson, 534 U.S. 204 (2002) (interpreting a provision of ERISA as not authorizing the relief sought because it did not constitute a classic form of "equitable relief"). For a critique of Great-West, see Meltzer, *The Supreme Court's Judicial Passivity*, 2002 Sup.Ct.Rev. 343, 346–51. And for eloquent support of the dissents in both the Grupo Mexicano and Great-West cases, see Resnik, *Constricting Remedies: The Rehnquist Judiciary, Congress, and Federal Power*, 78 Ind.L.J. 223 (2003).

[5]　For discussion of the role of state law in determining the authority of a district court to entertain a diversity case, see pp. 629–634, *infra*.

NOTE ON THE "OUTCOME" TEST AND ITS EVOLUTION TO HANNA V. PLUMER

(1) The "Outcome-Determinative" Test. Recall Justice Frankfurter's statement in Guaranty Trust that in diversity cases, "the outcome of the litigation in the federal court should be substantially the same, so far as legal rules determine the outcome of a litigation, as it would be if tried in a State court."

(a) Consider these interpretations of the concept of the same outcome:

(i) Federal courts should not take a view of the parties' primary legal relations that differs from the view that the state court would take.

(ii) Federal courts should not give any form of relief that differs from the relief the state court would give.

(iii) Federal courts should (A) not act at all if the state court would refuse to act, even though the state court's refusal would be without prejudice, and (B) not refuse to act, even by dismissing without prejudice, if the state court would be willing to act.

(b) In considering what the Guaranty Trust opinion meant by *"legal rules"* that "determine" the outcome of a lawsuit, note that any legal rule might determine the outcome if a litigant is sanctioned for violating it. But on that view, nearly any state rule could be outcome determinative in a particular case. Should *"legal rules"* be understood to exclude at least those rules whose application depends upon what the parties or counsel do after litigation begins and that might have been done differently under different rules of procedure?

(2) The 1949 Trilogy. Questions like those raised in Paragraph (1) have perplexed the federal courts at all levels ever since the Guaranty Trust decision. During the first 13 years after the decision, the Court disposed of a number of important cases without suggesting a stopping place for the outcome test. Of particular interest are three cases decided on the same day: Ragan v. Merchants Transfer & Warehouse Co., 337 U.S. 530 (1949); Woods v. Interstate Realty Co., 337 U.S. 535 (1949); and Cohen v. Beneficial Indus. Loan Corp., 337 U.S. 541 (1949). Only four members of the Court joined in all three decisions (and only Justice Rutledge dissented in all three).

The Cohen and Woods decisions are summarized in the footnote.[1] In Ragan, a diversity action for injuries suffered in a highway accident had been

---

[1]   In Cohen, a stockholder filed a derivative action in a New Jersey federal court; jurisdiction rested on diversity of citizenship. The question arose whether the federal court should apply a New Jersey statute whose general effect was "to make a plaintiff having so small an interest liable for the reasonable expenses and attorney's fees of the defense if he fails to make good his complaint and to entitle the corporation to indemnity before the case can be prosecuted". The Court held, 6–3, that the statute should be applied. Rejecting the contention that the statute conflicted with Fed.R.Civ.Proc. 23 (now 23.1), the Court said: "We do not think a statute which so conditions the stockholder's action can be disregarded by the federal court as a mere procedural device." The dissent argued that the statute "merely prescribes the method by which stockholders may enforce [a cause of action]".

In Woods, a Tennessee corporation had brought a diversity action in a Mississippi federal court against a Mississippi resident, seeking to recover a broker's commission allegedly due for the sale of real estate in Mississippi. The defense contended that since the plaintiff had not qualified to do business in the state, the action had to be dismissed under a state statute providing that any foreign corporation failing to qualify "shall not be permitted to bring or maintain any action or suit in any of the courts of this state." The Court held, 6–3, that the defense should be sustained, stating: "The York case was premised on the theory that a right

brought in a Kansas federal court. Kansas had a two-year statute of limitations; the action was filed within two years of the accident, but the summons and complaint were not served until after the two-year period had run. The Court held, 8–1, that summary judgment for the defendant should have been granted, on the basis of a state statute providing: "An action shall be deemed commenced * * *, as to each defendant, at the date of the summons which is served on him * * *." In a brief opinion that referred to but did not discuss the apparent conflict between the state statute and Fed.R.Civ.Proc. 3 (which provided that "[a] civil action is commenced by filing a complaint with the court"), the Court noted the holding of the court below that the Kansas statute was "an integral part" of its statute of limitations and said: "We can draw no distinction [from Guaranty Trust] in this case because local law brought the cause of action to an end after, rather than before, suit was started in the federal court. * * * We cannot give it longer life in the federal court than it would have had in the state court without adding something to the cause of action. We may not do that consistently with Erie R. Co. v. Tompkins."

(3) The Byrd v. Blue Ridge Decision: A New Approach.

(a) The first sign of a change of direction appeared in Byrd v. Blue Ridge Rural Elec. Coop., Inc., 356 U.S. 525 (1958). In a diversity action brought in a South Carolina federal court for injuries resulting from alleged negligence, the defendant asserted that it was the plaintiff's employer and that the plaintiff's exclusive remedy therefore lay before South Carolina's Industrial Commission under the state's Workers' Compensation Law. Although the state supreme court had ruled that such a defense was to be passed on by the judge, alone, the United States Supreme Court held that issues of fact relevant to the defense should be tried to the jury in the federal action. After noting that the state supreme court had given no reasons for its decision, the Court continued:

"We find nothing to suggest that this rule was announced as an integral part of the special relationship created by the statute. Thus the requirement appears to be merely a form and mode of enforcing the immunity, Guaranty Trust Co. v. York, 326 U.S. 99, 108 [1945], and not a rule intended to be bound up with the definitions of the rights and obligations of the parties. * * *

" * * * [C]ases following Erie have evinced a broader policy to the effect that the federal courts should conform as near as may be—in the absence of other considerations—to state rules even of form and mode where the state rules may bear substantially on the question whether the litigation would come out one way in the federal court and another way in the state court if the federal court failed to apply a particular local rule. [Citing Guaranty Trust and Bernhardt.] * * * It may well be that in the instant personal-injury case the outcome would be substantially affected by whether the issue [in question] * * * is decided by a judge or a jury. Therefore, were 'outcome' the only consideration, a strong case might appear for saying that the federal court should follow the state practice.

"But there are affirmative countervailing considerations at work here. The federal system is an independent system for administering justice to

---

which local law creates but which it does not supply with a remedy is no right at all for purposes of enforcement in a federal court in a diversity case; that where in such cases one is barred from recovery in the state court, he should likewise be barred in the federal court."

litigants who properly invoke its jurisdiction. An essential characteristic of that system is the manner in which, in civil common-law actions, it distributes trial functions between judge and jury and, under the influence— if not the command—of the Seventh Amendment, assigns the decisions of disputed questions of fact to the jury. The policy of uniform enforcement of state-created rights and obligations, see, *e.g.*, Guaranty Trust Co. v. York, *supra*, cannot in every case exact compliance with a state rule—not bound up with rights and obligations—which disrupts the federal system of allocating functions between judge and jury. Thus the inquiry here is whether the federal policy favoring jury decisions of disputed fact questions should yield to the state rule in the interest of furthering the objective that the litigation should not come out one way in the federal court and another way in the state court.

"We think that in the circumstances of this case the federal court should not follow the state rule."

(b) Note that in Byrd, perhaps for the first time since Erie, the Court sought to determine whether the policy behind a state rule would be frustrated if the federal court were not to follow it. At the same time, the Court said that even a state rule relating only to "form and mode"—if it might bear substantially on the outcome—should not be disregarded absent "affirmative countervailing considerations". Is that because there is no reason to adopt or follow a federal rule that encourages forum shopping but serves no other purpose?

The Court's analysis of the state's reason for assigning the issue in question to a judge rather than a jury was not particularly sympathetic. The South Carolina rule might be supported by arguments (a) that only a judge would be able to view the company's defense as an aspect of a comprehensive statutory scheme of liability without fault for industrial accidents, and (b) that a jury could not articulate the basis for its findings in a way that would help to assure predictability and consistency of decisions for litigants faced with many lawsuits raising the same issue. Wouldn't such bases for the state rule be undermined if the federal courts disregarded the rule?

As to the Court's reference to "affirmative countervailing considerations", it would have been simpler, and correct, to rest the result squarely on the Seventh Amendment. Instead the Court said that even if the Seventh Amendment does not apply to the trial of a particular issue, there is nevertheless a federal policy favoring trial by jury on that issue. What is the source of the policy?

(4) From Byrd to Hanna. Byrd plainly approached the Erie question much differently than had Guaranty Trust.[2] Seven years after Byrd, the Court again engaged with the Erie question. In doing so, it helped to resolve some of the tension between Byrd and Guaranty Trust, while also giving new importance to the question whether federal practice was required by a Federal Rule of Civil Procedure.

---

[2]   For discussions of the Erie doctrine during the period covered by this Note, see, *e.g.*, Smith, *Blue Ridge and Beyond: A Byrd's-Eye View of Federalism in Diversity Litigation*, 36 Tul.L.Rev. 443 (1962); Vestal, *Erie R.R. v. Tompkins: A Projection*, 48 Iowa L.Rev. 248 (1963).

Hanna v. Plumer

380 U.S. 460, 85 S.Ct. 1136, 14 L.Ed.2d 8 (1965).
Certiorari to the United States Court of Appeals for the First Circuit.

■ MR. CHIEF JUSTICE WARREN delivered the opinion of the Court.

The question to be decided is whether, in a civil action where * * * jurisdiction * * * is based upon diversity of citizenship between the parties, service of process shall be made in the manner prescribed by state law or that set forth in Rule 4(d)(1) of the Federal Rules of Civil Procedure.

[On February 6, 1963, an Ohio citizen filed a diversity action in federal court in Massachusetts, seeking damages for personal injuries resulting from an automobile accident in South Carolina, allegedly caused by the negligence of a Massachusetts citizen who was deceased when the complaint was filed. The decedent's executor, also a Massachusetts citizen, was named as defendant. On February 8, service was made by leaving copies of the summons and the complaint with the defendant's wife at his residence, concededly in compliance with Rule 4(d)(1) (now embodied in substantial part in Rule 4(e)(2)), which then provided:]

"The summons and complaint shall be served together. The plaintiff shall furnish the person making service with such copies as are necessary. Service shall be made as follows:

"(1) Upon an individual other than an infant or an incompetent person, by delivering a copy of the summons and of the complaint to him personally or by leaving copies thereof at his dwelling house or usual place of abode with some person of suitable age and discretion then residing therein * * *."

[The defendant] filed his answer on February 26, alleging, *inter alia*, that the action could not be maintained because it had been brought "contrary to and in violation of the provisions of Massachusetts General Laws (Ter.Ed.) Chapter 197, Section 9." That section provides:

"Except as provided in this chapter, an executor or administrator shall not be held to answer to an action by a creditor of the deceased which is not commenced within one year from the time of his giving bond for the performance of his trust, or to such an action which is commenced within said year unless before the expiration thereof the writ in such action has been served by delivery in hand upon such executor or administrator or service thereof accepted by him or a notice stating the name of the estate, the name and address of the creditor, the amount of the claim and the court in which the action has been brought has been filed in the proper registry of probate. * * *." Mass.Gen.Laws Ann., c. 197, § 9 (1958).

On October 17, 1963, the District Court granted [the defendant's] motion for summary judgment, citing Ragan v. Merchants Transfer & Warehouse Co., 337 U.S. 530, and Guaranty Trust Co. of New York v. York, 326 U.S. 99, in support of its conclusion that the adequacy of the service was to be measured by § 9, with which, the court held, [the plaintiff] had not complied. On appeal, [the plaintiff] admitted noncompliance with § 9, but argued that Rule 4(d)(1) defines the method by which service of process is to be effected in diversity actions. The Court of Appeals for the First Circuit, finding that "[r]elatively recent amendments [to § 9] evince a clear legislative purpose to require personal notification within the year,"[2] concluded that the conflict of state and federal rules was over "a substantive rather than a procedural matter," and unanimously affirmed. * * *

We conclude that the adoption of Rule 4(d)(1), designed to control service of process in diversity actions, neither exceeded the congressional mandate embodied in the Rules Enabling Act nor transgressed constitutional bounds, and that the Rule is therefore the standard against which the District Court should have measured the adequacy of the service. Accordingly, we reverse the decision of the Court of Appeals.

* * * Under the cases construing the scope of the Enabling Act, Rule 4(d)(1) clearly passes muster. Prescribing the manner in which a defendant is to be notified that a suit has been instituted against him, it relates to the "practice and procedure of the district courts." * * *

"The test must be whether a rule really regulates procedure,—the judicial process for enforcing rights and duties recognized by substantive law and for justly administering remedy and redress for disregard or infraction of them." Sibbach v. Wilson & Co., 312 U.S. 1, 14.

In Mississippi Pub. Corp. v. Murphree, 326 U.S. 438, this Court upheld [then] Rule 4(f), which permits service of a summons anywhere within the State (and not merely the district) in which a district court sits * * *.

Thus were there no conflicting state procedure, Rule 4(d)(1) would clearly control. * * * However, [the defendant], focusing on the contrary Massachusetts rule, calls to the Court's attention another line of cases, a line which—like the Federal Rules—had its birth in 1938. Erie R. Co. v. Tompkins, 304 U.S. 64, * * * held that federal courts sitting in diversity cases, when deciding questions of "substantive" law, are bound by state court decisions as well as state statutes. The broad command of Erie was therefore identical to that of the Enabling Act: federal courts are to apply state substantive law and federal procedural law. However, as subsequent cases sharpened the distinction between substance and procedure, the line of cases following Erie diverged markedly from the line construing the Enabling Act. Guaranty Trust Co. of New York v. York, 326 U.S. 99, made it clear that Erie-type problems were not to be solved by reference to any traditional or common-sense substance-procedure distinction * * *.

[The defendant], by placing primary reliance on York and Ragan, suggests that the Erie doctrine acts as a check on the Federal Rules of Civil Procedure, that despite the clear command of Rule 4(d)(1), Erie and its progeny demand the application of the Massachusetts rule. Reduced to essentials, the argument is: (1) Erie, as refined in York, demands that federal courts apply state law whenever application of federal law in its stead will alter the outcome of the case. (2) In this case, a determination

---

[1]   * * * The purpose of [the part of § 9 involved here] is, as the court below noted, to insure that executors will receive actual notice of claims. Actual notice is of course also the goal of Rule 4(d)(1); however, the Federal Rule reflects a determination that this goal can be achieved by a method less cumbersome than that prescribed in § 9. In this case the goal seems to have been achieved; although the affidavit filed by [defendant] in the District Court asserts that he had not been served in hand nor had he accepted service, it does not allege lack of actual notice.

that the Massachusetts service requirements obtain will result in immediate victory for [the defendant]. If, on the other hand, it should be held that Rule 4(d)(1) is applicable, the litigation will continue, with possible victory for [the plaintiff]. (3) Therefore, Erie demands application of the Massachusetts rule. The syllogism possesses an appealing simplicity, but is for several reasons invalid.

In the first place, it is doubtful that, even if there were no Federal Rule making it clear that in-hand service is not required in diversity actions, the Erie rule would have obligated the District Court to follow the Massachusetts procedure. "Outcome-determination" analysis was never intended to serve as a talisman. Byrd v. Blue Ridge Rural Elec. Cooperative, 356 U.S. 525, 537. Indeed, the message of York itself is that choices between state and federal law are to be made not by application of any automatic, "litmus paper" criterion, but rather by reference to the policies underlying the Erie rule. * * *

The Erie rule is rooted in part in a realization that it would be unfair for the character or result of a litigation materially to differ because the suit had been brought in a federal court. * * *

The decision was also in part a reaction to the practice of "forum-shopping" which had grown up in response to the rule of Swift v. Tyson. 304 U.S., at 73–74. That the York test was an attempt to effectuate these policies is demonstrated by the fact that the opinion framed the inquiry in terms of "substantial" variations between state and federal litigation. 326 U.S., at 109. Not only are nonsubstantial, or trivial, variations not likely to raise the sort of equal protection problems which troubled the Court in Erie; they are also unlikely to influence the choice of a forum. The "outcome-determination" test therefore cannot be read without reference to the twin aims of the Erie rule: discouragement of forum-shopping and avoidance of inequitable administration of the laws.[9]

The difference between the conclusion that the Massachusetts rule is applicable, and the conclusion that it is not, is of course at this point "outcome-determinative" in the sense that if we hold the state rule to apply, [the defendant] prevails, whereas if we hold that Rule 4(d)(1) governs, the litigation will continue. But in this sense *every* procedural variation is "outcome-determinative." For example, having brought suit in a federal court, a plaintiff cannot then insist on the right to file subsequent pleadings in accord with the time limits applicable in state courts, even though enforcement of the federal timetable will, if he continues to insist that he must meet only the state time limit, result in determination of the controversy against him. So it is here. Though choice of the federal or state rule will at this point have a marked effect upon the outcome of the litigation, the difference between the two rules would be of scant, if any, relevance to the choice of a forum. [The plaintiff] * * * was not presented with a situation where application of the state rule would wholly bar recovery; rather, adherence to the state rule would

---

9   * * * Erie and its progeny make clear that when a federal court sitting in a diversity case is faced with a question of whether or not to apply state law, the importance of a state rule is indeed relevant, but only in the context of asking whether application of the rule would make so important a difference to the character or result of the litigation that failure to enforce it would unfairly discriminate against citizens of the forum State, or whether application of the rule would have so important an effect upon the fortunes of one or both of the litigants that failure to enforce it would be likely to cause a plaintiff to choose the federal court.

have resulted only in altering the way in which process was served. Moreover, it is difficult to argue that permitting service of defendant's wife to take the place of in-hand service of defendant himself alters the mode of enforcement of state-created rights in a fashion sufficiently "substantial" to raise the sort of equal protection problems to which the Erie opinion alluded.

There is, however, a more fundamental flaw in respondent's syllogism: the incorrect assumption that the rule of Erie R. Co. v. Tompkins constitutes the appropriate test of the validity and therefore the applicability of a Federal Rule of Civil Procedure. The Erie rule has never been invoked to void a Federal Rule. It is true that there have been cases where this Court has held applicable a state rule in the face of an argument that the situation was governed by one of the Federal Rules. But the holding of each such case was not that Erie commanded displacement of a Federal Rule by an inconsistent state rule, but rather that the scope of the Federal Rule was not as broad as the losing party urged, and therefore, there being no Federal Rule which covered the point in dispute, Erie commanded the enforcement of state law. * * * [The Court here refers to Palmer v. Hoffman, p. 573, *supra*; Ragan v. Merchants Transfer & Whse Co., p. 607, *supra*; and Cohen v. Beneficial Indus. Loan Corp., p. 607, note 1, *supra*.] * * * At the same time, in cases adjudicating the validity of Federal Rules, we have not applied the York rule or other refinements of Erie, but have to this day continued to decide questions concerning the scope of the Enabling Act and the constitutionality of specific Federal Rules in light of the distinction set forth in Sibbach.

Nor has the development of two separate lines of cases been inadvertent. The line between "substance" and "procedure" shifts as the legal context changes. * * * When a situation is covered by one of the Federal Rules, the question facing the court is a far cry from the typical, relatively unguided Erie choice: the court has been instructed to apply the Federal Rule, and can refuse to do so only if the Advisory Committee, this Court, and Congress erred in their prima facie judgment that the Rule in question transgresses neither the terms of the Enabling Act nor constitutional restrictions.

We are reminded by the Erie opinion that neither Congress nor the federal courts can, under the guise of formulating rules of decision for federal courts, fashion rules which are not supported by a grant of federal authority contained in Article I or some other section of the Constitution; in such areas state law must govern because there can be no other law. But the opinion in Erie, which involved no Federal Rule and dealt with a question which was "substantive" in every traditional sense (whether the railroad owed a duty of care to Tompkins as a trespasser or a licensee), surely neither said nor implied that measures like Rule 4(d)(1) are unconstitutional. For the constitutional provision for a federal court system (augmented by the Necessary and Proper Clause) carries with it congressional power to make rules governing the practice and pleading in those courts, which in turn includes a power to regulate matters which, though falling within the uncertain area between substance and procedure, are rationally capable of classification as either. Cf. M'Culloch v. State of Maryland, 4 Wheat. 316, 421. Neither York nor the cases following it ever suggested that the rule there laid down for coping with situations where no Federal Rule applies is coextensive with the limitation on Congress to which Erie had adverted. Although this Court has never before been confronted with a case where the applicable Federal Rule is in direct collision with the law of the relevant State,[15] courts of appeals faced with such clashes have rightly discerned the implications of our decisions. * * *

Erie and its offspring cast no doubt on the long-recognized power of Congress to prescribe housekeeping rules for federal courts even though some of those rules will inevitably differ from comparable state rules. * * * Thus, though a court, in measuring a Federal Rule against the standards contained in the Enabling Act and the Constitution, need not wholly blind itself to the degree to which the Rule makes the character and result of the federal litigation stray from the course it would follow in state courts, it cannot be forgotten that the Erie rule, and the guidelines suggested in York, were created to serve another purpose altogether. To hold that a Federal Rule of Civil Procedure must cease to function whenever it alters the mode of enforcing state-created rights would be to disembowel either the Constitution's grant of power over federal procedure or Congress' attempt to exercise that power in the Enabling Act. Rule 4(d)(1) is valid and controls the instant case.

Reversed.

■ MR. JUSTICE BLACK concurs in the result.

■ MR. JUSTICE HARLAN, concurring.

It is unquestionably true that up to now Erie and the cases following it have not succeeded in articulating a workable doctrine governing choice of law in diversity actions. I respect the Court's effort to clarify the situation in today's opinion. However, in doing so I think it has misconceived the constitutional premises of Erie and has failed to deal adequately with those past decisions upon which the courts below relied.

Erie was something more than an opinion which worried about "forum-shopping and avoidance of inequitable administration of the laws," although to be sure these were important elements of the decision. I have always regarded that decision as one of the modern cornerstones of our federalism, expressing policies that profoundly touch the allocation of judicial power between the state and federal systems. Erie recognized that there should not be two conflicting systems of law controlling the primary activity of citizens, for such alternative governing authority must necessarily give rise to a debilitating uncertainty in the planning of everyday affairs. And it recognized that the scheme of our Constitution envisions an allocation of law-making functions between state and federal legislative processes which is undercut if the federal judiciary can make substantive law affecting state affairs beyond the bounds of congressional legislative powers in this regard. Thus, in diversity cases Erie commands that it be the state law governing primary private activity which prevails.

---

[15] In Sibbach v. Wilson & Co., *supra*, the law of the forum State (Illinois) forbade the sort of order authorized by Rule 35. However, Sibbach was decided before Klaxon Co. v. Stentor Electric Mfg. Co., *supra*, and the Sibbach opinion makes clear that the Court was proceeding on the assumption that if the law of any State was relevant, it was the law of the State where the tort occurred (Indiana), which, like Rule 35, made provision for such orders. 312 U.S., at 6–7, 10–11.

The shorthand formulations which have appeared in some past decisions are prone to carry untoward results that frequently arise from oversimplification. The Court is quite right in stating that the "outcome-determinative" test of Guaranty Trust Co. of New York v. York, 326 U.S. 99, if taken literally, proves too much, for any rule, no matter how clearly "procedural," can affect the outcome of litigation if it is not obeyed. In turning from the "outcome" test of York back to the unadorned forum-shopping rationale of Erie, however, the Court falls prey to like oversimplification, for a simple forum-shopping rule also proves too much; litigants often choose a federal forum merely to obtain what they consider the advantages of the Federal Rules of Civil Procedure or to try their cases before a supposedly more favorable judge. To my mind the proper line of approach in determining whether to apply a state or a federal rule, whether "substantive" or "procedural," is to stay close to basic principles by inquiring if the choice of rule would substantially affect those primary decisions respecting human conduct which our constitutional system leaves to state regulation.[2] If so, Erie and the Constitution require that the state rule prevail, even in the face of a conflicting federal rule.

The Court weakens, if indeed it does not submerge, this basic principle by finding, in effect, a grant of substantive legislative power in the constitutional provision for a federal court system, and through it, setting up the Federal Rules as a body of law inviolate. * * * So long as a reasonable man could characterize any duly adopted federal rule as "procedural," the Court * * * would have it apply no matter how seriously it frustrated a State's substantive regulation of the primary conduct and affairs of its citizens. Since the members of the Advisory Committee, the Judicial Conference, and this Court who formulated the Federal Rules are presumably reasonable men, it follows that the integrity of the Federal Rules is absolute. Whereas the unadulterated outcome and forum-shopping tests may err too far toward honoring state rules, I submit that the Court's "arguably procedural, *ergo* constitutional" test moves too fast and far in the other direction.

The courts below relied upon this Court's decisions in [Ragan and Cohen]. Those cases deserve more attention than this Court has given them, particularly Ragan which, if still good law, would in my opinion call for affirmance of the result reached by the Court of Appeals. Further, a discussion of these two cases will serve to illuminate the "diversity" thesis I am advocating.

* * * I think that the [Ragan] decision was wrong. At most, application of the Federal Rule would have meant that potential Kansas tort defendants would have to defer for a few days the satisfaction of knowing that they had not been sued within the limitations period. The choice of the Federal Rule would have had no effect on the primary stages of private activity from which torts arise, and only the most minimal effect on behavior following the commission of the tort. In such circumstances the interest of the federal system in proceeding under its own rules should have prevailed.

---

[2]   See Hart and Wechsler, The Federal Courts and the Federal System 678 [1st ed. 1953]. Byrd v. Blue Ridge Rural Elec. Coop., Inc., 356 U.S. 525, 536–540, indicated that state procedures would apply if the State had manifested a particularly strong interest in their employment. However, this approach may not be of constitutional proportions.

* * * The proper view of Cohen is in my opinion, that the statute was meant to inhibit small stockholders from instituting "strike suits," and thus it was designed and could be expected to have a substantial impact on private primary activity. * * * [E]ven had the Federal Rules purported to [deal with this problem], and in so doing provided a substantially less effective deterrent to strike suits, I think the state rule should still have prevailed. That is where I believe the Court's view differs from mine; for the Court attributes such overriding force to the Federal Rules that it is hard to think of a case where a conflicting state rule would be allowed to operate, even though the state rule reflected policy considerations which, under Erie, would lie within the realm of state legislative authority.

It remains to apply what has been said to the present case. * * * If the Federal District Court in Massachusetts applies Rule 4(d)(1) of the Federal Rules of Civil Procedure instead of the Massachusetts service rule, what effect would that have on the speed and assurance with which estates are distributed? As I see it, the effect would not be substantial. It would mean simply that an executor would have to check at his own house or the federal courthouse as well as the registry of probate before he could distribute the estate with impunity. As this does not seem enough to give rise to any real impingement on the vitality of the state policy which the Massachusetts rule is intended to serve, I concur in the judgment of the Court.

NOTE ON HANNA AND ITS AFTERMATH

A.   Introduction: Justice Harlan's Rationale in Hanna

Suppose the Court had adopted Justice Harlan's view that it should inquire whether "the choice of rule would substantially affect those primary decisions respecting human conduct which our constitutional system leaves to state regulation. If so, Erie and the Constitution require that the state rule prevail, even in the face of a conflicting federal rule." Consider rules of state law (a) allowing rescission or reformation of a contract for a mutual mistake of fact, (b) allocating the burden of proof with respect to comparative negligence, or (c) allowing the recovery of reliance damages for breach of a contract within the statute of frauds. Does any of these rules characteristically affect people's conduct at the stage of primary private activity? If not, should they be regarded as "quasi-procedural"—as rules that need not be followed in federal diversity actions? Isn't the more critical question whether the state rule embodies a significant state policy with respect to primary conduct and its effects?

B.   The Significance of Whether a Federal Rule of Civil Procedure Applies

To a significant extent, Hanna and later cases have distinguished between conflicts involving matters covered by a Federal Rule of Civil Procedure (or by another Federal Rule or statute) and conflicts to which no formal federal statute or rule applies. The following discussion is based on that distinction.

C. Matters Not Governed by a Federal Rule of Civil Procedure (or Other Federal Rule or Statute)

(1) The Analysis in Hanna. The Court in Hanna (in dictum) said that when the matter is *not* governed by a federal statute or Federal Rule of Civil Procedure, the question is whether failure to follow the state rule would make such an important difference as to "discriminate against citizens of the forum State" or as to lead the "plaintiff to choose the federal court". It is not clear why the courts should be unconcerned about discrimination against a *non-citizen* of the forum state, or whether the failure to follow the state rule leads the *defendant* to choose the federal court. But more fundamentally, the Court's emphasis on forum-shopping may make too short shrift of the Byrd analysis of the relationship between state and federal policies—an analysis that contemplates the presence of affirmative considerations justifying a uniform federal rule even in the absence of a statute or a Federal Rule of Civil Procedure.

Sharply contrasting views on these issues were expressed by Ely, p. 604, *supra,* at 714–17, and Redish & Phillips, *Erie and The Rules of Decision Act: In Search of the Appropriate Dilemma,* 91 Harv.L.Rev. 356, 394 (1977). Arguing that the Rules of Decision Act sought to mark out enclaves of exclusive state concern, Ely concludes that the Act requires state law to be followed whenever disregard of that law would be "likely to generate an outcome different from that which would result were the case litigated in the state court system and the state rules followed". "[I]n light of [the Act's] fairness rationale—or, for that matter in light of a desire either to minimize forum shopping or to avoid 'uncertainty in the planning of everyday affairs'— it becomes clear that there is no place in the analysis for the sort of balancing of federal and state interests contemplated by the Byrd opinion".

For Redish and Phillips, by contrast, Erie and the Rules of Decision Act warrant consideration not only of the interests of litigants in uniformity of outcome but also of the state's interest in enforcement of its substantive policies and of the federal interest in the fair and efficient administration of justice. Thus they urge a "refined balancing test" that considers, *inter alia,* the federal interest in "doing justice" and in avoiding unnecessary cost or inconvenience.[1]

(2) The Gasperini Decision. Gasperini v. Center for Humanities, Inc., 518 U.S. 415 (1996), was an especially difficult case involving the relation between state and federal law governing review of a jury damages award.[2] A New York law (N.Y. Civ. Prac. Law & Rules § 5501(c)) empowered appellate courts to review the size of a jury verdict and to order a new trial when the award "deviates materially from what would be reasonable compensation"— a standard inviting more rigorous judicial review of awards than the "shock the conscience" test followed in federal courts in New York. In a diversity action for the loss of certain slide transparencies, the jury in a New York federal court awarded the plaintiff $450,000. The district court denied the defendant's motion to set aside the verdict as excessive; the Second Circuit, after holding that § 5501(c) governed the controversy, reversed and

---

[1]   See also Doernberg, *The Unseen Track of Erie Railroad: Why History and Jurisprudence Suggest a More Straightforward Form of Erie Analysis,* 109 W.Va.L.Rev. 611, 644–48 (2007) (advocating a Byrd-style balancing of interests in which a presumption that state law applies can be rebutted only by showing that it conflicts with a "dominant federal interest").

[2]   For an earlier case following federal law on the question of sanctions for improper conduct in the course of litigation, see Chambers v. NASCO, Inc., 501 U.S. 32 (1991).

remanded the case for a new trial unless the plaintiff agreed to a reduced award of $100,000.

(a) The Supreme Court concluded that New York law should apply under the Erie doctrine. Writing for the majority, Justice Ginsburg ruled that if New York had enacted a "statutory cap" on damage awards, that cap would clearly control in a diversity case. She then stated that § 5501 did not differ from such a cap in its substantive objective (of controlling jury awards) but only in its use of a procedural technique to be applied on a case-by-case basis. Given the aims of Erie, its doctrine "precludes a recovery in federal court significantly larger than the recovery that would have been tolerated in state court".

The Court then considered whether the federal interest in the allocation of authority between judge and jury, especially as reflected in the Seventh Amendment, in any way undercut or modified the obligation to follow state law. The Court noted that, under New York precedent, § 5501 governed the standard to be applied by trial judges as well as by appellate courts, and held that the application of that standard by a federal trial judge would not run afoul of the Seventh Amendment. In light of the "re-examination clause" of that Amendment, however, *appellate review*, while not entirely precluded, was limited to the question whether the district court's determination was an abuse of discretion. The Court concluded that this resolution accommodated both the interests served by the Erie doctrine and those reflected in the Seventh Amendment, and ordered the case returned to the district court for its review of the award under the New York standard.[3]

Justice Scalia's dissent, joined by Chief Justice Rehnquist and Justice Thomas, argued that, under the Seventh Amendment, appellate courts may not review (even for abuse of discretion) district court refusals to set aside civil jury awards as contrary to the weight of the evidence. He added that the majority departed significantly from precedent in holding that federal courts must follow a state's allocation of authority between judges and juries. Quoting Byrd, Justice Scalia contended that "changing the standard by which trial judges review jury verdicts does disrupt the federal system, and is plainly inconsistent with 'the strong federal policy against allowing state rules to disrupt the judge-jury relationship in federal court' ". The analogy to a statutory cap on damages was misleading, he said, because of the difference "between a rule of law * * * [that] would ordinarily be imposed upon the jury in the trial court's instructions, and a rule of review, which simply determines how closely the jury verdict will be scrutinized for compliance with the instructions".

(b) Assuming that the Seventh Amendment itself does not bar application of the New York standard in a federal *trial* court, the Supreme Court's decision with respect to the task of the trial judge seems to reject the approach in the Byrd case. Instead, the Court appears to favor the analysis in Hanna discussed above in Paragraph C(1) and/or the outcome-determinative analysis of Guaranty Trust.[4] The Byrd rationale does appear to play a larger role in the Court's holding as to the scope of *appellate* review,

---

[3] The Court also rejected the argument that the result reached with respect to the standard to be applied by the trial court conflicted with Fed.R.Civ.Proc. 59. See p. 620–621, *infra.*

[4] See *The Supreme Court, 1995 Term—Leading Cases*, 110 Harv.L.Rev. 256, 265–66 (1996); Floyd, *Erie Awry: A Comment on Gasperini v. Center for Humanities, Inc.*, 1997 BYU L.Rev. 267, 303–04.

but that holding is also affected by the Court's understanding of the Seventh Amendment.[5]

D. Matters Governed by the Federal Rules of Civil Procedure (or by Other Federal Rules or Statutes)

(1) The Analysis in Hanna. In Hanna, Justice Harlan criticizes the majority for clothing the Federal Rules of Civil Procedure with virtually absolute immunity by adopting an "arguably procedural, ergo constitutional" test. That test is surely appropriate for measuring the constitutionality of a rule of procedure laid down for the federal courts by Congress. And Sibbach, p. 569, *supra*, seems to endorse application of essentially the same test in determining the validity under the Enabling Act of a rule promulgated by the Supreme Court. Hanna is of a piece with Sibbach. But was the Sibbach opinion sufficiently sensitive to state interests and to the language and purpose of the Enabling Act?[6]

The majority in Hanna did recognize that courts applying federal rules and statutes must interpret them, and that the process of interpretation should reflect an awareness of legitimate state interests. Indeed, that awareness may account for the fact that the Court did not squarely confront the issue posed in Hanna until 27 years after Erie and 25 years after Sibbach.

(2) Tension Between Hanna and Subsequent Decisions. After Hanna, the Supreme Court, in a number of cases, has interpreted the federal rules to avoid conflict with important state regulatory policies.[7]

(a) In Walker v. Armco Steel Corp., 446 U.S. 740 (1980), the Court unanimously decided that Ragan, p. 607, *supra*, was still good law, and that

---

[5] For an evaluation of Gasperini in the context of a comprehensive discussion of the Erie doctrine, see Rowe, *Not Bad for Government Work: Does Anyone Else Think the Supreme Court Is Doing a Halfway Decent Job in Its Erie-Hanna Jurisprudence?*, 73 Notre Dame L.Rev. 963, 1014–15 (1998). Rowe, taking his academic colleagues to task for their "hypercritical[ ]" approach to the Supreme Court's efforts, concludes that "in addition to being reasonably sensitive to federalist concerns and the nuances of a somewhat complex area", the Court's doctrine has been "fairly comprehensible and workable in its broad outlines" and "remarkably stable * * * over three decades". As for the Gasperini decision, it has left the "basic framework for analysis * * * very much intact", although it does suggest a greater willingness to construe potentially applicable Federal Rules to avoid "direct conflicts" with state policies and to preserve Byrd interest analysis "in a subset of cases involving judge-made federal procedural rules". Compare Freer, *Some Thoughts on the State of Erie After Gasperini*, 76 Tex.L.Rev. 1637, 1663 (1998) (arguing that the Court missed "perhaps its best [opportunity] in a generation—to make a meaningful contribution to [Rules of Decision Act] analysis * * *. Instead, the Court has left the field about as murky as it was before".).

[6] Ely, Paragraph C(1), *supra*, argues that the Court in Sibbach failed to give adequate scope to what was then the second sentence, and what is now subsection (b), of the Enabling Act. That provision, in his view, requires that a Federal Rule of Civil Procedure must yield in the face of a state rule that does not merely represent a procedural disagreement but embodies a substantive policy.

Professor Burbank, in *The Rules Enabling Act of 1934*, 130 U.Pa.L.Rev. 1015, 1025–26 (1982), also objects to the interpretation of the Enabling Act in Sibbach and Hanna, but on quite different grounds. Relying on his study of the pre-1934 history of the Act, he concludes (a) that the first two sentences of the original Act "were intended to allocate power between the Supreme Court as rulemaker and Congress and thus to circumscribe the delegation of legislative power, [(b) that those sentences] were thought to be equally relevant in all actions brought in a federal court, and [(c)] that the protection of state law was deemed a probable effect, rather than the primary purpose, of the allocation scheme established by the Act."

[7] For an arguable exception, see Burlington N.R.R. v. Woods, 480 U.S. 1 (1987) (state rule requiring imposition of a fixed penalty on an appellant who obtains a stay of a money judgment and then loses the appeal is preempted by the federal appellate rule giving discretion to impose a penalty).

state law rather than Rule 3 ("A civil action is commenced by filing a complaint with the court.") determined when a diversity action was commenced for the purpose of tolling the statute of limitations. Beyond relying upon stare decisis, the Court reasoned that significant state policy interests would be frustrated if Rule 3 were to supersede the state rule requiring actual service on the defendant in order to stop the running of the statute. The Court did not reach the question of the validity of Rule 3 in this context because the lack of any reference in the rule to the tolling of state limitations statutes meant that there was no "direct conflict between the Federal Rule and the state law".[8]

Does the Walker decision cast some doubt on the Hanna result? If the state law at issue in Hanna was essentially a provision for determining when and how the statute of limitations was tolled, should it have prevailed even though its requirements for valid service went beyond those of Rule 4?

(b) In Gasperini v. Center for Humanities, Inc., more fully discussed in Paragraph C(2), *supra*, Justice Scalia ended his dissent by contending that the decision to follow the state standard of review in ruling on a new trial motion in the district court was squarely in conflict with Fed.R.Civ.Proc. 59, which (as then worded) allowed a new trial "for any of the reasons for which new trials have heretofore been granted in actions at law in the courts of the United States". That provision, in his view, clearly imposed a federal standard. The majority (quoting the statement in the Fourth Edition of this book that the Court has "continued since Hanna to *interpret* the federal rules to avoid conflict with important state regulatory policies") responded that Rule 59 did not preclude reference to the only appropriate source of law for determining whether damages are excessive—the state law governing the cause of action.

(c) Finally, in Semtek Int'l, Inc. v. Lockheed Martin Corp., 531 U.S. 497 (2001) (more fully discussed at p. 1368, *infra*), a California federal court, applying a California statute of limitations, had dismissed a diversity suit "on the merits and with prejudice." The plaintiff then filed a new action on the same claim against the same defendant in a Maryland state court, because Maryland's statute of limitations had not yet run. The Maryland courts decided that the action was barred because under Rule 41(b) of the Federal Rules of Civil Procedure, the federal court dismissal "on the merits" had to be accorded claim preclusive effect. (Rule 41(b), as then worded, provided that "unless the dismissal order states otherwise," an involuntary dismissal (with certain exceptions not applicable in the Semtek case) "operates as an adjudication on the merits.")

A unanimous Supreme Court reversed. Justice Scalia's opinion stated first that a rule "governing the effect that must be accorded federal judgments * * * would arguably violate the jurisdictional limitation of the Rules Enabling Act" and in addition "would in many cases violate the federalism principle of [the Erie doctrine] by engendering 'substantial variations [in outcomes] between state and federal litigation' which would

---

[8]   The Court also stated, in a footnote: "We do not here address the role of Rule 3 as a tolling provision for a statute of limitations, whether set by federal law or borrowed from state law, if the cause of action is based on federal law". That question was addressed in West v. Conrail, 481 U.S. 35 (1987), where the Court held that "when the underlying cause of action is based on federal law and the absence of an express federal statute of limitations makes it necessary to borrow a limitations period from another statute, the action is not barred if it has been 'commenced' in compliance with Rule 3 within the borrowed period".

'[l]ikely influence the choice of a forum' " (quoting Hanna v. Plumer). He then concluded that the language of Rule 41(b) on which the Maryland court had relied simply meant "that, unlike a dismissal 'without prejudice,' the dismissal in the present case barred refiling of the same claim in the [same district court]." He added that the preclusive effect of the first judgment was governed by federal common law and that, in a diversity case, federal common law would usually refer to "the law that would be applied by state courts in the State in which the federal diversity court sits" (citing, *inter alia*, the decisions in Gasperini and Walker v. Armco).

Even in light of the decisions that sought, through interpretation, to avoid difficult questions under the Enabling Act and the principles underlying the Erie doctrine, was the interpretation of Rule 41(b) in Semtek nevertheless too much of a stretch? The Court might more plausibly have construed the rule as rendering a dismissal falling within its terms eligible for claim preclusive effect in *any* court, but only if that effect was required by the governing law of preclusion (which in Semtek would be federal common law). That interpretation would have avoided a novel and confusing distinction between the preclusive effect in the rendering court and in other courts.[9]

The Semtek decision could be read to cast doubt on the rationale of Hanna—that a valid and applicable Federal Rule of Civil Procedure trumps conflicting state law even in a diversity case. Justice Scalia's opinion in Semtek cited Hanna as supporting the proposition that even if the rejected interpretation of Rule 41(b) was consistent with the Enabling Act, it would "violate the federalism principle of Erie". Significantly, the portion of the Hanna opinion cited on this point dealt with the hypothetical case in which there was *no* conflicting Federal Rule of Civil Procedure. But note that Semtek's discussion of this point was essentially dictum, given the Court's ultimate decision to adopt an interpretation of Rule 41(b) that rendered the Erie issue moot.[10]

(3) The Shady Grove Decision. The Court's latest decision in this line, Shady Grove Orthopedic Associates, P.A. v. Allstate Ins. Co., 559 U.S. 393 (2010), suggests that the Court has yet to develop a consistent and predictable approach to determining when a Federal Rule is valid and should be read to govern the matter at hand. In striking contrast to the Walker, Gasperini, and Semtek decisions, a fractured Supreme Court decided that the provisions of Fed.R.Civ.Proc. 23 (on class actions) conflicted with, and trumped, state law.

The state law in question, N.Y.Civ.Prac. Law Ann. (CPLR) § 901(b), precludes the bringing of a class action to recover a "penalty", which the federal courts understood to include statutory interest. Notwithstanding this state law prohibition, Shady Grove filed a diversity class action in a New York federal district court to recover certain statutory interest on behalf of

---

[9] In a comment generally approving the Semtek result, Professor Burbank concludes that the Court's effort to cabin the rule was unpersuasive and that "[i]t might have been better, after all, to decide the Enabling Act question" (i.e., the question whether a federal rule of civil procedure that dictates the preclusive effect of a dismissal is valid under the Enabling Act). Burbank, *Semtek, Forum Shopping, and Federal Common Law*, 77 Notre Dame L.Rev. 1027, 1047 (2002). For a similar view, see Dudley & Rutherglen, *Deforming the Federal Rules: An Essay on What's Wrong with the Recent Erie Decisions*, 92 Va.L.Rev. 707, 708 (2006).

[10] For consideration of the relevance of state policy to a motion to transfer under § 1404, see Stewart Org., Inc. v. Ricoh Corp., 487 U.S. 22 (1988), p. 628, *infra*.

itself and a similarly situated class. The trial court decided, and the court of appeals agreed, that whether or not the action met the criteria for class certification under Rule 23, it could not be maintained as a class action in view of the prohibition in New York law, and since Shady Grove's individual claim was for less than the jurisdictional amount, dismissed the case.[11] The Supreme Court reversed.

(a) The Lead Opinion. A majority of the Court, in an opinion by Justice Scalia (joined by Chief Justice Roberts and Justices Stevens, Thomas, and Sotomayor), held that Federal Rule 23 conflicted with the New York law. The Court stated that Rule 23—in providing that a class action "may be maintained" if certain conditions are met—confers "categorical permission" to maintain such an action. Justice Scalia rejected the Second Circuit's view that federal and state law do not conflict, because Rule 23 governs the "certifiability" of a class action with respect to a claim while the New York law governs the antecedent question of the eligibility of the claim for class treatment. And while agreeing that the federal courts should read ambiguous rules to avoid substantial variations in the outcome in federal and state litigation, Justice Scalia saw no ambiguity here: "there is only one reasonable reading of Rule 23."

Justice Scalia, now speaking only for himself, Chief Justice Roberts and Justices Thomas and Sotomayor, went on to determine that because Rule 23 was a valid exercise of the authority granted by the Enabling Act, it trumped the conflicting state prohibition. Relying heavily on the holding of Sibbach v. Wilson, p. 569, as well as its language (to the effect that the test of validity is whether the rule really regulates procedure—"the judicial process for enforcing rights and duties recognized by substantive law"), he concluded that "[a] class action * * * merely enables a federal court to adjudicate claims of multiple parties at once, instead of in separate suits." Whether or not New York's prohibition of class actions in this context had a "substantive nature" or "substantive purpose", he insisted, "*makes no difference.*" (Emphasis in original.) As long as the rule itself is procedural, it is "valid in all jurisdictions, regardless of its incidental effect upon state-created rights."

(b) The Concurrence. Justice Stevens, whose concurrence in part and concurrence in the judgment supplied the fifth vote for the outcome, contended that Rule 23 prevailed over New York law because the state law "is a procedural rule that is not part of New York's substantive law." Disagreeing with Justice Scalia's view that in the event of conflict, the sole question was the validity of the federal rule as a rule of procedure, Justice Stevens emphasized that the rule also had to satisfy the limitation of subsection (b) of the Enabling Act, i.e., it could not "abridge, enlarge, or modify any substantive right."[12] Thus, a federal rule "cannot govern a particular case in which the rule would displace a state law that is procedural in the ordinary use of the term but is so intertwined with a state right or remedy that it functions to define the scope of the state-created right." He concluded, however, that the "high" bar for finding a violation of

---

[11] Under the Class Action Fairness Act, pp. 1426–1429, *infra,* it might have been possible to meet the jurisdictional amount threshold by aggregating the damages of class members. But an individual action could not meet § 1332's general threshold in diversity actions.

[12] Justice Scalia, responding to Justice Stevens in a portion of his opinion joined by only Chief Justice Roberts and Justice Thomas, again relied heavily on the rationale of Sibbach. He conceded that "Sibbach's exclusive focus on the challenged federal rule—driven by the very real fear that Federal Rules which vary from State to State would be chaos—is hard to square with § 2072(b)'s terms."

the Enabling Act had not been surmounted in this case. "The text of [New York's law] expressly and unambiguously applies not only to claims based on New York law but also to claims based on federal law or the law of any other State. * * * It is therefore hard to see how [the law] could be understood as a rule that, though procedural in form, serves the function of defining New York's rights or remedies." "In order to displace a federal rule, there must be more than just a possibility that a state rule is different than it appears."

(c) The Dissent. Justice Ginsburg (joined by Justices Kennedy, Breyer, and Alito) dissented. Her central theme was that Rule 23 need not, and should not, be read "to collide with New York's legitimate interest in keeping certain awards reasonably bounded." After discussing a number of earlier decisions in which the Court had avoided such conflicts by interpreting the federal rules "with awareness of, and sensitivity to, important state regulatory policies", she analyzed the history and purpose of the New York limitation and concluded that the state's decision "to block class-action proceedings for statutory damages * * * makes scant sense, except as a means to a manifestly substantive end: Limiting a defendant's liability in a single lawsuit in order to prevent the exorbitant inflation of penalties". Implementation of the state's substantive purpose, she contended, did not conflict with Rule 23 because that rule only "prescribes the considerations relevant to class certification and postcertification proceedings—but it does not command that a particular remedy be available when a party sues in a representative capacity." Justice Ginsburg also rejected as not in any way dispositive the placement of the New York limitation in the state's Civil Practice Law. And as to the fact that the provision was not expressly limited to claims under New York law, she said that "the most likely explanation for the absence of limiting language [was that] New York legislators make law with New York plaintiffs and defendants in mind". As in Gasperini, she said, the remedial provision could have been written, and should be understood, as a statutory cap.

(d) Questions and Comments About Shady Grove.

(i) The Nature of Class Actions. Justice Scalia asserts that a class action is only a procedural device for aggregating individual claims. Compare Shapiro, *Class Actions: The Class as Party and Client*, 73 Notre Dame L.Rev. 913 (1998), arguing that the availability of a class action has significant purposes and consequences that transcend the notion of joinder or aggregation. If Professor Shapiro is correct, how does that affect the appropriate scope of Rule 23 under the Enabling Act? If Justice Scalia is correct, do you agree that his reading of the rule is the only "reasonable" one? Is the dissent's reading of Rule 23 any more of a stretch than the Court's reading of other rules in the cases discussed earlier in this Chapter (particularly its reading of Rule 41(b) in Semtek)?

(ii) The Tension Between Erie Concerns and the Uniform Application of the Federal Rules. Note that both Justice Stevens (in his understanding of the Rules Enabling Act) and Justice Ginsburg (in her reading of Rule 23) must inquire into the substantive purposes of state law. Is such an inquiry at odds with the notion that the Federal Rules of Civil Procedure are trans-substantive and should be uniformly applied (in both federal question and diversity cases)?[13] Could either of their approaches

---

[13] As a sign of the uncertain effect of the Shady Grove decision, several Justices disagreed on the appropriateness of the Court's subsequent per curiam decision granting certiorari, and summarily vacating and remanding for reconsideration in light of Shady Grove, the Second

result in a Federal Rule's being applicable in some cases (in states that lack New York's policy, and in federal question cases) but not in others (cases like Shady Grove)? Does that explain why the plurality (and the Sibbach decision itself) brushed aside arguments that the federal rule was invalid under the Enabling Act and did not delve extensively into what the state's substantive policy was? What weight should the Justices have given, in interpreting the Rule, to the obvious incentive that the Court's decision gives to class representatives to file actions seeking "penalties" under New York law in federal rather than state court?[14]

(iii) The Reach of the Decision. If New York were to replace CPLR § 901(b) with a provision, inserted into every law authorizing recovery of a statutory penalty, that "the remedy herein provided may not be sought on behalf of a class but only on behalf of an individual plaintiff", doesn't the majority accept that such a provision would have to be honored in a federal diversity action? If so, the long-term importance of the Shady Grove decision may be quite limited.

(iv) The State of the Law. In cases that implicate a federal rule, questions can arise both as to its meaning and its validity. On the question of meaning, Shady Grove takes an approach quite different from that in earlier cases. Indeed, the precedent closest in time was Gasperini, in which the Court narrowly interpreted a federal rule, and in that case Justice Ginsburg wrote for the Court and Justice Scalia dissented.

On the question of validity, it remains true, more than 75 years after the adoption of the Federal Rules of Civil Procedure, that no rule has been held invalid, on its face or as applied, under the Rules Enabling Act.

(v) Commentary. Shady Grove stimulated an outpouring of scholarly comment, which highlighted disagreement among scholars on such basic questions as the meaning and scope of the Erie decision, the proper approach to questions arising under the Rules of Decision and Rules Enabling Acts, and the question whether the validity of a Federal Rule of Civil Procedure should ever be considered on an "as applied" basis. Much of that scholarship is cited and briefly summarized in the footnote below.[15]

Circuit's refusal to permit a class action in another suit. See Holster v. Gatco, Inc., 559 U.S. 1060 (2010). In the view of Justice Ginsburg, whom Justice Breyer joined in dissent, the decision to vacate and remand was not warranted because the particular class action had been brought under a federal law (the Telephone Consumer Protection Act (TCPA)) that allowed a private action to be brought only if it was "otherwise permitted by the laws or rules of court of a State". But in the view of Justice Scalia, concurring in the per curiam, the remand was appropriate because the "independent ground" *may* have rested on an assumption (a) that Rule 23 did not "address whether class actions are available for specific claims" or (b) that the TCPA superseded Rule 23 because CPLR § 901(b) precludes an action under state law. In either event, he contended, the Shady Grove decision would affect the outcome in view of its holding that CPLR § 901(b) did not bar an *action* to recover a penalty but only the use of a procedural joinder device, and thus was trumped by Rule 23.

Recall, also, West v. Conrail, p. 620, n. 8, *supra*, where the Court held that Rule 3 does govern the tolling of limitations periods in federal question cases, though not (under the Walker decision) in diversity cases resting on state law.

[14] For data confirming that the decision has led class representatives seeking a "penalty" to choose federal over state court, see Hubbard, *An Empirical Study of the Effect of Shady Grove v. Allstate on Forum Shopping in the New York Courts*, 10 J.L. Econ. & Pol'y 151 (2013).

[15] Leading articles include Burbank & Wolff, *Redeeming the Missed Opportunities of Shady Grove*, 159 U.Pa.L.Rev. 17 (2010) (arguing that Shady Grove was erroneous because Rule 23 is a *mechanism* for implementing aggregate liability policy, and not itself the source of that policy; in Shady Grove the source was the law of New York); and Tidmarsh, *Procedure, Substance, and Erie*, 64 Vand.L.Rev. 877 (2011) (defending the result in Shady Grove on the

(4) Hanna and the Rulemaking Process. To a significant extent, the result of Hanna's permissive standards for measuring the validity of the Federal Rules has been to remit important issues of federalism from the Court as a decider of cases to the participants in the rulemaking process: the Rules Committees, the Court as a promulgator of rules, and Congress in its review of those rules. A case in point is the evolution of the rules relating to privilege in the Federal Rules of Evidence. As proposed by the Rules Committee and promulgated by the Supreme Court, the rules set out a federally-defined set of privileges for all civil and criminal litigation in the federal courts. Responding to the argument that at least in cases governed by state substantive law these rules might run afoul of Erie and the Enabling Act, the Advisory Committee Note argued that Hanna gave a large measure of choice to the rulemakers, that state privileges had at most a "tenuous" substantive aspect, that they would have to give way in federal question cases in any event, and that the practical dimensions of the problem were not great. See Revised Draft of Proposed Rules of Evidence, 51 F.R.D. 315, 358–60 (1971).

Congress refused to accept this approach. Moved by concern for privacy interests and by a desire to safeguard substantive state policies, Congress enacted a statute providing that in Federal Rule of Evidence 501, federal "common law" is controlling on matters of privilege *only* with respect to claims or defenses governed by federal substantive law. When the claim or defense is governed by state law, the state law of privilege applies.

---

ground that the federal courts may properly apply their own rules to process a claim "as long as, in a world without transaction costs [including the costs of litigation], those rules do not affect the ex ante value of a claim").

In a Symposium in the Creighton Law Review, 44 Creighton L.Rev. 1–139 (2010), contributors were asked to rewrite one of the opinions in the case as they think it should have been written. The range of responses is striking: Bassett, *Enabling the Federal Rules, id.* at 7 (concurring in the judgment on the ground that under the broad test of a Federal Rule's validity, which should be determined as of the time of its promulgation, Rule 23 is valid under the Enabling Act and thus trumps a conflicting state rule); Borchers, *The Real Risk of Forum Shopping: A Dissent from Shady Grove, id.* at 29 (dissenting on the ground that because of the substantial risk of vertical forum shopping created by the clash between Rule 23 and the substantive goal of New York law, application of Rule 23 in the particular context violates the Enabling Act); Cox, *Putting Hanna to Rest in Shady Grove, id.* at 43 (dissenting, on the ground that application of Rule 23, when a conflicting state provision is part of the state's substantive tort reform policy, would violate Erie's constitutional mandate); Freer & Arthur, *The Irrepressible Influence of Byrd, id.* at 61 (arguing that the analysis in the Byrd decision should be relevant to the resolution of problems arising under the Rules Enabling Act as well as in other contexts, and concluding that application of Byrd's analysis in Shady Grove supports the approach in Justice Stevens' concurrence); Oakley, *Illuminating Shady Grove: A General Approach to Resolving Erie Problems, id.* at 79 (concurring on the ground that Rule 23 is a valid rule and expressly authorizes a class action in this case, and noting with approval the implicit rejection of the rationale of Gasperini); Rensberger, *Hanna's Unruly Family: An Opinion for * * * Shady Grove * * *, id.* at 89 (dissenting on the ground that, while Rule 23 is a valid rule, it is not applicable in this diversity case because it conflicts with a state rule that is intimately bound up with the state's substantive policy); Rowe, *Sonia, What's a Nice Person Like You Doing in Company Like That?, id.* at 107 (concurring in the judgment on the ground that Rule 23 is not invalid on its face *or* as applied, since the New York law with which it conflicts does not create a substantive right that would be abridged, enlarged, or modified by allowing a federal class action); Whitten, *Shady Grove * * *: Justice Whitten Nagging in Part and Declaring a Pox on All Houses, id.* at 115 (dissenting on the alternative grounds that (a) Rule 23 does not allow a class action in a diversity case such as this, where state law would not permit use of that remedy, and (b) since the state rule is bound up with substantive rights, application of Rule 23 to allow a class action would violate the Enabling Act).

For two symposia of particular interest, see 80 Notre Dame L.Rev. 939–1239 (2011); 44 Akron L.Rev. 897–1209 (2011).

4. THE EFFECT OF STATE LAW AND OF PRIVATE AGREEMENT ON THE EXERCISE OF FEDERAL JURISDICTION

Railway Co. v. Whitton's Administrator

80 U.S. (13 Wall.) 270, 20 L.Ed. 571 (1871).

Writ of Error to the Circuit Court for the Eastern District of Wisconsin.

[Henry Whitton, as administrator of his wife's estate, sued the railroad in a Wisconsin state court to recover damages for his wife's death. The action was brought under a Wisconsin statute which, after creating a right of action in favor of the decedent's personal representative, subjected it to the proviso that "such action shall be brought for a death caused in this State, and, in some court established by the constitution and laws of the same".

[The plaintiff removed the case to the federal court under an 1867 Act of Congress[1] and was ultimately awarded judgment for $5,000. The excerpt from the opinion that follows deals with one of the three grounds on which the jurisdiction of the circuit court was challenged on writ of error.]

■ MR. JUSTICE FIELD, having stated the case, delivered the opinion of the court as follows:

* * *

Second; as to the limitation to the State court of the remedy given by the statute of Wisconsin. * * *

It is undoubtedly true that the right of action exists only in virtue of the [Wisconsin wrongful death] statute * * *. The liability of the party, whether a natural or an artificial person, extends only to cases where, from certain causes, death ensues within the limits of the State. But when death does thus ensue from any of those causes, the relatives of the deceased named in the statute can maintain an action for damages. The liability within the conditions specified extends to all parties through whose wrongful acts, neglect, or default death ensues, and the right of action for damages occasioned thereby is possessed by all persons within the description designated. In all cases, where a general right is thus conferred, it can be enforced in any Federal court within the State having jurisdiction of the parties. It cannot be withdrawn from the cognizance of such Federal court by any provision of State legislation that it shall only

---

[1]   Enacted while Whitton's case was pending, the Act of March 2, 1867, 14 Stat. 558, provided that in any suit then pending or later brought in a state court "in which there is a controversy between a citizen of the State in which the suit is brought and a citizen of another State, and the matter in dispute exceeds the sum of $500, exclusive of costs, such citizen of another State, whether he be plaintiff or defendant, if he will make and file in such State court an affidavit stating that he has reason to, and does believe that, from prejudice or local influence, he will not be able to obtain justice in such State court, may, at any time before the final hearing or trial of the suit", remove the case to the federal circuit court.

be enforced in a State court. The statutes of nearly every State provide for the institution of numerous suits, such as for partition, foreclosure, and the recovery of real property in particular courts and in the counties where the land is situated, yet it never has been pretended that limitations of this character could affect, in any respect, the jurisdiction of the Federal court over such suits where the citizenship of one of the parties was otherwise sufficient. Whenever a general rule as to property or personal rights, or injuries to either, is established by State legislation, its enforcement by a Federal court in a case between proper parties is a matter of course, and the jurisdiction of the court, in such case, is not subject to State limitation. * * *

_____

NOTE ON AGREEMENTS NOT TO RESORT TO THE FEDERAL COURTS

(1) Agreements Not to Remove as a Statutory Condition of Doing Business. In Insurance Co. v. Morse, 87 U.S. (20 Wall.) 445 (1874), the Court held that an agreement by a foreign corporation, exacted by a state statute, not to remove state court actions to federal court could not prevent the corporation from later removing a case. The Court relied on the common law doctrine invalidating agreements in advance to oust courts of jurisdiction conferred by law, and said that the state statute added nothing, as the state lacked power to impose conditions repugnant to the Constitution and laws of the United States.

Then in Terral v. Burke Const. Co., 257 U.S. 529 (1922), the Court, overruling several earlier decisions, held that a state lacked power to revoke a foreign corporation's license to engage in intrastate business on the ground that it had violated a state statute by removing a case to federal court. The opinion stated: "The principle established by the more recent decisions of this court is that a state may not, in imposing conditions upon the privilege of a foreign corporation's doing business in the state, exact from it a waiver of the exercise of its constitutional right to resort to the federal courts * * *."

(2) Private Agreements Limiting Choice of Forum. A series of Supreme Court decisions, taken together, suggest receptivity to enforcement of a private agreement that precludes suit from being brought in a federal court originally or on removal, if that agreement is *not* exacted by state law.[1]

(a) The Court took a first step in The M/S Bremen v. Zapata Off-Shore Co., 407 U.S. 1 (1972). Zapata, an American corporation, had contracted with Unterweser, a German corporation, for towage of Zapata's ocean-going drilling rig from Louisiana to the Adriatic Sea. The contract specified that "[a]ny dispute arising must be treated before the London Court of Justice." After the rig sustained damage, Zapata brought an admiralty action in a Florida federal court seeking damages against Unterweser in personam and against Unterweser's deep sea tug, The Bremen, in rem. Unterweser moved to dismiss on the basis of the contract's forum selection clause or on forum non conveniens grounds, or, in the alternative, to stay the action pending submission of the dispute to the London Court of Justice.

_____

[1] The focus of the discussion in text is on an agreement that suit may be brought only in the court of another forum (*i.e.*, a court of a state or of another country). Agreements to submit disputes to arbitration, though once disfavored, are now generally enforced under a variety of state and federal statutes.

Reversing the lower courts, the Supreme Court upheld enforcement of the forum selection clause, stating that for federal courts sitting in admiralty, "such clauses are prima facie valid and should be enforced unless enforcement is shown by the resisting party to be 'unreasonable' under the circumstances * * *." The Court noted that much undesirable uncertainty in international transactions can be eliminated by an advance agreement as to forum and that the party seeking to avoid its impact on such grounds as fraud, undue influence, "overweening bargaining power", or, perhaps, serious inconvenience should have a heavy burden of proof.

Zapata also argued that enforcement of the forum selection clause would violate public policy because the contract also contained a clause, exculpating Unterweser from liability, that an English court would honor but a federal admiralty court presumably would not. See Bisso v. Inland Waterways Corp., 349 U.S. 85 (1955). The Supreme Court rejected this argument on the ground that the policy invoked did not reach "a freely negotiated international commercial transaction between a German and an American corporation for towage of a vessel from the Gulf of Mexico to the Adriatic Sea." Finally, the Court distinguished Insurance Co. v. Morse, Paragraph (1), *supra*, on the basis that in that case "a state statutory requirement was viewed as imposing an unconstitutional condition on the exercise of the federal right of removal."

(b) The rationale of The Bremen was extended beyond international transactions in Carnival Cruise Lines, Inc. v. Shute, 499 U.S. 585 (1991). At issue in this admiralty action was a forum-selection clause contained in a standard form passenger ticket. That the clause was undoubtedly not negotiated between the parties did not make it "unreasonable," the Court argued, stressing the advantages of such clauses. The Court did state, however, that such clauses "are subject to judicial scrutiny for fundamental fairness".[2]

(3) Private Agreements in Diversity Cases. The Bremen and Carnival Cruise Lines were both admiralty actions. In Stewart Org., Inc. v. Ricoh Corp., 487 U.S. 22 (1988), the Court considered a diversity action and the relevance of state law bearing on the enforceability of forum selection clauses.

There, an Alabama corporation signed a dealership agreement to market copier products of a nationwide manufacturer headquartered in New Jersey. The agreement's forum selection clause provided that any contractual dispute could be litigated only in a state or federal court located in Manhattan. The dealer nonetheless filed suit in federal court in Alabama, alleging primarily breach of contract but also fraud and federal antitrust violations. The manufacturer sought to transfer the case to the Southern District of New York under 28 U.S.C. § 1404(a), which provides that " * * * in the interest of justice, a district court may transfer any civil action to any other district or division where it might have been brought". The district court denied the motion, applying Alabama law, which disfavored forum selection clauses. But the Supreme Court ruled that the district court had erred. Justice Marshall's majority opinion stated that under Hanna v. Plumer the critical issue was whether § 1404(a) itself controlled the question

---

[2] For discussion of Carnival Cruise Lines, see, *e.g.*, Mullenix, *Another Easy Case, Some More Bad Law: Carnival Cruise Lines and Contractual Personal Jurisdiction*, 27 Tex.Int'l L.J. 323 (1992); Purcell, *Geography as a Litigation Weapon: Consumers, Forum-Selection Clauses, and the Rehnquist Court*, 40 UCLA L.Rev. 423 (1992).

of transfer. The Court said that it did, noting that § 1404(a) gives district courts discretion to decide transfer motions on a case-by-case basis, taking into account a range of factors, of which a forum selection clause is only one. To give such a clause either dispositive weight (as the defendant urged) or no weight at all (as Alabama law might have it) would interfere with the multi-factored balance set forth in § 1404(a). Accordingly, the case was remanded for the district court to determine the appropriate effect under federal law of the forum-selection clause on the defendant's motion to transfer.

In dissent, Justice Scalia offered two reasons why § 1404(a) should not supersede the forum selection clause. First, the statute is concerned with the just and convenient litigation of the case *after* it has been filed, not with the content and enforceability of an agreement made *before* suit. Before considering how much weight to give to a clause under § 1404(a), a court must first determine whether the clause is valid. The Court, he argued, had failed to consider whose law governs this prior question of validity; he found no reason to depart from the normal rule that state law governs the validity of a contract. Second, he suggested that "a broad reading [of a federal statute or rule] that would create significant disuniformity between state and federal courts should be avoided if the text permits" (citing, *inter alia*, Walker v. Armco Steel Corp., p. 619, *supra*). In his view, the text of § 1404(a) permitted such avoidance.[3]

NOTE ON THE VARIED EFFECTS OF STATE LAW ON FEDERAL JURISDICTION

(1) The Problem. The material in this Note considers whether state law can ever expand or limit the jurisdiction of the federal courts.[1]

(2) The Stude and Madisonville Cases. In Chicago, R.I. & P.R.R. v. Stude, 346 U.S. 574 (1954), the railroad sought to condemn certain lands owned by Stude, and a state commission awarded damages to Stude and others on the basis of its appraisal of the value of the property. The railroad then filed a diversity action in federal court, alleging that the assessment was excessive. Acting pursuant to state law, the railroad also filed an appeal in state court, which docketed the case with Stude as the plaintiff and the railroad as defendant. The railroad then sought to remove the state court action to federal district court. The district court granted Stude's motion to dismiss the original action and denied a motion to remand the removed action.

---

[3] For differing views of the Stewart decision, compare Freer, *Erie's Mid-Life Crisis*, 31 Tul.L.Rev. 1087, 1139–40 (1989) (arguing that forum selection clauses "are simply ancillary tools of choice of law" and that there is "no relevant federal interest" in enforcing such clauses), with Stein, *Erie and Court Access*, 100 Yale L.J. 1935, 1966 (1991) (arguing that the state rule reflected concerns about the administration of its own courts, that the asserted conflict with federal law was therefore a "false" one, and that "[n]o value of federalism would be sacrificed by nonconformity with state practice").

[1] In considering this question, note also cases like Smith v. Reeves, 178 U.S. 436 (1900), which held that in view of the Eleventh Amendment, a state may "give its consent to be sued in its own courts by private persons or by corporations in respect of any cause of action against it and at the same time exclude the jurisdiction of the Federal courts". For fuller discussion of Smith and related decisions, see p. 919, *infra*.

When the case reached the Supreme Court, it upheld dismissal of the federal court action and ruled that the state court action should be remanded. Justice Minton's majority opinion said that the railroad's filing in federal court was not a civil action but rather an action to review the state commission's assessment, and a federal district court "does not sit to review on appeal action taken administratively or judicially in a state proceeding". With respect to the removed action, the Court held that federal law determines who is a "defendant" entitled to remove under 28 U.S.C. § 1441, and here the railroad was plainly a plaintiff in the state action.

Justice Black, in dissent, argued that the action originally filed in federal court was a proper "civil action" under the diversity jurisdiction. Justice Frankfurter, in a separate dissent, expressed his agreement with Justice Black and argued that once the "judicial" phase of the proceedings had begun under state law, all the requirements for diversity jurisdiction had been fulfilled.

In Madisonville Traction Co. v. Saint Bernard Mining Co., 196 U.S. 239 (1905), on which Justice Frankfurter relied in his dissent in Stude, the traction company had filed an application in a Kentucky county court to condemn land belonging to the mining company. Pursuant to state law, commissioners awarded $100 as damages, and the county court issued an order to show cause why the commissioners' report should not be confirmed. State law gave either party a right of appeal to the state circuit court, and to a trial de novo, but the mining company instead removed the county court action to federal court, alleging diversity of citizenship. The Supreme Court upheld removal jurisdiction on the ground that the proceeding in the county court was "judicial" and that it could have been brought originally in a federal court. The Court said that a state could not confine the determination of the questions involved to its own judicial tribunals. The opinion recognized that the state might have established a nonjudicial process for determining the issue of condemnation, thus excluding concurrent federal diversity jurisdiction, but suggested that the state could not constitutionally do so with respect to the issue of compensation.

(3) The Significance of the Stude and Madisonville Decisions.

(a) Original and Removal Jurisdiction. Given the result in the Madisonville case, the state court appeal in Stude would evidently have been removable by Stude and the other defendants, as the Stude opinion assumes. But since removal jurisdiction depends on the existence of concurrent original jurisdiction, how could the Court in Stude have found jurisdiction to be lacking in the original federal court action? Was the railroad's failure in that action due only to a mistake of form in designating its complaint an "appeal"? Why can't a federal court review action taken administratively in a state proceeding?

(b) What Is a "Civil Action"? Federal courts have had difficulty over the years distinguishing between a "civil action", which may properly be brought in, or removed to, a federal court, and an administrative proceeding, which may not. Often the outcome will turn on a careful analysis both of the precise questions to be decided by the tribunal under the governing state law and of the character of the tribunal contemplated by that law.[2]

---

[2]   See, *e.g.*, Upshur County v. Rich, 135 U.S. 467, 472 (1890) (appeal to "county court" from an assessment for taxation is "not a suit within the meaning of the removal act"); Commissioners of Road Improvement Dist. No. 2 v. St. Louis S.W. Ry. Co., 257 U.S. 547 (1922) (proceeding

(c) Subsequent Supreme Court Decisions: Difficult Distinctions.

(i) In Horton v. Liberty Mut. Ins. Co., 367 U.S. 348 (1961), the Court held that an action to determine workers' compensation benefits under Texas law was properly brought in a federal court. The Court distinguished the Stude decision as follows: "Aside from many other relevant distinctions * * *, the Stude case is without weight here because, as shown by the Texas Supreme Court's interpretation of its compensation act: 'The suit to set aside an award of the board is in fact a suit, not an appeal * * *. * * * It is a trial *de novo* wholly without reference to what may have been done by the Board.'"

(ii) In City of Chicago v. International College of Surgeons, 522 U.S. 156 (1997), the Court held that the college's state court suit contesting local administrative action on federal constitutional grounds could be removed in its entirety to federal court, even though the complaint also contained state law claims, under Illinois' Administrative Review Act, requiring on-the-record review of the administrative proceedings. Justice O'Connor denied that Stude or other decisions suggested that federal district courts could never review state administrative action. Rather, insofar as these decisions "might be read to establish limits on the scope of federal jurisdiction [they] address only whether a cause of action for judicial review of a state administrative decision is within the district courts' original jurisdiction under the diversity statute". Given the existence of original jurisdiction over the federal claim in the case, the district court could exercise supplemental jurisdiction over related state law claims as to which original jurisdiction might be lacking. (For further discussion of the exercise of supplemental jurisdiction in this case, see p. 870, *infra*.)

(iii) A study of federal court challenges to state administrative action endorses the result in the Chicago v. ICS case but not the rationale, and is also critical of what it describes as the "murky" precedent in the Stude case itself. Woolhandler & Collins, *Judicial Federalism and the Administrative States*, 87 Calif.L.Rev. 613, 660–66 (1999). In the authors' view, there is good reason "to retain the historically grounded presumption that judicial review of agency action is an original judicial proceeding, even when review is deferential". But in light of the special state interests likely to inhere in provisions for *state court* judicial review of state administrative action, can a reasonable case be made for a federal statute excluding from the diversity jurisdiction (and from supplemental jurisdiction) claims seeking review of state administrative determinations? *Cf.* 28 U.S.C. § 1445(c), prohibiting removal of state court actions arising under the workers' compensation laws of that state.

NOTE ON THE EFFECT OF STATE DOOR-CLOSING AND "SCREENING" RULES

(1) Introduction. In Whitton and the cases discussed in the Note following that case, state laws authorized litigation in state tribunals. Different considerations arise when the doors of the state tribunal are closed, and the claim in federal court is that a federal doctrine, rule, or statute referring to state law (notably the Rules of Decision Act) requires that the doors of the

---

before "county court" to review assessment on railroad for benefits from projected improvements may be removed to a federal court).

federal court must also be closed. This problem has already been explored in cases like Guaranty Trust and Ragan (pp. 598, 607, *supra*), and is pursued further in this Note.

(2) A Point of Departure: The Szantay Case. In Szantay v. Beech Aircraft Corp., 349 F.2d 60 (4th Cir.1965), Szantay purchased a Beech airplane in Nebraska and flew it to Florida, and then to South Carolina, where it was serviced by Dixie Aircraft, a South Carolina corporation. On the next leg of the journey, the plane crashed in Tennessee, killing all the occupants. The plaintiffs (all citizens of Illinois) brought wrongful death actions in a South Carolina federal court against Dixie and Beech (a Delaware corporation with its principal place of business in Kansas), basing jurisdiction on diversity of citizenship. Beech moved to dismiss on the ground that a South Carolina "door-closing" statute deprived the state's courts of jurisdiction over a suit brought by a nonresident against a foreign corporation on a "foreign cause of action".

After an extensive analysis of Supreme Court precedent, the court of appeals upheld the district court's refusal to dismiss the action. The parties agreed that the South Carolina statute was "procedural" and was not "intimately bound up with" the substantive rights in the case, rights that allegedly arose (at least as against Beech) under the laws of another state. The court of appeals proceeded to consider whether important South Carolina policies would nevertheless be frustrated by disregard of the state statute and concluded that no such frustration would occur. On the other hand, militating against dismissal were significant federal interests, including the existence of the grant of diversity jurisdiction, the possibility that the state rule discriminated against out-of-state plaintiffs, and the virtues of joining Beech in the only court in which (the court assumed) Dixie was subject to personal jurisdiction. At the end of its opinion, the court noted that "[t]he superficiality of the South Carolina policy is demonstrated in this case by the fact that the plaintiffs could have gained access to a South Carolina court by simply qualifying as administrators under South Carolina law."

Suppose that a South Carolina state court, in discussing the state statute, had said: "The clear purpose of this provision is to encourage foreign corporations to do business in this state without fear of being subjected to lawsuits brought by nonresidents on foreign causes of action." On the Szantay facts, what effect, if any, should a federal court give to such a statement?[1]

(3) The Source of the Right Affected by the State Door-Closing Rule. Does it matter if, unlike in the Szantay case, a state door-closing rule operates on a right created by the laws of the forum? In David Lupton's Sons Co. v. Automobile Club, 225 U.S. 489 (1912), a pre-Erie decision, the Court resisted having a federal court in New York enforce a New York door-closing rule in a breach of contract action probably governed by New York law. The plaintiff was a Pennsylvania corporation, and a New York statute precluded a foreign corporation that had not qualified to do business in the state from bringing suit in the state. (The statute did not purport to render void the local contracts of such a corporation.) The Supreme Court held that the statute did not bar the federal action, saying: "The State could not prescribe

---

[1] On several occasions, notably in Piper Aircraft Co. v. Reyno, 454 U.S. 235, 248 n. 13 (1981), the Supreme Court has expressly left open the question whether "state or federal law of *forum non conveniens* applies in a diversity case."

the qualifications of suitors in the courts of the United States, and could not deprive of their privileges those who were entitled under the Constitution and laws of the United States to resort to the federal courts for the enforcement of a valid contract."

But in Angel v. Bullington, 330 U.S. 183 (1947), the Court relied on the intervening Erie decision as a reason to view decisions like David Lupton's Sons as "obsolete" and in turn to hold that a North Carolina door-closing statute did apply in a federal diversity action. The statute forbade deficiency judgments in favor of a mortgagee who had resorted to a foreclosure sale of the mortgaged property. A North Carolina state court had refused to award such a judgment to a Virginia plaintiff in connection with a sale of Virginia land. (The state court had said: "The statute operates upon the adjective law of the State, which pertains to the practice and procedure, or legal machinery by which the substantive law is made effective, and not upon the substantive law itself. It is a limitation of the jurisdiction of the courts of this State."). The plaintiff then tried to obtain a similar judgment in a diversity action in a North Carolina federal court. Although the matter was complicated by the question of the res judicata effect of the prior state action, the Supreme Court made it clear that by virtue of Erie, North Carolina's rule applied in a federal court sitting in that state. Distinguishing pre-Erie decisions like David Lupton's Sons, the Court said that Erie "drastically limited the power of federal district courts to entertain suits in diversity cases that could not be brought in the respective State courts or were barred by defenses controlling in the State courts".

Did Angel v. Bullington involve a significant state substantive policy, even though it was not articulated by the state court?

(4) State "Screening" Statutes and Other State Laws Mandating Resort to Alternative Dispute Resolution Techniques. One especially perplexing question has been the applicability in federal diversity actions of state statutes mandating resort to "screening" or "arbitration" panels. These statutes vary considerably in their terms. Some require resort as a condition to suit, while others constitute the panel as an arm of the court itself—akin to a master in the federal courts. Though one purpose of these panels is to relieve court congestion, another purpose—in medical malpractice cases, for example—is to cut back on large jury verdicts and resulting high insurance costs.

The question whether federal court plaintiffs can be required to comply with such state law mechanisms has grown in importance with the increasing efforts to channel disputes into alternative fora. Surely, these efforts have limits under the Erie doctrine, the Rules of Decision Act, and the boundaries of Congress' power under Article III, but those limits have yet to be clearly delineated.

An example of a malpractice screening statute is Mass.Gen.Laws ch. 231, § 60B, which provides for a panel consisting of a state judge, a physician, and an attorney. The panel is required to determine whether "the evidence presented if properly substantiated is sufficient to raise a legitimate question of liability appropriate for judicial inquiry * * *." A plaintiff wishing to sue for medical malpractice may do so even in the event of a negative determination, but the determination is admissible in evidence, and the plaintiff must post a bond (now $6000) for costs, including witness, expert, and attorney's fees, payable to defendant "if the plaintiff does not prevail in the final judgment."

In Feinstein v. Massachusetts General Hosp., 643 F.2d 880 (1st Cir.1981), the court ruled that a diversity action for malpractice filed in a Massachusetts federal court must be referred to the state Superior Court for a § 60B hearing. After concluding that the state law was designed to serve substantive policy objectives that would be undermined if the law were not observed in a federal diversity action, the court rejected the argument that the Whitton case, p. 626, *supra*, precluded the application of § 60B. Section 60B, the court said, does not attempt to confine medical malpractice actions to state courts: "Rather, [it] creates a screening mechanism through which every malpractice claim must proceed before being pursued in court. No ouster of federal jurisdiction results when, by reason of the policies expressed in Erie, a federal court requires that a state's rule barring an action from proceeding in its courts must be applied to bar the action from the federal court."

Most federal courts have followed Feinstein in requiring plaintiffs bringing medical malpractice claims to comply with varying state screening requirements. But in Hibbs v. Yashar, 522 F.Supp. 247 (D.R.I. 1981), a diversity action decided shortly after Feinstein, the federal court ruled that to require compliance with the state screening regime there at issue would run afoul of the Whitton principle. The case involved a Rhode Island law requiring that within 90 days of the filing of the answer in a malpractice case, the state court judge was to hold a preliminary hearing. The judge was given broad discretion to subpoena witness or documents to supplement the evidence presented by the parties, as well as to appoint experts. After the hearing, the judge was to determine whether the evidence (viewed favorably to the plaintiff) would suffice "to raise a legitimate question of liability appropriate for judicial inquiry or whether the plaintiff's case is merely an unfortunate medical result"; if the latter, the action must be dismissed with prejudice.

In Hibbs, the federal court said that if the state law were interpreted to require federal court plaintiffs to comply with the hearing requirement before a state court judge, it would conflict with the congressional policy embodied in the grant of diversity jurisdiction. (In so ruling the court relied on its own decision in an earlier case, which in turn had relied on Whitton's Administrator.) If, on the other hand, the state law were interpreted to require federal courts to conduct the prescribed hearing, it would contravene "the important federal interest in preserving the judge-jury relationship" (citing Byrd); the court added that "the federal interest in efficient administration of cases and in controlling the administrative burdens associated with implementation of the State's mechanism in the Federal Courts" justified disregarding the law.

CHAPTER VII

FEDERAL COMMON LAW

INTRODUCTION

No one today would seriously dispute that the body of federal law includes judge-made law. Most would further agree that such law involves the exercise of some degree of judicial policymaking discretion, rather than the straightforward application of federal statutory or constitutional enactments. Although varied in its nature, source, and scope, such judge-made law is frequently analyzed under the catch-all rubric of "federal common law."

Commentators have offered a range of definitions of federal common law.[1] This book uses the term loosely to refer to federal rules of decision whose content cannot be traced directly by traditional methods of interpretation to federal statutory or constitutional commands. While that definition captures the conventional understanding of federal common law as judge-made law, the fact is that common lawmaking often cannot be sharply distinguished from statutory or constitutional interpretation. As specific evidence of legislative purpose with respect to the issue at hand attenuates, much interpretation shades into judicial lawmaking. Similarly, because constitutional interpretation routinely entails value judgments of sorts, some matters that are conventionally viewed as "federal common law" may also be treated, in the alternative, as implications from a constitutional provision or from the structure and relationship among clusters of such provisions. Hence, questions about the legitimacy of federal common lawmaking may overlap with those concerning the legitimacy of particular interpretive techniques.

The broad topic of federal common law has a miscellaneous quality, in view of the wide variety of subject matters in which power to formulate such law has been or might be recognized. As in many areas of law, moreover, the doctrine here gives the distinct impression of path dependence. Rather than

---

[1]   Professor Field's "broad" definition—"any rule of federal law created by a court * * * when the substance of that rule is not clearly suggested by federal enactments—constitutional or congressional"—includes a good deal of what most would call statutory or constitutional interpretation. Field, *Sources of Law: The Scope of Federal Common Law*, 99 Harv.L.Rev. 881, 890 (1986) (italics omitted). See also Merrill, *The Common Law Powers of Federal Courts*, 52 U.Chi.L.Rev. 1, 5 (1985) (defining federal common law as "*any* federal rule of decision that is not mandated on the face of some authoritative federal text—whether or not that rule can be described as the product of 'interpretation' "). By contrast, Professor Hill defines federal common lawmaking more narrowly, implicitly distinguishing it from interpretation: While recognizing that the idea of "construing" a text is strained when courts interpret general standards like "restraint of trade" in the Sherman Act or determine what remedies should be provided in implementing a statutory program, he would include these and similar cases within the reach of interpretation because "the text provides at least a sense of direction in which the courts should go". See Hill, *The Law-Making Power of the Federal Courts: Constitutional Preemption*, 67 Colum.L.Rev. 1024, 1026 (1967).

attempting an exhaustive survey, this Chapter focuses on some of the major areas of judicial lawmaking in actions in the federal district courts.[2]

The Chapter draws a rough organizational distinction between common lawmaking that (i) defines primary legal obligations (Section 1) and (ii) shapes remedies to enforce primary obligations (Section 2). The boundary, however, is difficult to maintain, as the nature of the remedy may have much to do with determining the significance and, at least as a practical matter, the very existence of the right. Indeed, some questions—like capacity to sue or the availability of a right of contribution—are hard to place on either side of the divide. Further, some developments are noted in passing whenever they seem most relevant, even at the risk of straining the distinction.

---

1. DEFINING PRIMARY OBLIGATIONS

A. CRIMINAL PROSECUTIONS

INTRODUCTORY NOTE

The discussion of federal common law begins with criminal prosecutions. To the modern ear, it sounds unnatural to hear that federal courts could define federal crimes and their elements. Our constitutional culture today regards that function as a legislative one. Nothing in the Constitution, however, foreordained that outcome. Neither the constitutional text nor the common law tradition that framed its meaning nor the early history of the Republic precluded the recognition of a federal common law of crimes. Rather, as discussed below, the historical practice up to the beginning of the early nineteenth century cut decidedly in favor of such common law power. The case below, which forswears federal judicial power to define crimes, represents the culmination of a lengthy political and legal struggle, in the early days of the Republic, that brought into sharper focus the separation of powers and federalism implications of federal common lawmaking.

United States v. Hudson & Goodwin
11 U.S. (7 Cranch) 32, 3 L.Ed. 259 (1812).
On Certificate from the United States Circuit Court for the District of Connecticut.

[The defendants were indicted for criminal libel for having stated, in the *Connecticut Currant* of May 7, 1806, that the President and Congress of the United States had secretly voted $2,000,000 as a present to

---

[2]   Federal common law is also formulated and applied in actions originating in the state courts. See, *e.g.*, Reconstruction Fin. Corp. v. Beaver County, p. 678, *infra*; Farmers Educ. & Co-op. Union v. WDAY, Inc., p. 676, *infra;* Ward v. Love County, p. 752, *infra.* See also Bellia, *State Courts and the Making of Federal Common Law*, 153 U.Pa.L.Rev. 825 (2005); Meltzer, *State Court Forfeitures of Federal Rights*, 99 Harv.L.Rev. 1128 (1986).

Bonaparte, for leave to make a treaty with Spain. The question whether the federal circuit court has a common law jurisdiction in cases of criminal libel divided that court's judges, who certified that question to the Supreme Court.]

■ * * * [T]he following opinion was delivered * * * by JOHNSON, J.

The only question which this case presents is, whether the Circuit Courts of the United States can exercise a common law jurisdiction in criminal cases. We state it thus broadly because a decision on a case of libel will apply to every case in which jurisdiction is not vested in those Courts by statute.

Although this question is brought up now for the first time to be decided by this Court, we consider it as having been long since settled in public opinion. In no other case for many years has this jurisdiction been asserted; and the general acquiescence of legal men shews the prevalence of opinion in favor of the negative of the proposition.

The course of reasoning which leads to this conclusion is simple, obvious, and admits of but little illustration. The powers of the general Government are made up of concessions from the several states— whatever is not expressly given to the former, the latter expressly reserve. The judicial power of the United States is a constituent part of those concessions * * *. * * * [Only the Supreme Court] possesses jurisdiction derived immediately from the constitution, and of which the legislative power cannot deprive it. All other Courts created by the general Government possess no jurisdiction but what is given them by the power that creates them, and can be vested with none but what the power ceded to the general Government will authorize them to confer.

It is not necessary to inquire, whether the general Government * * * possesses the power of conferring on its Courts a jurisdiction in cases similar to the present; it is enough that such jurisdiction has not been conferred by any legislative act, if it does not result to those Courts as a consequence of their creation.

And such is the opinion of the majority of this Court: For, the power which congress possess to create Courts of inferior jurisdiction, necessarily implies the power to limit the jurisdiction of those Courts to particular objects; and when a Court is created, and its operations confined to certain specific objects, with what propriety can it assume to itself a jurisdiction—much more extended—in its nature very indefinite—applicable to a great variety of subjects—varying in every state in the Union—and with regard to which there exists no definite criterion of distribution between the district and Circuit Courts of the same district?

The only ground on which it has ever been contended that this jurisdiction could be maintained is, that, upon the formation of any political body, an implied power to preserve its own existence and promote the end and object of its creation, necessarily results to it. But, without examining how far this consideration is applicable to the peculiar character of our constitution, it may be remarked that it is a principle by no means peculiar to the common law. It is coeval, probably, with the first formation of a limited Government; belongs to a system of universal law, and may as well support the assumption of many other powers as those more peculiarly acknowledged by the common law of England.

But if admitted as applicable to the state of things in this country, the consequence would not result from it which is here contended for. If it may communicate certain implied powers to the general Government, it would not follow that the Courts of that Government are vested with jurisdiction over any particular act done by an individual, in supposed violation of the peace and dignity of the sovereign power. The legislative authority of the Union must first make an act a crime, affix a punishment to it, and declare the Court that shall have jurisdiction of the offence.

Certain implied powers must necessarily result to our Courts of justice from the nature of their institution. But jurisdiction of crimes against the state is not among those powers. To fine for contempt—imprison for contumacy—enforce the observance of order, & c. are powers which cannot be dispensed with in a Court, because they are necessary to the exercise of all others: and so far our Courts no doubt possess powers not immediately derived from statute; but all exercise of criminal jurisdiction in common law cases we are of opinion is not within their implied powers.

NOTE ON FEDERAL COMMON LAW CRIMES

(1) Hudson and the Early Debate over Federal Common Law. In rejecting federal judicial power to recognize common law crimes, Hudson treated the question "as having been long since settled in public opinion" and by "the general acquiescence of legal men".[1] This oblique statement almost surely refers to the political and ultimately legal resolution of a wide-ranging debate between Federalists and Jeffersonians over federal common law in the early years of the Republic. To oversimplify, prominent Federalists invoked a common law of the United States to advance their commitment to national power, whereas Jeffersonians opposed it in furtherance of their belief in limited national government and robust state sovereignty. The federal common law of crimes provided the platform for the broader debate between the two groups over the existence of a common law of the United States, enforceable by the federal courts. See Jay, *Origins of Federal Common Law: Part One*, 133 U.Pa.L.Rev. 1003 (1985); Jay, *Origins of Federal Common Law: Part Two*, 133 U.Pa.L.Rev. 1231, 1323 (1985).

Although Hudson represented the Supreme Court's first pronouncement on the subject, its holding cut against the almost uniform view of prior circuit court precedents.[2] See, *e.g.*, Williams' Case, 29 F.Cas.

---

[1] Section 11 of the Judiciary Act of 1789 granted federal courts "exclusive cognizance of all crimes and offenses cognizable under the authority of the United States". 1 Stat. 73, 79. Charles Warren concluded that Hudson might have been decided differently had the Court reviewed a manuscript of a draft bill that gave the district courts jurisdiction over crimes and offenses "cognizable under the authority of the United States *and defined by the laws of the same*" (emphasis added). He suggested that Congress, in eliminating the italicized words, "did not intend to limit criminal jurisdiction to crimes specifically defined by it." Warren, *New Light on the History of the Federal Judiciary Act of 1789*, 37 Harv.L.Rev. 49, 73 (1923). How much can one tell from that kind of legislative history, especially if the record does not disclose the reason for the change?

[2] But see Preyer, *Jurisdiction to Punish: Federal Authority, Federalism and the Common Law of Crimes in the Early Republic*, 4 L. & Hist.Rev. 223 (1986) (arguing that even in the early

1330 (C.C.D.Conn. 1799) (No. 17,708) (upholding conviction of expatriate for hostilities against the United States); United States v. Ravara, 27 F.Cas. 714 (C.C.D.Pa. 1794) (No. 16,122a) (upholding common law indictment of foreign consul for sending letters seeking to extort money); Henfield's Case, 11 F.Cas. 1099 (C.C.D.Pa. 1793) (17,708) (grand jury charge based on common law crime of violating neutrality); United States v. Smith, 27 F.Cas. 1147 (C.C.D.Mass. 1792) (No. 16,323) (conviction for counterfeiting United States bank notes); see generally Goebel, History of the Supreme Court of the United States: Antecedents and Beginnings to 1801, at 623ff (1971). By the turn of the nineteenth century, all but one of the Justices had approved the practice while riding circuit. See Note, 101 Yale L.J. 919, 920 (1992). Indeed, among the early Federalist Justices, only Justice Chase denied the legitimacy of federal common law crimes. See United States v. Worrall, 28 F. Cas. 774, 779 (C.C.D.Pa. 1798) (16,766), in which he argued that "the United States did not bring [the common law] with them from England; [that] the Constitution does not create it; and [that] no act of Congress has assumed it."

The federal judiciary's enforcement of a common law of crimes became a source of intense political controversy between the Jeffersonians and Federalists when the Federalist-dominated Congress passed the Alien and Sedition Acts, 1 Stat. 596 (1798). The issue arose in an odd way. In response to Jeffersonian opposition to the Sedition Act (which codified the crime of seditious libel), Federalist supporters argued that federal courts already possessed the authority to punish seditious libel as common law crime, and that the Act imposed various safeguards absent from the common law, including the requirement of intent and the availability of truth as a defense. Federalists claimed that common law decisionmaking was a standard method of exercising judicial power, familiar to those who adopted the Constitution, and prevalent in every state. They added that given the impossibility of codifying every wrong, a federal common law of crimes was needed to protect the lawful operations of the federal government from wrongdoing. Jeffersonians denied the possibility of identifying *a* body of common law for the nation because each state had modified the common law of England by adapting it to its own circumstances. More fundamentally, Jeffersonians argued that because the common law was a complete system of law, recognition of a common law of the United States would circumvent the limitations on federal power embodied in Article I of the Constitution. See Jay, *supra*, at 1077–83 (Part I) (summarizing the congressional debates about federal common law).

When the Alien and Sedition Acts were passed over Jeffersonian objections, federal common law became a major point of political contention outside Congress. The Jeffersonian opposition to federal common law crimes was crystallized in a report prepared by Madison for the Virginia legislature in connection with (its half of) the Virginia and Kentucky Resolutions, both of which were passed to protest the asserted unconstitutionality of the Alien and Sedition Acts. See Jay, *supra*, at 1089–91 (Part I). First, Madison contended that if the Constitution itself adopted the common law, "it follows that no part can be altered by the legislature", thereby undermining the sovereignty of the people. Second, if Congress could alter or displace federal common law, Madison argued that it would destroy "the limitations marked

years of the Republic, evidence of judicial acceptance of the common law of crimes was inconclusive, and non-statutory criminal charges were relatively rare).

out in the Constitution", because "some branch or other of the common law" extends to "every object of legislation". Third, Madison added that "whether the common law be admitted as of legal or constitutional obligation, it would confer on the judicial department a discretion little short of a legislative power", thus contravening the separation of powers. Madison's Report on the Virginia Resolutions, reprinted in 4 The Debates in the Several State Conventions on the Adoption of the Federal Constitution 565–66 (Elliot ed. 1888).

Many historians believe that a backlash against federal common law crimes helped to elect Jefferson in 1800. See, *e.g.*, 1 Warren, The Supreme Court in United States History 158–64 (1922); Wilmarth, *Elusive Foundation: John Marshall, James Wilson, and the Problem of Reconciling Popular Sovereignty and Natural Law Jurisprudence in the New Federal Republic*, 72 Geo.Wash.L.Rev. 113, 187–88 (2003). Although the prosecution of federal common law crimes did not entirely cease with Jefferson's election, several prominent decisions by the Administration to forgo such prosecutions confirmed its disapproval of such practice. See Preyer, note 2, *supra*, at 239–41. Presumably, Justice Johnson's reference to "public opinion" and "the general acquiescence of legal men" referred to the Jeffersonian triumph and the apparent ratification of the Jeffersonian position on federal common law. See Jay, *supra*, at 1017–18 (Part I). See also Casto, The Supreme Court in the Early Republic: The Chief Justiceships of John Jay and Oliver Ellsworth 162 (1995).

Even if one assumes that early practical interpretations of the Constitution can sometimes properly settle the meaning of ambiguous constitutional terms, see, *e.g.*, Stuart v. Laird, 5 U.S. (1 Cranch) 299, 309 (1803), how much, if anything, did Hudson settle about the common law authority of federal courts? Although Jeffersonians framed their critique of federal common law crimes broadly enough to sweep in the exercise of all common law powers by federal courts, Hudson did not produce that result. See Jay, *supra*, at 1323 (Part II) (noting that a "survey of jurisdictional theory from the Hudson period" shows a general awareness that "federal courts had what we would term significant common-law powers"). To be sure, in rejecting a common law copyright claim, the Court in Wheaton v. Peters, 33 U.S. (8 Pet.) 591, 658 (1834), broadly declared that "there can be no common law of the United States" and that "[t]he common law could be made a part of our federal system, only by legislative adoption." But the Court in that era also endorsed the application of "general principles and doctrines of commercial jurisprudence", rather than state or federal law, to resolve a contract dispute brought within the diversity jurisdiction. Swift v. Tyson, 41 U.S. (16 Pet.) 1, 18–19 (1842). The Court also recognized that the exercise of jurisdiction under the Admiralty Clause involves reliance on the "law of nations"—a series of principles applied by the common consent and practice of sovereigns that included norms of admiralty and maritime law. See American Ins. Co. v. Canter, 26 U.S. (1 Pet.) 511, 545–46 (1828). Insofar as those examples presupposed the existence of "general law" practices that did not emanate from any given sovereign, do they have much bearing on the dispute between the Federalists and the Jeffersonians over the "common law of the United States"? What is their relevance after Erie's rejection of "general law"? See pp. 688–689, 695, *infra*.

(2) The Coolidge Decision. Was Hudson correct in asserting that the legal community had come to a consensus against federal common law crimes?

Four years later, in United States v. Coolidge, 14 U.S. (1 Wheat.) 415 (1816), the Court followed Hudson, though not without some expression of doubt. Coolidge and a codefendant were indicted in the circuit court for having forcibly rescued a vessel that had been captured as a prize. The indictment charged the offense as one committed upon the high seas. In his opinion ("riding circuit") upholding the indictment, Justice Story expressed the view that "all offences against the sovereignty, the public rights, the public justice, the public peace, the public trade and the public police of the United States, are crimes and offences against the United States." Accordingly, he concluded that traditional "public offenses" at common law, such as "treasons, and conspiracies to commit treason, embezzlement of the public records, bribery and resistance of the judicial process, riots and misdemeanors on the high seas, frauds and obstructions of the public laws of trade, and robbery and embezzlement of the mail of the United States, would be offences against the United States."

In the Supreme Court, the Attorney General declined to argue the case, treating Hudson as having settled the matter. Several Justices, however, indicated a willingness at least to reconsider Hudson. Ultimately, the Court granted a "certificate for the defendant" requiring dismissal of the indictment. Justice Johnson delivered the following opinion for the Court: "Upon the question now before the court a difference of opinion has existed, and still exists, among the members of the court. We should, therefore, have been willing to have heard the question discussed upon solemn argument. But the attorney-general has declined to argue the cause; and no counsel appears for the defendant. Under these circumstances the court would not choose to review their former decision in the case of the United States v. Hudson and Goodwin, or draw it into doubt."

(3) Contemporary Common Lawmaking in Criminal Cases. Although nonstatutory prosecutions ended with Coolidge, the federal courts continue to make law in criminal cases.

(a) Federal courts have continued to enforce law by use of the contempt power—a role the Court approved in the last paragraph of the Hudson opinion—and to use a variety of common law techniques, forms, and writs in the enforcement of congressionally defined crimes.

(b) The Supreme Court has recognized that federal courts may exercise a "supervisory power to formulate and apply proper standards for enforcement of the criminal law in the federal courts". That statement is from Marshall v. United States, 360 U.S. 310, 313 (1959), in which the Court, invoking this "supervisory power", set aside a jury verdict when the jurors had been exposed to potentially prejudicial publicity. Is judicial lawmaking with respect to methods of enforcement and remediation, as distinguished from the definition of legal rights and duties, easier to defend against a charge that it usurps the legislative prerogative?[3]

Recent Supreme Court decisions have narrowed the scope of the supervisory power. For example, in United States v. Williams, 504 U.S. 36 (1992), the Court ruled that the supervisory power did not extend to prescribing standards of prosecutorial conduct before a federal grand jury; the opinion distinguished, however, (i) the power of federal courts to fashion doctrines that enforce rules of conduct prescribed by the Constitution,

---

[3]   See generally Levy, *Federal Common Law of Crimes*, 4 Encyclopedia of the American Constitution 693 (1986).

statutes, or court rules, and (ii) their power with respect to rules governing the conduct of litigants before the courts themselves.

(c) In the face of Congress' failure, in general, to prescribe the scope or even the existence of defenses (*e.g.*, self-defense or duress) to federal crimes, federal courts have freely crafted such defenses. See, *e.g.*, Brown v. United States, 256 U.S. 335 (1921) (self-defense); but *cf.* United States v. Oakland Cannabis Buyers' Cooperative, 532 U.S. 483, 490 (2001) (stating in dictum that it "is an open question whether courts ever have *authority* to recognize a necessity defense not provided by statute") (emphasis added). Why are federal courts competent to recognize defenses but not new offenses? Judge Easterbrook has argued that Congress passes criminal statutes in the light of well-established common law norms of defense. Easterbrook, *The Case of the Speluncean Explorers: Revisited*, 112 Harv.L.Rev. 1913, 1914 (1999). According to Easterbrook, because familiar norms of "justification" have been applied to criminal statutes for "thousands of years," they simply form part of the legislators' background social and linguistic assumptions, in much the same way that rules of "grammar or diction" do. Given the varied formulations—and, frequently, also the vagueness—of "established" defenses, does Easterbrook's theory adequately answer the question of judicial authority?

(d) Finally, consider the thesis of Professor Kahan in *Lenity and Federal Common Law Crimes*, 1994 Sup.Ct.Rev. 345, 347–48, "that Congress may *delegate* criminal lawmaking power to the courts"; "that federal criminal law, no less than other statutory domains, is dominated by judge-made law crafted to fill the interstices of open-textured statutory provisions"; and that "a regime of delegated criminal lawmaking is much more * * * effective than one in which Congress is obliged to make criminal law without judicial assistance". One illustration Kahan offers is the Crimes Act of 1790, 1 Stat. 112, whose text "merely identified" without defining various offenses on the high seas and in federal enclaves. He also mentions a number of modern statutes; for example, the offense of mail fraud, 18 U.S.C. § 1341, has been interpreted to encompass many forms of misconduct not generally recognized as fraud at common law—including public corruption and misappropriation of confidential information.

Is a statute like § 1341 fairly viewed as an implicit delegation? Can the interpretation of statutory provisions—especially very open-textured ones—be distinguished from common lawmaking? The last two questions are explored at greater length in the next Subsection, which addresses judicial lawmaking in civil actions. See especially pp. 645–656, *infra*. Consider whether, notwithstanding Kahan's argument, Hudson's and Coolidge's limits on judicial definition of primary duties in criminal cases are stricter than the parallel limits in civil cases—and if so, whether the difference in approach is justified.

———————

B. Civil Actions

Introductory Note

Recall that Erie R. Co. v. Tompkins, p. 584, *supra,* announced that "[t]here is no federal general common law." It did not, however, hold that there is no federal common law at all. Rather, Erie held that there was no federal *general* common law of the sort applied in Swift v. Tyson, p. 575. Erie's holding spoke only to the question of what law applies in diversity cases. It said nothing about the law to be applied to fill in the gaps inevitably left in any complex federal statutory scheme. Not long after Erie, in a case involving the financial rights and responsibilities created by a federal statutory program, the Court had occasion to address whether such gap-filling calls for the application of state law or, instead, allows the federal judiciary to craft federal rules of decision to supply the omission. Specifically, the case that follows resolved that question by determining what law governs the rights and obligations of the United States in disputes involving federal paychecks.

Clearfield Trust Co. v. United States

318 U.S. 363, 63 S.Ct. 573, 87 L.Ed. 838 (1943).
Certiorari to the Circuit Court of Appeals for the Third Circuit.

■ Mr. Justice Douglas delivered the opinion of the Court.

On April 28, 1936, a check was drawn on the Treasurer of the United States through the Federal Reserve Bank of Philadelphia to the order of Clair A. Barner in the amount of $24.20 * * *[,] for services rendered by Barner to the Works Progress Administration. The check was placed in the mail addressed to Barner * * * [, who] never received the check. Some unknown person obtained it in a mysterious manner and presented it to the J.C. Penney Co. store in Clearfield, Pa., representing that he was the payee and identifying himself to the satisfaction of the employees of J.C. Penney Co. He endorsed the check in the name of Barner and transferred it to J.C. Penney Co. in exchange for cash and merchandise. * * * J.C. Penney Co. endorsed the check over to the Clearfield Trust Co. which accepted it as agent for the purpose of collection and endorsed it as follows: "Pay to the order of Federal Reserve Bank of Philadelphia, Prior Endorsements Guaranteed."[1] Clearfield Trust Co. collected the check from the United States through the Federal Reserve Bank of Philadelphia and paid the full amount thereof to J.C. Penney Co. Neither the Clearfield Trust Co. nor J.C. Penney Co. had any knowledge or suspicion of the forgery. Each acted in good faith. On or before May 10, 1936, Barner advised the timekeeper and the foreman of the W.P.A. project on which he was employed that he had not received the check in question. This information was duly communicated to other agents of the United States and on November 30, 1936, Barner executed an affidavit

---

[1] Guarantee of all prior endorsements on presentment for payment of such a check to Federal Reserve banks or member bank depositories is required by Treasury Regulations.

alleging that the endorsement of his name on the check was a forgery. No notice was given the Clearfield Trust Co. or J.C. Penney Co. of the forgery until January 12, 1937, at which time the Clearfield Trust Co. was notified. The first notice received by Clearfield Trust Co. that the United States was asking reimbursement was on August 31, 1937.

This suit was instituted in 1939 by the United States against the Clearfield Trust Co. * * *. The cause of action was based on the express guaranty of prior endorsements made by the Clearfield Trust Co. J.C. Penney Co. intervened as a defendant. * * * The District Court held that the rights of the parties were to be determined by the law of Pennsylvania and that since the United States unreasonably delayed in giving notice of the forgery to the Clearfield Trust Co., it was barred from recovery under the rule of Market Street Title & Trust Co. v. Chelten T. Co., 296 Pa. 230, 145 A. 848. It accordingly dismissed the complaint. * * * [T]he Circuit Court of Appeals reversed. * * *

We agree with the Circuit Court of Appeals that the rule of Erie R. Co. v. Tompkins, 304 U.S. 64, does not apply to this action. The rights and duties of the United States on commercial paper which it issues are governed by federal rather than local law. When the United States disburses its funds or pays its debts, it is exercising a constitutional function or power. This check was issued for services performed under the Federal Emergency Relief Act of 1935. The authority to issue the check had its origin in the Constitution and the statutes of the United States and was in no way dependent on the laws of Pennsylvania or of any other state. The duties imposed upon the United States and the rights acquired by it as a result of the issuance find their roots in the same federal sources.[2] In absence of an applicable Act of Congress it is for the federal courts to fashion the governing rule of law according to their own standards. * * *

In our choice of the applicable federal rule we have occasionally selected state law. But reasons which may make state law at times the appropriate federal rule are singularly inappropriate here. The issuance of commercial paper by the United States is on a vast scale and transactions in that paper from issuance to payment will commonly occur in several states. The application of state law, even without the conflict of laws rules of the forum, would subject the rights and duties of the United States to exceptional uncertainty. It would lead to great diversity in results by making identical transactions subject to the vagaries of the laws of the several states. The desirability of a uniform rule is plain. And while the federal law merchant developed for about a century under the regime of Swift v. Tyson, 16 Pet. 1, represented general commercial law rather than a choice of a federal rule designed to protect a federal right, it nevertheless stands as a convenient source of reference for fashioning federal rules applicable to these federal questions.

United States v. National Exchange Bank, 214 U.S. 302, falls in that category. The Court held that the United States could recover as drawee from one who presented for payment a pension check on which the name

---

[2] Various Treasury Regulations govern the payment and endorsement of government checks and warrants and the reimbursement of the Treasurer of the United States by Federal Reserve banks and member bank depositories on payment of checks or warrants bearing a forged endorsement. Forgery of the check was an offense against the United States. Criminal Code § 148, 18 U.S.C. § 262.

of the payee had been forged, in spite of a protracted delay on the part of the United States in giving notice of the forgery. * * *

The National Exchange Bank case went no further than to hold that prompt notice of the discovery of the forgery was not a condition precedent to suit. It did not reach the question whether lack of prompt notice might be a defense. We think it may. If it is shown that the drawee on learning of the forgery did not give prompt notice of it and that damage resulted, recovery by the drawee is barred. [Citing lower federal court decisions.] The fact that the drawee is the United States and the laches those of its employees are not material. The United States as drawee of commercial paper stands in no different light than any other drawee. As stated in United States v. National Exchange Bank, 270 U.S. 527, 534, "The United States does business on business terms." It is not excepted from the general rules governing the rights and duties of drawees "by the largeness of its dealings and its having to employ agents to do what if done by a principal in person would leave no room for doubt." Id. [at 535]. But the damage occasioned by the delay must be established and not left to conjecture. Cases such as Market St. Title & Trust Co. v. Chelten Trust Co., *supra*, place the burden on the drawee of giving prompt notice of the forgery—injury to the defendant being presumed by the mere fact of delay. But we do not think that he who accepts a forged signature of a payee deserves that preferred treatment. It is his neglect or error in accepting the forger's signature which occasions the loss. He should be allowed to shift that loss to the drawee only on a clear showing that the drawee's delay in notifying him of the forgery caused him damage. No such damage has been shown by Clearfield Trust Co. who so far as appears can still recover from J.C. Penney Co. The only showing on the part of the latter is contained in the stipulation to the effect that if a check cashed for a customer is returned unpaid or for reclamation a short time after the date on which it is cashed, the employees can often locate the person who cashed it. It is further stipulated that when J.C. Penney Co. was notified of the forgery in the present case none of its employees was able to remember anything about the transaction or check in question. The inference is that the more prompt the notice the more likely the detection of the forger. But that falls short of a showing that the delay caused a manifest loss. It is but another way of saying that mere delay is enough.

Affirmed.

■ [JUSTICES MURPHY and RUTLEDGE did not participate.]

NOTE ON THE EXISTENCE, SOURCES, AND SCOPE OF FEDERAL COMMON LAW

(1) Erie and the "New" Federal Common Law. As the Brief for the United States in Clearfield points out, in cases involving the proprietary interests of the government prior to Erie, the choice between federal and state law rarely presented itself: "Under the regime of Swift v. Tyson, since the law of commercial contracts and negotiable instruments was of course regarded as 'general law', the courts found it unnecessary to consider separately the applicability of state decisional law to contracts or negotiable instruments involving the United States. The law merchant as interpreted by the federal courts was as a rule applied without discussion. Prior to Erie R. Co. v. Tompkins, an issue in regard to governing law insofar as the United States was concerned could have arisen only where the state law took the form of a state statute or state decisions interpreting such statutes. Such an issue seems to have been rarely presented and cannot be said to have been clearly considered or determined." Once Erie denied the existence of general law unattached to any sovereign, it became necessary to determine whether—and under what criteria—federal or state law would apply in such cases.

In a famous article—entitled, *In Praise of Erie—And of the New Federal Common Law*, 39 N.Y.U.L.Rev. 383, 405, 421–22 (1964)—Judge Henry Friendly offered the following defense of the Court's choice to adopt federal common law in cases such as Clearfield: "[B]y banishing the spurious uniformity of Swift v. Tyson—what Mr. Justice Frankfurter was to call 'the attractive vision of a uniform body of federal law' but a vision only—and by leaving to the states what ought to be left to them, Erie led to the emergence of a federal decisional law in areas of national concern that is truly uniform because, under the Supremacy Clause, it is binding in every forum, and therefore is predictable and useful as its predecessor, more general in subject matter but limited to the federal courts, was not. The clarion yet careful pronouncement of Erie, 'There is no federal general common law,' opened the way to what, for want of a better term, we may call specialized federal common law. * * *

"So, as it seems to me, the Supreme Court, in the years since Erie, has been forging a new centripetal tool incalculably useful to our federal system. It has employed a variety of techniques—spontaneous generation as in the cases of government contracts or interstate controversies, implication of a private federal cause of action from a statute providing other sanctions, construing a jurisdictional grant as a command to fashion federal law, and the normal judicial filling of statutory interstices. * * *

"The complementary concepts—that federal courts must follow state decisions on matters of substantive law appropriately cognizable by the states whereas state courts must follow federal decisions on subjects within national legislative power where Congress has so directed or the basic scheme of the Constitution demands—seem so beautifully simple, and so simply beautiful, that we must wonder why a century and a half was needed to discover them, and must wonder even more why anyone should want to shy away once the discovery was made."

(2) Theories of Federal Common Law: A Road Map. The remainder of this Note will consider certain prominent justifications for and critiques of the new federal common law typified by Clearfield. At least two major lines of justification have emerged. The first and broadest position—advanced in commentary but never adopted by the Court—states that federal courts possess general authority to craft common law whenever federal interests are at stake. Critics argue that the broad position cannot be squared with constitutional principles of federalism and separation of powers or with statutory norms derived from the Rules of Decision Act, as discussed in Erie. A second justification treats the new federal common law as legitimate when traceable, in some degree, to a source of federal authority derived from a statute or the Constitution. Those who subscribe to the latter position differ largely over the question of how clearly the relevant source of federal law must authorize the derivation of the common law norm by federal courts.

(One version of the second position, which will be discussed in greater detail in conjunction with admiralty, interstate disputes, and foreign relations, presupposes that the Constitution establishes certain uniquely federal enclaves, in which federal courts possess common lawmaking powers to the exclusion of the states.)

(3) The Broad Position. The broad position on the new federal common law is most closely associated with Professor Weinberg, who argues that "there are no fundamental constraints on the fashioning of rules of decision" by federal courts. For her, just as state courts have general lawmaking power in areas of state concern such as torts or contracts, federal courts have similar power in areas in which the Constitution authorizes federal legislative or executive action. As long as federal courts act "within their constitutional and statutory jurisdiction", she argues, the source of judicial lawmaking power "is the existence of a legitimate national governmental interest". Finally, aligning herself with the legal realist view that statutory interpretation inevitably involves judicial policymaking, Professor Weinberg finds it artificial to differentiate statutory interpretation, which all agree is an inherent judicial function, from "pure" federal common lawmaking, which, she says, the Court has rejected. See Weinberg, *Federal Common Law*, 83 Nw.U.L.Rev. 805 (1989).

(4) Objections to the Broad Position. Few decisions or commentators support the broad view. Commentators have advanced three major arguments against that position, two constitutional and one statutory.

(a) The first objection rests on the premise that policy decisions generally should be made by politically accountable branches of government. See, *e.g.*, Redish, The Federal Courts in the Political Order 29–46 (1991); Merrill, *The Common Law Powers of Federal Courts*, 52 U.Chi.L.Rev. 1 (1985). As the Court has said, "the federal lawmaking power is vested in the legislative, not the judicial, branch of government". Northwest Airlines v. Transport Workers Union, 451 U.S. 77, 95 (1981). But if common law judges traditionally exercised broad lawmaking authority before and after 1789, why shouldn't Article III's grant of judicial power be interpreted as giving federal judges similar latitude?[1] The separation-of-powers objection also seems to presuppose that federal common lawmaking *dis*serves legislative purposes. Does that premise necessarily follow if the federal courts, as in Clearfield, fill in the details of a statutory scheme in a way that furthers the legislative design by supplying a busy legislature's apparent omission? Compare Paragraph (7)(a), *infra*.

(b) A second objection sounds in federalism. Because the national government now has something approaching plenary legislative power by virtue of the post–New Deal understanding of the Commerce Power, the objection no longer centers on fears that federal common law will reach beyond the federal government's enumerated powers—a concern that strongly animated the Jeffersonians in the debate over federal common law crimes. See pp. 639–640, *supra*. Rather, the modern federalism objection emphasizes the ways in which the cumbersome lawmaking procedures prescribed by the Constitution—for example, bicameral enactment and either presidential assent or a legislative supermajority—protect state interests. By constitutional design, congressional action is restrained by the

---

[1] Much (though not all) of the post-1789 state common lawmaking was authorized by state "reception" statutes, for which there is no federal analogue. See Kramer, *The Lawmaking Power of the Federal Courts*, 12 Pace L.Rev. 263, 280–81 (1992).

"political safeguards of federalism"—the responsiveness of national legislators to the interests of the states. See Wechsler, *The Political Safeguards of Federalism: The Role of the States in the Composition and Selection of the National Government*, 54 Colum.L.Rev. 543 (1954). Lawmaking by federal courts, by contrast, is free of these important restraints.[2]

Supremacy Cl.

In an elaboration of the federalism position, Clark, *Separation of Powers as a Safeguard of Federalism*, 79 Tex.L.Rev. 1321 (2001), contends that the Supremacy Clause, U.S. Const. Art. VI, implicitly limits federal lawmaking to three carefully chosen procedural methods.[3] In identifying "the supreme Law of the Land", the Supremacy Clause specifies "[t]his Constitution, and the Laws * * * made in Pursuance thereof; and all Treaties made, or which shall be made, under the Authority of the United States." In turn, the constitutionally prescribed processes for adopting or amending the "Constitution" (Articles VII and V), enacting "a Law" (Article I, § 7), and making "Treaties" (Article II, § 2, cl. 2) all condition lawmaking on the assent of a majority or supermajority of the Senate, a supermajority of the states, or both. Noting that the Philadelphia Convention adopted the Supremacy Clause the day after the delegates agreed to the Great Compromise giving states equal representation in the Senate, Clark maintains that the Supremacy Clause was meant to prescribe an exclusive, state-protective set of preemptive lawmaking procedures.[4]

How convincing is the federalism position and the related Supremacy Clause thesis? One line of criticism contests the textual basis for the Supremacy Clause thesis, arguing that it is unlikely that the term "Laws" in the previously quoted passage of the Supremacy Clause refers only to *enacted* federal law rather than federal common law. On that account, if "Laws" is given the narrower reading, the clause may produce the anomalous result of preempting only state statute law, since it makes federal law supreme, "any Thing in the Constitution or *Laws* of any State to the Contrary notwithstanding." See, *e.g.*, Strauss, *The Perils of Theory*, 83 Notre Dame L.Rev. 1567, 1568–73 (2008). Another objection suggests that while Professor Clark's Supremacy Clause thesis has a textual basis, it cannot fully explain the history of the founding or account for subsequent developments in public law. See Monaghan, *Supremacy Clause Textualism*, 110 Colum.L.Rev. 731, 750–51 (2010). Monaghan claims that the history surrounding the clause's adoption belies any contention that it was framed to promote federalism. Its evident purpose, he adds, was to rectify weaknesses in the Articles of Confederation. Monaghan also argues that the assumptions underlying Clark's Supremacy Clause thesis—that the Clause implicitly limits federal lawmaking to three procedural methods using certain constitutionally prescribed processes—cannot account for the vast expanse of federal practice in the modern administrative state. If Monaghan is correct that the Supremacy Clause thesis has a textual basis but finds little support in

---

[2]   See, *e.g.*, Mishkin, *Some Further Last Words on Erie—The Thread*, 87 Harv.L.Rev. 1682, 1685 (1974); Field, *The Legitimacy of Federal Common Law*, 12 Pace L.Rev. 303, 305–06 (1992); Merrill, *supra*, at 349–50.

[3]   This article was the subject of Symposium, *Separation of Powers as a Safeguard of Federalism*, 83 Notre Dame L.Rev. 1417 (2008).

[4]   Prior to the Seventeenth Amendment, Senators were selected by their state legislatures, making them directly accountable to the states. See U.S. Const. Art. I, § 2, cl. 1.

historical practice, should that thesis have any relevance in assessing novel assertions of federal lawmaking power?

(c) The Rules of Decision Act, 28 U.S.C. § 1652, discussed in Erie R Co. v. Tompkins, p. 584, *supra*, provides: "The laws of the several states, except where the Constitution or treaties of the United States or Acts of Congress otherwise require or provide, shall be regarded as rules of decision in civil actions in the courts of the United States, in cases where they apply." Both Redish, *Federal Common Law, Political Legitimacy, and the Interpretive Process: An "Institutionalist" Perspective*, 83 Nw.U.L.Rev. 761 (1989), and Merrill, *supra*, at 27–32, argue that the Act generally prohibits federal court lawmaking. Wouldn't reading § 1652 in that way require drawing a line between permissible statutory interpretation and prohibited common lawmaking? Can such a line be drawn with adequate precision? Compare Weinberg, *The Curious Notion That the Rules of Decision Act Blocks Supreme Federal Common Law*, 83 Nw.U.L.Rev. 860 (1989) (arguing that it cannot); Westen & Lehman, *Is There Life For Erie After the Death of Diversity*, 78 Mich.L.Rev. 311, 331–36 (1980) (same).

Clearfield and numerous cases thereafter have fashioned federal common law while ignoring the Rules of Decision Act. A rare decision discussing the Act's pertinence to federal common lawmaking is DelCostello v. International Bhd. of Teamsters, 462 U.S. 151, 158–59 & n.13 (1983), p. 750, *infra*, in which the Court rejected the view that the Act barred judicial creation of a statute of limitations for a federal right of action. Noting that the Act "authorizes application of state law only when federal law does not 'otherwise require or provide' ", the Court found no barrier to formulation of a federal rule of decision when called for by "the policies and requirements of the underlying cause of action". One can also argue that the statutory phrase "in cases where [state rules] apply" means "in cases in which there is no federal common law preempting state rules of decision." See Meltzer, *State Court Forfeitures of Federal Rights*, 99 Harv.L.Rev. 1128, 1168 n.194 & sources cited (1986); Weinberg, *supra*. Does either of those readings of the Act render it a nullity? Compare, *e.g.*, Guaranty Trust Co. v. York, 326 U.S. 99, 103–04 (1945), p. 598, *supra*, stating that the Act is "merely declaratory of what would in any event have governed the federal courts".

(d) Insofar as any of these constitutional and statutory objections to the broad position is convincing, to what extent might it allow narrower theories of federal common lawmaking?

(5) Federal Common Law as Constitutional or Statutory Interpretation. An alternative theory of federal common law argues that even if it cannot be defended as the product of a generalized judicial lawmaking power, much of it is traceable to some identifiable constitutional or statutory source—even if a given common law norm does not flow from recognizably conventional approaches to statutory interpretation. On that theory, aspects of federal common law may be justifiable, for example, as an implication from the constitutional structure, as the product of an implicit delegation of power from Congress to supply an apparent omission in a statutory scheme, or as a tool for addressing a conflict between state law and federal statutory policy. Consider the following versions of this theory:

(a) Professor Hill would limit federal common lawmaking to particular federal enclaves. He argues that the Constitution preempts state lawmaking, and thus authorizes federal common lawmaking, in four areas—interstate controversies, admiralty, proprietary transactions of the United States, and international relations. Hill, *The Law-Making Power of the Federal Courts: Constitutional Preemption*, 67 Colum.L.Rev. 1024 (1967); see also Texas Indus., Inc. v. Radcliff Materials, Inc., 451 U.S. 630, 641 (1981) (following this approach).[5] However, Hill approves of many decisions, outside of these enclaves, that are sometimes viewed as making federal common law but that he sees as falling within his broad view of statutory or constitutional interpretation—for example, those involving the judicial elaboration of the broad standards of the federal securities laws, as well as the judicial prescription of remedial consequences for the violation of those laws.

(b) Professor Merrill's view, though narrow, is not restricted to particular domains. He argues that Congress is the "exclusive repository" of the so-called "disposing power," the power to decide "who has the authority to make law and under what circumstances." See Merrill, *The Disposing Power of the Legislature*, 110 Colum.L.Rev. 452 (2010). On Merrill's view, therefore, "neither the executive nor the judiciary has autonomous power to make law * * * unless delegated authority to do so by the legislature." From that starting point, the legitimacy of federal common law depends on identifying "authority grounded in an implied delegation, or the need to preempt state law to preserve the integrity of federal law." In Merrill's view, the recognized judicial lawmaking authority in admiralty and in interstate disputes is harder to justify, but still not overly troublesome if confined to circumstances in which the purpose of granting exclusive jurisdiction to the federal courts would be undermined if state law governed. See Merrill, *The Judicial Prerogative*, 12 Pace L.Rev. 327, 345–49 (1992). How strict is Merrill's approach as compared with others outlined in this Note?

(c) Professor Field's view of the power is arguably broader, permitting lawmaking so long as the court can "point to a federal enactment, constitutional or statutory, that it interprets as authorizing the federal common law rule." Field, *Sources of Law: The Scope of Federal Common Law*, 99 Harv.L.Rev. 881, 887 (1986).[6]

Critics of the new federal common law frequently invoke the following passage in Erie R. Co. v. Tompkins, 304 U.S. 64, 78 (1938): "Except in matters governed by the Federal Constitution or by acts of Congress, the law to be applied in any case is the law of the state." Do the theories of federal common law discussed in this Paragraph undermine such reliance on Erie? Do they refocus the question of legitimacy onto whether a given exercise of "federal common lawmaking" authority can be justified according to accepted methods of constitutional or statutory interpretation?

(6) Implied Delegation. One question raised by the foregoing theories of federal common law is the extent to which courts may derive the necessary statutory or constitutional authority for federal common lawmaking by implication rather than express grant. In D'Oench, Duhme & Co. v. FDIC, 315 U.S. 447 (1942), Justice Jackson's concurring opinion at least hinted that

---

[5]   See also Clark, *Federal Common Law: A Structural Reinterpretation*, 144 U.Pa.L.Rev. 1245 (1996) (suggesting that many of the rules currently regarded as federal common law—such as the act of state doctrine, rules governing prize cases, and rules governing interstate disputes—are actually consistent with, and frequently required by, the constitutional structure and thus are consistent with the Supremacy Clause).

[6]   Professor Kramer's views can be roughly characterized as a hybrid of the views of Professors Field and Hill: "federal courts can make common law * * * so long as whatever rules the courts fashion are consistent with and further an underlying federal enactment", or fall within areas (such as admiralty, foreign relations, and interstate disputes) in which the Constitution makes federal sovereignty exclusive. Kramer, note 1, *supra*, at 289.

federal common lawmaking may be justified as a form of implied statutory delegation of power to federal courts to complete a federal program in light of its apparent purpose.[7]

The FDIC sued D'Oench Duhme in federal district court in Missouri to recover on a note the defendant had executed and that was payable to an Illinois bank. The defendant initially had sold the bank some bonds that had become past due; the defendant then gave the bank the note in 1933, "with the understanding it will not be called for payment", to replace the bonds—so that they would not appear as assets of the bank. The FDIC insured the bank in 1934, and acquired the note in 1938 as collateral for a loan made in connection with the assumption of the bank's deposit liabilities by another bank.

Bckgrd.

On review, the Supreme Court found it unnecessary to determine whether the court of appeals had correctly applied Illinois rather than Missouri law, declaring instead that "the liability of [D'Oench Duhme] on the note involves decision of a federal, not a state, question". The Court found in various federal statutes "a federal policy to protect [the FDIC], and the public funds which it administers, against misrepresentations as to the securities or other assets in the portfolios of the banks which [the FDIC] insures or to which it makes loans."

Holdg

In a frequently cited concurring opinion, Justice Jackson noted that under the relevant jurisdictional statute, cases to which the FDIC was a party were deemed to arise under the laws of the United States. Yet because "no federal statute purports to define the Corporation's rights" on the facts before the Court, he wrote, the Court had to determine whether to apply state law or to resolve the question as a matter of federal common law. Although acknowledging that there was no "general common law," Jackson added that "this is not to say that wherever we have occasion to decide a federal question which cannot be answered from federal statutes alone we may not resort to all the source materials of the common law, or that when we have fashioned an answer it does not become a part of the federal non-statutory or common law".

Concurrence

Justice Jackson linked the Court's authority to make federal common law with the realities of the legislative process: "Were we bereft of the common law, our federal system would be impotent. This follows from the recognized futility of attempting all-complete statutory codes, and is apparent from the terms of the Constitution itself." Although noting that the Court sometimes supplied an apparent federal statutory omission by using state law as the rule of decision, Jackson believed that where a federal proprietary interest was at stake, any decision concerning the choice of law

---

[7] In rare cases, Congress expressly delegates lawmaking authority to the federal courts. See Fed.R.Evid. 501 (codified at 88 Stat. 1933 (1975)) ("Except as otherwise required * * * [by federal law], the privilege of a witness, person, government, State, or political subdivision thereof shall be governed by the principles of the common law as they may be interpreted by the courts of the United States in the light of reason and experience.") Moreover, where a statute adopts open-ended language that necessitates the exercise of substantial judicial discretion, it is hard to avoid concluding that Congress delegated implied lawmaking powers. See National Soc'y of Professional Eng'rs v. United States, 435 U.S. 679, 688 (1978) (holding that the broad language of the Sherman Act, 15 U.S.C. § 1, invites the courts to fashion a common law of anti-competitive practices); Merrill, Paragraph (4)(a), *supra*, at 43–46. But see Posner, The Problems of Jurisprudence 289 (1990) (questioning that view). Cases involving the Clearfield doctrine involve a much less explicit basis for inferring delegation.

necessarily "turns upon the law of the United States". For him, a federal judge-made rule of decision was appropriate in this case:

"The law which we apply to this case consists of principles of established credit in jurisprudence, selected by us because they are appropriate to effectuate the policy of the governing Act. The Corporation was created and financed in part by the United States to bolster the entire banking and credit structure. * * * Under the Act, the Corporation has a dual relation of creditor or potential creditor and of supervising authority toward insured banks. The immunity of such a corporation from schemes concocted by the cooperative deceit of bank officers and customers is not a question to be answered from considerations of geography."

Many commentators read the Clearfield-D'Oench Duhme line of cases to rest on the idea that a statute establishing a federal program can be understood to include an implied delegation to judges to supply necessary omissions. See, *e.g.*, Friendly, *The Gap in Lawmaking—Judges Who Can't and Legislators Who Won't*, 63 Colum.L.Rev. 787, 789 (1963); Mishkin, *The Variousness of "Federal Law": Competence and Discretion in the Choice of National and State Rules for Decision*, 105 U.Pa.L.Rev. 797, 800 (1957); Young, *Preemption and Federal Common Law*, 83 Notre Dame L.Rev. 1639, 1642–43 (2008). If that rationale is sound, does it negate concerns about the separation of powers?

Would such a theory of "implied" delegation leave the judiciary without an intelligible principle to guide the resultant development of federal common law? See Nielson, *Erie as Nondelegation*, 72 Ohio St.L.J. 239, 296–301 (2011) (arguing that grants of federal common lawmaking authority are subject to the strictures of the nondelegation doctrine). At least one commentator suggests that when federal courts formulate federal rules of decision that are not clearly specified by statute, such courts typically do not cut the rules out of whole cloth, but rather seek guidance in the background doctrines and practices of multiple jurisdictions. See Nelson, *The Persistence of General Law*, 106 Colum.L.Rev. 503 (2006); see also Nelson, *The Legitimacy of (Some) Federal Common Law*, 101 Va.L.Rev. 1, 7 (2015) (suggesting that the legitimacy of different forms of federal common law may depend on the mode of their formulation). If federal courts resort to off-the-rack legal doctrines and assumptions to fill in the gaps in federal law, does that approach mitigate separation-of-powers concerns with federal common law?

(7) Theories of Statutory Interpretation. Justice Jackson's concurrence rests upon three apparent assumptions: (i) Congress passed the governing Act to serve a public purpose; (ii) courts can identify that purpose; and (iii) courts permissibly fashion judge-made rules to implement the congressional purpose. How well do those assumptions fare under modern theories of statutory interpretation?[8] Although the modern statutory interpretation debate is too extensive and varied to address in detail here, it is possible to sketch the approaches most directly relevant to the theory that

---

[8]   For discussion of the current debate, see generally Bressman, Rubin, & Stack, The Regulatory State (2d ed. 2013); Eskridge, Frickey, Garrett, & Brudney, Cases and Materials on Legislation and Regulation: Statutes and the Creation of Public Policy (5th ed. 2014); Eskridge, Gluck, & Nourse, Statutes, Regulation, and Interpretation: Legislation and Administration in the Republic of Statutes (2014); Manning & Stephenson, Legislation and Regulation (2d ed. 2013); Nelson, Statutory Interpretation (2010); Mikva & Lane, Legislative Process (3d ed. 2009); Popkin, Materials on Legislation: Political Language and the Political Process (5th ed. 2009).

federal common law reflects an implied delegation of power to judges to complete federal statutes in a way that implements their purpose.

(a) Statutory Purpose and the Legal Process School. When Clearfield was decided, the approach of interpreting statutes to fulfill the overall statutory purpose was superseding the "plain meaning" approach as the dominant approach to interpretation.[9] In the leading case, United States v. American Trucking Ass'ns, 310 U.S. 534, 543–44 (1940), the Court announced that when the literal or semantic meaning of a statute was " 'plainly at variance with the policy of the legislation as a whole' ", the Court's duty was to "follow[ ] that purpose, rather than the literal words." This statement reflected—and contributed to—a post–New Deal trend in statutory interpretation theory that posited (a) that legislatures enact all statutes for a purpose; and (b) that courts in our system of government act appropriately—indeed, advance the goal of legislative supremacy—when they interpret statutes to further the legislation's overall purpose, rather than hewing literally to texts often drafted in haste. See, *e.g.*, Cox, *Judge Learned Hand and the Interpretation of Statutes*, 60 Harv.L.Rev. 370, 370–71 (1947); Frankfurter, *Some Reflections on the Reading of Statutes*, 47 Colum.L.Rev. 527, 536–37 (1947); Radin, A *Short Way with Statutes*, 56 Harv.L.Rev. 388 (1942).

This "purposivist" approach was later captured in the canonical teaching materials prepared by Professors Hart and Sacks: The Legal Process: Basic Problems in the Making and Application of Law (tent.ed.1958) (Eskridge & Frickey eds., 1994). Hart and Sacks wrote that "[t]he idea of a statute without an intelligible purpose is foreign to the idea of law and inadmissible." *Id.* at 1124. Accordingly, they believed that judges should use various tools of construction—including the overall policy evinced by the statutory text, the legislative history, and public knowledge of the mischief sought to be addressed—to determine what "purpose ought to be attributed to the statute" and to interpret the words "to carry out the purpose as best it can." *Id.* at 1374. They famously emphasized that, in doing so, judges "should assume, unless the contrary unmistakably appears, that the legislature was made up of reasonable persons pursuing reasonable purposes reasonably." *Id.* at 1378.

Courts applying the Legal Process approach could supply apparently omitted statutory terms by asking, in light of the available contextual evidence, how a "reasonable legislator" would have implemented the purposes underlying the statute. Such an approach, if accepted, would easily account for a federal court's authority to decide (a) whether an apparent omission should be addressed with a federal rather than a state rule of decision because of the need for uniformity or of the inconsistency of a state rule of decision with overall federal statutory policy; and (b) what federal rule of decision to prescribe when state law was deemed inappropriate.

---

[9]   For examples of the earlier, "plain meaning" approach, see, *e.g.*, Caminetti v. United States, 242 U.S. 470, 490 (1917); White v. United States, 191 U.S. 545, 551 (1903); United States v. Hartwell, 73 U.S. (6 Wall.) 385, 396 (1867). Of course, the Court had long since recognized that federal courts may deviate from plain meaning when sources such as the legislative history offer clear evidence of contrary legislative intent or when a statute, literally construed, would produce an absurd result. See, *e.g.*, Church of the Holy Trinity v. United States, 143 U.S. 457 (1892). But the relative emphasis on purpose became considerably more pronounced in the era in which the Court decided Clearfield.

(b) The New Textualism. Beginning in the late twentieth century, an approach that came to be known as the "new textualism"[10] challenged the Legal Process school's purposive assumptions as inconsistent with the constitutional structure and the realities of the legislative process. First, the leading judicial proponent of textualism (Justice Scalia) emphasized that Article I, § 7 of the Constitution prescribes the elaborate and cumbersome requirements of bicameralism and presentment and that judges must therefore pay close attention to the details of the enacted text, which is the only expression of policy that has made its way through that process.[11] Conroy v. Aniskoff, 507 U.S. 511, 519 (1993) (Scalia, J., concurring). Second, relying on the insights of a branch of political science known as public choice theory, other leading textualists maintained that the legislative process—which is marked by multiple veto gates (*e.g.*, committees), high procedural hurdles (*e.g.*, the Senate filibuster), and often hard-to-detect deals (*e.g.*, logrolling)—is simply too complex, opaque, and path dependent to allow judges to reconstruct what Congress would have intended to do about a matter that the text itself does not conclusively resolve. See, *e.g.*, Easterbrook, *Statutes' Domains*, 50 U.Chi.L.Rev. 533, 547 (1983); Shepsle, *Congress Is a "They," Not an "It": Legislative Intent as Oxymoron*, 12 Int'l Rev.L. & Econ. 239, 244 (1992). Third, textualists stressed that the framing of statutory policy entails not merely the articulation of legislative purposes, but also the specification of the *means* for carrying out those purposes. Since the choice of means may be the product of hard-fought legislative compromise, textualists argued that abstracting from a statute's textual details to the broader purposes behind them "dishonors the legislative choice as effectively as expressly refusing to follow the law." Easterbrook, *Text, History, and Structure in Statutory Interpretation*, 17 Harv.J.L. & Pub.Pol'y 61, 68 (1994).

Although the Supreme Court has not fully embraced modern textualism, by the late twentieth century elements of the Court's reasoning came to reflect certain assumptions underlying that approach. In Board of Governors of the Fed. Reserve Sys. v. Dimension Fin. Corp., 474 U.S. 361, 374 (1986), the Court thus explained that "Congress may be unanimous in its intent to stamp out some vague social or economic evil; however, because its Members may differ sharply on the means for effectuating that intent, the final language of the legislation may reflect hard-fought compromises. Invocation of the 'plain purpose' of legislation at the expense of the terms of the statute itself takes no account of the processes of compromise."

Such themes about the legislative process are now common in the Court's decisions. See Manning, *What Divides Textualists from Purposivists?*, 106 Colum.L.Rev. 70, 109 n.141 (2006) (collecting cases). Are they in tension with the Clearfield-D'Oench Duhme doctrine? If federal courts now emphasize that legislative compromises may not pursue a

---

[10] See Eskridge, *The New Textualism*, 37 UCLA L.Rev. 621 (1990).

[11] Textualism of course presupposes that legislators can use words to communicate with judges, administrators, and the public—an assumption that rests on the idea that members of a social and linguistic community have shared conventions for decoding language in context. See, *e.g.*, Schauer, *Statutory Construction and the Coordinating Function of Plain Meaning*, 1990 Sup.Ct.Rev. 231, 251; Waldron, *Legislators' Intentions and Unintentional Legislation*, in Law and Interpretation 339 (Marmor ed. 1995). For more skeptical opinions about that possibility, see, *e.g.*, Singer, *The Player and the Cards: Nihilism and Legal Theory*, 94 Yale L.J. 1, 19–21 (1984); Tushnet, *Following the Rules Laid Down: A Critique of Interpretivism and Neutral Principles*, 96 Harv.L.Rev. 781, 822–23 (1983).

statute's background purpose to its fullest, is it sound to presume that a statute has implicitly delegated authority to supply apparent omissions in light of the statutory purpose? If not, can federal courts simply rely on state law to supply the omission? Compare Hart, *The Relations Between State and Federal Law*, 54 Colum.L.Rev. 489, 498 (1954) (arguing that, in important respects, federal law is "obviously interstitial" and depends upon the existence of an "underlying body of state law" for its effectiveness); Mishkin, Paragraph (6), *supra*, at 811 (arguing that in our system of federalism, "Congress legislates against a background of existing state law").

Consider a competing view of the legislative process, which attributes omissions to the fallibility of the legislative process rather than to deliberate legislative compromise: "[J]udges * * * know that statutes are purposive utterances and that language is a slippery medium in which to encode a purpose. They know that legislatures, including the Congress of the United States, often legislate in haste, without considering fully the potential application of their words to novel settings." Friedrich v. City of Chicago, 888 F.2d 511, 514 (7th Cir. 1989) (Posner, J.). How should one choose between the conflicting accounts of the way the legislative process works? For an argument that the choice can be made only through empirical study, see Sunstein, *Must Formalism Be Defended Empirically?*, 66 U.Chi.L.Rev. 636 (1999). For interesting studies of congressional drafting practice, see Gluck & Bressman, *Statutory Interpretation from the Inside—An Empirical Study of Congressional Drafting, Delegation, and Canons: Part I*, 65 Stan.L.Rev. 901 (2013); Bressman & Gluck, *Statutory Interpretation from the Inside—An Empirical Study of Congressional Drafting, Delegation, and Canons: Part II*, 66 Stan.L.Rev. 727, 781 (2014); Nourse & Schacter, *The Politics of Legislative Drafting: A Congressional Case Study*, 77 N.Y.U.L.Rev. 575 (2002).

(c) Common Law Theories of Statutory Interpretation. Even assuming that the Court's new emphasis accurately depicts the legislative process, does it necessarily follow that the role of the federal courts in our constitutional system is to enforce legislative compromise rather than to make statute law more coherent and complete? An important strain of legal thought has long maintained that American judicial power should be understood to include common law powers in relation to statutes. See, *e.g.*, Landis, *Statutes and the Sources of Law*, in Harvard Legal Essays 213, 214–18 (Pound ed. 1934); Stone, *The Common Law in the United States*, 50 Harv.L.Rev. 4, 13, 15 (1936). Modern legal scholars have offered numerous arguments—some historical, some philosophical, and some pragmatic—to support the idea that courts should have robust inherent authority to make enacted law more coherent, adaptable, and/or just. See, *e.g.*, Dworkin, Law's Empire (1986); Eskridge, Dynamic Statutory Interpretation (1994); Aleinikoff, *Updating Statutory Interpretation*, 87 Mich.L.Rev. 20 (1988); Sunstein, *Interpreting Statutes in the Regulatory State*, 103 Harv.L.Rev. 405, 414–51 (1989); Strauss, *The Common Law and Statutes*, 70 U.Colo.L.Rev. 225 (1999).

In a direct challenge to modern textualists' reliance on the constitutional structure to support their theory of statutory interpretation, Professor Eskridge argues that the original understanding of "the judicial Power of the United States" would have included the power to engage in equitable interpretation, a form of inherent authority that, as relevant here, empowered English judges to extend a statute to cover omitted cases that fell within the statute's reason or purpose. See Eskridge, *Textualism, The*

Unknown Ideal?, 96 Mich.L.Rev. 1509 (1998); Eskridge, *All About Words: Early Understandings of the "Judicial Power" in Statutory Interpretation, 1776–1806*, 101 Colum.L.Rev. 990 (2001). According to Eskridge, it would have been natural for the founders—who had grown up within the English legal system—to assume that the judicial power included such authority. He adds that early state court practice routinely relied on equitable interpretation. Although acknowledging that early federal judicial practice— at least by the Marshall Court—was more ambiguous, Eskridge argues that even Chief Justice Marshall, who professed to look for the intended meaning of the statutory text, frequently interpreted statutes creatively to achieve purposive results not easily found in the text.

If Eskridge is correct, then the statutory completion power claimed in Clearfield and D'Oench Duhme would be consistent with the original understanding of Article III. Is it clear, however, that English judicial practice—which involved considerable commingling of legislative and judicial functions (*e.g.*, the Upper House of Parliament was the court of last resort)—provides an appropriate model for understanding the American system of separated powers? Similarly, given the varied structural arrangements in the early states, how relevant is the practice of state courts to determining the meaning of federal judicial power? Compare Manning, *Textualism and the Equity of the Statute*, 101 Colum.L.Rev. 1 (2001); Manning, *Deriving Rules of Statutory Interpretation from the Constitution*, 101 Colum.L.Rev. 1648 (2001). Whatever the original meaning, has our legal culture now embraced the assumption that federal judges must act as Congress' faithful agents, whose duty is to ascertain and enforce legislative commands with accuracy? Compare Zeppos, *Legislative History and the Interpretation of Statutes: Toward a Fact-Finding Model of Statutory Interpretation*, 76 Va.L.Rev. 1295, 1313 (1990) (discussing the central role of the faithful agent model), with Eskridge, *Spinning Legislative Supremacy*, 78 Geo.L.J. 319 (1988) (arguing that the model is too vague to do any work).

INTRODUCTORY NOTE ON KIMBELL FOODS

In his article on federal common law, p. 646, *supra*, Judge Friendly wrote that, properly understood, "Clearfield decided not one issue but two." The first issue, he wrote, was whether "the right of the United States to recover for conversion of a government check is a federal right"—one that gives judicial authority to establish the rule of decision. At the same time, the Court in Clearfield elided a second issue—specifically, whether a federal court exercising such authority should (a) adopt a single, uniform federal common law rule or (b) exercise its lawmaking discretion to leave the matter to state law. Because the Court in Clearfield did not disaggregate the two questions, Judge Friendly worried that it never explained why the benefit of assuring uniformity for "federal fiscal" matters outweighed the cost of creating disuniformity in the rules governing commercial transactions occurring within Pennsylvania.[1]

------

[1] To highlight the point, Judge Friendly explored a secondary effect of the Court's adopting a uniform federal rule that made Clearfield liable to the United States for having cashed the stolen check. See Clearfield Trust Co. v. United States, p. 643, *supra*. In view of that liability, Clearfield would itself presumably wish to go against J.C. Penney as the endorser of the stolen check. As Judge Friendly pointed out, however, that second action would likely be

A number of decisions have since disaggregated the two issues to which Judge Friendly's analysis refers. The first is the question of "competence": Do the federal courts have authority to apply a federal common law rule in the particular context? The second is the question of "discretion": If such authority exists, is its exercise appropriate? In the case that follows, the Court addresses both.

———

United States v. Kimbell Foods, Inc.

440 U.S. 715, 99 S.Ct. 1448, 59 L.Ed. 711 (1979).
Certiorari to the Circuit Court of Appeals for the Fifth Circuit.

■ MR. JUSTICE MARSHALL delivered the opinion of the Court.

[This decision arose out of two cases. The facts of the first give the necessary context for the Court's decision. O.K. Super Markets ("O.K.") took out a $27,000 loan from Kimbell Foods that was secured by interests in O.K.'s equipment and merchandise. The security agreements were executed in compliance with the Texas Uniform Commercial Code. Subsequently, O.K. took out a $300,000 loan from Republic National Bank. That loan was secured by the same collateral as the Kimbell Foods loan. The Small Business Administration (SBA), a federal agency, guaranteed Republic's loan. When O.K. defaulted on its obligations, Kimbell Foods brought suit to recover its debt. Republic assigned its security interest to the SBA, which sued to recover from O.K. At issue was whether Kimbell Foods' or the SBA's security interest took priority and whether federal common law or state law governed the case. No provision of the Small Business Act—the statute under which the SBA guaranteed the loan—spoke to the question of priority. In holding that state law rules should govern, the Supreme Court established the following frame of analysis:]

II

This Court has consistently held that federal law governs questions involving the rights of the United States arising under nationwide federal programs. As the Court explained in Clearfield Trust Co. v. United States, [318 U.S. 363,] 366–367 [(1943):]

> "When the United States disburses its funds or pays its debts, it is exercising a constitutional function or power. . . . The authority [to do so] had its origin in the Constitution and the statutes of the United States and was in no way dependent on

governed by state law under the reasoning of Bank of America Nat. Trust & Savings Ass'n v. Parnell, 352 U.S. 29 (1956). Parnell involved a suit between private parties concerning funds obtained by cashing United States bearer bonds that had been stolen. On the question whether Parnell had taken the bonds in good faith, the Court ruled that state law governed, distinguishing Clearfield on the ground that "[t]he present litigation is purely between private parties and does not touch the rights and duties of the United States." The implication, Judge Friendly suggested, is that a suit by Clearfield against J.C. Penney would likewise be governed by Pennsylvania law, which bars recovery. This would leave Clearfield liable to the United States but unable to recoup against J.C. Penney. On Judge Friendly's view, the Court in Clearfield should have taken that consideration into account before exercising its discretion to adopt a federal common law rule rather than embrace the state rule that would otherwise have governed Clearfield's liability.

the laws [of any State]. The duties imposed upon the United States and the rights acquired by it . . . find their roots in the same federal sources. In absence of an applicable Act of Congress it is for the federal courts to fashion the governing rule of law according to their own standards." (Citations and footnote omitted.)

Guided by these principles, we think it clear that the priority of liens stemming from federal lending programs must be determined with reference to federal law. The SBA * * * unquestionably perform[s] federal functions within the meaning of Clearfield. Since the [agency derives its] authority to effectuate loan transactions from specific Acts of Congress passed in the exercise of a "constitutional function or power," Clearfield Trust Co. v. United States, *supra*, at 366, their rights, as well, should derive from a federal source. When Government activities "aris[e] from and bea[r] heavily upon a federal . . . program," the Constitution and Acts of Congress " 'require' otherwise than that state law govern of its own force." United States v. Little Lake Misere Land Co., 412 U.S. 580, 592, 593 (1973). In such contexts, federal interests are sufficiently implicated to warrant the protection of federal law.

That the statutes authorizing these federal lending programs do not specify the appropriate rule of decision in no way limits the reach of federal law. It is precisely when Congress has not spoken " 'in an area comprising issues substantially related to an established program of government operation,' " id., at 593, quoting Mishkin [*The Variousness of 'Federal Law': Competence and Discretion in the Choice of National and State Rules for Decision*, 105 U.Pa.L.Rev. 797, 800 (1957)], that Clearfield directs federal courts to fill the interstices of federal legislation "according to their own standards." Clearfield Trust Co. v. United States, *supra*, 318 U.S., at 367.

Federal law therefore controls the Government's priority rights. The more difficult task, to which we turn, is giving content to this federal rule.

III

Controversies directly affecting the operations of federal programs, although governed by federal law, do not inevitably require resort to uniform federal rules. See Clearfield Trust Co. v. United States, *supra*, at 367; United States v. Little Lake Misere Land Co., *supra*, 412 U.S., at 594–595. Whether to adopt state law or to fashion a nationwide federal rule is a matter of judicial policy "dependent upon a variety of considerations always relevant to the nature of the specific governmental interests and to the effects upon them of applying state law." United States v. Standard Oil Co., 332 U.S. 301, 310 (1947).

Undoubtedly, federal programs that "by their nature are and must be uniform in character throughout the Nation" necessitate formulation of controlling federal rules. United States v. Yazell, 382 U.S. 341, 354 (1966); [citing additional cases]. Conversely, when there is little need for a nationally uniform body of law, state law may be incorporated as the federal rule of decision. Apart from considerations of uniformity, we must also determine whether application of state law would frustrate specific objectives of the federal programs. If so, we must fashion special rules solicitous of those federal interests. Finally, our choice-of-law inquiry must consider the extent to which application of a federal rule would disrupt commercial relationships predicated on state law.

The Government argues that effective administration of its lending programs requires uniform federal rules of priority. It contends further that resort to any rules other than first in time, first in right and choateness would conflict with protectionist fiscal policies underlying the programs. We are unpersuaded that, in the circumstances presented here, nationwide standards favoring claims of the United States are necessary to ease program administration or to safeguard the Federal Treasury from defaulting debtors. Because the state commercial codes "furnish convenient solutions in no way inconsistent with adequate protection of the federal interest[s]," United States v. Standard Oil Co., *supra*, 332 U.S., at 309, we decline to override intricate state laws of general applicability on which private creditors base their daily commercial transactions.

A

Incorporating state law to determine the rights of the United States as against private creditors would in no way hinder administration of the SBA * * * loan programs. In United States v. Yazell, *supra*, this Court rejected the argument, similar to the Government's here, that a need for uniformity precluded application of state coverture rules to an SBA loan contract. Because SBA operations were "specifically and in great detail adapted to state law," the federal interest in supplanting "important and carefully evolved state arrangements designed to serve multiple purposes" was minimal. Our conclusion that compliance with state law would produce no hardship on the agency was also based on the SBA's practice of "individually negotiat[ing] in painfully particularized detail" each loan transaction. These observations apply with equal force here and compel us again to reject generalized pleas for uniformity as substitutes for concrete evidence that adopting state law would adversely affect administration of the federal programs. * * *

[T]he Government maintains that requiring [federal] agencies to assess security arrangements under local law would dictate close scrutiny of each transaction and thereby impede expeditious processing of loans. We disagree. Choosing responsible debtors necessarily requires individualized selection procedures, which the agencies have already implemented in considerable detail. Each applicant's financial condition is evaluated under rigorous standards in a lengthy process. Agency employees negotiate personally with borrowers, investigate property offered as collateral for encumbrances, and obtain local legal advice on the adequacy of proposed security arrangements. In addition, they adapt the terms of every loan to the parties' needs and capabilities. Because each application currently receives individual scrutiny, the agencies can readily adjust loan transactions to reflect state priority rules, just as they consider other factual and legal matters before disbursing Government funds. As we noted in [Yazell], these lending programs are distinguishable from "nationwide act[s] of the Federal Government, emanating in a single form from a single source." Since there is no indication that variant state priority schemes would burden current methods of loan processing, we conclude that considerations of administrative convenience do not warrant adoption of a uniform federal law.

B

The Government argues that applying state law to [such federal] lending programs would undermine its ability to recover funds disbursed and therefore would conflict with program objectives. In the Government's view, it is difficult "to identify a material distinction between a dollar received from the collection of taxes and a dollar returned to the Treasury on repayment of a federal loan." Therefore, the agencies conclude, just as "the purpose of the federal tax lien statute to insure prompt and certain collection of taxes" justified our imposition of the first-in-time and choateness doctrines in the tax lien context, the federal interest in recovering on loans compels similar legal protection of the agencies' consensual liens. However, we believe significant differences between federal tax liens and consensual liens counsel against unreflective extension of rules that immunize the United States from the commercial law governing all other voluntary secured creditors. These differences persuade us that deference to customary commercial practices would not frustrate the objectives of the lending programs.

That collection of taxes is vital to the functioning, indeed existence, of government cannot be denied. Congress recognized as much over 100 years ago when it authorized creation of federal tax liens. Act of July 13, 1866, ch. 184, § 9, 14 Stat. 107, recodified as amended in 26 U.S.C. §§ 6321–6323. The importance of securing adequate revenues to discharge national obligations justifies the extraordinary priority accorded federal tax liens through the choateness and first-in-time doctrines. By contrast, when the United States operates as a moneylending institution under carefully circumscribed programs, its interest in recouping the limited sums advanced is of a different order. Thus, there is less need here than in the tax lien area to invoke protective measures against defaulting debtors in a manner disruptive of existing credit markets.

To equate tax liens with these consensual liens also misperceives the principal congressional concerns underlying the respective statutes. The overriding purpose of the tax lien statute obviously is to ensure prompt revenue collection. The same cannot be said of the SBA and FHA lending programs. They are a form of social welfare legislation, primarily designed to assist farmers and businesses that cannot obtain funds from private lenders on reasonable terms. We believe that had Congress intended the private commercial sector, rather than taxpayers in general, to bear the risks of default entailed by these public welfare programs, it would have established a priority scheme displacing state law. * * *

The Government's ability to safeguard its interests in commercial dealings further reveals that the rules developed in the tax lien area are unnecessary here, and that state priority rules would not conflict with federal lending objectives. The United States is an involuntary creditor of delinquent taxpayers, unable to control the factors that make tax collection likely. In contrast, when the United States acts as a lender or guarantor, it does so voluntarily, with detailed knowledge of the borrower's financial status. The agencies evaluate the risks associated with each loan, examine the interests of other creditors, choose the security believed necessary to assure repayment, and set the terms of every agreement. By carefully selecting loan recipients and tailoring each transaction with state law in mind, the agencies are fully capable of establishing terms that will secure repayment. * * *

C

In structuring financial transactions, businessmen depend on state commercial law to provide the stability essential for reliable evaluation of the risks involved. *Cf.* National Bank v. Whitney, 103 U.S. 99, 102 (1881). However, subjecting federal contractual liens to the doctrines developed in the tax lien area could undermine that stability. Creditors who justifiably rely on state law to obtain superior liens would have their expectations thwarted whenever a federal contractual security interest suddenly appeared and took precedence.

Because the ultimate consequences of altering settled commercial practices are so difficult to foresee, we hesitate to create new uncertainties, in the absence of careful legislative deliberation. Of course, formulating special rules to govern the priority of the federal consensual liens in issue here would be justified if necessary to vindicate important national interests. But neither the Government nor the Court of Appeals advanced any concrete reasons for rejecting well-established commercial rules which have proven workable over time. Thus, the prudent course is to adopt the readymade body of state law as the federal rule of decision until Congress strikes a different accommodation.

IV

Accordingly, we hold that, absent a congressional directive, the relative priority of private liens and consensual liens arising from these Government lending programs is to be determined under nondiscriminatory state laws. * * *

NOTE ON CHOICE OF LAW GOVERNING THE LEGAL RELATIONS OF THE UNITED STATES

(1) Kimbell Foods and the Presumption in Favor of State Law. Though many decisions coming on the heels of Clearfield followed its approach of not only recognizing federal lawmaking power but also fashioning a distinctive federal law rule to govern the government's proprietary interests,[1] decisions such as Kimbell Foods make clear that uniform federal law need not be applied to all questions in federal government litigation. Notice that Kimbell Foods does not question the *competence* of the federal courts to fashion a federal rule of decision to govern such matters. But it does suggest that, even in such cases, application of state law is the proper default position for federal courts. The Court's opinion was marked by careful analysis of the asserted need for interstate uniformity, concern that a federal rule of decision will generate intrastate disuniformity, and a preference for incorporation of state law absent a demonstrated need for a uniform federal rule of decision. And Kimbell Foods' conclusion that, as a matter of *discretion*, the particular matter in question

---

[1] See Priebe & Sons v. United States, 332 U.S. 407 (1947); United States v. Standard Rice Co., 323 U.S. 106 (1944); National Metropolitan Bank v. United States, 323 U.S. 454 (1945).

did not require formulation of a federal rule is one that the Court has frequently reached in more recent decisions.[2]

(2) The Need for a Federal Rule of Decision. Under the Kimbell Foods approach, what factors might justify displacing state law as the governing rule of decision? In a case decided before Kimbell Foods—United States v. 93.970 Acres of Land, 360 U.S. 328 (1959)—the U.S. Army, having leased an airfield to a private company, wished to use the property for military purposes. The lease was revocable by the government in specified circumstances, but the company disputed the government's right to revoke on the facts presented. In order to obtain immediate use of the land rather than awaiting an adjudication of its right to revoke, the government filed a federal court action to condemn whatever interest the company might have. The lower courts applied the state's election-of-remedies law, which treated the United States, in electing to condemn, as having abandoned its claim of a lawful right to revoke. Thus interpreted, state law required recognition of a remaining property interest in the company, whether or not in the circumstances involved the government in fact had the right to revoke. The Supreme Court unanimously reversed, holding that the government had the right to revoke under the lease and owed no compensation. To follow the state's election-of-remedies law would put the government to the "Hobson's choice" of giving up either its right to immediate possession under condemnation law or its right to revoke the lease; under governing federal law, no such election was to be imputed.[3]

(3) An Alternative Formulation: State Conflicts with Federal Policy. Courts virtually never claim that as a matter of discretion, federal common law should be formulated but that they lack competence to do so. Does this suggest that the two-step analysis collapses into a single question whether federal law should apply? Professor Young suggests that collapsing the inquiry into a single step—one that predicates federal common lawmaking power on a finding of incompatibility between state and federal law—puts the doctrine on firmer ground. Starting from the premise that any genuine link between federal common lawmaking and implied congressional authorization is "tenuous indeed", he argues that "competence" to make federal common law must come, if anywhere, "from the existence of a conflict between state law and some preexisting federal policy"—a circumstance that gives rise to preemption under the Supremacy Clause. Citing familiar federalism concerns (see pp. 647–649, *supra*), he contends that federal courts may craft a federal common law rule only "to fill a gap created by finding

---

[2]   In United States v. Yazell, 382 U.S. 341 (1966), a decision relied upon in Kimbell Foods, the government sued on a Small Business Administration loan to a married couple; the question was whether the wife's separate property was exempt from recovery under a Texas law limiting the contractual powers of married women. The Court held (6–3) that state law governed, stressing that (1) the loan was individually negotiated, so that the government was chargeable with knowledge of Texas law; (2) there was no need for uniformity; (3) the financial consequences to the Treasury were small, as the Texas statute had been repealed; and (4) solicitude for state interests, particularly in the family-property area, was desirable.

More recently, in two lawsuits brought by a federal agency as receiver of a failed bank, the Court followed the approach of Kimbell Foods and ruled that state law governed the liability of both the failed bank's former law firm, see O'Melveny & Myers v. FDIC, 512 U.S. 79, 83–86 (1994), and the bank's former officers and directors, see Atherton v. FDIC, 519 U.S. 213 (1997).

[3]   See also, *e.g.*, United States v. Little Lake Misere Land Co., Inc., 412 U.S. 580, 594–97 (1973) (rejecting state law in connection with mineral rights reserved in federal government contracts, partly on the ground that the specific state law was "hostile to the interests of the United States").

that state law is preempted in a particular case." On this view, in cases such as Kimbell Foods, state law would apply of its own force, not because federal courts choose to adopt it as a federal rule of decision. Young, *Preemption and Federal Common Law*, 83 Notre Dame L.Rev. 1639, 1660, 1664–65 (2008).

The Court's formulations in recent cases mostly support that view. While Kimbell Foods uses a two-step formula (federal law governs, but it incorporates state law), leading cases now often assert that state law applies unless displaced by a conflict with federal policy or interests. See O'Melveny & Myers, note 2, *supra*, at 87, in which the Court wrote: "[J]udicial creation of a special federal rule * * * is limited to situations where there is a 'significant conflict between some federal policy or interest and the use of state law.' Wallis v. Pan American Petroleum Corp., 384 U.S. 63, 68 (1966). Our cases uniformly require the existence of such a conflict as a precondition for recognition of a federal rule of decision. Not only the permissibility but also the scope of judicial displacement of state rules turns upon such a conflict." See also Atherton, note 2, *supra*, at 218–19; Boyle v. United Technologies Corp. (1988), p. 666, *infra*, at 507–08 & n.3. But see Semtek Int'l, Inc. v. Lockheed Martin Corp., 531 U.S. 497, 508 (2001) (applying the Kimbell Foods two-step framework). Note that despite the foregoing analysis, the Court in O'Melveny & Myers also declared that "if [state law] *is* applied it is of only theoretical interest whether the basis for that application is [the state's] own sovereign power or federal adoption of [the state's] disposition." Is the Court correct that the distinction is only of "theoretical interest"?[4]

(4) Tort Suits Involving the Federal Government. Although tort actions *against* the United States are governed by statute, see Federal Tort Claims Act, 28 U.S.C. § 1346(b); see generally pp. 899–902, *infra*, tort actions brought by the United States typically are not. In United States v. Standard Oil Co., 332 U.S. 301 (1947), after a Standard Oil truck injured a soldier, the government sued the company. The somewhat novel tort theory sought damages for the military's loss of the soldier's services while he was convalescing and for its expenses for his hospitalization—by analogy to "the master's rights of recovery for loss of the services of his servant or apprentice; the husband's similar action for interference with the marital relation, including loss of consortium as well as the wife's services; and the parent's right to indemnity for loss of a child's services, including his action for a daughter's seduction".

The Supreme Court held that the United States was not entitled to recover. Relying on Clearfield and similar cases, Justice Rutledge's opinion began by declaring that "the creation or negation of such a liability is not a matter to be determined by state law". Then, noting that " 'in our choice of

---

[4] The Court's rationale for applying state law in the context of a federal program may, for example, determine the existence of federal question jurisdiction. Compare Empire HealthChoice Assurance, Inc. v. McVeigh, 547 U.S. 677, 690–93 (2006) (in interpreting private contracts between federal employees and private carriers who administer federal health benefits pursuant to an antecedent contract with the federal government, in an area heavily saturated with federal regulatory requirements, state contract law applies of its own force unless it conflicts with federal policy), with *id.* at 712–13 (Breyer, J., dissenting) (arguing that even if the Court correctly determined that state law applies, a federal question exists because, in the context of such a federal program, the proper inquiry under Kimbell Foods is whether the Court should adopt state law as a matter of federal common law). For another potential distinction, see Young, *supra*, at 1651, which argues that if state law is incorporated as a federal common law rule of decision, then "the content or application of that rule can be appealed to the United States Supreme Court."

the applicable federal rule we have occasionally selected state law' ", it rejected any such reference. When it came to crafting a federal rule, however, the Court concluded that the question was one of "fiscal policy" for determination by Congress rather than by a federal court:

"We would not deny the Government's basic premise of the law's capacity for growth, or that it must include the creative work of judges. * * * But in the federal scheme our part in that work, and the part of the other federal courts, outside the constitutional area is more modest than that of state courts, particularly in the freedom to create new common-law liabilities, as Erie R. Co. v. Tompkins itself witnesses.

"Moreover, * * * we have not here simply a question of creating a new liability in the nature of a tort. For * * * the issue comes down in final consequence to a question of federal fiscal policy, coupled with considerations concerning the need for and the appropriateness of means to be used in executing the policy sought to be established. * * *

"Whatever the merits of the policy, its conversion into law is a proper subject for congressional action, not for any creative power of ours. Congress, not this Court or the other federal courts, is * * * the primary and most often the exclusive arbiter of federal fiscal affairs. * * *

"When Congress has thought it necessary to take steps to prevent interference with federal funds, property or relations, it has taken positive action to that end. We think it would have done so here, if that had been its desire. This it still may do, if or when it so wishes."

Justice Jackson's lone dissent argued: "If there is one function which I should think we would feel free to exercise under a Constitution which vests in us judicial power, it would be to apply well-established common law principles to a case whose only novelty is in facts. The courts of England, whose scruples against legislating are at least as sensitive as ours normally are, have not hesitated to say that His Majesty's Treasury may recover outlay to cure a British soldier from injury by a negligent wrongdoer and the wages he was meanwhile paid. Attorney General v. Valle-Jones, [1935] 2 K.B. 209. I think we could hold as much without being suspected of trying to usurp legislative function."

Despite all its talk of deference to Congress, didn't the Court in Standard Oil in fact render a decision—that federal law precludes recovery in these circumstances? Absent that decision, the United States might have been free, in a similar future case, to prevail in a different state whose law would permit recovery. But a decision that federal law governs a problem excludes both state courts and state legislatures from contributing to its solution. Was it wise and practicable for the Court to rely so heavily on Congress to address the problem? Is Congress equipped, with respect to matters of the order of magnitude involved in Standard Oil, to assume sole responsibility for the constructive elaboration and application of legal principles?[5] See generally Hart & Sacks, The Legal Process: Basic Problems

---

[5]   For cases exhibiting similar diffidence in fashioning rules of decision, see United States v. Gilman, 347 U.S. 507 (1954) (United States as employer may not seek indemnity from an employee whose negligence resulted in a judgment against the United States under the Federal Tort Claims Act); Francis v. Southern Pac. Co., 333 U.S. 445 (1948) (federal law governs and precludes interstate railroad's liability for ordinary negligence in an action by a railroad employee who was killed while riding on a free pass).

in the Making and Application of Law 522–27 (tent.ed. 1958) (Eskridge & Frickey eds. 1994).

(5) The Various Ways in Which State Law Applies. The general proposition that state law "applies" as the rule of decision for a particular issue can have a variety of meanings, including these:

(a) The federal government (Congress as well as the federal courts) lacks lawmaking authority.

(b) Congress has lawmaking authority, but in the absence of legislative action, state law governs. (Wasn't that so on the facts of Erie itself?)

(c) Federal legislation calls for the application of state law as part of a federal scheme. (The Federal Tort Claims Act is an example.)

(d) Although federal common law governs a given question, state law furnishes an appropriate and convenient measure of the content of this federal law. See, *e.g.*, Kimbell Foods, p. 657, *supra*.

Does the particular way in which state law applies make any difference with regard to (i) the nature or extent of the applicability of state law, (ii) the rules for ascertaining the content of state law,[6] or (iii) the choice of which state's law governs?[7] See generally von Mehren & Trautman, The Law of Multistate Problems 1049–59 (1965); Mishkin, *The Variousness of "Federal Law": Competence and Discretion in the Choice of National and State Rules for Decision*, 105 U.Pa.L.Rev. 797, 802 –10 (1957).

––––––––

INTRODUCTORY NOTE

The question of what law governs disputes concerning proprietary interests created by the United States arises not only when the United States is a party to the lawsuit, as in the preceding cases, but also in litigation between private parties. The next case—a tort suit between private parties that relates to a federal government contract—is an example, although its conclusion that the courts should fashion a distinctive federal common law rule, rather than borrow state law, is anything but typical. As you read the opinion that follows, consider whether the Court's approach comports with broader trends in federal common law cases.

––––––––

–––––––––––––––––––

[6] If state law applies of its own force absent any conflict with federal policy, then presumably the rules for "finding" state law developed under Erie R. Co. v. Tompkins, 304 U.S. 64 (1938), p. 584, *supra*, should apply. But if, under Kimbell Foods, state law applies in federal proprietary interest cases only where a court chooses to adopt it as the appropriate federal common law rule, then the content of "state law" arguably becomes a federal question, subject to review by the Supreme Court. See note 4, *supra*.

[7] When questions of state law arise in federal question actions, courts have followed different approaches in determining which state's law applies. Some follow Klaxon Co. v. Stentor Elec. Mfg. Co., 313 U.S. 487 (1941), p. 591, *supra*, and apply the choice-of-law rules of the forum state; others have fashioned federal common law to govern choice of law. See Recent Case, 109 Harv.L.Rev. 1156 (1996).

Boyle v. United Technologies Corp.

487 U.S. 500, 108 S.Ct. 2510, 101 L.Ed.2d 442 (1988).
Certiorari to the United States Court of Appeals for the Fourth Circuit.

■ JUSTICE SCALIA delivered the opinion of the Court.

This case requires us to decide when a contractor providing military equipment to the Federal Government can be held liable under state tort law for injury caused by a design defect.

I

[David A. Boyle, a United States Marine helicopter copilot, died when his military helicopter crashed and he drowned. His father, petitioner in the Supreme Court, filed a diversity action in federal court against the Sikorsky Division of United Technologies Corporation (Sikorsky), alleging under Virginia tort law that defective repairs had caused the crash and that a defective design of the emergency escape system had prevented Boyle from exiting the helicopter. The jury found Sikorsky liable and awarded petitioner $725,000. The court of appeals reversed, finding that petitioner had not met his burden of proof under state law on the defective repair claim and, as relevant here, that Sikorsky was not liable for the alleged design defect because it was entitled, on the facts, to invoke a newly recognized federal common law "military contractor defense."]

II

Petitioner's broadest contention is that, in the absence of legislation specifically immunizing Government contractors from liability for design defects, there is no basis for judicial recognition of such a defense. We disagree. In most fields of activity, to be sure, this Court has refused to find federal pre-emption of state law in the absence of either a clear statutory prescription or a direct conflict between federal and state law. But we have held that a few areas, involving "uniquely federal interests," Texas Industries, Inc. v. Radcliff Materials, Inc., 451 U.S. 630, 640 (1981), are so committed by the Constitution and laws of the United States to federal control that state law is pre-empted and replaced, where necessary, by federal law of a content prescribed (absent explicit statutory directive) by the courts—so-called "federal common law." See, e.g., United States v. Kimbell Foods, Inc., 440 U.S. 715, 726–729 (1979); Banco Nacional v. Sabbatino, 376 U.S. 398, 426–427 (1964); Howard v. Lyons, 360 U.S. 593, 597 (1959); Clearfield Trust Co. v. United States, 318 U.S. 363, 366–367 (1943); D'Oench, Duhme & Co. v. FDIC, 315 U.S. 447, 457–458 (1942).

The dispute in the present case borders upon two areas that we have found to involve such "uniquely federal interests." We have held that obligations to and rights of the United States under its contracts are governed exclusively by federal law. See, e.g., Clearfield Trust, supra. The present case does not involve an obligation to the United States under its contract, but rather liability to third persons. That liability may be styled one in tort, but it arises out of performance of the contract * * *.

Another area that we have found to be of peculiarly federal concern, warranting the displacement of state law, is the civil liability of federal officials for actions taken in the course of their duty. We have held in many contexts that the scope of that liability is controlled by federal law.

See, *e.g.*, Howard v. Lyons, *supra*, 360 U.S., at 597. The present case involves an independent contractor performing its obligation under a procurement contract, rather than an official performing his duty as a federal employee, but there is obviously implicated the same interest in getting the Government's work done.

We think the reasons for considering these closely related areas to be of "uniquely federal" interest apply as well to the civil liabilities arising out of the performance of federal procurement contracts. * * *

[It] is plain that the Federal Government's interest in the procurement of equipment is implicated by suits such as the present one—even though the dispute is one between private parties. It is true that where "litigation is purely between private parties and does not touch the rights and duties of the United States," Bank of America Nat. Trust & Sav. Assn. v. Parnell, 352 U.S. 29, 33 (1956), federal law does not govern. Thus, for example, in Miree v. DeKalb County, 433 U.S. 25, 30 (1977), which involved the question whether certain private parties could sue as third-party beneficiaries to an agreement between a municipality and the Federal Aviation Administration, we found that state law was not displaced because "the operations of the United States in connection with FAA grants such as these . . . would [not] be burdened" by allowing state law to determine whether third-party beneficiaries could sue, and because "any federal interest in the outcome of the [dispute] before us '[was] far too speculative, far too remote a possibility to justify the application of federal law to transactions essentially of local concern.' " But the same is not true here. The imposition of liability on Government contractors will directly affect the terms of Government contracts: either the contractor will decline to manufacture the design specified by the Government, or it will raise its price. Either way, the interests of the United States will be directly affected.

That the procurement of equipment by the United States is an area of uniquely federal interest does not, however, end the inquiry. That merely establishes a necessary, not a sufficient, condition for the displacement of state law.[3] Displacement will occur only where, as we have variously described, a "significant conflict" exists between an identifiable "federal policy or interest and the [operation] of state law," [Wallis v. Pan American Petroleum Corp., 384 U.S. 63, 68 (1966)], or the application of state law would "frustrate specific objectives" of federal legislation, Kimbell Foods, *supra*, 440 U.S., at 728. The conflict with federal policy need not be as sharp as that which must exist for ordinary pre-emption when Congress legislates "in a field which the States have traditionally occupied." Rice v. Santa Fe Elevator Corp., 331 U.S. [218, 230 (1947)]. Or to put the point differently, the fact that the area in question *is* one of unique federal concern changes what would otherwise

---

[3] We refer here to the displacement of state law, although it is possible to analyze it as the displacement of federal-law reference to state law for the rule of decision. Some of our cases appear to regard the area in which a uniquely federal interest exists as being entirely governed by federal law, with federal law deigning to "borro[w]," United States v. Little Lake Misere Land Co., 412 U.S. 580, 594 (1973), or "incorporat[e]" or "adopt[,]" United States v. Kimbell Foods, Inc., 440 U.S. 715, 728, 729, 730 (1979), state law except where a significant conflict with federal policy exists. We see nothing to be gained by expanding the theoretical scope of the federal pre-emption beyond its practical effect, and so adopt the more modest terminology. If the distinction between displacement of state law and displacement of federal law's incorporation of state law ever makes a practical difference, it at least does not do so in the present case.

be a conflict that cannot produce pre-emption into one that can. But conflict there must be. In some cases, for example where the federal interest requires a uniform rule, the entire body of state law applicable to the area conflicts and is replaced by federal rules. See, *e.g.*, Clearfield Trust, 318 U.S., at 366–367. In others, the conflict is more narrow, and only particular elements of state law are superseded. See, *e.g.*, Little Lake Misere Land Co., 412 U.S. at 595 (even assuming state law should generally govern federal land acquisitions, particular state law at issue may not).

In Miree, *supra*, the suit was not seeking to impose upon the person contracting with the Government a duty contrary to the duty imposed by the Government contract. Rather, it was the contractual duty *itself* that the private plaintiff (as third party beneficiary) sought to enforce. Between Miree and the present case, it is easy to conceive of an intermediate situation, in which the duty sought to be imposed on the contractor is not identical to one assumed under the contract, but is also not contrary to any assumed. If, for example, the United States contracts for the purchase and installation of an air conditioning unit, specifying the cooling capacity but not the precise manner of construction, a state law imposing upon the manufacturer of such units a duty of care to include a certain safety feature would not be a duty identical to anything promised the Government, but neither would it be contrary. The contractor could comply with both its contractual obligations and the state-prescribed duty of care. No one suggests that state law would generally be pre-empted in this context.

The present case, however, is at the opposite extreme from Miree. Here the state-imposed duty of care that is the asserted basis of the contractor's liability (specifically, the duty to equip helicopters with the sort of escape-hatch mechanism petitioner claims was necessary) is precisely contrary to the duty imposed by the Government contract (the duty to manufacture and deliver helicopters with the sort of escape-hatch mechanism shown by the specifications). Even in this sort of situation, it would be unreasonable to say that there is always a "significant conflict" between the state law and a federal policy or interest. If, for example, a federal procurement officer orders, by model number, a quantity of stock helicopters that happen to be equipped with escape hatches opening outward, it is impossible to say that the Government has a significant interest in that particular feature. That would be scarcely more reasonable than saying that a private individual who orders such a craft by model number cannot sue for the manufacturer's negligence because he got precisely what he ordered. * * *

There is * * * a statutory provision that demonstrates the potential for, and suggests the outlines of, "significant conflict" between federal interests and state law in the context of government procurement. In the Federal Tort Claims Act (FTCA), Congress authorized damages to be recovered against the United States for harm caused by the negligent or wrongful conduct of Government employees, to the extent that a private person would be liable under the law of the place where the conduct occurred. 28 U.S.C. § 1346(b). It excepted from this consent to suit, however,

"[a]ny claim . . . based upon the exercise or performance or the failure to exercise or perform a discretionary function or duty on the part of a federal agency or an employee of the Government, whether or not the discretion involved be abused." 28 U.S.C. § 2680(a).

We think that the selection of the appropriate design for military equipment to be used by our Armed Forces is assuredly a discretionary function within the meaning of this provision. It often involves not merely engineering analysis but judgment as to the balancing of many technical, military, and even social considerations, including specifically the trade-off between greater safety and greater combat effectiveness. And we are further of the view that permitting "second-guessing" of these judgments through state tort suits against contractors would produce the same effect sought to be avoided by the FTCA exemption. The financial burden of judgments against the contractors would ultimately be passed through, substantially if not totally, to the United States itself, since defense contractors will predictably raise their prices to cover, or to insure against, contingent liability for the Government-ordered designs. * * * In sum, we are of the view that state law which holds Government contractors liable for design defects in military equipment does in some circumstances present a "significant conflict" with federal policy and must be displaced.

We agree with the scope of displacement adopted by the Fourth Circuit here * * *. Liability for design defects in military equipment cannot be imposed, pursuant to state law, when (1) the United States approved reasonably precise specifications; (2) the equipment conformed to those specifications; and (3) the supplier warned the United States about the dangers in the use of the equipment that were known to the supplier but not to the United States. The first two of these conditions assure that the suit is within the area where the policy of the "discretionary function" would be frustrated—*i.e.*, they assure that the design feature in question was considered by a Government officer, and not merely by the contractor itself. The third condition is necessary because, in its absence, the displacement of state tort law would create some incentive for the manufacturer to withhold knowledge of risks, since conveying that knowledge might disrupt the contract but withholding it would produce no liability. We adopt this provision lest our effort to protect discretionary functions perversely impede them by cutting off information highly relevant to the discretionary decision. * * *

III

[Finding some ambiguity in the court of appeals' opinion, the Court remanded to permit that court to determine whether there was sufficient evidence to submit the case to the jury under a proper formulation of the contractor's defense.]

■ JUSTICE BRENNAN, with whom JUSTICE MARSHALL and JUSTICE BLACKMUN join, dissenting.

* * * We may assume, for purposes of this case, that Lt. Boyle was trapped under water and drowned because respondent * * * negligently designed the helicopter's escape hatch. * * * Had respondent designed such a death trap for a commercial firm, Lt. Boyle's family could sue under Virginia tort law * * *. But respondent designed the helicopter for the Federal Government, and that, the Court tells us today, makes all the difference: Respondent is immune from liability so long as it obtained

approval of "reasonably precise specifications"—perhaps no more than a rubberstamp from a federal procurement officer who might or might not have noticed or cared about the defects, or even had the expertise to discover them.

If respondent's immunity "bore the legitimacy of having been prescribed by the people's elected representatives," we would be duty bound to implement their will, whether or not we approved. United States v. Johnson, 481 U.S. 681, 703 (1987) (dissenting opinion of Scalia, J.). Congress, however, has remained silent—and conspicuously so, having resisted a sustained campaign by Government contractors to legislate for them some defense.[1] The Court—unelected and unaccountable to the people—has unabashedly stepped into the breach to legislate a rule denying Lt. Boyle's family the compensation that state law assures them. This time the injustice is of this Court's own making.

Worse yet, the injustice will extend far beyond the facts of this case, for the Court's newly discovered Government contractor defense is breathtakingly sweeping. It applies not only to military equipment * * *, but (so far as I can tell) to any made-to-order gadget that the Federal Government might purchase after previewing plans—from NASA's Challenger space shuttle to the Postal Service's old mail cars. The contractor may invoke the defense in suits brought * * * by anyone injured by a Government contractor's negligent design, including, for example, the children who might have died had respondent's helicopter crashed on the beach. It applies even if the Government has not intentionally sacrificed safety for other interests like speed or efficiency, and, indeed, even if the equipment is not of a type that is typically considered dangerous; thus, the contractor who designs a Government building can invoke the defense when the elevator cable snaps or the walls collapse. And the defense is invocable regardless of how blatant or easily remedied the defect, so long as the contractor missed it and the specifications approved by the Government, however unreasonably dangerous, were "reasonably precise."

In my view, this Court lacks both authority and expertise to fashion such a rule * * *. * * * I would leave that exercise of legislative power to Congress, where our Constitution places it * * *.

I

* * * [Erie R. Co. v. Tompkins, 304 U.S. 64, 78 (1938), proclaimed]: "Except in matters governed by the Federal Constitution or by Acts of Congress, the law to be applied in any case is the law of the State." The Court explained that the expansive power that federal courts had theretofore exercised was an unconstitutional "invasion of the authority of the State and, to that extent, a denial of its independence." Thus, Erie was deeply rooted in notions of federalism, and is most seriously implicated when, as here, federal judges displace the state law that would ordinarily govern with their own rules of federal common law. * * *

Accordingly, we have emphasized that * * * "absent some congressional authorization to formulate substantive rules of decision, federal common law exists only in such narrow areas as those concerned with the rights and obligations of the United States, interstate and international disputes implicating conflicting rights of States or our

---

[1]   [Citing numerous bills introduced in Congress between 1979 and 1987.]

relations with foreign nations, and admiralty cases." Texas Industries, Inc. v. Radcliff Materials, Inc., 451 U.S. 630, 641 (1981) (footnotes omitted). * * * State laws "should be overridden by the federal courts only where clear and substantial interests of the National Government, which cannot be served consistently with respect for such state interests, will suffer major damage if the state law is applied." United States v. Yazell, 382 U.S. 341, 352 (1966).

II

Congress has not decided to supersede state law here (if anything, it has decided not to, see n.1, *supra*) and the Court does not pretend that its newly manufactured "Government contractor defense" fits within any of the handful of "narrow areas," Texas Industries, *supra*, 451 U.S., at 641, of "uniquely federal interests" in which we have heretofore done so. Rather, the Court creates a new category of "uniquely federal interests" out of a synthesis of two whose origins predate Erie itself: the interest in administering the "obligations to and rights of the United States under its contracts," and the interest in regulating the "civil liability of federal officials for actions taken in the course of their duty." * * * We have steadfastly declined[, however,] to impose federal contract law on relationships that are collateral to a federal contract, or to extend the federal employee's immunity beyond federal employees. * * *

A

The proposition that federal common law continues to govern the "obligations to and rights of the United States under its contracts" is nearly as old as Erie itself. * * * But it is by now established that our power to create federal common law controlling the *Federal Government's* contractual rights and obligations does not translate into a power to prescribe rules that cover all transactions or contractual relationships collateral to Government contracts.

In Miree v. DeKalb County, *supra*, for example, the county was contractually obligated under a grant agreement with the Federal Aviation Administration (FAA) to "restrict the use of land adjacent to . . . the Airport to activities and purposes compatible with normal airport operations including landing and takeoff of aircraft." At issue was whether the county breached its contractual obligation by operating a garbage dump adjacent to the airport, which allegedly attracted the swarm of birds that caused a plane crash. Federal common law would undoubtedly have controlled in any suit by the Federal Government to enforce the provision against the county or to collect damages for its violation. The diversity suit, however, was brought not by the Government, but by assorted private parties injured in some way by the accident. We observed that * * * "the United States has a substantial interest in regulating aircraft travel and promoting air travel safety." Nevertheless, we held that state law should govern the claim because "only the rights of private litigants are at issue here," and the claim against the county "will have *no direct effect upon the United States or its Treasury*" (emphasis added).

Miree relied heavily on [Bank of America Nat. Trust & Sav. Assn. v. Parnell, 352 U.S. 29, 33 (1956)], and [Wallis v. Pan American Petroleum Corp., 384 U.S. 63, 68 (1966)] * * *. In the former case, Parnell cashed certain government bonds that had been stolen from their owner, a bank.

It is beyond dispute that federal law would have governed the United States' duty to pay the value bonds [sic] upon presentation; we held as much in Clearfield Trust, *supra*. But the central issue in Parnell, a diversity suit, was whether the victim of the theft could recover the money paid to Parnell. That issue, we held, was governed by state law, because the "litigation [was] purely between private parties and [did] *not touch the rights and duties of the United States*." (emphasis added).

The same was true in Wallis, which also involved a Government contract. * * *

Here, as in Miree, Parnell, and Wallis, a Government contract governed by federal common law looms in the background. But here, too, the United States is not a party to the suit and the suit neither "touch[es] the rights and duties of the United States," Parnell, *supra*, 352 U.S., at 33, nor has a "direct effect upon the United States or its Treasury," Miree, *supra*, 433 U.S., at 29. * * *

That the Government might have to pay higher prices for what it orders if delivery in accordance with the contract exposes the seller to potential liability does not distinguish this case. Each of the cases just discussed declined to extend the reach of federal common law despite the assertion of comparable interests that would have affected the terms of the Government contract—whether its price or its substance—just as "directly" (or indirectly). * * * As in each of the cases declining to extend the traditional reach of federal law of contracts beyond the rights and duties of the *Federal Government*, "any federal interest in the outcome of the question before us 'is far too speculative, far too remote a possibility to justify the application of federal law to transactions essentially of local concern.'" Miree, 433 U.S., at 32–33.

B

Our "uniquely federal interest" in the tort liability of affiliates of the Federal Government is equally narrow. * * * Never before have we so much as intimated that [official] immunity (or the "uniquely federal interest" that justifies it) might extend * * * to cover also nongovernment employees * * *.

The historical narrowness of the federal interest and the immunity is hardly accidental. A federal officer exercises statutory authority, which not only provides the necessary basis for the immunity in positive law, but also permits us confidently to presume that interference with the exercise of discretion undermines congressional will. In contrast, a Government contractor acts independently of any congressional enactment. Thus, immunity for a contractor lacks both the positive law basis and the presumption that it furthers congressional will.

* * * The extension of immunity to Government contractors skews the balance we have historically struck. On the one hand, whatever marginal effect contractor immunity might have on the "effective administration of policies of government," its "harm to individual citizens" is more severe than in the Government-employee context. Our observation that "there are . . . other sanctions than civil tort suits available to deter the executive official who may be prone to exercise his functions in an unworthy and irresponsible manner," [Barr v. Matteo, 360 U.S. 564, 576 (1959)], offers little deterrence to the Government contractor. On the other hand, a grant of immunity to Government

contractors could not advance "the fearless, vigorous, and effective administration of policies of government" nearly as much as does the current immunity for Government employees. *Id.*, at 571. In the first place, the threat of a tort suit is less likely to influence the conduct of an industrial giant than that of a lone civil servant, particularly since the work of a civil servant is significantly less profitable, and significantly more likely to be the subject of a vindictive lawsuit. * * * More importantly, inhibition of the Government official who actually sets Government policy presents a greater threat to the "administration of policies of government," than does inhibition of a private contractor, whose role is devoted largely to assessing the technological feasibility and cost of satisfying the Government's predetermined needs. Similarly, unlike tort suits against Government officials, tort suits against Government contractors would rarely "consume time and energies" that "would otherwise be devoted to governmental service." 360 U.S., at 571.

In short, because the essential justifications for official immunity do not support an extension to the Government contractor, it is no surprise that we have never extended it that far. * * *

III

* * * [T]he Court invokes the discretionary function exception of the Federal Tort Claims Act (FTCA), 28 U.S.C. § 2680(a). The Court does not suggest that the exception has any direct bearing here, for petitioner has sued a private manufacturer (not the Federal Government) under Virginia law (not the FTCA). * * *

[T]he Court * * * [reasons] that federal common law must immunize Government contractors from state tort law to prevent erosion of the discretionary function exception's *policy* of foreclosing judicial "second-guessing" of discretionary governmental decisions. The erosion the Court fears apparently is rooted not in a concern that suits against Government contractors will prevent them from designing, or the Government from commissioning the design of, precisely the product the Government wants, but in the concern that such suits might preclude the Government from purchasing the desired product at the price it wants: "The financial burden of judgments against the contractors," the Court fears, "would ultimately be passed through, substantially if not totally, to the United States itself."

Even granting the Court's factual premise, which is by no means self-evident, the Court cites no authority for the proposition that burdens imposed on Government contractors, but passed on to the Government, burden the Government in a way that justifies extension of its immunity. * * *

* * * [Moreover,] the Government's immunity for discretionary functions is not even "a product of" the FTCA. Before Congress[, in 1946,] enacted the FTCA (when sovereign immunity barred any tort suit against the Federal Government) we perceived no need for a rule of federal common law to reinforce the Government's immunity by shielding also parties who might contractually pass costs on to it. Nor did we * * * identify a special category of "discretionary" functions for which sovereign immunity was so crucial that a government contractor who exercised discretion should share the Government's immunity from state tort law.

* * * There is no more reason for federal common law to shield contractors now that the Government is liable for some torts than there was when the Government was liable for none. * * *

IV

At bottom, the Court's analysis is premised on the proposition that any tort liability indirectly absorbed by the Government so burdens governmental functions as to compel us to act when Congress has not. That proposition is by no means uncontroversial. The tort system is premised on the assumption that the imposition of liability encourages actors to prevent any injury whose expected cost exceeds the cost of prevention. If the system is working as it should, Government contractors will design equipment to avoid certain injuries (like the deaths of soldiers or Government employees), which would be certain to burden the Government. The Court therefore has no basis for its assumption that tort liability will result in a net burden on the Government (let alone a clearly excessive net burden) rather than a net gain.

Perhaps tort liability is an inefficient means of ensuring the quality of design efforts, but "[w]hatever the merits of the policy" the Court wishes to implement, "its conversion into law is a proper subject for congressional action, not for any creative power of ours." [United States v.] Standard Oil, 332 U.S. [301,] 314–315 [(1947)]. It is, after all, "Congress, not this Court or the other federal courts, [that] is the custodian of the national purse. By the same token [Congress] is the primary and most often the exclusive arbiter of federal fiscal affairs. And these comprehend, as we have said, securing the treasury or the Government against financial losses *however inflicted*. . . . " *Ibid.* (emphasis added). * * *

Were I a legislator, I would probably vote against any law absolving multibillion dollar private enterprises from answering for their tragic mistakes, at least if that law were justified by no more than the unsupported speculation that their liability might ultimately burden the United States Treasury. Some of my colleagues here would evidently vote otherwise (as they have here), but that should not matter here. We are judges not legislators, and the vote is not ours to cast. * * *

■ JUSTICE STEVENS, dissenting.

When judges are asked to embark on a lawmaking venture, I believe they should carefully consider whether they, or a legislative body, are better equipped to perform the task at hand. There are instances of so-called interstitial lawmaking that inevitably become part of the judicial process. But when we are asked to create an entirely new doctrine—to answer "questions of policy on which Congress has not spoken," United States v. Gilman, 347 U.S. 507, 511 (1954)—we have a special duty to identify the proper decisionmaker before trying to make the proper decision.

When the novel question of policy involves a balancing of the conflicting interests in the efficient operation of a massive governmental program and the protection of the rights of the individual—whether in the social welfare context, the civil service context, or the military procurement context—I feel very deeply that we should defer to the expertise of the Congress. * * *

NOTE ON CHOICE OF LAW IN PRIVATE LITIGATION THAT INVOLVES FEDERALLY CREATED INTERESTS

(1) The Presumption That State Law Governs. When the United States grants a property right—for example, to land or to intellectual property—federal law governs the scope of the right (what are the boundaries of a land grant? when does a patent expire?). See, *e.g.*, Hughes v. Washington, 389 U.S. 290 (1967) (federal law governs the ownership of "rights in accretion" to ocean-front lands conveyed by the United States to a private owner before statehood).

But ordinarily, federal law does not govern other questions arising in litigation between private parties—for example, the validity of subsequent transfers or of rights under contracts pertaining to such property interests. An example is Wallis v. Pan American Petroleum Corp., 384 U.S. 63 (1966), distinguished in Boyle. The questions in Wallis were the validity of an oral contract, and the interpretation of a written contract, allegedly assigning a share in an oil and gas lease issued by the United States under the Mineral Leasing Act of 1920. The Court held that these questions were governed by state law—under which, the district court had ruled, the oral contract was not valid and the written contract did not effect an assignment: "In deciding whether rules of federal common law should be fashioned, normally the guiding principle is that a significant conflict between some federal policy or interest and the use of state law * * * must first be specifically shown. * * * We find nothing in the Mineral Leasing Act of 1920 expressing policies inconsistent with state law in the area that concerns us here." Although it suggested that the federal statutory provision that leases shall be assignable might require a federal rule of decision if the state "interpose[d] unreasonable conditions on assignability", the Court found that Louisiana provided a quite feasible method (written instruments) for transferring leases.

(2) Boyle's Analogies. The immunities that federal officials enjoy from damage liability are discussed in detail at pp. 1030–1055, *infra*. When Boyle was decided, federal common law conferred absolute immunity from state-law tort liability on federal officials taking discretionary action within the scope of their employment. (Congress has since codified that immunity and extended it to ministerial conduct.)

Boyle also relies on a provision of the Federal Tort Claims Act (FTCA) that creates an exception, for "discretionary functions", to the Act's general recognition of governmental tort liability and concomitant waiver of the United States' sovereign immunity. See generally pp. 899–901, *infra*. Before invoking the "policy" of the FTCA, should the Court in Boyle have considered whether the exception in question was part of a legislative bargain that was tied to the waiver of sovereign immunity? Compare Pound, *Common Law and Legislation*, 21 Harv.L.Rev. 383, 385 (1908) (urging courts to incorporate statutes "fully into the body of the law as affording not only a rule to be applied but a principle from which to reason"); Strauss, *On Resegregating the Worlds of Statute and Common Law*, 1994 Sup.Ct.Rev. 429, 431 (same). Whatever the merits of relying on statutes as a source of common law generally, note that Boyle's reliance on the FTCA's discretionary function exception paradoxically invokes a statute designed to broaden government responsibility in tort to narrow private responsibility in tort.

(3) An Implied Structural Immunity. Instead of understanding Boyle as a federal common law decision, is it possible to read it as the implementation of a structural immunity against state interference with a federal constitutional function? Professor Clark argues that, properly understood, Boyle fits in a long line of precedents recognizing such implied immunity. See Clark, *Federal Common Law: A Structural Reinterpretation*, 144 U.Pa.L.Rev. 1245, 1368–75 (1996). In McCulloch v. Maryland, 17 U.S. (4 Wheat.) 316, 436 (1819), the Court invalidated a state tax on the Bank of the United States on the ground that states may not, "by taxation or otherwise, * * * retard, impede, burden, or in any manner control, the operations of the constitutional laws enacted by Congress to carry into execution the powers vested in the general government." Similarly, in Osborn v. Bank of the United States, 22 U.S. (9 Wheat.) 738, 867 (1824), Chief Justice Marshall wrote: "Can a contractor for supplying a military post with provisions, be restrained from making purchases within any State, or from transporting the provisions to the place at which the troops were stationed? or could he be fined or taxed for doing so? We have not yet heard these questions answered in the affirmative." According to Clark, allowing the state to impose liability for alleged design defects in Boyle would have intruded upon military functions that the Constitution assigns to the federal political branches. How convincing is that rationale for Boyle? What limiting principle distinguishes permissible from impermissible state regulations of private activity serving a federal purpose?

(4) The Scope of the Immunity. Are the United States' interests necessarily threatened by a private contractor's tort liability whenever there is a design defect in reasonably precise contractual specifications? Should the Court have required clearer proof that the design of the escape hatch in fact implicated "judgment as to the balancing of many technical, military, and even social considerations"? Consider also the holding in Boyle that immunity attaches only if the contractor warns of known dangers of which the United States is unaware. Why shouldn't contractors also be liable for failure to warn about dangers of which they *should* have known?[1]

(5) The WDAY Case. None of the Boyle opinions mentioned Farmers Educ. & Co-op. Union v. WDAY, Inc., 360 U.S. 525 (1959). The case involved a federal law requiring radio and television stations that permitted broadcasts by a political candidate to give equal time to competing candidates. Stations were forbidden to censor such "equal time" broadcasts. WDAY was sued for defamation for having broadcast a reply by one Townley to earlier broadcasts by rival candidates. The Court held that the station was immune from defamation liability arising from equal time broadcasts. A contrary holding would "sanction the unconscionable result of permitting civil and perhaps criminal liability to be imposed for the very conduct the statute demands of the licensee"—liability that might lead broadcasters to refuse to broadcast any candidates' speeches in the first instance, thereby "hamper[ing] the congressional plan to develop broadcasting as a political outlet". Justice Frankfurter's lone dissent argued that the Court should not "stifle" state

---

[1] For critical analyses of Boyle, see Cass & Gillette, *The Government Contractor Defense: Contractual Allocation of Public Risk*, 77 Va.L.Rev. 257 (1991); Green & Matasar, *The Supreme Court and the Products Liability Crisis: Lessons from Boyle's Government Contractor Defense*, 63 S.Cal.L.Rev. 637 (1990).

action unless it "would truly entail contradictory duties or make actual, not argumentative, inroads on what Congress has commanded or forbidden." Wasn't the WDAY case—involving immunity from tort liability arising from the defendant's adherence to federal rules—closely on point in Boyle? Indeed, was the case for federal common law *a fortiori* in Boyle, because WDAY involved no risk that, absent immunity, costs would be shifted to the United States? Or is WDAY distinguishable because recognition of immunity left a different private party (Townley) whom the plaintiff could sue? Because, in contrast to the legal duty imposed on the defendant in WDAY, the defendant in Boyle was under no legal duty to do business with the government?

———

NOTE ON FEDERAL PREEMPTION OF STATE LAW

(1) The Range of Issues. Many of the cases in the preceding Note raise the general question whether, in interpreting federal statutes or "filling in" their gaps, courts should fashion a distinctive federal rule of decision or should instead resort to state law. That question arises under a multitude of federal statutes; this Note discusses only a few of these situations in order to raise some general issues.[1]

Reconsider Farmers Educ. & Co-op. Union v. WDAY, Inc., discussed immediately above. In that case, one might frame the question before the Court as involving (a) an interpretation of a federal statute, (b) the appropriateness of federal common lawmaking, or (c) whether federal legislation preempts state law. Does (should) the framing of the issue affect the outcome? See generally Dinh, *Reassessing the Law of Preemption*, 88 Geo.L.J. 2085 (2000).

(2) The Meaning of Federal Statutory Terms. Many cases declare that "in the absence of a plain indication to the contrary, * * * Congress when it enacts a statute is not making the application of the federal act dependent on state law." Jerome v. United States, 318 U.S. 101, 104 (1943). Jerome held that under a federal bank robbery statute that prohibits entering a bank with intent to commit a "felony", federal rather than state law governs whether particular conduct is a "felony". Similarly, in Drye v. United States, 528 U.S. 49 (1999), the question was whether an insolvent taxpayer's right to inherit his mother's estate constituted either "property" or "a right to property" to which federal tax liens attached—even though the taxpayer had, in accordance with state law, disclaimed his right to inherit. In holding that the disclaimer did not defeat the attachment of federal tax liens, the Court reasoned that the federal lien provisions "look to state law for delineation of the taxpayer's rights or interests" but "leave to federal law the determination whether those rights or interests constitute 'property' or 'rights to property'".[2]

---

[1] For a wide-ranging discussion of preemption, see Symposium, *Ordering State-Federal Relations Through Preemption Doctrine*, 102 Nw.U.L.Rev. 503 (2008).

[2] For other cases in which the application of a federal law definition may require analysis of state law, see, *e.g.*, Dickerson v. New Banner Inst., Inc., 460 U.S. 103 (1983) (question whether someone whose state conviction had been expunged could be prosecuted for violating federal law banning a person "convicted" of a felony from dealing in guns); Helvering v. Stuart, 317 U.S. 154 (1942) (question whether there is "power to revest" title to trust corpus in grantor); Morgan v. Commissioner, 309 U.S. 78, 80 (1940) (definition of "general power of appointment" under tax statute).

Sometimes, however, a federal statutory term is interpreted as embodying a state law definition. In Reconstruction Fin. Corp. v. Beaver County, 328 U.S. 204 (1946), a *state* court action, a federal statute barred state or local taxation of the personal property of the RFC (a federal agency) but permitted non-discriminatory taxation of its real property. The county had taxed an RFC subsidiary on certain heavy machines. Most were not attached to the building but were held in place by their weight; others were attached by easily removable screws and bolts; and some could be moved within the manufacturing plant. Challenging the county's treatment of the machines as real property, the RFC relied "on the generally accepted principle that Congress normally intends that its laws shall operate uniformly throughout the nation". But the Court found uniformity unattainable under the statute, which permitted taxation of real property at the varying tax rates of different localities. More broadly, local taxation was geared to "[c]oncepts of real property [that] are deeply rooted in state traditions * * * and laws", and to require tax authorities to define real property differently for the RFC than for other taxpayers would hamper local tax administration. Thus, real property should be defined under state law, "so long as it is plain, as it is here, that the state rules do not effect a discrimination against the government, or patently run counter to the terms of the Act."

The decision in Beaver County was made easier by Congress' apparent purpose of maintaining uniformity in the treatment of taxpayers *within* each taxing authority. But in De Sylva v. Ballentine, 351 U.S. 570 (1956), the Court followed Beaver County without as strong an indication of legislative purpose. There, in a suit between private parties, the question was whether the right under the federal copyright law of "children" of a deceased author to renew the copyright included those born out of wedlock. The Court declared that "[t]he scope of a federal right is, of course, a federal question, but that does not mean that its content is not to be determined by state, rather than federal law. [Citing, *inter alia*, Beaver County.] This is especially true where a statute deals with a familial relationship; there is no federal law of domestic relations, which is primarily a matter of state concern." Thus, the Court held that state law (specifically, the rules defining whether a child takes as an heir) governs, at least when the state's definition of children is not "entirely strange to those familiar with its ordinary usage". Compare Mississippi Band of Choctaw Indians v. Holyfield, 490 U.S. 30 (1989) (applying federal standards to determine whether, for purposes of the Indian Child Welfare Act, a Native American child "is domiciled within the reservation of [a] tribe", thereby giving the tribal court exclusive jurisdiction over the child's adoption).

(3) Conflict with Federal Purposes and Preemption. What is the relationship between federal common lawmaking and implied federal preemption of state law? The remainder of this Note offers a brief overview of the large body of preemption jurisprudence.[3]

(a) A standard recitation of preemption doctrine is found in Crosby v. National Foreign Trade Council, 530 U.S. 363, 373 (2000):

"Even without an express provision for preemption, we have found that state law must yield to a congressional Act in at least two circumstances.

---

[3]   In addition to sources cited elsewhere in this Note, see 1 Tribe, American Constitutional Law §§ 6–28 to 6–32 (3d ed. 2000); Weinberg, *The Federal-State Conflict of Laws: "Actual Conflicts,"* 70 Tex.L.Rev. 1743 (1992).

When Congress intends federal law to 'occupy the field,' state law in that area is preempted. [California v. ARC America Corp., 490 U.S. 93, 100 (1989)]. And even if Congress has not occupied the field, state law is naturally preempted to the extent of any conflict with a federal statute. We will find preemption where it is impossible for a private party to comply with both state and federal law, and where 'under the circumstances of [a] particular case, [the challenged state law] stands as an obstacle to the accomplishment and execution of the full purposes and objectives of Congress.' Hines [v. Davidowitz, 312 U.S. 52,] 67 [(1941)]. What is a sufficient obstacle is a matter of judgment, to be informed by examining the federal statute as a whole and identifying its purpose and intended effects * * *."

Preemption Doctrine

In addition, the Court has said that "we start with the assumption that the historic police powers of the States were not to be superseded by the Federal Act unless that was the clear and manifest purpose of Congress." Rice v. Santa Fe Elevator Corp., 331 U.S. 218, 230 (1947). Some decisions describe this presumption as a general one, see, *e.g.*, Building & Constr. Trades Council v. Associated Builders & Contractors, 507 U.S. 218, 224 (1993), while others suggest that its application is confined to fields that the states have traditionally occupied, see, *e.g.*, United States v. Locke, 529 U.S. 89, 108 (2000).[4]

(b) Field preemption, though of notable importance in some areas (for example, labor-management relations[5]), is not easily established, see, *e.g.*, Hillsborough County v. Automated Med. Labs., Inc., 471 U.S. 707, 717 (1985), and, when it is recognized, the field is often narrowly defined, see, *e.g.*, PG & E Co. v. State Energy Res. Conservation & Dev. Comm'n, 461 U.S. 190, 212 (1983) (federal law occupies only the field of nuclear safety, not all nuclear matters).[6] For the suggestion that the Court's standards for field preemption have become stricter in recent years, see Kurns v. Railroad Friction Products Corp., 132 S.Ct. 1261, 1270 (2012) (Kagan, J., concurring).

(c) Conflict preemption, as the discussion in Crosby indicates, embraces two distinct situations. In the easier but far rarer case, compliance with both federal and state duties is simply impossible. See, *e.g.*, Southland Corp. v. Keating, 465 U.S. 1 (1984) (state law requiring judicial determination of certain claims preempted by federal law requiring arbitration of those

---

[4] Professor Hills argues that the presumption against preemption can be justified as a preference-eliciting default rule. (On such rules generally, see Elhauge, Statutory Default Rules 149–223 (2008).) Relying on insights from the political science literature, Hills suggests "that, in most cases, the interests *favoring* preemption are best suited for promoting an open and vigorous debate on the floor of Congress." Hills, *Against Preemption: How Federalism Can Improve the National Legislative Process*, 82 N.Y.U.L.Rev. 1, 28 (2007) (emphasis added). Accordingly, he believes that a presumption *disfavoring* preemption will more likely provoke Congress to address preemption issues explicitly. But see Note, 120 Harv.L.Rev. 1604, 1612–13 (2007) (examining 127 preemption cases decided by the Supreme Court between the 1983 and 2003 Terms and finding that "Congress has virtually always accepted the Court's preemption decisions").

[5] See, *e.g.*, Garner v. Teamsters Union, 346 U.S. 485 (1953) (state courts may not grant injunctions against activities prohibited by the National Labor Relations Act); Local 926, IUOE v. Jones, 460 U.S. 669 (1983) (state law damage action by supervisory employee against union for tortious interference with his employment contract was preempted because conduct was arguably prohibited by NLRA).

[6] Gardbaum, *The Nature of Preemption*, 79 Cornell L.Rev. 767, 801–07 (1994), contends that before the 1930s, preemption generally was viewed as field preemption, and congressional legislation was routinely taken to divest state power over the subject in question—a view that became untenable as the reach of federal legislation expanded.

claims). In the second and more common situation, compliance with both laws is possible, yet state law poses an obstacle to the achievement of federal purposes.

(d) Crosby and other decisions (*e.g.*, English v. General Elec. Co., 496 U.S. 72, 79 n.5 (1990)) have recognized that field and conflict preemption are not "rigidly distinct." Field preemption, for example, can be recharacterized as conflict preemption (any state regulation of the field conflicts with a congressional decision to exclude state regulation). Relatedly, in any field preemption case, an important question is just how broadly the field should be defined; the narrower the definition, the more the case resembles conflict preemption.

(4) Preemption of Parallel State Law. Generally, federal law permits parallel or supplemental state law to co-exist. In California v. ARC America Corp., 490 U.S. 93 (1989), for example, the Court, without dissent, held that the federal antitrust laws—which the Court has interpreted as generally precluding suit by "indirect purchasers" of products whose price has been illegally fixed—do not preempt state antitrust laws that do permit suit by indirect purchasers.

But sometimes federal regulation displaces parallel state law on the basis that Congress intended federal regulation to be exclusive. For example, in Sears, Roebuck & Co. v. Stiffel Co., 376 U.S. 225 (1964), and Compco Corp. v. Day-Brite Lighting, Inc., 376 U.S. 234 (1964), the Court held that state unfair competition law could not proscribe the copying of products not entitled to federal patent protection: "[T]he patent system is one in which uniform federal standards are carefully used to promote invention while at the same time preserving free competition. Obviously a State could not * * * extend the life of a patent beyond its expiration date or give a patent on an article which lacked the level of invention required for federal patents. * * * Just as a State cannot encroach upon the federal patent laws directly, it cannot, under some other law, such as that forbidding unfair competition, give protection of a kind that clashes with the objectives of the federal patent laws.

" * * * To allow a State by use of its law of unfair competition to prevent the copying of an article which represents too slight an advance to be patented would be to permit the State to block off from the public something which federal law has said belongs to the public. The result would be that while federal law grants only 14 or 17 years' protection to genuine inventions, States could allow perpetual protection to articles too lacking in novelty to merit any patent at all under federal constitutional standards."

(5) Express Preemption Clauses. In theory, an express preemption clause presents a standard question of statutory interpretation. Recent decisions interpreting such clauses, however, have suggested that such clauses do not preclude consideration of implied preemption as well, and some decisions find implied preemption without even reaching the question of express preemption. See generally Geier v. American Honda Motor Co., 529 U.S. 861, 869–74 (2000); Jordan, *The Shifting Preemption Paradigm: Conceptual and Interpretive Issues*, 51 Vand.L.Rev. 1149 (1998). Compare, *e.g.*, Boggs v. Boggs, 520 U.S. 833 (1997) (ignoring ERISA's broad and explicit preemption clause and holding instead that applying Louisiana community property law to determine the disposition of a decedent's ex-spouse's undistributed pension benefits would conflict with the purpose of particular substantive ERISA provisions), with Egelhoff v. Egelhoff, 532 U.S. 141 (2001) (holding that ERISA's express preemption clause displaced state law establishing a default provision that the designation of a spouse as the beneficiary of a pension and life insurance policy was automatically revoked upon divorce). In addition, the Court has now made clear that the presumption against preemption applies with full force to the interpretation of express preemption clauses. See Altria Group, Inc. v. Good, 555 U.S. 70, 77 (2008) ("[W]hen the text of a pre-emption clause is susceptible of more than one plausible reading, courts ordinarily 'accept the reading that disfavors preemption.'") (quoting Bates v. Dow Agrosciences LLC, 544 U.S. 431, 449 (2005)).[7]

When Congress has adopted an express preemption clause, does it threaten to disrupt the balance that Congress meant to strike if the Court invokes implied preemption principles? Are there still sound reasons to apply the presumption against preemption, rather than ordinary rules of construction, when Congress has expressed an explicit intention to preempt, leaving only the question of scope to be decided by the courts?

(6) Preemption, the Supremacy Clause, and Textualism. Because the "obstacle" component of conflict preemption rests on judicial attribution of legislative purpose to Congress, it can be viewed as depending on the assumption that such purposes can be ascertained, and as being in tension with more text-focused theories of statutory interpretation. See generally pp. 652–656, *supra.* Indeed, Professor Nelson suggests it is inappropriate to interpret every congressional enactment (as implied preemption doctrine effectively does) as if it included a textual provision preempting any state law that is an obstacle to accomplishing the statutory purposes. See Nelson, *Preemption,* 86 Va.L.Rev. 225 (2000). Yet the Court, despite its increasing emphasis on textual interpretation, continues to invoke implied preemption principles to invalidate state legislation as contrary to federal purposes. See Meltzer, *The Supreme Court's Judicial Passivity,* 2002 Sup.Ct.Rev. 343.

Indeed, even among the most textually inclined Justices, only Justice Thomas has forsworn "obstacle" preemption. Wyeth v. Levine, 555 U.S. 555, 582 (2009) (Thomas, J., concurring in the judgment). Describing the Court's "entire body of 'purposes and objectives' pre-emption jurisprudence [as] inherently flawed", Justice Thomas' separate opinion in Wyeth argued that obstacle preemption cases "improperly rely on legislative history, broad atextual notions of congressional purpose, and even congressional inaction in order to pre-empt state law." To find preemption based on those indicia of unenacted statutory purpose, he reasoned, contradicts the safeguards of federalism found in the Supremacy Clause, U.S. Const. Art. VI, cl. 2, which "gives 'supreme' status only to those [laws] that are 'made in Pursuance' of '[t]his Constitution.'" To respect that condition, he said, the Court may find preemption only when a state law conflicts with a statutory text (or a regulation authorized by such a text) that has cleared the hurdles of bicameralism and presentment set forth by Article I, § 7. How convincing is Justice Thomas' reading of the Supremacy Clause? Compare pp. 647–649, *supra.*

Justice Thomas has further stressed that the Court's finding preemption merely because a state law impedes a federal statutory purpose disregards the fact that federal often require compromise that may not

"Obstacle" preemption critique

---

[7] For a decision that broadly interpreted an awkwardly worded preemption clause without any mention of the presumption against preemption, see Bruesewitz v. Wyeth LLC, 562 U.S. 223 (2011).

pursue the legislative majority's goals " 'at all costs' " (quoting Geier v. American Honda Motor Co., 529 U.S. 861, 904 (2000) (Stevens, J., dissenting)); see also AT & T Mobility LLC v. Concepcion, 131 S.Ct. 1740, 1754 (2011) (Thomas, J., concurring) (renewing his objection to "purposes-and-objectives preemption"); Williamson v. Mazda Motor of America, Inc., 131 S.Ct. 1131, 1142–43 (2011) (Thomas, J., concurring in the judgment) (same).[8] Apart from the Supremacy Clause, Justice Thomas' position seems to rest on views concerning legislative compromise and bicameralism that the Court has embraced in some of its recent opinions. See pp. 654–655, *supra.* Given that the other Justices who associate themselves in some degree with textualism (Justices Scalia and Kennedy) frequently emphasize legislative compromise in other contexts, why haven't they joined Justice Thomas in rejecting obstacle preemption? In view of the challenges Congress would face if it were to try to anticipate, specify, and accurately express the proper resolution to all of the preemption questions that would arise in the lifetime of even a moderately complex regulatory statute, can textualism plausibly supply a workable approach to preemption questions? *See* Meltzer, *Textualism and Preemption,* 112 Mich.L.Rev. 1 (2013) (arguing that the answer is no).[9]

(7) Preemption and Federalism. The continued success of preemption challenges is noteworthy, in part, because it cuts against the Court's broader trend toward reinvigorating constitutional federalism. By one tally, in the ten years following Justice Thomas' ascension to the Court to produce a pro-federalism majority, the Court found preemption in whole or in part in roughly two-thirds of the thirty-five preemption cases before it. See Fallon, *The Conservative Paths of the Rehnquist Court's Federalism Decisions,* 69 U.Chi.L.Rev. 429, 462 (2002). Consistent with these statistics, moreover, conventional wisdom holds that the Court applies the presumption against preemption   spottily   at   best.   See,   *e.g.,*   Manning,   *Lessons   from   a*

---

[8]   Williamson highlights the judicial lawmaking discretion inherent in obstacle preemption. In that case, the Court held that a Department of Transportation regulation giving auto manufacturers the choice to install lap or shoulder belts in certain rear positions in a vehicle did not preempt a state tort action alleging that Mazda acted negligently by using a shoulder rather than a lap belt in such a position. By contrast, the Court in Geier v. American Honda Motor Co., *supra,* had previously held that, by giving manufacturers the choice between airbags or passive restraints, a prior version of the same regulation *did* preempt a state tort action alleging that an auto manufacturer had negligently failed to equip its vehicles with airbags. In Williamson, the majority distinguished Geier on the ground that both the drafting history and subsequent agency interpretations of the amended regulation revealed no agency intent to give manufacturers an *affirmative* choice between shoulder and lap belts. In his opinion concurring in the judgment in Williamson, Justice Thomas argued that the Court's reasoning, which he described as free-ranging "psychoanalysis" of the agency's goals, confirmed that "[p]urposes-and-objectives pre-emption" necessarily "roams beyond statutory or regulatory text" and "is thus wholly illegitimate."

[9]   In contrast with his views on "obstacle" preemption, Justice Thomas would not hesitate to find preemption in a case resting on a true conflict—one in which a party cannot simultaneously comply with state and federal law. See Paragraph (3), *supra.* In a plurality opinion in PLIVA, Inc. v. Mensing, 131 S.Ct. 2567 (2011), Justice Thomas (joined by Chief Justice Roberts and Justices Scalia and Alito) relied on historical analysis found in Nelson, *supra,* to conclude that the Supremacy Clause was modeled on *non obstante* clauses that eighteenth century legislatures had inserted into statutes to signal their intention to repeal earlier statutes on the same subject. In particular, legislatures used *non obstante* clauses to signal the inapplicability of the traditional strong presumption against implied repeal—a presumption that required interpreters to strain to read potentially conflicting statutes as being in harmony. From that starting point, the plurality concluded that the *non obstante* language in the Supremacy Clause meant that courts should not strain to find ways to avoid an evident conflict between state and federal law.

Nondelegation Canon, 83 Notre Dame L.Rev. 1541, 1560 n.58 (2008) (collecting sources); Hoke, *Preemption Pathologies and Civic Republican Values*, 71 B.U.L.Rev. 685, 733 (1991). Indeed, at least one scholar believes that the Court has shifted to a "centralization default"—a marked disposition toward finding preemption in cases of doubt. Sharpe, *Legislating Preemption*, 53 Wm. & Mary L.Rev. 163 (2011); see also Metzger, *Federalism and Federal Agency Reform*, 111 Colum.L.Rev. 1 (2011).

Consider a case like Boggs v. Boggs, Paragraph (5), *supra*, in which the Court found that the purposes underlying ERISA impliedly preempted state community property law. Do such cases—which quietly invoke statutory purpose to find implied preemption on mundane matters of local concern— ultimately have a greater effect on the federal-state balance than the Court presently acknowledges? Consider Justice Breyer's contention that "in today's world, filled with legal complexity, the true test of federalist principle may lie, not in the occasional constitutional effort to trim Congress' commerce power at its edges, United States v. Morrison, 529 U.S. 598 (2000), or to protect a State's treasury from a private damages action, Board of Trustees of Univ. of Ala. v. Garrett, 531 U.S. 356 (2001), but rather in those many statutory cases where courts interpret the mass of technical detail that is the ordinary diet of the law." Egelhoff v. Egelhoff, Paragraph (5), *supra*, at 160–61 (Breyer, J., dissenting).

(8) Preemption Through Agency Decisionmaking. What difference, if any, should it make if a federal court addressing regulatory preemption is reviewing an agency decision in favor of preemption? Should the Court apply its usual rule under Chevron U.S.A. v. Natural Resources Defense Council, Inc., 467 U.S. 837 (1984), which requires a reviewing court to accept an agency's "reasonable" interpretation of an ambiguous organic act? Although the Supreme Court ducked the question in Watters v. Wachovia Bank, 550 U.S. 1 (2007), three dissenting Justices (Chief Justice Roberts and Justices Stevens and Scalia) indicated their willingness to find that Chevron does not apply.

Some recent commentary supports the position taken in the Watters dissent. Forgoing Chevron deference to an agency's preemption decision is said to promote the political safeguards of federalism by ensuring that Congress does not displace state law through means that fall short of bicameralism and presentment—that is, by delegating to an agency the decision of whether and how much to preempt state law. See, *e.g.*, Sunstein, *Nondelegation Canons*, 67 U.Chi.L.Rev. 331 (2000) (describing the presumption against preemption as "an important requirement in light of the various safeguards against cavalier disregard of state interests created by the system of state representation in Congress"); Clark, *Process-Based Preemption*, in Preemption Choice: The Theory, Law, and Reality of Federalism's Core Question 192 (Buzbee ed. 2009) (arguing that the Supremacy Clause requires the presumption against preemption as a judicially manageable way to prevent Congress from using delegation to bypass the political safeguards of federalism). Other commentators, however, suggest that even if the presumption against preemption precludes Chevron's application by courts, the decision of expert agencies to preempt state law should at least receive the more modest, intermediate form of deference prescribed by Skidmore v. Swift & Co., 323 U.S. 134, 140 (1944), which instructs judges to give an agency interpretation of an organic statute the "weight" warranted by "the thoroughness evident in its consideration, the validity of its reasoning, its consistency with earlier and later pronouncements, and all those factors which give it power to persuade, if lacking power to control." See, *e.g.*, Mendelson, *Chevron and Preemption*, 102 Mich.L.Rev. 737, 789, 797–98 (2004);[10] Sharkey, *Products Liability Preemption: An Institutional Approach*, 76 Geo.Wash.L.Rev. 449, 491–98 (2008). See also Merrill, *Preemption and Institutional Choice*, 102 Nw.U.L.Rev. 727 (2008) (arguing that courts should give significant and, under some circumstances, perhaps conclusive weight to agency assessments of the impact of state rules on the implementation of federal regulation). Not all, however, are persuaded. See Young, *Executive Preemption*, 102 Nw.U.L.Rev. 869, 870–71 (2008), which contends that the presumption against preemption "is sufficiently important and sufficiently tied to constitutional values that it should override even agency interpretations that might otherwise be persuasive." See also Sharpe, *Toward (a) Faithful Agency in the Supreme Court's Preemption Jurisprudence*, 18 Geo. Mason L.Rev. 367 (2011) (arguing that the Court should find preemption only when Congress has included a preemption clause in a statute or has expressly delegated to an agency the power to preempt state law).

(9) Variable Preemption and Federal Common Lawmaking. Recall Justice Scalia's statement, in the Boyle decision, that for federal common lawmaking to be justified, "[t]he conflict with federal policy need not be as sharp as that which must exist for ordinary pre-emption when Congress legislates 'in a field which the States have traditionally occupied.' Rice v. Santa Fe Elevator Corp., 331 U.S. [218, 230 (1947)]. Or to put the point differently, the fact that the area in question *is* one of unique federal concern changes what would otherwise be a conflict that cannot produce pre-emption into one that can."

The Supreme Court has similarly indicated that preemption analysis operates differently in different areas. While the presumption against preemption most plainly applies in areas of traditional state regulatory authority, preemption is more easily inferred in areas in which "the federal interest is so dominant that the federal system will be assumed to preclude enforcement of state laws on the same subject." Rice, *supra*, at 230. See also, *e.g.*, United States v. Locke, 529 U.S. 89, 114 (2000) (state regulation of the operation of oil tankers preempted by federal law; in national and international maritime commerce, "there is no beginning assumption that concurrent regulation by the State is a valid exercise of its police powers"); Ramah Navajo Sch. Bd., Inc. v. Bureau of Revenue, 458 U.S. 832, 838 (1982) (question of preemption of state regulation of Navajo Tribe members "is not controlled by standards * * * developed in other areas," but is informed by "traditional notions of tribal sovereignty, and the recognition and

---

[10] More broadly, Professor Mendelson has suggested that the administrative process may take state interests into account no less effectively than the legislative process. In particular, she argues that administrative agencies, which are subject to presidential and congressional oversight, have political incentives to consider the interests of states. She further notes that the Administrative Procedure Act's general provisions give states the opportunity to participate in certain regulatory processes, and that a succession of executive orders specifically require agencies to take state interests into account in framing regulation. See Mendelson, *supra*, at 759–79. Despite these considerations, however, Professor Mendelson would limit agencies to Skidmore deference because they "lack both institutional expertise on important issues of state autonomy and federalism and adequate statutory guidance regarding preemption questions." Mendelson, *A Presumption Against Agency Preemption*, 102 Nw.U.L.Rev. 695, 698 (2008).

encouragement of this sovereignty in congressional Acts promoting tribal independence and economic development").

What criteria should the Court use to determine whether the federal interest predominates? Consider Arizona v. United States, 132 S.Ct. 2492 (2012), in which a divided Court held that Arizona could not (a) make it a crime for an alien to fail to comply with federal registration requirements; (b) make it a crime for an unauthorized alien to work or apply for employment in the state; and (c) authorize state law enforcement authorities to arrest a person on probable cause that he or she has committed an offense that makes that individual removable. At the outset of its analysis, the Court emphasized the federal government's "broad, undoubted power" over immigration and the potential foreign relations implications of the treatment of foreign nationals within U.S. borders. The Court also noted the pervasiveness of federal regulation of immigration. From that starting point, the Court found it relatively straightforward to conclude that the three provisions of state law mentioned above either entered a field that federal law had fully occupied or stood as an obstacle to the purposes of federal law.

Justices Scalia, Thomas, and Alito filed separate partial dissents. Of interest here, Justice Scalia argued that states have a traditional sovereign interest in the preservation of the integrity of their borders, and that courts should insist on a clear statement of legislative intent before reading a statute to abrogate that sovereign authority. Because none of the Arizona provisions squarely conflicted with federal law, Justice Scalia would have upheld them all. The fact that state laws strike a different balance from the federal laws on some issues, he argued, should not alone provide a ground for preemption.

Notice that both the majority and Justice Scalia's dissent relied upon broad structural presumptions to determine how to approach preemption in the context of immigration law.[11] Where do these presumptions come from and how far do they go?[12] Does the complexity of the competing arguments in this case lend any support to Justice Thomas's more general concerns about relying on implied preemption? See Paragraph (6), *supra*.

---

[11] See Abrams, *Plenary Power Preemption*, 99 Va.L.Rev. 601 (2013) (arguing that, in areas of overriding national interest such as alienage, the Court has consistently shown itself willing to find preemption even when conventional applications of conflict or obstacle preemption would not produce such a result).

[12] For another example of variable preemption, consider Arizona v. Inter-Tribal Council of Arizona, Inc., 133 S.Ct. 2247 (2013), in which the Court held that the presumption against preemption does not apply when Congress regulates the manner of voting for federal office. In an opinion by Justice Scalia (joined by Chief Justice Roberts and Justices Ginsburg, Breyer, Sotomayor, and Kagan), the Court held that the National Voter Registration Act of 1993 (NVRA), 42 U.S.C. § 1973gg *et seq.*, which requires states to "accept and use" a uniform federal voter registration form, preempted a state law requirement that voters submit proof of citizenship with their registration. According to Justice Scalia, "*all* [congressional] action under the Elections Clause displaces some element of a preexisting state regulatory regime, because the text of the Clause confers the power to do exactly (and only) that. By contrast, even laws enacted under the Commerce Clause * * * will not always implicate concurrent state power". In dissent, Justice Alito argued that the presumption against preemption applies "with full force" to election law, given the states' compelling interest in preserving the integrity of their elections. Are such canons, like the presumption against preemption itself, a form of federal common law? See Gluck, *The Federal Common Law of Statutory Interpretation: Erie for the Age of Statutes*, 54 Wm. & Mary.L.Rev.753 (2013).

INTRODUCTORY NOTE ON FEDERAL COMMON LAW IMPLIED BY JURISDICTIONAL GRANTS AND STRUCTURAL INFERENCE

In previous cases in this Chapter, federal common law is generally fashioned in support of statutory regulation enacted by Congress, and the judge-made law is interstitial, addressing matters allied to a legislative program that are not specifically addressed by any statutory provision. By contrast, the next principal case concerns federal common lawmaking in an area (admiralty matters) in which federal courts, exercising the admiralty jurisdiction granted by Article III and congressional legislation, initially provided an entire corpus juris without prior congressional regulation. Thus, common lawmaking cannot be justified as filling the gaps in a legislative program, nor can it be characterized merely as interstitial; and if it is viewed as field preemption, the only enactments on which it is based are constitutional and statutory grants of federal jurisdiction.

Chelentis v. Luckenbach S. S. Co.

247 U.S. 372, 38 S.Ct. 501, 62 L.Ed. 1171 (1918).
Certiorari to the United States Circuit Court of Appeals for the Second Circuit.

■ MR. JUSTICE MCREYNOLDS delivered the opinion of the Court.

* * * [P]etitioner was employed by respondent * * * on board the steamship J. L. Luckenbach * * *. While at sea, * * * petitioner undertook to perform certain duties on deck during a heavy wind; a wave came aboard, knocked him down and broke his leg. * * * [W]hen the vessel arrived [in New York] he was taken to the marine hospital, where he remained for three months; during that time it became necessary to amputate his leg. After discharge from the hospital, claiming that his injuries resulted from the negligence and an improvident order of a superior officer, he instituted a common-law action in Supreme Court, New York county, demanding full indemnity for damage sustained. The cause was removed to the United States District Court because of diverse citizenship. Counsel did not question [the] seaworthiness of [the] ship or her appliances, and announced that no claim was made for maintenance, cure, or wages.* At [the] conclusion of plaintiff's evidence the court directed verdict for respondent, and judgment thereon was affirmed by the Circuit Court of Appeals. [The court of appeals noted that "[t]he contract of a seaman is maritime, and has written into it those peculiar features of the maritime law that were considered in the case of The Osceola[, 189 U.S. 158]."] * * *

In The Osceola, a libel in rem to recover damages for personal injuries to a seaman while on board and alleged to have resulted from the master's negligence, * * * we held:

"1. That the vessel and her owners are liable, in case a seaman falls sick, or is wounded, in the service of the ship, to the extent of his

------

*   [Ed.] " 'Maintenance' is the right of a seaman to food and lodging if he falls ill or becomes injured while in the service of the ship. 'Cure' is the right to necessary medical services." Schoenbaum, Admiralty and Maritime Law, § 4–28, at 334 (5th ed. 2012).

maintenance and cure, and to his wages, at least so long as the voyage is continued.

."2. That the vessel and her owner are * * * liable to an indemnity for injuries received by seamen in consequence of the unseaworthiness of the ship * * *.

"3. That all the members of the crew, except perhaps the master, are, as between themselves, fellow servants, and hence seamen cannot recover for injuries sustained through the negligence of another member of the crew beyond the expense of their maintenance and cure.

"4. That the seaman is not allowed to recover an indemnity for the negligence of the master, or any member of the crew, but is entitled to maintenance and cure, whether the injuries were received by negligence or accident."

After reference to article 1, § 8, and article 3, § 2, of the Constitution, we declared in Southern Pacific Co. v. Jensen, 244 U. S. 205, 215, 216: "Considering our former opinions, it must now be accepted as settled doctrine that, in consequence of these provisions, Congress has paramount power to fix and determine the maritime law which shall prevail throughout the country. * * * And further, that in the absence of some controlling statute, the general maritime law, as accepted by the federal courts, constitutes part of our national law, applicable to matters within the admiralty and maritime jurisdiction." Concerning extent [sic] to which the general maritime law may be changed, modified or affected by state legislation, this was said: "No such legislation is valid if it contravenes the essential purpose expressed by an act of Congress, or works material prejudice to the characteristic features of the general maritime law, or interferes with the proper harmony and uniformity of that law in its international and interstate relations. This limitation, at the least, is essential to the effective operation of the fundamental purposes for which such law was incorporated into our national laws by the Constitution itself. These purposes are forcefully indicated in the foregoing quotations from The Lottawanna, 21 Wall. 558, 575." Among such quotations is the following: "One thing, however, is unquestionable; the Constitution must have referred to a system of law coextensive with, and operating uniformly in, the whole country. It certainly could not have been the intention to place the rules and limits of maritime law under the disposal and regulation of the several states, as that would have defeated the uniformity and consistency at which the Constitution aimed on all subjects of a commercial character affecting the intercourse of the states with each other or with foreign states."

* * * [T]he parties' rights and liabilities were matters clearly within the admiralty jurisdiction. * * * Under the doctrine approved in Southern Pacific Co. v. Jensen, no state has power to abolish the well-recognized maritime rule concerning measure of recovery and substitute therefor the full indemnity rule of the common law. Such a substitution would distinctly and definitely change or add to the settled maritime law; and it would be destructive of the "uniformity and consistency at which the Constitution aimed on all subjects of a commercial character affecting the intercourse of the states with each other or with foreign states."

* * * [Petitioner argues that he has the right to recover full indemnity according to the common law under s]ection 9, Judiciary Act of 1789,

whereby District Courts of the United States were given exclusive original cognizance of all civil causes of admiralty and maritime jurisdiction, "saving to suitors, in all cases, the right of a common-law remedy, where the common law is competent to give it" * * *.

The precise effect of the quoted clause of the original Judiciary Act has not been delimited by this court and different views have been entertained concerning it. In Southern Pacific Co. v. Jensen we definitely ruled that it gave no authority to the several states to enact legislation which would work "material prejudice to the characteristic features of the general maritime law or interfere with the proper harmony and uniformity of that law in its international and interstate relations." In The Moses Taylor, 4 Wall. 411, 431, we said: "That clause only saves to suitors 'the right of a common-law remedy, where the common law is competent to give it.' It is not a remedy in the common-law courts which is saved, but a common-law remedy. A proceeding in rem, as used in the admiralty courts, is not a remedy afforded by the common law; it is a proceeding under the civil law." And in Knapp, Stout & Co. v. McCaffrey, 177 U. S. 638, 644, 648: "Some of the cases already cited recognize the distinction between a common-law action and a common-law remedy. * * * 'If the suit be in personam against an individual defendant, with an auxiliary attachment against a particular thing, or against the property of the defendant in general, it is essentially a proceeding according to the course of the common law, and within the saving clause of the statute * * * of a common-law remedy. The suit in this case being one in equity to enforce a common-law remedy, the state courts were correct in assuming jurisdiction'."

The distinction between rights and remedies is fundamental. A right is a well founded or acknowledged claim; a remedy is the means employed to enforce a right or redress an injury. Plainly, we think, under the saving clause a right sanctioned by the maritime law may be enforced through any appropriate remedy recognized at common law; but we find nothing therein which reveals an intention to give the complaining party an election to determine whether the defendant's liability shall be measured by common-law standards rather than those of the maritime law. Under the circumstances here presented, without regard to the court where he might ask relief, petitioner's rights were those recognized by the law of the sea. * * *

The judgment of the court below is

Affirmed.

■ [MR. JUSTICE HOLMES concurred in the result. MR. JUSTICE PITNEY, MR. JUSTICE BRANDEIS, and MR. JUSTICE CLARKE dissented without opinion.]

NOTE ON FEDERAL COMMON LAW IMPLIED BY JURISDICTIONAL GRANTS

A. Introduction

Erie R. Co. v. Tompkins made clear that, as the Court later said, "[t]he vesting of jurisdiction in the federal courts does not in and of itself give rise to authority to formulate federal common law". Texas Indus., Inc. v. Radcliff

Materials, Inc., 451 U.S. 630, 640–41 (1981). Chelentis exemplifies one area—admiralty—in which the federal courts' lawmaking power is often viewed as based, at least substantially, on the grant of jurisdiction in Article III and federal statutes. Indeed, this exercise of lawmaking power is particularly dramatic not only because it arose in the absence of statutory regulation but also because the recognition of judicial lawmaking power was in turn deemed to be a source of Congress' power to legislate on admiralty matters.[1] A second area in which federal court lawmaking power is often viewed as grounded, at least in part, on a grant of jurisdiction is that involving controversies between two states. A third example—the Lincoln Mills case, see p. 700, *infra*—involves the implication of substantive lawmaking power from a labor statute granting federal jurisdiction over collective bargaining disputes between unions and management.

Given Erie's holding that the grant of federal jurisdiction over diversity actions does not authorize formulation of federal common law, should such grants of jurisdiction be treated as sources of lawmaking authority? As you read this Note, consider whether lawmaking authority in these areas rests on factors other than a jurisdictional grant—and, indeed, whether it is a mistake to think of lawmaking in admiralty and in interstate disputes as resting (exclusively? primarily?) on jurisdictional grants rather than on a structural inference that the area is inherently federal.[2]

Finally, consider how the Court should treat the fact that founding-era assumptions about the nature of law have changed over time. Although it is sometimes difficult for modern lawyers to appreciate the concept, late-eighteenth and early-nineteenth century lawyers subscribed to the idea of "general law" embodied in the "law of nations"—a set of rules and norms that did not emanate from the will of a particular sovereign, but rather emerged over a long period of time from "common practice and consent among a number of sovereigns." Fletcher, *The General Common Law and Section 34 of the Judiciary Act of 1789: The Example of Marine Insurance*, 97 Harv.L.Rev. 1513, 1517 (1984). To the extent that certain jurisdictional grants (such as those governing admiralty and maritime matters and state-state disputes) presupposed that certain branches of the law of nations (the law maritime and law of inter-sovereign relations) would supply uniform rules of decision, how should a modern Court maintain fidelity to the original purposes of those jurisdictional grants after Erie rejected the concept of general law on which they were premised?[3]

B. Admiralty[4]

(1) The Origins of Admiralty Jurisdiction and Admiralty Law. Article III's conferral of admiralty and maritime jurisdiction was among the least

---

[1]   For an account of the historical development, see Note, 67 Harv.L.Rev. 1214 (1954).

[2]   See Meltzer, *Customary International Law, Foreign Affairs, and Federal Common Law*, 42 Va.J.Int'l.L. 513, 540–41 (2002). *Cf.* Hill, *The Law-Making Power of the Federal Courts: Constitutional Preemption*, 67 Colum.L.Rev. 1024 (1967) (viewing these areas as ones in which the Constitution preempts state lawmaking, leaving federal common law to govern).

[3]   For discussion of the idea of translation, see generally Lessig, *Understanding Changed Readings: Fidelity and Theory*, 47 Stan.L.Rev. 395 (1995).

[4]   For extensive accounts of the development of the law, see Robertson, Admiralty and Federalism (1970); Currie, *Federalism and the Admiralty: "The Devil's Own Mess"*, 1960 Sup.Ct.Rev. 158. Other valuable sources include Gilmore & Black, The Law of Admiralty (2d ed. 1975); Lucas & Schmidt, Admiralty: Cases and Materials (6th ed. 2012); Robertson, Friedell & Sturley, Admiralty and Maritime Law in the United States (2d ed. 2008); Schoenbaum, Admiralty and Maritime Law (5th ed. 2012).

controversial of those in Article III. See, *e.g.*, The Federalist No. 80, at 478 (Hamilton) (Rossiter ed. 1961) ("The most bigoted idolizers of State authority have not thus far shown a disposition to deny the national judiciary the cognizance of maritime causes."). A central concern involved the relationship of admiralty matters to international affairs; consider, for example, the possible implications of prize cases, which adjudicated the legality under the law of nations of captures of one nation's ships and cargo by the nationals of another. These cases involved determination of the rights and status of foreign claimants and nations, neutral and belligerent. Accordingly, the proper disposition of such cases was a matter of obvious national concern. In addition, the emerging American states lacked a well-developed body of maritime law on which courts could rely.

However, admiralty and maritime law has come to govern not only the high seas and tidal waters, but also navigable waters generally, and thus embraces matters—such as a collision between two pleasure boats on Lake Michigan—far removed from foreign affairs or international commerce. Policy support for the broader understanding has been found in the perceived value of uniformity in admiralty and maritime law—a notion reflecting the traditional view of the law of the sea as an independent and international body of rules transcending the power of territorial jurisdictions—and in the contemporary federal interest in furthering maritime commerce. For all of these reasons, admiralty and maritime law developed as a freestanding body of judge-made law.

(2) From General Law to Preemptive Federal Law. As noted, early Americans understood admiralty and maritime law to be of the same genus of "general law" as the "law merchant" applied in diversity in Swift v. Tyson, 41 U.S. 1, 19 (1842), originating not in the will of a particular sovereign but in the commonly shared customs and practices that made up the law of nations. See Fletcher, p. 689, *supra*, at 1517. See also, *e.g.*, Clark, *Federal Common Law: A Structural Reinterpretation*, 144 U.Pa.L.Rev. 1245, 1280–81 (1996); Gilmore & Black, note 4, *supra* § 1–3, at 6; Jay, *Origins of Federal Common Law: Part Two*, 133 U.Pa.L.Rev. 1231, 1309–11 (1985); Young, *Preemption at Sea*, 67 Geo.Wash.L.Rev. 273, 318–22 (1999). Given the character of the law of nations, neither federal nor state courts had the authority to bind the other to its view of its content in cases within their respective jurisdictions. See, *e.g.*, Clark, *supra*, at 1283–86; Hill, note 2, *supra*, at 1034. Nonetheless, reliance on such law supplied (albeit imperfectly) a degree of needed uniformity. See Fletcher, p. 689, *supra*, at 1518–21, 1532, 1538.

The modern doctrine that admiralty and maritime law is a uniform body of substantive *federal* law, applicable not only in federal admiralty courts but also binding upon the state courts, is conventionally thought to have originated in Chelentis and in the decision one year earlier in Southern Pac. Co. v. Jensen, 244 U.S. 205 (1917).[5] Although predating by more than two decades the post-Erie emergence of modern federal common law, the Jensen Court viewed admiralty law, in a similar vein, as the product of an implicit grant of constitutional authority, derived from the Admiralty Clause of

---

[5]   See Robertson, Friedell & Sturley, note 4, *supra*, ch. 9, for a detailed analysis of the nineteenth-century cases. They challenge as an oversimplification the conventional view that until the Jensen decision the federal admiralty courts applied uniform maritime law, whereas state courts and federal courts (on the "law side") applied state law when acting under the "saving" clause.

Article III, to adopt a body of preemptive federal law that could serve the evident purpose of ensuring " 'the uniformity and consistency at which the Constitution aimed on all subjects of a commercial character affecting the intercourse of the states with each other or with foreign states' " (quoting The Lottawanna, p. 687, *supra*). Jensen involved a longshoreman killed while loading a vessel in the port of New York. His next of kin obtained a workers' compensation award under the New York Compensation Law, which the state courts sustained. However, the Supreme Court reversed. Recognizing that "it would be difficult, if not impossible, to define with exactness just how far the general maritime law may be changed, modified, or affected by state legislation" but that "this may be done to some extent", Justice McReynolds declared that "no such legislation is valid if it * * * works material prejudice to the characteristic features of the general maritime law or interferes with the proper harmony and uniformity of that law in its international or interstate relations." Without explaining why a workers' compensation law would be more destructive of "harmony and uniformity" than state wrongful death statutes (which could be relied on to remedy maritime deaths, see The Hamilton, 207 U.S. 398 (1907)), he concluded that "freedom of navigation between the States and with foreign countries would be seriously hampered" if the compensation law applied.

Famously asserting that "[t]he common law is not a brooding omnipresence in the sky, but the articulate voice of some sovereign or quasi sovereign that can be identified", Justice Holmes dissented from the Court's decision preempting state law. He considered it "too late to say that the mere silence of Congress excludes the statute or common law of a state from supplementing the wholly inadequate maritime law of the time of the Constitution". His dissent and that of Justice Pitney were approved by Justices Brandeis and Clarke.[6]

Note that the Jensen case came to the Supreme Court on review of a state court decision. As the Chelentis opinion notes, ever since 1789 Congress has conferred on the federal courts exclusive jurisdiction over all civil cases in admiralty and maritime jurisdiction, "saving to suitors, in all cases, the right of a common law remedy, where the common law is competent to give it."[7] The saving clause limits not federal jurisdiction but rather the scope of federal exclusivity, which is restricted to admiralty and maritime actions brought in rem, see The Moses Taylor, 71 U.S. (4 Wall.) 411 (1867). A plaintiff may institute an in personam action as a federal admiralty proceeding or, where state law provides a remedy, as a state law action by virtue of the saving clause. (Such a state law action may be litigated on the "law" side of a federal court if it has subject matter jurisdiction—*e.g.*, diversity or supplemental jurisdiction. See pp. 872–876, *infra*.) However, the "uniformity" doctrine of Jensen and Chelentis, insofar as it applies, governs a case whether litigated in a federal admiralty court, a state court, or on the

---

[6] After Jensen, Congress twice explicitly authorized states to provide workers' compensation schemes for maritime workers, but the Court held that both statutes had unconstitutionally delegated authority to the states to impair maritime uniformity. See Knickerbocker Ice Co. v. Stewart, 253 U.S. 149 (1920); Washington v. W.C. Dawson & Co., 264 U.S. 219 (1924). Subsequent decisions cast doubt on that view of congressional incapacity. See Wilburn Boat Co. v. Fireman's Fund Ins. Co., 348 U.S. 310, 321 n.29 (1955); Askew v. American Waterways Operators Inc., 411 U.S. 325, 344 (1973). For a defense of the earlier position, see Bederman, *Uniformity, Delegation and the Dormant Admiralty Clause*, 28 J.Mar.L. & Com. 1 (1997).

[7] For the present wording and further discussion, see p. 873, *infra*.

"law" side of a federal court; if uniform federal law must be applied, any conflicting state law is preempted.

(3) The Remaining Scope of State Law. Ever since Jensen and Chelentis, courts have faced vexing questions in trying to define what matters are governed by uniform federal admiralty law and in what areas state law remains free to operate. See Currie, note 4, *supra*, at 164–65. Jensen's formulation—whether application of state law "works material prejudice to" or "interferes with the proper harmony and uniformity of" federal maritime law—is not easy to apply. Nor are the other formulations the Court has supplied over time: that state law may (a) provide remedies but not rights (Chelentis); (b) fill gaps in federal maritime law (Western Fuel Co. v. Garcia, 257 U.S. 233, 242 (1921)); (c) regulate matters maritime but local (*id.*); (d) govern when state interests outweigh federal interests (Kossick v. United Fruit Co., 365 U.S. 731, 738–42 (1961)); or (e) govern procedure but not substance (American Dredging Co. v. Miller, 510 U.S. 443, 453–54 (1994)).[8] In American Dredging, the Court conceded that the "line separating permissible from impermissible state regulation" is neither "readily discernible" nor "entirely consistent" in the Court's decisions, and Justice Stevens' separate opinion argued that Jensen's assertion of judicial authority to preempt state law was unwarranted—and, in view of the Commerce Clause's broad grant of legislative authority and its dormant effect, unnecessary.

(4) The Relevance of Federal Legislation. Though originally governed by judicially defined common law rules, maritime matters are increasingly regulated by federal enactments, making for a complex mixture of statutory and common law. Federal statutes, of course, prevail over contrary federal common law,[9] but the appropriate relationship between judge-made and statutory law has presented challenging questions. A notable example is found in the area of wrongful death.

Although maritime law long recognized a right of action for harm suffered as the result of negligence or unseaworthiness, The Harrisburg, 119 U.S. 199 (1886), adopted for maritime law the longstanding rule at common law that, absent a wrongful death statute, no remedy exists for wrongful death. A later decision in The Tungus v. Skovgaard, 358 U.S. 588 (1959), held that when neither general maritime law and nor any federal statute provides a remedy, a wrongful death remedy may be provided under an applicable state statute.

The question whether federal admiralty law should recognize a wrongful death remedy was revisited in Moragne v. States Marine Lines, Inc., 398 U.S. 375 (1970), an action by the widow of a longshoreman killed while working on a vessel on navigable waters. After removing the case to federal court on the basis of diversity, the defendants successfully moved to dismiss the wrongful death claim based on unseaworthiness, on the ground that state law did not encompass unseaworthiness as a basis for liability.

The Supreme Court unanimously reversed. Justice Harlan's opinion noted that whatever the correctness of The Harrisburg at the time of its

---

[8]   See generally Robertson, *Displacement of State Law by Federal Maritime Law*, 26 J.Mar.L. & Com. 325, 338–46 (1995) (finding all the approaches unsuccessful); Force, *Choice of Law in Admiralty Cases: "National Interests" and the Admiralty Clause*, 75 Tul.L.Rev. 1421 (2001). See also Robertson & Sturley, *The Admiralty Extension Act Solution*, 34 J.Mar.L. & Comm. 209 (2003).

[9]   But *cf.* note 6, *supra*.

decision, legislative developments had changed the legal background against which the Court must assess the common law of admiralty. In particular, Justice Harlan's opinion observed:

"In the United States, every State today has enacted a wrongful-death statute. The Congress has created actions for wrongful deaths of railroad employees, Federal Employers' Liability Act, 45 U.S.C. §§ 51–59; of merchant seamen, Jones Act, 46 U.S.C. § 688; and of persons on the high seas, Death on the High Seas Act, 46 U.S.C. §§ 761, 762. Congress has also, in the Federal Tort Claims Act, 28 U.S.C. § 1346(b), made the United States subject to liability in certain circumstances for negligently caused wrongful death to the same extent as a private person.

"These numerous and broadly applicable statutes, taken as a whole, make it clear that there is no present public policy against allowing recovery for wrongful death. The statutes evidence a wide rejection by the legislatures of whatever justifications may once have existed for a general refusal to allow such recovery. This legislative establishment of policy carries significance beyond the particular scope of each of the statutes involved. The policy thus established has become itself a part of our law, to be given its appropriate weight not only in matters of statutory construction but also in those of decisional law."

The action in Moragne fell within a gap in what had become an extensive system of state and federal remedies for wrongful death. The Jones Act provided no remedy because the decedent was not a merchant seaman. The Death on the High Seas Act did not apply because the death did not occur outside the Act's three-mile limit. And, as noted, the accident happened within the territorial limits of a state whose wrongful death action happened not to extend to seaworthiness. The resultant gap highlighted certain discrepancies in coverage under existing maritime law. For example, although federal admiralty law required "the furnishing of a seaworthy vessel," identical violations of that duty "within territorial waters" would give rise to liability "if the victim is merely injured, but frequently not if he is killed." Similarly, "identical breaches of the duty to provide a seaworthy ship, resulting in death, produce liability outside the three-mile limit—since a claim under the Death on the High Seas Act may be founded on unseaworthiness—but not within the territorial waters of a State whose local statute excludes unseaworthiness claims." In light of the statutory developments since The Harrisburg and the discrepancies in coverage that now resulted from that precedent, the Court found The Harrisburg rule to be "such an unjustifiable anomaly in the present maritime law that it should no longer be followed." See also Norfolk Shipbuilding & Drydock Corp. v. Garris, 532 U.S. 811 (2001) (extending Moragne to wrongful death actions based on negligence and finding that negligence "is no less a distinctively maritime duty than seaworthiness"); Miles v. Apex Marine Corp., 498 U.S. 19 (1990) (recognizing a general maritime cause of action, based on unseaworthiness, for the wrongful death of a sailor, rather than a longshore worker like Moragne, killed in territorial waters).[10]

---

[10] In limiting the permissible ratio of punitive to compensatory damages in an admiralty action arising out of the Exxon Valdez oil spill, a sharply divided Court in Exxon Shipping Co. v. Baker, 554 U.S. 471, 508 n.21 (2008), noted that although an admiralty court should look primarily to pertinent legislation in formulating common law rules, "we may not slough off our responsibilities for common law remedies because Congress has not made a first move, and the absence of federal legislation constraining punitive damages does not imply a congressional

Central to Justice Harlan's opinion was the conviction that it is "the duty of the common-law court to perceive the impact of major legislative innovations and to interweave the new legislative policies with the inherited body of common-law principles". Does that approach fully account for the limits that statutes such as the Death on the High Seas Act place upon the reach of the legislative policies they embody? Was Justice Harlan's discussion of congressional purpose persuasive? Compare Posner, *Legal Formalism, Legal Realism, and the Interpretation of Statutes and the Constitution*, 37 Case W.Res.L.Rev. 179, 203 (1986): "Essentially the Court deleted the word 'High' from the Death on the High Seas Act. Congress thought it was legislating for the high seas. It thought wrong."[11]

(5) Contemporary Debate About the Sources of Law in Admiralty. A number of scholars have come to question the justification for federal judicial lawmaking in admiralty. See, *e.g.*, Redish, Federal Jurisdiction: Tensions in the Allocation of Judicial Power 138–47 (2d ed. 1990); Clark, Paragraph B(2), *supra*; Young, Paragraph B(2), *supra*. Critics of the Court's approach argue that post-Jensen federal common law attributes to the Admiralty Clause an unjustifiably broad purpose. Historically, they say, such jurisdiction was designed principally to deal with concerns arising out of certain classes of cases—crimes on the high seas, prize cases, and revenue cases.[12] And because those categories touched on questions involving foreign relations and the war power, they lay outside the competence of the states and posed few federalism concerns. Acknowledging that the Admiralty Clause historically also covered private maritime claims, the modern critics add that, insofar as uniformity was desired for such cases, this goal was to be implemented through the judicial application of "general maritime law"— the analogue to the law merchant applied in Swift v. Tyson. See Paragraph B(2), *supra*. Given the resultant similarity of the pre-Jensen regime to the Swift regime in diversity, critics of admiralty preemption maintain that the Jensen-Chelentis doctrine should not survive Erie, whose federalism and

---

decision that there should be no quantified rule". In partial dissent, Justice Stevens emphasized that some federal maritime statutes limit liability in other contexts, and treated the absence of an applicable statutory limitation as evidence "that Congress would *not* wish us to create a new rule restricting the liability of a wrongdoer like Exxon." Justice Ginsburg, also in partial dissent, agreed with Justice Stevens "that Congress is the better equipped decisionmaker" to determine any needed limits on punitive damages. Is the Stevens position—which infers a limit on federal admiralty authority from congressional inaction—consistent with Moragne?

[11] In some tension with its earlier position in Moragne, the Court in Atlantic Sounding Co. v. Townsend, 557 U.S. 404 (2009), held that the common law of admiralty authorizes the recovery of punitive damages when a shipowner willfully denies a crew member maintenance and cure after an injury. See p. 686 n.*, *supra* (defining maintenance and cure). In so holding, the Court (5–4, per Justice Thomas) concluded that the traditional punitive damages remedy remained available despite the fact that such damages would *not* be recoverable in an action brought pursuant to the Jones Act, 46 U.S.C. § 30104, which allows someone in the plaintiff's position to elect between a common law and statutory remedy. In contrast with its approach in Moragne, the Court in Townsend did not use the policy reflected in a federal statute to define a parallel common law admiralty claim. A dissent written by Justice Alito and joined by the Chief Justice and Justices Scalia and Kennedy would have followed the Jones Act's policy in determining the availability of punitive damages under the common law of admiralty. If Congress often passes compromise bills whose provisions go so far and no farther, is it dangerous for the Court to extend the "policy" from a statute to a context in which that statute does not apply? For an argument that courts possessing common law authority may properly use that power to broaden a statute's reach to new cases that text itself does not reach, see Pojanowski, *Statutes in Common Law Courts*, 91 Tex.L.Rev. 479 (2013).

[12] See generally Casto, *The Origins of Federal Admiralty Jurisdiction in an Age of Privateers, Smugglers, and Pirates*, 37 Am.J. Legal Hist. 117 (1993).

separation-of-powers concerns apply no less to most admiralty and maritime claims than to diversity cases. See Clark, Paragraph B(2), *supra*, at 1332–60; Young, Paragraph B(2), *supra*, at 312–28.

Is the foregoing argument a convincing translation of the original understanding of admiralty and maritime jurisdiction to the post-Erie context in which general law is no longer recognized? Insofar as the purpose of the Diversity Clause was to ensure a neutral forum while that of the Admiralty Clause was to assure uniformity in maritime commerce, does Erie's insistence upon the application of state law in diversity cases necessarily extend to the admiralty and maritime context? See Currie, The Constitution in the Supreme Court: The Second Century, 1888–1986, at 243 (1990) (suggesting such a distinction).

Professor Young further contends that today maritime commerce no more requires uniform rules than do other forms of commerce. He adds (along with Professor Clark) that even if the Court abandoned the Jensen-Chelentis doctrine, judge-made federal maritime law would be appropriate for cases that fall outside state competence (*e.g.*, those arising beyond territorial waters) or that implicate a compelling federal interest (*e.g.*, the conduct of foreign affairs). And while taking seriously the concern that overruling Jensen and Chelentis would subject maritime commerce to "a crazy-quilt" of state laws, Young finds it sufficient to rely on "Congress's power to impose uniformity by statute" and on the dormant Commerce Clause "prohibition on measures that discriminate against or unduly burden commerce." Young, Paragraph B(2), *supra*, at 349. See also American Dredging Co. v. Miller, 510 U.S. 443, 461–62 (1994) (Stevens, J., dissenting) (outlining similar grounds for overruling Jensen).

Consider the following responses to the modern critique of the Jensen-Chelentis doctrine: (1) the original understanding of admiralty and maritime jurisdiction treated private law cases (whether brought in state or federal court) as governed by a single body of judge-made law;[13] (2) admiralty law often involves relations with other nations, in which uniformity is an international objective; (3) any effort today to de-federalize admiralty law would generate chaos, for often there exists no corresponding state law that could be substituted; (4) creation of a body of federal admiralty law is consistent with the original wording of the Rules of Decision Act, whose directive to apply state law extended only to "trials at common law" and not to admiralty; and (5) admiralty jurisprudence already leaves considerable room for the application of state law. See Force, *An Essay on Federal Common Law and Admiralty*, 43 St. Louis U.L.Rev. 1367 (1999). See also, *e.g.*, Gutoff, *Federal Common Law and Congressional Delegation: A Reconceptualization of Admiralty*, 61 U.Pitt.L.Rev. 367, 405 (2000) (arguing, *inter alia*, that admiralty is properly viewed as an instance of congressional delegation of authority, and that congressional extensions of admiralty jurisdiction in various statutes enacted between 1845 and 1994 were "premised on the existence of a body of supreme federal maritime law that the federal courts had articulated").[14]

---

[13] See Gutoff, *Original Understandings and the Private Law Origins of the Federal Admiralty Jurisdiction: A Reply to Professor Casto*, 30 J.Mar.L. & Comm. 361 (1999).

[14] For criticism of Professor Gutoff's argument that congressional grants of jurisdiction delegated lawmaking authority to the federal courts, see Young, *It's Just Water: Toward the Normalization of Admiralty*, 35 J.Mar.L. & Comm. 469, 485–507 (2004).

C. Interstate Disputes

(1) The Law Governing Interstate Disputes. A second area in which lawmaking power is recognized despite the absence of federal substantive legislation is that involving interstate disputes. Article III gives the Supreme Court original jurisdiction of suits between states, and the implementing legislation, 28 U.S.C. § 1251, makes such jurisdiction exclusive. The Court has fashioned a body of federal common law in interstate disputes as an implication of the jurisdictional grant and the obvious difficulty with applying the law of either disputant. See generally Hill, note 2, *supra*, at 1031–32.

For example, in Connecticut v. Massachusetts, 282 U.S. 660 (1931), a suit to enjoin Massachusetts from diverting waters from the watershed of the Connecticut River, Connecticut asked the Court to follow the common law of both states, which, it argued, gave riparian owners a vested right in the use of the flowing waters unimpaired by such a diversion. The Court replied:

"For the decision of suits between States, federal, state and international law are considered and applied by this Court as the exigencies of the particular case may require. The determination of the relative rights of contending States in respect of the use of streams flowing through them does not depend upon the same considerations and is not governed by the same rules of law that are applied in such States for the solution of similar questions of private right. And, while the municipal law relating to like questions between individuals is to be taken into account, it is not to be deemed to have controlling weight. * * * [T]he principles of right and equity shall be applied having regard to the 'equal level or plane on which all the States stand * * * under our constitutional system' and * * *, upon a consideration of the pertinent laws of the contending States and all other relevant facts, this Court will determine what is an equitable apportionment of the use of such waters."

(2) The Hinderlider Decision and the Problem of Translation. Hinderlider v. La Plata River & Cherry Creek Ditch Co., 304 U.S. 92 (1938), handed down on the same day as Erie R. Co. v. Tompkins and, like Erie, authored by Justice Brandeis, made clear that the law applicable to interstate disputes was *federal* common law. The action was brought by a private company against Colorado officials whose actions, the company alleged, deprived it of water rights under an 1898 Colorado decree. The state supreme court had ruled for the plaintiff, finding that an interstate compact pursuant to which the defendants had acted was invalid because it deprived the company of its rights in violation of the Fourteenth Amendment. The Supreme Court reversed, finding that private parties are bound by a decree or compact to which their state is a party, and that "whether the water of an interstate stream must be apportioned between the two States is a question of 'federal common law' upon which neither the statutes nor the decisions of either State can be conclusive."[15]

Previously, the Court had not been so self-conscious in identifying the basis for its choice of law in interstate disputes. See Kansas v. Colorado, 206 U.S. 46, 97 (1907) ("Sitting, as it were, as an international, as well as a domestic tribunal, we apply Federal law, state law, and international law,

---

[15] For a later decision applying the federal common law of equitable apportionment of interstate waters, see Colorado v. New Mexico, 459 U.S. 176 (1982), 467 U.S. 310 (1984).

as the exigencies of the particular case may demand."). The Court could often draw upon general law principles because many disputes between the (formerly independent and still partly sovereign) states—such as border or water rights disputes—had pertinent analogues in the law of nations that governs relations among sovereigns. See, *e.g.*, Weisburd, *State Courts, Federal Courts, and International Cases*, 20 Yale J.Int'l L. 1, 51 (1995); Nelson, *The Persistence of General Law*, 106 Colum.L.Rev. 503, 508–09 (2006).[16]

But once Erie rejected the notion of general common law, wasn't it obvious that the law to be applied in suits between states would have to be treated as federal rather than state law? Several commentators have suggested that the Hinderlider doctrine represents a necessary implication of the constitutional structure. As Professor Monaghan has put it: "Some tribunal must exist for settling interstate controversies; but it is a basic presumption of the Constitution that the state courts may be too parochial to administer fairly disputes in which important state interests are at issue. Nor does it seem appropriate to restrict the choice of controlling substantive law to that of one of the contending states. * * * Thus the authority to create federal common law springs of necessity from the structure of the Constitution, from its basic division of authority between the national government and the states." Monaghan, *Foreword: Constitutional Common Law*, 89 Harv.L.Rev. 1, 14 (1975); see also Hill, note 2, *supra*, at 1076 (Hinderlider's lawmaking authority is "established not by Congress but by the Constitution"). Does it matter for any practical purpose if the Hinderlider doctrine is treated as an implication from the jurisdictional grant or from some deeper understanding of the federal structure?[17]

(3) Interstate Compacts. Federal common law governs questions about the obligations created by compacts between states. While not all interstate compacts require congressional approval, where such approval is provided, interpretation of the compact in effect requires interpretation of an act of Congress. See generally Engdahl, *Construction of Interstate Compacts: A Questionable Federal Question*, 51 Va.L.Rev. 987 (1965). In such a case, is there any role for state law? Compare Petty v. Tennessee-Missouri Bridge Comm'n, 359 U.S. 275, 285 (1959) (Frankfurter, J., dissenting) (contending

---

[16] Some commentators believe that by the early twentieth century the law of interstate disputes had effectively taken on the cast of federal common law, even if the Court was not calling it that. See, *e.g.*, Stephens, *The Law of Our Land: Customary International Law as Federal Law after Erie*, 66 Fordham L.Rev. 393, 419–20 (1997).

[17] Compare Clark, Paragraph B(2), *supra*, at 1322–31, which argues that the federal common law of interstate disputes, properly understood, rests on a structural constitutional inference from the admission of states on an "equal footing", which permitted the Court to draw on extant law-of-nations principles that implemented the corresponding principle of "perfect equality" of sovereigns. Sachs, *Constitutional Backdrops*, 80 Geo.Wash.L.Rev. 1813 (2012), offers yet another take on the problem. Professor Sachs argues that a considerable body of common law predating the Constitution survived its adoption without having been formally incorporated into the document. He argues, for example, that no provision of the Constitution formally adopted the preexisting law of nations rules governing the resolution of interstate boundary disputes. At the same time, nothing in the document displaced those rules. Accordingly, they survived the Constitution's adoption and became the relevant source of law for cases brought pursuant to the grant of jurisdiction for controversies between states. Professor Sachs adds, however, that even though the Constitution does not adopt the common law of interstate disputes, it makes those rules unalterable. Because U.S. Const. Art. IV, § 3, preserves the territorial integrity of the states, except insofar as the legislatures of the affected states and Congress agree, Sachs argues that the Court may not retroactively alter the preexisting common law rules for determining state boundaries without undermining territorial integrity.

that, at least where the states do not disagree, the language of a compact, which Congress had not modified, should be given the legal significance that the member states placed upon it, just as the interpretation of an ordinary contract depends on the meaning that the parties attribute to its words).

(4) Interstate Pollution. Does federal common law have a special role in disputes that pit interests from two different states against each other, even if the states themselves are not parties? The problem has arisen in the context of interstate water pollution, in which the Court has traveled up and down the hill on the role of federal common law—though in this area, unlike most interstate disputes, congressional legislation exists and has been taken as a source of guidance.

(a) A rather casual dictum in Ohio v. Wyandotte Chems. Corp., 401 U.S. 493, 498–99 n.3 (1971), suggested that state law would govern in an action by Ohio to abate, as a nuisance, the pollution of Lake Erie by private corporations in Michigan and Ontario. But a year later, in an action in the Court's original jurisdiction by Illinois against four Wisconsin cities and two sewer commissions to enjoin pollution of Lake Michigan, the Court held that federal common law governed (and then proceeded to dismiss on the ground that the suit should be filed in federal district court). Illinois v. Milwaukee, 406 U.S. 91 (1972). After noting a variety of federal statutes asserting an interest in the problem, Justice Douglas said:

"The Federal Water Pollution Control Act in § 1(b) declares that it is federal policy 'to recognize, preserve, and protect the primary responsibilities and rights of the States in preventing and controlling water pollution.' But the Act makes clear that it is federal, not state, law that in the end controls the pollution of interstate or navigable waters. * * *

"The remedy sought by Illinois is not within the precise scope of remedies prescribed by Congress. Yet the remedies which Congress provides are not necessarily the only federal remedies available. * * * When we deal with air or water in their ambient or interstate aspects, there is a federal common law * * *.

"The application of federal common law to abate a public nuisance in interstate or navigable waters is not inconsistent with the Water Pollution Control Act. Congress provided in § 10(b) of that Act that, save as a court may decree otherwise in an enforcement action, '[s]tate and interstate action to abate pollution of interstate and navigable waters shall be encouraged and shall not * * * be displaced by federal enforcement action.'"

(b) After this decision, Congress enacted the extensive Water Pollution Control Amendments of 1972, 33 U.S.C. § 1311 *et seq.*, which, among other things, made it illegal to discharge pollutants into the nation's waters without a permit. Illinois, meanwhile, re-filed its action in a federal district court in Illinois and served the defendants, who had obtained such permits. The district court held that a nuisance had been established under federal common law and issued an elaborate decree. The court of appeals affirmed in part. However, the Supreme Court reversed, 6–3. Milwaukee v. Illinois, 451 U.S. 304 (1981):

"Congress has not left the formulation of appropriate federal standards to the courts through application of often vague and indeterminate nuisance concepts and maxims of equity jurisprudence, but rather has occupied the field through the establishment of a comprehensive regulatory program supervised by an expert administrative agency. The 1972 Amendments to the Federal Water Pollution Control Act were not merely another law 'touching interstate waters' of the sort surveyed in Illinois v. Milwaukee, and found inadequate to supplant federal common law. Rather, the Amendments were viewed by Congress as a 'total restructuring' and 'complete rewriting' of the existing water pollution legislation considered in that case."

The 1972 amendments had explicitly preserved more stringent remedies under state law. For the majority, however, a less clear showing sufficed to establish that Congress had displaced federal common law—a matter that did not implicate the concerns underlying the reluctance to displace state authority. "Indeed, * * * 'we start with the assumption' that it is for Congress, not federal courts, to articulate the appropriate standards to be applied as a matter of federal law."

Justice Blackmun, for the dissenters, thought that the 1972 Act meant to preserve the federal common law of nuisance. The Court, he complained, "in effect is encouraging recourse to state law wherever the federal statutory scheme is perceived to offer inadequate protection against pollution from outside the State," a prospect that would lead states to turn to their own courts and would disserve the objective of uniformity.[18] See also Epstein, *Federal Preemption, and Federal Common Law, in Nuisance Cases*, 102 Nw.U.L.Rev. 551, 573 (2008) ("[T]he entire thrust of the [1972 Amendments] is to toughen the laws, so it seems gratuitous to knock out the extra protections that the federal common law offered.").

(c) In American Elec. Power Co. v. Connecticut, 131 S.Ct. 2527 (2011), the Court again addressed the criteria for statutory displacement of the federal common law of interstate pollution, this time in the context of air pollution. The plaintiffs—a number of states, the city of New York, and several private land trusts—filed public nuisance actions against several large power companies, alleging that the companies' carbon dioxide emissions contributed to global warming. The Second Circuit held that the plaintiffs had stated a claim under the federal common law of nuisance and that the Clean Air Act did not displace that federal common law right of action.

In an opinion by Justice Ginsburg, joined in full by Chief Justice Roberts and Justices Scalia, Kennedy, Breyer, and Kagan, the Court reversed. Given its previous holding in Massachusetts v. EPA, pp. 149–151, *supra*, that the Clean Air Act authorized the EPA to regulate greenhouse gases, the Court concluded that the Act displaced any federal common law right of action that the plaintiffs might otherwise have had.[19] Emphasizing that the standard for such displacement was lower than the standard for preemption of state law, the Court stated that "[t]he test for whether congressional legislation excludes the declaration of federal common law is simply whether the statute 'speak[s] directly to [the] question at issue' " (quoting Mobil Oil Corp. v. Higginbotham, 436 U.S. 618, 625 (1978)). Since Massachusetts v. EPA "made plain that emissions of carbon dioxide qualify as air pollution subject to regulation under the [Clean Air] Act," the Court held that the Act "speaks directly" to the claims brought by the plaintiffs. It made no difference that the EPA had not yet fully implemented its previously recognized regulatory

---

[18] For a comprehensive history of the role of federal common law in interstate pollution disputes, see Percival, *The Clean Water Act and the Demise of the Federal Common Law of Interstate Nuisance*, 55 Ala.L.Rev. 717 (2004).

[19] The Court declined to reach the question of whether the plaintiffs would have had a federal common law right of action if the Clean Air Act did not address the question at issue.

authority. If the EPA declined to set emissions standards for a particular pollutant or pollution source, the remedy would lie in the judicial review prescribed by the Act itself. The important point, for the Court, was that Congress entrusted the "complex balancing" of environmental, energy, and economic considerations, in the first instance, to an expert agency. For that reason, the Court found it inappropriate to attribute parallel authority to inexpert, unelected federal judges.

In Milwaukee v. Illinois, Paragraph C(4)(b), *supra*, the Court emphasized that the Clean Water Act "occupied the field through the establishment of a comprehensive regulatory program supervised by an expert administrate agency." In contrast, the American Elec. Power Court found displacement simply because the Clean Air Act authorized the EPA to address the subject matter of the lawsuit. Does this apparent relaxation of the displacement standard signal a broader reticence on the part of the Court about the federal common law of interstate pollution?

D.   Lincoln Mills and § 301 of the Taft Hartley Act

(1) The Lincoln Mills Decision. Can lawmaking authority be implied from a statutory grant of jurisdiction? The decision in Textile Workers Union v. Lincoln Mills, 353 U.S. 448 (1957), is sometimes viewed as an example of such a phenomenon.[20]

There, the union sued the employer to compel arbitration of grievances, as called for by the collective bargaining agreement. Section 301(a) of the Labor Management Relations Act of 1947 (the Taft-Hartley Act), 29 U.S.C. § 185, confers federal court jurisdiction on suits for violation of a collective bargaining agreement between union and employer. Section 301(b) provides a few slivers of substantive federal law: a union and employer shall be bound by the acts of their agents; a union may sue or be sued as an entity in a federal court; and any money judgment against a union in a federal district court is enforceable only against the organization, not against individual members. The Act does not indicate whose law governs the enforceability of collective bargaining agreements.

Justice Douglas' opinion for the Court noted the holdings of a majority of lower courts that § 301(a) was more than jurisdictional—that it authorized federal courts to fashion federal common law to enforce collective bargaining agreements, including the promise to arbitrate. Analyzing the legislative history, he reasoned that under the Act, the enforceability of the agreement to arbitrate grievances was the quid pro quo for an agreement not to strike and that the purpose of § 301 was to promote labor peace. Thus, in suits under § 301(a), federal courts should apply federal law, fashioned from national labor policy: "The range of judicial inventiveness will be determined by the nature of the problem. Federal interpretation of the federal law will govern, not state law. But state law, if compatible with the purpose of § 301, may be resorted to in order to find the rule that will best effectuate the federal policy. See Board of Commissioners v. United States, 308 U.S. [343], 351–52 [(1939)]. Any state law applied, however, will be absorbed as federal law and will not be an independent source of private rights." He proceeded to rule that federal law permitted suit to enforce the agreement to arbitrate.

---

[20]   For discussion of other areas sometimes viewed in this way, see pp. 717–722, *infra* (the Alien Tort Statute); pp. 602–603, *supra* (federal equity jurisdiction); Brilmayer, *State Forfeiture Rules and Federal Review of State Criminal Convictions*, 49 U.Chi.L.Rev. 741, 765–70 (1982) (federal habeas corpus jurisdiction).

A lengthy dissent by Justice Frankfurter took issue with the Court's reading of the legislative history. He also argued, *inter alia*, that (a) history and federal statutes reflected labor's historic mistrust of the use of familiar legal remedies by federal courts in labor disputes; (b) the time needed for litigation will exceed the brief specific terms of arbitration agreements; (c) "[t]here are severe limits on 'judicial inventiveness'" when, as here, no guides exist to fashioning "a whole industrial code"; and (d) even were federal law to govern, it does not follow that arbitration agreements should be enforceable. Reading § 301(a) merely as a jurisdictional grant and not as a source of lawmaking authority, he proceeded to argue that it was unconstitutional because it purported to confer jurisdiction beyond the scope of Article III. See p. 802, *infra*.

(2) The Meaning of Lincoln Mills. Quite apart from the uncertain claim that Congress had delegated lawmaking authority, there was a strong argument that federal law, which fosters the negotiation of collective bargaining agreements and the use of arbitration to forestall industrial strife, would be undermined if, as was true under the law of some states, agreements to arbitrate could not be enforced. Arguments have also been made that a uniform federal law was needed to avoid difficult choice-of-law problems for interstate agreements, or to forestall a "race to the bottom" by states seeking to attract businesses with anti-labor provisions, see Posner, The Federal Courts: Challenge and Reform 294–95 (rev.ed. 1996). Isn't federal common lawmaking in Lincoln Mills best viewed as rooted in the need to carry out the substantive policies of the federal labor laws rather than as an implication from the jurisdictional grant?[21] Can that position be reconciled with the Court's more recent approach to statutory interpretation? See pp. 654–655, *supra*.

(3) Lincoln Mills and State Court Actions. In Local 174 v. Lucas Flour Co., 369 U.S. 95 (1962), the Court held that federal common law governs in suits within the scope of § 301 that are brought in state court.[22] How can *state court* application of federal common law in labor-management disputes be justified by reference to § 301, a grant of jurisdiction to the *federal courts*? Does that question reinforce concerns about grounding federal common lawmaking power in a jurisdictional grant alone? The problem also exists in admiralty and interstate matters: federal admiralty law governs in state court actions under the saving clause; and while disputes between two states are subject to the exclusive original jurisdiction of the Supreme Court, federal common law also governs in state court disputes between a private company and state officials concerning interstate matters, as in Hinderlider, p. 696, *supra*.

---

[21] For discussion of Lincoln Mills and its aftermath, see Bickel & Wellington, *Legislative Purpose and the Judicial Process: The Lincoln Mills Case*, 71 Harv.L.Rev. 1 (1957); Shapiro, The Story of Lincoln Mills: Jurisdiction and the Source of Law, in Federal Courts Stories 389 (Jackson & Resnik eds., 2009); Pfander, *Judicial Purpose and the Scholarly Process: The Lincoln Mills Case*, 69 Wash.U.L.Q. 243 (1991).

[22] See Charles Dowd Box Co. v. Courtney, 368 U.S. 502 (1962) (§ 301 does not by implication divest state courts of concurrent jurisdiction).

INTRODUCTORY NOTE ON FEDERAL COMMON LAW AND PUBLIC INTERNATIONAL LAW

One area of potential judicial lawmaking that has drawn particular attention—and generated strong debate—is that of public international law. Article III creates several heads of jurisdiction that touch directly upon the foreign relations of the United States. Article III, § 2, clause 1, for example, extends federal jurisdiction "to all cases * * * arising under * * * treaties"; "to all cases affecting ambassadors, other public ministers and consuls;" and "to controversies * * * between a state, or the citizens thereof, and foreign states, citizens or subjects." In cases arising under treaties, the federal source of law—and of federal jurisdiction—is straightforward. But the history of the federal courts has generated many cases involving foreign relations that do not arise under any specific treaty. Those cases present their own set of questions. In cases involving foreign diplomats or foreign diversity, is the source of law state law, federal common law, or something else? More generally, when if ever do international law norms that are not embodied in U.S. treaties constitute federal rules of decision that can support federal question jurisdiction? Banco Nacional De Cuba v. Sabbatino frames just such issues.

Banco Nacional De Cuba v. Sabbatino

376 U.S. 398, 84 S.Ct. 923, 11 L.Ed.2d 804 (1964).
Certiorari to the United States Court of Appeals for the Second Circuit.

■ MR. JUSTICE HARLAN delivered the opinion of the Court.

The question which brought this case here * * * is whether the so-called act of state doctrine serves to sustain petitioner's claims in this litigation. * * * The act of state doctrine in its traditional formulation precludes the courts of this country from inquiring into the validity of the public acts a recognized foreign sovereign power committed within its own territory.

I.

[A New York corporation contracted to buy sugar from a subsidiary of a Cuban corporation, whose stock was owned primarily by Americans.* After President Eisenhower reduced the sugar quota for Cuba, the Cuban government expropriated the sugar under a decree that passed title to petitioner, a Cuban governmental agency. Although the decree purported to provide a system of compensation, the prospect of adequate recovery was dim. The New York corporation secured a Cuban export license for the sugar by promising to pay the proceeds to the petitioner, but after export it refused to honor this promise and transferred the funds to Sabbatino, a receiver for the Cuban corporation that had sold the sugar. Petitioner then brought a diversity action in federal district court against the purchaser for conversion of the proceeds. Finding the taking to be invalid under principles of international law, the district court held that the Cuban decree had not conveyed good title to the petitioner. The court of appeals affirmed, relying in part "on two letters * * * written by State

---

*   [Ed.] The summary of the case has been simplified in minor respects.

Department officers which it took as evidence that the Executive Branch had no objection to a judicial testing of the Cuban decree's validity."]

II.

[The Court first considered whether the Banco Nacional, an instrumentality of an unfriendly power that does not permit American nationals to obtain relief in its courts, should be permitted to sue in American courts. The Court refused to hold that America's severance of diplomatic relations with and commercial embargo on Cuba, along with the freezing of Cuban assets in this country, manifested such hostility that American courts should be closed to the Cuban government. The Court concluded that it lacked competence to assess the state of relations with a recognized sovereign power and that any relationship short of war permitted resort to American courts. It added that "[p]olitical recognition is exclusively a function of the Executive."] * * *

IV.

The classic American statement of the act of state doctrine * * * is found in Underhill v. Hernandez, 168 U.S. 250, p. 252 [1897] * * *:

> "Every sovereign state is bound to respect the independence of every other sovereign state, and the courts of one country will not sit in judgment on the acts of the government of another, done within its own territory. Redress of grievances by reason of such acts must be obtained through the means open to be availed of by sovereign powers as between themselves."

Following this precept the Court in that case refused to inquire into acts of Hernandez, a revolutionary Venezuelan military commander whose government had been later recognized by the United States, which were made the basis of a damage action in this country by Underhill, an American citizen, who claimed that he had been unlawfully assaulted, coerced, and detained in Venezuela by Hernandez.

* * * [T]he doctrine as announced in Underhill was [later] reaffirmed in unequivocal terms. [The Court here discussed Oetjen v. Central Leather Co., 246 U.S. 297 (1918), and Ricaud v. American Metal Co., 246 U.S 304 (1918).]

In deciding the present case the Court of Appeals relied in part upon an exception to the unqualified teachings of Underhill, Oetjen, and Ricaud which that court had earlier indicated. In Bernstein v. Van Heyghen Freres Societe Anonyme, 2 Cir., 163 F.2d 246, suit was brought to recover from an assignee property allegedly taken, in effect, by the Nazi Government because plaintiff was Jewish. Recognizing the odious nature of this act of state, the court, through Judge Learned Hand, nonetheless refused to consider it invalid on that ground. Rather, it looked to see if the Executive had acted in any manner that would indicate that United States Courts should refuse to give effect to such a foreign decree. Finding no such evidence, the court sustained dismissal of the complaint. In a later case involving similar facts the same court again assumed examination of the German acts improper, Bernstein v. N.V. Nederlandsche-Amerikaansche Stoomvaart-Maatschappij, 2 Cir., 173 F.2d 71, but, quite evidently following the implications of Judge Hand's opinion in the earlier case, amended its mandate to permit evidence of alleged invalidity, 2 Cir., 210 F.2d 375, subsequent to receipt by plaintiff's attorney of a letter from the Acting Legal Adviser to the

State Department written for the purpose of relieving the court from any constraint upon the exercise of its jurisdiction to pass on that question.[18]

This Court has never had occasion to pass upon the so-called Bernstein exception, nor need it do so now. For whatever ambiguity may be thought to exist in the two letters from State Department officials on which the Court of Appeals relied, is now removed by the position which the Executive has taken in this Court on the act of state claim; respondents do not indeed contest the view that these letters were intended to reflect no more than the Department's then wish not to make any statement bearing on this litigation.

The outcome of this case, therefore, turns upon whether any of the contentions urged by respondents against the application of the act of state doctrine in the premises is acceptable: (1) that the doctrine does not apply to acts of state which violate international law, as is claimed to be the case here; (2) that the doctrine is inapplicable unless the Executive specifically interposes it in a particular case; and (3) that, in any event, the doctrine may not be invoked by a foreign government plaintiff in our courts.

V.

* * * We do not believe that [the act of state] doctrine is compelled either by the inherent nature of sovereign authority * * * or by some principle of international law. * * * While historic notions of sovereign authority do bear upon the wisdom of employing the act of state doctrine, they do not dictate its existence.

* * * The traditional view of international law is that it establishes substantive principles for determining whether one country has wronged another. Because of its peculiar nation-to-nation character the usual method for an individual to seek relief is to exhaust local remedies and then repair to the executive authorities of his own state to persuade them to champion his claim in diplomacy or before an international tribunal. Although it is, of course, true that United States courts apply international law as a part of our own in appropriate circumstances, The Paquete Habana, 175 U.S. 677, 700, the public law of nations can hardly dictate to a country which is in theory wronged how to treat that wrong within its domestic borders.

Despite the broad statement in Oetjen that "The conduct of the foreign relations of our government is committed by the Constitution to the Executive and Legislative * * * Departments," 246 U.S. at 302, it cannot of course be thought that "every case or controversy which touches foreign relations lies beyond judicial cognizance." Baker v. Carr, 369 U.S. 186, 211. The text of the Constitution does not require the act of state

---

[18]   The letter stated:

"1. This government has consistently opposed the forcible acts of dispossession of a discriminatory and confiscatory nature practiced by the Germans on the countries or peoples subject to their controls.

"3. The policy of the Executive, with respect to claims asserted in the United States for the restitution of identifiable property (or compensation in lieu thereof) lost through force, coercion, or duress as a result of Nazi persecution in Germany, is to relieve American courts from any restraint upon the exercise of their jurisdiction to pass upon the validity of the acts of Nazi officials."

doctrine; it does not irrevocably remove from the judiciary the capacity to review the validity of foreign acts of state.

The act of state doctrine does, however, have "constitutional" underpinnings. It arises out of the basic relationships between branches of government in a system of separation of powers. * * * The doctrine as formulated in past decisions expresses the strong sense of the Judicial Branch that its engagement in the task of passing on the validity of foreign acts of state may hinder rather than further this country's pursuit of goals both for itself and for the community of nations as a whole in the international sphere. Many commentators disagree with this view; they have striven * * * to stimulate a narrowing of the apparent scope of the rule. Whatever considerations are thought to predominate, it is plain that the problems involved are uniquely federal in nature. If federal authority, in this instance this Court, orders the field of judicial competence in this area for the federal courts, and the state courts are left free to formulate their own rules, the purposes behind the doctrine could be as effectively undermined as if there had been no federal pronouncement on the subject.

We could perhaps in this diversity action avoid the question of deciding whether federal or state law is applicable to this aspect of the litigation. New York has enunciated the act of state doctrine in terms that echo those of federal decisions decided during the reign of Swift v. Tyson, 16 Pet. 1. * * *

However, we are constrained to make it clear that an issue concerned with a basic choice regarding the competence and function of the Judiciary and the National Executive in ordering our relationships with other members of the international community must be treated exclusively as an aspect of federal law.[23] It seems fair to assume that the Court did not have rules like the act of state doctrine in mind when it decided Erie R. Co. v. Tompkins. Soon thereafter, Professor Philip C. Jessup, now a judge of the International Court of Justice, recognized the potential dangers were Erie extended to legal problems affecting international relations.[24] He cautioned that rules of international law should not be left to divergent and perhaps parochial state interpretations. His basic rationale is equally applicable to the act of state doctrine.

The Court in the pre-Erie act of state cases, although not burdened by the problem of the source of applicable law, used language sufficiently strong and broadsweeping to suggest that state courts were not left free to develop their own doctrines (as they would have been had this Court merely been interpreting common law under Swift v. Tyson, *supra*). The Court of Appeals in the first Bernstein case, *supra*, a diversity suit, plainly considered the decisions of this Court, despite the intervention of Erie, to be controlling in regard to the act of state question, at the same time indicating that New York law governed other aspects of the case. We are not without other precedent for a determination that federal law governs; there are enclaves of federal judge-made law which bind the

---

[23] At least this is true when the Court limits the scope of judicial inquiry. We need not now consider whether a state court might, in certain circumstances, adhere to a more restrictive view concerning the scope of examination of foreign acts than that required by this Court.

[24] The Doctrine of Erie Railroad v. Tompkins Applied to International Law, 33 Am.J.Int'l L. 740 (1939).

States. A national body of federal-court-built law has been held to have been contemplated by § 301 of the Labor Management Relations Act, Textile Workers Union of America v. Lincoln Mills, 353 U.S. 448. Principles formulated by federal judicial law have been thought by this Court to be necessary to protect uniquely federal interests, Clearfield Trust Co. v. United States, 318 U.S. 363. Of course the federal interest guarded in all these cases is one the ultimate statement of which is derived from a federal statute. Perhaps more directly in point are the bodies of law applied between States over boundaries and in regard to the apportionment of interstate waters.

In Hinderlider v. La Plata River Co., 304 U.S. 92, 110, in an opinion handed down the same day as Erie and by the same author, Mr. Justice Brandeis, the Court declared, "For whether the water of an interstate stream must be apportioned between the two States is a question of 'federal common law' upon which neither the statutes nor the decisions of either State can be conclusive." Although the suit was between two private litigants and the relevant States could not be made parties, the Court considered itself free to determine the effect of an interstate compact regulating water apportionment. The decision implies that no State can undermine the federal interest in equitably apportioned interstate waters even if it deals with private parties. * * * The problems surrounding the act of state doctrine are, albeit for different reasons, as intrinsically federal as are those involved in water apportionment or boundary disputes. The considerations supporting exclusion of state authority here are much like those which led the Court in United States v. California, 332 U.S. 19, to hold that the Federal Government possessed paramount rights in submerged lands though within the three-mile limit of coastal States. We conclude that the scope of the act of state doctrine must be determined according to federal law.[25]

VI.

If the act of state doctrine is a principle of decision binding on federal and state courts alike but compelled by neither international law nor the Constitution, its continuing vitality depends on its capacity to reflect the proper distribution of functions between the judicial and political branches of the Government on matters bearing upon foreign affairs. It should be apparent that the greater the degree of codification or consensus concerning a particular area of international law, the more appropriate it is for the judiciary to render decisions regarding it, since the courts can then focus on the application of an agreed principle to circumstances of fact rather than on the sensitive task of establishing a principle not inconsistent with the national interest or with international justice. It is also evident that some aspects of international law touch much more sharply on national nerves than do others; the less important the implications of an issue are for our foreign relations, the weaker the justification for exclusivity in the political branches. The balance of relevant considerations may also be shifted if the government which perpetrated the challenged act of state is no longer in existence * * * for

---

[25] Various constitutional and statutory provisions indirectly support this determination, see U.S.Const., Art, I, § 8, cls. 3, 10; Art. II, §§ 2, 3; Art. III, § 2; 28 U.S.C. §§ 1251(a)(2), (b)(1), (b)(3), 1332(a)(2), 1333, 1350, 1351, by reflecting a concern for uniformity in this country's dealings with foreign nations and indicating a desire to give matters of international significance to the jurisdiction of federal institutions.

the political interest of this country may, as a result, be measurably altered. Therefore, rather than laying down or reaffirming an inflexible and all-encompassing rule in this case, we decide only that the Judicial Branch will not examine the validity of a taking of property within its own territory by a foreign sovereign government, extant and recognized by this country at the time of suit, in the absence of a treaty or other unambiguous agreement regarding controlling legal principles, even if the complaint alleges that the taking violates customary international law. * * *

The possible adverse consequences of a conclusion to the contrary * * * is highlighted by contrasting the practices of the political branch with the limitations of the judicial process in matters of this kind. Following an expropriation of any significance, the Executive engages in diplomacy aimed to assure that United States citizens who are harmed are compensated fairly. Representing all claimants of this country, it will often be able, either by bilateral or multilateral talks, by submission to the United Nations, or by the employment of economic and political sanctions, to achieve some degree of general redress. Judicial determinations of invalidity of title can, on the other hand, have only an occasional impact, since they depend on the fortuitous circumstance of the property in question being brought into this country. Such decisions would, if the acts involved were declared invalid, often be likely to give offense to the expropriating country; since the concept of territorial sovereignty is so deep seated, any state may resent the refusal of the courts of another sovereign to accord validity to acts within its territorial borders. Piecemeal dispositions of this sort involving the probability of affront to another state could seriously interfere with negotiations being carried on by the Executive Branch and might prevent or render less favorable the terms of an agreement that could otherwise be reached. Relations with third countries which have engaged in similar expropriations would not be immune from effect.

The dangers of such adjudication are present regardless of whether the State Department has, as it did in this case, asserted that the relevant act violated international law. If the Executive Branch has undertaken negotiations with an expropriating country, but has refrained from claims of violation of the law of nations, a determination to that effect by a court might be regarded as a serious insult, while a finding of compliance with international law would greatly strengthen the bargaining hand of the other state with consequent detriment to American interests.

Even if the State Department has proclaimed the impropriety of the expropriation, the stamp of approval of its view by a judicial tribunal, however impartial, might increase any affront and the judicial decision might occur at a time, almost always well after the taking, when such an impact would be contrary to our national interest. Considerably more serious and far-reaching consequences would flow from a judicial finding that international law standards had been met if that determination flew in the face of a State Department proclamation to the contrary. When articulating principles of international law in its relations with other states, the Executive Branch speaks not only as an interpreter of generally accepted and traditional rules, as would the courts, but also as an advocate of standards it believes desirable for the community of nations and protective of national concerns. In short, whatever way the matter is cut, the possibility of conflict between the Judicial and Executive Branches could hardly be avoided. * * *

It is suggested that if the act of state doctrine is applicable to violations of international law, it should only be so when the Executive Branch expressly stipulates that it does not wish the courts to pass on the question of validity. We should be slow to reject the representations of the Government that such a reversal of the Bernstein principle would work serious inroads on the maximum effectiveness of United States diplomacy. Often the State Department will wish to refrain from taking an official position, particularly at a moment that would be dictated by the development of private litigation but might be inopportune diplomatically. * * * We do not now pass on the Bernstein exception, but even if it were deemed valid, its suggested extension is unwarranted. * * *

VII.

* * * The judgment of the Court of Appeals is reversed and the case is remanded to the District Court for proceedings consistent with this opinion. It is so ordered.

■ MR. JUSTICE WHITE, dissenting.

[Justice White's lengthy dissent did not question the view that federal law governed. However, he argued that the act of state doctrine does not require American courts to disregard international law and the rights of litigants to a full determination on the merits. "As stated in The Paquete Habana, 175 U.S. 677, 700, '[i]nternational law is part of our law, and must be ascertained and administered by the courts of justice of appropriate jurisdiction as often as questions of right depending upon it are duly presented for their determination.' Principles of international law have been applied in our courts to resolve controversies not merely because they provide a convenient rule for decision but because they represent a consensus among civilized nations on the proper ordering of relations between nations and the citizens thereof. Fundamental fairness to litigants as well as the interest in stability of relationships and preservation of reasonable expectations call for their application whenever international law is controlling in a case or controversy."

[As for the Court's concern about embarrassing the Executive Branch, he responded: "Without doubt political matters in the realm of foreign affairs are within the exclusive domain of the Executive Branch * * *.[20] But this is far from saying that the Constitution vests in the executive exclusive absolute control of foreign affairs or that the validity of a foreign act of state is necessarily a political question. * * * And it cannot be contended that the Constitution allocates this area to the exclusive jurisdiction of the executive, for the judicial power is expressly extended by that document to controversies between aliens and citizens or States, aliens and aliens, and foreign states and American citizens or States."]

---

[20] These issues include whether a foreign state exists or is recognized by the United States, the status that a foreign state or its representatives shall have in this country (sovereign immunity), the territorial boundaries of a foreign state, and the authorization of its representatives for state-to-state negotiation.

———

NOTE ON FEDERAL COMMON LAW RELATING TO FOREIGN AFFAIRS

(1) The Basis for Federal Common Law. What is the basis for judicial lawmaking in Sabbatino? Does it implement statutory or constitutional provisions? See footnote 25 of the opinion. Does the Constitution impliedly preempt state lawmaking related to foreign affairs? See Professor Hill's views, p. 649–650, *supra.* Or is Sabbatino another example of "spontaneous generation", based on considerations of constitutional structure? See Friendly, p. 646, *supra.*

The decision, insofar as it was inspired by the Constitution, did not announce a "pure" constitutional rule of decision, in the sense that Congress could not override it. Indeed, Congress promptly did enact overriding legislation, see 22 U.S.C. § 2370(e), barring judicial invocation of the act of state doctrine except under specified circumstances.

(2) The Implications of Sabbatino for Federal Common Lawmaking. Should Sabbatino be read narrowly as addressing the allocation of powers between the judiciary and the political branches on matters implicating foreign relations—that is, as a decision calling for judicial self-restraint and deference to the Executive Branch? Or does it suggest a broader role for federal common law (which would preempt conflicting state law) in at least some areas relating to foreign affairs? Consider the following post-Sabbatino Supreme Court decisions:

(a) The high water mark for federal common lawmaking came four years after Sabbatino in Zschernig v. Miller, 389 U.S. 429, 432 (1968). There, the Court invalidated—as "an intrusion by the State into the field of foreign affairs which the Constitution entrusts to the President and the Congress"— an Oregon statute that, as interpreted and administered, barred foreigners from inheriting if their country did not (a) grant U.S. citizens reciprocal rights to inherit and (b) permit foreign legatees or heirs to enjoy the inherited property without confiscation. "The statute as construed seems to make unavoidable judicial criticism of nations established on a more authoritarian basis than our own" and could "impair the effective exercise of the Nation's foreign policy."[1] Justice Harlan concurred on the basis that the Oregon statute conflicted with a federal treaty, but disagreed with the Court's rationale, noting, *inter alia*, that American courts often inquire into the administration of foreign law. As examples, he pointed to doctrines refusing to enforce foreign judgments rendered without an impartial tribunal or procedures compatible with due process, or refusing to apply the law of a country shown to be "uncivilized". Justice White's dissent agreed with Justice Harlan's criticism of the Court's rationale.

(b) In subsequent cases, the Court has shown greater reluctance to displace state law based on the raw judicial assessment that enforcement of such law would interfere with the foreign relations of the United States. In Barclays Bank, PLC v. Franchise Tax Bd., 512 U.S. 298 (1994), the Court found unmeritorious a federal constitutional challenge to California's

---

[1] In distinguishing Clark v. Allen, 331 U.S. 503 (1947), which had upheld a similar California "reciprocity" statute, the Court reasoned that such statutes were not unconstitutional "on their face" but only if their application required state courts to appraise the quality of justice in foreign countries.

method of apportioning taxes on multinational corporations. In rejecting arguments that the challenged method impaired national uniformity in international trade and was likely to provoke international retaliation, the Court stressed that the nuances of foreign policy " 'are much more the province of the Executive Branch and Congress than of this Court' " and that "[t]he judiciary is not vested with power to decide 'how to balance a particular risk of retaliation against the sovereign right of the United States as a whole to let the States tax as they please' " (quoting Container Corp. of America v. Franchise Tax Bd., 463 U.S. 159, 194, 196 (1983)). The Court did not mention Zschernig. See also W.S. Kirkpatrick & Co. v. Environmental Tectonics Corp., Int'l, 493 U.S. 400 (1990) (declining to extend the act of state doctrine to a case that would not require invalidating the act of a foreign sovereign within its own territory, even though the lawsuit in question might otherwise "embarrass [a] foreign government[ ]").

Indeed, even though Crosby v. National Foreign Trade Council, 530 U.S. 363 (2000), displaced a Massachusetts law restricting the power of state agencies to purchase goods or services from companies doing business with Myanmar, the Court's opinion eschewed reliance on freestanding foreign affairs preemption doctrine. Instead, the Court held that the state statute was preempted by a federal statute that imposed upon Myanmar a similar set of sanctions. Should the Court more readily find preemption when the statutes at issue touch upon foreign relations? See Paragraph (3), *infra*.

(c) Despite the Court's increased reluctance to displace state laws based on perceived interference with foreign relations, it has shown continued willingness to do so in order to enforce the nation's foreign relations interests as defined by the political branches.[2] In American Ins. Ass'n v. Garamendi, 539 U.S. 396 (2003), the Court, dividing 5–4, held that certain executive agreements with Germany and other European nations preempted California's Holocaust Victim Insurance Relief Act (HVIRA). That Act, a response to the widespread confiscation of and refusal to honor life insurance

---

[2]   The issue of judicial deference to the political branches in foreign relations has also arisen in the context of determining foreign immunities from suit. Prior to 1976, the federal courts enforced common law immunities from suit for both foreign sovereigns and foreign officials. Foreign sovereign immunity cases were the more common of the two. Traditionally, if the State Department granted a "suggestion of immunity" requested by a foreign sovereign, district courts would dismiss for lack of jurisdiction. Ex parte Peru, 318 U.S. 578, 581 (1943). If the State Department did not recognize immunity, the district court remained free to decide the question itself under the common law. Although rare, cases involving suits against foreign *officials* employed a similar set of procedures. See Samantar v. Yousuf, 560 U.S. 305, 312 (2010).

For foreign sovereigns, the Foreign Sovereign Immunities Act of 1976 (FSIA), 28 U.S.C. §§ 1330, 1602 *et seq.*, "replac[ed] the old executive-driven, factor-intensive, loosely common-law-based immunity regime with [a] * * * 'comprehensive set of legal standards governing claims of immunity in every civil action against a foreign state.' " Republic of Argentina v. NML Capital, Ltd., 134 S.Ct. 2250, 2256 (2014) (quoting Verlinden B.V. v. Central Bank of Nigeria, 461 U.S. 480, 488 (1983)). As the Court in Samantar explained, the availability of immunity for foreign sovereigns now depends upon the district court's determination of whether the claimed immunity satisfies the criteria set forth in the FSIA itself.

Samantar also held, however, that the enactment of comprehensive statutory criteria for foreign *sovereign* immunity did not displace the preexisting common law of foreign *official* immunity. Yet, in so holding, Samantar left unresolved key questions about the present scope and implementation of foreign official immunity doctrine. To what extent should federal courts, in enforcing that doctrine, defer to executive determinations about the appropriateness of immunity in particular cases? Even though the FSIA does not directly apply to official immunity, should the approach taken by the FSIA to foreign sovereign immunity also inform the approach federal courts take in shaping the common law of official immunity? *Cf.* Moragne v. States Marine Lines, p. 692, *supra*.

policies held by Jews in Europe before and during the Second World War, required insurance companies, as a condition of doing business in California, to disclose information about all insurance policies sold in Europe from 1920–45. In an opinion by Justice Souter, the Court found that the HVIRA had been preempted by an executive agreement in 2000 between President Clinton and German Chancellor Schröder, in which Germany agreed to create a foundation to compensate victims of Nazi persecution, funded with 10 billion Deutsche marks contributed equally by the German Government and German companies. In agreeing to create the fund, Germany bargained for a measure of security against American lawsuits. Accordingly, the so-called Foundation Agreement called for the U.S. Government to submit, in any Holocaust-era claim against a German company in an American court, a statement that "it would be in the foreign policy interests of the United States for the Foundation to be the exclusive forum and remedy for the resolution of all asserted claims against German companies" arising from the Nazi regime and World War II and "that U.S. policy interests favor dismissal on any valid legal ground."

Although the relevant executive agreements contained no express preemption provision, Justice Souter's opinion for the Court found preemption based on a "clear conflict" between the policies adopted by the President and those adopted by California. Justice Ginsburg's dissent (joined by Justices Stevens, Scalia, and Thomas) argued not that the President lacked authority to preempt state law by executive agreement, but rather that the agreement here did not do so. Does preemption based on an executive agreement raise the same concerns as the dormant foreign affairs preemption concerns that underlay a case such as Zschernig? Compare Clark, *Domesticating Sole Executive Agreements*, 91 Va.L.Rev. 1573 (2007) (arguing that displacing state law based on an executive agreement violates the Supremacy Clause, which provides that only "treaties" and "laws" (along with the Constitution) constitute "supreme" federal law), with Note, 107 Colum.L.Rev. 746 (2007) (arguing that problems of institutional competence are less acute when preemption is based on a decision of the political branches that foreign affairs interests are implicated).

(3) Dormant Preemption of State Intrusions into Foreign Affairs?
Some commentators view the decision in Crosby, Paragraph (2)(b), *supra*, that a federal statute preempted Massachusetts sanctions against Myanmar as sufficiently different from standard preemption analysis as to constitute a kind of dormant foreign affairs preemption "in disguise", in which the driving force for invalidation was less the federal statute and more the foreign affairs subject matter. Thus, Professor Young, in *Dual Federalism, Concurrent Jurisdiction, and the Foreign Affairs Exception*, 69 Geo.Wash.L.Rev. 139, 172 (2001), states: "As the Court conceded, the state and federal laws shared common goals, and it was possible for private actors to comply with both sets of rules. Certainly, a non-exclusive reading of the federal statute was possible, and under some formulations of the presumption against preemption that would be enough to sustain the state law."[3]

---

[3] See also Cleveland, *Crosby and the One-Voice Myth in U.S. Foreign Relations*, 46 Vill.L.Rev. 975 (2001) (criticizing the "myth" that the nation has one voice in foreign affairs and Crosby's reliance on that myth to improvidently preempt the Massachusetts law); Goldsmith, *Statutory Foreign Affairs Preemption*, 2000 Sup.Ct.Rev. 175, 215–21 & n.159 (arguing against

Had there been no federal statute concerning relations with Myanmar, should the Massachusetts law at issue in Crosby have been invalidated on the ground that it invaded national prerogatives with regard to foreign affairs?[4]

Professor Goldsmith, in *Federal Courts, Foreign Affairs, and Federalism*, 83 Va.L.Rev. 1617 (1997), challenges the premise that foreign affairs constitute an inherently federal enclave in which federal common lawmaking is appropriate. He contends that nothing in the constitutional text reserves foreign affairs power exclusively to the federal sovereign. Rather, Article I, § 10 carefully specifies which external matters lie beyond the states' authority (*e.g.*, no treaties, no alliances, no granting letters of marque and reprisal), and Articles I and II adopt explicit mechanisms for the political branches to displace state laws that interfere with national interests. To the extent that the Constitution creates procedural obstacles to the exercise of the political branches' authority to displace state law (for example, the high hurdles set by the Treaty Clause), Goldsmith contends that such hurdles were in fact designed to *protect* state prerogatives. Turning to history, he contends that Sabbatino represented a sharp break with nearly 200 years of practice. In functional terms, moreover, he adds that any distinction between foreign and domestic matters is increasingly problematic in the face of growing global integration and the involvement of the fifty states in such transnational activities as trade, investment, tourism, border issues, and environmental cooperation. Finally, Goldsmith argues that Congress and the President have appropriate resources to monitor and, when necessary, to override state practices affecting foreign relations, while the federal courts lack the capacity to determine when international interests call for preempting state law.

Few would disagree with Professor Henkin's observation that "[j]udge-made law * * * can serve foreign policy only interstitially, grossly, and spasmodically; [judges'] attempts to draw lines and make exceptions must be bound in doctrine and justified in reasoned opinions, and they cannot provide flexibility, completeness, and comprehensive coherence." Henkin, Foreign Affairs and the United States Constitution 140 (2d ed. 1996). But how does the limited capacity of federal courts compare with the capacity of state courts (or of state legislatures, as in Crosby)? Should state courts be free, for example, to deny foreign diplomats or heads of state immunity from suit except to the extent that a federal enactment confers such immunity? See Koh, *Is International Law Really State Law?*, 111 Harv.L.Rev. 1824, 1855 (1998) (raising concerns about such a scenario).

(4) Customary International Law and Federal Common Law. Sabbatino can be viewed as an example of domestic federal common law

---

differing presumptions with regard to local and international matters, given the overlap between the two categories); Vázquez, *W(h)ither Zschernig?*, 46 Vill.L.Rev. 1259, 1304 (2001).

    4   See generally Restatement (Third) of the Foreign Relations Law of the United States §§ 111 & cmt. d, 112 & cmt. a (1987); Brilmayer, *Federalism, State Authority, and the Preemptive Power of International Law*, 1994 Sup.Ct.Rev. 295; Edwards, *The Erie Doctrine in Foreign Affairs Cases*, 42 N.Y.U.L.Rev. 674 (1967); Hill, *The Law-Making Power of the Federal Courts: Constitutional Preemption*, 67 Colum.L.Rev. 1024 (1967); Moore, *Federalism and Foreign Relations*, 1965 Duke L.J. 248. See also Weisburd, *State Courts, Federal Courts, and International Cases*, 20 Yale J.Int.L. 1, 59 (1995) (criticizing broad claims that federal law governs all matters of foreign relations, and arguing that federal common law displaces state law only in cases that (i) require a decision about what counts as a foreign state, (ii) require formal judicial evaluation of a foreign state's public policy, or (iii) involve immigration matters).

doctrine (albeit one of uncertain contours) rooted in the separation of powers. A distinct question concerns the status in the American legal system of customary international law (CIL)—which is found not in treaties but rather in the consistent practice of nations, followed from a sense of legal obligation. Should American courts view CIL as a kind of federal common law, which preempts conflicting state law and provides the basis for federal question jurisdiction? That question is difficult in part because the matters regulated by CIL vary widely: they include the immunity of governmental officials, human rights, limits on legislative and adjudicative jurisdiction, the enforcement of foreign judgments, the law of the sea, and the law of the environment.[5]

Older federal decisions are full of statements like that from The Paquete Habana, 175 U.S., at 700, quoted by Justice White in Sabbatino: "International Law is part of our law, and must be ascertained and administered by the courts of justice of appropriate jurisdiction, as often as questions of right depending upon it are duly presented for their determination." Some legal scholars read such statements, as well as similar utterances by prominent members of the founding generation, to indicate that from the early days of the Republic, CIL was understood to be federal common law.[6] But nearly all recent scholarship—including most of the work endorsing the "modern position" that CIL is federal common law—starts from the proposition that CIL was applied, in the years before Erie, as part of the *general* common law, rather than as either state or federal law.[7] And the Supreme Court has now endorsed that position. See Sosa v. Alvarez-Machain, 542 U.S. 692 (2004), discussed in *Note on the Alien Tort Statute and Customary International Law*, p. 717, *infra*. Accordingly, at the heart of the current debate lies the familiar question of translation that has arisen in contexts such as admiralty and the law of interstate disputes: Once Erie rejected the idea of general law and insisted that, in our system, law must emanate from the authority of a (state or federal) sovereign, how should one understand the status of CIL?

---

[5]   See, *e.g.*, 1 Restatement (Third) of Foreign Relations 456–57 (1987) (discussing CIL regarding the immunity of government officials); 2 *id.* 144–47, § 701 cmt. b, at 152–53, § 701 reporters' note 2, at 153–55 (discussing CIL and human rights law); 1 *id.* 235–37 (discussing jurisdiction to prescribe); 1 *id.* 304–05 (discussing jurisdiction to adjudicate); 2 *id.* 5–7 (discussing CIL sources of law of the sea); 2 *id.* 99–102 (discussing CIL sources of environmental law).

[6]   See, *e.g.*, Paust, International Law as the Law of the United States 7–8 (2d ed. 2003); Glennon, *Raising The Paquete Habana: Is Violation of Customary International Law by the Executive Unconstitutional?*, 80 Nw.U.L.Rev. 321, 343–47 (1985).

[7]   That pre-Erie CIL was "general law" is a central tenet of the "revisionist position", discussed below. See Paragraph (4)(b), *infra*. For leading proponents of the modern position who acknowledge the general law status of pre-Erie law, see, *e.g.*, Koh, Paragraph (3), *supra*, at 1830–31; Henkin, *International Law as Law in the United States*, 82 Mich.L.Rev. 1555, 1557–58 (1984); Neuman, *Sense and Nonsense About Customary International Law: A Response to Professors Bradley and Goldsmith*, 66 Fordham L.Rev. 371, 373–74 (1997). For an excellent account of the relevant history, see Jay, *The Status of the Law of Nations in Early American History*, 42 Vand.L.Rev. 819 (1989).

In a variant of this position, Professor Stephens argues that while CIL was considered general law in the early days of the Republic, certain areas involving the law of nations—such as admiralty and interstate dispute cases—had, by the late nineteenth century, begun to take on the character of federal common law, even though the Court did not say so in terms. See Stephens, *The Law of Our Land: Customary International Law as Federal Law After Erie*, 66 Fordham L.Rev. 393, 418–25 (1997).

The Sabbatino decision does not provide a definitive answer. On the one hand, footnote 24 of the opinion cited with approval an article by Professor Jessup, *The Doctrine of Erie Railroad v. Tompkins Applied to International Law*, 33 Am.J.Int'l L. 740 (1939). Jessup wrote: "If the dictum of Mr. Justice Brandeis in the Tompkins case is to be applied broadly, it would follow that hereafter a state court's determination of a rule of international law would be a finding regarding the law of the state and would not be reviewed by the Supreme Court of the United States. * * * [A]ny attempt to extend the doctrine of the Tompkins case to international law should be repudiated by the Supreme Court. * * * Any question of applying international law in our courts involves the foreign relations of the United States and can thus be brought within a federal power." On the other hand, the Sabbatino ruling *precluded* the application of CIL to the matter at hand, and Justice Harlan's opinion is reasonably clear that the rule of decision there announced implements "the basic relationships between branches of government in a system of separation of powers", rather than international law. See W.S. Kirkpatrick, Paragraph (2)(b), *supra*, at 404 ("We once viewed the [act of state] doctrine as an expression of international law * * *. We have more recently described it, however, as a consequence of domestic separation of powers * * * [citing Sabbatino]").

Commentators have extensively debated the post-Erie status of CIL.[8] Although the relevant literature is too copious to capture fairly in its entirety, it is possible to describe some of the high points of the competing positions:

(a) The Modern Position. Many international law scholars argue that CIL is presumptively incorporated into the American legal system and given effect as federal law—a view reflected in the Restatement (Third) of Foreign Relations § 111, editors' note 3 (1987). Support for the so-called "modern position" rests on several closely related historical, structural, and functional propositions:[9] First, the historical record reveals that the founders, chastened by the inadequacies of the Articles of Confederation, sought to ensure uniform and effective federal implementation of the law of nations, in part, by giving the federal courts jurisdiction over those cases most likely to implicate foreign relations (those concerning foreign envoys, admiralty cases, and alienage-based diversity jurisdiction). And even though Erie itself rejected the concept of "general law" that underlay the law of nations, nothing in that decision "require[d] that federal courts stop citing cases decided before 1938 and reinvent federal common law from scratch. * * * [Rather,] [f]ormer doctrines of 'general common law' have been reconceptualized as doctrines of federal common law that continue to govern in areas of dominant federal concern," Neuman, note 7, *supra*, at 380. Second, state-by-state variation in the content of CIL would undermine the goals underlying the constitutional structure and contradict embedded understandings about the national character of foreign relations. Third, treating customary international law as federal common law does not pose the federalism concerns highlighted by Erie because the Constitution does not reserve power to the states over foreign relations, but rather vests it

---

[8]   For a superb review of the debate, see Young, *Sorting Out the Debate Over Customary International Law*, 42 Va.J.Int'l.L. 365 (2002), which also cites the voluminous commentary on this matter.

[9]   The summary in this paragraph derives primarily from Henkin, note 7, *supra*, at 1651–52; Koh, Paragraph (3), *supra*, at 1831–32, 1853–58; Neuman, note 7, *supra*, at 382–83; and Stephens, note 7, *supra*, at 402–08.

exclusively in the federal government. Fourth, separation-of-powers concerns about the judiciary's exercising legislative discretion are addressed by the fact that judges *find* CIL based on an existing body of law derived from the common consent and practice of sovereigns.[10] And fifth, certain anomalies that would occur if post-Erie CIL were regarded as state, rather than federal, law. As Professor Koh writes, "how would the President's lawyers advise a visiting head of state about her chances of civil immunity while traveling on a classic State visit from Hawaii, to Williamsburg, Virginia, to Washington, D.C., and to New York (and the U.N. headquarters district)?" Koh, Paragraph (3), *supra*, at 1851.

Under the modern position, could a state law permitting the imposition of capital punishment in certain contexts be invalidated by a court if it were shown to violate a CIL norm? What if the United States, in assenting to various international agreements relating to human rights, expressed reservations or understandings that the agreements would not preempt state law?

(b) The Revisionist Position. The prevailing or "modern" position is challenged in Bradley & Goldsmith, *Customary International Law as Federal Common Law: A Critique of the Modern Position*, 110 Harv.L.Rev. 815 (1997).[11] First, they emphasize that prior to Erie the Court had never suggested that CIL was federal common law, and that Sabbatino did not alter that result, having invoked the act of state doctrine as an off-the-rack rule to implement the separation-of-powers principle of limited "judicial involvement in foreign affairs". Second, they say that treating CIL as federal common law is inconsistent with Erie, noting Erie's positivist insistence that law be associated with a particular sovereign and its realist recognition that judicial decisionmaking is a form of lawmaking. Third, in the absence of any textual source of constitutional or statutory authorization for courts to adopt CIL as federal common law,[12] they suggest that the modern position departs from constitutional norms of democratic self-governance. CIL is not "generated by U.S. lawmaking processes", but rather "is derived from the views and practices of the international community", which is not representative of the American polity. Finally, these difficulties, they say, have become more acute as CIL has evolved beyond its traditional concern with relations among nations to embrace a nation's relations with its citizens (as in human rights law), thus increasing the likelihood that CIL will conflict with domestic law.

---

[10] Professor Koh adds that the political branches, *in fact*, play a large role in formulating the federal common law that federal courts apply. First, he argues that a multiplicity of federal statutes and treaties now provide the "positive law framework" for international relations, with the federal common law of CIL "filling the interstices." Second, the political branches have a direct opportunity to influence the development of CIL through participation in "multilateral treaty drafting processes and fora such as the United Nations, regional fora, standing and ad hoc intergovernmental organizations, and diplomatic conferences"—which "have become the driving forces in the creation and shaping of contemporary international law." Koh, Paragraph (3), *supra*, at 1838, 1854.

[11] Some elements of the following critique of the modern position are foreshadowed in Trimble, *A Revisionist View of Customary International Law*, 33 UCLA L.Rev. 665 (1986), and Weisburd, note 4, *supra*.

[12] Bradley and Goldsmith note that in contrast with the Admiralty Clause and interstate dispute clause, "Article III of the Constitution does not even list CIL as a basis for the exercise of federal judicial power, much less authorize federal courts to incorporate CIL wholesale into federal law. Nor does [the Supremacy Clause of] Article VI list CIL as a source of supreme federal law." Bradley & Goldsmith, *supra*, at 856.

Consider a *federal* cause of action that presents an issue relating to international relations—*e.g.*, the immunity of a foreign head of state, or the extraterritorial application of a statute—that is not addressed by a federal statute. Isn't there a strong argument for viewing that issue as governed by federal common law? See Meltzer, *Customary International Law, Foreign Affairs, and Federal Common Law*, 42 Va.J.Int'l.L. 513, 536–37 (2002).

(c) Intermediate Positions. Do the modern position and the revisionist position exhaust the possibilities for understanding the role and status of CIL in the American legal system? Professors Weisburd and Young contend that CIL should be viewed as neither state nor federal law: Weisburd, note 4, *supra*, suggests an analogy to the law of a foreign nation, while Young, note 8, *supra*, views CIL as a contemporary and valid analogue of the general common law of the pre-Erie variety. That approach has some attractions, including a greater capacity for achieving uniformity, and a greater role for federal courts in formulating CIL, than would be true if CIL were merely state law. However, it raises some tricky questions about choice of law and about how to distinguish CIL from state law. For critical examinations, see Meltzer, Paragraph (4)(b), *supra*; Ramsey, *International Law as Non-preemptive Federal Law*, 42 Va.J.Int'l.L. 555 (2002).

Professors Bellia and Clark, in turn, have argued that neither the modern position nor the revisionist critique adequately explains the role of CIL in the federal system. See Bellia & Clark, *The Federal Common Law of Nations*, 109 Colum.L.Rev. 1 (2009); see also Bellia & Clark, *The Law of Nations as Constitutional Law*, 98 Va.L.Rev. 729 (2012). They maintain that early statements characterizing the law of nations (the precursor to modern customary international law) as part of the law of the land were carried over from England (where the common law incorporated the law of nations) and thus were not addressed to the distinctly American question whether the law of nations qualified as the *supreme* law of the land in the technical sense of the Supremacy Clause. They argue that, beginning in early prize cases and continuing through Sabbatino, the Supreme Court applied a subset of the law of nations—the so-called "perfect rights" of sovereigns—as a means of preserving the constitutional prerogatives of the Congress and the President to recognize foreign nations, conduct foreign relations, and decide momentous questions of war and peace. Under the law of nations, a violation of perfect rights gave a nation just cause for waging war. Bellia and Clark argue that courts used perfect rights as a baseline (even in the absence of federal incorporation by statute or treaty) that served to preserve the Constitution's allocation of powers. This approach ties the application of such rules to Articles I and II, but stops short of endorsing broad Article III power to create federal common law.[13]

Even assuming that one or more of the foregoing accounts find support in the historical record, has too much water passed over the dam to return to an eighteenth-century understanding of general law? Or would treating CIL as general law or incorporating certain aspects of it selectively into our

---

[13] Professor Vázquez argues that Bellia and Clark's position is "thoroughly convincing" but that it "actually provides substantial support for most of the modern position." Vázquez, *Customary International Law as U.S. Law: A Critique of the Intermediate Positions and a Defense of the Modern Position*, 86 Notre Dame L.Rev. 1495 (2011). To the extent that Bellia and Clark's analysis simply seeks to put existing CIL cases on firmer conceptual footing, what practical implications attach to treating CIL as implied constitutional law rather federal common law?

understanding of separated powers resolve some of the anomalies produced by both the modern and revisionist positions?

NOTE ON THE ALIEN TORT STATUTE AND CUSTOMARY INTERNATIONAL LAW

(1) Introduction: Filartiga and the Alien Tort Statute. The debate over the domestic legal status of CIL has been informed by doctrinal developments concerning the Alien Tort Statute (ATS), 28 U.S.C. § 1350, which confers jurisdiction in a "civil action by an alien for a tort only, committed in violation of the law of nations". The ATS was described by Judge Friendly as "a kind of legal Lohengrin; although it has been with us since the First Judiciary Act, no one seems to know whence it came." IIT v. Vencap, Ltd., 519 F.2d 1001, 1015 (2d Cir.1975). For a time, the ATS became a fount of international human rights litigation, typically for acts committed outside of the United States.[1] The decision that gave the ATS its modern prominence was Filartiga v. Pena-Irala, 630 F.2d 876 (2d Cir.1980), which held that § 1350 afforded jurisdiction over a claim brought by Paraguayan citizens against a former Paraguayan official (served while in the United States) for acts of torture allegedly committed in Paraguay. The court rejected the argument that § 1350 violated Article III because there was neither a federal question nor the requisites for party-based jurisdiction: "The constitutional basis for the Alien Tort Statute is the law of nations, which has always been part of the federal common law." A number of other lower courts followed suit.[2]

Filartiga and its progeny provoked a wide-ranging debate over the proper basis for federal jurisdiction in ATS cases that did not present distinctive grounds for federal question jurisdiction.[3] At least some proponents of the modern position on CIL have thus endorsed Filartiga's conclusion that federal jurisdiction under the ATS attaches because "the law of nations" counts among the "Laws of the United States" for purposes of federal question jurisdiction. See, *e.g.*, Dodge, *The Constitutionality of the Alien Tort Statute: Some Observations on Text and Context*, 42 Va.J.Int'l.L.

---

[1]   Two developments have now limited the generative capacity of ATS litigation. The first, discussed in greater detail below, see pp. 718–720, *infra*, is the cautious approach the Court in Sosa v. Alvarez-Machain, Paragraph (2), *infra*, took toward the recognition of new federal common law rights of action under the ATS. The second development is the Court's determination in Kiobel v. Royal Dutch Petroleum Co., Paragraph (6), *infra*, that the ATS does not reach "violations of the law of nations occurring within the territory of a sovereign other than the United States".

[2]   See cases cited in Goodman & Jinks, *Filartiga's Firm Footing: International Human Rights and Federal Common Law*, 66 Fordham L.Rev. 463, 467 n.21 (1997). Some lower courts took a more cautious approach. See, e.g., Tel-Oren v. Lybian Arab Republic, 726 F.2d 774 (D.C. Cir. 1984).

[3]   Among other things, a subset of ATS cases arose under the Torture Victim Protection Act of 1991 (TVPA), 106 Stat. 73 (1992) (codified at 28 U.S.C. § 1350 note), which provides for a damages action against "an individual who, under actual or apparent authority, or color of law, of any foreign nation, subjects an individual to torture" or "to extrajudicial killing". The TVPA is a substantive, not a jurisdictional, provision, but suits under it may ordinarily be brought in federal court under § 1331 or § 1350. The TVPA is broader than § 1350 in some respects (*e.g.*, it permits suit by American citizens as well as by aliens), but narrower in others (*e.g.*, it limits actionable violations to torture or extrajudicial killing under color of law). In cases to which it applies, the TVPA moots issues raised by the ATS by providing an unquestionable basis for federal question jurisdiction.

687 (2002). Conversely, adherents of the revisionist position have rejoined that (in the absence of an independent basis for federal question jurisdiction) § 1350 supports federal jurisdiction only in cases that fall within Article III's party-based jurisdiction. See, *e.g.*, Bradley, *The Alien Tort Statute and Article III*, 42 Va.J.Int'l.L. 587 (2002).[4] Others have developed intermediate approaches suggesting, for example, that § 1350 effects a delegation to federal courts to fashion federal common law rules from CIL, see Koh, *Is International Law Really State Law?*, 111 Harv.L.Rev. 1824, 1835 n.60 (1998), or that § 1350 itself recognizes private rights of action for *certain* violations of the law of nations, see, *e.g.*, In re Estate of Marcos, 25 F.3d 1467, 1474–75 (9th Cir.1994).[5] After allowing the debate over Filartiga to unfold for almost a quarter century, the Court resolved many of the questions about the ATS's meaning in Sosa v. Alvarez-Machain, 542 U.S. 692 (2004), discussed immediately below.[6]

(2) Sosa v. Alvarez-Machain. Sosa v. Alvarez-Machain, 542 U.S. 692 (2004), involved a claim brought under the ATS by Alvarez-Machain, a Mexican citizen who alleged that he had been abducted from Mexico and taken, in violation of the law of nations, to the United States by Sosa (also a citizen of Mexico) and others, under a plan developed by the U.S. Drug Enforcement Administration. The plaintiff prevailed in the lower courts on his ATS claim of arbitrary arrest and detention. The Supreme Court unanimously reversed. Justice Souter's opinion for the Court took a somewhat confusing middle position that reads the ATS as a jurisdictional statute but also recognizes a relatively narrow judicial power under the ATS to enforce certain elements of the eighteenth-century "law of nations" as well as carefully delimited modern-day analogues under CIL.

In a portion of his opinion joined by all members of the Court, Justice Souter rejected the view that the ATS was "authority for the creation of a new cause of action for torts in violation of international law." Instead, he found that the ATS was merely a grant of subject matter jurisdiction.[7] This conclusion, however, brought into focus the harder question of what substantive law was to be applied under the ATS. Sosa himself argued that the ATS provided no relief "without a further statute expressly authorizing adoption of causes of action." A law professors' amicus brief, in contrast, argued that the ATS alone would have authorized relief at the time of its enactment "because torts in violation of the law of nations would have been recognized within the common law of the time." After reviewing the historical materials, the Court identified a "sphere in which * * * rules [of the law of nations] binding individuals for the benefit of other individuals overlapped with the norms of state relationships. * * * It was this narrow set

---

[4]   For a contrary view, see, *e.g.*, Collins, *The Diversity Theory of the Alien Tort Statute*, 42 Va.J.Int'l.L. 649 (2002) (finding more confusion than does Bradley about whether cases involving the law of nations would have been thought to arise under federal law).

[5]   For criticism of both the cause of action and delegation theories, see Bradley & Goldsmith, *The Current Illegitimacy of International Human Rights Litigation*, 66 Fordham L.Rev. 319, 357–63 (1997); see also Casto, *The Federal Courts' Protective Jurisdiction over Torts Committed in Violation of the Law of Nations*, 18 Conn.L.Rev. 467 (1986).

[6]   Pre-Sosa commentary on § 1350 was voluminous. See The Alien Tort Claims Act: An Analytical Anthology (Steinhardt & D'Amato eds., 1999), which includes an extensive bibliography.

[7]   As support for the jurisdictional nature of the statute, Justice Souter noted that the language "bespoke a grant of jurisdiction, not power to mold substantive law", and added that its placement as one section "of the Judiciary Act, a statute otherwise exclusively concerned with federal-court jurisdiction, is itself support for its strictly jurisdictional nature".

of violations of the law of nations, admitting of a judicial remedy and at the same time threatening serious consequences in international affairs, that was probably on minds of the men who drafted the ATS". Justice Souter mentioned in particular three examples given by Blackstone of offenses against the law of nations that were criminal in England: violation of safe conducts, infringement of the rights of ambassadors, and piracy. The Court read the ATS as having been enacted "on the understanding that the common law would provide a cause of action for the modest number of international law violations with a potential for personal liability at the time."

In the final portion of the Court's opinion (joined by five other Justices), Justice Souter said that while no evidence indicated that Congress had in mind any torts beyond those corresponding to Blackstone's three offenses, no development between 1789 and the Filartiga decision in 1980 "has categorically precluded federal courts from recognizing a claim under the law of nations as an element of common law". However, he listed five reasons "for a restrained conception of the discretion a federal court should exercise in considering a new cause of action of this kind": (i) the modern conception of the common law as made, rather than found, which highlights the substantial discretion involved when a judge recognizes an international norm; (ii) the decision in Erie, which sharply limits the range of federal judicial lawmaking; (iii) the Court's general reluctance to create a private right of action; (iv) the risk of adverse foreign policy consequences, especially regarding modern international law norms that regulate the power of foreign governments over their own citizens; and (v) the lack of a congressional mandate for recognizing "new and debatable violations of the law of nations". Refusing, however, to "close the door to further independent judicial recognition of actionable international norms", Justice Souter explained why he thought "the door is still ajar subject to vigilant doorkeeping": post-Erie decisions recognize limited enclaves of judge-made law; "[f]or two centuries we have affirmed that the domestic law of the United States recognizes the law of nations"; ever since the Filartiga decision, the federal courts have agreed with that position; and Congress has expressed no disagreement. Accordingly, in an effort to balance preserving the original purposes of the ATS against recognizing an appropriately limited sphere of judicial power, the Court held that "federal courts should not recognize private claims under federal common law for violations of any international law norm with less definite content and acceptance among civilized nations than the historical paradigms familiar when § 1350 was enacted"—the norms concerning safe conducts, the rights of ambassadors, and piracy.[8]

Justice Scalia, joined by Chief Justice Rehnquist and Justice Thomas, concurring in part and in the judgment, would have closed the door altogether on the recognition of new causes of action, and viewed the last part of the Court's opinion as "commit[ting] the Federal Judiciary to a task

---

[8]   Measured against these standards, the Court held that the plaintiff's claim of an arbitrary arrest and detention, in violation of the Universal Declaration of Human Rights and the International Covenant on Civil and Political Rights, fell short. "[T]he Declaration does not of its own force impose obligations as a matter of international law." While the Covenant does bind the United States as a matter of international law, "the United States ratified [it] on the express understanding that it was not self-executing and so did not itself create obligations enforceable in the federal courts". More generally, Alvarez's claim that his arrest and abduction were unauthorized by positive law (here of the United States) was far broader than "any binding customary rule having the specificity we require."

it is neither authorized nor suited to perform." He stressed that after Erie, a grant of jurisdiction does not ordinarily carry with it lawmaking authority, and " 'the fact that a rule has been recognized as [customary international law], by itself, is not an adequate basis for viewing that rule as part of federal common law.' " (quoting Meltzer, *Customary International Law, Foreign Affairs, and Federal Common Law*, 42 Va.J.Int'l.L. 513, 519 (2002)). The Court, he said, focused too much on whether Congress had precluded federal courts from recognizing new claims under § 1350, when the real question was what authorizes the federal courts to recognize such claims in the first place. He added that post-Erie federal common lawmaking is so different from the general common law adjudication through which the law of nations was thought to apply in 1789 that "it would be anachronistic to find authorization to do the former in a statutory grant of jurisdiction that was thought to enable the latter." Finally, he expressed concern that the Court bestowed too much latitude upon lower federal courts, noting that the decision below, which the Court unanimously reversed, rested on a verbal formulation very similar to the narrow one endorsed by the last part of the Court's opinion.

(3) Sosa and the Problem of Translation. In view of the profound shift in jurisprudential assumptions occasioned by Erie, the Court in Sosa faced difficult issues concerning the nature of the common law to be applied under the ATS. The Court stressed that the ATS appears to have assumed the existence of a body of customary international law (CIL) that would be part of "the common law" as applied by the federal courts before Erie—that is, the kind of "general common law" of which Erie disapproved. Modern, post-Erie premises about federal common lawmaking—particularly the association of common law rules with the lawmaking authority of a particular jurisdiction (*e.g.*, the federal government, or one of the fifty states)—make the appropriateness of absorbing CIL into federal common law quite uncertain. Should § 1350 be interpreted as a relic that preserves, in the domain in which it operates, a pre-Erie approach under which federal courts recognize a "spurious" federal common law applicable only in the federal courts? (For an argument that the answer is no, see Bradley, Goldsmith & Moore, *Sosa, Customary International Law, and the Continuing Relevance of Erie*, 120 Harv.L.Rev. 869 (2007).)

(4) Sosa and the Status of CIL. What, if anything, does Sosa tell us about the debate over the status of CIL? With respect to the debate about the relationship of CIL to federal common law, the Sosa decision seems to provide a mixed if opaque verdict. The Court's statement that § 1350 is entirely jurisdictional suggests that the substantive law applied in actions properly brought under that statute is a preexisting federal common law of CIL. See, *e.g.*, Koh, *The Ninth Annual John W. Hager Lecture, The 2004 Term: The Supreme Court Meets International Law*, 12 Tulsa J.Comp.&Int'l L. 1 (2005) (reading Sosa to endorse the modern position); Flaherty, *The Future and Past of U.S. Foreign Relations Law*, 67 Law & Contemp.Probs. 169, 174 (2004) (same). But isn't it unlikely that, had the ATS never been enacted, the Court would have ruled that those violations of CIL that Sosa does recognize state good claims under the federal common law? Insofar as the Court relies on the fact that "the ATS was meant to underwrite litigation of a narrow set of common law actions derived from the law of nations", doesn't it give the ATS more than jurisdictional significance? Bradley, Goldsmith, and Moore, Paragraph (3), *supra*, view Sosa as reading the ATS also to be a source of authority under which the federal courts may recognize at least some federal common law rights of action (whose recognition would be inappropriate absent that statutory authorization). If that is correct, then the Court would seem to be rejecting the view that some urged, prior to Sosa, that § 1350 neither establishes a federal cause of action for violations of CIL nor authorizes the federal courts to do so. See, *e.g.*, Bradley & Goldsmith, *The Current Illegitimacy of International Human Rights Litigation*, 66 Fordham L.Rev. 319, 357–63 (1997).

On the other hand, the Court's caution in setting forth the kinds of CIL claims that can be brought under the ATS, and its linking the validity of those CIL claims to the action of Congress in 1789, appears to reject the modern view that all CIL is, by its nature, federal common law. In that regard, should the ATS be viewed, notwithstanding the language in Sosa that it is only jurisdictional, as authorizing the federal courts within a limited domain to fashion federal common law whose creation would be inappropriate without that statutory authorization—much like the jurisdictional grant in the Lincoln Mills case? Compare Sosa v. Alvarez-Machain, Paragraph (2), *supra*, at 731 n.19: "Our position does not * * * imply that every grant of jurisdiction to a federal court carries with it an opportunity to develop common law (so that the grant of federal-question jurisdiction would be equally as good for our purposes as § 1350). Section 1350 was enacted on the congressional understanding that courts would exercise jurisdiction by entertaining some common law claims derived from the law of nations; and we know of no reason to think that federal-question jurisdiction was extended subject to any comparable congressional assumption." Is there an intelligible way to understand the ATS without assuming that Congress meant to authorize the federal courts to develop a specialized federal common law of international torts?[9]

(5) The Extraterritorial Application of the ATS. In Kiobel v. Royal Dutch Petroleum Co., 133 S.Ct. 1659 (2012), the Supreme Court unanimously affirmed the dismissal of an Alien Tort Statute (ATS) suit by a foreign national against foreign corporations for conduct that occurred in a foreign country. In an opinion by Chief Justice Roberts (joined by Justices Scalia, Kennedy, Thomas, and Alito), the Court held that a familiar canon of construction—the presumption against extraterritorial application of U.S. law—governs claims brought pursuant to the ATS. The Court acknowledged that the presumption, which serves to prevent the U.S. from becoming embroiled in international disputes that might arise from conflicts between

---

[9] Professors Bellia and Clark argue that the original meaning of the ATS did not authorize the development of a CIL of torts; rather, in their view, the First Congress understood the statute to permit an alien to sue a U.S. citizen for any intentional tort to person or personal property because *any such tort* would have violated the law of nations in 1789. See Bellia & Clark, *The Alien Tort Statute and the Law of Nations*, 78 U.Chi.L.Rev. 445 (2011). Under law of nations principles, a nation became responsible for its citizens' intentional torts against an alien unless it extradited the offender, imposed criminal punishment, or gave the alien a civil remedy. Bellia and Clark maintain that by granting federal courts jurisdiction to hear alien tort claims against U.S. citizens, the ATS merely sought to establish a self-executing means of satisfying the United States' obligations under the law of nations. Bellia and Clark add that the tort law causes of action under the ATS would have come from the Process Act of 1789, which required federal courts to apply the forms of action and modes of process then used or allowed in the supreme courts of the states in which they sat. Act of Sept. 29, 1789, ch. 21, 1 Stat. 93. See Bellia & Clark, *The Process Acts and the Alien Tort Statute*, 101 Va.L.Rev. __ (forthcoming 2015). According to Bellia and Clark, the Process Act of 1789—and its successor, the Process Act of 1792, Act of May 8, 1792, ch. 36, 1 Stat. 275—would have made the relevant state forms of action applicable in federal court. If correct, how (if at all) should this conclusion affect our understanding of the ATS today?

U.S. and foreign law, ordinarily reaches only the extraterritorial application of statutes that "regulat[e] conduct". The ATS, in contrast, is strictly jurisdictional and thus "does not directly regulate conduct or afford relief." Still, the Court found that "the principles underlying the canon of interpretation similarly constrain courts considering causes of action that may be brought under the ATS." In particular, because Sosa v. Alvarez-Machain, Paragraph (2), *supra*, concluded that the ATS authorizes federal courts "to recognize certain causes of action based on * * * international law," the Court in Kiobel asserted that the risk of "unwarranted judicial interference" in U.S. foreign policy is, if anything, "magnified".

Justice Breyer, joined by Justices Ginsburg, Sotomayor, and Kagan, concurred only in the judgment and disputed the majority's reliance on the presumption against extraterritoriality. Justice Breyer emphasized that the presumption was inapt as applied to a statute that "was enacted with 'foreign matters' in mind." Indeed, noting that Congress passed the ATS "to permit recovery of damages from pirates and others who violated basic international law norms as understood in 1789," Justice Breyer emphasized that piracy was extraterritorial and often required the application of U.S. law to ships that flew the flag of foreign nations and thus lay within their jurisdiction. Invoking the jurisdictional principles of foreign relations law, Justice Breyer concluded that jurisdiction should lie under the ATS "where (1) the alleged tort occurs on American soil, (2) the defendant is an American national, or (3) the defendant's conduct substantially and adversely affects an important American national interest, and that includes a distinct interest in preventing the United States from becoming a safe harbor (free of civil as well as criminal liability) for a torturer or other common enemy of mankind." He added that he would rely on doctrines such as exhaustion, comity, and *forum non conveniens* to ensure the workability of the invocation of any such jurisdiction relating to events occurring abroad. Because the facts of Kiobel did not satisfy any of the criteria for jurisdiction, he would have dismissed the case.

Two centuries after the fact, it is obviously difficult to reconstruct the purposes of a statute with very little legislative history, especially when one can find but few interpretations of the statute before modern times. Is the majority's reliance on a presumption against extraterritoriality itself a form of federal common law? Does the Court convincingly explain why it makes sense to apply that presumption to a statute enacted, in part, to deal with piracy?

———

2. Enforcing Primary Obligations

A. Civil Actions

Introductory Note on Implied Private Rights of Action

Federal statutes do not always fully specify the means by which the rights or duties they create are to be effectuated. Some such statutes, for example, do not articulate the burden of persuasion upon plaintiffs or the order of proof. Others might not state whether a cause of action survives a plaintiff's death. Sometimes, moreover, federal statutes lack any statute of limitations, raising the question whether Congress could really have meant for the legal peril created by the statute to continue indefinitely. Some federal statutes create rights without specifying whether or how private litigants may bring federal lawsuits to vindicate those rights. The presence of these gaps poses the inevitable question of the proper judicial role in filling them. In some of these contexts—for example, the order of proof and burden of persuasion—the courts must inevitably supply what Congress has omitted; a case cannot proceed without the courts' articulating standards of proof. In other areas, the role of the federal courts is less obvious. To what extent should the federal judiciary supply a missing statute of limitations or even the right of action itself?

The question of implied private rights of action—or of private rights to sue to enforce statutes that do not expressly authorize private suits—offers the best and most thoroughly debated example of this phenomenon. Federal statutes sometimes state explicitly that private parties may sue to redress harm suffered as the result of another's violation of statutory duties. For example, the patent laws expressly authorize patentholders to sue infringers for damages and injunctive relief. But many federal statutes do not expressly authorize suit by persons injured as the result of statutory violations. Some statutes say nothing about remedies; others provide criminal sanctions but are silent about the availability of civil remedies; still others establish certain civil remedies (for example, by authorizing a federal administrative agency to take specified measures to enforce the statute) but say nothing about private actions. In each of these instances, if a private person seeks legal redress against another who has violated the statute, the courts may have to determine whether to recognize remedies not expressly authorized by the governing statute. The next two principal cases, and the Note that follows, address the appropriate role of the federal courts in implying private remedies for violations of federal statutes.

Cannon v. University of Chicago
441 U.S. 677, 99 S.Ct. 1946, 60 L.Ed.2d 560 (1979).
Certiorari to the United States Court of Appeals for the Seventh Circuit.

■ MR. JUSTICE STEVENS delivered the opinion of the Court.

[Cannon alleged that the University of Chicago's medical school, which receives federal funds, denied her admission on account of her sex. She sued the university under § 901(a) of Title IX of the Education Amendments of 1972, as amended, 20 U.S.C. § 1681, which provides in relevant part: "No person * * * shall, on the basis of sex, be excluded from participation in, be denied the benefits of, or be subjected to discrimination under any education program or activity receiving Federal financial assistance * * *." Cannon sought declaratory, injunctive, and monetary relief. Section 901, however, does not expressly authorize a private right of action by an injured person. The district court refused to infer such a right of action and dismissed the action. The court of appeals affirmed.]

* * * As our recent cases—particularly Cort v. Ash, 422 U.S. 66 [(1975)]—demonstrate, the fact that a federal statute has been violated and some person harmed does not automatically give rise to a private cause of action in favor of that person. Instead, before concluding that Congress intended to make a remedy available to a special class of litigants, a court must carefully analyze the four factors that Cort identifies as indicative of such an intent.[9] Our review of those factors persuades us, however, that * * * petitioner does have a statutory right to pursue her claim that respondents rejected her application on the basis of her sex. * * *

I

First, the threshold question under Cort is whether the statute was enacted for the benefit of a special class of which the plaintiff is a member. That question is answered by looking to the language of the statute itself. Thus, the statutory reference to "any employee of any such common carrier" in the 1893 legislation requiring railroads to equip their cars with secure "grab irons or handholds," made "irresistible" the Court's earliest "inference of a private right of action"—in that case in favor of a railway employee who was injured when a grab iron gave way. Texas & Pacific R. Co. v. Rigsby, 241 U.S. 33, 40 [(1916)].

Similarly, it was statutory language describing the special class to be benefited by § 5 of the Voting Rights Act of 1965 that persuaded the Court that private parties within that class were implicitly authorized to seek a declaratory judgment against a covered State. Allen v. State Board of Elections, 393 U.S. 544, 554–555 [(1969)]. The dispositive language in that statute—"no person shall be denied the right to vote for failure to

---

9   "In determining whether a private remedy is implicit in a statute not expressly providing one, several factors are relevant. First, is the plaintiff 'one of the class for whose *especial* benefit the statute was enacted,' Texas & Pacific R. Co. v. Rigsby, 241 U.S. 33, 39 (1916) (emphasis supplied)—that is, does the statute create a federal right in favor of the plaintiff? Second, is there any indication of legislative intent, explicit or implicit, either to create such a remedy or to deny one? Third, is it consistent with the underlying purposes of the legislative scheme to imply such a remedy for the plaintiff? See, *e.g.,* [National R.R. Passenger Corp. v. National Ass'n of R.R. Passengers, 414 U.S. 453 (1974)]. And finally, is the cause of action one traditionally relegated to state law, in an area basically the concern of the States, so that it would be inappropriate to infer a cause of action based solely on federal law?" 422 U.S., at 78.

comply with [a new state enactment covered by, but not approved under, § 5]"—is remarkably similar to the language used by Congress in Title IX.

The language in these statutes—which expressly identifies the class Congress intended to benefit—contrasts sharply with statutory language customarily found in criminal statutes, such as that construed in Cort, *supra*, and other laws enacted for the protection of the general public. There would be far less reason to infer a private remedy in favor of individual persons if Congress, instead of drafting Title IX with an unmistakable focus on the benefited class, had written it simply as a ban on discriminatory conduct by recipients of federal funds or as a prohibition against the disbursement of public funds to educational institutions engaged in discriminatory practices.

Unquestionably, therefore, the first of the four factors identified in Cort favors the implication of a private cause of action. * * *

Second, the Cort analysis requires consideration of legislative history. We must recognize, however, that the legislative history of a statute that does not expressly create or deny a private remedy will typically be equally silent or ambiguous on the question. Therefore, in situations such as the present one "in which it is clear that federal law has granted a class of persons certain rights, it is not necessary to show an intention to *create* a private cause of action, although an explicit purpose to *deny* such cause of action would be controlling." Cort, 422 U.S., at 82 (emphasis in original). But this is not the typical case. Far from evidencing any purpose to *deny* a private cause of action, the history of Title IX rather plainly indicates that Congress intended to create such a remedy.

Title IX was patterned after Title VI of the Civil Rights Act of 1964. Except for the substitution of the word "sex" in Title IX to replace the words "race, color, or national origin" in Title VI, the two statutes use identical language to describe the benefited class.* Both statutes provide the same administrative mechanism for terminating federal financial support for institutions engaged in prohibited discrimination. * * * The drafters of Title IX explicitly assumed that it would be interpreted and applied as Title VI had been during the preceding eight years.

In 1972 when Title IX was enacted, the critical language in Title VI had already been construed as creating a private remedy. Most particularly, in 1967, a distinguished panel of the Court of Appeals for the Fifth Circuit squarely decided this issue in an opinion that was repeatedly cited with approval and never questioned during the ensuing five years. In addition, at least a dozen other federal courts reached similar conclusions in the same or related contexts during those years. It is always appropriate to assume that our elected representatives, like other citizens, know the law; in this case, because of their repeated references to Title VI and its modes of enforcement, we are especially justified in presuming both that those representatives were aware of the

---

*   [Ed.] Section 601 of Title VI of the Civil Rights Act of 1964, 78 Stat. 252, 42 U.S.C. § 2000d, provides: "No person in the United States shall, on the ground of race, color, or national origin, be excluded from participation in, be denied the benefits of, or be subjected to discrimination under any program or activity receiving Federal financial assistance."

prior interpretation of Title VI and that that interpretation reflects their intent with respect to Title IX.

Moreover, * * * during the period between the enactment of Title VI in 1964 and the enactment of Title IX in 1972, this Court had consistently found implied remedies [under other statutory schemes]—often in cases much less clear than this. It was after 1972 that this Court decided Cort v. Ash * * *. We, of course, adhere to the strict approach followed in our recent cases, but our evaluation of congressional action in 1972 must take into account its contemporary legal context. In sum, it is not only appropriate but also realistic to presume that Congress was thoroughly familiar with these unusually important precedents from this and other federal courts and that it expected its enactment to be interpreted in conformity with them.

It is not, however, necessary to rely on these presumptions. The package of statutes of which Title IX is one part also contains a provision * * * that authorizes federal courts to award attorney's fees to the prevailing parties, other than the United States, in private actions brought against public educational agencies to enforce Title VI in the context of elementary and secondary education. The language of this provision explicitly presumes the availability of private suits to enforce Title VI in the education context. For many such suits, no express cause of action was then available; hence Congress must have assumed that one could be implied under Title VI itself. * * *

Finally, the very persistence—before 1972 and since, among judges and executive officials, as well as among litigants and their counsel, and even implicit in decisions of this Court[33]—of the assumption that both Title VI and Title IX created a private right of action for the victims of illegal discrimination and the absence of legislative action to change that assumption provide further evidence that Congress at least acquiesces in, and apparently affirms, that assumption. * * *

Third, under Cort, a private remedy should not be implied if it would frustrate the underlying purpose of the legislative scheme. On the other hand, when that remedy is necessary or at least helpful to the accomplishment of the statutory purpose, the Court is decidedly receptive to its implication under the statute.

Title IX, like its model Title VI, sought to accomplish two related, but nevertheless somewhat different, objectives. First, Congress wanted to avoid the use of federal resources to support discriminatory practices; second, it wanted to provide individual citizens effective protection against those practices. * * *

The first purpose is generally served by the statutory procedure for the termination of federal financial support for institutions engaged in discriminatory practices. That remedy is, however, severe and often may not provide an appropriate means of accomplishing the second purpose if merely an isolated violation has occurred. In that situation, the violation might be remedied more efficiently by an order requiring an institution to accept an applicant who had been improperly excluded. Moreover, in

---

[33] [The Court here cited Lau v. Nichols, 414 U.S. 563, 566–69 (1974), and Hills v. Gautreaux, 425 U.S 284, 286 (1976), both private actions to enforce Title VI in which the Court, without discussing whether the statute confers a private right of action, reached the merits and granted relief.] * * *

that kind of situation it makes little sense to impose on an individual, whose only interest is in obtaining a benefit for herself, or on [the Department of Health, Education, and Welfare], the burden of demonstrating that an institution's practices are so pervasively discriminatory that a complete cutoff of federal funding is appropriate. * * *

The Department of Health, Education, and Welfare, which is charged with the responsibility for administering Title IX, * * * takes the unequivocal position that the individual remedy will provide effective assistance to achieving the statutory purposes. The agency's position is unquestionably correct.[42]

Fourth, the final inquiry suggested by Cort is whether implying a federal remedy is inappropriate because the subject matter involves an area basically of concern to the States. No such problem is raised by a prohibition against invidious discrimination of any sort, including that on the basis of sex. * * * Moreover, it is the expenditure of federal funds that provides the justification for this particular statutory prohibition. * * *

In sum, there is no need in this case to weigh the four Cort factors; all of them support the same result. * * *

II

Respondents' principal argument against implying a cause of action under Title IX is that it is unwise to subject admissions decisions of universities to judicial scrutiny at the behest of disappointed applicants on a case-by-case basis. * * *

This argument * * * addresses a policy issue that Congress has already resolved.

History has borne out the judgment of Congress. Although victims of discrimination on the basis of race, religion, or national origin have had private Title VI remedies available at least since 1965, respondents have not come forward with any demonstration that Title VI litigation has been so costly or voluminous that either the academic community or the courts have been unduly burdened. * * *

III

[The Court here discussed, *inter alia*, the university's argument that a comparison of Title VI with other Titles of the Civil Rights Act of 1964 demonstrated that Congress created express private remedies whenever it found them desirable. The Court responded that "[e]ven if these arguments were persuasive with respect to Congress' understanding in 1964 when it passed Title VI, they would not overcome the fact that in 1972 when it passed Title IX, Congress was under the impression that Title VI could be enforced by a private action and that Title IX would be similarly enforceable." It added that "[t]he fact that other provisions of a complex statutory scheme create express remedies has not been accepted as a sufficient reason for refusing to imply an otherwise appropriate remedy under a separate section. See, *e.g.*, J.I. Case Co. v. Borak, 377 U.S. 426 [(1964)]."]

---

[42]   * * * HEW has candidly admitted that it does not have the resources necessary to enforce Title IX in a substantial number of circumstances * * *. * * *

IV

When Congress intends private litigants to have a cause of action to support their statutory rights, the far better course is for it to specify as much when it creates those rights. But * * * under certain limited circumstances the failure of Congress to do so is not inconsistent with an intent on its part to have such a remedy available to the persons benefited by its legislation. Title IX presents the atypical situation in which *all* of the circumstances that the Court has previously identified as supportive of an implied remedy are present. We therefore conclude that petitioner may maintain her lawsuit * * *.

The judgment of the Court of Appeals is reversed, and the case is remanded for further proceedings consistent with this opinion.

■ MR. CHIEF JUSTICE BURGER concurs in the judgment.

■ MR. JUSTICE REHNQUIST, with whom MR. JUSTICE STEWART joins, concurring.

* * * The question of the existence of a private right of action is basically one of statutory construction. And while state courts of general jurisdiction still enforcing the common law as well as statutory law may be less constrained than are federal courts enforcing laws enacted by Congress, the latter must surely look to those laws to determine whether there was an intent to create a private right of action under them.

We do not write on an entirely clean slate, however, and the Court's opinion demonstrates that Congress, at least during the period of the enactment of the several Titles of the Civil Rights Act, tended to rely to a large extent on the courts to *decide* whether there should be a private right of action, rather than determining this question for itself. * * *

I fully agree with the Court's statement that "[when] Congress intends private litigants to have a cause of action to support their statutory rights, the far better course is for it to specify as much when it creates those rights." It seems to me that the factors to which I have here briefly adverted apprise the lawmaking branch of the Federal Government that the ball, so to speak, may well now be in its court. Not only is it "far better" for Congress to so specify when it intends private litigants to have a cause of action, but for this very reason this Court in the future should be extremely reluctant to imply a cause of action absent such specificity on the part of the Legislative Branch.

■ MR. JUSTICE WHITE, with whom MR. JUSTICE BLACKMUN joins, dissenting. * * *

■ MR. JUSTICE POWELL, dissenting.

I agree with Mr. Justice White that even under the standards articulated in our prior decisions, it is clear that no private action should be implied here. * * * But as mounting evidence from the courts below suggests, and the decision of the Court today demonstrates, the mode of analysis we have applied in the recent past cannot be squared with the doctrine of the separation of powers. The time has come to reappraise our standards for the judicial implication of private causes of action.

* * * Congress * * * should determine when private parties are to be given causes of action under legislation it adopts. As countless statutes demonstrate, including Titles of the Civil Rights Act of 1964, Congress recognizes that the creation of private actions is a legislative function and

frequently exercises it. When Congress chooses not to provide a private civil remedy, federal courts should not assume the legislative role of creating such a remedy and thereby enlarge their jurisdiction.

* * * The "four factor" analysis of [Cort] is an open invitation to federal courts to legislate causes of action not authorized by Congress. It is an analysis not faithful to constitutional principles and should be rejected. Absent the most compelling evidence of affirmative congressional intent, a federal court should not infer a private cause of action.

I

The implying of a private action from a federal regulatory statute has been an exceptional occurrence in the past history of this Court. * * *

A

The origin of implied private causes of actions in the federal courts is said to date back to Texas & Pacific R. Co. v. Rigsby, 241 U.S. 33 (1916). * * * The narrow question presented for decision was whether the standards of care defined by the Federal Safety Appliance Act's penal provisions applied to a tort action brought against an interstate railroad by an employee not engaged in interstate commerce at the time of his injury. The jurisdiction of the federal courts was not in dispute, the action having been removed from state court on the ground that the defendant was a federal corporation. Under the regime of Swift v. Tyson, 16 Pet. 1 (1842), then in force, the Court was free to create the substantive standards of liability applicable to a common-law negligence claim brought in federal court. The practice of judicial reference to legislatively determined standards of care was a common expedient to establish the existence of negligence. Rigsby did nothing more than follow this practice * * *.

For almost 50 years after Rigsby, this Court recognized an implied private cause of action in only one other statutory context.[3] Four decisions held that various provisions of the Railway Labor Act of 1926 could be enforced in a federal court. * * * [The case for implication of judicial remedies in these cases was especially strong in view of (i) particular evidence of congressional intent, (ii) the absence of an express administrative or judicial enforcement mechanism, and/or (iii) a 1934 amendment to the Act indicating congressional approval of the initial decision in this line.] In each of these cases enforcement of the Act's various requirements could have been restricted to actions brought by the Board of Mediation (later the Mediation Board), rather than by

---

[3]　During this period, the Court did uphold the implication of civil remedies in favor of the Government, see Wyandotte Transportation Co. v. United States, 389 U.S. 191 (1967); United States v. Republic Steel Corp., 362 U.S. 482 (1960), and strongly suggested that private actions could be implied directly from particular provisions of the Constitution, Bell v. Hood, 327 U.S. 678, 684 (1946). Both of these issues are significantly different from the implication of a private remedy from a federal statute. In Wyandotte and Republic Steel, the Government already had a "cause of action" in the form of its power to bring criminal proceedings under the pertinent statutes. Thus, the Court was confronted only with the question whether the Government could exact less drastic civil penalties as an alternative means of enforcing the same obligations. And this Court's traditional responsibility to safeguard constitutionally protected rights, as well as the freer hand we necessarily have in the interpretation of the Constitution, permits greater judicial creativity with respect to implied constitutional causes of action. Moreover, the implication of remedies to enforce constitutional provisions does not interfere with the legislative process in the way that the implication of remedies from statutes can.

private parties. But whatever the scope of the judicial remedy, the implication of some kind of remedial mechanism was necessary to provide the enforcement authority Congress clearly intended.

During this same period, the Court frequently turned back private plaintiffs seeking to imply causes of action from federal statutes. Throughout these cases, the focus of the Court's inquiry generally was on the availability of means other than a private action to enforce the statutory duty at issue. * * *

A break in this pattern occurred in J.I. Case Co. v. Borak, 377 U.S. 426 (1964). There the Court held that a private party could maintain a cause of action under § 14(a) of the Securities Exchange Act of 1934, in spite of Congress' express creation of an administrative mechanism for enforcing that statute. I find this decision both unprecedented and incomprehensible as a matter of public policy. The decision's rationale, which lies ultimately in the judgment that "[p]rivate enforcement of the proxy rules provides a necessary supplement to Commission action," 377 U.S., at 432, ignores the fact that Congress, in determining the degree of regulation to be imposed on companies covered by the Securities Exchange Act, already had decided that private enforcement was unnecessary. More significant for present purposes, however, is the fact that Borak, rather than signaling the start of a trend in this Court, constitutes a singular and, I believe, aberrant interpretation of a federal regulatory statute.

Since Borak, this Court has upheld the implication of private causes of actions derived from federal statutes in only three extremely limited sets of circumstances. First, the Court in Jones v. Alfred H. Mayer Co., 392 U.S. 409 (1968); Sullivan v. Little Hunting Park, Inc., 396 U.S. 229 (1969); and Johnson v. Railway Express Agency, Inc., 421 U.S. 454 (1975), recognized the right of private parties to seek relief for violations of 42 U.S.C. §§ 1981 and 1982. But to say these cases "implied" rights of action is somewhat misleading, as Congress at the time these statutes were enacted expressly referred to private enforcement actions. Furthermore, as in the Railway Labor Act cases, Congress had provided no alternative means of asserting these rights. Thus, the Court was presented with the choice between regarding these statutes as precatory or recognizing some kind of judicial proceeding.

Second, the Court in Allen v. State Board of Elections, 393 U.S. 544 (1969), permitted private litigants to sue to enforce the preclearance provisions of § 5 of the Voting Rights Act of 1965. As the Court seems to concede, this decision was reached without substantial analysis, and in my view can be explained only in terms of this Court's special and traditional concern for safeguarding the electoral process. In addition * * * the remedy implied was very limited, thereby reducing the chances that States would be exposed to frivolous or harassing suits.

Finally, the Court in Superintendent of Insurance v. Bankers Life & Cas. Co., 404 U.S. 6 (1971), ratified 25 years of lower-court precedent that had held a private cause of action available under the Securities and Exchange Commission's Rule 10b–5. As the Court concedes, this decision reflects the unique history of Rule 10b–5, and did not articulate any standards of general applicability.

These few cases applying Borak must be contrasted with the subsequent decisions where the Court refused to imply private actions. * * *

B

It was against this background of almost invariable refusal to imply private actions, absent a complete failure of alternative enforcement mechanisms and a clear expression of legislative intent to create such a remedy, that Cort v. Ash, 422 U.S. 66 (1975), was decided. In holding that no private action could be brought to enforce 18 U.S.C. § 610 (1970 ed. and Supp. III), a criminal statute, the Court referred to four factors said to be relevant to determining generally whether private actions could be implied. * * * But, as the opinion of the Court today demonstrates, the Cort analysis too easily may be used to deflect inquiry away from the intent of Congress, and to permit a court instead to substitute its own views as to the desirability of private enforcement.

Of the four factors mentioned in Cort, only one refers expressly to legislative intent. The other three invite independent judicial lawmaking. Asking whether a statute creates a right in favor of a private party, for example, begs the question at issue. What is involved is not the mere existence of a legal right, but a particular person's right to invoke the power of the courts to enforce that right. Determining whether a private action would be consistent with the "underlying purposes" of a legislative scheme permits a court to decide for itself what the goals of a scheme should be, and how those goals should be advanced. Finally, looking to state law for parallels to the federal right simply focuses inquiry on a particular policy consideration that Congress already may have weighed in deciding not to create a private action. * * *

II

* * * Cort allows the Judicial Branch to assume policymaking authority vested by the Constitution in the Legislative Branch. It also invites Congress to avoid resolution of the often controversial question whether a new regulatory statute should be enforced through private litigation. * * * Because the courts are free to reach a result different from that which the normal play of political forces would have produced, the intended beneficiaries of the legislation are unable to ensure the full measure of protection their needs may warrant. For the same reason, those subject to the legislative constraints are denied the opportunity to forestall through the political process potentially unnecessary and disruptive litigation. * * *

The Court's implication doctrine encourages, as a corollary to the political default by Congress, an increase in the governmental power exercised by the federal judiciary. * * *

It is true that the federal judiciary necessarily exercises substantial powers to construe legislation, including, when appropriate, the power to prescribe substantive standards of conduct that supplement federal legislation. But this power normally is exercised with respect to disputes over which a court already has jurisdiction, and in which the existence of the asserted cause of action is established. Implication of a private cause of action, in contrast, involves a significant additional step. By creating a private action, a court of limited jurisdiction necessarily extends its authority to embrace a dispute Congress has not assigned it to resolve.[17] This runs contrary to the established principle that "[t]he jurisdiction of the federal courts is carefully guarded against expansion by judicial interpretation . . . [.]" American Fire & Cas. Co. v. Finn, 341 U.S. 6, 17 (1951) * * *.

The facts of this case illustrate how the implication of a right of action not authorized by Congress denigrates the democratic process. * * * Arming frustrated applicants with the power to challenge in court his or her rejection inevitably will have a constraining effect on admissions programs. The burden of expensive, vexatious litigation upon institutions whose resources often are severely limited may well compel an emphasis on objectively measured academic qualifications at the expense of more flexible admissions criteria that bring richness and diversity to academic life. If such a significant incursion into the arena of academic polity is to be made, it is the constitutional function of the Legislative Branch, subject as it is to the checks of the political process, to make this judgment.

Congress already has created a mechanism for enforcing the mandate found in Title IX against gender-based discrimination. * * * The current position of the Government notwithstanding, overlapping judicial and administrative enforcement of these policies inevitably will lead to conflicts and confusion * * *. * * *

III

* * * I would start afresh. Henceforth, we should not condone the implication of any private action from a federal statute absent the most compelling evidence that Congress in fact intended such an action to exist. Where a statutory scheme expressly provides for an alternative mechanism for enforcing the rights and duties created, I would be especially reluctant ever to permit a federal court to volunteer its services for enforcement purposes. Because the Court today is enlisting the federal judiciary in just such an enterprise, I dissent.

---

[17] * * * [A] private action implied from a federal statute * * * universally has been considered to present a federal question over which a federal court has jurisdiction under 28 U.S.C. § 1331. Thus, when a federal court implies a private action from a statute, it necessarily expands the scope of its federal-question jurisdiction.

It is instructive to compare decisions implying private causes of action to those cases that have found nonfederal causes of action cognizable by a federal court under § 1331. E.g., Smith v. Kansas City Title & Trust Co., 255 U.S. 180 (1921). Where a court decides both that federal-law elements * * * present in a state-law cause of action * * * predominate to the point that the action can be said to present a "federal question" cognizable in federal court, the net effect is the same as implication of a private action directly from the constitutional or statutory source of the federal-law elements. To the extent an expansive interpretation of § 1331 permits federal courts to assume control over disputes which Congress did not consign to the federal judicial process, it is subject to the same criticisms of judicial implication of private actions discussed in the text.

Alexander v. Sandoval

532 U.S. 275, 121 S.Ct. 1511, 149 L.Ed.2d 517 (2001).
Certiorari to the United States Court of Appeals for the Eleventh Circuit.

■ JUSTICE SCALIA delivered the opinion of the Court.

This case presents the question whether private individuals may sue to enforce disparate-impact regulations promulgated under Title VI of the Civil Rights Act of 1964.

I

[The Alabama Department of Public Safety (Department) receives federal funds from the Department of Justice (DOJ) and the Department of Transportation (DOT), and thus is subject to the restrictions of Title VI of the Civil Rights Act of 1964. Section 601 of that Title provides that no person shall, "on the ground of race, color, or national origin, be excluded from participation in, be denied the benefits of, or be subjected to discrimination under any program or activity" covered by Title VI. Section 602 authorizes federal agencies "to effectuate the provisions of [§ 601] . . . by issuing rules, regulations, or orders of general applicability," and DOJ promulgated a regulation forbidding funding recipients to "utilize criteria or methods of administration which have the effect of subjecting individuals to discrimination because of their race, color, or national origin. . . ." 28 CFR § 42.104(b)(2) (1999).

[Sandoval brought a class action to enjoin the Department's policy—adopted after an amendment to the Alabama Constitution declared English "the official language of the state"—of administering driver's license examinations only in English. The federal district court and court of appeals agreed with Sandoval's position that the English-only policy violated the DOJ regulation because its *effect* was to subject non-English speakers to discrimination based on national origin.] Both courts rejected petitioners' argument that Title VI did not provide respondents a cause of action to enforce the regulation.

We do not inquire here whether the DOJ regulation was authorized by § 602 * * *. The petition for writ of certiorari raised, and we agreed to review, only the question * * * whether there is a private cause of action to enforce the regulation.

II

* * * [T]hree aspects of Title VI must be taken as given. First, private individuals may sue to enforce § 601 of Title VI and obtain both injunctive relief and damages. [Cannon upheld a private right of action under Title IX, and its reasoning embraced Title VI.] Congress has since ratified Cannon's holding. * * * We recognized in Franklin v. Gwinnett County Public Schools, 503 U.S. 60[, 72] (1992), that [Section 1003 of the Rehabilitation Act Amendments of 1986, 42 U.S.C. § 2000d–7,] "cannot be read except as a validation of Cannon's holding." It is thus beyond dispute that private individuals may sue to enforce § 601.

Second, it is similarly beyond dispute—and no party disagrees—that § 601 prohibits only intentional discrimination. * * *

Third, we must assume for purposes of deciding this case that regulations promulgated under § 602 of Title VI may validly proscribe activities that have a disparate impact on racial groups, even though such activities are permissible under § 601. [Though no prior opinion of the Court has so held, and although the stated assumption is in considerable tension with other decisions,] petitioners have not challenged the regulations here. We therefore assume for the purposes of deciding this case that the * * * regulations proscribing activities that have a disparate impact on the basis of race are valid.

* * * [Cannon] *held* that Title IX created a private right of action to enforce its ban on intentional discrimination, but had no occasion to consider whether the right reached regulations barring disparate-impact discrimination.[2] * * *

Nor does it follow straightaway from the three points we have taken as given that Congress must have intended a private right of action to enforce disparate-impact regulations. We do not doubt that regulations applying § 601's ban on intentional discrimination are covered by the cause of action to enforce that section. Such regulations, if valid and reasonable, authoritatively construe the statute itself, see Chevron U.S.A. Inc. v. Natural Resources Defense Council, Inc., 467 U.S. 837, 843–844 (1984), and it is therefore meaningless to talk about a separate cause of action to enforce the regulations apart from the statute. A Congress that intends the statute to be enforced through a private cause of action intends the authoritative interpretation of the statute to be so enforced as well. The many cases that respondents say have "assumed" that a cause of action to enforce a statute includes one to enforce its regulations illustrate * * * only this point; each involved regulations of the type we have just described * * *. See National Collegiate Athletic Assn. v. Smith, 525 U.S. 459, 468 (1999) (regulation defining who is a "recipient" under Title IX); School Bd. of Nassau Cty. v. Arline, 480 U.S. 273, 279–281 (1987) (regulations defining the terms "physical impairment" and "major life activities" in § 504 of the Rehabilitation Act of 1973) * * *. Our decision in Lau v. Nichols, 414 U.S. 563 (1974), falls within the same category. The Title VI regulations at issue in Lau, similar to the ones at issue here, forbade funding recipients to take actions which had the effect of discriminating on the basis of race, color, or national origin. Unlike our later cases, however, the Court in Lau interpreted § 601 itself to proscribe disparate-impact discrimination * * *.

* * * [W]e have since rejected Lau's interpretation of § 601 as reaching beyond intentional discrimination. It is clear now that the disparate-impact regulations do not simply apply § 601—since they indeed forbid conduct that § 601 permits—and therefore clear that the private right of action to enforce § 601 does not include a private right to enforce these regulations. That right must come, if at all, from the independent force of § 602. As stated earlier, we assume for purposes of this decision that § 602 confers the authority to promulgate disparate-impact regulations;[6] the question remains whether it confers a private right of action to enforce them. If not, we must conclude that a failure to

---

[2]   Although the dissent acknowledges that "the breadth of [Cannon's] precedent is a matter upon which reasonable jurists may differ," it disagrees with our reading of Cannon's holding because it thinks the distinction we draw between disparate-impact and intentional discrimination was "wholly foreign" to that opinion * * *.

[6]   For this reason, the dissent's extended discussion of the scope of agencies' regulatory authority under § 602 is beside the point. We cannot help observing, however, how strange it is to say that disparate-impact regulations are "inspired by, at the service of, and inseparably intertwined with" § 601, when § 601 permits the very behavior that the regulations forbid. * * *

comply with regulations promulgated under § 602 that is not also a failure to comply with § 601 is not actionable.

Implicit in our discussion thus far has been a particular understanding of the genesis of private causes of action. Like substantive federal law itself, private rights of action to enforce federal law must be created by Congress. Touche Ross & Co. v. Redington, 442 U.S. 560, 578 (1979) (remedies available are those "that Congress enacted into law"). The judicial task is to interpret the statute Congress has passed to determine whether it displays an intent to create not just a private right but also a private remedy. Transamerica Mortgage Advisors, Inc. v. Lewis, 444 U.S. 11, 15 (1979). Statutory intent on this latter point is determinative. Without it, a cause of action does not exist and courts may not create one, no matter how desirable that might be as a policy matter, or how compatible with the statute. "Raising up causes of action where a statute has not created them may be a proper function for common-law courts, but not for federal tribunals." Lampf, Pleva, Lipkind, Prupis & Petigrow v. Gilbertson, 501 U.S. 350, 365 (1991) (Scalia, J., concurring in part and concurring in judgment).

Respondents would have us revert in this case to the understanding of private causes of action that held sway 40 years ago when Title VI was enacted. That understanding is captured by the Court's statement in J.I. Case Co. v. Borak, 377 U.S. 426, 433 (1964), that "it is the duty of the courts to be alert to provide such remedies as are necessary to make effective the congressional purpose" expressed by a statute. We abandoned that understanding in Cort v. Ash, 422 U.S. 66, 78 (1975)— which itself interpreted a statute enacted under the *ancien regime*—and have not returned to it since. * * * Having sworn off the habit of venturing beyond Congress's intent, we will not accept respondents' invitation to have one last drink.

Nor do we agree with the Government that our cases interpreting statutes enacted prior to Cort v. Ash have given "dispositive weight" to the "expectations" that the enacting Congress had formed "in light of the 'contemporary legal context.'" Brief for United States 14. Only three of our legion implied-right-of-action cases have found this sort of "contemporary legal context" relevant,* and two of those involved Congress's enactment (or reenactment) of the verbatim statutory text that courts had previously interpreted to create a private right of action. See Merrill Lynch, Pierce, Fenner & Smith, Inc. v. Curran, 456 U.S. 353, 378–379 (1982); Cannon v. University of Chicago, 441 U.S., at 698–699. In the third case, this sort of "contemporary legal context" simply buttressed a conclusion independently supported by the text of the statute. See Thompson v. Thompson, 484 U.S. 174 (1988). We have never accorded dispositive weight to context shorn of text. In determining whether statutes create private rights of action, as in interpreting

---

*   [Ed.] Neither majority nor dissent cited Morse v. Republican Party of Virginia, 517 U.S. 186 (1996), a suit alleging that the Republican Party of Virginia's imposition of a registration fee for delegates to a nominating convention for the party's candidate for the U.S. Senate constituted a poll tax prohibited by § 10 of the Voting Rights Act of 1965. Although there was no opinion for the Court, five Justices recognized a private right of action to enforce § 10, and two of those Justices noted that the Voting Rights Act was passed the year after the Borak decision, in a legal context in which generous standards were applied.

statutes generally, legal context matters only to the extent it clarifies text.

We therefore begin (and find that we can end) our search for Congress's intent with the text and structure of Title VI. Section 602 authorizes federal agencies "to effectuate the provisions of [§ 601] . . . by issuing rules, regulations, or orders of general applicability." It is immediately clear that the "rights-creating" language so critical to the Court's analysis in Cannon of § 601 is completely absent from § 602. Whereas § 601 decrees that "[n]o person . . . shall . . . be subjected to discrimination," the text of § 602 provides that "[e]ach Federal department and agency . . . is authorized and directed to effectuate the provisions of [§ 601]." Far from displaying congressional intent to create new rights, § 602 limits agencies to "effectuat[ing]" rights already created by § 601. And the focus of § 602 is twice removed from the individuals who will ultimately benefit from Title VI's protection. Statutes that focus on the person regulated rather than the individuals protected create "no implication of an intent to confer rights on a particular class of persons." California v. Sierra Club, 451 U.S. 287, 294 (1981). Section 602 is yet a step further removed: it focuses neither on the individuals protected nor even on the funding recipients being regulated, but on the agencies that will do the regulating. Like the statute found not to create a right of action in Universities Research Assn., Inc. v. Coutu, 450 U.S. 754 (1981), § 602 is "phrased as a directive to federal agencies engaged in the distribution of public funds," id., at 772. When this is true, "[t]here [is] far less reason to infer a private remedy in favor of individual persons," Cannon v. University of Chicago, *supra*, at 690–691. * * *

Nor do the methods that § 602 goes on to provide for enforcing its authorized regulations manifest an intent to create a private remedy; if anything, they suggest the opposite. Section 602 empowers agencies to enforce their regulations either by terminating funding to the "particular program, or part thereof," that has violated the regulation or "by any other means authorized by law." No enforcement action may be taken, however, "until the department or agency concerned has advised the appropriate person or persons of the failure to comply with the requirement and has determined that compliance cannot be secured by voluntary means." And every agency enforcement action is subject to judicial review. If an agency attempts to terminate program funding, still more restrictions apply. The agency head must "file with the committees of the House and Senate having legislative jurisdiction over the program or activity involved a full written report of the circumstances and the grounds for such action." And the termination of funding does not "become effective until thirty days have elapsed after the filing of such report." Whatever these elaborate restrictions on agency enforcement may imply for the private enforcement of rights created *outside* of § 602, compare Cannon, they tend to contradict a congressional intent to create privately enforceable rights through § 602 itself. The express provision of one method of enforcing a substantive rule suggests that Congress intended to preclude others. * * *

Both the Government and respondents argue that the *regulations* contain rights-creating language and so must be privately enforceable, but that argument skips an analytical step. Language in a regulation may invoke a private right of action that Congress through statutory text created, but it may not create a right that Congress has not. * * *

[Finally the Court rejected the argument that the Rehabilitation Act Amendments of 1986, § 1003, 42 U.S.C. § 2000d–7, and the Civil Rights Restoration Act of 1987, § 6, 42 U.S.C. § 2000d–4a, ratified Supreme Court decisions finding an implied private right of action to enforce the disparate-impact regulations. First, the Court said, no such decisions existed; second, at best the statutes speak to suits for violation of a *statute*, like § 601, rather than one, like this one, for violation of a *regulation*.] Respondents point to Merrill Lynch, Pierce, Fenner & Smith, Inc. v. Curran, 456 U.S., at 381–382, which inferred congressional intent to ratify lower court decisions regarding a particular statutory provision when Congress comprehensively revised the statutory scheme but did not amend that provision. But we recently criticized Curran's reliance on congressional inaction, saying that "[a]s a general matter . . . [the] argumen[t] deserve[s] little weight in the interpretive process." Central Bank of Denver, N.A. v. First Interstate Bank of Denver, N. A., 511 U.S., at 187. * * *

Neither as originally enacted nor as later amended does Title VI display an intent to create a freestanding private right of action to enforce regulations promulgated under § 602. We therefore hold that no such right of action exists. Since we reach this conclusion applying our standard test for discerning private causes of action, we do not address petitioners' additional argument that implied causes of action against States (and perhaps nonfederal state actors generally) are inconsistent with the clear statement rule of Pennhurst State School and Hospital v. Halderman, 451 U.S. 1 (1981).

The judgment of the Court of Appeals is reversed.

■ JUSTICE STEVENS, with whom JUSTICE SOUTER, JUSTICE GINSBURG, and JUSTICE BREYER join, dissenting.

[Justice Stevens' lengthy dissent is only summarized here. He first asserted, contrary to the majority, that prior Supreme Court decisions had already recognized a private right of action to enforce the disparate impact regulation, as had every court of appeals to address the question.

[Beyond relying on precedent, he criticized the majority's treatment of § 601 and § 602 as entirely separate provisions; instead, he argued that the two sections are part of an integrated scheme and that § 602 has the "sole purpose of forwarding the antidiscrimination ideals laid out in § 601." He added: "On its own terms, the statute supports an action challenging policies of federal grantees that explicitly or unambiguously violate antidiscrimination norms (such as policies that on their face limit benefits or services to certain races). With regard to more subtle forms of discrimination (such as schemes that limit benefits or services on ostensibly race-neutral grounds but have the predictable and perhaps intended consequence of materially benefiting some races at the expense of others), the statute does not establish a static approach but instead empowers the relevant agencies to evaluate social circumstances to determine whether there is a need for stronger measures.[13]"

---

[13] "It is important, in this context, to note that regulations prohibiting policies that have a disparate impact are not necessarily aimed only—or even primarily—at unintentional discrimination. Many policies whose very intent is to discriminate are framed in a race-neutral

[Justice Stevens also disputed the Court's textual analysis, contending that there was no reason to repeat in § 602 the rights-creating language of § 601, as the two sections were obviously designed to protect the same people. Whether the disparate impact regulation was viewed as an interpretation of discrimination in § 601 or a prophylactic measure broader than § 601, it made no sense to differentiate private actions under § 601 from those under § 602.

[More generally, Justice Stevens criticized the majority's approach to implied rights of action: "The majority couples its flawed analysis of the structure of Title VI with an uncharitable understanding of the substance of the divide between those on this Court who are reluctant to interpret statutes to allow for private rights of action and those who are willing to do so if the claim of right survives a rigorous application of the criteria set forth in Cort v. Ash, 422 U.S. 66 (1975). As the majority narrates our implied right of action jurisprudence, the Court's shift to a more skeptical approach represents the rejection of a common-law judicial activism in favor of a principled recognition of the limited role of a contemporary 'federal tribunal.' According to its analysis, the recognition of an implied right of action when the text and structure of the statute do not absolutely compel such a conclusion is an act of judicial self-indulgence.

[" * * * [I]t is the majority's approach that blinds itself to congressional intent. While it remains true that, if Congress intends a private right of action to support statutory rights, 'the far better course is for it to specify as much when it creates those rights,' Cannon, 441 U.S., at 717, its failure to do so does not absolve us of the responsibility to endeavor to discern its intent. In a series of cases since Cort v. Ash, we have laid out rules and developed strategies for this task." He proceeded to explain how in Cannon, the Court applied those factors to find an "implicit intent" to create a private right of action.

[Finally, he contended that the Court's argument that provision of an express statutory remedy suggests that Congress intends to preclude other remedies was squarely inconsistent with Cannon's reasoning.]

NOTE ON IMPLIED RIGHTS OF ACTION[1]

(1) The Evolution of the Court's Approach. Whether or not Justice Scalia is persuasive that the questions in Cannon and Sandoval differ

---

manner. It is often difficult to obtain direct evidence of this motivating animus. Therefore, an agency decision to adopt disparate-impact regulations may very well reflect a determination by that agency that substantial intentional discrimination pervades the industry it is charged with regulating but that such discrimination is difficult to prove directly. As I have stated before: 'Frequently the most probative evidence of intent will be objective evidence of what actually happened rather than evidence describing the subjective state of mind of the actor.' Washington v. Davis, 426 U.S. 229, 253 (1976) (concurring opinion). On this reading, Title VI simply accords the agencies the power to decide whether or not to credit such evidence."

[1] In addition to sources cited elsewhere in this Note, see, *e.g.*, Brown, *Of Activism and Erie—Implication Doctrine's Implications for the Nature and Role of the Federal Courts*, 69 Iowa L.Rev. 617, 627–49 (1984); Foy, *Some Reflections on Legislation, Adjudication, and Implied Private Actions in the State and Federal Courts*, 71 Cornell L.Rev. 501 (1986); Frankel, *Implied Rights of Action*, 67 Va.L.Rev. 553 (1981); Marcanel, *Abolishing Implied Private Rights of Action Pursuant to Federal Statutes*, 39 J.Legis. 251 (2013); Steinberg, *Implied Private Rights of Action*

sharply, probably more important to the differing results in the two cases was the change between 1979 and 2001 in the Court's general approach to implying rights of action. Even before Cannon, however, the Court had begun to toughen its stance on implied right of action claims.

(a) The Borak Approach. The high water mark of judicially inferred remedies may have been J.I. Case Co. v. Borak, 377 U.S. 426 (1964), in which a unanimous Court upheld a private party's right to sue under § 14(a) of the Securities Exchange Act of 1934, which prohibits fraud in the solicitation of proxy material. The Court adopted a broad, purposive rationale for embracing an implied right of action. Noting that "it is the duty of the courts to be alert to provide such remedies as are necessary to make effective the congressional purpose", the Court concluded that "[w]hile [§ 14(a)] makes no specific reference to a private right of action, among its chief purposes is 'the protection of investors,' which certainly implies the availability of judicial relief where necessary to achieve that result." The 1934 Act provided for SEC enforcement, but Borak emphasized the value of private enforcement as a "necessary supplement" to SEC action. Reflecting what was then the dominant Legal Process approach to statutes (see p. 653, *supra*), Borak's framework was followed, in cases in other statutory settings, by the Supreme Court and by lower federal courts.

(b) Retrenchment and Cort v. Ash. Beginning in 1974, the Court started to narrow the Borak approach. Particularly significant was its decision in Cort v. Ash, 422 U.S. 66 (1975). In Cort, the Court refused to infer—from a provision of the Federal Election Campaign Act making it a crime for a corporation to make certain campaign contributions—a shareholder's right to bring a derivative action against corporate directors alleged to have violated the criminal prohibition.[2] The decision was especially noteworthy for its effort, through its four-part test (quoted in footnote 9 of Cannon), to harmonize and rationalize the law.[3] Though stricter than Borak, Cort stated (in language on which Cannon relied) that when "federal law has granted a class of persons certain rights, it is not necessary to show an intention to *create* a private cause of action, although an explicit purpose to *deny* such cause of action would be controlling."

(c) Post-Cannon Developments. Justice Powell lost the battle in Cannon, but he won the war. The very same year, the Court further tightened its approach, and ever since has generally rejected claims of implied federal remedies. Although the Cort test occasionally reappears, many decisions view the question of implied remedies, as Sandoval does, in a narrower frame, requiring proof that Congress intended to create a private right of action. A leading, and typical, decision is Touche Ross & Co. v. Redington, 442 U.S. 560, 578 (1979), in which the Court refused to imply a right of action under § 17(a) of the Securities Act of 1934—which imposes

---

Under Federal Law, 55 Notre Dame Law. 33 (1979); Zeigler, *Rights Require Remedies: A New Approach to the Enforcement of Rights in the Federal Courts*, 38 Hastings L.J. 665 (1987).

   2   See also National R.R. Passenger Corp. v. National Ass'n of R.R. Passengers (the Amtrak case), 414 U.S. 453 (1974) (Amtrak Act provides exclusive remedies for breaches of obligations created by Act, and no additional private actions to enforce compliance may be inferred); Securities Investor Protection Corp. v. Barbour, 421 U.S. 412 (1975) (customers of broker-dealers do not have implied right of action under Securities Investor Protection Act to compel SIPC to exercise its statutory authority for their benefit).

   3   Several post-1975 decisions, applying that test, refused to infer a private right of action. See, *e.g.*, Piper v. Chris-Craft Indus., Inc., 430 U.S. 1 (1977) (§ 14(e) of the Securities Exchange Act); Santa Clara Pueblo v. Martinez, 436 U.S. 49 (1978) (Indian Civil Rights Act of 1968).

recordkeeping and reporting requirements on broker-dealers and others—against an accounting firm that had audited and prepared the required reports for a securities firm that became insolvent. Justice Rehnquist, for the majority, carried through on the warning he issued in Cannon: "Here, the statute by its terms grants no private rights to any identifiable class and proscribes no conduct as unlawful. And * * * the legislative history of the 1934 Act simply does not speak to the issue of private remedies under § 17(a). At least in such a case as this, the inquiry ends there * * *."

The Court has not, however, taken the step of overturning earlier decisions that had recognized a private right of action under a more liberal approach. Thus, in Herman & MacLean v. Huddleston, 459 U.S. 375 (1983), the Court reaffirmed the private right of action under § 10(b) of the Securities Exchange Act of 1934 for violation of Rule 10b–5, the anti-fraud regulation promulgated by the SEC pursuant to § 10(b). The lower courts had long recognized that right of action, as had the Court itself in Superintendent of Ins. v. Bankers Life & Cas. Co., 404 U.S. 6, 13 n.9 (1971).

But post-Cannon decisions recognizing a new implied right of action are extremely rare. In Merrill Lynch, Pierce, Fenner & Smith, Inc. v. Curran, 456 U.S. 353, 381 (1982), the Court, by a 5–4 vote, inferred a private cause of action under the Commodity Exchange Act, primarily on the theory that such a remedy was part of the "contemporary legal context" that was preserved when Congress undertook a comprehensive revision of the Act in 1974. Merrill Lynch, like Cannon itself, thus rested on the premise that courts should more easily recognize rights of action under statutes enacted during a period when Congress' expectations may have been influenced by the Borak line of decisions.

(d) **The Role of Contemporaneous Legal Context.** Merrill Lynch's approach has since been called into question. First, in Central Bank of Denver v. First Interstate Bank of Denver, 511 U.S. 164 (1994), the Court (5–4) refused to imply a right of action for aiding and abetting a violation of § 10(b) of the Securities Exchange Act and, in so doing, disagreed with the SEC and the eleven courts of appeals that had considered the question. In some tension with Merrill Lynch, the Court rejected the contention that Congress had acquiesced in the courts of appeals' recognition of aiding and abetting liability under § 10(b) of the Securities Exchange Act, even though Congress had left those interpretations untouched while otherwise amending the Act on several occasions. The Court explained that even in the face of serial amendments, "Congress' failure to overturn a statutory precedent" cannot be equated with " 'affirmative congressional approval of the [courts'] statutory interpretation' ", which can be effected only through bicameral passage and presentment to the President (quoting Patterson v. McLean Credit Union, 491 U.S. 164, 175, n.1 (1989)).[4]

Second, and more important, Sandoval more generally held that courts should interpret a statute of any vintage according to *current* principles

---

[4]   The following year, Congress partially restored enforcement authority against aiders and abettors, by giving the SEC (but not private parties) the right to sue those who knowingly provide substantial assistance to principal violators. See Private Securities Litigation Act of 1995, § 104, codified as amended at 15 U.S.C. § 78t(e) (2006).

For criticism of Central Bank, see Strauss, *On Resegregating the Worlds of Statute and Common Law*, 1994 Sup.Ct.Rev. 429, 509–13; Eisenberg, *Strict Textualism*, 29 Loyola L.A.L.Rev. 1 (1995); compare Grundfest, *We Must Never Forget That It Is an Inkblot We Are Expounding: Section 10(b) as Rorschach Test*, 29 id. 41.

governing the implication of private rights of action, rather than reverting to those that prevailed when the statute was enacted.

Given the Court's working presumption that Congress enacts statutes against the backdrop of the Court's well-known canons of interpretations, does the Sandoval approach compromise the reliability of background expectations that are essential to effective communication between Congress and the judiciary? See p. 654 n. 11, *supra* (discussing the coordinating function of language). Compare Foster, *Should Courts Give Stare Decisis Effect to Statutory Interpretation Methodology?*, 96 Geo.L.J. 1863 (2008).[5]

(e) Cannon and Sandoval. The Sandoval opinion treats Cannon as good law. But it is difficult to square the Cannon decision with two propositions that Justice Scalia embraces in Sandoval: (i) a private right of action must be based on legislative intent, and "legal context matters only to the extent it clarifies text"; and (ii) "the express provision of one method of enforcing a substantive rule [the fund cutoff mechanism under Titles VI and IX] suggests that Congress intended to preclude others." With respect to the second proposition, can the outcomes be harmonized on the basis that the fund cutoff mechanism is contained in § 602, and that, as the Sandoval Court said, "[w]hatever these elaborate restrictions on agency enforcement may imply for the private enforcement of rights created *outside* of § 602, compare *Cannon*, they tend to contradict a congressional intent to create privately enforceable rights through § 602 itself"?

Doesn't the tenor of the Sandoval opinion (see especially footnote 6) suggest that the Court might well have held the disparate impact regulations to be substantively invalid had the issue been properly presented? If so, does that help explain the Court's efforts to treat §§ 601 and 602 as virtually unrelated provisions?[6]

(2) Arguments of Principle and Policy. Allowing a private plaintiff to sue for a violation of a federal statute always adds force to the deterrent effect of a statutory prohibition. Because Congress must have meant the prohibition to be taken seriously, why shouldn't courts always imply private remedies to promote the statutory purpose?

Note the following five objections to this argument—and possible responses to each, focusing on the context of the Cannon case.

---

[5] Note that the Court's post-Sandoval decisions have not uniformly rejected reliance on contemporaneous legal context to resolve questions about private rights of action. In Jackson v. Birmingham Bd. of Educ., 544 U.S. 167 (2005), the Court held (5–4) that Title IX's implied right of action embraced a suit by a male teacher who alleged discrimination "on the basis of sex" stemming from the school board's retaliation for his protest of sex discrimination in school athletics. Writing for the majority, Justice O'Connor relied in part on the fact that three years before the enactment of Title IX, the Court had construed 42 U.S.C. § 1982's basic prohibition against race discrimination to cover an analogous retaliation claim. Justice O'Connor described that earlier decision as "valuable context for understanding" how Congress would have understood Title IX. Does this reasoning signal, as Justice Thomas' dissent suggested, some retrenchment from Sandoval's strict approach? Or does it merely recognize the continuing effects of a decision from an earlier era, with the majority simply delineating the scope of the right of action recognized in Cannon—a right of action that might not have been recognized at all had the question first arisen in 2005 rather than in 1979?

[6] For a thoughtful discussion criticizing Supreme Court decisions that have narrowly construed statutory grants of equity jurisdiction, see Resnik, *Constricting Remedies: The Rehnquist Judiciary, Congress, and Federal Power*, 78 Ind.L.J. 223 (2003). Resnik links those decisions not only to the Court's restrictiveness in implying private rights of action but also to lobbying positions taken by the federal judiciary (through its Judicial Conference) urging congressional hesitation in creating federal rights enforceable in federal court.

First, the argument assumes that a statutory prohibition is motivated by a one-dimensional purpose to deter or require certain kinds of conduct. In fact, a statute is often the product of a pitched battle between competing interest groups, one outcome of which may be a compromise that the available remedies would be limited—that full compliance was neither desired nor desirable.[7] *And modern federal statutes tend to be attentive to remedial detail, making it more likely that when no express remedy exists, an implied remedy will be in tension with congressional objectives.*[8]

Were Titles VI and IX parts of such a compromise, and if so what were the terms? Can a court reliably answer such questions?

Second, even when full compliance with the prohibition is the statutory goal, private enforcement in the courts leads to serious problems of overinclusion or excessive deterrence that discourage socially productive conduct outside the scope of the prohibition.

Did the right of action recognized in Cannon pose such a threat? Does the force of the objection depend on how meritorious most such actions are? The likely response of universities to the threat of lawsuits? The costs of litigation?

Third, Congress may have wished to give an administrative agency authority to flesh out statutory meaning and to determine appropriate levels of enforcement. Indeed, regulatory statutes frequently issue commands to administrative officials rather than directly to regulated parties, and judicial recognition of a private remedy may thwart congressional efforts to centralize enforcement in an administrative body.[9]

Did Congress wish to give federal agencies a monopoly over enforcement of Titles VI and IX? If so, does it follow that a state law remedy for violation of federal regulatory statutes like those provisions should be held to be preempted—even if, in Cannon, the majority was correct that the government's only remedy, a fund cutoff, is too draconian to be regularly enforced?[10]

---

[7]   See Easterbrook, *Foreword: The Court and the Economic System*, 98 Harv.L.Rev. 4, 45–51 (1984).

[8]   Mashaw, *Textualism, Constitutionalism, and the Interpretation of Federal Statutes*, 32 Wm. & Mary L.Rev. 827, 842 (1991).

[9]   See generally Stewart & Sunstein, *Public Programs and Private Rights*, 95 Harv.L.Rev. 1193 (1982). The authors consider private rights of action as one of several available forms of private initiative in the operation of regulatory programs. They suggest that such a private remedy is of greatest worth in programs emphasizing "entitlement values"—for example, the value of being treated with respect and without invidious discrimination—and is considerably more problematic in programs designed primarily to increase productive efficiency. In the latter cases, however, they argue that a remedy limited to damages for injuries suffered is far less likely than broader remedies (sweeping injunctions or damages not tied to harm suffered) to generate overdeterrence.

[10]   It has been argued that federal agencies have authority, by administrative rule, to "dis-imply" private rights of action, see Grundfest, *Disimplying Private Rights of Action Under the Federal Securities Laws: The Commission's Authority*, 107 Harv.L.Rev. 961 (1994), and to specify the scope of private rights of action, see Pierce, *Agency Authority To Define the Scope of Private Rights of Action*, 48 Admin.L.Rev. 1 (1996). But if, as the Court subsequently argued in the Sandoval decision, private rights of action are always creatures of statute and a regulation may not create a right of action when Congress did not do so by statute, wouldn't a rule purporting to dis-imply a right of action ordinarily conflict with the statutory provision implicitly establishing that right of action?

Perhaps that would not be so *if* the initial judicial recognition of the right of action were based on deference to the agency's view that an ambiguous statute should be interpreted as

Fourth, whether and to what extent to provide a private remedy is an important question that the legislature should decide. Treating it as left to judicial implication makes it too easy for Congress to dodge the question and unduly taxes the ingenuity and capacity of the federal courts.

If this objection is valid, is it equally valid as to a congressional failure to provide, for example, a statute of limitations for federal causes of action? Does the objection depend upon the assumption that Congress (or the Constitution) does not contemplate judges' acting as junior partners of the legislature, helping to implement its statutory purposes? That courts cannot reliably determine what the statutory purposes were or their implications with respect to private rights of action? See generally the discussion of theories of statutory interpretation, pp. 652–656, *supra.*

Fifth, even if private remedies are desirable, a federal remedy may not be necessary or appropriate if state remedies are adequate to the task.

Before deciding whether to formulate a federal remedy in Cannon, should the Justices have asked whether Illinois provided a private right of action against universities for sex discrimination? Whether the other forty-nine states did so?

(3) Common Lawmaking Versus Statutory Interpretation. Consider the Court's recent insistence that the question whether to imply a remedy should be regarded essentially as a conventional question of statutory interpretation, viewed in terms of "legislative intent". Does that insistence—especially if it relies heavily on the absence of textual warrant for an implied remedy—create a danger that effectuation of congressional purpose, more broadly and sympathetically viewed, will be thwarted? Or does it implement the competing premise that Congress does not merely enact purposes, but commonly also specifies particular means by which those purposes are to be carried out? Compare, *e.g.*, Zuni Public School Dist. No. 89 v. Department of Education, 550 U.S. 81, 98 (2007) (emphasizing that courts should not read "statutory language" in a way "that ignores its basic purpose and history"), with Rodriguez v. United States, 480 U.S. 522, 525–26 (1987) (contending that "no legislation pursues its purposes at all costs" and that "it frustrates rather than effectuates legislative intent simplistically to assume that *whatever* furthers the statute's primary objective must be the law"). See also pp. 653–655, *supra.*

Indeed, a broader conception of legislative purpose might itself lead to rejection of any private remedy, at least when Congress has established a comprehensive scheme for administration of a regulatory program. Thus, while Stewart and Sunstein, note 9, *supra*, criticize the Court's tendency to engage in simplistic analysis of statutory text and legislative intent, they regard the Court's retrenchment since 1974 as, in the main, consistent with their view of the values and policies at stake.

Do courts have the capacity to make intelligent judgments about which statutory schemes call for implication of private remedies? If not, then if Congress has not addressed the question in a particular statute, should the

---

providing that remedy, see Chevron U.S.A., Inc. v. Natural Resources Defense Council, Inc., 467 U.S. 837 (1984), and the agency later changed its mind. For a sophisticated argument that the wisdom of recognizing a private right of action requires context-specific evaluation of the costs and benefits of using that approach to achieve appropriate deterrence, and that agencies may be better equipped than courts (or, indeed, Congress) to make such a determination, see Stephenson, *Public Regulation of Private Enforcement: The Case for Expanding the Role of Administrative Agencies*, 91 Va.L.Rev. 93 (2005).

default rule be (i) a refusal to recognize a right of action (the Court's current position) or (ii) implication (as in Borak)? Either default rule would have the virtue of providing Congress with a clear and predictable baseline against which to legislate. Should the choice depend on which is more likely to induce Congress to address the problem and overcome the attributes of the legislative process (inertia, lack of time, lack of foresight, sloppiness, incapacity or unwillingness to reach agreement on various matters) that give rise to uncertainties in the first place? See generally Elhauge, Statutory Default Rules 149–223 (2008) (discussing the conditions under which courts should craft "preference-eliciting default rules").

(4) The Range of Remedies. Should the appropriateness of recognizing an implied right of action depend on just what remedy is sought? Note that Justice Powell, in Cannon, distinguished Allen v. State Board of Elections, 393 U.S. 544 (1969)—in which the Court had permitted private litigants to seek a declaratory judgment that certain legislation had to be submitted for preclearance under § 5 of the Voting Rights Act of 1965—on the ground that "the remedy implied was very limited, thereby reducing the chances that States would be exposed to frivolous or harassing suits."

Are those chances greater when actions for compensatory (or punitive) damages are recognized? More generally, might the Court's increased restrictiveness reflect, in part, changes in the Justices' view, for example, of the extent to which discrimination lawsuits or securities class actions constitute (i) an important enforcement tool or (ii) meritless strike suits instituted by unscrupulous plaintiffs' lawyers?

(a) The post-Cannon decision in Transamerica Mortgage Advisors, Inc. (TAMA) v. Lewis, 444 U.S. 11 (1979), involved § 206 of the Investment Advisers Act of 1940, which makes it unlawful for an investment adviser to "employ any device, scheme, or artifice to defraud", as well as § 215, which renders "void" any contract made in violation of the Act. Treating the remedial issue as one of legislative intent, the Court construed § 215 as implying a private remedy for rescission of the void contract and restitution of money paid, but refused (over four dissents) to recognize a right of action for damages under § 206.

(b) The TAMA decision appears, however, to be limited to the specifics of the Investment Advisers Act. In Franklin v. Gwinnett County Pub. Schools, 503 U.S. 60 (1992), all nine Justices agreed that when a private right of action exists, "[t]he general rule * * * is that absent clear direction to the contrary by Congress, the federal courts have the power to award any appropriate relief". Thus, the Court held that in a private action under the same statute involved in Cannon—Title IX of the Education Amendments of 1972—a damages remedy was available.

(c) Franklin's holding that "any appropriate relief" may be afforded in actions under Title IX and similar statutes imposing conditions on recipients of federal funds was narrowly construed in Barnes v. Gorman, 536 U.S. 181 (2002). In that case, an action alleging that the municipal defendant had discriminated on the basis of disability, the Court held, without dissent, that punitive damages were unavailable under the Americans with Disabilities Act and the Rehabilitation Act, which incorporate by reference the remedies available under Title VI. Noting that Title VI's remedial scheme originates in Congress's Spending Power, the Court's opinion (per Scalia, J.) stressed that spending programs are similar in nature to a contract; that " 'if Congress intends to impose a condition on the grant of federal moneys, it must do so unambiguously' " (quoting Pennhurst State Sch. & Hosp. v. Halderman, 451 U.S. 1, 17 (1981)); and that because punitive damages are generally unavailable for contractual breach, funding recipients are not on notice that they might be subject to such damages. Justice Stevens, joined by Justices Ginsburg and Breyer, concurred in the judgment on the narrower basis that a municipality is not ordinarily subject to punitive damages. See City of Newport v. Fact Concerts, Inc., 453 U.S. 247 (1981), p. 1000, *infra*. He objected, *inter alia*, to the Court's extension of the Pennhurst decision from the question of the scope of conduct for which recipients are liable to the question of the scope of remedies.

(5) Implied Rights of Action to Enjoin Preempted State Regulation. A different body of decisions routinely permits private parties to sue without express statutory authorization to prevent state officials from enforcing state laws on the ground that they are preempted by a federal statute. For example, the Court in Shaw v. Delta Air Lines, Inc., 463 U.S. 85, 96 (1983), p. 844, *infra*, unanimously upheld the availability of injunctive relief against a state law banning discrimination on the basis of pregnancy, on the ground that it was preempted by ERISA. Without citing Touche Ross, Transamerica Mortgage, or other decisions refusing to imply rights of action, the Court simply declared that "[i]t is beyond dispute that federal courts have jurisdiction over suits to enjoin state officials from interfering with federal rights." (Although many if not most such actions could today be brought under 42 U.S.C. § 1983, that was not the basis for Shaw or for many other decisions.[11])

What accounts for the seemingly disparate evolution of this line of decisions recognizing an implied right of action in the preemption context? (a) The limited relief typically sought (negative injunctions or declaratory relief rather than damages)? But *cf.* Franklin, Paragraph (4), *supra*. (b) A stronger argument for an implied right of action when regulations of different governments conflict and the Supremacy Clause is implicated? (But is that clause a source of rights to sue or merely a rule of priority?) (c) Greater sympathy for the plaintiffs in these cases (typically businesses seeking to avoid state regulation) than in "standard" implied right of action cases (typically individuals suing businesses or, as in Cannon, nonprofit organizations)? For thorough discussion of these questions, see Sloss, *Constitutional Remedies for Statutory Violations*, 89 Iowa L.Rev. 355 (2004).[12]

---

[11] See, *e.g.*, cases cited in Franchise Tax Bd. v. Construction Laborers Vacation Trust, 463 U.S. 1, 20 n.20 (1983), p. 846, *infra*.

[12] In Armstrong v. Exceptional Child Center, Inc., 135 S.Ct. 1378 (2015), the Court held that the Supremacy Clause, U.S. Const. Art. IV, cl. 2, does not create a right of action for plaintiffs seeking to enjoin the enforcement of state laws alleged to be preempted by federal law. In an opinion by Justice Scalia (that was joined, in relevant part, by Chief Justice Roberts and Justices Thomas, Breyer, and Alito), the Court emphasized that the Necessary and Proper Clause, U.S. Const. Art. I, § 2, cl. 1, gives Congress "broad discretion over the manner of implementing its enumerated powers". From that starting point, the Court found it implausible that the Supremacy Clause "*requires* Congress to permit the enforcement of its laws by private actors, significantly curtailing its ability to guide the implementation of federal law." The Court, however, added that, to the extent that prior cases had authorized injunctive relief against state (or federal) officers for violations of federal law, those cases reflected the traditions of equity and "a long history of judicial review of illegal executive action, tracing back to England."

Armstrong does not appear to threaten the holding of Shaw v. Delta Airlines, *supra*. Injunctions to bar anticipated suits seeking to impose criminal and civil penalties for violations of state law appear to have fallen comfortably within the equitable traditions to which

(6) Implied Rights of Contribution. The Court has held that an express statutory right of action does not authorize judges to recognize an implied right of contribution, but that an implied primary right of action does carry with it that further authority. In Texas Industries, Inc. v. Radcliff Materials, Inc., 451 U.S. 630 (1981), the Court held that a company sued for conspiring to fix prices under the Sherman Act cannot seek contribution against other alleged participants in the scheme in the absence of express statutory recognition of such a right. First, applying the Cort v. Ash test, the Court found that Congress had neither expressly nor implicitly intended to create such a right, stressing that alleged conspirators were not "beneficiaries" of the antitrust laws. Second, turning to what it saw as the distinct question of whether it was appropriate to fashion a right of contribution as a matter of federal common law, the Court found that the claim for contribution did not implicate the narrow class of "uniquely federal interests" that justify federal common lawmaking. (Some of the language is quoted in Justice Brennan's dissent in the Boyle case, p. 666, *supra*.) Finally, the Court ruled that although Congress had delegated broad authority to the courts to develop substantive rules specifying what conduct violates the antitrust laws, that delegation did not extend to the development of remedial rules like contribution. See also Northwest Airlines, Inc. v. Transport Workers Union, 451 U.S. 77 (1981) (refusing to recognize a right of contribution in an employment discrimination case and noting that, in the face of a comprehensive statutory scheme of remedies, the "judiciary may not * * * fashion new remedies that might upset carefully considered legislative programs").

In contrast, the Court was willing to fashion a right of contribution in Musick, Peeler & Garrett v. Employers Ins. of Wausau, 508 U.S. 286 (1993) (6–3). That suit was based on the implied private right of action, previously recognized by the Court, under § 10(b) of the Securities Exchange Act of 1934 and SEC Rule 10b–5. See Paragraph (1)(c), *supra*. The Court found Texas Industries to be distinguishable, because its central inquiries—whether Congress " 'expressly or by clear implication' envisioned" a right to contribution, or "whether Congress 'intended courts to have the power to alter or supplement the remedies enacted' "—are not helpful in the context of a *judicially* created private right of action like the one under Rule 10b–5. Rather, in that context, the Court must ask "how the 1934 Congress would have addressed the issue had the 10b–5 action been included as an express provision in the 1934 Act." Because analogous provisions in the Act that do create express private rights of action also provide a right to contribution, the Court concluded that Congress would have wanted a similar contribution right in 10b–5 actions.

Viewed from the standpoint of protecting Congress' policymaking prerogatives, does its specification of *express* rights and remedies carry negative implications concerning the right of contribution that are absent when the right of contribution would supplement an *implied* right of action?

Armstrong referred. With respect to the specific preemption question at issue in Armstrong, however, the Court concluded that the plaintiff's suit for an injunction requiring a state agency to make payments allegedly compelled by federal law was impliedly foreclosed by an alternative remedy (involving a cutoff of federal funds) provided by the Medicaid Act. For a discussion of contrasting perspectives on the question whether litigants should be able to use constitutional provisions not only as shields but also as swords against state action, see Shapiro, *Ex Parte Young and the Uses of History*, 67 NYU Ann.Surv.Am.L. 69 (2011). For further discussion of Armstrong, see pp. 845, 934, & 1012–1013, *infra*.

Or does Musick, Peeler just reflect the old adage, "in for a penny, in for a pound"?[13]

(8) Implied Rights of Action on Behalf of the United States. It has been long settled law that the United States needs no specific statutory authorization to bring common law actions of a kind that private citizens could also bring—for example, for trespass or breach of contract. See, *e.g.* United States v. San Jacinto Tin Co., 125 U.S. 273, 285 (1888) (noting that "the right of the government of the United States to institute such a suit depends upon the same general principles which would authorize a private citizen to apply to a court of justice for relief"). But the Court has, at times, recognized a much broader governmental authority to sue, without statutory authorization, to vindicate the public interest against federal law infractions or, on rarer occasion, against intrusion upon federal interests. See, *e.g.*, United States v. American Bell Tel. Co., 128 U.S. 315, 367 (1888) (concluding that the government need not have a "direct pecuniary interest" in a case, but may sue "to protect the public from the monopoly of the patent which was procured by fraud"); In re Debs, 158 U.S. 564 (1895) (holding that the United States could sue for a labor injunction against a railroad strike and observing that the government has "all the attributes of sovereignty," which include the power to go to court to seek injunctive relief "to remove all obstructions upon highways, natural or artificial, to the passage of interstate commerce or the carrying of the mail"); Sanitary Dist. of Chicago v. United States, 266 U.S. 405 (1925) (relying on a similar theory to uphold an injunction against an Illinois corporation from diverting more water from Lake Michigan than the Secretary of War had authorized).

Note that these are *not* recent cases. To the extent that they fail to insist upon prior congressional creation of an actionable right, do they suggest that a different rule obtains with respect to the government's ability to invoke common law principles to impose civil—as opposed to criminal—liability? Compare United States v. Hudson & Goodwin, 11 U.S. (7 Cranch) 32, 3 L.Ed. 259 (1812), p. 636, *supra*. Even if the defendant has violated a preexisting federal statutory duty, is it consistent with the private-right-of-action cases discussed above to recognize a non-statutory right, on behalf of the federal government, to sue to enforce that duty?[14]

NOTE ON "BORROWING" STATUTES OF LIMITATIONS

(1) Introduction. Just as Congress sometimes enacts a right without a remedy, so too does it at times neglect to provide a limitations period when creating an express cause of action. Prior to 1990, Congress had never enacted a general statute of limitations for civil actions not governed by a

---

[13] Compare Lampf, Pleva, Lipkind, Prupis & Petigrow v. Gilbertson, 501 U.S. 350, 365–66 (1991) (Scalia, J., concurring) (arguing that while the Court should ordinarily address an omitted federal statute of limitations by applying the analogous state limitations period, it appropriately borrows an analogous *federal* limitations period for an implied right of action, since Congress never had "the opportunity * * * to consider whether it is content with the state limitations or would prefer to craft its own rule").

[14] For a range of views, compare, e.g., Monaghan, *The Protective Power of the Presidency*, 93 Colum.L.Rev. 1 (1993), with Yackle, *A Worthy Champion for Fourteenth Amendment Rights: The United States in Parens Patriae*, 92 Nw.U.L.Rev. 111 (1997), and Hartnett, *The Standing of the United States: How Criminal Prosecutions Show That Standing Doctrine Is Looking for Answers in All the Wrong Places*, 97 Mich.L.Rev. 2239 (1999). For an in-depth analysis of federal and state public authorities' standing to bring both private and public actions, see Davis, *Implied Public Rights of Action*, 114 Colum.L.Rev. 1 (2014).

specific limitations period. In 1990, Congress enacted a general four-year statute of limitations (absent a specific limitations period) for all civil actions "arising under an Act of Congress enacted after the date of enactment of this section." 28 U.S.C. § 1658.

Section 1658 does not address the limitations period for civil actions brought under federal statutes on the books before December 1, 1990 (the date of enactment) that do not themselves specify any limitations period.[1] In dealing with such a situation, a court can (a) apply a limitations period from state law; (b) borrow a limitations period from a different federal statute; (c) itself decide how long the limitations period should be; or (d) provide that there is no limitations period whatever. The last two options have been almost universally rejected.[2] Instead, the Court has developed an elaborate and sometimes-shifting set of doctrines that either apply the most closely applicable state law limitations periods or, more infrequently, borrow a federal statute of limitations. In reading the material that follows, consider whether the Court's attitude toward "implied" statutes of limitations differs from its approach to implied private rights of action. If the two differ, is the distinction in approach justified?

(2) The Presumption That State Law Is Borrowed. In the absence of an applicable federal statute of limitations, the Court traditionally applied or borrowed an analogous limitation period from state law. See, *e.g.*, Cope v. Anderson, 331 U.S. 461 (1947); Chattanooga Foundry v. Atlanta, 203 U.S. 390 (1906). The doctrine was initially formulated in a case applying a state tort law statute of limitations to a patent infringement suit, an action for which the federal patent statute supplied no limitations period. See Campbell v. City of Haverhill, 155 U.S. 610, 614–15, 618–20 (1895). The Court there emphasized that if the relevant state tort statute did not apply, "we have the anomaly of a distinct class of actions subject to no limitations whatever"—a result that "cannot have been within the contemplation of [Congress]." As long as the applicable state statute did not discriminate against the federal patent rights, the Court found its application to fall within the principle "that rights created by congress are subject to the police power * * * of the several states." In other words, a generally applicable state statute of limitations—in this example, in tort—simply applied of its own force to a federal tort action prosecuted within the state.

Subsequent cases, however, interpreted Campbell as holding not that a relevant state limitations period applies of its own force in the absence of an applicable federal one, but rather that Congress intended to authorize federal courts, in those circumstances, to borrow a state limitations period

---

[1] One obvious interpretive problem is how § 1658 applies when an amendment to an existing statute creates a new cause of action (or significantly expands an existing one) but contains no specific limitations period. In Jones v. R.R. Donnelley & Sons Co., 541 U.S. 369 (2004), the Court unanimously held that § 1658's four-year period governed the plaintiffs' civil rights claim under 42 U.S.C. § 1981, which would have lacked merit prior to 1991, when § 1981 was amended to extend to such a claim. After finding § 1658's text to be unclear about the statute's application in such a situation, the Court stressed § 1658's apparent purpose of eliminating the complexities involved in borrowing state limitations periods: "The history that led to the enactment of § 1658 strongly supports an interpretation that fills more rather than less of the void that has created so much unnecessary work for federal judges." Therefore, the Court concluded, a cause of action "aris[es] under an Act of Congress enacted after December 1, 1990 * * * if the plaintiff's claim * * * was made possible by a post-1990 enactment."

[2] But *cf.* Occidental Life Ins. Co. v. EEOC, 432 U.S. 355, 367 (1977).

as a matter of federal law. See Holmberg v. Armbrecht, 327 U.S. 392, 395 (1946).

The Court has, at times, strictly applied the resultant presumption that congressional silence reflects an intent to borrow state law limitations periods. Even in a case arising under § 301 of the Labor Management Relations and Disclosure Act—the statute that Lincoln Mills, p. 700, *supra*, had read to authorize a *uniform* federal common law of labor contract interpretation—the Court found that state law provided the limitations period omitted from the Act. Noting that "state statutes have repeatedly supplied the periods of limitations for federal causes of action when federal legislation has been silent on the question", the Court declined to "take the omission in the [LMRDA] as a license to judicially devise a uniform time limitation". Automobile Workers v. Hoosier Cardinal Corp., 383 U.S. 696, 704 (1966). Hence, the Court applied the presumption in favor of looking to the relevant state limitations period, even though it seemed to conflict with a previously recognized federal statutory policy—in this case, uniformity. Is uniformity less important with respect to limitations periods than with respect to primary duties?

Similarly, in Johnson v. Railway Express Agency, Inc., 421 U.S. 454 (1975), the Court applied the state law limitations period, despite a strong argument that doing so violated a federal statutory policy. In Johnson, the Court held that a restrictive state tolling rule barred a claim for employment discrimination under 42 U.S.C. § 1981, which prohibits racial discrimination in "mak[ing] or enforc[ing] contracts" but does not define a limitations period for bringing such a claim. Under analogous provisions of Title VII of the Civil Rights Act of 1964, a plaintiff must exhaust administrative remedies with the Equal Employment Opportunity Commission before filing a lawsuit claiming discrimination in employment "because of race". After exhausting his administrative remedies as required by Title VII, Johnson sought to file an employment discrimination suit under both § 1981 and Title VII. Johnson's Title VII claim was timely under the applicable federal statute of limitations. But his § 1981 claim was untimely under the borrowed state statute, which did not toll the limitations period for plaintiff's § 1981 claim while he exhausted his administrative remedies under Title VII. Although the Court acknowledged that its holding would induce some plaintiffs to go straight to court with their § 1981 claims before their corresponding Title VII claims were exhausted, that difficulty, it said, arose from Congress' decision to retain § 1981 as a remedy "separate from and independent of the more elaborate and time-consuming procedures of Title VII." The dissent argued that by pressuring plaintiffs to file their § 1981 claims so early, the application of state tolling rules undercut the federal policy, embodied in Title VII, of seeking to "avoid unnecessary and costly litigation by making the informal investigatory and conciliatory offices of EEOC readily available to victims of unlawful discrimination".

If the default rule, in the absence of a federal limitations period, is to borrow the applicable state limitations period, could there be any sound justification for applying the state limitations period but not the accompanying state rules of tolling and revival?[3]

---

[3]　For reaffirmation of Johnson's holding that state law ordinarily supplies not only the time period but also the rules on closely related matters like tolling or revival, see Board of Regents v. Tomanio, 446 U.S. 478 (1980). While tolling and revival are ordinarily governed by

(3) Which State Statute of Limitations? When federal courts decide to borrow a state limitations period, they frequently encounter difficulty in deciding *which* statute to select—or, as Judge Posner put it, "which round peg to stuff in a square hole." Short v. Belleville Shoe Mfg. Co., 908 F.2d 1385, 1393 (7th Cir.1990) (concurring opinion). Many decisions concerning the choice among a state's various statutes of limitations have arisen under federal civil rights statutes, especially 42 U.S.C. §§ 1981 and 1983. Section 1983, in particular, presents vexing problems because it comprehends a wide variety of claims—from discrimination in public employment to illegal arrests or searches to violations of freedom of speech or religion—many of which lack precise analogues in state law. If a plaintiff alleges that the police unconstitutionally arrested and beat him, should the court adopt the state statute governing actions for false arrest? For battery? For suits against public officials? For violation of state civil rights laws? For personal injuries generally? In Wilson v. Garcia, 471 U.S. 261 (1985), which involved just such allegations, the Court held that (1) as a matter of federal law, "a simple, broad characterization of all § 1983 claims best fits the statute's remedial purpose", and (2) such claims are "best characterized as personal injury actions" for purposes of selecting the applicable statute of limitations.[4]

(4) Borrowing Federal Statutes. Despite the presumption in favor of state limitations law, a handful of Supreme Court decisions have now applied a limitations period drawn from federal rather than state law sources. Two arguments are commonly made (but not often found persuasive) for overcoming the presumption in favor of state limitations law and instead fashioning a federal rule of decision. The first is that state limitations law conflicts with federal policy. The second is that subjecting plaintiffs in different states to different rules governing limitations periods will create injustice and complexity. Consider how those arguments influenced the outcomes in the following cases.

(a) In DelCostello v. International Bhd. of Teamsters, 462 U.S. 151 (1983), an employee's "hybrid action" against his employer for breach of the collective bargaining agreement and against his union for breach of the duty of fair representation, the Court applied the National Labor Relations Act's six-month period covering the distinct matter of filing unfair labor practice charges before the NLRB. A hybrid action, the Court reasoned, had no close parallel in state law; the analogies that had been suggested raised problems of "legal substance" (because they were generally only 90 days) and "practical application". In so holding, the Court described "the general preference for borrowing state limitations periods" as a "fallback rule of thumb" that "rests on the assumption that, absent some sound reason to do otherwise, Congress would likely intend that the courts follow their previous practice of borrowing state provisions." But when state statutes of limitations prove to be "unsatisfactory vehicles for the enforcement of federal law", the Court found it "inappropriate to conclude that Congress would choose to adopt state

---

state law, the Court held in Wallace v. Kato, 549 U.S. 384 (2007), that the accrual date of a § 1983 action is governed by federal law, which is drawn from common law tort principles.

[4]   What happens when a state has different limitations periods for different kinds of personal injury actions? In Owens v. Okure, 488 U.S. 235 (1989), a § 1983 suit involving allegations similar to those in Wilson, the Court again opted for an approach stressing ease of application. Passing over the state's one-year statute of limitations for actions alleging assault, battery, false imprisonment and several other intentional torts, the Court ruled broadly that in § 1983 actions, courts should borrow the state's general or residual statute for personal injury actions.

rules at odds with the purpose or operation of federal substantive law."[5] In dissent, Justice O'Connor said: "I do not think that federal law implicitly rejects the practice of borrowing state periods of limitation in this situation."[6]

(b) The rationale of DelCostello was extended in Agency Holding Corp. v. Malley-Duff & Associates, Inc., 483 U.S. 143 (1987), a civil suit under the Racketeer Influenced and Corrupt Organizations Act (RICO). RICO makes enterprises liable when they engage in racketeering activity, which is defined to include nine state felonies and over twenty-five federal crimes. Because each RICO action involves a distinct subset of predicate crimes, the Court found that a uniform statute was needed to avoid "intolerable 'uncertainty and time-consuming litigation' " (quoting Wilson v. Garcia, 471 U.S. 261 (1985)). Not only were satisfactory state analogues lacking, but because "RICO cases commonly involve interstate transactions," "the use of state statutes would present the danger of forum shopping" and guarantee complex litigation about which state's law applies. The Court also expressed concern that the applicable state statute might be so short as to thwart federal purposes. In the end, the Court decided that because RICO's civil enforcement provisions—authorizing recovery of treble damages and attorney's fees—were patterned after those in a different federal statute, the Clayton Antitrust Act, RICO should import that Act's four-year limitations period.

Justice Scalia, concurring in the judgment, argued that early decisions involving omitted limitations periods in federal statutes suggested that state limitations statutes applied of their own force unless preempted by federal law. The later treatment of congressional silence as authorizing courts to "borrow" state law was an analytical error, which, he said, was now compounded by the Court's willingness to depart from the practice of borrowing state law and to "prowl[ ] hungrily through the Statutes at Large for an appetizing federal limitations period". He concluded that "if [as in the case at hand] we determine that the state limitations period that would apply under state law is pre-empted because it is inconsistent with the federal statute, that is the end of the matter, and there is no limitation on the federal cause of action."

(c) Given the Court's routine assumption that "Congress legislates with knowledge of our basic rules of statutory construction," McNary v. Haitian Refugee Ctr., 498 U.S. 479, 496 (1991), was it legitimate for the Court to begin borrowing from analogous federal statutes when Congress had long enacted federal legislation against the background assumption that the Court would fill in the relevant gaps in federal coverage with state limitations periods? Is the content of the relevant rule of construction as important as whether the Court picks and adheres to a clear and predictable rule against—or around—which Congress may legislate?

(d) The Court has now reasserted the proposition that borrowing state statutes is the norm. See, *e.g.*, Graham County Soil & Water Conservation Dist. v. United States ex rel. Wilson, 545 U.S. 409 (2005) (stating that the Court "generally 'borrow[s]' the most closely analogous state limitations

---

[5] For further examples of this approach, see Oscar Mayer & Co. v. Evans, 441 U.S. 750 (1979); County of Oneida v. Oneida Indian Nation, 470 U.S. 226 (1985); Occidental Life Ins. Co. v. EEOC, 432 U.S. 355 (1977); McAllister v. Magnolia Petroleum Co., 357 U.S. 221 (1958).

[6] In a separate dissent, Justice Stevens relied heavily on the Rules of Decision Act, 28 U.S.C. § 1652, which, he argued, called for application of state law. For the majority's response, see p. 649, *supra*.

period" and that borrowing an analogous federal statute of limitations occurs only in "the rare case"); North Star Steel Co. v. Thomas, 515 U.S. 29, 35 (1995) (explaining that borrowing from federal law "is the exception, and we decline to follow a state limitations period 'only when a rule from elsewhere in federal law clearly provides a closer analogy than available state statutes, and when the federal policies at stake and the practicalities of litigation make that rule a significantly more appropriate vehicle for interstitial lawmaking' ") (quoting Reed v. United Transp. Union, 488 U.S. 319, 324 (1989) (internal quotation omitted)). Does this apparent development sufficiently address concerns about Congress' need for a clear background principle against which to legislate?

(5) Congressional Specification: Desirability and Alternatives. Given the difficulties surrounding the selection of limitations periods from other sources, one might wonder why Congress did not extend § 1658 to *all* federal causes of action that fail to specify a limitations period.[7] If one worries that a one-size-fits-all four-year limitations period might not be appropriate to all causes of action, could Congress have properly delegated power to some entity (such as the Judicial Conference of the United States) to fashion the most appropriate limitations period for statutes lacking express limitations periods? See Short v. Belleville Shoe Mfg. Co., 908 F.2d 1385, 1393 (7th Cir.1990) (Posner, J., concurring); Note, 44 Vand.L.Rev. 1355 (1991).

B. REMEDIES FOR CONSTITUTIONAL VIOLATIONS

Ward v. Love County
253 U.S. 17, 40 S.Ct. 419, 64 L.Ed. 751 (1920).
Certiorari to the Supreme Court of Oklahoma.

■ MR. JUSTICE VAN DEVANTER delivered the opinion of the Court.

[Ward and sixty-six other members of the Choctaw Tribe sought to recover taxes that, they alleged, had been coercively collected from them in violation of federal law. After the county commissioners disallowed the claim, the claimants appealed to the state district court, which entered judgment for the claimants. That judgment, however, was reversed by the Oklahoma Supreme Court.]

The claimants, who were members of the Choctaw Tribe and wards of the United States, received their allotments out of the tribal domain under a congressional enactment of 1898, which subjected the right of alienation to certain restrictions and provided that "the lands allotted shall be nontaxable while the title remains in the original allottee, but not to exceed twenty-one years from date of patent." In the act of 1906, enabling Oklahoma to become a state, Congress made it plain that no impairment of the rights of property pertaining to the Indians was intended; and the state included in its Constitution a provision

---

[7]   See Norwood, *28 U.S.C. § 1658: A Limitation Period with Real Limitations*, 69 Ind.L.J. 477, 502–08 (1994); Mikva & Pfander, *On the Meaning of Congressional Silence: Using Federal Common Law To Fill the Gap in Congress's Residual Statute of Limitations*, 107 Yale L.J. 393 (1997).

exempting from taxation "such property as may be exempt by reason of treaty stipulations, existing between the Indians and the United States government, or by federal laws, during the force and effect of such treaties or federal laws." Afterwards Congress, by an act of 1908, removed the restrictions on alienation as to certain classes of allottees, including the present claimants, and declared that all land from which the restrictions were removed "shall be subject to taxation, * * * as though it were the property of other persons than allottees."

Following the last enactment the officers of Love and other counties began to tax the allotted lands from which restrictions on alienation were removed. [In previous litigation, allottees brought suit in state court to enjoin the threatened taxation, arguing "that the tax exemption was a vested property right which could not be abrogated or destroyed" without violating the Constitution. "[O]ne of the suits [was] prosecuted by some 8,000 allottees against the officers of Love and other counties. When the case was reviewed by the United States Supreme Court, it held that the exemption was a vested property right which Congress could not repeal consistently with the Fifth Amendment, that it was binding on the taxing authorities in Oklahoma, and that the state courts had erred in refusing to enjoin them from taxing the lands."]

While those suits were pending the officers of Love county, with full knowledge of the suits, and being defendants in one, proceeded with the taxation of the allotments, demanded of these claimants that the taxes on their lands be paid to the county, threatened to advertise and sell the lands unless the taxes were paid, did advertise and sell other lands similarly situated, and caused these claimants to believe that their lands would be sold if the taxes were not paid. So, to prevent such a sale and to avoid the imposition of a penalty of eighteen per cent, for which the local statute provided, these claimants paid the taxes. They protested and objected at the time that the taxes were invalid, and the county officers knew that all the allottees were pressing the objection in the pending suits.

* * * In reversing the judgment which the district court had given for the claimants the [Oklahoma] Supreme Court held, first, that the taxes were not collected by coercive means, but were paid voluntarily, and could not be recovered back as there was no statutory authority therefor; and, secondly, that there was no statute making the county liable for taxes collected and then paid over to the state and municipal bodies other than the county—which it was assumed was true of a portion of these taxes—and that the petition did not show how much of the taxes was retained by the county, or how much paid over to the state and other municipal bodies, and therefore it could not be the basis of any judgment against the county.

The county challenges our jurisdiction * * * [and] insists that the [Oklahoma] Supreme Court put its judgment entirely on independent nonfederal grounds which were broad enough to sustain the judgment.

* * * [I]t is certain that the lands were nontaxable. This was settled in [this Court's earlier decisions]; and it also was settled in those cases that the exemption was a vested property right arising out of a law of Congress and protected by the Constitution of the United States. This being so, the state and all its agencies and political subdivisions were bound to give effect to the exemption. It operated as a direct restraint on

Love county, no matter what was said in local statutes. The county did not respect it, but, on the contrary, assessed the lands allotted to these claimants, placed them on the county roll, and there charged them with taxes like other property. * * *

We accept so much of the [Oklahoma] Supreme Court's decision as held that, if the payment was voluntary, the moneys could not be recovered back in the absence of a permissive statute, and that there was no such statute. But we are unable to accept its decision in other respects.

The right to the exemption was a federal right * * *. Whether the right was denied, or not given due recognition, by the [Oklahoma] Supreme Court is a question as to which the claimants were entitled to invoke our judgment. It therefore is within our province to inquire not only whether the right was denied in express terms, but also whether it was denied in substance and effect, as by putting forward nonfederal grounds of decision that were without any fair or substantial support. [Citing numerous Supreme Court decisions.] * * *

The facts set forth in the petition * * * make it plain, as we think, that the finding or decision that the taxes were paid voluntarily was without any fair or substantial support. The claimants were Indians just emerging from a state of dependency and wardship. Through the pending suits and otherwise they were objecting and protesting that the taxation of their lands was forbidden by a law of Congress. But, notwithstanding this, the county demanded that the taxes be paid, and by threatening to sell the lands of these claimants and actually selling other lands similarly situated made it appear to the claimants that they must choose between paying the taxes and losing their lands. To prevent a sale and to avoid the imposition of a penalty of eighteen per cent, they yielded to the county's demand and paid the taxes, protesting and objecting at the same time that the same were illegal. The moneys thus collected were obtained by coercive means—by compulsion. The county and its officers reasonably could not have regarded it otherwise; much less the Indian claimants. Atchison, Topeka & Santa Fe Ry. Co. v. O'Connor, 223 U.S. 280; Gaar, Scott & Co. v. Shannon, 223 U.S. 471.

As the payment was not voluntary, but made under compulsion, no statutory authority was essential to enable or require the county to refund the money. It is a well-settled rule that "money got through imposition" may be recovered back; and, as this court has said on several occasions, "the obligation to do justice rests upon all persons, natural and artificial, and if a county obtains the money or property of others without authority, the law, independent of any statute, will compel restitution or compensation." Marsh v. Fulton County, 10 Wall. 676, 684. To say that the county could collect these unlawful taxes by coercive means and not incur any obligation to pay them back is nothing short of saying that it could take or appropriate the property of these Indian allottees arbitrarily and without due process of law. Of course this would be in contravention of the Fourteenth Amendment, which binds the county as an agency of the state.

If it be true, as the Supreme Court assumed, that a portion of the taxes was paid over, after collection, to the state and other municipal bodies, we regard it as certain that this did not alter the county's liability to the claimants. The county had no right to collect the money, and it took the same with notice that the rights of all who were to share in the taxes were disputed by these claimants and were being contested in the pending suits. In these circumstances it could not lessen its liability by paying over a portion of the money to others whose rights it knew were disputed and were no better than its own. In legal contemplation it received the money for the use and benefit of the claimants and should respond to them accordingly.

The county calls attention to the fact that * * * the [state] statute of limitation * * * was relied on [by Love County below]. This point was not discussed by the [Oklahoma] Supreme Court and * * * when the case is remanded it will be open to that court to deal with the point as to the whole claim or any item in it as any valid local law in force when the claim was filed may require.

Judgment reversed.

NOTE ON REMEDIES FOR FEDERAL CONSTITUTIONAL RIGHTS

(1) The Sources of Constitutional Remedies. Historically, in an action to enforce a legal duty *other* than one imposed by the Constitution itself, a litigant could invoke the Constitution to nullify that duty. Thus, if state or county officials had sued Ward and his fellow tribe members to enforce tax obligations imposed by state or local law, Ward and those similarly situated could have defended on the ground that assessment of the tax was unconstitutional.

But what was the source of the affirmative refund remedy in Ward? State law apparently provided a refund for taxes paid involuntarily. Perhaps the Supreme Court, in finding no fair or substantial support for the state court's conclusion that the taxes had been paid voluntarily, was seeking to ensure that the state courts were applying *state* remedial rules on a nondiscriminatory basis to claims based on federal law. See generally Chap. V, Sec. 2(B), *supra*. But how does that reading square with the Supreme Court's statement: "As the payment was not voluntary * * *, no statutory authority was essential to enable or require the county to refund the money"?

In any event, the Supreme Court did not assert that fair or substantial support was lacking for the state court's alternative holding that state law afforded no remedy against the county with respect to monies already paid over to the state. The Act of Congress did not explicitly create a right of action to recover taxes paid under compulsion. Did it create such a right by implication? Did such a right exist as a matter of the general common law, as then understood? Of federal common law? Or did it arise from the Constitution itself? Consider the Court's observation that "[t]o say that the county could collect these unlawful taxes by coercive means and not incur any obligation to pay them back is nothing short of saying that it could take * * * property * * * arbitrarily and without due process of law."

When, if ever, might the Constitution afford affirmative remedies against injurious government action? The text refers explicitly to remedies in only two instances. First, the remedy of habeas corpus is safeguarded against "suspension" by Congress. See p. 1200, *infra*. Second, the Just Compensation Clause of the Fifth Amendment "dictates the remedy for interference with property rights amounting to a taking"—compensation for the impairment of value. First English Evangelical Lutheran Church v.

County of Los Angeles, 482 U.S. 304, 316 n.9 (1987).[1] More broadly, "[t]o the framers, special provision for constitutional remedies probably appeared unnecessary, because the Constitution presupposed a going legal system, with ample remedial mechanisms, in which constitutional guarantees would be implemented." Fallon & Meltzer, *New Law, Non-Retroactivity, and Constitutional Remedies*, 104 Harv.L.Rev. 1731, 1779 (1991). Those mechanisms were the recognized forms of action at common law and in equity.[2]

(2) Remedies for Equal Protection Violations. Should an equal protection violation be redressed by granting better treatment to the previously disfavored class or by imposing harsher burdens on the previously favored class? In Iowa-Des Moines Nat'l Bank v. Bennett, 284 U.S. 239 (1931), taxpayers, alleging a denial of equal protection, sought a refund of taxes levied on the plaintiffs' stock at a higher rate than was applied to the shares of competing domestic corporations. Without denying that systematic discrimination existed, the Supreme Court of Iowa affirmed a judgment denying relief, holding that the auditor had violated state law in reducing taxes on the competitors, and that the plaintiffs' remedy was to await (or to initiate proceedings to compel) collection of the higher tax from their competitors. The Supreme Court (per Brandeis, J.) reversed, holding that the taxpayers were entitled to a refund of the excess of taxes exacted from them: "It may be assumed that all ground for a claim for refund would have fallen if the State, promptly upon discovery of the discrimination, had removed it by collecting the additional taxes from the favored competitors. * * * The right invoked is that to equal treatment; and such treatment will be attained if either their competitors' taxes are increased or their own reduced. But it is well settled that a taxpayer who has been subjected to discriminatory taxation * * * cannot be required himself to assume the burden of seeking an increase of the taxes which the others should have paid. Nor may he be remitted to the necessity of awaiting such action by the state officials upon their own initiative."[3]

---

[1] Brauneis, *The First Constitutional Tort: The Remedial Revolution in Nineteenth-Century State Just Compensation Law*, 52 Vand.L.Rev. 57 (1999), suggests that in the nineteenth century, the remedy for a violation of just compensation clauses in *state* constitutions was not an award of compensation but rather a declaration that the offending act was a nullity. That approach left property owners free to seek common law remedies (like trespass) against individual officers, who could be held liable once any purported legislative justification had been nullified as unconstitutional. Brauneis contends that state courts began, in the post-bellum period, to view just compensation provisions as the source of a right to bring an action for damages, and that beginning in the 1920s, some state courts also viewed those provisions as abrogating state sovereign immunity.

[2] For the radical thesis that the only constitutionally mandated remedy for constitutional violations is nullification of a void enactment—and that Congress accordingly may eliminate all affirmative federal remedies now provided, leaving persons harmed by constitutional violations to state law remedies for violation of "private rights"—see Harrison, *Jurisdiction, Congressional Power and Constitutional Remedies*, 86 Geo.L.J. 2513 (1998). For a critical reply, which both questions the textual and historical premises underlying Harrison's claims and disputes the appropriateness of his originalist framework, see Meltzer, *Congress, Courts, and Constitutional Remedies*, 86 Geo.L.J. 2537, 2549–65 (1998).

[3] Compare Heckler v. Mathews, 465 U.S. 728 (1984), p. 119, *supra* (upholding plaintiff's standing to challenge sex discrimination in the award of social security benefits—even though a congressional mandate limited relief to reducing benefits received by others rather than increasing plaintiff's benefits).

(3) The McKesson and Reich Decisions.

(a) The source of the remedial obligation in Ward and Bennett was clarified in McKesson Corp. v. Division of ABT, 496 U.S. 18 (1990), a state court action seeking a refund of state taxes paid under a discriminatory tax that was held to violate the dormant Commerce Clause. The state court had enjoined future enforcement of the tax but had refused, on the basis of "equitable considerations", to award a refund of taxes previously paid. A unanimous Supreme Court held that if (as in this case) a state requires taxpayers to pay first and obtain review of the tax's validity later, the Due Process Clause requires the state to afford a meaningful opportunity to secure postpayment relief. The Court held that the state must either refund to the complaining taxpayer the constitutionally excessive portion of the taxes paid, or (to the extent consistent with other constitutional restrictions[4]) assess and collect back taxes from the taxpayer's competitors to eliminate the discrimination. The opinion considered and rejected several arguments made by the state that such a requirement would cause serious economic dislocation and heavy administrative burdens. Concluding that the state's interest in financial stability did not justify a refusal to provide relief, the Court observed that there are procedural measures that states could take in the future to "protect [their] fiscal security when weighed against their obligation to provide meaningful relief for their unconstitutional taxation."

(b) Was it significant that the Court treated the remedial obligation as arising not from the constitutional provision that was violated (the dormant Commerce Clause) but from the Due Process Clause?

(c) In McKesson, the Court placed some emphasis on the fact that Florida had opened its courts to refund actions and did not contend that they were barred by sovereign immunity. But in Reich v. Collins, 513 U.S. 106 (1994), also a state court action for a state tax refund, the Supreme Court unanimously stated the constitutional obligation more unqualifiedly. It cited, *inter alia*, McKesson, Bennett, and Ward, as support for the proposition that due process requires that a state provide a "clear and certain" remedy for taxes collected in violation of federal law, and that while the state may choose between predeprivation and postdeprivation remedies, it must provide one or the other. Thus, exaction of taxes in violation of a federal statute or the Constitution, by compulsion, violated the Fourteenth Amendment. The Court added that the obligation exists notwithstanding "the sovereign immunity States traditionally enjoy in their own courts". (That statement was dictum, as the state court's denial of a refund did not rest on immunity grounds.)

(d) The Court has more recently recast the required refund remedy in light of its sovereign immunity jurisprudence. In Alden v. Maine, 527 U.S. 706 (1999), p. 967, *infra*, the Supreme Court held that state sovereign immunity does not derive simply from the Eleventh Amendment (whose text addresses only federal judicial power) but rather is embedded in the Constitution and is generally co-extensive in state and federal courts. In so holding, the Alden Court reaffirmed Reich v. Collins on narrow grounds: "We held [in Reich] that, despite its immunity from suit in federal court, a State

---

[4] On the permissible scope of retroactive taxation of the favored class as a remedy for discrimination, see Rakowski, *Harper and Its Aftermath*, 1 Fla.Tax.Rev. 445, 489–99 & authorities cited (1993); *cf.* United States v. Carlton, 512 U.S. 26 (1994) (applying doctrine that retroactive tax legislation is constitutional so long as there is a rational basis for retroactive application).

which holds out what plainly appears to be 'a clear and certain' postdeprivation remedy for taxes collected in violation of federal law may not declare, after disputed taxes have been paid in reliance on this remedy, that the remedy does not in fact exist. This case arose in the context of tax-refund litigation, where a State may deprive a taxpayer of all other means of challenging the validity of its tax laws by holding out what appears to be a 'clear and certain' postdeprivation remedy. In this context, due process requires the State to provide the remedy it has promised. The obligation arises from the Constitution itself; Reich does not speak to the power of Congress to subject States to suits in their own courts."

Does Alden suggest that a state is merely prohibited from using bait-and-switch tactics and that no remedy would be required if the state clearly provides that no remedy for the exaction of unconstitutional taxes exists? For further discussion, see p. 975, *infra*.

(4) Retroactivity and Remedies. A series of cases has addressed the question whether the remedial obligation recognized in McKesson and Reich extends to claims for tax refunds based upon "new" principles of federal law not clearly established at the time the tax was collected.

In Harper v. Virginia Dept. of Taxation, 509 U.S. 86, 113 (1993) (5–4), the Court determined that its decision in Davis v. Michigan Dept. of Treasury, 489 U.S. 803 (1989)—which held unconstitutional a state tax on federal pension income—should be applied retroactively. The Court relied, in part, on the narrow ground that in Davis itself, the new rule was applied retroactively, leaving no basis for denying retroactive relief to similarly situated taxpayers in Virginia. But some language in Justice Thomas' majority opinion indicated that retroactive relief must be afforded even in situations in which the new constitutional rule had not already been applied retroactively in a prior case, reasoning that the Court lacks the constitutional authority, in effect, to disregard substantive law when deciding a case or controversy or to treat similarly situated litigants differently by denying a new rule retroactive effect.

Following an argument made by Fallon & Meltzer, Paragraph (1), *supra*, at 1764–70, Justice O'Connor tried in her Harper dissent to recast the question of retroactivity as one of remedial discretion, allowing courts in appropriate circumstances to deny a full refund even where no predeprivation process was provided. Certainly, courts often consider factors like surprise, arguable injustice from retroactive application of unforeseeable rulings, and relative hardship to litigants, in framing remedies. May they consider such factors in framing remedies for *constitutional* violations?

A subsequent decision outside the tax context, Reynoldsville Casket Co. v. Hyde, 514 U.S. 749 (1995), cast doubt on the permissibility of invoking remedial discretion to deny relief for the violation of a "novel" constitutional rule. In retroactively applying an earlier precedent that had invalidated Ohio's statute of limitations, the Court emphasized, in particular, that Harper's nonretroactivity principle should not be avoidable simply by asserting that the denial of relief was "based on 'remedy' rather than 'non-retroactivity' ".

The plaintiff had drawn an analogy to the law of qualified immunity in constitutional tort actions, under which courts will deny damages if an official's conduct, though illegal, did not violate "clearly established" law. Conceding that that doctrine "does reflect certain remedial considerations", the Court attempted to distinguish it on the ground that "a set of special federal policy considerations have led to the creation of a well-established, independent rule of law", whereas Ohio had tried to create "what amounts to an ad hoc exemption from retroactivity." (Is that an adequate distinction?) The Court also found wanting a second analogy offered by the plaintiff—the general unavailability of habeas corpus relief when sought on the basis of "new" rulings of constitutional law. That doctrine, the Court said, was not a "remedial" limitation on retroactivity but rather a limitation inherent in retroactivity itself, and one based on special concerns about the finality of criminal convictions. (But because the Court's decisions had authorized habeas relief based on new law in exceptional circumstances, see generally Teague v. Lane, p. 1295, *infra*, isn't there in fact a remedial calculus at work in such cases?)

The opinion recognized, however, that sometimes a new rule of law will not require a retroactive remedy, pointing to the "well-established general legal rule" of official immunity, which, the Court said, "reflects *both* reliance interests and other significant policy justifications", and which "trumps the new rule of [constitutional] law".

(5) Claims for Injunctive Relief. When does the Constitution give rise to an implied right to injunctive relief? Is such relief sometimes not only appropriate but constitutionally required?

(a) The Crain Decision. In General Oil Co. v. Crain, 209 U.S. 211 (1908), suit was brought in Tennessee state court to enjoin a state official from enforcing a tax alleged, *inter alia*, to burden interstate commerce. The claim that anticipatory injunctive relief was necessary was premised on the heavy penalties for violation, doubts that payments under protest could be recovered, and concern that a multiplicity of refund actions would be necessary in order to obtain complete recovery.

The Supreme Court of Tennessee held that the state courts lacked jurisdiction to grant the injunction sought, holding that the suit was one against the state and thus could not be entertained. On appeal to the U.S. Supreme Court, Tennessee urged that the judgment "involved no Federal question, but only the powers and jurisdiction of the courts of the State of Tennessee, in respect to which the Supreme Court of Tennessee is the final arbiter." But the U.S. Supreme Court affirmed its jurisdiction (although it sustained the tax upon the merits). Justice McKenna said:

"It seems to be an obvious consequence that as a State can only perform its functions through its officers, a restraint upon them is a restraint upon its sovereignty from which it is exempt without its consent in the state tribunals, and exempt by the Eleventh Amendment of the Constitution of the United States, in the national tribunals. The error is in the universality of the conclusion, as we have seen. Necessarily to give adequate protection to constitutional rights a distinction must be made between valid and invalid state laws, as determining the character of the suit against state officers. And the suit at bar illustrates the necessity. If a suit against state officers is precluded in the national courts by the Eleventh Amendment to the Constitution, and may be forbidden by a state to its courts, * * * without power of review by this court, * * * an easy way is open to prevent the enforcement of many provisions of the Constitution, and the Fourteenth Amendment, which is directed at state action, could be nullified as to much of its operation * * *."

⌣   Justice Harlan dissented, finding that the Supreme Court lacked jurisdiction because of the presence of an adequate state ground—namely, the decision of the Tennessee Supreme Court that the state courts lacked jurisdiction to take cognizance of a suit like the one at bar.

(b) The Implications of Crain. The majority's suggestion that the Eleventh Amendment would have prevented the oil company from obtaining an injunction in federal court is puzzling, for on the very same day the Court decided Ex parte Young, p. 922, *infra*, holding that the Amendment did not bar a similar federal court action to enjoin state officials from enforcing a state law that was challenged on federal constitutional grounds.[5]

Whatever the proper reading of Crain, doesn't the decision plainly indicate that, if the tax were unconstitutional, the oil company had a federal right to injunctive relief?[6] Traditionally, injunctions were available only when there was no adequate remedy at law. If Tennessee had clearly made a refund remedy available, would its refusal to provide an injunctive remedy then have been an adequate state ground? See McCoy v. Shaw, 277 U.S. 302 (1928) (affirming a state's denial of anticipatory equitable relief against a state tax on the ground that the state could properly require payment and a suit for refund). Reread the excerpt from Professor Hart's Dialogue, quoted at pp. 330–333, *supra*, stressing the broad discretion that Congress has in choosing among alternative remedies for constitutional violations, and more particularly, that it is "hard to hold that anybody has a constitutional right to an injunction or a declaratory judgment."

(c) A Constitutional Right to Injunctive Relief? The notion that injunctive relief is exceptional has considerably less force today than it did when Crain was decided, or when Professor Hart wrote in 1953. Indeed, at least since Brown v. Board of Education was decided in 1954, injunctive remedies for constitutional violations have become the rule and actions at law (at least for damages) the exception in many areas of public law litigation—*e.g.*,   suits   attacking   school   segregation,   legislative

---

[5]   In Alden v. Maine, Paragraph (3)(d), *supra*, the Supreme Court, after quoting the language from Crain reproduced above, read Crain as premised on the idea that sovereign immunity bars suit against states, and in some cases their officers, in state as well as federal court—and on the consequent need to permit anticipatory relief to enforce the Constitution as supreme law of the land. Isn't that a distortion of the reasoning in Crain?

[6]   Compare Crain with Georgia R.R. & Banking Co. v. Musgrove, 335 U.S. 900 (1949), in which the Georgia Supreme Court had dismissed an action for injunctive relief against certain state taxes on the ground that the suit was an unconsented action against the state; the opinion suggested that other (unspecified) state remedies might be available. The Supreme Court, in one sentence, dismissed the appeal on the ground that there was an adequate nonfederal ground for decision. (A later Supreme Court decision held that in view of the inadequacy of state court remedies, an injunction *was* available in *federal* court. Georgia R.R. & Banking Co. v. Redwine, 342 U.S. 299 (1952).)

The meaning of the dismissal in Musgrove has been the subject of debate. Does Musgrove suggest that the Crain obligation will not be enforced unless it is first demonstrated that no federal court remedy exists (and if so, should the state's obligation to grant a remedy be contingent on the hypothetical availability of a federal action)? Justice Souter explicitly rejected that view in his dissent (joined by Justices Stevens, Ginsburg, and Breyer) in Idaho v. Coeur d'Alene Tribe, p. 931, *infra*. He added that Crain's holding was not undermined by the dismissal in Musgrove, which may have rested on the view that the state court's dismissal was based on a valid state law regarding the timing, but not the existence, of state remedies. In a footnote, Justice Souter reported that quite apart from any federal obligation, all fifty states permit private suit in state court for declaratory and injunctive relief "in circumstances where relief would be available in federal court under [Ex parte] Young." For criticism of Justice Souter's explanation, see Seamon, *The Sovereign Immunity of States in Their Own Courts*, 37 Brandeis L.J. 319, 341–46 (1998–99).

malapportionment, or prison conditions.[7] The question whether, or to what extent, particular injunctive remedies (for example, a busing order in a school desegregation case) might be constitutionally required has not been sharply presented in these cases, as it might be if Congress purported to prohibit such a remedy.[8] Controversy has focused instead on whether the courts have appropriately exercised a general grant of equity jurisdiction.

One important question is whether a person subject to civil or criminal sanctions has a constitutional right to anticipatory relief—*i.e.*, the right to bring a declaratory or injunctive action challenging the constitutionality of some statutory or other duty, before having to choose between (i) forgoing conduct believed to be constitutionally protected, or (ii) engaging in that conduct and suffering the specified penalties if the claim of constitutional protection is found to lack merit. In Ex parte Young, p. 922, *infra*, an anticipatory action was brought to enjoin the state attorney general from enforcing state statutes regulating railroad rates alleged to be confiscatory in violation of the Fourteenth Amendment. Each statutory violation constituted a separate offense, for which railroad employees would be criminally liable. The Court deemed those sanctions so enormous "as to intimidate the company and its officers from resorting to the courts to test the validity of the legislation," just "as if the law in terms prohibited the company from seeking judicial construction of laws which deeply affect its rights". The Court thus held that because of the harsh sanctions imposed, the acts "are unconstitutional on their face, without regard to the question of the insufficiency of those rates."

Despite some echoes in other rate cases decided not long after Young[9]— and the desirability of permitting litigants to determine in advance whether a statutory prohibition can validly be enforced against them[10]—there is little clear authority for a general right to obtain anticipatory relief. *Cf.* Thunder Basin Coal Co. v. Reich, 510 U.S. 200, 216–18 (1994), in which the Court upheld congressional preclusion of an anticipatory challenge to an administrative order claimed to violate a federal *statute*. The Court stated that the case was not one in which the "practical effect of coercive penalties for non-compliance was to foreclose all access to the courts. Nor does this approach a situation in which compliance is sufficiently onerous and coercive penalties sufficiently potent that a constitutionally intolerable choice might be presented."[11]

---

[7] See Laycock, The Death of the Irreparable Injury Rule 3–7, 41–42, 196, 223 (1991).

[8] An exception is tax refund cases, where the Tax Injunction Act, 28 U.S.C. § 1341, generally precludes federal court injunctions, and state law generally prohibits state court injunctions. Thus, taxpayers generally have the choice of refusing to pay (where that is permitted) or, more commonly, of seeking a refund after payment.

[9] See Pacific Tel. & Tel. Co. v. Kuykendall, 265 U.S. 196 (1924); Oklahoma Operating Co. v. Love, 252 U.S. 331 (1920); Missouri Pac. Ry. Co. v. Tucker, 230 U.S. 340 (1913).

[10] See Note, 80 Harv.L.Rev. 1490 (1967).

[11] Compare Kontorovich, *Liability Rules for Constitutional Rights: The Case of Mass Detentions*, 56 Stan.L.Rev. 755 (2004) (arguing that treating constitutional rights as property rules, which presumptively authorize injunctive relief, will sometimes offer less robust protection than liability rules, which involve *ex post* compensation, because courts may, in some contexts, be more reluctant to find an underlying violation if it results in injunctive relief), with Monaghan, *First Amendment "Due Process"*, 83 Harv.L.Rev. 518, 543–51 (1970) (arguing for a right to prospective relief in cases arising under the First Amendment).

Bivens v. Six Unknown Named Agents of Federal Bureau of Narcotics

403 U.S. 388, 91 S.Ct. 1999, 29 L.Ed.2d 619 (1971).
Certiorari to the United States Court of Appeals for the Second Circuit.

■ MR. JUSTICE BRENNAN delivered the opinion of the Court.

* * * In Bell v. Hood, 327 U.S. 678 (1946), we reserved the question whether violation of [the Fourth Amendment] by a federal agent acting under color of his authority gives rise to a cause of action for damages consequent upon his unconstitutional conduct. Today we hold that it does.

* * * Petitioner's complaint alleged that * * * respondents, agents of the Federal Bureau of Narcotics acting under claim of federal authority, entered his apartment and arrested him for alleged narcotics violations. The agents manacled petitioner in front of his wife and children, and threatened to arrest the entire family. They searched the apartment from stem to stern. Thereafter petitioner was taken to the federal courthouse in Brooklyn, where he was interrogated, booked, and subjected to a visual strip search.

* * * [P]etitioner brought suit in Federal District Court. In addition to the allegations above, his complaint asserted that the arrest and search were effected without a warrant, and that unreasonable force was employed in making the arrest; fairly read, it alleges as well that the arrest was made without probable cause. Petitioner claimed to have suffered great humiliation, embarrassment, and mental suffering as a result of the agents' unlawful conduct, and sought $15,000 damages from each of them. The District Court * * * dismissed the complaint on the ground, *inter alia*, that it failed to state a cause of action. The Court of Appeals * * * affirmed on that basis. We granted certiorari. We reverse.

I

Respondents do not argue that petitioner should be entirely without remedy for an unconstitutional invasion of his rights by federal agents. In respondents' view, however, the rights which petitioner asserts—primarily rights of privacy—are creations of state and not of federal law. Accordingly, they argue, petitioner may obtain money damages to redress invasion of these rights only by an action in tort, under state law, in the state courts. In this scheme the Fourth Amendment would serve merely to limit the extent to which the agents could defend the state law tort suit by asserting that their actions were a valid exercise of federal power: if the agents were shown to have violated the Fourth Amendment, such a defense would be lost to them and they would stand before the state law merely as private individuals. Candidly admitting that it is the policy of the Department of Justice to remove all such suits from the state to the federal courts for decision, respondents nevertheless urge that we uphold dismissal of petitioner's complaint in federal court, and remit him to filing an action in the state courts in order that the case may properly be removed to the federal court for decision on the basis of state law.

We think that respondents' thesis rests upon an unduly restrictive view of the Fourth Amendment's protection against unreasonable searches and seizures by federal agents, a view that has consistently been rejected by this Court. Respondents seek to treat the relationship between a citizen and a federal agent unconstitutionally exercising his authority as no different from the relationship between two private citizens. In so doing, they ignore the fact that power, once granted, does not disappear like a magic gift when it is wrongfully used. An agent acting—albeit unconstitutionally—in the name of the United States possesses a far greater capacity for harm than an individual trespasser exercising no authority other than his own. Accordingly, as our cases make clear, the Fourth Amendment operates as a limitation upon the exercise of federal power regardless of whether the State in whose jurisdiction that power is exercised would prohibit or penalize the identical act if engaged in by a private citizen. It guarantees to citizens of the United States the absolute right to be free from unreasonable searches and seizures carried out by virtue of federal authority. And "where federally protected rights have been invaded, it has been the rule from the beginning that courts will be alert to adjust their remedies so as to grant the necessary relief." Bell v. Hood, 327 U.S., at 684. * * *

First. Our cases have long since rejected the notion that the Fourth Amendment proscribes only such conduct as would, if engaged in by private persons, be condemned by state law. * * * In light of these cases, respondents' argument that the Fourth Amendment serves only as a limitation on federal defenses to a state law claim, and not as an independent limitation upon the exercise of federal power, must be rejected.

Second. The interests protected by state laws regulating trespass and the invasion of privacy, and those protected by the Fourth Amendment's guarantee against unreasonable searches and seizures, may be inconsistent or even hostile. Thus, we may bar the door against an unwelcome private intruder, or call the police if he persists in seeking entrance. The availability of such alternative means for the protection of privacy may lead the State to restrict imposition of liability for any consequent trespass. A private citizen, asserting no authority other than his own, will not normally be liable in trespass if he demands, and is granted, admission to another's house. But one who demands admission under a claim of federal authority stands in a far different position. The mere invocation of federal power by a federal law enforcement official will normally render futile any attempt to resist an unlawful entry or arrest by resort to the local police; and a claim of authority to enter is likely to unlock the door as well. * * *

Nor is it adequate to answer that state law may take into account the different status of one clothed with the authority of the Federal Government. For just as state law may not authorize federal agents to violate the Fourth Amendment, * * * neither may state law undertake to limit the extent to which federal authority can be exercised. The inevitable consequence of this dual limitation on state power is that the federal question becomes not merely a possible defense to the state law action, but an independent claim both necessary and sufficient to make out the plaintiff's cause of action. * * *

Third. That damages may be obtained for injuries consequent upon a violation of the Fourth Amendment by federal officials should hardly seem a surprising proposition. * * * See Nixon v. Condon, 286 U.S. 73 (1932); Nixon v. Herndon, 273 U.S. 536, 540 (1927); Swafford v. Templeton, 185 U.S. 487 (1902); Wiley v. Sinkler, 179 U.S. 58 (1900). Of course the Fourth Amendment does not in so many words provide for its enforcement by an award of money damages for the consequences of its violation. But "it is also well settled that where legal rights have been invaded, and a federal statute provides for a general right to sue for such invasion, federal courts may use any available remedy to make good the wrong done." Bell v. Hood, 327 U.S., at 684 (1946) (footnote omitted). The present case involves no special factors counselling hesitation in the absence of affirmative action by Congress. We are not dealing with a question of "federal fiscal policy," as in United States v. Standard Oil Co., 332 U.S. 301, 311 (1947). * * * Nor are we asked in this case to impose liability upon a congressional employee for actions contrary to no constitutional prohibition, but merely said to be in excess of the authority delegated to him by the Congress. Wheeldin v. Wheeler, 373 U.S. 647 (1963). Finally, we cannot accept respondents' formulation of the question as whether the availability of money damages is necessary to enforce the Fourth Amendment. For we have here no explicit congressional declaration that persons injured by a federal officer's violation of the Fourth Amendment may not recover money damages from the agents, but must instead be remitted to another remedy, equally effective in the view of Congress. The question is merely whether petitioner, if he can demonstrate an injury consequent upon the violation by federal agents of his Fourth Amendment rights, is entitled to redress his injury through a particular remedial mechanism normally available in the federal courts. "The very essence of civil liberty certainly consists in the right of every individual to claim the protection of the laws whenever he receives an injury." Marbury v. Madison, 1 Cranch 137, 163 (1803). Having concluded that petitioner's complaint states a cause of action under the Fourth Amendment, we hold that petitioner is entitled to recover money damages for any injuries he has suffered as a result of the agents' violation of the Amendment.

II

In addition to holding that petitioner's complaint had failed to state facts making out a cause of action, the District Court ruled that in any event respondents were immune from liability by virtue of their official position. This question was not passed upon by the Court of Appeals, and accordingly we do not consider it here. The judgment of the Court of Appeals is reversed and the case is remanded for further proceedings consistent with this opinion.

■ MR. JUSTICE HARLAN, concurring in the judgment.

My initial view of this case was that the Court of Appeals was correct in dismissing the complaint, but for reasons stated in this opinion I am now persuaded to the contrary. * * *

I am of the opinion that federal courts do have the power to award damages for violation of "constitutionally protected interests" and I agree with the Court that a traditional judicial remedy such as damages is appropriate to the vindication of the personal interests protected by the Fourth Amendment.

I

I turn first to the contention that the constitutional power of federal courts to accord Bivens damages for his claim depends on the passage of a statute creating a "federal cause of action." Although the point is not entirely free of ambiguity, I do not understand either the Government or my dissenting Brothers to maintain that Bivens' contention that he is entitled to be free from the type of official conduct prohibited by the Fourth Amendment depends on a decision by the State in which he resides to accord him a remedy. Such a position would be incompatible with the presumed availability of federal equitable relief, if a proper showing can be made in terms of the ordinary principles governing equitable remedies. See Bell v. Hood, 327 U.S. 678, 684 (1946). However broad a federal court's discretion concerning equitable remedies, it is absolutely clear—at least after Erie R. Co. v. Tompkins, 304 U.S. 64 (1938)—that in a nondiversity suit a federal court's power to grant even equitable relief depends on the presence of a substantive right derived from federal law. Compare Guaranty Trust Co. v. York, 326 U.S. 99, 105–107 (1945), with Holmberg v. Armbrecht, 327 U.S. 392, 395 (1946). See also H. Hart and H. Wechsler, The Federal Courts and the Federal System 818–819 (1953).

Thus the interest which Bivens claims—to be free from official conduct in contravention of the Fourth Amendment—is a federally protected interest.[3] Therefore, the question of judicial *power* to grant Bivens damages is not a problem of the "source" of the "right"; instead, the question is whether the power to authorize damages as a judicial remedy for the vindication of a federal constitutional right is placed by the Constitution itself exclusively in Congress' hands.

II

The contention that the federal courts are powerless to accord a litigant damages for a claimed invasion of his federal constitutional rights until Congress explicitly authorizes the remedy cannot rest on the notion that the decision to grant compensatory relief involves a resolution of policy considerations not susceptible of judicial discernment. Thus, in suits for damages based on violations of federal statutes lacking any express authorization of a damage remedy, this Court has authorized such relief where, in its view, damages are necessary to effectuate the congressional policy underpinning the substantive provisions of the statute. J.I. Case Co. v. Borak, 377 U.S. 426 (1964); [citing two other decisions.][4]

---

[3] The Government appears not quite ready to concede this point. Certain points in the Government's argument seem to suggest that the "state-created right—federal defense" model reaches not only the question of the power to accord a federal damages remedy, but also the claim to any judicial remedy in any court. * * *

In truth, the legislative record as a whole behind the Bill of Rights is silent on the rather refined doctrinal question whether the framers considered the rights therein enumerated as dependent in the first instance on the decision of a State to accord legal status to the personal interests at stake. That is understandable since the Government itself points out that general federal question jurisdiction was not extended to the federal district courts until 1875. The most that can be drawn from this historical fact is that the authors of the Bill of Rights assumed the adequacy of common law remedies to vindicate the federally protected interest. One must first combine this assumption with contemporary modes of jurisprudential thought which appeared to link "rights" and "remedies" in a 1:1 correlation, *cf.* Marbury v. Madison, 1 Cranch 137, 163 (1803), before reaching the conclusion that the framers are to be understood today as having created no federally protected interests. And, of course, that would simply require the conclusion that federal equitable relief would not lie to protect those interests guarded by the Fourth Amendment. * * *

[4] The Borak case is an especially clear example of the exercise of federal judicial power to accord damages as an appropriate remedy in the absence of any express statutory authorization

If it is not the nature of the remedy which is thought to render a judgment as to the appropriateness of damages inherently "legislative," then it must be the nature of the legal interest offered as an occasion for invoking otherwise appropriate judicial relief. But I do not think that the fact that the interest is protected by the Constitution rather than statute or common law justifies the assertion that federal courts are powerless to grant damages in the absence of explicit congressional action authorizing the remedy. Initially, I note that it would be at least anomalous to conclude that the federal judiciary—while competent to choose among the range of traditional judicial remedies to implement statutory and common-law policies, and even to generate substantive rules governing primary behavior in furtherance of broadly formulated policies articulated by statute or Constitution, see Textile Workers Union v. Lincoln Mills, 353 U.S. 448 (1957); United States v. Standard Oil Co., 332 U.S. 301, 304–311 (1947); Clearfield Trust Co. v. United States, 318 U.S. 363 (1943)—is powerless to accord a damage remedy to vindicate social policies which, by virtue of their inclusion in the Constitution, are aimed predominantly at restraining the Government as an instrument of the popular will.

More importantly, the presumed availability of federal equitable relief against threatened invasions of constitutional interests appears entirely to negate the contention that the status of an interest as constitutionally protected divests federal courts of the power to grant damages absent express congressional authorization. * * *

If explicit congressional authorization is an absolute prerequisite to the power of a federal court to accord compensatory relief regardless of the necessity or appropriateness of damages as a remedy simply because of the status of a legal interest as constitutionally protected, then it seems to me that explicit congressional authorization is similarly prerequisite to the exercise of equitable remedial discretion in favor of constitutionally protected interests. Conversely, if a general grant of jurisdiction to the federal courts by Congress is thought adequate to empower a federal court to grant equitable relief for all areas of subject-matter jurisdiction enumerated therein, see 28 U.S.C. § 1331(a), then it seems to me that statute is sufficient to empower a federal court to grant a traditional remedy at law. Of course, the special historical traditions governing the federal equity system might still bear on the comparative appropriateness of granting equitable relief as opposed to money damages. That possibility, however, relates not to whether the federal courts have the power to afford one type of remedy as opposed to the other, but rather to the criteria which should govern the exercise of our power. To that question, I now pass.

---

of a federal cause of action. There we "implied"—from what can only be characterized as an "exclusively procedural provision" affording access to a federal forum—a private cause of action for damages for violation of § 14(a) of the Securities Act of 1934. We did so in an area where federal regulation has been singularly comprehensive and elaborate administrative enforcement machinery had been provided. The exercise of judicial power involved in Borak simply cannot be justified in terms of statutory construction; nor did the Borak Court purport to do so. The notion of "implying" a remedy, therefore, as applied to cases like Borak, can only refer to a process whereby the federal judiciary exercises a choice among *traditionally available* judicial remedies according to reasons related to the substantive social policy embodied in an act of positive law.

III

The major thrust of the Government's position is that, where Congress has not expressly authorized a particular remedy, a federal court should exercise its power to accord a traditional form of judicial relief at the behest of a litigant, who claims a constitutionally protected interest has been invaded, only where the remedy is "essential," or "indispensable for vindicating constitutional rights." Govt. Brief, 19, 24. * * *

These arguments for a more stringent test to govern the grant of damages in constitutional cases seem to be adequately answered by the point that the judiciary has a particular responsibility to assure the vindication of constitutional interests such as those embraced by the Fourth Amendment. To be sure, "it must be remembered that legislatures are ultimate guardians of the liberties and welfare of the people in quite as great a degree as the courts." Missouri, Kansas & Texas R. Co. of Texas v. May, 194 U.S. 267, 270 (1904). But it must also be recognized that the Bill of Rights is particularly intended to vindicate the interests of the individual in the face of the popular will as expressed in legislative majorities; at the very least, it strikes me as no more appropriate to await express congressional authorization of traditional judicial relief with regard to these legal interests than with respect to interests protected by federal statutes.

The question then, is, as I see it, whether compensatory relief is "necessary" or "appropriate" to the vindication of the interest asserted. * * * In resolving that question, it seems to me that the range of policy considerations we may take into account are at least as broad as those a legislature would consider with respect to an express statutory authorization of a traditional remedy. In this regard I agree with the Court that the appropriateness of according Bivens compensatory relief does not turn simply on the deterrent effect liability will have on federal official conduct.[8] * * *

I think it is clear that Bivens advances a claim of the sort that, if proved, would be properly compensable in damages. The personal interests protected by the Fourth Amendment are those we attempt to capture by the notion of "privacy"; while the Court today properly points out that the type of harm which officials can inflict when they invade protected zones of an individual's life are different from the types of harm private citizens inflict on one another, the experience of judges in dealing with private trespass and false imprisonment claims supports the conclusion that courts of law are capable of making the types of judgment

---

[8]   And I think it follows from this point that today's decision has little, if indeed any, bearing on the question whether a federal court may properly devise remedies—other than traditionally available forms of judicial relief—for the purpose of enforcing substantive social policies embodied in constitutional or statutory policies. Compare today's decision with Mapp v. Ohio, 367 U.S. 643 (1961), and Weeks v. United States, 232 U.S. 383 (1914). The Court today simply recognizes what has long been implicit in our decisions concerning equitable relief and remedies implied from statutory schemes; i.e., that a court of law vested with jurisdiction over the subject matter of a suit has the power—and therefore the duty—to make principled choices among traditional judicial remedies. Whether special prophylactic measures—which at least arguably the exclusionary rule exemplifies—are supportable on grounds other than a court's competence to select among traditional judicial remedies to make good the wrong done is a separate question.

concerning causation and magnitude of injury necessary to accord meaningful compensation for invasion of Fourth Amendment rights.

On the other hand, the limitations on state remedies for violation of common law rights by private citizens argue in favor of a federal damage remedy. The injuries inflicted by officials acting under color of law, while no less compensable in damages than those inflicted by private parties, are substantially different in kind, as the Court's opinion today discusses in detail. See Monroe v. Pape, 365 U.S. 167, 195 (1961) (Harlan, J., concurring). It seems to me entirely proper that these injuries be compensable according to uniform rules of federal law, especially in light of the very large element of federal law which must in any event control the scope of official defenses to liability. See Monroe v. Pape, 365 U.S. 167, 194–195 (Harlan, J., concurring); Howard v. Lyons, 360 U.S. 593 (1959). Certainly, there is very little federalism interest in preserving different rules of liability for federal officers dependent on the State where the injury occurs.

Putting aside the desirability of leaving the problem of federal official liability to the vagaries of common law actions, it is apparent that damages in some form is the only possible remedy for someone in Bivens' alleged position. It will be a rare case indeed in which an individual in Bivens' position will be able to obviate the harm by securing injunctive relief from any court. However desirable a direct remedy against the Government might be as a substitute for individual official liability, the Sovereign still remains immune to suit. Finally, assuming Bivens' innocence of the crime charged, the "exclusionary rule" is simply irrelevant. For people in Bivens' shoes, it is damages or nothing. * * *

Of course, for a variety of reasons, the remedy may not often be sought. And the countervailing interests in efficient law enforcement of course argue for a protective zone with respect to many types of Fourth Amendment violations. *Cf.* Barr v. Matteo, 360 U.S. 564 (1959) (opinion of Harlan, J.). But, while I express no view on the immunity defense offered in the instant case, I deem it proper to venture the thought that at the very least such a remedy would be available for the most flagrant and patently unjustified sorts of police conduct. Although litigants may not often choose to seek relief, it is important, in a civilized society, that the judicial branch of the Nation's government stand ready to afford a remedy in these circumstances. * * *

For these reasons, I concur in the judgment of the Court.

■ MR. JUSTICE BLACK, dissenting.

* * * There can be no doubt that Congress could create a federal cause of action for damages for an unreasonable search in violation of the Fourth Amendment. Although Congress has created such a federal cause of action against *state* officials acting under color of state law,* it has never created such a cause of action against federal officials. * * * [T]he fatal weakness in the Court's judgment is that neither Congress nor the State of New York has enacted legislation creating such a right of action. For us to do so is, in my judgment, an exercise of power that the Constitution does not give us.

---

*   [Ed.] Justice Black's reference is to 42 U.S.C. § 1983, a statute that affords a private right of action against state officials who violate federal constitutional rights. See generally Chap. IX, Sec. 2(C), *infra*.

Even if we had the legislative power to create a remedy, there are many reasons why we should decline to create a cause of action where none has existed since the formation of our Government. * * *

We sit at the top of a judicial system accused by some of nearing the point of collapse. Many criminal defendants do not receive speedy trials and neither society nor the accused are assured of justice when inordinate delays occur. Citizens must wait years to litigate their private civil suits. Substantial changes in correctional and parole systems demand the attention of the lawmakers and the judiciary. If I were a legislator I might well find these and other needs so pressing as to make me believe that the resources of lawyers and judges should be devoted to them rather than to civil damage actions against officers who generally strive to perform within constitutional bounds. There is also a real danger that such suits might deter officials from the *proper* and honest performance of their duties.

All of these considerations make imperative careful study and weighing of the arguments both for and against the creation of such a remedy under the Fourth Amendment. I would have great difficulty for myself in resolving the competing policies, goals, and priorities in the use of resources, if I thought it were my job to resolve those questions. But that is not my task. The task of evaluating the pros and cons of creating judicial remedies for particular wrongs is a matter for Congress and the legislatures of the States. * * *

[CHIEF JUSTICE BURGER also dissented, arguing that the Court's prescription of a remedy had usurped a legislative function, in violation of the separation of powers. JUSTICE BLACKMUN's separate dissent contended that the Court's "judicial legislation" would produce an "avalanche of new federal cases."]

NOTE ON BIVENS AND THE FORMULATION OF REMEDIES IN CONSTITUTIONAL CASES

(1) Introduction. The Bivens case and the materials in this Note deal with damages actions against *federal officials* as an implied remedy for constitutional violations. Should officer suits for monetary relief be seen as different from suits against the government itself—because the relief does not come from the treasury—or instead as a functionally necessary surrogate for governmental immunity, without which such immunity would not be tolerable? Should the Court's willingness to imply a remedy depend on whether the suit challenges *state* or *federal* official action? On the latter point, what significance should the Bivens Court have attached to the absence of any broad statutory authorization of private remedies against federal officials, comparable to 42 U.S.C. § 1983, which authorizes suits against *state* officials who violate federal rights? The absence of any such statutory provision highlights the central question of the respective roles of Congress and the courts in fashioning remedies for constitutional violations.[1]

(2) Antecedents. The question of the availability of a damages remedy for violation of a constitutional right had been mooted ever since the 1946

---

[1]   See pp. 775–776, *infra*.

decision in Bell v. Hood, p. 818, *infra*. There, the Supreme Court held that a federal district court had jurisdiction under § 1331 over a claim for damages against federal officers for allegedly unconstitutional arrests and searches, but reserved the question whether there was a good claim on the merits under federal (as opposed to state) law. Why do you think that the question was not resolved until the Bivens decision in 1971?[2] Does the explanation lie in part in the availability of state damages remedies for a substantial range of violations and of federal statutory remedies against the United States (under such statutes as the Federal Tort Claims Act) for others? Recall that state court authority to issue *injunctions* against federal officers is not clearly established. See Chap. IV, Sec. 3, *supra*. Does that uncertainty help to account for the much earlier development of federal equitable remedies for constitutional violations?

(3) Official Immunity Doctrines. In Bivens, the Court left open whether the defendants might enjoy immunity from damages liabilities. A series of Supreme Court opinions has subsequently recognized that federal officials sued for constitutional violations do enjoy an official immunity from liability in damages. That immunity, which is designed primarily to avoid dampening the vigor of officials in the performance of their duties, prevents recovery against federal officials even when they have in fact violated constitutional rights. Accordingly, federal officials sued with respect to the exercise of judicial, prosecutorial, or legislative functions enjoy an *absolute* immunity from damages. Otherwise, federal officials generally enjoy a broad qualified immunity, which shields them from damages liability so long as their conduct did not violate "clearly established" federal law. See generally Chap. IX, Sec. 3, *infra*.

(4) Initial Extension of the Bivens Approach. The Bivens opinion suggested that implication of a damages remedy might be inappropriate in a case presenting (i) "special factors counselling hesitation in the absence of affirmative action by Congress" or (ii) "an explicit congressional declaration that * * * [plaintiff should be] remitted to another remedy, equally effective in the view of Congress." But the Court's next two decisions in the Bivens line—Davis v. Passman and Carlson v. Green—suggested a narrow compass for those limitations on the Bivens remedy.

(a) In Davis v. Passman, 442 U.S. 228 (1979), the Court held (5–4) that Davis could bring a Bivens action alleging that she had been fired from her job as administrative assistant to Congressman Passman because of her sex, in violation of the "equal protection" component of the Due Process Clause of the Fifth Amendment. Starting from the premise that "the judiciary is clearly discernible as the primary means through which [constitutional] rights may be enforced", Justice Brennan's opinion for the Court emphasized that "unless such rights are to become merely precatory," litigants with "no

---

[2]   Dellinger, *Of Rights and Remedies: The Constitution as a Sword*, 85 Harv.L.Rev. 1532, 1544–45 (1972), contends that the Court's assertion in Bivens that "[h]istorically, damages have been regarded as the ordinary remedy for an invasion of personal interests in liberty" was not supported by the four cases there cited. Compare Collins, *"Economic Rights," Implied Constitutional Actions, and the Scope of Section 1983*, 77 Geo.L.J. 1493, 1507–33 (1989) (arguing that a number of nineteenth- and early twentieth-century decisions, in suits against state and local officials for constitutional violations, provided some recognition of implied damages remedies). Professor Kian argues that familiar common law remedies that would have been used early in the Republic either withered or became inadequate to vindicate new forms of constitutional rights, thereby provoking the Court to derive implied federal remedies for constitutional violations. Kian, *The Path of the Constitution: The Original System of Remedies, How It Changed, and How the Court Responded*, 87 N.Y.U.L.Rev. 132 (2012).

[other] effective means [to] * * * enforce these rights[ ] must be able to invoke the existing jurisdiction of the courts for the protection of their justiciable constitutional rights." Because Passman was no longer in Congress, the Court concluded that "for Davis, as for Bivens, 'it is damages or nothing.'"

Perhaps the most significant aspect of Davis v. Passman is the set of concerns that the Court found unpersuasive in reaching its result: (a) In 1972, Congress extended Title VII of the Civil Rights Act of 1964 to certain federal employees, but excluded personal staff of members of Congress from protection;[3] (b) the action was against a high official of a coordinate branch making personnel decisions concerning his personal staff, raising (as Chief Justice Burger wrote in dissent) "grave questions of separation of powers"; and (c) as Justice Stewart's dissent noted, the action would require resolution of difficult and sensitive constitutional issues under the Speech and Debate Clause.

(b) The next year, in Carlson v. Green, 446 U.S. 14 (1980), the Court upheld the availability of a damages remedy in an action alleging that the failure of federal prison officials to provide medical attention to plaintiff's deceased son constituted cruel and unusual punishment in violation of the Eighth Amendment. The Court, again per Justice Brennan, stated flatly that "the victims of a constitutional violation by a federal agent have a right to recover damages against the official in federal court despite the absence of any statute conferring such a right," unless (1) the defendant demonstrates "special factors counselling hesitation", or (2) "Congress has provided an alternative remedy which it explicitly declared to be a *substitute* for recovery directly under the Constitution and viewed as equally effective" (emphasis in original). Although Congress had in 1974 amended the Federal Tort Claims Act (FTCA) to permit recovery against the United States for intentional torts of the kind at issue in Carlson, the Court found nothing in the legislative text or history to indicate that Congress intended the amendment to be a substitute rather than an alternative remedy. And the Court suggested four ways in which the Bivens remedy might be more effective than the FTCA remedy: (a) an action against the individual wrongdoer is a more effective deterrent than an action against the government; (b) unlike the FTCA, the Bivens remedy permits punitive damages; (c) a Bivens plaintiff can opt for jury trial, unavailable under the FTCA; and (d) the FTCA applies only to conduct that would be actionable under state law if committed by a private person, whereas uniform federal rules govern the extent of Bivens liability.

(5) Retrenchment in the Face of Congressional Provision of Alternative Remedies. Not long after Davis and Carlson, the tide began to run the other way. In three important decisions, discussed in this Paragraph, the Court's refusal was based primarily on the existence of alternative remedies provided by Congress.

(a) In Bush v. Lucas, 462 U.S. 367 (1983), Bush, an aerospace engineer employed by the federal government, sued his superior for damages, alleging, *inter alia*, that he had been demoted in retaliation for exercising his First Amendment rights. The Civil Service Commission's Appeals Review

---

[3]   Sixteen years after Davis v. Passman, the Congressional Accountability Act of 1995, 109 Stat. 3, extended coverage of Title VII to employees of the House and the Senate. Claimants are required to exhaust administrative remedies before bringing suit in court, and may recover compensatory (but not punitive) damages. Should that Act be viewed as precluding resort to the implied right of action recognized in Davis?

Board had previously restored him to his former position and awarded him back pay. Although assuming that the civil service remedy was "less than complete", the Court held (per Stevens, J.) that in this matter of "federal personnel policy" the "elaborate remedial system" constructed by Congress should not be "augmented by the creation of a new judicial remedy". The Court also stated that the remedy afforded by Congress was "constitutionally adequate", even though it was not an "equally effective substitute" for the judicial remedy sought. Justice Marshall, joined by Justice Blackmun, wrote a separate concurrence.

(b) The Court extended Bush v. Lucas in Schweiker v. Chilicky, 487 U.S. 412 (1988). The plaintiffs there had been improperly denied disability benefits under the Social Security Act, but subsequently were awarded, or had pending administrative applications for, full retroactive benefits. They sued federal and state policymaking officials, alleging that the defendants had denied them due process by adopting policies that resulted in the improper denials. The complaint sought equitable relief and damages for "emotional distress and for loss of food, shelter and other necessities proximately caused by [defendants'] denial of benefits". The Supreme Court refused to permit a Bivens action for the alleged due process violation, stressing that the Social Security Act provided an elaborate administrative and judicial remedy. While acknowledging that the statutory remedy permitted only the restoration of improperly denied benefits and that a Bivens remedy would offer the prospect of recovering damages for emotional distress or other hardships caused by the delay in awarding benefits, the Act nonetheless "provide[d] meaningful safeguards or remedies for the rights of persons situated as [plaintiffs] were." Justice Brennan (joined by Justices Marshall and Blackmun) dissented.

(c) In Hui v. Castaneda, 559 U.S. 799 (2010), the Court rejected a Bivens claim alleging that Public Health Service (PHS) officials had shown "deliberate indifference" to Casteneda's "serious medical needs," in violation of the Fifth, Eighth, and Fourteenth Amendments, while he was in the custody of U.S. Immigration and Customs Enforcement (ICE). In a unanimous opinion for the Court, Justice Sotomayor held that the Bivens action was precluded by 42 U.S.C. § 233(a), which provides: "The Federal Tort Claims [FTCA] remedy against the United States * * * for damage for personal injury, including death, resulting from the performance of medical * * * or related functions * * * by any [PHS] commissioned officer or employee * * * while acting within the scope of his office or employment, shall be exclusive of any other civil action or proceeding by reason of the same subject-matter against the officer or employee." Although Carlson v. Green, Paragraph 4(b), *supra*, had extended Bivens to Eighth Amendment claims and held that the remedies supplied by the FTCA did *not* provide an equally effective alternative to a Bivens action, the Court in Castaneda nonetheless found it dispositive that § 233(a) "grants absolute immunity to PHS officers and employees" in the circumstances of the case. No defendant in Carlson had invoked that immunity. Hence, the Court's recognition of a Bivens action in Carlson did not govern the question in Castaneda. Does Castaneda eliminate Carlson's requirement of an "equally effective" alternative remedy where Congress has expressly made the alternative remedy exclusive?

(6) Special Factors Counseling Hesitation. The Court has also declined to recognize Bivens actions when "special factors [might] counsel[ ] hesitation [even] in the absence of affirmative action by Congress".

(a) The most prominent cases implicating "special factors" involved claims against military officers. In Chappell v. Wallace, 462 U.S. 296 (1983), Navy enlisted men sued their superior officers, alleging racial discrimination in violation of the Constitution and federal civil rights legislation. The Court unanimously held that the constitutional claim could not be maintained, stating that "the unique disciplinary structure of the Military Establishment and Congress' activity in the field constitute 'special factors' which dictate that it would be inappropriate to provide enlisted military personnel a Bivens-type remedy against their superior officers." The activity of Congress to which the Court referred embraced "a comprehensive internal system of justice to regulate military life" that included procedures "for the review and remedy of complaints and grievances such as those presented by respondents." The Court said nothing about that system's effectiveness.

In United States v. Stanley, 483 U.S. 669 (1987), a former servicemember sued military officers and civilians for injuries resulting from the administration to him of the drug LSD, without his consent, as part of an army experiment. The Court held, 5–4, that the special factors found in Chappell "extend beyond the situation in which an officer-subordinate relationship exists, and require abstention in the inferring of Bivens actions * * * for injuries that 'arise out of or are in the course of activity incident to [military] service'" (quoting Feres v. United States, 340 U.S. 135 (1950)). Dissenting in part, Justice O'Connor contended that "conduct of the type alleged in this case is so far beyond the bounds of human decency that as a matter of law it simply cannot be considered a part of the military mission". In a lengthy partial dissent, Justice Brennan (joined by Justice Marshall and in part by Justice Stevens) argued that, in contrast to the situation in Chappell, no intramilitary system " 'provides for the * * * remedy' of Stanley's complaint" (quoting Chappell).

(b) The Court in Wilkie v. Robbins, 551 U.S. 557 (2007), applied the "special factors" analysis to encompass the judicial manageability of particular Bivens claims and the potential for disruption of government administration generally. At issue were claims brought by a rancher (Robbins) against federal Bureau of Land Management (BLM) officials. Robbins alleged that after he refused to re-grant an easement that the BLM had forfeited by failing to record it, the government retaliated against his property rights through selective enforcement of federal law and through various forms of harassment against him. After noting the existence of "administrative" and "ultimately judicial" remedies for the government's alleged wrongs, the Court stressed the "difficulty in defining a workable cause of action" to describe Robbins' claim. Because the BLM could legitimately make some efforts to induce Robbins to grant an easement, the Court concluded that Robbins' claim boiled down to the proposition "that defendants simply demanded too much and went too far." The relative unworkability of that standard, the Court said, "counts against recognizing freestanding liability in a case like this." Finally, the Court emphasized that "a Bivens action to redress retaliation against those who resist Government impositions on their property rights would invite claims in every sphere of legitimate governmental action affecting property interests, from negotiating tax claim settlements to enforcing Occupational Safety and Health Administration regulations." Justice Ginsburg, joined by Justice Stevens, dissented, objecting that the Court had established "a special factor counseling hesitation quite unlike any we have recognized before."

(7) Further Limitations on Bivens. The Court in Wilkie v. Robbins, Paragraph (6)(b), *supra*, characterized its approach to Bivens cases as one of "weighing reasons for and against the creation of a new cause of action, the way common law judges have always done." In doing so, the Court takes a number of different factors into consideration. For example, the Court has held that Bivens does not extend to public or private corporations charged with implementing federal programs. See Correctional Services Corp. v. Malesko, 534 U.S. 61 (2001) (no Bivens action against private contractor housing federal prisoners under contract with the Bureau of Prisons); Federal Deposit Insurance Corp. v. Meyer, 510 U.S. 473 (1994) (rejecting a Bivens action against the Federal Deposit Insurance Corporation despite a broad statutory waiver of sovereign immunity). Those decisions stressed, among other things, that suits against corporate entities would not serve the purposes, articulated in Bivens, of deterring federal *officers* from constitutional misconduct. In Minneci v. Pollard, 132 S.Ct. 617 (2012), the Court went one step further and held that although Carlson had extended Bivens to Eighth Amendment claims, a Bivens action was not available against *employees* of a private prison contractor alleged to have violated the Eighth Amendment. The Court reasoned that even though state tort law and Eighth Amendment requirements were not congruent, "state tort law remedies provide[d] roughly similar incentives for potential defendants to comply with the Eighth Amendment while also providing roughly similar compensation to victims of violations." Finally, in Ashcroft v. Iqbal, 556 U.S. 662 (2009) (also discussed in Chapter IX, *infra*), the Court relied on analogies to § 1983 in rejecting *respondeat superior* liability under Bivens.

Though each one of the cases, in some meaningful sense, reflects the type of case-specific analysis often associated with common law reasoning, it is striking that the Court has not extended Bivens to new fact situations since Carlson v. Green was decided more than three decades ago. Does this trend bespeak an implicit rejection of Bivens itself? Justices Scalia and Thomas have stated: "Bivens is a relic of the heady days in which this Court assumed common-law powers to create causes of action * * *. * * * [W]e have abandoned that power to invent 'implications' in the statutory field, see Alexander v. Sandoval, 532 U.S. 275, 287 (2000). There is even greater reason to abandon it in the constitutional field, since an 'implication' imagined in the Constitution can presumably not even be repudiated by Congress. I would limit Bivens and [Davis and Carlson] to the precise circumstances that they involved."[4] While not embracing that broad position,

---

[4]   Despite the change in surrounding doctrine, Pfander and Baltmanis argue that Bivens has become more firmly grounded over time because Congress effectively "ratified" the doctrine. See Pfander & Baltmanis, *Rethinking Bivens: Legitimacy and Constitutional Adjudication*, 98 Geo.L.J. 117 (2009). First, in amending the FTCA in 1974, Congress rejected legislation proposed by the Justice Department that would have substituted the government for individual defendants on constitutional tort claims. Second, in 1988, the Westfall Act, Pub. L. No. 100–694, 102 Stat. 4563 (1988), made the FTCA the exclusive remedy for certain nonconstitutional torts by federal officials and expressly assumed the continuing existence of Bivens actions for constitutional torts. See also Vázquez & Vladeck, *State Law, the Westfall Act, and the Nature of the Bivens Question*, 161 U.Pa.L.Rev. 509 (2013) (drawing similar inferences from the Westfall Act).

How convincing are these claims of ratification? Recall that the authors' contention runs up against the Court's general view that failed legislation may tell us little because "[a] bill can be proposed for any number of reasons, and it can be rejected for just as many others." Solid Waste Agency of Northern Cook County v. U.S. Army Corps of Engineers, 531 U.S. 159, 170 (2001). And if the Westfall Act affirmatively "ratified" the Bivens framework, should the Court assume that the Act ratified the framework as of 1971, when Bivens was decided, or as of 1988,

the Court itself has nonetheless acknowledged that "[b]ecause implied causes of action are [now] disfavored, the Court has been reluctant to extend Bivens liability 'to any new context or new category of defendants.' " Ashcroft v. Iqbal, *supra*, at 676 (quoting Malesko, *supra*, at 68).

Has the pattern of the Court's decisions since the early 1980s cut into Bivens' core? See Tribe, *Death by a Thousand Cuts: Constitutional Wrongs Without Remedies After Wilkie v. Robbins*, 2007 Cato Sup.Ct.Rev. 23, 70. So long as Bivens is not squarely overruled, is it sufficiently alive that it is capable of reinvigoration? See Shapiro, *The Role of Precedent in Constitutional Adjudication: An Introspection*, 86 Tex.L.Rev. 929, 940 n.41 (2008).[5]

(8) Is the Bivens Remedy Constitutionally Required? Suppose that Congress purported to eliminate the remedy recognized in Bivens. Given that, for Mr. Bivens, it was damages or nothing, such action would not be justified as merely a choice among remedies. Would the preclusion necessarily be unconstitutional? If so, would the unconstitutionality of providing no remedy whatsoever for someone in Bivens' shoes rest on the absence of adequate mechanisms to deter constitutional violations?[6] The absence of adequate compensation for Bivens himself? How strong is the latter claim in light of the decisions in Chilicky, Chappell, and especially Stanley? Compare Nichol, *Bivens, Chilicky, and Constitutional Damages Claims*, 75 Va.L.Rev. 1117 (1989).

In thinking about these questions, consider the following analysis (from Fallon & Meltzer, *New Law, Non-Retroactivity, and Constitutional Remedies*, 104 Harv.L.Rev. 1731, 1778–79 (1991)):

" * * * Within our constitutional tradition, * * * the Marbury dictum [that there must be a remedy for every right] reflects just one of two principles supporting remedies for constitutional violations. Another principle, whose focus is more structural, demands a system of constitutional remedies adequate to keep government generally within the bounds of law. Both principles sometimes permit accommodation of competing interests, but in different ways. The Marbury principle that calls for individually effective remediation can sometimes be outweighed; the principle requiring an overall system of remedies that is effective in maintaining a regime of

---

when the Court had already begun its retrenchment in cases such as Bush v. Lucas, p. 771, *supra*; Chappell v. Wallace, p. 773, *supra*; and United States v. Stanley, p. 773, *supra*?

    [5]   What light do broader litigation statistics cast on the continued availability of Bivens actions as an effective constitutional remedy? A former Justice Department lawyer reported that from 1971–86, more than 12,000 Bivens actions had been filed; that only thirty had resulted in judgments for plaintiffs at the trial level (some of which were reversed on appeal); that only four judgments had actually been paid; and that settlements are rare. Rosen, *The Bivens Constitutional Tort: An Unfulfilled Promise*, 67 N.C.L.Rev. 337, 343–44 (1989). For a contrasting view of the efficacy of Bivens actions, see Reinert, *Measuring the Success of Bivens Litigation and its Consequences for the Individual Liability Model*, 62 Stan.L.Rev. 809 (2010) (arguing, based on data collected from five district courts over three years, that "Bivens cases are much more successful than has been assumed" and that "[d]epending on the procedural posture, presence of counsel, and type of case, success rates for Bivens suits range from 16% to more than 40%").

    [6]   Remedies besides damages obviously have deterrent force—including the exclusion of illegally obtained evidence and injunctions against unconstitutional practices by law enforcement officials. For an examination of the constitutional and practical considerations surrounding judicial provision of deterrent remedies in the absence of legislative direction, see Meltzer, *Deterring Constitutional Violations by Law Enforcement Officials: Plaintiffs and Defendants as Private Attorneys General*, 88 Colum.L.Rev. 247 (1988).

lawful government is more unyielding in its own terms, but can tolerate the denial of particular remedies, and sometimes of individual redress."[7]

Recall that the Court appears to have recognized a constitutional obligation on the part of the government (rather than government officials) to provide a monetary remedy in at least two settings: (a) actions under the Just Compensation Clause, see First English Evangelical Lutheran Church v. County of Los Angeles, California, pp. 755–756, *supra*, and (b) actions seeking a refund of unconstitutionally exacted taxes, see McKesson Corp. v. Division of ABT, and Reich v. Collins, pp. 757–758, *supra*—at least when no adequate predeprivation remedy exists.[8]

Although neither obligation is quite as clear-cut as it might be, see p. 758, *supra*, insofar as those two lines of decision establish a constitutional right to compensatory relief, on what basis can the Court justify a refusal to provide a monetary remedy in a Bivens suit (especially when no other relief is available)?

(9) Bivens as Constitutional Common Law. If damages remedies are *not* constitutionally compelled in cases like Bivens, Davis v. Passman, and Carlson v. Green—even when other effective remedies are lacking—then by what authority do the federal courts recognize Bivens remedies in the absence of legislative authorization? Professor Monaghan, in an important article (*Foreword: Constitutional Common Law*, 89 Harv.L.Rev. 1 (1975)), views Bivens as one example of what he terms "constitutional common law"—a body of judge-made law that implements constitutional guarantees rather than statutory provisions.[9] Unlike simple interpretations of the Constitution, which Congress cannot overturn, constitutional common law is subject to legislative modification or repeal precisely because it is not constitutionally required.

What source of lawmaking power authorizes judicial development of a penumbra of supplemental, quasi-constitutional protection? If there is a valid source for constitutional common law, can that body of law adequately be distinguished from "real" constitutional law? (The problem arises sharply, of course, only when Congress attempts to modify a constitutional common law decision.) For a critical response to Monaghan, see Schrock & Welsh, *Reconsidering the Constitutional Common Law*, 91 Harv.L.Rev. 1117 (1978). Given that Carlson v. Green, p. 771, *supra*, held that an action under the FTCA is not an equally effective alternative to a Bivens remedy, does Hui v. Castaneda, p. 772, *supra*—which held that Congress made the FTCA the exclusive remedy in certain types of actions—make plain that Congress has the authority to prescribe an exclusive substitute remedy even if that remedy is *not* equally effective? At the same time, if Monaghan is correct that Bivens actions are at least constitutionally inspired, should the Court require a clear statement from Congress before finding legislative preclusion of a Bivens action? See Grey, *Preemption of Bivens Claims: How Clearly Must Congress Speak?*, 70 Wash.U.L.Q. 1087 (1992) (so arguing). See also Brown, *Letting*

---

[7]　For a general discussion rejecting a distinction between constitutional rights and remedies, see Levinson, *Rights Essentialism and Remedial Equilibration*, 99 Colum.L.Rev. 857 (1999).

[8]　And with the further possible qualification, not greatly significant in practice, that in cases of unconstitutional discrimination, retroactive tax increases on the favored class might substitute for refunds to the disfavored class.

[9]　Other examples noted by Monaghan include the Fourth Amendment's exclusionary rule and the invalidation of state statutes under the dormant Commerce Clause.

Statutory Tails Wag Constitutional Dogs—Have the Bivens Dissenters Prevailed?, 64 Ind.L.J. 263, 265 (1988–89).

CHAPTER VIII

THE FEDERAL QUESTION JURISDICTION OF THE DISTRICT COURTS

———

1. INTRODUCTION

———

PRELIMINARY NOTE ON THE PURPOSES OF FEDERAL QUESTION JURISDICTION

What purposes underlie the constitutional grant in Article III of power to confer original federal court jurisdiction, and the various statutory grants under that power? (Might the answer differ for the constitutional and statutory grants, or for particular statutory grants?) Put differently, why not leave federal question litigation in the state courts, subject to Supreme Court review? Consider the following possible justifications: compared to state courts, federal courts are: (1) more expert in adjudicating federal law; (2) more sympathetic to federal purposes when resolving federal questions or factual disputes underlying those questions; (3) more faithful to Supreme Court rulings and more responsive to Supreme Court supervision; (4) less susceptible to pressure (because their judges enjoy tenure and salary protection) and thus better able to protect unpopular rights; (5) better able to achieve uniformity in interpreting federal law; and (6) governed by uniform procedural rules whose content and fairness Congress controls.[1] To what extent does the current federal judicial structure achieve some or all of these purposes in practice?

NOTE ON THE STATUTORY DEVELOPMENT OF THE JURISDICTION[1]

Although a primary purpose for establishing a system of federal courts was to protect federal rights, the Judiciary Act of 1789 did not include a

---

[1]   See also Seinfeld, *The Federal Courts as a Franchise: Rethinking the Justifications for Federal Question Jurisdiction*, 97 Calif.L.Rev. 95 (2009). Professor Seinfeld is skeptical about many of the asserted justifications, contending that (a) federal judges cannot be viewed as expert, given the enormous range of federal statutes and issues they encounter; (b) over time, federal judges have not always proved more sympathetic than state judges to federal rights; and (c) the lower federal courts have limited capacity to achieve uniformity. In his view, federal courts provide a high quality "franchise" with a basic set of commonalities, and the key question for Congress is which cases should be given the benefit of that franchise.

See generally American Law Institute, Study of the Division of Jurisdiction Between State and Federal Courts 162–68 (1969); Chemerinsky & Kramer, *Defining the Role of the Federal Courts*, 1990 BYU L.Rev. 67; Mishkin, *The Federal "Question" in the District Courts*, 53 Colum.L.Rev. 157 (1953).

[1]   For discussion of the history of admiralty jurisdiction, see Section 6, pp. 872–876, *infra*.

general grant of jurisdiction over cases "arising under" the federal Constitution, laws, and treaties.[2] That Act conferred federal question jurisdiction only over suits for "penalties and forfeitures incurred" under federal laws[3] and cases in which "an alien sues for a tort only in violation of the law of nations or a treaty of the United States."[4] Early Congresses thus did not approach the limits of their authority under Article III to confer federal question jurisdiction.[5]

In 1801, the Federalist Party, having lost the 1800 election, pushed the Act of Feb. 13, 1801, § 11, 2 Stat. 89, 92 through a lame-duck Congress. That Act conferred jurisdiction in virtually the same language as the "arising under" clause of Article III and also authorized removal of state court actions, *id.* § 13.[6] The following year, however, the new Jeffersonian Congress repealed the Federalist statute.[7] Thus, absent diversity jurisdiction, private litigants in the antebellum period generally had to look

---

This Chapter discusses criminal jurisdiction only in connection with specialized grants of removal jurisdiction. The relevant history can, however, be briefly summarized.

The First Judiciary Act (1789), §§ 9, 11, 1 Stat. 73, 76, 79, gave the district and circuit courts exclusive jurisdiction over crimes and offenses "cognizable under the authority of the United States"; the district courts were restricted to cases involving less serious punishment. Beginning with the Carriage Tax Act of June 5, 1794, ch. 45, § 10, 1 Stat. 373, Congress occasionally authorized state court enforcement of federal criminal legislation, although federal court enforcement remained the rule, see generally Warren, *Federal Criminal Laws and the State Courts*, 38 Harv.L.Rev. 545 (1925), and doubts about the practicality or even constitutionality of the state court role have been voiced, see p. 432, *supra*. Today, the district courts have *exclusive* jurisdiction over "all offenses against the laws of the United States." 18 U.S.C. § 3231.

Congress has enacted a special jurisdictional provision governing geographical areas—for example, areas within federal maritime jurisdiction but outside the territorial jurisdiction of any state, or federal enclaves like military reservations or national parks—in which state criminal law does not operate. Specified acts are made federal crimes when committed within the "special maritime and territorial jurisdiction of the United States," which is defined in 18 U.S.C. § 7 to include the high seas and waters within the admiralty jurisdiction but outside any state's jurisdiction (including any American aircraft in flight over these areas), lands reserved or acquired for the use of the United States, any U.S. space vehicle in flight, and "[a]ny place outside the jurisdiction of any nation 'with respect to an offense by or against a national of the United States.'"

Recognition of the need for more complete specification of criminal conduct in these areas led to enactment of § 3 of the Federal Crimes Act of March 3, 1825, 4 Stat. 115, known as the Assimilative Crimes Act and today codified at 18 U.S.C. § 13. The Act makes it a federal crime to engage, in any place within the scope of 18 U.S.C. § 7, in conduct "not made punishable by any enactment of Congress" that would be a crime if committed within the jurisdiction of the state (or territory or the District of Columbia) in which that place is located.

[2] See Casto, *An Orthodox View of the Two-Tier Analysis of Congressional Control Over Federal Jurisdiction*, 7 Const. Commentary 89, 93 (1990). But see Engdahl, *Federal Question Jurisdiction Under the 1789 Judiciary Act*, 14 Okla. City U.L.Rev. 521, 522 (1989).

[3] Act of Sept. 24, 1789, § 9, 1 Stat. 73, 77.

[4] *Id.* § 9 (codified at 28 U.S.C. § 1350); see p. 717, *supra*.

[5] The first patent law gave the district courts limited authority in proceedings to revoke wrongfully secured patents. Act of April 10, 1790, § 5, 1 Stat. 109, 111. The Act of Feb. 21, 1793, § 6, 1 Stat. 318, 322, extended jurisdiction to infringement suits. See also Act of Feb. 15, 1819, 3 Stat. 481. Originally concurrent, the jurisdiction is now exclusive. 28 U.S.C. § 1338(a).

[6] See Turner, *Federalist Policy and the Judiciary Act of 1801*, 22 Wm. & Mary Q. 3 (1965) (contending that the Act was not simply a partisan effort to entrench Federalist power after electoral defeat but instead an integral part of Federalist policy); LaCroix, *Federalists, Federalism, and Federal Jurisdiction*, 30 Law & Hist.Rev. 205 (2012) (discussing the connection of law and politics in early debates about the federal judiciary).

[7] Act of Mar. 8, 1802, 2 Stat. 132.

to the state courts in the first instance for vindication of federal claims, subject to limited review by the Supreme Court.[8]

Until the second half of the nineteenth century, Congress made no important additions to the original jurisdiction of the federal courts. However, several acts sought to protect federal interests from hostile state action by authorizing removal of state court proceedings against federal officers (or against private persons for acts done under federal authority).[9]

The Civil War generated a major expansion of national political and economic activity. In response, Congress significantly expanded jurisdiction of the federal courts, which became the primary tribunals for the vindication of federal rights.[10] The process began during the war, when Congress authorized removal of all suits and prosecutions "for any arrest or imprisonment made, or other trespasses or wrongs * * * committed * * * [during the rebellion], by virtue or under color of any authority derived from * * * the President * * * or any Act of Congress."[11] In the period that followed, Congress turned to the federal courts to secure blacks' newly granted civil rights, enacting a series of jurisdictional and remedial provisions, most of which survive.[12] The first Civil Rights Act conferred federal jurisdiction (original and removal) over "all causes, civil and criminal, affecting persons who are denied or cannot enforce in the courts * * * of the state or locality where they may be any of the rights secured to them by the first section of this act."[13] Any defendant sued or prosecuted "for any arrest or imprisonment, trespasses, or wrongs done * * * under color of authority derived from this act * * * or for refusing to do any act upon the ground that it would be inconsistent with this act" could remove.[14] The Act of 1870 conferred federal jurisdiction over "all causes, civil and criminal, arising under" it.[15]

The following year Congress enacted a major civil rights provision, codified today as amended, as 42 U.S.C. § 1983, which authorized actions (including those for damages) against persons who, when acting under color of state law, deprived individuals of their constitutional rights.[16] The federal courts were granted jurisdiction to entertain such actions.[17] Anyone sued in state court for an act done under color of the statute could remove the action

---

[8]   Act of Sept. 24, 1789, § 25, 1 Stat. 73, 85. See pp. 461–462, *supra.*

For an argument that the federal courts, when exercising diversity jurisdiction in the antebellum period, often declined to follow state rules that might prevent vindication of federal rights, and thus were a more important forum for the vindication of federal rights than is commonly supposed, see Woolhandler, *The Common Law Origins of Constitutionally Compelled Remedies,* 107 Yale L.J. 77, 162 (1997). See also Collins, *Before Lochner—Diversity Jurisdiction and the Development of General Constitutional Law,* 74 Tul.L.Rev. 1263 (2000).

[9]   See pp. 853–855, *infra.*

[10]   See Frankfurter & Landis, The Business of the Supreme Court 64–65 (1928).

[11]   Act of Mar. 3, 1863, § 5, 12 Stat. 755, 756, amended by Act of May 11, 1866, 14 Stat. 46. Also during the war, Congress conferred jurisdiction over suits against national banks. Act of June 3, 1864, § 57, 13 Stat. 99, 116.

[12]   See 28 U.S.C. §§ 1343, 1344, 1443. See also 42 U.S.C. § 1983, discussed in Chap. IX, Sec. 2C, *infra.*

[13]   Act of Apr. 9, 1866, § 3, 14 Stat. 27.

[14]   *Id.* What survives of these provisions is now found in 28 U.S.C. § 1443.

[15]   Act of May 31, 1870, § 8, 16 Stat. 140, 142.

[16]   Act of Feb. 28, 1871, § 15, 16 Stat. 433, 438.

[17]   Act of Apr. 20, 1871, §§ 1, 2, 6, 17 Stat. 13–15.

to federal court.[18] The Civil Rights Act of 1875, the last in this series, enlarged the available remedies and again provided federal jurisdiction.[19]

In 1868, Congress authorized removal of suits against "any corporation, organized under a law of the United States."[20] And an 1874 enactment that regulated the Pacific railroads gave the federal courts cognizance of treble damage suits for injuries resulting from violations of the act.[21]

The expansion of federal court jurisdiction culminated with enactment of the 1875 Judiciary Act, which gave federal trial courts (specifically, the circuit courts) concurrent jurisdiction, subject to a $500 amount in controversy requirement, of "all suits of a civil nature at common law or in equity, * * * arising under the Constitution or laws of the United States, or treaties made, or which shall be made, under their authority."[22] Either party could remove such a case.[23] In its one cautionary note, the Act directed the circuit court to dismiss or remand if it appeared at any time "that such suit does not really and substantially involve a dispute or controversy properly within [its] jurisdiction."[24] Although this legislation revolutionized the nature of the federal judiciary, it passed almost unnoticed inside or outside Congress.[25]

In the 1870s and 1880s, the federal courts were flooded with litigation; among the causes were the growth of American business, new cases brought under Reconstruction legislation, and the broad removal authorized under the Pacific Railroad Removal Act[26] in 1874 and under the general removal provision of the 1875 Judiciary Act.[27] Congress responded: first, by beginning a long process of restricting the jurisdiction it had granted in 1868 based solely on federal incorporation,[28] and more significantly, in 1887, by raising the jurisdictional amount to $2,000, eliminating removal by plaintiffs, and providing that orders remanding removed cases to the state courts were not appealable.[29]

The Judicial Code of 1948 made few significant changes in the district courts' jurisdiction; the changes made centered on removal. The privilege of removal was extended to all federal officers sued or prosecuted "for any act under color of * * * office."[30] In addition, a provision extended removal jurisdiction over "separable" controversies, permitting removal of some cases in which a removable federal question claim was joined with a non-removable claim.[31] (The considerable confusion that this provision generated

---

[18] Act of Feb. 28, 1871, § 16, 16 Stat. 433, 439.

[19] Act of Mar. 1, 1875, §§ 2, 3, 18 Stat. 335–36.

[20] Act of July 27, 1868, § 2, 15 Stat. 226–27.

[21] Act of June 20, 1874, 18 Stat. 111–12.

[22] Act of Mar. 3, 1875, § 1, 18 Stat. 470.

[23] *Id.* § 2, 18 Stat. at 471.

[24] *Id.* § 5, 18 Stat. at 472.

[25] For discussion of the legislative history, see pp. 807–808, *infra*.

[26] Pacific Railroad Removal Cases, 115 U.S. 1 (1885).

[27] See Frankfurter & Landis, *supra* note 10, at 60–69.

[28] Today, jurisdiction is limited to cases in which the United States owns more than half the corporation's stock. 28 U.S.C. § 1349.

[29] Act of Mar. 3, 1887, 24 Stat. 552, corrected by Act of Aug. 13, 1888, 25 Stat. 433. For the current removal provisions, see 28 U.S.C. §§ 1441(a), 1447(d).

[30] *Id.* § 1442(a)(1). In 1996, Congress amended § 1442(a)(1) to authorize removal by the United States and federal agencies, not merely by federal officers. See pp. 855–856, *infra*.

[31] *Id.* § 1441(c).

has been largely dispelled by a 2011 enactment.[32]) Amendments to the Judicial Code since 1948 have not significantly altered the framework for federal court jurisdiction.[33]

Both before and after 1948, Congress created myriad new federal rights and enacted specific jurisdictional provisions authorizing the enforcement of these rights in the national courts, ordinarily without regard to jurisdictional amount.[34] These specialized jurisdictional provisions are generally codified in the particular substantive statutes rather than in the Judicial Code. Before 1980, their primary significance was to permit suits to be brought without regard to the amount in controversy, which, under the general federal question jurisdiction, 28 U.S.C. § 1331, was raised to $3,000 in 1911 and to $10,000 in 1958.[35] The importance of § 1331's amount in controversy requirement gradually declined, beginning in 1962 with the conferral of jurisdiction, without regard to amount in controversy, of actions "in the nature of mandamus" to compel federal officials to carry out their duties. 28 U.S.C. § 1361. That provision was overtaken by a 1976 amendment of § 1331 eliminating the jurisdictional amount requirement in any civil action "brought against the United States, any agency thereof, or any officer or employee thereof in his official capacity."[36] Finally, in 1980, Congress eliminated altogether any amount in controversy requirement in federal question cases brought under § 1331.[37]

The elimination of § 1331's amount in controversy requirement made the numerous specific grants of federal question jurisdiction mostly but not entirely irrelevant. The specific grants that make jurisdiction *exclusive* retain obvious significance, as jurisdiction under § 1331 is concurrent. Other questions of interpretation may arise because § 1331 is encrusted with a complex gloss of interpretive doctrines; the extent to which that gloss applies to more specific jurisdictional grants can itself be an important and difficult question.[38]

---

[32] See Federal Courts Jurisdiction and Venue Clarification Act of 2011, Pub.L. 112–63, 125 Stat. 758, 759. From 1948–2011, § 1441(c) embraced some cases in which a removable federal question claim was joined with a non-removable claim. See generally p. 870 n.8, *infra*.

Another provision in the 1948 Code, § 1338(b), seemed to expand pendent jurisdiction in patent, copyright, and trademark cases, but the Reviser's note stated that it merely codified the rule of Hurn v. Oursler, 289 U.S. 238 (1933). See p. 868, note 4, *infra*.

[33] A number of amendments conferred jurisdiction over specialized subject matters without any required amount in controversy. An important 1990 amendment (§ 1367) delineates the scope of supplemental jurisdiction. See Chap. VIII, Sec. 5, and Chap. XIII, Sec. 3, *infra*. And a 2011 amendment extended the exclusivity of jurisdiction over claims arising under the federal intellectual property laws to embrace a claim appearing anywhere in the case (for example, a counterclaim), rather than only a claim in the plaintiff's complaint. See p. 870, note 8, *infra*.

[34] For discussion of the proliferation of specialized grants that accompanied the surge in legislative activity in the 1960s and 1970s, see Friendly, Federal Jurisdiction: A General View 22–26 & n.53 (1973).

[35] The Judicial Code of 1911, § 24, 36 Stat. 1087, 1091; Act of July 25, 1958, 72 Stat. 415, 415.

[36] Act of Oct. 21, 1976, § 2, 90 Stat. 2721, 2721.

[37] Federal Question Jurisdictional Amendments Act of 1980, Pub. L. 96–486, § 2, 94 Stat. 2369, 2369. A few remaining statutes condition the exercise of federal question jurisdiction over specified claims on an amount in controversy. See p. 1437, note 10, *infra*.

[38] Compare Sparta Surgical Corp. v. NASD, Inc., 159 F.3d 1209 (9th Cir. 1998) (treating a specific grant of jurisdiction in the securities laws as broader than that in § 1331) with, *e.g.*, Barbara v. New York Stock Exchange, Inc., 99 F. 3d 49 (2nd Cir. 1996) (viewing the specific grant as no broader than § 1331).

* * *

Since 1789, the federal courts have possessed a related, and overlapping, jurisdiction over civil actions instituted by the United States. The First Judiciary Act gave the district courts concurrent jurisdiction "of all suits at common law where the United States shall sue," subject to a $100 jurisdictional amount requirement, and gave the circuit courts concurrent jurisdiction "of all suits at common law or in equity," subject to a $500 jurisdictional amount requirement.[39] After making various changes to this jurisdiction in the nineteenth century,[40] in 1911 Congress conferred on the district courts a broad jurisdiction over all civil actions brought by federal officers "authorized by law to sue".[41] The 1948 revision of the Judicial Code extended that grant to embrace actions by "any agency" as well as by officers of the United States.[42] 28 U.S.C. § 1345.

2. THE SCOPE OF THE CONSTITUTIONAL GRANT OF FEDERAL QUESTION JURISDICTION

INTRODUCTORY NOTE

Although Article III and the general federal question statute, 28 U.S.C. § 1331, use nearly identical language in conferring jurisdiction over actions arising under the Constitution, laws, or treaties of the United States, it is now well-established that the constitutional language reaches considerably more broadly than does the language of § 1331.

There is no doubt that a suit falling within § 1331 also falls within the scope of the constitutional grant. But occasionally, Congress enacts particular jurisdictional statutes that authorize the federal courts to hear cases that would not fall under § 1331 and in which federal law figures less centrally than it does in cases that do fall under § 1331. Some of these jurisdictional grants embrace cases in which a question of federal law is uncontested or subsidiary, and on rare occasions a statute may appear to confer jurisdiction in cases in which federal law is absent altogether. Statutes such as these raise the question of the outer limits of Article III's "arising under" jurisdiction, and hence of the limits of Congress' power to

---

[39] Act of Sept. 24, 1789, §§ 9, 11, 1 Stat. 73, 77–78.

[40] The Act of Mar. 3, 1815, § 4, 3 Stat. 244, 245, gave both the district and circuit courts jurisdiction of "all suits at common law" where either "the United States, or any officer thereof, under the authority of an act of Congress, shall sue," and dropped the requirement of a jurisdictional amount.

The Judiciary Act of 1875 restored the jurisdictional amount requirement of $500 in the circuit courts in suits at common law or in equity "in which the United States are plaintiffs or petitioners," and for the first time authorized removal in such cases. Act of Mar. 3, 1875, §§ 1, 2, 18 Stat. 470, 470–71. Twelve years later, Congress limited removal to nonresident defendants and permanently eliminated the requirement of a jurisdictional amount. Act of Mar. 3, 1887, 24 Stat. 552, corrected by Act of Aug. 13, 1888, 25 Stat. 433.

[41] Act of March 3, 1911, § 24, 36 Stat. 1087, 1091.

[42] As neither § 1345 nor § 1331 has a jurisdictional amount requirement, several more specific provisions conferring jurisdiction over suits by particular officers or agencies—some codified in the Judicial Code and some in substantive statutes—may serve no purpose.

authorize the federal courts to hear cases on the basis that they "arise under" federal law. That question is the subject of this Section.

The materials that follow present a range of understandings about the scope of Article III. The decision in Osborn v. Bank of the United States, and the following Note on the Scope of the Constitutional Grant, discuss just what kind of federal issue must be present for a case to arise under federal law within the meaning of Article III. There follows a Note on Protective Jurisdiction, addressing the question whether Congress may constitutionally assign to a federal court jurisdiction to hear a case under a theory called "protective jurisdiction", which is premised not on the need to adjudicate an issue of federal law but instead simply on the need to protect federal interests in a case governed by state law.

Osborn v. Bank of the United States

22 U.S. (9 Wheat.) 738, 6 L.Ed. 204 (1824).
Appeal from the Circuit Court of Ohio.

[The Bank of the United States sued to enjoin Ralph Osborn, auditor of the State of Ohio, from enforcing an Ohio statute that, after reciting that the Bank's operations violated an Ohio law, provided that the Bank, if it continued to transact business in Ohio after September 1, 1819, would be liable for an annual tax of $50,000 on each office of discount and deposit. In September of 1819—six months after the Bank's immunity from state taxation had been recognized in M'Culloch v. Maryland, 17 U.S. (4 Wheat.) 316—the federal circuit court issued the requested injunction, which was served upon Osborn and also upon Harper, whom Osborn had allegedly employed to collect the tax.

[An amended bill charged that Harper, after service of the injunction, took $100,000 in specie and bank notes from a Bank office in Ohio. Sullivan, the State treasurer, was apparently holding $98,000 of this money separately, with notice of the circumstances; the location of the remaining $2,000 was unclear. The circuit court ordered Osborn and Harper to restore $100,000 to the bank, with interest on $19,830 (the amount of specie held by Sullivan).]

■ MR. CHIEF JUSTICE MARSHALL delivered the opinion of the Court.

* * * The appellants contest the jurisdiction of the Court on two grounds:

1st. That the act of Congress has not given it.

2d. That, under the constitution, Congress cannot give it.

1.   The first part of the objection depends entirely on the language of the act. The words are, that the Bank shall be "made able and capable in law," "to sue and be sued, plead and be impleaded, answer and be answered, defend and be defended, in all State Courts having competent jurisdiction, and in any Circuit Court of the United States."

These words seem to the Court to admit of but one interpretation. * * * They give, expressly, the right "to sue and be sued," "in every Circuit Court of the United States," and it would be difficult to substitute other terms which would be more direct and appropriate for the purpose. The argument of the appellants is founded on the opinion of this Court, in The Bank of the United States v. Deveaux (5 Cranch 85). In that case it was decided, that the former Bank of the United States was not enabled, by the act which incorporated it, to sue in the federal Courts. The words of the 3d section of that act are, that the Bank may "sue and be sued," & c., "in Courts of record, or any other place whatsoever". The Court was of opinion, that these general words, which are usual in all acts of incorporation, gave only a general capacity to sue, not a particular privilege to sue in the Courts of the United States * * *. Whether this decision be right or wrong, it amounts only to a declaration, that a general capacity in the Bank to sue, without mentioning the Courts of the Union, may not give a right to sue in those Courts. To infer from this, that words expressly conferring a right to sue in those Courts, do not give the right, is surely a conclusion which the premises do not warrant.

The act of incorporation, then, confers jurisdiction on the Circuit Courts of the United States, if Congress can confer it.

2.   We will now consider the constitutionality of the clause in the act of incorporation, which authorizes the Bank to sue in the federal Courts.

In support of this clause, it is said, that the legislative, executive, and judicial powers of every well constructed government, are co-extensive with each other; that is, they are potentially co-extensive. The executive department may constitutionally execute every law which the Legislature may constitutionally make, and the judicial department may receive from the Legislature the power of construing every such law. All governments which are not extremely defective in their organization, must possess, within themselves, the means of expounding, as well as enforcing, their own laws. If we examine the constitution of the United States, we find that its framers kept this great political principle in view. * * * [T]he 3d article declares, "that the judicial power shall extend to all cases in law and equity, arising under this constitution, the laws of the United States, and treaties made, or which shall be made, under their authority".

This clause enables the judicial department to receive jurisdiction to the full extent of the constitution, laws, and treaties of the United States, when any question respecting them shall assume such a form that the judicial power is capable of acting on it. * * *

The suit of The Bank of the United States v. Osborn and others, is a case, and the question is, whether it arises under a law of the United States?

The appellants contend, that it does not, because several questions may arise in it, which depend on the general principles of the law, not on any act of Congress.

If this were sufficient to withdraw a case from the jurisdiction of the federal Courts, almost every case, although involving the construction of a law, would be withdrawn; and a clause in the constitution, relating to a subject of vital importance to the government, and expressed in the most comprehensive terms, would be construed to mean almost nothing. There is scarcely any case, every part of which depends on the constitution, laws, or treaties of the United States. The questions, whether the fact alleged as the foundation of the action, be real or fictitious; whether the conduct of the plaintiff has been such as to entitle him to maintain his action; whether his right is barred; whether he has received satisfaction, or has in any manner released his claims, are questions, some or all of which may occur in almost every case; and if their existence be sufficient to arrest the jurisdiction of the Court, words which seem intended to be as extensive as the constitution, laws, and treaties of the Union, which seem designed to give the Courts of the government the construction of all its acts, so far as they affect the rights of individuals, would be reduced to almost nothing.

In those cases in which original jurisdiction is given to the Supreme Court, the judicial power of the United States cannot be exercised in its appellate form. In every other case, the power is to be exercised in its original or appellate form, or both, as the wisdom of Congress may direct. With the exception of these cases, in which original jurisdiction is given to this Court, there is none to which the judicial power extends, from which the original jurisdiction of the inferior Courts is excluded by the constitution. * * *

The constitution establishes the Supreme Court, and defines its jurisdiction. It enumerates cases in which its jurisdiction is original and exclusive; and then defines that which is appellate, but does not insinuate, that in any such case, the power cannot be exercised in its original form, by Courts of original jurisdiction. It is not insinuated, that the judicial power, in cases depending on the character of the cause, cannot be exercised, in the first instance, in the Courts of the Union, but must first be exercised in the tribunals of the State; tribunals over which the government of the Union has no adequate control, and which may be closed to any claim asserted under a law of the United States.

We perceive, then, no ground on which the proposition can be maintained, that Congress is incapable of giving the Circuit Courts original jurisdiction, in any case to which the appellate jurisdiction extends.

We ask, then, if it can be sufficient to exclude this jurisdiction, that the case involves questions depending on general principles? A cause may depend on several questions of fact and law. Some of these may depend on the construction of a law of the United States; others on principles unconnected with that law. If it be a sufficient foundation for jurisdiction, that the title or right set up by the party, may be defeated by one construction of the constitution or law of the United States, and sustained by the opposite construction, provided the facts necessary to support the action be made out, then all the other questions must be decided as incidental to this, which gives that jurisdiction. * * * On the opposite construction, the judicial power never can be extended to a whole case, as expressed by the constitution, but to those parts of cases only which present the particular question involving the construction of the constitution or the law. * * * [I]f the circumstance that other points are involved in it, shall disable Congress from authorizing the Courts of the Union to take jurisdiction of the original cause, it equally disables Congress from authorizing those Courts to take jurisdiction of the whole cause, on an appeal, and thus will be restricted to a single question in that cause; and words obviously intended to secure to those who claim rights under the constitution, laws or treaties of the United States, a trial in the federal Courts, will be restricted to the insecure remedy of an appeal, upon an insulated point, after it has received that shape which may be given to it by another tribunal, into which he is forced against his will.

We think, then, that when a question to which the judicial power of the Union is extended by the constitution, forms an ingredient of the original cause, it is in the power of Congress to give the Circuit Courts jurisdiction of that cause, although other questions of fact or of law may be involved in it.

The case of the Bank is, we think, a very strong case of this description. The charter of incorporation not only creates it, but gives it every faculty which it possesses. The power to acquire rights of any description, to transact business of any description, to make contracts of any description, to sue on those contracts, is given and measured by its charter, and that charter is a law of the United States. This being can acquire no right, make no contract, bring no suit, which is not authorized by a law of the United States. It is not only itself the mere creature of a law, but all its actions and all its rights are dependent on the same law. Can a being, thus constituted, have a case which does not arise literally, as well as substantially, under the law?

Take the case of a contract, which is put as the strongest against the Bank.

When a Bank sues, the first question which presents itself, and which lies at the foundation of the cause, is, has this legal entity a right to sue? Has it a right to come, not into this Court particularly, but into any Court? This depends on a law of the United States. The next question is, has this being a right to make this particular contract? If this question be decided in the negative, the cause is determined against the plaintiff; and this question, too, depends entirely on a law of the United States. These are important questions, and they exist in every possible case. The right to sue, if decided once, is decided for ever; but the power of Congress was exercised antecedently to the first decision on that right, and if it was constitutional then, it cannot cease to be so, because the particular question is decided. It may be revived at the will of the party, and most probably would be renewed, were the tribunal to be changed. But the question respecting the right to make a particular contract, or to acquire a particular property, or to sue on account of a particular injury, belongs to every particular case, and may be renewed in every case. The question forms an original ingredient in every cause. Whether it be in fact relied on or not, in the defence, it is still a part of the cause, and may be relied on. The right of the plaintiff to sue, cannot depend on the defence which the defendant may choose to set up. His right to sue is anterior to that defence, and must depend on the state of things when the action is brought. The questions which the case involves, then, must determine its character, whether those questions be made in the cause or not.

The appellants say, that the case arises on the contract; but the validity of the contract depends on a law of the United States, and the plaintiff is compelled, in every case, to show its validity. The case arises emphatically under the law. The act of Congress is its foundation. The contract could never have been made, but under the authority of that act. The act itself is the first ingredient in the case, is its origin, is that from which every other part arises. That other questions may also arise, as the execution of the contract, or its performance, cannot change the case, or give it any other origin than the charter of incorporation. The action still originates in, and is sustained by, that charter. * * *

It is said, that a clear distinction exists between the party and the cause; that the party may originate under a law with which the cause has no connexion; and that Congress may, with the same propriety, give a naturalized citizen, who is the mere creature of a law, a right to sue in the Courts of the United States, as give that right to the Bank.

This distinction is not denied; and, if the act of Congress was a simple act of incorporation, and contained nothing more, it might be entitled to great consideration. But the act does not stop with incorporating the Bank. It proceeds to bestow upon the being it has made, all the faculties and capacities which that being possesses. Every act of the Bank grows out of this law, and is tested by it. * * *

A naturalized citizen is indeed made a citizen under an act of Congress, but the act does not proceed to give, to regulate, or to prescribe his capacities. He becomes a member of the society, possessing all the rights of a native citizen, and standing, in the view of the constitution, on the footing of a native. The constitution does not authorize Congress to enlarge or abridge those rights. The simple power of the national legislature is, to prescribe a uniform rule of naturalization, and the exercise of this power exhausts it, so far as respects the individual. The constitution then takes him up, and, among other rights, extends to him the capacity of suing in the Courts of the United States, precisely under the same circumstances under which a native might sue. He is distinguishable in nothing from a native citizen, except so far as the constitution makes the distinction. The law makes none.

There is, then, no resemblance between the act incorporating the Bank, and the general naturalization law.

* * * [W]e are of opinion, that the clause in the act of incorporation, enabling the Bank to sue in the Courts of the United States, is consistent with the constitution, and to be obeyed in all Courts. * * *

[The Court affirmed the circuit court's order that Sullivan return $98,000, and that Osborn and Harper pay the remaining $2,000, to the Bank, but the Court reversed the award of interest on the specie.]

■ MR. JUSTICE JOHNSON [dissenting]. * * *

I have very little doubt that the public mind will be easily reconciled to the decision of the Court here rendered; for, whether necessary or unnecessary originally, a state of things has now grown up, in some of the States, which renders all the protection necessary, that the general government can give to this Bank. The policy of the decision is obvious, that is, if the Bank is to be sustained; and few will bestow upon its legal correctness, the reflection, that it is necessary to test it by the constitution and laws, under which it is rendered.

The Bank of the United States, is now identified with the administration of the national government. * * * Attempts have been made to dispense with it, and they have failed; serious and very weighty doubts have been entertained of its constitutionality, but they have been abandoned; and it is now become the functionary that collects, the depository that holds, the vehicle that transports, the guard that protects, and the agent that distributes and pays away, the millions that pass annually through the national treasury; and all this, not only without expense to the government, but after paying a large bonus, and sustaining actual annual losses to a large amount; furnishing the only possible means of embodying the most ample security for so immense a charge.

[If the Bank had been confined to fiscal uses, this lawsuit and the law that gave rise to it, would probably not have arisen. But the Bank served another important objective. The expiration of the first Bank's charter had led to a proliferation of state banks, from which the states derived emoluments, and the country was soon inundated with new bills of credit, against which the constitution imposed no adequate inhibition. A specie-paying national Bank, with overwhelming capital and the aid of federal government deposits, was the only way for the nation to restore its power over the currency, which the framers intended to give to Congress alone. But that approach required restraint upon individual cupidity and upon State power, and in the nature of things the effort met great resistance.]

In the present instance, I cannot persuade myself, that the constitution sanctions the vesting of the right of action in this Bank, in cases in which the privilege is exclusively personal, or in any case, merely on the ground that a question might *possibly* be raised in it, involving the constitution, or constitutionality of a law, of the United States.

When laws were heretofore passed for raising a revenue by a duty on stamped paper, the tax was quietly acquiesced in, notwithstanding it entrenched so closely on the unquestionable power of the States over the law of contracts; but had the same law which declared void contracts not written upon stamped paper, declared, that every person holding such paper should be entitled to bring his action "in any Circuit Court" of the United States, it is confidently believed that there could have been but one opinion on the constitutionality of such a provision. The whole jurisdiction over contracts, might thus have been taken from the State Courts, and conferred upon those of the United States. Nor would the evil have rested there; by a similar exercise of power, imposing a stamp on deeds generally, jurisdiction over the territory of the State, whoever might be parties, even between citizens of the same State—jurisdiction of suits instituted for the recovery of legacies or distributive portions of intestates' estates—jurisdiction, in fact, over almost every possible case, might be transferred to the Courts of the United States. Wills may be required to be executed on stamped paper; taxes may be, and have been, imposed upon legacies and distributions; and, in all such cases, there is not only a possibility, but a probability, that a question may arise, involving the constitutionality, construction, & c. of a law of the United States. If the circumstance, that the questions which the case involves, are to determine its character, whether those questions be made in the case or not, then every case here alluded to, may as well be transferred to the jurisdiction of the United States, as those to which this Bank is a party. But still farther, as was justly insisted in argument, there is not a tract of land of the United States, acquired under laws of the United States, whatever be the number of mesne transfers that it may have undergone, over which the jurisdiction of the Courts of the United States might not be extended by Congress, upon the very principle on which the right of suit in this Bank is here maintained. Nor is the case of the alien, put in argument, at all inapplicable. The one acquires its character of individual property, as the other does his political existence, under a law of the United States; and there is not a suit which may be instituted to recover the one, nor an action of ejectment to be brought by the other, in which a right acquired under a law of the United States, does not lie as essentially at the basis of the right of action, as in the suits brought by this Bank. It is no answer to the argument, to say, that the law of the United States is but ancillary to the constitution, as to the alien; for the constitution could do nothing for him without the law: and, whether the question be upon law or constitution, still if the possibility of its arising be a sufficient circumstance to bring it within the jurisdiction of the United States Courts, that possibility exists with regard to every suit affected by alien disabilities; to real actions, in time of peace—to all actions in time of war.

I cannot persuade myself, then, that, with these palpable consequences in view, Congress ever could have intended to vest in the Bank of the United States, the right of suit to the extent here claimed. * * *

* * * I next proceed to consider, more distinctly, the constitutional question, on the right to vest the jurisdiction to the extent here contended for.

And here I must observe, that I altogether misunderstood the counsel, who argued the cause for the plaintiff in error, if any of them contended against the jurisdiction, on the ground that the cause involved questions depending on general principles. No one can question, that the Court which has jurisdiction of the principal question, must exercise jurisdiction over every question. Neither did I understand them as denying, that if Congress could confer on the Circuit Courts appellate, they could confer original jurisdiction. The argument went to deny the right to assume jurisdiction on a mere hypothesis. It was one of description, identity, definition; they contended, that until a question involving the construction or administration of the laws of the United States did actually arise, the *casus federis* was not presented, on which the constitution authorized the government to take to itself the jurisdiction of the cause. That until such a question actually arose, until such a case was actually presented, *non constat*, but the cause depended upon general principles, exclusively cognizable in the State Courts; that neither the letter nor the spirit of the constitution sanctioned the assumption of jurisdiction on the part of the United States at any previous stage. * * *

Efforts have been made to fix the precise sense of the constitution, when it vests jurisdiction in the general government, in "cases arising under the laws of the United States." To me, the question appears susceptible of a very simple solution; that all depends upon the identity of the case supposed; according to which idea, a case may be such in its very existence, or may become such in its progress. An action may "live, move and have its being," in a law of the United States; such is that given for the violation of a patent-right, and four or five different actions given by this act of incorporation; particularly that against the President and Directors for over-issuing; in all of which cases the plaintiff must count upon the law itself as the ground of his action. And of the other description, would have been an action of trespass, in this case, had remedy been sought for an actual levy of the tax imposed. Such was the case of the former Bank against Deveaux, and many others that have occurred in this Court, in which the suit, in its form, was such as occur in ordinary cases, but in which the pleadings or evidence raised the question on the law or constitution of the United States. In this class of cases, the occurrence of a question makes the case, and transfers it, as provided for under the twenty-fifth section of the Judiciary Act, to the jurisdiction of the United States. And this appears to me to present the only sound and practical construction of the constitution on this subject; for no other cases does it regard as necessary to place under the control of the general government. It is only when the case exhibits one or the other of these characteristics, that it is acted upon by the constitution. Where no question is raised, there can be no contrariety of construction; and what else had the constitution to guard against? As to cases of the first description, *ex necessitate rei*, the Courts of the United States must be susceptible of original jurisdiction; and as to all other cases, I should hold them, also, susceptible of original jurisdiction, if it were practicable, in the nature of things, to make out the definition of the case, so as to bring it under the constitution judicially, upon an original suit. But until the plaintiff can control the defendant in his pleadings, I see no practical mode of determining when the case does occur, otherwise than by permitting the cause to advance until the case for which the constitution provides shall actually arise. If it never occurs, there can be nothing to complain of; and such are the provisions of the twenty-fifth section. The cause might be transferred to the Circuit Court before an adjudication takes place; but I can perceive no earlier stage at which it can possibly be predicated of such a case, that it is one within the constitution; nor any possible necessity for transferring it then, or until the Court has acted upon it to the prejudice of the claims of the United States. It is not, therefore, because Congress may not vest an *original* jurisdiction, where they can constitutionally vest in the Circuit Courts *appellate* jurisdiction, that I object to this general grant of the right to sue; but, because that the peculiar nature of this jurisdiction is such, as to render it impossible to exercise it in a strictly original form, and because the principle of a possible occurrence of a question as a ground of jurisdiction, is transcending the bounds of the constitution, and placing it on a ground which will admit of an *enormous accession*, if not an *unlimited assumption*, of jurisdiction. * * *

NOTE ON THE SCOPE OF THE CONSTITUTIONAL GRANT

(1) Federal Question Jurisdiction and the Planters' Bank Case. Article III authorizes Congress to confer jurisdiction over controversies to which the United States is a party. However, neither the Bank's federal charter nor the national government's ownership of shares made the United States a "party" to suits by or against the Bank for this purpose. See Lebron v. National R.R. Passenger Corp., 513 U.S. 374, 398–99 (1995). Thus, to uphold the constitutionality of the statutory grant of jurisdiction in Osborn, the Court had to find that the case was one arising under federal law within the meaning of Article III.

The "arising under" question may have been easier in Osborn than in a companion case, in which the Court upheld federal court jurisdiction over an action by the Bank to collect on negotiable notes issued by a state bank. Bank of the United States v. Planters' Bank of Ga., 22 U.S. (9 Wheat.) 904 (1824). In both Osborn and Planters' Bank, the existence of the Bank of the United States as a federal corporation was only a relatively minor premise of the claim for relief. But in Osborn, it is arguable that the major premise—namely, the right under the Constitution and laws of the United States to be free from state taxation—was also federal. (One must say "arguable," because the case may have been viewed as one in which state tort law furnished the Bank with a cause of action to enjoin the seizure of its property and to recover funds seized, and if the defendants answered that state law authorized their actions, federal law entered the case by preempting any such defense. It may be anachronistic to try to characterize the right of action, with our post-Erie consciousness, as being either federal or state in character.) By contrast, in Planters' Bank, state law plainly governed the dispute over the negotiable note.

(2) The Pacific Railroad Removal Cases. Osborn's reasoning was applied to uphold the constitutionality of a grant of jurisdiction allowing the removal to federal court of actions against federally chartered railroad corporations. Pacific Railroad Removal Cases, 115 U.S. 1 (1885) (7–2). The Court said that "the corporations now before us not only derive their existence, but their powers, their functions, their duties, and a large portion of their resources, from [Acts of Congress], and by virtue thereof sustain important relations to the government of the United States." Two dissenters disagreed with the Court's interpretation of the statutory grant but did not question the Court's constitutional reasoning.

Unlike the Bank of the United States, these railroads were not federal instrumentalities primarily carrying out government policy, a difference that Justice Frankfurter viewed as significant. See Textile Workers Union v. Lincoln Mills, 353 U.S. 448, 471 n.4 (1957) (Frankfurter, J., dissenting).

(3) Original and Appellate Federal Question Jurisdiction. Consider Marshall's proposition that original jurisdiction "is coextensive with judicial power" and that Congress is capable of "giving the Circuit Courts original jurisdiction, in any case to which the appellate jurisdiction extends." Can this be right? Consider, for example, a state court action in which a federal issue is raised for the first time by the opinion of the state's highest court; contrary to Marshall's proposition, wouldn't the Supreme Court have appellate jurisdiction over the case even though there could not have been original federal court jurisdiction?

Marshall's formulation also suggests that appellate jurisdiction may be exercised in any case over which there would have been original jurisdiction. Can that be right? Consider a case in which a proposition of federal law "forms an ingredient" of the cause, even though the proposition is unchallenged and unchallengeable. Osborn apparently holds that Congress may constitutionally confer arising under jurisdiction over such a case. But if such a case were litigated in state court, and no question of federal law was ever disputed or decided, could the Supreme Court constitutionally be given appellate jurisdiction to review the state court judgment?

These examples illustrate the important point that appellate jurisdiction can be tailored to the case as it actually develops: the presence (or absence) of a federal "ingredient" is known by the time Supreme Court review is sought. The original jurisdiction, on the other hand, must often be based on conjecture: it cannot be known with certainty which issues will turn out to be decisive. Doesn't this difference have implications for the question whether the constitutional scope of the appellate jurisdiction is wholly congruent with that of the original jurisdiction? See also the Note on Murdock v. Memphis, p. 485, *supra*.

(4) The Purposes of Arising Under Jurisdiction. What light do the opinions in Osborn shed on the purposes of Article III's grant of arising under jurisdiction?

(a) Exposition of Federal Law. Justice Johnson believed that federal tribunals must be available to ensure that federal law is properly construed. This purpose can be fully served by authorizing federal appellate review of state court decisions upon determinative points of federal law—at least if (as was more true when Osborn was decided than today) the Supreme Court's appellate capacity is adequate to the task.

(b) Enforcement of Federal Law. But surely a further, constitutionally permissible function of federal courts is to enforce federal law—to establish the facts determinative of the application of federal law, even if the law's content and applicability are undisputed, and to enter and enforce the appropriate judgment. This purpose can be served by giving federal trial courts original jurisdiction in cases necessarily involving federal law, and removal jurisdiction whenever a determinative federal issue emerges. See Vázquez, *The Federal "Claim" in the District Courts: Osborn, Verlinden, and Protective Jurisdiction*, 95 Cal.L.Rev. 1731 (2007).

(c) Hypothetical Future Enforcement of Federal Law. Is there a further purpose in providing federal jurisdiction to assure a federal forum in the event that a federal question is raised in the future? In a dissenting opinion in Textile Workers Union v. Lincoln Mills, 353 U.S. 448 (1957), discussed more fully at p. 797, *infra*, Justice Frankfurter may have read Osborn, a decision he criticized, that way: he stated that "we would not be justified in perpetuating a principle that permits assertion of original federal jurisdiction on the remote possibility of presentation of a federal question." Frankfurter suggested that Osborn involved a distinctive historical setting and a juristic entity that was completely created by federal law and engaged in essential governmental functions. He thus resisted relying on Osborn even if a case presented some "analytic similarity".

Bellia, *Article III and the Cause of Action*, 89 Iowa L.Rev. 777 (2004), argues that Frankfurter misread Osborn insofar as he suggested that it construes Article III as permitting Congress to confer jurisdiction over any case in which a federal issue *might* possibly arise. (Indeed, on Frankfurter's reading, would any case fall outside the scope of the "arising under" jurisdiction of Article III?) Is it more sound to read Osborn as upholding jurisdiction when the plaintiff must affirm the federal ingredient (even if the defendant does not contest it) in order to obtain relief?

On that reading, however, jurisdiction depends on whether the plaintiff has the burden of pleading the federal issue in question, a burden that Congress can alter. Could Congress require federal court plaintiffs to plead that state law tort actions are not preempted by any federal statute, and then give the federal courts jurisdiction over all state law tort actions?

(5) Jurisdiction in Bankruptcy Proceedings. The Supreme Court has repeatedly upheld the statutory grant of federal court jurisdiction over bankruptcy proceedings. In such proceedings, much of the law—for example, concerning the marshaling of assets, the priority of various classes of creditors, and the effect of a discharge in bankruptcy—is federal. But many bankruptcy proceedings include disputes between the representative of the bankrupt's estate (formerly called the assignee in bankruptcy, now called the trustee) and a third party, and such disputes may turn entirely on state tort, contract, or property law. Absent diversity of citizenship, what is the basis for the exercise of federal subject matter jurisdiction over these state law claims?

That question has arisen under bankruptcy schemes at least since the Bankruptcy Act of 1867, 14 Stat. 517. Statutes enacted in 1898, 1978, and 1984 have changed some features of the bankruptcy system, but in every case Congress extended federal subject matter jurisdiction over bankruptcy cases to disputes, between the estate in bankruptcy and third parties, even when those disputes were founded on state law and no diversity of citizenship existed.

Jurisdiction under the 1867 Act was particularly broad, as any federal district throughout the nation (not merely the district in which the bankruptcy proceeding was filed) could exercise concurrent jurisdiction of an action by creditors against the assignee in bankruptcy or by the assignee against third parties. (The scope of that concurrent jurisdiction of federal courts other than the one in which bankruptcy action was filed has narrowed over time.) In Lathrop v. Drake, 91 U.S. 516, 517–18 (1875), the Court resolved a case brought under this concurrent jurisdiction, without directly considering its constitutionality, stressing that "a uniform system of bankruptcy, national in its character, ought to be capable of execution in the national tribunals, without dependence upon those of the States in which it is possible that embarrassments might arise." Other decisions have upheld bankruptcy jurisdiction without expressing a clear rationale for the holding.[1]

Note three distinct rationales on the basis of which broad bankruptcy jurisdiction might be upheld as constitutionally valid.

(a) Supplemental Jurisdiction. The jurisdiction could be seen as a version of supplemental jurisdiction. There plainly is federal question jurisdiction over the federal law issues that arise in bankruptcy, and jurisdiction over the adverse claims between trustee and third parties could be considered to be sufficiently related to the federal law proceeding as to be a single case or controversy. The four-Justice plurality opinion in Northern

---

[1]   See Schumacher v. Beeler, 293 U.S. 367, 374 (upholding the Bankruptcy Act of 1898). See also Williams v. Austrian, 331 U.S. 642 (1947) (upholding a similar jurisdiction over actions by the trustee in reorganization under the Chandler Act of 1938).

For commentary, see Brubaker, *On the Nature of Federal Bankruptcy Jurisdiction: A General Statutory and Constitutional Theory*, 41 Wm. & Mary L.Rev. 743 (2000) (arguing that claims by or against the bankrupt's estate satisfy the federal ingredient approach and that a "related" proceeding to which the estate is not a party falls within supplemental jurisdiction); Cross, *Viewing Federal Jurisdiction Through the Looking Glass of Bankruptcy*, 23 Seton Hall L.Rev. 530 (1993) (contending that such jurisdiction is best explained as a species of "ancillary jurisdiction"); Cross, *Congressional Power to Extend Federal Jurisdiction to Disputes Outside Article III: A Critical Analysis from the Perspective of Bankruptcy*, 87 Nw.U.L.Rev. 1188 (1993) (same); Galligan, *Article III and the "Related To" Bankruptcy Jurisdiction: A Case Study in Protective Jurisdiction*, 11 U. Puget Sound L.Rev. 1 (1987) (criticizing the "essential ingredient" and "ancillary jurisdiction" approaches and arguing that bankruptcy is a valid form of protective jurisdiction); Pathak, *Breaking the "Unbreakable Rule": Federal Courts, Article I, and the Problem of "Related To" Bankruptcy Jurisdiction*, 85 Or.L.Rev. 59 (2006) (finding all of the theories wanting).

Pipeline Constr. Co. v. Marathon Pipe Line Co., 458 U.S. 50, 72 n.26 (1982), p. 356, *supra*, may have embraced such a theory when it stated that the state law claim bought in that case by the trustee in bankruptcy against a third party could have been "adjudicated in federal court on the basis of its relationship to the petition for reorganization." (The other five Justices did not address subject matter jurisdiction.)

This rationale for upholding bankruptcy jurisdiction requires a capacious understanding of supplemental jurisdiction. In a large corporate bankruptcy, for example, one creditor's claim that it is owed money by the bankrupt company on a construction contract in Texas will have no factual connection with another creditor's claim that it is owed money because its property was damaged in Iowa by a vehicle of the bankrupt company. The strain on notions of supplemental jurisdiction was particularly severe under the 1867 Act, when the two claims could have been brought in different federal courts (and the bankruptcy proceeding might be in a third federal court).

On the supplemental jurisdiction view, how far might bankruptcy jurisdiction extend? In connection with the bankruptcy of Enron Corporation, a federal bankruptcy court permitted removal of state court tort actions against financial institutions alleged to have facilitated Enron's commission of fraud. Although these actions were based on state law and Enron was not a party to them, the court upheld jurisdiction, under 28 U.S.C. § 1334(b)'s extension of bankruptcy jurisdiction to civil actions "related to" bankruptcy proceedings, on the basis that the defendants, if found liable, might seek contribution or indemnity from Enron. See In re Enron Corp. Securities, Derivative & "ERISA" Litigation, 314 B.R. 354, 357 (S.D.Tex. 2004).[2]

(b) Federal Ingredient. Alternatively, the bankruptcy jurisdiction might be upheld on a theory similar to that in Osborn: in bankruptcy, the capacity of the trustee to stand in the shoes of the bankrupt party, and as such to sue and be sued, is bestowed by federal law and is an ingredient of every claim. But that theory raises additional complexities in certain bankruptcy cases,[3] and it does not easily justify the exercise of "related to" jurisdiction in disputes in which the trustee is not a party (as, for instance, in the Enron example just discussed).

(c) Protective Jurisdiction. A third theory rests on the concept of protective jurisdiction, which is discussed in the next Note.

(6) Verlinden B.V. v. Central Bank of Nigeria and the Foreign Sovereign Immunities Act. Verlinden B.V. v. Central Bank of Nigeria, 461 U.S. 480 (1983), was a rare case requiring the Supreme Court to consider a federal statutory grant of jurisdiction that seemed to approach the outer limits of Article III. The Court unanimously found that the case contained a sufficient federal ingredient to fall within the scope of Osborn.

---

[2]   On whether supplemental jurisdiction under 28 U.S.C. § 1367 may be superimposed on top of the "related to" jurisdiction in § 1334, see p. 869, note 7, *infra*.

[3]   In some bankruptcy proceedings, no trustee is appointed and the debtor serves as "debtor-in-possession". For an argument that even in such proceedings, there is a federal ingredient, because the debtor takes on a new, federally created, representative role when serving as debtor-in-possession, see Brubaker, note 1, *supra*. For a contrasting view, see Cross, note 1, *supra* (viewing Brubaker's approach as mere semantics and as conferring unbridled power on Congress); accord, Galligan, note 1, *supra*.

The Verlinden case involved a federal court action by a Dutch corporation against an instrumentality of the Government of Nigeria for breach of a contract. Statutory jurisdiction over the action was provided by the Foreign Sovereign Immunities Act (FSIA),[4] which confers on federal district courts original jurisdiction over "any nonjury civil action against a foreign state * * * as to any claim * * * with respect to which the foreign state is not entitled to immunity" under either the FSIA or any applicable international agreement. 28 U.S.C. § 1330(a). (The FSIA also confers removal jurisdiction over such action if initially filed in state court. 28 U.S.C. § 1441(d).) The main thrust of the FSIA is to establish substantive standards and procedural rules governing suits brought against foreign nations in the federal and state courts. The Act details when foreign states are immune from suit and specifies a number of instances in which such immunity does not exist; in the Verlinden case, the plaintiff alleged that Nigeria's conduct caused effects within the United States, within the meaning of one of the FSIA's provisions recognizing an exception to foreign sovereign immunity.

Before filing an answer (which might have asserted foreign sovereign immunity and thus clearly injected a federal issue into the case), the defendant moved to dismiss the complaint, *inter alia*, for want of subject matter jurisdiction. The court of appeals held that the Act was unconstitutional insofar as it purported to authorize the federal courts to entertain an action when the substantive claim is not based on federal law and when diversity jurisdiction was absent (because neither party was a citizen of the United States).

In a unanimous opinion by Chief Justice Burger, the Supreme Court reversed, upholding the FSIA's jurisdictional grant. The Court stated that the "controlling decision" is Osborn, which "reflects a broad conception of 'arising under' jurisdiction, according to which Congress may confer on the federal courts jurisdiction over any case or controversy that might call for the application of federal law." The Court continued: "The breadth of that conclusion has been questioned. It has been observed that, taken at its broadest, Osborn might be read as permitting 'assertion of original federal jurisdiction on the remote possibility of presentation of a federal question.' Textile Workers Union v. Lincoln Mills, 353 U.S. 448, 482 (1957) (Frankfurter, J., dissenting). See, *e.g.*, P. Bator, P. Mishkin, D. Shapiro, & H. Wechsler, Hart & Wechsler's The Federal Courts and the Federal System 866–867 (2d ed. 1973). We need not now resolve that issue or decide the precise boundaries of Art. III jurisdiction, however, since the present case does not involve a mere speculative possibility that a federal question may arise at some point in the proceeding. Rather, a suit against a foreign state under this Act necessarily raises questions of substantive federal law at the very outset, and hence clearly 'arises under' federal law, as that term is used in Art. III.

"By reason of its authority over foreign commerce and foreign relations, Congress has the undisputed power to decide, as a matter of federal law, whether and under what circumstances foreign nations should be amenable to suit in the United States. Actions against foreign sovereigns in our courts raise sensitive issues concerning the foreign relations of the United States, and the primacy of federal concerns is evident.

---

[4]   Act of Oct. 1, 1976, 90 Stat. 2891–98, codified at 28 U.S.C. §§ 1330, 1332(a)(2)–(4), 1391(f), 1441(d), & 1602–11.

"To promote these federal interests, Congress exercised its Art. I powers by enacting a statute comprehensively regulating the amenability of foreign nations to suit in the United States. The statute must be applied by the district courts in every action against a foreign sovereign, since subject-matter jurisdiction in any such action depends on the existence of one of the specified exceptions to foreign sovereign immunity, 28 U.S.C. § 1330(a). At the threshold of every action in a district court against a foreign state, therefore, the court must satisfy itself that one of the exceptions applies— and in doing so it must apply the detailed federal law standards set forth in the Act. Accordingly, an action against a foreign sovereign arises under federal law, for purposes of Art. III jurisdiction.

"In reaching a contrary conclusion, the Court of Appeals relied heavily upon decisions construing 28 U.S.C. § 1331 * * *[—particularly] on the so-called 'well-pleaded complaint' rule, which provides, for purposes of *statutory* 'arising under' jurisdiction, that the federal question must appear on the face of a well-pleaded complaint and may not enter in anticipation of a defense. * * *

* * * "Art. III 'arising under' jurisdiction is broader than federal-question jurisdiction under § 1331, and the Court of Appeals' heavy reliance on decisions construing that statute was misplaced. * * *

" * * * Congress deliberately sought to channel cases against foreign sovereigns away from the state courts and into federal courts, thereby reducing the potential for a multiplicity of conflicting results among the courts of the 50 States. The resulting jurisdictional grant is within the bounds of Art. III, since every action against a foreign sovereign necessarily involves application of a body of substantive federal law, and accordingly 'arises under' federal law, within the meaning of Art. III."

What is the rule of Verlinden? After that decision, how far may Congress go in enacting jurisdictional provisions that by their terms authorize federal courts to adjudicate a claim (even though not based on federal law) if, and only if, the claim is not subject to a valid federal defense?[5] Is it relevant that

---

[5]   In Gutierrez de Martinez v. Lamagno, 515 U.S. 417 (1995), a plurality of the Court discussed the meaning of Verlinden. This was a state law diversity action against a federal official. Under the Westfall Act, 28 U.S.C. § 2679(d)(1), the Attorney General certified that the official had been acting within the scope of his employment at the time of the alleged wrong. Under the Act, that certification required substituting the United States for the official as the defendant and transforming the suit into one under the Federal Tort Claims Act. However, because the relevant events occurred abroad, the Federal Tort Claims Act precluded liability. For that reason, the plaintiff sought judicial review of the certification, hoping to have the original suit against the official reinstated.

The Court ruled, 5–4, that the Attorney General's certification was subject to judicial review. Four members of the majority went on to discuss whether, if the certification were set aside and the state law action against the federal official reinstated, the federal court would still have subject matter jurisdiction over the case. Because diversity of citizenship provided an independent basis for jurisdiction, the question was only hypothetical, but in dictum the plurality, citing Verlinden, found that no "grave" Article III problem would be presented were the original state law action to proceed in federal court even absent diversity of citizenship. Any such action would present, at the outset, a significant federal question under the Westfall Act— whether the official was acting within the scope of employment—that Congress plainly wanted to be "aired" in a federal forum. Even if that question were resolved against the certification, it was appropriate for the federal court, having invested time on the federal question of the scope of employment, to proceed to final judgment. The fifth member of the majority, Justice O'Connor, declined to consider a "difficult constitutional question" that might arise in the future but that was not presented here in view of the existence of diversity jurisdiction.

in Verlinden, the FSIA adopted a restrictive view of immunity and thus opened the federal courts to many suits that had formerly been barred under federal judicial decisions recognizing a broader foreign sovereign immunity? See Vázquez, Paragraph (4)(b), *supra*.

(7) The Significance of a "Sue and Be Sued" Clause. In Osborn (and the companion Planters' Bank case) the constitutional issue arose only if the statutory "sue and be sued" clause was interpreted as conferring federal court jurisdiction. In the absence of a congressional grant of general federal question jurisdiction, John Marshall may have strained to interpret the statutory provision at issue in Osborn as a specific grant of federal question jurisdiction, given the serious threats to national supremacy. See pp. 785–786, *supra*.

A similar question of how to interpret a "sue and be sued" clause was presented in American Nat'l Red Cross v. S.G., 505 U.S. 247 (1992), a tort suit alleging that one of the plaintiffs had contracted AIDS from a blood transfusion. In upholding the Red Cross' removal of the action from state court, the Court ruled that the congressional charter authorizing the Red Cross "to sue and be sued in courts of law and equity, State or Federal, within the jurisdiction of the United States" conferred federal question jurisdiction. The Court viewed Deveaux, Osborn, and other precedents as supporting "the rule that a congressional charter's 'sue and be sued' provision may be read to confer federal court jurisdiction if, but only if, it specifically mentions the federal courts." The Court distinguished the Deveaux decision, discussed in the Osborn Court's opinion, principally on the ground that there, the act of incorporation did not mention the federal courts but simply referred to all "courts of record".

Four dissenting Justices contended that the Red Cross' charter did not confer jurisdiction. The statute in Osborn, they noted, provided that the Bank could be sued in state courts having competent jurisdiction and in the federal *circuit courts* but did not mention the federal *district courts*, and thus conferred jurisdiction on a particular set of federal trial courts. Because the Red Cross' charter, like the statute at issue in Deveaux, applies to suits in

---

Justice Souter, writing for the four dissenters, construed the Westfall Act as precluding judicial review, thereby avoiding what he viewed as a serious Article III problem. The plaintiff's challenge to certification, he argued, was a challenge to jurisdiction itself, and thus the Court's reasoning was "tantamount to saying the authority to determine whether a court has jurisdiction over the cause of action supplies the very jurisdiction that is subject to challenge."

Does Justice Souter fairly describe the plurality's hypothetical, which involves removal only after the official-defendant's assertion of a substantive federal defense to the initial action and the substitution of the United States as a party? At that point, subject matter jurisdiction could rest on both the existence of a federal defense and the presence of the United States as a party. Indeed, the hypothetical presents an easier case than Verlinden, in which federal question jurisdiction was based on the plaintiff's claim of the *absence* of a substantive federal defense to the action, even before the defendant had asserted such a defense.

A more recent decision under the Westfall Act expressed less anxiety about continuing to exercise jurisdiction were a certification overturned. In Osborn v. Haley, 549 U.S. 225 (2007), a state court action against a federal official was removed to federal court after the Attorney General certified that the official was acting within the scope of employment. The district court, however, held that certification was invalid because the government denied that the conduct had even occurred. On review, the Supreme Court held that denial that conduct occurred did not invalidate a certification. Justice Ginsburg's opinion for the Court said that an Article III question would arise only if, on remand, the district court ruled that the official's conduct fell outside the scope of employment. "Because a significant federal question (whether [the defendant] has Westfall Act immunity) would have been raised at the outset, the case would 'aris[e] under' federal law, as that term is used in Article III" (citing Verlinden).

all courts, the dissent concluded that it merely established the Red Cross as a juridical entity.

Is seems doubtful that over the years, members of Congress realized that the jurisdictional consequences of a federal charter would depend on whether it referred to "all state and federal courts" or to "all courts of record". No doubt, political exigencies help to account for the broad interpretation of the statute in Osborn. But why should charters like that in the Red Cross case be interpreted to permit federal court litigation of state law actions, without regard to diversity of citizenship—especially given the dissent's entirely plausible basis for distinguishing Osborn?

NOTE ON THE VALIDITY OF A PROTECTIVE JURISDICTION

(1) The Theory of Protective Jurisdiction. The opinions in Osborn, and the discussion of Osborn in the preceding Note, assume that federal question jurisdiction rests on the presence in the case of a question of federal law—even if only a sliver—that must be applied to the case in order to resolve the dispute. Is there, however, a convincing understanding of Article III that permits Congress to confer federal court jurisdiction over a case, quite apart from any need to resolve or apply any proposition of federal law?

Consider litigation by or against the Bank. Congress in 1819 could surely have thought that the Bank, if required to litigate in state court, faced risks beyond the state court's possible shortcomings in interpreting or enforcing substantive federal law. Thus, in Osborn, Congress might have been concerned not principally about the risk that a state court would hold that the Bank lacked the capacity to sue or to contract, but rather about state court hostility to the Bank that might manifest itself in discriminatory application of state law or unfavorable treatment of evidence. In such a case, proponents of protective jurisdiction contend that Congress should not have to enact federal substantive law that provides an ingredient of a particular lawsuit in order to bring that lawsuit into a federal forum.

In Osborn, the statutory grant of jurisdiction may have been motivated by a protective purpose, but cases falling within that statutory grant nonetheless did include a federal ingredient. But in its broadest form, the theory of protective jurisdiction suggests that Article III permits Congress to vest jurisdiction in the federal courts to prevent discrimination against or hostility toward federal instrumentalities or interests—even when a particular case involves only state substantive law.[1]

(2) The Debate about Protective Jurisdiction. The Supreme Court has never been required explicitly to endorse or repudiate the theory of protective jurisdiction. Thus, the debate about its persuasiveness has been largely conducted in the law reviews.

(a) Professor Wechsler offered the first articulation of this theory in one paragraph of a longer article. Wechsler, *Federal Jurisdiction and the Revision of the Judicial Code*, 13 Law & Contemp. Probs. 216, 224–225 (1948). He contended whenever Congress possessed authority to create federal rules of decision over a subject matter—which in turn would permit

---

[1]   Consider whether an analogous theory might have buttressed Justice Jackson's argument in the Tidewater case, p. 410, *supra*.

it to confer federal question jurisdiction based on those rules of decision—Congress also possessed the lesser power simply to confer federal jurisdiction over the subject matter, without enacting any federal rules of decision, permitting the federal courts to adjudicate a matter that might be governed entirely by state law. Thus, in his view the power of Congress to confer federal question jurisdiction "should extend * * * to all cases in which Congress has authority to make the rule to govern disposition of the controversy but is content instead to let the states provide the rule so long as jurisdiction to enforce it has been vested in a federal court. * * * A grant of jurisdiction is in short, one mode by which the Congress may assert its regulatory powers. A case is one 'arising under' federal law within the sense of Article III whenever it is comprehended in a valid grant of jurisdiction * * *."

(b) Professor Mishkin elaborated the idea of protective jurisdiction somewhat differently. See Mishkin, *The Federal "Question" in the District Courts*, 53 Colum.L.Rev. 157, 184–96 (1953).[2] The situation in Osborn, he suggested, exemplified the risk that state courts might enforce state law in a fashion that would compromise federal interests. And he thought that Chief Justice Marshall's contention that Supreme Court review of state court judgments was an "insecure remedy * * *, upon an insulated point, after it has received the shape which may be given to it by another tribunal, into which [one] has been forced against his will" was particularly apt with respect to a state court's enforcement of state law.

Mishkin criticized Wechsler's formulation because he doubted that Congress had the authority to legislate on all matters relating to the Bank (at least as that authority was understood in the early nineteenth century). Instead, Mishkin contended that "where there is an articulated and active federal policy regulating a field, the 'arising under' clause of Article III apparently permits the conferring of jurisdiction on the national courts of all cases in the area—including those substantively governed by state law." In such circumstances, the protection offered was not to a particular party (as in diversity cases) but rather to the legislative program, and the case can be said to arise under the law establishing that program. A second congressional program that he viewed as fitting his theory is bankruptcy. In his view, federal jurisdiction over state law claims between nondiverse parties is conferred not primarily to ensure correct determination of the question of the trustee's capacity to sue or be sued, but rather to protect the operation of the congressional program from the risks posed by state court adjudication.

In one respect Mishkin's theory is broader than Wechsler's: Mishkin would not require that Congress possess legislative authority to regulate the subject matter presented in a particular case. In another respect, however, Mishkin's theory is narrower than Wechsler's: Mishkin would require that Congress have already enacted legislation that establishes an "articulated and active federal policy" in the field.

(c) Three Supreme Court Justices opined on the validity of protective jurisdiction in Textile Workers Union v. Lincoln Mills, 353 U.S. 448 (1957). There, a labor union sued to compel an employer to submit to arbitration of grievances, as called for under the collective bargaining agreement between

---

[2] See also Forrester, *The Jurisdiction of Federal Courts in Labor Disputes,* 13 Law & Contemp. Probs. 114, 128–31 (1948).

the union and employer. The suit was filed under § 301(a) of the Taft-Hartley Act, 29 U.S.C. § 185(a), which confers jurisdiction on the federal courts over actions for violation of labor-management contracts in industries affecting commerce. A majority of the Court concluded that federal substantive law governs suits under § 301(a); on that understanding, the grant of jurisdiction raises no serious constitutional question.

Justice Burton, joined by Justice Harlan, concurred in the result. In a brief and unilluminating opinion, he disagreed with the Court that federal substantive law governed the action. In then turning to the constitutionality of the statutory grant of jurisdiction, he stated "that some federal rights may necessarily be involved in a § 301 case, and hence that the constitutionality of § 301 can be upheld as a congressional grant to Federal District Courts of what has been called 'protective jurisdiction.' "

In a lone dissent, Justice Frankfurter, like Justice Burton, disagreed with the Court that federal substantive law governed actions alleging a violation of a collective bargaining agreement. He then discussed at length the constitutionality of the statutory grant of jurisdiction.

In considering but rejecting the idea of protective jurisdiction as a basis for upholding the statute, he said: "Surely the truly technical restrictions of Article III are not met or respected by a beguiling phrase that the greater power here must necessarily include the lesser. In the compromise of federal and state interests leading to distribution of jealously guarded judicial power in a federal system, it is obvious that very different considerations apply to cases involving questions of federal law and those turning solely on state law." He objected to the breadth of congressional power under Wechsler's theory, noting that it would permit conferral of federal court jurisdiction over every state law contract or tort affecting commerce. Frankfurter also suggested that insofar as protective jurisdiction rested on mistrust of state tribunals, Article III confined the grant of jurisdiction on this basis to cases falling within its party-based clauses, notably the diversity clause. He added that Chief Justice Marshall's failure to rely on a theory of protective jurisdiction "at a time when conditions might have presented more substantial justification strongly suggests its lack of constitutional merit." Finally, as to Mishkin's theory, he said dismissively that it "has the dubious advantage of limiting incursions on state judicial power to situations in which the State's feelings may have been tempered by early substantive federal invasions."[3]

(d) Further skepticism about protective jurisdiction is found in Young, *Stalking the Yeti: Protective Jurisdiction, Foreign Affairs Removal, and Complete Preemption*, 95 Calif.L.Rev. 1775 (2007). Young argues that recognition of protective jurisdiction undermines valuable diversification in the political control of the judiciary, by permitting Congress more broadly to assign cases to federal rather than state courts, which are subject to different methods of selection and political control. He suggests, additionally, that the supposedly "lesser" power of Congress to confer protective jurisdiction may be more worrisome than the supposedly "greater" power to enact substantive federal rules and confer jurisdiction, for it may be easier in the national political process to reach agreement on jurisdiction than on substance. Young

---

[3] For further discussion of Justice Frankfurter's opinion in Lincoln Mills, and of the broader significance of the case, see Shapiro, *The Story of Lincoln Mills: Jurisdiction and the Source of Law,* in Federal Courts Stories 389 (Jackson & Resnik, eds., 2009).

adds that protective jurisdiction threatens to reduce state control over the content of state law for entire categories of cases.[4]

(e) Is protective jurisdiction a theory of nearly unbridled congressional power to vest jurisdiction in the federal courts? If so, is that a cause for concern?[5]

(3) Mesa v. California and the Federal Officer Removal Statute. In the few cases in which the theory of protective jurisdiction has been advanced, the Supreme Court has neither recognized nor rejected the validity of the theory. Thus, for example, in the Verlinden decision, p. 796, *supra*, the Court said: "[i]n view of our conclusion that proper actions by foreign plaintiffs under the Foreign Sovereign Immunities Act are within Article III 'arising under' jurisdiction, we need not consider petitioner's alternative argument that the Act is constitutional as an aspect of so-called

---

[4] Are these kinds of objections to protective jurisdiction blunted by an approach, advocated by Professor Vázquez, p. 794, *supra*, that starts with Professor Wechsler's theory, but adds to it the requirement that Congress "formally" adopt state law as federal law? Admitting that the difference between this approach and Wechsler's is largely formal, Vázquez nonetheless argues that it responds to the concern that under Wechsler's approach, there is no federal law (other than the jurisdictional statute) under which the case can be said to arise. Professor Young responds that under Vázquez's approach, Congress could vastly expand federal jurisdiction without agreeing on or articulating any federal policy. Young also asks whether, if the adopted state law is treated as real federal law, federal courts would no longer be required to follow state court interpretations of the law's content.

[5] In *Article I, Article III, and the Limits of Enumeration*, 108 Mich.L.Rev. 1389 (2010), Professor Seinfeld considers the relationship between the limited enumerated powers in Article I and the enumerated heads of jurisdiction in Article III, and argues that Congress has very broad power to assign cases to the federal courts, notwithstanding the enumeration of limited categories of subject matter jurisdiction in Article III, Section 2.

Seinfeld presents what he describes as two conventional stories. The first is that the enumeration of legislative power in Article I has failed; the Court's decisions have given Congress almost plenary authority to legislate. The second is that the enumeration of limited categories of federal judicial power in Article III has succeeded. Seinfeld views the second story as false. Surveying the decisions, he doubts that they significantly restrict congressional power to assign cases to the federal courts.

Seinfeld then sketches what he calls the congressional power model of jurisdiction, which posits that Congress may vest jurisdiction in the federal courts whenever the jurisdictional legislation can be viewed as within the scope of an enumerated power in Article I and the Necessary and Proper Clause. His approach, he suggests, is a "cousin" of theories of protective jurisdiction; what distinguishes it is his acknowledgment that the enumerated categories in Article III don't matter; by contrast, theories of protective jurisdiction contend (unpersuasively in his view) that a case still falls within the arising under jurisdiction. (How significant is that difference?) He notes that the Supreme Court has not found any statute to fall outside the scope of the nine heads of jurisdiction, while numerous decisions have stretched conceptions of "arising under" in order to uphold statutory grants of jurisdiction. (He acknowledges that the decision in Mesa v. California, discussed in the next Paragraph in text, narrowly construed a jurisdictional statute in order to avoid the need to determine the constitutional limits of Article III, but he explains the result as resting on the lack of any federal interest, under Article I, in enacting a broader grant of jurisdiction.)

Seinfeld's theory is very similar to that of Justice Jackson in his plurality opinion in National Mut. Ins. Co. of D.C. v. Tidewater Transfer Co., 337 U.S. 582 (1949). Tidewater upheld a statute granting jurisdiction over a state law claim brought by a citizen of the District of Columbia against a citizen of Virginia. Viewing the plaintiff as not being a citizen of a "State" within the meaning of Article III's diversity clause, Justice Jackson, joined by Justices Black and Burton, nonetheless voted to uphold the statute, on the theory that Congress, acting under its authority in Article I to make rules governing the District of Columbia, may assign to the federal courts cases or controversies that fall outside the nine heads of subject matter jurisdiction enumerated in Article III. Six of the nine Justices rejected Justice Jackson's view (although two of the six voted to uphold the statutory grant on the distinct ground, rejected by Justice Jackson, that a citizen of the District of Columbia was a citizen of a "State" within the meaning of Article III's diversity clause). For fuller discussion, see pp. 410–411. *supra*.

'protective jurisdiction.' " And as already noted, the statutory grants both in Osborn and in the bankruptcy decisions can be justified on grounds others than protective jurisdiction.[6]

Several years after Verlinden, in Mesa v. California, 489 U.S. 121 (1989), the Court again avoided the question of the constitutionality of protective jurisdiction, this time by narrowly construing a jurisdictional statute. There, two Postal Service employees faced state criminal prosecutions arising out of traffic violations committed in connection with their jobs. The prosecutions were removed to federal court under 28 U.S.C. § 1442(a)(1), which authorizes removal of any civil or criminal action against an officer of the United States for any act "under color of such office". The government, relying in part on its interpretation of Tennessee v. Davis, p. 423, *supra*, argued that removal was proper even though the defendants asserted no colorable federal defense to the state charges. The Supreme Court rejected that view, ruling instead that § 1442(a) permits federal officer removal only when the defendant-officer avers a federal defense.

Though relying primarily on precedent, the Court also stated that the government's view would "unnecessarily present grave constitutional problems. * * * At oral argument the Government urged upon us a theory of 'protective jurisdiction' to avoid these Art. III difficulties. * * * The Government insists that the full protection of federal officers from interference by hostile state courts cannot be achieved if the averment of a federal defense must be a predicate to removal, * * * [and] that this generalized congressional interest in protecting federal officers from state court interference suffices to support Art. III 'arising under' jurisdiction.

"We have, in the past, not found the need to adopt a theory of 'protective jurisdiction' to support Art. III 'arising under' jurisdiction, and we do not see any need for doing so here because we do not recognize any federal interests that are not protected by limiting removal to situations in which a federal defense is alleged. In these prosecutions, no state court hostility or interference has even been alleged by petitioners * * *." At the end of its opinion, the Court quoted language from Maryland v. Soper (No. 2), 270 U.S. 36, 43–44 (1926), stating that if state prosecutions come to be used to obstruct enforcement of federal law, " 'it will be for Congress in its discretion to amend [the earlier version of the officer removal statute] so that * * * any prosecution of a federal officer * * * which can be shown by evidence to have had its motive in a wish to hinder him in the enforcement of federal law, may be removed for trial to the proper federal court. We are not now considering * * * whether such an enlargement would be valid; but * * * the present language * * * can not be broadened by fair construction to give it such a meaning.' "

Could a narrow statute of the kind discussed at the end of the Mesa opinion—permitting officers to remove, absent a federal defense, upon a showing of efforts to hinder federal enforcement—be upheld without reference to protective jurisdiction? Or should Mesa be viewed as a warning that, if pressed, the Court would not uphold protective jurisdiction?[7]

---

[6]   Indeed, Professor Goldberg-Ambrose would reserve the concept of protective jurisdiction for cases in which federal law governs none of the legal relationships in the case. Goldberg-Ambrose, *The Protective Jurisdiction of the Federal Courts*, 30 UCLA L.Rev. 542, 549 (1983).

[7]   For further discussions of protective jurisdiction in addition to authorities already cited, see Segall, *Article III as a Grant of Power: Protective Jurisdiction, Federalism and the Federal Courts*, 54 Fla.L.Rev. 361 (2002); Note, 57 N.Y.U.L.Rev. 933 (1982).

(4) Some Testing Cases. The question of the validity of protective jurisdiction (and, if valid, its scope), as well as the question of the reach of Osborn, are not merely academic. The following jurisdictional statutes, which push against the limits of Article III, illustrate that these questions remain live ones. Are these statutes constitutional—and if so, on what theory?

(a) The Diplomatic Relations Act of 1978. Pub.L.No. 95–393, as amended in 1987 by Pub.L.No. 100–204, 28 U.S.C. § 1364, was designed to facilitate recovery of damages, particularly from automobile accidents, caused by foreign diplomats who are themselves immune from suit, by permitting suit, in some circumstances, against an insurer of members of diplomatic missions or their families. In such direct actions, the insurer may not defend on the ground that the insured is immune from suit or is an indispensable party, nor (absent fraud or collusion) on the ground that the insured has breached the insurance contract. The Senate Report accompanying the bill (S.Rep. No. 1108, 95th Cong., 2d Sess. 5 (1978)) made clear that state law would govern such suits.

Many members of diplomatic missions, as defined by the Act, are not ambassadors, ministers, or consuls, see *id.* at 6–7, and thus direct actions involving their conduct would probably not be considered "Cases affecting Ambassadors, other public Ministers and Consuls" within the meaning of that grant of jurisdiction in Article III. May such actions nonetheless be heard under the federal courts' "arising under" jurisdiction?

(b) The Clean Air Act. Under 42 U.S.C. § 7604, the district courts have jurisdiction over private civil actions against any person alleged to be in violation of any "emission standard or limitation" issued under the Act. "Emission standards" appear to include standards contained in state-promulgated "Implementation Plans"; these plans must meet federal requirements and be approved by EPA, but otherwise constitute detailed programs of implementation, maintenance, and enforcement of air quality standards as a matter of state law. The lower courts have heard cases based on violations of state plans without raising any question about jurisdiction. *E.g.,* Save Our Health Org. v. Recomp of Minnesota, Inc., 37 F.3d. 1334, 1336 (8th Cir.1994).

(c) The Air Transportation Safety and System Stabilization Act. A statute passed shortly after 9/11 creates a "Federal cause of action for damages" arising from the four terrorist-related airline crashes on that date. Pub.L.No. 107–42, § 408(b)(1), 115 Stat. 230, 240–41 (2001). The Act provides that the new federal cause of action is the exclusive remedy, and declares that the substantive law to be applied "shall be derived from the law, including choice of law principles, of the State in which the crash occurred unless such law is inconsistent with or preempted by Federal law." § 408(b)(2). The only substantive rule of decision that the statute prescribes is that an air carrier's liability for all claims arising out of the four crashes shall not exceed the limits of the carrier's liability insurance coverage. § 408(a).

The Act confers on the federal district court in the Southern District of New York "original and exclusive jurisdiction over all actions brought for any claim [including property and personal injury claims] resulting from or relating to the terrorist-related aircraft crashes of September 11, 2001." § 408(b)(3). Absent diversity, would that grant of jurisdiction be constitutional in a damage action against an air carrier? Insofar as the provision limiting the liability of air carriers might help to sustain jurisdiction in such a case, what about a damage action against some other defendant (for example, a security firm alleged to have been lax in operating airport metal detectors), in which the statute would not appear to supply any ingredient of federal law?

---

3. THE SCOPE OF THE STATUTORY GRANT OF FEDERAL QUESTION JURISDICTION

A. THE STRUCTURE OF "ARISING UNDER" JURISDICTION UNDER THE FEDERAL QUESTION STATUTE

Louisville & Nashville R.R. Co. v. Mottley

211 U.S. 149, 29 S.Ct. 42, 53 L.Ed. 126 (1908).
Appeal from the Circuit Court of the United States for the
Western District of Kentucky.

■ MR. JUSTICE MOODY delivered the opinion of the Court.

[Mr. and Mrs. Mottley sued the railroad for specific performance of a contract under which the railroad agreed to issue free passes to the Mottleys for life, in exchange for their release of damage claims arising from a collision. The complaint alleged that, beginning in 1907, the railroad refused to renew the passes, relying on a 1906 Act of Congress forbidding free passes, and further alleged that (i) the 1906 Act did not prohibit free passes pursuant to contracts made before its enactment, but (ii) if construed retroactively to invalidate the Mottleys' contract, the Act deprived them of property without due process. After the federal circuit court entered a decree of specific performance, the railroad appealed to the Supreme Court.]

* * * We do not deem it necessary, however, to consider either of [the questions raised by the bill of complaint,] because, in our opinion, the court below was without jurisdiction of the cause. Neither party has questioned that jurisdiction, but it is the duty of this court to see to it that the jurisdiction of the Circuit Court, which is defined and limited by statute, is not exceeded. This duty we have frequently performed of our own motion. [*E.g.,*] Mansfield, C & L.M. Railway Company v. Swan, 111 U.S. 379, 382.

There was no diversity of citizenship and it is not and cannot be suggested that there was any ground of jurisdiction, except that the case was a "suit * * * arising under the Constitution and laws of the United States." It is the settled interpretation of these words, as used in this statute, conferring jurisdiction, that a suit arises under the Constitution and laws of the United States only when the plaintiff's statement of his own cause of action shows that it is based upon those laws or that

Constitution. It is not enough that the plaintiff alleges some anticipated defense to his cause of action and asserts that the defense is invalidated by some provision of the Constitution * * *. Although such allegations show that very likely, in the course of the litigation, a question under the Constitution would arise, they do not show that the suit, that is, the plaintiff's original cause of action, arises under the Constitution. In Tennessee v. Union & Planters' Bank, 152 U.S. 454, the plaintiff, the State of Tennessee, brought suit * * * to recover from the defendant certain taxes alleged to be due under the laws of the State. The plaintiff alleged that the defendant claimed an immunity from the taxation by virtue of its charter, and that therefore the tax was void, because in violation of the provision of the Constitution of the United States, which forbids any State from passing a law impairing the obligation of contracts. The cause was held to be beyond the jurisdiction of the Circuit Court, the court saying, by Mr. Justice Gray (p. 464), "a suggestion of one party, that the other will or may set up a claim under the Constitution or laws of the United States, does not make the suit one arising under that Constitution or those laws." * * *

The interpretation of the act which we have stated was first announced in Metcalf v. Watertown, 128 U.S. 586, and has since been repeated and applied in * * * [citing 17 cases]. The application of this rule to the case at bar is decisive against the jurisdiction of the Circuit Court.

It is ordered that the *Judgment be reversed and the case remitted to the Circuit Court with instructions to dismiss the suit for want of jurisdiction.*

NOTE ON THE MOTTLEY CASE AND THE WELL-PLEADED COMPLAINT RULE

(1) The Interpretation of the Jurisdictional Statute.

(a) The 1875 Act conferring general federal question jurisdiction and its successors—including today's 28 U.S.C. § 1331—have always used the language of the Constitution to describe the statutory jurisdiction.[1] The 1875 Act originated as a Senate amendment to a House bill concerning the removal jurisdiction in diversity actions; the Act was hurriedly enacted at the close of a session without substantial debate.[2] The most significant portion of the legislative history was a statement by the bill's sponsor, Senator Carpenter. Following a debate about the scope of diversity jurisdiction, he referred to the views of Justice Story that Congress is obliged

---

[1] The only possibly significant departure in the 1875 Act from the language of the Constitution was the use of the word "suits" instead of "cases". Justice Miller, dissenting in New Orleans, M. & T. Railroad Co. v. Mississippi, 102 U.S. 135, 143 (1880), seized upon this difference in arguing that under the statute, jurisdiction depended on the law under which the plaintiff claimed and could not rest on a federal defense. The conclusion, though not the argument, was adopted in Tennessee v. Union & Planters' Bank, 152 U.S. 454 (1894), and was not affected by the substitution, in the Act of Mar 3, 1911, ch. 231,§ 24, 36 Stat. 1087, 1091, of the phrase "matter in controversy" for "suits". Today, § 1331 confers jurisdiction over "civil actions".

[2] See Frankfurter & Landis, The Business of the Supreme Court 65–69 (1928); Chadbourn & Levin, *Original Jurisdiction of Federal Questions*, 90 U.Pa.L.Rev. 639, 642–45 (1942); Forrester, *The Nature of a "Federal Question"*, 16 Tul.L.Rev. 362, 374–77 (1942).

to vest all of Article III's judicial power in the federal courts, see pp. 308–310, *supra*. He then said: "The act of 1789 did not confer the whole power which the Constitution conferred; it did not do what the Supreme Court has said Congress ought to do; it did not perform what the Supreme Court has declared to be the duty of Congress. This bill does. * * * This bill gives precisely the power which the Constitution confers—nothing more, nothing less." 2 Cong.Rec. 4986–87 (1874). Senator Carpenter's invocation of Justice Story, however, was in response to objections that the Senate amendment authorized suit in whatever federal district a defendant might be found and thereby eliminated the requirement, dating from 1789, that one of the parties in a diversity case must reside in the district in which suit was brought.

(b) Relying on Senator Carpenter's statement and on the identity of language, Dean Forrester, note 2, *supra*, argued that the statutory and constitutional "arising under" provisions should be "considered synonymous".[3] But Carpenter's statement did not directly address the federal question jurisdiction. And in light of the manifest differences between the functions of the constitutional grant and the statutory grant, there is strong reason to doubt the appropriateness of treating the common language as encompassing identical territory. Indeed, the expansive approach of Osborn would not be tenable as a measure of the statutory jurisdiction.

(c) The Pacific Railroad Removal Cases, 115 U.S. 1 (1885), p.793, *supra*, go further than any decision before or since in applying the general federal question statute and in suggesting that the 1875 Act filled the whole of the constitutional space provided for "arising under" cases.[4] The Court there held that federal incorporation of a party to a case by itself made the case one "arising under" federal law within the meaning of the 1875 Act. At the time of the decision, the requirements for removal jurisdiction were not tied, as they are today, to those for original jurisdiction; the 1875 Act permitted removal by either party of any suit, involving the requisite amount, "arising under the Constitution or laws of the United States".

But the equation of statutory and constitutional jurisdiction posited by the Pacific Railroad Removal Cases is no longer authoritative in light of subsequent decisions; the opinion in Verlinden, *supra*, is particularly clear on this point. And Congress has overruled the more specific holding of the Pacific Railroad Removal Cases that the general federal question statute embraces suits by or against federally incorporated bodies. See 28 U.S.C. § 1349.

---

[3]   Professors Chadbourn and Levin, *supra* note 2, at 649–50, agree that the 1875 Act should have been read as conferring all of the federal question jurisdiction permissible under the Constitution, or at least all of it permissible under the Osborn opinion. But, they say, the draftsmen recognized the need to protect the federal courts from a "flood of litigation technically within the broad limits staked out by Marshall, but actually unrelated to the purpose of the Act". They argue that § 5 of the Act was such a provision: it required dismissal or remand if "it shall appear * * * at any time after such suit has been brought or removed * * * that such suit does not really and substantially involve a dispute or controversy properly within the jurisdiction of said circuit court". In only one case does the Supreme Court seem to have applied the act in this fashion. See Robinson v. Anderson, 121 U.S. 522, 524 (1887).

[4]   For cases antedating the Pacific Railroad Removal Cases that appeared to construe the 1875 removal provision more narrowly (and which the Court has continued to treat as authoritative), see, *e.g.*, Albright v. Teas, 106 U.S. 613 (1883); Little York Gold-Washing & Water Co. v. Keyes, 96 U.S. 199 (1877).

(2) The Merits of the Well-Pleaded Complaint Rule. The holding of Mottley is universally known as the well-pleaded complaint rule. How effective is that rule in defining federal question jurisdiction so as to reach cases, and only cases, in which a dispute "really" turns on federal law?[5]

(a) Mottley is an example of a case that falls outside the statutory grant but turns on resolution of a federal question; indeed, after the Supreme Court's decision, the case was adjudicated in the state courts, where the federal questions proved decisive, and ultimately were reviewed by the Supreme Court, see 219 U.S. 467 (1911). It is also true that in some cases squarely within the statutory grant of federal jurisdiction, the only decisive questions may involve state law—for example, when the dispute centers on whether there was a valid settlement and release pertaining to a federal claim, or in a suit for patent or copyright infringement where the only dispute concerns the validity or meaning of a licensing contract.

But no rule is likely to be a perfect filter that permits the federal courts to hear all the federal question cases that are deemed to be appropriate for federal adjudication, and only those cases. Consider, as you read the remainder of this Paragraph, whether the well-pleaded complaint rule—especially as it interacts with the scope of removal jurisdiction—is a reasonably good filter or a highly imperfect one.

(b) The well-pleaded complaint rule could be viewed as a rule of convenience, which avoids making original jurisdiction turn on speculation about which issues will be decisive in the litigation. But the rule has a broader impact because, ever since 1887, the general removal statute (now 28 U.S.C. § 1441) reaches only cases that fall within the original jurisdiction of the district courts. Except when permitted by a more specialized removal statute (for example, 28 U.S.C. § 1442, governing suits against federal officers), removal based on a federal defense is not authorized. Thus, a case like Mottley, if brought in a state court, could not be removed to federal court even after federal issues were raised by the railroad's answer and in turn by the Mottleys' reply.[6]

(c) The rule tying removal to original jurisdiction has a profound effect on the jurisdictional structure and even on our ways of thinking about that structure. Debates about the "need for a federal forum" frequently focus only on whether plaintiffs with a claim of federal right should have access to a federal court. But doesn't this overlook defendants with a federal defense? See Bator, *The State Courts and Federal Constitutional Litigation*, 22 Wm. & Mary L.Rev. 605, 608–11 (1981). Why should they be forced to litigate in a state court? Is the point that the federal ingredient, when contained in the plaintiff's case, is likely to predominate, while a federal defense is more likely to be only one element in a case dominated by state-law issues? (But what

---

[5]   For criticism of the well-pleaded complaint rule, see Doernberg, *There's No Reason for It; It's Just Our Policy: Why the Well-Pleaded Complaint Rule Sabotages the Purposes of Federal Question Jurisdiction*, 38 Hastings L.J. 597 (1987).

[6]   Until 1986, subject matter jurisdiction in cases removed under § 1441 turned not only on the existence of original federal court jurisdiction in the removed case but also on the existence of state subject matter jurisdiction. Thus, if the state court lacked jurisdiction because the case was one within exclusive federal jurisdiction, it could not be removed to federal court. See, *e.g.*, Lambert Run Coal Co. v. Baltimore & Ohio R.R. Co., 258 U.S. 377 (1922). This rule was much-criticized, and Congress overturned it in 1986 by adding a new subsection [now subsection (f)] to § 1441 (100 Stat. 637 (1986)): "The court to which a civil action is removed * * * is not precluded from hearing and determining any claim in such civil action because the State court from which such civil action is removed did not have jurisdiction over that claim."

about cases like Mottley, in which the only issues actually in dispute were federal?) Or is the point that considerations of federalism make it appropriate to give the state court—the "enforcement" court—the first crack when the claimant seeks to enforce state law and federal law merely limits the extent to which state law may be validly enforced?

Note, however, that federal statutory or constitutional defenses can frequently be recast as affirmative claims of federal right. For example, suppose that a company sued by state regulators for violating a state regulation of cigarette advertising defends on the grounds that a federal statute preempts the state regulation and that the state statute violates the First Amendment; whatever the merits of the defenses, the case would not be removable. But the company, before being sued, might first bring a federal court action to enjoin enforcement of the state regulation on the grounds that it is preempted and is unconstitutional. And if, as is generally true, the relevant federal remedial law (express or implied) gives the company a federal cause of action for injunctive relief against conflicting state law, the company's action for an injunction would fall within the federal question jurisdiction. See, *e.g.*, Shaw v. Delta Airlines, p. 844, *infra*, and the line of cases flowing from Ex parte Young, 209 U.S. 123 (1908), discussed in Chap. IX, Section 2, *infra*. Thus, existing law does not generally exclude from federal court all litigants whose contention is that state-law claims are rendered *pro tanto* invalid by federal law.[7]

Isn't the underlying difficulty that litigants do not come labeled as "plaintiffs" and "defendants" as a matter of preexisting Platonic reality? Whether one is a plaintiff or a defendant—when the law is a sword and when it is a shield—is itself contingent, a product of our remedial and substantive rules.

(d) Consider again the cigarette advertising example. As noted, if the company is sued in state court, it cannot remove after filing a federal defense. By contrast, suppose that the company had struck first and sued, in *state court*, to enjoin the state law as violating both a federal statute and the First Amendment; in that case, the defendant could remove the case to federal court.

Is this pair of results backwards? Professor Wechsler, in *Federal Jurisdiction and the Revision of the Judicial Code*, 13 Law & Contemp.Probs. 216, 233–34 (1948), advocated allowing removal "by the party who puts forth the federal right". He argued that "the reason for providing the initial federal forum is the fear that state courts will view the federal right ungenerously. That reason is quite plainly absent in * * * the case where the *defendant* may remove because the *plaintiff's* case is federal. If in any case the reason can be present, it is only in the situations where [under § 1441] removal is denied."

Recall that until 1914, the Supreme Court could review state court judgments only if the state court failed to uphold a claim of a federal right or

---

7　But *cf.* Southland Corp. v. Keating, 465 U.S. 1 (1984), which held (in a case coming from a state court) that the Federal Arbitration Act preempts a California statute that rendered certain claims unarbitrable. In a puzzling footnote the Court said: "While the Federal Arbitration Act creates federal substantive law requiring the parties to honor arbitration agreements, it does not create any independent federal-question jurisdiction under 28 U.S.C. § 1331 or otherwise." The Court apparently read the Arbitration Act—which makes agreements to arbitrate "valid, irrevocable, and enforceable" (9 U.S.C. § 2)—as a substantive provision that negates a defense of unenforceability but that does not give rise to a federal right of action.

immunity; in that year, Congress expanded the Court's appellate jurisdiction to permit review of state court judgments that did uphold a claim of federal right or immunity. See p. 462, *supra*. Although that history suggests that federal review to avoid overprotection of federal rights is important, it also suggests that review to avoid underprotection of federal rights was historically viewed as *more* important. If so, it could be seen as odd that a defendant may remove a case because of concern that the state court will overprotect the federal rights of the plaintiff but not because of concern that the state court will underprotect the defendant's own federal defense.

(e) Compare Judge Posner's defense of existing law: "In many [cases] the federal defense would have little merit—would, indeed, have been concocted purely to confer federal jurisdiction—yet this fact might be impossible to determine with any confidence without having a trial before the trial. I grant that frivolous federal claims are also a problem when only plaintiffs can use them to get into court, but a less serious problem. If the plaintiff gets thrown out of federal court because his claim is frivolous, and he must therefore start over in state court, he has lost time, and the loss may be fatal if meanwhile the statute of limitations has run. But the defendant may be delighted to see the plaintiff's case thrown out of federal court when the court discovers that the federal defense is frivolous. Thus, it would not be a complete solution to the problem of the frivolous federal defense to allow removal on the basis of a federal question first raised by way of defense but to give the district court discretion to remand the case back to the state court." Posner, The Federal Courts: Challenge and Reform 302–03 (1996).

(f) Professor Field proposes expanding removal jurisdiction so that, subject to some possible exceptions, it would embrace cases in which the defendant's answer, or possibly further pleadings, "reveal that the case is likely to turn upon federal law." Field, *Removal Reform: A Solution for Federal Question Jurisdiction, Forum Shopping, and Duplicative State Litigation*, 88 Ind.L.J. 611, 642 (2013). As her title suggests, one advantage that she claims for that approach is that it would reduce the number of cases in which pending suits in federal and state court overlap, for under her scheme the party that prefers federal court would likely be able to remove an overlapping state court action.

(3) Counterclaims and the Well-Pleaded Complaint Rule. In Holmes Group, Inc. v. Vornado Air Circulation Systems, Inc., 535 U.S. 826 (2002), the Court held without dissent that a federal counterclaim, even when compulsory, does not establish "arising under" jurisdiction. Justice Scalia's opinion for the Court reasoned that a contrary rule would (i) permit the defendant to defeat the plaintiff's forum choice by raising a federal counterclaim, (ii) "radically expand the class of removable cases" and thereby fail to respect "the rightful independence of state governments", and (iii) undermine administrative simplicity by making jurisdictional determinations depend on the content not only of the complaint but also of responsive pleadings.[8]

---

[8]   The case actually involved the interpretation of 28 U.S.C. § 1295(a)(1), which, with certain exceptions not pertinent here, gives the Court of Appeals for the Federal Circuit exclusive appellate jurisdiction over the decision of a district court whose jurisdiction "was based, in whole or in part, on [28 U.S.C.] § 1338". Section 1338 confers exclusive district court jurisdiction over, *inter alia*, cases "arising under" any Act of Congress relating to patents. In Holmes Group, the plaintiff's complaint raised a federal claim but not one relating to patents; the defendant counterclaimed for patent infringement. The Supreme Court ruled that the case

(4) The Well-Pleaded Complaint Rule and Cases of Exclusive Federal Jurisdiction. Section 1331's grant of federal question jurisdiction is concurrent with the state courts, giving the plaintiff a forum choice. If the plaintiff chooses to file a case falling within § 1331 in state court, the defendant may remove. Thus, such a case will be litigated in state court only if both plaintiff and defendant so choose. See generally p. 422, *supra*.

By contrast, some more specialized jurisdictional provisions both within and outside of the Judicial Code (Title 28) make federal court jurisdiction exclusive. See, *e.g.*, 28 U.S.C. § 1337 (antitrust cases); *id.* § 1338 (patent and copyright cases); 15 U.S.C. § 78aa (certain securities cases). See generally pp. 418–422, *supra*. Typically, these provisions use the same statutory phrase ("arising under") as does § 1331. See, *e.g.*, 28 U.S.C. § 1338 (providing in part for exclusive federal jurisdiction "of any civil action arising under any Act of Congress relating to patents").

(a) These grants of exclusive jurisdiction have generally been interpreted as embodying the well-pleaded complaint rule. See, *e.g.*, Holmes Group, Inc. v. Vornado Air Circulation Systems, Inc., 535 U.S. 826, 829–30 (2002). As a result, when important questions of (for example) federal antitrust, patent, or copyright law arise as defenses to state law claims, the case lies outside of original federal question jurisdiction. Suppose, for example, that a plaintiff sues a non-diverse party for breach of the defendant's promise to pay royalties in exchange for a patent license; the defendant concedes the failure to pay but defends on the ground that the patent is invalid and as a result the promise is unenforceable. Although the case will turn exclusively on the federal issue of patent validity, that issue will be litigated entirely in state court.[9]

(b) In one important area of exclusive jurisdiction, cases arising under federal intellectual property laws, Congress altered the regime to restrict the role of state courts. The Leahy-Smith America Invents Act, Pub. L. No. 112–29, § 19, 125 Stat. 284, 331 (2011), a major patent reform measure, amended

---

did not "arise under" the patent laws by virtue of the patent counterclaim, and hence held that the Federal Circuit lacked appellate jurisdiction under § 1295(a)(1).

In reaching that decision, the Court's opinion rested more broadly on the premises that (i) the meaning of "arising under" in § 1331 and § 1338 is the same, and (ii) a counterclaim, because it appears in the answer, cannot provide the basis for "arising under" jurisdiction consistently with the well-pleaded complaint rule. The Court specifically noted that its approach also governs whether a case is removable from state court under § 1441(a). But *cf.* Horton v. Liberty Mut. Ins. Co., p. 631, *supra*.

With respect to patent and other cases embraced by § 1338, Congress has overturned the specific holding of the Holmes Group decision. See Paragraph (4)(b), *infra*. But the decision's rationale remains the law with respect to the interpretation of § 1331 and of other statutes using the "arising under" language.

[9] Sometimes plaintiffs have a choice of theories on which to bring suit for what is essentially the same complaint, and that choice determines where the litigation can occur. Consider disputes about whether the licensee of a patent or copyright has exploited the intellectual property right in a fashion unauthorized by the license. If the licensor alleges infringement, the federal courts plainly have jurisdiction, even if the only dispute is whether the licensee's action exceeded the scope of the license contract. See, *e.g.*, The Fair v. Kohler Die & Specialty Co., 228 U.S. 22 (1913). See also Medtronic, Inc. v. Mirowski Family Ventures, LLC, 132 S.Ct. 843 (2014) (if a licensee and a licensor dispute whether the licensee's product infringes the licensor's patent, and the licensee fails to pay royalties under license agreement, the licensor may sue for patent infringement). Indeed, 28 U.S.C. § 1338(a) makes federal jurisdiction over such an infringement action *exclusive*. On the other hand, if the licensor frames its claim as one for breach of contract—because the defendant violated an agreement to use the licensed property in only a specified way—the case would not arise under federal law. See, *e.g.*, Luckett v. Delpark, Inc., 270 U.S. 496, 510–11 (1926).

28 U.S.C. § 1338, the statute conferring exclusive federal court jurisdiction over patent, plant variety protection, and copyright cases, to read as follows:

> "(a) The district courts shall have original jurisdiction of any civil action arising under any Act of Congress relating to patents, plant variety protection, copyrights and trademarks. No State court shall have jurisdiction over any claim for relief arising under any Act of Congress relating to patents, plant variety protection, or copyrights. For purposes of this subsection, the term 'State' includes any State of the United States, the District of Columbia, the Commonwealth of Puerto Rico, the United States Virgin Islands, American Samoa, Guam, and the Northern Mariana Islands."

The first sentence is unchanged; the second and third sentences substitute for the second sentence of the previous provision.[10]

Note that while the first sentence of section § 1338(a), like § 1331 and many other jurisdictional provisions, speaks of federal court jurisdiction over *a civil action*, the second sentence of § 1338(a) excludes state court jurisdiction over *a claim for relief*. Federal Rule of Civil Procedure 8(a) makes clear that a claim for relief is not limited to claims in a plaintiff's complaint; it includes, for example, counterclaims. As amended, § 1338(a) thus appears to preclude a state court from hearing a patent, plant variety, or copyright counterclaim. The jurisdictional provisions of the Leahy-Smith Act appear to contemplate that a state court defendant may file a patent, plant variety, or copyright counterclaim in state court (and perhaps must if the counterclaim is compulsory under state law)—even though under § 1338(a) the state courts lack jurisdiction to decide that counterclaim—and then the defendant or the plaintiff may, under § 1454, remove the action to federal court.[11]

---

[10] Before 2011, the second sentence read: "Such jurisdiction shall be exclusive of the courts of the states in patent, plant variety protection and copyright cases."

[11] The 2011 Act also contains a new provision, codified as 28 U.S.C. § 1454, that authorizes *any party* to remove a civil action in state court in which any party asserts a claim for relief under the patent, plant variety, or copyright laws; by contrast, the general removal statute, 28 U.S.C. § 1441, which previously governed removal of civil actions filed under § 1338(a), authorizes only the defendant to remove. New § 1454 also specifies that removal is not precluded because the state court lacked jurisdiction over the claim.

The 2011 Act also changes the jurisdiction of the Court of Appeals for the Federal Circuit. Under 28 U.S.C. § 1295(a)(1), that court was initially given exclusive appellate jurisdiction over patent and plant variety cases arising under § 1338, in order to centralize appellate resolution of such matters in a specialized court. The Holmes Group case held that a civil action in which a defendant asserted a patent counterclaim did not arise under the patent laws within the meaning of § 1338, and hence, appellate jurisdiction lay in the regional court of appeals, not in the Court of Appeals for the Federal Circuit. As amended in 2011, 28 U.S.C. § 1295(a)(1) now gives the Federal Circuit exclusive jurisdiction "in any civil action arising under, *or in any civil action in which a party has asserted a compulsory counterclaim arising under,* any Act of Congress relating to patents or plant variety protection." The pre-2011 grant of appellate jurisdiction to the Federal Circuit was too narrow to ensure centralized review of patent cases, see note 8, *supra,* and the grant in 2011 of appellate jurisdiction over counterclaims makes enormous sense. (Indeed, what is the reason, under current law, to exclude from the Federal Circuit's appellate jurisdiction review of patent counterclaims that are not *compulsory?*).

But the jurisdiction that remains after the 2011 Act is also too broad. Imagine a case in which a plaintiff files a patent infringement action in federal court, the defendant counterclaims for a state law business tort, and the only issue raised on appeal concerns the trial court's decision of the business tort counterclaim. Under § 1295(a)(1), both before and after 2011, the Federal Circuit would have exclusive jurisdiction over the appeal, because the civil action arose under the patent laws. But it makes little sense to direct that appeal, which includes no patent law issue, to the Federal Circuit rather than to the regional court of appeals.

Note, however, that the Leahy-Smith Act did not completely strip state courts of authority to decide patent issues: a patent law defense (as distinguished from a counterclaim or other claim for relief) still does not provide a basis for removal. Does this power of state courts to decide issues of federal law embraced by a scheme of exclusive jurisdiction undermine the justification for such exclusivity?[12] Should the Leahy-Smith Act have authorized removal of cases in which a federal patent law defense has been raised?

More broadly, is there any reason of policy why the jurisdictional approach of the Leahy-Smith Act should not extend to claims for relief arising under other schemes where federal jurisdiction is exclusive (for example, the antitrust laws, or ERISA)? Indeed, should Congress more broadly permit removal on the basis of any compulsory counterclaim that itself arises under federal law, without regard to its relationship to schemes of exclusive federal jurisdiction? On the basis of any counterclaim that arises under federal law?

(5) Jurisdiction over Actions to Compel Arbitration. In Vaden v. Discover Bank, 556 U.S. 49 (2009), the Court divided 5–4 on a difficult issue involving a federal court action seeking to compel arbitration. The litigation began when Discover Bank (through an affiliate) sued Vaden under state law in state court to recover past-due charges on a credit card. Vaden counterclaimed that the charges and fees in question violated state law, though both parties later agreed, and the Supreme Court assumed, that the counterclaims were entirely based on federal law, because a provision of the Federal Deposit Insurance Act (FDIA) "completely preempted" any applicable state law and supplied the only possible basis for relief. (See pp. 850–853, *infra*.) At this point in the litigation, Discover filed a federal court action against Vaden under § 4 of the Federal Arbitration Act (FAA) (discussed at pp. 604–605, *supra*.), seeking to compel arbitration, which it contended was prescribed by the credit card agreement. Section 4 authorizes a party to seek federal district court enforcement of an agreement to arbitrate if "save for such agreement, [the district court] would have jurisdiction * * * of the subject matter of a suit arising out of the controversy between the parties".

On review, the Supreme Court held that the federal district court lacked jurisdiction over Discover's petition to compel arbitration. First, the Court unanimously agreed that the quoted language in § 4 did not refer to a "controversy" concerning an arbitration agreement (even though such a controversy might be governed by federal law under the FAA), but rather directed the federal court to "look through" the dispute over arbitrability to see whether the court would have had subject matter jurisdiction over the underlying controversy between the parties. Then the majority, per Justice Ginsburg, went on to hold that the "whole" controversy between the parties was one arising under state law (based as it was on Discover's claim for unpaid charges and fees), and that under the well-pleaded complaint rule as interpreted in Holmes Group, Vaden's counterclaim did not give rise to federal question jurisdiction under § 1331.

Dissenting in part, Chief Justice Roberts (joined by Justices Stevens, Breyer, and Alito) contended that the "controversy" referred to in § 4 was the controversy allegedly subject to arbitration, which in this instance was Vaden's federal law counterclaim, as Discover was not seeking arbitration of

---

[12] *Cf.* pp. 835–836, *infra* (discussing whether state court determinations of issues arising under schemes of exclusive federal jurisdiction should have issue-preclusive effect in federal court).

its state law claim against Vaden. He argued that federal question jurisdiction would clearly have existed had the only litigation been an original action by Vaden for violation of the FDIA (or, perhaps, by Discover for a declaratory judgment that the FDIA had not been violated), and that the sequence of the actual litigation in the case should not control. That Discover could also have sought arbitration of the counterclaim in state court (a point made by the majority) should not, the Chief Justice argued, deprive it of access to a federal forum.[13]

(6) The Standard for Congressional Divestment of § 1331 Jurisdiction. In Mims v. Arrow Financial Services, LLC, 132 S.Ct. 740 (2012), the Court held that an explicit congressional grant of *state court* jurisdiction over a federal cause of action did not oust federal court jurisdiction under § 1331. The Telephone Consumer Protection Act of 1991 (TCPA) (codified as amended at 42 U.S.C. § 227), which prohibits some telemarketing practices, authorizes States to bring civil actions on behalf of their citizens when there is a pattern or practice of violation; the federal courts have exclusive jurisdiction over such actions. The TCPA also authorizes private parties to seek judicial redress "if otherwise permitted by the laws or rules of court of a State, * * * in an appropriate court of that State".

In Mims, a unanimous Supreme Court held that Congress' express grant of state court jurisdiction did not preclude private parties from suing in federal court. Justice Ginsburg's opinion noted the deeply rooted presumption that an explicit grant of federal court jurisdiction does not oust concurrent state court jurisdiction—a presumption that can be overcome only " 'by an explicit statutory directive, by unmistakable implication from legislative history, or by a clear incompatibility between state-court jurisdiction and federal interests' " (quoting Gulf Offshore Co. v. Mobil Oil Corp., 453 U.S. 473, 478 (1981), p. 413, *supra*). " '[D]ivestment of district court jurisdiction,' " she stated, "should be found no more readily than 'divestmen[t] of state court jurisdiction,' given 'the longstanding and explicit grant of federal question jurisdiction in 28 U.S.C. § 1331' " (quoting ErieNet, Inc. v. Velocity Net, Inc., 156 F.3d 513, 523 (3d Cir.1998) (Alito, J., dissenting)). The defendant argued that in view of the presumption of concurrent state court jurisdiction, the Act's specific acknowledgment of state court jurisdiction would be superfluous if it merely gave state courts a non-exclusive jurisdiction. Justice Ginsburg responded that given the exclusive federal jurisdiction provided by the Act over suits by States, "Congress may simply have wanted to avoid any argument that" federal court jurisdiction over private actions is also exclusive.

---

[13] The Court's approach bears some resemblance to that followed in the context of declaratory judgment actions, as in both settings the determination of jurisdiction over the pending federal court action requires the court to "look through" that action to assess whether there would be jurisdiction over the dispute between the parties as framed in some other way. See pp. 841–843, *infra*. However, under the majority's opinion in Vaden, in "looking through," the court considers only whether there would be jurisdiction over the actual litigation already pending, whereas under the Declaratory Judgment Act, the court looks through the declaratory action to assess whether there is *any* hypothetical non-declaratory action (whether or not yet filed) between the parties that raises the same federal issue as the declaratory action. And in the declaratory judgment context, the plaintiff in the hypothetical action could be either the plaintiff or the defendant in the pending declaratory action.

INTRODUCTORY NOTE ON THE SCOPE OF FEDERAL QUESTION JURISDICTION UNDER 28 U.S.C. § 1331

The Mottley decision tells us that under § 1331, jurisdiction cannot depend on federal questions not contained in the well-pleaded complaint. But in order for jurisdiction to exist under § 1331, just what kind of federal question must a well-pleaded complaint contain? Although Article III might permit Congress to pass a statute conferring federal court jurisdiction over any case in which there is a federal ingredient within the meaning of Osborn, § 1331 has been understood to require more than that. Exactly what § 1331 does require is the focus of the remainder of this Section.

American Well Works Co. v. Layne & Bowler Co.

241 U.S. 257, 36 S.Ct. 585, 60 L.Ed. 987 (1916).
Error to the District Court of the United States for the Eastern District of Arkansas.

■ MR. JUSTICE HOLMES delivered the opinion of the Court.

[The question presented is whether the district court properly concluded that the cause of action arises under the federal patent laws.] * * *

Of course the question depends upon the plaintiff's declaration. That may be summed up in a few words. The plaintiff alleges that it owns, manufactures and sells a certain pump, has or has applied for a patent for it, and that the pump is known as the best in the market. It then alleges that the defendants have falsely and maliciously libeled and slandered the plaintiff's title to the pump by stating that the pump and certain parts thereof are infringements upon the defendants' pump and certain parts thereof and that without probable cause they have brought suits against some parties who are using the plaintiff's pump, and that they are threatening suits against all who use it. * * *

It is evident that the claim for damages is based upon conduct, or, more specifically, language, tending to persuade the public to withdraw its custom from the plaintiff and having that effect to its damage. Such conduct having such effect is equally actionable whether it produces the result by persuasion, by threats or by falsehood, and it is enough to allege and prove the conduct and effect, leaving the defendant to justify if he can. If the conduct complained of is persuasion, it may be justified by the fact that the defendant is a competitor, or by good faith and reasonable grounds. If it is a statement of fact, it may be justified, absolutely or with qualifications, by proof that the statement is true. But all such justifications are defences and raise issues that are no part of the plaintiff's case. In the present instance it is part of the plaintiff's case that it had a business to be damaged; whether built up by patents or without them does not matter. It is no part of it to prove anything concerning the defendants' patent or that the plaintiff did not infringe the same—still less to prove anything concerning any patent of its own. The material statement complained of is that the plaintiff infringes— which may be true notwithstanding the plaintiff's patent. That is merely a piece of evidence. Furthermore, the damage alleged presumably is rather the consequence of the threat to sue than of the statement that the plaintiff's pump infringed the defendants' rights.

A suit for damages to business caused by a threat to sue under the patent law is not itself a suit under the patent law. And the same is true when the damage is caused by a statement of fact—that the defendant has a patent which is infringed. What makes the defendants' act a wrong is its manifest tendency to injure the plaintiff's business, and the wrong is the same whatever the means by which it is accomplished. But whether it is a wrong or not depends upon the law of the State where the act is done, not upon the patent law, and therefore the suit arises under the law of the State. A suit arises under the law that creates the cause of action. The fact that the justification may involve the validity and infringement of a patent is no more material to the question under what law the suit is brought than it would be in an action of contract. If the State adopted for civil proceedings the saying of the old criminal law: the greater the truth, the greater the libel, the validity of the patent would not come in question at all. In Massachusetts the truth would not be a defence if the statement was made from disinterested malevolence. The State is master of the whole matter, and if it saw fit to do away with actions of this type altogether, no one, we imagine, would suppose that they still could be maintained under the patent laws of the United States.

Judgment reversed.

■ MR. JUSTICE MCKENNA dissents, being of the opinion that the case involves a direct and substantial controversy under the patent laws.

———

NOTE ON "ARISING UNDER" JURISDICTION AND THE CAUSE OF ACTION TEST

(1) The Cause of Action Test. The "cause of action" test that Justice Holmes announced should not be viewed as a canonical statement of the reach of § 1331. As Judge Friendly famously remarked, "Justice Holmes' formula is more useful for inclusion than for the exclusion for which it was intended." T.B. Harms Co. v. Eliscu, 339 F.2d 823, 827 (2d Cir.1964). Holmes' formula does, however, remain helpful as a rule of inclusion. With only the most uncertain and limited exceptions (see Paragraph (4), *infra*), § 1331 confers federal question jurisdiction when the plaintiff's complaint pleads a non-frivolous federal cause of action. That is so even when the only dispute between the parties is about the facts (or indeed when there is no dispute about facts or law, as may be true, for example, when a default judgment is entered).

But Holmes' test fails as a rule of exclusion. As is explored more fully in the next principal case, Grable & Sons Metal Prods., Inc. v. Darue Eng'g & Mfg., p. 825, *infra*, and in the Notes that precede and follow that opinion, jurisdiction under § 1331 has been upheld in some cases not involving a federal cause of action, on the basis that a state law cause of action incorporates a question of federal law in a fashion that merits the exercise of federal question jurisdiction.[1]

---

[1] Professors Woolhandler & Collins, in *Federal Question Jurisdiction and Justice Holmes*, 84 Notre Dame L.Rev. 2151 (2009), contend that cases in which federal law was a substantial ingredient but not the source of the cause of action may well have constituted the "paradigm" of

(2) The Substantiality of the Asserted Federal Cause of Action.
Complaints alleging doubtful or frivolous federal causes of action pose
distinctive problems. The Court addressed this issue in Bell v. Hood, 327
U.S. 678 (1946), a suit against FBI agents, seeking damages for arrests,
searches, and seizures in violation of the Fourth and Fifth Amendments. The
theory of the complaint was at that time novel—that those constitutional
provisions gave victims of the violations an implied federal right of action for
damages. With Justice Black writing, the Court upheld the district court's
jurisdiction, reasoning that "[j]urisdiction * * * is not defeated * * * by the
possibility that the averments might fail to state a cause of action on which
petitioners could actually recover"; that question "must be decided after and
not before the court has assumed jurisdiction". If there is no ground for relief,
then, Justice Black said, the complaint should be dismissed on the merits.
His opinion did, however, note "previously carved out exceptions" in which
"a suit may sometimes be dismissed for want of jurisdiction"—where the
claim "appears to be immaterial and made solely for the purpose of obtaining
jurisdiction or where such a claim is wholly insubstantial and frivolous." But
those exceptions, he said, did not apply, as the Court had never decided
whether the federal courts can award compensation for violations of the
Fourth and Fifth Amendments by federal officers, a question depending on
the scope of those constitutional provisions and on the interpretation of the
statute conferring federal question jurisdiction. "Thus, the right of the
petitioners to recover * * * will be sustained if the Constitution and laws of
the United States are given one construction and will be defeated if they are
given another. For this reason the district court has jurisdiction."

Some years later, Justice Rehnquist, dissenting from the denial of
certiorari in Yazoo County Indus. Dev. Corp. v. Suthoff, 454 U.S. 1157 (1982),
urged reexamination of the approach set forth in Bell v. Hood, which, he said,
requires a "three tiered analysis" of motions to dismiss: a complaint may
(i) be so wanting that it is dismissed for want of jurisdiction, (ii) establish
jurisdiction but be dismissed for failure to state a claim, or (iii) state a proper
claim not subject to dismissal. He suggested that Bell was wrong to treat a
frivolous claim as falling outside the district courts' jurisdiction, and favored
recognizing only two tiers: complaints whose allegations state a good claim
(category (iii)) and those that do not (categories (i) and (ii)).

In assessing this critique, note that under Bell v. Hood, if the federal
claim is so wanting as to be "wholly frivolous and insubstantial", then no
jurisdiction exists, precluding the exercise of supplemental jurisdiction over
any state claim averred in the complaint; Justice Rehnquist's approach, by
contrast, would not categorically preclude supplemental jurisdiction. But
this difference is more theoretical than real: at least when a dismissal for
failure to state a claim comes early in the proceeding, a district court would
probably decline to exercise supplemental jurisdiction even under Justice
Rehnquist's approach. See 28 U.S.C. § 1367(c)(3) (authorizing a district court
that "has dismissed all claims over which it has original jurisdiction" to
decline to exercise supplemental jurisdiction). But see Mackey v. Pioneer
Nat'l Bank, 867 F.2d 520, 523 (9th Cir.1989) (upholding the decision of the

---

"arising under" cases both before and after passage of the general federal question jurisdiction
statute in 1875 . They conclude, however, that allowing all such cases into federal court today
might prove unworkable and suggest that "federal ingredient" cases might appropriately be
limited to those in which the ingredient was a constitutional (and not merely a statutory) one.

district court, after granting a dismissal under Rule 12(b)(6) of the federal claim, to retain jurisdiction over the pendent state law claims).

Under Bell v. Hood, a frivolous claim triggers the rule that a federal court must dismiss a case sua sponte for lack of subject matter jurisdiction. But under Justice Rehnquist's approach, few defendants would fail to move to dismiss (under Rule 12(b)(6)) a claim that would be deemed "frivolous" under Bell, and so in practice, again, the differences in approach may matter little.[2]

(3) Causes of Action Created by Federal Common Law. Although most federal causes of action are created expressly by statute, it is now settled that causes of action that are properly "implied" from federal statutes or from the federal Constitution, or that are otherwise recognized by federal common law, do "arise under" federal law within the meaning of § 1331.[3] No plausible reason was ever advanced why—once a claim was determined to rest on federal rather than state law—the appropriateness of and need for a federal forum should turn on whether the claim arose under a federal statute or under federal common law. The proposition that § 1331 embraces actions based on federal common law was implicit in Bell v. Hood, and it was made explicit in Illinois v. City of Milwaukee, 406 U.S. 91 (1972), p. 274, *supra*. There, the Court denied a motion for leave to file an original action in the Supreme Court, seeking to enjoin pollution of Lake Michigan, on the ground that a district court would be a more appropriate forum. As a predicate for its decision, the Court determined that pollution of navigable interstate waters is governed by federal common law (as well as by statutes) and that the district courts had jurisdiction because actions asserting such common law rights arise under the "laws" of the United States.

(4) Do All Federal Causes of Action Arise under Federal Law? A rare if not unique case that appears to be an exception to the general rule that a case alleging a non-frivolous federal cause of action arises under federal law within the meaning of § 1331 is Shoshone Mining Co. v. Rutter, 177 U.S. 505 (1900). A federal law established conditions for issuance of federal patents (exclusive grants) for mining claims. The law provided that if, after notice of an application, an adverse claim were filed, "it shall be the duty of the adverse claimant, within thirty days after filing his claim, to commence proceedings in a court of competent jurisdiction, to determine the question of the right of possession"; in turn, the patent should issue in accordance with the judgment in those proceedings. Congress provided that this right of possession could be determined by "local customs or rules of miners in the several mining districts, so far as the same are applicable and not inconsistent with the laws of the United States", or "by the statute of limitations for mining claims of the state or territory where the same may be situated."

In Shoshone, the Court held that such an adverse suit to determine the right to possession fell outside the general grant of federal question jurisdiction, as it "may not involve any question as to the construction or

---

[2] For a decision taking a narrow view of when a federal question is so insubstantial as to fail to provide a basis for federal question jurisdiction, see Hagans v. Lavine, 415 U.S. 528 (1974). For further criticism of the "substantiality" requirement as a jurisdictional rule, see Matasar, *Rediscovering "One Constitutional Case": Procedural Rules and the Rejection of the Gibbs Test for Supplemental Jurisdiction*, 71 Calif.L.Rev. 1399, 1417–46 (1983).

[3] For a partial exception to that rule in the distinctive area of admiralty jurisdiction, see Sec. 6, *infra*.

effect of the Constitution or laws of the United States, but may present simply a question of fact as to the time of the discovery of mineral, the location of the claim on the ground, or a determination of the meaning and effect of certain local rules and customs prescribed by the miners of the district, or the effect of state statutes, it would seem to follow that it is not one which necessarily arises under the Constitution and laws of the United States." Earlier in its opinion the Court had said: "[It is] well settled that a suit to enforce a right which takes its origin in the laws of the United States is not necessarily one arising under the Constitution or laws of the United States, within the meaning of the jurisdiction clauses; for if it did, every action to establish title to real estate (at least in the newer states) would be such a one, as all titles in those states come from the United States or by virtue of its laws."

Note the ambiguity of the phrase "a suit to enforce a right which takes its origin in the laws of the United States." The "for if it did" clause in the rest of that sentence shows that the Court was thinking of a vast range of cases in which the chain of title includes a federal grant but there is no federal question in the forefront of the case and the right of action is entirely state-created. But many have understood the statutory scheme in Shoshone as one in which Congress created the right to sue. If that understanding is correct, why wasn't that decisive? As a general matter, there is federal jurisdiction when a federal statute creates a federal right of action, even if the statute incorporates state law standards of liability in substantial part; a leading example is the Federal Tort Claims Act, 28 U.S.C. §§ 1346(b), 2671–80, which creates a right of action in tort against the United States for actions of its employees, but borrows state tort law as the measure of liability.

Several recent Supreme Court decisions have described the Shoshone decision as an extremely rare exception to the rule that the presence of a federal right of action suffices to establish subject matter jurisdiction under the statutory grant of arising under jurisdiction.[4] For an argument that this exception is justified as a matter of statutory interpretation, see Shapiro, *Jurisdiction and Discretion*, 60 N.Y.U.L.Rev. 543, 569–70 (1985).[5]

---

[4]   See, *e.g.*, footnote 5 of the next principal case, Grable & Sons Metal Prods., Inc. v. Darue Eng'g & Mfg,, p. 825, *infra*; see also Gunn v. Minton, 133 S.Ct. 1059, 1064 (2013); Mims v. Arrow Fin. Services, LLC, 132 S.Ct. 740, 748 n.8 (2012); Merrell Dow Pharmaceuticals v. Thompson, 478 U.S. 804, 814 n.12 (1986).

Professor Oakley, by contrast, contends that the Shoshone case did not in fact present a federal cause of action; he suggests that the statute did not confer a federal right (and thus a basis for federal question jurisdiction) until after the invocation of non-federal judicial processes or the expiration of time for initiating such processes. See American Law Institute, Judicial Code Revision Project, Tentative Draft No. 2, at 138 (1998). On this view, no federal right of action would exist at the time of filing, and thus Shoshone would not stand as an exception to the general rule that there is "arising under" jurisdiction over federal causes of action.

[5]   With Shoshone, compare Oneida Indian Nation v. County of Oneida, 414 U.S. 661, 677 (1974), upholding jurisdiction under § 1331 over the Indian Nation's action for ejectment. The Court found that "the assertion of a federal controversy does not rest solely on the claim of a right to possession derived from a federal grant of title whose scope will be governed by state law. Rather, it rests on the not insubstantial claim that federal law now protects, and has continuously protected from the time of the formation of the United States, possessory rights to tribal lands, wholly apart from the application of state law principles which normally and separately protect a valid right of possession." Thus, the Court upheld jurisdiction on the theory that in the unique area of Indian affairs, the matter of competing claims to land, which would ordinarily be thought to arise under state law (even where some of the claims are based on a grant of federal title), is governed entirely by federal law.

_____

INTRODUCTORY NOTE ON JURISDICTION UNDER § 1331 BASED ON THE PRESENCE OF A FEDERAL ELEMENT

(1) Federal Causes of Action versus Federal Elements. If the Shoshone decision raises the question whether some cases averring federal causes of action fall outside of § 1331, what about the converse question: are there some cases that do not allege a federal cause of action but that nonetheless arise under federal law within the meaning of § 1331? The answer plainly is yes, although only a handful of Supreme Court decisions address this question. The Court's decisions here are not based upon a simple rule but instead on a more complex evaluation of when the presence of a federal element does—and does not—suffice to establish "arising under" jurisdiction.

(2) Smith v. Kansas City Title & Trust Co. Smith v. Kansas City Title & Trust Co., 255 U.S. 180 (1921), decided just five years after American Well Works, remains a leading decision upholding jurisdiction, under the general federal question statute, over a case alleging a state law cause of action that incorporates an element of federal law. The case involved a shareholder's suit to enjoin a trust company from investing in federal bonds issued by Federal Land Banks or Joint-Stock Land Banks under authority of an Act of Congress. That Act explicitly provided that these federal bonds constituted lawful investments for all fiduciary and trust funds. The shareholder claimed a right to relief on the ground that state law prohibited the trust company from investing in bonds not issued pursuant to a valid law, and that the federal statute under which the bonds were issued was invalid under the federal Constitution.

Despite the fact that state law supplied both the claimed right and the claimed remedy, the Supreme Court upheld the district court's jurisdiction, on the ground that "the controversy concerns the constitutional validity of an act of Congress, which is directly drawn in question. The decision depends upon the determination of this issue." More broadly, the Court said: "The general rule is that, where it appears from the bill or statement of the plaintiff that the right to relief depends upon the construction or application of the Constitution or laws of the United States, and that such federal claim is not merely colorable, and rests upon a reasonable foundation, the District Court has jurisdiction under this provision."

Not surprisingly, Justice Holmes dissented, relying in significant part on his own opinion for the Court in American Well Works. He argued that "a suit cannot be said to arise under any other law than that which creates the cause of action." He then discussed Osborn, which he could have distinguished as arising under a special jurisdictional statute rather than under the predecessor to § 1331. Instead, he viewed Osborn as suggesting that "[i]t may be enough that the law relied upon creates a part of the cause of action," but he insisted that even that minimal standard had not been met in the case at hand.[1]

_____

[1] For a fascinating study of the Smith case, see Yackle, *Federal Banks and Federal Jurisdiction in the Progressive Era: A Case Study of Smith v. K.C. Title & Trust Co.*, 62 U.Kan.L.Rev. 255 (2013). Among other things, Professor Yackle finds that (1) the mere institution of the suit in Smith "wrecked the rural financial system established by the Act" of Congress; (2) the lawsuit was a "friendly matter," as Smith was not a disgruntled shareholder but a vice president of the Trust Company, and, moreover, he was a "shill for the mortgage

(3) Merrell Dow Pharmaceuticals Inc. v. Thompson. An important decision applying the approach of Smith, but finding that § 1331 did not reach a state law cause of action incorporating a federal element, is Merrell Dow Pharmaceuticals Inc. v. Thompson, 478 U.S. 804 (1986). In two state law tort actions, the plaintiffs alleged that the defendants had misbranded a drug in violation of the Federal Food, Drug, and Cosmetic Act (FDCA). Under Ohio law, such a violation created a rebuttable presumption of negligence. Thus, embedded within a state law claim was a federal issue about the meaning and application of the FDCA. The defendant removed the actions from state to federal court, but on review, the Supreme Court, by 5–4, held the removal improper because the case did not arise under federal law within the meaning of § 1331.

(a) The Court's Opinion. Justice Stevens' majority opinion acknowledged that "a case may arise under federal law 'where the vindication of a right under state law necessarily turned on some construction of federal law,'" but he stressed that "this statement must be read with caution", as "in exploring the outer reaches of § 1331, determinations about federal jurisdiction require sensitive judgments about congressional intent, judicial power, and the federal system."

He began by noting the parties' agreement that the FDCA does not afford an implied *federal* remedy permitting injured parties like the plaintiffs to sue for damages. Summarizing the reasons underlying the Court's modern and restrictive doctrine on implying such remedies—"the 'increased complexity of federal legislation and the increased volume of federal litigation,' as well as 'the desirability of a more careful scrutiny of legislative intent,' Merrill Lynch, Pierce, Fenner & Smith, Inc. v. Curran, 456 U.S. 353, 377 (1982) (footnote omitted)"—he said that they "are precisely the kind of considerations that should inform the concern for 'practicality and necessity' * * * when jurisdiction is asserted because of the presence of a federal issue in a state cause of action." He continued by saying: "The significance of the necessary assumption that there is no federal private cause of action thus cannot be overstated. For the ultimate import of such a conclusion * * * is that it would flout congressional intent to provide a private federal remedy for the violation of the federal statute. We think it would similarly flout, or at least undermine, congressional intent to conclude that the federal courts might nevertheless exercise federal-question jurisdiction and provide remedies for violations of that federal statute solely because the violation of the federal statute is said to be a 'rebuttable presumption' or a 'proximate cause' under state law * * *."

In an important footnote, the Court added: "Several commentators have suggested that our § 1331 decisions can best be understood as an evaluation

---

banks sponsoring the suit"; (3) the jurisdictional holding in Smith was unexceptional, as "jurisdiction was commonly sustained when plaintiffs raised federal questions in actions that were almost certainly conceived to be warranted by nonfederal law."

Yackle distinguishes two readings of the Smith decision and Justice Holmes' dissent. One reading of the dissent is that Holmes found jurisdiction wanting "because federal law supplied no 'remedies' for shareholders in Smith's position." But a different reading is that both the majority and dissent "treated the substantive legal claim and the shareholder's ability to take it to court as one and the same." On this account, the majority and the dissent disagreed about whether the shareholder's claim was genuinely federal, but did not view the source of the plaintiff's authority to sue as the key issue. Under the second account, the idea "that a private litigant's entitlement to pursue judicial relief constitutes a separate, threshold issue distinct from a legal claim is an artifact of the administrative state," in which a legal claim might be enforced not by private litigants but by an administrative agency.

of the *nature* of the federal interest at stake. See, *e.g.*, Shapiro, *Jurisdiction and Discretion*, 60 N.Y.U.L.Rev. 543, 568 (1985); * * * Cohen, *The Broken Compass: The Requirement That A Case Arise "Directly" Under Federal Law*, 115 U.Pa.L.Rev. 890, 916 (1967). * * *

"The importance of the nature of the federal issue in federal-question jurisdiction is highlighted by the fact that, despite the usual reliability of the Holmes test as an inclusionary principle, this Court has sometimes found that formally federal causes of action were not properly brought under federal-question jurisdiction because of the overwhelming predominance of state-law issues. * * * See * * * Shoshone Mining Co. v. Rutter, 177 U.S. 505, 507 (1900)".

In response to Merrell Dow's contention that federal court adjudication would help to promote uniform interpretation of the FDCA, the Court said that if state court interpretation of the FDCA threatens the regulatory regime, the defendant should be arguing not for federal jurisdiction but for FDCA preemption of state court jurisdiction. Justice Stevens added that the concern about uniformity was "considerably mitigated" by the existence of Supreme Court review of issues of federal law decided by the state courts. In response to Merrell Dow's argument that the case presented a novel question about whether the FDCA applies to extraterritorial sales (the plaintiffs were foreign citizens), the Court said that jurisdiction under § 1331 does not depend on, and the judicial system would be "ill served" by, a case-by-case appraisal of novelty.

Thus, the Court "conclude[d] that a complaint alleging a violation of a federal statute as an element of a state cause of action, when Congress has determined that there should be no private, federal cause of action for the violation, does not state a claim" arising under federal law for purposes of § 1331.

(b) Justice Brennan's Dissent. Joined by Justices White, Marshall, and Blackmun, Justice Brennan wrote a vigorous dissent. His starting point was Smith v. Kansas City Title & Trust Co., a decision, he said, that the Court had cited approvingly on numerous occasions, the lower courts have widely followed, and most commentators have endorsed. Because the plaintiffs' " 'right to relief depend[ed] upon the construction or application of the Constitution or laws of the United States' " (quoting Smith) and was not frivolous, Justice Brennan concluded that their claims arose under federal law. And he objected to the Court's approach of evaluating the strength of the federal interest, contending that the Court's effort to reconcile decisions upholding or rejecting jurisdiction on that basis could be made to work "only because a test based upon an ad hoc evaluation of the importance of the federal issue is infinitely malleable * * *. * * * However, the inevitable—and undesirable—result of [such] a test * * * is that federal jurisdiction turns in every case on an appraisal of the federal issue, its importance and its relation to state-law issues. Yet it is precisely because the Court believes that federal jurisdiction would be 'ill served' by such a case-by-case appraisal that it rejects petitioner's claim that the difficulty and importance of the statutory issue presented by its claim suffices to confer jurisdiction under § 1331. The Court cannot have it both ways."

Justice Brennan then argued that Congress' failure to create a private damages remedy under the FDCA did not imply that federal jurisdiction should not be exercised over a state law claim incorporating an issue under the FDCA. He stressed the federal courts' expertise, sympathy to federal purposes, and capacity to generate uniform interpretation and application of federal law, and he declared that his 30 years' experience as a Justice had convinced him that Supreme Court review of state court decisions cannot come close to assuring correct and uniform interpretation of federal law. He added that interpretation of the FDCA, even when incorporated in a state law cause of action, will shape behavior and thus implicates the concerns underlying the grant of federal question jurisdiction in the same way as if federal law created the cause of action.

Finally, Justice Brennan contended that the reasons underlying the Court's stringent approach to implying private rights of action argued for, rather than against, the exercise of federal jurisdiction. Greater complexity of federal law, for example, made the greater expertise of federal courts especially important. And without disagreeing that concern over the number of lawsuits may inform "reasoned arguments" for limiting the reach of § 1331, he argued that the Court should not "trim a statute solely because it thinks that Congress made it too broad." Noting that the FDCA regime is typical of regulatory schemes, in which an administrative agency like the FDA may seek a broad range of remedies to combat violations in federal court, he contended that "it seems rather strange to conclude that it either 'flout[s]' or 'undermine[s]' congressional intent for the federal courts to adjudicate a private state-law remedy that is based upon violating the FDCA." He concluded that Congress, if it has not preempted a state law remedy for violation of the FDCA, should not be understood to have foreclosed federal jurisdiction over that state law remedy.

(c) The Meaning and Impact of Merrell Dow. Merrell Dow left considerable uncertainty about when § 1331 conferred jurisdiction in the absence of a federal cause of action. On the one hand, the majority carefully refrained from overruling Smith,[2] purporting instead to find the lack of a private federal remedy under the FDCA to be a special reason militating against jurisdiction. But in virtually all cases in which jurisdiction depends upon application of the Smith rule, no federal right of action is available. Thus, on one reading of Merrell Dow, little would be left of the Smith approach—except in the unusual situation in which a federal right of action does exist but the plaintiff chooses to sue only on a state cause of action with a federal ingredient.[3] Some lower courts read Merrell Dow as taking this

---

[2]   Two years after Merrell Dow, in Christianson v. Colt Industries Operating Corp., 486 U.S. 800, 808 (1988), the Court, per Justice Brennan, said that a case arises under federal law if "the plaintiff's right to relief necessarily depends on resolution of a substantial question of federal law".

[3]   That unusual situation seems to have been present in City of Chicago v. International College of Surgeons, 522 U.S. 156 (1997). The plaintiff filed a state court action under Illinois' Administrative Review Law, seeking judicial review of a municipal agency's land use decision. The plaintiff claimed that both the municipal law and the conduct of the proceedings violated the Fourteenth Amendment; the plaintiff also alleged various violations of state law.

The Supreme Court ruled that the case had been properly removed to federal court under §§ 1331 and 1441. The brief jurisdictional discussion did not even mention Smith and cited Merrell Dow only for an unrelated point (that insubstantial claims do not confer federal jurisdiction). The Court stated that " '[e]ven though state law [here the Illinois Administrative Review Law] creates [a party's] cause of action, its case might still 'arise under' the laws of the United States if a well-pleaded complaint established that its right to relief under state law requires resolution of a substantial question of federal law' " (quoting Franchise Tax Bd. v. Construction Laborers Vacation Trust, 463 U.S. 1, 13 (1983)). The Court appeared to acknowledge that the plaintiff could have filed a federal cause of action under 42 U.S.C. § 1983 against the local agency and its officials for alleged violations of federal constitutional rights, but did not rely on that observation in upholding jurisdiction over the actual case before it.

highly restrictive view of § 1331, while others had viewed the approach of Smith as more vital and broadly important. The next principal case addresses this conflict.

———

Grable & Sons Metal Products, Inc. v. Darue Engineering and Manufacturing

545 U.S. 308, 125 S.Ct. 2363, 162 L.Ed.2d 257 (2005).
Certiorari to the United States Court of Appeals for the Sixth Circuit.

■ JUSTICE SOUTER delivered the opinion of the Court.

The question is whether want of a federal cause of action to try claims of title to land obtained at a federal tax sale precludes removal to federal court of a state action with non-diverse parties raising a disputed issue of federal title law. We answer no, and hold that the national interest in providing a federal forum for federal tax litigation is sufficiently substantial to support the exercise of federal question jurisdiction over the disputed issue on removal, which would not distort any division of labor between the state and federal courts, provided or assumed by Congress.

I

[The Internal Revenue Service seized real property belonging to Grable to satisfy a federal tax delinquency. Grable received notice, by certified mail, of the seizure before the IRS sold the property to Darue. Grable also received notice of the sale but did not exercise its statutory right to redeem the property within 180 days of the sale, and after that period had passed, the Government gave Darue a quitclaim deed.]

Five years later, Grable brought a quiet title action in state court, claiming that Darue's record title was invalid because the IRS had failed to notify Grable of its seizure of the property in the exact manner required by [26 U.S.C.] § 6335(a), which provides that written notice must be "given * * * to the owner of the property [or] left at his usual place of abode or business." Grable said that the statute required personal service, not service by certified mail.

Darue removed the case to Federal District Court as presenting a federal question, because the claim of title depended on the interpretation of the notice statute in the federal tax law. The District Court declined to remand the case * * *. On the merits, the court granted summary judgment to Darue, holding that although § 6335 by its terms required personal service, substantial compliance with the statute was enough.

The Court of Appeals for the Sixth Circuit affirmed. * * * We granted certiorari on the jurisdictional question alone, to resolve a split within the Courts of Appeals on whether Merrell Dow Pharmaceuticals Inc. v. Thompson, 478 U.S. 804 (1986), always requires a federal cause of action as a condition for exercising federal-question jurisdiction. We now affirm.

II

Darue was entitled to remove the quiet title action if Grable could have brought it in federal district court originally, 28 U.S.C. § 1441(a), as a civil action "arising under the Constitution, laws, or treaties of the United States," § 1331. This provision for federal-question jurisdiction is invoked by and large by plaintiffs pleading a cause of action created by federal law * * *. There is, however, another longstanding, if less frequently encountered, variety of federal "arising under" jurisdiction, this Court having recognized for nearly 100 years that in certain cases federal question jurisdiction will lie over state-law claims that implicate significant federal issues. *E.g.*, Hopkins v. Walker, 244 U.S. 486, 490–491 (1917). The doctrine captures the commonsense notion that a federal court ought to be able to hear claims recognized under state law that nonetheless turn on substantial questions of federal law, and thus justify resort to the experience, solicitude, and hope of uniformity that a federal forum offers on federal issues.

The classic example is Smith v. Kansas City Title & Trust Co., 255 U.S. 180 (1921), a suit by a shareholder claiming that the defendant corporation could not lawfully buy certain bonds of the National Government because their issuance was unconstitutional. Although Missouri law provided the right to sue the trust company, the Court recognized federal-question jurisdiction because the principal issue in the case was the federal constitutionality of the bond issue. Smith thus held, in a somewhat generous statement of the scope of the doctrine, that a state-law claim could give rise to federal-question jurisdiction so long as it "appears from the [complaint] that the right to relief depends upon the construction or application of [federal law]." *Id.*, at 199.

The Smith statement has been subject to some trimming to fit earlier and later cases recognizing the vitality of the basic doctrine, but shying away from the expansive view that mere need to apply federal law in a state-law claim will suffice to open the "arising under" door. As early as 1912, this Court had confined federal-question jurisdiction over state-law claims to those that "really and substantially involv[e] a dispute or controversy respecting the validity, construction or effect of [federal] law." Shulthis v. McDougal, 225 U.S. 561, 569 (1912). This limitation was the ancestor of Justice Cardozo's later explanation that a request to exercise federal-question jurisdiction over a state action calls for a "common-sense accommodation of judgment to [the] kaleidoscopic situations" that present a federal issue, in "a selective process which picks the substantial causes out of the web and lays the other ones aside." Gully v. First Nat. Bank in Meridian, 299 U.S. 109, 117–118 (1936). It has in fact become a constant refrain in such cases that federal jurisdiction demands not only a contested federal issue, but a substantial one, indicating a serious federal interest in claiming the advantages thought to be inherent in a federal forum. *E.g.*, Chicago v. International College of Surgeons, 522 U.S. 156, 164 (1997); Merrell Dow, *supra*, at 814, and n. 12; Franchise Tax Bd. of Cal. v. Construction Laborers Vacation Trust for Southern Cal., 463 U.S. 1, 28 (1983).

But even when the state action discloses a contested and substantial federal question, the exercise of federal jurisdiction is subject to a possible veto. For the federal issue will ultimately qualify for a federal forum only if federal jurisdiction is consistent with congressional judgment about the sound division of labor between state and federal courts governing the application of § 1331. Thus, Franchise Tax Bd. explained that the appropriateness of a federal forum to hear an embedded issue could be evaluated only after considering the "welter of issues regarding the interrelation of federal and state authority and the proper management of the federal judicial system." *Id.*, at 8. Because arising-under jurisdiction to hear a state-law claim always raises the possibility of upsetting the state-federal line drawn (or at least assumed) by Congress, the presence of a disputed federal issue and the ostensible importance of a federal forum are never necessarily dispositive; there must always be an assessment of any disruptive portent in exercising federal jurisdiction.

These considerations have kept us from stating a "single, precise, all-embracing" test for jurisdiction over federal issues embedded in state-law claims between nondiverse parties. Christianson v. Colt Industries Operating Corp., 486 U.S. 800, 821 (1988) (Stevens, J., concurring). We have not kept them out simply because they appeared in state raiment, as Justice Holmes would have done, see Smith, *supra*, at 214 (dissenting opinion), but neither have we treated "federal issue" as a password opening federal courts to any state action embracing a point of federal law. Instead, the question is, does a state-law claim necessarily raise a stated federal issue, actually disputed and substantial, which a federal forum may entertain without disturbing any congressionally approved balance of federal and state judicial responsibilities.

test

III

A

This case warrants federal jurisdiction. Grable's state complaint must specify "the facts establishing the superiority of [its] claim," Mich. Ct. Rule 3.411(B)(2)(c) (West 2005), and Grable has premised its superior title claim on a failure by the IRS to give it adequate notice, as defined by federal law. Whether Grable was given notice within the meaning of the federal statute is thus an essential element of its quiet title claim, and the meaning of the federal statute is actually in dispute; it appears to be the only legal or factual issue contested in the case. The meaning of the federal tax provision is an important issue of federal law that sensibly belongs in a federal court. The Government has a strong interest in the "prompt and certain collection of delinquent taxes," United States v. Rodgers, 461 U.S. 677, 709 (1983), and the ability of the IRS to satisfy its claims from the property of delinquents requires clear terms of notice to allow buyers like Darue to satisfy themselves that the Service has touched the bases necessary for good title. The Government thus has a direct interest in the availability of a federal forum to vindicate its own administrative action, and buyers (as well as tax delinquents) may find it valuable to come before judges used to federal tax matters. Finally, because it will be the rare state title case that raises a contested matter of federal law, federal jurisdiction to resolve genuine disagreement over federal tax title provisions will portend only a microscopic effect on the federal-state division of labor. See n. 3, *infra*.

This conclusion puts us in venerable company, quiet title actions having been the subject of some of the earliest exercises of federal-question jurisdiction over state-law claims. In Hopkins, the question was federal jurisdiction over a quiet title action based on the plaintiffs' allegation that federal mining law gave them the superior claim. Just as in this case, "the facts showing the plaintiffs' title and the existence and invalidity of the instrument or record sought to be eliminated as a cloud upon the title are essential parts of the plaintiffs' cause of action."[3] [244 U.S.] at 490. As in this case again, "it is plain that a controversy respecting the construction and effect of the [federal] laws is involved and is sufficiently real and substantial." *Id.*, at 489. This Court therefore upheld federal jurisdiction in Hopkins, as well as in * * * similar quiet title matters * * *. Consistent with those cases, the recognition of federal jurisdiction is in order here.

B

Merrell Dow Pharmaceuticals Inc. v. Thompson, 478 U.S. 804 (1986), on which Grable rests its position, is not to the contrary. Merrell Dow considered a state tort claim resting in part on the allegation that the defendant drug company had violated a federal misbranding prohibition, and was thus presumptively negligent under Ohio law. The Court assumed that federal law would have to be applied to resolve the claim, but after closely examining the strength of the federal interest at stake and the implications of opening the federal forum, held federal jurisdiction unavailable. Congress had not provided a private federal cause of action for violation of the federal branding requirement, and the Court found "it would . . . flout, or at least undermine, congressional intent to conclude that federal courts might nevertheless exercise federal-question jurisdiction and provide remedies for violations of that federal statute solely because the violation . . . is said to be a . . . 'proximate cause' under state law." *Id.*, at 812.

Because federal law provides for no quiet title action that could be brought against Darue, Grable argues that there can be no federal jurisdiction here, stressing some broad language in Merrell Dow (including the passage just quoted) that on its face supports Grable's position. But an opinion is to be read as a whole, and Merrell Dow cannot be read whole as overturning decades of precedent, as it would have done by effectively adopting the Holmes dissent in Smith, and converting a federal cause of action from a sufficient condition for federal-question jurisdiction[5] into a necessary one.

In the first place, Merrell Dow disclaimed the adoption of any bright-line rule, as when the Court reiterated that "in exploring the outer reaches of § 1331, determinations about federal jurisdiction require sensitive judgments about congressional intent, judicial power, and the federal system." 478 U.S., at 810. The opinion included a lengthy footnote explaining that questions of jurisdiction over state-law claims require "careful judgments," *id.*, at 814, about the "nature of the federal interest at stake," *id.*, at 814, n. 12 (emphasis deleted). And as a final indication that it did not mean to make a federal right of action mandatory, it

---

[3]   The quiet title cases also show the limiting effect of the requirement that the federal issue in a state-law claim must actually be in dispute to justify federal-question jurisdiction. In Shulthis v. McDougal, 225 U.S. 561 (1912), this Court found that there was no federal question jurisdiction to hear a plaintiff's quiet title claim in part because the federal statutes on which title depended were not subject to "any controversy respecting their validity, construction, or effect." *Id.*, at 570. As the Court put it, the requirement of an actual dispute about federal law was "especially" important in "suit[s] involving rights to land acquired under a law of the United States," because otherwise "every suit to establish title to land in the central and western states would so arise [under federal law], as all titles in those States are traceable back to those laws." *Id.*, at 569–570.

[5]   For an extremely rare exception to the sufficiency of a federal right of action, see Shoshone Mining Co. v. Rutter, 177 U.S. 505, 507 (1900).

expressly approved the exercise of jurisdiction sustained in Smith, despite the want of any federal cause of action available to Smith's shareholder plaintiff. Merrell Dow then, did not toss out, but specifically retained the contextual enquiry that had been Smith's hallmark for over 60 years. At the end of Merrell Dow, Justice Holmes was still dissenting.

Accordingly, Merrell Dow should be read in its entirety as treating the absence of a federal private right of action as evidence relevant to, but not dispositive of, the "sensitive judgments about congressional intent" that § 1331 requires. The absence of any federal cause of action affected Merrell Dow's result two ways. The Court saw the fact as worth some consideration in the assessment of substantiality. But its primary importance emerged when the Court treated the combination of no federal cause of action and no preemption of state remedies for misbranding as an important clue to Congress's conception of the scope of jurisdiction to be exercised under § 1331. The Court saw the missing cause of action not as a missing federal door key, always required, but as a missing welcome mat, required in the circumstances, when exercising federal jurisdiction over a state misbranding action would have attracted a horde of original filings and removal cases raising other state claims with embedded federal issues. For if the federal labeling standard without a federal cause of action could get a state claim into federal court, so could any other federal standard without a federal cause of action. And that would have meant a tremendous number of cases.

One only needed to consider the treatment of federal violations generally in garden variety state tort law. "The violation of federal statutes and regulations is commonly given negligence per se effect in state tort proceedings."[6] Restatement (Third) of Torts § 14, Reporters' Note, p.195. Tent. Draft No.1, Mar. 28, 2001 * * * Comment a. A general rule of exercising federal jurisdiction over state claims resting on federal mislabeling and other statutory violations would thus have heralded a potentially enormous shift of traditionally state cases into federal courts. Expressing concern over the "increased volume of federal litigation," and noting the importance of adhering to "legislative intent," Merrell Dow thought it improbable that the Congress, having made no provision for a federal cause of action, would have meant to welcome any state-law tort case implicating federal law "solely because the violation of the federal statute is said to [create] a rebuttable presumption [of negligence] . . . under state law." 478 U.S., at 811–812 (internal quotation marks omitted). In this situation, no welcome mat meant keep out. Merrell Dow's analysis thus fits within the framework of examining the importance of having a federal forum for the issue, and the consistency of such a forum with Congress's intended division of labor between state and federal courts.

As already indicated, however, a comparable analysis yields a different jurisdictional conclusion in this case. Although Congress also indicated ambivalence in this case by providing no private right of action to Grable, it is the rare state quiet title action that involves contested issues of federal law, see n. 3, *supra*. Consequently, jurisdiction over

---

[6]   Other jurisdictions treat a violation of a federal statute as evidence of negligence or, like Ohio itself in Merrell Dow * * *, as creating a rebuttable presumption of negligence. Restatement [(Third) of Torts (proposed final draft)], § 14, Reporters' Note, Comment c at 196. Either approach could still implicate issues of federal law.

actions like Grable's would not materially affect, or threaten to affect, the normal currents of litigation. Given the absence of threatening structural consequences and the clear interest the Government, its buyers, and its delinquents have in the availability of a federal forum, there is no good reason to shirk from federal jurisdiction over the dispositive and contested federal issue at the heart of the state-law title claim.[7]

IV

The judgment of the Court of Appeals, upholding federal jurisdiction over Grable's quiet title action, is affirmed.

It is so ordered.

■ JUSTICE THOMAS, concurring.

The Court faithfully applies our precedents interpreting 28 U.S.C. § 1331 * * *. In this case, no one has asked us to overrule those precedents and adopt the rule Justice Holmes set forth in American Well Works Co. v. Layne & Bowler Co., 241 U.S. 257 (1916), limiting § 1331 jurisdiction to cases in which federal law creates the cause of action * * *. In an appropriate case, and perhaps with the benefit of better evidence as to the original meaning of § 1331's text, I would be willing to consider that course.

Jurisdictional rules should be clear. Whatever the virtues of the Smith standard, it is anything but clear. *Ante*, at 313 (the standard "calls for a 'common-sense accommodation of judgment to [the] kaleidoscopic situations' that present a federal issue, in 'a selective process which picks the substantial causes out of the web and lays the other ones aside' " (quoting Gully v. First Nat. Bank in Meridian, 299 U.S. 109, 117–118 (1936))); *ante*, at 314 ("[T]he question is, does a state-law claim necessarily raise a stated federal issue, actually disputed and substantial, which a federal forum may entertain without disturbing any congressionally approved balance of federal and state judicial responsibilities"); *ante*, at 317, 318 (" '[D]eterminations about federal jurisdiction require sensitive judgments about congressional intent, judicial power, and the federal system' "; "the absence of a federal private right of action [is] evidence relevant to, but not dispositive of, the 'sensitive judgments about congressional intent' that § 1331 requires" (quoting Merrell Dow, *supra*, at 810)).

Whatever the vices of the American Well Works rule, it is clear. Moreover, it accounts for the " 'vast majority' " of cases that come within § 1331 under our current case law, Merrell Dow, *supra*, at 808 (quoting Franchise Tax Bd. of Cal. v. Construction Laborers Vacation Trust for Southern Cal., 463 U.S. 1, 9 (1983))—further indication that trying to sort out which cases fall within the smaller Smith category may not be worth the effort it entails. See R. Fallon, D. Meltzer, & D. Shapiro, Hart and Wechsler's The Federal Courts and the Federal System 885–886 (5th

---

[7] * * * Grable's counsel espoused the position that after Merrell Dow, federal-question jurisdiction over state-law claims absent a federal right of action could be recognized only where a constitutional issue was at stake. There is, however, no reason in text or otherwise to draw such a rough line. As Merrell Dow itself suggested, constitutional questions may be the more likely ones to reach the level of substantiality that can justify federal jurisdiction. But a flat ban on statutory questions would mechanically exclude significant questions of federal law like the one this case presents.

ed.2003). Accordingly, I would be willing in appropriate circumstances to reconsider our interpretation of § 1331.

———

NOTE ON THE SCOPE OF "ARISING UNDER" JURISDICTION UNDER 28 U.S.C. § 1331

(1) Cases Involving Disputes Over Land Originally Owned by the United States. Like Grable, some of the oldest cases considering whether § 1331 embraces state law causes of action incorporating a federal ingredient involved disputes about real property rights, in which one or more of the chains of title included a grant from the United States. In nearly all such real property disputes, state law creates the plaintiff's right of action, and thus federal jurisdiction cannot be justified under the Holmes cause of action test.

An early example of such a dispute, noted in Grable, is Hopkins v. Walker, 244 U.S. 486 (1917). There, the Court upheld jurisdiction over an action to remove a cloud on title, after finding that under both "general" and Montana law, "the facts showing the plaintiff's title and the existence and invalidity of the instrument or record sought to be eliminated as a cloud upon the title are essential parts of the plaintiff's cause of action." It is noteworthy that the complaint in Hopkins left no doubt that the validity of the competing federal grants was in dispute, and thus, the case was not one in which the federal grant was merely an old and uncontested link in the plaintiff's chain of title.

As the Grable Court notes, however, other decisions have refused to recognize federal question jurisdiction over land disputes involving a federal ingredient. Thus, five years before Hopkins, jurisdiction was denied in Shulthis v. McDougal, 225 U.S. 561 (1912), an action to quiet title. The Court in Grable (see footnote 3) explains Shulthis on the basis that although the complainant's claim of right was derived from federal law, his averments made no reference to "any controversy respecting [the] validity, construction, or effect" of federal statutes. Thus, for all one could tell, the actual dispute might have had nothing to do with the fact that the complainant derived his title from federal law.

Jurisdiction was also denied in Joy v. City of St. Louis, 201 U.S. 332 (1906), an action for ejectment. There too, the Court noted that although the plaintiff's chain of title involved federal law, the actual dispute in the case might not. But the decision in Joy also rested in part on pleading conventions: in an ejectment action, a plaintiff need not allege the source of its title or that there is a dispute about the validity of that title.[1] Joy thus illustrates a distinct aspect of the well-pleaded complaint rule: a plaintiff may not unlock the door to federal court by including allegations about issues of federal law not required by pleading rules. This aspect of the rule, though beside the point when the plaintiff pleads a federal cause of action, may have bite when a state law claim incorporates a federal element; there, whether a "well-pleaded" complaint raises a federal issue depends on the niceties of pleading requirements.

---

[1] It is possible that Shulthis also rested in part on what was and was not viewed as a necessary allegation in an action to quiet title. (Although the Grable Court describes Hopkins as a quiet title action, the case was actually one *to remove a cloud on title*.)

The decisions in Hopkins, Shulthis, and Joy all predate Erie R.R. Co. v. Tompkins. Today, state law generally governs the allocation of the burden of pleading with respect to a state law claim in federal court.[2] It surely makes sense to distinguish cases in which a grant of title under federal law is in the background but not in controversy, as may have been true in Shulthis, from those in which a genuine dispute exists about the existence or validity of a grant of title under federal law, as in Grable and Hopkins. But can a convincing case be made that the appropriateness of federal adjudication depends on whether pleading conventions require the plaintiff to include allegations about a dispute respecting the federal title claimed by one of the disputants? In Grable, the Court noted that Michigan required a plaintiff to allege the superiority of its title to the competing title of the IRS; if another state did not require such allegations in a quiet title action, would (should) federal jurisdiction be lacking?

(2) Discretion and Federal Interests. Both in upholding jurisdiction in Grable and in refusing it in Merrell Dow, the Court sought to reserve discretion to tailor jurisdiction to the practical needs of the particular situation. What is the proper role of discretion in determining the reach of § 1331?

(a) In Merrell Dow, Justice Stevens cited Cohen, *The Broken Compass: The Requirement That a Case Arise "Directly" Under Federal Law*, 115 U.Pa.L.Rev. 890, 916 (1967), which argued against the use of any analytic formula for determining when a case "arises under" federal law for purposes of § 1331 and in favor of "pragmatic standards," including "the extent of the caseload increase * * * if jurisdiction is recognized"; the extent to which cases "of this class" turn on federal versus state law; "the extent of the necessity for an expert federal tribunal"; and "the extent of the necessity for a sympathetic federal tribunal." His position appears to be that *district* courts should exercise a case-by-case pragmatic discretion, unguided by any "formulation". Would such a regime be tolerable? (Note that it would both narrow and complicate Supreme Court supervision of this area.)

(b) Justice Stevens's opinion in Merrell Dow also cited Shapiro, *Jurisdiction and Discretion*, 60 N.Y.U.L.Rev. 543, 568–70 (1985). Professor Shapiro disassociates himself from the *ad hoc* approach of Professor Cohen, stressing that the range of discretion under § 1331, "though extremely broad at the outset, has been significantly narrowed by the course of decisions since the jurisdictional statute was enacted." He explains: "The discretion I advocate relates primarily to the existence of a range of permissible choices under the relevant grants of jurisdiction. It is entirely consistent with this view for judicial precedent to narrow the scope of discretion and even to generate predictable rules." In Shapiro's view, "no formulation can possibly explain or even begin to account for the variety of outcomes unless it accords sufficient room for the federal courts to make a range of choices based on considerations of judicial administration and the degree of federal concern." He continues:

"[The] cases suggest that the Court's authority, but not its obligation, is very broad indeed. In Smith, the presence of a federal ingredient made relevant by state law was sufficient to confer jurisdiction, but in Shoshone, a federally created claim that turned on issues of state law was not. Both cases,

---

[2]   However, federal statutes or rules that prescribe pleading requirements on particular issues arising in a state law cause of action (*e.g.*, Fed. R. Civ. P. 8(c)) may override state pleading rules. *Cf.* Palmer v. Hoffman, 318 U.S. 109 (1943).

however, may be better understood if viewed in terms of the federal interest at stake and the effect on the federal docket. Cases like Smith arise infrequently, but the issue—the ability of a party to invest in federally authorized securities—was a matter of great federal moment. Cases like Shoshone must have arisen with monotonous regularity at the turn of the century, but the degree of federal interest in an outcome dependent on local custom was marginal at best."

The Court's analysis in Grable appears to track rather closely the approach advocated by Professor Shapiro.

(c) Smith's recognition of jurisdiction might seem to depend on the fact that the federal question there was one of constitutional law.[3] The Grable opinion states that "constitutional questions may be the more likely ones to reach the level of substantiality that can justify federal jurisdiction. But a flat ban on statutory questions would mechanically exclude significant questions of federal law like the one this case presents."[4]

(d) Can Merrell Dow and Smith be distinguished on a different basis? If Congress' failure to provide an express private remedy in the FDCA argues against "arising under" jurisdiction in Merrell Dow, is the parallel argument about the lack of a private remedy under the statute in issue in Smith less forceful, given the absence of a comprehensive scheme of federal enforcement? Put differently, it is entirely conceivable that Congress might have enacted a private right of action under the FDCA (and thus Congress' assumed failure to do so is significant); but it is difficult to imagine that Congress might have enacted a statute authorizing shareholders to sue a corporation for having purchased bonds issued under an invalid federal statute (and hence the failure to do so has little significance).

(e) Is the statutory issue in Grable more appropriate for federal adjudication than the statutory issue in Merrell Dow?

(i) Grable says that upholding jurisdiction in Merrell Dow would have opened the federal courts to a horde of cases—all those in which a federal regulatory standard is embedded in a state law action. (Although that concern may have motivated the majority in Merrell Dow, the Court's opinion barely adverted to it.) And the concern goes beyond state tort actions like Merrell Dow; consider, for example, disputes about a state's "piggyback" income tax, in which a state chooses to base state tax liability on federal tax liability. Is it a persuasive response to that concern to say that the mere fact that a set of cases is numerous does not show that the cases in that set are less appropriate for federal adjudication?

(ii) The issue in Grable is close to a pure issue of law that could be settled once and for all and thereafter would govern numerous tax sale cases. The issue in Merrell Dow, by contrast, was more fact-specific; a determination

---

[3] So, too, was the issue in the College of Surgeons case, p. 824, note 3, *supra*, in which the Court also upheld jurisdiction.

[4] Reconsider the facts of American Well Works. Justice Holmes assumed that the plaintiff's complaint need not refer to federal law, as the defendant had the burden of proving the truth of its statements concerning alleged patent infringement. Today, some states would require the plaintiff to plead and prove falsity. See Restatement (Second) of Torts § 651 comment. In such a state, would (should) that affect the outcome? Suppose, further, that the federal First Amendment now requires, in a trade libel case like Well Works, that the plaintiff shoulder the burden of proving falsity. *Cf.* Philadelphia Newspapers, Inc. v. Hepps, 475 U.S. 767 (1986) (recognizing such a requirement in personal defamation actions). Would that strengthen the case for exercising jurisdiction today in a case like American Well Works?

whether the particular drug there at issue was misbranded might provide little guidance about the application of FDCA labeling requirements to other drugs. But on this dimension, did the Court in Merrell Dow do justice to the argument that the question whether the FDCA applies extraterritorially merited federal adjudication—not because of its novelty but because it too was a relatively pure legal issue whose resolution would thereafter govern many cases?

If federal jurisdiction is ill-served by assessment of the novelty of a federal issue, as the Merrell Dow majority suggested, is it ill-served by assessment of the nature or strength of the federal interest, as the Grable decision requires? Or is such an assessment necessary if the Court is to avoid two undesirable poles: (1) holding, with Justice Holmes, that § 1331 reaches no state law cause of action, no matter how strong the federal interest in adjudication of the federal ingredient in a particular case (an approach that would require overruling a decision like Smith, as well as Hopkins and Grable), or (2) accepting jurisdiction over every state law case in which a federal issue, no matter how unimportant, or uncontested, must be alleged as part of a well-pleaded complaint? Does the answer to these questions depend on whether the assessment must be made in each individual case (e.g., only the Merrell Dow lawsuit) or can instead be made for a larger class of cases (e.g., all state law tort actions incorporating a federal regulatory standard)?

(iii) In Grable, the Solicitor General filed an amicus brief supporting the recognition of jurisdiction, and, as the opinion noted, the government has an obvious interest in its ability to satisfy its tax claims and to confer secure title upon purchasers at tax sales. Should a court be more willing to exercise jurisdiction when the government has a direct interest in how the federal ingredient is interpreted and applied?[5]

(f) Grable views the likely impact on federal court workload, and on the federal-state balance, to be significant considerations in making jurisdictional determinations. Are both of those considerations sound? Does reliance upon them undervalue litigants' claim to a federal forum when resolution of a claim turns on federal law?

(3) Post-Grable Decisions. In both of the decisions it has handed down applying Grable's framework, the Court has suggested that Grable's recognition of jurisdiction absent a federal cause of action is of quite limited scope.

(a) In Empire Healthchoice Assurance, Inc. v. McVeigh, 547 U.S. 677 (2006), a federal statute authorized creation of a health insurance plan for federal employees. The government negotiated a master contract with insurance carriers. The agreement between one of the insurers and its enrollees required an enrollee who obtains a tort recovery to reimburse the insurer for payments made for the enrollee's medical care. In this case, after an enrollee's estate obtained a settlement of a state court tort action against

---

[5] The United States, in its brief in Grable, distinguished the situation in Grable from Merrell Dow on the ground that the question of federal law at issue in Grable required resolution because of the Supremacy Clause, whereas Ohio's decision to incorporate the FDCA's misbranding standard was voluntary and "did not fundamentally change the state law character of the plaintiff's tort action". Brief for the United States as Amicus Curiae at 9, Grable & Sons Metal Prods., Inc. v. Darue Eng'g & Mfg., 545 U.S. 308 (2005) (No. 04–608), 2005 WL 736815, at *9. Would that distinction, had it been endorsed by the Court in Grable, have cast doubt on Smith?

a third party, the insurer brought a federal court action to enforce its right to reimbursement.

After determining that the reimbursement claim was governed by state law, Justice Ginsburg, writing for the Court, considered and rejected the argument that the case nonetheless fell under § 1331 because federal law is a necessary element of the claim for relief. "This case," she said, "is poles apart from Grable." She stressed that the federal issue in Grable was triggered by the action of a federal agency (the IRS) and was "a nearly 'pure issue of law,' one 'that could be settled once and for all and thereafter would govern numerous tax sale cases' " (quoting Hart and Wechsler 65 (2005 Supp.)). The instant claim, by contrast, is "fact-bound and situation specific." She described with some skepticism the argument that federal law would govern the extent to which reimbursement "should take account of attorney's fees expended," saying that the state court was competent to apply federal law "to the extent it is relevant." She concluded: "In sum, Grable emphasized that it takes more than a federal element 'to open the "arising under" door.' This case cannot be squeezed into the slim category Grable exemplifies" (quoting Grable). (The four dissenters' approach to the case did not require them to address Grable.)

(b) In Gunn v. Minton, 133 S.Ct. 1059 (2013), the Court considered a case that was similar to Merrell Dow—a state law tort action in which the determination of the defendant's negligence turned on an issue of federal law. However, the incorporated federal issue was one of patent law, and under 28 U.S.C. § 1338(a), federal courts have exclusive jurisdiction over cases arising under the patent laws. Indeed, in 2011, Congress departed from the well-pleaded complaint rule in patent cases, providing that federal jurisdiction (and federal exclusivity) extends even to patent claims (such as a counterclaim) not asserted in the plaintiff's complaint. See pp. 812–814, *supra*. Nonetheless, in Gunn the Court unanimously ruled that the action fell outside the scope of § 1331.

The story began when, in Minton's action for patent infringement, the federal district court found Minton's patent invalid, on the basis that the invention had been on sale more than a year prior to the patent application. In a motion for reconsideration, Gunn, the lawyer for Minton, raised for the first time an argument that the prior uses of the invention were "experimental" and thus, under the patent laws, did not render the patent invalid. The district court denied the motion, and the U.S. Court of Appeals for the Federal Circuit affirmed, ruling that the district court had properly found Minton's experimental-use argument to have been waived by its belated assertion.

Minton then sued Gunn for malpractice in Texas state court, complaining of Gunn's tardiness in raising the experimental-use argument. After losing on the merits in the trial court, Minton argued on appeal that the state courts lacked subject matter jurisdiction, contending that his malpractice claim, because it was founded on a question of patent law, arose under federal patent law and hence was within the exclusive jurisdiction of the federal courts. On review, the Supreme Court held that the case did not arise under federal law and that the state courts had therefore properly entertained the malpractice action. (In so holding, the Court reaffirmed that the standard for arising under jurisdiction is the same under § 1331 and § 1338(a).)

Chief Justice Roberts' opinion observed that the Court has identified a "slim category" in which claims originating under state law nonetheless arise under federal law. The Grable decision sought "to bring some order to" a doctrine that had previously been "unruly" by providing that federal jurisdiction lies over a state claim "if a federal issue is: (1) necessarily raised, (2) actually disputed, (3) substantial, and (4) capable of resolution in federal court without disrupting the federal-state balance approved by Congress." Applying those requirements, the Court acknowledged that the federal patent issue was necessarily raised and actually disputed, but it concluded that the last two requirements were not satisfied.

As to the third criterion, the Court said that an issue was not "substantial" just because it was important to the plaintiff's case; rather, the relevant question was "the importance of the issue to the federal system as a whole." In both Grable and Smith v. Kansas City Title & Trust, the issue of federal law embedded in the state law claim for relief was of general importance to the federal government. Here, the federal question—whether timely presentation of the experimental-use argument would have changed the outcome of the patent infringement lawsuit—would not change the outcome of the patent action, nor would it threaten the uniformity of federal law. The Chief Justice also noted that a state court determination of the patent issue would not bind the federal courts and that state courts addressing patent issues could be expected to "hew closely to the pertinent federal precedents." And he expressed some doubt that a possibly erroneous state court decision would have preclusive effect; at most, he said, it could bind the parties with regard to the patents at issue.

Finally, as to Grable's fourth requirement, the Court noted that it was the states' responsibility to maintain standards of practice for members of their bars. Accordingly, "state legal malpractice claims based on underlying patent matters will rarely, if ever, arise under federal patent law for purposes of § 1338(a)." (Note that the result of the Gunn decision is that the standards of practice before a federal administrative agency (the Patent and Trademark Office) and the federal courts, for lawyers whose practice may be almost exclusively before those bodies, will be regulated by state law, and enforced by state courts whose jurisdiction to consider issues of patent law is unusually restricted. See pp. 812–814, *supra*. Is that a cause for concern?)

(4) Simple Versus Refined Jurisdictional Rules. In cases lacking a federal cause of action, the Supreme Court has clearly upheld jurisdiction under § 1331 in only four instances—Hopkins and similar cases, Smith, Grable, and College of Surgeons, p. 824, note 3, *supra*.[6] Even in the lower courts, rather few decisions uphold jurisdiction in such cases.

Justice Thomas' concurrence in Grable cites the Fifth Edition of this book as raising this question: assuming that the exercise of federal question jurisdiction over state law causes of action is desirable in some cases (like Grable and Smith), is the game worth the candle? Powerful arguments have been made that rules of subject matter jurisdiction should be subject to a "bright line" test. See Chafee, Some Problems of Equity 1–102 (1950). Justice Holmes' cause of action test is simpler and clearer—and while excluding cases like Smith or Grable, it avoids the need in a much larger number of cases to engage in what can be a refined and uncertain analysis, which some

---

[6]   See also De Sylva v. Ballentine, 351 U.S. 570 (1956) (deciding on the merits—without discussing any jurisdictional question—a federal court action involving a state law claim to partial ownership of copyright renewal terms).

courts may not handle successfully. See Meltzer, *Jurisdiction and Discretion Revisited*, 79 Notre Dame L.Rev. 1891, 1913 (2004) (suggesting that the lower court decisions after Merrell Dow and before Grable contain "some surprising statements" and, overall, raise a question "whether federal judges, as intelligent and dedicated as most of them are, can in fact establish a coherent framework for the boundaries of subject matter jurisdiction predicated not upon a federal claim for relief but instead upon a federal ingredient in a state law claim for relief"). Thus, a law review note cited by the majority in Grable found that since 1994, the courts of appeals had discussed Smith jurisdiction in 69 reported cases and in 45 of them had reversed the district court. See Note, 115 Harv.L.Rev. 2272, 2280 (2002).

To be sure, reported appeals are often an unrepresentative sample of cases generally. Moreover, Professor Meltzer's assessment, and a reversal rate of 65%, may have been the product of the unusual uncertainty generated by Merrell Dow, which the Grable decision could have reduced. In the Court's most recent decision, Gunn v. Minton, no Justice advocated return to Justice Holmes' "cause of action" test as the exclusive measure of arising under jurisdiction.[7]

B. STATUTORY JURISDICTION OVER DECLARATORY JUDGMENT ACTIONS

INTRODUCTORY NOTE ON THE FEDERAL DECLARATORY JUDGMENT ACT

Congress enacted the Federal Declaratory Judgment Act (28 U.S.C. §§ 2201–02) in 1934 after a long campaign by legal reformers to have a declaratory remedy provided in both state and federal courts. As explained in Doernberg & Mushlin, *The Trojan Horse: How the Declaratory Judgment Act Created a Cause of Action and Expanded Federal Jurisdiction While the Supreme Court Wasn't Looking*, 36 UCLA L.Rev. 529, 552–53 (1989), the campaigners viewed traditional remedies like damages or an injunction as inadequate because: "social equilibrium can be disturbed not only by direct violations of rights, but also by actions that leave persons in 'grave doubt and uncertainty' about their legal positions. In their view, the existing remedial structure failed in three ways. First, it failed to address the plight of a person embroiled in a dispute who, limited by traditional remedies, could not have the controversy adjudicated because the opposing party had the sole claim to traditional relief and chose not to use it. [For example, a party accused of breach of contract lacked a means to initiate a suit to determine whether in fact a breach had occurred, and the resulting uncertainty could be very damaging.] Second, the traditional system of remedies harmed parties by

---

[7]   For the view that the Holmes test lacks the "nuance and balancing" needed for sound jurisdictional determinations and is too grudging given the Court's limited capacity to review state court judgments, see Freer, *Of Rules and Standards: Reconciling Statutory Limitations on "Arising Under" Jurisdiction*, 82 Ind.L.J. 309, 320 (2007). For a thorough analysis of the Court's decisions from Smith v. Kansas City Title & Trust through Empire Healthcase, see Field, p. 811, *supra*.

forcing them to wait an unnecessarily long time before seeking relief. [A common example would be a contractor who agreed to construct a building using the 'highest grade' materials. If before construction the client contends that the builder's proposed materials are not of the highest quality, at common law the contractor would have to either accede to what may be an illegitimate objection, use the material selected and risk being found liable for breach, or refuse to build until the dispute is resolved, perhaps triggering a suit for nonperformance.] Third, the reformers criticized the harshness of damage and injunctive awards. Even when they could be invoked, they were thought to hamper litigants who did not need or desire coercive relief.

"For the reformers the declaratory judgment was the procedural innovation that would solve these problems."

Congress, in considering whether to create a declaratory remedy, faced concerns that a suit seeking only a declaration was tantamount to rendering a prohibited advisory opinion. The Supreme Court put those concerns to rest in Nashville, C. & St. Louis Ry. v. Wallace, 288 U.S. 249 (1933), in which it reviewed a state court decision in a suit under a state declaratory judgment provision, and in Aetna Life Insurance Co. v. Haworth, 300 U.S. 227 (1937), which upheld the federal Act. See pp. 57–58, *supra*.

The key provision of the Declaratory Judgment Act, 28 U.S.C. § 2201, authorizes a federal court to issue a declaratory judgment "[i]n a case of actual controversy *within its jurisdiction*" (emphasis added). Suppose that on the facts of the Mottley case, the plaintiffs sought a declaration that (1) the Act of Congress did not retroactively invalidate railroad passes previously issued by contract, or (2) if it did, the Act was unconstitutional. Both questions are ones of federal law, and an "actual controversy" exists between the parties. There is little doubt that Congress *could* confer federal court jurisdiction to entertain such a declaratory action; the case would "arise under" federal law within the meaning of Article III. But the question whether Congress *has* conferred jurisdiction over such an action—whether such an action falls within the "arising under" jurisdiction defined by statute—is the subject of the next case.

Skelly Oil Co. v. Phillips Petroleum Co.

339 U.S. 667, 70 S.Ct. 876, 94 L.Ed. 1194 (1950).
Certiorari to the United States Court of Appeals for the Tenth Circuit.

■ MR. JUSTICE FRANKFURTER delivered the opinion of the Court.

In 1945, Michigan-Wisconsin Pipe Line Company sought from the Federal Power Commission a certificate of public convenience and necessity, required by § 7(c) of the Natural Gas Act, for the construction and operation of a pipe line to carry natural gas from Texas to Michigan and Wisconsin. A prerequisite for such a certificate is adequate reserves of gas. To obtain these reserves Michigan-Wisconsin entered into an agreement with Phillips Petroleum Company * * * whereby the latter undertook to make available gas * * * which it produced or purchased from others. Phillips had contracted with petitioners, Skelly Oil Company, Stanolind Oil and Gas Company, and Magnolia Petroleum Company, to purchase gas produced by them * * * for resale to Michigan-Wisconsin. Each contract provided that "in the event Michigan-

Wisconsin Pipe Line Company shall fail to secure from the Federal Power Commission on or before (October 1, 1946) a certificate of public convenience and necessity for the construction and operation of its pipe line, Seller (a petitioner) shall have the right to terminate this contract by written notice to Buyer (Phillips) delivered to Buyer at any time after December 1, 1946, but before the issuance of such certificate." The legal significance of this provision is at the core of this litigation.

The Federal Power Commission * * * on November 30, 1946, ordered that "A certificate of public convenience and necessity be and it is hereby issued to applicant [Michigan-Wisconsin], upon the terms and conditions of this order," listing among the conditions [that gas not be transported to Detroit and Ann Arbor] except with due regard for the rights and duties of Panhandle Eastern Pipe Line Company * * * in its established service for resale in these areas, such rights and duties to be set forth in a supplemental order. It was also provided that Michigan-Wisconsin should have fifteen days from the issue of the supplemental order to notify the Commission whether the certificate "as herein issued is acceptable to it." Finally, the Commission's order provided that for purposes of computing the time within which applications for rehearing could be filed, "the date of issuance of this order shall be deemed to be the date of issuance of the opinions, or of the supplemental order referred to herein, whichever may be the later."

News of the Commission's action was released on November 30, 1946, but the actual content of the order was not made public until December 2, 1946. Petitioners * * *, on December 2, 1946, gave notice to Phillips of termination of their contracts on the ground that Michigan-Wisconsin had not received a certificate of public convenience and necessity. Thereupon Michigan-Wisconsin and Phillips brought suit against petitioners in the District Court for the Northern District of Oklahoma. Alleging that a certificate of public convenience and necessity, "within the meaning of said Natural Gas Act and said contracts" had been issued prior to petitioners' attempt at termination of the contracts, they invoked the Federal Declaratory Judgment Act for a declaration that the contracts were still "in effect and binding upon the parties thereto." * * * [T]he District Court decreed that the contracts between Phillips and petitioners have not been "effectively terminated and that each of such contracts remain (sic) in full force and effect." The Court of Appeals for the Tenth Circuit affirmed, and we brought the case here because it raises in sharp form the question whether a suit like this "arises under the Constitution, laws or treaties of the United States," 28 U.S.C. § 1331, so as to enable District Courts to give declaratory relief under the Declaratory Judgment Act, * * * 28 U.S.C. § 2201.

"[T]he operation of the Declaratory Judgment Act is procedural only." Aetna Life Ins. Co. v. Haworth, 300 U.S. 227, 240. Congress enlarged the range of remedies available in the federal courts but did not extend their jurisdiction. * * * Prior to [the Declaratory Judgment] Act, a federal court would entertain a suit on a contract only if the plaintiff asked for an immediately enforceable remedy like money damages or an injunction, but such relief could only be given if the requisites of jurisdiction, in the sense of a federal right or diversity, provided foundation for resort to the federal courts. The Declaratory Judgment Act allowed relief to be given by way of recognizing the plaintiff's right even though no immediate enforcement of it was asked. But the requirements of jurisdiction—the limited subject matters which alone Congress had authorized the District Courts to adjudicate—were not impliedly repealed or modified.

If Phillips sought damages from petitioners or specific performance of their contracts, it could not bring suit in a United States District Court on the theory that it was asserting a federal right. * * * Whatever federal claim Phillips may be able to urge would in any event be injected into the case only in anticipation of a defense to be asserted by petitioners. * * * [But it has long been settled that t]he plaintiff's claim itself must present a federal question "unaided by anything alleged in anticipation of avoidance of defenses which it is thought the defendant may interpose." Taylor v. Anderson, 234 U.S. 74, 75–76.

These decisions reflect the current of jurisdictional legislation since the Act of March 3, 1875, 18 Stat. 470, first entrusted to the lower federal courts wide jurisdiction in cases "arising under this Constitution, the Laws of the United States, and Treaties." * * * With exceptions not now relevant Congress has narrowed the opportunities for entrance into the federal courts, and this Court has been more careful than in earlier days in enforcing these jurisdictional limitations.

To be observant of these restrictions is not to indulge in formalism or sterile technicality. It would turn into the federal courts a vast current of litigation indubitably arising under State law, in the sense that the right to be vindicated was State-created, if a suit for a declaration of rights could be brought into the federal courts merely because an anticipated defense derived from federal law. Not only would this unduly swell the volume of litigation in the District Courts but it would also embarrass those courts—and this Court on potential review—in that matters of local law may often be involved, and the District Courts may either have to decide doubtful questions of State law or hold cases pending disposition of such State issues by State courts. To sanction suits for declaratory relief as within the jurisdiction of the District Courts merely because, as in this case, artful pleading anticipates a defense based on federal law would contravene the whole trend of jurisdictional legislation by Congress, disregard the effective functioning of the federal judicial system and distort the limited procedural purpose of the Declaratory Judgment Act. Since the matter in controversy as to which Phillips asked for a declaratory judgment is not one that "arises under the * * * laws * * * of the United States" and since as to Skelly and Stanolind jurisdiction cannot be sustained on the score of diversity of citizenship, the proceedings against them should have been dismissed.

[The Court proceeded to reach the merits as to Magnolia because, based on its citizenship and that of Phillips, diversity jurisdiction existed.]

■ MR. JUSTICE BLACK agrees with the Court of Appeals and would affirm
its judgment.

■ MR. JUSTICE DOUGLAS took no part in the consideration or disposition
of this case.

■ MR. CHIEF JUSTICE VINSON, with whom MR. JUSTICE BURTON joins,
dissenting in part.

I concur in that part of the Court's judgment that directs dismissal
of the cause as to Skelly and Stanolind. I have real doubts as to whether
there is a federal question here at all, even though interpretation of the
contract between private parties requires an interpretation of a federal
statute and the action of a federal regulatory body. But the Court finds
it unnecessary to reach that question because it holds that the federal
question, if any, is not a part of the plaintiff's claim and that jurisdiction
does not, therefore, attach. While this result is not a necessary one, I am
not prepared to dissent from it at this time. * * *

NOTE ON THE JURISDICTIONAL SIGNIFICANCE OF THE DECLARATORY JUDGMENT ACT

(1) The Basis for the Skelly Decision. Were Chief Justice Vinson's doubts
about "whether there is a federal question here at all" well founded? Did the
fact that federal law was "incorporated" into the case *by private contract*
differentiate the case from cases like Grable and Smith v. Kansas City Title
& Trust, p. 821, *supra*? If two Nevada citizens make a bet, valid and
enforceable under state law, about whether a transaction, in which neither
has any personal interest, is legal under federal law, should they be able to
file in federal court to obtain a declaratory judgment on the federal question
involved?

However one answers the preceding questions, Skelly Oil's refusal to
uphold jurisdiction did not rest on the specifics of the federal question in that
case; instead, the opinion articulated a much broader rule. The Court
interpreted the Declaratory Judgment Act as not conferring jurisdiction over
declaratory actions when the underlying dispute could not *otherwise* have
been heard in federal court. Under that interpretation, the existence of
jurisdiction over a declaratory action depends on the answer to a
hypothetical question: had the Declaratory Judgment Act not been enacted,
would there have been a nondeclaratory action (i) concerning the same issue,
(ii) between the same parties, (iii) that itself would have been within the
federal courts' subject matter jurisdiction? In Skelly Oil, there was no such
hypothetical nondeclaratory action (at least as to the non-diverse parties),
and as a result, there was no jurisdiction over the declaratory action. And if,
as is supposed above on p. 838, *supra*, in a case like Mottley, the individuals
had filed a declaratory judgment action against the railroad, there, too, no
§ 1331 jurisdiction would exist under the approach of Skelly Oil.

Skelly Oil's test for federal jurisdiction over declaratory actions has been
much criticized.[1] After all, the drafters and advocates of the Declaratory
Judgment Act clearly saw it as an innovation that permitted suit by parties

---

[1]   See, *e.g.*, Doernberg & Mushlin, p. 837, *supra*; see also Mishkin, *The Federal "Question"
in the District Courts*, 53 Colum.L.Rev. 157, 178 n.99 (1953).

who previously would not have had access to any forum. Chief among those whom the Act sought to authorize to sue were persons who would be defendants in traditional coercive actions if and when their adversaries brought suit. But Skelly Oil's interpretation often bars such prospective defendants from seeking declaratory relief in federal court on matters of federal law.

There is legislative history supporting the proposition, relied upon by Justice Frankfurter, that the Act was not meant to expand federal jurisdiction. But Professors Doernberg and Mushlin, p. 837, *supra*, argue persuasively that the concern underlying that history was along a different dimension—concern about ensuring that federal courts continue to decide only genuine cases or controversies, rather than about limiting federal courts to cases or controversies that, before 1934, would have been within federal subject matter jurisdiction.[2]

Under the rule of Skelly Oil, a complaint that turns exclusively on the meaning of federal law may be outside the federal question jurisdiction. Thus, the rule's division of cases between state and federal courts often disserves the purposes of the "arising under" jurisdiction.[3] Moreover, the rule is extremely complex, making jurisdiction turn on an analysis of all of the *hypothetical* nondeclaratory claims for relief that might relate to the same dispute and whether any of these hypothetical actions would have arisen under federal law.

(2) Reach of Skelly Oil. Skelly Oil clearly rejected the view that jurisdiction exists merely because a federal question is properly set forth in the complaint for a declaratory judgment, when that question would have arisen only by way of defense or reply in a nondeclaratory action between the same parties. But the scope of the jurisdiction that Skelly Oil permitted was not entirely clear. A narrow reading of Skelly Oil would permit the exercise of jurisdiction over a declaratory action only if jurisdiction would also exist in a hypothetical nondeclaratory action brought by the declaratory judgment *plaintiff*. A broader reading of Skelly Oil would uphold jurisdiction over a declaratory action if jurisdiction would exist in a hypothetical nondeclaratory action brought *by either party* against the other. See Note, *Developments in the Law—Declaratory Judgments—1941–1949*, 62 Harv.L.Rev. 787, 802–03 (1949) (discussing, before the Skelly Oil decision, various approaches and favoring the broader view).

The broader interpretation is in some tension with a premise of Skelly Oil, because it would permit defendants to sue in federal court when they could not have done so before enactment of the Declaratory Judgment Act. But the Supreme Court has nonetheless endorsed the broader view. In Franchise Tax Board v. Construction Laborers Vacation Trust, 463 U.S. 1 (1983), p. 846, *infra*, the Court stated that federal courts have "regularly"

---

[2]   For evidence that then-Professor Frankfurter opposed enactment of the Declaratory Judgment Act, primarily because he thought it would facilitate adjudication of constitutional issues without an adequate factual record or adequate experience under the statute—an approach that he feared would aggravate the judicial tendency of the era to declare social and economic legislation to be unconstitutional—see Doernberg & Mushlin, *History Comes Calling: Dean Griswold Offers New Evidence About the Jurisdictional Debate Surrounding the Enactment of the Declaratory Judgment Act*, 37 UCLA L.Rev. 139 (1989). The authors suggest that Professor Frankfurter's concerns about justiciability evolved into Justice Frankfurter's concerns in Skelly Oil about subject matter jurisdiction.

[3]   Recall the Court's similar approach to the question of arising under jurisdiction over actions to compel arbitration, pp. 814–815, *supra*.

assumed jurisdiction over declaratory judgment actions in which the declaratory *defendant* could have brought a coercive federal action against the declaratory plaintiff.

An important example of suits falling within this broader view are those in which an alleged patent infringer (who would, of course, be the defendant in any coercive action for patent infringement) asks a federal court for a declaration of noninfringement or of the invalidity of the patent. Apart from seeking declaratory relief, the alleged infringer would have no way to bring the dispute before a federal court; only the patent holder could have done so. But the leading and widely followed decision in E. Edelmann & Co. v. Triple-A Specialty Co., 88 F.2d 852 (7th Cir.1937), held that an alleged infringer's claim for declaratory relief "arises under" the patent laws. In the Franchise Tax Board case, the Court approved of the Edelmann holding, and in other decisions the Court has reached the merits of such actions for a declaratory judgment without raising any question of jurisdiction. See, *e.g.*, Calmar, Inc. v. Cook Chem. Co., decided *sub nom.* Graham v. John Deere Co., 383 U.S. 1 (1966).

A different question about the reach of Skelly Oil arises from the fact that sometimes more than one possible coercive action can be imagined. For example, suppose that a patent licensor and licensee disagree about whether a product made by the licensee infringes the licensor's patent; the licensee refuses to pay royalties with respect to that product; and then one of the disputants seeks a declaration about the scope of the patent. The licensor could have brought either of two coercive actions, one for breach of contract and one for patent infringement. In such a case, the Supreme Court has held that it suffices to establish arising under jurisdiction over the declaratory action that *one* hypothetical coercive action—that for patent infringement— would arise under federal law. See Medtronic, Inc. v. Mirowski Family Ventures, LLC, 134 S.Ct. 843 (2014).

NOTE ON ACTIONS FOR DECLARATORY AND INJUNCTIVE RELIEF CONCERNING STATE AND LOCAL LAWS ALLEGED TO BE PREEMPTED BY FEDERAL LAW

(1) Federal Complaints Asserting That State Laws Are Preempted. Litigants often sue state or local officials, claiming that a state statute, regulation, or other action is preempted by a federal statute or by the federal Constitution and seeking injunctive relief. If federal law gives a right of action (express or implied) to a plaintiff to bring such an action, there is no doubt that the lawsuit "arises under" federal law within the meaning of § 1331. The harder questions concern the source and scope of any federal right of action.

(a) Express Statutory Rights of Action. Sometimes a federal statute confers an express right to sue a state official for injunction against a state law that the plaintiff contends is preempted. Consider, for example, the Employee Retirement Income Security Act (ERISA), which provides protection for employee benefit plans; § 502(a) of the Act, 29 U.S.C. § 1132(a), expressly authorizes suit by participants, beneficiaries, and fiduciaries of benefit plans to enjoin conduct that violates the Act. Section 502(a) has been construed as including the right to sue state officials for an injunction against enforcing state laws that are inconsistent with ERISA.

(b) The Shaw Decision and Implied Rights of Action. The Supreme Court has suggested more broadly that an action seeking to enjoin preempted state regulation may be brought even if the federal statute alleged to have preemptive effect does not expressly authorize such a suit. The leading authority for the proposition that there is, in effect, an implied right of action to bring such an action is Shaw v. Delta Air Lines, Inc., 463 U.S. 85 (1983). In the Shaw case, private plaintiffs, alleging that ERISA preempted provisions of New York's Human Rights Law and Disability Benefits Law, sued state officials for declaratory and injunctive relief. In upholding federal question jurisdiction, the Court did not rest on the narrow ground that § 502(a) of ERISA specifically authorized the action. See Paragraph 1(a), *supra*. Instead, the Court relied on general principles seemingly applicable to any claim that a federal statute preempts state law:

"It is beyond dispute that federal courts have jurisdiction over suits to enjoin state officials from interfering with federal rights. See Ex parte Young, 209 U.S. 123, 160–62 (1908). A plaintiff who seeks injunctive relief from state regulation, on the ground that such regulation is pre-empted by a federal statute which, by virtue of the Supremacy Clause of the Constitution, must prevail, thus presents a federal question which the federal courts have jurisdiction under 28 U.S.C. § 1331 to resolve. This Court, of course, frequently has resolved pre-emption disputes in a similar jurisdictional posture."

The decision in Ex parte Young, p. 922, *infra*, cited by the Shaw opinion, upheld an injunction against a state statute regulating railroad rates on the ground that the statute was confiscatory and denied due process. The Due Process Clause does not expressly confer on individuals a right to enjoin unconstitutional state laws; it might have been interpreted as relegating rightholders to defending an enforcement proceeding on the ground that the state law is invalid. Young has often been interpreted as having recognized a judicially implied federal cause of action for injunctive relief under the Due Process Clause—although in recent years, some scholars and judges have advocated a narrower reading of the Young decision. See pp. 931–935, *infra*. But insofar as Young recognized an implied federal cause of action for injunctive relief under the Due Process Clause, could the Court have refused to recognize a similar cause of action under a federal statute?

(2) Questions about Implied Rights of Action on Grounds of Preemption. Under the Court's holdings that an implied right of action exists to enjoin state regulation as preempted, it is a simple matter to conclude that § 1331 confers arising under jurisdiction. The more difficult question is how the implied right of action recognized by cases like Shaw and Ex parte Young can be squared with recent Supreme Court decisions taking the view that if Congress did not provide an express right of action to a regulatory beneficiary, no implied right should be recognized. See Chapter VII, Sec. 2(A). Is there any reason why courts should be more willing to recognize implied rights of action claiming preemption of state law—for example, to permit a drug company to assert an implied right of action to enjoin a state regulation that, the company asserts, is preempted by the federal food and drug laws—than to permit an implied right of action by injured drug users against the drug company?[1]

Notwithstanding some lack of harmony in the case law,[2] the rule that there is an implied right of action to enjoin state or local regulation that is preempted by a federal statutory or constitutional provision—and that such an action falls within the federal question jurisdiction—long appeared to be well-established. Thus, in Verizon Maryland, Inc. v. Public Serv. Comm'n, 535 U.S. 635, 642 (2002), the Court stated: "Verizon seeks relief from the Commission's order 'on the ground that such regulation is pre-empted by a federal statute which, by virtue of the Supremacy Clause of the Constitution, must prevail,' and its claim 'thus presents a federal question which the federal courts have jurisdiction under 28 U.S.C. § 1331 to resolve'" (quoting Shaw).[3]

More recently, in Armstrong v. Exceptional Child Center, Inc., 135 S.Ct. 1378 (2015), which is discussed in greater detail at p. 745, note 12, *supra*, and pp. 934, 1012–1013, *infra*, the Court raised questions about the circumstances in which an implied cause of action for preemption will exist. Contrary to indications in several prior decisions, Armstrong held that no cause of action for preemption will lie directly under the Supremacy Clause. The Justices in Armstrong reaffirmed that a cause of action for preemption has long existed as a form of judicially recognized common law, cognizable pursuant to the traditions of equity jurisprudence. The Court, however, further ruled (5-4) that a specific remedy supplied by the relevant statute (in this case, the Medicaid Act) may foreclose a traditional equitable remedy. At the same time, Armstrong reaffirms Ex parte Young and other decisions establishing that a cause of action to enjoin state law on federal preemption grounds, where it exists, falls within the federal "arising under" jurisdiction.[4]

(3) A General, Express Federal Right of Action? The Relevance of 42 U.S.C. § 1983. A possible answer to any uncertainty about *implied* rights of action to obtain declaratory or injunctive relief against preempted state regulation was given, several years after the Shaw decision, in Golden State Transit Corp. v. City of Los Angeles, 493 U.S. 103 (1989), discussed at p. 1012, *infra*. There, the Court ruled that 42 U.S.C. § 1983, which provides an express right of action to obtain relief against action taken under color of state law in violation of federal statutory or constitutional rights, can embrace actions by a federal rightholder contending that state or local

---

[1] For an argument that historically the federal courts possessed equitable power to issue injunctive relief in constitutional cases, which has not been withdrawn by congressional enactments, see Preis, *In Defense of Implied Injunctive Relief in Constitutional Cases*, 22 Wm. & Mary Bill of Rts. L.J. 1 (2013).

[2] For an expression of doubts about decisions such as Shaw, see Monaghan, *Federal Statutory Review Under Section 1983 and the APA*, 91 Colum.L.Rev. 233, 239–40 (1991). *Cf.* Southland Corp. v. Keating, 465 U.S. 1 (1984), discussed at p. 810, note 7, *supra*.

[3] Although the majority treated the Verizon case as one, like Shaw, involving a claim that state law was preempted, in fact the claim was (in the words of Justice Souter's concurring opinion) that "the Maryland Public Service Commission has wrongly decided a question of federal law under a decisional power conferred by" a federal statute.

[4] In Sprint Communications, Inc. v. Jacobs, 134 S.Ct. 584 (2013), a unanimous Court had re-affirmed the Verizon decision, holding that federal question jurisdiction extends to a claim that federal law preempts a state administrative adjudication. Justice Ginsburg's opinion for the Court said little more than this: "Neither party has questioned the District Court's jurisdiction to decide whether federal law preempted the [state agency's] decision, and rightly so." Sprint, like Ex parte Young and Shaw, involved a plaintiff's pre-emptive assertion of a federal defense to an enforcement action.

regulation is preempted by federal law. It appears that § 1983 also contemplates the award of declaratory relief, for that statute states that an injunction against a judicial officer shall not be granted "unless a declaratory decree was violated or declaratory relief was unavailable." Insofar as § 1983 creates an express federal right of action to declaratory relief, the existence of federal jurisdiction over that right of action seems clear. But note that even after the Golden State decision, federal courts (including the Supreme Court) have continued to uphold their jurisdiction under § 1331 over actions to enjoin preempted state or local regulations without relying on § 1983. (Thus, the Verizon decision, cited in Paragraph (2), makes no reference to § 1983.)

(4) Declaratory Judgments that a State or Local Law is Preempted. Decisions like Shaw or the Golden State Transit decision seem to suggest that, at least in many cases, federal courts have jurisdiction over a complaint by a private party seeking nothing more than a declaration that a state or local regulation to which it is subject is preempted by federal law. Often, such a complaint satisfies the jurisdictional requirements established by Skelly Oil: the complaint presents a question of federal law, and there is a hypothetical nondeclaratory action between the same parties that presents the same issue and that would arise under federal law—an action seeking to enjoin the allegedly preempted law. (In Shaw, the plaintiff sought both declaratory and injunctive relief.)

But it may not always be the case that there is a valid hypothetical action for an injunction. (After all, one purpose of the Declaratory Judgment Act was to authorize relief in circumstances in which the requirements for issuance of an injunction have not been met.) And the absence of a plausible claim for injunctive relief might seem, under Skelly Oil, to cast doubt on the existence of federal question jurisdiction. Nonetheless, the Supreme Court, in a dictum in Lawrence County v. Lead-Deadwood School Dist. No. 40–1, 469 U.S. 256, 259 n.6 (1985), suggested more generally that there is § 1331 jurisdiction over an action seeking a declaration that state law is preempted. The Court relied on Shaw, but did not mention whether the plaintiff could have filed a coercive action for an injunction. Even if the Court thought it was merely applying Shaw, doesn't this dictum at least raise the possibility that any implied right of action to challenge a state regulation as preempted includes a right to not only injunctive relief (as in Shaw) but also to declaratory relief? See also Schneidewind v. ANR Pipeline Co., 485 U.S. 293 (1988).

(5) The Franchise Tax Board Decision. In a case decided the same day as Shaw, the Court unanimously declined to exercise jurisdiction under the Declaratory Judgment Act over a claim that federal law did *not* preempt state law. Franchise Tax Board v. Construction Laborers Vacation Trust, 463 U.S. 1 (1983). The opinion's reasoning is complex and not entirely persuasive.

(a) The Facts. The case involved a trust established to provide paid vacation benefits earned by construction employees in California. Some of the employee-beneficiaries of the trust were delinquent in paying their California state income taxes. The Franchise Tax Board, the California agency charged with enforcement of the income tax, filed a complaint in state court against the trust. The first claim sought to enforce three levies against the trust, which would require the trust to pay to the Board amounts equal to the tax delinquencies of employee beneficiaries of the trust. The second claim sought a declaration that the Board's regulatory authority was *not* preempted by ERISA.

After the trust removed the case to federal court under 28 U.S.C. § 1441, the Board moved to remand. The first claim in the complaint simply rested on California tax law, and hence could not, under the well-pleaded complaint rule, support jurisdiction. The difficulty in the case concerned whether the second claim arose under federal law.

(b) Removability of State Declaratory Judgment Actions. Justice Brennan's opinion noted that the case initially presented a question of first impression: "whether the doctrine of Skelly Oil limits original federal court jurisdiction under § 1331—and by extension removal jurisdiction under § 1441—when a question of federal law appears on the face of a well-pleaded complaint for a state law declaratory judgment." He reasoned that "while Skelly Oil itself is limited to the federal Declaratory Judgment Act, fidelity to its spirit leads us to extend it to state declaratory judgment actions as well." To hold otherwise would make the rule of Skelly Oil a "dead letter", for "litigants could get into federal court for a declaratory judgment despite our interpretation of § 2201, simply by pleading an adequate state claim for a declaration of federal law. * * * Therefore, we hold that * * * federal courts do not have original jurisdiction, nor do they acquire jurisdiction on removal, when a federal question is presented by a complaint for a state declaratory judgment, but Skelly Oil would bar jurisdiction if the plaintiff had sought a federal declaratory judgment."

(c) The Application of Skelly Oil. In applying Skelly Oil, the Court first acknowledged that the Board's request for a declaratory judgment presented an issue—and only an issue—of federal law. Moreover, there did appear to be a hypothetical nondeclaratory action between the same parties that raised the same issue of federal law, for the Court appeared willing to assume that the Trust "could have sought an injunction under ERISA against application to it of state regulations that require acts inconsistent with ERISA". On that assumption, this was not a case prohibited by Skelly Oil.

(d) The Franchise Tax Board Exception. Nonetheless, the Court refused to exercise jurisdiction, creating a new exception to the rules for arising under jurisdiction set forth in Skelly Oil. The discussion is worth quoting at length. "We have always interpreted what Skelly Oil called 'the current of jurisdictional legislation since the Act of March 3, 1875,' 339 U.S., at 673, with an eye to practicality and necessity. 'What is needed is something of that common-sense accommodation of judgment to kaleidoscopic situations which characterizes the law in its treatment of problems of causation * * * a selective process which picks the substantial causes out of the web and lays the other ones aside.' Gully v. First National Bank, 299 U.S.[109,] 117–18. There are good reasons why the federal courts should not entertain suits by the States to declare the validity of their regulations despite possibly conflicting federal law. States are not significantly prejudiced by an inability to come to federal court for a declaratory judgment in advance of a possible injunctive suit by a person subject to federal regulation. They have a variety of means by which they can enforce their own laws in their own courts, and they do not suffer if the preemption questions such enforcement may raise are tested there. [Footnote 22, appended at this point, added: 'Indeed, as appellant's strategy in this case shows, they may often be willing to go to great lengths to avoid federal-court resolution of a preemption question. Realistically, there is little prospect that States will flood the federal courts with declaratory judgment actions; most questions will arise, as in this case, because a State has sought a declaration in state court and the defendant has removed the case to federal court. Accordingly, it is perhaps appropriate to note that considerations of comity make us reluctant to snatch cases which a State has brought from the courts of that State, unless some clear rule demands it.'] The express grant of federal jurisdiction in ERISA is limited to suits brought by certain parties, as to whom Congress presumably determined that a right to enter federal court was necessary to further the statute's purposes. It did not go so far as to provide that any suit *against* such parties must also be brought in federal court when they themselves did not choose to sue. The situation presented by a State's suit for a declaration of the validity of state law is sufficiently removed from the spirit of necessity and careful limitation of district court jurisdiction that informed our statutory interpretation in Skelly Oil and Gully to convince us that, until Congress informs us otherwise, such a suit is not within the original jurisdiction of the United States district courts. Accordingly, the same suit brought originally in state court is not removable either."

(6) The Basis for Declining Jurisdiction in Franchise Tax Board.

(a) The Majority's Reasoning. The Court's reasoning is difficult to accept at face value. It should not matter that the *state* would not be prejudiced by a remand to state court, when the notice of removal was filed by *the Trust*, which sought a federal court adjudication of the preemption question and may have feared that the state court would give an unduly narrow scope to federal preemption. Moreover, given that federal jurisdiction over nearly all ERISA actions is exclusive, see 29 U.S.C. § 1132(e)(1), it is hard to justify the Court's ad hoc exception, which leaves an important question concerning ERISA preemption to the state courts. It is equally hard to justify the odd state of the law after Franchise Tax Board and Shaw—that a federal court may entertain a private litigant's action, against a government agency or official, seeking a determination that state regulation *is preempted* by federal law (Shaw), but may not entertain an action by the government agency or official against the private litigant, seeking a determination that the state regulation *is not preempted* (Franchise Tax Board).

(b) An Alternative Rationale. Consider, however, a different rationale for the Court's outcome. Suppose that the state had filed only Count I of its complaint—a simple state court enforcement action against the Trust for a tax lien, without including Count II (the request for a declaration of nonpreemption). Had the Trust then filed a separate federal court action seeking declaratory or injunctive relief against enforcement of state tax law on the ground that it was preempted by ERISA, the federal court would have had subject matter jurisdiction under § 1331. However, under established principles the federal district court would have abstained from exercising that jurisdiction, in order to prevent federal interference with important state interests implicated in the enforcement action. See generally Chap. X, Sec. 2(c), *infra*.

In the actual Franchise Tax Board case, the Trust's effort to remove the state court declaratory action, if successful, would have had much the same effect as a prohibited separate federal action for a declaratory judgment. Indeed, because the Trust sought to invoke supplemental jurisdiction so as to remove not only the state's declaratory judgment action but also its claim for a tax lien, to have upheld removal jurisdiction would have interfered more radically with the state's power to enforce its tax laws in its own courts than would a separate federal declaratory or injunctive action. For removal, if successful, would have brought into federal court not only the federal preemption issues in the dispute but also the tax lien claim, which was governed entirely by state law. Thus, if the abstention doctrine would have precluded the Trust from litigating a separate federal court action to enjoin the state court proceeding as preempted, it would seem to follow a fortiori that the Trust was precluded from removing the entire state court action and thereby totally obstructing state court enforcement of the tax lien provision.

This analysis, though perhaps hinted at by Justice Brennan's reference in footnote 22 to "comity", is hardly put forward clearly. Wouldn't it have provided a sounder basis for the Court's outcome?[5]

---

4. FEDERAL QUESTION REMOVAL

NOTE ON THE REMOVAL STATUTES

A. The General Removal Provision, 28 U.S.C. § 1441, and the "Complete Preemption" Rationale for Removal Under § 1441

(1) Statutory History of the General Removal Provision. As in the case of original jurisdiction, no general grant of removal jurisdiction in "arising under" cases existed until 1875. The Act of Mar. 3, 1875, 18 Stat. 470, went to the opposite extreme: subject to a $500 jurisdictional amount requirement, virtually every civil case removable under Article III was made removable by either plaintiff or defendant.

The present structure of federal question removal in civil cases was set by the Act of Mar. 3, 1887, 24 Stat. 552, corrected by the Act of Aug. 13, 1888, 25 Stat. 433. It gave the right to remove only to defendants and only in cases that could originally have been filed in federal court; no general

---

[5] The majority in both Grable and Merrell Dow endorsed basing jurisdictional decisions on judicial attributions of congressional purpose or evaluations of the federal interest in federal court adjudication. By contrast, Justice Thomas' concurrence in Grable and Justice Brennan's dissent in Merrell Dow both expressed concern about what they viewed as the ad hoc and malleable quality of that approach, although those two Justices would have moved in opposite directions: Justice Thomas urged limiting § 1331 to federal causes of action, while Justice Brennan suggested broadly entertaining state law claims incorporating an issue of federal law.

But then Justice Brennan's opinion for the Court in Franchise Tax Board discerned, and rested on, a congressional purpose to exclude states from seeking a declaration of non-preemption. That approach might appear to be vulnerable to the objections he raised in dissent in Merrell Dow. Perhaps, however, Justice Brennan could have distinguished Franchise Tax Board from Merrell Dow on the basis that Franchise Tax Board involved jurisdiction over a declaratory judgment action. The Declaratory Judgment Act, 28 U.S.C. § 2201, says that in a case within its jurisdiction, a federal court "*may* declare the rights and other legal relations of any interested party" (emphasis added); that language gives district courts a broad measure of discretion in determining whether to entertain a declaratory judgment action; and the Court might deem it appropriate to exercise a similar measure of discretion when deciding whether to entertain a state law declaratory judgment action that is removed to federal court.

authorization was included for removal based on a federal defense.[1] The current statute, 28 U.S.C. § 1441(a), preserves those features. Also preserved is the requirement that, in cases in which multiple defendants are sued on a claim, all the defendants must join in or consent to the petition for removal. 28 U.S.C. § 1446(b)(2)(A). Finally, some statutory provisions qualify § 1441(a)'s general right of removal by making actions under particular federal statutes non-removable.[2]

(2) Complete Preemption: The Avco Decision. Because removal jurisdiction is tied to original jurisdiction, and original jurisdiction rests on the well-pleaded complaint rule, a federal preemption *defense* to a state-law action typically does not furnish a basis for removal under § 1441.[3] But if the plaintiff's claim, though cast as resting on state law, is "really" a federal claim, removal will be permitted on the ground that the plaintiff should not, by artful pleading, be allowed to negate the defendant's removal rights.

The leading case for this proposition is Avco Corp. v. Aero Lodge No. 735, 390 U.S. 557 (1968). There, the company sued the union in state court, alleging that the union had violated the terms of a collective bargaining agreement, under which the union had agreed to submit all grievances to binding arbitration and not to cause or sanction any "work stoppages, strikes, or slowdowns." Although the company pled only a violation of state contract law, the union removed the case to federal court. On review, the Supreme Court held that the company's claim, although labeled a state law contract claim in the complaint, necessarily arose under § 301 of the federal Taft-Hartley Act, and thus, because it arose under federal law, was removable.

Justice Douglas' unanimous opinion noted that under § 301, substantive federal law governs a claim for breach of a collective bargaining agreement between union and employer, whether the case is filed in federal or state court. The opinion's reasoning is brief and not altogether clear. As elaborated in Franchise Tax Bd. v. Construction Laborers Vacation Trust, 463 U.S. 1, 23–24 (1983), Avco held that "the pre-emptive force of § 301 is so powerful as to displace entirely any state cause of action [for breach of contract.] * * * Avco stands for the proposition that if a federal cause of action completely preempts a state cause of action, any complaint that comes within the scope of the federal cause of action necessarily 'arises under' federal law."

(3) Complete Preemption Under ERISA. In Metropolitan Life Ins. Co. v. Taylor, 481 U.S. 58 (1987), the Court extended the approach of the Avco decision to federal regulation of employee benefit plans under ERISA. There, the Court upheld removal of a state court suit by an employee alleging that his employer had violated state tort and contract law in terminating

---

[1] For detailed discussion of the background of federal question removal, see Collins, *The Unhappy History of Federal Question Removal*, 71 Iowa L.Rev. 717 (1986).

[2] These include (i) damage actions under the Federal Employers' Liability Act, see Act of Apr. 22, 1908, 35 Stat. 65, amended by Act of Apr. 5, 1910, 36 Stat. 291, now codified as 28 U.S.C. § 1445(a); (ii) actions under the Jones Act, which made the FELA applicable to seamen by generic reference, see 46 U.S.C. App. § 688; (iii) actions against railroads sued under federal law for damages to goods shipped of less than $3,000, Act of Jan. 20, 1914, 38 Stat. 278 (a threshold since raised to $10,000, see 28 U.S.C. § 1445(b)); and (iv) actions under the 1933 Securities Act, Act of May 27, 1933, § 22(a), 48 Stat. 74. 87, now codified as amended at 15 U.S.C. § 77v.

For discussion of removal of maritime cases, see p. 873, note 3, *infra.*

[3] On whether the All Writs Act may be used to effect removal in certain cases not covered by the removal statutes, see p. 1085, note 12, *infra.*

disability benefits due under a plan regulated by ERISA. After determining that ERISA preempted the state law claims, the Court examined whether ERISA's civil enforcement provision, § 502(a)(1)(B), "also displaced" the employee's claims. The Court indicated that it was "reluctant to find that extraordinary preemptive power, such as has been found with respect to § 301 of the [Taft-Hartley Act], that converts an ordinary state common law complaint into one stating a federal claim for purposes of the well-pleaded complaint rule." But, the Court concluded, ERISA's legislative history strongly indicated that Congress intended the preemptive sweep of the statute to replicate that of § 301, showing that Congress wished "to make § 502(a)(1)(B) suits brought by participants or beneficiaries federal questions for the purposes of federal court jurisdiction in like manner as § 301 of the [Taft-Hartley Act]."

(4) The Reach of Complete Preemption: The Beneficial National Bank Decision. The Supreme Court's less than pellucid explanation, in Avco and Metropolitan Life, of the complete preemption doctrine generated some confusion about both the rationale and scope of the doctrine.[4] Much of the confusion, however, was dispelled by the decision in Beneficial Nat'l Bank v. Anderson, 539 U.S. 1 (2003). There, plaintiffs' state court action alleged that a bank chartered under the National Bank Act had violated state usury law. The Court, with Justice Stevens writing, upheld removal on the complete preemption theory. The Court's discussion of Avco and Metropolitan Life summarized those decisions as permitting removal "when a federal statute wholly displaces the state-law cause of action through complete pre-emption", and noted that in both instances "the federal statutes at issue provided the exclusive cause of action for the claim asserted and also set forth procedures and remedies governing that cause of action."

The Court found that the National Bank Act "unquestionably pre-empts any [state-law] rule that would treat * * * as usurious" rates that were lawful under the Act. But a federal preemption defense would not alone justify removal; "[o]nly if Congress intended [the pertinent provision of the federal Act] to provide the exclusive cause of action for usury claims against national banks would the statute be comparable to the provisions" in Avco and Metropolitan Life. Analyzing the federal scheme, the Court found that provisions of the National Bank Act "supersede both the substantive and the remedial provisions of state usury laws and create a federal remedy for overcharges that is exclusive," and that therefore the claim in this case could arise only under federal law. A footnote added that "the proper inquiry

---

4   Contributing to the lack of clarity was the Court's decision in Federated Dep't Stores, Inc. v. Moitie, 452 U.S. 394, 397 n.27 (1981). There, the plaintiffs, after a federal court dismissed their antitrust action, filed a state court action under state laws (concededly not preempted) regulating competition. Upholding removal of the action, the Supreme Court, in a surprising departure from the traditional view that the plaintiff is the master of the complaint, said in a footnote that it would not disturb the "factual finding" of the court below that plaintiffs had attempted by "artful pleading" to disguise the federal nature of their complaint. The Court proceeded to find the removed action barred by claim preclusion.

In Rivet v. Regions Bank of La., 522 U.S. 470 (1998), the Court appears to have effectively overruled Moitie's holding on removal. Stating that the "enigmatic footnote" in Moitie "did not create a preclusion exception to the rule * * * that a defendant could not remove on the basis of a federal defense", the Court unanimously ruled that a state court action removed on the basis that the state-law claim was precluded by a prior federal judgment should have been remanded to the state court. See generally Miller, *Artful Pleading: A Doctrine in Search of a Definition*, 76 Tex.L.Rev. 1781, 1824–25 (1998) (praising the Rivet decision and concluding that the Court's language "[c]onfining Moitie to its context" is simply a courteous way of saying that the "footnote has gone gently into the night").

focuses on whether Congress intended the federal cause of action to be exclusive rather than on whether Congress intended that the cause of action be removable."

Insofar as Avco and Metropolitan Life included language referring to the extraordinary preemptive effect of a statute or to an intent in the legislative history to permit removal, Beneficial National Bank seems to make clear that neither is required to invoke complete preemption. Instead, the Beneficial National Bank opinion suggests that any federal statute that both preempts state law and provides a substitute federal remedy creates an "exclusive cause of action" that falls within the complete preemption doctrine. The substitute federal remedy need not be as complete as that provided by the preempted state law cause of action. Thus, the only remedy available for usury by the National Bank Act is compensation in twice the amount of any unlawful interest charge. In some cases, the remedy that state law, if not preempted, would have provided would have been more generous (for example, compensatory and punitive damages). Nonetheless, federal law is said to provide a substitute remedy.

Justice Scalia (joined by Justice Thomas), dissenting in Beneficial National Bank, attacked the foundations of the complete preemption doctrine, characterizing Avco as a radical departure from the well-pleaded complaint rule and Metropolitan Life simply as following suit because ERISA was modeled on § 301 of the Taft-Hartley Act. To observe that federal preemption may render a state cause of action non-viable did not, he contended, "magically transform[ ]" it into a claim arising under federal law. Criticizing the entire doctrine as illogical, he urged that it be confined to cases under the Taft Hartley Act or statutes modeled on it.

If Justice Scalia's criticism is correct, isn't his intermediate position—to retain the doctrine but confine it to cases under the Taft-Hartley Act or statutes modeled on it—an odd resting point? On the one hand, given the procedural character of the issue and the absence of any significant reliance interests, stare decisis concerns don't appear to militate strongly against scrapping the doctrine altogether. On the other hand, if Avco and Metropolitan Life are to be retained, can one fairly distinguish cases under the National Bank Act?

(5) Exception to or Application of the Well-Pleaded Complaint Rule. The Supreme Court has found the complete preemption doctrine to apply only in the Avco, Metropolitan Life, and Beneficial National Bank decisions. Do you agree with Justice Scalia that these decisions (a) depart from the well-pleaded complaint rule[5] and (b) are illogical?

(a) Professor Seinfeld argues that the critical factor determining whether the doctrine applies—the presence of an exclusive federal cause of action—should not have determinative significance, but may have acquired centrality because of the Court's unwillingness to acknowledge that complete preemption removal is an exception to the well-pleaded complaint rule. He contends that the key policy implicated by federal defense removal is promoting what he calls regulatory uniformity—a congressional policy of "subjecting regulated entities to a single set of legal standards, so as to avoid the burdens that might accompany compliance with a multitude of rules

---

[5] One year after the Beneficial decision, in Aetna Health Inc. v. Davila, 542 U.S. 200 (2004), a case involving ERISA, the Court unanimously upheld removal under the complete preemption doctrine, which it described as "an exception" to the well-pleaded complaint rule.

enacted by different sovereigns." That interest is more likely to be implicated when federal law is more broadly preemptive, and "it would therefore make sense to tether a rule of federal defense removal to the scope of federal preemption". While he would not limit removal to instances of field preemption (a concept whose boundaries, he acknowledges, are blurry), he suggests that when Congress has established "both a regulatory floor and ceiling", removal is particularly appropriate. See Seinfeld, *The Puzzle of Complete Preemption*, 155 U.Pa.L.Rev. 537, 566–77 (2007).

(b) Professor Morrison agrees with much of Professor Seinfeld's analysis, but objects that any complete preemption doctrine is a wholly judge-made expansion of federal jurisdiction that reaches beyond what Congress authorized in § 1441 and that the necessary policy-based balancing that underlies it should be undertaken by Congress. Morrison, *Complete Preemption and the Separation of Powers*, 156 U.Pa.L.Rev. PENNumbra 186 (2007).

(c) In turn, Professor McGreal defends the doctrine as a corollary of rather than an exception to the well-pleaded complaint rule. He suggests that the plaintiffs in National Beneficial Bank were hoping, despite relatively clear law pointing to preemption of state usury claims, that elected state judges might find to the contrary, whether by mistake or out of local bias. McGreal argues that the content of a "well-pleaded" complaint depends not on how the lawyer drafted the allegations but on how a *reasonable* lawyer would characterize plaintiff's allegations, an approach that protects the federal interest in not permitting lawyers, by manipulating the pleading, to avoid federal jurisdiction and prospect for a state court error. McGreal, *In Defense of Complete Preemption*, 155 U.Pa.L.Rev. PENNumbra 147 (2007).

B. Removal Under 28 U.S.C. § 1442 of Actions Against Federal Officials, Federal Agencies, and Private Persons Acting Under Federal Officers

(1) The 1948 Revision and Its Antecedents. From 1815 on, specialized grants of removal jurisdiction, enacted in times of sharp federal-state conflict, permitted particular federal officials to remove state court actions to federal court. These grants were originally limited to removal by officers enforcing the customs laws and later extended to officers enforcing the revenue laws and certain other circumstances involving official federal action.[6] In 1948, Congress generalized this approach. The Revision of the

---

[6]   The major statutory developments can be summarized as follows:

1. In 1815, responding to New England's resistance to the War of 1812, Congress inserted into an act for the collection of customs duties a provision—of limited duration—authorizing removal of all suits or prosecutions against federal officers or other persons as a result of enforcement of the act. Act of Feb. 4, 1815, § 8, 3 Stat. 195, 198–99. See also Act of Mar. 3, 1815, § 6, 3 Stat. 231, 233–34, extended for one year by the Act of Apr. 27, 1816, § 3, 3 Stat. 315, and for another four years by the Act of Mar. 3, 1817, § 6, 3 Stat. 396, 397.

2. The "Force Bill" of 1833, which was prompted by South Carolina's threats of nullification, generalized the earlier provision, authorizing removal of all suits or prosecutions against officers of the United States or other persons on account of any acts done under the customs laws. Act of Mar. 2, 1833, § 3, 4 Stat. 632, 633–34.

3. The Civil War brought a wave of removal acts. In 1863, Congress authorized, for the period only of the rebellion, the removal of cases brought against federal officers or others for acts committed during the rebellion and justified under the authority of the President or Congress. Act of Mar. 3, 1863, § 5, 12 Stat. 756–57, amended by Act of May 11, 1866, §§ 3–4, 14 Stat. 46; Act of Feb. 5, 1867, 14 Stat. 385. See also Act of July 28, 1866, § 8, 14 Stat. 328, 329–30; Act of July 27, 1868, § 1, 15 Stat. 243.

Judicial Code enacted that year included a provision, 28 U.S.C. § 1442(a)(1), that in sweeping terms authorized removal of any civil action or criminal prosecution against "[a]ny officer of the United States or any agency thereof, or person acting under him, for any act under color of such office or on account of any right, title or authority claimed under any Act of Congress for the apprehension or punishment of criminals or the collection of the revenue."[7]

Section 1442(a)(1), unlike § 1441, permits removal of criminal as well as civil cases. And when it applies, § 1442(a)(1) permits something that § 1441 does not—removal of a state law action that could not have been filed originally in federal court, on the basis of a federal defense. However, in Mesa v. California, 489 U.S. 121 (1989), the Court held that § 1442(a)(1) does not permit removal of a state law action when the defendant officer has not alleged any colorable federal defense. See p. 803, *supra*.[8]

From 1864–66, Congress passed a confusing set of enactments whose net result was to extend the removal provisions of the "Force Bill" to cases involving the collection of internal revenues. See Act of Mar. 7, 1864, § 9, 13 Stat. 14, 17; Act of June 30, 1864, § 50, 13 Stat. 218, 241; Act of July 13, 1866, §§ 67–68, 14 Stat. 98, 171–72. See generally Frankfurter & Landis, The Business of the Supreme Court 61–62 (1928). These enactments were the antecedent for two current provisions of § 1442(a): (i) the last clause of § 1442(a)(1), which continued through successive codifications to be limited to cases growing out of the revenue laws, see Rev.Stat. § 643; Act of March 3, 1911, § 33, 36 Stat. 1087, 1097; 28 U.S.C. (1940 ed.) § 76, until the 1948 revision added a reference to acts "for the apprehension or punishment of criminals"; and (ii) § 1442(a)(2), providing for the removal of cases brought against a property holder claiming title derived from a federal official where the case affects the validity of an act of Congress—an authorization that, until 1948, was restricted to cases involving the validity of a revenue law.

4. In 1875, Congress enacted a provision authorizing removal of cases against an officer of either House of Congress for an act done under an order of the House. Act of Mar. 3, 1875, § 8, 18 Stat. 371, 401. The provision is now found in § 1442(a)(4).

5. In 1916, a provision was enacted authorizing the removal of proceedings against an officer of a United States court for acts done under color of office. Act of Aug. 23, 1916, 39 Stat. 532. It is presently found in § 1442(a)(3).

In Jefferson County v. Acker, 527 U.S. 423 (1999), the Court ruled, 5–4, that § 1442(a)(3) permitted federal judges to remove state court actions seeking to collect an occupational tax levied by the county. The judges alleged that tax's application to them was unconstitutional. The majority ruled that the action was "for" an act "under color of office" because the tax provision prohibited the defendants from serving as federal judges without paying the tax; the dissenters on this question contended that the requisite causal connection was lacking because the judges' refusal to pay was "not an action required by [their] official duties".

6. Also in 1916, Congress authorized removal by any member of the armed forces of a state court action brought "on account of any act done under color of his office or status, or in respect to which he claims any right, title, or authority under any law of the United States respecting the military forces thereof, or under the law of war". Act of Aug. 29, 1916, § 3, Art. 117, 39 Stat. 619, 669; Act of June 4, 1920, Art. 117, 41 Stat. 759, 811; Act of June 24, 1948, § 242, 62 Stat. 604, 642; Act of May 5, 1950, § 9, 64 Stat. 107, 146, superseded by Act of Aug. 10, 1956, § 1970A Stat. 626. This protection is now codified in § 1442a.

[7]   Act of June 25, 1948, Pub.L.No. 80–773, ch. 646, § 1442, 62 Stat. 869, 938.

[8]   When is a private defendant "acting under" a federal officer, so as to permit removal under § 1442(a)(1)? In Watson v. Philip Morris Companies, Inc., 551 U.S. 142 (2007), a state court action alleging false advertising by the defendant tobacco company in violation of state law, the Court unanimously rejected the defendant's effort to remove the case under § 1442(a)(1) on the ground that the plaintiffs were attacking a testing process that was mandated and supervised by the Federal Trade Commission. After discussing the history and purpose of the statute, the Court concluded that a private person's acting under a federal officer or agency, within the meaning of § 1442(a)(1), requires more than compliance with federal regulations; rather, the private person seeking to remove must have been engaged in "an effort to *assist*, or to help *carry out*, the duties or tasks of the federal superior."

Some courts have held that § 1442(a)(1) authorizes removal of a state court suit against a private contractor asserting the "government contractor" defense recognized in Boyle v. United

The more specialized provision for removal in the last clause of § 1442(a)(1), pertaining to officers engaged in criminal enforcement or revenue collection, is the residue of the earlier, more specialized grants, as are the provisions of §§ 1442(a)(2)–(4).[9] None of them appears to serve any purpose today in view of the general language of § 1442(a)(1).[10]

(2) Removal of Tort Actions Against Federal Officers. The Federal Employees Liability Reform and Tort Compensation Act of 1988, § 5, 102 Stat. 4563–64, amended 28 U.S.C. § 2679(b) to make the Federal Tort Claims Act (FTCA) the exclusive remedy for torts committed by federal employees in the course of their official duties. Under § 2679(d), as amended, if the Attorney General certifies that an employee who has been sued was acting within the scope of employment, the proceeding shall be redesignated as a suit against the United States; if pending in state court, the suit shall be removed to federal court; and the plaintiff may recover only if the United States is liable under the FTCA.[11]

(3) Removal of Actions Against Federal Agencies. In International Primate Protection League v. Administrators of Tulane Educational Fund, 500 U.S. 72 (1991), a unanimous Court ruled that § 1442(a)(1), as enacted in 1948, did not permit removal of suits against federal agencies (rather than against federal officers). Carefully examining the text—which authorized removal by "[a]ny officer of the United States or any agency thereof, or person acting under him, [in a suit challenging] any act under color of such office"— the Court stressed the failure to set off the phrase "or any agency thereof" by commas, and the use of the phrases "acting under him" and "under color of such office." Rejecting the argument that its construction of the statute would lead to absurd results, the Court suggested that Congress might well have thought officer removal particularly important, because the question of the scope of officers' immunity was complicated, while the immunity of a federal agency "was sufficiently straightforward that a state court, even if hostile to the federal interest, would be unlikely to disregard the law."

Did the statutory text compel the Court's result? If so, why was it necessary to explain that the result made at least some sense? If not, don't the considerations underlying the removal statute weigh strongly in favor of removal?

Five years later, Congress overrode the Primate Protection decision, amending § 1442(a)(1) to expressly authorize removal by the United States or federal agencies. See Federal Courts Improvement Act of 1996, Pub.L.No. 104–317, § 206, 110 Stat. 3847, 3480. After subsequent amendment by the Removal Clarification Act of 2011, Pub.L.No. 112–51, § 2, 125 Stat. 545, the provision authorizes removal by "[t]he United States or any agency thereof"

Technologies Corp., 487 U.S. 500 (1988), p. 666, *supra. E.g.,* Isaacson v. Dow Chem. Co., 517 F.3d 129 (2d Cir.2008).

[9] See note 6, *supra.*

[10] The same could be said about § 1442(b)'s peculiar grant of removal jurisdiction of personal actions brought by an alien against a nonresident who is, or was at the time the action accrued, a civil officer of the United States. This grant originated in the Act of Mar. 30, 1872, 17 Stat. 44, and in 1948 was placed in § 1442(b). Since then, no reported case has invoked the provision, see American Law Institute, Federal Judicial Code Revision Project 406 (2004), which appears to be subsumed by the general provisions permitting removal in diversity cases (28 U.S.C. §§ 1332(a)(2), 1441(b)) except to the extent that § 1442(b) lacks the jurisdictional amount requirement found in the general diversity provision.

[11] For discussion of constitutional questions that have arisen in litigation under the Act, see p. 798, note 5, *supra.*

as well as by "any officer (or any person acting under that officer) of the United States or of any agency thereof, in an official or individual capacity, for or relating to any act under color of such office * * *."

C.   Civil Rights Removal Under 28 U.S.C. § 1443

(1) Statutory Origins and History. The provisions of 28 U.S.C. § 1443 derive from the Reconstruction era.[12] Subsection (1) authorizes defendants to remove a case if they can show both that the right upon which they rely is a "right under any law providing for * * * equal civil rights" and that they are "denied or cannot enforce" that right in the state courts. (Subsection (2), which, unlike subsection (1), limits removal to persons acting under color of law, has largely been subsumed by § 1442.)

(2) Early Decisions. In Strauder v. West Virginia, 100 U.S. 303 (1880), and Virginia v. Rives, 100 U.S. 313 (1880), decided on the same day, the Court elaborated when pre-trial removal will be permitted. Strauder, a black man indicted for murder, based removal on the existence of a state law limiting jury service to white males. The Supreme Court held that removal was available: because of the state statute, it appeared before trial that he would be unable to enforce his right to have his jurors selected without regard to race, a right conferred by a law providing for equal rights—specifically, the Civil Rights Act of 1870 (codified today at 42 U.S.C. § 1981).

In the Rives case, defendants charged with murder alleged racial prejudice against them, and, more specifically, that only whites had been summoned as jurors and blacks had never been allowed to serve on juries in the county. However, because the only pertinent Virginia statute required service by all males of a specified age, the Court found no basis for removal, concluding that the provision "speaks * * * primarily, if not exclusively, [of] a denial of such rights, or an inability to enforce them, resulting from the Constitution or laws of the State, rather than a denial first made manifest at the trial of the case." If a state official discriminated in selecting the jury, it "can hardly be said that [the defendant] is denied, or cannot enforce, 'in the judicial tribunals of the State' the rights which belong to him".

(3) The Civil Rights Era Decisions: Rachel and Peacock. Seven years after Strauder and Rives, Congress enacted a provision (now codified in 28 U.S.C. § 1447(d)) precluding appeals from remand orders. Thereafter, the Supreme Court did not again encounter the civil rights removal provision for nearly 80 years. But the Civil Rights Act of 1964, Pub.L.No. 88–352, § 901, 78 Stat. 241, 266, amended § 1447(d) to create an exception to its general ban on review of remand orders for cases removed under § 1443. Within two years, two cases involving civil rights protests made their way to the Supreme Court.

(a) In Georgia v. Rachel, 384 U.S. 780 (1966), 20 defendants sought to remove criminal trespass cases pending against them in Georgia state court.

---

[12]   The original civil rights removal provision appeared in section 3 of the Civil Rights Act of 1866, which authorized removal in cases involving the statutory rights of racial equality guaranteed in Section 1 of that Act. See Act of Apr. 9, 1866, § 3, 14 Stat. 27; Act of May 31, 1870, § 18, 16 Stat. 140, 144. The present language originated in § 641 of the Revised Statutes of 1874, which unlike the earlier Acts, expressly stated that removal was permitted only "before the trial or final hearing of the cause." In 1977, Congress amended what was then 28 U.S.C. § 1446(c) to restore post-trial removal, but only in criminal cases and "for good cause shown". See Pub.L.No. 95–78, § 3, 91 Stat 319. The Federal Courts Jurisdiction and Venue Clarification Act of 2011 moved the language governing the procedure for removal of criminal cases to a new statutory section, 28 U.S.C. § 1455(b)(1).

The petition alleged that the defendants had been arrested when seeking service at restaurants that refused to serve black patrons, and initially asserted rights under the Due Process Clause and the First Amendment. The district court remanded the cases. While their appeals from the remand were pending, Congress enacted the Civil Rights Act of 1964, and later that year, the decision in Hamm v. City of Rock Hill, 379 U.S. 306 (1964), held that the Civil Rights Act bars state trespass prosecutions for peaceful attempts to be served on an equal basis in public accommodations regulated by the Act.

In Rachel, the Court first held that the 1964 Act was "plainly * * * a 'law providing for * * * equal civil rights,' " which it defined as "specific civil rights stated in terms of racial equality."[13] The Court added that the right relied on as the basis for removal was a "right under" a law providing for equal civil rights—a law that confers an immunity not merely from conviction but from even being brought to trial on the racially-motivated trespass charges.

The Court then considered whether the defendants were "denied or cannot enforce" that right in the Georgia courts. The Court stated that "Strauder and Rives * * * teach that removal is not warranted by an assertion that a denial of rights of equality may take place and go uncorrected at trial. Removal is warranted only if it can be predicted by reference to a law of general application that the defendant will be denied or cannot enforce the specified federal rights in the state courts. A state statute authorizing the denial affords an ample basis for such a prediction." Thus, the Strauder-Rives doctrine required that the removal petition allege that "denial be manifest in a formal expression of state law. This requirement served two ends. It ensured that removal would be available only in cases where the predicted denial appeared with relative clarity prior to trial. It also ensured that the task of prediction would not involve a detailed analysis by a federal judge of the likely disposition of particular federal claims by particular state courts. That task not only would have been difficult, but it also would have involved federal judges in the unseemly process of prejudging their brethren of the state courts."

The Court stressed, however, that under the Rives decision, "the denial of which the removal provision speaks 'is primarily, *if not exclusively*, a denial * * * resulting from the Constitution or laws of the State * * *' (Emphasis supplied)." Thus, "removal might be justified, even in the absence of a discriminatory state enactment, if an equivalent basis could be shown for an equally firm prediction that the defendant would be 'denied or cannot enforce' the specified federal rights in the state court. Such a basis for prediction exists in the present case.

"In the narrow circumstances of this case, *any* proceedings in the courts of the State will constitute a denial of the rights conferred by the Civil Rights Act of 1964, as construed in Hamm v. City of Rock Hill, if the allegations of the removal petition are true. * * * [I]f * * * the defendants were asked to leave solely for racial reasons, then the mere pendency of the prosecutions enables the federal court to make the clear prediction that the defendants will be 'denied or cannot enforce in the courts of [the] State' the right to be free of any 'attempt to punish' them for protected activity. It is no answer * * * that the defendants might eventually prevail in the state court. The burden of having to defend the prosecutions is itself the denial of a right

---

[13] On just what counts as a "specific civil right stated in terms of equality," see 14C Wright, Miller & Cooper, Federal Practice and Procedure § 3727.

explicitly conferred by the Civil Rights Act of 1964 as construed in Hamm v. City of Rock Hill". The court remanded the case to permit the district court to determine whether the defendants "were ordered to leave the restaurant facilities solely for racial reasons."

(b) In a companion decision to Rachel, City of Greenwood v. Peacock, 384 U.S. 808 (1966) (6–3), the Court refused to uphold removal. There, 29 state criminal defendants, alleging that they were working to encourage black voter registration in Mississippi, sought to remove their prosecutions to federal court. Their removal petitions claimed that the state courts and state law enforcement officers were prejudiced against them because of their race or their association with blacks; that the sole purpose of their arrests and prosecutions was to punish them for, and deter them from, exercising their constitutional rights to protest racial discrimination; that they would be tried in segregated courtrooms in which blacks would be excluded from the juries; that the judges and prosecutors had gained office at elections at which black voters had been excluded; and that the statutes and ordinances under which they were charged were unconstitutional and unconstitutionally vague as applied to their conduct.

In ruling that § 1443(1) did not permit removal,[14] the Court distinguished Rachel "in two significant respects. First, no federal law confers an absolute right on private citizens * * * to obstruct a public street, to contribute to the delinquency of a minor, to drive an automobile without a license, or to bite a policeman. [These were among the offenses charged.] Second, no federal law confers immunity from state prosecution on such charges. * * * It is *not* enough to support removal under § 1443(1) to allege or show that the defendant's federal equal civil rights have been illegally and corruptly denied by state administrative officials in advance of trial, that the charges * * * are false, or that the defendant is unable to obtain a fair trial in a particular state court. The motives of the officers bringing the charges may be corrupt, but that does not show that the state trial court will find the defendant guilty if he is innocent, or that * * * the defendant will be 'denied or cannot enforce in the courts' of the State any right under a federal law providing for equal civil rights. The civil rights removal statute does not require and does not permit the judges of the federal courts to put their brethren of the state judiciary on trial."

The Court noted that remedies other than removal—including, in appropriate cases, injunctions, actions for damages under 42 U.S.C. § 1983, and habeas corpus—were available to vindicate defendants' constitutional rights. A broad construction of § 1443 would cause an explosion of state criminal litigation in the federal courts, a change that, the Court said, raised fundamental issues of policy for Congress to consider: "Has the historic practice of holding state criminal trials in state courts * * * been such a failure that the relationship of the state and federal courts should now be revolutionized? Will increased responsibility of the state courts in the area of federal civil rights be promoted and encouraged by denying those courts any power at all to exercise that responsibility?"

(4) The Aftermath: Johnson v. Mississippi. A decade after Rachel and Peacock, the Court again construed the "murky language" of § 1443(1) narrowly. In Johnson v. Mississippi, 421 U.S. 213 (1975), the Court held that

---

[14] The Court also held that § 1443(2) did not apply: its first phrase covers only federal officials or those authorized to act with them in "affirmatively executing duties under any federal law providing for equal civil rights," while its second phrase covers only state officials.

a provision of the 1968 Civil Rights Act (18 U.S.C. § 245) prohibiting interference with certain federal rights "by force or threat of force" did not permit removal under § 1443(1) of a state criminal prosecution for conspiracy and unlawful boycott. (The petitioners had been picketing and urging the boycott of certain Vicksburg, Mississippi merchants for alleged racial discrimination in their hiring practices.) "Whether or not § 245 * * * provides for 'specific civil rights stated in terms of racial equality . . .' [within the meaning of Rachel] * * * it evinces no intention to interfere in any manner with state criminal prosecutions".

In dissent, Justices Marshall and Brennan argued that "[t]he use of force or the threat of force to intimidate or interfere with persons engaged in protected activity fairly describes an 'attempt to punish' the same persons" by arrest and prosecution. Commenting on the Court's observation that "varied avenues of relief" remained available to vindicate any federal rights that might be violated in the state prosecution, the dissent, citing Younger v. Harris, p. 1127, *infra*, concluded: "I only hope that the recent instances in which this Court has emphasized the values of comity and federalism in restricting the issuance of federal injunctions against state criminal * * * proceedings will not mislead the district courts into forgetting that at times these values must give way to the need to protect federal rights from being irremediably trampled."

(5) Can the Rachel and Peacock Decisions Be Reconciled? Consider the first basis on which the Court distinguished Peacock from Rachel—that no federal law conferred on defendants the right to obstruct a street or bite a policeman. One might infer from that distinction that a case is not removable unless the conduct *charged as violating state law* (rather than merely the conduct engaged in) is protected by a federal law providing for equal civil rights. That understanding would leave little if any room in which § 1443(1) can operate—a conclusion supported by the small number of cases successfully removed under this provision.

The second ground of distinction advanced in Peacock—that "no federal law confers immunity from prosecution"—was further elaborated in Johnson v. Mississippi, Paragraph (4), *supra*, in which the Court found that the petitioners did not possess a statutory right not to be proceeded against in the state courts at all. But it isn't clear that the circumstances in Rachel itself meet this test. Note that the defendants in Rachel had never moved to dismiss their cases. If the state courts would have promptly dismissed under Hamm, then the conclusion that the defendants' rights could not be enforced is not obvious. Does the Civil Rights Act of 1964 give a distinctive immunity—of a kind different from, for example, the Equal Protection Clause or the First Amendment—from even being named in a suit that violates its terms? In the end, perhaps the Rachel decision can be understood only in the context of the intransigent reaction of many Southern governments and judicial systems to the Civil Rights movement of the 1950s and 1960s.

(6) Removal and Alternative Federal Intervention. Writing before the Rachel and Peacock decisions, Professor Amsterdam urged a broader construction of § 1443 than the Court adopted. Amsterdam, *Criminal Prosecutions Affecting Federally Guaranteed Civil Rights: Federal Removal and Habeas Corpus Jurisdiction To Abort State Court Trial*, 113 U.Pa.L.Rev. 793 (1965). Exploring in depth the history and interpretation of the statute, which he called "a text of exquisite obscurity", Amsterdam emphasized the deep distrust of state courts on the part of "bad Tad Stevens and his rads"—the principal architects of the 1866 legislation. He also stressed the harm to the civil rights movement caused by groundless and discriminatory prosecutions, even if all convictions were ultimately set aside.[15] Thus, he contended that removal under § 1443 should be available to a defendant who makes "a colorable showing that the conduct for which he is prosecuted was conduct protected by the federal constitutional guarantees of civil rights * * * without regard to whether he also claims that the state courts are hostile, biased, conspiratorial, or incompetent."

Among the other possible remedies alluded to by the Court in Peacock were federal injunction against state proceedings, see Chap. X, Sec. 2(C), *infra*, and federal habeas corpus, see Chap. XI, Sec. 2, *infra*. For a civil rights protestor, removal is ordinarily a preferable option, as it comes early in the case (unlike habeas corpus, where exhaustion of state remedies is ordinarily required) and brings not only the federal issue but the entire case into the preferred federal forum. For the state, by contrast, removal is a far more dramatic intrusion, as it—unlike the other remedies—precludes the state from enforcing its own criminal or civil laws in its own courts. For a fuller discussion of the advantages and disadvantages of these remedies, see Bator, *The State Courts and Federal Constitutional Litigation*, 22 Wm. & Mary L.Rev. 605, 611–21 (1981).

D.   Miscellaneous Provisions

Beyond the general provisions just discussed, various statutory provisions authorize removal in specific circumstances. Some are found in the Judicial Code,[16] including the provision permitting removal of claims, alleged as counterclaims or otherwise outside of plaintiff's complaint, arising under the intellectual property laws. Others are codified elsewhere in the U.S. Code, including the Securities Litigation Uniform Standards Act of 1998 (SLUSA), which authorizes removal, on the basis of a federal defense of preemption, of certain state law class actions alleging fraud in the purchase or sale of securities.[17]

---

[15]   See also Goldstein, *Blyew: Variations on a Jurisdictional Theme*, 41 Stan.L.Rev. 469 (1989) (discussing the origins and development of § 1443 in the context of the original 1866 Act, whose protections Goldstein contends Congress and the federal courts have virtually eliminated—beginning with the Supreme Court's 1868 decision in the little-known federal prosecution of John Blyew); Redish, *Revitalizing Civil Rights Removal Jurisdiction*, 64 Minn.L.Rev. 523 (1980) (also arguing for a broader, though different, reading of § 1443).

[16]   See, *e.g.* § 1441(d) (authorizing removal of actions against foreign states); § 1444 (authorizing removal of actions, to which the United States has consented, to quiet title or otherwise establish ownership of property in which the United States has an interest or claim).

[17]   Pub.L.No. 105–353, 112 Stat. 3227. The background to SLUSA is found in the enactment in 1995 of the Private Securities Litigation Reform Act (PSLRA), which addressed what Congress viewed as abuses in private securities class actions by imposing a variety of restrictions (such as heightened pleading requirements and limits on discovery) on securities class actions filed under federal law. Some observers contended that plaintiffs sought to circumvent these procedural restrictions by filing state law actions in state court, which the PSLRA did not regulate. In enacting SLUSA, Congress responded to these concerns by preempting most state law class actions alleging that a defendant made a misrepresentation or omission of a material fact, or employed any manipulative or deceptive device, in connection with the purchase or sale of a federally-regulated security. 15 U.S.C. § 78bb(f)(1). (Where it applies, SLUSA preempts only class actions, not individual actions, brought under state law.) SLUSA further provides that a state court class action that is within the scope of the preemption provision may be removed to federal court. *Id.* § 78bb(f)(2). Since only preempted actions are removable, removal will inevitably be followed by dismissal, unless the action can be recast as

5. SUPPLEMENTAL (PENDENT) JURISDICTION

INTRODUCTORY NOTE

If a claim for relief falls within the "arising under" jurisdiction, how broad is the district court's "supplemental" jurisdiction to adjudicate related claims not independently within the court's subject matter jurisdiction? That question has both constitutional aspects (how broad is Congress' power under Article III to authorize the exercise of supplemental jurisdiction?) and nonconstitutional ones (has the exercise of supplemental jurisdiction in particular circumstances been authorized by the jurisdictional statutes and is it otherwise appropriate?).

Until 1990, no general statutory provision expressly conferred supplemental jurisdiction, but the courts had recognized the doctrine (previously called pendent or ancillary jurisdiction). The leading decision was United Mine Workers of America v. Gibbs, which follows. In 1990, Congress codified and modified the doctrine in 28 U.S.C. § 1367, discussed in the Note following Gibbs.

United Mine Workers of America v. Gibbs

383 U.S. 715, 86 S.Ct. 1130, 16 L.Ed.2d 218 (1966).
Certiorari to the United States Court of Appeals for the Sixth Circuit.

■ MR. JUSTICE BRENNAN delivered the opinion of the Court.

Respondent Paul Gibbs was awarded * * * damages in this action against petitioner United Mine Workers of America (UMW) for alleged violations of § 303 of the Labor Management Relations Act, 1947, as amended, and of the common law of Tennessee. The case grew out of the rivalry between the United Mine Workers and the Southern Labor Union over representation of workers in the southern Appalachian coal fields. Tennessee Consolidated Coal Company, not a party here, laid off 100 miners of the UMW's Local 5881 when it closed one of its mines * * *. * * * Grundy Company, a wholly owned subsidiary of Consolidated, hired respondent as mine superintendent to attempt to open a new mine on Consolidated's property * * * through use of members of the Southern Labor Union. As part of the arrangement, Grundy also gave respondent a contract to haul the mine's coal to the nearest railroad loading point.

On August 15 and 16, 1960, armed members of Local 5881 forcibly prevented the opening of the mine, threatening respondent and beating an organizer for the rival union. * * * [At that point the UMW international union intervened.] There was no further violence at the

---

based on federal law. The practical effect of the removal provision is to permit the removing defendant(s) to have the preemption defense determined in federal rather than in state court.

mine site; a picket line was maintained there for nine months; and no further attempts were made to open the mine during that period.

[Gibbs lost his job as superintendent, never entered into performance of his haulage contract, and testified that he began to lose other trucking contracts and mine leases he held. Claiming these harms resulted from a concerted union plan, he sued the UMW in federal court;] jurisdiction was premised on allegations of secondary boycotts under § 303. The state law claim, for which jurisdiction was based upon the doctrine of pendent jurisdiction, asserted "an unlawful conspiracy and an unlawful boycott aimed at him and [Grundy] to maliciously, wantonly and willfully interfere with his contract of employment and with his contract of haulage."

The trial judge refused to submit to the jury the claims of pressure intended to cause mining firms other than Grundy to cease doing business with Gibbs; he found those claims unsupported by the evidence. The jury's verdict was that the UMW had violated both § 303 and state law. Gibbs was awarded $60,000 * * * under the employment contract and $14,500 under the haulage contract; he was also awarded $100,000 punitive damages. On motion, the trial court set aside the award of damages with respect to the haulage contract on the ground that damage was unproved. It also held that union pressure on Grundy to discharge respondent as supervisor would constitute only a primary dispute with Grundy, as respondent's employer, and hence was not cognizable as a claim under § 303. Interference with the employment relationship was cognizable as a state claim, however, and a remitted award was sustained on the state law claim. The Court of Appeals for the Sixth Circuit affirmed. * * * We reverse.

I.

A threshold question is whether the District Court properly entertained jurisdiction of the claim based on Tennessee law. * * *

* * * The Court held in Hurn v. Oursler, 289 U.S. 238, that state law claims are appropriate for federal court determination if they form a separate but parallel ground for relief also sought in a substantial claim based on federal law. [There, plaintiffs, who had shown their play to the defendants, alleged that defendants had taken an idea and used it in their own play. Plaintiffs sought to enjoin production of the defendants' play, claiming (i) infringement of plaintiffs' copyrighted play, (ii) unfair competition through use of the plaintiffs' copyrighted play, and (iii) unfair competition with the plaintiffs' revised, uncopyrighted version of the same play. The Court upheld pendent jurisdiction over the state law unfair competition claim with respect to the copyrighted play, which was "but [a] different ground[ ] asserted in support of the same cause of action [as that stated in the federal claim]", but refused jurisdiction over the state law claim with regard to the uncopyrighted version, which asserted a "separate and distinct" cause of action "entirely outside the federal jurisdiction".] * * *

Hurn was decided in 1933, before the unification of law and equity by the Federal Rules of Civil Procedure. At the time, the meaning of "cause of action" was a subject of serious dispute * * *. The Court in Hurn identified what it meant by the term by citation of Baltimore S.S. Co. v. Phillips, 274 U.S. 316, a case in which "cause of action" had been used to identify the operative scope of the doctrine of *res judicata*. In that case the Court had noted that "the whole tendency of our decisions is to require a plaintiff to try his whole cause of action and his whole case at one time." 274 U.S., at 320. * * * Had the Court found a jurisdictional bar to reaching the state claim in Hurn, we assume that the doctrine of *res judicata* would not have been applicable in any subsequent state suit. But the citation of Baltimore S.S. Co. shows that the Court found that the weighty policies of judicial economy and fairness to parties reflected in *res judicata* doctrine were in themselves strong counsel for the adoption of a rule which would permit federal courts to dispose of the state as well as the federal claims.

With the adoption of the Federal Rules of Civil Procedure and the unified form of action, much of the controversy over "cause of action" abated. The phrase remained as the keystone of the Hurn test, however, and, as commentators have noted, has been the source of considerable confusion. Under the Rules, the impulse is toward entertaining the broadest possible scope of action consistent with fairness to the parties; joinder of claims, parties and remedies is strongly encouraged. Yet because the Hurn question involves issues of jurisdiction as well as convenience, there has been some tendency to limit its application to cases in which the state and federal claims are, as in Hurn, "little more than the equivalent of different epithets to characterize the same group of circumstances." 289 U.S., at 246.

This limited approach is unnecessarily grudging. Pendent jurisdiction, in the sense of judicial *power*, exists whenever there is a claim "arising under [the] Constitution, the Laws of the United States, and Treaties made, or which shall be made, under their Authority . . . ," U.S. Const., Art. III, § 2, and the relationship between that claim and the state claim permits the conclusion that the entire action before the court comprises but one constitutional "case." The federal claim must have substance sufficient to confer subject matter jurisdiction on the court. The state and federal claims must derive from a common nucleus of operative fact. But if, considered without regard to their federal or state character, a plaintiff's claims are such that he would ordinarily be expected to try them all in one judicial proceeding, then, assuming substantiality of the federal issues, there is *power* in federal courts to hear the whole.[13]

That power need not be exercised in every case in which it is found to exist. It has consistently been recognized that pendent jurisdiction is a doctrine of discretion, not of plaintiff's right. Its justification lies in considerations of judicial economy, convenience and fairness to litigants; if these are not present a federal court should hesitate to exercise jurisdiction over state claims, even though bound to apply state law to them, Erie R. Co. v. Tompkins, 304 U.S. 64. Needless decisions of state law should be avoided both as a matter of comity and to promote justice between the parties, by procuring for them a surer-footed reading of applicable law. Certainly, if the federal claims are dismissed before trial, even though not insubstantial in a jurisdictional sense, the state claims

---

[13] * * * While it is commonplace that the Federal Rules of Civil Procedure do not expand the jurisdiction of federal courts, they do embody "the whole tendency of our decisions * * * to require a plaintiff to try his . . . whole case at one time," Baltimore S.S. Co. v. Phillips, *supra*, and to that extent emphasize the basis of pendent jurisdiction.

should be dismissed as well. Similarly, if it appears that the state issues substantially predominate, whether in terms of proof, of the scope of the issues raised, or of the comprehensiveness of the remedy sought, the state claims may be dismissed without prejudice and left for resolution to state tribunals. There may, on the other hand, be situations in which the state claim is so closely tied to questions of federal policy that the argument for exercise of pendent jurisdiction is particularly strong. In the present case, for example, the allowable scope of the state claim implicates the federal doctrine of pre-emption; while this interrelationship does not create statutory federal question jurisdiction, Louisville & N.R. Co. v. Mottley, 211 U.S. 149, its existence is relevant to the exercise of discretion. Finally, there may be reasons independent of jurisdictional considerations, such as the likelihood of jury confusion in treating divergent legal theories of relief, that would justify separating state and federal claims for trial. If so, jurisdiction should ordinarily be refused.

The question of power will ordinarily be resolved on the pleadings. But the issue whether pendent jurisdiction has been properly assumed is one which remains open throughout the litigation. Pretrial procedures or even the trial itself may reveal a substantial hegemony of state law claims, or likelihood of jury confusion, which could not have been anticipated at the pleading stage. Although it will of course be appropriate to take account in this circumstance of the already completed course of the litigation, dismissal of the state claim might even then be merited. For example, it may appear that the plaintiff was well aware of the nature of his proofs and the relative importance of his claims; recognition of a federal court's wide latitude to decide ancillary questions of state law does not imply that it must tolerate a litigant's effort to impose upon it what is in effect only a state law case. Once it appears that a state claim constitutes the real body of a case, to which the federal claim is only an appendage, the state claim may fairly be dismissed.

We are not prepared to say that in the present case the District Court exceeded its discretion in proceeding to judgment on the state claim. We may assume for purposes of decision that the District Court was correct in its holding that the claim of pressure on Grundy to terminate the employment contract was outside the purview of § 303. Even so, the § 303 claims based on secondary pressures on Grundy relative to the haulage contract and on other coal operators generally were substantial. Although § 303 limited recovery to compensatory damages based on secondary pressures, and state law allowed both compensatory and punitive damages, and allowed such damages as to both secondary and primary activity, the state and federal claims arose from the same nucleus of operative fact and reflected alternative remedies. Indeed, the verdict sheet sent in to the jury authorized only one award of damages, so that recovery could not be given separately on the federal and state claims.

It is true that the § 303 claims ultimately failed and that the only recovery allowed respondent was on the state claim. We cannot confidently say, however, that the federal issues were so remote or played such a minor role at the trial that in effect the state claim only was tried. Although the District Court dismissed as unproved the § 303 claims that petitioner's secondary activities included attempts to induce coal operators other than Grundy to cease doing business with respondent, the court submitted the § 303 claims relating to Grundy to the jury. The jury returned verdicts against petitioner on those § 303 claims, and it was only on petitioner's motion for a directed verdict and a judgment *n.o.v.* that the verdicts on those claims were set aside. The District Judge considered the claim as to the haulage contract proved as to liability, and held it failed only for lack of proof of damages. Although there was some risk of confusing the jury in joining the state and federal claims— especially since * * * differing standards of proof of UMW involvement applied—the possibility of confusion could be lessened by employing a special verdict form, as the District Court did. Moreover, the question whether the permissible scope of the state claim was limited by the doctrine of pre-emption afforded a special reason for the exercise of pendent jurisdiction; the federal courts are particularly appropriate bodies for the application of pre-emption principles. We thus conclude that although it may be that the District Court might, in its sound discretion, have dismissed the state claim, the circumstances show no error in refusing to do so. * * *

[On the merits, the judgment was reversed.]

NOTE ON SUPPLEMENTAL JURISDICTION IN FEDERAL QUESTION AND OTHER NONDIVERSITY CASES

(1) The Rationale and Consequences of the Gibbs Rule. What is the justification for supplemental jurisdiction over state law claims? A federal trial court often could not function as a court, and decide the whole case, in the absence of the jurisdiction over state law questions that Chief Justice Marshall asserted in Osborn v. Bank of the United States—the jurisdiction to decide state law questions intermingled with questions of federal law in a single claim for relief. No such justification is available, however, for the pendent jurisdiction at issue in Gibbs, for decision of the federal claim under § 303 did not necessitate decision of the separate state law claims. Nor can Gibbs be justified solely by the policy of avoiding piecemeal litigation, because at least when federal jurisdiction is not exclusive, consolidated litigation of federal and state claims is available in state court.

Consider, however, the effect of a contrary rule under which federal courts could not exercise jurisdiction over pendent state law claims. A litigant like Gibbs could bring separate state court and federal court actions; but doing so would be costly and could create claim preclusion problems if the state case comes to judgment first. Alternatively, Gibbs could consolidate his claims in a single action in state court—but then he must give up his right to a federal forum on the federal claim. And when a plaintiff's federal claim falls within exclusive federal jurisdiction, then, absent supplemental jurisdiction, pursuit of both claims would require separate federal and state court actions. Do these concerns establish a persuasive argument for the result in Gibbs?[1]

---

[1] Professor Bone thinks not. He notes that most cases settle; contends that absent two trials, the cost of litigating in different courts is not so great (*e.g.*, discovery in one action may be usable in the other); and suggests that claim preclusion difficulties could be addressed

(2) Pendent Jurisdiction and Constitutional Avoidance. Some cases (typically those challenging official action) present an additional justification for pendent jurisdiction: to permit the avoidance of constitutional questions. (For general discussion of constitutional avoidance, see pp. 79–81, *supra*.) This rationale was prominent in Siler v. Louisville & Nashville R.R. Co., 213 U.S. 175 (1909), which predated the decision in Hurn v. Oursler, discussed in Gibbs. Siler was an action to enjoin enforcement of a state administrative order setting intrastate railroad rates. The Court upheld the exercise of pendent jurisdiction over a claim that the order violated state law, which was joined with the claim that the order violated the federal Constitution. Indeed, the Court went further, stating that the case should be disposed of, if possible, on state law grounds in order to avoid the need to reach the federal constitutional question.

The Siler approach was significantly affected by the Court's ruling in Pennhurst State School & Hospital v. Halderman, 465 U.S. 89 (1984), p. 737, *infra*, that the Eleventh Amendment, which has been interpreted as a constitutional recognition of state sovereign immunity, prohibits the federal courts from ordering state officials to conform their conduct to state law. Thus, for example, a suit seeking to order state officials to comply with a state statutory or constitutional provision is ordinarily barred by Pennhurst, and therefore could not be joined with a federal constitutional claim against the same officials. In Pennhurst, the Court acknowledged that Siler and numerous subsequent decisions had approved the exercise of pendent jurisdiction in such a situation, but stated that none of them had discussed the Eleventh Amendment. In the Court's view, the resulting problem of "bifurcation of claims" raised a policy consideration that could not outweigh the constraints of the Eleventh Amendment.

The Pennhurst decision still allows the exercise of jurisdiction over a pendent state law claim (and leaves in place the preference for resolving the case, when possible, on that basis) in situations in which the Eleventh Amendment poses no barrier to federal court relief against state or local officials for a violation of state law. Those situations include suits (i) against states whose consent to suit waives any Eleventh Amendment claim, (ii) against state officials when the plaintiff seeks only damages from the officials personally, and (iii) against local governments or their officials, who lack Eleventh Amendment protection.

(3) The Statutory and Constitutional Bases of the Gibbs Holding. The Gibbs opinion focuses on whether Article III permits the exercise of pendent jurisdiction; if so, the Court assumes that the federal courts have "discretion" whether to hear the case. But this assumption elides the question whether the statute granting subject matter jurisdiction—§ 303(b) in the Gibbs case; § 1331 in most other cases—should be read to authorize the exercise of pendent jurisdiction. The opinion does not even mention either provision.[2]

---

directly by eliminating interjurisdictional preclusion. See Bone, *Revisiting the Policy Case for Supplemental Jurisdiction*, 74 Ind.L.J. 139 (1998).

[2] Is it at all significant that § 1331 speaks of "civil actions" while Article III speaks of "cases"? The American Law Institute's Federal Judicial Code Revision Project 5–7 (2004), for which Professor Oakley served as Reporter, argues that although the new supplemental jurisdiction statute, 28 U.S.C. § 1367, like § 1331 (and like the diversity statute, § 1332), refers to jurisdiction over "civil actions", in fact subject matter jurisdiction attaches to particular claims in an action, although that action may consist of multiple claims. The ALI suggests that a court should ask not whether it has jurisdiction over an entire action, but instead (i) whether it has jurisdiction over a "freestanding" federal question claim and (ii) if so, whether another

(4) "Pendent Party" Jurisdiction Before the Enactment of 28 U.S.C. § 1367. Some lower courts took the Gibbs decision to authorize the exercise of "pendent party jurisdiction"—in which a plaintiff with a federal claim against one defendant appends a state law claim, arising from a common nucleus of facts, against *another defendant*, who could not otherwise be sued in a federal court. But in Finley v. United States, 490 U.S. 545 (1989) (5–4), the Court broadly rejected pendent party jurisdiction. There, the plaintiff sued the United States under the Federal Tort Claims Act (FTCA), alleging that the FAA's negligence caused a plane crash in which her husband and two of her children died. Under the FTCA, federal jurisdiction is exclusive. The question presented was whether the federal district court could exercise jurisdiction over a state law tort claim against the local electric company (whose transmission lines the plane had struck) and the city of San Diego.

Justice Scalia's majority opinion rested on the broad principle that federal court jurisdiction must be within the bounds of Article III and also conferred by act of Congress. On the Article III question, the Court "assume[d], without deciding, that the constitutional criterion for pendent-party jurisdiction is analogous to the constitutional criterion for pendent-claim jurisdiction, and that [plaintiff's] state-law claims pass that test." But in the Court's view, Gibbs' assertion of jurisdiction over pendent claims, "without specific examination of jurisdictional statutes," was in tension with the principle that jurisdiction must be conferred by Congress. The Court continued: "Our cases show * * * that with respect to the addition of parties, as opposed to the addition of only claims, we will not assume that the full constitutional power has been congressionally authorized, and will not read jurisdictional statutes broadly."[3] Justice Scalia recognized that because of the exclusivity of federal jurisdiction over FTCA actions against the federal government, the Court's decision would require plaintiff to file two suits, one in state court and one in federal court.

(5) Legislative Response: 28 U.S.C. § 1367. Following considerable criticism of Finley, the Federal Courts Study Committee recommended that the decision be legislatively overruled, and Congress responded by adding

---

claim not within federal question jurisdiction may be adjudicated based on its relationship to the freestanding claim. Despite the statutory phrase "civil actions", the ALI suggests that in practice courts determine the existence of subject matter jurisdiction on this claim-specific basis. See, in this regard, 28 U.S.C. §§ 1338(a), 1454, pp. 812–814, *supra*, provisions enacted in 2011 that move in the direction of asking whether a claim for relief arises under federal law.

[3]   The Court relied heavily on two diversity cases: Zahn v. Int'l Paper Co., 414 U.S. 291, 301 (1973), p. 1447, *infra* (holding that a federal court, in a class action, lacks jurisdiction over any plaintiff whose claim falls short of the jurisdictional amount), and Owen Equip. & Erection Co. v. Kroger, 437 U.S. 365, 374 (1978), p. 1449, *infra* (holding that there is no ancillary jurisdiction over a plaintiff's claim against a non-diverse third-party defendant).

In distinguishing pendent party from pendent jurisdiction, Justice Scalia placed considerable reliance upon Aldinger v. Howard, 427 U.S. 1 (1976), in which the Court refused, on a much narrower basis, to permit pendent party jurisdiction in the circumstances there presented. Aldinger was an action under 42 U.S.C. § 1983 against county officials for violating the plaintiff's constitutional rights. At the time, a county, as distinguished from its officials, was not subject to liability under § 1983, and thus the county was not a defendant on the federal claim. However, the plaintiff included a pendent state-law claim against the county. In Aldinger, the Court held that the claim against the county must be dismissed, reasoning that the Court's 1961 ruling that local governments could not be sued under § 1983 would be undermined by allowing them to be sued in federal court on the pendent claim. (In 1978, the Court partially overruled its 1961 decision and held that in some circumstances local governments could be sued under § 1983. See pp. 998–999, *infra*.) Unlike in Gibbs, where Congress' silence left the Court free to fashion its own rules, the context in Aldinger was not "congressional silence or tacit encouragement, but * * * quite the opposite * * *."

§ 1367 to Title 28 as part of the Judicial Improvements Act of 1990. See Mengler, Burbank & Rowe, *Congress Accepts Supreme Court's Invitation to Codify Supplemental Jurisdiction*, 74 Judicature 213 (1991). This provision substitutes the term "supplemental" jurisdiction for the prevailing (and often confusing) references to pendent, ancillary, and even "tag-along" jurisdiction. Section 1367 broadly confers supplemental jurisdiction, including pendent party jurisdiction, while otherwise seeking to codify existing decisional law.[4]

Subsection (a) provides in sweeping terms that (except as stated in subsections (b) and (c) or in another federal law) a district court with original jurisdiction over a case "shall have supplemental jurisdiction over all other claims" that "form part of the same case or controversy under Article III"— including claims involving additional parties (thus overruling Finley). Subsection (b), which applies to diversity cases, excepts from the scope of subsection (a) a variety of claims by plaintiffs against additional parties, or by persons proposed to be joined or seeking to intervene, when adding such claims would violate the requirement of complete diversity under the general diversity jurisdiction statute, 28 U.S.C. § 1332.

(6) The Scope of Supplemental Jurisdiction in Nondiversity Cases. Section § 1367 plainly applies broadly to nondiversity litigation, and thus governs admiralty as well as "arising under" cases. (See pp. 874–876, *infra*, as to the distinction. And see Chap. XIII, Sec. 3, *infra*, for discussion of § 1367's application to diversity litigation.) Section 1367 also clearly contemplates the availability of supplemental jurisdiction with respect to such devices as counterclaims, cross-claims, intervention, and permissive and necessary joinder, so long as the specified criteria are met. See generally McLaughlin, *The Federal Supplemental Jurisdiction Statute—A Constitutional and Statutory Analysis*, 24 Ariz.St.L.J. 849, 925–34 (1992).

There remain, however, a number of other questions concerning the application of § 1367 in federal question and other nondiversity litigation, only some of which have been resolved by decisions to date.

(a) The Constitutional Reach of § 1367. What is the permissible reach of jurisdiction over "all other claims that are so related to claims in the action within * * * original jurisdiction that they form part of the same case or controversy under Article III"?[5] Must there be a "common nucleus of operative fact", as required by Gibbs, or are the constitutional bounds broad enough to reach other kinds of relationships?

Permissive counterclaims by definition do not arise "out of the transaction or occurrence that is the subject matter of the opposing party's claim," Fed.R.Civ.Proc. 13(a), and thus generally will not share a common nucleus of operative fact with the plaintiff's claim. But Professor McLaughlin argues that a "logical relationship" to the claim over which arising under jurisdiction does exist is constitutionally sufficient, and thus he argues that in some instances permissive counterclaims, as well as some permissive

---

[4]   Prior to enactment of § 1367, 28 U.S.C. § 1338(b), as set forth by the 1948 Revision of the Judicial Code, had conferred jurisdiction over "a claim of unfair competition when joined with a substantial and related claim under the copyright, patent or trade-mark laws". That provision was designed to codify the decision in Hurn v. Oursler, 289 U.S. 238 (1933), discussed in the Gibbs opinion. See generally 13B Wright, Miller & Cooper, Federal Practice and Procedure § 3582.

[5]   The Ninth Circuit, alone among the courts of appeals, once doubted the constitutionality of pendent party jurisdiction, but in a decision post-dating the enactment of § 1367, eventually changed its mind. See Mendoza v. Zirkle Fruit Co., 301 F.3d 1163 (9th Cir.2002).

joinder, may qualify. See McLaughlin, *supra*. And three circuits have held that at least some permissive counterclaims, which once were thought to require an independent basis of jurisdiction (like diversity), fall within the scope of § 1367.[6]

Professor Matasar takes a still broader view of the permissible scope of § 1367. Arguing that Gibbs' conflation of statutory and constitutional tests unduly restricted the latter, he contends that the only limit to supplemental jurisdiction under Article III is the existence of a case or controversy as defined under lawfully adopted procedural rules for the joinder of claims and parties, and that no common nucleus of operative fact is constitutionally required. Matasar, *Rediscovering "One Constitutional Case": Procedural Rules and the Rejection of the Gibbs Test for Supplemental Jurisdiction*, 71 Calif.L.Rev. 1399 (1983).

Professor Floyd responds that Matasar's approach would give Congress essentially unlimited power. Supplemental jurisdiction, he argues, should extend only as far as is necessary to permit the federal courts to perform the tasks assigned to them by Article III. Applying that standard, he approves of supplemental jurisdiction over permissive counterclaims, without which, he contends, defendants would be unfairly deprived of security for the payment of their own claims. But he disapproves of supplemental jurisdiction over claims filed under Fed.R.Civ.P. 18, which permits a party asserting one claim against another party to join with that claim any other claim, no matter how unrelated, against the same party. See Floyd, *Three Faces of Supplemental Jurisdiction After the Demise of United Mine Workers v. Gibbs*, 60 Fla.L.Rev. 277 (2008).

Recall the question of the constitutionality of the grant of bankruptcy jurisdiction discussed at pp. 794–796, *supra*. May the existing grant of jurisdiction over claims between the bankrupt's estate and nondiverse parties—disputes governed by state law—be justified on a supplemental jurisdiction theory, based on their relationship to the bankruptcy proceedings that are governed by federal law? Does supplemental jurisdiction justify the further reach of jurisdiction under 28 U.S.C. § 1334 over a proceeding "related to cases under [the Bankruptcy Code]" even when the bankrupt's estate is not a party to the additional proceeding?[7]

---

[6] See Jones v. Ford Motor Credit Co., 358 F.3d 205, 213 (2d Cir. 2004); Channell v. Citicorp Nat'l Servs., Inc., 89 F.3d 379, 384–87 (7th Cir. 1996); Global Naps, Inc. v. Verizon New Eng. Inc., 603 F.3d 71, 76 (1st Cir. 2010).

[7] Assuming that § 1334's broad grant of jurisdiction over matters related to bankruptcy cases is constitutionally valid, may federal jurisdiction pertaining to bankruptcy be expanded still further, by superimposing § 1367 on § 1334—to embrace claims related to a "related to" proceeding under § 1334? Suppose, for example, that a creditor files a claim against the bankrupt's estate based on a loan agreement with the debtor; the debtor defends by asserting that the loan agreement violates state usury law. Assuming that § 1334 would extend that far, suppose the creditor files a third-party claim against its lawyers, alleging that if the usury objections are upheld, the lawyers are liable for malpractice. If the malpractice claim does not "relate to" a case under the Bankruptcy Code—and thus falls outside of § 1334—may a federal court nonetheless hear that claim under § 1367? For a negative answer and an argument that to avoid serious constitutional questions, § 1334 should be viewed as covering the full range of federal court jurisdiction in bankruptcy matters, see Block-Lieb, *The Case Against Supplemental Bankruptcy Jurisdiction: A Constitutional, Statutory, and Policy Analysis*, 62 Fordham L.Rev. 721 (1994). See also Brubaker, *On the Nature of Federal Bankruptcy Jurisdiction: A General Statutory and Constitutional Theory*, 41 Wm. & Mary L.Rev. 743, 926–33 (2000) (arguing that § 1367 enhances the scope of jurisdiction of the Article III district courts but not of the non-Article III bankruptcy courts, but that § 1334's "related to" jurisdiction is itself a grant of supplemental jurisdiction that the bankruptcy courts may exercise).

(b) Removed Cases. Although § 1367(a) does not apply explicitly to cases removed from state court, the decision in City of Chicago v. International College of Surgeons, 522 U.S. 156 (1997), squarely held that § 1367 authorizes the exercise of supplemental jurisdiction in such cases.[8]

(7) Other Issues in the Application of § 1367.

(a) Discretion to Decline. Section 1367(c) clearly rejects the language in Gibbs appearing to *require* dismissal of the supplemental claim if the federal claim is disposed of before trial. But does the statute alter the criteria that a district court should consider in deciding whether to exercise supplemental jurisdiction? The legislative history can be read to suggest that Congress meant to codify the judge-made principles set forth in Gibbs and other decisions.[9] However, some courts have read the specific list of four factors in § 1367(c) as narrowing the scope of district court discretion by excluding consideration of the "fairness" or "efficiency" concerns articulated in Gibbs or of any other concern not set forth in the statute. See Sherry, *Logic Without Experience: The Problem of Federal Appellate Courts*, 82 Notre Dame L.Rev. 97, 125–26 (2006).[10]

(b) Tolling the Statute of Limitations. When a state law claim is timely filed in federal court under § 1367 but thereafter the limitations period expires, a federal court that would otherwise dismiss the state claim might once have retained jurisdiction instead in order to avoid extinguishing the claim. The tolling provision of § 1367(d) now permits the court to dismiss such a claim where otherwise appropriate without fear of such hardship, for

---

[8]   Justice Ginsburg, joined by Justice Stevens, did not disagree with this aspect of the holding, but argued that judicial review of a state agency's administrative findings (which the pendent state-law claim called for in this case) is appellate in nature and that § 1367 should not be used as a vehicle for such "cross-system appeals" absent explicit congressional authorization. See the Reporter's Note to the American Law Institute, Federal Judicial Code Revision Project 73–77 (2004) (citing articles with contrasting evaluations of Justice Ginsburg's position, and expressing the Reporter's view that recognition of jurisdiction over cross-system appeals, though yet to have "widespread effects on the district courts", is "like an unstable dam from which a trickle may suddenly become a flood"). See also Chapter VI, p. 631, *supra*.

A different provision governing removal that dated from the 1948 Revision, 28 U.S.C. § 1441(c), appeared to authorize a form of supplemental jurisdiction in removed cases. For decades, § 1441(c) had generated confusion and serious questions about whether it reached beyond what Article III permitted. (The history is summarized at pp. 1441–44 of the Sixth Edition of this casebook.) However, a 2011 amendment to § 1441(c), included in the Federal Courts Jurisdiction and Venue Clarification Act of 2011, Pub.L.No. 112–63, 125 Stat.758, eliminated the confusion and constitutional doubts. Section 1441(c) now permits removal of a state court action containing both a removable claim falling within the district court's original federal question jurisdiction (within the meaning of § 1331) and a claim *not* within the original or supplemental jurisdiction (for example, a state law claim that is entirely unrelated to the federal question claim)—but then *requires* severance, and remand to the state court, of any claim falling outside the federal court's original or supplemental jurisdiction.

[9]   Possibly supporting this view is language in the Supreme Court's decision in City of Chicago v. International College of Surgeons, Paragraph (6)(b), *supra*: "The supplemental jurisdiction statute codifies these principles [*i.e.*, the principles of 'economy, convenience, fairness, and comity' set forth in Gibbs with respect to the exercise of discretion]".

[10]   The House Report accompanying the bill states, cryptically, that when a district court dismisses a supplemental claim under subsection (c) and the party refiles the claim in state court, the federal court "in deciding the party's claims over which the court has retained jurisdiction, should accord no claim preclusive effect to a state court judgment on the supplemental claim." H.R.Rep. No. 101–734, 101st Cong., 2d Sess. 29–30 (1990). This result could certainly have been provided in the statute itself, but can it be squared with the requirements of § 1738, as interpreted in the Marrese case, p. 1388, *infra*? If not, is this statement in the committee report sufficient to warrant an exception? *Cf.* England v. Louisiana State Bd. of Medical Examiners, 375 U.S. 411 (1964), p. 1115, *infra*.

the statute gives a claimant an additional 30 days within which to refile in state court. The validity of that tolling provision, even where it would open the doors of a state court that would otherwise be closed, was upheld in Jinks v. Richland County, 538 U.S. 456 (2003). Justice Scalia's opinion reasoned that the provision was "necessary and proper" for carrying out Congress' power to establish inferior federal courts in a fair and efficient manner. Absent such a provision, district courts could either (1) condition dismissal on the defendant's waiver of a limitations defense, which the defendant might refuse to give; (2) continue to exercise supplemental jurisdiction over the state law claim, when state-court adjudication might be more appropriate; or (3) dismiss while permitting the plaintiff to re-open the federal case should the state court hold the claim to be time-barred. The Court concluded that § 1367(d) provides a preferable, more efficient alternative to any of those options and ensures that plaintiffs can avail themselves of federal court jurisdiction without the risk that a related state law claim might, if dismissed by the federal court, ultimately be held to be time-barred.[11]

(c) Remand: Total or Partial? Section 1367(c) states that a federal court may refuse to exercise supplemental jurisdiction, but leaves open the question whether the court may remand to state court the *entire* case or only the state law claims. Most decisions have held that a federal court must retain jurisdiction over properly removed federal claims. See, *e.g.*, In re City of Mobile, 75 F.3d 605 (11th Cir.1996); Borough of West Mifflin v. Lancaster, 45 F.3d 780 (3d Cir.1995); accord, Steinman, *Crosscurrents: Supplemental Jurisdiction, Removal, and the ALI Revision Project*, 74 Ind.L.J. 76, 107–09 (1998).

(8) The Role of the Courts and of Congress. Was the Finley decision and the legislature's response to it an example of successful dialogue between the Court and Congress? Or should the statute be understood as a specific remonstrance to a Court that had taken too crabbed a view of the scope of federal jurisdiction? Justice Scalia's approach in the Finley case reduced judicial flexibility to shape the contours of supplemental jurisdiction, requiring Congress to take on that responsibility. Was that a desirable shift in course?

---

[11] The Jinks Court also rejected arguments that § 1367(d) infringed state sovereignty both by regulating the procedures that state courts use to adjudicate state law claims and by extending the liability of a political subdivision.

A narrower question concerning § 1367(d) was presented the prior year in Raygor v. Regents of the Univ. of Minnesota, 534 U.S. 533 (2002), in which plaintiffs' federal court action against their state employer asserted a federal age discrimination claim and a pendent state-law claim. The federal claim was dismissed as barred by the Eleventh Amendment's protection of state sovereign immunity. See generally Chap. IX, Sec. 2(A), *infra*. Within 30 days of the dismissal but after expiration of the state limitations period, the plaintiffs refiled their state-law claim in state court (the state had waived its immunity from suit on that claim in state court but not in federal court). On review, a majority of the Supreme Court affirmed the state courts' dismissal on limitation grounds, holding that § 1367(d)'s tolling provision does not extend to federal court suits *against a non-consenting state* that are dismissed under the Eleventh Amendment. Justice O'Connor's opinion reasoned that a contrary holding would affect the constitutional balance between nation and state, and hence was not warranted when, as here, the statute did not clearly indicate that Congress meant to change that balance. She added that "it is unclear if the tolling provision was meant to apply to dismissals for reasons unmentioned by [§ 1367(c)], such as dismissals on Eleventh Amendment grounds"; Justice Ginsburg, concurring in part and in the judgment, thought it unnecessary and unwise to raise that question. Justice Stevens (joined by Justices Souter and Breyer) dissented.

If Congress wished to take some kind of action to correct what it viewed as the unwarranted restrictiveness of Finley, it had a choice about whether to enact a general provision or one with a much greater degree of specification. Section 1367 is a reasonably detailed provision.[12] Did the approach of Finley, together with the Supreme Court's growing emphasis on the importance of statutory text, give Congress reason to opt for detailed specification of rules? Or do the uncertainties raised by the statute, as well as some of its unanticipated consequences, cast doubt upon the wisdom of such detailed efforts to codify? (To answer that question fully, one needs to explore some of § 1367's unanticipated consequences in diversity litigation. See pp. 1447–1461, *infra*.) Should Congress, instead, have followed Professor Shapiro's suggestion—that it "enact a law establishing the principle of supplemental jurisdiction, and then * * * leave all or most of the details to be worked out by the courts"? See Shapiro, *Supplemental Jurisdiction: A Confession, an Avoidance, and a Proposal*, 74 Ind.L.J. 211, 218 (1998); see also Meltzer, *The Supreme Court's Judicial Passivity*, 2002 Sup.Ct.Rev. 343, 396–403. It may be that some provisions in § 1367—for example, the 30-day tolling provision in § 1367(d)—would be hard for courts to develop. As to others—for example, the specification in § 1367(b) of the appropriate reach of supplemental jurisdiction over differing kinds of claims and joinder, or in § 1367(c) of the criteria for dismissing supplemental claims—it may be easier, and perhaps desirable, for Congress to enact only a general directive, on the assumption that courts are better suited to flesh out the details.

---

6. ADMIRALTY JURISDICTION

NOTE ON THE ADMIRALTY JURISDICTION

(1) Introduction. This Note briefly surveys the admiralty jurisdiction.[1] The closely-related question of the choice between federal and state law in maritime matters is discussed at pp. 689–695, *supra*.

(2) The Purposes of Admiralty Jurisdiction. The need for federal tribunals exercising admiralty jurisdiction was a key reason for establishing a system of lower federal courts. The Founders were particularly concerned with the relationship of maritime matters to international affairs—for example, prize cases required adjudication of the rights and status of foreign claimants and nations, both neutral and belligerent. See The Federalist, No. 80 (Hamilton). Indeed, Professor Casto, in *The Origins of Federal Admiralty Jurisdiction in an Age of Privateers, Smugglers, and Pirates*, 37 Am.J. Legal Hist. 117 (1993), contends that the original vision of the jurisdiction focused

---

[12] For a still more detailed proposal for a supplemental jurisdiction statute, see American Law Institute, Federal Judicial Code Revision Project 5–136 (2004).

For a bibliography of the more than ample literature on § 1367, see *id.* at 33–37. See also McFarland, *Viewing the "Same Case or Controversy" of Supplemental Jurisdiction Through the Lens of the "Common Nucleus of Operative Fact" of Pendent Jurisdiction*, 45 Tex. Tech L. Rev. 905 (2013) (urging an approach that is "fact-based and economy-driven", not preoccupied with legal categories, under which § 1367(a) is satisfied whenever "the facts of the litigation present a natural grouping that a lay person would expect to be tried together in one proceeding").

[1] For comprehensive accounts, see sources cited p. 689, note 4, *supra*.

not on private claims but on such "public" matters as prize cases, revenue cases, and criminal prosecutions. But the Admiralty Clause in Article III has given rise to a broader jurisdiction that includes a large area of private law. Policy support for the broader scope has been found in the perceived value of uniformity in maritime law—a notion reflecting the traditional view of the law of the sea as an independent and international body of rules, transcending the reach of territorial jurisdictions—and in the contemporary federal interest in furthering maritime commerce. See Gutoff, *Original Understandings and the Private Law Origins of the Federal Admiralty Jurisdiction: A Reply to Professor Casto*, 30 J.Mar.L. & Com. 361 (1999) (contending that this broader view squares with the original understanding). This broader understanding is deeply rooted in the case law, although some academics have criticized its soundness. See pp. 694–695, *supra*.

(3) Statutory History. Section 9 of the Judiciary Act of 1789 gave the district courts exclusive maritime jurisdiction. 1 Stat. 73, 76–77. At the same time, Congress preserved the traditional role of the common law courts of the original states in providing some remedies in maritime cases, by including § 9 the "Saving Clause". This clause grants federal jurisdiction while "saving to suitors, in all cases, the right of a common law remedy, where the common law is competent to give it". These common law remedies could be enforced in state courts, or, when diversity jurisdiction existed, in federal courts.

The admiralty jurisdiction has remained unchanged in substance to the present day. The current provision, 28 U.S.C. § 1333(1), reads: "The district courts shall have original jurisdiction, exclusive of the courts of the States, of * * * [a]ny civil case of admiralty or maritime jurisdiction, saving to suitors in all cases all other remedies to which they are otherwise entitled."

(4) The Scope of Exclusivity, the Saving Clause and the Role of State Law. In general, the exclusivity of federal admiralty jurisdiction under § 1333 is limited to maritime actions brought in rem against a vessel or its cargo. See The Moses Taylor, 71 U.S. (4 Wall.) 411 (1867).[2] An in personam action may be brought in federal admiralty court, or, where state law provides a remedy, in state court by virtue of the Saving Clause. And under the traditional division among cases in equity, at law, or in admiralty, state law actions permitted by the Saving Clause may be brought on the "law" side of the federal court if otherwise within the court's jurisdiction—*e.g.*, if diversity or supplemental jurisdiction exists. See 14A Wright, Miller & Cooper, Federal Practice and Procedure § 3672.[3]

---

[2] The in rem/in personam distinction has been criticized as without historical support. See Casto, Paragraph (2), *supra*, at 140–42.

Certain other maritime actions are committed by statute to exclusive federal jurisdiction. *E.g.*, suits against the United States arising from the operation of government vessels, 46 U.S.C. App. §§ 741–42, 781–82; proceedings under the Limitation of Liability Act, 46 U.S.C. App. §§ 181–96; actions under the Ship Mortgage Act, 46 U.S.C. §§ 31010, 31301–43. See also Offshore Logistics, Inc. v. Tallentire, 477 U.S. 207 (1986) (stating in dictum, contrary to some lower court holdings, that the Death on the High Seas Act, 46 U.S.C. App. § 761, does not confer exclusive federal jurisdiction).

[3] The question of the removability of a state court action under the Saving Clause has presented some perplexity. For disagreement about whether removal should be permitted only on the basis of diversity jurisdiction, compare 14A Wright, Miller & Cooper, *supra*, § 3674 (yes), with Friedell, *The Disappearing Act: Removal Jurisdiction of An Admiralty Claim*, 30 Tul.Mar.L.J. 75 (2006) (no).

The Supreme Court interpreted the original Saving Clause as permitting a state court to order specific performance of a maritime contract—an equitable remedy unknown to the common law courts of 1789. See Red Cross Line v. Atlantic Fruit Co., 264 U.S. 109 (1924). The current language ("saving to suitors * * * all other remedies to which they are otherwise entitled"), which dates from enactments in 1948 and 1949,[4] has been understood to preserve the holding in the Red Cross decision. See Madruga v. Superior Court, 346 U.S. 556, 560 n.12 (1954).

On the utility of state court jurisdiction under the Saving Clause, in Romero v. International Terminal Operating Co., 358 U.S. 354 (1959), Justice Brennan's dissent noted that in the five year period from 1953–57, the state courts rendered "only about 150 decisions in Saving Clause actions * * *. * * * Saving Clause suitors seem long ago to have deserted the state courts" (358 U.S. at 409). See also Black, *Admiralty Jurisdiction: Critique and Suggestions*, 50 Colum.L.Rev. 259, 276–80 (1950) (proposing exclusive federal jurisdiction in maritime industry contract and commercial matters and exclusive state court jurisdiction over personal injury claims).

(5) The Romero Decision.

(a) Actions in Admiralty Versus Actions at Law. Historically, admiralty was considered to be a distinct body of jurisprudence separate from law or equity, just as law and equity were historically thought to be distinct from each other. But may a claim in admiralty also be brought on the "law" side of the federal courts, under the "arising under" jurisdiction? That question seems highly conceptual, but its resolution could have important consequences; for example, in admiralty actions, unlike actions at law brought under 28 U.S.C. § 1331, jury trials are generally unavailable.

This issue was presented in Romero v. International Terminal Operating Co., 358 U.S. 354 (1959) (5–4). There, an injured seaman sued for damages, asserting a statutory claim under the Jones Act, 46 U.S.C. App. § 688, and claims under general judge-made maritime law for unseaworthiness and maintenance and cure. His complaint attempted to invoke federal jurisdiction under § 1331 as well as under the Jones Act, which explicitly confers jurisdiction on the district courts over actions under the Act for a seaman's injury. Romero's complaint did not invoke § 1333.

Justice Frankfurter, writing for the Court, concluded that § 1331 did not confer federal question jurisdiction over claims arising out of judge-made maritime law. Stressing the distinctness of Article III's grants of admiralty jurisdiction and of federal question jurisdiction, he saw no reason for assuming that Congress, when it conferred general federal question jurisdiction in 1875, meant to change the historic operation of admiralty jurisdiction. If § 1331 were to embrace admiralty claims, "the sole remaining justification for the federal admiralty courts which have played such a vital role in our federal judicial system for 169 years will be to provide a federal forum for the small number of maritime claims which derive from state law, and to afford the ancient remedy of a libel *in rem* in those limited instances when an *in personam* judgment would not suffice to satisfy a claim." He objected that the expanded view of § 1331 would remove "the historic option of a maritime suitor pursuing a common-law remedy to select his forum, state or federal," since saving-clause actions would then be freely removable under § 1441 of Title 28. And he added that "[i]f jurisdiction of maritime

---

4   See 62 Stat. 931 (1948); 63 Stat. 101 (1949).

claims were allowed to be invoked under § 1331, it would become necessary for courts to decide whether the action 'arises under federal law,' and this jurisdictional decision would largely depend on whether the governing law is state or federal. Determinations of this nature are among the most difficult and subtle that federal courts are called upon to make."

But the Court did uphold § 1331 jurisdiction over the Jones Act claim, which was based on the negligence of the employer.[5] The Court then proceeded to hold that Romero's unseaworthiness and maintenance and cure claims, although they did not arise under federal law, could be heard under the district court's pendent jurisdiction, given its jurisdiction over the Jones Act claim.

Justice Brennan's dissent argued that because the causes of action for unseaworthiness and for maintenance and cure were created by federal law, Romero's case arose under federal law within the meaning of § 1331. The issue before the Court, he stressed, was narrow: it did not involve a remedy that the common law could not provide and in which suit under § 1333 was exclusive, but only actions at law under the Saving Clause, and only actions based on federal substantive law. "The issue before us is only whether the fact that an action is a Saving Clause action excludes it from § 1331 where it would otherwise be maintainable thereunder." Noting that § 1333 does not exclude the exercise of diversity jurisdiction over actions under the Saving Clause, he saw no reason why § 1333 should exclude the exercise of § 1331 jurisdiction over Romero's general maritime law claims that were based on federal law.

(b) Romero and Jury Trial. In Romero, the Court ruled on the merits that the Jones Act and unseaworthiness and maintenance and cure doctrines were inapplicable, on the facts presented, to a foreign seaman like Romero. That ruling avoided any need to reach the question whether the "pendent" claims under the general maritime law could be submitted to the jury. Four years later, the Court held that when (as is the usual case) a seaman's claims for unseaworthiness and for maintenance and cure are joined in an action under the Jones Act on the "law side" of the district court, the general maritime claims must be submitted to the jury with the Jones Act claim as a matter of trial convenience. Fitzgerald v. United States Lines, 374 U.S. 16 (1963).

Given that holding, what is the ultimate significance of the Romero decision? Is the elaborateness of treatment explained by the suggestion that its question "wakes echoes in the deepest metaphysics of admiralty"? Gilmore & Black, The Law of Admiralty 33 n.118 (1st ed.1957).[6] See also Bederman, *Romero's Enduring Legacy*, 39 J.Mar.L. & Com. 27 (2008).

(6) The Scope of the Jurisdiction. There has been considerable controversy over the years about the proper scope of admiralty jurisdiction. For example, admiralty tort jurisdiction traditionally turned on the location of the tort: maritime law governed torts occurring on navigable waters, but if a vessel collided with a bridge, or someone was injured on docks or piers,

---

[5]   Notwithstanding Romero's holdings that actions under the Jones Act against employers for personal injuries can be brought under § 1331, some have argued that Romero does not apply to statutory claims generally. See Wetherington, *Jurisdictional Bases of Maritime Claims Founded on Acts of Congress*, 18 U.Miami L.Rev. 163 (1963).

[6]   For thorough analyses, see Currie, *The Silver Oar and All That: A Study of the Romero Case*, 27 U.Chi.L.Rev. 1 (1959); Kurland, *The Romero Case and Some Problems of Federal Jurisdiction*, 73 Harv.L.Rev. 817 (1960).

an action for personal injuries fell outside the admiralty jurisdiction. In 1948, Congress, dissatisfied with some decisions that had found claims to fall outside of admiralty jurisdiction, enacted the Admiralty Extension Act of 1948, 62 Stat. 496, 46 U.S.C. App. § 740, providing that "[t]he admiralty and maritime jurisdiction of the United States shall extend to and include all cases of damage or injury, to person or property, caused by a vessel on navigable water, notwithstanding that such damage or injury be done or consummated on land."[7]

Numerous decisions, before and after the 1948 Act, have discussed the scope of admiralty jurisdiction, not only in tort cases, but also in maritime contract disputes and other maritime matters. For general discussion of the scope of admiralty jurisdiction see 1 Benedict on Admiralty § 106 (7th rev.ed. 2007); 14A Wright, Miller & Cooper, Federal Practice & Procedure § 3671.

---

[7]   Constitutional attacks on the statute failed in lower federal courts, *e.g.*, United States v. Matson Navigation Co., 201 F.2d 610, 614–16 (9th Cir.1953). In Gutierrez v. Waterman Steamship Corp., 373 U.S. 206 (1963), the Supreme Court took jurisdiction under the Extension Act without discussing its constitutionality.

CHAPTER IX

SUITS CHALLENGING OFFICIAL ACTION

---

1. SUITS CHALLENGING FEDERAL OFFICIAL ACTION

PRELIMINARY NOTE ON THE SOVEREIGN IMMUNITY OF THE UNITED STATES AND THE ENFORCEMENT OF THE LAW AGAINST FEDERAL OFFICIALS AND FEDERAL AGENCIES[1]

(1) Introduction. The doctrine of sovereign immunity bars unconsented suits against the United States. In the absence of direct suits against the government, however, plaintiffs have traditionally been permitted to seek alternative redress in "officer suits" against the officials through whom the government acted. See generally Jaffe, *Suits Against Governments and Officers: Sovereign Immunity*, 77 Harv.L.Rev. 1 (1963). This Note explores the historical and conceptual foundations of sovereign immunity, on the one hand, and of "officer suits", on the other.

As will be made clear below, much of the current law governing the availability of suits against the federal government and its officers is statutory, with the United States having broadly waived its sovereign immunity and authorized suits for relief from unlawful official conduct. But nearly all of the modern law builds on, reacts to, or embodies tensions originating in a historical tradition that distinguished between suits against the sovereign, which were barred by sovereign immunity, and suits against the officers through whom the sovereign acted, which were frequently, but not always, permitted.

Among the questions to be considered throughout this Section is the extent to which officer suits have historically provided an effective substitute for direct actions against the sovereign.

(2) The Foundations of Sovereign Immunity.

(a) Despite the Constitution's omission of any reference to sovereign immunity (and, indeed, Article III's grant of jurisdiction over "Controversies to which the United States shall be a Party"), early Supreme Court decisions assumed that the United States could not be sued in its own name absent congressional consent. See, *e.g.*, Chisholm v. Georgia, 2 U.S. (2 Dall.) 419, 478 (1793) (Jay, C.J.); Cohens v. Virginia, 19 U.S. (6 Wheat.) 264, 383, 392, 411–12 (1821). In The Federalist No. 81, Alexander Hamilton expressly disavowed any suggestion that the Constitution's jurisdictional provisions

---

[1] For a survey of the purposes and historical evolution of federal sovereign immunity, as well as of current doctrine, see Sisk, *A Primer on the Doctrine of Federal Sovereign Immunity*, 58 Okla.L.Rev. 439 (2006).

should be read as implicitly displacing sovereign immunity: "It is inherent in the nature of sovereignty not to be amenable to the suit of an individual *without its consent*." The Court's view appears to have accorded wholly with the prevailing assumptions of the time. The 1789 Judiciary Act gave the lower federal courts jurisdiction over cases in which the United States appeared as a plaintiff or petitioner, but not over cases involving the government as a defendant.[2] And Justice Story, in his famous Commentaries on the Constitution, described the Article III grant of jurisdiction as intended to permit the United States to sue while making no reference to any possibility of its being subject to suit without its consent.[3] Yet the doctrine of federal sovereign immunity developed in the Supreme Court largely in dicta, without careful scrutiny of its underpinnings.

The earliest cases upholding a plea of immunity by the United States appear to be United States v. McLemore, 45 U.S. (4 How.) 286 (1846), and Hill v. United States, 50 U.S. (9 How.) 386 (1850). Both rejected bills in equity to enjoin the enforcement of judgments at law in favor of the United States, though the first pointed out that the relief sought could be obtained in the law action, and the second suggested that it might have been. Still, in 1882 Justice Miller could state in United States v. Lee, 106 U.S. 196, 207 (1882), p. 883, *infra*, that "the principle has never been discussed or the reasons for it given, but it has always been treated as an established doctrine."

(b) The foundation for the assumption that the United States enjoys sovereign immunity from unconsented suits undoubtedly lay partly in the British doctrine of sovereign immunity and in the practices of a number of the colonies and states in the pre-constitutional era. Yet many scholars have argued that the doctrine of sovereign immunity, as it had evolved in England prior to 1789, was less about *whether* the Crown or its agents could be sued than about *how*. See, *e.g.*, Jaffe, *supra*, at 18–19.

In addition to authorizing suits in many instances against the Crown's agents, British practice included a device called "the petition of right", which permitted suits directly against the Crown.[4] The petition of right originated in medieval England, when Edward I invited those with complaints or requests to come before him. Jaffe, *supra*, at 5. Although many petitioners sought favors not premised on a legal claim, others asserted wrongs that would have merited a legal remedy against anyone other than the King. The petition of right evolved to address these latter claims. See Holdsworth, *The History of Remedies Against the Crown*, 38 L.Quart.Rev. 141, 147–48 (1922). If the King supplied the requisite endorsement on the petition—"let right be done to the parties"—the Chancery would further investigate the claim and, if it seemed legitimate, would forward the petition to a court for litigation. See Pfander, *Sovereign Immunity and the Right to Petition: Toward a First Amendment Right to Pursue Judicial Claims Against the Government*, 91 Nw.U.L.Rev. 899, 909 (1997). Over time the King's personal role in endorsing

---

[2] Jackson, *Suing the Federal Government: Sovereignty, Immunity, and Judicial Independence*, 35 Geo.Wash.Int'l L.Rev. 521, 546–47 (2003).

[3] Story, Familiar Exposition of the Constitution of the United States § 332 (New York, America Book Co. 1840).

[4] For detailed discussions of English practice, see Chitty, A Treatise on the Law of the Prerogatives of the Crown and the Relative Duties and Rights of the Subject (1968); Ehrlich, *No. XII: Proceedings Against the Crown (1216–1377)*, in 6 Oxford Studies in Social and Legal History (Vinogradoff ed. 1921); 9 Holdsworth, A History of English Law (3d ed. 1944); Borchard, *Governmental Responsibility in Tort*, 36 Yale L.J. 1 (1926).

petitions disappeared; instead, a "fictional consent was substituted for the genuine consent of the King" and was routinely granted. *Id.* at 912. Eventually, Parliament enacted the Petition of Right Act of 1860, which "provided that courts of ordinary jurisdiction could hear petitions of right as a matter of course." Jaffe, *supra*, at 8.[5] Although obtaining relief upon a petition of right was cumbersome, remedies were available to address a variety of claims including, critically, land use and contract claims. According to Professor Jaffe, "[t]he one serious deficiency [in English law] was the nonliability of the government for torts of its servants." *Id. at* 18–19.

(c) The notion of popular sovereignty, the existence of a written constitution, and the institution of judicial review all might be thought to suggest a different role for sovereign immunity in this country than in England, but do not necessarily do so. Does adequate reason for the doctrine inhere: (i) In the affront to the dignity of the sovereign resulting from the "supposition that the government will not pay its debts, or will not do justice" absent the availability of a private action against it? See Gibbons v. United States, 75 U.S. 269, 274 (1868); see also Federal Maritime Comm'n v. South Carolina State Ports Auth., 535 U.S. 743 (2002), p. 977, *infra* (advancing a "dignity"-based rationale for state sovereign immunity). (ii) In the inability of the courts to enforce a judgment? See Chisholm v. Georgia, 2 U.S. (2 Dall.) 419, 478 (1793) (Jay, C.J.), p. 905, *infra*. (iii) In Article I, § 9, cl. 7, which provides that "No money shall be drawn from the Treasury, but in Consequence of Appropriations made by Law"? See Reeside v. Walker, 52 U.S. 272, 291 (1850); Figley & Tidmarsh, *The Appropriations Power and Sovereign Immunity*, 107 Mich.L.Rev. 1207 (2009). (iv) In the "logical and practical ground that there can be no legal right as against the authority that makes the law on which the right depends"? See Kawananakoa v. Polyblank, 205 U.S. 349, 353 (1907) (Holmes, J.). (v) In the avoidance of interference with governmental functions and with the government's control over its instrumentalities, funds, and property?[6] See United States v. Shearer, 473 U.S. 52, 58–59 (1985).

In reading the materials that follow, and especially United States v. Lee, consider to what extent each of these possible purposes of sovereign immunity is worthy, squares with the decided cases, or might better be served through other doctrines.

(d) Although the Supreme Court appears never to have questioned that the government generally enjoys sovereign immunity from suit even on constitutional claims (absent waiver), the Court has equivocated on several occasions about the availability of sovereign immunity in actions under particular constitutional provisions. Most notably, First English Evangelical Lutheran Church v. County of Los Angeles, 482 U.S. 304 (1987), suggested, albeit without holding, that sovereign immunity might not apply in a suit under the Takings Clause. On its facts, First English was a takings suit against a *county* that, as explained at pp. 921–922, *infra*, did not enjoy the sovereign immunity accorded to the states under federal law. But in the course of holding that the Fifth Amendment's Just Compensation Clause required compensation for a regulatory taking even before a challenged

---

[5] The Crown Proceedings Act of 1947 abolished the petition of right and empowered individuals to sue the Crown just as they would any other party. See Hogg, Monahan & Wright, Liability of the Crown 8–9 (4th ed. 2011).

[6] For a critical discussion of the historical foundations of sovereign immunity's survival, see Jackson, note 2, *supra*, at 545–47.

regulation had been judicially determined to constitute a "taking", the Court said: "The Solicitor General urges that the prohibitory nature of the Fifth Amendment, combined with principles of sovereign immunity, establishes that the Amendment itself is only a limitation on the power of the Government to act, not a remedial provision. The cases cited in the text, we think, refute the argument of the United States that 'the Constitution does not, of its own force, furnish a basis for a court to award money damages against the government.' Though arising in various factual and jurisdictional settings, these cases make clear that it is the Constitution that dictates the remedy for interference with property rights amounting to a taking."

Consider also the series of decisions culminating in Reich v. Collins, 513 U.S. 106 (1994) (discussed in detail in Chap. VII, pp. 757–758, *supra*), involving state court actions against state officials for refund of taxes allegedly exacted in violation of the federal Constitution. The Court in Reich, relying in part on its earlier decisions, stated that due process requires the state to afford a clear and certain remedy in such cases, and added (in dictum) that this obligation exists notwithstanding "the sovereign immunity States traditionally enjoy in their own courts".

Subsequent Supreme Court decisions, however, have cast doubt on the implications of both the First English and Reich decisions. City of Monterey v. Del Monte Dunes at Monterey, Ltd., 526 U.S. 687, 714 (1999), suggested that the defense of sovereign immunity may be available with respect to a just compensation claim against a state or state entity, and Alden v. Maine, 527 U.S. 706, 740 (1999), explained the decision in Reich as resting on the narrow ground that the state was constitutionally obligated to satisfy its promise to provide a post-deprivation remedy. See pp. 334, *supra,* 967, *infra*.

In determining whether the United States (or a state) is immune from damages liability, is there a basis in the constitutional text or in other considerations for treating an action under the Takings Clause, or for refund of taxes allegedly exacted in violation of the Constitution, differently from actions claiming other constitutional violations?

(3) Damages Against Federal Officers. While the King enjoyed at least a formal sovereign immunity, his officers did not.[7] They could be required, for example, to pay damages to private persons injured by illegal acts, on the theory that officials, like other wrongdoers, were subject to the law. Like the British tradition of sovereign immunity, officer suits became a fixture in American law.

For example, in Little v. Barreme, 6 U.S. (2 Cranch) 170, 179 (1804), the Supreme Court affirmed a damages judgment against an American naval captain who, in seizing a Danish vessel, had acted under presidential orders issued through the Secretary of Navy and purportedly pursuant to an act of Congress. The Court (per Marshall, C.J.) found that the orders had been based upon a misconstruction of the statute and that the seizure was thus a trespass unauthorized by federal law. Despite the presidential direction, the need for military obedience, and the harshness of holding the officer personally liable, the Court ruled that the captain's claim of official authority

---

[7] For an informative historical study of the development of official accountability in England, with emphasis on the period from the thirteenth century through the seventeenth, see Seidman, *The Origins of Accountability: Everything I Know About the Sovereign's Immunity, I Learned from King Henry III*, 49 St.Louis U.L.J. 393 (2004). Professor Seidman concludes that "[c]ommon law jurists and parliamentarians rejected the idea of divine rights of kings in favor of popular sovereignty and the more balanced regime of a constitutional monarchy".

could not shield an act that, absent lawful authorization, constituted a simple trespass.

Note the theory on which Little v. Barreme proceeded: An officer who committed an act for which the common law provided a right to relief—in that case, a trespass—was not shielded from liability merely because he or she purported to act in an official capacity. See generally Attorney General's Committee on Administrative Procedure, Administrative Procedure in Government Agencies, S.Doc. No. 8, 77th Cong, 1st Sess. 81 (1941): "[T]he basic judicial remedy for the protection of the individual against illegal official action [was historically] a private action for damages against the official in which the court determine[d], in the usual common-law manner and with the aid of a jury, whether or not the officer was legally authorized to do what he did in the particular case. The plaintiff [could not] sue to redress merely any unauthorized action by an officer. To maintain the suit the plaintiff [had to] allege conduct by the officer which, if not justified by his official authority, [was] a private wrong to the plaintiff, entitling the latter to recover damages." (On the absolute and qualified immunities that today broadly shield officials from personal liability in damages, even when they remain suable in theory, see Sec. 3, *infra*.)

Despite the Court's provision of a common law damages remedy in Little v. Barreme, the early cases involving claims to relief against federal officials do not follow a wholly consistent pattern. Woolhandler, *Patterns of Official Immunity and Accountability*, 37 Case W.Res.L.Rev. 396 (1987), identifies two competing models for evaluating actions seeking such remedies: a "legality" model, which focuses on whether harm to the citizen has been caused by an unlawful act, and a "discretion" model, which focuses on the harm posed by potential liability to "the decisionmaking processes of the official". She suggests that the former model was predominant during the era of the Marshall Court, and the latter during the era of the Taney Court.

Pfander & Hunt, *Public Wrongs and Private Bills: Indemnification and Government Accountability in the Early Republic*, 85 N.Y.U.L.Rev 1862 (2010), maintain that the seeming harshness of officer liability in tort actions was ameliorated in practice by congressional enactment of private bills indemnifying officials—such as Captain Little in Little v. Barreme—who were held liable for good faith efforts to discharge their official duties. According to the authors, Congress relied on a special House Committee on Claims to determine entitlements to indemnification, and the Committee developed criteria for decision that it applied with remarkable consistency. Those criteria generally followed common law agency rules, under which principals were liable for the actions of agents acting within the scope of their instructions and in good faith. The petition-and-indemnification practice became so well known, Pfander and Hunt report, that courts during the antebellum years routinely decided tort actions against federal officials on the assumption that the government, not the nominal defendant, would pay adverse judgments. On this account, sovereign immunity was little more than a formalism, except in cases in which common law agency rules would have adjudged any principal not responsible for the misconduct of an agent. Although Pfander and Hunt do not precisely date the demise of what they refer to as the antebellum system, they characterize modern doctrines, under which government officers frequently possess "official immunity" from damages liability, as reflecting "a remarkable feat of judicial creativity" by the modern-day Supreme Court. According to the authors, "[o]ne can fairly ask whether victims of positive government wrongdoing would fare better in 1810 or 2010."

(4) Writs Available Against Federal Officers. In addition to seeking damages, litigants aggrieved by federal official action could avail themselves, in appropriate cases, of such other common law remedies as ejectment or replevin. See, *e.g.*, United States v. Lee, p. 883, *infra*.

Equitable remedies included injunctions, which "rest[ed] on the same theory [as private actions for damages], namely, the answerability of a Government officer as a private individual for conduct injurious to another". Attorney General's Committee on Administrative Procedure, Paragraph (3), *supra*, at 81.[8]

Also available were the prerogative writs—quo warranto, habeas corpus, prohibition, certiorari, and mandamus—that were issued by the King's Bench in England,[9] though each was subject to distinctive limitations.[10]

(5) Transitional Questions. Although it was historically taken for granted that sovereign immunity did not always or perhaps even typically bar suits against governmental officers for legal wrongs, questions remained about whether some claims to relief—though nominally pleaded against a government officer—sufficiently implicated inherently sovereign interests to

---

[8] The Supreme Court suggested in Panama Canal Co. v. Grace Line, Inc., 356 U.S. 309, 318 (1958), that a suit for a mandatory injunction should be judged by the same principles as a suit seeking a writ of mandamus.

[9] See generally Jaffe, Judicial Control of Administrative Action 165–93 (1965); Smith, *The Prerogative Writs*, 11 Cambridge L.J. 40 (1951).

[10] The writ of quo warranto ("by what authority?") inquires into the authority by which a public office is held or power to act is claimed. Historically, it was used to discover whether an official (such as a sheriff) or state-chartered corporation was acting without authorization. If so, the remedy was to oust the relevant party from power. See Black's Law Dictionary 1371 (9th ed. 2011).

The writ of habeas corpus ("that you have the body") is available primarily to test the legality of official detention or custody. Its contemporary uses include challenges to the detention of aliens, of individuals in military service, and of persons confined pursuant to arrest or criminal conviction. For detailed discussion, see Chap. XI, *infra*.

The writ of prohibition is usually directed to an inferior judicial or quasi-judicial body, to bar it from exceeding its jurisdiction. This writ generally does not permit review of actions (even if unlawful) of a tribunal that does have jurisdiction, or of actions that are deemed to be purely administrative or ministerial. Moreover, the writ is discretionary, and is not to be awarded if another remedy is available. For these reasons, prohibition has been of limited importance in reviewing action by federal officials.

The writ of certiorari ("to be more fully informed") directs a lower tribunal to certify its record to a superior court (in England, the King's Bench) for review. It is generally limited to review of judicial or quasi-judicial action, and it too is available as a matter of discretion rather than right. Congress has never authorized its use in the federal district courts, and even in the District of Columbia courts—long regarded as common law courts—certiorari fell into disuse as a means of reviewing administrative action. See Degge v. Hitchcock, 229 U.S. 162 (1913).

The related writ of scire facias ("you are to show cause") was historically used to vacate a matter of record, such as an official's commission or a corporation's charter, due to an illegal action or abuse of power by the holder.

FRCP 81(b) abolished both the writ of scire facias and the writ of mandamus in the district courts: "The writs of scire facias and mandamus are abolished. Relief previously available through them may be obtained by appropriate action or motion under these rules." By its own language, however, the Rule preserves each writ's remedy. And the writ of mandamus remains available in the Supreme Court and the appellate courts. *Cf.* The Mandamus and Venue Act of 1962, p. 893, *infra*.

trigger the doctrine's application. The next principal case, United States v. Lee, presented such a question.

United States v. Lee

106 U.S. 196, 1 S.Ct. 240, 27 L.Ed. 171 (1882).
Appeal from the Circuit Court for the Eastern District of Virginia.

[The United States purchased the Arlington, Virginia estate of General Robert E. Lee's wife, after an alleged failure to pay a $92 assessment under a tax to support the Civil War. The tax commissioners had refused a proffer of payment on behalf of the owner, under a rule (later held invalid) that only the owner in person could pay overdue taxes. The United States proceeded to use part of the estate for Arlington National Cemetery and a fort.

[The Lees' son (who claimed title under his grandfather's will) filed an ejectment action in state court against the two federal officers who, under authority of the Secretary of War, had charge of the property. The defendants removed the action to the Circuit Court of the United States for the Eastern District of Virginia. Though the United States was not a party, the Attorney General filed a pleading in the Circuit Court seeking dismissal of the suit, stating that the United States possessed the property in the exercise of its sovereign and constitutional powers, and that "the court has no jurisdiction of the subject in controversy." Plaintiff's demurrer to this pleading was sustained, and after a jury trial, judgment for the plaintiff was entered.

[Both the individual defendants and the United States filed a writ of error in the Supreme Court. The Solicitor General argued the case for the individual defendants and for the United States.]

■ MR. JUSTICE MILLER delivered the opinion of the Court.

[The Court expressed doubt that the United States, a non-party, could file a writ of error, but noted that the defendants' writ raised all the issues pressed by the United States. After upholding the jury's determination that the United States did not acquire valid title under the tax sale proceeding because of the illegal refusal to accept payment on behalf of the owner, the Court turned to the question of sovereign immunity.]

The counsel for plaintiffs in error and in behalf of the United States assert the proposition, that though it has been ascertained by the verdict of the jury, in which no error is found, that the plaintiff has the title to the land in controversy, and that what is set up in behalf of the United States is no title at all, the court can render no judgment in favor of the plaintiff against the defendants in the action, because the latter hold the property as officers and agents of the United States, and it is appropriated to lawful public uses.

This proposition rests on the principle that the United States cannot be lawfully sued without its consent in any case, and that no action can be maintained against any individual without such consent, where the judgment must depend on the right of the United States to property held by such persons as officers or agents for the government.

The first branch of this proposition is conceded to be the established law of this country and of this court at the present day; the second, as a necessary or proper deduction from the first, is denied.

In order to decide whether the inference is justified from what is conceded, it is necessary to ascertain, if we can, on what principle the exemption of the United States from a suit by one of its citizens is founded, and what limitations surround this exemption. In this, as in most other cases of like character, it will be found that the doctrine is derived from the laws and practices of our English ancestors; and * * * it is beyond question that from the time of Edward the First until now the King of England was not suable in the courts of that country, except where his consent had been given on petition of right * * *.

There is in this country, however, no such thing as the petition of right, as there is no such thing as a kingly head to the nation, or to any of the States which compose it. There is vested in no officer or body the authority to consent that the State shall be sued except in the law-making power, which may give such consent on the terms it may choose to impose. Congress has created a court [the Court of Claims] in which it has authorized suits to be brought against the United States, but has limited such suits to those arising on contract, with a few unimportant exceptions.

What were the reasons which forbid that the King should be sued in his own court, and how do they apply to the political body corporate which we call the United States of America? As regards the King, one reason given by the old judges was the absurdity of the King's sending a writ to himself to command the King to appear in the King's court. No such reason exists in our government, as process runs in the name of the President, and may be served on the Attorney-General, as was done in Chisholm v. Georgia, 2 Dall. 419. Nor can it be said that the government is degraded by appearing as a defendant in the courts of its own creation, because it is constantly appearing as a party in such courts, and submitting its rights as against the citizen to their judgment. * * *

That the doctrine [of sovereign immunity] met with a doubtful reception in the early history of this court may be seen from the opinions of two of its justices in the case of Chisholm v. Georgia, where Mr. Justice Wilson, a member of the convention which framed the Constitution, after a learned examination of the laws of England and other states and kingdoms, sums up the result by saying: "We see nothing against, but much in favor of, the jurisdiction of this court over the State of Georgia, a party to this cause." Mr. Chief Justice Jay also considered the question as affected by the difference between a republican State like ours and a personal sovereign, and held that there is no reason why a state should not be sued, though doubting whether the United States would be subject to the same rule.

The first recognition of the general doctrine by this court is to be found in the case of Cohens v. Virginia, 6 Wheat. 264.

The terms in which Mr. Chief Justice Marshall there gives assent to the principle does not add much to its force. "The counsel for the defendant," he says, "has laid down the general proposition that a sovereign independent State is not suable except by its own consent." This general proposition, he adds, will not be controverted.

* * * [W]hile acceding to the general proposition that in no court can the United States be sued directly by original process as a defendant, there is abundant evidence in the decisions of this court that the doctrine, if not absolutely limited to cases in which the United States are made defendants by name, is not permitted to interfere with the judicial enforcement of the established rights of plaintiffs when the United States is not a defendant or a necessary party to the suit.

But little weight can be given to the decisions of the English courts on this branch of the subject, for two reasons:—

1. In all cases where the title to property came into controversy between the crown and a subject, whether held in right of the person who was king or as representative of the nation, the petition of right presented a judicial remedy,—a remedy which this court, on full examination in a case which required it, held to be practical and efficient. There has been, therefore, no necessity for suing the officers or servants of the King who held possession of such property, when the issue could be made with the King himself as defendant.

2. Another reason of much greater weight is found in the vast difference in the essential character of the two governments as regards the source and the depositaries of power. * * *

Under our system the *people*, who are there called *subjects*, are the sovereign. Their rights, whether collective or individual, are not bound to give way to a sentiment of loyalty to the person of a monarch. The citizen here knows no person, however near to those in power, or however powerful himself, to whom he need yield the rights which the law secures to him when it is well administered. When he, in one of the courts of competent jurisdiction, has established his right to property, there is no reason why deference to any person, natural or artificial, not even the United States, should prevent him from using the means which the law gives him for the protection and enforcement of that right. * * *

The earliest case in this court in which the true rule is laid down, and which, bearing a close analogy to the one before us, seems decisive of it, is United States v. Peters, 5 Cranch, 115. In an admiralty proceeding, * * * the District Court of the United States for Pennsylvania * * * had decided that the libellants were entitled to the proceeds of the sale of a vessel condemned as prize of war, which had come to the possession of David Rittenhouse as treasurer of Pennsylvania. * * * [O]n an application therefor, a writ of *mandamus* to compel the judge of the District Court to proceed in the execution of his decree was granted. In delivering the opinion, Mr. Chief Justice Marshall says: "The State cannot be made a defendant to a suit brought by an individual, but it remains the duty of the courts of the United States to decide all cases brought before them by citizens of one State against citizens of a different State, when a State is not necessarily a defendant. In this case, the suit was not instituted against the State or its treasurer, but against the executrixes of David Rittenhouse, for the proceeds of a vessel condemned in the Court of Admiralty, which were admitted to be in their possession. If these proceeds had been the actual property of Pennsylvania, however wrongfully acquired, the disclosure of that fact would have presented a case on which it was unnecessary to give an opinion; *but it certainly can never be alleged that a mere suggestion of title in a State to property in possession of an individual must arrest the proceedings of the court, and* *prevent their looking into the suggestion and examining the validity of the title."* * * *

It may be said—in fact it is said—that the present case differs from the one in 5 Cranch, because the officers who are sued assert no personal possession, but are holding as the mere agents of the United States, while the executors of Rittenhouse held the money until a better right was established. But the very next case in this court of a similar character, Meigs v. McClung's Lessee, 9 Cranch, 11, shows that this distinction was not recognized as sound. [In Meigs, the plaintiff brought an action against military officers in possession of property and prevailed over the objection that the action could not be maintained against the officers because they were acting for the benefit of the United States and under their direction. The lower court held that since title was in the plaintiff, he was entitled to recover possession, and the Supreme Court upheld the judgment.]

Osborn v. Bank of United States, 9 Wheat. 738, is a leading case, remarkable in many respects, and in none more than in those resembling the one before us.

It was this: The State of Ohio having levied a tax upon the branch of the Bank of the United States located in that State, which the bank refused to pay, Osborn, auditor of the State, was about to proceed to collect said tax by a seizure of the money of the bank in its vaults, and an amended bill alleged that he had so seized $100,000, and while aware that an injunction had been issued by the Circuit Court of the United States on the prayer of the bank, the money so seized had been delivered to the treasurer of the State, Curry, and afterwards came to the possession of Sullivan, who had succeeded Curry as treasurer. Both Curry and Sullivan were made defendants as well as Osborn and his assistant, Harper.

One of the objections pressed with pertinacity all through the case to the jurisdiction of the court was the conceded fact that the State of Ohio, though not made a defendant to the bill, was the real party in interest. That all the parties sued were her officers,—her auditor, her treasurer, and their agents,—concerning acts done in their official character, and in obedience to her laws. It was conceded that the State could not be sued, and it was earnestly argued there, as here, that what could not be done directly could not be done by suing her officers. And it was insisted that while the State could not be brought before the court, it was a necessary party to the relief sought, namely, the return of the money and obedience to the injunction, and that the bill must be dismissed.

A few citations from the opinion of Mr. Chief Justice Marshall will show the views entertained by the court on the question thus raised. * * *

[Chief Justice Marshall stated]: " * * * In cases where a State is a party on the record, the question of jurisdiction is decided by inspection. If jurisdiction depend not on this plain fact, but on the interest of the State, what rule has the Constitution given by which this interest is to be measured? If no rule is given, is it to be settled by the court? If so, the curious anomaly is presented of a court examining the whole testimony of a cause, inquiring into and deciding on the extent of a State's interest, without having a right to exercise any jurisdiction in the case. Can this inquiry be made without the exercise of jurisdiction?"

The decree of the Circuit Court ordering a restitution of the money was affirmed.

* * * [A]s late as the case of Davis v. Gray, 16 Wall. 203, the case of Osborn v. Bank of United States is cited with approval as establishing these among other propositions: "Where the State is concerned, the State should be made a party, if it can be done. That it cannot be done, is a sufficient reason for the omission to do it, and the court may proceed to decree against the officers of the State in all respects as if the State were a party to the record. In deciding who are parties to the suit, the court will not look beyond the record. Making a State officer a party does not make the State a party, *although her law may have prompted his action, and the State may stand behind him as a real party in interest.* A State can be made a party only by shaping the bill expressly with that view, as where individuals or corporations are intended to be put in that relation to the case."

Though not prepared to say now that the court can proceed against the officer in "all respects" as if the State were a party, this may be taken as intimating in a general way the views of the court at that time. * * *

The objection [of sovereign immunity] is also inconsistent with the principle involved in the last two clauses of article 5 of the amendments to the Constitution of the United States, whose language is: "That no person * * * shall be deprived of life, liberty, or property without due process of law, nor shall private property be taken for public use without just compensation."

Conceding that the property in controversy in this case is devoted to a proper public use, and that this has been done by those having authority to establish a cemetery and a fort, the verdict of the jury finds that it is and was the private property of the plaintiff, and was taken without any process of law and without any compensation. Undoubtedly those provisions of the Constitution are of that character which it is intended the courts shall enforce, when cases involving their operation and effect are brought before them. The instances in which the life and liberty of the citizen have been protected by the judicial writ of *habeas corpus* are too familiar to need citation, and many of these cases, indeed almost all of them, are those in which life or liberty was invaded by persons assuming to act under the authority of the government. Ex parte Milligan, 4 Wall. 2.

If this constitutional provision is a sufficient authority for the court to interfere to rescue a prisoner from the hands of those holding him under the asserted authority of the government, what reason is there that the same courts shall not give remedy to the citizen whose property has been seized without due process of law, and devoted to public use without just compensation? * * *

No man in this country is so high that he is above the law. No officer of the law may set that law at defiance with impunity. All the officers of the government, from the highest to the lowest, are creatures of the law, and are bound to obey it. * * *

Courts of justice are established, not only to decide upon the controverted rights of the citizens as against each other, but also upon rights in controversy between them and the government; and the docket of this court is crowded with controversies of the latter class.

Shall it be said, in the face of all this, and of the acknowledged right of the judiciary to decide in proper cases, statutes which have been passed by both branches of Congress and approved by the President to be unconstitutional, that the courts cannot give a remedy when the citizen has been deprived of his property by force, his estate seized and converted to the use of the government without lawful authority, without process of law, and without compensation, because the President has ordered it and his officers are in possession?

If such be the law of this country, it sanctions a tyranny which has no existence in the monarchies of Europe, nor in any other government which has a just claim to well-regulated liberty and the protection of personal rights. * * *

The evils supposed to grow out of the possible interference of judicial action with the exercise of powers of the government essential to some of its most important operations, will be seen to be small indeed compared to this evil, and much diminished, if they do not wholly disappear, upon a recurrence to a few considerations.

* * * [One such] consideration is, that since the United States cannot be made a defendant to a suit concerning its property, and no judgment in any suit against an individual who has possession or control of such property can bind or conclude the government, * * * the government is always at liberty, notwithstanding any such judgment, to avail itself of all the remedies which the law allows to every person, natural or artificial, for the vindication and assertion of its rights. Hence, taking the present case as an illustration, the United States may proceed by a bill in chancery to quiet its title, in aid of which, if a proper case is made, a writ of injunction may be obtained. Or it may bring an action of ejectment, in which, on a direct issue between the United States as plaintiff, and the present plaintiff as defendant, the title of the United States could be judicially determined. Or, if satisfied that its title has been shown to be invalid, and it still desires to use the property, or any part of it, for the purposes to which it is now devoted, it may purchase such property by fair negotiation, or condemn it by a judicial proceeding, in which a just compensation shall be ascertained and paid according to the Constitution.

If it be said that the proposition here established may subject the property, the officers of the United States, and the performance of their indispensable functions to hostile proceedings in the State courts, the answer is, that no case can arise in a State court, where the interests, the property, the rights, or the authority of the Federal government may come in question, which cannot be removed into a court of the United States under existing laws. * * *

The Circuit Court was competent to decide the issues in this case between the parties that were before it; in the principles on which these issues were decided no error has been found; and its judgment is

Affirmed.

■ MR. JUSTICE GRAY, with whom concurred MR. CHIEF JUSTICE WAITE, MR. JUSTICE BRADLEY, and MR. JUSTICE WOODS, dissenting.

* * * The case so deeply affects the sovereignty of the United States, and its relations to the citizen, that it is fit to announce the grounds of our dissent. * * *

This [action] * * * is brought to recover possession of land which the United States have for years held, and still hold, for military and other public purposes, claiming title under a certificate of sale for direct taxes, which is declared by the act of Congress of June 7, 1862, to be *prima facie* evidence of the regularity and validity of the sale and of the title of the purchaser * * *.

The principles upon which we are of opinion that the court below had no authority to try the question of the validity of the title of the United States in this action, and that this court has therefore no authority to pass upon that question, may be briefly stated.

The sovereign is not liable to be sued in any judicial tribunal without its consent. The sovereign cannot hold property except by agents. To maintain an action for the recovery of possession of property held by the sovereign through its agents, not claiming any title or right in themselves, but only as the representatives of the sovereign and in its behalf, is to maintain an action to recover possession of the property against the sovereign; and to invade such possession of the agents, by execution or other judicial process, is to invade the possession of the sovereign, and to disregard the fundamental maxim that the sovereign cannot be sued.

That maxim is not limited to a monarchy, but is of equal force in a republic. In the one, as in the other, it is essential to the common defense and general welfare that the sovereign should not, without its consent, be dispossessed by judicial process of forts, arsenals, military posts, and ships of war, necessary to guard the national existence against insurrection and invasion; of custom-houses and revenue cutters, employed in the collection of the revenue; or of light-houses and light-ships, established for the security of commerce with foreign nations and among the different parts of the country.

These principles appear to us to be axioms of public law, which would need no reference to authorities in their support, were it not for the exceeding importance and interest of the case, the great ability with which it has been argued, and the difference of opinion that has been manifested as to the extent and application of the precedents.

The exemption of the United States from being impleaded without their consent is, as has often been affirmed by this court, as absolute as that of the Crown of England or any other sovereign. * * *

To maintain this action, independently of any legislation by Congress, is to declare that the exemption of the United States from being impleaded without their consent does not embrace lands held by a disputed title; to defeat the exemption from judicial process in the very cases in which it is of the utmost importance to the public that it should be upheld; and to compel the United States to submit to the determination of courts and juries the validity of their title to any land held and used for military, naval, commercial, revenue, or police purposes.

[Justice Gray then argued that several precedents relied upon by the plaintiff, including Chisholm, Osborn, and Meigs, were distinguishable—Chisholm because the case did not hold that the United States could be sued without its consent, Osborn because the money in issue was in the personal possession of the defendants and the suit was one to enjoin federal constitutional violations, and Meigs because "no objection to the exercise of jurisdiction was made by the defendants or by the United States, or noticed by the Court".] * * *

NOTE ON SOVEREIGN IMMUNITY IN SUITS AGAINST FEDERAL OFFICERS

(1) Pertinent Authority. In discussing the sovereign immunity of the United States, the Court in United States v. Lee relied on a number of cases involving *state* immunity from suit. Because the Court frequently treats state and federal sovereign immunity as reflecting identical or at least closely analogous principles, this Note will also discuss state cases that the Court has treated as bearing on the scope of federal sovereign immunity—even though state immunity from at least some federal court actions has a specific textual basis, in the Eleventh Amendment, that federal sovereign immunity does not. State sovereign immunity and the Eleventh Amendment are discussed more comprehensively in Section 2 of this Chapter.

(2) Basis for the Holding in Lee. In applying the distinction between suits against the sovereign that are barred by sovereign immunity and officer suits that are not, the Lee majority says that upholding a claim of sovereign immunity would be "inconsistent with" the Fifth Amendment guarantee that no one "shall be deprived of life, liberty, or property without due process of law." Pressed for all that it might be worth, would this view turn the doctrine of sovereign immunity into an empty shell that plaintiffs could always evade in suits alleging constitutional violations by simply taking care to name government officials, rather than the government, as defendants? Would this result be desirable? Is there any principled stopping point short of it?

(3) Rejection of the Party-of-Record Rule. In Osborn v. Bank of the United States, 22 U.S. (9 Wheat.) 738, 857 (1824), a case cited in Lee involving state immunity from suit under the Eleventh Amendment, Chief Justice Marshall stated that the availability of the immunity did indeed depend on whether the government was the party of record: "It may, we think, be laid down as a rule which admits of no exception, that, in all cases where jurisdiction depends upon the party, it is the party named in the record. Consequently, the 11th amendment * * * is, of necessity, limited to those suits in which a State is a party on the record."[1] As late as Davis v. Gray, 83 U.S. 203, 220 (1872), the Court suggested adherence to the party-of-record rule.

United States v. Lee, while finding no barrier to suit, suggests that immunity may not be "absolutely limited to cases in which the United States are made defendants by name." The Court clearly rejected the party-of-record test in In re Ayers, 123 U.S. 443, 487 (1887), p. 928, *infra*, which held

---

[1]   Marshall had signaled a retreat from the broad party-of-record rule, however, in the complicated proceedings in Governor of Georgia v. Madrazo, 26 U.S. (1 Pet.) 110 (1828), p. 908, *infra*.

that the doctrine of state sovereign immunity and the Eleventh Amendment precluded a federal court from entering an injunction against state officials "the object of which is * * * indirectly to compel the specific performance of [a] contract." Since Lee and Ayers, the Supreme Court has consistently rejected the party-of-record rule as the sole determinant of whether sovereign immunity bars an action nominally against an official.

Nevertheless, as in Lee, rejection of the party-of-record rule as the exclusive measure of whether sovereign immunity applied left in place a broad scope for suits against officers, as long as it could be shown that the officer had personally committed an actionable wrong. Subsequent decisions thus confirm that government officials not only can be enjoined from causing harm, *e.g.*, Philadelphia Co. v. Stimson, 223 U.S. 605 (1912), but also compelled to perform affirmative acts if they are required by law to discharge some duty, see, *e.g.*, Wilbur v. United States ex rel. Krushnic, 280 U.S. 306 (1930).

In contrast to the liability of officers engaging in tortious conduct, officers agreeing to contracts on behalf of the government would not, under common law principles, be personally liable if the government committed a breach. Thus, suit for breach of contract could be brought only against the government—and such an action was barred by immunity. See, *e.g.*, Louisiana ex rel. Elliott v. Jumel, 107 U.S. 711, 721, 727 (1883); see also In re Ayers, *supra*.

Denial of relief in these cases was consistent with what Professor Jaffe found to be the general pattern of judicial responses to officer suits: "[T]he sensitive areas—the areas where consent to suit [was] likely to be required—[were] those involving the enforcement of contracts, treasury liability for tort, and the adjudication of interests in property which [had] come unsullied by tort into the bosom of the government." Jaffe, *Suits Against Governments and Officers: Sovereign Immunity*, 77 Harv.L.Rev. 1, 29 (1963). But the cases are by no means easy to square.[2]

In thinking about whether sovereign immunity should bar suits to enforce government contracts, note that the particular sensitivity of suits involving breach of *state* government contracts was clear from the resistance to such suits brought by bondholders of state governments following both the Revolutionary and Civil Wars. As explained on p. 906, *infra*, the Eleventh Amendment was enacted following the Supreme Court's decision enforcing a contract against a state in Chisholm v. Georgia, 2 U.S. (2 Dall.) 419 (1793), and has since been interpreted to protect state governments from federal jurisdiction to impose liability for breach of contract. See generally Section 2, *infra*.

Should it be assumed that the federal and state governments enjoy identical immunities from unconsented suit? That the federal government should enjoy a sovereign immunity at least as broad as that enjoyed by the states?

(4) The Impact of Ex parte Young. In Ex parte Young, 209 U.S. 123 (1908), p. 922, *infra*, the Supreme Court upheld the authority of a federal

---

[2] For further helpful discussions, see Cramton, *Nonstatutory Review of Federal Administrative Action: The Need for Statutory Reform of Sovereign Immunity, Subject Matter Jurisdiction, and Parties Defendant*, 68 Mich.L.Rev. 387, 402–04 (1970), and Engdahl, *Immunity and Accountability for Positive Government Wrongs*, 44 U.Colo.L.Rev. 1, 20–21, 32–34 (1972).

circuit court to enjoin a state attorney general from instituting suits to impose sanctions for violation of a state statute that allegedly conflicted with the Fourteenth Amendment. In doing so, the Court plainly assumed that the plaintiffs had a judicially cognizable cause of action. Reasoning that a state could not authorize its officials to violate the federal Constitution, and that state officials therefore could not act with state authority in doing so, the Court also held that the Eleventh Amendment did not apply.

Based partly on an assumption that Attorney General Young's announced readiness to bring a prosecution for violation of state law would not have been tortious at common law,[3] some commentators have assumed that the plaintiffs' cause of action for injunctive relief must have arisen directly from or otherwise been grounded in the Fourteenth Amendment. See Hart, *The Relations Between State and Federal Law*, 54 Colum.L.Rev. 489, 524 & n.124 (1954); Purcell, *Ex parte Young and the Transformation of the Federal Courts, 1890–1917*, 40 U.Tol.L.Rev. 931, 962–63 (2009). As discussed on p. 933, *infra*, Harrison, Ex Parte Young, 60 Stan.L.Rev. 989, 990 (2008), argues to the contrary. According to Professor Harrison, Ex parte Young involved a traditional equitable cause of action to enjoin a threatened lawsuit based on what otherwise would have been a legally valid defense. Whether or not Ex parte Young was a watershed, at the very least it represents a notable point on a continuum along which the federal courts began to recognize rights to sue state officials for injunctive relief for constitutional violations, regardless of whether the officials' conduct would traditionally have been actionable at common law or provided the basis for a traditionally actionable suit in equity. See Shapiro, *Ex parte Young and the Uses of History*, 67 N.Y.U.Ann.Surv.Am.L. 69, 82–83 (2011). The principle that the Constitution creates a cause of action against governmental officials for injunctive relief from non-tortious governmental action, and that sovereign immunity erects no general bar to such relief (outside of suits seeking, *e.g.*, unconsented payments out of the federal treasury), has also come to apply in suits challenging *federal* official action. See, *e.g.*, Shields v. Utah Idaho Cent. R.R., 305 U.S. 177, 183–84 (1938). (This principle possesses limited current practical significance, however, as a result of waivers by Congress of federal sovereign immunity in the Administrative Procedure Act and other statutes. See pp. 896–904, *infra*.)

(5) The Role of Mandamus. The Supreme Court has held that mandamus actions are not barred by sovereign immunity. See Houston v. Ormes, 252 U.S. 469, 472–74 (1920); Minnesota v. Hitchcock, 185 U.S. 373, 386 (1902). Why should this be? Part of the answer may lie in history: In England, mandamus and the other prerogative writs were issued by the King's Bench, over which the King once presided. His presence eventually became only a fiction, but the writ was still regarded as an indirect command of the sovereign himself.[4]

In Vishnevsky v. United States, 581 F.2d 1249, 1255–56 (7th Cir.1978), the court, in approving a writ of mandamus to compel IRS officials to credit plaintiffs with an overpayment of taxes, noted a long line of Supreme Court and lower court cases issuing mandamus to compel payment of funds out of the federal treasury, even absent consent by Congress. Consider how the

---

[3]   See Jacobs, The Eleventh Amendment and Sovereign Immunity 138–42 (1972).

[4]   See Note, 70 Harv.L.Rev. 827, 846 (1957). Although FRCP Rule 81(b) abolished the writ in federal civil proceedings, appellate courts and the Supreme Court can still issue writs of mandamus by virtue of the All Writs Act.

traditional treatment of mandamus bears on arguments that Article I, § 9, cl. 7—which provides that "[n]o money shall be drawn from the treasury, but in consequence of appropriations made by law"—explains or requires the doctrine of federal sovereign immunity.

Although mandamus was a traditional mechanism of nonstatutory review of official action, by 1838 it was established that, largely as the result of historical accident, neither the state courts nor the federal courts generally, but only the Circuit Court for the District of Columbia, possessed jurisdiction to issue the writ against federal officials. See Kendall v. United States ex rel. Stokes, 37 U.S. (12 Pet.) 524, 619–26 (1838).[5] In an important reform, the Mandamus and Venue Act of 1962, 28 U.S.C. § 1361, gave jurisdiction, without regard to amount in controversy, to all federal district courts over actions "in the nature of mandamus" to compel a federal officer to perform his or her duty. See generally Byse, *Proposed Reforms in Federal "Nonstatutory" Judicial Review: Sovereign Immunity, Indispensable Parties, Mandamus*, 75 Harv.L.Rev. 1479 (1962).[6]

(6) Retrenchment: Larson and Its Progeny. In several twentieth century decisions, the Supreme Court retreated to a significant extent from the broad implications of United States v. Lee with respect to the availability of specific relief against federal officers.

(a) In the first and perhaps the most controversial of these cases, Larson v. Domestic & Foreign Commerce Corp., 337 U.S. 682 (1949), a sharply divided Court upheld the defense of sovereign immunity in a suit by a plaintiff who claimed to have purchased some coal from the United States and sought to enjoin federal officers from transferring it to any other person. Writing for the Court, Chief Justice Vinson reasoned that the suit was "in substance, a suit against the Government over which the court, in the absence of consent, has no jurisdiction." In a suit against a government officer, "the question is * * * whether, by obtaining relief against the officer, relief will not, in effect, be obtained against the sovereign. For the sovereign can act only through agents and, when an agent's actions are restrained, the sovereign itself may, through him, be restrained."

Officer suits seeking to compel official action should be treated as *not* barred by sovereign immunity, the Chief Justice said, only when they are *ultra vires*, either because they exceed statutory bounds on official authority such that the officer is "not doing the business which the sovereign has empowered him to do or he is doing it in a way which the sovereign has forbidden." Deeming action in violation of the Constitution to be necessarily

---

[5]   Section 13 of the First Judiciary Act—purporting to vest in the Supreme Court an original jurisdiction to issue writs of mandamus to any persons holding office under the authority of the United States—was held unconstitutional in Marbury v. Madison, p. 59, *supra.*

Efforts to obtain mandamus in the inferior federal courts also failed. In McIntire v. Wood, 11 U.S. (7 Cranch) 504 (1813), the Supreme Court held that § 11 of the Judiciary Act did not authorize a federal circuit court to issue mandamus to a local federal official. Then, in McClung v. Silliman, 19 U.S. (6 Wheat.) 598, 604–05 (1821), the Court held that the state courts did not possess power to issue writs of mandamus to federal officials because Congress had not given that power to the federal courts.

[6]   In response to this enactment and to a more general movement toward expanded review of administrative action, two differing views of mandamus have emerged in the case law: the "traditional" view that the writ is appropriate only "to compel the performance of a 'clear, nondiscretionary duty,' " In re DRC, Inc., 358 F.App'x 193, 194 (D.C.Cir.2009), and the alternative view that mandamus is a more flexible remedy available whenever an official acts beyond the scope of lawful authority. See Strauss, Rakoff, Farina & Metzger, Gellhorn & Byse's Administrative Law 1200–01 (11th ed. 2011).

ultra vires, the Court distinguished Lee as a case involving official action in violation of the Takings Clause.

Applying these principles to the case at hand, Chief Justice Vinson concluded that although the defendant official might have violated the substantive law by failing to deliver coal to which the plaintiff had a legal right, the decision whether to deliver the coal lay within the bounds of his statutory authority, and he had not violated the Constitution by failing to deliver it.

Justice Frankfurter dissented, writing: "[T]he policy behind the immunity of the sovereign from suit without his consent does not call for disregard of a citizen's right to pursue an agent of the government for a wrongful invasion of a recognized legal right unless the legislature deems it appropriate to displace the right of suing the individual defendant with the right to sue the Government."

How useful is it to ask whether a particular action against government officials is "really" against the government? Government interests were fully implicated in Lee and other actions not barred by sovereign immunity. Is it a fiction that such suits against officers are not against the state even when they implicate important government interests? Or is the fiction that there ever existed a broad doctrine of sovereign immunity that, outside of a few specific areas, barred relief at the behest of individuals complaining of government illegality?

(b) Subsequent decisions upholding a sovereign immunity defense in suits nominally against officials include Malone v. Bowdoin, 369 U.S. 643 (1962), in which the plaintiffs sought to eject a federal forest service officer from certain land to which both plaintiffs and the federal government claimed title, and Dugan v. Rank, 372 U.S. 609 (1963), a suit to enjoin federal officers from impounding waters behind a federally financed dam, on the ground that the impoundment interfered with the plaintiffs' downstream uses of the water. Although Malone was otherwise similar on its facts to United States v. Lee, the cases were distinguishable, the Court reasoned, because Lee involved an alleged violation of the Takings Clause and Malone—in which subsequent changes in the statutory law would have authorized a suit against the government for just compensation—did not.

For now, issues involving the availability of an immunity defense in cases such as these have been essentially mooted, or at least transformed, by the enactment of statutes waiving the government's sovereign immunity, especially including the 1976 amendment to the Administrative Procedure Act, discussed at p. 902, *infra*, which waived immunity in all federal court actions seeking relief other than money damages. Nevertheless, Larson and its progeny appear to state the currently controlling law on the conditions under which a suit against a government officer that has not been authorized by statute may be barred on the ground that it is really one against the sovereign and thus falls under the doctrine of federal sovereign immunity. Sisk, *A Primer on the Doctrine of Federal Sovereign Immunity*, 58 Okla.L.Rev. 439, 457 (2006), offers this summary:

"[U]nder the Larson-Malone sovereign immunity doctrine, a suit may be maintained directly against a governmental officer under two circumstances. First, if the officer allegedly acted outside of the authority conferred on his or her office by Congress, that is, beyond delegated statutory authority, then his or her conduct will be treated as individual in nature and will be neither attributed to the sovereign nor barred by sovereign immunity. Second, if the officer acted within the conferred statutory limits of the office, but his or her conduct allegedly offended a provision of the Constitution, then sovereign immunity will be lifted."

Note that the law of federal sovereign immunity, as thus summarized, assumes that Congress not only can, but does, authorize federal officials to violate otherwise applicable law establishing statutory or common law rights in private citizens. Keeping in mind that Congress can always waive the sovereign immunity of the United States, when if ever should we assume that Congress has decided to deny a remedy for lawbreaking by federal officials?

(7) Preclusion Against the United States. Is it material, in determining if an action is in substance against the United States, whether the United States will be bound by the judgment? As the Lee case notes, the traditional rule held that the United States is not bound by a judgment in an in personam suit against one of its officers. See, *e.g.*, Carr v. United States, 98 U.S. 433 (1878); Hussey v. United States, 222 U.S. 88 (1911).[7]

Under modern preclusion law, however, an interested person who is active in the conduct of litigation is ordinarily bound by the judgment, at least by way of issue preclusion, even though that person is not a party. Applying this rule in a case in which the government had employed special counsel to prosecute an action concerning title to Indian lands, the Eighth Circuit held that "the United States is as effectually concluded as if it were a party to the judgment." United States v. Candelaria, 16 F.2d 559, 562–63 (8th Cir.1926), following United States v. Candelaria, 271 U.S. 432, 444 (1926). Accord Montana v. United States, 440 U.S. 147 (1979) (United States is bound, in its federal court challenge to a state tax, by a state court judgment in a suit filed by a private party but in which the United States had the "laboring oar"); see also Drummond v. United States, 324 U.S. 316, 318 (1945).

_____

NOTE ON STATUTORILY AUTHORIZED REVIEW OF FEDERAL OFFICIAL ACTION AND ON LEGISLATION WAIVING THE SOVEREIGN IMMUNITY OF THE UNITED STATES

The importance of federal sovereign immunity has declined substantially over time as Congress has enacted a variety of measures authorizing federal courts to hear suits that would otherwise be barred. This Note, which offers a partial survey of the most important enactments, is divided into two Parts. Part A deals with legislation establishing specific statutory authorizations of and mechanisms for judicial review of federal action, especially by administrative agencies and their officials. When Congress provides for specific review mechanisms, it has typically been taken for granted that the authorizing legislation constitutes a waiver of sovereign immunity. Part B considers more general enactments, not tied to

_____

[7]   There appears to be little doubt that a subordinate federal official may be precluded by a prior judgment either against another federal official (with whom the defendant in the subsequent action is deemed to be in privity), see Tait v. W. Md. Ry., 289 U.S. 620, 627 (1933), or against the United States or one of its agencies, see Sunshine Anthracite Coal Co. v. Adkins, 310 U.S. 381, 402–03 (1940).

a particular regulatory program, in which Congress has waived the United States' immunity. In reviewing the system that has arisen, consider whether it lives up to reasonable standards of rationality and comprehensiveness.

A. Statutorily Authorized Review of Federal Official Action

Statutory review, largely a development of the twentieth century, has become the predominant method of reviewing federal official action, though it has not wholly displaced the nonstatutory "officer suits" traditionally available at common law and in equity.

(1) Specific Statutory Provisions Authorizing Judicial Review. Regulatory statutes often authorize judicial review at the instance of a private person who wishes to challenge official action. Though these statutory review provisions vary widely, probably the most common authorize a petition in a federal court of appeals to set aside an administrative order. Thus, the National Labor Relations Act specifies that final orders of the NLRB may be reviewed in an appropriate court of appeals, see 29 U.S.C. § 160(f), and similar provisions govern other agencies. Other statutes authorize review in a federal district court. An important example is § 205(g) of the Social Security Act, 42 U.S.C. § 405(g), which provides for district court review of final and adverse administrative decisions on claims for social security benefits.

(2) The Administrative Procedure Act. In addition to specific statutory review provisions, Congress in 1946 enacted the Administrative Procedure Act (APA), which in § 10, 5 U.S.C. §§ 701–06, generally authorizes judicial review at the behest of a person who suffers legal wrong because of final agency action or who is adversely affected by such action.[1] Though review under the APA may be denied, *inter alia*, when (1) the action is committed to agency discretion, (2) the governing regulatory statute expressly or impliedly precludes judicial review, (3) the challenge is not ripe, or (4) the petitioner has failed to meet specific requirements for the exhaustion of administrative remedies, the decisions have established a strong presumption that federal agency action is reviewable.

Although the lower courts were once divided on whether the APA constituted a waiver of sovereign immunity, in 1976, Congress amended § 702 to effect a broad waiver of immunity in federal court suits seeking relief other than money damages against federal agencies. See Part B, Paragraph (3), *infra*.

B. Federal Legislation Waiving the Sovereign Immunity of the United States

Although the statutory review mechanisms discussed in Part A routinely authorize review of the lawfulness of federal official action, they do not always provide for relief in the form of payments of money out of the Treasury, and especially for damages for past official misconduct. The resulting gap is filled, at least in part, by general enactments in which the Congress has waived the sovereign immunity of the United States.

---

[1] In 1977 the Supreme Court held that the Act does not give the federal courts subject matter jurisdiction. Califano v. Sanders, 430 U.S. 99 (1977). But since Congress amended § 1331 the year before to eliminate the amount-in-controversy requirement in suits against federal agencies or federal officials in their official capacity, there is now virtually always subject matter jurisdiction under § 1331 for a review proceeding under the APA.

This Part discusses the three most important statutory waivers: the Tucker Act, governing non-tort monetary claims against the United States; the Federal Tort Claims Act, governing tort suits against the United States; and a 1976 statute governing all claims against the United States, its agencies, and its officials for relief other than money damages.[2] It also briefly addresses provisions for attorneys' fees against the United States and some of the remaining obstacles to plaintiffs wishing to sue the government.

In cases presenting the question whether Congress in fact intended to waive sovereign immunity, the Court has failed to settle on a clear interpretive approach. The traditional view held that waivers must be clearly expressed. See, *e.g.*, Borchard, *Government Liability in Tort*, 34 Yale L.J. 1, 28–41 (1924). But other decisions treat sovereign immunity as disfavored. See, *e.g.*, Keifer & Keifer v. Reconstr. Fin. Corp., 306 U.S. 381, 391 (1939); United States v. Yellow Cab Co., 340 U.S. 543 (1951); FDIC v. Meyer, 510 U.S. 471 (1994). According to Sisk, *Twilight for the Strict Construction of Waivers of Federal Sovereign Immunity*, 92 N.C.L.Rev. 1245 (2014), the twenty-first century trend limits strict construction, at most, to the threshold "question of whether Congress has clearly consented to a type of claim and form of remedy" against the United States and not to subsequent, ancillary questions involving such matters as "exceptions, definitional terms, limitations periods, * * * measurement of damages, or role and compensation of attorneys."[3]

As you read the remainder of this Part, consider again when if ever Congress should be presumed *not* to want to authorize a remedy against the United States for violations of citizens' rights.

(1) The Tucker Act.

(a) History. Before 1855, no statute gave consent to suit against the United States on claims for money damages; such claims were disposed of, if at all, by "private" acts of Congress. Because reliance on private acts had proved burdensome and inequitable, Congress created the Court of Claims in 1855 and authorized it to determine all claims against the government founded upon any statute, executive regulation, or express or implied contract with the United States.

In 1887, the Tucker Act broadened the Court of Claims' jurisdiction to include all "claims founded upon the Constitution of the United States or any law of Congress, except for pensions, or upon any regulation of an Executive

---

[2] Other important measures consenting to suit against the United States include legislation authorizing district court jurisdiction over specified land disputes, 28 U.S.C. §§ 2409–2410, and provisions authorizing jurisdiction of the United States Court of Federal Claims over (i) patent and copyright infringement cases, 28 U.S.C. § 1498, (ii) disputes with government contractors arising under the Contract Disputes Act of 1978, *id.* § 1491(a)(2), and (iii) specified claims of Indian tribes, *id.* § 1505. See generally *id.* §§ 1491–1509; Sisk, Litigation with the Federal Government (4th ed.2006); 14 Wright & Miller et al., Federal Practice and Procedure § 3656 (4th ed.2013).

[3] The line that Professor Sisk seeks to draw can be a thin and wavering one, as illustrated by FAA v. Cooper, 132 S.Ct. 1441 (2012), which held, by 5–3, that an authorization of suits for "actual damages" under the Federal Privacy Act did not waive immunity from suits to recover for mental and emotional distress. Writing for the Court, Justice Alito concluded that "[a]mbiguity exists", and thus precludes the conclusion that Congress has waived immunity under the rule requiring that waivers must be unequivocally expressed, "if there is a plausible interpretation of the statute that would not authorize money damages against the Government." Justice Sotomayor, joined by Justices Ginsburg and Breyer, dissenting, argued that "both as a term of art and in its plain meaning, 'actual damages' connotes compensation for proven injuries or losses" regardless of whether they are "pecuniary in nature."

Department, or upon any contract, expressed or implied, with the Government of the United States, or for damages, liquidated or unliquidated, in cases not sounding in tort, in respect of which claims the party would be entitled to redress against the United States either in a court of law, equity, or admiralty if the United States were suable." 24 Stat. 505. Concurrent jurisdiction of claims not exceeding $1,000 was given to the district courts, and of claims of $1,000 to $10,000 to the circuit courts. The basic structure established by the Tucker Act, now codified at 28 U.S.C. §§ 1346(a)(2), 1491(a)(1), remains. (On the history of the court's constitutional status, and the problem of legislative revision of its judgments, see pp. 89–91, *supra*.)

(b) United States Court of Federal Claims. In 1982 Congress established the United States Claims Court, an Article I court, to assume the trial jurisdiction formerly possessed by the Court of Claims. Renamed the United States Court of Federal Claims in 1992, this tribunal has jurisdiction over all claims governed by the Tucker Act. Its jurisdiction over claims (other than for a tax refund) in excess of $10,000 is exclusive, while the district courts have concurrent jurisdiction of claims not exceeding $10,000. There is no right in either forum to jury trial. 28 U.S.C. § 2402.

(c) Limits of the Tucker Act. The Tucker Act is merely a grant of jurisdiction and a concomitant waiver of sovereign immunity; it does not itself create any substantive rights. A suit under the Tucker Act must therefore demonstrate that the source of substantive law relied upon " 'can fairly be interpreted as mandating compensation by the Federal Government.' " United States v. Navajo Nation, 556 U.S. 287, 290 (2009). Constitutional claims founded on the Takings Clause satisfy this standard. See, *e.g*, United States v. Causby, 328 U.S. 256 (1946).[4] The lower courts have consistently rejected Tucker Act suits based on violations of other constitutional provisions, however, on the ground that these provisions do not "command the payment of money", United States v. Connolly, 716 F.2d 882, 887 (Fed.Cir.1983) (First Amendment claim); accord, *e.g.*, Hohri v. United States, 782 F.2d 227, 244–45 (D.C.Cir.1986) (claims based, *inter alia*, on Fourth Amendment, Due Process Clause, Sixth Amendment's counsel and fair trial provisions, and Cruel and Unusual Punishments Clause), *vacated on other grounds*, 482 U.S. 64 (1987). The Act also does not extend to claims based on quasi-contract or restitution claims. See generally Sisk, note 2, *supra*, §§ 4.02, 4.08.

The Tucker Act is strictly limited to claims for money. It gives no jurisdiction to hear claims for specific performance, delivery of property in kind, or injunctive relief,[5] although other provisions give the Court of Federal Claims a limited power to award equitable remedies.[6]

Judgments in cases under the Tucker Act, both in the Court of Federal Claims and (except for cases based on the internal revenue laws) in the

---

[4] In Preseault v. ICC, 494 U.S. 1, 11 (1990), the Court noted that "taking claims against the Federal Government are premature until the property owner has availed itself of the process provided by the Tucker Act" (quoting Williamson Cnty. Reg'l Planning Comm'n v. Hamilton Bank, 473 U.S. 172, 195 (1985)).

[5] See Richardson v. Morris, 409 U.S. 464 (1973) (per curiam) (refusing injunctive relief). See generally United States v. Mitchell, 463 U.S. 206, 218 (1983).

[6] To limit the need for claimants to bring two actions, one in district court seeking specific relief and one in the Court of Federal Claims seeking monetary relief, the latter has authority, in cases in which a judgment for damages is entered under the Tucker Act, to provide incidental and collateral relief "directing restoration to office or position, placement in appropriate duty or retirement status, and correction of applicable records." 28 U.S.C. § 1491(a)(2).

district courts, are appealable only to the Court of Appeals for the Federal Circuit, a specialized Article III tribunal established in 1982. See 28 U.S.C. § 1295(a); United States v. Hohri, 482 U.S. 64 (1987).

(2) The Federal Tort Claims Act.[7] The exclusion of tort claims from coverage under the Tucker Act left tort victims without any general damages remedy against the government itself (rather than against individual officers) until 1946, when Congress enacted the Federal Tort Claims Act (FTCA).[8] The FTCA establishes federal district court jurisdiction and waives sovereign immunity in suits against the United States "for injury or loss of property, or personal injury or death caused by the negligent or wrongful act or omission of any employee of the Government while acting within the scope of his office or employment, under circumstances where the United States, if a private person, would be liable to the claimant in accordance with the law of the place [which is typically a state] where the act or omission occurred." 28 U.S.C. § 1346(b). Though it contains significant exceptions and limitations, the FTCA for the first time recognized the general principle of governmental liability in tort.[9]

    (a) Procedures and Remedies. Procedure under the FTCA differs from that in ordinary tort suits in important respects. No suit may be filed unless (1) the claimant has made a timely application to the involved agency for administrative settlement, and (2) the claim has been denied or not acted upon for six months. 28 U.S.C. § 2675. Trial is de novo, however, and is without jury. Relief is limited to money damages, and punitive damages are barred.

    (b) The "Discretionary Function" Exception. There are a number of express exceptions to the FTCA. The most important, which has caused difficulty from the outset, excludes any claim "based upon the exercise or performance or the failure to exercise or perform a discretionary function or duty on the part of a federal agency or an employee of the Government, whether or not the discretion involved be abused." 28 U.S.C. § 2680(a).

    (i) The Dalehite Case. The Supreme Court first considered the scope of this exception in Dalehite v. United States, 346 U.S. 15 (1953). Pursuant to a high-level government decision, agents of the federal government manufactured large quantities of an ammonium nitrate fertilizer for

---

[7]   See generally Jayson & Longstreth, Handling Federal Tort Claims (2013).

[8]   60 Stat. 842 (1946). The FTCA's grant of jurisdiction is codified in 28 U.S.C. § 1346(b); procedures for tort claims are set forth in *id.* §§ 1402, 2401–02, 2412, 2671–79; exceptions to the rule of liability are contained in *id.* § 2680.

Dozens of other statutes provide remedies against the government in particular circumstances for the tortious conduct of its employees. See 1 Jayson & Longstreth, note 7 *supra*, § 2.05.

[9]   The Federal Employees Liability Reform and Tort Compensation Act of 1988, 102 Stat. 4563, amended 28 U.S.C. § 2679(b), (d), to make the FTCA the *exclusive* remedy for torts committed by federal officials in the course of their official duties. Under § 2679(d) as amended, if the Attorney General certifies that an employee who has been sued was acting within the scope of his employment, the proceeding shall be redesignated as a suit against the United States; if pending in state court, the suit shall be removed to federal court, *id.* § 2679(d)(2); and the plaintiff may recover only if the United States is liable under the FTCA, *id.* § 2679(d)(4).

The 1988 Act also amended 28 U.S.C. § 2671 to extend the FTCA's coverage to injuries caused by employees of the judicial and legislative branches, but provided (in an amendment to 28 U.S.C. § 2674) that the United States may assert any defense of judicial or legislative immunity that would have been available to the employee. These amendments do not appear to disturb the rule that the United States may not assert in an FTCA action an immunity that would have been available to an *executive* official whose conduct gave rise to the lawsuit.

← Westfall Act

shipment to occupied Germany, Japan, and Korea. The material was being loaded on ships at Texas City when spontaneous combustion led to an explosion that killed 560 people, injured some 3,000, and leveled a portion of the city.

The District Court awarded damages in a test case, finding negligence in the manufacture, coating, and packaging of the fertilizer as well as in the failure to give warning of the danger of fire and explosion. Sustaining a reversal of the judgment by the Court of Appeals, the Supreme Court, per Justice Reed, relied upon the fact that the entire program, including the aspects of the operation held to involve negligence, had been planned "at a high level under a direct delegation of plan-making authority from the apex of the Executive Department". The "discretionary function or duty" exception "includes more than the initiation of programs and activities. It also includes determinations made by executives or administrators in establishing plans, specifications or schedules of operations. Where there is room for policy judgment and decision there is discretion. It necessarily follows that acts of subordinates in carrying out the operations of government in accordance with official directions cannot be actionable. If this were not so, the protection of § 2680(a) would fail at the time it would be needed, that is, when a subordinate performs or fails to perform a causal step, each action or nonaction being directed by the superior, exercising, perhaps abusing, discretion".[10]

Justice Jackson, joined by Justices Black and Frankfurter, filed a powerful dissent, arguing:

"We do not predicate liability on any decision taken at 'Cabinet level' or on any other high-altitude thinking. * * * However, if decisions are being made at Cabinet levels as to the temperature of bagging explosive fertilizer, whether paper is suitable for bagging hot fertilizer, and how the bags should be labeled, perhaps an increased sense of caution and responsibility even at that height would be wholesome. The common sense of this matter is that a policy adopted in the exercise of an immune discretion was carried out carelessly by those in charge of the detail. We cannot agree that all the way down the line there is immunity for every balancing of care against cost, of safety against production, of warning against silence".

(ii) The Berkovitz Decision. A later decision, Berkovitz v. United States, 486 U.S. 531 (1988), clarified the application of the discretionary function exception in the context of federal regulatory programs. Berkovitz held unanimously that the exception does not preclude liability for all acts arising out of such programs, even though they involve activities that private persons do not perform.[11] The plaintiff alleged that federal health officials had violated specific federal regulatory directives when they licensed the sale of a vaccine that injured the plaintiff. The Court stressed that the

---

[10] The Court also rejected the plaintiff's contention that the FTCA permitted recovery against the Coast Guard for negligence in fighting the fire. "The Act did not create new causes of action where none existed before", and "if anything is doctrinally sanctified in the law of torts it is the immunity of communities and other public bodies for injuries due to fighting fire". This part of Dalehite was overruled four years later in Rayonier Inc. v. United States, 352 U.S. 315, 319 (1957), which held that the United States could be liable for the Forest Service's negligence in fighting a fire, and stated that "the very purpose of the Tort Claims Act [was] to establish novel and unprecedented governmental liability".

[11] In Indian Towing Co. v. United States, 350 U.S. 61 (1955), the Court had previously rejected an argument that the FTCA excluded liability for activities that private parties do not perform.

discretionary function exception does not apply when "the employee has no rightful option but to adhere to the directive", and that even where the conduct involves the exercise of judgment, the exception shields "only governmental actions and decisions based on considerations of public policy". The plaintiff's claim that the officials had wrongfully issued a product license, without receiving data required by statute as a precondition to licensing, was not barred, because the officials had no discretion under federal law to act as they had. And the claim that the officials wrongfully authorized the distribution of a particular lot of vaccine without first testing it survived a motion to dismiss, since the plaintiff had alleged that the applicable regulations gave the responsible officials no policy discretion to release untested lots.

(c) Other Exceptions. Of the numerous other exceptions to the FTCA,[12] two bear highlighting.

(i) Due Care in Implementing Invalid Statutes and Regulations. In addition to excluding claims arising from discretionary functions, § 2680 excludes claims based upon the action of a government employee "exercising due care, in the execution of a statute or regulation, whether or not * * * valid." Note the contrasting rule of Monell v. Department of Social Services, 436 U.S. 658 (1978), p. 998, *infra*, under which local government bodies are liable under 42 U.S.C. § 1983 for constitutional torts of their employees only when the allegedly unconstitutional conduct "implements or executes a policy statement, ordinance, regulation, or decision officially adopted and promulgated by that body's officers".

(ii) Arising out of Military Service. Numerous cases have considered the FTCA's application to injuries suffered by military personnel. In 1950, the Court unanimously held the Act inapplicable to injuries to service members that "arise out of or are in the course of activity incident to service", notwithstanding the absence of any statutory language supporting that result. Feres v. United States, 340 U.S. 135, 146 (1950). The Court later explained this doctrine as based primarily upon three considerations: the distinctively federal character of military relationships, the existence of alternative compensation systems, and the deleterious effect that tort suits could have upon military discipline. Stencel Aero Eng'g Corp. v. United States, 431 U.S. 666, 673 (1977).[13] Some years later, the Court stressed that the last of these considerations is the most important, and that "[t]he Feres doctrine cannot be reduced to a few bright-line rules." United States v. Shearer, 473 U.S. 52 (1985).

With Congress having created numerous specific exceptions to FTCA liability, is there any justification for judicial creation of an additional exception? See United States v. Johnson, 481 U.S. 681, 693–701 (1987) (Scalia, J., dissenting) (arguing that there is not).

(d) The Relation Between the FTCA and the Bivens Doctrine. Carlson v. Green, 446 U.S. 14 (1980), p. 771, *supra*, held that the FTCA does not preclude a Bivens action against individual officers.[14] In subsequent

---

[12] See generally 28 U.S.C. § 2680; 2 Jayson & Longstreth, note 7, *supra*, §§ 13.01–13.12.

[13] Note that the first rationale is in some tension with Rayonier v. United States, note 10, *supra*, while the second cannot explain the differing outcomes of Feres and of United States v. Brown, 348 U.S. 110 (1954) (holding that a *discharged* veteran may sue for negligent treatment in a VA Hospital for a service-connected disability).

[14] Nevertheless, the Feres doctrine, which was developed under the FTCA, has had an impact on the availability of Bivens remedies. In United States v. Stanley, 483 U.S. 669 (1987),

cases, however, the Court has tightened the requirements for Bivens actions, see pp. 771–775, *supra*, thereby heightening the significance of the FTCA and its exceptions.

(3) Suits for Relief Other than Money Damages. In a statute enacted in 1976, 90 Stat. 2721, Congress eliminated three barriers to federal court actions seeking specific relief against federal official action. First, the statute amended 28 U.S.C. § 1331 to abolish any jurisdictional minimum in suits thereunder "brought against the United States, any agency thereof, or any officer or employee thereof in his official capacity." Second, the statute waived sovereign immunity in federal court suits seeking relief other than money damages against federal agencies or officials. Third, the statute allowed the United States to be named as a defendant and to have judgment entered against it, provided that any mandatory or injunctive order specify the officer(s) responsible for compliance.

The language waiving sovereign immunity is codified as the last three sentences of section 10(b) of the Administrative Procedure Act, 5 U.S.C. § 702. The last of these sentences sets out two provisos: "Nothing herein (1) affects other limitations on judicial review or the power or duty of the court to dismiss any action or deny relief on any other appropriate legal or equitable ground; or (2) confers authority to grant relief if any other statute that grants consent to suit expressly or impliedly forbids the relief which is sought." The House Report accompanying that legislation remarks that it does not change existing limitations on specific relief, if any, derived from statutes dealing with such matters as government contracts, patent infringement, tort claims, and tax claims.

(a) Scope of the Waiver. Though codified in the APA, the waiver applies to any suit, whether or not brought under the APA. But § 702 applies only to suits in federal court and covers only actions of an "agency" of the United States as that term is defined in 5 U.S.C. § 701(b)(1), thereby excluding, for example, suits against Congress, the federal courts, the District of Columbia, and the territories.

(b) The Effect of the Waiver on Pre-existing Supreme Court Authority. As indicated above, the 1976 amendment to the APA has essentially mooted the question of the availability of the defense of immunity in such cases as Larson v. Domestic & Foreign Commerce Corp. and Malone v. Bowdoin, both briefly described at pp. 893–895, *supra*. Note, however, that the absence of a sovereign immunity bar does not necessarily eliminate all statutory and jurisdictional obstacles to suit. An illustration comes from

---

the Court held that a former serviceman could not maintain a Bivens action against military officers and civilians who had administered the drug LSD to him, without his consent, as part of an army experiment. Justice Scalia, writing for the Court, applied the approach of Chappell v. Wallace, 462 U.S. 296 (1983), p. 773, *supra*, which was held to require "abstention in the inferring of Bivens actions" whenever the injury is "incident to [military] service". (The court of appeals had ruled that Stanley's injury was incident to service, and the Supreme Court refused to reexamine that ruling.)

Justice Brennan (joined by Justices Marshall and Stevens) dissented, as did Justice O'Connor. In Justice O'Connor's view, "conduct of the type alleged in this case is so far beyond the bounds of human decency that as a matter of law it simply cannot be considered a part of the military mission".

Although the FTCA does not bar Bivens claims altogether, the lower courts have held consistently that the judgment in an FTCA action will preclude any subsequent Bivens claim based on the same underlying facts. For an argument that this result overreaches Congress' assumptions and purposes in enacting the FTCA, see Pfander & Aggarwal, *Bivens, the Judgment Bar, and the Perils of Dynamic Textualism*, 8 U.St.Thomas L.J. 417 (2011).

Spectrum Leasing Corp. v. United States, 764 F.2d 891 (D.C.Cir.1985), in which the plaintiff, as in Larson, was attempting to enforce the provisions of an alleged contract of sale. Dismissing the action, the D.C. Circuit held (i) that in requesting an injunction to compel the Government to continue making payments under a contract on the ground that failure to pay violated the Debt Collection Act of 1982, Spectrum was seeking "the classic contractual remedy of specific performance," and (ii) that the Tucker Act impliedly precludes contractual remedies other than money damages. Does Spectrum suggest that it may often be difficult to distinguish specific performance from review of the legality of administrative action?

(c) The Significance of the Exception for "Money Damages" in § 702 of the APA. Section 702 requires determining whether a particular form of monetary relief constitutes "money damages" and thus falls outside the scope of the waiver of sovereign immunity. Bowen v. Massachusetts, 487 U.S. 879 (1988), involved a dispute between Massachusetts and the Department of Health and Human Services (HHS) about whether certain state-provided services qualified for reimbursement under Medicaid. The Court sustained the prospective declaratory and injunctive relief permitted by the court of appeals, and also ruled that the court of appeals had erred in refusing to uphold the district court's order reversing HHS's disallowance of reimbursement for past services. The Court noted that this order did not require payment by the United States; to the extent that an order reversing the agency's disallowance of reimbursement leads to monetary relief, it is "a mere by-product of [the district court's] primary function of reviewing the Secretary's interpretation of federal law". The Court also endorsed the position that monetary relief for past disallowances was not "money damages", thus implying that § 702 would not have barred a money judgment against the United States.

The government argued in Bowen that in view of the availability of a monetary remedy in the Claims Court under the Tucker Act, APA review was unavailable in light of § 10(c), 5 U.S.C. § 704, which provides that agency action "for which there is no other adequate remedy in any court shall be subject to judicial review." The Supreme Court rejected that argument: even if the Claims Court could award monetary relief—a question about which the Court expressed some doubt—the Claims Court's lack of general equitable powers prevented it from providing the kind of "special and adequate review" that, under the APA, will foreclose district court jurisdiction.

Justice Scalia, joined by Chief Justice Rehnquist and Justice Kennedy, dissented. He criticized, as exalting form over substance, the Court's holdings that the district court's reversal of the HHS order was not a money judgment and that the monetary aspects of the relief were not money damages. Both of these propositions, he objected, would permit inventive lawyers to escape the Claims Court's exclusive jurisdiction simply by denominating damage claims as suits for specific relief against the government for its refusal to pay, or as suits for monetary relief not constituting damages. Justice Scalia also argued that in any event, the state could bring suit under the Medicaid Act for damages in the Claims Court, and that in all but the most unusual circumstances, such relief would constitute an "adequate remedy" under § 704, thereby precluding suit under § 702.[15]

---

[15] Compare Sisk, *The Tapestry Unravels: Statutory Waivers of Sovereign Immunity and Money Claims Against the United States*, 71 Geo.Wash.L.Rev. 602, 706 (2003) (criticizing the

(4) Attorney's Fees. The Equal Access to Justice Act of 1980, codified at 28 U.S.C. § 2412(b), authorizes the award of attorney's fees to a party who prevails against the United States in the same circumstances in which courts would award fees against private parties. In addition, § 2412(d) provides that courts *shall* award attorney's fees to certain persons who prevail against the United States in non-tort civil actions, unless the United States' position was "substantially justified" or "special circumstances make an award unjust."[16] There are, moreover, many statutory provisions authorizing the award of attorney's fees in particular kinds of actions. See generally Bennett, Winning Attorneys' Fees from the U.S. Government (rev.ed.2014); Rossi, Attorneys' Fees (3d ed.2002).

(5) Remaining Problems Confronting Litigants. As the issues in cases such as Bowen v. Massachusetts, Paragraph (3)(c), *supra*, and Spectrum Leasing Corp v. United States, Paragraph (3)(b), *supra*, illustrate, litigants suing the government must navigate statutory schemes that can be complex and confusing and are not always gap-free. It may not always be clear whether a suit seeking specific relief should be filed in district court, or, because it is "really" a disguised suit for breach of contract, in the Court of Federal Claims. Similar uncertainty may arise concerning whether a suit for monetary relief is for money damages, and thus outside § 702 (though perhaps cognizable in the Court of Federal Claims), or for some other kind of monetary relief, and therefore within the district court's jurisdiction under § 702. Further examples could be multiplied.[17]

To eliminate such problems, should Congress abolish the Court of Federal Claims and give the district courts jurisdiction to entertain all claims against the United States under the Tucker Act, the FTCA, and every other statute consenting to suit? Should it instead expand the Court of Federal Claims' jurisdiction? Compare 28 U.S.C. § 1631 (permitting, in the interest of justice, transfer of a civil action from a court without jurisdiction to one in which the case could have been filed). Is there any sound basis for determining that suits against the United States for money damages should be tried before a semi-specialized non-Article III tribunal?

Bowen decision as having "sown jurisdictional chaos" and urging that it be repudiated), with Sisk, *The Jurisdiction of the Court of Federal Claims and Forum Shopping in Money Claims Against the Federal Government,* 88 Ind.L.J. 83 (2013) (maintaining that more recent decisions by both the Supreme Court and the Court of Appeals for the Federal Circuit resolve uncertainties created by Bowen and establish that when a plaintiff ultimately wants monetary relief, and the Court of Federal Claims can provide an adequate remedy, suit must be brought in that court).

[16] The Supreme Court has consistently held that in the absence of an authorizing statute, the United States is not liable for costs or attorney's fees. See, *e.g.*, United States v. Bodcaw Co., 440 U.S. 202, 203–04 n.3 (1979) (per curiam).

[17] Similar jurisdictional uncertainties can arise on appeal. See United States v. Hohri, 482 U.S. 64 (1987). See also United States v. Tohono O'Odham Nation, 131 S.Ct. 1723 (2011) (holding that a statute bars Court of Federal Claims jurisdiction whenever a suit in another court is based on substantially the same operative facts, even if neither court alone could provide the plaintiff with complete relief).

2.   SUITS CHALLENGING STATE OFFICIAL ACTION

———

A.   THE ELEVENTH AMENDMENT AND STATE SOVEREIGN IMMUNITY

———

INTRODUCTORY NOTE ON STATE SOVEREIGN IMMUNITY AND THE ELEVENTH AMENDMENT

(1) The Text of the Constitution. Just as the Constitution makes no reference to federal sovereign immunity, it says nothing about state sovereign immunity—neither that the common law immunity previously enjoyed by the states in their own courts had been divested, nor that the Constitution preserved that immunity or elevated it to the status of a constitutional guarantee. Several headings of Article III jurisdiction—including those for cases arising under the Constitution and laws of the United States and for "Controversies between two or more States"—appear to contemplate and possibly even authorize suits against the states in federal court. But when opponents of the Constitution charged during the ratification debates that the proposed Constitution would subject the states to unconsented suits on their debts, a number of defenders—most famously Alexander Hamilton, in The Federalist No. 81, p. 877, *supra*—maintained that it would not. (At least a few defenders disagreed on this point.) According to Hamilton, "[i]t is inherent in the nature of sovereignty not to be amenable to the suit of an individual without its consent".

(2) The Decision in Chisholm. A question involving state sovereign immunity arose in Chisholm v. Georgia, 2 U.S. (2 Dall.) 419 (1793), when a South Carolina citizen filed an assumpsit claim against the State of Georgia as an original action in the Supreme Court. Jurisdiction was predicated on a statute authorizing the Court to entertain actions against a state by citizens of another state pursuant to the customs and usages of law. Rejecting Georgia's protest that an unconsenting state was immune from suit, the Court upheld its jurisdiction as consistent with Article III's grant of judicial power over controversies "between a State and Citizens of another State." Each of the five Justices wrote separately. Justices Blair and Cushing both relied on the clear language of Article III, noting that its grant of jurisdiction over controversies between two states contemplated that an unconsenting state could be a defendant. Chief Justice Jay likewise relied on Article III's language, but argued in addition that the "feudal" doctrine of sovereign immunity was incompatible with popular sovereignty. Troubled, though, that this argument implied that the United States itself could be sued, notwithstanding the difficulty of enforcing a judgment against it, he ultimately left that question open. Justice Wilson argued most fully that the doctrine of sovereign immunity was incompatible with principles of public law and with a republican form of government, reasoning that a state was no more sovereign, and no less subject to the law, than a free man.

Justice Iredell's lone dissent proceeded from the premise that the Supreme Court could exercise only that jurisdiction conferred by Congress. He contended that the First Judiciary Act's grant of original jurisdiction should be interpreted in light of common law principles. English law would have permitted an action like Chisholm's only by petition of right, with the sovereign's consent. When the Constitution and First Judiciary Act took effect, no state permitted "a compulsory suit for the recovery of money against a State". Though acknowledging that he strongly opposed "any construction of [the Constitution] which will admit, under any circumstances, a compulsive suit against a State for the recovery of money", he rested his conclusion on statutory grounds.[1]

(3) The Adoption of the Eleventh Amendment. Chisholm provoked a strongly adverse reaction that subsequent opinions of the Supreme Court have characterized as "a shock of surprise." *E.g.*, Seminole Tribe v. Florida, 517 U.S. 44 (1996).[2] A constitutional amendment to overrule Chisholm was introduced in the Senate only two days after the decision. In due course, both Houses of Congress proposed, and in 1798 the states ratified, the Eleventh Amendment. It provides:

> "The Judicial power of the United States shall not be construed to extend to any suit in law or equity, commenced or prosecuted against one of the United States by Citizens of another State, or by Citizens or Subjects of any Foreign State."

As history has revealed, the meaning of these words is hardly self-evident. All agree that the Eleventh Amendment was intended and originally understood to overrule the Supreme Court's decision in Chisholm, which had "construed" Article III to "extend to [a] * * * suit in law * * * against one of the United States by Citizens of another State." But the Amendment does not refer to state sovereign immunity from suit—and does not in terms even preclude the exercise of federal jurisdiction over suits against the states by their own citizens or of suits in admiralty against the states. (As will be discussed on p. 915, *infra*, some Justices and commentators have concluded, in addition, that the Amendment's otherwise peculiar language should not be read to exclude federal jurisdiction of a suit against a state by a citizen of another state on the basis of a federal question.) It is, accordingly, fair to say that the text of the Eleventh Amendment raises as many questions as it answers.[3]

---

[1] For an informative analysis of the Chisholm opinions, see Casto, The Supreme Court in the Early Republic 188–97 (1995). For a discussion of Justice Iredell's dissent, see Orth, *The Truth About Justice Iredell's Dissent in Chisholm v. Georgia (1793)*, 73 N.C.L.Rev. 255 (1994).

For an in-depth historical study of the case and its background, see Desan, *Contesting the Character of Political Economy in the Early Republic*, in The House and Senate in the 1790s: Petitioning, Lobbying, and Institutional Development 178 (Bowling & Kennon eds. 2002). Professor Desan suggests that "two aspects of the constitutional controversy have so far escaped sufficient notice". The first is the contention over "what kind of remedy was appropriate", since it was generally recognized that resort could and should be had to the legislature to assert a claim for money owing, while resort to a judicial forum was viewed as a radical departure from the accepted approach. The second, and related, aspect derived from the type of claim at issue— a claim in contract against the public fisc. Such a claim, she contends, was in the slow process of "moving from one politically mediated to one judicially defined".

[2] But see Gibbons, *The Eleventh Amendment and State Sovereign Immunity: A Reinterpretation*, 83 Colum.L.Rev. 1889, 1926 (1983) (contending that "Congress's initial reaction to the Chisholm decision hardly demonstrates the sort of outrage so central to the profound shock thesis").

[3] Important commentary on the history and purpose of the Amendment includes Amar, *Of Sovereignty and Federalism*, 96 Yale L.J. 1425, 1481–84 (1987); Casto, note 1, *supra*, at 197–212; Fletcher, *A Historical Interpretation of the Eleventh Amendment: A Narrow Construction of an Affirmative Grant of Jurisdiction Rather than a Prohibition Against Jurisdiction*, 35 Stan.L.Rev. 1033, 1058–59 (1983); Gibbons, note 2, *supra*; Jacobs, The Eleventh Amendment

(4) The Eleventh Amendment and the Marshall Court. The Marshall Court generally construed the Eleventh Amendment narrowly.[4]

(a) In Cohens v. Virginia, 19 U.S. (6 Wheat.) 264 (1821), defendants, convicted in Virginia state court for violating Virginia law by selling District of Columbia lottery tickets, sought review in the Supreme Court, asserting that under the Supremacy Clause they were immune from prosecution because the lottery was authorized by Congress.[5] Although the Court affirmed the convictions on the merits, it rejected the state's contention that it was being sued without its consent. Because the defendants' petition for the writ of error was entirely defensive and sought no affirmative relief, Chief Justice Marshall concluded that it was not a "suit" within the meaning of the Amendment.[6]

(b) In Osborn v. Bank of the United States, 22 U.S. (9 Wheat.) 738 (1824), pp. 785, 890, *supra*, after the federal circuit court enjoined state officials from collecting an unconstitutional tax from the plaintiff Bank, an official seized $100,000 from a Bank office. The Supreme Court upheld a second decree ordering one official to return the $98,000 held in his possession but credited to the state, and ordering two others to repay the remaining $2,000 (the location of which was not discussed in the opinion), all over defendants' objection that the order violated the Eleventh Amendment.[7] The Court said:

> "It may, we think, be laid down as a rule which admits of no exception, that, in all cases where jurisdiction depends on the party, it is the party named in the record. Consequently, the 11th amendment * * * is, of necessity, limited to those suits in which a State is a party on the record. The amendment has its full effect, if the constitution be construed as it would have been construed, had the jurisdiction of the Court never been extended to suits brought against a State, by the citizens of another State, or by aliens."[8]

---

and Sovereign Immunity 67–74 (1972); Lash, *Leaving The Chisholm Trail: The Eleventh Amendment and the Background Principle of Strict Construction,* 50 Wm. & Mary L.Rev. 1577 (2009); and Pfander, *History and State Suability: An "Explanatory" Account of the Eleventh Amendment,* 83 Cornell L.Rev. 1269 (1998).

[4] Smith, *The Marshall Court and the Originalist's Dilemma,* 90 Minn.L.Rev. 612 (2006), maintains that the Justices who favor broad application of the Eleventh Amendment tend to reconcile their originalist approach with the Marshall Court's narrow interpretations of the Amendment by disregarding those interpretations or labeling them as dicta, while Justices favoring a narrow application frequently rely on the same pronouncements.

[5] For illuminating discussion of the Cohens case, see Jackson, *The Supreme Court, the Eleventh Amendment, and State Sovereign Immunity,* 98 Yale L.J. 1, 13–25 (1988).

[6] Following this analysis, Marshall added a brief alternative holding: If "we in this be mistaken, the error does not affect the case now before the Court", as the defendants were citizens of Virginia. (A decade later, in Worcester v. Georgia, 31 U.S. (6 Pet.) 515 (1832), the party seeking a writ of error against the state was a noncitizen; the Supreme Court exercised jurisdiction without discussing the Eleventh Amendment issue.)

[7] While a state has no immunity from suit brought by the United States, see p. 921, *infra,* the Bank was treated as a private party rather than as an arm of the United States.

[8] According to Pfander & Hunt, *Public Wrongs and Private Bills: Indemnification and Government Accountability in the Early Republic,* 85 N.Y.U.L.Rev. 1862 (2010), the "party of record" rule followed naturally from the assumption, which prevailed in antebellum suits for damages against federal officials, that sovereign immunity was "a matter of mere form" and that the government would indemnify its officers against liability incurred in the discharge of official responsibility.

Is it plausible to think that the Eleventh Amendment could always be evaded by the expedient of pleading an action as one against a state officer, rather than the state itself?

(c) Compare Governor of Georgia v. Madrazo, 26 U.S. (1 Pet.) 110 (1828), in which the Court dismissed a libel in admiralty brought in federal district court by Madrazo against the governor for possession of certain slaves (and the proceeds of the sale of others) seized under a state statute after the slaves had allegedly been brought to this country in violation of federal law. The Court reasoned that "[t]he demand made upon [the Governor], is not made personally, but officially" because he was sued "not by his name, but by his title". Therefore, "the state itself may be considered as a party on the record". Even if the governor were treated as if he had been sued personally, "no case is made which justifies a decree against him personally" since he "acted in obedience to a law of the state, made for the purpose of giving effect to an Act of Congress; and has done nothing in violation of any law of the United States". Because the suit was against the state, it fell within the Supreme Court's, rather than the district court's, original jurisdiction.

Madrazo subsequently filed a libel in admiralty against the State of Georgia as an original action in the Supreme Court. In a one paragraph opinion in Ex parte Madrazzo [sic], 32 U.S. (7 Pet.) 627, 632 (1833), Chief Justice Marshall dismissed the suit: it was not within the admiralty jurisdiction, as the "property" was not in the custody of either the court or any private person. "It is a mere personal suit against a state to recover proceeds in its possession, and in such a case no private person has a right to commence an original suit in this court against a state."

Note that Ex parte Madrazzo—the only case prior to the Civil War in which the Court based a dismissal on Eleventh Amendment grounds—was held not to fall within admiralty jurisdiction and involved no federal cause of action.

(5) Open Questions. Among the open questions about the Eleventh Amendment at the end of the Marshall era and nearly until the end of the nineteenth century was whether the Amendment barred a federal court suit against a state (a) by one of the state's own citizens (recall that the Amendment's language refers to suits against "one of the United States by Citizens of another State") or (b) by a plaintiff asserting a claim that arose under the Constitution or laws of the United States. The next principal case, Hans v. Louisiana, involved a suit with both of these characteristics.

Hans v. Louisiana
134 U.S. 1, 10 S.Ct. 504, 33 L.Ed. 842 (1890).
Error to the Circuit Court of the United States for the Eastern District of Louisiana.

[This was an action brought in the Circuit Court of the United States against the State of Louisiana by Hans, a citizen of that State, to recover the amount of certain coupons annexed to bonds of the State, issued under the provisions of an act of the legislature approved January 24, 1874. The coupons sued on were for interest accrued as of January 1, 1880. Hans alleged that an amendment to the state constitution barring the state from paying the interest owing was an impairment of the obligation of contract in violation of the U.S. Constitution. The lower court dismissed the action for lack of jurisdiction, and Hans appealed to the Supreme Court.]

■ MR. JUSTICE BRADLEY delivered the opinion of the court.

The question is presented, whether a State can be sued in a Circuit Court of the United States by one of its own citizens upon a suggestion that the case is one that arises under the Constitution or laws of the United States.

The ground taken is, that under the Constitution, as well as under the act of Congress passed to carry it into effect, a case is within the jurisdiction of the federal courts, without regard to the character of the parties, if it arises under the Constitution or laws of the United States * * * It is conceded that where the jurisdiction depends alone upon the character of the parties, a controversy between a State and its own citizens is not embraced within it; but it is contended that though jurisdiction does not exist on that ground, it nevertheless does exist if the case itself is one which necessarily involves a federal question; and with regard to ordinary parties this is undoubtedly true. The question now to be decided is, whether it is true where one of the parties is a State, and is sued as a defendant by one of its own citizens.

That a State cannot be sued by a citizen of another State, or of a foreign state, on the mere ground that the case is one arising under the Constitution or laws of the United States, is clearly established by the decisions of this court in several recent cases. Louisiana v. Jumel, 107 U.S. 711; Hagood v. Southern, 117 U.S. 52; In re Ayers, 123 U.S. 443. Those were cases arising under the Constitution of the United States, upon laws complained of as impairing the obligation of contracts, one of which was the constitutional amendment of Louisiana complained of in the present case. Relief was sought against state officers who professed to act in obedience to those laws. This court held that the suits were virtually against the States themselves and were consequently violative of the Eleventh Amendment of the Constitution, and could not be maintained. It was not denied that they presented cases arising under the Constitution; but, notwithstanding that, they were held to be prohibited by the amendment referred to.

In the present case the plaintiff in error contends that he, being a citizen of Louisiana, is not embarrassed by the obstacle of the Eleventh Amendment, inasmuch as that amendment only prohibits suits against a State which are brought by the citizens of another State, or by citizens or subjects of a foreign State. It is true, the amendment does so read: and if there were no other reason or ground for abating his suit, it might be maintainable; and then we should have this anomalous result, that in cases arising under the Constitution or laws of the United States, a State may be sued in the federal courts by its own citizens, though it cannot be sued for a like cause of action by the citizens of other States, or of a foreign state; and may be thus sued in the federal courts, although not allowing itself to be sued in its own courts. If this is the necessary consequence of the language of the Constitution and the law, the result is no less startling and unexpected than was the original decision of this court, that under the language of the Constitution and of the judiciary act of 1789, a State was liable to be sued by a citizen of another State, or of a foreign country. That decision was made in the case of Chisholm v. Georgia, 2 Dall. 419, and created such a shock of surprise throughout the country that, at the first meeting of Congress thereafter, the Eleventh Amendment to the Constitution was almost unanimously proposed, and was in due course adopted by the legislatures of the States. This amendment, expressing the will of the ultimate sovereignty of the whole country, superior to all legislatures and all courts, actually reversed the decision of the Supreme Court. It did not in terms prohibit suits by individuals against the States, but declared that the Constitution should not be construed to import any power to authorize the bringing of such suits. The language of the amendment is that "the judicial power of the United States shall *not be construed to extend* to any suit in law or equity, commenced or prosecuted against one of the United States by citizens of another State or by citizens or subjects of any foreign state." The Supreme Court had construed the judicial power as extending to such a suit, and its decision was thus overruled. The court itself so understood the effect of the amendment * * * [as shown by its later decisions].

This view of the force and meaning of the amendment is important. It shows that, on this question of the suability of the States by individuals, the highest authority of this country was in accord rather with the minority than with the majority of the court in the decision of the case of Chisholm v. Georgia; and this fact lends additional interest to the able opinion of Mr. Justice Iredell on that occasion. The other justices were more swayed by a close observance of the letter of the Constitution, without regard to former experience and usage; and because the letter said that the judicial power shall extend to controversies "between a State and citizens of another State;" and "between a State and foreign states, citizens or subjects," they felt constrained to see in this language a power to enable the individual citizens of one State, or of a foreign state, to sue another State of the Union in the federal courts. Justice Iredell, on the contrary, contended that it was not the intention to create new and unheard of remedies, by subjecting sovereign States to actions at the suit of individuals, (which he conclusively showed was never done before,) but only, by proper legislation, to invest the federal courts with jurisdiction to hear and determine controversies and cases, between the parties designated, that were properly susceptible of litigation in courts.

Looking back from our present standpoint at the decision in Chisholm v. Georgia, we do not greatly wonder at the effect which it had upon the country. Any such power as that of authorizing the federal judiciary to entertain suits by individuals against the States, had been expressly disclaimed, and even resented, by the great defenders of the Constitution whilst it was on its trial before the American people. As some of their utterances are directly pertinent to the question now under consideration, we deem it proper to quote them.

The eighty-first number of the Federalist, written by Hamilton, has the following profound remarks:

"It has been suggested that an assignment of the public securities of one State to the citizens of another, would enable them to prosecute that State in the federal courts for the amount of those securities; a suggestion which the following considerations prove to be without foundation:

"It is inherent in the nature of sovereignty not to be amenable to the suit of an individual without its consent. This is the general sense and the general practice of mankind; and the exemption, as one of the attributes of sovereignty, is now enjoyed by the government of every State in the Union. Unless, therefore, there is a surrender of this immunity in the plan of the convention, it will remain with the States, and the danger intimated must be merely ideal. * * * [T]here is no color to pretend that the state governments would, by the adoption of that plan, be divested of the privilege of paying their own debts in their own way, free from every constraint but that which flows from the obligations of good faith. The contracts between a nation and individuals are only binding on the conscience of the sovereign, and have no pretension to a compulsive force. They confer no right of action independent of the sovereign will. To what purpose would it be to authorize suits against States for the debts they owe? How could recoveries be enforced? It is evident that it could not be done without waging war against the contracting State; and to ascribe to the federal courts by mere implication, and in destruction of a pre-existing right of the state governments, a power which would involve such a consequence, would be altogether forced and unwarrantable."

* * * [L]ooking at the subject as Hamilton did, and as Mr. Justice Iredell did [in Chisholm], in the light of history and experience and the established order of things, the[ir] views * * * were clearly right,—as the people of the United States in their sovereign capacity subsequently decided.

But Hamilton was not alone in protesting against the construction put upon the Constitution by its opponents. In the Virginia convention the same objections were raised by George Mason and Patrick Henry, and were met by Madison and Marshall as follows. Madison said: "Its jurisdiction [the federal jurisdiction] in controversies between a State and citizens of another State is much objected to, and perhaps without reason. It is not in the power of individuals to call any State into court. The only operation it can have is that, if a State should wish to bring a suit against a citizen, it must be brought before the federal court. This will give satisfaction to individuals, as it will prevent citizens on whom a State may have a claim being dissatisfied with the state courts. . . . It appears to me that this [clause] can have no operation but this—to give a citizen a right to be heard in the federal courts; and if a State should condescend to be a party, this court may take cognizance of it." 3 Elliott's Debates, 2d ed. 533. Marshall, in answer to the same objection, said: "With respect to disputes between a State and the citizens of another State, its jurisdiction has been decried with unusual vehemence. I hope that no gentleman will think that a State will be called at the bar of the federal court. . . . It is not rational to suppose that the sovereign power should be dragged before a court. The intent is to enable States to recover claims of individuals residing in other States. . . . But, say they, there will be partiality in it if a State cannot be defendant—if an individual cannot proceed to obtain judgment against a State, though he may be sued by a State. It is necessary to be so, and cannot be avoided. I see a difficulty in making a State defendant which does not prevent its being plaintiff." *Id.* 555.

It seems to us that these views of those great advocates and defenders of the Constitution were most sensible and just; and they apply equally to the present case as to that then under discussion. The letter is appealed to now, as it was then, as a ground for sustaining a suit brought by an individual against a State. The reason against it is as strong in this case as it was in that. It is an attempt to strain the Constitution and the law to a construction never imagined or dreamed of. Can we suppose that, when the Eleventh Amendment was adopted, it was understood to be left open for citizens of a State to sue their own state in the federal courts, whilst the idea of suits by citizens of other states, or of foreign states, was indignantly repelled? Suppose that Congress, when proposing the Eleventh Amendment, had appended to it a proviso that nothing therein contained should prevent a State from being sued by its own citizens in cases arising under the Constitution or laws of the United States: can we imagine that it would have been adopted by the States? The supposition that it would is almost an absurdity on its face. * * *

The suability of a State without its consent was a thing unknown to the law. This has been so often laid down and acknowledged by courts and jurists that it is hardly necessary to be formally asserted. It was fully shown by an exhaustive examination of the old law by Mr. Justice Iredell in his opinion in Chisholm v. Georgia; and it has been conceded in every case since, where the question has, in any way been presented, even in the cases which have gone farthest in sustaining suits against the officers or agents of States. Osborn v. Bank of United States, 9 Wheat. 738; Davis v. Gray, 16 Wall. 203; Board of Liquidation v. McComb, 92 U.S. 531; United States v. Lee, 106 U.S. 196; Poindexter v. Greenhow, 109 U.S. 63; Virginia Coupon Cases, 114 U.S. 269. In all these cases the effort was to show, and the court held, that the suits were not against the State or the United States, but against the individuals; conceding that if they had been against either the State or the United States, they could not be maintained. * * *

Undoubtedly a State may be sued by its own consent, as was the case in Curran v. Arkansas et al., 15 How. 304, 309, and in Clark v. Barnard, 108 U.S. 436, 447. * * *

[B]esides the presumption that no anomalous and unheard-of proceedings or suits were intended to be raised up by the Constitution—anomalous and unheard of when the Constitution was adopted—an additional reason why the jurisdiction claimed for the Circuit Court does not exist, is the language of the act of Congress by which its jurisdiction is conferred. The words are these: "The circuit courts of the United States shall have original cognizance, concurrent with the courts of the several States, of all suits of a civil nature at common law or in equity, . . . arising under the Constitution or laws of the United States, or treaties," etc.—"Concurrent with the courts of the several States." Does not this qualification show that Congress, in legislating to carry the Constitution into effect, did not intend to invest its courts with any new and strange jurisdictions? The state courts have no power to entertain suits by individuals against a State without its consent. Then how does the Circuit Court, having only concurrent jurisdiction, acquire any such power? It is true that the same qualification existed in the judiciary act of 1789, which was before the court in Chisholm v. Georgia, and the majority of the court did not think that it was sufficient to limit the jurisdiction of the Circuit Court. Justice Iredell thought differently. In view of the manner in which that decision was received by the country, the adoption of the Eleventh Amendment, the light of history and the reason of the thing, we think we are at liberty to prefer Justice Iredell's views in this regard.

Some reliance is placed by the plaintiff upon the observations of Chief Justice Marshall, in Cohens v. Virginia, 6 Wheat. 264, 410. The

Chief Justice was there considering the power of review exercisable by this court over the judgments of a state court, wherein it might be necessary to make the State itself a defendant in error. He showed that this power was absolutely necessary in order to enable the judiciary of the United States to take cognizance of all cases arising under the Constitution and laws of the United States. He also showed that making a State a defendant in error was entirely different from suing a State in an original action in prosecution of a demand against it, and was not within the meaning of the Eleventh Amendment; that the prosecution of a writ of error against a State was not the prosecution of a suit in the sense of that amendment, which had reference to the prosecution, by suit, of claims against a State. * * *

After * * * showing by incontestable argument that a writ of error to a judgment recovered by a State, in which the State is necessarily the defendant in error, is not a suit commenced or prosecuted against a State in the sense of the amendment, he added, that if the court were mistaken in this, its error did not affect that case, because the writ of error therein was not prosecuted by "a citizen of another State" or "of any foreign state," and so was not affected by the amendment; but was governed by the general grant of judicial power, as extending "to all cases arising under the Constitution or laws of the United States, without respect to parties".

It must be conceded that the last observation of the Chief Justice does favor the argument of the plaintiff. But the observation was unnecessary to the decision, and in that sense *extra judicial*, and though made by one who seldom used words without due reflection, ought not to outweigh the important considerations referred to which lead to a different conclusion. With regard to the question then before the court, it may be observed, that writs of error to judgments in favor of the crown, or of the State, had been known to the law from time immemorial; and had never been considered as exceptions to the rule, that an action does not lie against the sovereign. * * *

It is not necessary that we should enter upon an examination of the reason or expediency of the rule which exempts a sovereign State from prosecution in a court of justice at the suit of individuals. This is fully discussed by writers on public law. It is enough for us to declare its existence. The legislative department of a State represents its polity and its will; and is called upon by the highest demands of natural and political law to preserve justice and judgment, and to hold inviolate the public obligations. Any departure from this rule, except for reasons most cogent, (of which the legislature, and not the courts, is the judge,) never fails in the end to incur the odium of the world, and to bring lasting injury upon the State itself. But to deprive the legislature of the power of judging what the honor and safety of the State may require, even at the expense of a temporary failure to discharge the public debts, would be attended with greater evils than such failure can cause.

The judgment of the Circuit Court is

Affirmed.

■ MR. JUSTICE HARLAN, concurring.

I concur with the court in holding that a suit directly against a State by one of its own citizens is not one to which the judicial power of the

United States extends, unless the State itself consents to be sued. Upon this ground alone I assent to the judgment. But I cannot give my assent to many things said in the opinion. The comments made upon the decision in Chisholm v. Georgia do not meet my approval. They are not necessary to the determination of the present case. Besides, I am of opinion that the decision in that case was based upon a sound interpretation of the Constitution as that instrument then was.

———————

NOTE ON THE ORIGIN, MEANING, AND SCOPE OF THE ELEVENTH AMENDMENT

(1) Eleventh Amendment Immunity and Constitutional Obligation. Note the effect of Hans v. Louisiana: The Court does not doubt that the state is legally bound by the Contract Clause or other provisions of the Constitution, but it holds that the Eleventh Amendment bars the enforcement of the Constitution in a suit against the state. And Hans can be read to intimate, though it does not hold, that a state could also claim immunity from a suit on the Contract Clause in its own courts.[1] Is this a constitutionally tenable situation?

In answering this question, recall that the federal government enjoys a similar immunity from unconsented suits alleging constitutional violations. Is it any more troubling for states than it is for the federal government to enjoy an immunity from unconsented suits? Recall, too, the long tradition under which plaintiffs who are barred from suing the sovereign can frequently obtain relief in "officer suits" against governmental officials. Traditionally, officer suits have been as readily available against state as against federal officials—as, for example, in Osborn v. Bank of the United States, pp. 785, 890, *supra*.

(2) Dismissal of the Language of the Eleventh Amendment. Was the Hans Court warranted in dismissing the language of the Eleventh Amendment as a virtual irrelevancy? Consider Manning, *The Eleventh Amendment and the Reading of Precise Constitutional Texts*, 113 Yale L.J. 1663, 1669–70 (2004), arguing that "at least where the Constitution speaks in precise, rule-like terms, as the Eleventh Amendment does", the Court should apply it as written, rather than adopting a "strongly purposive" approach.

In rejecting a literal interpretation, the Hans Court essentially concludes that reading the Eleventh Amendment literally would make no sense—that it would conflict with the Amendment's manifest purpose. But isn't the language relevant in discerning the Amendment's purpose?

Clark, *The Eleventh Amendment and the Nature of the Union*, 123 Harv.L.Rev. 1817 (2010), argues that, contrary to the Supreme Court's assumption in Hans, the narrow language of the Eleventh Amendment made perfect sense in the historical context in which it was written. According to Professor Clark, the founding generation understood it as implicit in the nature of the union created by the Constitution—which, unlike the Articles of Confederation, authorized the federal government to issue commands

———————

[1] The holding of Hans and its implications for suits in state court are analyzed and disputed in the majority and dissenting opinions in Alden v. Maine, 527 U.S. 706 (1999), p. 967, *infra*.

directly to individuals—that Congress could not impose statutory duties on the sovereign states and that states could not be sued for constitutional violations. With the possibility of suits against the states based on federal law being ruled out by a widely shared original understanding, Professor Clark argues, the Eleventh Amendment had the clear, limited purpose of correcting Chisholm's mistaken (and anomalous) conclusion that Article III permitted out-of-state citizens to sue states in federal court based on diversity of citizenship. In other words, by barring federal suits against the states by out-of-state citizens, the Eleventh Amendment closed the only possible loophole that might have permitted any kind of suit against unconsenting states.[2]

(3) The "Diversity" Interpretation of the Eleventh Amendment.

(a) In a dissenting opinion in Atascadero State Hosp. v. Scanlon, 473 U.S. 234 (1985), Justice Brennan, drawing on the work of several commentators,[3] attempted to make sense of the language of the Eleventh Amendment as reflecting a historical purpose that would have permitted federal jurisdiction in cases such as Hans in which plaintiffs assert federal causes of action. Justice Brennan's "diversity theory" rested on two central distinctions. First, he sharply differentiated "sovereign immunity"—a traditional concept barring uncontested suit against the sovereign in any court—from the jurisdictional bar to suit in *federal* court erected by the Eleventh Amendment. The Eleventh Amendment, he argued, had nothing to do with sovereign immunity (in suits in state court, for example); it was designed exclusively to regulate the scope of federal judicial power.

Second, Justice Brennan distinguished between two grounds of federal jurisdiction under Article III: jurisdiction based on subject matter (such as suits arising under federal law) and that dependent on party status (such as citizen-state diversity). The Eleventh Amendment, he contended, barred federal jurisdiction in suits based on party status, but not those based on subject matter. More specifically, it barred jurisdiction in suits against an unconsenting state brought under the state-citizen diversity clause, in which state rather than federal law would ordinarily supply the plaintiff's cause of action, but did not restrict suits against an unconsenting state brought under admiralty or federal question jurisdiction.

According to Justice Brennan, "in most of the States in 1789, the doctrine of sovereign immunity formally forbade the maintenance of suits against States in state courts". To permit federal court jurisdiction based on party status "was a particularly troublesome prospect to the States that had incurred debts, some of which dated back to the Revolutionary War. The debts would naturally find their way into the hands of noncitizens and aliens, who at the first sign of default could be expected promptly to sue the State

---

[2] *Cf.* Vazquez, *The Unsettled Nature of the Union,* 123 Harv.L.Rev. Forum 79 (2011) (maintaining that most of the evidence that Professor Clark cites to support his claim that the federal government lacked the power to regulate the states unequivocally supports only the narrower conclusion that Congress could not subject the states (rather than their officers) to coercive suits).

[3] *E.g.,* Fletcher, *A Historical Interpretation of the Eleventh Amendment: A Narrow Construction of an Affirmative Grant of Jurisdiction Rather than a Prohibition Against Jurisdiction,* 35 Stan.L.Rev. 1033, 1058–59 (1983); Gibbons, *The Eleventh Amendment and State Sovereign Immunity: A Reinterpretation,* 83 Colum.L.Rev. 1889 (1983); Orth, *The Interpretation of the Eleventh Amendment, 1798–1908: A Case Study of Judicial Power,* 1983 U.Ill.L.Rev. 423; see also Lee, *Making Sense of the Eleventh Amendment: International Law and State Sovereignty,* 96 Nw.U.L.Rev. 1027 (2002).

in federal court. The State's effort to retain its sovereign immunity in its own courts would turn out to be futile".

In tracing the Eleventh Amendment's historical background, Justice Brennan reviewed at length the ratification debates over Article III, including the comments of Hamilton, Madison, and Marshall that are discussed in the Hans opinion:

"The various references to state sovereign immunity all appear in discussions of the state-citizen diversity clause. Virtually all of the comments were addressed to the problem created by state debts that predated the Constitution, when the State's creditors may often have had meager judicial remedies in the case of default. Yet, even in this sensitive context, a number of participants in the debates welcomed the abrogation of sovereign immunity that they thought followed from the state-citizen and state-alien clauses.[4] The debates do not directly address the question of suits against States in admiralty or federal question cases, where federal law and not state law would govern. Nonetheless, the apparent willingness of many delegates to read the state-citizen clause as abrogating sovereign immunity in state-law causes of action suggests that they would have been even more willing to permit suits against States in federal question cases, where Congress had authorized such suits in the exercise of its Article I or other powers."

Justice Brennan then examined the drafting of the Eleventh Amendment by Congress. He concluded that the language chosen "would have been a particularly cryptic way to embody" in the Constitution a consensus that the doctrine of state sovereign immunity would apply in federal court in, for example, cases brought to enforce the Constitution and laws of the United States. Rather, the language chosen—"The Judicial power of the United States shall not be construed to extend * * * "—parallels the phrasing of Article III, and was meant merely to abandon the construction of Article III in Chisholm, which permitted federal court suit against a state based simply upon party status. The Amendment, accordingly, bars only suits against a state brought by aliens or citizens of another state, in order to track (and restrict) the party-based jurisdiction in Article III.

Recall that Chisholm was an assumpsit action. In drafting a provision to overrule it, the Framers of the Eleventh Amendment gave little if any explicit consideration to the question of an unconsenting state's liability under federal law. Are the justifications for a state's claim of sovereign immunity as weighty in that context?

The Atascadero case involved a claim that a state was liable in damages under a federal statute, while Hans involved a claim for a judicially-implied remedy directly under the Constitution. Justice Brennan's dissent did not specifically address the question whether the federal courts' power to imply damage remedies for violations of federal constitutional provisions (as in the Bivens line of cases) or of federal statutes should extend to remedies against

---

[4]   [Ed.] The view that the Constitution abrogated immunity was advanced as an argument against ratification by some opponents (such as George Mason and Patrick Henry in Virginia) and various anti-Federalist publicists, but the view was also held by proponents of ratification (like Edmund Pendleton and Edmund Randolph of Virginia and Timothy Pickering and James Wilson of Pennsylvania). See Atasacadero, 473 U.S. at 263–80 (Brennan, J., dissenting). See generally Gibbons, note 3, *supra*, at 1902–08.

the states themselves. (He did suggest, however, that the *result* in Hans, denying relief, might be justified.)[5]

Suppose Justice Brennan's view—that the Eleventh Amendment merely restricts party-based jurisdiction—had been adopted. Might the states nonetheless enjoy some form of immunity (derived from the common law rather than the Constitution) in federal court actions under the Constitution and laws of the United States unless either (i) a state chose to waive its immunity or (ii) Congress, in the exercise of its constitutional powers, withdrew the immunity that the states otherwise would possess?[6]

(b) Recall that in the Hans opinion, the Court notes that the Eleventh Amendment had previously been held to bar a suit against a state by a citizen of another state, even when the claim was based on a question of federal law.[7] How then, the Court asked, could a federal court suit on such grounds be permitted by a citizen of the defendant state? Several scholars (disagreeing on this point with both the Hans majority and with Justice Brennan) have maintained that the Amendment should be read literally to bar *all* suits against a state by citizens of other states (even if their causes of action arise under federal law) and to bar *no* suits against a state by citizens of that state. See, *e.g.*, Marshall, *Fighting the Words of the Eleventh Amendment*, 102 Harv.L.Rev. 1342 (1989); Massey, *State Sovereignty and the Tenth and Eleventh Amendments*, 56 U.Chi.L.Rev. 61 (1989).[8]

(4) Hans and the Enforcement of Contracts. Several authors have suggested that the Hans decision may best be understood in the context of factors to which the Court did not explicitly advert. See, *e.g.*, Shapiro, *Wrong Turns: The Eleventh Amendment and the Pennhurst Case*, 98 Harv.L.Rev. 61, 69–70 (1984); Strasser, *Hans, Ayers, and Eleventh Amendment Jurisprudence: On Justification, Rationalization, and Sovereign Immunity*, 10 Geo. Mason L.Rev. 251, 289 (2001).

First, Hans involved a suit to enforce a contract. As discussed in connection with federal sovereign immunity and the availability of officer suits, see p. 891, *supra*, efforts to enforce contracts against the sovereign have historically been regarded as especially sensitive and problematic.

Second, Hans arose in a period in which a number of southern states were defaulting on their bonds and there existed no political will on the part of the national government to force insolvent states to pay their debts. Accordingly, judgments against the states or their officials in the series of bond cases that came before the Court in the late nineteenth century might well have proven unenforceable. See Orth, The Judicial Power of the United

---

[5]　Later in his opinion, Justice Brennan observed: "Most likely, Chisholm could not have been brought directly under the Contracts Clause of the Constitution. Prior to Fletcher v. Peck, 6 Cranch 87 (1810), it was not at all clear that the Contracts Clause applied to contracts to which a state was a party. Moreover, the case involved a simple breach of contract, not a law impairing the obligation of the contract to which the Clause would have applied. Finally, it was certainly not clear at the time of Chisholm that the Contracts Clause provided a plaintiff with a private right of action for damages."

[6]　See Jackson, *The Supreme Court, the Eleventh Amendment, and State Sovereign Immunity*, 98 Yale L.J. 1, 72–104 (1988) (advocating this view).

[7]　In those cases, however, the Court may well have viewed the claims as "arising under" general contract law rather than under the Contracts Clause of the Constitution.

[8]　For responses by defenders of a "diversity" theory similar to Justice Brennan's, see Amar, *Marbury, Section 13, and the Original Jurisdiction of the Supreme Court*, 56 U.Chi.L.Rev. 443, 496 (1989); Fletcher, *The Diversity Explanation of the Eleventh Amendment: A Reply to Critics*, 56 U.Chi.L.Rev. 1261 (1989).

States: The Eleventh Amendment in American History 47–120 (1987); Gibbons, note 3, *supra*, at 1978–2002.

Would these considerations, either singly or in conjunction, *justify* the decision in Hans?[9]

(5) Legacy of Non-Literalism. Since Hans the Supreme Court has rejected arguments for a "literal" reading of the Eleventh Amendment in a variety of contexts. Despite earlier dicta to the contrary, see, *e.g.*, Cherokee Nation v. Georgia, 30 U.S. (5 Pet.) 1, 15–16 (1831), the Court held in Monaco v. Mississippi, 292 U.S. 313, 322 (1934), that the effect of the Amendment is to bar suit against a state by a foreign country.[10] In Ex parte New York, 256 U.S. 490 (1921), the Court applied the Amendment to bar a suit in admiralty, despite the textual limitation to suits "in law or equity".[11] More recently, and more significantly, the Court barred an unconsented private action against a state brought on a federal claim in a *state* court, Alden v. Maine, p. 967, *infra*, and an action against a state before a federal *administrative* agency, Fed. Maritime Comm'n v. S.C. State Ports Auth., p. 977, *infra*.[12]

---

[9]   Professor Purcell, in *The Particularly Dubious Case of Hans v. Louisiana: An Essay on Law, Race, History, and "Federal Courts"*, 81 N.C.L.Rev. 1927 (2003), argues that Hans should not be given weight as precedent precisely because the decision was "an integral part of the nation's surrender to southern intransigence and racial oppression" and constituted a "rejection of both established Eleventh Amendment doctrine and the principles of the new post-Civil War Constitution".

[10]   Lee, *The Supreme Court of the United States as Quasi-International Tribunal: Reclaiming the Court's Original and Exclusive Jurisdiction over Treaty-Based Suits by Foreign States Against States*, 104 Colum.L.Rev. 1765 (2004), criticizes the rationale of the Monaco case and argues that it should at least be limited to its facts (involving jurisdiction based solely on diversity) because the states, in ratifying the Constitution, gave up their immunity to suits against them by foreign states, particularly those based on alleged treaty violations. Such suits, however, must in his view be confined to the original and exclusive jurisdiction of the Supreme Court.

[11]   The Court's subsequent forays into the Eleventh Amendment in the admiralty context have not been models of clarity. In Florida Department of State v. Treasure Salvors, Inc., 458 U.S. 670 (1982), the Court determined that the Eleventh Amendment did not preclude a federal district court from issuing a warrant, directed against state officials, for property from a wreckage that was the subject of an in rem admiralty suit. But at the same time, the opinion for a plurality of four Justices suggested that the Eleventh Amendment might bar adjudication of the state's ownership of the wreckage.

Revisiting the issue of state sovereign immunity in the admiralty context in California v. Deep Sea Research, Inc., 523 U.S. 491 (1998), the Court held that the Eleventh Amendment did not bar federal jurisdiction over an in rem admiralty suit where the state did not possess the res to which it claimed title. The Court concluded that because of the state's lack of possession, any intimations from Treasure Salvors that the Eleventh Amendment barred the adjudication of the state's interest in the property were inapposite.

[12]   The Court has addressed the pertinency of the Eleventh Amendment to suits against multi-state agencies in several cases. In Lake Country Estates, Inc. v. Tahoe Regional Planning Agency, 440 U.S. 391 (1979), the Court held that a bi-state regional agency created by a congressionally approved interstate compact between California and Nevada to coordinate development of the Lake Tahoe area was not immune from suit in federal court: "Unless there is good reason to believe that the States structured the new agency to enable it to enjoy the special constitutional protection of the States themselves, and that Congress concurred in that purpose, there would appear to be no justification for reading additional meaning into the limited language of the Amendment". See also Hess v. Port Authority Trans-Hudson Corp. [PATH], 513 U.S. 30 (1994), in which injured railroad workers brought an FELA action against PATH, a bi-state railway created by a congressionally approved interstate compact. In a 5–4 decision, the Court held that PATH was not entitled to Eleventh Amendment immunity. Despite the formal elements of state control over PATH, there were significant elements pointing away from immunity for an entity that was not itself a state—notably the lack of state financial responsibility for the Authority's liabilities.

(6) State Waivers of Sovereign Immunity. Hans did not purport to question the rule that a state, like any sovereign entity, may waive its immunity and consent to suit. See, *e.g.*, Clark v. Barnard, 108 U.S. 436, 447 (1883); Petty v. Tenn.-Mo. Bridge Comm'n, 359 U.S. 275 (1959). Is this an anomaly (however well-established) in light of the ordinary rule that the parties lack power to confer subject matter jurisdiction on the federal courts? Or, despite the constitutional text, is the question of Eleventh Amendment immunity not a true question of subject matter jurisdiction at all, but one more analogous to personal jurisdiction? See Nelson, *Sovereign Immunity as a Doctrine of Personal Jurisdiction*, 115 Harv.L.Rev. 1561 (2002) (arguing, *inter alia*, that historically, sovereign immunity was premised on the lack of *personal* jurisdiction over non-consenting states but that the Eleventh Amendment itself created an additional, and non-waivable, *subject matter* immunity in cases falling within the terms of its specific text).[13]

The Court has taken a range of positions on this issue, indicating, for example, in Edelman v. Jordan, 415 U.S. 651 (1974), that the matter is jurisdictional, but stating in Patsy v. Board of Regents, 457 U.S. 496, 515–16 n. 19 (1982), that an Eleventh Amendment question is not jurisdictional "in the sense that it must be raised and decided by this Court on its own motion". In Wisconsin Department of Corrections v. Schacht, 524 U.S. 381, 391 (1998), the Court said that the issue has yet to be resolved.

      (a) Consent to Suit Confined to State Tribunals. Smith v. Reeves, 178 U.S. 436, 441 (1900), held that a state may waive sovereign immunity as to suits for tax refunds in its own courts, while retaining its Eleventh Amendment immunity from such lawsuits in federal court. Earlier cases looked the other way, see, *e.g.*, Reagan v. Farmers' Loan & Trust Co., 154 U.S. 362, 391 (1894), but Smith reasoned that a limitation upon tax refund actions could not be seen as "hostile to the General Government, or as touching upon any right granted or secured by the Constitution of the United States". Subsequent cases have permitted selective waiver by the state without regard to Smith's qualifications. See, *e.g.*, Edelman v. Jordan, *supra*. Should they have, especially when other efforts by states to restrict lawsuits to the state courts have been held unlawful? See, *e.g.*, Railway Co. v. Whitton's Adm'r, 80 U.S. (13 Wall.) 270 (1871), p. 626, *supra*, holding that a state statute purporting to permit enforcement of a state wrongful death action only in state court could not prevent the exercise of federal diversity jurisdiction. See also Shapiro, Paragraph (4), *supra*.

      (b) On the Basis of the State's Conduct in Litigation.

      (i) When a state files suit in federal court, it necessarily waives its sovereign immunity from the court's jurisdiction to determine the validity of its claims and of any defenses that might be asserted against those claims. See, *e.g.*, Gardner v. New Jersey, 329 U.S. 565 (1947). The circuits are divided on whether a state's voluntary appearance as a plaintiff in federal court waives the state's sovereign immunity with respect to compulsory (or permissive) counterclaims, and if so whether the relief sought must be of the same kind and not in an amount greater than that sought by the state. See 71 U.S.L.W. 2592 (2003).

---

[13] See also Lee, *The Dubious Concept of Jurisdiction*, 54 Hastings L.J. 1613, 1632–35 (2003) (suggesting that understanding subject matter jurisdiction not as referring to a court's physical "power" but to its legal authority may help to explain several doctrinal anomalies, including the waivability of a state's Eleventh Amendment immunity).

(ii) In Lapides v. Board of Regents, 535 U.S. 613 (2002), the Court addressed the question whether a state that removes a state court action against it to a federal court under § 1441 or some other removal provision thereby waives its Eleventh Amendment immunity. Lapides had filed a state court damages action against state officials and the Board (a state agency), complaining of violations of both federal and state law. (The federal claims were based on 42 U.S.C. § 1983.) All defendants joined in removing the case to federal court, which dismissed the action against the individual defendants on grounds of qualified immunity and held that by removing the case to federal court, the state agency had waived any Eleventh Amendment immunity with respect to the claims against it. The Supreme Court, in a unanimous opinion authored by Justice Breyer, first noted that under Will v. Michigan Dep't of State Police, 491 U.S. 58 (1989), p. 1004, *infra*, the state agency could not be sued on a federal claim under § 1983, and then held that "in the context of state-law claims, in respect to which the state has explicitly waived immunity from state-court proceedings", the "State's act of removing a lawsuit from state court to federal court" constitutes a waiver of any claim of Eleventh Amendment immunity.[14]

The "motive" for the removal was irrelevant, as was the question whether the state's attorney general, who had been responsible for the removal and who had authority to represent the state in civil litigation, had the further authority under state law to waive the state's Eleventh Amendment immunity. The Court also stated that the question whether particular litigation activities amount to a waiver is a question of federal law, and expressly overruled any indication to the contrary in Ford Motor Co. v. Department of Treasury, 323 U.S. 459 (1945).[15] Cases involving the ability of the United States to claim sovereign immunity after voluntarily entering a case were distinguished as not involving the Eleventh Amendment—"a specific text with a history that focuses on the State's immunity vis-a-vis the Federal Government".[16]

(7) "Exceptions" to Hans. Although Hans continues to establish the states' immunity against a range of unconsented actions, it has never been understood to bar all actions through which the Constitution and laws of the United States might be enforced against states, their subdivisions, and their officers—notwithstanding efforts by the defendants to claim immunity from such actions.

(a) Appeals of Actions Initiated by the States in State Court. Hans accepted the ruling of Cohens v. Virginia, p. 907, *supra*, that appeals

---

[14] The Court had held previously, in Wisconsin Dep't of Corrections v. Schacht, 524 U.S. 381 (1998), that the presence in an otherwise removable case of one or more claims barred by the Eleventh Amendment does not deprive the federal court of jurisdiction to hear the remaining claims. Justice Kennedy, concurring, wrote separately to suggest the possibility—not considered below and not argued or briefed by the parties—that by removing the case to a federal court, the state may have waived its Eleventh Amendment immunity.

[15] For pre-Lapides discussion of the inconsistency between the "waiver in litigation" doctrine and the holding of Ford Motor Co. that a state defendant does not constructively waive sovereign immunity by litigating on the merits in trial court, see Seinfeld, *Waiver-In-Litigation: Eleventh Amendment Immunity and the Voluntariness Question*, 63 Ohio St.L.J. 871 (2002).

[16] For an in-depth discussion of the history of the Court's waiver doctrine, including an analysis of which actions (and by whom) give rise to a waiver, see Siegel, *Waivers of State Sovereign Immunity and the Ideology of the Eleventh Amendment*, 52 Duke L.J. 1167 (2003) (arguing that until 1945 the Court was more willing to find a waiver than during later years, when the waiver doctrine has "ebbed and flowed with the overall ideological tide of the Eleventh Amendment").

to the Supreme Court of state criminal convictions are not suits against the state within the meaning of the Eleventh Amendment. Neither are appeals of civil actions instituted by the states.

(b) Suits by Other States and the United States. The Supreme Court has declined to bar either suits against a state by another state, see, *e.g.*, Kansas v. Colorado, 206 U.S. 46, 83 (1907),[17] or suits against a state by the United States, see, *e.g.*, United States v. Mississippi, 380 U.S. 128, 140–41 (1965); Idaho v. United States, 533 U.S. 262, 272 n.4 (2001). In Monaco v. Mississippi, the Court explained that the former holding "was essential to the peace of the Union" and "a necessary feature of the formation of a more perfect Union", while the latter was "inherent in the constitutional plan".[18]

(c) Waiver and Abrogation. Beyond the waiver doctrine discussed in Paragraph (6), *supra*, the Court has held that in certain limited circumstances, Congress may abrogate, or strip a state of, Eleventh Amendment immunity. See pp. 957–967, *infra*.

(d) Suits Against Local Governments. Lincoln County v. Luning, 133 U.S. 529 (1890), decided the same day as Hans, held that the Eleventh Amendment does not bar an individual's suit in federal court against a county for nonpayment of a debt. (By contrast, a suit against a statewide agency is considered a suit against the state under the Eleventh Amendment. See, *e.g.*, Edelman v. Jordan, 415 U.S. 651 (1974); Ford Motor Co. v. Department of Treasury, 323 U.S. 459 (1945)). In allowing suits against counties and municipalities, the Court was unanimous, relying in part on its "general acquiescence" in such suits over the prior thirty years. The Court has adhered to this position as to local government bodies ever since. See, *e.g.*, Mount Healthy City School Dist. Bd. of Educ. v. Doyle, 429 U.S. 274, 280–81 (1977); Northern Ins. Co. v. Chatham County, Georgia, 547 U.S. 189 (2006).

Does it make sense for local governments to be treated differently from state agencies for Eleventh Amendment purposes when both are creatures of the state?[19] William Fletcher explains the different treatment on the ground that in the nineteenth century, a municipal corporation was viewed as more closely analogous to a private corporation than to a state government. Fletcher, note 3, *supra*, at 1099–1107. By contrast, Professor Orth, Paragraph (4) *supra*, traces the opposing outcomes in Hans and Lincoln County to practical limits on judicial power: in Hans and other cases against debt-ridden southern states, the Court chose not to issue orders that, in the post-Reconstruction political environment, could never have been enforced; by contrast, enforcement of court orders was far easier against

---

[17]　But cf. New Hampshire v. Louisiana, 108 U.S. 76 (1883), p. 279, *supra*.

[18]　In Alabama v. North Carolina, 560 U.S. 330 (2010), a case within the Supreme Court's original jurisdiction, the majority, in an opinion by Justice Scalia, held that the Eleventh Amendment and principles of state sovereign immunity did not bar an interstate commission's suit against a state insofar as the commission "makes the same claims and seeks the same relief" as co-plaintiff states whose actions were concededly not barred. Chief Justice Roberts, joined by Justice Thomas, dissented. Although acknowledging that Arizona v. California, 460 U.S. 605 (1983), supported the Court's decision, the Chief Justice argued that subsequent cases, including Federal Maritime Commission v. South Carolina Ports Authority, p. 977, *infra*, showed the error of the earlier ruling: "Our Constitution does not countenance such 'no harm, no foul' jurisdiction."

[19]　For a spirited defense of the Lincoln County decision on both historical and functional grounds, see Durschlag, *Should Political Subdivisions Be Accorded Eleventh Amendment Immunity?*, 43 DePaul L.Rev. 577 (1994).

counties, especially western counties (such as Lincoln County, Nevada) that depended upon maintaining their credit to permit further borrowing.

(e) Officer Suits. Hans had no occasion to address the availability of "officer suits" as a device for ensuring state compliance with the Constitution and laws of the United States. The consistency of officer suits with the Eleventh Amendment was one of the issues before the Court in the next principal case, Ex parte Young.

Ex parte Young

209 U.S. 123, 28 S.Ct. 441, 52 L.Ed. 714 (1908).
Petition for Writs of Habeas Corpus and Certiorari.

[Shareholders of various railroads brought derivative actions in federal circuit court in Minnesota, alleging that state legislation regulating railroad rates was confiscatory and violated the Fourteenth Amendment. The companies' managements, plaintiffs alleged, had refused their demands that the companies not comply with the legislation.

[The trial court entered a temporary restraining order prohibiting Edward Young, the state's Attorney General, from enforcing the legislation, and after denying Young's motion under the Eleventh Amendment to dismiss, entered a preliminary injunction to the same effect. Young then defied the injunction by filing a state court action seeking to enforce the legislation against the railroads.

[The circuit court held Young in contempt, again rejecting his Eleventh Amendment defense. He then filed an application in the Supreme Court for leave to file a petition for writs of habeas corpus and certiorari.]

■ MR. JUSTICE PECKHAM * * * delivered the opinion of the court.

[The Court first concluded that the circuit court had "arising under" jurisdiction, as the suit raised several federal questions: (i) whether enforcement of the rates would take property without due process of law, (ii) whether the penalties for violation were so enormous as to deny equal protection and due process, and (iii) whether the legislation interfered with interstate commerce.]

Coming to the inquiry regarding the alleged invalidity of these acts, we take up the contention that they are invalid on their face on account of the penalties. For disobedience to the freight act the officers, directors, agents and employés of the company are made guilty of a misdemeanor, and upon conviction each may be punished by imprisonment in the county jail for a period not exceeding ninety days. Each violation would be a separate offense, and, therefore, might result in imprisonment of the various agents of the company who would dare disobey for a term of ninety days each for each offense. Disobedience to the passenger rate act renders the party guilty of a felony and subject to a fine not exceeding five thousand dollars or imprisonment in the state prison for a period not exceeding five years, or both fine and imprisonment. The sale of each ticket above the price permitted by the act would be a violation thereof. * * * The company, in order to test the validity of the acts, must find some agent or employé to disobey them at the risk stated. The necessary effect and result of such legislation must be to preclude a resort to the courts (either state or Federal) for the purpose of testing its validity. * * * It may therefore be said that when the penalties for disobedience are by fines so enormous and imprisonment so severe as to intimidate the company and its officers from resorting to the courts to test the validity of the legislation, the result is the same as if the law in terms prohibited the company from seeking judicial construction of laws which deeply affect its rights.

* * * Ordinarily a law creating offenses in the nature of misdemeanors or felonies relates to a subject over which the jurisdiction of the legislature is complete in any event. In the case, however, of the establishment of certain rates without any hearing, the validity of such rates necessarily depends upon whether they are high enough to permit at least some return upon the investment (how much it is not now necessary to state), and an inquiry as to that fact is a proper subject of judicial investigation. If it turns out that the rates are too low for that purpose, then they are illegal. Now, to impose upon a party interested the burden of obtaining a judicial decision of such a question (no prior hearing having ever been given) only upon the condition that if unsuccessful he must suffer imprisonment and pay fines as provided in these acts, is, in effect, to close up all approaches to the courts, and thus prevent any hearing upon the question whether the rates as provided by the acts are not too low, and therefore invalid. * * *

We hold, therefore, that the provisions of the acts relating to the enforcement of the rates, either for freight or passengers, by imposing such enormous fines and possible imprisonment as a result of an unsuccessful effort to test the validity of the laws themselves, are unconstitutional on their face, without regard to the question of the insufficiency of those rates. * * *

* * * The question that arises is whether there is a remedy that the parties interested may resort to, by going into a Federal court of equity, in a case involving a violation of the Federal Constitution, and obtaining a judicial investigation of the problem, and pending its solution obtain freedom from suits, civil or criminal, by a temporary injunction, and if the question be finally decided favorably to the contention of the company, a permanent injunction restraining all such actions or proceedings.

This inquiry necessitates an examination of the most material and important objection made to the jurisdiction of the Circuit Court, the objection being that the suit is, in effect, one against the State of Minnesota * * *. This objection is to be considered with reference to the Eleventh and Fourteenth Amendments to the Federal Constitution. * * *

We may assume that each [Amendment] exists in full force, and that we must give to the Eleventh Amendment all the effect it naturally would have, without cutting it down or rendering its meaning any more narrow than the language, fairly interpreted, would warrant. It applies to a suit brought against a State by one of its own citizens as well as to a suit brought by a citizen of another State. Hans v. Louisiana, 134 U.S. 1. * * *

The cases * * * [following adoption of the Eleventh Amendment] were reviewed, and it was held, In re Ayers, 123 U.S. 443, that a bill in equity brought against officers of a State, who, as individuals, have no personal interest in the subject-matter of the suit, and defend only as representing the State, where the relief prayed for, if done, would constitute a performance by the State of the alleged contract of the State, was a suit against the State (page 504), following in this respect Hagood v. Southern, [117 U.S. 52, 67].

A suit of such a nature was simply an attempt to make the State itself, through its officers, perform its alleged contract, by directing those officers to do acts which constituted such performance. The State alone had any interest in the question, and a decree in favor of plaintiff would affect the treasury of the State.

[The Court then discussed a number of its recent decisions that it viewed as "ample justification" for determining that a state official who is about to commence civil or criminal proceedings to enforce unconstitutional state legislation may be enjoined from such action by a federal court of equity. Those cases included Reagan v. Farmers' Loan & Trust Co., 154 U.S. 362 (1894) and Smyth v. Ames, 169 U.S. 466, 518 (1898). The Court continued:]

* * * In those cases the only wrong or injury or trespass involved was the threatened commencement of suits to enforce the statute as to rates, and the threat of such commencement was in each case regarded as sufficient to authorize the issuing of an injunction to prevent the same. The threat to commence those suits under such circumstances was therefore necessarily held to be equivalent to any other threatened wrong or injury to the property of a plaintiff which had theretofore been held sufficient to authorize the suit against the officer.

* * * It is contended that the complainants do not complain and they care nothing about any action which Mr. Young might take or bring as an ordinary individual, but that he was complained of as an officer, to whose discretion is confided the use of the name of the State of Minnesota so far as litigation is concerned, and that when or how he shall use it is a matter resting in his discretion and cannot be controlled by any court.

The answer to all this is the same as made in every case where an official claims to be acting under the authority of the State. The act to be enforced is alleged to be unconstitutional, and if it be so, the use of the name of the State to enforce an unconstitutional act to the injury of complainants is a proceeding without the authority of and one which does not affect the State in its sovereign or governmental capacity. It is simply an illegal act upon the part of a state official in attempting by the use of the name of the State to enforce a legislative enactment which is void because unconstitutional. If the act which the state Attorney General seeks to enforce be a violation of the Federal Constitution, the officer in proceeding under such enactment comes into conflict with the superior authority of that Constitution, and he is in that case stripped of his official or representative character and is subjected in his person to the consequences of his individual conduct. The State has no power to impart to him any immunity from responsibility to the supreme authority of the United States. * * *

It is further objected (and the objection really forms part of the contention that the State cannot be sued) that a court of equity has no jurisdiction to enjoin criminal proceedings, by indictment or otherwise, under the state law. This, as a general rule, is true. But there are exceptions. When such indictment or proceeding is brought to enforce an alleged unconstitutional statute, which is the subject matter of inquiry in a suit already pending in a Federal court, the latter court having first obtained jurisdiction over the subject matter, has the right, in both civil and criminal cases, to hold and maintain such jurisdiction, to the exclusion of all other courts, until its duty is fully performed. But the Federal court cannot, of course, interfere in a case where the proceedings were already pending in a state court. * * *

It is proper to add that the right to enjoin an individual, even though a state official, from commencing suits under circumstances already stated, does not include the power to restrain a court from acting in any case brought before it, either of a civil or criminal nature, nor does it include power to prevent any investigation or action by a grand jury. The latter body is part of the machinery of a criminal court, and an injunction against a state court would be a violation of the whole scheme of our Government. * * *

It is further objected that there is a plain and adequate remedy at law open to the complainants and that a court of equity, therefore, has no jurisdiction in such case. It has been suggested that the proper way to test the constitutionality of the act is to disobey it, at least once, after which the company might obey the act pending subsequent proceedings to test its validity. But in the event of a single violation the prosecutor might not avail himself of the opportunity to make the test, as obedience to the law was thereafter continued, and he might think it unnecessary to start an inquiry. If, however, he should do so while the company was thereafter obeying the law, several years might elapse before there was a final determination of the question, and if it should be determined that the law was invalid the property of the company would have been taken during that time without due process of law, and there would be no possibility of its recovery.

Another obstacle to making the test on the part of the company might be to find an agent or employé who would disobey the law, with a possible fine and imprisonment staring him in the face if the act should be held valid. Take the passenger rate act, for instance: A sale of a single ticket above the price mentioned in that act might subject the ticket agent to a charge of felony, and upon conviction to a fine of five thousand dollars and imprisonment for five years. It is true the company might pay the fine, but the imprisonment the agent would have to suffer personally. It would not be wonderful if, under such circumstances, there would not be a crowd of agents offering to disobey the law. The wonder would be that a single agent should be found ready to take the risk.

* * * [I]t must be remembered that jurisdiction of this general character has, in fact, been exercised by Federal courts from the time of Osborn v. United States Bank up to the present; the only difference in regard to the case of Osborn and the case in hand being that in this case the injury complained of is the threatened commencement of suits, civil or criminal, to enforce the act, instead of, as in the Osborn case, an actual and direct trespass upon or interference with tangible property. A bill filed to prevent the commencement of suits to enforce an unconstitutional act, under the circumstances already mentioned, is no new invention, as we have already seen. The difference between an actual and direct

interference with tangible property and the enjoining of state officers from enforcing an unconstitutional act, is not of a radical nature, and does not extend, in truth, the jurisdiction of the courts over the subject matter. * * * The sovereignty of the State is, in reality, no more involved in one case than in the other. The State cannot in either case impart to the official immunity from responsibility to the supreme authority of the United States.

This supreme authority, which arises from the specific provisions of the Constitution itself, is nowhere more fully illustrated than in the series of decisions under the Federal *habeas corpus* statute, in some of which cases persons in the custody of state officers for alleged crimes against the State have been taken from that custody and discharged by a Federal court or judge, because the imprisonment was adjudged to be in violation of the Federal Constitution. The right to so discharge has not been doubted by this court, and it has never been supposed there was any suit against the State by reason of serving the writ upon one of the officers of the State in whose custody the person was found. * * *

The rule to show cause is discharged and the petition for writs of *habeas corpus* and certiorari is dismissed. * * *

■ MR. JUSTICE HARLAN, dissenting.

* * * Let it be observed that the suit * * * in the Circuit Court of the United States was, as to the defendant Young, one against him *as, and only because he was*, Attorney General of Minnesota. No relief was sought against him individually but only in his capacity *as* Attorney General. And the manifest, indeed the avowed and admitted, object of seeking such relief was *to tie the hands* of the *State* so that it could not in any manner or by any mode of proceeding, *in its own courts*, test the validity of the statutes and orders in question. It would therefore seem clear that within the true meaning of the Eleventh Amendment the suit brought in the Federal court was one, in legal effect, against the State—as much so as if the State had been formally named on the record as a party—and therefore it was a suit to which, under the Amendment, so far as the State or its Attorney General was concerned, the judicial power of the United States did not and could not extend.

* * * [T]he intangible thing, called a State, however extensive its powers, can never appear or be represented or known in any court in a litigated case, except by and through its officers. When, therefore, the Federal court forbade the defendant Young, as Attorney General of Minnesota, from taking any action, suit, step or proceeding whatever looking to the enforcement of the statutes in question, it said in effect to the State of Minnesota: " * * * the Federal court adjudges that you, the State, although a sovereign for many important governmental purposes, shall not appear in your own courts, by your law officer, with the view of enforcing, or even for determining the validity of the state enactments which the Federal court has, upon a preliminary hearing, declared to be in violation of the Constitution of the United States."

This principle, if firmly established, would work a radical change in our governmental system. It would inaugurate a new era in the American judicial system and in the relations of the National and state governments. It would enable the subordinate Federal courts to supervise and control the official action of the States as if they were "dependencies" or provinces. It would place the States of the Union in a condition of inferiority never dreamed of when the Constitution was adopted or when the Eleventh Amendment was made a part of the Supreme Law of the Land. * * * Too little consequence has been attached to the fact that the courts of the States are under an obligation equally strong with that resting upon the courts of the Union to respect and enforce the provisions of the Federal Constitution as the Supreme Law of the Land, and to guard rights secured or guaranteed by that instrument. We must assume—a decent respect for the States requires us to assume—that the state courts will enforce every right secured by the Constitution. If they fail to do so, the party complaining has a clear remedy for the protection of his rights; for, he can come by writ of error, in an orderly, judicial way, from the highest court of the State to this tribunal for redress in respect of every right granted or secured by that instrument and denied by the state court. * * *

NOTE ON EX PARTE YOUNG AND SUITS AGAINST STATE OFFICERS

(1) The Significance of Ex parte Young. At the time of the Court's decision in Ex parte Young, the tradition of "officer suits" as a means of redress for official misconduct was already well established. Apart from affirming that the Eleventh Amendment in no way displaced this tradition, commentators have long regarded Young as significant because it (a) recognized a cause of action for injunctive relief directly under the Fourteenth Amendment[1] and (b) strengthened the idea of breach of legal duty as a basis for equitable relief[2] by extending it into a context in which the challenged official action—Attorney General Young's announced readiness to prosecute for conduct in violation of state law—would probably not have been tortious at common law.[3] Although recent commentary has questioned the historical accuracy of interpreting Young as having upheld a constitutionally based cause of action (and instead argued that it rested on traditional equitable principles, as discussed in Paragraph (5), *infra*), there is no doubt that a long and important string of subsequent cases has built on the understanding that the Constitution of its own force gives rise to causes of action to enjoin state officials engaged in constitutional violations— including those involving school segregation and suppression of voting rights—against which state tort law would have provided no protection.

(2) The Possible "Paradox" of Ex parte Young. Consider whether Ex parte Young—if interpreted as upholding a cause of action based directly on the Fourteenth Amendment—rests on a paradox. On the one hand, State Attorney General Young acted to enforce the challenged Minnesota statute

---

[1]   See Hart, *The Relations Between State and Federal Law*, 54 Colum.L.Rev. 489, 524 & n.124 (1954); Purcell, *Ex parte Young and the Transformation of the Federal Courts, 1890–1917*, 40 U.Tol.L.Rev. 931, 962–63 (2009). Woolhandler, *The Common Law Origins of Constitutionally Compelled Remedies*, 107 Yale L.J. 77, 99–111 (1997), notes that prior to Young, federal court actions against state officials were not uncommon, but that they were frequently founded on diversity jurisdiction, even when they raised federal questions. According to Professor Woolhandler, the remedies imposed by the federal courts in these actions often diverged from those available in state courts.

[2]   See Woolhandler, *Patterns of Official Immunity and Accountability*, 37 Case W.Res.L.Rev. 396, 441 (1987).

[3]   See Jacobs, The Eleventh Amendment and Sovereign Immunity 138–42 (1972).

solely in his role as an officer of the state. Accordingly, he was a state actor for purposes of the Fourteenth Amendment. On the other hand, the Court deemed Young not to be the state for purposes of the Eleventh Amendment.

Does this juxtaposition make sense? In thinking about this question, recall that the Eleventh Amendment was enacted against the background of a long historical tradition in which unconsented suits against the sovereign were barred by the doctrine of sovereign immunity, but suits against government officers frequently, and indeed perhaps typically, were not. See pp. 878–882, *supra*. Consider, too, whether constitutional government would be workable if neither the states nor their officials were suable for constitutional violations.

As is discussed at length in Section 3, *infra*, state officials who are sued for damages typically enjoy either absolute or "qualified" official immunity from damages liability. For discussion of the limits that state sovereign immunity may impose on suits for injunctive relief that are nominally pleaded against state officials, see pp. 929–931, *infra*.

(3) The Limits of Ex parte Young. In holding that the Eleventh Amendment interposed no bar against a suit against a state officer seeking a remedy for an alleged constitutional violation, Young differed from both some earlier and some subsequent cases.

(a) In re Ayers. Ex parte Young did not purport to question the holding of In re Ayers, 123 U.S. 443 (1887), that the Eleventh Amendment barred an award of injunctive relief "the object of which is * * * to compel the specific performance of a contract"[4] Instead, consistent with the historic pattern of sovereign immunity decisions holding that officer suits cannot be used to enforce government contract actions, see p. 891, *supra,* the Young Court distinguished Ayers as follows: "[the suit] was one against the state, to enforce its alleged contract. * * * It was not stated that the suit or the injunction was necessarily confined to a case of a threatened direct trespass upon or injury to property."

But cf. Ga. R.R. & Banking Co. v. Redwine, 342 U.S. 299 (1952), which held that the Eleventh Amendment did not bar a federal court action, based on the Contracts Clause, seeking to enjoin the state revenue commissioner from imposing taxes upon property claimed to be exempt pursuant to a state charter. The Court purported to distinguish Ayers on the ground that there the "complainant had not alleged that officers threatened to tax its property in violation of its constitutional rights", while in Redwine the plaintiff sought "to enjoin [the commissioner] from a threatened and allegedly unconstitutional invasion of its property".

---

[4]   A tort-contract distinction in gauging the permissible scope of officer suits has been defended by some as consistent with the historically prevailing idea that an official could be enjoined only from the commission (or threatened commission) of a wrong for which the official would be personally liable at common law. *E.g.*, Engdahl, *Immunity and Accountability for Positive Government Wrongs*, 44 U.Colo.L.Rev. 1, 15–16, 37–38 (1972). But the distinction has been attacked by Woolhandler, *Patterns of Official Immunity and Accountability*, note 2, *supra*, at 436–45, on the basis that the historical pattern of decisions was mixed and that given "the flexibility of the common law, the legal duty strand easily merges with the tort strand". See also Vázquez, *Night and Day: Coeur D'Alene, Breard, and the Unraveling of the Prospective-Retrospective Distinction in Eleventh Amendment Doctrine*, 87 Geo.L.J. 1 (1998) (urging an approach—represented, in his view, by Edelman—in which a suit against an officer for a violation of federal law does not run afoul of the Eleventh Amendment if it seeks only nonmonetary relief).

(b) Edelman v. Jordan. In Edelman v. Jordan, 415 U.S. 651 (1974), Jordan had brought an individual and class action against various state officers, including Edelman, seeking "declaratory and injunctive relief" on the basis that the defendants "were administering the federal-state programs of Aid to the Aged, Blind, or Disabled (AABD) in a manner inconsistent with various federal regulations and with the Fourteenth Amendment". The district court granted a permanent injunction "requiring compliance with the federal time limits for processing and paying AABD applicants" and also ordered the defendants to release AABD benefits "wrongfully withheld" from certain AABD applicants during a specified period. Following affirmance by the court of appeals, the Supreme Court, in a 5–4 decision, reversed in part, holding that while the rationale of Ex parte Young permitted the part of the judgment that constituted a *prospective* injunction, the provision for the payment of funds "wrongfully withheld" in the past was *retrospective* relief barred by the Eleventh Amendment.

Writing for the majority, Justice Rehnquist cited Ford Motor Co. v. Department of Treasury, 323 U.S. 459, 464 (1945), for the proposition that "when the action is in essence one for the recovery of money from the state, the state is the real, substantial party in interest and is entitled to invoke its sovereign immunity from suit even though individual officials are nominal defendants".[5] That the payment in the case at bar had been described as "equitable restitution" did not affect the result; the state's immunity derived from the fact that the judgment mandated "a form of compensation"—a "retroactive award of monetary relief" that would "to a virtual certainty be paid from state funds, and not from the pockets of the individual state officials who were the defendants in the action".[6] Acknowledging that the "necessary result of compliance" with a purely prospective decree permitted under Ex parte Young could be a substantial burden on the state's treasury, Justice Rehnquist reasoned that "such an *ancillary* effect on the state treasury is a permissible and often an inevitable consequence" of application of the Young principle (emphasis added).

Justice Brennan, dissenting, argued that when the states entered the federal union, they surrendered their immunity with respect to matters falling within the enumerated powers delegated to Congress. And Justice Marshall, joined by Justice Blackmun, dissented on the ground that the states' participation in the AABD program constituted a waiver of "whatever immunity they might otherwise have from federal court orders requiring retroactive payment of welfare benefits".[7]

Prior to Edelman, federal courts had issued writs ordering state officials to perform ministerial duties—the traditional office of the writ of

---

[5] In the Ford Motor Co. case, a taxpayer had brought a federal action against state officials for the recovery of taxes allegedly imposed in violation of the federal Constitution. The Supreme Court held that the action was barred by the Eleventh Amendment.

[6] It is not clear from this language, or from the opinion as a whole, whether Justice Rehnquist meant that the plaintiffs had made a mistake in failing to seek recovery from the individual defendants in their *personal* capacity (see p. 996 *infra*), that all parties simply assumed that any monetary recovery would come directly from the state treasury, or that in the circumstances, no recovery *could* be had from the individual defendants.

[7] The Court rejected the argument that the state had waived its immunity from suit by accepting federal funds. Mere participation in a funding program was insufficient to constitute a waiver in the absence of "the most express language or * * * such overwhelming implications from the text [of the state's agreement to participate] as [will] leave no room for any other reasonable construction" (quoting Murray v. Wilson Distilling Co., 213 U.S. 151, 171 (1909)).

mandamus[8]—and some writs of mandamus issued against *federal* officials had required payments from the federal treasury.[9] Should Edelman be read to bar mandamus requiring state officers to perform ministerial duties that involve the payment of "compensation" out of public funds? Why should a state's immunity be broader in this respect than that of the United States?

(c) The Elusiveness of the Prospective-Retrospective Distinction. In Milliken v. Bradley, 433 U.S. 267 (1977) (Milliken II), after the Supreme Court had disapproved an interdistrict busing remedy to desegregate the Detroit schools, the district court ordered the provision of remedial education for pupils and in-service training for teachers and administrators, as well as the hiring of more counselors. The state, which shared responsibility for the segregation, was ordered to pay half the cost of these programs; though the order ran only against state officials, it contemplated payment from the state treasury. The Supreme Court unanimously held that the decree "fits squarely within the prospective-compliance exception reaffirmed by Edelman. * * * The educational components * * * are plainly designed to wipe out continuing conditions of inequality produced by the inherently unequal dual school system long maintained by Detroit.

" * * * That the programs are also 'compensatory' in nature does not change the fact that they are part of a plan that operates *prospectively* to bring about the delayed benefits of a unitary school system".

Wasn't the decree in Milliken II just as much an effort to redress past violations as the award of retroactive benefits in Edelman? Is Milliken distinguishable because the order required the state to purchase services for (rather than to pay cash to) the plaintiffs? Because the payments in Milliken would be made over a long period, giving more time for budgetary planning? Because of the continuing effects of past violations?[10]

Consider whether it helps in understanding Milliken II to recall the history of the Supreme Court's efforts to eradicate school segregation and that the order that was upheld took the place of an earlier multidistrict busing order.[11]

(d) The Special Treatment of Attorney's Fees Awards. In Hutto v. Finney, 437 U.S. 678 (1978), the district court—after finding that conditions in the Arkansas penal system constituted cruel and unusual punishment and issuing various injunctive orders over the course of seven years—had ruled

---

[8]   See, *e.g.*, Board of Liquidation v. McComb, 92 U.S. 531 (1875); Tindal v. Wesley, 167 U.S. 204 (1897); Rolston v. Mo. Fund Comm'rs, 120 U.S. 390 (1887).

[9]   See, *e.g.*, Kendall v. United States, 37 U.S. (12 Pet.) 524 (1838); Roberts v. United States ex rel. Valentine, 176 U.S. 221 (1900).

[10]   In Papasan v. Allain, 478 U.S. 265 (1986), Mississippi officials were sued for allegedly underfunding certain public schools. The Court held, 5–4, that a theory of recovery based on a long-standing and continuing breach of trust, in violation of federal law, was barred by the Eleventh Amendment, but held unanimously that another theory—that the State's *current* school funding methods denied equal protection—was not barred.

[11]   Decisions subsequent to Edelman have struggled to draw the line between retrospective relief that is barred by the Eleventh Amendment, even when a suit names a state official as the defendant, and prospective relief that is not barred. Compare Quern v. Jordan, 440 U.S. 332 (1979) (finding no bar to requiring defendants to apprise class members of state administrative procedures through which they might seek retroactive benefits), with Green v. Mansour, 474 U.S. 64 (1985) (ruling that plaintiffs' request for a declaratory judgment that the defendants' past conduct was unlawful, together with notice relief as in Quern, was barred by the Eleventh Amendment after the defendants had come into compliance with federal law).

that defendant officials had acted in bad faith and ordered them to pay $20,000 "out of Department of Correction funds" to plaintiffs' attorneys. In upholding that fee award, the Supreme Court stressed the importance of enforcing federal court orders, and held that "[t]he power to impose a fine is properly treated as ancillary to the federal court's power to impose injunctive relief. In this case, the award of attorney's fees for bad faith served the same purpose as a remedial fine imposed for civil contempt. It vindicated the District Court's authority over a recalcitrant litigant." The Court also observed that the compensatory effect of the award did not distinguish it from a fine for civil contempt, and the award was not so large "that it interfered with the State's budgeting process". In a footnote, the Court added: "We do not understand the Attorney General to urge that the fees should have been awarded against the officers personally; that would be a remarkable way to treat individuals who have relied on the Attorney General to represent their interests throughout this litigation."

Hutto also upheld a second award of attorneys' fees on the distinct theory that Congress, in authorizing fee awards to plaintiffs prevailing in actions under federal civil rights legislation enacted (in part) pursuant to § 5 of the Fourteenth Amendment, had abrogated any Eleventh Amendment immunity. See pp. 958–962, *infra.* But in so ruling, the Court noted that "[c]osts have traditionally been awarded without regard for the States' Eleventh Amendment immunity," and though the precedents predate Edelman, such awards "do not seriously strain" the retrospective-prospective distinction; "[w]hen a State defends a suit for prospective relief, it is not exempt from the ordinary discipline of the courtroom".

Hutto

    (e) States as Named Defendants. Although Ex parte Young held the Eleventh Amendment inapplicable to a suit seeking injunctive relief against a state officer, the Eleventh Amendment does bar unconsented suits against the states themselves, including those in which the plaintiffs seek injunctive relief only. See, *e.g.,* Alabama v. Pugh, 438 U.S. 781 (1978) (per curiam). In other words, the doctrine and rationale of Ex parte Young require plaintiffs to sue state officials, not the state in its own name, in order to avoid the Eleventh Amendment's prohibition.

(4) The Continuing Vitality of Ex parte Young.

    (a) Although Young has been a feature of the constitutional landscape since 1908, and one that many have regarded as being as important as if not more important than Hans v. Louisiana—see, *e.g.,* Monaghan, *The Sovereign Immunity "Exception,"* 110 Harv.L.Rev. 102 (1996)—its continuing force came into question in Idaho v. Coeur d'Alene Tribe, 521 U.S. 261 (1997). The plaintiffs (an Indian Tribe and several of its members) brought a federal court action against state officials and agencies, and the state itself, seeking declaratory and injunctive relief based on a claim of ownership of certain submerged and related lands. As the case came to the Supreme Court, only the state officers, who had been sued in their individual capacities, remained as defendants, but the majority held (5–4) that suit against them was barred by the Eleventh Amendment.

    In what the Justices referred to as the "principal opinion", Justice Kennedy contended that over the years, the doctrine of Ex parte Young had become an essentially discretionary one in which the federal courts—in determining whether suit against an officer was permitted—looked to a variety of factors in striking an appropriate balance. But the relevant sections of Justice Kennedy's opinion were joined only by Chief Justice

Rehnquist, and seven other Justices expressly rejected them. Justice O'Connor, in a concurring opinion joined by Justices Scalia and Thomas, took pains to disavow Justice Kennedy's effort to "recharacterize[ ] and narrow[ ] much of our Young jurisprudence". And Justice Souter, writing for four Justices in dissent, argued vigorously that the case was governed by a long tradition of allowing suits for prospective relief against government officers as a means of testing whether those officers were complying with federal law.

Nevertheless, four other Justices joined Justice Kennedy in Part III of his opinion, in which he found "the Young exception inapplicable" under the "particular circumstances" that the case presented, involving the state's special concern—deeply rooted in English history—for its sovereign control of submerged lands and the extraordinarily intrusive effect on state interests that a judgment for the plaintiffs would have.[12]

How convincing was Justice Kennedy's effort—which was embraced and expanded upon by Justice O'Connor's concurring opinion—to create a special categorical exception to Ex parte Young? In thinking about this question, consider whether it has not always been the case that at least some officer suits have been deemed to be barred by sovereign immunity.

(b) The Court's later decision in Verizon Maryland Inc. v. Public Service Commission, 535 U.S. 635 (2002), confirmed that the core of the Young doctrine is still alive and well, even in cases involving federal statutory rights. Verizon had filed a federal court action against a state agency, its members (in their official capacity), and others, seeking declaratory and injunctive relief on the basis that an agency decision violated both a federal statute and a federal agency ruling. A unanimous Supreme Court, in an opinion by Justice Scalia, held that the Young doctrine allowed Verizon to proceed against the individual commissioners. In a short concurring opinion speaking this time only for himself, Justice Kennedy reiterated the view he had expressed in Coeur d'Alene that "our Ex parte Young jurisprudence requires careful consideration of the sovereign interests of the State as well as the obligations of state officials to respect the supremacy of federal law".[13]

---

[12] Dissenting, Justice Souter commented that "Idaho indisputably has a significant sovereign interest in regulating its submerged lands, but it has no legitimate sovereign interest in regulating submerged lands located outside state borders".

[13] In Virginia Office for Protection and Advocacy v. Stewart, 131 S.Ct. 1632 (2011), the Court relied on Ex parte Young to hold, by 6–2, that sovereign immunity did not bar a suit for prospective relief brought against a state official by an agency of the same state. Although acknowledging that "the relative novelty" of the lawsuit "does give us pause", Justice Scalia's opinion for the Court concluded that "there is no warrant in our cases for making the validity of an Ex parte Young action turn on the identity of the plaintiff." Justice Kennedy, joined by Justice Thomas, concurred in the Court's opinion but also wrote separately to reiterate his view that correct application of Ex parte Young required a balancing test sensitive to "the need to preserve 'the dignity and respect afforded a State, which [sovereign] immunity is designed to protect' " (quoting Idaho v. Coeur d'Alene Tribe, supra). Among pertinent considerations, Justice Kennedy emphasized that "state law must authorize an agency or official to sue another arm of the State" in order for a state agency to sue a state official.

Chief Justice Roberts, joined by Justice Alito, dissented. In his view, the "fiction" of Ex parte Young constituted " 'a narrow exception' to a State's sovereign immunity", the extension of which was unjustified. In Alden v. Maine, p. 967, infra, the Court had held that Congress could not force an unconsenting state to defend itself in a suit in its own courts: "Here extending Young" subjected the state to the greater indignity of being required "to defend itself against itself in federal court." Chief Justice Roberts did not question, however, that a state court would need to entertain a suit by a state agency against a state official seeking prospective relief under federal law. Is the Chief Justice's concession of that point consistent with his reliance on Alden to oppose the "extension" of Ex parte Young?

(5) Revisionist Interpretations of Ex parte Young and Their Possible Implications. (a) In a forceful attack on the conventional wisdom concerning Ex parte Young, Harrison, *Ex Parte Young*, 60 Stan.L.Rev. 989 (2008), argues that Young did not "rest on a novel cause of action derived from the Fourteenth Amendment." Rather, he writes, the plaintiff asserted a traditional, equitable cause of action to enjoin a prosecution on the basis of what would have been a valid defense at law; that equitable cause of action would today be classified as arising under state law; and federal jurisdiction was proper, despite the absence of diversity, only because equity pleading rules required the plaintiff to recite his Fourteenth Amendment defense at law on the face of his well-pleaded complaint in equity.[14]

Taking stock of the debate about the source of the cause of action in Ex parte Young as it is now framed, Shapiro, *Ex parte Young and the Uses of History*, 67 N.Y.U.Ann.Surv.Am.L. 69 (2011), hypothesizes that scholars who have characterized Young as either dramatically pathbreaking or as marking no extension of traditional federal equitable practice have done so based on ideologically charged preferences and expectations. Relying heavily on the work of Professor Woolhandler, cited in notes 1 and 2, *supra*, as well as on case law and treatises available at the time of the Young decision, Shapiro depicts Young as being situated in but not the culmination of "two gradual transitions: (1) from the granting of relief against wrongs to tangible property to the granting of relief against the constitutional wrong of enforcing an invalid law, and (2) from the development of remedies without concern over the source of law to the federalization, and even constitutionalization, of those same forms of relief." He concludes: "[A]rguments about the case have become a proxy for a more important debate: To what extent, if any, should federal law (especially the Constitution) be available for use not only as a shield against state action but as a sword, and to what extent should litigants be able to unsheathe that sword in a suit against a state or local government, or its officers, in federal court? Young is certainly not irrelevant to that debate, but its significance should not be exaggerated." Notably, even Professor Harrison does not deny that a number of post-Young cases have upheld causes of action for injunctive relief directly under the Constitution (without adverting to 42 U.S.C. § 1983, which is discussed in Section 2(B), *infra*, and would today supply an alternative basis for the cause of action). Rather, his thesis appears to be that the generative force of Ex parte Young in supporting

---

[14] Harrison's argument that the Young recognized no cause of action directly under the Fourteenth Amendment depends heavily on his claim that federal question jurisdiction over the case could be supported based on the presence of a federal element in Young's well-pleaded complaint asserting a common law cause of action. The idea that federal question jurisdiction could exist in the absence of a federal cause of action would be incompatible with what Justice Holmes stated to be the controlling standard eight years later in American Well Works Co. v. Layne & Bowler Co., 241 U.S. 257 (1916), p. 816, *supra*, but consistent with the Court's position five years after that in Smith v. Kansas City Title & Trust Co., 255 U.S. 180 (1921), p. 821, *supra*.

Note, *Pleading Sovereign Immunity: The Doctrinal Underpinnings of Hans v. Louisiana and Ex Parte Young,* 61 Stan.L.Rev. 1233 (2009), echoes Professor Harrison's assertion that Ex parte Young reflected a standard application of nineteenth century pleading conventions but offers a different account of those conventions. The Note also argues more broadly that pleading conventions—rather than concerns about state treasuries or a tort/contract distinction—were the "mainspring" that drove sovereign immunity doctrine up to and including Hans v. Louisiana and Ex parte Young.

constitutional causes of action has rested on a misunderstanding of the original decision.[15]

(b) Whereas the plaintiffs in Ex parte Young alleged that a state statute conflicted with the Fourteenth Amendment, in other cases plaintiffs have alleged that state officials' violation of federal statutory law is also necessarily a violation of the Supremacy Clause. In Douglas v. Independent Living Center of Southern California, 132 S.Ct. 1204 (2012), Chief Justice Roberts, in a dissenting opinion joined by three other Justices, maintained that no cause of action would lie under the Supremacy Clause. Quoting an earlier opinion that cited Professor Harrison's article, the Chief Justice distinguished Ex parte Young and similar subsequent cases on the ground that they "present[ed] quite different questions involving 'the pre-emptive assertion in equity of a defense that would otherwise have been available in the State's enforcement proceedings at law.' " Justice Breyer's majority opinion did not reach the Supremacy Clause issue that the Court had granted certiorari to address, but instead remanded the case to the lower court to consider the pertinence of intervening developments in framing the question presented. For further discussion, see p. 1012, *infra*.

Either the position of the Douglas dissent or a close analogue commanded a majority of the Court in Armstrong v. Exceptional Child Center, Inc., 135 S.Ct. 1378 (2015), in which Justice Scalia, joined by the Chief Justice and Justices Thomas, Breyer, and Alito, rejected a direct suit under the Supremacy Clause to enforce purported state obligations to increase payments to care providers under the Medicaid Act: "The ability to sue to enjoin unconstitutional actions by state and federal officers is the creation of courts of equity, and reflects a long history of judicial review of illegal executive action, tracing back to England. It is a judge-made remedy, and we have never held or even suggested that, in its application to state officers, it rests upon an implied right of action contained under the Supremacy Clause." The Armstrong majority further concluded that the Medicaid Act impliedly precluded any equitable cause of action that otherwise might have existed through its authorization of an alternative remedy, the withholding of Medicaid funds by the Secretary of Health and Human Services. In a dissenting opinion joined by Justices Kennedy, Ginsburg, and Kagan, Justice Sotomayor acknowledged that "it is somewhat misleading to speak of 'an implied right of action contained in the Supremacy Clause,'" but she also maintained that the suit before the Court "falls comfortably within th[e] doctrine", exemplified by Ex parte Young, under which "parties may call upon the federal courts to enjoin unconstitutional government action." She also quoted a prior decision asserting that "[a] claim that a state law contravenes a federal statute is 'basically constitutional in nature, deriving its force from the operation of the Supremacy Clause'". She further noted that "we have characterized 'the availability of prospective relief of the sort awarded in Ex parte Young' as giving 'life to the Supremacy Clause.'"

If the cause of action in Ex parte Young were grounded in the Fourteenth Amendment, it might be argued that suits to enforce the Supremacy Clause present distinctive considerations. But much of the Court's language appears to contemplate that all suits for injunctive relief

---

[15] For a variety of perspectives on Young and its significance, see *Ex parte Young Symposium: A Centennial Recognition*, 40 U.Tol.L.Rev. 819 (2009) (including articles by Professors Bobroff, Copeland, Leonard, McCormick, Purcell, Sloss, and Solimine).

against unconstitutional official action, whether state or federal, seek a "judge-made remedy" that is the creation of courts of equity, not the Constitution. What implications, if any, might adoption of that broad position hold for the future of injunctive actions to enforce the First or Fourteenth Amendment when Congress has failed to authorize suits for injunctions or has provided alternative remedies such as a funds cut-off to state agencies that violate constitutional rights or a suit for damages under the Federal Tort Claims Act? Note, too, that the Supreme Court has frequently recognized causes of action directly under the Supremacy Clause to enjoin the coercive enforcement of a state statute that is allegedly preempted by federal statutory law. See pp. 810, 844–845, *supra*.[16]

NOTE ON THE PENNHURST CASE AND THE BEARING OF THE ELEVENTH AMENDMENT ON FEDERAL COURT RELIEF FOR VIOLATIONS OF STATE LAW

(1) The Facts and Opinions in the Pennhurst Case. In Pennhurst State School & Hosp. v. Halderman, 465 U.S. 89 (1984), the Court sharply restricted federal court authority in suits against state officials for violations of *state* law. In this case, a resident of a Pennsylvania state institution for the developmentally disabled (Pennhurst) filed a federal class action seeking injunctive relief against the institution and various state and county officials, alleging that conditions at Pennhurst violated federal statutory and constitutional requirements, as well as state law.

On its initial review in 1981, the Supreme Court held that there was no basis for relief under one provision of federal law, but remanded for determination whether plaintiffs might be entitled to relief on other grounds. Pennhurst State School & Hosp. v. Halderman, 451 U.S. 1 (1981). On remand, the Third Circuit en banc affirmed its prior judgment, ruling that state law required the award of certain injunctive relief (ordering the placement of residents in the least restrictive setting).

In 1984, the Supreme Court again reversed, holding (5–4) that the Eleventh Amendment barred injunctive relief based on state law. Justice Powell wrote for the Court:

"The Eleventh Amendment bars a suit against state officials when 'the state is the real substantial party in interest' [quoting Ford Motor Co. v. Department of Treasury, 323 U.S. 459, 464 (1945)]. * * *

"The Court has recognized an important exception to this general rule: a suit challenging the constitutionality of a state official's action is not one against the State. This was the holding in Ex parte Young * * *. The theory of the case was that an unconstitutional enactment is 'void' and therefore does not 'impart to [the officer] any immunity from responsibility to the supreme authority of the United States.' Since the State could not authorize the action, the officer was 'stripped of his official or representative character and [was] subjected to the consequences of his individual conduct.' * * * [T]he Young doctrine has been accepted as necessary to permit the federal courts

-----

See also Yackle, *Young Again*, 35 U.Haw.L.Rev. 51, 58 (2013) ("It is arguable that Young proceeded from the premise that a claim that state rail rates conflicted with the Federal Constitution could be advanced under the authority of the Supremacy Clause.").

to vindicate federal rights and hold state officials responsible to 'the supreme authority of the United States.' Young, 209 U.S., at 160. * * *

"The Court also has recognized, however, that the need to promote the supremacy of federal law must be accommodated to the constitutional immunity of the States. This is the significance of Edelman v. Jordan * * *, [where] we declined to extend the fiction of Young to encompass retroactive relief, for to do so would effectively eliminate the constitutional immunity of the States. * * *

"This need to reconcile competing interests is wholly absent, however, when a plaintiff alleges that a state official has violated *state* law. * * * [Relief in such a case] does not vindicate the supreme authority of federal law. On the contrary, it is difficult to think of a greater intrusion on state sovereignty than when a federal court instructs state officials on how to conform their conduct to state law. Such a result conflicts directly with the principles of federalism that underlie the Eleventh Amendment. We conclude that Young and Edelman are inapplicable in a suit against state officials on the basis of state law."

The Court then discussed the impact of its ruling on the doctrine of pendent (now supplemental) jurisdiction:

"As the Court of Appeals noted, in Siler [v. Louisville & Nashville R.R., 213 U.S. 175 (1909)], and subsequent cases concerning pendent jurisdiction, relief was granted against state officials on the basis of state-law claims that were pendent to federal constitutional claims. In none of these cases, however, did the Court so much as mention the Eleventh Amendment in connection with the state-law claim". As for plaintiffs' argument that the Court's ruling "may cause litigants to split causes of action between state and federal courts" and could undercut the policy of constitutional avoidance by denying federal courts the opportunity to premise relief on state law grounds, Justice Powell responded that pendent jurisdiction was a "judge-made doctrine of expediency and efficiency" and that "neither pendent jurisdiction nor any other basis of jurisdiction may override the Eleventh Amendment".

Justice Stevens, joined by Justices Brennan, Marshall, and Blackmun, filed an unusually long and bitter dissent. He discussed a number of prior decisions supporting the proposition that the Eleventh Amendment does not bar suits alleging that state officials have acted tortiously as a matter of state law, or in violation of state statutes, and then turned to the relevance of Ex parte Young:

"The majority states that the holding of Ex parte Young is limited to cases in which relief is provided on the basis of federal law, and that it rests entirely on the need to protect the supremacy of federal law. That position overlooks the foundation of the rule of Young * * *.

"The pivotal consideration in Young was that it was not conduct of the sovereign that was at issue. The rule that unlawful acts of an officer should not be attributed to the sovereign has deep roots in the history of sovereign immunity and makes Young reconcilable with the principles of sovereign immunity found in the Eleventh Amendment, rather than merely an unprincipled accommodation between federal and state interests that ignores the principles contained in the Eleventh Amendment.

"This rule plainly applies to conduct of state officers in violation of state law. Young states that the significance of the charge of unconstitutional conduct is that it renders the state official's conduct 'simply an illegal act,' and hence the officer is not entitled to the sovereign's immunity. Since a state officer's conduct in violation of state law is certainly no less illegal than his violation of federal law, in either case the official, by committing an illegal act, is 'stripped of his official or representative character.' * * *

"That the doctrine of sovereign immunity does not protect conduct which has been prohibited by the sovereign is clearly demonstrated by the [Larson case, see p. 893, *supra*], on which petitioners chiefly rely. The Larson opinion teaches that the actions of state officials are not attributable to the state— are *ultra vires*—in two different types of situations: (1) when the official is engaged in conduct that the sovereign has not authorized, and (2) when he has engaged in conduct that the sovereign has forbidden. A sovereign, like any other principal, cannot authorize its agent to violate the law. * * *

" * * * Under the second track of the Larson analysis, petitioners were acting *ultra vires*, because they were acting in a way that the sovereign, by statute, had forbidden."

Finally, Justice Stevens objected to the overruling of cases exercising pendent jurisdiction over state law claims against state officials. Such jurisdiction, he argued, not only serves the policy of constitutional avoidance, but "enhances the decisionmaking autonomy of the States * * * [by directing] the federal court to turn first to state law, which the State is free to modify or repeal." By contrast, under the Court's opinion, "federal courts are required to resolve cases on federal grounds that no state authority can undo".

(2) The Holding of Pennhurst. What exactly is the holding of Pennhurst? The majority opinion does not appear to question that the state, if it chose, could waive any immunity that might otherwise protect its officials from suit, either in state or in federal court. But it establishes a rigid presumption that states would wish to clothe their officials with immunity from suits in federal court that seek to enjoin compliance with state law unless the legislature has expressly said otherwise. Is this an appropriate allocation of the burden of proof?

(3) The Implications of Pennhurst.

(a) Consider the options open after Pennhurst to a litigant who has plausible claims under both state and federal law for equitable relief against a course of ongoing state action. She is free, of course, to file in state court under both state and federal law—but to do so she must forgo her right under § 1331 to a federal forum for her federal cause of action.[1] A plaintiff may instead file the federal claim in federal court. But to do so, she must either forgo her state law claim altogether, or file a second lawsuit in state court asserting the state law claim. Even if she can afford to file two separate lawsuits, the result is patently inefficient for the judicial system and the litigants, and it may deprive the federal court of the chance to avoid a constitutional decision. And it raises further complications:

(i) Should one court stay its hand while the other proceeds? See generally Chap. X, Sec. 2(D), *infra*. If so, what standards govern whether the federal court, or the state court, should abstain? See Werhan, *Pullman*

---

[1]   On the consequences if the defendant then removes the case to federal court, see p. 920, *supra* (discussing Lapides v. Board of Regents, 535 U.S. 613 (2002), and Wisconsin Dep't of Corrections v. Schact, 524 U.S. 381 (1998)).

Abstention After Pennhurst: A Comment on Judicial Federalism, 27 Wm. & Mary L.Rev. 449 (1986).

(ii) Suppose the state court action comes to judgment first. At a minimum, the doctrine of issue preclusion may prevent the plaintiff from obtaining an independent federal court adjudication of issues in her federal lawsuit. It is also possible that the entire federal action might be barred by a plea of claim preclusion. See Chap. XII, pp. 1377–1387, *infra*.

Is any satisfactory option left open after Pennhurst? If not, consider the suggestion of Professor Shapiro that "the eleventh amendment and sovereign immunity are inappropriately blunt instruments for dealing with" collisions of state and individual interests when "[o]ther, more precise * * * nonconstitutional doctrines of restraint" are available. Shapiro, *Wrong Turns: The Eleventh Amendment and the Pennhurst Case*, 98 Harv.L.Rev. 61, 79 (1984).

(b) Will it always be clear whether a federal injunction should be characterized as resting on state law (and hence barred by Pennhurst) or federal law (and hence permissible under Young and Edelman)? Consider, for example, the Individuals with Disabilities Education Act, 20 U.S.C. §§ 1400–82, which conditions federal assistance upon a state's adopting a plan (that must be federally approved) for ensuring to handicapped children the right to a free public education. May a district court award prospective relief upon a finding that state officials have not complied with state law requirements in a federally approved plan, even if that plan provides greater protection to handicapped pupils than is minimally required under federal law?[2]

(4) Suits Against Local Officers. Though local governments and their officials have no Eleventh Amendment immunity, see pp. 921–922, *supra*, the Court in Pennhurst refused to leave standing a judgment against the defendant county officials: "[e]ven assuming" that they have no immunity, the relief ordered relates to an institution run and funded by the state; the state law under which relief had been ordered "contemplates that the state and county officials will cooperate in operating mental retardation programs"; and any relief against the county officials would be partial and incomplete. But the Court has not read Pennhurst as casting doubt upon courts' authority to award relief under state law against local government officials absent some significant effect on the *state* treasury. See Regents of the Univ. of Cal. v. Doe, 519 U.S. 425, 431 (1997).[3]

---

[2]   For an exploration of Pennhurst's impact on suits to enforce federal requirements in cooperative state-federal programs, see Babcock, *The Effect of the Supreme Court's Eleventh Amendment Jurisprudence on Clean Water Act Citizen's Suits*, 83 Or.L.Rev. 47 (2004). Noting that the Clean Water Act gives the states primary responsibility for implementing certain federal policies, Professor Babcock suggests that Pennhurst may effectively thwart use of the Act's citizen suit provision, in either state or federal court, to remedy state violations of federal policies.

[3]   For discussion of Pennhurst, in addition to the articles already cited, see Althouse, *How to Build a Separate Sphere: Federal Courts and State Power*, 100 Harv.L.Rev. 1485 (1987); Brown, *Beyond Pennhurst: Protective Jurisdiction, the Eleventh Amendment, and the Power of Congress to Enlarge Federal Jurisdiction in Response to the Burger Court*, 71 Va.L.Rev. 343 (1985); Dwyer, *Pendent Jurisdiction and the Eleventh Amendment*, 75 Cal.L.Rev. 129 (1987); Rudenstine, *Pennhurst and the Scope of Federal Judicial Power to Reform Social Institutions*, 6 Cardozo L.Rev. 71 (1984).

PRELIMINARY NOTE ON CONGRESSIONAL POWER TO ABROGATE STATE IMMUNITY FROM SUIT

(1) Distinguishing "Abrogation" from "Waiver". Although Hans v. Louisiana held that the states' sovereign or Eleventh Amendment immunity constitutes a barrier to unconsented suits in federal court seeking to enforce the Constitution and laws of the United States, Hans had no occasion to consider whether Congress has power to remove or "abrogate" that barrier. In thinking about that question, recall the long-settled understanding that the states can voluntarily "waive" their Eleventh Amendment immunity. When, if ever, should an immunity that is subject to waiver by the state also be subject to abrogation by the national government, over the states' objection? The Supreme Court has confronted this question in a number of cases.

(2) A False Start: The Parden Case. The Court framed the question whether Congress has the power to abrogate the states' Eleventh Amendment immunity, but then failed to give a clear answer, in Parden v. Terminal Ry., 377 U.S. 184 (1964). Parden rejected (5–4) Alabama's claim of immunity from an employee's federal court negligence action under the Federal Employers' Liability Act (FELA) against a state-owned railway. Writing for the majority, Justice Brennan began by stating that the case presented two questions: "(1) Did Congress in enacting the FELA intend to subject a State to suit in these circumstances? (2) Did it have power to do so, as against the State's claim of immunity?" The Court clearly answered the first question in the affirmative. It then purported to answer the second in the affirmative as well, but its analysis confusingly conflated an abrogation theory ("imposition of the FELA right of action upon interstate railroads * * * cannot be precluded by sovereign immunity") with a theory of waiver or implied state consent ("Alabama, when it began operation of an interstate railroad * * * [after enactment of the FELA] necessarily consented to such suit as was authorized by that Act"). Parden thus left it uncertain whether, in the absence of actual or some kind of implied consent, Congress could strip the states of their immunity from suit when legislating under Article I. (The Supreme Court has subsequently overruled Parden. See p. 966, *infra*).

(3) Congressional Power to Abrogate Under § 5 of the Fourteenth Amendment: Fitzpatrick v. Bitzer. The Court did deal squarely with the power of Congress to abrogate state immunity in Fitzpatrick v. Bitzer, 427 U.S. 445 (1976), a federal court action alleging that Connecticut's retirement plan discriminated against male employees in violation of Title VII of the 1964 Civil Rights Act. (Title VII regulates any "person" employing the requisite number of employees in interstate commerce; in 1972 Congress amended the definition of "person" to include state and local "governments, governmental agencies, [and] political subdivisions.") The Supreme Court, per Rehnquist, J., held that the Eleventh Amendment did not bar an award of retroactive retirement benefits and attorney's fees under Title VII, to be paid from the state treasury, as long as "the 'threshold fact of congressional authorization' * * * is clearly present", as it was in this case.

In explaining the Court's ruling, Justice Rehnquist emphasized that the 1972 amendment was enacted pursuant to § 5 of the Fourteenth Amendment. That Amendment as a whole represented a "shift in the federal-state balance [that] has been carried forward by more recent decisions of this Court," and past decisions had "sanctioned intrusions by Congress, acting under the Civil War Amendments, into the judicial, executive, and legislative spheres of autonomy previously preserved to the States". Justice Rehnquist continued:

"It is true that none of these previous cases presented the question of the relationship between the Eleventh Amendment and the enforcement power granted to Congress under § 5 of the Fourteenth Amendment. But we think that the Eleventh Amendment, and the principle of state sovereignty which it embodies, are necessarily limited by the enforcement provisions of § 5 of the Fourteenth Amendment. In that section Congress is expressly granted authority to enforce 'by appropriate legislation' the substantive provisions of the Fourteenth Amendment, which themselves embody significant limitations on state authority. When Congress acts pursuant to § 5, not only is it exercising legislative authority that is plenary within the terms of the constitutional grant, it is exercising that authority under one section of a constitutional Amendment whose other sections by their own terms embody limitations on state authority. We think that Congress may, in determining what is 'appropriate legislation' for the purpose of enforcing the provisions of the Fourteenth Amendment, provide for private suits against States or state officials which are constitutionally impermissible in other contexts."

(4) Union Gas. In Pennsylvania v. Union Gas, 491 U.S. 1 (1989), the Court held (5–4) that Congress can abrogate state immunity from federal court suit in the exercise of its power under the Commerce Clause—and that it had done so in the environmental statutes there at issue. Justice Brennan, who wrote for the plurality, argued that the states had ceded their sovereignty to Congress insofar as the Constitution vests Congress with power to regulate the states, and he concluded that the Eleventh Amendment posed no bar to suits to enforce federal law when Congress has abrogated the states' immunity.

The necessary fifth vote for the Court's ruling concerning Congress' abrogation power came from Justice White, who, in a cryptic opinion, declined to endorse the theory advanced by the plurality, or indeed any other theory, of Congress' power to abrogate the states' Eleventh Amendment immunity. He stated only that he concurred in the plurality's conclusion but did not agree "with much of [its] reasoning".

Seven years later, in the next principal case, the Court revisited the question of Congress' power to abrogate the states' immunity when legislating pursuant to Article I.

Seminole Tribe of Florida v. Florida

517 U.S. 44, 116 S.Ct. 1114, 134 L.Ed.2d 252 (1996).
Certiorari to the United States Court of Appeals for the Eleventh Circuit.

■ CHIEF JUSTICE REHNQUIST delivered the opinion of the Court.

The Indian Gaming Regulatory Act provides that an Indian tribe may conduct certain gaming activities only in conformance with a valid compact between the tribe and the State in which the gaming activities are located. 25 U.S.C. § 2710(d)(1)(C). The Act, passed by Congress under the Indian Commerce Clause, imposes upon the States a duty to negotiate in good faith with an Indian tribe toward the formation of a compact, § 2710(d)(3)(A), and authorizes a tribe to bring suit in federal court against a State in order to compel performance of that duty, § 2710(d)(7). We hold that notwithstanding Congress' clear intent to abrogate the States' sovereign immunity, the Indian Commerce Clause does not grant Congress that power, and therefore § 2710(d)(7) cannot grant jurisdiction over a State that does not consent to be sued. We further hold that the doctrine of Ex parte Young, 209 U.S. 123 (1908), may not be used to enforce § 2710(d)(3) against a state official.

I

Congress passed the Indian Gaming Regulatory Act in 1988 in order to provide a statutory basis for the operation and regulation of gaming by Indian tribes. The Act [provides that certain types of gaming on Indian lands, including that involved in this case, are lawful only if they are authorized by a tribe, satisfy federal statutory requirements, and are] "conducted in conformance with a Tribal-State compact entered into by the Indian tribe and the State under paragraph (3) that is in effect." § 2710(d)(1).

The "paragraph (3)" to which the last prerequisite of § 2710(d)(1) refers is § 2710(d)(3), which describes the permissible scope of a Tribal-State compact, and provides that the compact is effective "only when notice of approval by the Secretary [of the Interior] of such compact has been published by the Secretary in the Federal Register." More significant for our purposes, however, is that § 2710(d)(3) describes the process by which a State and an Indian tribe begin negotiations toward a Tribal-State compact:

> "(A) Any Indian tribe having jurisdiction over the Indian lands upon which a class III gaming activity is being conducted, or is to be conducted, shall request the State in which such lands are located to enter into negotiations for the purpose of entering into a Tribal-State compact governing the conduct of gaming activities. Upon receiving such a request, the State shall negotiate with the Indian tribe in good faith to enter into such a compact."

The State's obligation to "negotiate with the Indian tribe in good faith," is made judicially enforceable by §§ 2710(d)(7)(A)(i) and (B)(i):

> "(A) The United States district courts shall have jurisdiction over—

> "(i) any cause of action initiated by an Indian tribe arising from the failure of a State to enter into negotiations with the Indian tribe for the purpose of entering into a Tribal-State compact under paragraph (3) or to conduct such negotiations in good faith. . . .

> "(B)(i) An Indian tribe may initiate a cause of action described in subparagraph (A)(i) only after the close of the 180-day period beginning on the date on which the Indian tribe requested the State to enter into negotiations under paragraph (3)(A)."

Sections 2710(d)(7)(B)(ii)–(vii) describe an elaborate remedial scheme designed to ensure the formation of a Tribal-State compact. A tribe that brings an action under § 2710(d)(7)(A)(i) must show that no Tribal-State compact has been entered and that the State failed to respond in good faith to the tribe's request to negotiate * * *. If the district court concludes that the State has failed to negotiate in good faith toward the formation of a Tribal-State compact, then it "shall order the State and Indian tribe to conclude such a compact within a 60-day period." § 2710(d)(7)(B)(iii). If no compact has been concluded 60 days after the court's order, then "the Indian tribe and the State shall each submit to a mediator appointed by the court a proposed compact that represents their last best offer for a compact." The mediator chooses from between the two proposed compacts the one "which best comports with the terms of [the Act] and any other applicable Federal law and with the findings and order of the court," and submits it to the State and the Indian tribe. If the State consents to the proposed compact within 60 days of its submission by the mediator, then the proposed compact is "treated as a Tribal-State compact entered into under paragraph (3)." If, however, the State does not consent within that 60-day period, then the Act provides that the mediator "shall notify the Secretary [of the Interior]" and that the Secretary "shall prescribe . . . procedures . . . under which class III gaming may be conducted on the Indian lands over which the Indian tribe has jurisdiction."

In September 1991, the Seminole Tribe * * * sued the State of Florida and its Governor * * *. [P]etitioner alleged that respondents had * * * violat[ed] the "requirement of good faith negotiation" contained in § 2710(d)(3). Respondents moved to dismiss the complaint, arguing that the suit violated the State's sovereign immunity from suit in federal court. The District Court denied respondents' motion * * * [and on interlocutory appeal, the Eleventh Circuit reversed], holding that the Eleventh Amendment barred petitioner's suit against respondents. * * *

* * * [W]e granted certiorari, in order to consider two questions: (1) Does the Eleventh Amendment prevent Congress from authorizing suits by Indian tribes against States for prospective injunctive relief to enforce legislation enacted pursuant to the Indian Commerce Clause?; and (2) Does the doctrine of Ex parte Young permit suits against a State's governor for prospective injunctive relief to enforce the good faith bargaining requirement of the Act? * * *

Although the text of the [Eleventh] Amendment would appear to restrict only the Article III diversity jurisdiction of the federal courts, "we have understood the Eleventh Amendment to stand not so much for what it says, but for the presupposition . . . which it confirms." Blatchford v. Native Village of Noatak, 501 U.S. 775, 779 (1991). That presupposition, first observed over a century ago in Hans v. Louisiana, 134 U.S. 1 (1890), has two parts: first, that each State is a sovereign entity in our federal system; and second, that " 'it is inherent in the nature of sovereignty not to be amenable to the suit of an individual without its consent.' " Id., at 13 (emphasis deleted), quoting The Federalist No. 81 * * *. For over a century we have reaffirmed that federal jurisdiction over suits against unconsenting States "was not contemplated by the Constitution when establishing the judicial power of the United States." Hans, supra, at 15 [additional citations omitted]. * * *

II

Petitioner argues that Congress through the Act abrogated the States' immunity from suit. In order to determine whether Congress has abrogated the States' sovereign immunity, we ask two questions: first, whether Congress has "unequivocally expressed its intent to abrogate the immunity," Green v. Mansour, 474 U.S. 64, 68 (1985); and second, whether Congress has acted "pursuant to a valid exercise of power." *Ibid.*

A

* * * [W]e agree * * * that Congress has in § 2710(d)(7) provided an "unmistakably clear" statement of its intent to abrogate. * * *.

B

Having concluded that Congress clearly intended to abrogate the States' sovereign immunity through § 2710(d)(7), we turn now to consider whether the Act was passed "pursuant to a valid exercise of power." Green v. Mansour, 474 U.S. at 68. Before we address that question here, however, we think it necessary first to define the scope of our inquiry.

Petitioner suggests that one consideration weighing in favor of finding the power to abrogate here is that the Act authorizes only prospective injunctive relief rather than retroactive monetary relief. * * * [But] the Eleventh Amendment does not exist solely in order to "prevent federal court judgments that must be paid out of a State's treasury," Hess v. Port Authority Trans-Hudson Corporation, 513 U.S. 30 (1994); it also serves to avoid "the indignity of subjecting a State to the coercive process of judicial tribunals at the instance of private parties," Puerto Rico Aqueduct and Sewer Authority, 506 U.S. at 146 (internal quotation marks omitted). * * *

Thus our inquiry into whether Congress has the power to abrogate unilaterally the States' immunity from suit is narrowly focused on one question: Was the Act in question passed pursuant to a constitutional provision granting Congress the power to abrogate? See, *e.g.*, Fitzpatrick v. Bitzer, 427 U.S. 445, 452–456 (1976). Previously, in conducting that inquiry, we have found authority to abrogate under only two provisions of the Constitution. In Fitzpatrick, we recognized that the Fourteenth Amendment, by expanding federal power at the expense of state autonomy, had fundamentally altered the balance of state and federal power struck by the Constitution. We noted that § 1 of the Fourteenth Amendment contained prohibitions expressly directed at the States and that § 5 of the Amendment expressly provided that "The Congress shall have the power to enforce, by appropriate legislation, the provisions of this article." See *id.*, at 453 (internal quotation marks omitted). We held that through the Fourteenth Amendment, federal power extended to intrude upon the province of the Eleventh Amendment and therefore that § 5 of the Fourteenth Amendment allowed Congress to abrogate the immunity from suit guaranteed by that Amendment.

In only one other case has congressional abrogation of the States' Eleventh Amendment immunity been upheld. In Pennsylvania v. Union Gas Co., 491 U.S. 1 (1989), a plurality of the Court found that the Interstate Commerce Clause, granted Congress the power to abrogate state sovereign immunity, stating that the power to regulate interstate commerce would be "incomplete without the authority to render States liable in damages." Union Gas, 491 U.S. at 19–20. Justice White added the fifth vote necessary to the result in that case, but wrote separately in order to express that he "[did] not agree with much of [the plurality's] reasoning." *Id.*, at 57.

* * * [P]etitioner does not challenge the Eleventh Circuit's conclusion that the Act was passed pursuant to neither the Fourteenth Amendment nor the Interstate Commerce Clause. Instead, * * * petitioner now asks us to consider whether [the Indian Commerce] clause grants Congress the power to abrogate the States' sovereign immunity.

Both parties make their arguments from the plurality decision in Union Gas,* and we, too, begin there. * * * We agree with the petitioner that the plurality opinion in Union Gas allows no principled distinction in favor of the States to be drawn between the Indian Commerce Clause and the Interstate Commerce Clause.

Respondents argue, however, that * * * if we find the rationale of the Union Gas plurality to extend to the Indian Commerce Clause, then "Union Gas should be reconsidered and overruled." * * *

The Court in Union Gas reached a result without an expressed rationale agreed upon by a majority of the Court. * * * Justice White, who provided the fifth vote for the result, wrote separately in order to indicate his disagreement with the majority's [sic] rationale, and four Justices joined together in a dissent that rejected the plurality's rationale. Since it was issued, Union Gas has created confusion among the lower courts that have sought to understand and apply the deeply fractured decision. * * *

The plurality's rationale also deviated sharply from our established federalism jurisprudence and essentially eviscerated our decision in Hans. * * *

Never before the decision in Union Gas had we suggested that the bounds of Article III could be expanded by Congress operating pursuant to any constitutional provision other than the Fourteenth Amendment. Indeed, it had seemed fundamental that Congress could not expand the jurisdiction of the federal courts beyond the bounds of Article III. Marbury v. Madison, 5 U.S. 137, 1 Cranch 137 (1803). The plurality's citation of prior decisions for support was based upon what we believe to be a misreading of precedent. The plurality claimed support for its decision from a case holding the unremarkable, and completely unrelated, proposition that the States may waive their sovereign immunity, and cited as precedent propositions that had been merely assumed for the sake of argument in earlier cases, see 491 U.S. at 15.

The plurality's extended reliance upon our decision in Fitzpatrick v. Bitzer, that Congress could under the Fourteenth Amendment abrogate the States' sovereign immunity was also, we believe, misplaced. Fitzpatrick was based upon a rationale wholly inapplicable to the Interstate Commerce Clause, viz., that the Fourteenth Amendment, adopted well after the adoption of the Eleventh Amendment and the ratification of the Constitution, operated to alter the pre-existing balance

---

* [Ed.] Petitioner contended that "there is no principled basis for finding that congressional power under the Indian Commerce Clause is less than that conferred by the Interstate Commerce Clause", while respondents asserted that since the Indian Commerce Clause gives Congress *complete* authority over the Indian tribes, the abrogation power is not "necessary" to the exercise of authority under that clause.

between state and federal power achieved by Article III and the Eleventh Amendment. * * *

* * * Reconsidering the decision in Union Gas, we conclude that none of the policies underlying stare decisis require our continuing adherence to its holding. * * * We feel bound to conclude that Union Gas was wrongly decided and that it should be, and now is, overruled.

The dissent makes no effort to defend the decision in Union Gas, but nonetheless would find congressional power to abrogate in this case.[11] Contending that our decision is a novel extension of the Eleventh Amendment, the dissent chides us for "attending" to dicta. We adhere in this case, however, not to mere obiter dicta, but rather to the well-established rationale upon which the Court based the results of its earlier decisions. * * * [The Court at this point discussed Principality of Monaco v. Mississippi (p. 918, *supra*), Pennhurst State School & Hosp. v. Halderman (p. 935, *supra*), and Ex parte New York (p. 918, *supra*).] It is true that we have not had occasion previously to apply established Eleventh Amendment principles to the question whether Congress has the power to abrogate state sovereign immunity (save in Union Gas). But consideration of that question must proceed with fidelity to this century-old doctrine.

The dissent, to the contrary, disregards our case law in favor of a theory cobbled together from law review articles and its own version of historical events. The dissent cites not a single decision since Hans (other than Union Gas) that supports its view of state sovereign immunity, instead relying upon the now-discredited decision in Chisholm v. Georgia, 2 U.S. (2 Dall.) 419 (1793). Its undocumented and highly speculative extralegal explanation of the decision in Hans is a disservice to the Court's traditional method of adjudication.

The dissent mischaracterizes the Hans opinion. That decision found its roots not solely in the common law of England, but in the much more fundamental " 'jurisprudence in all civilized nations.' " Hans, 134 U.S. at 17, quoting Beers v. Arkansas, 61 U.S. (20 How.) 527, 529 (1858); see also The Federalist No. 81 (A. Hamilton) (sovereign immunity "is the general sense and the general practice of mankind"). The dissent's proposition that the common law of England, where adopted by the States, was open to change by the legislature, is wholly unexceptionable and largely beside the point: that common law provided the substantive rules of law rather than jurisdiction. * * * It also is noteworthy that the principle of state sovereign immunity stands distinct from other principles of the common law in that only the former prompted a specific constitutional amendment.

Hans—with a much closer vantage point than the dissent—recognized that the decision in Chisholm was contrary to the well-understood meaning of the Constitution. The dissent's conclusion that the decision in Chisholm was "reasonable," certainly would have struck the Framers of the Eleventh Amendment as quite odd: that decision created "such a shock of surprise that the Eleventh Amendment was at once proposed and adopted." Monaco, *supra*, at 325. The dissent's lengthy analysis of the text of the Eleventh Amendment is directed at a straw

---

[11] Unless otherwise indicated, all references to the dissent are to the dissenting opinion authored by Justice Souter.

man—we long have recognized that blind reliance upon the text of the Eleventh Amendment is " 'to strain the Constitution and the law to a construction never imagined or dreamed of.' " Monaco, 292 U.S. at 326, quoting Hans, 134 U.S. at 15. The text dealt in terms only with the problem presented by the decision in Chisholm; in light of the fact that the federal courts did not have federal question jurisdiction at the time the Amendment was passed (and would not have it until 1875), it seems unlikely that much thought was given to the prospect of federal question jurisdiction over the States.

That same consideration causes the dissent's criticism of the views of Marshall, Madison, and Hamilton to ring hollow. The dissent cites statements made by those three influential Framers, the most natural reading of which would preclude all federal jurisdiction over an unconsenting State.[12] Struggling against this reading, however, the dissent finds significant the absence of any contention that sovereign immunity would affect the new federal-question jurisdiction. But the lack of any statute vesting general federal question jurisdiction in the federal courts until much later makes the dissent's demand for greater specificity about a then-dormant jurisdiction overly exacting.

In putting forward a new theory of state sovereign immunity, the dissent develops its own vision of the political system created by the Framers, concluding with the statement that "the Framer's principal objectives in rejecting English theories of unitary sovereignty . . . would have been impeded if a new concept of sovereign immunity had taken its place in federal question cases, and would have been substantially thwarted if that new immunity had been held untouchable by any congressional effort to abrogate it."[14] This sweeping statement ignores the fact that the Nation survived for nearly two centuries without the question of the existence of such power ever being presented to this Court. And Congress itself waited nearly a century before even conferring federal question jurisdiction on the lower federal courts.

In overruling Union Gas today, we reconfirm that the background principle of state sovereign immunity embodied in the Eleventh Amendment is not so ephemeral as to dissipate when the subject of the suit is an area, like the regulation of Indian commerce, that is under the exclusive control of the Federal Government. Even when the Constitution vests in Congress complete law-making authority over a particular area, the Eleventh Amendment prevents congressional

---

[12] * * * [T]he dissent quotes selectively from the Framers' statements that it references. The dissent cites the following, for instance, as a statement made by Madison: "the Constitution 'gives a citizen a right to be heard in the federal courts; and if a state should condescend to be a party, this court may take cognizance of it.' " But that statement, perhaps ambiguous when read in isolation, was preceded by the following: "Jurisdiction in controversies between a state and citizens of another state is much objected to, and perhaps without reason. It is not in the power of individuals to call any state into court. The only operation it can have, is that, if a state should wish to bring a suit against a citizen, it must be brought before the federal courts. It appears to me that this can have no operation but this." See 3 Elliot, Debates on the Federal Constitution 67 (1866).

[14] This argument wholly disregards other methods of ensuring the States' compliance with federal law: the Federal Government can bring suit in federal court against a State; an individual can bring suit against a state officer in order to ensure that the officer's conduct is in compliance with federal law; and this Court is empowered to review a question of federal law arising from a state court decision where a State has consented to suit.

authorization of suits by private parties against unconsenting States.[16] * * * Petitioner's suit against the State of Florida must be dismissed for a lack of jurisdiction.

III

Petitioner argues that we may exercise jurisdiction over its suit to enforce § 2710(d)(3) against the Governor notwithstanding the jurisdictional bar of the Eleventh Amendment. Petitioner notes that since our decision in Ex parte Young, we often have found federal jurisdiction over a suit against a state official when that suit seeks only prospective injunctive relief in order to "end a continuing violation of federal law." Green v. Mansour, 474 U.S. at 68. The situation presented here, however, is sufficiently different from that giving rise to the traditional Ex parte Young action so as to preclude the availability of that doctrine.

* * * Where [as here] Congress has created a remedial scheme for the enforcement of a particular federal right, we have, in suits against federal officers, refused to supplement that scheme with one created by the judiciary. Schweiker v. Chilicky, 487 U.S. 412, 423 (1988) * * *. Here, of course, the question is not whether a remedy should be created, but instead is whether the Eleventh Amendment bar should be lifted, as it was in Ex parte Young, in order to allow a suit against a state officer. Nevertheless, we think that the same general principle applies * * *.

[After summarizing the statutory scheme described above, the Court continued:] By contrast with this quite modest set of sanctions, an action brought against a state official under Ex parte Young would expose that official to the full remedial powers of a federal court, including, presumably, contempt sanctions. If § 2710(d)(3) could be enforced in a suit under Ex parte Young, § 2710(d)(7) would have been superfluous; it is difficult to see why an Indian tribe would suffer through the intricate scheme of § 2710(d)(7) when more complete and more immediate relief would be available under Ex parte Young.[17]

Here, of course, we have found that Congress does not have authority under the Constitution to make the State suable in federal court under § 2710(d)(7). Nevertheless, the fact that Congress chose to impose upon the State a liability which is significantly more limited than would be the liability imposed upon the state officer under Ex parte Young strongly indicates that Congress had no wish to create the latter under § 2710(d)(3). Nor are we free to rewrite the statutory scheme in order to approximate what we think Congress might have wanted had it known

---

[16] Justice Stevens understands our opinion to prohibit federal jurisdiction over suits to enforce the bankruptcy, copyright, and antitrust laws against the States. He notes that federal jurisdiction over those statutory schemes is exclusive, and therefore concludes that there is "no remedy" for state violations of those federal statutes.

That conclusion is exaggerated both in its substance and in its significance. First, * * * [w]e have already seen that several avenues remain open for ensuring state compliance with federal law. See *supra*, at n. [14]. * * * Second, contrary to the implication of Justice Stevens' conclusion, it has not been widely thought that the federal antitrust, bankruptcy, or copyright statutes abrogated the States' sovereign immunity. * * * [T]here is no established tradition in the lower federal courts of allowing enforcement of those federal statutes against the States. * * *

[17] Contrary to the claims of the dissent, we do not hold that Congress cannot authorize federal jurisdiction under Ex parte Young over a cause of action with a limited remedial scheme. We find only that Congress did not intend that result in the Indian Gaming Regulatory Act. * * *

that § 2710(d)(7) was beyond its authority. If that effort is to be made, it should be made by Congress, and not by the federal courts. We hold that Ex parte Young is inapplicable to petitioner's suit against the Governor of Florida, and therefore that suit is barred by the Eleventh Amendment and must be dismissed for a lack of jurisdiction. * * *

■ JUSTICE STEVENS, dissenting.

This case is about power—the power of the Congress of the United States to create a private federal cause of action against a State, or its Governor, for the violation of a federal right. In Chisholm v. Georgia, the entire Court—including Justice Iredell whose dissent provided the blueprint for the Eleventh Amendment—assumed that Congress had such power. In Hans v. Louisiana—a case the Court purports to follow today—the Court again assumed that Congress had such power. In Fitzpatrick v. Bitzer and Pennsylvania v. Union Gas Co., the Court squarely held that Congress has such power. In a series of cases beginning with Atascadero State Hospital v. Scanlon, the Court formulated a special "clear statement rule" to determine whether specific Acts of Congress contained an effective exercise of that power. Nevertheless, in a sharp break with the past, today the Court holds that with the narrow and illogical exception of statutes enacted pursuant to the Enforcement Clause of the Fourteenth Amendment, Congress has no such power.

The importance of the majority's decision to overrule the Court's holding in Pennsylvania v. Union Gas Co. cannot be overstated. The majority's opinion does not simply preclude Congress from establishing the rather curious statutory scheme under which Indian tribes may seek the aid of a federal court to secure a State's good faith negotiations over gaming regulations. Rather, it prevents Congress from providing a federal forum for a broad range of actions against States, from those sounding in copyright and patent law, to those concerning bankruptcy, environmental law, and the regulation of our vast national economy.

There may be room for debate over whether, in light of the Eleventh Amendment, Congress has the power to ensure that such a cause of action may be enforced in federal court by a citizen of another State or a foreign citizen. There can be no serious debate, however, over whether Congress has the power to ensure that such a cause of action may be brought by a citizen of the State being sued. Congress' authority in that regard is clear. * * *

I

* * * Justice Brennan has persuasively explained that the Eleventh Amendment's jurisdictional restriction is best understood to apply only to suits premised on diversity jurisdiction, see Atascadero State Hospital v. Scanlon, 473 U.S. 234, 247 (1985) (dissenting opinion), and Justice Scalia has agreed that the plain text of the Amendment cannot be read to apply to federal-question cases. See Pennsylvania v. Union Gas, 491 U.S. at 31 (dissenting opinion).[8] Whatever the precise dimensions of the

---

8   Of course, even if the Eleventh Amendment applies to federal-question cases brought by a citizen of another State, its express terms pose no bar to a federal court assuming jurisdiction in a federal-question case brought by an in-state plaintiff pursuant to Congress' express authorization. As that is precisely the posture of the suit before us, and as it was also precisely the posture of the suit at issue in Pennsylvania v. Union Gas, there is no need to decide here

Amendment, its express terms plainly do not apply to all suits brought against unconsenting States. The question thus becomes whether the relatively modest jurisdictional bar that the Eleventh Amendment imposes should be understood to reveal that a more general jurisdictional bar implicitly inheres in Article III. * * *

II

The majority appears to acknowledge that one cannot deduce from either the text of Article III or the plain terms of the Eleventh Amendment that the judicial power does not extend to a congressionally created cause of action against a State brought by one of that State's citizens. Nevertheless, the majority asserts that precedent compels that same conclusion. I disagree. The majority relies first on our decision in Hans v. Louisiana, which involved a suit by a citizen of Louisiana against that State for a claimed violation of the Contracts Clause. The majority suggests that by dismissing the suit, Hans effectively held that federal courts have no power to hear federal question suits brought by same-state plaintiffs.

Hans does not hold, however, that the Eleventh Amendment, or any other constitutional provision, precludes federal courts from entertaining actions brought by citizens against their own States in the face of contrary congressional direction. * * * Hans instead reflects, at the most, this Court's conclusion that, as a matter of federal common law, federal courts should decline to entertain suits against unconsenting States. Because Hans did not announce a constitutionally mandated jurisdictional bar, one need not overrule Hans, or even question its reasoning, in order to conclude that Congress may direct the federal courts to reject sovereign immunity in those suits not mentioned by the Eleventh Amendment. Instead, one need only follow it. * * *

* * * Hans deduced its rebuttable presumption in favor of sovereign immunity largely on the basis of its extensive analysis of cases holding that the sovereign could not be forced to make good on its debts via a private suit. * * *

In Hans, the plaintiff asserted a Contracts Clause claim against his State and thus asserted a federal right. To show that Louisiana had impaired its federal obligation, however, Hans first had to demonstrate that the State had entered into an enforceable contract as a matter of state law. That Hans chose to bring his claim in federal court as a Contract Clause action could not change the fact that he was, at bottom, seeking to enforce a contract with the State. * * *

The view that the rule of Hans is more substantive than jurisdictional comports with Hamilton's famous discussion of sovereign immunity in The Federalist Papers. Hamilton offered his view that the federal judicial power would not extend to suits against unconsenting States only in the context of his contention that no contract with a State could be enforceable against the State's desire. He did not argue that a State's immunity from suit in federal court would be absolute. * * *

---

whether Congress would be barred from authorizing out-of-state plaintiffs to enforce federal rights against States in federal court. * * *

III

* * * The fundamental error that continues to lead the Court astray is its failure to acknowledge that its modern embodiment of the ancient doctrine of sovereign immunity "has absolutely nothing to do with the limit on judicial power contained in the Eleventh Amendment." Pennsylvania v. Union Gas Co., 491 U.S. at 25 (Stevens, J., concurring). It rests rather on concerns of federalism and comity that merit respect but are nevertheless, in cases such as the one before us, subordinate to the plenary power of Congress. * * *

For these reasons, as well as those set forth in Justice Souter's opinion, I respectfully dissent.

■ JUSTICE SOUTER, with whom JUSTICE GINSBURG and JUSTICE BREYER join, dissenting.

* * * [T]he Court today holds for the first time since the founding of the Republic that Congress has no authority to subject a State to the jurisdiction of a federal court at the behest of an individual asserting a federal right. * * *

It is useful to separate three questions: (1) whether the States enjoyed sovereign immunity if sued in their own courts in the period prior to ratification of the National Constitution; (2) if so, whether after ratification the States were entitled to claim some such immunity when sued in a federal court exercising jurisdiction either because the suit was between a State and a non-state litigant who was not its citizen, or because the issue in the case raised a federal question; and (3) whether any state sovereign immunity recognized in federal court may be abrogated by Congress.

[Justice Souter here stated that the answer to the first question is not clear and that the Hans Court had premised its answer to the second on erroneous reasoning.]

The Court's answer today to the third question is likewise at odds with the Founders' view that common law, when it was received into the new American legal systems, was always subject to legislative amendment. * * *

Whatever the scope of sovereign immunity might have been in the Colonies * * * or during the period of Confederation, the proposal to establish a National Government under the Constitution drafted in 1787 presented a prospect unknown to the common law prior to the American experience: the States would become parts of a system in which sovereignty over even domestic matters would be divided or parceled out between the States and the Nation, the latter to be invested with its own judicial power and the right to prevail against the States whenever their respective substantive laws might be in conflict. With this prospect in mind, the 1787 Constitution might have addressed state sovereign immunity by eliminating whatever sovereign immunity the States previously had, as to any matter subject to federal law or jurisdiction; by recognizing an analogue to the old immunity in the new context of federal jurisdiction, but subject to abrogation as to any matter within that jurisdiction; or by enshrining a doctrine of inviolable state sovereign immunity in the text, thereby giving it constitutional protection in the new federal jurisdiction.

The 1787 draft in fact said nothing on the subject, and it was this very silence that occasioned some, though apparently not widespread, dispute among the Framers and others over whether ratification of the Constitution would preclude a State sued in federal court from asserting sovereign immunity as it could have done on any matter of nonfederal law litigated in its own courts. As it has come down to us, the discussion gave no attention to congressional power under the proposed Article I but focused entirely on the limits of the judicial power provided in Article III. * * *

It may have been reasonable to contend (as we will see that Madison, Marshall, and Hamilton did) that Article III would not alter States' pre-existing common-law immunity despite its unqualified grant of jurisdiction over diversity suits against States. But then, as now, there was no textual support for contending that Article III or any other provision would "constitutionalize" state sovereign immunity, and no one uttered any such contention.

B

The argument among the Framers and their friends about sovereign immunity in federal citizen-state diversity cases * * * ended when this Court, in Chisholm v. Georgia, chose between the constitutional alternatives of abrogation and recognition of the immunity enjoyed at common law. * * *

C

The Eleventh Amendment, of course, repudiated Chisholm * * *. There are two plausible readings of this provision's text. Under the first, it simply repeals the Citizen-State Diversity Clauses of Article III for all cases in which the State appears as a defendant. Under the second, it strips the federal courts of jurisdiction in any case in which a state defendant is sued by a citizen not its own, even if jurisdiction might otherwise rest on the existence of a federal question in the suit. Neither reading of the Amendment, of course, furnishes authority for the Court's view in today's case * * *.

The history and structure of the Eleventh Amendment convincingly show that it reaches only to suits subject to federal jurisdiction exclusively under the Citizen-State Diversity Clauses. In precisely tracking the language in Article III providing for citizen-state diversity jurisdiction, the text of the Amendment does, after all, suggest to common sense that only the Diversity Clauses are being addressed. If the Framers had meant the Amendment to bar federal question suits as well, they could not only have made their intentions clearer very easily, but could simply have adopted the first post-Chisholm proposal, introduced in the House of Representatives by Theodore Sedgwick of Massachusetts on instructions from the Legislature of that Commonwealth. Its provisions would have had exactly that expansive effect:

"No state shall be liable to be made a party defendant, in any of the judicial courts, established, or which shall be established under the authority of the United States, at the suit of any person or persons, whether a citizen or citizens, or a foreigner or foreigners, or of any body politic or corporate, whether within or without the United States." Gazette of the United States 303 (Feb. 20, 1793). * * *

Congress took no action on Sedgwick's proposal, however, and the Amendment as ultimately adopted two years later could hardly have been meant to limit federal question jurisdiction, or it would never have left the states open to federal question suits by their own citizens. * * *

It should accordingly come as no surprise that the weightiest commentary following the amendment's adoption described it simply as constricting the scope of the Citizen-State Diversity Clauses. [Discussion of Cohens v. Virginia and Osborn v. Bank of the United States omitted.]

The good sense of this early construction of the Amendment as affecting the diversity jurisdiction and no more has the further virtue of making sense of this Court's repeated exercise of appellate jurisdiction in federal question suits brought against states in their own courts by out-of-staters. Exercising appellate jurisdiction in these cases would have been patent error if the Eleventh Amendment limited federal question jurisdiction, for the Amendment's unconditional language ("shall not be construed") makes no distinction between trial and appellate jurisdiction. And yet, again and again we have entertained such appellate cases, even when brought against the State in its own name by a private plaintiff for money damages. * * *

II

* * * Hans v. Louisiana * * * was indeed a leap in the direction of today's holding, even though it does not take the Court all the way. * * * Although the Court invoked a principle of sovereign immunity to cure what it took to be the Eleventh Amendment's anomaly of barring only those state suits brought by noncitizen plaintiffs, the Hans Court had no occasion to consider whether Congress could abrogate that background immunity by statute. * * * [But since, as shown below, Hans was wrongly decided,] [i]t follows that the Court's further step today of constitutionalizing Hans's rule against abrogation by Congress compounds and immensely magnifies the century-old mistake of Hans itself and takes its place with other historic examples of textually untethered elevations of judicially derived rules to the status of inviolable constitutional law. * * *

B

The majority does not dispute the point that Hans v. Louisiana had no occasion to decide whether Congress could abrogate a State's immunity from federal question suits. * * *

The majority * * * would read the "rationale" of Hans and its line of subsequent cases as answering the further question whether the "postulate" of sovereign immunity that "limits and controls" the exercise of Article III jurisdiction, Monaco [v. Mississippi, 292 U.S.] at 322, is constitutional in stature and therefore unalterable by Congress. It is true that there are statements in the cases that point toward just this conclusion. * * * These statements, however, are dicta * * * [and] are counterbalanced by many other opinions that have either stated the immunity principle without more, or have suggested that the Hans immunity is not of constitutional stature. * * *

The most damning evidence for the Court's theory that Hans rests on a broad rationale of immunity unalterable by Congress, however, is the Court's proven tendency to disregard the post-Hans dicta in cases where that dicta would have mattered. If it is indeed true that "private suits against States [are] not permitted under Article III (by virtue of the understanding represented by the Eleventh Amendment)," Union Gas, 491 U.S., at 40 (Scalia, J., concurring in part and dissenting in part), then it is hard to see how a State's sovereign immunity may be waived any more than it may be abrogated by Congress. * * *

If these examples were not enough to distinguish Hans's rationale of a pre-existing doctrine of sovereign immunity from the post-Hans dicta indicating that this immunity is constitutional, one would need only to consider a final set of cases: those in which we have assumed, without deciding, that congressional power to abrogate state sovereign immunity exists even when § 5 of the Fourteenth Amendment has no application. * * * Although the Court in each of these cases failed to find abrogation for lack of a clear statement of congressional intent, the assumption that such power was available would hardly have been permissible if, at that time, today's majority's view of the law had been firmly established. * * *

III

Three critical errors in Hans weigh against constitutionalizing its holding as the majority does today. The first we have already seen: the Hans Court misread the Eleventh Amendment. It also misunderstood the conditions under which common-law doctrines were received or rejected at the time of the Founding, and it fundamentally mistook the very nature of sovereignty in the young Republic that was supposed to entail a State's immunity to federal question jurisdiction in a federal court. While I would not, as a matter of stare decisis, overrule Hans today, an understanding of its failings on these points will show how the Court today simply compounds already serious error in taking Hans the further step of investing its rule with constitutional inviolability against the considered judgment of Congress to abrogate it.

A

* * * [Justice Souter argued that the sovereign immunity known to the Founding generation was a common law immunity.] An examination of the States' experience with common-law reception will shed light on subsequent theory and practice at the national level, and demonstrate that our history is entirely at odds with Hans's resort to a common-law principle to limit the Constitution's contrary text. [Justice Souter then argued that the reception of English common law in the states was subject to limitation and adaptation in the light of local circumstances and that the Constitution made no provision for the reception of English common law at the national level.]

B

Given the refusal to entertain any wholesale reception of common law, given the failure of the new Constitution to make any provision for adoption of common law as such, and given the protests already quoted that no general reception had occurred, the Hans Court and the Court today cannot reasonably argue that something like the old immunity doctrine somehow slipped in as a tacit but enforceable background principle. The evidence is even more specific, however, that there was no pervasive understanding that sovereign immunity had limited federal question jurisdiction.

1

As I have already noted briefly, the Framers and their contemporaries did not agree about the place of common-law state sovereign immunity even as to federal jurisdiction resting on the Citizen-State Diversity Clauses. Edmund Randolph argued in favor of ratification on the ground that the immunity would not be recognized, leaving the States subject to jurisdiction. Patrick Henry opposed ratification on the basis of exactly the same reading. On the other hand, James Madison, John Marshall, and Alexander Hamilton all appear to have believed that the common-law immunity from suit would survive the ratification of Article III, so as to be at a State's disposal when jurisdiction would depend on diversity. This would have left the States free to enjoy a traditional immunity as defendants without barring the exercise of judicial power over them if they chose to enter the federal courts as diversity plaintiffs or to waive their immunity as diversity defendants. See [3 Elliot's Debates] at 533 (Madison: the Constitution "gives a citizen a right to be heard in the federal courts; and if a state should condescend to be a party, this court may take cognizance of it");[39] *id.*, at 556 (Marshall: "I see a difficulty in making a state defendant, which does not prevent its being plaintiff"). * * *

[Justice Souter here quoted from and discusses Hamilton's view of sovereignty in two Federalist Papers: Nos. 32 and 81. He concluded from these materials that Hamilton did not address the question of a state's immunity "when a congressional statute not only binds the States but even creates an affirmative obligation on the State as such, as in this case". Thus, he contended, Hamilton "is no authority for the Court's position."]

2

* * * While there is no need here to calculate exactly how close the American States came to sovereignty in the classic sense prior to ratification of the Constitution, it is clear that the act of ratification affected their sovereignty in a way different from any previous political event in America or anywhere else. For the adoption of the Constitution made them members of a novel federal system that sought to balance the States' exercise of some sovereign prerogatives delegated from their own people with the principle of a limited but centralizing federal supremacy. * * *

[In light of] the Framers' general concern with curbing abuses by state governments, it would be amazing if the scheme of delegated powers embodied in the Constitution had left the National Government powerless to render the States judicially accountable for violations of federal rights. * * *

Today's majority discounts this concern. Without citing a single source to the contrary, the Court dismisses the historical evidence regarding the Framers' vision of the relationship between national and

---

[39] The Court accuses me of quoting this statement out of context, but the additional material included by the Court makes no difference. I am conceding that Madison, Hamilton, and Marshall all agreed that Article III did not of its own force abrogate the states' pre-existing common-law immunity, at least with respect to diversity suits. None of the statements offered by the Court, however, purports to deal with federal question jurisdiction or with the question whether Congress, acting pursuant to its Article I powers, could create a cause of action against a State. * * *

state sovereignty, and reassures us that "the Nation survived for nearly two centuries without the question of the existence of [the abrogation] power ever being presented to this Court." But we are concerned here not with the survival of the Nation but the opportunity of its citizens to enforce federal rights in a way that Congress provides. * * * In the end, is it plausible to contend that the plan of the convention was meant to leave the National Government without any way to render individuals capable of enforcing their federal rights directly against an intransigent state?

C

[In this section, Justice Souter developed the theme that the majority's decision, "constitutionalizing common-law rules at the expense of legislative authority," could not be squared with the Framers' "abhorrence" of the notion that any common law rules received into the new legal systems would be beyond legislative power to change or reject. He concluded by analogizing the decision to the "practice in the century's early decades that brought this Court to the nadir of competence that we identify with Lochner v. New York, 198 U.S. 45 (1905)."]

IV

The Court's holding that the States' Hans immunity may not be abrogated by Congress leads to the final question in this case, whether federal question jurisdiction exists to order prospective relief enforcing IGRA against a state officer [the Governor], who is said to be authorized to take the action required by the federal law. * * *. The answer to this question is an easy yes, the officer is subject to suit under the rule in Ex parte Young, and the case could, and should, readily be decided on this point alone.

* * * I do not in theory reject the Court's assumption that Congress may bar enforcement by suit even against a state official. But because in practice, in the real world of congressional legislation, such an intent would be exceedingly odd, it would be equally odd for this Court to recognize an intent to block the customary application of Ex parte Young without applying the rule recognized in our previous cases, which have insisted on a clear statement before assuming a congressional purpose to "affect the federal balance," United States v. Bass, 404 U.S. 336, 349 (1971). * * *

IGRA's jurisdictional provision reads as though it had been drafted with the specific intent to apply to officer liability under Young. * * * The door is so obviously just as open to jurisdiction over an officer under Young as to jurisdiction over a State directly that it is difficult to see why the statute would have been drafted as it was unless it was done in anticipation that Young might well be the jurisdictional basis for enforcement action.

* * *

It may be that even the Court agrees, for it falls back to the position that only a State, not a state officer, can enter into a compact. This is true but wholly beside the point. The issue is whether negotiation should take place as required by IGRA and an officer (indeed, only an officer) can negotiate. * * *

Finally, one must judge the Court's purported inference by stepping back to ask why Congress could possibly have intended to jeopardize the enforcement of the statute by excluding application of Young's traditional jurisdictional rule, when that rule would make the difference between success or failure in the federal court if state sovereign immunity was recognized. Why would Congress have wanted to go for broke on the issue of state immunity in the event the State pleaded immunity as a jurisdictional bar? Why would Congress not have wanted IGRA to be enforced by means of a traditional doctrine giving federal courts jurisdiction over state officers, in an effort to harmonize state sovereign immunity with federal law that is paramount under the Supremacy Clause? There are no plausible answers to these questions. * * *

V

Absent the application of Ex parte Young, I would, of course, follow Union Gas in recognizing congressional power under Article I to abrogate Hans immunity. Since the reasons for this position, as explained in Parts II–III, *supra*, tend to unsettle Hans as well as support Union Gas, I should add a word about my reasons for continuing to accept Hans's holding as a matter of stare decisis.

The Hans doctrine was erroneous, but it has not previously proven to be unworkable or to conflict with later doctrine or to suffer from the effects of facts developed since its decision (apart from those indicating its original errors). I would therefore treat Hans as it has always been treated in fact until today, as a doctrine of federal common law. For, as so understood, it has formed one of the strands of the federal relationship for over a century now, and the stability of that relationship is itself a value that stare decisis aims to respect.

In being ready to hold that the relationship may still be altered, not by the Court but by Congress, I would tread the course laid out elsewhere in our cases. The Court has repeatedly stated its assumption that insofar as the relative positions of States and Nation may be affected consistently with the Tenth Amendment, they would not be modified without deliberately expressed intent. * * *

When judging legislation passed under unmistakable Article I powers, no further restriction could be required. Nor does the Court explain why more could be demanded. In the past, we have assumed that a plain statement requirement is sufficient to protect the States from undue federal encroachments upon their traditional immunity from suit. It is hard to contend that this rule has set the bar too low, for (except in Union Gas) we have never found the requirement to be met outside the context of laws passed under § 5 of the Fourteenth Amendment. The exception I would recognize today proves the rule, moreover, because the federal abrogation of state immunity comes as part of a regulatory scheme which is itself designed to invest the States with regulatory powers that Congress need not extend to them. This fact suggests to me that the political safeguards of federalism are working, that a plain statement rule is an adequate check on congressional overreaching, and that today's abandonment of that approach is wholly unwarranted. * * *

NOTE ON CONGRESSIONAL POWER TO ABROGATE STATE IMMUNITY

(1) The Stakes.

(a) In holding that Congress lacks power to abrogate the states' Eleventh Amendment immunity under the Indian Commerce Clause, the Court does not question that Congress, when legislating under that clause, can impose valid and binding legal obligations on the states.[1] Accordingly, the effect of Seminole Tribe, in theory anyway, is not to free the states from congressionally imposed restraints, but only to exempt them from unconsented suits in federal court to enforce their federal legal obligations. In practical terms, as long as prospective injunctive relief is available against state officials, what plaintiffs are denied is monetary or other retrospective relief from the state itself for past statutory and constitutional violations.

(b) The abrogation question is undoubtedly an important one in its own right, but exactly how important it is in affecting congressional capacity to provide for the enforcement of federal law against the states depends in significant part on the availability of—or Congress' capacity to provide for—suits against state officers under the theory of Ex parte Young, p. 922, *supra*.

How convincing was the Court's explanation in Seminole Tribe of why an officer suit was unavailable on the facts of the case? Couldn't equitable remedies under Young and § 1983 be crafted to reflect specific statutory limitations imposed by the legislature? Perhaps the Young doctrine may not be used to compel a state to enter into a contract, *see* p. 928, *supra*, but Congress in IGRA stopped short of such coercion; rather, the core of IGRA's approach is to impose a requirement on the state (acting through its officers, of course) to bargain in good faith.[2]

Although Seminole Tribe initially raised questions about whether the Court might be prepared to question the Ex parte Young theory that suits for injunctive relief against state officers are not generally barred by the Eleventh Amendment,[3] subsequent decisions largely dispel that concern. See p. 932, *supra*.

(2) The Continuing Historical Debate.

(a) The majority and dissenting opinions in Seminole Tribe disagreed sharply both about the original understanding of pertinent constitutional language and about the rationale and holding of Hans v. Louisiana. Especially when there is such sharp disagreement over historical questions,

---

[1] As the Seminole majority observed in footnote 10, the state's argument that the statutory scheme also violated the Tenth Amendment was not considered by the Court.

[2] Meltzer, *The Seminole Decision and State Sovereign Immunity*, 1996 Sup.Ct.Rev. 1, 36–41, argues that the Seminole Tribe "should have been afforded a declaratory or injunctive remedy against Governor Chiles" under the rationale of Young and the specific statutory remedy afforded by § 1983, and that the Court's denial of such relief rests on a "mischaracterization" of Young, "a disregard of § 1983, and a misapplication of familiar principles of congressional primacy in shaping remedies for federal statutory violations". See also Jackson, *Seminole Tribe, The Eleventh Amendment, and the Potential Evisceration of Ex Parte Young*, 72 N.Y.U.L.Rev. 495 (1997) (contending, *inter alia*, that the Seminole Court failed to establish that the injunctive relief sought would have been broader than the statutory remedy, and that the holding threatens the future availability of relief under the doctrine of Ex parte Young)."

[3] *But cf.* Monaghan, *The Sovereign Immunity "Exception,"* 110 Harv.L.Rev. 102 (1996) (arguing forcefully that the Seminole case in no way compromised Young's logic and rationale).

how great a role should they play—and how great a role do you believe they play in fact—in determining the vote of each Justice?[4]

(b) Granted that Justice Bradley's opinion in Hans is not a model of lucidity, and that it could have rested on narrow grounds (especially in light of the tenuous nature of the "federal" claim of impairment of contract), can it reasonably be read—as the Seminole dissenters contended—as stating only a rule of "federal common law"?[5] Bear in mind, in thinking about this question, that explicit recognition of true federal common law (as distinct from the "general" law of Swift v. Tyson) is in large part a twentieth-century development.

(3) Congressional Power to Abrogate Eleventh Amendment Immunity Under the Fourteenth Amendment: The Continuing Validity of Fitzpatrick v. Bitzer. The Seminole majority affirmed the rationale of Fitzpatrick v. Bitzer, p. 939, *supra*, which had upheld congressional power to abrogate the states' Eleventh Amendment immunity when legislating pursuant to section 5 of the Fourteenth Amendment.

Is it readily apparent why the authority granted by § 5 of the Fourteenth Amendment differs from Congress' authority to regulate state activity under other provisions of the Constitution? True, the Fourteenth Amendment was enacted after the Eleventh Amendment, but surely § 5 does not authorize Congress to abrogate individual rights—such as, for example, rights under First or Eighth Amendments—that it might wish to sweep aside in order to enforce the Fourteenth Amendment more effectively. If the states have a constitutional right to immunity from suit, why should the Eleventh Amendment give way in § 5 cases—and if they don't have such a right, then why should Congress not be able to subject them to suit when legislating under the Commerce Clause?[6]

---

[4]   Post-Seminole studies that re-examine the history and criticize the majority's conclusions include Hovenkamp, *Judicial Restraint and Constitutional Federalism: The Supreme Court's Lopez and Seminole Tribe Decisions*, 96 Colum.L.Rev. 2213 (1996), and Pfander, *History and State Suability: An "Explanatory" Account of the Eleventh Amendment*, 83 Cornell L.Rev. 1269 (1998), with the latter finding strong historical support for the "revisionist challenges to the sweeping immunity of Hans and Seminole Tribe".

[5]   Meltzer, note 2, *supra*, quotes extensively from Justice Bradley's opinion—including his statement that "cognizance of suits and actions unknown to the law, and forbidden by the law, was not contemplated by the Constitution when establishing the judicial power of the United States"; concludes that Bradley's opinion clearly contains an "alternative constitutional holding"; and suggests that Justice Souter's view of the Hans decision as resting only on federal common law may have been animated at least in part by a desire to "foreclose the response" that he was no different from the majority in his willingness to overrule precedent.

[6]   Meltzer, note 2, *supra*, at 20–24, criticizes the Court's distinction between abrogation under § 5 and abrogation pursuant to Article I on several grounds. With respect to the "temporal argument", he notes the long-established practice of viewing an amended enactment as a whole and observes that the argument rests in significant part on the purely stylistic convention of reproducing constitutional amendments after the text of the original document. He then points out that the Civil War and its aftermath had a profound impact on all aspects of constitutional theory and practice—an impact not limited to the post–Civil War amendments—and that the distinction drawn by the Court between § 5 and other constitutional provision is especially ironic, coming as it did in a case involving Indian affairs, where the limitation on state sovereignty is particularly stringent.

Harrison, *State Sovereign Immunity and Congress's Enforcement Powers*, 2006 Sup.Ct.Rev. 353, agrees with Professor Meltzer that Fitzpatrick and Seminole Tribe cannot be reconciled persuasively, but argues on originalist grounds that Fitzpatrick was the erroneous decision. According to Harrison, congressional debates surrounding several Reconstruction statutes suggest that Congress did not understand the enforcement provisions of the Reconstruction

In thinking about congressional power to abrogate the states' Eleventh Amendment immunity pursuant to § 5 of the Fourteenth Amendment, keep in mind that any attempted congressional abrogation, in order to be valid, must satisfy what the Court in Seminole Tribe—in reliance on prior authorities—described as an "unmistakably clear" manifestation of intent to do so on the face of the statute.

(4) The Limits of Congressional Power to Abrogate Under § 5. Although Congress retains authority to abrogate the states' immunity when legislating pursuant to § 5, decisions subsequent to Seminole have emphasized the limits on Congress' § 5 power. The most important decision is City of Boerne v. Flores, 521 U.S. 507 (1997), in which the Court held the Religious Freedom Restoration Act unconstitutional insofar as it attempted to overrule a Supreme Court decision interpreting the First Amendment as it applied to the States through the Fourteenth Amendment. The Court reasoned that although Congress' power under § 5 extends to the creation of remedies, it does not include the power to alter substantive rights. Although Boerne did not involve an abrogation issue, it laid down the principles that also govern Congress' abrogation power: For § 5 legislation to be valid, it must exhibit "congruence and proportionality between the [constitutional violations] to be prevented or remedied and the means"—including abrogation of the states' immunity—"adopted to that end."

Note that the congruence and proportionality inquiry inherently involves a comparison. But what, exactly, is to be compared with what? On the statutory side, does a court look to the statute on its face? To a particular provision of a multi-part statute? Or to a statute as applied? On the other side, insofar as abrogation is in issue, does the court look to the entire universe of violations of the constitutional provision in issue, including those committed by agents and agencies of local governments (that are not protected by sovereign immunity), or just to those committed by the states? Keep these questions in mind as you read the remainder of this Paragraph, and consider the extent to which the Court has adopted a consistent approach to them.

(a) In Florida Prepaid Postsecondary Education Expense Board v. College Savings Bank, 527 U.S. 627 (1999), the Court, by 5–4, held unconstitutional provisions of the Patent Remedy Act, 35 U.S.C. §§ 271(h), 296(a), that purported to strip the states of immunity and to authorize suits for patent infringement against "[a]ny State" and "any instrumentality of a State". Writing for the majority, Chief Justice Rehnquist cited Boerne as establishing that for Congress to invoke § 5, "it must identify conduct transgressing the Fourteenth Amendment's substantive provisions, and must tailor its legislative scheme to remedying or preventing such conduct". He then concluded that this standard had not been met.[7] Congress had "identified no pattern of patent infringement by the States, let alone a pattern of constitutional violations"; there was "no evidence that unremedied patent infringement by States had become a problem of national import". Moreover, any argument that a state's infringement of a patent constituted a deprivation of property without due process was undercut by decisions such

---

Amendments to authorize Congress to abrogate state sovereign immunity, but only to provide statutory remedies against individual government officers who violated federal rights.

   [7]   Before reaching the question of § 5 power, the Chief Justice held that Congress could not abrogate the state's immunity in the exercise of its Article I powers and that Florida had not waived its immunity.

as Parratt v. Taylor, p. 1016, *infra*, Hudson v. Palmer, pp. 1025–1026, *infra*, and Daniels v. Williams, p. 1026, *infra*, which collectively supported the propositions that a due process violation can occur (a) only when there is an intentional act that causes injury to property, and (b) only when state law provides insufficient remedies. Since the Patent Remedy Act reached unintentional infringements and cases in which an adequate state remedy was available, the Act exceeded Congress' power under § 5.[8]

Justice Stevens, dissenting for himself and Justices Souter, Ginsburg, and Breyer, spoke first of the recognized need for uniformity in the administration of the national patent laws as establishing the validity of the decision by Congress to vest exclusive jurisdiction over patent infringement cases in the federal courts. Then, after noting the majority's concession that patents are property, he questioned the application of the "willful-negligent" distinction to a patent case, and pointed out that in any event, the bank in this case had alleged that the defendant's infringement was "willful". Justice Stevens then challenged the majority's conclusion of insufficient congressional findings, citing legislative history to show that Congress did have ample evidence that state remedies were inadequate to deal with patent infringement and noting that in any event, in view of federal preemption of state jurisdiction over patent infringement, "it was surely reasonable for Congress to assume that such remedies simply did not exist".

(b) Following Florida Prepaid, the Court decided a string of cases, all by 5–4, in which it took a stringent view of the congruence and proportionality test. Two specifically addressed congressional power to abrogate and found it lacking. See Kimel v. Fla. Bd. of Regents, 528 U.S. 62 (2000) (ruling that § 5 could not furnish a basis for overcoming a state's immunity from private suit under the Age Discrimination in Employment Act because "the substantive requirements the ADEA imposes on state and local governments are disproportionate to any unconstitutional conduct that conceivably could be targeted by the Act"); Univ. of Ala. v. Garrett, 531 U.S. 356 (2001) (holding that Congress' abrogation of state immunity from damages actions for violation of Title I of the Americans with Disabilities Act—the Title prohibiting discrimination in employment—could not be sustained because there was insufficient evidence of state discrimination in violation of the Fourteenth Amendment; the record of discrimination by *local* governments was irrelevant).

(c) Compare Nevada Dep't of Human Resources v. Hibbs, 538 U.S. 721 (2003), which upheld, by a vote of 6–3, the abrogation of state sovereign immunity in the Family and Medical Leave Act of 1993 (FMLA). This Act, *inter alia*, entitles eligible employees (including certain employees of public agencies) to up to twelve weeks of unpaid leave annually for any of several reasons, including the onset of a "serious health condition" in the employee's spouse, child, or parent. The Act also creates a private right of action "against any employer (including a public agency)" for equitable and monetary relief. The Court, per Chief Justice Rehnquist, held that Congress had met its burden under § 5: it had satisfied the requirement that the statement of abrogation be clearly made and, in light of the relevant evidence of gender-based discrimination in the legislative record, had sufficient evidence of a "pattern of constitutional violations on the part of the States in this area" to warrant the provision of the FMLA's private rights and remedies as

---

[8] Since Congress had not invoked the Just Compensation Clause, the Court declined to consider the latter provision as a basis for upholding the Act.

"appropriate prophylactic legislation". The Court noted that it had subjected gender-based discrimination to heightened judicial scrutiny and pointed to evidence that women had been disadvantaged in both private and public employment because of mutually enforcing, prevailing stereotypes that women are responsible for family care-giving and that men lack domestic responsibilities.

Justice Souter, joined by Justices Ginsburg and Breyer, concurred on the ground that the validity of the challenged provisions followed a fortiori from his understanding of § 5 as conferring a broader congressional power to prevent and remedy discrimination than recent decisions (from which he had dissented) had recognized. He also noted his continuing adherence to the dissenting views expressed in Seminole. Justice Kennedy, joined by Justices Scalia and Thomas, dissented. Justice Scalia, also dissenting separately, stressed his conviction that in order to justify the application of "prophylactic legislation" to a particular state, it was insufficient to rely on a notion of collective guilt; the question must be "whether the State has itself engaged in discrimination sufficient to support the exercise of Congress's prophylactic power".

(d) In two decisions since Hibbs, the Court has upheld the application of immunity-abrogating legislation enacted under § 5 *as applied* to particular conduct or patterns of conduct.

(i) Tennessee v. Lane, 541 U.S. 509 (2004), per Justice Stevens, rejected (5–4) a motion to dismiss a damages claim against Tennessee by two paraplegics, one a criminal defendant and the other a court reporter, alleging a denial of physical access to the state's courts in violation of Title II of the Americans with Disabilities Act (ADA): "[T]he question presented in this case is not whether Congress can validly subject the States to private suits for money damages for failing to provide reasonable access to hockey rinks, or even to voting booths, but whether Congress has the power under § 5 to enforce the constitutional right of access to courts." Justice Stevens found ample evidence of "pervasive unequal treatment" of the disabled in the administration of both state and local services and programs generally, and with respect to access to courthouses in particular. "To operate on [the] premise [that only the action of the states themselves should be considered] would be particularly inappropriate", the Court said, "because this case concerns the provision of judicial services, an area in which local governments are typically treated as 'arms of the State' for Eleventh Amendment purposes [citing cases]". In addition, it was significant that the constitutional claim asserted—the due process right of access to courts—triggered an elevated standard of review; in this respect the case was analogous to the Court's treatment of sex-based classifications in Hibbs. "Because we find that Title II unquestionably is valid § 5 legislation as it applies to the class of cases implicating the accessibility of judicial services, we need go no further".

Writing in dissent, Chief Justice Rehnquist, joined by Justices Kennedy and Thomas, objected vigorously to the Court's reliance on evidence of discrimination by local entities and to its as-applied approach to the constitutionality of Title II: "[T]he majority posits a hypothetical statute, never enacted by Congress, that applies only to courthouses. * * * Our § 5 cases do not support this as-applied approach."

Justice Scalia, dissenting separately, argued for abandonment of the "flabby" congruence and proportionality test for the validity of prophylactic legislation, except in matters of racial discrimination, and even there, he urged, the legislation should be confined to "those particular States in which there has been an identified history of relevant constitutional violations".

(ii) In United States v. Georgia, 546 U.S. 151 (2006), in which a paraplegic prison inmate sought damages under Title II of the ADA based on conduct that allegedly included violations of his right to be free from cruel and unusual punishment, a unanimous Court, per Justice Scalia, ruled that the allegations of constitutional violations differentiated this from "our other cases" involving Congress' § 5 power. According to Justice Scalia, "no one doubts" Congress' power under § 5 to create "private remedies against the States for *actual* violations of the Constitution." The Court remanded the case for the lower courts to determine in the first instance which aspects of the state's alleged conduct violated the Constitution and whether the purported abrogation of sovereign immunity for conduct that did not violate the Constitution was nevertheless valid.

(e) Deep divisions about the scope of Congress' § 5 power were again on display, however, in Coleman v. Court of Appeals of Maryland, 132 S.Ct. 1327 (2012), in which the Court, without a majority opinion, held that Congress had no authority under the Fourteenth Amendment to abrogate the states' immunity from suit under a provision of the FMLA that required employers to provide up to twelve weeks of unpaid leave per year for an employee's *own* health issues. (Hibbs had upheld provisions of the FMLA regarding the health issues of an employee's *family member*.) Writing for a four-Justice plurality, Justice Kennedy found that Congress had not adequately linked the provision to a pattern of constitutional violations and, in particular, had not shown it to be a response to sex discrimination in sick leave policies. Justice Thomas joined the plurality opinion but wrote separately to state his view that Hibbs, which the plurality distinguished, was wrongly decided. Justice Scalia concurred in the judgment only: "[O]utside of the context of racial discrimination (which is different for *stare decisis* reasons)," he "would limit Congress's § 5 power to the regulation of conduct that *itself* violates the Fourteenth Amendment."

In a vigorous dissenting opinion, Justice Ginsburg, joined in full by Justice Breyer and in pertinent parts by Justices Sotomayor and Kagan, relied heavily on the FMLA's legislative history in arguing that the contested provision was directed at the exclusion of women from the workplace based on pregnancy-related health issues, even though it was deliberately framed in gender-neutral terms. In light of the record before Congress, Justice Ginsburg concluded that the statute was congruent and proportional to an identified pattern of sex discrimination. (She also argued at length that the Court should revisit and overrule the holding of Geduldig v. Aiello, 417 U.S. 484 (1974), that discrimination on the basis of pregnancy does not constitute discrimination on the basis of sex. But she maintained that the Court erred in its § 5 analysis "even if Aiello"—which the plurality did not discuss— "senselessly holds sway".)

(f) Note that, with the exceptions of Hibbs and United States v. Georgia, all of the post-City of Boerne cases summarized in this Paragraph have been decided by shifting majorities of 5–4. Have consistent principles emerged?[9]

---

[9]   For deeper analysis of the Court's § 5 cases, see, *e.g.*, Bandes, *Fear and Degradation in Alabama: The Emotional Subtext of University of Alabama v. Garrett*, 5 U.Pa.J.Const.L. 520 (2003) (focusing on "the emotive cast of the majority's language about the states" in the Court's opinion in Garrett as suggestive of the majority's "emotional commitments and blind spots:

(5) Eleventh Amendment Immunity and Congressional Power Under Article I: General Principles. After Seminole, there was some disagreement in the lower federal courts about whether Congress might be able to abrogate the states' immunity under *any* of its Article I powers, including that involving patents and copyrights. But Florida Prepaid Postsecondary Education Expense Board v. College Savings Bank, 527 U.S. 627, 636 (1999), Paragraph (4), *supra*, appeared to dispel any doubts, as the majority stated flatly that "Congress may not abrogate state sovereign immunity pursuant to its Article I powers".[10]

(6) Congressional Power to Subject the States to Suit: Developments in the Area of Bankruptcy. To the surprise of many observers, however, the Court has found that somewhat different rules may apply to congressional efforts to subject the states to suit in the domain of federal bankruptcy law. The key case is Central Virginia Community College v. Katz, 546 U.S. 356 (2006), which involved a proceeding initiated by the federally appointed trustee of a bankrupt's estate to set aside, and recover for the estate, certain allegedly preferential transfers made by the debtor to several state agencies. (A "preferential [and therefore voidable] transfer" under federal bankruptcy law is defined to include certain transfers made by the debtor before filing of the bankruptcy petition and at a time when the debtor was already insolvent.) The state agencies moved to dismiss the proceedings on grounds of state sovereign immunity; the motions were denied by the bankruptcy court, the district court, and the court of appeals, and the Supreme Court affirmed.

Justice Stevens, writing for a majority of five (including Justice O'Connor, in one of her last cases before retirement, and Justices Souter, Ginsburg, and Breyer), referred to the rationale of an earlier, narrower bankruptcy decision, but relied more broadly on the nature of the bankruptcy

---

toward Congress, toward civil rights plaintiffs and civil rights statutes, and toward its own prerogatives"); Kaczorowski, *Congress's Power To Enforce Fourteenth Amendment Rights: Lessons from Federal Remedies the Framers Enacted*, 42 Harv.J.Legis. 187 (2005) (supporting with historical evidence the author's criticism of the Supreme Court's § 5 jurisprudence as insufficiently sensitive to the framers' intent to endow Congress with broad remedial powers); Post & Siegel, *Legislative Constitutionalism and Section Five Power: Policentric Interpretation of the Family and Medical Leave Act*, 112 Yale L.J. 1943 (2003) (contrasting the Court's "enforcement model" view of the § 5 power with the authors' proposed "policentric model", in which Congress—within limits believed by the Court to be needed to protect individual rights and such structural values as separation of powers and federalism—may exercise its § 5 power to enact legislation based on its own interpretation of constitutional rights); Symposium, *The Eleventh Amendment, Garrett, and Protection for Civil Rights*, 53 Ala.L.Rev. 1183 (2002).

[10] Do different considerations apply in determining whether a treaty—which is not an exercise of Congress's Article I power but rather of the President's Article II power, subject to the advice and consent of the Senate—may abrogate state sovereign immunity? Compare Vázquez, *Treaties and the Eleventh Amendment*, 42 Va.J.Int'l Law 713 (2002) (contending that there should be no difference), with Bandes, *Treaties, Sovereign Immunity, and "The Plan of the Convention"*, 42 Va.J.Int'l Law 743 (2002) (contending that the special nature of treaties requires special consideration of the question of abrogation).

For consideration of the relation between the Treaty Power and state sovereign immunity as an aspect of broader questions of American federalism, see Swaine, *Does Federalism Constrain the Treaty Power?*, 103 Colum.L.Rev. 403, 433–41, 487–92, 524–32 (2003). Professor Swaine concludes that, although the Court is unlikely to hold that the Treaty Power can serve as a basis for abrogating state immunity, there are significant "arcane loopholes" (*e.g.* the doctrine of Ex parte Young) that are relevant to effective implementation of international agreements, and perhaps more significantly, that practical solutions to the problem may be found through creative use of state and national authority relating to foreign and interstate compacts.

power vested in Congress under Article I.[11] The question, he stated, was not whether Congress could "abrogate" state sovereign immunity in the Bankruptcy Act (as Congress had attempted to do), because the history and justification of the Bankruptcy Clause, as well as legislation enacted immediately following ratification, "demonstrate that [the Bankruptcy Clause] was intended not just as a grant of legislative authority to Congress, but also to authorize limited subordination of state sovereign immunity in the bankruptcy arena". In reaching this conclusion, he acknowledged that the Court's decisions in Seminole Tribe and succeeding cases had assumed that those holdings would apply to the Bankruptcy Clause, but stated that the Court was convinced by "[c]areful study and reflection" that "that assumption was erroneous".

In its discussion of the history of the Bankruptcy Clause, the Court noted that the concept of "discharge" of a bankrupt, at a time when debtor's prisons were in common use, referred to both "release of debts and release of the debtor from prison". And because the colonies, and later the states, had "wildly divergent" schemes for discharging debtors, one problem confronting the new union was that a debtor discharged from debts in one state could nevertheless be imprisoned in another state for non-payment of those same debts. As a result, it was proposed in the Constitutional Convention that insolvency laws be brought within the coverage of the Full Faith and Credit Clause, and that Congress be given specific authority "to establish uniform laws upon the subject of bankruptcies".

The Court noted that bankruptcy jurisdiction is now, and has traditionally been, principally in rem jurisdiction, but added that the power granted by the Bankruptcy Clause is a "unitary concept" that embraces the authority to issue "ancillary orders" enforcing in rem adjudications—even those ancillary orders that might in themselves involve some sort of in personam process. Thus, whether or not an action to recover a preferential transfer is itself in rem, it is concededly a "core aspect of the administration of bankrupt estates", and even if such orders do implicate state sovereign immunity, "the States agreed in the plan of the Convention" not to assert that immunity.

The Court found strong evidence of this agreement in the first Bankruptcy Act, enacted in 1800, which "specifically granted federal courts

---

[11] Tennessee Student Assistance Corp. (TSAC) v. Hood, 541 U.S. 440 (2004), held that the states' Eleventh Amendment immunity does not apply in the context of a bankruptcy court's discharge of a debtor's debts due to the in rem nature of the proceeding. The case arose from a bankruptcy proceeding in which a student sought a discharge from loans that had been assigned to TSAC, a state agency. Writing for a 7–2 majority, Chief Justice Rehnquist relied on prior holdings establishing the power of a federal court to determine the nature of a state's interest in property in an in rem proceeding in admiralty, as well as on several pre-Seminole bankruptcy decisions, in concluding that "the [bankruptcy] court's jurisdiction is premised on the debtor and his estate, and not on the creditors". (In distinguishing an earlier bankruptcy decision refusing to allow an injunction against a state court action in which the state sought to establish ownership of property that conflicted with an earlier federal court determination, the Chief Justice said that even though a bankruptcy discharge operates by federal law as an injunction against creditors seeking to collect a discharged debt, "the enforcement of such an injunction against the State by a federal court is not before us".)

Justice Thomas, joined by Justice Scalia, dissented. He argued, inter alia, that questions involving the Court's in rem approach—which had not been considered by the court of appeals and had apparently been suggested only in an amicus brief—should be considered by the lower court before the Court resolved them: " '[W]e have never applied an in rem exception to the sovereign-immunity bar against monetary recovery, and have suggested that no such exception exists' " quoting United States v. Nordic Village Inc., 503 U.S. 30, 38 (1992).

the authority to issue writs of habeas corpus effective to release debtors from state prisons". (Comparable authority to entertain federal habeas petitions brought by *state* prisoners in other contexts was—with a very few exceptions—not conferred on the federal courts until after the Civil War.)

"This history", the Court continued, "strongly supports the view that the Bankruptcy Clause * * * simply did not contravene the norms this Court has understood the Eleventh Amendment to exemplify". On the contrary, the Framers "plainly intended to give Congress the power to redress the rampant injustice resulting from States' refusal to respect one another's discharge orders". And while the Court declined to rest on the "peculiar text" of the Clause (especially the reference to "uniform" laws), this language "supports the historical evidence showing that the States agreed not to assert their sovereign immunity" in such proceedings. But the Court added this cryptic caveat: it did not "mean to suggest that every law labeled a 'bankruptcy' law could, consistent with the Bankruptcy Clause, properly impinge upon state sovereign immunity".

Justice Thomas, joined by Chief Justice Roberts and Justices Scalia and Kennedy, dissented. Stressing the Court's line of decisions establishing that the powers conferred by Article I do not constitute a surrender of state sovereign immunity, he went on to note that "there is nothing special about the Bankruptcy Clause in this regard". He charged the majority with improperly conflating "two distinct attributes of sovereignty: the authority of a sovereign to enact legislation regulating its own citizens, and sovereign immunity against suit by private citizens. Nothing in the history of the Bankruptcy Clause suggests that, by including that clause in Article I, the founding generation intended to waive the latter aspect of sovereignty". Indeed, the grant of authority was essentially the same as that empowering Congress to regulate patents and copyrights, a subject already dealt with in prior Court decisions. Nor, in his view, did the States' immunity from suit undermine the objective of a uniform national law of bankruptcy.

Justice Thomas also criticized the majority for exaggerating the depth of national concern with the problem, noting that federal bankruptcy laws were in effect for only 16 of the first 109 years of the Republic, and that the very Act relied on by the Court was repealed only three years after its enactment. He then sought to refute arguments advanced by the majority. First, with respect to the authority to issue habeas corpus to a state officer, the availability of the writ "was well established by the time of the Framing and [on the theory recognized in Ex parte Young] consistent with then-prevailing notions of sovereignty". Second, he said, the concern that discharge orders issued by one state would not be recognized in other states was fully resolved by the Full Faith and Credit obligation imposed on every state by Article IV.

Concluding, Justice Thomas said: "It would be one thing if the majority simply wanted to overrule Seminole Tribe altogether. That would be wrong, but at least the terms of our disagreement would be transparent. The majority's action today, by contrast, is difficult to comprehend. Nothing in the text, structure, or history of the Constitution indicates that the Bankruptcy Clause, in contrast to all the other provisions of Article I, manifests the States' consent to be sued by private citizens".

Isn't Justice Thomas correct that Katz is not persuasively reconcilable with Seminole Tribe and its progeny? If so, what accounts for Justice

O'Connor's decision to vote with the majority? Is the viability of Katz threatened by Justice O'Connor's departure?[12]

(7) Congressional Power Under Article I to Induce, Identify, or Compel State "Consent" to Suit.

(a) In College Savings Bank v. Florida Prepaid Postsecondary Education Expense Board, 527 U.S. 666 (1999), the Supreme Court rejected the so-called "constructive waiver" theory traceable to Parden v. Terminal Ry., 377 U.S. 184 (1964), p. 939, *supra*, as inconsistent with Seminole Tribe and held that Congress lacks power under Article I to deem a state to have waived its sovereign immunity simply because the state engaged in otherwise lawful conduct. College Savings Bank arose when the bank brought a federal court action against a state entity under the federal Lanham Act, claiming that the defendant had falsely promoted its product (a tuition savings plan) in violation of the Act, and in doing so had caused competitive injury to the bank. In a 5–4 decision, Justice Scalia, writing for the Court, recognized that Congress had provided for such conduct to count as a "constructive waiver" of the state's immunity, as Parden suggested that it could do. But, the Court said, "[w]hatever may remain of our decision in Parden is expressly overruled".[13] Consent, the opinion continued, cannot be based "upon the State's mere presence in a field subject to congressional regulation"; to recognize congressional power to "exact constructive waivers through the exercise of Article I powers would * * * permit Congress to circumvent the antiabrogation holding of Seminole Tribe". In sum, when it comes to sovereign immunity, "the point of coercion is automatically passed—and the voluntariness of waiver destroyed—when what is attached to the refusal to waive is the exclusion of the State from otherwise lawful activity".

Justice Breyer's dissent, joined by Justices Stevens, Souter, and Ginsburg, expressed continuing disagreement with the Seminole decision. He also argued that in order to avoid giving the states a strong competitive advantage over regulated private entities, Congress must have "the power to condition entry into the market upon a waiver of sovereign immunity * * * for to deny Congress that power would deny Congress the power effectively to regulate *private* conduct". Accordingly, the authority to impose such a condition was "necessary and proper" to the effective exercise of the commerce power.

(b) Does College Savings Bank threaten the holding of South Dakota v. Dole, 483 U.S. 203 (1987), that Congress, in exercising its Spending Clause power, can condition financial grants on a state's agreement to do something that Congress could not compel the state to do under other provisions of Article I? In considering this question, note that the Court has held that the conditions Congress imposes on the states pursuant to federal spending programs must not be "coercive"—a limit that it found exceeded for the first

---

[12] In thinking about these questions, consider carefully how far Katz's rationale extends. Would it apply, for example, to a suit by the trustee in bankruptcy in a personal bankruptcy proceeding against a university, seeking to recover damages for patent infringement? For discussion of this question and a more general consideration of the Justices' obligation to follow precedent, see Shapiro, *The Role of Precedent in Constitutional Adjudication: An Introspection*, 86 Tex.L.Rev. 929, 947–56 (2008). See also Plank, *State Sovereignty in Bankruptcy After Katz*, 15 Am.Bankr.Inst.L.Rev. 59, 94 (2007) (asserting that Katz should not bar a sovereign immunity defense to an action by a bankruptcy trustee "to collect a debt owed by the state that the debtor in bankruptcy could not collect outside of bankruptcy").

[13] Insofar as Parden rested on an abrogation theory, it had been implicitly overruled by Seminole Tribe.

time, post-Dole, in National Federation of Independent Business v. Sebelius, 132 S.Ct. 2566 (2012). There, Congress threatened to withhold all Medicaid funds from states that refused to expand their Medicaid coverage in accordance with the Patient Protection and Affordable Care Act (ACA). The Court, per Chief Justice Roberts, found this threat of withheld funds coercive because "Medicaid spending account[ed] for over 20 percent of the average State's total budget, with federal funds covering 50 to 83 percent of those costs."

Short of the prohibition against coercive exercises of the Spending Power, what is the principle that allows Congress to condition the "gift" of funds on a state's waiver of immunity but denies it the ability to condition the "gift" of entry into a "preemptable" activity (or one subject to extensive regulation) on a similar waiver?[14]

_____

NOTE ON ALDEN V. MAINE AND STATE IMMUNITY FROM SUIT ON FEDERAL CLAIMS IN STATE COURT

(1) Introduction. Hans v. Louisiana and Seminole Tribe both dealt expressly with the states' Eleventh Amendment immunity from suit in federal court. It is a separate question whether either the Constitution of its own force, or Congress through the enactment of legislation, might compel *state courts* to accept and exercise jurisdiction over federal causes of action against the states, notwithstanding the states' wish to claim immunity. The Eleventh Amendment, on which the Hans and Seminole opinions were based, refers solely to a limitation on the construction of "the judicial Power of the United States". In addition, a number of pre-Seminole decisions had either held or suggested that federal law may sometimes require state courts to exercise jurisdiction that state law purports to deny them, see, *e.g.*, Testa v. Katt, 330 U.S. 386 (1947), p. 437, *supra*, even when the state would otherwise treat the action as barred by state sovereign immunity, see, *e.g.*, General Oil Co. v. Crain, 209 U.S. 211 (1908), p. 759, *supra*.

(2) The Alden Case. The Supreme Court addressed the question whether Congress has power under Article I to subject an unconsenting state to private suits for damages in its own courts in Alden v. Maine, 527 U.S. 706 (1999). In Alden, a group of Maine probation officers filed suit against the state in a Maine court, alleging that the state had violated the overtime provisions of the Fair Labor Standards Act of 1938 (FLSA), 29 U.S.C. § 201

_____

[14] For discussion of the authority of Congress to induce a "waiver" of state sovereign immunity through use of the spending and (possibly) other powers, see, *e.g.*, Baker & Berman, *Getting off the Dole: Why the Court Should Abandon Its Spending Doctrine, and How a Too-Clever Congress Could Provoke It To Do So*, 78 Ind.L.J. 459, 461 (2003) (arguing that the "Dole test" for judging Congress's power to condition aid to the states on waiver of various sovereign rights is "substantively and conceptually infirm"); Childers, *State Sovereign Immunity and the Protection of Intellectual Property: Do Recent Congressional Attempts to "Level the Playing Field" Run Afoul of Current Eleventh Amendment Jurisprudence and Other Constitutional Doctrines?*, 82 N.C.L.Rev. 1067 (2004) (questioning the constitutionality of proposed legislation designed to protect against state infringement of intellectual property rights and suggesting more moderate measures); Meltzer, *Overcoming Immunity: The Case of Federal Regulation of Intellectual Property*, 53 Stan.L.Rev. 1331, 1386–89 (2001) (discussing issues of waiver or constructive consent through conduct other than the enactment of state legislation when Congress has expressly stated that such conduct constitutes waiver); Zietlow, *Federalism's Paradox: The Spending Power and Waiver of Sovereign Immunity*, 37 Wake Forest L.Rev. 141 (2002) (defending a broad authority of Congress to condition federal funding on waiver of immunity).

et seq., and seeking money damages. (The plaintiffs had initially filed their action in federal district court; they turned to the state court only after the federal court, following the Supreme Court's decision in Seminole Tribe, had dismissed their case.)

The state responded to the state court action by invoking its sovereign immunity from suit. (It did not dispute Alden's showing that Maine law allows suits against the state by state employees for wage claims based on state law even though it denies those same employees the ability to enforce wage claims based on federal law. The sole difference is that state law does not require overtime pay, while the FLSA does.) The state courts dismissed the action on sovereign immunity grounds, and the Supreme Court affirmed by 5–4, with Justice Kennedy writing for the majority.

(3) The Majority Opinion. Justice Kennedy began by characterizing the immunity claimed by the state as an incident of the constitutional plan: The phrase " 'Eleventh Amendment immunity' * * * is convenient shorthand but something of a misnomer, for the sovereign immunity of the States neither derives from, nor is limited by, the terms of the Eleventh Amendment. Rather, as the Constitution's structure, its history, and the authoritative interpretations by this Court make clear, the States' immunity from suit is a fundamental aspect of the sovereignty which the States enjoyed before the ratification of the Constitution, and which they retain today (either literally or by virtue of their admission into the Union upon an equal footing with the other States) except as altered by the plan of the Convention or certain constitutional Amendments."

"Although the Constitution establishes a National Government with broad, often plenary authority over matters within its recognized competence," Justice Kennedy continued, the Constitution " 'specifically recognizes the States as sovereign entities' " (quoting Seminole Tribe of Fla. v. Florida, *supra*) and accords the States "the dignity, though not the full authority, of sovereignty". Consistent with this position, "[t]he generation that designed and adopted our federal system considered immunity from private suits central to sovereign dignity." When the Constitution was drafted and ratified, "the doctrine that the sovereign could not be sued without its consent was universal in the states," and the ratification debates reflected an intent to retain it. In the succeeding paragraphs, the Court quoted from statements by Alexander Hamilton in The Federalist No. 81, from statements by James Madison and John Marshall—all of which also appear in Hans v. Louisiana, p. 908, *supra*—and from the records of state ratifying conventions in Rhode Island and New York. The Court then turned to a discussion of the decision in Chisholm v. Georgia, p. 905, *supra*, and the "profound shock" that greeted that decision. The Court then described the proposal and ratification of the Eleventh Amendment.

"The text and history of the Eleventh Amendment also suggest that Congress acted not to change but to restore the original constitutional design." The dissenting opinion, Justice Kennedy conceded, offered some evidence to the contrary, but, he concluded, the more persuasive evidence supported the majority view. The discussions in a number of prior decisions, including Hans and Seminole Tribe, were also consistent with this assessment, Justice Kennedy said.

Against this background, Justice Kennedy continued, that the Eleventh Amendment spoke only of federal judicial power was irrelevant. The petitioners claimed that "the text of the Constitution and our recent sovereign immunity decisions establish that the States" surrendered their sovereign immunity from state court actions authorized by Congress, but their arguments were unpersuasive. "[T]he Supremacy Clause enshrines as 'the supreme Law of the Land' only those Federal Acts that accord with the constitutional design * * * [and thus] merely raises the question whether a law is a valid exercise of the national power. * * * Nor can we conclude that the specific Article I powers delegated to Congress necessarily include, by virtue of the Necessary and Proper Clause or otherwise, the incidental authority to subject the States to private suits as a means of achieving objectives otherwise within the scope of the enumerated powers."

The Court had previously concluded that "neither the Supremacy Clause nor the enumerated powers of Congress confer authority to abrogate the States' immunity from suit in federal court", and their logic "does not turn on the forum in which the suits were prosecuted but extends to state-court suits as well. * * * Although the sovereign immunity of the States derives at least in part from the common-law tradition, the structure and history of the Constitution make clear that the immunity exists today [not as a result of the common law or 'natural law' but] by constitutional design. * * * [Furthermore,] [t]he dissent has offered no evidence that the founders believed sovereign immunity extended only to cases where the sovereign was the source of the right asserted."

Justice Kennedy acknowledged isolated statements in some cases suggesting that the Eleventh Amendment is inapplicable in state courts, but the question did not turn on "the literal terms of the Eleventh Amendment" for, as the Court had explained, it "is not an exhaustive description of the States' constitutional immunity from suit."

Justice Kennedy then distinguished a series of cases. In Hilton v. South Carolina Public Railways Comm'n, 502 U.S. 197 (1991), the Court had held that an injured employee of a state-owned railroad could sue his employer (an arm of the State) in state court under the Federal Employers' Liability Act (FELA), but Hilton was argued and decided on the assumption that Congress could either abrogate the states' immunity outright, under Pennsylvania v. Union Gas, p. 940, *supra*, or could condition their operation of railroads on consent to suit, under Parden v. Terminal Ry., p. 939, *supra*. The overruling of Union Gas and Parden thus rendered Hilton irrelevant.

Nevada v. Hall, 440 U.S. 410 (1979), which held that the Constitution did not bar California from subjecting Nevada to suit in a California state court, was also off-point. The Court "determined the Constitution did not reflect an agreement between the States to respect the sovereign immunity of one another", but did not speak to whether the Constitution authorized Congress to force the states to submit to suit in their own courts.

It was similarly unavailing for the petitioners to rely on Reich v. Collins, 513 U.S. 106 (1994), which, according to Justice Kennedy, held that "despite its immunity from suit in federal court, a State which holds out what plainly appears to be 'a clear and certain' postdeprivation remedy for taxes collected in violation of federal law may not declare, after disputed taxes have been paid in reliance on this remedy, that the remedy does not in fact exist. * * * In this context, due process requires the State to provide the remedy it has promised. The obligation arises from the Constitution itself; Reich does not speak to the power of Congress to subject States to suits in their own courts."

With the cases on which the petitioners relied all being distinguishable, Justice Kennedy reasoned that "[w]hether Congress has authority under Article I to abrogate a State's immunity from suit in its own courts is, then, a question of first impression" appropriately answered in the negative.

Looking "first to evidence of the original understanding of the Constitution", the Court found no express discussion of the states' immunity in their own courts, but immunity was so well established, and its preservation of such concern to the ratifiers, that to read "the Founders' silence" as "permitting the inference that the Constitution stripped the States of immunity in their own courts and allowed Congress to subject them to suit there would turn on its head the concern of the founding generation".

Early congressional practice supported this conclusion. "The first statute we confronted that even arguably purported to subject the States to private actions was the FELA [in 1908]." Turning then to "the theory and reasoning of our earlier cases", the Court found abundant support for upholding the state's claim of immunity from suit in its own courts: "We have often described the States' immunity in sweeping terms, without reference to whether the suit was prosecuted in state or federal court. See, *e.g.*, Briscoe v. Bank of Kentucky, 11 Pet. 257, 321–322 (1837) ('No sovereign state is liable to be sued without her consent'); Board of Liquidation v. McComb, 92 U.S. 531, 541 (1875) ('A State, without its consent, cannot be sued by an individual')." Indeed, the Court had "relied on the States' immunity in their own courts as a premise in our Eleventh Amendment rulings. See Hans."

The Court continued: "In particular, the exception to our sovereign immunity doctrine recognized in Ex parte Young, 209 U.S. 123 (1908), is based in part on the premise that sovereign immunity bars relief against States and their officers in both state and federal courts, and that certain suits for declaratory or injunctive relief against state officers must therefore be permitted if the Constitution is to remain the supreme law of the land. As we explained in General Oil Co. v. Crain, 209 U.S. 211 (1908), a case decided the same day as Ex parte Young and extending the rule of that case to state-court suits:

"* * * If a suit against state officers is precluded in the national courts by the Eleventh Amendment to the Constitution, and may be forbidden by a State to its courts, as it is contended in the case at bar that it may be, without power of review by this court, it must be evident that an easy way is open to prevent the enforcement of many provisions of the Constitution." * * *

"Had we not understood the States to retain a constitutional immunity from suit in their own courts, the need for the Ex parte Young rule would have been less pressing, and the rule would not have formed so essential a part of our sovereign immunity doctrine."

Satisfied that "settled doctrine" supported "the conclusion that Congress lacks the Article I power to subject the States to private suits" in state court, Justice Kennedy found similar support for the same conclusion in the structure of the Constitution, which made clear that Congress must "treat the States in a manner consistent with their status as residuary sovereigns and joint participants in the governance of the Nation. * * *

"Petitioners contend that immunity from suit in federal court suffices to preserve the dignity of the States. Private suits against nonconsenting States, however, present 'the indignity of subjecting a State to the coercive process of judicial tribunals at the instance of private parties,' regardless of the forum. Not only must a State defend or default but also it must face the prospect of being thrust, by federal fiat and against its will, into the disfavored status of a debtor, subject to the power of private citizens to levy on its treasury or perhaps even government buildings or property which the State administers on the public's behalf.

"In some ways, of course, a congressional power to authorize private suits against nonconsenting States in their own courts would be even more offensive to state sovereignty than a power to authorize the suits in a federal forum", for it would be a "power first to turn the State against itself and ultimately to commandeer the entire political machinery of the State against its will and at the behest of individuals. * * * It is unquestioned that the Federal Government retains its own immunity from suit not only in state tribunals but also in its own courts. In light of our constitutional system recognizing the essential sovereignty of the States, we are reluctant to conclude that the States are not entitled to a reciprocal privilege."

Practical concerns were also at stake: "Private suits against nonconsenting States—especially suits for money damages—may threaten the financial integrity of the States. It is indisputable that, at the time of the founding, many of the States could have been forced into insolvency but for their immunity from private suits for money damages. Even today, an unlimited congressional power to authorize suits in state court to levy upon the treasuries of the States for compensatory damages, attorney's fees, and even punitive damages could create staggering burdens, giving Congress a power and a leverage over the States that is not contemplated by our constitutional design. The potential national power would pose a severe and notorious danger to the States and their resources." It would also "place unwarranted strain on the States' ability to govern in accordance with the will of their citizens. Today, as at the time of the founding, the allocation of scarce resources among competing needs and interests lies at the heart of the political process. While the judgment creditor of the State may have a legitimate claim for compensation, other important needs and worthwhile ends compete for access to the public fisc. * * * If the principle of representative government is to be preserved to the States, the balance between competing interests must be reached after deliberation by the political process established by the citizens of the State, not by judicial decree mandated by the Federal Government and invoked by the private citizen."

The Court acknowledged that Congress may, under Testa v. Katt, 330 U.S. 386 (1947), p. 437, *supra*, require state courts of competent jurisdiction to enforce valid federal laws, but it would be unprecedented and unwarranted to infer that "Congress' authority to pursue federal objectives through the state judiciaries exceeds not only its power to press other branches of the State into its service but even its control over the federal courts themselves. * * * The Supremacy Clause does impose specific obligations on state judges. There can be no serious contention, however, that the Supremacy Clause imposes greater obligations on state-court judges than on the Judiciary of the United States itself."

Having concluded that Congress had no authority to strip the state of immunity from FLSA actions in its own courts, Justice Kennedy paused to mark some bounds on the Court's decision: "The constitutional privilege of a State to assert its sovereign immunity in its own courts does not confer upon the State a concomitant right to disregard the Constitution or valid federal law. The States and their officers are bound by obligations imposed by the

Constitution and by federal statutes that comport with the constitutional design. We are unwilling to assume the States will refuse to honor the Constitution or obey the binding laws of the United States."

Moreover, sovereign immunity did not bar all suits to enforce federal law against the states. Suits could proceed in cases of consent, and consent to some actions was implicit in the constitutional plan: "In ratifying the Constitution, the States consented to suits brought by other States or by the Federal Government. A suit which is commenced and prosecuted against a State in the name of the United States * * * differs in kind from the suit of an individual: While the Constitution contemplates suits among the members of the federal system as an alternative to extralegal measures, the fear of private suits against nonconsenting States was the central reason given by the founders who chose to preserve the States' sovereign immunity. Suits brought by the United States itself require the exercise of political responsibility for each suit prosecuted against a State, a control which is absent from a broad delegation to private persons to sue nonconsenting States."

The states similarly had no immunity against suits duly authorized by Congress under § 5 of the Fourteenth Amendment. Moreover, the states' immunity does not extend to local governments. "Nor does sovereign immunity bar all suits against state officers * * * [including] certain actions against state officers for injunctive or declaratory relief. Even a suit for money damages may be prosecuted against a state officer in his individual capacity for unconstitutional or wrongful conduct fairly attributable to the officer himself, so long as the relief is sought not from the state treasury but from the officer personally."

The last question to be addressed was whether Maine had waived its immunity from FLSA actions, and Justice Kennedy concluded that it had not: Maine retained its immunity under state law, and "[a]lthough petitioners contend the State has discriminated against federal rights by claiming sovereign immunity from this FLSA suit, there is no evidence that the State has manipulated its immunity in a systematic fashion to discriminate against federal causes of action. To the extent Maine has chosen to consent to certain classes of suits while maintaining its immunity from others, it has done no more than exercise a privilege of sovereignty concomitant to its constitutional immunity from suit."

The Court then concluded as follows: "The State of Maine has not questioned Congress' power to prescribe substantive rules of federal law to which it must comply. Despite an initial good-faith disagreement about the requirements of the FLSA, it is conceded by all that the State has altered its conduct so that its compliance with federal law cannot now be questioned. The Solicitor General of the United States has appeared before this Court, however, and asserted that the federal interest in compensating the States' employees for alleged past violations of federal law is so compelling that the sovereign State of Maine must be stripped of its immunity and subjected to suit in its own courts by its own employees. Yet, despite specific statutory authorization, see 29 U.S.C. § 216(c), the United States apparently found the same interests insufficient to justify sending even a single attorney to Maine to prosecute this litigation. The difference between a suit by the United States on behalf of the employees and a suit by the employees implicates a rule that the National Government must itself deem the case of sufficient importance to take action against the State; and history, precedent, and the structure of the Constitution make clear that, under the plan of the Convention, the States have consented to suits of the first kind but not of the second."

(4) The Dissenting Opinion. Justice Souter, joined by Justices Stevens, Ginsburg, and Breyer, filed a long and passionate dissenting opinion. He began by objecting to the Court's characterization of the relationship between the concept of state sovereign immunity and the text of the Eleventh Amendment: "[T]he Court * * * confronts the fact that the state forum renders the Eleventh Amendment beside the point, and it has responded by discerning a simpler and more straightforward theory of state sovereign immunity than it found in Seminole Tribe: a State's sovereign immunity from all individual suits is a 'fundamental aspect' of state sovereignty 'confirm[ed]' by the Tenth Amendment. As a consequence, Seminole Tribe's contorted reliance on the Eleventh Amendment and its background was presumably unnecessary; the Tenth would have done the work with an economy that the majority in Seminole Tribe would have welcomed." But the Court's analysis, he said, was "mistaken" on "each point".

In the first part of his opinion, Justice Souter examined the sovereign immunity that had existed at the time of the Founding: "While sovereign immunity entered many new state legal systems as a part of the common law selectively received from England, it was not understood to be indefeasible or to have been given any such status by the new National Constitution, which did not mention it. Had the question been posed, state sovereign immunity could not have been thought to shield a State from suit under federal law on a subject committed to national jurisdiction by Article I of the Constitution. Congress exercising its conceded Article I power may unquestionably abrogate such immunity."

For the common law immunity that the Founders had known, Justice Souter argued, the majority had substituted what it took to be "a conception necessarily implied by statehood itself. The conception is thus not one of common law so much as of natural law, a universally applicable proposition discoverable by reason." But the historical evidence did not support this view of state sovereign immunity. "To the extent that States were thought to possess immunity, it was perceived as a prerogative of the sovereign under common law. And where sovereign immunity was recognized as barring suit, provisions for recovery from the State were in order, just as they had been at common law in England."

The same understanding prevailed at the Constitutional Convention and in the ratifying debates. "The controversy over the enforceability of state debts subject to state law produced emphatic support for sovereign immunity from eminences as great as Madison and Marshall, but neither of them indicated adherence to any immunity conception outside the common law." Nor did the ratification of the Eleventh Amendment suggest that sovereign immunity was understood, then or earlier, to be any more than a common law prerogative. "The federal citizen-state diversity jurisdiction was settled by the Eleventh Amendment; Article III was not 'restored.' "

Continuing to characterize the majority as espousing a "natural law theory of sovereign immunity," Justice Souter wrote that the closest historical analogue to that view was Justice Holmes's opinion in Kawananakoa v. Polyblank, 205 U.S. 349 (1907), p. 879, *supra*, in which Holmes, although not "a natural law jurist", said: "A sovereign is exempt from suit, not because of any formal conception or obsolete theory, but on the logical and practical ground that there can be no legal right as against the authority that makes the law on which the right depends." But even on Holmes' view, when there are "multiple sovereignties, the subordinate sovereign will not be immune where the source of the right of action is the sovereign that is dominant." His view thus "yields the clear conclusion that even in a system of 'fundamental' state sovereign immunity, a State would be subject to suit *eo nomine* in its own courts on a federal claim."

Apart from its reliance on a natural law conception of sovereignty, the majority, according to Justice Souter, misunderstood the structure of the Constitution and of constitutional federalism. Under the Constitution, the states are sovereign with respect to the matters committed to them, but not with respect to matters committed to the national government. Accordingly, "[t]he State of Maine is not sovereign with respect to the national objective of the FLSA." And it was "sheer circularity for the Court to talk of the 'anomaly' that would arise if the State could be sued on federal law in its own courts, when it may not be sued under federal law in federal court" under Seminole Tribe: "The short and sufficient answer is that the anomaly is the Court's own creation: The Eleventh Amendment was never intended to bar federal-question suits against the States in federal court."

Nor could it be argued, Justice Souter continued, "that because the State of Maine creates its own court system, it has authority to decide what sorts of claims may be entertained there", for "the Supremacy Clause of the Constitution * * * requires the Maine courts to entertain this federal cause of action" under cases such as Testa v. Katt.

Justice Souter also found the majority's policy arguments unconvincing. The Court cited the need to protect the states' dignity, but this idea was "inimical to the republican conception, which rests on the understanding of its citizens precisely that the government is not above them, but of them, its actions being governed by law just like their own. * * * Least of all does the Court persuade by observing that 'other important needs' than that of the 'judgment creditor' compete for public money. The 'judgment creditor' in question is not a dunning bill collector, but a citizen whose federal rights have been violated, and a constitutional structure that stints on enforcing federal rights out of an abundance of delicacy toward the States has substituted politesse in place of respect for the rule of law."

Justice Souter then returned to historical matters and their contemporary relevance: "The Court apparently believes that because state courts have not historically entertained Commerce Clause based federal-law claims against the States, such an innovation carries a presumption of unconstitutionality." But the premise was out of touch with contemporary understandings of congressional regulatory power, under which it "is settled that federal legislation enacted under the Commerce Clause may bind the States without having to satisfy a test of undue incursion into state sovereignty. * * * If the Framers would be surprised to see States subjected to suit in their own courts under the commerce power, they would be astonished by the reach of Congress under the Commerce Clause generally. The proliferation of Government, State and Federal, would amaze the Framers, and the administrative state with its reams of regulations would leave them rubbing their eyes. But the Framers' surprise at, say, the FLSA, or the Federal Communications Commission, or the Federal Reserve Board is no threat to the constitutionality of any one of them, for a very fundamental reason:

"[W]hen we are dealing with words that also are a constituent act, like the Constitution of the United States, we must realize that they have called into life a being the development of which could not have been foreseen completely by the most gifted of its begetters. It was enough for them to realize or to hope that they had created an organism; it has taken a century and has cost their successors much sweat and blood to prove that they created a nation. The case before us must be considered in the light of our whole experience and not merely in that of what was said a hundred years ago.' Missouri v. Holland, 252 U.S. 416, 433 (1920) (Holmes, J.)."

Absent any doubt of Congress' authority to enact the FLSA and make it binding on the states, Justice Souter continued, it was wholly unpersuasive for the majority to suggest that enforcement actions by the Secretary of Labor would suffice to ensure state compliance. And there was irony in the Court's purported respect for tradition, for it "abandons a principle nearly as inveterate, and much closer to the hearts of the Framers: that where there is a right, there must be a remedy."

(5) Securing State Compliance with Federal Law. Is the majority consistent in suggesting, on the one hand, that it is "unwilling to assume the states will refuse to honor the Constitution or obey the binding laws of the United States" and, on the other hand, that "[p]rivate suits against the States—especially suits for money damages—may threaten the financial integrity of unconsenting States"?

(6) The Court's Treatment of Precedent. The majority's treatment of precedent raised a number of questions.

(a) How persuasive was the majority's distinction of General Oil Co. v. Crain, p. 759, *supra*? The majority invoked this case for the proposition that where the doctrine of Ex parte Young allows a federal court action against a state officer to enjoin a constitutional violation, a state court must allow a similar remedy. But in the very excerpt quoted by the majority, doesn't the Court appear to say that if *both* federal and state courts are closed to a claim of constitutional right, the impermissible result would be a denial of that right?

(b) In Reich v. Collins, p. 757, *supra*, the Court, in the course of holding that due process requires a "clear and certain" remedy for taxes collected in violation of federal law, added, in dictum, that if a state fails to provide adequate predeprivation remedies, it must provide a damages or restitution remedy in state court, notwithstanding "the sovereign immunity States traditionally enjoy in their own courts." Alden narrows Reich's rationale by saying the former case stands only for the proposition that when state law appears to provide a tax-refund remedy (and only a refund remedy), the "Constitution itself" (*i.e.*, the Due Process Clause) requires the state to provide the remedy it has promised. Is there any good reason why the Constitution would require a remedy against a state in its own courts only when it withholds a promised remedy? After Alden, could a state invoke sovereign immunity as a defense against an action in state court seeking just compensation for a violation of the Takings Clause? Dictum in First English Evangelical Lutheran Church v. County of Los Angeles, p. 334, *supra*, had suggested a negative answer, but does its analysis survive Alden?

(c) The Alden majority distinguishes Nevada v. Hall, 440 U.S. 410 (1979), which held that a California state court need not honor Nevada's claim of sovereign immunity in a suit against it by a private party,[1] on the grounds that it dealt with the immunity of a state in the courts of another state, not in its own courts, and that "an implied constitutional limit on the power of the States cannot be construed * * * to support an analogous reluctance to find implied constitutional limits on the power of the Federal Government". How convincing is that distinction? If a state's sovereign immunity affords it constitutional protection from suit in a federal court that does not depend on the text of the Eleventh Amendment, why doesn't the Constitution afford at least as much protection against suit in the courts of a sister state?

Following Alden, it was widely speculated that the Court might be prepared to overrule Nevada v. Hall, but the Justices explicitly declined to reconsider the earlier decision in rejecting a state's claim of immunity from being sued in the courts of another state in Franchise Tax Board of California [CFTB] v. Hyatt, 538 U.S. 488 (2003).[2]

(7) The Court's Sovereignty and Dignity Rationales and Their Implications.

(a) To a significant extent, the states may be regulated by the national government acting in the exercise of its delegated powers, and (after considerable oscillation) the Court now recognizes that such regulation may include matters relating to the wages paid by the state to certain employees. Is there any justification, then, for a free-standing notion of state sovereign immunity from suit that exceeds the substantive scope of state sovereignty (or autonomy) with respect to those matters? Does it make sense for states to be subject to federal regulation but to enjoy immunity with respect to

---

[1] For presentation of the historical, doctrinal, textual, and practical arguments against the Court's decision in Nevada v. Hall and in support of Justice Rehnquist's dissent, see Woolhandler, *Interstate Sovereign Immunity*, 2006 Sup.Ct.Rev. 249 (2007). Professor Woolhandler notes that the result in Hall gives rise to a question of the enforceability of a judgment for the plaintiff. Could a judgment against Nevada be enforced against the state in either a state or a federal court?

[2] In the CFTB case, Hyatt, a Nevada resident at the time of filing, brought an action against CFTB in a Nevada state court, alleging that the defendant had committed negligent and intentional torts in the course of auditing Hyatt's California state tax returns. Holding that California's sovereign interests warranted recognition of CFTB's claim of immunity with respect to negligence but that they did not outweigh Nevada's interests with respect to intentional torts, the Nevada Supreme Court rejected CFTB's claim of immunity with respect to the latter aspect of the complaint, and the U.S. Supreme Court unanimously affirmed.

The Court stated that petitioner CFTB "does not ask us to reexamine [the holding of Hall summarized above] and we therefore decline the invitation of petitioner's amici States * * * to do so". The Court then went on to consider CFTB's claim, said to implicate "Hall's second holding: that the Full Faith and Credit Clause did not require California to apply Nevada's sovereign immunity statutes where such application would violate California's own legitimate public policy". Relying heavily on Hall, the Court rejected CFTB's claim that the Full Faith and Credit Clause required a determination that California's sovereign interest in enforcing its tax laws outweighed Nevada's interests in providing a remedy for an intentional tort allegedly injuring one of its citizens within its borders. After noting that "[t]he Nevada Supreme Court sensitively applied principles of comity with a healthy regard for California's sovereign status," the Court "decline[d] to embark on the constitutional course of balancing coordinate States' competing sovereign interests to resolve conflicts of laws under the Full Faith and Credit Clause".

The Court has not always been loath to reconsider a decision when no party has asked it to do so (see, *e.g.*, Erie R.R. v. Tompkins, 304 U.S. 64 (1938)), especially when it does not find an alternative ground for reaching the result that overruling the prior decision would achieve. Does the CFTB case thus suggest that despite the difficulty of reconciling Hall's rationale with that of Alden, Hall is not likely to be overruled?

major techniques of enforcement of that regulation? If so, why should such immunity apply only to suits against states and not against local governments? (Recall that the immunity from substantive regulation of employee wages, which was recognized by the Court from 1976 until its decision in Garcia v. San Antonio Metropolitan Transit Authority, 469 U.S. 528 (1985), p. 447, *supra*, extended to local as well as state governments.)[3]

(b) As a justification for a free-standing concept of state immunity, the majority in Seminole and (especially) in Alden relied in part on the notion that an unconsented suit against a state was an "affront" to its "dignity". Although the dissenters in those cases vigorously challenged this rationale—partly on the ground that it derived from notions of "divine right" that had no place in a democracy—this justification became the mainstay of the Court's reasoning in Federal Maritime Commission [FMC] v. South Carolina State Ports Authority, 535 U.S. 743 (2002), which held that state sovereign immunity precluded a federal *administrative agency* from adjudicating a private party's complaint against an unconsenting state. In this case, a private company filed a complaint with a federal agency (the FMC), seeking injunctive relief and reparations on the basis that the Ports Authority, a state agency, had violated federal law when it denied the complainant berthing rights at the agency's port facilities in South Carolina. The agency, in response to the complaint, claimed that as an arm of the state it was entitled to sovereign immunity, and, in a 5–4 decision, the Supreme Court agreed.

Justice Thomas, for the majority, reiterated the view that the Eleventh Amendment "is but one particular exemplification" of state sovereign immunity,[4] and then went on to address the specific arguments raised by the FMC and its amici. First, assuming that the FMC was not exercising the "judicial power" conferred by Article III, he concluded that the "Hans presumption" of immunity came into play because "FMC adjudications * * * are the type of proceedings from which the Framers would have thought the States possessed immunity when they agreed to enter the Union". Second, in view of this similarity, and the fact that "the *preeminent purpose* [of immunity] is to accord States the dignity that is consistent with their status as sovereign entities", the affront to that dignity "does not lessen when an adjudication takes place in an administrative tribunal as opposed to an Article III court" (emphasis added). Moreover, it did not matter that the FMC's orders were not self-executing, but could only be enforced in a judicial proceeding (which in certain instances could be brought by the federal government) because of the many pressures on the state to appear and defend itself in the administrative proceedings. Given the consequences of non-compliance with an FMC order, and the limited scope of judicial review, for the Court to conclude that the state was not coerced to participate at the agency level "would [be to] blind ourselves to reality. And the argument that

---

[3]   Fallon, *The "Conservative" Paths of the Rehnquist Court's Federalism Decisions*, 69 U.Chi.L.Rev. 429 (2002), ascribes the Court's hesitancy to extend sovereign immunity to local governments partly to a long historical tradition. He notes, however, that the Court has developed a number of sub-constitutional barriers to suits against local governments, including a requirement that in order for a plaintiff in a § 1983 action against a local government to succeed, the plaintiff must establish the local government's causal responsibility for the wrongful acts of its officials (see pp. 999–1003, *infra*.).

[4]   In addition to this acknowledgment (that the principle of sovereign immunity applied here did not fall within the scope of the Eleventh Amendment itself), Justice Thomas later stated that "[t]he principle of state sovereign immunity enshrined in our constitutional framework * * * is not rooted in the Tenth Amendment".

FMC proceedings did not threaten the financial integrity of the states in the same way as private judicial suits was not only incorrect as a practical matter but also 'reflects a fundamental misunderstanding of the purposes of sovereign immunity'—to 'accord the states the respect owed them as' joint sovereigns".

Justice Breyer, joined by Justices Stevens, Souter, and Ginsburg, dissented.[5] He began by noting that even "independent agencies" like the FMC should be "considered to be part of the Executive Branch". He then argued that agency adjudication, like agency rulemaking and other forms of agency action, was in essence a form of executive activity that was designed to evaluate complaints, not finally adjudicate them, and thus was not subject to any Eleventh Amendment or other sovereign immunity constraint. Therefore, he continued, a claim of state sovereign immunity should be evaluated only in the context, and at the time, of any judicial enforcement proceeding that might ultimately be brought. As for the argument that the administrative adjudicatory proceeding was an unacceptable affront to the state's dignity, he contended that this position was impossible to reconcile with the conceded ability of an agency, on the complaint of a private citizen, to initiate an investigation or to promulgate a rule that would "place a State under far greater practical pressures" than the proceeding in the case at bar. After disagreeing with the majority's contention that the consequences of its decision would be minor because other enforcement techniques were available, Justice Breyer concluded that the FMC case was the latest in a series of decisions that had "set loose an interpretive principle that restricts far too severely the authority of the federal government to regulate innumerable relationships between State and citizen".

Given the range of regulatory techniques that are admittedly open to the Executive, do you agree with the majority that the choice of the "adjudicatory" approach at the administrative level is more of an affront to the state than the others? Doesn't the majority's own insistence that its decision does not seriously interfere with the prevention and remediation of state violations of federal law (whether correct or not) undermine its own "dignity" rationale?[6]

(c) Sossamon v. Texas, 131 S.Ct. 1651 (2011), affirmed that Congress can condition grants of federal funds on state waivers of sovereign immunity, but held that statutory language authorizing suits for "appropriate relief against a government" that accepts federal money did not constitute a waiver

---

[5] Justice Stevens also wrote a brief separate dissent in which he attacked the Court's "dignity" rationale as stemming from the now irrelevant interests of the English monarchs and concluded that by applying that "untethered" rationale to "routine federal administrative proceedings," the Court's decision was "even more anachronistic than Alden".

[6] For critical discussion of the Court's reliance on the concept of "dignity" as a basis for state immunity from suit, see *e.g.*, Meltzer, *State Sovereign Immunity: Five Authors in Search of a Theory*, 75 Notre Dame L.Rev. 1011, 1038 (2000); Resnik & Suk, *Adding Insult to Injury: Questioning the Role of Dignity in Conceptions of Sovereignty*, 55 Stan.L.Rev. 1921, 1962 (2003) (arguing that although the concept of "institutional dignity" has value in many contexts, it should not be used as a justification for immunizing states from accounting for their behavior: "requiring governments to participate in litigation * * * enhanc[es], rather than diminish[es] the role-dignity appropriate to sovereignty"); Smith, *States as Nations: Dignity in Cross-Doctrinal Perspective*, 89 Va.L.Rev. 1, 7 (2003) (suggesting that the "dignity" rationale is implicitly drawn from the Court's long recognition of the dignity of foreign nations and urging that (1) this notion should not apply to the constituent states of our federal union, and (2) to the extent that it is applied, "the doctrinal consequence ought to be that Congress has authority [as it does with respect to foreign nations] to abrogate the states' immunity").

of immunity from suits for money damages. Writing for the majority, Justice Thomas echoed prior admonitions that "[a] State's consent to suit must be 'unequivocally expressed'" and that the scope of any waiver "'will be strictly construed * * * in favor of the sovereign.'" The term "appropriate relief", he then concluded, was too "open-ended and ambiguous" to elicit a waiver of immunity from damages actions.

Justice Sotomayor dissented in an opinion joined by Justice Breyer. According to her, it was "self-evident" that "money damages are 'appropriate relief'". Even the majority, she noted, "appears to accept" that by taking federal funds Texas had waived its immunity from suits for equitable relief. She continued: "But sovereign immunity is not simply a defense against certain classes of remedies—it is a defense against being sued at all. As a result, there is no inherent reason why the phrase 'appropriate relief' would provide adequate notice as to equitable remedies but not as to monetary ones. In fact, * * * in light of general remedies principles the presumption arguably should be the reverse."[7]

(8) The "Commandeering" of State Courts and Their Nondiscrimination Obligation. The Alden majority rejected the notion that Congress could require state courts to adjudicate claims against the states arising under federal law partly on the basis that the power to press a state's courts into federal service to coerce other branches of the state "is the power * * * ultimately to commandeer the entire political machinery of the State against its will and at the behest of individuals." If the "commandeering" argument has persuasive force in this context, why isn't it a similarly unacceptable commandeering for state courts of otherwise competent jurisdiction to be required to entertain federal claims against private parties under Testa v. Katt, p. 437, *supra*?

Does Alden weaken the obligation on state courts, as defined by Testa and other cases, not to discriminate against federal claims? Without disputing that the Maine courts would have entertained state employees' claims for back wages based on state law, the majority says first that there is no evidence that Maine engaged in "systematic" manipulation of its immunity to discriminate against federal claims. It then concludes that as "a privilege of sovereignty concomitant to its constitutional immunity from suit" the state may choose "to consent to certain classes of suits while maintaining its immunity from others". If the only significant distinction between these two classes of cases is the source of law on which the plaintiff relies, what more would be needed to demonstrate the discrimination against federal claims that Testa forbids?

(9) Congress' Options After Alden and the Scope and Significance of the Court's Rulings. Consider the options available to Congress in the wake of Alden to achieve effective judicial enforcement of federal law against the states, including: (a) suits for injunctive relief against state officials; (b) suits for damages against state officials in their individual capacities;[8]

---

[7] For critical commentary on the relatively recently minted rule that a general waiver of sovereign immunity will not encompass suits for money relief absent clear authorization of that remedy, see Tang, *Double Immunity,* 65 Stan.L.Rev. 279 (2013).

[8] For a discussion of the issue of individual liability for damages under the FLSA and other federal statutes affecting employees, see Meltzer, *supra* note 6, at 1018–19 & n. 37. (Would an individual supervisor who may be sued for damages in such a case have a defense of qualified immunity?)

(c) suits for damages or injunctive relief by the United States;[9] (d) abrogation of state sovereign immunity under § 5 of the Fourteenth Amendment in suits alleging constitutional violations; and (e) provision for federal jurisdiction in many if not all actions under federal bankruptcy law. In light of these possibilities, how seriously does Alden impede the effective enforcement of federal law?

Consider the suggestion of Professor Shapiro—a severe critic of the Court's rulings conferring constitutional status on the concept of state sovereign immunity—that "the doctrine as it has evolved has so many loopholes and limitations that it seldom if ever stands in the way of implementing federal policy or vindicating federal rights." Shapiro, *The Role of Precedent in Constitutional Adjudication: An Introspection*, 86 Tex.L.Rev. 929 (2008). (For arguments to the same effect, see Choper & Yoo, *Who's Afraid of the Eleventh Amendment? The Limited Impact of the Court's Sovereign Immunity Rulings*, 106 Colum.L.Rev. 213 (2006), and Jeffries, *In Praise of the Eleventh Amendment and Section 1983*, 84 Va.L.Rev. 47 (1998).)

How persuasive do you find this view? In weighing it, consider that (a) injunctive relief leaves the compensatory purpose of statutory and constitutional remedies unfulfilled; moreover, in the absence of the prospect of damages recovery, many victims of rights violations may not bring suit at all, see, *e.g.*, Colker, *The Section Five Quagmire*, 47 UCLA L.Rev. 653 (2000); (b) although plaintiffs can sue officials for damages in their individual capacities, doctrines of "official immunity" typically bar recovery unless an official has violated "clearly established" law and sometimes protect even those who violate well settled rights, see Section 3, *infra*; (c) suits by the

---

[9]   Could Congress also circumvent the limitation on its abrogation power by authorizing individuals to sue in the name of the United States to seek compensation for a state's violation of its duty under federal law? (And must such actions be limited to cases where the duty is one owing to the federal government?) Actions of this type, in which a private citizen brings suit in the name of the government (the caption usually describes the government as plaintiff and the citizen as "relator"), and in which the private citizen is awarded a percentage of the recovery if the suit is successful, have long been recognized and are known as "*qui tam*" actions.

The False Claims Act, 31 U.S.C. §§ 3729–33, provides for a *qui tam* action against "any person" who, *inter alia*, "knowingly presents" to the federal government "a false or fraudulent claim for payment" (§ 3729 (a)). Writing for the Court in Vermont Agency of Natural Resources v. United States ex rel. Stevens, 529 U.S. 765 (2000) (7–2 decision), Justice Scalia first held, in a portion of the opinion discussed *supra*, p. 155, that a *qui tam* relator enjoys Article III standing. Then, employing the "longstanding interpretive presumption that 'person' does not include the sovereign" as well as the "the doctrine that statutes should be construed so as to avoid difficult constitutional questions", the Court concluded that Congress had not clearly expressed its intent to bring states within the definition of "any person" and therefore had not subjected the states to liability under the Act. The majority thus had no occasion to address the further question whether a contrary interpretation would withstand constitutional challenge, though it did note that "there is 'a serious doubt' on that score". Justice Ginsburg, in a brief concurring opinion joined by Justice Breyer, stressed two points: (1) that the "Court has no cause to engage in an Eleventh Amendment inquiry, and appropriately leaves that issue open," and (2) that the Court's opinion also leaves open "the question whether the word 'person' encompasses States when the United States itself sues under the False Claims Act". (Can the majority's method of interpretation support a conclusion that the same word in the same provision (*i.e.*, "person") means two different things depending on who is suing that person?)

For arguments that Congress may authorize such qui tam actions against a state, see Siegel, *The Hidden Source of Congress's Power to Abrogate State Sovereign Immunity*, 73 Tex.L.Rev. 539 (1995); Caminker, *State Immunity Waivers for Suits by the United States*, 98 Mich.L.Rev. 92 (1999). For the view that such arguments are unlikely to convince the Supreme Court, see Meltzer, *Overcoming Immunity: The Case of Federal Regulation of Intellectual Property*, 53 Stan.L.Rev. 1331, 1365–70 (2001). Professor Meltzer's article also explores other means of melding private initiative and public enforcement.

United States are rare; (d) the Court has construed Congress' § 5 relatively narrowly, see, *e.g.,* City of Boerne v. Flores, p. 959, *supra*; and (e) the relief available in bankruptcy cases provides cold comfort to those victims of rights violations whose claims fall outside the bankruptcy jurisdiction.

———

B.   FEDERAL CONSTITUTIONAL PROTECTION AGAINST STATE OFFICIAL ACTION

As has been noted repeatedly in this Chapter, state officers often can be sued for violating the law even when sovereign immunity or the Eleventh Amendment would bar a direct action against the state. But suits against state officers for violating the federal Constitution pose a conceptual issue in cases in which the officials' alleged acts also violate state law: How could conduct in violation of state law count as "state action" in violation of the Constitution? The next principal case addresses this issue.

———

Home Telephone & Telegraph Co. v. City of Los Angeles

227 U.S. 278, 33 S.Ct. 312, 57 L.Ed. 510 (1913).
Appeal from the United States District Court for the Southern District of California.

■ MR. CHIEF JUSTICE WHITE delivered the opinion of the Court.

The appellant, a California corporation furnishing telephone service in the city of Los Angeles, sued the city and certain of its officials to prevent the putting into effect of a city ordinance establishing telephone rates for the year commencing July 1, 1911.

It was alleged that by the Constitution and laws of the state the city was given a right to fix telephone rates, and had passed the assailed ordinance in the exercise of the general authority thus conferred. It was charged that the rates fixed were so unreasonably low that their enforcement would bring about the confiscation of the property of the corporation, and hence the ordinance was repugnant to the due process clause of the 14th Amendment. * * *

Being of the opinion that no jurisdiction was disclosed by the bill, the court refused to grant a restraining order or allow a preliminary injunction, and thereafter, on the filing of a formal plea to the jurisdiction the bill was dismissed for want of power as a Federal court to consider it. This direct appeal was then taken. * * *

The ground of challenge to the jurisdiction advanced by the plea may be thus stated: As the acts of the state officials (the city government) complained of were alleged to be wanting in due process of law, and therefore repugnant to the 14th Amendment,—a ground which, on the face of the bill, if well founded, also presumptively caused the action complained of to be repugnant to the due-process clause of the state Constitution,—there being no diversity of citizenship, there was no Federal jurisdiction. In other words, the plea asserted that where, in a given case, taking the facts averred to be true, the acts of state officials violated the Constitution of the United States, and likewise, because of the coincidence of a state constitutional prohibition, were presumptively repugnant to the state Constitution, such acts could not be treated as acts of the state within the 14th Amendment, and hence no power existed in a Federal court to consider the subject until, by final action of an appropriate state court, it was decided that such acts were authorized by the state, and were therefore not repugnant to the state Constitution. * * *

Coming to consider the real significance of this doctrine, we think it is so clearly in conflict with the decisions of this court as to leave no doubt that plain error was committed in announcing and applying it. In view, however, of the fact that the proposition was sanctioned by the court below, and was by it deemed to be supported by the persuasive authority of two opinions of the circuit court of appeals for the ninth circuit, before coming to consider the decided cases we analyze some of the conceptions upon which the proposition must rest, in order to show its inherent unsoundness, to make its destructive character manifest, and to indicate its departure from the substantially unanimous view which has prevailed from the beginning.

In the first place, the proposition addresses itself not to the mere distribution of the judicial power granted by the Constitution, but substantially denies the existence of power under the Constitution over the subject with which the proposition is concerned. It follows that the limitation which it imposes would be beyond possible correction by legislation. Its restriction would, moreover, attach to the exercise of Federal judicial power under all circumstances, whether the issue concerned original jurisdiction or arose in the course of a controversy to which otherwise jurisdiction would extend. Thus, being applicable equally to all Federal courts, under all circumstances, in every stage of a proceeding, the enforcement of the doctrine would hence render impossible the performance of the duty with which the Federal courts are charged under the Constitution. Such paralysis would inevitably ensue, since the consequence would be that, at least in every case where there was a coincidence between a national safeguard or prohibition and a state one, the power of the Federal court to afford protection to a claim of right under the Constitution of the United States, as against the action of a state or its officers, would depend on the ultimate determination of the state courts, and would therefore require a stay of all action to await such determination. * * * [Moreover,] it would come to pass that in every case where action of a state officer was complained of as violating the Constitution of the United States, the Federal courts, in any form of procedure, or in any stage of the controversy, would have to await the determination of a state court as to the operation of the Constitution of the United States. It is manifest that, in necessary operation, the doctrine which was sustained would, in substance, cause the state courts to become the primary source for applying and enforcing the constitution of the United States in all cases covered by the 14th Amendment.

* * * [I]f there be no right to exert [Federal judicial] power until, by the final action of a state court of last resort, the act of a state officer has been declared rightful and to be the lawful act of the state as a governmental entity, the inquiry naturally comes whether, under such

circumstances, a suit against the officer would not be a suit against the state, within the purview of the 11th Amendment. The possibility of such a result, moreover, at once engenders a further inquiry; that is, whether the effect of the proposition would not be to cause the 14th Amendment to narrow Federal judicial power instead of enlarging it and making it more efficacious. It must be borne in mind, also, that the limitations which the proposition, if adopted, would impose upon Federal judicial power, would not be in reason solely applicable to an exertion of such power as to the persons and subjects covered by the 14th Amendment, but would equally govern controversies concerning the contract and possibly other clauses of the Constitution.

The vice which not only underlies but permeates the proposition is not far to seek. It consists, first, in causing by an artificial construction the provisions of the 14th Amendment not to reach those to whom they are addressed when reasonably construed; and, second, in wholly misconceiving the scope and operation of the 14th Amendment, thereby removing from the control of that Amendment the great body of rights which it was intended it should safeguard, and in taking out of reach of its prohibitions the wrongs which it was the purpose of the Amendment to condemn.

Before demonstrating the accuracy of the statement just made as to the essential result of the proposition relied upon by a reference to decided cases, in order that the appreciation of the cases may be made more salient, we contrast the meaning as above stated, which the 14th Amendment would have if the proposition was maintained, with the undoubted significance of that Amendment as established by many decisions of this court.

By the proposition the prohibitions and guaranties of the Amendment are addressed to and control the states only in their complete governmental capacity, and as a result give no authority to exert Federal judicial power until, by the decision of a court of last resort of a state, acts complained of under the 14th Amendment have been held valid, and therefore state acts in the fullest sense. To the contrary, the provisions of the Amendment as conclusively fixed by previous decisions are generic in their terms, are addressed, of course, to the states, but also to every person, whether natural or juridical, who is the repository of state power. By this construction the reach of the Amendment is shown to be coextensive with any exercise by a state of power, in whatever form exerted. * * *

To speak broadly, the difference between the proposition insisted upon and the true meaning of the Amendment is this: that the one assumes that the Amendment virtually contemplates alone wrongs authorized by a state, and gives only power accordingly, while in truth the Amendment contemplates the possibility of state officers abusing the powers lawfully conferred upon them by doing wrongs prohibited by the Amendment. In other words, the Amendment, * * * [conceiving] that state powers might be abused by those who possessed them, and as a result might be used as the instrument for doing wrongs, provided against all and every such possible contingency. * * * [A] state officer cannot, on the one hand, as a means of doing a wrong forbidden by the Amendment, proceed upon the assumption of the possession of state power, and at the same time, for the purpose of avoiding the application of the Amendment, deny the power, and thus accomplish the wrong. * * *

Let us consider the decided cases in order to demonstrate how plainly they refute the contention here made by the court below, and how clearly they establish the converse doctrine which we have formulated in the two propositions previously stated. * * *

Although every contention pressed and authority now relied upon in favor of affirmance is disposed of by the general principles which we have previously stated, before concluding we specially advert to some of the contentions urged to the contrary. * * * Much reliance is placed upon the decisions in Barney v. New York, [193 U.S. 430 (1904)], and Memphis v. Cumberland Teleph. & Teleg. Co., 218 U.S. 624 [1910]. The latter we at once put out of view with the statement that, on its face, the question involved was one of pleading, and in no sense of substantive Federal power. As to the other,—the Barney Case,—it might suffice to say * * * [that] if it conflicted with the doctrine * * * of the subsequent and leading case of Ex parte Young, [it] is now so distinguished or qualified as not to be here authoritative or even persuasive. But on the face of the Barney Case it is to be observed that * * * [since] the decision there rendered proceeded upon the hypothesis that the facts presented took the case out of the established rule, there is no ground for saying that that case is authority for overruling the settled doctrine which, abstractly, at least, it recognized. If there were room for such conclusion, in view of what we have said, it would be our plain duty to qualify and restrict the Barney Case in so far as it might be found to conflict with the rule here applied. * * *

Reversed.

NOTE ON THE SCOPE OF FEDERAL CONSTITUTIONAL PROTECTION AGAINST UNAUTHORIZED STATE ACTION

(1) The Relation Between the Eleventh and Fourteenth Amendments. Despite the Court's reliance on Ex parte Young, is Home Telephone's construction of the Fourteenth Amendment inconsistent with the construction of the Eleventh Amendment in Young? In other words, if an official counts as a "state" capable of violating the Fourteenth Amendment, why does the official not also count as the "state" for purposes of the Eleventh Amendment? In considering this question, note that (as pointed out on pp. 927–928, *supra*) a similar though not identical question about state officials' status under the Eleventh and Fourteenth Amendments could be raised with respect to Young itself.

(2) The Barney Case and Its Aftermath.

(a) In Barney v. City of New York, 193 U.S. 430 (1904), discussed in Home Telephone, the plaintiff sued to enjoin the city from proceeding with construction of the Park Avenue subway tunnel, alleging that the construction deprived him of his property without due process in violation of the Fourteenth Amendment and also violated state law. The Supreme Court affirmed a dismissal of the bill for want of jurisdiction.

The bill of complaint seems to have relied principally on the theory that the acts of the defendants denied due process not because of their intrinsic nature but simply because they violated state law. If so, the Court's substantive interpretation of the Fourteenth Amendment would surely be unexceptionable. But the bill also alleged that state law denied due process insofar as it authorized construction without the consent of abutting owners and without compensation to them. It is doubtful, however, that this allegation raised a substantial federal question, and the Court did not specifically address it.

(b) A few years later, in Siler v. Louisville & Nashville R.R., 213 U.S. 175 (1909), a railroad sought to enjoin enforcement of a state administrative order fixing maximum rates, on the grounds that it was unauthorized under state law and that it violated various provisions of the federal Constitution. Relying upon Barney, the defendants argued that if the order was unauthorized, it was "not the action of the State" and hence there could be no constitutional violation. The Supreme Court responded that if the bill alleged *only* "that the order was invalid because it was not authorized by the State * * * the objection might be good," but since the bill also asserted several distinct federal questions, "there can be no doubt that the Circuit Court obtained jurisdiction over the case by virtue of [those] Federal questions." See also United States v. Raines, 362 U.S. 17, 25–26 (1960) (discriminatory voting practices that violated state law were unlawful under the Fifteenth Amendment and federal civil rights legislation: "Barney must be regarded as having been 'worn away by the erosion of time' * * * and of contrary authority.").

(c) Justice Frankfurter attempted to resuscitate the Barney doctrine in his concurrence in Snowden v. Hughes, 321 U.S. 1 (1944). There, a complaint for damages under 42 U.S.C. § 1983 alleged that defendants (members of a state agency), in refusing to file a certificate of plaintiff's selection as a Republican candidate for the state legislature, had violated Illinois law as well as both the Privileges and Immunities and Equal Protection Clauses of the Fourteenth Amendment. The Court (per Stone, C.J.) held that plaintiff had failed to state a cause of action due to the absence of any allegation of "intentional or purposeful discrimination."

Justice Frankfurter concurred, saying: "Our question is not whether a remedy is available for * * * illegality, but whether it is available in the first instance in a federal court. Such a problem of federal judicial control must be placed in the historic context of the relationship of the federal courts to the states, with due regard for the natural sensitiveness of the states and for the appropriate responsibility of state courts to correct the action of lower state courts and state officials. * * * I am clear * * * that the action of the Canvassing Board taken, as the plaintiff himself acknowledges, in defiance of the duty of that Board under Illinois law, cannot be deemed the action of the State, certainly not until the highest court of the State confirms such action and thereby makes it the law of the State."

(3) The Implications of Justice Frankfurter's View. Would the guarantees of the Fourteenth Amendment be adequately protected by a constitutional interpretation that treated the prohibitions of the Amendment as addressed only to the state as a whole after it has spoken with its final judicial voice? Could Justice Frankfurter's proposed jurisdictional doctrine have been accepted without rethinking the whole course of constitutional history since the Home Telephone case?[1]

(4) The Relationship Between the Home Telephone Doctrine and the Materials That Follow. The question whether federal law should be construed to regulate the conduct of state officials acting without authorization under or contrary to state law has proven to be a persistent one. In the next subsection, this question (or some variant of it) resurfaces in two contexts: (i) as a question of the proper interpretation of the Civil Rights Act of 1871, 42 U.S.C. § 1983, see Monroe v. Pape, which follows immediately, and Monell v. Department of Soc. Servs., p. 998, *infra*; and (ii) in cases considering whether the existence of state-law remedies to redress a state official's deprivation of liberty or property provides "due process of law" so as to preclude any constitutional claim under the Due Process Clause, see Parratt v. Taylor, p. 1016, *infra*, and the following Note.

C. FEDERAL STATUTORY PROTECTION AGAINST STATE OFFICIAL ACTION: HEREIN OF 42 U.S.C. § 1983

In 1871, in response to an ongoing pattern of violence and intimidation against former slaves and those in sympathy with them, especially in the former Confederacy, Congress enacted the Ku Klux Klan Act, 17 Stat. 13. But while the Act's most immediate target was the KKK, its first section created a federal cause of action that was not so limited:

> "Every person who, under color of any statute, ordinance, regulation, custom, or usage, of any State or Territory or the District of Columbia, subjects, or causes to be subjected, any citizen of the United States or other person within the jurisdiction thereof to the deprivation of any rights, privileges, or immunities secured by the Constitution and laws, shall be liable to the party injured in an action at law, suit in equity, or other proper proceeding for redress."

This provision, which today is codified as 42 U.S.C. § 1983, spawned relatively few cases for many decades, apparently because its language partly tracks the wording of the Fourteenth Amendment's Privileges or Immunities Clause, which the Supreme Court rendered a near constitutional dead letter in The Slaughter-House Cases, 83 U.S. (16. Wall.) 36 (1873). (One commentator reports that there were only 19 cases in the U.S.C.A. annotations under § 1983 in its first 65 years. See Note, 82 Harv.L.Rev. 1486, 1486 n. 4 (1969).) Note, however, that during this period, many suits that might have been brought under § 1983 as it has more recently been interpreted were treated instead as actions for a remedy (usually an injunction) that was already available under the common law, governing traditions of equity, or the Constitution. See, *e.g.*, General Oil Co. v. Crain, 209 U.S. 211 (1908), p. 759, *supra*; Ex parte Young, 209 U.S. 123 (1908), p. 922, *supra*; Ward v. Love County, 253 U.S. 17 (1920), p. 752, *supra*.

---

[1]   *But cf., e.g.*, Hooe v. United States, 218 U.S. 322 (1910), holding that damages for an unconstitutional taking by the federal government are available under the Tucker Act only if the taking was "authorized".

Since the 1960s, § 1983 has emerged as easily the most important statute authorizing suits against state officials for violations of the Constitution and laws of the United States. This Subsection examines the scope of the § 1983 cause of action, the interpretive issues to which the statute has given rise,[1] and the evolving course of the Supreme Court's implementing decisions.

Monroe v. Pape

365 U.S. 167, 81 S.Ct. 473, 5 L.Ed.2d 492 (1961).
Certiorari to the United States Court of Appeals for the Seventh Circuit.

■ MR. JUSTICE DOUGLAS delivered the opinion of the Court.

This case presents important questions concerning the construction of 42 U.S.C. § 1983 * * * : * * *

The complaint alleges that 13 Chicago police officers broke into petitioners' home in the early morning, routed them from bed, made them stand naked in the living room, and ransacked every room, emptying drawers and ripping mattress covers. It further alleges that Mr. Monroe was then taken to the police station and detained on "open" charges for 10 hours, while he was interrogated about a two-day-old murder, that he was not taken before a magistrate, though one was accessible, that he was not permitted to call his family or attorney, that he was subsequently released without criminal charges being preferred against him. It is alleged that the officers had no search warrant and no arrest warrant and that they acted "under color of the statutes, ordinances, regulations, customs and usages" of Illinois and of the City of Chicago. Federal jurisdiction was asserted under [§ 1983], which we have set out above, and 28 U.S.C. § 1343 and 28 U.S.C. § 1331.

The City of Chicago moved to dismiss the complaint on the ground that it is not liable under the Civil Rights Acts nor for acts committed in performance of its governmental functions. All defendants moved to dismiss, alleging that the complaint alleged no cause of action under those Acts or under the Federal Constitution. The District Court dismissed the complaint. The Court of Appeals affirmed * * *. * * *

I.

Petitioners claim that the invasion of their home and the subsequent search without a warrant and the arrest and detention of Mr. Monroe without a warrant and without arraignment constituted a deprivation of their "rights, privileges, or immunities secured by the Constitution" within the meaning of [§ 1983]. * * *

Section [1983] came onto the books as § 1 of the Ku Klux Act of April 20, 1871. 17 Stat. 13. * * *

Its purpose is plain from the title of the legislation, "An Act to enforce the Provisions of the Fourteenth Amendment to the Constitution of the United States, and for other Purposes." 17 Stat. 13. Allegation of facts

---

[1] A valuable introduction to issues of interpretive methodology arising under § 1983 is Eisenberg, *Section 1983: Doctrinal Foundations and An Empirical Study*, 67 Cornell L.Rev. 482 (1982).

constituting a deprivation under color of state authority of a right guaranteed by the Fourteenth Amendment satisfies to that extent the requirement of [§ 1983]. So far petitioners are on solid ground. For the guarantee against unreasonable searches and seizures contained in the Fourth Amendment has been made applicable to the States by reason of the Due Process Clause of the Fourteenth Amendment. Wolf v. Colorado, 338 U.S. 25.

II.

There can be no doubt at least since Ex parte Virginia, 100 U.S. 339, 346–347, that Congress has the power to enforce provisions of the Fourteenth Amendment against those who carry a badge of authority of a State and represent it in some capacity, whether they act in accordance with their authority or misuse it. See Home Tel. & Tel. Co. v. Los Angeles, 227 U.S. 278, 287–296. The question with which we now deal is the narrower one of whether Congress, in enacting § [1983], meant to give a remedy to parties deprived of constitutional rights, privileges and immunities by an official's abuse of his position. We conclude that it did so intend.

It is argued that "under color of" enumerated state authority excludes acts of an official or policeman who can show no authority under state law, state custom, or state usage to do what he did. In this case it is said that these policemen, in breaking into petitioners' apartment, violated the Constitution and laws of Illinois. It is pointed out that under Illinois law a simple remedy is offered for that violation and that, so far as it appears, the courts of Illinois are available to give petitioners that full redress which the common law affords for violence done to a person; and it is earnestly argued that no "statute, ordinance, regulation, custom or usage" of Illinois bars that redress. * * *

The legislation—in particular the section with which we are now concerned—had several purposes. * * * One who reads [the debates] in their entirety sees that the present section had three main aims.

First, it might, of course, override certain kinds of state laws. * * *

Second, it provided a remedy where state law was inadequate. * * *

But the purposes were much broader. The *third* aim was to provide a federal remedy where the state remedy, though adequate in theory, was not available in practice. * * *

This Act of April 20, 1871, sometimes called "the third 'force bill,' " was passed by a Congress that had the Klan "particularly in mind." The debates are replete with references to the lawless conditions existing in the South in 1871. * * * It was not the unavailability of state remedies but the failure of certain States to enforce the laws with an equal hand that furnished the powerful momentum behind this "force bill." Mr. Lowe of Kansas said:

"While murder is stalking abroad in disguise, while whippings and lynchings and banishment have been visited upon unoffending American citizens, the local administrations have been found inadequate or unwilling to apply the proper corrective. * * * Immunity is given to crime, and the records of the public tribunals are searched in vain for any evidence of effective redress." * * *

There was, it was said, no quarrel with the state laws on the books. It was their lack of enforcement that was the nub of the difficulty. [Further excerpts from the legislative history are omitted.]

The debates were long and extensive. It is abundantly clear that one reason the legislation was passed was to afford a federal right in federal courts because, by reason of prejudice, passion, neglect, intolerance or otherwise, state laws might not be enforced and the claims of citizens to the enjoyment of rights, privileges, and immunities guaranteed by the Fourteenth Amendment might be denied by the state agencies. * * *

Although the legislation was enacted because of the conditions that existed in the South at that time, it is cast in general language and is as applicable to Illinois as it is to the States whose names were mentioned over and again in the debates. It is no answer that the State has a law which if enforced would give relief. The federal remedy is supplementary to the state remedy, and the latter need not be first sought and refused before the federal one is invoked. Hence the fact that Illinois by its constitution and laws outlaws unreasonable searches and seizures is no barrier to the present suit in the federal court.

We had before us in United States v. Classic, [313 U.S. 299 (1941)], § 20 of the Criminal Code, 18 U.S.C. § 242, which provides a criminal punishment for anyone who "under color of any law, statute, ordinance, regulation, or custom" subjects any inhabitant of a State to the deprivation of "any rights, privileges, or immunities secured or protected by the Constitution or laws of the United States." Section 242 first came into the law as § 2 of the Civil Rights Act, Act of April 9, 1866, 14 Stat. 27. After passage of the Fourteenth Amendment, this provision was re-enacted and amended by §§ 17, 18, Act of May 31, 1870, 16 Stat. 140, 144. The right involved in the Classic case was the right of voters in a primary to have their votes counted. The laws of Louisiana required the defendants "to count the ballots, to record the result of the count, and to certify the result of the election." United States v. Classic, *supra*, 325–326. But according to the indictment they did not perform their duty. In an opinion written by Mr. Justice (later Chief Justice) Stone, in which Mr. Justice Roberts, Mr. Justice Reed, and Mr. Justice Frankfurter joined, the Court ruled, "Misuse of power, possessed by virtue of state law and made possible only because the wrongdoer is clothed with the authority of state law, is action taken 'under color of' state law." *Id.*, 326. There was a dissenting opinion; but the ruling as to the meaning of "under color of" state law was not questioned.

That view of the meaning of the words "under color of" state law, 18 U.S.C. § 242, was reaffirmed in Screws v. United States, *supra*, * * * [and] in Williams v. United States, [341 U.S. 97. 99 (1951)] * * *.

Mr. Shellabarger, reporting out the bill which became the Ku Klux Act, said of the provision with which we now deal:

"The model for it will be found in the second section of the act of April 9, 1866, known as the 'civil rights act.' . . . This section of this bill, on the same state of facts, not only provides a civil remedy for persons whose former condition may have been that of slaves, but also to all people where, under color of State law, they or any of them may be deprived of rights. . . . "

Thus, it is beyond doubt that this phrase should be accorded the same construction in both statutes—in § [1983] and in 18 U.S.C. § 242. * * *

So far, then, the complaint states a cause of action. There remains to consider only a defense peculiar to the City of Chicago.

III.

The City of Chicago asserts that it is not liable under § [1983]. We do not stop to explore the whole range of questions tendered us on this issue at oral argument and in the briefs. For we are of the opinion that Congress did not undertake to bring municipal corporations within the ambit of § [1983]. [The Court concluded that the complaint was properly dismissed against the city, but reversed dismissal of the complaint against the officials.]

■ MR. JUSTICE HARLAN, whom MR. JUSTICE STEWART joins, concurring.

Were this case here as one of first impression, I would find the "under color of any statute" issue very close indeed. However, in Classic and Screws this Court considered a substantially identical statutory phrase to have a meaning which, unless we now retreat from it, requires that issue to go for the petitioners here. * * *

Those aspects of Congress' purpose which are quite clear in the earlier congressional debates, as quoted by my Brothers Douglas and Frankfurter in turn, seem to me to be inherently ambiguous when applied to the case of an isolated abuse of state authority by an official. * * * If attention is directed at the rare specific references to isolated abuses of state authority, one finds them neither so clear nor so disproportionately divided between favoring the positions of the majority or the dissent as to make either position seem plainly correct. * * *

The dissent considers that the "under color of" provision of § 1983 distinguishes between unconstitutional actions taken without state authority, which only the State should remedy, and unconstitutional actions authorized by the State, which the Federal Act was to reach. If so, then the controlling difference for the enacting legislature must have been either that the state remedy was more adequate for unauthorized actions than for authorized ones or that there was, in some sense, greater harm from unconstitutional actions authorized by the full panoply of state power and approval than from unconstitutional actions not so authorized or acquiesced in by the State. I find less than compelling the evidence that either distinction was important to that Congress.

I.

If the state remedy was considered adequate when the official's unconstitutional act was unauthorized, why should it not be thought equally adequate when the unconstitutional act was authorized? * * *

Since the suggested narrow construction of § 1983 presupposes that state measures were adequate to remedy unauthorized deprivations of constitutional rights and since the identical state relief could be obtained for state-authorized acts with the aid of Supreme Court review, this narrow construction would reduce the statute to having merely a jurisdictional function, shifting the load of federal supervision from the Supreme Court to the lower courts and providing a federal tribunal for fact findings in cases involving authorized action. Such a function could be justified on various grounds. It could, for example, be argued that the state courts would be less willing to find a constitutional violation in cases involving "authorized action" and that therefore the victim of such action would bear a greater burden in that he would more likely have to carry his case to this Court, and once here, might be bound by unfavorable state court findings. But the legislative debates do not disclose congressional concern about the burdens of litigation placed upon the victims of "authorized" constitutional violations contrasted to the victims of unauthorized violations. Neither did Congress indicate an interest in relieving the burden placed on this Court in reviewing such cases.

The statute becomes more than a jurisdictional provision only if one attributes to the enacting legislature the view that a deprivation of a constitutional right is significantly different from and more serious than a violation of a state right and therefore deserves a different remedy even though the same act may constitute both a state tort and the deprivation of a constitutional right. This view, by no means unrealistic as a common-sense matter,[5] is, I believe, more consistent with the flavor of the legislative history than is a view that the primary purpose of the statute was to grant a lower court forum for fact findings. * * *

II.

I think [the] limited interpretation of § 1983 fares no better when viewed from the other possible premise for it, namely that state-approved constitutional deprivations were considered more offensive than those not so approved. For one thing, the enacting Congress was not unaware of the fact that there was a substantial overlap between the protections granted by state constitutional provisions and those granted by the Fourteenth Amendment. * * * I hesitate to assume that the proponents of the present statute, who regarded it as necessary even though they knew that the provisions of the Fourteenth Amendment were self-executing, would have thought the remedies unnecessary whenever there were self-executing provisions of state constitutions also forbidding what the Fourteenth Amendment forbids. * * *

These difficulties in explaining the basis of a distinction between authorized and unauthorized deprivations of constitutional rights fortify my view that the legislative history does not bear the burden which *stare decisis* casts upon it. For this reason and for those stated in the opinion of the Court, I agree that we should not now depart from the holdings of the Classic and Screws cases.

---

[5] There will be many cases in which the relief provided by the state to the victim of a use of state power which the state either did not or could not constitutionally authorize will be far less than what Congress may have thought would be fair reimbursement for deprivation of a constitutional right. * * * Even the remedy for such an unauthorized search and seizure as Monroe was allegedly subjected to may be only the nominal amount of damages to physical property allowable in an action for trespass to land. It would indeed be the purest coincidence if the state remedies for violations of common-law rights by private citizens were fully appropriate to redress those injuries which only a state official can cause and against which the Constitution provides protection.

■ MR. JUSTICE FRANKFURTER, dissenting except insofar as the Court holds that this action cannot be maintained against the City of Chicago. * * *

III.

* * * [A]lthough this Court has three times found that conduct of state officials which is forbidden by state law may be "under color" of state law for purposes of the Civil Rights Acts, it is accurate to say that that question has never received here the consideration which its importance merits. * * *

The issue in the present case concerns directly a basic problem of American federalism: the relation of the Nation to the States in the critically important sphere of municipal law administration. In this aspect, it has significance approximating constitutional dimension. * * * This imposes on this Court a corresponding obligation to exercise its power within the fair limits of its judicial discretion. * * *

IV.

* * * [Plaintiffs] assert that they have been deprived of due process of law and of equal protection of the laws under color of state law, although from all that appears the courts of Illinois are available to give them the fullest redress which the common law affords for the violence done them, nor does any "statute, ordinance, regulation, custom, or usage" of the State of Illinois bar that redress. Did the enactment by Congress of § 1 of the Ku Klux Act of 1871 encompass such a situation? * * *

The original text of the present § [1983] contained words, left out in the Revised Statutes, which clarified the objective to which the provision was addressed:

> "That any person who, under color of any law, statute, ordinance, regulation, custom, or usage of any State, shall subject, or cause to be subjected, any person within the jurisdiction of the United States to the deprivation of any rights, privileges, or immunities secured by the Constitution of the United States, shall, *any such law, statute, ordinance, regulation, custom, or usage of the State to the contrary notwithstanding*, be liable to the party injured. . . ."

* * *

The Court now says, however, that "It was not the unavailability of state remedies but the failure of certain States to enforce the laws with an equal hand that furnished the powerful momentum behind this 'force bill.'" Of course, if the notion of "unavailability" of remedy is limited to mean an absence of statutory, paper right, this is in large part true. Insofar as the Court undertakes to demonstrate—as the bulk of its opinion seems to do—that § [1983] was meant to reach some instances of action not specifically authorized by the avowed, apparent, written law inscribed in the statute books of the States, the argument knocks at an open door. No one would or could deny this, for by its express terms the statute comprehends deprivations of federal rights under color of any "statute, ordinance, regulation, *custom, or usage*" of a State. (Emphasis added.) The question is, *what* class of cases other than those involving state statute law were meant to be reached. And, with respect to this question, the Court's conclusion is undermined by the very portions of the legislative debates which it cites. For surely the misconduct of individual municipal police officers, subject to the effective oversight of appropriate state administrative and judicial authorities, presents a situation which differs *toto coelo* from one in which "Immunity is given to crime, and the records of the public tribunals are searched in vain for any evidence of effective redress," or in which murder rages while a State makes "no successful effort to bring the guilty to punishment or afford protection or redress," or in which the "State courts . . . [are] unable to enforce the criminal laws . . . or to suppress the disorders existing," or in which, in a State's "judicial tribunals one class is unable to secure that enforcement of their rights and punishment for their infraction which is accorded to another" * * *. These statements indicate that Congress— made keenly aware by the post-bellum conditions in the South that States through their authorities could sanction offenses against the individual by settled practice which established state law as truly as written codes—designed § [1983] to reach, as well, official conduct which, because engaged in "permanently and as a rule," or "systematically," came through acceptance by law-administering officers to constitute "custom, or usage" having the cast of law. They do not indicate an attempt to reach, nor does the statute by its terms include, instances of acts in defiance of state law and which no settled state practice, no systematic pattern of official action or inaction, no "custom, or usage, of any State," insulates from effective and adequate reparation by the State's authorities.

* * * [A]ll the evidence converges to the conclusion that Congress by § [1983] created a civil liability enforceable in the federal courts only in instances of injury for which redress was barred in the state courts because some "statute, ordinance, regulation, custom, or usage" sanctioned the grievance complained of. This purpose, manifested even by the so-called "Radical" Reconstruction Congress in 1871, accords with the presuppositions of our federal system. The jurisdiction which Article III of the Constitution conferred on the national judiciary reflected the assumption that the state courts, not the federal courts, would remain the primary guardians of that fundamental security of person and property which the long evolution of the common law had secured to one individual as against other individuals. The Fourteenth Amendment did not alter this basic aspect of our federalism.

Its commands were addressed to the States. Only when the States, through their responsible organs for the formulation and administration of local policy, sought to deny or impede access by the individual to the central government in connection with those enumerated functions assigned to it, or to deprive the individual of a certain minimal fairness in the exercise of the coercive forces of the State, or without reasonable justification to treat him differently than other persons subject to their jurisdiction, was an overriding federal sanction imposed. * * *

* * * Suppose that a state legislature or the highest court of a State should determine that within its territorial limits no damages should be recovered in tort for pain and suffering, or for mental anguish, or that no punitive damages should be recoverable. * * * Should an unlawful intrusion by a policeman in Chicago entail different consequences than an unlawful intrusion by a hoodlum? These are matters of policy in its

strictly legislative sense, not for determination by this Court. And if it be, as it is, a matter for congressional choice, the legislative evidence is overwhelming that § [1983] is not expressive of that choice. * * *

[Justice Frankfurter concluded that the general allegation that the police intrusion was under color of Illinois law failed to state a claim under § 1983 in the face of Illinois decisions holding such intrusions unlawful. However, the averment that it was the "custom or usage" of the Chicago police department to detain individuals for long periods on "open charges" did state a valid claim of unlawful detention.]

NOTE ON 42 U.S.C. § 1983: AN OVERVIEW[1]

In the decades since Monroe v. Pape, litigation under § 1983 has been extremely controversial and extremely important. All agree that that § 1983 litigation has grown rapidly since Monroe,[2] though the statistics kept by the Administrative Office of the United States Courts make it hard to disaggregate § 1983 actions from suits filed under other civil rights statutes. But the overall number of civil rights actions has risen markedly, with § 1983 cases accounting for a large if uncertain percentage of the increase. In 1961 there were 296 civil rights cases filed in federal courts (the 1961 records do not indicate whether the plaintiffs were prisoners[3]); in 1986 there were over 40,000, with 20,846 filed by prisoners and 20,128 by nonprisoners.[4] The most

---

[1] For further discussion of § 1983 in these materials, see, in addition to the remainder of this chapter, Chapters X and XII. For extensive treatment of § 1983 and related civil rights statutes in other sources, as well as additional references to secondary materials, see Schwartz, Section 1983 Litigation: Claims and Defenses (4th ed.2008 & Supp.2013).

[2] Professor Weinberg contends that the large increase in civil rights cases after Monroe was caused not so much by Monroe's holding as by the Warren Court's expansion of protections afforded by the Bill of Rights—especially those relating to the criminal process. See Weinberg, *The Monroe Mystery Solved: Beyond the "Unhappy History" Theory of Civil Rights Litigation*, 1991 BYU L.Rev. 737.

[3] The term "prisoner", as here used, includes inmates of both prisons and jails.

[4] More refined analysis of data available during this period suggests that § 1983 actions account for less of the increase than some have assumed. Eisenberg & Schwab, *The Reality of Constitutional Tort Litigation*, 72 Cornell L.Rev. 641 (1987), conducted a detailed review of one federal judicial district, and concluded that (i) only 50% of the Administrative Office's "civil rights cases" were constitutional tort actions brought under § 1983 or the Bivens line of cases; (ii) much of the increase reflected in the Administrative Office's data was attributable to the burgeoning of other kinds of actions, such as employment discrimination actions under Title VII of the 1964 Civil Rights Act; (iii) from 1975–84, the number of nonprisoner civil rights cases outside the employment area increased by 94%, while the number of all other civil cases increased more rapidly, by 125%; and (iv) though prisoner civil rights cases rose by nearly 200% between 1975 and 1984, from less than 7,000 to more than 18,000, when one adjusts for increases in prison population, the rate of increase was only 101%, compared with a 119% increase in all civil cases other than prisoner civil rights actions.

For additional data on § 1983 litigation and on the correlation between the number of state prisoners and the number of suits, the types of issues raised, and the average disposition time of such suits, see Hanson & Daley, U.S. Dep't of Justice, Challenging the Conditions of Prisons and Jails: A Report on Section 1983 Litigation (1995); Kreimer, *Exploring the Dark Matter of Judicial Review: A Constitutional Census of the 1990s*, 5 Wm. & Mary Bill Rts.J. 427, 485–90 (1997) (reporting that (a) from 1984 to 1994, prisoner civil rights cases and habeas petitions increased from 1/10 to almost 1/5 of the federal civil docket (an increase "largely attributable to the growth in the American prison population") and (b) probably between four and seven of every thousand prisoners have their claims to obtain relief "seriously considered" by the federal courts).

recent available figures show a total of 35,307 civil rights actions filed in federal court in 2013 (17,793 nonprisoner actions and 17,514 prisoner suits[5]).

Because § 1983 provides a cause of action for violations of constitutional and statutory rights, it raises a myriad of issues about the meaning of the Constitution and of other federal statutes. Some of these issues will be addressed later in this Chapter, as will the important question of the "official immunity"—which is distinct from the states' "sovereign immunity" that was discussed in Subsection A, *supra*—that governmental officers typically enjoy when they are sued for damages in their individual capacities. See Section 3, *infra*.

This introductory Note is divided into three parts. Part A considers when official action occurs "under color of" state law and thus is actionable under § 1983. Part B addresses issues involving suable defendants under § 1983. Part C surveys some of the jurisdictional, procedural, and related issues that arise in § 1983 litigation.

A. The Meaning of "Under Color of" Law

(1) "Under Color of Law" and "State Action". Monroe construes § 1983's language, authorizing a cause of action for violations of the Fourteenth Amendment occurring "under color of" state law, as being coextensive with the "state action" requirement necessary to establish a constitutional violation. Conduct that satisfies the latter necessarily satisfies the former. Lugar v. Edmondson Oil Co., 457 U.S. 922, 928, 930 (1982).

(2) The Relationship of Monroe to Home Telephone. In equating action "under color of" state law with the state action requirement, Monroe establishes that § 1983 remedies are available even in cases in which a state official *violates* state law. Does this construction make sense?[6]

In answering this question, consider the alternatives. Justice Frankfurter's position in Monroe (which permits immediate resort to federal court when the defendant's acts have formal sanction in state law) allows a somewhat greater role to the federal courts than they would have had under the argument of the defendants in the Home Telephone case (which maintained there is no state action until the particular defendant's acts in the very case have been passed on by the highest state court). Consider also the question raised by Justice Harlan: if state court remedies are deemed adequate to redress federal constitutional violations when the officer's acts violate state law, why should immediate resort to a federal court be allowed—as Justice Frankfurter concedes it is—when the officer's act is formally sanctioned by a state law or practice? Recall that in the latter case,

---

[5]   The filing of prisoner civil rights petitions peaked at 39,008 in 1995, see Schlanger, *Inmate Litigation*, 116 Harv.L.Rev. 1555 (2003), just before the enactment of the Prisoner Litigation Reform Act (PLRA), 110 Stat. 1321 (1996), see pp. 1008, 1099, *infra*. Since the passage of that Act, there has been a dramatic decline in such filings (which consist primarily but not exclusively of actions based on § 1983). The decline appears to be due to several aspects of the PLRA, including a nonwaivable filing fee requirement and provisions limiting the amount of lawyer's fees that may be awarded to prevailing plaintiffs. (The requirement of the exhaustion of administrative remedies, discussed at p. 1099, *infra*, while undoubtedly affecting outcomes, may not have significantly affected the number of filings.)

[6]   See Achtenberg, *A "Milder Measure of Villainy": The Unknown History of 42 U.S.C. § 1983 and the Meaning of "Under Color of" Law*, 1999 Utah L.Rev. 1 (tracing in great detail previously unexplored aspects of the legislative history of § 1983, and concluding that "this history should dispel the remarkably persistent myth that the Forty-second Congress never intended the provision to cover constitutional wrongs unless those wrongs were actually authorized by state law").

too, the state courts are obliged under the Supremacy Clause to disregard state law if it conflicts with federal law, and that failure to do so is subject to review in the Supreme Court.

Note, finally, the awkward inquiry that Justice Frankfurter's test would force on the federal courts in determining whether state "custom or usage" sanctions an individual defendant's unconstitutional acts. Do the difficulties of such an inquiry argue for the reading of § 1983 given in Monroe—a reading that makes the inquiry unnecessary in actions against state officials?[7]

B.   Suable "Persons"

(1) Natural Persons Engaging in State Action. As Monroe makes clear, government officials are suable persons under § 1983 insofar as they engage in state action.[8] So are non-officials in the rare circumstances in which they satisfy the "state action" requirement. See, *e.g.*, Lugar, *supra*.

(2) Individual Officers as Defendants in Damages Actions: Personal Capacity Suits. When damages are sought from a governmental official, the officer is ordinarily sued in a "personal" or "individual" capacity. This designation indicates that any judgment will be assessed against the officer personally, rather than against the government employer. Similarly, in a personal capacity action, attorney's fees can be awarded only against the officer, not against the government. Kentucky v. Graham, 473 U.S. 159 (1985). The Eleventh Amendment is inapplicable, since the relief does not directly affect the state. (This rule applies even when a state chooses to indemnify the officer.)

(a) Ever since Tenney v. Brandhove, 341 U.S. 367 (1951), however, it has been clear that officials sued under § 1983 in their personal capacity may avail themselves of "official immunity" doctrines—which are wholly distinct from the sovereign immunity doctrines considered in Sections 1 and 2(A), *supra*—shielding them in many cases from damages liability. These doctrines are discussed in detail in Section 3, *infra*, and for present purposes a summary of their broadest outlines will suffice. Most executive officials have a "qualified immunity" that shields them from damages liability unless their conduct violated "clearly established statutory or constitutional rights of which a reasonable person would have knowledge." Harlow v. Fitzgerald, 457 U.S. 800, 812 (1982). Officials acting in a legislative, judicial, or prosecutorial capacity enjoy "absolute immunity" from damages liability. As a result, it frequently happens that even plaintiffs who have a cause of action under § 1983 may be unable to collect damages. (Official immunity doctrines do not typically bar suits for injunctions, except against legislators acting in a legislative capacity.)

(b) Ashcroft v. Iqbal, 556 U.S. 662 (2009), also discussed at p. 774, *supra*, and p. 1006, *infra*, a Bivens action against federal officials, held that there can be no "supervisory liability" in Bivens and § 1983 actions, and that "each

---

[7]   But a similar inquiry must, in essence, be made today—under post-Monroe decisions that extend § 1983 liability to local government entities but limit the basis of such liability—in ruling whether the governmental entity itself is liable. The determination has not proved easy to make. See pp. 998–1003, *infra*.

[8]   The question whether a governmental employee has engaged in state action is not always a simple one. Compare Polk County v. Dodson, 454 U.S. 312, 319 (1981) (state public defender was not acting under color of law because she undertook an "essentially * * * private function * * * for which state office and authority are not needed"), with West v. Atkins, 487 U.S. 42 (1988) (physician who was under part-time contract with state and who treated inmates at a prison hospital was acting under color of state law).

Government official, his or her title notwithstanding, is only liable for his or her own misconduct." In an opinion by Justice Kennedy, the Court, by a 5–4 vote, ordered the dismissal of claims against a former Attorney General and FBI Director predicated, *inter alia*, on their " 'knowledge and acquiescence in' " lower officials' alleged violations of the rights of a Pakistani Muslim arrested and detained in the aftermath of 9/11. "[M]ere knowledge" is not enough to establish a constitutional violation, Justice Kennedy wrote: "In a § 1983 suit or a Bivens action * * * the term 'supervisory liability' is a misnomer."

Dissenting, Justice Souter, joined by Justices Stevens, Ginsburg, and Breyer, protested that the majority had ruled ill-advisedly on a question that the petitioner defendants had not presented: "[T]hey conceded * * * that they would be liable if they had 'actual knowledge' of [unconstitutional] discrimination by their subordinates and exhibited 'deliberate indifference' to that discrimination." The Court, Justice Souter continued, "is not narrowing the scope of supervisory liability; it is eliminating * * * supervisory liability entirely" based on a false assumption that the only two possible standards are respondeat superior liability and "no supervisory liability at all. * * * In fact, there is quite a spectrum of possible tests for supervisory liability: it could be imposed where a supervisor has actual knowledge of a subordinate's constitutional violation and acquiesces; or where supervisors 'know about the conduct and facilitate it, approve it, condone it, or turn a blind eye for fear of what they might see'; or where the supervisor has no actual knowledge of the violation but was reckless in his supervision of the subordinate; or where the supervisor was grossly negligent. I am unsure what the general test for supervisory liability should be, and in the absence of briefing and argument I am in no position to choose or devise one." (Citations and some internal quotations omitted.)

Justice Souter seems correct that "supervisory liability" is not necessarily an all-or-nothing proposition. If so, should the Court have distinguished between the questions (1) when, if ever, supervisors violate the Constitution by failing to exercise adequate control over their subordinates and (2) when, if ever, state officials should be deemed to have "cause[d]" a constitutional violation within the meaning of § 1983? Was the Court justified in deciding the second question in the context of a Bivens action? See Levinson, *Who Will Supervise the Supervisors? Establishing Liability for Failure to Train, Supervise, or Discipline Subordinates in a Post-Iqbal/Connick World,* 47 Harv.C.R.-C.L.L.Rev. 273 (2012) (answering in the negative).

(3) Individual Officers as Defendants: Official Capacity Suits. Some damages actions under § 1983 are filed against an officer in the officer's "official" capacity. When an official is sued for damages in an "official" (as opposed to an "individual") capacity, the suit will be treated as one against the official's employer. Accordingly, damages actions pleaded against state officials in their "official capacity" will ordinarily be dismissed as barred by the state's sovereign immunity. Damages actions against local government officers in their official capacities can go forward only in accordance with the rules governing local governmental liability described in Paragraphs (4)–(6), *infra.*

When officials are *properly* sued in their official capacities, the government can be ordered to pay damages and attorney's fees, provided that it had adequate notice and opportunity to defend. Brandon v. Holt, 469 U.S. 464 (1985).

When *equitable relief* is sought, the defendant official is ordinarily named in an official capacity. See, *e.g.*, Hutto v. Finney, 437 U.S. 678, 693 (1978). Even in a suit thus captioned, the Eleventh Amendment ordinarily interposes no bar if the relief is deemed prospective in character. See pp. 929–930, *supra*. (Don't be confused by the fact that even in an official capacity suit, the authority-stripping rationale of Ex parte Young applies, so that for purposes of the Eleventh Amendment defendants are treated as stripped of their official character and are subject, like any private tortfeasor, to an injunction against continuing harm).[9]

In Kentucky v. Graham, *supra*, the Supreme Court observed that the distinction between personal and official capacity suits "continues to confuse lawyers and confound lower courts." 473 U.S. at 165. Wouldn't it make sense, instead of using the somewhat elusive labels of official and personal capacity, simply to require the plaintiff to set forth in the complaint, or soon thereafter, the particular person or entity from which monetary relief is sought?[10]

(4) Local Governments as Defendants: The Monell Decision. Between 1961 and 1978 the Court reaffirmed and extended the subsidiary holding of Monroe v. Pape that municipalities are not "persons" within the meaning of § 1983. But in Monell v. Department of Social Services, 436 U.S. 658 (1978), the Court shifted course, holding that Monroe v. Pape had misread the legislative history of § 1983, and that Congress did intend to include local governments among the "persons" it rendered liable. In Monell, a class of female employees sued municipal agencies for back pay and injunctive relief, challenging defendants' policy of requiring pregnant employees to take unpaid leaves of absence. Reversing the lower courts, the Supreme Court, per Justice Brennan, ruled that cities and counties may be sued directly under § 1983 for damages or for declaratory and injunctive relief "where * * * the action that is alleged to be unconstitutional implements or executes a policy statement, ordinance, regulation or decision officially adopted and promulgated by that body's officers. Moreover * * * local governments * * * may be sued for constitutional deprivations visited pursuant to governmental 'custom' even though such a custom has not received formal approval through the body's official decisionmaking channels".

The opinion determined that Monroe v. Pape had misinterpreted the import of the 42d Congress' rejection of the so-called Sherman Amendment. That amendment would have made municipalities liable not simply for violations of federal rights by municipal officials, but also for certain wrongful acts of *private citizens* within the municipality. In the view of the

---

[9]   Under the theory of Young, it is not clear that a suit seeking prospective relief against an officer in that officer's "personal capacity" is defective. Even if such a pleading were adjudged erroneous, the defect is sufficiently technical that it should be remediable by amendment, which may in fact be required in circumstances within the scope of Fed.R.Civ.P. 25(d)(1) (providing that when a public officer who is a party to an action "in an official capacity" ceases to hold office, "the action does not abate and the officer's successor is automatically substituted as a party").

[10]   When plaintiff seeks attorney's fees, "fee liability runs with merits liability", Kentucky v. Graham, *supra*, at 168. The government is not liable for attorney's fees in a damages action unless the plaintiff has prevailed against it, and presumably an individual is not liable for fees in an "official capacity" suit. See Bender v. Williamsport Area Sch. Dist., 475 U.S. 534, 543 n. 6 (1986) (by implication).

Monell Court, rejection of the Sherman Amendment could not justify an inference that Congress sought to exclude municipal liability for the conduct of *officials*. The Court found support for municipal liability in the legislative debates, and in the general understanding in 1871 that the term "person" included municipal corporations.

But the Court clearly stated, albeit in dictum, that "a municipality cannot be held liable *solely* because it employs a tortfeasor—or, in other words, a municipality cannot be held liable under § 1983 on a *respondeat superior* theory". The language of the statute (in particular, "[a]ny person who * * * shall subject, or causes to be subjected," a person to the deprivation of federal rights) "cannot be easily read to impose liability vicariously on governing bodies solely on the basis of the existence of an employer-employee relationship". The Court viewed the primary rationales for *respondeat superior* liability—loss-spreading and reduction of harm—as too close to the justifications for the Sherman Amendment to be the predicate for municipal liability. Thus, "it is [only] when execution of a government's policy or custom, whether made by its lawmakers or by those whose edicts or acts may fairly be said to represent official policy, inflicts the injury that the government as an entity is responsible under § 1983".

Justice Stevens concurred in part, refusing to join the Court's dictum rejecting *respondeat superior* liability. He later expressed his views on this question in a lone dissent in Oklahoma City v. Tuttle, 471 U.S. 808 (1985). Section 1983 was enacted, he argued, against a recognized background of *respondeat superior* liability in tort suits in general and specifically in tort suits against municipal corporations. He suggested that the policy considerations supporting the application of *respondeat superior* in common law tort suits against municipal corporations—compensation of victims, deterrence of misconduct, and fairness to individual officers "performing difficult and dangerous work"—also apply in constitutional tort actions. The fear that broadened liability would bankrupt municipalities, though legitimate, was in Justice Stevens' view a matter primarily for Congress to consider, and in any event such a concern related to the question of damages rather than to the question of which classes of defendants could be held liable.[11]

(5) The Scope of Municipal Damages Liability After Monell. The important consequence of Monell was to render city, county, and school board treasuries liable in § 1983 damages actions for violations of constitutional and statutory rights by their officials—but only when the violation had occurred pursuant to government policy or custom. Monell thus adopts the same line that Justice Frankfurter argued should govern officer liability under § 1983 liability—a view the Court rejected in Monroe v. Pape. Is that

---

[11] Kramer & Sykes, *Municipal Liability Under § 1983: A Legal and Economic Analysis*, 1987 Sup.Ct.Rev. 249, lend support to Justice Stevens' position. The authors argue that the Court in Monell read the language and history of § 1983 incorrectly: in their view, Congress intended to create a full-fledged federal tort remedy for deprivations of federal rights under color of state law. They add that the Monell approach has proven "extremely difficult to apply coherently", and that conventional *respondeat superior* liability (perhaps exonerating the municipality when the individual who was at fault enjoys an immunity defense) would be economically efficient.

See also Achtenberg, *Taking History Seriously: Municipal Liability Under 42 U.S.C. § 1983 and the Debate over Respondeat Superior*, 73 Fordham L.Rev. 2183 (2005) (contending that an understanding of 19th century principles of the common law, and of the methods of implementing those principles, supports the respondeat superior liability of municipalities in § 1983 actions).

line more appropriate for measuring local government liability than for measuring the liability of individual officers?

Note that the imposition of governmental liability in damages *always* creates vicarious liability, in the sense that the taxpayers foot the bill. Does this fact call for hesitation in holding local governments liable?

The Court addressed one aspect of this question in Owen v. City of Independence, 445 U.S. 622, 638 (1980). There, the Court held, 5–4, that a municipality sued under Monell for violations committed by its officials does not have a qualified immunity from damages liability under § 1983, even if it can show that the officials would themselves be entitled to such an immunity in a § 1983 action against them in their personal capacity. Justice Brennan's opinion for the Court argued that the concept of official immunity was already deeply embedded in the common law when § 1983 was passed, so that the 42d Congress should be deemed to have enacted § 1983 in contemplation of such a defense; by contrast, there existed at the time no common-law tradition of immunity in actions against municipalities. Moreover, allowing the municipality to avail itself of the immunity of its officials would interfere with both the compensatory and the deterrent purposes of § 1983. The Court concluded by asserting that its holding, together with its previous decisions, "properly allocates [the costs of federal violations] among the three principals in the scenario of the § 1983 cause of action: the victim of the constitutional deprivation; the officer whose conduct caused the injury; and the public, as represented by the municipal entity. The innocent individual who is harmed by an abuse of governmental authority is assured of compensation. The offending official who conducts himself in good faith may go about his business secure in the knowledge that a qualified immunity will preclude personal liability for damages that are more appropriately chargeable to the populace as a whole. And the public will be forced to bear only the costs of injury inflicted by the 'execution of a government's policy or custom, whether made by its lawmakers or by those whose edicts or acts may fairly be said to represent official policy' [citing Monell]".[12]

Justice Powell's dissent, which was joined by Chief Justice Burger and Justices Stewart and Rehnquist, objected to the imposition of municipal liability in damages in a case in which government officials had violated "a constitutional right that was unknown when the events in this case occurred".

Is Justice Brennan's reasoning in Owen consistent with his rejection of *respondeat superior* liability in Monell? Do you agree with the Court that there is nothing unfair about imposing liability on taxpayers for official conduct where there was insufficient reason at the time the conduct occurred to believe that the conduct violated constitutional norms? *Cf.* City of Newport v. Fact Concerts, Inc., 453 U.S. 247, 258–71 (1981), holding that municipalities may not be held liable under § 1983 for *punitive* damages. The Court in Newport stressed that the common law did not subject municipalities to punitive damages awards, and also expressed the view that such an award would be a windfall to the plaintiff, while unfairly punishing

---

[12] Owen did not squarely decide whether local governments may be liable for acts by officials who are themselves shielded by an absolute (rather than merely a qualified) immunity. The major thrust of the opinion, however, is that all individual immunity defenses are irrelevant to suits against governmental entities, and the cases distinguished include holdings that an official is absolutely immune.

"blameless or unknowing taxpayers". Consider also the argument of Jeffries, *Compensation for Constitutional Torts: Reflections on the Significance of Fault*, 88 Mich.L.Rev. 82, 101 (1989), that the "corrective justice" rationale for liability does not apply in the absence of "fault" on the part of the defendant. See also Jeffries, *The Right-Remedy Gap in Constitutional Law*, 109 Yale L.J. 87, 98–101 (1999) (arguing that "limitations on money damages for constitutional violations facilitate constitutional change" and noting that it would have been more difficult for the Supreme Court to decide Brown v. Board of Education, 347 U.S. 483 (1954), as it did if a ruling for the plaintiffs had entailed an obligation of local governments to pay damages for their "policy" of maintaining segregated schools).

Note that Monell dealt only with municipalities' formal legal liability for their officials torts. According to a recent empirical study, Schwartz, *Police Indemnification,* 89 N.Y.U.L.Rev. 885 (2014), nearly all state and local governments routinely pay judgments and settlements in suits in which their officers are sued in their individual capacities for constitutional violations. In light of this practice—which neither the Constitution nor § 1983 mandates—Professor Schwartz concludes that "[r]eplacing Monell with vicarious liability would align doctrine with actual practice." As will be discussed below, however, officials who are sued in their official capacities frequently enjoy "official immunity", and any vicarious liability that results is therefore limited by the availability of an official immunity defense.

(6) The Meaning of "Policy" or "Custom". The Supreme Court has dealt with the meaning of Monell's "policy or custom" standard in a number of subsequent cases.

(a) In Pembaur v. City of Cincinnati, 475 U.S. 469 (1986), the Court ruled that a single decision of a high official like the county prosecutor, who had authority under state law to decide whether police officers should enter a premises and whose decision "may fairly be said to represent official policy", was an adequate basis for imposing governmental liability under § 1983 (quoting Monell).

(b) In City of St. Louis v. Praprotnik, 485 U.S. 112 (1988), the Court confronted the question of *which* officials' decisions can render a municipality liable under § 1983. Praprotnik, a municipal employee, brought suit contending that the Director of Urban Design (UD) (to whom plaintiff reported) in the St. Louis Community Development Agency (CDA), and CDA's Director, had violated the First Amendment by discharging plaintiff in retaliation for earlier appeals to the city's Civil Service Commission. The Supreme Court ruled, 7–1, that the city could not be held liable for these acts. Justice O'Connor's plurality opinion—later endorsed by a majority in Jett v. Dallas Independent School District, 491 U.S. 701 (1989)—affirmed that state law determines who is a policymaking official; found that under state and local regulations, only the mayor and aldermen of St. Louis, and the Civil Service Commission, had policymaking authority over personnel decisions; and concluded that no policymaker had adopted an unconstitutional municipal policy authorizing retaliatory discharges. The mere fact that policymakers had delegated to the Directors of UD and of CDA discretion to act did not give the subordinate officials policymaking authority so as to make the municipality liable for their conduct.[13]

---

[13] State law is significant not only in determining who is a policymaking official, but also in determining the entity that the official represents when exercising a policymaking function.

Justice Brennan (joined by Justices Marshall and Blackmun) concurred in the judgment, agreeing that the record showed that the two subordinate officials lacked final authority to establish city policy. He questioned, however, the plurality's exclusive reliance on state statutory law in determining who the policymakers were. Justice Brennan disagreed in particular with the plurality's view that an official whose decisions are formally subject to review by others cannot be deemed a policymaker when, because that review is never exercised, the official effectively makes final policy.

Since Monell, there have been no Supreme Court decisions elaborating on the meaning of "custom" as used in the Court's opinion in that case. Has the Praprotnik decision effectively eliminated that ground for the imposition of municipal liability—at least where those establishing the custom lack policymaking authority?

(c) In City of Canton v. Harris, 489 U.S. 378 (1989), the Court dealt with the much-mooted question of the existence and extent of municipal liability for constitutional violations resulting from "failure to train" employees. In the Canton case, which involved a complaint that the due process rights of a person under arrest had been violated because he had been given inadequate medical attention by the police, the Court held that municipal liability for inadequate training is permitted by § 1983, but "only where the failure to train amounts to deliberate indifference to the rights of persons with whom the police (the officials involved in the particular case) come into contact". Thus, the Court said, "the focus must be on [the] adequacy of the training program in relation to the tasks the particular officers must perform". The question, in other words, is the adequacy of the training program itself and its relation to the injury caused, not simply the mistake or indifference of the individual officer.[14]

In McMillian v. Monroe County, 520 U.S. 781 (1997), a § 1983 action against an Alabama county (and others) alleging that the county sheriff had suppressed exculpatory evidence in a criminal case, the Court held, 5–4, that under Alabama law, county sheriffs acting in their law enforcement capacity represent the state and not their counties. Thus there could be no local government liability under the Monell rule.

[14] The Court, by 5–4, once again rejected a claim of local governmental liability predicated on a failure-to-train theory in Connick v. Thompson, 131 S.Ct. 1350 (2011). The petitioner Orleans Parish District Attorney's Office, for which Connick was at relevant times the sole policymaker, conceded that assistant district attorneys had failed to disclose potentially exculpatory physical evidence (a blood sample) to the plaintiff, who spent 18 years in prison on robbery and murder convictions (14 of them on death row), before both convictions were vacated. In his § 1983 action, Thompson alleged that the failure of District Attorney Connick to train his subordinates regarding their obligations to disclose exculpatory evidence under Brady v. Maryland, 373 U.S. 83 (1963), manifested "deliberate indifference" to plainly foreseeable constitutional violations and was causally responsible for his wrongful convictions. In an opinion by Justice Thomas, the Court emphasized that Thompson "did not contend that he proved a pattern of * * * Brady violations" that were "similar" to the one that occurred in his case. Although Louisiana courts had overturned four convictions obtained by the Orleans Parish District Attorney's Office in the 10 years preceding Thompson's prosecution, the previous incidents had not involved failures to disclose physical evidence, and thus "could not have put Connick on notice that the office's Brady training was inadequate with respect to the sort of Brady violation at issue here." Nor should Connick have anticipated that in the absence of training, prosecutors would commit Brady violations of the kind at issue. Although other officials might require constitutional training, attorneys not only have legal educations, but also possess the tools to perform legal research when uncertain of their obligations.

In a dissent joined by Justices Breyer, Sotomayor, and Kagan, Justice Ginsburg argued that "the evidence demonstrated that misperception and disregard of Brady's disclosure requirements were pervasive in Orleans Parish" and that, under the circumstances, failure to

(d) In Board of County Commissioners v. Brown, 520 U.S. 397 (1997), the Court continued to draw fine distinctions for purposes of determining municipal liability, but in this instance the dissenters urged that the time had come to reexamine the Monell rule itself.

In Brown, the plaintiff brought a § 1983 damages action against the county, alleging that a deputy had arrested her with excessive force and that the county was liable for her injuries because the sheriff—a policymaking official—had hired the deputy without adequate review of his background (which included a conviction for assault and battery). The Court, per Justice O'Connor, reversed a judgment for the plaintiff, noting the absence of any claim that action by a policymaking official directly violated federal law or directed or authorized the deprivation of federal rights. In the absence of such a claim, the plaintiff must establish deliberate indifference on the part of the policymaking representative of the municipality, not merely to the risk of *any* constitutional injury, but to the risk of the *particular* injury suffered by the plaintiff. To cross that threshold on the basis of a single instance of inadequate screening might not be possible, and in any event, is far more difficult than the showing required by the Court in City of Canton, *supra*, to establish municipal liability on the basis of a failure to train. On the present record, Justice O'Connor concluded that the requisite deliberate indifference had not been shown.

Justice Souter, joined by Justices Stevens and Breyer, dissented. He contended that in cases involving a single act that neither violates nor directs a violation of federal law, the Court had raised the requirements for establishing deliberate indifference far too high. Justice Breyer's dissent, joined by Justices Stevens and Ginsburg, suggested that since the Monell rule that municipalities cannot be liable on a *respondeat superior* basis was "leading us to spin ever finer distinctions[,] we should reexamine the soundness of [Monell's] basic distinction itself". Justice Breyer contended that all the prerequisites for such a reexamination were present: the doubtfulness of the original principle, the complex body of interpretive law that the principle had generated, developments that had divorced the Monell rule from its apparent original purposes, and the lack of significant reliance on the rule itself.

Do you agree?[15] Note that criticisms of the Monell regime can come either from those who believe that it should be easier for plaintiffs to recover damages from local governments or from those who believe that any local governmental liability, especially when coupled with the no-municipal-immunity rule of Owen v. City of Independence, was a mistake in the first place. Consider whether the Monell regime is a sensible compromise, the worst of all possible worlds, or something in between.

---

provide training reflected actionable "deliberate indifference" to the kind of wrong that Thompson suffered.

For an argument in favor of a broader interpretation of "custom or usage" in § 1983—one including "fusion of both pervasive private practices and official acquiescence"—as well as a similar broadening of the interpretation of congressional authority under § 5 of the Fourteenth Amendment, see Rutherglen, *Custom and Usage as Action Under Color of State Law: An Essay on the Forgotten Terms of Section 1983*, 89 Va.L.Rev. 925, 927, 967 (2003).

[15] In a 1999 symposium, *Section 1983 Municipal Liability in Civil Rights Litigation*, 48 DePaul L.Rev. 619 (1999), the contributors expressed near unanimity in criticizing the Monell decision and in decrying the unworkability of the regime to which it has given rise. See also Bandes, *Not Enough Blame To Go Around: Reflections on Requiring Purposeful Government Conduct*, 68 Brook.L.Rev. 1195 (2003).

(7) States and State Agencies as Defendants: The Will Decision.
Quern v. Jordan, 440 U.S. 332 (1979), held that Congress did not clearly
manifest an intention in § 1983 to override the states' Eleventh Amendment
immunity. But Quern held only that a *federal* court lacks power to impose
such a remedy against an unconsenting state. It did not answer the question
whether § 1983 itself creates a remedy against a state.

That question was resolved in Will v. Michigan Department of State
Police, 491 U.S. 58 (1989), a state court § 1983 action seeking damages from
a state agency. (The action preceded the Court's ruling in Alden v. Maine, p.
967, *supra,* that states enjoy sovereign immunity in their own courts from
federal causes of action.) The Supreme Court ruled, 5–4, that neither a state
nor a state official acting in an official capacity is a "person" within the
meaning of § 1983, at least when sued for retrospective relief. Justice White's
opinion for the Court stated that in common usage, the term "person" does
not include the sovereign. Invoking the "clear statement" requirement
developed in Eleventh Amendment cases, he insisted on application of a
similar approach to the question presented and concluded that the language
of § 1983 did not satisfy such a requirement. The Court also noted its holding
in Quern that § 1983 does not abrogate state sovereign immunity and that a
federal court therefore cannot award retrospective relief against a state
under § 1983. Given that a principal reason for enacting § 1983 was to
provide a federal forum, the Court found it implausible that Congress meant
to create a liability under § 1983 that was enforceable only in a state court.[16]

(8) Native American Tribes as Plaintiffs and Defendants. In Inyo
County v. Paiute-Shoshone Indians, 538 U.S. 701 (2003), a Native American
tribe sought injunctive and declaratory relief under § 1983 against a county
and certain county officials. The complaint asserted that because of the
tribe's sovereign status, it was immune from the processes of the county—in
particular, from execution of search warrants against the tribe and tribal
property. The Supreme Court assumed without deciding "that Native
American tribes, like States of the Union, are not subject to suit under
§ 1983". The Court then held that "in the situation here presented [in which
the tribe was not complaining of any conduct that would have violated the
federal rights of a private individual or entity but rather was objecting to an
interference with its sovereign status], the Tribe does not qualify as a 'person'
who may sue under § 1983". "Section 1983", the Court said, "was designed to
secure private rights against government encroachment, not to advance a
sovereign's prerogative to withhold evidence relevant to a criminal
investigation". Justice Stevens, concurring in the judgment, contended that
a tribe is always a "person" for purposes of defining who may sue under
§ 1983, but stated that a claim "based entirely on the Tribe's sovereign status
[ ] is not one for which the § 1983 remedy was enacted".

C.   Jurisdictional, Procedural, and Related Issues

(1) Jurisdiction Over § 1983 Actions. Section 1 of the Civil Rights Act of
1871 contained not only a remedial provision, now codified as § 1983, but
also a grant of what appeared to be exclusive jurisdiction to the federal courts
(without regard to the amount in controversy). When the Act was revised in
1874, the jurisdictional portion was cut loose from the remedial provision
and was itself divided into several provisions dealing with the circuit and

---

[16] In Hafer v. Melo, 502 U.S. 21 (1991), the Court unanimously rejected the defendant's
claim that Will bars damages actions against state officers sued in their personal capacities
when the conduct in question was part of the defendant's official duties.

district courts. When the original jurisdiction of the circuit and district courts was merged in 1911, the jurisdictional provisions of the Civil Rights Act were also merged, and eventually came to rest in what is now 28 U.S.C. § 1343(3).[17] That provision, which has been rendered superfluous by the elimination of the jurisdictional amount requirement in the general federal question statute (§ 1331), was not written in terms suggesting that federal jurisdiction was exclusive, and thus the Supreme Court has held that state courts have concurrent jurisdiction in actions under § 1983. See Martinez v. California, 444 U.S. 277, 283–84 n. 7 (1980); Maine v. Thiboutot, 448 U.S. 1, 3 n. 1 (1980).

(2) Remedial and Procedural Doctrine in § 1983 Actions. Section 1983 provides a barebones cause of action, without specifying such important matters as the measure of damages, the immunities of official defendants, and the statute of limitations. From what sources should the courts fashion rules of decision to govern issues such as these?

One approach, which the Court has sometimes followed in developing doctrines governing official immunities and the measure of damages in § 1983 actions, is to establish a federal common law rule of decision that is designed to promote the statutory purposes.[18] A second approach—borrowing analogous rules of decisions of the applicable state (at least so long as those rules do not interfere with federal purposes)—has been followed in selecting the appropriate statute of limitations and in deciding whether a § 1983 action survives if the plaintiff dies during the lawsuit and an executor is substituted.[19] A third possible approach, which the Court has not taken, would be to borrow analogous doctrines from other federal civil rights statutes.

To the extent the Court has discretion to choose, is its election to follow different approaches as to different issues a sound one? For discussion of this question, see Chap. VII, Sec. 2(B), pp. 769–777, *supra.*

(3) Preclusion. Another important issue in § 1983 actions that was much mooted for several years involves the extent to which preclusion doctrines apply in determining the res judicata effect of a prior state court proceeding. In Allen v. McCurry, 449 U.S. 90 (1980), and subsequent decisions, the Court held that normal preclusion rules apply. See Chap. XII, Sec. 1, *infra.*

(4) Pleading Requirements. A number of lower federal courts responded to the growth in § 1983 cases (and the corresponding growth in Bivens actions against federal officials) by imposing on plaintiffs a "heightened pleading standard" in order to survive a motion to dismiss for failure to state a claim. But in Leatherman v. Tarrant County Narcotics Intelligence and Coordination Unit, 507 U.S. 163 (1993), the Supreme Court held that such a demanding standard could not be squared with the liberal system of notice pleading established by the Federal Rules of Civil Procedure.

---

[17] This complicated story is told in fuller detail in Justice Powell's dissent in Maine v. Thiboutot, 448 U.S. 1, 15–16 (1980), pp. 1009–1010, *infra.*

[18] See, *e.g.*, Memphis Comm. Sch. Dist. v. Stachura, 477 U.S. 299 (1986) (rules governing the measure of compensatory damages); Smith v. Wade, 461 U.S. 30 (1983) (punitive damages may be awarded on a showing of recklessness by an official defendant); Felder v. Casey, 487 U.S. 131 (1988), p. 455, *supra* (state notice-of-claim statute was preempted in a state court action under § 1983); Town of Newton v. Rumery, 480 U.S. 386 (1987) (enforceability of agreement releasing § 1983 claims is governed by federal law); see also Sec. 3, *infra* (on official immunity doctrines).

[19] See pp. 747–750, *supra.*

Nevertheless, without purporting to augment the requirement of the Federal Rules of Civil Procedure, the Court found that the plaintiffs' pleadings were inadequate to survive a motion to dismiss in Ashcroft v. Iqbal, 556 U.S. 662 (2009), also discussed at pp. 774, 996, *supra*, which involved claims against former Attorney General John Ashcroft and FBI Director Robert Mueller based on alleged unconstitutional acts in the period following September 11, 2001. Iqbal, a Pakistani Muslim who was arrested for and pleaded guilty to fraud and subsequently was removed to Pakistan, alleged that Ashcroft and Mueller adopted a policy of discriminatorily designating Arab Muslims as persons of "high interest" to the 9/11 investigation and of detaining them in a maximum security facility—in which detainees were kept in lockdown for 23 hours a day and spent the sole hour outside their cells in handcuffs and leg irons—on account of their race, religion, or national origin. The complaint further averred that Ashcroft and Mueller knew of and condoned Iqbal's subjection to the policy. In finding Iqbal's complaint insufficient to survive a motion to dismiss under Rule 8 of the Federal Rules of Civil Procedure, which says that a pleading must contain a "short and plain statement of the claim showing that the pleader is entitled to relief," the Court (5–4) relied on its earlier interpretation in Bell Atlantic Corp. v. Twombly, 550 U.S. 544 (2007), a case that had ordered dismissal of an antitrust complaint.

Twombly, Justice Kennedy wrote for the majority, had established two pertinent principles. First, "the tenet that a court must accept as true all of the allegations contained in a complaint is inapplicable to legal conclusions. Threadbare recitals of the elements of a cause of action, supported by mere conclusory statements, do not suffice." Applying this principle, the Court rejected as inadequate Iqbal's averments that the petitioners knew of and condoned his alleged mistreatment; that the mistreatment reflected a policy of discrimination based on race, religion, or national origin; "that Ashcroft was the 'principal architect' of this invidious policy"; and that "Mueller was 'instrumental' in adopting and executing it." Justice Kennedy explained that "we do not reject these bald allegations on the ground that they are unrealistic or nonsensical. * * * It is the conclusory nature of respondent's allegations, rather than their extravagantly fanciful nature, that disentitles them to the presumption of truth."

The second principle that the Court extracted from Twombly was that "only a complaint that states a plausible claim to relief survives a motion to dismiss. Determining whether a complaint states a plausible claim for relief will * * * be a context-specific task that requires the reviewing court to draw on its judicial experience and common sense." Applying this principle both to Iqbal's conclusory averments and to more specific assertions intended to support them, Justice Kennedy found Iqbal's claim that the defendants had "adopted a policy of classifying post-September-11 detainees as 'of high interest' because of their race, religion, or national origin" not to be sufficiently plausible to survive a motion to dismiss "given more likely explanations" for the defendants' alleged conduct: "The September 11 attacks were perpetrated by 19 Arab Muslim hijackers * * *. It should come as no surprise that a legitimate policy directing law enforcement to arrest and detain individuals because of their suspected link to the attacks would produce a disparate, incidental impact on Arab Muslims, even though the purpose of the policy was to target neither Arabs nor Muslims." Even on the assumption that the defendants had adopted a policy of subjecting some terrorist suspects to the rigors of maximum security facilities, "the complaint does not show, or even intimate," that they did so for invidiously discriminatory reasons. The more plausible inference was that "the Nation's top law enforcement officers, in the aftermath of a devastating terrorist attack, sought to keep suspected terrorists in the most secure conditions available until the suspects could be cleared of terrorist activity. * * * [Iqbal] would need to allege more by way of factual content to 'nudg[e]' his claim of purposeful discrimination 'across the line from conceivable to plausible.' Twombly, 550 U.S., at 570."

Justice Souter, joined by Justices Stevens, Ginsburg, and Breyer, dissented. Twombly, he said, made clear that "a court must take the allegations [in a complaint] as true, no matter how skeptical the court may be", subject to a "sole exception" for "allegations that are sufficiently fantastic to defy reality as we know it: claims about little green men, or the plaintiff's recent trip to Pluto, or experiences in time travel. That is not what we have here." Nor was this a case, like Twombly, in which the plaintiff's factual allegations, although " 'consistent with' " alleged illegality, were " 'just as much in line with' " a lawful course of conduct (quoting Twombly). "[T]he allegations in the complaint are neither confined to naked legal conclusions nor consistent with legal conduct. The complaint alleges that FBI officials discriminated against Iqbal solely on account of his race, religion, and national origin, and it alleges * * * knowledge and deliberate indifference [by the defendants.] * * * Iqbal's complaint therefore contains 'enough facts to state a claim to relief that is plausible on its face' " (quoting Twombly).

In a separate dissenting opinion, Justice Breyer wrote that he, "like the Court, believe[d] it important to prevent unwarranted litigation from interfering with" government operations, but that he could not "find in that need adequate justification for the Court's interpretation" of the pleading requirements of the Federal Rules of Civil Procedure. According to Justice Breyer, trial judges already have other mechanisms for preventing unwarranted discovery: "A district court, for example, can begin discovery with lower level government defendants before determining whether a case can be made to allow discovery related to higher level government officials."

Whatever its wisdom as a matter of policy, can the Court's ruling be justified as an interpretation of Rule 8 of the Federal Rules of Civil Procedure?[20] What does it mean to say that a court must "draw on its judicial

---

[20] Consider the pertinence of Form 11, which at the time Iqbal was decided was attached to the Rules and which, under Rule 84 as it then read, "suffice[d] under these rules". The Form was entitled a "Complaint for Negligence", which, on the question of liability stated simply "On *date* and *place*, the defendant negligently drove a motor vehicle against the plaintiff."

Iqbal has been widely criticized. See, e.g., Meier, *Why Twombly Is Good Law (But Poorly Drafted) and Iqbal Will Be Overturned*, 87 Ind.L.J. 709 (2012); Miller, *From Conley to Twombly to Iqbal: A Double Play on the Federal Rules of Civil Procedure*, 60 Duke L.J. 1 (2010); Steinman, *The Pleading Problem*, 62 Stan.L.Rev. 1293 (2010). For a rare defense, see Moline, *Nineteenth-Century-Principles for Twenty-First Century-Pleading*, 60 Emory L.J. 159 (2010).

Fitzpatrick, *Twombly and Iqbal Reconsidered*, 87 Notre Dame L.Rev. 1621 (2012), characterizes Iqbal (and the prior decision in Twombly) as sensibly aimed "to recalibrate plaintiffs' discovery rights in light of the exponential increases in discovery costs that have developed in the years since the Federal Rules of Civil Procedure were first promulgated in 1938". Among the purposes of the qualified immunity doctrine of Harlow v. Fitzgerald, p. 1030, *infra*, is to facilitate the dismissal of insubstantial suits against governmental officials prior to discovery. If the Court believes that discovery costs have gotten out of hand, is the "recalibrat[ion]" of pleading standards an appropriate response?

experience and common sense" in assessing whether the allegations of a complaint are sufficiently "plausible" to survive a motion to dismiss?[21]

(5) Attorney's Fees. The Civil Rights Attorney's Fees Awards Act of 1976, codified in 42 U.S.C. § 1988, provides that a court "in its discretion, may allow the prevailing party, other than the United States, a reasonable attorney's fee as part of the costs." This provision is applicable to § 1983 actions in state as well as federal courts. Maine v. Thiboutot, 448 U.S. 1, 8–11 (1980). Despite the statutory language, it is established that (i) absent special circumstances, the "prevailing party" language applies to plaintiffs whose litigation terminates in judicially approved consent decrees, Maher v. Gagne, 448 U.S. 122 (1980)[22] ; and (ii) defendants may not automatically recover whenever they prevail, but only when the plaintiff's action was frivolous or vexatious, see Hughes v. Rowe, 449 U.S. 5 (1980) (per curiam).

The essentially one-way shifting of fees may well have contributed to efforts to fit claims for relief under § 1983, and may also have increased the total number of civil rights actions filed. See Rowe, *Predicting the Effects of Attorney Fee Shifting*, 47 Law & Contemp.Prob. 139, 147 (1984). But see Schwab & Eisenberg, *Explaining Constitutional Tort Litigation: The Influence of the Attorney Fees Statute and the Government as Defendant*, 73 Cornell L.Rev. 719, 780 (1988) ("attorney fees statutes may have less of an effect on filing rates than is commonly believed"). Is a one-way approach warranted by the importance of the rights asserted in § 1983 actions?

D.   Prisoner Litigation

(1) The Prison Litigation Reform Act. In 1996, Congress responded to concern about mounting numbers of prisoner civil rights actions, many of which were frivolous, by enacting the Prisoner Litigation Reform Act (PLRA), 110 Stat. 1321–66 to 1321–77. The PLRA imposes restrictions on prisoner suits that do not apply to nonprisoner § 1983 actions. Among the innovations are:

1.   A requirement that plaintiffs, for whom filing fees had previously been waived, pay the customary filing fee (if necessary, in installments from the small prison financial account that they would otherwise use to pay for sundries).

2.   A requirement that before filing suits challenging prison conditions, plaintiffs must first exhaust administrative remedies.

3.   A provision addressed to "frequent filers" that prohibits a prisoner who has brought three or more previous actions that were dismissed as frivolous or malicious or for failure to state a claim from filing additional actions unless in imminent danger of serious physical injury.

4.   A prohibition on the award of damages for mental and emotional distress unaccompanied by physical injury.

5.   Limits on the permissible scope of consent decrees and injunctive orders, designed to keep judicial intrusion into prison management to the minimum required by the Constitution.

---

[21]   Beinart, *The Burdens of Pleading,* 162 U.Pa.L.Rev. 1768 (2014), criticizes Iqbal's regime of "plausibility pleading" as especially troubling in light of psychological research on cognitive biases.

[22]   But see Buckhannon Bd. & Care v. West Va. DHHR, 532 U.S. 598 (2001) (holding that identical language in two other statutes does not extend to plaintiffs who achieve settlements that are not judicially ratified).

6.   Special limits on attorney's fees.

Schlanger, *Inmate Litigation*, 116 Harv.L.Rev. 1555, 1559–60 (2003), describes the PLRA as having had "an impact on inmate litigation that is hard to exaggerate; to set out the most obvious effect, 2001 filings by inmates were down forty-three percent since their peak in 1995 [from 39,008 to 22,206], notwithstanding a simultaneous twenty-three percent increase in the number of people incarcerated nationwide." Without contesting the Act's success in reducing strain on federal dockets, critics express concern that it poses traps for legally unsophisticated prisoners (notably through its "exhaustion" requirement) and precludes the filing of meritorious as well as frivolous claims. For discussion of the effect of the exhaustion requirement in reducing filings, see p. 1099, *infra*.

(2) The Relationship Between the Remedy Under § 1983 and the Writ of Federal Habeas Corpus. The Supreme Court, in Preiser v. Rodriguez, 411 U.S. 475 (1973), and Heck v. Humphrey, 512 U.S. 477 (1994), has effectively subordinated the § 1983 remedy to the writ of habeas corpus when the remedies would overlap (and to some extent, even when they do not), holding that § 1983 may not be resorted to if the direct or indirect effect of granting relief would be to invalidate an existing state court conviction. For analysis of these and related decisions, see Chap. XII, Sec. 2, *infra*.

———

NOTE ON § 1983 AS A REMEDY FOR THE VIOLATION OF A FEDERAL STATUTE

(1) Historical Background. As originally enacted in 1871 (17 Stat. 13), the provision that is now § 1983 created a cause of action only for the deprivation of *constitutional* rights. The phrase "and laws" was added, without helpful explanation, as part of a revision of the statutes in 1874, at the same time that the jurisdictional provisions of the 1871 Act were severed from its remedial provisions (see p. 1004–1005, *supra*). The Supreme Court did not fully explore the significance of this revision and the scope of § 1983's application to federal statutory violations until over a century later.

(2) Maine v. Thiboutot. Section 1343(a)(3) of Title 28—the jurisdictional counterpart of § 1983—refers only to rights secured by the Constitution or "by any Act of Congress *providing for equal rights*" (emphasis added). In Chapman v. Houston Welfare Rights Org., 441 U.S. 600 (1979), the Court interpreted that jurisdictional provision as not providing a basis for a federal court suit challenging the deprivation of welfare benefits as unlawful under the federal Social Security Act. But since the elimination in 1980 of the amount-in-controversy requirement in 28 U.S.C. § 1331, § 1343(a)(3) has been superfluous even in federal court actions.

Unlike § 1343(a)(3), § 1983 itself speaks generally of violations of federal law. The question whether that provision should also be interpreted as limited to actions claiming violations of "equal rights" statutes was resolved in Maine v. Thiboutot, 448 U.S. 1 (1980), a similar challenge to the denial of welfare benefits, but one filed in state court, to which § 1343(a)(3) had no application. The Supreme Court, per Justice Brennan, held that the complaint (which asserted no denial of equal rights) stated a good claim under § 1983. The Court reasoned that prior decisions had upheld the provision of relief in such cases, and concluded that there was no contrary legislative history sufficiently clear to warrant departure from the plain statutory language.

Justice Powell (joined by Chief Justice Burger and Justice Rehnquist) wrote a lengthy dissent, arguing that the legislative history showed an intention to encompass only rights secured by the Constitution and by laws providing for equal rights. He further maintained that the omission of this limitation on the coverage of statutory rights from the 1874 predecessor to § 1983 resulted from an accident in the process of recodifying the United States statutes. (See the discussion at p. 1004–1005, *supra*.) Justice Powell also criticized the Court for imposing upon state and local governments and officials "liability whenever a person believes he has been injured by the administration of *any* federal-state cooperative program * * *. * * * [L]iterally hundreds of cooperative regulatory and social welfare enactments may be affected".

(3) The Aftermath of the Thiboutot Decision: Suits for Violation of Federal Statutes. In its decision in Thiboutot, the Court did not consider the relationship between its construction of § 1983 and case law on whether to imply a private right of action under a federal statute that does not expressly provide one. See generally Chap. VII, Sec. 2(B), *supra*. Suppose that, in the absence of § 1983, no private remedy would be implied under a particular federal statute—as is generally the case under the recent implied right of action precedents. Did Thiboutot indicate that § 1983 will supply the missing remedy whenever the offender is a state official?

The problem is a complex one, raising two specific, and interrelated, questions: (1) Has the statute created a private right within the meaning of § 1983? (2) Has the scheme of remedies created by Congress implicitly excluded a private remedy under § 1983?[1] The two questions have not always been rigorously distinguished in judicial analysis, and underlying them both is the issue whether a private remedy should be available under a federal statute applicable to both public and private action *only* when the offender is a state officer. Consider whether the Court, through its answers to these questions, has retreated from any promise of broadly available federal remedies against state officials that Thiboutot might have offered.

(a) Has Congress Created a Private Right? The question whether Congress has created a statutory "right" enforceable under § 1983 typically arises only when Congress did not afford the plaintiff an express statutory cause of action to enforce the asserted right.

(i) The Court's General Approach. The Court's course of decisions on this aspect of the problem has not been wholly consistent, but the general tenor—exhibited, for example, in Gonzaga University v. Doe, 536 U.S. 273 (2002)—has reflected skepticism that Congress intends federal statutes to create "rights" when it fails to provide statutory remedies.[2] In the Gonzaga

---

[1]   Recall that in the Seminole decision, p. 940, *supra*, the Supreme Court held that an action against state officers under the doctrine of Ex parte Young was unavailable because such an action could not be reconciled with the statutory scheme. What significance, if any, should be attached to the Court's silence with respect to the § 1983 remedy as a basis for the requested relief? See Meltzer, *The Seminole Decision and State Sovereign Immunity*, 1996 Sup.Ct.Rev. 1, 40 n. 185 (Seminole Tribe's failure to rely on § 1983 "does not justify the Court's failure to consider that provision's implications").

[2]   Cases in which the Court has declined to find that federal statutes created rights enforceable under § 1983 include Pennhurst State Sch. & Hosp. v. Halderman (Pennhurst I), 451 U.S. 1 (1981) (involving a "bill of rights" for persons with developmental disabilities); Suter v. Artist M., 503 U.S. 347 (1992) (involving an alleged failure to make "reasonable efforts"

case, the plaintiff brought suit under § 1983 claiming that defendants, acting under color of state law, had disclosed his educational records in violation of his rights under the Family Educational Rights and Privacy Act (FERPA). The Supreme Court held, 7–2, that the action was foreclosed because the relevant FERPA provisions created no personal rights enforceable under § 1983. The most specific of those provisions, 20 U.S.C. § 1232g(b)(1), provides that "No funds shall be made available under any applicable program to any educational agency or institution which has a policy or practice of permitting the release of education records * * * of students without the written consent of their parents to any individual, agency, or organization". In the course of an opinion for five Justices, Chief Justice Rehnquist noted that FERPA had been enacted under the federal spending power, that the sole remedy prescribed by FERPA for failure to comply was the withholding of federal funds, and that "FERPA's nondisclosure provisions * * * speak only in terms of institutional policy and practice, not individual instances of disclosure". Thus, the nondisclosure provisions of the Act have an " 'aggregate' focus" that does not " 'give rise to individual rights' ".

The Court recognized that unlike an implied right of action case, in which the plaintiff must establish Congress' intent to create *both* a private right and a private remedy, a plaintiff in a § 1983 case need only show an intent to create a private right. But the Court explicitly rejected "the notion that our cases permit anything short of an unambiguously conferred right to support a cause of action under § 1983". The Court "further reject[ed] the notion that our implied right of action cases are separate and distinct from our § 1983 cases", at least to this extent: "[O]ur implied right of action cases should guide the determination of whether a statute confers rights enforceable under § 1983".

Justices Breyer and Souter, concurring in the judgment, disagreed with the requirement that a private right must be "unambiguously" conferred, but agreed that in this case Congress did not intend private judicial enforcement. Justice Stevens, joined by Justice Ginsburg, dissented vigorously, arguing that the "right at issue is more specific and clear than rights previously found enforceable under § 1983". He went on to criticize the Court for paying lip service to the distinction between the implied right of action cases and § 1983 cases but at the same time collapsing the two parts of the implied right of action test ("is there a right?" and "is it enforceable?") into one by "circularly defining a right actionable under § 1983 as, in essence, 'a right which Congress intended to make enforceable' ". The Court, he concluded, has "eroded—if not eviscerated—the long-established principle of presumptive enforceability of rights under § 1983".[3]

---

required as a condition for federal reimbursement for foster care and adoption services); and Blessing v. Freestone, 520 U.S. 329 (1997) (involving failure of a state agency to achieve reasonable compliance with a provision of the Social Security Act dealing with child support services). *But cf.* Wilder v. Virginia Hosp. Ass'n, 496 U.S. 498 (1990) (holding that § 1983 permitted a suit by a health care provider who claimed a violation of its right to have the state provide "reasonable and adequate" payments as required by federal law).

[3] May a private person obtain relief under § 1983 for a violation by a defendant of federal *regulations* rather than of a federal statute? In Alexander v. Sandoval, p. 733, *supra*, Justice Stevens' dissent contended that the majority's refusal to recognize a private right of action directly under § 602 of Title VI and its implementing regulations was "something of a sport"; the plaintiffs "neglected to mention 42 U.S.C. § 1983 in framing their Title VI claim," but, he continued, a new lawsuit could be filed under § 1983 challenging the same official conduct as a

(ii) The Special Problem of the Application of § 1983 to Preemption Claims. In Golden State Transit Corp. v. City of Los Angeles, 493 U.S. 103 (1989), the question involved the application of § 1983 to a claim of federal statutory preemption of state law. The plaintiff, Golden State, had challenged Los Angeles' effort to condition renewal of its taxicab franchise on settlement of a labor dispute. The Court upheld Golden State's ability to sue under § 1983 for both injunctive and compensatory relief for interference with a federally protected bargaining relationship. The Court reasoned that (a) the National Labor Relations Act did not benefit private parties merely "as an incident" of federal regulation; rather the Act "creates rights in labor and management both against one another and against the State"; and (b) those rights are secured against state interference by the Supremacy Clause. The availability of a § 1983 remedy in such cases, the Court said, "turns on whether the statute, by its terms or as interpreted, creates obligations 'sufficiently specific and definite' to be within 'the competence of the judiciary to enforce,' is intended to benefit the putative plaintiff, and is not foreclosed 'by express provision or other specific evidence from the statute itself' ".

Dissenting for himself, Chief Justice Rehnquist, and Justice O'Connor, Justice Kennedy argued that plaintiff's only remedy was for declaratory and injunctive relief (but not damages) in an action under 28 U.S.C. § 1331. Although he recognized that § 1983 extended to interests secured by various federal statutes, he observed that "[n]one of these secured statutory interests * * * has been the sole result of a statute's pre-emptive effect * * *. Pre-emption concerns the federal structure of the Nation rather than the securing of rights, privileges, and immunities to individuals".

Is the Court's approach in Golden State Transit consistent with its approach in cases involving purely statutory claims unconnected to the Supremacy Clause? For a perceptive analysis, see Monaghan, *Federal Statutory Review Under Section 1983 and the APA*, 91 Colum.L.Rev. 233 (1991).

(iii) The Bearing of the Supremacy Clause and Equity Jurisprudence as a Possible Alternative to Suit Under § 1983. In both Douglas v. Independent Living Center of Southern California, p. 934, *supra,* and Armstrong v. Exceptional Child Center, Inc., pp. 845, 934, *supra,* the plaintiffs argued that they had a direct cause of action under the Supremacy Clause—and thus did not need to rely on § 1983—in seeking injunctions compelling state officials to make payments allegedly owed to them under federal law. In Armstrong, however, the Court, in an opinion by Justice Scalia, ruled squarely that the Supremacy Clause "does not create a cause of action" and characterized "the ability to sue to enjoin unconstitutional actions by state and federal officers", where it exists, as "the creation of courts of equity". Justice Sotomayor's dissenting opinion, in which Justices Kennedy, Ginsburg, and Kagan joined, appeared to accept the majority's conclusion that the right to injunctive relief recognized in cases such as Ex parte Young, p. 922, *supra,* lay in principles of equity, not the requirements of the Supremacy Clause.

---

violation of federal regulations. Yet the Gonzaga decision would seem to require that a regulation, like a statute, unambiguously confer a private right on the plaintiff.

On the question whether § 1983 creates a cause of action for violations of treaty rights, see Parry, *A Primer on Treaties and § 1983 After Medellin v. Texas*, 13 Lewis & Clark L.Rev. 35 (2009) (arguing that it does).

Having rejected a claim to relief under the Supremacy Clause, the Armstrong majority also found that the plaintiffs' asserted equitable cause of action was "implicitly preclude[d]" by the combined operation of two aspects of the Medicaid Act. First, the statute provided an alternative remedy for state non-compliance with statutory obligations by authorizing the Secretary of Health and Human Services to withhold funds. Second, the provision under which the plaintiffs sought increased payments was so vague and non-specific as to be "judicially unadministrable". Writing for the dissenters, Justice Sotomayor argued that the vagueness of the statute's payment mandate counseled deference and flexibility in interpretation of the states' obligations, but did not preclude a traditional equitable cause of action to compel official compliance with federal law.

Armstrong clearly appears to shift the theoretical basis for suits to enjoin state statutes that are allegedly preempted by federal law, which some previous cases had suggested were founded directly on the Supremacy Clause, see p. 745, *supra,* to the traditions of equity jurisprudence. The full implications of that shift remain to be seen. One possibility, suggested by Chief Justice Roberts' dissenting opinion in the Douglas case, is that the shift may have further reaching ramifications for suits seeking to enforce states' affirmative obligations under federal law (as in Douglas and Armstrong) than in suits to enjoin coercive violations of federal law, which the Court has routinely upheld. According to the Chief Justice, to allow suits to enforce states' affirmative obligations under federal funding statutes when Congress has failed to provide a statutory cause of action "would effect a complete end-run around this Court's implied right of action" jurisprudence, which "would serve no purpose if a plaintiff could overcome the absence of a statutory right of action by invoking a right of action under the Supremacy Clause to exactly the same effect." The Chief Justice distinguished Ex parte Young, p. 922, *supra,* and similar subsequent cases that had recognized rights to sue for injunctive relief to enforce the Constitution on the ground that they "present[ed] quite different questions involving 'the pre-emptive assertion in equity of a defense that would otherwise have been available in the State's enforcement proceedings at law.' " (For discussion of this interpretation of Ex parte Young, see pp. 933–935, *supra.*)

Vladeck, *Douglas and the Fate of Ex Parte Young*, 122 Yale L.J. Online 13 (2012), rejects the Chief Justice's analysis: "[I]f the Supremacy Clause divests state officers of the power to act in violation of *any* federal law (as Ex parte Young holds), then a plaintiff who seeks injunctive relief in a case like Douglas" or presumably Armstrong "is seeking as much to enforce the Constitution against the state officer as he or she is seeking to enforce the relevant federal statute. An inability to bring such a suit would leave plaintiffs without a remedy for an ongoing constitutional violation." Consider once more the suggestion of Shapiro, *Ex parte Young and the Uses of History*, 67 N.Y.U.Ann.Surv.Am.L. 69 (2011), that modern interpretations of Ex parte Young tend to reflect the ideological predispositions of the interpreter. According to Professor Shapiro, "arguments about the case have become a proxy for" debates about the extent to which litigants should be able to invoke the Constitution "not only as a shield against state action [that coercively invades their rights] but [also] as a sword" with which to seek affirmative redress "against a state or local government, or its officers, in federal court". If the debate is thus characterized, is an ideologically neutral stance possible?

(b) Statutory Supersession of the § 1983 Remedy. Even if the Court determines that a particular statute creates an enforceable private right, the question remains whether Congress has created a system of remedies in that statute that implicitly excludes an action under § 1983. The decisions are not wholly consistent.

(i) In Wright v. Roanoke Redev. & Hous. Auth., 479 U.S. 418 (1987) (5–4), in which tenants of a federally-funded public housing project brought a § 1983 damages action against the municipal housing authority for violating a rent ceiling established under a federal statute and implementing regulations, the Court ruled that the suit could go forward. The majority reasoned that federal law created enforceable rights in the tenants *and* that HUD's powers to audit its contract with the public housing authority and to cut off funds were insufficient to indicate congressional intent to foreclose enforcement under § 1983: " 'We do not lightly conclude that Congress intended to preclude reliance on § 1983 as a remedy' for the deprivation of a federally secured right" (quoting Smith v. Robinson, 468 U.S. 992 (1984)).

(ii) By contrast, in City of Rancho Palos Verdes v. Abrams, 544 U.S. 113 (2005), the Court built on an earlier, pre-Wright case to hold that Congress' provision of express statutory remedies barred a § 1983 action for violation of a federal statute.[4] The Abrams case involved an attempt to use § 1983 to enforce a provision of the federal Telecommunications Act limiting the authority of state and local governments to impede the installation of facilities for wireless communications. The Act itself authorizes a private remedy for violation of this provision, and the Court held that this private remedy superseded any remedy under § 1983. Noting that the statutory remedy was in several respects more restrictive than that provided by § 1983, Justice Scalia, in an opinion for the Court, first rejected the argument that such a specific statutory remedy should *conclusively* establish an intent to preclude § 1983 relief. But he then stated that "[t]he provision of an express, private means of redress in the statute itself is *ordinarily* an indication that Congress did not intend to leave open a more expansive remedy under § 1983" (emphasis added)—an inference that can be overcome "by textual indication, express or implicit, that the remedy is to complement, rather than supplant, § 1983".

---

[4] The earlier decision, Middlesex County Sewerage Auth. v. National Sea Clammers Ass'n, 453 U.S. 1 (1981), involved a § 1983 action for an injunction and damages brought by commercial fishermen against state and local governments and their officials. Plaintiffs alleged that defendants' discharge of sewage and pollutants violated the Federal Water Pollution Control Act (FWPCA) and the Marine Protection, Research, and Sanctuaries Act of 1972 (MPRSA). Both statutes provided what the Court termed "elaborate enforcement provisions", expressly authorizing suits by federal administrators to impose sanctions, suits by private persons to obtain judicial review of federal administrative decisions, and citizen suits against polluters for injunctive relief. (Injunctive relief under the two statutes' citizen suit provisions was unavailable in the actual case because the plaintiffs had not given the requisite 60-day notice to federal and state officials). The Supreme Court held that the plaintiffs could not obtain remedies other than those expressly provided in the two regulatory statutes. After rejecting plaintiffs' argument that they were entitled to implied remedies under the two Acts, the Court ruled that Congress intended, in providing these "quite comprehensive enforcement mechanisms", not only to foreclose implied private actions, but also "to supplant any remedy that otherwise would be available under § 1983". However, the majority denied the charge made by the dissenters that the decision placed on plaintiffs, in § 1983 actions based on rights created by Congress, the burden of demonstrating congressional intent to preserve the § 1983 remedy.

Had Middlesex come out the other way, could plaintiffs have brought suit without giving 60-days' notice and obtained both damages and injunctive relief? If so, wouldn't that have effectively read the notice requirement in such actions out of the statute?

Justice Breyer, concurring in an opinion joined by Justices O'Connor, Souter, and Ginsburg, agreed with the creation of an "ordinary inference" of remedial exclusivity resulting from a specific private remedy in the governing statute and praised the Court for "wisely reject[ing]" the conclusive presumption urged by the Government. But he added that the inference should in his view be rebuttable on the basis not only of the text but also of the overall context.[5]

(iii) In Fitzgerald v. Barnstable Sch. Comm., 555 U.S. 246 (2009), the Court held unanimously that Title IX of the Education Amendments of 1972 does not preclude a § 1983 action alleging *unconstitutional* gender discrimination in the public schools. In reaching this conclusion, Justice Alito made clear that congressional intent was the touchstone. In gauging intent, he emphasized two points. First, the only remedies provided by Title IX— withdrawal of federal funds and an implied cause of action—are not as elaborate or restrictive as those in cases in which the Court has found that Congress intended to preclude § 1983 remedies. Second, there is considerable divergence between the scope of the protections provided by Title IX (which, for example, extends to non-state institutions that receive federal funds, but does not create any cause of action against school administrators or other individuals) and by § 1983.

In fitting Fitzgerald into the framework of prior decisions, Justice Alito repeatedly grouped precedents finding implied preclusion of § 1983 actions involving *statutory* violations with the single Supreme Court case that had held that a statutory cause of action impliedly precluded *constitutional* claims under § 1983, Smith v. Robinson, 468 U.S. 992 (1984). For an argument that the Court should not apply the same standards in these two situations, see Levinson, *Misinterpreting "Sounds of Silence": Why Courts Should Not "Imply" Congressional Preclusion of § 1983 Claims*, 77 Fordham L.Rev. 775 (2008).

INTRODUCTORY NOTE ON THE RELATIONSHIP BETWEEN COMMON LAW TORTS AND CONSTITUTIONAL TORTS IN ACTIONS AGAINST STATE AND LOCAL OFFICIALS

In the materials that follow, we turn from a consideration of the application of § 1983 in the context of federal statutory violations to questions in which the availability of relief under that provision turns on the meaning of the Fourteenth Amendment. Nearly every common law tort deprives the injured party of liberty or property. The question thus arises whether every common law tort committed by an official acting under color of law does or should give rise to a constitutional tort action under § 1983 for a deprivation of liberty or property without due process.

In a series of otherwise unrelated decisions, the Supreme Court has recoiled from the notion that either § 1983 or the Due Process Clause should function as a "font of tort law." *E.g.*, Castle Rock v. Gonzales, 545 U.S. 748,

---

[5]   Justice Stevens, concurring only in the judgment, criticized the Court's opinion on two grounds: its assumption "that the legislative history of the statute is totally irrelevant" and its failure to "properly acknowledge[ ] the strength of our normal presumption that Congress intended to preserve, rather than preclude, the availability of § 1983 as a remedy for the enforcement of federal statutory rights".

768 (2005); Daniels v. Williams, 474 U.S. 327, 332 (1986); Parratt v. Taylor, 451 U.S. 527, 544 (1981); Paul v. Davis, 424 U.S. 693, 701 (1976). In resisting this idea, the Court has explored three possibilities.

First, the Court has entertained arguments that although § 1983 creates a cause of action for some constitutional violations, it does not create a cause of action for other, possibly less serious ones. But the Court concluded that § 1983 will not bear this interpretation in the next principal case, Parratt v. Taylor.

Second, the Court once appeared open to the possibility that some common law torts—maybe many—do not deprive the victim of "liberty" or "property" in the constitutional sense of those terms. Paul v. Davis exemplifies this approach. In Paul, police officials had circulated to local merchants a list of "active shoplifters" that included Davis' name, and Davis filed a § 1983 action, contending that this conduct, taken without a prior hearing, denied him liberty and property without due process. The Supreme Court held that the plaintiff's interest in his reputation was not an interest in liberty or property protected by the Constitution. The decision was widely criticized. See, *e.g.*, Monaghan, *Of "Liberty" and "Property"*, 62 Cornell L.Rev. 405, 423–29 (1977); Shapiro, *Mr. Justice Rehnquist: A Preliminary View*, 90 Harv.L.Rev. 293, 322–38 (1976).

Nevertheless, the approach taken in Davis was followed a few years later in Baker v. McCollan, 443 U.S. 137 (1979), a case in which the plaintiff had been mistakenly held in custody for eight days by the police, who confused him with his brother. The mistake could have been remedied had the police more promptly checked their records. The Supreme Court ruled that though the plaintiff might have a state law action for false imprisonment, he had not suffered a deprivation of liberty under the Fourteenth Amendment.

Third, the Court has ruled that some common law torts that deprive a plaintiff of liberty or property do so without thereby depriving the plaintiff of due process of law and, thus, do not violate the Due Process Clause. This approach, which was pioneered in Parratt v. Taylor, the case immediately following this Note, has proved to be generative, controversial, and also somewhat confusing.

Parratt v. Taylor

451 U.S. 527, 101 S.Ct. 1908, 68 L.Ed.2d 420 (1981).
Certiorari to the United States Court of Appeals for the Eighth Circuit.

■ JUSTICE REHNQUIST delivered the opinion of the Court.

The respondent is an inmate at the Nebraska Penal and Correctional Complex who ordered by mail certain hobby materials valued at $23.50. The hobby materials were lost and respondent brought suit under 42 U.S.C. § 1983 to recover their value. At first blush one might well inquire why respondent brought an action in federal court to recover damages of such a small amount for negligent loss of property, but because 28 U.S.C. § 1343, the predicate for the jurisdiction of the United States District Court, contains no minimum dollar limitation, he was authorized by Congress to bring his action under that section if he met its requirements and if he stated a claim for relief under 42 U.S.C. § 1983. Respondent claimed that his property was negligently lost by prison officials in violation of his rights under the Fourteenth Amendment to the United States Constitution. More specifically, he claimed that he had been deprived of property without due process of law.

The United States District Court for the District of Nebraska entered summary judgment for respondent, and the United States Court of Appeals for the Eighth Circuit affirmed in a *per curiam* order. We granted certiorari.

I

The facts underlying this dispute are not seriously contested. Respondent paid for the hobby materials he ordered with two drafts drawn on his inmate account by prison officials. The packages arrived at the complex and were signed for by two employees who worked in the prison hobby center. One of the employees was a civilian and the other was an inmate. Respondent was in segregation at the time and was not permitted to have the hobby materials. Normal prison procedures for the handling of mail packages is that upon arrival they are either delivered to the prisoner who signs a receipt for the package or the prisoner is notified to pick up the package and to sign a receipt. No inmate other than the one to whom the package is addressed is supposed to sign for a package. After being released from segregation, respondent contacted several prison officials regarding the whereabouts of his packages. The officials were never able to locate the packages or to determine what caused their disappearance.

In 1976, respondent commenced this action against the petitioners, the Warden and Hobby Manager of the prison, in the District Court seeking to recover the value of the hobby materials which he claimed had been lost as a result of the petitioners' negligence. Respondent alleged that petitioners' conduct deprived him of property without due process of law in violation of the Fourteenth Amendment of the United States Constitution. Respondent chose to proceed in the United States District Court under 28 U.S.C. § 1343 and 42 U.S.C. § 1983, even though the State of Nebraska had a tort claims procedure which provided a remedy to persons who suffered tortious losses at the hands of the State. * * *

II

* * * Nothing in the language of § 1983 or its legislative history limits the statute solely to intentional deprivations of constitutional rights. * * * Section 1983, unlike its criminal counterpart, 18 U.S.C. § 242, has never been found by this Court to contain a state-of-mind requirement.[2] The Court recognized as much in Monroe v. Pape, 365 U.S. 167 (1961), when we explained after extensively reviewing the legislative history of § 1983, that

> "[i]t is abundantly clear that one reason the legislation was passed was to afford a federal right in federal courts because, by

---

[2]   Title 18 U.S.C. § 242 provides in pertinent part: "Whoever, under color of any law, statute, ordinance, regulation, or custom, *willfully* subjects any inhabitant of any State, Territory, or District to the deprivation of any rights, privileges, or immunities secured or protected by the Constitution or laws of the United States * * * shall be fined not more than $1,000 or imprisoned not more than one year, or both; and if death results shall be subject to imprisonment for any term of years or for life." (Emphasis supplied.)

reason of prejudice, passion, neglect, intolerance or otherwise, state laws might not be enforced and the claims of citizens to the enjoyment of rights, privileges and immunities guaranteed by the Fourteenth Amendment might be denied by the state agencies." *Id.*, at 180. * * *

[Thus] Monroe v. Pape suggest[s] that § 1983 affords a "civil remedy" for deprivations of federally protected rights caused by persons acting under color of state law without any express requirement of a particular state of mind. Accordingly, in any § 1983 action the initial inquiry must focus on whether the two essential elements to a § 1983 action are present: (1) whether the conduct complained of was committed by a person acting under color of state law; and (2) whether this conduct deprived a person of rights, privileges, or immunities secured by the Constitution or laws of the United States.

III

Since this Court's decision in Monroe v. Pape, *supra*, it can no longer be questioned that the alleged conduct by the petitioners in this case satisfies the "under color of state law" requirement. Petitioners were, after all, state employees in positions of considerable authority. They do not seriously contend otherwise. Our inquiry, therefore, must turn to the second requirement—whether respondent has been deprived of any right, privilege, or immunity secured by the Constitution or laws of the United States.

The only deprivation respondent alleges in his complaint is that "his rights under the Fourteenth Amendment of the Constitution of the United States were violated. That he was deprived of his property and Due Process of Law." As such, respondent's claims differ from the claims which were before us in Monroe v. Pape, *supra*, which involved violations of the Fourth Amendment, and the claims presented in Estelle v. Gamble, 429 U.S. 97 (1976), which involved alleged violations of the Eighth Amendment. Both of these Amendments have been held applicable to the States by virtue of the adoption of the Fourteenth Amendment. Respondent here refers to no other right, privilege, or immunity secured by the Constitution or federal laws other than the Due Process Clause of the Fourteenth Amendment *simpliciter*. * * *

Unquestionably, respondent's claim satisfies three prerequisites of a valid due process claim: the petitioners acted under color of state law; the hobby kit falls within the definition of property; and the alleged loss, even though negligently caused, amounted to a deprivation. Standing alone, however, these three elements do not establish a violation of the Fourteenth Amendment. Nothing in that Amendment protects against all deprivations of life, liberty, or property by the State. The Fourteenth Amendment protects only against deprivations "without due process of law." Our inquiry therefore must focus on whether the respondent has suffered a deprivation of property without due process of law. In particular, we must decide whether the tort remedies which the State of Nebraska provides as a means of redress for property deprivations satisfy the requirements of procedural due process.

This Court has never directly addressed the question of what process is due a person when an employee of a State negligently takes his property. In some cases this Court has held that due process requires a predeprivation hearing before the State interferes with any liberty or property interest enjoyed by its citizens. In most of these cases, however, the deprivation of property was pursuant to some established state procedure and "process" could be offered before any actual deprivation took place. For example, in Mullane v. Central Hanover Trust Co., 339 U.S. 306 (1950), the Court struck down on due process grounds a New York statute that allowed a trust company, when it sought a judicial settlement of its trust accounts, to give notice by publication to all beneficiaries even if the whereabouts of the beneficiaries were known. The Court held that personal notice in such situations was required and stated that "when notice is a person's due, process which is a mere gesture is not due process." *Id.*, at 315. * * * See also Boddie v. Connecticut, 401 U.S. 371 (1971); Goldberg v. Kelly, 397 U.S. 254 (1970); and Sniadach v. Family Finance Corp., 395 U.S. 337 (1969). In all these cases, deprivations of property were authorized by an established state procedure and due process was held to require predeprivation notice and hearing in order to serve as a check on the possibility that a wrongful deprivation would occur.

We have, however, recognized that postdeprivation remedies made available by the State can satisfy the Due Process Clause. In such cases, the normal predeprivation notice and opportunity to be heard is pretermitted if the State provides a postdeprivation remedy. * * * These cases recognize that either the necessity of quick action by the State or the impracticality of providing any meaningful predeprivation process, when coupled with the availability of some meaningful means by which to assess the propriety of the State's action at some time after the initial taking, can satisfy the requirements of procedural due process. * * *

Our past cases mandate that some kind of hearing is required at some time before a State finally deprives a person of his property interests. The fundamental requirement of due process is the opportunity to be heard and it is an "opportunity which must be granted at a meaningful time and in a meaningful manner." Armstrong v. Manzo, 380 U.S. 545, 552 (1965). However, as many of the above cases recognize, we have rejected the proposition that "at a meaningful time and in a meaningful manner" *always* requires the State to provide a hearing prior to the initial deprivation of property. This rejection is based in part on the impracticability in some cases of providing any preseizure hearing under a state-authorized procedure, and the assumption that at some time a full and meaningful hearing will be available.

The justifications which we have found sufficient to uphold takings of property without any predeprivation process are applicable to a situation such as the present one involving a tortious loss of a prisoner's property as a result of a random and unauthorized act by a state employee. In such a case, the loss is not a result of some established state procedure and the State cannot predict precisely when the loss will occur. It is difficult to conceive of how the State could provide a meaningful hearing before the deprivation takes place. The loss of property, although attributable to the State as action under "color of law," is in almost all cases beyond the control of the State. Indeed, in most cases it is not only impracticable, but impossible, to provide a meaningful hearing before the deprivation. That does not mean, of course, that the State can take property without providing a meaningful postdeprivation hearing. The prior cases which have excused the prior-hearing requirement have rested in part on the availability of some meaningful opportunity subsequent to the initial taking for a determination of rights and liabilities.

A case remarkably similar to the present one is Bonner v. Coughlin, 517 F.2d 1311 (C.A.7 1975), modified en banc, 545 F.2d 565 (1976), cert. denied, 435 U.S. 932 (1978). There, a prisoner alleged that prison officials "made it possible by leaving the door of Plaintiff's cell open, for others without authority to remove Plaintiff's trial transcript from the cell." 517 F.2d, at 1318. The question presented was whether negligence may support a recovery under § 1983. Then Judge Stevens, writing for a panel of the Court of Appeals for the Seventh Circuit, recognized that the question that had to be decided was "whether it can be said that the deprivation was 'without due process of law.'" *Ibid.* He concluded:

> "It seems to us that there is an important difference between a challenge to an established state procedure as lacking in due process and a property damage claim arising out of the misconduct of state officers. In the former situation the facts satisfy the most literal reading of the Fourteenth Amendment's prohibition against 'State' deprivations of property; in the latter situation, however, even though there is action 'under color of' state law sufficient to bring the amendment into play, the state action is not necessarily complete. For in a case such as this the law of Illinois provides, in substance, that the plaintiff is entitled to be made whole for any loss of property occasioned by the unauthorized conduct of the prison guards. We may reasonably conclude, therefore, that the existence of an adequate state remedy to redress property damage inflicted by state officers avoids the conclusion that there has been any constitutional deprivation of property without due process of law within the meaning of the Fourteenth Amendment." *Id.,* at 1319.

We believe that the analysis recited above in Bonner is the proper manner in which to approach a case such as this. * * *

IV

Application of the principles recited above to this case leads us to conclude the respondent has not alleged a violation of the Due Process Clause of the Fourteenth Amendment. Although he has been deprived of property under color of state law, the deprivation did not occur as a result of some established state procedure. Indeed, the deprivation occurred as a result of the unauthorized failure of agents of the State to follow established state procedure. There is no contention that the procedures themselves are inadequate nor is there any contention that it was practicable for the State to provide a predeprivation hearing. Moreover, the State of Nebraska has provided respondent with the means by which he can receive redress for the deprivation. The State provides a remedy to persons who believe they have suffered a tortious loss at the hands of the State. See Neb.Rev.Stat.§ 81–8,209 et seq. (1976). Through this tort claims procedure the State hears and pays claims of prisoners housed in its penal institutions. This procedure was in existence at the time of the loss here in question but respondent did not use it. It is argued that the State does not adequately protect the respondent's interests because it provides only for an action against the State as opposed to its individual employees, it contains no provisions for punitive damages, and there is no right to a trial by jury. Although the state remedies may not provide the respondent with all the relief which may have been available if he could have proceeded under § 1983, that does not mean that the state remedies are not adequate to satisfy the requirements of due process. The remedies provided could have fully compensated the respondent for the property loss he suffered, and we hold that they are sufficient to satisfy the requirements of due process.

Our decision today is fully consistent with our prior cases. To accept respondent's argument that the conduct of the state officials in this case constituted a violation of the Fourteenth Amendment would almost necessarily result in turning every alleged injury which may have been inflicted by a state official acting under "color of law" into a violation of the Fourteenth Amendment cognizable under § 1983. It is hard to perceive any logical stopping place to such a line of reasoning. Presumably, under this rationale any party who is involved in nothing more than an automobile accident with a state official could allege a constitutional violation under § 1983. Such reasoning "would make of the Fourteenth Amendment a font of tort law to be superimposed upon whatever systems may already be administered by the States." Paul v. Davis, 424 U.S. 693, 701 (1976). We do not think that the drafters of the Fourteenth Amendment intended the Amendment to play such a role in our society. * * *

Reversed.

■ JUSTICE STEWART, concurring.

It seems to me extremely doubtful that the property loss here, even though presumably caused by the negligence of state agents, is the kind of deprivation of property to which the Fourteenth Amendment is addressed. If it is, then so too would be damages to a person's automobile resulting from a collision with a vehicle negligently operated by a state official. To hold that this kind of loss is a deprivation of property within the meaning of the Fourteenth Amendment seems not only to trivialize, but grossly to distort the meaning and intent of the Constitution.

But even if Nebraska has deprived the respondent of his property in the constitutional sense, it has not deprived him of it without due process of law. By making available to the respondent a reparations remedy, Nebraska has done all that the Fourteenth Amendment requires in this context.

On this understanding, I join the opinion of the Court.

■ JUSTICE WHITE, concurring.

I join the opinion of the Court but with the reservations stated by my Brother Blackmun in his concurring opinion.

■ JUSTICE BLACKMUN, concurring.

While I join the Court's opinion in this case, I write separately to emphasize my understanding of its narrow reach. This suit concerns the deprivation only of property and was brought only against supervisory personnel, whose simple "negligence" was assumed but, on this record, not actually proved. I do not read the Court's opinion as applicable to a case concerning deprivation of life or of liberty. *Cf.* Moore v. East

Cleveland, 431 U.S. 494 (1977). I also do not understand the Court to intimate that the sole content of the Due Process Clause is procedural regularity. I continue to believe that there are certain governmental actions that, even if undertaken with a full panoply of procedural protection, are, in and of themselves, antithetical to fundamental notions of due process. See, *e.g.*, Boddie v. Connecticut, 401 U.S. 371 (1971); Roe v. Wade, 410 U.S. 113 (1973).

Most importantly, I do not understand the Court to suggest that the provision of "postdeprivation remedies" within a state system would cure the unconstitutional nature of a state official's intentional act that deprives a person of property. While the "random and unauthorized" nature of negligent acts by state employees makes it difficult for the State to "provide a meaningful hearing before the deprivation takes place," it is rare that the same can be said of intentional acts by state employees. When it is possible for a State to institute procedures to contain and direct the intentional actions of its officials, it should be required, as a matter of due process, to do so. See Sniadach v. Family Finance Corp., 395 U.S. 337 (1969); Fuentes v. Shevin, 407 U.S. 67 (1972); Goldberg v. Kelly, 397 U.S. 254 (1970). In the majority of such cases, the failure to provide adequate process prior to inflicting the harm would violate the Due Process Clause. The mere availability of a subsequent tort remedy before tribunals of the same authority that, through its employees, deliberately inflicted the harm complained of, might well not provide the due process of which the Fourteenth Amendment speaks.

■ JUSTICE POWELL, concurring in the result.

* * * Unlike the Court, I do not believe that * * * negligent acts by state officials constitute a deprivation of property within the meaning of the Fourteenth Amendment, regardless of whatever subsequent procedure a State may or may not provide. I therefore concur only in the result.

The Court's approach begins with three "unquestionable" facts concerning respondent's due process claim: "the petitioners acted under color of state law; the hobby kit falls within the definition of property; and the alleged loss, even though negligently caused, amounted to a deprivation." It then goes on to reject respondent's claim on the theory that procedural due process is satisfied in such a case where a State provides a "postdeprivation" procedure for seeking redress-here a tort claims procedure. I would not decide this case on that ground for two reasons. First, the Court passes over a threshold question—whether a negligent act by a state official that results in loss of or damage to property constitutes a deprivation of property for due process purposes.[1] Second, in doing so, the Court suggests a narrow, wholly procedural view of the limitation imposed on the States by the Due Process Clause.

The central question in this case is whether unintentional but negligent acts by state officials, causing respondent's loss of property, are actionable under the Due Process Clause. In my view, this question requires the Court to determine whether intent is an essential element

---

[1]   Assuming that there was a "deprivation" of the hobby kit under color of state law in this case, I would agree with the Court's conclusion that state tort remedies provide adequate procedural protection. *Cf.* Ingraham v. Wright, 430 U.S. 651, 674–682 (1977) (common-law remedies are adequate to afford procedural due process in cases of corporal punishment of students).

of a due process claim, just as we have done in cases applying the Equal Protection Clause and the Eighth Amendment's prohibition of "cruel and unusual punishment." The intent question cannot be given "a uniform answer across the entire spectrum of conceivable constitutional violations which might be the subject of a § 1983 action," Baker v. McCollan, 443 U.S. 137, 139–140 (1979). Rather, we must give close attention to the nature of the particular constitutional violation asserted, in determining whether intent is a necessary element of such a violation.

In the due process area, the question is whether intent is required before there can be a "deprivation" of life, liberty, or property. In this case, for example, the negligence of the prison officials caused respondent to lose his property. Nevertheless, I would not hold that such a negligent act, causing unintended loss of or injury to property, works a deprivation in the *constitutional sense*. Thus, no procedure for compensation is constitutionally required.

A "deprivation" connotes an intentional act denying something to someone, or, at the very least, a deliberate decision not to act to prevent a loss. The most reasonable interpretation of the Fourteenth Amendment would limit due process claims to such active deprivations. * * * [S]uch a rule would avoid trivializing the right of action provided in § 1983. That provision was enacted to deter real *abuses* by state officials in the exercise of governmental powers. It would make no sense to open the federal courts to lawsuits where there has been no affirmative abuse of power, merely a negligent deed by one who happens to be acting under color of state law.

The Court appears unconcerned about this prospect, probably because of an implicit belief in the availability of state tort remedies in most cases. In its view, such remedies will satisfy procedural due process, and relegate cases of official negligence to nonfederal forums. But the fact is that this rule would "make of the Fourteenth Amendment a font of tort law," Paul v. Davis, 424 U.S. 693, 701 (1976), whenever a State has failed to provide a remedy for negligent invasions of liberty or property interests. Moreover, despite the breadth of state tort remedies, such claims will be more numerous than might at first be supposed. * * *

Such an approach has another advantage; it avoids a somewhat disturbing implication in the Court's opinion concerning the scope of due process guarantees. The Court analyzes this case solely in terms of the procedural rights created by the Due Process Clause. Finding state procedures adequate, it suggests that no further analysis is required of more substantive limitations on state action located in this Clause. *Cf.* Paul v. Davis, *supra*, at 712–714 (assessing the claim presented in terms of the "substantive aspects of the Fourteenth Amendment"); Ingraham v. Wright, 430 U.S. 651, 679, n. 47 (1977) (leaving open the question whether "corporal punishment of a public school child may give rise to an independent federal cause of action to vindicate substantive rights under the Due Process Clause").

The Due Process Clause imposes substantive limitations on state action, and under proper circumstances these limitations may extend to intentional and malicious deprivations of liberty and property, even where compensation is available under state law. The Court, however, fails altogether to discuss the possibility that the kind of state action alleged here constitutes a violation of the substantive guarantees of the

Due Process Clause. As I do not consider a negligent act the kind of deprivation that implicates the procedural guarantees of the Due Process Clause, I certainly would not view negligent acts as violative of these substantive guarantees. But the Court concludes that there has been such a deprivation. And yet it avoids entirely the question whether the Due Process Clause may place substantive limitations on this form of governmental conduct.

In sum, it seems evident that the reasoning and decision of the Court today, even if viewed as compatible with our precedents, create new uncertainties as well as invitations to litigate under a statute that already has burst its historical bounds.

■ JUSTICE MARSHALL, concurring in part and dissenting in part.

I join the opinion of the Court insofar as it holds that negligent conduct by persons acting under color of state law may be actionable under 42 U.S.C. § 1983. I also agree with the majority that in cases involving claims of *negligent* deprivation of property without due process of law, the availability of an adequate postdeprivation cause of action for damages under state law may preclude a finding of a violation of the Fourteenth Amendment. I part company with the majority, however, over its conclusion that there was an adequate state-law remedy available to respondent in this case. My disagreement with the majority is not because of any shortcomings in the Nebraska tort claims procedure. Rather, my problem is with the majority's application of its legal analysis to the facts of this case.

It is significant, in my view, that respondent is a state prisoner whose access to information about his legal rights is necessarily limited by his confinement. Furthermore, there is no claim that either petitioners or any other officials informed respondent that he could seek redress for the alleged deprivation of his property by filing an action under the Nebraska tort claims procedure. This apparent failure takes on additional significance in light of the fact that respondent pursued his complaint about the missing hobby kit through the prison's grievance procedure. In cases such as this, I believe prison officials have an affirmative obligation to inform a prisoner who claims that he is aggrieved by official action about the remedies available under state law. If they fail to do so, then they should not be permitted to rely on the existence of such remedies as adequate alternatives to a § 1983 action for wrongful deprivation of property. Since these prison officials do not represent that respondent was informed about his rights under state law, I cannot join in the judgment of the Court in this case.

Thus, although I agree with much of the majority's reasoning, I would affirm the judgment of the Court of Appeals.

NOTE ON THE PARRATT DOCTRINE: ITS RATIONALE, IMPLICATIONS, AND AFTERMATH

(1) **Parratt's Conceptual Foundations.** The predicate for the Court's holding in Parratt v. Taylor appears to be that the State of Nebraska could not be said to have deprived the inmate plaintiff of property without due process of law, in a context in which no pre-deprivation process was feasible,

until the state had had the opportunity to provide adequate post-deprivation remedies. But Taylor did not sue the state of Nebraska; if he had, the suit would have been barred by the state's sovereign immunity. Instead, he sued various state officials who had no capacity to provide him with post-deprivation process. In trying to make sense of the Court's decision, Professor Monaghan thus characterizes Parratt as a "state action" decision, holding that the defendant state officials could not be said to have acted with the authority of the state until the state had had an opportunity to provide post-deprivation remedies. See Monaghan, *State Law Wrongs, State Law Remedies, and the Fourteenth Amendment*, 86 Colum.L.Rev. 979, 990–91 (1986). Consider whether this is a helpful analysis and, if so, whether it justifies the Court's decision.

In refusing to allow Taylor's suit to proceed in federal court until the state's responsibility for any constitutional wrong had been established, Parratt looks superficially analogous to the position championed by Justice Frankfurter in his dissenting opinion in Monroe v. Pape. But whereas Justice Frankfurter rested his case on an interpretation of § 1983, Parratt reflects an interpretation of the Fourteenth Amendment. Insofar as plaintiffs seek relief against state officials based on alleged violations of procedural due process, does Parratt come close to adopting the position rejected by a unanimous Court in Home Telephone & Telegraph Co. v. City of Los Angeles, 227 U.S. 278 (1913), p. 981, *supra*?

(2) Adequate Post-Deprivation Remedies. When are state post-deprivation remedies adequate to satisfy the requirements of procedural due process? Consider Fallon, *Some Confusions About Due Process, Judicial Review, and Constitutional Remedies*, 93 Colum.L.Rev. 309, 356 (1993): "It seems unthinkable * * * that a state should have to furnish broader remedies for officials' torts than would be available under the [sovereign and official] immunity doctrines applicable to constitutional actions in federal court. Those doctrines generally hold unconsenting states immune from damages liability, and state officers often enjoy simultaneous immunity from damages claims" against them in their individual capacities, as is discussed in Section 3, *infra*.

Does Parratt imply that the opportunity to file a lawsuit in state court that would be dismissed on the pleadings under sovereign and official immunity doctrines furnishes a plaintiff who has been deprived of liberty or property by random and unauthorized state action all the process that he or she is due under the Due Process Clause? Anticipating a similar question in Hudson v. Palmer, 468 U.S. 517, 535 (1984), which is more fully discussed in Paragraph (3), *infra*, the Court said simply: "that Palmer might not be able to recover under these [state] remedies the full amount which he might receive in a § 1983 action is not * * * determinative of the adequacy of the state remedies".[1]

---

[1]　In Davidson v. Cannon, 474 U.S. 344 (1986), in which the majority held that a state prisoner could not bring a § 1983 action for the failure of prison officials to protect him from another inmate, Justice Blackmun (joined by Justice Marshall) and Justice Stevens each found that a deprivation of liberty had occurred, and, accordingly, proceeded to consider whether the state had provided an adequate postdeprivation remedy. The question revolved around a state statute that immunized all public officials and entities from liability in an action by one prisoner claiming injury inflicted on him by another prisoner. For Justice Stevens, this statute did not render the state's postdeprivation procedure constitutionally invalid so as to permit a § 1983 action. Just as "defenses such as contributory negligence or statutes of limitations may defeat recovery in particular cases without raising any question about the constitutionality of a State's

What, then, should be determinative of the adequacy of state remedies? For discussion of lower court cases, see Schwartz, Section 1983 Litigation: Claims and Defenses § 307[F] (4th ed.2008 & Supp. 2013) (reporting that lower courts have found "a wide variety of state remedies to be adequate, including judicial review, tort, breach of contract, statutory and administrative remedies," but that uncertainty still surrounds "the impact of potential immunity defenses").

(3) Scienter Requirements in § 1983 Actions Based on Asserted Deprivations of Liberty or Property Without Due Process. In a § 1983 action, three separate issues of scienter may arise: (i) Does § 1983 itself require any distinctive scienter? (ii) Is proof of scienter necessary in order to establish a violation (for which relief under § 1983 is sought) of the constitutional provision in question? (iii) Does an official sued have a qualified immunity from damages liability if the official's conduct did not violate clearly established legal norms? (On the last of these issues, see Sec. 3, *infra*.)

With respect to the second question, decisions after Parratt moved in two directions. First, in Hudson v. Palmer, Paragraph (2), *supra*, the Court extended the Parratt doctrine to intentional deprivations claimed to violate the Due Process Clause. In this case, plaintiff, also a state prison inmate, brought a § 1983 action against a prison official for intentionally and unjustifiably destroying some of his personal property during a prison shakedown. Summary judgment for the defendant was unanimously affirmed by the Supreme Court. The Court declined to distinguish Parratt on the ground that the deprivation in Hudson was intentional. The underlying rationale of Parratt, it said, was that an adequate postdeprivation remedy satisfies the demands of due process whenever deprivation occurs "through random and unauthorized conduct of a state employee". In such a situation, "predeprivation procedures are simply 'impracticable' since the state cannot know when such deprivations will occur".

The second direction followed after Parratt involved the Court's holding—contrary to what the Court had said in Parratt itself—that merely negligent acts do not constitute a deprivation within the meaning of the Due Process Clause of the Fourteenth Amendment. In Daniels v. Williams, 474 U.S. 327 (1986), still another state prisoner brought a § 1983 action alleging a deprivation without due process after he tripped over a pillow negligently left on a staircase by a prison official. The Supreme Court held that, whether or not the prisoner had an adequate post-injury state remedy, there was no constitutional violation because (overruling Parratt on the point) mere lack of due care by a state officer cannot constitute a deprivation of liberty or property under the Fourteenth Amendment.[2]

---

procedures for disposing of tort litigation", so the provision of an immunity defense "does not justify the conclusion that [the state's] remedial system is constitutionally inadequate".

Justice Blackmun, disagreeing with Justice Stevens, argued that the state remedy was obviously inadequate: "Conduct that is wrongful under § 1983 surely cannot be immunized by state law." Does Justice Blackmun put the cart before the horse by assuming the conduct was wrongful under § 1983 without first establishing that it constituted a denial of due process?

[2] The prisoner in Daniels, in support of the argument that negligent conduct can deny due process, posited a case in which the state negligently failed to provide an inmate with a hearing before revoking his good time credit, as required by Wolff v. McDonnell, 418 U.S. 539, 558 (1974). The Court responded that "the relevant action of the prison officials in that situation is their deliberate decision to deprive the inmate of good-time credit, not their hypothetically

(4) Conduct Pursuant to Established State Procedures Versus Random, Unauthorized Conduct. The Court's opinion in Hudson v. Palmer stated that "postdeprivation remedies do not satisfy due process where a deprivation of property is caused by conduct pursuant to established state procedure, rather than random and unauthorized action". The Hudson Court cited Logan v. Zimmerman Brush Co., 455 U.S. 422 (1982), as supporting that proposition. In Logan, an individual claiming employment discrimination—in accordance with the requirements of state law for the pursuit of a state remedy—filed a charge with the state equal opportunity commission. By statute, the commission had 120 days to schedule a factfinding conference, but, apparently due to inadvertence, it failed to do so within that time. Ruling on a motion of the employer, the Illinois Supreme Court held that because the 120-day limit was jurisdictional, the commission must dismiss the charge. The Supreme Court unanimously reversed, holding that Logan's cause of action was a property interest of which he had been deprived without due process. The employer argued that, because Logan could sue the commission in state court for damages, there was no deprivation without due process under Parratt, but the Court was unconvinced: "Here * * * it is the state system itself that destroys a complainant's property interest, by operation of law, whenever the Commission fails to convene a timely conference * * *. Unlike the complainant in Parratt, Logan is challenging not the Commission's error, but the 'established state procedure' that destroys his entitlement without according him proper procedural safeguards."

Recall the Court's stated worry that the Due Process Clause not become a font of tort law. Is it somehow more important for the federal courts to be open to challenges to the constitutionality of state statutes, such as that involved in Logan, than to challenges to random and unauthorized official acts, as in Parratt? See Fallon, Paragraph (2), *supra*, at 326–27, 348–51 (suggesting that a perceived difference in the importance of the cases may underlie the Court's framework).

(5) The Zinermon Case. The analysis of Parratt v. Taylor requires courts to distinguish between alleged random and unauthorized deprivations of liberty and property, such that no pre-deprivation process is feasible, and deprivations that are the result of an established state procedure, as in Logan v. Zimmerman Brush Co. The difficulty in drawing that distinction was evident in Zinermon v. Burch, 494 U.S. 113 (1990). Burch had voluntarily committed himself to a state mental hospital but, after his release, brought a § 1983 action against state hospital officials, alleging that he had been deprived of liberty without due process. He contended that the defendants should have known that he was incompetent to give informed consent to his admission and should have confined him only if justified in doing so by the state's involuntary commitment processes. In a 5–4 decision, the Court decided that the complaint should not have been dismissed. The Court first held that the Parratt and Hudson decisions were applicable to deprivations of liberty as well as to deprivations of property. But it then found those cases distinguishable on other grounds:

"[The general rule of Monroe v. Pape—that overlapping state remedies are irrelevant to the existence of a cause of action under § 1983—] applies in a straightforward way to two of the three kinds of § 1983 claims that may be

---

negligent failure to accord him the procedural protections of the Due Process Clause". Compare Logan v. Zimmerman Brush Co., Paragraph (4), *infra*.

brought against the State under the Due Process Clause of the Fourteenth Amendment. First, the Clause incorporates many of the specific protections defined in the Bill of Rights. A plaintiff may bring suit under § 1983 for state officials' violation of his rights to, *e.g.*, freedom of speech or freedom from unreasonable searches and seizures. Second, the Due Process Clause contains a substantive component that bars certain arbitrary, wrongful government actions 'regardless of the fairness of the procedures used to implement them.' Daniels v. Williams, 474 U.S., at 331. As to these two types of claims, the constitutional violation actionable under § 1983 is complete when the wrongful action is taken. *Id.*, at 338 (Stevens, J., concurring in the judgment). A plaintiff, under Monroe v. Pape, may invoke § 1983 regardless of any state-tort remedy that might be available to compensate him for the deprivation of these rights.

"The Due Process Clause also encompasses a third type of protection, a guarantee of fair procedure. A § 1983 action may be brought for a violation of procedural due process, but here the existence of state remedies *is* relevant in a special sense. In procedural due process claims, the deprivation by state action of a constitutionally protected interest in 'life, liberty, or property' is not in itself unconstitutional; what is unconstitutional is the deprivation of such an interest *without due process of law*. Parratt, 451 U.S., at 537. The constitutional violation actionable under § 1983 is not complete when the deprivation occurs; it is not complete unless and until the State fails to provide due process. Therefore, to determine whether a constitutional violation has occurred, it is necessary to ask what process the State provided, and whether it was constitutionally adequate. This inquiry would examine the procedural safeguards built into the statutory or administrative procedure of effecting the deprivation, and any remedies for erroneous deprivations provided by statute or tort law.

"In this case, Burch does not claim that his confinement * * * violated any of the specific guarantees of the Bill of Rights. Burch's complaint could be read to include a substantive due process claim, but that issue was not raised in the petition for certiorari, and we express no view on whether the facts Burch alleges could give rise to such a claim. The claim at issue falls within the third, or procedural, category of § 1983 claims based on the Due Process Clause. * * *

"[But this case] is not controlled by Parratt and Hudson, for three basic reasons:

"First, petitioners cannot claim that the deprivation of Burch's liberty was unpredictable. * * *. It is hardly unforeseeable that a person requesting treatment for mental illness might be incapable of informed consent, and that state officials with the power to admit patients might take their apparent willingness to be admitted at face value and not initiate voluntary placement procedures. * * *

"Second, we cannot say that predeprivation process was impossible here. Florida already has an established procedure for involuntary placement. * * *

"Third, petitioners cannot characterize their conduct as 'unauthorized' in the sense the term is used in Parratt and Hudson. The State delegated to them the power and authority to effect the very deprivation complained of here. * * *

"We conclude that petitioners cannot escape § 1983 liability by characterizing their conduct as a 'random, unauthorized' violation of Florida law which the State was not in a position to predict or avert, so that all the process Burch could possibly be due is a postdeprivation damages remedy".

Justice O'Connor, joined by the Chief Justice and Justices Scalia and Kennedy, dissented: "Application of Parratt and Hudson indicates that respondent has failed to state a claim allowing recovery under 42 U.S.C. § 1983. Petitioners' actions were unauthorized: they are alleged to have wrongly and without license departed from established state practices. * * * The wanton or reckless nature of the failure indicates it to be random. The State could not foresee the particular contravention and was hardly 'in a position to provide for predeprivation process' [quoting Hudson]". Justice O'Connor concluded by protesting that "the Court has gone some measure to 'make of the Fourteenth Amendment a font of tort law to be superimposed upon whatever systems may already be administered by the States.' Parratt, *supra*, at 544".

(6) The Significance of the Zinermon Decision.

(a) Despite the sharp division within the Court on the proper result, the Zinermon case appeared to put some issues to rest. First, the Court ruled unanimously that the Parratt doctrine applies to a claimed deprivation of liberty as well as of property. Second, the Court appeared to rule, again unanimously, that the Parratt doctrine does not apply to alleged violations of "substantive" (as opposed to procedural) due process or of specific guarantees of the Bill of Rights—violations that are viewed as complete when the conduct complained of occurs.

(b) Left uncertain by Zinermon was how a court should distinguish between a case in which challenged official action that causes the deprivation of liberty or property is wholly "random", and thus falls under the rule of Parratt, and one in which the action complained of is sufficiently "predictable" in light of the authority granted by state law to be governed by Zinermon. According to Schwartz, Section 1983 Litigation: Claims and Defenses § 3.07[E][1]–[2] (4th ed.2008 & Supp.2013), the lower courts are inconsistent in their approaches, with the circuits expressly split on the issue of whether actions by high-ranking officials endowed with discretionary authority can be "random and unauthorized". At least one lower court judge has opined that the distinction that Zinermon requires courts to draw in determining Parratt's applicability is inherently unworkable. See Easter House v. Felder, 910 F.2d 1387, 1408–12 (7th Cir.1990) (Easterbrook, J., concurring).

(7) The Pertinence of Parratt and Its Progeny to Constitutional Tort Actions Against Federal Officials.

How should a federal court deal with a Bivens-type action seeking damages, under the Fifth Amendment, for a procedural due process violation arising from the random and unauthorized conduct of *federal* officials? In Weiss v. Lehman, 676 F.2d 1320 (9th Cir.1982), the Supreme Court had vacated and remanded, "for further consideration in light of Parratt v. Taylor", a prior judgment of the court of appeals that had upheld a damages award in such a case. On remand, the court of appeals ruled that because the plaintiff had an adequate remedy under the Federal Tort Claims Act, no due process violation had occurred. Recall that the FTCA (i) makes actionable wrongs as defined by state law rather than by the federal Constitution, (ii) affords no jury trial, (iii) establishes governmental but not individual liability, and (iv) forbids punitive damages. These were the very "defects" that the Court held in Carlson v. Green, 446 U.S. 14 (1980), p. 771, *supra*, made the FTCA less effective than a Bivens suit, and therefore made it appropriate to infer a Bivens remedy in an action directly under the Eighth Amendment. On the other hand, the state remedy that Parratt found adequate to redress a deprivation of property under the Fourteenth Amendment's Due Process Clause had all four of these "defects".

Parratt's concerns about excessive federal interference with state officials and state courts have little direct applicability in suits against federal officials, but does that difference justify giving divergent interpretations to the Due Process Clauses of the Fifth and Fourteenth Amendments? See Smolla, *The Displacement of Federal Due Process Claims by State Remedies: Parratt v. Taylor and Logan v. Zimmerman Brush*, 1982 U.Ill.L.Rev. 831, 881–83.

---

3. OFFICIAL IMMUNITY

Harlow v. Fitzgerald

457 U.S. 800, 102 S.Ct. 2727, 73 L.Ed.2d 396 (1982).
Certiorari to the United States Court of Appeals for the District of Columbia Circuit.

■ JUSTICE POWELL delivered the opinion of the Court.

The issue in this case is the scope of the immunity available to the aides and advisers of the President of the United States in a suit for damages based upon their official acts.

I

In this suit for civil damages, petitioners Bryce Harlow and Alexander Butterfield are alleged to have participated in a conspiracy to violate the constitutional and statutory rights of the respondent * * *. Respondent avers that petitioners entered the conspiracy in their capacities as senior White House aides to former President Richard M. Nixon. [The] alleged conspiracy is the same as that involved in Nixon v. Fitzgerald [decided the same day, see p. 1046, *infra*. In both cases, Fitzgerald, a well-known "whistleblower", sought damages for the elimination of his federal job, claiming that this action and his ensuing dismissal violated the First Amendment and several federal statutes.]

Respondent claims that Harlow joined the conspiracy in his role as the Presidential aide principally responsible for congressional relations. At the conclusion of discovery the supporting evidence remained inferential. As evidence of Harlow's conspiratorial activity respondent relies heavily on a series of conversations in which Harlow discussed Fitzgerald's dismissal with Air Force Secretary Robert Seamans. The other evidence most supportive of Fitzgerald's claims consists of a recorded conversation in which the President later voiced a tentative recollection that Harlow was "all for canning" Fitzgerald. * * *

Petitioner Butterfield also is alleged to have entered the conspiracy not later than May 1969. * * *

Together with their codefendant Richard Nixon, petitioners Harlow and Butterfield moved for summary judgment on February 12, 1980. In denying the motion the District Court upheld the legal sufficiency of Fitzgerald's Bivens (Bivens v. Six Unknown Fed. Narcotics Agents, 403 U.S. 388 (1971)) claim under the First Amendment and his "inferred" statutory causes of action * * *.[10] * * *

Independently of former President Nixon, petitioners * * * appealed the denial of their immunity defense to the Court of Appeals for the District of Columbia Circuit. The Court of Appeals dismissed the appeal without opinion. Never having determined the immunity available to the senior aides and advisers of the President of the United States, we granted certiorari.

II

As we reiterated today in Nixon v. Fitzgerald, our decisions consistently have held that government officials are entitled to some form of immunity from suits for damages. As recognized at common law, public officers require this protection to shield them from undue interference with their duties and from potentially disabling threats of liability.

Our decisions have recognized immunity defenses of two kinds. For officials whose special functions or constitutional status requires complete protection from suit, we have recognized the defense of "absolute immunity." The absolute immunity of legislators, in their legislative functions, see, *e.g.*, Eastland v. United States Servicemen's Fund, 421 U.S. 491 (1975), and of judges, in their judicial functions, see, *e.g.*, Stump v. Sparkman, 435 U.S. 349 (1978), now is well settled. Our decisions also have extended absolute immunity to certain officials of the Executive Branch. These include prosecutors and similar officials, see Butz v. Economou, 438 U.S. 478, 508–512 (1978), executive officers engaged in adjudicative functions, *id.*, at 513–517, and the President of the United States, see Nixon v. Fitzgerald.

For executive officials in general, however, our cases make plain that qualified immunity represents the norm. In Scheuer v. Rhodes, 416 U.S. 232 (1974), we acknowledged that high officials require greater protection than those with less complex discretionary responsibilities. Nonetheless, we held that a governor and his aides could receive the requisite protection from qualified or good-faith immunity. *Id.*, at 247–248. In Butz v. Economou, *supra*, we extended the approach of Scheuer to high federal officials of the Executive Branch. Discussing in detail the considerations that also had underlain our decision in Scheuer, we explained that the recognition of a qualified immunity defense for high executives reflected an attempt to balance competing values: not only the importance of a damages remedy to protect the rights of citizens, 438 U.S., at 504–505, but also "the need to protect officials who are required to exercise their discretion and the related public interest in encouraging the vigorous exercise of official authority." *Id.*, at 506. Without discounting the adverse consequences of denying high officials an absolute immunity from private lawsuits alleging constitutional violations—consequences found sufficient in Spalding v. Vilas, 161 U.S. 483 (1896), and Barr v. Matteo, 360 U.S. 564 (1959), to warrant extension

---

[10] * * * The legal sufficiency of respondent's asserted causes of action is not, however, a question that we view as properly presented for our decision in the present posture of this case.

to such officials of absolute immunity from suits at common law—we emphasized our expectation that insubstantial suits need not proceed to trial:

> "Insubstantial lawsuits can be quickly terminated by federal courts alert to the possibilities of artful pleading. Unless the complaint states a compensable claim for relief . . . , it should not survive a motion to dismiss. * * * In responding to such a motion, plaintiffs may not play dog in the manger; and firm application of the Federal Rules of Civil Procedure will ensure that federal officials are not harassed by frivolous lawsuits." 438 U.S., at 507–508 (citations omitted). * * *

III

A

Petitioners argue that they are entitled to a blanket protection of absolute immunity as an incident of their offices as Presidential aides. In deciding this claim we do not write on an empty page. In Butz v. Economou, *supra*, the Secretary of Agriculture—a Cabinet official directly accountable to the President—asserted a defense of absolute official immunity from suit for civil damages. We rejected his claim. In so doing we did not question the power or the importance of the Secretary's office. Nor did we doubt the importance to the President of loyal and efficient subordinates in executing his duties of office. Yet we found these factors, alone, to be insufficient to justify absolute immunity. "[T]he greater power of [high] officials," we reasoned, "affords a greater potential for a regime of lawless conduct." 438 U.S., at 506. Damages actions against high officials were therefore "an important means of vindicating constitutional guarantees." *Ibid.* Moreover, we concluded that it would be "untenable to draw a distinction for purposes of immunity law between suits brought against state officials under § 1983 and suits brought directly under the Constitution against federal officials." *Id.*, at 504.

Having decided in Butz that Members of the Cabinet ordinarily enjoy only qualified immunity from suit, we conclude today that it would be equally untenable to hold absolute immunity an incident of the office of every Presidential subordinate based in the White House. Members of the Cabinet are direct subordinates of the President, frequently with greater responsibilities, both to the President and to the Nation, than White House staff. The considerations that supported our decision in Butz apply with equal force to this case. It is no disparagement of the offices held by petitioners to hold that Presidential aides, like Members of the Cabinet, generally are entitled only to a qualified immunity.

B

In disputing the controlling authority of Butz, petitioners rely on the principles developed in Gravel v. United States, 408 U.S. 606 (1972). In Gravel we endorsed the view that "it is literally impossible . . . for Members of Congress to perform their legislative tasks without the help of aides and assistants" and that "the day-to-day work of such aides is so critical to the Members' performance that they must be treated as the latter's alter egos. . . . " *Id.*, at 616–617. Having done so, we held the Speech and Debate Clause derivatively applicable to the "legislative acts" of a Senator's aide that would have been privileged if performed by the Senator himself. *Id.*, at 621–622. * * *

Petitioners' [reliance on Gravel] is not without force. Ultimately, however, it sweeps too far. If the President's aides are derivatively immune because they are essential to the functioning of the Presidency, so should the Members of the Cabinet—Presidential subordinates some of whose essential roles are acknowledged by the Constitution itself—be absolutely immune. Yet we implicitly rejected such derivative immunity in Butz. Moreover, in general our cases have followed a "functional" approach to immunity law. We have recognized that the judicial, prosecutorial, and legislative functions require absolute immunity. But this protection has extended no further than its justification would warrant. In Gravel, for example, we emphasized that Senators and their aides were absolutely immune only when performing "acts legislative in nature," and not when taking other acts even "in their official capacity." 408 U.S., at 625. Our cases involving judges[15] and prosecutors[16] have followed a similar line. The undifferentiated extension of absolute "derivative" immunity to the President's aides therefore could not be reconciled with the "functional" approach that has characterized the immunity decisions of this Court, indeed including Gravel itself.[17]

C

Petitioners also assert an entitlement to immunity based on the "special functions" of White House aides. This form of argument accords with the analytical approach of our cases. For aides entrusted with discretionary authority in such sensitive areas as national security or foreign policy, absolute immunity might well be justified to protect the unhesitating performance of functions vital to the national interest. But a "special functions" rationale does not warrant a blanket recognition of absolute immunity for all Presidential aides in the performance of all their duties. This conclusion too follows from our decision in Butz, which establishes that an executive official's claim to absolute immunity must be justified by reference to the public interest in the special functions of his office, not the mere fact of high station.

* * * In order to establish entitlement to absolute immunity a Presidential aide first must show that the responsibilities of his office embraced a function so sensitive as to require a total shield from liability. He then must demonstrate that he was discharging the protected function when performing the act for which liability is asserted.

Applying these standards to the claims advanced by petitioners Harlow and Butterfield, we cannot conclude on the record before us that either has shown that "public policy requires [for any of the functions of his office] an exemption of [absolute] scope." Butz, 438 U.S., at 506. Nor, assuming that petitioners did have functions for which absolute immunity would be warranted, could we now conclude that the acts

---

[15] See, e.g., Supreme Court of Virginia v. Consumers Union of United States, 446 U.S. 719, 731–737 (1980); Stump v. Sparkman, 435 U.S. 349, 362 (1978).

[16] In Imbler v. Pachtman, 424 U.S. 409, 430–431 (1976), this Court reserved the question whether absolute immunity would extend to "those aspects of the prosecutor's responsibility that cast him in the role of an administrator or investigative officer." * * * [For later Supreme Court decisions dealing with this question, see pp. 1044–1045, infra.]

[17] Our decision today in Nixon v. Fitzgerald in no way abrogates this general rule. As we explained in that opinion, the recognition of absolute immunity for all of a President's acts in office derives in principal part from factors unique to his constitutional responsibilities and station. Suits against other officials—including Presidential aides—generally do not invoke separation-of-powers considerations to the same extent as suits against the President himself.

charged in this lawsuit—if taken at all—would lie within the protected area. We do not, however, foreclose the possibility that petitioners, on remand, could satisfy the standards properly applicable to their claims.

IV

Even if they cannot establish that their official functions require absolute immunity, petitioners assert that public policy at least mandates an application of the qualified immunity standard that would permit the defeat of insubstantial claims without resort to trial. We agree.

A

The resolution of immunity questions inherently requires a balance between the evils inevitable in any available alternative. In situations of abuse of office, an action for damages may offer the only realistic avenue for vindication of constitutional guarantees. It is this recognition that has required the denial of absolute immunity to most public officers. At the same time, however, it cannot be disputed seriously that claims frequently run against the innocent as well as the guilty—at a cost not only to the defendant officials, but to society as a whole. These social costs include the expenses of litigation, the diversion of official energy from pressing public issues, and the deterrence of able citizens from acceptance of public office. Finally, there is the danger that fear of being sued will "dampen the ardor of all but the most resolute, or the most irresponsible [public officials], in the unflinching discharge of their duties." Gregoire v. Biddle, 177 F.2d 579, 581 (C.A.2 1949), cert. denied, 339 U.S. 949 (1950).

In identifying qualified immunity as the best attainable accommodation of competing values, in Butz, *supra*, at 507–508, as in Scheuer, 416 U.S., at 245–248, we relied on the assumption that this standard would permit "[i]nsubstantial lawsuits [to] be quickly terminated." 438 U.S., at 507–508. Yet petitioners advance persuasive arguments that the dismissal of insubstantial lawsuits without trial—a factor presupposed in the balance of competing interests struck by our prior cases—requires an adjustment of the "good faith" standard established by our decisions.

B

Qualified or "good faith" immunity is an affirmative defense that must be pleaded by a defendant official. Gomez v. Toledo, 446 U.S. 635 (1980). Decisions of this Court have established that the "good faith" defense has both an "objective" and a "subjective" aspect. The objective element involves a presumptive knowledge of and respect for "basic, unquestioned constitutional rights." Wood v. Strickland, 420 U.S. 308, 322 (1975). The subjective component refers to "permissible intentions." *Ibid.* Characteristically the Court has defined these elements by identifying the circumstances in which qualified immunity would *not* be available. Referring both to the objective and subjective elements, we have held that qualified immunity would be defeated if an official "*knew or reasonably should have known* that the action he took within his sphere of official responsibility would violate the constitutional rights of the [plaintiff], *or* if he took the action *with the malicious intention* to cause a deprivation of constitutional rights or other injury. . . . " *Ibid.* (emphasis added).

The subjective element of the good-faith defense frequently has proved incompatible with our admonition in Butz that insubstantial claims should not proceed to trial. Rule 56 of the Federal Rules of Civil Procedure provides that disputed questions of fact ordinarily may not be decided on motions for summary judgment. And an official's subjective good faith has been considered to be a question of fact that some courts have regarded as inherently requiring resolution by a jury.

In the context of Butz' attempted balancing of competing values, it now is clear that substantial costs attend the litigation of the subjective good faith of government officials. Not only are there the general costs of subjecting officials to the risks of trial—distraction of officials from their governmental duties, inhibition of discretionary action, and deterrence of able people from public service. There are special costs to "subjective" inquiries of this kind. Immunity generally is available only to officials performing discretionary functions. In contrast with the thought processes accompanying "ministerial" tasks, the judgments surrounding discretionary action almost inevitably are influenced by the decisionmaker's experiences, values, and emotions. These variables explain in part why questions of subjective intent so rarely can be decided by summary judgment. Yet they also frame a background in which there often is no clear end to the relevant evidence. Judicial inquiry into subjective motivation therefore may entail broad-ranging discovery and the deposing of numerous persons, including an official's professional colleagues. Inquiries of this kind can be peculiarly disruptive of effective government.

Consistently with the balance at which we aimed in Butz, we conclude today that bare allegations of malice should not suffice to subject government officials either to the costs of trial or to the burdens of broad-reaching discovery. We therefore hold that government officials performing discretionary functions, generally are shielded from liability for civil damages insofar as their conduct does not violate clearly established statutory or constitutional rights of which a reasonable person would have known. See Procunier v. Navarette, 434 U.S. 555, 565 (1978); Wood v. Strickland, 420 U.S., at 322.[30]

Reliance on the objective reasonableness of an official's conduct, as measured by reference to clearly established law, should avoid excessive disruption of government and permit the resolution of many insubstantial claims on summary judgment. On summary judgment, the judge appropriately may determine, not only the currently applicable law, but whether that law was clearly established at the time an action occurred.[32] If the law at that time was not clearly established, an official could not reasonably be expected to anticipate subsequent legal developments, nor could he fairly be said to "know" that the law forbade

---

[30] This case involves no issue concerning the elements of the immunity available to state officials sued for constitutional violations under § 1983. We have found previously, however, that it would be "untenable to draw a distinction for purposes of immunity law between suits brought against state officials under 42 U.S.C. § 1983 and suits brought directly under the Constitution against federal officials." Butz v. Economou, 438 U.S., at 504.

Our decision in no way diminishes the absolute immunity currently available to officials whose functions have been held to require a protection of this scope.

[32] As in Procunier v. Navarette, 434 U.S., at 565, we need not define here the circumstances under which "the state of the law" should be "evaluated by reference to the opinions of this Court, of the Courts of Appeals, or of the local District Court."

conduct not previously identified as unlawful. Until this threshold immunity question is resolved, discovery should not be allowed. If the law was clearly established, the immunity defense ordinarily should fail, since a reasonably competent public official should know the law governing his conduct. Nevertheless, if the official pleading the defense claims extraordinary circumstances and can prove that he neither knew nor should have known of the relevant legal standard, the defense should be sustained. But again, the defense would turn primarily on objective factors.

By defining the limits of qualified immunity essentially in objective terms, we provide no license to lawless conduct. The public interest in deterrence of unlawful conduct and in compensation of victims remains protected by a test that focuses on the objective legal reasonableness of an official's acts. Where an official could be expected to know that certain conduct would violate statutory or constitutional rights, he should be made to hesitate; and a person who suffers injury caused by such conduct may have a cause of action. But where an official's duties legitimately require action in which clearly established rights are not implicated, the public interest may be better served by action taken "with independence and without fear of consequences." Pierson v. Ray, 386 U.S. 547, 554 (1967).[34]

C

In this case petitioners have asked us to hold that the respondent's pretrial showings were insufficient to survive their motion for summary judgment.[35] We think it appropriate, however, to remand the case to the District Court for its reconsideration of this issue in light of this opinion. The trial court is more familiar with the record so far developed and also is better situated to make any such further findings as may be necessary. * * *

■ JUSTICE BRENNAN, with whom JUSTICE MARSHALL and JUSTICE BLACKMUN join, concurring.

I agree with the substantive standard announced by the Court today, imposing liability when a public-official defendant "knew or should have known" of the constitutionally violative effect of his actions. This standard would not allow the official who *actually knows* that he was violating the law to escape liability for his actions, even if he could not "reasonably have been expected" to know what he actually did know. Thus the clever and unusually well-informed violator of constitutional rights will not evade just punishment for his crimes. I also agree that this standard applies "across the board," to all "government officials performing discretionary functions." I write separately only to note that given this standard, it seems inescapable to me that some measure of discovery may sometimes be required to determine exactly what a public-official defendant did "know" at the time of his actions. * * * Of course, as the Court has already noted, summary judgment will be readily available to public-official defendants whenever the state of the law was so

---

[34] We emphasize that our decision applies only to suits for civil *damages* arising from actions within the scope of an official's duties and in "objective" good faith. We express no view as to the conditions in which injunctive or declaratory relief might be available.

[35] In Butz, we admonished that "insubstantial" suits against high public officials should not be allowed to proceed to trial. 438 U.S., at 507. We reiterate this admonition. * * *

ambiguous at the time of the alleged violation that it could not have been "known" then, and thus liability could not ensue. * * *

■ CHIEF JUSTICE BURGER, dissenting.

The Court today decides in Nixon v. Fitzgerald what has been taken for granted for 190 years, that it is implicit in the Constitution that a President of the United States has absolute immunity from civil suits arising out of official acts as Chief Executive. I agree fully that absolute immunity for official acts of the President is, like executive privilege, "fundamental to the operation of Government and inextricably rooted in the separation of powers under the Constitution." United States v. Nixon, 418 U.S. 683, 708 (1974).

In this case the Court decides that senior aides of the President do not have derivative immunity from the President. I am at a loss, however, to reconcile this conclusion with our holding in Gravel v. United States, 408 U.S. 606 (1972). * * *

In Gravel we held that it is implicit in the Constitution that aides of Members of Congress have absolute immunity for acts performed for Members in relation to their legislative function. We viewed the aides' immunity as deriving from the Speech or Debate Clause * * *. * * * The Clause says nothing about "legislative acts" outside the Chambers, but we concluded that the Constitution grants absolute immunity for legislative acts not only "in either House" but in committees and conferences and in reports on legislative activities.

Nor does the Clause mention immunity for congressional aides. Yet, going far beyond any words found in the Constitution itself, we held that a Member's aides who implement policies and decisions of the Member are entitled to the same absolute immunity as a Member. It is hardly an overstatement to say that we thus avoided a "literalistic approach," Gravel, *supra*, at 617, and instead looked to the structure of the Constitution and the evolution of the function of the Legislative Branch. In short, we drew this immunity for legislative aides from a functional analysis of the legislative process in the context of the Constitution taken as a whole and in light of 20th-century realities. Neither Presidents nor Members of Congress can, as they once did, perform all their constitutional duties personally.

We very properly recognized in Gravel that the central purpose of a Member's absolute immunity would be "diminished and frustrated" if the legislative aides were not also protected by the same broad immunity. * * *

The Court has made this reality a matter of our constitutional jurisprudence. How can we conceivably hold that a President of the United States, who represents a vastly larger constituency than does any Member of Congress, should not have "alter egos" with comparable immunity? * * *

I challenge the Court * * * to say that the effectiveness of Presidential aides will not "inevitably be diminished and frustrated," Gravel, *supra*, at 617, if they must weigh every act and decision in relation to the risks of future lawsuits. The Gravel Court took note of the burdens on congressional aides: the stress of long hours, heavy responsibilities, constant exposure to harassment of the political arena. Is the Court suggesting the stresses are less for Presidential aides? By construing the Constitution to give only qualified immunity to senior Presidential aides we give those key "alter egos" only lawsuits, winnable lawsuits perhaps, but lawsuits nonetheless, with stress and effort that will disperse and drain their energies and their purses. * * *

We—judges collectively—have held that the common law provides us with absolute immunity for ourselves with respect to judicial acts, however erroneous or ill-advised. See, *e.g.*, Stump v. Sparkman, 435 U.S. 349 (1978). Are the lowest ranking of 27,000 or more judges, thousands of prosecutors, and thousands of congressional aides—an aggregate of not less than 75,000 in all—entitled to greater protection than two senior aides of a President?

Butz v. Economou, 438 U.S. 478 (1978), does not dictate that senior Presidential aides be given only qualified immunity. Butz held only that a Cabinet officer exercising discretion was not entitled to absolute immunity; we need not abandon that holding. A senior Presidential aide works more intimately with the President on a daily basis than does a Cabinet officer, directly implementing Presidential decisions literally from hour to hour. * * *

The Court's analysis in Gravel demonstrates that the question of derivative immunity does not and should not depend on a person's rank or position in the hierarchy, but on the *function* performed by the person and the relationship of that person to the superior. Cabinet officers clearly outrank United States Attorneys, yet qualified immunity is accorded the former and absolute immunity the latter; rank is important only to the extent that the rank determines the function to be performed. The function of senior Presidential aides, as the "alter egos" of the President, is an integral, inseparable part of the function of the President. * * *

By ignoring Gravel and engaging in a wooden application of Butz, the Court significantly undermines the functioning of the Office of the President. Under the Court's opinion in Nixon today it is clear that Presidential immunity derives from the Constitution as much as congressional immunity comes from that source. Can there rationally be one rule for congressional aides and another for Presidential aides simply because the initial absolute immunity of each derives from different aspects of the Constitution? I find it inexplicable why the Court makes no effort to demonstrate why the Chief Executive of the Nation should not be assured that senior staff aides will have the same protection as the aides of Members of the House and Senate.

NOTE ON OFFICERS' ACCOUNTABILITY IN DAMAGES FOR OFFICIAL MISCONDUCT

(1) Introduction: Basic Distinctions. In appraising the law governing official immunity, it is important to keep a number of basic distinctions in mind.

    (a) Absolute v. Qualified Immunity. Officials protected by absolute immunity—such as judges acting in a judicial capacity—cannot be held liable for damages under any circumstances, even if they intentionally or maliciously violate clearly established federal rights. Because an official with absolute immunity has no obligation to justify action taken, a suit barred by the doctrine can ordinarily be dismissed on a Rule 12(b)(6) motion. Absolute immunity thus eliminates nearly all of the possible burden, expense, and anxiety of litigation.

By contrast, "qualified immunity" will result in the dismissal of a lawsuit on a Rule 12(b)(6) motion only if the defendant is not alleged to have violated "clearly established statutory or constitutional rights of which a reasonable person would have known." In qualified immunity cases, complex questions frequently arise concerning whether a right was "clearly established". See Paragraph (7), *infra*.

(b) Functions v. Offices. Although judicial and prosecutorial immunity are absolute, and officials engaging in executive functions are protected only by qualified immunity, Harlow makes clear that immunity attaches to functions, not offices. Accordingly, executive officials enjoy absolute judicial immunity from suit for actions taken in a judicial capacity. See, *e.g.*, Butz v. Economou, 438 U.S. 478 (1978). By contrast, judges have only qualified immunity when sued for non-judicial actions such as firing a probation officer. See Forrester v. White, 484 U.S. 219 (1988).

(c) Individual Capacity v. Official Capacity. The "official" immunities discussed in Harlow apply only in suits in which officials are sued in their "individual" capacities, meaning that damages are at least nominally sought from the officials themselves, rather than from government treasuries. (Damages actions against state and federal officials in their "official" capacities will normally be barred by sovereign immunity. See pp. 996–998, *supra*.)

(d) Damages v. Other Relief. The Supreme Court's discussion in Harlow, and the doctrine of qualified immunity in particular, apply only to suits for damages. On the immunities applicable in suits for injunctive relief, see *Note On the Immunity of Government Officers From Relief Other Than Damages*, p. 1056, *infra*. Generally speaking, however, the doctrine of qualified immunity has no bearing whatsoever in suits for injunctive relief. If injunctions are not barred either by sovereign immunity or by absolute official immunity, they are not barred by any immunity doctrine at all (though they might of course be inappropriate for other reasons).

(e) Federal Law Actions v. State Law Actions. The immunities discussed in Harlow apply only in suits alleging violations of federal, rather than state, law. On the immunities applicable in suits predicated on state law, see Paragraph (9), *infra*.

(2) The Basis for Official Immunity.

(a) Origins and Policy Rationale. Official immunity originated as a common law doctrine available to defendants sued on common law causes of action. A classic statement of the policy rationale came in Gregoire v. Biddle, 177 F.2d 579 (2d Cir.1949) (L. Hand, J.), which upheld the absolute immunity not only of the Attorney General, but also of mid-level Justice Department officials, in a suit claiming that the defendants had, with malice and without justification, falsely imprisoned the plaintiff. The court wrote:

"It does indeed go without saying that an official, who is in fact guilty of using his powers to vent his spleen upon others, or for any other personal motive not connected with the public good, should not escape liability for the injuries he may so cause; and, if it were possible in practice to confine such complaints to the guilty, it would be monstrous to deny recovery. The justification for doing so is that it is impossible to know whether the claim is well founded until the case has been tried, and that to submit all officials, the innocent as well as the guilty, to the burden of a trial and to the inevitable danger of its outcome, would dampen the ardor of all but the most resolute, or the most irresponsible, in the unflinching discharge of their duties. Again and again the public interest calls for action which may turn out to be founded on a mistake, in the face of which an official may later find himself hard put to it to satisfy a jury of his good faith. There must indeed be means of punishing public officers who have been truant to their duties; but that is quite another matter from exposing such as have been honestly mistaken to suit by anyone who has suffered from their errors. As is so often the case, the answer must be found in a balance between the evils inevitable in either alternative. In this instance it has been thought in the end better to leave unredressed the wrongs done by dishonest officers than to subject those who try to do their duty to the constant dread of retaliation. Judged as res nova, we should not hesitate to follow the path laid down in the books."

The view that executive actions were entitled to some form of "discretionary immunity" from actions for damages—a view expressed by the Supreme Court at the turn of the last century in Spalding v. Vilas, 161 U.S. 483 (1896)—represented a major shift from earlier nineteenth century practice. See Woolhandler, *Patterns of Official Immunity and Accountability*, 37 Case W.Res.L.Rev. 396, 453–57 (1986–87). Under the earlier view, officials sued in tort generally were treated like private tortfeasors and not shielded by any distinctive immunity—although pockets of immunity did evolve, as for judges and high federal officials.

(b) Extension of Immunity to § 1983 Actions. The Court first confronted the question whether official immunity doctrine applied in § 1983 actions in Tenney v. Brandhove, 341 U.S. 367 (1951), a case involving state legislators sued for actions taken in a legislative capacity: "Did Congress by the general language of its 1871 statute mean to overturn the tradition of legislative freedom achieved in England by Civil War and carefully preserved in the formation of State and National Governments here? * * * The limits of [§ 1983's reach] were not spelled out in debate. We cannot believe that Congress—itself a staunch advocate of legislative freedom—would impinge on a tradition so well grounded in history and reason by covert inclusion in the general language before us." See also Pierson v. Ray, 386 U.S. 547, 554–55 (1967) (stating that the legislative history of the Civil Rights Act did not support the notion that Congress meant to abrogate the common law doctrine of judicial immunity). The Court subsequently characterized Tenney as "establish[ing] that § 1983 is to be read in harmony with general principles of tort immunities and defenses rather than in derogation of them." Imbler v. Pachtman, 424 U.S. 409, 418 (1976).

Is the Court right in assuming (as it consistently has) that if the 42d Congress had intended § 1983 to abrogate any and all immunities recognized at common law, that intent would have been more clearly signaled in the statute? See Matasar, *Personal Immunities Under Section 1983: The Limits of the Court's Historical Analysis*, 40 Ark.L.Rev. 741 (1987).

(c) Origins and Evolution of Qualified Immunity. Although recognizing that judges enjoyed an absolute immunity from suit, Pierson v. Ray held that police officers sued for false arrest had a less absolute defense of "good faith and probable cause", which it characterized as available to police officers sued for the analogous common law tort. The Court did not use the term "qualified immunity" until Scheur v. Rhodes, 416 U.S. 232, 243 (1974). Citing Monroe v. Pape, the Scheur Court held that "government officials, as a class, could not be totally exempt, by virtue of some absolute immunity, from liability under [§ 1983's] terms." At the same time, the Court again asserted that § 1983 should not be interpreted to overturn common law doctrines existing in 1871. Looking to public policy as the guiding star, the Court held: "These considerations suggest that, in varying scope, a qualified immunity is available to officers of the executive branch of government, the variation being dependent upon the scope of discretion and responsibilities of the office and all the circumstances as they reasonably appeared at the time of the action on which liability is sought to be based".

(d) **Parallelism of State and Federal Officials' Immunity.** Footnote 30 of Harlow assumes that the immunities of state officials in § 1983 actions and of federal officials in Bivens actions should be co-extensive.[1] Is this assumption justified?

(e) **Sources of Immunity Law.** In Tower v. Glover, 467 U.S. 914 (1984), a § 1983 action, the Court described the appropriate inquiry for determining the scope of officials' immunity as follows: "If an official was accorded immunity from tort actions at common law when the Civil Rights Act was enacted in 1871, the Court next considers whether § 1983's history or purposes nonetheless counsel against recognizing the same immunity in § 1983 actions." Both of these inquiries may be quite open-ended. The common law history may be inapposite to the distinctive functions and organization of modern governments, or may simply be unclear. See generally Matasar, *supra*. And analysis of policy considerations may be quite indeterminate in view of the complexity of the competing goals, the paucity of pertinent empirical data, and the need to consider damages suits as just one of many remedies for official misconduct.

With the inquiry prescribed by Tower v. Glover, compare the Court's analysis in Harlow, a Bivens action in which the Court formulated a new standard for qualified immunity broader than that recognized at common law. As discussed in Paragraph (7)(b), *infra*, subsequent decisions have arguably extended the protective reach of qualified immunity even further. Could Congress narrow or abolish immunities in § 1983 actions? In Bivens actions? Conversely, could Congress constitutionally provide all officials with absolute immunity in all constitutional tort actions without making other remedies available?

(f) **Indemnification and Its Relevance.** Note the assumption by Judge Hand in Gregoire v. Biddle, by the Court in Harlow v. Fitzgerald, and by nearly all courts and commentators that government officials sued in their personal capacity are threatened with potentially ruinous personal liability. But is this assumption warranted? An important empirical study, Schwartz, *Police Indemnification,* 89 N.Y.U.L.Rev. 885 (2014), concludes that it is not, due to a widespread governmental practice of indemnifying officers sued for tortious misconduct. Based on a survey involving forty-four of the nation's seventy largest law enforcement agencies and thirty-seven of seventy randomly selected smaller jurisdictions, Professor Schwartz found that between 2006 and 2011, in the over 9200 suits against officers in the larger jurisdictions that ended in either damages awards or settlements

---

[1] A limited exception to this parity is the absolute immunity of the President, see Paragraph (5), *infra*; state governors have only a qualified immunity under Scheuer v. Rhodes, *supra*.

(which collectively totaled over $730 million), "officers paid just .02% of the dollars awarded to plaintiffs in police misconduct suits. In thirty-seven small and mid-sized law enforcement agencies, officers never contributed to settlements or judgments [that totaled over $9 million]. No officer in any of the eighty-one jurisdictions satisfied a punitive damages judgment entered against him. * * * And officers were indemnified even when they were disciplined, terminated, or prosecuted for their misconduct."[2]

An earlier study by Professor Schuck, which was based largely on statutes and formally promulgated policies, found indemnification of state and local officials sued under § 1983 to be "neither certain nor universal". Schuck, Suing the Government: Citizen Remedies for Official Wrongs 85 (1983). According to Professor Schwartz, however, "[d]espite the wide variation in indemnification statutes, there is little variation in outcome—officers almost never pay"—though she acknowledges that "government attorneys may strategically employ the threat that officers will be denied indemnification" and seek to negotiate favorable settlements on that basis.

Based on her findings, Professor Schwartz argues that qualified immunity is unnecessary to protect officials from unfair liability or to avoid overdeterrence and concludes that it should be "eliminated or restricted." According to her, "[w]hen officers are indemnified * * * there is less injustice in 'subjecting to liability an officer who is required, by the legal obligations of his position, to exercise discretion' " (quoting Owen v. City of Independence, 445 U.S. 622, 654 (1980)). Compare Jeffries, *Compensation for Constitutional Torts: Reflections on the Significance of Fault*, 88 Mich.L.Rev. 82 (1989) (arguing that policy reasons make damages relief appropriate only in cases of "fault" and that Harlow's test for qualified immunity is a reasonable measure of fault. See also Fallon, *Asking the Right Questions About Officer Immunity*, 80 Fordham L.Rev. 479 (2011): "[O]fficial immunity is not a variable among constants but * * * one potential variable among others. * * * In the absence of official immunity, even some currently well-established constitutional rights and authorizations to sue to enforce them would likely *shrink*, and sometimes appropriately so." (For example, if there were no official immunity, the Court might hold that searches are not unreasonable under the Fourth Amendment unless no reasonable official could have thought them unreasonable, or that no cause of action runs against judges whose only constitutional violation is to rule erroneously on constitutional claims.)[3]

---

[2] Professor Schwartz reports, although she did not test, what she describes as a "general consensus" that, despite their effective vicarious liability, "most governments are not taking aggressive enough action to investigate and discipline their officers and no not effectively manage their law enforcement agencies." She adds: "[A]necdotal evidence suggests that police litigation costs are often paid from a city's general budget or insurer with limited or no direct impact on the finances of the police department. So, in many departments, there is not just indemnification, but double indemnification—the individual officers are indemnified and the police department itself is indemnified by the city."

[3] Nevertheless, Professor Fallon is equivocal about existing immunity doctrine. Viewing immunity as "a potential mechanism for achieving the best overall bundle of rights and correspondingly calibrated remedies," he maintains that "there has been too little thinking about" alternatives to official immunity (such as non-retroactivity doctrines applicable to path-breaking rulings recognizing new rights or straitened pleading requirements as a way of weeding out frivolous suits) and the distinctive features of immunity, if any, that might make it—"in comparison with other potentially adjustable variables"—the best "tool for defining or redefining packages of rights and enforcement mechanisms that confer meaningful guarantees but are not intolerably [socially] costly". In thinking about policy variables such as these, consider the potential relevance of the historical argument of Pfander & Hunt, *Public Wrongs*

(3) Absolute Immunities Associated with the Judicial Process.

(a) Judicial Immunity. The considerations offered by the Court as justifications for absolute judicial immunity have been summarized as follows: "(1) the need for a judge to 'be free to act upon his own conviction, without apprehension of personal consequences to himself'; (2) the controversiality and importance of the competing interests adjudicated by judges and the likelihood that the loser, feeling aggrieved, would wish to retaliate; (3) the record-keeping to which self-protective judges would be driven in the absence of immunity; (4) the availability of alternative remedies, such as appeal and impeachment, for judicial wrongdoing; and (5) the ease with which bad faith can be alleged and made the basis for 'vexatious litigation.' " Schuck, Paragraph (2)(f), *supra*, at 90.

The only way to circumvent judicial immunity is to show that a judge was acting "in the clear absence of all jurisdiction" or was not performing a "judicial act". These tests, dating back at least to Bradley v. Fisher, 80 U.S. (13 Wall.) 335, 351 (1871), were applied in Stump v. Sparkman, 435 U.S. 349 (1978), in which an Indiana judge had approved *ex parte* a petition filed by parents of a fifteen-year-old girl to have her sterilized without her knowledge. When she later sued the judge for damages under § 1983, the Supreme Court ruled that he was absolutely immune: since he presided over a court of general jurisdiction, he had not acted wholly outside his jurisdiction, and he did not lose his immunity simply because no state statute specifically authorized his conduct.

The Court also rejected the argument that because the petition was never docketed or filed with the clerk, no hearing was held, and no guardian *ad litem* was appointed, the judge's approval of the petition was not a "judicial act". In the Court's view, whether a judge's action is a "judicial act" depends on whether (i) it is a function normally performed by a judge, and (ii) the parties' expectations revealed that they were dealing with the judge in his judicial capacity. The Court found both criteria to be met, noting as to the former that Indiana judges are often called upon to approve petitions about minors' affairs.

Justice Stewart, joined by Justices Marshall and Powell, wrote an angry dissent, arguing that *ex parte* approval of a parent's petition was not an act normally performed by Indiana judges. He continued by insisting that "false illusions as to a judge's power can hardly convert a judge's response to those illusions into a judicial act", and that "[a] judge is not free, like a loose cannon, to inflict indiscriminate damage whenever he announces that he is acting in his judicial capacity." Justice Powell's separate dissent emphasized that "[t]he complete absence of normal judicial process" made inoperative the assumption underlying judicial immunity that "there exist alternative forums and methods for vindicating [private] rights."

Since Stump, most of the cases finding judges not to have acted in a judicial capacity have involved off-beat situations. Compare Mireles v. Waco, 502 U.S. 9 (1991) (per curiam) (extending absolute immunity to a state judge

---

and Private Bills: Indemnification and Government Accountability in the Early Republic, 85 N.Y,U.L.Rev. 1862 (2010), that federal officials generally enjoyed no immunity from suit during the Antebellum Era and that Congress routinely provided indemnification for official action taken in good faith discharge of official duties. Although the authors assert that "[n]o one would argue for a return to the world of the early republic and * * * an indemnity practice managed through petitions to Congress", they see considerable virtues in a regime in which "[c]ourts evaluated legality" and Congress took responsibility for "adjust[ing] official incentives".

who allegedly ordered police officers to seize "with excessive force", and bring to the judge's chambers, a public defender who had missed a calendar call, since it was a properly judicial function to direct officers to bring a person in the courthouse before a judge) with Zarcone v. Perry, 572 F.2d 52 (2d Cir.1978) (judge who ordered court officials to bring "in front of me in cuffs" the vendor of coffee that the judge thought tasted "putrid", and who then interrogated the vendor and threatened his "livelihood", acted outside his judicial capacity). But in Forrester v. White, Paragraph (1), *supra*, the Supreme Court unanimously ruled that a judge was acting in an administrative rather than a judicial capacity, and hence was not entitled to absolute immunity, when he fired a probation officer, allegedly on account of her sex and thus in violation of the Fourteenth Amendment.

(b) Prosecutorial Immunity. The purposes and scope of prosecutorial immunity are similar to those of judicial immunity. In Imbler v. Pachtman, 424 U.S. 409 (1976), a § 1983 action alleging that a state prosecutor had knowingly introduced perjured testimony, the Court found that prosecutorial immunity was well-established at common law and that absolute rather than qualified immunity was appropriate. Otherwise, a criminal defendant could "transform his resentment * * * into the ascription of improper and malicious actions to the State's advocate", and suits "could be expected with some frequency". These suits would require a retrial of the criminal case, could discourage the prosecutor from presenting relevant evidence, and might skew postconviction procedures because of a judge's subconscious knowledge that a decision favorable to the accused could lead to a prosecutor's civil liability. There was "no occasion", the Court added, "to consider whether like or similar reasons require immunity for those aspects of the prosecutor's responsibility that cast him in the role of an administrator or investigative officer rather than that of advocate".[4]

In subsequent cases the Court has made clear that prosecutorial immunity extends only to prosecutorial functions related to courtroom advocacy and not to administrative tasks. In Mitchell v. Forsyth, 472 U.S. 511 (1985), the Court thus held with little discussion that former Attorney General John N. Mitchell, in authorizing a warrantless wiretap for reasons of national security, was not acting in a prosecutorial capacity and hence was not shielded by absolute immunity. Burns v. Reed, 500 U.S. 478 (1991), then further limited the reach of a prosecutor's absolute immunity. In Burns, the plaintiff alleged, *inter alia*, that the defendant had violated her constitutional rights (i) by improperly advising the police that they could question her under hypnosis and that they "probably had probable cause" to arrest her and (ii) by presenting false and misleading evidence at a court appearance in support of an application for a search warrant. The Supreme Court held that the defendant's court appearance and his presentation of evidence at the hearing on the search warrant were protected by absolute immunity, but that his acts of providing advice to the police were subject only to a qualified immunity defense. The Court noted the lack of any historical or common law support for extending absolute immunity to the provision of

---

[4] Jurors and witnesses in judicial proceedings also enjoy absolute immunity. See Briscoe v. LaHue, 460 U.S. 325 (1983). Rehberg v. Paulk, 132 S.Ct. 1497 (2012), held unanimously that a witness in a grand jury proceeding enjoys the same absolute immunity from suit as a witness at trial. Public defenders, who do not ordinarily act under color of state law, see Polk County v. Dodson, 454 U.S. 312 (1981), are likely to be liable under § 1983 only if they conspire with state officials, and Tower v. Glover, 467 U.S. 914 (1984), held that in such a § 1983 action a defender has *no* immunity.

advice and stressed the rationale behind absolute prosecutorial immunity—
"to free the *judicial process* from the harassment and intimidation associated
with litigation". Moreover, one significant check on constitutional violations
in the course of the judicial process—the availability of appellate review—
"will not necessarily restrain out-of-court activities by a prosecutor that
occur prior to the initiation of a prosecution", particularly "if a suspect is not
eventually prosecuted".[5]

Compare Van de Kamp v. Goldstein, 555 U.S. 335 (2009), which held
that absolute prosecutorial immunity barred claims based on the
prosecution's non-disclosure of impeachment material, which was allegedly
due to the defendants' failure to (1) train and supervise prosecutors and (2)
establish an information system containing potential impeachment material
concerning informants. Although the alleged constitutional violations
involved "administrative activities", absolute prosecutorial immunity
applied, Justice Breyer reasoned for a unanimous Court, because "[t]he
management tasks at issue * * * concern how and when to make
impeachment information available at trial" and "are thereby directly
connected with the prosecutor's basic trial advocacy responsibilities". It
would "prove difficult", the Court said, "to draw a line between *general* office
supervision or office training * * * and *specific* supervision or training related
to a particular case."

The Court added: "[B]ecause better training or supervision might
prevent most, if not all, prosecutorial errors at trial, permission to bring such
a suit here would grant permission to criminal defendants to bring claims in
other similar instances, in effect claiming damages for (trial-related)
training or supervisory failings."

Is the Court's reluctance to grant "permission" for the filing of claims
based on inadequate training and supervision better understood as a concern
about the proper reach of prosecutorial immunity, the limits of the § 1983
cause of action, or the scope of the underlying constitutional right? How
successfully can these considerations be kept apart?

(4) The Absolute Immunity of Legislators. The only explicit source in
the Constitution for official immunity of any kind appears in Article I,
Section 6, which states that Senators and Representatives "shall in all Cases,
except Treason, Felony, and Breach of Peace, be privileged from Arrest

---

[5]   In Buckley v. Fitzsimmons, 509 U.S. 259 (1993), the plaintiff alleged that prosecutors
had fabricated evidence during the preliminary investigation of a crime by obtaining testimony
about a bootprint from an expert known to be unreliable. The suit also alleged that prosecutors
had made false statements at a press conference announcing the return of an indictment. The
Court ruled that the prosecutors were entitled only to qualified immunity with respect to both
the press conference (on this point, the Court was unanimous) and the alleged fabrication (here,
the Court divided 5–4). See also Kalina v. Fletcher, 522 U.S. 118 (1997) (holding that a
prosecutor who allegedly filed a false "Certification of Determination of Probable Cause" in
support of an application for an arrest warrant was not entitled to absolute immunity from suit
because, in filing the certification, the prosecutor was acting as a complaining witness, not as a
lawyer).

For a forceful argument that neither history nor considerations of policy lend support to
absolute prosecutorial immunity, see Johns, *Reconsidering Absolute Prosecutorial Immunity*,
2005 BYU L.Rev. 53. For further attacks on absolute prosecutorial immunity, largely predicated
on the claim that current law includes too few deterrents to prosecutorial misconduct, see Johns,
Unsupportable and Unjustified: A Critique of Absolute Prosecutorial Immunity, 80 Fordham
L.Rev. 509 (2011); Rudin, *The Supreme Court Assumes Errant Prosecutors Will Be Disciplined
by Their Offices or the Bar: Three Case Studies that Prove that Assumption Wrong*, 80 Fordham
L.Rev. 537 (2011).

during their Attendance at the Session of their respective Houses, and in going to and returning from the same; and for any Speech or Debate in either House, they shall not be questioned in any other Place."

The Supreme Court first considered the Speech or Debate Clause in Kilbourn v. Thompson, 103 U.S. 168, 200–05 (1880). Relying on the English tradition of parliamentary privilege, the Court held that federal legislators who had voted for a resolution ordering the plaintiff to be imprisoned for contempt of Congress were immune from damages liability in a suit for false imprisonment. Subsequent cases have interpreted the Speech or Debate Clause to shield all "legislative acts"—matters that are "an integral part of the deliberative and communicative processes by which Members participate in committee and House proceedings with respect to the consideration and passage or rejection of proposed legislation or with respect to other matters which the Constitution places within the jurisdiction of either House". Gravel v. United States, 408 U.S. 606, 625 (1972).[6] The Gravel case—discussed at length in the Harlow opinions—also held, contrary to prior authority, that the immunity extends not only to members of Congress but also to their aides.

Although the Speech or Debate Clause extends only to members of Congress, Tenney v. Brandhove, Paragraph (2)(b), *supra*, held a state legislator absolutely immune from damages liability in a § 1983 action that alleged that the defendant had called a hearing not for a legitimate legislative purpose but instead to deprive plaintiff of his constitutional rights.[7]

(5) Absolute Immunity of the President. In Nixon v. Fitzgerald, 457 U.S. 731 (1982), Fitzgerald (the plaintiff in the Harlow case) sought damages from President Nixon, who allegedly shared responsibility for the loss of his federal job. Justice Powell's opinion for the Court ruled that the President enjoyed an absolute immunity from damages liability for all acts within the "outer perimeter" of his official responsibilities. This immunity, he argued, was a "functionally mandated incident of the President's unique office, rooted in the constitutional tradition of the separation of powers".[8] The Court stressed that the President's prominence made the Chief Executive an easy target for damages actions, and that if Presidents had only a qualified immunity, the resulting diversion of their energies in defending themselves would jeopardize the effective functioning of government. Justice White wrote a vigorous dissent, in which Justices Brennan, Marshall, and Blackmun joined, accusing the Court of mistakenly conferring immunity on

---

6   Compare Doe v. McMillan, 412 U.S. 306 (1973) (House Members responsible for preparing a committee report were absolutely immune in a suit for invasion of privacy filed by schoolchildren identified in the report, though the Superintendent of Documents and the Public Printer, who publicly disseminated the report, were not immune), with Hutchinson v. Proxmire, 443 U.S. 111 (1979) (Senator was not immune from a defamation action arising out of his publicizing his "Golden Fleece" award—for wasteful federal spending—in a press release, newsletter, and television program).

7   In Bogan v. Scott-Harris, 523 U.S. 44 (1998), the Court held that local legislators are entitled to the same absolute immunity from § 1983 civil liability as are state and regional legislators. The Court then determined that a mayor's preparation of a budget eliminating the plaintiff's position and his signing of the ordinance so providing, as well as the city council vice president's vote on the measure, were legislative actions entitled to absolute immunity. In its opinion, the Court stated that the determination whether a particular activity should be classified as legislative hinges on the nature of the activity, not the subjective intent of the actor.

8   The Court left open the question whether the President could be subjected to damages liability by explicit and affirmative congressional action.

an office rather than a function, and finding nothing in the nature of executive personnel decisions to warrant absolute rather than qualified immunity.[9]

(6) National Security Functions. Although Harlow held that absolute immunity might be appropriate for presidential aides with discretionary authority in national security matters or foreign affairs, the Court rejected a claim of absolute immunity in Mitchell v. Forsyth, 472 U.S. 511 (1985), Paragraph 3(b), *supra*, a Bivens action against former Attorney General John N. Mitchell for having authorized a warrantless wiretap for the purpose of protecting national security. The Court reasoned that the secrecy of national security matters reduced both the likelihood of unfounded and burdensome lawsuits and the effectiveness of other possible mechanisms of restraining misconduct.

(7) Qualified Immunity: Clearly Established Law. Harlow makes the availability of qualified immunity turn on whether the plaintiff has alleged a violation of "clearly established" federal law. But how does one tell whether an asserted right was "clearly established" at the time of the asserted violation?[10]

    (a) Courts Capable of "Clearly Establishing" the Law. In many situations, the Supreme Court may not have ruled on a claimed federal right, but lower federal or state courts may have. In United States v. Lanier, 520 U.S. 259 (1997), a criminal case brought under 18 U.S.C. § 242, the Court stated that it was possible for a right to be "clearly established" even in the absence of a Supreme Court decision so holding, but that disparate decisions in the lower courts might preclude such a determination.

    In Camreta v. Greene, 131 S.Ct. 2020 (2011), the Court posited that a Ninth Circuit ruling that a defendant had violated a constitutional right would not be "mere dictum" in subsequent cases within the circuit, even if the court ordered the suit dismissed on qualified immunity grounds. The Court also asserted that "district court decisions—unlike those from the courts of appeals—do not necessarily settle constitutional standards or prevent repeated claims of qualified immunity." In conjunction, do these

---

    [9]   A different question is that of the ability of a litigant to bring a civil suit against a sitting President for conduct occurring prior to the President's taking office. In Clinton v. Jones, 520 U.S. 681 (1997), a case involving sexual harassment claims against President Clinton that arose out of alleged conduct prior to his Presidency (when he was governor of Arkansas), the Supreme Court denied a claim of broad Presidential "temporary immunity" from civil damages actions relating to events outside the scope of his Presidential duties. The Court did not decide whether a *state* court could entertain a private action in such a case, or whether the trial court in the case at hand could compel the President's appearance at any specific time or place. The Court held that the trial court had broad discretion to control its own docket and that the respect owed the Presidency should inform the exercise of that discretion, but that staying the action was premature. Justice Breyer, concurring in the judgment, argued at length that "ordinary case-management principles" must be "supplemented with a constitutionally based requirement that district courts schedule proceedings so as to avoid significant interference with the President's ongoing discharge of his official responsibilities".

    [10] Jeffries, *The Liability Rule for Constitutional Torts,* 99 Va.L.Rev. 207 (2012), argues for shifting the immunity inquiry "from whether the defendant violated a 'clearly established' right to whether the defendant's actions were 'clearly unconstitutional.' " According to Professor Jeffries, the latter standard would "signal a less technical requirement, less tied to specific precedent, and more accommodating of notice through 'common social duty' " in cases involving egregious official misconduct but no closely on-point judicial precedents clearly establishing constitutional rights. See also Jeffries, *What's Wrong With Qualified Immunity?*, 62 Fla.L.Rev. 851 (2010) (discussing lower courts' difficulties in applying the "clearly established" standard and offering "modest" suggestions for doctrinal clarification).

assertions imply that a squarely on-point court of appeals decision suffices to "clearly establish" the law within the circuit in which it was issued? Would it matter if other circuits or state supreme courts had decided the same question differently?

The Court also addressed the significance of district court rulings in Ashcroft v. al-Kidd, 131 S.Ct. 2074 (2011), holding that dictum in a single district court decision could not "clearly establish" that a course of action by the Attorney General violates the Constitution: "[A] district judge's * * * holding is not 'controlling authority' in any jurisdiction, much less in the entire United States; and his *ipse dixit* of a footnoted dictum falls far short of what is necessary absent controlling authority: a robust 'consensus of cases of persuasive authority.' Wilson v. Layne, 526 U.S. 603, 617 (1999)."

In a concurring opinion in al-Kidd, Justice Kennedy argued that the criteria for identifying clearly established law might vary with the office that an official holds: "In contrast [with officials operating within a single jurisdiction,] the Attorney General occupies a national office and so sets policies implemented in many jurisdictions throughout the country. * * * A national officer intent on retaining qualified immunity need not abide by the most stringent standard adopted anywhere in the United States." Imagine that the Attorney General and a county sheriff are both sued in the Ninth Circuit for ordering seizures that would be unreasonable under Ninth Circuit precedent. Is it possible that the latter has violated clearly established law but the former has not?

(b) Specific Applications of Generally Defined Rights. A recurring scenario involves the application of well established *general* principles of law to particular facts. The leading case is Anderson v. Creighton, 483 U.S. 635 (1987), involving the unquestioned Fourth Amendment rule that a warrantless search of a home is impermissible absent probable cause and exigent circumstances. Reversing a ruling by the court of appeals, the Supreme Court held (6–3) that the availability of qualified immunity should turn not on the general right, but on its application to particular facts: "The contours of the right must be sufficiently clear that a reasonable official would understand that *what he is doing* violates that right" (emphasis added). The Court also rejected the plaintiff's argument that since the Fourth Amendment prohibits "unreasonable searches and seizures", it is logically impossible to find an officer immune under Harlow, for to do so would imply that an officer "reasonably" acted unreasonably. A court must conduct a two-step process: (1) determining whether a constitutional violation had occurred because of the officer's unreasonable behavior and, if so, (2) determining whether it was "reasonable" for the officer to have been unaware of the legal significance of his conduct.[11]

---

[11] The Court applied a similar analysis in addressing an immunity defense against a complaint of excessive force in making an arrest in Saucier v. Katz, 533 U.S. 194 (2001) (more fully discussed at pp. 1051–1052, *infra*): If the officer was reasonably mistaken about "whether a particular amount of force [was] legal" on the case's particular facts, "the officer is entitled to the immunity defense". In Reichle v. Howards, 132 S.Ct. 2088 (2012), the Court upheld a claim of qualified immunity by Secret Service agents who were alleged to have violated the First Amendment by arresting a suspect, admittedly with probable cause (for making a materially false statement to a federal official), but purportedly in retaliation for speech uttered in an encounter with Vice President Cheney. In an opinion joined by five other Justices, Justice Thomas held that the question was not whether there is a "general right to be free from retaliation for one's speech", but whether there was a clearly established "right to be free from a retaliatory arrest that is otherwise supported by probable cause." After concluding that Supreme Court cases had not established such a right, he overturned the Tenth Circuit's holding

In Anderson, the Court said that for qualified immunity to be defeated, "[t]he contours of the right must be sufficiently clear that a reasonable official would understand that what he is doing violates that right." In Ashcroft v. al-Kidd, *supra*, Justice Scalia's Court opinion quoted that language but interrupted the quotation to replace "a reasonable official" with "every 'reasonable official.' " See also Reichle v. Howards, 132 S.Ct. 2088, 2093 (2012) (quoting the al-Kidd formulation). How large a change in the law, if any, does that substitution make?

(c) **Disagreement Among Courts.** The Court cited disagreement among lower court judges as its principal ground for upholding a qualified immunity defense in Safford Unified School District #1 v. Redding, 557 U.S. 364 (2009). In an opinion by Justice Souter, the Court first held that the defendant school officials had violated the Fourth Amendment when they strip-searched a thirteen-year-old middle school student without adequate reason to suspect her of hiding dangerous contraband in her underwear. But the defendants possessed qualified immunity, the Court said, largely because lower courts had "reached divergent conclusions regarding how" the controlling precedent allowing school searches under a reasonableness standard, New Jersey v. T.L.O., 469 U.S. 325 (1985), applied to strip searches: "We would not suggest that entitlement to qualified immunity is the guaranteed product of disuniform views of the law in the other federal, or state, courts, and the fact that a single judge, or even a group of judges, disagrees about the contours of a right does not automatically render the law unclear. That said, however, the cases viewing strip searches differently from the way we see them are numerous enough, with well-reasoned majority and dissenting opinions, to counsel doubt that we were sufficiently clear in the prior statement of the law." Justice Stevens, joined by Justice Ginsburg, dissented, asserting that "the clarity of a well-established right should not depend on whether jurists have misread our precedents".

When, if ever, would "disuniform views" among lower courts fail to demonstrate that the law was not "clearly established"? In thinking about this question, note that in Groh v. Ramirez, 540 U.S. 551 (2004), a five-Justice majority held that the defendant had violated clearly established rights, even though Justices Scalia and Thomas concluded that the defendants had not violated the Constitution at all.

(d) **Factual Similarity to Decided Cases.** In Hope v. Pelzer, 536 U.S. 730 (2002), a state prisoner brought an action against state officers under § 1983, alleging violations of his Eighth Amendment right not to be subjected to cruel and unusual punishment. More specifically, the plaintiff asserted that on two occasions, while working on a chain gang, he had been handcuffed to a hitching post for disruptive conduct. He further alleged that on the first occasion, he was handcuffed above shoulder height for a two-hour period during which the cuffs cut into his wrists, causing pain; on the second, he was made to take off his shirt, then hitched for seven hours in the hot sun, and was given only one or two water breaks and no bathroom breaks. The lower courts thought the action barred by qualified immunity because the facts of Hope's situation were not "materially similar" to those of previous cases, but the Supreme Court, per Justice Stevens, reversed (6–3).

---

that one of its cases had done so. An intervening Supreme Court decision had created reasonable uncertainty about the Tenth Circuit precedent's continuing validity, he ruled. Justices Ginsburg and Breyer concurred in the judgment only. Justice Kagan did not participate.

After holding (as had the court below) that the plaintiff's treatment violated the Eighth Amendment, Justice Stevens rejected the idea that the facts of prior cases must be "materially similar" to the case at hand for qualified immunity to be overcome. Quoting Anderson v. Creighton, he said that a plaintiff need not show "that the very action in question has previously been held unlawful" so long as "in the light of pre-existing law, the unlawfulness [was] apparent". The purpose of qualified immunity is to give "fair warning" to government officials, and in some instances "a general constitutional rule already identified in the decisional law may apply with obvious clarity to the specific conduct in question," even though that conduct itself has not been previously held unlawful. In this case, the clarity of the violation was established by several factors: (a) the Supreme Court's holding, in Whitley v. Albers, 475 U.S. 312, 319 (1986), that the "unnecessary and wanton infliction of pain" violated the Eighth Amendment; (b) two of the Eleventh Circuit's own precedents handed down in 1987 and 1974, the latter condemning various forms of punishment, including handcuffing an inmate to a fence for a long period of time; (c) a state regulation, restricting the use of the hitching post, that had not been followed, at least in one of the instances complained of; and (d) a U.S. Department of Justice report advising the state department of corrections to stop using the practice in order to meet constitutional standards.

In a dissent joined by Chief Justice Rehnquist and Justice Scalia, Justice Thomas challenged the majority's explicit grounds for rejecting the qualified immunity defense by (a) noting that the Court itself apparently did not regard the broad statement in Whitley as sufficient; (b) maintaining that the law of the Eleventh Circuit was far from clear (even looking only at appellate cases but especially in view of several more recent Alabama district court cases upholding very similar practices); (c) stating (as the majority acknowledged) that the Department of Justice report had never been seen by any of the guards at the prison in question and in any event, taken in context, revealed only a dispute between federal and state authorities; and (d) contending that the state regulation cited by the majority may well not have been violated.

Did the majority's reliance on a conjunction of factors suggest that the judicial precedents, by themselves, might not have sufficed to create "clearly established" rights?[12] Under the subtle reformulation of the qualified immunity test in Paragraph (7)(a), how would (and should) Hope v. Pelzer come out?

(e) Advice of Counsel. Suppose a lawyer advises an official that contemplated action would be lawful even though under judicial precedents it clearly would not be. Jack Goldsmith, a former head of the Justice Department's Office of Legal Counsel (OLC), reports in his book The Terror Presidency: Law and Judgment Inside the Bush Administration (2007) that officials implementing the Bush Administration's antiterrorism policies regarded OLC memos adjudging those policies to be constitutional as providing a reliable shield against subsequent legal actions seeking to impose criminal or civil liability. Insofar as constitutional tort actions are concerned, would an official who acted on legal advice be governed by Harlow's statement that even an official whose conduct violates clearly

---

[12] Failure to follow the state regulation invoked by the Court would apparently not have sufficed by itself in light of the earlier decision in Davis v. Scherer, 468 U.S. 183 (1984), that to overcome a defense of qualified immunity, it is not enough to show a clear violation of *state* law.

established law is still immune if the official "claims extraordinary circumstances and can prove that he neither knew nor should have known of the relevant legal standard"?

In thinking about this question, consider the partial analogy presented by cases in which police officers are alleged to have violated clearly established rights while executing warrants issued by magistrates. In Malley v. Briggs, 475 U.S. 335 (1986), a police officer presented arrest warrants to a state judge, who approved and signed them. The officer was later sued under § 1983 for having caused the arrest of individuals without probable cause. The Supreme Court refused to hold that the officer was absolutely immune because he had relied "on the judgment of a judicial officer in finding that probable cause exist[ed] and hence issuing the warrant". Though in an ideal system no judge would approve a defective application, it was not unreasonable to minimize the risk of error by holding an officer liable if "the warrant application is so lacking in indicia of probable cause as to render official belief in its existence unreasonable". The Court remanded for application of the Harlow standard.[13]

The Court appeared to attach greater significance to a magistrate's issuance of a search warrant in Messerschmidt v. Millender, 132 S.Ct. 1235 (2012), in which it characterized "the fact that a neutral magistrate has issued a warrant" as a legally relevant indicator that "the officers acted in an objectively reasonable manner". Chief Justice Roberts' majority opinion described Malley as establishing an "exception" to the principle that a magistrate's decision to issue a warrant normally establishes the objective legal reasonableness of its execution. That exception applied, he said, only when "the magistrate so obviously erred that any reasonable officer would have recognized the error." Justice Sotomayor, in a dissenting opinion joined by Justice Ginsburg, and Justice Kagan, in an opinion concurring in part and dissenting in part, protested that the majority misread Malley. According to the dissenting Justices, an officer's unreasonable decision to seek an overbroad warrant could not be rendered objectively reasonable by a magistrate's issuance of such a warrant.

(8) Order of Decision in Qualified Immunity Cases. In cases in which the defendant pleads qualified immunity, it will sometimes be clear that the defendant violated no "clearly established" right, but less clear whether the defendant violated a right at all. The question then arises whether a court should nevertheless resolve the latter question with the aim—which the Supreme Court can realize, but lower courts may fail to achieve—of "clearly establish[ing]" the law for future cases.

(a) In Saucier v. Katz, 533 U.S. 194 (2001), the Court said that whenever a claim of qualified immunity was asserted, courts must proceed in two steps, with the first question being: "Taken in the light most favorable to the party asserting the injury, do the facts alleged show that the officer's conduct violated a constitutional right? *This must be the initial inquiry*" (emphasis

---

[13] A closely divided Court has refused to recognize immunity for private parties acting under color of law. See Wyatt v. Cole, 504 U.S. 158 (1992); Richardson v. McKnight, 521 U.S. 399 (1997). In Filarsky v. Delia, 132 S.Ct. 1657 (2012), however, a unanimous Court held that a person hired directly by the government to work on its behalf need not be a permanent or full-time employee in order to claim official immunity.

added). If the answer is yes, the court must then inquire whether the right was "clearly established".[14]

(b) Saucier's mandated order of decision encountered resistance from lower court judges as well as commentators,[15] however, and the Court unanimously reversed itself in Pearson v. Callahan, 555 U.S. 223 (2009), which held that lower court judges "should be permitted to exercise their sound discretion in deciding which of the two prongs of the qualified immunity analysis should be addressed first in light of the particular circumstances in the particular case at hand."

In discussing the considerations that a court should take into account in determining whether to rule first on whether a defendant's conduct violated any constitutional right at all or whether an asserted right was "clearly established" at the time of an alleged violation, the opinion in Pearson took note of a variety of conflicting considerations:

"Although we now hold that the Saucier protocol should not be regarded as mandatory in all cases, we continue to recognize that it is often beneficial. * * * [T]here are cases in which there would be little if any conservation of judicial resources to be had by beginning and ending with * * * the 'clearly established' prong. * * * In addition, * * * the two-step procedure promotes the development of constitutional precedent and is especially valuable with respect to questions that do not frequently arise * * *.

"At the same time, however, the rigid Saucier procedure comes with a price. The procedure sometimes results in a substantial expenditure of scarce judicial resources on difficult questions that have no effect on the case. * * * District courts and courts of appeals with heavy caseloads are often understandably unenthusiastic about what may seem to be an essentially academic exercise. Unnecessary litigation of constitutional issues also wastes the parties' resources. * * *

"Adherence to Saucier's two-step protocol [also] departs from the general rule of constitutional avoidance and runs counter to the older, wiser judicial counsel not to pass on questions of constitutionality * * * unless such adjudication is unavoidable" (internal quotation marks and citations omitted).

Is the Court's praise for the Saucier approach of resolving constitutional issues at the outset reconcilable with its endorsement of constitutional avoidance as the "wiser judicial counsel"?[16]

---

[14] Saucier's holding on this issue mandated what County of Sacramento v. Lewis, 523 U.S. 833, 841 n.5 (1998), had previously described as "the better approach" (over the objections of Justices Stevens and Breyer). According to Lewis, the alternative of asking first whether an alleged right was clearly established, and thus avoiding the unresolved constitutional question in cases in which the defendants were entitled to prevail on immunity grounds, would tend to leave standards of official conduct "uncertain, to the detriment both of officials and individuals".

[15] See, *e.g.*, Leval, *Judging Under the Constitution: Dicta About Dicta*, 81 N.Y.U. L.Rev. 1249 (2007).

[16] For defense of the Saucier approach, see Wells, *The "Order-of-Battle" in Constitutional Litigation,* 60 SMU L.Rev. 539 (2007). Empirical studies disagree sharply about whether Saucier's order-of-decision rule had a significant impact in promoting the identification of new constitutional rights. Compare Leong, *The Saucier Qualified Immunity Experiment: An Empirical Analysis*, 36 Pepperdine L.Rev. 667, 670 (2009) (finding the "the decline in avoidance" mandated by Saucier "was accompanied only by a sharp increase in the percentage of cases in which courts explicitly held that no constitutional violation had occurred") and Healy, *The Rise of Unnecessary Constitutional Rulings,* 83 N.C.L.Rev. 847, 930 (2005) (reporting similar findings), with Note, *An Empirical Analysis of Section 1983 Qualified Immunity Actions and*

On its facts, Pearson upheld a claim of immunity on the ground that the asserted right was not clearly established; the Court did not reach the question whether the defendant's alleged conduct violated the Constitution at all.

(c) The Court's struggle with issues involving the proper order of decision in qualified immunity cases took a series of further, tortuous turns in Camreta v. Greene, 131 S.Ct. 2020 (2011) Paragraph 7(a), *supra*, with Justice Kagan's Court opinion pronouncing at one point that "[i]n general, courts should think hard, and then think hard again, before turning small cases into large ones" by ruling on the merits when a case could be easily dismissed on qualified immunity grounds. In early 2003, Camreta, a child services worker, and a deputy sheriff interviewed the respondent Greene's then 9-year-old daughter, S.G., at her Oregon elementary school about allegations that her father had sexually abused her. In a § 1983 action brought on her daughter's behalf, Greene alleged that the interview, conducted in the absence of parental consent, judicial authorization, or exigent circumstances, constituted an unreasonable seizure forbidden by the Fourth Amendment. Affirming the district court, the Ninth Circuit held for the defendants on the ground of qualified immunity, but also determined that "government officials investigating allegations of child abuse" should not assume "that a 'special need' automatically justifies dispensing with traditional Fourth Amendment protections in this context." It said that it had decided the merits before reaching the qualified immunity issue in order to "provide guidance to those charged with the difficult task of protecting child welfare within the confines of the Fourth Amendment". Although the plaintiff Greene did not seek review in the Supreme Court, Camreta, the prevailing defendant, did, alleging that the court of appeals' ruling on the merits of the Fourth Amendment issue interfered with his capacity as a child services worker to protect his clients against abuse.

Writing for the majority, Justice Kagan ultimately dismissed the case as moot. Because S.G. was nearly 18 and had moved out of state, she faced no realistic prospect of ever again being subjected to interrogation as a suspected victim of child abuse within the Ninth Circuit. The proper disposition, the Court held, was to vacate the part of the judgment holding that the defendants' conduct violated the Constitution (even though the part of the judgment involving qualified immunity should remain intact), in order to prevent Camreta from being bound by a lower court decision of which he had no opportunity to seek review.

Implications of Pearson v. Callahan, 62 Stan.L.Rev. 523 (2010) (concluding that the frequency of rights-affirming outcomes—in which courts found that the plaintiffs had alleged the violation of a constitutional right—"jumped from 34.2% of all pre-Saucier dispositions to 50.4% of all post-Saucier dispositions").

Examining circuit court practice in the wake of Pearson v. Callahan, Sampsell-Jones & Yauch, *Measuring Pearson in the Circuits*, 80 Fordham L.Rev. 623 (2011), conclude that circuit courts that had the option of ruling only on the immunity question followed the Saucier approach of deciding the merits question anyway in over 68 percent of all cases that cited Pearson in the calendar years 2009 and 2010.

See also Beermann, *Qualified Immunity and Constitutional Avoidance,* 2009 S.Ct.Rev. 139 (criticizing Pearson for giving lower courts "standardless, unreviewable discretion" about the order of decision in qualified immunity cases and urging a presumption in favor of ruling on the merits first); Jeffries, *Reversing the Order of Battle in Constitutional Torts,* 2009 S.Ct.Rev. 115 (arguing for a merits-first approach in cases involving constitutional rights that are difficult to enforce except through suits for money damages).

On its way to that determination, however, the Court pronounced on a number of issues potentially relevant to future qualified immunity cases presenting order-of-decision issues:

(1) The language of 28 U.S.C. § 1254(1), authorizing a petition for certiorari by "any party", permitted Camreta and a co-defendant to seek Supreme Court review even though they were prevailing parties in the Ninth Circuit.

(2) Camreta retained a continuing "personal stake" sufficient to satisfy the Article III case-or-controversy requirement: because he "regularly engages" in conduct that the court of appeals found to be illegal, "he suffers injury caused by the adverse constitutional ruling."

(3) The policy of avoidance of constitutional issues did not bar review on the unusual facts of the case. Nor did the policy of avoidance preclude the court of appeals from deciding the merits issue before holding for the defendants on qualified immunity grounds. In response to a suggestion that the court's ruling could not have the intended law-settling effect, the Court pronounced that the merits ruling was "[n]o mere dictum". (Why not?)

(4) Although the Court held that it had jurisdiction to review the Ninth Circuit's decision, it expressly left open the question whether a court of appeals could review a district court decision in an appeal taken by a prevailing defendant since "district court decisions—unlike those from courts of appeals—do not necessarily settle constitutional standards or prevent repeated claims of qualified immunity."

Justice Scalia, who cast a necessary fifth vote for the majority opinion, said that he did so because it "reasonably applies our precedents, strange though they may be". He added, however, that he would be willing to consider in an appropriate case whether it might be better "to end the extraordinary practice of ruling upon constitutional questions unnecessarily when the defendant possesses qualified immunity."

Justice Sotomayor, joined by Justice Breyer, agreed with the Court that the case was moot and that vacatur was the appropriate disposition but thought it improper to reach the "difficult" question of whether a prevailing party was entitled to seek review of a court of appeals decision.

Justice Kennedy, joined by Justice Thomas, dissented. In his view, review at the behest of a prevailing party violated the fundamental precept that appellate review will lie only to correct judgments, not to revise statements in lower-court opinions. According to him, Camreta had no more standing to prosecute an appeal than would any other social worker or police officer. The Court, he concluded, had erred by providing the lower courts with "special permission to reach the merits" in qualified immunity cases when "settled principles of constitutional avoidance would [otherwise] apply."

Does the unusual posture of the Camreta case expose the Court's recent order-of-decision cases as resting on untenably shaky jurisprudential foundations?[17]

---

[17] In assessing the Court's commitment to the current order-of-decision regime, note that less than one week after the decision in Camreta, the Court, in Ashcroft v. al-Kidd, 131 S.Ct. 2074 (2011)—in an opinion written by Justice Scalia and joined by Justices Kennedy and Thomas—accepted "that lower courts have discretion to decide which of the two prongs of qualified-immunity analysis to tackle first" and reasserted its own authority, when a court of appeals has ruled on both, to reverse erroneous rulings that a constitutional right exists even when upholding a defendant's entitlement to qualified immunity: "Although not necessary to

(9) Official Immunity in State Law Actions. The immunity of *state* officials in actions based on state law is itself governed by state law, for absent wholly arbitrary action by the state, there is no distinctive federal interest. See Martinez v. California, 444 U.S. 277 (1980). This rule applies even in actions that fall within the federal courts' jurisdiction. See, *e.g.*, Oyler v. National Guard Ass'n, 743 F.2d 545 (7th Cir.1984).

State law actions against federal officials raise more complicated issues. Prior to 1988, in state law tort actions against a federal officer, federal common law had established a shield of absolute immunity from damages liability for actions within the "outer perimeter of [the official's] line of duty". Barr v. Matteo, 360 U.S. 564 (1959) (plurality opinion). In 1988, the Federal Employees Liability Reform and Tort Compensation Act, 102 Stat. 4563, amended 28 U.S.C. § 2679(b), (d) to make the Federal Tort Claims Act (FTCA) the *exclusive* remedy for common law torts committed by federal officials in the course of their official duties. Under § 2679(d) as amended, if the Attorney General or a designee certifies that an employee who has been sued was acting within the scope of employment, the proceeding will be re-designated as a suit against the United States; if pending in state court, the suit will be removed to federal court, and the plaintiff may recover only if the United States is liable under the FTCA.

---

reverse an erroneous judgment, doing so ensures that courts do not insulate constitutional decisions at the frontiers of the law from our review or inadvertently undermine the values qualified immunity seeks to promote. The former occurs when the constitutional law question is wrongly decided; the latter when what is not clearly established is held to be so."

In al-Kidd, a unanimous Court (Justice Kagan did not participate) agreed that the alleged actions of former Attorney General John Ashcroft in causing the detention of suspected terrorists as "material witnesses" to crimes (as authorized by a federal statute), even in the absence of any intent actually to call them as witnesses, did not violate any clearly established constitutional rights. All participating Justices also accepted that the Court had jurisdiction to decide whether any actual right was violated, even though it would suffice to hold that Ashcroft deserved to prevail on immunity grounds. Justices Ginsburg, Breyer, and Sotomayor nevertheless concurred in the judgment only. In their view, the merits issue involved a number of complexities that the majority had not adequately reckoned with and that were better left for another case.

Following al-Kidd, would it be fair to say that the Justices view the problems presented in Camreta as limited to cases in which a defendant who has successfully asserted a qualified immunity defense seeks review of an adverse merits decision *and* the plaintiff does not seek review of the qualified immunity ruling?

Pfander, *Resolving the Qualified Immunity Dilemma: Constitutional Tort Claims for Nominal Damages*, 111 Colum.L.Rev. 1601 (2011), argues that courts should allow plaintiffs in § 1983 and Bivens cases to avoid both the qualified immunity defense and worries about order-of-battle issues by seeking only nominal damages on the order of $1. Given the unavailability of significant attorneys' fees when a plaintiff recovers nominal damages only, see, *e.g.*, Farrar v. Hobby, 506 U.S. 103 (1992), how many parties could afford to pursue the type of action that Pfander proposes? With district court decisions generally having no binding precedential effect, and apparently being unable to create "clearly established" law, what incentives would defendants or their employers have to mount defenses against such suits as might be brought?

NOTE ON THE IMMUNITY OF GOVERNMENT OFFICERS FROM RELIEF OTHER THAN DAMAGES

A. Civil Actions Against Officers Exercising Legislative Functions

(1) The Eastland and Consumers Union Cases. In Eastland v. United States Servicemen's Fund, 421 U.S. 491 (1975), a Senate Committee subpoenaed the bank records of an organization that was critical of the Vietnam War. The organization sued the Chair of the Subcommittee and others to enjoin enforcement of the subpoenas as a violation of the First Amendment. The Supreme Court, without extended consideration, held that the suit was barred by the Speech or Debate Clause: "Just as a criminal prosecution infringes upon the independence which the Clause is designed to preserve, a private civil action, whether for an injunction or damages, creates a distraction and forces Members to divert their time, energy, and attention from their legislative tasks to defend the litigation".

Immunity from injunctive relief was extended to state officials acting in a legislative capacity in Supreme Court of Virginia v. Consumers Union of the U.S., Inc., 446 U.S. 719 (1980). There a consumer group sued, *inter alia*, the Supreme Court of Virginia and its Chief Justice under § 1983, seeking to enjoin (as inconsistent with the First Amendment) state bar rules restricting plaintiffs' ability to gather information about lawyers' fees. A three-judge federal court ultimately awarded the injunctive relief sought, as well as attorney's fees under 42 U.S.C. § 1988, against the Supreme Court of Virginia and the Chief Justice in his official capacity. On appeal, the Supreme Court ruled that officials acting in a legislative capacity could not be enjoined.

The Court first reasoned that "in promulgating the disciplinary rules the Virginia Supreme Court acted in a legislative capacity". Given the decision in Eastland, and the Court's general practice of "equat[ing] the legislative immunity to which state legislators are entitled under § 1983 to that accorded Congressmen under the Constitution", there was little doubt that a state legislator would be immune from suit seeking an injunction. Even conceding that not all officials exercising delegated rulemaking power are necessarily immune from suit, the Court rejected the contention that "in *no* circumstances do those who exercise delegated legislative power enjoy legislative immunity". The Supreme Court of Virginia was "exercising the State's entire legislative power"; its members were the state's legislators with respect to regulation of the Bar, and they could not be enjoined in that capacity.

The injunction was upheld, however, under a different theory. The Supreme Court noted that the Virginia court performed non-legislative functions in connection with attorney discipline—it both adjudicated (on appeal) violations of bar disciplinary rules and had independent enforcement authority. "We need not decide whether judicial immunity would bar prospective relief, for we believe that the Virginia Court and its chief justice properly were held liable in their enforcement capacities", much as prosecutors—who enjoy absolute immunity from damages liability—may be enjoined from enforcing laws that violate the Constitution.

Was the Court in Eastland justified in extending Speech or Debate Clause immunity to actions seeking prospective relief? To what extent do such lawsuits threaten to inhibit legislators from the fearless discharge of their duties, or to create injustice for individual legislators, given that Congress employs a legal staff to defend these actions?

As Consumers Union itself shows, the extension of legislative immunity is relatively unimportant in suits seeking relief from unconstitutional legislation, precisely because enforcement officials are amenable to suit. But in legislative investigations, there may be no potential defendants other than legislators and their aides. Does Eastland mean that the only way to obtain judicial review of the constitutionality of committee process is to risk contempt?[1] Contrast the Court's argument in Consumers Union that prosecutors must be amenable to prospective relief, for otherwise "putative plaintiffs would have to await the institution of state-court proceedings against them in order to assert their federal constitutional claims". If an individual is held in contempt of Congress and detained, would legislators be immune from an action seeking a writ of habeas corpus? If so, is there no remedy whatsoever? If not, can habeas relief after contempt and injunctive relief before contempt really be distinguished with respect to their impact on legislative independence?

(2) The Yonkers Litigation. Some of the issues discussed in Paragraph (1) were presented, but not resolved, in Spallone v. United States, 493 U.S. 265 (1990). In this case, arising out of a civil rights action brought against the city of Yonkers, both the city and four members of the city council were held in civil contempt (and fines were imposed) for failing to enact a public housing ordinance required by a consent decree. After affirmance by the court of appeals, the Supreme Court denied the city's petition for certiorari but granted the petitions of the individual members. The members argued, *inter alia*, that under the doctrine of legislative immunity, they could not be held in contempt for voting against the ordinance. Without ruling on that argument, the Court held, 5–4, that "in view of the 'extraordinary' nature of" a civil contempt sanction against local legislative officers for refusing to vote as ordered, the district court "should have proceeded with such contempt sanctions first against the city alone in order to secure compliance with the remedial order. Only if that approach failed to produce compliance within a reasonable time should the question of imposing contempt sanctions against petitioners even have been considered".

The four dissenters argued that the district court had not abused its remedial discretion by imposing civil contempt fines on the individual members. With respect to the claim of legislative immunity, the dissenters distinguished the question presented from the question of the immunity of legislators from suit by a private plaintiff. Once the district court found, in an action brought against the city, "that the city (through acts of its council) had engaged in a pattern and practice of racial discrimination in housing and [the court] had issued a valid remedial order, the members of the city council became obliged to respect the limits thereby placed on their legislative independence".

Does the Court's later decision in New York v. United States, discussed at p. 447, *supra*, have any bearing on the issues presented in the Yonkers litigation?

---

[1]   Indeed, in Eastland itself, because the subpoenas were directed at the bank, the plaintiff lacked even that option.

B.   Civil Actions Against Officers Exercising Judicial Functions

The question left open in Consumers Union—whether judicial immunity bars suits for prospective relief—was dealt with in Pulliam v. Allen, 466 U.S. 522 (1984). Pulliam, a state magistrate, had a practice in criminal cases involving nonjailable offenses of setting bail and incarcerating persons who could not post it. Two arrestees subjected to this policy brought suit against the magistrate under § 1983, seeking injunctive and declaratory relief. The district court ruled that the practice was unconstitutional and enjoined Pulliam from continuing it. The court also awarded the plaintiffs $7,691 in costs, of which $7,038 was attorney's fees awarded under 42 U.S.C. § 1988. Dividing 5–4, the Supreme Court upheld the injunction and the fee award.

Subsequently, Congress overruled the Court's decision in The Federal Courts Improvement Act of 1996, Pub.L.No. 104–317, § 309(b)–(c), 110 Stat. 3847. That act amended § 1988 to bar the collection of any costs, including attorney's fees, from judicial officers in suits against them arising from actions taken in their judicial capacity, and also amended § 1983 to bar suits against judicial officers for injunctive relief, except when declaratory relief was unavailable or the officer was acting contrary to a prior declaratory decree.

C.   Civil Actions Against Officers Exercising Executive Functions

(1) General Principles. Consumers Union indicates that executive officials in general have no immunity from suit for prospective relief—a conclusion supported by the entire history of suits against officers as a means of ensuring governmental accountability.

(2) The Case of the President. The Supreme Court has addressed questions involving possible presidential immunity from non-damages relief in only a few cases, but has suggested that just as the President's "unique office" mandates a special presidential immunity from damages liability, Nixon v. Fitzgerald, p. 1046, *supra*, it might support some form of presidential immunity from other judicial remedies.

(a) In Mississippi v. Johnson, 71 U.S. (4 Wall.) 475 (1866), the state, in an original action in the Supreme Court, sought to restrain the President from executing provisions of the Reconstruction Acts that it alleged to be unconstitutional. Without ruling on the constitutionality of the challenged acts, the Court dismissed the action. After referring to cases on mandamus against executive officers, and expressly reserving the question whether the President may be ordered to perform a purely ministerial act, Chief Justice Chase said:

"Very different is the duty of the President in the exercise of the power to see that the laws are faithfully executed, and among these laws the acts named in the bill. By the first of these acts he is required to assign generals to command in the several military districts, and to detail sufficient military force to enable such officers to discharge their duties under the law. By the supplementary act, other duties are imposed on the several commanding generals, and these duties must necessarily be performed under the supervision of the President as commander-in-chief. The duty thus imposed on the President is in no just sense ministerial. It is purely executive and political. * * *

"It is true that in the instance before us the interposition of the court is not sought to enforce action by the Executive under constitutional legislation, but to restrain such action under legislation alleged to be unconstitutional. But we are unable to perceive that this circumstance takes the case out of the general principles which forbid judicial interference with the exercise of Executive discretion. * * *

"The impropriety of such interference will be clearly seen upon consideration of its possible consequences.

"Suppose the bill filed and the injunction prayed for allowed. If the President refuse obedience, it is needless to observe that the court is without power to enforce its process. If, on the other hand, the President complies with the order of the court and refuses to execute the acts of Congress, is it not clear that a collision may occur between the executive and legislative departments of the government?"

As is evident from the quoted language, the Court's analysis in Johnson subsumed the question of presidential immunity under concerns involving the scope of unreviewable executive discretion and the hazards of creating a direct conflict between Congress and the President—hazards that may have achieved a historical zenith in the face-off between President Johnson and a Republican-dominated Reconstruction Congress.

(b) In United States v. Nixon, 418 U.S. 683 (1974), the Supreme Court unanimously affirmed an order requiring President Nixon to respond to a grand jury subpoena seeking, *inter alia*, tape recordings of presidential conversations. The Court stressed the special importance of the government's demonstrated need for evidence in a criminal trial. It did not cite Mississippi v. Johnson, and the question of presidential immunity from process was submerged in a discussion of the merits of the President's claim of executive privilege.

(c) In Franklin v. Massachusetts, 505 U.S. 788 (1992), plaintiffs challenging the reapportionment of congressional seats following the 1990 census named President Bush as well as various other federal officials as defendants. In an opinion for a plurality of four Justices, Justice O'Connor stated: "We have left open the question whether the President might be subject to a judicial injunction requiring the performance of a purely 'ministerial' duty, Mississippi v. Johnson, *supra*, at 498–99, and we have held that the President may be subject to a subpoena to provide information relevant to an ongoing criminal prosecution, United States v. Nixon, *supra*, but in general 'this court has no jurisdiction of a bill to enjoin the President in the performance of his official duties' " (quoting Mississippi v. Johnson).

Justice Scalia concurred in the judgment. He noted that Mississippi v. Johnson "left open the question whether the President might be subject to a judicial injunction requiring the performance of a purely 'ministerial' duty", but argued that "no court has authority to direct the President to take an official act" or to enter a declaratory judgment with respect to the concededly nonministerial function presented in the case at bar.

(d) Several habeas corpus cases litigated in the Supreme Court have included the President as a named respondent, apparently without triggering any immunity-based objection. See Rasul v. Bush, 542 U.S. 466 (2004); Boumediene v. Bush, 553 U.S. 723 (2008).

(3) The Pertinence of Available Relief Against Presidential Subordinates. In Youngstown Sheet & Tube Co. v. Sawyer, 343 U.S. 579

(1952), the Supreme Court affirmed a decision by the district court to order the Secretary of Commerce to terminate a seizure of the nation's steel mills that had been ordered by President Truman. According to the Court, the President lacked constitutional authority to take over the mills in the absence of congressional authorization. If a mandatory injunction could be entered against the Secretary of Commerce, how often is it likely to make a practical difference whether the President has an immunity not shared by other executive officials from suits for non-damages relief?

CHAPTER X

JUDICIAL FEDERALISM: LIMITATIONS ON DISTRICT COURT JURISDICTION OR ITS EXERCISE

1. INTRODUCTION: THE COORDINATION OF CONCURRENT JURISDICTION IN A FEDERAL SYSTEM

Kline v. Burke Construction Company

260 U.S. 226, 43 S.Ct. 79, 67 L.Ed. 226 (1922).
Certiorari to the Circuit Court of Appeals for the Eighth Circuit.

■ MR. JUSTICE SUTHERLAND delivered the opinion of the Court.

[On February 16, 1920, Burke Construction Company, a Missouri corporation, brought an action in law in federal district court in Arkansas against petitioners (citizens of Arkansas), invoking diversity jurisdiction. The suit alleged breach of a contract under which Burke was to pave certain streets in the town of Texarkana.]

[On March 19, 1920, petitioners brought a suit in equity in an Arkansas Chancery Court against Burke and the sureties on the bond given for the faithful performance of the contract. The bill alleged that Burke had abandoned the contract; it sought an accounting for the work that had been done and that remained, and prayed for judgment in the sum of $88,000. Burke removed the equity suit to federal district court, which remanded the case to the Arkansas Chancery Court.]

[Both actions were in personam and sought money judgments; they presented substantially the same issues; and the defendant's answer and cross-complaint in each alleged, in substance, the matters set forth as complainant in the other. The principal difference between the suits was the addition of the sureties as defendants in the equitable action.

[In the federal action, following a mistrial, Burke sought to enjoin petitioners from further prosecuting the state court action. The federal district court denied the injunction, but the court of appeals reversed and remanded with instructions to issue the injunction.] From that decree the case comes here upon writ of certiorari.

Section 265 of the Judicial Code [the Anti-Injunction Act, now codified, as amended, as 28 U.S.C. § 2283] provides: "The writ of injunction shall not be granted by any court of the United States to stay

1061

proceedings in any court of a State, except in cases where such injunction may be authorized by any law relating to proceedings in bankruptcy." But this section is to be construed in connection with § 262 [the All Writs Act, now codified, as amended, as 28 U.S.C. § 1651], which authorizes the United States courts "to issue all writs not specifically provided for by statute, which may be necessary for the exercise of their respective jurisdictions, and agreeable to the usages and principles of law." It is settled that where a federal court has first acquired jurisdiction of the subject-matter of a cause, it may enjoin the parties from proceeding in a state court of concurrent jurisdiction where the effect of the action would be to defeat or impair the jurisdiction of the federal court. Where the action is *in rem* the effect is to draw to the federal court the possession or control, actual or potential, of the *res*, and the exercise by the state court of jurisdiction over the same *res* necessarily impairs, and may defeat, the jurisdiction of the federal court already attached. The converse of the rule is equally true, that where the jurisdiction of the state court has first attached, the federal court is precluded from exercising its jurisdiction over the same *res* to defeat or impair the state court's jurisdiction. * * *

But a controversy * * * over a mere question of personal liability does not involve the possession or control of a thing, and an action brought to enforce such a liability does not tend to impair or defeat the jurisdiction of the court in which a prior action for the same cause is pending. Each court is free to proceed in its own way and in its own time, without reference to the proceedings in the other court. Whenever a judgment is rendered in one of the courts and pleaded in the other, the effect of that judgment is to be determined by the application of the principles of *res adjudicata* by the court in which the action is still pending * * *. The rule, therefore, has become generally established that where the action first brought is *in personam* and seeks only a personal judgment, another action for the same cause in another jurisdiction is not precluded. [Citing numerous cases.]

* * * In the case now under consideration, however, the court below held otherwise, upon the ground that: "By the Constitution of the United States (article 3, § 2, and the acts of Congress) the constitutional right was granted to the Burke Company to ask and to have a trial and adjudication . . . by the federal court." * * * The force of the cases above cited is sought to be broken by the suggestion that in none of them was this question of constitutional right presented or considered.

The right of a litigant to maintain an action in a federal court on the ground that there is a controversy between citizens of different States is not one derived from the Constitution of the United States, unless in a very indirect sense. * * * Only the jurisdiction of the Supreme Court is derived directly from the Constitution. Every other court created by the general government derives its jurisdiction wholly from the authority of Congress. * * * A right which thus comes into existence only by virtue of an act of Congress * * * cannot well be described as a constitutional right. The Construction Company, however, had the undoubted right under the statute to invoke the jurisdiction of the federal court and that court was bound to take the case and proceed to judgment. It could not abdicate its authority or duty in favor of the state jurisdiction. But, while this is true, it is likewise true that the state court had jurisdiction of the suit instituted by petitioners. Indeed, since the case presented by that suit was such as to preclude its removal to the federal jurisdiction, the state jurisdiction in that particular suit was exclusive. It was, therefore, equally the duty of the state court to take the case and proceed to judgment. There can be no question of judicial supremacy, or of superiority of individual right. * * * The rank and authority of the courts are equal but both courts cannot possess or control the same thing at the same time, and any attempt to do so would result in unseemly conflict. The rule, therefore, that the court first acquiring jurisdiction shall proceed without interference from a court of the other jurisdiction is a rule of right and of law based upon necessity, and where the necessity, actual or potential, does not exist, the rule does not apply. Since that necessity does exist in actions *in rem* and does not exist in actions *in personam*, involving a question of personal liability only, the rule applies in the former but does not apply in the latter.

The decree of the Circuit Court of Appeals is therefore reversed and the case remanded to the District Court for further proceedings in conformity with this opinion.

———

NOTE ON THE COORDINATION OF OVERLAPPING STATE COURT AND FEDERAL COURT JURISDICTION

(1) The Prevalence of Overlapping Jurisdiction. State and federal jurisdiction overlap pervasively. The overlap emerges most clearly from 28 U.S.C. §§ 1331–32, which give the federal courts jurisdiction, *concurrently* with the state courts, over federal question and diversity cases. But it extends even to matters that at first glance appear to fall within the exclusive jurisdiction of the state or the federal courts. Consider, for example, a contractual dispute in which the defaulting party contends that the contract violates the federal antitrust or patent laws. If the promisee sues for breach of contract, then (if there is no diversity of citizenship) the state courts have exclusive jurisdiction. But if the promisor sues, under the federal statute in question, for declaratory or injunctive relief against contractual liability, then the federal courts have exclusive jurisdiction. Similarly, a claim that a state criminal statute is unconstitutional might be a defense to a state criminal prosecution (over which the state courts have exclusive jurisdiction) or the basis for a federal § 1983 action seeking declaratory or injunctive relief against the statute's enforcement (which would fall within the concurrent jurisdiction of the federal courts). More generally, whether an asserted federal right is a "defense" or provides an "affirmative claim for relief" cannot be determined *a priori*. The answer depends on a variety of remedial and substantive rules.

(2) Accommodation of Jurisdictional Overlap. The question of how to accommodate overlapping proceedings in state and federal courts raises complex issues of legislative and judicial policy.

(a) Kline suggests one solution: Apart from actions *in rem*, there is no barrier to overlapping litigations, but the law of preclusion will apply once one of the actions has come to judgment. Is that approach sound in view of the duplication that it invites? Consider, *e.g.*, Burns v. Watler, 931 F.2d 140 (1st Cir.1991), where the court of appeals reversed, as an abuse of discretion, a federal district court's stay of a diversity action for personal injuries—even though a virtually identical state court action, filed by plaintiff one day after filing the federal action, was much further along.

(b) A different solution would give priority (absolute or presumptive) to the suit first filed. See, *e.g.*, Rehnquist, *Taking Comity Seriously: How to Neutralize the Abstention Doctrine*, 46 Stan.L.Rev. 1049, 1068 (1994) (advocating replacement of all of the various abstention doctrines—under which a federal court may dismiss or stay proceedings within its statutory jurisdiction—with the rule that "[a] federal court should abstain if, and only if, the federal plaintiff has an adequate opportunity to litigate his federal claim in a duplicative suit already pending in state court").[1]

Without doubt, a first-filed approach would sometimes generate a race to the courthouse, but that race might be less wasteful than the race to judgment that current doctrine invites. Still, should the dice be loaded so heavily in favor of the first-filed action? Rehnquist's affirmative answer is based on the contention that the Constitution is neutral as between state and federal forums. Even if this is so, can the same be said of the federal jurisdictional statutes? Though §§ 1331–32 confer concurrent jurisdiction in federal question and diversity cases, they operate, in conjunction with the removal statute (§ 1441), to favor federal court adjudication—for when the parties disagree about forum, the preference of either party for a federal court generally prevails.

(c) Still another approach might attempt to determine, either in particular cases or in general categories, which forum should be preferred, and to require the other to desist (perhaps even via an anti-suit injunction, if necessary). See, *e.g.*, Redish, *Intersystemic Redundancy and Federal Court Power: Proposing a Zero Tolerance Solution to the Duplicative Litigation Problem*, 75 Notre Dame L.Rev. 1347 (2000) (arguing that a federal court, after determining that parallel suits are pending, should decide which of the cases will go forward and then either enjoin the state court action or abstain from adjudication and permit the state court action to proceed).[2] See also Field, *Removal Reform: A Solution for Federal Question Jurisdiction, Forum Shopping, and Duplicative State Litigation*, 88 Ind.L.J. 611 (2013) (proposing to reduce duplicative litigation by authorizing removal to federal court of cases that involve federal defenses or are otherwise "likely to turn upon federal law").

(d) A distinct question of accommodation is whether federal courts should in some circumstances decline to exercise jurisdiction in order to permit state court adjudication of a state law issue, even when no state proceeding is yet pending. See Sections 3(A–C), 3(E), *infra*.

(3) Special Problems in Class Actions and Complex Litigation. Class actions and multi-party, multi-forum litigation—involving, for example, hazardous products or mass disasters—give rise to especially acute and sometimes distinctive problems of jurisdictional overlap. Because there are

---

[1] See also Currie, *The Federal Courts and the American Law Institute (II)*, 36 U.Chi.L.Rev. 268, 335 (1969).

[2] Although the Anti-Injunction Act, 28 U.S.C. § 2283, generally bars federal injunctions against state proceedings, Professor Redish suggests that they might be permissible under a broad reading of the "in aid of jurisdiction" exception to the Act. Compare pp. 1083–1086, *infra*, suggesting that this exception has been given a far narrower range.

For discussion of the accommodation of overlapping jurisdiction between federal courts and courts of another nation, see Treviro de Coale, *Stay, Dismiss, Enjoin, or Abstain? A Survey of Foreign Parallel Litigation in the Federal Courts of the United States*, 17 B.U.Int'l L.J. 79 (1999).

as many potential plaintiffs in class actions as there are class members, lawyers have great flexibility to determine when and where to file class actions. Multiple filings are apparently the norm, with the same lawyers initiating the parallel suits in some cases and other groups of plaintiffs' attorneys filing competing lawsuits in other jurisdictions in other instances. The resulting problems can be considerable for all concerned. From the perspective of defendants, some state courts are too willing to certify inappropriate and even frivolous class actions and thereby subject them to unreasonable risks of liability and pressures to enter settlements. From the perspective of plaintiffs, the possibility of multiple suits in multiple jurisdictions—a judicially approved settlement in any of which would typically have preclusive effect in all of the others—creates incentives for class counsel in the various actions to want to be the first to settle so that they can collect their contingent fees. In this context, "reverse auctions" can result in which the plaintiffs' lawyers in the dueling lawsuits compete with one another to offer the lowest settlement price to the defendants. See Coffee, *Class Wars: The Dilemma of the Mass Tort Class Action*, 95 Colum.L.Rev. 1343, 1370–72 (1995) (describing the incentives that produce "reverse auctions").

A number of commentators have argued that in this context the traditional approach of Kline v. Burke is misplaced. Wholly apart from being wasteful, competing class actions give rise to fundamental problems of fairness, especially but not exclusively to plaintiff class members who have no effective control of the litigation to which they are parties and whose interests may be poorly represented by class counsel. Given the problems generated by multi-party, multi-forum litigation, the chair of the Civil Rules Advisory Committee of the Judicial Conference of the United States, Judge David Levi, concluded in an April 2002 memorandum to the Advisory Committee that "[t]he question is not whether something should be done, but what should be done and by whom." Levi, *Perspectives on Rule 23, Including the Problem of Overlapping Classes*, reprinted in *Class Action Reform Gets a Shot in the Arm*, 69 Def.Couns.J. 263 (2002).[3]

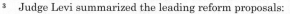

---

[3] Judge Levi summarized the leading reform proposals:

"One means of doing something about the problems created by overlapping class actions might be through new provisions in the Civil Rules. * * * Rule 23, for example, might address the effect one federal court should give to the refusal by another federal court to certify a class action or to approve a class-action settlement. * * * [But p]rovisions that might address overlapping class actions in state courts [would invite serious objections under the Enabling Act and the Anti-Injunction Act, discussed pp. 1068–1089, *infra*].

" * * * [Another] approach, exemplified in several of the bills that have been before Congress, would establish minimal diversity jurisdiction [based on diversity between at least one plaintiff class member and at least one defendant] in federal court for class actions of a certain size or scope. [A version of this approach has now been enacted and is discussed in text.] * * *

"Another approach would be to rely on case-specific determinations whether a particular litigation pattern is better brought into federal court control. This approach could be implemented by authorizing the Judicial Panel on Multidistrict Litigation to determine whether a particular set of litigations should be removed to federal court. * * *

"Yet another approach would be to authorize individual federal courts to coordinate federal litigation with overlapping state court actions, by enjoining state court actions, if necessary, when the state court actions threaten to disrupt litigation filed under one of the present subject-matter jurisdiction statutes. While this approach may have the apparent advantage of leaving federal jurisdiction where it is, it also has

Congress responded to some of the problems that can confront defendants in multiple class actions in the Class Action Fairness Act of 2005 (CAFA), which is more comprehensively discussed in Chap. XIII, pp. 1426–1430, *infra.* The central innovation of CAFA is to allow certain class actions to be brought in, or removed to, federal court based on minimal, rather than complete, diversity of citizenship. Under CAFA, defendants that fear state court certification of class actions in inappropriate cases can thus alleviate the threat by removing to federal court. A 2008 study concluded, however, that the federal courts "have embraced CAFA with coolness." Clermont & Eisenberg, *CAFA Judicata: A Tale of Waste and Politics*, 156 U.Pa.L.Rev. 1553, 1592 (2008); see also Lee & Willging, *The Impact of the Class Action Fairness Act on the Federal Courts: An Empirical Analysis of Filings and Removals,* 156 U.Pa.L.Rev. 1723, 1724–25 (2008) (finding "an increase in diversity class action filings and removals in the federal courts * * * [though] a less dramatic increase than some anticipated").

CAFA notably contains no provision conferring comparable protections on "absent class members"—those who are not named plaintiffs in class actions in state court—for it gives them no comparable removal option and, accordingly, leaves them vulnerable to the risk of reverse auctions. (If class counsel behave self-interestedly and offer bargain-rate settlements, then defendants cannot be counted on to remove a state court action against them to federal court.) Although an earlier version of CAFA would have permitted absent class members to remove state court class actions to federal court, the relevant provision was deleted in the final Senate bill.

Noting that CAFA lists among its purposes the goal of protecting "absent class members from the faithless or collusive behavior of their class counsel" while failing to provide "a mechanism by which absent class plaintiffs can act independently of class counsel to move their lawsuits into federal court," Wolff, *Federal Jurisdiction and Due Process in the Era of the Nationwide Class Action*, 156 U.Pa.L.Rev. 2035, 2038–39 (2008), argues that the Act should be read as impliedly authorizing federal courts with jurisdiction over a class action to enjoin any parallel state court class actions where necessary to protect the interests of the plaintiff class. How significant is it that Congress, when enacting CAFA, failed to provide any express statutory mechanism by which absent class members in state court actions could insist upon a resolution of their claims by a federal court? In the absence of legislation, the lower federal courts have continued to struggle with the questions whether and when they may issue injunctions against competing state court class actions within the structure of existing doctrine. For further discussion, see pp. 1084–1086, *infra.*

(4) The Subjects of Federal Deference. At least prior to modern concerns about class actions, the central disputes about how to handle overlapping state and federal jurisdiction have not involved private suits, as in Kline, but suits against state and local officials. Exercise of the jurisdiction that was sanctioned in Ex parte Young, p. 922, *supra*, and the Home Telephone case,

---

the obvious disadvantage of potential conflict and tension between the court systems. * * *

"But the problems that persist with respect to overlapping and competing class actions are precisely the problems of multi-state coordination that can claim high priority in allocating work to the federal courts. * * * The apparent need is for a single, authoritative tribunal that can definitively resolve those problems that have eluded resolution and that affect litigation that is nationwide or multi-state in scope."

p. 981, *supra*, brought about a major shift in the distribution of power between state and nation. Because of its association with decisions enjoining state laws as unconstitutional under the jurisprudence of the Lochner era, the power sanctioned by Ex parte Young became, in Judge Friendly's words, "the *bête noire* of liberals" until the Lochner era had decisively passed. Friendly, Federal Jurisdiction: A General View 3 n. 7 (1973). That power became more salient, and also more attractive to liberals, with the expansion of non-economic individual rights beginning under the Warren Court.

(5) Statutory and Judicial Limitations on the Exercise of Federal Jurisdiction. The judicial power upheld in Young and Home Telegraph—which made possible federal injunctions against the enforcement of state laws, including state laws not yet construed by state courts—led to both congressional and, significantly, judicial responses that continue to dominate the doctrinal structure in cases in which they apply.

(a) The early congressional response was embodied in three provisions of the Judicial Code:

(i) a requirement (all but a fragment of which was repealed in 1976) that a district court of three judges be convened to hear actions seeking injunctive relief against state statutes or administrative orders alleged to be unconstitutional;

(ii) the Johnson Act of 1934, now 28 U.S.C. § 1342, limiting federal district court jurisdiction to enjoin state public utility rate orders; and

(iii) the Tax Injunction Act of 1937, now 28 U.S.C. § 1341, limiting federal district court jurisdiction to enjoin the collection of state taxes.

These provisions are considered in Section 2 of this Chapter, which begins with consideration of the Anti-Injunction Act, first enacted in 1793.

(b) The federal courts themselves have formulated additional doctrines under which they will abstain from adjudicating cases that fall within the literal terms of congressional grants of jurisdiction, so as to permit adjudication in state tribunals. Section 3 of this Chapter considers these abstention doctrines.

(c) Both the statutory and judge-made doctrines raise important and diverse questions, including: (i) How can courts promote effective judicial administration in light of the pervasiveness of overlap and potential duplication? (ii) What are the distinctive qualities of federal and of state courts, and in which cases should those respective qualities be viewed as (in)dispensable?[4] and (iii) What is the appropriate role of the federal courts in interpreting statutes, and in formulating judge-made doctrines, limiting the exercise of broad congressional grants of jurisdiction?

---

[4] When the limitations on federal district court jurisdiction described in this Chapter were created, state court decisions striking down a treaty or Act of Congress, or holding valid a state or local statute challenged on federal grounds, were reviewable as of right in the Supreme Court. In 1988, Congress eliminated mandatory appeals from state court decisions. See Chap. V, Sec. 1, *supra*. Does the disappearance of guaranteed federal review by the Supreme Court affect the appropriateness of statutory or judicially fashioned limits on the original jurisdiction of the district courts, especially to entertain constitutional challenges to state laws?

2. STATUTORY LIMITATIONS ON FEDERAL COURT JURISDICTION

A. THE ANTI-INJUNCTION ACT

Atlantic Coast Line R.R. v. Brotherhood of Locomotive Engineers

398 U.S. 281, 90 S.Ct. 1739, 26 L.Ed.2d 234 (1970).
Certiorari to the United States Court of Appeals for the Fifth Circuit.

■ MR. JUSTICE BLACK delivered the opinion of the Court.

Congress in 1793 * * * provided that in federal courts "a writ of injunction [shall not] be granted to stay proceedings in any court of a state." Act of March 2, 1793, § 5, 1 Stat. 335. Although certain exceptions to this general prohibition have been added, that statute, directing that state courts shall remain free from interference by federal courts, has remained in effect until this time. Today that amended statute provides:

> "A court of the United States may not grant an injunction to stay proceedings in a State court except as expressly authorized by Act of Congress, or where necessary in aid of its jurisdiction, or to protect or effectuate its judgments." 28 U.S.C. § 2283.

Despite the existence of this longstanding prohibition, in this case a federal court did enjoin the petitioner, Atlantic Coast Line Railroad Co. (ACL), from invoking an injunction issued by a Florida state court which prohibited certain picketing by respondent Brotherhood of Locomotive Engineers (BLE). The case arose in the following way.

In 1967 BLE began picketing the Moncrief Yard, a switching yard located near Jacksonville, Florida, and wholly owned and operated by ACL.[2] As soon as this picketing began ACL went into federal court seeking an injunction. When the federal judge denied the request, ACL immediately went into state court and there succeeded in obtaining an injunction. No further legal action was taken in this dispute until two years later in 1969, after this Court's decision in Brotherhood of Railroad Trainmen v. Jacksonville Terminal Co., 394 U.S. 369. In that case the Court considered the validity of a state injunction against picketing by the BLE and other unions at the Jacksonville Terminal, located immediately next to Moncrief Yard. The Court * * * concluded that the unions had a federally protected right to picket under the Railway Labor Act, 45 U.S.C. § 151 et seq., and that that right could not be interfered with by state court injunctions. Immediately after a petition for

---

[2] There is no present labor dispute between the ACL and the BLE or any other ACL employees. ACL became involved in this case as a result of a labor dispute between the Florida East Coast Railway Co. (FEC) and its employees. FEC cars are hauled into and out of Moncrief Yard and switched around to make up trains in that yard. The BLE picketed the yard, encouraging ACL employees not to handle any FEC cars. * * *

rehearing was denied in that case, 394 U.S. 1024 (1969), the respondent BLE filed a motion in state court to dissolve the Moncrief Yard injunction, arguing that under the Jacksonville Terminal decision the injunction was improper. The state judge refused to dissolve the injunction, holding that this Court's Jacksonville Terminal decision was not controlling. The union did not elect to appeal that decision directly, but instead went back into the federal court and requested an injunction against the enforcement of the state court injunction. The District Judge granted the injunction * * *. The Court of Appeals summarily affirmed on the parties' stipulation * * *.

I

* * * While all the reasons that led Congress to adopt [the anti-injunction statute in 1793] are not wholly clear, it is certainly likely that one reason stemmed from the essentially federal nature of our national government. When this Nation was established by the Constitution each State surrendered only a part of its sovereign power to the national government. But those powers that were not surrendered were retained by the States and unless a State was restrained by "the supreme Law of the Land" as expressed in the Constitution, laws or treaties of the United States, it was free to exercise those retained powers as it saw fit. One of the reserved powers was the maintenance of state judicial systems for the decision of legal controversies. * * *

While the lower federal courts were given certain powers in the [Judiciary Act of 1789], they were not given any power to review directly cases from state courts, and they have not been given such powers since that time. Only the Supreme Court was authorized to review on direct appeal the decisions of state courts. Thus from the beginning we have had in this country two essentially separate legal systems. Each system proceeds independently from the other with ultimate review in this Court of the federal questions raised in either system. Understandably this dual court system was bound to lead to conflicts and frictions. Litigants who foresaw the possibility of more favorable treatment in one or the other system would predictably hasten to invoke the powers of whichever court it was believed would present the best chance of success. Obviously this dual system could not function if state and federal courts were free to fight each other for control of a particular case. Thus, in order to make the dual system work and "to prevent needless friction between state and federal courts," Oklahoma Packing Co. v. Oklahoma Gas & Electric Co., 309 U.S. 4, 9 (1940), it was necessary to work out lines of demarcation between the two systems. Some of these limits were spelled out in the 1789 Act. Others have been added by later statutes as well as judicial decisions. The 1793 anti-injunction Act was at least in part a response to these pressures.

On its face the present Act is an absolute prohibition against enjoining state court proceedings, unless the injunction falls within one of three specifically defined exceptions. The respondent here has intimated that the Act only establishes a "principle of comity," not a binding rule on the power of the federal courts. The argument implies that in certain circumstances a federal court may enjoin state court proceedings even if that action cannot be justified by any of the three exceptions. We cannot accept any such contention. In 1954 when this Court interpreted this statute, it stated: "This is not a statute conveying a broad general policy for appropriate *ad hoc* application. Legislative policy is here expressed in a clear-cut prohibition qualified only by specifically defined exceptions." Amalgamated Clothing Workers v. Richman Brothers, 348 U.S. 511, 515–516 (1955). * * * [W]e * * * adhere to that position and hold that any injunction against state court proceedings otherwise proper under general equitable principles must be based on one of the specific statutory exceptions to § 2283 if it is to be upheld. Moreover since the statutory prohibition against such injunctions in part rests on the fundamental constitutional independence of the States and their courts, the exceptions should not be enlarged by loose statutory construction. Proceedings in state courts should normally be allowed to continue unimpaired by intervention of the lower federal courts, with relief from error, if any, through the state appellate courts and ultimately this Court.

II

In this case the Florida Circuit Court enjoined the union's intended picketing, and the United States District Court enjoined the railroad "from giving effect to or availing themselves of the benefits of" that state court order. Both sides agree that although this federal injunction is in terms directed only at the railroad it is an injunction "to stay proceedings in a state court." It is settled that the prohibition of § 2283 cannot be evaded by addressing the order to the parties or prohibiting utilization of the results of a completed state proceeding. * * * Thus if the injunction against the Florida court proceedings is to be upheld, it must be "expressly authorized by Act of Congress," "necessary in aid of [the District Court's] jurisdiction," or "to protect or effectuate [that court's] judgments."

Neither party argues that there is any express Congressional authorization for injunctions in this situation and we agree with that conclusion. The respondent union does contend that the injunction was proper either as a means to protect or effectuate the District Court's 1967 order, or in aid of that court's jurisdiction. We do not think that either alleged basis can be supported.

A

The argument based on protecting the 1967 order is not clearly expressed, but in essence it appears to run as follows: In 1967 the railroad sought a temporary restraining order which the union opposed. In the course of deciding that request, the United States District Court determined that the union had a federally protected right to picket Moncrief Yard and that this right could not be interfered with by state courts. When the Florida Circuit Court enjoined the picketing, the United States District Court could, in order to protect and effectuate its prior determination, enjoin enforcement of the state court injunction. Although the record on this point is not unambiguously clear, we conclude that no such interpretation of the 1967 order can be supported.

When the railroad initiated the federal suit it filed a complaint with three counts, each based entirely on alleged violations of federal law. The first two counts alleged violations of the Railway Labor Act, and the third alleged a violation of that Act and the Interstate Commerce Act as well. Each of the counts concluded with a prayer for an injunction against the picketing. * * * [T]he union * * * appeared at a hearing on a motion for a temporary restraining order and argued against the issuance of such an order. The union argued that it was a party to a labor dispute with the FEC,* that it had exhausted the administrative remedies required by the Railway Labor Act, and that it was thus free to engage in "self-help," or concerted economic activity. Then the union argued that such activity could not be enjoined by the federal court. In an attempt to clarify the basis of this argument the District Judge asked: "You are basing your case solely on the Norris-LaGuardia Act?" The union's lawyer replied: "Right. I think at this point of the argument, since Norris-LaGuardia is clearly in point here." At no point during the entire argument did either side refer to state law, the effects of that law on the picketing, or the possible preclusion of state remedies as a result of overriding federal law. The next day the District Court entered an order denying the requested restraining order. In relevant part that order included these conclusions of law:

"3. The parties of the BLE-FEC 'major dispute,' having exhausted the procedures of the Railway Labor Act, are now free to engage in self-help. * * *

"4. The conduct of the FEC pickets and that of the responding ACL employees are a part of the FEC-BLE major dispute. * * *

"7. The Norris-LaGuardia Act, 29 U.S.C. § 101, and the Clayton Act, 29 U.S.C. § 52, are applicable to the conduct of the defendants here involved."

In this Court the union asserts that the determination that it was "free to engage in self-help" was a determination that it had a federally protected right to picket and that state law could not be invoked to negate that right. The railroad, on the other hand, argues that the order merely determined that the *federal* court could not enjoin the picketing, in large part because of the general prohibition in the Norris-LaGuardia Act, against issuance by federal courts of injunctions in labor disputes. * * *

[After reviewing the record, the Court stated that it] conclusively shows that neither the parties themselves nor the District Court construed the 1967 order as the union now contends it should be construed. Rather we are convinced that the union in effect tried to get the Federal District Court to decide that the state court judge was wrong in distinguishing the Jacksonville Terminal decision. Such an attempt to seek appellate review of a state decision in the Federal District Court cannot be justified as necessary "to protect or effectuate" the 1967 order. * * *

B

This brings us to the second prong of the union's argument in which it is suggested that * * * once the decision in Jacksonville Terminal was announced, the District Court was then free to enjoin the state court on the theory that such action was "necessary to aid [the District Court's] jurisdiction." Again the argument is somewhat unclear, but it appears to go in this way: The District Court had acquired jurisdiction over the labor controversy in 1967 when the railroad filed its complaint, and it determined at that time that it did have jurisdiction. The dispute involved the legality of picketing by the union and the Jacksonville

---

*   [Ed.] See footnote 2.

Terminal decision clearly indicated that such activity was not only legal, but was protected from state court interference. The state court had interfered with that right, and thus a federal injunction was "necessary in aid of its jurisdiction." For several reasons we cannot accept the contention.

First, a federal court does not have inherent power to ignore the limitations of § 2283 and to enjoin state court proceedings merely because those proceedings interfere with a protected federal right or invade an area preempted by federal law, even when the interference is unmistakably clear. * * * This conclusion is required because Congress itself set forth the only exceptions to the statute, and those exceptions do not include this situation. Second, if the District Court does have jurisdiction, it is not enough that the requested injunction is related to that jurisdiction, but it must be "*necessary in aid of*" that jurisdiction. While this language is admittedly broad, we conclude that it implies something similar to the concept of injunctions to "protect or effectuate" judgments. Both exceptions to the general prohibition of § 2283 imply that some federal injunctive relief may be necessary to prevent a state court from so interfering with a federal court's consideration or disposition of a case as to seriously impair the federal court's flexibility and authority to decide that case. Third, no such situation is presented here. * * * [T]he state and federal courts had concurrent jurisdiction in this case, and neither court was free to prevent either party from simultaneously pursuing claims in both courts. Kline v. Burke Constr. Co., 260 U.S. 226 (1922); *cf.* Donovan v. City of Dallas, 377 U.S. 408 (1964). Therefore the state court's assumption of jurisdiction over the state law claims and the federal preclusion issue did not hinder the federal court's jurisdiction so as to make an injunction *necessary* to aid that jurisdiction. An injunction was no more necessary because the state court may have taken action which the federal court was certain was improper under the Jacksonville Terminal decision. * * * If the union was adversely affected by the state court's decision, it was free to seek vindication of its federal right in the Florida appellate courts and ultimately, if necessary, in this Court. Similarly if, because of the Florida Circuit Court's action, the union faced the threat of immediate irreparable injury sufficient to justify an injunction under usual equitable principles, it was undoubtedly free to seek such relief from the Florida appellate courts, and might possibly in certain emergency circumstances seek such relief from this Court as well. * * *

III

This case is by no means an easy one. The arguments in support of the union's contentions are not insubstantial. But * * * [a]ny doubts as to the propriety of a federal injunction against state court proceedings should be resolved in favor of permitting the state courts to proceed in an orderly fashion to finally determine the controversy. The explicit wording of § 2283 itself implies as much, and the fundamental principle of a dual system of courts leads inevitably to that conclusion.

The injunction issued by the District Court must be vacated. * * *

■ [Justice Marshall did not participate. Justice Harlan wrote a concurring opinion.]

■ Mr. Justice Brennan, with whom Mr. Justice White joins, dissenting.

My disagreement with the Court in this case is a relatively narrow one. I do not disagree with much that is said concerning the history and policies underlying 28 U.S.C. § 2283. * * * Nevertheless, in my view the District Court had discretion to enjoin the state proceedings in the present case because it acted pursuant to an explicit exception to the prohibition of § 2283, that is, "to protect or effectuate [the District Court's] judgments." * * *

In my view, what the District Court decided in 1967 was that BLE had a federally protected right to picket at the Moncrief Yard and, by necessary implication, that this right could not be subverted by resort to state proceedings. I find it difficult indeed to ascribe to the District Judge the views which the Court now says he held, namely, that ACL, merely by marching across the street to the state court, could render wholly nugatory the District Judge's declaration that BLE had a federally protected right to strike at the Moncrief Yard. * * *

Accordingly, I would affirm the judgment of the Court of Appeals sustaining the District Court's grant of injunctive relief against petitioner's giving effect to, or availing itself of, the benefit of the state injunction.

Mitchum v. Foster

407 U.S. 225, 92 S.Ct. 2151, 32 L.Ed.2d 705 (1972).
Appeal from the United States District Court for the Northern District of Florida.

■ Mr. Justice Stewart delivered the opinion of the Court.

The federal anti-injunction statute provides that a federal court "may not grant an injunction to stay proceedings in a State court except as expressly authorized by Act of Congress, or where necessary in aid of its jurisdiction, or to protect or effectuate its judgments." An Act of Congress, 42 U.S.C. § 1983, expressly authorizes a "suit in equity" to redress "the deprivation," under color of state law, "of any rights, privileges, or immunities secured by the Constitution. . . . " The question before us is whether this "Act of Congress" comes within the "expressly authorized" exception of the anti-injunction statute so as to permit a federal court in a § 1983 suit to grant an injunction to stay a proceeding pending in a state court. * * *

I

The prosecuting attorney of Bay County, Florida, brought a proceeding in a Florida court to close down the appellant's bookstore as a public nuisance under the claimed authority of Florida law. The state court entered a preliminary order prohibiting continued operation of the bookstore. After further inconclusive proceedings in the state courts, the appellant filed a complaint in the United States District Court for the Northern District of Florida, alleging that the actions of the state judicial and law enforcement officials were depriving him of rights protected by the First and Fourteenth Amendments. Relying upon 42 U.S.C. § 1983, he asked for injunctive and declaratory relief against the state court proceedings, on the ground that Florida laws were being unconstitutionally applied by the state court * * *. * * *

II

In denying injunctive relief, the District Court relied on this Court's decision in Atlantic Coast Line R. Co. v. Brotherhood of Locomotive Engineers, 398 U.S. 281. The * * * Court's opinion in that case * * * made clear that the statute imposes an absolute ban upon the issuance of a federal injunction against a pending state court proceeding, in the absence of one of the recognized exceptions * * *.

It follows, in the present context, that if 42 U.S.C. § 1983 is not within the "expressly authorized" exception of the anti-injunction statute, then a federal equity court is wholly without power to grant any relief in a § 1983 suit seeking to stay a state court proceeding.

Last Term, in Younger v. Harris, 401 U.S. 37, and its companion cases, the Court dealt at length with the subject of federal judicial intervention in pending state criminal prosecutions. In Younger a three-judge federal district court in a § 1983 action had enjoined a criminal prosecution pending in a California court. In asking us to reverse that judgment, the appellant argued that the injunction was in violation of the federal anti-injunction statute. But the Court carefully eschewed any reliance on the statute in reversing the judgment, basing its decision instead upon what the Court called "Our Federalism"—upon "the national policy forbidding federal courts to stay or enjoin pending state court proceedings except under special circumstances."

* * * At the same time, however, the Court clearly left room for federal injunctive intervention in a pending state court prosecution in certain exceptional circumstances—where irreparable injury is "both great and immediate," where the state law is "flagrantly and patently violative of express constitutional prohibitions," or where there is a showing of "bad faith, harassment, or * * * other unusual circumstances that would call for equitable relief." * * *

While the Court in Younger and its companion cases expressly disavowed deciding the question now before us—whether § 1983 comes within the "expressly authorized" exception of the anti-injunction statute—it is evident that our decisions in those cases cannot be disregarded in deciding this question. In the first place, if § 1983 is not within the statutory exception, then the anti-injunction statute would have absolutely barred the injunction issued in Younger, as the appellant in that case argued, and there would have been no occasion whatever for the Court to decide that case upon the "policy" ground of "Our Federalism." Secondly, if § 1983 is not within the "expressly authorized" exception of the anti-injunction statute, then we must overrule Younger and its companion cases insofar as they recognized the permissibility of injunctive relief against pending criminal prosecutions in certain limited and exceptional circumstances. * * *

The Atlantic Coast Line and Younger cases thus serve to delineate both the importance and the finality of the question now before us. And it is in the shadow of those cases that the question must be decided.

III

* * * In 1793, Congress enacted a law providing that no "writ of injunction be granted [by any federal court] to stay proceedings in any court of a state. . . . " Act of March 2, 1793; 1 Stat. 335. The precise origins of the legislation are shrouded in obscurity,[10] but the consistent understanding has been that its basic purpose is to prevent "needless friction between state and federal courts." Oklahoma Packing Co. v. Gas Co., 309 U.S. 4, 9. The law remained unchanged until 1874, when it was amended to permit a federal court to stay state court proceedings that interfered with the administration of a federal bankruptcy proceeding. The present wording of the legislation was adopted with the enactment of Title 28 of the United States Code in 1948.

Despite the seemingly uncompromising language of the anti-injunction statute prior to 1948, the Court soon recognized that exceptions must be made to its blanket prohibition if the import and purpose of other Acts of Congress were to be given their intended scope. So it was that, in addition to the bankruptcy law exception that Congress explicitly recognized in 1874, the Court through the years found that federal courts were empowered to enjoin state court proceedings, despite the anti-injunction statute, in carrying out the will of Congress under at least six other federal laws. These covered a broad spectrum of congressional action: (1) legislation providing for removal of litigation from state to federal courts,[12] (2) legislation limiting the liability of shipowners,[13] (3) legislation providing for federal interpleader actions,[14] (4) legislation conferring federal jurisdiction over farm mortgages,[15] (5)

---

[10] "The history of this provision in the Judiciary Act of 1793 is not fully known. We know that on December 31, 1790, Attorney General Edmund Randolph reported to the House of Representatives on desirable changes in the Judiciary Act of 1789. * * * A section of the proposed bill submitted by him provided that 'no injunction in equity shall be granted by a district court to a judgment at law of a State court.' Randolph explained * * *[:] 'it is enough to split the same suit into one at law, and another in equity, without adding a further separation, by throwing the common law side of the question into the State courts, and the equity side into the federal courts.' * * * No action was taken until after Chief Justice Jay and his associates wrote the President that their circuit-riding duties were too burdensome. In response to this complaint, which was transmitted to Congress, the Act of March 2, 1793, was passed, containing in § 5, *inter alia*, the prohibition against staying state court proceedings.

"There is no record of any debates over the statute. It has been suggested that the provision reflected the then strong feeling against the unwarranted intrusion of federal courts upon state sovereignty. * * * Much more probable is the suggestion that the provision reflected the prevailing prejudices against equity jurisdiction. * * * " Toucey v. New York Life Ins. Co., 314 U.S. 118, 130–132.

[12] See French v. Hay, 22 Wall. 250; Kline v. Burke Construction Co., 260 U.S. 226. The federal removal provisions, both civil and criminal, 28 U.S.C. §§ 1441–1450, provide that once a copy of the removal petition is filed with the clerk of the state court, the "State court shall proceed no further unless and until the case is remanded." 28 U.S.C. § 1446(e).

[13] See Providence & N.Y.S.S. Co. v. Hill Mfg. Co., 109 U.S. 578. The Act of 1851, as amended, provides that once a shipowner has deposited with the court an amount equal to the value of his interest in the ship, "all claims and proceedings against the owner with respect to the matter in question shall cease." 46 U.S.C. § 185.

[14] See Treinies v. Sunshine Mining Co., 308 U.S. 66. The Interpleader Act of 1926 as currently written provides that in "any civil action of interpleader * * * a district court may * * * enter its order restraining [all claimants] * * * from instituting or prosecuting any proceeding in any State or United States court affecting the property, instrument or obligation involved in the interpleader action." 28 U.S.C. § 2361.

[15] See Kalb v. Feuerstein, 308 U.S. 433. The Frazier-Lemke Farm-Mortgage Act, as amended in 1935, provides that in situations to which it is applicable a federal court shall "stay all judicial or official proceedings in any court." 11 U.S.C. § 203(s)(2) (1940 ed.).

legislation governing federal habeas corpus proceedings,[16] and (6) legislation providing for control of prices.[17]

In addition to the exceptions to the anti-injunction statute found to be embodied in these various Acts of Congress, the Court recognized other "implied" exceptions to the blanket prohibition of the anti-injunction statute. One was an *"in rem"* exception, allowing a federal court to enjoin a state court proceeding in order to protect its jurisdiction of a res over which it had first acquired jurisdiction. Another was a "relitigation" exception, permitting a federal court to enjoin relitigation in a state court of issues already decided in federal litigation. Still a third exception, more recently developed, permits a federal injunction of state court proceedings when the plaintiff in the federal court is the United States itself, or a federal agency asserting "superior federal interests."

In Toucey v. New York Life Ins. Co., 314 U.S. 118, the Court in 1941 issued an opinion casting considerable doubt upon the approach to the anti-injunction statute reflected in its previous decisions. The Court's opinion expressly disavowed the "relitigation" exception to the statute, and emphasized generally the importance of recognizing the statute's basic directive "of 'hands off' by the federal courts in the use of the injunction to stay litigation in a state court." The congressional response to Toucey was the enactment in 1948 of the anti-injunction statute in its present form in 28 U.S.C. § 2283, which, as the Reviser's Note makes evident, served not only to overrule the specific holding of Toucey, but to restore "the basic law as generally understood and interpreted prior to the Toucey decision."

We proceed, then, upon the understanding that in determining whether § 1983 comes within the "expressly authorized" exception of the anti-injunction statute, the criteria to be applied are those reflected in the Court's decisions prior to Toucey. A review of those decisions makes reasonably clear what the relevant criteria are. In the first place, it is evident that, in order to qualify under the "expressly authorized" exception of the anti-injunction statute, a federal law need not contain an express reference to that statute. * * * Indeed, none of the previously recognized statutory exceptions contains any such reference.[24] Secondly, a federal law need not expressly authorize an injunction of a state court proceeding in order to qualify as an exception. Three of the six previously recognized statutory exceptions contain no such authorization.[25] Thirdly, it is clear that, in order to qualify as an "expressly authorized" exception to the anti-injunction statute, an Act of Congress must have created a specific and uniquely federal right or remedy, enforceable in a federal court of equity, that could be frustrated if the federal court were not empowered to enjoin a state court proceeding. This is not to say that in order to come within the exception an Act of Congress must, on its face

---

[16] See Ex parte Royall, 117 U.S. 241, 248–249. The Federal Habeas Corpus Act provides that a federal court before which a habeas corpus proceeding is pending may "stay any proceeding against the person detained in any State Court * * * for any matter involved in the habeas corpus proceeding." 28 U.S.C. § 2251.

[17] Section 205(a) of the Emergency Price Control Act of 1942 provided that the Price Administrator could request a federal district court to enjoin acts that violated or threatened to violate the Act. In Porter v. Dicken, 328 U.S. 252, we held that this authority was broad enough to justify an injunction to restrain state court proceedings. * * *

[24] See nn. 12, 13, 14, 15, 16, and 17, *supra.*

[25] See nn. 12, 13, and 17, *supra.* * * *

and in every one of its provisions, be totally incompatible with the prohibition of the anti-injunction statute. The test, rather, is whether an Act of Congress, clearly creating a federal right or remedy enforceable in a federal court of equity, could be given its intended scope only by the stay of a state court proceeding. * * *

With these criteria in view, we turn to consideration of 42 U.S.C. § 1983.

IV

Section 1983 was originally § 1 of the Civil Rights Act of 1871. * * * The predecessor of § 1983 was thus an important part of the basic alteration in our federal system wrought in the Reconstruction era through federal legislation and constitutional amendment. As a result of the new structure of law that emerged in the post-Civil War era—and especially of the Fourteenth Amendment, which was its centerpiece—the role of the Federal Government as a guarantor of basic federal rights against state power was clearly established. * * *

It is clear from the legislative debates surrounding passage of § 1983's predecessor that the Act was intended to enforce the provisions of the Fourteenth Amendment "against State action, * * * whether that action be executive, legislative, or *judicial*." Ex parte Virginia, 100 U.S. 339, 346 (emphasis supplied). Proponents of the legislation noted that state courts were being used to harass and injure individuals, either because the state courts were powerless to stop deprivations or were in league with those who were bent upon abrogation of federally protected rights.

As Representative Lowe stated, the "records of the [state] tribunals are searched in vain for evidence of effective redress [of federally secured rights]. * * * What less than this [the Civil Rights Act of 1871] will afford an adequate remedy? The Federal Government cannot serve a writ of mandamus upon State Executives or upon State courts to compel them to protect the rights, privileges and immunities of citizens. * * * The case has arisen * * * when the Federal Government must resort to its own agencies to carry its own authority into execution. Hence this bill throws open the doors of the United States courts to those whose rights under the Constitution are denied or impaired." Cong. Globe, 42d Cong., 1st Sess., 374–376 (1871). This view was echoed by [other legislators]. * * *

This legislative history makes evident that Congress clearly conceived that it was altering the relationship between the States and the Nation with respect to the protection of federally created rights; it was concerned that state instrumentalities could not protect those rights; it realized that state officers might, in fact, be antipathetic to the vindication of those rights; and it believed that these failings extended to the state courts.

V

Section 1983 was thus a product of a vast transformation from the concepts of federalism that had prevailed in the late 18th century when the anti-injunction statute was enacted. The very purpose of § 1983 was to interpose the federal courts between the States and the people, as guardians of the people's federal rights—to protect the people from unconstitutional action under color of state law, "whether that action be executive, legislative, or judicial." Ex parte Virginia, 100 U.S., at 346. In carrying out that purpose, Congress plainly authorized the federal courts to issue injunctions in § 1983 actions, by expressly authorizing a "suit in equity" as one of the means of redress. And this Court long ago recognized that federal injunctive relief against a state court proceeding can in some circumstances be essential to prevent great, immediate, and irreparable loss of a person's constitutional rights. Ex parte Young, 209 U.S. 123 * * *. For these reasons we conclude that, under the criteria established in our previous decisions construing the anti-injunction statute, § 1983 is an Act of Congress that falls within the "expressly authorized" exception of that law.

Holdy

In so concluding, we do not question or qualify in any way the principles of equity, comity, and federalism that must restrain a federal court when asked to enjoin a state court proceeding. These principles, in the context of state criminal prosecutions, were canvassed at length last Term in Younger v. Harris, 401 U.S. 37, and its companion cases. * * * Today we decide only that the District Court in this case was in error in holding that, because of the anti-injunction statute, it was absolutely without power in this § 1983 action to enjoin a proceeding pending in a state court under any circumstances whatsoever.

The judgment is reversed and the case is remanded to the District Court for further proceedings consistent with this opinion.

■ [JUSTICES POWELL and REHNQUIST did not participate. CHIEF JUSTICE BURGER, joined by JUSTICES WHITE and BLACKMUN, filed a concurring opinion stressing that the Court had not yet decided whether the principles of equity, comity, and federalism set forth in Younger v. Harris. p. 1127, *infra,* restricted federal injunctive relief against pending state *civil* proceedings. He urged the district court on remand to consider that question before proceeding to the merits.]

NOTE ON THE ANTI-INJUNCTION ACT (28 U.S.C. § 2283)

A. Background, Purpose, and Interpretation of the Act

(1) History and Purpose. Both Atlantic Coast Line and Mitchum describe the original Anti-Injunction Act (AIA) as having the purpose of preventing tension between state and federal courts. Disputing that assumption, Professor Mayton marshals considerable support for the view that the original Act of 1793 was designed merely to prohibit a *single Justice* of the Supreme Court from enjoining such proceedings while riding circuit. Mayton, *Ersatz Federalism under the Anti-Injunction Statute*, 78 Colum.L.Rev. 330 (1978). The original meaning was lost, Mayton argues, when, in Peck v. Jenness, 48 U.S. (7 How.) 612 (1849), the Supreme Court asserted without discussion that the Act barred federal injunctions against state court proceedings. That view was followed in an 1874 statutory revision when the anti-injunction language was separated from its surrounding context governing the powers of a single Justice.[1] Even Mayton concedes that

---

[1] Although section 5 of the 1793 Act dealt generally with the powers of a single Justice, Mayton has some difficulty explaining the statute's syntax and its use at one point of the phrase "court or judge". He also observes that for over fifty years, the federal courts did not rely on the statute in considering requests for injunctions against state court proceedings, disposing of such

the 1948 revision had a broader purpose, though he argues that its true intent was to authorize the exercise of sound discretion to protect the exercise of federal court jurisdiction.

Pfander & Nazemi, *The Anti-Injunction Act and the Problem of Federal-State Jurisdictional Overlap,* 92 Tex.L.Rev. 1 (2013), offer an alternative account of the historical purpose of the Anti-Injunction Act. According to the authors, the original AIA tracked historical practice by forbidding the "writ of injunction," which would have been sought to enjoin an already-pending state court action based on a federal defense, but did not prohibit ancillary relief in the "nature of an injunction," which would have issued to protect previously established federal equitable jurisdiction and to effectuate federal decrees.[2]

History aside, why should federal injunctions against state proceedings be disfavored when a federal court may enjoin proceedings in a different federal court, and a state court may enjoin proceedings in the court of a different state? Note the contrasting rhetoric of Atlantic Coast Line (stressing the independence of state legal systems) and Mitchum (arguing that Reconstruction worked a "vast transformation" in the concept of federalism and that federal jurisdiction is needed to protect federal rights that state courts may be unable or unwilling to protect). Must the Court ultimately choose one of these perspectives and reject the other? As you read the remainder of this Note, consider whether "the goal of a bright-line anti-injunction standard may be doomed never to succeed, because it attempts to incorporate two mutually inconsistent imperatives". Wood, *Fine-Tuning Judicial Federalism: A Proposal for Reform of the Anti-Injunction Act,* 1990 B.Y.U.L.Rev. 289, 290. See generally Fallon, *The Ideologies of Federal Courts Law,* 74 Va.L.Rev. 1141 (1988) (elaborating two conflicting models of the relation of state and federal courts: a "Federalist" model exemplified by Atlantic Coast Line and a "Nationalist" model reflected in Mitchum).

(2) Pre-1948 Exceptions. A number of pre-1948 decisions recognized limitations to the anti-injunction statute, some not founded on congressional enactments.

(a) The Res Exception. As Mitchum notes, a line of cases beginning with Hagan v. Lucas, 35 U.S. (10 Pet.) 400 (1836), announced an implied exception to the statute by declaring that the court (state or federal) that first assumes jurisdiction over property may exercise that jurisdiction to the exclusion of any other court—if necessary by enjoining another court's proceedings. But no Supreme Court case actually has upheld an injunction against state proceedings on this basis.[3] In assessing the res exception and

_____

cases instead on "equitable principles, * * * standards of comity * * *, and on general principles of federalism".

  [2] In a separate article, *Morris v. Allen and the Lost History of the Anti-Injunction Act of 1793,* 108 Nw.U.L.Rev. 187 (2014), the authors argue that much of the impetus for adopting the AIA stemmed from a high-profile federal suit by financier and Senator Robert Morris that largely duplicated a pending state court equitable action and from a report by Attorney General Edmund Randolph (which the AIA follows only in part) recommending congressional action to avoid bifurcated proceedings.

  [3] In Colorado River Water Conservation Dist. v. United States, p. 1171, *infra,* however, the Court held that the district court should have declined to exercise jurisdiction in favor of a pending state action that was analogized to an in rem proceeding. See also Princess Lida of Thurn and Taxis v. Thompson, 305 U.S. 456 (1939), which held that the filing of trust accounts gave a state court *quasi in rem* jurisdiction and empowered it to enjoin a later federal action against the trustees for an accounting and other relief. Compare Mandeville v. Canterbury, 318

its boundaries, keep in mind that the traditional distinction between *in rem* and *in personam* jurisdiction has for some decades been criticized as standing in the way of useful analysis, see, *e.g.*, Mullane v. Central Hanover Bank & Trust Co., 339 U.S. 306 (1950); von Mehren & Trautman, *Jurisdiction to Adjudicate: A Suggested Analysis*, 79 Harv.L.Rev. 1121 (1966), and has suffered significant erosion, see, *e.g.*, Shaffer v. Heitner, 433 U.S. 186 (1977).

(b) Fraudulent State Court Judgments. Several Supreme Court decisions sustained the power of federal courts to enjoin litigants from enforcing judgments fraudulently obtained in state courts. See, *e.g.*, Wells Fargo & Co. v. Taylor, 254 U.S. 175, 184–86 (1920); Simon v. S. Ry. Co., 236 U.S. 115, 128 (1915); Marshall v. Holmes, 141 U.S. 589, 601 (1891).

(3) The Toucey Decision. In Toucey v. New York Life Ins. Co., 314 U.S. 118 (1941), the Court (per Frankfurter, J.) broke with the tradition of implying exceptions to the statute, holding that the federal courts lacked authority to enjoin state relitigation of issues settled in a prior federal action. The opinion found the precedents upholding such injunctions to be at most "a tenuous basis for the exception which we are now asked explicitly to sanction"; "[w]e must be scrupulous in our regard for the limits within which Congress has confined the authority of the courts of its own creation". While acknowledging the existence of the "res" exception, the Court argued that "[t]he fact that one exception has found its way into [the statute] is no justification for making another".[4]

(4) The 1948 Revision. Section 2283, the current embodiment of the Anti-Injunction Act, dates from the 1948 revision of the judicial code. The only legislative history is found in the Revisers' Notes:

"An exception as to acts of Congress relating to bankruptcy was omitted and the general exception substituted to cover all exceptions.

"The phrase 'in aid of its jurisdiction' was added to conform to section 1651 of this title and to make clear the recognized power of the Federal courts to stay proceedings in State cases removed to the district courts.

"The exceptions specifically include the words 'to protect or effectuate its judgments,' for lack of which the Supreme Court held that the Federal courts are without power to enjoin relitigation of cases and controversies fully adjudicated by such courts. (See Toucey v. New York Life Ins. Co. * * *. A vigorous dissenting opinion * * * notes that at the time of the 1911 revision of the Judicial Code, the power of the courts of the United States to protect their judgments was unquestioned and that the revisers of that code noted no change and Congress intended no change).

U.S. 47 (1943) (holding that because federal court action concerning a trust was in personam, related state court action could not be enjoined).

4   Compare Pfander & Nazemi, Paragraph (1), *supra:* "[C]ontrary to Justice Frankfurter's view, the AIA exceptions were often well grounded in the Act's qualified language [barring suits for 'the writ of injunction' but not relief in the 'nature of an injunction' to protect previously established federal jurisdiction or prior federal decrees]. In the main, federal courts granted injunctive relief against state proceedings when the former had first obtained authority over the dispute, when the relief was ancillary to the federal action, and when the relief sought to defend the federal court's equitable priority. Indeed, in many of the leading cases, the Supreme Court expressly invoked the distinction between original and ancillary injunctive relief in support of federal authority." *Id.* at 8.

"Therefore the revised section restores the basic law as generally understood and interpreted prior to the Toucey decision.

"Changes were made in phraseology."

(5) Interpretative Approaches to § 2283. In light of the statement in the Reviser's Notes that the purpose of the 1948 revision was to "restore[ ] the basic law as generally understood and interpreted prior to the Toucey decision", how convincing are the statements in Atlantic Coast Line and Mitchum that § 2283's ban should be viewed as absolute unless the case falls within one of the three stated exceptions?

In fact, the Court has not been quite as strict as those statements would suggest. In Leiter Minerals, Inc. v. United States, 352 U.S. 220 (1957), the Court recognized an additional exception for injunctions sought by the United States. Leiter sued lessees of the United States in state court, seeking a declaration that it owned certain mineral rights and an accounting. The United States subsequently brought a federal action against Leiter and others to quiet title to the mineral rights and sought to enjoin the state proceedings. In upholding the injunction, Justice Frankfurter's opinion for the Court declared that the policy of preventing conflict between federal and state courts "is much more compelling" in litigation between private parties than "when * * * the United States * * * seeks a stay to prevent a threatened irreparable injury to a national interest. The frustration of superior federal interests * * * from precluding the Federal Government from obtaining a stay of state court proceedings except under the severe restrictions of 28 U.S.C. § 2283 would be so great that we cannot reasonably impute such a purpose to Congress from the general language of § 2283 alone".[5]

Although the expansive view expressed in Leiter appeared to foreshadow further judicial creativity, subsequent decisions, including Atlantic Coast Line and Mitchum, seem to have closed the door on efforts to create additional exceptions to § 2283.

B.   The Three Statutory Exceptions

(1) Expressly Authorized by Congress.

(a) The Scope of Mitchum. The significance of the Mitchum decision, which holds § 1983 to be an expressly authorized exception to § 2283, plainly depends on the reach of the underlying § 1983 cause of action. One question about § 1983's scope concerns its requirement that the challenged action be taken "under color of law"—specifically, whether that requirement is satisfied by state court litigation between private parties. In Lugar v. Edmondson Oil Co., Inc., 457 U.S. 922 (1982), a creditor sued in state court on a debt and, pursuant to a state statute, obtained ex parte a prejudgment attachment of the defendant's property. The Court held (5–4) that though "a private party's mere invocation of state legal procedures" was not action under color of law, the ex parte attachment was and hence could be challenged under § 1983.[6] And the issuance of a state court injunction surely constitutes action "under color of law." See, *e.g.*, Henry v. First Nat. Bank,

---

[5]   In NLRB v. Nash-Finch Co., 404 U.S. 138 (1971), the Court extended the Leiter rationale to an application for an injunction by the National Labor Relations Board, an "independent" federal agency.

[6]   See also Pennzoil Co. v. Texaco, Inc., 481 U.S. 1 (1987), p. 1166, *infra*, in which four Justices, concurring in the judgment, stated that a judgment creditor's invocation of state post-judgment collection procedures constitutes action under color of state law. The majority did not reach the issue.

595 F.2d 291, 299–300 (5th Cir.1979); *cf.* Shelley v. Kraemer, 334 U.S. 1 (1948).

A different question as to the scope of § 1983 was resolved in Maine v. Thiboutot, 448 U.S. 1 (1980), Chap. IX, Sec. 2(C), p. 1009–1010, *supra*, which held that § 1983 provides a remedy for violations of federal rights conferred not only by the Constitution or by legislation relating to equal rights, but also by federal statutes generally.

How helpful is the legislative history of the Reconstruction era, on which Mitchum placed great weight, in determining whether a federal court should enjoin a state court proceeding on the ground that the Railway Labor Act bars state court injunctions?

(b) Mitchum's Interpretation of the Act. Mitchum came perilously close to reading "expressly authorized" to mean "impliedly authorized". With regard to supporting precedent, a careful look at footnotes 12–17 of the Mitchum opinion shows that in five of the six statutes that had previously been found expressly to authorize injunctive relief against state proceedings, Congress clearly indicated that state proceedings should cease. (The exception is the Emergency Price Control Act of 1942.) Whether or not such an indication necessarily authorizes such federal intervention—the Supremacy Clause, after all, obliges a state court to stay its own proceedings if federal law so dictates—Mitchum represents a further step.

(c) The Vendo Decision. Vendo Co. v. Lektro-Vend Corp., 433 U.S. 623 (1977) signaled that the Court would not necessarily apply Mitchum's broad construction of the "expressly authorized" exception to other federal statutes. Vendo sued Lektro-Vend (and others) in state court for breach of an agreement not to compete. Lektro-Vend countered with a federal court action against Vendo, alleging that the agreement violated the federal antitrust laws and that the state court suit was designed to stifle competition and to harass. After a state court judgment against Lektro-Vend for over $7 million was affirmed, the federal district court enjoined enforcement of the judgment, holding that § 16 of the Clayton Act, 15 U.S.C. § 26 (which authorizes private suits for injunctive relief against antitrust violations) was an "expressly authorized" exception to § 2283. The Seventh Circuit affirmed.

A splintered Supreme Court reversed. Justice Rehnquist, for himself and Justices Stewart and Powell, argued that, unlike § 1983, § 16 of the Clayton Act could be given "its intended scope" without a stay of state court proceedings; there was no indication that Congress "was concerned with the possibility that state-court proceedings would be used to violate the Sherman or Clayton Acts". To rule otherwise would "eviscerate" § 2283 "since the ultimate logic of this position can mean no less than that virtually *all* federal statutes authorizing injunctive relief are exceptions to § 2283".

Justice Blackmun, joined by Chief Justice Burger, concurred, but on the very different theory that § 16 was an "expressly authorized" exception only in the "narrowly limited circumstances", not found in the present case, where state court proceedings "are themselves part of a 'pattern of baseless, repetitive claims' that are being used as an anticompetitive device". Justice Stevens, for the four dissenters, contended that prosecution of even a single state-court proceeding could (and in this case did) violate the antitrust laws; that to deny an injunction would deprive § 16 of its intended scope; and thus that § 16 was an "expressly authorized" exception.

The key disagreement between the four dissenting and the two concurring Justices concerned the circumstances when state court litigation violates the federal antitrust laws. Does it follow that, after Vendo, any federal statute providing for injunctive relief against unlawful action is an "expressly authorized" exception to § 2283 whenever the prosecution of a state court suit is at least a significant part of such unlawful action?

Unsurprisingly, the lower court decisions since Vendo do not form a coherent pattern. See generally 17A Wright, Miller & Cooper, Federal Practice & Procedure § 4224. See also Redish, *The Anti-Injunction Statute Reconsidered*, 44 U.Chi.L.Rev. 717 (1977), arguing, *inter alia*, that the three opinions in Vendo demonstrate the unworkability of the Mitchum test.

(2) "In Aid of Its Jurisdiction". The exception for injunctions "in aid of [the federal court's] jurisdiction" has been taken to have two primary objectives. First, most courts have viewed the language as confirming the "res" exception, see Paragraph A(2)(a), *supra*—despite the failure of the Reviser's Notes so to indicate.[7] The Reviser's Notes do mention the second purpose—to confirm the power of the federal courts to stay proceedings in state cases that have been removed. Compare footnote 12 of Mitchum, which viewed the power to enjoin in removed cases as "expressly authorized by act of Congress" rather than "in aid of jurisdiction".

(a) Richman Brothers. The principal Supreme Court decision discussing this exception is Amalgamated Clothing Workers v. Richman Brothers, 348 U.S. 511 (1955). There, a union sought to enjoin a state-court suit as preempted by the NLRB's exclusive jurisdiction. The Supreme Court affirmed the district court's refusal to issue an injunction: because no statute authorized the union to file the federal court suit, the federal injunction was not ancillary to an independently-based, ongoing proceeding; and the Court refused to permit an injunction merely because state court jurisdiction had allegedly been preempted.[8]

(b) Exclusive Jurisdiction. If the "in aid of jurisdiction" exception permits an injunction to protect federal court jurisdiction after removal, does it authorize an injunction against a state proceeding that falls within the federal courts' exclusive jurisdiction? There is some force to the analogy, but most lower courts have viewed Richman Brothers' refusal to authorize an injunction to protect the NLRB's exclusive jurisdiction as applying equally to protection of the federal courts' exclusive jurisdiction. See, *e.g.*, Piambino v. Bailey, 610 F.2d 1306, 1333–34 (5th Cir.1980). The existence of exclusive jurisdiction may be one relevant factor, however, in determining whether a statute constitutes an "express" exception within the meaning of Mitchum.

---

[7]   For a collection of cases, see 17A Wright, Miller & Cooper, *supra*, § 4225.

[8]   The Court had to distinguish Capital Service, Inc. v. NLRB, 347 U.S. 501 (1954). There, an employer, having obtained a state court injunction against a union's secondary boycott, filed an unfair labor practice charge with the NLRB. After issuing a complaint, the NLRB obtained a federal court injunction against enforcement of the state court injunction, on the ground that federal law preempts state court jurisdiction over unfair labor practices. The Supreme Court affirmed the order as "necessary in aid of jurisdiction": to make effective its statutory power to seek injunctions, the NLRB "must have authority to take all steps necessary to preserve its case".

Richman Brothers distinguished Capital Service on the ground that the NLRB had a statutory right to file the federal action in which injunctive relief was sought. But perhaps Capital Service is best understood in light of the decisions, rendered only later, permitting anti-suit injunctions in actions by the United States or its agencies. See Paragraph A(5), *supra*.

(c) Complex Litigation. May a federal court enjoin state court actions that threaten to interfere with administration of a pending federal class action?[9] As noted on pp. 1064–1066, *supra*, the underlying policy concern is not simply that competing class actions cause wasteful duplication. The existence of overlapping class actions can actually compromise class members' interests by triggering "reverse auctions", in which class counsel in rival actions compete to become the first to settle, thereby ensuring an award of attorney's fees. See Wasserman, *Dueling Class Actions*, 80 B.U.L.Rev. 461, 470–74 (2000).

Some lower courts have read the "in aid of jurisdiction" exception broadly to permit anti-suit injunctions in class actions, with a number of decisions relying on the statement in Atlantic Coast Line that some injunctive relief may be necessary "to prevent a state court from so interfering with a federal court's consideration or disposition of a case as to seriously impair the federal court's flexibility and authority to decide that case." See, *e.g.*, In re Diet Drugs Prods. Liab. Litig., 282 F.3d 220, 234–35 (3d Cir.2002) (citing Carlough v. Amchem Prods., Inc., 10 F.3d 189, 202 (3d Cir.1993)).[10] A few others have analogized the subject matter of a class suit

---

[9]   The question of injunctive authority "in aid of" federal jurisdiction in class action cases is not necessarily a unitary one. Relevant factors may include (i) the kind of federal class action (Rule 23(b)(1), (b)(2), or (b)(3)); (ii) whether the state court action was brought by members of the federal class; and (iii) whether the injunction is sought before certification, after certification but before the time for opting-out in (b)(3) actions, after formulation of a proposed settlement, or after entry of judgment. See also Note, 75 N.Y.U.L.Rev. 1085 (2000) (offering several criteria that a federal court should consider in deciding whether to issue an injunction, including whether federal jurisdiction is exclusive and whether the claim is based on federal or state law; the complexity of the matter; the relative stage of each action; and the extent of potential overlap).

[10]   The decision in Carlough is criticized in Monaghan, *Antisuit Injunctions and Preclusion Against Absent Nonresident Class Members*, 98 Colum.L.Rev. 1148 (1998), in which the author considers a range of issues relating to the ability of class members to avoid being bound by a class action judgment. When class members seek to litigate in a second forum claims purportedly resolved by the class action judgment, ordinarily the second forum would apply principles of res judicata, to which the plaintiff in the second forum might respond by contending that the former judgment was unconstitutional because the court lacked jurisdiction or because there was a failure of adequate representation. But when federal courts rendering class judgments also issue injunctions barring class members from bringing such claims in other courts, they require any attack on the constitutionality of the former judgment to be litigated in the court that rendered the judgment, rather than in a forum more convenient to the litigant.

While recognizing that the complex problems presented may call for legislation, Monaghan contends that in the present landscape, absent class members should be permitted to choose the forum in which to attack a class action judgment on due process grounds—an opportunity foreclosed in Carlough. But Professors Kahan and Silberman argue that collateral attacks on class actions lead to wasteful relitigation and, more importantly, impede settlement by subjecting defendants to increased litigation risk, undermining the very purposes that class actions are meant to serve. Kahan & Silberman, *The Inadequate Search for "Adequacy" in Class Actions: A Critique of Epstein v. MCA, Inc.*, 73 N.Y.U.L.Rev. 765, 779 (1998). For more recent perspectives on the question of collateral attacks in class actions, see Rubenstein, *Finality in Class Action Litigation: Lessons from Habeas*, 82 N.Y.U.L.Rev. 790 (2007) (comparing the finality problem in class actions with habeas corpus); Issacharoff & Nagareda, *Class Settlements Under Attack*, 156 U.Pa.L.Rev. 1649, 1659 (2008) (arguing that the availability of collateral attacks should turn on a case by case determination of the alleged defect and the "status of the rendering court").

The Supreme Court appeared resolved to clarify the pertinent law when it granted certiorari to review a Second Circuit decision that permitted a collateral attack on the adequacy of representation in the Agent Orange litigation. But the Second Circuit's decision was affirmed by an equally divided Court, Dow Chemical Co. v. Stephenson, 539 U.S. 111 (2003). The American Law Institute's Principles of the Law of Aggregate Litigation § 3.14(a)(2) (2010) would limit collateral attacks to cases in which the court rendering a class action judgment lacked subject

to a "res",[11] Most have concluded, however, that in most circumstances federal courts have no authority under current law to enjoin rival class actions.[12] See, *e.g.*, Ret. Sys. of Ala. v. J.P. Morgan Chase & Co., 386 F.3d 419, 425–31 (2d Cir. 2004); In re Gen. Motors Corp. Pick-Up Truck Fuel Tank Prods. Liab. Litig., 134 F.3d 133, 143–46 (3d Cir.1998); see generally Kerr, *Cleaning Up One Mess to Create Another: Duplicative Class Actions, Federal Courts' Injunctive Power, and the Class Action Fairness Act of 2005*, 29 Hamline L.Rev. 218 (2006).

Wolff, *Federal Jurisdiction and Due Process in the Era of the Nationwide Class Action*, 156 U.Pa.L.Rev. 2035, 2069–73 (2008), argues that federal courts with jurisdiction over a class action should be able to enjoin parallel state court actions "in aid of" their jurisdiction under the Class Action Fairness Act, which is discussed at p. 1066 *supra*, and pp. 1426–1430, *infra*. Although acknowledging that the "in aid of jurisdiction" exception typically does not apply in cases under such general grants of federal jurisdiction as §§ 1331 and 1332, Professor Wolff argues that CAFA—like other "targeted" grants of jurisdiction to protect discretely identified federal interests— should be read to authorize injunctions to protect those interests. Professor Wolff points to language in CAFA's statement of purposes as supporting the conclusion that the Act is intended to protect "absent" class members who are not named parties from reverse auctions. In light of the Act's purposes, he says that plaintiffs in a federal court class action brought under CAFA should be entitled to an injunction against parallel state court litigation upon a showing "that they are threatened with the type of harm that [CAFA's] jurisdictional provision was designed to prevent—a state proceeding tainted by collusion [between plaintiffs' counsel and the defendants in a state class action] or malfeasance [by plaintiffs' counsel in the state action]—and that there is a concomitant need for an antisuit injunction to prevent that harm."

---

matter or personal jurisdiction, "failed to make the necessary findings of adequate representation, or failed to afford class members reasonable notice and an opportunity to be heard". For criticism of the ALI's proposal, and especially the narrowness of its definition of "adequacy of representation" exclusively in terms of "structural defects", *id.*, § 2.07 cmt. d, see Woolley, *Collateral Attack and the Role of Adequate Representation in Class Suits for Money Damages*, 58 U.Kan.L.Rev. 917 (2010).

[11] See In re Baldwin-United Corp., 770 F.2d 328 (2d Cir.1985) (observing, in upholding an anti-suit injunction to aid the district court's jurisdiction over a class settlement, that "[i]n effect * * * the district court had before it a class action proceeding so far advanced that it was the virtual equivalent of a res over which the district judge required full control"). That analogy would seem especially strong in an action under Rule 23(b)(1)(B), which authorizes class suit (without a right to opt-out) when separate actions would effectively dispose of the interests of nonparties or substantially impair their ability to protect their interests. But in In re Federal Skywalk Cases, 680 F.2d 1175 (8th Cir.1982), the court held impermissible an order enjoining class members, including those with pending actions in state court, from settling their punitive damage claims until the federal court had resolved the issue.

[12] Prior to the Supreme Court's decision in Syngenta Crop Protection, Inc. v. Henson, 537 U.S. 28 (2002), several courts of appeals had upheld an alternative technique for preventing a rival state court class action from interfering with the administration of a federal class action settlement: removal of the rival action under the All Writs Act (28 U.S.C. § 1651). In Syngenta, however, the Court held unanimously that the All Writs Act is not a grant of jurisdiction and thus "cannot confer the original jurisdiction required to support removal jurisdiction" under 28 U.S.C. § 1441. Nor, the Court ruled, could removal be supported on an "ancillary jurisdiction" theory, even though the plaintiff in the state action was a party to the federal action and had allegedly violated the terms of a federal settlement. In many of the cases in which Syngenta would bar removal under the All Writs Act, the Class Action Fairness Act, which is discussed at p. 1066 *supra*, and pp. 1426–1430, *infra*, would now provide a basis for removal.

As Professor Wolff notes, the original version of CAFA would have protected absent class members by allowing them (or their lawyers) to remove state court class actions to federal court, and thus to avoid the threat that dueling actions pose to plaintiffs' interests, but the pertinent provision was removed prior to final Senate action. Is the Senate's failure to enact language protecting plaintiffs against the threat of reverse auctions in dueling state court class actions relevant to how CAFA's purposes should be described? See generally pp. 652–656, *supra* (discussing theories of statutory interpretation).

(3) The Relitigation Exception.

(a) Purpose. The relitigation exception permits a federal court to enjoin a state court to respect the preclusive effect of a federal judgment. But why shouldn't the litigant relying on that judgment be relegated to a plea of res judicata in state court? Is it because the federal court is better able to determine the effect of a prior federal judgment?

(b) The Chick Kam Choo Decision. In Chick Kam Choo v. Exxon Corp., 486 U.S. 140 (1988), a federal district court in Texas had dismissed plaintiff's wrongful death action, finding that (i) choice of law doctrine called for application of the law of Singapore rather than of Texas, and (ii) forum non conveniens called for dismissal of the suit so long as the defendants submitted to jurisdiction in Singapore. The plaintiff then filed suit in Texas state court, asserting claims under the laws of Texas and Singapore. The defendants returned to federal court and obtained an injunction against the state court action. The Supreme Court ruled that § 2283 did not preclude the injunction insofar as it barred re-litigation of the Texas law claim, which the federal court had previously held not to be actionable when it determined that the law of Singapore applied. But the Court overturned the injunction insofar as it barred state court litigation of the claim based on the law of Singapore: because federal and state forum non conveniens law might differ, the state court would not necessarily be asked to relitigate the federal court's forum non conveniens ruling; and (per Atlantic Coast Line) even if federal maritime law preempted Texas' application of its own forum non conveniens law, no injunction could issue on that basis because that preemption issue had not been decided by the federal court.[13]

---

[13] The Court unanimously held the relitigation exception to the Anti-Injunction Act inapplicable in Smith v. Bayer Corp., 131 S.Ct. 2368 (2011). After a federal district court had denied class certification in a suit under a West Virginia consumer protection statute that was removed to federal court on the basis of diversity jurisdiction, the court, at the defendant Bayer's request, issued an injunction barring the named plaintiff in a parallel action in a West Virginia court from seeking class certification. In an opinion by Justice Kagan, the Supreme Court found two flaws in the district court's conclusion that the relitigation exception applied. First, in holding that a class could not be certified under federal law, the district court had not determined whether a class could be certified under West Virginia law, which differs from federal law in some respects. Second, since no federal class action was ever certified, the named plaintiff in the West Virginia action was not a party to the federal suit and thus could not be bound by the district court's judgment. (Justice Thomas joined only in the first of these holdings, which the Court termed "little more than a rerun of Chick Kam Choo", but recorded no dissent from the second.) Twice in the course of its opinion, the Court quoted precedents establishing that "[a]ny doubts" in Anti-Injunction Act cases "should be resolved in favor of permitting the state courts to proceed."

Some language in the Chick Kam Choo opinion ("an essential prerequisite for applying the relitigation exception is that the claims or issues which the federal injunction insulates from litigation in state proceedings actually have been decided by the federal court") has led some federal circuits to conclude that that exception permits enforcement on the basis of issue preclusion but not of claim preclusion. See generally Martinez, *The Anti-Injunction Act: Fending*

(c) The Parsons Steel Decision. In Parsons Steel, Inc. v. First Alabama Bank, 474 U.S. 518 (1986), plaintiffs sued the bank in separate actions in federal and state court. The federal action came to judgment first, with the bank prevailing. The bank's assertion in state court of res judicata defenses, based on the federal judgment, was rejected, leading to a $4 million state court verdict against the bank.

The bank returned to federal court and obtained an injunction against the state court proceeding on the ground that the state court claims could have been raised as pendent claims in the prior federal action and thus should have been held by the state court to have been precluded by the federal judgment. The Supreme Court unanimously overturned the injunction. The Court noted that 28 U.S.C. § 1738 (the full faith and credit statute) generally requires a federal court to give a state court judgment the same effect that it would have under state law, see Chap. XII, Sec. 1, pp. 1377–1391, *infra*; that § 2283 was not an exception to § 1738; and that the relitigation exception was limited "to those situations in which the state court has not yet ruled on the merits of the res judicata issue. Once the state court has finally rejected a claim of res judicata, * * * federal courts must turn to state law to determine the preclusive effect of the state court's decision".

Doesn't Parsons Steel encourage a litigant who has obtained a favorable federal judgment to seek an immediate federal injunction against state court relitigation if there is any doubt that the state court will recognize the judgment's effect and thereby risk an increase in federal-state friction?[14]

C. Questions of Coverage

(1) Introduction. Even where there is no exception to § 2283's prohibition, the question remains whether the particular "interference" by the federal court with state court proceedings is one that the Act forbids.

(2) The Meaning of "Proceedings".

(a) Commencement of Proceedings. When do the state court "proceedings" referred to in § 2283 begin? Ex parte Young, 209 U.S. 123 (1908), p. 922, *supra*, held the Act inapplicable to an injunction against criminal proceedings not yet instituted.[15] Consider how critical that holding has been to the vindication of federal rights.

Off the New Attack on the Relitigation Exception, 72 Neb.L.Rev. 643 (1993). Should one sentence in an opinion that involved only the question of issue preclusion be read as having such significance? Is there any reason to treat claim preclusion differently? Compare the Parsons Steel case, immediately following.

[14] For a generally critical discussion of federal injunctions against state court judicial proceedings asserted to be in violation of contractual arbitration provisions—injunctions that a number of courts have entered, sometimes without careful attention to § 2283—see Sternlight, *Forum Shopping for Arbitration Decisions: Federal Courts' Use of Antisuit Injunctions Against State Courts*, 147 U.Pa.L.Rev. 91 (1998).

[15] Note that the question can arise even when a federal action is filed first. Dombrowski v. Pfister, 380 U.S. 479, 484 n. 2 (1965), appears to hold (in the alternative) that when state grand jury indictments are returned after the filing of a federal complaint but before injunctive relief is issued, "no state 'proceedings' are pending within the intendment of § 2283." Nevertheless, the circuits appear to be split on the question whether the Anti-Injunction Act bars injunctions against state court litigation commenced subsequent to the filing of a federal action. See Denny's, Inc. v. Cake, 364 F.3d 521, 529 (4th Cir.2004). *Cf.* Hicks v. Miranda, 422 U.S. 332 (1975), p. 1158, *infra*, holding that the equitable restraint doctrine of Younger v. Harris applies "in full force" when a state prosecution is filed after the federal action but "before any proceedings of substance on the merits" in federal court.

In Lynch v. Household Finance Corp., 405 U.S. 538 (1972), the Court held (6–3) that a prejudgment garnishment was not a "proceeding" in state court within the scope of § 2283, and hence could be enjoined by a federal court, even though the garnishment might be necessary to obtain satisfaction of any subsequent judgment obtained by the creditor. The opinion emphasized that the garnishment could be instituted by the creditor's attorney, without judicial order, before filing suit.

(b) Termination of Proceedings and Proceedings Against Different Parties. In County of Imperial v. Munoz, 449 U.S. 54 (1980), the county obtained a state court injunction against a landowner barring him from selling water from a well on his property for use outside the county. Three persons who had agreements to buy water from the landowner for use in Mexico then sued the county in federal court, alleging that the state court injunction violated the Commerce Clause. The Supreme Court reversed a grant of preliminary injunctive relief, relying on Atlantic Coast Line in rejecting the view that the state court proceedings had terminated.

The federal plaintiffs sought to avoid § 2283 by relying on Hale v. Bimco Trading, Inc., 306 U.S. 375 (1939). There, after one party obtained a state court order requiring a state agency to enforce a state statute, a different person obtained a federal court injunction barring the agency's enforcement of the statute. The Hale opinion upheld that injunction, rejecting the view that the Anti-Injunction Act in effect bars federal suit by strangers to a state court proceeding who seek to enjoin a statute that was the subject of that proceeding. In Munoz, the Court ruled that unless the federal plaintiffs were "strangers," the injunction they sought was barred by § 2283; the case was remanded for an appropriate determination. Justice Blackmun, concurring in the result, was disturbed by the Court's implication that § 2283 does not apply when the state litigation involves different parties.[16]

Wouldn't acceptance of Justice Blackmun's view effectively transform a state court proceeding like that in Munoz into a defendant class action, without any due process safeguards? See Vestal, *Protecting A Federal Court Judgment*, 42 Tenn.L.Rev. 635, 661–63 (1975).[17]

(3) Declaratory Judgments. When § 2283 bars an injunction, may a federal plaintiff obtain declaratory relief? This question was once of particular importance in suits challenging state or local official action as unlawful under federal law. But because those suits fall under § 1983, under Mitchum even injunctions are no longer barred by the Anti-Injunction Act.[18]

---

[16] Justices Brennan and Stevens dissented, finding no reason to believe that two of the three plaintiffs were strangers. Justice Marshall would have dismissed the writ of certiorari as improvidently granted.

[17] Justice Blackmun's view is also in tension with the Supreme Court's disapproval of "virtual representation," a doctrine developed by the lower courts that would subject nonparties to issue and claim preclusion where they have a sufficiently close relationship to the parties in a prior suit. See Taylor v. Sturgell, 553 U.S. 880 (2008). In Taylor, the Court explained that due process requires "at a minimum" that "the interests of the nonparty and her representative [be] aligned" and that "either the party [understands] herself to be acting in a representative capacity or the original court [takes] care to protect the interests of the nonparty", usually by applying special procedures. How significant is the gap between Taylor's requirements and Munoz's "stranger" standard?

[18] A year before Mitchum, Justice Brennan (joined by Justices White and Marshall) opined that § 2283 does not extend to declarations. See Perez v. Ledesma, 401 U.S. 82, 128–29 n. 18 (1971) (separate opinion).

D.   Rules Versus Standards

A 1969 study by the ALI proposed a revision of § 2283 specifying seven exceptions to the general statutory prohibition (intended largely as a restatement of the pre-Mitchum law).[19] Commenting on that proposal, Professor Currie argued instead for a statute providing not specific rules but a general standard: "The federal courts shall not enjoin pending or threatened proceedings in state courts unless there is no other effective means of avoiding grave and irreparable harm." See Currie, *The Federal Courts and the American Law Institute, Part II,* 36 U.Chi.L.Rev. 268, 329 (1969). Under such a standard, how should a court deal, for example, with Atlantic Coast Line? Bear in mind that, in labor disputes, the timing of economic pressure by either side may be critical, and a state court's preliminary injunction may effectively moot the controversy.

The ALI called on Congress to assume a larger and more detailed role in specifying outcomes. Currie's alternative proposal would give the courts greater latitude in making ultimate decisions. What are the pros and cons of each approach?

Would it be preferable in a case like Atlantic Coast Line to retain a bar on injunctions but to authorize removal to federal court based on a federal defense, at least if the defense is one of federal preemption?

———

B.   OTHER STATUTORY RESTRICTIONS ON FEDERAL COURT JURISDICTION

———

NOTE ON THREE-JUDGE DISTRICT COURTS, THE JOHNSON ACT OF 1934, AND THE TAX INJUNCTION ACT OF 1937

Introduction

This Note considers three congressional responses to the recognition, in Ex parte Young and Home Telephone, of the federal courts' jurisdiction to enjoin state officials: the three-judge court requirement; the Johnson Act of 1934; and the Tax Injunction Act of 1937.

A.   The Rise and Decline of Three-Judge District Courts

(1) The Reaction to Ex parte Young. A storm of controversy following Ex parte Young centered on the power of a single federal judge to stop the implementation of state legislation in its tracks.[1] Responding to the particular abuses of *ex parte* restraining orders and interlocutory injunctions, Congress in 1910 required that applications for interlocutory injunctions against enforcement of state statutes on constitutional grounds be heard by a district court of three judges (at least one of whom had to be a

———

[19] See ALI Study of the Division of Jurisdiction Between State and Federal Courts, proposed § 1372.

[1] See generally Frankfurter, *Distribution of Judicial Power Between United States and State Courts,* 13 Cornell L.Q. 499, 519 (1928); Lilienthal, *The Federal Courts and State Regulation of Public Utilities,* 43 Harv.L.Rev. 379 (1930); Lockwood, Maw, & Rosenberry, *The Use of the Federal Injunction in Constitutional Litigation,* 43 Harv.L.Rev. 426 (1930); Hutcheson, *A Case for Three Judges,* 47 Harv.L.Rev. 795 (1934).

judge of the court of appeals), with appeal as of right directly to the Supreme Court.[2] The statute was extended in 1913 to cover interlocutory injunctions against state administrative orders, and in 1925 and 1948 to encompass permanent injunctions. From 1948–76, this three-judge court requirement was codified as 28 U.S.C. § 2281. A parallel provision, enacted in 1937 and codified from 1948–76 as 28 U.S.C. § 2282, required a three-judge court in suits seeking to enjoin federal statutes as unconstitutional.

(2) Near Abolition of the Requirement. The burdens of conducting three-judge court hearings proved substantial. Moreover, the mandatory appeals from three-judge courts proved taxing for the Supreme Court; in some years they constituted more than 20% of the argued cases.[3]

Responding to these problems, Congress in 1976 abolished nearly all three-judge courts. It repealed 28 U.S.C. §§ 2281–82, while enacting a new provision (codified as 28 U.S.C. § 2284) that calls for three-judge courts only in suits "challenging the constitutionality of the apportionment of congressional districts or the apportionment of any statewide legislative body"[4] or "when otherwise required by Act of Congress." 90 Stat. 1119 (1976).[5]

B.   The Johnson Act of 1934

(1) Origins. The Johnson Act of 1934, 48 Stat. 775, now 28 U.S.C. § 1342, which was enacted in response to concerns about the sensitivity of federal judicial interference with the operation of state regulatory schemes, deprives the district courts of jurisdiction to enjoin the operation of, or compliance with, any order of a state administrative agency or local body fixing rates for a public utility, whenever four conditions are met:

"(1) Jurisdiction is based solely on diversity of citizenship or repugnance of the order to the Federal Constitution; and,

"(2) The order does not interfere with interstate commerce; and,

"(3) The order has been made after reasonable notice and hearing; and,

"(4) A plain, speedy and efficient remedy may be had in the courts of such State."

The Johnson Act overrides traditional doctrines of federal equity by barring federal injunctive relief not only, as before, when an adequate remedy is available on the law side of the federal court (which seldom happens in rate

---

[2]   36 Stat. 557. Three-judge courts had previously been used in certain antitrust cases, see 32 Stat. 823 (1903), and in suits challenging ICC orders, see 34 Stat. 584, 592 (1906).

[3]   S.Rep.No. 201, 94th Cong., 2d Sess. 4 (1976).

[4]   This language eliminates the distinction between suits for declaratory judgments, which the Supreme Court had held could be heard by a single judge under the former § 2282 (in Kennedy v. Mendoza-Martinez, 372 U.S. 144 (1963)), and suits for injunctions subject to the three-judge requirement.

The requirement of three-judge courts in certain antitrust actions, see note 2, *supra*, was abolished in 1974, 88 Stat. 1706, and the following year, the requirement in suits to enjoin ICC orders was also repealed, 88 Stat. 1918.

[5]   The latter phrase refers primarily to provisions of the Civil Rights Act of 1964, 42 U.S.C. §§ 1971(g), 2000a–5(b), 2000e–6(b), and the Voting Rights Act of 1965, as amended, *id.* §§ 1973b(a), 1973c, 1973h(c), 1973aa–2, 1973bb(a)(2)—although other statutes occasionally employ the device. See generally Williams, *The New Three-Judge Courts of Reapportionment and Continuing Problems of Three-Judge-Court Procedure*, 65 Geo.L.J. 971 (1977); Solimine, *Congress, Ex parte Young, and the Fate of the Three-Judge District Court*, 70 U.Pitt.L.Rev. 101 (2008) (tracing the history of political support for three-judge district courts and attributing their near abolition in 1976 to considerations involving judicial workload).

cases), but also when there is a sufficient remedy in the state courts (whether in equity, in an action at law, or via statutory review of the order).

(2) Exceptions. The Johnson Act does not govern a challenge to a utility rate order as preempted by a federal statute. See, *e.g.*, IBEW v. Public Serv. Comm'n, 614 F.2d 206, 211 (9th Cir.1980). The Act has also been held not to apply to suits brought by the United States. See, *e.g.*, PUC of Cal. v. United States, 355 U.S. 534 (1958).

C.   The Tax Injunction Act of 1937

(1) Origins. The Tax Injunction Act of 1937, 50 Stat. 738, now 28 U.S.C. § 1341, states: "The district courts shall not enjoin, suspend or restrain the assessment, levy or collection of any tax under State law where a plain, speedy and efficient remedy may be had in the courts of such State." The Act's legislative history reveals purposes of avoiding federal interference with state revenue collection—in order to challenge a tax levy in state courts, plaintiffs frequently had to pay first and then sue for a refund—and of preventing out-of-state businesses from forum-shopping in their decisions about where to challenge state taxes. Previous language restricting the district courts' "jurisdiction" was removed in the 1948 statutory revision. For purposes of the Act, local taxes have uniformly been held to be collected "under State law." See 17A Wright, Miller & Cooper, Federal Practice & Procedure § 4237.

In early decisions under the Act, the Supreme Court often seemed to treat the phrase "a plain, speedy, and efficient remedy" as synonymous with an "adequate" remedy in pre-1937 equity practice.[6] But the argument that Congress meant to establish a more stringent standard for federal intervention in tax cases was found persuasive in Rosewell v. LaSalle Nat. Bank, 450 U.S. 503, 524–27 (1981).[7] There, after reviewing statistics showing the serious delays in state and federal urban trial courts, the Court, in an opinion by Justice Brennan, held that a customary delay of two years from payment under protest until receipt of a refund after state court litigation was not so unusual as to make the remedy not "speedy." Adopting a purely "procedural interpretation" of "plain, speedy and efficient", the Court also found it immaterial that the refund remedy available in state court excluded interest. Justice Stevens, joined by Justices Stewart, Marshall, and Powell, filed a vigorous dissent, arguing that the Tax Injunction Act must include a standard of substantive adequacy that the failure to pay interest violated.

(2) Declaratory Judgments. California v. Grace Brethren Church, 457 U.S. 393 (1982), squarely ruled that § 1341 bars the issuance of declaratory judgments. In so holding, the Court relied on language from an earlier decision, in Great Lakes Dredge & Dock Co. v. Huffman, 319 U.S. 293 (1943), that equated the practical effect of a declaration with that of an injunction and on the Act's prohibition of actions that not only "enjoin" but also "suspend or restrain" collection of state taxes.

(3) Damages Actions. An even greater limitation on federal court remedies for illegal state taxation emerges from Fair Assessment in Real Estate Ass'n,

---

[6]   See, *e.g.*, Great Lakes Dredge & Dock Co. v. Huffman, 319 U.S. 293 (1943).

[7]   But *cf.* Fair Assessment in Real Estate Ass'n v. McNary, 454 U.S. 100, 117 n. 8 (1981), Paragraph (3), *infra* (discerning no significant difference between remedies that are "plain, speedy and efficient" under § 1341, and those that are "plain, adequate, and complete" under the equitable restraint doctrine, Sec. 3(C), *infra*).

Inc. v. McNary, 454 U.S. 100 (1981), decided one year before Grace Brethren Church. The plaintiffs sued under 42 U.S.C. § 1983, alleging that local officials had violated the Fourteenth Amendment by taxing real property unequally and by targeting for reassessment taxpayers who had successfully appealed prior assessments. Plaintiffs sought actual and punitive damages for past over-assessments and for expenses incurred in combating them. The Court (per Justice Rehnquist) deemed it unnecessary to decide whether § 1341 barred plaintiffs' action, as "the principle of comity" that had been held to bar declaratory relief in Great Lakes applied in the instant case as well. That principle, the Court said, barred any federal intervention whose practical effect was to suspend collection of state taxes, regardless of the form of relief sought.[8]

The taxpayers argued that their § 1983 suit did not disrupt the collection of taxes, because they sought damages from individual officers rather than from the county, and those officers would be shielded by a qualified immunity. But the Court rejected that argument, stating that in a damages action, the district court must "in effect * * * first enter a declaratory judgment like that barred in Great Lakes"—a prospect as disruptive as an equitable remedy. Moreover, the Court feared the disruptive effect of the litigation itself: plaintiffs' suit, hauling virtually every county tax official into federal court, with the risk of punitive damages and attorney's fees liability, could have a chilling effect upon the officials' conduct of their duties.

Justice Brennan, joined by Justices Marshall, Stevens, and O'Connor, concurred in the judgment. He rejected the majority's reliance on the principle of comity because he associated that principle with the discretion of a court of equity in exercising its extraordinarily intrusive powers, a view that he believed Great Lakes had followed. "There is little room for the 'principle of comity' in actions at law where, apart from matters of administration, judicial discretion is at a minimum". In enacting § 1983, Congress clearly intended federal adjudication of damages actions for constitutional violations by state officials; the precedents prior to passage of the Tax Injunction Act supported federal court power to award damages in actions for wrongful collection of state taxes; and the Act's legislative history expressly suggested that refund actions would be permitted.

Justice Brennan noted, however, that in First Nat. Bank of Greeley v. Board of County Comm'rs, 264 U.S. 450, 456 (1924), the Court held that a federal refund action based on an alleged violation of the Fourteenth Amendment was barred by the taxpayers' failure to exhaust state administrative remedies. He acknowledged that in general exhaustion should not be required in § 1983 actions. (On this point, see Sec. 3(A), infra.) But he argued that whether or not the Tax Injunction Act itself created an exception to the no exhaustion rule under § 1983, congressional policy called for an exhaustion requirement in suits challenging state taxes. Thus, "[w]here administrative remedies are a precondition to suit for monetary relief in state court, absent some substantial consideration compelling a contrary result in a particular case, those remedies should be deemed a precondition to suit in federal court as well".

---

[8]   The Court reserved the question "whether * * * comity * * * would also bar a claim under § 1983 which requires no scrutiny whatever of state tax assessment practices, such as a facial attack on tax laws colorably claimed to be discriminatory as to race".

Can McNary be squared with the view of § 1983 articulated in Monroe v. Pape and Mitchum v. Foster? If the majority's concerns are implicated in a suit in which the taxpayer has already paid, are they implicated in every § 1983 action?

(4) Section 1983 Actions in State Courts. By its terms, the Tax Injunction Act governs only the federal district courts. Is a state court obliged to entertain a suit under 42 U.S.C. § 1983 that asserts that a state tax violates federal law—and, if the tax is found invalid, to provide injunctive or declaratory relief of the sort ordinarily available in § 1983 actions? (The issue has practical importance no matter how complete the state law remedies, for relief under § 1983 carries with it the right to attorney's fees under 42 U.S.C. § 1988.)

In National Private Truck Council, Inc. v. Oklahoma Tax Comm'n, 515 U.S. 582 (1995), the state court had ordered tax refunds as authorized by state law, but had refused to award an injunction or attorney's fees under § 1983. A unanimous Supreme Court affirmed, declaring that the Tax Injunction Act was but "one manifestation of" a longstanding "aversion to federal interference with state tax administration" that dated back to the time of § 1983's enactment during Reconstruction. Among other examples of that aversion, Justice Thomas's opinion noted the "particular relevance" of the McNary decision, which it read as holding "that because of principles of comity and federalism, Congress never authorized federal courts to entertain damages actions under § 1983 against state taxes when state law furnishes an adequate remedy". Assuming without deciding that state courts generally must hear § 1983 suits, the Court ruled that "the background presumption that federal law generally will not interfere with administration of state taxes leads us to conclude that Congress did not authorize injunctive or declaratory relief under § 1983 in state tax cases when there is an adequate [state] remedy at law".[9] Because no relief was available under § 1983, there was no basis for an award of attorney's fees under § 1988.

(5) Suits Between States or Suits Filed by the United States. In Department of Employment v. United States, 385 U.S. 355 (1966), the Court held that the Act does not bar suits by the United States, or by a federal instrumentality, to enjoin state taxation of the instrumentality's employees, who asserted a federal immunity from taxation.[10]

---

9 The Court added: "[T]here may be extraordinary circumstances under which injunctive or declaratory relief is available even when a legal remedy exists. For example, if the 'enforcement of the tax would lead to a multiplicity of suits, or produce irreparable injury, [or] throw a cloud upon the title,' equity might be invoked. Dows v. City of Chicago, 78 U.S. 108, 11 Wall. 108, 110 (1871)."

10 See also Moe v. Confederated Salish and Kootenai Tribes, 425 U.S. 463 (1976), holding that § 1341 does not bar a suit by an Indian tribe that could have been brought by the United States on behalf of the tribe.

3. JUDICIALLY DEVELOPED LIMITATIONS ON FEDERAL COURT JURISDICTION: DOCTRINES OF EQUITY, COMITY, AND FEDERALISM

INTRODUCTORY NOTE

The central issue of this Section is whether, and if so in what circumstances, it is appropriate for federal courts to abstain from entertaining actions that fall within the literal terms of congressional grants of jurisdiction. (That question has previously been raised by the decisions in McNary and in Great Lakes Dredge & Dock, pp. 1091–1093, *supra*, notably in Justice Brennan's separate opinion in the former case.) These materials consider the courts' response to continuing and conflicting pressures. Militating on one side are the desires to avoid premature constitutional determinations, to defer to state tribunals on questions of state law, to avoid duplicative proceedings, and to interfere as little as possible with state processes. Competing impulses are to uphold a litigant's choice of a federal forum, to respect the policies of the jurisdictional grants, and to vindicate federal rights without undue delay.

This Section divides the judicially developed doctrines limiting district court jurisdiction into five groupings: (1) the requirement of exhaustion of state administrative and other nonjudicial remedies; (2) the doctrine derived from the Pullman case, often referred to as "Pullman abstention", and related abstention doctrines; (3) the doctrine, derived from equity practice and frequently labeled "Younger abstention", restricting the availability of federal equitable relief from pending state enforcement actions and particularly from pending criminal prosecutions; (4) the doctrine calling for a federal court to stay its hand in exceptional circumstances because of the pendency of a parallel proceeding in state court; and (5) the rules restricting the exercise of federal jurisdiction in probate and domestic relations matters.

The primary though not exclusive focus of the materials that follow is on federal actions against state officials.

A. EXHAUSTION OF STATE NONJUDICIAL REMEDIES

NOTE ON EXHAUSTION OF STATE NONJUDICIAL REMEDIES

(1) The Prentis Case. In the same year that Ex parte Young was decided, the Supreme Court, in Prentis v. Atlantic Coast Line Co., 211 U.S. 210 (1908), laid the foundation for the general doctrine that (subject to important exceptions discussed below) a plaintiff may not sue in federal court for redress of allegedly unlawful state action without first invoking or "exhausting" available state *administrative* (as opposed to judicial) remedies. The underlying principle, in a nutshell, is that plaintiffs should not run to a federal court until it has become clear that their grievances cannot be resolved through nonjudicial, administrative processes.

Although "exhaustion" doctrine requires plaintiffs to avail themselves of state administrative remedies, but not to sue in state court, before proceeding to federal court, some of the generative cases, including Prentis, are potentially confusing because they arose from circumstances in which state courts acted in administrative rather than judicial capacities. In (anomalous) situations of that kind, the doctrine requiring exhaustion of state administrative remedies can require a would-be plaintiff in federal court to exhaust administrative remedies available in a state court (but not judicial remedies available in state court) before suing in federal court.

Prentis arose when the plaintiffs asked a federal court to enjoin the enforcement of a rate order of the Virginia State Corporation Commission. On appeal from a lower court decision granting the injunction, the appellants argued that under state law the commission had the characteristics and powers of a court and that the Anti-Injunction Act, now 28 U.S.C. § 2283, forbade a federal injunction. The Court, speaking through Justice Holmes, dismissed that objection to the exercise of federal jurisdiction: Whatever the status of the commission in other types of proceedings, "[t]he establishment of a rate is the making of a rule for the future, and therefore is an act legislative not judicial in kind", to which the Anti-Injunction Act did not apply. Having characterized the Commission's role under the statute as legislative rather than judicial, Justice Holmes then noted that state law provided an appeal as of right to the Supreme Court of Appeals of Virginia, upon the record made in the commission, and that "that court, if it reverses what has been done, is to substitute such order as in its opinion the commission should have made". According to Justice Holmes, the role of the court, in substituting an order for that of the commission, would be acting as much in a *legislative* capacity as the Commission itself, and a federal court of equity should not intervene until the legislative or administrative process was complete:

"We should hesitate to say, as a general rule, that a right to resort to the courts could be made always to depend upon keeping a previous watch upon the bodies that make laws, and using every effort and all the machinery available to prevent unconstitutional laws from being passed. * * * But this case hardly can be disposed of on purely general principles. The question that we are considering may be termed a question of equitable fitness or propriety, and must be answered on the particular facts. * * * The State of Virginia has endeavored to impose the highest safeguards possible upon the exercise of the great power given to the State Corporation Commission * * * by making its decisions dependent upon the assent of the same historic body that is entrusted with the preservation of the most valued constitutional rights, if the railroads see fit to appeal. It seems to us only a just recognition of the solicitude with which their rights have been guarded, that they should make sure that the State in its final legislative action would not respect what they think their rights to be, before resorting to the courts of the United States.

"If the rate should be affirmed by the Supreme Court of Appeals and the railroads still should regard it as confiscatory, * * * they will be at liberty then to renew their application to the [federal] Circuit Court, without fear of being met by a plea of res judicata."[1]

---

[1]   Accord, Porter v. Investors' Syndicate, 286 U.S. 461 (1932), 287 U.S. 346 (1932), holding that a legislative remedy in a state district court against an administrative order under a state blue sky law must be exhausted before resort to a federal court.

(2) The Legislative/Judicial Distinction. Bacon v. Rutland R.R., 232 U.S. 134 (1914), marked the limits of the Prentis doctrine and made its rationale unmistakable. There, in a suit to enjoin the Public Service Commission of Vermont from enforcing an order concerning a passenger station, the defendants invoked the Prentis case in objecting that the railroad had failed to appeal to the state supreme court. But the Court, speaking again through Justice Holmes, held that at the judicial stage the railroads had a right to resort to the federal courts at once. Finding that no legislative powers had been conferred upon the Supreme Court of Vermont, it sustained the federal court's jurisdiction.

Following Prentis, whether a state court's role is characterized as legislative or judicial determines not only whether a litigant must exhaust state remedies—by taking an appeal in the state courts before mounting a federal challenge—but also the proper forum in which to seek federal review. If the state court acts in a legislative capacity, a federal district court will have jurisdiction of a timely challenge, and the state court's findings will lack res judicata effect. By contrast, if the decision by a state's highest court is judicial, the only review is by the Supreme Court. See pp. 1409–1411, *infra*, discussing the "Rooker-Feldman" doctrine.

The characterization of state proceedings as legislative or judicial appears to be governed by state law. In Oklahoma Packing Co. v. Oklahoma Gas & Elec. Co., 309 U.S. 4 (1940), the Supreme Court, after first upholding a plea of res judicata, withdrew its former opinion and overruled the plea in light of an intervening state court opinion characterizing the review as legislative.

(3) The Traditional Requirement to Exhaust Administrative Remedies. Analogous to the Prentis doctrine is the traditional, judicially developed principle that a federal court will not entertain an action against a state officer if the plaintiff has failed to exhaust remedies before a state administrative agency. As explained by courts and commentators, the exhaustion requirement is calculated to avoid premature interruption of agency procedures, to permit proper factual development, to take advantage of the agency's expertise, to give the agency the chance to correct its own errors, and to promote efficiency in both the judicial and administrative processes. See generally Fuchs, *Prerequisites to Judicial Review of Administrative Agency Action*, 51 Ind.L.J. 817, 859–911 (1976). At least until the developments discussed in Paragraphs (4) and (7), *infra*, it had become the norm that prospective plaintiffs must exhaust administrative remedies as a precondition to raising federal challenges.[2]

But cf. Pacific Tel. & Tel. Co. v. Kuykendall, 265 U.S. 196 (1924), where the utility alleged that existing rates were confiscatory and that no stay was available: "Under such circumstances comity yields to constitutional right, and the fact that the procedure on appeal in the legislative fixing of rates has not been concluded will not prevent a federal court of equity from suspending the daily confiscation, if it finds the case to justify it."

[2] See, *e.g.*, Pacific Live Stock Co. v. Lewis, 241 U.S. 440 (1916); First Nat. Bank of Greeley v. Board of County Comm'rs, 264 U.S. 450 (1924); Illinois Commerce Comm'n v. Thomson, 318 U.S. 675, 686 (1943).

The exhaustion doctrine has always been subject to important limits. For example, exhaustion has not generally been required when undue delay would result, when the state remedy is inadequate, or when exhaustion would be futile. See generally 17A Wright, Miller & Cooper, Federal Practice & Procedure § 4233.

For discussion of the legitimacy under the separation of powers of courts declining to exercise jurisdiction of cases within their jurisdictional grants, see pp. 1105–1106, *infra*.

(4) Inapplicability of Exhaustion Requirements to § 1983 Actions. In Patsy v. Board of Regents of the State of Florida, 457 U.S. 496 (1982), the Supreme Court ruled that exhaustion of state administrative remedies is not required in actions under 42 U.S.C. § 1983.

(a) **The Patsy Case.** Alleging that her employer, a state university, had discriminated against her on the basis of race and gender, Patsy filed a civil rights action in federal district court. The district court dismissed, based on Patsy's failure to exhaust administrative remedies provided by the university itself. The en banc court of appeals reversed, ruling that a § 1983 plaintiff was required to exhaust administrative remedies when (but only when): (i) an orderly system of review is provided by statute or agency rule; (ii) the agency can grant relief more or less commensurate with the claim; (iii) relief is available without undue delay; (iv) the procedures are fair, not burdensome, and are not used to harass those with legitimate claims; and (v) interim relief is available in appropriate cases. It remanded for the district court to determine whether exhaustion was appropriate under those standards.

The Supreme Court, per Justice Marshall, reversed. The Court noted its ruling in McNeese v. Board of Education, 373 U.S. 668 (1963), that exhaustion should not be required in § 1983 actions and its adherence to that view in seven subsequent cases. That position was also supported by the legislative history of § 1 of the Civil Rights of 1871, the precursor to § 1983, whose "very purpose * * * was to interpose the federal courts between the States and the people, as guardians of the people's federal rights * * *" (quoting Mitchum v. Foster, Sec. 2(A), *supra*). Though Congress in 1871 did not consider the question of exhaustion, the Court believed that the "tenor of the debates" did not support an exhaustion requirement. The Court based this conclusion on three recurring themes in the legislative history: Congress' assignment "to the federal courts [of] a paramount role in protecting constitutional rights"; Congress' belief "that the state authorities had been unable or unwilling to protect the constitutional rights of individuals or to punish those who violated those rights"; and "the fact that many legislators interpreted the bill to provide dual or concurrent forums in the state and federal system, enabling the plaintiff to choose the forum in which to seek relief".

Justice Marshall also found support for the Court's holding in a 1980 amendment to the Civil Rights of Institutionalized Persons Act, 42 U.S.C. § 1997 *et seq.* That amendment requires adult prisoners, before seeking relief under § 1983, to exhaust administrative remedies that satisfy statutorily specified conditions. In the Court's view, "[t]his detailed scheme is inconsistent with discretion to impose, on an ad hoc basis, a judicially developed exhaustion rule in other cases".

Justice Powell, joined by Chief Justice Burger, dissented. The court of appeals' exhaustion requirement was based, he said, on "sound considerations. It does not defeat federal-court jurisdiction, it merely defers it. It permits the States to correct violations through their own procedures, and it encourages the establishment of such procedures. It is consistent with the principles of comity that apply whenever federal courts are asked to review state action or supersede state proceedings". A rule requiring exhaustion also conserves federal court resources, Justice Powell argued, a matter particularly important given the rapid growth of § 1983 litigation.

In Justice Powell's view, many of the Court's past decisions suggesting that exhaustion was not required in a § 1983 action "can be explained as applications of traditional exceptions to the exhaustion requirement. Other decisions speak to the question in an offhand and conclusory fashion without full briefing and argument". Nor did § 1997e support the Court's decision: that provision focused on the particular question of prisoners' suits, and simply did not bear on the general question of exhaustion in § 1983 actions.[3]

(b) The Soundness of the Decision. To assess the soundness of the Patsy decision, it is necessary to appraise the significance of the distinction between exhaustion of state judicial remedies (which Monroe v. Pape, 365 U.S. 167 (1961), p. 987, *supra*, held is not required) and exhaustion of distinctively administrative remedies. Some state administrative regimes were created in response to federal court decisions holding that the failure to provide administrative procedures denied due process. On the one hand, it may seem ironic that Patsy authorizes litigants to bypass these regimes altogether. On the other hand, an exhaustion requirement would have been difficult to square with the rationale of Monroe v. Pape (even if not with its actual holding), as well as with the results in a number of prior cases. Consider, too, Justice Powell's assertion that exhaustion does not heavily burden the federal plaintiff: "[I]t does not defeat federal-court jurisdiction, it merely defers it." Compare University of Tennessee v. Elliott, 478 U.S. 788 (1986), p. 1387, *infra*, which held that when a state administrative agency acting in a judicial capacity makes factual findings after the parties have had a fair opportunity to litigate, a federal court in a § 1983 action must give those findings the same preclusive effect that they would have in the state's courts. On the facts of Patsy, a rule requiring exhaustion might not have resulted in preclusion, but that would not be true under many other administrative regimes governed by the rule of Patsy. In cases in which administrative decisions would have preclusive effect in federal litigation, wouldn't a contrary decision have been difficult to reconcile with Monroe v. Pape?

(5) Exceptions to the Patsy Rule. Patsy's general rule that exhaustion of administrative remedies is not required in § 1983 actions is subject to important limitations.

(a) Plain, Adequate, and Complete Tax Remedies. In Fair Assessment in Real Estate Ass'n v. McNary, 454 U.S. 100 (1981), pp. 1091–1092, *supra*, the Court applied principles of comity to require federal courts to decline jurisdiction in suits seeking a damages remedy for state taxation whenever the state provides a plain, adequate, and complete remedy. Though the four concurring Justices would not have required the federal court to decline jurisdiction where state *judicial* remedies were available, they agreed that when the state courts would require exhaustion of *administrative* remedies before entertaining a challenge to state taxes in

---

[3]   Justice O'Connor wrote a concurring opinion, in which Justice Rehnquist joined, endorsing an exhaustion requirement as sound policy, but noting that, "for the reasons set forth in the Court's opinion", that view had already been rejected by prior decisions. Justice White concurred in part, expressing his disagreement with the Court's view that Congress' enactment of § 1997e supported the Court's decision.

which monetary relief was sought, a federal court entertaining a § 1983 action should ordinarily do likewise.[4]

(b) Actions by Prisoners. The Prison Litigation Reform Act of 1995 ("PLRA"), 110 Stat. 1321 (1996), requires the exhaustion of "such administrative remedies as are available" prior to the filing of federal suits by prisoners challenging prison conditions under § 1983 "or any other Federal law". 42 U.S.C. § 1997e(a). The court may, however, dismiss the underlying claim without requiring exhaustion "[i]n the event that a claim, on its face, is frivolous or malicious, fails to state a claim on which relief can be granted, or seeks monetary relief from a defendant who is immune from such relief". § 1997e(c)(2).

When a prisoner fails to comply with state administrative requirements—including time limits for filing grievances or administrative appeals—a number of circuits have held that suit in federal court is foreclosed, unless stringent conditions are satisfied, on the theory that no sanction for noncompliance with state procedures would otherwise exist. The net result can be not only to defer federal court jurisdiction, but to defeat it altogether. See generally Schlanger, *Inmate Litigation*, 116 Harv.L.Rev. 1555 (2003).

Booth v. Churner, 532 U.S. 731 (2001), applied the exhaustion requirement to a prisoner seeking only money damages, despite the unavailability of monetary relief in the administrative forum. The Court unanimously concluded that "one 'exhausts' processes, not forms of relief". It also attached significance to the PLRA's failure to require the exhaustion only of "effective" remedies, as had a prior version of § 1997(e).[5]

In Jones v. Bock, 549 U.S. 199 (2007), however, the Court held that a court of appeals had overstepped its authority by erecting procedural barriers to prisoner suits that went beyond the requirements of the PLRA. More specifically, the Court rejected rulings that had required inmates to plead exhaustion in their complaints (rather than treating non-exhaustion as an affirmative defense), barred suits against a defendant who had not been specifically named in an administrative grievance, and mandated total dismissal of complaints in which petitioners had failed to exhaust some, but not all, of their claims.

(c) Administrative Remedies, the Merits, and Ripeness. Although not "exceptions" to Patsy in the technical sense, substantive doctrines and the "finality" requirement may sometimes compel plaintiffs to complete administrative processes prior to bringing a § 1983 action.

In "taking" cases, the demand for "finality" very often compels a resort to administrative remedies. See, *e.g.*, Williamson County Regional Planning Comm'n v. Hamilton Bank of Johnson City, 473 U.S. 172 (1985) (finding a Takings Clause challenge to the action of a zoning board premature because the plaintiff had not sought a variance from the agency). The Court distinguished the finality and exhaustion doctrines, as follows: "[T]he

---

[4]   National Private Truck Council, Inc. v. Oklahoma Tax Comm'n, 515 U.S. 582 (1995), builds on Fair Assessment by holding that § 1983 does not authorize equitable or injunctive relief against state taxes, either in federal or state court, when state law provides an adequate legal remedy.

[5]   The Court also construed the PLRA broadly in Porter v. Nussle, 534 U.S. 516 (2002), which unanimously held the exhaustion requirement applicable to all inmate suits based on conditions of prison life, including actions alleging use of excessive force and those involving discrete acts rather than general conditions.

finality requirement is concerned with whether the initial decision-maker has arrived at a definitive position on the issue that inflicts an actual, concrete injury; the exhaustion requirement generally refers to administrative * * * procedures by which an injured party may seek review of an adverse decision and obtain a remedy if the decision is found to be unlawful or otherwise inappropriate. Patsy concerned the latter, not the former".[6]

Under Parratt v. Taylor, p. 1016, *supra*, adequate postdeprivation *judicial* remedies can sometimes provide all the process that is constitutionally due and thus eliminate the basis for a federal suit under the Due Process Clause. Can postdeprivation *administrative* remedies have the same effect? See pp. 1025–1026, *supra*.

(6) Section 1983 Actions in State Court. Does Patsy's rule of non-exhaustion apply to § 1983 suits filed in the state courts? Although the state courts were initially divided, the issue appears to have been resolved in Felder v. Casey, 487 U.S. 131 (1988), also discussed at pp. 445, 455–456, *supra*. There, the Wisconsin Supreme Court had dismissed a state court § 1983 suit because of plaintiff's noncompliance with the state's notice-of-claim statute, which required, as a condition of bringing suit in state court, provision of written notice, within 120 days of the injury, of any claim against state or local governments (or their officials). The Supreme Court reversed, reasoning that "[g]iven the evil at which the federal civil rights legislation was aimed, there is simply no reason to suppose that Congress * * * contemplated that those who sought to vindicate their federal rights in state courts could be required to seek redress in the first instance from the very state officials whose hostility to those rights precipitated their injuries" (quoting Patsy, 457 U.S. at 504). The "dominant characteristic" of a § 1983 action—that it is "judicially enforceable *in the first instance*"—holds as true in state court as in federal court suits. Dissenting, Justice O'Connor (joined by Chief Justice Rehnquist) distinguished Patsy as resting on legislative history indicating that § 1983 was meant to provide access to a *federal* forum.

(7) Exhaustion Requirements in Challenges to Federal Administrative Action. The requirement that plaintiffs exhaust administrative remedies traditionally applied to challenges to federal as well as state administrative action. But in Darby v. Cisneros, 509 U.S. 137 (1993), the Supreme Court held unanimously that when judicial review is authorized by the Administrative Procedure Act, a litigant who has exhausted all administrative remedies expressly prescribed by the governing regulatory statute or by agency rules has a right, under § 10(c) of the APA, to judicial review. In the Court's view, § 10(c) modified the judge-made exhaustion doctrine in cases governed by the APA and precludes the federal courts from requiring a litigant to exhaust *optional* federal administrative appeals before seeking judicial review. The Court noted that "the exhaustion doctrine continues to apply as a matter of judicial discretion in cases not governed by the APA". For sharply critical comment on Darby, see Schwartz, *Timing of Judicial Review—A Survey of Recent Cases*, 8 Admin.L.J. 261, 285–88 (1994).

Note the partial symmetry of Darby with the Supreme Court's earlier decision in Patsy v. Board of Regents, Paragraph (4), *supra*, holding judge-

---

[6] In an alternate holding, the Court ruled that the claim was not ripe because plaintiff had not availed itself of state procedures for obtaining compensation.

made exhaustion rules displaced in cases brought under § 1983. Is the case that exhaustion requirements are statutorily precluded stronger or weaker in Darby than it was in Patsy? Has the Court grown more skeptical of the benefits of requiring exhaustion of administrative remedies? More reluctant to craft or apply jurisdiction-limiting doctrines not explicitly authorized by Congress?

B. ABSTENTION: PULLMAN AND RELATED DOCTRINES

Railroad Commission of Texas v. Pullman Co.

312 U.S. 496, 61 S.Ct. 643, 85 L.Ed. 971 (1941).
Appeal from the United States District Court for the Western District of Texas.

■ MR. JUSTICE FRANKFURTER delivered the opinion of the Court.

In those sections of Texas where the local passenger traffic is slight, trains carry but one sleeping car. These trains, unlike trains having two or more sleepers, are without a Pullman conductor; the sleeper is in charge of a porter who is subject to the train conductor's control. As is well known, porters on Pullmans are colored and conductors are white. Addressing itself to this situation, the Texas Railroad Commission after due hearing ordered that "no sleeping car shall be operated on any line of railroad in the State of Texas * * * unless such cars are continuously in the charge of an employee * * * having the rank and position of Pullman conductor". Thereupon, the Pullman Company and the railroads affected brought this action in a federal district court to enjoin the Commission's order. Pullman porters were permitted to intervene as complainants, and Pullman conductors entered the litigation in support of the order. Three judges having been convened, the court enjoined enforcement of the order. From this decree, the case came here directly.

The Pullman Company and the railroads assailed the order as unauthorized by Texas law as well as violative of the Equal Protection, the Due Process and the Commerce Clauses of the Constitution. The intervening porters adopted these objections but mainly objected to the order as a discrimination against Negroes in violation of the Fourteenth Amendment.

The complaint of the Pullman porters undoubtedly tendered a substantial constitutional issue. It is more than substantial. It touches a sensitive area of social policy upon which the federal courts ought not to enter unless no alternative to its adjudication is open. Such constitutional adjudication plainly can be avoided if a definitive ruling on the state issue would terminate the controversy. It is therefore our duty to turn to a consideration of questions under Texas law.

The Commission found justification for its order in a Texas statute * * *.[1] It is common ground that if the order is within the Commission's

---

[1] Vernon's Anno. Texas Civil Statutes, Article 6445:

"Power and authority are hereby conferred upon the Railroad Commission of Texas over all railroads, and suburban, belt and terminal railroads, and over all public

authority its subject matter must be included in the Commission's power to prevent "unjust discrimination * * * and to prevent any and all other abuses" in the conduct of railroads. Whether arrangements pertaining to the staffs of Pullman cars are covered by the Texas concept of "discrimination" is far from clear. What practices of the railroads may be deemed to be "abuses" subject to the Commission's correction is equally doubtful. Reading the Texas statutes and the Texas decisions as outsiders without special competence in Texas law, we would have little confidence in our independent judgment regarding the application of that law to the present situation. The lower court did deny that the Texas statutes sustained the Commission's assertion of power. And this represents the view of an able and experienced circuit judge of the circuit which includes Texas and of two capable district judges trained in Texas law. Had we or they no choice in the matter but to decide what is the law of the state, we should hesitate long before rejecting their forecast of Texas law. But no matter how seasoned the judgment of the district court may be, it cannot escape being a forecast rather than a determination. The last word on the meaning of Article 6445 of the Texas Civil Statutes, and therefore the last word on the statutory authority of the Railroad Commission in this case, belongs neither to us nor to the district court but to the supreme court of Texas. In this situation a federal court of equity is asked to decide an issue by making a tentative answer which may be displaced tomorrow by a state adjudication. The reign of law is hardly promoted if an unnecessary ruling of a federal court is thus supplanted by a controlling decision of a state court. The resources of equity are equal to an adjustment that will avoid the waste of a tentative decision as well as the friction of a premature constitutional adjudication.

An appeal to the chancellor, as we had occasion to recall only the other day, is an appeal to the "exercise of the sound discretion, which guides the determination of courts of equity". Beal v. Missouri Pacific R.R., 312 U.S. 45, decided January 20, 1941. The history of equity jurisdiction is the history of regard for public consequences in employing the extraordinary remedy of the injunction. There have been as many and as variegated applications of this simple principle as the situations that have brought it into play. Few public interests have a higher claim upon the discretion of a federal chancellor than the avoidance of needless friction with state policies, whether the policy relates to the enforcement of the criminal law, Fenner v. Boykin, 271 U.S. 240; Spielman Motor Co. v. Dodge, 295 U.S. 89; or the administration of a specialized scheme for liquidating embarrassed business enterprises, Pennsylvania v. Williams, 294 U.S. 176; or the final authority of a state court to interpret doubtful regulatory laws of the state, Gilchrist v. Interborough Co., 279 U.S. 159;

---

wharves, docks, piers, elevators, warehouses, sheds, tracks and other property used in connection therewith in this State, and over all persons, associations and corporations, private or municipal, owning or operating such railroad, wharf, dock, pier, elevator, warehouse, shed, track or other property to fix, and it is hereby made the duty of the said Commission to adopt all necessary rates, charges and regulations, to govern and regulate such railroads, persons, associations and corporations, and to correct abuses and prevent unjust discrimination in the rates, charges and tolls of such railroads, persons, associations and corporations, and to fix division of rates, charges and regulations between railroads and other utilities and common carriers where a division is proper and correct, and to prevent any and all other abuses in the conduct of their business and to do and perform such other duties and details in connection therewith as may be provided by law."

cf. Hawks v. Hamill, 288 U.S. 52, 61. These cases reflect a doctrine of abstention appropriate to our federal system whereby the federal courts, "exercising a wise discretion", restrain their authority because of "scrupulous regard for the rightful independence of the state governments" and for the smooth working of the federal judiciary. See Cavanaugh v. Looney, 248 U.S. 453, 457; Di Giovanni v. Camden Ins. Ass'n., 296 U.S. 64, 73. This use of equitable powers is a contribution of the courts in furthering the harmonious relation between state and federal authority without the need of rigorous congressional restriction of those powers. * * *

Regard for these important considerations of policy in the administration of federal equity jurisdiction is decisive here. If there was no warrant in state law for the Commission's assumption of authority there is an end of the litigation; the constitutional issue does not arise. The law of Texas appears to furnish easy and ample means for determining the Commission's authority. Article 6453 of the Texas Civil Statutes gives a review of such an order in the state courts. Or, if there are difficulties in the way of this procedure of which we have not been apprised, the issue of state law may be settled by appropriate action on the part of the State to enforce obedience to the order. Beal v. Missouri Pacific R.R., *supra*; Article 6476, Texas Civil Statutes. In the absence of any showing that these obvious methods for securing a definitive ruling in the state courts cannot be pursued with full protection of the constitutional claim, the district court should exercise its wise discretion by staying its hands. Compare Thompson v. Magnolia Co., 309 U.S. 478.

We therefore remand the cause to the district court, with directions to retain the bill pending a determination of proceedings, to be brought with reasonable promptness, in the state court in conformity with this opinion.

not "dismiss"

Reversed and remanded.

■ MR. JUSTICE ROBERTS took no part in the consideration or decision of this case.

NOTE ON ABSTENTION IN CASES INVOLVING A FEDERAL QUESTION

(1) The Basis of the Pullman Doctrine. In explaining its decision to order abstention in the Pullman case, the Supreme Court cited a number of considerations, including the following: resolution of a state law question in a particular way would avoid the necessity to decide a federal constitutional question; the relevant state law was unclear; resolution of the federal constitutional question adversely to the defendants might generate "needless friction" with state policies; and "the federal constitutional question 'touche[d] a sensitive area of social policy upon which the federal courts ought not to enter unless no alternative to adjudication is open' ". Do these factors, individually or jointly, justify the decision to abstain?[1]

---

[1]   Even before Pullman, the Supreme Court had endorsed federal court abstention on difficult, unsettled questions of state law. See, *e.g.*, Gilchrist v. Interborough Rapid Transit Co., 279 U.S. 159 (1929) (federal court action to prevent state commission from interfering with fare increase; action was filed only a few hours before commission sued in state court to compel compliance with existing fare); Railroad Comm'n v. Rowan & Nichols Oil Co., 310 U.S. 573

(a) Recall that, in Siler v. Louisville & N. R.R., 213 U.S. 175 (1909), p. 866, *supra*, the Court held that if a controverted question of state law was presented in an action that also presented a federal constitutional issue, the federal district court should decide the state question first (even though the court had only pendent jurisdiction with respect to that question) in order to avoid, if possible, a constitutional decision. (This background to the Pullman case was importantly modified by Pennhurst State School & Hosp. v. Halderman, 465 U.S. 89 (1984), p. 935, *supra*, the consequences of which are discussed in Paragraph (4), *infra*.) Is Pullman inconsistent with Siler? Or does Pullman simply implement Siler's injunction to avoid unnecessary constitutional decisions by a mechanism that also satisfies other legitimate concerns?

(b) How significant is the worry that a federal court's decision of a difficult state law issue, in a case such as Pullman, might be "supplanted by a controlling decision of a state court"? If a state court decision in a suit between other parties was contrary to that of the federal court, the federal court would need to withdraw or modify any injunction that it had issued previously. Although this result might be embarrassing, federal courts are frequently called upon to resolve hard questions of state law that they could potentially decide erroneously.[2]

(c) In suggesting that the friction generated by a federal remedy for unconstitutional state action might be "needless", Justice Frankfurter appeared to assume that it is preferable for a state court, rather than a federal court, to invalidate a state law or state policy. Although Pullman was decided prior to Monroe v. Pape, consider whether this aspect of the Pullman rationale is consistent with the policy judgment subsequently held to have been reflected in § 1983.

(d) What did Justice Frankfurter mean in suggesting that the constitutional question "touche[d] a sensitive area of state policy"? According to Resnik, *Rereading "The Federal Courts:" Revising the Domain of Federal Courts Jurisprudence at the End of the Twentieth Century*, 47 Vand.L.Rev. 1021, 1039 (1994) (footnotes omitted): "The testimony [in the record] in Pullman is filled with discussion of how white women feel 'a little bit safer . . . with a white man conductor in charge of that car.' * * * Further, in an effort to prop up the porters' claims, the record also includes testimony aimed

---

(1940), *reh'g denied*, 311 U.S. 614 (1940) (rejecting on the merits a federal due process challenge to a regulatory order, and refusing to decide whether under state law there was a "reasonable basis" for the commission's order, so as to avoid supplanting the commission's expert judgment). See also Thompson v. Magnolia Petroleum Co., 309 U.S. 478 (1940) (although federal bankruptcy court had jurisdiction to determine the title to property in trustee's possession, trustee should be directed to bring state court proceeding to settle the issue).

[2]   See generally Shapiro, *State Courts and Federal Declaratory Judgments*, 74 Nw.U.L.Rev. 759 (1979) (suggesting that after a federal court has resolved a dispute in an action for equitable relief, its decision should have claim and issue preclusive effect in subsequent litigation between the same parties, but that issue preclusion ought not apply against the state with regard to other parties). For specific discussion of the effect of federal judgments that state statutes are overbroad and therefore unenforceable—judgments that necessarily rest on a possibly erroneous determination of the meaning of those statutes as a matter of state law—see Fallon, *Making Sense of Overbreadth*, 100 Yale L.J. 853, 877–83, 898–903 (1991).

One of the situations in which federal courts may be asked to resolve difficult state law questions is specifically addressed by the supplemental jurisdiction statute, 28 U.S.C. § 1367, under which a federal court may refuse jurisdiction over a pendent state law claim in a federal question case if it "raises a novel or complex issue of State law". On the relationship between § 1367(c) and abstention, see Schapiro, *Polyphonic Federalism: State Constitutions in the Federal Courts*, 87 Cal.L.Rev. 1409, 1421–22 (1999).

at distinguishing 'the Pullman porter[s],' as 'pretty high-classed colored men,' from those other kinds of 'colored men.'

" * * * In 1941 it was, I take it, not obvious how federal constitutional law would decide [the equal protection] question [that Pullman presented]. It was not easy because national norms did not readily trump local customs and prejudices, indeed because national norms may well have shared such prejudices. [As Professor Resnik observes in a footnote, the United States Army remained segregated in 1941.] Thus the case was 'sensitive,' the engagement between federal and state law fraught with anxiety, and if some other point of law could determine the outcome without having to consider announcing federal constitutional rules about discrimination based on race, more the better."

Was Pullman a wise avoidance of a question better faced after prevailing social understandings had undergone further evolution? Was it an abdication of judicial responsibility?

(2) Abstention and the Separation of Powers. The federal district court possessed undoubted statutory jurisdiction over the Pullman case. In his much-quoted opinion in Cohens v. Virginia, 19 U.S. (6 Wheat.) 264 (1821), Chief Justice Marshall wrote: "We have no more right to decline the exercise of a jurisdiction which is given, than to usurp that which is not given. The one or the other would be treason to the constitution." Did the Court in Pullman commit "treason to the constitution"?

In approaching this question, recall Justice Frankfurter's invocation of the tradition of judicial discretion in the award of equitable remedies. But the traditions of equity developed in England, and considerations of federalism therefore had no role in early equitable practice. Under these circumstances, Professor Redish argues that reference to equity simply begs the question whether the federal courts possess authority under the separation of powers to decline to exercise a congressionally authorized jurisdiction based on their own federalism-based notions of sound policy. Redish, The Federal Courts in the Political Order: Judicial Jurisdiction and American Political Theory 59–60 (1991). In his view, there is no demonstrated justification for assuming that Congress would have intended courts to retain discretionary authority to decline jurisdiction based on federalism-related concerns. He sees a judicial claim of power to abstain as a power grab—a usurpation of congressional power to define the jurisdiction of the federal courts—that is incompatible with basic premises of constitutional democracy.[3]

Compare Shapiro, *Jurisdiction and Discretion*, 60 N.Y.U.L.Rev. 543, 543–45, 574–75 (1985) (some paragraphing omitted):

"Judges and lawyers have often said that the federal courts are obligated to exercise the jurisdiction conferred on them by the Constitution and by Congress. * * * [S]uggestions of an overriding obligation, subject only and at most to a few narrowly drawn exceptions, are far too grudging in their recognition of judicial discretion in matters of jurisdiction. * * * [T]he existence of this discretion is much more pervasive than is generally realized, and * * * it has ancient and honorable roots at common law as well as in equity. * * *

---

[3] To the suggestion that Pullman abstention merely delays rather than declines the exercise of federal jurisdiction, Professor Redish responds that "even a delay * * * may be considered a violation of the separation of powers if it has not been contemplated by Congress".

"My point is not that the Constitution expressly 'provides' that a grant of jurisdiction carries with it certain discretion not to proceed, or that Congress necessarily 'intends' to confer such discretion when it authorizes the exercise of jurisdiction. Rather, I submit that, as experience and tradition teach, the question whether a court must exercise jurisdiction and resolve a controversy on its merits is difficult, if not impossible, to answer in gross. And the courts are functionally better adapted to engage in the necessary fine tuning than is the legislature. * * *

"A grant of jurisdiction obligates the court to receive and consider the plaintiff's complaint and, on appropriate occasions, to determine whether the ends of justice will be served best by declining to proceed. At the same time, nothing in our history or traditions permits a court to interpret a normal grant of jurisdiction as conferring unbridled authority to hear cases simply at its pleasure. * * * [W]hen jurisdiction is conferred, I believe that there is at least a 'principle of preference' that a court should entertain and resolve on its merits an action within the scope of the jurisdictional grant. For this preference to yield in a particular case, the court must provide an explanation based on the language of the grant, the historical context in which the grant was made, or the common law tradition behind it."

In Shapiro's view, experience suggests that the criteria for channeling discretion in matters of jurisdiction may be grouped under four headings— "equitable discretion, federalism and comity, separation of powers, and judicial administration"—that "in general, are to be weighed against the presumption favoring the assertion and exercise of jurisdiction". Compare Friedman, *A Different Dialogue: The Supreme Court, Congress and Federal Jurisdiction*, 85 Nw.U.L.Rev. 1 (1990) (arguing that the Constitution authorizes a dialogic interaction between Congress and the courts in fixing the bounds of federal jurisdiction).[4]

---

[4]   The question whether judicially crafted abstention doctrines are permissible under the jurisdictional statutes and the separation of powers is a general one, by no means limited to Pullman abstention, and it has stimulated a broad debate. Professor Redish remains the leading proponent of the view that, in the absence of clear statutory authorization, abstention violates separation-of-powers principles. *E.g.*, Redish, *supra*, at 47–74; Redish, *Abstention, Separation of Powers, and the Limits of the Judicial Function*, 94 Yale L.J. 71 (1984). See also Doernberg, *"You Can Lead a Horse to Water . . . ": The Supreme Court's Refusal to Allow the Exercise of Original Jurisdiction Conferred by Congress*, 40 Case W.Res.L.Rev. 999 (1989–90). For critical analyses of this view, in addition to Shapiro, *supra*, see Wells, *Why Professor Redish is Wrong About Abstention*, 19 Ga.L.Rev. 1097 (1985); Althouse, *The Humble and the Treasonous: Judge-Made Jurisdiction Law*, 40 Case W.Res.L.Rev. 1035 (1989–90); Beerman, *"Bad" Judicial Activism and Liberal Federal-Courts Doctrine: A Comment on Professor Doernberg and Professor Redish*, 40 Case W.Res.L.Rev. 1053 (1989–90); Brown, *When Federalism and Separation of Powers Collide—Rethinking Younger Abstention*, 59 Geo.Wash.L.Rev. 114 (1990); and Marshall, *Abstention, Separation of Powers, and Recasting the Meaning of Judicial Restraint*, 107 Nw.U.L.Rev. 881 (2013). For an argument that abstention doctrines do not merely involve questions of policy, but are rooted in the Constitution, see Massey, *Abstention and the Constitutional Limits of the Judicial Power of the United States*, 1991 B.Y.U.L.Rev. 811.

Fallon, *Why Abstention Is Not Illegitimate: An Essay on the Distinction Between "Legitimate" and "Illegitimate" Statutory Interpretation and Judicial Lawmaking*, 107 Nw.U.L.Rev. 847 (2013), argues that if abstention involves an illegitimate judicial usurpation of congressional prerogatives (as Professor Redish maintains), then so do a number of other federal courts doctrines discussed by Professors Shapiro and Friedman, with whom he agrees in rejecting Redish's characterization. But Fallon also rejects the view, which he ascribes to Professors Shapiro and Friedman, that past latitudinarian interpretations of jurisdictional statutes would necessarily legitimate future judicial claims of comparably broad interpretive and lawmaking prerogative.

(3) The Evolution of Pullman Abstention.

(a) Early Years. In the early years after Pullman, the Supreme Court frequently required abstention on unsettled state law issues when resolution of those issues was preliminary to consideration of a federal constitutional question. See, *e.g.*, Spector Motor Serv., Inc. v. McLaughlin, 323 U.S. 101 (1944); Albertson v. Millard, 345 U.S. 242 (1953); City of Meridian v. Southern Bell Tel. & Tel. Co., 358 U.S. 639 (1959). In Propper v. Clark, 337 U.S. 472 (1949), however, the Court made clear that abstention was inappropriate to avoid decision of *nonconstitutional* federal issues.[5]

(b) Extension to Actions at Law. Despite Pullman's equitable foundations, the Court, without further discussion (and indeed without citation to Pullman), ordered abstention in actions at law, not equity, in several significant cases that involved both difficult state law issues and potentially avoidable federal constitutional issues. See Clay v. Sun Ins. Office, Ltd., 363 U.S. 207 (1960); United Gas Pipe Line Co. v. Ideal Cement Co., 369 U.S. 134 (1962); Fornaris v. Ridge Tool Co., 400 U.S. 41 (1970).

The Court appeared at least partially to change course with respect to the permissibility of abstention in actions at law in Quackenbush v. Allstate Ins. Co., 517 U.S. 706 (1996), which affirmed a court of appeals decision holding an abstention-based order to remand a removed case to state court inappropriate in a suit for damages. In doing so, the Court ruled that "federal courts have the power to dismiss or remand cases based on abstention principles only where the relief being sought is equitable or otherwise discretionary".[6] Writing for a unanimous Court, Justice O'Connor viewed prior decisions as establishing that "the authority of a federal court to abstain from exercising its jurisdiction extends to all cases in which the court has discretion to grant or deny relief", but concluded that "we have not previously addressed whether the principles underlying our abstention cases would support the remand or dismissal of a common-law action for damages." She distinguished Clay, United Gas Pipe Line, and Fornaris as involving a "stay" or "postponement", rather than the dismissal or remand, of the federal action.[7] The Court acknowledged that "federal courts have discretion to dismiss damage actions * * * under the common-law doctrine of forum non conveniens", but concluded that the abstention doctrine was "of a distinct

---

[5] Most lower courts have resisted efforts to circumvent Propper by characterizing federal statutory challenges to state action as constitutional challenges under the Supremacy Clause. See, *e.g.*, United Servs. Auto. Ass'n v. Muir, 792 F.2d 356, 363–64 (3d Cir.1986), *cert. denied*, 479 U.S. 1031 (1987); 17A Wright, Miller, & Cooper, Federal Practice and Procedure § 4242.

[6] Petitioner Quackenbush, California's Insurance Commissioner, was appointed trustee of an insurance company ordered into liquidation by a California court. On behalf of that company, Quackenbush filed a common law damages suit against Allstate in state court, alleging breach of reinsurance agreements. Allstate removed to federal court on diversity grounds and moved to compel arbitration under the Federal Arbitration Act. Quackenbush then sought to remand the suit to state court, arguing that federal abstention was appropriate under the doctrine of Burford v. Sun Oil Co., p. 1120, *infra*, because federal adjudication might interfere with California's resolution of the underlying insolvency and because the viability of Allstate's set-off claims depended on a disputed question of state law pending before the California courts in another case arising out of the same insolvency. Presumably, the Court's pronouncements concerning the limits of "abstention principles" apply equally to cases involving the Pullman doctrine.

[7] The Court distinguished Fair Assessment in Real Estate Ass'n, Inc. v. McNary, p. 1091, *supra*, which held that a federal court should not entertain a § 1983 action for damages arising from a state tax scheme, on the ground that it had been construed by the subsequent decision in National Private Truck Council, Inc., p. 1093, *supra*, as "a case about the scope of the § 1983 cause of action, not the abstention doctrines".

historical pedigree" and that it more narrowly circumscribed judicial discretion to dismiss or remand a case. Although abstention principles "might support a federal court's decision to postpone adjudication of a damages action", dismissal or remand was inappropriate.[8]

Do persuasive reasons support the distinction between a stay or postponement of a federal damages action, which Quackenbush treats as permissible under abstention principles, and a dismissal or remand, which Quackenbush holds impermissible?[9] Suppose a plaintiff files a damages action in federal court and the federal defendant files a parallel state court action presenting the same issues. If the federal action is stayed pending resolution of the state action, the state court's determination may dictate the outcome of the federal action under doctrines of claim and issue preclusion. If so, the practical effect of a stay may be identical to that of an order dismissing the federal action. See Moses H. Cone Memorial Hosp. v. Mercury Constr. Corp., p. 1179, *infra*.[10] Consider next a case, such as Quackenbush, in which a plaintiff files suit in state court and a defendant removes to federal court on diversity grounds. How useful is a stay or postponement likely to be under this scenario?

Is the notion that a federal court may not dismiss or remand a case that does not involve discretionary remedies consistent with judicial practice declining to exercise jurisdiction in other cases? Compare Shapiro, Paragraph (2), *supra*, at 555–61 (discussing exercises of discretion to decline jurisdiction including, *inter alia*, the forum non conveniens doctrine and the Supreme Court's assumption of discretion to decline jurisdiction of cases—including suits for damages—within its original jurisdiction). Should the considerations of convenience and judicial administration that underlie forum non conveniens doctrine be treated as more important than the considerations of comity and federalism that support abstention doctrines?[11]

The Court, in Quackenbush, did not consider the circumstances under which a stay of a suit for damages in federal court might be appropriate under abstention principles. Imagine that the plaintiffs in Pullman itself had claimed damages as well as injunctive relief under the federal Constitution. How should the Court have dealt with the damages claim? If it is assumed, anachronistically, that the defendants would have enjoyed official immunity unless they had violated "clearly established" federal rights, see Harlow v. Fitzgerald, p. 1030, *supra*, it seems clear that ultimate liability should not

---

[8]   Justice Kennedy, concurring, noted that he would "not rule out * * * the possibility that a federal court might dismiss a suit for damages in a case where a serious affront to the interests of federalism could be averted in no other way". In response, Justice Scalia, also concurring, said that he "would not have joined [the Court's] opinion if [he] believed it left such discretionary dismissal available".

[9]   Compare the similar distinction drawn by Frankfurter, J., in Louisiana Power & Light Co. v. City of Thibodaux, pp. 1123–1126, *infra*.

[10]   In ruling that the district court's remand order was appealable, Quackenbush relied on the holding of Moses H. Cone that a stay order was immediately appealable under the collateral order doctrine because it " 'amount[ed] to a refusal to adjudicate' the case in federal court" that would not be effectively reviewable on appeal from a final judgment in the federal action, "because the district court would be bound, as a matter of res judicata, to honor the state court's judgment". The stay in Moses H. Cone, the Court said, was "functionally indistinguishable" from the remand order in Quackenbush. If a stay and a remand order are "functionally indistinguishable" for purposes of collateral order doctrine, why aren't they equally so for purposes of abstention?

[11]   *Cf.* Shreve, *Pragmatism Without Polics—A Half Measure of Authority for Jurisdictional Common Law,* 1991 BYU L.Rev. 767.

attach. But in Pearson v. Callahan, 555 U.S. 223 (2009), discussed p. 1052, *supra*, the Court stated that the lower federal courts have discretion to determine whether a constitutional right was violated before determining whether it was previously established with clarity. Can this approach be reconciled with the avoidance policy prescribed in Pullman?

(c) **Diversity Cases.** The early cases extending Pullman from equitable to legal actions also crossed a second divide, again without discussion from the Court. Whereas jurisdiction in the Pullman case rested on the general federal jurisdiction statute, 28 U.S.C. § 1331, Clay, United Gas Pipe Line, and Fornaris were all diversity cases (even though all presented federal questions as well). A major purpose of the diversity jurisdiction—to provide a neutral forum for the determination of state law issues, both hard and easy—is at least attenuated by abstention, whether or not the state law issue is preliminary to a federal question. According to Redish, *supra,* this extension of Pullman flouts the congressional policy expressed in the grant of diversity jurisdiction. Is congressional intent with respect to the precise question raised by these cases sufficiently clear to be flouted?

(d) **Section 1983 Actions.** Over the dissent of Justice Douglas (joined by Chief Justice Warren and Justice Brennan), the Supreme Court, in Harrison v. NAACP, 360 U.S. 167 (1959), found Pullman abstention doctrine applicable to cases under § 1983. The dissenters emphasized the suspicion of state courts evinced in the legislative history of the Civil Rights Act of 1871 and asserted the special importance of a federal forum in civil rights cases. Note, however, that an "exception" for § 1983 cases would nearly swallow the rule, as that section extends to all constitutional violations by those acting under color of state law.

(e) **Decline and Resurgence.** The Supreme Court's enthusiasm for Pullman abstention appeared to wane during the 1960s, as the Court expressed concern about the delays that abstention entails. See Paragraph (7), *infra.* The doctrine enjoyed a resurgence in the Burger Court, see, *e.g.,* Babbitt v. United Farm Workers Nat. Union, 442 U.S. 289 (1979); Harris County Com'rs Court v. Moore, 420 U.S. 77 (1975); Lake Carriers' Ass'n v. MacMullan, 406 U.S. 498 (1972), only to recede again as an express ground of Supreme Court decision-making. Despite the relative dearth of recent, supportive cases in the Supreme Court, the doctrine continues to be applied by the lower federal courts, although with some uncertainty and confusion. See generally 17A Wright, Miller & Cooper, Federal Practice & Procedure § 4242.

(4) **The Impact of Pennhurst.** In Pennhurst State School & Hosp. v. Halderman, 465 U.S. 89 (1984), p. 935, *supra*, the Supreme Court held that the Eleventh Amendment denies federal courts jurisdiction to award injunctive relief against state officials based upon state law. Pennhurst does not bar federal court suits challenging state action under both state and federal law if the relief is not of the kind barred by the Eleventh Amendment—as is true of relief against a local government or its officials and of damages to be paid out of a state or local official's pocket. Nor is Pennhurst relevant to cases in which a plaintiff attempts to attack a state statute and the validity of the attack depends on how the statute would be construed by the state's courts.[12] But if the Pullman case were filed today in

---

[12] In cases presenting First Amendment overbreadth and vagueness challenges, the question frequently arises whether abstention is appropriate pending a state court determination of a statute's actual reach. In City of Houston v. Hill, 482 U.S. 451 (1987), in

federal court, under Pennhurst the court would lack power altogether to entertain a claim to enjoin the order as unauthorized by Texas law.

Following Pennhurst, suppose that a plaintiff who would have colorable claims to injunctive relief against state officials on both state law and federal constitutional grounds files suit in federal court seeking relief on the federal constitutional grounds only. Should the federal court stay its hand in order to permit state court resolution of the state law issue? In Askew v. Hargrave, 401 U.S. 476 (1971), Florida citizens filed a federal class action challenging a state school financing program under the Equal Protection Clause. A pending state court action by a school board challenged the same law under the Florida constitution. The Court remanded for consideration whether to abstain, noting that the "claims under the Florida Constitution * * *, if sustained, will obviate the necessity of determining the [federal equal protection] question." Note that in Askew, unlike Pullman itself, abstention could be justified only to avoid a federal constitutional question, and not to prevent misconstruction of state law or unjustified interference with a state program. Werhan, *Pullman Abstention After Pennhurst: A Comment on Judicial Federalism*, 27 Wm. & Mary L.Rev. 449, 490–99 (1986). Should abstention be allowed on this basis?

Imagine that a federal plaintiff raises only federal claims in a federal court action, and neither the federal plaintiff nor anyone else has raises parallel state law claims in a state court action. Should a federal court abstain on the ground that the plaintiff *must* go to state court with claims that, if resolved favorably, might moot or modify the federal issue? A few have done so. See, *e.g.*, Muskegon Theatres, Inc. v. City of Muskegon, 507 F.2d 199 (6th Cir.1974) (refusing to permit the "simple expedient" of not raising the state law claim at all to "frustrate the policies underlying the doctrine of abstention"); International Brotherhood of Elec. Workers v. Public Serv. Comm'n of Nevada, 614 F.2d 206 (9th Cir.1980) (noting that union's decision not to raise state law claims "does not affect our determination of the abstention issue"). Is it reasonable to compel plaintiffs, at their own expense, to make state law claims they do not wish to make in a forum in which they do not wish to litigate, when resolution of the state claim is not *necessary* to consideration of the federal claim?

(5) The Meaning of Unsettled State Law. When is an issue of state law sufficiently "unsettled" or "unclear" to warrant abstention under the Pullman doctrine? The answer does not emerge easily from the decisions, since the Court frequently announces only its conclusion with little elaboration of its reasons.

---

which the plaintiff challenged a municipal ordinance making it a misdemeanor "to assault, strike, or in any manner oppose, molest, abuse or interrupt any policeman in the execution of his duty * * * ", the Supreme Court stated that "abstention * * * is inappropriate for cases [where] * * * statutes are justifiably attacked on their face as abridging free expression" (quoting Dombrowski v. Pfister, 380 U.S. 479 (1965)), and that "the delay of state-court proceedings might itself effect the impermissible chilling of the very constitutional right [plaintiff] seeks to protect," (quoting Zwickler v. Koota, 389 U.S. 241 (1967)). (Justice Powell, joined by Chief Justice Rehnquist and Justices Scalia and O'Connor, concurred in the judgment, but did not agree that abstention is generally inappropriate in facial challenges under the First Amendment.) In contrast with Hill, the Court declined to consider First Amendment challenges to state statutes before the state courts had the chance to construe them in Babbitt v. United Farm Workers Nat. Union, 442 U.S. 289 (1979), and Virginia v. American Booksellers Ass'n, Inc., 484 U.S. 383 (1988). See also Harrison v. NAACP, 360 U.S. 167 (1959) (ordering abstention). For general discussion of the relationship between the Pullman abstention and First Amendment overbreadth doctrines, see Fallon, note 2, *supra*, at 901–02.

Harrison v. NAACP, 360 U.S. 167 (1959), which involved a First Amendment challenge to Virginia statutes dealing with litigation and lobbying, especially with respect to racial matters, found abstention appropriate where the Court was "unable to agree that [there was] * * * no reasonable room" for a limiting construction. Similar language appears in Fornaris v. Ridge Tool Co., 400 U.S. 41, 44 (1970), and Reetz v. Bozanich, 397 U.S. 82, 86–87 (1970). Other cases have articulated a narrower standard. See, *e.g.*, Hawaii Housing Auth. v. Midkiff, 467 U.S. 229 (1984), in which the Court stated without dissent that although "[i]n the abstract" the possibility of a limiting construction always exists, "the relevant inquiry is not whether there is a bare, though unlikely possibility that state courts *might* render adjudication of the federal question unnecessary. Rather, '[w]e have frequently emphasized that abstention is not to be ordered unless the statute is of an uncertain nature, and is obviously susceptible of a limiting construction' " (quoting Zwickler v. Koota, 389 U.S. 241 (1967)).

The newness of a state statute and the total absence of judicial precedent are clearly significant considerations. See, *e.g.*, the Pullman case itself; Lake Carriers' Ass'n v. MacMullan, Paragraph (3)(e), *supra*; Harrison, *supra*. On the other hand, the mere presence of judicially unconstrued state law does not automatically require abstention. See, *e.g.*, Brockett v. Spokane Arcades, Inc., 472 U.S. 491 (1985); Wisconsin v. Constantineau, 400 U.S. 433, 439 (1971); Toomer v. Witsell, 334 U.S. 385 (1948).

Most important, the uncertainty in state law must be such that construction by the state court might obviate the need for decision (or at least help to limit the scope) of the federal constitutional question. See, *e.g.*, Baggett v. Bullitt, 377 U.S. 360 (1964) (rejecting an argument for abstention in a case challenging a statute as unconstitutionally vague where it was "fictional to believe that anything less than extensive adjudications, under the impact of a variety of factual situations", would cure the vagueness).

(6) Unsettled State Constitutional Provisions. Do different considerations govern the appropriateness of abstention due to the unclarity of state *constitutional* provisions—when, for example, a statute or official action is (or might be) attacked under both the state and federal constitutions? In Reetz v. Bozanich, 397 U.S. 82 (1970), the plaintiff sought a declaration that Alaska fishing laws and regulations, which limited eligibility to receive certain commercial fishing licenses, violated (i) the Fourteenth Amendment of the federal Constitution and (ii) two provisions of the Alaska constitution—one reserving fishing rights to the people, and the other proscribing exclusive fishing rights. A three-judge court upheld these contentions, but the Supreme Court vacated and remanded with directions to abstain, emphasizing that the Alaska constitutional provisions "have never been interpreted by an Alaska court" and that management of fish resources was "a matter of great state concern". See also Askew v. Hargrave, Paragraph (4), *supra*.

By contrast, in Wisconsin v. Constantineau, 400 U.S. 433 (1971), the Court upheld a lower court decision invalidating, under the Fourteenth Amendment's Due Process Clause, a Wisconsin statute providing for the public posting, without notice or hearing to the person affected, of the name of any person whose excessive drinking produced specified social problems. (The statute prohibited the provision of intoxicating beverages to any such person.) The Court declined to abstain, notwithstanding the dissenting protest of Chief Justice Burger and Justices Black and Blackmun that "[f]or all we know, the state courts would find this statute invalid under the State Constitution". Chief Justice Burger added: "Although Wisconsin has no due process clause as such, Art. I, § 1, of the Wisconsin Constitution has been held by the Wisconsin Supreme Court to be substantially equivalent to the limitation on state action contained in the Due Process and Equal Protection Clauses of the Fourteenth Amendment".[13]

The Court sought to reconcile these decisions in Harris County Comm'rs Court v. Moore, 420 U.S. 77 (1975), which ordered abstention to obtain a state court construction of the state constitution. The Court said that in Constantineau, "we declined to order abstention where the federal due process claim was not complicated by an unresolved state-law question, even though the plaintiffs might have sought relief under a similar provision of the state constitution. But where the challenged statute is part of an integrated scheme of related constitutional provisions, statutes, and regulations, and where the scheme as a whole calls for clarifying interpretation by the state courts, we have regularly required the district courts to abstain [citing Reetz]."[14]

Since most state constitutions contain guarantees analogous to those in the Bill of Rights, the stakes of this point are relatively high. Consider Professor Currie's response: "If the doctrine itself is sound, it should be applied to all cases within its purpose. Perhaps the Court's unprincipled limitation of abstention indicates a healthy dissatisfaction with the doctrine itself. If so, it would be more consistent to abolish abstention altogether." Currie, *The Supreme Court and Federal Jurisdiction: 1975 Term*, 1976 Sup.Ct.Rev. 183, 212. Consider, too, Professor Schapiro's suggestion that the Court's hesitancy to order abstention to obtain state court interpretations of state constitutional provisions underestimates the possibility that state courts may construe even identically worded state constitutional provisions differently from the parallel federal provisions. See Schapiro, note 2, *supra* at 1430. In light of this possibility, should federal courts inquire into state interpretive practices before deciding whether to abstain?

(7) The Problem of Delay. During the early years of the Pullman doctrine, pursuit of the prescribed procedure sometimes occasioned delays of six or eight years before the final resolution of litigation,[15] and critics cited the problem of delay in urging that the doctrine be abolished.[16] For discussion of the extent to which the widespread availability of certification procedures,

---

[13] If that analysis of Wisconsin constitutional law was correct, would a state decision invalidating the state law under the state constitution necessarily have been reviewable by the Supreme Court? See Chap. V, Sec. 2(A), *supra*. Is the answer to that question relevant to the decision whether to abstain?

[14] The Court sounded a similar theme in Examining Board of Engineers v. Flores de Otero, 426 U.S. 572, 597–98 (1976), in which it refused to abstain simply because a challenged Puerto Rico statute might violate Puerto Rico's constitutional guarantees of equal protection and nondiscrimination. To require abstention because of the "broad and sweeping" provisions of the Puerto Rico constitution "would convert abstention from an exception into a general rule". See also Hawaii Housing Auth. v. Midkiff, 467 U.S. 229, 237 n. 4 (1984).

[15] See, *e.g.*, Spector Motor Serv., Inc. v. O'Connor, 340 U.S. 602 (1951) (eight years); United States v. Leiter Minerals, Inc., 381 U.S. 413 (1965) (dismissed as moot eight years after abstention was ordered).

[16] See, *e.g.*, Kurland, *Toward a Co-operative Judicial Federalism: The Federal Court Abstention Doctrine*, 24 F.R.D. 481 (1959); Field, The Abstention Doctrine Today, 125 U.Pa.L.Rev. 590, 605 (1977); Currie, *The Federal Courts and the American Law Institute, Part II*, 36 U.Chi.L.Rev. 268, 317 (1969). See also England v. Louisiana State Bd. of Medical Exam'rs, 375 U.S. 411, 423 (1964) (Douglas, J., concurring) (urging that the doctrine be reconsidered).

which have proliferated since that time, might avoid the problem, see *Note on Procedural Aspects of Pullman Abstention*, immediately following this Note.

(8) Discretionary or Mandatory? As the Pullman case itself shows, a federal court may decide to abstain on its own motion.[17] But is the decision discretionary or mandatory?

The Supreme Court has occasionally cited protracted delay as an equitable factor supporting a refusal to abstain in particular cases. See, *e.g.*, Harman v. Forssenius, 380 U.S. 528, 537 (1965); Hostetter v. Idlewild Bon Voyage Liquor Corp., 377 U.S. 324, 329 (1964); Griffin v. County School Bd. of Prince Edward County, 377 U.S. 218, 228–29 (1964). Cases such as these imply that Pullman abstention is a discretionary doctrine that should be applied only after a balancing of competing considerations in the particular case. So, arguably, does the Court's reference to the Pullman dispute as touching a "sensitive area of social policy". In other instances, however, Supreme Court decisions have not devoted much attention to the sensitivity of the state program, see, *e.g.*, Hawaii Housing Auth. v. Midkiff, note 14, *supra*, and it is not obvious that the issue in Clay v. Sun Ins. Office, Paragraph (3)(b), *supra*, for example, which involved contract damages in a diversity action between private parties, was particularly sensitive or affected an important state program.

Would some of the objections to Pullman be mooted if the doctrine were framed in explicitly prudential terms and the costs exacted only where they could be justified on a fact-specific basis?[18]

NOTE ON PROCEDURAL ASPECTS OF PULLMAN ABSTENTION

(1) Stay of Federal Proceedings. When invoking the Pullman abstention doctrine, a federal court typically retains jurisdiction to permit it to resolve the federal question if a decision is ultimately necessary.[1] Retaining jurisdiction also enables the federal court to guard against unreasonable delay or an unforeseen bar to relief in the state courts, and, where appropriate, to provide interim relief pending the outcome of the state court litigation.[2]

(2) Commencing a State Proceeding. If a federal court decides to abstain on an issue of state law and to remit the plaintiff to state court to seek a resolution of that issue, a variety of issues and obstacles may immediately present themselves.

---

[17] See also Ohio Bureau of Emp't Servs. v. Hodory, 431 U.S. 471, 480 n. 11 (1977); Bellotti v. Baird, 428 U.S. 132, 143 n. 10 (1976).

[18] In Frost & Lindquist, *Countering the Majoritarian Difficulty*, 96 Va.L.Rev. 719 (2010), the authors cite evidence that state court judges who must run for reelection are sometimes under pressure to rule in accordance with majority preferences and argue that "federal courts should refuse to abstain in cases where it appears justice may be hard to find in state court".

[1] For a discussion of the limited exceptions, see Paragraph (2), *infra*.

[2] On the latter point, consider Babbitt v. United Farm Workers Nat. Union, 442 U.S. 289 (1979). There, the Court found abstention appropriate in a First Amendment challenge to state law. In responding to plaintiff's request for an injunction against enforcement of the statute at issue pending the state court proceeding, the Court said simply that "this is a matter that is best addressed by the District Court in the first instance." See generally Wells, *Preliminary Injunctions and Abstention: Some Problems in Federalism*, 63 Cornell L.Rev. 65 (1977).

(a) A state proceeding raising the issue may already be pending, as in Askew v. Hargrave, p. 1110, *supra*, but if (again as in Askew) the state proceeding involves different parties, the federal plaintiff may be unhappy with the adequacy of presentation of the issue and may be denied intervention. If so, the plaintiff may have to file an independent action in a state court.

(b) In some cases, the plaintiff may be able to seek a state declaratory judgment limited to the precise issue on which abstention was ordered. But there is no assurance that the state courts will entertain an action in the abstention context. In United Serv. Life Ins. Co. v. Delaney, 328 F.2d 483 (5th Cir.1964), after the Fifth Circuit abstained (reserving jurisdiction to enter final judgment), the Texas Supreme Court held that declaratory relief was unavailable because the decision of the issue of state law would be only an "advisory opinion." 396 S.W.2d 855 (Tex.1965).[3]

(c) As an alternative to requiring plaintiffs to commence a declaratory judgment action at the bottom of the state judicial ladder and to go up as far as they can, nearly all states now have certification procedures that permit a federal court to certify an unsettled question directly to the state's highest court. Certification and procedure in certified cases are discussed in Paragraph (5), *infra*. The discussion in all other Paragraphs of this Note primarily involves cases in which, following a federal court's decision to abstain under the Pullman doctrine, the parties themselves had to commence litigation in state court.

(3) Resolution of the Federal Questions. Whether or not the federal court retains jurisdiction, the parties may present their federal as well as their state contentions to the state court for decision, and the loser may seek Supreme Court review. A party may elect, however, not to submit the federal questions for state court decision. At least where the federal questions involve constitutional challenges to the state statute being construed, the state court must be apprised of the federal challenges, even if the plaintiff wishes to reserve the federal questions for federal court adjudication. In Government & Civic Employees Organizing Committee, CIO v. Windsor, 353 U.S. 364 (1957), the district court first abstained, and then, following a state court's construction of a state statute, ruled that the statute was constitutional. The Supreme Court vacated that ruling: "The bare adjudication by the Alabama Supreme Court * * * does not suffice, since that court was not asked to interpret the statute in light of the constitutional objections presented to the District Court. If appellants' freedom-of-expression and equal protection arguments had been presented to the state court, it might have construed the statute in a different manner. Accordingly, the judgment of the District Court is vacated, and this cause is remanded to

---

[3] What options remain available if a state court adopts the position of the Texas Supreme Court in Delaney? In Harris County Comm'rs Court v. Moore, 420 U.S. 77 (1975), the Court ordered abstention in a case arising in Texas and, in view of the Delaney case, ruled that the district court should dismiss instead of retaining jurisdiction. "The dismissal", the Court specified, "should be without prejudice so that any remaining federal claim may be raised in a federal forum after the Texas courts have been given the opportunity to address the state law questions in this case". This approach has since been followed by the federal courts in Texas cases. See, *e.g.*, Nationwide Mut. Ins. Co. v. Unauthorized Practice of Law Committee, 283 F.3d 650 (5th Cir.2002). Although adhering to the Delaney rule in Pullman cases, the Texas Supreme Court will decide questions certified to it by federal appellate courts under a specifically authorizing provision of the Texas constitution, Art. V, § 3–c.

it with directions to retain jurisdiction until efforts to obtain an appropriate adjudication in the state courts have been exhausted."

(4) The England Case. Suppose the state supreme court, having been apprised of the federal questions, chooses to decide them, and the litigant prefers not to seek Supreme Court review (or review is denied). May the litigant return to the federal court, or is the state decision res judicata? The Court answered this question in England v. Louisiana State Bd. of Medical Examiners, 375 U.S. 411 (1964), holding that a party is bound by the state court determination *only* if the party did in fact elect, in the words of NAACP v. Button, 371 U.S. 415 (1963), "to seek a complete and final adjudication of his rights in a state court". The Court said:

> "There are fundamental objections to any conclusion that a litigant who has properly invoked the jurisdiction of a Federal District Court to consider federal constitutional claims can be compelled, without his consent and through no fault of his own, to accept instead a state court's determination of those claims. * * * [A] party may readily forestall any conclusion that he has elected not to return to the District Court. He may accomplish this by making on the state record the 'reservation to the disposition of the entire case by the state courts' that we referred to in Button. That is, he may inform the state courts that he is exposing his federal claims there only for the purpose of complying with Windsor, and that he intends, should the state courts hold against him on the question of state law, to return to the District Court for disposition of his federal contentions. Such an explicit reservation is not indispensable; the litigant is in no event to be denied his right to return to the District Court unless it clearly appears that he voluntarily did more than Windsor required and fully litigated his federal claims in the state courts. When the reservation has been made, however, his right to return will in all events be preserved."[4]

Although the England procedure is now well entrenched in Pullman abstention doctrine, the Supreme Court attached an important limitation to its availability in San Remo Hotel, L.P. v. City and County of San Francisco, 545 U.S. 323 (2005). The plaintiff hotel operators initiated litigation in both state and federal court asserting both facial and as-applied challenges to a city ordinance requiring them to pay a $567,000 fee for converting residential rooms to tourist rooms. After the Ninth Circuit held the as-applied challenge unripe and abstained under Pullman from ruling on the facial claims, the plaintiffs returned to state court. There, seeking to reserve their federal claims, they argued that the ordinance was unconstitutional both on its face and as-applied under California law. When the state courts ruled against the plaintiffs on the merits, the plaintiffs sought to revive their federal claims in federal court, but the Supreme Court held that preclusion doctrine barred them from doing so, despite their efforts to reserve their federal claims under England. The Court, in an opinion by Justice Stevens, began by observing that " '[t]ypical' England cases generally involve federal constitutional challenges to a state statute that can be avoided if a state court construes the statute in a particular manner. In such cases, the purpose of abstention

---

[4] In the specific case before it, the Court found that the litigants had submitted the federal question to the state court, but only in the belief that the Windsor case required them to do so; the Court therefore declined to apply its new rule to them, and held that the district court should pass on the merits of their federal contention.

Is the judicial pronouncement of a rule with purely prospective effect consistent with Article III? See Chap. II, Sec. 1, pp. 50–58, *supra*.

is not to afford state courts an opportunity to adjudicate an issue that is functionally identical to the federal question".

Having described the purpose of the England reservation procedure in these terms, the Court reasoned that although the plaintiffs "were entitled to insulate from preclusive effect one federal issue—their facial constitutional challenge to the [city ordinance]"—they had advanced broad facial challenges under the California constitution on the same legal theory that supported their challenge under the federal Constitution. By doing so, "petitioners effectively asked the state court to resolve the same federal issues they asked it to reserve. England does not support the exercise of any such right". Nor had the plaintiffs successfully reserved their as-applied takings claims. Because unripe, those claims "were never properly before the District Court, and there was no reason to expect that they could be relitigated in full if advanced in the state proceedings". Chief Justice Rehnquist, joined by Justices O'Connor, Kennedy, and Thomas, concurring in the judgment, did not discuss the pertinence of England.

Could the plaintiffs have successfully reserved their facial challenge under the federal Constitution if they had asked the state court to rule the ordinance facially invalid under the state constitution, but on a different legal theory from that supporting their federal claim (due to relevant differences between state and federal constitutional law)?[5]

(5) The Option of Certification. In the decades since Pullman, nearly all states have adopted procedures that permit federal courts, while retaining jurisdiction of a case, to certify uncertain state law issues to the state's supreme court for authoritative resolution.[6] Although state procedures vary somewhat,[7] the federal court invariably drafts the questions of which it seeks resolution (often with the aid of the parties) and submits those questions directly to the state court. In certifying a question, the federal court is expected to state all pertinent facts, so that the state supreme court can answer a pure question of law.

State certification statutes are not limited to cases fitting the criteria for Pullman abstention. But in such cases, certification, when available, frequently furnishes a more expeditious method of obtaining state court resolution of state issues than would classic Pullman abstention.[8]

---

[5] If pressing in state court a state law claim identical in substance to a federal claim counts as presenting the federal claim to a state court for purposes of Pullman abstention, does it also count as presenting a federal claim to a state court for other purposes—for example, when a criminal defendant explicitly raises a federal claim for the first time in the Supreme Court or in federal habeas proceedings, but had raised a substantively identical state law claim in state court? *Cf.* Howell v. Mississippi, 543 U.S. 440 (2005), p. 527, *supra*.

[6] As of 2010, all of the states except North Carolina had authorized certification (as had the District of Columbia and Puerto Rico). See Acquaviva, *The Certification of Unsettled Questions of State Law to State High Courts: The Third Circuit's Experience*, 115 Penn.St.L.Rev. 377, 384–85 (2010).

[7] As of 2008, 30 states and the District of Columbia had adopted a version of the Uniform Certification of Questions of State Law Act, the most recent version of which was adopted by the National Conference of Commissioners on Uniform State Laws in 1995. See Uniform Certification of Questions of Law [Act] (1995), 12 U.L.A. 45 (2008); Uniform Certification of Questions of Law Act (1967), 12 U.L.A. 61 (2008). See also *Appellate Court Certification of Legal Issue to State High Court*, Fed. Litigator (Thomson Reuters), Apr. 2013, at 19.

[8] In a study of 48 cases, Seron, Certifying Questions of State Law: Experience of Federal Judges 16 (Federal Judicial Center 1983), found a median of six months from certification to the state's provision of an answer, with the range extending from less than one month to two and one-half years.

(a) Doctrinal History. The Supreme Court first ordered a lower federal court to avail itself of state certification procedures in Clay v. Sun Ins. Office, Ltd., 363 U.S. 207 (1960), p. 1107, *supra*. (The Clay case arose in Florida, which from 1945–1965 was the only state with a statute authorizing its courts to answer certified questions.) The Court also endorsed the certification option in Lehman Brothers v. Schein, 416 U.S. 386 (1974), a case involving a difficult question of state law but no federal question. (On the doctrines governing abstention in cases not presenting a federal question, see *Note on Burford and Thibodaux Abstention*, immediately following this Note.)

Again exhibiting enthusiasm for certification, in Arizonans for Official English v. Arizona, 520 U.S. 43, 80 (1997), a unanimous Court, per Justice Ginsburg, held that a federal court should not have ruled on the constitutionality of an Arizona constitutional amendment prescribing that the State "shall act in English and in no other language" without first certifying the question of the amendment's meaning to the Arizona Supreme Court. The Court quoted Justice O'Connor's concurring opinion in Brockett v. Spokane Arcades, Inc., 472 U.S. 491 (1985): " 'Speculation by a federal court about the meaning of a state statute in the absence of prior state adjudication is particularly gratuitous when * * * the state courts stand willing to address questions of state law on certification from a federal court' " (omission in original). The Court also emphasized the importance of the policy of avoiding or narrowing unsettled questions of federal constitutional law and the absence under certification procedures of "the delays, expense, and procedural complexity that generally attend abstention decisions". Under the circumstances, the Court ruled, the court of appeals erred in suggesting that "unique circumstances" were necessary to justify certification. In concluding otherwise, it said, the Ninth Circuit had improperly "[b]lended abstention with certification".[9]

(b) Mechanics. All states with certification procedures authorize the submission of certified questions by the Supreme Court or a federal court of appeals. Most, but not all, also authorize the certification of questions by federal district courts.[10] If a state supreme court will answer certified questions only from a federal court of appeals, should a district court feel encouraged to attempt to resolve a difficult state law issue, knowing that certification will be possible on appeal? Or would classic Pullman abstention be a better option?

Certification sometimes occurs at the request of one of the parties, but responsibility for the decision rests with the federal court, which can also decide to certify sua sponte. Most states require that the certified question be potentially determinative of the case. Thus, in Abrams v. West Virginia Racing Comm'n, 263 S.E.2d 103 (W.Va.1980), the state court refused to decide a certified question because it believed that federal law would control regardless of the answer. Some states, moreover, impose the stricter

---

[9]   In Fiore v. White, 528 U.S. 23 (1999), a habeas corpus case, the Supreme Court itself certified a question to the Pennsylvania Supreme Court, as it had previously done in Aldrich v. Aldrich, 378 U.S. 540 (1964).

[10]   As of 2003, 36 states permitted district courts to certify questions directly to their supreme courts. See Cochran, *Federal Court Certification of Questions of State Law to State Courts: A Theoretical and Empirical Study*, 29 J. Legis. 157, 223 (2003).

requirement that the answer will certainly determine the case.[11] How often will an answer *either way* determine the outcome? Apart from the requirement that a certified question be actually or potentially dispositive of the case, most if not all state supreme courts retain discretion to refuse to answer certified questions that they adjudge inappropriate for their decision.

(c) Certification in Practice. Formal and informal studies confirm that the use of certification is increasingly widespread,[12] and the trend seems almost certain to continue. In response to a survey conducted by the American Judicature Society, "[a]lmost all of the [responding] circuit judges (93%), district judges (86%), and state justices (87%) *agree[d]* that certification improves federal-state comity." Goldschmidt, Certification of Questions of Law 66 (1995). The literature, which includes numerous articles by both state and federal judges, is also generally supportive of certification as a model of cooperative federal-state judicial interaction.[13]

But the literature is by no means monolithic. In addition to tributes, it includes a number of negative assessments of certification's operation in practice, including some by both federal judges and state supreme court justices. There are well-documented instances in which state courts have declined to respond to certified questions, either because they were badly drafted[14] or for other reasons. See, *e.g.*, Schneider, *"But Answer Came There None": The Michigan Supreme Court and the Certified Question of State Law*, 41 Wayne L.Rev. 273, 316–22 (1995). Presumably based on his experience on the First Circuit, Judge Selya complains that certification "frequently adds time and expense to litigation that is already overlong and overly expensive" without achieving its intended purposes. Selya, *Certified Madness: Ask a Silly Question . . .* , 29 Suffolk U.L.Rev. 677, 681 (1995). The chief justice of Indiana's supreme court has also sounded notes of caution: "There are at least three difficulties with certification that affect the law-giving function. First, the procedural posture of certified questions forces a state court's collective hand to answer yes or no on complicated and often fact-sensitive issues. Second, judges are required to resolve constitutional issues when the case would be better decided on statutory grounds. Third, the creation of precedent-setting law without a well-developed factual background before the state supreme court may very well undermine and dilute state case law." Shepard, *Is Making State Constitutional Law Through Certified Questions a Good Idea or a Bad Idea?*, 38 Val.U.L.Rev. 327, 346 (2004).

(d) Considerations Governing the Use of Certification. Despite the Supreme Court's suggestion in Arizonans for Official English, p. 1117, *supra*, that the standards for certification are somehow more relaxed than

---

[11] See Newman, *Certification of State Law Questions: Pennsylvania's Experience in the First Five Years*, 75 Penn. Bar Assoc.Q. 47, 53 (2004) (reporting 13 states in this category).

[12] See, *e.g.*, Prefatory Note, Uniform Certification of Questions of Law [Act], note 7, *supra*. An informal search of an electronic database revealed 78 federal cases handed down in 2007 in which federal courts considered certifying a state law question. Within that sample, federal courts ordered certification in 31 cases and declined to do so in 47. A comparable search in 2001 found 62 reported cases in which federal courts considered certifying questions to a state supreme court and 24 in which they actually did so.

[13] See Nash, *Examining the Power of Federal Courts to Certify Questions of State Law*, 88 Cornell L.Rev. 1672, 1699–1700 (2003) (collecting sources).

[14] See, *e.g.*, Eley v. Pizza Hut of America, 500 N.W.2d 61 (Iowa 1993), in which the Supreme Court of Iowa declined to answer a certified question on the ground that, because the question was poorly drafted and did not include sufficient facts, the court could respond in a variety of ways and had no basis to choose the right answer.

those necessary for Pullman abstention,[15] the Court has not laid down a clear test for when federal courts should avail themselves of the certification option, and patterns appear to vary among the circuits. See generally 17A Wright, Miller & Cooper, Federal Practice & Procedure § 4248. There is an obvious threshold question of how uncertain a state law issue should be in order for a federal court to hesitate to decide it. Further questions involve how important and difficult the potentially avoidable federal question ought to be in order for the parties to be asked to bear the expense and delay of certification. Clark, *Ascertaining the Laws of the Several States: Positivism and Judicial Federalism After Erie*, 145 U.Pa.L.Rev. 1459 (1997), argues that the federal courts should employ a presumption in favor of certifying unsettled questions of state law to state courts in order to avoid inequitable administration of state law and encroachment on states' lawmaking powers, on the one hand, and separation-of-powers objections to abstention, on the other hand.[16] *Cf.* Glassman, *Making State Law in Federal Court*, 41 Gonz.L.Rev. 237, 254–55 (2005–06), maintaining that while state supreme courts are likely to welcome the opportunity to resolve "political hot-button issue[s]", they may appropriately prefer to postpone decision of more mundane state law issues until they have the benefit of being able to review lower court opinions. Should it matter whether a state court is likely to welcome the certified question?

Would Congress have the power to require states to entertain certified questions in cases in which state courts currently either cannot or will not do so? In thinking about this question, consider, *inter alia*, the pertinence of Testa v. Katt, 330 U.S. 386 (1947), p. 437, *supra*, and Alden v. Maine, 527 U.S. 706 (1999), p. 967, *supra*.

(6) Appealability of Decisions Whether to Abstain. An order denying a request to abstain is not immediately appealable. Gulfstream Aerospace Corp. v. Mayacamas Corp., 485 U.S. 271 (1988). On the circumstances under which abstention orders are and are not immediately appealable, see 15A Wright, Miller & Cooper § 3914.14.

NOTE ON BURFORD AND THIBODAUX ABSTENTION

(1) Departures from the Pullman Paradigm. In its paradigmatic applications, the Pullman doctrine involves challenges to state action in which resolution of an unsettled state law issue could eliminate the need to decide (or at least narrow) a difficult federal constitutional question. Is abstention ever justified when constitutional avoidance is not at issue?

The cases discussed in this Note respond to this question. One, Burford v. Sun Oil Co., 319 U.S. 315 (1943), is conventionally viewed as the leading case establishing a form of so-called "Burford" or "administrative"

---

[15] See also Bellotti v. Baird, 428 U.S. 132 (1976) ("Although we do not mean to intimate that abstention would be improper in this case were certification not possible, the availability of certification greatly simplifies the analysis."). But cf. Houston v. Hill, 482 U.S. 451 (1987) (the availability of certification, though important in deciding whether to abstain, "is not in itself sufficient to render abstention appropriate").

[16] See also Calabresi, *Federal and State Courts: Restoring a Workable Balance*, 78 N.Y.U.L.Rev. 1293 (2003) (arguing, *inter alia*, for increased use of certification and suggesting congressional authorization of state court appellate review of federal appellate decisions on issues of state law).

abstention. Another, Louisiana Power & Light Co. v. City of Thibodaux, 360 U.S. 25 (1959), is thought to have launched another abstention doctrine applicable to at least some cases otherwise within the federal courts' diversity jurisdiction and not presenting any federal question at all.

Although often cited, the Burford and Thibodaux cases have produced few if any progeny in the Supreme Court, and attempts to apply them in the lower courts have frequently spawned confusion. As you read through the remainder of this Note, consider (i) whether the Burford and Thibodaux decisions can be justified, (ii) whether they truly have given rise to sufficiently clear principles and bodies of law to constitute "doctrines", and if so, (iii) how those doctrines ought to be defined.

(2) Burford Abstention.

(a) The Burford Case. Burford v. Sun Oil Co., 319 U.S. 315 (1943), was an action to enjoin the execution of an order of the Railroad Commission of Texas granting a neighboring leaseholder a permit to drill new wells. The plaintiffs principally attacked the order on state law grounds, but also alleged an unlawful deprivation of property under the federal Due Process Clause. Jurisdiction rested on both diversity of citizenship and the presence in the case of a federal question. The Court held, 5–4, that the federal district court "as a matter of sound equitable discretion" should have declined to exercise jurisdiction and dismissed the case.

Justice Black's opinion cited Pullman, but he gave no indication that the Court thought the federal question especially difficult or sensitive, nor did he refer to the policy of constitutional avoidance. Instead, he emphasized the complexity of the problems of oil and gas regulation and the role of state courts as collaborators with a state administrative agency in administering the state's regulatory scheme:

"Since * * * oil moves through the entire field, one operator can not only draw oil from under his own surface area, but can also, if he is advantageously located, drain oil from the most distant parts of the reservoir. * * * For these and many other reasons based on geologic realities, each oil and gas field must be regulated as a unit for conservation purposes. * * *

"Texas' interests in this matter are more than that very large one of conserving gas and oil, two of our most important natural resources. It must also weigh the impact of the industry on the whole economy of the State and must consider its revenue, much of which is drawn from taxes on industry and from mineral lands preserved for the benefit of its educational and eleemosynary institutions. * * * The primary task of attempting adjustment of these diverse interests is delegated to the Railroad Commission, which Texas has vested with 'broad discretion' in administering the law."

Justice Black condemned the results of previous federal court injunctions, particularly those that had proved to be based on "misunderstanding of local law". He continued:

"In describing the relation of the Texas court to the Commission, no useful purpose will be served by attempting to label the court's position as legislative, Prentis v. Atlantic Coast Line Co., [p. 1094, *supra*] * * *, or judicial, Bacon v. Rutland Railroad Co., [p. 1096, *supra*] * * *—suffice it to say that the Texas courts are working partners with the Railroad Commission in the business of creating a regulatory system for the oil industry. * * *

"The State provides a unified method for the formation of policy and determination of cases by the Commission and by the state courts. The judicial review of the Commission's decisions in the state courts is expeditious and adequate. Conflicts in the interpretation of state law, dangerous to the success of state policies, are almost certain to result from the intervention of the lower federal courts. On the other hand, if the state procedure is followed from the Commission to the State Supreme Court, ultimate review of the federal questions is fully preserved here. * * * Under such circumstances, a sound respect for the independence of state action requires the federal equity court to stay its hand."

Justice Frankfurter, joined by three other Justices, dissented vigorously. He found no uncertainty in state law akin to that in the Pullman case. Rather, he said, the case depended upon "narrowly defined standards of law established by Texas for review of the orders of its Railroad Commission", which federal judges "are certainly not incompetent to apply". Apparently regarding the federal issues as minor, he distinguished Pullman as "merely illustrative of one phase of the basic constitutional doctrine that substantial constitutional issues should be adjudicated only when no alternatives are open".

(b) The Burford Doctrine in the Supreme Court. The Supreme Court has applied the rationale of Burford to order abstention only once, in Alabama Pub. Serv. Comm'n v. Southern Ry., 341 U.S. 341 (1951). After the Commission denied the railroad's request to discontinue two intrastate trains, the railroad sued in federal court. Jurisdiction was based on diversity of citizenship and on a federal question, since the railroad alleged that the Commission's order constituted confiscation of property in violation of the Fourteenth Amendment. A three-judge court granted the requested injunction, but the Supreme Court reversed, ordering dismissal of the complaint. Chief Justice Vinson, writing for the Court, apparently conceded that the case presented no issues of unsettled state law and no challenge to the constitutionality of the state statute on its face. But, he said:

"This Court has held that regulation of intrastate railroad service is 'primarily the concern of the state.' North Carolina v. United States, 325 U.S. 507, 511 (1945). Statutory appeal from an order of the Commission is an integral part of the regulatory process under the Alabama Code. Appeals, concentrated in one circuit court, are 'supervisory in character.' * * * As adequate state court review of an administrative order based upon predominantly local factors is available to appellee, intervention of a federal court is not necessary for the protection of federal rights."

Justice Frankfurter, joined by Justice Jackson, concurred in the result on the basis that the complaint failed to state a substantial claim, but again dissented from the abstention rationale.

Although the Supreme Court has not invoked Burford abstention since the Southern Railway decision, the Court has distinguished Burford in a number of cases in terms that appear to imply its continuing validity. See, *e.g.*, Colorado River Water Conserv. Dist. v. United States, 424 U.S. 800 (1976), Sec. 3(D), *infra*; New Orleans Public Service, Inc. ("NOPSI") v. Council of New Orleans, 491 U.S. 350 (1989), p. 1166, *infra*; Ankenbrandt v. Richards, 504 U.S. 689 (1992), p. 1181, *infra*; and Quackenbush v. Allstate Ins. Co., 517 U.S. 706 (1996), p. 1107, *supra*.

In the NOPSI case, the Court summarized the Burford doctrine as follows: "Where timely and adequate state court review is available, a federal court sitting in equity must decline to interfere with the proceedings or orders of state administrative agencies: (1) when there are 'difficult questions of state law bearing on policy problems of substantial public import whose importance transcends the result in the case then at bar'; or (2) where the 'exercise of federal review * * * would be disruptive of state efforts to establish a coherent policy with respect to a matter of substantial public concern' " (quoting Colorado River, *supra*, 424 U.S. at 814).

This formulation would appear to suggest, and some commentators have maintained, that Burford abstention applies most sensibly to cases in which a particular state court, through its exclusive appellate jurisdiction, works as a de facto partner of a state administrative agency in developing state regulatory policy, and review of the agency's decision by a federal district court would disrupt the partnership relationship.[1] But how well does that understanding cohere with the decision in Patsy v. Board of Regents, Sec. 3(A), *supra*, which held that plaintiffs need not exhaust available administrative remedies before bringing suit under 42 U.S.C. § 1983?[2]

In Quackenbush, the Court observed that the balance of state and federal interests contemplated by the Burford doctrine "only rarely favors abstention".[3] Quackenbush also limits the Burford doctrine by holding expressly that "federal courts have the power to dismiss or remand cases based on abstention principles only where the relief being sought is equitable or otherwise discretionary".

(c) Burford and the Judicial Power. In both Burford and Southern Railway, Justice Frankfurter protested that abstention was incompatible with the expressed policy of the jurisdictional statutes. But was abstention

---

[1] See Rehnquist, *Taking Comity Seriously: How to Neutralize the Abstention Doctrine*, 46 Stan.L.Rev. 1049, 1077–78 (1994). See also Young, *Federal Court Abstention and State Administrative Law From Burford to Ankenbrandt: Fifty Years of Judicial Federalism Under Burford v. Sun Oil Co. and Kindred Doctrines*, 42 DePaul L.Rev. 859, 886–99 (1993) (arguing that the decision in Burford reflected concerns such as these).

[2] If Burford abstention is premised on the notion that a state reviewing court acts in a policymaking partnership with the state administrative agency, would it follow that the state court's decision should be deemed legislative rather than judicial, and that ordinary res judicata principles should not apply? Compare Young, note 1, *supra*, at 877–78.

[3] The abstention issue arose in Quackenbush when the California Insurance Commissioner (Quackenbush), acting in his capacity as trustee of a California insurance company that was in state liquidation proceedings, brought a damages action against Allstate in state court. Allstate removed the case to federal court on diversity grounds and filed a motion to compel arbitration, but the district court ordered the case remanded under the Burford doctrine without ruling on the arbitration motion. According to the district court, federal adjudication could interfere with the state's " 'overriding interest in regulating insurance insolvencies and litigations in a uniform and orderly manner' " and, in particular, risked erroneous federal decision of the important and unresolved state law issue whether Allstate was entitled to set off its own contract claims against any recovery by the commissioner. The court of appeals reversed on the ground that federal courts can abstain under the Burford doctrine only in cases in which equitable relief is sought.

The Supreme Court affirmed, 9–0, on a somewhat narrower basis: although Burford abstention principles might permit a federal court, in exceptional cases, to stay or postpone its action in a suit for damages pending resolution of relevant state court proceedings, the dismissal or remand of an action in federal court, though "not strictly limited" to "equitable" cases, is permissible only when "a federal court is asked to provide some form of discretionary relief". Having held remand improper on this ground, the Court declined to consider whether "this case presents the sort of 'exceptional circumstance' in which Burford abstention * * * [in the form of a stay of the federal action] might be appropriate".

in those cases any more at odds with the policy of the jurisdictional statutes than abstention in Pullman (in which Justice Frankfurter wrote the majority opinion)?[4]

Note that there are at least two differences between the cases. First, jurisdiction in Burford and Southern Railway rested on *both* federal question and diversity grounds, whereas in Pullman there was federal question jurisdiction only. Is abstention more problematic under the diversity than under the federal question grant? Nash, *Examining the Power of Federal Courts to Certify Questions of State Law*, 88 Cornell L.Rev. 1672, 1698 (2003), so suggests on the ground that the grant of diversity jurisdiction reflects a congressional judgment that federal courts should resolve state law questions as a guarantee against state court bias. But *cf.* Colorado River Water Conserv. Dist., p. 1171, *infra*, a case presenting only state law issues, in which the Court, in ordering a federal court to stay its proceedings in deference to a parallel state proceeding in state court, observed in a footnote that Burford involved a federal constitutional question and stated that "the presence of a federal basis for jurisdiction may raise the level of justification needed for abstention". Second, in Burford abstention, the federal court defers to the state court on federal as well as state issues, and unless the Supreme Court reviews the case, res judicata would preclude federal litigation of the federal issues. In Pullman abstention, by contrast, the plaintiff retains the right, following an excursion to state court, to litigate federal claims in federal court.

(d) Burford in the Lower Courts. Are the criteria that govern Burford's application sufficiently clear to permit reasonable predictability? The lower courts have generally applied Burford narrowly and cautiously. For a survey of lower court decisions, see 17A Wright, Miller, Cooper & Amar § 4244.

(3) Thibodaux Abstention.

(a) The Thibodaux Case. Louisiana Power & Light Co. v. City of Thibodaux, 360 U.S. 25 (1959), was a proceeding by the city to take by eminent domain property owned by Louisiana Power & Light. As pleaded, the case included no federal question, but turned entirely on whether, as a matter of Louisiana law, municipalities had the authority to condemn public utility properties (and, if so, on the amount of compensation due). After the company removed the proceeding to federal court on the basis of diversity of citizenship, the district court stayed the action pending the institution and resolution of a state declaratory judgment action. The court of appeals reversed, but was in turn reversed by the Supreme Court.

Writing for the majority, Justice Frankfurter acknowledged that the Court had held previously in cases such as Meredith v. City of Winter Haven, 320 U.S. 228 (1943), that a federal court could not refuse to exercise diversity jurisdiction merely because state law was unsettled or difficult to determine.[5] But Justice Frankfurter identified two grounds of distinction.

---

[4]   *Cf.* McManamon, *Felix Frankfurter: The Architect of "Our Federalism"*, 27 Ga.L.Rev. 697 (1993) (arguing generally that much of modern abstention law and its underlying notions of comity and federalism reflect Frankfurter's influence).

[5]   In a few cases prior to Meredith, however, the Supreme Court had indicated that under certain circumstances a federal court should refrain from deciding a case governed entirely by state law. See Hawks v. Hamill, 288 U.S. 52 (1933) (concluding that a federal court should not enjoin legal actions by a state attorney general and county attorneys where jurisdiction rested on "no other basis than the accidents of residence"); Pennsylvania v. Williams, 294 U.S. 176

*Thibodaux:
"sovereign
prerogatives"*

First, he stressed that eminent domain proceedings are "special and peculiar" and "intimately involved with sovereign prerogative", particularly where the issue "concerns the apportionment of governmental powers between City and State": "The special nature of eminent domain justifies a district judge, when his familiarity with the problems of local law so counsels him, to ascertain the meaning of a disputed state statute from the only tribunal empowered to speak definitively—the courts of the State under whose statute eminent domain is sought to be exercised—rather than himself make a dubious and tentative forecast."

Second, Justice Frankfurter maintained that for a district court to stay an action "does not constitute abnegation of judicial duty. On the contrary, it is a wise and productive discharge of it. There is only postponement of decision for its best fruition. Eventually the District Court will award compensation if the taking is sustained. If for some reason a declaratory judgment is not promptly sought from the state courts and obtained within a reasonable time, the District Court, having retained complete control of the litigation, will doubtless assert it to decide also the question of the meaning of the state statute. The justification for this power, to be exercised within the indicated limits, lies in regard for the respective competence of the state and federal court systems and for the maintenance of harmonious federal-state relations in a matter close to the political interests of a State."

Justice Brennan, joined by Chief Justice Warren and Justice Douglas, filed a long and vehement dissent, in the course of which he said:

"Until today, the standards for testing this order of the District Court sending the parties to this diversity action to a state court for decision of a state law question might have been said to have been reasonably consistent with the imperative duty of a District Court, imposed by Congress under 28 U.S.C. §§ 1332 and 1441, to render prompt justice in cases between citizens of different States. * * * The doctrine of abstention, in proper perspective, is an extraordinary and narrow exception to this duty, and abdication of the obligation to decide cases can be justified under this doctrine only in the exceptional circumstances where the order to the parties to repair to the state court would clearly serve one of two important countervailing interests: either the avoidance of a premature and perhaps unnecessary decision of a serious federal constitutional question, or the avoidance of the hazard of unsettling some delicate balance in the area of federal-state relationships. * * *

"[N]either of the two recognized situations justifying abstention is present in the case before us. * * * [M]ere difficulty of construing the state statute is not justification for running away from the task."

Note that Justice Brennan appears to concede that, in principle, the avoidance of friction with significant state policies is an independent justification for abstention. Doesn't this concession seriously weaken his argument that abstention reflects a "plain disregard of [an] imperative duty"?[6]

(1935) (federal diversity court should defer to impending state statutory proceeding for liquidating insolvent building and loan association); *cf.* Thompson v. Magnolia Petroleum Co., 309 U.S. 478 (1940).

[6] Justice Frankfurter, who in the Burford and Southern Railway cases had offered anti-abstention arguments similar to those of Justice Brennan's dissent, supported abstention in Thibodaux (as he had in Pullman). Is there any thread of consistency among his positions?

(b) The Thibodaux Rationale. Although Justice Frankfurter's Thibodaux opinion emphasized "the special nature of eminent domain", in another case decided the same day, County of Allegheny v. Frank Mashuda Co., 360 U.S. 185 (1959), the Court declined (5–4) to abstain from deciding whether land taken by the county and then leased to a private party was validly condemned under state law. Like Thibodaux, the Mashuda case was brought under the diversity jurisdiction, and Justice Brennan's majority opinion was an almost verbatim gloss of parts of his dissent in Thibodaux, which rejects any notion that federal adjudication of cases involving the eminent domain power of the states presents any special risks of friction with state authority.

Justice Clark's dissent was joined by Justices Black, Frankfurter, and Harlan, all of whom were in the Thibodaux majority. Thus, of the nine Justices, seven evidently felt that Thibodaux and Mashuda were indistinguishable and dissented in either one or the other of the cases. Justices Stewart and Whittaker alone were in the majority in both cases, and only Justice Stewart attempted an explanation. He said in a concurring opinion that in Mashuda, unlike Thibodaux, "the controlling state law is clear and only factual issues need be resolved".

Consider, too, the ground of distinction asserted in Quackenbush v. Allstate Ins. Co., 517 U.S. 706 (1996), p. 1107, *supra*: Thibodaux involved a permissible "stay" of the federal suit pending state court action, whereas Mashuda involved an outright dismissal of the federal suit.[7]

(c) Current Status. Thibodaux's subsequent history is much like that of Burford: although the Supreme Court has not decided any cases based on Thibodaux's authority,[8] it has nevertheless continued to cite Thibodaux approvingly. In Colorado River Water Conserv. Dist. v. United States, 424 U.S. 800 (1976), p. 1171, *infra*, the Court characterized Thibodaux as supporting abstention "where there have been presented difficult questions of state law bearing on policy problems of substantial public import whose importance transcends the result in the case at bar."

In New Orleans Public Service, Inc. v. New Orleans ("NOPSI"), 491 U.S. 350, 361 (1989), this formulation reappeared, but as a description of one of two prongs of Burford abstention doctrine. See p. 1122, *supra* (quoting

---

[7] The page of the Mashuda opinion cited to establish the centrality of this distinction, 360 U.S. at 190, provides somewhat less than straightforward support. Justice Stewart's concurring opinion in Thibodaux can be read as resting squarely on this ground, see 360 U.S. at 31, but it was not joined by any other member of the Court. Query, too, whether the distinction will bear the weight assigned to it, given that resolution of the state court action in Thibodaux would effectively determine the outcome of the federal suit under normal principles of claim and issue preclusion. See p. 1108, *supra*.

[8] Although the Supreme Court did not cite Thibodaux, Kaiser Steel Corp. v. W.S. Ranch Co., 391 U.S. 593 (1968), might be regarded as a Thibodaux abstention case. In Kaiser Steel, a diversity action involving a dispute over rights to water on private land, the question was whether a New Mexico statute had authorized the defendant to take water, and, if so, whether the statute was valid under the state constitution, which permits takings only for "public use". In a per curiam decision, the Supreme Court held that the suit should be stayed pending adjudication of the central issues in a state declaratory judgment action. The Court explained: "The state law issue which is crucial in this case is one of vital concern in the arid State of New Mexico, where water is one of the most valuable natural resources. The issue, moreover, is a truly novel one. The question will eventually have to be resolved by the New Mexico courts, and since a declaratory judgment action is actually pending there, in all likelihood that resolution will be forthcoming soon. Sound judicial administration requires that the parties in this case be given the benefit of the same rule of law which will apply to all other businesses and landowners concerned with the use of this vital state resource".

doctrinal fusion?

NOPSI's formulation). Although NOPSI might seem to imply that Thibodaux abstention has now been subsumed by Burford abstention, might it be more accurate to say that both reflect an amorphous notion that when state issues are sufficiently difficult, sufficiently important, and sufficiently bound up with other state law issues and state administration, federal courts should sometimes abstain?

(4) Certification as an Alternative to Abstention in Diversity Cases.

certification alternative

In Lehman Brothers v. Schein, 416 U.S. 386 (1974), a diversity case presenting no federal question, a unanimous Supreme Court vacated the Second Circuit's decision of a difficult question of Florida law and directed the lower court to certify that question to the Florida supreme court. Without reference to Thibodaux or the appropriate criteria for its application, the Court said that the decision whether to certify "rests in the sound discretion of the federal courts", but pronounced certification "particularly appropriate in view of the novelty of the question and the great unsettlement of Florida law". The Court has not addressed the appropriate criteria for certification in diversity cases in any subsequent case.

Challener, *Distinguishing Certification From Abstention in Diversity Cases: Postponement Versus Abdication of the Duty to Exercise Jurisdiction*, 38 Rutgers L.J. 847, 874 (2007), reports that the circuits are divided over the significance of Lehman Brothers. According to her, roughly half "tend to rely on abstention principles derived from * * * Thibodaux and Burford" and, "[i]n particular, * * * require 'exceptional circumstances' before they will certify" an uncertain question of state law in a diversity case; only a minority adopt what the author calls "the Lehman approach" of certification in diversity cases "where state law is unclear". Given the reference in Lehman Brothers to "the sound discretion of the federal courts", it might be doubted whether the case mandates any reasonably determinate approach to certification in diversity cases. But *should* federal courts apply the same criteria in determining whether to stay federal proceedings pending the completion of state adjudication, on the one hand, as to certify a question of law to a state supreme court, on the other hand? (On certification procedures, see pp. 1117–1119, *supra*.) Note that in the partly parallel cases in which resolution of an uncertain state law issue by a state court might moot a federal constitutional question, the Court has suggested that certification might sometimes be appropriate even if abstention under Pullman criteria would not. See Arizonans for Official English v. Arizona, 520 U.S. 43 (1997), p. 1117, *supra*, in which a unanimous Court held that the court of appeals had "[b]lend[ed] abstention with certification" when it ruled erroneously that "unique circumstances" were necessary to justify certification.

Nash, Paragraph (2), *supra*, at 1740–48, urges special wariness of certification in diversity (as compared with federal question) cases. Appealing to the underlying policies of the diversity jurisdiction, he emphasizes that a state court bent on discriminating against an out-of-stater would be able to frame its response to a certified question accordingly and that the state court's answer is overwhelmingly likely to be outcome-determinative. *Cf.* Challener, *supra*, at 849, arguing that certification does little to undermine the significance of federal jurisdiction since the certifying courts continue to find all relevant facts and ultimately apply law to fact.

(5) The Burford and Thibodaux Rationales Re-examined. Consider the validity of each of the following propositions:

(i) A necessary and desirable function of state courts, as of state administrative agencies, is to make law.

(ii) Burford counsels abstention in order not to disrupt coordinated policymaking by state agencies and state courts; Thibodaux takes the logical, parallel step of authorizing abstention, even in the absence of action by an administrative agency, when a federal court believes that adjudication of a state law issue would require "sensitive and uncertain decisions of policy better made by the state judiciary." Young, note 1, *supra*, at 945.

(iii) The rationales of the Burford and Thibodaux doctrines are therefore closely linked, with Thibodaux being broader in that it omits the apparent Burford requirement of decisionmaking by a state administrative agency and unified review in the state court. It would thus be as true to say that Thibodaux subsumes, as that Thibodaux is an extension of, Burford.

(iv) A major difficulty with both Burford and Thibodaux lies in developing a metric to compare state interests favoring abstention with federal interests counseling against abstention and to weigh those interests in a reasonably predictable way.

(v) When factors exist that would tend to support Burford or Thibodaux abstention, the availability of certification, which permits a federal court to retain jurisdiction and ultimately to engage in pertinent fact-finding and to apply the law to facts, may introduce a further relevant consideration.

C. EQUITABLE RESTRAINT

Younger v. Harris

401 U.S. 37, 91 S.Ct. 746, 27 L.Ed.2d 669 (1971).
Appeal from the United States District Court for the Central District of California.

■ MR. JUSTICE BLACK delivered the opinion of the Court.

Appellee, John Harris, Jr., was indicted in a California state court, charged with violation of the California Penal Code §§ 11400 and 11401, known as the California Criminal Syndicalism Act * * *. He then filed a complaint in the Federal District Court, asking that court to enjoin the appellant, Younger, the District Attorney of Los Angeles County, from prosecuting him, and alleging that the prosecution and even the presence of the Act inhibited him in the exercise of his rights of free speech and press, rights guaranteed him by the First and Fourteenth Amendments. Appellees Jim Dan and Diane Hirsch intervened as plaintiffs in the suit, claiming that the prosecution of Harris would inhibit them as members of the Progressive Labor Party from peacefully advocating the program of their party, which was to replace capitalism with socialism and to abolish the profit system of production in this country. Appellee Farrell Broslawsky, an instructor in history at Los Angeles Valley College, also intervened claiming that the prosecution of Harris made him uncertain as to whether he could teach about the doctrines of Karl Marx or read from the Communist Manifesto as part of his classwork. All claimed that unless the United States court restrained the state prosecution of Harris each would suffer immediate and irreparable injury. A three-judge Federal District Court, convened pursuant to 28 U.S.C. § 2284, held that it had jurisdiction and power to restrain the District Attorney from prosecuting, held that the State's Criminal Syndicalism Act was void for vagueness and overbreadth in violation of the First and Fourteenth Amendments, and accordingly restrained the District Attorney from "further prosecution of the currently pending action against plaintiff Harris for alleged violation of the Act."

The case is before us on appeal by the State's District Attorney Younger, pursuant to 28 U.S.C. § 1253. In his notice of appeal and his jurisdictional statement appellant presented two questions: (1) whether the decision of this Court in Whitney v. California, 274 U.S. 357, holding California's law constitutional in 1927 was binding on the District Court and (2) whether the State's law is constitutional on its face. In this Court the brief for the State of California, filed at our request, also argues that only Harris, who was indicted, has standing to challenge the State's law, and that issuance of the injunction was a violation of a longstanding judicial policy and of 28 U.S.C. § 2283 * * *. Without regard to the questions raised about Whitney v. California, *supra*, since overruled by Brandenburg v. Ohio, 395 U.S. 444 (1969), or the constitutionality of the state law, we have concluded that the judgment of the District Court, enjoining appellant Younger from prosecuting under these California statutes, must be reversed as a violation of the national policy forbidding federal courts to stay or enjoin pending state court proceedings except under special circumstances.[2] We express no view about the circumstances under which federal courts may act when there is no prosecution pending in state courts at the time the federal proceeding is begun.

I

Appellee Harris has been indicted, and was actually being prosecuted by California for a violation of its Criminal Syndicalism Act at the time this suit was filed. He thus has an acute, live controversy with the State and its prosecutor. But none of the other parties plaintiff in the District Court, Dan, Hirsch, or Broslawsky, has such a controversy. None has been indicted, arrested, or even threatened by the prosecutor. * * *

Whatever right Harris, who is being prosecuted under the state syndicalism law may have, Dan, Hirsch, and Broslawsky cannot share it with him. If these three had alleged that they would be prosecuted for the conduct they planned to engage in, and if the District Court had found this allegation to be true—either on the admission of the State's district attorney or on any other evidence—then a genuine controversy might be said to exist. But here appellees, Dan, Hirsch, and Broslawsky do not claim that they have ever been threatened with prosecution, that a prosecution is likely, or even that a prosecution is remotely possible. They

---

[2] Appellees did not explicitly ask for a declaratory judgment in their complaint. They did, however, ask the District Court to grant "such other and further relief as to the Court may seem just and proper," and the District Court in fact granted a declaratory judgment. For the reasons stated in our opinion today in Samuels v. Mackell, 401 U.S. 66, we hold that declaratory relief is also improper when a prosecution involving the challenged statute is pending in state court at the time the federal suit is initiated.

claim the right to bring this suit solely because, in the language of their complaint, they "feel inhibited." We do not think this allegation even if true, is sufficient to bring the equitable jurisdiction of the federal courts into play to enjoin a pending state prosecution. A federal lawsuit to stop a prosecution in a state court is a serious matter. And persons having no fears of state prosecution except those that are imaginary or speculative, are not to be accepted as appropriate plaintiffs in such cases. See Golden v. Zwickler, 394 U.S. 103 (1969). Since Harris is actually being prosecuted under the challenged laws, however, we proceed with him as a proper party.

II

Since the beginning of this country's history Congress has, subject to few exceptions, manifested a desire to permit state courts to try state cases free from interference by federal courts. In 1793 an Act unconditionally provided: "[N]or shall a writ of injunction be granted to stay proceedings in any court of a state * * *." A comparison of the 1793 Act with 28 U.S.C. § 2283, its present-day successor, graphically illustrates how few and minor have been the exceptions granted from the flat, prohibitory language of the old Act. During all this lapse of years from 1793 to 1970 the statutory exceptions to the 1793 congressional enactment have been only three: (1) "except as expressly authorized by Act of Congress"; (2) "where necessary in aid of its jurisdiction"; and (3) "to protect or effectuate its judgments." In addition, a judicial exception to the longstanding policy evidenced by the statute has been made where a person about to be prosecuted in a state court can show that he will, if the proceeding in the state court is not enjoined, suffer irreparable damages. See Ex parte Young, 209 U.S. 123 (1908).

The precise reasons for this longstanding public policy against federal court interference with state court proceedings have never been specifically identified but the primary sources of the policy are plain. One is the basic doctrine of equity jurisprudence that courts of equity should not act, and particularly should not act to restrain a criminal prosecution, when the moving party has an adequate remedy at law and will not suffer irreparable injury if denied equitable relief. The doctrine may originally have grown out of circumstances peculiar to the English judicial system and not applicable in this country, but its fundamental purpose of restraining equity jurisdiction within narrow limits is equally important under our Constitution, in order to prevent erosion of the role of the jury and avoid a duplication of legal proceedings and legal sanctions where a single suit would be adequate to protect the rights asserted. This underlying reason for restraining courts of equity from interfering with criminal prosecutions is reinforced by an even more vital consideration, the notion of "comity," that is, a proper respect for state functions, a recognition of the fact that the entire country is made up of a Union of separate state governments, and a continuance of the belief that the National Government will fare best if the States and their institutions are left free to perform their separate functions in their separate ways. This, perhaps for lack of a better and clearer way to describe it, is referred to by many as "Our Federalism," and one familiar with the profound debates that ushered our Federal Constitution into existence is bound to respect those who remain loyal to the ideals and dreams of "Our Federalism." The concept does not mean blind deference to "States'

Rights" any more than it means centralization of control over every important issue in our National Government and its courts. The Framers rejected both these courses. What the concept does represent is a system in which there is sensitivity to the legitimate interests of both State and National Governments, and in which the National Government, anxious though it may be to vindicate and protect federal rights and federal interests, always endeavors to do so in ways that will not unduly interfere with the legitimate activities of the States. It should never be forgotten that this slogan, "Our Federalism," born in the early struggling days of our Union of States, occupies a highly important place in our Nation's history and its future.

This brief discussion should be enough to suggest some of the reasons why it has been perfectly natural for our cases to repeat time and time again that the normal thing to do when federal courts are asked to enjoin pending proceedings in state courts is not to issue such injunctions. In Fenner v. Boykin, 271 U.S. 240 (1926), suit had been brought in the Federal District Court seeking to enjoin state prosecutions under a recently enacted state law that allegedly interfered with the free flow of interstate commerce. The Court, in a unanimous opinion made clear that such a suit, even with respect to state criminal proceedings not yet formally instituted, could be proper only under very special circumstances:

> "Ex parte Young, 209 U.S. 123, and following cases have established the doctrine that, when absolutely necessary for protection of constitutional rights, courts of the United States have power to enjoin state officers from instituting criminal actions. But this may not be done, except under extraordinary circumstances, where the danger of irreparable loss is both great and immediate. Ordinarily, there should be no interference with such officers; primarily, they are charged with the duty of prosecuting offenders against the laws of the state, and must decide when and how this is to be done. The accused should first set up and rely upon his defense in the state courts, even though this involves a challenge of the validity of some statute, unless it plainly appears that this course would not afford adequate protection." *Id.*, at 243–244.

These principles, made clear in the Fenner case, have been repeatedly followed and reaffirmed in other cases involving threatened prosecutions. See, *e.g.*, Spielman Motor Sales Co. v. Dodge, 295 U.S. 89 (1935); Beal v. Missouri Pac. R. Co., 312 U.S. 45 (1941); Watson v. Buck, 313 U.S. 387 (1941); Williams v. Miller, 317 U.S. 599 (1942); Douglas v. City of Jeannette, 319 U.S. 157 (1943).

In all of these cases the Court stressed the importance of showing irreparable injury, the traditional prerequisite to obtaining an injunction. In addition, however, the Court also made clear that in view of the fundamental policy against federal interference with state criminal prosecutions, even irreparable injury is insufficient unless it is "both great and immediate." Fenner, *supra*. Certain types of injury, in particular, the cost, anxiety, and inconvenience of having to defend against a single criminal prosecution, could not by themselves be considered "irreparable" in the special legal sense of that term. Instead, the threat to the plaintiff's federally protected rights must be one that cannot be eliminated by his defense against a single criminal prosecution. * * *

This is where the law stood when the Court decided Dombrowski v. Pfister, 380 U.S. 479 (1965), and held that an injunction against the enforcement of certain state criminal statutes could properly issue under the circumstances presented in that case.[4] In Dombrowski, unlike many of the earlier cases denying injunctions, the complaint made substantial allegations that: "the threats to enforce the statutes against appellants are not made with any expectation of securing valid convictions, but rather are part of a plan to employ arrests, seizures, and threats of prosecution under color of the statutes to harass appellants and discourage them and their supporters from asserting and attempting to vindicate the constitutional rights of Negro citizens of Louisiana."

The appellants in Dombrowski had offered to prove that their offices had been raided and all their files and records seized pursuant to search and arrest warrants that were later summarily vacated by a state judge for lack of probable cause. They also offered to prove that despite the state court order quashing the warrants and suppressing the evidence seized, the prosecutor was continuing to threaten to initiate new prosecutions of appellants under the same statutes, was holding public hearings at which photostatic copies of the illegally seized documents were being used, and was threatening to use other copies of the illegally seized documents to obtain grand jury indictments against the appellants on charges of violating the same statutes. These circumstances, as viewed by the Court sufficiently establish the kind of irreparable injury, above and beyond that associated with the defense of a single prosecution brought in good faith, that had always been considered sufficient to justify federal intervention. See, *e.g.*, Beal, *supra*, 312 U.S., at 50. Indeed, after quoting the Court's statement in Douglas [v. City of Jeannette, *supra*] concerning the very restricted circumstances under which an injunction could be justified, the Court in Dombrowski went on to say:

"But the allegations in this complaint depict a situation in which defense of the State's criminal prosecution will not assure adequate vindication of constitutional rights. They suggest that a substantial loss of or impairment of freedoms of expression will occur if appellants must

---

[4] Neither the cases dealing with standing to raise claims of vagueness or overbreadth, *e.g.*, Thornhill v. Alabama, 310 U.S. 88 (1940), nor the loyalty oath cases, *e.g.*, Baggett v. Bullitt, 377 U.S. 360 (1964), changed the basic principles governing the propriety of injunctions against state criminal prosecutions. In the standing cases we allowed attacks on overly broad or vague statutes in the absence of any showing that the defendant's conduct could not be regulated by some properly drawn statute. But in each of these cases the statute was not merely vague or overly broad "on its face"; the statute was held to be vague or overly broad as construed and *applied* to a particular defendant in a particular case. If the statute had been too vague as written but sufficiently narrow as applied, prosecutions and convictions under it would ordinarily have been permissible. See Dombrowski, *supra*, 380 U.S., at 491 n. 7.

In Baggett and similar cases we enjoined state officials from discharging employees who failed to take certain loyalty oaths. We held that the States were without power to exact the promises involved, with their vague and uncertain content concerning advocacy and political association, as a condition of employment. Apart from the fact that any plaintiff discharged for exercising his constitutional right to refuse to take the oath would have had no adequate remedy at law, the relief sought was of course the kind that raises no special problem—an injunction against allegedly unconstitutional state action (discharging the employees) that is not part of a criminal prosecution.

await the state court's disposition and ultimate review in this Court of any adverse determination. These allegations, if true, clearly show irreparable injury." 380 U.S., at 485–486.

And the Court made clear that even under these circumstances the District Court issuing the injunction would have continuing power to lift it at any time and remit the plaintiffs to the state courts if circumstances warranted. 380 U.S., at 491, 492. * * *

It is against the background of these principles that we must judge the propriety of an injunction under the circumstances of the present case. Here a proceeding was already pending in the state court, affording Harris an opportunity to raise his constitutional claims. There is no suggestion that this single prosecution against Harris is brought in bad faith or is only one of a series of repeated prosecutions to which he will be subjected. In other words, the injury that Harris faces is solely "that incidental to every criminal proceeding brought lawfully and in good faith," Douglas, *supra*, and therefore under the settled doctrine we have already described he is not entitled to equitable relief "even if such statutes are unconstitutional," Buck, *supra*.

The District Court, however, thought that the Dombrowski decision substantially broadened the availability of injunctions against state criminal prosecutions and that under that decision the federal courts may give equitable relief, without regard to any showing of bad faith or harassment, whenever a state statute is found "on its face" to be vague or overly broad, in violation of the First Amendment. We recognize that there are some statements in the Dombrowski opinion that would seem to support this argument. But, as we have already seen, such statements were unnecessary to the decision of that case, because the Court found that the plaintiffs had alleged a basis for equitable relief under the long-established standards. In addition, we do not regard the reasons adduced to support this position as sufficient to justify such a substantial departure from the established doctrines regarding the availability of injunctive relief. It is undoubtedly true, as the Court stated in Dombrowski, that "[a] criminal prosecution under a statute regulating expression usually involves imponderables and contingencies that themselves may inhibit the full exercise of First Amendment freedoms." 380 U.S., at 486. But this sort of "chilling effect," as the Court called it, should not by itself justify federal intervention. In the first place, the chilling effect cannot be satisfactorily eliminated by federal injunctive relief. In Dombrowski itself the Court stated that the injunction to be issued there could be lifted if the State obtained an "acceptable limiting construction" from the state courts. The Court then made clear that once this was done, prosecutions could then be brought for conduct occurring before the narrowing construction was made, and proper convictions could stand so long as the defendants were not deprived of fair warning. 380 U.S., at 491 n. 7. The kind of relief granted in Dombrowski thus does not effectively eliminate uncertainty as to the coverage of the state statute and leaves most citizens with virtually the same doubts as before regarding the danger that their conduct might eventually be subjected to criminal sanctions. The chilling effect can, of course, be eliminated by an injunction that would prohibit any prosecution whatever for conduct occurring prior to a satisfactory rewriting of the statute. But the States would then be stripped of all power to prosecute even the socially dangerous and constitutionally unprotected conduct that had been covered by the statute, until a new statute could be passed by the state legislature and approved by the federal courts in potentially lengthy trial and appellate proceedings. Thus, in Dombrowski itself the Court carefully reaffirmed the principle that even in the direct prosecution in the State's own courts, a valid narrowing construction can be applied to conduct occurring prior to the date when the narrowing construction was made, in the absence of fair warning problems. * * *

Beyond all this is another, more basic consideration. Procedures for testing the constitutionality of a statute "on its face" in the manner apparently contemplated by Dombrowski, and for then enjoining all action to enforce the statute until the State can obtain court approval for a modified version, are fundamentally at odds with the function of the federal courts in our constitutional plan. The power and duty of the judiciary to declare laws unconstitutional is in the final analysis derived from its responsibility for resolving concrete disputes brought before the courts for decision; a statute apparently governing a dispute cannot be applied by judges, consistently with their obligations under the Supremacy Clause, when such an application of the statute would conflict with the Constitution. Marbury v. Madison, 5 U.S. (1 Cranch) 137 (1803). But this vital responsibility, broad as it is, does not amount to an unlimited power to survey the statute books and pass judgment on laws before the courts are called upon to enforce them. Ever since the Constitutional Convention rejected a proposal for having members of the Supreme Court render advice concerning pending legislation it has been clear that, even when suits of this kind involve a "case or controversy" sufficient to satisfy the requirements of Article III of the Constitution, the task of analyzing a proposed statute, pinpointing its deficiencies, and requiring correction of these deficiencies before the statute is put into effect, is rarely if ever an appropriate task for the judiciary. The combination of the relative remoteness of the controversy, the impact on the legislative process of the relief sought, and above all the speculative and amorphous nature of the required line-by-line analysis of detailed statutes ordinarily results in a kind of case that is wholly unsatisfactory for deciding constitutional questions, whichever way they might be decided. In light of this fundamental conception of the Framers as to the proper place of the federal courts in the governmental processes of passing and enforcing laws, it can seldom be appropriate for these courts to exercise any such power of prior approval or veto over the legislative process.

For these reasons, fundamental not only to our federal system but also to the basic functions of the Judicial Branch of the National Government under our Constitution, we hold that the Dombrowski decision should not be regarded as having upset the settled doctrines that have always confined very narrowly the availability of injunctive relief against state criminal prosecutions. We do not think that opinion stands for the proposition that a federal court can properly enjoin enforcement of a statute solely on the basis of a showing that the statute "on its face" abridges First Amendment rights. There may, of course, be extraordinary circumstances in which the necessary irreparable injury can be shown even in the absence of the usual prerequisites of bad faith and harassment. For example, as long ago as the Buck case, supra, we indicated:

"It is of course conceivable that a statute might be flagrantly and patently violative of express constitutional prohibitions in every clause, sentence and paragraph, and in whatever manner and against whomever an effort might be made to apply it." 313 U.S., at 402.

Other unusual situations calling for federal intervention might also arise, but there is no point in our attempting now to specify what they might be. It is sufficient for purposes of the present case to hold, as we do, that the possible unconstitutionality of a statute "on its face" does not in itself justify an injunction against good-faith attempts to enforce it, and that appellee Harris has failed to make any showing of bad faith, harassment, or any other unusual circumstance that would call for equitable relief. Because our holding rests on the absence of the factors necessary under equitable principles to justify federal intervention, we have no occasion to consider whether 28 U.S.C. § 2283, which prohibits an injunction against state court proceedings "except as expressly authorized by Act of Congress" would in and of itself be controlling under the circumstances of this case.

The judgment of the District Court is reversed, and the case is remanded for further proceedings not inconsistent with this opinion.

■ MR. JUSTICE BRENNAN with whom MR. JUSTICE WHITE and MR. JUSTICE MARSHALL join, concurring in the result.

I agree that the judgment of the District Court should be reversed. Appellee Harris had been indicted for violations of the California Criminal Syndicalism Act before he sued in federal court. He has not alleged that the prosecution was brought in bad faith to harass him. His constitutional contentions may be adequately adjudicated in the state criminal proceeding, and federal intervention at his instance was therefore improper. * * *

■ MR. JUSTICE STEWART, with whom MR. JUSTICE HARLAN joins, concurring.

The questions the Court decides today are important ones. Perhaps as important, however, is a recognition of the areas into which today's holdings do not necessarily extend. In all of these cases, the Court deals only with the proper policy to be followed by a federal court when asked to intervene by injunction or declaratory judgment in a criminal prosecution which is contemporaneously pending in a state court.

In basing its decisions on policy grounds, the Court does not reach any questions concerning the independent force of the federal anti-injunction statute, 28 U.S.C. § 2283. Thus we do not decide whether the word "injunction" in § 2283 should be interpreted to include a declaratory judgment, or whether an injunction to stay proceedings in a state court is "expressly authorized" by § 1 of the Civil Rights Act of 1871, now 42 U.S.C. § 1983. And since all these cases involve state criminal prosecutions, we do not deal with the considerations that should govern a federal court when it is asked to intervene in state civil proceedings, where, for various reasons, the balance might be struck differently.[2]

---

[2]   Courts of equity have traditionally shown greater reluctance to intervene in criminal prosecutions than in civil cases. See Younger v. Harris, 401 U.S., at 43–44; Douglas v. City of Jeannette, 319 U.S. 157, 163–164. The offense to state interests is likely to be less in a civil proceeding. A State's decision to classify conduct as criminal provides some indication of the

Finally, the Court today does not resolve the problems involved when a federal court is asked to give injunctive or declaratory relief from *future* state criminal prosecutions.

The Court confines itself to deciding the policy considerations that in our federal system must prevail when federal courts are asked to interfere with pending state prosecutions. Within this area, we hold that a federal court must not, save in exceptional and extremely limited circumstances, intervene by way of either injunction or declaration in an existing state criminal prosecution.[3] Such circumstances exist only when there is a threat of irreparable injury "both great and immediate." A threat of this nature might be shown if the state criminal statute in question were patently and flagrantly unconstitutional on its face * * * or if there has been bad faith and harassment—official lawlessness—in a statute's enforcement * * *. * * *

■ MR. JUSTICE DOUGLAS, dissenting.

* * * Dombrowski represents an exception to the general rule that federal courts should not interfere with state criminal prosecutions. The exception does not arise merely because prosecutions are threatened to which the First Amendment will be the proffered defense. Dombrowski governs statutes which are a blunderbuss by themselves or when used *en masse*—those that have an "overbroad" sweep. * * * Harris is charged only with distributing leaflets advocating political action toward his objective. He tried unsuccessfully to have the state court dismiss the indictment on constitutional grounds. He resorted to the state appellate court for writs of prohibition to prevent the trial, but to no avail. He went to the federal court as a matter of last resort in an effort to keep this unconstitutional trial from being saddled on him. * * *

NOTE ON YOUNGER V. HARRIS AND THE DOCTRINE OF EQUITABLE RESTRAINT

(1) The History of Equitable Restraint Doctrine. The pre-Younger history of equitable restraint doctrine is complex and multi-faceted. Within the leading cases, one prominent theme—which you should bear in mind in reading the material that follows—involves a distinction between actions in which plaintiffs seek injunctions against pending criminal prosecutions based on their past conduct, in which equitable relief has almost invariably been denied, and actions in which plaintiffs seek injunctions to protect them from prosecution for future conduct that they believe to be constitutionally protected, in which injunctive relief has much more often been available. You should, accordingly, consider whether that distinction reflects a sound accommodation of competing practical considerations, including interests in both protecting parties claiming constitutional rights against the threat of

---

importance it has ascribed to prompt and unencumbered enforcement of its law. By contrast, the State might not even be a party in a proceeding under a civil statute.

These considerations would not, to be sure, support any distinction between civil and criminal proceedings should the ban of 28 U.S.C. § 2283, which makes no such distinction, be held unaffected by 42 U.S.C. § 1983.

[3] The negative pregnant in this sentence—that a federal court may, as a matter of policy, intervene when such "exceptional and extremely limited circumstances" are found—is subject to any further limitations that may be placed on such intervention by 28 U.S.C. § 2283.

multiple prosecutions and in avoiding the friction that is likely to attend a
court of equity's interference with a pending prosecution. You should be
aware from the outset, however, that the leading cases are hard to reconcile
in all of their particulars and that the distinction between suits to enjoin
pending prosecutions and suits to enjoin future threatened prosecutions has
not always been observed. Among the confounding factors, a plaintiff who
has been charged with a past violation of a statute may also wish to continue
violating that statute in the future. When this is so, it may be impossible for
a court to entertain a suit to enjoin the future enforcement of an allegedly
unconstitutional statute without also determining—and thus forcing a
prosecutor to litigate in the equitable action—whether a pending prosecution
under that statute can go forward.

(a) **English Origins.** A venerable maxim, which apparently originated
in the English Court of Chancery, holds that equity will not enjoin a criminal
prosecution.[1] Also of English origin are the complementary maxims that
equity will not provide relief unless (i) there is no adequate remedy at law
and (ii) the plaintiff is threatened with irreparable injury. Because the legal
remedy of defending a criminal proceeding was ordinarily considered
adequate, the irreparable injury requirement also established a barrier to
injunctions against criminal proceedings. From the beginning, however, the
bar against injunction of criminal prosecutions admitted exceptions. For
example, a court of equity would enjoin a party from litigating the same
matter in a later-commenced criminal action,[2] and some American cases
permitted an injunction against a criminal prosecution that would infringe
property rights, see Davis & Farnum Mfg. Co. v. Los Angeles, 189 U.S. 207,
217 (1903); Fitts v. McGhee, 172 U.S. 516, 531–32 (1899).

(b) **Early Reception in the United States.** Section 16 of the First
Judiciary Act stated that "suits in equity shall not be sustained in * * * the
courts of United States, in any case where plain, adequate, and complete
remedy may be had at law," 1 Stat. 82—a limitation repealed in 1948, see p.
603, *supra*. That provision defeated the plaintiff's case for equitable relief,
however, only if the remedy was available on the law side of a *federal* court;
it was not intended to affect the plaintiff's right to a federal—as against a
state—forum. See Atlas Life Ins. Co. v. W.I. Southern, Inc., 306 U.S. 563, 569
(1939).

(c) **Background to Modern Doctrine: Ex Parte Young.** In Ex parte
Young, p. 922, *supra*, a case best known for its Eleventh Amendment holding,
the Supreme Court sustained a federal injunction forbidding the Minnesota
Attorney General to enforce railroad rate regulations alleged to deny due
process. The Court noted that the "general rule" that "equity has no
jurisdiction to enjoin [state] criminal proceedings * * * [was subject to]
exceptions. When such * * * [a] proceeding is brought to enforce an alleged
unconstitutional statute, which is the subject matter of inquiry in a suit
already pending in a Federal court, the latter court having first obtained
jurisdiction over the subject matter, has the right, in both civil and criminal
cases, to hold and maintain such jurisdiction, to the exclusion of all other
courts, until its duty is fully performed. But the Federal court cannot, of

---

[1] See Shapiro, *Jurisdiction and Discretion*, 60 N.Y.U.L.Rev. 543, 550 n. 37 (1985);
Whitten, *Federal Declaratory and Injunctive Interference with State Court Proceedings: The
Supreme Court and the Limits of Judicial Discretion*, 53 N.C.L.Rev. 591, 597–600 (1975).

[2] See Whitten, note 1, *supra*, at 598.

course, interfere in a case where the proceedings were already pending in a state court".

The Court in Young also rejected the Attorney General's argument that the railroads had an adequate remedy at law—namely, to disobey the statute and then challenge its constitutionality in a subsequent prosecution. In part, this conclusion was based on the difficulty for the railroad of finding an employee willing to risk imprisonment in order to set up a test case. But the Court also advanced a broader argument: To force the railroad "[t]o await proceedings against the company in a state court, grounded upon a disobedience of the act, [and then if necessary seek Supreme Court review,] would place the company in peril of large loss and its agents in great risk of fines and imprisonment if it should be finally determined that the act was valid. This risk the company ought not to be required to take".[3]

(d) Restriction, Exceptions, and the Decision in Douglas v. City of Jeannette. In the years following Ex parte Young, federal courts seldom if ever enjoined pending criminal prosecutions, but while "a few prominent cases said that injunctions against *future* prosecutions [as in Ex parte Young] should be hard to get, in practice they become routine." Laycock, *Federal Interference with State Prosecutions: The Need for Prospective Relief*, 1977 Sup.Ct.Rev. 193, 193; see Soifer & MacGill, *The Younger Doctrine: Reconstructing Reconstruction*, 55 Tex.L.Rev. 1141, 1158 (1977).

Whatever the normal pattern in the years following Ex parte Young, there is no doubt about the generative significance of cases such as Douglas v. City of Jeannette, 319 U.S. 157 (1943), which not only denied equitable relief, but also forged the link between equitable concepts and a vision of American federalism in which federal courts should frequently defer to state institutions and especially state courts. In the Douglas case, the Supreme Court, per Stone, C.J., ordered dismissal, for want of equity, of a class action by Jehovah's Witnesses (whose religious practice was to distribute books door-to-door) seeking to restrain, as a violation of the First Amendment, their prosecution under a city ordinance forbidding solicitation of orders for merchandise without a license. The Chief Justice noted first that Congress had adopted a deliberate policy of "leaving generally to the state courts the trial of criminal cases arising under state laws, subject to review by this Court of any federal questions involved." He then deployed equitable concepts to implement that policy, reasoning that a criminal prosecution, "even though alleged to be in violation of constitutional guarantees, is not a ground for equity relief since the lawfulness or constitutionality of the statute or ordinance on which the prosecution is based may be determined as readily in the criminal case as in the suit for an injunction".[4]

---

[3] For discussion of the precedents prior to Young, see Isseks, *Jurisdiction of the Lower Federal Courts to Enjoin Unauthorized Action of State Officials*, 40 Harv.L.Rev. 969 (1927); Taylor & Willis, *The Power of Federal Courts to Enjoin Proceedings in State Courts*, 42 Yale L.J. 1169, 1190–92 (1942); Warren, *Federal and State Court Interference*, 43 Harv.L.Rev. 345, 372–74 (1930); B. Wechsler, *Federal Courts, State Criminal Law and the First Amendment*, 49 N.Y.U.L.Rev. 740, 753–62 (1974); Whitten, note 1, *supra*, at 629–30.

[4] But *cf.* Laycock, *Federal Interference with State Prosecutions: The Cases Dombrowski Forgot*, 46 U.Chi.L.Rev. 636, 666 & n. 201 (1979). Professor Laycock notes that both before and after the Douglas case, the Supreme Court approved federal injunctions against threatened prosecution for future conduct, even when the federal plaintiff wishing to engage in a continuous course of conduct was already the subject of a pending state prosecution for past conduct. For example, in Cline v. Frink Dairy Co., 274 U.S. 445, 452–53, 466 (1927), a three-judge court had permanently enjoined state officials from bringing criminal prosecutions under an unconstitutional state statute. The Supreme Court reversed the grant of relief as to a

Is it appropriate to use "doctrines of equity—doctrines forged in the battles of English Chancery—to further views of federalism, a political principle central to American Government"? See Fiss, *Dombrowski*, 86 Yale L.J. 1103, 1107 (1977), for a negative view.

(e) The Warren Era and the Dombrowski Case. The Warren Court's expansion of constitutional rights in the sphere of criminal procedure and the events surrounding the civil rights movement conjoined to put new strains on doctrines demanding federal judicial deference to state court proceedings. The case most clearly exhibiting the emerging tension was Dombrowski v. Pfister, 380 U.S. 479 (1965), discussed at length in Younger. Suit was brought by a civil rights group and affiliated individuals to enjoin state officials from prosecuting or threatening to prosecute the plaintiffs for alleged violations of two Louisiana statutes criminalizing subversive activities. A divided Supreme Court, per Justice Brennan, purported to accept the position of the Douglas case that "the mere possibility of erroneous initial application of constitutional standards will usually not amount to the irreparable injury necessary to justify a disruption of orderly state proceedings". But in the Court's view, the plaintiffs' allegations that the statutes were overbroad, if true, would establish the threat of "irreparable injury" warranting relief. The majority argued that when statutes are overbroad, "[t]he assumption that defense of a criminal prosecution will generally assure ample vindication of constitutional rights is unfounded * * *. * * * The chilling effect upon the exercise of First Amendment rights may derive from the fact of the prosecution, unaffected by the prospects of its success or failure". The Court noted that the repeated invocation (and threatened invocation) of state criminal prosecutions, and concomitant searches and seizures, had frightened off potential members of the organization and "paralyzed operations", making the need for "immediate resolution" of the First Amendment claims especially pressing.

The Court also concluded that the district court "erred in holding that it should abstain pending authoritative interpretation of the statutes in state court * * *. We hold the abstention doctrine is inappropriate for cases such as the present one where, unlike Douglas v. City of Jeannette, statutes are justifiably attacked on their face as abridging free expression, or as applied for the purpose of discouraging protected activities".

Justice Harlan, joined by Justice Clark, dissented: "[U]nderlying the Court's major premise that enforcement of an overly broad statute affecting speech and association is itself a deterrent to the free exercise thereof seems to be the unarticulated assumption that state courts will not be as prone as federal courts to vindicate constitutional rights promptly and effectively". The Court, he thought, had departed from healthy traditions of federalism by creating a situation in which "[i]n practical effect * * * a State may no

---

prosecution already pending when the federal suit was filed, but affirmed the grant as to the institution of future prosecutions.

Although Douglas is often read as barring any injunctions against state criminal enforcement actions, the previous cases had distinguished between pending and threatened prosecutions, see the articles by Laycock, *supra*, and the facts of Douglas were themselves somewhat exceptional. On the same day Douglas was decided, the Court, in reviewing the criminal convictions of some Jehovah's Witnesses who had already violated the ordinance, held it unconstitutional. Murdock v. Pennsylvania, 319 U.S. 105 (1943). In view of that authoritative ruling, the plaintiffs in Douglas did not face the same dilemma as to their continuing conduct faced by the plaintiffs in Ex parte Young. The Douglas opinion recognizes this point, see 319 U.S. at 165, though much of its language sweeps far more broadly.

longer carry on prosecutions under statutes challengeable * * * on 'First Amendment' grounds without the prior approval of the federal courts".[5]

(2) Younger's Near Unanimity. Given Younger's controversiality, it is striking that eight of the nine Justices—including Justice Brennan, who had authored the opinion in Dombrowski, *supra*—concurred in the judgment. How do you account for the virtual unanimity? Consider the following suggestions:

(a) Younger involved a claim for an injunction against a *pending* criminal prosecution. *Cf.* Stefanelli v. Minard, 342 U.S. 117 (1951), in which a district court was asked to enjoin the use, in a state criminal proceeding, of evidence seized by state police officers in violation of the federal Constitution, and the Court held that the equity rule of Douglas v. City of Jeannette applies *a fortiori* where the request is "to intervene piecemeal to try collateral issues" in a criminal proceeding.[6] Especially in light of the revolution wrought by the Warren Court, it is hard to imagine a criminal prosecution in which a constitutional claim could not be raised; and most observers have thought that it would be unworkable if every prosecution could be interrupted by suit for a federal injunction at any stage in the proceedings. Although § 1983 includes no express exception for suits to enjoin pending prosecutions, it is at least arguable that it should be interpreted in light of the general body of background law, including the traditional maxim that equity will not enjoin a criminal prosecution.[7]

(b) Whatever may have been the case in other eras, by 1971 there was less reason to think state courts generally untrustworthy in cases involving claimed federal rights, especially given the availability of federal habeas corpus as well as Supreme Court review. See, *e.g.*, Friedman, *A Revisionist Theory of Abstention*, 88 Mich.L.Rev. 530, 561–63 (1989).[8] Nor did the facts of Younger exhibit any special factors that might justify federal interference with a pending judicial action, such as a pattern of bad faith or harassment in which state courts were arguably complicit.

(c) Given the Court's holding that plaintiffs other than Harris lacked standing, Younger did not involve a claim to class relief and did not implicate the federal interest in avoiding the chill of *future*, constitutionally protected

---

[5]   Justices Black and Stewart did not participate.

[6]   For the subsequent, often complex, development of the Stefanelli principle, see Rea v. United States, 350 U.S. 214 (1956) (federal officers enjoined from testifying in state criminal proceeding as to evidence obtained by them in violation of Fed.R.Crim.P. 41); Wilson v. Schnettler, 365 U.S. 381 (1961) (upholding refusal to enjoin federal officers from testifying where allegation that the evidence was illegally obtained was insufficient); Pugach v. Dollinger, 365 U.S. 458 (1961) (refusing to enjoin state officer from testifying as to illegal wiretap); Cleary v. Bolger, 371 U.S. 392 (1963) (reversing grant of injunction prohibiting state officer from testifying as to evidence illegally gathered by federal officers).

[7]   See Bator, *The State Courts and Federal Constitutional Litigation*, 22 Wm. & Mary L.Rev. 605, 622 n. 49 (1981); see generally Shapiro, *Jurisdiction and Discretion*, 60 N.Y.U.L.Rev. 543 (1985), *quoted* pp. 1105–1106, *supra*. Even most advocates of a textualist approach to statutory interpretation appear to have accepted this conclusion. For a discussion of the application of textualist theories to § 1983, see Fallon, *Three Symmetries Between Textualist and Purposivist Theories of Statutory Interpretation—and the Irreducible Roles of Values and Judgment Within Both,* 99 Corn.L.Rev. 685 (2014).

[8]   But *cf.* Bright, *Can Judicial Independence Be Attained in the South? Overcoming History, Elections, and Misperceptions About the Role of the Judiciary,* 14 Ga.St.U.L.Rev. 817 (1998) (arguing that southern state courts, in particular, have continued to reflect legacies of racism and have remained subject to political pressures, including those stemming from judicial elections).

conduct, which might deserve to be weighed in the scale against the state interest in avoiding disruption of a pending criminal prosecution.[9] (Even in such a case, the actual or prospective defendants might seek injunctive and class remedies in a state court of equity, but if a separate suit for such relief is to proceed, why shouldn't the plaintiff have a forum choice?)

(3) Companion Cases. On the day that Younger was decided, the Supreme Court denied federal equitable relief in several companion cases, the most important of which was Samuels v. Mackell, 401 U.S. 66 (1971). In Samuels, the Court held that the Younger doctrine applies not only to injunctive but also to declaratory relief against a pending state criminal prosecution.[10] Writing for the Court, Justice Black conceded that there might be "unusual circumstances" in which, despite a plaintiff's "strong claim for relief", an injunction would be withheld because it would have been "particularly intrusive or offensive", but in which "a declaratory judgment might be appropriate". In general, however, he thought that a declaratory judgment would "result in precisely the same interference with" state proceedings as an injunction, especially since a declaratory judgment could be enforced, if necessary, with a subsequent injunction. Justice Black "express[ed] no views on the propriety of declaratory relief when no state proceeding is pending at the time the federal suit is begun".

(4) The Relationship of Younger to Mitchum v. Foster. The question reserved in Younger—whether the Anti-Injunction Act, 28 U.S.C. § 2283, would bar an injunction in that case—was decided a year later in Mitchum v. Foster, 407 U.S. 225 (1972) (p. 1073, *supra*). Was it appropriate for the Court in Younger to decide the case on the basis of a judge-made doctrine of equitable restraint without first determining the reach of § 2283?

There is an obvious tension between Younger's trust in state enforcement of federal rights and the parallel distrust, coupled with a demand for federal court jurisdiction in § 1983 actions, expressed in Mitchum and in cases such as Patsy v. Board of Regents of the State of Florida, p. 1097, *supra*. In appraising the disparity, consider whether the Court would clearly have decided Mitchum the same way if, as a consequence of that decision, cases such as Younger necessarily could have been litigated in federal court.

(5) The Relationship of Younger to Pullman Abstention. Note the differences between the Pullman "abstention" doctrine and the equitable restraint doctrine of Younger. In conventional Pullman-type cases, the issue is whether federal plaintiffs—as a necessary condition of having the federal court adjudicate their federal claims—should be forced to obtain a state court resolution of state law issues. In the normal Younger-type case, on the other hand, the whole point is that a state proceeding either has been or is about to be commenced by the state authorities, and that the entire case should be

---

[9] For further discussion of distinctions among suits that seek relief from prosecution based on (i) past, (ii) future, and (iii) continuing conduct, see pp. 1153–1155, *infra*.

[10] The Court relied heavily on Great Lakes Dredge & Dock Co. v. Huffman, 319 U.S. 293 (1943), p. 1091, *supra*, which, though not literally extending the Tax Injunction Act to restrict declaratory judgments, had, as an exercise of equitable discretion, refused federal declaratory relief against the imposition of state taxes. (The Court subsequently held that the Tax Injunction Act itself bars federal declaratory relief. See California v. Grace Brethren Church, 457 U.S. 393 (1982), p. 1091, *supra*.)

Samuels did not refer to Kennedy v. Mendoza-Martinez, 372 U.S. 144 (1963), p. 1090 n. 4, *supra*, in which the Court refused to equate declaratory and injunctive relief for purposes of the three-judge court requirement.

litigated in that proceeding. The two doctrines thus have sharply different impacts on federal plaintiffs' ability to obtain federal court resolution of their federal claims. The Pullman doctrine ordinarily entails postponement, not relinquishment, of federal jurisdiction to pass on claims of federal right. In Younger cases, by contrast, the federal court dismisses the suit, and the underlying federal claims must typically be adjudicated in the context of a state criminal case, subject only to Supreme Court review. As the Court later held in Allen v. McCurry, 449 U.S. 90 (1980), p. 1377, *infra*, the state court adjudication will have full res judicata effect in subsequent federal court proceedings, including those brought under 42 U.S.C. § 1983.

Notwithstanding Younger, some state criminal defendants may ultimately reach federal court by filing a federal habeas corpus petition, but important limits applied to this remedy in 1971, and they have grown more stringent since. See generally Chapter XI, Sec. 2, *infra*.

(6) Criticisms of Younger. Three criticisms of Younger are especially common.

First, numerous commentators have objected that Younger fails to respect congressional policy by requiring abstention in suits under 42 U.S.C. § 1983—a statute whose purpose (according to Mitchum v. Foster, p. 1073, *supra*) "was to interpose the federal courts between the States and the people, as guardians of the people's federal rights".[11] See, *e.g.,* Redish, *Abstention, Separation of Powers, and the Limits of the Judicial Function*, 94 Yale L.J. 71 (1984). For further discussion of abstention and the separation of powers, see pp. 1105–1106, *supra*. Consider, however, whether the alternative outcome in Younger might have been in tension with Congress' having given the state courts exclusive jurisdiction over state criminal prosecutions that involve federal defenses (apart from prosecutions of federal officers covered by § 1442).

A second, related complaint is that Younger relegates plaintiffs claiming constitutional rights violations to state forums that they, at least, expect to be less sympathetic to their claims than the federal court in which they would prefer to litigate. For discussion of the "parity" or "disparity" of state and federal courts, see Chap. IV, Sec. 1, *supra*.

A third objection is that Younger erects a frequently insuperable barrier to prospective and class relief—remedies typically unavailable from a criminal court. See, *e.g.,* Laycock, Paragraph (1)(d), *supra*.

(7) Exceptions to the Younger Doctrine. Younger suggested that there might be exceptional cases warranting federal equitable relief against pending state criminal prosecutions. Subsequent decisions have stressed the narrowness of the possible openings. (As is discussed in detail in the *Note on Further Extensions of the Equitable Restraint Doctrine*, pp. 1165–1171, *infra*, the Younger doctrine has been extended to bar federal interference in some kinds of state *civil* proceedings, and many of the cases discussed in this Paragraph involve intervention in civil matters.)

(a) Bad Faith Prosecution or Harassment. The Supreme Court has never authorized intervention under this exception. Among the cases in which the Court has refused to find bad faith are Cameron v. Johnson, 390 U.S. 611 (1968) (rejecting the notion that bad faith could be inferred from the innocence of the accused and framing the question as whether enforcement

bad faith never used

---

[11] For further discussion of the relation of Younger and Mitchum, see Paragraph (4), *supra*.

was undertaken "with no expectation of convictions but only to discourage exercise of protected rights"), and Hicks v. Miranda, 422 U.S. 332 (1975), p. 1158, *infra* (finding that the districts court's "vague and conclusory" findings concerning the "pattern of seizure" of the adult movie "Deep Throat" did not make out bad faith and harassment since each step in the pattern was authorized by judicial order, and even a showing "that the state courts were in error on some one or more issues of state or federal law" would not necessarily establish bad faith or harassment).

If Younger itself is sound, why should there be such an exception? Is a state court unable to determine whether a prosecutor is acting in bad faith? Or is the real problem one of harassment—of repeated, unfounded prosecutions that are dismissed before the defendant can obtain a favorable ruling?

(b) Patent and Flagrant Unconstitutionality. Younger also suggested that federal courts might be justified in restraining prosecutions under statutes that are "flagrantly and patently violative of express constitutional prohibitions in every clause, sentence, and paragraph, and in whatever manner and against whomever an effort might be made to apply it." The language is from Watson v. Buck, 313 U.S. 387 (1941), which refused to enjoin an entire statute when parts could be severed or the legislation could be given a narrowing construction. Why might an exception for patently and flagrantly unconstitutional statutes be warranted at all? Isn't it a particular insult to the state courts to suggest that they will be unable to detect patent unconstitutionality in state statutes?

Whatever the rationale, not much is left of this "exception" after Trainor v. Hernandez, 431 U.S. 434, 446–47 (1977).[12] There, the defendants in a state court action filed a federal suit challenging the constitutionality of a state court attachment against their property that had been obtained without any prior hearing, as authorized by state law. The lower court, in enjoining the attachment, held that the state's attachment procedure was "on its face patently violative of the due process clause." 405 F.Supp. 757 (N.D.Ill. 1975). Dividing 5–4, the Supreme Court reversed. Without clearly stating whether there was an exception to Younger for statutes found to be flagrantly unconstitutional, the majority simply said that if the lower court's statement constituted such a finding, it "would have not been warranted in light of our cases. Compare North Georgia Finishing, Inc. v. Di-Chem, Inc., 419 U.S. 601 (1975), with Mitchell v. W.T. Grant Co., 416 U.S. 600 (1974)."[13]

See also New Orleans Public Serv., Inc. v. Council of New Orleans, 491 U.S. 350 (1989) (concluding that an allegation that "requires further factual inquiry can hardly be deemed" to have satisfied the test for flagrant unlawfulness "for purposes of a threshold abstention determination").

---

[12] Indeed, what was left of this exception after Younger itself? Two years earlier, Brandenburg v. Ohio, 395 U.S. 444 (1969), had invalidated a statute almost identical to the one under which Harris was being prosecuted.

[13] Justices Brennan, Stewart, Marshall, and Stevens dissented. Justice Brennan's dissent argued that "a requirement that the * * * formulation [defining this exception] must be literally satisfied renders the exception meaningless". Analyzing the statute in some detail, Justice Brennan found it clearly unconstitutional under North Georgia Finishing and clearly distinguishable from the statute upheld in W.T. Grant. Justice Stevens' dissent objected that the majority's view made the exception inapplicable whenever the statute had a separability clause, and argued that there was no reason "why all sections of any statute must be considered invalid in order to justify an injunction against a portion that is itself flagrantly unconstitutional".

(c) Other Extraordinary Circumstances. What else might constitute "extraordinary circumstances" meriting an exception to Younger's policy of non-interference? In Gibson v. Berryhill, 411 U.S. 564 (1973), the Court refused to apply Younger to require deference to administrative proceedings before a state agency that the lower court had found to be "incompetent by reason of bias to adjudicate the issues pending before it. If the District Court's conclusion was correct in this regard, it was also correct that it need not defer to the Board. Nor, in these circumstances, would a different result be required simply because judicial review, de novo or otherwise, would be forthcoming at the conclusion of the administrative proceedings".[14]

Should the applicability of Younger, like the applicability of the Tax Injunction Act's bar on federal interference, depend on the existence of a "plain, speedy, and effective" remedy in state court? See Rosenfeld, *The Place of State Courts in the Era of Younger v. Harris*, 59 B.U.L.Rev. 597, 655–58 (1979).[15]

(8) Equitable Restraint—Mandatory or Permissive? In Ohio Bureau of Employment Servs. v. Hodory, 431 U.S. 471 (1977), the state, in appealing a three-judge court's injunction against the enforcement of a state statute, argued for reversal on the merits but not for dismissal under Younger. The Supreme Court reached the merits and reversed, over the suggestion of an amicus that Younger called for dismissal. On this point, the Court said: "If the State voluntarily chooses to submit to a federal forum, principles of comity do not demand that the federal court force the case back into the State's own system." Accord, Brown v. Hotel & Rest. Employees & Bartenders Local 54, 468 U.S. 491, 500 n. 9 (1984).[16]

---

[14] In Kugler v. Helfant, 421 U.S. 117 (1975), the Court described Gibson as an example of an "extraordinary circumstance", other than bad faith/harassment or patent unconstitutionality, but concluded that the case was distinguishable because the plaintiff's claim (in Kugler) that he could not obtain a fair hearing in the state courts was without merit.

[15] A number of courts of appeals have recognized an exception to Younger principles for cases in which plaintiffs seek to enjoin state prosecutions on double jeopardy grounds. See, *e.g.*, Gilliam v. Foster, 75 F.3d 881, 903–05 (4th Cir.1996) (en banc); Mannes v. Gillespie, 967 F.2d 1310, 1312 (9th Cir.1992). Beginning with the well-settled premise that the Double Jeopardy Clause prohibits not merely subsequent convictions but also subsequent prosecutions, the decisions reason that because the Clause's "full protection would be irretrievably lost if it could not be asserted before the occurrence of the subsequent prosecution that it prohibits, the comity concerns behind Younger must yield to the paramount right of the individual." Carter v. Medlock, No. 93–7221, 1994 WL 687287, at *3 n. 9 (4th Cir. Dec. 9, 1994) (unpublished opinion). Is this reasoning consistent with Younger? Even if the premise is granted that the Double Jeopardy Clause creates a special right to be free from trial and not just conviction (could the same not be said of other constitutional rights?), why should state courts be viewed as less competent to vindicate rights under the Double Jeopardy Clause than under other constitutional provisions? (Note, however, that the Supreme Court relies on similar reasoning to allow appeal before trial of denial of motions to dismiss indictments on double jeopardy grounds. See Abney v. United States, 431 U.S. 651 (1977).)

[16] In Ohio Civil Rights Comm'n v. Dayton Christian Schools, 477 U.S. 619 (1986), the federal plaintiff contended that the defendant had waived any claim for equitable restraint under Younger, because though the claim was raised in the federal district court and in oral argument before the Supreme Court, the defendant conceded in the district court that that court had jurisdiction. The Supreme Court ruled that this waiver argument "misconceive[d] the nature of Younger abstention", which is founded not on lack of jurisdiction but on "strong policies" of noninterference. Hodory and Brown showed, the Court said, that a state may voluntarily submit to federal jurisdiction even though it could have invoked Younger, but in those two cases the state had expressly urged federal court adjudication of the merits; "there was no similar consent or waiver here, and we therefore address the [Younger issue]".

By contrast, in Hodory the Court stated that it was not required to defer to the parties' wishes regarding Pullman abstention, which may result in avoidance of a constitutional question, though on the facts it found Pullman abstention inappropriate. Is the distinction valid? (Note that the Supreme Court has occasionally upheld the desirability of Younger abstention as a means of allowing state courts to provide narrowing constructions that might avoid constitutional questions. See, *e.g.*, Pennzoil Co. v. Texaco, Inc., 481 U.S. 1, 11–12 (1987); Moore v. Sims, 442 U.S. 415, 429–30 (1979).)

(9) Appealability. Decisions dismissing a federal action on Younger grounds are plainly appealable. On the appealability of the refusal to dismiss an action, see 15A Wright, Miller & Cooper § 3914.14.

Steffel v. Thompson

415 U.S. 452, 94 S.Ct. 1209, 39 L.Ed.2d 505 (1974).
Certiorari to the United States Court of Appeals for the Fifth Circuit.

■ MR. JUSTICE BRENNAN delivered the opinion of the Court.

* * * This case presents the important question reserved in Samuels v. Mackell, 401 U.S. 66, 73–74 (1971), whether declaratory relief is precluded when a state prosecution has been threatened, but is not pending, and a showing of bad-faith enforcement or other special circumstances has not been made.

Petitioner, and others, filed a complaint in the District Court for the Northern District of Georgia, invoking the Civil Rights Act of 1871, 42 U.S.C. § 1983, and its jurisdictional implementation, 28 U.S.C. § 1343. The complaint requested a declaratory judgment pursuant to 28 U.S.C. §§ 2201–2202, that Ga.Code Ann. § 26–1503 (1972) was being applied in violation of petitioner's First and Fourteenth Amendment rights, and an injunction restraining respondents—the Solicitor of the Civil and Criminal Court of DeKalb County, the chief of the DeKalb County Police, the owner of the North DeKalb Shopping Center, and the manager of that shopping center—from enforcing the statute so as to interfere with petitioner's constitutionally protected activities.

The parties stipulated to the relevant facts: On October 8, 1970, while petitioner and other individuals were distributing handbills protesting American involvement in Vietnam on an exterior sidewalk of the North DeKalb Shopping Center, shopping center employees asked them to stop handbilling and leave. They declined to do so, and police officers were summoned. The officers told them that they would be arrested if they did not stop handbilling. The group then left to avoid arrest. Two days later petitioner and a companion returned to the shopping center and again began handbilling. The manager of the center called the police, and petitioner and his companion were once again told that failure to stop their handbilling would result in their arrests. Petitioner left to avoid arrest. His companion stayed, however, continued handbilling, and was arrested and subsequently arraigned on a charge of criminal trespass in violation of § 26–1503. Petitioner alleged in his complaint that, although he desired to return to the shopping center to distribute handbills, he had not done so because of his concern that he, too, would be arrested for violation of § 26–1503; the parties stipulated that, if petitioner returned and refused upon request to stop handbilling, a warrant would be sworn out and he might be arrested and charged with a violation of the Georgia statute.

After hearing, the District Court denied all relief and dismissed the action, finding that "no meaningful contention can be made that the state has [acted] or will in the future act in bad faith," and therefore "the rudiments of an active controversy between the parties * * * [are] lacking." Petitioner appealed only from the denial of declaratory relief. The Court of Appeals for the Fifth Circuit, one judge concurring in the result, affirmed the District Court's judgment refusing declaratory relief. * * *

We granted certiorari, and now reverse.

I

At the threshold we must consider whether petitioner presents an "actual controversy," a requirement imposed by Art. III of the Constitution and the express terms of the Federal Declaratory Judgment Act, 28 U.S.C. § 2201.

Unlike three of the appellees in Younger v. Harris, 401 U.S. [37, 41 (1971)], petitioner has alleged threats of prosecution that cannot be characterized as "imaginary or speculative," *id.*, at 42. He has been twice warned to stop handbilling that he claims is constitutionally protected and has been told by the police that if he again handbills at the shopping center and disobeys a warning to stop he will likely be prosecuted. The prosecution of petitioner's handbilling companion is ample demonstration that petitioner's concern with arrest has not been "chimerical," Poe v. Ullman, 367 U.S. 497, 508 (1961). In these circumstances, it is not necessary that petitioner first expose himself to actual arrest or prosecution to be entitled to challenge a statute that he claims deters the exercise of his constitutional rights. See, *e.g.*, Epperson v. Arkansas, 393 U.S. 97 (1968). Moreover, petitioner's challenge is to those specific provisions of state law which have provided the basis for threats of criminal prosecution against him. *Cf.* Boyle v. Landry, 401 U.S. 77, 81 (1971); Watson v. Buck, 313 U.S. 387, 399–400 (1941). * * *

II

We now turn to the question of whether the District Court and the Court of Appeals correctly found petitioner's request for declaratory relief inappropriate.

Sensitive to principles of equity, comity, and federalism, we recognized in Younger v. Harris, *supra*, that federal courts should ordinarily refrain from enjoining ongoing state criminal prosecutions. * * * In Samuels v. Mackell, *supra*, the Court also found that the same principles ordinarily would be flouted by issuance of a federal declaratory judgment when a state proceeding was pending, since the intrusive effect of declaratory relief "will result in precisely the same interference with and disruption of state proceedings that the long-standing policy limiting injunctions was designed to avoid." 401 U.S., at 72.[11] * * *

---

[11] The Court noted that under 28 U.S.C. § 2202 a declaratory judgment might serve as the basis for issuance of a later injunction to give effect to the declaratory judgment, and that a declaratory judgment might have a res judicata effect on the pending state proceeding. 401 U.S., at 72.

Neither Younger nor Samuels, however, decided the question whether federal intervention might be permissible in the absence of a pending state prosecution. * * * These reservations anticipated the Court's recognition that the relevant principles of equity, comity, and federalism "have little force in the absence of a pending state proceeding." Lake Carriers' Assn. v. MacMullan, 406 U.S. 498, 509 (1972). When no state criminal proceeding is pending at the time the federal complaint is filed, federal intervention does not result in duplicative legal proceedings or disruption of the state criminal justice system; nor can federal intervention, in that circumstance, be interpreted as reflecting negatively upon the state court's ability to enforce constitutional principles. In addition, while a pending state prosecution provides the federal plaintiff with a concrete opportunity to vindicate his constitutional rights, a refusal on the part of the federal courts to intervene when no state proceeding is pending may place the hapless plaintiff between the Scylla of intentionally flouting state law and the Charybdis of forgoing what he believes to be constitutionally protected activity in order to avoid becoming enmeshed in a criminal proceeding. *Cf.* Dombrowski v. Pfister, 380 U.S. 479, 490 (1965).

When no state proceeding is pending and thus considerations of equity, comity, and federalism have little vitality, the propriety of granting federal declaratory relief may properly be considered independently of a request for injunctive relief. Here, the Court of Appeals held that, because injunctive relief would not be appropriate since petitioner failed to demonstrate irreparable injury—a traditional prerequisite to injunctive relief, *e.g.*, Dombrowski v. Pfister, *supra*—it followed that declaratory relief was also inappropriate. Even if the Court of Appeals correctly viewed injunctive relief as inappropriate—a question we need not reach today since petitioner has abandoned his request for that remedy,[12] the court erred in treating the requests for injunctive and declaratory relief as a single issue. "[W]hen no state prosecution is pending and the only question is whether declaratory relief is appropriate[,] * * * the congressional scheme that makes the federal courts the primary guardians of constitutional rights, and the express congressional authorization of declaratory relief, afforded because it is a less harsh and abrasive remedy than the injunction, become the factors of primary significance." Perez v. Ledesma, 401 U.S. 82, 104 (1971) (Brennan, J., concurring in part and dissenting in part).

The subject matter jurisdiction of the lower federal courts was greatly expanded in the wake of the Civil War. A pervasive sense of nationalism led to enactment of the Civil Rights Act of 1871, empowering the lower federal courts to determine the constitutionality of actions, taken by persons under color of state law, allegedly depriving other individuals of rights guaranteed by the Constitution and federal law, see 42 U.S.C. § 1983, 28 U.S.C. § 1343(3). Four years later, in the Judiciary

---

[12] We note that, in those cases where injunctive relief has been sought to restrain an imminent, but not yet pending, prosecution *for past conduct*, sufficient injury has not been found to warrant injunctive relief, see Beal v. Missouri Pacific R. Co., 312 U.S. 45 (1941); Spielman Motor Sales Co. v. Dodge, 295 U.S. 89 (1935); Fenner v. Boykin, 271 U.S. 240 (1926). There is some question, however, whether a showing of irreparable injury might be made in a case where, although no prosecution is pending or impending, an individual demonstrates that he will be required to *forego* constitutionally protected activity in order to avoid arrest. Compare Dombrowski v. Pfister, 380 U.S. 479 (1965).

Act of March 3, 1875, Congress conferred upon the lower federal courts, for but the second time in their nearly century-old history, general federal-question jurisdiction subject only to a jurisdictional-amount requirement, see 28 U.S.C. § 1331. With this latter enactment, the lower federal courts "ceased to be restricted tribunals of fair dealing between citizens of different states and became the *primary* and powerful reliances for vindicating every right given by the Constitution, the laws, and treaties of the United States." F. Frankfurter & J. Landis, The Business of the Supreme Court 65 (1928) (emphasis added). These two statutes, together with the Court's decision in Ex parte Young, 209 U.S. 123 (1908)—holding that state officials who threaten to enforce an unconstitutional state statute may be enjoined by a federal court of equity and that a federal court may, in appropriate circumstances, enjoin future state criminal prosecutions under the unconstitutional Act—have "established the modern framework for federal protection of constitutional rights from state interference." Perez v. Ledesma, *supra*, 401 U.S., at 107 (separate opinion of Brennan, J.).

A "storm of controversy" raged in the wake of Ex parte Young, focusing principally on the power of a single federal judge to grant *ex parte* interlocutory injunctions against the enforcement of state statutes, H. Hart & H. Wechsler, The Federal Courts and the Federal System 967 (2d ed. 1973). This uproar was only partially quelled by Congress' passage of legislation requiring the convening of a three-judge district court before a preliminary injunction against enforcement of a state statute could issue, and providing for direct appeal to this Court from a decision granting or denying such relief. See 28 U.S.C. §§ 2281, 1253. From a State's viewpoint the granting of injunctive relief—even by these courts of special dignity—"rather clumsily" crippled state enforcement of its statutes pending further review. Furthermore, plaintiffs were dissatisfied with this method of testing the constitutionality of state statutes, since it placed upon them the burden of demonstrating the traditional prerequisites to equitable relief—most importantly, irreparable injury. See, *e.g.*, Fenner v. Boykin, 271 U.S. 240, 243 (1926).

To dispel these difficulties, Congress in 1934 enacted the Declaratory Judgment Act, 28 U.S.C. §§ 2201–2202. That Congress plainly intended declaratory relief to act as an alternative to the strong medicine of the injunction and to be utilized to test the constitutionality of state criminal statutes in cases where injunctive relief would be unavailable is amply evidenced by the legislative history of the Act, traced in full detail in Perez v. Ledesma, *supra*, at 111–115 (separate opinion of Brennan, J.). The highlights of that history, particularly pertinent to our inquiry today, emphasize that:

"* * *

"The express purpose of the Federal Declaratory Judgment Act was to provide a milder alternative to the injunction remedy. * * * Of particular significance on the question before us, the Senate report makes it even clearer that the declaratory judgment was designed to be available to test state criminal statutes in circumstances where an injunction would not be appropriate. * * *

"* * * Moreover, the Senate report's clear implication that declaratory relief would have been appropriate in Pierce v.

Society of Sisters, 268 U.S. 510 (1925), and Village of Euclid v. Ambler Realty Co., 272 U.S. 365 (1926), both cases involving federal adjudication of the constitutionality of a state statute carrying criminal penalties, and the report's quotation from Terrace v. Thompson, 263 U.S. 197 (1923), which also involved anticipatory federal adjudication of the constitutionality of a state criminal statute, make it plain that Congress anticipated that the declaratory judgment procedure would be used by the federal courts to test the constitutionality of state criminal statutes."

It was this history that formed the backdrop to our decision in Zwickler v. Koota, 389 U.S. 241 (1967), where a state criminal statute was attacked on grounds of unconstitutional overbreadth and no state prosecution was pending against the federal plaintiff. There, we found error in a three-judge district court's considering, as a single question, the propriety of granting injunctive and declaratory relief. Although we noted that injunctive relief might well be unavailable under principles of equity jurisprudence canvassed in Douglas v. City of Jeannette, 319 U.S. 157 (1943), we held that "a federal district court has the duty to decide the appropriateness and the merits of the declaratory request irrespective of its conclusion as to the propriety of the issuance of the injunction." 389 U.S., at 254. Only one year ago, we reaffirmed the Zwickler v. Koota holding in Roe v. Wade, 410 U.S. 113 (1973), and Doe v. Bolton, 410 U.S. 179 (1973). * * *

The "different considerations" entering into a decision whether to grant declaratory relief have their origins in the preceding historical summary. First, as Congress recognized in 1934, a declaratory judgment will have a less intrusive effect on the administration of state criminal laws. As was observed in Perez v. Ledesma, 401 U.S., at 124–126 (separate opinion of Brennan, J.):

> " * * * [W]here the highest court of a State has had an opportunity to give a statute regulating expression a narrowing or clarifying construction but has failed to do so, and later a federal court declares the statute unconstitutionally vague or overbroad, it may well be open to a state prosecutor, after the federal court decision, to bring a prosecution under the statute if he reasonably believes that the defendant's conduct is not constitutionally protected and that the state courts may give the statute a construction so as to yield a constitutionally valid conviction. * * * [E]ven though a declaratory judgment has 'the force and effect of a final judgment,' 28 U.S.C. § 2201, it is a much milder form of relief than an injunction. Though it may be persuasive, it is not ultimately coercive; noncompliance with it may be inappropriate, but is not contempt."[19]

Second, engrafting upon the Declaratory Judgment Act a requirement that all of the traditional equitable prerequisites to the

---

[19] The pending prosecution of petitioner's handbilling companion does not affect petitioner's action for declaratory relief. In Roe v. Wade, 410 U.S. 113 (1973), while the pending prosecution of Dr. Hallford under the Texas Abortion law was found to render his action for declaratory and injunctive relief impermissible, this did not prevent our granting plaintiff Roe, against whom no action was pending, a declaratory judgment that the statute was unconstitutional.

issuance of an injunction be satisfied before the issuance of a declaratory judgment is considered would defy Congress' intent to make declaratory relief available in cases where an injunction would be inappropriate. * * *

Thus, the Court of Appeals was in error when it ruled that a failure to demonstrate irreparable injury * * * precluded the granting of declaratory relief.

The only occasions where this Court has disregarded these "different considerations" and found that a preclusion of injunctive relief inevitably led to a denial of declaratory relief have been cases in which principles of federalism militated altogether against federal intervention in a class of adjudications. See Great Lakes Dredge & Dock Co. v. Huffman, 319 U.S. 293 (1943) (federal policy against interfering with the enforcement of state tax laws); Samuels v. Mackell, 401 U.S. 66 (1971). In the instant case, principles of federalism not only do not preclude federal intervention, they compel it. Requiring the federal courts totally to step aside when no state criminal prosecution is pending against the federal plaintiff would turn federalism on its head. When federal claims are premised on 42 U.S.C. § 1983 and 28 U.S.C. § 1343(3)—as they are here— we have not required exhaustion of state judicial or administrative remedies, recognizing the paramount role Congress has assigned to the federal courts to protect constitutional rights. See, e.g., McNeese v. Board of Education, 373 U.S. 668 (1963); Monroe v. Pape, 365 U.S. 167 (1961). But exhaustion of state remedies is precisely what would be required if both federal injunctive and declaratory relief were unavailable in a case where no state prosecution had been commenced.

III

Respondents, however, relying principally upon our decision in Cameron v. Johnson, 390 U.S. 611 (1968), argue that, although it may be appropriate to issue a declaratory judgment when no state criminal proceeding is pending and the attack is upon the *facial validity* of a state criminal statute, such a step would be improper where, as here, the attack is merely upon the constitutionality of the statute as applied, since the State's interest in unencumbered enforcement of its laws outweighs the minimal federal interest in protecting the constitutional rights of only a single individual. We reject the argument. * * *

Indeed, the State's concern with potential interference in the administration of its criminal laws is of lesser dimension when an attack is made upon the constitutionality of a state statute as applied. A declaratory judgment of a lower federal court that a state statute is invalid *in toto*—and therefore incapable of any valid application—or is overbroad or vague—and therefore no person can properly be convicted under the statute until it is given a narrowing or clarifying construction—will likely have a more significant potential for disruption of state enforcement policies than a declaration specifying a limited number of impermissible applications of the statute. While the federal interest may be greater when a state statute is attacked on its face, since there exists the potential for eliminating any broad-ranging deterrent effect on would-be actors, see Dombrowski v. Pfister, 380 U.S. 479 (1965), we do not find this consideration controlling. The solitary individual who suffers a deprivation of his constitutional rights is no less deserving of redress than one who suffers together with others.

We therefore hold that, regardless of whether injunctive relief may be appropriate, federal declaratory relief is not precluded when no state prosecution is pending and a federal plaintiff demonstrates a genuine threat of enforcement of a disputed state criminal statute, whether an attack is made on the constitutionality of the statute on its face or as applied. The judgment of the Court of Appeals is reversed, and the case is remanded for further proceedings consistent with this opinion.

It is so ordered.

■ MR. JUSTICE STEWART, with whom THE CHIEF JUSTICE joins, concurring.

While joining the opinion of the Court, I add a word by way of emphasis.

Our decision today must not be understood as authorizing the invocation of federal declaratory judgment jurisdiction by a person who thinks a state criminal law is unconstitutional, even if he genuinely feels "chilled" in his freedom of action by the law's existence, and even if he honestly entertains the subjective belief that he may now or in the future be prosecuted under it. * * *

The petitioner in this case has succeeded in objectively showing that the threat of imminent arrest, corroborated by the actual arrest of his companion, has created an actual concrete controversy between himself and the agents of the State. He has, therefore, demonstrated "a genuine threat of enforcement of a disputed state criminal statute * * *." Cases where such a "genuine threat" can be demonstrated will, I think, be exceedingly rare.

■ MR. JUSTICE WHITE, concurring.

I offer the following few words in light of Mr. Justice Rehnquist's concurrence in which he discusses the impact on a pending federal action of a later filed criminal prosecution against the federal plaintiff, whether a federal court may enjoin a state criminal prosecution under a statute the federal court has earlier declared unconstitutional at the suit of the defendant now being prosecuted, and the question whether that declaratory judgment is res judicata in such a later filed state criminal action.

It should be noted, first, that his views on these issues are neither expressly nor impliedly embraced by the Court's opinion filed today. Second, my own tentative views on these questions are somewhat contrary to my Brother's.

At this writing at least, I would anticipate that a final declaratory judgment entered by a federal court holding particular conduct of the federal plaintiff to be immune on federal constitutional grounds from prosecution under state law should be accorded res judicata effect in any later prosecution of that very conduct. There would also, I think, be additional circumstances in which the federal judgment should be considered as more than a mere precedent bearing on the issue before the state court.

Neither can I at this stage agree that the federal court, having rendered a declaratory judgment in favor of the plaintiff, could not enjoin a later state prosecution for conduct that the federal court has declared immune. The Declaratory Judgment Act itself provides that a

"declaration shall have the force and effect of a final judgment or decree,"
28 U.S.C. § 2201; eminent authority anticipated that declaratory
judgments would be res judicata, E. Borchard, Declaratory Judgments
10–11 (2d ed. 1941); and there is every reason for not reducing
declaratory judgments to mere advisory opinions. Toucey v. New York
Life Insurance Co., 314 U.S. 118 (1941), once expressed the view that 28
U.S.C. § 2283 forbade injunctions against relitigation in state courts of
federally decided issues, but the section was then amended to overrule
that case, the consequence being that "[i]t is clear that the Toucey rule is
gone, and that to protect or effectuate its judgment a federal court may
enjoin relitigation in the state court." C. Wright, Federal Courts 180 (2d
ed. 1970). I see no more reason here to hold that the federal plaintiff must
always rely solely on his plea of res judicata in the state courts. The
statute provides for "[f]urther necessary or proper relief * * * against any
adverse party whose rights have been determined by such judgment," 28
U.S.C. § 2202, and it would not seem improper to enjoin local prosecutors
who refuse to observe adverse federal judgments.

Finally, I would think that a federal suit challenging a state criminal
statute on federal constitutional grounds could be sufficiently far along
so that ordinary consideration of economy would warrant refusal to
dismiss the federal case solely because a state prosecution has
subsequently been filed and the federal question may be litigated there.

■ MR. JUSTICE REHNQUIST, with whom THE CHIEF JUSTICE joins,
concurring.

I concur in the opinion of the Court. Although my reading of the
legislative history of the Declaratory Judgment Act of 1934 suggests that
its primary purpose was to enable persons to obtain a definition of their
rights before an actual injury had occurred, rather than to palliate any
controversy arising from Ex parte Young, 209 U.S. 123 (1908), Congress
apparently was aware at the time it passed the Act that persons
threatened with state criminal prosecutions might choose to forego the
offending conduct and instead seek a federal declaration of their rights.
Use of the declaratory judgment procedure in the circumstances
presented by this case seems consistent with that congressional
expectation. * * *

The Court quite properly leaves for another day whether the
granting of a declaratory judgment by a federal court will have any
subsequent res judicata effect or will perhaps support the issuance of a
later federal injunction. But since possible resolutions of those issues
would substantially undercut the principles of federalism reaffirmed in
Younger v. Harris, 401 U.S. 37 (1971), and preserved by the decision
today, I feel it appropriate to add a few remarks.

First, the legislative history of the Declaratory Judgment Act and
the Court's opinion in this case both recognize that the declaratory
judgment procedure is an alternative to pursuit of the arguably illegal
activity. There is nothing in the Act's history to suggest that Congress
intended to provide persons wishing to violate state laws with a federal
shield behind which they could carry on their contemplated conduct.
Thus I do not believe that a federal plaintiff in a declaratory judgment
action can avoid, by the mere filing of a complaint, the principles so firmly
expressed in Samuels, supra. The plaintiff who continues to violate a
state statute after the filing of his federal complaint does so both at the

risk of state prosecution and at the risk of dismissal of his federal lawsuit. For any arrest prior to resolution of the federal action would constitute a pending prosecution and bar declaratory relief under the principles of Samuels.

Second, I do not believe that today's decision can properly be raised to support the issuance of a federal injunction based upon a favorable declaratory judgment. The Court's description of declaratory relief as "a milder alternative to the injunction remedy," having a "less intrusive effect on the administration of state criminal laws" than an injunction, indicates to me critical distinctions which make declaratory relief appropriate where injunctive relief would not be. It would all but totally obscure these important distinctions if a successful application for declaratory relief came to be regarded, not as the conclusion of a lawsuit, but as a giant step toward obtaining an injunction against a subsequent criminal prosecution. * * *

A declaratory judgment is simply a statement of rights, not a binding order supplemented by continuing sanctions. State authorities may choose to be guided by the judgment of a lower federal court, but they are not compelled to follow the decision by threat of contempt or other penalties. If the federal plaintiff pursues the conduct for which he was previously threatened with arrest and is in fact arrested, he may not return the controversy to federal court, although he may, of course, raise the federal declaratory judgment in the state court for whatever value it may prove to have.[3] In any event, the defendant at that point is able to present his case for full consideration by a state court charged, as are the federal courts, to preserve the defendant's constitutional rights. Federal interference with this process would involve precisely the same concerns discussed in Younger and recited in the Court's opinion in this case.

Third, attempts to circumvent Younger by claiming that enforcement of a statute declared unconstitutional by a federal court is *per se* evidence of bad faith should not find support in the Court's decision in this case. * * *

If the declaratory judgment remains, as I think the Declaratory Judgment Act intended, a simple declaration of rights without more, it will not be used merely as a dramatic tactical maneuver on the part of any state defendant seeking extended delays. Nor will it force state officials to try cases time after time first in the federal courts and then in the state courts. * * * If the federal court finds that the threatened prosecution would depend upon a statute it judges unconstitutional, the State may decide to forgo prosecution of similar conduct in the future, believing the judgment persuasive. Should the state prosecutors not find the decision persuasive enough to justify forbearance, the successful federal plaintiff will at least be able to bolster his allegations of unconstitutionality in the state trial with a decision of the federal district court in the immediate locality. The state courts may find the reasoning convincing even though the prosecutors did not. Finally, of course, the state legislature may decide, on the basis of the federal decision, that the statute would be better amended or repealed. All these possible avenues of relief would be reached voluntarily by the States and would be

---

[3] The Court's opinion notes that the possible res judicata effect of a federal declaratory judgment in a subsequent state court prosecution is a question "not free from difficulty." * * * I express no opinion on that issue here. * * *

completely consistent with the concepts of federalism discussed above. Other more intrusive forms of relief should not be routinely available. * * *

NOTE ON STEFFEL V. THOMPSON AND ANTICIPATORY RELIEF

(1) The Pending/Non-Pending Distinction. Do you agree with the Court's conclusion in Steffel that the "principles of equity, comity, and federalism" that underlay Younger v. Harris "have little or no force in the absence of a pending state proceeding"? Consider Redish, Federal Jurisdiction: Tensions in the Allocation of Judicial Power 356 (2d ed.1990) : "[Steffel] appears to contradict two * * * recognized bases of Younger deference—the desire to avoid interference with state substantive legislative policies and with state prosecutorial discretion. For whether or not a prosecution has been filed, federal relief tells the prosecutor 'when and how'—and indeed if—he or she is to bring a prosecution.'"

If there is a disparity of outlooks between Younger and Steffel,[1] how do you account for the Supreme Court's nearly total unanimity in *both* cases? (The decision in Steffel was unanimous, while eight of the nine Justices concurred in the result in Younger.) Note that the distinction between pending and non-pending actions, on which Justice Brennan's opinion relied so heavily, is not necessarily a stable one, since prosecutors will frequently have the option to file charges after the filing of a declaratory judgment complaint. See generally Hicks v. Miranda, 422 U.S. 332 (1975), p. 1158, *infra*.

(2) Interests in Anticipatory Relief. Apart from any desire to litigate their federal rights in federal rather than state court, plaintiffs such as Steffel may have powerful interests in obtaining anticipatory relief from what they believe to be unconstitutional applications of state laws. To clarify the interests at stake, and to evaluate the extent to which they are in tension with the values underlying Younger v. Harris, it is useful to distinguish claims to federal relief against state prosecution for future, past, and continuing conduct.

(a) Future Conduct. Suppose that Steffel had never violated the Georgia anti-trespassing statute, but that he had definite plans to do so, and was deterred from carrying out those plans only by the threat of a criminal prosecution. As Justice Brennan points out in Steffel, to allow plaintiffs to obtain a declaration of their rights in such cases would appear to be a central purpose of the Declaratory Judgment Act. Exposing oneself to criminal prosecution is a perilous business; anticipatory federal relief is important to relieve parties acting in good faith from having to choose between forgoing conduct they believe to be constitutionally protected and risking criminal liability.

For a declaratory judgment to be available under these circumstances, the standing and ripeness barriers must of course be surmounted, as they

---

[1]   Compare Fallon, *The Ideologies of Federal Courts Law*, 74 Va.L.Rev. 1141, 1164–72 (1988) (suggesting that Steffel's acceptance of the "Nationalist" premise that Congress intended the federal courts to be "the primary and powerful reliances for vindicating every right given by the Constitution" is dissonant with Younger's "Federalist presumption that Congress would wish to show deference to state courts or that rules of equitable restraint should be crafted to do so").

were in Steffel. Although the Supreme Court's standing and ripeness decisions have taken a sometimes perplexing path, on the whole Justice Stewart's forecast in Steffel—that cases where a genuine threat of prosecution can be demonstrated will be "exceedingly rare"—has not been borne out. See, *e.g.*, Laycock, Modern American Remedies 596 (4th ed.2010) (observing that "[m]ost of the Court's cases hold or assume that a suit to enjoin enforcement is ripe when the statute is on the books and plaintiff wants to violate it"). See generally Chap. II, Sec. 3 and Sec. 5, *supra*.

(b) Past Conduct. Consider now the case of someone who has engaged in conduct in the past, but has no plan to continue that conduct in the future, and who seeks a federal declaration that the past conduct was constitutionally protected. Declaratory relief designed to immunize past, noncontinuing conduct from state prosecution cannot spare a litigant the choice between violating the statute and forgoing possibly lawful activity; that choice has already been made. And if the state prevails in the federal action, a subsequent prosecution is likely to be highly duplicative, since the federal litigation will have at best very limited res judicata effect against the state criminal defendant.[2]

Friedman, *Under the Law of Federal Jurisdiction: Allocating Cases Between State and Federal Courts*, 104 Colum.L.Rev. 1211, 1248–54 (2004), argues that our constitutional tradition includes a "don't break the law" principle and that litigants who have violated a state statute have less of a claim to federal adjudication than litigants who have not yet violated a state statute, but wish to do so and believe that the Constitution would protect them. Do you agree?

(c) Continuing Conduct. Consider now the case of a plaintiff, like Steffel, engaged in a continuing course of conduct—someone who has already violated a criminal statute, but who seeks federal equitable relief from prosecution for similar actions not yet undertaken. In such a case, anticipatory federal intervention offers the federal plaintiff distinctive advantages over defending against a state prosecution. First, in appropriate cases interlocutory relief may be available, thereby largely eliminating the need for the federal plaintiff to choose, *pendente lite*, between desisting from conduct that the plaintiff believes to be constitutionally protected and risking additional criminal penalties. Second, if the federal court awards equitable relief based upon the protected nature of the plaintiff's conduct, the plaintiff has protection against prosecution for similar conduct undertaken in the future.[3] By contrast, a defendant's victory in the pending state criminal case will not necessarily preclude prosecution for engaging thereafter in the same conduct: an acquittal, or even a trial judge's dismissal of the charges, may not have preclusive effect, especially where the state could not appeal. See generally Laycock, *Federal Interference With State Prosecutions: The Need for Prospective Relief*, 1977 Sup.Ct.Rev. 193.

---

[2]   Although preclusion might apply to a pure issue of law—such as the facial validity of a statute—differences in the burden of proof in civil and criminal cases would ordinarily require relitigation of the application of law to fact. See generally Restatement (Second) of Judgments §§ 27, 28 (1982).

Does this suggest that there may be a stronger argument for federal intervention in cases involving past conduct if the federal plaintiff is challenging the state statute on its face rather than as applied?

[3]   This assumes a federal declaratory judgment would be accorded res judicata effect in a subsequent state prosecution. For an examination of this assumption, see Paragraph (3), *infra*.

On the other hand, in cases of continuing conduct as in cases of past conduct only, the availability of a federal suit for equitable relief may force the state prosecutor's hand about when and where to litigate. In addition, if the federal claim fails, duplicative litigation may ensue.

Even so, aren't the arguments for allowing federal equitable intervention much stronger in a case involving continuing conduct than in a case involving past conduct only?

(3) Declaratory v. Injunctive Relief. Justice Brennan's opinion in Steffel places considerable weight on the distinction between declaratory and injunctive relief. How well does that distinction bear up?

(a) Intended Effect. The intended effect of a declaratory judgment will ordinarily be the same as that of an injunction—to forestall and protect against a threatened prosecution. Of course, if a state prosecutor subsequently brings an action that "violates" a declaration, the prosecutor would not be in contempt, as would be the case had an injunction issued. But the plaintiff would surely seek and presumably would be entitled to a supplementary injunction under 28 U.S.C. §§ 2201–2202.

It might be suggested that a declaration leaves the state with more freedom than it would have under an injunction to prosecute other persons under the statute and thereby to salvage its constitutional applications. But if such flexibility is desired, a court could craft an injunction to permit it.

(b) The Res Judicata Effect of a Federal Declaratory Judgment on an Issue of Federal Law. In his concurring opinion in Steffel, Justice Rehnquist suggests that a declaratory judgment interferes with state interests less than an injunction because it lacks the same res judicata effect. Suppose that, on remand in Steffel, the district court entered a declaratory judgment that the plaintiff's leafletting was constitutionally protected, and thereafter the state indicted him for criminal trespass. Wouldn't "[t]he very purpose of the declaratory judgment proceeding * * * be thwarted were this determination to be regarded * * * as no more than the view of a coordinate court"? Shapiro, *State Courts and Federal Declaratory Judgments*, 74 Nw.U.L.Rev. 759, 764 (1979); see also Shapiro, Preclusion in Civil Actions 63 (2001); accord, Restatement (Second) of Judgments § 33.[4] Indeed, if a federal declaratory judgment lacked any significant preclusive effect, mightn't it

---

[4] There should be no problem with binding the state in the criminal case on the basis of a federal action that, because of Eleventh Amendment constraints, named an official rather than the state as a defendant. See Shapiro, *supra*, 74 Nw.U.L.Rev. at 764. But *cf.* Idaho v. Coeur d'Alene Tribe, 521 U.S. 261, 305–06 (1997) (Souter, J., dissenting) (suggesting that a holding concerning ownership of property, rendered in a suit against government officials, would not necessarily bind the government itself in a subsequent action).

The res judicata effect of a federal judgment that a state statute is invalid due to overbreadth, which rests in part on a state law determination concerning the challenged statute's meaning, raises different and more complex issues. A dictum in Dombrowski v. Pfister, 380 U.S. 479, 491 n. 7 (1965), clearly suggested that even the beneficiaries of a federal declaratory judgment would subsequently become vulnerable to prosecution, the declaratory judgment notwithstanding, if a state court subsequently gave a constitutionally valid narrowing construction in a state declaratory judgment action. Shapiro, *supra*, 74 Nw.U.L.Rev. at 769–70, finds the dictum unpersuasive due to problems of inadequate notice. Compare Fallon, *Making Sense of Overbreadth*, 100 Yale L.J. 853, 878, 884–903 (1991) (asserting that the notice argument "is circular" and arguing that the preclusive effect of a federal determination of unconstitutional overbreadth is largely a question of federal common law that should be determined based on a range of policy considerations).

constitute a constitutionally forbidden advisory opinion? See Chapter II, Sec. 1, *supra*.[5]

Suppose instead that the federal district court declared that the statute was *constitutional* as applied to Steffel's conduct. Should Steffel be precluded in the criminal case from relitigating the constitutional question? See generally Restatement (Second) of Judgments § 27 ("When an issue of fact or law is actually litigated and determined by a valid and final judgment, and the determination is essential to the judgment, the determination is conclusive in a subsequent action between the parties, whether on the same or a different claim.").

(c) Prohibitory Intent and Preclusive Effect Conjoined. If the intended effect of a declaratory judgment is the same as that of an injunction, and if a federal declaratory judgment would enjoy the same preclusive effect as an injunction in subsequent state litigation, then the distinction between the two types of remedy is a good deal less significant than Justice Brennan suggested in Steffel.[6] It would not necessarily follow, however, that the distinction is wholly chimerical.[7] Does the distinction help to effect a workable, if somewhat arbitrary, accommodation of the interests that underlay Younger on the one hand and those supporting Steffel on the other? Or, like most arbitrary lines, is the distinction between injunctive and declaratory relief inherently vulnerable to erosion?

(4) After Steffel: Injunctions Against Threatened Actions. In Wooley v. Maynard, 430 U.S. 705 (1977), the Court upheld a permanent injunction barring New Hampshire officials from enforcing against the plaintiffs a state law making it a misdemeanor to "obscure" the phrase "Live Free or Die" on state license plates. Maynard had previously been convicted three times for violating the statute, but his federal action did not seek to attack his past convictions, only to enjoin future prosecutions. The Court held that "[t]he threat of repeated prosecutions in the future against both [Maynard] and his wife, and the effect of such a continuing threat on their ability to perform the ordinary tasks of daily life which require an automobile, is sufficient to justify injunctive relief". Justice White, joined by Justices Blackmun and Rehnquist, dissented on the Younger issue, arguing that there was no reason to believe that the state officials—who had simply been performing their jobs in obtaining the three prior convictions—would not comply with a declaration, and hence there was no special need for injunctive relief.

In subsequent cases involving threatened prosecution for future conduct, the Court has sometimes approved final injunctions (rather than

---

[5]   Even if Steffel could invoke the preclusive effect of a favorable federal judgment, does it follow that a fellow protester who was not a party to the federal proceeding should be able to do so? See Shapiro, *supra*, 74 Nw.U.L.Rev. at 770–76, arguing that to permit nonmutual preclusion could prevent the full ventilation of issues of law regarding matters of public importance. See also Chap. XII, Sec. 1, *infra*. (If, however, the federal suit can be and is filed as a class action, there may be no one outside the class against whom the state could bring an enforcement action.)

[6]   Compare California v. Grace Brethren Church, p. 1091, *supra* (Tax Injunction Act bars a federal action for declaratory judgment as to state taxes).

[7]   See generally Bray, *The Myth of the Mild Declaratory Judgment,* 63 Duke L.J. 1091 (2014) (rejecting the "standard" view that "the injunction is the stronger remedy and the declaratory judgment is the milder one" but identifying features of injunctions—such as a requirement of specificity, rules governing modification and dissolution, and potential contempt sanctions for violation—that the author says "make it easier for a judge to observe and respond to violations").

declaratory judgments) without comment or dissent. See, *e.g.*, Bellotti v. Baird, 443 U.S. 622, 651 (1979); Ray v. Atlantic Richfield Co., 435 U.S. 151, 156–57 (1978); Zablocki v. Redhail, 434 U.S. 374, 377 (1978).

The Justices took a slightly more cautious position in Morales v. TWA, Inc., 504 U.S. 374 (1992). The district court had enjoined the Texas Attorney General from bringing enforcement proceedings against various airlines under certain state advertising regulations held to be preempted by the federal Airline Deregulation Act. No enforcement actions were pending, but the Attorney General's office had sent several putative violators a letter that served "as formal notice of intent to sue." In affirming part of the injunction, the Court found that the requirements of irreparable injury and of no adequate remedy at law were satisfied "[w]hen enforcement actions are imminent[,] * * * at least when repetitive penalties attach to continuing or repeated violations and the moving party lacks the realistic option of violating the law once and raising its federal defenses". The Court nevertheless overturned the injunction insofar as it barred the Attorney General from enforcing *any* regulation regarding airline advertising, rates, routes, or services, finding this "blunderbuss" prohibition invalid in the absence of any imminent enforcement action.

In the wake of Wooley and its successor cases, how disparate are the standards for declaratory and injunctive relief against non-pending enforcement actions?

(5) Exhaustion of State Remedies and Res Judicata. Once the doctrine of equitable restraint closes the door to the federal courthouse because a state proceeding is pending, does there ever come a time—for example, after the state trial court has rendered judgment—when access to a federal court is no longer barred? The answer to this question may depend on whether further state-court remedies are available at the time the federal suit is filed.

    (a) State Remedies Still Available. In Huffman v. Pursue, Ltd., 420 U.S. 592 (1975), the state had brought a civil action under its obscenity laws to "abate" the showing of obscene movies by Pursue. After the state trial court had issued a final order of abatement, Pursue filed a § 1983 action in federal court challenging the validity of the state obscenity statute. The Supreme Court first ruled that Younger applied when this form of *civil* proceeding was pending in state court—a question discussed at pp. 1165–1170, *infra*. The Court then ruled that a party in Pursue's position "must exhaust his state appellate remedies before seeking relief in the District Court, unless he can bring himself within one of the exceptions specified in Younger", and noted that at the time the federal action was commenced Pursue still had the right to appeal the state trial court's order. Refusing to "assum[e] that state judges will not be faithful to their constitutional responsibilities", the Court held that the exhaustion requirement is not excused merely because the prospects for success in the state courts are poor.

    (b) State Remedies No Longer Available. Suppose that at the time a federal action is filed, the federal plaintiff has forfeited state court appellate remedies that would have been available at an earlier point. This may have been the case in Huffman: the Court was not sure whether, at the time the federal district court issued its injunction, Pursue could still have appealed the state court's order, but said that it "may not avoid the standards of Younger by simply failing to comply with the procedures of perfecting its appeal within the Ohio judicial system".

(Must exhaust state app. remedies)

A similar question was presented in Ellis v. Dyson, 421 U.S. 426 (1975), decided two months after Huffman. On the basis of their pleas of *nolo contendere*, several defendants were convicted in a Texas municipal court of loitering and fined $10 each. Under Texas law, they were entitled to trial de novo in a county court and thereafter to appellate review. But, fearing higher fines on reconviction, they allowed the municipal court convictions to become final. They then brought suit in federal district court, seeking (a) a declaratory judgment that the loitering ordinance was unconstitutional and could not be applied to them in the future, and (b) an order "expunging" the records of the municipal court convictions. The court of appeals affirmed the district court's holding that the federal plaintiffs were not entitled to relief absent a showing of bad faith. The Supreme Court, in a confusing and opaque opinion, reversed and remanded for reconsideration in light of the intervening decision in Steffel. Justice Powell, dissenting, argued that the collateral attack on the convictions raised an issue not of equitable restraint, but of res judicata.

Wasn't Justice Powell right that if a federal § 1983 suit challenges the validity of a state statute under which a conviction has already become final, the real issue is res judicata rather than Younger and exhaustion?[8]

Hicks v. Miranda

422 U.S. 332, 95 S.Ct. 2281, 45 L.Ed.2d 223 (1975).
Appeal from the United States District Court for the Central District of California.

■ MR. JUSTICE WHITE delivered the opinion of the Court.

* * *

I

On November 23 and 24, 1973 * * * the police seized four copies of the film "Deep Throat," each of which had been shown at the Pussycat Theatre in Buena Park, Orange County, California. On November 26 an eight-count criminal misdemeanor charge was filed in the Orange County Municipal Court against two employees of the theater, each film seized being the subject matter of two counts in the complaint. Also on

---

[8]   On this point, consider Wooley v. Maynard, 430 U.S. 705 (1977), Paragraph (4), *supra*. There, Maynard, who had not appealed any of his three state convictions for obscuring his license plate, later joined with his wife in bringing a § 1983 action to enjoin enforcement of the state law under which he had been convicted. In finding no bar to the action, the Court, in distinguishing Huffman, said that the plaintiff in that case was trying to "annul the results of a state trial"; by contrast, Maynard sought relief that was "wholly prospective, to preclude further prosecution", and did not seek expungement of his prior convictions or relief from their consequences. Federal intervention was appropriate to avoid the dilemma of either risking punishment under state law or forgoing conduct that might be constitutionally protected.

The Court proceeded to award the Maynards federal injunctive relief without discussing whether the prior state judgment deserved issue preclusive effect in the federal action. The three-judge district court in Wooley had addressed this question, ruling that the Maynards were not precluded from challenging the statute's constitutionality because that issue was not actually litigated in the criminal prosecutions. 406 F.Supp. 1381, 1385 n. 6 (D.N.H. 1976). Moreover, although the district court did not say so, claim preclusion could not be invoked, since in a misdemeanor prosecution Maynard could not have counterclaimed for an injunction against enforcement of a state statute. But see Currie, *Res Judicata: The Neglected Defense*, 45 U.Chi.L.Rev. 317, 336–47, 349–50 (1978), questioning the lower court's reasoning, though not necessarily its result.

November 26, the Superior Court of Orange County ordered [the owners of the theaters] to show cause why "Deep Throat" should not be declared obscene, an immediate hearing being available to appellees, who appeared that day, objected on state law grounds to the court's jurisdiction to conduct such a proceeding, purported to "reserve" all federal questions and refused further to participate. Thereupon, on November 27 the Superior Court held a hearing, viewed the film, took evidence and then declared the movie to be obscene and ordered seized all copies of it that might be found at the theater. This judgment and order were not appealed by appellees.

Instead, on November 29, they filed this suit in the District Court against appellants—four police officers of Buena Park and the District Attorney and Assistant District Attorney of Orange County. The complaint recited the seizures and the proceedings in the Superior Court, stated in the body of the complaint that the action was for an injunction against the enforcement of the California obscenity statute, prayed for judgment declaring the obscenity statute unconstitutional and for an injunction ordering the return of all copies of the film, but permitting one of the films to be duplicated before its return.

A temporary restraining order was requested and denied, the District Judge finding the proof of irreparable injury to be lacking and an insufficient likelihood of prevailing on the merits to warrant an injunction. He requested the convening of a three-judge court, however, to consider the constitutionality of the statute. Such a court was then designated on January 8, 1974.

Service of the complaint was completed on January 14, 1974, and answers and motions to dismiss, as well as a motion for summary judgment, were filed by appellants. Appellees moved for a preliminary injunction. None of the motions was granted and no hearings held, all of the issues being ordered submitted on briefs and affidavits. * * *

Meanwhile, on January 15, the criminal complaint pending in the Municipal Court had been amended by naming appellees as additional parties defendant and by adding four conspiracy counts, one relating to each of the seized films. * * *

(next day)

On June 4, 1974, the three-judge court issued its judgment and opinion declaring the California obscenity statute to be unconstitutional * * * and ordering appellants to return to appellees all copies of "Deep Throat" which had been seized as well as to refrain from making any additional seizures. Appellants' claim that Younger v. Harris, *supra*, and Samuels v. Mackell, *supra*, required dismissal of the case was rejected, the court holding that no criminal charges were pending in the state court against appellees and that in any event the pattern of search warrants and seizures demonstrated bad faith and harassment on the part of the authorities, all of which relieved the court from the strictures of Younger v. Harris, *supra*, and its related cases. * * *

III

The District Court committed error in reaching the merits of this case despite the State's insistence that it be dismissed under Younger v. Harris, *supra*, and Samuels v. Mackell, *supra*. When they filed their federal complaint, no state criminal proceedings were pending against appellees by name; but two employees of the theater had been charged and four copies of "Deep Throat" belonging to appellees had been seized, were being held and had been declared to be obscene and seizable by the Superior Court. Appellees had a substantial stake in the state proceedings, so much so that they sought federal relief, demanding that the state statute be declared void and their films be returned to them. Obviously, their interest and those of their employees were intertwined; and as we have pointed out, the federal action sought to interfere with the pending state prosecution. Absent a clear showing that appellees, whose lawyers also represented their employees, could not seek the return of their property in the state proceedings and see to it that their federal claims were presented there, the requirements of Younger v. Harris could not be avoided on the ground that no criminal prosecution was pending against appellees on the date the federal complaint was filed. The rule in Younger v. Harris is designed to "permit state courts to try state cases free from interference by federal courts," 401 U.S., at 43, particularly where the party to the federal case may fully litigate his claim before the state court. Plainly, "the same comity considerations apply," Allee v. Medrano, 416 U.S. 802, 831 (Burger, C.J., concurring), where the interference is sought by some, such as appellees, not parties to the state case.

What is more, on the day following the completion of service of the complaint, appellees were charged along with their employees in Municipal Court. Neither Steffel v. Thompson, 415 U.S. 452, nor any other case in this Court has held that for Younger v. Harris to apply, the state-criminal proceedings must be pending on the day the federal case is filed. Indeed, the issue has been left open;[17] and we now hold that where state criminal proceedings are begun against the federal plaintiffs after the federal complaint is filed but before any proceedings of substance on the merits have taken place in the federal court, the principles of Younger v. Harris should apply in full force. Here, appellees were charged on January 15, prior to answering the federal case and prior to any proceedings whatsoever before the three-judge court. Unless we are to trivialize the principles of Younger v. Harris, the federal complaint should have been dismissed on the State's motion absent satisfactory proof of those extraordinary circumstances calling into play one of the limited exceptions to the rule of Younger v. Harris and related cases.

[The Court then rejected the district court's finding of official harassment and bad faith. See p. 1141, *supra*.][20]

* * * The District Court should have dismissed the complaint before it and we accordingly reverse its judgment.

---

[17] At least some Justices have thought so. Perez v. Ledesma, 401 U.S. 82, at 117 n. 9 (opinion of Mr. Justice Brennan, joined by Justices White and Marshall). Also, Steffel v. Thompson, *supra*, did not decide whether an injunction, as well as a declaratory judgment, can be issued when no state prosecution is pending.

[20] It has been noted that appellees did not appeal the Superior Court's order of November 27, 1973, declaring "Deep Throat" obscene and ordering all copies of it seized. It may be that under Huffman v. Pursue, 420 U.S. 592, decided March 18, 1975, the failure of appellees to appeal the Superior Court order of November 27, 1973, would itself foreclose resort to federal court, absent extraordinary circumstances bringing the case within some exception to Younger v. Harris. Appellees now assert, seemingly contrary to their prior statement before Judge Ferguson, that the November 27 order was not appealable. In view of our disposition of the case, we need not pursue the matter further.

■ MR. CHIEF JUSTICE BURGER, concurring.

* * *

■ MR. JUSTICE STEWART, with whom MR. JUSTICE DOUGLAS, MR. JUSTICE BRENNAN, and MR. JUSTICE MARSHALL join, dissenting.

* * * In Steffel v. Thompson, 415 U.S. 452, the Court unanimously held that the principles of equity, comity, and federalism embodied in Younger v. Harris, 401 U.S. 37, and Samuels v. Mackell, 401 U.S. 66, do not preclude a federal district court from entertaining an action to declare unconstitutional a state criminal statute when a state criminal prosecution is threatened but not pending at the time the federal complaint is filed. Today the Court holds that the Steffel decision is inoperative if a state criminal charge is filed at any point after the commencement of the federal action "before any proceedings of substance on the merits have taken place in the federal court." Any other rule, says the Court, would "trivialize" the principles of Younger v. Harris. I think this ruling "trivializes" Steffel, decided just last Term, and is inconsistent with those same principles of equity, comity, and federalism.[1]

There is, to be sure, something unseemly about having the applicability of the Younger doctrine turn solely on the outcome of a race to the courthouse. The rule the Court adopts today, however, does not eliminate that race; it merely permits the State to leave the mark later, run a shorter course, and arrive first at the finish line. This rule seems to me to result from a failure to evaluate the state and federal interests as of the time the state prosecution was commenced. * * *

The Court's new rule creates a reality which few state prosecutors can be expected to ignore. It is an open invitation to state officials to institute state proceedings in order to defeat federal jurisdiction. * * *

The doctrine of Younger v. Harris reflects an accommodation of competing interests. The rule announced today distorts that balance beyond recognition.

FURTHER NOTE ON ENJOINING STATE CRIMINAL PROCEEDINGS

(1) Hicks and Traditional Equity Practice. Hicks is contrary to the settled rule that equity jurisdiction is not destroyed because an adequate legal remedy has become available after the equitable action was filed. See,

---

[1] There is the additional difficulty that the precise meaning of the rule the Court today adopts is a good deal less than apparent. What are "proceedings of substance on the merits"? Presumably, the proceedings must be both "on the merits" and "of substance." Does this mean, then, that months of discovery activity would be insufficient, if no question on the merits is presented to the court during that time? What proceedings "on the merits" are sufficient is also unclear. An application for a temporary restraining order or a preliminary injunction requires the court to make an assessment about the likelihood of success on the merits. Indeed, in this case, appellees filed an application for a temporary restraining order along with six supporting affidavits on November 29, 1973. Appellants responded on December 3, 1973, with six affidavits of their own as well as additional documents. On December 28, 1973, Judge Lydick denied the request for a temporary restraining order, in part because appellees "have failed totally to make that showing of * * * likelihood of prevailing on the merits needed to justify the issuance of a temporary restraining order." These proceedings, the Court says implicitly, were not sufficient to satisfy the test it announces. Why that should be, even in terms of the Court's holding, is a mystery.

e.g., American Life Ins. Co. v. Stewart, 300 U.S. 203, 215 (1937) (Cardozo, J.); Dawson v. Kentucky Distilleries & Whse. Co., 255 U.S. 288, 296 (1921) (Brandeis, J.).[1]

(2) The Meaning of "Proceedings of Substance on the Merits". What suffices to constitute "proceedings of substance on the merits" in the federal action? The not insignificant proceedings on the motion for a temporary restraining order in Hicks obviously did not suffice—a result that Justice Stewart deemed a "mystery".

Ordinarily, if a plaintiff obtains a temporary restraining order or preliminary injunction, the State will be barred from instituting suit. But suppose any injunctive order is later vacated, or is limited in scope, or indeed is defied; are the federal proceedings leading to the issuance of that order substantial enough to permit the federal court to retain jurisdiction notwithstanding a subsequently filed state proceeding? In Hawaii Housing Auth. v. Midkiff, 467 U.S. 229 (1984), the Supreme Court found that Younger did not bar consideration of a federal action seeking injunctive relief against a state land reform scheme, stating: "Whether issuance of the February temporary restraining order was a substantial federal court action or not, issuance of the June preliminary injunction certainly was"; the court had by then "proceeded well beyond the 'embryonic stage' ", and no state judicial proceedings had yet been filed.

(3) The Pertinence of Doran v. Salem Inn. A week after the decision in Hicks v. Miranda, the Court decided Doran v. Salem Inn, Inc., 422 U.S. 922 (1975). Consider the pertinence of Doran to the issues raised by Hicks.

(a) Doran's Facts and Holding. The Doran case arose from a dispute about the constitutionality of a municipal ordinance that prohibited topless dancing in bars. Three local bars that had previously featured topless dancing initially complied with the ordinance, but their corporate owners (M & L, Salem, and Tim-Robb) brought suit in federal court seeking a declaration that the ordinance was unconstitutional as well as a temporary restraining order and a preliminary injunction against its enforcement. The day after the complaint was filed, M & L (but not the other two plaintiffs) resumed topless dancing; a criminal prosecution against M & L was commenced immediately. The district court granted plaintiffs' prayer for a preliminary injunction, and the court of appeals affirmed.

The Supreme Court first concluded that the three plaintiffs should not "be thrown into the same hopper for Younger" purposes, although there "may be some circumstances in which legally distinct parties are so closely related

---

[1]   Neither the majority nor dissent in Hicks paid attention to the alternate holding in Dombrowski v. Pfister, 380 U.S. 479 (1965), that when grand jury indictments are returned after the filing of a federal complaint seeking interlocutory and permanent injunctive relief but before such relief is issued, "no state 'proceedings' were pending within the intendment of [the Anti-Injunction Act, 28 U.S.C. § 2283]." In Texas Ass'n of Business v. Earle, 388 F.3d 515, 519–21 (5th Cir. 2004), the Fifth Circuit joined two other courts of appeals in deciding that Younger abstention was appropriate when a state grand jury proceeding was pending because the grand jury's functions related to the enforcement of the state's criminal laws. By contrast, in Monaghan v. Deakins, 798 F.2d 632 (3d Cir.1986), the court of appeals found that Younger's non-interference policy did not apply to grand jury proceedings, but the issue was mooted in that case before it could be decided by the Supreme Court. See Deakins v. Monaghan, 484 U.S. 193 (1988). In Morales v. TWA, Inc., 504 U.S. 374 (1992), the Court, although not relying on the Younger doctrine (because it had not been invoked), described it as "impos[ing] heightened requirements for an injunction to restrain an already-pending *or an about-to-be-pending* state criminal action" (emphasis added).

that they should all be subjected to the Younger considerations which govern any one of them, this is not such a case".[2] The court then held that M & L was barred from securing an injunction by Younger and a declaratory judgment by Samuels v. Mackell, p. 1140, *supra*. "When the criminal summonses issued against M & L on the days immediately following the filing of the federal complaint, the federal litigation was in an embryonic stage". With regard to Salem and Tim-Robb, the Court held their prayers for declaratory relief squarely governed by Steffel, since they were not subject to state criminal prosecution at any time. Further, the Court held that under the circumstances the issuance of a preliminary injunction barring enforcement of the ordinance was not subject to the restrictions of Younger. The Court reasoned that, at the end of trial on the merits, the plaintiffs' interests can generally be protected by a declaratory judgment; but "prior to final judgment there is no established declaratory remedy comparable to a preliminary injunction; unless preliminary relief is available upon a proper showing, plaintiffs in some situations may suffer unnecessary and substantial irreparable harm".

(b) The Relationship Among Steffel, Hicks, and Doran. Steffel permits federal intervention as long as no state prosecution is pending. Under Hicks, however, if a federal plaintiff has violated a state statute, the state can preempt the federal action by commencing a prosecution before substantial proceedings occur in the federal case, and thereby bar federal relief even as to future conduct; that, indeed, is what happened to M & L in Doran.[3] But under Doran, the district court may issue a preliminary injunction against enforcement of the statute if the requisites for such relief have been satisfied.

Of course merely filing a motion for a preliminary injunction does not constitute "proceedings of substance on the merits", and a prosecutor can often file charges before much has happened in connection with such a motion. A plaintiff might seek still earlier federal intervention by way of a temporary restraining order, but even then would have to give prior notice to the defendant, unless it were clear that irreparable injury would result before notice could be provided. See Fed.R.Civ.Proc. 65(b). In many if not most cases, Fiss, *Dombrowski*, 86 Yale L.J. 1103, 1136 (1977), thus concludes that Hicks gives alert prosecutors a "reverse removal power".

(4) Doran and Issues Involving Federal Relief Pendente Lite. Doran raises a number of questions about the availability and effect of federal injunctive relief *pendente lite*.

(a) The Availability of Interim Relief. In Doran, M & L, during the pendency of the state prosecution against it, presumably had just as much need as the other plaintiffs to avoid having either to suffer economic injury from suspending topless dancing or to run the risk of multiple prosecutions if the dancing continued. Given a proper showing of likely success on the merits and irreparable injury, why wasn't the district judge in Doran right, then, to grant M & L a preliminary injunction restraining the enforcement of the ordinance with respect to violations by M & L occurring *after* the

---

[2]   The Court noted that, although the plaintiffs were represented by common counsel, they were unrelated in terms of ownership or management.

[3]   See also Roe v. Wade, 410 U.S. 113, 125–27 (1973), where a doctor who had already been indicted for performing abortions sought an injunction against further prosecution for performing additional abortions. The Supreme Court held that under Younger, this request for prospective relief was barred in view of the pending prosecution.

injunction was granted and before the constitutional issues were settled on the merits?[4] This approach would have allowed the state to prosecute the single *past violation* without being preempted by the federal action; on the other hand, the preliminary injunction would have permitted M & L to continue the disputed activity while the issue of constitutionality was being settled (either in the state prosecution or, if none were brought, in federal court).[5]

(b) The Effect of Preliminary Relief. When preliminary relief is awarded—as it was in Doran to Salem and Tri-Robb—does it immunize the plaintiff from criminal prosecution for acts taken after the injunction issued, even if the statute is ultimately held constitutional? This view was urged in Edgar v. MITE Corp., 457 U.S. 624 (1982), as part of an argument that a federal action seeking to restrain enforcement of a state statute was moot because (i) the only past violation occurred during the pendency of a preliminary injunction forbidding the statute's enforcement, and (ii) the plaintiff did not plan any future violations of the challenged statute. The Court brushed aside the mootness argument, concluding that the effect of the preliminary injunction "is an issue to be decided when and if the [state official charged with enforcing the statute] initiates an action".

Of the five Justices in the majority, only Justice Stevens reached the immunity question. In his concurring opinion he contended that whether or not such immunity would be wise, federal judges were not empowered to confer it. He suggested that even a final judgment declaring a state law unconstitutional would not confer immunity from prosecution for post-judgment conduct if the judgment were later reversed on appeal.

Justice Marshall's dissent on the mootness point—which Justice Brennan joined and with which Justice Powell expressed general agreement—argued that federal courts have the power to confer such immunity; that "whether a particular injunction provides temporary or permanent protection becomes a question of interpretation"; and that "in the ordinary case * * * it should be presumed that an injunction secures permanent protection from penalties for violations that occurred during the period it was in effect". He insisted that people will be "reluctant to challenge [the validity of state statutes] unless they can obtain permanent immunity from penalties", and that "short-term protection is often only marginally better than no protection at all".[6]

None of the opinions cited Oklahoma Operating Co. v. Love, 252 U.S. 331 (1920) (Brandeis, J.), where, in unanimously affirming the award of a preliminary injunction against allegedly confiscatory rate regulation, the

---

[4] For suggestions along this line, see Laycock, *Federal Interference with State Prosecutions: The Need for Prospective Relief*, 1977 Sup.Ct.Rev. 193, 238; *The Supreme Court, 1974 Term-Leading Cases*, 89 Harv.L.Rev. 151–69 (1975).

[5] Should the federal court's role be so limited, or should it be permitted, while the state prosecution is pending (but before it has come to judgment), to enter a *final* judgment declaring the ordinance invalid and *permanently* enjoining the institution of prosecutions? Note that a final injunction could presumably be entered, in an appropriate case, as to Salem and Tri-Robb, which had not yet violated the statute. Although the award of permanent federal injunctive relief to M & L might be difficult to reconcile with Younger itself, recall that in Cline v. Frink Dairy Co., 274 U.S. 445, 452–53, 466 (1927), p. 1137, n. 4, *supra*, the Supreme Court, per Brandeis, J., affirmed the issuance of final injunctive relief against the institution of *future* prosecutions even though a state prosecution was pending when the federal action was filed.

[6] Justice Rehnquist found the case moot on other grounds without reaching the immunity issue.

Court said: "If upon final hearing the maximum rates fixed should be found not to be confiscatory, a permanent injunction should, nevertheless, issue to restrain enforcement of penalties accrued *pendente lite*, provided that it also be found that the plaintiff had reasonable ground to contest them as being confiscatory." See also Paragraph (3) of the *Note on Steffel v. Thompson and Anticipatory Relief*, pp. 1155–1156, *supra*.

(5) The Pertinence of Pending Actions Against Nonparties. Notice the contrary indications in Hicks and Doran with respect to whether Younger ever bars one party (X) from obtaining federal relief because of the pendency of state proceedings against another party (Y).[7] Did the Court in Hicks really mean to hold so casually (albeit in the alternative) that for Younger purposes a criminal prosecution against Y can oust X's right to litigate a constitutional claim in federal court because X and Y's interests are "intertwined", X and Y share the same lawyer, and X has not made a "clear showing" that his or her rights cannot be protected in state court? Compare the Court's refusal in Doran to withhold federal relief in favor of two bar owners because of the pending prosecution of the third: "while [the three owners] are represented by common counsel, * * * they are apparently unrelated in terms of ownership, control, and management". Hicks, decided one week earlier, was not cited.

The interests of employees and owners would appear to be potentially divergent in Hicks. Suppose, for example, that the prosecutor were to offer a favorable plea to the employees if they would agree to implicate the owners. See Wood v. Georgia, 450 U.S. 261 (1981), discussed in Chap. V, p. 528, *supra*. Shouldn't X (and other federal plaintiffs) be barred from seeking federal relief only if they would be deemed to be in privity with state defendant Y (and hence to have their day in court) in the state court proceeding against Y?[8]

NOTE ON FURTHER EXTENSIONS OF THE EQUITABLE RESTRAINT DOCTRINE

(1) Civil Actions to Which the State Is a Party. In Huffman v. Pursue, Ltd., 420 U.S. 592 (1975) (also discussed at p. 1157, *supra*), the state brought a civil action under its obscenity laws to "abate" the showing of obscene movies by Pursue. Dividing 6–3, the Supreme Court held that Younger applies to bar federal relief when "[t]he State is a party to the * * *

---

[7]   In Steffel the Court dismissed the argument that the pendency of a prosecution against Steffel's handbilling companion barred Steffel's federal action. 415 U.S. at 471 n. 19. See also Roe v. Wade, 410 U.S. 113, 126–27 (1973) (pending prosecution against a physician who was a plaintiff-intervenor does not bar challenge to same statute by a different plaintiff). *But cf.* Kowalski v. Tesmer, 543 U.S. 125 (2004), p. 165, *supra* (holding that plaintiffs challenging a state statute in federal court lacked third-party standing to assert the rights of defendants in state court criminal actions who would have been unable to appear as parties in the federal litigation on account of the Younger doctrine).

[8]   Taylor v. Sturgell, 553 U.S. 880 (2008), rejects subjecting nonparties to preclusion except "at a minimum" where "the interests of the nonparty and her representative are aligned" and "either the party understood herself to be acting in a representative capacity or the original court took care to protect the interests of the nonparty." Compare County of Imperial v. Munoz, 449 U.S. 54 (1980), p. 1088, *supra*, holding that the plaintiffs' federal action challenging on federal grounds a state court injunction against a different person was barred under the Anti-Injunction Act, 28 U.S.C. § 2283, unless the federal plaintiffs were "strangers" to the state court litigation.

proceeding, and the proceeding is both in aid of and closely related to criminal statutes".

(a) The Huffman Opinions and Rationale. In the view of the Huffman majority, the federalism strain of Younger—its policies of avoiding interference with state officials, duplicative proceedings, and negative reflection upon the state courts—all counseled restraint. The Court conceded that Younger's equitable component—the traditional reluctance to enjoin criminal proceedings—was not "strictly" on point. "But whatever may be the weight attached to this factor in civil litigation involving private parties, we deal here with a state proceeding which in important respects is more akin to a criminal prosecution than are most civil cases".

Justice Brennan's dissent, joined by Justices Douglas and Marshall, complained that the Court was taking a "first step toward extending to state *civil* proceedings generally the holding of Younger v. Harris". He argued that such a course would undermine Mitchum v. Foster, which, on virtually identical facts, held that a federal court § 1983 action was not barred by the Anti-Injunction Act, 28 U.S.C. § 2283.[1] Justice Brennan also cited functional differences between civil and criminal proceedings: while many safeguards are provided against the initiation of unwarranted criminal proceedings, state civil proceedings may be initiated "merely upon the filing of a complaint, whether or not well founded". (The ease of filing a civil complaint may also facilitate a state official's exercise of the "reverse removal power" later established by Hicks v. Miranda.)

One other difference between pending civil and criminal cases deserves mention. Unlike a criminal defendant, a civil defendant in state court will often be able to counterclaim for relief against enforcement of the challenged enactment—including declaratory relief, class relief, and relief *pendente lite*. But if a civil defendant fails to counterclaim, compulsory counterclaim and claim preclusion rules may bar later federal court consideration of the federal constitutional claim, even if the constitutional issue was not raised or decided in state court. Compare Wooley v. Maynard, p. 1156, *supra*.

(b) Subsequent Developments. The Court, dividing 5–4, appeared to extend Younger more broadly to encompass all civil enforcement actions brought by the state in Trainor v. Hernandez, 431 U.S. 434 (1977), which involved a state court civil action by the State of Illinois to recover welfare payments that the defendants had allegedly obtained by fraud.

And in two cases—Juidice v. Vail, 430 U.S. 327 (1977), and Pennzoil Co. v. Texaco, Inc., 481 U.S. 1 (1987)—the Court held Younger abstention to be justified by important state interests even though the state had not initiated an enforcement action in the former, and was not a party at all in the latter. (Both cases involved constitutional challenges to the mechanisms through which states enforce the orders and judgments of their courts—in Juidice, New York's civil contempt procedures and, in Pennzoil, a Texas statute that effectively required civil defendants who sought to appeal judgments against them to post a bond that was exorbitant on the facts of the case.)

But more recent cases emphasize the narrow and exceptional character of Younger doctrine. The first signal of a change in direction came in New Orleans Public Service, Inc. v. Council of City of New Orleans ("NOPSI"), 491

---

[1]   Does § 2283 support the Court's holding? After all, (i) Younger relied heavily upon that Act as a source of the federal policy of noninterference, and (ii) the Act does not distinguish between criminal and civil proceedings.

U.S. 350 (1989), a case arising from the efforts of NOPSI, a regulated utility, to procure federal injunctive and declaratory relief from the city council's denial to it of a rate increase, allegedly in violation of a federal statute. Fearful that the district court might abstain (as it had in two prior suits filed by NOPSI during the city council's consideration of the proposed rate increase), NOPSI also filed a petition for review of the city council's order in state court. The city council also filed its own state court action seeking a declaratory judgment of the lawfulness of its order, which was consolidated with NOPSI's state court action. Relying partly on the pendency of the state court actions, the district court dismissed, and the court of appeals upheld the dismissal, *inter alia*, on Younger grounds.

The Supreme Court reversed. Justice Scalia's majority opinion reasoned: "NOPSI's challenge must stand or fall upon the answer to the question whether the Louisiana court action is the type of proceeding to which Younger applies. Viewed in isolation, it plainly is not. Although our concern for comity and federalism has led us to expand the protection of Younger beyond state criminal prosecutions, to civil enforcement proceedings, [citing, *inter alia,* Huffman,] and even to civil proceedings involving certain orders that are uniquely in furtherance of the state courts' ability to perform their judicial functions, see Juidice * * *; Pennzoil * * *, it has never been suggested that Younger requires abstention in deference to a state judicial proceeding reviewing legislative or executive action. Such a broad abstention requirement would make a mockery of the rule that only exceptional circumstances justify a federal court's refusal to decide a case in deference to the States".

Viewing the suit as a challenge to "completed legislative action", the Court found that, "insofar as our policies of federal comity are concerned, [it was] no different in substance from a facial challenge to an allegedly unconstitutional statute or zoning ordinance—which we would assuredly not require to be brought in state courts".[2]

NOPSI thus appears to establish that the rationale of cases such as Huffman and Trainor—which calls for abstention when the state brings a civil enforcement action in its sovereign capacity—does not extend to challenges to completed legislative or executive actions that do not require, or have not yet led to, enforcement suits. This is surely an important distinction, but also one that (like many distinctions) may have blurry margins. Suppose that Louisiana amended its laws so that the city council's rate orders were not self-executing, but instead had to be enforced by a judicial decree in the state courts, which were obliged to issue the decree unless they found that the rate order was contrary to law or arbitrary or capricious. If a utility such as NOPSI brought a federal action challenging a rate order while there was a pending enforcement proceeding in state court, should the federal court abstain?

More recently, in Sprint Communications, Inc. v. Jacobs, 134 S.Ct. 584 (2013), also discussed p. 1169, *infra,* the Court quoted NOPSI as having recognized three "exceptional" categories to which Younger applies—involving criminal prosecutions, civil enforcement proceedings brought by a state, and "civil proceedings involving certain orders * * * uniquely in

---

[2]   All members of the Court joined the section of the opinion dealing with Younger abstention except Justice Blackmun, who concurred in the result.

furtherance of the state courts' ability to perform their judicial functions"—
and held that these three categories "define Younger's scope."[3]

(2) Administrative Proceedings of a Judicial Nature.

Although Steffel v. Thompson, *supra,* characterized Younger as a doctrine uniquely concerned with deference to state courts, later cases have extended it to state administrative proceedings of a judicial nature (that otherwise fall within the categories approved in NOPSI and Sprint Communications, *supra*).

(a) Middlesex County Ethics Comm. v. Garden State Bar Ass'n, 457 U.S. 423 (1982), involved New Jersey's system for the discipline of attorneys, for which the state supreme court had ultimate responsibility. By rule, the court had established local district ethics committees to investigate complaints and hold hearings on any charges issued, subject to review by a statewide board and in some cases by the state supreme court. A lawyer who had referred to a pending murder trial as "a travesty", a "legalized lynching", and a "kangaroo court" was charged with violating a bar rule prohibiting conduct "prejudicial to the administration of justice". Rather than defend himself before the local ethics committee, the lawyer filed a federal action challenging the rule under the First Amendment, but the Supreme Court held the suit barred by Younger.

The Court first noted that under state law, a local committee was "an arm of the [New Jersey Supreme Court]" and its disciplinary proceedings were "judicial in nature". Because those proceedings implicated the state's extremely important interests in assuring the professional conduct of attorneys, federal interference was inappropriate, as long as the lawyer had an adequate opportunity to raise his First Amendment claim. The Court rejected his argument that the local ethics committee lacked authority to consider that claim. In addition, citing Hicks v. Miranda, p. 1158, *supra*, the Court held that it could take account of the fact that the New Jersey Supreme Court had recently undertaken review of the disciplinary case, leaving no doubt that the First Amendment issue could be raised in the pending state proceeding.

Justice Marshall, joined by Justices Brennan, Blackmun, and Stevens, concurred in the judgment, finding Younger applicable only because of the state supreme court's recent intervention. In a separate concurrence, Justice Brennan said that "[t]he traditional * * * responsibility of state courts for [bar discipline] and the quasi-criminal nature of bar disciplinary procedures call for exceptional deference by the federal courts".

(b) The significance of Middlesex County in extending Younger doctrine to state administrative proceedings of a judicial nature became clear in Ohio Civil Rights Comm'n v. Dayton Christian Schools, Inc., 477 U.S. 619 (1986). There, the Ohio Civil Rights Commission had filed a formal administrative complaint against a religious school for terminating the employment of a pregnant teacher. The school then filed a federal court § 1983 action to enjoin the administrative proceedings as a violation of the Religion Clauses of the First Amendment. Relying in part upon Middlesex County, the Court ruled that Younger bars interference with a pending state administrative proceeding involving sufficiently important state interests, of which

---

[3] Fallon, *Why Abstention Is Not Illegitimate: An Essay on the Distinction Between "Legitimate" and "Illegitimate" Statutory Interpretation and Judicial Lawmaking*, 107 Nw.U.L.Rev. 847 (2013), attributes the current Supreme Court's discomfit with an expansive Younger doctrine partly to an increased attentiveness by the Justices to methodological issues involving permissible statutory interpretation and the limits of acceptable judicial lawmaking.

combatting discrimination was one. The Court rejected on the merits the school's argument that the investigation itself was prohibited by the First Amendment. It then found that the school had an adequate opportunity to raise its First Amendment objections in a state tribunal; even if they could not be raised in the administrative hearing, it sufficed that they could be heard in state court judicial review of any administrative decision.

The case was consistent, in the Court's view, with the rule that § 1983 plaintiffs need not exhaust state administrative remedies, see Patsy v. Board of Regents of the State of Florida, 457 U.S. 496 (1982), p. 1097, *supra*: "Unlike Patsy, the administrative proceedings here are coercive rather than remedial, began before any substantial advancement in the federal action took place, and involve an important state interest".

Finding the school's challenge not ripe, Justice Stevens, joined by Justices Brennan, Marshall, and Blackmun, concurred in the judgment, but criticized the Court's reliance on Younger: "That disposition would presumably deny the School a federal forum to adjudicate the constitutionality of a provisional administrative remedy, such as reinstatement pending resolution of the complainant's charges, even though * * * the Commission refuses to address the merits of the constitutional claims".

(c) The Court unanimously rebuffed an argument for abstention in deference to state administrative proceedings and an appeal therefrom in Sprint Communications, Inc. v. Jacobs, *supra*. After Windstream, an Iowa communications company, threatened to block all calls to and from Sprint customers unless Sprint resumed making payments to it for a subset of calls to Windstream customers, Sprint filed a complaint with the Iowa Utilities Board (IUB). Windstream responded by retracting its threat, and Sprint then successfully withdrew its complaint. Despite the withdrawal, the IUB decided to continue proceedings to determine whether the calls in question remained subject to intrastate access charges or whether state regulation was preempted by the federal Telecommunications Act of 1996. Following the Board's decision that intrastate fees continued to apply, Sprint petitioned for review in Iowa state court, but also filed suit in federal district court, alleging that the Board's members had violated the federal Telecommunications Act.

In her opinion for the Court, Justice Ginsburg assumed without deciding that "an administrative adjudication and the subsequent state court's review of it count as a 'unitary process' for Younger purposes" (quoting NOPSI, *supra*). But NOPSI recognized Younger abstention as appropriate only in three "exceptional" circumstances (listed in Paragraph (1)(b), *supra*), none of which applied.

The court of appeals had read Middlesex to say that "Younger abstention was warranted" whenever * * * [t]here is (1) 'an ongoing state judicial proceeding, which (2) implicates important state interests, and (3) . . . provide[s] an adequate opportunity to raise [federal] challenges.' " But those conditions were "not dispositive; they were, instead, *additional* factors appropriately considered by the federal court before invoking Younger. Divorced from their quasi-criminal context, the three Middlesex conditions would extend Younger to virtually all parallel state and federal proceedings, at least where a party could identify a plausibly important state interest. That result is irreconcilable with our dominant instruction that, even in the presence of parallel state proceedings, abstention from the exercise of federal jurisdiction is the 'exception, not the rule.' "

(3) Equitable Restraint and State Executive Functions. In Rizzo v. Goode, 423 U.S. 362 (1976), a lawsuit under § 1983 charging the mayor and other high officials of the City of Philadelphia with responsibility for a wide variety of discriminatory and arbitrary police practices, the Supreme Court held that there was no justification for equitable relief against the named defendants, since there was no showing that they had themselves invaded or authorized any invasions of the plaintiffs' constitutional rights. The opinion then went on, quite unnecessarily, to suggest that "principles of federalism" would independently bar relief. After citing Doran v. Salem Inn, p. 1162, *supra*, and Huffman, Paragraph (1), *supra*, the Court said: "[T]he principles of federalism which play such an important part in governing the relationship between federal courts and state governments, though initially expounded and perhaps entitled to their greatest weight in cases where it was sought to enjoin a criminal prosecution in progress * * * likewise have applicability where injunctive relief is sought, not against the judicial branch of the state government, but against those in charge of an executive branch of an agency of state or local governments such as petitioners here."[4] Accord, City of Los Angeles v. Lyons, 461 U.S. 95 (1983), p. 232, *supra*. Cf. Missouri v. Jenkins, 515 U.S. 70 (1995) (suggesting that, due to "federalism concerns", federal courts should be more hesitant to award equitable relief against a state than against a federal agency).

The Younger-based aspect of Rizzo, which appears to conflict with a long line of federal cases including Ex parte Young, 209 U.S. 123 (1908), p. 922, *supra,* drew scathing commentary, see, *e.g.*, Weinberg, *The New Judicial Federalism*, 29 Stan.L.Rev. 1191, 1219–27 (1977); Eisenberg & Yeazell, *The Ordinary and the Extraordinary in Institutional Litigation*, 93 Harv.L.Rev. 465, 503–06 (1980); Fiss, *Dombrowski*, 86 Yale L.J. 1103, 1159 (1977), and was applied very cautiously by the lower federal courts. Sprint Communications, Inc. v. Jacobs, *supra*, which holds Younger to be limited to three narrow and exceptional categories of cases, seems to repudiate Rizzo's Younger-based analysis.

(4) Damages Actions Involving State Officials. In Juidice v. Vail, 430 U.S. at 339 n. 16, the Supreme Court noted but reserved the question "as to the applicability of Younger-Huffman principles to a § 1983 suit seeking only [damages] relief." Quackenbush v. Allstate Ins. Co., 517 U.S. 706 (1996), also discussed at p. 1107, *supra*, stated unequivocally that "federal courts have the power to dismiss * * * cases based on abstention principles only where the relief being sought is equitable or otherwise discretionary", but it left open the possibility that a suit for damages might be stayed pending the outcome of state court litigation. According to Estrada, *Pushing Doctrinal Limits: The Trend Toward Applying Younger Abstention to Claims for Monetary Damages and Raising Younger Sua Sponte on Appeal*, 81 N.D.L.Rev. 475 (2005), a plurality of the circuits have applied the Younger doctrine to suits seeking only money damages.

(5) Application in Non-Article III Federal Proceedings. The Court has relied on Younger in holding that federal courts often (though not invariably)

---

[4]   Just two years before Rizzo, in Allee v. Medrano, 416 U.S. 802 (1974), the Court had approved a district court decree barring certain law enforcement practices, observing that it "creates no interference with prosecutions pending in the state courts, so that the special considerations relevant to cases like Younger v. Harris, 401 U.S. 37, do not apply here."

should abstain when asked to intervene prior to the completion of federal criminal prosecutions before courts martial or military commissions and of appeals therefrom within the executive branch. For discussion, see pp. 1242–1245, *infra*.

D. PARALLEL PROCEEDINGS

Colorado River Water Conservation District v. United States

424 U.S. 800, 96 S.Ct. 1236, 47 L.Ed.2d 483 (1976).
Certiorari to the United States Court of Appeals for the Tenth Circuit.

■ MR. JUSTICE BRENNAN delivered the opinion of the Court.

The McCarran Amendment, 43 U.S.C. § 666, provides that "consent is hereby given to join the United States as a defendant in any suit (1) for the adjudication of rights to the use of water of a river system or other source, or (2) for the administration of such rights, where it appears that the United States is the owner of or is in the process of acquiring water rights by appropriation under State law, by purchase, by exchange, or otherwise, and the United States is a necessary party to such suit." The questions presented by this case concern the effect of the McCarran Amendment upon the jurisdiction of the federal district courts under 28 U.S.C. § 1345 over suits for determination of water rights brought by the United States as trustee for certain Indian tribes and as owner of various non-Indian Government claims.

I

It is probable that no problem of the Southwest section of the Nation is more critical than that of scarcity of water. * * * [S]everal Southwestern States have established elaborate procedures for allocation of water and adjudication of conflicting claims to that resource. In 1969, Colorado enacted its Water Rights Determination and Administration Act in an effort to revamp its legal procedures for determining claims to water within the State.

Under the Colorado Act, the State is divided into seven Water Divisions, each Division encompassing one or more entire drainage basins for the larger rivers in Colorado. * * * Each month, Water Referees in each Division rule on applications for water rights filed within the preceding five months or refer those applications to the Water Judge of their Division. Every six months, the Water Judge passes on referred applications and contested decisions by Referees. A State Engineer and engineers for each Division are responsible for the administration and distribution of the waters of the State according to the determinations in each Division.

Colorado applies the doctrine of prior appropriation in establishing rights to the use of water. Under that doctrine, one acquires a right to water by diverting it from its natural source and applying it to some beneficial use. Continued beneficial use of the water is required in order to maintain the right. In periods of shortage, priority among confirmed rights is determined according to the date of initial diversion.

The reserved rights of the United States extend to Indian reservations and other federal lands, such as national parks and forests. The reserved rights claimed by the United States in this case affect waters within Colorado Water Division No. 7. On November 14, 1972, the Government instituted this suit in the United States District Court for the District of Colorado, invoking the court's jurisdiction under 28 U.S.C. § 1345. The District Court is located in Denver, some 300 miles from Division 7. The suit, against some 1,000 water users, sought declaration of the Government's rights to waters in certain rivers and their tributaries located in Division 7. In the suit, the Government asserted reserved rights on its own behalf and on behalf of certain Indian tribes, as well as rights based on state law. It sought appointment of a water master to administer any waters decreed to the United States. Prior to institution of this suit, the Government had pursued adjudication of non-Indian reserved rights and other water claims based on state law in Water Divisions 4, 5, and 6, and the Government continues to participate fully in those Divisions.

Shortly after the federal suit was commenced, one of the defendants in that suit filed an application in the state court for Division 7, seeking an order directing service of process on the United States in order to make it a party to proceedings in Division 7 for the purpose of adjudicating all of the Government's claims, both state and federal. On January 3, 1973, the United States was served pursuant to authority of the McCarran Amendment. Several defendants and intervenors in the federal proceeding then filed a motion in the District Court to dismiss on the ground that under the Amendment, the court was without jurisdiction to determine federal water rights. Without deciding the jurisdictional question, the District Court, on June 21, 1973, granted the motion * * *, stating that the doctrine of abstention required deference to the proceedings in Division 7. On appeal, the Court of Appeals for the Tenth Circuit reversed, holding that the suit of the United States was within district-court jurisdiction under 28 U.S.C. § 1345, and that abstention was inappropriate. * * * We reverse.

II

[Under 28 U.S.C. § 1345, the district courts have jurisdiction over all civil actions brought by the Federal Government "[e]xcept as otherwise provided by Act of Congress." The Court determined that the McCarran Amendment is not an Act of Congress excepting jurisdiction under § 1345 (or under § 1331, on which jurisdiction might also have been based), but that the Amendment merely provides for concurrent state and federal court jurisdiction over the actions that it encompasses.]

III

We turn next to the question whether this suit nevertheless was properly dismissed in view of the concurrent state proceedings in Division 7.

A

[The Court here concluded that the McCarran Amendment provided consent for the state courts to determine federal reserved rights held on behalf of Indians.]

B

Next, we consider whether the District Court's dismissal was appropriate under the doctrine of abstention. We hold that the dismissal cannot be supported under that doctrine in any of its forms.

Abstention from the exercise of federal jurisdiction is the exception, not the rule. "The doctrine of abstention, under which a District Court may decline to exercise or postpone the exercise of its jurisdiction, is an extraordinary and narrow exception to the duty of a District Court to adjudicate a controversy properly before it. Abdication of the obligation to decide cases can be justified under this doctrine only in the exceptional circumstances where the order to the parties to repair to the State court would clearly serve an important countervailing interest." County of Allegheny v. Frank Mashuda Co., 360 U.S. 185, 188–189 (1959). "[I]t was never a doctrine of equity that a federal court should exercise its judicial discretion to dismiss a suit merely because a State court could entertain it." Alabama Pub. Serv. Comm'n v. Southern R. Co., 341 U.S. 341, 361 (1951) (Frankfurter, J., concurring in result). Our decisions have confined the circumstances appropriate for abstention to three general categories.

(a) Abstention is appropriate "in cases presenting a federal constitutional issue which might be mooted or presented in a different posture by a state court determination of pertinent state law." County of Allegheny v. Frank Mashuda Co., *supra*, at 189. See, *e.g.*, Railroad Comm'n of Texas v. Pullman Co., 312 U.S. 496 (1941). This case, however, presents no federal constitutional issue for decision.

(b) Abstention is also appropriate where there have been presented difficult questions of state law bearing on policy problems of substantial public import whose importance transcends the result in the case then at bar. Louisiana Power & Light Co. v. City of Thibodaux, 360 U.S. 25 (1959), for example, involved such a question. In particular, the concern there was with the scope of the eminent domain power of municipalities under state law. See also Kaiser Steel Corp. v. W.S. Ranch Co., 391 U.S. 593 (1968). In some cases, however, the state question itself need not be determinative of state policy. It is enough that exercise of federal review of the question in a case and in similar cases would be disruptive of state efforts to establish a coherent policy with respect to a matter of substantial public concern. In Burford v. Sun Oil Co., 319 U.S. 315 (1943), for example, the Court held that a suit seeking review of the reasonableness under Texas state law of a state commission's permit to drill oil wells should have been dismissed by the District Court. The reasonableness of the permit in that case was not of transcendent importance, but review of reasonableness by the federal courts in that and future cases, where the State had established its own elaborate review system for dealing with the geological complexities of oil and gas fields, would have had an impermissibly disruptive effect on state policy for the management of those fields. See also Alabama Pub. Serv. Comm'n v. Southern R. Co., *supra*.

The present case clearly does not fall within this second category of abstention. While state claims are involved in the case, the state law to be applied appears to be settled. No questions bearing on state policy are presented for decision. Nor will decision of the state claims impair efforts to implement state policy as in Burford. To be sure, the federal claims that are involved in the case go to the establishment of water rights which may conflict with similar rights based on state law. But the mere potential for conflict in the results of adjudications, does not, without more, warrant staying exercise of federal jurisdiction. See Meredith v. Winter Haven, 320 U.S. 228 (1943); Kline v. Burke Constr. Co., 260 U.S. 226 (1922); McClellan v. Carland, 217 U.S. 268 (1910). * * *

(c) Finally, abstention is appropriate where, absent bad faith, harassment, or a patently invalid state statute, federal jurisdiction has been invoked for the purpose of restraining state criminal proceedings, Younger v. Harris, 401 U.S. 37 (1971); state nuisance proceedings antecedent to a criminal prosecution, which are directed at obtaining the closure of places exhibiting obscene films, Huffman v. Pursue, Ltd., 420 U.S. 592 (1975); or collection of state taxes, Great Lakes Dredge & Dock Co. v. Huffman, 319 U.S. 293 (1943). Like the previous two categories, this category also does not include this case. * * *23 * * *

C

Although this case falls within none of the abstention categories, there are principles unrelated to considerations of proper constitutional adjudication and regard for federal-state relations which govern in situations involving the contemporaneous exercise of concurrent jurisdictions, either by federal courts or by state and federal courts. These principles rest on considerations of "[w]ise judicial administration, giving regard to conservation of judicial resources and comprehensive disposition of litigation." Kerotest Mfg. Co. v. C-O-Two Fire Equipment Co., 342 U.S. 180, 183 (1952). Generally, as between state and federal courts, the rule is that "the pendency of an action in the state court is no bar to proceedings concerning the same matter in the Federal court having jurisdiction. * * * " McClellan v. Carland, supra, at 282. As between federal district courts, however, though no precise rule has evolved, the general principle is to avoid duplicative litigation. See Kerotest Mfg. Co. v. C-O-Two Fire Equipment Co., supra. This difference in general approach between state-federal concurrent jurisdiction and wholly federal concurrent jurisdiction stems from the virtually unflagging obligation of the federal courts to exercise the jurisdiction given them. England v. Medical Examiners, 375 U.S. 411, 415 (1964); Cohens v. Virginia, 6 Wheat. 264, 404 (1821) (dictum). Given this obligation, and the absence of weightier considerations of constitutional adjudication and state-federal relations, the circumstances permitting the dismissal of a federal suit due to the presence of a concurrent state proceeding for reasons of wise judicial administration are considerably more limited than the circumstances appropriate for abstention. The former circumstances, though exceptional, do nevertheless exist.

It has been held, for example, that the court first assuming jurisdiction over property may exercise that jurisdiction to the exclusion of other courts. Donovan v. City of Dallas, [377 U.S. 408, 412 (1964)]; Princess Lida v. Thompson, 305 U.S. 456, 466 (1939). But cf. Markham v. Allen, 326 U.S. 490 (1946). This has been true even where the Government was a claimant in existing state proceedings and then sought to invoke district-court jurisdiction under the jurisdictional

---

23 Our reasons for finding abstention inappropriate in this case make it unnecessary to consider when, if at all, abstention would be appropriate where the Federal Government seeks to invoke federal jurisdiction. Cf. Leiter Minerals, Inc. v. United States, 352 U.S. 220 (1957).

provision antecedent to 28 U.S.C. § 1345. In assessing the appropriateness of dismissal in the event of an exercise of concurrent jurisdiction, a federal court may also consider such factors as the inconvenience of the federal forum, *cf.* Gulf Oil Corp. v. Gilbert, 330 U.S. 501 (1947); the desirability of avoiding piecemeal litigation, *cf.* Brillhart v. Excess Ins. Co., 316 U.S. 491, 495 (1942); and the order in which jurisdiction was obtained by the concurrent forums, Pacific Live Stock Co. v. Lewis, 241 U.S. 440, 447 (1916). No one factor is necessarily determinative; a carefully considered judgment taking into account both the obligation to exercise jurisdiction and the combination of factors counselling against that exercise is required. Only the clearest of justifications will warrant dismissal.

Turning to the present case, a number of factors clearly counsel against concurrent federal proceedings. The most important of these is the McCarran Amendment itself. The clear federal policy evinced by that legislation is the avoidance of piecemeal adjudication of water rights in a river system. This policy is akin to that underlying the rule requiring that jurisdiction be yielded to the court first acquiring control of property, for the concern in such instances is with avoiding the generation of additional litigation through permitting inconsistent dispositions of property. This concern is heightened with respect to water rights, the relationships among which are highly interdependent. Indeed, we have recognized that actions seeking the allocation of water essentially involve the disposition of property and are best conducted in unified proceedings. The consent to jurisdiction given by the McCarran Amendment bespeaks a policy that recognizes the availability of comprehensive state systems for adjudication of water rights as the means for achieving these goals.

As has already been observed, the Colorado Water Rights Determination and Administration Act established such a system for the adjudication and management of rights to the use of the State's waters. * * *

Beyond the congressional policy expressed by the McCarran Amendment and consistent with furtherance of that policy, we also find significant (a) the apparent absence of any proceedings in the District Court, other than the filing of the complaint, prior to the motion to dismiss, (b) the extensive involvement of state water rights occasioned by this suit naming 1,000 defendants, (c) the 300-mile distance between the District Court in Denver and the court in Division 7, and (d) the existing participation by the Government in Division 4, 5, and 6 proceedings. We emphasize, however, that we do not overlook the heavy obligation to exercise jurisdiction. We need not decide, for example, whether, despite the McCarran Amendment, dismissal would be warranted if more extensive proceedings had occurred in the District Court prior to dismissal, if the involvement of state water rights were less extensive than it is here, or if the state proceeding were in some respect inadequate to resolve the federal claims. But the opposing factors here, particularly the policy underlying the McCarran Amendment, justify the District Court's dismissal in this particular case.[26]

---

[26] Whether similar considerations would permit dismissal of a water suit brought by a private party in federal district court is a question we need not now decide.

The judgment of the Court of Appeals is reversed and the judgment of the District Court dismissing the complaint is affirmed for the reasons here stated.

■ MR. JUSTICE STEWART, with whom MR. JUSTICE BLACKMUN and MR. JUSTICE STEVENS concur, dissenting.

The Court says that the United States District Court for the District of Colorado clearly had jurisdiction over this lawsuit. I agree. The Court further says that the McCarran Amendment "in no way diminished" the District Court's jurisdiction. I agree. The Court also says that federal courts have a "virtually unflagging obligation * * * to exercise the jurisdiction given them." I agree. And finally, the Court says that nothing in the abstention doctrine "in any of its forms" justified the District Court's dismissal of the Government's complaint. I agree. These views would seem to lead ineluctably to the conclusion that the District Court was wrong in dismissing the complaint. Yet the Court holds that the order of dismissal was "appropriate." With that conclusion I must respectfully disagree.

* * * [T]he Court relies principally on cases reflecting the rule that where "control of the property which is the subject of the suit [is necessary] in order to proceed with the cause and to grant the relief sought, the jurisdiction of one court must of necessity yield to that of the other." Penn General Casualty Co. v. Pennsylvania ex rel. Schnader, 294 U.S. 189, 195. See also Donovan v. City of Dallas, 377 U.S. 408; Princess Lida v. Thompson, 305 U.S. 456. But, as those cases make clear, this rule applies only when exclusive control over the subject matter is necessary to effectuate a court's judgment. Here the federal court did not need to obtain *in rem* or *quasi in rem* jurisdiction in order to decide the issues before it. The court was asked simply to determine as a matter of federal law whether federal reservations of water rights had occurred, and, if so, the date and scope of the reservations. The District Court could make such a determination without having control of the river.

The rule invoked by the Court thus does not support the conclusion that it reaches. In the Princess Lida case, for example, the reason for the surrender of federal jurisdiction over the administration of a trust was the fact that a state court had already assumed jurisdiction over the trust estate. But the Court in that case recognized that this rationale "ha[d] no application to a case in a federal court * * * wherein the plaintiff seeks merely an adjudication of his right or his interest as a basis of a claim against a fund in the possession of a state court. * * *" * * * Similarly, in [United States v. Bank of New York & Trust Co., 296 U.S. 463 (1936)], the Court stressed that the "object of the suits is to take the property from the depositaries and from the control of the state court, and to vest the property in the United States. * * * " "The suits are not merely to establish a debt or a right to share in property, and thus to obtain an adjudication which might be had without disturbing the control of the state court." * * *

The precedents cited by the Court thus not only fail to support the Court's decision in this case, but expressly point in the opposite direction. The present suit, in short, is not analogous to the administration of a trust, but rather to a claim of a "right to participate," since the United States in this litigation does not ask the court to control the administration of the river, but only to determine its specific rights in the flow of water in the river. This is an almost exact analogue to a suit seeking a determination of rights in the flow of income from a trust.

The Court's principal reason for deciding to close the doors of the federal courthouse to the United States in this case seems to stem from the view that its decision will avoid piecemeal adjudication of water rights.[6] * * * To the extent that the Court's view is based on the realistic practicalities of this case, it is simply wrong, because the relegation of the Government to the state courts will not avoid piecemeal litigation.

The Colorado courts are currently engaged in two types of proceedings under the State's water-rights law. First, they are processing new claims to water based on recent appropriations. Second, they are integrating these new awards of water rights with all past decisions awarding such rights into one all-inclusive tabulation for each water source. The claims of the United States that are involved in this case have not been adjudicated in the past. Yet they do not involve recent appropriations of water. In fact, these claims are wholly dissimilar to normal state water claims, because they are not based on actual beneficial use of water but rather on an intention formed at the time the federal land use was established to reserve a certain amount of water to support the federal reservations. The state court will, therefore, have to conduct separate proceedings to determine these claims. And only after the state court adjudicates the claims will they be incorporated into the water source tabulations. If this suit were allowed to proceed in federal court the same procedures would be followed, and the federal court decree would be incorporated into the state tabulation, as other federal court decrees have been incorporated in the past. * * * Whether the virtually identical separate proceedings take place in a federal court or a state court, the adjudication of the claims will be neither more nor less "piecemeal." * * *

As the Court says, it is the virtual "unflagging obligation" of a federal court to exercise the jurisdiction that has been conferred upon it. Obedience to that obligation is particularly "appropriate" in this case, for at least two reasons.

First, the issues involved are issues of federal law. A federal court is more likely than a state court to be familiar with federal water law and to have had experience in interpreting the relevant federal statutes, regulations, and Indian treaties. * * *

---

[6] The Court lists four other policy reasons for the "appropriateness" of the District Court's dismissal of this lawsuit. All of those reasons are insubstantial. First, the fact that no significant proceedings had yet taken place in the federal court at the time of the dismissal means no more than that the federal court was prompt in granting the defendants' motion to dismiss. At that time, of course, no proceedings involving the Government's claims had taken place in the state court either. Second, the geographic distance of the federal court from the rivers in question is hardly a significant factor in this age of rapid and easy transportation. Since the basic issues here involve the determination of the amount of water the Government intended to reserve rather than the amount it actually appropriated on a given date, there is little likelihood that live testimony by water district residents would be necessary. In any event, the Federal District Court in Colorado is authorized to sit at Durango, the headquarters of Water Division 7. Third, the Government's willingness to participate in some of the state proceedings certainly does not mean that it had no right to bring this action, unless the Court has today unearthed a new kind of waiver. Finally, the fact that there were many defendants in the federal suit is hardly relevant. It only indicates that the federal court had all the necessary parties before it in order to issue a decree finally settling the Government's claims. * * *

Second, some of the federal claims in this lawsuit relate to water reserved for Indian reservations. It is not necessary to determine that there is no state-court jurisdiction of these claims to support the proposition that a federal court is a more appropriate forum than a state court for determination of questions of life-and-death importance to Indians. * * *

I would affirm the judgment of the Court of Appeals.

■ MR. JUSTICE STEVENS, dissenting.

[While agreeing with Justice Stewart, Justice Stevens added three points: (1) "the holding that United States may not litigate a federal claim in a federal court having jurisdiction thereof [is] particularly anomalous"; (2) the Court's holding would restrict private water users' access to federal courts—a "surprising byproduct of the McCarran Amendment"— since private persons could hardly have greater access than the United States to a federal court; and (3) the Court should defer to the judgment of the Court of Appeals, rather than evaluate itself the balance of factors for and against the exercise of jurisdiction.]

NOTE ON FEDERAL COURT DEFERENCE TO PARALLEL STATE COURT PROCEEDINGS

(1) Earlier Examples of Deference to Pending State Court Proceedings. Both the majority and the dissent in Colorado River accepted (i) the principle set forth in the Kline case, p. 1061, *supra*, that the pendency of a state court action does not require a federal court to stay proceedings concerning the same matter, and (ii) the exception to that principle that applies when the state court has already exercised jurisdiction over a *res*— although the Justices differed over that exception's applicability to the circumstances at bar.

Apart from the *res* exception and the Younger line of cases (involving pending state enforcement actions), the Court had approved federal deference to pending state proceedings in only a few instances before Colorado River. One of the earlier cases, like Colorado River, had involved federal abstention in favor of a state court determination of water rights. See Kaiser Steel Corp. v. W.S. Ranch Co., 391 U.S. 593 (1968), p. 1125, *supra*. Another, Scott v. Germano, 381 U.S. 407 (1965) (per curiam), involved a challenge to a state legislative apportionment—a matter that the Court has subsequently described as "primarily the duty and responsibility of the state." Growe v. Emison, 507 U.S. 25 (1993). In a third case of potentially broader import, Brillhart v. Excess Ins. Co., 316 U.S. 491 (1942), the Court had emphasized that the district courts have discretion in determining whether to grant relief under the Declaratory Judgment Act: "Although the District Court had jurisdiction of the suit under the Federal Declaratory Judgments Act, it was under no compulsion to exercise that jurisdiction. * * * Ordinarily it would be uneconomical as well as vexatious for a federal court to proceed in a declaratory judgment suit where another suit is pending in a state court presenting the same issues, not governed by federal law, between the same parties." In determining whether to abstain, however, the district court should consider "whether the claims of all parties in interest can satisfactorily be adjudicated in" the state proceeding. For further discussion of abstention in cases under the Declaratory Judgment Act, see Paragraph (3), *infra*.

Does any general principle emerge from Colorado River when it is read against the background of these precedents? The Court apparently regards at least some disputes over water rights as presenting special claims to abstention, and it may view reapportionment challenges similarly. Note that Colorado River also seemed to rest in part on the specific purpose of the McCarran Amendment and on a policy of avoiding piecemeal litigation.[1]

(2) The Moses Cone Decision. The Court elaborated on the Colorado River holding seven years later in Moses H. Cone Memorial Hosp. v. Mercury Constr. Corp., 460 U.S. 1 (1983).[2] The case revolved around a construction contract between the hospital and a contractor, which provided that disputed claims, after initial referral to the architect, were subject to arbitration. After the contractor filed with the architect a claim against the hospital, the hospital sued the contractor and architect in state court, seeking declarations (i) that the hospital was not liable to the contractor, (ii) that if the hospital were liable, it would be entitled to indemnity from the architect, and (iii) that the contractor had no present right to arbitration. The hospital also sought a stay of arbitration. Soon thereafter, the contractor filed a federal diversity action to compel arbitration under the Federal Arbitration Act (FAA), 9 U.S.C. § 4. The district court stayed the suit in view of the pending state court action, but the court of appeals reversed and instructed the district court to issue an order compelling arbitration.

In an opinion by Justice Brennan, the Supreme Court affirmed. Although "the decision whether to defer to the state courts is necessarily left to the discretion of the district court in the first instance", that discretion must be exercised in accordance with "Colorado River's exceptional circumstances test, as elucidated by the factors discussed in that case". Applying that test, the Court found that the district court had abused its discretion. Of the four factors supporting dismissal in Colorado River, the first two—the state court's assumption of jurisdiction over a *res*, and that court's greater convenience—were inapplicable. Nor did the suit implicate the third and "paramount" Colorado River consideration, avoidance of piecemeal litigation: because the contractor's claim against the hospital was arbitrable but the hospital's indemnity claim against the architect was not, piecemeal litigation was inevitable. With respect to the fourth, the order of suit did not support the stay: though the state action had been filed first, the hospital's claim of priority was "too mechanical"; "[t]his factor, as with the other Colorado River factors, is to be applied in a pragmatic, flexible manner", and here "the federal suit was running well ahead of the state suit * * *".

Justice Brennan also found it pertinent that the federal action in Moses Cone was governed by federal law (the FAA's provisions governing

---

[1] For discussions of the Colorado River case itself, see Mullenix, *A Branch Too Far: Pruning the Abstention Doctrine*, 75 Geo.L.J. 99 & authorities cited at 107 n. 33 (1986).

[2] Will v. Calvert Fire Ins. Co., 437 U.S. 655 (1978), in which the Court could not muster a majority opinion, did little to clarify the meaning of Colorado River. Although the Court reversed a decision of the court of appeals granting mandamus to compel an exercise of jurisdiction by the district court, the Justices disagreed, *inter alia*, over (i) whether the district court's decision could appropriately be reviewed on mandamus, and (ii) whether the broad discretion recognized in Brillhart, Paragraph (1), *supra*, was limited to suits based on state law or to those seeking declaratory relief.

arbitrability of the dispute); this "must always be a major consideration weighing against surrender".[3] Moreover, because of uncertainty whether the FAA obliges state as well as federal courts to issue orders compelling arbitration,[4] the state court proceeding was "probabl[y] inadequa[te]" to protect the contractor's rights.

Finally, the Court rejected the hospital's argument that a *stay* of a federal action could be justified more easily than a *dismissal* (as in Colorado River). In either event, Justice Brennan reasoned, the district court must conclude "that the parallel state-court litigation will be an adequate vehicle for the complete and prompt resolution of the issues between the parties" and must contemplate "that the federal court will have nothing further to do in resolving any substantive part of the case".

Moses Cone's functionally based rejection of a distinction between the standards governing stays and those governing dismissals is inconsistent with and may not survive Quackenbush v. Allstate Ins. Co., 517 U.S. 706 (1996), discussed more fully at p. 1107, *supra*. Quackenbush held that federal courts generally have no authority to dismiss actions otherwise within their jurisdiction unless the relief sought is itself discretionary, but contemplated a discretion of at least some scope to stay actions at law. The Court did not, however, reach the question of what substantive standards govern issuance of a stay in a common law damages action. As a result, Quackenbush does not appear to modify Moses Cone's analysis of the circumstances in which a federal court should defer to state proceedings, but only addresses the form (stay versus dismissal or remand) that such deference should take.

(3) Declaratory Judgment Actions. In Wilton v. Seven Falls Co., 515 U.S. 277 (1995), the Court faced a declaratory judgment action very similar to that in Brillhart, Paragraph (1), *supra*. In Wilton, as in Brillhart, there were pending (i) an insurer's federal diversity action seeking a declaratory judgment of non-coverage and (ii) a state court action seeking to recover from the insurer. (But in Wilton, unlike Brillhart, the federal suit had been filed first.)

Without dissent, the Court upheld the district court's dismissal of the federal action, finding that the "exceptional circumstances" test of Colorado River and Moses Cone did *not* govern a federal declaratory judgment action, in which a district court's discretion whether to proceed is far broader. Justice O'Connor noted that the Declaratory Judgment Act, 28 U.S.C. § 2201, says that a district court "*may* declare the rights and other legal relations of any interested party * * * ", 28 U.S.C. § 2201. She concluded that the Act's "textual commitment to discretion, and the breadth of leeway we have always understood it to suggest, distinguish the declaratory judgment context from other areas of the law in which concepts of discretion surface. See generally Shapiro, *Jurisdiction and Discretion*, 60 N.Y.U.L.Rev. 543 (1985)." Here, "the normal principle that federal courts should adjudicate claims within their jurisdiction yields to considerations of practicality and

---

[3]   Justice Brennan noted the "anomaly" that the FAA creates a federal right to arbitration that cannot be enforced under the federal question jurisdiction. "But * * * our task * * * is not to find some substantial reason for the *exercise* of federal jurisdiction, [but rather] * * * to ascertain whether there exist 'exceptional' circumstances, 'the clearest of justifications,' that can suffice under Colorado River to justify the *surrender* of that jurisdiction".

[4]   The Court subsequently ruled in Southland Corp. v. Keating, 465 U.S. 1 (1984), that the FAA preempts a state law purporting to limit state court power to enforce arbitration agreements.

wise judicial administration". Without trying "to delineate the outer boundaries of [the district court's] discretion in other cases, for example, cases raising issues of federal law or cases in which there are no parallel state proceedings", the Court found no abuse of discretion.

When a claim is based on federal law, should a district court have less leeway to decline to exercise declaratory judgment jurisdiction (much as it has less leeway to abstain under Colorado River and Moses Cone when the claim is federal)?

(4) Criticisms of Colorado River. The practice of deferring to pending state proceedings has been criticized on various grounds.

(a) The most fundamental challenge asserts that federal courts may not legitimately decline to exercise jurisdiction conferred by Congress. Recall the discussion of that position, and of responses to it, in connection with other judge-made doctrines in this Chapter—particularly Pullman and Younger abstention.

(b) Whatever the justification for the Pullman and Younger doctrines, Professor Mullenix argues that Colorado River extended abstention beyond its justified purpose of promoting comity and federalism into the realm of "an unprincipled judicial self-help remedy", assertedly in response to Congress' failure to restrict diversity jurisdiction. Mullenix, note 1, *supra*, at 101, 103–04. *Compare* Shreve, *Pragmatism Without Politics—A Half Measure of Authority for Jurisdictional Common Law*, 1991 B.Y.U.L.Rev. 767 (approving abstention when based on concerns about judicial administration, but not when based on matters requiring "political choices").

(5) Appealability. A refusal to stay or dismiss an action is not appealable. Gulfstream Aerospace Corp. v. Mayacamas Corp., 485 U.S. 271 (1988). An order staying or dismissing a federal action in favor of state court proceedings is appealable—at least where the judgment in that proceeding will be res judicata. See Moses Cone, Paragraph (2), *supra*; Wilton v. Seven Falls Co., Paragraph (3), *supra*.

E. MATTERS OF DOMESTIC RELATIONS AND PROBATE

Ankenbrandt v. Richards

504 U.S. 689, 112 S.Ct. 2206, 119 L.Ed.2d 468 (1992).
Certiorari to the Circuit Court of Appeals for the Fifth Circuit.

■ JUSTICE WHITE delivered the opinion of the Court.

* * *

I

Petitioner Carol Ankenbrandt, a citizen of Missouri, brought this lawsuit * * * on behalf of her daughters L. R. and S. R. against respondents Jon A. Richards and Debra Kesler * * *. Alleging federal jurisdiction based on the diversity of citizenship provision of § 1332, Ankenbrandt's complaint sought monetary damages for alleged sexual and physical abuse of the children committed by Richards and Kesler.

Richards is the divorced father of the children and Kesler his female companion. * * * [T]he District Court granted respondents' motion to dismiss this lawsuit. Citing In re Burrus, 136 U.S. 586, 593–594 (1890), for the proposition that "[t]he whole subject of the domestic relations of husband and wife, parent and child, belongs to the laws of the States and not to the laws of the United States," the court concluded that this case fell within what has become known as the "domestic relations" exception to diversity jurisdiction, and that it lacked jurisdiction over the case. The court also invoked the abstention principles announced in Younger v. Harris, 401 U.S. 37 (1971), to justify its decision to dismiss the complaint without prejudice. The Court of Appeals affirmed * * *.

We granted certiorari limited to the following questions: "(1) Is there a domestic relations exception to federal jurisdiction? (2) If so, does it permit a district court to abstain from exercising diversity jurisdiction over a tort action for damages? (3) Did the District Court in this case err in abstaining from exercising jurisdiction under the doctrine of Younger v. Harris, [*supra*]?". We address each of these issues in turn.

II

The domestic relations exception * * * has been invoked often by the lower federal courts. The seeming authority for doing so originally stemmed from the announcement in Barber v. Barber, 21 How. 582 (1859), that the federal courts have no jurisdiction over suits for divorce or the allowance of alimony. [There, a woman who had obtained a New York state award of divorce and alimony sued in equity in a federal district court in Wisconsin (to which her former husband had moved) and won an order enforcing the New York judgment.] * * *

On appeal, it was argued that the District Court lacked jurisdiction on two grounds: first, that there was no diversity of citizenship because although divorced, the wife's citizenship necessarily remained that of her former husband; and second, that the whole subject of divorce and alimony * * * was exclusively ecclesiastical at the time of the adoption of the Constitution and that the Constitution therefore placed the whole subject * * * beyond the jurisdiction of the United States courts. Over the dissent of three Justices, the Court rejected both arguments. After an exhaustive survey of the authorities, the Court concluded that * * * a suit to enforce an alimony decree rested within the federal courts' equity jurisdiction. * * * In so stating, however, the Court also announced the following limitation on federal jurisdiction:

"Our first remark is—and we wish it to be remembered—that this is not a suit asking the court for the allowance of alimony. That has been done by a court of competent jurisdiction. The court in Wisconsin was asked to interfere to prevent that decree from being defeated by fraud.

"We disclaim altogether any jurisdiction in the courts of the United States upon the subject of divorce, or for the allowance of alimony, either as an original proceeding in chancery or as an incident to divorce *a vinculo*, or to one from bed and board." Barber, *supra*, at 584. * * *

The statements disclaiming jurisdiction over divorce and alimony decree suits, though technically dicta, formed the basis for excluding "domestic relations" cases from the jurisdiction of the lower federal courts, a jurisdictional limitation those courts have recognized ever since. The Barber Court, however, cited no authority and did not discuss the foundation for its announcement. Since that time, the Court has dealt only occasionally with the domestic relations limitation on federal-court jurisdiction, and it has never addressed the basis for such a limitation. Because we are unwilling to cast aside an understood rule that has been recognized for nearly a century and a half, we feel compelled to explain why we will continue to recognize this limitation on federal jurisdiction.

A

[In this section of its opinion, the Court held that "the Constitution does not exclude domestic relations cases from the jurisdiction otherwise granted by statute to the federal courts." The Court noted, *inter alia*, that it had heard appeals from territorial courts involving divorce, see *e.g.*, De La Rama v. De La Rama, 201 U.S. 303 (1906); Simms v. Simms, 175 U.S. 162 (1899), and had upheld the jurisdiction of the federal courts in the District of Columbia to decide divorce actions, see, *e.g.*, Glidden Co. v. Zdanok, 370 U.S. 530, 581 n. 54 (1962).][3]

B

* * * We thus turn our attention to the relevant jurisdictional statutes.

The Judiciary Act of 1789 [gave the circuit courts concurrent jurisdiction] "*of all suits of a civil nature at common law or in equity* [where the amount in controversy exceeds five hundred dollars], and . . . an alien is a party, or the suit is *between a citizen of the State where the suit is brought, and a citizen of another State.*" Act of Sept. 24, 1789, § 11, 1 Stat. 73, 78. (Emphasis added.) The defining phrase, "all suits of a civil nature at common law or in equity," remained a key element of statutory provisions demarcating the terms of diversity jurisdiction until 1948, when Congress amended the diversity jurisdiction provision to eliminate this phrase and replace in its stead the term "all civil actions." 28 U.S.C. § 1332.

The Barber majority itself did not expressly refer to the diversity statute's use of the limitation on "suits of a civil nature at common law or in equity." The dissenters in Barber, however, implicitly made such a reference, for they suggested that the federal courts had no power over certain domestic relations actions because * * * " * * * the jurisdiction of the chancery in England does not extend to or embrace the subjects of divorce and alimony, and * * * the jurisdiction of the courts of the United States in chancery is bounded by that of the chancery in England * * *." Barber, *supra*, at 605 (Daniel, J., dissenting). * * * Because the Barber Court did not disagree with this reason for accepting the jurisdictional limitation over the issuance of divorce and alimony decrees, it may be inferred fairly that the jurisdictional limitation recognized by the Court rested on this statutory basis and that the disagreement between the Court and the dissenters thus centered only on the extent of the limitation.

We have no occasion here to join the historical debate over whether the English court of chancery had jurisdiction to handle certain domestic

---

[3] We read Ohio ex rel. Popovici v. Agler, 280 U.S. 379 (1930), as in accord with this conclusion. In that case, the Court referenced the language in In re Burrus, 136 U.S. 586 (1890), regarding the domestic relations exception and then held that a state court was not precluded by the Constitution and relevant federal statutes from exercising jurisdiction over a divorce suit brought against the Roumanian vice-consul.

relations matters, though we note that commentators have found some support for the Barber majority's interpretation. * * * We * * * are content to rest our conclusion that a domestic relations exception exists * * * on Congress' apparent acceptance of this construction of the diversity jurisdiction provisions in the years prior to 1948, when the statute limited jurisdiction to "suits of a civil nature at common law or in equity." * * *

When Congress amended the diversity statute in 1948 to replace the law/equity distinction with the phrase "all civil actions," we presume Congress did so with full cognizance of the Court's nearly century-long interpretation of the prior statutes * * *. * * * [W]here Congress made substantive changes to the statute in other respects, see 28 U.S.C. § 1332 note, we presume, absent any indication that Congress intended to alter this exception, that Congress "adopt[ed] that interpretation" when it reenacted the diversity statute. Lorillard v. Pons, 434 U.S. 575, 580 (1978).

III

In the more than 100 years since this Court laid the seeds for the development of the domestic relations exception, the lower federal courts have applied it in a variety of circumstances. Many of these applications go well beyond the circumscribed situations posed by Barber and its progeny. * * *

The Barber Court * * * did not intend to strip the federal courts of authority to hear cases arising from the domestic relations of persons unless they seek the granting or modification of a divorce or alimony decree. * * *

Subsequently, this Court expanded the domestic relations exception to include decrees in child custody cases. In a child custody case brought pursuant to a writ of habeas corpus, for instance, the Court held void a writ issued by a Federal District Court to restore a child to the custody of the father. "As to the right to the control and possession of this child, as it is contested by its father and its grandfather, it is one in regard to which neither the Congress of the United States nor any authority of the United States has any special jurisdiction." In re Burrus, 136 U.S. 586, 594 (1890).

Although In re Burrus technically did not involve a construction of the diversity statute, as we understand Barber to have done, its statement that "[t]he whole subject of the domestic relations of husband and wife, parent and child, belongs to the laws of the States and not to the laws of the United States," id., at 593–594, has been interpreted by the federal courts to apply with equal vigor in suits brought pursuant to diversity jurisdiction. [Citing numerous authorities.] * * * We conclude, therefore, that the domestic relations exception, as articulated by this Court since Barber, divests the federal courts of power to issue divorce, alimony, and child custody decrees. * * *

* * * [O]ur conclusion * * * is also supported by sound policy considerations. Issuance of decrees of this type not infrequently involves retention of jurisdiction by the court and deployment of social workers to monitor compliance. As a matter of judicial economy, state courts are more eminently suited to work of this type than are federal courts, which lack the close association with state and local government organizations

dedicated to handling issues that arise out of conflicts over divorce, alimony, and child custody decrees. Moreover, * * * [the state courts have developed special proficiency] * * * over the past century and a half in handling issues that arise in the granting of such decrees.

By concluding, as we do, that the domestic relations exception encompasses only cases involving the issuance of a divorce, alimony, or child custody decree, we necessarily find that the Court of Appeals erred by affirming the District Court's invocation of this exception. This lawsuit in no way seeks such a decree; rather, it alleges that respondents Richards and Kesler committed torts against L. R. and S. R., Ankenbrandt's children by Richards. * * * We now address whether, even though subject-matter jurisdiction might be proper, sufficient grounds exist to warrant abstention from the exercise of that jurisdiction.

IV

The Court of Appeals, as did the District Court, stated abstention as an alternative ground for its holding. * * * Abstention rarely should be invoked, because the federal courts have a "virtually unflagging obligation . . . to exercise the jurisdiction given them." [Colorado River Water Conservation Dist. v. United States, 424 U.S. 800,] 817 [(1976)].

The courts below cited Younger v. Harris, 401 U.S. 37 (1971), to support their holdings to abstain in this case. * * * Though we have extended Younger abstention to the civil context, we have never applied the notions of comity so critical to Younger's "Our Federalism" when no state proceeding was pending nor any assertion of important state interests made. [Because no state proceedings were pending when Ankenbrandt filed suit,] * * * application by the lower courts of Younger abstention was clearly erroneous.

It is not inconceivable, however, that in certain circumstances, the abstention principles developed in Burford v. Sun Oil Co., 319 U.S. 315 (1943), might be relevant in a case involving elements of the domestic relationship even when the parties do not seek divorce, alimony, or child custody. This would be so when a case presents "difficult questions of state law bearing on policy problems of substantial public import whose importance transcends the result in the case then at bar." Colorado River Water Conservation Dist., *supra*, at 814. Such might well be the case if a federal suit were filed prior to effectuation of a divorce, alimony, or child custody decree, and the suit depended on a determination of the status of the parties. Where, as here, the status of the domestic relationship has been determined as a matter of state law, and in any event has no bearing on the underlying torts alleged, we have no difficulty concluding that Burford abstention is inappropriate in this case.

V

* * * Accordingly, we reverse the decision of the Court of Appeals and remand the case for further proceedings consistent with this opinion.

It is so ordered.

■ JUSTICE BLACKMUN, concurring in the judgment.

I agree with the Court that the District Court had jurisdiction over petitioner's claims in tort. Moreover, I agree that the federal courts should not entertain claims for divorce, alimony, and child custody. I am unable to agree, however, that the diversity statute contains any "exception" for domestic relations matters. * * * In my view, the longstanding, unbroken practice of the federal courts in refusing to hear domestic relations cases is precedent at most for continued discretionary abstention rather than mandatory limits on federal jurisdiction. * * *

I

* * * I do not see how [the 1948 change in the wording of the diversity statute] that, if anything, expands the jurisdictional scope of the statute can be said to constitute evidence of approval of a prior narrow construction.[1] Any inaction on the part of Congress in 1948 in failing expressly to mention domestic relations matters in the diversity statute reflects the fact * * * that Congress likely had no idea until the Court's decision today that the diversity statute contained an exception for domestic relations matters.

This leads to my primary concern: the Court's conclusion that Congress understood Barber as an interpretation of the diversity statute. Barber did not express any intent to construe the diversity statute * * *. As the Court puts it, it may only be "inferred" that the basis for declining jurisdiction was the diversity statute. It is inferred not from anything in the Barber majority opinion. Rather, it is inferred from the comments of a dissenting justice and the absence of rebuttal by the Barber majority. The Court today has a difficult enough time arriving at this unlikely interpretation of the Barber decision. I cannot imagine that Congress ever assembled this construction on its own.

[Justice Blackmun then discussed three decisions that, in his view, "seriously undermine any inference that Barber's recognition of a domestic relations 'exception' traces to a 'common law or equity' limitation of the diversity statute."] * * * Even assuming the Court today correctly interprets Barber, its extension of any domestic relations "exception" to the diversity statute for child custody matters is not warranted by any known principles of statutory construction. The Court relies on In re Burrus, 136 U.S. 586 (1890), in which the Court denied the "jurisdiction" of a federal district court to issue a writ of habeas corpus in favor of a father to recover the care and custody of his child from the child's grandfather. That case * * * involve[d] * * * the habeas corpus statute, and the Court expressly declined to address the diversity statute. * * *

II

A

To reject the Court's construction of the diversity statute is not, however, necessarily to reject the federal courts' longstanding practice of declining to hear certain domestic relations cases. * * * [T]he common concern reflected in these earlier cases is, in modern terms, abstentional—and not jurisdictional—in nature. These cases are premised not upon a concern for the historical limitation of equity

---

[1]   To be sure, this modification in language was part of a wholesale revision of the Judicial Code in 1948, and this Court has recognized that "no changes in law or policy are to be presumed from changes of language in the revision unless an intent to make such changes is clearly expressed." Fourco Glass Co. v. Transmirra Products Corp., 353 U.S. 222, 227 (1957). This principle may negate an inference that the change in language expanded the scope of the statute, but it does not affirmatively authorize an inference that Congress' recodification was designed to approve of prior constructions of the statute.

jurisdiction of the English courts, but upon the virtually exclusive primacy at that time of the States in the regulation of domestic relations. * * *

Whether the interest of States remains a sufficient justification today for abstention is uncertain in view of the expansion in recent years of federal law in the domestic relations area.[8] I am confident, nonetheless, that the unbroken and unchallenged practice of the federal courts since before the War Between the States of declining to hear certain domestic relations cases provides the very rare justification for continuing to do so. It is not without significance, moreover, that, because of this historical practice of the federal courts, the States have developed specialized courts and institutions in family matters, while Congress and the federal courts generally have not done so. Absent a contrary command of Congress, the federal courts properly should abstain, at least from diversity actions traditionally excluded from the federal courts, such as those seeking divorce, alimony, and child custody.

* * * Although there is no occasion to resolve the issue in definitive fashion in this case, I would suggest that principles of abstention provide a more principled basis for the Court's continued disinclination to entertain domestic relations matters.[9]

B

Whether or not the domestic relations "exception" is properly grounded in principles of abstention or principles of jurisdiction, I do not believe this case falls within the exception. * * *

■ [JUSTICE STEVENS, joined by JUSTICE THOMAS, concurred in the judgment, finding that the case fell outside the scope of any plausible "domestic relations exception", and leaving for another day consideration of whether such an exception in fact exists.]

_____

NOTE ON FEDERAL JURISDICTION IN MATTERS OF DOMESTIC RELATIONS

(1) History. The view, repudiated in Ankenbrandt, that Article III excludes jurisdiction in domestic relations cases was bound up with the assertion that certain matters were beyond the historical scope of law and equity. See, *e.g.*,

_____

[8]   See, *e.g.*, Victims of Child Abuse Act of 1990, 104 Stat. 4792, 42 U.S.C. § 13001 *et seq.*; Family Violence Prevention and Services Act, 98 Stat. 1757, 42 U.S.C. § 10401 *et seq.*; Parental Kidnaping Prevention Act of 1980, 94 Stat. 3568, 28 U.S.C. § 1738A; Adoption Assistance and Child Welfare Act of 1980, 94 Stat. 500, 42 U.S.C. §§ 620–628, 670–679a; Child Abuse Prevention and Treatment and Adoption Reform Act of 1978, 92 Stat. 205, 42 U.S.C. § 5111 *et seq.*; Child Abuse Prevention and Treatment Act, 88 Stat. 4, 42 U.S.C. § 5101 *et seq.*

Like the diversity statute, the federal-question grant of jurisdiction in Article III * * * limits the judicial power in federal-question cases to "Cases, in Law and Equity." Assuming this limitation applies with equal force in the constitutional context as the Court finds today that it does in the statutory context, the Court's decision today casts grave doubts upon Congress' ability to confer federal-question jurisdiction (as under 28 U.S.C. § 1331) on the federal courts in any matters involving divorces, alimony, and child custody.

[9]   As this Court has previously observed that the various types of abstention are not "rigid pigeonholes," Pennzoil Co. v. Texaco Inc., 481 U.S. 1, 11, n. 9 (1987), there is no need to affix a label to the abstention principles I suggest. Nevertheless, I fully agree with the Court that Younger abstention is inappropriate on the facts before us, because of the absence of any pending state proceeding.

Fontain v. Ravenel, 58 U.S. (17 How.) 369 (1854) (Taney, C.J., dissenting) (arguing that the federal courts lacked power to enforce a charitable bequest, as the "chancery jurisdiction" of the federal courts conferred by Article III extended only to matters of which chancery had jurisdiction "in its judicial character as a court of equity", and not to the "prerogative powers, which the king, as *parens patriae*, in England, exercised through the courts", and which remained with the States as sovereigns).

(2) The Spindel Decision. In Spindel v. Spindel, 283 F.Supp. 797 (E.D.N.Y.1968), Judge Weinstein offered a searching analysis and criticism of the whole development of the federal domestic relations exception. On the historical point, he challenged the premise that matrimonial matters were handled exclusively in the ecclesiastical courts and not in chancery acting in its judicial capacity. He also noted that Article III requires only a "controversy" (not a "case in law or equity") between citizens of different states for federal jurisdiction to exist and that Congress could therefore confer on the federal courts authority to grant divorces in such cases. The force of his critique was broadly recognized.[1]

(3) The Justification for Ankenbrandt. Note that the Ankenbrandt opinion eschews historical arguments about the scope of chancery vs. ecclesiastical jurisdiction in matrimonial matters and relies instead on precedents and on Congress' failure to object to them. Do other circumstances support continued observance of the exception, including "the strong state interest in domestic relations matters, the competence of state courts in settling family disputes,[2] the possibility of incompatible federal and state court decrees in cases of continuing judicial supervision by the state, and the problem of congested dockets in the federal courts", Crouch v. Crouch, 566 F.2d 486 (5th Cir.1978)?[3]

Professor Resnik argues that the exception marginalizes the domestic sphere, based on an assumption that it is dominated by women: "[W]omen and the families they sometimes inhabit are not only assumed to be outside the federal courts, they also are assumed not to be related to the 'national issues' to which the federal judiciary is to devote its interests. Jurisdictional lines have not been drawn according to the laws of nature but by men, who today are seeking to confirm their prestige as members of the most important judiciary in the country * * *. Dealing with women * * * is not how they want to frame their job." Resnik, *"Naturally" Without Gender: Women, Jurisdiction, and the Federal Courts*, 66 N.Y.U.L.Rev. 1682, 1749 (1991). See also Cahn, *Family Law, Federalism, and the Federal Courts*, 79 Iowa L.Rev. 1073 (1994); Stein, *The Domestic Relations Exception to Federal Jurisdiction: Rethinking an Unsettled Federal Courts Doctrine*, 36 B.C.L.Rev. 669 (1995).

Should federal courts be especially reluctant to refuse jurisdiction insofar as studies suggest that gender bias is found in *state* family courts?

---

[1]   Some commentators suggested outright abolition of the exception. See Wand, *A Call for the Repudiation of the Domestic Relations Exception to Federal Jurisdiction*, 30 Vill.L.Rev. 307 (1985); Note, 24 B.C.L.Rev. 661 (1983).

[2]   *Cf.* Currie, *Suitcase Divorce in the Conflict of Laws: Simons, Rosenstiel, and Borax*, 34 U.Chi.L.Rev. 26, 49–53 (1966), arguing that a state whose divorce law is to be applied may properly confine divorce litigation to its own (often specialized) courts to avoid the serious risk of error in adjudication in other fora.

[3]   In Begum v. Miner, No. 99–20027, 2000 WL 554953, at *1 (5th Cir. Apr. 20, 2000) (unpublished opinion), the Fifth Circuit questioned whether its reasoning in Crouch survived the Supreme Court's analysis in Ankenbrandt and thus declined to rely on Crouch to support its decision to abstain in a case involving family law issues.

Or is diversity jurisdiction meant to protect against state court prejudice against non-citizens rather than against gender bias? See Jackson, *Empiricism, Gender, and Legal Pedagogy: An Experiment in a Federal Courts Seminar at Georgetown University Law Center*, 83 Geo.L.J. 461, 494–95 & n. 113 (1994).

(4) The Scope of the Exception. Ankenbrandt defines the domestic relations exception rather narrowly. Before the decision, it was less certain whether the exception extended to suits arising in a domestic relations context but involving claims traditionally adjudicated in federal courts—for example, tort or contract claims—though the majority of cases had held that it did not. See Note, 83 Colum.L.Rev. 1824, 1828 & nn. 29–31 (1983). On whether Ankenbrandt does and should exclude disputes about other matters such as child support, pre-nuptial agreements, and domestic partnership agreements, see Cahn, Paragraph (3), *supra*, at 1084–85.

(5) Lack of Jurisdiction Versus Abstention.

Note that while Ankenbrandt adopts the "jurisdictional" view of the domestic relations exception, Part IV of the opinion leaves open the possibility of "abstention" in cases that fall outside the jurisdictional exception. But Quackenbush v. Allstate Ins. Co., 517 U.S. 706 (1996), more fully discussed at p. 1107, *supra*, suggests that where the suit is not one for a discretionary remedy such as an injunction or declaratory judgment, a federal court may not refuse to exercise jurisdiction altogether; at most it can stay the action pending the resolution of state court proceedings.

(6) Jurisdictional Grants Other than Diversity. What implications does Ankenbrandt have for cases in which federal jurisdiction does not rest on the diversity statute (§ 1332)?

(a) Recall that the Ankenbrandt Court's interpretation of § 1332 relied in part (over Justice Blackmun's protest) on In re Burrus, a case that arose under the habeas corpus jurisdiction. *Cf.* Lehman v. Lycoming County Children's Services Agency, 458 U.S. 502 (1982), in which a mother filed a federal habeas corpus action on behalf of her children challenging, as a denial of due process, a state court's termination of her parental rights. Custody had been awarded to a county agency, which placed the children in a private foster home. In ruling (6–3) that there was no federal habeas jurisdiction, the Supreme Court distinguished the children's situation from that of a petitioner whose custody arises from a criminal conviction. Though it did not advert to the domestic relations exception per se, the Court stressed the special solicitude that federal courts have traditionally shown in "family and family-property arrangements" and the importance to the state of certainty and finality in child custody disputes. The Court reserved the question of jurisdiction when the child is confined in a state institution.

(b) Following Ankenbrandt, the predominant view among the lower courts is that the domestic relations exception applies only to the diversity jurisdiction. See, *e.g.*, Reale v. Wake Cnty. Human Servs., 480 F. App'x 195, 197 (4th Cir.2012); Atwood v. Fort Peck Tribal Court Assiniboine, 513 F.3d 943, 946–47 (9th Cir.2008); United States v. Bailey, 115 F.3d 1222, 1231 (5th Cir.1997).[4]

---

[4] The Parental Kidnapping Prevention Act of 1980, 94 Stat. 3568–73 (1980), codified in pertinent part as 28 U.S.C. § 1738A, generally requires that a state enforce child custody decrees rendered by other states in accordance with the Act's provisions. Resolving a circuit conflict, the Supreme Court ruled in Thompson v. Thompson, 484 U.S. 174 (1988), that the Act does not

———

NOTE ON FEDERAL JURISDICTION IN MATTERS OF PROBATE AND ADMINISTRATION

(1) Development of the Exception. Perhaps reflecting a heritage in which the probate of wills was vested in special courts in England—first the ecclesiastical courts and then chancery courts—nineteenth century decisions of the Supreme Court recognized a "probate exception" to federal jurisdiction that was in some ways analogous to the domestic relations exception. At its core, the decisions barred efforts by lower federal courts to take over, generally, the administration of a decedent's estate. *E.g.*, Hook v. Payne, 81 U.S. (14 Wall.) 252 (1872); Byers v. McAuley, 149 U.S. 608 (1893). Cf. Waterman v. Canal-Louisiana Bank & Trust Co., 215 U.S. 33 (1909) (denying jurisdiction, in an otherwise proper case, over a prayer for an accounting of an estate). Like the domestic relations exception, the probate exception has generated uncertainties in application and triggered controversy. See generally Nicolas, *Fighting the Probate Mafia: A Dissection of the Probate Exception to Federal Court Jurisdiction*, 74 S.Cal.L.Rev. 1479 (2001) (discussing and critically analyzing a variety of proffered justifications for the exception). Consider Dragan v. Miller, 679 F.2d 712 (7th Cir.1982) (Posner, J.): "If there is diversity of citizenship among the claimants to an estate, the possible bias that a state court might have in favor of citizens of its own state might frustrate the decedent's intentions; it is just such bias, of course, that the diversity jurisdiction of the federal courts was intended to counteract." Dragan concludes, however, that "however shoddy the historical underpinnings of the probate exception, it is too well established a feature of our federal system to be lightly discarded, and by an inferior court at that".

(2) The Marshall Decision. The Court undertook "to resolve the apparent confusion among federal courts concerning the scope of the probate exception" in Marshall v. Marshall, 547 U.S. 293 (2006). The case arose from a dispute between Vickie Lynn Marshall (to whom the Court referred as "Vickie", though she was also widely known as "Anna Nicole Smith"), the widow of J. Howard Marshall II ("J. Howard"), and the decedent's son, E. Pierce Marshall ("Pierce"), following J. Howard's death. Although J. Howard had lavished gifts on the much-younger Vickie during their brief marriage, his will—of which Pierce was the ultimate beneficiary—gave her nothing. With probate proceedings occurring in the Texas state courts, Vickie filed for bankruptcy in a federal bankruptcy court in California, and Pierce filed a proof of claim in the bankruptcy proceeding, seeking to recover from Vickie for an alleged libel. Vickie responded, also in the bankruptcy court, with a counterclaim against Pierce asserting tortious interference by him with a gift to her that J. Howard would otherwise have made in his will. The bankruptcy court entered a judgment for Vickie on the tortious interference claim, as the district court ultimately did also (after finding that her counterclaim against Pierce involved a non-core matter concerning which the bankruptcy court could only issue proposed findings of fact and conclusions of law). The court

———

create an implied federal right of action permitting federal court suit to enjoin state court proceedings in violation of the Act. The Court noted that Congress, when enacting this statute, had rejected a proposal to extend the diversity jurisdiction to actions seeking enforcement of state custody orders. Federal court determination of which of two conflicting decrees should be given effect, the Court added, would offend the "longstanding tradition of reserving domestic-relations matters to the States".

of appeals reversed on the ground that the case came within the probate exception to federal jurisdiction, but the Supreme Court unanimously held otherwise.

In an opinion by Justice Ginsburg, the Court began by quoting language from Cohens v. Virginia, 19 U.S. (6 Wheat.) 264 (1821), admonishing that the Court has "no more right to decline the exercise of jurisdiction which is given, than to usurp that which is not given". It then reviewed its decision in Ankenbrandt v. Richards, p. 1181, *supra*, in which it had held that the "domestic relations exception" to federal jurisdiction applied only to divorce, alimony, and child custody decrees. Coming then to the question of the probate exception, Justice Ginsburg carefully reviewed "enigmatic" language from Markham v. Allen, 326 U.S. 490 (1946),[1] that had proscribed federal courts from " 'disturb[ing] or affect[ing] the possession of property in the possession of a state court' ", and construed it as no more than "a reiteration of the general principle that, when one court is exercising *in rem* jurisdiction over a *res*, a second court will not assume *in rem* jurisdiction over the same *res*": "Thus, the probate exception reserves to state probate courts the probate or annulment of a will and the administration of a decedent's estate; it also precludes federal courts from endeavoring to dispose of property that is in the custody of a state probate court. But it does not bar federal courts from adjudicating matters outside those confines and otherwise within federal jurisdiction".

Applying those principles to the case before it, the Court upheld the jurisdiction of the federal courts: "Vickie seeks an *in personam* judgment against Pierce, not the probate or annulment of a will. Nor does she seek to reach a *res* in the custody of a state court".[2]

Concurring in part and concurring in the judgment, Justice Stevens would have renounced the idea of a "probate exception" to federal jurisdiction altogether: "Rather than preserving whatever vitality that the 'exception' has retained as a result of the Markham dicta, I would provide the creature with a decent burial in a grave adjacent to the resting place of the Rooker-Feldman doctrine [discussed pp. 1409–1411, *infra*]".

Is Justice Stevens persuasive that there is no sensible stopping point short of abolishing the probate exception altogether? Note that even Justice Stevens recognizes that there should be some restrictions on the exercise of federal jurisdiction over "probate and annulment of wills and the administration of decedents' estates" arising from "generally applicable jurisdictional rules" such as, presumably, the *res* exception.

(3) Abstention. In Rice v. Rice Foundation, 610 F.2d 471 (7th Cir.1979), the court of appeals remanded for consideration of whether the

---

[1] On its facts, Markham held that a federal district court properly exercised jurisdiction over a suit by the federal Alien Property Custodian, suing under a statutory provision authorizing suits by federal officers, to declare that the administrator was "entitled to receive [the decedent's] net estate". Because the declaration left "undisturbed the orderly administration of decedent's estate in the state probate court", it was "not an exercise of probate jurisdiction or an interference with property in the possession or custody of a state court".

[2] In an apparent rejection of the approach of Sutton v. English, 246 U.S. 199 (1918), which held that an action fell outside federal jurisdiction because state law would have made it "cognizable only by the probate court" even though its subject matter did not involve "pure probate", the Court also deemed it irrelevant that under Texas law the Texas Probate Court would have had exclusive jurisdiction of all of Vickie's claims against Pierce. Although Texas law created Vickie's cause of action, federal jurisdiction to hear her suit lay beyond Texas' capacity to control.

proceeding was within the probate exception and added that even if it were not, "the district court may, in its discretion, decline to exercise its jurisdiction. * * * Discretionary abstention in probate-related matters is suggested not only by the strong state interest in such matters generally but also by special circumstances in particular cases". Is this approach a tenable one following the Supreme Court's Marshall decision? Even if it is not, there may of course be cases involving probate-related matters that would come within one of the generally recognized abstention doctrines. For a helpful discussion, see Nicolas, Paragraph (1), *supra*, at 1528–37.

CHAPTER XI

FEDERAL HABEAS CORPUS

---

1. INTRODUCTION

INTRODUCTORY NOTE ON THE FUNCTION OF THE WRIT

The writ of *habeas corpus ad subjiciendum*—the so-called Great Writ[1]—played an historic part in the English struggle with royal prerogative.[2] The writ's underlying premise is that only legal authority can justify detention. Thus, an individual whose liberty is restrained may file a petition seeking issuance of the writ, and thereby require a custodian (usually an official, though occasionally a private citizen[3]) to respond in court and justify the restraint as lawful. If that justification cannot be made, the court will order the discharge of the petitioner.[4]

---

[1] Other forms of the writ of habeas corpus at common law were: (1) *ad respondendum* (to remove a prisoner confined by process of an inferior court to answer to an action in a higher court); (2) *ad satisfaciendum* (to remove a prisoner to a higher court to be charged with process of execution); (3) *ad prosequendum, testificandum, deliberandum* (to remove a prisoner to enable prosecution, testimony, or trial in the proper jurisdiction); and (4) *ad faciendum et recipiendum* (to remove a cause at the prisoner's behest from an inferior court to Westminster). 3 Blackstone Commentaries 129–32.

[2] See Duker, A Constitutional History of Habeas Corpus (1980); Halliday, Habeas Corpus: From England to Empire (2010); Walker, The Constitutional and Legal Development of Habeas Corpus as the Writ of Liberty (1960); Farbey, Sharpe & Atrill, The Law of Habeas Corpus (3d ed.2011). For other sources, see 1 Hertz & Liebman, Federal Habeas Corpus Practice & Procedure § 2.3, at 22 n.1 (6th ed.2011).

[3] See Wales v. Whitney, 114 U.S. 564, 571 (1885) (including, within forms of custody subject to the writ, "arbitrary custody by private individuals"). The court in Neale v. Pfeiffer, 523 F.Supp. 164, 165–66 (S.D.Ohio), *aff'd without opinion*, 665 F.2d 1046 (6th Cir.1981), reviewed a variety of situations in which the writ had been sought against private custodians—parents (in child custody cases), persons operating mental institutions, ship officials holding persons forbidden to enter the country—and concluded that the writ could issue only when a private custodian acts pursuant to a court decree or other government intervention.

That state involvement, even if necessary, is not sufficient was made clear in Lehman v. Lycoming County Children's Servs. Agency, 458 U.S. 502 (1982). There the Court held that federal habeas jurisdiction does not embrace a petition challenging an adjudication terminating parental rights and awarding custody of petitioner's children to a county agency, which placed the children in a private foster home. See also Chap. X, Sec. 3(E), *supra* (discussing the domestic relations exception to diversity jurisdiction and its implications for other grants of federal subject matter jurisdiction).

[4] Professor Halliday, note 2, *supra*, provides a rich account of the writ from 1500–1800. One of his important themes is that by 1605, the writ had become "fundamentally an instrument of judicial power derived from the king's prerogative, a power more concerned with the wrongs of jailers than with the rights of prisoners". His other themes with particular relevance to material in this Chapter include: (1) the King's Bench used procedural innovations in "transform[ing] habeas corpus from an instrument for moving around bodies as part of routine court business into an instrument for controlling other jurisdictions"; (2) the writ was not limited to citizens but was available to aliens who came under the King's protection; (3) courts administering the writ had power over people, not places, and habeas corpus could follow those subject to the King's protection

The primary contemporary use of federal habeas corpus is as a postconviction remedy for prisoners claiming that an error of federal law—almost always of constitutional law—infected the judicial proceedings that resulted in detention. But postconviction relief was not the original office of habeas corpus, which focused instead on whether extra-judicial detention—most often by the executive—was authorized by law. That historic use of habeas corpus became less important as other procedures arose through which one could seek judicial review of the legality of extra-judicial detention. But in recent years, inquiry into the legality of extra-judicial detention has regained prominence in connection with the government's detention of "enemy combatants" following 9/11.

Other uses of the writ include challenges to (i) the legality of detention (including confinement, exclusion, and deportation) in immigration matters, see p. 336, *supra*; (ii) the holding of individuals for military service, the conduct of trials before military commissions,[5] and the relocation and detention of Japanese citizens during World War II;[6] (iii) the determination of preliminary matters in criminal cases, involving, for example, the sufficiency of cause for detention on the basis of a criminal complaint[7] or for removal to another federal district,[8] the legality of interstate rendition[9] or of extradition to a foreign country,[10] the denial of bail,[11] the failure to provide a prompt post-arrest hearing[12] or a speedy trial,[13] or a claim under the Double Jeopardy Clause;[14] and (iv) according to some authorities, the legality of conditions of confinement.[15] In cases potentially falling within the scope of the writ, habeas review may not be available where a distinct and adequate

---

wherever they traveled, limited only by the practicalities created by distance; (4) though not strictly an equitable writ, habeas was administered equitably to do justice; and (5) although a petitioner could not challenge the factual accuracy of the return (the custodian's response to the petition), judges evaded this limitation by looking to counsel, court officers, and affidavits for additional information not contained in the return.

See also Freedman, *Habeas Corpus in Three Dimensions, Dimension I: Habeas Corpus as a Common Law Writ*, 46 Harv.C.R.-C.L.L.Rev. 591 (2011) (arguing that in the colonial and early national period, demands for release from unlawful custody were made not merely through habeas corpus, but also through a variety of other common law writs, and that the full range of cases reflects a shared approach of treating a possibly wrongful detention as an emergency warranting swift and pragmatic resolution).

[5]   See, *e.g.*, Ex parte Quirin, 317 U.S. 1 (1942); Ex parte Milligan, 71 U.S. (4 Wall.) 2 (1866).

[6]   See Ex parte Endo, 323 U.S. 283 (1944).

[7]   See, *e.g.*, Ex parte Bollman, 8 U.S. (4 Cranch) 75 (1807), p. 1195, *infra*. See also Jurney v. MacCracken, 294 U.S. 125 (1935) (power of Senate to order arrest for contempt of a committee).

[8]   See, *e.g.*, Tinsley v. Treat, 205 U.S. 20 (1907); United States ex rel. Kassin v. Mulligan, 295 U.S. 396 (1935).

[9]   See, *e.g.*, Roberts v. Reilly, 116 U.S. 80 (1885); Biddinger v. Commissioner of Police, 245 U.S. 128 (1917). But *cf.* Sweeney v. Woodall, 344 U.S. 86 (1952) (escaped prisoner).

[10]   See, *e.g.*, Fernandez v. Phillips, 268 U.S. 311 (1925); Factor v. Laubenheimer, 290 U.S. 276 (1933).

[11]   This historic use of habeas has been displaced, in the federal courts, by the statutory right to apply for bail, see 18 U.S.C. §§ 3142, 3144; Fed.R.Crim.Proc. 46, and the right to move in court for a reduction of excessive bail, see Stack v. Boyle, 342 U.S. 1 (1951).

[12]   See, *e.g.*, Gerstein v. Pugh, 420 U.S. 103 (1975).

[13]   See, *e.g.*, Braden v. 30th Judicial Cir. Ct., 410 U.S. 484 (1973), pp. 1245, 1353, *infra*.

[14]   See Justices of Boston Municipal Ct. v. Lydon, 466 U.S. 294 (1984), p. 1353, *infra*.

[15]   See, *e.g.*, Aamer v. Obama, 742 F.3d 1023 (D.C.Cir.2014) (finding that D.C. Circuit precedent "establishes that one in custody may challenge the conditions of his confinement in a petition for habeas corpus", while recognizing that the Supreme Court has not resolved the issue and that the lower courts are divided).

form of judicial review has been provided. (For example, in most cases today, a denial of bail would be challenged under the rules of criminal procedure rather than via a habeas corpus petition.) See note 11, *supra*.

The Framers, aware of the English history—which included episodes in the seventeenth and eighteenth centuries in which the privilege of the writ was suspended—included in Article I, sec. 9, cl. 2 of the Constitution the Suspension Clause: "The Privilege of the Writ of Habeas Corpus shall not be suspended, unless when in Cases of Rebellion or Invasion the public Safety may require it."

NOTE ON THE JURISDICTIONAL STATUTES

(1) The First Judiciary Act. Section 14 of the First Judiciary Act (1 Stat. 81–82) provided:

"That all the before-mentioned courts of the United States, shall have power to issue writs of *scire facias, habeas corpus,* and all other writs not specially provided for by statute, which may be necessary for the exercise of their respective jurisdictions, and agreeable to the principles and usages of law. And that either of the justices of the supreme court, as well as judges of the district courts, shall have power to grant writs of *habeas corpus* for the purpose of an inquiry into the cause of commitment.—*Provided*, That writs of *habeas corpus* shall in no case extend to prisoners in gaol, unless where they are in custody, under or by colour of the authority of the United States, or are committed for trial before some court of the same, or are necessary to be brought into court to testify."

(2) Ex parte Bollman. Section 14 came before the Court in Ex parte Bollman, 8 U.S. (4 Cranch) 75 (1807). Bollman and Swartwout, who were linked to the mysterious expedition of Aaron Burr in the Louisiana Territory in 1805–06, had been arrested by military officials in New Orleans and taken to Washington, D.C. The U.S. Attorney obtained from the U.S. Circuit Court for the District of Columbia an arrest warrant to have the two committed to stand trial for treason; that court also denied bail. The prisoners then sought a writ of habeas corpus from the Supreme Court, which issued the writ, finding the evidence of treason insufficient. Chief Justice Marshall's opinion included several important rulings concerning the habeas jurisdiction.

First, he rejected the view that § 14 authorized issuance of the writ only as an auxiliary to jurisdiction otherwise conferred. Instead, he read § 14 as authorizing an independent action in habeas corpus. (The power expressly conferred on the *justices* and *judges* was held to be vested in the courts by implication.)

Second, he declared that when (as in Bollman) a petitioner applies for the writ directly in the Supreme Court, the Court may use the writ as a means of reviewing the legality of a commitment ordered by a lower federal court. Issuance of the writ by the Supreme Court in such circumstances was held to be an exercise of *appellate* jurisdiction, thus avoiding any difficulty under Marbury v. Madison's holding that Congress may not expand the scope of the Supreme Court's *original* jurisdiction.[1]

---

[1] The view that the Supreme Court had a duty to inquire into the cause of commitment, Ex parte Yarbrough, 110 U.S. 651, 653 (1884), gave way, by the time of Ex parte Abernathy,

Finally, he stated that the jurisdiction of the federal courts to issue the writ is not an "inherent" power but must be conferred by statute. At the same time, the Chief Justice's opinion in Bollman stated: "Acting under the immediate influence of [the Suspension Clause, the members of the First Congress] must have felt, with peculiar force, the obligation of providing efficient means by which this great constitutional privilege should receive life and activity; for if the means be not in existence, the privilege itself would be lost, although no law for its suspension should be enacted. Under the impression of this obligation, they give, to all the courts, the power of awarding writs of *habeas corpus*."

Commentators have offered a range of criticisms of Bollman's conclusion that the federal courts lack inherent power to issue the writ.[2] And there are evident difficulties in reconciling Bollman's insistence that jurisdiction be granted by statute with the apparent presupposition of the Suspension Clause that (absent a congressional act of suspension) habeas corpus review would be available. More recently, the Supreme Court has taken the view that the Suspension Clause itself affirmatively confers a right to habeas corpus review in some circumstances, even when Congress has not conferred statutory jurisdiction. See pp. 335–341, *supra,* 1201–1203, *infra.*

---

320 U.S. 219, 220 (1943), to the view that "this Court does not, save in exceptional circumstances, exercise [jurisdiction] in cases where an adequate remedy may be had in a lower federal court, or, if the relief sought is from the judgment of a state court, where the petitioner has not exhausted his remedies in the state courts". The current Sup.Ct.R. 20.4(a) states: "To justify the granting of a writ of habeas corpus, the petitioner must show that exceptional circumstances warrant the exercise of the Court's discretionary powers, and that adequate relief cannot be obtained in any other form or from any other court. This writ is rarely granted."

Since 1900, the Court appears to have granted relief in only three cases involving direct recourse to its habeas jurisdiction. See Ex parte Grossman, 267 U.S. 87 (1925); Ex parte Hudgings, 249 U.S. 378 (1919); In re Heff, 197 U.S. 488 (1905). See also In re Davis, 557 U.S. 952 (2009) (transferring a petition for an original writ of habeas jurisdiction, filed in the Supreme Court, to a district court). See generally Felker v. Turpin, 518 U.S. 651 (1996), p. 1292, *infra*; Oaks, *The "Original" Writ of Habeas Corpus in the Supreme Court*, 1962 Sup.Ct.Rev. 153.

²   Professor Freedman, in *Just Because John Marshall Said It Doesn't Make It So: Ex parte Bollman and the Illusory Prohibition on the Federal Writ of Habeas Corpus for State Prisoners in the Judiciary Act of 1789*, 51 Ala.L.Rev. 531 (2000), argues that the federal courts possessed common law and state law powers to issue writs of habeas corpus even absent statutory authority; he reads the ratification debates as assuming that all courts had power to issue the writ. Professor Paschal, in *The Constitution and Habeas Corpus*, 1970 Duke L.J. 605, had earlier argued that § 14 merely ratified a court's power to employ habeas corpus in aid of jurisdiction otherwise conferred; he added that the Constitution's Suspension Clause directs the courts to make habeas available. See pp. 1201–1205, *infra*. Both Paschal and Freedman contend that § 14's proviso does not limit the section's first sentence, which vests power in the courts of the United States, but only its second sentence, which vests power in individual judges.

Professor Neuman, in *The Habeas Corpus Suspension Clause After INS v. St. Cyr*, 33 Colum.Hum.Rts.L.Rev. 555, 580–81 (2002), suggests that the Constitution does not vest habeas jurisdiction in any particular federal court but obliges Congress to provide some effective means through which the writ can be made available—much as Article III does not set judicial salaries but implicitly requires Congress to provide for compensation. See also Halliday & White, *The Suspension Clause: English Text, Imperial Contexts, and American Implications*, 94 Va.L.Rev. 575, 683–98 (2008) (questioning Bollman's denial that federal courts possess common law habeas jurisdiction).

See also Kovarksy, *A Constitutional Theory of Habeas Power*, 99 Va.L.Rev. 753 (2013), discussed at p. 1291, *infra*.

(3) Ante-Bellum Legislation. Section 14 reached only persons held in *federal* custody. Subsequent enactments extended the federal courts' power to small categories of prisoners held in *state* custody.[3]

(a) The Force Act of 1833, countering South Carolina's resistance to the "Tariff of Abominations", conferred power to grant writs when prisoners were confined "for any act done, or omitted to be done, in pursuance of a law of the United States, or any order, process, or decree, of any judge or court thereof, any thing in any act of Congress to the contrary notwithstanding." Section 7, 4 Stat. 634–35.

(b) Nine years later, following British protests that the New York murder trial of a Canadian soldier violated the law of nations (the homicide was claimed to be an act of state),[4] Congress vested the federal courts with power to grant writs in certain cases involving prisoners who are "subjects or citizens of a foreign State, and domiciled therein". Act of Aug. 29, 1842, 5 Stat. 539–40.

(4) The Act of 1867. The most significant expansion of the writ—to encompass generally persons in *state* custody—came during Reconstruction with the Act of February 5, 1867, 14 Stat. 385. It conferred power on all federal courts, and the judges and Justices thereof, "within their respective jurisdictions, * * * to grant writs of habeas corpus in all cases where any person may be restrained of his or her liberty in violation of the constitution, or of any treaty or law of the United States", whether held in federal or in state custody.[5]

(5) The 1948 Revision. The foregoing provisions survived without important change until 1948, when they were codified in 28 U.S.C. §§ 2241–55. The revision placed the general grant of habeas corpus jurisdiction to the federal courts in § 2241, without significantly altering the bases for challenging the lawfulness of custody. But the revision did effect some procedural changes;[6] established a new provision (§ 2254) dealing specifically with challenges to custody resulting from conviction in state court; and gave statutory recognition to the judge-made rule requiring exhaustion of state remedies prior to seeking the writ, see § 2254(b–c), p. 1349, *infra*. In addition, the revision created, in § 2255, a new statutory motion for federal prisoners collaterally attacking their convictions, which is similar in substance but different in form from a habeas petition. See generally Sec. 3(B), *infra*.

(6) The Antiterrorism and Effective Death Penalty Act of 1996. The structure established in 1948 remained in effect for nearly 50 years, with

---

[3] In addition to the legislation described in text, the Bankruptcy Act of 1800 authorized federal courts exercising bankruptcy jurisdiction to issue writs of habeas corpus to state officials ordering the release of debtors arrested after having received a discharge in bankruptcy. See Central Virginia Community College v. Katz, 546 U.S. 356 (2006), p. 963, *supra*.

[4] See People v. McLeod, 25 Wend. 483 (N.Y. 1841); 2 Warren, The Supreme Court in United States History 98 (rev.ed.1947).

[5] Decisions under each of the foregoing statutory formulations are collected in 18 Fed. 68 (1884). For further discussion of the 1867 Act, see p. 1273, *infra*.

[6] Unlike prior law, the 1948 revision, without explanation, did not authorize district judges (as distinguished from courts) to issue the writ. Compare 28 U.S.C. § 452 (1940). The courts of appeals (as distinguished from their judges) have never had such authority, see Whitney v. Dick, 202 U.S. 132 (1906), except under the "all writs" provision, 28 U.S.C. § 1651, in aid of appellate jurisdiction in a pending case, see, *e.g.*, Price v. Johnston, 334 U.S. 266 (1948).

only minor changes.[7] Then, in 1996, Congress enacted the Antiterrorism and Effective Death Penalty Act of 1996 (AEDPA), 110 Stat. 1214, which contains numerous provisions restricting the availability of the writ in postconviction cases.[8] AEDPA's most important provision, codified in § 2254(d)(1), states that habeas relief cannot be awarded to a state prisoner solely because a federal court disagrees with the state court's application of established constitutional principles to the facts in a particular case; rather, relief may be issued only when the state court determination was "contrary to, or involved an unreasonable application of, clearly established Federal law, as determined by the Supreme Court of the United States". In addition, AEDPA sharply narrows the power of federal habeas courts to conduct evidentiary hearings, to disregard factfindings made in state court, and to entertain multiple petitions from a prisoner. The Act also establishes, for the first time, a statute of limitations (of one year) governing collateral attacks by both state and federal prisoners. §§ 2244(d), 2255(f).[9] The provisions added by AEDPA are discussed throughout Section 3, *infra*.

(7) The Detainee Treatment Act of 2005 and the Military Commissions Act of 2006. Following the 9/11 terrorist attacks, Congress modified the habeas corpus jurisdiction as it applies to suspected terrorists. The first of these enactments responded to the decision in Rasul v. Bush, 542 U.S. 466 (2004), which had interpreted the basic grant of habeas corpus jurisdiction in 28 U.S.C. § 2241 as extending to aliens detained as suspected terrorists at the American military base at Guantánamo Bay, Cuba. One year later, Congress passed the Detainee Treatment Act of 2005 (DTA), 119 Stat. 2739, codified at 10 U.S.C. § 801 note. The DTA, in § 1005(e)(1), added a new subsection (§ 2241(e)) to the jurisdictional statute, providing that, except as authorized by the DTA, no federal court or judge may entertain a habeas petition or any other form of action by an alien detained at Guantánamo Bay as an enemy combatant. The following year, § 7(a) of the Military Commissions Act of 2006 (MCA of 2006), Pub.L.No. 109–366, 120 Stat. 2600, significantly broadened the scope of § 2241(e). As amended by the MCA of 2006, § 2241(e) reads:

enemy combatant excluded from HC

> "(e)(1) No court, justice, or judge shall have jurisdiction to hear or consider an application for a writ of habeas corpus filed by or on behalf of an alien detained by the United States who has been determined by the United States to have been properly detained as an enemy combatant or is awaiting such determination.

> "(2) Except as provided in paragraphs (2) and (3) of section 1005(e) of the Detainee Treatment Act of 2005 (10 U.S.C. 801 note), no court, justice, or judge shall have jurisdiction to hear or consider any other action against the United States or its agents relating to any aspect of the detention, transfer, treatment, trial, or conditions of confinement of an alien who is or was detained by the United

---

[7] In 1966, Congress added §§ 2244(b–c) (further specifying the effect of previous federal adjudications on a federal habeas petition) and § 2254(d) (providing that state court factfindings made in a procedurally fair manner must be treated as presumptively correct).

[8] See generally Yackle, *A Primer on the New Habeas Corpus Statute*, 44 Buff.L.Rev. 381 (1996); Tushnet & Yackle, *Symbolic Statutes and Real Laws: The Pathologies of the Antiterrorism and Effective Death Penalty Act and the Prison Litigation Reform Act*, 47 Duke L.J. 1 (1997).

[9] The Act also includes provisions designed to speed adjudication of capital cases. See 28 U.S.C. §§ 2261–66; pp. 1268–1269, 1271–1272, *infra*.

States and has been determined by the United States to have been properly detained as an enemy combatant or is awaiting such determination."

The DTA gave the D.C. Circuit jurisdiction (exclusive of all other courts) to entertain actions by aliens detained at Guantánamo Bay in two circumstances.

DC Cir. limited jur.

(a) Review of Enemy Combatant Status. First, the D.C. Circuit had "jurisdiction to determine the validity of any final decision of a Combatant Status Review Tribunal that an alien is properly detained as an enemy combatant", so long as the alien was still detained when review was sought. DTA § 1005(e)(2)(A–B). (A Combatant Status Review Tribunal (CSRT), described in more detail at pp. 1223, 1236, *infra*, is a panel of three military officers established to determine whether aliens may properly be detained as enemy combatants.) The court of appeals was authorized to review "(i) whether the status determination of the [CSRT] with regard to such alien was consistent with the standards and procedures specified by the Secretary of Defense for [CSRTs] (including the requirement that the conclusion of the Tribunal be supported by a preponderance of the evidence and allowing a rebuttable presumption in favor of the Government's evidence); and (ii) to the extent the Constitution and laws of the United States are applicable, whether the use of such standards and procedures to make the determination is consistent with the Constitution and laws of the United States." DTA § 1005(e)(2)(C).

In Boumediene v. Bush, 553 U.S. 723 (2008), pp. 1224, 1249, *infra*, the Supreme Court ruled that the DTA procedure was not an adequate substitute for habeas corpus; that the MCA's purported elimination of habeas corpus jurisdiction, codified at 28 U.S.C. § 2241(e)(1), violated the Suspension Clause; and hence that aliens detained at Guantánamo Bay as enemy combatants were constitutionally entitled to file a petition for a writ of habeas corpus. The following year, the D.C. Circuit ruled that Boumediene had invalidated § 2241(e)(1)'s effort to limit habeas corpus jurisdiction with respect to all claims by Guantánamo detainees, refusing to distinguish "core" form "ancillary" habeas petitions. Kiyemba v. Obama, 561 F.3d 509 (D.C.Cir.2009).[10]

No core/ ancillary distinctions

(b) Review of Military Commission Proceedings. The DTA also gave the D.C. Circuit jurisdiction to review a "final" decision of a military commission convened to try a war crime prosecution, with a scope of review similar to that for review of CSRT determinations.[11] DTA § 1005(e)(3). This provision has been replaced by a newer provision in the Military Commissions Act of 2009, discussed in Paragraph (8), *infra*.

(8) The Military Commissions Act of 2009. The Military Commissions Act of 2009 (MCA of 2009) amended the 2006 Act in a variety of ways, one of which was to establish a new system of postconviction review of military commission proceedings that replaced the system established under the DTA. See 10 U.S.C. §§ 950a–950j. A defendant convicted by a military commission may first seek review before the Defense Department's Convening Authority, who

---

[10] The D.C. Circuit has also held, however, that § 2241(e)(2)'s jurisdictional limits remain in effect in non-habeas actions. See Al-Zahrani v. Rodriguez, 669 F.3d 315 (D.C.Cir.2012).

[11] Initially, the DTA granted review as of right only in cases of capital punishment or imprisonment of at least 10 years; otherwise, review was within the discretion of the D.C. Circuit. A 2006 amendment made all review as of right. See MCA of 2006, § 9(2).

has complete discretion to dismiss or reduce charges or to reduce a sentence. Thereafter, defendants have a right to appellate review—unusually, of fact as well as of law—by the United States Court of Military Commission Review, an Article I court. The appellate panels of that court have at least three military judges, but can have additional military or civilian judges; the latter are appointed by the President with the advice and consent of the Senate. Thereafter, review by an Article III court is available in the D.C. Circuit, which has jurisdiction "only with respect to matters of law, including the sufficiency of the evidence to support the verdict". Finally, there is certiorari review before the Supreme Court. The 2009 Act repealed a provision of the 2006 Act—former 10 U.S.C. § 950j(b)—which had restricted the availability of habeas jurisdiction for persons prosecuted under the Military Commissions Act.

Despite (i) the Supreme Court's invalidation of Congress' effort to substitute DTA review of detainees' status for habeas corpus review with respect to detainees at Guantánamo Bay, and (ii) the establishment by the Military Commissions Act of 2009 of new review provisions for aliens subject to military commission proceedings, the 2006 MCA's amendments to the habeas statute have continuing relevance. Section 5(a) of the 2006 MCA expressly precludes litigants from relying on the Geneva Conventions and their protocols as a source of rights in any civil action (specifically including a habeas corpus action) against the United States or its officials. (Compare the general provision in § 2241(c), stating, in somewhat negative phrasing, that habeas jurisdiction does not exist unless the prisoner alleges "custody in violation of the Constitution or laws or treaties of the United States.") And because the 2009 MCA did not purport to amend 28 U.S.C. § 2241(e), discussed at p. 1198, *supra*, section 5(a) presumably continues to preclude the actions that it specifies, but only to the extent that the Constitution permits. For example, while the Boumediene decision held that § 2241(e)(1) could not constitutionally prelude challenges to detention brought by aliens at Guantánamo Bay, § 2241(e) might validly bar at least some habeas petitions filed on behalf of aliens detained abroad. See p. 1259, *infra*. Similarly, § 2241(e)(2) might validly bar some actions complaining about conditions of confinement or about transfers, to the extent that the substance of the complaints falls outside the protection of the Suspension Clause and of other constitutional provisions.

---

2. HABEAS CORPUS AND EXECUTIVE DETENTION

NOTE ON THE SUSPENSION CLAUSE OF THE CONSTITUTION

A. Introduction

The Suspension Clause (Art. I, § 9, cl. 2) provides: "The Privilege of the Writ of Habeas Corpus shall not be suspended, unless when in Cases of Rebellion or Invasion the public Safety may require it."[1] That the Constitution included this Clause testifies that the Founding generation viewed the writ as an established and fundamental guarantee of liberty. Yet

---

[1]   On the significance of the reference to the "Privilege of the Writ" rather than simply the Writ itself, see Ex parte Milligan, 71 U.S. (4 Wall.) 2, 130–31 (1866) (dictum).

neither the proceedings of the Convention nor the ratification debates cast much light on just what the Founders assumed the "Privilege of the Writ" to be.

The wording of the Clause presents an immediate puzzle, as it appears to presuppose the existence of habeas corpus jurisdiction without affirmatively guaranteeing a right to habeas corpus—a failing to which four of the state ratifying conventions objected. See Collings, *Habeas Corpus for Convicts—Constitutional Right or Legislative Grace?*, 40 Calif.L.Rev. 335, 340–41 (1952).[2] And Ex parte Bollman, p. 1195, *supra*, held (controversially) that the federal courts' habeas jurisdiction must be given by statute. Since enactment of the Judiciary Act of 1789, however, Congress has affirmatively vested habeas corpus jurisdiction in the federal courts, and in 1867 Congress broadened the jurisdiction to embrace individuals in state as well as federal custody. Consequently, for more than two hundred years, the Supreme Court was not required to address what power, if any, the federal courts could exercise by virtue of the Suspension Clause in the absence of statutory habeas jurisdiction.

That situation changed as a result of two clusters of legislation—one enacted in 1996 and the other in 2005–06—that either withdrew habeas corpus jurisdiction over a particular set of cases or might be interpreted as having done so. Subsequent decisions assessing that legislation have established that the Suspension Clause does not merely limit power to suspend the writ but also confers an affirmative right to habeas corpus review.

B. The Suspension Clause as an Affirmative Guarantee of Judicial Review

(1) Immigration and the St. Cyr Decision. In INS v. St. Cyr, 533 U.S. 289 (2001), p. 336, *supra*, the INS ordered St. Cyr to be removed from the United States. Provisions of 1996 amendments to the immigration laws broadly precluded recourse to state or federal court to challenge the legality of the INS' action, and the government contended that the preclusion of judicial review was total and barred the exercise of habeas corpus jurisdiction. The Supreme Court disagreed, construing the amendments as not precluding the exercise of federal habeas corpus jurisdiction under the general grant in § 2241, and stating that "a serious Suspension Clause issue would be presented if we were to accept the INS' submission that the 1996 statutes have withdrawn [the power to issue the writ] from federal judges and provided no adequate substitute for its exercise." Justice Stevens' majority opinion did not read Chief Justice Marshall's opinion in Ex parte Bollman, p. 1195, *supra*, as having interpreted the Suspension Clause to "proscribe a temporary abrogation of the writ, while permitting its permanent suspension. Indeed, Marshall's comment expresses the far more sensible view that the Clause was intended to preclude any possibility that 'the privilege itself would be lost' by either the inaction or the action of Congress." Justice Stevens said that "at the absolute minimum, the Suspension Clause protects the writ 'as it existed in 1789' " and that "[a]t its historical core, the writ of habeas corpus has served as a means of reviewing

---

[2]   See also Paschal, *The Constitution and Habeas Corpus*, 1970 Duke L.J. 605, who reads the negative phraseology as "only a circumlocution to propose a suspending power in the least offensive way" and asserts that the Clause "is a direction to all superior courts of record, state as well as federal, to make the habeas privilege routinely available".

the legality of Executive detention * * * " (quoting Felker v. Turpin, 518 U.S. 651 (1996)).

Turning to the scope of the right protected by the Suspension Clause, Justice Stevens first concluded that aliens had always been protected by the writ.[3] He then declared that historically, habeas review extended not only to constitutional claims but also to "errors of law, including the erroneous application or interpretation of statutes." The writ thus embraced St. Cyr's legal claim that the INS had erred in interpreting amendments to the immigration laws as having withdrawn, in this case, the Attorney General's discretionary power to waive deportation.

In dissent, Justice Scalia (joined on this issue by Chief Justice Rehnquist and Justice Thomas) took issue with the majority's reading of the Suspension Clause. Relying in part on the statement in Ex parte Bollman that the power to issue the writ must be given by written law, he argued that the Clause was designed only to limit temporary suspension of the writ as it existed under the statutory law in effect at the time—an abuse he said was well known to the Founders. Thus, the Clause did not "guarantee[ ] any particular habeas right that enjoys immunity from suspension". To guard only against suspension was no more irrational, he said, than to prevent denials of equal protection. And even if one assumed that the Suspension Clause protected some right to review, it surely would not extend to "the right to judicial compulsion of the exercise of Executive *discretion*".[4]

In the end, St. Cyr rested on statutory interpretation. But the textual argument that Congress had indeed withdrawn federal habeas corpus jurisdiction was very powerful, see p. 336, *supra,* and the statutory ruling was plainly driven by the Court's desire to avoid the constitutional question that would have been presented had the Court determined that Congress had withdrawn habeas corpus jurisdiction in the circumstances presented.

(2) "Enemy Combatants" Detained at Guantánamo Bay and the Boumediene Decision. Seven years after St. Cyr, the Court again confronted the question whether the Suspension Clause guarantees an affirmative right to habeas corpus review. This time, none of the Justices doubted that Congress had indeed purported to abolish habeas corpus review. And in Boumediene v. Bush, 553 U.S. 723 (2008) (5–4), the Court, for the first time, clearly *held* that the Suspension Clause does confer an affirmative right to habeas review, and in turn struck down as unconstitutional a federal statutory provision purporting to preclude any federal or state court from exercising habeas corpus jurisdiction.

Boumediene involved provisions of the Detainee Treatment Act of 2005 and the Military Commissions Act of 2006, which purported to limit judicial review of challenges by aliens held at Guantánamo Bay as suspected enemy combatants to the legality of their detention. The four dissenters argued that the petitioners fell outside the scope of the Suspension Clause's protection (because they were aliens detained as enemy combatants beyond the territorial sovereignty of the United States) and that, in any event, the

---

[3]   On this point, see especially Neuman, *Habeas Corpus, Executive Detention, and the Removal of Aliens*, 98 Colum.L.Rev. 961 (1998).

[4]   In a separate dissent, Justice O'Connor said: "assuming, *arguendo*, that the Suspension Clause guarantees some minimum extent of habeas review, the right asserted by the alien in this case falls outside the scope of that review * * *."

For discussion of St. Cyr, see Neuman, *The Habeas Corpus Suspension Clause After INS v. St. Cyr*, 33 Colum.Hum.Rts.L.Rev. 555 (2002).

substitute procedure that Congress had provided, involving limited judicial review in the D.C. Circuit, was a constitutionally adequate substitute for habeas review. Unlike in St. Cyr, however, none of the dissenters (who included Justices Scalia and Thomas) questioned the premise that for persons who do fall within its ambit, the Suspension Clause confers an affirmative right to habeas corpus review or to an adequate substitute. See pp. 1232–1236, 1256–1258, *infra.*

(3) Federal Versus State Court. Is the affirmative right to habeas review guaranteed by the Suspension Clause a right to *federal* habeas corpus review? In both St. Cyr and Boumediene, the government argued that the jurisdictional statutes precluded all review in federal or state court; finding such a total preclusion constitutionally suspect or invalid, the Court, without real discussion, assumed that any constitutionally required review should be provided in federal court.

Does that assumption cast doubt on Professor Hart's position that the state courts are the ultimate guardians of constitutional rights? Or can the Court's assumption that review should occur in federal court be explained on a narrower basis? In both cases, that assumption seems entirely justified as a matter of statutory construction and severability analysis. Had Congress realized that judicial review of executive action was required in either federal or state court, surely it would have preferred that review of immigration matters and of federal military detention occur in federal court. The point is only reinforced by the language (much criticized, but never repudiated) in Tarble's Case, p. 427, *supra,* stating that state courts lack authority to entertain habeas actions against federal custodians. And in both cases, once the Court had dealt with the jurisdiction-stripping provisions (invalidating them in Boumediene, narrowly construing them in St. Cyr), there remained in place the pre-existing general grant of habeas corpus jurisdiction in § 2241, under which the petitions could be entertained.

But in light of the Madisonian Compromise and the possibility that Congress might never have established federal courts at all (or might never have conferred on them any habeas corpus jurisdiction), must any right to review conferred by the Clause be afforded in federal court? It has been argued that the Clause, at its core, precludes Congress, where it has not established the requisite habeas jurisdiction in federal court, from interfering with the power of the state courts to issue habeas relief. See Duker, p. 1193, note 2, *supra;* see generally pp. 431–435, *supra.* On this view, Congress could presumably eliminate federal review for a particular class of detainees while leaving them free to seek habeas corpus relief in state court. In such a circumstance, would a state court be obliged to entertain a habeas action—even one against a federal custodian?

C.   The Power to Suspend the Writ

Whether federal court power rests on a statutory grant of jurisdiction, inherent common law authority, or the Suspension Clause, the Constitution clearly contemplates that the writ may be suspended—the only explicit grant of an emergency power in the Constitution. But the Suspension Clause leaves open a welter of questions.

(1) Which Branch of Government Has the Power to Suspend the Writ? There seems little question that Congress has the power to suspend the writ. Congress has authorized suspension of the writ four times in the nation's history—twice within the United States (during the Civil War and later in Reconstruction), once in the Philippines in 1905, and once, during World War II, in what was then the territory of Hawaii. On each occasion, rather than declaring a suspension itself, Congress delegated to executive officials authority to suspend the writ under specified circumstances. See Barrett, *Suspension and Delegation*, 99 Cornell L.Rev. 251, 270–92 (2014). Is there a limit on Congress' authority to delegate the power to suspend the writ? See *id.* at 325 (acknowledging some power to delegate, but arguing that Congress must itself decide that an invasion or rebellion has occurred and that protecting the public safety may require suspension—a standard not satisfied by three of the four acts of suspension).

May the President suspend the writ without any delegation of authority by Congress? Prior to legislative action during the Civil War, President Lincoln purported to suspend the writ, but his claim that the President could do so without congressional authorization was rejected in Ex parte Merryman, 17 F.Cas. 144, 151–52 (C.C.D.Md.1861) (No. 9487), by Chief Justice Taney, sitting as a Circuit Judge. For agreement with Taney, see Hamdi v. Rumsfeld, 542 U.S. 507, 562 (2004) (Scalia, J., dissenting) (noting both English practice and the Suspension Clause's placement in Article I, which defines Congress' power). See generally Jackson, *The Power to Suspend Habeas Corpus: An Answer from the Arguments Surrounding Ex parte Merryman*, 34 U.Balt.L.Rev. 11 (2004).

(2) What Constitutes a Suspension of the Writ? The Supreme Court has repeatedly recognized that Congress may replace habeas corpus with a different form of judicial review, so long as the substitute is adequate. See, *e.g.*, Boumediene v. Bush, pp. 1224, 1249, *infra*; Swain v. Pressley, 430 U.S. 372 (1977); United States v. Hayman, 342 U.S. 205 (1952). But whether a limitation on habeas jurisdiction, or on a substitute remedy, constitutes a suspension is bound up with the question of what scope of habeas corpus review is required by the Suspension Clause.

That question is a complex one on which there is little authority. While the basic office of the writ is clear, history reveals that habeas courts exercised a considerable measure of discretion. Moreover, the writ has evolved along many dimensions, including: (i) the purpose for which the writ was exercised (protecting individuals, permitting one court in England to exercise *jurisdictional* primacy over another, or permitting the common law courts to contest royal power);[5] (ii) the scope of the courts' territorial jurisdiction; (iii) the extent of explanation required to justify detention; (iv) the scope of inquiry (which often turned on whether detention was pursuant to executive action, to action of an "inferior" court or a court of limited jurisdiction, or to action of a superior court of general jurisdiction); and (v) the breadth of the understanding of "custody".

In the United States, expansions of the writ along various dimensions occurred under the *statutory* grant of jurisdiction that has existed since 1789. Professor Shapiro says that "[s]urely, the guarantee is not a one-way ratchet, in which every advance in the availability of the writ becomes part of the [Suspension Clause] guarantee itself," but that "the guarantee would be stripped of virtually all meaning if it did not include what might fairly be viewed as the essence of the writ at the time of ratification". Shapiro, *Habeas Corpus, Suspension, and Detention: Another View*, 82 Notre Dame L.Rev. 59,

[5] Halliday & White, p. 1196, note 2, *supra*, contend that the writ originated as a means by which the king asserted royal prerogative over officials acting in his name, but over time an understanding of the writ as a protection of individual liberty took hold.

74 (2006). Shapiro suggests, *inter alia*, that the heart of the writ involves a determination of the adequacy of the custodian's return—that is, the custodian's response to the allegations in the petition—but not necessarily of the accuracy of factual statements in the return. He suggests that the essence of the writ did not necessarily permit the court to probe behind the competency of the committing authority to order the commitment. Shapiro notes that the review for lawfulness was especially rigorous when the committing authority was the executive or an inferior court and when the commitment was not pursuant to conviction by a competent superior court.

(3) Interpretation of Congressional Statutes. In the Boumediene case, there was no doubt that Congress had eliminated habeas corpus jurisdiction. The government did not argue, and the Supreme Court did not conclude, however, that the congressional action purported to suspend the writ; instead, the Court treated the absence of habeas jurisdiction as a violation of the affirmative right guaranteed by the Suspension Clause.

Congress clearly did not want cases like Boumediene heard in federal court (or indeed in any court). Was the Supreme Court correct in refusing to treat the relevant legislation as an effort to suspend the writ? Given that the right to a habeas court's intervention to review the legality of custody can be viewed as the most fundamental protection of liberty conferred by the Constitution, isn't there warrant for a clear statement rule, requiring Congress to be very explicit when purporting to exercise its emergency power to suspend the privilege of the writ? In each of the four instances in which Congress authorized suspension of the writ, the statutory authorization was clear (and also limited to the period in which the requisite rebellion or invasion existed). See Hamdan v. Rumsfeld, 464 F.Supp.2d 9, 14 (D.D.C.2006).

(4) Is the Act of Suspension Subject to Judicial Review? Some opinions have broadly asserted that the courts may not review a congressional decision to suspend. See, *e.g.*, Hamdi v. Rumsfeld, 542 U.S. 507, 577–78 (2004) (Scalia, J., dissenting); *id.* at 594 n. 4 (Thomas, J., dissenting); Ex parte Merryman, 17 F.Cas. 144, 152 (C.C.D.Md.1861) (No. 9487) (Taney, C.J.) (dictum). Note, however, that a detainee confronting a measure that allegedly suspends the writ might object that (i) there was no rebellion or invasion, (ii) the public safety did not require suspension, (iii) the measure in question was not in fact an exercise of the power to suspend, (iv) the branch that purported to suspend the writ lacked the constitutional authority to do so, or (v) the terms of the suspension were limited by time, geography, or in some other respect and did not extend to the detention at issue.

Is there any reason why the last three of these issues should not be subject to judicial review? Indeed, Ex parte Milligan, 71 U.S. (4 Wall.) 2 (1866), determined that Milligan's custody was illegal only after concluding that it fell outside the scope of the suspension that Congress had authorized. Ex parte Merryman, Paragraph (1), *supra*, reviewed (and found wanting) the President's power, acting without congressional authorization, to suspend the writ. And in Hamdi v. Rumsfeld, the next principal case, Justice Scalia's dissenting opinion addressed the question of whether the Force Resolution passed by Congress shortly after 9/11 constituted a suspension of the writ (he determined that it did not).

What about judicial review of the existence of a rebellion or invasion? In suggesting that the issue is not immune from all review, Professor Shapiro,

Paragraph (2), *supra*, offers the example of a suspension based on a legislative determination that the flow of undocumented immigrants crossing from Mexico into the United States constitutes an "invasion". As for reviewability of a determination that "the public Safety may require" suspension, Professor Shapiro suggests that the text of the Suspension Clause indicates that Congress has, at a minimum, very broad discretion on that question. For a forceful argument that the validity of a suspension does not present a political question, see Tyler, *Is Suspension a Political Question?*, 59 Stan.L.Rev. 333 (2006).

(5) What is the Effect of a Suspension? Does a valid suspension merely withdraw the privilege of the writ (thereby requiring dismissal of habeas petitions falling within its scope)? Or does it go further, so that the detainee may not assert the right to be free from unlawful detention through other procedural vehicles? (The issue might arise, for example, were a detainee subject to a suspension of the writ later to seek damages for an illegal detention.) For an argument that other remedies remain available, see Morrison, *Hamdi's Habeas Puzzle: Suspension as Authorization?*, 91 Cornell L.Rev. 411 (2006), and Morrison, *Suspension and the Extrajudicial Constitution*, 107 Colum.L.Rev. 1533 (2007); for criticism of that view, see Shapiro, Paragraph (2), *supra*, and Tyler, *Suspension as an Emergency Power*, 118 Yale L.J. 600 (2009).[6]

INTRODUCTORY NOTE ON HAMDI V. RUMSFELD

In 2004, the Supreme Court decided three habeas cases involving alleged enemy combatants. Two of them reached only the question whether habeas jurisdiction existed. But in the third, Hamdi v. Rumsfeld, the Court considered a case in which habeas jurisdiction was not in doubt. Hamdi presented the question whether detention was legally authorized, which in turn required consideration of the procedural protections that a habeas court must afford a petitioner when making a determination of enemy combatant status.

Hamdi v. Rumsfeld

542 U.S. 507, 124 S.Ct. 2633, 159 L.Ed.2d 578 (2004).
Certiorari to the United States Court of Appeals for the Fourth Circuit.

■ JUSTICE O'CONNOR announced the judgment of the Court and delivered an opinion, in which THE CHIEF JUSTICE, JUSTICE KENNEDY, and JUSTICE BREYER join.

* * * [W]e are called upon to consider the legality of the Government's detention of a United States citizen on United States soil as an "enemy combatant" and to address the process that is constitutionally owed to one who seeks to challenge his classification as such. * * * We hold that although Congress authorized the detention of combatants in the narrow

---

[6]   Consider in this connection the argument of Professor Harrison, p. 1221, n. 1, *infra*, that the Suspension Clause is primarily a protection not of the remedy of habeas corpus but rather of a substantive right to natural liberty.

circumstances alleged here, due process demands that a citizen held in the United States as an enemy combatant be given a meaningful opportunity to contest the factual basis for that detention before a neutral decisionmaker.

I

* * * [One week after the 9/11 attacks,] Congress passed a resolution authorizing the President to "use all necessary and appropriate force against those nations, organizations, or persons he determines planned, authorized, committed, or aided the terrorist attacks" or "harbored such organizations or persons, in order to prevent any future acts of international terrorism against the United States by such nations, organizations or persons." Authorization for Use of Military Force (AUMF), 115 Stat. 224. Soon thereafter, the President ordered United States Armed Forces to Afghanistan, with a mission to subdue al Qaeda and quell the Taliban regime that was known to support it.

[Yaser Hamdi, an American citizen who resided in Afghanistan in 2001, was seized by members of the Northern Alliance (a coalition of military groups opposed to the Taliban government) and turned over to the United States military. After authorities learned that he was an American citizen, he was transferred to a naval brig in South Carolina. The government designated him as an "enemy combatant" and took the position that he could be detained indefinitely on that basis.

[Hamdi's father filed a habeas corpus petition, alleging that his son's detention was unlawful and that as an American citizen, Hamdi was entitled to an impartial tribunal, the assistance of counsel, and the full protections of the Constitution. The petition alleged that Hamdi went to Afghanistan to do relief work and had received no military training. It requested an evidentiary hearing should the government contest those allegations.

[The government did not contest the district court's jurisdiction. After various proceedings in the lower courts, the government filed a motion to dismiss the petition, supported by a declaration from a Defense Department official, Michael Mobbs. He stated that he was generally familiar with the war against al Qaeda and the Taliban, and that "based upon my review of the relevant records and reports, I am also familiar with the facts and circumstances related to the capture of * * * Hamdi and his detention by U.S. military forces." In the only evidentiary support for Hamdi's detention that the government submitted, Mobbs stated that after Hamdi traveled to Afghanistan in July or August of 2001, he "affiliated with a Taliban military unit and received weapons training", that he remained with his Taliban unit following September 11, that his unit surrendered in battle to the Northern Alliance, and that Hamdi himself surrendered his assault rifle. Mobbs also stated that a series of "U.S. military screening team[s]" determined that Hamdi met the "criteria for enemy combatants" and that "a subsequent interview of Hamdi has confirmed that he surrendered and gave his firearm to Northern Alliance forces".

[The district court found that Mobbs' declaration, given its "generic and hearsay nature", fell "far short" of supporting Hamdi's detention. The court ordered the government to turn over, for *in camera* review, numerous materials, including copies of Hamdi's statements and notes from his interviews; the names and addresses of all of Hamdi's interrogators; statements by members of the Northern Alliance regarding Hamdi's capture; and the identity of the American officials who determined that Hamdi was an enemy combatant. The Fourth Circuit reversed, concluding "that because it was 'undisputed that Hamdi was captured in a zone of active combat in a foreign theater of conflict,' no factual inquiry or evidentiary hearing allowing Hamdi to be heard or to rebut the Government's assertions was necessary or proper. Concluding that the factual averments in the Mobbs Declaration, 'if accurate,' provided a sufficient basis upon which to conclude that the President had constitutionally detained Hamdi pursuant to the President's war powers, it ordered the habeas petition dismissed."]

II

The threshold question before us is whether the Executive has the authority to detain citizens who qualify as "enemy combatants." * * * [The government] has made clear * * * that, for purposes of this case, the "enemy combatant" that it is seeking to detain is an individual who, it alleges, was " 'part of or supporting forces hostile to the United States or coalition partners' " in Afghanistan and who " 'engaged in an armed conflict against the United States' " there. Brief for Respondents 3. We therefore answer only the narrow question before us: whether the detention of citizens falling within that definition is authorized.

The Government maintains that no explicit congressional authorization is required, because the Executive possesses plenary authority to detain pursuant to Article II of the Constitution. We do not reach the question whether Article II provides such authority, however, because we agree with the Government's alternative position, that Congress has in fact authorized Hamdi's detention, through the AUMF.

* * * [Hamdi] * * * posits that his detention is forbidden by 18 U.S.C. § 4001(a). Section 4001(a) states that "[n]o citizen shall be imprisoned or otherwise detained by the United States except pursuant to an Act of Congress." * * * [W]e conclude that the AUMF is explicit congressional authorization for the detention of individuals in the narrow category we describe * * * and that the AUMF satisfied § 4001(a)'s requirement that a detention be "pursuant to an Act of Congress" (assuming, without deciding, that § 4001(a) applies to military detentions).

* * * There can be no doubt that individuals who fought against the United States in Afghanistan as part of the Taliban, an organization known to have supported the al Qaeda terrorist network responsible for those attacks, are individuals Congress sought to target in passing the AUMF. We conclude that detention of individuals falling into the limited category we are considering, for the duration of the particular conflict in which they were captured, is so fundamental and accepted an incident to war as to be an exercise of the "necessary and appropriate force" Congress has authorized the President to use.

The capture and detention of lawful combatants and the capture, detention, and trial of unlawful combatants, by "universal agreement and practice," are "important incident[s] of war." *Ex parte Quirin*, [317 U.S. 1, 28, 30 (1942)]. The purpose of detention is to prevent captured individuals from returning to the field of battle and taking up arms once again. * * *

There is no bar to this Nation's holding one of its own citizens as an enemy combatant. In *Quirin,* one of the detainees, Haupt, alleged that he was a naturalized United States citizen. 317 U.S., at 20.[1]

* * * While Haupt was tried for violations of the law of war, nothing in *Quirin* suggests that his citizenship would have precluded his mere detention for the duration of the relevant hostilities. * * * A citizen, no less than an alien, can be "part of or supporting forces hostile to the United States or coalition partners" and "engaged in an armed conflict against the United States," Brief for Respondents 3; such a citizen, if released, would pose the same threat of returning to the front during the ongoing conflict.

In light of these principles, it is of no moment that the AUMF does not use specific language of detention. Because detention to prevent a combatant's return to the battlefield is a fundamental incident of waging war, in permitting the use of "necessary and appropriate force," Congress has clearly and unmistakably authorized detention in the narrow circumstances considered here.

Hamdi objects, nevertheless, that Congress has not authorized the *indefinite* detention to which he is now subject. * * * As the Government concedes, "given its unconventional nature, the current conflict is unlikely to end with a formal cease-fire agreement." *Ibid.* * * *

It is a clearly established principle of the law of war that detention may last no longer than active hostilities. Hamdi contends that the AUMF does not authorize indefinite or perpetual detention. Certainly, we agree that indefinite detention for the purpose of interrogation is not authorized. Further, we understand Congress' grant of authority for the use of "necessary and appropriate force" to include the authority to detain for the duration of the relevant conflict * * *. If the practical circumstances of a given conflict are entirely unlike those of the conflicts that informed the development of the law of war, that understanding may unravel. But that is not the situation we face as of this date. Active combat operations against Taliban fighters apparently are ongoing in Afghanistan. The United States may detain, for the duration of these hostilities, individuals legitimately determined to be Taliban combatants who "engaged in an armed conflict against the United States." * * *

Ex parte Milligan, 4 Wall. 2, 125 (1866), does not undermine our holding about the Government's authority to seize enemy combatants, as we define that term today.[2] In that case, the Court made repeated reference to the fact that its inquiry into whether the military tribunal had jurisdiction to try and punish Milligan turned in large part on the fact that Milligan was not a prisoner of war, but a resident of Indiana arrested while at home there. That fact was central to its conclusion. Had Milligan been captured while he was assisting Confederate soldiers by carrying a rifle against Union troops on a Confederate battlefield, the holding of the Court might well have been different. The Court's repeated explanations that Milligan was not a prisoner of war suggest that had these different circumstances been present he could have been detained

---

[1] [Ed.] For a fuller description of the Quirin decision than the plurality provides, see pp. 405–408, *supra.*

[2] [Ed.] For a fuller description of the Milligan decision than the plurality provides, see pp. 405–408, *supra.*

under military authority for the duration of the conflict, whether or not he was a citizen.

Moreover, as Justice Scalia acknowledges, the Court in *Ex parte Quirin* dismissed the language of *Milligan* that the petitioners had suggested prevented them from being subject to military process. * * * Haupt * * * was accused of being a spy. The Court in *Quirin* found him "subject to trial and punishment by [a] military tribuna[l]" for those acts, and held that his citizenship did not change this result. 317 U.S., at 31, 37–38.

Quirin was a unanimous opinion. It both postdates and clarifies *Milligan,* providing us with the most apposite precedent that we have on the question of whether citizens may be detained in such circumstances. Brushing aside such precedent—particularly when doing so gives rise to a host of new questions never dealt with by this Court—is unjustified and unwise.

To the extent that Justice Scalia accepts the precedential value of *Quirin,* he argues that it cannot guide our inquiry here because "[i]n *Quirin* it was uncontested that the petitioners were members of enemy forces," while Hamdi challenges his classification as an enemy combatant. But it is unclear why, in the paradigm outlined by Justice Scalia, such a concession should have any relevance. Justice Scalia envisions a system in which the only options are congressional suspension of the writ of habeas corpus or prosecution for treason or some other crime. He does not explain how his historical analysis supports the addition of a third option—detention under some other process after concession of enemy-combatant status—or why a concession should carry any different effect than proof of enemy-combatant status in a proceeding that comports with due process. * * *

Further, Justice Scalia largely ignores the context of this case: a United States citizen captured in a *foreign* combat zone. Justice Scalia refers to only one case involving this factual scenario—a case in which a United States citizen-prisoner of war (a member of the Italian army) from World War II was seized on the battlefield in Sicily and then held in the United States. The court in that case held that the military detention * * * was lawful. See *In re Territo* [156 F.2d 142, 148 (9th Cir. 1946)].

* * *

Moreover, Justice Scalia presumably would come to a different result if Hamdi had been kept in Afghanistan or even Guantanamo Bay. This creates a perverse incentive. Military authorities faced with the stark choice of submitting to the full-blown criminal process or releasing a suspected enemy combatant captured on the battlefield will simply keep citizen-detainees abroad. * * *

III

Even in cases in which the detention of enemy combatants is legally authorized, there remains the question of what process is constitutionally due to a citizen who disputes his enemy-combatant status. Hamdi argues that he is owed a meaningful and timely hearing and that "extra-judicial detention [that] begins and ends with the submission of an affidavit based on third-hand hearsay" does not comport with the Fifth and Fourteenth Amendments. Brief for Petitioners 16. The Government counters that any more process than was provided below would be both unworkable and "constitutionally intolerable." Brief for Respondents 46. Our resolution of this dispute requires a careful examination both of the writ of habeas corpus * * * and of the Due Process Clause, which informs the procedural contours of that mechanism in this instance.

A

* * * All agree that, absent suspension, the writ of habeas corpus remains available to every individual detained within the United States. * * * All agree suspension of the writ has not occurred here. Thus, * * * Hamdi was properly before an Article III court to challenge his detention under 28 U.S.C. § 2241. Further, all agree that § 2241 and its companion provisions provide at least a skeletal outline of the procedures to be afforded a petitioner in federal habeas review. Most notably, § 2243 provides that "the person detained may, under oath, deny any of the facts set forth in the return or allege any other material facts," and § 2246 allows the taking of evidence in habeas proceedings by deposition, affidavit, or interrogatories.

The simple outline of § 2241 makes clear both that Congress envisioned that habeas petitioners would have some opportunity to present and rebut facts and that courts in cases like this retain some ability to vary the ways in which they do so as mandated by due process. The Government recognizes the basic procedural protections required by the habeas statute, but asks us to hold that, given both the flexibility of the habeas mechanism and the circumstances presented in this case, the presentation of the Mobbs Declaration * * * completed the required factual development. It suggests two separate reasons for its position that no further process is due.

B

First, the Government urges the adoption of the Fourth Circuit's holding below—that because it is "undisputed" that Hamdi's seizure took place in a combat zone, the habeas determination can be made purely as a matter of law, with no further hearing or factfinding necessary. This argument is easily rejected. * * * [The Court here stressed that Hamdi had not been permitted to respond to the government's allegations, and that the habeas petition states only that "[w]hen seized by the United States Government, Mr. Hamdi resided in Afghanistan"—which is "not a concession that one was '*captured* in a zone of active combat' operations in a foreign theater of war, and certainly is not a concession that one was 'part of or supporting forces hostile to the United States or coalition partners' and 'engaged in an armed conflict against the United States.' "]

C

The Government's second argument requires closer consideration. * * * Under the Government's most extreme rendition of this argument, "[r]espect for separation of powers and the limited institutional capabilities of courts in matters of military decision-making in connection with an ongoing conflict" ought to eliminate entirely any individual process, restricting the courts to investigating only whether legal authorization exists for the broader detention scheme. Brief for Respondents 26. At most, the Government argues, courts should review its determination that a citizen is an enemy combatant under a very deferential "some evidence" standard. Under this review, a court would assume the accuracy of the Government's articulated basis for Hamdi's detention, as set forth in the Mobbs Declaration, and assess only whether that articulated basis was a legitimate one.

In response, Hamdi emphasizes that this Court consistently has recognized that an individual challenging his detention may not be held at the will of the Executive without recourse to some proceeding before a neutral tribunal to determine whether the Executive's asserted justifications for that detention have basis in fact and warrant in law. * * *

Both of these positions highlight legitimate concerns. * * * The ordinary mechanism that we use for balancing such serious competing interests, and for determining the procedures that are necessary to ensure that a citizen is not "deprived of life, liberty, or property, without due process of law," U.S. Const., Amdt. 5, is the test that we articulated in *Mathews v. Eldridge,* 424 U.S. 319 (1976). *Mathews* dictates that the process due in any given instance is determined by weighing "the private interest that will be affected by the official action" against the Government's asserted interest, "including the function involved" and the burdens the Government would face in providing greater process. 424 U.S., at 335. The *Mathews* calculus then contemplates a judicious balancing of these concerns, through an analysis of "the risk of an erroneous deprivation" of the private interest if the process were reduced and the "probable value, if any, of additional or substitute procedural safeguards." *Ibid.* We take each of these steps in turn.

1

* * * Hamdi's "private interest . . . affected by the official action," *ibid.,* is the most elemental of liberty interests—the interest in being free from physical detention by one's own government.

Nor is the weight on this side of the *Mathews* scale offset by the circumstances of war or the accusation of treasonous behavior, for "[i]t is clear that commitment for *any* purpose constitutes a significant deprivation of liberty that requires due process protection," *Jones v. United States,* 463 U.S. 354, 361 (1983) (emphasis added; internal quotation marks omitted), and at this stage in the *Mathews* calculus, we consider the interest of the *erroneously* detained individual. Indeed, * * * the risk of erroneous deprivation of a citizen's liberty in the absence of sufficient process here is very real. Moreover, as critical as the Government's interest may be in detaining those who actually pose an immediate threat to the national security of the United States during ongoing international conflict, history and common sense teach us that an unchecked system of detention carries the potential to become a means for oppression and abuse of others who do not present that sort of threat. * * *

2

On the other side of the scale are the weighty and sensitive governmental interests in ensuring that those who have in fact fought with the enemy during a war do not return to battle against the United States. * * * Without doubt, our Constitution recognizes that core strategic matters of warmaking belong in the hands of those who are best positioned and most politically accountable for making them.

The Government also argues at some length that its interests in reducing the process available to alleged enemy combatants are heightened by the practical difficulties that would accompany a system of trial-like process. In its view, military officers who are engaged in the serious work of waging battle would be unnecessarily and dangerously distracted by litigation half a world away, and discovery into military operations would both intrude on the sensitive secrets of national defense and result in a futile search for evidence buried under the rubble of war. To the extent that these burdens are triggered by heightened procedures, they are properly taken into account in our due process analysis.

3

* * *

With due recognition of these competing concerns, we believe that * * * "the risk of an erroneous deprivation" of a detainee's liberty interest is unacceptably high under the Government's proposed rule, while some of the "additional or substitute procedural safeguards" suggested by the District Court are unwarranted in light of their limited "probable value" and the burdens they may impose on the military in such cases. *Mathews,* 424 U.S., at 335, 96 S.Ct. 893.

We therefore hold that a citizen-detainee seeking to challenge his classification as an enemy combatant must receive notice of the factual basis for his classification, and a fair opportunity to rebut the Government's factual assertions before a neutral decisionmaker. These essential constitutional promises may not be eroded.

At the same time, the exigencies of the circumstances may demand that, aside from these core elements, enemy-combatant proceedings may be tailored to alleviate their uncommon potential to burden the Executive at a time of ongoing military conflict. Hearsay, for example, may need to be accepted as the most reliable available evidence from the Government in such a proceeding. Likewise, the Constitution would not be offended by a presumption in favor of the Government's evidence, so long as that presumption remained a rebuttable one and fair opportunity for rebuttal were provided. Thus, once the Government puts forth credible evidence that the habeas petitioner meets the enemy-combatant criteria, the onus could shift to the petitioner to rebut that evidence with more persuasive evidence that he falls outside the criteria. * * *

We think it unlikely that this basic process will have the dire impact on the central functions of warmaking that the Government forecasts. The parties agree that initial captures on the battlefield need not receive the process we have discussed here; that process is due only when the determination is made to *continue* to hold those who have been seized. The Government has made clear in its briefing that documentation regarding battlefield detainees already is kept in the ordinary course of military affairs. Any factfinding imposition created by requiring a knowledgeable affiant to summarize these records to an independent tribunal is a minimal one. Likewise, arguments that military officers ought not have to wage war under the threat of litigation lose much of their steam when factual disputes at enemy-combatant hearings are limited to the alleged combatant's acts. This focus meddles little, if at all, in the strategy or conduct of war, inquiring only into the appropriateness of continuing to detain an individual claimed to have taken up arms against the United States. * * *

* * *

D

In so holding, we necessarily reject the Government's assertion that separation of powers principles mandate a heavily circumscribed role for the courts in such circumstances. Indeed, the position that the courts must forgo any examination of the individual case and focus exclusively on the legality of the broader detention scheme cannot be mandated by any reasonable view of separation of powers, as this approach serves only to *condense* power into a single branch of government. We have long since made clear that a state of war is not a blank check for the President when it comes to the rights of the Nation's citizens. *Youngstown Sheet & Tube* [343 U.S. 579, 587 (1952)]. * * * Likewise, we have made clear that, unless Congress acts to suspend it, the Great Writ of habeas corpus allows the Judicial Branch to play a necessary role in maintaining [the] delicate balance of governance, serving as an important judicial check on the Executive's discretion in the realm of detentions. Thus, while we do not question that our due process assessment must pay keen attention to the particular burdens faced by the Executive in the context of military action, it would turn our system of checks and balances on its head to suggest that a citizen could not make his way to court with a challenge to the factual basis for his detention by his Government, simply because the Executive opposes making available such a challenge. * * *

Because we conclude that due process demands some system for a citizen-detainee to refute his classification, the proposed "some evidence" standard is inadequate. Any process in which the Executive's factual assertions go wholly unchallenged or are simply presumed correct without any opportunity for the alleged combatant to demonstrate otherwise falls constitutionally short. As the Government itself has recognized, * * * the "some evidence" standard * * * has been employed by courts in examining an administrative record developed after an adversarial proceeding—one with process at least of the sort that we today hold is constitutionally mandated in the citizen enemy-combatant setting. This standard therefore is ill suited to the situation in which a habeas petitioner has received no prior proceedings before any tribunal and had no prior opportunity to rebut the Executive's factual assertions before a neutral decisionmaker.

* * *

There remains the possibility that the standards we have articulated could be met by an appropriately authorized and properly constituted military tribunal. Indeed, it is notable that military regulations already provide for such process in related instances, dictating that tribunals be made available to determine the status of enemy detainees who assert prisoner-of-war status under the Geneva Convention. In the absence of such process, however, a court that receives a petition for a writ of habeas corpus from an alleged enemy combatant must itself ensure that the minimum requirements of due process are achieved. * * *

IV

* * * Since our grant of certiorari in this case, Hamdi has been appointed counsel * * *. He unquestionably has the right to access to counsel in connection with the proceedings on remand. No further consideration of this issue is necessary at this stage of the case.

* * *

The judgment of the United States Court of Appeals for the Fourth Circuit is vacated, and the case is remanded for further proceedings.

It is so ordered.

■ JUSTICE SOUTER, with whom JUSTICE GINSBURG joins, concurring in part, dissenting in part, and concurring in the judgment.

[Unlike the plurality, Justice Souter concluded that the AUMF was not the kind of clearly expressed congressional authorization to detain a citizen that he believed was required by the Non-Detention Act. He argued that while the AUMF "is fairly read to authorize the use of armies and weapons * * * it never so much as uses the word detention, and there is no reason to think Congress might have perceived any need to augment Executive power to deal with dangerous citizens within the United States, given the well-stocked statutory arsenal of defined criminal offenses covering the gamut of actions that a citizen sympathetic to terrorists might commit." Justice Souter rejected the government's position that the AUMF confers authority to deal with enemy belligerents according to the laws of war; whatever the merits of that position in other circumstances, he stated, the government, in holding Hamdi incommunicado, has not been treating him as a prisoner of war under the Geneva Convention, and thus "has not made out its claim that * * * it is acting in accord with the laws of war".

[Thus concluding that Hamdi's detention violated the Non-Detention Act, Justice Souter found no need to address what process was due; he thought it appropriate to simply vacate and remand on the basis that detention was unauthorized. However, "[s]ince this disposition does not command a majority of the Court, * * * the need to give practical effect to the conclusions of eight members of the Court rejecting the Government's position calls for me to join with the plurality in ordering remand on terms closest to those I would impose."]

■ JUSTICE SCALIA, with whom JUSTICE STEVENS joins, dissenting.

　　　* * *

Where the Government accuses a citizen of waging war against it, our constitutional tradition has been to prosecute him in federal court for treason or some other crime. Where the exigencies of war prevent that, the Constitution's Suspension Clause, Art. I, § 9, cl. 2, allows Congress to relax the usual protections temporarily. Absent suspension, however, the Executive's assertion of military exigency has not been thought sufficient to permit detention without charge. No one contends that the congressional Authorization for Use of Military Force * * * is an implementation of the Suspension Clause. Accordingly, I would reverse the judgment below.

I

The very core of liberty secured by our Anglo-Saxon system of separated powers has been freedom from indefinite imprisonment at the will of the Executive.

　　　* * *

[Quoting Blackstone, Justice Scalia continued:] "To make imprisonment lawful, it must either be, by process from the courts of judicature, or by warrant from some legal officer, having authority to commit to prison; which warrant must be in writing, under the hand and seal of the magistrate, and express the causes of the commitment, in order to be examined into (if necessary) upon a *habeas corpus.* If there be no cause expressed, the gaoler is not bound to detain the prisoner. For the law judges in this respect, . . . that it is unreasonable to send a prisoner, and not to signify withal the crimes alleged against him." 1 W. Blackstone, Commentaries on the Laws of England 131–133 (1765) (hereinafter Blackstone).

These words were well known to the Founders. * * * The two ideas central to Blackstone's understanding—due process as the right secured, and habeas corpus as the instrument by which due process could be insisted upon by a citizen illegally imprisoned—found expression in the Constitution's Due Process and Suspension Clauses.

The gist of the Due Process Clause, as understood at the founding and since, was to force the Government to follow those common-law procedures traditionally deemed necessary before depriving a person of life, liberty, or property. When a citizen was deprived of liberty because of alleged criminal conduct, those procedures typically required committal by a magistrate followed by indictment and trial.

To be sure, certain types of permissible *non* criminal detention * * * did not require the protections of criminal procedure. However, these fell into a limited number of well-recognized exceptions—civil commitment of the mentally ill, for example, and temporary detention in quarantine of the infectious. It is unthinkable that the Executive could render otherwise criminal grounds for detention noncriminal merely by disclaiming an intent to prosecute, or by asserting that it was incapacitating dangerous offenders rather than punishing wrongdoing.

[Justice Scalia recounted the outrage that followed after the Crown had argued that detention was a matter of state, leading Parliament to respond to an English court's denial of relief in 1627] with the Petition of Right, accepted by the King in 1628, which expressly prohibited imprisonment without formal charges, see 3 Car. 1, ch. 1, §§ 5, 10.

The struggle between subject and Crown continued, and culminated in the Habeas Corpus Act of 1679, 31 Car. 2, ch. 2, described by Blackstone as a "second *magna carta,* and stable bulwark of our liberties." 1 Blackstone 133. [The act provided, *inter alia,* that for felony or treason, criminal proceedings must begin within a specified time, in practice not more than three to six months.]

> * * *

II

The allegations here, of course, are no ordinary accusations of criminal activity. * * * [T]he Government believes [Hamdi] participated in the waging of war against the United States. The relevant question, then, is whether there is a different, special procedure for imprisonment of a citizen accused of wrongdoing *by aiding the enemy in wartime.*

A

Justice O'Connor, writing for a plurality of this Court, asserts that captured enemy combatants (other than those suspected of war crimes) have traditionally been detained until the cessation of hostilities and then released. That is probably an accurate description of wartime practice with respect to enemy *aliens.* The tradition with respect to

American citizens, however, has been quite different. Citizens aiding the enemy have been treated as traitors subject to the criminal process.

[Justice Scalia discussed English sources supporting his position. He also noted that during World Wars I and II, American citizens were tried in the Article III courts for acts of war against the United States (other than Haupt in the Quirin case) and that the only American citizen other than Hamdi imprisoned in connection with military hostilities against the United States in Afghanistan was charged in an Article III court.]

B

* * *

Where the Executive has not pursued the usual course of charge, committal, and conviction, it has historically secured the Legislature's explicit approval of a suspension. * * *

* * *

III

* * * Even if suspension of the writ on the one hand, and committal for criminal charges on the other hand, have been the only *traditional* means of dealing with citizens who levied war against their own country, it is theoretically possible that the Constitution does not *require* a choice between these alternatives.

I believe, however, that substantial evidence does refute that possibility. First, the text of the 1679 Habeas Corpus Act makes clear that indefinite imprisonment on reasonable suspicion is not an available option of treatment for those accused of aiding the enemy, absent a suspension of the writ. In the United States, this Act was read as "enforc[ing] the common law," *Ex parte Watkins,* 3 Pet. 193, 202, and shaped the early understanding of the scope of the writ. * * * The Act does not contain any exception for wartime. That omission is conspicuous, since § 7 explicitly addresses the offense of "High Treason," which often involved offenses of a military nature.

[Justice Scalia then discussed writing from the founding generation, and three New York state decisions from the War of 1812, which he viewed as supporting his position.]

Further evidence comes from this Court's decision in *Ex parte Milligan, supra.* There, the Court issued the writ to an American citizen who had been tried by military commission for offenses that included conspiring to overthrow the Government, seize munitions, and liberate prisoners of war. The Court rejected in no uncertain terms the Government's assertion that military jurisdiction was proper "under the 'laws and usages of war,' ":

"It can serve no useful purpose to inquire what those laws and usages are, whence they originated, where found, and on whom they operate; they can never be applied to citizens in states which have upheld the authority of the government, and where the courts are open and their process unobstructed," *ibid.*[1]

---

[1]   As I shall discuss presently, the Court purported to limit this language in *Ex parte Quirin,* 317 U.S. 1, 45. Whatever *Quirin's* effect on *Milligan's* precedential value, however, it cannot undermine its value as an indicator of original meaning.

* * * The Government justifies imprisonment of Hamdi on principles of the law of war and admits that, absent the war, it would have no such authority. But if the law of war cannot be applied to citizens where courts are open, then Hamdi's imprisonment without criminal trial is no less unlawful than Milligan's trial by military tribunal.

* * *

Thus, criminal process was viewed as the primary means—and the only means absent congressional action suspending the writ—not only to punish traitors, but to incapacitate them.

* * *

IV

The Government * * * places primary reliance upon *Ex parte Quirin*, 317 U.S. 1 (1942), a World War II case upholding the trial by military commission of eight German saboteurs, one of whom, Herbert Haupt, was a U.S. citizen. The case was not this Court's finest hour. The Court * * * denied relief in a brief *per curiam* issued the day after oral argument concluded; a week later the Government carried out the commission's death sentence upon six saboteurs, including Haupt. The Court eventually explained its reasoning in a written opinion issued several months later.

Only three paragraphs of the Court's lengthy opinion dealt with the particular circumstances of Haupt's case. * * * *Quirin* purported to interpret the language of *Milligan* quoted above (the law of war "can never be applied to citizens in states which have upheld the authority of the government, and where the courts are open and their process unobstructed") in the following manner:

"Elsewhere in its opinion . . . the Court was at pains to point out that Milligan, a citizen twenty years resident in Indiana, who had never been a resident of any of the states in rebellion, was not an enemy belligerent either entitled to the status of a prisoner of war or subject to the penalties imposed upon unlawful belligerents. We construe the Court's statement as to the inapplicability of the law of war to Milligan's case as having particular reference to the facts before it. From them the Court concluded that Milligan, not being a part of or associated with the armed forces of the enemy, was a non-belligerent, not subject to the law of war . . . ." 317 U.S., at 45.

In my view this seeks to revise *Milligan* rather than describe it. *Milligan* had involved (among other issues) two separate questions: (1) whether the military trial of Milligan was justified by the laws of war, and if not (2) whether the President's suspension of the writ, pursuant to congressional authorization, prevented the issuance of habeas corpus. The Court's categorical language about the law of war's inapplicability to citizens where the courts are open * * * was contained in its discussion of the first point. The factors pertaining to whether Milligan could reasonably be considered a belligerent and prisoner of war, while mentioned earlier in the opinion, were made relevant and brought to bear in the Court's later discussion of whether Milligan came within the statutory provision that effectively made an exception to Congress's authorized suspension of the writ for (as the Court described it) "all parties, not prisoners of war, resident in their respective jurisdictions, . . . who were citizens of states in which the administration of the laws in the

Federal tribunals was unimpaired," *id.,* at 116. *Milligan* thus understood was in accord with the traditional law of habeas corpus I have described: Though treason often occurred in wartime, there was, absent provision for special treatment in a congressional suspension of the writ, no exception to the right to trial by jury for citizens who could be called "belligerents" or "prisoners of war."[2]

But even if *Quirin* gave a correct description of *Milligan,* or made an irrevocable revision of it, *Quirin* would still not justify denial of the writ here. In *Quirin* it was uncontested that the petitioners were members of enemy forces. * * * The specific holding of the Court was only that, "upon the *conceded* facts," the petitioners were "plainly within [the] boundaries" of military jurisdiction, *id.,* at 46 (emphasis added).[3] But where those jurisdictional facts are *not* conceded—where the petitioner insists that he is *not* a belligerent—*Quirin* left the pre-existing law in place: Absent suspension of the writ, a citizen held where the courts are open is entitled either to criminal trial or to a judicial decree requiring his release.[4]

V

* * * [T]he plurality finishes up by transmogrifying the Great Writ— * * * by remanding for the District Court to "engag[e] in a factfinding process that is both prudent and incremental". * * * This judicial remediation of executive default is unheard of. The role of habeas corpus is to determine the legality of executive detention, not to supply the omitted process necessary to make it legal. * * *

VI

Several limitations give my views * * * a relatively narrow compass. They apply only to citizens, accused of being enemy combatants, who are detained within the territorial jurisdiction of a federal court. This is not likely to be a numerous group; currently we know of only two, Hamdi and

---

[2] Without bothering to respond to this analysis, the plurality states that *Milligan* "turned in large part" upon the defendant's lack of prisoner-of-war status, and that the *Milligan* Court explicitly and repeatedly *said* so. Neither is true. To the extent, however, that prisoner-of-war status was relevant in *Milligan,* it was only because prisoners of war *received different statutory treatment* under the conditional suspension then in effect.

[3] The only two Court of Appeals cases from World War II cited by the Government in which citizens were detained without trial likewise involved petitioners who were conceded to have been members of enemy forces. See *In re Territo,* 156 F.2d 142, 143–145 (C.A.9 1946); *Colepaugh v. Looney,* 235 F.2d 429, 432 (C.A.10 1956). The plurality complains that *Territo* is the only case I have identified in which "a United States citizen [was] captured in a *foreign* combat zone". Indeed it is; such cases must surely be rare. But given the constitutional tradition I have described, the burden is not upon me to find cases in which the writ was *granted* to citizens in this country *who had been captured on foreign battlefields;* it is upon those who would carve out an exception for such citizens (as the plurality's complaint suggests it would) to find a single case (other than one where enemy status was admitted) in which habeas was *denied.*

[4] The plurality's assertion that *Quirin* somehow "clarifies" *Milligan* is simply false. * * * [T]he *Quirin* Court propounded a mistaken understanding of *Milligan;* but nonetheless its holding was limited to "the case presented by the present record," and to "*the conceded facts,*" and thus avoided conflict with the earlier case. See 317 U.S., at 45–46 (emphasis added). The plurality, ignoring this expressed limitation, thinks it "beside the point" whether belligerency is conceded or found "by some other process" (not necessarily a jury trial) "that verifies this fact with sufficient certainty." But the whole point of the procedural guarantees in the Bill of Rights is to limit the methods by which the Government can determine facts that the citizen disputes and on which the citizen's liberty depends. The plurality's claim that *Quirin's* one-paragraph discussion of *Milligan* provides a "[c]lear . . . disavowal" of two false imprisonment cases from the War of 1812 thus defies logic; unlike the plaintiffs in those cases, Haupt was concededly a member of an enemy force. * * *

Jose Padilla. Where the citizen is captured outside and held outside the United States, the constitutional requirements may be different. Moreover, even within the United States, the accused citizen-enemy combatant may lawfully be detained once prosecution is in progress or in contemplation. * * *

I frankly do not know whether these tools are sufficient to meet the Government's security needs, including the need to obtain intelligence through interrogation. * * * If the situation demands it, the Executive can ask Congress to authorize suspension of the writ—which can be made subject to whatever conditions Congress deems appropriate, including even the procedural novelties invented by the plurality today. To be sure, suspension is limited by the Constitution to cases of rebellion or invasion. But whether the attacks of September 11, 2001, constitute an "invasion," and whether those attacks still justify suspension several years later, are questions for Congress rather than this Court.[6] * * *

                      * * *

■ JUSTICE THOMAS, dissenting.

[Justice Thomas was the only member of the Court voting to uphold the government's authority to detain Hamdi without further process. Agreeing with the plurality that the AUMF authorized the detention of enemy combatants generally, he thought that the determination by the Executive Branch, within the scope of its war powers, that Hamdi was an enemy combatant sufficed to establish the legality of detention. Stressing the breadth of the President's power to protect national security and conduct foreign affairs, he reasoned that while Congress too has a substantial role to play, "*judicial* interference in these domains destroys the purpose of vesting primary responsibility in a unitary Executive." Because much intelligence is appropriately secret, courts lack the information needed to make judgments in these domains, and even if they could require some form of disclosure, " 'the very nature of executive decisions as to foreign policy is political, not judicial' " (quoting Chicago & Southern Air Lines, Inc. v. Waterman S.S. Corp., 333 U.S. 103, 111 (1948)). Thus, resolution of the question whether Hamdi is an enemy combatant "is committed to other branches."]

──────────

NOTE ON HAMDI V. RUMSFELD AND THE SCOPE OF HABEAS INQUIRY OVER PETITIONS FILED BY ALLEGED ENEMY COMBATANTS

(1) The Function of Habeas Corpus Jurisdiction. The range of views about the legality of Hamdi's detention—from Justice Scalia's view that Hamdi was entitled to immediate release to Justice Thomas' view that continued detention was lawful without further process—is considerable. But all nine Justices agreed that the federal courts' role was to examine the legality of Hamdi's detention; their disagreements rested on divergent substantive views about the interpretation of relevant statutes (particularly

──────────

[6]   Justice Thomas worries that the constitutional conditions for suspension of the writ will not exist "during many . . . emergencies during which . . . detention authority might be necessary". It is difficult to imagine situations in which security is so seriously threatened as to justify indefinite imprisonment without trial, and yet the constitutional conditions of rebellion or invasion are not met.

the AUMF), the scope of executive war power, and the meaning of due process.[1]

(2) Agency Versus Common Law Approaches to Adjudication. It is a commonplace that the kind of armed conflict authorized by the AUMF differs in important respects from traditional wars. In the words of Professors Bradley and Goldsmith, "[t]he enemy intermingles with civilians and attacks civilian and military targets alike. The traditional concept of 'enemy alien' is inapplicable in this conflict; instead of being affiliated with particular states that are at war with the United States, terrorist enemies are predominantly citizens and residents of friendly states or even the United States. The battlefield lacks a precise geographic location and arguably includes the United States. It is unclear how to conceptualize the defeat of terrorist organizations, and thus unclear how to conceptualize the end of the conflict. Uncertainty about whether and when the conflict will end, in turn, raises questions about the applicability of traditional powers to detain and try the enemy." Bradley & Goldsmith, *Congressional Authorization and the War on Terrorism*, 118 Harv.L.Rev. 2047, 2048–49 (2005).

Neither Justice Scalia nor Justice Thomas emphasized these differences from traditional wars. Instead, both of their dissents can be viewed as following an "agency" model of interpretation of the requirements of habeas corpus and due process, under which the judicial role is to carry out the Founding understanding. See Fallon & Meltzer, *Habeas Corpus Jurisdiction, Substantive Rights, and the War on Terror*, 120 Harv.L.Rev. 2029, 2040–42, 2080 (2007). But they reached diametrically opposed conclusions about the relevant history and about the requirements of due process.

The plurality, by contrast, adopted what might be viewed as a common law model, viewing Hamdi's detention as raising distinctive issues calling for a flexible adaptation of due process requirements to the circumstances presented by the armed conflict with al Qaeda and the Taliban. Justice O'Connor also noted a number of other contexts in which the Constitution authorizes detention outside of the criminal process. For a defense of the common law approach, see Fallon and Meltzer, *supra*.

---

[1]   The disagreement among the Justices is echoed by disagreement among scholars. Tyler, in *The Forgotten Core Meaning of the Suspension Clause*, 125 Harv.L.Rev. 901 (2012), reviews the history of the writ, and its suspension, from the Stuart period in England through the American Founding and up to the Civil War and Reconstruction. She concludes that persons owing allegiance to the government and thereby enjoying the protection of its laws—most especially citizens—could not, absent suspension, be detained domestically except by the normal criminal process. That understanding extended, she argues, to persons suspected of aiding the enemy. She supports her argument by noting instances in which suspension was undertaken to permit the seizure and detention, outside of the criminal process, of persons accused of "adhering to the king's enemies" or taking up arms against the King. Although most of her evidence involves persons seized within a nation's sovereign territory, she contends that the extraterritorial seizure of Hamdi did not deprive him of protection.

Professor Harrison, in *The Habeas Corpus Suspension Clause and the Right to Natural Liberty* (forthcoming), offers a quite different conclusion. He contends that neither the text of the Suspension Clause nor historical practice places citizens outside the scope of permissible detention, noting in particular that during the Revolutionary War, both the British and the Americans held captured citizens as prisoners of war. He also contends, based on his review of English and early American history, that the Suspension Clause, despite its language, is not primarily about habeas corpus but rather about a substantive right to natural liberty. At the Founding, he argues, the central concept of a suspension was a law that conferred on the executive extremely broad discretion to detain—whether or not the judicial remedy of habeas corpus remained intact, and whether or not the detainee was a citizen.

(3) Variations on a Theme: Aliens Versus Citizens, the Circumstances of Seizure, and the Location of Detention. The Hamdi case involved only one of a range of situations in which persons alleged to be enemy terrorists might contest the legality of their custody. The existence of habeas jurisdiction or the appropriate scope of habeas review may depend on (a) the location of detention, see pp. 1245–1249, *infra*; (b) whether the detainee is a citizen or an alien;[2] and (c) the location of seizure—for example, on or off a battlefield, or within or outside of the United States. For an effort to outline how these kinds of factors influence the exercise of habeas jurisdiction, see Fallon & Meltzer, *supra*.

(a) The Padilla Case. Jose Padilla, one of the few American citizens detained in connection with the war on terror, was arrested not on a foreign battlefield but rather when he arrived at O'Hare Airport from Pakistan. The government alleged that he had been armed in a combat zone in Afghanistan during fighting between the American military and Taliban and al Qaeda forces, and that, upon his escape to Pakistan, he was involved with al Qaeda operatives. Padilla's case engaged the attention of two different courts of appeals. One year before the Hamdi decision, the Second Circuit found Padilla's detention to be unlawful, holding that the President lacked inherent constitutional authority to detain Padilla, that the Non-Detention Act prohibited detention of a citizen captured on American soil absent specific statutory authorization, and that the AUMF did not provide such authorization. That decision, however, was vacated the following year by the Supreme Court for want of jurisdiction, see Rumsfeld v. Padilla, 542 U.S. 426 (2004), p. 1262, *infra*. Justice Stevens' dissent (joined by Justices Souter, Ginsburg, and Breyer) argued that jurisdiction existed, and then said briefly: "I believe that the Non-Detention Act, 18 U.S.C. § 4001(a), prohibits—and the [AUMF] does not authorize—the protracted, incommunicado detention of American citizens arrested in the United States."

Padilla's habeas proceedings then continued in South Carolina, and when the matter reached the Fourth Circuit, it ruled that there was no difference in principle between Hamdi and Padilla, both of whom allegedly fought against the United States in Afghanistan; although Padilla escaped capture on the battlefield, he would pose the same threat of returning to battle if not detained. Padilla v. Hanft, 423 F.3d 386, 391–92 (4th Cir.2005).

(b) The Al-Marri Case. In Al-Marri v. Pucciarelli, 534 F.3d 213 (4th Cir.2008) (en banc) (per curiam), a lawful resident alien seized in the United States and held by the military challenged the legality of his custody. Al-Marri disputed a government affidavit asserting that he was closely associated with al Qaeda and had come to this country as a sleeper agent. (Unlike Padilla and Hamdi, al-Marri was not alleged to have directly engaged in hostilities.) When his case reached the Fourth Circuit, sitting en banc, it held, 5–4, that the government's allegations, if true, established an adequate basis for detention.

The five judges in the majority expressed overlapping but differing points of view in four separate opinions. Among the themes voiced were these: neither the language nor the purpose of the AUMF is limited to

---

[2] For an argument that recent decisions considering military detention have focused unduly on whether a petitioner has legally cognizable rights, rather than on whether the custodian had lawful authority to detain, see Goldstein, *Habeas Without Rights*, 2007 Wis.L.Rev. 1165. Goldstein offers considerable evidence that historically the latter question was the focus of courts exercising habeas jurisdiction in both England and the United States.

persons who took hostile action on a battlefield; the scope of detention authorized by the AUMF, even if broader than that traditionally recognized by the laws of war, was justified in view of the dangers posed by stateless actors who target innocent civilians; and the opposing view would have prevented the government, had it apprehended the 9/11 hijackers in the United States before they could carry out their plans, from detaining them militarily. The four dissenters argued that detention was not authorized by the AUMF (or by principles of the laws of war that inform its interpretation); Al-Marri, they stressed, was neither a citizen of, nor affiliated with the armed forces of, any nation at war with the United States and never directly participated in hostilities against the United States; thus, al-Marri was a civilian, very much like Milligan.

(4) The Establishment of Combatant Status Review Tribunals (CSRTs). At the end of its opinion in Hamdi, the plurality stated: "There remains the possibility that the standards we have articulated could be met by an appropriately authorized and properly constituted military tribunal." Nine days after the Supreme Court's decision in Hamdi, the Department of Defense established Combatant Status Review Tribunals (CSRTs)—panels of three "neutral" military officers charged with reviewing, in the case of each alien detained at Guantánamo Bay, the government's initial determination that the individual could lawfully be detained as an enemy combatant.

In a decision handed down the same day as Hamdi, the Court held that the statutory grant of habeas jurisdiction in 28 U.S.C. § 2241 extended to aliens detained as enemy combatants at Guantánamo Bay. Rasul v. Bush, 542 U.S. 466 (2004), p. 1247, *infra*. But in 2005 and 2006, Congress enacted legislation designed to override the Rasul decision and to strip federal (and state) courts of habeas or other jurisdiction to entertain challenges by aliens to the legality of their detention as enemy combatants, except as provided under a review procedure established by the Detainee Treatment Act of 2005. That Act authorized limited review, in the D.C. Circuit, of decisions of the CSRTs. See pp. 1198–1199, *supra*. Apart from such review, § 7 of the Military Commission Act of 2006 purported to strip the federal and state courts of habeas or other jurisdiction to review the legality of detention.

After enactment of the jurisdiction-stripping provisions, the government moved to dismiss pending habeas petitions that had been filed by detainees. The question of the effect of the jurisdiction-stripping provisions reached the Supreme Court in the next principal case, Boumediene v. Bush, in which the Court faced two principal issues. The first was whether the Suspension Clause's guarantee of habeas review (or of an adequate substitute therefor) extended to aliens detained as enemy combatants at the U.S. Naval Base in Guantánamo Bay, Cuba, located as it is outside the de jure territorial sovereignty of the United States. Dividing 5–4, the Supreme Court held that the Suspension Clause did reach those aliens. That aspect of the decision is discussed at pp. 1249–1261, *infra*.

The second question was whether the legal structure in place for those detainees—limited review by the D.C. Circuit of CSRT determinations—provided an adequate substitute for the review guaranteed by the Suspension Clause. The following presents those portions of the Boumediene opinion addressing that second question.

Boumediene v. Bush

553 U.S. 723, 128 S.Ct. 2229, 171 L.Ed.2d 41 (2008).
Certiorari to the United States Court of Appeals for the District of Columbia Circuit.

■ JUSTICE KENNEDY delivered the opinion of the Court.

Petitioners are aliens designated as enemy combatants and detained at the United States Naval Station at Guantánamo Bay, Cuba. * * *

Petitioners present a question not resolved by our earlier cases * * * : whether they have the constitutional privilege of habeas corpus, a privilege not to be withdrawn except in conformance with the Suspension Clause, Art. I, § 9, cl. 2. We hold these petitioners do have the habeas corpus privilege. Congress has enacted a statute, the Detainee Treatment Act of 2005 (DTA), 119 Stat. 2739, that provides certain procedures for review of the detainees' status. We hold that those procedures are not an adequate and effective substitute for habeas corpus. Therefore § 7 of the Military Commissions Act of 2006 (MCA), 28 U.S.C.A. § 2241(e) [(Supp. 2007), which purports to strip the federal and state courts of habeas corpus jurisdiction,] operates as an unconstitutional suspension of the writ. * * *

I

* * * [All of the petitioners] are foreign nationals, but none is a citizen of a nation now at war with the United States. Each denies he is a member of the al Qaeda terrorist network that carried out the September 11 attacks or of the Taliban regime that provided sanctuary for al Qaeda. Each petitioner appeared before a separate CSRT; was determined to be an enemy combatant; and has sought a writ of habeas corpus in the United States District Court for the District of Columbia.

[After the Supreme Court's decision in Rasul v. Bush, 542 U.S. 466 (2004), which had interpreted the basic grant of habeas corpus jurisdiction in 28 U.S.C. § 2241 as extending to petitions filed by aliens detained as suspected terrorists at the American military base at Guantánamo Bay, Cuba, petitioners' cases were remanded. In 2005, Congress passed the DTA, subsection 1005(e) of which amended § 2241] to provide that "no court, justice, or judge shall have jurisdiction to hear or consider . . . an application for a writ of habeas corpus filed by or on behalf of an alien detained by the Department of Defense at Guantánamo Bay, Cuba." Section 1005 further provides that the Court of Appeals for the District of Columbia Circuit shall have "exclusive" jurisdiction to review decisions of the CSRTs.

[In 2006, Congress enacted the MCA, 10 U.S.C.A. § 948a et seq. (Supp. 2007), which again amended § 2241 so as to eliminate habeas corpus jurisdiction for cases like those of petitioners. * * *]

[* * * The Court of Appeals held that MCA § 7 must be read to strip it, and all federal courts, of jurisdiction to consider petitioners' habeas corpus petitions; that petitioners are not entitled to the privilege of the writ or the protections of the Suspension Clause; and, as a result, that it was unnecessary to consider whether Congress provided an adequate and effective substitute for habeas corpus in the DTA.]

We granted certiorari.

* * *

[In Parts II–IV of its opinion, which are found at pp. 1249–1258, *infra*, the Court held that although Congress purported to withdraw habeas corpus jurisdiction from the federal courts, aliens detained at Guantánamo Bay as suspected enemy combatants have a right under the Suspension Clause to habeas corpus review of the legality of their detention.]

V

In light of this holding the question becomes whether * * * Congress has provided adequate substitute procedures for habeas corpus. The Government submits there has been compliance with the Suspension Clause because the [review process in the D.C. Circuit authorized by the Detainee Treatment Act] provides an adequate substitute. Congress has granted that court jurisdiction to consider

"(i) whether the status determination of the [Combatant Status Review Tribunal] . . . was consistent with the standards and procedures specified by the Secretary of Defense . . . and (ii) to the extent the Constitution and laws of the United States are applicable, whether the use of such standards and procedures to make the determination is consistent with the Constitution and laws of the United States." § 1005(e)(2)(c), 119 Stat. 2742.

The Court of Appeals * * * found it unnecessary to consider whether an adequate substitute has been provided. [Although our normal practice would be to remand to permit the Court of Appeals to consider this question in the first instance, in exceptional circumstances we may appropriately depart from that practice.]

The gravity of the separation-of-powers issues raised by these cases and the fact that these detainees have been denied meaningful access to a judicial forum for a period of years render these cases exceptional. * * *

A

Our case law does not contain extensive discussion of standards defining suspension of the writ or of circumstances under which suspension has occurred. * * *

The two leading cases addressing habeas substitutes, Swain v. Pressley, 430 U.S. 372 (1977), and United States v. Hayman, 342 U.S. 205 (1952) * * * provide little guidance here. [Those cases considered statutory procedures designed as a substitute for *postconviction* habeas review; the procedures sought to mirror the scope of inquiry on habeas, while prescribing, for administrative reasons, a different procedural form that funneled applications into a different court. Moreover, both statutes provided that habeas jurisdiction remained available if the alternative process proved inadequate or ineffective.]

Unlike in Hayman and Swain, * * * the DTA and the MCA * * * were intended to circumscribe habeas review. * * *

[Under the DTA, t]he Court of Appeals has jurisdiction not to inquire into the legality of the detention generally but only to assess whether the CSRT complied with the "standards and procedures specified by the Secretary of Defense" and whether those standards and procedures are lawful. If Congress had envisioned DTA review as coextensive with traditional habeas corpus, it would not have drafted the statute in this manner. [And instead of preserving habeas review as a last resort, as in

Swain and Hayman,] MCA § 7 eliminates habeas review for these petitioners.

[The Court noted that a habeas court can engage in factfinding, and that even a petition initially filed with a Justice or a circuit judge can be transferred to a district court for factfinding.] By granting the Court of Appeals "exclusive" jurisdiction over petitioners' cases, Congress has foreclosed that option. This choice indicates Congress intended the Court of Appeals to have a more limited role in enemy combatant status determinations than a district court has in habeas corpus proceedings. The DTA should be interpreted to accord some latitude to the Court of Appeals to fashion procedures necessary to make its review function a meaningful one, but, if congressional intent is to be respected, the procedures adopted cannot be as extensive or as protective of the rights of the detainees as they would be in a § 2241 proceeding. Otherwise there would have been no, or very little, purpose for enacting the DTA.

* * *

B

We do not endeavor to offer a comprehensive summary of the requisites for an adequate substitute for habeas corpus. We do consider it uncontroversial, however, that the privilege of habeas corpus entitles the prisoner to a meaningful opportunity to demonstrate that he is being held pursuant to "the erroneous application or interpretation" of relevant law. St. Cyr, 533 U.S., at 302. And the habeas court must have the power to order the conditional release of an individual unlawfully detained * * *. * * * [D]epending on the circumstances, more may be required.

Indeed, common-law habeas corpus was, above all, an adaptable remedy. Its precise application and scope changed depending upon the circumstances. It appears the common-law habeas court's role was most extensive in cases of pretrial and noncriminal detention, where there had been little or no previous judicial review of the cause for detention. Notably, the black-letter rule that prisoners could not controvert facts in the jailer's return was not followed (or at least not with consistency) in such cases. [Citing authorities.]

[Evidence from 19th-century American sources indicates that habeas courts] routinely allowed prisoners to introduce exculpatory evidence that was either unknown or previously unavailable to the prisoner. [Citing authorities.] * * *

The idea that the necessary scope of habeas review in part depends upon the rigor of any earlier proceedings accords with our test for procedural adequacy in the due process context. See Mathews v. Eldridge, 424 U.S. 319, 335 (1976) (noting that the Due Process Clause requires an assessment of, *inter alia*, "the risk of an erroneous deprivation of [a liberty interest;] and the probable value, if any, of additional or substitute procedural safeguards"). This principle has an established foundation in habeas corpus jurisprudence as well, as Chief Justice Marshall's opinion in Ex parte Watkins, 3 Pet. 193 (1830), demonstrates. * * * Watkins sought a writ of habeas corpus after being imprisoned pursuant to a judgment of a District of Columbia court. In holding that the judgment stood on "high ground," 3 Pet., at 209, the Chief Justice emphasized [that the original judgment had been issued by] a "court of record, having general jurisdiction over criminal cases."

Id., at 203. In contrast to "inferior" tribunals of limited jurisdiction, ibid., courts of record had broad remedial powers, which gave the habeas court greater confidence in the judgment's validity.

* * *

Where a person is detained by executive order, rather than, say, after being tried and convicted in a court, the need for collateral review is most pressing. A criminal conviction in the usual course occurs after a judicial hearing before a tribunal disinterested in the outcome and committed to procedures designed to ensure its own independence. These dynamics are not inherent in executive detention orders or executive review procedures. * * * The intended duration of the detention and the reasons for it bear upon the precise scope of the inquiry. Habeas corpus proceedings need not resemble a criminal trial, even when the detention is by executive order. But * * * [t]he habeas court must have sufficient authority to conduct a meaningful review of both the cause for detention and the Executive's power to detain.

To determine the necessary scope of habeas corpus review, therefore, we must assess the CSRT process * * *. Whether one characterizes the CSRT process as direct review of the Executive's battlefield determination that the detainee is an enemy combatant—as the parties have and as we do—or as the first step in the collateral review of a battlefield determination makes no difference in a proper analysis of whether the procedures Congress put in place are an adequate substitute for habeas corpus. * * *

[Earlier in his opinion, Justice Kennedy had emphasized the limited procedural protections afforded to detainees in CSRT hearings, including the fact that the "Personal Representative" assigned to assist a detainee does not serve as counsel or even as an advocate and that the government's evidence is given a presumption of validity.]

Petitioners identify what they see as myriad deficiencies in the CSRTs. The most relevant for our purposes are the constraints upon the detainee's ability to rebut the factual basis for the Government's assertion that he is an enemy combatant. As already noted, at the CSRT stage the detainee has limited means to find or present evidence to challenge the Government's case against him. He does not have the assistance of counsel and may not be aware of the most critical allegations that the Government relied upon to order his detention. The detainee can confront witnesses that testify during the CSRT proceedings. But given that there are in effect no limits on the admission of hearsay evidence—the only requirement is that the tribunal deem the evidence "relevant and helpful"—the detainee's opportunity to question witnesses is likely to be more theoretical than real.

The Government [argues that the CSRT] was designed to conform to the procedures suggested by the plurality in Hamdi. Setting aside the fact that the relevant language in Hamdi did not garner a majority of the Court, it does not control the matter at hand. * * * [There, t]he § 2241 habeas corpus process remained in place. Accordingly, the plurality concentrated on whether the Executive had the authority to detain and, if so, what rights the detainee had under the Due Process Clause. True, there are places in the Hamdi plurality opinion where it is difficult to tell where its extrapolation of § 2241 ends and its analysis of the petitioner's

Due Process rights begins. But the Court had no occasion to define the necessary scope of habeas review, for Suspension Clause purposes, in the context of enemy combatant detentions. The closest the plurality came to doing so was in discussing whether, in light of separation-of-powers concerns, § 2241 should be construed to forbid the District Court from inquiring beyond the affidavit Hamdi's custodian provided in answer to the detainee's habeas petition. The plurality answered this question with an emphatic "no."

Even if we were to assume that the CSRTs satisfy due process standards, it would not end our inquiry. Habeas corpus is a collateral process that exists, in Justice Holmes' words, to "cu[t] through all forms and g[o] to the very tissue of the structure. It comes in from the outside, not in subordination to the proceedings, and although every form may have been preserved opens the inquiry whether they have been more than an empty shell." Frank v. Mangum, 237 U.S. 309, 346 (1915) (dissenting opinion). Even when the procedures authorizing detention are structurally sound, the Suspension Clause remains applicable and the writ relevant. * * *

Although we make no judgment as to whether the CSRTs, as currently constituted, satisfy due process standards, we agree with petitioners that * * * there is considerable risk of error in the tribunal's findings of fact. * * * And given that the consequence of error may be detention of persons for the duration of hostilities that may last a generation or more, this is a risk too significant to ignore.

For the writ of habeas corpus, or its substitute, to function as an effective and proper remedy in this context, the court that conducts the habeas proceeding must have the means to correct errors that occurred during the CSRT proceedings. This includes some authority to assess the sufficiency of the Government's evidence against the detainee. It also must have the authority to admit and consider relevant exculpatory evidence that was not introduced during the earlier proceeding. Federal habeas petitioners long have had the means to supplement the record on review, even in the postconviction habeas setting. Here that opportunity is constitutionally required.

Consistent with the historic function and province of the writ, habeas corpus review may be more circumscribed if the underlying detention proceedings are more thorough than they were here. In two habeas cases involving enemy aliens tried for war crimes, In re Yamashita, 327 U.S. 1 (1946), and Ex parte Quirin, 317 U.S. 1 (1942), for example, this Court limited its review to determining whether the Executive had legal authority to try the petitioners by military commission. * * * [However,] the proceedings in Yamashita and Quirin, like those in Eisentrager, had an adversarial structure that is lacking here.

The extent of the showing required of the Government in these cases is a matter to be determined. We need not explore it further at this stage. We do hold that when the judicial power to issue habeas corpus properly is invoked the judicial officer must have adequate authority to make a determination in light of the relevant law and facts and to formulate and issue appropriate orders for relief, including, if necessary, an order directing the prisoner's release.

C

We now consider whether the DTA allows the Court of Appeals to conduct a proceeding meeting these standards. [We must construe the statute to avoid constitutional problems where possible, but we] cannot ignore the text and purpose of a statute in order to save it.

The DTA does not explicitly empower the Court of Appeals to order the applicant * * * released * * *. Yet, for present purposes, we can assume congressional silence permits a constitutionally required remedy. In that case it would be possible to hold that a remedy of release is impliedly provided for. The DTA might be read, furthermore, to allow the petitioners to assert most, if not all, of the legal claims they seek to advance, including their most basic claim: that the President has no authority under the AUMF to detain them indefinitely. * * *

* * * The more difficult question is whether the DTA permits the Court of Appeals to make requisite findings of fact. * * *

Assuming the DTA can be construed to allow the Court of Appeals to review or correct the CSRT's factual determinations, as opposed to merely certifying that the tribunal applied the correct standard of proof, we see no way to construe the statute to allow what is also constitutionally required in this context: an opportunity for the detainee to present relevant exculpatory evidence that was not made part of the record in the earlier proceedings.

On its face the statute allows the Court of Appeals to consider no evidence outside the CSRT record. In the parallel litigation, however, the Court of Appeals determined that the DTA allows it to order the production of all " 'reasonably available information in the possession of the U.S. Government bearing on the issue of whether the detainee meets the criteria to be designated as an enemy combatant,' " regardless of whether this evidence was put before the CSRT. See Bismullah v. Gates (I), 501 F.3d 178, 180 (D.C. Cir. 2007). * * * [Even assuming the correctness of that determination,] the DTA review proceeding falls short of being a constitutionally adequate substitute, for the detainee still would have no opportunity to present evidence discovered after the CSRT proceedings concluded.

* * * [N]ewly discovered evidence * * * may be critical to the detainee's argument that he is not an enemy combatant and there is no cause to detain him.

This is not a remote hypothetical. One of the petitioners, Mohamed Nechla, requested at his CSRT hearing that the Government contact his employer. The petitioner claimed the employer would corroborate Nechla's contention he had no affiliation with al Qaeda. Although the CSRT determined this testimony would be relevant, it also found the witness was not reasonably available to testify at the time of the hearing. Petitioner's counsel, however, now represents the witness is available to be heard. If a detainee can present reasonably available evidence demonstrating there is no basis for his continued detention, he must have the opportunity to present this evidence to a habeas corpus court. * * *

[In postconviction cases, where the prisoner had a full and fair opportunity to develop the factual predicate of his claims, foreclosing consideration of evidence not previously presented may be appropriate. But here,] where the underlying detention proceedings lack the necessary adversarial character, the detainee cannot be held responsible for all deficiencies in the record.

The Government * * * [points out] that if a detainee obtains such evidence, he can request that the Deputy Secretary of Defense convene a new CSRT. Whatever the merits of this procedure, it is an insufficient replacement for the factual review these detainees are entitled to receive through habeas corpus. The Deputy Secretary's determination whether to initiate new proceedings is wholly a discretionary one. And we see no way to construe the DTA to allow a detainee to challenge the Deputy Secretary's decision not to open a new CSRT * * *. * * *

We do not imply DTA review would be a constitutionally sufficient replacement for habeas corpus but for these limitations on the detainee's ability to present exculpatory evidence. For even if it were possible * * * to read into the statute each of the necessary procedures we have identified, * * * the cumulative effect of [holding] that the detainees at Guantánamo may, under the DTA, challenge the President's legal authority to detain them, contest the CSRT's findings of fact, supplement the record on review with exculpatory evidence, and request an order of release would come close to reinstating the § 2241 habeas corpus process Congress sought to deny them. The language of the statute, read in light of Congress' reasons for enacting it, cannot bear this interpretation. * * *

Although we do not hold that an adequate substitute must duplicate § 2241 in all respects, it suffices that the Government has not established that the detainees' access to the statutory review provisions at issue is an adequate substitute for the writ of habeas corpus. MCA § 7 thus effects an unconstitutional suspension of the writ. In view of our holding we need not discuss the reach of the writ with respect to claims of unlawful conditions of treatment or confinement.

VI

A

* * * [T]he question remains whether there are prudential barriers to habeas corpus review under these circumstances.

The Government argues petitioners must seek review of their CSRT determinations in the Court of Appeals before they can proceed with their habeas corpus actions in the District Court. [We have required exhaustion of alternative remedies not only by state prisoners, whose cases present federalism concerns, but also by defendants in federal court-martial proceedings.]

[It likely would be an impractical and unprecedented extension of judicial power to make habeas corpus available at the moment a foreign citizen is detained abroad by the Executive.] * * * [P]roper deference can be accorded to reasonable procedures for screening and initial detention under lawful and proper conditions of confinement and treatment for a reasonable period of time. * * *

The cases before us, however, do not involve detainees who have been held for a short period of time while awaiting their CSRT determinations. * * * To require these detainees to complete DTA review before proceeding with their habeas corpus actions would be to require additional months, if not years, of delay. The first DTA review applications were filed over a year ago, but no decisions on the merits have been issued. While some delay in fashioning new procedures is unavoidable, the costs of delay can no longer be borne by those who are held in custody. The detainees in these cases are entitled to a prompt habeas corpus hearing.

* * * The only law we identify as unconstitutional is MCA § 7. Accordingly, both the DTA and the CSRT process remain intact. Our holding with regard to exhaustion should not be read to imply that a habeas court should intervene the moment an enemy combatant steps foot in a territory where the writ runs. The Executive is entitled to a reasonable period of time to determine a detainee's status before a court entertains that detainee's habeas corpus petition. The CSRT process is the mechanism Congress and the President set up to deal with these issues. Except in cases of undue delay, federal courts should refrain from entertaining an enemy combatant's habeas corpus petition at least until after the Department, acting via the CSRT, has had a chance to review his status.

B

[The Suspension Clause permits accommodations to reduce the burden habeas corpus proceedings place on the military without impermissibly diluting the protections of the writ. The DTA sought to consolidate review in the D.C. Circuit, and consolidating future cases in one district would reduce burdens on the government. This legitimate objective might be advanced even without an amendment to § 2241, and should a detainee file a petition in another district with jurisdiction, the Government can move to change venue to the District of Columbia.]

* * * We make no attempt to anticipate all of the evidentiary and access-to-counsel issues that will arise during the course of the detainees' habeas corpus proceedings. We recognize, however, that the Government has a legitimate interest in protecting sources and methods of intelligence gathering; and we expect that the District Court will use its discretion to accommodate this interest to the greatest extent possible.

* * *

[In considering the procedural and substantive standards used to impose detention in order to prevent terrorist acts, the Executive, which, unlike the judiciary, has access to intelligence, should be accorded substantial deference. But security depends not only on the actions of intelligence and military officials, but also on] fidelity to freedom's first principles. Chief among these are freedom from arbitrary and unlawful restraint and the personal liberty that is secured by adherence to the separation of powers. * * *

* * *

* * * The judgment of the Court of Appeals is reversed. The cases are remanded to the Court of Appeals with instructions that it remand the cases to the District Court for proceedings consistent with this opinion.

It is so ordered.[*]

---

[*] [Ed.] In a concurring opinion joined by Justices Ginsburg and Breyer, Justice Souter said that in light of the duration for which some of the petitioners had already been detained, the dissents had a "hollow ring" when suggesting "that the Court is somehow precipitating the Judiciary into reviewing claims that the military (subject to appeal to the Court of Appeals for the District of Columbia Circuit) could handle within some reasonable period of time."

■ CHIEF JUSTICE ROBERTS, with whom JUSTICE SCALIA, JUSTICE THOMAS, and JUSTICE ALITO join, dissenting.

Today the Court strikes down as inadequate the most generous set of procedural protections ever afforded aliens detained by this country as enemy combatants, * * * without bothering to say what due process rights the detainees possess, without explaining how the statute fails to vindicate those rights, and before a single petitioner has even attempted to avail himself of the law's operation. And to what effect? The majority merely replaces a review system designed by the people's representatives with a set of shapeless procedures to be defined by federal courts at some future date. One cannot help but think, after surveying the modest practical results of the majority's ambitious opinion, that this decision is not really about the detainees at all, but about control of federal policy regarding enemy combatants.

* * * I regard the issue [whether the detainees are entitled to the protections of habeas corpus] as a difficult one, primarily because of the unique and unusual jurisdictional status of Guantánamo Bay. * * * The important point for me, however, is that the Court should have resolved these cases on other grounds. * * * The critical threshold question in these cases * * * is whether the system the political branches designed protects whatever rights the detainees may possess. If so, there is no need for any additional process * * *.

* * * [T]he habeas process the Court mandates will most likely end up looking a lot like the DTA system it replaces, as the district court judges shaping it will have to reconcile review of the prisoners' detention with the undoubted need to protect the American people from the terrorist threat—precisely the challenge Congress undertook in drafting the DTA. All that today's opinion has done is shift responsibility for those sensitive foreign policy and national security decisions from the elected branches to the Federal Judiciary.

I believe the system the political branches constructed adequately protects any constitutional rights aliens captured abroad and detained as enemy combatants may enjoy. I therefore would dismiss these cases on that ground. * * *

I

[The Court should have declined to intervene until petitioners had exhausted their remedies in the D.C. Circuit under the DTA. In Hamdi v. Rumsfeld, 542 U.S. 507, 533 (2004), a case involving detention of a citizen, the plurality stated that constitutionally adequate process could be provided "by an appropriately authorized and properly constituted military tribunal."] * * *

If the CSRT procedures meet the minimal due process requirements outlined in Hamdi, and if an Article III court is available to ensure that these procedures are followed in future cases, there is no need to reach the Suspension Clause question. * * *

[In response to the Court's concern that exhausting DTA review could cause undue delay, Chief Justice Roberts contended that the unsettled nature of the habeas remedy ordered by the Court will generate litigation followed by appeals to the D.C. Circuit]—exactly where judicial review *starts* under Congress's system. * * *

II

The majority's overreaching is particularly egregious given the weakness of its objections to the DTA. * * * [The existing system] is adequate to vindicate whatever due process rights petitioners may have.

A

[The CSRTs are a means for challenging the Government's initial determination of enemy combatant status, based on the very Army Regulation that] the plurality in Hamdi said provided the type of process an enemy combatant could expect from a habeas court. The CSRTs operate much as habeas courts would if hearing the detainee's collateral challenge for the first time * * *. * * *

* * * The majority attempts to dismiss Hamdi's relevance by arguing that because the availability of § 2241 federal habeas was never in doubt in that case, "the Court had no occasion to define the necessary scope of habeas review * * *." Hardly. Hamdi was all about the scope of habeas review in the context of enemy combatant detentions. * * *

B

* * *

By virtue of its refusal to allow the D.C. Circuit to assess petitioners' statutory remedies, and by virtue of its own refusal to consider, at the outset, the fit between those remedies and due process, the majority now finds itself in the position of evaluating whether the DTA system is an adequate substitute for habeas review without knowing what rights either habeas or the DTA is supposed to protect. * * *

The scope of federal habeas review is traditionally more limited in some contexts than in others, depending on the status of the detainee and the rights he may assert. See St. Cyr, 533 U.S., at 306 ("In [immigration cases], other than the question whether there was some evidence to support the [deportation] order, the courts generally did not review factual determinations made by the Executive" (footnote omitted)); Burns v. Wilson, 346 U.S. 137, 139 (1953) (plurality opinion) ("[I]n military habeas corpus the inquiry, the scope of matters open for review, has always been more narrow than in civil cases"); In re Yamashita, 327 U.S. 1, 8 (1946) (" * * * If the military tribunals have lawful authority to hear, decide and condemn, their action is not subject to judicial review"); Ex parte Quirin, 317 U.S. 1, 25 (1942) (federal habeas review of military commission verdict limited to determining commission's jurisdiction).

* * * We have said that "at the absolute minimum," the Suspension Clause protects the writ " 'as it existed in 1789.' " St. Cyr, supra, at 301 (quoting Felker v. Turpin, 518 U.S. 651, 663–664 (1996)). The majority admits that a number of historical authorities suggest that at the time of the Constitution's ratification, "common-law courts abstained altogether from matters involving prisoners of war." If this is accurate, the process provided prisoners under the DTA is plainly more than sufficient * * *.

Assuming the constitutional baseline is more robust, the DTA still provides adequate process * * *. * * *

C

[The Court complains that (i) the right to confront witnesses before the CSRT is "more theoretical than real" because hearsay evidence may be admitted, (ii) petitioners lack the assistance of counsel, and (iii) petitioners may be unaware, because of their restricted access to classified information, of the most critical allegations against them.] None of these complaints is persuasive.

[Detainees may call any witness who is "reasonably available", a standard drawn from Army Regulations that permits the government to avoid a futile search for evidence that might burden the military. And Hamdi expressly approved the use of hearsay evidence.]

[The access to classified information afforded to the detainee's Personal Representative, and to counsel on appeal, is broader than that ever before provided to alleged alien enemy combatants. Prisoners of war who challenge status determinations under the Geneva Convention enjoy no such access and have no right to assistance from counsel or from a personal representative.]

Keep in mind that all this is just at the CSRT stage. [Before the D.C. Circuit, detainees have counsel and the right to challenge the factual and legal bases of their detentions.] * * *

D

Despite these guarantees, the Court finds the DTA system an inadequate habeas substitute, for one central reason: Detainees are unable to introduce at the appeal stage exculpatory evidence discovered after the conclusion of their CSRT proceedings. The Court hints darkly that the DTA may suffer from other infirmities, but it does not bother to name them, making a response a bit difficult. * * *

[If new evidence materializes after the CSRT's determination but before review in the Court of Appeals, the DTA permits the D.C. Circuit to remand for a new CSRT determination.]

If that sort of procedure sounds familiar, it should. Federal appellate courts reviewing factual determinations follow just such a procedure in a variety of circumstances.

A remand is not the only relief available for detainees caught in the Court's hypothetical conundrum. The DTA expressly directs the Secretary of Defense to "provide for periodic review of any new evidence that may become available relating to the enemy combatant status of a detainee." DTA § 1005(a)(3). Regulations issued by the Department of Defense provide that when a detainee puts forward new, material evidence "not previously presented to the detainee's CSRT, the Deputy Secretary of Defense 'will direct that a CSRT convene to reconsider the basis of the detainee's . . . status in light of the new information.' " * * *[2]

* * *

The Court's hand wringing over the DTA's treatment of later-discovered exculpatory evidence is the most it has to show after a roving search for constitutionally problematic scenarios. * * * The Court today invents a sort of reverse facial challenge and applies it with gusto: If

---

[2] The Court wonders what might happen if the detainee puts forward new material evidence but the Deputy Secretary refuses to convene a new CSRT. The answer is that the detainee can petition the D.C. Circuit for review. The DTA directs that the procedures for review of new evidence be included among "[t]he procedures submitted under paragraph (1)(A)" governing CSRT review of enemy combatant status[.] § 1405(a)(3), 119 Stat. 3476. It is undisputed that the D.C. Circuit has statutory authority to review and enforce these procedures.

there is *any* scenario in which the statute *might* be constitutionally infirm, the law must be struck down. * * *

E

[The DTA can and should be read to authorize the Court of Appeals to order release, which is consistent with the text and avoids serious constitutional difficulty.] * * *

The basis for the Court's [conclusion that the DTA system is not an adequate substitute for habeas] is summed up in the following sentence near the end of its opinion: "To hold that the detainees at Guantánamo may, under the DTA, challenge the President's legal authority to detain them, contest the CSRT's findings of fact, supplement the record on review with newly discovered or previously unavailable evidence, and request an order of release would come close to reinstating the § 2241 habeas corpus process Congress sought to deny them." In other words, any interpretation of the statute that would make it an adequate substitute for habeas must be rejected, because Congress could not possibly have intended to enact an adequate substitute for habeas. The Court could have saved itself a lot of trouble if it had simply announced this Catch-22 approach at the beginning rather than the end of its opinion.

III

For all its eloquence about the detainees' right to the writ, the Court makes no effort to elaborate how exactly the remedy it prescribes will differ from the procedural protections * * * under the DTA. * * * [The Court] simply ignores the many difficult questions its holding presents. What, for example, will become of the CSRT process? The majority says federal courts should generally refrain from entertaining detainee challenges until after the petitioner's CSRT proceeding has finished. But to what deference, if any, is that CSRT determination entitled?

There are other problems. Take witness availability. What makes the majority think witnesses will become magically available when the review procedure is labeled "habeas"? Will the location of most of these witnesses change—will they suddenly become easily susceptible to service of process? Or will subpoenas issued by American habeas courts run to Basra? * * * [W]ill detainees be able to call active-duty military officers as witnesses? If not, why not?

The majority has no answers for these difficulties. What it does say leaves open the distinct possibility that its "habeas" remedy will, when all is said and done, end up looking a great deal like the DTA review it rejects. * * *

* * *

So who has won? Not the detainees. The Court's analysis leaves them with only the prospect of further litigation to determine the content of their new habeas right, followed by further litigation to resolve their particular cases, followed by further litigation before the D.C. Circuit— where they could have started had they invoked the DTA procedure. Not Congress, whose attempt to "determine—through democratic means— how best" to balance the security of the American people with the detainees' liberty interests, has been unceremoniously brushed aside. Not the Great Writ, whose majesty is hardly enhanced by its extension to a jurisdictionally quirky outpost, with no tangible benefit to anyone. Not the rule of law, unless by that is meant the rule of lawyers, who will now arguably have a greater role than military and intelligence officials in shaping policy for alien enemy combatants. And certainly not the American people, who today lose a bit more control over the conduct of this Nation's foreign policy to unelected, politically unaccountable judges.

I respectfully dissent.

NOTE ON BOUMEDIENE V. BUSH AND THE CONSTITUTIONALLY REQUIRED SCOPE OF HABEAS REVIEW

(1) The Adequacy of DTA Review. Chief Justice Roberts complains that while the majority "hints darkly" that the DTA may have other infirmities, the only one plainly found was the inability of the D.C. Circuit to consider exculpatory evidence that materializes after conclusion of the CSRT process. Was that a sufficient basis for a broad holding that the DTA is not an adequate substitute for habeas corpus—even for petitioners who do not wish to present such evidence? When a petitioner seeks to proffer such evidence, the Court could have interpreted § 1005(a)(3) of the DTA, which requires that CSRT procedures "shall provide for periodic review of any new evidence that may become available relating to the enemy combatant status of a detainee," as *requiring* reconsideration by a CSRT—thereby overriding the Defense Department's regulation that made the decision to reconsider discretionary.

Alternatively, the majority might have held that exculpatory evidence could be presented to a special master in accordance with Fed.R.App.Proc. 48, which specifically authorizes a court of appeals to appoint a special master to recommend factual findings in matters ancillary to proceedings in the appellate court, and expressly contemplates that the master can be a judge. Does the exclusivity of the D.C. Circuit's jurisdiction under the DTA plainly foreclose reliance on the normal rules of appellate procedure—especially if such foreclosure raises constitutional concerns?

(2) The Quality of CSRT Proceedings. Although the Court focused on the detainee's inability to introduce exculpatory evidence, it may have had broader concerns about the process by which enemy combatant status was determined.

(a) Two critical descriptions of that process, both publicly available, raised numerous objections to the CRST proceedings, including the following:

(1) The information used to prepare files for CSRT proceedings was often generic, outdated intelligence not relating to individual detainees, prepared by officials who sometimes lacked access to pertinent information and often lacked the capacity to evaluate the information they did have;

(2) Evidence presented lacked detail, was generalized, and was presented in passive form without identifying the source, but the government's evidence was nonetheless presumed to be reliable and valid;

(3) There was reason to doubt whether other government agencies met their obligation to furnish exculpatory information for use before the CSRTs;

(4) In almost every case, the government's evidence was exclusively documentary but was not presented to the detainee before the hearing, and the detainee was given only a conclusory summary of classified evidence;

(5) The detainee's personal representative did not participate in any meaningful way; and

(6) When a panel found an individual was not an enemy combatant, it was questioned and ordered to re-open the hearing, or the government convened a new CSRT (and in one case, a third CSRT after two negative determinations), and the second (or third) CSRT found the detainee to be an enemy combatant. See Declaration of Lt. Col. Stephen Abraham, an intelligence officer assigned to the Office for the Administrative Review of the Detention of Enemy Combatants, found in Reply to Opposition to Petition for Rehearing at i-viii, Al Odah v. United States, 551 U.S. 1161 (2007); Denbeaux et al., *No-Hearing Hearings—CSRT: The Modern Habeas Corpus? An Analysis of the Proceedings of the Government's Combatant Status Review Tribunals at Guantánamo*, http://law.shu.edu/news/final_no_ hearing_hearings_report.pdf, later published as edited in Denbeaux et al., *No-Hearing Hearings: An Analysis of the Proceedings of the Combatant Status Review Tribunals at Guantánamo*, 41 Seton Hall L.Rev. 1231 (2011). There is reason to believe that at least one of these descriptions may have influenced the Court.[1]

(b) Chief Justice Roberts says that federal appellate courts reviewing factual determinations routinely remand cases to permit the tribunal that initially decided the case to consider new evidence in the first instance. The examples that he provides, however, involve remands to district courts. Doesn't the attractiveness of the remand option depend upon the faith one has that the tribunal to which the case is being returned will respond appropriately to any court order?

In this regard, Chief Justice Roberts mentions more than once that the procedures followed by CSRTs are rooted in the plurality's decision in the Hamdi case, which suggested that due process might be provided by an appropriately constituted military panel. The majority's effort to respond is a bit hard to understand. But might Justices Kennedy and Breyer, who both joined the plurality opinion in Hamdi and were in the majority in Boumediene, have lost faith over the course of four years in the approach that Hamdi described and, more particularly, in the reliability of the CSRT determinations? Would concerns like these adequately answer the dissenters' accusations that the majority was essentially engaged in a power grab?

For discussion of these issues, see Meltzer, *Habeas Corpus, Suspension, and Guantánamo: The Boumediene Decision*, 2008 Sup.Ct.Rev. 1.

(3) Unanswered Questions About the Scope of Habeas Review. The Court's opinion leaves unanswered a large number of questions concerning the scope of the constitutional entitlement to habeas corpus.

(a) At various times the Court refers to practice under § 2241 in assessing the adequacy of review under the DTA. Note, however, that

---

[1] On April 2, 2007, the Supreme Court denied the petition for certiorari filed by the detainees—over the dissent of Justice Breyer, joined by Justice Souter and in part by Justice Ginsburg. 549 U.S. 1328. In an extraordinary reversal, on June 29, 2007, the Court granted rehearing, vacated the April 2 order, and granted certiorari. The petitioners' Reply Brief in support of their Petition for Rehearing prominently featured the Abraham declaration.

Congress may vest broader jurisdiction by statute than is required by the Suspension Clause—a point the Court seemed to acknowledge when stating: "we do not hold that an adequate substitute must duplicate § 2241 in all respects". Is the constitutional entitlement to be measured by practice at the time of the Founding (to the extent that can be determined)? By evolving practice over time in dealing with captives during wartime? By a judicial calculus that might view the struggle against terrorism as not necessarily fitting neatly within the paradigms of either war or crime?

(b) Although the historical materials concerning the scope of review are anything but clear, several themes emerge from the history. First, precedents often state that habeas review is limited to questions of jurisdiction. However, decisional law, especially in recent times, has stretched the notion of jurisdiction, thereby making it difficult at times to distinguish jurisdiction from the legal merits. Second, as the majority notes, the scope of review has often turned on the quality of any prior determination concerning the legality of custody: the more trustworthy the prior determination, the more limited subsequent habeas review might be. Third, review of questions of law, where courts generally are thought to have comparative expertise, has generally been broader than review of questions of fact. In the context of collateral review of criminal convictions, however, some cases have suggested that not all legal errors—only those that are fundamental, that involve exceptional circumstances, or that would create a complete miscarriage of justice if not redressed—are cognizable on habeas. See, *e.g.*, Hill v. United States, 368 U.S. 424, 428 (1962); Sunal v. Large, 332 U.S. 174 (1947). A broader view was expressed in INS v. St. Cyr, pp. 336, 1201, *supra*, an immigration case, where the Court said that historically, habeas review extended to "errors of law, including the erroneous application or interpretation of statutes." Fourth, as to review of fact, while some English and early American decisions barred petitioners from introducing evidence to contest the facts presented by a custodian in a return to the writ, the practice was not consistent, the limitation was sometimes evaded,[2] and it eventually eroded in the nineteenth century. Finally, the scope of review has varied in different circumstances, and as Chief Justice Roberts noted, has often been considerably narrower when reviewing military decisions and matters arising out of war. See generally Fallon & Meltzer, p. 1221, *supra*, at 2096–99.

(c) In considering the appropriate scope of review by a habeas court, does the DTA have any relevance? The year after Boumediene, the D.C. Circuit held that DTA review is no longer available, reasoning that the DTA's provision for review in the D.C. Circuit could not be severed from the provision purporting to preclude habeas jurisdiction, which Boumediene had invalidated. The court did not view the Supreme Court's statement in Boumediene that the DTA remained intact as a barrier to its ruling, as the Court had not addressed the issue of severability. Bismullah v. Gates, 551 F.3d 1068 (D.C.Cir.2009).

In at least one respect, however, the Boumediene Court drew on the DTA: noting that the Act sought to channel cases into the D.C. Circuit, the Court stated that it would be appropriate for all habeas petitions from Guantánamo detainees to be heard in (or transferred to) the District Court for the District of Columbia.

---

[2]   See pp. 1193–1194, note 4, *supra*.

The DTA appears to preclude the D.C. Circuit from entertaining a challenge based on an alleged violation of a treaty, and § 5(a) of the MCA precludes a habeas petitioner from invoking the Geneva Convention as a source of rights. If, apart from those provisions, detainees could have relied upon the Geneva Convention in habeas proceedings, what is the statutes' effect in habeas proceedings under Boumediene?[3]

(4) Unanswered Questions About the Conduct of Future Habeas Proceedings. Apart from questions about scope of review, an enormous number of procedural issues have arisen in the numerous habeas cases filed by Guantánamo detainees.[4] In addressing those questions, are the courts implicitly determining what the Suspension Clause does, and does not, require when habeas courts review the detention of aliens, asserted to be subject to detention under the laws of war? Or does the invalidation of the jurisdiction stripping provisions in Boumediene leave the courts with their normal jurisdiction under § 2241, which might provide more procedural protection than the Constitution requires?

Examples of the procedural questions include:

(a) Admissibility of Hearsay Evidence. In Al-Bihani v. Obama, 590 F.3d 866, 879 (D.C.Cir.2010), the court held that hearsay is always admissible in these cases and that the only question is "what probative weight to ascribe to whatever indicia of reliability it exhibits."

(b) Burden of Proof. The Al-Bihani decision also ruled that the district court had permissibly adopted a preponderance of the evidence standard in reviewing the factual determinations of a CSRT. Thereafter, in Al-Adahi v. Obama, 613 F.3d 1102 (D.C.Cir.2010), the court of appeals doubted that the Suspension Clause requires the government to meet the preponderance of the evidence standard, citing cases from other contexts (review of deportation orders, selective service decisions, court martial convictions, and arrests) in which habeas courts applied a lesser standard—in the first two instances, a requirement only that there be "some evidence" to support the decision. But since both parties agreed that the preponderance standard governed, the court adhered to it arguendo in upholding the legality of the particular detention.

In at least some of the other settings noted by the court, an adversary hearing had been provided prior to the habeas proceeding. As the Hamdi plurality noted, the difference between such a hearing and one before a CSRT is a key factor in assessing the relevance of those precedents.

(c) Presumption of Regularity. In Latif v. Obama, 666 F.3d 746 (D.C.Cir.2011), the D.C. Circuit held that Government intelligence reports merit a presumption of regularity, permitting courts to presume, absent clear contrary evidence, that officials have properly discharged their official duties.

---

[3] The statutory limitations might be challenged on the ground that, without substantively amending the Geneva Convention, they preclude the federal courts from enforcing applicable sub-constitutional law, thereby violating a principle of judicial integrity associated with Marbury v. Madison, p. 59, *supra*, and Klein v. United States, p. 323, *supra*—that a federal court must decide a case in accordance with all applicable law. See Vázquez, *The Military Commissions Act, the Geneva Conventions, and the Courts: A Critical Guide*, 101 Am.J.Intl.L. 73 (2007). Is it an adequate answer that Congress has simply determined, as it may, that the Geneva Convention does not confer privately enforceable rights?

[4] For developments in the D.C. federal courts, see Wittes, Chesney, & Reynolds, The Emerging Law of Detention 2.0: The Guantánamo Habeas Cases as Lawmaking (2011), http://www.brookings.edu/papers/2011/05_guantanamo_wittes.aspx; Hafetz, *Calling the Government to Account: Habeas Corpus in the Aftermath of Boumediene*, 57 Wayne L.Rev. 99 (2011); Vladeck, *The D.C. Circuit After Boumediene*, 41 Seton Hall L.Rev. 1451 (2011).

The court justified the presumption by arguing that "courts have no special expertise in evaluating the nature and reliability of * * * wartime records" and therefore should defer to the Executive Branch. The court stressed, however, that "[t]he presumption of regularity * * * presumes the government official accurately identified the source and accurately summarized his statement, but it implies nothing about the truth of the underlying non-government source's statement." Judge Tatel's dissent argued that the presumption of regularity applies only when government documents are the product of reliable processes. Here, however, the report was issued "in the fog of war by a clandestine method that we know almost nothing about", and he emphasized that it was, in the majority's own words, "prepared in stressful and chaotic conditions, filtered through interpreters, subject to transcription errors, and heavily redacted for national security purposes." Judge Tatel said he would presume the report was authentic, but would permit the factfinder to decide how much probative weight to accord the evidence.[5]

NOTE ON THE SCOPE OF REVIEW IN IMMIGRATION CASES

(1) The Pre-1996 Practice. Questions about the scope of review required by the Suspension Clause have also arisen in deportation cases (now labeled removal cases). In INS v. St. Cyr, 533 U.S. 289, 306–09 (2001), the Court described the pre-1996 practice this way (most citations are omitted).

> Until the enactment of the 1952 Immigration and Nationality Act, the sole means by which an alien could test the legality of his or her deportation order was by bringing a habeas corpus action in district court. In such cases, other than the question whether there was some evidence to support the order, the courts generally did not review factual determinations made by the Executive. However, * * * [i]n case after case, courts answered questions of law in habeas corpus proceedings brought by aliens challenging Executive interpretations of the immigration laws.

> Habeas courts also regularly answered questions of law that arose in the context of discretionary relief. Traditionally, courts recognized a distinction between eligibility for discretionary relief * * * and the favorable exercise of discretion * * *. Eligibility that was "governed by specific statutory standards" provided "a right to a ruling on an applicant's eligibility," even though the actual granting of relief was "not a matter of right under any circumstances, but rather is in all cases a matter of grace." * * *

>   * * *

> [Beginning in 1952, Congress established procedures other than habeas corpus for federal court review of immigration matters. Under the 1952 Immigration and Nationality Act, Pub.L.No. 82–414, 66 Stat. 163,] district courts had broad authority to grant declaratory and injunctive relief in immigration cases, including orders adjudicating deportability and those denying suspensions of deportability. The [Act of Sept. 26, 1961, Pub.L.No.

---

[5]   For a review of these and other decisions, which concludes that the D.C. Circuit has "effectively reversed" Boumediene, see Alexander, *The Law-Free Zone and Back Again*, 2013 U.Ill.L.Rev. 551.

87–301, 75 Stat. 650,] withdrew that jurisdiction from the district courts and provided that the procedures set forth in the Hobbs Act [governing direct review in the federal circuits of agency actions] would be the "sole and exclusive procedure" for judicial review of final orders of deportation, subject to a series of exceptions. See 75 Stat. 651. The last of those exceptions stated that "any alien held in custody pursuant to an order of deportation may obtain review thereof by habeas corpus proceedings." See *id.*, at 652, codified at 8 U.S.C. § 1105a(10) (repealed Sept. 30, 1996).

(2) The Effect of Statutory Changes in 1996 and 2005. In 1996, Congress enacted a set of statutory provisions that, in the government's view, precluded all judicial review (including habeas review) in federal and state courts of the Attorney General's decision that the 1996 amendments had eliminated her discretion to waive deportation in specified circumstances. In the St. Cyr decision, pp. 336, 1201, *supra*, and the companion decision in Calcano-Martinez v. INS, 533 U.S. 348 (2001), the Court agreed that the 1996 amendments did strip the courts of appeals of the reviewing jurisdiction they had been given in 1961, but held that that Congress had not precluded the exercise of habeas corpus jurisdiction to review the legality of removal decisions. In the aftermath of St. Cyr, Congress enacted the REAL ID Act of 2005, Pub.L.No. 109–13, 119 Stat. 302 (2005), which eliminated habeas corpus jurisdiction in removal cases, substituting a review procedure in the federal courts of appeals. A provision of the Act, codified at 8 U.S.C. § 1252(a)(2)(D), authorizes review of "constitutional claims or questions of law". The legislative history indicates that this section was designed to "permit judicial review over those issues that were historically reviewable on habeas." H.R. Rep. No. 109–72, 175 (2005). In immigration matters, however, the relevant history is particularly tortured. See, *e.g.*, the articles by Neuman, p. 338, n. 4, *supra*.

The courts of appeals have agreed that § 1252(a)(2)(D) does not authorize review of the exercise of discretion or of determinations of fact by agency officials. (Is a failure to exercise any review of factual determinations, even to ascertain if they are supported by "some evidence," consistent with St. Cyr?[1]) The circuits have disagreed, however, about whether, especially in light of St. Cyr, § 1252(a)(2)(D) limits review to "pure" issues of law or instead embraces the application of the governing legal standard to the facts as found.[2] Those disagreements sometimes intersect with disagreements about whether a particular determination under the immigration laws involves the

---

[1]   *Cf.* Xiao Ji Chen v. U.S. Dep't of Justice, 471 F.3d 315 (2d Cir.2006) (explaining that a "question of law" might arise if administrative factfinding "is flawed by an error of law, such as * * * where the IJ states that his decision was based on petitioner's failure to testify to some pertinent fact when the record of the hearing reveals unambiguously that the petitioner *did* testify to that fact").

[2]   On this question, compare Ramadan v. Gonzales, 479 F.3d 646 (9th Cir.2007) (invoking "principles of constitutional avoidance" to support its interpretation of § 1252(a)(2)(D) as embracing review of the application of law to undisputed facts), with Viracacha v. Mukasey, 518 F.3d 511, 515–16 (7th Cir.2008) (criticizing the Ninth Circuit's use of the constitutional avoidance canon and reading § 1252(a)(2)(D) as "limited to 'pure' questions of law—situations in which a case comes out one way if the Constitution or statute means one thing, and the other way if it means something different").

For a highly critical review of both the REAL ID Act and actions by the Executive Branch in modifying the processes of administrative adjudication in immigration cases, see Legomsky, *Deportation and the War on Independence*, 91 Cornell L.Rev. 369 (2006).

application of law to fact or, instead, either a factual question or an exercise of the government's discretion.

In most cases, won't the application of law to fact be as or more critical to the individual than broad questions of statutory meaning? On the other hand, would upholding jurisdiction to review the application of law to fact risk bringing in routine questions of administration, rather than the kind of fundamental questions to which habeas jurisdiction is sometimes thought to be limited? In any event, can pure questions of law easily be distinguished from the applications of law to fact, or do the categories blend into each other?

_____

NOTE ON EXHAUSTION OF NON-HABEAS REMEDIES

(1) Timing of Habeas Review. A court possessing habeas jurisdiction may nonetheless sometimes abstain from exercising it until other legal processes have concluded. For example, the rule that state prisoners seeking postconviction federal habeas corpus review must first exhaust state court remedies was developed as judge-made law before it was codified. See generally pp. 1349–1354, *infra*. As the Boumediene opinion illustrates, the question of exhaustion of non-habeas remedies has arisen in other contexts, notably when habeas courts are asked to intervene in federal military proceedings.

(2) Exhaustion and Courts Martial. In Schlesinger v. Councilman, 420 U.S. 738 (1975) (6–3), an army captain facing court martial proceedings for sale and possession of marijuana sought immediate federal court review, alleging that the offense was not service-connected and that therefore, under the decisional law then governing, the military courts could not constitutionally exercise jurisdiction.[1] The Supreme Court, relying on decisions calling on federal courts to abstain from exercising jurisdiction to enjoin state court proceedings, held that the lower federal courts should have abstained: "While the peculiar demands of federalism are not implicated, the deficiency is supplied by factors equally compelling"—the need for deference to the military and the federal courts' respect for Congress' judgment that "the military court system will vindicate servicemen's constitutional rights."

The Court distinguished habeas decisions that had permitted anticipatory relief against courts-martial acting in excess of their constitutionally permissible jurisdiction on the basis that (a) those decisions involved civilian petitioners and (b) the jurisdictional question "turned on the status of the persons as to whom the military asserted its power." By contrast, here the petitioner was unquestionably subject to military authority, and the question whether the marijuana charges were service-related depended on judgments about which "the expertise of military courts is singularly relevant".

(3) Abstention and Military Commission Trials. In Hamdan v. Rumsfeld, 548 U.S. 557 (2006), p. 408, *supra*, the government, alleging that Hamdan, a Yemeni national, had, in violation of the laws of war, conspired

_____

[1]   See O'Callahan v. Parker, 395 U.S. 258 (1969), *overruled*, Solorio v. United States, 483 U.S. 435 (1987). Captain Councilman sought to enjoin further proceedings, but the Court made clear it was applying principles equally applicable to, and indeed drawn from, habeas corpus practice.

with members of al Qaeda to attack civilians and commit acts of terrorism, brought criminal charges against him in a military commission. Before trial, Hamdan sought writs of habeas corpus and mandamus, challenging the authority of the military commission to try him. In upholding Hamdan's challenge, the Supreme Court rejected, 5–3, the contention that the federal courts should have abstained until completion of the military proceedings. For the majority, Justice Stevens reasoned that "neither of the comity considerations identified in Councilman weighs in favor of abstention * * *. First, Hamdan is not a member of our Nation's Armed Forces, so concerns about military discipline do not apply. Second, the tribunal convened to try Hamdan is not part of the integrated system of military courts, complete with independent review panels, that Congress has established." He added that the Court had not abstained from providing pre-conviction review of war crimes trials before military commission proceedings in Ex parte Quirin, 317 U.S. 1, 19 (1942), where the Court justified intervention by the importance of the questions and the judicial duty in war as in peacetime to preserve constitutional liberties. Without foreclosing the possibility that some military commission proceedings (such as those convened on the battlefield) might call for abstention, Justice Stevens said that the government had not identified any important reason for abstention in this case, and that both the government and Hamdan had "a compelling interest in knowing in advance whether Hamdan may be tried by a military commission that arguably is without any basis in law".[2]

In dissent, Justice Scalia (joined by Justices Thomas and Alito) offered three reasons supporting abstention. First, if "military necessities" required abstention in Councilman, surely the necessities recognized by the political branches "relating to the * * * terrorists of September 11 require abstention all the more here." Second, the absence of an integrated scheme and independent review stressed by the Court was more than compensated for by the provision in the Detainee Treatment Act (DTA) for review of any final decision by the D.C. Circuit—a form of review not available in Quirin. Third, "considerations of *interbranch* comity * * * weigh heavily against" judicial intervention, which would create a "direct conflict with the Executive in an area where the Executive's competence is maximal and ours is virtually nonexistent."

(4) Exhaustion and Boumediene. In Boumediene, the Court said that ordinarily a habeas court should not entertain a petition from a detainee at Guantánamo until a CSRT had completed its status determination but held that the petitioners need not exhaust DTA review in the D.C. Circuit. The Court stressed that some of the petitioners had been detained for six years without judicial oversight and doubted that DTA review could be performed expeditiously. But if those conditions do not hold, might exhaustion be warranted? Recall this language in the majority opinion: "The cases before us, however, do not involve detainees who have been held for a short period of time while awaiting their CSRT determinations. Were that the case, or were it probable that the Court of Appeals could complete a prompt review

---

[2] The government also objected, more specifically, to the Court's consideration of any challenges to the commission's procedures, contending that Hamdan could obtain review of any procedural issue after final decision and that there was no reason to presume that a violation would occur. In response, Justice Stevens said, *inter alia*, that procedural harm was not conjectural as Hamdan had already been excluded from proceedings in his own case.

of their applications, the case for requiring temporary abstention or exhaustion of alternative remedies would be much stronger."

(5) Reconciling the Decisions. The Hamdan opinion found abstention inappropriate when there is a substantial question about a military tribunal's personal jurisdiction over a defendant. Does the "jurisdictional" label provide a clear benchmark for the appropriate scope of abstention? If not, note the multiplicity of factors on which the Court's judgments about whether to abstain have rested.[3] And in the end, isn't there an inherent tension between any kind of abstention, on the one hand, and the language in Boumediene that habeas corpus is meant to "cu[t] through all forms and g[o] to the very tissue of the structure" (quoting Justice Holmes' dissent in Frank v. Mangum, 237 U.S. 309, 346 (1915))?[4]

(6) Exhaustion and Military Trials Today: Congressional Power and Constitutional Limits. Four months after the Hamdan decision, Congress enacted the Military Commissions Act of 2006 (MCA of 2006), and three years later, the Military Commissions Act of 2009. Together these acts were designed to alter the procedures followed in military commission proceedings against aliens charged criminally for law of war violations and in doing so to address the defects that the Supreme Court had found in the Hamdan decision. As noted on p. 1199, *supra,* under current law a conviction by military commission is subject to review within the Department of Defense, then to review of law and fact before the United States Court of Military Commission Review, an Article I court staffed by military and civilian judges, and then to further review in the U.S. Court of Appeals for the D.C. Circuit, see 10 U.S.C. § 950f, whose decisions can be reviewed on certiorari by the Supreme Court.

Does that structure effectively undercut a key basis for Hamdan's holding on exhaustion—namely, that Congress had not created an integrated system of review? Even if so, does the Suspension Clause permit withholding habeas review until all remedies under that elaborate review procedure have been exhausted? Consider this language in the Boumediene opinion: "This Court may not impose a *de facto* suspension by abstaining from these controversies. See Hamdan, 548 U.S., at 585, n. 16 ('[A]bstention is not appropriate in cases . . . in which the legal challenge "turn[s] on the status of the persons as to whom the military asserted its power" (quoting Schlesinger v. Councilman, 420 U.S. 738, 759 (1975))).' "[5]

---

[3] Following Hamdan, the District Court for the District of Columbia has rebuffed petitioners' efforts to avoid the exhaustion requirement by arguing that their cases fall within the scope of Hamdan's. In Khadr v. Bush, 587 F.Supp.2d 225 (D.D.C.2008), the district court emphasized that Hamdan's exception to the courts' general stance of abstaining while military proceedings are pending applies only when the case presents a substantial *constitutional* question that turns on the status of the detainee. See also Khadr v. Obama, 724 F.Supp.2d 61 (D.D.C.2010); Al Odah v. Bush, 593 F.Supp.2d 53 (D.D.C.2009).

[4] Compare the material on pre-trial intervention by habeas courts into state criminal proceedings, p. 1353, *infra.*

[5] In Obaydullah v. Obama, 609 F.3d 444 (D.C.Cir.2010), the court refused to abstain in a habeas action filed by a Guantánamo detainee who did not yet face a prosecution before a military commission. Although charges had been sworn against the petitioner, under the Defense Department rules, the "Convening Authority"—either the Secretary of Defense or his designee—had to decide whether to dismiss the charges or instead to refer them to a military commission. The Convening Authority had made no decision and faced no deadline for doing so. In ruling that the detainee's habeas action challenging the lawfulness of his detention could proceed, the D.C. Circuit relied on Steffel v. Thompson, 415 U.S. 452 (1974), p. 1144, *supra,* which held that in a federal court action under 42 U.S.C. § 1983 challenging the constitutionality

In Hamdan's case itself, after the Supreme Court decision and Congress' enactment of the MCA of 2006, the government pursued war crimes charges against him under the framework set forth in the Act. Following various proceedings before a military commission (which found Hamdan to be an unlawful enemy combatant), he sought to enjoin commencement of his military trial, asserting that the commission lacked jurisdiction over him because (a) he had not yet had the opportunity to obtain habeas review, under Boumediene, of the determination that he was an unlawful enemy combatant, and (b) his trial would violate a range of constitutional protections (including the Ex Post Facto and Due Process Clauses). The district court denied the motion, noting, *inter alia*, that Hamdan's challenge to the military commission was further removed from the historic core of habeas corpus than the issue in Boumediene, that Hamdan had already had not only a CSRT hearing but also a two-day adversarial hearing, with counsel, before the commission, and that he would have an adversarial trial. Noting that Hamdan could raise all of his jurisdictional arguments at a later time in the D.C. Circuit, the court said: "Where both Congress and the President have expressly decided when Article III review is to occur, the courts should be wary of disturbing their judgment." Hamdan v. Gates, 565 F.Supp.2d 130 (D.D.C.2008).

———

NOTE ON THE TERRITORIAL REACH OF THE WRIT

(1) Territorial Jurisdiction: Location of the Petitioner. Section 2241(a) vests authority to grant the writ in the Supreme Court and the district courts, any Justice of the Supreme Court and any circuit judge, but only "within their respective jurisdictions". In Ahrens v. Clark, 335 U.S. 188 (1948), the Court held that the District Court for the District of Columbia could not issue the writ because the petitioners, who were held at Ellis Island, New York, by order of the Attorney General, were not within the district court's territorial jurisdiction. It did not suffice, the Court held, that a custodian was within the district court's jurisdiction; instead, it was fatal to jurisdiction that the petitioners were not. Over time, however, amendments to the habeas statute and judicial decisions have eroded Ahrens' restriction.

(2) Statutory and Judicial Expansion of Territorial Jurisdiction.

(a) Legislative Revisions. In 1948, Congress added a provision (§ 2255) that, for persons "in custody under sentence of a court established by Act of Congress"—ordinarily those convicted of federal crimes—requires filing a motion in the sentencing court rather than a habeas petition in the district of incarceration. See Section 3(B), *infra*. Then in 1966 Congress added a provision, codified in § 2241(d), that permits state prisoners attacking convictions in states containing more than one federal district to file in the district either of conviction or of confinement. Neither provision required that the petitioner be located in the district in which relief was sought.

(b) The Braden Decision. Neither of the amendments just described applied to the facts in Braden v. 30th Judicial Cir. Ct., 410 U.S. 484 (1973)

---

of a state criminal statute, abstention in deference to the state courts was inappropriate when no state criminal proceeding against the federal court plaintiff had been commenced.

(6–3). But there, the Court sharply limited Ahrens' interpretation of § 2241(a) and recognized the jurisdiction of a district court to entertain a petition from a prisoner physically confined in another state. In Braden, a detainer had been filed against an Alabama prisoner on behalf of the state of Kentucky, to assure that he would be turned over to Kentucky for trial when his Alabama sentence expired. He filed a petition in federal court in Kentucky against his future Kentucky custodians, alleging denial of his constitutional right to a speedy trial in Kentucky and seeking an order compelling his immediate trial there. The Supreme Court upheld the district court's jurisdiction, concluding that § 2241(a) requires only that the court "have jurisdiction over the custodian". The Court pointed to §§ 2255 and 2241(d) as exemplifying Congress' recognition of the desirability of resolving habeas cases in a court closely connected to the underlying controversy, while acceptance of "a more expansive definition of the 'custody' requirement", see pp. 1354–1355, *infra*, permitted new forms of challenge, including Braden's challenge to a detainer lodged against him by a state in which he was not physically confined. The Court concluded that Ahrens should be confined to its facts—on which it was correctly decided, since in that case both the prisoners and those holding them were in New York and no showing had been made that the District of Columbia was a more convenient forum.

(3) Persons Detained Outside of the United States. The foregoing discussion concerns detainees located within American territory. What is the reach of habeas jurisdiction over detainees held by the federal government outside of the United States?

    (a) Aliens Detained in Foreign Nations: Johnson v. Eisentrager. In Johnson v. Eisentrager, 339 U.S. 763 (1950), the Court held that the federal district court in the District of Columbia (and, by implication, all other district courts) could not issue a writ sought by German citizens detained abroad. The petitioners had been captured in China and convicted by a U.S. military tribunal there of violating the laws of war by continuing hostilities against the United States after the surrender of Germany in 1945. After conviction, they were sent to an American military prison in occupied Germany, where they were being held when the petitions were filed. The precise basis for the Supreme Court's decision—how far it rested on a lack of statutory jurisdiction, and how far it was based on a determination on the merits that the petitioners had suffered no violation of their constitutional rights—was not clear. The meaning of Eisentrager was the subject of elaborate debate in Rasul v. Bush, Paragraph (4), *infra*, and Boumediene v. Bush, p. 1249, *infra*.

    (b) Citizens Detained Abroad. In Burns v. Wilson, 346 U.S. 137 (1953), two American servicemen detained overseas, after having been convicted by court martial of crimes committed in Guam, filed habeas petitions in federal court in the District of Columbia, naming the Secretary of Defense as respondent. Although in the end it refused to grant the writ, the Supreme Court did not question the district court's jurisdiction, even though both the petitioners and their immediate custodian were abroad and thus outside the territorial jurisdiction of any district court. The jurisdictional issue, though not mentioned in the opinion, was discussed several months later by Justice Frankfurter in an opinion dissenting from the denial of rehearing, 346 U.S. 844 (1953).

In United States ex rel. Toth v. Quarles, 350 U.S. 11 (1955), habeas relief against the Secretary of the Air Force was granted to an ex-serviceman arrested in the United States and taken to Korea for military trial. The jurisdictional issue, though again not discussed, could hardly have been overlooked in view of Justice Frankfurter's opinion two years earlier.

Professors Fallon and Meltzer, in *Habeas Corpus Jurisdiction, Substantive Rights, and the War on Terror*, 120 Harv.L.Rev. 2029, 2053–55 (2007), view Burns and Toth as exemplifying what they call the Common Law Model, an approach that they believe courts have traditionally, and appropriately, used in interpreting the habeas jurisdiction. Under this approach, courts, while agents of the legislature, may assume a creative role in adapting the statute to new circumstances, and in doing so, seeking to avoid possible constitutional difficulties. The Burns and Toth decisions, they note, were nearly contemporaneous with a recognition that citizens detained abroad could assert constitutional rights in challenging court martial convictions. See Reid v. Covert, 354 U.S. 1 (1957). A strict territorial limitation on jurisdiction could have left the petitioners with no chance to reach an Article III court in which to assert their constitutional challenges to the legality of custody—a circumstance that might itself have raised a serious constitutional question. By contrast, it was at best uncertain whether the Constitution confers rights on aliens held abroad, as in the Eisentrager case.

Is it justifiable for extraterritorial jurisdiction to turn on a distinction between citizens and aliens not found in the text of § 2241? In answering that question, is it relevant that the extent to which particular constitutional provisions have extraterritorial application—and thus whether a habeas petitioner has substantive constitutional rights to invoke—may depend on citizenship?

(4) Detention at Guantánamo Bay: The Rasul Decision. Insofar as Eisentrager was interpreted as barring habeas jurisdiction over aliens held outside of territory over which the United States exercises de jure sovereignty, it was limited by Rasul v. Bush, 542 U.S. 466 (2004). The case involved two Australians and twelve Kuwaitis captured during hostilities between the United States and the Taliban regime in Afghanistan and held at the United States Naval Base at Guantánamo Bay in Cuba. The United States' agreements with Cuba, dating from 1903 and 1934, recognize the ultimate sovereignty of Cuba over the leased areas but grant the United States, as long as it retains a naval base there, "complete jurisdiction and control". Actions on petitioners' behalf were filed in federal court in the District of Columbia. Treating all of the filings as habeas petitions, the lower courts ruled that under Eisentrager, they lacked jurisdiction. The Supreme Court reversed.

(a) Justice Stevens' opinion for the Court began by closely examining the Eisentrager decision, in which the court of appeals had upheld habeas jurisdiction. "In reversing that determination, this Court summarized the six critical facts in the case:

"We are here confronted with a decision whose basic premise is that these prisoners are entitled, as a constitutional right, to sue in some court of the United States for a writ of *habeas corpus*. To support that assumption we must hold that a prisoner of our military authorities is constitutionally entitled to the writ, even though he (a) is an enemy alien; (b) has never been or resided in the United

States; (c) was captured outside of our territory and there held in military custody as a prisoner of war; (d) was tried and convicted by a Military Commission sitting outside the United States; (e) for offenses against laws of war committed outside the United States; (f) and is at all times imprisoned outside the United States" (quoting Eisentrager, 339 U.S. at 777).

The Guantánamo detainees, Justice Stevens reasoned, differed from the Eisentrager petitioners in important respects: "They are not nationals of countries at war with the United States, and they deny that they have engaged in or plotted acts of aggression against the United States; they have never been afforded access to any tribunal, much less charged with and convicted of wrongdoing; and for more than two years they have been imprisoned in territory over which the United States exercises exclusive jurisdiction and control."

The Court then stated a critical premise of its opinion: that the six factors mentioned in Eisentrager "were relevant only to the question of the prisoners' *constitutional* entitlement to habeas corpus". On this view, the court of appeals in Eisentrager "implicitly conceded" that under Ahrens, statutory jurisdiction was lacking, but held that the Suspension Clause conferred a constitutional right to habeas review that could not be denied by a statutory gap.

That "statutory gap" had since been filled, Justice Stevens argued, by the Braden decision, Paragraph (2)(b), *supra*. Braden overruled Ahrens and held that "the prisoner's presence within the territorial jurisdiction of the district court is not an 'invariable prerequisite' " to a district court's jurisdiction under § 2241, which exists so long as the custodian can be reached by service of process (quoting Braden). "Because Braden overruled the statutory predicate to Eisentrager's holding, Eisentrager plainly does not preclude the exercise of § 2241 jurisdiction over petitioner's claims."

The principle that federal statutes (including § 2241) are presumed to lack extraterritorial application, Justice Stevens reasoned, was inapposite because given the terms of the lease agreements, the Guantánamo detainees were within the territorial jurisdiction of the United States. Noting that the government conceded that habeas jurisdiction would lie over a petition by an American citizen held at Guantánamo, he observed that § 2241 does not distinguish citizens from aliens. "No party questions the District Court's jurisdiction over petitioners' custodians. Section 2241, by its terms, requires nothing more."

(b) Justice Scalia, joined by Chief Justice Rehnquist and Justice Thomas, filed a lengthy dissent. He argued that the court of appeals in Eisentrager, though motivated by the policy of constitutional avoidance, had upheld statutory jurisdiction, and the Supreme Court, in reversing the court of appeals, necessarily held that § 2241 conferred no jurisdiction. The Braden decision, he contended, had not "overruled the statutory predicate to Eisentrager's holding" but merely resolved the question, not foreseen by the Ahrens decision, whether a prisoner in custody in multiple American jurisdictions may file in the district within which the challenged confinement originates, even if he is physically confined elsewhere.

For Justice Scalia, the text of § 2241 "could not be clearer that a necessary requirement for issuing the writ is that *some* federal district court have territorial jurisdiction over the detainee."[1] He acknowledged that enforcing that limitation so as to deny any habeas review to a *citizen* detained abroad might raise constitutional doubts, thereby "justifying a strained construction of the habeas statute, or (more honestly) a determination of [the] constitutional right to habeas. * * * [B]ut the possibility of one atextual exception thought to be required by the Constitution is no justification for abandoning the clear application of the text to a situation [involving an *alien* petitioner] in which it raises no constitutional doubt." He then rehearsed what he thought were the untoward consequences of the majority's decision and included a long quotation from Eisentrager highlighting the practical difficulties that could ensue.

(c) Concurring in the judgment, Justice Kennedy agreed with Justice Scalia that Braden had not overruled the statutory predicate to Eisentrager and thus rejected the Court's recognition of "automatic statutory authority" to entertain petitions from persons held outside the United States. But he distinguished Eisentrager on two grounds: "First, Guantánamo Bay is in every practical respect a United States territory, and it is one far removed from any hostilities." Second, the detainees were being held indefinitely without trial or other proceedings, which suggests a weaker case of military necessity and "much greater alignment with the traditional function of habeas corpus."

INTRODUCTORY NOTE ON BOUMEDIENE V. BUSH

Reprinted at p. 1224, *supra*, is one portion of the decision in Boumediene v. Bush, discussing whether the process that Congress established as a substitute for habeas corpus review—an initial determination of enemy combatant status made within the military by a Combatant Status Review Tribunal, followed by limited judicial review in the D.C. Circuit—provided an adequate substitute for habeas review. But that question arose only if the petitioners—aliens seized abroad and detained as enemy combatants at Guantánamo Bay, Cuba—fell within the group of individuals who enjoy protection under the Constitution's Suspension Clause. The portions of the Boumediene majority opinion and Justice Scalia's dissent below address that question. Before reading them, please review Section I of the Boumediene opinion, reprinted at p. 1224, *supra*.

Boumediene v. Bush

553 U.S. 723, 128 S.Ct. 2229, 171 L.Ed.2d 41 (2008).
Certiorari to the United States Court of Appeals for the District of Columbia Circuit.

■ JUSTICE KENNEDY delivered the opinion of the Court.

    * * *

---

[1]   Justice Scalia also relied on § 2242, which states that if an application is "addressed to the Supreme Court, a justice thereof or a circuit judge it shall state the reasons for not making application to *the district court of the district in which the applicant is held.*" (Emphasis added by Justice Scalia.)

III

* * * [W]e must determine whether petitioners are barred from seeking the writ or invoking the protections of the Suspension Clause either because of their status, *i.e.*, petitioners' designation by the Executive Branch as enemy combatants, or their physical location, *i.e.*, their presence at Guantánamo Bay. The Government contends that noncitizens designated as enemy combatants and detained in territory located outside our Nation's borders have no constitutional rights and no privilege of habeas corpus. [Petitioners dispute both of those contentions.]

We begin with a brief account of the history and origins of the writ. Our account proceeds from two propositions. First, * * * [i]n the system conceived by the Framers the writ had a centrality that must inform proper interpretation of the Suspension Clause. Second, to the extent there were settled precedents or legal commentaries in 1789 regarding the extraterritorial scope of the writ or its application to enemy aliens, those authorities can be instructive for the present cases.

A

The Framers viewed freedom from unlawful restraint as a fundamental precept of liberty * * *. Experience taught, however, that the common-law writ all too often had been insufficient to guard against the abuse of monarchial power. That history counseled the necessity for specific language in the Constitution to secure the writ * * *.

[The Court discussed the history of the writ in England, noting that the practice of suspension of the writ by Parliament, and protests against suspension, were known to the Framers and confirmed their mistrust of undivided government power.]

That the Framers considered the writ a vital instrument for the protection of individual liberty is evident from the care taken to specify the limited grounds for its suspension: "The Privilege of the Writ of Habeas Corpus shall not be suspended, unless when in Cases of Rebellion or Invasion the public Safety may require it." Art. I, § 9, cl. 2. * * *

* * * The [Suspension] Clause * * * ensures that, except during periods of formal suspension, the Judiciary will have a time-tested device, the writ, to maintain the "delicate balance of governance" that is itself the surest safeguard of liberty. See Hamdi [v. Rumsfeld, 542 U.S. 507, 536 (2004)] (plurality opinion). The Clause protects the rights of the detained by affirming the duty and authority of the Judiciary to call the jailer to account. The separation-of-powers doctrine, and the history that influenced its design, therefore must inform the reach and purpose of the Suspension Clause.

B

* * * The Court has been careful not to foreclose the possibility that the protections of the Suspension Clause have expanded along with post-1789 developments that define the present scope of the writ. See INS v. St. Cyr, 533 U.S. 289, 300–301 (2001). But the analysis may begin with precedents as of 1789, for the Court has said that "at the absolute minimum" the Clause protects the writ as it existed when the Constitution was drafted and ratified. *Id.*, at 301.

* * * The Government argues the common-law writ ran only to those territories over which the Crown was sovereign. Petitioners argue that jurisdiction followed the King's officers. * * * In none of the cases cited [by the parties] do we find that a common-law court would or would not have granted, or refused to hear for lack of jurisdiction, a petition for a writ of habeas corpus brought by a prisoner deemed an enemy combatant, under a standard like the one the Department of Defense has used in these cases, and when held in a territory, like Guantánamo, over which the Government has total military and civil control.

We know that at common law a petitioner's status as an alien was not a categorical bar to habeas corpus relief. See, *e.g.*, Sommersett's Case, 20 How. St. Tr. 1, 80–82 (1772). We know as well that common-law courts entertained habeas petitions brought by enemy aliens detained in England—"entertained" at least in the sense that the courts held hearings to determine the threshold question of entitlement to the writ. See Case of Three Spanish Sailors, 2 Black. W. 1324, 96 Eng. Rep. 775 (C. P. 1779); King v. Schiever, 2 Burr. 765, 97 Eng. Rep. 551 (K. B. 1759); Du Castro's Case, Fort. 195, 92 Eng. Rep. 816 (K. B. 1697).

[Relief was denied in Schiever and the Spanish Sailors' case, but it is unclear whether the denial was for lack of jurisdiction or because the detention was lawful. In Du Castro's Case, although relief was granted, the prisoner was detained in England.

[As to the geographic scope of the writ at common law, Petitioners cite cases granting relief to prisoners held in areas outside the realm of England though under the Crown's control, but those areas, unlike Guantánamo, may have been considered sovereign territory. Petitioners also cite cases involving detainees held in territory in India within the sovereignty and control of the Moghul Emperor, but there relief was granted not by an English common law court but by a special statutory court located in Calcutta; by contrast, no American court sits in Guantánamo.

[The Government points to cases denying the power to issue writs to Scotland and Hanover, territories controlled by the English Monarch in his capacity as King of Scotland and Elector of Hanover. But in view of England's delicate relationship with those territories and the fact that they maintained their own laws, the refusal to issue the writ may have rested on prudential concerns.

[Those prudential concerns] are not relevant here. We have no reason to believe an order from a federal court would be disobeyed at Guantánamo. No Cuban court has jurisdiction to hear these petitioners' claims, and no law other than the laws of the United States applies at the naval station. The modern-day relations between the United States and Guantánamo thus differ in important respects from the 18th-century relations between England and the kingdoms of Scotland and Hanover. * * *

* * * [G]iven the unique status of Guantánamo Bay and the particular dangers of terrorism in the modern age, the common-law courts simply may not have confronted cases with close parallels to this one. We decline, therefore, to infer too much, one way or the other, from the lack of historical evidence on point.

IV

* * * [T]he Government says the Suspension Clause affords petitioners no rights because the United States does not claim sovereignty over the place of detention.

Guantánamo Bay is not formally part of the United States. And under the terms of the lease between the United States and Cuba, Cuba retains "ultimate sovereignty" over the territory while the United States exercises "complete jurisdiction and control." [Citing Lease Agreement.] Under the terms of the 1934 Treaty, however, Cuba effectively has no rights as a sovereign until the parties agree to modification of the 1903 Lease Agreement or the United States abandons the base.

[It is not improper "to inquire into the objective degree of control the Nation asserts over foreign territory." Although Cuba "retains *de jure* sovereignty over Guantánamo Bay," we note, as we did in Rasul, the] uncontested fact that the United States, by virtue of its complete jurisdiction and control over the base, maintains *de facto* sovereignty over this territory.

* * * [T]he history of common-law habeas corpus provides scant support for [the proposition that *de jure* sovereignty is the touchstone of habeas corpus jurisdiction, and] that position would be inconsistent with our precedents and contrary to fundamental separation-of-powers principles.

A

* * *

Fundamental questions regarding the Constitution's geographic scope first arose at the dawn of the 20th century when the Nation acquired * * * Puerto Rico, Guam, and the Philippines * * * at the conclusion of the Spanish-American War [and then annexed Hawaii in 1898.] * * *

In a series of opinions later known as the Insular Cases, the Court addressed whether the Constitution, by its own force, applies in any territory that is not a State. [Citing six decisions from the early twentieth century.] The Court held that the Constitution has independent force in these territories, a force not contingent upon acts of legislative grace. [Yet the Court was wary of applying the Anglo-American legal tradition (for example, the use of grand and petit juries) to territories that followed the civil law system, especially when, as with the Philippines, the United States intended to grant independence to the territory.]

These considerations resulted in the doctrine of territorial incorporation, under which the Constitution applies in full in incorporated Territories surely destined for statehood but only in part in unincorporated Territories. * * * [T]he Court took for granted that even in unincorporated Territories the * * * United States was bound to provide to noncitizen inhabitants "guaranties of certain fundamental personal rights declared in the Constitution" [Balzac v. Porto Rico, 258 U.S. 298, 312 (1922), while recognizing] the inherent practical difficulties of enforcing all constitutional provisions "always and everywhere" * * *. * * *

Practical considerations likewise influenced the Court's analysis a half-century later in Reid [v. Covert, 354 U.S. 1 (1957). There, spouses of

American servicemen living on military bases overseas were tried by military courts for crimes committed abroad. In upholding their claim of a right to jury trial, the Court placed great weight on their status as citizens. But] practical considerations, related not to the petitioners' citizenship but to the place of their confinement and trial, were relevant to each Member of the Reid majority. * * *

Practical considerations weighed heavily as well in Johnson v. Eisentrager, 339 U.S. 763 (1950) * * *. The prisoners were detained at Landsberg Prison in Germany during the Allied Powers' postwar occupation. The Court stressed the difficulties of ordering the Government to produce the prisoners in a habeas corpus proceeding. It "would require allocation of shipping space, guarding personnel, billeting and rations" and would damage the prestige of military commanders at a sensitive time. *Id.*, at 779. * * *

True, the Court in Eisentrager denied access to the writ, and it noted the prisoners "at no relevant time were within any territory over which the United States is sovereign, and [that] the scenes of their offense, their capture, their trial and their punishment were all beyond the territorial jurisdiction of any court of the United States." 339 U.S., at 778. The Government seizes upon this language as proof positive that the Eisentrager Court adopted a formalistic, sovereignty-based test for determining the reach of the Suspension Clause. We reject this reading for three reasons.

First, we do not accept the idea that the above-quoted passage from Eisentrager is the only authoritative language in the opinion and that all the rest is dicta. * * *

Second, because the United States lacked both *de jure* sovereignty and plenary control over Landsberg Prison, it is far from clear that the Eisentrager Court used the term sovereignty only in the narrow technical sense * * *. * * * That the Court devoted a significant portion of Part II to a discussion of practical barriers to the running of the writ suggests that the Court was not concerned exclusively with the formal legal status of Landsberg Prison but also with the objective degree of control the United States asserted over it. * * *

Third, * * * [the Government's reading] of Eisentrager overlooks what we see as a common thread uniting the Insular Cases, Eisentrager, and Reid: the idea that questions of extraterritoriality turn on objective factors and practical concerns, not formalism.

B

[The Government's formal sovereignty-based test would permit the political branches to escape constitutional restraints by surrendering formal sovereignty over any unincorporated territory to another country while executing a lease granting total control back to the United States.] * * *

Our basic charter cannot be contracted away like this. * * * [To hold otherwise] would permit a striking anomaly in our tripartite system of government, leading to a regime in which Congress and the President, not this Court, say "what the law is." Marbury v. Madison, 1 Cranch 137, 177 (1803). * * *

C

As we recognized in Rasul, the outlines of a framework for determining the reach of the Suspension Clause are suggested by the factors the Court relied upon in Eisentrager * * *[—that] each petitioner:

"(a) is an enemy alien; (b) has never been or resided in the United States; (c) was captured outside of our territory and there held in military custody as a prisoner of war; (d) was tried and convicted by a Military Commission sitting outside the United States; (e) for offenses against laws of war committed outside the United States; (f) and is at all times imprisoned outside the United States." 339 U.S., at 777.

Based on this language * * * and the reasoning in our other extraterritoriality opinions, we conclude that at least three factors are relevant in determining the reach of the Suspension Clause: (1) the citizenship and status of the detainee and the adequacy of the process through which that status determination was made; (2) the nature of the sites where apprehension and then detention took place; and (3) the practical obstacles inherent in resolving the prisoner's entitlement to the writ.

Applying this framework, we note at the onset that the status of these detainees is a matter of dispute[, for they, unlike the detainees in Eisentrager, deny they are enemy combatants.] They have been afforded some process in CSRT proceedings to determine their status; but, unlike in Eisentrager, there has been no trial by military commission for violations of the laws of war. The difference is not trivial. [The Eisentrager petitioners were afforded a rigorous adversarial process to test the legality of their detention, in which they were represented by counsel and could introduce evidence and cross-examine the prosecution's witnesses.]

In comparison the procedural protections afforded to the detainees in the CSRT hearings are far more limited, and * * * fall well short of the procedures and adversarial mechanisms that would eliminate the need for habeas corpus review. Although the detainee is assigned a "Personal Representative" to assist him during CSRT proceedings, * * * that person is not the detainee's lawyer or even his "advocate." The Government's evidence is accorded a presumption of validity. The detainee is allowed to present "reasonably available" evidence, but his ability to rebut the Government's evidence against him is limited by the circumstances of his confinement and his lack of counsel at this stage. And although the detainee can seek review of his status determination in the Court of Appeals, that review process cannot cure all defects in the earlier proceedings. See Part V, *infra*.

As to the second factor relevant to this analysis, [the sites of apprehension and detention], * * * there are critical differences between Landsberg Prison, circa 1950, and the United States Naval Station at Guantánamo Bay in 2008. * * * [T]he United States' control over the prison in Germany was neither absolute nor indefinite. [The United States was answerable to the combined Allied Forces, which did not intend to occupy Germany indefinitely or even to displace all German institutions during the occupation.] Guantánamo Bay, on the other hand, is no transient possession. In every practical sense Guantánamo is not abroad; it is within the constant jurisdiction of the United States.

As to the third factor, we recognize, as the Court did in Eisentrager, that there are costs to holding the Suspension Clause applicable in a case of military detention abroad. * * * While we are sensitive to these concerns, we do not find them dispositive. * * * The Government presents no credible arguments that the military mission at Guantánamo would be compromised if habeas corpus courts had jurisdiction to hear the detainees' claims. * * *

The situation in Eisentrager was far different * * *. [The United States was responsible for an occupation zone in Germany exceeding 57,000 square miles, with a population of 18 million. American forces faced potential security threats from a defeated enemy. By contrast, Guantánamo is a secure prison facility located on an isolated and heavily fortified military base consisting of 45 square miles of land and water, where the only long-term residents are American military personnel, their families, and a small number of workers.]

There is no indication, furthermore, that adjudicating a habeas corpus petition would cause friction with the host government. * * * Under the facts presented here * * * there are few practical barriers to the running of the writ. To the extent barriers arise, habeas corpus procedures likely can be modified to address them. See Part VI–B, *infra*.

It is true that before today the Court has never held that noncitizens detained by our Government in territory over which another country maintains *de jure* sovereignty have any rights under our Constitution. But the cases before us lack any precise historical parallel. They involve individuals detained by executive order for the duration of a conflict that, if measured from September 11, 2001, to the present, is already among the longest wars in American history. The detainees, moreover, are held in a territory that * * * is under the complete and total control of our Government. * * *

We hold that Art. I, § 9, cl. 2, of the Constitution has full effect at Guantánamo Bay. * * * This Court may not impose a *de facto* suspension by abstaining from these controversies. The MCA does not purport to be a formal suspension of the writ; and the Government * * * has not argued that it is. Petitioners, therefore, are entitled to the privilege of habeas corpus to challenge the legality of their detention.

[The Court proceeded to hold that the judicial review procedures established by the DTA were not an adequate substitute for habeas corpus review and need not be exhausted before habeas jurisdiction could be exercised. (For that portion of the Court's opinion, and Chief Justice Roberts' dissent taking issue with it, see pp. 1224–1236, *supra*.) Accordingly, the Court reversed the lower courts' dismissal of the habeas petitions and remanded for further proceedings.]*

---

* [Ed.] In a concurring opinion joined by Justices Ginsburg and Breyer, Justice Souter stated that "no one who reads the Court's opinion in Rasul could seriously doubt that the jurisdictional question must be answered the same way in purely constitutional cases, given the Court's reliance on the historical background of habeas generally in answering the statutory question."

■ JUSTICE SCALIA, with whom THE CHIEF JUSTICE, JUSTICE THOMAS, and JUSTICE ALITO join, dissenting.

* * * The writ of habeas corpus does not, and never has, run in favor of aliens abroad; the Suspension Clause thus has no application, and the Court's intervention in this military matter is entirely *ultra vires*. * * *

I

America is at war with radical Islamists. * * * [The Court's opinion "will almost certainly cause more Americans to be killed." At least 30 of the prisoners that the military had chosen to release from Guantánamo Bay have returned to the battlefield. Despite the "incredible difficulty" of assessing who is and is not an enemy combatant, "[a]stoundingly, the Court raises the bar" by requiring the military to defend its decisions in civilian courts under rules beyond those specified by Congress.]

* * * During the 1995 prosecution of Omar Abdel Rahman, federal prosecutors gave the names of 200 unindicted co-conspirators to the "Blind Sheik's" defense lawyers; that information was in the hands of Osama Bin Laden within two weeks. In another case, trial testimony revealed to the enemy that the United States had been monitoring their cellular network, whereupon they promptly stopped using it, enabling more of them to evade capture and continue their atrocities.

* * * The Court today decrees that no good reason to accept the judgment of the other two branches is "apparent." * * * What competence does the Court have to second-guess the judgment of Congress and the President on such a point? None whatever. But the Court blunders in nonetheless. Henceforth, as today's opinion makes unnervingly clear, how to handle enemy prisoners in this war will ultimately lie with the branch that knows least about the national security concerns that the subject entails.

II

A

* * * The Court admits that it cannot determine whether the writ historically extended to aliens held abroad, and it concedes (necessarily) that Guantánamo Bay lies outside the sovereign territory of the United States. Together, these two concessions establish that it is (in the Court's view) perfectly ambiguous whether the common-law writ would have provided a remedy for these petitioners. If that is so, the Court has no basis to strike down the Military Commissions Act * * *.[2]

[Justice Scalia then criticized the Court's reliance on separation-of-powers principles to interpret the Suspension Clause. Those principles are simply the sum total, he said, of particular constitutional provisions, whose content must be considered one by one.] And if the understood scope of the writ of habeas corpus was "designed to restrain" (as the Court says) the actions of the Executive, the understood *limits* upon that scope

---

[2]   The opinion seeks to avoid this straightforward conclusion by saying that the Court has been "careful not to foreclose the possibility that the protections of the Suspension Clause have expanded along with post-1789 developments that define the present scope of the writ" (citing INS v. St. Cyr, 533 U.S. 289 300–301 (2001)). But not foreclosing the possibility that they have expanded is not the same as demonstrating (or at least holding without demonstration, which seems to suffice for today's majority) that they have expanded. The Court must either hold that the Suspension Clause has "expanded" in its application to aliens abroad, or acknowledge that it has no basis to set aside the actions of Congress and the President. It does neither.

were (as the Court seems not to grasp) just as much "designed to restrain" the incursions of the Third Branch. * * *

B

[The most pertinent precedent, Johnson v. Eisentrager, clearly found a lack of] habeas jurisdiction: "We are cited to [sic] no instance where a court, in this or any other country where the writ is known, has issued it on behalf of an alien enemy who, at no relevant time and in no stage of his captivity, has been within its territorial jurisdiction. Nothing in the text of the Constitution extends such a right, nor does anything in our statutes." [Eisentrager, 339 U.S., at 768.] * * *

The Court would have us believe that Eisentrager rested on "[p]ractical considerations," such as the "difficulties of ordering the Government to produce the prisoners in a habeas corpus proceeding." * * * This is a sheer rewriting of the case. Eisentrager mentioned practical concerns, to be sure—* * * to support *its holding* that the Constitution does not empower courts to issue writs of habeas corpus to aliens abroad *in any circumstances*. * * *

[Nor, Justice Scalia argued, can a "functional" reading of Eisentrager be supported by the Insular Cases, which concerned sovereign territories of the United States, or by the decision in Reid v. Covert, which concerned only the rights of citizens abroad.]

The category of prisoner comparable to these detainees are not the Eisentrager criminal defendants, but the more than 400,000 prisoners of war detained in the United States alone during World War II. Not a single one was accorded the right to have his detention validated by a habeas corpus action in federal court—and that despite the fact that they were present on U.S. soil. The Court's analysis produces a crazy result: Whereas those convicted and sentenced to death for war crimes are without judicial remedy, all enemy combatants detained during a war, at least insofar as they are confined in an area away from the battlefield over which the United States exercises "absolute and indefinite" control, may seek a writ of habeas corpus in federal court. * * *

C

[Today's decision is driven by "an inflated notion of judicial supremacy." The Court's concern that a test resting on formal sovereignty would permit the political branches to govern without legal constraint and would thus undercut this Court's duty "to say what the law is" is question-begging, as o]ur power "to say what the law is" is circumscribed by the limits of our statutorily and constitutionally conferred jurisdiction. And that is precisely the question in these cases: whether the Constitution confers habeas jurisdiction on federal courts to decide petitioners' claims. It is both irrational and arrogant to say that the answer must be yes, because otherwise we would not be supreme. * * *

III

Putting aside the conclusive precedent of Eisentrager, it is clear that the original understanding of the Suspension Clause was that habeas corpus was not available to aliens abroad * * *.

[The Suspension Clause should be given the meaning it was understood to have at the time of its adoption—a particularly important approach "when (as here) the Constitution limits the power of Congress to infringe upon a pre-existing common-law right." English common law made clear that the writ did not extend beyond the Crown's sovereign territory, and the Habeas Corpus Act of 1679, codifying the common law, maintained that limit. The Court's arguments that the writ did not run to Scotland because Scotland had its own judicial system and because enforcement there was impractical are mistaken: the former was not a basis for denying the writ, and enforcement was no more difficult in Scotland than in other locations, like the Channel Islands, to which the writ did run.] * * *

In sum, *all* available historical evidence points to the conclusion that the writ would not have been available at common law for aliens captured and held outside the sovereign territory of the Crown. * * *

What history teaches is confirmed by the nature of the limitations that the Constitution places upon suspension of the common-law writ. It can be suspended only "in Cases of Rebellion or Invasion." Art. I, § 9, cl. 2. * * * If the extraterritorial scope of habeas turned on flexible, "functional" considerations, as the Court holds, why would the Constitution limit its suspension almost entirely to instances of domestic crisis? Surely there is an even greater justification for suspension in foreign lands where the United States might hold prisoners of war during an ongoing conflict. And correspondingly, there is less threat to liberty when the Government suspends the writ's (supposed) application in foreign lands, where even on the most extreme view prisoners are entitled to fewer constitutional rights. * * *

[The limited reach of the writ, Justice Scalia said, was not disproved by its availability for citizens held abroad, for the common law writ, when absorbed into the Constitution, took on those changes demanded by a system in which] citizens (not "subjects") are afforded defined protections against the Government. * * *

NOTE ON BOUMEDIENE AND THE TERRITORIAL REACH OF HABEAS CORPUS

(1) Interpretive Methodology in Boumediene. Justice Scalia's dissent argues that fidelity to original intent is especially important "when (as here) the Constitution limits the power of Congress to infringe upon a pre-existing common-law right." Is that argument convincing, given that other constitutional guarantees have similar effect? (Consider, for example, the rights to a jury trial and to be free from unreasonable searches and seizures.) Indeed, one might respond that Justice Scalia's claim is undercut given that the Constitution gives Congress the power (which it lacks as to other constitutional guarantees) to suspend the privilege afforded by the common law.

Is the majority's view of the relevance of original understanding clear? Justice Kennedy says both that "[t]he Court has been careful not to foreclose the possibility that the protections of the Suspension Clause have expanded" since the Founding and that "the analysis may begin with precedents as of 1789, for the Court has said that 'at the absolute minimum' the Clause protects the writ as it existed when the Constitution was drafted and ratified" (quoting St. Cyr). In turn, Justice Scalia's dissent (see footnote 2) takes the Court to task for not being explicit about whether the Suspension Clause's protection is broader today than it was two centuries ago.

One might view the majority's extensive historical discussion (of which only a summary is provided) as having accepted, at least to some extent, an originalist approach, only to determine that history yields no definitive answer. But the majority's emphases on functional assessments, the particularities of the detention site, and prudential and practical considerations together seem to depart from originalism, for that cluster of factors will have quite different significance today than it did two centuries ago. (Could a federal court in the nation's capital have effectively exercised jurisdiction over a location like Guantánamo Bay in the eighteenth century?) Or should the Court's opinion be read as holding that the original understanding of the Suspension Clause was a functional one? Does the Suspension Clause's reference to a common law writ implicitly contemplate a continued common law-like development of constitutional meaning? In any event, isn't the Court's opinion consistent with what has been called a "common law" approach to interpretation of the scope of the writ, under which courts have "a creative, discretionary function in adapting constitutional and statutory language—which is frequently vague, and even more frequently reflects imperfect foresight—to novel circumstances"? Fallon & Meltzer, p. 1247, *supra*, at 2033.

In his dissent, Justice Scalia argued that the Court should provide great deference to Congress' determination that a law is constitutional, especially with respect to a law involving foreign and military affairs. He complained that the Court was second-guessing the political branches on the question whether the exercise of habeas jurisdiction would compromise the military mission at Guantánamo Bay. In response, the majority acknowledged the concept of deference, but found it inapplicable, in part because the challenged detention here was by executive order rather than by judicial trial, in part because the political branches should not be able, by disclaiming sovereignty over territory, to "switch the Constitution on or off", and most fundamentally, because of the majority's view that "habeas corpus is itself an indispensable mechanism for monitoring the separation of powers."

(2) The Suspension Clause and Aliens Abroad.

(a) The reasoning of the Rasul decision on the reach of § 2241 (before that statute's amendment by the DTA and the MCA of 2006) was profoundly ambiguous about whether the writ extended generally to detentions throughout the world. Some language in the Boumediene decision could be viewed as opening up arguments that habeas jurisdiction can reach aliens detained by the U.S. in foreign countries—for example, the statement that questions of extraterritoriality turn on objective factors and practical concerns, not formalism, and the concern about efforts by the government to avoid habeas jurisdiction. But the majority sharply distinguished the circumstances in Eisentrager from those in Boumediene, and the Court emphasized American "de facto sovereignty" at Guantánamo Bay: "In every practical sense Guantánamo is not abroad; it is within the constant jurisdiction of the United States." Those features of the opinion strongly suggest (as did Justice Kennedy himself in his concurrence in Rasul) that its reach is limited to what the Court itself calls the "unique status" of Guantánamo Bay.

(b) Whether aliens detained abroad enjoy any rights under the Suspension Clause (or the Constitution more generally) is a much-debated question. Among arguments supporting constitutional protection are these: (1) historically, habeas corpus was concerned with the actions of the officials, wherever located, and with their fidelity to the King's prerogative (in England) or to the law (in the United States), see Halliday & White, p. 1196, note 2, *supra*; (2) the Suspension Clause clearly protects aliens (when detained in the United States) and persons detained overseas (when they are citizens) and should therefore protect aliens detained overseas; (3) modern transportation and communication permit the extraterritorial exercise of habeas jurisdiction; and (4) a variety of normative arguments supporting such constitutional protection. Professor Neuman has classified these normative arguments as including (a) universalism—the view that the Constitution provides all persons with natural rights against the American government; (b) global due process—a balancing framework in which constitutional protections remain, though in diminished force, when (as with overseas detentions) the government has a more limited claim to obedience and capacity for enforcement;[1] and (c) his preferred view, "mutuality of obligation"—a presumption that the Constitution protects aliens abroad when the United States seeks to impose and enforce its own law. See generally Neuman, Strangers to the Constitution 5–8 (1996). Others are far more skeptical about extraterritorial application of constitutional protections. See, *e.g.*, Kent, *A Textual and Historical Case Against a Global Constitution*, 95 Geo.L.J. 463 (2007). But it should be clear that questions about the territorial reach of habeas corpus are bound up with broader questions about the extraterritorial reach of the Constitution.

(c) One might argue that the functional approach of Boumediene at least opens up the possibility that aliens abroad are protected under the Suspension Clause—at least in those instances in which the exercise of habeas jurisdiction is functionally justified. But that argument depends on the level of generality at which a functional approach is applied. Indeed, a critic of Boumediene like Justice Scalia could offer a functional argument that, as a general matter, habeas jurisdiction is more awkward for detentions outside sovereign territory than those inside such territory—without distinguishing Guantánamo from other areas beyond American sovereignty.

Alternatively, one could establish three categories: sovereign American territory, areas with the distinctive attributes of Guantánamo, and "truly" foreign areas, where in general the functional arguments against the exercise of habeas corpus jurisdiction are stronger than is true at Guantánamo. See Fallon & Meltzer, *supra*, at 2057: "[I]f habeas were available to noncitizens worldwide, it could in theory (if not always in practice) be pressed both in conventional wars, in which there might be thousands of alien captives, and with respect to such sensitive activities as foreign espionage. Moreover, efforts even to entertain petitions by aliens abroad would present practical problems. We have no constituted courts (other than military tribunals) that sit abroad. Notwithstanding modern transportation and communications, there could be considerable difficulties in litigating, in the United States, claims pertaining to detentions in distant areas over which American control rests on a temporary and possibly fragile

---

[1]   See, *e.g.*, United States v. Verdugo-Urquidez, 494 U.S. 259, 277–78 (1990) (Kennedy, J., concurring); Reid v. Covert, 354 U.S. 1, 74 (1957) (Harlan, J., concurring).

military balance. (Imagine moving detainees, witnesses, or lawyers around in Baghdad [in 2007] to develop evidence for a habeas proceeding.)"

Or one could subdivide still further, asking in each individual case whether the exercise of habeas jurisdiction is practicable in the circumstances presented—which might depend, for example, on whether the detention was on a battlefield or in an area over which American de facto control was secure, or on whether habeas inquiry would reveal sensitive intelligence.

(d) Even if in general the Suspension Clause does not reach aliens detained abroad, might some cases call for an exception? See *id.* at 2058 (imagining "a resident alien who ventured abroad to serve the United States as a military translator and was detained [overseas] on allegations of complicity with terrorists").

(e) In Al Maqaleh v. Gates, 605 F.3d 84 (D.C.Cir.2010), the court of appeals considered whether, in light of the Boumediene decision, the Suspension Clause grants a right to habeas review to detainees held by the United States in Afghanistan. Habeas petitions were filed on behalf of three individuals suspected of being enemy combatants, who had been seized outside of Afghanistan and then transported there for detention at the American-operated Bagram Theater Internment Facility outside Kabul. The district court denied the government's motion to dismiss for want of jurisdiction, viewing the degree of American control over the Bagram facility as little different from that at Guantánamo, and giving little weight to practical barriers to the exercise of jurisdiction since the Executive had chosen to move petitioners there. The court concluded that, as in Boumediene, the statutory prohibition on the exercise of habeas jurisdiction was unconstitutional as applied to the petitioners.

On an interlocutory appeal, the D.C. Circuit reversed, applying the three factors that the Boumediene Court had found relevant: "(1) the citizenship and status of the detainee and the adequacy of the process through which that status determination was made; (2) the nature of the sites where apprehension and then detention took place; and (3) the practical obstacles inherent in resolving the prisoner's entitlement to the writ." As to the first factor, citizenship and status were the same as in Boumediene, and because the administrative hearing afforded at Bagram was more rudimentary than the CSRT hearings afforded Guantánamo detainees, the first factor weighed in the petitioners' favor. The second factor weighed in the government's favor, as the U.S. had no intention to occupy Bagram permanently and did not exercise the kind of de facto sovereignty present at Guantánamo. Most important, however, and also favoring the government, was the third factor, in view of Afghanistan's status as an active war zone and Bagram's exposure to all of the vagaries of war. The court acknowledged that a government transfer of detainees to an active theater of war for the purpose of evading habeas jurisdiction might in some cases be a factor relevant to jurisdiction, but found it unnecessary to assess the significance of that factor given the lack of evidence that the government had been so motivated in this case.[2]

---

[2]　See also Al Maqaleh v. Hagel, 738 F.3d 312 (D.C.Cir.2013) (reaffirming the lack of jurisdiction).

NOTE ON PROPER RESPONDENTS

(1) The Padilla Decision. When a prisoner challenges the lawfulness of custody, who is the proper respondent? The official who operates the detention facility? That official's supervisor? How far up the chain of authority may a detainee go in naming a respondent?

In Rumsfeld v. Padilla, 542 U.S. 426 (2004), an American citizen, Padilla, was being held in New York City as a material witness in connection with a federal grand jury investigation of the 9/11 attacks. While his motion to vacate the material witness warrant was pending in federal court in New York, the government designated him as an "enemy combatant", took him into military custody, and transferred him to the Naval Brig in Charleston, South Carolina. All that action was taken without notice to his counsel—who two days later filed a federal habeas corpus petition in New York, naming as respondents President Bush, Secretary of Defense Rumsfeld, and Melanie Marr, Commander of the Naval Brig. When the case reached the Supreme Court, it held, 5–4, that (a) only Commander Marr, the immediate custodian, was a proper respondent, and (b) the district court in New York lacked jurisdiction over her.

(a) On the former point, Chief Justice Rehnquist's opinion emphasized that the habeas statute consistently refers to "the" custodian, and cited longstanding authority and practice confirming "that in habeas challenges to present physical confinement—'core challenges'—the default rule is that the proper respondent is the warden of the facility where the prisoner is being held, not the Attorney General or some other remote supervisory official." Cases departing from that rule involved challenges to something other than present physical confinement—as, for example, in Braden, p. 1245, *supra*, where the petitioner challenged future confinement.

(b) In finding a lack of jurisdiction, the Court invoked the "traditional rule" that the writ may be issued only in the district in which the immediate custodian is located. The Court relied in part on precedent and in part on a variety of statutory provisions that presupposed that a petition must be filed in the district of confinement,[1] which, "[i]n habeas challenges to *present* physical confinement * * * is *synonymous* with the district court that has territorial jurisdiction over the proper respondent."[2]

(c) In a concurring opinion joined by Justice O'Connor, Justice Kennedy said that the rules set forth by the Court were more like personal jurisdiction

---

[1]   Those provisions include §§ 2241(d) and 2255, which in some circumstances permit state or federal convicts to file in districts other than the district of confinement; both would have been unnecessary, the Court said, if § 2241 generally permitted a prisoner to do so.

[2]   Padilla relied on Strait v. Laird, 406 U.S. 341 (1972), where an inactive Army reservist petitioned for habeas (to review a failure to grant discharge as a conscientious objector) in California, where he was domiciled. The Court ruled that the petitioner's superior officers, though located in Indiana, were "present" in California because Strait's discharge application was processed through Army personnel there. Padilla argued that Secretary of Defense Rumsfeld was present in New York through his subordinates who took Padilla into custody there.

The majority in Padilla distinguished Strait as involving no challenge to present physical confinement and "*no* immediate physical custodian with respect to the 'custody' being challenged"; only in the "limited circumstances" there, "when Strait had always resided in California and had his only meaningful contacts with the Army there * * * did we invoke concepts of personal jurisdiction to hold that the custodian was 'present' in California through the actions of his agents." There was no need to do so here, as both Padilla and Commander Marr were in South Carolina.

or venue than subject matter jurisdiction, and thus were subject to exceptions and to waiver by the government. He would recognize an exception, he said, if the government were not forthcoming about the location of detention or if it moved a detainee in order to impede filing in the proper district.

(d) Justice Stevens, joined by Justices Souter, Ginsburg, and Breyer, dissented. While agreeing that "the immediate custodian rule should control in the ordinary case", he noted that the government had moved *ex parte* to vacate the material witness warrant and transfer custody to the military on June 9, two days before a scheduled hearing on Padilla's motion challenging the legality of his detention under that warrant. On June 10, the Attorney General announced Padilla's transfer to the Defense Department, and when on June 11 Padilla's lawyer filed a habeas petition, she apparently had not received official notice of Padilla's whereabouts. Justice Stevens objected that if the government had notified her of its intention to transfer Padilla to military custody, she would presumably have filed immediately, when both Padilla and his immediate custodian were in New York; the government should not, he contended, be able to obtain an advantage by having proceeded *ex parte*.

Justice Stevens stressed that the Court's "bright line rule" admits many exceptions—including when physical custody is not at issue (as in Braden),[3] when citizens are confined overseas, see Paragraph (2), *infra*, and when the petitioner is transferred from a judicial district after having filed a petition.[4] Padilla's detention, rather than being run-of-the-mill, in fact "is singular not only because it calls into question decisions made by [Secretary Rumsfeld] himself, but also because those decisions have created a unique and unprecedented threat to the freedom of every American citizen." Justice Stevens would have upheld jurisdiction in New York over Secretary Rumsfeld on the basis of his order to military personnel to seize Padilla and remove him to South Carolina.

(2) Custodians of Persons Held Overseas.

(a) **Citizens Held by U.S. Officials.** In Padilla, the Court acknowledged that "[w]e have long implicitly recognized an exception to the immediate custodian rule in the military context where an American citizen is detained outside the territorial jurisdiction of any district court." The Court cited Burns v. Wilson, 346 U.S. 137 (1953), and United States ex rel. Toth v. Quarles, 350 U.S. 11 (1955), both discussed at pp. 1246–1247, *supra*, in which the Court did not question the district court's jurisdiction to consider petitions on behalf of servicemen, detained abroad, who challenged the constitutionality of their convictions by courts martial. Both cases appear to hold, albeit implicitly, that at least when the immediate custodian is outside the jurisdiction of any federal district court, a petitioner may name

---

[3]   Justice Stevens also relied on Strait v. Laird, note 2, *supra*.

[4]   Justice Stevens referred here to Ex parte Endo, 323 U.S. 283 (1944), where the petitioner sought the writ in the Northern District of California while being held there during the relocation and internment of persons of Japanese ancestry during World War II. The Court held that the district court retained jurisdiction, despite petitioner's subsequent removal to Utah, because a custodian—the assistant director of the War Relocation Authority—remained within the district. In Padilla, the majority said that "Endo stands for the important but limited proposition that when the Government moves a habeas petitioner after she properly files a petition naming her immediate custodian, the District Court retains jurisdiction and may direct the writ to any respondent within its jurisdiction who has legal authority to effectuate the prisoner's release."

as the respondent a high official located within the United States—in Burns, the Secretary of Defense, and in Toth, the Secretary of the Air Force.

(b) Citizens Detained Under Multinational Auspices. Munaf v. Geren, 553 U.S. 674 (2008), involved petitions filed on behalf of American citizens who, after allegedly committing crimes in Iraq, were detained by American forces there. The government relied on Hirota v. MacArthur, 338 U.S. 197 (1948), p. 292, *supra*, for the proposition that American courts lack habeas jurisdiction when, as in Iraq, American military forces are part of a multinational force. In rejecting that view, a unanimous Court, per Roberts, C.J., said that in Hirota, it was not clear that the multinational tribunal whose decision was at issue was subject to plenary United States authority; here, by contrast, the government conceded that American forces were subject to plenary control by the American chain of command. The Court also emphasized that the petitioners, unlike those in Hirota, were American citizens.[5]

(c) Aliens Detained Abroad by U.S. Officials. Does the recognized exception to the immediate custodian rule when *citizens* are held abroad apply equally to *aliens*? In Rasul v. Bush, p. 1247, *supra*, the Guantánamo detainees named as respondents the President, the Secretary of Defense, the Chairman of the Joint Chiefs of Staff, the Commandant of Camp X-Ray/Camp Delta at Guantánamo, and other military officials. The Supreme Court did not address the question of who was a proper respondent, saying only that no challenge had been made to the district court's jurisdiction over the petitioner's custodians. In Boumediene v. Bush, pp. 1224, 1249, *supra*, the Court, in upholding habeas jurisdiction, did not even discuss the identity of the respondents.

———

[5] In Munaf, the Court proceeded, again unanimously, to deny relief on the merits. The petitioners sought an order barring their transfer for criminal prosecution to the Iraqi government, which the petitioners alleged would likely torture them. The Court said that the Executive's policy is not to transfer individuals when torture will likely result, that the State Department had found that the Iraqi Justice Ministry "generally met internationally accepted standards for basic prisoner needs", and that the judiciary was not well suited to second-guess such determinations. More broadly, the Court rejected the notion that the judiciary should shelter petitioners from a sovereign government seeking to hold them accountable for alleged crimes committed within the sovereign's borders.

For discussion of the Hirota decision, see generally Huq, *The Hirota Gambit*, 63 N.Y.U. Ann.Surv.Am.L. 63 (2007); Vladeck, *Deconstructing Hirota: Habeas Corpus, Citizenship, and Article III*, 95 Geo.L.J. 1497 (2007).

3. COLLATERAL ATTACK ON CRIMINAL CONVICTIONS

A. COLLATERAL ATTACK ON STATE CONVICTIONS

INTRODUCTORY NOTE ON THE OPERATION OF FEDERAL HABEAS CORPUS JURISDICTION FOR STATE PRISONERS

In 1867, Congress extended federal court habeas corpus jurisdiction so that it generally reached cases challenging the lawfulness of *state* custody. From 1867 to 1996, Congress did not fundamentally reshape the jurisdiction, but decisional law wove an intricate web of rules that changed significantly over time. In 1867 it was hardly clear that habeas corpus courts had power to entertain petitions from state prisoners seeking to relitigate, in federal court, federal issues decided adversely to them by a state criminal court of competent jurisdiction. Over time, Supreme Court decisions interpreted the statutory grant of jurisdiction as conferring such power.

The Warren Court generally defined the habeas jurisdiction broadly. In turn, the Burger and Rehnquist Courts narrowed the jurisdiction and tightened procedural requirements. Then Congress, in the Antiterrorism and Effective Death Penalty Act of 1996 (AEDPA), p. 1197, *supra*, enacted provisions significantly restricting the writ's availability, while leaving intact many judge-made doctrines that pre-date that Act. Both those doctrines and the provisions of AEDPA are complex, erecting a maze of requirements through which almost no petitions successfully emerge. The following overview of the operation of the habeas jurisdiction in actions commenced by prisoners convicted in state court may therefore be useful.

A. Cognizable Issues

(1) The Statutory Grant. In practice, habeas relitigation for state prisoners involves almost exclusively questions of federal *constitutional* law, as few state prosecutions implicate federal statutes or treaties.[1] For emphatic reaffirmation that federal habeas corpus does not reach errors of *state* law, see Estelle v. McGuire, 502 U.S. 62 (1991).

Under the Warren Court, a habeas court could review all constitutional issues that the Supreme Court could have considered on direct review of a state criminal conviction. The Burger and Rehnquist Courts created two key exceptions to that general rule: (i) one precluded claims that the state court erred in refusing to suppress evidence under the Fourth Amendment, so long as the state court provided a full and fair opportunity to litigate that question, see pp. 1285–1286, *infra*; (ii) the second, subject only to extraordinarily narrow exceptions, excluded claims founded on "new law"— *i.e.*, a constitutional rule that was not dictated by precedent at the time that

---

[1] In Reed v. Farley, 512 U.S. 339 (1994), five Justices indicated that a non-constitutional violation must constitute a "fundamental defect" to be cognizable, and that a violation of an interstate compact requiring commencement of trial within 120 days of a prisoner's transfer from one state to another did not qualify, at least when the prisoner had not made a timely objection and had suffered no prejudice. Two of the five Justices in the majority stated that few if any nonconstitutional violations constitute "fundamental defects".

the prisoner's conviction became final on direct review, see pp. 1295–1300, *infra*.

B.   Prerequisites to Review

A prisoner seeking federal habeas relief must satisfy two pre-conditions.

(1) Custody. Because habeas corpus is a remedy for unlawful custody, the prisoner must be in custody when the petition is filed. See 28 U.S.C. § 2241(c)(3); pp. 1354–1355, *infra*. "Custody" includes not only physical detention but also being subject to parole or probation conditions. But a convict who has served the entire sentence (including parole or probation terms) before filing a habeas petition, or whose only penalty was a fine, is not in custody.

(2) Exhaustion of State Remedies. Before seeking habeas relief, a prisoner must exhaust state remedies, including direct appellate review in the state courts (but not Supreme Court review of the state court conviction). See 28 U.S.C. § 2254(b–c); pp. 1349–1354, *infra*. Ordinarily, state postconviction remedies must be exhausted only as to issues not previously presented to the state courts (as might be true of claims of ineffective assistance of counsel or of failure to disclose exculpatory evidence). Studies suggested that in the 1970s and 1980s, 37–53% of habeas petitions were dismissed for failure to exhaust; a more recent study put the figure at 11%.[2]

Note the interaction of the custody and exhaustion requirements: in cases involving short sentences, a prisoner may no longer be in custody by the time state remedies have been exhausted.

C.   Initiation and Nature of the Proceedings

(1) Filing a Petition. A habeas petition (sometimes called an "application") names as the respondent a state officer having custody of the petitioner— ordinarily the prison warden or the director of the state correctional system. A habeas petition is not an appeal from, but rather a collateral attack upon, the state criminal conviction. Although most state prisoners are convicted by guilty plea, a recent study found that 97% of habeas petitioners sentenced to death, and 65% of non-capital habeas petitioners, were convicted at trial.[3]

(2) Civil Nature of Proceedings and Applicable Rules. Habeas corpus actions are *civil* proceedings. Since 1977, they have been subject to the "Rules Governing Section 2254 Cases in the United States District Courts" ("§ 2254 Rules"), Rule 12 of which states: "The Federal Rules of Civil Procedure, to the extent that they are not inconsistent with any statutory provisions or these rules, may be applied to a proceeding under these rules."

(3) Time Limits. No statute of limitations existed until 1996, when AEDPA added a one-year limitations period running from the latest of four specified dates. Ordinarily, the operative date is that "on which the judgment became final by the conclusion of direct review or the expiration of the time for

---

[2]   See pp. 1353–1354, *infra*.

[3]   See King, Cheesman & Ostrom, *Final Technical Report: Habeas Litigation in U.S. District Courts*, National Center for State Courts, Aug. 21, 2007, at 20. For earlier studies, see Flango, Habeas Corpus in State and Federal Courts 36 (1994); Robinson, An Empirical Study of Federal Habeas Corpus Review of State Court Judgments 7 (1979); Faust, Rubenstein & Yackle, *The Great Writ in Action: Empirical Light on the Federal Habeas Corpus Debate*, 18 N.Y.U.Rev.L. & Soc. Change 637, 678 (1991). Petitions from prisoners convicted by guilty plea may become even rarer if a relatively new practice—requiring defendants, as a condition of plea agreements, to waive the right to seek habeas relief—grows. See Malani, *Habeas Settlements*, 92 Va.L.Rev. 1, 7–10 (2006).

seeking such review." 28 U.S.C. § 2244(d)(1)(A). The other three are the dates on which (a) an impediment to filing, created by state action in violation of the Constitution or federal law, was removed; (b) the Supreme Court initially recognized a new constitutional right, retroactively applicable to cases on collateral review, see p. 1318, *infra*; and (c) the factual predicate of the claim could have been discovered with due diligence. § 2244(d). In addition, the Supreme Court has indicated that petitions filed more than one year after the dates specified in § 2244(d) are nonetheless not time-barred if the claim falls within the doctrine of equitable tolling or if the petitioner can satisfy an exacting standard of actual innocence.[4] The limitations period is tolled during the pendency of properly filed state postconviction proceedings, but not during the pendency of a prior federal habeas proceeding. Duncan v. Walker, 533 U.S. 167 (2001).

Many other complexities have arisen in the application of the limitations period.[5] Roughly one-fifth of non-capital cases (but a smaller percentage of capital cases) are dismissed as time-barred.[6]

(4) Availability of Counsel. Prisoners, the great majority of whom are indigent, generally have no *constitutional* right to appointed counsel in state or federal collateral attacks on their convictions.[7] Any federal right to counsel derives from statutes or court rules.

(a) Capital Cases. In 1988, Congress conferred a right to appointed counsel upon indigent federal habeas petitioners attacking a capital sentence

---

[4] On equitable tolling, see Holland v. Florida, 560 U.S. 631 (2010) (finding equitable tolling available in appropriate cases because § 2244(d) is properly considered "nonjurisdictional", equitable principles have traditionally governed habeas corpus, and equitable tolling would not undermine statutory purposes). On actual innocence, see McQuiggin v. Perkins, 133 S.Ct. 1924 (2013) (5–4) (holding that a petitioner who can demonstrate that in light of new evidence, no juror, acting reasonably, would have found the petitioner guilty beyond a reasonable doubt is not time-barred).

In both cases, Justice Scalia dissented, contending that § 2244(d) had spelled out how equitable considerations bear on the timeliness of a petition and that the Court lacked authority to create additional qualifications or exceptions to the limitations period.

[5] See, *e.g.*, Day v. McDonough, 547 U.S. 198 (2006) (5–4) (district court may raise a limitations defense sua sponte); Wood v. Milyard, 132 S.Ct. 1826 (2012) (by contrast, when the state expressly disclaimed reliance on a limitations defense of which it was aware, the court of appeals abused its discretion by resurrecting the defense); Lawrence v. Florida, 549 U.S. 327 (2007) (5–4) (limitations period is not tolled by filing a petition for certiorari seeking review of an otherwise final state postconviction proceeding); Mayle v. Felix, 545 U.S. 644 (2005) (amended petition, filed outside limitation period, that seeks to add a claim to a pending timely petition does not relate back when claims lack common core of operative facts); Pace v. DiGuglielmo, 544 U.S. 408 (2005) (5–4) (state postconviction petition dismissed as untimely by the state court is not "properly filed" under § 2244(d) and hence does not toll the federal limitations period). See also Dodd v. United States, 545 U.S. 353 (2005) (5–4), p. 1319, note 6, *infra* (in a § 2255 action brought by a federal prisoner, the one-year period from initial recognition by the Supreme Court of a new constitutional right, retroactively applicable to cases on collateral review, runs from the date on which the Supreme Court recognizes the new right, rather than the date on which the right is made retroactive).

[6] King, Cheesman & Ostrom, note 3, *supra*, at 46.

[7] See, *e.g.*, Pennsylvania v. Finley, 481 U.S. 551, 554–55 (1987); Johnson v. Avery, 393 U.S. 483, 488 (1969).

or conviction.[8] Only about 7% of capital petitioners proceed pro se.[9] (Nearly every state provides counsel to indigent capital defendants in state postconviction proceedings, although there is little monitoring of their performance.)

(b) Non-Capital Cases. In non-capital cases, the § 2254 Rules require appointment of counsel for an indigent petitioner if an evidentiary hearing is warranted (Rule 8(c)) or when necessary to utilize effectively discovery authorized by the court (Rule 6(a)); both circumstances are extraordinarily rare. Otherwise, counsel may be appointed if "the interests of justice so require". 18 U.S.C. § 3006A. More than 90% of non-capital petitioners proceed pro se.[10]

D.   Processing of Cases

(1) Petition and Response. Many petitions are frivolous, and more than 40% of non-capital petitions are dismissed without the state's even filing a response.[11] A state's response, when filed, often establishes a basis for dismissal without further proceedings. Discovery proceeds only as authorized by the judge for good cause shown, § 2254 Rules, Rule 6(a), and in practice is extremely limited. Evidentiary hearings to develop the facts are also rare[12]: in the twelve months ending September 30, 2013, of 13,370 petitions on which court action was taken, 13,312 were terminated "Before Pretrial", 54 "During or After Pretrial", and only 4 "During or After Trial".[13]

(2) The Role of Magistrate Judges. In many districts, federal magistrate judges have primary responsibility for handling habeas petitions. If a party objects to the magistrate judge's proposed findings and recommendations, the district judge must make a "de novo determination" with respect to any contested matter. 28 U.S.C. § 636(b)(1).

(3) Deference to State Court Determinations. Although res judicata does not apply in habeas proceedings, the federal court's role in reviewing the facts was sharply limited in 1996 by the new § 2254(d)(2), which precludes relief unless the court finds that the state court made an unreasonable determination of the facts based on the evidence in the state court record. See pp. 1320–1321, *infra*.

Traditionally, a habeas court was not bound to defer to a state court's decision on a question of law or the application of law to the facts. But § 2254(d)(1)—the most significant restriction that Congress added in 1996—now requires deference, by precluding habeas relief unless the state court's determination was "contrary to, or involved an unreasonable application of,

    8   See Anti-Drug Abuse Act of 1988, Pub.L.No. 100–690, § 7001(b), 102 Stat. 4393–94, codified at 21 U.S.C. § 848(q)(4)(B), repealed and recodified without change at 18 U.S.C. § 3599 by the Terrorist Death Penalty Enhancement Act of 2005, Pub.L.No. 109–177, Tit. II, § 222, 120 Stat. 231–32 (2006). This statutory right to counsel applies both before a habeas petition is filed, to provide assistance in preparing the petition, see McFarland v. Scott, 512 U.S. 849 (1994), and also during state clemency proceedings, see Harbison v. Bell, 556 U.S. 180 (2009).

    9   King, Cheesman & Ostrom, note 3, *supra*, at 23.

    10   *Id.*

    11   *Id.* at 34.

    12   See Weisselberg, *Evidentiary Hearings in Federal Habeas Corpus Cases*, 1990 B.Y.U.L.Rev. 131, 165–68.

    13   Annual Report of the Director of the Administrative Office of the United States Courts, Table C–4 (2013).

clearly established Federal law, as determined by the Supreme Court of the United States". See generally pp. 1301–1319, *infra*.

E.   Procedural Default

(1) Forfeiture of Federal Claims. When a claim raised in a federal habeas petition was not presented to the state courts, or was not presented in accordance with state procedural rules (*e.g.*, was not raised on a timely basis), ordinarily the state courts will not have reached the merits of the claim. When that is so, subject to only the narrowest exceptions, the federal habeas court will not consider the defaulted claim. See pp. 1323–1346, *infra*. (A procedural default involves a failure to pursue opportunities to litigate in state court that once were but no longer are available; a failure to exhaust state remedies, by contrast, involves a failure to pursue opportunities to litigate in state court that *remain* available.) About 13% of non-capital petitions are dismissed because of procedural default, and in nearly half of capital habeas proceedings, at least one claim is dismissed on this basis.[14]

[margin note:] claim usually can't make its first appearance in fed. ct.

F.   Remedy, Appeals, and Successive Petitions

(1) Relief. Ordinarily the only remedy awarded is release from custody, but the remedy is tailored to the nature of the constitutional violation. Thus, a petitioner convicted for conduct that is constitutionally protected (for example, burning the American flag) would obtain unconditional release from custody; a prisoner who established a procedural error (for example, admission of a confession in violation of the Miranda rules) would in practice obtain a retrial (through award of a conditional remedy, requiring release only if a retrial is not commenced within a specified period); and a prisoner who established a sentencing error would in practice be granted a new sentencing hearing.

(2) Appeals. The custodian may appeal a district court's grant of relief. A prisoner, before appealing a denial of relief, must obtain, from either the district court or the court of appeals,[15] a "certificate of appealability," which issues upon "a substantial showing of the denial of a constitutional right" and which must indicate the specific issue(s) satisfying that standard. 28 U.S.C. § 2253(c).[16]

[margin note:] need certificate to appeal (as prisoner)

(3) Successive Petitions. A prisoner may file more than one habeas petition only in exceedingly narrow circumstances. See pp. 1346–1349, *infra*.

---

[14]   King, Cheesman & Ostrom, note 3, *supra*, at 48.

[15]   See, *e.g.*, Tiedeman v. Benson, 122 F.3d 518, 522 & cases cited (8th Cir.1997).

[16]   In Slack v. McDaniel, 529 U.S. 473, 483 (2000), the Court ruled that § 2253(c)(2), added in 1996, codified precedent calling for issuance of a certificate if the appeal presented a federal question of substance that was "debatable among jurists of reason" or not "squarely foreclosed by statute, rule or authoritative court decision", Barefoot v. Estelle, 463 U.S. 880, 893 n.4, 894 (1983) (internal quotations omitted), except that § 2253(c)(2) substitutes "constitutional" for "federal". For discussion of the application of that standard in light of § 2254(d)(1)'s rule that, in order to grant relief, a habeas court must find that the state court's determination was not merely erroneous but was contrary to, or an unreasonable application of, law clearly established by the Supreme Court, see Medellín v. Dretke, 544 U.S. 660 (2005) (O'Connor, J., dissenting); Miller-El v. Cockrell, 537 U.S. 322 (2003).

G.   Filing and Success Rates

(1) Number of Petitions Filed. The trend in filings is as follows:

	Number of State Prisoner Habeas Corpus Petitions[17]	Number of State Prisoners[18]	State Prisoner Habeas Petitions as % of State Prisoners	Number of Private Civil Cases Filed in the Federal Courts[19]	State Prisoner Habeas Petitions as % of Private Civil Cases
1950	560	149,031	0.38%	32,193	1.74%
1955	660	165,692	0.40%	39,225	1.68%
1960	871	189,735	0.46%	38,444	2.27%
1965	4,845	189,855	2.55%	46,027	10.53%
1970	9,063	176,403	5.14%	62,356	14.53%
1975	7,843	216,462	3.62%	85,541	9.17%
1980	7,031	305,458	2.30%	105,161	6.69%
1985	8,534	462,284	1.85%	156,182	5.46%
1990	10,823	708,393	1.53%	161,579	6.70%
1995	13,632	1,025,624	1.33%	205,177	6.64%
2000	21,349	1,248,815	1.71%	188,408	11.33%
2005	19,190	1,338,292	1.43%	200,887	9.55%
2010	17,042	1,404,032	1.21%	239,958	7.11%
2013	16,919	1,358,375	1.25%	236,765	7.16%

---

[17] See Annual Report of the Director of the Administrative Office of the United States Courts, Table C–3, for the years indicated. Where numbers have been revised, the most recent figure is used. Through 1990, statistics are for a June 30 fiscal year and thereafter for a September 30 fiscal year. The figures include the very small number of petitions listed (a) under "local jurisdiction" and (b) in 2000, 2005, 2010, 2012, and 2013, in a separate category of death penalty cases.

Studies have found that roughly four of five habeas petitions attacked convictions or sentences; the rest related to pretrial matters, conditions of confinement, or revocation of probation or parole. Allen, Schachtman & Wilson, *Federal Habeas Corpus and its Reform: An Empirical Analysis*, 13 Rutgers L.J. 675, 755 n.367 (1982); King, Cheesman & Ostrom, note 3, *supra*, at 26–27. One study found a relationship between state prisoner population in a given year and the number of habeas petitions filed six years later. Cheesman, Hanson, & Ostrom, *A Tale of Two Laws: The U.S. Congress Confronts Habeas Corpus Petitions and Section 1983 Lawsuits*, 22 Law & Pol'y 89 (2000).

[18] See Bureau of Justice Statistics (BJS), *Historical Statistics on Prisoners in State and Federal Institutions, Yearend 1925–86* (May 1988) (1950–1975 figures); BJS, *Prisoners in State and Federal Institutions on December 31, 1981*, Table 1 (1980 figure); BJS, *Correctional Populations in the United States*, 1986, 1991, and 1996, respectively, Table 5 (1985–95 figures); BJS, *Bulletin: Prisoners in 2011* (December 2012), at 1 (2000–10 figure); BJS, *Bulletin: Prisoners in 2013* (September 2014), at 2 (2013 figure). Where numbers have been revised, the most recent figure is used. Statistics are as of December 31 for the indicated year.

The figures through 1975 are of prisoners "in custody", which refers to the direct physical control by the state of a confined person. Beginning in 1978, BJS published statistics of prisons "under jurisdiction", which refers to the legal power to incarcerate the person, and includes persons confined but not in the state's own prisons—for example, prisoners housed in local jails, in other states or in federal prisons, or in hospitals outside the correctional system, and inmates on work release, furlough, or bail. Beginning with 1980, the table uses the "under jurisdiction" statistic.

[19] See Annual Report, note 13, *supra*, Table C–2. Statistics through 1990 are based on a fiscal year ending June 30, and thereafter for a fiscal year ending September 30.

(2) Success Rates. Studies conducted during the 1970s and early 1980s found that only 3–4% of state prisoners who filed a petition obtained any kind of relief in the district courts[20]—and relief may result only in a further hearing or retrial that sustains the conviction. As judge-made and statutory restrictions on the exercise of habeas jurisdiction tightened, success rates in the district courts declined: to 1% in a study of petitions filed in 1990 and 1992,[21] and then, in a study of petitions filed in 2003–04 (when the 1996 amendments were fully operative), to less than 0.6% for non-capital petitioners.[22] (As noted below in Section H of this Note, relief is far more common in capital cases.)

(3) The Impact of the System. One commentator estimated that of state prisoners committed to custody each year, no more than 0.4% file habeas petitions—and (assuming a 3.2% success rate), no more than 0.003%, or 30 of every 100,000, obtain relief. See Meltzer, *Habeas Corpus Jurisdiction: The Limits of Models*, 66 S.Cal.L.Rev. 2507, 2523–24 (1993). (Recall that in the most recent study, the success rate had declined from 3.2% to less than 1%.) Do these statistics suggest that habeas review is a waste of time? That the jurisdiction exacts few costs while providing the valuable promise of federal review of federal questions arising in state criminal cases? (Consider the finding by Professor Shapiro, note 20, *supra*, at 340–42, that in a significant number of cases in which no relief is awarded, habeas review nonetheless serves useful functions—including aid in getting state processes that have been derailed back on track.) That uncounseled prisoners cannot navigate the procedural complexities or surmount the strict limits on the scope of federal review? That it is doubtful that any purpose that one might posit for habeas review is substantially fulfilled in practice?

H. Procedures in Capital Cases

Capital cases, although they constituted only 161 of the 13,370 habeas cases on which the district courts took action in the twelve months ending September 30, 2013,[23] pose special difficulties. On the one hand, the finality of execution calls for special solicitude, and the complexity of capital cases provides fertile ground for constitutional errors. One study found that petitioners obtained some relief in roughly 40% of the cases in which a death sentence was imposed between 1973 and 1995. Liebman, Fagan, & West, *A Broken System: Error Rates in Capital Cases, 1973–1995* (http://www2. law.columbia.edu/instructionalservices/liebman/liebman_final.pdf). A more recent study of capital petitions in 2000–02 found that 33 of 368 petitioners in the sample, or roughly 9%, obtained some form of relief, which two-thirds of the time was from the sentence rather than from conviction.[24] That rate, though dramatically lower than 40%, was nearly 30 times higher than the

---

[20] See Faust, Rubenstein & Yackle, note 3, *supra*, at 681; Robinson, note 3, *supra*, at 23; Shapiro, *Federal Habeas Corpus: A Study in Massachusetts*, 87 Harv.L.Rev. 321, 333 (1973). Capital cases aside, very few petitioners who lose in the district court obtain relief on appeal. See, *e.g.*, King, *Non-Capital Habeas Cases After Appellate Review: An Empirical Analysis*, 24 Fed. Sent'g Rep. 308, 310 (2012) (in a study in which 2,188 cases terminated in the district courts, only 18 petitioners received favorable rulings on appeal).

[21] Flango, note 3, *supra*, at 62–63.

[22] King, Cheesman & Ostrom, note 3, *supra*, at 52, as modified by King, note 20, *supra*. King's article found that after appeals were resolved, another 0.3% of petitioners obtained relief.

[23] See Annual Report, note 13, *supra*, Table C–4.

[24] See King, Cheesman & Ostrom, note 3, *supra*, at 51–52.

rate for non-capital cases. (Recall that only capital petitioners are entitled by statute to counsel in federal habeas proceedings.)

On the other hand, critics of capital habeas litigation have expressed concern about what they view as abuses and unnecessary delays (such as filing multiple petitions and/or petitions at the eleventh hour and then seeking a stay of execution). The AEPDA, enacted in 1996, provides that if a state has established a mechanism for providing counsel in state postconviction proceedings brought by indigent prisoners under sentence of death, 28 U.S.C. § 2261(b), various additional procedural restrictions take effect.[25] To date, no state has qualified,[26] perhaps because most find the benefits not worth the cost of supplying counsel in state postconviction proceedings. See Blume, *AEDPA: The "Hype" and the "Bite"*, 91 Cornell L.Rev. 259, 274–76 (2006).

INTRODUCTORY NOTE ON THE HISTORICAL DEVELOPMENT OF FEDERAL RELITIGATION IN CRIMINAL CASES

Many scholars have discussed the historic scope of the writ of habeas corpus as a postconviction remedy and the implications of the history for contemporary interpretation of the jurisdictional grant. Drawing lessons

---

[25] One such restriction is a limitations period of 180 days rather than one year. § 2263. A second is the specification of deadlines within which courts must render decisions: for the district courts, the initial deadline of 180 days after filing (with one 30-day extension possible) was amended in 2006 to the earlier of (i) 450 days after filing or (ii) 60 days after the case was submitted for decision; for the courts of appeals, the deadline is 120 days after the reply brief is filed. § 2266. A third restriction limits the issuance of stays of execution. Pre-AEDPA decisions had come close to laying down a rule that a petitioner under death sentence is entitled to a stay of execution in connection with a first habeas petition, see Lonchar v. Thomas, 517 U.S. 314, 324 (1996), while suggesting that a stay in connection with a successive petition will be far more difficult to obtain, see Bowersox v. Williams, 517 U.S. 345 (1996) (per curiam). AEDPA does not disturb this approach, but provides that any stay of execution shall expire if the prisoner (a) fails to file a timely petition, (b) "fails to make a substantial showing of the denial of a Federal right", or (c) "is denied relief in the district court or at any subsequent stage of review". § 2262(b). Upon expiration, "no Federal court thereafter shall have the authority to enter a stay of execution in the case, unless the court of appeals approves the filing of a second or successive application under section 2244(b)". § 2262(c). For a detailed analysis of the entire set of provisions that govern petitions filed by prisoners under sentence of death in a qualifying state, see Yackle, *The New Habeas Corpus in Death Penalty Cases*, 63 Am.U.L.Rev. 1791 (2014).

[26] See Blume et al., *In Defense of Noncapital Habeas: A Response to Hoffman and King*. 96 Cornell L.Rev. 435 (2011). In Spears v. Stewart, 283 F.3d 992 (9th Cir.2002), the panel found that Arizona's system could qualify, but refused to enforce the provisions of §§ 2261–64 in the case at bar because Arizona had not complied with its own rules requiring timely appointment of counsel.

Section 507 of the USA PATRIOT Improvement and Reauthorization Act of 2005, Pub.L.No. 109–177, 120 Stat. 192, 250 (2006), amended the habeas statute by shifting from the federal courts to the Attorney General the authority initially to certify that states have established mechanisms for providing counsel in state postconviction proceedings and by specifying that no additional requirements for certification shall be imposed beyond those set forth in the statute: "whether the State has established a mechanism for the appointment, compensation, and payment of reasonable litigation expenses of competent counsel in State postconviction proceedings brought by indigent prisoners who have been sentenced to death" and "whether the State provides standards of competency for the appointment" (§ 2265(a)(1)). In 2013, the Attorney General issued a final rule implementing the certification procedure. See 78 Fed. Reg. 58,160 (Sept. 23, 2013) (to be codified at 28 C.F.R. pt. 26). Three months later, a federal court issued a preliminary injunction against the rule. See Habeas Corpus Res. Ctr. v. U.S. Dep't of Justice, No. C 13–4517 CW, 2013 WL 6326618 (N.D.Cal. Dec. 4, 2013).

from the history is difficult, as the precedents involve a broad range of variables—federal vs. state prisoners; pre-trial vs. post-trial detention; ordinary criminal cases vs. contempt proceedings; unfamiliar and shifting conceptions of jurisdiction; evolving conceptions of due process; and changes in the Supreme Court's appellate jurisdiction—whose significance is not always discussed. Moreover, many decisions do not articulate a clear understanding of habeas corpus—particularly one that corresponds to modern categories and perceptions.[1] Nonetheless, it is worth noting several key points about the historical development and debate.

(1) The Historical Limits of Postconviction Review. Numerous authorities suggest that both before and after the Founding, a prisoner held pursuant to a criminal conviction could challenge, in a habeas corpus petition, only the jurisdiction of the court that rendered the judgment of conviction. See, *e.g.*, Ex parte Watkins, 28 U.S. (3 Pet.) 193 (1830).[2]

(2) The Habeas Corpus Act of 1867. The Act of February 5, 1867, 14 Stat. 385, extended the federal writ to a new class of prisoners—all of those in state custody—but scholars dispute whether the Reconstruction Congress, mistrustful as it was of state courts, also broadened the scope of the writ to reach not merely jurisdictional defects but violations of federal law more broadly.[3]

(3) Evolution in the Nineteenth Century. After 1867, the Court held that the writ embraced claims by federal prisoners that the statute under which a criminal conviction had been obtained was unconstitutional, *e.g.*, Ex parte Siebold, 100 U.S. 371, 376–77 (1879), or that the sentence imposed exceeded what the statute authorized, *e.g.*, Ex parte Lange, 85 U.S. (18 Wall.) 163, 176 (1873). Some view these decisions as merely "softening", but not departing from, the jurisdictional concept.[4] Others view them as part of a trend in

---

[1]   Thus, Arkin, *The Ghost at the Banquet: Slavery, Federalism, and Habeas Corpus for State Prisoners*, 70 Tulane L.Rev. 1 (1995), notes that in the ante-bellum period, (i) postconviction habeas petitions were rare because imprisonment was not a common sanction, and (ii) the most prominent use of federal habeas jurisdiction to promote federal supremacy was in enforcing the Fugitive Slave Act—hardly a comfortable foundation for modern understandings.

[2]   See Bator, *Finality in Criminal Law and Federal Habeas Corpus for State Prisoners*, 76 Harv.L.Rev. 441 (1963); Oaks, *Habeas Corpus in the States—1776–1865*, 32 U.Chi.L.Rev. 243, 258–61 (1965). For discussion of the British development, see the authorities cited at p. 1193, note 2, *supra*.

Professor Peller explains decisions like Watkins differently. He contends that it would have been anomalous for the Supreme Court, which until 1891 lacked jurisdiction to review federal criminal convictions directly, to review convictions indirectly on habeas; by contrast, he contends that lower federal courts exercised plenary power to relitigate constitutional claims. Peller, *In Defense of Federal Habeas Corpus Relitigation*, 16 Harv.C.R.–C.L.L.Rev. 579 (1982). For doubts about this explanation, see Woolhandler, *Demodeling Habeas*, 45 Stan.L.Rev. 575, 585–96 & n. 67 (1993); Liebman, *Apocalypse Next Time?: The Anachronistic Attack on Habeas Corpus/Direct Review Parity*, 92 Colum.L.Rev. 1997, 2046 (1992).

Kovarsksy, *A Constitutional Theory of Habeas Power*, 99 Va.L.Rev. 753, 768–69 (2013), contends that the King's Bench in England did use habeas proceedings to review criminal convictions, and that Chief Justice Marshall's statement in Watkins that review was limited to the question of jurisdiction has contributed to "one of the most pervasive falsehoods in the habeas literature."

[3]   Compare Bator, note 2, *supra*, at 465–66 (no expansion of the writ); Forsythe, *The Historical Origins of Broad Federal Habeas Review Reconsidered*, 70 Notre Dame L.Rev. 1079, 1101–24 (1995) (same); and Mayers, *The Habeas Corpus Act of 1867: The Supreme Court as Legal Historian*, 33 U.Chi.L.Rev. 31 (1965) (same), with Peller, note 2, *supra*, at 618–20 (Congress expanded the writ).

[4]   See Bator, note 2, *supra*.

which habeas courts reached beyond jurisdictional defects to consider most constitutional claims. On one interpretation, for much of the nineteenth century, constitutional claims were generally limited to challenges to statutes, but as the understanding of constitutional wrongs expanded to encompass ad hoc or unauthorized actions of state officials, the effective scope of habeas relitigation expanded.[5]

(4) Early Twentieth Century Precedents. Two decisions from the early twentieth century involved due process claims arising from alleged mob domination of state trial proceedings. In Frank v. Mangum, 237 U.S. 309 (1915), the Court refused to grant the writ; eight years later, in Moore v. Dempsey, 261 U.S. 86 (1923), the writ was granted. One explanation for the differing results is that in Frank, the state appellate court, in reviewing the trial proceedings, had already provided fair corrective process, whereas in Moore, the Court may have held that the state appellate review of the alleged mob domination had been so perfunctory as not to constitute an adequate state corrective process, therefore permitting federal habeas review.[6] Others view Moore as overruling Frank on either the scope of the writ[7] or on the meaning of due process.[8]

(5) The 1953 Decision in Brown v. Allen. The next principal case, Brown v. Allen, is one landmark whose holding is not in dispute. Brown clearly ruled that a federal court should routinely relitigate the merits of federal constitutional issues that the state court had decided adversely to the state prisoner. Some commentators viewed Brown as a dramatic expansion of the historic role of habeas,[9] while others saw Brown as merely confirming a trend by which violations of fundamental law—a term that encompassed evolving notions of due process—could be reviewed by a habeas court.[10] Whatever its consistency with the history, Brown ushered in a regime of broad federal relitigation during the Warren Court years and in the early years of the Burger Court. That same era witnessed the incorporation of virtually all of the provisions of the Bill of Rights through the Fourteenth Amendment so as

---

[5] See Woolhandler, note 2, *supra*, at 596–630.

[6] See Bator, note 2, *supra*, at 483–93.

[7] See Wechsler, *Habeas Corpus and the Supreme Court: Reconsidering the Reach of the Great Writ*, 59 U.Colo.L.Rev. 167, 173 (1988).

[8] See Peller, note 2, *supra*, at 646. A distinct explanation of the expansion of the writ exemplified by Moore rests on the premise that "[s]ince 1789, Congress has entitled federal and state prisoners incarcerated in violation of any fundamental legal (typically, any constitutional) principle to one meaningful federal court review as of right"; when, in 1914, the Supreme Court's jurisdiction to review state court judgments became discretionary rather than mandatory, federal habeas corpus jurisdiction expanded to fill the gap. Liebman, note 2, *supra*, at 2081, 2096. See also Freedman, *Leo Frank Lives: Untangling the Historical Roots of Meaningful Federal Habeas Corpus Review of State Convictions*, 51 Ala.L.Rev. 1467 (2000).

[9] The leading proponent of that view was Bator, note 2, *supra*. Accord, *e.g.*, Duker, A Constitutional History of Habeas Corpus (1980); Mayers, note 3, *supra*; Oaks, *Legal History in the High Court—Habeas Corpus*, 64 Mich.L.Rev. 451 (1966). See also, *e.g.*, Felker v. Turpin, 518 U.S. 651, 663 (1996); Wright v. West, 505 U.S. 277, 285–86 (1992) (opinion of Thomas, J., joined by Rehnquist, C.J., and Scalia, J.); McCleskey v. Zant, 499 U.S. 467, 477–79 (1991); Stone v. Powell, 428 U.S. 465, 475–76 (1976).

[10] That view was taken by Justice Brennan, for the Court, in Fay v. Noia, 372 U.S. 391 (1963). See also Yackle, *Form and Function in the Administration of Justice: The Bill of Rights and Federal Habeas Corpus*, 23 U.Mich.J.L.Reform 685, 695–702 (1990). Freedman, *Brown v. Allen: The Habeas Corpus Revolution That Wasn't*, 51 Ala.L.Rev. 1541 (2000), concludes, after examining internal Court documents, that the Justices did not perceive Brown to be revolutionary. (The documents do reveal the Court's recognition of considerable uncertainty about the scope of habeas jurisdiction.)

to make them applicable to the states, as well as a dramatic expansion of the reach of constitutional rights concerning criminal procedure. Many observers believe that without the broad scope of habeas review authorized by Brown, the federal judiciary could not have effectively supervised the compliance by state courts (particularly in Southern states) with Supreme Court decisions recognizing new and controversial federal constitutional rights governing state criminal processes.

Judicial decisions from the 1970s on, and in turn the 1996 congressional amendments to the habeas jurisdiction, together sharply limited the scope of relitigation that Brown had recognized. Though Brown no longer states the governing law, the current scope of review and the issues it raises cannot be understood without studying the Brown regime.

———

Brown v. Allen

344 U.S. 443, 73 S.Ct. 397, 97 L.Ed. 469 (1953).
Certiorari to the United States Court of Appeals for the Fourth Circuit.

[Brown involved three consolidated cases (those of Brown, Speller, and Daniels), all involving black defendants sentenced to death in North Carolina for interracial rape or murder. All three habeas petitions alleged unconstitutional racial discrimination in the selection of the petit jury; Brown and Daniels also complained of discrimination in the selection of the grand jury and of the admission at trial of a coerced confession.

[In the Daniels case, the Supreme Court of North Carolina, on direct appeal from the conviction, refused to consider the merits of the constitutional claims because the appeal had been filed one day late. The U.S. Supreme Court held that this state court procedural default precluded federal habeas review.[1]

[Brown's and Speller's petitions raised constitutional issues that had been fully litigated with the aid of counsel at trial, rejected on the merits on appeal, and set forth in an unsuccessful petition for certiorari. In considering their habeas petitions, the federal district court examined the state court record, and, in Speller's case, took additional evidence. It then denied relief, essentially on the basis that the state court's determinations were supported by the evidence and should not be relitigated. In Speller's case, the district judge stated that a "habeas corpus proceeding is not available * * * for the purpose of raising the identical question passed upon in [the state] Courts", but added, as an alternative ground, that Speller had failed to substantiate his constitutional claims. The Fourth Circuit affirmed in both cases.

[In the Supreme Court, eight opinions were filed. The Justices divided both on the central question presented by the Brown and Speller petitions—whether a federal court exercising habeas jurisdiction may re-examine the merits of federal constitutional claims that were denied by the state courts—and on the merits of those claims.

---

[1]   For discussion of Daniels and the effect of state court procedural defaults on habeas corpus jurisdiction, see pp. 1323–1346, *infra*.

[The Court's handling of the case was unusual. Justice Reed delivered the "opinion of the Court"—even though on one issue, he spoke for a minority.[2] His opinion, joined by Chief Justice Vinson and Justices Burton, Clark, and Minton, sends conflicting signals on whether federal courts should defer to the state court's substantive determinations. In the end, Justice Reed reached the merits of Brown's and Speller's constitutional claims and found them wanting. Justice Frankfurter filed an elaborate opinion that no other Justice formally joined, but with which four other Justices (Black, Douglas, Burton, and Clark) indicated their agreement in separate opinions. Justice Frankfurter described his opinion as "designed to make explicit and detailed matters that are also the concern of Mr. Justice Reed's opinion", and he stated that "[t]he views of the Court * * * may thus be drawn from the two opinions jointly." Because Justice Frankfurter's opinion reflects the way that Brown v. Allen has subsequently been understood, substantial portions of it are presented here.]

■ Opinion of Frankfurter, J.

* * *

II

* * * I deem it appropriate to begin by making explicit some basic considerations underlying the federal habeas corpus jurisdiction. Experience may be summoned to support the belief that most claims in these attempts to obtain review of State convictions are without merit. Presumably they are adequately dealt with in the State courts. Again, no one can feel more strongly than I do that a casual, unrestricted opening of the doors of the federal courts to these claims not only would cast an undue burden upon those courts, but would also disregard our duty to support and not weaken the sturdy enforcement of their criminal laws by the States. That wholesale opening of State prison doors by federal courts is, however, not at all the real issue before us is best indicated by a survey recently prepared in the Administrative Office of the United States Courts for the Conference of Chief Justices: of all federal question applications for habeas corpus, some not even relating to State convictions, only 67 out of 3,702 applications were granted in the last seven years. And "only a small number" of these 67 applications resulted in release from prison: "a more detailed study over the last four years * * * shows that out of 29 petitions granted, there were only 5 petitioners who were released from state penitentiaries."[11] The meritorious claims are few, but our procedures must ensure that those few claims are not stifled by undiscriminating generalities. * * *

For surely it is an abuse to deal too casually and too lightly with rights guaranteed by the Federal Constitution, even though they involve limitations upon State power and may be invoked by those morally unworthy. Under the guise of fashioning a procedural rule, we are not justified in wiping out the practical efficacy of a jurisdiction conferred by Congress on the District Courts. Rules which in effect treat all these

---

[2] That issue was whether the Supreme Court's denial of certiorari should be treated as a determination that there was no constitutional violation. The majority said no.

[11] Habeas Corpus Cases in the Federal Courts Brought by State Prisoners, Administrative Office of the United States Courts 4 (Dec. 16, 1952). * * *

cases indiscriminately as frivolous do not fall far short of abolishing this head of jurisdiction.

Congress could have left the enforcement of federal constitutional rights governing the administration of criminal justice in the States exclusively to the State courts. These tribunals are under the same duty as the federal courts to respect rights under the United States Constitution. Indeed, * * * [i]t was not until the Act of 1867 that the power to issue the writ was extended to an applicant under sentence of a State court. It is not for us to determine whether this power should have been vested in the federal courts. As Mr. Justice Bradley * * * commented not long after the passage of that Act, "although it may appear unseemly that a prisoner, after conviction in a state court, should be set at liberty by a single judge on *habeas corpus*, there seems to be no escape from the law." Ex parte Bridges, 2 Woods (5th Cir.) 428, 432. * * * By giving the federal courts [habeas] jurisdiction, Congress has embedded into federal legislation the historic function of habeas corpus adapted to reaching an enlarged area of claims.

In exercising the power thus bestowed, the District Judge must take due account of the proceedings that are challenged by the application for a writ. All that has gone before is not to be ignored as irrelevant. But the prior State determination of a claim under the United States Constitution cannot foreclose consideration of such a claim, else the State court would have the final say which the Congress, by the Act of 1867, provided it should not have. * * * That most claims are frivolous has an important bearing upon the procedure to be followed by a district judge. The prior State determination may guide his discretion in deciding upon the appropriate course to be followed in disposing of the application before him. The State record may serve to indicate the necessity of further pleadings or of a quick hearing to clear up an ambiguity, or the State record may show the claim to be frivolous or not within the competence of a federal court because solely dependent on State law.

It may be a matter of phrasing whether we say that the District Judge summarily denies an application for a writ by accepting the ruling of the State court or by making an independent judgment, though he does so on the basis of what the State record reveals. But since phrasing mirrors thought, it is important that the phrasing not obscure the true issue before a federal court. * * * If we are to give effect to the statute and at the same time avoid improper intrusion into the State criminal process by federal judges * * *[,] we must direct them to probe the federal question while drawing on available records of prior proceedings to guide them in doing so.

Of course, experience cautions that the very nature and function of the writ of habeas corpus precludes the formulation of fool-proof standards which the 225 District Judges can automatically apply. * * * But it is important, in order to preclude individualized enforcement of the Constitution in different parts of the Nation, to lay down as specifically as the nature of the problem permits the standards or directions that should govern the District Judges in the disposition of applications for habeas corpus by prisoners under sentence of State courts.

First. Just as in all other litigation, a prima facie case must be made out by the petitioner. The application should be dismissed when it fails to state a federal question, or fails to set forth facts which, if accepted at face value, would entitle the applicant to relief. * * *

Second. Failure to exhaust an available State remedy is an obvious ground for denying the application. * * *

Third. If the record of the State proceedings is not filed, the judge is required to decide * * * whether it is more desirable to call for the record or to hold a hearing. * * *

Fourth. When the record of the State court proceedings is before the court, it may appear that the issue turns on basic facts and that the facts (in the sense of a recital of external events and the credibility of their narrators) have been tried and adjudicated against the applicant. Unless a vital flaw be found in the process of ascertaining such facts in the State court, the District Judge may accept their determination in the State proceeding * * *. On the other hand, State adjudication of questions of law cannot, under the habeas corpus statute, be accepted as binding. It is precisely these questions that the federal judge is commanded to decide. * * *

Fifth. Where the ascertainment of the historical facts does not dispose of the claim but calls for interpretation of the legal significance of such facts, the District Judge must exercise his own judgment on this blend of facts and their legal values. Thus, so-called mixed questions or the application of constitutional principles to the facts as found leave the duty of adjudication with the federal judge.

For instance, the question whether established primary facts underlying a confession prove that the confession was coerced or voluntary cannot rest on the State decision. * * * Although there is no need for the federal judge, if he could, to shut his eyes to the State consideration of such issues, no binding weight is to be attached to the State determination. * * * The State court cannot have the last say when it, though on fair consideration and what procedurally may be deemed fairness, may have misconceived a federal constitutional right. * * *

These standards, addressed as they are to the practical situation facing the District Judge, recognize the discretion of judges to give weight to whatever may be relevant in the State proceedings, and yet preserve the full implication of the requirement of Congress that the District Judge decide constitutional questions presented by a State prisoner even after his claims have been carefully considered by the State courts. Congress has the power to distribute among the courts of the States and of the United States jurisdiction to determine federal claims. It has seen fit to give this Court power to review errors of federal law in State determinations, and in addition to give to the lower federal courts power to inquire into federal claims, by way of habeas corpus. Such power is in the spirit of our inherited law. It accords with, and is thoroughly regardful of, "the liberty of the subject" * * *.

The reliable figures of the Administrative Office of the United States Courts, showing that during the last four years five State prisoners, all told, were discharged by federal district courts, prove beyond peradventure that it is a baseless fear, a bogey man, to worry lest State convictions be upset by allowing district courts to entertain applications for habeas corpus on behalf of prisoners under State sentence. Insofar as this jurisdiction enables federal district courts to entertain claims that

State Supreme Courts have denied rights guaranteed by the United States Constitution, it is not a case of a lower court sitting in judgment on a higher court. It is merely one aspect of respecting the Supremacy Clause of the Constitution whereby federal law is higher than State law. It is for the Congress to designate the member in the hierarchy of the federal judiciary to express the higher law. * * *

The uniqueness of habeas corpus in the procedural armory of our law cannot be too often emphasized. It differs from all other remedies in that it is available to bring into question the legality of a person's restraint and to require justification for such detention. Of course this does not mean that prison doors may readily be opened. It does mean that explanation may be exacted why they should remain closed. * * *

■ Mr. JUSTICE JACKSON, concurring in the result.

Controversy as to the undiscriminating use of the writ of habeas corpus by federal judges to set aside state court convictions is traceable to three principal causes: (1) this Court's use of the generality of the Fourteenth Amendment to subject state courts to increasing federal control, especially in the criminal law field; (2) *ad hoc* determination of due process of law issues by personal notions of justice instead of by known rules of law; and (3) the breakdown of procedural safeguards against abuse of the writ. * * *

The fact that the substantive law of due process is and probably must remain so vague and unsettled as to invite farfetched or borderline petitions makes it important to adhere to procedures which enable courts readily to distinguish a probable constitutional grievance from a convict's mere gamble on persuading some indulgent judge to let him out of jail. Instead, this Court has sanctioned progressive trivialization of the writ until floods of stale, frivolous and repetitious petitions inundate the docket of the lower courts and swell our own. Judged by our own disposition of habeas corpus matters, they have, as a class, become peculiarly undeserving. It must prejudice the occasional meritorious application to be buried in a flood of worthless ones. He who must search a haystack for a needle is likely to end up with the attitude that the needle is not worth the search. Nor is it any answer to say that few of these petitions in any court really result in the discharge of the petitioner. That is the condemnation of the procedure which has encouraged frivolous cases. In this multiplicity of worthless cases, states are compelled to default or to defend the integrity of their judges and their official records, sometimes concerning trials or pleas that were closed many years ago. State Attorneys General recently have come habitually to ignore these proceedings, responding only when specially requested and sometimes not then. Some state courts have wearied of our repeated demands upon them and have declined to further elucidate grounds for their decisions. The assembled Chief Justices of the highest courts of the states have taken the unusual step of condemning the present practice by resolution.[13]

It cannot be denied that the trend of our decisions is to abandon rules of pleading or procedure which would protect the writ against abuse. Once upon a time the writ could not be substituted for appeal * * * but

---

[13] Conference of Chief Justices—1952, 25 State Government, No. 11, p. 249 (Nov.1952) [.]
* * *

challenged only the legal competence or jurisdiction of the committing court. We have so departed from this principle that the profession now believes that the issues we *actually consider* on a federal prisoner's habeas corpus are substantially the same as would be considered on appeal.

Conflict with state courts is the inevitable result of giving the convict a virtual new trial before a federal court sitting without a jury. Whenever decisions of one court are reviewed by another, a percentage of them are reversed. That reflects a difference in outlook normally found between personnel comprising different courts. However, reversal by a higher court is not proof that justice is thereby better done. There is no doubt that if there were a super-Supreme Court, a substantial proportion of our reversals of state courts would also be reversed. We are not final because we are infallible, but we are infallible only because we are final. * * *

It is sometimes said that *res judicata* has no application whatever in habeas corpus cases and surely it does not apply with all of its conventional severity. Habeas corpus differs from the ordinary judgment in that, although an adjudication has become final, the application is renewable, at least if new evidence and material is discovered or if, perhaps as the result of a new decision, a new law becomes applicable to the case. This is quite proper so long as its issues relate to jurisdiction. But call it *res judicata* or what one will, courts ought not to be obliged to allow a convict to litigate again and again exactly the same question on the same evidence. Nor is there any good reason why an identical contention rejected by a higher court should be reviewed on the same facts in a lower one. * * *

My conclusion is that * * * no lower federal court should entertain a petition except on the following conditions: (1) that the petition raises a jurisdictional question involving federal law on which the state law allowed no access to its courts, either by habeas corpus or appeal from the conviction, and that he therefore has no state remedy; or (2) that the petition shows that although the law allows a remedy, he was actually improperly obstructed from making a record upon which the question could be presented, so that his remedy by way of ultimate application to this Court for certiorari has been frustrated. There may be circumstances so extraordinary that I do not now think of them which would justify a departure from this rule, but the run-of-the-mill case certainly does not. * * *

NOTE ON THE RULE OF BROWN V. ALLEN AND ON HABEAS CORPUS POLICY

A.   The Scope of Federal Relitigation

The basic principle of Brown v. Allen—that federal habeas courts should relitigate questions of federal constitutional law that were fully and fairly litigated in state court—was controversial from its inception.[1] But as Justice

---

[1]   In 1955, the Judicial Conference of the United States recommended restricting habeas review to claims presenting a constitutional question "(1) which was not theretofore raised and determined (2) which there was no fair and adequate opportunity theretofore to raise and have determined and (3) which cannot thereafter be raised and determined in a proceeding in the

Frankfurter noted, the scope of relitigation did not routinely extend to the basic, or historical, facts. Thus, for example, if in Brown the admissibility of the confession turned on the length of the interrogation, or on whether certain threats had been made, Brown permitted (though it did not require) a federal court to accept the state court's factfindings about what happened.[2] The federal obligation was limited to determining the appropriate standard for deciding whether a confession was admissible (a question of legal principle), and applying that standard to the facts as found (an application of law to fact, or a "mixed" question). As a result, the vast majority of cases were always resolved on the state court record without evidentiary proceedings in federal court.

A distinct set of cases addresses efforts to litigate in federal court claims that, unlike those in Brown, were not resolved on the merits in state court, ordinarily because of a procedural default by the petitioner. A companion case to Brown, Daniels v. Allen, p. 1323, *infra*, announced a general rule that defaulted claims could not be heard by federal habeas courts. For discussion of Daniels and of subsequent developments in procedural default cases, see pp. 1323–1346, *infra*.

B. Justifications for Federal Relitigation

(1) A Surrogate for Appellate Review. One justification for Brown v. Allen rests on the inability of the Supreme Court adequately to protect constitutional rights through its direct review of state court judgments. On this view, habeas jurisdiction, though not technically appellate review by district courts, serves as a substitute for Supreme Court review to ensure that federal constitutional claims are heard by a federal court.[3] Consider these questions:

(a) If state courts can be trusted to find the facts, why can't they be trusted to apply the law? Compare Townsend v. Sain, 372 U.S. 293, 312 (1963) ("It is the typical, not the rare, case in which constitutional claims turn upon the resolution of contested factual issues.")

(b) If habeas courts are a surrogate for Supreme Court review, why should they (unlike the Supreme Court) be limited to reviewing only state court decisions that deny, rather than that uphold, claims of federal constitutional right?

(c) Why should federal relitigation of constitutional issues be limited to criminal cases leading to custody—thereby excluding issues arising in state

---

State court * * * to review by the Supreme Court of the United States on writ of certiorari." See Hearings on H.R. 5649 Before Subcomm. No. 3 of the House Comm. on the Judiciary, 84th Cong., 1st Sess., § 6, at 89–90 (1955). This bill twice passed the House but never the Senate. See 102 Cong.Rec. 940 (84th Cong.1956); 104 Cong.Rec. 4675 (85th Cong.1958). Other bills to limit Brown were introduced in succeeding decades; two passed the Senate but went no further. See S. 1763, 98th Cong., 1st Sess. (1984); S. 1241, 102d Cong., 1st Sess. (1991).

[2] Statutory amendments in 1966 and 1996 narrowed the district courts' discretion by making state court factfindings presumptively binding. See pp. 1319–1321, *infra*.

[3] See, *e.g.*, Justice Brennan's dissent in Stone v. Powell, p. 1286, *infra*; Hart, *The Supreme Court, 1958 Term—Foreword: The Time Chart of the Justices*, 73 Harv.L.Rev. 84, 105–07 (1959); Friedman, *A Tale of Two Habeas*, 73 Minn.L.Rev. 247 (1988); Liebman, *Apocalypse Next Time?: The Anachronistic Attack on Habeas Corpus/Direct Review Parity*, 92 Colum.L.Rev. 1997 (1992).

Judge Friendly, in *Is Innocence Irrelevant? Collateral Attack on Criminal Judgments*, 38 U.Chi.L.Rev. 142, 166–67 (1970), raised the possibility of substituting for habeas a system of appeals in state criminal cases to an intermediate federal court of appeals. See also Meador, *Straightening Out Federal Review of State Criminal Cases*, 44 Ohio St.L.J. 273 (1983).

court civil cases or in the many state criminal cases in which the defendant is never in custody (because the punishment was only by a fine) or is no longer in custody by the time state remedies have been exhausted?[4]

(2) Independent Inquiry into Detention. A different justification for federal relitigation was offered by Justice Brennan for the Court in Fay v. Noia, 372 U.S. 391, 430–31 (1963), p. 1324, *infra*: "The jurisdictional prerequisite [in habeas] is not the judgment of a state court but detention *simpliciter.* * * * And the broad power of the federal courts under 28 U.S.C. § 2243 * * * to 'determine the facts, and dispose of the matter as law and justice require,' is hardly characteristic of an appellate jurisdiction. Habeas lies to enforce the right of personal liberty * * *. * * * [I]t cannot revise the state court judgment; it can act only on the body of the petitioner."[5]

In support of this understanding, Professor Yackle argues: (a) in principle, federal courts should have original or removal jurisdiction over all cases in which federal issues are raised (whether as part of the complaint or by defense); (b) that principle is not observed in state criminal cases, where there is no general removal provision; (c) the absence of removal jurisdiction is justifiable because federal issues often arise only late in the game and also because removal would concentrate excessive coercive power in the federal courts; but (d) habeas review must be available after conviction to provide the needed federal forum for federal constitutional issues. See Yackle, *Explaining Habeas Corpus*, 60 N.Y.U.L.Rev. 991 (1985); Yackle, *The Habeas Hagioscope*, 66 S.Cal.L.Rev. 2331 (1993).

(a) Is Professor Yackle's premise—that a party should always be able to litigate a federal question in federal court—convincing? If accepted, wouldn't it require abolition of the custody requirement—which blocks many state convicts from federal court—as well as full relitigation of the facts? Compare Meltzer, *Habeas Corpus Jurisdiction: The Limits of Models*, 66 S.Cal.L.Rev. 2507, 2507–13 (1993), with Yackle, Reclaiming the Federal Courts 287–88 n. 157 (1994).[6]

---

[4] For a response to this question, see Friedman, *Pas de Deux: The Supreme Court and the Habeas Courts*, 66 S.Cal.L.Rev. 2467, 2485–90 (1993).

[5] See also Townsend v. Sain, p. 1321, *infra*; Reitz, *Federal Habeas Corpus: Postconviction Remedy for State Prisoners*, 108 U.Pa.L.Rev. 461 (1960); Amsterdam, *Search, Seizure and Section 2255: A Comment*, 112 U.Pa.L.Rev. 378 (1964); Wright & Sofaer, *Federal Habeas Corpus for State Prisoners: The Allocation of Fact-Finding Responsibility*, 75 Yale L.J. 895 (1966).

[6] According to Cover & Aleinikoff, *Dialectical Federalism: Habeas Corpus and the Court*, 86 Yale L.J. 1035 (1977), habeas jurisdiction generates a healthy dialogue between state and federal courts about the scope of federal constitutional rights. State courts tend to possess the pragmatic perspective (and narrow view of rights) of everyday law enforcement, while federal habeas courts, which consider constitutional issues in relative isolation from evidence of guilt, tend to have a "utopian", rights-protective perspective. Neither system has the power to enforce its view upon the other: although federal courts may effectively nullify a conviction by granting habeas relief, their decisions are not binding precedents for the state courts, which thus remain free to follow a narrower view of constitutional rights in future cases.

Do state and federal courts' perspectives differ in this way? Doesn't the adversary process inject both pragmatic and utopian perspectives into state prosecutions and habeas proceedings alike? And are habeas courts truly unaware of the likely guilt of the prisoner, or inattentive to concerns about the impact on law enforcement of recognizing a constitutional right? Insofar as the perspectives do differ, will the result in fact be dialogue or simply an accommodation of opposing power? See Meltzer, *State Court Forfeitures of Federal Rights*, 99 Harv.L.Rev. 1128, 1233–34 n. 505 (1986). In any event, Cover and Aleinikoff's argument rested on at least the premise that federal habeas review was relatively broad, as it was when they wrote; the sharp contraction in the scope of review since then, see pp. 1292–1346, *infra*, undercuts that premise.

(b) If state courts do not adequately protect federal rights, can habeas relief—which comes only after conviction and incarceration—undo the damage? *Cf.* Amsterdam, *Criminal Prosecutions Affecting Federally Guaranteed Civil Rights: Federal Removal and Habeas Corpus Jurisdiction to Abort State Court Trial*, 113 U.Pa.L.Rev. 793, 801 (1965) ("The battle is for the streets, and on the streets conviction now is worth a hundred times reversal later.").

(c) Does Justice Brennan's notion of an independent inquiry justify habeas courts in disregarding limits on the scope of review that would apply on direct review by the Supreme Court? Justice Harlan's dissent in Fay v. Noia said that the answer was no, reasoning that "[i]n habeas as on direct review, ordering the prisoner's release invalidates the judgment of conviction" on which the detention was based.

(3) Finality in the Criminal Process. In Sanders v. United States, 373 U.S. 1, 8 (1963), Justice Brennan declared: "Conventional notions of finality of litigation have no place where life or liberty is at stake and infringement of constitutional rights is alleged." Judge Friendly responded: "Why do they have *no* place? One will readily agree that * * * different rules should govern the determination of guilt than when only property is at issue * * *. * * * But this shows only that 'conventional notions of finality' should not have as *much* place in criminal as in civil litigation, not that they should have *none.*" Friendly, note 3, *supra*, at 149–50.

C. Objections to Federal Relitigation: The Process View

(1) Professor Bator's Argument. A celebrated article by Professor Bator, *Finality in Criminal Law and Federal Habeas Corpus for State Prisoners*, 76 Harv.L.Rev. 441 (1963), built on Justice Jackson's opinion in Brown v. Allen and articulated a narrow conception, often called the "process" view, of the appropriate scope of habeas review. Among Bator's objections to routine federal relitigation were these: (a) "[I]f a job can be well done once, it should not be done twice"; (b) "I could imagine nothing more subversive of a [state] judge's sense of responsibility, of the inner subjective conscientiousness which is so essential a part of the difficult and subtle art of judging well, than an indiscriminate acceptance of the notion that all the shots will always be called by someone else"; (c) Broad habeas review undermines the swiftness and certainty of punishment, and thus the educative, deterrent, and rehabilitative functions of the criminal law; and (d) "There comes a point where a procedural system which leaves matters perpetually open no longer reflects humane concern but merely anxiety and a desire for immobility."

Bator rested in part upon an epistemological skepticism, arguing that no legal process can assure the ultimate correctness of the results reached. He doubted that when state and federal court decisions differed, the latter were necessarily correct, and he resisted "the notion that sound remedial institutions can be built on the premise that state judges are not in sympathy with federal law." He thus concluded that habeas jurisdiction should be limited to determining whether the state provided a fair process for resolving constitutional claims—"whether the conditions and tools of inquiry were such as to assure a reasonable probability that the facts were correctly found and the law correctly applied" (emphasis omitted). Thus, habeas review would be appropriate, for example, to consider an alleged deprivation of the effective assistance of counsel or a claim that evidence discovered only after a conviction was affirmed shows that the trial judge had been bribed.[7]

(a) Is any approach to the scope of habeas review necessarily appropriate for all eras? Some have argued that postconviction habeas served an important role through the 1970s to force defiant state court judges to obey the federal Constitution but is no longer needed, in view of the improvement of state courts processes. See, *e.g.*, Hoffman & King, *Rethinking the Federal Role in State Criminal Justice*, 84 N.Y.U.L.Rev. 791 (2009). For a critical response, see Blume, Johnson & Weyble, *In Defense of Noncapital Habeas: A Response to Hoffman and King*, 96 Cornell L.Rev. 435 (2011) (contending, *inter alia*, that in many state court systems there are impediments to meaningful appellate and postconviction review; that review by a tenured Article III judge is important; that racial discrimination persists; and that the prospect of habeas review affects state court behavior).

(b) The reasonably broad habeas review recognized in Brown has been sharply narrowed by subsequent judicial and legislative developments. But how realistic is it to view habeas review, whatever it scope, as significantly affecting state court behavior, given that most convicts plead guilty (thereby waiving most rights), that most do not receive sufficiently long sentences to file a proper habeas petition, that the success rate for those who do file is minuscule, and that post-hoc litigation has inherent limitations, particularly in addressing claims of ineffective assistance of counsel? Should federal efforts be redirected to address the greatest barrier to the enforcement of constitutional rights for state criminal defendants—the lack of adequate defense representation? See King & Hoffman, Habeas for the Twenty-First Century (2011) (so arguing). Compare Meltzer, *Habeas Corpus Jurisdiction: The Limits of Models,* 66 S.Cal.L.Rev. 2507, 2526 (1993) ("(1) those most critical of habeas relitigation are not usually the most supportive of improving the quality of defense representation, and (2) the resources devoted to habeas do not approach those required to provide adequate defense representation in the state courts.").

D.   The Relevance of Guilt or Innocence to the Scope of the Writ

(1) Is Innocence Irrelevant? In an influential article, *Is Innocence Irrelevant? Collateral Attack on Criminal Judgments*, 38 U.Chi.L.Rev. 142 (1970), Judge Friendly contended that, subject to limited exceptions, a petitioner who received a fair hearing in state court should not be able collaterally to attack a criminal conviction without making "a colorable showing that an error, whether 'constitutional' or not, may be producing the continued punishment of an innocent" person. He defined the necessary showing as "a fair probability that, in light of all the evidence, including that alleged to have been illegally admitted (but with due regard to any unreliability of it) and evidence tenably claimed to have been wrongly excluded or to have become available only after the trial, the trier of the facts would have entertained a reasonable doubt of [the defendant's] guilt."[8] He

---

[7]   However, for Bator, if an allegation of bribery at the trial level had been rejected by a state appellate court after a fair hearing, no habeas relief should follow.

[8]   He advocated exceptions to his proposed requirement where (i) the original tribunal lacked jurisdiction or the criminal process had broken down; (ii) the constitutional claim was based on facts outside the record and only collateral attack could vindicate the claim; (iii) the state failed to provide a proper procedure for making a defense; or (iv) the governing constitutional law had changed.

added that after the Warren Court's criminal procedure decisions, "the 'constitutional' label no longer assists in appraising how far society should go in permitting relitigation of criminal convictions. It carries a connotation of outrage—the mob-dominated jury, the confession extorted by the rack, the defendant deprived of counsel—which is wholly misplaced when, for example, the claim is a pardonable but allegedly mistaken belief that probable cause existed for an arrest or that a statement by a person not available for cross-examination came within an exception to the hearsay rule. A judge's overly broad construction of a [state] penal statute can be much more harmful to a defendant than unwarranted refusal to compel a prosecution witness on some peripheral element of the case to reveal his address. If a second round on the former is not permitted, and no one suggests it should be, I see no justification for one on the latter in the absence of a colorable showing of innocence."

(2) Justice Powell's Approach. In Schneckloth v. Bustamonte, 412 U.S. 218 (1973), Justice Powell's concurrence (joined by Chief Justice Burger and Justice Rehnquist)[9] echoed many of Judge Friendly's concerns, and would have held that a Fourth Amendment claim was cognizable on habeas only where the petitioner did not have a fair opportunity to litigate in state court: "I am aware that history reveals no exact tie of the writ of habeas corpus to a constitutional claim relating to innocence or guilt. * * * We are now faced, however, with the task of accommodating the historic respect for the finality of the judgment of a committing court with recent Court expansions of the role of the writ. This accommodation can best be achieved * * * by recourse to the central reason for habeas corpus: the affording of means, through an extraordinary writ, of redressing an unjust incarceration."

Justice Powell's approach differed subtly from Judge Friendly's. Justice Powell favored limiting habeas based on the general nature of the claim; coerced confession claims would be permitted, Fourth Amendment exclusionary rule claims would not. Judge Friendly favored a focus on the specific facts of the prisoner's case: upon a proper showing of innocence, the prisoner could raise any constitutional claim (even a Fourth Amendment claim); absent the requisite showing, habeas would be unavailable (even on a coerced confession claim).

(3) Questions About Guilt and Innocence. Would petitioners simply plead around any innocence-based limitation, by alleging innocence and/or including innocence-related claims in their petitions? Insofar as state court underenforcement of federal constitutional norms may be greatest when conviction of the innocent is not at issue, would any innocence limitation eliminate federal oversight in exactly the cases in which it is most important? Would acceptance of Judge Friendly's position burden habeas courts by requiring threshold, fact-specific inquiries into prisoners' innocence?

(4) Stone v. Powell. In Stone v. Powell, 428 U.S. 465 (1976) (6–3), the Court, overturning prior authority, held that a state prisoner generally cannot obtain federal habeas corpus relief on the ground that evidence obtained in an unconstitutional search or seizure was introduced at his trial. Relying on the premise that the exclusionary rule is not a personal constitutional right of the defendant but rather a judicially created remedy designed to safeguard Fourth Amendment rights by deterring police misconduct, Justice Powell argued that enforcing the rule on habeas imposed serious costs while

No habeas for 4am claims

---

[9]   Justice Blackmun agreed with "nearly all" of, but did not join, Justice Powell's opinion.

providing little incremental deterrence of Fourth Amendment violations. Thus, the Court ruled "that where the State has provided an opportunity for full and fair litigation of a Fourth Amendment claim, a state prisoner may not be granted federal habeas corpus relief on the ground that evidence obtained in an unconstitutional search or seizure was introduced at his trial."

Despite the Court's statement that "[o]ur decision today is not concerned with the scope of the habeas corpus statute as authority for litigating constitutional claims generally", some observers feared that the majority was laying the groundwork for the elimination of all claims unrelated to guilt or innocence. Although the Court's holding rested on distinctive features of the exclusionary remedy, some the opinion's reasoning appeared to reach more broadly. For example, the Court dismissed the argument that state courts cannot be trusted to enforce Fourth Amendment rights: whatever was true of those courts in the past, "we are unwilling to assume" that they now lack "appropriate sensitivity to constitutional rights". And the opinion stressed that habeas relitigation imposes resource costs, erodes finality, generates friction between federal and state courts, and threatens the constitutional balance on which federalism rests. "We nevertheless afford broad habeas corpus relief, recognizing the need in a free society for an additional safeguard against compelling an innocent man to suffer an unconstitutional loss of liberty." But relitigation on habeas of a typical Fourth Amendment claim, the Court said, "has no bearing on the basic justice" of incarceration.

Justice Brennan, joined by Justice Marshall, wrote an angry dissent. Declaring that a state court that admits evidence obtained in violation of the Fourth Amendment "has committed a constitutional error," he argued that it follows that a petitioner would be " 'in custody in violation of the Constitution' within the comprehension of 28 U.S.C. § 2254." That is the basis for Supreme Court review of a state court judgment, and "Congress, which has the power to do so under Art. III of the Constitution, has effectively cast the district courts sitting in habeas in the role of surrogate Supreme Courts." He concluded that the "real ground" for the Court's decision must be its "novel reinterpretation of the habeas statutes * * *. I am therefore justified in apprehending that the groundwork is being laid today for a drastic withdrawal of federal habeas jurisdiction * * * at least for claims—for example, of double jeopardy, entrapment, self-incrimination, Miranda violations, and use of invalid identification procedures—that this Court later decides are not 'guilt-related.' "[10]

(5) The Limitation of Stone. Despite Justice Brennan's fears, decisions since Stone v. Powell have not adopted a general rule limiting habeas corpus to matters relating to guilt or innocence.[11]

---

[10] Justice White dissented separately "[f]or many of the reasons stated by Mr. Justice Brennan".

Articles critical of Stone v. Powell include Seidman, *Factual Guilt and the Burger Court: An Examination of Continuity and Change in Criminal Procedure*, 80 Colum.L.Rev. 436, 449–59 (1980), and Tushnet, *Constitutional and Statutory Analyses in the Law of Federal Jurisdiction*, 25 UCLA L.Rev. 1301, 1316–18 (1978). More supportive is Halpern, *Federal Habeas Corpus and the Mapp Exclusionary Rule After Stone v. Powell*, 82 Colum.L.Rev. 1 (1982).

[11] The Court did rely on Stone in re-shaping the harmless error doctrine applied in habeas proceedings. In Brecht v. Abrahamson, 507 U.S. 619 (1993) (5–4), the Court held that habeas courts should not apply the rule followed by state and federal courts on direct review—that upon finding a constitutional violation, a court should grant relief unless the government can prove

(a) Rose v. Mitchell, 443 U.S. 545 (1979), involved an allegation of racial discrimination in selection of the grand jury. When, as in that case, an untainted trial jury finds the prisoner guilty beyond a reasonable doubt, discrimination in selection of the grand jury—which typically has to find only a prima facie case of guilt—is highly unlikely to have led to conviction of an innocent person. But Justice Blackmun, writing for the Court, reached the merits of the discrimination claim, confining Stone to "cases involving the judicially created exclusionary rule" and distinguishing grand jury discrimination from the exclusionary remedy on a number of grounds. Justice Powell (joined by Justice Rehnquist) wrote separately, reiterating many of the arguments in his Bustamonte opinion in support of the conclusion that the claim should not be cognizable on habeas review.[12]

(b) A key decision refusing to extend Stone was Withrow v. Williams, 507 U.S. 680 (1993), where the petitioner claimed a violation of the Miranda rules. Justice Souter's majority opinion argued that unlike the Fourth Amendment's exclusionary rule, the Miranda decision "safeguards 'a fundamental *trial* right' " that is not "necessarily divorced from the correct ascertainment of guilt." Most importantly, eliminating habeas review of Miranda claims would not significantly unburden the courts: petitioners would simply allege instead that their confessions were involuntary and thus inadmissible under the Due Process Clause, which would require difficult determinations under a totality of the circumstances test rather than under Miranda's "brighter-line" rules. Dissenting from this portion of the decision, Justice O'Connor (joined by Chief Justice Rehnquist) argued, *inter alia*, that (1) confessions obtained in violation of Miranda, but that are not involuntary under the Due Process Clause, are reliable, and (2) any impact of habeas review in improving police compliance with Miranda is slight and, under the approach of Stone v. Powell, is outweighed by considerations of finality, equity, and federalism.[13]

The exception to habeas review set forth in Stone v. Powell, even though it was not extended to the facts of Withrow, remains good law today.

---

that the error was harmless beyond a reasonable doubt, see Chapman v. California, 386 U.S. 18 (1967). Instead, echoing some of Stone's reasoning, the majority in Brecht stated that application on collateral review of the Chapman standard was unnecessary to give incentives for state courts faithfully to apply that standard on direct review, and hence habeas courts should apply a less stringent standard under which an error is harmless unless it "had substantial and injurious effect or influence in determining the jury's verdict" (quoting Kotteakos v. United States, 328 U.S. 750, 776 (1946)).

[12] Justice Stewart (joined by Justice Rehnquist) concurred in the judgment on the ground that a grand jury discrimination claim by a defendant convicted beyond a reasonable doubt by an untainted petit jury is "harmless error", whether on collateral or on direct review.

[13] She also argued, consistently with much language in Supreme Court decisions, that Miranda announced a set of prophylactic rules, not a core constitutional right. That position was later rejected in Dickerson v. United States, 530 U.S. 428 (2000) (7–2).

Justice Scalia (joined by Justice Thomas) would have denied relief on the ground that the equitable discretion possessed by habeas courts is abused by granting relief to a petitioner who had a full and fair opportunity to litigate in state court, unless the claim "goes to the fairness of the trial process or to the accuracy of the ultimate result." He noted that federal prisoners ordinarily may not relitigate federal constitutional claims in collateral attacks under § 2255, and argued that to treat state prisoners differently, in order to give them access to a federal forum, was inconsistent with the history of federal habeas corpus in the nineteenth century and with the presumption, drawn from Article III's failure to mandate creation of lower federal courts, that state courts will faithfully apply federal law.

E. The Cognizability of Claims of Innocence in Habeas Corpus Proceedings

(1) Claims Relating to Innocence. The decisions just discussed indicate that the Court has not limited habeas review to claims that suggest that the prisoner is innocent. For example, a claim of that the state court failed to exclude a coerced confession remains cognizable in habeas even if the evidence (apart from the confession) overwhelmingly establishes the petitioner's guilt.

But how far does the habeas jurisdiction extend to a claim that alleges no specific constitutional violation (like introduction of a coerced confession) but simply asserts that the petitioner is in fact innocent?

(2) Jackson v. Virginia. In Jackson v. Virginia, 443 U.S. 307 (1979), the Court held that the due process requirement of proof beyond a reasonable doubt means not only that a jury must be so instructed, but also that the question whether a properly instructed jury could reasonably have found the evidence in the record to establish guilt beyond a reasonable doubt is itself a federal constitutional question cognizable on habeas. The Court for the most part treated the case as a routine exercise of habeas jurisdiction, in which the habeas court reviews applications of a federal constitutional standard (proof beyond a reasonable doubt) to the historical facts (the evidence in the state court record). But the Court did note that unlike the Fourth Amendment issue in Stone, "[t]he question whether a defendant has been convicted upon inadequate evidence is central to the basic question of guilt or innocence."

(3) Freestanding Claims of Innocence. A different question arises when the record at trial suffices to uphold the finding of guilt, but a petitioner claims that evidence obtained after conviction establishes innocence.

(a) In Herrera v. Collins, 506 U.S. 390 (1993), the evidence at Herrera's murder trial included two eyewitness identifications and a handwritten letter in which Herrera appeared to admit his guilt. Ten years after his conviction and death sentence, his habeas petition contended that newly discovered evidence (affidavits declaring that Herrera's now-dead brother had confessed to the murder) showed that Herrera was actually innocent and argued that his execution would violate the Eighth and Fourteenth Amendments. Holding that his petition should be denied, the Court ruled that "[c]laims of actual innocence based on newly discovered evidence have never been held to state a ground for federal habeas relief absent an independent constitutional violation occurring in the underlying state criminal proceeding." The function of habeas review, the Court submitted, was to redress *constitutional* violations, not to correct factual errors, and review of freestanding innocence claims would severely disrupt the strong state interest in finality. The Court resisted petitioner's formulation of the question—whether it is constitutional to execute the innocent—stressing that Herrera, having been convicted after a fair trial, was to be treated as guilty. The Court distinguished the claim in Jackson v. Virginia because it (i) established an independent constitutional violation; (ii) could be adjudicated by reviewing the adequacy of the record evidence, without new factfinding; and (iii) asked only if the verdict of guilt was rational, not whether it was correct.

The Court added: "We may assume, for the sake of argument * * *, that in a capital case a truly persuasive demonstration of 'actual innocence' " would warrant habeas relief "if there were no state avenue open to process such a claim." However, Herrera's showing fell far short of the "extraordinarily high" threshold for such an "assumed right". Four Justices (White, Blackmun, Stevens, and Souter), in separate concurring or dissenting opinions, assumed, in Justice White's words, "that a persuasive showing of 'actual innocence' * * * would render unconstitutional the execution of petitioner"; Justices O'Connor and Kennedy said they would not reach that "sensitive" and "troubling" issue given the strong evidence of Herrera's guilt; and Justices Scalia and Thomas criticized the Court for failing to declare firmly that there is no constitutional right to consideration of evidence of innocence discovered after conviction.

(b) The Court has yet to resolve the uncertainty generated by the array of views expressed in Herrera about the circumstances (if any) in which freestanding claims of innocence are cognizable—either in capital cases or more generally. In House v. Bell, 547 U.S. 518 (2006), p. 1343, *infra*, a unanimous Court said that *if* a freestanding innocence claim may be brought on habeas, relief was not warranted by the evidence presented, even though five Justices concluded that it was more likely than not that no reasonable juror would have found the prisoner guilty beyond a reasonable doubt. Then in In re Davis, 557 U.S. 952 (2009), p. 291, *supra*, the Court transferred an original petition for habeas corpus to a district court, with instructions that it should hold an evidentiary hearing on a freestanding innocence claim raised in the petition. Dissenting from the order, Justice Scalia, joined by Justice Thomas, emphasized that the Court had never held, and indeed had expressed considerable doubt, that a freestanding innocence claim is constitutionally cognizable.

Few habeas petitions in fact advance freestanding claims of innocence.[14] One review of 173 reported decisions involving such claims found no outright grants of relief and only seven instances in which some relief (*e.g.*, an evidentiary hearing or required DNA testing) was provided. Note, 42 Am.Crim.L.Rev. 121 (2005).

(4) Questions About Freestanding Claims of Innocence. Is any purpose of postconviction review more central than overturning the conviction of an innocent person? Even if federal habeas jurisdiction exists only when custody violates the federal Constitution or some other fundamental federal law, can it be persuasively argued that the Court has always reshaped the writ based on its evaluation of competing concerns—as illustrated, for example, by the evolution of the writ over the centuries into a regime of federal relitigation, and by the qualification to that regime established in Stone v. Powell? See Steiker, *Innocence and Federal Habeas*, 41 UCLA L.Rev. 303, 309 (1993).

Consider, however, these countervailing arguments: (i) the burdens of entertaining "actual innocence" claims would be high, for such claims can be raised in every case and their adjudication can be labor-intensive; and (ii) federal review of such claims may be relatively less important because state courts care about not convicting the innocent, and less appropriate because their resolution often requires interpretation of the elements of the offense, a question of state law. Would these points be persuasive in the context of a capital conviction for a heinous murder in an area where pro-death penalty

---

[14] See King, Cheesman & Ostrom, p. 1266, note 3, *supra*, at 29–30 (finding such claims asserted in 11% of capital cases and 4% of non-capital cases).

sentiment is strong and resources for defense representation are seriously inadequate?

(5) The Availability of State Court Postconviction Remedies. As the Herrera opinion noted, every state permits motions for a new trial based on new evidence, but such motions are subject to a number of limitations. When Herrera was decided in 1993, 17 states (including Texas, where Herrera was convicted) required such a motion to be made within 60 days after judgment, while another 18 had time limits of one to three years. In addition, many states require the evidence to have come to light after trial, not to have been obtainable earlier in the exercise of due diligence, and to be likely to lead to a different result upon retrial. See Berger, *Herrera v. Collins: The Gateway of Innocence for Death-Sentenced Prisoners Leads Nowhere*, 35 Wm. & Mary L.Rev. 943, 958 (1994). Judges are often skeptical about such motions, and success is rare.

Instead of claiming simply that he was innocent, could Herrera have argued that Texas' short time period for filing a new trial motion based on new evidence denied due process?[15] Framed that way, the petition does assert a federal constitutional claim. See Thomas et al., *Is It Ever Too Late for Innocence? Finality, Efficiency, and Claims of Innocence*, 64 U.Pitt.L.Rev. 263 (2003) (arguing that due process "require[s] courts to be open to powerful claims of innocence without regard to whether procedural deadlines for challenging a conviction have expired" and noting a trend in recent decisions toward "finding a basis to allow powerful claims of innocence to be heard even if filed too late under the rules of procedure"); Berger, *supra* (arguing for a right to state postconviction relief in some circumstances).[16] But were such a claim upheld, should the remedy be an inquiry by the habeas court itself into the petitioner's innocence, or instead an order requiring the state court to conduct such an inquiry?

NOTE ON THE SUSPENSION CLAUSE AND POSTCONVICTION REVIEW

(1) Executive Detention Versus Postconviction Cases. The Constitution's Suspension Clause guarantees access to habeas corpus (or an adequate substitute) in some cases involving executive detention. See p. 1201, *supra*. But it is uncertain whether the Clause confers a right to habeas corpus as a means of postconviction review. Such review was not the original office of the writ, and numerous decisions state that "at common law a

---

[15] In Case v. Nebraska, 381 U.S. 336 (1965), the state courts had held that they lacked jurisdiction to entertain a postconviction motion asserting ineffective assistance of counsel. The Supreme Court granted certiorari but ultimately remanded in light of a supervening state statute that appeared to afford a hearing.

[16] Forty-four states have enacted statutes giving convicts the right (which can be more or less broadly defined) to obtain post-conviction DNA testing. Such tests are now quite inexpensive and the evidence of innocence can be (though often is not) conclusive.

Note, however, that even when favorable DNA results are obtained, it is a separate question whether relief from criminal conviction is available, and the limitations in state postconviction proceedings, noted above, may create hurdles hard to overcome.

Insofar as Herrera rested on the importance of finality, on the premise that post-hoc determinations are less reliable than those at trial, and on the resource costs of relitigating innocence after conviction, does the availability of DNA testing substantially change the calculus? For a comprehensive discussion, see Garrett, *Claiming Innocence*, 92 Minn.L.Rev. 1629 (2008).

judgment of conviction rendered by a court of general criminal jurisdiction was conclusive proof that confinement was legal. Such a judgment prevented issuance of the writ without more." United States v. Hayman, 342 U.S. 205, 211 (1952).[1] Indeed, absent some limiting conception, no decision denying relief could be immune from a further claim that the decision was in error and the detention therefore illegal.[2]

Over time, *statutory* authority to issue the writ reached well beyond the common law limit on postconviction review. See pp. 1272–1280, *supra*. Might the scope of the Suspension Clause similarly evolve over time to afford a constitutional right to postconviction review? *Cf.* Boumediene v. Bush, p. 1249, *supra*.

(2) The Right of *State* Prisoners to Federal Postconviction Review. Any argument that the Suspension Clause gives petitioners complaining of *state* custody pursuant to a criminal conviction a right to *federal* habeas review faces two hurdles beyond the general question about whether or when the Suspension Clause guarantees postconviction review. First, the Suspension Clause appears to have been directed only to detention under *federal* authority, as was the grant of habeas jurisdiction in the Judiciary Act of 1789. See pp. 1193–1196, *supra*. Second, a claimed right to habeas review in *federal* court must take account of the Madisonian Compromise—the constitutional understanding, reflected in the text of Article III, that it was for Congress to decide whether to create lower federal courts at all. See pp. 7–9, *supra*.[3]

(3) Supreme Court Interpretation. Supreme Court decisions in the postconviction setting contain little discussion of the Suspension Clause.[4]

---

[1] See Collings, *Habeas Corpus for Convicts—Constitutional Right or Legislative Grace?*, 40 Calif.L.Rev. 335, 340–41 (1952) (concluding that suspension of the writ historically was not aimed at convicts, but rather at suspects deprived of their right to a speedy trial).

For a survey of the historical materials on the Suspension Clause, see the authorities cited at p. 1193, note 2, and p. 1196, note 2, *supra*. See also Freedman, *The Suspension Clause in the Ratification Debates*, 44 Buff.L.Rev. 451 (1996); Neuman, p. 1196, note 2, *supra*; Neuman, p. 1202, note 3, *supra*; Oaks, *The "Original" Writ of Habeas Corpus in the Supreme Court*, 1962 Sup.Ct.Rev. 153.

For a dramatic challenge to the conventional view of the role of Congress in shaping the writ, see Kovarsky, *A Constitutional Theory of Habeas Power*, 99 Va.L.Rev. 753 (2013). He contends that the Constitution guarantees all federal prisoners, whatever the basis for their detention, some habeas review before an Article III judge, and that absent an act of suspension, Congress lacks power to restrict judicial power to decide whether custody is lawful.

[2] See generally Bator, *Finality in Criminal Law and Federal Habeas Corpus for State Prisoners*, 76 Harv.L.Rev. 441, 447 (1963).

[3] Professor Jordan Steiker, while acknowledging the foregoing difficulties, argues that state prisoners do enjoy a constitutional right to habeas review in federal court of constitutional challenges to their criminal convictions. See Steiker, *Incorporating the Suspension Clause: Is There a Constitutional Right to Federal Habeas Corpus for State Prisoners?*, 92 Mich.L.Rev. 862, 874–78 (1994). He finds that by the time the Fourteenth Amendment was ratified, the writ had evolved far beyond its common law origins and that the Fourteenth Amendment's Due Process Clause incorporated the "privilege" of that broadened writ against *state authority*. But even accepting those conclusions, the hardest part of his argument is the further claim that the Fourteenth Amendment, a provision directed to the *states*, implicitly obliges the *federal* government to vest federal courts with habeas corpus jurisdiction.

For an effort to surmount that and other difficulties while arguing that the Fourteenth Amendment's Privileges and Immunities Clause guarantees state prisoners a right to habeas review in federal court, see Kovarsky, *Prisoners and Habeas Privileges under the Fourteenth Amendment*, 67 Vand.L.Rev. 609 (2014).

[4] Besides the decisions discussed in text, see Sanders v. United States, 373 U.S. 1, 11–12 (1963), and Fay v. Noia, 372 U.S. 391, 406 (1963), both providing liberal interpretations of the

(a) In Swain v. Pressley, 430 U.S. 372 (1977), the Court upheld a provision of the District of Columbia Code that, for persons convicted of local crimes in the District, replaced federal habeas corpus with a statutory motion in the local D.C. courts. The majority noted that the statutory motion was "commensurate" with habeas corpus and was not inadequate merely because the local judges who administer it are not Article III judges. Chief Justice Burger, joined by Justices Blackmun and Rehnquist, concurred on the broader ground that the Suspension Clause protects only the writ as known to the Framers and does not require collateral review after conviction by a court of competent jurisdiction.

(b) Felker v. Turpin, 518 U.S. 651 (1996), involved a statutory provision added in 1996 that sharply restricts the ability of state prisoners to file more than one habeas petition in federal court. Chief Justice Rehnquist's opinion for a unanimous Court began by stating that before 1867, habeas jurisdiction was not generally available for persons in state custody and that collateral attacks on judgments of conviction rendered by courts of competent jurisdiction were not permitted until well into the twentieth century. Nonetheless, he said that "we assume, for purposes of decision here, that the Suspension Clause * * * refers to the writ as it exists today, rather than as it existed in 1789." The Court proceeded to find no suspension of the writ. Quoting Ex parte Bollman for the proposition that a federal court's power to award the writ must be given by positive law, the Court declared that judgments about the proper scope of the writ are normally left to Congress and concluded that the restrictions on filing multiple petitions "are well within the compass of this evolutionary process * * *."[5]

NOTE ON RETROACTIVITY AND NEW LAW IN HABEAS CORPUS

A.   The Warren Court and the Background to Teague v. Lane

(1) The Problem. Traditionally, judicial decisions, no matter how novel, apply retroactively to the parties in the litigation and to other litigants in all pending cases that have not yet become "final" on direct review. (For these purposes, "final" means that certiorari has been denied or that the time for seeking further appellate review has expired.) Should that tradition of full retroactivity also apply to all pending or future cases of *collateral attack* on a final conviction? If so, the decision in Miranda v. Arizona, 384 U.S. 436 (1966), would have permitted every state prisoner whose trial had not been conducted in accordance with the Miranda rules to file a habeas petition and, unless the error was harmless, to obtain relief. (Until 1996, no federal statute of limitations applied in habeas corpus. And while today a prisoner who had not raised a claim in state court would ordinarily be barred from pursuing it

---

scope of the jurisdiction while suggesting in dictum that narrower interpretations might raise constitutional questions. Both decisions have been overruled. See pp. 1344, 1346 note 1, *infra*. For other judicial statements about the Suspension Clause, see Yackle, *Form and Function in the Administration of Justice: The Bill of Rights and Federal Habeas Corpus*, 23 U.Mich.J.L.Ref. 685, 694 nn. 39–40 (1990).

   [5] In INS v. St. Cyr, 533 U.S. 289 (2001), pp. 336, 1201, *supra*, the Court remarked: "[T]his case involves an alien subject to a federal removal order rather than a person confined pursuant to a state-court conviction. * * * At its historical core, the writ * * * has served as a means of reviewing the legality of Executive detention".

on habeas corpus, that was not the law when Miranda was decided. See generally pp. 1323–1346, *infra*.)

The retroactivity question grew in significance during the 1960s as a result of the sharp increase in the number of habeas petitions filed, the expansive scope of habeas review recognized by the Warren Court, and that Court's broad and novel criminal procedure decisions, of which Miranda is an example. In the decades that followed, the sharp rise in state prisoner population—a nearly eight-fold increase between 1970 and 2010—also gave the question great significance.[1]

Ever since 1965, the Supreme Court has been unwilling to treat all constitutional criminal procedure decisions as fully retroactive in postconviction habeas corpus cases. The Warren Court adopted one approach that limited the retroactive applicability of some decisions; in 1989, the Rehnquist Court adopted a different approach to retroactivity that sharply limited the effective reach of federal collateral relitigation.

Then in 1996, Congress enacted a provision, codified as 28 U.S.C. § 2254(d)(1), that bars federal habeas courts from granting relief on a claim that was adjudicated on the merits by a state court, unless the state court's decision "was contrary to, or involved an unreasonable application of, clearly established Federal law, as determined by the Supreme Court of the United States" as of the time of the state court decision. As a result of § 2254(d)(1), today habeas claims seeking retroactive application of new federal constitutional norms are excluded from habeas jurisdiction if they were decided on the merits by state courts. And as a result, there is no need for the federal courts to apply any doctrine of non-retroactivity when the petitioner is relying on new law.

However, the non-retroactivity doctrines that governed between 1965 and 1996 form an important backdrop to the enactment and understanding of § 2254(d)(1). Moreover, the non-retroactivity doctrine still applies in the rare habeas case in which a federal claim, not decided by the state courts on the merits and not barred procedurally, rests on a new rule of constitutional law.

(2) The Warren Court's Approach: Non-Retroactivity.[2] In Linkletter v. Walker, 381 U.S. 618 (1965), the Court for the first time asserted the power to render a constitutional decision that was not fully retroactive, ruling that its decision in Mapp v. Ohio, 367 U.S. 643 (1961), which applied the Fourth Amendment's exclusionary remedy to the states, would not be retroactively applied to state court convictions that had become final before Mapp was decided. A year later, in Johnson v. New Jersey, 384 U.S. 719, 733–35 (1966), the Court held that the Miranda rules did not apply to trials that commenced before the date of the Miranda decision. Eventually, the Court held that the retroactivity of new constitutional rulings depended on three factors: the purpose of the new rule, the extent of reliance on the old rule, and the effect on the administration of justice of retroactive application of the new rule. See Stovall v. Denno, 388 U.S. 293, 297 (1967).

Under this approach, a new rule like that in Miranda always applied to the case in which it was announced, whether that case reached the Supreme Court on direct or collateral review. When a subsequent case implicating the

---

[1]   See p. 1270, *supra*.

[2]   See generally Fallon & Meltzer, *New Law, Non-Retroactivity, and Constitutional Remedies*, 104 Harv.L.Rev. 1731, 1838–44 (1991), which cites much bibliographic material.

new rule reached the Supreme Court (again, whether on direct or collateral review), the Court applied the three-factor test to determine whether the new decision applied retroactively. A decision determined to be non-retroactive would not apply in any subsequent case, whether that case was pending on direct review or habeas review, when the conduct being regulated (*e.g.*, introduction of a confession or conduct of a lineup) predated the new decision. By contrast, a rule held to be fully retroactive (*e.g.*, the Sixth Amendment right to the assistance of counsel recognized in Gideon v. Wainwright, 372 U.S. 335 (1963)) was enforced in all proceedings, whether on direct review or on habeas review. Thus, the Warren Court's non-retroactivity doctrine did not treat cases on habeas review differently from those on direct review.

(3) Justice Harlan's Critique. Justice Harlan's separate opinions in Desist v. United States, 394 U.S. 244, 256–69 (1969), and Mackey v. United States, 401 U.S. 667, 675–702 (1971), strongly criticized the Warren Court's approach to retroactivity. In his view, cases still subject to adjudication or on appeal differed importantly from cases on habeas review. On direct review, he argued, courts must apply all decisions retroactively; to do otherwise would suggest that their function was not one of adjudication but of legislation. But because habeas corpus is an extraordinary remedy, no such judicial obligation exists, and the state's interest in finality called for a narrower judicial inquiry. In Desist, he argued that habeas review must be adequate to "serve[ ] as a necessary additional incentive for trial and appellate courts throughout the land to conduct their proceedings in a manner consistent with established constitutional standards." That purpose did not require the retroactive application of *new* rules, which, he said in Mackey, should apply retroactively only when they (i) held previously punishable conduct to be constitutionally protected, or (ii) recognized constitutional rights of procedure so fundamental as to be " 'implicit in the concept of ordered liberty' ".

(4) Griffith v. Kentucky. In Griffith v. Kentucky, 479 U.S. 314 (1987), a divided Supreme Court endorsed Justice Harlan's view that new rules should be fully retroactive on direct review. Justice Blackmun wrote for the Court that the "failure to apply a newly declared constitutional rule to criminal cases pending on direct review violates basic norms of constitutional adjudication." He stressed that "the integrity of judicial review" requires the application of the new rule to "all similar cases pending on direct review" and that "selective application of new rules violates the principle of treating similarly situated defendants the same." Justice White, joined by Chief Justice Rehnquist and Justice O'Connor, dissented, contending that the majority's concerns about judicial legislation "go more to the substance of the Court's decisions than to whether or not they are retroactive." He deemed the concern about inequality to be "hollow", because the Court will tolerate comparable inequalities between defendants, based on whether their cases come up on direct or collateral review—inequalities that depend on how long ago the unconstitutional conduct occurred and how quickly cases move through the judicial system.

Since 1987, the Court has adhered to the approach of Griffith in deciding cases on direct review.[3]

---

[3] In Davis v. United States, 131 S.Ct. 2419 (2011), the dissent accused the majority of departing from Griffith's approach. In the Davis case, evidence obtained in a search that was lawful under the decisions of the federal circuit in question was admitted at trial. While Davis'

B. The Approach of Teague v. Lane

(1) The Teague Decision. In Teague v. Lane, 489 U.S. 288 (1989), the Court completed its rejection of the Warren Court's approach, holding that, with only the most limited exceptions, new constitutional rules do not apply retroactively on collateral review. Although Justice O'Connor's opinion announcing the Court's judgment spoke only for a plurality of four, in numerous subsequent decisions, the Court endorsed and followed Justice O'Connor's approach.

Justice O'Connor began by stating that "[r]etroactivity is properly treated as a threshold question, for, once a new rule is applied to the defendant in the case announcing the rule, evenhanded justice requires that it be applied retroactively to all who are similarly situated." Accordingly, she said that "before deciding [the merits of the petitioner's claim—whether the prosecution violated the Sixth Amendment's fair cross section requirement by its racially motivated exercise of peremptory challenges—] we should ask whether such a rule would be applied retroactively to the case at issue." Endorsing Justice Harlan's views, she stated that, subject to two exceptions, new constitutional rules of criminal procedure will not apply to cases that "have become final before the new rules are announced." To provide state judges with the incentive to comply with established constitutional principles requires only that habeas courts apply constitutional standards prevailing when the state proceedings took place; to apply new rules on habeas undermines finality and unfairly burdens states that provided trials that were entirely fair under then-governing standards.

Conceding the difficulty of determining whether a case announces a new rule, she suggested as the measure whether "it breaks new ground or imposes a new obligation on the States or the Federal Government. * * * To put it differently, a case announces a new rule if the result was not *dictated* by precedent existing at the time the defendant's conviction became final." The claim here presented, she found, was "new" under this standard.

Turning to the exceptions, she endorsed the first exception identified by Justice Harlan—that a new rule does apply retroactively if it provides that the conduct for which the defendant was prosecuted is constitutionally protected. Her second exception, drawing on two different formulations that Justice Harlan had advanced, provided that a habeas court may apply a new rule (a) that implicates the fundamental fairness of the trial and (b) without which the likelihood of an accurate conviction is seriously diminished. She

---

appeal was pending, the Supreme Court decided, in a different case, that the kind of search of which Davis complained violated the Fourth Amendment. When Davis' case reached the Supreme Court, it acknowledged that under Griffith, the search must be found to be unlawful. But Justice Alito's majority opinion went on to say that whether that violation required suppression of the evidence was a distinct question of the appropriate remedy. Here, the officer had acted in accordance with binding judicial precedent and so suppression would serve no useful deterrent purpose and was therefore inappropriate. In dissent, Justice Breyer (joined by Justice Ginsburg) said that the distinction between application of a new rule and the availability of a remedy was highly artificial and "re-creates the very problems that led the Court to abandon Linkletter's approach to retroactivity in favor of Griffith's." He added that in many cases (unlike the present one) the question whether the officer's conduct was consistent with precedent will be unclear and contested, and the majority's approach creates the risk that similarly situated defendants will be treated differently.

The Davis decision appears to depend on the distinctive nature of the Fourth Amendment's exclusionary remedy, which the Supreme Court has repeatedly held not to be a right of the particular defendant but rather a deterrent remedy. See p. 1285, *supra*. As a result, any tension with Griffith is likely to be confined to the search and seizure area.

doubted that many components of due process fitting the second exception have yet to emerge, and offered as examples domination of the proceeding by mob violence, the prosecution's knowing use of perjured testimony, and the introduction of a confession extorted by brutal methods.

Turning back to the situation in Teague, Justice O'Connor concluded that because the rule sought by the petitioner was new and fit neither exception, the claim in the habeas petition was not cognizable on collateral review.

Justice Stevens, joined by Justice Blackmun, also generally endorsed Justice Harlan's approach, but differed with the plurality on two points. First, he disputed that retroactivity is a threshold issue, so that once a habeas court determined that a rule is new, it could not reach the merits. Instead, he suggested following the approach of harmless error decisions, which frequently first decide the constitutional merits and only thereafter assess whether relief should nonetheless be denied because the error was harmless. Second, he would have defined the second exception as reaching all claims of fundamental error, without regard to the likelihood of diminishing accuracy.

In dissent, Justice Brennan, joined by Justice Marshall, objected that the plurality "would erect a formidable new barrier to relief. * * * Few decisions on appeal or collateral review are '*dictated*' by what came before. Most such cases involve a question of law that is at least debatable * * *. Virtually no case that prompts a dissent on the relevant legal point, for example, could be said to be '*dictated*' by prior decisions. By the plurality's test, therefore, a great many cases could only be heard on habeas if the rule urged by the petitioner fell within one of the two exceptions the plurality has sketched. Those exceptions, however, are narrow. * * * The plurality's approach today can thus be expected to contract substantially the Great Writ's sweep." He concluded that the Court should have followed the Stovall approach, under which it would decide Teague's claim and grant relief if the claim were meritorious, while waiting for a subsequent case in which to determine whether the right applied retroactively.

(2) The Meaning of "New" Law. Teague generally precludes habeas review of a petitioner's claim if the claim falls within a range in which reasonable jurists could differ—whether or not the state court's resolution of that claim was correct. But just how broad that range is depends on the definition of "new" law. Subsequent decisions gave a wide definition to the concept of new law, thereby sharply contracting the scope of federal postconviction review.

A notable example is Butler v. McKellar, 494 U.S. 407 (1990). The background to Butler lay in two decisions elaborating the Miranda rules: Edwards v. Arizona, 451 U.S. 477 (1981), which held that after a suspect has requested counsel, the police may not initiate further interrogation until counsel has been made available, and Arizona v. Roberson, 486 U.S. 675 (1988), which held that Edwards applies equally when the second interrogation concerns a different crime from the one that was the subject of the initial questioning.

Butler's claim was similar to that in Roberson, but Butler's conviction had become final in 1982, before Roberson was decided. The Supreme Court ruled, 5–4, that Butler could not obtain habeas relief because the Roberson decision, on which Butler's claim depended, had established a new rule.

Chief Justice Rehnquist wrote that "[t]he 'new rule' principle * * * validates reasonable, good-faith interpretations of existing precedents made by state courts even though they are shown to be contrary to later decisions." The fact that the Court, in Roberson, had viewed the case as within the scope of its Edwards decision "is not conclusive * * *. Courts frequently view their decisions as being 'controlled' or 'governed' by prior opinions even when aware of reasonable contrary conclusions reached by other courts. * * * [Differing positions taken by judges in the courts of appeals indicate that] the outcome in Roberson was susceptible to debate among reasonable minds * * *." The four dissenters in Butler objected that under the Court's approach, "a state prisoner can secure habeas relief only by showing that the state court's rejection of the constitutional challenge was *so* clearly invalid under then-prevailing legal standards that the decision could not be defended by any reasonable jurist."

(3) Application of Law to Fact. When a habeas petition rests on a well-established constitutional principle, but the application of that principle to the facts of the case is uncertain, does the petition rest on a "new rule"? That question was raised in **Wright v. West**, 505 U.S. 277 (1992), in which petitioner sought relief under the rule (well-established before his conviction became final) of Jackson v. Virginia, 443 U.S. 307 (1979), p. 1288, *supra*, that due process is denied if no rational juror could have found that all of the elements of the crime had been proven beyond a reasonable doubt. In Wright, the state characterized Teague as requiring deference to state court determinations of legal principles, and submitted that habeas courts should also defer to "reasonable" state court decisions of "mixed" questions of law and fact—that is, to reasonable applications of established legal rules to the facts as found.

All the Justices voted to deny relief on the ground that the prisoner's claim lacked merit. But Justice Thomas (joined by Chief Justice Rehnquist and Justice Scalia) described the state's interpretation of Teague in sympathetic detail. Justice Souter's separate opinion appeared to endorse the state's position, while Justice White did not discuss it. The other Justices rejected the state's invitation to extend Teague in this case: Justice O'Connor, joined by Justices Blackmun and Stevens, asserted that precedent foreclosed the state's argument, while Justice Kennedy said that Teague did not establish a rule of deference to state courts but a principle of retroactivity, based on objective review of the precedents at the time of the state court's determination (a point that Justice O'Connor echoed).

Aren't the categories "legal rules" and "application of legal rules to fact" points on a continuum rather than sharply differentiated concepts? Did Butler v. McKellar, Paragraph (2), *supra*, involve application of the rule of Edwards v. Arizona to a new set of facts (in which the second interrogation related to a different crime)? Or did Butler ask for recognition of a new rule—that police may not initiate an interrogation as to a different crime after the suspect has requested counsel? And even if a distinction between legal rules and mixed questions can be drawn, why—in view of the theory of Teague—should it matter?[4]

---

[4] In Chaidez v. United States, 133 S.Ct. 1103 (2013), the Court, in deciding that its decision in Padilla v. Kentucky, 559 U.S. 356 (2010), had announced a new rule, articulated a distinction between "threshold" issues about whether a constitutional right applies and "garden-variety" applications of established law to new facts.

(4) The Teague Exceptions.

(a) Constitutionally Protected Primary Conduct. Does Teague's first exception echo the historic notion that habeas lies when the sentencing court lacked jurisdiction—and that jurisdiction is lacking when the statute under which the defendant was convicted is unconstitutional? See p. 1273, *supra.* Is relief less prejudicial to state interests because no trial should have been held and no retrial can be commenced?

The question how Teague's first exception applies to constitutional challenges to *sentences* arose in Penry v. Lynaugh, 492 U.S. 302 (1989), where the claim was that execution of a prisoner with the mental capacity of a seven-year old violated the Eighth Amendment. A unanimous Court ruled that the first exception extends to new rules "prohibiting a certain category of punishment for a class of defendants because of their status or offense."[5] However, in another challenge to the lawfulness of a sentence, Caspari v. Bohlen, 510 U.S. 383 (1994), the Court found the first exception inapplicable. There, the petitioner claimed that providing the state a chance, at resentencing, to prove prior convictions (for purposes of sentence enhancement) that the state had failed to prove at the initial sentencing violated the Double Jeopardy Clause. The Court said that the petitioner's primary conduct was not beyond punishment because he could be sentenced to prison (whether as a repeat offender or not) on the underlying convictions. Is that an adequate response?

(b) Rules That Implicate Fundamental Fairness and Bear on Guilt or Innocence. The Supreme Court has yet to find a claim that fits within Teague's second exception, for fundamental or bedrock procedures "without which the likelihood of an accurate conviction is seriously diminished."[6] (Recall Justice O'Connor's statement that it is "unlikely that many such components of basic due process have yet to emerge".)

In Padilla, the Court held that an attorney's failure to provide competent advice about the risk of deportation resulting from a guilty plea denies the effective assistance of counsel, in violation of the Sixth Amendment. Relying on Padilla, Chaidez, a *federal* prisoner, filed a collateral attack on her conviction. Applying the principles of Teague v. Lane, the Supreme Court ruled that the Padilla decision did not apply retroactively. Justice Kagan's opinion for the Court acknowledged that a decision does not announce a new rule when it merely applies a governing principle to a new set of facts. But the Court found that "Padilla did something more." It "considered a threshold question: Was advice about deportation 'categorically removed' from the scope of the Sixth Amendment right to counsel because it involved only a 'collateral consequence' of a conviction, rather than a component of the criminal sentence?" Before the Padilla decision, the Supreme Court had explicitly left that question open, and nearly all state and federal appellate courts to consider the question had found no Sixth Amendment violation. Padilla held otherwise, but, Justice Kagan said, "[i]f that does not count as 'break[ing] new ground' or 'impos[ing] a new obligation,' we are hard pressed to know what would."

Justice Sotomayor's dissent (joined by Justice Ginsburg) viewed Padilla as a more straightforward application of Sixth Amendment standards. Justice Thomas concurred in the judgment on the ground that Padilla was wrongly decided.

The majority's emphasis on the "threshold" nature of the Sixth Amendment issue seems designed to leave intact the principle that the application of established constitutional principles to a distinctive set of facts is not "new". But doesn't the force of the "threshold" argument depend upon the state of precedent in the Supreme Court and courts below?

[5] On the merits, a 5–4 majority rejected Penry's claim—a decision later overruled in Atkins v. Virginia, 536 U.S. 304 (2002) (holding that the Eighth Amendment precluded imposition of a death sentence on a developmentally disabled defendant).

[6] Cases finding it inapplicable include Whorton v. Bockting, 549 U.S. 406 (2007) (rule of Crawford v. Washington, 541 U.S. 36 (2004), that the Confrontation Clause prohibits the admission of hearsay that is "testimonial", whether or not it would be deemed reliable, unless the declarant is unavailable and the defendant had a prior opportunity to cross-examine);

(c) Substantive Rights Versus Procedural Rights. In Schriro v. Summerlin, 542 U.S. 348 (2004), the Court recharacterized the first Teague exception as follows: "New *substantive* rules generally apply retroactively. This includes decisions that narrow the scope of a [federal] criminal statute by interpreting its terms, see Bousley v. United States, [p. 1358, *infra*], as well as constitutional determinations that place particular conduct or persons covered by the statute beyond the State's power to punish". A footnote added: "We have sometimes referred to rules of this latter type as falling under an exception to Teague's bar on retroactive application of procedural rules; they are more accurately characterized as substantive rules not subject to the bar." Given this recharacterization, and so long as Teague's second exception remains a null set, it would be accurate to restate Teague and its exceptions this way: new substantive rules apply retroactively; new procedural rules do not.

C. Questions About Teague

(1) Criticisms. A common criticism of Teague is that the Court's conception of "new law" is too broad: by including rules that reflect ordinary legal evolution, it reduces the incentives for state courts, and state law enforcement officials, to take account of the direction of legal developments. See, *e.g.*, Fallon & Meltzer, note 2, *supra*, at 1816–17.[7] Others question any effort to distinguish old from new rules. See Meyer, *"Nothing We Say Matters": Teague and New Rules*, 61 U.Chi.L.Rev. 423 (1994) (treating some rules as new is incompatible with the common law tradition, in which the meaning of precedents emerges only when they are characterized by subsequent cases); Feldman, *Diagnosing Power: Postmodernism in Legal Scholarship and Judicial Practice (with an Emphasis on the Teague Rule Against New Rules in Habeas Corpus Cases)*, 88 Nw.U.L.Rev. 1046, 1065 (1994) (every rule is both new, because reconstructed whenever applied, and old, because grounded in existing traditions).

(2) Equal Treatment of Litigants. Justice O'Connor's opinion in Teague objected that the Warren Court's approach to retroactivity treated similarly situated litigants differently. But, as Justice White's dissent in Griffith noted, an approach turning on when a conviction became final on direct review merely redirects any inequality. Consider two prisoners who filed habeas petitions in 2014, relying on a new Supreme Court decision rendered in 2012. Both prisoners were tried in 2010; one's case moved swiftly on appeal and the conviction became final in 2011, while the other's case progressed more slowly and the conviction became final only in 2013. Teague bars the first but not the second prisoner from relying on the 2012 decision in habeas proceedings. More generally, any approach that is neither fully retroactive nor fully prospective necessarily treats some litigants differently

---

Caspari v. Bohlen, Paragraph (4)(a), *supra*; Sawyer v. Smith, 497 U.S. 227, 244 (1990) (rule of Caldwell v. Mississippi, 472 U.S. 320 (1985), that the Eighth Amendment bars imposition of death sentence by a sentencer that has been led to the false belief that responsibility for determining the appropriateness of such a sentence lies elsewhere); Gilmore v. Taylor, 508 U.S. 333 (1993) (claim that homicide instructions denied due process because they permitted a jury to convict for murder rather than voluntary manslaughter without considering whether killing was in the heat of passion).

[7] See also, *e.g.*, Liebman, *More Than "Slightly Retro": The Rehnquist Court's Rout of Habeas Corpus Jurisdiction in Teague v. Lane*, 18 N.Y.U.Rev.L. & Soc.Change 537 (1990–91); Hoffman, *Retroactivity and the Great Writ: How Congress Should Respond to Teague v. Lane*, 1990 B.Y.U.L.Rev. 183.

from others. Which dividing line makes greater sense—that of the Warren Court or that of Teague?

(3) Teague and Constitutional Remedies. Fallon & Meltzer, note 2, *supra*, argue that habeas corpus is a remedy for constitutional wrongdoing and that Teague is an adjustment of the scope of that remedy. They offer a general argument that the novelty of a constitutional right is relevant to the appropriate scope of remediation and has been recognized as such not only in habeas actions but also in actions seeking damages for violations of constitutional rights (in which officials' immunity from damages liability often depends on whether their conduct violated "clearly established" law, see Chap. IX, Sec. 3, *supra*).[8] They agree that the newness of a rule of decision should have greater significance on collateral than on direct review, but they object not only to the breadth of the definition of "new law" but also to the application of the same standards in capital and non-capital cases and to the narrowness of Teague's exceptions.

Consider Jeffries, *The Right-Remedy Gap in Constitutional Law*, 109 Yale L.J. 87 (1999) (doctrines like Teague and official immunity, which withhold remedies for violations of new constitutional rules, enable courts more easily to develop rights-protective doctrines—an approach that redistributes constitutional benefits from past to future claimants).

(4) A Threshold Issue? Does deciding whether a habeas petition rests on "new law" at the threshold make sense, given how intertwined that question is with the merits? A different approach might sometimes help establish more promptly the contours of new constitutional protections, thereby providing useful guidance for state officials and state courts. See generally Fallon & Meltzer, note 2, *supra*, at 1797–1807. And as Justice Stevens noted in discussing the harmless error doctrine, courts often discuss the merits even if relief is ultimately denied on other grounds.

For discussion of whether a habeas court must always determine whether Teague precludes relief before reaching the constitutional merits, see Campiti v. Matesanz, 333 F.3d 317, 321 & n. 4 (1st Cir.2003) ("Only as a last resort should the circuit courts read Supreme Court decisions to create * * * mandatory priorities. * * * Anything that precludes judges from taking the shortest distance to a result impairs their ability to give truly difficult cases the time they require."). Compare the Court's quite different, and shifting, approach to a similar problem in constitutional tort actions seeking damages—whether first to decide if there was a constitutional violation before determining whether the case should be dismissed because the defendant enjoys official immunity. See pp. 1051–1054, *supra*.

D.   The Application of Teague in State Court

Does Teague govern state postconviction proceedings? That issue arose in Danforth v. Minnesota, 552 U.S. 264 (2008). After Danforth's conviction became final, the Supreme Court decided Crawford v. Washington, 541 U.S. 36 (2004), which reshaped a defendant's rights under the Confrontation Clause. Crawford announced a "new" rule not retroactively applicable in federal habeas corpus proceedings. Whorton v. Bockting, 549 U.S. 406 (2007). When Danforth filed a state postconviction petition relying on Crawford, the state supreme court ruled that it could not give retroactive

---

[8]   See also Kinports, *Habeas Corpus, Qualified Immunity, and Crystal Balls: Predicting the Course of Constitutional Law*, 33 Ariz.L.Rev. 115 (1991).

effect to a federal constitutional ruling that, under Teague, does not apply retroactively in federal habeas corpus proceedings.

The Supreme Court reversed. Justice Stevens' majority opinion reasoned that the Court's retroactivity jurisprudence "is primarily concerned, not with the question whether a constitutional violation occurred, but with the availability or nonavailability of remedies." Teague rested on an interpretation of the federal habeas corpus statute in light of equitable and prudential considerations, including concern about comity and respect for the finality of state convictions, which are distinctive to the exercise of federal court power. The state courts, he reasoned, should be free to evaluate whether the state's interest in finality calls for precluding reliance on new law in state postconviction proceedings. He added that it would be anomalous to bar state courts from extending the retroactive applicability of new rulings, given that the state political branches may waive a Teague defense—the effect of which was similarly to extend retroactive applicability.

In dissent, Chief Justice Roberts, joined by Justice Kennedy, argued that retroactivity is a question not of remedies but of what law, old or new, will apply. State courts, he contended, may not depart from the Supreme Court's determination of when federal constitutional law applies.

INTRODUCTORY NOTE ON 28 U.S.C. § 2254(D)(1)

The Antiterrorism and Effective Death Penalty Act of 1996 (AEDPA) includes a provision, codified at 28 U.S.C. § 2254(d)(1), that was motivated by concerns similar to those underlying the Teague decision. Unlike Teague, § 2254(d)(1) applies only when a state court has decided the constitutional issue. But when it does apply, § 2254(d)(1) curtails the scope of federal habeas review even more sharply than does Teague.

The next principal case, Terry Williams v. Taylor, provides the Supreme Court's first and fullest discussion of § 2254(d)(1). (During its 2000 Term, the Court decided two habeas cases against Virginia's Warden, Taylor, in which the prisoner's surname was Williams; hence, in discussing each, we include the prisoner's first name as well.) Although Justice Stevens delivers the majority opinion in Terry Williams, note that on the key issue in the case, the interpretation of § 2254(d)(1), he is in the minority, while Justice O'Connor speaks for the majority.

Terry Williams v. Taylor

529 U.S. 362, 120 S.Ct. 1495, 146 L.Ed.2d 389 (2000).
Certiorari to the United States Court of Appeals for the Fourth Circuit.

■ JUSTICE STEVENS announced the judgment of the Court and delivered the opinion of the Court with respect to Parts I, III, and IV, and an opinion with respect to Parts II and V.*

The questions presented are whether Terry Williams' constitutional right to the effective assistance of counsel as defined in Strickland v. Washington, 466 U.S. 668 (1984), was violated, and whether the judgment of the Virginia Supreme Court refusing to set aside his death sentence "was contrary to, or involved an unreasonable application of, clearly established Federal law, as determined by the Supreme Court of the United States," within the meaning of 28 U.S.C. § 2254(d)(1) (1994 ed., Supp. III). We answer both questions affirmatively.

I

[Having been sentenced to death, Williams alleged, in a state postconviction proceeding, that his lawyers denied him the effective assistance of counsel at the sentencing hearing by failing to introduce mitigating evidence of Williams' childhood neglect and abuse, borderline mental retardation, repeated head injuries, and possible mental impairment that was organic in origin. Williams also complained that after the government's experts testified to a "high probability" that he would pose a continuing threat to society, his counsel failed on cross-examination to elicit the experts' view that Williams would not pose such a threat if kept in a structured environment.]

[Applying the Strickland standard, the state trial judge ruled that Williams had been denied his right to counsel, finding that (a) his lawyer's performance fell below the range of competent assistance, and (b) that deficiency was prejudicial, as there was a reasonable probability that the sentencing outcome would have differed had counsel been effective. The Virginia Supreme Court disagreed, reasoning that, even assuming that counsel's performance was deficient, there was no prejudice. The state supreme court read Lockhart v. Fretwell, 506 U.S. 364 (1993), as having modified the Strickland standard of prejudice.]

[Lockhart was an unusual case in which the prisoner's lawyer failed to raise a constitutional objection based on an established lower court precedent that the Supreme Court later rejected. Ruling against the prisoner, the Supreme Court held that no prejudice results from a lawyer's failure to have made an objection that is no longer meritorious.]

[In Terry Williams' case, the Virginia Supreme Court ruled that, in light of Lockhart, the trial judge erred in relying on "mere outcome determination" when assessing prejudice under the Sixth Amendment. The state supreme court also found no reasonable possibility that the omitted mitigating evidence would have changed the jury's recommendation, as it "barely would have altered the profile of this defendant".]

---

*   JUSTICE SOUTER, JUSTICE GINSBURG, and JUSTICE BREYER join this opinion in its entirety. JUSTICE O'CONNOR and JUSTICE KENNEDY join Parts I, III, and IV of this opinion.

[Williams then sought federal habeas corpus relief. The district judge upheld the claim of ineffective assistance of counsel. The Fourth Circuit reversed, construing § 2254(d)(1) as barring relief unless the state court "decided the question by interpreting or applying the relevant precedent in a manner that reasonable jurists would all agree is unreasonable".] It explained that the evidence that Williams presented a future danger to society was "simply overwhelming," it endorsed the Virginia Supreme Court's interpretation of Lockhart, and it characterized the state court's understanding of the facts in this case as "reasonable".

We granted certiorari, and now reverse.

II

* * * The warden here contends that federal habeas corpus relief is prohibited by the amendment to 28 U.S.C. § 2254, enacted as a part of the Antiterrorism and Effective Death Penalty Act of 1996 (AEDPA). The relevant portion of that amendment provides:

> "(d) An application for a writ of habeas corpus on behalf of a person in custody pursuant to the judgment of a State court shall not be granted with respect to any claim that was adjudicated on the merits in State court proceedings unless the adjudication of the claim—

> "(1) resulted in a decision that was contrary to, or involved an unreasonable application of, clearly established Federal law, as determined by the Supreme Court of the United States. . . . "

* * * The inquiry mandated by the amendment relates to the way in which a federal habeas court exercises its duty to decide constitutional questions; the amendment does not alter the underlying grant of jurisdiction in § 2254(a). When federal judges exercise their federal-question jurisdiction under the "judicial Power" of Article III of the Constitution, it is "emphatically the province and duty" of those judges to "say what the law is." Marbury v. Madison, 1 Cranch 137, 177 (1803). At the core of this power is the federal courts' independent responsibility * * * to interpret federal law. A construction of AEDPA that would require the federal courts to cede this authority to the courts of the States would be inconsistent with the practice that federal judges have traditionally followed in discharging their duties under Article III of the Constitution. If Congress had intended to require such an important change in the exercise of our jurisdiction, we believe it would have spoken with much greater clarity than is found in the text of AEDPA.

This basic premise informs our interpretation of both parts of § 2254(d)(1): first, the requirement that the determinations of state courts be tested only against "clearly established Federal law, as determined by the Supreme Court of the United States," and second, the prohibition on the issuance of the writ unless the state court's decision is "contrary to, or involved an unreasonable application of," that clearly established law. We address each part in turn.

The "clearly established law" requirement

In Teague v. Lane, 489 U.S. 288 (1989), we held that the petitioner was not entitled to federal habeas relief because he was relying on a rule of federal law that had not been announced until after his state conviction became final. The antiretroactivity rule recognized in *Teague*, which prohibits reliance on "new rules," is the functional equivalent of a statutory provision commanding exclusive reliance on "clearly established law." Because there is no reason to believe that Congress intended to require federal courts to ask both whether a rule sought on habeas is "new" under Teague—which remains the law—and also whether it is "clearly established" under AEDPA, it seems safe to assume that Congress had congruent concepts in mind. It is perfectly clear that AEDPA codifies Teague to the extent that Teague requires federal habeas courts to deny relief that is contingent upon a rule of law not clearly established at the time the state conviction became final.[12]

* * * [Under Teague,] a federal habeas court operates within the bounds of comity and finality if it applies a rule "dictated by precedent existing at the time the defendant's conviction became final." 489 U.S., at 301 (emphasis deleted). A rule that "breaks new ground or imposes a new obligation on the States or the Federal Government," *ibid.*, falls outside this universe of federal law.

To this, AEDPA has added, immediately following the "clearly established law" requirement, a clause limiting the area of relevant law to that "determined by the Supreme Court of the United States." * * * [T]he lower federal courts cannot themselves establish such a principle with clarity sufficient to satisfy the AEDPA bar. * * *

* * *

In the context of this case, we also note that * * * rules of law may be sufficiently clear for habeas purposes even when they are expressed in terms of a generalized standard rather than as a bright-line rule. As Justice Kennedy has explained:

"If the rule * * * requires a case-by-case examination of the evidence, then we can tolerate a number of specific applications without saying that those applications themselves create a new rule. . . . [When a general rule is] * * * designed for the specific purpose of evaluating a myriad of factual contexts, it will be the infrequent case that yields a result so novel that it forges a new rule, one not dictated by precedent." *Wright v. West*, 505 U.S. 277 (1992) (opinion concurring in judgment). * * *

It has been urged, in contrast, that we should read Teague and its progeny to encompass a broader principle of deference requiring federal courts to "validat[e] 'reasonable, good-faith interpretations' of the law" by state courts. * * * This presumption of deference was in essence the position taken by three Members of this Court in Wright, 505 U.S., at 290–291 (opinion of Thomas, J.) ("[A] federal habeas court 'must defer to

---

[12] We are not persuaded by the argument that because Congress used the words "clearly established law" and not "new rule," it meant * * * to codify an aspect of the doctrine of executive qualified immunity rather than Teague's antiretroactivity bar. The warden refers us specifically to § 2244(b)(2)(A) and 28 U.S.C. § 2254(e)(2), in which the statute does in so many words employ the "new rule" language familiar to Teague and its progeny. * * * [But] the verbatim adoption of the Teague language in these other sections bolsters our impression that Congress had Teague—and not any unrelated area of our jurisprudence—specifically in mind in amending the habeas statute. * * * We will not assume that in a single subsection of an amendment entirely devoted to the law of habeas corpus, Congress made the anomalous choice of reaching into the doctrinally distinct law of qualified immunity for a single phrase that just so happens to be the conceptual twin of a dominant principle in habeas law of which Congress was fully aware.

the state court's decision rejecting the claim unless that decision is patently unreasonable' ") (quoting Butler [v. McKellar], 494 U.S. [407], 422 [(1990)] (Brennan, J., dissenting)).

Teague, however, does not extend this far. The often repeated language that Teague endorses "reasonable, good-faith interpretations" by state courts is an explanation of policy, not a statement of law. * * * [W]e have long insisted that federal habeas courts attend closely to [considered decisions of state courts], and give them full effect when their findings and judgments are consistent with federal law. See Thompson v. Keohane, 516 U.S. 99, 107–116 (1995). But as Justice O'Connor explained in Wright:

> "[T]he duty of the federal court in evaluating whether a rule is 'new' is not the same as deference * * *.

> "We have always held that federal courts, even on habeas, have an independent obligation to say what the law is." 505 U.S., at 305 (opinion concurring in judgment).

We are convinced that in the phrase, "clearly established law," Congress did not intend to modify that independent obligation.

The "contrary to, or an unreasonable application of," requirement

The message that Congress intended to convey by using the phrases "contrary to" and "unreasonable application of" is not entirely clear. The prevailing view in the Circuits is that the former phrase requires *de novo* review of "pure" questions of law and the latter requires some sort of "reasonability" review of so-called mixed questions of law and fact.

We are not persuaded that the phrases define two mutually exclusive categories of questions. Most constitutional questions that arise in habeas corpus proceedings * * * require the federal judge to apply a rule of law to a set of facts * * *. For example, an erroneous conclusion that particular circumstances established the voluntariness of a confession, or that there exists a conflict of interest when one attorney represents multiple defendants, may well be described either as "contrary to" or as an "unreasonable application of" the governing rule of law. In constitutional adjudication, as in the common law, rules of law often develop incrementally as earlier decisions are applied to new factual situations. But rules that depend upon such elaboration are hardly less lawlike than those that establish a bright-line test.

Indeed, our pre-AEDPA efforts to distinguish questions of fact, questions of law, and "mixed questions," and to create an appropriate standard of habeas review for each, generated some not insubstantial differences of opinion as to which issues of law fell into which category of question, and as to which standard of review applied to each. * * *

The statutory text likewise does not obviously prescribe a specific, recognizable standard of review for dealing with either phrase. * * * Rather, the text is fairly read simply as a command that a federal court not issue the habeas writ unless the state court was wrong as a matter of law or unreasonable in its application of law in a given case. The suggestion that a wrong state-court "decision" * * * may no longer be redressed through habeas (because it is unreachable under the "unreasonable application" phrase) is based on a mistaken insistence that the § 2254(d)(1) phrases have not only independent, but mutually exclusive, meanings. Whether or not a federal court can issue the writ "under [the] 'unreasonable application' clause," the statute is clear that habeas may issue under § 2254(d)(1) if a state-court "decision" is "contrary to . . . clearly established Federal law." We thus anticipate that there will be a variety of cases, like this one, in which both phrases may be implicated.

Even though we cannot conclude that the phrases establish "a body of rigid rules," they do express a "mood" that the Federal Judiciary must respect. Universal Camera Corp. v. NLRB, 340 U.S. 474, 487 (1951). * * * [I]t seems clear that Congress intended federal judges to attend with the utmost care to state-court decisions, including all of the reasons supporting their decisions, before concluding that those proceedings were infected by constitutional error * * *. * * *

On the other hand, it is significant that the word "deference" does not appear in the text of the statute itself. Neither the legislative history nor the statutory text suggests any difference in the so-called "deference" depending on which of the two phrases is implicated. Whatever "deference" Congress had in mind with respect to both phrases, it surely is not a requirement that federal courts actually defer to a state-court application of the federal law that is, in the independent judgment of the federal court, in error. * * *[14]

Our disagreement with the Court about the precise meaning of the phrase "contrary to," and the word "unreasonable," is, of course, important, but should affect only a narrow category of cases. The simplest and first definition of "contrary to" as a phrase is "in conflict with." Webster's Ninth New Collegiate Dictionary 285 (1983). * * * [W]e think the phrase surely capacious enough to include a finding that the state-court "decision" is simply "erroneous" or wrong. * * * And there is nothing in the phrase "contrary to"—as the Court appears to agree—that implies anything less than independent review by the federal courts. * * * Our difference is as to the cases in which, at first blush, a state-court judgment seems entirely reasonable, but thorough analysis by a federal court produces a firm conviction that that judgment is infected by

---

[14] [Justice Stevens found unpersuasive the three reasons advanced by Justice O'Connor in support of the majority's interpretation of the phrase "unreasonable application of."

[As to the suggestion that Congress, in using the word "unreasonable", was directly influenced by the "patently unreasonable" standard advocated by Justice Thomas' opinion in Wright v. West, 505 U.S. 277, 287 (1992), Justice Stevens responded that the debate in Wright was "not about the *standard of review* habeas courts should use for law-application questions, but about whether a rule is 'new' or 'old' " for purposes of Teague. * * * "Teague, of course, as Justice O'Connor correctly pointed out, 'did not establish a standard of review at all,' 505 U.S., at 303–304; rather than instructing a court *how* to review a claim, it simply asks, in absolute terms, *whether* a rule was clear at the time of a state-court decision. We thus do not think *Wright* 'confirms' anything about the meaning of § 2254(d)(1) * * *."

[As to the suggestion that the legislative history supports the Court's interpretation, Justice Stevens said that the only two passages on which the Court relies "do no more than beg the question. One merely quotes the language of the statute without elaboration, and the other goes to slightly greater length in stating that state-court judgments must be upheld unless 'unreasonable.' "

[Finally, as to the claim that Congress must have intended to change the law more substantially than his reading of 28 U.S.C. § 2254(d)(1) permits, he responded that although AEDPA "wrought substantial changes in habeas law, [citing various provisions], there is an obvious fallacy in the assumption that because the statute changed pre-existing law in some respects, it must have rendered this specific change here."]

constitutional error. In our view, such an erroneous judgment is "unreasonable" within the meaning of the Act * * *.

In sum, the statute directs federal courts to attend to every state-court judgment with utmost care, but it does not require them to defer to the opinion of every reasonable state-court judge on the content of federal law. If, after carefully weighing all the reasons for accepting a state court's judgment, a federal court is convinced that a prisoner's custody—or, as in this case, his sentence of death—violates the Constitution, that independent judgment should prevail. Otherwise the federal "law as determined by the Supreme Court of the United States" might be applied by the federal courts one way in Virginia and another way in California. In light of the well-recognized interest in ensuring that federal courts interpret federal law in a uniform way, we are convinced that Congress did not intend the statute to produce such a result.

III

[To prevail on his claim of ineffective assistance of counsel at his sentencing hearing, Williams must show, under Strickland v. Washington, (a) that "counsel's representation fell below an objective standard of reasonableness", and (b) "that there is a reasonable probability that, but for counsel's unprofessional errors, the result of the proceeding would have been different."] * * *

It is past question that the rule set forth in Strickland qualifies as "clearly established Federal law, as determined by the Supreme Court of the United States." * * * Williams is therefore entitled to relief if the Virginia Supreme Court's decision rejecting his ineffective-assistance claim was either "contrary to, or involved an unreasonable application of," that established law. It was both.

IV

[The Virginia Supreme Court's understanding of Lockhart v. Fretwell was contrary to clearly established law. Lockhart dealt only with the unusual case in which a lawyer failed to make an objection that had merit under the law as it then stood but that subsequent decisions have held to be invalid. Lockhart did not change the law in a case, like Williams', in which counsel's ineffectiveness "*does* deprive the defendant of a substantive or procedural right to which the law entitles him." * * *

[Justice Stevens proceeded to find that Williams' counsel was ineffective at the sentencing phase. The opinion pointed to numerous investigatory failures that could have uncovered "extensive records graphically describing Williams' nightmarish childhood", which would have permitted the jury to learn] that Williams' parents had been imprisoned for the criminal neglect of Williams and his siblings, that Williams had been severely and repeatedly beaten by his father, [and] that he had been committed to the custody of the social services bureau for two years during his parents' incarceration (including one stint in an abusive foster home). * * *

[Counsel also failed to introduce evidence of Williams' borderline mental retardation, * * * his limited education, and the aid he had provided officials in cracking a prison drug ring. Counsel failed to seek testimony of prison officials who described Williams as among the inmates] least likely to act in a violent, dangerous or provocative way. * * *

We are also persuaded * * * that counsel's unprofessional service prejudiced Williams within the meaning of Strickland. * * *

The Virginia Supreme Court's own analysis of prejudice reaching the contrary conclusion was * * * unreasonable in at least two respects. First, * * * the court's decision turned on its erroneous view that a "mere" difference in outcome is not sufficient to establish constitutionally ineffective assistance of counsel. Its analysis in this respect was thus not only "contrary to," but also, inasmuch as the Virginia Supreme Court relied on the inapplicable exception recognized in Lockhart, an "unreasonable application of" the clear law as established by this Court.

Second, the State Supreme Court's prejudice determination was unreasonable insofar as it failed to evaluate the totality of the available mitigation evidence—both that adduced at trial, and the evidence adduced in the habeas proceeding in reweighing it against the evidence in aggravation. * * * [I]t correctly emphasized the strength of the prosecution evidence supporting the future dangerousness aggravating circumstance.

But the state court failed even to mention the sole argument in mitigation that trial counsel did advance—Williams turned himself in, alerting police to a crime they otherwise would never have discovered, expressing remorse for his actions, and cooperating with the police after that. While this, coupled with the prison records and guard testimony, may not have overcome a finding of future dangerousness, the graphic description of Williams' childhood, filled with abuse and privation, or the reality that he was "borderline mentally retarded," might well have influenced the jury's appraisal of his moral culpability. * * * Mitigating evidence unrelated to dangerousness may alter the jury's selection of penalty, even if it does not undermine or rebut the prosecution's death-eligibility case. The Virginia Supreme Court did not entertain that possibility. It thus failed to accord appropriate weight to the body of mitigation evidence available to trial counsel.

V

* * * [T]he Virginia Supreme Court rendered a "decision that was contrary to, or involved an unreasonable application of, clearly established Federal law." * * *

Accordingly, the judgment of the Court of Appeals is reversed, and the case is remanded for further proceedings.

■ JUSTICE O'CONNOR delivered the opinion of the Court with respect to Part II (except as to the footnote), concurred in part, and concurred in the judgment.*

[I agree with the Court's determination that the Virginia Supreme Court's decision was contrary to, or involved an unreasonable application of, clearly established federal law, as determined by the Supreme Court of the United States,] and join Parts I, III, and IV of the Court's opinion. Because I disagree, however, with the interpretation of § 2254(d)(1) set forth in Part II of Justice Stevens' opinion, I write separately to explain my views.

---

* JUSTICE KENNEDY joins this opinion in its entirety. The CHIEF JUSTICE and JUSTICE THOMAS join this opinion with respect to Part II. JUSTICE SCALIA joins this opinion with respect to Part II, except as to the footnote.

I

Before 1996, this Court held that a federal court entertaining a state prisoner's application for habeas relief must exercise its independent judgment when deciding both questions of constitutional law and mixed constitutional questions (*i.e.*, application of constitutional law to fact). *See, e.g.*, Miller v. Fenton, 474 U.S. 104, 112 (1985). * * * In 1991, in the case of Wright v. West, 502 U.S. 1021, we revisited our prior holdings by asking the parties to address the following question in their briefs:

"In determining whether to grant a petition for writ of habeas corpus by a person in custody pursuant to the judgment of a state court, should a federal court give deference to the state court's application of law to the specific facts of the petitioner's case or should it review the state court's determination *de novo?*" *Ibid.*

Although our ultimate decision did not turn on the answer to that question, our several opinions did join issue on it.

Justice Thomas * * * acknowledged that our precedents had "treat[ed] as settled the rule that mixed constitutional questions are 'subject to plenary federal review' on habeas." *Id.*, at 289 (quoting Miller, *supra*, at 112). * * * Justice Thomas suggested that the time to revisit our decisions may have been at hand, given that our more recent habeas jurisprudence in the nonretroactivity context, *see, e.g.*, Teague v. Lane, 489 U.S. 288 (1989), had called into question the then-settled rule of independent review of mixed constitutional questions.

I wrote separately in Wright because I believed Justice Thomas had "understate[d] the certainty with which Brown v. Allen rejected a deferential standard of review of issues of law." *Id.*, at 300. * * * I noted that "Teague did not establish a 'deferential' standard of review" because "[i]t did not establish a standard of review at all." 505 U.S., at 303–304. * * *

Finally, * * * I stated my disagreement with Justice Thomas' suggestion that *de novo* review is incompatible with the maxim that federal habeas courts should "give great weight to the considered conclusions of a coequal state judiciary," Miller, *supra*, at 112. Our statement in Miller signified only that a state-court decision is due the same respect as any other "persuasive, well-reasoned authority." Wright, 505 U.S., at 305. "But this does not mean that * * * federal courts must presume the correctness of a state court's legal conclusions on habeas, or that a state court's incorrect legal determination has ever been allowed to stand because it was reasonable." * * *

II

A

* * *

Justice Stevens' opinion in Part II essentially contends that § 2254(d)(1) does not alter the previously settled rule of independent review. Indeed, the opinion concludes its statutory inquiry with the somewhat empty finding that § 2254(d)(1) does no more than express a " 'mood' that the Federal Judiciary must respect." For Justice Stevens, the congressionally enacted "mood" has two important qualities. First, "federal courts [must] attend to every state-court judgment with utmost care" by "carefully weighing all the reasons for accepting a state court's judgment." Second, if a federal court undertakes that careful review and yet remains convinced that a prisoner's custody violates the Constitution, "that independent judgment should prevail."

One need look no further than our decision in Miller to see that Justice Stevens' interpretation of § 2254(d)(1) gives the 1996 amendment no effect whatsoever. The command that federal courts should now use the "utmost care" by "carefully weighing" the reasons supporting a state court's judgment echoes our pre-AEDPA statement in Miller that federal habeas courts "should, of course, give great weight to the considered conclusions of a coequal state judiciary." 474 U.S., at 112. Similarly, the requirement that the independent judgment of a federal court must in the end prevail essentially repeats the conclusion we reached in the very next sentence in Miller with respect to the specific issue presented there: "But, as we now reaffirm, the ultimate question whether, under the totality of the circumstances, the challenged confession was obtained in a manner compatible with the requirements of the Constitution *is a matter for independent federal determination.*" *Ibid.* (emphasis added).

* * *

Justice Stevens arrives at his erroneous interpretation by means of one critical misstep. He fails to give independent meaning to both the "contrary to" and "unreasonable application" clauses of the statute. * * *

The word "contrary" is commonly understood to mean "diametrically different," "opposite in character or nature," or "mutually opposed." Webster's Third New International Dictionary 495 (1976). The text of § 2254(d)(1) therefore suggests that the state court's decision must be substantially different from the relevant precedent of this Court. * * * A state-court decision will certainly be contrary to our clearly established precedent if the state court applies a rule that contradicts the governing law set forth in our cases. Take, for example, our decision in Strickland v. Washington, 466 U.S. 668 (1984). If a state court were to reject a prisoner's claim of ineffective assistance of counsel on the grounds that the prisoner had not established by a preponderance of the evidence that the result of his criminal proceeding would have been different, that decision would be "diametrically different," "opposite in character or nature," and "mutually opposed" to our clearly established precedent because we held in Strickland that the prisoner need only demonstrate a "reasonable probability that . . . the result of the proceeding would have been different." *Id.*, at 694. A state-court decision will also be contrary to this Court's clearly established precedent if the state court confronts a set of facts that are materially indistinguishable from a decision of this Court and nevertheless arrives at a result different from our precedent. * * *

On the other hand, a run-of-the-mill state-court decision applying the correct legal rule from our cases to the facts of a prisoner's case would not fit comfortably within § 2254(d)(1)'s "contrary to" clause. Assume, for example, that a state-court decision on a prisoner's ineffective-assistance claim correctly identifies Strickland as the controlling legal authority and, applying that framework, rejects the prisoner's claim. * * * [E]ven assuming the federal court considering the prisoner's habeas application might reach a different result applying the Strickland framework itself[, i]t is difficult * * * to describe such a run-of-the-mill state-court decision as "diametrically different" from, "opposite in character or nature" from, or "mutually opposed" to *Strickland*, our clearly established precedent. * * *

Justice Stevens would instead construe § 2254(d)(1)'s "contrary to" clause to encompass such a routine state-court decision. That construction, however, saps the "unreasonable application" clause of any meaning. * * *

The Fourth Circuit's interpretation of the "unreasonable application" clause of § 2254(d)(1) is generally correct. * * * [The Fourth Circuit correctly reasoned that] a state-court decision can involve an "unreasonable application" of this Court's clearly established precedent * * * if the state court identifies the correct governing legal rule from this Court's cases but unreasonably applies it to the facts of the particular state prisoner's case. * * **

The Fourth Circuit also held * * * that state-court decisions that unreasonably extend a legal principle from our precedent to a new context where it should not apply (or unreasonably refuse to extend a legal principle to a new context where it should apply) should be analyzed under § 2254(d)(1)'s "unreasonable application" clause. Although that holding may perhaps be correct, the classification does have some problems of precision. Just as it is sometimes difficult to distinguish a mixed question of law and fact from a question of fact, it will often be difficult to identify separately those state-court decisions that involve an unreasonable application of a legal principle (or an unreasonable failure to apply a legal principle) to a new context. Indeed, on the one hand, in some cases it will be hard to distinguish a decision involving an unreasonable extension of a legal principle from a decision involving an unreasonable application of law to facts. On the other hand, in many of the same cases it will also be difficult to distinguish a decision involving an unreasonable extension of a legal principle from a decision that "arrives at a conclusion opposite to that reached by this Court on a question of law," *supra*, at 405. Today's case does not require us to decide how such "extension of legal principle" cases should be treated under § 2254(d)(1). For now it is sufficient to hold that when a state-court decision unreasonably applies the law of this Court to the facts of a prisoner's case, a federal court applying § 2254(d)(1) may conclude that the state-court decision falls within that provision's "unreasonable application" clause.

B

There remains the task of defining what exactly qualifies as an "unreasonable application" of law under § 2254(d)(1). The Fourth Circuit held * * * that a state-court decision involves an "unreasonable application of . . . clearly established Federal law" only if the state court has applied federal law "in a manner that reasonable jurists would all agree is unreasonable." The placement of this additional overlay on the "unreasonable application" clause was erroneous. * * *

---

   *   The legislative history of § 2254(d)(1) also supports this interpretation. See, *e.g.*, 142 Cong. Rec. 7799 (1996) (remarks of Sen. Specter) ("[U]nder the bill deference will be owed to State courts' decisions on the application of Federal law to the facts. Unless it is unreasonable, a State court's decision applying the law to the facts will be upheld") * * *.

* * * Stated simply, a federal habeas court making the "unreasonable application" inquiry should ask whether the state court's application of clearly established federal law was objectively unreasonable. The federal habeas court should not transform the inquiry into a subjective one by resting its determination instead on the simple fact that at least one of the Nation's jurists has applied the relevant federal law in the same manner the state court did in the habeas petitioner's case. * * *

The term "unreasonable" is no doubt difficult to define. * * * For purposes of today's opinion, the most important point is that an *unreasonable* application of federal law is different from an *incorrect* application of federal law. Our opinions in Wright, for example, make that difference clear. [Justice O'Connor noted that Justice Thomas' opinion in Wright argued that Brown v. Allen did not indicate whether a habeas court must grant relief unless the state court's decision was deemed to be *correct*, as opposed to merely *reasonable*. Her own opinion in Wright maintained that "a state court's *incorrect* legal determination has [never] been allowed to stand because it was *reasonable*. * * *"] In § 2254(d)(1), Congress specifically used the word "unreasonable," and not a term like "erroneous" or "incorrect." * * *

Justice Stevens turns a blind eye to the debate in Wright because he finds no indication in § 2254(d)(1) itself that Congress was "directly influenced" by Justice Thomas' opinion in Wright. * * * [H]owever, Congress need not mention a prior decision of this Court by name in a statute's text in order to adopt either a rule or a meaning given a certain term in that decision. In any event, whether Congress intended to codify the standard of review suggested by Justice Thomas in Wright is beside the point. Wright is important for the light it sheds on § 2254(d)(1)'s requirement that a federal habeas court inquire into the reasonableness of a state court's application of clearly established federal law. * * * The Wright opinions confirm what § 2254(d)(1)'s language already makes clear—that an *unreasonable* application of federal law is different from an *incorrect* or *erroneous* application of federal law.

Throughout this discussion the meaning of the phrase "clearly established Federal law, as determined by the Supreme Court of the United States" has been put to the side. That statutory phrase refers to the holdings, as opposed to the dicta, of this Court's decisions as of the time of the relevant state-court decision. In this respect, the "clearly established Federal law" phrase bears only a slight connection to our Teague jurisprudence. With one caveat, whatever would qualify as an old rule under our Teague jurisprudence will constitute "clearly established Federal law, as determined by the Supreme Court of the United States" under § 2254(d)(1). The one caveat, as the statutory language makes clear, is that § 2254(d)(1) restricts the source of clearly established law to this Court's jurisprudence.*

In sum, § 2254(d)(1) places a new constraint on the power of a federal habeas court * * * with respect to claims adjudicated on the merits in state court. Under § 2254(d)(1), the writ may issue only if * * * [(1)] the

---

* [Ed.] Are the third and fourth sentences in this paragraph consistent? How can both of the following propositions be true: (1) the standard in § 2254(d) "bears only a slight connection to our Teague jurisprudence"; and (2) "with one caveat [that § 2254(d)(1) restricts the source of clearly established law to this Court's jurisprudence,] whatever would qualify as an old rule under our Teague jurisprudence will constitute 'clearly established Federal law' "?

state court arrives at a conclusion opposite to that reached by this Court on a question of law or if the state court decides a case differently than this Court has on a set of materially indistinguishable facts[,] or (2) * * * the state court identifies the correct governing legal principle from this Court's decisions but unreasonably applies that principle to the facts of the prisoner's case.

III

Although I disagree with Justice Stevens concerning the standard we must apply under § 2254(d)(1) * * *, [the Court's discussion] in Parts III and IV is correct and * * * demonstrates the reasons that the Virginia Supreme Court's decision in Williams' case, even under the interpretation of § 2254(d)(1) I have set forth above, was both contrary to and involved an unreasonable application of our precedent. * * *

Accordingly, I join Parts I, III, and IV of the Court's opinion and concur in the judgment of reversal.

■ CHIEF JUSTICE REHNQUIST, with whom JUSTICE SCALIA and JUSTICE THOMAS join, concurring in part and dissenting in part.

I agree with the Court's interpretation of 28 U.S.C. § 2254(d)(1) but disagree with its decision to grant habeas relief in this case.

[The Chief Justice argued that the Virginia Supreme Court had, in fact, properly applied the prejudice standard of Strickland v. Washington; hence, the state court's decision was not contrary to clearly established precedent. Nor, he argued, was the decision an unreasonable application of Strickland, for given the strong evidence of the prisoner's dangerousness, the state court could reasonably have determined that evidence of the prisoner's terrible childhood and low IQ would not have swayed the jury.] * * *

Accordingly, * * * I would hold that habeas relief is barred by 28 U.S.C. § 2254(d).

NOTE ON TERRY WILLIAMS V. TAYLOR AND 28 U.S.C. § 2254(D)(1)

(1) The Significance of the Terry Williams Decision. The situation in the Terry Williams case—in which a state court is found to have misunderstood the meaning of a Supreme Court precedent—is unusual. More often, a state court decision will properly recite the applicable doctrine and the prisoner's complaint will be about the doctrine's application to the facts. Accordingly, the "unreasonable application" clause will typically be the critical one in determining whether § 2254(d)(1) bars relief.

Consider in this regard Lockyer v. Andrade, 538 U.S. 63 (2003) (5–4), where the prisoner claimed that the imposition, under California's "three strikes" law, of two consecutive sentences of 25 years to life for each of two thefts of a handful of videotapes violated the Cruel and Unusual Punishment Clause. Justice O'Connor's opinion stressed that the Court's decisions "in this area have not been a model of clarity" and "have not established a clear or consistent path for courts to follow." The only "clearly established" doctrine is a "gross disproportionality principle, the precise contours of which are unclear, applicable only in the 'exceedingly rare' and 'extreme' case." Finding that the sentence at issue fell between two Supreme Court precedents, one invalidating a life sentence without parole and the other upholding a life sentence with the possibility of parole, the Court held that the state court's application of the gross disproportionality principle was not unreasonable.

If the "precise contours" of an established principle must be clear, § 2254(d)(1) is especially likely to preclude habeas relief when the prisoner invokes constitutional doctrine framed as a standard rather than as a rule. The Court suggested as much in Yarborough v. Alvarado, 541 U.S. 652 (2004), where the state courts had found no error in the admission of a confession, on the basis that the suspect had not been "in custody" for purposes of the Miranda rules. The Court found that § 2254(d)(1) barred relief, observing that "[a]pplying a general standard to a specific case can demand a substantial element of judgment. As a result, evaluating whether a rule application was unreasonable requires considering the rule's specificity. The more general the rule, the more leeway courts have in reaching outcomes in case-by-case determinations."

(2) Section 2254(d)(1) in Operation. The hurdle interposed by § 2254(d)(1) has proved to be extremely difficult for petitioners to overcome. In Harrington v. Richter, 562 U.S. 86 (2011), the Court, after describing the § 2254(d) standard, stated: "If this standard is difficult to meet, that is because it was meant to be", as § 2254(d) was designed to be a " 'guard against extreme malfunctions in the state criminal justice systems,' not a substitute for ordinary error correction through appeal" (quoting Jackson v. Virginia, 443 U.S. 307, 332 n.5 (1979) (Stevens, J., concurring in judgment)). The Court added that to obtain relief, a prisoner must show that the state court ruling "was so lacking in justification that there was an error well understood and comprehended in existing law beyond any possibility for fairminded disagreement."

From the 2005 Term (the first for the Chief Justice and Justice Alito) through the end of the 2013 Term, the Court decided 35 habeas cases in which section § 2254(d)(1) figured. In 30 of the 35 cases, the Court found that § 2254(d)(1) barred relief. Of the 35 total decisions, 23 were unanimous. Twenty-five of the 30 decisions in which relief was barred originated in the Sixth or Ninth Circuits, which typically had ruled otherwise. The few cases in which the Court found that § 2254(d)(1) did not bar relief have tended to involve death sentences, often from Texas. Some Supreme Court opinions have expressed frustration with what the Justices view as disobedience to § 2254(d)(1) by the lower courts. See, *e.g.*, White v. Woodall, 134 S.Ct 1697, 1701 (2014) (the Sixth Circuit "disregarded the limitations of 28 U.S.C. § 2254(d)—a provision of law that some federal judges find too confining, but that all federal judges must obey".

Recall that Teague v. Lane was criticized for having defined new law so broadly that it reduced the incentive for state courts to faithfully enforce federal constitutional standards. If that criticism was persuasive, how strong is the incentive provided by habeas review after the enactment of § 2254(d)(1)?

(3) The Constitutionality of the Court's Interpretation. Justice Stevens' opinion in the Terry Williams case states that a deferential standard of review would be so extraordinary that Congress would surely have spoken with greater clarity than it did in § 2254(d)(1). That statement, together with his citation to Marbury v. Madison, carries a suggestion that the statute, as interpreted by the majority, raises a constitutional concern.

In an article predating the Terry Williams decision, Liebman & Ryan, *"Some Effectual Power": The Quantity and Quality of Decisionmaking Required of Article III Courts*, 98 Colum.L.Rev. 696 (1998), the authors contend that § 2254(d)(1) would violate Article III if read to require habeas courts to defer to a state court decision that was erroneous when rendered. In their view, Article III requires that a federal court given jurisdiction by Congress be able, *inter alia*, (1) to decide federal questions "based on the whole supreme law"—an obligation that extends to reviewing de novo all "mixed" questions of law (*i.e.*, application of legal principles to the facts) but not questions of historical fact—and (2) to make its judgment remedially effectual. On this view, the majority's interpretation of § 2254(d)(1) in Terry Williams is unconstitutional. The majority, of course, implicitly rejects any such constitutional objection.

Liebman and Ryan's argument is rich and complex but bristles with difficulties, some of which are highlighted by Scheidegger, *Habeas Corpus, Relitigation, and the Legislative Power*, 98 Colum.L.Rev. 888 (1998). Considerable tensions exists between Liebman & Ryan's approach and, *inter alia*, (1) the decision in Teague; (2) the qualified immunity doctrine in constitutional tort actions, which precludes damage awards when an officer acted unconstitutionally but did not violate "clearly established law"; (3) the occasional practice of the Supreme Court of limiting its review of state court judgments to determining whether the state court identified the correct constitutional standard and whether its application of that standard "was within the realm of permissible judgment";[1] (4) the Court's occasional practice of limiting a grant of certiorari to particular issues, effectively deferring entirely to the state court's determination of other issues; and (5) the res judicata doctrine, which limits the power of federal courts to relitigate constitutional questions that state courts may have decided incorrectly.

Do limitations on the judicial power exercised on collateral review stand on a different constitutional footing from similar limitations on direct review? *Cf.* Steiker, *Habeas Exceptionalism*, 78 Tex.L.Rev. 1703 (2000). Do self-imposed limitations on judicial power like those in Teague stand on a different footing from limitations imposed by Congress? See Note, 114 Harv.L.Rev. 1551 (2001).[2]

(4) Section 2254(d) and Summary State Court Decisions. In Harrington v. Richter, 562 U.S. 86 (2011), the Supreme Court considered the application of § 2254(d) to summary state court decisions that deny federal constitutional claims on the merits without explanation. After Richter's conviction became final on direct review, he petitioned directly to the California Supreme Court for a state writ of habeas corpus. That court denied the petition in a one sentence summary order. When Richter's federal habeas corpus case reached the Supreme Court, it ruled, without dissent, that the California Supreme Court's order was an adjudication on the merits within the meaning of § 2254(d). Justice Kennedy's opinion stressed that if

---

[1]   See, *e.g.*, Container Corp. of America v. Franchise Tax Bd., 463 U.S. 159 (1983).

[2]   For elaborate judicial discussion of the constitutionality of § 2254(d), see Lindh v. Murphy, 96 F.3d 856 (7th Cir.1996) (en banc), in which Judge Easterbrook's majority opinion found no constitutional defect, but Judge Wood's dissent marshaled the contrary arguments. For discussion of whether § 2254(d) is unconstitutional insofar as it requires determination of the relevant constitutional law by reference only to Supreme Court decisions rather than to all federal law, see Caminker, *Allocating the Judicial Power in a "Unified Judiciary"*, 78 Tex.L.Rev. 1513 (2000); Jackson, *Introduction: Congressional Control of Jurisdiction and the Future of the Federal Courts—Opposition, Agreement, and Hierarchy*, 86 Geo.L.J. 2445, 2470 (1998).

§ 2254(d) applied only when the state court provided a statement of reasons, state judiciaries could be prevented from concentrating resources on cases where opinions are most needed. He noted that the California Supreme Court disposes of nearly 10,000 cases annually, including more than 3400 original habeas petitions. Proceeding to apply § 2254(d), the Court said that a habeas court must determine what arguments or theories could have supported the state court's decision, and then ask whether fair-minded jurists could disagree about whether those arguments or theories are inconsistent with the holding in a prior Supreme Court decision.

Two Terms later, in Johnson v. Williams, 133 S.Ct. 1088 (2013), the Court extended Harrington. In Williams, the defendant had argued on appeal that the trial court's discharge of a particular juror violated both a California statute and the Sixth Amendment's right to jury trial. The state appellate court's extended discussion of the matter never expressly stated that the court was deciding the Sixth Amendment issue. On habeas review, the Court of Appeals for the Ninth Circuit held that § 2254(d) did not apply, deeming it "obvious" that the state appellate court had "overlooked or disregarded" the Sixth Amendment claim. The Supreme Court reversed. After noting that "Richter itself concerned a state-court order that did not address *any* of the defendant's claims," the Court said that there was "no reason why the Richter presumption should not also apply when a state-court opinion addresses some but not all of a defendant's claims." For the Court, Justice Alito noted several reasons why a state court may not expressly address one of many claims raised on appeal. But he refused to adopt an irrebuttable presumption that the state court must have rejected the federal claim on the merits. Justice Alito suggested that when a petitioner seeks relief under both state and federal law, if the state standard is less protective than, or very different from, the federal standard, the presumption may be rebutted, either by the petitioner (in order to obtain de novo federal review) or by the state (in order to show that the claim was not decided on the merits at all and hence might have been forfeited). Section 2254(d) does not apply, he stressed, if the federal claim was rejected because of "sheer inadvertence".[3] After examining the course of proceedings in the state courts, the Court found that it was hard to imagine that the California Supreme Court had overlooked the Sixth Amendment issue.

(5) When Must the Law Have Been Clearly Established? In Greene v. Fisher, 132 S.Ct. 38 (2011) (9–0), the Court ruled that "clearly established law", for purposes of § 2254(d), does not include Supreme Court decisions announced after the last decision on the merits in state court but before the defendant's conviction became final on direct review. A petitioner's claim that relies on such decisions would not be "new" under (and therefore would not be barred by) Teague v. Lane, but in Greene, the Court stressed that the inquiries under § 2254(d) and Teague are distinct and relied upon what it viewed as the plain meaning of § 2254(d).[4]

---

[3]   Concurring in the judgment, Justice Scalia argued that the presumption can be overcome only by a showing, based on the text of the state court order (or when the text is ambiguous, based on standard state practice) that the state court did not purport to decide the federal issue.

[4]   The Court said that the petitioner's predicament was one of his own creation, because he could have sought certiorari in the U.S. Supreme Court—which surely would have granted the petition and vacated the state court's judgment—or could have filed a state postconviction petition. Note, however, that defendants have no constitutional right to counsel before the U.S. Supreme Court or in state postconviction proceedings.

(6) The Relationship of § 2254(d)(1) to Teague. Section 2254(d)(1) does not by its terms override the judge-made doctrine of Teague v. Lane. Ordinarily, however, § 2254(d)(1)'s limitation on review will be the key question, as that limitation is broader than the limitation established in Teague. But unlike Teague, § 2254(d)(1) applies only when a habeas claim was adjudicated in state court. Cases in which there was no state court adjudication will rarely go far in federal court: if state remedies remain, the prisoner will not have satisfied the exhaustion requirement, see pp. 1349-1354, *infra*, while if the prisoner failed properly to present the federal claim in the state courts, that procedural default will ordinarily bar habeas review, see pp. 1323–1346, *infra*. But where there is neither a state court determination on the merits nor a procedural barrier to the exercise of habeas jurisdiction, the Teague doctrine (both its general bar on relying on "new" law and the exceptions to that bar) applies. See Horn v. Banks, 536 U.S. 266 (2002) (per curiam).

[margin note: where Teague still applies.]

(7) The Teague Exceptions and § 2254(d)(1). Unlike the Teague doctrine, the text of § 2254(d)(1) recognizes no exceptions. Suppose a state court "reasonably" decides that a prisoner's conduct is not constitutionally protected, but the Supreme Court later decides (in a different case) that the Constitution does protect the conduct in question. As the case fits Teague's first exception, Teague would not bar relief, but would § 2254(d)(1)? Recall that in the nineteenth century, when postconviction habeas relief was limited (at least in the view of some) to "jurisdictional" defects, that category embraced challenges to the constitutionality of the statute under which the prisoner was convicted. See Ex parte Siebold, p. 1273, *supra*.

In Whorton v. Bockting, 549 U.S. 406 (2007), the Ninth Circuit had found that in enacting § 2254(d), Congress impliedly preserved Teague's two exceptions; a contrary interpretation, the Ninth Circuit suggested, would raise serious constitutional questions. The Supreme Court unanimously reversed, finding that the new rule in question was not a watershed rule within the meaning of Teague's second exception; the Court therefore had no need to reach the question whether § 2254(d) implicitly incorporates Teague's two exceptions.[5]

[margin note: Whorton does not reach the issue of Teague in 2254, but overturns 9th Cir. doing so.]

(8) A Threshold Issue? Justice O'Connor's opinion in Teague stated that "newness" is a threshold issue that must be resolved before a federal court may reach the constitutional merits, although some lower courts have viewed themselves as having greater latitude to determine the proper order of decision. See p. 1300, *supra*. A parallel issue arises under § 2254(d)(1): must a habeas court first determine whether a state court decision was "contrary to, or involved an unreasonable application of, clearly established Federal law, as determined by the Supreme Court" under § 2254(d)(1)—and if it was not, refrain from discussing whether the state court's decision was correct?

The Supreme Court has rejected the view of one court of appeals that habeas courts *must* first review the state court decision de novo before applying § 2254(d)'s standard of review, stating: "AEDPA does not require a federal habeas court to adopt any one methodology in deciding the only question that matters under § 2254(d)(1)—whether a state court decision is contrary to, or involved an unreasonable application of, clearly established federal law." Lockyer v. Andrade, 538 U.S. 63 (2003), p. 1313, *supra*. And

[margin note: 2254 does not req. de novo review]

---

[5]   See also Greene v. Fisher, paragraph (5), *supra*.

"... but it may."

then in Berghuis v. Thompkins, 560 U.S. 370 (2010), the Court reached the merits of a petitioner's habeas claim and after finding it wanting, said that "[t]he state court's decision rejecting Thompkins's Miranda claim was * * * correct under *de novo* review and therefore necessarily reasonable under the more deferential AEDPA standard of review" (citing 28 U.S.C. § 2254(d)). Dissenting from that decision, Justice Sotomayor (joined by Justices Stevens, Ginsburg, and Breyer) disagreed with the Court's understanding of Miranda, but in addition complained that "[t]he broad rules the Court announces today are also troubling because they are unnecessary to decide this case, which is governed by the deferential standard of review set forth in the [AEDPA]."

Certainly, Justice Sotomayor is correct that the Court needed only to decide whether the state court had made an "unreasonable application of * * * clearly established Federal law, as determined by the Supreme Court of the United States." But is there a systemic interest in having the Court resolve unsettled legal questions *de novo* in § 2254(d)(1) cases? For a discussion of similar issues in the context of determining whether an officer violated "clearly established" constitutional rights for qualified immunity purposes, see pp. 1051–1054, *supra*.

(9) AEDPA and the Meaning of "Made Retroactively Applicable to Cases on Collateral Review." One puzzle under AEDPA involves the interaction of § 2254(d)(1) with other provisions added by the same Act. Some provisions of AEDPA, after setting forth procedural restrictions on the exercise of habeas jurisdiction, create exceptions to those restrictions when the prisoner relies on a new constitutional rule that the Supreme Court has "made" retroactive to cases on collateral review. See, *e.g.*, § 2244(b)(2)(A) (limits on successive petitions), p. 1346, *infra*; § 2254(e)(2)(a)(i) (availability of federal evidentiary hearings), p. 1321, *infra*. See also § 2244(d)(1)(C) (statute of limitations provision, requiring that the provision have been made retroactively applicable on collateral review without specifying that the Supreme Court itself must have done so), p. 1266, *supra*. But given that § 2254(d)(1) generally bars habeas courts from relying on new law, when will it be the case that the Supreme Court, or any federal habeas court, has made new law retroactive on habeas review? When a habeas case implicates one of the Teague exceptions—and then only on the assumption either that § 2254(d)(1) does not apply or that it implicitly recognizes the Teague exceptions?

The Court faced this question in Tyler v. Cain, 533 U.S. 656 (2001). After Tyler's federal habeas petition was denied, he filed a second petition, contending that the jury instruction on proof beyond a reasonable doubt was substantively identical to one later invalidated in Cage v. Louisiana, 498 U.S. 39 (1990). Under § 2244(b)(2)(A), in order to raise this claim in a second federal habeas petition, Tyler had to demonstrate that the ruling in Cage had been "made retroactive to cases on collateral review by the Supreme Court."

petitioner must demonstrate retroactivity beyond a reasonable doubt.

The Court (per Justice Thomas) held that Tyler could not make that showing, reasoning that it is not enough that the Court has "establishe[d] principles of retroactivity [as it did in Teague] and leaves the application of those principles to lower courts." Nor was § 2244(b)(2)(A)'s requirement satisfied by the Court's later holding, in Sullivan v. Louisiana, 508 U.S. 275 (1993), that a "Cage error" is "structural" in the sense that it is not amenable to harmless error analysis and thus always invalidates a conviction; structural error does not necessarily fall within the second Teague exception for bedrock procedural requirements whose violation seriously diminishes the likelihood of an accurate conviction. Although the Court acknowledged that it could "make a rule retroactive over the course of two cases" without actually saying so, through the logical implications of a "combination of holdings" that "dictate" the retroactivity of the new rule, the Sullivan decision had not done so with respect to Cage. In the end, the Court saw no need to decide whether the Cage rule is retroactive on collateral review, given that the petitioner could not show that, at the time of his habeas petition, "this Court already had made Cage retroactive."

Justice O'Connor joined the Court's opinion but added in a concurrence that, as to the first Teague exception (for rules that place particular conduct beyond the power of the criminal law to proscribe), it "necessarily follows" from the very decision declaring the new rule that it has been "made" retroactive under Teague. By contrast, the second exception, at issue in Tyler, necessarily calls for a judgment beyond the mere fact that the new rule was created.

Dissenting for four Justices, Justice Breyer argued that "[t]he Court made Cage retroactive" through the conjunction of Teague and Sullivan, as there was no meaningful difference "between the definition of a watershed rule under Teague and the standard that we have articulated in the handful of instances in which we have held errors structural". He complained that under the majority's approach, "the only way in which this Court can make a rule such as Cage's retroactive is to repeat its Sullivan reasoning in a case triggered by a prisoner's filing a first habeas petition * * * or in some other case that presents the issue in a posture that allows such language to have the status of a 'holding.' "[6]

NOTE ON RELITIGATING THE FACTS IN HABEAS CORPUS PROCEEDINGS

Although Brown v. Allen required de novo relitigation of issues of law (including so-called mixed questions—*i.e.*, application of legal principles to the facts)—it permitted, though it did not require, a habeas court to defer to state court factfindings.[1] And both Justice Reed's and Justice Frankfurter's opinions stated that a habeas court generally had discretion whether to hold an evidentiary hearing, being obliged to do so only if there were "unusual circumstances" (Reed) or a "vital flaw" (Frankfurter) in the state proceedings.

---

[6] Note that even this route is made more difficult still by a subsequent decision interpreting the statute of limitations. In Dodd v. United States, 545 U.S. 353 (2005) (5–4), a § 2255 action by a federal prisoner, the Court held that the one-year period from initial recognition by the Supreme Court of a new constitutional right, retroactively applicable to cases on collateral review, runs from the date on which the Supreme Court recognizes the new right, rather than the date on which the right is made retroactive. The language of § 2255(f) (governing federal prisoners) does not differ materially from that in § 2244(d)(1) (governing state prisoners).

[1] Distinguishing questions of fact from mixed questions was anything but an exact science, as the categories are really points on a spectrum. And judicial decisions may have been motivated less by a priori analysis of the platonic essence of the issue and more by a functional judgment about how decisional authority with respect to a particular issue should be allocated between state and federal tribunals. See, *e.g.*, Thompson v. Keohane, 516 U.S. 99 (1995). The new § 2254(d) added by AEDPA in 1996 requires deference to state court determinations, whether of law or fact, and so federal habeas courts no longer need to draw this distinction.

Over time, these flexible standards were modified by judicial decisions and statutory amendments that narrowed the power of federal courts both to reject state court factfindings and to hold evidentiary hearings. Then, in 1996, AEDPA included provisions that further limit the power of habeas courts to rest on factual determinations other than those made by the state courts.

A.   Deference to State Court Factfindings

(1) The 1966 Amendment. A 1966 amendment, codified in former § 2254(d), began the shift from Brown's approach, which *permitted* deference to state court factfindings, to an approach *requiring* such deference. The amendment required a federal habeas court to presume that a state court's written determination of fact was correct, unless one of eight specified circumstances, relating generally to procedural defects in the state court proceeding, was present. If no exception applied, the petitioner had the burden of establishing by clear and convincing evidence that the state court's factual determination was erroneous.

(2) The AEDPA Amendments. In 1996, AEDPA replaced former § 2254(d) with two different provisions mandating deference to state court factfindings, neither of which included the limitations found in the earlier provision.

(a) Current § 2254(d) precludes habeas relief unless the federal court finds that a state court decision was either (i) contrary to or an unreasonable application of clearly established *law* (subsection (d)(1), the provision at issue in Terry Williams), or (ii) "based on an unreasonable determination of the *facts* in light of the evidence presented in the State court proceeding" (subsection (d)(2)) (emphasis added). Thus, state court determinations, whether characterized as legal or factual, today enjoy comparable deference from habeas courts.

(b) Section 2254(e)(1) provides that "a determination of a factual issue made by a State court shall be presumed to be correct. The applicant shall have the burden of rebutting the presumption of correctness by clear and convincing evidence."

(c) The relationship between §§ 2254(d)(2) and 2254(e)(1) is not entirely clear. The lower courts generally recite them together without suggesting that they differ.[2] Notably, however, neither § 2254(d)(2) nor § 2254(e)(1) includes any exception for findings resulting from state court determinations that were in some way procedurally defective.

(3) Determining What Facts the State Court Found. Not infrequently, a state court decision simply denies relief or otherwise makes no explicit finding on a factual issue relevant to a habeas claim. In LaVallee v. Delle Rose, 410 U.S. 690 (1973), the petitioner argued that a state court's decision that his confession was voluntary was not entitled to a presumption of correctness because the state court had made no finding as to the credibility of the petitioner's testimony that the confession had been coerced—and thus had failed to resolve the merits of the factual dispute. The Court disagreed, ruling that the determination of voluntariness obviously, if implicitly, rested on a finding (to which the federal court must defer) that the petitioner's

---

[2]   For discussion of decisions that have found subtle differences between the provisions, see Marceau, *Deference and Doubt: The Interaction of AEDPA § 2254(d)(2) and (e)(1)*, 82 Tul.L.Rev. 385 (2007).

testimony was not credible. *Cf.* Harrington v. Richter, p. 1315, *supra* (holding that § 2254(d)(1) applies to summary state court decisions).

B. The Availability of a Federal Evidentiary Hearing

(1) Pre-AEDPA Law and Practice. The power of federal courts to conduct evidentiary hearings, like its power to override state court factfindings, has narrowed over time. In Townsend v. Sain, 372 U.S. 293 (1963), the Warren Court, after stating that "[i]t is the typical, not the rare, case in which constitutional claims turn upon the resolution of contested factual issues", spelled out six circumstances in which a defect in the state factfinding procedures made a federal hearing mandatory—without limiting the power to hold a hearing in other circumstances. Despite that broad language, the percentage of habeas cases in which a hearing was conducted has always been low: after reaching 11% in the 1960s, by 1988 it had declined to roughly 1%.[3]

In Keeney v. Tamayo-Reyes, 504 U.S. 1 (1992), the Rehnquist Court shifted gears, forbidding federal courts from holding hearings unless strict criteria were satisfied.[4]

(2) Evidentiary Hearings and the 1996 Act. In 1996, AEDPA prescribed, for the first time, a statutory standard restricting federal court power to conduct evidentiary hearings. Section 2254(e)(2) precludes an evidentiary hearing when the prisoner "failed to develop the factual basis of a claim in State court proceedings" unless the prisoner shows that—

"(A) the claim relies on (i) a new rule of constitutional law, made retroactive to cases on collateral review by the Supreme Court, that was previously unavailable; or (ii) a factual predicate that could not have been previously discovered through the exercise of due diligence; and

"(B) the facts underlying the claim would be sufficient to establish by clear and convincing evidence that but for constitutional error, no reasonable factfinder would have found the applicant guilty of the underlying offense."

Would evidence that petitioner's conduct was constitutionally protected, or that a death sentence was constitutionally defective, establish that the prisoner did not commit *the underlying offense*, within the meaning of (B)? If not, is a habeas court barred from holding an evidentiary hearing on such a claim?

(3) The Meaning of "Failed to Develop." In Michael Williams v. Taylor, 529 U.S. 420 (2000), Justice Kennedy's opinion for a unanimous Court rejected the state's argument that non-development of the facts in state court was in itself enough to bar a federal evidentiary hearing. Section 2254(e)(2) applies only if the prisoner "failed to develop" the facts, and the Court said that the word "fail" typically "connotes some omission, fault, or negligence on the part of the person who has failed to do something." Thus, "a failure to develop the factual basis of a claim is not established unless there is lack of

---

[3] See Weisselberg, *Evidentiary Hearings in Federal Habeas Corpus Cases*, 1990 B.Y.U.L.Rev. 131, 165–68.

[4] In Tamayo-Reyes, the Court viewed a prisoner's effort to establish in a federal habeas court facts not developed in state court as implicating the same policies as an effort to adjudicate in federal habeas proceedings a claim not raised in state court. Accordingly, the Court held that an evidentiary hearing may be afforded only if the prisoner shows that (i) there was "cause and prejudice" for the failure to present the evidence in state court, or (ii) a "fundamental miscarriage of justice" would occur were relitigation foreclosed. (Those standards are discussed at pp. 1337–1344, *infra*; both have been given extremely narrow scope.)

diligence, or some greater fault, attributable to the prisoner or the prisoner's counsel."

The Court proceeded to find a lack of diligence as to one of the three claims asserted, but not as to the other two, both of which related to the questioning at voir dire. One prospective juror, when asked if she was related to any of the witnesses, failed to reveal that she had been married to a prosecution witness, and when asked if any of the lawyers involved had ever represented her, said nothing, although one of the prosecutors had done so in her divorce. The Court found that "[t]he trial record contains no evidence which would have put a reasonable attorney on notice that [the juror's] nonresponse was a deliberate omission of material information", and that as a result, § 2254(e)(2) did not bar a hearing.

(4) Section 2254(d)(1) and Evidentiary Hearings. The Court sharply limited the significance of evidentiary hearings in Cullen v. Pinholster, 131 S.Ct. 1388 (2011), where it considered whether, when determining if § 2254(d)(1) bars habeas relief, the habeas court may consider evidence introduced in an evidentiary hearing permitted by § 2254(e)(2). In this case, a prisoner claimed a denial of the effective assistance of counsel at his capital sentencing hearing, a claim rejected on the merits in state courts. In his federal habeas action, the district court held an evidentiary hearing and granted relief. In affirming, the Ninth Circuit en banc ruled that a habeas court could consider evidence adduced in a federal evidentiary hearing permitted by § 2254(c)(2) when determining, under § 2254(d)(1), whether the state court's rejection of a constitutional claim was contrary to, or an unreasonable application of, clearly established federal law.

The Supreme Court reversed. Justice Thomas' majority opinion reasoned that § 2254(d)(1)'s use of the past tense—in referring to a state court determination that "resulted" in a decision that was contrary to, or "involved" an unreasonable application of, clearly established law—required an examination of the record when the state court decision was made. "It would be strange to ask federal courts to analyze whether a state court's adjudication resulted in a decision that unreasonably applied federal law to facts not before the state court." Justice Thomas asserted that this approach did not render § 2254(e)(2) superfluous; that section's limits on the authority to conduct a hearing continue to have force where § 2254(d)(1) does not bar federal habeas relief.

Justice Sotomayor's dissent stressed that evidentiary hearings are held in only 4 of every 1000 non-capital cases and 9.5 of every 100 capital cases and are permitted by § 2254(e)(2) only when the prisoner was diligent or when very restrictive requirements are satisfied. In these limited circumstances, consideration of new evidence does not upset the balance established by AEDPA. She contested the majority's linguistic argument by noting that § 2254(d) expressly requires district courts to base their review on the state court record—a direction that would be unnecessary if the use of the past tense in § 2254(d) required the same result. When § 2254(e)(2) permits a hearing, some courts of appeals had held (incorrectly, she declared) that § 2254(d)(1) simply does not apply; others had followed the approach of the Ninth Circuit. No court of appeals, however, had followed the majority's approach, which, she said, could prevent diligent petitioners from having any court available to resolve their claims based on the relevant evidence available.

Justice Alito's separate opinion agreed with Justice Sotomayor's conclusion, although he would add a gloss to § 2254(e)(2) by precluding an evidentiary hearing unless the evidence was not and could not have been introduced in state court—a standard that he found the petitioner did not meet.

After the Pinholster decision, how much remains of the federal evidentiary hearing? Indeed, under the majority's view, isn't the next logical step to bar evidentiary hearings altogether until the habeas court has first determined that § 2254(d)(1) does not preclude relief? And the rare case in which § 2254(d)(1) is not a barrier to relief is likely to be one in which (a) the state court determination is plainly wrong on the merits (in which case no evidentiary hearing is likely to be necessary), or (b) no state court determination was rendered on the claim (in which case it is likely that the petitioner will run into a procedural bar for having failed to raise the claim in state court, a matter discussed immediately below).

INTRODUCTORY NOTE ON FEDERAL HABEAS CORPUS AND STATE PROCEDURAL DEFAULT

(1) Introduction. Some habeas petitions include a claim that was not raised in state court at all or that was not raised in accordance with state procedural requirements. Typically, a state court will treat a procedural default—*i.e.*, a failure to have raised a claim in accordance with state procedural rules—as forfeiting the prisoner's right to an adjudication on the merits. And so long as the state procedural ground is "adequate", it will bar Supreme Court review of the state court judgment. See Chap. V, Sec. 2(B), *supra*.

If the prisoner then files a habeas corpus petition, ordinarily state remedies no longer are available; hence, there is no question of exhaustion of state remedies. The question, rather, is whether a procedural default that would preclude the Supreme Court from exercising appellate jurisdiction should also preclude the exercise of federal habeas jurisdiction. In dealing with this question, the Supreme Court has shifted ground more than once. Two cases decided ten years apart—Daniels v. Allen, 344 U.S. 443 (1953), and Fay v. Noia, 372 U.S. 391 (1963)—took sharply different approaches to that question, and they provide the backdrop to the next principal case, Wainwright v. Sykes.

(2) Daniels v. Allen. In Daniels v. Allen, a companion case to Brown v. Allen, 344 U.S. 443 (1953), p. 1275, *supra*, two prisoners had been sentenced to death for murder. At their trial they raised federal claims (concerning jury discrimination and the introduction of coerced confessions) similar to those raised in Brown v. Allen. But the North Carolina Supreme Court refused to consider the merits of their appeals, because their lawyer had been tardy in serving the "statement of the case on appeal" on the prosecutor. According to Justice Frankfurter's dissent (which was unchallenged on this point), "if petitioners' lawyer had mailed his 'statement of the case on appeal' on the 60th day and the prosecutor's office had received it on the 61st day the law of North Carolina would clearly have been complied with, but because he delivered it by hand on the 61st day", it was untimely. In petitioners' federal habeas corpus action, the Supreme Court ruled that the prisoners' failure to have made timely service of the statement of the case on appeal precluded federal habeas review.

(a) Justice Reed's opinion was not entirely clear whether the denial of relief rested on waiver, failure to exhaust state remedies, or the presence of an adequate state ground. He stated: "North Carolina has applied its law in refusing this out-of-time review. This Court applies its jurisdictional statute in the same manner. We cannot say that North Carolina's action * * * violates the Federal Constitution. A period of limitation accords with our conception of proper procedure.

" * * * A failure to use a state's available remedy, in the absence of some interference or incapacity * * * bars federal habeas corpus. The statute requires that the applicant exhaust available state remedies. To show that the time has passed for appeal is not enough to empower the Federal District Court to issue the writ."

(b) In dissent, Justice Black (joined by Justice Douglas) objected that the state supreme court's refusal to review the merits on state procedural grounds "is now held to cut off review in federal habeas corpus proceedings. But in the [cases of Brown and Speller, jointly decided in Brown v. Allen,] where the State Supreme Court did review the evidence, this Court has also reviewed it. I find it difficult to agree with the soundness of a philosophy which prompts this Court to grant a second review where the state has granted one but to deny any review at all where the state has granted none.

" * * * [T]he object of habeas corpus is to search records to prevent illegal imprisonments. * * * [I]t is never too late for courts in habeas corpus proceedings to look straight through procedural screens in order to prevent forfeiture of life or liberty in flagrant defiance of the Constitution. Perhaps there is no more exalted judicial function. I am willing to agree that it should not be exercised in cases like these except under special circumstances or in extraordinary situations. But I cannot join in any opinion that attempts to confine the Great Writ within rigid formalistic boundaries."

(c) Justice Frankfurter's separate dissent (joined by Justices Black and Douglas) emphasized that because North Carolina did not have a fixed period for taking an appeal, the North Carolina courts had discretion to hear the appeal. "The decisive question is whether a refusal to exercise * * * discretion * * * is an act so arbitrary and so cruel in its operation, considering that life is at stake, that in the circumstances of this case it constitutes a denial of due process in its rudimentary procedural aspect." In a separate opinion in the same case, Justice Frankfurter wrote: "Of course, nothing we have said suggests that the federal habeas corpus jurisdiction can displace a State's procedural rule requiring that certain errors be raised on appeal. Normally rights under the Federal Constitution may be waived at the trial, and may likewise be waived by failure to assert such errors on appeal. * * * However, this does not touch one of those extraordinary cases in which a substantial claim goes to the very foundation of a proceeding * * *."

(3) Fay v. Noia. Ten years later, in Fay v. Noia, 372 U.S. 391 (1963), the Court rejected the Daniels rule and greatly expanded habeas review of defaulted claims. Noia had been convicted of a capital crime but he avoided a death sentence. He then chose not to appeal. His subsequent motion for postconviction relief in state court, asserting that his conviction was based on a coerced confession, was denied because he had failed to appeal from his conviction. Meanwhile, Noia's two co-defendants, who had appealed from their convictions, did obtain postconviction relief in state court on the ground that their confessions were coerced. When Noia's federal habeas petition raising the coerced confession claim reached the Supreme Court, it held that his failure to have appealed from his conviction did not preclude the exercise of federal habeas jurisdiction.

(a) Justice Brennan, writing for the Court, rejected the contention that a procedural default that would block Supreme Court review of a state court's decision also bars the exercise of federal habeas corpus jurisdiction: "The fatal weakness of this contention is its failure to recognize that the adequate state-ground rule is a function of the limitations of *appellate* review. * * * [W]e have held that the adequate state-ground rule is a consequence of the Court's obligation to refrain from rendering advisory opinions or passing upon moot questions. * * * But while our appellate function is concerned only with the judgments or decrees of state courts, * * * [in habeas corpus cases t]he jurisdictional prerequisite is not the judgment of a state court but detention *simpliciter*. * * * Habeas lies to enforce the right of personal liberty; when that right is denied and a person confined, the federal court has the power to release him. Indeed, it has no other power; it cannot revise the state court judgment; it can act only on the body of the petitioner.

"To be sure, this may not be the entire answer to the contention that the adequate state-ground principle should apply to the federal courts on habeas corpus * * *. The [decision in Murdock v. City of Memphis, p. 477, *supra*, which held that the Supreme Court will not review state court decisions resting on an adequate state ground] may be supported not only by the factor of mootness, but in addition by certain characteristics of the federal system. * * * For the federal courts to refuse to give effect in habeas proceedings to state procedural defaults might conceivably have some effect upon the States' regulation of their criminal procedures. But the problem is crucially different from that posed in Murdock of the federal courts' deciding questions of substantive state law. In Noia's case the only relevant substantive law is federal—the Fourteenth Amendment. State law appears only in the procedural framework for adjudicating the substantive federal question. The paramount interest is federal. That is not to say that the States have not a substantial interest in exacting compliance with their procedural rules from criminal defendants asserting federal defenses. * * * But * * * the only concrete impact the assumption of federal habeas jurisdiction in the face of a procedural default has on the state interest we have described, is that it prevents the State from closing off the convicted defendant's last opportunity to vindicate his constitutional rights, thereby punishing him for his default and deterring others who might commit similar defaults in the future.

" * * * [I]f because of inadvertence or neglect [a prisoner] runs afoul of a state procedural requirement, and thereby forfeits his state remedies, appellate and collateral, as well as direct review thereof in this Court, those consequences should be sufficient to vindicate the State's valid interest in orderly procedure. Whatever residuum of state interest there may be under such circumstances is manifestly insufficient in the face of the federal policy * * * of affording an effective remedy for restraints contrary to the Constitution. * * * "

The Court did "recognize a limited discretion in the federal judge to deny relief to an applicant" who "has deliberately bypassed the orderly procedure of the state courts and in so doing has forfeited his state court remedies." Justice Brennan explained that if a habeas petitioner, after consulting with competent counsel, intentionally relinquishes a known right, "whether for strategic, tactical, or any other reasons * * *, then it is open to the federal court on habeas to deny him all relief if the state courts refused to entertain his federal claims on the merits * * *. * * * [T]he standard here put forth depends on the considered choice of the petitioner. A choice made by counsel not participated in by the petitioner does not automatically bar relief."

Although Noia's was one of the rare cases in which the defendant had in fact participated in a decision not to raise an issue in state court, the Court refused to find a deliberate bypass, stressing the "grisly choice" that Noia had faced—either forgoing an appeal from his conviction or running the risk that a successful appeal might lead to a death sentence on retrial.

(b) Justice Harlan, joined by Justices Clark and Stewart, dissented, stressing that "[t]he adequate state ground doctrine * * * finds its source in basic constitutional principles," and asking whether a federal habeas court is "constitutionally more free than the Supreme Court on direct review to 'ignore' the adequate state ground, proceed to the federal question, and order the prisoner's release?

"The answer must be that it is not. Of course, as the majority states, a judgment is not a 'jurisdictional prerequisite' to a habeas corpus application, but that is wholly irrelevant. The point is that if the applicant is detained *pursuant* to a judgment, termination of the detention necessarily nullifies the judgment. * * * In habeas as on direct review, ordering the prisoner's release invalidates the judgment of conviction and renders ineffective the state rule relied upon to sustain that judgment. * * *

" * * * [T]he Court exceeds its constitutional power if in fact the state ground relied upon to sustain the judgment of conviction is an adequate one. The effect of the approach adopted by the Court is, indeed, to do away with the adequate state ground rule entirely in every state case, involving a federal question, in which detention follows from a judgment."

(4) Wainwright v. Sykes. Fourteen years after the Warren Court's decision in Noia, the Burger Court, in Wainwright v. Sykes, once again sharply changed course in addressing the problem of procedural default.

Wainwright v. Sykes

433 U.S. 72, 97 S.Ct. 2497, 53 L.Ed.2d 594 (1977).
Certiorari to the United States Court of Appeals for the Fifth Circuit.

■ MR. JUSTICE REHNQUIST delivered the opinion of the Court.

We granted certiorari to consider the availability of federal habeas corpus to review a state convict's claim that testimony was admitted at his trial in violation of his rights under Miranda v. Arizona, 384 U.S. 436 (1966), a claim which the Florida courts have previously refused to consider on the merits because of noncompliance with a state contemporaneous-objection rule. * * *

Respondent Sykes was convicted of third-degree murder after a jury trial * * *. He testified at trial that on the evening of January 8, 1972, he told his wife to summon the police because he had just shot Willie Gilbert. Other evidence indicated that when the police arrived at respondent's trailer home, they found Gilbert dead of a shotgun wound, lying a few feet from the front porch. Shortly after their arrival, respondent came from across the road and volunteered that he had shot Gilbert, and a few minutes later respondent's wife approached the police and told them the same thing. Sykes was immediately arrested and taken to the police station.

Once there, it is conceded that he was read his Miranda rights * * *. He then made a statement, which was admitted into evidence at trial through the testimony of the two officers who heard it, to the effect that he had shot Gilbert * * *. There were several references during the trial to respondent's consumption of alcohol * * * and to his apparent state of intoxication * * *. At no time during the trial, however, was the admissibility of any of respondent's statements challenged by his counsel on the ground that respondent had not understood the Miranda warnings. * * *

[Respondent then] appealed his conviction, but apparently did not challenge the admissibility of the inculpatory statements. [He later filed a post-trial motion and state court petitions for habeas corpus, in which he,] apparently for the first time, challenged the statements made to police on grounds of involuntariness. In all of these efforts respondent was unsuccessful.

Having failed in the Florida courts, respondent initiated the present action under 28 U.S.C. § 2254, asserting the inadmissibility of his statements by reason of his lack of understanding of the Miranda warnings. * * *

The simple legal question before the Court calls for a construction of the language of 28 U.S.C. § 2254(a), which provides that the federal courts shall entertain an application for a writ of habeas corpus "in behalf of a person in custody pursuant to the judgment of a state court only on the ground that he is in custody in violation of the Constitution or laws or treaties of the United States." But, to put it mildly, we do not write on a clean slate in construing this statutory provision. * * *

* * * For more than a century since the [Act of 1867, which extended federal habeas corpus to persons held under *state* custody], this Court has grappled with the relationship between the classical common-law writ of habeas corpus and the remedy provided in 28 U.S.C. § 2254. * * * Where the habeas petitioner challenges a final judgment of conviction rendered by a state court, this Court has been called upon to decide no fewer than four different questions, all to a degree interrelated with one another: (1) What types of federal claims may a federal habeas court properly consider? (2) Where a federal claim is cognizable by a federal habeas court, to what extent must that court defer to a resolution of the claim in prior state proceedings? (3) To what extent must the petitioner who seeks federal habeas exhaust state remedies before resorting to the federal court? (4) In what instances will an adequate and independent state ground bar consideration of otherwise cognizable federal issues on federal habeas review?

Each of these four issues has spawned its share of litigation. * * *

There is no need to consider here in greater detail these first three areas of controversy * * *. Only the fourth area—the adequacy of state grounds to bar federal habeas review—is presented in this case. * * * [D]iscussion of the other three is pertinent here only as it illustrates this Court's historic willingness to overturn or modify its earlier views of the scope of the writ, even where the statutory language authorizing judicial action has remained unchanged.

As to the role of adequate and independent state grounds, it is a well-established principle of federalism that a state decision resting on an adequate foundation of state substantive law is immune from review in the federal courts. Fox Film Corp. v. Muller, 296 U.S. 207 (1935); Murdock v. Memphis, 20 Wall. 590 (1875). * * * The area of controversy which has developed has concerned the reviewability of federal claims which the state court has declined to pass on because they were not presented in the manner prescribed by its *procedural* rules. * * * The pertinent decisions marking the Court's somewhat tortuous efforts to deal with this problem are: Brown v. Allen, 344 U.S. 443 (1953); Fay v. Noia, [372 U.S. 391 (1963)]; Davis v. United States, 411 U.S. 233 (1973); and Francis v. Henderson, 425 U.S. 536 (1976).

[The Court here described the decisions in Daniels v. Allen and Fay v. Noia, noting that the Court in Noia effectively overruled Daniels when it held that the petitioner could raise his defaulted claim in a federal habeas corpus proceeding, even if the default would have constituted an adequate and independent state ground on direct review.]

As a matter of comity but not of federal power, the Court [in Noia] acknowledged "a limited discretion in the federal judge to deny relief . . . to an applicant who had deliberately by-passed the orderly procedure of the state courts and in so doing has forfeited his state court remedies." [372 U.S.], at 438. In so stating, the Court made clear that the waiver must be knowing and actual * * *. Noting petitioner's "grisly choice" between acceptance of his life sentence and pursuit of an appeal which might culminate in a sentence of death, the Court concluded that there had been no deliberate bypass of the right to have the federal issues reviewed through a state appeal.

A decade later we decided Davis v. United States, *supra*, in which a federal prisoner's application under 28 U.S.C. § 2255 sought for the first time to challenge the makeup of the grand jury which indicted him. The Government contended that he was barred by the requirement of Fed.Rule Crim.Proc. 12(b)(2) providing that such challenges must be raised "by motion before trial." The Rule further provides that failure to so object constitutes a waiver of the objection, but that "the court for cause shown may grant relief from the waiver." We * * * held that this standard contained in the Rule, rather than the Fay v. Noia concept of waiver, should pertain in federal habeas as on direct review. Referring to previous constructions of Rule 12(b)(2), we concluded that review of the claim should be barred on habeas, as on direct appeal, absent a showing of cause for the noncompliance and some showing of actual prejudice resulting from the alleged constitutional violation.

Last Term, in Francis v. Henderson, *supra*, the rule of Davis was applied to the parallel case of a state procedural requirement that challenges to grand jury composition be raised before trial. * * * While there was no counterpart provision of the state rule which allowed an exception upon some showing of cause, the Court concluded that the standard derived from the Federal Rule should nonetheless be applied in that context since "[t]here is no reason to . . . give greater preclusive effect to procedural defaults by federal defendants than to similar defaults by state defendants." [425 U.S.] at 542, quoting Kaufman v. United States, 394 U.S. 217, 228 (1969). As applied to the federal petitions of state convicts, the Davis cause-and-prejudice standard was thus incorporated directly into the body of law governing the availability of federal habeas corpus review.

To the extent that the dicta of Fay v. Noia may be thought to have laid down an all-inclusive rule rendering state contemporaneous-objection rules ineffective to bar review of underlying federal claims in federal habeas proceedings—absent a "knowing waiver" or a "deliberate bypass" of the right to so object—its effect was limited by Francis, which applied a different rule and barred a habeas challenge to the makeup of a grand jury. * * *

We * * * conclude that Florida procedure did, consistently with the United States Constitution, require that respondent's confession be challenged at trial or not at all, and thus his failure to timely object to its admission amounted to an independent and adequate state procedural ground which would have prevented direct review here. We thus come to the crux of this case. Shall the rule of Francis v. Henderson, *supra*, barring federal habeas review absent a showing of "cause" and "prejudice" attendant to a state procedural waiver, be applied to a waived objection to the admission of a confession at trial? We answer that question in the affirmative.

* * * [The rule of Brown v. Allen, 344 U.S. 443 (1953), permitting federal courts to determine the constitutional challenges raised in a habeas petition, without being bound by the state court's determination of the merits,] is in no way changed by our holding today. Rather, we deal only with contentions of federal law which were *not* resolved on the merits in the state proceeding due to respondent's failure to raise them there as required by state procedure. We leave open for resolution in future decisions the precise definition of the "cause"-and-"prejudice" standard, and note here only that it is narrower than the standard set forth in dicta in Fay v. Noia, 372 U.S. 391 (1963), which would make federal habeas review generally available to state convicts absent a knowing and deliberate waiver of the federal constitutional contention. It is the sweeping language of Fay v. Noia, going far beyond the facts of the case eliciting it, which we today reject.[12]

The reasons for our rejection of it are several. The contemporaneous-objection rule itself is by no means peculiar to Florida, and deserves greater respect than Fay gives it, both for the fact that it is employed by a coordinate jurisdiction within the federal system and for the many interests which it serves in its own right. A contemporaneous objection enables the record to be made with respect to the constitutional claim when the recollections of witnesses are freshest, not years later in a federal habeas proceeding. It enables the judge who observed the

---

[12] We have no occasion today to consider the Fay rule as applied to the facts there confronting the Court. Whether the Francis rule should preclude federal habeas review of claims not made in accordance with state procedure where the criminal defendant has surrendered, other than for reasons of tactical advantage, the right to have all of his claims of trial error considered by a state appellate court, we leave for another day.

The Court in Fay stated its knowing-and-deliberate-waiver rule in language which applied not only to the waiver of the right to appeal, but to failures to raise individual substantive objections in the state trial. Then, with a single sentence in a footnote, the Court swept aside all decisions of this Court "to the extent that [they] may be read to suggest a standard of discretion in federal habeas corpus proceedings different from what we lay down today * * *." 372 U.S., at 439 n. 44. We do not choose to paint with a similarly broad brush here.

demeanor of those witnesses to make the factual determinations necessary for properly deciding the federal constitutional question. * * *

A contemporaneous-objection rule may lead to the exclusion of the evidence objected to, thereby making a major contribution to finality in criminal litigation. Without the evidence claimed to be vulnerable on federal constitutional grounds, the jury may acquit the defendant, and that will be the end of the case; or it may nonetheless convict the defendant, and he will have one less federal constitutional claim to assert in his federal habeas petition. If the state trial judge admits the evidence in question after a full hearing, the federal habeas court pursuant to the 1966 amendment to § 2254 will gain significant guidance from the state ruling in this regard. [The amendment in question required federal habeas courts ordinarily to presume that state court factfindings were correct.] Subtler considerations as well militate in favor of honoring a state contemporaneous-objection rule. An objection on the spot may force the prosecution to take a hard look at its hole card, and even if the prosecutor thinks that the state trial judge will admit the evidence he must contemplate the possibility of reversal by the state appellate courts or the ultimate issuance of a federal writ of habeas corpus based on the impropriety of the state court's rejection of the federal constitutional claim.

We think that the rule of Fay v. Noia, broadly stated, may encourage "sandbagging" on the part of defense lawyers, who may take their chances on a verdict of not guilty in a state trial court with the intent to raise their constitutional claims in a federal habeas court if their initial gamble does not pay off. The refusal of federal habeas courts to honor contemporaneous-objection rules may also make state courts themselves less stringent in their enforcement. Under the rule of Fay v. Noia, state appellate courts know that a federal constitutional issue raised for the first time in the proceeding before them may well be decided in any event by a federal habeas tribunal. Thus, their choice is between addressing the issue notwithstanding the petitioner's failure to timely object, or else face the prospect that the federal habeas court will decide the question without the benefit of their views.

The failure of the federal habeas courts generally to require compliance with a contemporaneous-objection rule tends to detract from the perception of the trial of a criminal case in state court as a decisive and portentous event. * * * To the greatest extent possible all issues which bear on [the accusation of crime] should be determined in this proceeding * * *. * * * Any procedural rule which encourages the result that those proceedings be as free of error as possible is thoroughly desirable, and the contemporaneous-objection rule surely falls within this classification.

* * * The "cause"-and-"prejudice" exception of the Francis rule will afford an adequate guarantee, we think, that the rule will not prevent a federal habeas court from adjudicating for the first time the federal constitutional claim of a defendant who in the absence of such an adjudication will be the victim of a miscarriage of justice. Whatever precise content may be given those terms by later cases, we feel confident in holding without further elaboration that they do not exist here. Respondent has advanced no explanation whatever for his failure to object at trial, and, as the proceeding unfolded, the trial judge is certainly

not to be faulted for failing to question the admission of the confession himself. The other evidence of guilt presented at trial, moreover, was substantial to a degree that would negate any possibility of actual prejudice resulting to the respondent from the admission of his inculpatory statement.

We accordingly conclude that the judgment * * * must be reversed, and the cause remanded to the District Court with instructions to dismiss respondent's petition for a writ of habeas corpus.

■ MR. CHIEF JUSTICE BURGER, concurring.

* * * I write separately to emphasize one point * * *. In my view, the "deliberate bypass" standard enunciated in Fay v. Noia, 372 U.S. 391 (1963), was never designed for, and is inapplicable to, errors—even of constitutional dimension—alleged to have been committed during trial.

In Fay v. Noia, * * * the critical procedural decision—whether to take a criminal appeal—was entrusted to a convicted defendant. * * * [T]he role of the attorney was limited to giving advice and counsel. * * * Because * * * important rights hung in the balance of the *defendant's own decision*, the Court required that a waiver impairing such rights be a knowing and intelligent decision by the defendant himself. * * *

* * * In contrast, the claim in the case before us relates to events during the trial itself. * * * As a practical matter, a criminal defendant is rarely, if ever, in a position to decide, for example, whether certain testimony is hearsay and, if so, whether it implicates interests protected by the Confrontation Clause * * *.

Once counsel is appointed, the day-to-day conduct of the defense rests with the attorney. He, not the client, has the immediate—and ultimate—responsibility of deciding if and when to object, which witnesses, if any, to call, and what defenses to develop. * * *[1] The trial process simply does not permit the type of frequent and protracted interruptions which would be necessary if it were required that clients give knowing and intelligent approval to each of the myriad tactical decisions as a trial proceeds.

* * * The dissent in this case * * * implicitly recognizes as much. According to the dissent, Fay imposes the knowing-and-intelligent-waiver standard "where possible" during the course of the trial. In an extraordinary modification of Fay, Mr. Justice Brennan would now require "that the lawyer actually exercis[e] his expertise and judgment in his client's service, and with his client's knowing and intelligent participation *where possible*" * * *. What had always been thought the standard governing the *accused's* waiver of his own constitutional rights the dissent would change, in the trial setting, into a standard of conduct imposed upon the defendant's *attorney*. This vague "standard" would be unmanageable to the point of impossibility.

■ MR. JUSTICE STEVENS, concurring.

Although the Court's decision today may be read as a significant departure from the "deliberate bypass" standard announced in Fay v. Noia, 372 U.S. 391, I am persuaded that the holding is consistent with

---

[1]   Only such basic decisions as whether to plead guilty, waive a jury, or testify in one's own behalf are ultimately for the accused to make.

the way other federal courts have actually been applying Fay.[1] The notion that a client must always consent to a tactical decision not to assert a constitutional objection to a proffer of evidence has always seemed unrealistic to me. Conversely, if the constitutional issue is sufficiently grave, even an express waiver by the defendant himself may sometimes be excused. Matters such as the competence of counsel, the procedural context in which the asserted waiver occurred, the character of the constitutional right at stake, and the overall fairness of the entire proceeding, may be more significant than the language of the test the Court purports to apply. I therefore believe the Court has wisely refrained from attempting to give precise content to its "cause" and "prejudice" exception to the rule of Francis v. Henderson, 425 U.S. 536.[4]

In this case I agree with the Court's holding that collateral attack on the state-court judgment should not be allowed. The record persuades me that competent trial counsel could well have made a deliberate decision not to object to the admission of the respondent's in-custody statement. That statement was consistent, in many respects, with the respondent's trial testimony. It even had some positive value, since it portrayed the respondent as having acted in response to provocation, which might have influenced the jury to return a verdict on a lesser charge. To the extent that it was damaging, the primary harm would have resulted from its effect in impeaching the trial testimony, but it would have been admissible for impeachment in any event. Counsel may well have preferred to have the statement admitted without objection when it was first offered rather than making an objection which, at best, could have been only temporarily successful.

Moreover, since the police fully complied with Miranda, the deterrent purpose of the Miranda rule is inapplicable to this case. Finally, there is clearly no basis for claiming that the trial violated any standard of fundamental fairness. Accordingly, no matter how the rule is phrased, this case is plainly not one in which a collateral attack should be allowed. I therefore join the opinion of the Court.

■ MR. JUSTICE WHITE, concurring in the judgment. * * *

■ MR. JUSTICE BRENNAN, with whom MR. JUSTICE MARSHALL joins, dissenting.

* * * [Today's decision leaves unanswered] the thorny question that must be recognized to be central to a realistic rationalization of this area of law: How should the federal habeas court treat a procedural default in

---

[1]   The suggestion in Fay that the decision must be made personally by the defendant has not fared well * * *. Courts have generally found a "deliberate bypass" where counsel could reasonably have decided not to object, but they have not found a bypass when they consider the right "deeply embedded" in the Constitution, Frazier v. Roberts, 441 F.2d 1224, 1230 (C.A.8 1971), or when the procedural default was not substantial. Sometimes, even a deliberate choice by trial counsel has been held not to be a "deliberate bypass" when the result would be unjust. In short, the actual disposition of these cases seems to rest on the court's perception of the totality of the circumstances, rather than on mechanical application of the "deliberate bypass" test.

[4]   As Fay v. Noia makes clear, we are concerned here with a matter of equitable discretion rather than a question of statutory authority; and equity has always been characterized by its flexibility and regard for the necessities of each case.

a state court that is attributable purely and simply to the error or negligence of a defendant's trial counsel? * * *2 * * *

I

* * * If it could be assumed that a procedural default more often than not is the product of a defendant's conscious refusal to abide by the duly constituted, legitimate processes of the state courts, then I might agree that a regime of collateral review weighted in favor of a State's procedural rules would be warranted. Fay, however, recognized that such rarely is the case; and therein lies Fay's basic unwillingness to embrace a view of habeas jurisdiction that results in "an airtight system of [procedural] forfeitures." 372 U.S., at 432.

This, of course, is not to deny that there are times when the failure to heed a state procedural requirement stems from an intentional decision to avoid the presentation of constitutional claims to the state forum. * * * Indeed, the very purpose of [Fay's] bypass test is to detect and enforce such intentional procedural forfeitures of outstanding constitutionally based claims. * * *

But * * * Fay recognized that intentional, tactical forfeitures are not the norm upon which to build a rational system of federal habeas jurisdiction. In the ordinary case, litigants simply have no incentive to slight the state tribunal, since constitutional adjudication on the state and federal levels are not mutually exclusive. * * * [N]o rational lawyer would risk the "sandbagging" feared by the Court. * * *

II

What are the interests that Sykes can assert in preserving the availability of federal collateral relief in the face of his inadvertent state procedural default? Two are paramount.

As is true with any federal habeas applicant, Sykes seeks access to the federal court for the determination of the validity of his federal constitutional claim. * * *

With respect to federal habeas corpus jurisdiction, Congress explicitly chose to effectuate the federal court's primary responsibility for preserving federal rights and privileges by authorizing the litigation of constitutional claims and defenses in a district court after the State vindicates its own interest through trial of the substantive criminal offense in the state courts. * * * If the standard adopted today is later construed to require that the simple mistakes of attorneys are to be treated as binding forfeitures, it * * * would essentially leave it to the States, through the enactment of procedure and the certification of the competence of local attorneys, to determine whether a habeas applicant will be permitted the access to the federal forum that is guaranteed him by Congress.

* * * But federal review is not the full measure of Sykes' interest, for there is another of even greater immediacy: assuring that his constitutional claims can be addressed to *some* court. For the obvious

---

2   * * * This Court has never taken issue with the foundation principle established by Fay v. Noia—that [federal habeas courts] possess the *power* to look beyond a state procedural forfeiture in order to entertain the contention that a defendant's constitutional rights have been abridged. * * * Our disagreement, therefore, centers upon the standard that should govern a federal district court in the exercise of this power * * *. * * *

consequence of barring Sykes from the federal courthouse is to insulate Florida's alleged constitutional violation from any and all judicial review because of a lawyer's mistake. From the standpoint of the habeas petitioner, it is a harsh rule indeed that denies him "any review at all where the state has granted none," Brown v. Allen, 344 U.S., at 552 (Black, J., dissenting)—particularly when he would have enjoyed both state and federal consideration had his attorney not erred. * * *

III

A regime of federal habeas corpus jurisdiction that permits the reopening of state procedural defaults does not invalidate any state procedural rule as such; Florida's courts remain entirely free * * * to deny any and all state rights and remedies to a defendant who fails to comply with applicable state procedure. The relevant inquiry is whether more is required—specifically, whether the fulfillment of important interests of the State necessitates that federal courts be called upon to impose additional sanctions for inadvertent noncompliance with state procedural requirements such as the contemporaneous-objection rule involved here. * * *

Punishing a lawyer's unintentional errors by closing the federal courthouse door to his client is both a senseless and misdirected method of deterring the slighting of state rules. It is senseless because unplanned and unintentional action of any kind generally is not subject to deterrence; and, to the extent that it is hoped that a threatened sanction addressed to the defense will induce greater care and caution on the part of trial lawyers, * * * the potential loss of all valuable state remedies would be sufficient to this end. And it is a misdirected sanction because * * * the habeas applicant, as opposed to his lawyer, hardly is the proper recipient of such a penalty. Especially with fundamental constitutional rights at stake, no fictional relationship of principal-agent or the like can justify holding the criminal defendant accountable for the naked errors of his attorney. This is especially true when so many indigent defendants are without any realistic choice in selecting who ultimately represents them at trial. Indeed, if responsibility for error must be apportioned between the parties, it is the State, through its attorney's admissions and certification policies, that is more fairly held to blame for the fact that practicing lawyers too often are ill-prepared or ill-equipped to act carefully and knowledgeably when faced with decisions governed by state procedural requirements. * * *

IV

* * * [A]lthough some four years have passed since its introduction in Davis v. United States, 411 U.S. 233 (1973), the only thing clear about the Court's "cause"-and-"prejudice" standard is that it exhibits the notable tendency of keeping prisoners in jail without addressing their constitutional complaints. * * * Left unresolved is whether a habeas petitioner like Sykes can adequately discharge this burden by offering the commonplace and truthful explanation for his default: attorney ignorance or error beyond the client's control. The "prejudice" inquiry, meanwhile, appears to bear a strong resemblance to harmless-error doctrine. * * * [I]f this is what is meant by prejudice, respondent's constitutional contentions could be as quickly and easily disposed of in this regard by permitting federal courts to reach the merits of his complaint. * * *

One final consideration deserves mention. * * * [M]ost courts, this one included, traditionally have resisted any realistic inquiry into the competency of trial counsel. * * * [The conduct of a lawyer who unreasonably permits state procedural rules to bar the client's constitutional claims] may well fall below the level of competence that can fairly be expected of him. For almost 40 years it has been established that inadequacy of counsel undercuts the very competence and jurisdiction of the trial court and is always open to collateral review. Obviously, as a practical matter, a trial counsel cannot procedurally waive his own inadequacy. If the scope of habeas jurisdiction previously governed by Fay v. Noia is to be redefined so as to enforce the errors and neglect of lawyers with unnecessary and unjust rigor, the time may come when conscientious and fair-minded federal and state courts * * * will have to reconsider whether they can continue to indulge the comfortable fiction that all lawyers are skilled or even competent craftsmen in representing the fundamental rights of their clients.

NOTE ON FEDERAL HABEAS CORPUS AND STATE COURT PROCEDURAL DEFAULT

A. Introductory Questions

(1) The Relationship of Procedural Default to the Adequate State Ground Doctrine. What should be the relationship among the standards for forgiving procedural defaults applied by the state courts in the first instance, by the Supreme Court on direct review, and by federal habeas courts?

(a) A state procedural default that would not bar direct review by the Supreme Court (because the procedural ruling is not an "adequate" state ground) also does not bar federal habeas corpus review. Lee v. Kemna, 534 U.S. 362 (2002). In addition, some defaults that would bar Supreme Court review do not bar habeas review—for example, where "cause and prejudice" can be shown. But, as is elaborated below, the standards applied in habeas for excusing state court defaults are so difficult for petitioners to satisfy that in practice the standards applied on direct and collateral review differ very little.

(b) In Noia, the Court stated that a habeas court's refusal to give effect to a state court forfeiture did not bar the state from enforcing the underlying procedural requirement. The regime thus created, the Court contended, had several advantages: (i) it minimized federal interference with the state courts; (ii) it adequately deterred violations of state procedural rules by permitting forfeiture of remedies in state court and on direct review; and (iii) under the deliberate bypass standard, it ensured virtually all criminal defendants an ultimate federal adjudication of their federal claims.[1] But as noted in Meltzer, *State Court Forfeitures of Federal Rights*, 99 Harv.L.Rev. 1128, 1150–58, 1190–1202 (1986), Noia placed considerable pressure on

---

[1] Accord, Reitz, *Federal Habeas Corpus: Impact of an Abortive State Proceeding*, 74 Harv.L.Rev. 1315, 1347–48 (1961); Note, 39 N.Y.U.L.Rev. 78, 94 (1964). See also Justice Brennan, *Federal Habeas Corpus and State Prisoners: An Exercise in Federalism*, 7 Utah L.Rev. 423 (1961).

states to excuse defaults that would ultimately be excused on habeas, a course that many states followed.

(c) Professor Meltzer argues that the doctrines that permit defendants to obtain direct or collateral federal review of federal claims, notwithstanding noncompliance with state procedural rules, should be characterized as rules of federal common law. As such, like other forms of federal common law, they should be binding on the states and require state courts to forgive any defaults that would not block federal review: "If the state's interest in imposing a forfeiture * * * is not sufficiently weighty to bar the Supreme Court or a federal habeas court from reviewing the federal issue, that interest is also not weighty enough to bar review of the federal issue in state court in the first instance."

(2) Procedural Default and the Adversary Process. The procedural default cases vividly highlight the intractable difficulties that arise when lawyers are responsible for compliance with state procedural rules but their mistakes jeopardize the constitutional rights of their clients. How should the costs of the inevitable errors be allocated between the state and criminal defendants? Does the answer depend on whether Justice Rehnquist was correct, in Sykes, that broad excuse of procedural defaults creates a serious risk that defense lawyers will "sandbag" the prosecution? (For an argument that the risk is small, see Meltzer, Paragraph (1), *supra*, at 1196–1200.) Does it depend on the general quality of defense representation and on the strictness of constitutional standards of effective assistance of counsel? Note that under prevailing constitutional standards, many defaults resulting from lawyers' errors are not serious enough to constitute a violation of the defendant's Sixth Amendment rights.

(3) Alternatives. Should excuse of procedural default require a showing that the defaulted claim, if meritorious, would establish a reasonable probability that the prisoner was innocent of the crime on which custody is based? Jeffries & Stuntz, *Ineffective Assistance and Procedural Default in Federal Habeas Corpus*, 57 U.Chi.L.Rev. 679, 691–92 (1990), contend that if such a showing is made, procedural barriers to review should be swept aside so that a possibly innocent person can obtain federal review; absent such a showing, there is no reason to excuse a default. Without rejecting a more general limitation of habeas relief to claims related to innocence, they argue that barring habeas review of defaulted claims that are unrelated to innocence sacrifices little: because state courts do not reach the merits of defaulted claims, habeas review cannot help ensure that state courts properly applied federal standards.

(4) The Impact of Procedural Default. Studies prior to Sykes found that no more than 3% of *petitions* were denied on procedural default grounds.[2] A recent post-Sykes study found that at least one *claim* was barred by procedural default in 13% of non-capital cases and 42% of capital cases.[3]

---

[2] See Shapiro, p. 1271, note 20, *supra*, at 346–47; Faust, Rubenstein & Yackle, p. 1266, note 3, *supra*, at 692–93.

[3] King, Cheesman & Ostrom, p. 1266, note 3, *supra*, at 48. See also Flango p. 1266, note 3, *supra*, at 67 (finding, after Sykes, that 6.2% of claims were dismissed on the basis of procedural default).

B. The Meaning of the Sykes Standard

(1) Introduction. Sykes left "cause and prejudice" to be defined in later cases.[4] The 1996 AEDPA amendments contain no general provision dealing with state court procedural defaults, and thus, with one small exception, leave in place the judge-made doctrines just described.[5]

An elaborate series of decisions has given "cause" a very restricted meaning, embracing only these categories: (a) reliance on a novel constitutional claim, see Paragraph B(2), *infra;* (b) deficient performance by counsel that is serious enough to constitute ineffective assistance of counsel under the standards established by the Sixth Amendment, see Paragraphs B(3–5), *infra;*[6] and (c) the state's creation of an "external impediment" to presentation of the claim, see Paragraph B(6), *infra.* A prisoner who can establish "cause" must also establish "prejudice" to gain the right to have a habeas court reach the merits. See Paragraph B(7), *infra.*

The Court has also ruled that a habeas court may hear a defaulted claim, even where cause and prejudice cannot be shown, in one other, narrowly defined circumstance—when the petitioner makes an adequate showing of "actual innocence". See Paragraph B(8), *infra.*

(2) Novelty. In Reed v. Ross, 468 U.S. 1 (1984) (5–4), the jury instructions at Ross' trial in North Carolina placed on him the burden of proving provocation (which would mitigate murder to manslaughter). Ross did not challenge those instructions in his appeal, which was decided one year before the Supreme Court held in In re Winship, 397 U.S. 358, 364 (1970), that due process requires "proof beyond a reasonable doubt of every fact necessary to constitute the crime with which [a defendant] is charged." After the ruling in Hankerson v. North Carolina, 432 U.S. 233 (1977), that North Carolina's assignment of the burden of proof of provocation was unconstitutional under Winship, Ross sought federal habeas relief. The Court, with Justice Brennan writing, found that "the cause requirement may be satisfied under certain circumstances when a procedural failure is not attributable to an intentional decision by counsel made in pursuit of his client's interests." Here, at the time of appeal, counsel could not reasonably have been expected to know his client had a constitutional argument. In dissent, Justice Rehnquist first questioned whether novelty should ever constitute cause, and added that in any event Ross' claim was not novel, because the Winship approach had been adopted in one federal and one state decision handed down some months prior to Ross' appeal.

Ross was a narrow decision—both in its 5–4 margin and in its fine distinction of an earlier decision that found no cause on facts that differed

---

[4]   On the evolution from Noia to Sykes, see Hill, *The Forfeiture of Constitutional Rights in Criminal Cases*, 78 Colum.L.Rev. 1050, 1051–62 (1978); Tague, *Federal Habeas Corpus and Ineffective Representation of Counsel: The Supreme Court Has Work to Do*, 31 Stan.L.Rev. 1, 6–19 (1978).

[5]   AEDPA does have provisions that apply only in capital cases in states whose provision of counsel in state postconviction proceedings satisfies statutorily specified standards. See §§ 2261, 2264, p. 1272, *supra.* (So far, no states have qualified. See p. 1272, *supra.*) Under these provisions, a habeas court may not consider a defaulted claim unless the default resulted from (i) unconstitutional state action, (ii) the Supreme Court's recognition of a new right made retroactively applicable on collateral review, or (iii) the prisoner's inability, through the exercise of due diligence, to have discovered the factual predicate for the claim.

[6]   One Supreme Court decision addressed the unusual case of attorneys' abandonment of their client and deemed that to be cause. See note 8, *infra.*

only slightly.[7] But even this narrow opening was essentially closed off five years later, when the Court, in Teague v. Lane, held that a habeas court could virtually never entertain a petition (whether or not there had been a procedural default) based on "new law". A claim sufficiently novel to excuse a default will be barred by Teague, unless it fits within one of Teague's extraordinarily narrow exceptions—and even then it may be barred by § 2254(d)(1), see pp. 1295–1299, 1301–1319, *supra*. Thus, novelty as cause is of little present significance.

(3) Counsel's Inadvertence. In Murray v. Carrier, 477 U.S. 478 (1986), appellate counsel inadvertently failed to include in the brief on appeal one claim that was listed in the notice of appeal. In an opinion for five Justices, Justice O'Connor held that this state court procedural default barred federal habeas review of the claim, emphasizing that the "considerable costs" associated with habeas review "do not disappear when the default stems from counsel's ignorance or inadvertence rather than from a deliberate decision * * * to withhold a claim." These costs would increase, she argued, if the excuse of procedural defaults depended on whether they were unintentional, because "federal habeas courts would routinely be required to hold evidentiary hearings to determine what prompted counsel's failure to raise the claim in question." The Court thus held that a defendant who is "represented by counsel whose performance is not constitutionally ineffective under the standard established in Strickland v. Washington, [466 U.S. 668 (1984),]" bears "the risk of attorney error that results in a procedural default." But the Court said that "if the procedural default is the result of ineffective assistance of counsel, the Sixth Amendment itself requires that responsibility for the default be imputed to the State * * *. Ineffective assistance of counsel, then, is cause for a procedural default." The Court added, however, that a petitioner must first exhaust any available state remedies for the claim of ineffective assistance of counsel.[8]

---

[7] See Engle v. Isaac, 456 U.S. 107 (1982). The Engle decision is noteworthy also for its refusal to excuse a state court default on the basis that, in view of the state courts' consistent rejection of similar claims, objection was futile: "Even a state court that has previously rejected a constitutional argument may decide, upon reflection, that the contention is valid."

[8] In Maples v. Thomas, 132 S.Ct. 912 (2012), the Court addressed an unusual situation in which a death row inmate was abandoned by counsel of record. There, after a state trial court denied a postconviction petition, the court sent notices to two out-of-state lawyers who had been representing the petitioner. By then, however, the lawyers had left their former law firm, whose mailroom returned the unopened envelopes to the court with an indication that they could not be delivered at that address. The court clerk took no action in response to the returned mail. Local counsel also received a notice of the petition's denial but took no action, assuming that the out-of-state lawyers were responsible for the matter. No notice was sent to the petitioner, and no appeal was filed.

When petitioner's subsequent federal habeas corpus petition reached the Supreme Court, Justice Ginsburg, writing for the majority, said that the general principle that a lawyer's negligence does not by itself constitute cause rests on the principle of agency law that a principal bears the risk of negligent conduct by his agent. Here, by contrast, petitioner's attorneys had severed the agency relationship on whose existence that general principle depends. And given local counsel's failure even to call the two out-of-state lawyers when the notice of the decision arrived, the Court concluded that at that time, he was not "serving as [petitioner's] agent 'in any meaningful sense of that word'" (quoting Holland v. Florida, 560 U.S. 631, 659 (2010) (opinion of Alito, J.)).

In dissent, Justice Scalia, joined by Justice Thomas, agreed that default "may be excused when it is attributable to abandonment by his attorney", but he contended that on the facts there had not been an abandonment.

(4) Ineffective Assistance of Counsel as Cause.

(a) Does Carrier's statement that ineffective assistance of counsel constitutes cause add anything to the scope of habeas relief, since the prisoner could simply assert ineffectiveness directly as the basis for habeas relief?

(b) Litigation of ineffectiveness—whether as cause or as a claim in itself—is full of pitfalls. The first time when such claims can effectively be raised is often state postconviction proceedings,[9] where prisoners ordinarily lack counsel. Thus, prisoners in state postconviction proceedings who proceed pro se—and even those few who obtain legal representation—often fail to advance a claim of ineffective assistance of trial counsel, or fail to advance the claim in a fashion that complies with state time limits or other procedural requirements.

(c) Apart from all the difficulties prisoners face in satisfying the limitations period, the exhaustion requirement, and state procedural rules generally, claims of ineffective assistance of counsel rarely succeed on the merits. Despite (or perhaps because of) the widespread shortcomings of criminal defense representation, defendants have generally had great difficulty in persuading courts that a lawyer's performance fell below the constitutional minimum and that any shortcoming was prejudicial.[10]

(5) Procedural Defaults in State Postconviction Proceedings Challenging the Effectiveness of Counsel. Coleman v. Thompson, 501 U.S. 722 (1991), held that any right to counsel in state collateral proceedings, if it exists, would not extend to an appeal from the denial of relief in such a proceeding, and hence that the prisoner's failure to have appealed in the postconviction proceedings was a procedural default barring federal habeas review. The decision left open the possibility that a prisoner does have a constitutional right to counsel in a state collateral proceeding with respect to a claim of ineffective assistance of counsel during trial, sentencing, or direct appeal, when that claim could not have been raised earlier.

(a) In Martinez v. Ryan, 132 S.Ct. 1309 (2012), the Court faced such a situation. Arizona requires that ineffective assistance of counsel claims be litigated in state collateral proceedings rather than on direct review. After Martinez's conviction became final on direct review, his lawyer commenced

---

[9]   Indeed, in Massaro v. United States, 538 U.S. 500 (2003), where a *federal* prisoner filed a collateral attack, under 28 U.S.C. § 2255, asserting the ineffectiveness of his trial counsel, the Court unanimously rejected the government's argument that the failure of counsel on direct appeal to raise the ineffectiveness of trial counsel, even when that claim was based solely on the trial record, constituted a procedural default. The Court offered a variety of reasons why ineffectiveness claims are more appropriately litigated in collateral proceedings.

Those reasons are equally applicable to state prisoners, and the Court's opinion noted that "[a] growing majority of state courts now follow the rule we adopt today." But what of the states that don't and instead require new counsel on direct review to raise at least some ineffective assistance claims? See Note, 99 Colum.L.Rev. 1103 (1999) (noting, *inter alia*, that some states find such claims barred during state postconviction proceedings if not raised on direct appeal, even when the attorney on appeal also represented the defendant at trial). Would failure to comply with such a requirement bar direct review by the Supreme Court? Habeas review? See Dripps, *Ineffective Litigation of Ineffective Assistance Claims: Some Uncomfortable Reflections on Massaro v. United States*, 42 Brandeis L.J. 793 (2004).

[10]   See, *e.g.*, Primus, *Structural Reform in Criminal Defense: Relocating Ineffective Assistance of Counsel Claims*, 92 Cornell L.Rev. 679, 682–88 (2007); Bright, *Counsel for the Poor: The Death Sentence Not for the Worst Crime but for the Worst Lawyer*, 103 Yale L.J. 1835, 1850–51 (1994); Green, *Lethal Fiction: The Meaning of "Counsel" in the Sixth Amendment*, 78 Iowa L.Rev. 433, 499–507 (1993).

a state postconviction proceeding but made no claim that Martinez's trial counsel had been ineffective, instead stating that she could not identify any colorable claim to raise on Martinez's behalf. Martinez did not respond to the trial court's invitation to raise any claims he felt his lawyer had overlooked, and the court then denied postconviction relief. When a new lawyer launched a second state postconviction proceeding, alleging that Martinez's trial counsel had been ineffective, it was dismissed on the basis of a state rule barring a claim that could have been raised in a prior state postconviction proceeding. Martinez then filed a federal habeas corpus petition asserting the ineffectiveness of both his trial counsel and his counsel in the first state postconviction proceeding.

When the case reached the Supreme Court, it ruled, 7–2, that the lower federal courts had erred in ruling that Martinez had procedurally defaulted. Justice Kennedy's majority opinion declined to decide whether the Sixth Amendment guarantees the assistance of counsel in state postconviction proceedings that constitute the first opportunity for a defendant to allege the ineffectiveness of trial counsel. Instead, the Court qualified its general rule that attorney ignorance or inadvertence does not constitute cause for a procedural default unless it deprives the defendant of the *constitutional* right to counsel. The Court held in Martinez that "[i]nadequate assistance of counsel [in a state collateral proceeding that provides the first occasion at which the ineffectiveness of trial counsel may be litigated] may establish cause for a prisoner's procedural default of a claim of ineffective assistance at trial." Otherwise, the Court argued, no state court—and hence neither the Supreme Court on direct review nor a federal habeas court—could hear the claim.

The procedural default rules on habeas, the Court stated, "are elaborated in the exercise of the Court's discretion." Despite its refusal to decide whether Martinez had a Sixth Amendment right that might have been violated, the Court drew on Sixth Amendment jurisprudence in ruling that cause can be established "in two circumstances. The first is where the state courts did not appoint counsel in the initial-review collateral proceeding for a claim of ineffective assistance at trial. The second is where appointed counsel in the initial-review collateral proceeding, where the claim should have been raised, was ineffective under the standards of Strickland v. Washington, 466 U.S. 668 (1984). To overcome the default, a prisoner must also demonstrate that the underlying ineffective-assistance-of-trial-counsel claim is a substantial one, which is to say that the prisoner must demonstrate that the claim has some merit."[11]

Justice Scalia's dissent (joined by Justice Thomas) objected that the Court's decision was no different in effect from the recognition of a constitutional right to counsel in this postconviction setting. The Court, he claimed, may not have called into question the "lawfulness" of denying counsel in postconviction proceedings, only its "sanity", for if counsel is denied, the state risks having to defend the adequacy of trial counsel in a federal habeas corpus proceeding many years later. (But might not a state rationally choose that option, given that some prisoners will never file a federal habeas petition, while others will find their petitions blocked by other

---

[11]   AEDPA includes a provision, 28 U.S.C. § 2254(i), that states that "[t]he ineffectiveness * * * of counsel during Federal or State collateral post-conviction proceedings shall not be a ground for relief". The Court held that this provision did not bar relief, as recognizing ineffectiveness as "cause" to excuse a default differs from recognizing it as a ground for relief.

procedural rules limiting the exercise of habeas jurisdiction?)[12] Justice Scalia also accused the Court of giving insufficient weight to the value of finality and of ignoring the frequency with which claims of ineffective assistance of counsel can be made.

(b) In his Martinez dissent, Justice Scalia objected that the Court's limitation of its holding to cases in which the state has barred litigation on direct appeal of the ineffectiveness of trial counsel "lacks any principled basis, and will not last." His fear was realized the following Term in Trevino v. Thaler, 133 S.Ct. 1911 (2013). There, the prisoner set forth in a federal habeas proceeding a claim of ineffective trial counsel that he had not raised either on direct review or in state postconviction proceedings. Texas law did not bar the litigation of ineffective assistance of counsel claims on direct review, but the state courts had expressed a preference for litigating such claims in state collateral proceedings and had acknowledged that it was "virtually impossible for appellate counsel to adequately present an ineffective assistance [of trial counsel] claim."

In Trevino, the Court, with Justice Breyer writing for the majority, held, 5–4, that "where, as here, [a] state procedural framework, by reason of its design and operation, makes it highly unlikely in a typical case that a defendant will have a meaningful opportunity to raise a claim of ineffective assistance of trial counsel on direct appeal, our holding in Martinez applies". In a dissent joined by Justice Alito, Chief Justice Roberts objected that the narrow holding in Martinez was being greatly expanded. He complained that the Court's opinion was unclear about "how meaningful is meaningful enough, how meaningful-ness is to be measured, how unlikely highly unlikely is, * * * or what case qualifies as the 'typical' case." Justices Scalia and Thomas also dissented.

[handwritten margin note: ... or when direct is highly unlikely]

Justice Breyer's opinion in Trevino detailed some of the difficulties facing any effort in Texas to raise ineffective assistance of counsel claims on direct review. But one of the key problems that the Court identified—that the trial record often does not contain the information necessary to assess a claim of ineffectiveness—would commonly exist in any state system. Consider also whether the Court's approach in Martinez and Trevino can be limited to the right to effective assistance of counsel. In Martinez, the Court stressed that that right is a "bedrock principle" of the criminal justice system. But could a federal habeas court refuse to excuse an uncounseled prisoner's failure to raise, in state postconviction proceedings, a claim (not discoverable earlier) that the prosecutor failed to disclose exculpatory evidence?

(6) External Impediment as Cause. Of the very few Supreme Court decisions that have found cause to exist, three involved "external impediments" created by the state.

(a) In Amadeo v. Zant, 486 U.S. 214 (1988), while the defendant's direct appeal was pending, an independent voting rights lawsuit uncovered a handwritten memorandum from the District Attorney's Office to the jury commissioners, listing figures for the number of blacks and women to be placed on master jury lists. The document's apparent purpose was to ensure

---

[12] King, *Enforcing Effective Assistance After Martinez*, 122 Yale L.J. 2428 (2013), notes, *inter alia*, that state courts under fiscal constraints may refuse to appoint counsel in postconviction cases, that when defendants plead guilty, courts increasingly accept waivers of the right to pursue postconviction relief, and that even petitioners whose claims are resolved on the merits rarely prevail on ineffective assistance claims. For these and other reasons, she views the dissent's prediction that states will be forced to provide counsel in every case as "absurd".

that these groups were under-represented but not so much as to give rise to a prima facie case of discrimination. When the prisoner asserted a jury discrimination claim for the first time on appeal, the Georgia Supreme Court rejected it as untimely. On federal habeas corpus, the Supreme Court found cause for the default because the basis for the claim was "reasonably unknown" to the prisoner's lawyers as a result of "the 'objective factor' of 'some interference by officials' ".[13]

(b) In Strickler v. Greene, 527 U.S. 263 (1999), the Court extended the "external impediment" concept to the possibly inadvertent withholding of information by the government. In his federal habeas petition, Strickler for the first time claimed that the government had not disclosed exculpatory information, in violation of the Due Process Clause. Justice Stevens' opinion found cause for Strickler's failure to have sought the information either at trial or in a state habeas proceeding. Writing for a unanimous Court on this point, he stressed that the prosecution had maintained at trial an "open files policy" toward discovery. It was reasonable, he argued, for Strickler's lawyers to rely on the government's "implicit representation that [exculpatory materials that the government was obliged to disclose] would be included in the open files tendered to defense counsel", and he found no basis for concluding that Strickler or his counsel should have realized earlier that material was missing from those files.

(c) Strickler was followed in Banks v. Dretke, 540 U.S. 668 (2004), also involving a claim that the prosecution had withheld exculpatory evidence.

(7) Prejudice. The Sykes decision requires a prisoner to show cause *and* "prejudice", but the Supreme Court's subsequent decisions dealing with procedural default have not elaborated on just what constitutes a showing of prejudice.[14] The most pertinent statement came in United States v. Frady, 456 U.S. 152 (1982), a collateral postconviction attack brought by a *federal* prisoner under 28 U.S.C. § 2255, but applying the same cause and prejudice standard. There, the Court said that to establish prejudice, the prisoner must show that errors at trial "worked to his *actual* and substantial disadvantage, infecting his entire trial with error of constitutional dimensions."[15]

(8) Actual Innocence. In Murray v. Carrier, Paragraph B(3), *supra*, the Court mentioned one circumstance, other than where "cause and prejudice" are shown, in which a state court default could be excused: "in an

---

[13] Amadeo was read narrowly in McCleskey v. Zant, 499 U.S. 467 (1991), p. 1346, note 1, *infra*. In rejecting McCleskey's argument that the state's failure to turn over a document constituted cause for an earlier procedural default, the Court said: "This case differs from Amadeo in two crucial respects. First, there is no finding that the State concealed the evidence. And second, * * * [any concealment that might have occurred] would not establish cause here because, in light of McCleskey's knowledge of the information in the document, any initial concealment would not have prevented him from raising the claim [in the earlier proceeding]."

[14] In two cases in which the Supreme Court has found cause—Reed v. Ross, Paragraph B(2), *supra*, and Amadeo v. Zant, Paragraph (B)(6)(a), *supra*—there was no dispute that prejudice was present and thus no occasion for defining its meaning. Two other cases both involved claims that the prosecution had unconstitutionally suppressed exculpatory evidence in violation of Brady v. Maryland, 373 U.S. 83 (1963). See Paragraph B(6)(b–c), *supra*. The more recent of them, Banks v. Dretke, explained that in that situation, the meaning of prejudice essentially merges into the question whether the suppressed evidence "is 'material' for Brady purposes"—which in turn requires a " 'reasonable probability of a different result' " (quoting Kyles v. Whitley, 514 U.S. 419, 434 (1995)). In the Martinez and Trevino decisions, see Paragraph B(5), *supra*, as well as the Maples decision, see p. 1338, note 8, *supra,* the Court did not reach the prejudice question.

[15] See generally Jeffries & Stuntz, Paragraph A(3), *supra*, at 684–85 & n. 25.

extraordinary case, where a constitutional violation has probably resulted in the conviction of one who is actually innocent, a federal habeas court may grant the writ even in the absence of a showing of cause for the procedural default.' Cases satisfying that approach have been rare in the lower courts, see Steiker, *Innocence and Federal Habeas*, 41 UCLA L.Rev. 303, 341 (1993), and it was more than twenty years before the Supreme Court found a case satisfying that standard. But in House v. Bell, 547 U.S. 518 (2006), the Court, dividing 5–3, ruled that the prisoner was entitled to litigate claims of ineffective assistance of counsel and failure to disclose exculpatory evidence that would otherwise have been foreclosed because of his procedural default in state court.

House's conviction of capital murder rested on circumstantial evidence, including testimony that a semen sample taken from the victim was consistent with House's semen and that blood stains on House's pants were consistent with the blood of the victim. In his federal habeas corpus proceeding, House presented new evidence (i) establishing that the semen was that of the victim's husband, (ii) suggesting that the victim's blood might have been spilled from autopsy samples onto House's pants before the pants were tested, and (iii) indicating that the victim's husband had a history of abuse as well as the opportunity to have caused his wife's death, and had told two people that he had accidentally done so.

The Supreme Court (per Justice Kennedy) found that House was entitled to relief if he could show that "it is more likely than not that no reasonable juror would have convicted".[16] The Court concluded that House's was one of the "extraordinary" cases that meets this "demanding" standard: "Were House's challenge to the State's case limited to the questions he has raised about the blood and semen, the other evidence favoring the prosecution might well suffice to bar relief." But that evidence, together with the other testimony incriminating the victim's husband, made it more likely than not that no reasonable juror viewing all the evidence would lack reasonable doubt.

In dissent, Chief Justice Roberts (joined by Justices Scalia and Thomas) argued that the standard had not been met, objecting that the Court disregarded key findings of the district court: that the autopsy blood had spilled after, not before, the blood stains on House's pants had been tested, and that two witnesses who said that the victim's husband had admitted to causing his wife's death were not credible. Adding that the evidence about semen had not been central to the prosecution's case at trial and that the jury had been told that the semen was just as likely to have come from the husband as from House, the Chief Justice concluded that "the evidence before us now is not substantially different from that considered by House's

---

[16] That standard was borrowed from Schlup v. Delo, 513 U.S. 298 (1995), dealing with whether a prisoner could file a second or successive petition. In that context, the Court has discussed what it means to be "actually innocent" with respect to eligibility for the death penalty. See Sawyer v. Whitley, 505 U.S. 333 (1992), which requires proof "by clear and convincing evidence" that "no reasonable juror would find [the prisoner] eligible for the death penalty" under state law. Prisoners can meet this standard only by showing either that they are innocent of the crime itself or that no aggravating factor or "other condition of eligibility" for a capital sentence was present; the failure to have introduced mitigating evidence at sentencing does not satisfy this standard.

The circuits are divided on the applicability of the actual innocence exception to non-capital sentencing. See Note, 93 Ky.L.J. 531 (2004–05) (noting that some circuits find the exception inapplicable, one holds it generally applicable, and others hold it applicable only to sentences under habitual offender statutes).

jury. I therefore find it more likely than not that in light of this new evidence, at least one juror, acting reasonably, would vote to convict House."

House put forward a distinct argument—that the new evidence supported not only his "gateway" claim (permitting the habeas court to reach otherwise defaulted constitutional claims) but also a freestanding claim of innocence that could itself be the substantive basis for relief under Herrera v. Collins, p. 1288, *supra*. All eight Justices hearing the case rejected that contention. Justice Kennedy noted that Herrera had indicated that *if* a freestanding claim of innocence can ever be the basis for habeas relief (a question he left open), the standard would be higher than the standard for establishing a "gateway" claim—and "given the closeness of the [gate-way] question here," House had not established a freestanding claim of innocence.

Suppose that on remand the habeas court finds that the constitutional claims that House is now free to litigate lack merit. Wouldn't that leave the state free to execute House, despite the Supreme Court's having found it more likely than not that no reasonable juror could find him guilty beyond a reasonable doubt? Is that a comfortable resting place for the judicial system?

C.   The Extension of the Sykes Approach

(1) Introduction. In Sykes, the Court, declaring that it did "not choose to paint with a * * * broad brush" (footnote 12), left open whether the "cause and prejudice" standard, which it applied to a default at trial relating to a decision entrusted to the lawyer, governed other kinds of defaults (for example, the failure to file an appeal at all, as in Fay v. Noia). But over time, the approach in Sykes has been extended, through a series of smaller brush strokes, to cover virtually all state court procedural defaults.

(2) Defaults on Appeal: Murray v. Carrier. In Murray v. Carrier, Paragraph B(3), *supra*, where counsel, in appealing from the judgment of conviction, inadvertently failed to include one of several claims, the Court ruled that the cause and prejudice standard "should not vary depending on the timing of a procedural default or on the strength of an uncertain and difficult assessment of the relative magnitude of the benefits attributable to the state procedural rules that attach at each successive stage of the judicial process." Concurring in the judgment, Justice Stevens (joined by Justice Blackmun) argued that the procedural default standard requires consideration of the demands of justice, which in turn calls for consideration, *inter alia,* of the strength of the state's interest, which he argued, was weaker than at trial.

(3) Failure to Appeal: Coleman v. Thompson and the Overruling of Fay v. Noia. In Coleman v. Thompson, 501 U.S. 722, 749 (1991), the Court said that Fay v. Noia's deliberate bypass standard does not continue to apply "where a state prisoner has defaulted his entire appeal." In sweeping terms, the Court concluded that the Sykes regime governs all state court defaults.[17]

---

[17]   Does Coleman rule out the possibility that as a matter of substantive constitutional law, some basic rights—including the right to appeal the conviction itself—cannot validly be waived except by the defendant personally? Note that in Coleman, the default occurred at a stage—appeal from denial of *postconviction relief*—at which there is no right to counsel. Compare Roe v. Flores-Ortega, 528 U.S. 470 (2000), where the prisoner sought habeas relief on the ground that his lawyer's failure to consult him before deciding not appeal constituted ineffective assistance of counsel. Although the Justices varied in their formulations of when such a failure to consult violates the Sixth Amendment, all agreed that it was a violation "in the vast majority of cases" and reiterated earlier holdings that counsel must appeal when so instructed by the client.

(4) Discretionary State Appeals. In O'Sullivan v. Boerckel, 526 U.S. 838 (1999), the Court extended the Sykes regime to a defendant's failure to include claims in a petition seeking *discretionary* review before the Illinois Supreme Court, after the intermediate appellate court had affirmed his conviction. Most of Justice O'Connor's opinion was devoted to establishing that discretionary review was a state remedy that § 2254(c) requires a prisoner to exhaust. Having so ruled, the Court added that because discretionary review was now time-barred, the prisoner had procedurally defaulted by not having raised the claims in question at the appropriate time.[18]

Dissents by Justices Stevens and Breyer (joined by each other and by Justice Ginsburg) complained, *inter alia*, that discretionary review was not part of the regular appellate process and that omission of some claims may have been entirely consistent with state law; that the majority's approach would burden state supreme courts with an unwelcome influx of routine filings; that whether this kind of omission counts as a default should depend on the state's preference; and that the Court's opinion leaves open the proper approach if the state makes clear that it does not mean to require prisoners to seek such review. Justice Souter expressed agreement with this last point. And some lower courts have interpreted the Court's opinion as merely creating a default rule from which a state may opt out.[19]

(5) Procedural Default and Guilty Pleas. Most of the Court's procedural default decisions involve prisoners convicted after trial. For a case in which the Justices differed about the proper treatment of a *federal* prisoner's failure to appeal from his conviction by *guilty plea*, see Bousley v. United States, 523 U.S. 614 (1998), pp. 1358–1359 & note 4, *infra*.

D. The Grounds of a State Court Decision, the Problem of Ambiguity, and Waiver by the State

(1) State Court Excuse of Procedural Default. If the state courts overlook a procedural default and decide the federal claim on the merits, a federal court on habeas may also reach the merits. See, *e.g.*, Warden v. Hayden, 387 U.S. 294, 297 n. 3 (1967). (The Supreme Court follows a similar rule on direct review of state court decisions. See p. 546, *supra*.)

(2) Ambiguous Decisions. It is sometimes unclear whether a state court rejected a defendant's constitutional claim on the merits or because the defendant had defaulted. Similar ambiguities can arise on Supreme Court review of state court decisions, a matter addressed in Michigan v. Long, p. 494, *supra*. Decisions considering the implications of Long for federal habeas courts have established a presumption that an ambiguous state court

---

[18] Note, however, the apparent dissonance between procedural default doctrine and exhaustion doctrine on whether a defendant must pursue state remedies that appear to be futile. Compare Engle v. Isaac, p. 1338, note 7, *supra* (failure to pursue an apparently futile remedy constitutes a procedural default), with Lynce v. Mathis, p. 1350, *infra* (no need to exhaust when the state supreme court had previously rejected similar claims in other cases).

[19] For decisions ruling that a state had opted out of the requirement that prisoners exhaust discretionary review before that state's highest court, see Swoopes v. Sublett, 196 F.3d 1008, 1010 (9th Cir.1999) (per curiam) (Arizona); Randolph v. Kemna, 276 F.3d 401, 404 (8th Cir.2002) (Missouri); Adams v. Holland, 330 F.3d 398, 402 (6th Cir.2003) (Tennessee); Lambert v. Blackwell, 387 F.3d 210, 233 (3d Cir.2004) (Pennsylvania). For criticism of this approach, see Hills v. Washington, 441 F.3d 1374, 1378 (11th Cir.2006) (Carnes, J., concurring).

In opt-out states, could a prisoner seek U.S. Supreme Court review of the decision of a state intermediate appellate court without making any effort to present the issue to the state supreme court? See p. 558, *supra*.

decision rests on the merits and hence there is no procedural default barring habeas review, see Harris v. Reed, 489 U.S. 255 (1989), but the presumption can be rebutted, see Coleman v. Thompson, 501 U.S. 722 (1991), and Ylst v. Nunnemaker, 501 U.S. 797 (1991), pp. 506–507, *supra*. In considering the analogy to Supreme Court review via certiorari, is it relevant that a habeas court lacks discretion to refuse to hear a case? That a federal habeas court cannot vacate and remand to clarify an ambiguity?

(3) State Waiver of a Procedural Default Objection. In Trest v. Cain, 522 U.S. 87 (1997), the Court unanimously ruled that a procedural default does not deprive a federal habeas court of jurisdiction; rather, it is normally a defense that the state must raise. In Day v. McDonough, 547 U.S. 198, 206 (2006), the Court noted without comment the unanimous view of the courts of appeals that in habeas proceedings, district courts may, "in appropriate circumstances," raise a procedural default defense that the state neglected to raise. Is it ironic that petitioners (who generally lack counsel) are required to turn squarer corners than the state in order to avoid forfeiture?[20]

NOTE ON SUCCESSIVE AND ABUSIVE HABEAS PETITIONS

(1) Introduction. The preceding Note considered the consequences of a failure to properly raise a federal claim in *state court*. This Note considers the consequences of a failure to raise such a claim in a previous *federal habeas corpus petition*. Though not identical, the concerns in the two areas have important similarities, and the doctrinal evolution is broadly parallel: the Warren Court favored broad excuse of defaults, and some years later, a different Court sharply narrowed federal review.[1] With respect to successive petitions, however, in 1996 Congress stepped in and further limited federal power, amidst concerns that death row inmates were filing successive petitions (often at the eleventh hour) in order to delay their executions.

---

[20] Article 36 of the Vienna Convention on Consular Relations, to which the United States is a signatory, requires that an alien who is detained be informed without delay of the alien's right under the Convention to ask that authorities inform the consulate of the detainee's home country. For discussion of the Supreme Court decisions permitting states to apply their normal procedural default rules to claims based on alleged violations of the Convention, see pp. 399–402, *supra*.

[1] In Sanders v. United States, 373 U.S. 1 (1963) (7–2), the Warren Court first ruled that the standards under § 2255, governing successive applications by federal prisoners, are those set forth in § 2244, which governs successive applications by state prisoners. The Court then read §§ 2244 and 2255 as permitting (but not obliging) a habeas court to deny a successive application if on a prior application the court had rejected the present claim on the merits and if "the ends of justice would not be served by reaching the merits of the subsequent application." But claims in a successive petition that were not previously adjudicated had to be entertained, at least absent an abuse of the writ; to exemplify an abuse of the writ, the Court mentioned a "deliberate bypass" within the meaning of Fay v. Noia, p. 1324, *supra*.

Because Sanders' approach drew on Noia, it came under pressure after Noia's deliberate bypass standard was repudiated in Wainwright v. Sykes and successive cases. See pp. 1326–1345, *supra*. In McCleskey v. Zant, 499 U.S. 467 (1991), the Court overturned Sanders, and held that the standards set forth in Wainwright v. Sykes and successive cases governed the filing of successive petitions; under those standards, the failure to raise a claim in an earlier federal habeas petition would be excused only by showing (i) cause and prejudice, or (ii) "that a fundamental miscarriage of justice would result from a failure to entertain the claim."

(2) The 1996 Amendments.

(a) The Standards Governing Second or Successive Petitions. As amended in 1996, § 2244(b)(1) requires dismissal (without exception) of a claim that was presented in a prior petition. Section 2244(b)(2) requires dismissal of a claim not previously presented unless:

> "(A) * * * the claim relies on a new rule of constitutional law, made retroactive to cases on collateral review by the Supreme Court, that was previously unavailable; or
>
> "(B)(i) the factual predicate for the claim could not have been discovered previously through the exercise of due diligence; and (ii) the facts underlying the claim, if proven and viewed in light of the evidence as a whole, would be sufficient to establish by clear and convincing evidence that, but for constitutional error, no reasonable factfinder would have found the applicant guilty of the underlying offense."

Note that § 2244(b)(2) combines various elements of procedural default doctrine in a way that narrows the basis for excuse.[2] Thus, defaults in a prior federal proceeding, where a prisoner not under death sentence is unlikely to have had counsel, are harder to excuse than defaults in state court (where the prisoner had a right to counsel at trial and on the first appeal).

(b) The Procedure for Filing a Second or Successive Petition. The 1996 amendments require a prisoner, before filing a successive petition in district court, to first file a motion in the court of appeals, seeking authorization to file the petition in district court; the court of appeals is to act on the motion within 30 days, § 2244(b)(3)(D), and will grant the motion if the petition satisfies the criteria set forth in § 2244(b)(2). Without such authorization, a prisoner may not file a successive habeas petition in the district court.

Section 2244(b)(3)(E) provides that the grant or denial of authorization "by a court of appeals * * * shall not be appealable and shall not be the subject of a petition for rehearing or for a writ of certiorari." In Felker v. Turpin, 518 U.S. 651 (1996), p. 317, *supra*, the Court unanimously ruled that § 2244(b)(3)(E) did not preclude the prisoner whose request for authorization had been denied from filing a petition in the Supreme Court seeking an original writ of habeas corpus, but that the standards set forth in § 2244(b)(2) would inform the Court's decision whether to grant relief. The Court proceeded to find that neither of the prisoner's constitutional claims satisfied those standards, "let alone the requirement [in Sup.Ct.R. 20.4(a), governing original writs of habeas corpus,] that there be 'exceptional circumstances' justifying the issuance of the writ."[3]

Og. writ exception (handwritten marginalia)

---

[2] Consider these differences: (1) under the procedural default doctrine, "novelty" constitutes cause, while subsection (A) is considerably narrower (see Tyler v. Cain, p. 1318, *supra*); (2) subsection (B) requires that a successive claim satisfy both of two conditions which under procedural default doctrine are essentially alternatives; (3) subsection (B) also tightens the standard of "actual innocence", see p. 1342, *supra*; and (4) it is uncertain how subsection (B) applies to challenges to sentences rather than convictions, see p. 1343, n. 16, *supra*.

[3] For discussion of Felker, see Tushnet, *"The King of France with Forty Thousand Men": Felker v. Turpin and the Supreme Court's Deliberative Processes*, 1996 Sup.Ct.Rev. 163. See also Kovarsky, *Original Habeas Redux*, 97 Va.L.Rev. 61, 90–94 (2011) (finding that more than half of petitioners seeking an original writ in the Supreme Court, including 80% of capital petitioners, are trying to avoid restrictions on successive petitions).

(3) Unripe Claims and § 2244(b). If a claim was not ripe when a first habeas petition was filed, is a second petition containing the now ripe claim governed by the restrictions and authorization requirement of § 2244(b)? The Supreme Court has not charted a clear course on this question.

Two decisions have addressed the problem posed by the fact that a death row inmate's claim that he may not be executed because of his mental incompetence will be deemed premature if included in a first habeas petition that challenges the conviction or sentence. In Stewart v. Martinez-Villareal, 523 U.S. 637 (1998), the prisoner's claim of incompetency, filed in his first petition, was dismissed as premature. Then, after the other grounds for relief were denied, the prisoner, fearing that § 2244(b) might foreclose a second petition raising his incompetency claim, moved to re-open the earlier petition. Rejecting the state's argument that the incompetency claim now constituted a second petition, the Court found that the prisoner had filed only one petition and that a district court should rule on each claim presented at the time it becomes ripe.

In Panetti v. Quarterman, 551 U.S. 930 (2007), a death row inmate's first petition did not include an incompetency claim; after that petition was denied and an execution date was set, the prisoner filed a second petition raising that claim. The Court, per Justice Kennedy, held that the phrase "second or successive" takes its meaning from case law, including decisions pre-dating the enactment of § 2244(b) in 1996. Stating that it was "hesitant to construe a statute, implemented to further the principles of comity, finality, and federalism, in a manner that would require unripe * * * claims to be raised as a mere formality, to the benefit of no party", the Court concluded that "[t]he statutory bar on 'second or successive' applications does not apply to [a claim that one is incompetent to be executed] brought in an application filed when the claim is first ripe."

In dissent, Justice Thomas, joined by the Chief Justice and Justices Scalia and Alito, argued that "second or successive" means "second or successive" and hence under § 2244(b), Panetti's second petition must be dismissed. Justice Thomas relied on the unanimous per curiam decision in Burton v. Stewart, 549 U.S. 147 (2007), decided five months earlier. There, the petitioner's several convictions had been affirmed on direct review but his sentence was vacated. After the trial court resentenced him, and while an appeal of the new sentence was pending, he filed a federal habeas petition challenging his convictions, which was denied. After the state court rejected his appeal from the new sentence, he filed a second petition in federal court, challenging the new sentence. The Supreme Court ruled that the second petition was barred for non-compliance with § 2244(b).

In Panetti, Justice Thomas argued that the Burton decision indicated that a prisoner is not excused from § 2244(b)'s limitations merely because the claim in a second petition would have been unripe if filed in the first petition. He concluded that the majority's decision "stands only for the proposition that [claims of incompetency to be executed] somehow deserve a special (and unjustified) exemption from the statute's plain import." The

---

If a court of appeals denies authorization to file a successive petition and a prisoner seeks an original writ of habeas corpus, is the Supreme Court limited to deciding whether the denial of authorization was proper? If the Supreme Court itself could not dispose of the petition by ordering release, is the proceeding before the Court not really in the nature of habeas corpus? Is it a sufficient answer that the Court, after deciding the authorization issue, may transfer any proceedings on the merits to a district court (see 28 U.S.C. § 2241(b))?

majority did not directly address the dissent's discussion of Burton. Isn't Justice Thomas correct that the two decisions are difficult to reconcile?

(4) Exhaustion and Successive Petitions. In Slack v. McDaniel, 529 U.S. 473 (2000), a habeas petition included some claims that had not yet been presented to the state courts. The "total exhaustion" doctrine, p. 1351, *infra*, prevents a federal court from entertaining a petition that includes both exhausted and unexhausted claims. Therefore, upon the prisoner's motion and without objection from the state, the district court dismissed the petition without prejudice; the order granted leave to refile after completing the exhaustion of state remedies. After exhaustion, Slack filed a new habeas corpus petition.[4] The Supreme Court held, 7–2, that the second petition was not successive, stressing that "the complete exhaustion rule is not to 'trap the unwary *pro se* prisoner'" (quoting Rose v. Lundy, 455 U.S. 509, 520 (1982)). As for the state's concern that under the Court's ruling, a prisoner's new petition might contain still other unexhausted claims, "causing the process to repeat itself", the Court noted that states may limit multiple state postconviction filings and that federal courts may require, as a condition of dismissing the first petition, that any new filing contain only exhausted claims.

(5) The Effect of the 1996 Act. Studies that predate both the judicial and legislative restrictions imposed in the 1990s found that anywhere from 13% to 54% of petitioners were known to have filed one or more previous petitions.[5] A recent post-AEDPA study found that 41% of petitions contained four or more claims, compared to the 11–25% found in pre-AEDPA studies. That increase might be attributable in part to AEDPA's tightened restrictions on successive petitions and in part to the change in the law that now permits a court to deny a habeas petition on the merits without first requiring exhaustion.[6]

NOTE ON EXHAUSTION OF STATE COURT REMEDIES[1]

(1) Origins. The requirement that state prisoners exhaust state court remedies before seeking federal habeas corpus relief derives from Ex parte Royall, 117 U.S. 241 (1886), where a state prisoner detained for trial alleged that the state statute under which he was charged violated the federal Constitution. The Supreme Court affirmed the dismissal of his habeas

---

[4] Because the second petition was filed in 1995, the Supreme Court noted that it was not governed by the 1996 amendments, "though we do not suggest the definition of second or successive would be different under [§ 2244(b), as amended in 1996]."

[5] See Faust, Rubenstein & Yackle, p. 1266, note 3, *supra*, at 687 (15–20%); Flango, p. 1266, note 3, *supra*, at 37 (54%); Robinson, p. 1266, note 3, *supra*, at 15 (31%); Shapiro, p. 1271, note 20, *supra*, at 353–54 (13%).

[6] See King, Cheesman & Ostrom, p. 1266, note 3, *supra*, at 57. See also Cheesman, Hanson & Ostrom, *A Tale of Two Laws: The U.S. Congress Confronts Habeas Corpus Petitions and Section 1983 Lawsuits*, 22 Law & Pol'y 89, 92, 115 (2000) (finding that despite AEDPA's many restrictions, habeas filings increased by 40% between 1996 and 1998, and suggesting that many prisoners, rather than filing multiple challenges to a particular conviction, instead are serving long sentences for multiple convictions that they attack separately).

[1] See generally Yackle, *The Exhaustion Doctrine in Federal Habeas Corpus: An Argument for a Return to First Principles*, 44 Ohio St.L.J. 393 (1983); Amsterdam, *Criminal Prosecutions Affecting Federally Guaranteed Civil Rights: Federal Removal and Habeas Corpus Jurisdiction to Abort State Court Trial*, 113 U.Pa.L.Rev. 793, 884–96 (1965); 2 Hertz & Liebman, Federal Habeas Corpus Practice & Procedure, ch. 23 (6th ed.2011).

petition, ruling that although the trial court had *power* to inquire into the allegation in advance of trial, it should exercise its discretion to permit the state court to resolve the question in the normal course of trial. Despite Royall's emphasis on "discretion", from early on the Supreme Court routinely reversed grants of the writ before exhaustion of state remedies.[2]

In 1948, Congress codified some aspects of the exhaustion rule in 28 U.S.C. § 2254(b) and (c). The Reviser's note states that "[t]his new section is declaratory of existing law". H.R. Rep. No.308, 80th Cong., 1st Sess. A180 (1947). More recently, the Supreme Court has raised doubts about whether judges may fashion non-statutory exceptions to the exhaustion requirement. See Duckworth v. Serrano, 454 U.S. 1, 5 (1981) (per curiam) (refusing to recognize an exception for "clear violations" of federal law).

(2) The Import of Exhaustion. In Rose v. Lundy, 455 U.S. 509 (1982), the Court said that the exhaustion requirement serves to "protect the state courts' role in the enforcement of federal law", to "prevent disruption of state judicial proceedings", and to " 'minimize friction between our federal and state systems of justice by allowing the State an initial opportunity to pass upon and correct alleged violations of prisoners' federal rights' " (quoting Duckworth v. Serrano, Paragraph (1), *supra*, at 3). The Court also noted that exhaustion helps to generate a complete factual record to aid federal review and that over time it may make state courts more familiar with and hospitable to federal claims.[3]

Though it is often said that the exhaustion requirement merely postpones federal review until the state courts have had the chance to consider a federal claim, the requirement has always had broader effects. Most importantly today, exhaustion may lead to the generation of state court determinations of law or fact, to which federal courts are obliged, under § 2254(d), to defer.

(3) What Constitutes Exhaustion? A prisoner is required to exhaust only state remedies that remain available when the habeas petition is filed. If, for example, a prisoner did not appeal from a state court conviction and the time for doing so has expired, the exhaustion requirement (as distinguished from the procedural default doctrine) poses no barrier to habeas relief. Moreover, under § 2254(b), exhaustion is not required where a state remedy is "ineffective", which is true, the Court has ruled, where resort to the state courts would clearly be futile. See, *e.g.*, Lynce v. Mathis, 519 U.S. 433, 436 n. 4 (1997) (excusing the failure to have raised an ex post facto challenge to a state statute that canceled early release credits, because the Florida Supreme Court had previously rejected challenges to retrospective

---

[2]   See, *e.g.*, New York v. Eno, 155 U.S. 89 (1894); Urquhart v. Brown, 205 U.S. 179 (1907); Duncan v. Henry, 513 U.S. 364 (1995) (per curiam).

[3]   Compare Amsterdam, note 1, *supra*, arguing that federal habeas corpus should be available before trial whenever the defendant makes a "colorable showing that the conduct for which he is prosecuted [is] protected by the federal constitutional guarantees of civil rights". Writing in 1965 against the background of prosecutions of civil rights protesters in the South, he contended that state courts often flout the federal Constitution, and that even if convictions are ultimately overturned on direct or collateral review, in the interim defendants have suffered incarceration, been required to post bail, lost educational or employment opportunities, and been chilled in the exercise of federal rights. He recognized objections that his proposal disserves federalism and permits defendants to delay or disrupt state trials, but argued that such abuses can be minimized and that the price is one that Congress should be willing to pay.

cancellation of such credits and there was no reason to believe the Florida courts would have changed course).[4]

Among other issues that have arisen in the administration of the exhaustion requirement are the following:

(a) Proper Presentation of the Federal Claim. Proper exhaustion requires presentation to the state courts of the *same* claim being raised on habeas: "[t]he rule would serve no purpose if it could be satisfied by raising one claim in the state courts and another in the federal courts." Picard v. Connor, 404 U.S. 270, 276 (1971). And a mere claim of unconstitutionality in state court does not suffice; "ordinarily a state prisoner does not 'fairly present' a claim to a state court if that court must read beyond a petition or a brief (or a similar document) that does not alert it to the presence of a *federal* claim". Baldwin v. Reese, 541 U.S. 27, 32 (2004) (emphasis added).[5]

(b) Which Remedies Must Be Exhausted? A prisoner ordinarily must exhaust state remedies available at trial and on appeal.[6] The Court has also stated, over a strong dissent, that a prisoner whose conviction was affirmed by an intermediate court of appeals must exhaust discretionary review available in the state supreme court. O'Sullivan v. Boerckel, 526 U.S. 838 (1999), p. 1345, *supra*. However, a prisoner need not seek certiorari before the U.S. Supreme Court, for § 2254 requires exhaustion only of "remedies available in the courts of the State". See Fay v. Noia, 372 U.S. 391, 435–38 (1963).

Although § 2254(c) states that an applicant must exhaust "any available procedure" under state law, Justice Reed's opinion in Brown v. Allen, p. 1275, *supra*, relied on the legislative history in ruling that a prisoner who has properly presented a federal claim to the trial and appellate courts need not "ask the state for collateral relief, based on the same evidence and issues already decided by direct review". Nor must a prisoner resubmit the federal contention to the state courts because a change in their interpretation of federal law suggests that a second attempt would succeed. Francisco v. Gathright, 419 U.S. 59 (1974) (per curiam). However, exhaustion of state postconviction processes is required when they are open to a claim not previously raised in state court; the most common example is a claim of ineffective assistance of counsel.

(4) "Mixed" Petitions and the Total Exhaustion Rule. Habeas petitions frequently include both exhausted and unexhausted claims. In Rose v. Lundy, 455 U.S. 509 (1982), the Court adopted a "total exhaustion" rule that requires dismissal of such "mixed" petitions. That rule, Justice O'Connor argued for the Court, promotes the general purposes of exhaustion,

---

[4] Note the apparent dissonance between procedural default doctrine and exhaustion doctrine on whether a defendant must pursue state remedies that appear to be futile. See p. 1345, note 18, *supra*.

[5] Compare the analogous requirement that a litigant seeking Supreme Court review of a state court judgment must have properly presented the *federal* issue in state court. See pp. 526–527, *supra*.

[6] In Pitchess v. Davis, 421 U.S. 482 (1975) (per curiam), the Court reaffirmed the holding of Ex parte Hawk, 321 U.S. 114 (1944), that application to state appellate courts for an extraordinary writ does not exhaust state remedies when the denial of that writ could not be taken as a decision on the merits and when normal channels of appellate review remain open.

eliminates any temptation for district courts to consider unexhausted claims, and discourages piecemeal litigation in federal court.[7]

Some of the options for prisoners that Rose v. Lundy left open have become more hazardous because of provisions of the 1996 amendments. The prisoner may amend the petition to proceed with only the exhausted claims, but that course will generally forfeit the unexhausted claims, for even if the prisoner later exhausts remedies as to them, habeas review will ordinarily be barred by the statutory restrictions on second or successive petitions. Alternatively, the prisoner may dismiss the petition and return to state court to complete exhaustion, but in doing so may run afoul of the one-year limitations period; that period is tolled while state postconviction proceedings are pending, but not during the pendency of federal proceedings nor when shuttling back and forth between federal and state courts. See generally Duncan v. Walker, 533 U.S. 167, 182 (2001) (Stevens, J., concurring in part and concurring in the judgment).

In Rhines v. Weber, 544 U.S. 269 (2005), the Court gave qualified approval to a third option, under which district courts stay mixed petitions pending exhaustion. Rhines, who had been sentenced to death, filed a timely habeas petition, but by the time the district court found that eight of his thirty-five claims were unexhausted, the limitations period had run. The district court held Rhines' petition in abeyance, conditioned upon his commencing state court proceedings within 60 days and returning to federal court within 60 days of completing exhaustion. When the case reached the Supreme Court, Justice O'Connor's majority opinion concluded that the district court's stay could undermine AEDPA's purposes of reducing delays in executing sentences (especially capital sentences) and encouraging litigants to ensure that all claims are exhausted before filing in federal court. Accordingly, the Court held that the stay-and-abeyance procedure is appropriate only "when the district court determines there was good cause for the petitioner's failure to exhaust his claims first in state court", and, further, that a district court would abuse its discretion by issuing a stay with respect to "plainly meritless" unexhausted claims. The Court added that to avoid delay, district courts should impose "reasonable time limits on a petitioner's trip to state court and back", and should not grant a stay "if a petitioner engages in abusive litigation tactics or intentional delay". But the Court warned that a district court would abuse its discretion by denying a stay when a prisoner had good cause for a failure to exhaust potentially meritorious claims and had not engaged in intentional dilatory tactics. The Court remanded the case for decision under these newly-announced standards.

Concurring in part and concurring in the judgment, Justice Souter, joined by Justices Ginsburg and Breyer, would not have conditioned the availability of a stay on demonstration of good cause: given the difficulties that tricky exhaustion issues pose for pro se prisoners, he thought a threshold inquiry into good cause "will give the district courts too much trouble to be worth the time". He would instead have denied a stay only when "intentionally dilatory litigation tactics" have been shown. In another concurring opinion, Justice Stevens (joined by Justices Ginsburg and Breyer)

---

[7] Concurring only in the judgment, Justice Blackmun asserted that a district court should dismiss only the unexhausted claims in a mixed petition.

For criticism of Lundy, see Yackle, note 1, *supra*, at 424–40.

stated that he joined the Court on the understanding that the good cause requirement would not prove to be a trap for unwary pro se petitioners.

(5) "Special Circumstances" Justifying Prompt Federal Intervention. Section 2254(b) is limited to cases of custody pursuant to a "judgment of a state court". While exhaustion as a judge-made doctrine may still be required even when § 2254(b) does not apply, certain circumstances have been thought to warrant earlier federal intervention.[8]

(a) In Braden v. 30th Judicial Cir. Ct., 410 U.S. 484 (1973), the Court ruled that the petitioner, who was serving a sentence in Alabama while under detainer on a separate Kentucky charge, could seek relief premised on Kentucky's alleged denial of his right to a speedy trial. Acknowledging that the prisoner could "assert a speedy trial defense when, and if, he is finally brought to trial," the Court found that the Kentucky courts had already rejected his claim of a "present" denial of a speedy trial. The Court added that the petitioner was not trying to disrupt or forestall state prosecution but rather "to enforce the Commonwealth's obligation to provide him with a state court forum."

(b) What about a pre-trial claim of double jeopardy? In Justices of Boston Municipal Ct. v. Lydon, 466 U.S. 294 (1984), the defendant was convicted at a bench trial in municipal court; he had no right of appeal, but he invoked his right under state law to a de novo jury trial in superior court. He then moved to dismiss the charge, arguing that a new jury trial would violate the Double Jeopardy Clause absent a prior determination that the evidence at the bench trial sufficed to sustain a conviction. After the state courts rejected that claim, the defendant sought federal habeas review before his trial. Although finding no double jeopardy violation, the Supreme Court held that the petitioner had satisfied the exhaustion requirement, noting that the highest state court had rejected the double jeopardy claim on the merits. But the Court also pointed to "the unique nature of the double jeopardy right", which "cannot be fully vindicated on appeal following final judgment, since in part the Double Jeopardy Clause protects 'against being twice put to *trial* for the same offense.'"

(6) Waiver. The question whether a failure to exhaust always bars habeas review is now governed by two statutory provisions adopted in AEDPA in 1996. First, implementing a proposal made by Professor Shapiro,[9] § 2254(b)(2) provides that the failure to exhaust does not bar a court from *denying* a petition on the merits. Second, § 2254(b)(3) confirms that the exhaustion requirement can be waived by the state, although only if there is an express waiver by counsel.

(7) The Exhaustion Requirement in Action. Older empirical studies suggested that failure to exhaust state remedies was a major obstacle to adjudication of habeas petitions on the merits. In a pioneering study of Massachusetts habeas cases, Professor Shapiro found that more than half of the petitions filed from 1970–72 (135 out of 257) were dismissed wholly or in part on exhaustion grounds.[10] Another study of 1,899 petitions filed in six district courts and one court of appeals between 1975 and 1977 found that

---

[8] In addition to the cases discussed in text, see generally Amsterdam, note 1, *supra*, at 892–99.

[9] Shapiro, p. 1271, note 20, *supra*, at 359–61.

[10] See *id*. at 356–61.

37% were denied for failure to exhaust.[11] A more recent study found that in 2003–04, only 11% of non-capital petitions were dismissed on exhaustion grounds; the reduction may have resulted in part from the large number of petitions that, since the enactment of a limitations period in 1996, are now dismissed as time-barred.[12]

NOTE ON PROBLEMS OF CUSTODY AND REMEDY

(1) The Statutory Requirement of Custody. Echoing the common law, 28 U.S.C. § 2241(c) confers jurisdiction only when the petitioner is "in custody". Until the 1960s, courts interpreted the custody requirement strictly. See, *e.g.*, Wales v. Whitney, 114 U.S. 564 (1885) (naval officer's challenge to order confining him to city limits; no jurisdiction); Stallings v. Splain, 253 U.S. 339 (1920) (habeas will not lie if petitioner has been released on bail); Weber v. Squier, 315 U.S. 810 (1942) (habeas does not lie for convict released on parole).

(2) A Broadened Understanding of Custody. The understanding of "custody" was revolutionized in Jones v. Cunningham, 371 U.S. 236 (1963), which held that a petitioner free on parole could obtain habeas review of the original criminal conviction.[1] The Court said that parole release "imposes conditions which significantly confine and restrain his freedom"—including the threat of re-imprisonment for parole violations, the obligation to report monthly to a parole officer, and the need for official permission to leave the city, change residence, or drive an automobile. The opinion did not specify which of those constraints was essential to the finding of custody. But where all or most of these constraints accompany other forms of restraint (*e.g.*, probation[2] or release on a conditionally suspended sentence[3]), the lower courts have not hesitated since Jones to entertain applications for habeas corpus. See also Hensley v. Municipal Court, 411 U.S. 345 (1973) (petitioner who had exhausted all state remedies after having been sentenced to jail, but remained free on his own recognizance, awaiting execution of the sentence, was in custody).

Is Jones' relaxation of the custody requirement understandable insofar as habeas corpus was viewed as a means of ensuring federal review of state criminal convictions, and as a particularly important means during the period when the Warren Court was developing new (and often unwelcome) constitutional rules governing state criminal proceedings?

(3) Release from Custody. Broad language in Jones—"besides physical imprisonment, there are other restraints on a man's liberty, restraints not

---

[11] Allen, Schachtman & Wilson, *Federal Habeas Corpus and Its Reform: An Empirical Analysis*, 13 Rutgers L.J. 675, 695, 703 (1982).

[12] King, Cheesman & Ostrom, p. 1266, note 3, *supra*, at 48, 57.

[1] For criticism of the Court's use of history and precedent, see Oaks, *Legal History in the High Court—Habeas Corpus*, 64 Mich.L.Rev. 451 (1966). For an inquiry into the reasons for expansion of the custody concept, see Yackle, *Explaining Habeas Corpus*, 60 N.Y.U.L.Rev. 991, 998–1010 (1985).

[2] *E.g.*, Lawrence v. 48th Dist. Ct., 560 F.3d 475, 479–81 (6th Cir.2009).

[3] *E.g.*, Sammons v. Rodgers, 785 F.2d 1343, 1345 (5th Cir.1986) & authorities cited.

For criticism of decisions holding that a sex offender subject to post-release registration and community notification requirements is not in custody, see Logan, *Federal Habeas in the Information Age*, 85 Minn.L.Rev. 147 (2000).

shared by the public generally, which have been thought sufficient in the English-speaking world to support the issuance of habeas corpus"—had the potential to push the law even further. But Maleng v. Cook, 490 U.S. 488, 492 (1989) (per curiam), rejected the notion that when a sentence has been fully served, the prisoner may challenge the conviction on habeas on the basis that civil disabilities still adhered or that the prior conviction could be used in another criminal case to enhance the sentence.

Maleng did not disturb the decision in Carafas v. LaVallee, 391 U.S. 234 (1968), that a petition filed while a prisoner is in custody does not automatically become moot following the expiration of the sentence and the prisoner's unconditional release. Thus, petitions filed one day before and one day after release are treated differently. The Court in Carafas stressed that civil disabilities and burdens accompanied the petitioner after his release.[4] (Of course, such disabilities and burdens may persist in a case, like Maleng, in which release precedes filing.[5])

(4) The Nature of Relief: Release from Custody and the Rise and Fall of the Prematurity Rule. The correlative of the custody requirement is the notion that the only appropriate remedy is release from confinement. But in Peyton v. Rowe, 391 U.S. 54 (1968), the Court, overruling its decision in McNally v. Hill, 293 U.S. 131, 138 (1934), permitted a prisoner to challenge the validity of the second of two consecutive sentences while still serving the first.[6] Rejecting the view that the challenge was premature, the Court noted that if the first sentence is lengthy, it is impractical to wait to determine the validity of the second until the petitioner begins to serve it, when memories will have dimmed and witnesses may have disappeared. The Court added that the prematurity rule prejudices petitioners who ultimately succeed, by forcing them to commence the second confinement before litigating its validity.[7]

Garlotte v. Fordice, 515 U.S. 39 (1995) (7–2), was a case of Peyton in reverse: the petitioner, after completing a sentence for a drug offense, was serving a *consecutive* sentence for murder when he filed a habeas petition challenging the drug conviction. The warden argued that he was no longer in custody on the drug conviction, relying on Maleng v. Cook, Paragraph (3), *supra*. Rejecting the warden's contention, the Court ruled that the prisoner remained " 'in custody' under all of his sentences until all are served".

---

[4] Carafas was limited by Lane v. Williams, 455 U.S. 624 (1982), where a habeas petition challenging not conviction but only the re-confinement because of a parole violation was held to be moot after the prisoners, having served the full parole term, were released. See also Spencer v. Kemna, 523 U.S. 1 (1998).

[5] Maleng left open the question of the circumstances in which a court may consider a challenge to a prior conviction for which the petitioner is no longer in custody but which has been used to enhance the sentence that the petitioner is presently serving for a subsequent offense. The Court decided that issue in Lackawanna County Dist. Atty. v. Coss, 532 U.S. 394 (2001), ruling that, subject to only the narrowest exceptions, a habeas court may not entertain such a petition.

[6] Two months earlier, in Walker v. Wainwright, 390 U.S. 335 (1968), the Court had permitted attack on the validity of a sentence presently being served, even though another sentence awaited the prisoner.

[7] Prisoners have generally been permitted to mount attacks that, if successful, would shorten the total period of confinement but would not lead to immediate release. See, *e.g.*, Bostic v. Carlson, 884 F.2d 1267, 1269 (9th Cir.1989); Jensen v. Satran, 688 F.2d 76 (8th Cir.1982).

The Supreme Court's decisions do not clearly resolve whether the writ is available to test the validity of conditions of confinement in prison. See generally Aamer v. Obama, 742 F.3d 1023 (D.C.Cir.2014) (holding that circuit precedent authorizes such habeas petitions).

B. COLLATERAL ATTACK ON FEDERAL CONVICTIONS

NOTE ON 28 U.S.C. § 2255 AND ITS RELATIONSHIP TO FEDERAL HABEAS CORPUS

(1) The Enactment of § 2255. Before 1948, federal prisoners detained after criminal convictions could file a habeas corpus petition only in the district in which they were being confined. That rule caused serious administrative problems. The few federal districts within whose territorial jurisdiction the major federal correctional facilities were located were inundated with petitions. Facially meritorious applications were often found wholly wanting after consulting the records of the sentencing court, but those records were not readily available to the habeas court. Venue also proved inconvenient when hearings had to be conducted far from the locale of the underlying events. See generally United States v. Hayman, 342 U.S. 205, 210–14 (1952).

To address these difficulties, in 1948 Congress enacted 28 U.S.C. § 2255,[1] which provides that in postconviction review cases, federal prisoners must file any motion for collateral relief in the court that entered the sentence. Although entitled "Federal custody; remedies on motion attacking sentence", § 2255, like habeas corpus for state prisoners, is available to attack convictions or sentences resulting in custody in violation of the federal Constitution or, in some cases, federal statutes or treaties. In Hayman, the Court stressed that § 2255 was not meant to "impinge upon prisoners' rights of collateral attack upon their convictions" but only "to minimize the difficulties encountered in habeas corpus hearings by affording the same rights in another and more convenient forum."

This Note sketches the basic outlines of the § 2255 remedy, highlighting the ways in which it resembles, and differs from, collateral relief under § 2254 for state prisoners.

(2) The Exclusivity of § 2255. Although Congress, in enacting § 2255, did not repeal or limit the pre-existing grant of habeas corpus jurisdiction, § 2255 provides that a federal convict's habeas petition shall not be entertained unless the petitioner has first sought relief under § 2255 and "unless it also appears that the remedy by motion [under § 2255] is inadequate or ineffective to test the legality of his detention." In the Hayman case, the Supreme Court found no need to consider the petitioner's argument that § 2255 was an unconstitutional suspension of the writ, ruling that Hayman made no showing that the § 2255 remedy was inadequate, and that if he had, the statute would permit resort to the writ. Accord, Swain v. Pressley, 430 U.S. 372, 381 (1977), pp. 1204, 1292, *supra*.

Section 2255 applies only to persons "in custody under sentence of a court established by Act of Congress". It does not limit federal habeas corpus challenges to other kinds of federal detention—for example, court martial

---

[1] The provision was drafted by a committee of the Judicial Conference. See Parker, *Limiting the Abuse of Habeas Corpus*, 8 F.R.D. 171 (1948).

proceedings, military detention of terrorists, civil commitment of the mentally ill, extradition, and immigration matters.

(3) Proceedings Under § 2255. Unlike a state prisoner's habeas petition, a § 2255 motion is not a separate civil action but rather a continuation of the criminal proceeding. The motion will be opposed not by a prison warden but rather by the United States, which initiated the prosecution. Nonetheless, § 2255 motions are processed in much the same way as § 2254 petitions, and the Rules Governing § 2255 Proceedings in the United States District Courts are virtually identical to the parallel Rules Governing § 2254 Proceedings.[2] Rule 4 of the § 2255 Rules specifies that the motion shall be heard by the judge who presided at the original trial and sentencing (where possible)—although, as with state prisoner petitions, § 2255 motions are often referred initially to magistrate judges.

(4) The Analogy to Brown v. Allen. In Kaufman v. United States, 394 U.S. 217 (1969) (6–3), the Warren Court rejected the government's argument that the general approach of Brown v. Allen, permitting collateral attack on criminal convictions, was inapposite in § 2255 proceedings because federal petitioners, unlike their state counterparts, had already enjoyed the opportunity to litigate in a *federal* court. That opportunity, the Court said, "is clearly not the sole justification for federal post-conviction relief; otherwise there would be no need to make such relief available to federal prisoners at all. The provision of federal collateral remedies rests more fundamentally upon a recognition that adequate protection of constitutional rights relating to the criminal trial process requires the continuing availability of a mechanism for relief. * * *

" * * * Plainly the interest in finality is the same with regard to both federal and state prisoners. With regard to both, Congress has determined that the full protection of their constitutional rights requires the availability of a mechanism for collateral attack."

(5) Section 2255 in Practice. Despite Kaufman's assertion of an equivalence between state and federal prisoners, review under § 2255 is in practice considerably more restricted. Suppose that a prisoner's constitutional challenge to a conviction was rejected on the merits at trial and on appeal. A *state* prisoner can then seek a determination from a federal habeas court, which traditionally was not bound by the state court's determination (and, even after 1996, remains free to grant relief if it views the state court determination as in conflict with constitutional principles clearly established by the Supreme Court). But a federal prisoner's § 2255 motion will ordinarily be presented to the same judge who initially denied the claim, and who is likely to ask, "What's new?". If there was an appeal from the original conviction, the district judge in the § 2255 proceeding, even if not the judge before whom the petitioner was convicted, would ordinarily be bound by a decision of the court of appeals rejecting the claim on direct appeal. Indeed, most circuits require an appellate panel to follow circuit precedent, from which only the en banc court may depart; where that rule applies, only in the rare instance in which the en banc court of appeals, or the Supreme Court, reviews the denial of relief under § 2255 would a prior

---

[2] For a catalogue of minor differences, see the Advisory Committee Notes to the § 2255 Rules, particularly the Note to Rule 1. Rule 12 of the § 2255 Rules (which has no counterpart in the § 2254 Rules) authorizes a district court to apply the criminal as well as the civil rules, as the court deems appropriate.

circuit decision not be binding. See Potuto, *The Federal Prisoner Collateral Attack: Requiescat in Pace*, 1988 B.Y.U.L.Rev. 37, 41–47.[3]

When, then, might a federal prisoner obtain relief under § 2255?

(a) New Law. One situation is when legal standards have changed— for example, by virtue of a recent Supreme Court decision after the conviction became final. But although § 2255 contains no limitation on the scope of review similar to that added in 1996 by § 2254(d), the courts of appeals have held that the Supreme Court's decision in Teague v. Lane, p. 1295, *supra*— which precludes habeas courts from considering state prisoners' claims based on new law in all but the most exceptional cases—also governs § 2255 proceedings. See, *e.g.*, United States v. Sanchez-Cervantes, 282 F.3d 664, 667–68 & n.9 (9th Cir.2002) (citing cases). See also Chaidez v. United States, 133 S.Ct. 1103 (2013), p. 1297, n. 4, *supra* (applying Teague in a proceeding in which a federal prisoner sought a writ of coram nobis—a writ that in some circumstances permits someone no longer in custody to attack a conviction— and remarking that the parties agreed that nothing turned on any difference between coram nobis and relief under § 2255).

An important limit to the Teague doctrine was set forth in Bousley v. United States, 523 U.S. 614 (1998). Bousley, after pleading guilty to the federal crime of using a firearm during and in relation to a drug trafficking offense, had unsuccessfully appealed his sentence. Thereafter, the Supreme Court held in an unrelated case, Bailey v. United States, 516 U.S. 137 (1995), that "use" of a firearm requires not merely possession but "active employment" of the weapon—a narrower understanding of the elements of the crime than had been established at the plea allocution in Bousley's case. In a § 2255 motion, Bousley asserted the very claim that Bailey had upheld. On review, the Court, with Chief Justice Rehnquist writing, held that Bousley's motion stated a good due process claim that the guilty plea was not voluntary and intelligent. The Court stated that that claim was hardly new within the meaning of Teague, but then continued more broadly: "And because Teague by its terms applies only to procedural rules, we think it is inapplicable to the situation in which this Court decides the meaning of a criminal statute enacted by Congress.

"This distinction between substance and procedure is an important one in the habeas context. The Teague doctrine is founded on the notion that one of the 'principal functions of habeas corpus [is] "to assure that no man has been incarcerated under a procedure which creates an impermissibly large risk that the innocent will be convicted." ' Consequently, unless a new rule of criminal procedure is of such a nature that 'without [it] the likelihood of an accurate conviction is seriously diminished,' there is no reason to apply the rule retroactively on habeas review. By contrast, decisions of this Court holding that a substantive federal criminal statute does not reach certain conduct, like decisions placing conduct 'beyond the power of the criminal law- making authority to proscribe,' necessarily carry a significant risk that a defendant stands convicted of 'an act that the law does not make criminal' " (internal citations omitted).

---

[3]   The requirement that circuit precedent be followed may not apply when the panel in the § 2255 proceeding was also the panel on direct review. See 18B Wright, Miller & Cooper, Federal Practice and Procedure § 4478. Even so, there would have to be very strong reason to reopen an issue already decided on direct appeal.

The Court proceeded to state that Bousley could have attacked the voluntariness and intelligence of the plea in his initial appeal and that his failure to have done so constituted a procedural default, at least where, as here, decision of the issue on appeal would not have required further factual development. However, the Court added that he might be able to demonstrate "actual innocence" so as to excuse the default, and remanded to give him that opportunity.[4]

(b) New Evidence. Some cases suggest that § 2255 reaches claims based on new evidence that could not, with due diligence, have been discovered at trial, see, *e.g.*, United States v. Johnpoll, 748 F.Supp. 86, 91 n. 3 (S.D.N.Y.1990), *aff'd without opinion*, 932 F.2d 956 (2d Cir.1991)— although it is difficult to find decisions granting relief on this basis.

(c) No Previous Decision on the Merits. A § 2255 motion would not simply revisit ground already covered when it presents a claim not raised at trial or on direct review. However, the standards governing the effect of procedural defaults by state prisoners apply equally to federal prisoners,[5] and thus in the situation posed, relief under § 2255 will ordinarily be foreclosed. See generally pp. 1323–1346 *supra*. But some claims may appropriately be raised for the first time in § 2255 proceedings; the most important set of such claims are those alleging ineffective assistance of counsel. See Massaro v. United States, 538 U.S. 500 (2003), p. 1339, note 9,

---

[4] The Justices offered a range of views about whether there had been a procedural default and, if so, what effect it should have. Justice Scalia's dissent, joined by Justice Thomas, argued that a showing of actual innocence should not excuse a default in a guilty plea situation: no trial transcript exists, and thus the government, many years after the fact, would have to produce witnesses to establish that Bousley had committed the crime. Noting that most convictions are by guilty plea, Justice Scalia feared that the Court's ruling could produce a flood of collateral attacks. He also observed that pleas often are entered in exchange for dismissal of more serious charges.

Responding to Justice Scalia, the Court stressed that the government was free to introduce any admissible evidence of guilt, including evidence not presented at the plea colloquy, and added: "where the Government has forgone more serious charges in the course of plea bargaining, petitioner's showing of actual innocence must also extend to those charges."

What does this last statement mean? Surely if a prisoner is permitted to overturn a conviction, the government may re-open charges that had been dismissed as part of a plea agreement. But in order to establish his "actual innocence" of an offense whose elements he did not understand when he entered his plea, why must a prisoner like Bousley be required to show that he was also innocent of other charges of which he was never convicted?

Justice Stevens, dissenting in part, criticized the Court's holding that the failure to raise an issue on direct appeal from a plea constitutes a procedural default: "A layman who justifiably relied on incorrect advice from the court and counsel in deciding to plead guilty to a crime that he did not commit will ordinarily continue to assume that such advice was accurate during the time for taking an appeal." Thus, without requiring a showing of actual innocence, he would have vacated the conviction and remanded for Bousley to plead anew.

Suppose that on remand there is a dispute about whether Bousley did "use" a gun within the meaning of the statute as construed by the Bailey decision: Bousley cannot establish "actual innocence"—*i.e.*, that "it is more likely than not that no reasonable juror would have convicted" him of the offense—but the government cannot establish his guilt beyond a reasonable doubt. Under the Court's approach, the conviction remains in force; under Justice Stevens' approach, Bousley could not be convicted. Which result is preferable?

[5] See Bousley v. United States, Paragraph (5)(a), note 4, *supra*; Reed v. Farley, 512 U.S. 339, 354–55 (1994) (dictum); United States v. Frady, 456 U.S. 152 (1982). Whether or not one views state and federal prisoners as differently situated with respect to claims previously litigated, aren't the two classes of prisoners similarly situated with respect to defaulted claims? For both, a refusal to excuse the default forfeits the claim altogether, while excuse of the default permits a federal court decision on collateral review. See generally Meltzer, *State Court Forfeitures of Federal Rights*, 99 Harv.L.Rev. 1128, 1204–05 (1986).

supra (unanimously rejecting the government's contention that the failure of counsel on direct appeal to raise the ineffectiveness of trial counsel, even when that claim was based solely on the trial record, constituted a procedural default).

(6) Nonconstitutional Claims. Like § 2254, § 2255 refers to sentences "imposed in violation of the Constitution *or laws* of the United States". Federal prosecutions obviously involve federal nonconstitutional laws far more often than do state prosecutions; therefore, the reference to "laws" is far more significant in the § 2255 setting than in the § 2254 setting.

But not every claim alleging a violation of federal law provides the basis for collateral relief. In Hill v. United States, 368 U.S. 424 (1962), the Court held that § 2255 did not encompass a claim that the sentencing judge violated Rule 32(a) of the Criminal Rules by failing to ask whether the defendant (who was represented by counsel) had anything to say before sentence was imposed. The alleged error was "neither jurisdictional nor constitutional. It is not a fundamental defect which inherently results in a complete miscarriage of justice, nor an omission inconsistent with the rudimentary demands of fair procedure. It does not present 'exceptional circumstances where the need for the remedy afforded by the writ of habeas corpus is apparent'" (quoting Bowen v. Johnston, 306 U.S. 19, 27 (1939)).

That language from Hill, though hardly self-applying, was recited by the Court in holding that § 2255 also does not reach a claim of a purely "formal" violation of Fed.R.Crim.Proc. 11 (governing the taking of guilty pleas), see United States v. Timmreck, 441 U.S. 780 (1979), or a claim that in imposing a sentence, the judge had failed to foresee a change in parole regulations whose effect was to delay the prisoner's release, see United States v. Addonizio, 442 U.S. 178, 186 (1979).[6]

But the Court did find that the statutory claim in Davis v. United States, 417 U.S. 333 (1974), satisfied the Hill test and thus could provide the basis for relief. There, the Ninth Circuit had affirmed Davis' conviction for refusing to obey an order of induction into the armed forces, rejecting his claim that the federal regulation authorizing his induction for "delinquency" (failing to report for a physical examination) was invalid because not authorized by the statute. After a different Ninth Circuit panel, in an unrelated case, upheld the same claim that Davis had presented, Davis sought relief under § 2255.

Thus Davis, like Bousley, Paragraph (5)(a), *supra*, sought relief because of a change in the understanding of the criminal offense of which he was convicted. Unlike Bousley, Davis had gone to trial instead of pleading guilty, and therefore could not claim a due process violation in the submission of an involuntary or unintelligent plea. As a result, the Supreme Court treated Davis' claim as purely statutory. Concluding without discussion that the second panel's decision constituted "an intervening change in the law,"[7] the

---

[6]   *Cf.* Reed v. Farley, p. 1265, note 1, *supra* (applying the Hill standard in a § 2254 proceeding and finding not cognizable a prisoner's claim that the state had violated an interstate compact, approved by Congress, which requires the trial of a prisoner transferred from one state to another to commence within 120 days of the transfer).

[7]   Note that the only intervening "change" in the law resulted from a decision of another panel of the Ninth Circuit. Should collateral relitigation be permitted only when the asserted change in the law would be *authoritative* (*e.g.*, a ruling by the Supreme Court or by the court of appeals *en banc*)? Under Davis, may a federal prisoner collaterally relitigate a claim rejected on direct appeal if thereafter another *circuit* takes a different view of the law?

Court ruled that Davis' claim that he had been convicted "for an act that the law does not make criminal" was sufficiently fundamental to fall within § 2255.

(7) Limitations on § 2255 Relief. Much of the doctrine governing habeas relief for state prisoners has been imported into § 2255 proceedings.

(a) Sometimes doctrines found only in the statutory provisions governing state prisoners are read into § 2255. Thus, although § 2255 does not mention exhaustion of remedies, the Advisory Committee Note to Rule 5 notes that "courts have held that [a § 2255] motion is inappropriate if the movant is simultaneously appealing the [conviction]." (Recall that the exhaustion requirement was originally a judge-made doctrine. See pp. 1349–1350, *supra*.)

(b) Sometimes matters not expressly governed by statutory text under either § 2254 or § 2255 are treated similarly—as is true, for example, of the treatment of procedural defaults, see Paragraph (5)(c), *supra*.

(c) In 1996, AEDPA included a number of amendments to § 2255 that impose new restrictions on the availability of collateral relief and that generally parallel the restrictions that AEDPA established for state prisoners. These include (i) a one-year statute of limitations for § 2255 motions, similar to § 2244(d)'s limitations period for state prisoners, see p. 1266, *supra*,[8] and (ii) strict limits on the consideration of second or successive motions, similar to those governing state prisoners under § 2244(b), see pp. 1346–1349, *supra*.[9]

In addition, AEDPA established time limits within which federal courts must decide § 2255 motions filed by prisoners under sentence of death: for the district courts, the earlier of 450 days after filing or 60 days after the date on which the case is submitted for decision, with one 30 day extension

---

[8] Section 2255's limitations period, unlike that in § 2244, does not specify that a judgment becomes final on the date of "the conclusion of direct review or the expiration of the time for seeking such review." In Clay v. United States, 537 U.S. 522 (2003), the Court ruled unanimously that when a federal defendant whose conviction was affirmed on appeal does not petition for certiorari, the conviction becomes final when the time for filing a petition for a writ of certiorari expired.

Under § 2255, as under § 2244, the one-year period runs from the latest of four dates, one of which is "the date on which the right asserted was initially recognized by the Supreme Court, if that right has been newly recognized by the Supreme Court and made retroactively applicable to cases on collateral review". In Dodd v. United States, 545 U.S. 353 (2005) (5–4), the Court held that the one-year period runs from the date on which the Supreme Court recognizes the new right, rather than the date on which the right is made retroactive in a subsequent proceeding. The Court recognized that when, as is often true and was true in Dodd's case, more than a year passes between the Supreme Court's recognition of a new right and that right's being made retroactively applicable, a prisoner will be unable to file a timely claim invoking the new right, but held that the statutory language clearly required that result. In dissent, Justice Stevens (joined by Justices Souter, Ginsburg, and Breyer) refused to accept the view that Congress should be understood, "in the same provision, both to recognize a potential basis for habeas relief and also to make it highly probable that the statute of limitations would bar relief before the claim can be brought."

[9] In two respects, § 2255's treatment of successive petitions is less strict than that of § 2244(b). First, § 2255 contains no provision, like that in § 2244(b)(1), that unqualifiedly requires dismissal of a claim presented in a prior application. Second, § 2255 permits a successive petition based on newly discovered evidence of innocence, without § 2244(b)(2)(B)(i)'s further requirement that "the factual predicate for the claim could not have been discovered previously through the exercise of due diligence". Moreover, although § 2255 (like § 2244(b)) requires a prisoner, before filing a second or successive application, to obtain a ruling from a panel of the court of appeals that the conditions have been satisfied, § 2255, unlike § 2244(b)(3)(E), does not preclude appeal from the court of appeals' determination.

permitted; for the courts of appeals, 120 days after the reply brief is filed. 28 U.S.C. § 2266. (The parallel provisions for state prisoners under sentence of death apply only if the state's provision of counsel in *state* postconviction proceedings meets specified conditions. See pp. 1271–1272, *supra*.)[10]

(8) Problems Under the 1996 Act. The limitation on second or successive petitions for § 2255 petitioners largely tracks the similar limitation for state petitioners seeking habeas review. But Congress seems to have lost sight of the fact that federal convicts more often can raise federal *statutory* claims in their collateral attacks—notably in cases in which the federal criminal statute under which a prisoner was convicted has since been authoritatively interpreted more narrowly. See Paragraphs (5)(a) & (6), *supra*. Suppose that after a district court rejects a prisoner's initial § 2255 motion raising, for example, a Miranda claim, the Supreme Court, in a different case, interprets the criminal offense of which the prisoner was convicted more narrowly than did the convicting court. Is the prisoner foreclosed from filing a second § 2255 motion relying on the intervening Supreme Court decision, because the second motion does not fall under either of the exceptions to the general ban on multiple filings, as it neither rests on "a new rule of *constitutional* law, made retroactive * * * by the Supreme Court * * * " nor is it based on "newly discovered evidence" (emphasis added)?[11]

Could this claim, if foreclosed by § 2255's limits on successive petitions, instead be raised in a habeas corpus petition under § 2241? Recall that § 2255 contains a safety valve, under which § 2255 precludes habeas corpus review unless "the remedy by motion [under § 2255] is inadequate or ineffective to test the legality of [the prisoner's] detention." On the one hand, it cannot be that the restrictions on successive petitions make § 2255 "inadequate or ineffective" whenever a prisoner has already filed a § 2255 motion—for to so conclude would mean that any statutory restriction on § 2255 could be bypassed by filing under § 2241. On the other hand, if resort to § 2241 under the safety valve provision were precluded in this case, a prisoner convicted of an offense that has been found not to exist would have no remedy.

Virtually all of the circuits have stated that petitioners who were convicted for conduct that has been rendered non-criminal by a subsequent authoritative decision, and who are barred from resorting to § 2255, may resort to § 2241 in some circumstances. Indeed, some courts have suggested that a refusal to permit resort to § 2241 would raise serious constitutional issues. In formulating a standard, some decisions have specified that the petitioner must show that precedent foreclosed the argument earlier in the process, or, alternatively, that the petitioner had no prior opportunity to have raised the issue. See, *e.g.*, Triestman v. United States, 124 F.3d 361, 377 (2d Cir.1997); United States v. Tyler, 732 F.3d 241, 246 (3d Cir.2013); Brown v. Caraway, 719 F.3d 583, 586 (7th Cir.2013). But *cf.* Prost v. Anderson, 636 F.3d 578, 584, 593 (10th Cir.2011) (refusing to excuse a failure to have raised an argument earlier that was erroneously foreclosed by circuit precedent, but leaving open the possibility that a petitioner may resort to

---

[10] A last change made by AEPDA is to extend to federal prisoners (whether or not under sentence of death) the rule, which before 1996 applied only to state prisoners, that an appeal from a district court's denial of relief cannot be filed without having first obtained a certificate of appealability. See 28 U.S.C. § 2253, discussed at p. 1269, *supra*.

[11] The lower courts have rejected efforts to characterize the prisoner's claim as constitutional. See, *e.g.*, Triestman v. United States, 124 F.3d 361, 370–71 & cases cited (2d Cir.1997).

§ 2241 when the denial of collateral review "would seriously threaten to render the § 2255 remedial process unconstitutional").

CHAPTER XII

ADVANCED PROBLEMS IN JUDICIAL FEDERALISM

1. PROBLEMS OF RES JUDICATA

INTRODUCTORY NOTE

The general subject of the preclusive effect of judgments (often called "res judicata") is usually studied in first year courses in Civil Procedure. This section, which builds on that background, focuses on: (1) problems of preclusion arising in litigation with the federal government, and (2) issues of interjurisdictional preclusion—the effects of federal judgments in subsequent state court actions and the effects of state court judgments in subsequent federal actions. To aid in understanding these materials, a brief review of some basic principles of preclusion may be helpful—although considerable variation is found in the doctrines followed in different American jurisdictions. For a more exhaustive treatment of these and related principles, see the Restatement (Second) of Judgments (1982) (hereafter cited as Restatement 2d); Shapiro, Civil Procedure: Preclusion in Civil Actions (2001).

While the term "res judicata" is occasionally used in a narrower sense, we use it here to embrace the entire subject of the preclusive effects of a prior adjudicatory proceeding in a subsequent adjudicatory proceeding. Those effects are in turn divided into "claim" and "issue" preclusion.

(1) Claim Preclusion. Under the doctrine of claim preclusion, once a court has entered a valid final judgment, a subsequent action on the same claim by any party to that judgment, or by one in "privity" with a party, is normally precluded. The underlying intuition rests at least in part on waiver: the precluded party could and should have raised the matter in the earlier litigation and has now waived the opportunity to do so. Today, most courts embrace the Restatement 2d view that a claim should be defined in terms of the transaction or transactions that were the subject of the dispute, not in terms of the particular theory of recovery that was advanced. Another aspect of claim preclusion provides that a judgment is not subject to collateral attack on the basis of a defense that might have been, but was not, raised in the prior action. Here too, the operating premise is one of waiver: the precluded party could and should have presented the defense in the prior litigation.

A range of exceptions to the rule of claim preclusion covers such matters as the existence of "consent" to the splitting of a claim and instances in which the prior judgment rested on such preliminary grounds as lack of jurisdiction or improper venue. The exceptions for lack of jurisdiction or venue help to illustrate that the theory of claim preclusion is based on waiver. But if the claim could not have been heard in the prior proceeding—because the court there lacked jurisdiction or venue, or, to take another example, because the claim had not yet accrued—then claim preclusion does not apply, as the litigant can hardly be taxed for having failed to raise a claim that could not have been resolved in that proceeding.

The applicability of claim preclusion does not ordinarily depend on whether the claim or defense in question was actually litigated in a prior proceeding. Rather, the question is whether it could and should have been litigated.

(2) Issue Preclusion. When the doctrine of claim preclusion does not entirely bar a second action, the doctrine of issue preclusion (also frequently referred to as collateral estoppel) will normally bar a party to the first action from *relitigating* an issue of fact or law decided in the first action that was necessary to the judgment. The underlying theory of issue preclusion is that when an issue was fully and fairly litigated in an earlier proceeding, there ordinarily is insufficient reason to discard that presumptively reliable determination. Issue preclusion thereby avoids duplicative litigation and the risk of inconsistent adjudications. Note that the application of issue preclusion, unlike claim preclusion, does not require that the subject matter of the current action have any particular relationship to the subject matter of the prior adjudication; instead, the key question is whether the issue in the second action on which preclusion is invoked was resolved in the first action. Again, numerous exceptions are recognized in the Restatement 2d and in virtually all jurisdictions.

(3) Offensive and Defensive Preclusion. It is common to refer to preclusion as being offensive or defensive in nature. Offensive preclusion refers to invocation of issue preclusion by a plaintiff or other claimant who seeks to use the doctrine in order to help establish a claim for relief by invoking preclusion. Defensive preclusion simply refers to a party's reliance on issue preclusion when defending against a claim for relief.

(4) Limits on Issue Preclusion.

(a) Mutuality of Preclusion. Under the ancient doctrine of "mutuality," a party A could invoke issue preclusion against a party B only if B would also have had the right to invoke issue preclusion against A. Thus, under the mutuality approach, if a passenger on a bus proved that the bus company's negligence had caused a crash, a different passenger who was not a party to the first lawsuit could not, after filing an action, preclude the bus company on the basis of the earlier litigation—for had the earlier litigation found no liability, the bus company would not have been permitted to preclude the second passenger on the basis of a litigation to which the second passenger was not a party. But the requirement of mutuality has largely given way: most courts have extended issue preclusion beyond the parties to the initial action, so that a party to that action (like the bus company) who suffered an adverse determination on an issue may be barred from relitigating that issue with any other person in a subsequent proceeding.[1] But the abandonment of the requirement of mutuality is not complete; jurisdictions vary especially with respect to the conditions under which non-mutual *offensive* preclusion will be allowed.

---

[1] See, *e.g.*, Blonder-Tongue Laboratories, Inc. v. University of Illinois Foundation, 402 U.S. 313 (1971); Parklane Hosiery Co. v. Shore, 439 U.S. 322 (1979).

(b) Requirement that the Issue be the Same. A basic requirement for the application of issue preclusion is that the issue in the two adjudications be identical. But that requirement can be tricky when the burden of proof in the two proceedings differs. For example, suppose that in a civil proceeding, the SEC establishes by a preponderance of the evidence that a corporate official intentionally engaged in illegal insider trading. If the official were then criminally prosecuted for intentional insider trading, preclusion would be inappropriate, as the prior adjudication did not establish the elements of the offense *beyond a reasonable doubt*, as is required in a criminal case. But suppose the order of the proceedings was the reverse, and the government first secured a criminal conviction for intentional insider trading. In a subsequent proceeding by the SEC seeking sanctions for insider trading, the prior adjudication would have established what the SEC was attempting to prove—that the official had intentionally engaged in insider trading by at least a preponderance of the evidence—and hence the individual would be subject to preclusion, so long as other requirements were satisfied.

(5) Preclusion Between Criminal and Civil Cases. As the insider trading example illustrates, in principle there is no reason why a civil judgment cannot have issue preclusive effect in a subsequent criminal proceeding (or vice versa). The issue generally does not arise with regard to claim preclusion, as American jurisdictions generally do not permit litigation of civil claims and criminal charges in a single action. With respect to issue preclusion, as the prior Paragraph explains, one has to examine carefully the respective burdens of proof in the two adjudications. But there are situations in which the burden does not vary: examples might include questions about the suppression of evidence under the Fourth Amendment or the Miranda rules, or determinations whether the statute under which a defendant has been charged is constitutional.

(6) Preclusion of Non-Parties. The general rule is that a non-party to a prior litigation is not subject to claim or issue preclusion on the basis of the prior adjudication. See Taylor v. Sturgell, 553 U.S. 880 (2008). However, there are instances in which a non-party to a prior action may be precluded from litigating a claim or an issue in a subsequent proceeding. When preclusion is permitted, the precluded party is often said to be "in privity" with a party to the prior adjudication. But that characterization is largely a conclusion, based on the extent to which the non-party stood in the shoes of, or manifested significant control over, a party to the prior litigation. For discussion of the situations in which a non-party to the first action may be precluded, see the Restatement 2d §§ 39–42.[2]

NOTE ON THE RES JUDICATA EFFECTS OF FEDERAL JUDGMENTS

(1) Source of Law. The United States, like each of the fifty states, has its own law of res judicata; as in other areas of law, there are important commonalities but also notable differences among American jurisdictions.

---

[2]   Since the question of claim or issue preclusion is not regarded as going to the court's subject matter jurisdiction, it is generally agreed that the question may be waived (or indeed forfeited) by failure to raise it in a timely fashion. But since the question does involve the effective use of judicial resources, courts do, on occasion, raise the question *sua sponte*. See the discussion in Arizona v. California, 530 U.S. 392 (2000).

Res judicata law is almost entirely judge-made, and the Supreme Court has held that in the absence of a governing federal statute or rule, the res judicata effect of a federal judgment is determined by "federal common law". See Semtek Int'l, Inc. v. Lockheed Martin Corp., 531 U.S. 497 (2001).

(2) The Effect of a Federal Civil Judgment in a Subsequent State Proceeding. When a federal court decides a federal question, federal preclusion rules govern the preclusive effect of the judgment in subsequent state or federal court proceedings. See, *e.g.*, Deposit Bank v. Frankfort, 191 U.S. 499 (1903); Stoll v. Gottlieb, 305 U.S. 165 (1938). But when the federal judgment was rendered in a diversity case (or was based on state law in other situations governed by the Erie doctrine), the proper source of preclusion rules is more complicated. Until recently, Supreme Court precedent consisted only of pre-Erie decisions, in which the Conformity Act of 1872, 17 Stat. 196, which called for federal practice in actions at law to conform as closely as possible to the practice in the state in which the federal court was located, may have influenced the conclusion that state law controlled. In Dupasseur v. Rochereau, 88 U.S. (21 Wall.) 130, 135 (1874), for instance, the Court stated, with respect to the preclusive effect of a judgment in a diversity case: "The only effect that can be justly claimed for the [federal court] judgment * * * is such as would belong to judgments of the State courts [in the state in which the federal court was sitting] rendered under similar circumstances."

In 2001, the Court revisited this issue in Semtek, Paragraph (1), *supra*. There, a California federal court dismissed a diversity suit "on the merits and with prejudice" on the basis of California's statute of limitations. The plaintiff then filed a new action on the same claim against the same defendant in a Maryland state court, because Maryland's statute of limitations had not yet run. The Maryland courts decided—without looking either to their own law or the law of California—that the doctrine of claim preclusion barred the action, because under Rule 41(b) of the Federal Rules of Civil Procedure, the federal court dismissal "on the merits" had to be accorded claim preclusive effect.

A unanimous Supreme Court, speaking through Justice Scalia, reversed. First, the Court held that Dupasseur did not control because (as noted above) the since-repealed Conformity Act could have affected that decision. Then the Court concluded, for reasons discussed in detail at pp. 620–621, *supra*, that the case was not governed by the provisions of Rule 41(b). Since neither the Full Faith and Credit Clause of the Constitution nor the Full Faith and Credit Statute, 28 U.S.C. § 1738, applies to the judgments of a federal court, the Court continued, "federal common law governs the claim-preclusive effect of a dismissal by a federal court sitting in diversity". As to the content of the federal common law rule in this context, "we think the result decreed by Dupasseur continues to be correct for diversity cases. Since state, rather than federal, substantive law is at issue there is no need for a uniform federal rule. And indeed, nationwide uniformity in the substance of the matter is better served by having the same claim-preclusive rule (the state rule) apply whether the dismissal has been ordered by a state or a federal court. This is, it seems to us, a classic case for adopting, as the federally prescribed rule of decision, the law that would be applied by state courts in the State in which the federal diversity court sits." The Court noted, however, that "[t]his federal reference to state law will not obtain, of course, in situations in which the state law is incompatible with federal interests. If, for example, state law did not accord claim-preclusive effect to dismissals for willful violation of discovery orders, federal courts' interest in the integrity of their own processes might justify a contrary federal rule."

The Court's reliance on federal common law as the source of the governing rule in this case is discussed at p. 621, *supra*. Given the Court's determination that there was no controlling federal statute or Federal Rule of Civil Procedure, that reliance is not surprising in light of the clear federal interest in the integrity and effect of federal court judgments. And as to the decision that federal law would normally adopt state law by reference when the judgment in question had been rendered in a diversity case, the policies underlying the Erie decision and subsequent developments (see pp. 584–625, *supra*) seem to warrant such a reference. (There had, however, been considerable scholarly debate over this question prior to the Semtek decision.) But the Court's explicit statement that state law would be trumped if there were "incompatible" federal interests raises interesting and difficult questions. For example, what is the impact of specific federal rules, such as Rule 23 (class actions) and Rule 13(a) (compulsory counterclaims), which appear to contemplate that certain preclusive effects will flow from actions taken or not taken in the course of federal litigation? And does it matter whether the second action is brought in *state* court (as in Semtek) or *federal* court? See generally Shapiro, Civil Procedure: Preclusion in Civil Actions 147–53 (2001).[1]

(3) Federal Declaratory Judgments. As a general matter, principles of issue preclusion do apply to declaratory judgments, but principles of claim preclusion applicable to judgments in actions for coercive relief do not. Moreover, there are special problems in cases in which a federal declaratory judgment renders determinations on issues of state law. See Shapiro, *State Courts and Federal Declaratory Judgments*, 74 Nw.U.L.Rev. 759 (1979). See also the discussion in Chap. X, p. 1104, *supra*.

A. LITIGATION WITH THE FEDERAL GOVERNMENT

INTRODUCTORY NOTE

The case that follows raises one aspect of an important question: in what circumstances, if any, should the United States as a litigant not be subjected to the "normal" rules of res judicata that apply to private litigants?

---

[1]   For comments on Semtek, see Burbank, *Semtek, Forum Shopping, and Federal Common Law*, 77 Notre Dame L.Rev. 1027 (2002) (generally approving the result but noting the "exquisite complications" presented when a dismissal is based on the first forum's statute of limitations); Woolley, *The Sources of Federal Preclusion Law After Semtek*, 72 U.Cin.L.Rev. 527 (2003) (arguing in favor of limited reliance on the preclusion rules of the initial forum state).

United States v. Mendoza

464 U.S. 154, 104 S.Ct. 568, 78 L.Ed.2d 379 (1984).
Certiorari to the United States Court of Appeals for the Ninth Circuit.

■ JUSTICE REHNQUIST delivered the opinion of the Court.

In 1978 respondent Sergio Mendoza, a Filipino national, filed a petition for naturalization under a statute which by its terms had expired 32 years earlier. Respondent's claim for naturalization was based on the assertion that the Government's administration of the Nationality Act denied him due process of law. Neither the District Court nor the Court of Appeals for the Ninth Circuit ever reached the merits of his claim, because they held that the Government was collaterally estopped from litigating that constitutional issue in view of an earlier decision against the Government in a case brought by other Filipino nationals in the United States District Court for the Northern District of California. We hold that the United States may not be collaterally estopped on an issue such as this, adjudicated against it in an earlier lawsuit brought by a different party. We therefore reverse the judgment of the Court of Appeals.

The facts bearing on respondent's claim to naturalization are not in dispute. In 1942 Congress amended the Nationality Act, § 701 of which provided that noncitizens who served honorably in the Armed Forces of the United States during World War II were exempt from some of the usual requirements for nationality. * * * Congress later provided by amendment that all naturalization petitions seeking to come under § 701 must be filed by December 31, 1946. Section 702 of the Act provided for the overseas naturalization of aliens in active service who were eligible for naturalization under § 701 but who were not within the jurisdiction of any court authorized to naturalize aliens. In order to implement that provision, the Immigration and Naturalization Service from 1943 to 1946 sent representatives abroad to naturalize eligible alien servicemen.

Respondent Mendoza served as a doctor in the Philippine Commonwealth Army from 1941 until his discharge in 1946. Because Japanese occupation of the Philippines had made naturalization of alien servicemen there impossible before the liberation of the Islands, the INS did not designate a representative to naturalize eligible servicemen there until 1945. Because of concerns expressed by the Philippine Government to the United States, however, to the effect that large numbers of Filipinos would be naturalized and would immigrate to the United States just as the Philippines gained their independence, the Attorney General subsequently revoked the naturalization authority of the INS representative. Thus all naturalizations in the Philippines were halted for a 9-month period from late October 1945 until a new INS representative was appointed in August 1946.

Respondent's claim for naturalization is based on the contention that that conduct of the Government deprived him of due process of law in violation of the Fifth Amendment to the United States Constitution, because he was present in the Philippines during part, but not all, of the 9-month period during which there was no authorized INS representative there. The * * * District Court granted [Mendoza's] petition[,] * * *[concluding] that the Government could not relitigate the due process issue because that issue had already been decided against the Government in In re Naturalization of 68 Filipino War Veterans, 406 F.Supp. 931 (N.D.Cal.1975) (hereinafter 68 Filipinos), a decision which the Government had not appealed.

Noting that the doctrine of nonmutual offensive collateral estoppel has been conditionally approved by this Court in Parklane Hosiery Co. v. Shore, 439 U.S. 322 (1979), the Court of Appeals concluded that the District Court had not abused its discretion in applying that doctrine against the United States in this case. * * * For the reasons which follow, we agree with the Government that Parklane Hosiery's approval of nonmutual offensive collateral estoppel is not to be extended to the United States.

Under the judicially developed doctrine of collateral estoppel, once a court has decided an issue of fact or law necessary to its judgment, that decision is conclusive in a subsequent suit based on a different cause of action involving a party to the prior litigation. Montana v. United States, 440 U.S. 147, 153 (1979). Collateral estoppel [issue preclusion], like the related doctrine of res judicata [claim preclusion], serves to "relieve parties of the cost and vexation of multiple lawsuits, conserve judicial resources, and, by preventing inconsistent decisions, encourage reliance on adjudication." Allen v. McCurry, 449 U.S. 90, 94 (1980). In furtherance of those policies, this Court in recent years has broadened the scope of the doctrine of collateral estoppel beyond its common-law limits. It has done so by abandoning the requirement of mutuality of parties, Blonder-Tongue Laboratories, Inc. v. University of Illinois Foundation, 402 U.S. 313 (1971), and by conditionally approving the "offensive" use of collateral estoppel by a nonparty to a prior lawsuit. Parklane Hosiery, *supra*.

In Standefer v. United States, 447 U.S. 10, 24 (1980), however, we emphasized the fact that Blonder-Tongue and Parklane Hosiery involved disputes over private rights between private litigants. We noted that "[i]n such cases, no significant harm flows from enforcing a rule that affords a litigant only one full and fair opportunity to litigate an issue, and [that] there is no sound reason for burdening the courts with repetitive litigation." Here, as in Montana v. United States, the party against whom the estoppel is sought is the United States; but here, unlike in Montana, the party who seeks to preclude the Government from relitigating the issue was not a party to the earlier litigation.

We have long recognized that "the Government is not in a position identical to that of a private litigant," INS v. Hibi, 414 U.S. 5, 8 (1973) (*per curiam*), both because of the geographic breadth of Government litigation and also, most importantly, because of the nature of the issues the Government litigates. * * * [T]he Government is a party to a far greater number of cases on a nationwide basis than even the most litigious private entity; in 1982, the United States was a party to more than 75,000 of the 206,193 filings in the United States District Courts. In the same year the United States was a party to just under 30% of the civil cases appealed from the District Courts to the Court of Appeals. Government litigation frequently involves legal questions of substantial public importance; indeed, because the proscriptions of the United States Constitution are so generally directed at governmental action, many constitutional questions can arise only in the context of litigation to which the Government is a party. Because of those facts the Government is more likely than any private party to be involved in lawsuits against different parties which nonetheless involve the same legal issues.

A rule allowing nonmutual collateral estoppel against the Government in such cases would substantially thwart the development of important questions of law by freezing the first final decision rendered on a particular legal issue. Allowing only one final adjudication would deprive this Court of the benefit it receives from permitting several courts of appeals to explore a difficult question before this Court grants certiorari. Indeed, if nonmutual estoppel were routinely applied against the Government, this Court would have to revise its practice of waiting for a conflict to develop before granting the Government's petitions for certiorari.

The Solicitor General's policy for determining when to appeal an adverse decision would also require substantial revision. The Court of Appeals faulted the Government in this case for failing to appeal a decision that it now contends is erroneous. But * * * [u]nlike a private litigant who generally does not forgo an appeal if he believes that he can prevail, the Solicitor General considers a variety of factors, such as the limited resources of the Government and the crowded dockets of the courts, before authorizing an appeal. The application of nonmutual estoppel against the Government would force the Solicitor General to abandon those prudential concerns and to appeal every adverse decision in order to avoid foreclosing further review.

In addition to those institutional concerns traditionally considered by the Solicitor General, the panoply of important public issues raised in governmental litigation may quite properly lead successive administrations of the Executive Branch to take differing positions with respect to the resolution of a particular issue. While the Executive Branch must of course defer to the Judicial Branch for final resolution of questions of constitutional law, the former nonetheless controls the progress of Government litigation through the federal courts. It would be idle to pretend that the conduct of Government litigation in all its myriad features, from the decision to file a complaint in the United States district court to the decision to petition for certiorari to review a judgment of the court of appeals, is a wholly mechanical procedure which involves no policy choices whatever.

* * * The Government of course may not now undo the consequences of its decision not to appeal the District Court judgment in the 68 Filipinos case; it is bound by that judgment under the principles of res judicata. But we now hold that it is not further bound in a case involving a litigant who was not a party to the earlier litigation.

The Court of Appeals did not endorse a routine application of nonmutual collateral estoppel against the Government, because it recognized that the Government does litigate issues of far-reaching national significance which in some cases, it concluded, might warrant relitigation. But in this case it found no "record evidence" indicating that there was a "crucial need" in the administration of the immigration laws for a redetermination of the due process question decided in 68 Filipinos * * *. The Court of Appeals did not make clear what sort of "record evidence" would have satisfied it that there *was* a "crucial need" for redetermination of the question in this case, but we pretermit further discussion of that approach; we believe that the standard announced by the Court of Appeals for determining when relitigation of a legal issue is to be permitted is so wholly subjective that it affords no guidance to the courts or to the Government. * * *

We hold, therefore, that nonmutual offensive collateral estoppel simply does not apply against the Government in such a way as to preclude relitigation of issues such as those involved in this case. The conduct of Government litigation in the courts of the United States is sufficiently different from the conduct of private civil litigation in those courts so that what might otherwise be economy interests underlying a broad application of collateral estoppel are outweighed by the constraints which peculiarly affect the Government. We think that our conclusion will better allow thorough development of legal doctrine by allowing litigation in multiple forums. Indeed, a contrary result might disserve the economy interests in whose name estoppel is advanced by requiring the Government to abandon virtually any exercise of discretion in seeking to review judgments unfavorable to it. The doctrine of res judicata, of course, prevents the Government from relitigating the same cause of action against the parties to a prior decision, but beyond that point principles of nonmutual collateral estoppel give way to the policies just stated.

Our holding in this case is consistent with each of our prior holdings to which the parties have called our attention, and which we reaffirm. Today in a companion case we hold that the Government may be estopped under certain circumstances from relitigating a question when the parties to the two lawsuits are the same. United States v. Stauffer Chemical Co., [464 U.S.] 165; see also Montana v. United States, 440 U.S. 147 (1979); United States v. Moser, 266 U.S. 236 (1924). None of those cases, however, involve the effort of a party to estop the Government in the absence of mutuality.

The concerns underlying our disapproval of collateral estoppel against the Government are for the most part inapplicable where mutuality is present, as in Stauffer Chemical, Montana, and Moser. The application of an estoppel when the Government is litigating the same issue with the same party avoids the problem of freezing the development of the law because the Government is still free to litigate that issue in the future with some other party. And, where the parties are the same, estopping the Government spares a party that has already prevailed once from having to relitigate—a function it would not serve in the present circumstances. We accordingly hold that the Court of Appeals was wrong in applying nonmutual collateral estoppel against the Government in this case. Its judgment is therefore reversed.

NOTE ON RES JUDICATA IN FEDERAL GOVERNMENT LITIGATION AND ON THE PROBLEM OF ACQUIESCENCE

(1) The Reach of the Mendoza Decision. The Mendoza opinion states: "We hold, therefore, that nonmutual *offensive* collateral estoppel [issue preclusion] simply does not apply against the Government in such a way as to preclude relitigation of issues *such as those involved in this case*" (emphasis added). But among the questions left open are whether a party may invoke nonmutual preclusion against the government either

(a) defensively, or (b) on an issue of fact rather than law. See Kanter v. C.I.R., 590 F.3d 410 (7th Cir.2009) (rejecting a private defendant's arguments that Mendoza did not govern because preclusion was being invoked (a) defensively, and (b) on factual rather than legal issues).

(2) Mutual Preclusion in Government Litigation. As indicated at the end of the Mendoza opinion, the Supreme Court considered the applicability of *mutual* preclusion in government litigation in United States v. Stauffer Chemical Co., 464 U.S. 165 (1984), decided the same day as Mendoza. Stauffer had refused to allow private contractors hired by EPA to inspect one of its chemical plants in Wyoming. In the suit that followed, the Tenth Circuit held (in Stauffer I) that private contractors were not "authorized representatives" of the EPA with statutory authority to inspect the plant. A similar refusal by Stauffer, a short time later at its plant in Tennessee, led to an action by the EPA against it in a Tennessee federal court. The Sixth Circuit held (in Stauffer II) that the government was precluded from relitigating against Stauffer the question of statutory interpretation settled in Stauffer I. The Supreme Court affirmed. Writing for the Court, Justice Rehnquist said:

"[W]e concluded in United States v. Mendoza that [the argument that preclusion against the government will freeze development of the law] is persuasive only to prevent the application of collateral estoppel against the Government in the absence of mutuality. When estoppel is applied in a case where the Government is litigating the same issue arising under virtually identical facts against the same party, as here, the Government's argument loses its force."

Unlike the Tenth Circuit, the Ninth Circuit (in an unrelated case) had interpreted the relevant statute to authorize inspection by private contractors. Bunker Hill Company Lead & Zinc Smelter v. EPA, 658 F.2d 1280 (9th Cir.1981). The EPA argued in Stauffer II that "if it is foreclosed from relitigating the statutory issue with Stauffer, then Stauffer plants within the Ninth Circuit will benefit from a rule precluding inspections by private contractors while plants of Stauffer's competitors will be subject to the Ninth Circuit's contrary rule", and "an inequitable administration of the law" will result. Compare Restatement 2d § 28(2)(b) comment *c* (problems of inequality are particularly significant if "one of the parties is a government agency responsible for continuing administration of a body of law that affects members of the public generally, as in the case of tax law"). The Court, however, refused to address the question whether preclusion would operate against the EPA in an action against Stauffer in the Ninth Circuit.

Justice White, concurring, agreed that further litigation of the statutory interpretation issue was foreclosed between the EPA and Stauffer in the Tenth Circuit, and (though the question was more difficult) in the Sixth Circuit as well. But Justice White stated that he would not give Stauffer the benefit of estoppel in a circuit that had adopted a contrary rule on the merits, as had the Ninth Circuit. Moreover, preclusion in such circumstances would create inconsistency "more dramatic and more troublesome than a normal circuit split; by definition, it compounds that problem. It would be dubious enough were the EPA unable to employ private contractors to inspect Stauffer's plants within the Ninth Circuit even though it can use such contractors in inspecting other plants. But the disarray is more extensive. By the same application of mutual collateral estoppel, the EPA could presumably use private contractors to inspect Bunker Hill's plants in circuits like the Tenth, despite the fact that other companies are not subject to such inspections. Furthermore * * * the EPA can relitigate this matter as to other companies. As a result, in, say, the First Circuit, the EPA must follow one rule as to Bunker Hill, the opposite as to Stauffer, and, depending on any ruling by that Circuit, one or the other or a third as to other companies".

Would Justice White's solution cause complexities of its own? Suppose the Sixth Circuit were later to decide in the EPA's favor in a suit brought against a different defendant. Would Stauffer be able to rely on issue preclusion in the Sixth Circuit thereafter?

(3) The Question of Party Identity. Under Mendoza, there can be no issue preclusion against the government without mutuality. Questions can therefore arise whether the same government party was involved in both the prior and the current litigation. Sunshine Anthracite Coal Co. v. Adkins, 310 U.S. 381, 402–03 (1940), a case involving an IRS claim of issue preclusion resulting from a prior judgment in favor of the National Bituminous Coal Commission, held that "a judgment in a suit between a party and a representative of the United States is *res judicata* in relitigation of the same issue between that party and another officer of the government." Compare the materials discussing the question of when the United States is bound by judgments rendered in actions against its individual officials, Chap. IX, p. 895, *supra*.[1]

(4) Executive or Administrative Nonacquiescence. Difficult questions about the fair administration of justice can arise when the government is faced with lower court rulings it believes to be wrong. Mendoza established that res judicata does not bar the government from relitigating an issue against a new party. And the policy arguments that the Supreme Court relied on in Mendoza make it plain that the government may relitigate issues in order to persuade other courts that the first decision was erroneous.

Should there nevertheless be some limits on the government's privilege to relitigate? Suppose that the government loses on an issue in Circuit A. May it—and should it—take the position that, even in Circuit A, it will not "acquiesce" in the decision—that it will require other citizens to litigate the question in district courts even though those courts are bound to reject the government's position? Is this simply bullying, by putting pressure on those citizens who cannot afford litigation to forgo their rights? Can nonacquiescence be justified if the government's purpose is to generate either an intracircuit conflict or an *en banc* reconsideration by Circuit A—at least if subsequent, well-considered opinions elsewhere have rejected the views of Circuit A?

---

[1]   Parallel issues of privity can arise in litigation involving state officials. If a federal court, in an action brought against a state officer (on account of state sovereign immunity) rather than against the state itself, holds that a state statute is unconstitutional, is the state barred from prosecuting the federal plaintiff for violating the statute? Shapiro, *State Courts and Federal Declaratory Judgments*, 74 Nw.U.L.Rev. 759, 764 & n. 31 (1979), argues that the answer should be yes. See also Jackson, *The Supreme Court, the Eleventh Amendment, and State Sovereign Immunity*, 98 Yale L.J. 1, 67 n. 276 (1988) (supporting Shapiro's view and comparing Steffel v. Thompson, 415 U.S. 452, 477 (White, J., concurring) (judgment would be conclusive in subsequent prosecution against federal plaintiff), with *id.* at 482 n. 3 (Rehnquist, J., concurring) (reserving question)); *cf.* Idaho v. Coeur d'Alene Tribe, 521 U.S. 261, 305–06 (1997) (Souter, J., dissenting) (suggesting that a holding rendered in a suit against government officials might not bind the government itself in a later action).

Suppose that the government's position on an issue is rejected in three or four—or seven or eight—circuits. Is the government free to—and should it—relitigate the issue in the remaining circuits?

These issues have generated intense controversy. A number of federal agencies have regularly refused to acquiesce in circuit court decisions. Between 1981 and 1984, for example, the Social Security Administration (SSA)—acting at the instance of Congress in re-evaluating all cases where disability payments were being made—terminated an unusually high number of disability payments. By 1984, all but one circuit had struck down the SSA's termination criteria. The SSA nevertheless refused to acquiesce in these decisions, prompting at least one judge to threaten the Secretary with contempt proceedings, see Hillhouse v. Harris, 715 F.2d 428, 430 (8th Cir.1983) (McMillian, J., concurring), and at one point causing the Ninth Circuit to uphold a preliminary injunction ordering the Secretary to reinstate beneficiaries terminated pursuant to the nonacquiescence policy, Lopez v. Heckler, 725 F.2d 1489 (9th Cir.), *vacated and remanded*, 469 U.S. 1082 (1984). And in the Second Circuit, a class action led to a settlement agreement in which the SSA agreed, *inter alia*, to instruct all its adjudicators acting in cases falling within the circuit's jurisdiction to comply with holdings in Second Circuit disability decisions. Stieberger v. Sullivan, 792 F.Supp. 1376 (S.D.N.Y.), *modified by* 801 F.Supp. 1079 (S.D.N.Y.1992).[2]

In thinking about the practice of nonacquiescence, consider the impact of class actions. A judgment against the agency is res judicata as to the entire class; thus, as to class members, doesn't the government lose the ability not to "acquiesce"? If there are some valid reasons for nonacquiescence, should a federal court hesitate to certify a nationwide class action against the government?[3]

Consider also the relationship of nonacquiescence to the Chevron doctrine (see p. 357, *supra*). Insofar as Chevron requires courts to defer to agency interpretations of the law, doesn't it limit the occasions in which agencies have to consider whether to yield to judicial interpretations with

---

[2]   Several years later, SSA adopted regulations providing that when the agency's position on an issue of law is rejected by a court of appeals, the agency will promptly publish an intracircuit acquiescence ruling unless further review is sought or other conditions are met. See 20 C.F.R. § 404.985.

Whatever the case for intracircuit acquiescence, when the venue for judicial review is confined to a particular circuit, the argument for acquiescence at the administrative stage appears to collapse if there is a choice of venue for judicial review and at least one of the circuits in which review may be sought has not declared itself on the issue. But if review in such a case is sought in a circuit that has declared itself adversely to the agency, may the agency properly argue for a change in the circuit's law? Should the panel hearing the case be free—despite a rule or prevailing practice in the circuit in other kinds of cases—to disagree with another panel in the same circuit without an en banc hearing by the full bench? For an affirmative answer to both questions, see White, *Time for a New Approach: Why the Judiciary Should Disregard the "Law of the Circuit" When Confronting Nonacquiescence by the National Labor Relations Board*, 69 N.C.L.Rev. 639 (1991).

[3]   For further discussion of these problems, see Estreicher & Revesz, *Nonacquiescence by Federal Administrative Agencies*, 98 Yale L.J. 679 (1989); Diller & Morawetz, *Intracircuit Nonacquiescence and the Breakdown of the Rule of Law: A Response to Estreicher & Revesz*, 99 Yale L.J. 801 (1990); Estreicher & Revesz, *The Uneasy Case Against Intracircuit Nonacquiescence: A Reply*, 99 Yale L.J. 831 (1990); Coenen, *The Constitutional Case Against Nonacquiescence*, 75 Minn.L.Rev. 1339 (1991); Schwartz, *Nonacquiescence, Crowell v. Benson, and Administrative Adjudication*, 77 Geo.L.J. 1815 (1989).

which they disagree? See National Cable & Telecommunications Ass'n v. Brand X Internet Services, 545 U.S. 967 (2005).[4]

B. THE PRECLUSIVE EFFECTS OF STATE COURT JUDGMENTS IN FEDERAL COURT

INTRODUCTORY NOTE

The previous subsection focused on the preclusive effect of *federal* court judgments on issues of federal law. This subsection examines the preclusive effect of *state* court judgments on issues of or claims under federal law presented in a subsequent federal proceeding.

Allen v. McCurry

449 U.S. 90, 101 S.Ct. 411, 66 L.Ed.2d 308 (1980).
Certiorari to the United States Court of Appeals for the Eighth Circuit.

■ JUSTICE STEWART delivered the opinion of the Court.

At a hearing before his criminal trial in a Missouri court, the respondent, Willie McCurry, invoked the Fourth and Fourteenth Amendments to suppress evidence that had been seized by the police. The trial court denied the suppression motion in part, and McCurry was subsequently convicted after a jury trial. The conviction was later affirmed on appeal. Because he did not assert that the state courts had denied him a "full and fair opportunity" to litigate his search and seizure claim, McCurry was barred by this Court's decision in Stone v. Powell, 428 U.S. 465, from seeking a writ of habeas corpus in a federal district court. Nevertheless, he sought federal-court redress for the alleged constitutional violation by bringing a damages suit under 42 U.S.C. § 1983 against the officers who had entered his home and seized the evidence in question. We granted certiorari to consider whether the unavailability of federal habeas corpus prevented the police officers from raising the state courts' partial rejection of McCurry's constitutional claim as a collateral estoppel defense to the § 1983 suit against them for damages.

I

In April 1977, several undercover police officers, following an informant's tip that McCurry was dealing in heroin, went to his house in St. Louis, Mo., to attempt a purchase. Two officers, petitioners Allen and Jacobsmeyer, knocked on the front door * * *. When McCurry opened the door, the two officers asked to buy some heroin "caps." McCurry went back into the house and returned soon thereafter, firing a pistol at and seriously wounding Allen and Jacobsmeyer. After a gun battle with the other officers and their reinforcements, McCurry retreated into the house; he emerged again when the police demanded that he surrender.

---

[4] For discussion, see Modesitt, *The Hundred-Years War: The Ongoing Battle Between Courts and Agencies over the Right to Interpret Federal Law*, 74 Mo.L.Rev. 949 (2009).

Several officers then entered the house without a warrant, purportedly to search for other persons inside. One of the officers seized drugs and other contraband that lay in plain view, as well as additional contraband he found in dresser drawers and in auto tires on the porch.

McCurry was charged with possession of heroin and assault with intent to kill. At the pretrial suppression hearing, the trial judge excluded the evidence seized from the dresser drawers and tires, but denied suppression of the evidence found in plain view. McCurry was convicted of both the heroin and assault offenses.

McCurry subsequently filed the present § 1983 action for $1 million in damages against petitioners Allen and Jacobsmeyer, other unnamed individual police officers, and the city of St. Louis and its police department. The complaint alleged a conspiracy to violate McCurry's Fourth Amendment rights, an unconstitutional search and seizure of his house, and an assault on him by unknown police officers after he had been arrested and handcuffed. * * * The District Court apparently understood the gist of the complaint to be the allegedly unconstitutional search and seizure and granted summary judgment, holding that collateral estoppel prevented McCurry from relitigating the search-and-seizure question already decided against him in the state courts.

The Court of Appeals reversed the judgment and remanded the case for trial. The appellate court said it was not holding that collateral estoppel was generally inapplicable in a § 1983 suit raising issues determined against the federal plaintiff in a state criminal trial. But noting that Stone v. Powell, *supra*, barred McCurry from federal habeas corpus relief, and invoking "the special role of the federal courts in protecting civil rights," the court concluded that the § 1983 suit was McCurry's only route to a federal forum for his constitutional claim and directed the trial court to allow him to proceed to trial unencumbered by collateral estoppel.

II

The federal courts have traditionally adhered to the related doctrines of res judicata [claim preclusion] and collateral estoppel [issue preclusion]. * * *5 As this Court and other courts have often recognized, res judicata and collateral estoppel relieve parties of the cost and vexation of multiple lawsuits, conserve judicial resources, and, by preventing inconsistent decisions, encourage reliance on adjudication. * * *.7

The federal courts generally have also consistently accorded preclusive effect to issues decided by state courts. *E.g.*, Montana v. United States, *supra*; Angel v. Bullington, 330 U.S. 183. Thus, res

---

5   * * * Contrary to a suggestion in the dissenting opinion, n. 12, this case does not involve the question whether a § 1983 claimant can litigate in federal court an issue he might have raised but did not raise in previous litigation.

7   * * * Contrary to the suggestion of the dissent, our decision today does not "fashion" any new, more stringent doctrine of collateral estoppel, nor does it hold that the collateral-estoppel effect of a state-court decision turns on the single factor of whether the State gave the federal claimant a full and fair opportunity to litigate a federal question. Our decision does not "fashion" any doctrine of collateral estoppel at all. Rather, it construes § 1983 to determine whether the conventional doctrine of collateral estoppel applies to the case at hand. It must be emphasized that the question whether any exceptions or qualifications within the bounds of that doctrine might ultimately defeat a collateral-estoppel defense in this case is not before us.

judicata and collateral estoppel not only reduce unnecessary litigation and foster reliance on adjudication, but also promote the comity between state and federal courts that has been recognized as a bulwark of the federal system.

Indeed, * * * Congress has specifically required all federal courts to give preclusive effect to state-court judgments whenever the courts of the State from which the judgments emerged would do so:

> "[J]udicial proceedings [of any court of any State] shall have the same full faith and credit in every court within the United States and its Territories and Possessions as they have by law or usage in the courts of such State. * * * " 28 U.S.C. § 1738.

It is against this background that we examine the relationship of § 1983 and collateral estoppel, and the decision of the Court of Appeals in this case.

III

This Court has never directly decided whether the rules of res judicata and collateral estoppel are generally applicable to § 1983 actions. But in Preiser v. Rodriguez, 411 U.S. 475, 497, the Court noted with implicit approval the view of other federal courts that res judicata principles fully apply to civil rights suits brought under that statute. And the virtually unanimous view of the Courts of Appeals since Preiser has been that § 1983 presents no categorical bar to the application of res judicata and collateral estoppel concepts. * * *

Because the requirement of mutuality of estoppel was still alive in the federal courts until well into this century * * *, the drafters of the 1871 Civil Rights Act, of which § 1983 is a part, may have had less reason to concern themselves with rules of preclusion than a modern Congress would. Nevertheless, in 1871 res judicata and collateral estoppel could certainly have applied in federal suits following state-court litigation between the same parties or their privies, and nothing in the language of § 1983 remotely expresses any congressional intent to contravene the common-law rules of preclusion or to repeal the express statutory requirements of the predecessor of 28 U.S.C. § 1738. Section 1983 creates a new federal cause of action. It says nothing about the preclusive effect of state-court judgments.[12]

Moreover, the legislative history of § 1983 does not in any clear way suggest that Congress intended to repeal or restrict the traditional doctrines of preclusion. * * * [O]f course the debates show that one strong motive behind its enactment was grave congressional concern that the state courts had been deficient in protecting federal rights. But in the context of the legislative history as a whole, this congressional concern lends only the most equivocal support to any argument that, in cases where the state courts have recognized the constitutional claims asserted and provided fair procedures for determining them, Congress intended to override § 1738 or the common-law rules of collateral estoppel and res judicata. Since repeals by implication are disfavored, * * * much clearer

---

[12] * * * [T]he traditional exception to res judicata for habeas corpus review, see Preiser v. Rodriguez, 411 U.S. 475, 497, provides no analogy to § 1983 cases, since that exception finds its source in the unique purpose of habeas corpus—to release the applicant for the writ from unlawful confinement.

support than this would be required to hold that § 1738 and the traditional rules of preclusion are not applicable to § 1983 suits.[14] * * *

To the extent that it did intend to change the balance of power over federal questions between the state and federal courts, the 42d Congress was acting in a way thoroughly consistent with the doctrines of preclusion. In reviewing the legislative history of § 1983 in Monroe v. Pape[, 365 U.S. 167 (1961)], the Court inferred that Congress had intended a federal remedy in three circumstances: where state substantive law was facially unconstitutional, where state procedural law was inadequate to allow full litigation of a constitutional claim, and where state procedural law, though adequate in theory, was inadequate in practice. In short, the federal courts could step in where the state courts were unable or unwilling to protect federal rights. This understanding of § 1983 might well support an exception to res judicata and collateral estoppel where state law did not provide fair procedures for the litigation of constitutional claims, or where a state court failed to even acknowledge the existence of the constitutional principle on which a litigant based his claim. Such an exception, however, would be essentially the same as the important general limit on rules of preclusion that already exists: Collateral estoppel does not apply where the party against whom an earlier court decision is asserted did not have a full and fair opportunity to litigate the claim or issue decided by the first court. But the Court's view of § 1983 in Monroe lends no strength to any argument that Congress intended to allow relitigation of federal issues decided after a full and fair hearing in a state court simply because the state court's decision may have been erroneous.[17]

The Court of Appeals in this case * * * concluded that since Stone v. Powell had removed McCurry's right to a hearing of his Fourth Amendment claim in federal habeas corpus, collateral estoppel should not deprive him of a federal judicial hearing of that claim in a § 1983 suit.

Stone v. Powell does not provide a logical doctrinal source for the court's ruling. This Court in Stone assessed the costs and benefits of the judge-made exclusionary rule within the boundaries of the federal courts' statutory power to issue writs of habeas corpus, and decided that the incremental deterrent effect that the issuance of the writ in Fourth Amendment cases might have on police conduct did not justify the cost

---

[14] To the extent that Congress in the post-Civil War period did intend to deny full faith and credit to state-court decisions on constitutional issues, it expressly chose the very different means of postjudgment removal for state-court defendants whose civil rights were threatened by biased state courts and who therefore "are denied or cannot enforce [their civil rights] in the courts or judicial tribunals of the State." Act of Apr. 9, 1866, ch. 31, § 3, 14 Stat. 27.

[17] The dissent suggests that the Court's decision in England v. Medical Examiners, 375 U.S. 411, demonstrates the impropriety of affording preclusive effect to the state-court decision in this case. The England decision is inapposite to the question before us. In the England case, a party first submitted to a federal court his claim that a state statute violated his constitutional rights. The federal court abstained and remitted the plaintiff to the state courts * * *. This Court held that in such a circumstance, a plaintiff who properly reserved the federal issue by informing the state courts of his intention to return to federal court, if necessary, was not precluded from litigating the federal question in federal court. The holding in England depended entirely on this Court's view of the purpose of abstention in such a case: Where a plaintiff properly invokes federal court jurisdiction in the first instance on a federal claim, the federal court has a duty to accept that jurisdiction. Abstention may serve only to postpone, rather than to abdicate, jurisdiction, since its purpose is to determine whether resolution of the federal question is even necessary, or to obviate the risk of a federal court's erroneous construction of state law. These concerns have no bearing whatsoever on the present case.

the writ imposed upon the fair administration of criminal justice. The Stone decision concerns only the prudent exercise of federal-court jurisdiction under 28 U.S.C. § 2254. It has no bearing on § 1983 suits or on the question of the preclusive effect of state-court judgments.

The actual basis of the Court of Appeals' holding appears to be a generally framed principle that every person asserting a federal right is entitled to one unencumbered opportunity to litigate that right in a federal district court, regardless of the legal posture in which the federal claim arises. But the authority for this principle is difficult to discern. It cannot lie in the Constitution, which makes no such guarantee, but leaves the scope of the jurisdiction of the federal district courts to the wisdom of Congress. And no such authority is to be found in § 1983 itself. * * *

* * *

The only other conceivable basis for finding a universal right to litigate a federal claim in a federal district court is hardly a legal basis at all, but rather a general distrust of the capacity of the state courts to render correct decisions on constitutional issues. It is ironic that Stone v. Powell provided the occasion for the expression of such an attitude in the present litigation, in view of this Court's emphatic reaffirmation in that case of the constitutional obligation of the state courts to uphold federal law, and its expression of confidence in their ability to do so.

The Court of Appeals erred in holding that McCurry's inability to obtain federal habeas corpus relief upon his Fourth Amendment claim renders the doctrine of collateral estoppel inapplicable to his § 1983 suit.[25] Accordingly, the judgment is reversed, and the case is remanded to the Court of Appeals for proceedings consistent with this opinion.

It is so ordered.

■ JUSTICE BLACKMUN, with whom JUSTICE BRENNAN and JUSTICE MARSHALL join, dissenting.

* * *

* * * In my view, the Court * * * ignores the clear import of the legislative history of [42 U.S.C. § 1983] and disregards the important federal policies that underlie its enforcement. It also shows itself insensitive both to the significant differences between the § 1983 remedy and the exclusionary rule, and to the pressures upon a criminal defendant that make a free choice of forum illusory. I do not doubt that principles of preclusion are to be given such effect as is appropriate in a § 1983 action. In many cases, the denial of res judicata or collateral estoppel effect would serve no purpose and would harm relations between federal and state tribunals. Nonetheless, the Court's analysis in this particular case * * * works injustice on this § 1983 plaintiff, and it makes more difficult the consistent protection of constitutional rights, a consideration that was at the core of the enacters' intent. * * *

* * * Although the legislators of the 42d Congress did not expressly state whether the then existing common-law doctrine of preclusion would survive enactment of § 1983, they plainly anticipated more than the creation of a federal statutory remedy to be administered indifferently by

---

[25] We do not decide *how* the body of collateral-estoppel doctrine or 28 U.S.C. § 1738 should apply in this case.

either a state or a federal court. The legislative intent, as expressed by supporters and understood by opponents, was to restructure relations between the state and federal courts. * * * The availability of the federal forum was not meant to turn on whether, in an individual case, the state procedures were adequate. Assessing the state of affairs as a whole, Congress specifically made a determination that federal oversight of constitutional determinations through the federal courts was necessary to ensure the effective enforcement of constitutional rights.

[Justice Blackmun's analysis of the legislative history is omitted.]

I appreciate that the legislative history is capable of alternative interpretations. I would have thought, however, that our prior decisions made very clear which reading is required. The Court repeatedly has recognized that § 1983 embodies a strong congressional policy in favor of the federal courts' acting as the primary and final arbiters of constitutional rights. In Monroe v. Pape, 365 U.S. 167 (1961), the Court held that Congress passed the legislation in order to substitute a federal forum for the ineffective, though plainly available, state remedies. * * * In Mitchum v. Foster, 407 U.S. 225 (1972), the Court reiterated its understanding of the effect of § 1983 upon state and federal relations:

> "Section 1983 was thus a product of a vast transformation from the concepts of federalism that had prevailed in the late 18th century. . . . The very purpose of § 1983 was to interpose the federal courts between the States and the people, as guardians of the people's federal rights * * *." *Id.*, at 242.

At the very least, it is inconsistent now to narrow, if not repudiate, the meaning of Monroe and Mitchum and to alter our prior understanding of the distribution of power between the state and federal courts.

* * *

The Court now fashions a new doctrine of preclusion, applicable only to actions brought under § 1983, that is more strict and more confining than the federal rules of preclusion applied in other cases. * * *

* * * [T]he Court states that the collateral-estoppel effect of prior state adjudication should turn on only one factor, namely, what it considers the "one general limitation" inherent in the doctrine of preclusion: "that the concept of collateral estoppel cannot apply when the party against whom the earlier decision is asserted did not have a 'full and fair opportunity' to litigate that issue in the earlier case." If that one factor is present, the Court asserts, the litigant properly should be barred from relitigating the issue in federal court.[12] One cannot deny that this factor is an important one. I do not believe, however, that the doctrine of preclusion requires the inquiry to be so narrow, and my understanding of the policies underlying § 1983 would lead me to consider all relevant factors in each case before concluding that preclusion was warranted.

In this case, the police officers seek to prevent a criminal defendant from relitigating the constitutionality of their conduct in searching his house, after the state trial court had found that conduct in part violative of the defendant's Fourth Amendment rights and in part justified by the

---

[12] This articulation of the preclusion doctrine of course would bar a § 1983 litigant from relitigating any issue he *might* have raised, as well as any issue he actually litigated in his criminal trial.

circumstances. I doubt that the police officers, now defendants in this § 1983 action, can be considered to have been in privity with the State in its role as prosecutor. Therefore, only "issue preclusion" is at stake.

The following factors persuade me to conclude that this respondent should not be precluded from asserting his claim in federal court. First, at the time § 1983 was passed, a non-party's ability, as a practical matter, to invoke collateral estoppel was nonexistent. One could not preclude an opponent from relitigating an issue in a new cause of action, though that issue had been determined conclusively in a prior proceeding, unless there was "mutuality." Additionally, the definitions of "cause of action" and "issue" were narrow. As a result, and obviously, no preclusive effect could arise out of a criminal proceeding that would affect subsequent *civil* litigation. Thus, the 42d Congress could not have anticipated or approved that a criminal defendant, tried and convicted in state court, would be precluded from raising against police officers a constitutional claim arising out of his arrest.

Also, the process of deciding in a state criminal trial whether to exclude or admit evidence is not at all the equivalent of a § 1983 proceeding. The remedy sought in the latter is utterly different. In bringing the civil suit the criminal defendant does not seek to challenge his conviction collaterally. At most, he wins damages. In contrast, the exclusion of evidence may prevent a criminal conviction. A trial court, faced with the decision whether to exclude relevant evidence, confronts institutional pressures that may cause it to give a different shape to the Fourth Amendment right from what would result in civil litigation of a damages claim. Also, the issue whether to exclude evidence is subsidiary to the purpose of a criminal trial, which is to determine the guilt or innocence of the defendant, and a trial court, at least subconsciously, must weigh the potential damage to the truth-seeking process caused by excluding relevant evidence. * * *

A state criminal defendant cannot be held to have chosen "voluntarily" to litigate his Fourth Amendment claim in the state court. The risk of conviction puts pressure upon him to raise all possible defenses. He also faces uncertainty about the wisdom of forgoing litigation on *any* issue, for there is the possibility that he will be held to have waived his right to appeal on that issue. The "deliberate bypass" of state procedures, which the imposition of collateral estoppel under these circumstances encourages, surely is not a preferred goal. To hold that a criminal defendant who raises a Fourth Amendment claim at his criminal trial "freely and without reservation submits his federal claims for decision by the state courts," see England v. Medical Examiners, 375 U.S. [411, 419 (1964)], is to deny reality. The criminal defendant is an involuntary litigant in the state tribunal, and against him all the forces of the State are arrayed. To force him to a choice between forgoing either a potential defense or a federal forum for hearing his constitutional civil claim is fundamentally unfair.

I would affirm the judgment of the Court of Appeals.

———

NOTE ON 28 U.S.C. § 1738 AND THE RES JUDICATA EFFECT OF STATE JUDGMENTS[1]

(1) The Rationale of the McCurry Decision.

(a) Assuming that in general federal courts should give preclusive effect to state court determinations of federal issues, is the result in McCurry so easily squared with the jurisprudence that has evolved under § 1983? As developed in earlier chapters, and as emphasized in Justice Blackmun's dissent, that jurisprudence recognizes the right of a litigant asserting a cause of action under § 1983 ordinarily to resort to a federal court, state law and available state remedies notwithstanding. And as both opinions in McCurry recognize, when Pullman abstention is appropriate, the federal plaintiff can retain the ability to return to federal court for a determination of the federal claim. When the doctrine of Younger v. Harris requires abstention, should the principles of res judicata limit the person seeking federal relief to direct Supreme Court review (or such limited collateral review as may be available in habeas corpus in the case of a criminal conviction)? (Recall that the Supreme Court today reviews only in the range of 8–12 state court judgments annually.) Should the federal courts be permitted, consistently with the spirit of § 1983 and the context of its enactment, to make exceptions to general rules of preclusion in order to give special consideration to the interest of a litigant in obtaining a federal court determination of a federal claim?

(b) The McCurry Court left open a number of difficult questions. (i) The Court noted the relevance of § 1738 as "background", but at the same time insisted that it was not deciding exactly "how" res judicata applies in § 1983 actions. (ii) The Court reserved the question whether preclusion could or should apply to matters that could have been but were not raised in the state courts, and did not indicate whether this issue turned on federal or state law. (iii) Nor did the Court specify the source or content of the rule that res judicata does not apply when there was no "full and fair opportunity" to litigate in the prior adjudication.

Many of these questions have been resolved in the Court's later opinions—opinions that have in turn generated further controversy.[2]

(2) The Kremer Decision and the Role of State Law. Kremer v. Chemical Constr. Corp., 456 U.S. 461 (1982), squarely held, in a way that Allen v. McCurry does not, that it is the Full Faith and Credit Statute, 28 U.S.C. § 1738, that commands the federal courts to give state court resolutions of federal questions the same preclusive effect that the courts of the rendering state would give them—at least absent a countervailing command in another federal statute. Kremer involved not § 1983, but Title VII of the Civil Rights Act of 1964, which provides that employment discrimination charges must initially be filed with the state agency that administers state antidiscrimination laws. Thereafter, a complainant may file a claim with the federal EEOC, which is required to "accord substantial

---

[1]   This chapter does not focus on the effect to be given in the courts of one state to judicial proceedings in the courts of *another state*, a topic that is a major subject of study with respect to the Full Faith and Credit Clause and its implementation. Some of the issues raised in that context are the same as, or similar to, those discussed in this Note, which addresses the effects of a state judgment in a subsequent *federal* proceeding.

[2]   See, *e.g.*, Shreve, *Preclusion and Federal Choice of Law*, 64 Tex.L.Rev. 1209 (1986); Althouse, *Tapping the State Court Resource*, 44 Vand.L.Rev. 953, 995 (1991).

weight" to the state agency decision. Title VII also gives a complainant the right, after state and federal agency determinations of his claim, to a trial de novo in federal (or state) court. In Kremer the complainant had unsuccessfully appealed an unfavorable state agency determination to the New York courts before filing with the EEOC and, after failing there, bringing suit in a federal district court. By a bare majority, the Supreme Court held that neither the grant in Title VII of a right to a trial de novo in court following the completion of administrative proceedings, nor the provision that state agency findings be accorded "substantial weight" by the EEOC, effected an implied partial repeal of § 1738. As a result, the state court's judgment rejecting the claim precluded the federal action to the same extent that the judgment would preclude a second action in the New York state courts. Thus, Kremer's decision to appeal from the state agency to the state courts cost him his right to de novo federal review.

The state court in Kremer had determined only that the state agency's decision had not been "arbitrary or capricious". In dissent, Justice Blackmun argued that because "the Appellate Division made no finding one way or the other concerning the *merits*" of the discrimination claim, "although it claims to grant a state *court* decision preclusive effect, in fact the Court bars petitioner's suit based on the state *agency's* decision of no probable cause. The Court thereby disregards the express provisions of Title VII, for * * * Congress has decided that an adverse state agency decision will not prevent a complainant's subsequent Title VII suit".

Is there a convincing answer to Justice Blackmun's argument?

The Court in Kremer also considered the "full and fair opportunity to litigate" exception to preclusion. Noting that neither the source nor content of the exception had been specified in previous cases, the Court stated that "for present purposes, where we are bound by the statutory directive of § 1738, state proceedings need do no more than satisfy the minimum procedural requirements of the Fourteenth Amendment's Due Process Clause in order to qualify for the full faith and credit guaranteed by federal law".[3]

---

[3]   For a striking instance of the application of McCurry and Kremer, see San Remo Hotel, L.P. v. City and County of San Francisco, 545 U.S. 323 (2005), also discussed at pp. 224, 1115, *supra*. In this case, plaintiffs had brought a federal court action challenging a city ordinance as a violation, both on its face and as applied, of the federal Constitution's Takings Clause. The Ninth Circuit decided that Pullman abstention was appropriate with respect to the facial challenge, and that the as-applied challenge was unripe because the plaintiffs had not yet sought compensation under state law. The plaintiffs then went to state court and argued that the ordinance violated the Takings Clause of the California constitution. The state supreme court, noting that it had interpreted that clause to be co-extensive with the federal Takings Clause, upheld the ordinance both on its face and as applied. Plaintiffs then returned to federal court on their federal claims. But the Supreme Court held that the issues determined in the state proceedings were entitled to preclusive effect and, as a result, the federal suit was effectively barred.

On the facial challenge, the Court held that while the England case (discussed in both opinions in McCurry and at p. 1115, *supra*) allowed plaintiffs to renew their facial challenge following federal court abstention, it did not protect against issue preclusion on issues actually determined in the state courts. On the as-applied challenge, the rule of the England case was not relevant at all, since the original claim was dismissed for lack of ripeness, and the Court held that issue preclusion was required by § 1738 even though existing doctrine compelled the plaintiffs to seek compensation in state court before asserting their federal claim. In answer to plaintiffs' argument that they should not lose their ability to litigate their federal claim in federal court as a result of being forced to go to state court first, the Court responded: "We have repeatedly held * * * that issues actually decided in valid state-court judgments may well

(3) The Migra Decision. Further ambiguities in the Court's opinion in Allen v. McCurry were resolved in Migra v. Warren City School Dist., 465 U.S. 75 (1984), in an opinion—this time for a surprisingly unanimous Court—written by Justice Blackmun. Migra was an elementary school supervisor who had been fired from her job. She brought a successful suit in the Ohio courts for damages and reinstatement, alleging only breach of contract and tortious interference with an employment contract. Thereafter she filed a second action under § 1983 in federal court, alleging that her dismissal violated the First, Fifth, and Fourteenth Amendments and seeking, *inter alia*, punitive damages. The Supreme Court held that § 1738 governed and required *claim* preclusion to the same extent that the judgment would be given preclusive effect by the Ohio courts.

Justice White's concurrence, joined by Chief Justice Burger and Justice Powell, stated that it would be desirable to allow federal courts to use federal res judicata law to give state court judgments preclusive effect even if state res judicata doctrine would not bar relitigation in the state courts. However, in view of the "long standing" construction of § 1738 as allowing a federal court to give a state judgment "no greater efficacy" than would the judgment-rendering state, Justice White agreed with the Court's disposition.

(4) Arguments for Alternative Approaches. Several commentators have taken issue with the Court's assumption that under § 1738, the preclusive effect of a state court judgment on an issue of federal law is measured entirely by state preclusion law (subject only to due process limits or to congressional repeal of § 1738 with respect to particular matters). Thus, Professor Burbank has argued that while a state court determining the preclusive effect of a prior state judgment involving federal law would usually apply the forum state's res judicata law, in some cases federal common law rules governing preclusion should supervene. For example, even if, in a case like Allen v. McCurry, the subsequent § 1983 action had been filed in state court, a state court might be required to apply federal common law limiting the preclusive effect of a ruling on a search and seizure question in a suppression hearing in which no discovery is available and the rules of evidence do not apply. And because § 1738 mandates only that the federal court apply *the same law* that the state court would, a federal court should apply federal common law rules in those instances when a state court would be obligated to do so.[4]

Consider in this regard the reiteration, in ASARCO Inc. v. Kadish, 490 U.S. 605 (1989), p. 158, *supra*, of suggestions in earlier decisions (*e.g.*, Fidelity Nat'l Bank & Trust Co. v. Swope, 274 U.S. 123 (1927)) that if a state court decision on a question of federal law cannot be reviewed by the Supreme Court (because the state proceedings did not satisfy Article III's justiciability requirements), the state court decision might not have res judicata effect in a subsequent federal proceeding. ASARCO made no reference to the line of decisions, beginning with Allen v. McCurry, that read § 1738 as obliging the federal courts to adhere to state res judicata doctrine.

---

deprive plaintiffs of the 'right' to have their federal claims relitigated in federal court. This is so even when the plaintiff would have preferred not to litigate in state court, but was required to do so * * *. The relevant question * * * is whether the state court actually decided an issue of fact or law that was necessary to its judgment."

[4] See Burbank, *Interjurisdictional Preclusion, Full Faith and Credit and Federal Common Law: A General Approach*, 71 Cornell L.Rev. 733 (1986); Burbank, *Federal Judgments Law: Sources of Authority and Sources of Rules*, 70 Tex.L.Rev. 1551 (1992).

Don't ASARCO and the precedents on which it relies in effect recognize federal power, when federal policy so requires, to deny res judicata effect to state court decisions on questions of federal law—even when state res judicata doctrine would dictate otherwise?

(5) Nonmutual Issue Preclusion Against a State or its Officers. Recall the holding of Mendoza (p. 1370, *supra*), rejecting the use of nonmutual issue preclusion against the United States. What if a party in a federal court action asserts nonmutual issue preclusion with respect to an issue resolved against a state government in state court litigation involving a different party? Assuming that the question is one of the state's preclusion law, should a state adopt Mendoza's rationale, or should a different approach apply to state (and local) governmental entities? Note that many states have only one intermediate appellate court (and in at least one state, there is none), thus eliminating the relevance of conflicts among lower appellate courts as a factor in determining the availability of, and need for, review by the highest court. See generally Note, 109 Harv.L.Rev. 792 (1996) (arguing that nonmutual issue preclusion should be presumptively unavailable against states unless a multi-factor balancing test suggests otherwise).

(6) The Res Judicata Effect of State Administrative Decisions. In University of Tennessee v. Elliott, 478 U.S. 788 (1986), the Court extended the notion that the preclusive effect of state *judicial* proceedings on the federal courts is to be measured by state law, to embrace factual determinations in certain state *administrative* procedures. A state administrative law judge determined that Elliott's discharge from his university job had not been motivated by racial prejudice, a finding upheld on administrative appeal. Rather than seeking review of these agency determinations in the Tennessee courts, Elliott filed Title VII and § 1983 claims in a federal district court. The Supreme Court ruled that § 1738 did not apply because it governs only the preclusive effect of "judicial" proceedings. Nevertheless, the Court noted that it had "frequently fashioned federal common-law rules of preclusion in the absence of a governing statute", and that "because § 1738 antedates the development of administrative agencies it clearly does not represent a congressional determination that the decisions of state administrative agencies should not be given preclusive effect". The Court held that a rule giving unreviewed state administrative proceedings preclusive effect would be inconsistent with Title VII's provision for a trial de novo following agency action. As to § 1983 actions, however, the Court held that factfinding by a state agency acting in a judicial capacity was to be given the preclusive effect to which it would be entitled in the state's courts. Citing Allen v. McCurry for the proposition that Congress in § 1983 did not "repeal or restrict the traditional doctrines of preclusion", and United States v. Utah Constr. & Mining Co., 384 U.S. 394 (1966), for the proposition that federal agency factfinding has preclusive effect, the Court held that the traditional purposes of preclusion are "equally implicated whether factfinding is done by a federal or state agency".[5]

Recall that in Patsy v. Florida Bd. of Regents, p. 1097, *supra*, the Court held that a § 1983 plaintiff does not have to exhaust state administrative

---

[5] Although the courts of appeals are not unanimous, several of those courts have held that the Elliott decision does not require giving *claim* preclusive effect to a state administrative proceeding, at least in the context of a § 1983 action. See, *e.g.*, Gjellum v. City of Birmingham, 829 F.2d 1056 (11th Cir.1987); Dionne v. Mayor and City Council of Baltimore, 40 F.3d 677 (4th Cir.1994).

remedies. In light of that holding, was it wise for the Court to discourage voluntary resort to state administrative procedures by creating a risk that administrative factfindings may bar the § 1983 action entirely? On the other hand, recall also the holding in Ohio Civil Rights Comm'n v. Dayton Christian Schools, p. 1168, *supra*, that Younger requires a federal court to abstain when there is a pending state administrative enforcement proceeding. The consequences of that holding are intensified by the Elliott case.[6]

(7) Cases Involving Exclusive Federal Jurisdiction. Difficult questions arise when, after a state court judgment, the prevailing party argues for the preclusive effect of that judgment in a subsequent federal court action over which the federal courts have exclusive jurisdiction.

(a) The Marrese Case. Marrese v. American Academy of Orthopaedic Surgeons, 470 U.S. 373 (1985), involved the effect of a judgment in a state court action asserting that the Academy's denial of membership to plaintiff violated Illinois law. After a defeat in the state courts, plaintiff brought a new action in federal court, alleging a violation of the federal antitrust laws—a claim over which the federal courts have exclusive jurisdiction and which could not, therefore, have been joined in the state action. The Seventh Circuit applied federal res judicata doctrine in holding that the federal action was barred. In the Supreme Court, Justice O'Connor said that the lower courts had erred in not taking account of Illinois preclusion law, given that § 1738 "requires a federal court to look first to state preclusion law in determining the preclusive effect of a state court judgment". Acknowledging that Illinois law would have no "occasion to address the specific question whether a state judgment has issue or claim preclusive effect in a later action that can be brought only in federal court," the Court pointed out that Illinois res judicata law might nevertheless address the more general question whether claim preclusion forecloses related claims that were not within the jurisdiction of the rendering court. Ordinarily, the Court said, claim preclusion does not apply in such situations. If Illinois adheres to that rule, the federal courts under § 1738 must also do so and may not give preclusive effect to the Illinois judgment.

The Court remanded the case for an inquiry into Illinois law, but also noted that it would not now determine whether, if Illinois law called for preclusion of a closely related claim that was not within the jurisdiction of the rendering court, preclusion of that claim would ultimately be required. The Court stated that in deciding whether an exception is to be made to § 1738 for a particular class of federal claims (antitrust claims, for example), the question is "whether the concerns underlying a particular grant of exclusive jurisdiction justify a finding of an implied partial repeal of § 1738".

Does this last point lend support to the arguments of Professor Burbank, discussed in Paragraph (4)?

---

[6] Woolhandler and Collins, in *Judicial Federalism and the Administrative States*, 87 Cal.L.Rev. 613, 694–700 (1999), note that a § 1983 federal court challenge to state agency action could be combined (under the supplemental jurisdiction provisions of § 1367) with a petition for review of that same action under state law, and that in such a proceeding the agency decision would be entitled to deference but not preclusive effect. Thus, they argue that if no review is sought under state law but state agency action is challenged solely under federal law, the "maximum effect" that should be given to the agency's findings "as a matter of federal common law is the deference, if any, they would receive under state law".

The Restatement 2d § 26 provides that rules against splitting causes of action do not apply where the plaintiff was barred from submitting a "certain theory of the case" because of limitations on the subject matter jurisdiction of the rendering court, and a specific illustration states that if A sues B in a state court on a state antitrust claim and loses on the merits, A is not thereafter barred from bringing a federal antitrust action against B in federal court.[7]

(b) Matsushita: Settlement of a State Court Class Action. In Matsushita Elec. Indus. Co. v. Epstein, 516 U.S. 367 (1996), shareholders in an acquired corporation brought a state court class action, on behalf of all the corporation's shareholders, based purely on state-law grounds. Another group of shareholders in the same company brought a federal court class action—one that fell within the federal courts' exclusive jurisdiction—complaining of violation of the Securities Exchange Act of 1934 with respect to the same transaction. Matsushita, the acquiring company, was a defendant in both actions. While the federal action was pending, the state court entered a judgment approving a settlement that provided, *inter alia*, for release by all class members (who did not opt out of the class) of *all* claims arising out of the events in question, "including * * * claims arising under the federal securities laws".

The question presented to the Supreme Court was whether, under § 1738, the state court judgment embodying the settlement precluded those class members who had not opted out from prosecuting their federal securities claims in federal court. Although the Justices disagreed on what questions should be open to the Ninth Circuit on remand, the Court unanimously held that so long as the demands of due process are met and federal law does not provide otherwise, § 1738 requires reference to state law to determine whether such a judgment has preclusive effect—even with respect to a federal claim over which the state court had no jurisdiction.[8] The Court also ruled that nothing in the 1934 Exchange Act constituted a repeal, in whole or in part, of § 1738.

If the claim under the 1934 Exchange Act had been litigated in the state court class action, despite the state court's lack of subject matter jurisdiction over that claim, would a judgment with respect to the claim be entitled to preclusive effect? (*Cf.* the discussion of the Marrese case in subparagraph (a) of this Paragraph.) If not, then how can a judgment embodying a settlement of a claim over which the state court had no subject-matter jurisdiction be given broader preclusive effect?

One possible argument in support of the result in Matsushita is that, unlike an adjudication, a settlement is a contract that acquires the force of a

---

[7]   For an exploration in depth of the broad range of approaches to the questions of whether and to what extent state preclusion rules can be defeated by the policies that led Congress to provide for exclusive federal jurisdiction over a certain class of claims, see 18B Wright, Miller & Cooper, Federal Practice and Procedure § 4470–4470.3.

[8]   The majority analyzed the state cases and concluded that under state law, such "global settlements" operate to preclude litigation of any federal claims within the scope of the settlement. The majority also stated that any due process issue relating to the adequacy of representation in the state proceeding fell outside the scope of the question presented to the Supreme Court. In a separate opinion, Justice Ginsburg, joined by Justices Souter and Stevens on this point, stated explicitly that the court of appeals should be free on remand to consider issues relating to the adequacy of representation of the class in the state proceeding.

binding judgment when approved by a court.[9] Surely, that "contract" rationale would cause no difficulty if a judgment had been entered based on a consent agreement between two individuals or entities, both of whom were parties to the litigation. The problem becomes more difficult when the question is the effect of a class-wide settlement on class members who did not themselves participate in the settlement negotiations or in the judicial proceeding leading to its approval. But does that question differ in any way from any other question of the binding effect of a class action judgment, *i.e.*, one that turns on such due process issues as the adequacy of notice and opportunity to opt out, and the adequacy of representation of the class in the proceedings leading up to the settlement and its final approval?[10]

For an interesting analysis of the Matsushita case, see Kahan & Silberman, *Matsushita and Beyond: The Role of State Courts in Class Actions Involving Exclusive Federal Claims*, 1996 Sup.Ct.Rev. 219. The authors contend that state court class action settlements encompassing exclusive federal claims present special problems, that state courts should therefore take more than the usual precautions in determining whether to approve such settlements, but that if such precautions are taken, collateral attack (even on the question of the adequacy of representation of absent class members) should be barred. For a sharply contrasting analysis of the desirability of permitting collateral attack, see Monaghan, *Antisuit Injunctions and Preclusion Against Absent, Nonresident Class Members*, 98 Colum.L.Rev. 1148 (1998). Monaghan argues, *inter alia*, that given the conditions under which class actions are litigated, absent members should be permitted to choose the forum in which to attack a judgment on due process grounds (including inadequacy of representation).[11]

(c) Issue Preclusive Effect of State Judgments Relating to Regimes of Exclusive Federal Jurisdiction. In Gunn v. Minton, 133 S.Ct. 1059 (2013), also discussed at p. 835, *supra*, the Court held that the provision for exclusive federal jurisdiction over cases arising under the patent laws did not bar a state court from adjudicating a state legal malpractice claim based on the conduct of an attorney in a prior federal patent action. Responding to the argument that an important federal interest supporting the recognition of federal question jurisdiction could be found in the possible issue preclusive effect of a state court ruling on the scope of the relevant patent, the Court said: "It is unclear whether [the

---

[9] The majority purported not to consider this theory. The opinion stated that the issue whether the settlement could bar the federal suit "as a matter of contract law, as distinguished from § 1738 law[,] is outside the scope of the question on which we granted certiorari."

[10] On remand in Matsushita itself, a divided Ninth Circuit panel originally held that the state court judgment was not entitled to full faith and credit because the representation of the class had been inadequate. 126 F.3d 1235 (9th Cir.1997). After the resignation of one member of the panel, however, the opinion was withdrawn, and a reconstituted panel held, 2–1, on rehearing that since a determination of adequacy had been made in the state court proceeding, all members of the class were bound by that determination. 179 F.3d 641 (9th Cir.1999).

[11] The questions whether and under what circumstances an absent class member may litigate the issue of adequate representation in a *subsequent* proceeding were left open in an affirmance without opinion by an equally divided Court in Dow Chem. Co. v. Stephenson, 539 U.S. 111 (2003) (Stevens, J., not participating). The enactment in 2005 of the federal Class Action Fairness Act, discussed in Chapter 13, section 2, *infra*, has generated additional interest in the preclusive effects of class action determinations. See, *e.g.*, Issacharoff & Nagareda, *Class Settlements under Attack*, 156 U.Pa.L.Rev. 1649 (2008); Wolff, *Federal Jurisdiction and Due Process in the Era of the Nationwide Class Action*, 156 U.Pa.L.Rev. 2035 (2008); Woolley, *The Jurisdictional Nature of Adequate Representation in Class Litigation*, 79 Geo.Wash.L.Rev. 410 (2011).

possibility of issue preclusive effect] is true. * * * In fact, Minton has not identified any case finding such preclusive effect based on a state court decision. But even assuming that a state court's case-within-a-case adjudication may be preclusive under some circumstances, the result would be limited to the parties and patents that had been before the state court. Such 'fact-bound and situation-specific' effects are not sufficient to establish federal arising under jurisdiction."

Does this dictum suggest that even if the state court decision would have issue preclusive effect in subsequent federal patent litigation as between the parties, it could not be accorded *non-mutual* issue preclusive effect?

---

2. OTHER ASPECTS OF CONCURRENT OR SUCCESSIVE JURISDICTION

INTRODUCTORY NOTE ON THE RELATIONSHIP BETWEEN HABEAS CORPUS AND SECTION 1983

(1) The Problem. Allen v. McCurry focused on the question of the preclusive effect of a state judgment on a subsequent federal action for a claimed violation of federal rights. A further layer of complexity is added when the federal plaintiff seeks relief in an action under § 1983 but—because the basis on which relief is sought would invalidate the plaintiff's criminal conviction or shorten the period of incarceration—the plaintiff might also have sought relief in a habeas corpus action. There are, of course, significant differences between the two remedies, especially (but not exclusively) the requirement that before bringing a habeas action, the petitioner must have exhausted available state remedies. See p. 1349, *supra*.

The exhaustion requirement can have important effects on forum choice—in particular, on whether the federal plaintiff or petitioner can obtain a trial de novo of fact and law in federal court. In a § 1983 action, absent a prior state court judgment, the federal court would decide all relevant issues itself. In a habeas action, by contrast, the requirement of exhaustion of state remedies may generate a state court decision on the merits of the claim. The federal habeas regime has been treated, as Allen v. McCurry notes, as an exception to the command of § 1738, so that the state court decision would have not have strict res judicata effect in a habeas proceeding. But the state court decision is one to which habeas courts will nonetheless defer. Deference to factual findings has been common for decades, and since the enactment of AEDPA in 1996, the state court's determinations of law as well as fact are entitled to broad deference, often making the state court decision determinative of the outcome in federal court. See pp. 1301–1319, *supra*.

(2) The Preiser and Wolff Decisions. Preiser v. Rodriguez, 411 U.S. 475 (1973), was the first case raising the problem of overlap of habeas corpus and § 1983 to reach the Court. There, the majority held that a federal court could not entertain a § 1983 action in which state prisoners sought the restoration of good time credits—relief that, if granted, would result in their immediate release. The Court held that habeas was the only available federal remedy.

Justice Brennan, dissenting for himself and Justices Douglas and Marshall, argued that since the prisoners' actions did not focus on the relations between state and federal judiciaries, but rather on the constitutionality of the state's administrative treatment of the prisoners, habeas should not be regarded as the exclusive remedy and hence exhaustion should not be required.

The limits of Preiser were tested in Wolff v. McDonnell, 418 U.S. 539 (1974), in which state prisoners brought § 1983 actions challenging the constitutionality of certain state disciplinary proceedings (which had resulted in loss of good time credits), of the state legal aid program, and of the prison mail censorship system. Plaintiffs sought both damages and the restoration of good time credits. The Court allowed the § 1983 action to go forward but ruled that the restoration of good time credits in such an action was foreclosed under Preiser.

Neither Preiser nor Wolff considered the question of the availability of a § 1983 action for damages under comparable circumstances, *i.e.*, when a determination in favor of the federal plaintiff would rest on grounds that would necessarily imply the invalidity of his conviction or shorten the period of incarceration. That question was addressed in the following case.

Heck v. Humphrey

512 U.S. 477, 114 S.Ct. 2364, 129 L.Ed.2d 383 (1994).
Certiorari to the United States Court of Appeals for the Seventh Circuit.

■ JUSTICE SCALIA delivered the opinion of the Court.

This case presents the question whether a state prisoner may challenge the constitutionality of his conviction in a suit for damages under 42 U.S.C. § 1983.

I

[While petitioner's appeal from his conviction in Indiana was pending, he filed a § 1983 action in federal court against prosecutorial and police officials.] The complaint alleged that respondents, acting under color of state law, had engaged in an "unlawful, unreasonable, and arbitrary investigation" leading to petitioner's arrest; "knowingly destroyed" evidence "which was exculpatory in nature and could have proved [petitioner's] innocence"; and caused "an illegal and unlawful voice identification procedure" to be used at petitioner's trial. The complaint sought, among other things, compensatory and punitive monetary damages. It did not ask for injunctive relief, and petitioner has not sought release from custody in this action.

The District Court dismissed the action without prejudice, because the issues it raised "directly implicate the legality of [petitioner's] confinement." While petitioner's appeal to the Seventh Circuit was pending, the Indiana Supreme Court upheld his conviction and sentence on direct appeal; his first petition for a writ of habeas corpus in Federal District Court was dismissed because it contained unexhausted claims; and his second federal habeas petition was denied, and the denial affirmed by the Seventh Circuit.

[Thereafter, the Seventh Circuit affirmed the dismissal of petitioner's § 1983 complaint.] Heck filed a petition for certiorari, which we granted.[2]

II

This case lies at the intersection of the two most fertile sources of federal-court prisoner litigation—the Civil Rights Act of 1871, 42 U.S.C. § 1983, and the federal habeas corpus statute, 28 U.S.C. § 2254. Both of these provide access to a federal forum for claims of unconstitutional treatment at the hands of state officials, but they differ in their scope and operation. In general, exhaustion of state remedies "is *not* a prerequisite to an action under § 1983," Patsy v. Board of Regents of Fla., 457 U.S. 496, 501 (1982) (emphasis added), even an action by a state prisoner, *id.*, at 509. The federal habeas corpus statute, by contrast, requires that state prisoners first seek redress in a state forum.

Preiser v. Rodriguez, 411 U.S. 475 (1973), considered the potential overlap between these two provisions, and held that habeas corpus is the exclusive remedy for a state prisoner who challenges the fact or duration of his confinement and seeks immediate or speedier release, even though such a claim may come within the literal terms of § 1983. We emphasize that Preiser did not create an exception to the "no exhaustion" rule of § 1983; it merely held that certain claims by state prisoners are not cognizable under that provision, and must be brought in habeas corpus proceedings, which do contain an exhaustion requirement.

This case is clearly not covered by the holding of Preiser, for petitioner seeks not immediate or speedier release, but monetary damages, as to which he could not "have sought and obtained fully effective relief through federal habeas corpus proceedings." *Id.*, at 488. In dictum, however, Preiser asserted that since a state prisoner seeking only damages "is attacking something other than the fact or length of . . . confinement, and . . . is seeking something other than immediate or more speedy release[,] . . . a damages action by a state prisoner could be brought under [§ 1983] in federal court without any requirement of prior exhaustion of state remedies." 411 U.S., at 494. That statement may not be true, however, when establishing the basis for the damages claim necessarily demonstrates the invalidity of the conviction. In that situation, the claimant *can* be said to be "attacking the fact or length of confinement," bringing the suit within the other dictum of Preiser: "Congress has determined that habeas corpus is the appropriate remedy for state prisoners attacking the validity of the fact or length of their confinement, and that specific determination must override the general terms of § 1983." *Id.*, at 490. In the last analysis, we think the dicta of Preiser to be an unreliable, if not an unintelligible, guide: that opinion had no cause to address, and did not carefully consider, the damages question before us today.

---

[2] Neither in his petition for certiorari nor in his principal brief on the merits did petitioner contest the description of his monetary claims (by both the District Court and the Court of Appeals) as challenging the legality of his conviction. * * * Petitioner [contended in his reply brief] that findings validating his damages claims would not invalidate his conviction. That argument comes too late. We did not take this case to review such a fact-bound issue, and we accept the characterization of the lower courts. * * *

* * * [The Court also found that the question before it had not been resolved by Wolff v. McDonnell, 418 U.S. 539 (1974), which is discussed in Paragraph (2) of the Introductory Note preceding this case.]

Thus, the question posed by § 1983 damage claims that do call into question the lawfulness of conviction or confinement remains open. To answer that question correctly, we see no need to abandon * * * our teaching that § 1983 contains no exhaustion requirement beyond what Congress has provided. The issue with respect to monetary damages challenging conviction is not, it seems to us, exhaustion; but rather, the same as the issue was with respect to injunctive relief challenging conviction in Preiser: whether the claim is cognizable under § 1983 at all. We conclude that it is not.

* * *

The common-law cause of action for malicious prosecution provides the closest analogy to claims of the type considered here because, unlike the related cause of action for false arrest or imprisonment, it permits damages for confinement imposed pursuant to legal process. * * *

One element that must be alleged and proved in a malicious prosecution action is termination of the prior criminal proceeding in favor of the accused. Prosser & Keeton [on Torts] 874 [(5th ed. 1984)]. * * * "[T]o permit a convicted criminal defendant to proceed with a malicious prosecution claim would permit a collateral attack on the conviction through the vehicle of a civil suit." [8 S. Speiser, C. Krause, & A. Gans, American Law of Torts § 28:5, p. 24 (1991).][4] This Court has long expressed similar concerns for finality and consistency and has generally declined to expand opportunities for collateral attack. We think the hoary principle that civil tort actions are not appropriate vehicles for challenging the validity of outstanding criminal judgments applies to § 1983 damages actions that necessarily require the plaintiff to prove the unlawfulness of his conviction or confinement, just as it has always applied to actions for malicious prosecution.

We hold that, in order to recover damages for allegedly unconstitutional conviction or imprisonment, or for other harm caused by actions whose unlawfulness would render a conviction or sentence invalid, a § 1983 plaintiff must prove that the conviction or sentence has been reversed on direct appeal, expunged by executive order, declared invalid by a state tribunal authorized to make such determination, or called into question by a federal court's issuance of a writ of habeas corpus, 28 U.S.C. § 2254. A claim for damages bearing that relationship to a conviction or sentence that has *not* been so invalidated is not cognizable under § 1983. Thus, when a state prisoner seeks damages in a § 1983 suit, the district court must consider whether a judgment in favor of the plaintiff would necessarily imply the invalidity of his conviction or sentence; if it would, the complaint must be dismissed unless the plaintiff can demonstrate that the conviction or sentence has

---

4   * * * [E]ven if Justice Souter were correct [in his opinion concurring in the judgment] in asserting that a prior conviction, although reversed, "dissolved [a] claim for malicious prosecution," [and we do not believe he is,] our analysis would be unaffected. It would simply demonstrate that *no* common-law action, *not even* malicious prosecution, would permit a criminal proceeding to be impugned in a tort action, *even after* the conviction had been reversed. That would, if anything, strengthen our belief that § 1983, which borrowed general tort principles, was not meant to permit such collateral attack.

already been invalidated. But if the district court determines that the plaintiff's action, even if successful, will *not* demonstrate the invalidity of any outstanding criminal judgment against the plaintiff, the action should be allowed to proceed,[7] in the absence of some other bar to the suit.

Respondents had urged us to adopt a rule that was in one respect broader than this: exhaustion of state remedies should be required, they contended, not just when success in the § 1983 damages suit would necessarily show a conviction or sentence to be unlawful, but whenever "judgment in a § 1983 action would resolve a necessary element to a likely challenge to a conviction, even if the § 1983 court [need] not determine that the conviction is invalid." Such a broad sweep was needed, respondents contended, lest a judgment in a prisoner's favor in a federal-court § 1983 damage action claiming, for example, a Fourth Amendment violation, be given preclusive effect as to that sub-issue in a subsequent state-court post-conviction proceeding. Preclusion might result, they asserted, if the State exercised sufficient control over the officials' defense in the § 1983 action. See Montana v. United States, 440 U.S. 147, 154 (1979). While we have no occasion to rule on the matter at this time, it is at least plain that preclusion will not necessarily be an automatic, or even a permissible, effect.[9]

In another respect, however, our holding sweeps more broadly than the approach respondents had urged. We do not engraft an exhaustion requirement upon § 1983, but rather deny the existence of a cause of action. Even a prisoner who has fully exhausted available state remedies has no cause of action under § 1983 unless and until the conviction or sentence is reversed, expunged, invalidated, or impugned by the grant of a writ of habeas corpus. That makes it unnecessary for us to address the statute-of-limitations issue wrestled with by the Court of Appeals * * *. Under our analysis the statute of limitations poses no difficulty while the state challenges are being pursued, since the § 1983 claim has not yet arisen. * * *[10]

---

[7]   For example, a suit for damages attributable to an allegedly unreasonable search may lie even if the challenged search produced evidence that was introduced in a state criminal trial resulting in the § 1983 plaintiff's still-outstanding conviction. Because of doctrines like independent source and inevitable discovery, and especially harmless error, such a § 1983 action, even if successful, would not *necessarily* imply that the plaintiff's conviction was unlawful. * * *

[9]   State courts are bound to apply federal rules in determining the preclusive effect of federal-court decisions on issues of federal law. See P. Bator, D. Meltzer, P. Mishkin, & D. Shapiro, Hart and Wechsler's The Federal Courts and the Federal System 1604 (3d ed. 1988) ("It is clear that where the federal court decided a federal question, federal res judicata rules govern"). The federal rules on the subject of issue and claim preclusion, unlike those relating to exhaustion of state remedies, are "almost entirely judge-made." Hart & Wechsler, *supra*, at 1598. And in developing them the courts can, and indeed should, be guided by the federal policies reflected in congressional enactments. * * * [The policy underlying the exhaustion requirement of § 2254 is] that state courts be given the first opportunity to review constitutional claims bearing upon state prisoners' release from custody.

[10]   Justice Souter also adopts the common-law principle that one cannot use the device of a civil tort action to challenge the validity of an outstanding criminal conviction, but thinks it necessary to abandon that principle in those cases (of which no real-life example comes to mind) involving former state prisoners who, because they are no longer in custody, cannot bring post-conviction challenges. We think the principle barring collateral attacks—a longstanding and deeply rooted feature of both the common law and our own jurisprudence—is not rendered inapplicable by the fortuity that a convicted criminal is no longer incarcerated. Justice Souter opines that disallowing a damages suit for a former state prisoner framed by Ku Klux Klan-

Applying these principles to the present action, * * * we find that the dismissal of the action was correct. The judgment of the Court of Appeals for the Seventh Circuit is

Affirmed.

■ JUSTICE THOMAS, concurring.

* * * I write separately to note that it is we who have put § 1983 and the habeas statute on what Justice Souter appropriately terms a "collision course." It has long been recognized that we have expanded the prerogative writ of habeas corpus and § 1983 far beyond the limited scope either was originally intended to have. Expanding the two historic statutes brought them squarely into conflict in the context of suits by state prisoners, as we made clear in Preiser.

Given that the Court created the tension between the two statutes, it is proper for the Court to devise limitations aimed at ameliorating the conflict, provided that it does so in a principled fashion. Because the Court today limits the scope of § 1983 in a manner consistent both with the federalism concerns undergirding the explicit exhaustion requirement of the habeas statute, and with the state of the common law at the time § 1983 was enacted, I join the Court's opinion.

■ JUSTICE SOUTER, with whom JUSTICE BLACKMUN, JUSTICE STEVENS, and JUSTICE O'CONNOR join, concurring in the judgment.

* * * While I do not object to referring to the common law when resolving the question this case presents, I do not think that the existence of the tort of malicious prosecution alone provides the answer. Common-law tort rules can provide a "starting point for the inquiry under § 1983," Carey v. Piphus, 435 U.S. 247, 258 (1978), but we have relied on the common law in § 1983 cases only when doing so was thought to be consistent with ordinary rules of statutory construction * * *. At the same time, we have consistently refused to allow common-law analogies to displace statutory analysis, declining to import even well-settled common-law rules into § 1983 "if [the statute's] history or purpose counsel against applying [such rules] in § 1983 actions." Wyatt v. Cole, 504 U.S. 158, 164 (1992).

An examination of common-law sources arguably relevant in this case confirms the soundness of our hierarchy of principles for resolving questions concerning § 1983. * * * [A plaintiff in a malicious-prosecution action must prove both the absence of probable cause for the proceeding and malice. These requirements would mean that even a plaintiff whose] conviction was invalidated as unconstitutional (premised, for example, on a confession coerced by an interrogation-room beating) could not obtain damages for the unconstitutional conviction and ensuing confinement if [law enforcement officials] had probable cause to believe the plaintiff was guilty and intended to bring him to justice. Absent an

---

dominated state officials is "hard indeed to reconcile . . . with the purpose of § 1983." But if, as Justice Souter appears to suggest, the goal of our interpretive enterprise under § 1983 were to provide a remedy for all conceivable invasions of federal rights that freedmen may have suffered at the hands of officials of the former States of the Confederacy, the entire landscape of our § 1983 jurisprudence would look very different. We would not, for example, have adopted the rule that judicial officers have absolute immunity from liability for damages under § 1983, a rule that would prevent recovery by a former slave who had been tried and convicted before a corrupt state judge in league with the Ku Klux Klan.

independent statutory basis for doing so, importing into § 1983 the malicious-prosecution tort's favorable-termination requirement but not its probable-cause requirement would be particularly odd since it is from the latter that the former derives.

* * * Furthermore, * * * the Court overlooks a significant historical incongruity that calls into question the utility of the analogy to the tort of malicious prosecution insofar as it is used exclusively to determine the scope of § 1983: the damages sought in the type of § 1983 claim involved here, damages for unlawful conviction or postconviction confinement, were not available at all in an action for malicious prosecution at the time of § 1983's enactment. A defendant's conviction, under Reconstruction-era common law, dissolved his claim for malicious prosecution because the conviction was regarded as irrebuttable evidence that the prosecution never lacked probable cause. Thus the definition of "favorable termination" with which the framers of § 1983 were aware (if they were aware of any definition) included none of the events relevant to the type of § 1983 claim involved in this case ("revers[al] on direct appeal, expunge[ment] by executive order, [a] declaration [of] invalid[ity] by a state tribunal authorized to make such determination, or [the] call[ing] into question by a federal court's issuance of a writ of habeas corpus"), and it is easy to see why the analogy to the tort of malicious prosecution in this context has escaped the collective wisdom of the many courts and commentators to have previously addressed the issue, as well as the parties to this case. Indeed, relying on the tort of malicious prosecution to dictate the outcome of this case would logically drive one to the position, untenable as a matter of statutory interpretation (and, to be clear, disclaimed by the Court), that conviction of a crime wipes out a person's § 1983 claim for damages for unconstitutional conviction or postconviction confinement.

We are not, however, in any such strait, for our enquiry in this case may follow the interpretive methodology employed in Preiser v. Rodriguez. In Preiser, we read the "general" § 1983 statute in light of the "specific federal habeas corpus statute," which applies only to "person[s] in custody," 28 U.S.C. § 2254(a), and the habeas statute's policy, embodied in its exhaustion requirement, § 2254(b), that state courts be given the first opportunity to review constitutional claims bearing upon a state prisoner's release from custody. 411 U.S., at 489. Though in contrast to Preiser the state prisoner here seeks damages, not release from custody, the distinction makes no difference when the damages sought are for unconstitutional conviction or confinement. * * * Because allowing a state prisoner to proceed directly with a federal-court § 1983 attack on his conviction or sentence "would wholly frustrate explicit congressional intent" as declared in the habeas exhaustion requirement, Preiser, 411 U.S., at 489, the statutory scheme must be read as precluding such attacks. This conclusion flows not from a preference about how the habeas and § 1983 statutes ought to have been written, but from a recognition that "Congress has determined that habeas corpus is the appropriate remedy for state prisoners attacking the validity of the fact or length of their confinement, [a] specific determination [that] must override the general terms of § 1983." *Id.*, at 490.

That leaves the question of how to implement what statutory analysis requires. It is at this point that the malicious-prosecution tort's favorable-termination requirement becomes helpful, not in dictating the elements of a § 1983 cause of action, but in suggesting a relatively simple way to avoid collisions at the intersection of habeas and § 1983. A state prisoner may seek federal-court § 1983 damages for unconstitutional conviction or confinement, but only if he has previously established the unlawfulness of his conviction or confinement, as on appeal or on habeas. This has the effect of requiring a state prisoner challenging the lawfulness of his confinement to follow habeas's rules before seeking § 1983 damages for unlawful confinement in federal court, and it is ultimately the Court's holding today. * * * The favorable-termination requirement avoids the knotty statute-of-limitations problem that arises if federal courts dismiss § 1983 suits filed before an inmate pursues federal habeas, and (because the statute-of-limitations clock does not start ticking until an inmate's conviction is set aside) it does so without requiring federal courts to stay, and therefore to retain on their dockets, prematurely filed § 1983 suits.

It may be that the Court's analysis takes it no further than I would thus go, and that any objection I may have to the Court's opinion is to style, not substance. * * * The Court's opinion can be read as saying nothing more than that now, after enactment of the habeas statute and because of it, prison inmates seeking § 1983 damages in federal court for unconstitutional conviction or confinement must satisfy a requirement analogous to the malicious-prosecution tort's favorable-termination requirement.

That would be a sensible way to read the opinion, in part because the alternative would needlessly place at risk the rights of those outside the intersection of § 1983 and the habeas statute, individuals not "in custody" for habeas purposes. If these individuals (people who were merely fined, for example, or who have completed short terms of imprisonment, probation or parole, or who discover (through no fault of their own) a constitutional violation after full expiration of their sentences), like state prisoners, were required to show the prior invalidation of their convictions or sentences in order to obtain § 1983 damages for unconstitutional conviction or imprisonment, the result would be to deny any federal forum for claiming a deprivation of federal rights to those who cannot first obtain a favorable state ruling. The reason, of course, is that individuals not "in custody" cannot invoke federal habeas jurisdiction, the only statutory mechanism besides § 1983 by which individuals may sue state officials in federal court for violating federal rights. That would be an untoward result.

     * * *

In sum, while the malicious-prosecution analogy provides a useful mechanism for implementing what statutory analysis requires, congressional policy as reflected in enacted statutes must ultimately be the guide. I would thus be clear that the proper resolution of this case (involving, of course, a state prisoner) is to construe § 1983 in light of the habeas statute and its explicit policy of exhaustion. I would not cast doubt on the ability of an individual unaffected by the habeas statute to take advantage of the broad reach of § 1983.

NOTE ON THE PREISER-HECK DOCTRINE

In reading this Note, consider whether it is sensible to expect prisoners, who are usually acting pro se, to navigate the complexities of the Preiser-Heck doctrine.

(1) Some Questions Raised by the Heck Decision. The Court's unanimous agreement on the result in the Heck case masked some difficult questions.

(a) When is it sufficiently clear that upholding a damage claim under § 1983 would *necessarily* imply the invalidity of the prisoner's conviction, thus requiring resort to habeas corpus as the exclusive federal remedy? The Court stated in footnote 2 that it was no longer open to Heck to argue that his claim would not have such an effect, but had he been allowed to argue this point, should he have prevailed? After Heck, the availability of § 1983 in a number of instances appears to turn on a rather delicate analysis of the harmless error rule or some variant of it. If so, won't the state prisoner be caught between the Scylla of the Heck rule barring a § 1983 action and the Charybdis of negating whatever part of his claim for damages is based on an invalid conviction?[1]

(b) In Skinner v. Switzer, 562 U.S. 521 (2011) (6–3) the Court refused to extend Heck to a case presenting the question: "May a convicted state prisoner seeking DNA testing of crime-scene evidence assert that claim [under § 1983] or is such a claim cognizable in federal court only * * * in a petition for a writ of habeas corpus * * *?" After Skinner's conviction in Texas, the Texas courts found that he did not qualify for DNA testing under a Texas law permitting such testing in certain circumstances. Claiming that the state's law, as interpreted by the decisions rejecting his requests for testing, denied him procedural due process, Skinner filed a federal court action under § 1983 seeking an order that the testing be performed. When the case reached the Supreme Court, it ruled that the action could be maintained under § 1983".

For Justice Ginsburg, writing for the majority, it was crucial that "[s]uccess in [Skinner's] suit for DNA testing would not 'necessarily imply' [quoting Heck] the invalidity of his conviction." The test might well prove inconclusive or even further incriminate him. In no case, she observed, has the Court recognized habeas as the sole remedy—"or even an available one"— where the relief sought would not either terminate custody, reduce the level of custody, or accelerate release. And allowing such an action to be brought under § 1983 was not likely to result in a flood of litigation, because no such flood had occurred in the circuit that already allowed such actions and because the decision would not "spill over" to claims (under Brady v. Maryland, 373 U.S. 83 (1963)) that the prosecution had withheld exculpatory evidence to the prejudice of the defendant. Such evidence is, "by definition, always favorable to the defendant and material to his guilt or punishment."[2]

---

[1]   May a prisoner who is willing to stipulate that any relief would not impugn his conviction (or to waive any right to try to do so) obtain relief under § 1983?

[2]   Some of the Justices in the majority may have been comfortable with this holding given the decision two terms earlier, in District Attorney's Office for Third Judicial Dist. v. Osborne, 557 U.S. 52 (2009) (5–4), which suggested that it would be a rare case in which a prisoner could establish that a state's refusal of postconviction DNA testing is a due process violation that can in turn undergird a § 1983 claim. Thus, the door opened in Skinner may lead to a closed door on the merits under Osborne.

Justice Thomas, joined by Justices Kennedy and Alito, dissented. While accepting *arguendo* the majority's conclusion that the specific relief sought, if obtained, would not necessarily imply the invalidity of Skinner's conviction, Justice Thomas argued for an extension of the Preiser-Heck rule "to all constitutional challenges to procedures concerning the validity of a conviction." Failure to do so, he contended, would undermine federal-state comity as evidenced by the judicial and legislative restrictions that had in recent decades been imposed on the availability of the habeas remedy.

Should the Preiser-Heck doctrine have been extended as Justice Thomas urged? Isn't there a problem in holding that the existence of the habeas remedy preempts other avenues of relief when the relief sought falls so far outside the core of the traditional habeas remedy that, as Justice Ginsburg noted, it is not even clear that habeas would lie?

(c) If a state prisoner who is allowed to pursue a § 1983 claim relating to a prior conviction prevails on the merits, what is the res judicata effect of that determination in a later state post-conviction or federal habeas corpus proceeding? The question is not purely academic, since there are sure to be instances in which the issue determined has a bearing on the validity of the conviction, even though the determination does not *necessarily* imply the invalidity of the conviction.

(d) Heck clearly bars a § 1983 damages action for a confession obtained by torture if a conviction that depended on that confession has not been invalidated on direct or collateral attack. But as noted in subparagraph (a), above, it apparently does not bar a damages action for a constitutional violation that, under the harmless error doctrine, would not invalidate a conviction. (Even unconstitutionally obtained confessions can be harmless error.) A "harmless" constitutional error is likely (though not certain) to have been less egregious than one that is presumed or found to have affected the outcome. Is there a sound basis for a rule that may, as an empirical matter, be more permissive with respect to damages actions under § 1983 for *less serious* violations? (Note, however, that individual liability in damages for marginal violations may be precluded on the basis of qualified immunity.)

(e) Habeas corpus jurisdiction has been sharply limited by Supreme Court decisions and, in 1996, by congressional amendments to the statute. Suppose a constitutional claim in a prisoner's § 1983 action would not be cognizable in habeas corpus (for example, because the prisoner failed to raise it in state court, or, alternatively, because the state court rejected it on the merits and that determination, though erroneous, was not unreasonable and thus under the 1996 amendments could not provide a basis for relief). Is the prisoner then left with no remedy whatsoever, unless the state chooses to afford either a post-conviction remedy of its own or a damages action? Or can the prisoner escape Heck by arguing that a victory in a § 1983 action will not invalidate the prior conviction precisely because no court has jurisdiction to entertain a federal post-conviction attack?

(f) Does Justice Scalia adequately answer Justice Souter's argument that the majority's reasoning has no application to a state defendant who never was or no longer is in custody, because habeas corpus does not lie for such a defendant and thus § 1983 becomes the *only* form of available federal relief? Justice Scalia, in footnote 10, notes that in view of doctrines such as that of qualified or absolute official immunity, § 1983 is not a comprehensive remedy for all violations of federal law committed by state officers. But those doctrines are presumably based on a careful balancing of the interest in vindicating individual rights against the interest in not unduly undermining effective law enforcement. When the latter interest does not provide immunity from liability in damages, what factors might warrant denial of relief under § 1983?

In Spencer v. Kemna, 523 U.S. 1 (1998), it appeared that a majority of the Court agreed with Justice Souter. The case was a complicated one in which the Court held that a habeas petition was moot because the petitioner had been released. In a concurrence joined by three other Justices, Justice Souter agreed that the case was moot on the ground that the Heck decision did not bar a released inmate from bringing a § 1983 action based on the invalidity of his conviction. A fifth Justice (Justice Stevens in his dissent) agreed with Justice Souter on this point.

But six years later, in Muhammad v. Close, 540 U.S. 749, 752 n. 2 (2004) (Paragraph (3)(a), *infra*), the Court indicated that it was still an open question whether the Heck doctrine applies to an action by a former prisoner whose sentence has been fully served or by a defendant who had been fined but not imprisoned. Citing Spencer, and the expression there by "[m]embers of the Court" of the view that "unavailability of habeas for other reasons [i.e., reasons other than those in the Muhammad case] may also dispense with the habeas requirement", the Court went on to state that "[t]his case is no occasion to settle the issue."

(2) The Application of Preiser-Heck to the Accrual of the Statute of Limitations. The Preiser-Heck rule has generated difficult questions in determining the proper accrual date for a § 1983 damages action that might affect the validity of a criminal conviction. In Wallace v. Kato, 549 U.S. 384 (2007), petitioner Wallace was convicted of murder, but the state courts ultimately concluded that he had been arrested without probable cause and that the unlawful arrest rendered his subsequent statements inadmissible. Some eight years after the arrest, the charges were dropped, and one year later, Wallace brought a § 1983 damages action, seeking, among other things, damages arising from the unlawful arrest. The defendants obtained summary judgment in the courts below on the basis that the action was time-barred.

In the Supreme Court, all the Justices agreed that the applicable statute of limitations (under relevant state law) was two years, that the question of when the cause of action accrued was a matter of federal law, and that the relevant accrual date (by analogy to the common law tort of false imprisonment) was the date when the prisoner's detention without legal process ended, "when, for example, he is bound over by a magistrate or arraigned on charges." That period had long since run before the suit was filed.

Wallace contended, however, that the normal accrual date for such an action was displaced because of the Preiser-Heck rule, under which the action could not accrue until the conviction was invalidated and the charges dropped. The majority, in an opinion by Justice Scalia, held that the rule did not come into play because at the time of accrual, "there was in existence no criminal conviction that the cause of action would impugn; indeed there may not even have been an indictment". An extension of Heck to such facts would be "bizarre" and unnecessary: "If a plaintiff files a false-arrest claim before he has been convicted (or files any other claim relating to rulings that will likely be made in a pending or anticipated criminal trial), it is within the power of the district court, and in accord with common practice, to stay the civil action until the criminal case or the likelihood of a criminal case is ended." The court may then proceed, or, if the plaintiff is ultimately convicted and the "stayed civil suit would impugn that conviction, Heck will require dismissal."[3]

Justice Stevens (joined by Justice Souter) concurred on the ground that Preiser-Heck was simply inapplicable to the case at bar because under Stone v. Powell, p. 1285, *supra*, success in a § 1983 suit based on an alleged Fourth Amendment violation cannot be used in a habeas proceeding to impugn a conviction. The majority responded that the Stone decision would not bar habeas if the state were to deny the habeas petitioner a full and fair hearing, to which Justice Stevens replied that since Stone would operate as a bar in almost all cases, the majority "lets the perfect become the enemy of the good".[4]

Even after this decision, difficulties in applying the statute of limitations in the context of Heck-related issues are likely to persist. Does the Court's rationale apply, for example, to a claim of a violation of the Miranda rule, of a confession obtained by brutal means, of the prosecution's knowing use of perjured testimony, or of the prosecution's failure to disclose exculpatory evidence? Does the answer depend on whether the § 1983 plaintiff suffers any ascertainable harm prior to conviction? (The Court in Wallace did say that a cause of action accrues "when the wrongful act or omission results in damages.")

(3) The Application of Preiser-Heck in Other Contexts.

(a) Prison Disciplinary Proceedings. In Edwards v. Balisok, 520 U.S. 641 (1997), the Court unanimously extended the Heck rationale to § 1983 actions involving prison disciplinary proceedings. There, a state prisoner had been found guilty of violating prison rules, and among the sanctions imposed was the loss of 30 days of good-time credit that he had previously earned. Alleging procedural due process violations, the prisoner brought a § 1983 action for damages and declaratory and injunctive relief, preserving the right to seek restoration of the good-time credit in an appropriate proceeding. The Court held that Preiser-Heck barred the action because certain allegations, if proved, would necessarily imply the invalidity of the deprivation of the good-time credit.

Note that the Court in Edwards made no explicit effort (as it had in Heck) to analogize the prisoner's action to a common law claim for malicious prosecution or indeed to any other common law action. Note also that the Edwards decision appears to enable a prison authority to avoid a § 1983 action by attaching a very small sentencing sanction to an otherwise non-custodial penalty. If so, does that bear on the soundness of the decision?

---

[3] Suppose Wallace had filed suit a few days after his arrest, but upon his conviction the suit had been dismissed under Preiser-Heck, as this passage appears to require. If, eight years later but immediately after the conviction was set aside and the charges dropped, he had refiled, would the action be barred? If so, shouldn't the stay of the original § 1983 action be continued until all opportunities for invalidating the conviction have been exhausted?

[4] Justice Breyer (joined by Justice Ginsburg) dissented, arguing that when the possibility of a Preiser-Heck problem would justify a stay of the civil action, the principle of "equitable tolling" would be appropriate during the period when a filed civil action would be stayed. Whether or not tolling would be available in analogous cases under state law, "§ 1983, in my view, permits the federal courts to devise and impose" such a principle. In response, the majority said that equitable tolling was a "rare remedy to be applied in unusual circumstances" and was not appropriate simply "to avoid the risk of concurrent litigation".

Edwards was distinguished in Muhammad v. Close, 540 U.S. 749 (2004). In this case, Muhammad, a prisoner in a state institution, brought a § 1983 damages action against a prison guard for injuries allegedly caused by the guard's efforts to retaliate for earlier proceedings filed by Muhammad against the guard. (As one result of the incidents complained of, Muhammad had been disciplined, and the discipline included detention, but Muhammad did not challenge that detention or the determination of misconduct on which it was based.) In a per curiam decision, the Court held that the lower court's ruling barring a § 1983 action under Preiser-Heck was flawed "as a matter of fact and as a matter of law". The factual error lay in the assumption that Muhammad had sought expungement of the misconduct ruling from his prison record. The legal error lay in the view that Preiser-Heck "applies categorically" to all suits involving prison disciplinary proceedings. In this instance, the rule did not apply because the federal magistrate judge had "found or assumed that [as a matter of state law,] no good-time credits were eliminated by the prehearing action Muhammad called in question."

(b) Challenges to the Validity of Parole Procedures. In Wilkinson v. Dotson, 544 U.S. 74 (2005), Preiser-Heck was further confined. In this consolidated case involving two § 1983 actions, one prisoner challenged the validity of a parole officer's determination that he was not presently eligible for consideration for parole, and the other challenged the validity of a parole board determination that he was not suitable for parole. Both prisoners argued that the constitutional error consisted of the retroactive application of new, harsher guidelines, and each sought a parole hearing free from the alleged constitutional defect. In both cases, the lower federal courts decided that the prisoner could seek relief only in a habeas proceeding. The Supreme Court reversed, 8–1.

Writing for the Court, Justice Breyer summarized the prior holdings as focusing "on the need to ensure that state prisoners use only habeas corpus (or similar state) remedies when they seek to invalidate the duration of their confinement—either *directly* through an injunction compelling speedier release or *indirectly* through a judicial determination that necessarily implies the unlawfulness of the State's custody." Such cases, he observed, seek "core" habeas corpus relief. But in the present case, neither prisoner sought an injunction ordering immediate or speedier release, and a favorable judgment would not "necessarily imply" the invalidity of their convictions or sentences.

Concurring, Justice Scalia (joined by Justice Thomas) went further than Justice Breyer and argued that in the circumstances, a habeas remedy should not lie at all because the relief sought "neither terminates custody, accelerates the future date of release from custody, nor reduces the level of custody". Thus, "a contrary holding would require us to broaden the scope of habeas relief beyond recognition." Dissenting, Justice Kennedy argued that Preiser-Heck should govern because "[c]hallenges to parole proceedings are cognizable in habeas."

Isn't Justice Scalia correct, at least as a matter of precedent and the traditional conception of habeas? No case has been found in which the Supreme Court has recognized habeas as an available remedy even though the relief sought would neither require immediate or accelerated release nor reduce the level of custody.[5]

(c) Challenges to the Method of Execution. In Nelson v. Campbell, 541 U.S. 637 (2004), and Hill v. McDonough, 547 U.S. 573 (2006), the Court considered § 1983 actions challenging the constitutionality of a particular method of execution. (In both cases, a habeas petition would probably have been barred by 28 U.S.C. § 2244(b) as an improper successive petition.) Both actions were allowed to go forward under § 1983, but since it was not clear in either case that a successful challenge would prevent the use of alternative methods of execution under existing state law, the Court has yet to determine the availability of § 1983 under such circumstances. Could the allowance of such an action be squared with the rule that a § 1983 action is not a substitute for (or alternative to) habeas when the outcome of the action, if successful, would affect the "duration" of a sentence?

————

INTRODUCTORY NOTE ON THE IMPACT OF 28 U.S.C. § 1257 ON A SUBSEQUENT CIVIL ACTION IN A FEDERAL DISTRICT COURT

The availability of an action in a federal district court after (or during) proceedings in a state court is affected not only by preclusion doctrine, and the rules developed with relation to the availability of habeas corpus, but also by the provisions of 28 U.S.C. § 1257, authorizing direct Supreme Court review of certain state court judgments. The impact of that provision is the subject of the case that follows and of the remaining materials in this chapter.

————

Exxon Mobil Corporation v. Saudi Basic Industries Corporation

544 U.S. 280, 125 S. Ct. 1517, 161 L. Ed. 2d 454 (2005).
Certiorari to the United States Court of Appeals for the Third Circuit.

■ JUSTICE GINSBURG delivered the opinion of the Court:

This case concerns what has come to be known as the Rooker-Feldman doctrine, applied by this Court only twice, first in Rooker v. Fidelity Trust Co., 263 U.S. 413 (1923), then, 60 years later, in District of Columbia Court of Appeals v. Feldman, 460 U.S. 462 (1983). Variously interpreted in the lower courts, the doctrine has sometimes been construed to extend far beyond the contours of the Rooker and Feldman cases, overriding Congress' conferral of federal-court jurisdiction concurrent with jurisdiction exercised by state courts, and superseding the ordinary application of preclusion law pursuant to 28 U.S.C. § 1738.

Rooker was a suit commenced in Federal District Court to have a judgment of a state court, adverse to the federal court plaintiffs,

———————————

[5] Is Justice Scalia's point undermined by the fact that a habeas court upholding a petitioner's claim may issue a *conditional* writ ordering the petitioner released *unless* a new proceeding (*e.g.*, a trial on the merits or a sentencing proceeding) is conducted? Perhaps not, since a federal court would probably lack authority to require *release* of the petitioner unless the constitutional defect is remedied.

"declared null and void." In Feldman, parties unsuccessful in the District of Columbia Court of Appeals (the District's highest court) commenced a federal-court action against the very court that had rejected their applications. Holding the federal suits impermissible, we emphasized that appellate jurisdiction to reverse or modify a state-court judgment is lodged, initially by § 25 of the Judiciary Act of 1789, and now by 28 U.S.C. § 1257, exclusively in this Court. Federal district courts, we noted, are empowered to exercise original, not appellate, jurisdiction. Plaintiffs in Rooker and Feldman had litigated and lost in state court. Their federal complaints, we observed, essentially invited federal courts of first instance to review and reverse unfavorable state-court judgments. We declared such suits out of bounds, i.e., properly dismissed for want of subject-matter jurisdiction.

The Rooker-Feldman doctrine, we hold today, is confined to cases of the kind from which the doctrine acquired its name: cases brought by state-court losers complaining of injuries caused by state-court judgments rendered before the district court proceedings commenced and inviting district court review and rejection of those judgments. Rooker-Feldman does not otherwise override or supplant preclusion doctrine or augment the circumscribed doctrines that allow federal courts to stay or dismiss proceedings in deference to state-court actions.

In the case before us, the Court of Appeals for the Third Circuit misperceived the narrow ground occupied by Rooker-Feldman, and consequently erred in ordering the federal action dismissed for lack of subject-matter jurisdiction. We therefore reverse the Third Circuit's judgment.

I

In Rooker, the parties defeated in state court turned to a Federal District Court for relief. Alleging that the adverse state-court judgment was rendered in contravention of the Constitution, they asked the federal court to declare it "null and void." This Court noted preliminarily that the state court had acted within its jurisdiction. If the state-court decision was wrong, the Court explained, "that did not make the judgment void, but merely left it open to reversal or modification in an appropriate and timely appellate proceeding." Federal district courts, the Rooker Court recognized, lacked the requisite appellate authority, for their jurisdiction was "strictly original." Among federal courts, the Rooker Court clarified, Congress had empowered only this Court to exercise appellate authority "to reverse or modify" a state-court judgment. Accordingly, the Court affirmed a decree dismissing the suit for lack of jurisdiction.

Sixty years later, the Court decided District of Columbia Court of Appeals v. Feldman. The two plaintiffs in that case, Hickey and Feldman, neither of whom had graduated from an accredited law school, petitioned the District of Columbia Court of Appeals to waive a court Rule that required D.C. bar applicants to have graduated from a law school approved by the American Bar Association. After the D.C. court denied their waiver requests, Hickey and Feldman filed suits in the United States District Court for the District of Columbia. The District Court and the Court of Appeals for the District of Columbia Circuit disagreed on the question whether the federal suit could be maintained, and we granted certiorari.

Recalling Rooker, this Court's opinion in Feldman observed first that the District Court lacked authority to review a final judicial determination of the D.C. high court. "Review of such determinations," the Feldman opinion reiterated, "can be obtained only in this Court." The "crucial question," the Court next stated, was whether the proceedings in the D.C. court were "judicial in nature." Addressing that question, the Court concluded that the D.C. court had acted both judicially and legislatively.

In applying the accreditation Rule to the Hickey and Feldman waiver petitions, this Court determined, the D.C. court had acted judicially. As to that adjudication, Feldman held, this Court alone among federal courts had review authority. Hence, "to the extent that Hickey and Feldman sought review in the District Court of the District of Columbia Court of Appeals' denial of their petitions for waiver, the District Court lacked subject-matter jurisdiction over their complaints." But that determination did not dispose of the entire case, for in promulgating the bar admission rule, this Court said, the D.C. court had acted legislatively, not judicially. "Challenges to the constitutionality of state bar rules," the Court elaborated, "do not necessarily require a United States district court to review a final state-court judgment in a judicial proceeding." Thus, the Court reasoned, 28 U.S.C. § 1257 did not bar District Court proceedings addressed to the validity of the accreditation Rule itself. The Rule could be contested in federal court, this Court held, so long as plaintiffs did not seek review of the Rule's application in a particular case.

The Court endeavored to separate elements of the Hickey and Feldman complaints that failed the jurisdictional threshold from those that survived jurisdictional inspection. Plaintiffs had urged that the District of Columbia Court of Appeals acted arbitrarily in denying the waiver petitions of Hickey and Feldman, given that court's "former policy of granting waivers to graduates of unaccredited law schools." That charge, the Court held, could not be pursued, for it was "inextricably intertwined with the District of Columbia Court of Appeals' decisions, in judicial proceedings, to deny [plaintiffs'] petitions."

On the other hand, the Court said, plaintiffs could maintain "claims that the [bar admission] rule is unconstitutional because it creates an irrebuttable presumption that only graduates of accredited law schools are fit to practice law, discriminates against those who have obtained equivalent legal training by other means, and impermissibly delegates the District of Columbia Court of Appeals' power to regulate the bar to the American Bar Association," for those claims "do not require review of a judicial decision in a particular case." The Court left open the question whether the doctrine of res judicata foreclosed litigation of the elements of the complaints spared from dismissal for want of subject-matter jurisdiction.

Since Feldman, this Court has never applied Rooker-Feldman to dismiss an action for want of jurisdiction. The few decisions that have mentioned Rooker and Feldman have done so only in passing or to explain why those cases did not dictate dismissal. * * *

II

In 1980, two subsidiaries of petitioner Exxon Mobil Corporation * * * formed joint ventures with respondent Saudi Basic Industries Corp. (SABIC) to produce polyethylene in Saudi Arabia. Two decades later, the parties began to dispute royalties that SABIC had charged the joint ventures for sublicenses to a polyethylene manufacturing method.

SABIC preemptively sued the two ExxonMobil subsidiaries in Delaware Superior Court in July 2000 seeking a declaratory judgment that the royalty charges were proper under the joint venture agreements. About two weeks later, ExxonMobil and its subsidiaries countersued SABIC in the United States District Court for the District of New Jersey, alleging that SABIC overcharged the joint ventures for the sublicenses. * * *

In January 2002, the ExxonMobil subsidiaries answered SABIC's state-court complaint, asserting as counterclaims the same claims ExxonMobil had made in the federal suit in New Jersey. The state suit went to trial in March 2003, and the jury returned a verdict of over $400 million in favor of the ExxonMobil subsidiaries. SABIC appealed the judgment entered on the verdict to the Delaware Supreme Court.

Before the state-court trial, SABIC moved to dismiss the federal suit, alleging, *inter alia*, immunity under the Foreign Sovereign Immunities Act of 1976, 28 U.S.C. § 1602 et seq. The Federal District Court denied SABIC's motion to dismiss. SABIC took an interlocutory appeal, and the Court of Appeals heard argument in December 2003, over eight months after the state-court jury verdict.

The Court of Appeals, on its own motion, raised the question whether "subject matter jurisdiction over this case fails under the Rooker-Feldman doctrine because ExxonMobil's claims have already been litigated in state court." The court did not question the District Court's possession of subject-matter jurisdiction at the outset of the suit, but held that federal jurisdiction terminated when the Delaware Superior Court entered judgment on the jury verdict. The court rejected ExxonMobil's argument that Rooker-Feldman could not apply because ExxonMobil filed its federal complaint well before the state-court judgment. The only relevant consideration, the court stated, "is whether the state judgment precedes a federal judgment on the same claims." If Rooker-Feldman did not apply to federal actions filed prior to a state-court judgment, the Court of Appeals worried, "we would be encouraging parties to maintain federal actions as 'insurance policies' while their state court claims were pending." Once ExxonMobil's claims had been litigated to a judgment in state court, the Court of Appeals held, Rooker-Feldman "preclude[d] [the] federal district court from proceeding."

ExxonMobil, at that point prevailing in Delaware, was not seeking to overturn the state-court judgment. Nevertheless, the Court of Appeals hypothesized that, if SABIC won on appeal in Delaware, ExxonMobil would be endeavoring in the federal action to "invalidate" the state-court judgment, "the very situation," the court concluded, "contemplated by Rooker-Feldman's 'inextricably intertwined' bar."

We granted certiorari to resolve conflict among the Courts of Appeals over the scope of the Rooker-Feldman doctrine. We now reverse the judgment of the Court of Appeals for the Third Circuit.

III

Rooker and Feldman exhibit the limited circumstances in which this Court's appellate jurisdiction over state-court judgments, 28 U.S.C. § 1257, precludes a United States district court from exercising subject-matter jurisdiction in an action it would otherwise be empowered to adjudicate under a congressional grant of authority. In both cases, the losing party in state court filed suit in federal court after the state proceedings ended, complaining of an injury caused by the state-court judgment and seeking review and rejection of that judgment. Plaintiffs in both cases, alleging federal-question jurisdiction, called upon the District Court to overturn an injurious state-court judgment. Because § 1257, as long interpreted, vests authority to review a state court's judgment solely in this Court, the District Courts in Rooker and Feldman lacked subject-matter jurisdiction.[8]

When there is parallel state and federal litigation, Rooker-Feldman is not triggered simply by the entry of judgment in state court. This Court has repeatedly held that "the pendency of an action in the state court is no bar to proceedings concerning the same matter in the Federal court having jurisdiction." McClellan v. Carland, 217 U.S. 268, 282 (1910). Comity or abstention doctrines may, in various circumstances, permit or require the federal court to stay or dismiss the federal action in favor of the state-court litigation. But neither Rooker nor Feldman supports the notion that properly invoked concurrent jurisdiction vanishes if a state court reaches judgment on the same or related question while the case remains sub judice in a federal court.

Disposition of the federal action, once the state-court adjudication is complete, would be governed by preclusion law. * * * Preclusion, of course, is not a jurisdictional matter. In parallel litigation, a federal court may be bound to recognize the claim- and issue-preclusive effects of a state-court judgment, but federal jurisdiction over an action does not terminate automatically on the entry of judgment in the state court.

Nor does § 1257 stop a district court from exercising subject-matter jurisdiction simply because a party attempts to litigate in federal court a matter previously litigated in state court. If a federal plaintiff "present[s] some independent claim, albeit one that denies a legal conclusion that a state court has reached in a case to which he was a party . . . , then there is jurisdiction and state law determines whether the defendant prevails under principles of preclusion." GASH Assocs. v. Rosemont, 995 F.2d 726, 728 (CA7 1993).

* * * ExxonMobil plainly has not repaired to federal court to undo the Delaware judgment in its favor. Rather, it appears ExxonMobil filed suit in Federal District Court (only two weeks after SABIC filed in Delaware and well before any judgment in state court) to protect itself in the event it lost in state court on grounds (such as the state statute of limitations) that might not preclude relief in the federal venue. Rooker-Feldman did not prevent the District Court from exercising jurisdiction when ExxonMobil filed the federal action, and it did not emerge to vanquish jurisdiction after ExxonMobil prevailed in the Delaware courts.

---

[8]   Congress, if so minded, may explicitly empower district courts to oversee certain state-court judgments and has done so, most notably, in authorizing federal habeas review of state prisoners' petitions. 28 U.S.C. § 2254(a).

For the reason stated, the judgment of the Court of Appeals for the Third Circuit is reversed, and the case is remanded for further proceedings consistent with his opinion. It is so ordered.

NOTE ON THE ROOKER-FELDMAN DOCTRINE

(1) The Rooker and Feldman Decisions. The facts and holdings of Rooker and Feldman are set out by Justice Ginsburg in the Court's opinion in the Exxon Mobil case. Rooker, decided in 1923, was largely forgotten until revived in Chang, *Rediscovering the Rooker Doctrine: Section 1983, Res Judicata and the Federal Courts*, 31 Hastings L.J. 1337 (1980), and soon after, provided the basis for the Court's per curiam decision in Feldman. With respect to the plaintiffs' "general challenge" to the constitutionality of the D.C. bar membership rule in Feldman—a challenge the Court said was not barred by its holding—the opinion "expressly" did not reach the question "whether the doctrine of res judicata forecloses litigation". Justice Stevens, dissenting from the holding that the district court lacked jurisdiction to entertain the specific challenges to the denials of the plaintiffs' waiver applications, said: "If a challenge to a state court's decision is brought in United States district court and alleges violations of the United States Constitution, then by definition it does not seek appellate review. It is plainly within the federal-question jurisdiction of the federal court. There may be other reasons for denying relief to the plaintiff—such as failure to state a cause of action, claim or issue preclusion, or failure to prove a violation of constitutional rights. But it does violence to jurisdictional concepts for this Court to hold, as it does, that the federal district court has no *jurisdiction* to conduct independent review of a specific claim that a licensing body's action did not comply with federal constitutional standards."

If, as the Court stated in Feldman, the challenges to the denials of plaintiffs' petitions for waiver could not be pursued because they were "inextricably intertwined" with the prior decision of the D.C. Court of Appeals, why weren't the general challenges to the constitutionality of the admission rules similarly "intertwined" and thus also barred?

(2) The Relationship to Res Judicata Doctrine. The Rooker and Feldman decisions raised a number of questions centering on the issue of what, if anything, they added to the doctrine of res judicata and to § 1738.

(a) Suppose that under state res judicata doctrine, a collateral challenge to a state court judgment would be barred in the state's own courts. Wouldn't a collateral challenge in a federal court normally be barred by § 1738? If Rooker-Feldman means that § 1257 furnishes an independent statutory basis for that result, what turns on labeling the result a lack of jurisdiction in the district court to review the state court judgment, rather than an application of res judicata? (Since unlike lack of subject matter jurisdiction, res judicata is a waivable defense, the Rooker-Feldman reformulation apparently suggests that the case must be dismissed even if the defendant does not object to the action.)

(b) Now assume that an original action of the sort at issue in Feldman, challenging on constitutional grounds the state supreme court's denial of waiver, *could* be maintained in the state courts. Does the Rooker-Feldman doctrine mean that a federal action is impermissible nevertheless, and if so, how would this result square with the Court's insistence, in its § 1738 cases, that the preclusive effect in a federal court of a state court judgment must be measured by state law?

When a federal district court is asked to reopen issues already adjudicated by another *federal* district court, the law of res judicata ordinarily determines whether reopening is permissible. Does it help the analysis to ask, independently, whether the second inquiry is precluded by 28 U.S.C. § 1291—the statute governing the federal courts of appeals' "exclusive" jurisdiction to review final district court judgments?

(c) Rooker and Feldman both involved state court proceedings that were complete when district court challenges were initiated; there was no occasion to inquire whether state remedies should be exhausted before the federal action is entertained, or whether comity principles barred the action. But the "exclusive jurisdiction" notion underlying Rooker and Feldman may well be relevant when state proceedings are still underway and doctrines of comity, abstention, and exhaustion could also come into play.

(3) From Feldman to Exxon Mobil and Beyond. After Feldman, the lower courts—as Justice Ginsburg indicated in Exxon Mobil—often found the Rooker-Feldman doctrine relevant and even dispositive in situations "extend[ing] far beyond the contours" of that doctrine as the Supreme Court had articulated it.[1]

The Court's decision in the Exxon Mobil case, in both its holding and its general tone, undoubtedly has tempered the enthusiasm of many lower courts for applying the Rooker-Feldman doctrine. And the cabining of the doctrine continued in Lance v. Dennis, 546 U.S. 459 (2006), a case discussed in the footnote.[2] But there are still a number of unresolved questions,

---

[1] During this period, the doctrine attracted a good deal of scholarly attention. Of particular interest was a 1999 symposium in the Notre Dame Law Review, in which most (but not all) of the commentators were critical of the doctrine, in whole or in substantial part, as indicated by the title of the opening article. See Rowe, *Rooker-Feldman: Worth Only the Powder To Blow it Up?*, 74 Notre Dame L.Rev. 1081 (1999) (quoting David Shapiro and setting the stage for the debate). See also Sherry, *Judicial Federalism in the Trenches: The Rooker-Feldman Doctrine in Action*, id. at 1085, 1100, 1128 (defending the doctrine as a "valuable tool" for plugging gaps in the rules governing res judicata and Younger abstention "that would otherwise wreak havoc on our system of dual courts"); Friedman & Gaylord, *Rooker-Feldman, from the Ground Up*, id. at 1129 (analyzing the overlap of various doctrines and concluding that Rooker-Feldman performs a unique function only in situations in which the lower courts have extended the doctrine well beyond its precedential roots); Bandes, *The Rooker-Feldman Doctrine: Evaluating Its Jurisdictional Status*, id. at 1175 (tracing the jurisdictional lineage of the doctrine and arguing that it can properly be applied only in certain narrowly defined instances); Beermann, *Comments on Rooker-Feldman, or Why We Should Let State Law Be Our Guide*, id. at 1209 (joining with those who question both the value and significance of the doctrine).

[2] In this case, after a state court action brought by the state's attorney general against the secretary of state resulted in rejection of the state legislature's redistricting plan, several state citizens filed a federal court action seeking to require the secretary of state to use the legislature's plan. A three-judge district court held the federal action barred by Rooker-Feldman, even though the federal plaintiffs were not parties to the state proceeding, on the ground that the federal plaintiffs were in privity with the state general assembly, which had intervened in the state proceeding. The Supreme Court reversed in a per curiam opinion, holding that Rooker-Feldman "does not bar actions by nonparties to the earlier state court judgment simply because, for purposes of preclusion law, they could be considered in privity with a party to the judgment." The question of preclusion under state law, which the Court insisted should not be conflated with Rooker-Feldman, was left open on remand.

In its 2011 decision in Skinner v. Switzer, p. 1399, *supra*, the Court again refused to find that Rooker-Feldman defeated jurisdiction, unanimously ruling that Skinner's § 1983 action "[did] not

including some of those posed in Paragraph (2), *supra*. For example, does the doctrine apply to bar federal actions commenced after the grant of interlocutory relief in a state court proceeding, or after final judgment in a lower state court? And what is the precise relationship between the state court judgment and the subsequently commenced federal action that will bring the doctrine into play?[3]

Justice Stevens, writing for himself in Lance v. Dennis, stated that Rooker-Feldman had been "finally interred" by Exxon Mobil. Wasn't this an overstatement? But assuming that Justice Stevens was mistaken in suggesting that that Rooker-Feldman has been "interred," should it be? In what situations, if any, should § 1257 bar an original action in federal court when existing preclusion doctrine would not bar that action? Consider, for example, a case in which a state allows a person whose property has been condemned by a municipality in a judicial proceeding to collaterally attack the judgment in that proceeding on the ground that the notice given was constitutionally inadequate. Should a federal court have jurisdiction to entertain a § 1983 action brought by that person against the municipality for damages allegedly resulting from the failure to give constitutionally adequate notice? See Ritter v. Ross, 992 F.2d 750 (7th Cir.1993) (holding that Rooker-Feldman barred such an action).

Or consider a case in which state preclusion doctrine—applied in the federal courts through 28 U.S.C. § 1738—does not bar a federal court from proceeding with an independent action after a state court judgment has become final. Should there be an exception to Rooker-Feldman if the federal plaintiff can show that the challenged state court judgment was obtained by fraud? The question has arisen in the context of federal attacks on state court mortgage foreclosure judgments, and a number of circuits have disagreed on the answer. See Baker, *The Fraud Exception to Rooker-Feldman: How It Almost Wasn't (and Probably Shouldn't Be)*, 5 Fed.Cts.L.Rev. 139 (2011).

---

challenge the adverse [state court] decisions themselves; instead he target[ed] as unconstitutional the Texas statute they authoritatively construed."

[3] For a comprehensive analysis of the implications of the Exxon Mobil and Lance decisions, see Rowe & Baskauskas, *"Inextricably Intertwined" Explicable at Last? Rooker-Feldman Analysis After the Supreme Court's Exxon Mobil Decision*, 1 Fed.Cts.L.Rev. 367 (2006). The authors conclude by expressing the hope that these decisions will eliminate the "exuberant overgrowth that had sprung from the doctrine's modest roots".

CHAPTER XIII

THE DIVERSITY JURISDICTION OF THE FEDERAL DISTRICT COURTS

---

1. INTRODUCTION

STATUTORY DEVELOPMENT

Federal diversity jurisdiction has existed ever since the Judiciary Act of 1789. Section 11 of that Act, 1 Stat. 79, conferred jurisdiction when the "matter in dispute" exceeded the sum or value of $500 and (1) an alien was a party, or (2) the suit was between a citizen of the state where the action was brought and a citizen of another state. The requirement in the second category that one of the parties be a citizen of the forum state was eliminated in 1875, 18 Stat. 470. The 1875 Act also modified the first category by conferring jurisdiction in controversies between "citizens of a State and foreign states, citizens, or subjects."

A 1940 amendment extended diversity jurisdiction to suits "between * * * citizens of the District of Columbia, the Territory of Hawaii, or Alaska, and any State or Territory." 54 Stat. 143. In the general revision of the Judicial Code in 1948, the operative provisions were rewritten, codified in 28 U.S.C. § 1332, and subdivided to cover (in subsection (a)) suits between "(1) Citizens of different States; (2) Citizens of a State and foreign states or citizens or subjects thereof; [or] (3) Citizens of different States and in which foreign states or citizens or subjects thereof are additional parties." 62 Stat. 930. Subsection (b) defined "States" to include the Territories and the District of Columbia; in 1956, that definition was extended to the Commonwealth of Puerto Rico (70 Stat. 658).

In 1958, the definition of "States" was moved to subsection (d), and Congress added new subsections (b) and (c). 72 Stat. 415. Subsection (b), dealing with cases in which the plaintiff recovers less than the jurisdictional amount, has remained unchanged to the present day (except for the subsequent increases in the dollar amount). Subsection (c) provided as follows:

"(c) For the purposes of this section and section 1441 of this title, a corporation shall be deemed a citizen of any State by which it has been incorporated and of the State where it has its principal place of business."

In 1964, Congress added a proviso to subsection (c) designed to deal with "direct actions" against insurance companies. 78 Stat. 445. It stated that in such actions, when the insured is not joined as a party-defendant, the insurer "shall be deemed a citizen of the State of which the insured is a citizen, as well as of any State by which the insurer has been incorporated and of the State where it has its principal place of business."

In 1976, § 1332 was amended in connection with the Foreign Sovereign Immunities Act, 28 U.S.C. §§ 1602–11. The references to foreign states as parties were stricken from subsections (a)(2) and (a)(3), and a new subsection (a)(4) was added conferring jurisdiction over suits brought by foreign states as defined by the new Act. Suits against foreign states, as defined by the Act, were dealt with in a new § 1330 of Title 28.

In 1988, § 1332 was amended once again. 102 Stat. 4646. Congress provided that for purposes of § 1332 (as well as §§ 1335 and 1441), "an alien admitted to the United States for permanent residence shall be deemed a citizen of the State in which such alien is domiciled." In addition, the direct action proviso of subsection (c) was slightly changed and a second paragraph added to that subsection stating: "The legal representative of the estate of a decedent shall be deemed to be a citizen only of the same State as the decedent, and the legal representative of an infant or incompetent shall be deemed to be a citizen only of the same State as the infant or incompetent."

In 2005, Congress enacted the Class Action Fairness Act, 119 Stat. 4 (2005) (discussed in detail at pp. 1426–1430, *infra*). As part of this Act, § 1332 was amended, moving former subsection (d) (defining "States") to subsection (e), and adding a new subsection (d) significantly expanding federal court jurisdiction over certain class actions, as well as certain "mass action[s]" in which "monetary relief claims of 100 or more persons are proposed to be tried jointly".

In 2011, Congress enacted the Federal Courts Jurisdiction and Venue Clarification Act of 2011, Pub.L.No. 112–63, 125 Stat. 758, making a number of changes discussed in this Chapter. With respect to diversity jurisdiction, the Act substituted for the 1988 change relating to resident aliens the following language: "except that the district courts shall not have original jurisdiction under this subsection [1332(a)] of an action between citizens of a State and citizens or subjects of a foreign state who are lawfully admitted for permanent residence in the United States and are domiciled in the same State." (For further discussion of this provision, see pp. 1421–1422, *infra*.)

The 2011 Act also changed the words "any State" in § 1332(c)(1) to "every State and foreign state", thereby making it even clearer that diversity jurisdiction does not exist when, for example, a citizen of state A sues a corporation incorporated in states A and B. That change, along with corresponding changes in the "direct action" provision of subsection (c), also extended the reach of the subsection to corporations incorporated in other countries.

The requisite amount in controversy has been increased many times since 1789: to $2,000 in 1887 (24 Stat. 552), $3,000 in 1911 (36 Stat. 1091), $10,000 in 1958 (72 Stat. 415), $50,000 in 1988 (102 Stat. 4646), and $75,000 in 1996 (110 Stat. 3847).

Finally, several other statutes contain provisions allowing diversity jurisdiction in circumstances not covered by § 1332. These include the Interpleader Act, 28 U.S.C. § 1335 (discussed at pp. 1423, 1437, *infra*) and 28 U.S.C. § 1369, dealing with certain actions involving a large number of casualties and arising out of a single accident (discussed at p. 1426, *infra*).

NOTE ON THE HISTORICAL BACKGROUND AND CONTEMPORARY
UTILITY OF THE DIVERSITY JURISDICTION

A.   Historical Background

The conventional account of the diversity jurisdiction has found its roots
in fear of prejudice against out-of-state litigants in the state courts. The most
quoted statement is Chief Justice Marshall's in Bank of the United States v.
Deveaux, 9 U.S. (5 Cranch) 61, 87 (1809): "However true the fact may be,
that the tribunals of the states will administer justice as impartially as those
of the nation, to parties of every description, it is not less true that the
constitution itself either entertains apprehensions on this subject, or views
with such indulgence the possible fears and apprehensions of suitors, that it
has established national tribunals for the decision of controversies between
aliens and a citizen, or between citizens of different states."

Perhaps the best-known study of the origins of the diversity jurisdiction
is Friendly, *The Historic Basis of Diversity Jurisdiction*, 41 Harv.L.Rev. 483
(1928). As he noted, the principal discussion took place in the debates on
ratification, in which the proposed jurisdiction was bitterly denounced. What
Friendly found "astounding", however, was "not the vigor of the attack but
the apathy of the defense." Friendly questioned the "sincerity" of the
argument about apprehension of local prejudice because of the failure of
Madison and other proponents to adduce specific examples. Reviewing the
scanty reports of contemporary decisions, Friendly concluded that the
evidence "entirely fails to show the existence of prejudice on the part of the
state judges."

What Friendly did find was that "the real fear was not of state courts so
much as of state legislatures. * * * In summary, we may say that the desire
to protect creditors against legislation favorable to debtors was a principal
reason for the grant of diversity jurisdiction, and that as a reason it was by
no means without validity." To this he added a general lack of confidence in
state judges and fear of the practice of legislative review of judicial decisions
that prevailed in some states. (Note also state legislative control of judicial
salaries and, in many states, the removability of judges at the behest of
governors or on address of the legislatures.) "Not unnaturally the commercial
interests of the country were reluctant to expose themselves to the hazards
of litigation before such courts as these. They might be good enough for the
inhabitants of their respective states, but merchants from abroad felt
themselves entitled to something better. There was a vague feeling that the
new courts would be strong courts, creditors' courts, business men's courts."

Friendly's research and conclusions have not gone unchallenged.
Yntema & Jaffin, *Preliminary Analysis of Concurrent Jurisdiction*, 79
U.Pa.L.Rev. 869, 873–76 & n.13 (1931), argue that the available evidence
"precludes extensive inference" and that "the theory of no local prejudice is
presumptively improbable." Frank, *Historical Bases of the Federal Judicial
System*, 13 Law & Contemp.Probs. 3, 22–28 (1948), reviews the question and
concludes that the relevant considerations in creating the jurisdiction were
"1. The desire to avoid regional prejudice against commercial litigants, based
in small part on experience and in large part on common-sense anticipation.
2. The desire to permit commercial, manufacturing, and speculative interests
to litigate their controversies, and particularly their controversies with other
classes, before judges who would be firmly tied to their own interests. 3. The

desire to achieve more efficient administration of justice for the classes thus benefitted."

And most recently, Jones, *Finishing a Friendly Argument: The Jury and the Historical Origins of Diversity Jurisdiction*, 82 N.Y.U.L.Rev. 997 (2007), argues that (a) the Federalists' goal in creating the diversity jurisdiction transcended purely commercial matters and (b) the Federalists did not fear state legislatures but instead state court *juries*, whose primarily rural agrarian composition and power to decide issues of both law and fact had transformed them into powerful pro-debtor, quasi-legislative bodies. Jones posits that diversity jurisdiction was devised by the Federalists to present commercial (and other) cases instead to federal juries, which were designed to be composed primarily of urban merchants more sympathetic to commercial interests.[1]

B.   Contemporary Utility

(1) Pre-Erie Controversy. Diversity jurisdiction has always been controversial. During the era before the decision in Erie R.R. Co. v. Tompkins, 304 U.S. 64 (1938), see Chap. VI, Sec. 2, *supra*, opposition to the jurisdiction was buttressed by the belief that federal courts were using the diversity power to favor business interests and to exercise law-making authority that exceeded both federal and judicial bounds.[2]

(2) The Effect of the Erie Decision. Did the Erie decision weaken or strengthen the case for the diversity jurisdiction? Writing a decade later, Professor Wechsler argued that the jurisdiction could not be justified solely on the basis of the "original fear of prejudice against the litigant from out of state." Wechsler, *Federal Jurisdiction and the Revision of the Judicial Code*, 13 Law & Contemp.Probs. 216, 235–39 (1948). But he went on to say: "There is, I think, a solid case for preservation of the jurisdiction in any instance where a concrete showing of state prejudice can be established. There may be cases, too, where there is need for process that outruns state borders, as in the interpleader under present law." The challenge, he argued, is to limit federal intervention to the situations in which it in fact responds to such needs.

(3) The Possible Uses of the Diversity Jurisdiction. Consider the contemporary persuasiveness of the following possible justifications for the diversity jurisdiction.

---

[1]   For the view that alienage jurisdiction was "historically the single most important grant of national court jurisdiction embodied in the [First Judiciary] Act", and that the "poor record" of the state courts in enforcing the treaty obligations of the union was the main impetus behind the creation of national courts, see Holt, *The Origins of Alienage Jurisdiction*, 14 Okla. City U.L.Rev. 547, 548–49 (1989). For discussions of the origins of the diversity jurisdiction that emphasize the nationalizing functions it served, see Marbury, *Why Should We Limit Federal Diversity Jurisdiction?*, 46 A.B.A.J. 379 (1960); Moore & Weckstein, *Diversity Jurisdiction: Past, Present, and Future*, 43 Tex. L.Rev. 1 (1964).

[2]   For conflicting views in the decade prior to Erie, see Frankfurter, *Distribution of Judicial Power between United States and State Courts*, 13 Cornell L.Q. 499, 520–30 (1928); Yntema & Jaffin; *Limiting Jurisdiction of Federal Courts—Pending Bills—Comments by Members of Chicago University Law Faculty*, 31 Mich.L.Rev. 59 (1932); Clark, *Diversity of Citizenship Jurisdiction of the Federal Courts*, 19 A.B.A.J. 499 (1933). For a summary of earlier views, see Frankfurter & Landis, The Business of the Supreme Court 86–102, 136–41 (1928). And for a contemporary review of the pre-Erie period that focuses on the concerns of Justice Brandeis, see Purcell, Brandeis and the Progressive Constitution: Erie, the Judicial Power, and the Politics of the Federal Courts in Twentieth-Century America (2000), discussed at p. 583, *supra*.

(a) *As a vehicle for building up and administering a uniform body of judge-made law in areas in which Congress either has not legislated or could not.*

This was the goal of Swift v. Tyson on which, presumably, the books are now closed—absent a basis for the formulation of "genuine" federal common law. See Chaps. VI, VII, *supra*.

(b) *As a means of encouraging out-of-state individuals and enterprises to engage in local investment and other activities, by providing an assurance of impartial decision of disputes growing out of those activities.*

Notice the varying kinds of injustice against which a safeguard may be desired: *e.g.*, invocation of unjust or discriminatory rules of law; unjust factfinding or application of law to the facts; delays and inefficiencies in judicial administration. Should an in-state plaintiff be able to invoke the jurisdiction, especially given that an in-state defendant may not remove a state court action brought by an out-of-state plaintiff? See 28 U.S.C. § 1441(b)(2).

There are other federal protections against these evils: *e.g.*, the Privileges and Immunities Clause of Article IV, § 2; the Privileges or Immunities Clause of the Fourteenth Amendment; the Commerce Clause; the Due Process Clause of the Fourteenth Amendment; and the Equal Protection Clause. Do these constitutional provisions sufficiently protect against the potential injustices described above? Is the need for diversity jurisdiction decreased or eliminated by the lessening of provincialism and the improvement of state judicial systems?[3]

(c) *As a means of providing for the just resolution of conflicts of laws in controversies between citizens of different states.*

This purpose implicates the question whether Klaxon Co. v. Stentor Elec. Mfg. Co., 313 U.S. 487 (1941), p. 591, *supra*, was correctly decided. Should legislative or judicial action be taken under the Full Faith and Credit Clause to achieve this goal, in all or some specific area(s) of diversity jurisdiction?[4]

(d) *As a means of assuring out-of-state litigants and their lawyers that a familiar procedural system will be available for the resolution of disputes.*

The adoption of the Federal Rules of Civil Procedure in 1938 made it possible to think about this objective as a justification for the diversity jurisdiction. Has its value been undercut by the extent to which those very rules have influenced the development of procedural systems in virtually every state?

(e) *As a means of facilitating interchange between state and federal systems on matters of substance and procedure.*

---

[3] Some justification for the diversity jurisdiction may be based on "rational prejudice"—situations in which a state's residents (including the judges they have chosen) have an *economic* incentive to discriminate against nonresidents. See Posner, The Federal Courts: Challenge and Reform 215–16 (1996).

[4] In cases involving complex litigation, especially litigation likely to take the form of lawsuits brought in a number of courts (state and/or federal), are the arguments for such action especially strong? For proposed federal legislation governing choice of law in such cases, see American Law Institute, Complex Litigation: Statutory Recommendations and Analysis (1994). See also the extensive discussion of this and other aspects of the proposals made by the ALI Project in the Symposium appearing in 54 La.L.Rev. No. 4 (1994).

For discussion of the possible values of diversity jurisdiction in supporting the "migration of ideas" between state and federal courts, see Shapiro, *Federal Diversity Jurisdiction: A Survey and a Proposal*, 91 Harv.L.Rev. 317, 324–27 (1977). See also Posner, note 3, *supra*, at 216, concluding that "even in the years since the Erie decision eliminated or, more realistically, confined their creative lawmaking role in diversity cases, the federal courts have made a disproportionate contribution to the shaping of the common law * * *."

(f) *As a means of facilitating the settlement of controversies that, because of the multiplicity of parties and their diversity of citizenship, cannot be effectually settled in the courts of any one state.*

The notion that diversity jurisdiction should be available to resolve controversies that involve similar claims of many parties in a number of states (or class claims involving class members residing in many states) has gained increasing traction in recent decades. The first special enactment providing for such use was the Federal Interpleader Act of 1936, now codified in 28 U.S.C. §§ 1335, 1397, 2361, discussed at pp. 1425–1426, *infra*. Many years later, proposals for broader uses of diversity in multiparty litigation appeared. See, *e.g.*, American Law Institute, Study of the Division of Jurisdiction Between State and Federal Courts, proposed §§ 2371–76 (1969); Rowe & Sibley, *Beyond Diversity: Federal Multiparty, Multiforum Jurisdiction*, 135 U.Pa.L.Rev. 7 (1986). Legislation ensued, first in 2002 with the enactment of § 1369, providing for jurisdiction based on "minimal diversity" in certain mass tort cases, see p. 1426, *infra*, and most important, in the Class Action Fairness Act of 2005, see pp. 1426–1430, *infra*.[5]

Are there other justifications for the diversity jurisdiction to which consideration should be given? Should it matter if the federal courts of first instance are in fact, or are perceived to be, of higher quality than their state counterparts? (See Chap. IV, p. 299, *supra*.) For an argument that it should not, see Friendly, Federal Jurisdiction: A General View 145–47 (1973).[6]

Recent decades have seen much discussion of the desirability and proper scope of the diversity jurisdiction. Those favoring abolition suggest not only that local prejudice is no longer a serious concern,[7] but that diversity cases burden the federal courts, whose resources could better be devoted to cases turning on federal law, and that these cases pose complexities—including the need to ascertain jurisdiction, difficult questions of whether federal or state law applies, and, where state law does apply, to determine its content— that would be avoided were such cases litigated in state court.[8] In response, proponents of retention not only cite some of the foregoing possible justifications for the jurisdiction, but also argue that lightening federal court burdens will increase the burdens on state courts and that experience with the jurisdiction suggests that "[t]here is no widespread, obvious abuse to be

---

[5] For an analysis of these developments, and their implications for the federal courts, see Underwood, *The Late, Great Diversity Jurisdiction*, 57 Case W.Res.L.Rev. 179 (2006).

[6] Compare Professor Seinfeld's argument, p. 779 & n.1, *supra*, that the primary purpose of *federal question jurisdiction* is to provide litigants and their lawyers with a high quality "franchise" provided by federal courts.

[7] See, *e.g.*, Testimony of Professor Charles Allen Wright, Hearings on Federal Diversity of Citizenship Jurisdiction Before the Subcommittee on Improvements in Judicial Machinery of the Senate Committee on the Judiciary, 95th Cong. 45–49 (1978).

[8] See especially Rowe, *Abolishing Diversity Jurisdiction: Positive Side Effects and Potential for Further Reforms*, 92 Harv.L.Rev. 963 (1979).

corrected." Frank, *The Case for Diversity Jurisdiction*, 16 Harv.J. on Legis. 403, 409 (1979).[9]

(4) Diversity Filings in the District Courts. According to the annual reports of the Administrative Office of the United States Courts, the number of diversity cases filed in the district courts continued to rise prior to the 1988 increase in the jurisdictional amount, but the ratio of such cases to all civil actions filed in those courts declined—from approximately one-third in 1960 to one-quarter in 1988. After some fluctuation in the intervening years, the ratio of diversity filings to all civil filings had returned to slightly less than 25% in 1994. Following the 1996 increase in the jurisdictional amount threshold, diversity filings declined by approximately 15% during the next three years. Bak, Golmant & O'Conor, *Reducing Federal Diversity Jurisdiction Filings: A Qualified Success*, 39 Judges' J., Summer 2000, at 20, 24 tbl 1. But that trend did not continue, and in the 2006 fiscal year, a total of 80,370 diversity cases were filed, constituting a 29% spike from 2005 and 31% of all civil filings in 2006. Between fiscal 2006 and fiscal 2011, the number of diversity cases filed continued to rise, peaking in fiscal 2011 at 108,072, which represented 36.7% of all civil cases filed. See Table C–2 of Federal Judicial Caseload Statistics, available at www.uscourts.gov. In the fiscal year ending March 31, 2013, diversity filings declined to 81,203, representing 29.8% of all civil cases filed.

---

2. ELEMENTS OF DIVERSITY JURISDICTION

NOTE ON THE KINDS OF DIVERSE CITIZENSHIP THAT CONFER JURISDICTION

A. The Meaning of State Citizenship

State citizenship of an individual, for the purposes of diversity jurisdiction, has traditionally depended upon two elements: first, United States citizenship; and second, domicile in the state, in the accepted conflict-of-laws sense of the term "domicile." See, *e.g.*, Brown v. Keene, 33 U.S. (8 Pet.) 112 (1834). "Domicile" in this sense is usually a person's home, i.e., the place "where a person dwells and which is the center of his domestic, social and civil life." Also, "no person has more than one domicil at a time." Restatement (Second) of Conflict of Laws §§ 11, 12 (1971).

---

[9] Among those favoring abolition of general diversity jurisdiction have been Judge Friendly, in Federal Jurisdiction: A General View 3–4, 139–52 (1973), and then-Chief Justice Burger in *Annual Report on the State of the Judiciary*, 62 A.B.A.J. 443, 444 (1976). See also Rowe, note 7, *supra*; Kramer, *Diversity Jurisdiction*, 1990 B.Y.U.L.Rev. 97 (concluding that, with the exception of cases involving aliens, interpleader actions, and complex multistate litigation, the jurisdiction should be abolished, a conclusion that paralleled the contemporaneous recommendation of the Federal Courts Study Committee, which he served as a reporter).

With the foregoing, compare, *e.g.*, Arnold, *The Future of the Federal Courts*, 60 Mo.L.Rev. 533, 538–39 (1995) (noting that Congress "created the lower [federal] court[s] primarily to hear diversity cases"); Frank, cited above; Shapiro, Paragraph (3)(e), *supra*, at 319 (suggesting a " 'local option plan,' under which each federal district would have limited freedom to retain, curtail, or virtually eliminate diversity jurisdiction within its borders").

Innumerable cases hold that a mere allegation of residence in a state is insufficient to found diversity jurisdiction, since such an allegation may not connote domicile and hence state citizenship. *E.g.*, Wolfe v. Hartford Life & Annuity Ins. Co., 148 U.S. 389 (1893). This doctrine survived the Fourteenth Amendment, despite its statement that all persons born or naturalized in the United States are citizens of the United States and "the State wherein they reside." See Robertson v. Cease, 97 U.S. 646, 648–50 (1878).

The doctrine, of course, is initially one of pleading, but there is an underlying point of substance. It is possible to be a citizen of the United States without being a citizen of any state or federal territory. See Paragraph B(5) of this Note.

B.   The Kinds of Diverse Citizenship

(1) Actions Between a Citizen of the Forum State and a Citizen of Another State. From 1789 to 1875 the diversity jurisdiction (apart from aliens) extended only to cases of this type. It has never made a difference whether the out-of-state citizen was plaintiff or defendant. But if the plaintiff elected to sue in a state court, only an out-of-state defendant could, or now can, remove to a federal court. Is there a sound reason for this difference?

(2) Actions Between Citizens of Two Different Non-forum States. Jurisdiction in this class of cases was first conferred in 1875 and still exists. If the case is brought in a state court, the defendant can remove.

Did the Klaxon case, p. 591, *supra*, which rejected the possibility of federal choice-of-law rules in diversity cases, remove whatever justification there was for this jurisdiction? Or is it justified by the fact that one noncitizen often may have much closer ties to the forum state than another?

(3) Actions Between an Alien (or a Foreign State) and a Citizen of the Forum State. This jurisdiction has existed since 1789, but now excludes actions in which one party is an alien who has been admitted for permanent residence and is domiciled in the same state as an opposing party. The present statute also appears to exclude from the jurisdiction an alien who is "stateless" (at least if not domiciled in the United States and admitted here as a permanent resident). See, *e.g.*, Shoemaker v. Malaxa, 241 F.2d 129 (2d Cir.1957).

(4) Actions Between an Alien (or a Foreign State) and a Citizen of a Non-forum State. This jurisdiction has also existed since 1789 (but—as in (3), above—now excludes actions in which one party is an alien admitted for permanent residence and domiciled in the same state as his adversary). Are there special dangers of prejudice here that do not exist in class 2?

(5) Actions in Which One of the Parties Is a Citizen of the United States but Not of Any State or Territory or of the District of Columbia or Puerto Rico. This class of American citizens includes Americans domiciled abroad. See, *e.g.*, Smith v. Carter, 545 F.2d 909 (5th Cir.1977); Van Der Schelling v. U.S. News & World Report, Inc., 213 F.Supp. 756 (E.D.Pa.), *aff'd per curiam*, 324 F.2d 956 (3d Cir.1963). Both cases held that such persons are not within the grant of diversity jurisdiction. Is this result compelled by Article III?

(6) Actions Between a Citizen of the District of Columbia and Either (a) a Citizen of the Forum State; (b) a Citizen of a Non-forum State; (c) an Alien; (d) a Citizen of Puerto Rico; or (e) a Citizen of a Territory.

Actions Between a Citizen of a Territory and either (a) a Citizen of the Forum State; (b) a Citizen of a Non-forum State; (c) an Alien; (d) a Citizen of Puerto Rico; or (e) a Citizen of Another Territory.

Actions Between a Citizen of Puerto Rico and Either (a) a Citizen of the Forum State; (b) a Citizen of a Non-forum State; or (c) an Alien.

For many years, § 1332 conferred jurisdiction over all of the subclasses in this class (with parallel removal jurisdiction under § 1441, except when a citizen of the forum state is a defendant).

Does the decision in the Tidewater case, p. 410, *supra*—upholding the jurisdiction of a Maryland federal court over an action by a D.C. citizen against a Maryland citizen involving only issues of Maryland law—settle the constitutionality of every aspect of this grant? See, *e.g.*, Americana of Puerto Rico, Inc. v. Kaplus, 368 F.2d 431 (3d Cir.1966) (upholding jurisdiction in an action by a Puerto Rican corporation against New Jersey defendants brought in a New Jersey federal court). In which of the sub-classes is there substantial justification for the jurisdiction?[1]

(7) Actions (a) Between Aliens, or (b) Between a Foreign State and an Alien Who Is a Subject of That or of a Different State, or (c) Between Different Foreign States. At least until 1988, there was no statutory basis for jurisdiction in any of these cases. The language of the 1988 amendment (p. 1414, *supra*) providing that "an alien admitted to the United States for permanent residence shall be deemed a citizen of the State in which such alien is domiciled", appeared to authorize federal jurisdiction (on the basis of diversity) in an action between two aliens, at least one of whom is domiciled in a state and admitted to the U.S. as a permanent resident. Doubts were raised about whether such jurisdiction (or jurisdiction in any of the other categories in this part) was consistent with the limitations on diversity jurisdiction in Article III.[2] But that constitutional question was mooted by the 2011 amendment to § 1332(a), p. 1414, *supra*, which eliminated

---

[1] One commentator has argued that present § 1332(e) (until 2005, § 1332(d))—which purports to bring all these cases within the diversity jurisdiction by defining the District of Columbia, the territories, and Puerto Rico as "States" for purposes of that jurisdiction—should be conceived "less as a grant of diversity jurisdiction than as permissible legislation, adopted pursuant to Section 5 of the Fourteenth Amendment, to enforce the Privileges or Immunities Clause." Pfander, *The Tidewater Problem: Article III and Constitutional Change*, 79 Notre Dame L.Rev. 1925, 1930 (2004). Note that this theory, standing alone, would not support the result in the Tidewater case itself, since the litigants there were corporations not entitled to the benefits conferred by the Privileges or Immunities Clause. But Pfander suggests "work[ing] around the corporate gap * * * by relying upon this equal protection-based limit on discrimination against out-of-state corporations."

[2] For an analysis of the Article III concerns arising from the 1988 amendment, see Gill, *The Perfect Textualist Statute: Interpreting the Permanent Resident Alien Provision of 28 U.S.C. § 1332*, 75 Tul.L.Rev. 481 (2000); Bassett, *Statutory Interpretation in the Context of Federal Jurisdiction*, 76 Geo.Wash.L.Rev. 52 (2007). In Chavez-Organista v. Vanos, 208 F.Supp.2d 174, 176–77 (D.P.R. 2002), the court, citing cases, said that because of the constitutional problem "[s]everal Courts * * * have held that the plain language of [this amendment] could not govern [in] cases where a permanent resident alien residing in state A sues only a permanent resident alien residing in state B or a nonresident alien." See also Van Der Steen v. Sygen Int'l, PLC, 464 F.Supp.2d 931, 933–37 (N.D.Cal. 2006) (taking the same view).

that "deeming" provision and thus removed any textual basis for the exercise of jurisdiction in such a case.

———

Strawbridge v. Curtiss

7 U.S. (3 Cranch) 267, 2 L.Ed. 435 (1806).
Appeal from the Circuit Court for the District of Massachusetts.

■ MARSHALL, CH.J., delivered the opinion of the court.

[In this case, the question before the Court was whether a federal court could exercise diversity jurisdiction in a multi-party case in which one of the plaintiffs was a citizen of the same state as several of the defendants. The lower court had dismissed the action.]

The court has considered this case, and is of opinion that the jurisdiction cannot be supported.

The words of the act of congress are, "where an alien is a party; or the suit is between a citizen of a state where the suit is brought, and a citizen of another state."

The court understands these expressions to mean that each distinct interest should be represented by persons, all of whom are entitled to sue, or may be sued, in the federal courts. That is, that where the interest is joint, each of the persons concerned in that interest must be competent to sue, or liable to be sued, in those courts.

But the court does not mean to give an opinion in the case where several parties represent several distinct interests, and some of those parties are, and others are not, competent to sue, or liable to be sued, in the courts of the United States.

Decree affirmed.

———

State Farm Fire & Casualty Co. v. Tashire

386 U.S. 523, 87 S.Ct. 1199, 18 L.Ed. 2d 270 (1967).
Certiorari to the United States Court of Appeals for the Ninth Circuit.

[Following a collision between a bus and a pick-up truck in California, four injured passengers on the bus filed a suit for damages in excess of $1,000,000 in California state court against the bus company, the owner of the truck, and the drivers of the bus and the truck. Soon after, State Farm, which had insured the truck driver with a policy limit of $10,000 per person and $20,000 per accident, filed a federal interpleader action against the four state plaintiffs and all other potential claimants alleging that interpleader was appropriate because the aggregate damages in actions already pending and others it anticipated far exceeded the policy limits. It asked, *inter alia*, that (a) all claimants be required to establish their claims against the insured and State Farm in the interpleader proceeding and (b) State Farm be discharged from all further obligations under the policy. Several but not all of the claimants named as defendants were co-citizens, but there was diversity between some of the claimants and between all claimants and

State Farm. State Farm based federal jurisdiction on the Interpleader Act of 1935, codified in part in 28 U.S.C. § 1335, which confers jurisdiction on the district courts over "any civil action of interpleader * * * filed by any * * * [corporation having issued an insurance policy in the amount] of $500 or more * * * if * * * [t]wo or more adverse claimants, of diverse citizenship * * * are claiming or may claim to be entitled to [the benefits of that policy]."*

[On appeal from a preliminary injunction restraining all defendants from prosecuting any other action against State Farm and its insured relating to the accident, the Ninth Circuit reversed, holding that interpleader was not available in the circumstances of the case. The Supreme Court granted certiorari.]

■ MR. JUSTICE FORTAS delivered the opinion of the Court.

* * *

Before considering the issues presented by the petition for certiorari, we find it necessary to dispose of a question neither raised by the parties nor passed upon by the courts below. Since the matter concerns our jurisdiction, we raise it on our own motion. The interpleader statute, 28 U. S. C. § 1335, applies where there are "Two or more adverse claimants, of diverse citizenship. . . . " This provision has been uniformly construed to require only "minimal diversity," that is, diversity of citizenship between two or more claimants, without regard to the circumstance that other rival claimants may be cocitizens. The language of the statute, the legislative purpose broadly to remedy the problems posed by multiple claimants to a single fund, and the consistent judicial interpretation tacitly accepted by Congress, persuade us that the statute requires no more. There remains, however, the question whether such a statutory construction is consistent with Article III of our Constitution, which extends the federal judicial power to "Controversies . . . between Citizens of different States . . . and between a State, or the Citizens thereof, and foreign States, Citizens or Subjects." In Strawbridge v. Curtiss, 3 Cranch 267 (1806), this Court held that the diversity of citizenship statute required "complete diversity": where co-citizens appeared on both sides of a dispute, jurisdiction was lost. But Chief Justice Marshall there purported to construe only "The words of the act of congress," not the Constitution itself. And in a variety of contexts this Court and the lower courts have concluded that Article III poses no obstacle to the legislative extension of federal jurisdiction, founded on diversity, so long as any two adverse parties are not co-citizens.[7] Accordingly, we conclude that the present case is properly in the federal courts.

---

* [Ed.] Because there was complete diversity between State Farm and all the defendants, State Farm also alleged jurisdiction on the basis of the general diversity statute, 28 U.S.C. § 1332, but as the Court noted, jurisdiction had to be upheld under § 1335 in order for State Farm to take advantage of the other provisions of the Interpleader Act governing venue (§ 1397) and service of process (§ 2361).

[7] See, *e.g.*, American Fire & Cas. Co. v. Finn, 341 U.S. 6, 10, n. 3 (1951), and Barney v. Latham, 103 U.S. 205, 213 (1881), construing the removal statute, now 28 U.S.C. § 1441 (c); Supreme Tribe of Ben-Hur v. Cauble, 255 U.S. 356 (1921), concerning class actions; Wichita R. R. & Light Co. v. Public Util. Comm., 260 U.S. 48 (1922), dealing with intervention by co-citizens. Full-dress arguments for the constitutionality of "minimal diversity" in situations like interpleader, which arguments need not be rehearsed here, are set out in Judge Tuttle's opinion in Haynes v. Felder, 239 F.2d, at 875–876; in Judge Weinfeld's opinion in Twentieth Century-Fox Film Corp. v. Taylor, 239 F.Supp. 913, 918–921 (S.D.N.Y. 1965); and in ALI, Study of the

[The Court went on to hold that State Farm had properly invoked federal interpleader jurisdiction, but that it was not entitled to the injunctive relief granted by the district court. Justice Douglas, dissenting, expressed his agreement "with the Court's view as to 'minimal diversity' ", but disagreed with the holding that, in the particular circumstances, federal interpleader was available.]

NOTE ON COMPLETE VERSUS MINIMAL DIVERSITY AND ON ALIGNMENT OF PARTIES

(1) The Strawbridge Holding. The Strawbridge opinion is one of Marshall's more cryptic efforts. The case involved a suit brought by co-executors, neither of whom could bring suit without the other joining as a plaintiff. Strawbridge's requirement of complete diversity could have been read narrowly, as applying only to cases in which the interests of the several plaintiffs and/or defendants were "joint". But the decision has consistently been interpreted more broadly, under all the varying formulations of the general grant of diversity jurisdiction in successive judiciary acts, as requiring "complete" diversity—that is, diversity of citizenship as between each plaintiff and each defendant. Does the co-citizenship of two adverse parties always assure that the state court will be impartial in the disposition of every aspect of the litigation?[1]

(2) Realignment. In applying the doctrine of Strawbridge v. Curtiss, a court is not controlled by the plaintiff's alignment of the parties. The Court "will look beyond the pleadings and arrange the parties according to their sides in the dispute", whether the result is to establish or to defeat jurisdiction. City of Dawson v. Columbia Ave. Saving Fund, Safe Deposit, Title & Trust Co., 197 U.S. 178, 180 (1905) (realigning to defeat jurisdiction); see also City of Indianapolis v. Chase Nat'l Bank, 314 U.S. 63 (1941) (same).

Realignment is particularly important in stockholders' derivative suits, since the defendants are often directors or officers of the corporation and thus co-citizens of the corporation.[2] The circumstances in which realignment was required in such suits remained cloudy at least until Smith v. Sperling, 354 U.S. 91 (1957). The plaintiff in Smith brought a derivative action in federal court on behalf of Warner Bros. (a Delaware corporation), against United States Pictures, Inc. (another Delaware corporation), certain directors of Warner, and others, challenging the fairness of various agreements between Warner and United. Warner was joined as a defendant. The district court, after a 15-day hearing, ordered Warner realigned as a plaintiff and dismissed the action for lack of diversity, finding that the stockholders,

---

Division of Jurisdiction Between State and Federal Courts 180–190 (Official Draft, Pt. 1, 1965); 3 Moore, Federal Practice para. 22.09, at 3033–3037; Chafee, *Federal Interpleader Since the Act of 1936*, 49 Yale L.J. 377, 393–406 (1940); Chafee, *Interpleader in the United States Courts*, 41 Yale L.J. 1134, 1165–1169 (1932). * * *

[1]   For an argument that the complete diversity requirement contravenes the history and purposes of Article III's diversity clause and "rests on a construction of the diversity statute that the Supreme Court has acknowledged was erroneous", see Cooper & Nielson, Jr., *Complete Diversity and the Closing of the Federal Courts*, 37 Harv.J.L. & Pub.Pol'y. 295 (2014).

[2]   In determining diversity in derivative actions, the only shareholder whose citizenship is taken into account is the one in whose name the action is filed. See 7C Wright, Miller & Kane, Federal Practice and Procedure § 1822.

officers, and directors of Warner were not "antagonistic to the financial interests" of the company and that none of the officers and directors "wrongfully participated" in the acts complained of. After affirmance by the court of appeals, the Supreme Court reversed, 5–4, with both sides relying on existing precedent. Justice Douglas, for the majority, said:

"It seems to us that the proper course [for deciding the alignment question] is not to try out the issues presented by the charges of wrongdoing but to determine the issue of antagonism on the face of the pleadings and by the nature of the controversy. The bill and answer normally determine whether the management is antagonistic to the stockholder * * *. Whenever the management refuses to take action to undo a business transaction or whenever, as in this case, it so solidly approves it that any demand to rescind would be futile, antagonism is evident. The cause of action, to be sure, is that of the corporation. But the corporation has become through its managers hostile and antagonistic to the enforcement of the claim.

"Collusion to satisfy the jurisdictional requirements of the District Courts may, of course, always be shown; and it will always defeat jurisdiction. Absent collusion, there is diversity jurisdiction when the real collision of issues * * * is between citizens of different States."

Some commentators read the Smith decision as holding that an allegation of antagonism and satisfaction of the other pleading requirements of Rule 23.1 is sufficient to ensure that the corporation will be aligned as a defendant. See, *e.g.*, Wright & Kane, Federal Courts § 73 (7th ed. 2011). Indeed, it is hard to see what else the majority is asking the plaintiff to allege. Is there an acceptable alternative that does not involve a lengthy hearing that is bound to duplicate in part the hearing on the merits?

The possibility of realignment exists in other contexts. See, *e.g.*, Standard Oil Co. of California v. Perkins, 347 F.2d 379 (9th Cir.1965), holding that parties who had refused to join as plaintiffs and who had been added as defendants because they were "indispensable" ("Required to Be Joined if Feasible" under present Fed.R.Civ.Proc. 19(a)) should be realigned as plaintiffs, thus preserving diversity jurisdiction.[3]

(3) Statutory Jurisdiction in Cases of Less Than Complete Diversity.

(a) Interpleader. The Tashire case appeared to put to rest a debate over the constitutionality of diversity jurisdiction based on less than complete diversity between adversaries.[4] Does that decision stand for the

---

[3]　In Sherkow, *A Call for the End of the Doctrine of Realignment*, 107 Mich.L.Rev. 525 (2008), the author notes a division among the circuits on the proper test for applying the realignment doctrine laid down by the Supreme Court, argues that any test would be undesirable because it would necessarily force federal courts to examine the merits of jurisdictionally doubtful cases, and urges that the doctrine be abandoned altogether. Such provisions as 28 U.S.C. § 1359 (dealing with improper joinder) and § 1332(c)(1) (dealing with "direct actions"), he contends, are available to take up any slack.

A different critique is offered by Bassett & Perschacher, *Realigning Parties*, 2014 Utah L.Rev. 109, who contend that the courts have too often viewed realignment as a doctrine designed only to ensure correct application of the requirements of diversity jurisdiction. The authors contend that the doctrine extends to federal question cases as well and that its purpose is to ensure the adversariness demanded by Article III's case or controversy requirement.

[4]　For discussion prior to the decision, compare, *e.g.*, McGovney, *A Supreme Court Fiction: Corporations in the Diverse Citizenship Jurisdiction of the Federal Courts*, 56 Harv.L.Rev. 853, 1090, 1103–11 (1943) (arguing that Article III probably requires complete diversity), with ALI, Study of the Division of Jurisdiction Between State and Federal Courts, Supporting

proposition that minimal diversity is always enough to satisfy Article III? The question is especially relevant to the current debate over the constitutionality of the Class Action Fairness Act, discussed in subparagraph (d), below.

(b) 28 U.S.C. § 1369: "Multiparty, Multiforum Jurisdiction." In response to calls from several quarters for the use of "minimal diversity" as a basis of federal jurisdiction in cases involving claims of substantial harm to many people, Congress took a step in that direction in 2002 by adding a new provision to the Judicial Code (§ 1369), along with related provisions governing venue (new § 1391(g)), removal (new § 1441(e)), nationwide service of process (new § 1697), and subpoenas (new § 1785). See Pub.L.No. 107–273, § 11020. Section 1369 itself provides for original jurisdiction "of any civil action involving minimal diversity between adverse parties that arises from a single accident" if any one of three additional conditions is met (for example, if any two defendants reside in different states), and also requires that prompt notice of the action be given to the Judicial Panel on Multidistrict Litigation, which supervises transfers under § 1407. "Minimal diversity" between "adverse parties" exists if any party is a citizen of a state and any adverse party is a citizen of another state, a citizen or subject of a foreign state, or a foreign state. An "accident" is defined as a "sudden accident, or a natural event culminating in an accident that results in death incurred in a discrete location by at least 75 natural persons." There is no jurisdictional amount requirement, but the district court is required to "abstain" if (a) both the primary defendants and the substantial majority of all plaintiffs are citizens of a single state and (b) the claims will be governed primarily by the law of that state.

This new section, together with its related provisions, addresses only one of a range of instances in which harm may occur to a large number of people. It does not deal, for example, with claims of harm caused in many locations as a result of an allegedly defective product.

(c) The Class Action Fairness Act of 2005.

(i) Background and Summary. For a number of years, there had been intense debate, and lobbying, on the question whether federal court jurisdiction should be expanded with respect to class actions involving significant sums of money and class members and/or defendants from several states. Arguments favoring such expansion focused on claims that many state courts were too willing to certify inappropriate, even frivolous, class actions, and then to approve settlements that defendants felt compelled to accept in order to avoid litigation, or that benefitted the lawyers for the plaintiff class far more than the class members themselves, or both. Congress responded to these arguments by enacting the Class Action Fairness Act of 2005 (CAFA), Pub.L.No. 109–2, 119 Stat. 4. The Act considerably expanded the original and removal jurisdiction of the federal courts over certain class actions (and related actions) and adopted a number of special provisions regarding the settlement of such actions and the award of attorney's fees. Following is a brief summary of the Act's principal provisions as they relate to the diversity jurisdiction.[5]

Memorandum A, at 426–36 (1969) (arguing the opposite on the basis of both precedent and policy).

[5] Beyond its expansion of diversity jurisdiction, the Act added new §§ 1711–15 to Title 28. These provisions deal with the settlement of class actions in the federal courts. Section 1712 imposes substantive and procedural limitations on settlements that involve the recovery of

— Section 2 of the Act contains findings about the importance of class actions and abuses of the device that have adversely affected interstate commerce, plaintiff class members, and defendants, and includes among the purposes of the Act the assurance of prompt and fair recovery for class members and of "Federal court consideration of interstate cases of national importance under diversity jurisdiction."

— Section 4 inserted into the original jurisdiction provision of 28 U.S.C. § 1332 a new subsection (d), which is the heart of the expansion of federal diversity jurisdiction. It confers original federal court jurisdiction over class actions (as defined) in which the matter in controversy (after *aggregating* the claims of all class members) exceeds $5,000,000,[6] and in which any member of a class of plaintiffs is (i) a citizen of a state different from any defendant, *or* (ii) a foreign state or citizen of a foreign state if any defendant is a citizen of a state, *or* (iii) a citizen of a state if any defendant is a foreign state or citizen of a foreign state. The provision then goes on (a) to *authorize* the district court, after consideration of six enumerated factors, to decline to exercise jurisdiction in any case in which more than 1/3 but less than 2/3 of the plaintiff class members, as well as the "primary defendants", are citizens of the forum state; and (b) to *mandate* the decline of jurisdiction if more than 2/3 of the plaintiff class members are citizens of the forum state, if at least one defendant from whom significant relief is sought is also a citizen of the forum state, and if certain other conditions are met. Remaining provisions of new § 1332(d) serve, among other things, (a) to exempt certain class actions from the section's coverage (including classes consisting of fewer than 100 members), (b) to define, for purposes of CAFA only, an unincorporated association as a citizen of the state where it is organized and of the state where it has its principal place of business, and (c) to include in the definition of "class action" certain "mass action[s]" involving the joinder of 100 or more plaintiffs even if not formally certified as a class under Rule 23.[7]

"coupons" (to be used, for example, in purchasing the defendant's product(s)) and on the calculation of attorney's fees in such cases. Sections 1713 and 1714 provide protection against a net loss by class members as a result of a settlement and against discrimination in settlements based on the geographic locations of class members. Section 1715 provides that particular state and federal officials, and certain institutions, must be given notice of and opportunity for comment on certain proposed settlements.

In addition, the Act required the Judicial Conference to submit a report containing recommendations for ensuring fair settlements and fair attorney's fee awards and specifying the actions taken to achieve those goals; explicitly approved the 2003 Supreme Court amendments to Federal Rule 23 (on class actions); reaffirmed the role of the Judicial Conference and the authority of the Supreme Court in promulgating rules of practice and procedure; and provided that the Act shall apply to any civil action commenced on or after the date of enactment.

[6] In Standard Fire Ins. Co. v. Knowles, 133 S.Ct. 1345 (2013), the Court held that a state court stipulation by the class representative that he and absent class members would seek less than $5 million in damages does not prevent removal under CAFA, because the stipulation could not bind absent members.

[7] See Mullenix, *Class Actions Shrugged: Mass Actions and the Future of Aggregate Litigation*, 32 Rev. Litig. 591 (2013) (arguing that scholars' focus on CAFA's implications for state law class actions has obscured the law's significant changes to mass action litigation, which can be a more powerful tool for plaintiffs than the class action model).

In Mississippi ex rel. Hood v. AU Optronics Corp. 134 S.Ct. 736 (2014), the state had brought an action in state court to recover (under state law) restitution for purchases made by itself and by (more than 100 unnamed) citizens of the state. Resolving a circuit conflict, the Supreme Court held unanimously that the case was not removable under CAFA as a "mass action" because Mississippi was the only named plaintiff and the statutory definition of a mass action required 100 or more "actual named parties". In answer to the argument that the Court

— Section 5 added a new § 1453 to Title 28, authorizing removal of class actions (as defined in the Act) "by any defendant without the consent of all defendants" and "without regard to whether any defendant is a citizen of the State in which the action is brought". Section 1453 further provides that the one-year limitation on removal (in § 1446(c)) does not apply, and creates a specific exception to the general prohibition (in § 1447(d)) of appellate review of a remand order; instead, under new § 1453, "a court of appeals may accept an appeal from an order of a district court granting or denying a motion to remand * * * if application is made to the court of appeals not more than 10 days after entry of the order."[8]

The definition of "class action" in § 1332(d)(1), which is incorporated by reference in § 1453, is very broad: "any civil action filed under rule 23 of the Federal Rules of Civil Procedure or similar State statute or rule of judicial procedure authorizing an action to be brought by 1 or more representative persons as a class action". This definition contains none of CAFA's limitations on original jurisdiction, found in other provisions of § 1332(d)— although the legislative history leaves no doubt that the scope of the removal provision was intended to be co-extensive with that original jurisdiction.[9]

(ii) Comments and Questions. CAFA expands the diversity jurisdiction not only by requiring only minimal diversity, but also by departing from existing rules generally barring plaintiffs from aggregating their claims for purposes of satisfying a jurisdictional amount requirement, see Snyder v. Harris, p. 1445, *infra*, and by departing significantly from existing statutory limitations on removal (such as the bar on removal when a properly joined defendant is a citizen of the forum state).

Among the broad policy questions raised by this Act are: whether, and to what extent, the Act is warranted by state court abuses and overreaching in class action cases; whether the Act may overburden federal courts with the adjudication of matters not involving federal law; and whether Congress should have considered addressing not only procedural and remedial issues in class action cases significantly affecting commerce but also issues of substantive tort liability (particularly in the area of responsibility for defective products).

In addition, no consensus yet exists with respect to a number of more specific problems raised by these provisions. For example: Who is a "primary" defendant? How does a court determine—particularly in cases involving large classes, at least some of whose members are not known or may not even have been born—what percentage of class members are citizens of the forum

---

should consider whether the form of the action constituted an improper effort to defeat removal jurisdiction, the Court held that Congress did not intend that judge-made principle to apply to the mass action provision.

[8]   Section 1453 originally read "not less than 7 days after entry of the order." That drafting error was corrected by Pub.L.No. 111–16, 123 Stat. 1607, which changed the time for appeal to "not more than 10 days after entry of the order".

[9]   Professor Adam Steinman, in *Sausage-Making, Pigs' Ears, and Congressional Expansions of Federal Jurisdiction: Exxon Mobil v. Allapattah and Its Lessons for the Class Action Fairness Act*, 81 Wash.L.Rev. 279 (2006), proposes a resolution of the resulting tension based in part on the rationale and result of the Allapattah case (p. 1450, *supra*). Section 1453, he suggests, should be read not as conferring removal jurisdiction but only as providing more "defendant-friendly" removal provisions "for class actions that have an independent basis for removal elsewhere under federal law." He concedes that this approach does not square easily with either the text or the legislative history of the provision, but sees it as the best solution to a problem made especially difficult by the combination of poor legislative drafting and a growing judicial insistence on adherence to the statutory text.

state? To what extent, if any, should the Act be interpreted to modify the Erie doctrine (and especially the determination of which state's laws shall apply) in cases arising under it? Does the Act affect the authority of federal courts to enjoin state court proceedings, or the preclusive effects of judgments granting or denying certification, approving settlements, or entered after trial?

Moreover, since the Act applies "to any class action before or after the entry of a class certification order by the court", what happens if, for example, in a removed action, the federal court refuses to certify under Rule 23? Must the entire action be remanded to state court, or are there situations in which any remaining individual action(s) by the named plaintiff(s) may remain in federal court? In the event of remand, is it still open to the state court to certify the action as a class action under state rules? If so, would the result undermine one of the goals of CAFA? If not, would the result unconstitutionally interfere with state administration of a case not governed by federal law?[10]

---

[10] A large body of literature deals with CAFA. Studies of particular interest include Vairo, The Class Action Fairness Act of 2005: A Review and Preliminary Analysis (2005); Issacharoff, *Settled Expectations in a World of Unsettled Law: Choice of Law After the Class Action Fairness Act*, 106 Colum.L.Rev. 1839 (2006) (arguing that courts should not follow the Klaxon rule, p. 591, *supra*, in "national market" cases falling under the Act but should instead apply the law of the defendant's home state); Marcus, *Erie, the Class Action Fairness Act, and Some Federalism Implications of Diversity Jurisdiction*, 48 Wm. & Mary L.Rev. 1247 (2007) (discussing parallels between the debates that led to the enactment of CAFA and the debates over the diversity jurisdiction and applicable law that preceded the Erie decision); Nagareda, *Aggregation and Its Discontents: Class Settlement Pressure, Class-Wide Arbitration, and CAFA*, 106 Colum.L.Rev. 1872 (2006); Scribner, *Protecting Federalism Interests After the Class Action Fairness Act of 2005: A Reply to Professor Vairo*, 51 Wayne L.Rev. 1417 (2005); Burbank, *Aggregation on the Couch: The Strategic Uses of Ambiguity and Hypocrisy*, 106 Colum.L.Rev. 1924 (2006) (critiquing the articles by Issacharoff and Nagareda, *supra*, and arguing that in light of CAFA, the non-constitutional aspects of Erie that drove the Klaxon and Guaranty Trust decisions, pp. 591, 598, *supra*, are ripe for reexamination); Cabraser, *Just Choose: The Jurisprudential Necessity To Select a Single Governing Law for Mass Claims Arising from Nationally Marketed Consumer Goods and Services*, 14 Roger Williams U.L.Rev. 29 (2009); Richardson, *Class Dismissed, Now What? Exploring the Exercise of CAFA Jurisdiction After the Denial of Class Certification*, 39 N.M.L.Rev. 121 (2009) (contending, after discussing the confusion in the decided cases, that a federal court's denial of class certification in a CAFA case does not obviate jurisdiction already acquired, but that federal courts should have the ability to abstain in such cases); Silberman, *Choice of Law in National Class Actions: Should CAFA Make a Difference?*, 14 Roger Williams U.L.Rev. 54, 67 (2009) ("If one views CAFA as designating specific types of class actions appropriate for 'national treatment'—that is, in need of federal jurisdiction to ensure neutral and non-parochial assessments with respect to class viability—it follows that such cases are also deserving of independent 'federal' choice of law rules."); Wood, *The Changing Face of Diversity Jurisdiction*, 82 Temp.L.Rev. 593, 605 (2009) (commending Congress' adoption of "a more robust form of minimal diversity", particularly in CAFA, as a useful "tool for assuring a national approach to national problems that happen to be governed by state law"); Roosevelt, *Choice of Law in Federal Courts: From Erie and Klaxon to CAFA and Shady Grove*, 106 Nw.U.L.Rev. 1, 40–50 (2012) (arguing that federal courts should ordinarily follow state choice of law determinations, as Klaxon generally requires, but that CAFA authorizes federal courts to disregard determinations that depart from the state's ordinary choice of law approach in order to facilitate class actions that could not otherwise be maintained); Steinman, *Kryptonite for CAFA?*, 32 Rev. Litig. 649 (2013) (arguing that certain aspects of state law may be binding in federal court).

For broad-ranging discussions of these and other issues raised by CAFA, see Symposium, *Fairness to Whom?: Perspectives on the Class Action Fairness Act of 2005*, 156 U.Pa.L.Rev. 1439 (2008); Symposium, *Developments in the Law—The Class Action Fairness Act of 2005*, 39 Loy.L.A.L.Rev. 979 (2006).

For an analysis addressing the questions posed in the final sentences of this Paragraph and persuasively contending that, despite the holdings of several appellate courts, a case removed under CAFA must be remanded if class certification is denied and federal jurisdiction depends solely on CAFA, see Note, *Class Certification as a Prerequisite for CAFA Jurisdiction*, 96

(d) The Constitutional Question Renewed. For the view that in many of their applications, various enactments and proposals basing federal jurisdiction on "minimal diversity" (including § 1369 and CAFA) "present significant issues in terms both of congressional power to enact them, and the appropriateness of its doing so", see Floyd, *The Limits of Minimal Diversity*, 55 Hastings L.J. 613, 616 (2004). (Writing before CAFA was enacted, Floyd discussed legislative proposals similar to CAFA.) Part of the problem, Professor Floyd argues, is that substantial aspects of these enactments and proposals "baldly are predicated on the need to achieve judicial and litigant economy and consistent outcomes between federal and state litigation arising from the same events or transactions" and are not sufficiently focused on whether the expansion of jurisdiction is necessary and proper to achieve the purposes of the Diversity Clause. He extends the argument to the use of the concept of supplemental jurisdiction to reach non-diverse state law claims.[11] In appraising this thesis, consider how stringent the courts should be in assessing the authority of Congress to utilize the diversity jurisdiction (and related notions of supplemental jurisdiction) to achieve a wide range of goals consistent with a reasonable view of the needs of judicial federalism.

NOTE ON THE TREATMENT OF CORPORATIONS, UNINCORPORATED ENTITIES, AND LITIGATION CLASSES IN THE DETERMINATION OF DIVERSITY

A.   Corporations

(1) Historical Development and Constitutional Issues.

(a) The Current Approach to Corporate Citizenship. In 1958, Congress addressed for the first time the question of the status of corporations in determining diversity of citizenship. It provided, in 28 U.S.C. § 1332(c), that "a corporation shall be deemed a citizen of any State by which it has been incorporated and of the State where it has its principal place of business." A 2011 amendment changed the words "any state" to "every State and foreign state". See p. 1414, *infra*.

(b) Pre-1958 Historical Development. Before 1958, the question was controlled entirely by judicial decision. In the Supreme Court's first major pronouncement on the subject, Chief Justice Marshall said: "That invisible, intangible, and artificial being, that mere legal entity, a corporation

---

Minn.L.Rev. 1151 (2012) (also contending that upon remand, certification of a class in state court is not foreclosed). The Note argues that the lack of federal jurisdiction after denial is consistent with the principle that jurisdiction properly invoked is not ousted by later events because certification is itself an essential element of CAFA jurisdiction.

[11] Professor Floyd has pursued these issues in *The Inadequacy of the Interstate Commerce Justification for the Class Action Fairness Act of 2005*, 55 Emory L.J. 487 (2006). He acknowledges that CAFA, as enacted, "at least partially" addressed the questions that he had raised in 2004, but contends that they have not been satisfactorily resolved. He then goes on to reject the view that CAFA's validity may be upheld by equating the alleged interstate commerce effects of cases falling under the statute with the purposes of the diversity clause or by the claim that the Act is "necessary and proper" to achieve the purposes of the Commerce Clause. And in *Three Faces of Supplemental Jurisdiction After the Demise of United Mine Workers v. Gibbs*, 60 Fla.L.Rev. 277 (2008), Professor Floyd applies his "necessary and proper" standard in the context of the availability of supplemental jurisdiction over counterclaims lacking an independent basis of federal jurisdiction.

aggregate, is certainly not a citizen". Bank of the United States v. Deveaux, 9 U.S. (5 Cranch) 61, 86 (1809).

From this premise the Court might have moved to any of three conclusions: first, that despite its capacity to sue and be sued, a corporation was barred altogether from the diversity jurisdiction; second, that actions by and against corporations should be regarded as conducted, on behalf of the stockholders, by the president and directors, and that the citizenship of these managers controlled; or third, that because such actions should be treated as, in substance, actions by or against all the stockholders, the citizenship of all the stockholders controlled. In the Deveaux case, the Court reached the third conclusion. Together with the rule of Strawbridge v. Curtiss, this approach effectively barred the use of diversity jurisdiction in much corporate litigation.

Thirty-five years later, the Court yielded to the pressure of the bar for a different result. In Louisville, C. & C.R.R. v. Letson, 43 U.S. (2 How.) 497, 555 (1844), the Court said: "A corporation created by a state to perform its functions under the authority of that state and only suable there, though it may have members out of the state, seems to us to be a person, though an artificial one, inhabiting and belonging to that state, and therefore entitled, for the purpose of suing and being sued, to be deemed a citizen of that state."

While the Letson opinion said that a corporation was "entitled to be deemed" a citizen, and elsewhere that it was "substantially" a citizen, the Court carefully avoided saying that a corporation *was* a citizen. Under the hammering of a minority of the Justices, the Court later rephrased its position so as to bring it into closer accord with the Deveaux decision. Marshall v. Baltimore & O.R.R., 57 U.S. (16 How.) 314, 329 (1853). As Chief Justice Taney later explained, the Court decided "that where a corporation is created by the laws of a State, the legal presumption is, that its members are citizens of the State * * * and that a suit by or against a corporation, in its corporate name, must be presumed to be a suit by or against citizens of the State which created the corporate body * * *." Ohio & M.R.R. v. Wheeler, 66 U.S. (1 Black) 286, 296 (1861). See also National Steamship Co. v. Tugman, 106 U.S. 118 (1882), applying a similar presumption to corporations created by foreign states.

The story here summarized is told in detail, but from sharply conflicting points of view, in McGovney, *A Supreme Court Fiction*, 56 Harv.L.Rev. 853, 1090, 1225 (1943), and Green, *Corporations as Persons, Citizens, and Possessors of Liberty*, 94 U.Pa.L.Rev. 202 (1946).[1] Professor McGovney saw this judicial development as part of a larger effort by the federal courts to free business interests from state control. Speaking of the presumption of the Marshall case, he concluded:

"In this era of candor and intellectual integrity in judicial decision it is inconceivable that the present Court would now create the fiction. Nothing but *stare decisis* stands in the way of its recall, and *stare decisis* was ignored by the justices who adopted it. Is it not time for the Supreme Court to say of it, as Mr. Justice Holmes said of the doctrine of Swift v. Tyson, that it is 'an unconstitutional assumption of powers by the Courts of the United States

---

[1] See also Henderson, The Position of Foreign Corporations in American Constitutional Law (1918), particularly Chap. IV; Moore & Weckstein, *Corporations and Diversity of Citizenship Jurisdiction: A Supreme Court Fiction Revisited*, 77 Harv.L.Rev. 1426 (1964).

which no lapse of time or respectable array of opinion should make us hesitate to correct'?"

The following excerpts indicate Professor Green's position:

"A state which calls a corporation into being endows its members with corporate existence and capacities. * * * The fulfillment of the legitimate purposes of incorporation requires that if the corporation is looked upon as a body of members it be also recognized that the members in their organized capacity are the adopted citizens of the state that has made them into a body. To that state the incorporated group stands in a relation which for the purposes of the jurisdictional clauses of the Constitution seems identical with that of an individual citizen to his state. * * *

" * * * The so-called presumption of citizenship is not a fictitious presumption as to what the facts are, but a characterization of the actual facts. It is not a presumption about persons, who happen to be members of a corporation, to the effect that they are individually citizens of the state of incorporation; it is a doctrine about corporations, to the effect that their members, as members, are citizens of the corporation's state. * * *

"It was the Deveaux case and not the later cases that was founded on fiction, for a suit by or against a corporation is not a suit by or against its members."

Whoever has the better of the constitutional argument, it is clear that during the reign of Swift v. Tyson, the availability of diversity jurisdiction to multistate corporations, especially on removal from state courts, played a significant role in protecting those businesses from having to litigate in unfriendly state courts and, in many instances, from the application of uncongenial state law. See generally Purcell, Brandeis and the Progressive Constitution: Erie, the Judicial Power, and the Politics of the Federal Courts in Twentieth-Century America (2000), discussed at p. 583, *supra*.

(2) The 1958 Amendment. Prior to the 1958 amendment, the Supreme Court's treatment of the problem of the corporation incorporated in more than one state was not a model of clarity. After a per curiam opinion in Jacobson v. New York, N.H. & H.R.R., 347 U.S. 909 (1954), the chances were excellent that a corporation would be considered a citizen of the forum state, and *only* of the forum state, if it was incorporated there, at least if it had not been compelled to incorporate in that state as a condition of doing business.

The 1958 amendment made a corporation a citizen of "any" state in which it was incorporated. But some courts still held that diversity exists if a citizen of state *A* brings an action in state *B* against a corporation incorporated in both *A* and *B*, at least if the corporation's principal place of business was not in *A*. See Wright & Kane, Federal Courts § 27, at 168 and authorities cited nn. 22, 24 (7th ed. 2011).

As noted above at p. 1430, Congress took another crack at the problem in 2011, changing "any State" in § 1332(c)(1) to "every State and foreign state". That amendment made it clear that diversity jurisdiction does not exist when a citizen of state *A* sues a corporation incorporated in states *A* and *B*.

No matter how the statute is drafted, isn't there a problem if a corporation incorporated in state *A* is required to incorporate in *B* as a condition of doing business there and then is considered a citizen of *B* for diversity purposes? Can or should such a condition imposed by a state lead to the closing of the doors of the federal court for disputes between the corporation and the citizens of *B*? *Cf.* Terral v. Burke Constr. Co., 257 U.S. 529 (1922), p. 627, *supra.*

(3) Locating the Principal Place of Business. For many years, the most frequently litigated issue under what is now § 1332(c)(1) was the location of a corporation's "principal place of business". The language suggests that there is one and only one such place, and the legislative history so indicates. See S.Rep. No. 1830, 85th Cong., 2d Sess. 5 (1958); H.R.Rep. No. 1706, 85th Cong., 2d Sess. 4 (1958).

According to a leading treatise, the early cases "seemed to take two different views on how to determine the principal place of business of a corporation with significant activities in several states." On one view, the principal place was the one in which the "home office" was located, since this was "the nerve center" of the corporation. The other view looked to "the place where the corporation carried on the bulk of its activity." See Wright & Kane, Federal Courts § 27, at 169 (7th ed. 2011).

The Supreme Court ultimately resolved the question in Hertz Corp. v. Friend, 559 U.S. 77 (2010). Conceding that there is probably no ideal test, the Court concluded unanimously that the "nerve center" test should apply in all cases—an approach that it said was not only supported by the text and history of 28 U.S.C. § 1332(c)(1), but was easier to apply than any of the other tests that the lower courts had developed in seeking to locate the principal place of business.

(4) Corporations Incorporated in Other Countries. Does § 1332(c) have any impact on a corporation incorporated abroad with its principal place of business in the United States? What if, for example, a Panamanian corporation headquartered in Florida sues (or is sued by) a Florida citizen? Compare Chemical Transp. Corp. v. Metropolitan Petroleum Corp., 246 F.Supp. 563 (S.D.N.Y. 1964) (upholding jurisdiction on the basis that § 1332(c) does not apply to foreign corporations, because it capitalizes the word "State", while references in § 1332 to foreign "states" are in lower case) with, *e.g.*, Jerguson v. Blue Dot Inv., Inc., 659 F.2d 31 (5th Cir.1981); Danjaq, S.A. v. Pathe Communications Corp., 979 F.2d 772 (9th Cir.1992) (rejecting jurisdiction on the basis that § 1332(c) was meant to preclude an otherwise local corporation from invoking diversity jurisdiction just because it is incorporated in another state). If the latter cases are followed, could the Panamanian corporation in the hypothetical sue a Mexican national in a federal court? (Compare the question raised by the 1988 amendment to § 1332, discussed at p. 1421, *supra.*)

(5) Federally Chartered Corporations. What is the status for diversity purposes of a corporation incorporated under the laws of the United States but not of any state? Section 1348 of Title 28 provides that national banking associations shall "be deemed citizens of the States in which they are respectively located."[2] This provision codified a result that had previously been reached without the aid of statute, and has also been reached with respect to federal corporations other than national banks. Perhaps a similar result should be reached with respect to other nationally chartered corporations, at least if "localized" within one state. See generally 13F

---

[2] In Wachovia Bank, Nat'l Ass'n v. Schmidt, 546 U.S. 303 (2006), a unanimous Supreme Court held that for purposes of determining the state citizenship of a national bank, the word "located" in § 1348 refers to the state in which the bank has its main branch, and does not include any other states in which the bank has branch offices.

Wright, Miller & Cooper, Federal Practice and Procedure § 3627. The only effect of such a decision would be to expand the reach of the diversity jurisdiction. But would a decision sustaining jurisdiction in such a case be consistent with the provisions of 28 U.S.C. § 1349, which provides that "The district courts shall not have jurisdiction of any civil action by or against any corporation upon the ground that it was incorporated by or under an Act of Congress, unless the United States is the owner of more than one-half of its capital stock." Consider also, after you have read about the Bouligny decision below, whether such a decision could be squared with the approach of Bouligny.[3]

(6) State and Local Governments. A state itself is not a "citizen of a state". Postal Tel. Cable Co. v. Alabama, 155 U.S. 482, 487 (1894). But a political subdivision is, "unless it is merely an alter ego" of the state itself. See 13F Wright, Miller & Cooper, Federal Practice and Procedure § 3602. Note that the presumption of Marshall v. Baltimore & O.R.R., Paragraph (1)(b), *supra* (that all members of a corporation are citizens of the state of incorporation) has a real foundation of probability in such cases.

B.   Unincorporated Entities and Litigating Classes

(1) The Bouligny Decision. The leading decision on the citizenship of *unincorporated* entities is United Steelworkers v. R.H. Bouligny, Inc., 382 U.S. 145 (1965). There, the union was sued in a state court and sought to remove the case, on diversity grounds, to a federal court. The union argued that, like a corporation, it should be treated as a citizen for diversity purposes despite the absence of any statutory provision relating to unincorporated entities and despite the holding in Chapman v. Barney, 129 U.S. 677 (1889), that a joint stock company could not be treated as if it were a corporation. (As a result, jurisdiction for diversity purposes was determined in the Chapman case on the basis of the citizenship of all of the company's members.) The union contended that it was neither fair nor good judicial administration to remit it or any other unincorporated entity "to vagaries of jurisdiction determined by the citizenship of its members and to disregard the fact that [such entities] may exist and have an identity and a local habitation of their own."

The Court rejected these arguments, concluding that "however appealing, [they] are addressed to an inappropriate forum, and that pleas for extension of the diversity jurisdiction to hitherto uncovered broad categories of litigants ought to be made to the Congress and not to the courts." Moreover, the Court reasoned, acceptance of the union's invitation to "amend diversity jurisdiction" would create considerable difficulty for the Court in fashioning "a test for ascertaining of which State the labor union is a citizen".

The Bouligny Court noted that "in 1958 Congress thought it necessary to enact legislation providing that corporations are citizens both of the State of incorporation and of the State in which their principal place of business is located." However, the legislative history shows no consideration of the Bouligny problem, or of the rule of Chapman v. Barney. Would it have "amend[ed] diversity jurisdiction" for the Court to have overruled its own prior decision in Chapman? Did the Court exaggerate the difficulty of

---

[3]   See Lund, *Federally Chartered Corporations and Federal Jurisdiction*, 36 Fla.St.U.L.Rev. 317 (2009) (questioning the judicial recognition of a "localization" rule for federally chartered corporations and urging Congress to enact a statute defining the citizenship (for diversity purposes) of all such corporations).

formulating a test for determining citizenship that overruling would bring in its wake? Aside from any such difficulty, is there a rational basis for distinguishing between a corporation and a labor union?

In the Class Action Fairness Act, as noted at p. 1427, *supra*, Congress provided that for purposes of the act, "an unincorporated association shall be deemed to be a citizen of the State where it has its principal place of business and the State under whose laws it is organized." 28 U.S.C. § 1332(d)(10). Does the congressional overruling of Bouligny only in the class action setting preclude the Court from overruling Bouligny more broadly?

(2) Partnerships and Business Trusts. When a partnership sues or is sued, the citizenship of each of its members must be considered in determining diversity jurisdiction. See 13F Wright, Miller & Cooper, Federal Practice and Procedure § 3630. But in Navarro Sav. Ass'n v. Lee, 446 U.S. 458 (1980), the Court decided that individual trustees of a Massachusetts business trust could invoke diversity jurisdiction on the basis of their own citizenship without regard to the citizenship of the trust's beneficial shareholders. The Court began with the proposition that diversity jurisdiction should rest on the citizenship of the "real parties to the controversy" and took note of a line of decisions establishing that a trustee is such a party "when he possesses certain customary powers to hold, manage, and dispose of assets for the benefit of others." The business trust in Navarro, though different from a conventional trust in some respects, was one in which there were "active trustees whose control over the assets held in their names is real and substantial." The Court stressed the value of simplicity in determining jurisdictional issues, and observed that there was a rough correspondence between the test of citizenship it had applied and the test for determining capacity to sue under Fed.R.Civ.P. 17(a).

Did the Court in Navarro pay sufficient heed to the rationale of Bouligny? Or can it be said that Bouligny simply reaffirmed the unavailability of entity status to organizations other than corporations, leaving open the question of determining those individuals in an organization whose citizenship should be looked to when diversity jurisdiction is invoked? (For discussion of citizenship for diversity purposes when the party is the trust as an entity rather than one or more trustees, see note 6, *infra*.)

(3) Limited Partnerships. The question of the citizenship of limited partnerships, in which there are both "general" and "limited" partners, was resolved in Carden v. Arkoma Associates, 494 U.S. 185 (1990).[4] There, the Court held, 5–4, that a limited partnership is not itself a citizen and that in determining whether there is complete diversity, a federal court must look to the citizenship of the limited as well as the general partners. Justice Scalia, for the majority, said that the Navarro decision was "irrelevant, since it involved not a juridical person but the distinctive common-law institution of trustees." Citing Bouligny and Chapman v. Barney, he concluded that diversity jurisdiction in a suit by or against an artificial entity other than a

---

[4] Under the law prevailing in every state, limited partners have narrow rights with respect to management, do not have an interest in the property of the partnership but only a right to a distributive share of the profits, are not personally liable for the debts or torts of the partnership, and cannot sue or be sued on behalf of the partnership. See Comment, 45 U.Chi.L.Rev. 384, 403–04 (1978).

corporation "depends on the citizenship of 'all the members' " (quoting Chapman).[5]

Note that even after Navarro, the class action device may allow limited partnerships, or other unincorporated entities, to sue or be sued in a federal court on the basis of diversity, even though some of their members are co-citizens of the adverse party. See Paragraph (5) of this Note.

(4) Indian Tribes. For a discussion of the complex question of the citizenship, for diversity purposes, of Indian tribes or tribal entities, see Nicolas, *American-Style Justice in No Man's Land*, 36 Ga.L.Rev. 895, 942–47, 1072–73 (2002). Professor Nicolas sees this question as an aspect of a broad range of issues relevant to the solution of what he describes as the "no forum" and "biased forum" problems in Indian law. The former arises when "no court has jurisdiction over disputes involving Indian tribes, tribal entities, or tribal members", and the latter when a substantial risk exists that a state or tribal court with jurisdiction over a dispute will not treat the litigants fairly.

(5) Class Actions. Supreme Tribe of Ben-Hur v. Cauble, 255 U.S. 356 (1921), established that in a class action the citizenship of the named representatives is controlling. The courts are not of one view on whether the class action device may be successfully invoked to circumvent the limitations of the Chapman rule in all its manifestations. See authorities cited in 13F Wright, Miller & Cooper, Federal Practice and Procedure § 3630. Note also that Fed.R.Civ.P. 23.2, added in 1966, relates specifically to actions "by or against the members of an unincorporated association as a class".

The Class Action Fairness Act, discussed at pp. 1426–1430, *supra*, departed from the Ben-Hur approach in expanding access to federal court in diversity class actions. Section 1332(d)(2)(A) provides that, in class actions otherwise falling under the act, the diversity requirement is met if *"any member"* of a plaintiff class is a citizen of a State "different from any defendant."

---

3. JURISDICTIONAL AMOUNT

INTRODUCTORY NOTE[1]

(1) Statutory History. The Judiciary Act of 1789, 1 Stat. 73, 78, fixed the jurisdictional amount, in those cases in which some amount was requisite, at $500. Ninety-eight years later, 24 Stat. 552 (1887), this was raised to

---

[5] The question of the citizenship of a trust when it sues or is sued as an entity has divided the lower courts. Among the approaches taken are to treat the trust as a citizen of any state of which (1) a trustee is a citizen, (2) a beneficiary is a citizen, or (3) either a trustee or a beneficiary is a citizen. For a thoughtful analysis, see Nomura Asset Acceptance Corp. Alternative Loan Trust v. Nomura Credit & Capital, Inc., 27 F.Supp.3d 487 (S.D.N.Y. 2014). The court there relied upon Carden in following the second approach, distinguishing Navarro as a suit brought by individual trustees rather than by the trust as an entity.

[1] For a fuller review of the jurisdictional amount requirement, see Baker, *The History and Tradition of the Amount in Controversy Requirement: A Proposal To "Up the Ante" in Diversity Jurisdiction*, 102 F.R.D. 299 (1984).

$2,000. In 1911, 36 Stat. 1087, 1091, it was set at $3,000, in 1958, 72 Stat. 415, at $10,000, in 1988, 102 Stat. 4646, at $50,000, and in 1996, 110 Stat. 3847, at $75,000, where it remains today in diversity cases brought under 28 U.S.C. § 1332.[2] (Note that the amount in controversy must *exceed* the statutory figure in order to qualify for federal jurisdiction.) In interpleader the figure is far lower—$500, 28 U.S.C. § 1335—and there is no jurisdictional minimum in either the new "multiparty, multiforum" provision (§ 1369, see p. 1426, *supra*) or the jurisdictional provision of the Foreign Sovereign Immunities Act (§ 1330).[3]

(2) Amount in Controversy Requirements in Federal Question Cases.

From 1875, when general federal question jurisdiction was first enacted, to 1976, there was a jurisdictional amount requirement in such cases identical to that in diversity cases. But many statutes, *e.g.*, 28 U.S.C. § 1333 (admiralty), 28 U.S.C. § 1337 (cases arising under any act of Congress regulating commerce), 28 U.S.C. § 1343 (certain civil rights cases), authorized suits to be brought without regard to that requirement. And in cases involving constitutional claims in which federal jurisdiction could be based only on § 1331 (the general federal question statute), some decisions ignored the requirement,[4] or stretched it to accommodate the case,[5] or even questioned its constitutionality,[6] while others rigorously insisted that it be satisfied.[7] The difficulty was significantly alleviated in 1976, when Congress excepted actions against federal officers and agencies from the jurisdictional amount requirement of § 1331,[8] and was virtually eliminated in 1980 when the requirement was deleted from § 1331 altogether.[9] Only a few federal statutes remain in which federal question jurisdiction is conditioned on a specified amount in controversy.[10]

---

[2] The requisite amount in controversy in order to come within the jurisdictional provisions of the Class Action Fairness Act (§ 1332(d)) is $5,000,000, but the act also provides, in contrast to the general rule regarding aggregation, that in determining whether this requirement is satisfied, "the claims of the individual class members shall be aggregated". § 1332(d)(6). See p. 1427, *supra*.

[3] Inflation plainly causes the "real" value of the amount in controversy to decline during the long intervals between statutory increases. One set of commentators has proposed that legislation provide for the automatic revision of the amount in controversy each year, under a formula that is based upon (1) a measure of inflation and (2) the ratio of diversity filings to the number of federal judges (which is meant to capture the "burden" placed on the judiciary). Under this approach, the appropriate amount, if deemed to be $75,000 in 2001, would have risen to more than $130,000 by 2011. See Mohebbi *et al.*, *A Dynamic Formula for the Amount in Controversy*, 7 Fed.Cts.L.Rev. 95 (2013).

[4] See, *e.g.*, Flast v. Cohen, 392 U.S. 83 (1968); Kleindienst v. Mandel, 408 U.S. 753 (1972).

[5] See, *e.g.*, Spock v. David, 469 F.2d 1047 (3d Cir.1972).

[6] See, *e.g.*, Cortright v. Resor, 325 F.Supp. 797 (E.D.N.Y.1971), *reversed on other grounds*, 447 F.2d 245 (2d Cir.1971). See also Note, 71 Colum.L.Rev. 1474 (1971).

[7] See, *e.g.*, Goldsmith v. Sutherland, 426 F.2d 1395 (6th Cir.1970); McGaw v. Farrow, 472 F.2d 952 (4th Cir.1973).

[8] Act of Oct. 21, 1976, 90 Stat. 2721.

[9] Act of Dec. 1, 1980, 94 Stat. 2369.

[10] *E.g.*, 15 U.S.C. § 2072 (actions under Consumer Product Safety Act); 15 U.S.C. § 2310(d) (actions under Consumer Product Warranties Act); 28 U.S.C. §§ 1337, 1445(b) (suits under 49 U.S.C. § 11706 for freight damage or loss); 42 U.S.C. § 1395 ff(b) (judicial review of the denial of benefits under the Medicare Act). With respect to the last of these provisions, see Bartlett v. Bowen, 816 F.2d 695, 697 (D.C.Cir.1987) (holding that Congress "did not intend to bar judicial review [in cases falling below the jurisdictional amount] of constitutional challenges to the underlying Act").

Thus, the principal contemporary impact of the amount in controversy requirement occurs in diversity cases. Some of the relevant cases, however, are federal question cases decided under earlier versions of the grant of federal question jurisdiction, which is why these cases are discussed in this Chapter's review of diversity jurisdiction.

(3) Policy Considerations. If it was appropriate to abolish the jurisdictional amount requirement in federal question cases, should it be retained in diversity cases? Professor Currie at one time proposed eliminating the requirement across the board. Currie, *The Federal Courts and the American Law Institute (II)*, 36 U.Chi.L.Rev. 268, 292–98 (1969). But isn't there a greater justification for imposing on a federal court the burden of litigating a "small" case when it arises under federal rather than state law? Note too that state courts may be better equipped, through the use of special tribunals and procedures, to adjudicate small cases, especially those arising under state law. And consider the burden on a defendant who is forced to litigate a small case in a distant, unfamiliar federal court rather than in a nearby state court; isn't that burden easier to explain if the rights and liabilities at stake are themselves federal? Do the practical difficulties in administration of the amount requirement, the ease of circumventing it in many cases, and the possible unfairness of judging a case's importance in terms of a dollar figure outweigh these considerations? Keep these questions in mind in reading the materials that follow.

Burns v. Anderson

502 F.2d 970 (1974).
United States Court of Appeals for the Fifth Circuit.

■ JOHN R. BROWN, CHIEF JUDGE:

The question on this appeal is whether a district court may dismiss a personal injury diversity suit where it appears "to a legal certainty" that the claim was "really for less than the jurisdictional amount."[1]

The suit grew out of an auto accident in which plaintiff Burns' automobile was struck amidships by that of defendant Anderson. Burns' principal injury was a broken thumb. He brought the action in the Eastern District of Louisiana, claiming $1,026.00 in lost wages and medical expenses and another $60,000.00 for pain and suffering. After a pre-trial conference and considerable discovery, the District Court dismissed for want of jurisdiction. Plaintiff appeals.

The test for jurisdictional amount was established by the Supreme Court in St. Paul Mercury Indemnity Co. v. Red Cab Co.[2] There, the Court held that the determinant is plaintiff's good faith claim and that to justify dismissal it must appear to a legal certainty that the claim is really for less than the jurisdictional amount. There is no question but that this is a test of liberality, and it has been treated as such by this Court. This does not mean, however, that Federal Courts must function as small claims courts. The test is an objective one and, once it is clear

---

[1]   St. Paul Mercury Indemnity Co. v. Red Cab Co., 1938, 303 U.S. 283, 289.

[2]   *Id.*

that as a matter of law the claim is for less than $10,000.00 [the statutory figure at that time], the Trial Judge is required to dismiss.

In the instant case, the District Judge dismissed only after examination of an extensive record. * * * The accident occurred on May 26. The evidence is without contradiction that by the middle of August only very minimal disability remained. By December, even this minor condition had disappeared. Burns' actions speak even more strongly than the medical testimony. In his deposition he testified that he took a job as a carpenter's assistant on June 21 or 22—less than a month after the accident. He did heavy manual labor for the remainder of the summer with absolutely no indication of any difficulty with his thumb. It is equally clear that any pain he suffered was not of very great magnitude or lasting duration. Burns admitted that by the end of July there was no pain whatsoever. * * * [T]he evidence reveals that the only medication he ever received was a single prescription on the day of the accident for Empirin, a mild aspirin compound. Nor did his special damages take him a significant way down the road to the $10,000.00 minimum. His total medical bills were less than $250.00. Although he claims $800.00 in lost wages, it is difficult to see how this could have amounted to even $300.00 at Burns' rate of pay that summer.

The point of this fact recitation is that it really does appear to a legal certainty that the amount in controversy is less than $10,000. This is no Plimsoll case,[6] where dismissal was based on "bare bones pleadings" alone. The present situation differs from that case also in that this dismissal was for lack of subject matter jurisdiction not for failure to state a claim. Here the Trial Court examined an extensive record and determined as a matter of law that the requisite amount in controversy was not present. Indeed, had the case gone to trial and had the jury returned an award of $10,000, a Gorsalitz-girded Judge [see footnote 7] would have been compelled as a matter of law to order a remittitur. He would have inescapably found that the verdict was "so inordinately large as obviously to exceed the maximum of the reasonable range within which the jury may properly operate.[7]" * * *

Neither are we affected by plaintiff's plaintive plea that he is being deprived of a jury trial. The question in this case is not whether Burns is entitled to a trial by jury but rather where that trial is to be. We hold only that the case cannot be tried in the Federal Court because competence over it has not been granted to that Court by Congress.

Affirmed.

NOTE ON THE EFFECT OF PLAINTIFF'S AD DAMNUM IN UNLIQUIDATED DAMAGES CASES

(1) Questions About the Burns Decision. After the decision in Burns, was a state court jury still free to award plaintiff more than $10,000? Was plaintiff's jury trial argument in Burns properly disposed of?

----

[6] Cook & Nichol, Inc. v. Plimsoll Club, 5 Cir., 1971, 451 F.2d 505.

[7] Gorsalitz v. Olin Mathieson Chemical Corp., 5 Cir., 1970, 429 F.2d 1033, 1046.

(2) The St. Paul Decision. In St. Paul Mercury Indem. Co. v. Red Cab Co., 303 U.S. 283 (1938), cited in the Burns opinion, the Court held, in a case removed by the defendant to federal court, that federal jurisdiction, once it had attached by virtue of the plaintiff's good faith claim in excess of the jurisdictional threshold, was not defeated by the plaintiff's later amendment reducing the ad damnum below that amount. Would it ever be possible to find bad faith in a claim for unliquidated damages where, as in St. Paul, the defendant rather than the plaintiff had invoked federal jurisdiction?[1]

(3) Unliquidated Damages. A "short and plain statement" that a case satisfies the jurisdictional amount requirement suffices; the pleading need not include evidence backing up the allegation. Dart Cherokee Basin Operating Co. v. Owens, 135 S.Ct. 547 (2014). The lower federal courts had at one time taken the view that the plaintiff's claim in an action for unliquidated damages was virtually conclusive on the issue of amount in controversy. *E.g.*, Deutsch v. Hewes St. Realty Corp., 359 F.2d 96 (2d Cir.1966); Wade v. Rogala, 270 F.2d 280 (3d Cir.1959).[2] But a number of later decisions, of which Burns is representative, have taken a much closer look. See 14AA Wright, Miller & Cooper, Federal Practice and Procedure § 3707.

Despite a genuine concern over crowded federal dockets, is the game worth the candle? Might motions to dismiss on this ground, coupled with extensive discovery designed to show lack of a colorable claim, increase the net expenditure of judicial time?

(4) The Effect of a Recovery of Less than the Jurisdictional Amount. Suppose it is established at trial that any recovery to which plaintiff is entitled falls short of the jurisdictional amount, or that plaintiff is not entitled to recover at all. Should the action be dismissed for lack of jurisdiction? In Mt. Healthy City Sch. Dist. Bd. of Educ. v. Doyle, 429 U.S. 274, 277 (1977), at a time when the jurisdictional threshold was $10,000, the plaintiff had sought $50,000 damages and reinstatement but was awarded only $5,158 damages, together with reinstatement. In upholding jurisdiction, the Court said: "Even if the District Court had chosen to award only compensatory damages [of $5,158] and not reinstatement, it was far from a 'legal certainty' at the time of suit that Doyle would not have been entitled to more than $10,000." See also Rosado v. Wyman, 397 U.S. 397, 405 n. 6 (1970).

Section 1332(b), enacted in 1958, provides that a plaintiff who recovers less than the jurisdictional amount may be saddled with the opponent's court costs. The provision does not seem to have had much impact. See Wright & Kane, Federal Courts § 33, at 200 (7th ed. 2011). Note the difficulty of imposing such a sanction on the plaintiff when in all probability it was plaintiff's lawyer who chose the forum. Do the provisions of Fed.R.Civ.P. 11

---

[1]   There has been uncertainty in the lower courts about how to deal with a removed case in which the amount in controversy is unclear on the face of the plaintiff's complaint. The Clarification Act, p. 1414, *supra*, provides that the sum demanded in good faith in the state court pleading shall be deemed to be the amount in controversy, subject to certain exceptions (*e.g.*, the notice of removal may assert the amount in controversy if non-monetary relief is sought or if state law does not permit demand for a specific sum or allows recovery of a larger amount than that demanded (subsections (c)(2) and (c)(3)(a)).

[2]   For unliquidated damage cases in which the Supreme Court upheld the plaintiff's invocation of federal jurisdiction against a challenge to the amount in controversy, see, *e.g.*, Bell v. Preferred Life Assurance Soc'y, 320 U.S. 238, 243 (1943) (although actual damages could not exceed $1,000, evidence might justify a jury verdict for actual and punitive damages exceeding $3,000); Barry v. Edmunds, 116 U.S. 550 (1886).

(subjecting a lawyer to possible sanctions for filing a pleading or other paper that is without "evidentiary support") afford a more appropriate basis for relief? See generally Note, 27 B.C.L.Rev. 385 (1986).

NOTE ON THE ADMISSIBLE ELEMENTS IN VALUATION

(1) Introduction: The Rule of Healy v. Ratta. The Supreme Court addressed some important questions of valuation in Healy v. Ratta, 292 U.S. 263 (1934), in which the plaintiff sought to enjoin as unconstitutional the state's imposition of a license fee on peddlers and hawkers. The plaintiff alleged that the jurisdictional amount requirement (then $3,000) was met because the inability or unwillingness of his salesmen to pay the tax meant a loss to his business in excess of that amount. He alleged in the alternative that the jurisdictional amount requirement was met because the capitalized value of the tax that would have to be paid in order for him to stay in business (at least $350 per year) also exceeded $3,000.

The Court rejected both arguments. It said: "The disputed tax is the matter in controversy, and its value, not that of the penalty or loss which payment of the tax would avoid, determines the jurisdiction. * * * [Moreover, it does not follow from the requirement of annual payment] that capitalization of the tax is the method of determining the value of the matter in controversy." The Court declined to assume that the defendant (a city official) would seek to exact compliance in future years, that the plaintiff would wish to continue his business in that city, or indeed that the statute itself (or its allegedly objectionable features) would remain on the books. Further, since the defendant who had threatened to enforce the statute was an official of a particular city, the Court declined to consider the monetary effect of the tax in other parts of the state.

Finally, the Court distinguished such cases as Berryman v. Board of Trustees of Whitman College, 222 U.S. 334 (1912), which involved the validity of a *permanent* exemption by contract from an annual property tax. In such a case, the Court said, the value of the permanent immunity was "more than a limited number of the annual payments demanded. * * * [Thus] the burden which rests on a defendant who challenges the plaintiff's allegation of the jurisdictional amount may well not be sustained by the mere showing that the annual payment is less than the jurisdictional amount."

The Healy case applied doctrine that is standard in tax litigation: the amount in controversy is measured by the amount of the tax rather than the penalty. See, *e.g.*, Henneford v. Northern Pac. Ry., 303 U.S. 17 (1938). Can these cases be explained in part on the basis of a policy of avoiding undue friction with the administration of state tax laws—a policy now reflected in 28 U.S.C. § 1341? With these decisions, compare Hunt v. New York Cotton Exch., 205 U.S. 322 (1907) (in suit to enjoin unauthorized use of stock quotations, the amount in controversy is the value to the exchange of the right to control their distribution, not the cost of a subscription by the defendant).

Consider also the much-cited decision in Mississippi & M.R.R. v. Ward, 67 U.S. (2 Black) 485 (1862). Ward was a suit, based on the theory of abatement of nuisance, to enjoin the continued maintenance of a bridge over the Mississippi. The Court upheld jurisdiction and indicated that the damage to the plaintiff's navigation business was not controlling: "But the want of a sufficient amount of damage having been sustained to give the Federal Courts jurisdiction, will not defeat the remedy, as the removal of the obstruction is the matter of controversy, and the value of the object must govern."

(2) Capitalization of the Amount Due. The Healy decision—and its not entirely successful effort to distinguish Berryman v. Whitman College—created uncertainty about when it is proper to capitalize the amount currently due or to be expended.

In Aetna Casualty & Surety Co. v. Flowers, 330 U.S. 464 (1947), the Court in effect permitted capitalization of a future income stream. There, a widow sued for death benefits under a state workers' compensation statute, and the case was removed to a federal court. The statute provided for maximum payments of $18 per week, for a maximum of 400 weeks (but not to exceed $5,000). Payments were to end on the death or remarriage of the widow, or on the death or attainment of the age of eighteen by the children. The Court held that a remand for lack of the jurisdictional amount (then $3,000) was improper.

In decisions involving the right to recover on a policy of disability insurance, however, courts have generally refused to consider future installments in computing the amount in controversy unless the suit relates to the validity of the policy. *E.g.*, Mutual Life Ins. Co. v. Wright, 276 U.S. 602 (1928), *affirming* 19 F.2d 117 (5th Cir.1927); Lenox v. S.A. Healy Co., 463 F.Supp. 51 (D.Md.1978).[1] In the Flowers case, the Court distinguished these decisions on the ground that the state law creating liability for the award in Flowers "contemplates a single action for the determination of claimant's right to benefits and a single judgment for the award granted." Are you satisfied with the distinction? Is it like the difference between a contingent remainder and a vested remainder subject to divestment? *Cf.* Western & A.R.R. v. Railroad Comm'n, 261 U.S. 264, 267 (1923) (in a suit to enjoin an order to build a side track, the "permanent annual burden" of interest on the cost of construction, of depreciation, and of maintenance and operation of the side track, capitalized at a reasonable rate, should be taken into account in computing the amount in controversy).

The relevance of future harm to the determination of the amount in controversy was underscored in Hunt v. Washington State Apple Advertising Comm'n, 432 U.S. 333 (1977). There, an agency of the State of Washington sought a declaration of the unconstitutionality, and an injunction against enforcement, of a North Carolina law effectively prohibiting the use by Washington apple growers and dealers of their own state's system for grading apples destined for North Carolina. The requested relief was granted below. On appeal, the Supreme Court unanimously affirmed, holding that the jurisdictional amount requirement was satisfied on the basis of "the losses [to growers and dealers] that will follow from the statute's enforcement."

Note that Hunt was a federal question case—arising before the 1980 amendment to § 1331 eliminated the amount requirement. Moreover, the

---

[1] Nor does it appear to avail the plaintiff to seek a declaratory judgment that the plaintiff is permanently disabled and entitled to future installments. *E.g.*, Beaman v. Pacific Mut. Life Ins. Co., 369 F.2d 653 (4th Cir.1966). But *cf.* Goldberg, *The Influence of Procedural Rules on Federal Jurisdiction*, 28 Stan.L.Rev. 395, 424–27 (1976), discussing some of the older decisions.

decision below decided an important constitutional question in a way that allowed the loser to invoke the Supreme Court's mandatory appellate jurisdiction. Do you think these facts made the Court more receptive to the arguments favoring jurisdiction than it would have been in a diversity case?

(3) The Relevance of the "Res Judicata" Value of the Judgment. Closely related to the decisions on capitalization is the question whether the res judicata value of a decision—that is, the value of future judgments in which the pending decision would have preclusive effect—counts in calculating the amount in controversy. Is the Healy Court's refusal to take future taxes into account based simply on the uncertainty of the taxes or on a general principle that only the value of the relief *currently* sought can be counted and not the value of the issue preclusive effect of the decision in future litigation?

The Supreme Court's decisions have not endorsed consideration of the res judicata value. For example, Clark v. Paul Gray, Inc., 306 U.S. 583, 589 (1939), involved a suit to enjoin enforcement of a California statute imposing license fees aggregating $15 for each automobile "caravaned" into the state for sale. The Court noted that the complaint alleged that one of the litigants, Paul Gray, Inc., "causes to be caravaned into the said state * * * approximately one hundred fifty (150) automobiles each year' ", an allegation supported by the evidence. But the Court did not rely upon the value of relief from the fees far into the future, instead focusing on the period during which the case would be pending: "Since the amount in controversy in a suit to restrain illegal imposition of fees or taxes is the amount of the fees or taxes which would normally be collected during the period of the litigation, Healy v. Ratta, 292 U.S. 263, we cannot say, upon this state of the record, that jurisdiction was not established as to appellee Paul Gray, Inc."

The Court took a similar approach in Town of Elgin v. Marshall, 106 U.S. 578 (1883), an action to recover the amount due on certain coupons detached from bonds, the defense being that both the bonds and the coupons were void. The Court held that the amount in controversy was the value of the coupons in suit only, although it recognized that a decision would be res judicata as to other coupons and as to the bonds themselves. This approach echoes the cases discussed in Paragraph (2) concerning the right to recover on a policy of disability insurance.

(4) The Relevance of the "Good Faith" Test in Actions for Non-Monetary Relief. In an action for other than monetary relief, is the "good faith" test applicable to the amount alleged by the plaintiff to be in controversy? Several cases discussed in this Note indicate that good faith does not suffice; instead, the plaintiff must satisfy the court as to the objective facts. See also Justice Roberts' opinion in Hague v. CIO, 307 U.S. 496, 507–08 (1939).

(5) Value to the Plaintiff Versus Cost to the Defendant. Either the plaintiff or the defendant might argue that the amount in controversy depends not just on the value of relief to the plaintiff but also on the cost to the defendant of providing relief—which might be more or less than the value to the plaintiff.[2]

---

[2] Professor Currie suggests that the question—whether to look to either the value to the plaintiff or the cost to the defendant—may be meaningless: "If the * * * [right sought to be protected] is worth only $1000 to the plaintiff, cannot the defendant buy it from him for $1000.01?" Currie, Federal Courts 303–04 (4th ed. 1990). Wright & Kane reply that the answer

The decision in Glenwood Light & Water Co. v. Mutual Light, Heat & Power Co., 239 U.S. 121 (1915), held that the relatively low defendant's cost was irrelevant so long as the value to the plaintiff exceeded the jurisdictional threshold. In this suit to enjoin the defendant from maintaining its poles in a manner that interfered with the plaintiff's poles and wires, the Court, finding that the damage to the plaintiff from the interference exceeded $3,000, held it to be irrelevant that the defendant could remove the offending equipment for $500. See also Hunt v. New York Cotton Exch., Paragraph (1), *supra* (looking to potential damage to the plaintiff). But compare Mississippi & M.R.R. v. Ward, Paragraph (1), *supra* (looking to the value of the asset in controversy).

But the plaintiff's perspective is not always dispositive. In Ronzio v. Denver & Rio Grande W.R.R. Co., 116 F.2d 604 (10th Cir.1940), a suit to quiet title to water rights, the value of the water to the plaintiff for farming purposes appeared to be less than $3,000, but its value to the defendant railroad materially exceeded that amount. The court upheld jurisdiction.[3]

Glenwood and Ronzio can be reconciled if the principle at work is that jurisdiction exists if either the value to the plaintiff or the cost to the defendant exceeds the jurisdictional amount. If the major purpose of the jurisdictional amount limitation is to keep relatively small cases out of the federal courts, why shouldn't the value to either party suffice? Indeed, to the extent the limitation is designed to protect defendants against harassment by suit in distant courts, shouldn't the value to the defendant be critical? (Note that in some cases the presence of a readily ascertainable value to the defendant may eliminate the necessity of a highly speculative judgment as to the value to the plaintiff.) See Wright & Kane, Federal Courts § 34, at 206–07 (7th ed. 2011).

(6) Declaratory Judgments. How is the amount in controversy determined in a declaratory judgment action? "Usually the right or nonliability sought to be established in a declaratory suit might be adjudicated in a present or potential coercive action by one of the parties. The potential monetary value of the right, or amount of the liability, in such a coercive action, is normally considered to be the amount in controversy in the declaratory suit. * * * If breach of a contractual condition is in issue, the amount of the probable liability is the amount in controversy." *Developments in the Law— Declaratory Judgments*, 62 Harv.L.Rev. 787, 801 (1949).

(7) The Relevance of Counterclaims. For some time, commentators and lower courts discussed whether the jurisdictional amount requirement, if not satisfied by the plaintiff's claim, may be satisfied by a defendant's counterclaim. But the decision in Holmes Group, Inc. v. Vornado Air Circulation Sys., Inc., 535 U.S. 826 (2002), discussed at p. 811, *supra*, strongly implies that the counterclaim cannot do the trick. There, the Supreme Court relied heavily on the "well-pleaded complaint" rule in stating that "arising under" jurisdiction (under § 1331—or in Vornado itself, under

---

"will not always be 'Yes,' either because of stubbornness or because a right may have intangible value to a party, not included among the elements used in measuring the value of the right for purposes of amount in controversy." Wright & Kane, Federal Courts § 34, at 206 n. 12 (7th ed. 2011).

[3]   Ronzio and other authorities supporting an "either party" viewpoint were cited with approval in Illinois v. City of Milwaukee, 406 U.S. 91, 98 (1972). The citation followed the cryptic comment that the "considerable interests involved in the purity of interstate waters would seem to put beyond question the jurisdictional amount provided in § 1331(a)."

the patent law provision of § 1338) could not be based solely on a counterclaim. The Court's rationale would seem to apply equally to a diversity case where the sole basis for asserting the requisite amount in controversy rests on the value of a counterclaim.[4]

(8) Interest and Costs. Section 1332(a) explicitly excludes interest and costs from the determination of the jurisdictional amount. See generally Note, 45 Iowa L.Rev. 832 (1960). The interest exclusion has caused difficulty. In some cases, interest must be included in determining the amount in controversy—for example, in an action on a bond coupon. But if the purpose of the interest exclusion is to prevent the plaintiff from profiting from a delay in bringing suit, interest accruing *after* the cause of action arose should be excluded. Nonetheless, artful pleading sometimes enables the plaintiff to defeat this purpose. See cases cited in Wright & Kane, Federal Courts § 35, at 209 n. 21 (7th ed. 2011). See also Baron, *The "Amount in Controversy" Controversy: Using Interest, Costs, and Attorneys' Fees in Computing Its Value*, 41 Okla.L.Rev. 257 (1988).

NOTE ON JOINDER AND AGGREGATION OF CLAIMS

(1) Aggregation by an Individual Plaintiff. It has long been settled that in determining whether the jurisdictional amount requirement has been satisfied, a single plaintiff may aggregate two or more claims against a single defendant, even if the claims are unrelated. Does that approach serve the purpose of the jurisdictional amount requirement?

(2) Aggregation of the Claims of Two or More Plaintiffs or of a Plaintiff Class. In Snyder v. Harris, 394 U.S. 332 (1969)—a plaintiff class action—the named plaintiff sought only $8,740 in damages for herself, but the total of all 4,000 potential claims of the class would have been approximately $1,200,000. The Court stated that, under established law, two or more plaintiffs could aggregate their claims for purposes of satisfying the amount in controversy requirement [then $10,000] *only* "in cases in which [they] unite to enforce a single title or right in which they have a common or undivided interest." The Court went on to note that in Clark v. Paul Gray, Inc., 306 U.S. 583 (1939), "this doctrine * * * was applied to class actions under the then recently passed Federal Rules." The Court rejected the argument that because Rule 23, as amended in 1966, provided that all class members who did not opt out by a certain date would be included in the judgment, the rule of the Clark case was no longer controlling: "[I]t is equally true," the Court stated, "that where two or more plaintiffs join their claims under the joinder provisions of Rule 20, each and every joined plaintiff is bound by the judgment. And it was in joinder cases of this very kind that the doctrine that distinct claims could not be aggregated was originally enunciated. The fact that judgments under class actions formerly classified as spurious [under the original version of Rule 23] may now have the same effect as claims brought under the joinder provisions is certainly no reason

---

[4]   But *cf.* Horton v. Liberty Mut. Ins. Co., 367 U.S. 348 (1961) (holding—in a federal diversity action by a workers' compensation insurer against the claimant (Horton) to set aside an administrative award of less than the jurisdictional amount—that the amount threshold was satisfied in light of a pending state court action by Horton against the insurer, as well as a counterclaim by Horton in the federal action, both asserting a right to an award of more than the requisite amount).

to treat them *differently* from joined actions for purposes of aggregation." Upholding the district court's determination that class members' interests were "separate and distinct", the Court affirmed the dismissal for lack of jurisdiction.

Justices Fortas and Douglas dissented, arguing that the matter in controversy "in a class action found otherwise proper under the amended Rule 23" should be measured "by the monetary value of the claim of the whole class."

Recall the suggestion at p. 1444, *supra*, that the controlling amount is either the value to the plaintiff or the cost to the defendant, whichever is higher. If the suggestion is sound, why isn't the total potential liability of each defendant in a case like Snyder sufficient to meet the requirement? See Lonnquist v. J.C. Penney Co., 421 F.2d 597, 599 (10th Cir.1970), a class action in which the court refused to permit aggregation and attempted to distinguish Ronzio v. Denver & Rio Grande W.R.R. Co., 116 F.2d 604 (10th Cir.1940), p. 1444, *supra*, by stating: "Although the court [in Ronzio] said that the test was the pecuniary value to either party, the decision is not pertinent because a single right was asserted by a single plaintiff and the question was the value of that right. No problem of aggregation was presented."[1]

Unless a theory analogous to that adopted in Ronzio is used, how could federal jurisdiction have existed in a case like Flast v. Cohen, 392 U.S. 83 (1968), p. 128, *supra*, a case that was decided at a time when federal question cases were also subject to a jurisdictional amount requirement and that involved a challenge by federal taxpayers to the constitutionality of federal government aid to schools with religious affiliations? See Note, 79 Yale L.J. 1577 (1970). The problem was not alluded to in Flast itself, or in later decisions dealing with similar issues. *E.g.*, Lemon v. Kurtzman, 403 U.S. 602 (1971).

(3) "Joint and Common" Claims. The Snyder majority's discussion referred to "largely workable standards for determining when claims are joint and common". A review of the decisions dealing with aggregation of multiple claims offers a convincing basis for skepticism that such "workable standards" exist. See 14AA Wright, Miller & Cooper, Federal Practice and Procedure § 3704.

(4) The Relevance of Federal Rule 82. Rule 82 of the Federal Rules of Civil Procedure states that the Rules "do not extend or limit the jurisdiction of the district courts or the venue of actions in those courts." In the Snyder case, the Court relied on Rule 82 as a barrier to sustaining jurisdiction. Professor Goldberg, in *The Influence of Procedural Rules on Federal Jurisdiction*, 28 Stan.L.Rev. 395 (1976), challenges this reliance. Pointing to a number of areas in which the courts, resting in part on the federal rules, sustained federal jurisdiction on a theory of pendent or ancillary jurisdiction without even alluding to the prohibition of Rule 82, Goldberg argues that Rule 82 is not required by either the Enabling Act or the Constitution but

---

[1] One type of class action in which aggregation is not a problem is a stockholder's derivative action. The Court has held that the measure of the amount in controversy in such cases is not the possible benefit to the plaintiff shareholder but the damage asserted to have been sustained by the corporation. Koster v. (American) Lumbermens Mut. Cas. Co., 330 U.S. 518 (1947). Was the Koster holding inconsistent with the Court's observation in the same case that the corporation was properly aligned as a defendant for diversity purposes because it was in "antagonistic hands"?

rather is a rule of judicial self-restraint. She then urges that Rule 82 should be construed in harmony with Rule 1 with respect to changes in the Federal Rules that serve "some procedural purpose in one or more situations in which jurisdiction is not a barrier to the rule's implementation".

Do you agree that Rule 82 is not required by the Enabling Act or the Constitution? Absent Rule 82, could the rulemakers abolish the diversity jurisdiction? Eliminate the jurisdictional amount limitation under § 1332?[2]

(5) The Zahn Decision. After Snyder, the question arose whether federal jurisdiction existed in a class action in which (a) the interests were not joint and common, and (b) the named members of the class had the requisite amount in controversy but some other members of the class did not. In Zahn v. International Paper Co., 414 U.S. 291 (1973), the Supreme Court, 6–3, upheld the decision of the district court that in a Rule 23(b)(3) class action "[e]ach plaintiff * * * must satisfy the jurisdictional amount, and any plaintiff who does not must be dismissed from the case". The Court invoked the requirement of Clark v. Paul Gray, Inc., a decision on which the Court had relied in Snyder, that named plaintiffs in such a suit who did not meet the jurisdictional requirements had to be dismissed. Reasoning that unnamed members of a class should not "enjoy advantages not shared by named plaintiffs", the Court applied "the rule governing named plaintiffs joining in an action to the unnamed members of a class".

The enactment in 1990 of the supplemental jurisdiction provision (28 U.S.C. § 1367) threw the results of Zahn and of Clark v. Paul Gray, Inc. (but not of Snyder v. Harris) into doubt. The question was finally settled when the Supreme Court, in the Exxon Mobil case, the principal case in the section that follows, held that § 1367 overrode the Zahn decision.

---

4. SUPPLEMENTAL JURISDICTION

INTRODUCTORY NOTE ON THE DEVELOPMENT OF SUPPLEMENTAL JURISDICTION IN DIVERSITY CASES PRIOR TO THE ENACTMENT OF § 1367

Prior to the enactment in 1990 of the supplemental jurisdiction provision, 28 U.S.C. § 1367, the scope of what was usually called "ancillary" jurisdiction in diversity cases was essentially judge-made. This Note is a brief history of developments during that period.

(1) Origins. Freeman v. Howe, 65 U.S. (24 How.) 450 (1860), held that a state court lacked jurisdiction over a replevin action brought by claimants to obtain property that had previously been attached in a federal diversity action. Answering the objection that the claimants would then be "utterly remediless in the Federal courts, inasmuch as both parties were citizens of

---

[2] With respect to the limitations imposed by the Enabling Act, see Burbank, *The Rules Enabling Act of 1934*, 130 U.Pa.L.Rev. 1015 (1982). On the general question whether and to what extent Congress may delegate to the federal courts authority to regulate subject-matter jurisdiction, see Shapiro, *Federal Diversity Jurisdiction: A Survey and a Proposal*, 91 Harv.L.Rev. 317, 343–48 (1977).

Massachusetts" the Court said: "The principle is, that a bill filed on the equity side of the [federal] court to restrain or regulate judgments or suits at law in the same court, and thereby prevent injustice, or an inequitable advantage under mesne or final process, is not an original suit, but ancillary and dependent, supplementary merely to the original suit, out of which it had arisen, and is maintained without reference to the citizenship or residence of the parties."

(2) Jurisdiction Relating to Final Judgments. From Freeman and related holdings, the Court moved almost imperceptibly to the recognition of an ancillary jurisdiction to effectuate or to reexamine judgments after they had become final. See, *e.g.*, Dietzsch v. Huidekoper, 103 U.S. 494 (1880) (upholding district court jurisdiction, after judgment for the plaintiff in a removed action of replevin, to enjoin the prosecution of an action against the plaintiff in a state court on the plaintiff's replevin bond).

A key case in this development is Supreme Tribe of Ben-Hur v. Cauble, 255 U.S. 356 (1921). A class action had been brought in a federal court against a fraternal benefit association organized under the laws of Indiana; the plaintiffs (members of the association) were certificate holders from states other than Indiana, and a judgment was rendered favorable to the association. Indiana certificate holders then commenced a state court action against the association, seeking to litigate the same questions, and the association filed a bill in federal court against the Indiana plaintiffs seeking to enjoin them from prosecuting the state court action on the ground that they were bound by the federal decree. The Supreme Court reversed a dismissal of the federal action for lack of jurisdiction and held that the requested injunction should issue. The Court ruled that the Indiana certificate holders were bound by the judgment rendered in that action as members of the class represented, even though their joinder at the outset of the initial federal action would have defeated jurisdiction. "The intervention of the Indiana citizens in the suit [after it had begun]", the Court noted, "would not have defeated the jurisdiction already acquired." The Court then disposed of the remaining jurisdictional issue—that the adversaries in the second federal proceeding were not of diverse citizenship—in a single sentence: "As to the other question herein involved, holding, as we do, that the [Indiana certificate holders] * * * were concluded by the decree of the District Court, an ancillary bill may be prosecuted from the same court to protect the rights secured to all in the class by the decree rendered."

Was the determination that the Indiana certificate holders could have intervened in the initial action essential to the result? Consistent with Strawbridge's requirement of complete diversity? Was the need to uphold ancillary jurisdiction as great in Ben-Hur as in Freeman v. Howe?

(3) Effect of Intervention. Several Supreme Court decisions prior to the enactment of § 1367 dealt directly with the effect of intervention on diversity jurisdiction. *E.g.*, Phelps v. Oaks, 117 U.S. 236 (1886); Wichita R.R. & Light Co. v. Public Util. Comm'n, 260 U.S. 48 (1922). In Wichita, the Court said: "Jurisdiction once acquired on [the ground of diversity of citizenship] * * * is not divested by a subsequent change in the citizenship of the parties. Much less is such jurisdiction defeated by the intervention, by leave of the court, of a party whose presence is not essential to a decision of the controversy between the original parties."

During this period, however, the lower courts held that if intervention was needed to cure an otherwise fatal defect of parties (*i.e.*, the absence of an "indispensable" party under Rule 19), there was no preexisting jurisdiction to which the intervention could be regarded as ancillary. See, *e.g.*, Kentucky Natural Gas Corp. v. Duggins, 165 F.2d 1011 (6th Cir.1948); Chance v. County Bd., 332 F.2d 971 (7th Cir.1964). Also during this period, the lower courts generally held that permissive intervention under Rule 24(b) had to be supported by independent grounds of jurisdiction. Was this sound? Even in a case in which the applicant for intervention was trying only to prevent a judgment that would worsen the applicant's position?

(4) Class Actions. The Ben-Hur decision itself indicated that ancillary jurisdiction would support intervention in a class action (at least one that, under the rule prevailing at that time, was not "spurious") by a member of the class without regard to that member's citizenship. But *cf.* Snyder v. Harris, 394 U.S. 332 (1969), p. 1445, *supra* (relying in part on Rule 82 in disallowing aggregation of claims for purposes of satisfying the jurisdictional amount requirement in a class action).

(5) Claims Against Third Party Defendants. In Owen Equipment and Erection Co. v. Kroger, 437 U.S. 365 (1978), the Court addressed the issue whether, in a diversity action, the plaintiff could assert a non-federal claim against a third party defendant who was a co-citizen of the plaintiff. In a 7–2 decision, the Court, per Justice Stewart, held that there was no jurisdiction over such a claim. While conceding that Article III (which had been held not to preclude jurisdiction in cases of "incomplete diversity") was not a bar, the Court reasoned that to allow such a claim would "allow the [statutory] requirement of complete diversity to be circumvented". Moreover, the plaintiff (unlike, say, a defendant, who seeks to bring into a case a non-diverse third-party defendant) "cannot complain * * * since it is he who has chosen the federal rather than the state forum and must thus accept its limitations." Justice White, dissenting for himself and Justice Brennan, argued that the result was not required by any rule of constitutional or statutory jurisdiction, that it too casually brushed aside considerations of "convenience, judicial economy, and fairness", and that it could not be justified on the theory that the plaintiff was trying to circumvent the rule of complete diversity because the plaintiff has "absolutely no assurance that the defendant will decide or be able to implead a particular third-party defendant."

The Supreme Court did not foreclose the possibility that in a case like Kroger, the third-party defendant would be allowed to assert a claim, arising out of the subject matter of the original action, against the original plaintiff, even though the parties to such a claim would be co-citizens. Were such a claim allowed, could the plaintiff in turn assert a "compulsory" counterclaim against the third-party defendant? If your answer is yes, does your response cast doubt on the central distinction between parties drawn in Kroger itself?

(6) The Effect of § 1367. Some of the difficult questions of supplemental jurisdiction raised by the enactment of § 1367 in 1990—questions that had left the appellate courts almost evenly divided—were addressed by the Supreme Court in the case that follows.

Exxon Mobil Corporation v. Allapattah Services, Inc.

545 U.S. 546, 125 S.Ct. 2611, 162 L.Ed.2d 502 (2005).
Certiorari to the United States Court of Appeals for the Eleventh Circuit.

■ JUSTICE KENNEDY delivered the opinion of the Court.

These consolidated cases present the question whether a federal court in a diversity action may exercise supplemental jurisdiction over additional plaintiffs whose claims do not satisfy the minimum amount-in-controversy requirement, provided the claims are part of the same case or controversy as the claims of plaintiffs who do allege a sufficient amount in controversy. Our decision turns on the correct interpretation of 28 U.S.C. § 1367. * * *

We hold that, where the other elements of jurisdiction are present and at least one named plaintiff in the action satisfies the amount-in-controversy requirement, § 1367 does authorize supplemental jurisdiction over the claims of other plaintiffs in the same Article III case or controversy, even if those claims are for less than the jurisdictional amount specified in the statute setting forth the requirements for diversity jurisdiction. * * *

I

In 1991, about 10,000 Exxon dealers filed a class-action suit against the Exxon Corporation in the United States District Court for the Northern District of Florida. The dealers alleged an intentional and systematic scheme by Exxon under which they were overcharged for fuel purchased from Exxon. The plaintiffs invoked [diversity jurisdiction under § 1332.] After a unanimous jury verdict in favor of the plaintiffs, the District Court certified the case for interlocutory review, asking whether it had properly exercised § 1367 supplemental jurisdiction over the claims of class members who did not meet the jurisdictional minimum amount in controversy.

The Court of Appeals for the Eleventh Circuit upheld the District Court's extension of supplemental jurisdiction to these class members. * * *

In the other case now before us, the Court of Appeals for the First Circuit took a different position on the meaning of § 1367(a). In that case, a 9-year-old girl sued Star-Kist in a diversity action in the United States District Court for the District of Puerto Rico, seeking damages for unusually severe injuries she received when she sliced her finger on a tuna can. Her family joined in the suit, seeking damages for emotional distress and certain medical expenses. The District Court granted summary judgment to Star-Kist, finding that none of the plaintiffs met the minimum amount-in-controversy requirement. The Court of Appeals for the First Circuit, however, ruled that the injured girl, but not her family members, had made allegations of damages in the requisite amount.

The Court of Appeals then addressed whether * * * supplemental jurisdiction over the remaining plaintiffs' claims was proper under § 1367. The court held that § 1367 authorizes supplemental jurisdiction only when the district court has original jurisdiction over the action, and that in a diversity case original jurisdiction is lacking if one plaintiff fails to satisfy the amount-in-controversy requirement. Although the Court of Appeals claimed to "express no view" on whether the result would be the same in a class action, its analysis is inconsistent with that of the Court of Appeals for the Eleventh Circuit. * * *

II

A

* * * Although the district courts may not exercise jurisdiction absent a statutory basis, it is well established—in certain classes of cases—that, once a court has original jurisdiction over some claims in the action, it may exercise supplemental jurisdiction over additional claims that are part of the same case or controversy. The leading modern case for this principle is Mine Workers v. Gibbs, 383 U.S. 715 (1966) [p. 861, *supra*]. * * *

We have not, however, applied Gibbs' expansive interpretive approach to other aspects of the jurisdictional statutes. For instance, we have consistently interpreted § 1332 as requiring complete diversity * * *. The complete diversity requirement is not mandated by the Constitution, or by the plain text of § 1332(a). The Court, nonetheless, has adhered to the complete diversity rule in light of the purpose of the diversity requirement, which is to provide a federal forum for important disputes where state courts might favor, or be perceived as favoring, home-state litigants. * * *

In contrast to the diversity requirement, most of the other statutory prerequisites for federal jurisdiction, including the federal-question and amount-in-controversy requirements, can be analyzed claim by claim. True, it does not follow by necessity from this that a district court has authority to exercise supplemental jurisdiction over all claims provided there is original jurisdiction over just one. Before the enactment of § 1367, the Court declined in contexts other than the pendent-claim instance to follow Gibbs' expansive approach to interpretation of the jurisdictional statutes. The Court took a more restrictive view of the proper interpretation of these statutes in so-called pendent-party cases involving supplemental jurisdiction over claims involving additional parties—plaintiffs or defendants—where the district courts would lack original jurisdiction over claims by each of the parties standing alone.

Thus, with respect to plaintiff-specific jurisdictional requirements, the Court held in Clark v. Paul Gray, Inc., 306 U.S. 583 (1939), that every plaintiff must separately satisfy the amount-in-controversy requirement. * * * The Court reaffirmed this rule, in the context of a class action brought invoking § 1332(a) diversity jurisdiction, in Zahn v. International Paper Co., 414 U.S. 291 (1973). It follows "inescapably" from Clark, the Court held in Zahn, that "any plaintiff without the jurisdictional amount must be dismissed from the case, even though others allege jurisdictionally sufficient claims."

The Court took a similar approach with respect to supplemental jurisdiction over claims against additional defendants that fall outside the district courts' original jurisdiction. [Discussion of Aldinger v. Howard, p. 867, note 3, *supra*, and Finley v. United States, p. 867, *supra*, omitted.]

As the jurisdictional statutes existed in 1989, then, here is how matters stood: First, the diversity requirement in § 1332(a) required complete diversity * * *. Second, if the district court had original jurisdiction over at least one claim, the jurisdictional statutes implicitly authorized supplemental jurisdiction over all other claims between the same parties arising out of the same Article III case or controversy. Third, even when the district court had original jurisdiction over one or more claims between particular parties, the jurisdictional statutes did not authorize supplemental jurisdiction over additional claims involving other parties.

B

In Finley we emphasized that "[w]hatever we say regarding the scope of jurisdiction conferred by a particular statute can of course be changed by Congress." In 1990, Congress accepted the invitation. * * * Section 1367 provides, in relevant part:

"(a) Except as provided in subsections (b) and (c) or as expressly provided otherwise by Federal statute, in any civil action of which the district courts have original jurisdiction, the district courts shall have supplemental jurisdiction over all other claims that are so related to claims in the action within such original jurisdiction that they form part of the same case or controversy under Article III of the United States Constitution. Such supplemental jurisdiction shall include claims that involve the joinder or intervention of additional parties.

"(b) In any civil action of which the district courts have original jurisdiction founded solely on section 1332 of this title, the district courts shall not have supplemental jurisdiction under subsection (a) over claims by plaintiffs against persons made parties under Rule 14, 19, 20, or 24 of the Federal Rules of Civil Procedure, or over claims by persons proposed to be joined as plaintiffs under Rule 19 of such rules, or seeking to intervene as plaintiffs under Rule 24 of such rules, when exercising supplemental jurisdiction over such claims would be inconsistent with the jurisdictional requirements of section 1332."

All parties to this litigation and all courts to consider the question agree that § 1367 overturned the result in Finley. There is no warrant, however, for assuming that § 1367 did no more than to overrule Finley and otherwise to codify the existing state of the law of supplemental jurisdiction. We must not give jurisdictional statutes a more expansive interpretation than their text warrants, but it is just as important not to adopt an artificial construction that is narrower than what the text provides. * * *

Section 1367(a) is a broad grant of supplemental jurisdiction over other claims within the same case or controversy, as long as the action is one in which the district courts would have original jurisdiction. The last sentence of § 1367(a) makes it clear that the grant of supplemental jurisdiction extends to claims involving joinder or intervention of additional parties. The single question before us, therefore, is whether a diversity case in which the claims of some plaintiffs satisfy the amount-in-controversy requirement, but the claims of other plaintiffs do not, presents a "civil action of which the district courts have original jurisdiction." * * *

We now conclude the answer must be yes. When the well-pleaded complaint contains at least one claim that satisfies the amount-in-controversy requirement, and there are no other relevant jurisdictional defects, the district court, beyond all question, has original jurisdiction over that claim. The presence of other claims in the complaint, over which the district court may lack original jurisdiction, is of no moment. If the court has original jurisdiction over a single claim in the complaint, it has original jurisdiction over a "civil action" within the meaning of § 1367(a), even if the civil action over which it has jurisdiction comprises fewer claims than were included in the complaint. Once the court determines it has original jurisdiction over the civil action, it can turn to the question whether it has a constitutional and statutory basis for exercising supplemental jurisdiction over the other claims in the action.

* * *

If § 1367(a) were the sum total of the relevant statutory language, our holding would rest on that language alone. The statute, of course, instructs us to examine § 1367(b) to determine if any of its exceptions apply, so we proceed to that section. While § 1367(b) qualifies the broad rule of § 1367(a), it does not withdraw supplemental jurisdiction over the claims of the additional parties at issue here. The specific exceptions to § 1367(a) contained in § 1367(b), moreover, provide additional support for our conclusion that § 1367(a) confers supplemental jurisdiction over these claims. Section 1367(b), which applies only to diversity cases, withholds supplemental jurisdiction over the claims of plaintiffs proposed to be joined as indispensable parties under Federal Rule of Civil Procedure 19, or who seek to intervene pursuant to Rule 24. Nothing in the text of § 1367(b), however, withholds supplemental jurisdiction over the claims of plaintiffs permissively joined under Rule 20 * * * or certified as class-action members pursuant to Rule 23 * * *. The natural, indeed the necessary, inference is that § 1367 confers supplemental jurisdiction over claims by Rule 20 and Rule 23 plaintiffs. This inference, at least with respect to Rule 20 plaintiffs, is strengthened by the fact that § 1367(b) explicitly excludes supplemental jurisdiction over claims against defendants joined under Rule 20.

We cannot accept the view * * * that a district court lacks original jurisdiction over a civil action unless the court has original jurisdiction over every claim in the complaint. As we understand this position, it requires assuming either that all claims in the complaint must stand or fall as a single, indivisible "civil action" as a matter of definitional necessity—what we will refer to as the "indivisibility theory"—or else that the inclusion of a claim or party falling outside the district court's original jurisdiction somehow contaminates every other claim in the complaint, depriving the court of original jurisdiction over any of these claims—what we will refer to as the "contamination theory."

The indivisibility theory is easily dismissed, as it is inconsistent with the whole notion of supplemental jurisdiction. If a district court must have original jurisdiction over every claim in the complaint in order to have "original jurisdiction" over a "civil action," then in Gibbs there was no civil action of which the district court could assume original jurisdiction under § 1331, and so no basis for exercising supplemental jurisdiction over any of the claims. The indivisibility theory is further belied by our practice—in both federal-question and diversity cases—of allowing federal courts to cure jurisdictional defects by dismissing the offending parties rather than dismissing the entire action. * * *

We also find it unconvincing to say that the definitional indivisibility theory applies in the context of diversity cases but not in the context of federal-question cases. The broad and general language of the statute does not permit this result. The contention is premised on the notion that the phrase "original jurisdiction of all civil actions" means different things in §§ 1331 and 1332. It is implausible, however, to say that the identical phrase means one thing (original jurisdiction in all actions where at least one claim in the complaint meets the following requirements) in § 1331 and something else (original jurisdiction in all actions where every claim in the complaint meets the following requirements) in § 1332.

The contamination theory, as we have noted, can make some sense in the special context of the complete diversity requirement because the presence of nondiverse parties on both sides of a lawsuit eliminates the justification for providing a federal forum. The theory, however, makes little sense with respect to the amount-in-controversy requirement, which is meant to ensure that a dispute is sufficiently important to warrant federal-court attention. The presence of a single nondiverse party may eliminate the fear of bias with respect to all claims, but the presence of a claim that falls short of the minimum amount in controversy does nothing to reduce the importance of the claims that do meet this requirement.

It is fallacious to suppose, simply from the proposition that § 1332 imposes both the diversity requirement and the amount-in-controversy requirement, that the contamination theory germane to the former is also relevant to the latter. * * * After all, federal-question jurisdiction once had an amount-in-controversy requirement as well. If such a requirement were revived under § 1331, it is clear beyond peradventure that § 1367(a) provides supplemental jurisdiction over federal-question cases where some, but not all, of the federal-law claims involve a sufficient amount in controversy. In other words, § 1367(a) unambiguously overrules the holding and the result in Clark. If that is so, however, it would be quite extraordinary to say that § 1367 did not also overrule Zahn, a case that was premised in substantial part on the holding in Clark.

                    * * *

We also reject the argument * * * that while the presence of additional claims over which the district court lacks jurisdiction does not mean the civil action is outside the purview of § 1367(a), the presence of additional parties does. The basis for this distinction is not altogether clear, and it is in considerable tension with statutory text. * * * The argument that the presence of additional parties removes the civil action from the scope of § 1367(a) also would mean that § 1367 left the Finley result undisturbed. Finley, after all, involved a Federal Tort Claims Act suit against a federal defendant and state-law claims against additional defendants not otherwise subject to federal jurisdiction. Yet all concede that one purpose of § 1367 was to change the result reached in Finley.

                    * * *

C

The proponents of the alternative view of § 1367 insist that the statute is at least ambiguous and that we should look to other interpretive tools, including the legislative history of § 1367, which supposedly demonstrate Congress did not intend § 1367 to overrule Zahn. We can reject this argument at the very outset simply because § 1367 is not ambiguous. * * * Even if we were to stipulate, however, that the reading these proponents urge upon us is textually plausible, the legislative history cited to support it would not alter our view as to the best interpretation of § 1367.

* * *

First of all, the legislative history of § 1367 is far murkier than selective quotation from the House Report [reflecting an understanding that the text of § 1367 did not overrule the Zahn case] would suggest.
* * *

Second, the worst fears of critics who argue legislative history will be used to circumvent the Article I process were realized in this case. The telltale evidence is the statement, by three law professors who participated in drafting § 1367, see House Report, at 27, n. 13, that § 1367 "on its face" permits "supplemental jurisdiction over claims of class members that do not satisfy section 1332's jurisdictional amount requirement, which would overrule [Zahn]. [There is] a disclaimer of intent to accomplish this result in the legislative history. . . . It would have been better had the statute dealt explicitly with this problem, and the legislative history was an attempt to correct the oversight." Rowe, Burbank, & Mengler, *Compounding or Creating Confusion About Supplemental Jurisdiction? A Reply to Professor Freer*, 40 Emory L.J. 943, 960, n. 90 (1991). * * * So there exists an acknowledgment, by parties who have detailed, specific knowledge of the statute and the drafting process, both that the plain text of § 1367 overruled Zahn and that language to the contrary in the House Report was a post hoc attempt to alter that result. One need not subscribe to the wholesale condemnation of legislative history to refuse to give any effect to such a deliberate effort to amend a statute through a committee report.

* * *

D

Finally, we note that the Class Action Fairness Act (CAFA), enacted this year, has no bearing on our analysis of these cases. Subject to certain limitations, the CAFA confers federal diversity jurisdiction over class actions where the aggregate amount in controversy exceeds $5 million. It abrogates the rule against aggregating claims, a rule this Court recognized in Ben-Hur and reaffirmed in Zahn. The CAFA, however, is not retroactive * * *. The CAFA, moreover, does not moot the significance of our interpretation of § 1367, as many proposed exercises of supplemental jurisdiction, even in the class-action context, might not fall within the CAFA's ambit. * * *

* * *

The judgment of the Court of Appeals for the Eleventh Circuit is affirmed. The judgment of the Court of Appeals for the First Circuit is reversed, and the case is remanded for proceedings consistent with this opinion.

■ JUSTICE STEVENS, with whom JUSTICE BREYER joins, dissenting.

Justice Ginsburg's carefully reasoned opinion demonstrates the error in the Court's rather ambitious reading of this opaque jurisdictional statute. She also has demonstrated that "ambiguity" is a term that may have different meanings for different judges, for the Court has made the remarkable declaration that its reading of the statute is so obviously correct—and Justice Ginsburg's so obviously wrong—that the text does not even qualify as "ambiguous." * * * I remain convinced that it is unwise to treat the ambiguity vel non of a statute as determinative of whether legislative history is consulted. Indeed, I believe that we as judges are more, rather than less, constrained when we make ourselves accountable to all reliable evidence of legislative intent.

The legislative history of 28 U.S.C. § 1367 provides powerful confirmation of Justice Ginsburg's interpretation of that statute. [Justice Stevens' discussion of that history is omitted.]

The Court's reasons for ignoring this virtual billboard of congressional intent are unpersuasive. That a subcommittee of the Federal Courts Study Committee believed that an earlier, substantially similar version of the statute overruled Zahn only highlights the fact that the statute is ambiguous. What is determinative is that the House Report explicitly rejected that broad reading of the statutory text. Such a report has special significance as an indicator of legislative intent. In Congress, committee reports are normally considered the authoritative explication of a statute's text and purposes, and busy legislators and their assistants rely on that explication in casting their votes. * * *

The Court's second reason—its comment on the three law professors who participated in drafting § 1367—is similarly off the mark. In the law review article that the Court refers to, the professors were merely saying that the text of the statute was susceptible to an overly broad (and simplistic) reading, and that clarification in the House Report was therefore appropriate. See Rowe, Burbank, & Mengler, *Compounding or Creating Confusion About Supplemental Jurisdiction? A Reply to Professor Freer*, 40 Emory L.J. 943, 960, n. 90 (1991). * * * To suggest that these professors participated in a "deliberate effort to amend a statute through a committee report," reveals an unrealistic view of the legislative process, not to mention disrespect for three law professors who acted in the role of public servants. To be sure, legislative history can be manipulated. But, in the situation before us, there is little reason to fear that an unholy conspiracy of "unrepresentative committee members," law professors, and "unelected staffers and lobbyists," endeavored to torpedo Congress' attempt to overrule (without discussion) two longstanding features of this Court's diversity jurisprudence.

* * * Given Justice Ginsburg's persuasive account of the statutory text and its jurisprudential backdrop, and given the uncommonly clear legislative history, I am confident that the majority's interpretation of § 1367 is mistaken. I respectfully dissent.

■ JUSTICE GINSBURG, with whom JUSTICE STEVENS, JUSTICE O'CONNOR, and JUSTICE BREYER join, dissenting.

[In the initial portions of her dissent, Justice Ginsburg traced the history of the concepts of pendent and ancillary jurisdiction, and of the proposals leading up to the enactment of § 1367. Before turning to her reading of that section, she addressed some aspects of the Court's interpretation of the general diversity statute, § 1332.]

The statute today governing federal-court exercise of diversity jurisdiction in the generality of cases, § 1332, like all its predecessors, incorporates both a diverse-citizenship requirement and an amount-in-controversy specification.[5] * * * This Court has long held that, in determining whether the amount-in-controversy requirement has been satisfied, a single plaintiff may aggregate two or more claims against a single defendant, even if the claims are unrelated. But in multiparty cases, including class actions, we have unyieldingly adhered to the nonaggregation rule * * *.

* * *

The Court's reading [of § 1367(a)] is surely plausible, especially if one detaches § 1367(a) from its context and attempts no reconciliation with prior interpretations of § 1332's amount-in-controversy requirement. But § 1367(a)'s text * * * can be read another way, one that would involve no rejection of Clark and Zahn. * * * [Section 1367(a)] addresses "civil action[s] of which the district courts have original jurisdiction," a formulation that, in diversity cases, is sensibly read to incorporate the rules on joinder and aggregation tightly tied to § 1332 at the time of § 1367's enactment. On this reading, a complaint must first meet that "original jurisdiction" measurement. If it does not, no supplemental jurisdiction is authorized. If it does, § 1367(a) authorizes "supplemental jurisdiction" over related claims. In other words, § 1367(a) would preserve undiminished, as part and parcel of § 1332 "original jurisdiction" determinations, both the "complete diversity" rule and the decisions restricting aggregation to arrive at the amount in controversy.[9] Section 1367(b)'s office, then, would be "to prevent the erosion of the complete diversity [and amount-in-controversy] requirement[s] that might otherwise result from an expansive application of what was once termed the doctrine of ancillary jurisdiction." See Pfander, *Supplemental Jurisdiction and Section 1367: The Case for a Sympathetic Textualism*, 148 U.Pa.L.Rev. 109, 114 (1999). In contrast to the Court's construction of § 1367, which draws a sharp line between the diversity and amount-in-controversy components of § 1332, the interpretation presented here does not sever the two jurisdictional requirements.

* * *

The less disruptive view I take of § 1367 also accounts for the omission of Rule 20 plaintiffs and Rule 23 class actions in § 1367(b)'s text. If one reads § 1367(a) as a plenary grant of supplemental jurisdiction to

---

[5] Endeavoring to preserve the "complete diversity" rule first stated in Strawbridge v. Curtiss, the Court's opinion drives a wedge between the two components of 28 U.S.C. § 1332, treating the diversity-of-citizenship requirement as essential, the amount-in-controversy requirement as more readily disposable. Section 1332 itself, however, does not rank order the two requirements. * * * [T]he Court asserts that amount in controversy can be analyzed claim-by-claim, but the diversity requirement cannot. It is not altogether clear why that should be so. The cure for improper joinder of a nondiverse party is the same as the cure for improper joinder of a plaintiff who does not satisfy the jurisdictional amount. In both cases, original jurisdiction can be preserved by dismissing the nonqualifying party.

[9] On this reading of § 1367(a), it is immaterial that § 1367(b) "does not withdraw supplemental jurisdiction over the claims of the additional parties at issue here." Because those claims would not come within § 1367(a) in the first place, Congress would have had no reason to list them in § 1367(b).

federal courts sitting in diversity, one would indeed look for exceptions in § 1367(b). Finding none for permissive joinder of parties or class actions, one would conclude that Congress effectively, even if unintentionally, overruled Clark and Zahn. But if one recognizes that the nonaggregation rule delineated in Clark and Zahn forms part of the determination whether "original jurisdiction" exists in a diversity case, then plaintiffs who do not meet the amount-in-controversy requirement would fail at the § 1367(a) threshold. Congress would have no reason to resort to a § 1367(b) exception to turn such plaintiffs away from federal court, given that their claims, from the start, would fall outside the court's § 1332 jurisdiction.

Nor does the more moderate reading assign different meanings to "original jurisdiction" in diversity and federal-question cases. As the First Circuit stated [in the companion case under review]:

> " '[O]riginal jurisdiction' in § 1367(a) has the same meaning in every case: [An] underlying statutory grant of original jurisdiction must be satisfied. What differs between federal question and diversity cases is not the meaning of 'original jurisdiction' but rather the [discrete] requirements of sections 1331 and 1332. Under § 1331, the sole issue is whether a federal question appears on the face of the plaintiff's well-pleaded complaint; the [citizenship] of the parties and the amounts they stand to recover [do not bear on that determination]. Section 1332, by contrast, predicates original jurisdiction on the identity of the parties (i.e., [their] complete diversity) and their [satisfaction of the amount-in-controversy specification]. [In short,] the 'original jurisdiction' language in § 1367 operates differently in federal-question and diversity cases not because the meaning of that term varies, but because the [jurisdiction-granting] statutes are different."

What is the utility of § 1367(b) under my reading of § 1367(a)? Section 1367(a) allows parties other than the plaintiff to assert reactive claims once entertained under the heading ancillary jurisdiction. * * * [Section] 1367(b) stops plaintiffs from circumventing § 1332's jurisdictional requirements by using another's claim as a hook to add a claim that the plaintiff could not have brought in the first instance. Kroger is the paradigm case. * * * Section 1367(b), then, is corroborative of § 1367(a)'s coverage of claims formerly called ancillary, but provides exceptions to ensure that accommodation of added claims would not fundamentally alter "the jurisdictional requirements of section 1332." See Pfander, *supra*, at 135–137.

While § 1367's enigmatic text defies flawless interpretation,[13] the precedent-preservative reading, I am persuaded, better accords with the

---

[13] If § 1367(a) itself renders unnecessary the listing of Rule 20 plaintiffs and Rule 23 class actions in § 1367(b), then it is similarly unnecessary to refer, as § 1367(b) does, to "persons proposed to be joined as plaintiffs under Rule 19." On one account, Congress bracketed such persons with persons "seeking to intervene as plaintiffs under Rule 24" to modify pre-§ 1367 practice. Before enactment of § 1367, courts entertained, under the heading ancillary jurisdiction, claims of Rule 24(a) intervenors "of right," but denied ancillary jurisdiction over claims of "necessary" Rule 19 plaintiffs. Congress may have sought simply to underscore that those seeking to join as plaintiffs, whether under Rule 19 or Rule 24, should be treated alike, i.e., denied joinder when "inconsistent with the jurisdictional requirements of section 1332." See 370 F.3d at 140, and n. 15. * * *

historical and legal context of Congress' enactment of the supplemental jurisdiction statute, and the established limits on pendent and ancillary jurisdiction. It does not attribute to Congress a jurisdictional enlargement broader than the one to which the legislators adverted, and it follows the sound counsel that "close questions of [statutory] construction should be resolved in favor of continuity and against change." Shapiro, *Continuity and Change in Statutory Interpretation*, 67 N.Y.U. L.Rev. 921, 925 (1992).

* * *

For the reasons stated, I would hold that § 1367 does not overrule Clark and Zahn. * * *

NOTE ON THE EFFECT OF § 1367 ON THE AVAILABILITY OF SUPPLEMENTAL JURISDICTION IN DIVERSITY CASES

(1) Background. The genesis of the supplemental jurisdiction provision enacted in 1990 is described at pp. 867–868, *supra*, and the reader should refer to that discussion for consideration of a number of problems that arise in both the federal question and diversity contexts. The legislative history indicates, however, that the provision was designed primarily to deal with the "pendent party" question in the context of federal question litigation and, by and large, not to change the law dramatically in the diversity context. As it turned out, a number of questions arose involving the provision's application in diversity cases, and in the 15 years preceding the Exxon Mobil decision, the questions generated both vigorous debate in the law reviews and disagreement in the lower federal courts about the meaning (and wisdom) of the provision in that context. Some of those questions persist even after the decision.

(2) Comments and Questions on Exxon Mobil. The close division in the Exxon Mobil case reflects the difficulty of interpreting a statute that tried perhaps too hard to deal in elaborate detail with an area that did not easily yield to codification. Indeed, both sides had to confront several difficulties in reaching their conclusions.[1]

For the majority, perhaps the major problem lay in explaining why its "contamination theory" precluded subsection (a) from affecting the complete diversity requirement but did not preclude the overruling of Zahn and of Clark v. Paul Gray.[2] The majority's argument was that (unlike the absence of the requisite jurisdictional amount with respect to one plaintiff's claim) the presence of co-citizens as adversaries dispels the concern that underlies diversity jurisdiction because it obviates the danger that home state citizen(s) will be unfairly preferred. The statutory availability of diversity jurisdiction in the plaintiff's home state is difficult to square with this view, as is the strained definition of complete diversity in class actions under the Ben-Hur rule, p. 1436, *supra*. But even assuming the majority's premise, will the presence of citizens of the same state—even the forum state—on both

---

[1] Although the Court held that the Class Action Fairness Act was not relevant to the outcome, and did not moot the case, that Act, in authorizing aggregation in many diversity class actions, clearly reduced the significance of the decision.

[2] For forceful criticism of the majority's distinction between these aspects of the diversity jurisdiction, see Note, 81 Notre Dame L.Rev. 2013 (2006).

sides of a case guarantee that a party from another state will not be disfavored? Wouldn't it often be possible to prefer a forum-state defendant at the expense of an out-of-state defendant? Moreover, if the majority is right that the absence of complete diversity means that the entire action has been jurisdictionally contaminated from the start, how does one justify the decisions in cases like Newman-Green, Inc. v. Alfonzo-Larrain, 490 U.S. 826 (1989), allowing dismissal of a non-diverse party on appeal and affirmance of the relief awarded against the remaining defendants? And finally, how does the Court's decision apply in a case in which there is not one defendant (as in both Exxon Mobil and the companion case), but multiple defendants who have been joined under Rule 20? Doesn't the exception of § 1367(b) apply in that situation? Does that distinction make sense?

For the dissent, the principal problem was to distinguish between the meaning of subsection (a) in diversity cases and in federal question cases, for if the term "civil action over which the district courts have original jurisdiction" always requires reference to all claims in the case, then the provision does not even overrule Finley, given the holding in Finley itself that the district court lacked original jurisdiction. Justice Ginsburg grapples with this problem, but does her explanation account for the fact that, prior to the enactment of § 1367, had a case like Finley (i.e., one in which the plaintiff sued one defendant on a federal claim and joined another, non-diverse defendant on a state claim) been brought in a state court, it could not have been removed under § 1441(a) as a case over which the district courts had "original jurisdiction"? Moreover, her theory of subsection (b) is, as she recognizes, difficult to square with some of its provisions, e.g., the exception for claims by plaintiffs *against* persons made parties under Rule 20—even in the original complaint.[3]

(3) The Applicability of § 1367 to Removed Cases. Despite some uncertainty in the language of § 1367, the Supreme Court held, in City of Chicago v. International College of Surgeons, 522 U.S. 156 (1997), that the provision applies to removed cases. But the question remains whether the limitations in § 1367(b) apply to claims asserted in state court before removal. For a forceful argument that they do not, see Steinman, *Supplemental Jurisdiction in § 1441 Removed Cases: An Unsurveyed Frontier of Congress' Handiwork*, 35 Ariz.L.Rev. 305 (1993). Professor Steinman's argument is supported by the phrasing of § 1367(b) in terms of the relationship of the *Federal* Rules of Civil Procedure to the assertion of claims and the joinder of parties. Indeed, given this terminology, rejection of her argument might raise difficult questions of the application of subsection (b) to removed cases in which claims have been asserted and/or parties joined under state rules that differ significantly from the relevant federal rules.

(4) Preservation of the Kroger Rule. Both the wording of subsection (b) and the legislative history indicate that the drafters did not intend to change the result in Owen Equipment and Erection Co. v. Kroger, p. 1449, *supra*. But was that approach sound, in view of Justice White's powerful arguments,

---

[3] In a critique of the rationale of Exxon Mobil, Steinman, *Claims, Civil Actions, Congress & the Court: Limiting the Reasoning of Cases Construing Poorly Drawn Statutes*, 65 Wash. & Lee L.Rev. 1593 (2008), contends that the Court has redefined the terms "claim" and "civil action" by sometimes conflating them. Noting that the lower courts have not extended this redefinition to other statutory contexts though they may have a duty to do so under accepted notions of the effects of a binding Supreme Court precedent, Steinman argues that such an extension would have undesirable consequences, particularly in cases removed from state courts. She concludes by urging congressional action to clarify the law and to prevent such consequences.

in his Kroger dissent, that the majority's result disserved judicial economy, generated inconvenience, and rested on a concern that was improbable—that a plaintiff who could not sue a non-diverse person initially would rely on the defendant's impleading that person to permit the plaintiff in turn to file a claim against that person? Does the intent to preserve the Kroger result mean that a plaintiff cannot assert a direct claim against a third-party nondiverse defendant even if the action was originally brought in a state court and then removed? Does the statute affect the answer to the question asked at the end of Paragraph (5), p. 1449, *supra*, about the ability of a plaintiff to assert a claim against a nondiverse third party defendant if the claim is asserted as a *counterclaim* to a claim by the third party? As a *compulsory* counterclaim to such a claim?

(5) Additional Problems of Interpreting § 1367(b). Difficult questions also arise under subsection (b) with respect to the addition of parties under Rule 19 and intervention under Rule 24. For example, are *all* claims excluded if they are asserted by plaintiffs against persons made parties under these rules, or only those that "would be inconsistent" with the requirements of § 1332? (And what are those?) An aspect of this question is grammatical: does the final clause of subsection (b) relate to the entire subsection, or only to claims by persons joined as, or seeking to intervene as, plaintiffs? As another example, since subsection (b) does not purport to affect claims made by persons seeking to intervene as *defendants*, the problem of alignment, and possible realignment, becomes critical.

(6) Other Sources of Ancillary Jurisdiction. The doctrine of "ancillary jurisdiction" is not exhausted by the provisions of § 1367. Thus in Kokkonen v. Guardian Life Ins. Co., 511 U.S. 375 (1994), the Court first held that the doctrine did *not* confer authority on a federal court to enforce the terms of a settlement agreement in a diversity case, but then suggested (without reference to § 1367) that such authority would exist had the district court "embod[ied] the settlement contract in its dismissal order (or, what has the same effect, retain[ed] jurisdiction over the settlement contract) if the parties [had] agree[d]". The distinction drawn in Kokkonen between an independent action and an ancillary proceeding was buttressed by the decision two years later in Peacock v. Thomas, 516 U.S. 349 (1996). In that case the Court held, 8–1, that federal courts do not possess ancillary jurisdiction over a new action in which a federal judgment creditor sues to impose liability on a person who has not previously been held liable for a monetary judgment against another defendant. The Court noted, in passing, that "Congress codified much of the common-law doctrine of ancillary jurisdiction" in § 1367, and then went on to reject any common-law basis of ancillary jurisdiction on the facts presented.

5. DEVICES FOR CREATING OR AVOIDING DIVERSITY JURISDICTION

Kramer v. Caribbean Mills, Inc.

394 U.S. 823, 89 S.Ct. 1487, 23 L.Ed.2d 9 (1969).
Certiorari to the United States Court of Appeals for the Fifth Circuit.

■ MR. JUSTICE HARLAN delivered the opinion of the Court.

The sole question presented by this case is whether the Federal District Court in which it was brought had jurisdiction over the cause, or whether that court was deprived of jurisdiction by 28 U.S.C. § 1359. * * *

The facts were these. Respondent Caribbean Mills, Inc. (Caribbean) is a Haitian corporation. In May 1959 it entered into a contract with an individual named Kelly and the Panama and Venezuela Finance Company (Panama), a Panamanian corporation. The agreement provided that Caribbean would purchase from Panama 125 shares of corporate stock, in return for payment of $85,000 down and an additional $165,000 in 12 annual installments.

No installment payments ever were made, despite requests for payment by Panama. In 1964, Panama assigned its entire interest in the 1959 contract to petitioner Kramer, an attorney in Wichita Falls, Texas. The stated consideration was $1. By a separate agreement dated the same day, Kramer promised to pay back to Panama 95% of any net recovery on the assigned cause of action, "solely as a Bonus."

Kramer soon thereafter brought suit against Caribbean for $165,000 in the United States District Court for the Northern District of Texas, alleging diversity of citizenship between himself and Caribbean. The District Court denied Caribbean's motion to dismiss for want of jurisdiction. The case proceeded to trial, and a jury returned a $165,000 verdict in favor of Kramer.

On appeal, the Court of Appeals for the Fifth Circuit reversed, holding that the assignment was "improperly or collusively made" within the meaning of 28 U.S.C. § 1359, and that in consequence the District Court lacked jurisdiction. * * * For reasons which follow, we affirm the judgment of the Court of Appeals.

I

The issue before us is whether Kramer was "improperly or collusively made" a party "to invoke the jurisdiction" of the District Court, within the meaning of 28 U.S.C. § 1359. We look first to the legislative background.

Section 1359 has existed in its present form only since the 1948 revision of the Judicial Code. Prior to that time, the use of devices to create diversity was regulated by two federal statutes. The first, known as the "assignee clause," provided that, with certain exceptions not here relevant:

"No district court shall have cognizance of any suit . . . to recover upon any promissory note or other chose in action in favor of any

assignee. . . . unless such suit might have been prosecuted in such court
. . . if no assignment had been made."[3]

The second pre-1948 statute, 28 U.S.C. § 80 (1940 ed.), stated that a
district court should dismiss an action whenever: "it shall appear to the
satisfaction of the . . . court . . . that such suit does not really and
substantially involve a dispute or controversy properly within the
jurisdiction of [the] court, or that the parties to said suit have been
improperly or collusively made or joined . . . for the purpose of creating
[federal jurisdiction]."

As part of the 1948 revision, § 80 was amended to produce the
present § 1359. The assignee clause was simultaneously repealed. The
Reviser's Note describes the amended assignee clause as a "jumble of
legislative jargon," and states that "[t]he revised section changes this
clause by confining its application to cases wherein the assignment is
improperly or collusively made . . . . Furthermore, . . . the original purpose
of [the assignee] clause is better served by substantially following section
80." That purpose was said to be "to prevent the manufacture of Federal
jurisdiction by the device of assignment."

II

* * * Because the approach of the former assignee clause was to
forbid the grounding of jurisdiction upon *any* assignment, regardless of
its circumstances or purpose, decisions under that clause are of little
assistance. However, decisions of this Court under the other predecessor
statute, 28 U.S.C. § 80 (1940 ed.), seem squarely in point. These
decisions, together with the evident purpose of § 1359, lead us to conclude
that the Court of Appeals was correct in finding that the assignment in
question was "improperly or collusively made."

The most compelling precedent is Farmington v. Pillsbury, 114 U.S.
138 (1885). There Maine holders of bonds issued by a Maine village
desired to test the bonds' validity in the federal courts. In an effort to
accomplish this, they cut the coupons from their bonds and transferred
them to a citizen of Massachusetts, who gave in return a non-negotiable
two-year note for $500 and a promise to pay back 50% of the net amount
recovered above $500. The jurisdictional question was certified to this
Court, which held that there was no federal jurisdiction because the
plaintiff had been "improperly or collusively" made a party within the
meaning of the predecessor statute to 28 U.S.C. § 80 (1940 ed.). The Court
pointed out that the plaintiff could easily have been released from his
non-negotiable note, and found that apart from the hoped-for creation of
federal jurisdiction the only real consequence of the transfer was to
enable the Massachusetts plaintiff to "retain one-half of what he collects
for the use of his name and his trouble in collecting." The Court concluded
that "the transfer of the coupons was 'a mere contrivance, a pretence, the
result of a collusive arrangement to create'" federal jurisdiction.

We find the case before us indistinguishable from Farmington and
other decisions of like tenor. When the assignment to Kramer is
considered together with his total lack of previous connection with the
matter and his simultaneous reassignment of a 95% interest back to
Panama, there can be little doubt that the assignment was for purposes

---

[3]   28 U.S.C. § 41(1) (1940 ed.). The clause first appeared as § 11 of the Judiciary Act of
1789, 1 Stat. 79.

of collection, with Kramer to retain 5% of the net proceeds "for the use of his name and his trouble in collecting."[9] If the suit had been unsuccessful, Kramer would have been out only $1, plus costs. Moreover, Kramer candidly admits that the "assignment was in substantial part motivated by a desire by [Panama's] counsel to make diversity jurisdiction available . . . ."

The conclusion that this assignment was "improperly or collusively made" within the meaning of § 1359 is supported not only by precedent but also by consideration of the statute's purpose. If federal jurisdiction could be created by assignments of this kind, which are easy to arrange and involve few disadvantages for the assignor, then a vast quantity of ordinary contract and tort litigation could be channeled into the federal courts at the will of one of the parties. Such "manufacture of Federal jurisdiction" was the very thing which Congress intended to prevent when it enacted § 1359 and its predecessors.

III

Kramer nevertheless argues that the assignment to him was not "improperly or collusively made" within the meaning of § 1359, for two main reasons. First, he suggests that the undisputed legality of the assignment under Texas law necessarily rendered it valid for purposes of federal jurisdiction. We cannot accept this contention. * * * [To do so] would render § 1359 largely incapable of accomplishing its purpose; this very case demonstrates the ease with which a party may "manufacture" federal jurisdiction by an assignment which meets the requirements of state law.

Second, Kramer urges that this case is significantly distinguishable from earlier decisions because it involves diversity jurisdiction under 28 U.S.C. § 1332(a)(2), arising from the alienage of one of the parties, rather than the more common diversity jurisdiction based upon the parties' residence in different States. We can perceive no substance in this argument: by its terms, § 1359 applies equally to both types of diversity jurisdiction, and there is no indication that Congress intended them to be treated differently.

IV

In short, we find that this assignment falls not only within the scope of § 1359 but within its very core. It follows that the District Court lacked jurisdiction to hear this action, and that petitioner must seek his remedy in the state courts. The judgment of the Court of Appeals is affirmed.

---

[9]   Hence, we have no occasion to re-examine the cases in which this Court has held that where the transfer of a claim is absolute, with the transferor retaining no interest in the subject matter, then the transfer is not "improperly or collusively made," regardless of the transferor's motive.

Nor is it necessary to consider whether, in cases in which suit is required to be brought by an administrator or guardian, a motive to create diversity jurisdiction renders the appointment of an out-of-state representative "improper" or "collusive." *See, e.g.,* McSparran v. Weist, 402 F.2d 867 (3 Cir.1968); *cf.* Mecom v. Fitzsimmons Drilling Co., 284 U.S. 183 (1931). * * *

NOTE ON DEVICES FOR CREATING OR AVOIDING FEDERAL JURISDICTION

(1) Appointment of Legal Representatives.

(a) Footnote 9 of the Kramer opinion refers to the appointment of an administrator or guardian for the purpose of creating diversity jurisdiction. The problem presented by this practice had become particularly acute in the Eastern District of Pennsylvania, where it was common for lawyers to arrange for the appointment—as guardians, administrators, or executors—of secretaries or other office staff who commuted to work from New Jersey, thus laying the basis for a diversity action against a Pennsylvania defendant. In McSparran v. Weist, 402 F.2d 867 (3d Cir.1968), decided a few months before Kramer, the plaintiff conceded that the fiduciary (a guardian for a minor) was "a straw party, chosen solely to create diversity jurisdiction." The Third Circuit, overruling its own precedent, sustained a challenge to the jurisdiction, saying: "[A] nominal party designated simply for the purpose of creating diversity of citizenship, who has no real or substantial interest in the dispute or controversy, is improperly or collusively named."

(b) In 1988, Congress addressed the McSparran problem by adopting a "bright line" test for determining jurisdiction: 28 U.S.C. § 1332(c)(2) specifies that the representative of an estate shall be deemed to be a citizen only of the state of citizenship of the decedent, and the representative of an infant or incompetent shall be deemed to be a citizen only of the state of citizenship of the person represented.

(2) Variations on the Theme: Matters Not Covered by Kramer or by § 1332(c)(2).

The Kramer Court deliberately left open the status under § 1359 of a variety of events, thus casting doubt on a number of its own precedents. As stated in the Court's footnote 9, an absolute transfer not subject to the former assignee clause had been held not improper or collusive, regardless of the transferor's motive. *E.g.*, Cross v. Allen, 141 U.S. 528 (1891). And if the plaintiff effectively changed his domicile prior to the bringing of suit, it did not matter that his sole motive was to create jurisdiction. Williamson v. Osenton, 232 U.S. 619 (1914). Finally, although reincorporation would fail to create diversity jurisdiction if the old corporation continued in existence with power to control the new, *e.g.*, Lehigh Mining & Mfg. Co. v. Kelly, 160 U.S. 327 (1895), the device would succeed if the new corporation was a genuine one not subject to control by any predecessor, Black & White Taxicab & Transfer Co. v. Brown and Yellow Taxicab & Transfer Co., 276 U.S. 518 (1928).

Should any or all of these holdings be overruled? What is the effect, if any, of Congress' decision, in § 1332(c)(2), to deal specifically with the case of the legal representative?

(3) Direct Actions Against Insurers: § 1332(c)(1).

In its 1964 amendment to 28 U.S.C. § 1332(c), Congress dealt with another device for obtaining federal diversity jurisdiction. Statutes of a few states (notably, Louisiana) permitted an injured person to bring suit directly against a liability insurer without joining the insured. This made it possible, for example, for a case in which one Louisiana citizen had injured another to be litigated in a federal court if the alleged tortfeasor had an out-of-state insurer. Lumbermen's Mut. Cas. Co. v. Elbert, 348 U.S. 48 (1954). Such cases poured into the Louisiana federal courts until Congress provided that the insurer defendant in a direct action must be deemed a citizen of the insured's state as well as of its own.

Was Congress correct in concluding that such cases are less fitting for original diversity jurisdiction than other cases in which an in-state citizen sues an out-of-state citizen? See the criticism of the statute in Weckstein, *The 1964 Diversity Amendment: Congressional Indirect Action Against State "Direct Action" Laws*, 1965 Wis.L.Rev. 268.

(4) Avoidance Devices. No statutory provision aids a district court in disregarding devices to avoid federal jurisdiction, and such devices have often been successful. In Provident Savings Life Assurance Society v. Ford, 114 U.S. 635 (1885), the Court held that an assignment to the plaintiff made to prevent removal, even if only "merely colorable", raised at most a defense to the action in the state court, and thus the case could not be removed. See also Oakley v. Goodnow, 118 U.S. 43 (1886) (assignment to defeat jurisdiction precludes removal); Mecom v. Fitzsimmons Drilling Co., 284 U.S. 183 (1931) (appointment of co-citizen administrator to defeat jurisdiction precludes removal).

But in Gentle v. Lamb-Weston, Inc., 302 F.Supp. 161 (D.Me.1969), each of the plaintiffs, who were citizens of Maine, transferred 1% of his claim to an Oregon citizen (a law school classmate of their Maine attorney), and the Oregon citizen then joined as a plaintiff in an action against an Oregon defendant in a Maine state court. The admitted purpose of the transfer, to prevent removal, failed when Judge Gignoux denied a motion to remand the case to the state court. He managed to distinguish each of the Supreme Court cases cited above (as involving either total assignments or state-court approved appointments), and relied on the Kramer rationale as well as on cases in which "fraudulent joinder" of an in-state defendant failed to preclude removal. As to the partial transfer in the case before him, "the essential diversity of citizenship of the parties at bar has not been vitiated by plaintiffs' sham transaction." The case has been followed by other courts. See generally Wright & Kane, Federal Courts § 31, at 186–88 (7th ed. 2011).

INDEX

References are to Pages